Pronunciation Table

Vowels

Symbol	Key Word
i	beat, feed
ɪ	bit, did
eɪ	date, paid
ɛ	bet, bed
æ	bat, bad
ɑ	box, odd, father
ɔ	bought, dog
oʊ	boat, road
ʊ	book, good
u	boot, food, student
ʌ	but, mud, mother
ə	banana, among
ɚ	shirt, murder
aɪ	bite, cry, buy, eye
aʊ	about, how
ɔɪ	voice, boy
ɪr	beer
ɛr	bare
ɑr	bar
ɔr	door
ʊr	tour

/*t*/ means that /t/ may be dropped.
/*d*/ means that /d/ may be dropped.
/ˈ/ shows main stress.
/ˌ/ shows secondary stress.
/◂/ shows stress shift.

Consona

Symbol	
p	pack, happy
b	back, rubber
t	tie
d	die
k	came, key, quick
g	game, guest
tʃ	church, nature, watch
dʒ	judge, general, major
f	fan, photograph
v	van
θ	thing, breath
ð	then, breathe
i	sip, city, psychology
z	zip, please, goes
ʃ	ship, machine, station, special, discussion
ʒ	measure, vision
h	hot, who
m	men, some
n	sun, know, pneumonia
ŋ	sung, ringing
w	wet, white
l	light, long
r	right, wrong
y	yes, use, music
t̬	butter, bottle
t˺	button

American English Sounds – /t̬/, /t˺/, /*t*/, /*d*/, and /nʃ/

/t̬/

The /t/ in tap or sat is a voiceless sound. Many Americans, however, use a voiced sound like a quick /d/ for the *t* in words like *latter*, *party*, and *little*. The *t* in these words, shown in this Dictionary as /t̬/, sounds like the *d* in *ladder*, *hardy*, and *middle*. This sound usually occurs between vowels (especially before an unstressed vowel), between *r* and a vowel, or before a syllabic /l/.

/t˺/

This symbol means that many speakers pronounce a *glottal stop* in place of or together with /t/. A glottal stop is the sound in the middle of the expression *uh oh*. For example, in the words **button** /ˈbʌt˺n/ and **football** /ˈfʊt˺bɔl/, the *t* does not sound the same as in the word *ton* /tʌn/; it sounds more like a short period of silence. The glottal stop usually occurs before a syllabic /n/ or a consonant that begins the next syllable.

/*t*/ and /*d*/

These symbols mean that these consonants may either be pronounced or left out. For example, the *t* in **restless** /ˈrɛs*t*lɪs/ and the *d* in **grandfather** /ˈgræn*d*ˌfɑðɚ/ are usually dropped in normal connected speech, even though it is considered more correct in slow careful speech to pronounce the *t* and *d* in these words.

/nʃ/

Many speakers pronounce the sequence /nʃ/ as /ntʃ/. For example, **attention** /əˈtɛnʃən/, **conscious** /ˈkɑnʃəs/ may also be pronounced as /əˈtɛntʃən/, /ˈkɑntʃəs/. Only the pronunciation with /nʃ/ is shown.

Pronunciation

American English

This dictionary shows pronunciations used by speakers of the most common American English dialects. Sometimes more than one pronunciation is shown. For example, many Americans say the first vowel in *data* as /eɪ/, while many others say this vowel as /æ/. We show *data* as /ˈdeɪṭə, ˈdæṭə/. This means that both pronunciations are possible and are commonly used by educated speakers. We have not, however, shown all American dialects and all possible pronunciations. For example, *news* is shown only as /nuz/ even though a few Americans might pronounce this word as /nyuz/. In words like *caught* and *dog* we show the vowel /ɔ/, but many speakers use the vowel /ɑ/ in place of /ɔ/, so that *caught* and *cot* are both said as /kɑt/.

Use of the Hyphen

When more than one pronunciation is given for a word, we usually show only the part of the pronunciation that is different from the first pronunciation, replacing the parts that are the same with a hyphen: **economics** /ˌɛkəˈnɑmɪks, ˌi-/. The hyphen is also used for showing the division between syllables when this might not be clear: **boyish** /ˈbɔɪ-ɪʃ/, **drawing** /ˈdrɔ-ɪŋ/, **clockwise** /ˈklɑk-waɪz/.

Symbols

The symbols used in this dictionary are based on the symbols of the International Phonetic Alphabet (IPA) with a few changes. The symbol /y/, which is closer to English spelling than the /j/ used in the IPA, is used for the first sound in *you* /yu/. Other changes are described in the paragraph **American English Sounds**.

Abbreviations

No pronunciations are shown for most abbreviations. This is either because they are not spoken (and are defined as "written abbreviations"), or because they are pronounced by saying the names of the letters, with main stress on the last letter and secondary stress on the first: **VCR** /ˌvi si ˈɑr/. Pronunciations have been shown where an abbreviation is spoken like an ordinary word: **RAM** /ræm/.

Words that are Forms of Main Words

A form of a main word that is a different part of speech may come at the end of the entry for that word. If the related word is pronounced by saying the main word and adding an ending (see list on page A45), no separate pronunciation is given. If the addition of the ending causes a change in the pronunciation of the main word, the pronunciation for the related word is given. For example: **impossible** /ɪmˈpɑsəbəl/, **impossibility** /ɪmˌpɑsəˈbɪləṭi/. There are some pronuncation changes that we do not show at these entries, because they follow regular patterns: (1) When an *-ly* or *-er* ending is added to a main word ending in /-bəl/, /-kəl/, /-pəl/, /-gəl/, or /-dəl/, the /ə/ is usually omitted. For example, **practical** is shown as /ˈpræktɪkəl/. When *-ly* is added to it, it becomes **practically** /ˈpræktɪkli/. This difference is not shown. (2) When *-ly* or *-ity* is added to words ending in *-y* /i/, the /i/ becomes /ə/: **angry** /ˈæŋgri/ becomes **angrily** /ˈæŋgrəli/. This is not shown.

Stress

In English words of two or more syllables, at least one syllable is said with more force than the others. The sign /ˈ/ is put before the syllable with the most force. We say it has *main stress*: **person** /ˈpɚsən/, **percent** /pɚˈsɛnt/. Some words also have a stress on another syllable that is less strong than the main stress. We call this *secondary stress*, and the sign /ˌ/ is placed before such a syllable: **personality** /ˌpɚsəˈnæləṭi/, **personify** /pɚˈsɑnəˌfaɪ/. Secondary stress is not usually shown in the second syllable of a two-syllable word, unless it is necessary to show that the second syllable must not be shortened, as in **starlit** /ˈstɑrˌlɪt/ compared to **starlet** /ˈstɑrlɪt/.

Unstressed Vowels

/ə/ and /ɪ/

Many unstressed syllables in American English are pronounced with a very short unclear vowel. This vowel is shown as /ə/ or /ɪ/; however, there is very little difference between them in normal connected speech. For example, the word *affect* /əˈfɛkt/ and *effect* /ɪˈfɛkt/ usually sound the same. The word *rabbit* is shown as /ˈræbɪt/, but it may also be pronounced /ˈræbət/.

/ə/ and /ʌ/

These sounds are very similar. The symbol /ə/ is used in unstressed syllables, and /ʌ/, which is longer, is used in stressed and secondary stressed syllables. When people speak more quickly, secondary stressed syllables become unstressed so that /ʌ/ may be pronounced as /ə/. For example, *difficult* /ˈdɪfɪˌkʌlt/ and *coconut* /ˈkoʊkəˌnʌt/ may be pronounced as /ˈdɪfɪkəlt/ and /ˈkoʊkənət/. Only the pronunciation with /ʌ/ is shown.

Compound Words with a Space or Hyphen

Many compounds are written with either a space or a hyphen between the parts. When all parts of the compound appear in the dictionary as separate main words, the full pronunciation of the compound is not shown. Only its stress pattern is given. For example: **ˈbus stop**, **ˌtown ˈhall**. Sometimes a compound contains a main word with an ending. If the main word is in the dictionary and the ending is a common one, only a stress pattern is shown. For example: **ˈwashing ˌmachine**. *Washing* is not a main word in the Dictionary, but *wash* is; so only a stress pattern is shown because *-ing* is a common ending. But if any part is not a main word, the full pronunciation is given: **helter-skelter** /ˌhɛltɚ ˈskɛltɚ/.

Stress Shift

Some words may have a shift in stress. The secondary stress becomes the main stress when the word comes before a noun. The mark /◂ / shows this. For example: **artificial** /ˌɑrṭəˈfɪʃəl◂ /, **artificial intelligence** /ˌɑrṭəfɪʃəl ɪnˈtɛlədʒəns/.

Syllabic Consonants

The sounds /n/ and /l/ can be syllabic. That is, they can themselves form a syllable, especially when they are at the end of a word (and follow particular consonants, especially /t/ and /d/). For example, in **sudden** /ˈsʌdn/ the /n/ is syllabic; there is no vowel between the /d/ and the /n/, so no vowel is shown. In the middle of a word, a hyphen or stress mark after /n/ or /l/ shows that it is syllabic: **botanist** /ˈbɑtˀn-ɪst/ and **catalog** /ˈkæṭlˌɔg/ are three-syllable words.

The sound *r* can be either a consonant, /r/, or a vowel, /ɚ/. When /ɚ/ is followed by an unstressed vowel, it may be pronounced as a sequence of two vowels, /ɚ/ plus the following vowel, or as /ə/ followed by a syllable beginning with /r/. For example, the word *coloring* may be pronounced as /ˈkʌlɚɪŋ/ instead of /ˈkʌlərɪŋ/. Only the pronunciation, /ˈkʌlərɪŋ/, is shown.

Short Forms Used in the Dictionary

Parts of Speech

Some parts of speech have short forms:

adj.	adjective	*prep.*	preposition
adv.	adverb	*pron.*	pronoun
n.	noun	*v.*	verb
phr. v.	phrasal verb		

Other Short Forms

etc.	et cetera (=and so on)
U.S.	United States
s/he	she or he
sb	somebody/someone
sth	something
sb/sth	someone or something

Grammar Patterns

Grammar patterns are shown in ***dark letters*** in the example sentences.

Grammar Codes Used in the Dictionary

Nouns – to learn more about the grammar of nouns, see the LEARNER'S HANDBOOK on pages A46–A47.

[C]
COUNTABLE nouns such as **chair** and **store** are the most common type of noun in English. Their plural is usually formed by adding -s, and they are used with a plural verb:
Most of the smaller stores in the area have closed down.

[U]
an UNCOUNTABLE noun, such as **happiness** and **furniture**. Uncountable nouns cannot be used with *a* or *an*. They do not have plural forms, and are used with a singular verb:
The new furniture is being delivered on Saturday.
Some uncountable nouns can look like plurals, so be careful:
Economics is a difficult subject to study.

[C,U]
a noun that has both countable and uncountable uses, such as **wine**:
Our wines are specially chosen by our own buyer.
This is great wine – where did you buy it?

[singular]
a SINGULAR noun, such as **outcome**. Singular nouns can be used with *a*, *an*, or *the*, or without any determiner. They have no plural form, and they are used with a singular verb:
No one knew what the outcome of the discussion was.
We never dreamed there would be such a good outcome.

[plural]
a PLURAL noun, such as **pajamas**. Plural nouns do not have a singular form, and are used with a plural verb:
Your red pajamas are in the wash.

[C usually singular]
a noun such as **setting** that is countable, but is not used in the plural very often:
It was a lovely setting for a wedding.

[C usually plural]
a noun such as **resource** that is countable, and is usually used in the plural:
The country is rich in natural resources.

[singular, U]
a noun that has both singular and uncountable uses, such as **calm**:
The Harrisons preferred the calm of the country.
Marta reacted with amazing calm.

Verbs – to learn more about the grammar of verbs, see the LEARNER'S HANDBOOK on page A48.

[I]
an INTRANSITIVE verb, such as **exist**. Intransitive verbs are not followed by objects:
Only five railroads from the old network still exist.

[T]
a TRANSITIVE verb, such as **take**. Transitive verbs are followed by objects:
Will you take my jacket to the dry cleaners for me?

[I,T]
a verb that has both intransitive and transitive uses, such as **decide**:
It's so hard to decide.
I can't decide what to wear.

[linking verb]
a verb such as **be**, **become**, **seem**, etc.:
Jared's father is a teacher.
Dana seems really sorry.

Labels Used in the Dictionary

approving and disapproving	Words and phrases are labeled *approving* or *disapproving* if people use them in order to show that they approve or disapprove of someone or something. For example, both **childlike** and **childish** are used for describing behavior that is typical of a child, but **childlike** shows approval, and **childish** shows disapproval.
formal	Formal words and phrases such as **await** and **moreover** are used only in speech and writing that is formal or official, for example in essays or announcements.
humorous	Humorous words and phrases such as **clear as mud** are intended to be funny.
informal	Informal words and phrases such as **grungy** and **long shot** are used in informal conversations and unofficial writing such as letters to friends. Do not use these words and phrases in essays.
journalism	Words labelled journalism such as **parlay** and **heist** are typically used in newspapers and news reports.
law	Words and phrases labeled *law* have a special legal meaning.
literary	Literary words and phrases such as **foe** and **inferno** are used mostly in poetry and other types of literature. They are not usually suitable for essays.
nonstandard	Nonstandard words and phrases do not follow the rules of grammar, but are still used a lot. For example, many people use **real** instead of **really**. Do not use nonstandard language in essays.
offensive	Offensive words and phrases are likely to make someone upset if you use them. People often use them when they intend to insult other people, but these can also be words and phrases that only particular people consider to be offensive.
old-fashioned	Old-fashioned words and phrases are ones that people still know, but that are not used very often in modern speech or writing.
slang	Slang words and phrases are ones that are not acceptable in many situations, because they are only used by particular groups of people (such as young people), or because they are extremely informal or not very polite. Be very careful when using these words and phrases, and do not use them in essays.
spoken	Spoken words and phrases such as **I mean** and **by the way** are hardly ever used in writing. They are always informal, unless they have the label *spoken formal*. Do not use these words and phrases in essays.
taboo	Taboo words and phrases are extremely rude, offensive to everyone and should be avoided.
technical	Technical words and phrases such as **larynx** and **certificate of deposit** relate to particular subjects, such as science, medicine, language study etc.
trademark	A trademark is a special name for a product that a company owns. It must always be spelled in a particular way, and cannot be used by anyone else in the names of similar products.
written	Written words and phrases such as **ablaze** or **exclaim** are used only, or nearly always, in written English.

Pearson Education Limited
Edinburgh Gate
Harlow
Essex CM20 2JE
England
and Associated Companies throughout the world

www.longman.com/dictionaries

First edition published 1983
Second edition 1997
Third edition 2004

ISBN
Paper 0-13-192762-0
Paper 0-13-170344-7 (with CD-ROM)
Hardcover 0-13-192764-7
Hardcover 0-13-170343-9 (with CD-ROM)

Library of Congress Cataloging-in-Publication Data
A catalog record for this book is available from the Library of Congress.

British Library Cataloguing-in-Publication Data
A catalogue record for this book is available from the British Library.

Set in Times by Letterpart, UK
Printed in the United States of America

1 2 3 4 5 6 7 8 9 10 RRD 07 06 05 04 Paper
1 2 3 4 5 6 7 8 9 10 RRD 07 06 05 04 Paper + CD-Rom
1 2 3 4 5 6 7 8 9 10 RRD 07 06 05 04 Hardcover
1 2 3 4 5 6 7 8 9 10 RRD 07 06 05 04 Hardcover + CD-Rom

LONGMAN

Dictionary of American English

Longman

NEW EDITION

Table of Contents

Acknowledgements

Director
Della Summers

Senior Publisher
Laurence Delacroix

Projects Director
Michael Mayor

Managing Editor
Stephen Bullon

Editor
Michael Murphy

Lexicographers
Daniel Baron
Elizabeth Beizai
Karen Cleveland-Marwick

Project Manager
Alan Savill

Production Manager
Clive McKeough

Corpus and CD-ROM Development
Steve Crowdy

Computational Linguist and CD-ROM Project Management
Allan Ørsnes

Production Editor
Paola Rocchetti

Project and Database Administrator
Denise McKeough

Technical Support Manager
Trevor Satchell

Network Administrator
Kim Lee-Amies

Pronunciation Editor
Dinah Jackson

Language Notes
Stephen Handorf

Proofreaders
Johanna Chisholm
Meic Haines
Jane Horwood
Irene Lakhani
Mary Morton
Carole Murphy
Jane Tait

Design
Mick Harris

Keyboarder
Pauline Savill

Administrative Assistance
Janine Trainor

Artwork
Graham Humphries, Chris Paveley, Maltings Partnership, Oxford Designers and Illustrators

Photography credits
Hemera Technologies Inc "Copyright ©2004 (Pearson Education) and its licensors. All rights reserved"; **Brand X Pictures**; **DK Picture Library**; **IMS Communications Ltd.**; **Corbis**; **Gareth Bowden**; **PhotoDisc**; **Dorling Kindersley**; **Getty Images (Photodisc Blue)**

The Publishers would like to thank:

- Professor Jack du Bois of the University of California at Santa Barbara, for the development of the Longman Corpus of Spoken American English. This unique corpus, developed especially for the *Longman Dictionary of American English*, consists of 5 million words of everyday conversation by US speakers of English. The corpus was designed to provide a representative sample of the US population, by age, sex, region, educational attainment and ethnic origin. Volunteers were selected to wear a digital cassette recorder and record their conversations over a two-week period. The tapes were then transcribed and built into a computer system so that the lexicographic team could analyze exactly how native speakers use the language.
- the thousands of teachers and students from around the world who have contributed scripts for the Longman Learner's Corpus. This corpus consists of 8 million words of writing in English by learners, and helps lexicographers to analyze what students know and where they have difficulty.
- the Linguistic Data Consortium for texts included in the 80-million-word Longman Corpus of Written American English
- the many teachers and students who have taken part in the development of the second edition of the dictionary. This has included focus groups, questionnaires, student vocabulary notebooks (in which students kept a record of which words they looked up), classroom piloting of material, and written feedback on text by teachers.

Nancy Ackels, University of Washington Extension, Seattle. **Tom Adams**, University of Pennsylvania. **Monica Alvaraz**, California State University, Fullerton. **Isabella Anikst**, American Language Center, University of California, Los Angeles Extension. **Catherine Berg**, Drexel University, Philadelphia. **Gretchen Bitterlin**, San Diego Community College. **Donna Brinton**, University of California, Los Angeles. **Arlene Bublick**, William Rainey Harper College, Palatine, Illinois. **Christine Bunn**, City College of San Francisco. **Dorothy Burak**, University of California, San Diego. **Rand Burger**, California State Polytechnic, Pomona University. **Laura Cameron**, A.C.E. Language Institute, Seattle Pacific University. **Sarah Canady**, A.C.E. Language Institute, Seattle Pacific University. **Jane Cater**, Intensive English Language Institute, Seattle. **Rick Chapman**, California State University, Fullerton. **Martha Compton**, University of California, Irvine. **Jan Copeland**, Long Beach City College, Long Beach, California. **Patrick Cox**, Houston Community College. **Nick Crump**, Merritt College, Oakland. **Catherine Crystal**, Laney College, Oakland. **Kevin G. Curry**, Wichita State University, Kansas. **Susan Davis**, EF International. **Carlos C. Delgado**, North Valley Occupational Center, Mission Hills, California. **Carolyn Dupaquier**, California State University, Fullerton. **Nancy Dyer**, A.C.E. Language Institute, Seattle Pacific University. **Julie Easton**, Adult Education Center, Santa Monica. **Gerry Eldred**, Long Beach City College, Long Beach, California. **Rita Esquivel**, Adult Education Center, Santa Monica. **Mary Fitzpatrick**, College of Marin, Novato. **Annette Fruehan**, Orange Coast College, California. **Caroline Gibbs**, College of Marin, Novato. **Janet Goodwin**, University of California, Los Angeles. **Lisa Hale**, St Giles College, London. **James Harris**, Rancho Santiago College, Santa Ana. **Tamara Hefter**, Truman College, Chicago. **Patti Heiser**, University of Washington Extension. **Julie Herrmann**, A.C.E. Language Institute, Seattle Pacific University. **Wayne Heuple**, A.C.E. Language Institute, Seattle Pacific University. **Kathi Holper**, William Rainey Harper College, Palatine, Illinois. **Barbara Howard**, Daley College ALSP, Chicago. **Kathryn Howard**, Leann Howard, San Diego Community College. **Stephanie Howard**, American Language Center, University of California, Los Angeles Extension. **Gail Hutchins**, East San Jose College. **Susan Jamieson**, Bellevue Community College. **Jeff Janulis**, Daley College, Chicago. **Linda Jensen**, University of California, Los Angeles. **Winston Joffrion**, Bellevue Community College, Bellevue. **Deborah Jonas**, California State University, Long Beach. **Kathryn Curry Keesler**, Orange Coast College. **Barbara Logan**, A.C.E. Language Institute, Seattle Pacific University. **Walter Lowe**, Bellevue Community College, Seattle. **Lynne Lucas**, Daley College ALSP, Chicago. **Robyn Mann**, William Rainey Harper College, Palatine, Illinois. **Anne McGinley**, San Diego State University. **Elaine McVey**, San Diego State University. **Amy Meepoe**, University of California, Los Angeles. **Andy Muller**, A.C.E. Language Institute, Seattle Pacific University. **Jill Neely**, Merritt College, Oakland. **Maura Newberry**, University of California, Los Angeles. **Yvonne Nishio**, Evans Community Adult School, Los Angeles. **Roxanne Nuhaily**, University of California, San Diego. **Carla Nyssen**, California State University, Long Beach. **David Olsher**, University of California, Los Angeles. **Jorge Perez**, Southwestern College, San Diego. **Ellen Pentkowski**, Truman College, Chicago. **Eileen Prince Lou**, Northeastern University, Boston. **Nancy Quinn**, Truman College, Chicago. **Ralph Radell**, Bunker Hill Community College, Boston. **Eva Ramirez**, Laney College, Oakland. **Alison Rice**, Hunter College. **Lenore Richmond**, California State University, Fullerton. **Jane Rinaldi**, California State Polytechnic, Pomona. **Bruce Rindler**, CELOP, Boston University. **Shirley Roberts**, Long Beach City College, Long Beach. **William Robertson**, Northeastern University, Boston. **Bonnie Rose**, University of Denver. **Teresa Ross**, California State University, Long Beach. **Paul Safstrom**, South Seattle Community College. **Karen Santiago**, American Language Academy, Philadelphia. **Irene Schoenberg**, Hunter College, New York. **Esther Sunde**, South Seattle Community College, Seattle. **Barbara Swartz**, Northeastern University, Boston. **Priscilla Taylor**, California State University, Los Angeles. **Elizabeth Terplan**, College of Marin, Novato, California. **Bill Trimble**, Modesto Junior College. **Wendy Walsh**, College of Marin, Novato, California. **Colleen Weldele**, Palomar College, San Marcos, California. **Sabella Wells**, A.C.E. Language Institute, Seattle Pacific University. **Madeleine Youmans**, Long Beach City College, Long Beach. **Christine Zilkow**, California State University, Fullerton. **Janet Zinner**, Northeastern University, Boston. **Jean Zukowski**-Faust, Northern Arizona University.

Yuri Komuro, for assistance in compiling the results of teacher questionnaires and student word diaries.
Norma A. Register, PhD, for advice on coverage of socially sensitive language.

Preface

The new edition of the ***Longman Dictionary of American English*** has been specially researched and written to meet the real needs of students of English. It offers a completely up-dated text and **new thesaurus boxes** that give extra help with vocabulary acquisition.

Real Language

The new edition of the *Dictionary* is based on the authentic language data in the ***Longman Corpus Network***. This unique computerized language database now contains over 400 million words from all types of written texts, and from real conversations recorded across the U.S.

The Corpus tells us how frequently words and phrases are used, so there is no guesswork in deciding which ones students need to know most. The Corpus also shows which grammar patterns are the most important to illustrate, which important new words and idioms people use every day, and which words are frequently used together (*collocations*). We take our example sentences from the Corpus, and this makes the language come alive as never before.

Real Clarity

The definitions in the *Dictionary* are written using only the 2,000 most common English words – the **Longman American Defining Vocabulary**. Longman pioneered the use of a limited vocabulary as the best way to guarantee that definitions are clear and easy to understand.

The comprehensive grammatical information is easy to understand and use. Important patterns are highlighted in the example sentences, so that you can see at a glance how to use a word in a sentence.

The meaning you want is easy to find. Words that have a large number of meanings have short, clear **signposts** to guide you to the right meaning quickly.

Real Help

The new edition of the *Dictionary* is the result of extensive research into student needs and abilities. **New thesaurus boxes** explain thousands of synonyms and antonyms to help users expand their vocabulary, so that instead of using the same words all the time, such as the word *angry*, for example, they learn how to use related words such as *annoyed*, *irritated*, *furious*, etc.

The writers have also used their knowledge from years of teaching to analyze the **Longman Learner's Corpus**, which is a computerized collection of over 8 million words of writing in English by learners. By studying the errors students make in essays and exams, the writers were able to give clear, helpful usage information throughout the *Dictionary* – in the definitions, example sentences, usage notes, and in the **new Learner's Handbook** – to help students avoid common errors.

Use the exercises in the **Workbook** to learn how to get the most from your dictionary. The grammar codes and labels are on pages ii–iii, and the IPA (International Phonetic Alphabet) pronunciation table is inside the front cover, so they are always easy to find and use.

Whether you are writing a report, sending an e-mail, or talking with friends, the *Longman Dictionary of American English* will help you choose the right words, understand them clearly, and use them correctly.

Key to the Dictionary

Definitions explain the meaning of the word in clear simple language, using the 2000-word Longman American Defining Vocabulary.

The meanings of each word are listed in order of frequency. The most common meaning is shown first.

Part of speech is shown first, then information about whether a word is countable, uncountable, transitive, intransitive, etc.

Information about irregular forms of verbs and nouns is shown at the beginning of the entry.

Pronunciation is shown using the International Phonetic Alphabet.

Labels before the definition show if a word is used in informal, formal, literary, etc. English.

Usage boxes help you avoid the common mistakes people often make when using a word.

Synonyms (=words with the same meaning), opposites and related words are shown after the definition.

Phrasal verbs are listed in alphabetical order after the main verb.

ab·a·cus /ˈæbəkəs/ *n.* [C] a tool used for counting and calculating, consisting of a frame with small balls that can be slid along on thick wires

a·ban·don /əˈbændən/ *v.* [T] **1** to leave a person or thing, especially one that you are responsible for, and not go back: *How could she abandon her own child?* | *We had to abandon the car and walk the rest of the way.* **2** to stop doing or using something because of problems: *The policy had to be abandoned.* —**abandonment** *n.* [U]

ab·bey /ˈæbi/ *n.* [C] a large church, with buildings next to it where MONKS and NUNS live

ab·bre·vi·ate /əˈbriviˌeɪt/ *v.* [T] *formal* to make a word, story, etc. shorter: *"Street" is often* ***abbreviated as*** *"St.".*

ab·hor /əbˈhɔr, æb-/ *v.* past tense and past participle **abhorred**, present participle **abhorring** [T] *formal* to hate something, especially because you think it is morally wrong: *I abhor discrimination of any kind.*

a·bil·i·ty /əˈbɪləṭi/ *n.* plural **abilities** [C,U] the state of being able to do something, or your level of skill at doing something: *A manager must have the* ***ability to*** *communicate well.* | *a young girl with great* ***musical/athletic/acting, etc. ability*** | *She worked* ***to the best of her ability*** (=as well as she could) *in school.*

a·bun·dance /əˈbʌndəns/ *n.* [singular, U] *formal* a large quantity of something: *an* ***abundance of*** *information* | *Wild flowers grow* ***in abundance*** *on the hillsides.*

act² *n.* **1** [C] something that you do: *a criminal act* | ***acts of*** *cruelty* | *Police caught the suspect* ***in the act of*** *making a bomb.*

USAGE

Act is always countable, and is used when you mean a particular type of action: *an act of friendship* | *He was caught in the act of stealing.* **Action** can be countable or uncountable: *a kind action* | *What we need now is quick action.*

A.D. **Anno Domini** used in order to show that a date is a particular number of years after the birth of Christ [➡ **B.C.**]: *432 A.D.*

ad·di·tion·al /əˈdɪʃənəl/ *adj.* more than you already have, or more than was agreed or expected [= **extra**]: *We were charged an additional $50 in late fees.* | ***Additional information*** *is available on our website.*

ad·here /ədˈhɪr/ *v.* [I] *formal* to stick firmly to something

adhere to sth *phr. v. formal* to continue to behave according to a particular rule, agreement, or belief: *Not all the states adhered to the treaty.*

ad·mis·si·ble /ədˈmɪsəbəl/ *adj. formal* acceptable or allowed, especially in a court of law [≠ **inadmissible**]: *admissible evidence*

ad·mon·ish /əd'mɑnɪʃ/ *v.* [T] *literary* to tell someone that s/he has done something wrong —**admonishment** *n.* [C,U]

ad·vice /əd'vaɪs/ *n.* [U] an opinion you give someone about what s/he should do: *The book is full of **advice on/about** child care.* | *Can you **give** me some **advice** about buying a house?* | *If I were you, I'd **seek** (=get) some **legal/medical/financial advice**.* | *Did you **follow/take** your father's **advice**?* | *He offered them one **piece of advice**: Don't panic.*

THESAURUS

tip – a helpful piece of advice: *useful tips on healthy eating*
recommendation – advice given to someone, especially about what to do: *Do you have any recommendations about hotels in the city?*
guidance – helpful advice about work, education etc: *His parents should provide more guidance.*

ad·vis·er, **advisor** /əd'vaɪzə/ *n.* [C] someone whose job is to give advice about a particular subject: *a financial adviser*

alert[3] *n.* [C] **1 be on the alert** to be ready to notice and deal with a problem: *Police are **on the alert for** trouble.* **2** a warning to be ready for possible danger: *a flood alert*

an·chor·man /'æŋkə,mæn/, **an·chor·wom·an** /'æŋkə,wʊmən/ *n.* [C] plural **anchormen** /-,mɛn/, **anchorwomen** /-,wɪmɪn/ → ANCHOR[1]

an·y·way /'ɛni,weɪ/ *adv.* **1** in spite of something: *It was raining, but we went anyway.*

SPOKEN PHRASES

2 used in order to continue a story or change the subject of a conversation: *I think she's Lori's age, but anyway, she just had a baby.* | *Anyway, where do you want to go for lunch?* **3** used when you are ending a conversation: *Anyway, I guess I'd better go.* **4** used when you are saying something to support what you have just said:

ar·rears /ə'rɪrz/ *n.* [plural] **1 be in arrears** to owe someone money because your regular payment to him/her is late: *We're six weeks in arrears with the rent.* **2** money that is owed and should already have been paid: *The prime minister promised that all wage arrears would be paid in May.*

beat[1] /bit/ *v.* past tense **beat**, past participle **beaten** /'bit^n/
1 DEFEAT [T] to get more points, votes, etc. than other people in a game or competition: *New York beat Boston 4–1.* | *Stuart usually **beats** me **at** chess.* | *Hank Aaron finally **beat the record** for home runs set by Babe Ruth.*
2 HIT SB [T] to hit someone many times with your hand, a stick, etc.: *He used to come home and beat us.* | *The woman had been **beaten to death**.*

Derived words are shown at the end of an entry.

Useful natural examples show how you can use the word.

Thesaurus boxes help you to increase your vocabulary by showing you words related to the word you are using.

Different spellings are shown at the beginning of an entry.

Collocations are shown before the examples, or highlighted in bold in the examples.

Dots show how words are divided into syllables.

References to other words, and to pictures, are given.

Groups of phrases which are only used in spoken English are explained together, each with its own separate definition.

Idioms and phrases have their own definition, and the meaning of the whole phrase is explained.

Key words are printed in red letters. This shows you which are the most important words to know.

Signposts help you find the meaning you want quickly.

The TOEFL® Test

TOEFL® practice tests are available on the *Longman Dictionary of American English* CD-ROM.

The TOEFL® test is widely used to evaluate the English proficiency of people whose native language is not English.

Scores on the TOEFL test are required for purposes of admission by more than 2,400 colleges and universities in the United States and Canada and by institutions in other countries where English is the language of instruction. Government agencies, scholarship programs, and licensing/certification agencies also use TOEFL scores to evaluate English proficiency.

ISBN
0-13-040895-6 (with answer key)
0-13-040902-2 (without answer key)

A, a

A, a /eɪ/ **1** the first letter of the English alphabet **2** the best GRADE that a student can get in a class or on a test

A /eɪ/ *n.* [C] **1** the best GRADE that a student can get in a class or on a test: ***I got an A** on my math test!* | *Rick was an* ***A student*** (=always received the best grades) *in high school.* **2** the sixth note in the musical SCALE of C, or the musical KEY based on this note

a /ə; *strong* eɪ/ **also an** *indefinite article* **1** used before a noun to show that you are talking about a general type of thing, not a specific thing [➡ **the**]: *Do you have a car?* | *I'll find you a pencil.* **2 a)** one: *a thousand dollars* | *a dozen eggs* **b)** used before some words that show how much of something there is: *a few weeks from now* | *a little water* | *a lot of people* **3** used before a noun that is one of many similar things, people, events, times, etc.: *I'd like to be a teacher.* | *This is a very good wine.* **4** every or each: *A square has 4 sides.* **5 once a week/$100 a day etc.** one time each week, $100 a day, etc. [= **per**] **6** used before two nouns that are frequently mentioned together: *a cup and saucer* | *a knife and fork* **7 a)** used before the -ing form of some verbs when they are used as nouns: *a loud screeching of brakes* **b)** used before some singular nouns that are actions: *Take a look at that!*

GRAMMAR

a, an

If the word that follows starts with a consonant sound, use **a**: *a car* | *a white egg* | *a house* | *I bought a CD today.*

If the word that follows starts with a vowel sound (the sounds shown by the letters a, e, i, o, or u), use **an**: *an apple* | *an orange sweater* | *I waited an hour.*

➔ ANY

AA *n.* **1 Alcoholics Anonymous** an organization for ALCOHOLICS who want to stop drinking alcohol **2 Associate of Arts** a college degree given after two years of study, usually at a COMMUNITY COLLEGE

a·back /ə'bæk/ *adv.* **be taken aback** to be very surprised or shocked: *I was taken aback by her criticism.*

ab·a·cus /'æbəkəs/ *n.* [C] a tool used for counting and calculating, consisting of a frame with small balls that can be slid along on thick wires

a·ban·don /ə'bændən/ *v.* [T] **1** to leave a person or thing, especially one that you are responsible for, and not go back: *How could she abandon her own child?* | *We had to abandon the car and walk the rest of the way.* **2** to stop doing or using something because of problems: *The policy had to be abandoned.* —**abandonment** *n.* [U]

a·ban·doned /ə'bændənd/ *adj.* not being used or taken care of any longer: *an abandoned building*

a·bashed /ə'bæʃt/ *adj.* embarrassed or ashamed: *an abashed grin*

a·bate /ə'beɪt/ *v.* [I] *formal* to become less strong [➡ **unabated**]: *Public anger does not appear to be abating.*

ab·bey /'æbi/ *n.* [C] a large church, with buildings next to it where MONKS and NUNS live

ab·bre·vi·ate /ə'brivi,eɪt/ *v.* [T] *formal* to make a word, story, etc. shorter: *"Street" is often* ***abbreviated as*** *"St.".*

ab·bre·vi·a·tion /ə,brivi'eɪʃən/ *n.* [C] the short form of a word used in writing. For example, Mr. is the abbreviation of Mister

ABC *n.* **1 ABC's** [plural] the letters of the English alphabet as taught to children **2** [U] **American Broadcasting Company** one of the national companies that broadcasts television and radio programs in the U.S.

ab·di·cate /'æbdɪ,keɪt/ *v.* [I,T] **1** to officially give up the position of being king or queen **2 abdicate (your) responsibility** *formal* to refuse to continue being responsible for something —**abdication** /,æbdɪ'keɪʃən/ *n.* [C,U]

ab·do·men /'æbdəmən/ *n.* [C] *technical* the front part of your body between your chest and the top of your legs, including your stomach —**abdominal** /æb'dɑmənəl, əb-/ *adj.*

ab·duct /əb'dʌkt, æb-/ *v.* [T] to take someone away by force [= **kidnap**] —**abduction** /-'dʌkʃən/ *n.* [C,U]

a·ber·ra·tion /,æbə'reɪʃən/ *n.* [C,U] something that is completely different from what usually happens or from what someone usually does: *The coach said the team's poor performance was an aberration.*

a·bet /ə'bɛt/ *v.* past tense and past participle **abetted**, present participle **abetting** [T] ➔ **aid and abet** at AID²

ab·hor /əb'hɔr, æb-/ *v.* past tense and past participle **abhorred**, present participle **abhorring** [T] *formal* to hate something, especially because you think it is morally wrong: *I abhor discrimination of any kind.*

THESAURUS

hate, **can't stand**, **detest**, **loathe**, **despise**

➔ see Thesaurus box at HATE¹

ab·hor·rent /əb'hɔrənt, -'hɑr-, æb-/ *adj. formal* behavior or beliefs that are abhorrent are unacceptable because they are morally wrong —**abhorrence** *n.* [U]

a·bide /əˈbaɪd/ *v.* [T] **can't abide sb/sth** to hate someone or something very much: *I can't abide his stupid jokes.*

abide by sth *phr. v.* to obey a law, agreement, etc.: *If you're going to live here, you will abide by my rules.*

a·bid·ing /əˈbaɪdɪŋ/ *adj. literary* continuing for a long time and not likely to change: *Our father had an **abiding love** for nature.*

A

a·bil·i·ty /əˈbɪləṭi/ *n.* plural **abilities** [C,U] the state of being able to do something, or your level of skill at doing something: *A manager must have the **ability to** communicate well.* | *a young girl with great **musical/athletic/acting, etc. ability*** | *She worked **to the best of her ability*** (=as well as she could) *in school.*

THESAURUS

skill – something that you do very well because you have learned and practiced it: *a class that will help you improve your writing skills*
talent – a natural ability to do something well: *He has a remarkable musical talent.*
knack informal – a natural ability to do something well: *Kate has a knack for decorating.*

ab·ject /ˈæbdʒɛkt, æbˈdʒɛkt/ *adj.* **1 abject poverty/failure/terror/despair etc.** the state of being extremely poor, unsuccessful, frightened, unhappy, etc. **2 abject apology** an abject apology shows that you are ashamed of what you have done —**abjectly** *adv.*

a·blaze /əˈbleɪz/ *adj. written* burning strongly with a lot of flames: *During the riot, a police car was **set ablaze**.*

a·ble /ˈeɪbəl/ *adj.* **1 able to do sth a)** having the skill, strength, knowledge, etc. to do something: *I was just able to reach the handle.* **b)** in a situation in which it is possible for you to do something: *Will you be able to come tonight?* **2** smart or good at doing something: *an able student*

ab·nor·mal /æbˈnɔrməl/ *adj.* different from usual in a way that is strange, worrying, or dangerous [**≠ normal**]: *abnormal levels of chemicals in the water* | *abnormal behavior* —**abnormally** *adv.*: *an abnormally high heart rate* —**abnormality** /ˌæbnɔrˈmæləṭi, -nɚ-/ *n.* [C,U]

a·board /əˈbɔrd/ *adv., prep.* on or onto a ship, airplane, or train: *The plane crashed, killing all 200 people aboard.* | *They were prevented from **going aboard**.*

a·bode /əˈboʊd/ *n.* [C] *formal* the place where you live

a·bol·ish /əˈbɑlɪʃ/ *v.* [T] to officially end a law, system, etc.: *plans to abolish the death penalty* —**abolition** /ˌæbəˈlɪʃən/ *n.* [U] *the abolition of slavery* —**abolitionist** *n.* [C]

a·bom·i·na·ble /əˈbɑmənəbəl/ *adj.* extremely bad or of very bad quality

ab·o·rig·i·nal /ˌæbəˈrɪdʒənəl/ *adj.* **1 Aboriginal** relating to the Australian aborigines **2** relating to the people or animals that have existed in a place from the earliest times

ab·o·rig·i·ne, **Aborigine** /ˌæbəˈrɪdʒəni/ *n.* [C] a member of the people who have lived in Australia from the earliest times

a·bort /əˈbɔrt/ *v.* [T] **1** to stop an activity because it would be difficult or dangerous to continue: *The Reagan administration had to abort plans to sell public lands.* **2** to deliberately end a PREGNANCY when the baby is still too young to live

a·bor·tion /əˈbɔrʃən/ *n.* [C,U] the act of aborting a baby: *She decided to **have** an **abortion**.*

a·bor·tive /əˈbɔrṭɪv/ *adj.* an abortive action is not successful or not finished: *abortive attempts to learn a language*

a·bound /əˈbaʊnd/ *v.* [I] *literary* to exist in large numbers: *Coffee shops **abound in** American small towns.*

a·bout[1] /əˈbaʊt/ *prep.* **1** relating to a particular subject: *a book about horses* | *We were talking about the stock market.* | *I'll tell you **all about*** (=everything about) *it later.* | *About that CD. I need it back by tomorrow.*

THESAURUS

on – if a book, lecture, conference, etc. is **on** a particular subject, it relates to it: *a seminar on résumé writing*
concerning/regarding formal – about or relating to something: *The police want to ask you some questions concerning the night of April 4th.*
re – used in business letters to introduce the subject that you are going to write about: *Re your letter of June 10...*

2 in the nature or character of a person or thing: ***There's something** weird **about** that guy.* **3 what about/how about** *spoken* **a)** used in order to make a suggestion: *How about coming to my house after we're done here?* **b)** used to ask a question concerning another person or thing involved in a situation: *What about Jack? Should we invite him?*

about[2] *adv.* **1** a little more or less than a number or amount [**= approximately**]: *I live about 10 miles from here.* | *We need to leave at about 7:30.*

THESAURUS

approximately – a little more or a little less than a number, amount, distance, or time: *A kilo is approximately 2 pounds.*
around – used when guessing a number, amount, time, etc., without being exact: *Around 50 people came to the meeting.*
roughly – a little more or a little less than a number, used when you are saying a number you know is not exact: *Roughly 7,000 vehicles a day cross the border.*

or so – used when you cannot be exact about a number, amount, or period of time: *Every month or so he drives up to visit his parents.*

2 almost: *Dinner's **just about** ready.*

about[3] *adj.* **1 be about to do sth** if someone is about to do something, or if something is about to happen, s/he will do it or it will happen very soon: *I was about to step into the shower when the phone rang.* | *The parade is about to start.* **2 not be about to do sth** *informal* used to emphasize that you will not do something: *I'm not about to give him any more money!*

a·bove /ə'bʌv/ *adv., prep.* **1** in or to a higher position than something else [≠ **below**]: *Raise your arm above your head.* | *The sound came from the room above.* **2** more than a number, amount, or level [≠ **below**]: *Temperatures rose above freezing today.* | *Males aged 18 **and above** could be drafted.* **3** louder than other sounds: *He couldn't hear her voice above the noise.* **4** higher in rank, more powerful, or more important: *He never rose above the rank of corporal.* **5 above all** *formal* most importantly: *Above all, I would like to thank my parents.* **6 be above suspicion/criticism etc.** to be so honest or good that no one can doubt or criticize you **7** *formal* before, in the same piece of writing [≠ **below**]: *The graph above shows the growth in pollution levels.*

a·bove·board /ə'bʌvˌbɔrd/ *adj.* [not before noun] honest and legal: *The agreement seems to be aboveboard.*

a·bra·sion /ə'breɪʒən/ *n.* **1** [C] an area on your skin that has been injured by rubbing against something hard: *She was treated for cuts and abrasions.* **2** [U] the process of rubbing a surface very hard so that it becomes damaged

a·bra·sive /ə'breɪsɪv, -zɪv/ *adj.* **1** rude and annoying: *an abrasive personality* **2** having a rough surface that can be used to clean something or make it smooth —**abrasively** *adv.*

a·breast /ə'brɛst/ *adv.* **1 keep abreast of sth** to make sure that you know the most recent facts about a subject: *Please keep us abreast of his progress.* **2** next to someone or something, usually in a line, and facing the same direction: *Patrol cars were lined up four abreast.*

a·bridged /ə'brɪdʒd/ *adj.* an abridged form of a book, play, etc. has been made shorter [≠ **unabridged**]: *the **abridged version** of the dictionary*

a·broad /ə'brɔd/ *adv.* in or to a foreign country: *He suggested that his son **go abroad** for a year.* | *There are more than a million Americans **living abroad**.*

a·brupt /ə'brʌpt/ *adj.* **1** sudden and unexpected: *an **abrupt change** in the attitudes of voters* **2** not polite or friendly, especially because you do not want to waste time: *She was very abrupt on the phone.* —**abruptly** *adv.*: *The train stopped abruptly.*

abs /æbz/ *n.* [plural] *informal* the muscles on your ABDOMEN (=stomach): *exercises that strengthen your abs*

ABS *n.* [U] **anti-lock braking system** a type of car BRAKE that makes the car easier to control when you have to stop very suddenly

ab·scess /'æbsɛs/ *n.* [C] a swollen place on your body that is infected and contains a yellow liquid

ab·scond /əb'skɑnd, æb-/ *v.* [I] *formal* to leave a place without permission, or to leave somewhere after stealing something

ab·sence /'æbsəns/ *n.* **1** [C,U] an occasion when you are not in a place where people expect you to be, or the time that you are away: *The vice president will handle things **in** my **absence**.* | *frequent **absences from** work* **2** [U] the lack of something: *a complete **absence of** physical evidence*

ab·sent /'æbsənt/ *adj.* **1** not at work, school, a meeting, etc. because you are sick or decide not to go [≠ **present**]: *Ten children were **absent from** class today.* **2 absent look/smile/expression** a look, etc. that shows you are not thinking about what is happening

ab·sen·tee /ˌæbsən'ti/ *n.* [C] *formal* someone who is supposed to be in a place but is not there

ˌabsentee 'ballot *n.* [C] a process by which people can vote by mail before an election because they will be away during the election

ab·sen·tee·ism /ˌæbsən'tiɪzəm/ *n.* [U] regular absence from work or school without a good reason

ab·sent·ly /'æbsəntˀli/ *adv.* in a way that shows you are not interested in or not thinking about what is happening: *Jason patted his son absently.*

ˌabsent-'minded *adj.* often forgetting or not noticing things because you are thinking of something else —**absent-mindedly** *adv.*

ab·so·lute /'æbsəˌlut, ˌæbsə'lut/ *adj.* **1** complete or total: *The king has **absolute power**.* | *I have absolute confidence in you.* **2** used to emphasize your opinion: *The show was an absolute disaster.* | *He's talking absolute nonsense.* **3** definite and not likely to change: *I can't give you any absolute promises.*

ab·so·lute·ly /ˌæbsə'lutli, 'æbsəˌlutli/ *adv.* **1** completely or totally: *Are you absolutely sure?* | *We had **absolutely nothing** in common.*

THESAURUS

completely, **totally**, **entirely**, **utterly**
➔ see Thesaurus box at COMPLETELY

2 Absolutely *spoken* said when you agree completely with someone: *"Can I talk to you for a minute?" "Absolutely, come in."* **3 Absolutely not!** *spoken* said when you disagree completely with someone or when you do not want someone to do something

ab·solve /əb'zɑlv, -'sɑlv/ *v.* [T] *formal* to say publicly that someone should not be blamed for something, or to forgive him/her: *He cannot be* ***absolved of*** *all responsibility for the accident.*

ab·sorb /əb'sɔrb, -'zɔrb/ *v.* [T] **1** if something absorbs liquid, heat, etc., it takes it in through its surface: *The towel absorbed most of the water.* **2 be absorbed in sth** to be interested in something so much that you do not pay attention to other things: *He's completely absorbed in his job.* **3** to learn, understand, and remember new information: *She's a good student who absorbs ideas quickly.* —**absorption** /-ɔrpʃən/ *n.* [U]

A

ab·sorb·ent /əb'sɔrbənt, -'zɔr-/ *adj.* something that is absorbent can take in liquid through its surface: *absorbent paper towel*

ab·sorb·ing /əb'sɔrbɪŋ, -'zɔr-/ *adj.* so interesting that you do not notice or think about other things: *an absorbing article*

THESAURUS

interesting, **fascinating**, **intriguing**, **compelling**
➔ see Thesaurus box at INTERESTING

ab·stain /əb'steɪn/ *v.* [I] **1** to deliberately not vote for or against something: *Three members of the committee abstained.* **2** to not do something that you would normally enjoy doing: *For two weeks I* ***abstained from*** *alcohol.* —**abstention** /əb'stɛnʃən/ *n.* [C,U]

ab·sti·nence /'æbstənəns/ *n.* [U] the practice of not doing something you enjoy, especially for health or religious reasons —**abstinent** *adj.*

ab·stract¹ /əb'strækt, æb-, 'æbstrækt/ *adj.* **1** based on ideas rather than specific examples or real events: *Beauty is an* ***abstract idea.*** | *an abstract argument about justice* **2** abstract art is made of shapes and patterns that do not look like real things or people ➔ see picture at PAINTING —**abstraction** /əb'strækʃən/ *n.* [C,U]

ab·stract² /'æbstrækt/ *n.* [C] a short written statement containing only the most important ideas in a speech, article, etc.

ab·surd /əb'sɚd, -'zɚd/ *adj.* completely unreasonable or silly: *an absurd situation* | *It's absurd to pay all that money for something you're only going to use once.* —**absurdly** *adv.* —**absurdity** *n.* [C,U]

a·bun·dance /ə'bʌndəns/ *n.* [singular, U] *formal* a large quantity of something: *an* ***abundance of*** *information* | *Wild flowers grow* ***in abundance*** *on the hillsides.*

a·bun·dant /ə'bʌndənt/ *adj.* more than enough in quantity [**= plentiful**]: *an abundant supply of fresh fruit*

a·bun·dant·ly /ə'bʌndəntli/ *adv.* **1 abundantly clear** very easy to understand: *Kaplan* ***made it abundantly clear*** *that we weren't welcome.* **2** in large quantities: *Lavender will grow abundantly with little water.*

a·buse¹ /ə'byus/ *n.* **1** [U] cruel or violent treatment of someone: *accusations of* ***child abuse*** | *victims of* ***sexual abuse*** **2** [C,U] the use of something in a way it should not be used: *the President's* ***abuse of*** *power* | ***drug/alcohol abuse*** (=the practice of taking illegal drugs or drinking too much) **3** [U] cruel or offensive things someone says when s/he is angry: *People were* ***shouting abuse at*** *the soldiers.*

a·buse² /ə'byuz/ *v.* [T] **1** to do cruel or violent things to someone: *He used to get drunk and abuse his wife.* | *She was* ***sexually abused*** *as a child.* **2** to use something too much or in the wrong way: *He* ***abused*** *his* ***position*** *of authority by taking advantage of his students.* | *She had been* ***abusing drugs/alcohol*** *since she was 12.* **3** to say cruel or unkind things to someone

a·bu·sive /ə'byusɪv/ *adj.* using cruel words or physical violence: *an abusive husband*

a·bys·mal /ə'bɪzməl/ *adj.* very bad: *the country's abysmal record on human rights*

THESAURUS

bad, **awful**, **terrible**, **horrible**, **appalling**, **horrific**, **lousy**, **horrendous**, **atrocious**
➔ see Thesaurus box at BAD¹

a·byss /ə'bɪs/ *n.* [C] **1** *literary* a very dangerous or frightening situation: *The country might plunge into the* ***abyss of*** *economic ruin.* **2** a very deep hole or space that seems to have no bottom

AC *n.* [U] **1 alternating current** the type of electric current used in buildings for electrical equipment [➡ **DC**] **2** the abbreviation of AIR CONDITIONING

ac·a·de·mi·a /ˌækə'dimiə/ *n.* [U] the activities and work done at universities and colleges, or the teachers and students involved in it

ac·a·dem·ic¹ /ˌækə'dɛmɪk◂/ *adj.* relating to education, especially in a college or university: *The academic year starts September 3rd.* | *an attempt to raise academic standards*

academic² *n.* [C] a teacher in a college or university

a·cad·e·my /ə'kædəmi/ *n.* plural **academies** [C] **1** a school or college that trains students in a special subject or skill: *a military academy* **2** an organization of people who want to encourage the progress of art, science, literature, etc.

ac·cel·er·ate /ək'sɛləˌreɪt/ *v.* **1** [I] if a vehicle or its driver accelerates, it moves faster ➔ see Topic box at DRIVE¹ **2** [I,T] to happen at a faster rate than usual, or to make something do this: *We tried to accelerate the process by heating the chemicals.* —**acceleration** /əkˌsɛlə'reɪʃən/ *n.* [U]

ac·cel·er·a·tor /ək'sɛləˌreɪt̬ɚ/ *n.* [C] the part of a car that you press with your foot to make it go faster

ac·cent¹ /'æksɛnt/ *n.* **1** [C] a way of pronouncing words that someone has because of where s/he was born or lives: *a strong southern accent* | *a*

German/Korean etc. accent → see Thesaurus box at LANGUAGE **2** [C] the part of a word that you emphasize when you say it **3** [C] a mark, usually written above some letters (such as é or â), that shows how to pronounce that letter **4** [singular] the extra importance or emphasis given to something: *In this year's guide, there is an* ***accent on*** *restaurants that offer value for money.*

ac·cent² /ˈæksɛnt, ækˈsɛnt/ *v.* [T] to emphasize a word in speech

ac·cen·tu·ate /əkˈsɛntʃuˌeɪt, æk-/ *v.* [T] to make something easier to notice: *Her scarf accentuated the blue of her eyes.*

THESAURUS

emphasize, **stress**, **highlight**, **underline**, **underscore**
→ see Thesaurus box at EMPHASIZE

ac·cept /əkˈsɛpt/ *v.* **1** [I,T] to take something that someone offers you, or to agree to do something that someone asks you to do [≠ **refuse**]: *They offered him the job, and he accepted.* | *Mr. Ryan wouldn't* ***accept*** *any money* ***from*** *us.* | *They* ***accepted*** *our* ***invitation*** *to dinner.* | *She* ***accepted*** *his* ***offer*** *to repair the damage on her car.*

THESAURUS

When someone asks you to do something, you **agree** to do it. Do not say "accept to do something": *The U.S. has agreed to provide aid.* You **accept** an invitation, a job, an offer, etc.: *Schroeder accepted a job offer to teach at Princeton University.*

COMMUNICATION

Ways of accepting

yes, please: *"Would you like some wine?" "Yes, please."*
I'd love to: *"Why don't you come over for dinner?" "Thanks, I'd love to."*
that sounds nice/good/great/(like) fun: *"Let's go see a movie." "That sounds great."*
sure spoken: *"Do you want to come with us?" "Sure."*
why not? informal spoken: *"Try one of these chocolates." "Oh, why not."*
→ AGREE, OFFER, REFUSE

2 [T] to admit that something bad or difficult is true, and continue with your normal life: *He's not going to change, and you just have to accept it.* | *I* ***accept that*** *we've made mistakes.* | *It took Ann months to accept her son's death.*

THESAURUS

tolerate, **put up with**, **live with**
→ see Thesaurus box at TOLERATE

3 [T] to believe something, because someone has persuaded you to believe it: *The jury accepted his story.*

THESAURUS

believe, **take sb's word**, **swallow**, **fall for**, **buy**
→ see Thesaurus box at BELIEVE

4 [T] to let someone join an organization, university, etc. [≠ **reject**]: *I've been* ***accepted at/to*** *Harvard.* **5** [T] to let someone new become part of a group and to treat him/her in the same way as other members: *At first the kids at school didn't accept him.* **6** [T] to let customers pay for something in a particular way [= **take**]: *We don't accept credit cards.* **7 accept responsibility/blame for sth** *formal* to admit that you are responsible for something bad that has happened: *Benson accepts full responsibility for his crimes.*

ac·cept·a·ble /əkˈsɛptəbəl/ *adj.* **1** good enough for a particular purpose: *a deal that is* ***acceptable to*** *all sides* | *a cheap and acceptable substitute for rubber*

THESAURUS

satisfactory, **good enough**, **adequate**, **all right**, **okay**
→ see Thesaurus box at SATISFACTORY

2 acceptable behavior is considered morally or socially good enough: *Smoking used to be more* ***socially acceptable.*** | ***It is*** *now considered* ***acceptable for*** *mothers* ***to*** *work outside the home.* —**acceptability** /əkˌsɛptəˈbɪləti/ *n.* [U]

ac·cept·ance /əkˈsɛptəns/ *n.* [U] **1** the act of agreeing that something is right or true: *the* ***acceptance of*** *Einstein's theory* **2** the act of agreeing to accept something that is offered to you: *a candidate's* ***acceptance of*** *illegal contributions* **3** the process of allowing someone to become part of a group: *the immigrants' gradual* ***acceptance into*** *the community* **4** the act of deciding that there is nothing you can do to change a bad situation **5 gain/find acceptance** to become popular: *Home computers first gained wide acceptance in the 1980s.*

ac·cess¹ /ˈæksɛs/ *n.* [U] **1** the right to enter a place, use something, see someone, etc.: *Anyone with* ***access to*** *the Internet can visit our website.* | *Do you* ***have access to*** *a car?* **2** the way you enter a building or get to a place, or how easy this is: *The only* ***access to*** *the building is through the parking lot.* | *The law requires businesses to improve* ***access for*** *disabled customers.* → **gain access** at GAIN

access² *v.* [T] to find and use information, especially on a computer: *I couldn't access the file.*

ac·ces·si·ble /əkˈsɛsəbəl/ *adj.* **1** easy to reach or get into [≠ **inaccessible**]: *The park is not* ***accessible by*** *road.* **2** easy to obtain or use: *A college education wasn't* ***accessible to*** *women until the 1920s.* **3** easy to understand and enjoy: *I thought his last book was more accessible.* —**accessibility** /əkˌsɛsəˈbɪləti/ *n.* [U]

ac·ces·so·ry /əkˈsɛsəri/ *n.* plural **accessories** [C] **1** something such as a belt, jewelry, etc. that you wear or carry because it is attractive: *a dress with matching accessories* **2** something that you can add to a machine, tool, car, etc. which is not necessary but is useful or attractive **3** *law* someone who helps a criminal

ac·ci·dent /'æksədənt, -ˌdɛnt/ *n.* [C] **1** a situation in which someone is hurt or something is damaged without anyone intending it to happen: *She didn't do it on purpose, **it was an accident**.* | *Her parents were killed in a **car/traffic/auto, etc. accident**.* | *Ken **had** an **accident** on the way home from work.*

THESAURUS

crash/collision – an accident in which a vehicle hits something else
disaster – something that happens which causes a lot of harm or suffering
catastrophe – a very serious disaster
wreck – an accident in which a car or train is badly damaged
pile-up – an accident that involves several cars or trucks
mishap – a small accident that does not have a very serious effect
fender-bender informal – a car accident in which little damage is done

2 by accident in a way that is not intended or planned: *I discovered by accident that he'd lied to me.*

ac·ci·den·tal /ˌæksə'dɛntəl/ *adj.* happening without being planned or intended [≠ **deliberate**]: *He was killed in an accidental shooting.* —**accidentally** *adv.*: *I accidentally locked myself out of the house.*

'accident-ˌprone *adj.* someone who is accident-prone often has accidents

ac·claim[1] /ə'kleɪm/ *v.* [T] to praise someone or something publicly: *Landry was acclaimed as the best coach in football.*

acclaim[2] *n.* [U] strong praise for a person, idea, book, etc.: *Morrison's novels have won **critical acclaim**.*

ac·claimed /ə'kleɪmd/ *adj.* praised by a lot of people: *Rodzinki's latest film has been **highly/widely acclaimed**.*

ac·cli·mate /'ækləˌmeɪt/ **also ac·cli·ma·tize** /ə'klaɪməˌtaɪz/ *v.* [I,T] to become used to the weather, way of living, etc. in a new place, or to make someone do this: *It takes the astronauts a day to **get acclimated to** conditions in space.* —**acclimatization** /əˌklaɪmət̬ə'zeɪʃən/ *n.* [U]

ac·co·lade /'ækəˌleɪd/ *n.* [C] praise and approval given to someone, or a prize given to someone for his/her work

ac·com·mo·date /ə'kɑməˌdeɪt/ *v.* [T] **1** to have enough space for a particular number of people or things: *The hall can accommodate 300 people.* **2** to give someone a place to stay, live, or work: *A new dorm was built to accommodate students.* **3** *formal* to provide someone with what s/he needs, or do what s/he wants: *The new road will accommodate the extra traffic in summertime.*

ac·com·mo·dat·ing /ə'kɑməˌdeɪt̬ɪŋ/ *adj.* helpful and willing to do what someone else wants

ac·com·mo·da·tion /əˌkɑmə'deɪʃən/ *n.* **1 accommodations** [plural] a place to live, stay, or work: *hotel accommodations* **2** [singular, U] *formal* a way of solving a problem between two people or groups so that both are satisfied

ac·com·pa·ni·ment /ə'kʌmpənimənt/ *n.* [C] **1** music played while someone sings or plays another instrument: *a piano accompaniment* **2** *formal* something that is good to eat or drink with another food: *This wine makes a nice **accompaniment to** fish.*

ac·com·pa·nist /ə'kʌmpənɪst/ *n.* [C] someone who plays a musical instrument while another person sings or plays the main tune

ac·com·pa·ny /ə'kʌmpəni/ *v.* past tense and past participle **accompanied** [T] **1** *formal* to go somewhere with someone: *Children under 12 must be **accompanied by** an adult.* | *She needed someone to **accompany** her **to** the doctor.* **2** to happen or exist at the same time: *Tonight, heavy rains will be accompanied by high winds.* **3** to play music while someone is playing or singing the main tune

ac·com·plice /ə'kɑmplɪs/ *n.* [C] someone who helps a criminal do something wrong

ac·com·plish /ə'kɑmplɪʃ/ *v.* [T] to succeed in doing something: *We've accomplished our goal of raising $45,000.*

ac·com·plished /ə'kɑmplɪʃt/ *adj.* very skillful: *an accomplished musician*

ac·com·plish·ment /ə'kɑmplɪʃmənt/ *n.* **1** [U] the act of accomplishing something: *the **accomplishment of** policy goals* **2** [C] something you can do well: *Playing the piano is one of her many accomplishments.*

ac·cord[1] /ə'kɔrd/ *n.* **1 of sb's own accord** without being asked or forced to do something: *I didn't say anything. He left of his own accord.* **2** *formal* [C] an official agreement between countries **3 in accord (with sth)** *formal* in agreement with someone or something: *These results are **in accord with** earlier research.*

accord[2] *v. formal* [T] to give someone or something special attention or a particular type of treatment: *He was accorded the honor in 1972.*

ac·cord·ance /ə'kɔrdns/ *n.* **in accordance with sth** according to a system or rule: *He placed pebbles on the grave, in accordance with Jewish tradition.*

ac·cord·ing·ly /ə'kɔrdɪŋli/ *adv.* **1** in a way that is appropriate for a particular situation, or based on what someone has done or said: *If you break the rules, you will be punished accordingly.* **2** *formal* as a result of something [= **therefore**]: *He* *knows how the Democrats like to work. Accordingly, he can help the Republicans defeat them.*

ac'cording to *prep.* **1** as shown by something or said by someone: *According to our records, you still have six of our books.* | *The president is still very popular, according to recent public opinion polls.* **2** in a way that is directly affected or determined by something: *You will be paid according to the amount of work you do.* | *Everything* ***went according to plan.***

ac·cor·di·on /ə'kɔrdiən/ *n.* [C] a musical instrument that is played by pulling the sides and pushing buttons to produce different notes

ac·cost /ə'kɔst, ə'kɑst/ *v.* [T] *formal* to go up to someone you do not know and speak to him/her in an impolite or threatening way: *I was accosted by a man asking for money.*

ac·count[1] /ə'kaʊnt/ *n.* **1** [C] a written or spoken description of an event or situation: *Can you* ***give us an account of*** *what happened?* | *a* ***detailed account*** *of the attack* | ***By/from all accounts*** (=according to what everyone says), *Frank was once a great player.* **2** [C] **also bank account** an arrangement with a bank that allows you to keep your money there and take money out when you need it: *I don't have much money in my account.* | *I'd like to* ***open an account****, please.* | ***checking account*** (=one that you can take money out of at anytime) | ***savings account*** (=one in which you save money so that the amount increases)

TOPIC

You **open** an **account** at a **bank**. You **pay**, **put**, or **deposit money into** your **account**. You **take money out of** your **account** or **withdraw money from** your **account**. You can do this at a bank or you can use an **ATM** (=a machine that you use with a card). An ATM is also called a **cash machine**.
When there is money in your account, you **have a balance of** that amount of money, or you have that amount **in your account**. When the amount of money in your account is less than zero, you are **overdrawn**.
Many banks have an **online banking** service which allows you to check the balance in your account, make payments, etc. using a computer that is connected to the Internet.

THESAURUS

checking account – one that you use regularly for making payments, etc.
savings account – one where you leave money for longer periods of time, and which pays you a higher rate of interest than a checking account
joint account – one that is used by two people, usually a husband and wife
online account – one which allows you to check the balance in your account, make payments, etc. by using a computer that is connected to the Internet

3 take sth into account/take account of sth to consider particular facts when judging or deciding something: *The price does not take taxes into account.* **4** [C,U] an arrangement with a shop or company that allows you to buy goods and pay for them later: *buying a dishwasher* ***on account*** | *Please* ***settle your account*** (=pay all you owe) *as soon as possible.* | *I'd like to* ***charge*** *this* ***to*** *my* ***account*** (=pay using this arrangement). **5 accounts** [plural] a record of the money that a company has received and spent: *The accounts for last year showed a profit of $2 million.* **6** [C] a company or organization that regularly buys goods or a service from another company over a long period of time: *Our sales manager won five new accounts this year.* **7 not on my/his etc. account** *spoken* not for me or because of me: *Don't stay up late on my account.* **8 on no account** *formal* used in order to say that someone must not do something: *On no account should anyone go near the building.*

account[2] *v.* [T]

account for sth *phr. v.* to be the reason for something, or to explain the reason for something: *How do you account for the $20 that's missing?*

ac·count·a·ble /ə'kaʊntəbəl/ *adj.* [not before noun] responsible for what you do and willing to explain it: *If anything happens to Max, I'll* ***hold you accountable*** (=consider you responsible). —**accountability** /əˌkaʊntə'bɪləṭi/ *n.* [U]

ac·count·ant /ə'kaʊntənt, ə'kaʊnt̚nt/ *n.* [C] someone whose job is to write or check financial records

ac·count·ing /ə'kaʊntɪŋ/ *n.* [U] the job of being an accountant

ac·cred·it·ed /ə'krɛdɪṭɪd/ *adj.* having official approval: *an accredited college* —**accreditation** /əˌkrɛdə'teɪʃən/ *n.* [U]

ac·crue /ə'kru/ *v.* [I,T] to increase over a period of time: *tax benefits that* ***accrue to*** *investors*

ac·cu·mu·late /ə'kyumyəˌleɪt/ *v.* [I,T] to gradually increase in amount, or to make something do this: *Dust had accumulated in the corners of the room.* | *Myers accumulated almost $700,000.* —**accumulation** /əˌkyumyə'leɪʃən/ *n.* [C,U]

ac·cu·ra·cy /'ækyərəsi/ *n.* [U] the quality of being accurate: *The bombs can be aimed* ***with*** *amazing* ***accuracy.***

ac·cu·rate /'ækyərɪt/ *adj.* **1** correct in every detail [≠ **inaccurate**]: *the most accurate information available* | *These figures are no longer accurate.*

THESAURUS

right, correct
➔ see Thesaurus box at RIGHT[1]

2 an accurate shot, throw, etc. succeeds in hitting the thing that it is aimed at —**accurately** *adv.*: *He estimated the cost of repairs pretty accurately.*

A

ac·cu·sa·tion /ˌækyəˈzeɪʃən/ *n.* [C] a statement saying that someone has done something wrong or illegal: *Serious* ***accusations*** *have been made* ***against*** *the Attorney General.* | *The boy's parents* ***face accusations*** (=are accused of) *of neglect and abuse.*

A

> **THESAURUS**
>
> **allegation** – a statement that someone has done something illegal, which has not been proved: *He has denied the allegations of wrongdoing.*
> **charge** – a statement that says that someone has done something illegal or bad: *The charges against her were dismissed.*
> **indictment** law – an official written statement saying that someone has done something illegal: *He is under indictment for credit card fraud.*

ac·cuse /əˈkyuz/ *v.* [T] to say that someone has done something wrong or illegal: *Norton was* ***accused of*** *murder.* | *Are you accusing me of cheating?* —**accuser** *n.* [C]

> **THESAURUS**
>
> **allege** – to say that something is true though it has not been proved: *Ms. Ruiz alleges that she was harassed.*
> **charge** – to state officially that someone might be guilty of a crime: *He was charged with murder.* charged with murder.
> **indict** law – to officially charge someone with a crime: *He was indicted on charges of fraud.*

ac·cused /əˈkyuzd/ *n. law* **the accused** the person or people who are accused of a crime in a court of law

ac·cus·tomed /əˈkʌstəmd/ *adj. formal* **1 be accustomed to (doing) sth** to be used to something and accept it as normal: *Ed's eyes quickly* ***grew/became/got accustomed to*** *the dark.* **2** [only before noun] *formal* usual: *We sat at our accustomed table.* —**accustom** *v.* [T]

ace¹ /eɪs/ *n.* [C] **1** a PLAYING CARD with one mark on it, that has the highest or lowest value in a game: *the* ***ace of*** *spades* ➔ see picture at PLAYING CARD **2** a SERVE (=first hit) in tennis or VOLLEYBALL that is so good that your opponent cannot hit it back **3** someone who is extremely skillful at doing something: *motorcycle ace Jeremy McGrath* | *an ace pitcher* ➔ see Thesaurus box at GOOD¹

ace² *v.* [T] *spoken* to do very well on a test, a piece of written work, etc.: *Danny aced the spelling test.*

a·cer·bic /əˈsɚbɪk/ *adj.* criticizing someone or something in an intelligent but cruel way: *an acerbic wit*

ache¹ /eɪk/ *n.* [C] a continuous pain: *I* ***have a headache/backache/toothache etc.*** —**achy** *adj.*: *My arm feels all achy.*

ache² *v.* [I] **1** to feel a continuous pain: *I ache all over.*

> **THESAURUS**
>
> **hurt**, **throb**, **sting**
> ➔ see Thesaurus box at HURT¹

2 to want to do or have something very much: *Jenny was* ***aching to*** *go home.*

a·chieve /əˈtʃiv/ *v.* [T] to succeed in getting a good result or in doing something you want: *You'll never achieve anything if you don't work harder.* —**achiever** *n.* [C] *a high achiever* —**achievable** *adj.*

a·chieve·ment /əˈtʃivmənt/ *n.* **1** [C] something good and impressive that you succeed in doing: *Winning the championship is quite an achievement.* **2** [U] success in doing or getting what you worked for: *the* ***achievement of*** *a goal*

ac·id¹ /ˈæsɪd/ *n.* [C,U] a liquid chemical substance. Some types of acid can burn holes in things or damage your skin: *hydrochloric acid*

acid² *adj.* using humor in an unkind way or saying cruel things: *Everyone fears her acid tongue.*

a·cid·ic /əˈsɪdɪk/ *adj.* **1** having a very sour taste **2** containing acid —**acidity** /əˈsɪdəṭi/ *n.* [U]

ˌacid ˈrain *n.* [U] rain that can damage the environment because it contains acid from factory smoke, waste gases from cars and trucks, etc.

> **TOPIC**
>
> **environment**, **pollution**, **the greenhouse effect**, **global warming**, **deforestation**, **environmentally friendly**, **eco-friendly**, **recycle**, **biodegradable**, **organic**
> ➔ see Topic box at ENVIRONMENT

ac·knowl·edge /əkˈnɑlɪdʒ/ *v.* [T] **1** to accept or admit that something is true or official: *Angie* ***acknowledged (that)*** *she had made a mistake.* | *They are refusing to acknowledge the court's decision.* **2** to recognize how good or important someone or something is: *It is* ***acknowledged as*** *the finest restaurant in London.* | *He's widely* ***acknowledged to be*** *the best surgeon in his field.* **3** to let someone know that you have received something from him/her: *She never acknowledged my letter.* **4** to show someone that you have seen him/her or heard what s/he has said: *Tina didn't even acknowledge me.*

ac·knowl·edg·ment /əkˈnɑlɪdʒmənt/ *n.* **1** [C,U] the act of admitting or accepting that something is true: *Simons resigned following his* ***acknowledgment of*** *illegal trading.* **2** [C] a letter you write telling someone that you have received something s/he sent to you

ac·ne /ˈækni/ *n.* [U] a skin problem that causes spots to appear on the face and is common among young people

a·corn /ˈeɪkɔrn/ *n.* [C] the nut of an OAK tree ➔ see picture at PLANT¹

acoustic

a·cous·tic /ə'kustɪk/ *adj.* **1** relating to sound and the way people hear things **2** an acoustic musical instrument is not electric: *an acoustic guitar*

a·cous·tics /ə'kustɪks/ *n.* [plural] the way in which the shape and size of a room affect the quality of the sound you can hear in it

ac·quaint /ə'kweɪnt/ *v.* **acquaint yourself with sth** *formal* to deliberately find out about something: *We have already acquainted ourselves with the facts.*

ac·quaint·ance /ə'kweɪnt˺ns/ *n.* [C] someone you know, but not very well: *He's an old acquaintance of mine from school.*

ac·quaint·ed /ə'kweɪntɪd/ *adj.* if you are acquainted with someone, you know him/her, but not well: *Yes, I'm acquainted with Roger.* | *Why don't you two* ***get acquainted*** (=start to learn more about each other)*?*

ac·qui·esce /ˌækwi'ɛs/ *v.* [I] *formal* to agree to do what someone wants, or to allow something to happen, although you do not like it —**acquiescence** *n.* [U]

ac·quire /ə'kwaɪɚ/ *v.* [T] **1** to buy a company or property

THESAURUS

buy, **purchase**, **get**, **snap up**, **pick up**, **stock up**
→ see Thesaurus box at BUY[1]

2 to develop or learn a skill, or become known for a particular quality: *He* ***acquired a reputation for*** *honesty.* **3 an acquired taste** something that you only begin to like after you have tried it a few times: *Whiskey is often an acquired taste.*

ac·qui·si·tion /ˌækwə'zɪʃən/ *n. formal* **1** [U] the act of getting something: *the* ***acquisition of*** *new companies* **2** [C] something that you have gotten: *a recent acquisition*

ac·quit /ə'kwɪt/ *v.* past tense and past participle **acquitted**, present participle **acquitting** [T] to decide in a court of law that someone is not guilty of a crime: *Simmons was* ***acquitted of*** *murder.*

ac·quit·tal /ə'kwɪtl/ *n.* [C,U] an official statement in a court of law that someone is not guilty: *The trial ended with his acquittal.*

a·cre /'eɪkɚ/ *n.* [C] a unit for measuring an area of land, equal to 4,840 square yards or about 4,047 square meters

ac·rid /'ækrɪd/ *adj.* having a very strong and bad smell that hurts your nose or throat: *a cloud of acrid smoke*

ac·ri·mo·ni·ous /ˌækrə'moʊniəs/ *adj.* an acrimonious meeting, argument, etc. involves a lot of anger and disagreement: *an acrimonious divorce*

ac·ri·mo·ny /'ækrəˌmoʊni/ *n.* [U] *formal* very angry feelings between people, often strongly expressed

ac·ro·bat /'ækrəˌbæt/ *n.* [C] someone who does difficult physical actions to entertain people, such as balancing on a high rope —**acrobatic** /ˌækrə'bætɪk/ *adj.*

ac·ro·bat·ics /ˌækrə'bætɪks/ *n.* [plural] the skill or tricks of an acrobat

ac·ro·nym /'ækrənɪm/ *n.* [C] a word that is made from the first letters of a group of words. For example, NATO is an acronym for the North Atlantic Treaty Organization

a·cross /ə'krɔs/ *adv., prep.* **1** from one side of something to the other side: *The road's too busy to walk across.* | *Vince stared across the canyon.* | *flying across the Atlantic* **2 10 feet/5 miles etc. across** used to show how wide something is: *At its widest point, the river is 2 miles across.* **3** on the opposite side of something: *Ben lives* ***across the street*** *from us.* | *Andi* ***sat across from*** *me.* | *The school is all the way* ***across town***. **4** reaching or spreading from one side of an area to the other: *There was only one bridge across the bay.* | *a deep crack across the ceiling* **5 across the board** affecting everyone or everything: *Changes will have to be made across the board.*

a·cryl·ic /ə'krɪlɪk/ *adj.* acrylic paints, cloth, etc. are made from a chemical substance rather than a natural substance

act[1] /ækt/ *v.* **1** [I] to do something: *We must act now in order to protect American jobs.* | *The jury decided that Walker had acted in self-defense.* | *We're* ***acting on*** *the advice of our lawyer* (=doing what s/he says). **2** [I] to behave in a particular way: *Nick's been acting strangely recently.* | *Pam's* ***acting like*** *a baby.* | *Gabe* ***acted as if*** *nothing was wrong.* **3** [I,T] to perform as a character in a play or movie: *I started acting in high school.* **4** [I] to produce a particular effect: *Salt* ***acts as*** *a preservative.*

act sth ⇔ **out** *phr. v.* to show how an event happened by performing it like a play: *The children read the story and then acted it out.*

act up *phr. v.* to behave badly or not work correctly: *The car's acting up again.*

act[2] *n.* **1** [C] something that you do: *a criminal act* | ***acts of*** *cruelty* | *Police caught the suspect* ***in the act of*** *making a bomb.*

A

USAGE

Act is always countable, and is used when you mean a particular type of action: *an act of friendship* | *He was caught in the act of stealing.* **Action** can be countable or uncountable: *a kind action* | *What we need now is quick action.*

2 [C] **also Act** a law that has been officially accepted by the government: *the Civil Rights Act* **3** [C] **also Act** one of the main parts of a play, OPERA etc.: *Hamlet kills the king in Act 5.* **4** [C] a short piece of entertainment on television or stage: *a **comedy act*** **5** [singular] behavior that is not sincere: *He doesn't care, Laura – it's **just an act**.* **6 get your act together** *informal* to start to do things in a more organized or effective way: *If Julie doesn't get her act together, she'll never graduate.* **7 get in on the act** *informal* to become involved in a successful activity that someone else has started

act·ing[1] /ˈæktɪŋ/ *adj.* **acting manager/director etc.** someone who replaces the manager, etc. for a short time

acting[2] *n.* [U] the job or skill of performing in plays or movies

ac·tion /ˈækʃən/ *n.* **1** [U] the process of doing something for a particular purpose: *He realized the need for immediate action.* | *We must **take action*** (=start doing something) *before it's too late.* | *The best **course of action*** (=way of dealing with the situation) *is to resign immediately.* | *The president has threatened **military action**.*

USAGE

Act is always countable, and is used when you mean a particular type of action: *an act of friendship* | *He was caught in the act of stealing.* **Action** can be countable or uncountable: *a kind action* | *What we need now is quick action.*

2 [C] something that you do: *The child could not be held responsible for his actions.* | *His **quick actions** probably saved my life.* **3 out of action** *informal* not working because of damage or injury: *My car's out of action.* | *Jim will be out of action for two weeks.* **4** [U] *informal* exciting things that are happening: *New York's **where the action is**.* | *an **action movie*** (=one with a lot of fast, exciting scenes) **5 in action** doing a particular job or activity: *a chance to **see** ski jumpers **in action*** **6** [C,U] fighting in a war: *He was **killed in action**.* **7** [U] the effect a substance has on something: *The rock is worn down by the **action of** the falling water.*

ac·ti·vate /ˈæktəˌveɪt/ *v.* [T] *formal* to make something start working: *This switch activates the alarm.* —**activation** /ˌæktəˈveɪʃən/ *n.* [U]

ac·tive[1] /ˈæktɪv/ *adj.* **1** always doing things, or moving around a lot [≠ **inactive**]: *Grandpa's very active for his age.* | *games for active youngsters* **2** involved in an organization or activity by doing things for it: *an **active member** of the American Civil Liberties Union* | *Mahke is **active in** the Republican Party.* **3** *technical* something that is active is ready or able to work as expected: *an active volcano* | *The alarm is now active.* **4** *technical* an active verb or sentence has the person or thing doing the action as its SUBJECT. In "The boy kicked the ball," the verb "kick" is active. [≠ **passive**]

active[2] *n.* **the active (voice)** *technical* the active form of a verb [➡ **passive**]

ac·tive·ly /ˈæktɪvli/ *adv.* in a way that involves doing things or taking part in something: *My parents are **actively involved** with the church.*

ac·tiv·ist /ˈæktəvɪst/ *n.* [C] someone who works to achieve social or political change: *human rights activists* —**activism** *n.* [U]

ac·tiv·i·ty /ækˈtɪvət̬i/ *n.* plural **activities** **1** [C usually plural] things that you do for pleasure: *after-school activities* | *She loves nature and **outdoor activities**.* **2** [C,U] things that you do because you want to achieve something: *an increase in terrorist activity* | *anti-government **political activity*** **3** [U] a situation in which a lot of things are happening or a lot of things are being done: *the noise and activity of the city*

ac·tor /ˈæktɚ/ *n.* [C] someone who performs in a play or movie: *a leading Hollywood actor*

TOPIC

actress, **star**, **director**, **producer**, **film/movie crew**

➔ see Topic box at MOVIE

ac·tress /ˈæktrɪs/ *n.* [C] a woman who performs in a play or movie

ac·tu·al /ˈæktʃuəl, ˈækʃuəl/ *adj.* real or exact: *Were those his actual words?* | *Well, the actual cost is a lot higher than they say.*

ac·tu·al·ly /ˈæktʃuəli, -tʃəli, ˈækʃuəli, -ʃəli/ *adv.* **1** used to emphasize that something is true, especially when it is a little surprising or unexpected: *They were never actually married.* | *What actually happened?* | *Actually, it was a lot of fun.* **2** used in order to give more information, give your opinion, etc.: *The watch actually belonged to my father.* | *Actually, I think I'll stay home tonight.*

a·cu·men /əˈkyumən, ˈækyəmən/ *n.* [U] the ability to think quickly and make good judgments: ***business acumen***

ac·u·punc·ture /ˈækyəˌpʌŋktʃɚ/ *n.* [U] a way of treating pain or illness by putting thin needles into parts of the body

a·cute /əˈkyut/ *adj.* **1** very serious or severe: ***acute pain*** | ***acute shortages** of food* **2** quick to notice and understand things: *an acute observation* | *an **acute mind*** **3** showing an ability to notice small differences in sound, taste, etc.: *acute hearing* **4** *technical* an acute disease or illness quickly becomes dangerous [➡ **chronic**]:

acute tuberculosis **5** *technical* an acute angle is less than 90 degrees

a·cute·ly /ə'kyutli/ *adv.* feeling or noticing something very strongly: *We are* ***acutely aware*** *of the problem.*

ad /æd/ *n.* [C] *informal* ADVERTISEMENT

A.D. **Anno Domini** used in order to show that a date is a particular number of years after the birth of Christ [➡ **B.C.**]: *432 A.D.*

ad·age /'ædɪdʒ/ *n.* [C] a well-known phrase that says something wise about life

ad·a·mant /'ædəmənt/ *adj. formal* determined not to change your opinion, decision, etc. —**adamantly** *adv.*: *The chairman has remained adamantly opposed to the project.*

Ad·am's ap·ple /'ædəmz ˌæpəl/ *n.* [C] the lump at the front of a man's neck that moves when he talks or swallows

Adam's apple

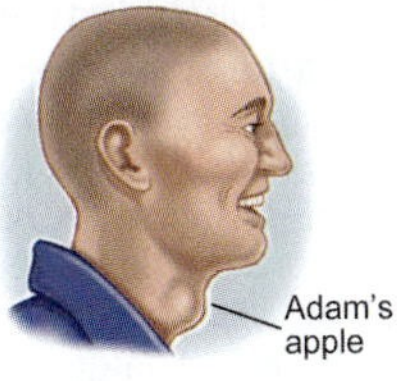

a·dapt /ə'dæpt/ *v.* **1** [I,T] to change your behavior or ideas to fit a new situation: *The kids are having trouble* ***adapting to*** *their new school.* | *These plants are able to adapt themselves to desert conditions.* **2** [T] to change something so that it is appropriate for a new purpose: *The car has been* ***adapted to*** *take unleaded gas.* | *The house was* ***adapted for*** *wheelchair users.*

THESAURUS

change, **alter**, **adjust**, **modify**, **reform**, **reorganize**, **restructure**, **transform**, **revolutionize**
➔ see Thesaurus box at CHANGE[1]

a·dapt·a·ble /ə'dæptəbəl/ *adj.* able to change and be successful in new and different situations —**adaptability** /əˌdæptə'bɪləṭi/ *n.* [U]

ad·ap·ta·tion /ˌædəp'teɪʃən, ˌædæp-/ *n.* **1** [C] a play, film, or television program that is based on a book **2** [U] the process of changing something so that it can be used in a different way or in different conditions

a·dapt·er /ə'dæptɚ/ *n.* [C] an object you use to connect two pieces of electrical equipment, or to connect more than one piece of equipment to the same power supply

add /æd/ *v.* [T] **1** to put something with something else, or with a group of other things: *Continue mixing, then add flour.* | *Do you want to* ***add*** *your name* ***to*** *the mailing list?* **2** to put numbers or amounts together and then calculate the total: *If you add 5 and 3 you get 8.* | *The interest will be added to your savings every six months.* **3** to say something extra about what you have just said: *The Judge* ***added that*** *this case was one of the worst she had ever tried.*

THESAURUS

say, **mention**, **express**, **point out**, **suggest**, **imply**, **whisper**, **mumble**, **mutter**, **murmur**
➔ see Thesaurus box at SAY[1]

4 add insult to injury to make a bad situation even worse for someone who has already been treated badly

add on ⇔ *phr. v.* to include or put on something extra: *Eating chocolate really adds on the calories.*

add to sth *phr. v.* to make a feeling or quality stronger and more noticeable: *The change of plans only added to our confusion.*

add up *phr. v.* **1 add** sth ⇔ **up** to put numbers or amounts together and then calculate the total: *We're now adding up the latest figures.* **2 not add up** to not seem true or reasonable: *Her* ***story*** (=explanation or account of what has happened) *just* ***doesn't add up.***

ad·dict /'ædɪkt/ *n.* [C] someone who is unable to stop taking drugs: *a heroin addict*

ad·dict·ed /ə'dɪktɪd/ *adj.* unable to stop taking a drug: *Marvin was* ***addicted to*** *sleeping pills.* —**addiction** /ə'dɪkʃən/ *n.* [C,U] ***addiction to*** *alcohol* —**addictive** /ə'dɪktɪv/ *adj.*: *a highly addictive drug*

ad·di·tion /ə'dɪʃən/ *n.* **1 in addition** used in order to add another fact to what has already been mentioned: *We installed a new security system. In addition, extra guards were hired.* | ***In addition to*** *his job, Harvey also coaches Little League.*

THESAURUS

extra- if something is **extra**, it is not included in the price of something and you have to pay more for it: *Dinner costs $15, but drinks are extra.*
on top of – in addition to something: *On top of everything else, I have to work on Saturday.*

2 [U] the process of adding together several numbers or amounts to get a total [➡ **subtraction**] **3** [C] something that is added: *She was an important addition to our group.*

THESAURUS

additive – a substance that is added to food to make it taste or look better or to keep it fresh: *food additives*
supplement – something that is added to something else to improve it: *vitamin supplements*

4 [C] an extra room that is added to a building

ad·di·tion·al /ə'dɪʃənəl/ *adj.* more than you already have, or more than was agreed or expected [= **extra**]: *We were charged an additional $50 in late fees.* | ***Additional information*** *is available on our website.*

THESAURUS

more, another, extra, further
→ see Thesaurus box at MORE[2]

ad·di·tive /'ædətɪv/ *n.* [C usually plural] a substance that is added to food to make it taste or look better or to keep it fresh

A

THESAURUS

addition, supplement
→ see Thesaurus box at ADDITION

ad·dress[1] /ə'drɛs, 'ædrɛs/ *n.* [C] **1** the details of where someone lives or works, including the number of a building, name of the street and town, etc.: *I forgot to give Damien my new address.* | *Write your* ***name and address*** *on a postcard.* | *Please notify us of any* ***change of address***. **2** a series of letters or numbers used to send an email to someone, or to reach a page of information on the Internet: *Give me your* ***email address***.

TOPIC

Internet, connect, modem, broadband, search engine, website, surfing the net, chat rooms, newsgroups, blogs, e-mail, work online
→ see Topic box at INTERNET

3 /ə'drɛs/ a formal speech: *the Gettysburg Address*

ad·dress[2] /ə'drɛs/ *v.* [T] **1** to write a name and address on an envelope, package, etc.: *There's a letter here* ***addressed to*** *you.* **2** *formal* to speak directly to a person or a group: *A guest speaker then addressed the audience.* | *You should* ***address*** *your question* ***to*** *the chairman.* **3 address a problem/question/issue etc.** *formal* to start trying to solve a problem: *Special meetings address the concerns of new members.* **4** to use a particular name or title when speaking or writing to someone: *The President should be* ***addressed as*** *"Mr. President."*

a·dept /ə'dɛpt/ *adj.* good at doing something that needs care or skill: *He has become* ***adept at*** *cooking.* —**adeptly** *adv.*

ad·e·quate /'ædəkwɪt/ *adj.* **1** enough in quantity or of a good enough quality for a particular purpose [≠ **inadequate**]: *We have not been given adequate information.* | *Her income is hardly* ***adequate to*** *pay the bills.*

THESAURUS

enough, plenty, sufficient
→ see Thesaurus box at ENOUGH

2 fairly good, but not excellent: *an adequate performance* —**adequacy** *n.* [U] —**adequately** *adv.*

THESAURUS

satisfactory, good enough, acceptable, all right, okay
→ see Thesaurus box at SATISFACTORY

ad·here /əd'hɪr/ *v.* [I] *formal* to stick firmly to something
adhere to sth *phr. v. formal* to continue to behave according to a particular rule, agreement, or belief: *Not all the states adhered to the treaty.*

ad·her·ence /əd'hɪrəns/ *n.* [U] the act of behaving according to particular rules, ideas, or beliefs: *a strict* ***adherence to*** *religious beliefs*

ad·her·ent /əd'hɪrənt/ *n.* [C] someone who agrees with and supports a particular idea, opinion, or political party

ad·he·sion /əd'hiʒən/ *n.* [U] the state of one thing sticking to another thing

ad·he·sive /əd'hisɪv, -zɪv/ *n.* [C] a substance such as glue that can stick things together —**adhesive** *adj.*: *adhesive tape*

ad hoc /ˌæd 'hɑk/ *adj., adv.* done when necessary, rather than planned or regular: *an ad hoc committee*

ad·ja·cent /ə'dʒeɪsənt/ *adj. formal* next to something: *the building* ***adjacent to*** *the library*

ad·jec·tive /'ædʒɪktɪv, 'ædʒətɪv/ *n.* [C] *technical* in grammar, a word that describes a noun or PRONOUN. In the sentence "I bought a new car," "new" is an adjective

ad·join·ing /ə'dʒɔɪnɪŋ/ *adj.* next to something, and connected to it: *a bedroom with an adjoining bathroom* —**adjoin** *v.* [T]

ad·journ /ə'dʒɚn/ *v.* [I,T] to stop a meeting or a legal process for a short time or until a later date: *This court is* ***adjourned until*** *2:30 p.m. tomorrow.* —**adjournment** *n.* [C,U]

ad·ju·di·cate /ə'dʒudɪˌkeɪt/ *v.* [I,T] *formal* to judge something such as a competition, or to make an official decision —**adjudication** /əˌdʒudɪ'keɪʃən/ *n.* [U]

ad·junct[1] /'ædʒʌŋkt/ *n.* [C] *formal* something that is added or joined to something else, but is not part of it.: *Medication can be a useful* ***adjunct to*** *physical therapy.*

adjunct[2] *adj.* **adjunct professor/instructor** a professor or instructor who works PART-TIME at a college

ad·just /ə'dʒʌst/ *v.* **1** [I,T] to gradually become familiar with a new situation: *Don't worry about the kids – they just need time to adjust.* | *It took a few seconds for her eyes to* ***adjust to*** *the darkness.* **2** [T] to change or move something slightly in order to improve it, make it more effective, etc.: *Adjust your seat and mirror before driving away.*—**adjustable** *adj.*

THESAURUS

change, alter, adapt, modify
→ see Thesaurus box at CHANGE[1]

ad·just·ment /ə'dʒʌstmənt/ *n.* [C,U] **1** a small change made to a machine, system, or calculation: *We've* ***made*** *some* ***adjustments to*** *our original calculations.* **2** a change in the way you behave or think: *Moving to the city has been a difficult adjustment for us.*

ad-lib /ˌæd'lɪb/ *v.* past tense and past participle **ad-libbed**, present participle **ad-libbing** [I,T] to say something in a speech or a performance without preparing or planning it —**ad lib** *n.* [C]

ad·min·is·ter /əd'mɪnəstɚ/ *v.* [T] **1** to manage and organize the affairs of a company, government, etc. **2** to provide or organize something officially as part of your job: *The test was **administered to** all high school seniors.* **3** *formal* to give someone a medicine or drug: *Painkillers were **administered to** the boy.*

ad·min·is·tra·tion /ədˌmɪnə'streɪʃən/ *n.* **1** [C] the government of a country at a particular time: *the Kennedy Administration* **2** [U] the activities that are involved in managing and organizing the affairs of a company, institution, etc.: *We're looking for someone with experience in administration.* **3 the administration** the people who manage a company, institution, etc.

ad·min·i·stra·tive /əd'mɪnəˌstreɪt̬ɪv/ *adj.* relating to the work of managing a company or organization: *The job is mainly administrative.*

adˌministrative as'sistant *n.* [C] someone who works in an office, typing (=type) letters, keeping records, answering telephone calls, arranging meetings, etc.

ad·min·is·tra·tor /əd'mɪnəˌstreɪt̬ɚ/ *n.* [C] someone whose job is related to the management and organization of a company, institution, etc.

ad·mi·ra·ble /'ædmərəbəl/ *adj.* having many good qualities that you respect and admire: *an admirable achievement* —**admirably** *adv.*

ad·mi·ral /'ædmərəl/ *n.* [C] a very high rank in the Navy, or an officer who has this rank

ad·mi·ra·tion /ˌædmə'reɪʃən/ *n.* [U] a feeling of approval and respect for something or someone: *She's always had a great **admiration for** her father.*

ad·mire /əd'maɪɚ/ *v.* [T] **1** to approve of and respect someone or something: *I really **admire the way** she brings up those kids.* | *I **admired** her **for** having the courage to tell the truth.*

> **THESAURUS**
>
> **respect** – to admire someone because of his/her knowledge, skill, personal qualities, etc.: *He is respected by his colleagues.*
> **look up to sb** – to admire and respect someone: *The other kids looked up to him.*
> **idolize** – to admire someone so much that you think s/he is perfect: *He's now competing with the players he idolized in high school.*

2 to look at something and think how beautiful or impressive it is: *We stopped to admire the view.* —**admirer** *n.* [C] —**admiring** *adj.*: *She drew **admiring glances** from all the men* (=the men were looking at her with approval because she is attractive). —**admiringly** *adv.*

ad·mis·si·ble /əd'mɪsəbəl/ *adj. formal* acceptable or allowed, especially in a court of law [≠ **inadmissible**]: *admissible evidence*

ad·mis·sion /əd'mɪʃən/ *n.* **1** [U] the price charged when you go to a movie, sports event, concert, etc.: *Admission is $6.50.* | *The museum has no **admission charge**.* **2** [C] a statement in which you admit that something is true or that you have done something wrong: *If he resigns, it will be an **admission of** guilt.* **3** [U] permission that is given to someone to enter a building or place, or to become a member of a school, club, etc.: *Tom has applied for **admission to** the university.* **4 admissions** [plural] the process of allowing people to enter a college, institution, hospital, etc., or the number of people who can enter

ad·mit /əd'mɪt/ *v.* past tense and past participle **admitted**, present participle **admitting** **1** [T] to accept or agree unwillingly that something is true or that someone else is right: *He was wrong, but he won't admit it.* | *You may not like her, but you have to **admit that** she is good at her job.* **2** [I,T] to say that you did something wrong or are guilty of a crime [= **confess**]: *She finally **admitted to** the murder.* | *In court, he **admitted** his **guilt**.*

> **THESAURUS**
>
> **own up** informal – to admit that you have done something wrong: *He finally owned up to the fact that he had lied to us.*
> **come clean** informal – to finally tell the truth about something you have been hiding: *Do you think she'll ever come clean about her past?*

3 [T] to allow someone to enter a building or place, or to become a member of a school, club, etc.: *Only members will be **admitted to** the club for tonight's performance.*

ad·mit·tance /əd'mɪt̚ns/ *n.* [U] permission to enter a place: *Most journalists were unable to **gain admittance** backstage.*

ad·mit·ted·ly /əd'mɪt̬ɪdli/ *adv.* used when admitting that something is true: *Our net profit this year is admittedly much smaller than we had expected.*

ad·mon·ish /əd'mɑnɪʃ/ *v.* [T] *literary* to tell someone that s/he has done something wrong —**admonishment** *n.* [C,U]

a·do·be /ə'doʊbi/ *n.* [U] a material made of clay and STRAW, used for building houses

a·do·les·cence /ˌædl'ɛsəns/ *n.* [U] the period of time, usually between the ages of 12 and 18, when a young person is developing into an adult

ad·o·les·cent[1] /ˌædl'ɛsənt/ *n.* [C] a young person who is developing into an adult

adolescent[2] *adj.* relating to or typical of a young person who is developing into an adult: *adolescent behavior*

> **THESAURUS**
>
> **young, small, little, teenage**
> → see Thesaurus box at YOUNG[1]

a·dopt /ə'dɑpt/ *v.* **1** [I,T] to take someone else's child into your home and legally become his or her parent: *Melissa was adopted when she was two.* | *couples who are hoping to adopt* **2** [T] to begin to have or use an idea, plan, or way of doing something: *The city has adopted a new approach to fighting crime.* —**adopted** *adj.*: *our adopted son*

A

a·dop·tion /ə'dɑpʃən/ *n.* [U] **1** the act or process of adopting a child: *She decided to* ***put*** *the baby* ***up for adoption****.* **2** the act of deciding to use an idea, plan, or way of doing something: *the* ***adoption of*** *new technology*

a·dop·tive /ə'dɑptɪv/ *adj.* [only before noun] an adoptive parent is one who has adopted a child

a·dor·a·ble /ə'dɔrəbəl/ *adj.* very attractive and easy to like: *What an adorable little puppy!*

a·dore /ə'dɔr/ *v.* [T] **1** to love and admire someone very much: *Betty adores her grandchildren.*

> **THESAURUS**
>
> **love, be infatuated with, have a crush on, be crazy about, be devoted to**
> ➔ see Thesaurus box at LOVE[1]

2 *informal* to like something very much —**adoring** *adj.*: *his adoring fans* —**adoration** /ˌædə'reɪʃən/ *n.* [U]

a·dorn /ə'dɔrn/ *v.* **be adorned with sth** *formal* to be decorated with something: *The church walls were adorned with religious paintings.* —**adornment** *n.* [C,U]

a·dren·a·line /ə'drɛnl-ɪn/ *n.* [U] a chemical produced by your body that makes your heart beat faster and gives you extra strength when you are afraid, excited, or angry

a·drift /ə'drɪft/ *adj., adv.* a boat that is adrift is not tied to anything, and is moved around by the ocean or wind

a·droit /ə'drɔɪt/ *adj.* smart and skillful, especially in the way you use words and arguments: *an adroit negotiator* —**adroitly** *adv.*

ad·u·la·tion /ˌædʒə'leɪʃən/ *n.* [U] *formal* praise and admiration for someone that is more than what s/he really deserves

a·dult[1] /ə'dʌlt, 'ædʌlt/ *n.* [C] a fully grown person or animal: *She's an adult – she can do what she pleases.* | *Admission is $8 for adults and $5 for children.*

adult[2] *adj.* [only before noun] **1** fully grown or developed: *an adult male frog* **2** typical of an adult: *You need to deal with your problems in an adult way.* **3 adult movies/magazines/bookstores etc.** movies, magazines, etc. that show sexual acts, etc.

a·dul·ter·ate /ə'dʌltəˌreɪt/ *v.* [T] to make something less pure by adding a substance of a lower quality to it —**adulteration** /əˌdʌltə'reɪʃən/ *n.* [U]

a·dul·ter·y /ə'dʌltəri/ *n.* [U] sex between someone who is married and someone who is not that person's husband or wife: *men who* ***commit adultery*** —**adulterous** *adj.*

a·dult·hood /ə'dʌlthʊd/ *n.* [U] the time when you are an adult [➡ **childhood**]

ad·vance[1] /əd'væns/ *n.* **1 in advance** before something happens or is expected to happen: *The airline suggests booking tickets 21 days in advance.* **2** [C,U] a change, discovery, or invention that brings progress: *medical advances* | ***advances in*** *technology* **3** [C] a movement forward to a new position, especially by an army [≠ **retreat**]: *Napoleon's advance towards Moscow* **4** [C usually singular] money paid to someone before the usual time: *I asked for an* ***advance on*** *my salary.* **5 advances** [plural] efforts to start a sexual relationship with someone

advance[2] *v.* **1** [I] to move forward to a new position [≠ **retreat**]: *Troops* ***advanced on*** (=moved forward while attacking) *the rebel forces.* **2** [I,T] to develop or progress, or to make something develop or progress: *a job that will* ***advance*** *his* ***career*** **3** [T] to give someone money before s/he has earned it: *Will they advance you some money until you get your first paycheck?* —**advancement** *n.* [U]

advance[3] *adj.* **advance planning/warning/notice etc.** planning, etc. that is done before something else happens: *We had no advance warning of the hurricane.*

ad·vanced /əd'vænst/ *adj.* **1** using the most modern ideas, equipment, and methods: *advanced weapon systems*

> **THESAURUS**
>
> **sophisticated** – made or designed well, and often complicated: *sophisticated software*
> **high-tech** – using the most modern machines and methods in industry, business, etc.: *high-tech weapons*
> **state-of-the-art** – using the newest methods, materials, or knowledge: *state-of-the-art technology*
> **cutting-edge** – using the newest design or the most advanced way of doing something: *cutting-edge medical research*

2 studying or relating to a school subject at a difficult level: *an advanced student* | *advanced physics* **3** having reached a late point in time or development: *By this time, the disease was too far advanced to be treated.*

ad·van·tage /əd'væntɪdʒ/ *n.* **1** [C,U] something that helps you to be better or more successful than others [≠ **disadvantage**]: *Her computer skills gave her an* ***advantage over*** *the other applicants.* | *He turns every situation* ***to*** *his* ***advantage****.* **2 take advantage of sth** to use a situation or thing to help you do or get something you want: *He* ***took advantage of*** *the* ***opportunity*** *given to him.* **3** [C] a good or useful quality that something has: *Good restaurants are one of the many* ***advantages of*** *living in a big city* **4 take**

advantage of sb to treat someone unfairly or to control a particular situation in order to get what you want

ad·van·ta·geous /ˌædvænˈteɪdʒəs, -vən-/ *adj.* helpful and likely to make you more successful [≠ **disadvantageous**]

ad·vent /ˈædvɛnt/ *n.* **the advent of sth** the time when something first begins to be widely used: *the advent of the computer*

ad·ven·ture /ədˈvɛntʃɚ/ *n.* [C,U] an exciting experience in which dangerous or unusual things happen

ad·ven·tur·er /ədˈvɛntʃərɚ/ *n.* [C] someone who enjoys traveling and doing exciting things

ad·ven·ture·some /ədˈvɛntʃɚsəm/ *adj.* enjoying exciting and slightly dangerous activities

ad·ven·tur·ous /ədˈvɛntʃərəs/ *adj.* **1** wanting to do new, exciting, or dangerous things: *adventurous travelers* **2** exciting and slightly dangerous: *an adventurous expedition up the Amazon*

ad·verb /ˈædvɚb/ *n. technical* [C] in grammar, a word or a group of words that describes or adds to the meaning of a verb, an adjective, another adverb, or a sentence. For example, "slowly" in "He walked slowly" and "very" in "It was a very nice day" are adverbs —**adverbial** /ədˈvɚbiəl/ *adj.*

ad·ver·sar·y /ˈædvɚˌsɛri/ *n.* plural **adversaries** [C] *formal* a country or person you are fighting or competing against [≠ **opponent**]

ad·verse /ədˈvɚs, æd-, ˈædvɚs/ *adj. formal* not good or favorable: *The recession will have an* ***adverse effect*** *on the building industry.* —**adversely** *adv.*

ad·ver·si·ty /ədˈvɚsəṭi, æd-/ *n.* plural **adversities** [C,U] difficulties or problems that seem to be caused by bad luck: *We remained hopeful* ***in the face of adversity.***

ad·ver·tise /ˈædvɚˌtaɪz/ *v.* **1** [I,T] to tell the public about a product or service in order to persuade them to buy it: *The new perfume is being* ***advertised in*** *women's magazines.* | *companies who* ***advertise on*** *TV*

THESAURUS

promote – to advertise a product or event: *She's in Atlanta to promote her new book.*
market – to try to persuade someone to buy something by advertising it in a particular way: *The clothes are marketed to teenagers.*
hype – to try to make people think something is good or important by advertising or talking about it a lot on television, the radio, etc: *The director is just using the controversy to hype his movie.*
plug – to advertise a book, movie, etc. by talking about it on a radio or television program: *Marc was on the show to plug his new play.*

2 [I] to make an announcement, for example in a newspaper, that a job is available, an event is going to happen, etc.: *They're* ***advertising for*** *an accountant.* —**advertiser** *n.* [C]

ad·ver·tise·ment /ˌædvɚˈtaɪzmənt/ *n.* [C] a picture, set of words, or a short movie, which is intended to persuade people to buy a product or use a service, or that gives information about a job that is available, an event that is going to happen, etc. [➡ **commercial**]: *an* ***advertisement for*** *laundry detergent*

THESAURUS

commercial – an advertisement on TV or radio
billboard – a very large sign at the side of a road or on a building, used as an advertisement
poster – an advertisement on a wall, often with a picture on it
want ads/classified ads – short advertisements in a newspaper, in which people offer things for sale
flier – a piece of paper with an advertisement on it, often given to you in the street
junk mail – unwanted letters that you receive in the mail containing advertisements
spam – unwanted e-mails containing advertisements

ad·ver·tis·ing /ˈædvɚˌtaɪzɪŋ/ *n.* [U] the business of advertising things on television, in newspapers, etc.

ad·vice /ədˈvaɪs/ *n.* [U] an opinion you give someone about what s/he should do: *The book is full of* ***advice on/about*** *child care.* | *Can you* ***give*** *me some* ***advice*** *about buying a house?* | *If I were you, I'd* ***seek*** (=get) *some* ***legal/medical/financial advice.*** | *Did you* ***follow/take*** *your father's* ***advice?*** | *He offered them one* ***piece of advice:*** *Don't panic.*

THESAURUS

tip – a helpful piece of advice: *useful tips on healthy eating*
recommendation – advice given to someone, especially about what to do: *Do you have any recommendations about hotels in the city?*
guidance – helpful advice about work, education etc: *His parents should provide more guidance.*

COMMUNICATION

you ought to...: *You ought to see the doctor.*
you should...: *I think you should write to her.*
if I were you, I'd...: *If I were you, I'd ask for my money back.*
why don't you...: *Why don't you take the bus?*
you'd better...: *You'd better ask your teacher.*
it would be a good idea to...: *It would be a good idea to make a reservation.*

ad·vise /ədˈvaɪz/ *v.* **1** [I,T] to tell someone what you think s/he should do: *Doctors* ***advised*** *her* ***to***

have the operation. | *We were* ***advised against*** *getting a cat because of Joey's allergies.*

THESAURUS

recommend – to advise someone to do something: *I recommend that you get some professional help.*
urge – to strongly advise someone to do something: *I urged Frida to reconsider her decision to drop out of school.*

2 [T] *formal* to officially tell someone something: *You will be advised when the shipment arrives.*

ad·vis·er, **advisor** /əd'vaɪzɚ/ *n.* [C] someone whose job is to give advice about a particular subject: *a financial adviser*

ad·vi·so·ry /əd'vaɪzəri/ *adj.* having the purpose of giving advice: *an advisory committee*

ad·vo·cate¹ /'ædvə,keɪt/ *v.* [T] to strongly support a particular way of doing things: *Extremists were openly advocating violence.* —**advocacy** /'ædvəkəsi/ *n.* [U]

ad·vo·cate² /'ædvəkət, -,keɪt/ *n.* [C] someone who publicly supports someone or something: *an* ***advocate for*** *prisoners' rights*

aerobics

aer·i·al /'ɛriəl/ *adj.* from the air or happening in the air: *aerial photographs* | *aerial stunts*

ae·ro·bic /ə'roʊbɪk, ɛ-/ *adj.* relating to exercises that make your heart and lungs stronger

ae·ro·bics /ə'roʊbɪks, ɛ-/ *n.* [U] a very active type of physical exercise done to music, usually in a class

TOPIC

exercise, **stay/keep/get in shape**, **jogging**, **lifting weights**, **gym**, **health club**, **workout**, **warm up**, **stretching**
➔ see Topic box at EXERCISE²

aer·o·dy·nam·ics /,ɛroʊdaɪ'næmɪks/ *n.* [U] the scientific study of how objects move through the air —**aerodynamic** *adj.*

aer·o·sol /'ɛrə,sɔl, -,sɑl/ *n.* [U] a small metal container from which a liquid can be forced out using high pressure

aer·o·space /'ɛroʊ,speɪs/ *adj.* involving the designing and building of aircraft and space vehicles: *the aerospace industry*

aes·thet·ic, **esthetic** /ɛs'θɛṭɪk, ɪs-/ *adj.* relating to beauty and the study of beauty —**aesthetically** *adv.*: *aesthetically pleasing*

aes·thet·ics, **esthetics** /ɛs'θɛṭɪks, ɪs-/ *n.* [U] the study of beauty, especially beauty in art

a·far /ə'fɑr/ *adv.* **from afar** *literary* from a long distance away

AFC, **American Football Conference** American Football Conference ; a group of teams that is part of the NFL

af·fa·ble /'æfəbəl/ *adj.* friendly and easy to talk to: *an affable guy* —**affably** *adv.*

af·fair /ə'fɛr/ *n.* [C] **1 affairs** [plural] **a)** public or political events and activities: *a* ***foreign affairs*** *correspondent for CNN* **b)** things connected with your personal life, your financial situation, etc.: *You need to get your financial affairs in order.* **2** an event or a set of related events, especially unpleasant ones: *the Watergate affair* **3** a secret sexual relationship between two people, when at least one of them is married to someone else: *Ed is* ***having an affair with*** *his boss's wife.* ➔ LOVE AFFAIR

af·fect /ə'fɛkt/ *v.* [T] **1** to do something that produces a change in someone or something [➡ **influence**]: *Help is being sent to areas affected by the floods.* | *decisions which* ***affect*** *our* ***lives***

USAGE

Use **affect** to talk about making changes, and use **effect** to talk about the results of those changes: *Do you think the changes in the law will affect us?* | *I don't know what effect they will have.*
Effect can be used as a verb to mean "to make something happen." This use is formal and not very common.: *No law is going to effect change in a parent who does not take his or her role seriously.*

2 to make someone feel strong emotions: *I was* ***deeply affected*** *by the news of Paul's death.*

af·fec·ta·tion /,æfɛk'teɪʃən/ *n.* [C,U] an action or type of behavior that is not natural or sincere

af·fect·ed /ə'fɛktɪd/ *adj.* not natural or sincere: *an affected laugh*

af·fec·tion /ə'fɛkʃən/ *n.* [C,U] a feeling of gentle love and caring: *Bart felt great* ***affection for*** *her.* | *He doesn't* ***show affection*** *easily.*

af·fec·tion·ate /ə'fɛkʃənɪt/ *adj.* showing that you like or love someone: *an affectionate child* | *an affectionate hug* —**affectionately** *adv.*

af·fi·da·vit /,æfə'deɪvɪt/ *n. law* [C] a written statement about something that you swear is true, used in a court of law

af·fil·i·ate¹ /ə'fɪli,eɪt/ *v.* **be affiliated with/to sth** if a group or organization is affiliated to a larger one, it is related to it or controlled by it: *a TV station affiliated to CBS* —**affiliation** /ə,fɪli'eɪʃən/ *n.* [C,U] *What are Jean's political affiliations?*

af·fil·i·ate² /ə'fɪliɪt, -,eɪt/ *n.* [C] a small company or organization that is related to or controlled by a larger one

af·fin·i·ty /ə'fɪnəṭi/ *n.* plural **affinities** **1** [singular] the feeling you have when you like and understand someone or something: *They had a natural **affinity for** each other.* **2** [C,U] a close similarity or relationship between two things because of qualities or features that they both have

af·firm /ə'fɚm/ *v.* [T] *formal* to state publicly that something is true: *The President affirmed his intention to reduce taxes.* —**affirmation** /ˌæfɚ'meɪʃən/ *n.* [C,U]

af·firm·a·tive /ə'fɚmət̬ɪv/ *adj. formal* a word, sign, etc. that is affirmative means "yes" [≠ **negative**] —**affirmative** *n.* [C] *She answered in the affirmative.* —**affirmatively** *adv.*

afˌfirmative 'action *n.* [U] the practice of choosing people for jobs, education, etc. who have been treated unfairly because of their race, sex, etc.

af·flict /ə'flɪkt/ *v.* [T usually passive] *formal* to make someone have a serious illness or experience serious problems: *a country **afflicted by** famine* | *people **afflicted with** AIDS* —**affliction** /ə'flɪkʃən/ *n.* [C,U]

af·flu·ent /'æfluənt/ *adj.* having a lot of money, nice houses, expensive things, etc. [➡ **rich, wealthy**]: *an affluent suburb of Baltimore* —**affluence** *n.* [U]

af·ford /ə'fɔrd/ *v.* [T] **1 can afford a)** to have enough money to buy or pay for something: *I can't **afford to** buy a new car.* | *Do you think we can afford a computer now?* **b)** to be able to do something without causing serious problems for yourself: *We can't **afford to** offend regular customers.* **c)** to have enough time to do something: *I really can't afford any more time away from work.* **2** *formal* to provide something or allow something to happen: *The walls afforded some protection from the wind.*

af·ford·a·ble /ə'fɔrdəbəl/ *adj.* not expensive: *affordable housing*

af·front /ə'frʌnt/ *n.* [C usually singular] a remark or action that offends or insults someone

a·float /ə'floʊt/ *adj.* [not before noun] **1** having enough money to operate or stay out of debt: *They're struggling to **stay afloat**.* **2** floating on water

a·fraid /ə'freɪd/ *adj.* [not before noun] **1** frightened because you think that you may get hurt or that something bad may happen [= **scared**]: *There's no need to be afraid.* | *Small children are often **afraid of** the dark.* | *Mary's **afraid to** walk home alone.*

> **THESAURUS**
>
> **frightened**, **scared**, **terrified**, **petrified**
> ➔ see Thesaurus box at FRIGHTENED

2 very worried that something bad will happen: *A lot of people are **afraid of** losing their jobs.* | *He was **afraid (that)** the other kids would laugh at him.* **3 I'm afraid** *spoken* used in order to politely tell someone something that may annoy, upset, or disappoint him/her: ***I'm afraid (that)** this is a "no smoking" area.* | *"Are we late?" **"I'm afraid so** (=yes)."* | *"Are there any tickets left?" **"I'm afraid not** (=no)."*

a·fresh /ə'frɛʃ/ *adv. formal* if you do something afresh, you do it again from the beginning: *We decided to move to Texas and **start afresh**.*

Af·ri·ca /'æfrɪkə/ *n.* one of the seven CONTINENTS, that includes land south of Europe and west of the Indian Ocean

A

Af·ri·can[1] /'æfrɪkən/ *adj.* relating to or coming from Africa

African[2] *n.* [C] someone from Africa

ˌAfrican A'merican *n.* [C] an American with dark skin, whose family originally came from the part of Africa south of the Sahara Desert —**African-American** *adj.*

af·ter[1] /'æftɚ/ *prep.* **1** when a particular time or event has happened: *I go swimming every day after work.* | *A **month/year after** the fire, the house was rebuilt.*

> **THESAURUS**
>
> **afterward** – after an event or time that has been mentioned: *He said afterward that it had been the scariest experience of his life.*
> **next** – immediately afterward: *What should we do next?*
> **later** – after the present time or a time you are talking about: *We can clean up later.*
> **subsequently** – after an event in the past: *Subsequently, the company filed for bankruptcy*

2 following someone or something else in a list or a piece of writing, or in order of importance: *Whose name is after mine on the list?* | *After baseball, tennis is my favorite sport.* **3 after 10 minutes/3 hours etc.** when a particular amount of time has passed: *After a while, the woman returned.* **4 day after day/year after year etc.** continuing for a very long time: *Day after day we waited, hoping she'd call.* **5** used when telling time to say how many minutes past the hour it is: *It's ten after five.* **6** because of something that happened earlier: *I'm not surprised he left her, after the way she treated him.* **7 after all a)** used in order to say that what you expected did not happen: *It didn't rain after all.* **b)** used in order to say that something should be remembered or considered because it helps to explain what you have just said: *Don't shout at him – he's only a baby, after all.* **8 one after the other also one after another** if a series of events, actions, etc. happen one after another, each one happens soon after the previous one: *Ever since we moved here, it's been one problem after another.* **9 be after sb** to be looking for someone and trying to catch him/her: *The FBI is after him for fraud.* **10 be after sth** *informal* to be trying to get something that belongs to someone else: *You're just after my money!* **11** in spite of: *After all the trouble I had, Reese didn't even say* *thank you.* ➔ see **one after the other/one after another** at ONE[2]

after² *conjunction* when a particular time has passed, or an event has happened: *Regan changed his name after he left Poland.* | *He discovered the jewel was fake **10 days/3 weeks after** he bought it.*

after³ *adv.* later than someone or something else: *Gina came on Monday, and I got here the day after.*

A

af·ter·ef·fect /'æftəə,fɛkt/ *n.* [C usually plural] a bad effect that remains after something has ended

af·ter·life /'æftɚ,laɪf/ *n.* [singular] the life that some people believe you have after death

af·ter·math /'æftɚ,mæθ/ *n.* [singular] the time after an important or bad event: *the danger of fire **in the aftermath of** the earthquake*

af·ter·noon /,æftɚ'nun◂ / *n.* [C,U] the period of time between 12 p.m. and the evening [➡ **morning, evening**]: *a class on Friday afternoon* | *We should get there about 3 **in the afternoon.*** | *Can you go swimming **this afternoon*** (=today in the afternoon)? —**afternoon** *adj.*: *an afternoon snack*

af·ter·shave /'æftɚ,ʃeɪv/ *n.* [C,U] a liquid with a pleasant smell that a man puts on his face after he SHAVES

af·ter·taste /'æftɚ,teɪst/ *n.* [C usually singular] a taste that stays in your mouth after you eat or drink something: *The wine has a bitter aftertaste.*

af·ter·thought /'æftɚ,θɔt/ *n.* [C usually singular] something that you mention or add later because you did not think of it before: *"Bring Claire too," he added **as an afterthought**.*

af·ter·ward /'æftɚwɚd/ **also afterwards** *adv.* after an event or time that has been mentioned: *We met at college but didn't get married until **two years afterward**.*

THESAURUS

after, next, later, subsequently
➔ see Thesaurus box at AFTER[1]

a·gain /ə'gɛn/ *adv.* **1** one more time: *Could you say that again? I couldn't hear you.* | *The cake burned so we had to start **all over again*** (=from the beginning). **2** back to the same condition, situation, or place as before: *Thanks for coming! Please come again.* | *He's home again, after studying in Europe.* **3 again and again** repeating many times: *I've tried again and again to contact her.* **4 then again** *spoken* used in order to add a fact that is different from what you have just said, or makes it seem less likely to be true: *She says she's thirty, **but then again** she might be lying.*

a·gainst /ə'gɛnst/ *prep.* **1** opposed to or disagreeing with an idea, belief, etc.: *John was against the idea of selling the house.* | *You can't do that! It's **against the law*** (=illegal). **2** in a way that has a bad or unfair effect: *discrimination against racial minorities* **3** fighting or competing with someone or something: *He was injured in the game against the Cowboys.* **4** touching a surface: *The cat's fur felt soft against her face.* **5** in the opposite direction from something: *At least my drive to work is against the traffic.* **6 have sth against sb/sth** to dislike or disapprove of someone or something: *I have nothing against dogs, but I don't want one myself.*

age¹ /eɪdʒ/ *n.* **1** [C,U] the number of years that someone has lived or something has existed: *Patrick is **my age*** (=the same age as me). | *Jamie won his first tournament **at the age of** 15.* | *Most kids start kindergarten **at age** 5.* | *girls who become mothers **at an early age*** (=very young) | *Stop messing around and **act your age*** (=behave in a way that is suitable for how old you are)! | *Judy's very smart **for her age*** (=compared to others of the same age). **2** [C,U] a period in someone's life: *Who will look after you in old age?* | *women of childbearing age* **3** [U] the age when you are legally old enough to do something: ***voting/drinking/retirement age*** (=when you can legally vote, drink alcohol, etc.) | *You can't buy alcohol – you're **under age**.* **4** [C usually singular] a particular period of history: *the modern age* | *the **age of** new technology* **5 be/come of age** to be or become old enough that you are considered to be a responsible adult **6** [U] the state of being old: *a letter that was brown with age* **7 ages** [plural] *informal* a long time: *I haven't been there **for ages**.* **8 age group/bracket** the people between two particular ages, considered as a group: *a book for children in the 8–12 age group*

age² *v.* [I,T] to become or look older, or to make someone look older: *Jim has really aged.* —**aging** *adj.*: *an aging movie star*

aged¹ /eɪdʒd/ *adj.* **aged 5/15/50 etc.** 5, 15, etc. years old: *a game for children aged 12 and over*

a·ged² /'eɪdʒɪd/ *adj.* **1** very old: *an aged man* **2 the aged** old people

age·less /'eɪdʒlɪs/ *adj.* never seeming old or old-fashioned: *an ageless song*

a·gen·cy /'eɪdʒənsi/ *n.* plural **agencies** [C] **1** a business that provides a particular service: *an employment agency* **2** an organization or department, especially within a government, that does a specific job: *the UN agency responsible for helping refugees*

a·gen·da /ə'dʒɛndə/ *n.* [C] **1** a list of the subjects to be discussed at a meeting: *Let's move on to item five **on the agenda**.* **2** a list of problems or subjects that a government, organization, etc. is planning to deal with: *Health care reforms are **high on the agenda*** (=very important).

a·gent /'eɪdʒənt/ *n.* [C] **1** a person or company that represents another person or company in business, in their legal problems, etc.: *a literary agent* **2** someone who works for a government or police department in order to get secret information about another country or an organization: *an FBI agent* ➔ REAL ESTATE AGENT ➔ TRAVEL AGENT

ag·gra·vate /'ægrə,veɪt/ *v.* [T] **1** to make a bad situation, illness, or injury worse: *The doctors say* *her condition is aggravated by stress.* **2** to annoy someone: *What really aggravates me is the way she won't listen.* —**aggravating** *adj.* —**aggravation** /ˌægrəˈveɪʃən/ *n.* [C,U]

aggregate /ægrɪgɪt/ *adj.* [only before noun] *technical* being the total amount of something, especially money: *aggregate income and investment* —**aggregate** *n.* [singular, U]

ag·gres·sion /əˈgrɛʃən/ *n.* [U] angry or threatening behavior, especially in which you attack someone: *an **act of aggression***

ag·gres·sive /əˈgrɛsɪv/ *adj.* **1** very determined to succeed: *aggressive sales tactics* **2** behaving in an angry or violent way toward someone: *aggressive behavior* —**aggressively** *adv.* —**aggressiveness** *n.* [U]

ag·gres·sor /əˈgrɛsɚ/ *n.* [U] a person or country that starts a fight or war

ag·grieved /əˈgrivd/ *adj.* angry or unhappy because you think you have been treated unfairly

a·ghast /əˈgæst/ *adj.* [not before noun] suddenly feeling or looking shocked

ag·ile /ˈædʒəl, ˈædʒaɪl/ *adj.* **1** able to move quickly and easily **2** someone who has an agile mind is able to think quickly and intelligently —**agility** /əˈdʒɪləṭi/ *n.* [U]

ag·i·tate /ˈædʒəˌteɪt/ *v.* [I] *formal* to protest in order to achieve social or political changes: *workers **agitating for** higher pay* —**agitator** *n.* [C]

ag·i·tat·ed /ˈædʒəˌteɪṭɪd/ *adj.* very anxious, nervous, or upset —**agitation** /ˌædʒəˈteɪʃən/ *n.* [U]

ag·nos·tic /ægˈnɑstɪk, əg-/ *n.* [C] someone who believes that it is impossible to know whether God exists or not —**agnostic** *adj.* —**agnosticism** /ægˈnɑstəˌsɪzəm, əg-/ *n.* [U]

a·go /əˈgoʊ/ *adj.* used in order to show how far back in the past something happened: *Jeff left for work **10 minutes/2 hours ago**.* | *We went to Maine once, but it was **a long time ago**.* | *I had the tickets **a minute ago**!* | *Scott's dad called **a little while ago**.*

> **GRAMMAR**
>
> **ago, for, since**
>
> **Ago**, **for**, and **since** are all used to talk about time.
>
> **Ago** is used with the simple past tense to say how far back in the past something happened. It follows a length of time: *My grandfather died two years ago.*
>
> **For** is used with the present perfect or simple past tense to say how long a situation or event has lasted. It is followed by a length of time: *She's been here for three days.* | *The party lasted for five hours.*
>
> **Since** is used with the present perfect tense to say when something started. It is followed by an exact day, date, or time: *He's been here since Sunday.* | *I've been working here since 1998.*

a·gon·ize /ˈægəˌnaɪz/ *v.* [I] to think about a decision very carefully and with a lot of effort: *For a long time she had **agonized about/over** what she should do.*

a·gon·iz·ing /ˈægəˌnaɪzɪŋ/ *adj.* extremely painful or difficult: *an agonizing decision* —**agonizingly** *adv.*

ag·o·ny /ˈægəni/ *n.* plural **agonies** [C,U] very severe pain or suffering: *The poor guy was **in agony**.*

a·gree /əˈgri/ *v.* **1** [I,T] to have the same opinion as someone else [≠ **disagree**]: *I **agree with** Karen. It's much too expensive.* ▶ Don't say "I am agree." ◀: *Most experts **agree that** global warming is a serious problem.* | *Mike and I certainly don't **agree on/about** everything.*

> **COMMUNICATION**
>
> **Ways of agreeing**
>
> **yes/yeah**: *"It's a really great film." "Yes, it is."*
> **you're right**: *I guess you're right, we should have left earlier.*
> **that's right**: *"I think San Diego's stadium is named after a sports writer." "That's right, the Jack Murphy Stadium is named in honor of the famous reporter."*
> **that's true**: *"I think people have to work a lot harder these days." "Unfortunately, that's true."*
> **exactly/absolutely/definitely**: *"So, you think we should sell the house and move to the coast." "Exactly."* | *"You think I should apply for the job?" "Absolutely, we need good teachers."*
> → ACCEPT, SUGGEST

2 [I,T] to say yes to a suggestion, plan, etc. [≠ **refuse**]: *She **agreed to** stay home with Charles.* **3** [I,T] to make a decision with someone after discussing something: *We **agreed to** meet next week.* | *We're still trying to **agree on** a date for the wedding.* **4** [I] if two pieces of information agree, they say the same thing: *Your story doesn't **agree with** what the police have said.*

agree with *phr. v.* **1 agree with sth** to think that something is the right thing to do: *I don't agree with the decision at all.* **2 not agree with sb** if something that you ate or drank does not agree with you, it makes you feel sick

a·gree·a·ble /əˈgriəbəl/ *adj.* **1** acceptable and able to be agreed on: *a solution that's **agreeable to** both parties* **2** *old-fashioned* pleasant —**agreeably** *adv.*: *I was agreeably surprised.*

a·greed /əˈgrid/ *adj.* **1** an agreed price, method, arrangement, etc. is one that people have discussed and accepted **2 be agreed** if people are agreed, they all agree about something: *Are we all **agreed on** the date for the meeting?*

a·gree·ment /əˈgrimənt/ *n.* **1** [C] an arrangement or promise to do something, made by two or more people, organizations, etc.: *a trade agreement* | *Lawyers on both sides finally **reached***

an agreement. **2** [U] a situation in which two or more people have the same opinion as each other [**≠ disagreement**]: *All of us were **in agreement**.*

ag·ri·cul·ture /ˈægrɪˌkʌltʃɚ/ *n.* [U] the science or practice of farming —**agricultural** /ˌægrɪˈkʌltʃərəl/ *adj.*

ah /ɑ/ *interjection* used in order to show surprise, happiness, etc. or that you have just understood something: *Ah, yes, I see what you mean.*

a·ha /ɑˈhɑ/ *interjection* said when you suddenly understand or realize something: *Aha! So that's where you've been hiding!*

a·head /əˈhɛd/ *adv.* **1** in front of someone or something: *Do you see that red convertible **ahead of** us?* | *We could see the lights of Las Vegas **up ahead**.* **2** in or into the future: *We **have** a busy day **ahead** of us.* | *The **days/weeks/months ahead** are going to be difficult.* | *You need to **plan ahead*** (=plan for the future). **3** arriving, waiting, finishing, etc. before other people: *There were two people **ahead of** me at the doctor's.* **4** making more progress or more developed than other people or things: *Jane is **ahead of** the rest of her class.* | *You need to work hard if you want to **get ahead**.* **5 ahead of schedule/time** earlier than planned: *The building was completed ahead of schedule.* **6 go ahead a)** *spoken* used in order to tell someone s/he can do something: *Go ahead and help yourself to some punch.* **b)** used in order to say you are going to start doing something: *I'll go ahead and start the coffee.* **7** winning in a game or competition: *The 49ers finished two games ahead of the Cowboys.* | *He's **ahead by** 17 points in the polls.*

aid¹ /eɪd/ *n.* **1** [U] money, food, or services that an organization or government gives to help people [**➡ financial aid**]: *The UN is sending aid to the earthquake victims.* **2 with/without the aid of sth** using or not using something such as a tool to help you do something: *The star can only be seen with the aid of a telescope.* **3 come/go to sb's aid** *formal* to help someone: *Several people came to the man's aid after he collapsed on the sidewalk.* **4** [C,U] a thing that helps you do something: *study aids*

aid² *v.* [T] **1** *formal* to help or give support to someone **2 aid and abet** *law* to help someone do something illegal

aide, aid /eɪd/ *n.* [C] someone whose job is to help someone in a more important position: *a nurse's aide*

AIDS /eɪdz/ *n.* [U] **Acquired Immune Deficiency Syndrome** a very serious disease that stops your body from defending itself against infection

ail·ing /ˈeɪlɪŋ/ *adj.* weak or sick: *the country's ailing economy* | *his ailing mother*

ail·ment /ˈeɪlmənt/ *n.* [C] an illness that is not very serious

aim¹ /eɪm/ *v.* **1** [I] to plan or intend to achieve something: *We **aim to** finish by Friday.* | *a program **aimed at** creating more jobs* **2 aim sth at sb** to do or say something that is intended for a particular person or group: *TV commercials aimed at children* **3** [I,T] to point a weapon at a person or thing you want to hit: *A gun was **aimed at** his head.*

aim

aim² *n.* **1** [C] something that you are trying to achieve: *What is the **aim of** their research?* | *Our **main aim** is to provide good service.* | *I flew to California **with the aim of** finding a job.*

THESAURUS

purpose, goal, objective
➔ see Thesaurus box at PURPOSE

2 take aim to point a weapon at someone or something: *He **took aim at** the target.* **3** [U] someone's ability to hit something by throwing or shooting something at it: *Mark's aim wasn't very good.*

aim·less /ˈeɪmlɪs/ *adj.* without a clear purpose or reason —**aimlessly** *adv.*: *We wandered aimlessly around the city.*

ain't /eɪnt/ *v. spoken nonstandard* a short form of "am not," "is not," "are not," "has not," or "have not"

air¹ /ɛr/ *n.* **1** [U] the gases around the Earth, which we breathe: *There was a smell of burning **in the air**.* | *Let's go outside and get some **fresh air**.* | ***air pollution*** **2** [U] the space above the ground or around things: *David threw the ball up into the air.* **3 by air** traveling by or using an airplane: *Are you shipping that box by air or by land?* **4 air travel/safety etc.** travel, safety, etc. involving or relating to airplanes: *the worst air disaster in the state's history* **5 be in the air** if a feeling is in the air, a lot of people have it: *There was tension in the air.* **6** [singular] a quality that someone or something seems to have: *There was an **air of** mystery **about** her.* **7 be up in the air** *spoken* used to say that something has not been decided yet: *Our trip is still very much up in the air.* **8** [U] *spoken* **air conditioning** **9 be on/off the air** to be broadcasting or to stop broadcasting **10 airs** [plural] a way of behaving that shows someone thinks s/he is more important than s/he really is: *You shouldn't have to **put on airs** with your own friends.*

air² *v.* **1** [T] to broadcast a program on television or radio: *Star Trek was first aired in 1966.* **2** [T] to express your opinions publicly: *You will all get* *a chance to **air** your **views**.* **3** [I,T] **also air out** to let fresh air into a room

air·bag /ˈɛrbæg/ *n.* [C] a bag in a car that fills with air to protect people in an accident

air·borne /ˈɛrbɔrn/ *adj.* flying or carried through the air

air·brush¹ /ˈɛrbrʌʃ/ *n.* [C] a piece of equipment that uses air to put paint onto a surface

airbrush² *v.* [T] to use an airbrush to make a picture or photograph look better

airbrush sb/sth ⇔ **out** *phr. v.* to remove someone or something from a picture or photograph using an airbrush

ˈair conˌditioner *n.* [C] a machine that makes the air in a room, car, etc. stay cool

ˈair conˌditioning *n.* [U] a system of machines that makes the air in a room, building, etc. stay cool —**air conditioned** *adj.*

air·craft /ˈɛrkræft/ *n.* plural **aircraft** [C] an airplane or other vehicle that can fly

ˈaircraft ˌcarrier *n.* [C] a ship that airplanes can fly from and land on

THESAURUS

ship, **cruise ship**, **liner**, **ferry**, **freighter**, **tanker**, **barge**, **battleship**, **cruiser**, **submarine**, **warship**
➔ see Thesaurus box at SHIP¹

air·fare /ˈɛrfɛr/ *n.* [U] the price of an airplane trip

air·field /ˈɛrfild/ *n.* [C] a place where military or small airplanes fly from

ˈAir Force *n.* **the Air Force** the military organization of the U.S. that uses airplanes when fighting a war

air·head /ˈɛrˌhɛd/ *n.* [C] *slang* someone who is stupid

air·i·ly /ˈɛrəli/ *adv.* in a way that shows you do not think something is important: *"I know all that," she said airily.*

air·less /ˈɛrlɪs/ *adj.* without fresh air

air·lift /ˈɛrlɪft/ *n.* [C] an occasion when people or things are taken to a place by airplane because it is too difficult or dangerous to get there by road —**airlift** *v.* [T]

air·line /ˈɛrlaɪn/ *n.* [C] a business that regularly flies passengers to different places by airplane

air·lin·er /ˈɛrˌlaɪnɚ/ *n.* [C] a large airplane for passengers

air·mail /ˈɛrmeɪl/ *n.* [U] letters, packages, etc. that are sent to another country by airplane, or the system of doing this —**airmail** *adj., adv.*

air·plane /ˈɛrpleɪn/ *n.* [C] a vehicle that flies by using wings and one or more engines [**= plane**]

air·port /ˈɛrpɔrt/ *n.* [C] a place where airplanes take off and land, that has buildings for passengers to wait in

TOPIC

At the airport you go into the **terminal**. You **check in** (=show your ticket, leave your bags, etc.) at the **check-in counter/desk**, usually one or two hours before your **flight** leaves. You go through **airport security** where passengers and their bags are checked for weapons, etc. You wait in the **departure lounge** until your **flight number** is called. You go through the **departure gate** before **boarding** (=getting on) the plane. The airplane **takes off** from the **runway**. When the airplane **lands**, you get off. You then go to the **baggage claim** to get your suitcases. If you have traveled from another country, you show your **passport** as you go through **immigration** and then you **go through customs** where your bags may be checked before leaving the airport.
➔ PASSPORT, TRAVEL

airplane

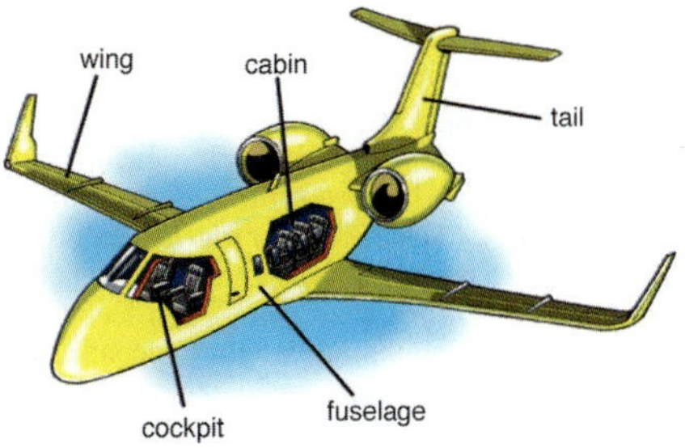

air·space /ˈɛrspeɪs/ *n.* [U] the sky above a particular country, considered to be controlled by that country

ˈair strike *n.* [C] an attack on a place in which military aircraft drop bombs on it

air·strip /ˈɛrstrɪp/ *n.* [C] a long narrow piece of land that airplanes can fly from and land on

air·tight /ˈɛrˌtaɪt, ˌɛrˈtaɪt/ *adj.* **1** not allowing air to get in or out: *airtight containers* **2** planned or done so carefully that there is no chance of any problems or mistakes: *an airtight alibi*

ˈair time *n.* [U] the amount of time that a radio or television station gives to a particular subject, advertisement, etc.

air·waves /ˈɛrweɪvz/ *n.* [plural] *informal* all the programs that are broadcast on radio and television

air·y /ˈɛri/ *adj.* an airy room, building, etc. has a lot of space and fresh air

aisle /aɪl/ *n.* [C] a long passage between rows of seats in a theater, airplane, church, etc.: *Frances **walked down the aisle** (=to get married) carrying a bouquet of flowers.*

a·jar /əˈdʒɑr/ *adj.* [not before noun] a door or window that is ajar is not completely closed

AK the written abbreviation of **Alaska**

a.k.a. *adv.* **also known as** used when giving

someone's real name together with the name s/he is known by: *John Phillips, a.k.a. The Mississippi Mauler*

a·kin /ə'kɪn/ *adj.* **akin to sth** *formal* similar to something: *His music is much more akin to jazz than rock.*

AL the written abbreviation of **Alabama**

A

a·larm¹ /ə'lɑrm/ *n.* [U] **1** a piece of equipment that makes a noise to warn people of danger: *a **fire/burglar** alarm* | *He **set off the alarm*** (=made it start ringing). | *Someone's car **alarm** was **going off*** (=making a noise). **2** *informal* an ALARM CLOCK: *I've **set the alarm** for six o'clock.* **3** a feeling of fear because something bad might happen: *Calm down! There's no **cause for alarm**.* **4 raise/sound the alarm** to warn everyone about something bad or dangerous that is happening: *They first sounded the alarm about the problem of nuclear waste in 1955.*

alarm² *v.* [T] to make someone feel very worried or frightened: *The news about Tony alarmed me.* —**alarmed** *adj.*

a'larm clock *n.* [C] a clock that will make a noise at a particular time to wake you up ➔ see picture at CLOCK¹

a·larm·ing /ə'lɑrmɪŋ/ *adj.* very frightening or worrying: *an alarming increase in violent crime*

a·larm·ist /ə'lɑrmɪst/ *adj.* making people feel worried about dangers that do not exist —**alarmist** *n.* [C]

a·las /ə'læs/ *interjection literary* said in order to express sadness

al·be·it /ɔl'biɪt, æl-/ *conjunction formal* although

al·bi·no /æl'baɪnoʊ/ *n.* plural **albinos** [C] a person or animal with a GENETIC condition that makes the skin and hair extremely pale or white

al·bum /'ælbəm/ *n.* [C] **1** a group of songs or pieces of music on a record, CD, or tape **2** a book in which you put photographs, stamps, etc. that you want to keep: *a photo album*

al·co·hol /'ælkəˌhɔl, -ˌhɑl/ *n.* **1** [U] drinks such as beer or wine that can make you drunk: *I don't drink alcohol anymore.* **2** [C,U] a chemical substance that can be used for cleaning medical or industrial equipment

al·co·hol·ic¹ /ˌælkə'hɔlɪk◂, -'hɑ-/ *n.* [C] someone who cannot stop the habit of drinking too much alcohol

alcoholic² *adj.* containing alcohol or relating to alcohol [≠ **non-alcoholic**]: *an alcoholic beverage*

al·co·hol·is·m /'ælkəhɔˌlɪzəm, -hɑ-/ *n.* [U] the medical condition of being an alcoholic

al·cove /'ælkoʊv/ *n.* [C] a small place in a wall of a room that is built further back than the rest of the wall

al·der·man /'ɔldɚmən/ *n.* plural **aldermen** /-mən/ [C] a city or town government official who is elected

ale /eɪl/ *n.* [U] a type of beer

a·lert¹ /ə'lɚt/ *adj.* **1** always watching and ready to notice anything strange, unusual, dangerous, etc.: *Cyclists must always be **alert to** the dangers on a busy road.* **2** able to think quickly and clearly: *I didn't feel alert enough to do any more work.*

alert² *v.* [T] to warn someone of a problem or of possible danger: *As soon as we suspected it was a bomb, we alerted the police.*

alert³ *n.* [C] **1 be on the alert** to be ready to notice and deal with a problem: *Police are **on the alert for** trouble.* **2** a warning to be ready for possible danger: *a flood alert*

al·fal·fa sprout /æl'fælfə spraʊt/ *n.* [C] a very small plant, eaten raw as a vegetable in SALADS

al·gae /'ældʒi/ *n.* [U] a very simple plant without stems or leaves that lives in or near water

al·ge·bra /'ældʒəbrə/ *n.* [U] a type of mathematics that uses letters and signs to represent numbers and values —**algebraic** /ˌældʒə'breɪ-ɪk/ *adj.*

al·go·rithm /'ælgəˌrɪðəm/ *n.* [C] a set of mathematical instructions that are done in a particular order

a·li·as¹ /'eɪliəs, 'eɪlyəs/ *prep.* used when giving a criminal's real name together with the name s/he uses: *the spy Margaret Zelle, alias Mata Hari*

alias² *n.* [C] a false name, usually used by a criminal

al·i·bi /'æləbaɪ/ *n.* [C] something that proves that someone was not where a crime happened and is therefore not guilty of the crime: *He **had** a perfect **alibi** and the police let him go.*

a·li·en¹ /'eɪliən, 'eɪlyən/ *adj.* **1** very different or strange: *The landscape was **alien to** me.* **2** relating to creatures from other worlds

alien² *n.* [C] **1** someone who lives or works in a country but is not a citizen: ***illegal aliens** entering the country* **2** in stories, a creature that comes from another world

a·li·en·ate /'eɪliəˌneɪt, 'eɪlyə-/ *v.* [T] to make someone stop feeling friendly or stop feeling like s/he belongs in a group: *policies that will alienate some voters* —**alienation** /ˌeɪliə'neɪʃən, ˌeɪlyə-/ *n.* [U]

a·light¹ /ə'laɪt/ *adj.* **1** burning: *Several cars were **set alight** by rioters.* **2** someone whose face or eyes are alight is happy or excited

alight² *v.* [I] *formal* if a bird, insect, etc. alights on something, it stops flying in order to stand on a surface

a·lign /ə'laɪn/ *v.* [I,T] **1** to work together with another person or group because you have the same aims: *Five Democrats have **aligned** themselves **with** the Republicans on this issue.* **2** to arrange something so that it is in the same line as something else: *It looks like your wheels need aligning.* —**alignment** *n.* [C,U]

a·like¹ /ə'laɪk/ *adj.* almost exactly the same [= **similar**]: *She and her sister are very alike.*

THESAURUS

similar, like, akin to, identical, matching
➔ see Thesaurus box at SIMILAR

alike² *adv.* **1** in a similar way, or in the same way: *The twins were dressed alike.* **2** in a way that includes both the people, groups, or things you have mentioned: *The rule was criticized by teachers and students alike.*

al·i·mo·ny /ˈæləˌmoʊni/ *n.* [U] money that someone has to pay regularly to his/her former wife or husband after a DIVORCE

a·live /əˈlaɪv/ *adj.* **1** living and not dead: *Only one passenger was still alive.* | *the food you need to **stay alive*** | *He called his mother to tell her he was **alive and well**.* **2** continuing to exist: *Let's **keep** the traditions of the Inuit **alive**.* **3** full of activity or interest: *The streets **come alive** after ten o'clock.* | *Her eyes were **alive with** mischief.*

al·ka·li /ˈælkəˌlaɪ/ *n.* [C,U] a substance that forms a chemical salt when combined with an acid —**alkaline** *adj.*

all¹ /ɔl/ *determiner, pron.* **1** the whole of an amount, time, or thing: *Have you done all your homework?* | *We've spent it all.* | *I've been waiting **all day/week**.* | *Bill talks about work **all the time*** (=very often or too much). | *Professor Ito explained **all of** this.* **2** every one of a group of things or people: *Answer all twenty questions.* | *Have you told them all?* | *This is important to **all of** us.* | *She makes **almost all (of)** her own clothes.*

USAGE

Each, **every**, and **all** are all used to talk about every person or thing in a group.
When you are considering them separately, use **each** or **every** with a singular noun: *Each/Every child at the party was given a balloon.*
When you are considering them together, use **all** with a plural noun: *All the children enjoyed the trip.*

3 the only thing or things: *All I want is a cup of coffee.* **4 all kinds/sorts of sth** very many different types of things, people, or places: *The students are reading all kinds of books.* **5 for all...** in spite of a particular fact or situation: *For all his faults, he's a good father.* **6 at all** used in questions to mean "in any way": *Did the new drugs help her at all?* **7 not at all** not in any way: *The snow didn't affect us at all.* **8 in all** including every thing or person: *In all, there were 28 people there.* **9 all in all** considering everything: *All in all, it was a successful event.*

GRAMMAR

Use **all** with a singular verb when you are using a U noun: *All the wine is gone.*
Use **all** with a plural verb when you are using a plural noun form: *All my friends are coming to the party.*
➔ EVERY

all² *adv.* **1** completely or entirely: *I walked all alone.* | *The judges were dressed all in black.* **2 all over a)** everywhere on a surface or in a place: *There was stuff all over the floor.* | *We looked **all over the place** for it.* **b)** finished: *Thank goodness it's all over; it was awful.* **3 all too** used in order to mean "very" when talking about a bad situation: *It's all too easy to blame parents for their children's problems.* **4** used in order to say that both sides have the same number of points in a game: *The score was 10-all at half time.* **5 all but** almost completely: *It was all but impossible to contact him.* **6 all along** from the beginning and all of the time after that: *I knew all along that I couldn't trust him.* **7 sb was all...** *spoken* used in order to report what someone said or did, when telling a story: *She was all, "don't do it that way!"* **8 sb/sth is not all that** *spoken* used in order to say that someone or something is not very attractive or desirable: *Why him? He's not all that.* ➔ **after all** at AFTER¹ ➔ **all of a sudden** at SUDDEN

Al·lah /ˈælə, ˈɑlə/ *n.* the name used in Islam for God

ˌall-Aˈmerican *adj.* **1** typical of America or Americans: *an all-American girl* **2** belonging to a group of players who have been chosen as the best in their sport in college

ˌall-aˈround *adj.* good at doing many different things, especially in sports: *the best all-around player*

al·lay /əˈleɪ/ *v.* **allay sb's fears/concerns/worries etc.** to make someone feel less afraid, worried, etc.

al·le·ga·tion /ˌæləˈgeɪʃən/ *n.* [C] a statement that someone has done something illegal, which has not been proved: ***allegations of** child abuse*

THESAURUS

accusation, charge, indictment
➔ see Thesaurus box at ACCUSATION

al·lege /əˈlɛdʒ/ *v.* [T] to say that something is true though it has not been proved: *Three students **alleged that** they had been expelled unfairly.*

THESAURUS

accuse, charge, indict
➔ see Thesaurus box at ACCUSE

al·leged /əˈlɛdʒd/ *adj.* supposed to be true, but not proven: *the group's alleged connections with organized crime*

al·leg·ed·ly /əˈlɛdʒɪdli/ *adv.* used when reporting what other people say is true, although it has not been proved: *Felix allegedly offered him a bribe.*

al·le·giance /əˈlidʒəns/ *n.* [C] loyalty to or support for a leader, country, belief, etc.: *The class stood up and **pledged allegiance** to the flag of the United States of America.*

al·le·go·ry /ˈæləˌgɔri/ *n.* plural **allegories** [C,U] a story, poem, painting, etc. in which the events and characters represent good and bad qualities —**allegorical** /ˌæləˈgɔrɪkəl/ *adj.*

al·le·lu·ia /ˌæləˈluyə/ *interjection* HALLELUJAH

al·ler·gic /əˈlɚdʒɪk/ *adj.* **1** having an ALLERGY: *Jess is **allergic to** milk.* **2** caused by an ALLERGY: *an **allergic reaction** to the bee sting*

A

al·ler·gy /ˈælɚdʒi/ *n.* plural **allergies** [C] a condition that makes you sick when you eat, touch, or breathe a particular thing: *He **has an allergy to** cats.*

al·le·vi·ate /əˈliviˌeɪt/ *v.* [T] to make something less bad or severe: *Aspirin should alleviate the pain.* | *The road was built to alleviate traffic problems.*

THESAURUS

reduce, **relieve**, **ease**, **lessen**
→ see Thesaurus box at REDUCE

al·ley /ˈæli/ **also al·ley·way** /ˈæliˌweɪ/ *n.* [C] a narrow street between buildings

al·li·ance /əˈlaɪəns/ *n.* [C] a close agreement or connection between people, countries, etc.: *the NATO alliance*

al·lied /əˈlaɪd, ˈælaɪd/ *adj.* joined or closely related, especially by a political or military agreement: *allied forces* | *The government was **allied with** oil companies.*

al·li·ga·tor /ˈæləˌgeɪt̬ɚ/ *n.* [C] a large REPTILE (=type of animal) with a long body, a long mouth, and sharp teeth that lives in hot wet areas of the U.S. and China

ˌall-inˈclusive *adj.* including everything: *an all-inclusive list*

al·lit·e·ra·tion /əˌlɪt̬əˈreɪʃən/ *n.* [U] the use of the same sound at the beginning of several words, to make a special effect, especially in poetry

ˌall-ˈnighter *n.* [C] *informal* an occasion when you spend the whole night studying or writing

al·lo·cate /ˈæləˌkeɪt/ *v.* [T] to decide to use a particular amount of money, time, etc. for a particular purpose: *the money **allocated to** low-income housing* —**allocation** /ˌæləˈkeɪʃən/ *n.* [U]

al·lot /əˈlɑt/ *v.* past tense and past participle **allotted**, present participle **allotting** [T] to use a particular amount of time for something, or give a particular share of something to someone or something: *Each person was allotted four tickets.* | *Two hours were **allotted to** each interview.* —**allotment** *n.* [C,U]

al·low /əˈlaʊ/ *v.* [T] **1** to give someone permission to do something, have something, or go somewhere: *Smoking is not allowed.* | *Reporters were allowed access to the files.* | *Those over 18 are **allowed to** vote.* | *The cat's not **allowed in** the bedroom.*

THESAURUS

Allow is used in both formal and informal English: *You're not allowed to use a calculator during the test.*

Let is informal and is used a lot in spoken English: *Will your Mom let you come to the party?*

Permit is formal and is mainly used in written English: *Smoking is not permitted in this building.*

2 to make it possible for something to happen or for someone to do something: *The plan preserves the state's wild areas while allowing economic growth.* | *The waiting period **allows for** a background check.* **3** to make sure you have enough time, money, etc. for a particular purpose: *Allow ten days for delivery.* | *I allow myself $75 a week for groceries.*

allow for sb/sth *phr. v.* to consider the possible effects of something and make plans to deal with it: *Even allowing for delays, we should finish early.*

al·low·a·ble /əˈlaʊəbəl/ *adj.* acceptable according to particular rules: *the allowable dosage of the drug*

al·low·ance /əˈlaʊəns/ *n.* **1** [C,U] money you are given regularly or for a special reason: *Do your kids get an allowance?* | *a travel allowance* **2** [C usually singular] an amount of something that is acceptable or safe: *a baggage allowance* | *the recommended daily allowance of Vitamin C* **3 make allowances (for sb)** to consider something when dealing with someone's behavior

al·loy /ˈælɔɪ/ *n.* [C] a metal made by mixing two or more different metals

all ˈright *adj., adv. spoken* **1** acceptable, but not excellent: *"How was the movie?" "It was all right."* **2** not hurt, not upset, or not having problems: *Sue, are you all right?* | *The press conference **went all right*** (=happened without any problems). **3** used in order to say you agree with a plan, suggestion, etc.: *"Let's go." "All right."* **4 that's all right a)** used in order to reply when someone thanks you: *"Thanks for your help!" "That's all right."* **b)** used in order to tell someone you are not angry when s/he says s/he is sorry: *"Sorry I'm late!" "That's all right."* **5** used in order to say or ask whether something is convenient for you: *Would Thursday morning be all right?* **6** used in order to ask or give permission to do something: ***Is it all right if** I close the window?* | *It's **all right with** me.* **7** used in order to ask if someone has understood something: *Put the cards into three piles, all right?* **8 it's all right** used in order to make someone feel less afraid or worried: *It's all right, Mommy's here.* **9** used in order to get someone's attention, introduce a new subject, or end a conversation: *All right, quiet down now.* **10** used in order to say you are happy about something: *"I got the job!" "All right!"* **11 be doing all right** to be successful in your job or life

USAGE

All right is the usual way of spelling this phrase: *Are you all right?* | *The movie was all right.* **Alright** is very informal and most teachers think that it is not correct.

al·lude /ə'lud/ *v.*
allude to sb/sth *phr. v. formal* to talk about something in a way that is not direct

al·lure /ə'lʊr/ *n.* [singular, U] a pleasant or exciting quality that attracts people: *the **allure of** travel* —**alluring** *adj.*

al·lu·sion /ə'luʒən/ *n.* [C,U] *formal* something said or written that mentions a subject, person, etc. in a way that is not direct: *His poetry is full of **allusions to** the Bible.* —**allusive** /ə'lusɪv/ *adj.*

al·ly[1] /ə'laɪ, 'ælaɪ/ *n.* plural **allies** [C] a person or country that helps another, especially in war: *the U.S. and its European allies*

ally[2] *v.* past tense and past participle **allied**, third person singular **allies** [I,T] **ally yourself to/with sb** to join with other people or countries to help each other

al·ma ma·ter /ˌælmə 'mɑt̬ɚ, ˌɑl-/ *n.* [singular, U] *formal* **1** the school, college, or university where you used to study **2** the official song of a school, college, or university

al·ma·nac /'ɔlməˌnæk/ *n.* [C] **1** a book giving a list of the days of a year, times the sun rises and sets, changes in the moon, etc. **2** a book giving information about a particular subject or activity: *the Almanac of American Politics*

al·might·y /ɔl'maɪt̬i/ *adj.* **1** having the power to do anything: *Almighty God* **2** very important or powerful: *the almighty dollar*

al·mond /'ɑmənd, 'æm-/ *n.* [C] a flat white nut with pale brown skin and a slightly sweet taste, or the tree on which these nuts grow

al·most /'ɔlmoʊst, ɔl'moʊst/ *adv.* nearly but not quite: *Are we almost there?* | *Supper's almost ready.* | *We've spent **almost all** the money.* | *They practice **almost every** day.*

a·loft /ə'lɔft/ *adv. literary* high up in the air

a·lo·ha /ə'loʊhɑ/ *interjection* used in order to say hello or goodbye in Hawaii

a·lone /ə'loʊn/ *adj., adv.* **1** without any other people: *She lives alone.* | *They had **left** their son **alone**.* | *I was **all alone** in a strange city.*

THESAURUS

on your own – without anyone helping you: *Finally the baby started breathing on her own.*
(all) by yourself – without anyone helping you: *She raised four children by herself.*
single-handedly – done by one person, with no help from anyone else: *He almost single-handedly is responsible for the business's success.*
solo – done alone, without anyone else helping you: *Lindbergh's solo flight across the Atlantic Ocean*

2 used in order to emphasize that only one person can do something, that something belongs to only one person, etc.: *He alone can do the job.* ➔ **leave sb alone** at LEAVE[1] ➔ **leave sth alone** at LEAVE[1] ➔ **let alone** at LET

a·long[1] /ə'lɔŋ/ *prep.* **1** from one place on something such as a line, road, or edge toward the other end of it: *We took a walk along the river.* | *She looked anxiously along the line of faces.* **2** in a line next to or on something: *a fence along the road* | *photographs arranged along the wall* **3** at a particular place on something, usually something long: *The house is somewhere along this road.* **4 along the way/line** during a process or experience, or during someone's life: *The company has had more successes than failures along the way.*

along[2] *adv.* **1** going forward: *I was driving along, listening to the radio.* **2 go/come/be along also take/bring sth along** to go to, come to, or be in the place where something is happening, or to take someone or something with you to that place: *You're welcome to come along.* | *Why don't you bring your guitar along?* **3 along with sb/sth** in addition to and at the same time: *Many heart patients now take aspirin, along with other drugs.* ➔ **all along** at ALL[2] ➔ **get along** at GET ➔ **come along** at COME

a·long·side /əˌlɔŋ'saɪd/ *adv., prep.* **1** close to and in line with the edge of something: *a boat tied up alongside the dock* **2** used in order to say that people or things do something or exist together: *The children were playing alongside each other.*

a·loof /ə'luf/ *adj., adv.* apart from other people and deliberately not doing things with them: *He **held himself** somewhat **aloof** from the others.*

a·loud /ə'laʊd/ *adv.* in a voice that you can hear: *Mama **read aloud** to us.* | *I was just **thinking aloud*** (=saying what I was thinking). | *The pain made him **cry aloud**.*

al·pha·bet /'ælfəˌbɛt/ *n.* [C] a set of letters in a particular order, used in writing a language: *the Greek alphabet*

al·pha·bet·i·cal /ˌælfə'bɛt̬ɪkəl/ *adj.* arranged according to the letters of the alphabet: *books **in alphabetical order*** —**alphabetically** *adv.*

al·pine /'ælpaɪn/ *adj.* being in or related to the Alps or other high mountains: *alpine flowers*

al·read·y /ɔl'rɛdi/ *adv.* **1** before a particular time: *By the time he arrived, the room was already crowded.* **2** before: *You already told me that.*

USAGE

Already is used in order to talk about something that has happened: *John has already seen the movie.*
All ready is used in order to say that someone is ready to do something, or that something is completely prepared: *We're all ready to go now.* | *Dinner is all ready.*

A

3 sooner than expected: *I've already forgotten her number.* | *Is he leaving already?* **4** *spoken* said in order to emphasize that you are annoyed: *Make up your mind already!*

al·right /ɔl'raɪt/ *adv.* ➔ ALL RIGHT

al·so /'ɔlsoʊ/ *adv.* **1** in addition [**= too**]: *Deming also criticized the policy.* | *This question is* ***not only*** *about writing* ***but also*** *about reading.*

A

USAGE

Also is more formal than **too**, and is used more often in writing than in speech: *Tom was also hungry.*
Too and **as well** are less formal and more often used in spoken English: *Tom's hungry, and I am too.*
In negative sentences, use **either** rather than **also** or **too**. Do not say "Tom was also not hungry." or "Tom was not hungry too." Say "Tom was not hungry either."

2 used in order to say that the same thing is true about another person or thing: *My father also died of a heart attack.*

GRAMMAR

Use **also** before a verb, unless the verb is "be": *Ron also speaks Italian.* Use **also** after the verb "be": *His wife is also a doctor.*
If there are two or more verbs together, one of which is an auxiliary verb, **also** comes after the first one: *Patty can also speak Italian.*

al·tar /'ɔltɚ/ *n.* [C] a table or raised structure used in a religious ceremony

al·ter /'ɔltɚ/ *v.* [I,T] to change, or to make someone or something change: *The design has been altered slightly.*

THESAURUS

change, **adapt**, **adjust**, **modify**, **reform**, **reorganize**, **restructure**, **transform**, **revolutionize**
➔ see Thesaurus box at CHANGE[1]

al·ter·a·tion /ˌɔltə'reɪʃən/ *n.* [C,U] a change in something, or the act of changing it: *We're planning to* ***make*** *a few* ***alterations to*** *the house.* | ***alterations in*** *the world's climate*

al·ter·ca·tion /ˌɔltɚ'keɪʃən/ *n.* [C] *formal* a noisy argument

al·ter e·go /ˌæltɚ 'igoʊ, ˌɔl-/ *n.* [C] a person or character in a book who represents part of someone's character or who has similar opinions, attitudes, etc.: *Gissing used his fictional alter ego to attack Victorian morals.*

al·ter·nate[1] /'ɔltɚˌneɪt/ *v.* [I,T] if two things alternate, or if you alternate them, they happen one after the other in a repeated pattern: *periods of laziness* ***alternating with*** *periods of frantic activity* | *Alternate the layers of pasta and meat sauce.* —**alternation** /ˌɔltɚ'neɪʃən/ *n.* [C,U]

al·ter·nate[2] /'ɔltɚnɪt/ *adj.* **1** able to be used instead of something or someone else [**= alternative**]: *an alternate route to the airport* **2** happening in a regular way, first one thing and then the other thing: *Davis and Zeller play on alternate nights.*

al·ter·na·tive[1] /ɔl'tɚnətɪv/ *adj.* **1** an alternative plan, idea, etc. can be used instead of another one: *an alternative way home* **2** different from what is usual or accepted: *alternative medicine* | *alternative sources of energy* —**alternatively** *adv.*

alternative[2] *n.* [C] something you can choose to do or use instead of something else: *This costs less than the other alternative.* | *There was no* ***alternative to*** *the use of force.*

al·though /ɔl'ðoʊ/ *conjunction* **1** in spite of the fact that [**= though**]: *Although the car's old, it runs well.* **2** but: *No, I'll do it, although I appreciate your offer.*

al·ti·tude /'æltəˌtud/ *n.* [C] the height of something above sea level: *flying* ***at high/low altitude***

al·to /'æltoʊ/ *n.* [C,U] a female singer with a low voice, or the line of a piece of music that this person sings

al·to·geth·er /ˌɔltə'gɛðɚ, 'ɔltəˌgɛðɚ/ *adv.* **1** completely – used in order to emphasize what you are saying: *He uses an altogether different method.* | *Smoking in public buildings is banned altogether.* **2** considering everything or the whole amount: *There were five people altogether.* | *It did rain a lot, but altogether it was a good trip.*

USAGE

Use **altogether** to talk about the total amount or number of something: *There were 50 guests altogether at their wedding.*
Use **all together** to say that things or people are together in a group: *Try to keep the puzzle pieces all together.*

al·tru·ism /'æltruˌɪzəm/ *n.* [U] the practice of caring about the needs of other people before dealing with your own needs —**altruist** *n.* [C] —**altruistic** /ˌæltru'ɪstɪk◂/ *adj.*

a·lu·mi·num /ə'lumənəm/ *n.* [U] a silver-white metal that is an ELEMENT, and that is light and easily bent

a·lum·ni /ə'lʌmnaɪ/ *n.* [plural] the former students of a school, college, or university

al·ways /'ɔlweɪz, -wiz, -wɪz/ *adv.* **1** at all times, or each time: *Always lock the doors.* | *We always want to improve our service.*

THESAURUS

permanently – every time or at all times: *The door is permanently locked.*
all the time/the whole time – continuously and often: *It rains here all the time.*

USAGE

Still is used to say that a situation that began in the past has not changed and is continuing: *He still lives with his parents.*
Always means "all the time" or "every time": *Her house is always clean.* | *I always see him on Tuesdays.*
Yet is used in negative sentences and questions to talk about something that you expect to happen, but which has not happened: *I haven't finished the book yet.* | *Is Mark back from lunch yet?*

2 for a very long time: *He said he'd always love her.* | *I've always wanted to go to China.*

THESAURUS

permanently – forever or for a very long time: *His eyesight may be permanently damaged.*
forever – for all time in the future: *I could stay here forever.*
for life – for the rest of your life: *Marriage is supposed to be for life.*
for good – used to say that a change is permanent: *I've given up smoking for good.*

3 happening often, especially in an annoying way: *The stupid car is always breaking down!* **4 as always** as is usual or expected: *Her singing, as always, was wonderful.* **5 you can/could always...** *spoken* said in order to make a polite suggestion: *You could always try calling her.*

GRAMMAR

Use **always** before a verb, unless the verb is "be": *We always go on vacation in August.* Use **always** after the verb "be": *Jeff's always late for school.*
If there are two or more verbs together, **always** comes after the first one: *I have always lived in this town.*

AM /ˌeɪ 'ɛm◂/ **amplitude modulation** a system of broadcasting radio programs in which the strength of the radio waves changes [➡ **FM**]

am /m, əm; *strong* æm/ the first person singular and present tense of the verb BE

a.m. /ˌeɪ 'ɛm/ used when talking about times that are between MIDNIGHT and NOON [➡ **p.m.**]: *I start work at 9:00 a.m.*

a·mal·gam·ate /ə'mælgəˌmeɪt/ *v. formal* **1** [I,T] to join in order to form one larger organization **2** [T] to combine two or more things to make one thing —**amalgamation** /əˌmælgə'meɪʃən/ *n.* [C,U]

a·mass /ə'mæs/ *v.* [T] to gather together or collect money or information in large amounts: *He had amassed a fortune.*

am·a·teur[1] /'æmətʃɚ/ *adj.* doing something for enjoyment, but not for money: *an amateur musician*

amateur[2] *n.* [C] **1** someone who does something because s/he enjoys it, but not for money [≠ **professional**] **2** someone who does not have experience or skill in a particular activity: *Don't have your tattoo done by an amateur.* —**amateurish** /ˌæmə'tʃʊrɪʃ/ *adj.*

a·maze /ə'meɪz/ *v.* [T] to surprise someone very much: *He made a shot that amazed everyone.* | *You **never cease to amaze me*** (=always surprise me).

a·mazed /ə'meɪzd/ *adj.* very surprised: *We were **amazed at** how quickly the kids learned.* | *I'm **amazed (that)** you remember him.* | *Many people were **amazed to** learn that he had grown up poor.*

THESAURUS

surprised, **shocked**, **astonished**, **astounded**, **flabbergasted**, **stunned**, **dumbfounded**, **nonplussed**
➔ see Thesaurus box at SURPRISED

a·maze·ment /ə'meɪzmənt/ *n.* [U] the state or feeling of being AMAZED: *We watched **in/with amazement**.*

a·maz·ing /ə'meɪzɪŋ/ *adj.* making someone feel very surprised, often because something is very good or very unexpected: *an amazing coincidence* | ***It's amazing how** many things have gone wrong.* —**amazingly** *adv.*

THESAURUS

surprising, **extraordinary**, **shocking**, **astonishing**, **astounding**, **staggering**, **stunning**
➔ see Thesaurus box at SURPRISING

am·bas·sa·dor /æm'bæsədɚ, əm-/ *n.* [C] an important official who represents his/her country in another country: *the Mexican **ambassador to** Canada* —**ambassadorial** /æmˌbæsə'dɔriəl/ *adj.*

am·bi·ance, **ambience** /'æmbiəns, 'ɑmbiɑns/ *n.* [U] the way a place makes you feel: *the restaurant's friendly ambiance*

am·bi·dex·trous /ˌæmbɪ'dɛkstrəs/ *adj.* able to use both hands with equal skill

am·bi·gu·i·ty /ˌæmbə'gyuəṭi/ *n.* plural **ambiguities** [C,U] the state of being AMBIGUOUS: *the ambiguity of her words*

am·big·u·ous /æm'bɪgyuəs/ *adj.* something that is ambiguous is confusing or not clear because it can be understood in more than one way: *Their response was somewhat ambiguous.*

am·bi·tion /æm'bɪʃən/ *n.* **1** [C] a strong desire to do or achieve something: *Her **ambition** is **to** climb Mount Everest.* | *She seems determined to **achieve** all her **ambitions**.* **2** [U] the quality of being determined to succeed: *Saul **has** no **ambition** at all.*

am·bi·tious /æm'bɪʃəs/ *adj.* **1** needing a lot of skill and effort to achieve something: *an ambitious mission to Mars* **2** having a strong desire to be successful or powerful: *a young and ambitious man* —**ambitiously** *adv.*

A

am·biv·a·lent /æm'bɪvələnt/ *adj.* not sure whether you want or like something or not: *His wife was* ***ambivalent about*** *having a child.* —**ambivalence** *n.* [U]

am·ble /'æmbəl/ *v.* [I] to walk slowly in a relaxed way: *We* ***ambled along/down*** *the beach.*

A

THESAURUS

walk, march, stride, stroll, wander, creep, sneak, trudge, limp, wade, hike
→ see Thesaurus box at WALK[1]

am·bu·lance /'æmbyələns/ *n.* [C] a special vehicle for taking sick or injured people to the hospital: *Somebody should* ***call an ambulance.***

am·bush[1] /'æmbʊʃ/ *n.* [C] a sudden attack on someone by people who have been hiding and waiting to attack: *Two soldiers were killed in an ambush.*

THESAURUS

attack, invasion, raid, assault, counterattack, assault, mugging, rape
→ see Thesaurus box at ATTACK[1]

ambush[2] *v.* [T] to attack someone from a place where you have been hiding

a·me·lio·rate /ə'milyə,reɪt/ *v.* [I,T] *formal* to make something better —**amelioration** /ə,milyə'reɪʃən/ *n.* [U]

a·men /,eɪ'mɛn, ,ɑ-/ *interjection* said at the end of a prayer to express agreement or the hope that it will be true

a·me·na·ble /ə'minəbəl, ə'mɛ-/ *adj.* **1** willing to listen to or do something: *a child who is* ***amenable to*** *your suggestions* **2** appropriate for a particular type of treatment: *jobs that are* ***amenable to*** *flexible scheduling*

a·mend /ə'mɛnd/ *v.* [T] to make small changes or improvements, especially in the words of a law: *The act was amended to protect wildlife.*

a·mend·ment /ə'mɛndmənt/ *n.* [C,U] a change, especially in the words of a law: *an* ***amendment to*** *the banking bill*

a·mends /ə'mɛndz/ *n.* **make amends** to do something that shows you are sorry for something: *There must be some way I can make amends.*

a·men·i·ty /ə'mɛnəṭi, ə'mi-/ *n.* plural **amenities** [C usually plural] something in a place that makes living there enjoyable and pleasant: *a housing development with a pool and other amenities*

A·mer·i·can[1] /ə'mɛrɪkən/ *n.* [C] someone from the U.S.

American[2] *adj.* relating to or coming from the U.S.: *American cars*

A·mer·i·ca·na /ə,mɛrə'kɑnə/ *n.* [U] objects, styles, stories, etc. that are typical of America

A,merican 'dream *n.* **the American Dream** the belief that everyone in the U.S. has the opportunity to be successful if s/he works hard

A,merican 'Indian *n.* [C] → NATIVE AMERICAN

A·mer·i·can·ize /ə'mɛrɪkə,naɪz/ *v.* [T] to change something or someone to make he, she, or it more American: *After ten years here, we've become very Americanized.* —**Americanization** /ə,mɛrɪkənə'zeɪʃən/ *n.* [U]

A·mer·i·cas /ə'mɛrɪkəz/ *n.* **the Americas** [plural] North, Central, and South America considered together as a whole

a·mi·a·ble /'eɪmiəbəl/ *adj.* friendly and pleasant: *an amiable child* —**amiably** *adv.*

am·i·ca·ble /'æmɪkəbəl/ *adj.* feeling friendly and doing things without arguments: *an amicable divorce*

a·mid /ə'mɪd/ **also a·midst** /ə'mɪdst/ *prep. formal* among or in the middle of: *life amid the horrors of war*

a·miss /ə'mɪs/ *adj.* **be amiss** *formal* to be a problem or to be wrong: *She sensed something was amiss.*

am·mo /'æmoʊ/ *n.* [U] *informal* ammunition

am·mo·nia /ə'moʊnyə/ *n.* [U] a gas or liquid with a strong unpleasant smell, used in cleaning

am·mu·ni·tion /,æmyə'nɪʃən/ *n.* [U] **1** things such as bullets, bombs, etc. that are fired from guns **2** information that can be used in order to criticize someone or win an argument against him or her: *The scandal has given his opponents plenty of ammunition.*

am·ne·sia /æm'niʒə/ *n.* [U] the medical condition of not being able to remember anything

am·ne·si·ac /æm'nizi,æk, -'niʒi-/ *n.* [C] someone with AMNESIA

am·nes·ty /'æmnəsti/ *n.* plural **amnesties** [C,U] an official order forgiving criminals or freeing prisoners, especially people who have opposed the government

a·moe·ba /ə'mibə/ *n.* [C] a very small creature that has only one cell

a·mok /ə'mʌk, ə'mɑk/ *adv.* **run amok** to behave or happen in an uncontrolled way

a·mong /ə'mʌŋ/ **also a·mongst** /ə'mʌŋst/ *prep.* **1** in a particular group of people or things: *unemployment among men under 25 | The university is among the top 10 in the nation. | Relax, you're* ***among friends.*** | *They were talking* ***amongst themselves*** (=a group of people were talking). **2** in the middle of, through, or between: *We walked among the huge redwood trees. | He stood among the huge piles of papers, frowning.*

USAGE

Between and **among** are both used to talk about the position of someone or something.
Use **between** when there is one other person or thing on each side of someone or something: *I sat between Alex and Sarah.*
Use **among** when there are two or more people or things on each side of someone or something: *The hut was hidden among the trees.*

3 used when mentioning one or two people or things from a larger group: *Swimming and diving are among the most popular Olympic events.* | *We discussed,* ***among other things****, ways to raise money.*

a·mor·al /eɪˈmɔrəl, -ˈmɑr-/ *adj.* not moral: *his amoral actions*

am·o·rous /ˈæmərəs/ *adj.* showing or relating to sexual love

a·mor·phous /əˈmɔrfəs/ *adj. formal* without a fixed form or shape, or without clear organization

a·mount[1] /əˈmaʊnt/ *n.* [C] how much of something there is, or how much is needed: *a large* ***amount of*** *money* | *Please pay the full amount.* | *a huge amount of time* | *Add a small amount of water.*

USAGE

Amount is used with uncountable nouns: *a large amount of money*
Number is used with countable nouns: *a large number of cities*

amount[2] *v.*

amount to sth *phr. v.* **1** to add up to a total of a particular amount: *Jenny's debts amount to over $1,000.* **2** to mean something without saying it directly: *What he said amounted to an apology.* **3 not amount to something/anything/much** to not be important, valuable, or successful: *His father never thought he'd amount to much.*

amp /æmp/ **also am·pere** /ˈæmpɪr, -pɛr/ *n.* [C] a unit for measuring an electric current

am·phet·a·mine /æmˈfɛt̬əˌmin, -mɪn/ *n.* [C,U] a drug that gives people more energy and makes them feel excited

am·phib·i·an /æmˈfɪbiən/ *n.* [C] an animal such as a FROG that can live on land and in water

am·phib·i·ous /æmˈfɪbiəs/ *adj.* **1** an amphibious vehicle can travel on land and water **2** an amphibious animal can live on land and in water

am·phi·the·a·ter /ˈæmfəˌθiət̬ɚ/ *n.* [C] a large structure with no roof and rows of seats that curve partly around a central space, used for performances

am·ple /ˈæmpəl/ *adj.* **1** more than enough: *There will be ample opportunity to ask questions.* **2 ample belly/bosom etc.** a big stomach, etc., in a way that is attractive or pleasant —**amply** *adv.*

am·pli·fi·er /ˈæmpləˌfaɪɚ/ *n.* [C] a piece of electronic equipment that makes an electrical sound signal stronger, so that it is loud enough to hear ➔ see picture at ACOUSTIC

am·pli·fy /ˈæmpləˌfaɪ/ *v.* past tense and past participle **amplified**, third person singular **amplifies** [T] **1** to make something louder or stronger: *an amplified guitar* **2** *formal* to explain something in more detail —**amplification** /ˌæmpləfəˈkeɪʃən/ *n.* [singular, U]

am·pu·tate /ˈæmpyəˌteɪt/ *v.* [I,T] to cut off a part of someone's body for medical reasons: *Doctors had to amputate his left leg.* —**amputation** /ˌæmpyəˈteɪʃən/ *n.* [C,U]

am·pu·tee /ˌæmpyəˈti/ *n.* [C] someone who has a part of his/her body cut off for medical reasons

a·muck /əˈmʌk/ *adv.* ➔ AMOK

a·muse /əˈmyuz/ *v.* [T] **1** to make someone laugh or smile: *The question seemed to amuse him.* **2** to make the time pass in an enjoyable way for someone: *the stories she tells to amuse her daughter*

a·mused /əˈmyuzd/ *adj.* **1** thinking something is funny: *He looked amused by my embarrassment.* **2 keep sb amused** to entertain or interest someone for a long time: *games to keep the kids amused*

a·muse·ment /əˈmyuzmənt/ *n.* **1** [U] the feeling you have when you think something is funny: *She looked at him* ***with/in amusement****.* **2** [C,U] something you do to make the time pass in an enjoyable way: *What do you do* ***for amusement****?*

a'musement ˌpark *n.* [C] a large park where people can play games of skill, go on rides, and see performances

a·mus·ing /əˈmyuzɪŋ/ *adj.* funny and entertaining: *Luckily, Joe* ***found*** *it* ***amusing*** (=thought it was funny). | *a* ***highly/mildly/fairly amusing*** *movie*

THESAURUS

funny, **hilarious**, **hysterical**, **witty**, **corny**, **humorous**
➔ see Thesaurus box at FUNNY[1]

an /ən; *strong* æn/ *indefinite article* a – used when the following word begins with a vowel sound: *an orange* | *an X-ray* | *an hour*

a·nach·ro·nism /əˈnækrəˌnɪzəm/ *n.* [C] someone or something that is or seems to be in the wrong historical time: *Today, small farmers are almost an anachronism.* —**anachronistic** /əˌnækrəˈnɪstɪk/ *adj.*

an·a·gram /ˈænəˌgræm/ *n.* [C] a word or phrase made by changing the order of the letters in another word or phrase: *"Silent" is an anagram of "listen."*

a·nal /ˈeɪnl/ *n.* [C] **1** relating to the ANUS **2** *disapproving* showing a lot of concern with small details: *Don't be so anal.*

an·al·ge·sic /ˌænlˈdʒizɪk◂/ *n.* [C] *technical* a drug that reduces pain

a·nal·o·gous /əˈnæləgəs/ *adj. formal* similar to another situation or thing: *The system works in a way that is* ***analogous to*** *a large clock.*

a·nal·o·gy /əˈnælədʒi/ *n.* plural **analogies** [C,U] something that seems similar in two situations, processes, etc.: *We can* ***draw/make an analogy*** *between the brain and a computer.*

a·nal·y·sis /əˈnæləsɪs/ *n.* [C,U] **1** the careful examination of something in order to understand it better or see what it consists of: *an* ***analysis of***

the data | *a blood sample sent* ***for analysis*** **2** PSYCHOANALYSIS

an·a·lyst /ˈænl-ɪst/ *n.* [C] **1** someone whose job is to analyze things: *a financial analyst* **2** PSYCHOANALYST

an·a·lyt·ic·al /ˌænlˈɪṭɪkəl/ **also** **an·a·lyt·ic** /ˌænlˈɪṭɪk/ *adj.* using methods that help you examine things carefully: *an analytical mind* | *analytic skills*

A

an·al·yze /ˈænlˌaɪz/ *v.* [T] **1** to examine or think about something carefully in order to understand it: *students learning to analyze literature* | *The patient's blood is then analyzed.* **2** to examine someone's mental or emotional problems using PSYCHOANALYSIS

an·ar·chy /ˈænɚki/ *n.* [U] **1** a situation in which no one obeys rules or laws: *the period of anarchy before and after the riots* **2** a situation in which there is no government in a country —**anarchist** *n.* [C] —**anarchic** /æˈnɑrkɪk/ *adj.*

a·nath·e·ma /əˈnæθəmə/ *n.* [singular, U] *formal* something that is completely the opposite of what you believe in: *ideas that are* ***anathema to*** *conservative voters*

a·nat·o·my /əˈnæṭəmi/ *n.* [U] the scientific study of the structure of the body —**anatomical** /ˌænəˈtɑmɪkəl/ *adj.*

an·ces·tor /ˈænˌsɛstɚ/ *n.* [C] a member of your family who lived in past times [➡ **descendant**]: *the traditions of their ancestors* —**ancestral** /ænˈsɛstrəl/ *adj.*

an·ces·try /ˈænˌsɛstri/ *n.* [U] the members of your family who lived in past times: *people* ***of*** *Scottish* ***ancestry***

an·chor¹ /ˈæŋkɚ/ *n.* [C] **1** someone who reads the news on television or radio and introduces news reports: *the local evening news anchor* **2** a heavy metal object that is lowered into the water to prevent a ship or boat from moving **3** someone or something that provides a feeling of support, strength, or safety: *He's the anchor for the team's defense.*

anchor² *v.* **1** [I,T] to lower the anchor on a ship or boat to keep it from moving: *Three tankers were anchored in the harbor.* **2** [T] to be the person who reads the news and introduces reports on television or radio: *Collins anchors the six o'clock news.* **3** [T] to fasten something firmly to something so that it cannot move: *The main rope* ***anchors*** *the tent* ***to*** *the ground.* **4** [T] to provide a feeling of support, safety, or help: *Travolta anchors a complicated plot with a strong performance.*

an·chor·man /ˈæŋkɚˌmæn/, **an·chor·wom·an** /ˈæŋkɚˌwʊmən/ *n.* [C] plural **anchormen** /-ˌmɛn/, **anchorwomen** /-ˌwɪmɪn/ ➔ ANCHOR¹

an·cho·vy /ˈænˌtʃoʊvi, -tʃə-, ænˈtʃoʊvi/ *n.* plural **anchovies** [C,U] a very small ocean fish that tastes very salty

an·cient /ˈeɪnʃənt/ *adj.* **1** happening or existing very far back in history: *ancient Rome*

THESAURUS

old, antique
➔ see Thesaurus box at OLD

2 *humorous* very old: *an ancient truck piled with furniture* ➔ OLD

and /n, ən, ənd; *strong* ænd/ *conjunction* **1** used in order to join two words or parts of sentences: *a peanut butter and jelly sandwich* | *They have two kids, a boy and a girl.* | *Martha cooks, and Tom does the dishes.* **2** used in order to say that one thing happens after another: *Grant knocked and went in.* **3** *spoken* used instead of "to" after "come," "go," "try," and some other verbs: *Try and finish your homework before dinner, okay?* | *We're going to go and play basketball.* **4** used when adding numbers: *Six and four make ten.* | *a hundred and thirty dollars* **5** used in order to say that one thing is caused by something else: *I missed supper and I'm starving!* **6** used between repeated words to emphasize what you are saying: *She spent more and more time alone.*

and·ro·gyn·ous /ænˈdrɑdʒənəs/ *adj.* **1** someone who is androgynous looks both female and male **2** an androgynous plant or animal has both male and female parts

an·droid /ˈændrɔɪd/ *n.* [C] a ROBOT that looks completely human

an·ec·dot·al /ˌænɪkˈdoʊṭl/ *adj.* consisting of stories based on someone's personal experience: *There is* ***anecdotal evidence*** *that this can help asthma sufferers.*

an·ec·dote /ˈænɪkˌdoʊt/ *n.* [C] a short interesting story about a particular person or event

a·ne·mi·a /əˈnimiə/ *n.* [U] a medical condition in which there are not enough red cells in your blood —**anemic** *adj.*

an·es·the·sia /ˌænəsˈθiʒə/ *n.* [U] the use of ANESTHETICS in medicine

an·es·thet·ic /ˌænəsˈθɛṭɪk/ *n.* [C,U] a drug that stops feelings of pain, used during a medical operation: *an operation done under a* ***local/general anesthetic*** (=affecting part or all of your body)

a·nes·thet·ist /əˈnɛsθəṭɪst/ *n.* [C] someone whose job is to give ANESTHETIC to people in hospitals

a·nes·the·tize /əˈnɛsθəˌtaɪz/ *v.* [T] to make someone unable to feel pain or strong emotions

a·new /əˈnu/ *adv. literary* in a new or different way: *She started life anew in New York.*

an·gel /ˈeɪndʒəl/ *n.* [C] **1** a spirit who lives with God in heaven, usually represented as a person with wings and dressed in white **2** *spoken* someone who is very kind or helpful: *Oh, thanks! You're an angel!* —**angelic** /ænˈdʒɛlɪk/ *adj.*

an·ger¹ /ˈæŋgɚ/ *n.* [U] a strong feeling of wanting to hurt or criticize someone because s/he has done something bad to you or been unkind to you: *his feelings of anger and frustration* | *Paul shouted at him* ***in anger.*** | *his* ***anger at*** *his mother*

anger[2] *v.* [T] to make someone feel angry: *The court's decision angered environmentalists.*

an·gle[1] /ˈæŋgəl/ *n.* [C] **1** the space between two lines or surfaces that meet or cross each other, measured in degrees [➡ **right angle**]: *an angle of 90 degrees | a 45-degree angle* **2 at an angle** not upright or straight: *The plant was growing at an angle.* **3** a way of considering a problem or situation: *We need to **look at** this **from a new angle**.*

angle[2] *v.* [T] to turn or move something so that it is not straight or upright: *a lamp angled to give the best light*

angle for sth *phr. v.* to try to get something without asking for it directly: *I think she's angling for an invitation.*

An·gli·can /ˈæŋglɪkən/ *adj.* relating to the official church of England or related churches, such as the Episcopal church —**Anglican** *n.* [C]

an·go·ra /æŋˈgɔrə/ *n.* [U] wool or thread made from the fur of some goats or rabbits

an·gry /ˈæŋgri/ *adj.* feeling or showing anger: *I'm so **angry with/at** her! | My parents were really **angry about** my grades. | Lerner **got angry** and started shouting.* —**angrily** *adv.*

THESAURUS

annoyed – a little angry: *I get annoyed with the kids.*
irritated – feeling annoyed and not patient with people or things: *I was getting irritated by all the noise.*
livid/furious – very angry: *My teacher will be furious if my essay's late again.*
mad informal – very angry: *Mom was mad at me for not cleaning up.*
➔ HAPPY, SAD

angst /ɑŋst, ˈæŋst/ *n.* [U] strong feelings of anxiety and sadness because you are worried about your life

an·guish /ˈæŋgwɪʃ/ *n.* [U] suffering caused by extreme pain or worry: *"No!" cried her mother, **in anguish**.* —**anguished** *adj.*: *her anguished parents*

an·gu·lar /ˈæŋgyələ˞/ *adj.* **1** having sharp corners: *an angular shape* **2** very thin, and without much flesh on your bones: *a tall, angular young man*

an·i·mal[1] /ˈænəməl/ *n.* [C] **1** a living creature such as a cow or dog, that is not a bird, insect, fish, or person: *farm animals | wild animals* **2** any living creature, including people: *Humans are highly intelligent animals.* **3** *informal* someone who behaves in a cruel, violent, or rude way: *He's an animal – stay out of his way.* ➔ **party animal** at PARTY

animal[2] *adj.* **1** relating to or made from animals: *animal fats* **2 animal urges/instincts etc.** human feelings, desires, etc. that relate to sex, food, and other basic needs

an·i·mate[1] /ˈænəˌmeɪt/ *v.* [T] to make something seem to have more life or energy: *Laughter animated his face.*

an·i·mate[2] /ˈænəmɪt/ *adj. formal* living [≠ **inanimate**]

an·i·mat·ed /ˈænəˌmeɪt̬ɪd/ *adj.* **1** full of interest and energy: *an animated debate* **2** an animated CARTOON, movie, etc. is one in which pictures, clay models, etc. seem to move and talk —**animatedly** *adv.*

an·i·ma·tion /ˌænəˈmeɪʃən/ *n.* [U] **1** the process of making ANIMATED movies, etc. **2** energy and excitement: *They were talking with animation.*

an·i·mos·i·ty /ˌænəˈmɑsət̬i/ *n.* plural **animosities** [C,U] *formal* strong dislike or hatred

an·kle /ˈæŋkəl/ *n.* [C] the joint between your foot and your leg: *The skirt came down to her ankles.* ➔ see picture on page A3

an·nals /ˈænlz/ *n.* **in the annals of history/science etc.** in the whole history of a particular subject

an·nex[1] /əˈnɛks, ˈænɛks/ *v.* [T] to take control of a country or area next to your own, especially by using force —**annexation** /ˌænɪkˈseɪʃən, ˌænɛk-/ *n.* [C,U]

annex[2] *n.* [C] a separate building that has been added to a larger one

an·ni·hi·late /əˈnaɪəˌleɪt/ *v.* [T] to destroy something or defeat someone completely —**annihilation** /əˌnaɪəˈleɪʃən/ *n.* [U]

an·ni·ver·sa·ry /ˌænəˈvə˞səri/ *n.* plural **anniversaries** [C] a date on which something important or special happened in an earlier year [➡ **birthday**]: *Our **wedding anniversary** is in June. | A parade was held on the **anniversary of** the revolution.*

an·nounce /əˈnaʊns/ *v.* [T] **1** to officially and publicly tell people about something: *The company announced plans to build 300 homes. | The Senator **announced that** he was running for a fourth term.* **2** to say something in a loud or confident way, especially something other people will not like: *Randy suddenly **announced (that)** he was leaving.*

an·nounce·ment /əˈnaʊnsmənt/ *n.* **1** [C] an official public statement: *School announcements are broadcast over the PA system. | Carter **made the announcement** on Wednesday. | the **announcement that** he had died* **2** [U] the act of telling people something publicly: *the announcement of the winners*

an·nounc·er /əˈnaʊnsə˞/ *n.* [C] someone who gives people news or tells them what is happening at an event, during a broadcast, etc.

an·noy /əˈnɔɪ/ *v.* [T] to make someone feel slightly angry about something [= **irritate**]: *His reaction annoyed her.*

an·noy·ance /əˈnɔɪəns/ *n.* **1** [U] the feeling of being slightly angry [= **irritation**]: *a look of annoyance | **To** her **annoyance**, he was late.*

2 [C] something that makes you slightly angry: *The noise was an annoyance.*

an·noyed /əˈnɔɪd/ *adj.* slightly angry [= **irritated**]: *I was* ***annoyed at*** *myself for telling him.* | *Joel is really* ***annoyed about*** *the mess.* | *My sister's* ***annoyed (that)*** *we didn't call.* | *Her father was* ***getting annoyed with*** *her.*

A

> **THESAURUS**
>
> **angry**, **irritated**, **livid**, **furious**, **mad**
> → see Thesaurus box at ANGRY

an·noy·ing /əˈnɔɪ-ɪŋ/ *adj.* making you feel slightly angry [= **irritating**]: *an annoying habit* | ***It's annoying that*** *we didn't know about this before.* —**annoyingly** *adv.*

an·nu·al[1] /ˈænyuəl/ *adj.* **1** happening once a year: *the annual conference*

> **THESAURUS**
>
> **regular**, **hourly**, **daily**, **weekly**, **monthly**, **yearly**, **annually**
> → see Thesaurus box at REGULAR[1]

2 calculated over a period of one year: *my annual income* —**annually** *adv.*: *The jazz festival is held annually in July.*

annual[2] *n.* [C] a plant that lives for one year or season

an·nu·i·ty /əˈnuət̬i/ *n.* plural **annuities** [C] an amount of money that is paid each year to someone from an INVESTMENT

an·nul /əˈnʌl/ *v.* past tense and past participle **annulled**, present participle **annulling** [T] *technical* to officially state that a marriage or legal agreement no longer exists: *Their marriage was annulled last year.* —**annulment** *n.* [C,U]

a·noint /əˈnɔɪnt/ *v.* [T] to put oil or water on someone's head or body during a religious ceremony —**anointment** *n.* [C,U]

a·nom·a·ly /əˈnɑməli/ *n.* plural **anomalies** [C,U] *formal* something that is very noticeable because it is so different from what is usual: *Women firefighters are still an anomaly in a largely male profession.*

a·non. /əˈnɑn/ the written abbreviation of **anonymous**

an·o·nym·i·ty /ˌænəˈnɪmɪt̬i/ *n.* [U] the state of not having your name known

a·non·y·mous /əˈnɑnəməs/ *adj.* **1** not known by name: *an anonymous writer* | *an official who wished to* ***remain anonymous*** **2** done, made, or given by someone whose name is not known: *an anonymous letter* **3** without interesting features or qualities: *an anonymous black car* —**anonymously** *adv.*

a·no·rex·i·a /ˌænəˈrɛksiə/ *n.* [U] a mental illness that makes people, especially young women, stop eating

a·no·rex·ic /ˌænəˈrɛksɪk/ *adj.* having anorexia, or relating to anorexia —**anorexic** *n.* [C]

an·oth·er /əˈnʌðɚ/ *determiner, pron.* **1** one more person or thing of the same kind: *Do you want another beer?* | *I'll cancel that check and send you another.*

> **THESAURUS**
>
> **more**, **extra**, **additional**, **further**
> → see Thesaurus box at MORE[2]

2 a different person or thing: *Is there another room we could use?* | *It is easy to send information from one place to another.* **3** something in addition to a particular amount, distance, period of time, etc.: *We'll wait another ten minutes.* → **one after the other/one after another** at ONE[2] → ONE ANOTHER

an·swer[1] /ˈænsɚ/ *v.* [I,T] **1** to reply to something that someone has asked or written: *Why don't you answer me?* | *She thought for a minute before answering.* | *The witness refused to* ***answer the question.*** | *He* ***answered that*** *he did not know.*

> **THESAURUS**
>
> **answer** – to say something to someone when s/he has asked you a question or spoken to you: *She reluctantly answered his question.*
> **reply** – to answer someone – used especially in written English: *"Are you coming?" "Yes," he replied.*
> **respond** formal – to answer someone, especially in a detailed way: *We would like to thank everyone who responded to our survey.*

2 to reply to a question in a test, competition, etc.: *Please answer questions 1–20.* **3 answer the telephone/door** to pick up the telephone when it rings or go to the door when someone knocks or rings a bell **4** to react to something that someone else has done: *The army answered by firing into the crowd.*

answer (sb) **back** *phr. v.* to reply to someone in a rude way: *Don't answer back, young man!*

answer for sth *phr. v.* **1** to explain why you did something or why something happened, and be punished if necessary: *Voters should make politicians answer for the damage to the environment.* **2 have a lot to answer for** to be responsible for causing a lot of trouble

answer to sb *phr. v.* to be judged by someone or have to explain your actions to him/her, especially someone you work for: *Wharton doesn't answer to anyone.*

answer[2] *n.* **1** [C,U] a reply to what someone asks or writes: *the* ***answer to*** *my question* | *Can you* ***give*** *me* ***an answer*** *as soon as possible?* | ***I get*** *a different* ***answer*** *every time I ask him.* | ***In answer to*** *reporters'* ***questions****, Wallace said they were looking into the matter.* **2** [C] a reply to a question in a test, competition, etc.: *What was the* ***answer to*** *question 7?* **3** [C] something that you get as a result of thinking or calculating with numbers: *The answer is 255.* **4** [C] something that solves a problem: *There are no **easy/simple/right** answers.* | *the **answer to** the illegal immigration problem* **5** [singular, U] if you get an answer when you call someone, knock on his/her door, etc., s/he picks up the telephone or comes to the door: *I knocked, but there was **no answer**.* ➔ see Topic box at TELEPHONE[1]

an·swer·a·ble /ˈænsərəbəl/ *adj.* **be answerable (to sb) for sth** to have to explain your actions to someone

ˈanswering maˌchine *n.* [C] a machine that records your telephone calls when you cannot answer them ➔ see Topic box at TELEPHONE[1]

ant /ænt/ *n.* [C] a common small black or red insect that lives in groups

an·tac·id /ˌæntˈæsɪd/ *n.* [C] a drug that gets rid of the burning feeling in your stomach when you have eaten too much, drunk too much alcohol, etc.

an·tag·o·nism /ænˈtægəˌnɪzəm/ *n.* [U] strong opposition to or hatred of someone else: *Polucci's **antagonism toward** the press*

THESAURUS

opposition, **objection**, **antipathy**
➔ see Thesaurus box at OPPOSITION

an·tag·o·nist /ænˈtægənɪst/ *n.* [C] your opponent in an argument, fight, etc.

an·tag·o·nis·tic /ænˌtægəˈnɪstɪk/ *adj.* showing opposition to or hatred of someone or something: *an antagonistic attitude* —**antagonistically** *adv.*

an·tag·o·nize /ænˈtægəˌnaɪz/ *v.* [T] to make someone feel angry with you: *The reaction of the police antagonized the black community.*

Ant·arc·tic /æntˈɑrktɪk, æn*t*ˈɑrtɪk/ *n.* **the Antarctic** the very cold, most southern part of the world —**antarctic** *adj.*

Ant·arc·tic·a /æntˈɑrktɪkə, æn*t*ˈɑrtɪkə/ *n.* one of the seven CONTINENTS that is the most southern area of land on earth

an·te[1] /ˈænti/ *n.* **up/raise the ante** to increase your demands or try to get more things from a situation

ante[2] *v.*
ante up (sth) *phr. v.* to pay an amount of money in order to be able to do or be involved in something

ant·eat·er /ˈæn*t*itər/ *n.* [C] an animal that has a very long nose and eats small insects

an·te·lope /ˈæn*t*əlˌoʊp/ *n.* [C] an animal that has long horns, can run very fast, and is very graceful

an·ten·na /ænˈtɛnə/ *n.* [C] **1** a piece of equipment on a television, car, roof, etc. for receiving or sending radio or television signals ➔ see picture on page A12 **2** plural **antennae** /-ni/ one of two long thin things on an insect's head that it uses to feel things ➔ see picture on page A2

an·them /ˈænθəm/ *n.* [C] **1** a formal or religious song **2** a song that a particular group of people consider to be very important to them: *The Rolling Stones' "Satisfaction" was an anthem for a generation.*

ant·hill /ˈæntˌhɪl/ *n.* [C] a small pile of dirt on the ground over the place where ANTS live

an·thol·o·gy /ænˈθɑlədʒi/ *n.* plural **anthologies** [C] a set of stories, poems, etc. by different people collected together in one book: *an **anthology of** American literature*

an·thrax /ˈænθræks/ *n.* [U] a serious disease that affects cattle and sheep, and that can affect people

an·thro·pol·o·gy /ˌænθrəˈpɑlədʒi/ *n.* [U] the scientific study of people, their societies, their beliefs, etc. —**anthropologist** *n.* [C] —**anthropological** /ˌænθrəpəˈlɑdʒɪkəl/ *adj.*

an·ti·air·craft /ˌæn*t*iˈɛrkræft/ *adj.* able to be used against enemy aircraft: *antiaircraft missiles*

an·ti·bi·ot·ic /ˌæn*t*ɪbaɪˈɑtɪk, ˌæntaɪ-/ *n.* [C usually plural] a drug that is used in order to kill BACTERIA and cure infections —**antibiotic** *adj.*

an·ti·bod·y /ˈæn*t*ɪˌbɑdi/ *n.* plural **antibodies** [C] a substance produced by your body to fight disease

an·tic·i·pate /ænˈtɪsəˌpeɪt/ *v.* [T] **1** to expect that something will happen, and do something to prepare for it or prevent it: *City officials are anticipating problems.* | *He **anticipates that** only 20% will finish the course.* **2** to think about something that is going to happen, especially something good: *Daniel was eagerly anticipating her arrival.*

an·tic·i·pa·tion /ænˌtɪsəˈpeɪʃən/ *n.* [U] the act of expecting something to happen: *They cleaned the church **in anticipation of** the bishop's visit.*

an·ti·cli·max /ˌæn*t*ɪˈklaɪmæks/ *n.* [C,U] something that seems disappointing because it happens after something that was much better: *After all the advertising, the concert itself was kind of an anticlimax.* —**anticlimactic** /ˌæn*t*ɪklaɪˈmæktɪk/ *adj.*

an·tics /ˈæn*t*ɪks/ *n.* [plural] behavior that seems strange, funny, silly, or annoying: *We're all growing tired of his childish antics.*

an·ti·de·pres·sant /ˌæn*t*ɪdɪˈprɛsənt, ˌæntaɪ-/ *n.* [C,U] a drug used for treating DEPRESSION (=a mental illness that makes people very unhappy) —**antidepressant** *adj.*

an·ti·dote /ˈæn*t*ɪˌdoʊt/ *n.* [C] **1** a substance that stops the effects of a poison: *an **antidote to** the bite of a rattlesnake* **2** something that makes an unpleasant situation better: *Laughter is one of the best **antidotes to** stress.*

an·ti·freeze /ˈæn*t*ɪˌfriz/ *n.* [U] a substance that is put in the water in car engines to stop it from freezing

an·ti·his·ta·mine /ˌæn*t*ɪˈhɪstəˌmin, -mɪn/ *n.* [C,U] a drug that is used for treating an ALLERGY or COLD (=common illness) —**antihistamine** *adj.*

an·tip·a·thy /ænˈtɪpəθi/ *n.* [U] *formal* a feeling of strong dislike or opposition

THESAURUS

opposition, objection, antagonism
➔ see Thesaurus box at OPPOSITION

an·ti·per·spi·rant /ˌæntɪˈpɚspərənt/ *n.* [U] a substance that you put under your arms to prevent you from SWEATING

A

an·ti·quat·ed /ˈæntɪˌkweɪt̬ɪd/ *adj.* old-fashioned and not appropriate for modern needs or conditions: *antiquated laws*

an·tique /ænˈtik/ *n.* [C] a piece of furniture, jewelry, etc. that is old and usually valuable [➡ **ancient**]: *priceless antiques* —**antique** *adj.*: *an antique table*

THESAURUS

old, ancient, vintage, classic
➔ see Thesaurus box at OLD

an·tiq·ui·ty /ænˈtɪkwət̬i/ *n.* **1** [U] ancient times: *a tradition that stretches back into antiquity* **2** [U] the state of being very old: *a building of great antiquity* **3** [C usually plural] a building or object made in ancient times: *a collection of Roman antiquities*

an·ti-Sem·i·tism /ˌæntiˈsɛməˌtɪzəm, ˌæntaɪ-/ *n.* [U] hatred of Jewish people —**anti-Semitic** /ˌæntisəˈmɪt̬ɪk, ˌæntaɪ-/ *adj.*

THESAURUS

racism, prejudice, discrimination, intolerance
➔ see Thesaurus box at PREJUDICE

an·ti·sep·tic /ˌæntəˈsɛptɪk/ *n.* [C] a chemical substance that prevents a wound from becoming infected —**antiseptic** *adj.*: *antiseptic lotion*

an·ti·so·cial /ˌæntiˈsoʊʃəl, ˌæntaɪ-/ *adj.* **1** not liking to meet people and talk to them: *Peter's colleagues regarded him as antisocial.*

THESAURUS

reserved, introverted, withdrawn
➔ see Thesaurus box at SHY[1]

2 not caring if you cause problems for or injuries to other people: *antisocial behavior among school children*

an·tith·e·sis /ænˈtɪθəsɪs/ *n.* [C] *formal* the exact opposite of something: *This chaotic, rigged election is the antithesis of democracy.*

an·ti·trust /ˌæntɪˈtrʌst, ˌæntaɪ-/ *adj.* preventing one company from unfairly controlling prices: *antitrust laws*

ant·ler /ˈæntˈlɚ/ *n.* [C] one of the two horns that look like tree branches on the head of animals such as DEER ➔ see picture on page A2

an·to·nym /ˈæntəˌnɪm/ *n.* [C] *technical* a word that means the opposite of another word. For example, "war" is the antonym of "peace" [≠ **synonym**]

a·nus /ˈeɪnəs/ *n.* [C] the hole in your body through which solid waste leaves your BOWELS

an·vil /ˈænvɪl/ *n.* [C] a heavy iron block on which pieces of metal are shaped using a hammer

anx·i·e·ty /æŋˈzaɪət̬i/ *n.* [U] a strong feeling of worry about something: *a lifestyle that creates stress and anxiety* | *parents' **anxiety about** violence in schools*

anx·ious /ˈæŋkʃəs, ˈæŋʃəs/ *adj.* **1** very worried about something, or showing that you are worried: *June's **anxious about** the results of her blood test.* | *an anxious look*

THESAURUS

worried, concerned, nervous, uneasy, stressed (out)
➔ see Thesaurus box at WORRIED

2 feeling strongly that you want something to happen, especially in order to improve a bad situation: *The Moores are **anxious to** adopt a child.* | *Company directors were **anxious for** a meeting.*

an·y[1] /ˈɛni/ *quantifier, pron.* **1** some – used in negative statements and questions: *Is there any coffee left?* | *Do you want any?* | *I don't think that will make any difference.* | *Are **any of** Norm's relatives coming for Christmas?* | *The Super Bowl is watched by more people than **any other** American sporting event.*

USAGE

Use **some** in questions when you think the answer will be "yes": *Would you like some coffee?*
Use **any** when you do not know what the answer will be: *Were there any letters for me?*

2 used in order to say that it does not matter which person or thing you choose from a group, or that something is true of all people or things from that group: ***Any of** the restaurants in Chinatown would be fine.* | *There are bad things about any job.* ➔ **in any case** at CASE[1] ➔ **at any rate** at RATE[1]

USAGE

Do not say "Any parents love their children." Say "All parents love their children."
Do not say "Any teacher must deal with these problems." Say "Every teacher must deal with these problems."

GRAMMAR

any, a
Use **any** with uncountable nouns or plural noun forms: *Do you have any money?*
Use **a** with singular noun forms: *Do you have a car?*
➔ A

any[2] *adv.* even a small amount or at all – used in negative statements or questions: *Are you feeling any better?* | *Sandra couldn't walk any farther.*

an·y·bod·y /ˈɛni,bɑdi, -,bʌdi, -bədi/ *pron. informal* ➔ ANYONE

an·y·how /ˈɛni,haʊ/ *adv. informal* ➔ ANYWAY

an·y·more, **any more** /,ɛniˈmɔr/ *adv.* **not anymore** used in order to say that something happened or was true before, but is not now: *Frank doesn't live here anymore.*

an·y·one /ˈɛni,wʌn, -wən/ *pron.* **1** any person or any people – used when it does not matter exactly who: *Anyone can learn to swim.* | *Why would anyone want to do that?* | *Have you told **anyone else**?* **2** a person or someone – used in questions and negative statements: *Is anyone home?* | *She'd just moved and didn't know anyone.*

an·y·place /ˈɛni,pleɪs/ *adv. informal* ➔ ANYWHERE

an·y·thing /ˈɛni,θɪŋ/ *pron.* **1** something or nothing – used in questions and negative statements: *Her dad didn't know anything about it.* | *Do you need **anything else** from the store?* **2** any thing, event, situation, etc., when it does not matter exactly which: *That cat will eat anything.* | *I was so worried it was hard to think about **anything else**.* **3 or anything** *spoken* said when there are several things or ideas that are possible: *Do you want a Coke or anything?* **4 anything like sb/sth** similar to someone or something: *Carrie doesn't look anything like her sister.* **5 anything but** used in order to emphasize that someone or something does not have a particular quality: *The book is anything but boring.* **6 anything goes** used in order to say that anything is acceptable: *Don't worry about what to wear – anything goes at Ben's parties.*

an·y·time /ˈɛni,taɪm/ *adv.* at any time: *Call me anytime.* | *Are you going to see him **anytime soon**?*

an·y·way /ˈɛni,weɪ/ *adv.* **1** in spite of something: *It was raining, but we went anyway.*

SPOKEN PHRASES

2 used in order to continue a story or change the subject of a conversation: *I think she's Lori's age, but anyway, she just had a baby.* | *Anyway, where do you want to go for lunch?* **3** used when you are ending a conversation: *Anyway, I guess I'd better go.* **4** used when you are saying something to support what you have just said: *We decided to sell it because nobody uses it anyway.* **5** used in order to add something that slightly changes what you have said: *Think about it a while – a few days, anyway.* **6** used in order to find out the real reason for something: *What were you doing at his house anyway?*

an·y·where /ˈɛni,wɛr/ *adv.* **1** in or to any place, when it does not matter exactly where: *Fly anywhere in the U.S. with this special offer.* | *I can't imagine living **anywhere else**.* **2** somewhere or nowhere – used in questions and negative statements: *I can't find my keys anywhere.* | *Are you going anywhere exciting?* **3 not anywhere near** not at all: *She doesn't consider her collection anywhere near complete.* **4 anywhere from one to ten** any age, number, amount, etc. between the two numbers: *He may get anywhere from 12 to 15% of the vote.* **5 not get anywhere** *spoken* to not be successful at something: *I'm trying to set up a meeting, but I don't seem to be getting anywhere.*

a·part /əˈpɑrt/ *adv.* **1** separated by distance or time: *The two towns are 15 miles apart.* | *Our birthdays are only two days apart.* | *The baby's never been **apart from** his mother.* **2** separated into many pieces: *He had to **take** the camera **apart** to fix it.* | *The book just **came apart** in my hands.* ➔ **fall apart** at FALL[1] **3 apart from a)** except for: *Apart from a couple of spelling mistakes, your paper looks fine.* **b)** in addition to: *What do you do for fun? Apart from volleyball, I mean.*

a·part·heid /əˈpɑrtaɪt, -teɪt, -taɪd/ *n.* [U] a system in which the different races in a country are separated from each other

a·part·ment /əˈpɑrt˺mənt/ *n.* [C] a place to live that consists of a set of rooms in a large building: *My apartment is really small.* | *She lives in a **studio/one-bedroom/two-bedroom apartment**.*

THESAURUS

house, **ranch house**, **ranch**, **cottage**, **row house**, **mansion**, **bungalow**, **duplex**, **condominium**, **condo**, **townhouse**, **mobile home**, **trailer**

➔ see Thesaurus box at HOUSE[1]

aˈpartment ˌbuilding also **aˈpartment ˌhouse** *n.* [C] a building that is divided into separate apartments

aˈpartment ˌcomplex *n.* [C] a group of apartment buildings built at the same time in the same area

ap·a·thet·ic /,æpəˈθɛt̮ɪk/ *adj.* not interested in something: *students who are apathetic about learning*

ap·a·thy /ˈæpəθi/ *n.* [U] the feeling of not being interested in something or not caring about life: *public apathy about the coming election*

ape /eɪp/ *n.* [C] a large monkey without a tail or with a very short tail, such as a GORILLA

a·per·i·tif /ə,pɛrəˈtif, ɑ-/ *n.* [C] a small alcoholic drink that you have before a meal

ap·er·ture /ˈæpɚtʃɚ/ *n.* [C] a small opening, especially one that lets light into a camera

a·pex /ˈeɪpɛks/ *n.* [C] **1** the top or highest part of something: *the apex of the pyramid* **2** the most successful part of something: *the apex of her career*

aph·o·rism /ˈæfə,rɪzəm/ *n.* [C] a short expression that says something true

aph·ro·dis·i·ac /,æfrəˈdizi,æk, -ˈdɪ-/ *n.* [C] a food or drug that makes someone feel sexual excitement —**aphrodisiac** *adj.*

A

a·piece /ə'pis/ *adv.* each: *Oranges are 20¢ apiece* (=for each one). | *We gave $10 apiece for the gift* (=each of us gave $10).

a·plomb /ə'plɑm, ə'plʌm/ *n. formal* **with aplomb** in a confident or skillful way, especially in a difficult situation: *She answered all their questions with aplomb.*

A

a·po·ca·lypse /ə'pɑkəlɪps/ *n.* [U] **1** a dangerous situation that results in great destruction, death, or harm **2 the Apocalypse** the religious idea of the destruction and end of the world —**apocalyptic** /əˌpɑkə'lɪptɪk/ *adj.*

a·po·lit·i·cal /ˌeɪpə'lɪṭɪkəl/ *adj.* not having any interest in or connection with politics

a·pol·o·get·ic /əˌpɑlə'dʒɛṭɪk/ *adj.* showing or saying that you are sorry about something: *Dave came in late, looking apologetic.* —**apologetically** *adv.*

a·pol·o·gize /ə'pɑləˌdʒaɪz/ *v.* [I] to say that you are sorry about something that you have done, said, etc.: *Harris* ***apologized for*** *being late.* | ***Apologize to*** *your sister now!*

COMMUNICATION

I'm sorry: *I'm sorry I was rude. I've had a bad day.*
I'm really/so sorry: *I'm really sorry that I hurt you.*
excuse me spoken: *"You're blocking the doorway." "Oh, excuse me."*
I apologize formal: *We apologize for the inconvenience.*
sb owes you an apology (=used especially when you think someone else should apologize to you): *I think they owe us an apology.*

a·pol·o·gy /ə'pɑlədʒi/ *n.* plural **-ies** [C] something that you say or write to show that you are sorry: *an* ***apology for*** *missing the meeting* | *The Senator* ***made*** *a formal* ***apology***. | *Please* ***accept*** *our* ***apologies***. | *I feel I* ***owe*** *you* ***an apology***.

ap·o·plec·tic /ˌæpə'plɛktɪk◂/ *adj.* **1** so angry you cannot control yourself **2** relating to a STROKE —**apoplexy** /'æpəˌplɛksi/ *n.* [U]

a·pos·tle /ə'pɑsəl/ *n.* [C] **1** one of the 12 men chosen by Christ to teach his message **2** someone who believes strongly in a new idea and tries to persuade other people to believe it —**apostolic** /ˌæpə'stɑlɪk/ *adj.*

a·pos·tro·phe /ə'pɑstrəfi/ *n.* [C] **a)** the mark (') used in writing to show that one or more letters or figures are missing, such as in don't (=do not) or '96 (=1896/1996, etc.) **b)** the same mark used before or after the letter "s" to show that something belongs or relates to someone: *Mandy's coat* | *the workers' strike* **c)** the same sign used before "s" to show the plural of letters and numbers: *4 A's and 2 B's on my report card*

ap·palled /ə'pɔld/ *adj.* very shocked and upset: *The boy's mother was* ***appalled at/by*** *the violence of the game.* —**appall** *v.* [T]

ap·pall·ing /ə'pɔlɪŋ/ *adj.* **1** shocking and terrible: *animals kept in appalling conditions* **2** *informal* very bad: *an appalling movie* —**appallingly** *adv.*

THESAURUS

bad, **awful**, **terrible**, **horrible**, **horrific**, **lousy**, **horrendous**, **atrocious**, **abysmal**
➔ see Thesaurus box at BAD[1]

ap·pa·rat·us /ˌæpə'ræṭəs, -'reɪṭəs/ *n.* plural **apparatus** or **apparatuses** **1** [U] a set of instruments, tools, machines, etc. used for a particular purpose: *an apparatus for breathing under water* **2** [C usually singular] the way in which a lot of people are organized to work together to do a job or control a country or company: *a large security apparatus*

ap·par·el /ə'pærəl/ *n.* [U] *formal* clothes: *men's apparel*

ap·par·ent /ə'pærənt, ə'pɛr-/ *adj.* **1** easily seen or understood: ***It was apparent that*** *the enemy was stronger than they had believed.* | *Her embarrassment was* ***apparent to*** *everyone in the room.* | ***For no apparent reason*** (=without a clear reason), *he began to shout at her.* **2** seeming to be true or real, although it may not really be: *his apparent lack of fear*

ap·par·ent·ly /ə'pærəntˀli, ə'pɛr-/ *adv.* **1** according to what you have heard is true, although you are not completely sure about it: *She apparently caught him in bed with another woman.* | *Apparently, the meeting went really well.* **2** according to the way something appears or someone looks, although it may not really be true: *We waited in apparently endless lines at the airport.*

ap·pa·ri·tion /ˌæpə'rɪʃən/ *n.* [C] ➔ GHOST

ap·peal[1] /ə'pil/ *v.* [I] **1** to make an urgent public request for help, money, information, etc.: *The water company* ***appealed to*** *everyone* ***to*** *save water.* | *charities* ***appealing for*** *money* **2 appeal to sb** to seem attractive or interesting to someone: *The program should appeal to older viewers.* **3** to make a formal request to a higher court or to someone in authority to change a decision: *We plan to appeal the verdict.*

appeal[2] *n.* **1** [C] an urgent public request for money, information, etc.: *Kennedy* ***made*** *a dramatic* ***appeal*** *for peace.* | *an* ***appeal for*** *food and medical aid* **2** [U] the quality that makes you like or want something: *her glamor and* ***sex appeal*** (=sexual attractiveness) | *Their music* ***has*** *a broad* ***appeal***. | *Romances have* ***appeal for*** *many readers.* **3** [C,U] a request to a higher court or to someone in authority to change a decision: *an* ***appeal to*** *the Supreme Court* | *His conviction was overturned* ***on appeal***.

ap·peal·ing /ə'pilɪŋ/ *adj.* attractive or interesting: *an appealing smile* | *O'Neal's playful nature makes him* ***appealing to*** *kids.* —**appealingly** *adv.*

ap·pear /ə'pɪr/ *v.* **1** [I] to begin to be seen: *Dark clouds began to appear in the sky. | A face appeared at the window.* **2** [linking verb] to seem: *The man **appeared to** be dead. | He tried hard to appear calm. | Light colors make a room appear bigger than it is.*

THESAURUS
seem, look
➔ see Thesaurus box at SEEM

3 [I] to take part in a movie, television program, play, etc.: *He'll be **appearing in** a new Broadway musical. | Davis **appeared on** Horn's breakthrough album.* **4** [I] to happen, exist, or become available for the first time: *Irving's novel is soon to **appear in** paperback.* **5** [I] to be present officially, especially in a court of law: *He failed to **appear in court**. | They were required to **appear before** a grand jury.*

ap·pear·ance /ə'pɪrəns/ *n.* [C] **1** the way someone or something looks or seems to other people: *He cared little about his appearance. | The Christmas lights gave the house a festive appearance.* **2** an arrival by someone or something: *the sudden **appearance of** several reporters* **3** the point at which something begins to exist or starts being used: *The industry has changed with the **appearance of** new technology.* **4** a public performance in a film, play, concert, etc.: *his first appearance on stage* **5** the act of arriving at or attending an event: *his first **public appearance** since the election | I **put in an appearance** at the wedding but did not stay long.*

ap·pease /ə'piz/ *v.* [T] to make someone less angry or stop him/her from attacking you by giving him/her what s/he wants: *A goat was killed to appease the spirits.* —**appeasement** *n.* [C]

ap·pel·late /ə'pɛlɪt/ *adj.* *law* an appellate court, judge, etc. is able to change a decision that was made earlier in a court of law

ap·pend /ə'pɛnd/ *v.* [T] *formal* to add something, especially a separate part, to a piece of writing: *The results of the survey are **appended to** this document.*

ap·pend·age /ə'pɛndɪdʒ/ *n.* [C] something that is added or attached to something larger or more important

ap·pen·di·ci·tis /əˌpɛndə'saɪt̬ɪs/ *n.* [U] an illness in which your APPENDIX swells and becomes painful

ap·pen·dix /ə'pɛndɪks/ *n.* [C] **1** a small organ in your body that has little or no use **2** plural **appendixes** or **appendices** /-dɪsiz/ a part at the end of a book that has additional information

ap·pe·tite /'æpəˌtaɪt/ *n.* [C,U] **1** a desire for food: *I seem to have **lost** my **appetite** lately. | Don't eat that cake now – you'll **ruin/spoil** your **appetite**.* **2** a desire or liking for a particular activity: *his **appetite for** books*

ap·pe·tiz·er /'æpəˌtaɪzɚ/ *n.* [C] a small dish of food served at the beginning of a meal

ap·pe·tiz·ing /'æpəˌtaɪzɪŋ/ *adj.* food that is appetizing looks or smells very good

ap·plaud /ə'plɔd/ *v.* [T] **1** to hit your open hands together to show that you have enjoyed a play, concert, speaker, etc. [= **clap**]: *As Maria walked onto the stage, the **audience applauded**.* **2** *formal* to express strong approval of an idea, plan, etc.: *We applaud the company's efforts to improve safety.*

ap·plause /ə'plɔz/ *n.* [U] the sound of people hitting their hands together in order to show that they enjoy or approve of something: *There was a burst of applause as the band came on stage. | Let's **give** Rodney **a big round of applause**!*

ap·ple /'æpəl/ *n.* [C] a hard round red or green fruit that is white inside, or the tree this fruit grows on: *apple pie* ➔ see picture at FRUIT

'apple ˌcider *n.* [C,U] CIDER

ap·ple·sauce /'æpəlˌsɔs/ *n.* [U] a thick smooth food made from cooked apples

ap·plet /'æplət/ *n.* [C] *technical* a computer program that is part of a larger program, and which performs a particular job, such as finding documents on the Internet

ap·pli·ance /ə'plaɪəns/ *n.* [C] a piece of electrical equipment such as a REFRIGERATOR or a DISHWASHER, used in people's homes: *kitchen appliances*

THESAURUS
machine, device, gadget
➔ see Thesaurus box at MACHINE[1]

ap·pli·ca·ble /'æplɪkəbəl, ə'plɪkəbəl/ *adj.* affecting or relating to a particular person, group, or situation: *These tax laws are not **applicable to** foreigners.*

ap·pli·cant /'æplɪkənt/ *n.* [C] someone who has formally asked for a job, place at a college, etc., especially by writing a letter: *There were 30 **applicants for** the job.*

ap·pli·ca·tion /ˌæplɪ'keɪʃən/ *n.* **1** [C] a formal, usually written, request for a job, place at a college, etc.: *an **application form** | a **job application** | The counselor will help students **fill out** college **applications**.* **2** [C] a piece of SOFTWARE: *multimedia applications* **3** [C,U] the use of a machine, idea, etc. for a practical purpose: *the **application of** fair housing laws | The research has many **practical applications**.* **4** [C,U] the act of putting something like paint, medicine, etc. on to a surface: *the **application of** fertilizer to the crops*

ap·pli·ca·tor /'æplɪˌkeɪt̬ɚ/ *n.* [C] a special brush or tool used for putting paint, glue, medicine, etc. on something

ap·plied /ə'plaɪd/ *adj.* a subject such as applied mathematics or applied science is studied for a practical purpose

A

A

ap·ply /ə'plaɪ/ *v.* past tense and past participle **applied**, third person singular **applies** **1** [I] to make a formal, especially written, request for a job, place at a college, permission to do something, etc.: *Fifteen people **applied for** the job.* | *He has **applied for** U.S. citizenship.* | *Anna **applied to** several colleges in California.* **2** [I,T] to have an effect on, involve, or concern a particular person, group, or situation: *The nutrition labeling requirements **apply to** most foods.* **3** [T] to use a method, idea, etc. in a particular situation, activity, or process: *Internships give students a chance to apply their skills in real situations.* **4** [T] to put something on a surface or press on the surface of something: *Apply the lotion evenly.* | ***Apply pressure** to the wound.* **5** [T] **apply yourself (to sth)** to work very hard and very carefully, especially for a long time: *He never really applied himself in school.*

ap·point /ə'pɔɪnt/ *v.* [T] **1** to choose someone for a job, position, etc.: *Palmer was **appointed to** the Board of Trustees.* | *Dr. Gordon was **appointed as** the local representative.* **2** *formal* to arrange or decide a time or place for something to happen: *Judge Bailey appointed a new time for the trial.* | *They met at the appointed time.*

ap·point·ee /ə,pɔɪn'ti/ *n.* [C] someone who is chosen to do a particular job: *a Presidential appointee*

ap·point·ment /ə'pɔɪnt˺mənt/ *n.* **1** [C] a meeting that has been arranged for a particular time and place: *an **appointment with** a reporter* | *I'd like to **make an appointment** with Dr. Hanson.* | *Lisa **has an appointment** at two.* | *She called a client to **cancel an appointment**.* **2** [C,U] the act of choosing someone for a job, position, etc.: *the **appointment of** a new Supreme Court Justice* **3 by appointment** after arranging to meet at a particular time: *Dr. Sutton will only see you by appointment.*

ap'pointment ,book *n.* [C] a book you keep at work with a CALENDAR in it, in which you write meetings, events, and other things you plan to do

ap·por·tion /ə'pɔrʃən/ *v.* [T] *formal* to decide how something should be divided between various people

ap·prais·al /ə'preɪzəl/ *n.* [C,U] an official judgment about how valuable, effective, or successful someone or something is: *an **appraisal of** a watch* (=finding out how much it is worth) | *a performance appraisal* (=judging how well someone does a job)

ap·praise /ə'preɪz/ *v.* [T] to make an APPRAISAL of someone or something: *The furniture was **appraised at** $14,000.* | *an appraising look*

THESAURUS

judge, evaluate, assess, gauge
➔ see Thesaurus box at JUDGE[2]

ap·pre·cia·ble /ə'priʃəbəl/ *adj.* large enough to be noticed, felt, or considered important: *There's no appreciable change in the patient's condition.* —**appreciably** *adv.*

ap·pre·ci·ate /ə'priʃi,eɪt/ *v.* **1** [T] to be grateful for something: *Mom really appreciated the flowers you sent.* | *Thanks for meeting with me. I **appreciate it**.* | ***I'd** really **appreciate it if** you'd turn that down.* **2** [T] to understand and enjoy the good qualities or value of something: *Dorm food made me appreciate Mom's home cooking.* **3** [T] to understand a difficult situation or problem: *I **appreciate that** many parents struggle to afford college fees.* | *You don't seem to **appreciate how** hard this is for us.* **4** [I] to gradually increase in value [≠ **depreciate**]

ap·pre·ci·a·tion /ə,priʃi'eɪʃən, ə,pri-/ *n.* [singular, U] **1** the feeling of being grateful for something: *I'd like to **show/express** my **appreciation** for everything you've done.* **2** an understanding of the importance or meaning of something: *an **appreciation of** the risks involved in rock climbing* **3** the enjoyment you feel when you recognize the good qualities of something: *a new **appreciation for** nature* | *an **appreciation of** fine food* **4** a rise in the value of something: *the **appreciation** of the dollar **against** the yen*

ap·pre·cia·tive /ə'priʃət̬ɪv/ *adj.* feeling or showing how much you enjoy, admire, or feel grateful for something or someone: *Appreciative laughter broke out in the room.* —**appreciatively** *adv.*

ap·pre·hend /,æprɪ'hɛnd/ *v.* [T] *formal* to find a criminal and take him/her to prison [= **arrest**]

ap·pre·hen·sion /,æprɪ'hɛnʃən/ *n.* [C,U] **1** anxiety or fear, especially about the future: *my sense of **apprehension about** flying* **2** *formal* the act of catching a criminal

ap·pre·hen·sive /,æprɪ'hɛnsɪv/ *adj.* worried or anxious, especially about the future: *She was **apprehensive about** the demands of the job.* —**apprehensively** *adv.*

ap·pren·tice /ə'prɛntɪs/ *n.* [C] someone who works for an employer for an agreed amount of time, usually for low pay, in order to learn a particular skill

ap·pren·tice·ship /ə'prɛntɪ,ʃɪp/ *n.* [C,U] the job of being an APPRENTICE, or the time spent as one

ap·prise /ə'praɪz/ *v.* [T] *formal* to formally or officially tell someone about something: *Mrs. Bellamy has been **apprised of** the situation.*

ap·proach[1] /ə'proʊtʃ/ *v.* **1** [I,T] to move closer to someone or something: *The plane began to approach Pittsburgh.* | *The hostess approached us.* **2** [T] to ask someone for something when you are not sure if s/he will do what you want: *She's been **approached** by two schools **about** teaching jobs.* **3** [I,T] to almost be a particular time, age, amount, temperature, etc.: *The temperature was approaching 100°.* | *Winter was **fast approaching**.* **4** [T] to begin to deal with something: *Different nations have approached the problem differently.*

approach[2] *n.* **1** [C] a way of doing something or dealing with a problem: *a creative* ***approach to*** *teaching science* **2** [U] the act of coming closer in time or distance: *the* ***approach of*** *winter* **3** [C] if an airplane makes an approach, it starts the process of landing on the ground **4** [C] a road or path leading to a place: *a traffic jam at the* ***approach to*** *the bridge*

ap·proach·a·ble /əˈproʊtʃəbəl/ *adj.* **1** friendly and easy to talk to: *Dr. Grieg is very approachable.* **2** able to be reached

ap·pro·ba·tion /ˌæprəˈbeɪʃən/ *n.* [U] *formal* praise or approval

ap·pro·pri·ate[1] /əˈproʊpriɪt/ *adj.* correct or good for a particular time, situation, or purpose [≠ **inappropriate**]: *a movie that is* ***appropriate for*** *all ages | books* ***appropriate to*** *elementary school children | There may come a time when* ***it is appropriate to*** *cut jobs. | an* ***appropriate time*** *to honor our veterans* —**appropriately** *adv.* —**appropriateness** *n.* [U]

THESAURUS

appropriate – used to talk about clothes or behavior that are right or acceptable for a particular situation: *an appropriate dress for the party*
suitable – used to talk about something that has the right qualities for a particular person or purpose: *a suitable school for the children*
suited – used to talk about someone who has the right qualities to do something: *He'd be well suited to the job.*

ap·pro·pri·ate[2] /əˈproʊpriˌeɪt/ *v.* [T] *formal* **1** to use or take something that does not belong to you: *He is suspected of appropriating company funds.* **2** to keep something such as money separate to be used for a particular purpose: *Congress* ***appropriated*** *$11.7 billion* ***for*** *anti-drug campaigns.*

ap·prov·al /əˈpruvəl/ *n.* [U] **1** official permission or acceptance: *The deal requires the* ***approval of*** *shareholders. | A two-thirds majority vote is required* ***for approval****. | The drug has* ***won*** *FDA* ***approval****. | The board never* ***gave*** *its* ***approval****.* **2** the belief that someone or something is good or doing something right: *a child trying to* ***win/earn*** *her father's* ***approval***

ap·prove /əˈpruv/ *v.* **1** [I] to believe that someone or something is good or acceptable [≠ **disapprove**]: *54% of voters* ***approve of*** *the president's performance. | Her parents did not* ***approve of*** *her marriage.*

THESAURUS

pass – to officially accept a law or proposal, especially by voting: *Many anti-smoking laws have been passed.*
ratify – to make a written agreement official by signing it: *Both sides are willing to ratify the treaty.*

2 [T] to officially agree to something: *Voters approved Proposition D.* —**approving** *adj.*: *an approving nod* —**approvingly** *adv.*

ap·prox *adv.* the written abbreviation of **approximately**

ap·prox·i·mate[1] /əˈprɑksəmɪt/ *adj.* an approximate number, amount, or time is not exact: *the approximate cost of the materials* —**approximately** *adv.*: *The plane will land in approximately 20 minutes.*

ap·prox·i·mate[2] /əˈprɑksəˌmeɪt/ *v.* [I, linking verb] *formal* to become similar to but not exactly the same as something else: *The animals' food approximates what they would eat in the wild.* —**approximation** /əˌprɑksəˈmeɪʃən/ *n.* [C,U]

APR *n.* [C usually singular] **annual percentage rate** the rate of INTEREST that you must pay when you borrow money

ap·ri·cot /ˈeɪprɪˌkɑt, ˈæ-/ *n.* [C] a small soft yellow-orange fruit with a single large seed

A·pril /ˈeɪprəl/ *n.* [C,U] the fourth month of the year: *Sometimes it snows* ***in April****. | The twins were born* ***on April 15th****. | Mira will begin her training* ***next April****. | The president signed the treaty* ***last April****.*

ˌApril ˈFool's ˌDay *n.* April 1, a day for playing funny tricks on people

a·pron /ˈeɪprən/ *n.* [C] a piece of clothing you wear to protect your clothes when you cook

ap·ro·pos /ˌæprəˈpoʊ, ˈæprəˌpoʊ/ *adv. formal* **apropos of sth** relating to something just mentioned: ***Apropos of nothing*** (=not relating to anything previously mentioned), *he suddenly asked me if I liked cats!*

apt /æpt/ *adj.* **1 apt to** likely to do something: *A sensitive child is apt to become overwhelmed in busy situations.* **2** exactly right for a particular situation or purpose: *an apt remark* **3** able to learn or understand things quickly: *an apt pupil* —**aptly** *adv.*

apt. *n.* the written abbreviation of **apartment**

ap·ti·tude /ˈæptəˌtud/ *n.* [C,U] a natural ability or skill, especially in learning: *He never had much* ***aptitude for*** *business.*

ˈaptitude ˌtest *n.* [C] a test used for finding out what someone's best skills are: *the Scholastic Aptitude Test*

aquarium

a·quar·i·um /əˈkwɛriəm/ *n.* [C] **1** a clear glass or plastic container for fish or other water animals to live in **2** a building where people go to look at fish or other water animals

A·quar·i·us /əˈkwɛriəs/ *n.* **1** [U] the ELEVENTH sign of the

ZODIAC, represented by a person pouring water **2** [C] someone born between January 20 and February 18

a·quat·ic /ə'kwætɪk, ə'kwɑtɪk/ *adj.* living or happening in water: *aquatic plants | aquatic sports*

A

aq·ue·duct /'ækwə,dʌkt/ *n.* [C] a structure like a bridge for carrying water across a valley

AR the written abbreviation of **Arkansas**

Ar·a·bic nu·me·ral /,ærəbɪk 'numərəl/ *n.* [C] the sign 1, 2, 3, 4, 5, 6, 7, 8, 9, or 0, or a combination of these signs, used as a number [➡ **Roman numeral**]

ar·a·ble /'ærəbəl/ *adj.* arable land is good for growing crops

ar·bi·ter /'ɑrbət̬ɚ/ *n.* [C] **1** a person or organization that settles an argument between two groups of people **2** an arbiter of style, fashion, taste, etc. influences society's opinions about what is fashionable

ar·bi·trar·y /'ɑrbə,trɛri/ *adj.* decided or arranged without any reason or plan, often unfairly: *arbitrary rules* —**arbitrarily** /,ɑrbə'trɛrəli/ *adv.* —**arbitrariness** /,ɑrbə'trɛrinɪs/ *n.* [U]

ar·bi·trate /'ɑrbə,treɪt/ *v.* [I,T] to be a judge in an argument because both sides have asked for this —**arbitrator** *n.* [C]

ar·bi·tra·tion /,ɑrbə'treɪʃən/ *n.* [U] the process in which someone tries to help two opposing sides settle an argument

arc /ɑrk/ *n.* [C] part of a circle or any curved line

ar·cade /ɑr'keɪd/ *n.* [C] **1** a special room or small building where people go to play VIDEO GAMES **2** a passage or side of a building that is covered with an ARCHed roof, and that often has small stores along it

arch[1] /ɑrtʃ/ *n.* plural **arches** [C] **1** a curved structure at the top of a door, window, bridge, etc., or something that has this curved shape **2** the curved middle part of the bottom of your foot —**arched** *adj.*: *an arched doorway*

arch[2] *v.* [I,T] to make something form an ARCH, or be in the shape of an arch: *The cat arched her back and hissed.*

ar·chae·ol·o·gy, **archeology** /,ɑrki'ɑlədʒi/ *n.* [U] the study of ancient societies by examining what remains of their buildings, GRAVES, tools, etc. —**archaeologist** *n.* [C] —**archaeological** /,ɑrkiə'lɑdʒɪkəl/ *adj.*

ar·cha·ic /ɑr'keɪ-ɪk/ *adj.* belonging to the past, or old-fashioned and no longer used

arch·bish·op /,ɑrtʃ'bɪʃəp◂/ *n.* [C] a priest with a very high rank

ar·cher·y /'ɑrtʃəri/ *n.* [U] the sport of shooting ARROWS from a BOW

ar·chi·pel·a·go /,ɑrkə'pɛlə,goʊ/ *n.* [C] a group of small islands

ar·chi·tect /'ɑrkə,tɛkt/ *n.* [C] someone whose job is to design buildings

ar·chi·tec·ture /'ɑrkə,tɛktʃɚ/ *n.* [U] **1** the style and design of a building or buildings: *medieval architecture | the architecture of Venice* **2** the art and practice of planning and designing buildings —**architectural** /,ɑrkə'tɛktʃərəl/ *adj.*

ar·chive /'ɑrkaɪv/ *n.* [C usually plural] **1** a large number of records, reports, letters, etc. relating to the history of a country, organization, family, etc., or the place where these records are stored: *an **archive of** the writer's unpublished work* **2** copies of a computer's FILES that are stored on a DISK or in the computer's memory in a way that uses less space than usual, so that the computer can keep them for a long time

arch·way /'ɑrtʃweɪ/ *n.* [C] a passage or entrance under an ARCH or arches

Arc·tic /'ɑrktɪk, 'ɑrt̬ɪk/ *n.* **the Arctic** the most northern part of the earth, including parts of Alaska and Greenland, and the sea called the Arctic Ocean —**arctic** *adj.*

ar·dent /'ɑrdnt/ *adj.* having very strong feelings of admiration or determination about someone or something: *the team's ardent fans* —**ardently** *adv.*

ar·dor /'ɑrdɚ/ *n.* [U] very strong feelings of admiration, excitement, or love: *the ardor of the reformers*

ar·du·ous /'ɑrdʒuəs/ *adj.* needing a lot of hard and continuous effort: *an arduous climb*

are /ɚ; *strong* ɑr/ the present tense plural of BE

ar·e·a /'ɛriə/ *n.* [C] **1** a particular part of a place, city, country, etc.: *Mom grew up **in** the Portland **area**. | people who live in **urban/rural areas*** (=in cities or the country)

THESAURUS

region – a large area of a country or the world: *the northwest region of Russia*
zone – an area that is different in a particular way from the areas around it: *a no-parking zone*
district – a particular area of a city or the country: *San Francisco's Mission District*
neighborhood – an area of a town where people live: *a friendly neighborhood*
suburb – an area outside the center of a city where people live: *a suburb of Boston*
slum – an area of a city that is in very bad condition, where many poor people live: *one of the city's worst slums*
ghetto – a very poor area of a city: *our urban ghettos*

2 a part of a house, office, park, etc. that is used for a particular purpose: *a large dining area | a no-smoking area* **3** a particular subject or type of activity: *Safety is a major **area of** concern. | experts in different **subject areas*** **4** the amount of space that a flat surface or shape covers

ˈarea ˌcode *n.* [C] the three numbers before a telephone number that you use when you telephone someone outside your local area in the U.S. and Canada

a·re·na /əˈrinə/ *n.* [C] **1** a building with a large flat central area surrounded by raised seats, used for sports or entertainment: *A new **sports arena** is under construction downtown.* **2 the political/public/national arena** all the people and activities relating to politics or public life: *More women are entering the political arena.*

aren't /ˈarənt/ **1** the short form of "are not": *They aren't here.* **2** the short form of "am not", used in questions: *I'm in big trouble, aren't I?*

ar·gu·a·ble /ˈargyuəbəl/ *adj.* if something is arguable, people can argue about it, because it is not certain

ar·gu·a·bly /ˈargyuəbli/ *adv.* used when giving your opinion to say that there are good reasons why something might be true: *Wagner is arguably the best athlete in the school.*

ar·gue /ˈargyu/ *v.* **1** [I] to disagree with someone, usually by talking or shouting in an angry way: *The kids are constantly arguing.* | *Two men at the bar were **arguing over/about** politics.* | *Rivera was **arguing with** the umpire.*

THESAURUS

argue or **have an argument**: *They started arguing over money.* | *We've had serious arguments before but never split up.*
fight or **have a fight**: *My mom and dad were always fighting.* | *The neighbors had a huge fight.*
quarrel or **have a quarrel** – to have an angry argument: *Let's not quarrel about money.* | *She had a quarrel with her boyfriend.*
squabble/bicker – to argue about unimportant things: *The kids were bickering over what program to watch.*

2 [I,T] to clearly explain or prove why you think something is true or should be done: *Democrats **argued that** the cuts would hurt the poor.* | *Some experts **argue for/against** sex education in schools.*

ar·gu·ment /ˈargyəmənt/ *n.* [C] **1** a disagreement, especially one in which people are angry and shout: *an **argument with** my husband* | *Jodie and I **had** a big **argument** last night.* | *Congressional **arguments about/over** the budget deficit* **2** a set of reasons you use to try to prove that something is right or wrong, true or false, etc.: *the **arguments for/against** becoming a vegetarian* | *the **argument that** the policy discriminates against women*

ar·gu·men·ta·tive /ˌargyəˈmɛntət̬ɪv/ *adj.* someone who is argumentative often argues or likes arguing

a·ri·a /ˈariə/ *n.* [C] a song that is sung by only one person in an OPERA

ar·id /ˈærɪd/ *adj.* getting very little rain, and therefore very dry: *arid land* | *an arid climate*

Ar·ies /ˈɛriz/ *n.* **1** [U] the first sign of the ZODIAC, represented by a RAM **2** [C] someone born between March 21 and April 19

a·rise /əˈraɪz/ past tense **arose** /əˈroʊz/ past participle **arisen** /əˈrɪzən/ present participle **arising** *v.* [I] **1** to happen or appear: *the questions that arose during the discussion* | *the problems that **arise from** losing a job* **2** *literary* to get up

ar·is·toc·ra·cy /ˌærəˈstakrəsi/ *n.* plural **aristocracies** [C] the people in the highest social class, who traditionally have a lot of land, money, and power —**aristocrat** /əˈrɪstəˌkræt/ *n.* [C] —**aristocratic** /əˌrɪstəˈkræt̬ɪk/ *adj.*

a·rith·me·tic /əˈrɪθmətɪk/ *n.* [U] the science of numbers involving adding, dividing, multiplying, etc. [➡ **mathematics**] —**arithmetic** /ˌærɪθˈmɛt̬ɪk◂/ *adj. technical*

arm¹ /arm/ *n.* [C] **1** one of the two long parts of your body between your shoulders and your hands: *He put his arm around her.* | *Marie touched her arm.* | *He had a tattoo on his **left/right arm**.* | *I had a pile of books **in my arms**.* | *She took him **by the arm*** (=holding his arm) *and pushed him out the door.* ➔ see picture on page A3 **2 arms** [plural] weapons used for fighting wars [➡ **armed**]: *sales of arms to the rebels* | ***nuclear arms*** | *the right to **bear arms*** (=keep weapons for protection) **3** the part of a chair, SOFA, etc. that you rest your arms on **4** a SLEEVE **5** a long part of an object that moves like an arm: *the arm of the record player* **6** a particular part of a group: *the political arm of the terrorist organization* **7 be up in arms** *informal* to be very angry and ready to argue or fight: *Parents should be up in arms about the quality of the schools.*

arm² *v.* [T] to give someone the weapons or information s/he needs [➡ **armed**]: *The ship was **armed with** 130 missiles.* | ***Armed with** a court order, Gilley moved the squatters off his land.*

ar·ma·dil·lo /ˌarməˈdɪloʊ/ *n.* [C] a small animal with a pointed nose and a hard shell that lives in hot dry parts of North and South America

ar·ma·ments /ˈarməmənts/ *n.* [plural] weapons and military equipment: *nuclear armaments*

arm·band /ˈarmbænd/ *n.* [C] a band of material that you wear around your arm, for example to show that someone you love has died

arm·chair /ˈarmtʃɛr/ *n.* [C] a chair with sides that you can rest your arms on ➔ see picture at SEAT¹

armed /armd/ *adj.* carrying one or more weapons: *an armed guard* | *a charge of **armed robbery*** (=stealing using guns) | *The fort was **heavily armed*** (=had a lot of weapons).

ˌarmed ˈforces *n.* **the armed forces** [plural] a country's military organizations

TOPIC

army, soldiers, troops, the military, the services
➔ see Topic box at ARMY

arm·ful /ˈɑrmfʊl/ *n.* [C] the amount of something that you can hold in one or both arms: *an **armful of** books*

ar·mi·stice /ˈɑrməstɪs/ *n.* [C] an agreement to stop fighting, usually for a specific period of time

ar·mor /ˈɑrmɚ/ *n.* [U] **1** metal or leather clothing worn in past times by men and horses in battle: *a suit of armor* **2** a strong layer of metal that protects vehicles, ships, and aircraft

ar·mored /ˈɑrmɚd/ *adj.* protected against bullets or other weapons by a strong layer of metal: *an armored car*

ar·mor·y /ˈɑrməri/ *n.* plural **armories** [C] a place where weapons are stored

arm·pit /ˈɑrmˌpɪt/ *n.* [C] the hollow place under your arm where it joins your body

ˈarms conˌtrol *n.* [U] the attempts by powerful countries to limit the number and types of war weapons that exist

ˈarms race *n.* [C usually singular] the competition between different countries to have a larger number of powerful weapons

ar·my /ˈɑrmi/ *n.* plural **armies** [C] **1** a military force that fights wars on land: *The two armies advanced across Europe.* | *Our son is **in the army**.* | *He dropped out of school to **join the army**.*

TOPIC

An army consists of **soldiers** or **troops**.
If you **join up** or **enlist**, you join the army.
If you are **drafted**, you are ordered to serve in the army by the government.
You can use **armed forces**, **the military**, or **the services** to talk in a general way about the army, navy, marines, and air force.

2 a large group of people or animals involved in the same activity: *an **army of** ants*

a·ro·ma /əˈroʊmə/ *n.* [C] a strong pleasant smell: *the **aroma of** fresh coffee*

THESAURUS

smell, scent, fragrance, perfume
➔ see Thesaurus box at SMELL²

—**aromatic** /ˌærəˈmætɪk◂/ *adj.*: *aromatic oils*

a·ro·ma·ther·a·py /əˌroʊməˈθɛrəpi/ *n.* [U] the use of pleasant-smelling oils to help you feel more healthy —**aromatherapist** *n.* [C]

a·rose /əˈroʊz/ *v.* the past tense of ARISE

a·round /əˈraʊnd/ *adv., prep.* **1** surrounding something or someone: *We put a fence around the yard.* | *Mario put his arms around her.* **2** to or in many parts of a place: *Stan showed me around the office.* | *an international company with offices **all around*** (=in all parts of) *the world* **3** in or near a particular place: *Is there a bank around here?* **4 also about** used when guessing a number, amount, time, etc., without being exact: *Dodger Stadium seats around 50,000 people.*

THESAURUS

about, approximately, roughly, or so
➔ see Thesaurus box at ABOUT²

5 in a circular movement: *Water pushes the wheel around.* | *Leaves were blowing **around and around*** (=in a continuous circular movement). **6** along the outside of a place, instead of through it: *We had to go around to the back of the house.* **7** toward or facing the opposite direction: *I'll turn the car around and pick you up at the door.* **8** present in the same place as you: *It was 11:30 at night, and nobody was around.* **9** existing: *That joke's been around for years.* **10 10 feet/3 inches etc. around** measuring a particular distance on the outside of a round object: *Redwood trees can measure 30 or 40 feet around.* ➔ **around the clock** at CLOCK¹

ˌaround-the-ˈclock *adj.* [only before noun] continuing or happening all the time, both day and night: *a station where you can get around-the-clock news* —**around the clock** *adv.*

a·rouse /əˈraʊz/ *v.* [T] **1** to make someone have a particular feeling: *Her behavior aroused the suspicions of the police.* **2** to make someone feel sexually excited —**arousal** *n.* [U]

ar·raign /əˈreɪn/ *v.* [T] *law* to make someone come to court to hear what his/her crime is —**arraignment** *n.* [C,U]

ar·range /əˈreɪndʒ/ *v.* **1** [I,T] to make plans for something to happen: *Jeff will arrange our flights.* | *We've **arranged to** go to the cabin this weekend.* | *I've **arranged for** Mark **to** join us.* | *We still have to **arrange where** to meet.* **2** [T] to put a group of things or people in a particular order or position: *The file is arranged alphabetically.*

ar·range·ment /əˈreɪndʒmənt/ *n.* **1** [C usually plural] the things that you must organize for something to happen: *travel arrangements* | *We're **mak-***

***ing arrangements for** the wedding.* **2** [C,U] something that has been organized or agreed on: *We **have** a special **arrangement with** the bank.* | *I'm sure we can **come to some arrangement**.* | *Maxine canceled our **arrangement to** meet.* **3** [C,U] a group of things in a particular order or position, or the activity of arranging things in this way: *a flower arrangement* **4** [C,U] a piece of music that has been written or changed for a particular instrument

THESAURUS

music, **tune**, **melody**, **song**, **composition**, **number**
➔ see Thesaurus box at MUSIC

ar·ray /ə'reɪ/ *n.* [C usually singular] a group of people or things, especially one that is large or impressive: *a dazzling **array of** acting talent*

ar·rears /ə'rɪrz/ *n.* [plural] **1 be in arrears** to owe someone money because your regular payment to him/her is late: *We're six weeks in arrears with the rent.* **2** money that is owed and should already have been paid: *The prime minister promised that all wage arrears would be paid in May.*

ar·rest[1] /ə'rɛst/ *v.* [T] **1** if the police arrest someone, the person is taken away because the police think s/he has done something illegal: *He was arrested and charged with murder.* | *The police **arrested** Eric **for** shoplifting.*

THESAURUS

catch, **capture**, **corner**, **trap**
➔ see Thesaurus box at CATCH[1]

2 *formal* to stop something happening or make it happen more slowly: *The drug is used to arrest the spread of the disease.*

arrest[2] *n.* [C,U] the act of taking someone away and guarding him/her because s/he may have done something illegal: *The police expect to **make an arrest** soon.* | *Don't move, you're **under arrest**!*

ar·riv·al /ə'raɪvəl/ *n.* **1** [U] the act of arriving somewhere [≠ **departure**]: *Porter spoke to reporters shortly after his arrival.* | *The **arrival of** our flight was delayed.* | *Shortly after our **arrival in** Toronto, Lisa got sick.* **2 the arrival of sth** the time when a new idea, method, product, etc. is first used or discovered: *The arrival of the personal computer changed the way we work.* **3** [C] a person or thing that has arrived recently: ***Late arrivals** will not be admitted to the theater.*

ar·rive /ə'raɪv/ *v.* [I] **1** to get to a place: *Your letter arrived last week.* | *What time does the plane **arrive in** New York?* | *We **arrived at** Mom's two hours late.* | *We **arrived home** at ten o'clock.*

THESAURUS

get to – to reach a particular place: *What time will you get to Atlanta?*
reach – to arrive at a particular place: *The climbers reached the top of Mt. Everest.*
come – if someone comes, s/he arrives at the place where you are: *She came home yesterday.*
turn up also **show up** – to arrive somewhere, used especially when someone is waiting for you: *Lee turned up an hour late for the meeting.*
get in – to arrive at a particular time or in a particular place: *What time did your plane get in?*
come in – if an airplane, train, or ship comes in, it arrives in the place where you are: *I'll be there to pick you up when the train comes in.*
land – to arrive somewhere in an airplane, boat, etc.: *The first U.S. Marines landed in Vietnam in 1965.*

2 to happen: *At last the big day arrived!* **3 arrive at a conclusion/decision** to finally decide what to do about something **4** to begin to exist, or start being used: *Our toy sales have doubled since computer games arrived.* **5** to be born: *It was just past midnight when the baby arrived.*

GRAMMAR

arrive in, arrive at
Use **arrive in** with the name of a country, city, town, etc.: *He arrived in Japan in July.* | *We arrived in Paris at four in the afternoon.*
Use **arrive at** with a building or place: *Paul arrived at the hotel just before ten.* | *I try to arrive at school half an hour early.*

ar·ro·gant /'ærəgənt/ *adj.* behaving in a rude way because you think you are more important than other people: *an arrogant, selfish man*—**arrogance** *n.* [U] *I couldn't believe her arrogance.* —**arrogantly** *adv.*

THESAURUS

proud, **conceited**, **big-headed**, **vain**
➔ see Thesaurus box at PROUD

ar·row /'æroʊ/ *n.* [C] **1** a thin straight weapon with a point at one end that you shoot from a BOW **2** a sign in the shape of an arrow, used in order to show the direction of something

ar·se·nal /'ɑrsənl/ *n.* [C] a large number of weapons, or the building where they are stored

ar·se·nic /'ɑrsənɪk, 'ɑrsnɪk/ *n.* [U] a very strong poison

ar·son /'ɑrsən/ *n.* [U] the crime of deliberately burning a building —**arsonist** *n.* [C]

art /ɑrt/ *n.* **1** [U] the activity or skill of producing paintings, photographs, etc., or paintings, etc. that are produced using this skill: *Steve's studying art at college.* | *modern art* | *an art exhibition* | *Several famous **works of art** were stolen from the museum.*

THESAURUS

Types of art
painting – the art or skill of making a picture using paint

drawing – the art or skill of making a picture using a pen or pencil
photography – the art or skill of producing photographs
sculpture – the art or skill of making objects out of stone, wood or clay
pottery – the activity of making pots, plates, etc. from clay
ceramics – the art or skill of making pots, plates, etc. from clay
➔ see Thesaurus box at ARTIST

2 the arts painting, music, literature, etc. all considered together: *government funding for the arts* **3 arts** [plural] subjects of study that are not considered scientific, such as history, languages, etc.: *an arts degree* **4** [C,U] the skill involved in making or doing something: *the* ***art of*** *writing*

ar·ter·y /ˈɑrt̬əri/ *n.* plural **arteries** [C] **1** one of the tubes that carries blood from your heart to the rest of your body [➡ **vein**] **2** *formal* a main road, railroad line, or river

ar·thri·tis /ɑrˈθraɪt̬ɪs/ *n.* [U] a disease that causes pain and swelling in the joints of your body —**arthritic** /ɑrˈθrɪt̬ɪk/ *adj.*: *arthritic fingers*

ar·ti·choke /ˈɑrt̬ɪˌtʃoʊk/ *n.* [C] a round green vegetable with thick pointed leaves and a firm base

ar·ti·cle /ˈɑrt̬ɪkəl/ *n.* [C] **1** a piece of writing in a newspaper, magazine, etc.: *Did you read that* ***article on/about*** *the space shuttle?* | *magazine articles*

TOPIC

story, column, front page, sports/ entertainment/ food etc. section, the comics page, the funnies, editorial page, headlines
➔ see Topic box at NEWSPAPER

2 a thing, especially one of a group of things: *an* ***article of*** *clothing*

THESAURUS

thing, object, item
➔ see Thesaurus box at THING

3 *technical* in grammar, the word "the" (=the definite article), or the word "a" or "an" (=the indefinite article)

ar·tic·u·late¹ /ɑrˈtɪkyəlɪt/ *adj.* able to express your thoughts and feelings clearly [≠ **inarticulate**]: *a bright and articulate child* —**articulately** *adv.*

ar·tic·u·late² /ɑrˈtɪkjyəˌleɪt/ *v.* [I,T] to put your thoughts or feelings into words: *It's hard to articulate what I'm feeling.* —**articulation** /ɑrˌtɪkyəˈleɪʃən/ *n.* [U]

ar·ti·fact /ˈɑrt̬ɪˌfækt/ *n.* [C] an object such as a tool, weapon, etc. that was made in the past and is historically important: *Egyptian artifacts*

ar·ti·fi·cial /ˌɑrt̬əˈfɪʃəl◂/ *adj.* **1** not real or natural, but made by people [≠ **natural**]: *artificial sweeteners* | *an artificial leg*

THESAURUS

synthetic – made from artificial substances, not natural ones: *synthetic fabrics*
fake – made to look or seem like something else in order to deceive people: *fake identity cards*
simulated – not real, but made to look, sound, or feel real: *a simulated space journey*
imitation – something that looks real, but that is a copy: *imitation leather*
false – not real, but intended to seem real: *He was using a false name.*
virtual – made, done, seen, etc. on the Internet, rather than in the real world: *virtual reality*
➔ see Thesaurus box at NATURAL¹

2 *disapproving* not natural or sincere: *an artificial smile* —**artificially** *adv.*: *artificially colored*

ˌartificial inˈtelligence *n.* [U] the science of how to make computers do things that people can do, such as make decisions or see things

ˌartificial respiˈration *n.* [U] a way of making someone breathe again when s/he has stopped, by blowing air into his/her mouth

ar·til·ler·y /ɑrˈtɪləri/ *n.* [U] large heavy guns, usually on wheels

ar·ti·san /ˈɑrt̬əzən, -sən/ *n.* [C] someone who does skilled work, making things by hand

art·ist /ˈɑrt̬ɪst/ *n.* [C] **1** someone who produces art, especially paintings: *an exhibition of paintings by local artists*

THESAURUS

Types of artists
painter – someone who paints pictures
photographer – someone who takes photographs
sculptor – someone who makes sculptures
potter – someone who makes objects out of baked clay
➔ ART

2 a professional performer such as a singer or dancer

ar·tis·tic /ɑrˈtɪstɪk/ *adj.* **1** good at painting, drawing, etc.: *I never knew you were so artistic.* **2** relating to art or culture: *artistic freedom* —**artistically** *adv.*

art·ist·ry /ˈɑrt̬əstri/ *n.* [U] skill in a particular artistic activity

art·sy /ˈɑrtsi/ *adj. informal* interested in art, or seeming to know a lot about art: *an artsy foreign film*

art·work /ˈɑrtˀwɚk/ *n.* **1** [U] pictures, photographs, etc. that are prepared for a book, magazine, etc. **2** [C,U] paintings and other pieces of art

as /əz; *strong* æz/ *adv., prep., conjunction* **1** used to compare people or things: *I can't run nearly* ***as*** *fast* ***as*** *I used to.* | *Tom works* ***just as*** *hard as the* *others.* | *Ask Carol to call me* ***as soon as possible*** (=very soon). **2** used to say what someone's job is or what purpose something has: *In the past, women were mainly employed as secretaries or teachers.* | *John used an old blanket as a tent.* **3** in a particular way or state: *Make sure you leave this room as you found it.* **4** while something is happening: *Be patient with your puppy as he adjusts to his new home.* | *The phone rang* ***just as*** *I was leaving.* **5** used when mentioning something that has been stated before: ***As you know****, I'm leaving at the end of this month.* | ***As I mentioned*** *in my letter, I plan to arrive on the 6th.* **6 as if/though** used when you are saying how someone or something seems: *She looked as if she had been crying.* **7 as for sb/sth** used when you are starting to talk about someone or something new that is related to what you were talking about before: *As for racism, much progress has been made, but there is still much to do.* **8 as of today/December 12th/next spring etc.** starting from a particular time: *The pay raise will come into effect as of January.* **9 as it is a)** already: *Keep quiet – we're in enough trouble as it is.* **b)** because of the situation that exists: *We were saving money to go to Hawaii, but as it is we can only afford a camping trip.* **10 as to** concerning: *The President asked for opinions as to the likelihood of war.* | *She offered no explanation as to why she'd left so suddenly.* **11** *formal* because: *James decided not to go out as he was still really tired.* ➔ **as long as** at LONG² ➔ **as a matter of fact** at MATTER¹ ➔ **as well (as sb/sth)** at WELL¹ ➔ **so as (not) to do sth** at SO¹ ➔ **such as** at SUCH

ASAP, **a.s.a.p.** *adv.* **as soon as possible**

as·bes·tos /æs'bɛstəs, æz-, əs-, əz-/ *n.* [U] a gray substance that does not burn easily and was used in some clothing and building material in the past

as·cend /ə'sɛnd/ *v.* [I,T] *formal* **1** to move to a higher position [≠ **descend**]: *The plane ascended rapidly.* **2 in ascending order** arranged so that each thing in a group is bigger, more important, etc. than the one before

as·cen·dan·cy, **ascendency** /ə'sɛndənsi/ *n.* [U] *formal* a position of increasing power, influence, or control: *the* ***ascendancy of*** *conservative values in American life*

as·cent /ə'sɛnt, 'æsɛnt/ *n.* **1** [C] the act of moving or climbing to a higher position [≠ **descent**]: *the first ascent of Everest* **2** [U] the process of becoming more important or successful: *Jerry's quick ascent into management surprised no one.* **3** [C] a path or road that goes gradually up [≠ **descent**]: *a* ***steep ascent***

as·cer·tain /ˌæsɚ'teɪn/ *v.* [T] *formal* to find out the truth about something: *The police have* ***ascertained that*** *the killer did not act alone.*

as·cet·ic /ə'sɛt̬ɪk/ *adj.* living a simple life with no physical comforts —**ascetic** *n.* [C] —**asceticism** /ə'sɛt̬əˌsɪzəm/ *n.* [U]

as·cribe /ə'skraɪb/ *v.* [T]
ascribe sth **to** sb/sth *phr. v. formal* to say that something is caused by a particular person or thing: *Carter ascribed his problems to a lack of money.*

a·sex·u·al /eɪ'sɛkʃuəl/ *adj.* **1** not having sexual organs or not involving sexual activity **2** not interested in sex

ash /æʃ/ *n.* **1** [C,U] the soft gray powder that remains after something has been burned: *cigarette ash* **2 ashes** [plural] the ash that remains after the body of a dead person has been CREMATED (=burned) **3** [C,U] a tree that is common in Britain and North America, or the wood from this tree

a·shamed /ə'ʃeɪmd/ *adj.* **1** feeling embarrassed or guilty about something: *I* ***felt ashamed of*** *the things I had said to him.* | *You should be* ***ashamed of yourself****, acting like that!* | *Fred was* ***ashamed to*** *admit his mistake.* | *We have* ***nothing to be ashamed of****.*

THESAURUS

guilty, embarrassed
➔ see Thesaurus box at GUILTY

2 be ashamed of sb feeling upset because someone's behavior embarrasses you: *Helen felt ashamed of her parents.*

ash·en /'æʃən/ *adj.* very pale because of shock or fear: *His face was ashen.*

a·shore /ə'ʃɔr/ *adv.* onto or toward the shore of a lake, river, sea, or ocean: *The body* ***washed ashore*** *on a remote beach.* | *We* ***came ashore*** *at Sagres.*

ash·tray /'æʃtreɪ/ *n.* [C] a small dish for used cigarettes and cigarette ASHES

A·sia /'eɪʒə/ *n.* one of the seven CONTINENTS that includes land between the Ural mountains and the Pacific Ocean

A·sian /'eɪʒən/ *adj.* someone who comes from Asia, or whose family came from Asia —**Asian** *adj.*

ˌAsian-A'merican *n.* [C] an American whose family originally came from Asia —**Asian-American** *adj.*

a·side¹ /ə'saɪd/ *adv.* **1** to the side or away from you: *Jim stepped aside to let me pass.* | *He* ***took/pulled/called*** *Kate* ***aside*** *so they could talk privately.* **2 put/set sth aside a)** to keep or not use something so that you can use it later: *I try to* ***put aside*** *$30 a week* ***for*** *my vacation.* **b)** to leave something to be dealt with at another time: *We* ***put aside*** *our* ***differences*** *to fight a common enemy.* **3 aside from** ➔ see **apart from** at APART

aside² *n.* [C] a remark you make in a quiet voice so that only a few people can hear

ask /æsk/ *v.* [I,T] **1** to make a request for someone to tell you something: *"What's your name?" she asked.* | *I asked him his phone number.* | *Can I*

ask** a **question**? | He **asked how** this could have happened. | **Ask** Elaine **if** she knows what time it is. | Visitors often **ask about** the place. | You should **ask around (=ask a lot of people) *before deciding.*

THESAURUS

order – to ask for food or drinks in a restaurant: *He ordered a club sandwich.*
demand – to ask for something in a firm or angry way: *They're demanding immediate payment.*
request – to ask for something officially: *I wrote to request information about the college.*
beg – to ask for something that you want very much: *"Please can I have one?" she begged. | I begged her to stay.*
question/interrogate – if the police question or interrogate someone, they ask them a lot of questions in order to get information: *The two men are being questioned by police about the robbery.*
inquire/enquire formal – to ask someone for information or facts about something: *I'm writing to inquire about the job you advertised.*

2 to make a request for help, advice, information, etc.: *If you need anything, just ask. | **Ask** Paula **to** mail the letters. | Some people don't like to **ask for** help. | I had to **ask** my parents **for** money. | **Ask** your Dad **if** we can borrow his car. | Karen **asked to** see the doctor.* **3** to invite someone to go somewhere: *Jerry would like to **ask** her **out*** (=invite her to a movie, restaurant, etc. because he likes her). | *Why don't you **ask** them **over*** (=invite them to your house) *for dinner?* **4** to want a particular amount of money for something you are selling: *He's asking $2,000 for that old car!* **5 Don't ask me!** *spoken* said when you do not know the answer to a question: *"When will Vicky get home?" "Don't ask me!"* **6 If you ask me** used in order to emphasize your opinion: *If you ask me, he should be in jail.* **7 be asking for trouble/it** *informal* to be behaving in a way that will probably cause problems: *Allowing campus police to have guns is just asking for trouble.*

a·skance /ə'skæns/ *adv.* **look askance (at sb/sth)** if you look askance at something, you do not approve of it or think it is good

a·skew /ə'skyu/ *adv.* not straight or level: *His coat was wrinkled and his hat was askew.*

a·sleep /ə'slip/ *adj.* sleeping [≠ **awake**]: *Be quiet. The baby is asleep. | I **fell asleep*** (=started sleeping) *in front of the TV. | **fast/sound asleep*** (=sleeping very deeply)

as·par·a·gus /ə'spærəgəs/ *n.* [U] a long thin green vegetable

as·pect /'æspɛkt/ *n.* [C] one part of a situation, plan, or subject: *The committee discussed several **aspects of** the traffic problem.*

aspen

as·pen /'æspən/ *n.* [C] a tall thin straight tree that grows in the western U.S.

as·per·sion /ə'spɚʒən, -ʃən/ *n. formal* **cast aspersions on sb/sth** to criticize someone or something, or make an unfair judgment

as·phalt /'æs,fɔlt/ *n.* [U] a hard black substance used on the surface of roads

as·phyx·i·ate /ə'sfɪksi,eɪt, æ-/ *v.* [I,T] *formal* to stop someone breathing [= **suffocate**] —**asphyxiation** /ə,sfɪksi'eɪʃən/ *n.* [U]

as·pi·ra·tion /,æspə'reɪʃən/ *n.* [C usually plural, U] a strong desire to have or achieve something: *a young man with **political aspirations***

as·pire /ə'spaɪɚ/ *v.* [I] to have a strong desire to achieve something: *Milligan **aspires to be** Governor of the state.* —**aspiring** *adj.*: *aspiring young actors*

as·pirin /'æsprɪn/ *n.* plural **aspirins** or **aspirin** [C,U] a drug that reduces pain and fever: *I **took** an **aspirin** and went to bed.*

ass /æs/ *n.* [C] *old-fashioned* DONKEY

as·sail·ant /ə'seɪlənt/ *n.* [C] *formal* someone who attacks someone else

as·sas·sin /ə'sæsən/ *n.* [C] someone who murders an important person

as·sas·si·nate /ə'sæsə,neɪt/ *v.* [T] to murder an important person: *a plot to assassinate the President* —**assassination** /ə,sæsə'neɪʃən/ *n.* [C,U]

THESAURUS

kill, **murder**, **commit manslaughter**, **execute**, **put to death**
→ see Thesaurus box at KILL[1]

as·sault[1] /ə'sɔlt/ *n.* [C,U] **1** *formal* the crime of attacking a person: *He served three years in prison for assault. | an increase in **sexual assaults** | He was charged with **assault on/against** a police officer.*

THESAURUS

crime, **theft**, **robbery**, **burglary**, **shoplifting**, **mugging**, **murder**, **rape**
→ see Thesaurus box at CRIME

2 an attack by an army to take control of a place: *the assault on Iwo Jima*

THESAURUS

attack, **invasion**, **raid**, **ambush**, **counterattack**
→ see Thesaurus box at ATTACK[1]

assault[2] *v.* [T] to attack someone violently: *Two men assaulted him after he left the bar.*

as·sem·ble /ə'sɛmbəl/ *v.* **1** [I,T] if you assemble people or things, or if people assemble, they are brought together in the same place: *A crowd had assembled in front of the White House.*

THESAURUS
meet, get together, gather, come together
➔ see Thesaurus box at MEET[1]

2 [T] to put the different parts of something together: *You'll need to assemble the grill yourself.* ➔ see picture at BUILD[1]

as·sem·bly /ə'sɛmbli/ *n.* plural **assemblies** **1** [C] a group of people who are elected to make laws or decisions for a country, state, or organization: *the New York State Assembly* **2** [C,U] a meeting of a group of people for a particular purpose: *an **assembly of** reporters* | ***freedom of assembly*** (=the right to gather as a group) **3** [C,U] a meeting of all the teachers and students of a school **4** [U] the process of putting something together: *The fan comes with assembly directions.*

as'sembly ˌline *n.* [C] a system for making things in a factory in which the products move past a line of workers who each make or check one part

as·sem·bly·man /ə'sɛmblimən/ *n.* plural **assemblymen** /-mən/ [C] a man who is a member of a state assembly

as·sem·bly·wom·an /ə'sɛmbliˌwʊmən/ *n.* plural **assemblywomen** /-ˌwɪmɪn/ [C] a woman who is a member of a state assembly

as·sent /ə'sɛnt/ *n.* [U] *formal* official agreement: *The court **gave** its **assent**.* —**assent** *v.* [I]

as·sert /ə'sɚt/ *v.* [T] **1** to state firmly that something is true: *Professor Ross **asserts that** American schools are not strict enough.* **2** to behave in a determined and confident way to make people respect you: *The president tried to assert his power over the military.* | *Don't be afraid to **assert yourself** in the interview.*

as·ser·tion /ə'sɚʃən/ *n.* [C,U] something that you say or write that you strongly believe: *He repeated his **assertion that** he was innocent.*

as·ser·tive /ə'sɚṭɪv/ *adj.* behaving confidently so that people pay attention to what you say: *She needs to be more assertive.* —**assertively** *adv.* —**assertiveness** *n.* [U]

as·sess /ə'sɛs/ *v.* [T] **1** to make a judgment about a person or situation after thinking carefully about it: *Psychologists will assess the child's behavior.* | *We're trying to **assess what** went wrong.*

THESAURUS
judge, evaluate, appraise, gauge
➔ see Thesaurus box at JUDGE[2]

2 to calculate the quality, amount, or value of something: *They **assessed** the house **at** $90,000.* —**assessment** *n.* [C,U]

as·set /'æsɛt/ *n.* **1 assets** [plural] a company's assets are the things it owns: *a firm with $1.3 billion in assets* **2** [C usually singular] something or someone that helps you to succeed [➡ **liability**]: *A sense of humor is a real asset.* | *You're an **asset to** the company, George.*

as·sign /ə'saɪn/ *v.* [T] **1** to give someone a job to do: *I've been assigned the task of looking after the new students.* | *Guards were **assigned to** the President.* **2** to give something to someone: *They assigned me a small room.*

as·sign·ment /ə'saɪnmənt/ *n.* **1** [C,U] a job or piece of work that is given to someone: *a homework assignment* | *The newspaper is sending her **on a** special **assignment to** Libya.* | *She was arrested while **on assignment** in China.* **2** [U] the act of giving people particular jobs to do

as·sim·i·late /ə'sɪməˌleɪt/ *v.* **1** [I,T] to accept someone completely as a member of a group, or to become an accepted member of a group: *Many ethnic groups have been **assimilated into** American society.* **2** [T] to learn and understand information: *We need someone who can assimilate new ideas quickly.* —**assimilation** /əˌsɪmə'leɪʃən/ *n.* [U]

as·sist /ə'sɪst/ *v.* [I,T] *formal* to help someone do something: *Two nurses **assisted** Dr. Bernard **in** performing the operation.*

THESAURUS
help, give a hand (with sth), lend a hand (with sth)
➔ see Thesaurus box at HELP[1]

as·sist·ance /ə'sɪstəns/ *n.* [U] help or support: *The company provides assistance for new computer users.* | *We offer **financial assistance** to students.* | *Can I **be of** any **assistance*** (=help you)? | *No one would **come to** her **assistance*** (=help her).

as·sist·ant /ə'sɪstənt/ *n.* [C] **1** someone whose job is to help someone who has a higher rank: *a sales assistant* **2 assistant manager/director/editor etc.** someone whose job is just below the position of manager, director, etc.

THESAURUS
senior, chief, high-ranking, top, junior
➔ see Thesaurus box at POSITION[1]

as·so·ci·ate[1] /ə'soʊʃiˌeɪt, -siˌeɪt/ *v.* **1** [T] if you associate two people or things, you see that they are connected in some way: *I always **associate** summer **with** travel.* **2 be associated (with sb/sth) a)** to be related to a particular subject, activity, group, etc.: *health problems associated with tobacco* **b) also associate yourself with sb/sth** to show support for someone or something: *I refuse to be friends with anyone who associates himself with racists.* **3 associate with**

sb to spend time with someone: *I don't like the people she associates with.*

as·so·ci·ate[2] /ə'souʃiɪt, -siɪt/ *n.* [C] someone that you work or do business with: *a business associate*

As,sociate of 'Arts also **As'sociate de,gree** *n.* [C] **A.A.** a degree given after two years of study at a COMMUNITY COLLEGE

A

as·so·ci·a·tion /ə,sousi'eɪʃən, -ʃi'eɪ-/ *n.* **1** [C] an organization for people who do the same kind of work or have the same interests: *the National Education Association*

> **THESAURUS**
>
> **organization, institution, (political) party, club, society, union**
> ➔ see Thesaurus box at ORGANIZATION

2 in association with sb/sth together with someone or something else: *Community groups are working in association with the schools.* **3** [C usually plural] a memory or feeling that is related to a particular place, event, etc.: *Los Angeles has happy associations for me.*

as·sort·ed /ə'sɔrṭɪd/ *adj.* of various different types: *a box of assorted cookies*

as·sort·ment /ə'sɔrt˺mənt/ *n.* [C] a mixture of different types of the same thing: *an **assortment of** chocolates*

as·sume /ə'sum/ *v.* [T] **1** to think that something is true although you have no proof: *Your light wasn't on so I **assumed (that)** you were out.* | ***Assuming (that)** Dad agrees, when do you want to shop for cars?* **2** *formal* to take control, power, or a particular position: *Stalin **assumed power/control** in 1941.* **3 assume an air/expression of sth** *formal* to pretend to feel something or be something you are not: *Andy assumed an air of innocence when the teacher walked by.* **4** to start having a particular quality or appearance: *Her family life assumed more importance after the accident.*

as·sumed /ə'sumd/ *adj.* **an assumed name/identity** a false name: *Davis applied for a loan **under an assumed name**.*

as·sump·tion /ə'sʌmpʃən/ *n.* [C] something that you think is true although you have no proof: *How can you **make an assumption** about her if you've never met her?* | *The budget is **based on the assumption** that the economy will grow at the same rate.*

as·sur·ance /ə'ʃurəns/ *n.* **1** [C] a promise that something is true or will happen: *We need an **assurance that** you can pay off your loan.* **2** [U] confidence in your own abilities or the truth of what you are saying: *Cindy answered their questions with quiet assurance.*

as·sure /ə'ʃur/ *v.* [T] **1** to tell someone that something will definitely happen or is definitely true so that s/he is less worried: *The doctors **assured** me **(that)** her life was not in danger.* | *The concert won't be canceled, **I can assure you**.* **2** to make something certain to happen or be achieved: *The new contract means that the future of the company is assured.*

as·sured /ə'ʃurd/ *adj.* **1** showing confidence in your abilities: *an assured manner* **2** certain to be achieved: *Victory was assured.* —**assuredly** /ə'ʃurɪdli/ *adv.*

as·ter·isk /'æstərɪsk/ *n.* [C] a mark like a star (*) used especially to show something interesting or important

as·ter·oid /'æstə,rɔɪd/ *n.* [C] a large object made of rock that moves around in space

> **TOPIC**
>
> **space, meteor, comet, moon, planet, star, sun, constellation, galaxy, black hole, spacecraft, spaceship, rocket, (space) shuttle, satellite, probe, astronaut**
> ➔ see Topic box at SPACE[1]

asth·ma /'æzmə/ *n.* [U] an illness that makes it difficult to breathe —**asthmatic** /æz'mæṭɪk/ *adj.*

as·ton·ish /ə'stɑnɪʃ/ *v.* [T] to surprise someone very much: *Einstein's work still astonishes physicists.*

as·ton·ished /ə'stɑnɪʃt/ *adj.* very surprised: *Parker seemed **astonished that** someone wanted to buy the house.* | *I was **astonished to** learn that she was only 22.*

> **THESAURUS**
>
> **surprised, amazed, shocked, astounded, flabbergasted, stunned, dumbfounded, nonplussed**
> ➔ see Thesaurus box at SURPRISED

as·ton·ish·ing /ə'stɑnɪʃɪŋ/ *adj.* very surprising: *astonishing news* —**astonishingly** *adv.*

> **THESAURUS**
>
> **surprising, extraordinary, amazing, shocking, astounding, staggering, stunning**
> ➔ see Thesaurus box at SURPRISING

as·ton·ish·ment /ə'stɑnɪʃmənt/ *n.* [U] great surprise: ***To our astonishment**, Sue won the race.* | *Ken looked at her **in astonishment**.*

as·tound /ə'staund/ *v.* [T] to make someone feel very surprised: *My brother's decision astounded us all.*

as·tound·ed /ə'staundɪd/ *adj.* very surprised: *I was **astounded at** what I saw.*

> **THESAURUS**
>
> **surprised, amazed, shocked, astonished, flabbergasted, stunned, dumbfounded, nonplussed**
> ➔ see Thesaurus box at SURPRISED

as·tound·ing /ə'staundɪŋ/ *adj.* so surprising that it is difficult to believe: *the band's astounding success* —**astoundingly** *adv.*

THESAURUS

surprising, extraordinary, amazing, shocking, astonishing, staggering, stunning
➔ see Thesaurus box at SURPRISING

a·stray /ə'streɪ/ *adv.* **1 go astray** *formal* to be lost: *One of the documents we sent them has gone astray.* **2 lead sb astray** to encourage someone to do bad or immoral things

a·stride /ə'straɪd/ *adv., prep.* having one leg on each side of something: *a young girl **sitting astride** a horse*

as·trin·gent /ə'strɪndʒənt/ *adj.* **1** criticizing someone very severely: *astringent remarks* **2** *technical* able to make your skin less oily or stop a wound from bleeding: *an astringent cream*

as·trol·o·gy /ə'strɑlədʒi/ *n.* [U] the study of the position and movements of stars and PLANETS and how they might affect people's lives —**astrologer** *n.* [C] —**astrological** /ˌæstrə'lɑdʒɪkəl/ *adj.*

as·tro·naut /'æstrəˌnɔt, -ˌnɑt/ *n.* [C] someone who travels in a spacecraft

TOPIC

space, meteor, asteroid, comet, moon, planet, star, sun, constellation, galaxy, black hole, spacecraft, spaceship, rocket, (space) shuttle, satellite, probe
➔ see Topic box at SPACE[1]

as·tro·nom·i·cal /ˌæstrə'nɑmɪkəl/ *adj.* **1** extremely large in amount: *astronomical prices*

THESAURUS

expensive, high, pricey, overpriced, be a ripoff, extortionate, exorbitant
➔ see Thesaurus box at EXPENSIVE

2 relating to the study of the stars and PLANETS

as·tron·o·my /ə'strɑnəmi/ *n.* [U] the scientific study of the stars and PLANETS —**astronomer** *n.* [C]

as·tute /ə'stut/ *adj.* quick to understand a situation and how to get an advantage from it: *an astute politician* —**astutely** *adv.*

a·sy·lum /ə'saɪləm/ *n.* **1** [U] protection that a government gives to someone who escapes from a country for political reasons: *He was granted **political asylum**.* **2** [C] *old-fashioned* a hospital for people with mental illness

a·sym·met·ri·cal /ˌeɪsɪ'mɛtrɪkəl/ **also a·sym·met·ric** /ˌeɪsɪ'mɛtrɪk◂/ *adj.* having two sides that are different in size and shape [≠ **symmetrical**]

at /ət; *strong* æt/ *prep.* **1** used to say where someone or something is or where something happens: *Meet me at my house.* | *There was a long line at the bank.* | *I parked my car **at the end of** the road.* | *John's at work* (=in the place where he works). | *I'll see you at Jane's* (=Jane's house). **2** used to say when something happens: *The movie starts at 8:00.* | *Alison gets lonely at Christmas.* **3** used to say what event or activity someone is taking part in: *I'm sorry, Mr. Rivers is **at lunch/dinner etc.*** (=eating lunch, etc.). **4** used to show who or what a particular action or feeling is directed toward: *Jake shot at the deer but missed.* | *Stop shouting at me!* | *Jenny, I'm surprised at you.* **5** used in order to show a price, rate, speed, level, age, etc.: *Gas is selling at about $1.25 a gallon.* | *I started school at age five.* **6** used in order to show what you are considering when making a judgment about someone's ability: *How's Brian doing at his new job?* | *Debbie is **good/bad at** math.* **7** in a particular state: *Many children are still at risk of disease.* | *The two nations are at war.* **8** the symbol @, used in email addresses ➔ **at all** at ALL[1] ➔ **at first** at FIRST[3] ➔ **at least** at LEAST[1]

ate /eɪt/ the past tense of EAT

a·the·ist /'eɪθiɪst/ *n.* [C] someone who does not believe in God [➥ **agnostic**] —**atheism** *n.* [U]

ath·lete /'æθlit/ *n.* [C] someone who is good at sports or who often plays sports: *a professional athlete*

ath·let·ic /æθ'lɛt̬ɪk/ *adj.* **1** physically strong and good at sports **2** relating to athletics: *the athletic department*

ath·let·ics /æθ'lɛt̬ɪks/ *n.* [U] sports in general

At·lan·tic O·cean /ət˺ˌlænt̬ɪk 'oʊʃən/ *n.* **the Atlantic Ocean, the Atlantic** the large ocean between North and South America in the west, and Europe and Africa in the east

at·las /'æt˺ləs/ *n.* [C] a book of maps: *a world atlas*

ATM *n.* [C] **Automated Teller Machine** a machine that you use with a card to get money from your bank account ➔ see Topic box at ACCOUNT[1]

ATM

at·mos·phere /'æt˺məsˌfɪr/ *n.* **1** [singular, U] the feeling that an event, situation, or place gives you: *The atmosphere in the bar was casual.* | *The restaurant has a nice friendly atmosphere.* | *an **atmosphere of** suspicion* **2** [singular] the mixture of gases that surrounds the Earth or another PLANET **3** [singular] the air in a room: *a smoky atmosphere* —**atmospheric** /ˌæt˺məs'fɪrɪk◂/ *adj.*

at·om /'æt̬əm/ *n.* [C] the smallest part of an ELEMENT that can exist alone

a·tom·ic /ə'tɑmɪk/ *adj.* relating to atoms and the energy produced by splitting them: *atomic energy*

aˌtomic 'bomb *n.* [C] a very powerful bomb that splits atoms to cause an extremely large explosion

a·tone /ə'toʊn/ *v.* [I] *formal* to do something to show that you are sorry for doing something wrong: *Reilly would like to* ***atone for*** *his mistakes.* —**atonement** *n.* [U]

a·tro·cious /ə'troʊʃəs/ *adj.* extremely bad: *atrocious weather* | *My spelling is atrocious.* —**atrociously** *adv.*

A

THESAURUS

bad, awful, terrible, horrible, appalling, horrific, lousy, horrendous, abysmal
➔ see Thesaurus box at BAD[1]

a·troc·i·ty /ə'trɑsət̬i/ *n.* plural **atrocities** [C,U] very cruel or violent action: *the atrocities of war*

at·tach /ə'tætʃ/ *v.* [T] **1** to fasten or join one thing to another: *Please* ***attach*** *a photograph* ***to*** *your application.*

THESAURUS

fasten, join, glue, tape, staple, clip, tie, button (up), zip (up)
➔ see Thesaurus box at FASTEN

2 be attached to sb/sth to like someone or something very much, especially because you have known him/her or had it for a long time: *As a doctor I cannot get too attached to my patients.* **3** to connect a document or FILE to an email so that you can send them together **4 attach importance/blame etc. to sth** to believe that something is important, valuable, guilty, etc.: *They seem to attach more importance to money than to happiness.*

at·tach·ment /ə'tætʃmənt/ *n.* **1** [C,U] a strong feeling of loyalty, love, or friendship: *a mother's deep* ***attachment to*** *her baby* **2** [C] a piece of equipment that you attach to a machine to make it do a particular job: *The vacuum cleaner has various attachments.* **3** [C] a FILE that you send with an email message: *I can't* ***open*** *the* ***attachment***.

at·tack[1] /ə'tæk/ *n.* **1** [C,U] a violent action that is intended to hurt a person or damage a place: *There have been several* ***attacks on*** *foreigners recently.* | *a* ***terrorist attack*** | *a* ***bomb/knife/missile, etc. attack*** | *The city is* ***under attack*** (=being attacked).

THESAURUS

Military attack
invasion – an occasion when an army enters a country and takes control of it
raid – a short surprise military attack on a place
assault – an attack by an army to take control of a place
ambush – a sudden attack by people who have been waiting and hiding
counterattack – an attack that you make against someone who has attacked you

Physical attack on a person
assault – the crime of attacking someone
mugging – the crime of attacking and robbing someone in a public place
rape – the crime of forcing someone to have sex
➔ CRIME

2 [C,U] strong criticism: *an* ***attack on*** *the government's welfare policy* | *The mayor is* ***under*** *heavy* ***attack for*** *his racist remarks.* **3** [C] a short period of time when you are sick, worried, afraid, etc.: *an* ***attack of*** *asthma* | ***panic attacks*** —**attacker** *n.*
➔ HEART ATTACK

attack[2] *v.* **1** [I,T] to try to hurt or kill someone: *Dan was attacked as he got into his car.* | *He was arrested for* ***attacking*** *his brother* ***with*** *a knife.* **2** [T] to criticize someone strongly: *Newspapers* ***attacked*** *the President* ***for*** *failing to cut taxes.* **3** [T] if a disease, insect, or substance attacks something, it damages it: *The virus attacks the body's immune system.*

at·tack·er /ə'tækɚ/ *n.* [C] someone who uses violence to hurt someone: *The police have been unable to identify her attacker.*

THESAURUS

offender, thief, robber, burglar, shoplifter, pickpocket, mugger, murderer, rapist
➔ see Thesaurus box at CRIMINAL[2]

at·tain /ə'teɪn/ *v.* [T] to achieve something after trying for a long time: *More women are attaining high positions in business.* —**attainable** *adj.* —**attainment** *n.* [C,U]

at·tempt[1] /ə'tɛmpt/ *v.* [T] to try to do something, especially something difficult: *The plane crashed while attempting an emergency landing.* | *He died when he* ***attempted to*** *rescue his wife.*

THESAURUS

try, do your best, make an effort, endeavor
➔ see Thesaurus box at TRY[1]

attempt[2] *n.* [C] **1** an act of trying to do something: *an* ***attempt to*** *be funny* | *Can't you* ***make an attempt to*** *be nice to your sister?* | *His early* ***attempts at*** *writing were a dismal failure.* | ***In an attempt to*** *save money, I offered to do the work myself.* **2** an act of trying to kill someone important or famous that fails: *the* ***assassination attempt*** *on President Reagan*

at·tend /ə'tɛnd/ *v.* [I,T] **1** to be present at an event, such as a meeting, class, etc.: *More than 1,000 people attended the conference.* | *Please let us know if you are unable to attend.* **2** to go regularly to a school, church, etc.: *Neither of my parents attended college.*
attend to sb/sth *phr. v. formal* to give attention to someone or something: *I have some business to attend to.*

THESAURUS

deal with, tackle, handle, take care of
→ see Thesaurus box at DEAL WITH

at·tend·ance /əˈtɛndəns/ *n.* [C,U] **1** the number of people who attend an event, such as a meeting, concert, etc.: *an average attendance of 4,000 fans per game* | *Be quiet while I* ***take attendance*** (=count how many students are in class today). **2** the act of regularly going to a meeting, class, etc.: *Daily* ***attendance at*** *physical education classes.*

at·tend·ant /əˈtɛndənt/ *n.* [C] someone whose job is to take care of customers in a public place: *a parking lot attendant*

at·ten·tion /əˈtɛnʃən/ *n.* [U] **1** the state of carefully watching, listening, or thinking about someone or something: *Sorry, what did you say? I wasn't* ***paying attention****.* | *My* ***attention wasn't*** *really* ***on*** *the game.* | *He ended his sports career and* ***turned*** *his* ***attention to*** *politics.* | *This assignment requires your* ***full/undivided/complete attention****.* | ***May/Can I have your attention, please*** (=used when asking a group of people to listen carefully to you)*?* | *Most children have a short* ***attention span*** (=period of time that they are interested in watching, listening, etc. to something). | *Her boss admired her* ***attention to detail****.* **2** the interest that people show in someone or something: *Charlie tried to* ***get/attract/catch*** *our* ***attention****.* | *The governor's race has* ***drawn the attention of*** *the nation's media.* | *Rob loves being* ***the center of attention*** (=the person everyone notices). **3** special care or treatment: *The back yard really needs some attention – it's full of weeds.* | *Some of the children required urgent* ***medical attention****.* **4 stand at/to attention** if soldiers stand to attention, they stand very straight, with their feet together

at·ten·tive /əˈtɛntɪv/ *adj.* listening or watching carefully: *an attentive audience* —**attentively** *adv.* —**attentiveness** *n.* [U]

at·test /əˈtɛst/ *v.* [I,T] to show or prove that something is true: *The crowd of people waiting outside his door* ***attests to*** *this young star's popularity.*

at·tic /ˈæt̬ɪk/ *n.* [C] a room at the top of a house, usually used for storing things: *I think the photos are* ***up in the attic****.*

at·tire /əˈtaɪɚ/ *n.* [U] *formal* clothes: *Reservations and* ***formal attire*** *are required.*

at·ti·tude /ˈæt̬əˌtud/ *n.* **1** [C,U] the opinions and feelings that you usually have about someone or something: *a* ***positive/negative attitude*** | *I don't like his* ***attitude toward*** *women.* | *The study examines teenagers'* ***attitudes about*** *drugs.*

THESAURUS

opinion, view, point of view, position
→ see Thesaurus box at OPINION

2 [C,U] the way that you behave toward someone or in a particular situation: *Their whole attitude changed once they found out Ron was rich.* | *Cathy has a real* ***attitude problem*** (=she is not helpful or pleasant to be with). **3** [U] *informal* the confidence to do unusual and exciting things without caring what other people think: *a young singer* ***with attitude***

at·tor·ney /əˈtɚni/ *n.* plural **attorneys** [C] LAWYER

at͵torney ˈgeneral *n.* [C] the chief lawyer in a state, or of the government in the U.S.

at·tract /əˈtrækt/ *v.* [T] **1** to make someone like something or feel interested in it: *The story* ***attracted*** *a lot of* ***attention*** *from the media.* | *What* ***attracted*** *you* ***to*** *Atlanta?* **2** to make someone come to a place: *Disneyland attracts millions of tourists each year.* **3 be attracted to sb** to like someone in a sexual way: *I was immediately attracted to him.* **4** to make someone or something move toward another thing: *Flowers attract bees.*

at·trac·tion /əˈtrækʃən/ *n.* **1** [C,U] a feeling of liking someone, especially in a sexual way: *I can't understand Beth's* ***attraction to*** *Stan.* **2** [C] something interesting or fun to see or do: *the attractions at the county fair* | *the city's top* ***tourist attraction*** (=place that many tourists visit)

at·trac·tive /əˈtræktɪv/ *adj.* **1** pretty or nice to look at: *an attractive young woman* | *an attractive location for a wedding* | *Women seem to* ***find*** *him* ***attractive****.*

THESAURUS

good-looking – used about anyone who is attractive
pretty – used about a girl or woman who is attractive
beautiful – used about a woman, girl, or baby who is extremely attractive
handsome – used about a man or boy who is attractive
gorgeous/stunning – used about anyone who is very attractive
nice-looking – used about anyone who is attractive
cute – used about a baby or young child who is attractive
cute – used about someone you think is sexually attractive
hot informal – used about someone you think is sexually attractive

2 interesting or exciting: *an attractive salary/offer* | *Advertising campaigns make alcohol* ***attractive to*** *young people.*

at·tri·but·a·ble /əˈtrɪbyət̬əbəl/ *adj. formal* likely to have been caused by something: *The price increase is* ***attributable to*** *a rise in the cost of paper.*

at·trib·ute¹ /əˈtrɪbyut/ *v.*
attribute sth **to** sb/sth *phr. v.* to believe or say

that someone or something is responsible for something: *Many diseases can be attributed to stress.* | *a painting attributed to Rembrandt* —**attribution** /ˌætrəˌbyuʃən/ *n.*

at·tri·bute[2] /ˈætrəˈbyut/ *n.* [C] a good or useful quality: *Kindness is just one of her many attributes.*

A

THESAURUS

characteristic, feature, quality, property
→ see Thesaurus box at CHARACTERISTIC[1]

at·trib·u·tive /əˈtrɪbyət̬ɪv/ *adj.* *technical* in grammar, an attributive adjective or noun comes before the noun or phrase it describes. In the sentence "I heard a funny story," the word "funny" is attributive

at·tuned /əˈtund/ *adj.* **be/become attuned to sth** to be so familiar with someone or something that you know how to deal with him, her, or it: *It took me a while to become attuned to the strong southern accent.*

a·typ·i·cal /eɪˈtɪpɪkəl/ *adj.* not typical or usual

au·burn /ˈɔbɚn/ *adj.* auburn hair is a reddish brown color —**auburn** *n.* [U]

auc·tion /ˈɔkʃən/ *n.* [C] an event at which things are sold to the person who offers the most money —**auction** *v.* [T]

THESAURUS

sell, put up, peddle, export
→ see Thesaurus box at SELL

auc·tion·eer /ˌɔkʃəˈnɪr/ *n.* [C] someone who is in charge of an auction

au·da·cious /ɔˈdeɪʃəs/ *adj.* brave and shocking: *audacious behavior* —**audaciously** *adv.*

au·dac·i·ty /ɔˈdæsət̬i/ *n.* [U] the quality of having enough courage to take risks or do things that are shocking or rude: *I can't believe he **had the audacity to** call your father at 3 a.m.*

au·di·ble /ˈɔdəbəl/ *adj.* loud enough to be heard [≠ **inaudible**]: *Her voice was **barely audible**.* | *an **audible sigh** of relief* —**audibly** *adj.*

au·di·ence /ˈɔdiəns/ *n.* [C] **1** the people watching or listening to a performance: *an **audience of** 300 people* | ***Members of the audience** were invited to ask questions.*

TOPIC

theater, go to the theater, see a play/musical/opera/ballet, reserve tickets, box office, seat, the floor, balcony, program, orchestra, stage, intermission
→ see Topic box at THEATER

2 the people who watch a particular television program, read a particular book or magazine, etc.: *The show attracts a regular **audience of** 20 million viewers.* **3** a formal meeting with someone who is very important: *an **audience with** the Pope*

au·di·o /ˈɔdioʊ/ *adj.* relating to recording and broadcasting sound [➡ **video**]: *audio equipment*

au·di·o·vis·u·al /ˌɔdioʊˈvɪʒuəl/ *adj.* using recorded pictures and sound: *an audiovisual presentation*

au·dit /ˈɔdɪt/ *v.* [T] **1** to officially examine a company's financial records in order to check that they are correct **2** to study a subject at college without getting a GRADE for it —**audit** *n.* [C] —**auditor** *n.* [C]

au·di·tion[1] /ɔˈdɪʃən/ *n.* [C] a short performance by an actor, singer, etc. to test whether s/he is good enough to perform in a play, concert, etc.: *The ballet company is **holding auditions for** "Swan Lake."*

audition[2] *v.* [I,T] to perform in an audition or judge someone in an audition: *He plans to **audition for** a part in "Oklahoma!"*

au·di·to·ri·um /ˌɔdɪˈtɔriəm/ *n.* [C] a large building used for concerts or public meetings

aug·ment /ɔgˈmɛnt/ *v.* [T] *formal* to increase the size or value of something

Au·gust /ˈɔgəst/ *written abbreviation* **Aug.** *n.* [C,U] the eighth month of the year: *The winner will be announced **on August 31st**.* | *They sold their house **in August**.* | ***Last August**, we traveled through Europe.* | *The changes will take effect **next August**.*

aunt /ænt, ɑnt/ *n.* [C] the sister of your mother or father, or the wife of your UNCLE: *Aunt Jean*

THESAURUS

relative, parents, father, mother, dad, daddy, mom, mommy, brother, sister, grandparents, grandfather, grandmother, grandpa, grandma, great-grandparents, uncle, nephew, niece, cousin
→ see Thesaurus box at RELATIVE[1]

au pair /oʊ ˈpɛr/ *n.* [C] a young person who stays with a family in a foreign country and looks after their children

au·ra /ˈɔrə/ *n.* [C] a quality or feeling that seems to come from a person or place: *There's an **aura of** mystery around the castle.*

au·ral /ˈɔrəl/ *adj.* related to the sense of hearing [➡ **oral**]: *aural skills*

aus·pic·es /ˈɔspəsɪz, -ˌsiz/ *n.* **under the auspices of sb/sth** *formal* with the help and support of a person or organization: *The research was done under the auspices of Harvard Medical School.*

aus·pi·cious /ɔˈspɪʃəs/ *adj.* showing that something is likely to be successful [➡ **inauspicious**]: *an **auspicious start/beginning** to her career*

aus·tere /ɔˈstɪr/ *adj.* **1** very strict and serious: *a cold, austere woman* **2** very plain and simple: *an austere style of painting* **3** without a lot of comfort or enjoyment: *They lived an austere life.*

aus·ter·i·ty /ɔˈstɛrət̬i/ *n.* [U] **1** bad economic conditions in which people do not have enough money to live: *the austerity of post-communist Eastern Europe* **2** the quality of being austere

Aus·tra·lia /ɑ'streɪliə/ *n.* one of the seven CONTINENTS that is also its own country

Aus·tra·li·an /ɑ'streɪliən/ *adj.* relating to Australia or its people

au·then·tic /ɔ'θɛntɪk/ *adj.* **1** done or made in a traditional way: *authentic Indian food* **2** proven to be made by a particular person [= **genuine**]: *an authentic Renoir painting* —**authentically** *adj.* /ˌɔθən'tɪsəṭi/ —**authenticity** *n.* [U] *Tests confirmed the book's authenticity.*

au·thor /'ɔθɚ/ *n.* [C] someone who writes a book, story, article, play, etc.: *Who is your favorite author?* | *Banville is the* ***author of*** *"The Book of Evidence."*

au·thor·i·tar·i·an /əˌθɔrə'tɛriən, əˌθɑr-/ *adj.* forcing people to obey strict rules or laws and not allowing any freedom: *an authoritarian government* —**authoritarian** *n.* [C] *Papa was a strict authoritarian.*

au·thor·i·ta·tive /ə'θɔrəˌteɪṭɪv, ə'θɑr-/ *adj.* **1** an authoritative book, account, etc. is respected because the person who wrote it knows a lot about the subject: *an authoritative account of the country's history* **2** behaving or speaking in a confident, determined way that makes people respect and obey you: *The captain spoke in a calm and authoritative voice.* —**authoritatively** *adv.*

au·thor·i·ty /ə'θɔrəṭi, ə'θɑr-/ *n.* **1** [U] the power someone has because of his/her official position: *You have no* ***authority over*** *me!* | *Could I speak to someone* ***in authority*** (=who has a position of power) *please?* | *She has the* ***authority to*** *sign checks.* | *people* ***in positions of authority*** **2 the authorities** the people or organizations that are in charge of a particular place: *Please report any suspicious activities to the authorities immediately.* **3** [C] someone who is respected because of his/her knowledge about a subject: *Dr. Ballard is a leading* ***authority on*** *tropical diseases.*

THESAURUS

expert, specialist, connoisseur
→ see Thesaurus box at EXPERT

au·thor·ize /'ɔθəˌraɪz/ *v.* [T] to give official permission for something: *Can you authorize my expenses?* | *No one* ***authorized*** *you* ***to*** *sign this.* —**authorization** /ˌɔθərə'zeɪʃən/ *n.* [C,U] *You'll need authorization from the Director to do that.*

au·tis·m /'ɔˌtɪzəm/ *n.* [U] a problem in the way the brain works that makes someone unable to communicate in a normal way, or to form normal relationships —**autistic** /ɔ'tɪstɪk/ *adj.*: *an autistic child*

au·to /'ɔṭoʊ/ *adj.* relating to cars: *auto parts*

au·to·bi·og·ra·phy /ˌɔṭəbaɪ'ɑgrəfi/ *n.* plural **autobiographies** [C] a book that someone writes about his/her own life —**autobiographical** /ˌɔṭəˌbaɪə'græfɪkəl/ *adj.*

THESAURUS

book, nonfiction, fiction, literature, reference book, text book, hardcover, hardback, paperback, novel, science fiction, biography
→ see Thesaurus box at BOOK[1]

au·toc·ra·cy /ɔ'tɑkrəsi/ *n.* plural **autocracies** [C,U] a system of government in which one person or group has unlimited power, or a country governed in this way

au·to·crat·ic /ˌɔṭə'kræṭɪk/ *adj.* **1** giving orders to people without considering their opinions: *an autocratic style of management* **2** having unlimited power to govern a country: *an autocratic government* —**autocrat** /'ɔṭəˌkræt/ *n.* [C]

au·to·graph /'ɔṭəˌgræf/ *n.* [C] a famous person's name, written in his/her own writing: *Can I have your autograph?* —**autograph** *v.* [T] *a jacket autographed by all the players*

au·to·mat·ed /'ɔṭəˌmeɪṭɪd/ *adj.* using computers and machines to do a job rather than people: *automated phone lines* —**automation** /ˌɔṭə'meɪʃən/ *n.* [U]

au·to·mat·ic[1] /ˌɔṭə'mæṭɪk◂/ *adj.* **1** an automatic machine is designed to operate by itself after you start it: *an automatic timer* **2** certain to happen: *We get an automatic pay increase every year.* **3** done without thinking: *At first, driving is hard, but then it just becomes automatic.* —**automatically** *adv.*: *She automatically assumed that he was guilty.*

automatic[2] *n.* [C] **1** a car with a system of GEARS that operate themselves **2** a gun that can shoot bullets continuously

au·to·mo·bile /ˌɔṭəmə'bil, 'ɔṭəməˌbil/ *n.* [C] a car

au·to·mo·tive /ˌɔṭə'moʊṭɪv/ *adj.* relating to cars: *the automotive industry*

au·ton·o·mous /ɔ'tɑnəməs/ *adj.* having the power to make your own decisions or rules: *an autonomous nation* —**autonomously** *adv.* —**autonomy** *n.* [U] *political autonomy*

au·top·sy /'ɔˌtɑpsi/ *n.* plural **autopsies** [C] an official examination of a dead body to discover the cause of death

au·to·work·er /'ɔṭoʊˌwɚkɚ/ *n.* [C] someone whose job is to make cars

au·tumn /'ɔṭəm/ *n.* [C,U] FALL —**autumnal** /ɔ'tʌmnəl/ *adj.*

aux·il·ia·ry /ɔg'zɪləri, -'zɪlyəri/ *adj.* giving extra help or support: *auxiliary police* —**auxiliary** *n.* [C]

auxˌiliary 'verb *n.* [C] *technical* a verb that is used with another verb to form questions, negative sentences, and tenses. In English the auxiliary verbs are "be," "do," and "have."

a·vail[1] /ə'veɪl/ *n.* **to no avail** without success: *We searched everywhere to no avail.*

avail[2] *v.* **avail yourself of sth** *formal* to accept an offer or use an opportunity: *Avail yourself of every chance to improve your English.*

a·vail·a·ble /ə'veɪləbəl/ *adj.* **1** if something is available, you can have it, buy it, or use it: *The database in the library is **available to** anyone.* | *Several thousand seats are **available for** tonight's show.* | *films **available on** video* | *The book is **available in** the museum's bookstore.* | ***readily/widely available*** (=easily available or available from many places) **2** [not before noun] someone who is available is not busy and has enough time to talk to you: *I'm available after lunch.* —**availability** /əˌveɪlə'bɪləṭi/ *n.* [U] *the easy availability of guns in the U.S.*

av·a·lanche /'ævəˌlæntʃ, -ˌlɑntʃ/ *n.* [C] **1** a large amount of snow, ice, and rocks that falls down the side of a mountain **2 an avalanche of sth** a very large number of things that happen or arrive at the same time: *The station received an avalanche of letters.*

a·vant-garde /ˌævɑnt'gɑrd◂ , ˌɑ-/ *adj.* avant-garde art, literature, or music is very modern and different from existing art, etc., often in a way that is strange or shocking

av·a·rice /'ævərɪs/ *n.* [U] *formal* an extreme desire for wealth [= **greed**] —**avaricious** /ˌævə'rɪʃəs/ *adj.*

Ave. the written abbreviation of **avenue**

a·venge /ə'vɛndʒ/ *v.* [T] *literary* to punish someone because s/he has harmed you, your family, or friends: *plans to avenge his father's death* —**avenger** *n.* [C]

av·e·nue /'ævəˌnu/ *n.* [C] **1 also Avenue** a street in a town or city: *Fifth Avenue* | *He lives on Melrose Avenue.*

THESAURUS

road, street, main street, lane, main road
➔ see Thesaurus box at ROAD

2 a possible way of achieving something: *We **explored every avenue**, but couldn't find a solution.*

av·erage¹ /'ævrɪdʒ/ *adj.* **1** [only before noun] the average amount is the amount you get when you add together several figures and divide this by the total number of figures: *the **average price** of a new home* | *The **average age** of teachers is rising steadily.* **2** [only before noun] having qualities that are typical of most people or things: *In an average week I drive about 250 miles.* | *The average American has not even thought about next year's election.*

THESAURUS

normal, ordinary, standard, routine, conventional
➔ see Thesaurus box at NORMAL¹

3 not very good but not very bad: *an average book*

average² *n.* **1** [C] the amount that you get by adding several figures together and then dividing the result by the number of figures: *The **average of** 3, 8, and 10 is 7.* **2 on average** based on a calculation of what usually happens: *On average, women live longer than men.* **3** [C,U] the usual level or amount: *an **above average/below average** student*

average³ *v.* [T] **1** to be a particular amount as an average: *I average about 10 cigarettes a day.* **2** to calculate the average of an amount

average out *phr. v.* to result in a particular average amount: *Our weekly profits **average out at** about $750.*

a·verse /ə'vɚs/ *adj.* **not be averse to sth** to like to do something: *I don't drink much, but I'm not averse to the occasional glass of wine.*

a·ver·sion /ə'vɚʒən/ *n.* [singular, U] a strong dislike of something or someone: *Mary **has an aversion to** cats.*

a·vert /ə'vɚt/ *v.* [T] **1** to prevent something bad from happening: *The whole thing could've been averted if you'd listened to us.* **2 avert your eyes/gaze** to look away from something

a·vi·a·tion /ˌeɪvi'eɪʃən/ *n.* [U] the science or activity of flying or making aircraft

a·vi·a·tor /'eɪviˌeɪṭɚ/ *n.* [C] *old-fashioned* a pilot

av·id /'ævɪd/ *adj.* [only before noun] doing something as much as possible: *an **avid reader*** | *an avid golfer*

av·o·ca·do /ˌævə'kɑdoʊ, ˌɑ-/ *n.* plural **avocados** [C,U] a firm, green fruit, eaten as a vegetable ➔ see picture at FRUIT

a·void /ə'vɔɪd/ *v.* [T] **1** to prevent something bad from happening: *Exercise will help you avoid heart disease.* | *He had to swerve to avoid being hit by the other car.* ▶ Don't say "avoid to do something." ◀ **2** to deliberately stay away from someone or something: *Paul's been avoiding me all day.* **3** to deliberately not do something: *To avoid paying tax, he moved to Canada.* —**avoidable** *adj.* —**avoidance** *n.* [U]

a·vow /ə'vaʊ/ *v.* [T] *formal* to say or admit something publicly

a·vowed /ə'vaʊd/ *adj.* said or admitted publicly: *an avowed atheist*

a·wait /ə'weɪt/ *v.* [T] *formal* **1** to wait for something: *Briggs is awaiting trial for murder.* **2** if a situation or event awaits someone, it is going to happen to him/her: *A terrible surprise awaited them.*

a·wake¹ /ə'weɪk/ *adj.* [not before noun] not sleeping: *Is she awake yet?* | *I couldn't **stay awake** during the movie.* | *I was **wide awake*** (=completely awake) *before dawn.* | *The baby **kept** us **awake*** (=stopped us from sleeping) *all night.*

awake² *v.* past tense **awoke** /ə'woʊk/ past participle **awoken** /ə'woʊkən/ [I,T] *literary* **1** to wake up, or to wake someone up: ***I awoke to** the sound of rain pounding on the roof.* **2** to suddenly begin to feel an emotion, or to make someone do this

a·wak·en /ə'weɪkən/ *v.* [I,T] AWAKE
awaken sb/sth **to** sth *phr. v. formal* to make someone begin to realize something: *Churches are awakening to the needs of their older members.*

a·wak·en·ing /ə'weɪkənɪŋ/ *n.* [C,U] a situation when you suddenly realize that you understand or feel something: *a spiritual awakening*

a·ward¹ /ə'wɔrd/ *n.* [C] **1** a prize or money given to someone for something that s/he has achieved: *the **award for** best actor | an **award of** $10,000 to each victim | an experienced reporter who has **won** many **awards*** **2** an amount of money that is given to someone because of a judge's decision: *an **award for** injuries suffered*

award² *v.* [T] to officially give someone an award: *He was awarded the Nobel Prize. | A large sum of money was **awarded to** the survivors.*

THESAURUS
give, donate, leave
→ see Thesaurus box at GIVE¹

a·ware /ə'wɛr/ *adj.* [not before noun] **1** realizing that something is true, exists, or is happening [≠ **unaware**]: *Are you **aware of** the dangers of smoking? | Were you **aware (that)** your son has been taking drugs? | "Are there any more problems?" "**Not that I'm aware of.**"* **2 politically/socially/environmentally etc. aware** interested in politics, etc. and knowing a lot about it

a·ware·ness /ə'wɛrnɪs/ *n.* [U] knowledge or understanding of a particular subject or situation: *The TV ads are meant to **raise** the public's **awareness of** environmental issues.*

a·wash /ə'wɑʃ, ə'wɔʃ/ *adj.* **1 awash with/in sth** having too much of something: *TV is awash with talk shows.* **2** covered with water

a·way¹ /ə'weɪ/ *adv.* **1** moving further from a place, or staying far from a place: *Go away! | Diane drove away quickly. | Move **away from** the fire!* **2** in a different direction: *She looked away and began to cry.* **3 3 miles/40 feet/2 weeks etc. away** used to say how far it is to a place, thing, or time in the future: *a town about 50 miles **away from** Chicago | Christmas is only a month away.* **4** into a safe place: *Put all your toys away now, please.* **5** not at home, at work, or in school: *I'm sorry, Ms. Parker is away this week.* **6** used to say that something disappears or is removed: *He gave his money away to charity. | The music died away.* **7** used to say how close someone is to achieving something or experiencing something: *At one point they were only two points **away from** victory.* **8** without stopping: *He's been working away on the patio all day.*

away² *adj.* **away team/game/match** a sports team that is playing at an opponent's field, or a game they are playing there [≠ **home**]

awe /ɔ/ *n.* [U] a feeling of great respect for someone or something: *We were **in awe of** our father.* —**awed** *adj.*: *an awed silence*

'awe-in,spiring *adj.* making you feel awe: *an awe-inspiring achievement*

THESAURUS
impressive, imposing, dazzling, breathtaking, majestic
→ see Thesaurus box at IMPRESSIVE

awe·some /'ɔsəm/ *adj.* **1** very impressive, serious, or difficult: *an awesome responsibility* **2** *spoken* extremely good: *That concert was awesome!*

awe·struck /'ɔstrʌk/ *adj.* feeling great awe: *We gazed awestruck at the pyramids.*

aw·ful¹ /'ɔfəl/ *adj.* **1** very bad: *an awful movie | The weather was awful. | This soup tastes awful!*

THESAURUS
bad, terrible, horrible, appalling, horrific, lousy, horrendous, atrocious, abysmal
→ see Thesaurus box at BAD¹, HORRIBLE

2 [only before noun] *spoken* used in order to emphasize how much, how good, how bad, etc. something is: *I have **an awful lot** (=a very large amount) of work to do.* **3 look/feel awful** to look or feel sick

awful² *adv. spoken nonstandard* very: *She's awful cute.*

aw·fully /'ɔfli/ *adv. spoken* very: *Helen looks awfully tired.*

a·while /ə'waɪl/ *adv.* for a short time: *I needed to be alone for awhile.*

awk·ward /'ɔkwɚd/ *adj.* **1** embarrassing: *This puts us in an **awkward position**. | For a few moments there was an **awkward silence**.* **2** moving or behaving in a way that does not seem relaxed or comfortable: *an awkward teenager*

THESAURUS
clumsy, gawky, inelegant
→ see Thesaurus box at CLUMSY

3 not convenient: *They came at an awkward time.* **4** difficult to use or handle: *The camera is awkward to use.* —**awkwardly** *adv.* —**awkwardness** *n.* [U]

awn·ing /'ɔnɪŋ/ *n.* [C] a sheet of material outside a store, tent, etc. used for protection from the sun or the rain

a·woke /ə'woʊk/ *v.* the past tense of AWAKE

a·wok·en /ə'woʊkən/ *v.* the past participle of AWAKE

AWOL /'eɪ,wɔl/ *adj.* **Absent Without Leave** absent from your military group without permission: *Private Ames has **gone AWOL**.*

a·wry /ə'raɪ/ *adj.* **go awry** to not happen in the way that was planned: *My carefully laid plans had already gone awry.*

ax¹, axe /æks/ *n.* [C] **1** a tool with a metal blade on a long handle, used for cutting wood **2 give sb/sth the ax** *informal* to dismiss someone from his/her job, or get rid of something: *The TV station gave Brown the ax.* **3 get the ax** *informal* to be dismissed from your job **4 have an ax to grind** to have a personal reason for doing something: *I have no political ax to grind.*

ax², **axe** *v.* [T] *informal* to get rid of a plan, service, or someone's job: *Did you hear they're axing 500 jobs?*

ax·i·om /ˈæksiəm/ *n.* [C] *formal* a rule or principle that is considered by most people to be true

B

ax·i·o·mat·ic /ˌæksiəˈmæṭɪk/ *adj.* a principle that is axiomatic does not need to be proved because people can see that it is true

ax·is /ˈæksɪs/ *n.* plural **axes** /ˈæksiz/ [C] **1** the imaginary line around which something turns, for example the Earth ➔ see picture at GLOBE **2** a line at the side or bottom of a GRAPH, used for marking measurements

ax·le /ˈæksəl/ *n.* [C] the bar that connects two wheels on a vehicle

aye /aɪ/ *adv. spoken formal* used in order to say yes, especially when voting

AZ the written abbreviation of **Arizona**

B, b

B, b /bi/ the second letter of the English alphabet

B /bi/ *n.* **1** [C] a GRADE that a teacher gives to a student's work, showing that it is good but not excellent: *Greg **got a B** in Chemistry.* **2** [C,U] the seventh note in the musical SCALE of C, or the musical KEY based on this note

b. the written abbreviation of **born**: *A. Lincoln, b. 1809*

B.A. *n.* [C] **Bachelor of Arts** a university degree in a subject such as history or literature [➡ **B.S.**]: *He graduated from Stanford with a **B.A. in** English.*

baa /bɑ, bæ/ *v.* [I] to make the sound a sheep makes

bab·ble /ˈbæbəl/ *v.* [I,T] to talk a lot in a way that does not make sense: *I couldn't understand what he was babbling about.* —**babble** *n.* [U]

babe /beɪb/ *n.* [C] **1** *spoken informal* an attractive young woman **2** *spoken* a way of speaking to a woman, often considered offensive **3** *literary* a baby

ba·boon /bæˈbun/ *n.* [C] a large monkey that lives in Africa and south Asia

ba·by /ˈbeɪbi/ *n.* plural **babies** [C] **1** a very young child: *A baby was crying upstairs.* | *Joyce **had a baby** (=gave birth to a baby) in September.* | *Pam **is expecting a baby** (=will have a baby).* | *a **baby boy/girl***

TOPIC

A baby that has just been born is called a **newborn**. A very young baby who cannot walk or talk yet is called an **infant**. A baby who has learned how to walk is called a **toddler**.
When babies **crawl**, they move around on their hands and knees. Babies usually crawl before they learn how to walk.
When you take a baby somewhere, you can push him/her there in a **baby carriage**, which is like a bed on wheels. You can push an older baby along in a **stroller**, which is like a chair on wheels.
Babies sleep in a special bed with bars on it, called a **crib**.
If a baby is being fed milk from its mother's breast, the baby is **nursing** or the mother is **breast-feeding** the baby. If a baby drinks milk from a bottle, s/he is being **bottle-fed**. When a baby is old enough to sit up and eat food, s/he sits in a **highchair**.
➔ see Thesaurus box at CHILD

2 a very young animal: *baby birds* **3** *spoken* someone, especially an older child, who is behaving in a stupid or silly way: *Don't be such a baby.* **4** *spoken* a way of speaking to someone you love: *Bye, baby. I'll be back by six.*

ˈbaby boom *n.* [C] a time when a lot of babies are born in a particular country, especially between 1946 and 1964

baby carriage

ˈbaby ˌboomer *n.* [C] *informal* someone born between 1946 and 1964

ˈbaby ˌcarriage, **ˈbaby ˌbuggy** *n.* [C] a thing like a bed on wheels, used for pushing a baby around

TOPIC

baby, **newborn**, **infant**, **toddler**, **crawl**, **stroller**, **crib**, **nursing**, **breast-feeding**, **bottle-fed**, **highchair**
➔ see Topic box at BABY

ba·by·sit /ˈbeɪbiˌsɪt/ *v.* past tense and past participle **babysat** /-ˌsæt/ present participle **babysitting** [I,T] to take care of children while their parents are not at home —**babysitter** *n.* [C] —**babysitting** *n.* [U]

bach·e·lor /ˈbætʃələ˞, ˈbætʃlə˞/ *n.* [C] a man who has never been married

ˈbachelor ˌparty *n.* [C] a party given for a man before he gets married

THESAURUS

party, **baby/wedding/bridal shower**, **reception**, **celebration**
➔ see Thesaurus box at PARTY¹

ˈbachelor's deˌgree *n.* [C] B.A.

back¹ /bæk/ *adv.* **1** where someone or something was before: ***Put*** *the milk* ***back*** *in the refrigerator.* | *Roger said he'd* ***be back*** (=return) *in an hour.* | *If the shirt doesn't fit,* ***take*** *it* ***back*** *to the store.* | *I was on my way* ***back home*** (=the place I come from or think of as my home). **2** into the condition that someone or something was in before: *I woke up at 5 a.m. and couldn't* ***get back to*** *sleep.* | *I never want to go back to being a waitress.* **3** in the direction that is behind you: *George glanced back to see if he was being followed.* **4** doing the same thing to someone that s/he has done to you: *Can you call me back later?* | *Sarah smiled, and the boy smiled back.* **5** away from someone or something: *Her hair was pulled back in a ponytail.* | *Stand* ***back from*** *the fire!* **6** in or toward an earlier time: *This all happened about three years back.* | *They were using computers that dated* ***back to*** *the 1980s.* **7 back and forth** in one direction and then in the opposite direction several times: *He walked back and forth across the floor.*

back² *n.*

1 BODY [C] **a)** the part of your body between your neck and legs, opposite your stomach and chest: *My back was really aching.* | *The cat arched its back and hissed.* | *He lay* ***on*** *his* ***back****, staring at the sky.* | *Mrs. Ducin stood* ***with*** *her* ***back to*** *the camera.* **b)** the bone that goes from your neck to your BUTTOCKS: *He broke his back in a motorcycle accident.*

2 PART OF STH [C usually singular, U] the part of something that is furthest from the front [≠ **front**]: *a grocery list* ***on the back of*** *an envelope* | *The index is* ***at the back of*** *the book.* | *The pool's* ***in back of*** *the house.* | *Kids should always wear seat belts, even* ***in back*** (=in the seats behind the driver). | *Tom's working on the car* ***out back*** (=behind a building).

3 SEAT [C] the part of a seat that you lean against when you are sitting: *Jack leaned against the* ***back of*** *the chair.*

4 behind sb's back if you do something bad or unkind behind someone's back, you do it without him/her knowing: *I can't believe she said that about me behind my back!*

5 at/in the back of your mind a thought or feeling at the back of your mind is influencing you even though you are not thinking about it: *There was always a slight fear in the back of his mind.*

6 get off my back *spoken* said when you want someone to stop annoying you or asking you to do something: *I'll do it in a minute. Just get off my back!*

7 be on sb's back *spoken* to keep telling someone to do something, in a way that annoys him/her: *The boss has been on my back about being late.*

8 have your back to/against the wall *informal* to be in a very difficult situation with no choice about what to do ➔ **turn your back (on)** at TURN

back³ *v.* **1** [I,T] to move backward, or to make a vehicle move backward: *Teresa backed the car into the garage.* | *We slowly* ***backed away*** *from the snake.* **2** [T] to support someone or something, especially by using your money or power: *The bill is backed by several environmental groups.* **3** [T] to risk money on the team, person, horse, etc. that you think will win something: *Which team did you back in the Superbowl?*

back down *phr. v.* to admit that you are wrong or that you have lost an argument or fight: *Neither side would back down.*

back off *phr. v.* **1** to move away from something: *Back off a little, you're too close.* **2** *spoken* said in order to tell someone to stop telling you what to do, or to stop criticizing you: *Back off! I don't need your advice.*

back onto sth *phr. v.* if a building backs onto a place, the back of the building faces it: *The house backs onto a busy road.*

back out *phr. v.* to decide not to do something you promised to do: *They* ***backed out of*** *the deal at the last minute.*

back up *phr. v.* **1 back** sb/sth ⇔ **up** to support what someone is doing or saying, or show that it is true: *He had evidence on video to back up his claim.* **2 back** sth ⇔ **up** to move backward, or to make a vehicle go backward: *Back up a little so they can get by.* **3 back** sth ⇔ **up** to make a copy of information on a computer **4 be backed up** traffic that is backed up is moving very slowly

back⁴ *adj.* [only before noun] **1** at the back of something [≠ **front**]: *the back door* | *We sat in the back row of the theater.* **2 back street/road** a street that is away from the main streets **3 back rent/taxes/pay** money that someone owes from an earlier date

back·ache /ˈbækeɪk/ *n.* [C,U] a pain in your back

back·bit·ing /ˈbækˌbaɪt̬ɪŋ/ *n.* [U] rude or cruel talk about someone who is not present

back·board /ˈbækbɔrd/ *n.* [C] the board behind the basket in the game of basketball

back·bone /ˈbækboʊn/ *n.* **1** [C] SPINE ➔ see picture on page A3 **2 the backbone of sth** the most important part of something: *The cocoa industry is the backbone of Ghana's economy.* **3** [U] courage and determination: *Stuart doesn't have the backbone to be a good manager.*

back·break·ing /ˈbækˌbreɪkɪŋ/ *adj.* backbreaking work is very difficult and tiring

back·date /ˈbækˌdeɪt/ *v.* [T] to write an earlier date on a document or check than the date when it was really written

back·drop /ˈbækdrɑp/ *n.* [C] **1** the conditions in which something happens: *a love story* ***set against the backdrop of*** *war* **2** the painted cloth at the back of a stage

back·er /ˈbækɚ/ *n.* [C] someone who supports a plan, especially by providing money: *We're still trying to find* ***backers for*** *the new enterprise.*

B

back·fire /ˈbækfaɪɚ/ *v.* [I] **1** if a plan or action backfires, it has the opposite effect to the one you wanted **2** if a car backfires, it makes a sudden loud noise because the engine is not working correctly

back·gam·mon /ˈbæk͵gæmən/ *n.* [U] a game for two players, using flat round pieces and DICE on a board

back·ground /ˈbækgraʊnd/ *n.* **1** [C] someone's education, family, and experience: *kids from very different **ethnic/religious/cultural backgrounds** | Steve **has a background in** computer engineering. | a writer **with a background in** television* **2** [C usually singular] the area that is behind the main things that you are looking at: *Palm trees swayed **in the background.*** **3 in the background** someone who keeps or stays in the background tries not to be noticed: *The president's wife preferred to stay in the background.* **4** [singular] sounds that are in the background are not the main ones that you can hear: *I could hear cars honking **in the background.** | soft lights and **background music*** **5** [singular, U] the general conditions in which something happens

back·hand /ˈbækhænd/ *n.* [C usually singular] a way of hitting the ball in tennis, etc. with the back of your hand turned toward the ball [➡ **forehand**]

back·hand·ed /ˈbæk͵hændɪd/ *adj.* **backhanded compliment** a statement that seems to express praise or admiration, but is actually insulting

back·ing /ˈbækɪŋ/ *n.* [U] support or help, especially with money: *The agency has provided **financial backing** for the project.*

back·lash /ˈbæklæʃ/ *n.* [singular] a strong reaction from people against an idea or person: *a political **backlash against** immigrants*

back·log /ˈbæklɔg, -lɑg/ *n.* [C] work that still needs to be done and should have been done earlier: *a huge **backlog of** orders*

back·pack¹ /ˈbækpæk/ *n.* [C] a bag used to carry things on your back, especially when you go walking ➔ see picture at BAG¹

backpack² *v.* [I] to go walking or traveling carrying a backpack —**backpacker** *n.* [C] —**backpacking** *n.* [U]

͵back ˈseat *n.* [C] **1** the seat behind where the driver sits in a car: *Holly and I were sitting **in the backseat.*** **2 back seat driver** someone who gives unwanted advice about how to drive to the driver of a car **3 take a back seat** to accept or be put in a less important position: *His career has taken a back seat while he raises his son.*

back·side /ˈbæksaɪd/ *n.* [C] *informal* the part of your body that you sit on

back·slash /ˈbækslæʃ/ *n.* [C] a line (\) used in writing to separate words, numbers, or letters

back·space /ˈbækspeɪs/ *n.* [singular] a button on a computer KEYBOARD or TYPEWRITER that you press to move backward toward the beginning of the line

back·stab·bing /ˈbæk͵stæbɪŋ/ *n.* [U] the act of secretly doing bad things to someone else, especially saying bad things about him/her, in order to gain an advantage for yourself —**backstabber** *n.* [C]

back·stage /͵bækˈsteɪdʒ/ *adv.* behind the stage in a theater

back·stroke /ˈbækstroʊk/ *n.* [singular] a style of swimming on your back ➔ see picture at SWIM¹

͵back-to-ˈback *adj., adv.* happening one after the other: *back-to-back wins*

back·track /ˈbæktræk/ *v.* [I] **1** to change something you have said so that it is not as strong as it was earlier: *The witness backtracked, adding some new facts to his story.* **2** to go back the way you have just come: *We had to backtrack about a mile.*

back·up /ˈbækʌp/ *n.* **1** [C] something or a copy of something that you can use if the original thing is lost or does not work: ***Make a backup of** any work you do on the computer. | Always have a backup plan.* **2** [C,U] extra help or support that can be used if it is needed: *Several police cars provided backup for the officers.*

back·ward¹ /ˈbækwɚd/ **also backwards** *adv.* **1** in the direction that is behind you [≠ **forward**]: *She took a step backwards.* **2** toward the beginning or the past [≠ **forward**]: *Can you say the alphabet backward?* **3** with the back part in front: *Your t-shirt is on backwards.* **4** toward a worse state [≠ **forward**]: *The new law is seen by some as a major step backward.*

backward² *adj.* **1** [only before noun] made toward the direction that is behind you [≠ **forward**]: *She left without a backward glance.* **2** developing slowly and less successfully than others: *a backward country*

back·wa·ter /ˈbæk͵wɔt̬ɚ, -͵wɑ-/ *n.* [C] a quiet town or place far away from cities, where not much happens

back·woods /ˈbæk͵wʊdz/ *n.* [plural] an area in the forest that is far from any towns —**backwoods** *adj.*: *a backwoods town*

back·yard, **back yard** /ˈbæk͵yɑrd/ *n.* [C] the area of land behind a house

ba·con /ˈbeɪkən/ *n.* [U] meat from a pig that has been put in salt and cut into thin pieces: *bacon and eggs*

THESAURUS

meat, **beef**, **veal**, **pork**, **ham**
➔ see Thesaurus box at MEAT

bac·te·ri·a /bækˈtɪriə/ *n.* [plural] very small living things that sometimes cause disease

bad¹ /bæd/ *adj.* comparative **worse**, superlative **worst** **1** not good or not nice [≠ **good**]: *I'm afraid I have some bad news for you. | a really bad smell*

THESAURUS

awful – very bad or unpleasant: *The weather was awful.*
terrible – extremely bad: *The hotel food was terrible.*
horrible – very bad or upsetting: *What a horrible thing to say!*
appalling/horrific formal – very bad and very shocking: *She suffered appalling injuries.* | *a horrific plane crash*
lousy informal – very bad in quality: *a lousy movie*
horrendous formal – very bad and very frightening or shocking: *a horrendous crash*
atrocious formal – extremely bad and often very severe: *Her driving is atrocious.* | *atrocious weather conditions*
abysmal formal – very bad, used especially to describe the standard of something: *The quality of care at the hospital was abysmal.*
→ GOOD, HORRIBLE

2 of a low quality or standard [≠ **good**]: *She was the worst teacher I ever had.* | *Brian is really* ***bad at*** *sports.* **3** morally wrong or evil [≠ **good**]: *He plays one of the bad guys in the movie.*

THESAURUS

evil/wicked – used to describe an evil person or his/her actions: *a fairy tale about a wicked witch* | *evil thoughts*
immoral/wrong – morally wrong, and not accepted by society: *It's wrong to steal.*
reprehensible – reprehensible behavior is very bad and deserves criticism: *His conduct was very reprehensible.*

4 damaging or harmful [≠ **good**]: *Smoking is* ***bad for*** *your health.* | *Pollution in the lake is having a bad effect on fish stocks.* **5** serious or severe: *a bad cold* | *Traffic in this city is getting worse by the day.* **6 too bad** *spoken* said when you are sorry about something that has happened: *It's too bad she had to give up teaching.* **7 feel bad** to feel ashamed or sorry about something: *I* ***felt bad about*** *missing your birthday.* **8 a bad time** a time that is not suitable or convenient: *Is this a bad time to call?* **9** food that is bad is not safe to eat because it is not fresh: *The milk has* ***gone bad.*** **10** permanently injured or not working correctly: *a bad heart* | *a bad back* **11 not bad** *spoken* good or acceptable: *"How are you?" "Oh, not bad."* **12 bad language/words** swearing or rude words **13** *slang* extremely good: *Now that's a bad car!*

bad² *adv. spoken nonstandard* BADLY

bade /bæd. beɪd/ *v.* past tense **bid**

badge /bædʒ/ *n.* [C] a small piece of metal, plastic, etc. that you wear or carry to show people that you work for a particular organization: *a police officer's badge*

badg·er /ˈbædʒɚ/ *n.* [C] an animal with black and white fur that lives under the ground

bad·lands /ˈbædˌlændz/ *n.* [plural] an area of rocks and hills where no crops can be grown

bad·ly /ˈbædli/ *adv.* comparative **worse**, superlative **worst** **1** in a way that is not good [≠ **well**]: *a badly written book* | *She* ***did badly*** *on the exam.* ► Don't say "I sing very bad." say "I sing badly." ◄ **2** to a great or serious degree: *The refugees* ***badly need*** *food and clean water.* | *Our house was badly damaged during the storm.*

bad·min·ton /ˈbædˌmɪntˀn, -ˌmɪntən/ *n.* [U] a game in which players hit a small object with feathers on it over a net

'bad-mouth *v.* [T] *informal* to criticize someone or something: *Divorced parents shouldn't bad-mouth each other in front of the kids.*

baf·fle /ˈbæfəl/ *v.* [T] if something baffles you, you cannot understand it: *Scientists are completely baffled by the results.* —**baffling** *adj.*

bags

bag¹ /bæg/ *n.* [C] **1 a)** a container made of paper, plastic, cloth, etc. that opens at the top: *a paper bag* | *a shopping bag* **b)** a large bag that you use to carry your clothes, etc. when you are traveling: *She* ***packed*** *her* ***bags*** *and left.* **c)** a PURSE **2** the amount a bag can hold: *two* ***bags of*** *rice* **3 in the bag** certain to be won or to be a success: *We knew the game was in the bag.* **4 bags under your eyes** dark circles or loose skin under your eyes

bag² *v.* past tense and past participle **bagged**, present participle **bagging** [T] **1** to put things in a bag: *He got a job bagging groceries at the supermarket.* **2** *informal* to manage to get something that a lot of people want: *I'll get there early and bag some seats.*

ba·gel /ˈbeɪgəl/ *n.* [C] a type of bread that is shaped like a ring → see picture at BREAD

bag·ful /ˈbægfʊl/ *n.* [C] the amount a bag can hold

bag·gage /ˈbægɪdʒ/ *n.* [U] **1** the bags that you carry when you are traveling [= **luggage**]

2 beliefs, opinions, and experiences from the past that influence the way a person behaves or thinks: *emotional baggage*

bag·gy /ˈbægi/ *adj.* baggy clothes are big and loose: *a baggy t-shirt*

ˈbag ˌlady *n.* [C] *informal* an impolite word for a woman who lives on the street and carries all her possessions with her

bag·pipes /ˈbægpaɪps/ *n.* [plural] a Scottish musical instrument which is played by blowing air into a bag and forcing it out through pipes

B

bail¹ /beɪl/ *n.* [U] money left with a court of law so that someone can be let out of prison while waiting for his/her TRIAL: *Marshall's father* ***posted bail*** (=paid the bail) *for him.* | *Harrell was* ***released on bail*** (=let out of prison when bail was paid) *until his trial.*

bail² *v.*

bail out *phr. v.* **1 bail** sb/sth **out** to help someone get out of trouble, especially by giving him/her money: *Young people often expect their parents to bail them out.* **2 bail** sb ⇔ **out** to give money to a court of law so that someone can leave prison until his/her TRIAL: *Clarke's family paid $500 to bail him out.* **3** *informal* to escape from a situation that you no longer want to be involved in: *After ten years in the business, McArthur is bailing out.* **4 bail** sth ⇔ **out** to remove water from the bottom of a boat

bail·out /ˈbeɪlaʊt/ *n.* [C] a situation in which a person or organization gives money to help someone who needs it

bait¹ /beɪt/ *n.* [singular, U] **1** food used for attracting fish or animals so that you can catch them **2** something that is offered to someone to persuade him/her to do something: *Plenty of people* ***took the bait*** (=accepted what was offered) *and lost their life savings.*

bait² *v.* [T] **1** to put food on a hook to catch fish, or in a trap to catch animals **2** to deliberately try to make someone angry by criticizing him/her, using rude names, etc.: *Goodman refused to be baited into saying anything bad about his co-star.*

bake /beɪk/ *v.* [I,T] to cook something such as bread or cakes in an OVEN: *I'm baking a cake.* | *baked potatoes*

THESAURUS

cook, fry, roast, broil, grill, sauté, boil, steam, deep fry
→ see Thesaurus box at COOK¹

bak·er /ˈbeɪkɚ/ *n.* [C] someone whose job is to bake bread, cakes, cookies, etc.

bak·er·y /ˈbeɪkəri/ *n.* plural **bakeries** [C] a place where bread, cakes, cookies, etc. are made or sold

THESAURUS

store, bookstore, clothes store, record store, grocery store, supermarket, delicatessen, deli, liquor store, drugstore, hardware store, nursery, garden center, newsstand, boutique, convenience store, department store, chain store, superstore, outlet store, warehouse store
→ see Thesaurus box at STORE¹

ˈbake sale *n.* [C] an occasion when the members of a school group, church organization, etc. make cookies, cakes, etc. and sell them in order to make money for the organization

bal·ance¹ /ˈbæləns/ *n.* **1** [U] the ability to stand and walk steadily, without falling: *Billy fell when he* ***lost*** *his* ***balance*** (=was unable to stay steady). | *Tricia could not* ***keep*** *her* ***balance*** (=could not stay steady), *and slipped on the ice.* | *He hit me when I was still* ***off balance*** (=not standing steady). **2** [singular, U] a state in which different or opposite qualities are given equal importance, or exist together in a way that is good: *Try to* ***keep a balance between*** *work and play.* | *The car's designers wanted to* ***strike a balance between*** *safety and style* (=make sure that two things have equal importance). | *We must not upset* ***the balance of*** *nature.* **3** [C] **a)** the amount of money that you have in your bank account: *a* ***balance of*** *$1,247* **b)** the amount of money that you owe for something: *The balance must be paid by the end of the month.* **4 on balance** used to tell someone your opinion after considering all the facts: *On balance, I'd say it was a fair decision.* **5 be/hang in the balance** to be in a situation where the result of something could be good or bad: *With the war still going on, thousands of lives hang in the balance.*

balance² *v.* **1** [I,T] to be in a steady position, without falling, or to put something in this position: *They walked past,* ***balancing*** *heavy loads* ***on*** *their head.* | *He turned around,* ***balancing*** *awkwardly* ***on*** *one foot.* **2 balance the budget/books** to make sure that you do not spend more money than you have **3** [T] to give the right amount of importance to two or more things: *A working mother has to* ***balance*** *her home life* ***with*** *a career.* | *The need for a new road must be* ***balanced against*** *the damage to the environment.* **4 also balance out** [I,T] if two or more things balance, or if one balances the other, the effect of one equals the effect of the other: *Job losses in some departments were balanced by increases in others.*

bal·anced /ˈbælənst/ *adj.* **1** fair and sensible: *balanced reporting of the election campaign*

THESAURUS

fair, just, reasonable, equitable, even-handed
→ see Thesaurus box at FAIR¹

2 including the right mixture of things: *a* ***balanced diet***

ˈbalance sheet *n.* [C] a written statement of how much a business has earned and how much it has spent

bal·co·ny /ˈbælkəni/ *n.* plural **balconies** [C] **1** a structure that you can stand on that is built above ground level onto an outside wall of a building

TOPIC

theater, **go to the theater**, **see a play/musical/opera/ballet**, **reserve tickets**, **box office**, **seat**, **the floor**, **program**, **audience**, **orchestra**, **stage**, **intermission**
➔ see Topic box at THEATER

2 the seats upstairs in a theater

bald /bɔld/ *adj.* **1** having little or no hair on your head: *I'm **going bald**.* | *a **bald spot/patch*** (=a small area with no hair) **2** not having enough of what usually covers something: *bald tires*

ˈbald ˌeagle *n.* [C] a large North American wild bird with a white head and neck that is the national bird of the U.S. ➔ see picture at EAGLE

bald·ing /ˈbɔldɪŋ/ *adj.* becoming bald: *a balding man in his mid-thirties*

bale /beɪl/ *n.* [C] a large amount of something such as paper or HAY that is tied tightly together

bale·ful /ˈbeɪlfəl/ *adj.* expressing a desire to harm someone: *a baleful look*

balk /bɔk/ *v.* [I] to not want to do something: *Customers **balked at** paying $25 for a hamburger.* —**balky** *adj.*

ball /bɔl/ *n.* [C] **1** a round object that you throw, hit, or kick in a game or sport: *tennis balls* | *Troy **threw/kicked** the **ball** to Michael.* | *Try to **catch** the **ball**.*

THESAURUS

dance, **prom**
➔ see Thesaurus box at DANCE[2]

2 something rolled into a round shape: *a **ball of** yarn* **3 on the ball** *informal* able to think or act quickly: *We need an assistant who's really on the ball.* **4 have a ball** *informal* to have a very good time **5** an occasion when a ball is thrown in baseball that the hitter does not try to hit because it is not within the correct area [➥ **strike**] **6 set/start the ball rolling** to start something happening: *Just a small donation will start the ball rolling.* **7** a large formal occasion where people dance **8 the ball of the foot** the rounded part of the foot at the base of the toes ➔ **play ball** at PLAY[1]

bal·lad /ˈbæləd/ *n.* [C] **1** a slow love song **2** a long song or poem that tells a story

bal·le·ri·na /ˌbæləˈrinə/ *n.* [C] a woman who dances in ballets

bal·let /bæˈleɪ, ˈbæleɪ/ *n.* **1** [C] a performance in which a story is told using dance and music, without any speaking: *the ballet "Swan Lake"* | *a **ballet dancer***

TOPIC

play, **musical**, **opera**
➔ see Topic box at THEATER

2 [U] this type of dancing **3** [C] a group of ballet dancers who work together: *the Bolshoi Ballet*

ˈball game *n.* [C] **1** a game of baseball, basketball, or football **2 a whole new ball game/a different ball game** a situation that is very different from the one you were in before

bal·lis·tic /bəˈlɪstɪk/ *adj.* **go ballistic** *spoken* to suddenly become very angry

bal·lis·tics /bəˈlɪstɪks/ *n.* [U] the study of how objects move through the air when they are thrown or shot from a gun

B

bal·loon[1] /bəˈlun/ *n.* [C] **1** a small brightly colored rubber bag that can be filled with air: *Can you **blow up** these **balloons**?* **2** HOT AIR BALLOON

balloon[2] *v.* [I] to suddenly become much larger

bal·lot /ˈbælət/ *n.* **1** [C] a piece of paper that you use to vote **2** [C,U] a system of voting in secret, or an occasion when you vote in this way: *He won 54% of **the ballot*** (=the number of votes in an election). | *There were 17 propositions **on the ballot*** (=17 things to be voted on).

ˈballot box *n.* [C] **1 the ballot box** the system of voting in an election: *The issue will be decided **at the ballot box**.* **2** a box that ballot papers are put in during the vote

ˈball park *n.* [C] **1** a field for playing baseball, with seats for people to watch the game **2 a ball park figure/estimate** a number or amount that is almost but not exactly correct

ball·point pen /ˌbɔlpɔɪnt ˈpɛn/ *n.* [C] a pen with a small ball at the end that rolls ink onto the paper

ball·room /ˈbɔlrum/ *n.* [C] a large room for formal dances

balm /bɑm/ *n.* [U] an oily liquid that you rub onto your skin to reduce pain

balm·y /ˈbɑmi/ *adj.* balmy weather or air is warm and pleasant: *a balmy summer night*

ba·lo·ney /bəˈloʊni/ *n.* [U] **1** *informal* something that is silly or not true: *His explanation sounded like a bunch of baloney to me.* **2** *nonstandard* BOLOGNA

bam·boo /ˌbæmˈbu◂/ *n.* [C,U] a tall plant with hard hollow stems, often used for making furniture

bam·boo·zle /bæmˈbuzəl/ *v.* [T] *informal* to trick or confuse someone

ban[1] /bæn/ *n.* [C] an official order saying that people must not do something: *a global **ban on** nuclear testing* | *a movement to **lift*** (=end) *the **ban** on illegal drugs*

ban[2] *v.* past tense and past participle **banned**, present participle **banning** [T] to officially say that people must not do something or that something is not allowed: *The city council banned smoking in public areas in 1995.* | *The government **banned** Zhang **from** making films.*

THESAURUS

forbid, not allow/permit/let, prohibit, bar
➔ see Thesaurus box at FORBID

ba·nal /bəˈnæl, bəˈnɑl, ˈbeɪnl/ *adj.* ordinary and not interesting [➡ **boring**]: *a banal love song* —**banality** /bəˈnæləṭi/ *n.* [C,U]

ba·nan·a /bəˈnænə/ *n.* [C] **1** a long curved yellow fruit ➔ see picture at FRUIT **2 go bananas** *informal* to become very angry or excited: *The kids went bananas and tore open the boxes.*

B

band¹ /bænd/ *n.* [C] **1** a group of musicians, especially a group that plays popular music: *a **rock/jazz, etc.** band | Solem **played in a band** called "Great Buildings." | The **band** was **playing** old Beatles songs.* **2** a group of people who work together to achieve the same aims: *a small **band of** terrorists* **3** a narrow piece of something, with one end joined to the other to form a circle: *Her hair was pulled back with a **rubber band**.* **4** a narrow area of color or light that is different from the areas around it: *a fish with a black band along its back*

THESAURUS

line, stripe, streak
➔ see Thesaurus box at LINE¹

band² *v.*
band together *phr. v.* to work with other people in order to achieve something: *Neighbors banded together to fight for a health clinic.*

ban·dage¹ /ˈbændɪdʒ/ *n.* [C] a long piece of cloth that you tie around a wound or injury

bandage² *v.* [T] to tie a bandage around a wound or injury

ˈBand-Aid *n.* [C] *trademark* a small piece of material that you stick over a small cut on your skin

ban·dan·na /bænˈdænə/ *n.* [C] a square piece of colored cloth that you can wear around your head or neck

ban·dit /ˈbændɪt/ *n.* [C] someone who robs people who are traveling

band·stand /ˈbændstænd/ *n.* [C] a structure in a park, used by a band playing music

band·wag·on /ˈbændˌwægən/ *n.* **jump/get/climb on the bandwagon** *disapproving* to start doing something because a lot of other people are doing it: *Many companies have jumped on the environmental bandwagon* (=started to give attention to the environment).

band·width /ˈbændˌwɪdθ/ *n.* [U] *technical* the amount of information that can be carried through a telephone wire or computer connection at one time

ban·dy /ˈbændi/ *v.* past tense and past participle **bandied**, third person singular **bandies**, **be bandied about/around** to be mentioned by a lot of people: *Her name was bandied about in connection with the recent scandal.*

bane /beɪn/ *n.* **be the bane of sth** to be the thing that causes trouble or makes people unhappy: *Locusts are **the bane of** farmers.*

bang¹ /bæŋ/ *v.* **1** [I,T] to make a loud noise, especially by hitting something against something hard: *Larren was **banging on** the wall with his fist. | The screen door banged shut behind him.*

THESAURUS

hit, punch, slap, beat, smack, whack, strike, knock, tap, pound, rap, hammer
➔ see Thesaurus box at HIT¹

2 [T] to hit a part of your body against something by accident: *I banged my knee on the corner of the bed.*

THESAURUS

hit, bump, knock, collide, strike
➔ see Thesaurus box at HIT¹

bang² *n.* [C] **1** a sudden loud noise such as an explosion or something hitting a hard surface: *There was a loud bang outside the kitchen door.* ➔ see picture on page A7 **2** a painful blow to the body when you hit against something or something hits you: *a nasty **bang on** the head* **3 with a bang** in a way that is very exciting or noticeable: *He began his presidential campaign with a bang.* **4 bangs** [plural] hair that is cut straight across the front of your head, above your eyes ➔ see picture at HAIR

bang³ *adv. informal* directly or exactly: *They've built a parking lot bang in the middle of town.*

bang⁴ *interjection* said in order to make the sound of a gun or bomb: *Bang! Bang! You're dead!*

ˌbanged-ˈup *adj. informal* damaged or injured: *a banged-up old car*

ban·ish /ˈbænɪʃ/ *v.* [T] to make someone leave a place as a punishment: *The king **banished** Roderigo **from** the court.*

ban·is·ter /ˈbænəstɚ/ *n.* [C] a row of wooden posts with a BAR along the top that you hold onto when you use stairs

ban·jo /ˈbændʒoʊ/ *n.* plural **banjos** [C] a musical instrument like a GUITAR, with four or more strings, a circular body, and a long neck ➔ see picture on page A6

bank¹ /bæŋk/ *n.* [C] **1** the company or place where you can keep your money or borrow money: *I went to the bank at noon to deposit my check. | a bank loan | We have very little money **in the bank**.*

TOPIC

account, open an account, pay/put/deposit money into an account, take money out of an account, withdraw money from an account, ATM, cash machine, overdrawn, online banking
➔ see Topic box at ACCOUNT¹

2 land along the side of a river or lake: *the river*

bank | *the* ***banks of*** *the Charles River* **3 blood/sperm/organ etc. bank** a place where human blood, etc. is stored until someone needs it **4** a large number of machines, etc. arranged close together in a row: *a* ***bank of*** *TV monitors* **5** a large pile of snow, sand, etc.: *a snow bank* **6 cloud/fog etc. bank** a mass of cloud, fog, etc.

bank² *v.* **1** [T] to put or keep money in a bank: *She's managed to bank more than $300,000.* **2** [I] to use a particular bank: *Do you* ***bank with/at*** *First National?* **3** [I] if an airplane, MOTORCYCLE, etc. banks, it slopes to one side when it is turning **4** [I] to have steep sides like a hill: *The race track banks steeply in the third turn.*

bank on sb/sth *phr. v.* to depend on something happening: *We were banking on Jesse being here to help.*

bank·er /'bæŋkɚ/ *n.* [C] someone who has an important job in a bank

bank·ing /'bæŋkɪŋ/ *n.* [U] the business of a bank

bank·rupt¹ /'bæŋkrʌpt/ *adj.* unable to pay your debts: *Many small businesses* ***went bankrupt*** *during the recession.*

bankrupt² *v.* [T] to make someone become bankrupt: *The deal nearly bankrupted us.*

bank·rupt·cy /'bæŋkˌrʌptsi/ *n.* plural **bankruptcies** [C,U] the state of being unable to pay your debts: *The company was forced to* ***declare bankruptcy****.*

'bank ˌteller *n.* [C] TELLER

ban·ner¹ /'bænɚ/ *n.* [C] **1** a long piece of cloth with writing on it: *voters waving election banners* **2** a belief or principle: *Civil rights groups have achieved a lot* ***under the banner of*** *fair and equal treatment.*

banner² *adj.* excellent or successful: ***a banner year for*** *American soccer*

ban·quet /'bæŋkwɪt/ *n.* [C] a formal meal for many people

ban·ter /'bæntɚ/ *n.* [U] friendly conversation with a lot of jokes in it: *lighthearted banter* —**banter** *v.* [I]

bap·tism /'bæptɪzəm/ *n.* [C,U] a religious ceremony in which a priest puts water on someone to make him/her a member of the Christian church —**baptismal** /bæp'tɪzməl/ *adj.*

Bap·tist /'bæptɪst/ *adj.* relating to the Protestant church that believes baptism is only for people old enough to understand its meaning —**Baptist** *n.* [C]

bap·tize /'bæptaɪz, bæp'taɪz/ *v.* [T] to perform a baptism

bar¹ /bɑr/ *n.* [C] **1** a place where alcoholic drinks are sold and can be drunk: *a cocktail bar* **2** a COUNTER where alcoholic drinks are served: *O'Keefe and I stood* ***at the bar****.* | *He ordered a drink from the woman* ***behind the bar****.* **3** a long narrow piece of metal or wood: *iron bars* **4 a salad/coffee/sushi etc. bar** a place where a particular kind of food or drink is served **5** a small block of something: *a* ***bar of*** *soap* | *a candy bar* **6 bar to (doing) sth** something that prevents something else from happening: *His lack of a formal education was not a bar to his success.* **7 behind bars** *informal* in prison: *He spent the night behind bars.* **8 the bar** the profession of being a lawyer, or lawyers considered as a group → SALAD BAR → SNACK BAR

bar² *v.* past tense and past participle **barred**, present participle **barring** [T] **1** to officially prevent someone from doing something: *Photographers are* ***barred from*** *taking pictures inside the courtroom.*

> **THESAURUS**
> **forbid, not allow/permit/let, ban, prohibit**
> → see Thesaurus box at FORBID

2 to prevent people from going somewhere by placing something in their way: *She stood in the hall,* ***barring*** *my* ***way****.* **3** to put a piece of wood or metal across a door or window to prevent people from going in or out

bar·bar·i·an /bɑr'bɛriən/ *n.* [C] someone who is rough, violent, and uneducated and does not respect art, education, etc.

bar·bar·ic /bɑr'bærɪk, -'bɛrɪk/ *adj.* violent and cruel: *a barbaric act of terrorism* —**barbarism** /'bɑrbərɪzəm/ *n.* [U] —**barbarous** *adj.*

bar·be·cue¹ /'bɑrbɪˌkyu/ *n.* [C] **1** an occasion when you cook and eat food outdoors: *We're* ***having a barbecue*** *on Saturday.*

> **THESAURUS**
> **meal, breakfast, lunch, brunch, dinner, supper, picnic**
> → see Thesaurus box at MEAL

2 a metal frame for cooking food on outdoors

barbecue² *v.* [T] to cook food outdoors on a barbecue: *barbecued ribs*

barbed /bɑrbd/ *adj.* barbed humor or a barbed remark is unkind

ˌbarbed 'wire *n.* [U] wire with short sharp points on it, usually used for making fences

bar·bell /'bɑrbɛl/ *n.* [C] a metal bar with weights at each end, which you lift to make you stronger

bar·ber /'bɑrbɚ/ *n.* [C] a man whose job is to cut men's hair

bar·bi·tu·rate /bɑr'bɪtʃərɪt/ *n.* [C,U] a drug that makes people calm and helps them to sleep

'bar code *n.* [C] a row of black lines on a product that a computer can read to get information such as the price

bard /bɑrd/ *n.* [C] *literary* a poet

bare¹ /bɛr/ *adj.* **1** not covered by clothes [➡ **naked**]: *children running around in bare feet* | *bare-chested/bare-legged, etc.*

> **THESAURUS**
> **naked, nude, undressed**
> → see Thesaurus box at NAKED

2 empty, or not covered by anything: *bare and treeless hills* | *Except for a few cans, the shelves were bare.*

THESAURUS

empty, **deserted**, **uninhabited**, **free**, **hollow**
➔ see Thesaurus box at EMPTY¹

3 basic and with nothing extra: *The refugees took only the* ***bare necessities/essentials*** (=the most necessary things they owned). | *a report giving just the* ***bare facts*** **4 with your bare hands** without using a weapon or tool: *It is said that Daniel Boone killed a bear with his bare hands.*

B

bare² *v.* [T] **1** to let people see part of your body by removing something that is covering it: *The dog* ***bared*** *its* ***teeth*** *and growled.* **2 bare your soul** to tell your most secret feelings to someone

bare·back /ˈbɛrbæk/ *adj., adv.* on the back of a horse, without a SADDLE: *riding bareback*

ˌbare ˈbones *n.* **the bare bones** *informal* the most basic things, information, qualities, etc. that are needed: *He reduced his company to the bare bones.* —**bare-bones** *adj.*: *a bare-bones existence*

bare·foot /ˈbɛrfʊt/ *adj., adv.* not wearing any shoes or socks: *We walked barefoot in the sand*

bare·ly /ˈbɛrli/ *adv.* **1** used in order to say that something only just happens, exists, etc.: *She was barely 18 when she had her first child.* | *I could barely stay awake.* **2** used in order to emphasize that something happens immediately after something else: *He'd barely sat down when she started asking questions.*

barf /bɑrf/ *v.* [I] *informal* VOMIT —**barf** *n.* [U]

bar·gain¹ /ˈbɑrgən/ *n.* [C] **1** something bought for less than its usual price: *Check the advertisements for bargains.* | *At $8,500, this car is a* ***(real) bargain.*** | *The stores were packed with* ***bargain hunters*** (=people looking for things that are cheap).

THESAURUS

cheap, **inexpensive**, **reasonable**, **a good/great/excellent deal**, **good/great/excellent value**
➔ see Thesaurus box at CHEAP¹

2 an agreement to do something in return for something else: *Management and unions have* ***struck a bargain*** *over wage increases.* | *The company* ***drove a hard bargain*** *in the negotiations* (=they made sure the agreement was favorable to them).

bargain² *v.* [I] to discuss the conditions of a sale, agreement, etc. in order to get a fair deal: *auto workers* ***bargaining with*** *management* | *teachers* ***bargained for*** *higher pay* | *union leaders* ***bargaining over*** *wages*

bargain for/on sth *phr. v.* to expect that something will happen: *I hadn't really bargained on things being so expensive there.* | ***I got more than I bargained for*** *in this job.*

ˈbargaining ˌchip *n.* [C] something that one person or group in a business deal or political agreement has that can be used in order to gain an advantage in the deal

barge¹ /bɑrdʒ/ *n.* [C] a boat with a flat bottom, used for carrying goods on a CANAL or river

THESAURUS

ship, **cruise ship**, **liner**, **ferry**, **freighter**, **tanker**, **aircraft carrier**, **battleship**, **cruiser**, **submarine**, **warship**
➔ see Thesaurus box at SHIP¹

barge² *v.* [I] *informal* to walk somewhere so quickly or carelessly that you push people or hit things: *Dana* ***barged past*** *the guards at the door.* | *She* ***barged*** *her* ***way*** *through the crowds.*

barge in also barge into sth *phr. v.* to interrupt someone or go into a place when you were not invited: *The police just barged in.*

bar·i·tone /ˈbærəˌtoʊn/ *n.* [C,U] a male singing voice that is fairly low, but not the lowest, or a man with a voice like this [➡ **bass**]

bark¹ /bɑrk/ *v.* **1** [I] to make the sound that a dog makes **2** [I,T] **also bark out** to say something in a loud angry voice: *Perry* ***barked at*** *his assistant.* **3 be barking up the wrong tree** *informal* to be doing something that will not get the result you want: *I realize now that I was barking up the wrong tree.*

bark² *n.* **1** [C] the sound a dog makes **2** [U] the outer covering of a tree ➔ see picture at PLANT¹

bar·ley /ˈbɑrli/ *n.* [U] a grain used for making food and alcohol

barn /bɑrn/ *n.* [C] a large building on a farm for storing crops or keeping animals in

bar·na·cle /ˈbɑrnəkəl/ *n.* [C] a small sea animal with a hard shell that sticks firmly to rocks, boats, etc.

barn·yard /ˈbɑrnyɑrd/ *n.* [C] the area on a farm around a barn

ba·rom·e·ter /bəˈrɑmət̬ɚ/ *n.* [C] **1** an instrument for measuring changes in the air pressure and weather **2** something that shows any changes in a situation: *The election is seen as a* ***barometer of*** *the nation's mood.* —**barometric** /ˌbærəˈmɛtrɪk◂/ *adj.*

ba·roque /bəˈroʊk/ *adj.* relating to the very decorated style of art, music, buildings, etc. popular in Europe in the 17th century

bar·racks /ˈbærɪks/ *n.* [plural] a group of buildings in which soldiers live

bar·rage /bəˈrɑʒ/ *n.* **1** [singular] a lot of complaints, questions, etc.: *a* ***barrage of*** *insults/abuse* **2** [C usually singular] the continuous shooting of guns

bar·rel¹ /ˈbærəl/ *n.* [C] **1** a large container with curved sides and a flat top and bottom: *a* ***barrel of*** *beer* **2** the part of a gun that the bullets are shot through **3 have sb over a barrel** *informal* to put someone in a situation where s/he is forced to do something: *I didn't really want to work overtime, but my boss had me over a barrel.* **4** a unit used for measuring oil, equal to about 42 gallons or 159 liters

barrel[2] *v.* [I] to move very fast, especially in an uncontrolled way: *We were **barreling down** the road at 90 miles an hour.*

bar·ren /ˈbærən/ *adj.* land that is barren cannot grow plants: *a barren desert*

bar·rette /bəˈrɛt/ *n.* [C] a small metal or plastic object used to keep a woman's hair in place

bar·ri·cade[1] /ˈbærəˌkeɪd/ *n.* [C] something that is put across a road, door, etc. to prevent people from going past: *Protesters were kept behind barricades.*

barricade[2] *v.* [T] to use a barricade to prevent someone or something from going somewhere: *They **barricaded** themselves **in** and the police had to storm the building.*

bar·ri·er /ˈbæriə/ *n.* [C] **1** something that prevents people from doing something: *an attempt to reduce **trade barriers** | The **language barrier** prevents many people from working abroad. | A lack of education is a **barrier to** many good jobs.* **2** a type of fence that keeps people or things separate or prevents people from entering a place: *The police put up barriers to hold back the crowds.* **3** a physical object that separates two areas, groups of people, etc.: *The Alps form a **natural barrier** across Europe.*

bar·ring /ˈbɑrɪŋ/ *prep.* unless something happens: *Barring any last minute problems, we should finish Friday.*

bar·ri·o /ˈbæriˌoʊ/ *n.* plural **barrios** [C] an area in a city where many poor, Spanish-speaking people live

bar·room /ˈbɑrˌrum/ *n.* [C] *informal* a BAR

bar·tend·er /ˈbɑrˌtɛndə/ *n.* [C] someone whose job is to make and serve drinks in a bar

bar·ter /ˈbɑrt̬ə/ *v.* [I,T] to exchange goods or services instead of money: *I had to **barter with** the locals for food.*

base[1] /beɪs/ *v.* [T] to use somewhere as your main place of business: *a law firm **based in** Denver | Ohio-based/Miami-based, etc.*

base sth **on/upon** sth *phr. v.* to use something as the model from which you develop something else: *Discrimination based on race or sex is forbidden by law. | The movie was based on Amelia Earhart's life.*

base[2] *n.* [C]

1 LOWEST PART the lowest part or surface of something: *a black vase with a round base | Waves crashed against **the base of** the cliff. | the base of the skull*

2 MAIN PART all the people, companies, money, etc. that form the main part of something: *Roosevelt had a broad base of political support. | the city's **economic base** (=things that produce jobs and money) | Japan's **manufacturing base** (=companies that make things)*

3 COMPANY the main place where someone works or stays, or from which work is done: *Microsoft's base is in Redmond. | The hotel is an ideal **base for** sightseeing.*

4 MILITARY a place where people in the army, navy, etc. live and work: *an army base*

5 IDEAS the most important part of something, from which new ideas develop: *Both French and Spanish come from a Latin base.*

6 off base *informal* completely wrong: *The estimate for painting the house seems **way off base**.*

7 cover/touch all the bases to prepare for or deal with a situation thoroughly: *The police have called in experts to make sure they've covered all the bases.*

8 SUBSTANCE/MIXTURE the main part of a substance, to which other things can be added: *paints with a water base*

9 BASEBALL one of the four places that a player must touch in order to score a point

baseball

base·ball /ˈbeɪsbɔl/ *n.* **1** [U] a game in which two teams try to score points by hitting a ball and running around four bases **2** [C] the ball used in this game

base·ment /ˈbeɪsmənt/ *n.* [C] the room or rooms in a building that are below the level of the ground

bas·es /ˈbeɪsiz/ *n.* the plural of BASIS

bash[1] /bæʃ/ *v.* [I,T] **1** to hit someone or something hard, causing pain or damage: *He **bashed** his toe **on** the coffee table. | Police bashed down the door to get in.* **2** *informal* to criticize someone or something very strongly: *Hodge took every opportunity to bash the media.*

bash[2] *n.* [C] *informal* a party: *an anniversary bash*

THESAURUS

party, get-together, dinner party, birthday party, house-warming party, cocktail party, bachelor party, baby/wedding/bridal shower, reception, celebration
→ see Thesaurus box at PARTY[1]

bash·ful /ˈbæʃfəl/ *adj.* shy

THESAURUS

shy, timid, reserved, introverted, withdrawn, antisocial, retiring
→ see Thesaurus box at SHY[1]

bash·ing /ˈbæʃɪŋ/ *n.* **gay-bashing/immigrant-bashing/media-bashing etc.** the act of physically attacking or strongly criticizing a particular group of people or businesses

ba·sic /ˈbeɪsɪk/ *adj.* **1** forming the main or most necessary part of something: *the* ***basic principles*** *of mathematics* | *a soldier's* ***basic training*** | *There are two basic problems here.*

THESAURUS

fundamental – relating to the most basic and important parts of something: *The fundamental problem is a lack of resources.*
essential – the essential parts, qualities, or features of something are the ones that are most important, typical, or easily noticed: *Religion is an essential part of their lives.*
central – more important than anything else: *Linda played a central role in the negotiations.*

B

2 at the simplest or least developed level: *basic health care* | *The farm lacks even basic equipment.* ➔ BASICS

ba·si·cally /ˈbeɪsɪkli/ *adv.* **1** *spoken* used to give a simple explanation of something: *Well, basically the teacher said he'll need extra help with math.* **2** in the main or most important ways, without considering small details: *Norwegian and Danish are basically the same.* | *I believe that human beings are basically good.*

ba·sics /ˈbeɪsɪks/ *n.* [plural] **1 the basics** the most important facts or things that you need: *We were taught* ***the basics of*** *sailing.* | *It will take you awhile to master the basics.* **2 get/go back to basics** to return to teaching or doing the most important or the simplest part of something: *A lot of parents want schools to get back to basics.*

ba·sin /ˈbeɪsən/ *n.* [C] **1** a large area of land that is lower in the center than at the edges: *the Amazon basin* **2** a large bowl, especially one for water

ba·sis /ˈbeɪsɪs/ *n.* plural **bases** /ˈbeɪsiz/ [C] **1 on a weekly/informal/freelance etc. basis** happening at a particular time or in a particular way: *Meetings are held on a monthly basis.* | *She still works, but on a part-time basis.* **2** the information or ideas from which something develops: *The video will provide a* ***basis for*** *class discussion.* | *The fear of Communism* ***formed the basis of*** *American foreign policy at that time.* **3 on the basis of sth** because of a particular fact or situation: *Employers may not discriminate on the basis of race or sex.*

bask /bæsk/ *v.* [I] **1** to enjoy sitting or lying somewhere warm: *a snake* ***basking in*** *the sun* **2** to enjoy the attention or approval you receive from someone: *She* ***basked in*** *her mother's praise.*

bas·ket /ˈbæskɪt/ *n.* [C] **1** a container made of thin pieces of dried plants, wire, etc. used for carrying or holding things: *a picnic basket* | *a* ***laundry basket*** (=for putting dirty clothes in) | *a* ***basket of*** *fruit* **2** the net in basketball: *Bird* ***scored/made a basket*** (=threw the ball into the basket) *with just under a minute to play.*

basketball

bas·ket·ball /ˈbæskɪtˌbɔl/ *n.* **1** [U] a game between two teams, in which each team tries to throw a ball through a net **2** [C] the ball used in this game

ˈbasket case *n. informal* [C] someone who you think is crazy: *Mom was a complete basket case at our wedding.*

bass¹ /beɪs/ *n.* **1** [C] **also bass guitar** a GUITAR that plays low notes **2** [C,U] the lowest male singing voice, or a man with a voice like this **3** [U] the lower half of the whole range of musical notes **4** [C] DOUBLE BASS

bass² /bæs/ *n.* [C,U] a fish that lives both in the sea and in rivers, lakes, etc., or the meat from this fish

bas·si·net /ˌbæsɪˈnɛt/ *n.* [C] a small bed that looks like a basket, used for a very young baby

bas·soon /bəˈsun, bæ-/ *n.* [C] a very long wooden musical instrument with a low sound that you play by blowing into it ➔ see picture on page A6

bas·tard /ˈbæstɚd/ *n.* [C] *old-fashioned* someone whose parents were not married when s/he was born

baste /beɪst/ *v.* [T] to pour liquid fat over food that is cooking

bas·tion /ˈbæstʃən/ *n.* [C] a place, organization, etc. that protects old beliefs or ways of doing things: *a* ***bastion of*** *free speech*

bat¹ /bæt/ *n.* [C] **1** a long wooden stick used for hitting the ball in baseball **2** a small animal like a mouse with wings that flies at night **3 right off the bat** *informal* immediately: *He got into trouble right off the bat.* **4 be at bat** to be the person who is trying to hit the ball in baseball

bat² *v.* past tense and past participle **batted**, present participle **batting** [I,T] **1** to hit a ball with a bat: *Brent is* ***up to bat*** *next* (=he will try to hit the ball next). **2 bat your eyes/eyelashes** if a woman bats her eyes, she opens and closes them several times quickly in order to look attractive to men **3 not bat an eye/eyelash** *informal* without showing any emotion or guilty feelings: *He used to tell the worst lies without batting an eye.* **4 go to bat for sb** *informal* to help and support someone: *Andy really went to bat for me with my* *manager.* **5 bat a thousand** *informal* to be very successful

batch /bætʃ/ *n.* [C] a group of things or people that are made, arrive, or are dealt with at the same time: *She's just baked another **batch of** cookies*

bat·ed /ˈbeɪt̬ɪd/ *adj.* **with bated breath** in a very excited and anxious way: *I **waited** for her answer **with bated breath**.*

bath /bæθ/ *n.* plural **baths** /bæðz, bæθs/ [C] **1** an act of washing your body in the water that you put in a bathtub: *You need to **take a bath** before you go to bed. | Dan, will you **give** the kids **a bath*** (=wash them) *tonight?* **2** a bathroom, used especially in advertising: *a three-bedroom, two-bath house* **3** water that you sit or lie in to wash yourself: *I love to sit and soak in a hot bath. | Lisa **ran a bath*** (=put water in a bathtub) *for herself.*

bathe /beɪð/ *v.* **1** [I,T] to wash yourself or someone else in a bath: *Water was scarce, and we only bathed once a week. | He bathed the children and put them to bed.* **2** [T] to put water or another liquid on part of your body as a medical treatment **3 be bathed in light** if something is bathed in light, a lot of light is shining on it

bathing suit /ˈbeɪðɪŋ ˌsut/ *n.* [C] a piece of clothing you wear for swimming

bath·robe /ˈbæθroʊb/ *n.* [C] a loose piece of clothing like a coat that you especially wear before or after a bath

bath·room /ˈbæθrum/ *n.* [C] **1** a room where there is a toilet and usually a bathtub or a SHOWER and SINK [➡ **restroom**]

> **THESAURUS**
>
> **toilet**, **restroom**, **women's/ladies' room**, **men's room**, **lavatory**, **latrine**
> ➔ see Thesaurus box at TOILET

2 go to the bathroom to use the toilet: *Mommy, I have to go to the bathroom!*

bath·tub /ˈbæθtʌb/ *n.* [C] a long container in which you wash yourself

ba·ton /bəˈtɑn/ *n.* [C] **1** a short stick used by the leader of a group of musicians to direct the music **2** a metal stick that you spin and throw into the air **3** a stick that a police officer uses as a weapon **4** a stick passed from one runner to another in a race

bat·tal·ion /bəˈtælyən/ *n.* [C] a cheap piece of jewelry

bat·ter¹ /ˈbæt̬ɚ/ *n.* **1** [C,U] a mixture of flour, eggs, milk, etc. used for making cakes, some types of bread, etc.: *pancake batter* **2** [C] the person who is trying to hit the ball in baseball

batter² *v.* [I,T] to hit someone or something very hard many times: *He was **battered to death**. | Waves were **battering against** the rocks.* —**battering** *n.* [C,U]

bat·tered /ˈbæt̬ɚd/ *adj.* **1** old and slightly damaged: *a battered old guitar* **2 battered woman/child** a woman who has been attacked by her husband/boyfriend etc., or a child who has been attacked by a parent

bat·ter·y /ˈbæt̬əri/ *n.* plural **batteries** **1** [C] an object that provides electricity for something such as a radio or car: *a **dead battery*** (=one with no power) **2** [U] *law* the crime of beating someone **3** [C] a set of many things of the same type: *a **battery of** medical tests*

bat·tle¹ /ˈbæt̬l/ *n.* **1** [C,U] a fight between two armies or groups, especially during a war: *the Battle of Bunker Hill | Thousands of soldiers were killed **in battle*** (=during a war or battle). **2** [C] a situation in which people or groups compete or argue with each other: *the **battle for** control of Congress | a long and costly **legal battle*** **3** [C] an attempt to stop something happening or to achieve something difficult: *the **battle against** racial discrimination | a long **battle with** lung cancer | Gina **fought** a **losing battle** to hold back the tears.*

> **THESAURUS**
>
> **fight**, **campaign**, **struggle**
> ➔ see Thesaurus box at FIGHT²

battle² *v.* [I,T] to try very hard to achieve something difficult: *My mother **battled** bravely **against** breast cancer. | Doctors **battled to** save his life.*

bat·tle·ground /ˈbæt̬lˌgraʊnd/ **also** **bat·tle·field** /ˈbæt̬lˌfild/ *n.* [C] **1** a subject that people argue about: *Prayer in schools has become a **political battleground**.* **2** a place where a battle is fought

bat·tle·ship /ˈbæt̬lˌʃɪp/ *n.* [C] a very large ship used in wars

> **THESAURUS**
>
> **ship**, **cruise ship**, **liner**, **ferry**, **freighter**, **tanker**, **barge**, **aircraft carrier**, **cruiser**, **submarine**, **warship**
> ➔ see Thesaurus box at SHIP¹

bawd·y /ˈbɔdi/ *adj.* bawdy songs, jokes, etc. are about sex

bawl /bɔl/ *v.* [I] *informal* to shout or cry loudly: *By the end of the movie I was bawling.*

bawl sb ⇔ **out** *phr. v. informal* to speak angrily to someone because s/he has done something wrong: *Mom bawled me out for not cleaning my room.*

bay /beɪ/ *n.* [C] **1** a place where the coast curves around the sea: *Chesapeake Bay* **2 keep/hold sth at bay** to prevent something dangerous or bad from happening or from coming too close: *The dogs kept the intruder at bay.* **3** a small area used for a special purpose: *the plane's cargo bay*

bay·o·net /ˈbeɪənɪt, -ˌnɛt, ˌbeɪəˈnɛt/ *n.* [C] a long knife attached to the end of a long gun

bay·ou /ˈbaɪu, ˈbaɪoʊ/ *n.* [C] a large area of water in the southeast U.S. that moves very slowly and has many water plants

B

ˌbay ˈwindow *n.* [C] a window that sticks out from the wall of a house, with glass on three sides

ba·zaar /bəˈzɑr/ *n.* [C] **1** an event at which a lot of people sell various things to collect money for an organization: *a church bazaar* **2** a market in Asian or Middle Eastern countries

BB gun /ˈbibi ˌgʌn/ *n.* [C] a gun that uses air pressure to shoot small metal balls

BBQ /ˈbɑrbɪˌkyu/ **barbecue**

B.C. *adv.* **Before Christ** used after a date to show that it was before the birth of Christ [➡ **A.D.**]: *2600 B.C.*

B

be¹ /bi/ *auxiliary verb* past tense **was, were**, past participle **been** **1** used with a present participle to form the continuous tenses of verbs: *Jane was reading by the fire.* | *Don't talk to me while I'm* (=I am) *working.* **2** used with a PAST PARTICIPLE to form the PASSIVE: *Smoking is not permitted on this flight.* | *I was shown a copy of the contract.* **3** used in CONDITIONAL sentences to talk about an imagined situation: ***If I were*** *rich, I'd buy myself a Rolls Royce.* | *He could lose his job* ***if*** *he* ***were to*** *be charged with a crime.* **4 sb is to do sth** *formal* **a)** used in order to say what will happen: *I'll be* (=I will be) *leaving tomorrow.* **b)** used in order to say what must happen: *The children are to go to bed by 8:00.* **5 sb/sth is to be seen/found/heard etc.** *formal* used to say that someone or something can be seen, etc.: *The money was* ***nowhere to be found.*** ➔ IS ➔ AM ➔ ARE ➔ BEEN

be² *v.* [linking verb] **1** used in order to give or ask for information about someone or something, or to describe that person or thing in some way: *January is the first month of the year.* | *The concert was last night.* | *Julie wants to be a doctor.* | *Where are my shoes?* | *Is this your coat?* | *It's* (=it is) *going to be hot today.* | *I'm* (=I am) *cold.* **2 there is/are/were etc.** used in order to show that something exists or happens: *There were only eight people at choir practice.* | *There's* (=there is) *a hole in your jeans.* **3** to behave in a particular way: *Be careful.* | *He was just being silly.* **4** used to give your opinion about something: *"We won't be able to make it tomorrow night." "That's too bad."* | ***It's*** *strange* ***that*** *she hasn't phoned.* **5 be yourself** to behave in a natural way: *Don't worry about impressing them – just be yourself.* **6 not be yourself** to be behaving in a way that is unusual for you, especially because you are sick or upset: *She hasn't been herself lately.* ➔ **let sb/sth be** at LET

beach /bitʃ/ *n.* [C] an area of sand or small stones at the edge of an ocean or a lake: *We spent the day* ***at the beach.*** | *children playing* ***on the beach*** | *a beach house*

THESAURUS

shore, coast, seashore, bank
➔ see Thesaurus box at SHORE¹

ˈbeach ball *n.* [C] a large plastic ball that you fill with air and play with at the beach

beach

bea·con /ˈbikən/ *n.* [C] a light or electronic signal used to guide boats, airplanes, etc.

bead /bid/ *n.* [C] **1** a small ball of plastic, wood, glass, etc. used for making jewelry **2** a small drop of liquid: *beads of sweat*

bead·y /ˈbidi/ *adj.* beady eyes are small and shiny

bea·gle /ˈbigəl/ *n.* [C] a dog with large ears, short legs, and smooth fur, sometimes used in hunting

beak /bik/ *n.* [C] the hard pointed mouth of a bird ➔ see picture on page A2

beak·er /ˈbikɚ/ *n.* [C] a glass cup with straight sides, used in a LABORATORY (=place where people do scientific tests)

beam¹ /bim/ *n.* [C] **1** a line of light or energy: *a* ***laser beam*** | *the* ***beam of*** *the flashlight* **2** a long piece of wood or metal used in building houses, bridges, etc.

beam² *v.* **1** [I] to smile in a very happy way: *Uncle Willie* ***beamed at*** *us proudly.*

THESAURUS

smile, grin, smirk
➔ see Thesaurus box at SMILE

2 [I,T] to send out energy, light, radio, or television signals, etc.: *the first broadcast* ***beamed across*** *the Atlantic* | *The sun beamed through the clouds.*

bean /bin/ *n.* [C] **1** a seed or a case that seeds grow in, cooked as food: *green beans* | *baked beans* **2** a plant that produces beans **3 coffee/cocoa bean** a seed used in making coffee or COCOA, and food such as chocolate

bear¹ /bɛr/ *v.* past tense **bore** /bɔr/ past participle **borne** /bɔrn/ [T]

1 BE RESPONSIBLE *formal* to be responsible for something: *In this case, you must* ***bear the blame/responsibility*** *yourself.* | *The federal government will* ***bear the cost*** *of the program.*

2 DEAL WITH STH to bravely accept or deal with a painful or difficult situation: *She didn't think she could bear the pain.* | *Make the water as hot as you* ***can bear.*** | *The pressure was* ***more than*** *he* ***could bear.***

3 can't bear sb/sth to dislike someone or something very much, or to feel unable to do something because it upsets you [**= can't stand**]: *I can't bear that woman.* | *He can't bear people watching him* *eat.* | *She can't* **bear to** *throw anything away.* | ***I couldn't bear the thought of*** *working on Christmas.*

4 bear a resemblance/relation to sb/sth to be similar to or related to someone or something: *He* ***bears a striking resemblance to*** *his father* (=looks very like his father). | *The facts* ***bear little relation to*** (=are not similar to) *reality.*

5 bear (sth) in mind to consider a fact when you are deciding or judging something: ***Bear in mind that*** *this method might not work.*

6 HAVE FEELINGS *formal* to have bad feelings toward someone: *I don't* ***bear*** *a* ***grudge*** (=still feel angry about something).

7 bear fruit if a plan or decision bears fruit, it is successful: *The project may not begin to bear fruit for at least two years.*

8 WEIGHT to support the weight of something: *The ice wasn't thick enough to* ***bear*** *his* ***weight****.*

9 sth doesn't bear thinking about used to say that something is very upsetting or shocking: *The long-term effects don't bear thinking about.*

10 MARK/NAME *formal* to have a particular name or appearance: *the company that* ***bore*** *her father's* ***name*** | *He bore the scars for the rest of his life.*

11 bear with me *spoken* used in order to politely ask someone to wait while you do something: *Bear with me for a minute while I check the files.*

12 bear right/left to turn toward the right or left: *Bear left where the road divides.*

13 BABY *formal* to give birth to a baby

14 CARRY *formal* to bring or carry something: *They came* ***bearing gifts****.*

THESAURUS

carry, tote, lug, cart, haul, schlep
→ see Thesaurus box at CARRY

→ **bring sth to bear (on)** at BRING

bear down on sb/sth *phr. v.* to move quickly toward someone or something in a threatening way: *We ran as the truck bore down on us.*

bear sb/sth **out** *phr. v.* to show that something is true: *The study's findings were borne out by further research.*

bear up *phr. v.* to succeed in being brave and determined during a difficult or upsetting time

bear

bear² *n.* [C] a large strong animal with thick fur → POLAR BEAR, TEDDY BEAR

bear·a·ble /ˈbɛrəbəl/ *adj.* a situation that is bearable is difficult but can be accepted or dealt with: *His friendship was the one thing that made life bearable.*

beard /bɪrd/ *n.* [C] the hair that grows on a man's chin —**bearded** *adj.* → see picture at HAIR

bear·er /ˈbɛrɚ/ *n.* [C] someone who brings or carries something: *the* ***bearer of bad news*** | *a flag bearer* → PALLBEARER

bear·ing /ˈbɛrɪŋ/ *n.* **1 have a bearing on sth** to have some influence on or effect on something: *The new information* ***has no/some bearing on*** *the case.* **2 get your bearings** to find out where you are or what you should do **3 lose your bearings** to become confused about where you are **4** [singular, U] the way someone moves or stands: *an elderly man with a military bearing*

ˈbear ˌmarket *n.* [C] a situation in which the value of STOCKS is decreasing [➡ **bull market**]

beast /bist/ *n.* [C] **1** *literary* a wild animal **2** *old-fashioned* a cruel person

beat¹ /bit/ *v.* past tense **beat**, past participle **beaten** /ˈbit˺n/

1 DEFEAT [T] to get more points, votes, etc. than other people in a game or competition: *New York beat Boston 4–1.* | *Stuart usually* ***beats*** *me* ***at*** *chess.* | *Hank Aaron finally* ***beat the record*** *for home runs set by Babe Ruth.*

2 HIT SB [T] to hit someone many times with your hand, a stick, etc.: *He used to come home and beat us.* | *The woman had been* ***beaten to death****.*

THESAURUS

hit, punch, slap, smack, whack, strike
→ see Thesaurus box at HIT¹

3 HIT STH [I, T] to hit against the surface of something continuously, or to make something do this: *waves* ***beating on/against*** *the shore*

4 FOOD [I, T] to mix foods together quickly using a fork or a kitchen tool: *Beat the eggs and add them to the sugar mixture.* → see picture on page A4

THESAURUS

mix, combine, stir, blend
→ see Thesaurus box at MIX¹

5 SOUND [I, T] to make a regular sound or movement, or to make something do this: *She could feel her* ***heart beating****.* | *I could hear* ***drums beating****.*

6 beat around the bush to avoid talking about something embarrassing or upsetting: *Stop beating around the bush, and say it!*

7 AVOID [T] to do something early in order to avoid problems because later everyone will be doing it: *We left at 5:00 to* ***beat the traffic****.* | *Shop early and* ***beat the*** *Christmas* ***rush****!*

SPOKEN PHRASES

8 [T] to be better or more enjoyable than something else: *It's not the greatest job, but **it beats** waitressing.* | ***You can't beat*** (=nothing is better than) *San Diego for good weather.*
9 (it) beats me used in order to say that you do not understand or know something: *"Where's Myrna?" "Beats me."*
10 beat it! an impolite way to tell someone to leave at once

B

→ **off the beaten track/path** at BEATEN

beat down *phr. v.* **1** if the sun beats down, it shines brightly and is hot **2** if the rain beats down, it rains very hard

beat sb/sth ⇔ **off** *phr. v.* to hit someone who is attacking you until s/he goes away

beat sb ⇔ **out** *phr. v. informal* to defeat someone in a competition: *Lange **beat out** Foster **for** the award.*

beat sb **to** sth *phr. v.* to get or do something before someone else: *I wanted the car, but someone **beat** me **to it**.*

beat sb ⇔ **up** *phr. v.* **1** to hit someone until s/he is badly hurt: *My boyfriend went crazy and beat me up.* **2 beat yourself up** *informal* to blame yourself too much for something: *Don't beat yourself up over this!*

beat² *n.* **1** [C] one of a series of regular movements or sounds: *a heart rate of 80 **beats per minute** | the **beat of** the drum* **2** [singular] the pattern of sounds in a piece of music **3** [singular] a subject or area of a city that someone is responsible for as his/her job: *journalists covering the political beat | a police officer **on the beat*** (=walking around the streets in a particular area)

beat³ *adj. informal* very tired: *You look beat!*

THESAURUS

defeat – to win a victory over someone: *I don't think anybody will be able to defeat Kennedy.*
trounce – to defeat someone completely: *The Bears trounced Nebraska 44–10.*
clobber/cream informal – to defeat someone easily: *We got creamed in the finals.*

beat·en /ˈbitˀn/ *adj.* **off the beaten track/path** far away from places that people usually visit: *a little hotel off the beaten track*

beat·er /ˈbit̬ɚ/ *n.* [C] **1** a kitchen tool that is used for mixing foods together **2 wife/child beater** someone who hits his wife or his/her child

beat·ing /ˈbit̬ɪŋ/ *n.* [C] **1** an act of hitting someone many times as a punishment or in a fight: *a severe beating* **2 take a beating** to lose very badly in a game or competition

ˈbeat-up *adj. informal* old and slightly damaged: *a beat-up old car*

beau·ti·cian /byuˈtɪʃən/ *n.* [C] *old-fashioned* HAIRDRESSER

beau·ti·ful /ˈbyut̬əfəl/ *adj.* **1** extremely attractive to look at: *She was the most beautiful woman I've ever seen. | a beautiful baby | The views from the mountaintop were beautiful.*

THESAURUS

attractive, good-looking, pretty, handsome, gorgeous, stunning, nice-looking, cute
→ see Thesaurus box at ATTRACTIVE

2 very good or giving you great pleasure: *beautiful music | The weather was beautiful.*

beau·ty /ˈbyut̬i/ *n.* plural **beauties** **1** [U] a quality that people, places, or things have that makes them very attractive to look at: *a woman of **great beauty** | the **beauty of** Yosemite* **2** [U] a quality that something such as a poem, song, etc. has that gives you pleasure: *the **beauty of** Keats' poetry* **3** [C] *informal* something that is very good or impressive: *His new car's a beauty.* **4 the beauty of sth is...** used to explain why something is especially good: *The beauty of this exercise is that you can do it anywhere.* **5** [C] *old-fashioned* a woman who is very beautiful

ˈbeauty saˌlon also **ˈbeauty ˌparlor** *n.* [C] SALON

bea·ver /ˈbivɚ/ *n.* [C] a North American animal that has thick fur, a wide flat tail, and cuts down trees with its teeth

be·bop /ˈbibɑp/ *n.* [U] a style of JAZZ music

be·came /bɪˈkeɪm/ *v.* the past tense of BECOME

be·cause /bɪˈkɔz, -ˈkʌz/ *conjunction* used when you are giving the reason for something: *You can't go because you're too young. | We weren't able to have the picnic **because of** the rain. | They liked him **simply because** he could play basketball. | He moved to Florida **partly/largely/mainly because** he liked the weather.* → **just because ... (it) doesn't mean ...** at JUST¹

beck·on /ˈbɛkən/ *v.* [I,T] to move your hand to show that you want someone to move toward you: *He beckoned her to join him. | He **beckoned to** her.*

be·come /bɪˈkʌm/ *v.* past tense **became** /-ˈkeɪm/ past participle **become** **1** [linking verb] to begin to be something, or to develop in a particular way: *The weather had become warmer. | In 1960 Kennedy became the first Catholic president. | It is becoming harder to find good housing for low-income families. | It became clear that she was lying. | She started to become anxious about her son.* ▶ Don't say "She started to be anxious about her son." ◀ **2 become of sb/sth** to happen to someone or something: ***Whatever became of** Grandma's dishes? | No one knows **what will become of** him when his mother dies.*

USAGE

Become is used in both written and spoken English: *He's becoming very successful. | Canada has become popular with tourists.*
Get and **go** are less formal than **become**, and

are used more often in spoken English: *I got very hungry.* | *Have you gone crazy?*
Become can be used in front of an adjective or a noun, but **get** and **go** are only used in front of an adjective: *The noise from the airport is becoming a problem.* | *It became clear that the company would lose the contract.* | *It's getting dark.* | *Beethoven went deaf when he was 40 years old.*

be·com·ing /bɪˈkʌmɪŋ/ *adj. old-fashioned* a piece of clothing, HAIRSTYLE, etc. that is becoming makes you look attractive

beds

bed[1] /bɛd/ *n.* **1** [C,U] a piece of furniture for sleeping on: *a **double bed*** (=a bed for two people) | *a **single bed*** (=a bed for one person) | *I was lying **in bed** reading.* | *She looked like she had just **gotten out of bed.*** | *What time do you usually **put** the kids **to bed?*** | *Jamie usually **goes to bed** around seven o'clock.* | *Sara, have you **made** your **bed** yet* (=pulled the sheets, etc. into place)*?* | *Come on, it's **time for bed*** (=time to go to sleep). **2 go to bed with sb** *informal* to have sex with someone **3** [C] the ground at the bottom of the ocean, a river, or a lake: *a river bed* **4** [C] an area of ground that has been prepared for plants to grow in: ***flower beds*** **5 a bed of sth** a layer of something that is a base for something else: *potato salad on a bed of lettuce*

bed[2] *v.* past tense and past participle **bedded**, present participle **bedding**
bed down *phr. v.* to make yourself comfortable and sleep in a place where you do not usually sleep: *I'll just bed down on the sofa.*

ˌbed and ˈbreakfast, **B&B** *n.* [C] a house or a small hotel where you pay to sleep and have breakfast: *We plan to stay at a bed and breakfast while we're in England.*

bed·clothes /ˈbɛdkloʊz, -kloʊðz/ *n.* [plural] BEDDING

bed·ding /ˈbɛdɪŋ/ *n.* [U] **1** the sheets, BLANKETS, etc. that you put on a bed **2** soft material that an animal sleeps on

bed·lam /ˈbɛdləm/ *n.* [singular, U] a situation where there is a lot of noise and confusion: *When the bomb exploded, there was bedlam.*

bed·pan /ˈbɛdpæn/ *n.* [C] a container used as a toilet by someone who is too sick or old to get out of bed

be·drag·gled /bɪˈdrægəld/ *adj.* looking dirty, wet, and messy: *bedraggled hair*

bed·rid·den /ˈbɛdˌrɪdn/ *adj.* not able to get out of bed because you are old or very sick

bed·room /ˈbɛdrum/ *n.* [C] a room for sleeping in: *a four-bedroom house* | *We use the **spare bedroom** as an office.*

bed·side /ˈbɛdsaɪd/ *n.* [C] the area around a bed: *His family has been **at** his **bedside*** (=stayed with him because he was very ill) *all night.* | *a bedside table*

bed·spread /ˈbɛdsprɛd/ *n.* [C] a large cover that goes on top of a bed

bed·time /ˈbɛdtaɪm/ *n.* [C,U] the time when you usually go to bed: *It's way past your bedtime!*

bee /bi/ *n.* [C] a yellow and black insect that flies, makes HONEY, and can sting you: *James was stung by a bee.* ➔ SPELLING BEE

beech /bitʃ/ *n.* [C,U] a large tree with smooth gray branches, or the hard wood of this tree

beef[1] /bif/ *n.* **1** [U] meat from a cow: *roast beef*

THESAURUS

meat, **veal**, **pork**, **ham**, **bacon**
➔ see Thesaurus box at MEAT

2 [C] *informal* a complaint: *The guy **had a beef with** the manager and yelled at him for about 15 minutes.*

beef[2] *v.* [I] *informal* to complain: *They're always **beefing about** something.*
beef sth ⇔ **up** *phr. v. informal* to improve something, especially to make it stronger or more interesting: *Security around the White House has been beefed up since the attack.*

beef·y /ˈbifi/ *adj.* a beefy man is big and strong

bee·hive /ˈbihaɪv/ *n.* [C] HIVE

bee·line /ˈbilaɪn/ *n.* **make a beeline for sb/sth** *informal* to go quickly and directly toward someone or something: *The bear made a beeline for the woods.*

been /bɪn/ *v.* **1** the past participle of BE **2 have been to (do) sth** used in order to say that someone has gone to a place and come back: *Sandy has just been to Japan.* | *Have you been to see Katrina's new house?*

beep /bip/ *v.* **1** [I] if a machine beeps, it makes a short high sound: *The computer beeps when you push the wrong key.* **2** [I,T] if a horn beeps, or if you beep it, it makes a loud sound —**beep** *n.* [C]

beep·er /ˈbipɚ/ *n.* [C] a small machine that you carry with you that makes a sound to tell you to telephone someone [= **pager**]

B

beer /bɪr/ *n.* [C,U] an alcoholic drink made from grain, or a glass, can, or bottle of this drink: *a pitcher of beer* | *Would you like a beer?* ➔ ROOT BEER

beet /bit/ *n.* [C] a dark red vegetable that is the root of a plant

bee·tle /ˈbit̬l/ *n.* [C] an insect with a hard round back

be·fall /bɪˈfɔl/ *v.* past tense **befell** /-ˈfɛl/ past participle **befallen** /-ˈfɔlən/ [T] *formal* if something bad or dangerous befalls you, it happens to you: *We prayed that no harm should befall them.*

B

be·fit /bɪˈfɪt/ *v.* past tense and past participle **befitted**, present participle **befitting** [T] *formal* to be appropriate or seem right for someone: *a funeral befitting a national hero* —**befitting** *adj.*

be·fore¹ /bɪˈfɔr/ *prep.* **1** earlier than something or someone [≠ **after**]: *I usually shower before breakfast.* | *Denise got there before me.* | *He arrived **the day before yesterday*** (=two days ago).

THESAURUS

prior to sth – before: *Please be at the gate at least 30 minutes prior to departure.*
earlier – during the first part of a period of time, event, or process: *I saw Kim earlier today.*
previously – before now, or before a particular time: *Jim previously worked for Apple Bank.*

2 ahead of someone or something else in a list or order [≠ **after**]: *There were ten people before us in line.* | *S **comes before** T in the alphabet.* **3** used to say that one thing or person is considered more important than another: *His wife and children **come before** his job.* | *companies who **put** profit **before** people* **4** if one place is before another as you go toward it, you will reach it first [≠ **after**]: *Turn right just before the stop light.* **5** if something is put before a person or group of people, they must consider it and make a decision about it: *The case is now before the Supreme Court.* **6** *formal* in front of: *The priest knelt before the altar.*

before² *adv.* at an earlier time: *They'd met before, at one of Sandra's parties.* | *Sales were up 14% from **the year/month/day etc. before*** (=the previous year, etc.).

before³ *conjunction* **1** earlier than the time when something happens: *It will be several days before we know the results.* | *John wants to talk to you before you go.* **2** so that something bad does not happen: *You'd better lock your bike before it gets stolen.* **3 before you know it** *spoken* used in order to say that something will happen very soon: *We'd better get going – it'll be dark before you know it.*

be·fore·hand /bɪˈfɔrˌhænd/ *adv.* before something happens: *Never eat a piece of fruit without washing it beforehand.*

be·friend /bɪˈfrɛnd/ *v.* [T] *formal* to become someone's friend, especially someone who needs your help: *An old woman befriended me and made me dinner.*

be·fud·dled /bɪˈfʌdld/ *adj.* completely confused

beg /bɛg/ *v.* past tense and past participle **begged**, present participle **begging** [I,T] **1** to ask for something in a way which shows you want it very much: *I **begged** him **to** stay, but he wouldn't.* | *a prisoner begging to be released* | *He **begged for** forgiveness.*

THESAURUS

ask, **order**, **demand**, **request**
➔ see Thesaurus box at ASK

2 to ask someone for food, money, etc. because you are very poor: *children begging in the streets* | *homeless families **begging for** food* **3 I beg your pardon** *spoken* **a)** used in order to ask someone politely to repeat something: *"It's 7:00." "I beg your pardon?" "It's 7:00."* **b)** *formal* used in order to say you are sorry: *Oh, I beg your pardon, did I hurt you?* **c)** *formal* used in order to show that you strongly disagree: *"You never had to work hard in your life!" "I beg your pardon!"*

be·gan /bɪˈgæn/ *v.* the past tense of BEGIN

beg·gar /ˈbɛgɚ/ *n.* [C] **1** someone who lives by asking people for food and money **2 beggars can't be choosers** *spoken* used in order to say that when you have no money, no power to choose, etc., you have to accept whatever is available

be·gin /bɪˈgɪn/ *v.* past tense **began** /-ˈgæn/ past participle **begun** /-ˈgʌn/ present participle **beginning** **1** [I,T] to start doing something, or to start to happen or exist: *The meeting will **begin at** 10:00.* | *He began his career 30 years ago.* | *She began painting when she was a child.* | ***I began to** realize that he was lying.* **2** [I] **a)** if you begin with something or begin by doing something, you do it first: *Let's **begin with** exercise 5.* | *May I **begin by** thanking you all for coming.* **b)** if a book, film, word, etc. begins with something, that is how it starts: *"Pharmacy" **begins with** a "p."* **3 to begin with a)** used in order to introduce the first or most important point: *To begin with, photography is not really an art form at all.* **b)** used in order to say what something was like before something else happened: *If his hands weren't dirty to begin with, they certainly are now.* **c)** in the first part of an activity or process: *The children helped me to begin with, but they soon got bored.*

be·gin·ner /bɪˈgɪnɚ/ *n.* [C] someone who has just started to do or learn something: *a class for beginners*

be·gin·ning /bɪˈgɪnɪŋ/ *n.* [C usually singular] **1** the start or first part of something: *the **beginning of** the book* | *Placement tests are given **at the beginning of** the year.* | *He didn't take me seriously **in the beginning**.* | *The whole trip was a disaster **from beginning to end**.* **2 beginnings** [plural] the early part or signs of something that later develops into something bigger or more important: *I think I* ***have the beginnings of*** *a cold.*

be·grudge /bɪ'grʌdʒ/ *v.* [T] to feel upset or JEALOUS about something: *Honestly, I don't begrudge him his success.*

be·guile /bɪ'gaɪl/ *v.* [T] to interest and attract someone: *She was beguiled by his smooth talk.* —**beguiling** *adj.*

be·gun /bɪ'gʌn/ *v.* the past participle of BEGIN

be·half /bɪ'hæf/ *n.* **on behalf of sb/on sb's behalf** instead of someone: *He agreed to speak on her behalf.*

be·have /bɪ'heɪv/ *v.* **1** [I] to do or say things in a particular way: *Lions in a zoo do not* ***behave like*** *lions in the wild.* | *He began* ***behaving*** *differently* ***towards*** *me.* | *We were* ***behaving as if/though*** *nothing was wrong.* **2** [I,T] to be polite and not cause trouble [≠ **misbehave**]: *Will you boys please behave!* | *If you* ***behave yourself****, you can stay up late.* | *a* ***well-behaved*** *child*

be·hav·ior /bɪ'heɪvyɚ/ *n.* [U] **1** the things that a person or animal does, or the way in which they do them: *I'm not very pleased with your behavior.* | *criminal behavior* | *Reward your pet for* ***good behavior.*** | *We've noticed a change in his* ***behavior toward*** *the other children.*

THESAURUS

conduct formal – the way someone behaves: *The chairman has denied any improper conduct.*
manner – the way in which someone talks or behaves with other people: *They were teasing her in a friendly manner.*
demeanor formal – the way someone behaves, dresses, speaks etc. that shows what his/her character is like: *her cheerful demeanor*

2 *technical* the things that a substance, material, etc. normally does: *the* ***behavior of*** *cancer cells*

be·head /bɪ'hɛd/ *v.* [T] to cut off someone's head as a punishment

be·held /bɪ'hɛld/ *v.* the past tense and past participle of BEHOLD

be·hind[1] /bɪ'haɪnd/ *prep.* **1** at the back of something: *I was driving behind a truck on the freeway.* | *The liquor store is* ***right behind*** (=just behind) *the supermarket.* **2** not as successful or advanced as someone or something else: *The Lakers were four points behind the Celtics at half time.* | *Work on the new building is three months* ***behind schedule*** (=later than it should be). **3** supporting a person, idea, etc.: *Congress is behind the President on this issue.* **4** responsible for something, or causing something to happen: *The police believe a local gang is behind the killings.* **5 behind the times** old-fashioned

behind[2] *adv.* **1** at or toward the back of something: *Several other runners followed* ***close behind.*** | *The car was bumped* ***from behind.*** **2** in the place where someone or something was before: *I got there and realized I'd* ***left*** *the tickets* ***behind.*** | *Barb* ***stayed behind*** *to wait for Tina.* **3 be/get behind** to be late or slow in doing something: *We are three months behind with the rent.*

behind[3] *n.* [C] *informal* the part of your body that you sit on

be·hold /bɪ'hoʊld/ *v.* past tense and past participle **beheld** /bɪ'hɛld/ [T] *literary* to see something —**beholder** *n.* [C]

beige /beɪʒ/ *n.* [U] a pale brown color —**beige** *adj.*

B

be·ing /'biɪŋ/ *n.* [C] **1** a living thing or imaginary creature [➡ **human being**]: *strange beings from outer space* **2 come into being** to begin to exist: *Their political system came into being in the early 1900s.*

be·lat·ed /bɪ'leɪt̬ɪd/ *adj.* happening or arriving late: *a belated birthday card* | *a belated effort to apologize*

belch /bɛltʃ/ *v.* **1** [I] to let air from your stomach come out loudly through your mouth [= **burp**] **2** [T] to send out a large amount of smoke, flames, etc.: *factories belching blue smoke*

be·lea·guered /bɪ'ligɚd/ *adj. formal* having a lot of problems: *the beleaguered tobacco industry*

be·lie /bɪ'laɪ/ *v.* past tense and past participle **belied**, present participle **belying** [T] *formal* to give you a wrong idea about something: *With a quickness that belied her age, she ran across the road.*

be·lief /bə'lif/ *n.* **1** [singular, U] the feeling that something is definitely true or definitely exists: *the medieval* ***belief that*** *the sun went around the earth* | *a strong* ***belief in*** *God* | ***Contrary to popular belief*** (=despite what most people believe), *eating carrots does not improve your eyesight.*

THESAURUS

faith, religion, creed
➔ see Thesaurus box at FAITH

2 [singular] the feeling that someone or something is good and can be trusted: *a strong* ***belief in*** *the importance of education* **3** [C usually plural] an idea or set of ideas that you think are true: *religious beliefs* **4 beyond belief** used to emphasize that something is very bad, good, strange, etc.: *It seemed cruel beyond belief.*

be·liev·a·ble /bə'livəbəl/ *adj.* able to be believed because it seems possible, likely, or real: *There's not a single believable character in the book.*

be·lieve /bə'liv/ *v.* **1** [T] to be sure that something is true or that someone is telling the truth: *Do you believe her?* | *You shouldn't believe everything you read.* | *Young children often* ***believe (that)*** *animals can understand them.* | *I* ***found*** *his excuse* ***hard to believe.*** ▶ Don't say "...no one believed in him." Say "...no one believed him." ◀

THESAURUS

accept/take sb's word – to believe what someone says is true
swallow informal – to believe a story or explanation that is not actually true: *Did he really think we'd swallow that story?*
fall for sth informal – to be tricked into believing something that is not true
buy – to believe an explanation or reason for something

B

2 [T] to think that something is true, although you are not completely sure: *I* ***believe (that)*** *she'll be back on Monday.* | ***It is believed that*** *the victim knew his killer.* | *Lane is* ***believed to be*** *about 60.*

THESAURUS

think, **suspect**, **consider**, **figure**, **guess**
→ see Thesaurus box at THINK

3 [I] to have religious faith

SPOKEN PHRASES

4 [T] used in some phrases to show that you are surprised or shocked: *I* ***can't believe*** *you lied to me!* | ***Would you believe it***, *he even remembered my birthday!* **5 believe it or not** said when something is true but surprising: *Believe it or not, we work hard around here.*

believe in sth *phr. v.* **1** to be sure that something or someone definitely exists: *Do you believe in ghosts?* **2** to think that someone or something is good, important, or right: *He believes in the democratic system.*

be·liev·er /bəˈlivɚ/ *n.* [C] **1** someone who believes that a particular idea or thing is very good: *I'm a* ***firm/great believer in*** *healthy eating.* **2** someone who believes in a particular religion

be·lit·tle /bɪˈlɪtl/ *v.* [T] *formal* to make someone or something seem small or unimportant: *I don't like the way he belittles his children.*

bell /bɛl/ *n.* [C] **1** a metal object that makes a ringing sound when you hit it or shake it: *church bells* | *The bell rang for school to start.* **2** a piece of electrical equipment that makes a ringing sound: *We ran out of the classroom as soon as the bell rang.* | *She walked up the path and* ***rang*** *the* ***door bell.***

ˈbell ˌbottoms *n.* [plural] a pair of pants with legs that are wide at the bottom

bel·lig·er·ent /bəˈlɪdʒərənt/ *adj.* wanting to fight or argue —**belligerence** *n.* [U]

bel·low /ˈbɛloʊ/ *v.* [I,T] to shout loudly in a deep voice: *Tony was bellowing orders from upstairs.*

THESAURUS

shout, **call (out)**, **scream**, **yell**, **cry out**, **raise your voice**, **cheer**, **holler**
→ see Thesaurus box at SHOUT[1]

ˈbell ˌpepper *n.* [C] PEPPER

bel·ly /ˈbɛli/ *n.* plural **bellies** [C] *informal* **1** your stomach, or the part of your body between your chest and the top of your legs **2 go belly up** *informal* to fail: *The store went belly up in 1969.*

ˈbelly ˌbutton *n.* [C] *informal* the small hole or raised place in the middle of your stomach [= **navel**]

be·long /bɪˈlɔŋ/ *v.* [I] **1** to be in the right place or situation: *Please put the chair back where it belongs.* | *Books like that don't* ***belong in*** *the classroom.* **2** if you belong somewhere, you feel happy and comfortable there: *I'm going back to Colorado where I belong.*

belong to *phr. v.* **1 belong to sth** to be a member of a group or organization: *Mary and her husband belong to the yacht club.* **2 belong to sb** if something belongs to you, you own it: *Who does this umbrella belong to?*

be·long·ings /bɪˈlɔŋɪŋz/ *n.* [plural] the things that you own, especially things that you are carrying with you

THESAURUS

property, **possessions**, **things**, **stuff**, **effects**
→ see Thesaurus box at PROPERTY

be·loved /bɪˈlʌvd, bɪˈlʌvɪd/ *adj. literary* loved very much: *his beloved wife, Kelly* —**beloved** *n.* [singular]

be·low /bɪˈloʊ/ *adv., prep.* **1** in a lower place or position than someone or something else [≠ **above**]: *Jake lives in the apartment below.* | *Can you read the writing below the picture?* **2** less than a particular number or amount [≠ **above**]: *Sales for this year are below last year's.* | *It was 10 below outside* (=10 below zero in temperature). | *Tom's spelling is* ***well below*** *average* (=much worse than the normal standard). **3** on a later page, or lower on the same page [≠ **above**]: *For more information,* ***see below.*** **4** lower in rank [≠ **above**]: *There are people below him to handle that type of thing.*

belt[1] /bɛlt/ *n.* [C] **1** a band of leather or cloth that you wear around your waist → see picture at CLOTHES **2** a circular band of material such as rubber that moves parts of a machine: *the car's fan belt* **3** a large area of land that has particular qualities: *America's farm belt* **4 have sth under your belt** to have already done something useful or important: *At 25, she already has two novels under her belt.* → SEAT BELT

belt[2] *v.* [T] *informal* to hit someone or something hard

belt sth ⇔ **out** *phr. v.* to sing a song loudly

belt·way /ˈbɛltˀweɪ/ *n.* [C] **1** a road that goes around a city to keep traffic away from the center **2 the Beltway** the U.S. government in Washington, D.C., and the politicians, lawyers, LOBBYISTS, etc. who are involved in it

be·mused /bɪˈmyuzd/ *adj.* slightly confused: *a bemused expression*

bench[1] /bɛntʃ/ *n.* [C] **1** a long seat for two or more people, especially outdoors **2 the bench a)** the job of a judge in a court of law: *He was appointed to the bench in 1974.* **b)** the place where a judge sits in a court

bench[2] *v.* [T] to make a sports player stay out of a game for a period of time

bench·mark /ˈbɛntʃmɑrk/ *n.* [C] something that is used for comparing and measuring other things: *The test results provide a* ***benchmark for*** *measuring student achievement.*

bend[1] /bɛnd/ *v.* past tense and past participle **bent** /bɛnt/ [I,T] **1** to move a part of your body so that it is not straight or so that you are not standing upright: *He* ***bent down/over*** *to tie his shoelace.* | *Bend your knees slightly.* ➔ see picture on page A9 **2** to push or press something so that it is no longer flat or straight: *You've bent the handle.* **3 bend over backwards** to try very hard to help someone: *The neighbors bent over backwards to help when we moved into the house.* **4 bend the rules** to allow someone to do something that is not normally allowed: *Can't we bend the rules just this one time?*

bend[2] *n.* [C] a curve in something, especially a road or river: *a sharp bend in the road*

be·neath /bɪˈniθ/ *adv., prep. formal* **1** under or below something: *the warm sand beneath her feet* **2** if someone or something is beneath you, you think that he, she, or it is not good enough for you: *She seemed to think that talking to us was beneath her.*

ben·e·dic·tion /ˌbɛnəˈdɪkʃən/ *n.* [C] a prayer that asks God to protect and help someone

ben·e·fac·tor /ˈbɛnəˌfæktɚ/ *n. formal* [C] someone who gives money or help to someone else

ben·e·fi·cial /ˌbɛnəˈfɪʃəl/ *adj.* good or useful: *The agreement will be* ***beneficial to*** *both groups.*

ben·e·fi·ci·ar·y /ˌbɛnəˈfɪʃiˌɛri, -ˈfɪʃəri/ *n.* plural **beneficiaries** [C] **1** someone who gets advantages from an action or change: *The rich were the main* ***beneficiaries of*** *the tax cut.* **2** someone who gets money when someone dies

ben·e·fit[1] /ˈbɛnəfɪt/ *n.* **1** [C] the money or other advantages that you get from something such as insurance or the government, or as part of your job: *The company provides medical benefits.* | *social security benefits* **2** [C,U] an advantage, improvement, or help that you get from something: *What are the* ***benefits of*** *contact lenses?* | *The new credit cards will* ***be of*** *great* ***benefit to*** *our customers.* | *Marc translated what the minister said* ***for*** *my* ***benefit*** (=to help me). **3** [C] a performance, concert, etc. that is done in order to make money for a CHARITY **4 give sb the benefit of the doubt** to believe or trust someone even though it is possible that s/he is lying or is wrong: *His story was a little hard to believe, but I gave him the benefit of the doubt.*

benefit[2] *v.* past tense and past participle **benefitted** or **benefited**, present participle **benefitting** or **benefiting** [I,T] if you benefit from something or if it benefits you, it helps you: *These policy changes mainly benefit small companies.* | *Most of these children would* ***benefit from*** *an extra year at school.*

be·nev·o·lent /bəˈnɛvələnt/ *adj. formal* kind and generous —**benevolence** *n.* [U]

be·nign /bɪˈnaɪn/ *adj.* **1** *technical* a benign TUMOR is not caused by CANCER [≠ **malignant**] **2** *formal* kind and gentle

bent[1] /bɛnt/ *v.* the past tense and past participle of BEND

bent

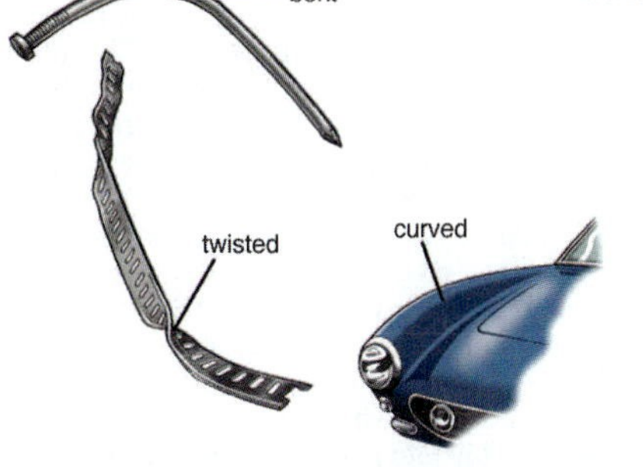

bent[2] *adj.* **1** curved and no longer flat or straight: *a bent nail*

THESAURUS

twisted – bent in many directions or turned many times: *a cable made of twisted strands of wire*
curved – bent in the shape of part of a circle, or having this shape: *curved wooden coathangers*
warped – bent or twisted into the wrong shape: *The window frame was old and warped.*
crooked – not straight, but bending sharply in one or more places: *the crooked streets in the old part of the city*
wavy – having even curved shapes: *She had wavy black hair.*

2 be bent on (doing) sth to be determined to do something or have something: *Mendez was bent on getting a better job.*

bent[3] *n.* [singular] a natural skill or ability: *Rebecca has an artistic bent.*

be·queath /bɪˈkwiθ, bɪˈkwið/ *v.* [T] *formal* to arrange for someone to get something that belongs to you after your death

be·quest /bɪˈkwɛst/ *n.* [C] *formal* money or property that you BEQUEATH to someone

be·rate /bəˈreɪt/ *v.* [T] *formal* to speak angrily to someone because s/he has done something wrong: *Dunn berated Kelly in front of his staff.*

be·reaved /bəˈrivd/ *adj. formal* if someone is bereaved, someone s/he loves has died —**bereavement** *n.* [C,U]

be·reft /bəˈrɛft/ *adj. formal* completely without something: ***bereft of*** *all hope*

be·ret /bəˈreɪ/ *n.* [C] a soft round hat that is almost flat ➔ see picture at HAT

ber·ry /ˈbɛri/ *n.* plural **berries** [C] one of several types of small soft fruits with very small seeds

ber·serk /bɚˈsɚk, -ˈzɚk/ *adj.* **go berserk** *informal* to become very angry and violent in a crazy way: *The guy went berserk and started hitting Paul.*

berth /bɚθ/ *n.* [C] **1** a place to sleep on a train or boat **2** a place near land where a ship can be kept

B

be·seech /bɪˈsitʃ/ *v.* past tense and past participle **besought** /-ˈsɔt/ or **beseeched** [T] *literary* to ask for something in an eager or anxious way

be·set /bɪˈsɛt/ *v.* past tense and past participle **beset**, present participle **besetting** [T] *formal* to make someone have a lot of trouble or problems: *The family was beset by financial difficulties.*

be·side /bɪˈsaɪd/ *prep.* **1** next to or very close to someone or something: *Gary sat down beside me.* | *a cabin beside the lake* **2** used in order to compare two people or things: *Pat looked big and clumsy beside her sister.* **3 be beside the point** to not be important compared to something else: *"I'm not hungry." "That's beside the point; you need to eat!"* **4 be beside yourself (with anger/fear/grief/joy etc.)** to feel a particular emotion very strongly: *Matt was beside himself with excitement.*

be·sides /bɪˈsaɪdz/ *prep., adv.* **1** in addition to something or someone: *Besides going to college, she works 15 hours a week.* | *Who's going to be there besides David and me?* **2** *spoken* said when giving another reason: *I wanted to help her out. Besides, I needed the money.*

be·siege /bɪˈsidʒ/ *v.* **1 be besieged by people/worries/thoughts etc.** to be surrounded by a lot of people or to be very worried, etc.: *a rock star besieged by fans* **2 be besieged with letters/questions/demands etc.** to receive a lot of letters, be asked a lot of questions, etc.: *The radio station was besieged by letters of complaint.* **3** [T] to surround a place with an army

be·sought /bɪˈsɔt/ *v.* the past tense and past participle of BESEECH

best¹ /bɛst/ *adj.* [the superlative of "good"] better than anyone or anything else: *the best player on the team* | *What's **the best way** to get to El Paso?* | ***The best thing** to do is to stop worrying.* | *my **best friend*** (=the one I know and like the most)

best² *adv.* [the superlative of "well"] **1** more than anyone else or anything else: *Helene knows him best.* | *Which song do you like best?* **2** in a way that is better than any other: *It works best if you warm it up first.* **3 as best you can** *spoken* as well as you can: *I'll deal with the problem as best I can.*

best³ *n.* **1 the best a)** someone or something that is better than any others: *Which stereo is the best?* **b)** the most successful situation or results you can achieve: *All parents want the best for their children.* **2 do/try your best** to try very hard to achieve something: *I did my best, but I still didn't pass.* **3 to the best of your ability/knowledge/belief etc.** used in order to say that something is as much as you know, believe, or are able to do: *I'm sure he'll do the work to the best of his ability.* **4 at best** used in order to emphasize that something is not very good, even when you consider it in the best possible way: *At best, sales have been good but not great.* **5 at your/its best** performing as well or as effectively as you are able to: *The movie shows Hollywood at its best.* **6 make the best of sth** to accept a bad situation and do what you can to make it better: *It's not going to be fun, but we'll have to make the best of it.* **7 be for the best** used in order to say that a particular event may seem bad now, but might have a good result later: *She's upset that they broke up, but it's probably for the best.*

bes·tial /ˈbɛstʃəl, ˈbis-/ *adj.* behaving like an animal, especially in a cruel way —**bestially** *adv.*

ˌbest ˈman *n.* [singular] a friend of a BRIDEGROOM (=man who is getting married), who helps him to get ready and stands next to him during the wedding

TOPIC

wedding, **wedding ceremony/service**, **bride**, **groom**, **maid of honor**, **bridesmaids**, **reception**, **go on a honeymoon**
➔ see Topic box at WEDDING

be·stow /bɪˈstoʊ/ *v.* [T] *formal* to give someone something valuable or important

best·sell·er /ˌbɛstˈsɛlɚ/ *n.* [C] a new book that a lot of people have bought —**best-selling** *adj.* [only before noun] *a best-selling novel*

THESAURUS

blockbuster, **hit**, **craze**, **fad**, **cult**
➔ see Thesaurus box at POPULAR

bet¹ /bɛt/ *v.* past tense and past participle **bet**, present participle **betting** **1** [I, T] to risk money on the result of a race, game, competition, or other future event [➡ **gamble**]: *She **bet** all her money **on** a horse that came in last.* | *I **bet** him $20 **that** he wouldn't do it.*

SPOKEN PHRASES

2 I/I'll bet a) said when you think something is true or likely to happen: *I bet they'll be late.* | *I'll bet that made her mad!* **b)** said in order to show that you agree with someone or understand how s/he feels: *"I was furious." "I bet you were!"*
3 you bet! a) said in order to agree with someone, or to say that you are definitely going to do something: *"Would you like to come?" "You bet!"* **b)** used in order to reply to someone when s/he thanks you for something: *"Thanks for all your help, Bob." "You bet."*

bet² *n.* **1** [C] an agreement to risk money on the

result of a race, game, competition, or other future event, or the money that you risk: *Higgins **had a bet on** the World Series.* | *I **lost/won** the **bet**.* | *a $10 bet* **2 your best bet** *spoken* said in order to give someone advice about the best thing to do: *Your best bet would be to take Highway 9.* **3 a good/safe bet** an action, situation, or thing that is likely to be successful or produce the results you want: *The earrings seemed like a good bet for a birthday present.*

bet·cha /ˈbɛtʃə/ a short form of "bet you", used in writing to show how people sound when they speak: *You betcha.*

be·tray /bɪˈtreɪ/ *v.* [T] **1** to behave dishonestly toward someone who loves you or trusts you: *He felt that she had betrayed him.* **2** to be disloyal to your country, company, etc., for example by giving secret information to its enemies **3** to show feelings that you are trying to hide: *Keith's voice betrayed his nervousness.*

be·tray·al /bɪˈtreɪəl/ *n.* [C,U] the act of betraying your country, friends, or someone who trusts you

bet·ter¹ /ˈbɛt̬ɚ/ *adj.* **1** [the comparative of "good"] higher in quality, or more useful, appropriate, interesting, etc. than something or someone else [≠ **worse**]: *He's applying for a better job.* | *Your stereo is **better than** mine.* | *My sister's **better at** math than I am.* | *The Mexican place across the street has **much better** food.* | *Your English is **getting better*** (=improving). **2** [the comparative of "well"] less sick than you were, or no longer sick [≠ **worse**]: *He's much better today.* | *I hope your sore throat **gets better** soon.* | *Are you **feeling better**?* → see Thesaurus box at HEALTHY **3 it is better/it would be better** used in order to give advice: *It's better to get a written agreement.* | *It would be **better if** you stayed here.* **4 have seen better days** *informal* to be in a bad condition: *The sofa had definitely seen better days.*

better² *adv.* [the comparative of "well"] **1** to a higher standard or degree: *He can speak French a lot **better than** I can.* | *She knows this town better than you do.* **2 better late than never** used in order to say that it is better for something to happen late rather than not happen at all **3 the sooner/bigger etc., the better** used in order to emphasize that something should happen as soon as possible, that it should be as big as possible, etc.: *He needs a wife, and the sooner the better.* **4 had better (do sth) a)** used in order to say that you or someone else should do something: *I think I'd better leave now.* **b)** said when threatening someone: *You'd better keep your mouth shut about this.* **5 do better** to perform better or reach a higher standard: *We **did better than** all the other schools.* → BETTER OFF

better³ *n.* **1 the better** the one that is the higher in quality, more appropriate, etc. when you are comparing two similar people or things: *It's hard to decide which one is the better.* **2 get the better of sb a)** if a feeling gets the better of you, you do not control it when you should: *His curiosity got the better of him and he opened the letter.* **b)** to defeat someone **3 for the better** in a way that improves the situation: *Smaller classes are definitely **a change for the better.***

better⁴ *v.* [T] *formal* to achieve something that is higher in quality, amount, etc. than something else

ˌbetter ˈoff *adj.* **1** more successful, richer, or having more advantages than you did before: *The more prepared you are, the better off you'll be.* **2 sb is better off doing sth** *spoken* said when giving advice about what someone should do: *You're better off leaving early.*

be·tween¹ /bɪˈtwin/ *prep.* **1** in or into the space or time that separates two things, people, events, etc.: *Jay was sitting between Kate and Lisa.* | *You know I don't want you to eat between meals.* → IN-BETWEEN **2** used in order to show a range of amounts, distances, times, etc.: *Why don't you come over between seven and eight?* | *The project will cost between 10 and 12 million dollars.* ► Don't say "between 10 to 12 million dollars." ◄ **3** used in order to show that something is divided or shared by two people, places, or things: *We had about two loads of laundry between us.* | *Linda and Dave split a milkshake between them.* **4** used in order to show a relationship between two people, things, events, etc.: *What's the difference between the two computers?* | *Trade relations between the countries have improved.* **5** used in order to show how two places are connected: *the highway between Fresno and Visalia* **6 between you and me** *spoken* said before you tell someone a secret or a private opinion: *Between you and me, I don't think she has a chance of getting that promotion.*

between² *adv.* in or into the space that separates two things, people, etc., or in or into the time that separates two events: *two yards with a fence between*

USAGE

Between and **among** are both used to talk about the position of someone or something.
Use **between** when there is one other person or thing on each side of someone or something: *I sat between Alex and Sarah.*
Use **among** when there are two or more people or things on each side of someone or something: *The hut was hidden among the trees.*

→ IN-BETWEEN

bev·er·age /ˈbɛvrɪdʒ, ˈbɛvərɪdʒ/ *n. formal* [C] a drink: *alcoholic beverages*

bev·y /ˈbɛvi/ *n.* plural **bevies** [C] a large group of people: *a **bevy of** teenagers*

be·ware /bɪˈwɛr/ *v.* [I,T] used in order to warn someone to be careful: ***Beware of** the dog!*

be·wil·dered /bɪˈwɪldɚd/ *adj.* very confused and not sure what to do or think: *a bewildered expression* —**bewilderment** *n.* [U]

be·wil·der·ing /bɪ'wɪldərɪŋ/ *adj.* making you feel very confused: *a bewildering number of choices*

be·witched /bɪ'wɪtʃt/ *adj.* so interested in or attracted by someone or something that you cannot think clearly —**bewitching** *adj.*

be·yond /bɪ'yɑnd/ *prep., adv.* **1** on or to the farther side of something: *There was a forest beyond the river.* | *a view from the mountains with the plains beyond* **2** later than a particular time, date, etc.: *The ban has been extended beyond 2005.* | *planning for the year 2010 and beyond* **3** more than a particular amount, level, or limit: *The population has grown beyond estimated levels.* **4** outside the range or limits of someone or something: *an apple just beyond my reach* | *Chemistry was beyond my understanding.* **5 beyond belief/doubt/recognition etc.** used in order to say that you cannot believe something, doubt something, etc.: *In just six years, the town had changed beyond all recognition.* | *The car has been damaged beyond repair.* **6 it's beyond me why/what etc.** *spoken* said when you do not understand something: *It's beyond me why they ever got married at all.* **7** used in order to mean "except" in negative sentences: *Santa Fe doesn't have much industry beyond tourism.*

bi·as /'baɪəs/ *n.* [singular, U] an opinion about whether a person, group, or idea is good or bad, which influences how you deal with it: *Some employers have a **bias against** women.* —**bias** *v.* [T]

bi·ased /'baɪəst/ *adj.* unfairly preferring one person or group over another: *The referee was definitely biased.* | *biased news reporting*

bib /bɪb/ *n.* [C] a piece of cloth that you tie under a baby's chin to protect his/her clothes while s/he eats

bi·ble /'baɪbəl/ *n.* [C] **1 the Bible** the holy book of the Christian religion **2** a copy of the Bible

bib·li·og·ra·phy /ˌbɪbli'ɑgrəfi/ *n.* plural **bibliographies** [C] a list of all the books and articles used in the preparation of another book, or a list of books and articles on a particular subject

bi·cen·ten·ni·al /ˌbaɪsɛn'tɛniəl/ *n.* [C] the day or year exactly 200 years after an important event: *the **bicentennial of** the Declaration of Independence*

bi·cep /'baɪsɛps/ *n.* [C usually plural] the large muscle on the front of your upper arm

bick·er /'bɪkɚ/ *v.* [I] to argue about something that is not very important: *The kids were **bickering about/over** who would sleep in the top bunk.*

THESAURUS

argue, have an argument, fight, have a fight, quarrel, have a quarrel, squabble
→ see Thesaurus box at ARGUE

bi·cy·cle¹ /'baɪsɪkəl/ *n.* [C] a vehicle with two wheels that you ride by pushing the PEDALS with your feet [= **bike**]: *She usually **rides** her **bicycle** to work.*

bicycle² *v.* [I] to go somewhere by bicycle [= **bike**]

bid¹ /bɪd/ *n.* [C] **1** an offer to pay a particular price for something: *They put in a **bid for** the house.* **2** an offer to do work for someone at a particular price: *The company accepted the lowest **bid for** the project.* **3** an attempt to achieve or gain something: *Clinton's successful **bid for** the presidency in 1992*

bid² *v.* past tense and past participle **bid**, present participle **bidding** **1** [I,T] to offer to pay a particular price for something: *Foreman **bid** $150,000 **for** an antique table.* | *The two men ended up **bidding against** each other at the auction.* **2** [I] to offer to do work for someone at a particular price: *Four companies were invited to **bid for** the contract.* —**bidder** *n.* [C] *There are five bidders for the contract.*

bid³ *v.* past tense **bade** /bæd, beɪd/ or **bid**, past participle **bid** or **bidden** /'bɪdn/ present participle **bidding** *literary* **bid sb good morning/goodbye etc.** to say good morning, etc. to someone

bid·ding /'bɪdɪŋ/ *n.* [U] **1** the activity of offering to pay a particular price for something, or offering to do work **2 do sb's bidding** *literary* to do what someone tells you to do

bide /baɪd/ *v.* **bide your time** to wait until the right time to do something

bi·en·ni·al /baɪ'ɛniəl/ *adj.* happening once every two years

bi·fo·cals /'baɪˌfoʊkəlz, baɪ'foʊkəlz/ *n.* [plural] a pair of special glasses made so that you can look through the upper part to see things that are far away and through the lower part to see things that are close

big /bɪg/ *adj.* comparative **bigger**, superlative **biggest** **1** more than average size or amount [≠ **small**]: *a big house* | *Los Angeles is the biggest city in California.* | *That boy **gets bigger** every time I see him.*

THESAURUS

large – big or bigger than usual in size or amount: *the largest city in America* | *People are now watching the program in large numbers.*
huge – extremely big: *He died owing a huge sum of money.*
enormous – extremely big: *an enormous cake*
vast – extremely big: *The birds nest here in vast numbers.*
gigantic – extremely big or tall: *gigantic waves*
massive – very big, solid, and heavy: *a massive stone fireplace*
immense – extremely large or great: *We still have an immense amount of work to do.*
colossal – very large: *We have made a colossal mistake.*
substantial – large in number or amount: *He earns a substantial amount of money.*

bicycle

Big and **large** mean the same thing, but **large** is slightly more formal: *That's a big piece of cake!* | *It's the largest hotel in the city.*
Use **large**, not **big**, to describe amounts: *They have borrowed a large amount of money.*
Use **big**, not **large**, to describe something that is important: *a big opportunity* | *That's the big question.*
➔ see Thesaurus box at FAT[1]

2 important or serious: *a big decision* | *He has big plans for the house.* | *I'm having big problems with my PC.* **3** successful or popular: *The song was a big hit.* | *I knew I'd never **make it big*** (=become very successful) *as a professional golfer.* **4 big sister/big brother** *informal* your older sister or brother **5** [only before noun] *informal* doing something to a large degree: *I've never been a big baseball fan.* | *Both the girls are **big eaters*** (=they eat a lot). **6 big money/big bucks** a lot of money: *They are willing to pay big bucks to attract the best players.* **7 be big on sth** *spoken* to like something very much: *I'm not big on kids.*

big·a·my /ˈbɪgəmi/ *n.* [U] the crime of being married to two people at the same time —**bigamist** *n.* [C] —**bigamous** *adj.*

ˌBig ˈApple *n.* **the Big Apple** *informal* a name for New York City

ˌbig ˈbrother *n.* [C] any person, organization, or system that seems to control people's lives and restrict their freedom

ˌbig ˈbusiness *n.* [U] very large companies, considered as a group with a lot of influence

ˌbig ˈdeal *n. spoken* [C] **1** said when you do not think something is as important as someone else thinks it is: *It's just a game. If you lose, big deal.* | ***It's no big deal.*** *Everybody forgets things sometimes.* **2** an important event or situation: *This audition is a big deal for Joey.* **3 make a big deal of/out of/about sth** to get too excited or upset about something, or make something seem more important than it is: *She's making a big deal out of nothing.*

ˌBig ˈDipper *n.* [C] a group of seven bright stars seen in the northern sky in the shape of a bowl with a long handle

big·gie /ˈbɪgi/ *n.* **no biggie** *spoken* said when something is not important, or when you are not upset or angry about something: *"Oh, I'm sorry." "That's okay, no biggie."*

ˈbig ˌgovernment *n.* [U] government, when people think it is controlling their lives too much

big·head·ed /ˈbɪgˌhɛdɪd/ *adj.* someone who is bigheaded thinks s/he is better than other people

ˈbig-league *adj. informal* ➔ MAJOR-LEAGUE

ˈbig mouth *n.* [C] *informal* someone who cannot be trusted to keep secrets

ˌbig ˈname *n.* [C] a famous person, especially an actor, musician, etc. —**big name** *adj.*

big·ot /ˈbɪgət/ *n.* [C] someone who is bigoted

big·ot·ed /ˈbɪgət̬ɪd/ *adj.* having strong opinions that most people think are unreasonable, especially about race, religion, or politics

big·ot·ry /ˈbɪgətri/ *n.* [U] bigoted behavior or beliefs: *religious bigotry*

ˈbig shot *n.* [C] *informal* someone who is very important or powerful

B

ˌbig-ˈticket *adj.* very expensive: ***big-ticket items*** *such as houses and cars*

ˈbig time¹ *adv. spoken* a lot or very much: *He messed up big time.*

ˈbig time² *n.* **the big time** *informal* the position of being very famous or important: *The author has finally* ***hit the big time****.* —**big-time** *adj.* [only before noun] *big-time drug dealers*

big·wig /ˈbɪgwɪg/ *n.* [C] *informal* an important person

bike¹ /baɪk/ *n.* [C] *informal* **1** a bicycle: *The kids were* ***riding*** *their* ***bikes****. | Do you want to* ***go for a bike ride****?* **2** a MOTORCYCLE

bike² *v.* [I] to ride a bicycle

> **THESAURUS**
>
> **travel**, **drive**, **go by car**, **fly**, **go by plane**, **sail**, **go by boat/ship**, **take a train/bus/taxi/cab**, **go by train/bus etc.**, **walk**, **hike**, **go on foot**, **go by bike**
>
> ➔ see Thesaurus box at TRAVEL¹

bik·er /ˈbaɪkɚ/ *n.* [C] someone who rides a MOTORCYCLE

bi·ki·ni /bɪˈkini/ *n.* [C] a piece of clothing in two parts that women wear for swimming

bi·lat·er·al /baɪˈlæt̬ərəl/ *adj.* **bilateral agreement/treaty etc.** an agreement, etc. between two groups or countries: *bilateral Mideast peace talks* —**bilaterally** *adv.*

bile /baɪl/ *n.* [U] a liquid produced by the LIVER to help the body DIGEST food

bi·lin·gual /baɪˈlɪŋgwəl/ *adj.* **1** able to speak two languages: *Their children are completely bilingual.* **2** written or spoken in two languages: *a bilingual dictionary*

bill¹ /bɪl/ *n.* [C] **1** a written list showing how much you have to pay for services you have received, work that has been done, etc.: *I have to remember to* ***pay*** *the phone* ***bill*** *this week. | The* ***bill for*** *the repairs came to $600.*

> **THESAURUS**
>
> **check** – a bill that you are given in a restaurant: *Can I have the check, please?*
>
> **invoice** – a document that shows how much you owe for goods, work, etc.: *Payment is due 10 days after receipt of the invoice.*
>
> **tab** – an amount of money that you owe for a meal or drinks you have had, but have not yet paid for: *I ordered a rum and Coke and had the bartender put it on my tab.*

> **TOPIC**
>
> **restaurant**, **waiter**, **waitress**, **menu**, **appetizer**, **main course**, **entrée**, **dessert**, **check**, **leave a tip**, **service**
>
> ➔ see Topic box at RESTAURANT

2 a piece of paper money: *a ten-dollar bill*

> **THESAURUS**
>
> **money**, **coin**, **penny**, **nickel**, **dime**, **quarter**, **cash**, **change**, **currency**
>
> ➔ see Thesaurus box at MONEY

3 a plan for a law that is written down for a government to decide on: *The House of Representatives* ***passed*** *a new gun-control* ***bill*** (=made it a law). **4 fit/fill the bill** to be exactly what you need: *This car fits the bill perfectly.* **5** a program of entertainment at a theater, concert, etc., with details of who is performing, what is being shown, etc. **6** a wide or long beak on a bird such as a duck ➔ **foot the bill** at FOOT²

bill² *v.* [T] **1** to send a bill to someone: *They've* ***billed*** *me* ***for*** *things I didn't order.* **2 bill sth as sth** to advertise or describe something in a particular way: *The boxing match was billed as "the fight of the century."*

bill·board /ˈbɪlbɔrd/ *n.* [C] a very large sign used for advertising, especially next to a road

> **THESAURUS**
>
> **advertisement**, **commercial**, **poster**, **want ad**, **classified ad**, **flier**, **junk mail**, **spam**
>
> ➔ see Thesaurus box at ADVERTISEMENT

bill·fold /ˈbɪlfoʊld/ *n.* [C] a WALLET

bil·liards /ˈbɪlyɚdz/ *n.* [plural] a game like POOL in which the balls go into the holes in a special order

bil·lion /ˈbɪlyən/ *number* plural **billion** or **billions** 1,000,000,000: *$7 billion |* ***Billions of*** *dollars have been invested.* —**billionth** *number*

ˌbill of ˈrights *n.* [singular] an official written list of the most important rights of the citizens of a country

bil·low /ˈbɪloʊ/ *v.* [I] **1** if something made of cloth billows, it moves in the wind and fills with air: *Her long skirt billowed in the breeze.* **2** if a cloud or smoke billows, it rises in a round mass

bim·bo /ˈbɪmboʊ/ *n.* plural **bimbos** [C] *informal* an insulting word meaning an attractive but stupid woman

bi·month·ly /baɪˈmʌnθli/ *adj., adv.* happening or being done every two months, or twice each month: *a bimonthly magazine*

bin /bɪn/ *n.* [C] a large container for storing things

bi·na·ry /ˈbaɪnəri/ *adj.* **the binary system** *technical* a system of counting, used in computers, in which only the numbers 0 and 1 are used

bind¹ /baɪnd/ past tense and past participle **bound** /baʊnd/ *v.* **1** [T] to tie something firmly with string or rope: *His legs were bound with rope.* **2 also bind together** [T] to form a strong relationship between two people, countries, etc.: *Religious belief binds the community together.* **3** [T] if you are bound by an agreement or promise, you must do what you agreed or promised to do: *Each country is bound by the treaty.* **4** [I,T] *technical* to stick together in a mass, or to make small pieces of something stick together **5** [T] to fasten the pages of a book together and put them in a cover: *The book was printed and bound in Spain.*

bind² *n.* [C] an annoying or difficult situation: *I'm so mad at him for **putting** me **in** this **bind**!*

bind·er /ˈbaɪndɚ/ *n.* [C] a cover for holding loose sheets of paper, magazines, etc. together ➔ see picture on page A11

bind·ing¹ /ˈbaɪndɪŋ/ *adj.* a contract or agreement that is binding must be obeyed: *The contract isn't binding until you sign it.*

binding² *n.* **1** [C] the cover of a book **2** [U] material sewn along the edge of a piece of cloth for strength or decoration

binge /bɪndʒ/ *n.* [C] *informal* a short period of time when you do too much of something, especially drinking alcohol: *He **went on a** drinking **binge** last week.* —**binge** *v.* [I] *Whenever she's depressed, she **binges on** chocolate.*

bin·go /ˈbɪŋgoʊ/ *n.* [U] a game played for money or prizes in which you win if a set of numbers chosen by chance are the same as one of the lines of numbers on your card

bin·oc·u·lars /bɪˈnɑkyəlɚz, baɪ-/ *n.* [plural] a pair of special glasses that you hold up and look through to see things that are far away

bi·o·chem·is·try /ˌbaɪoʊˈkɛmɪstri/ *n.* [U] the scientific study of the chemistry of living things —**biochemist** *n.* [C] —**biochemical** /ˌbaɪoʊˈkɛmɪkəl/ *adj.*

bi·o·de·grad·a·ble /ˌbaɪoʊdɪˈgreɪdəbəl/ *adj.* a material, product, etc. that is biodegradable is able to change or decay naturally so that it does not harm the environment: *Most plastic is not biodegradable.*

TOPIC

environment, pollution, the greenhouse effect, global warming, acid rain, deforestation, environmentally friendly, eco-friendly, recycle, organic
➔ see Topic box at ENVIRONMENT

bi·og·ra·pher /baɪˈɑgrəfɚ/ *n.* [C] someone who writes a biography of someone else

bi·og·ra·phy /baɪˈɑgrəfi/ *n.* plural **biographies** [C] a book about a person's life: *a **biography of** Louis Armstrong*

THESAURUS

book, nonfiction, fiction, literature, reference book, text book, hardcover, hardback, paperback, novel, science fiction, autobiography
➔ see Thesaurus box at BOOK¹

bi·o·log·i·cal /ˌbaɪəˈlɑdʒɪkəl/ *adj.* **1** relating to the natural processes performed by living things: *a biological process* **2** [only before noun] relating to BIOLOGY: *the biological sciences* **3 biological weapons/warfare/attack etc.** weapons, attacks, etc. that involve the use of living things, including BACTERIA, to harm people —**biologically** *adv.*

bi·ol·o·gy /baɪˈɑlədʒi/ *n.* [U] the scientific study of living things —**biologist** *n.* [C]

bi·op·sy /ˈbaɪˌɑpsi/ *n.* plural **biopsies** [C] a medical test in which cells, TISSUE, etc. are removed from someone's body in order to find out more about a disease s/he may have

bi·o·tech·nol·o·gy /ˌbaɪoʊtɛkˈnɑlədʒi/ *n.* [U] the use of living things such as cells and BACTERIA in science and industry to make drugs, chemicals, etc.

bi·par·ti·san /baɪˈpɑrt̬əzən/ *adj.* involving two political parties: *a bipartisan committee in the Senate*

birch /bɚtʃ/ *n.* [C,U] a tree with BARK like paper that comes off easily, or the wood of this tree

bird /bɚd/ *n.* [C] an animal with wings and feathers that lays eggs and can usually fly ➔ **early bird** at EARLY¹ ➔ **kill two birds with one stone** at KILL¹

ˈbird-brained *adj. informal* silly or stupid

bird·ie /ˈbɚdi/ *n.* [C] *informal* a small light object that you hit over the net in the game of BADMINTON

ˌbird of ˈprey *n.* plural **birds of prey** [C] any bird that kills other birds and small animals for food

bird·seed /ˈbɚdsid/ *n.* [U] a mixture of seeds for feeding birds

ˌbird's eye ˈview *n.* [singular] a view from a very high place: *a bird's eye view over the city*

birth /bɚθ/ *n.* **1 give birth** if a woman gives birth, she produces a baby from her body: *Jo **gave birth to** a baby girl at 6:20 a.m.* **2** [C,U] the time when a baby comes out of its mother's body: *The baby weighed 7 pounds **at birth**.* | *What is your **birth date*** (=the date on which you were born)? **3** [U] someone's family origin: *Her grandfather was French **by birth**.* **4 the birth of sth** the time when something begins to exist: *the birth of a nation*

ˈbirth cerˌtificate *n.* [C] an official document that shows when and where you were born

ˈbirth conˌtrol *n.* [U] the practice of controlling the number of children you have, or the methods used [= **contraception**]

birth·day /ˈbɚθdeɪ/ *n.* [C] the date on which someone was born, usually celebrated each year: *When is your birthday?* | *It's my 18th birthday* *next week.* | *a* ***birthday present/card/party*** | ***Happy Birthday!*** (=said to someone on his/her birthday)

birth·mark /ˈbɚθmɑrk/ *n.* [C] a permanent mark on someone's skin that s/he has had since birth

birth·place /ˈbɚθpleɪs/ *n.* [C usually singular] the place where someone was born: *Cézanne's birthplace*

birth·rate /ˈbɚθreɪt/ *n.* [C] the average number of babies born during a particular period of time in a country or area

B

birth·right /ˈbɚθreɪt/ *n.* [C usually singular] a basic right that you have because of your family or country you come from: *Freedom is every American's birthright.*

bis·cuit /ˈbɪskɪt/ *n.* [C] a type of bread that is baked in small round shapes: *a plate of homemade biscuits*

bi·sect /ˈbaɪsɛkt, baɪˈsɛkt/ *v.* [T] *technical* to divide something, especially a line or angle, into two equal parts —**bisection** /ˈbaɪˌsɛkʃən, baɪˈsɛkʃən/ *n.* [U]

bi·sex·u·al /baɪˈsɛkʃuəl/ *adj.* sexually attracted to both men and women —**bisexual** *n.* [C] —**bisexuality** /ˌbaɪsɛkʃuˈæləṭi/ *n.* [U]

bish·op /ˈbɪʃəp/ *n.* [C] a Christian priest with a high rank who is in charge of the churches and priests in a large area

bison

bi·son /ˈbaɪsən/ *n.* plural **bison** or **bisons** [C] a BUFFALO

bis·tro /ˈbistroʊ/ *n.* plural **bistros** [C] a small restaurant or bar: *a French bistro on the Upper East Side*

bit¹ /bɪt/ *n.* [C]
1 a (little) bit slightly, but not very: *I'm a little bit tired.* | *Enrollment is down a bit from last year.*
2 quite a bit a fairly large amount: *He owes me quite a bit of money.*
3 SMALL PIECE a small piece of something: *The floor was covered with tiny* ***bits of*** *glass.* | *I tore the letter* ***to bits*** (=into small pieces) *and threw it away.*
4 a bit of sth a small amount of something that is not a physical object: *We just need* ***a bit of luck.***
5 COMPUTER the smallest unit of information that can be used by a computer [➡ **byte**]
6 TIME a short amount of time: *We'll talk about the Civil War* ***in*** *just* ***a bit.*** | *I could see that she was learning,* ***bit by bit*** (=gradually).
7 every bit as... just as: *Ray was every bit as good-looking as his brother.*
8 TOOL the sharp part of a tool for cutting or making holes: *a drill bit*
9 HORSE a piece of metal that is put in the mouth of a horse to control its movements

bit² *v.* the past tense of BITE

bitch /bɪtʃ/ *n.* [C] a female dog

bite¹ /baɪt/ *v.* past tense **bit** /bɪt/ past participle **bitten** /ˈbɪt̚n/ present participle **biting** **1** [I,T] to cut or crush something with your teeth: *The dog bit him and made his hand bleed.* | *I had just* ***bitten into*** *the apple.* | *I wish I could stop* ***biting*** *my* ***nails*** (=biting the nails on my fingers). **2** [I,T] if an insect or snake bites you, it injures you by making a hole in your skin [➡ **sting**]: *I think I've been bitten.* | *She was bitten by a rattlesnake.* **3 bite the bullet** to start dealing with a bad situation because you can no longer avoid it: *I finally bit the bullet and called her.* **4 bite sb's head off** *spoken* to speak to someone very angrily, especially when there is no good reason to do this: *I asked if she wanted help, and she bit my head off!* **5 bite your tongue** to not say what you really think, even though you want to **6 bite the dust** *informal* to die, fail, be defeated, or stop working **7 bite off more than you can chew** to try to do more than you are able to do **8** [I] to start having the effect that was intended, especially a bad effect: *The new tobacco taxes have begun to bite.* **9** [I] if a fish bites, it takes food from a hook

bite² *n.* [C] **1** the act of cutting or crushing something with your teeth: *He* ***took a bite*** *of the cheese.* **2** a wound made when an animal or insect bites you [= **sting**]: *I'm covered in mosquito bites!* **3 a bite (to eat)** *informal* a quick meal: *We can* ***grab a bite*** *at the airport before we go.*

ˈbite-size also **ˈbite-sized** *adj.* the right size to fit in your mouth easily: *bite-size pieces of chicken*

bit·ing /ˈbaɪṭɪŋ/ *adj.* **1** a biting wind feels very cold **2** biting criticism or remarks are very unkind

bit·ten /ˈbɪt̚n/ *v.* the past participle of BITE

bit·ter /ˈbɪṭɚ/ *adj.* **1** angry and upset because you feel something bad or unfair has happened to you: *I* ***feel*** *very* ***bitter about*** *what happened.* | *a bitter old man* **2** [only before noun] making you feel very unhappy and upset: *a* ***bitter disappointment*** | *She knew* ***from bitter experience*** *that they wouldn't agree.* **3** a bitter argument, battle, etc. is one in which people oppose or criticize each other with strong feelings of hate or anger: *a bitter legal battle over custody of the children* **4** having a strong taste, like coffee without sugar **5** extremely cold: *a bitter wind* | *We had to walk home in* ***the bitter cold.*** **6 to/until the bitter end** continuing until the end even though this is difficult: *We will **fight until the bitter end** to defend our land.* —**bitterness** *n.* [U]

bit·ter·ly /ˈbɪt̬ɚli/ *adv.* **1** with a lot of anger or sadness: *I was **bitterly disappointed**.* **2 bitterly cold** very cold

bit·ter·sweet /ˌbɪt̬ɚˈswit◂/ *adj.* feelings, memories, or experiences that are bittersweet are happy and sad at the same time: *a bittersweet goodbye*

bi·week·ly /baɪˈwikli/ *adj., adv.* happening or being done every two weeks or twice a month: *a biweekly meeting*

bi·zarre /bɪˈzɑr/ *adj.* very unusual and strange: *a bizarre coincidence*

THESAURUS

strange, **funny**, **peculiar**, **mysterious**, **odd**, **weird**, **eccentric**
→ see Thesaurus box at STRANGE[1]

blab /blæb/ *v.* past tense and past participle **blabbed**, present participle **blabbing** [I] *spoken* to talk too much about something, often something that should be secret: *This is not something you go **blabbing to** your friends about.*

blab·ber·mouth /ˈblæbɚˌmaʊθ/ *n.* [C] *spoken* someone who always talks too much and often says things that should be secret

black[1] /blæk/ *adj.* **1** having a color that is darker than every other color, like the sky at night: *a black dress* | *Outside, it was **pitch black*** (=completely dark). **2 also Black** someone who is black has dark skin, and is from a family that was originally from Africa [➡ **African American**] **3** black coffee does not have milk in it: *I take my coffee black.* **4** sad and without hope for the future: *a mood of black despair* **5 black humor/comedy** humor that makes jokes about serious subjects —**blackness** *n.* [U]

black[2] *n.* **1** [U] the color of the sky at night: *She was wearing black.* **2** [C] **also Black** someone who has dark skin, and whose family originally came from Africa **3 be in the black** to have money in your bank account [≠ **in the red**]

black[3] *v.*

black out *phr. v.* to suddenly become unconscious: *Sharon blacked out and fell to the floor.*

ˌblack and ˈblue *adj.* skin that is black and blue has BRUISES (=dark marks) on it as a result of being hit or injured: *Her leg was black and blue where she had fallen.*

ˌblack and ˈwhite *adj.* **1** showing pictures of images in black, white, and gray [≠ **color**]: *old black and white movies* **2 in black and white a)** written or printed: *The rules are there in black and white.* **b)** in a very simple way, as if there are clear differences between good and bad: *He tends to see the issues in black and white.*

ˈblack belt *n.* [C] a high rank in JUDO or KARATE, or someone who has this rank

black·ber·ry /ˈblækˌbɛri/ *n.* plural **blackberries** [C] a very sweet black or dark purple BERRY

black·bird /ˈblækbɚd/ *n.* [C] a common American and European bird, the male of which is completely black

black·board /ˈblækbɔrd/ *n.* [C] a board with a dark smooth surface, usually in a school, which you write on with CHALK

ˌblack ˈbox *n.* [C] a piece of equipment on an airplane that records what happens on a flight and can be used to discover the cause of accidents

black·en /ˈblækən/ *v.* [I,T] **1** to become black, or to make something black: *Smoke had blackened the kitchen walls.* **2 blacken sb's name/character/reputation etc.** to say unpleasant things about someone so that other people will have a bad opinion of him/her

ˌblack ˈeye *n.* [C] if you have a black eye, you have a dark area around your eye because you have been hit

black·head /ˈblækhɛd/ *n.* [C] a small spot on someone's skin that has a black center

ˌblack ˈhole *n.* [C] *technical* an area in outer space into which everything near it is pulled, including light

TOPIC

space, **meteor**, **asteroid**, **comet**, **moon**, **planet**, **star**, **sun**, **constellation**, **galaxy**, **spacecraft**, **spaceship**, **rocket**, **(space) shuttle**, **satellite**, **probe**, **astronaut**
→ see Topic box at SPACE[1]

black·jack /ˈblækdʒæk/ *n.* [U] a card game, usually played for money, in which you try to get as close to 21 points as possible

black·list /ˈblækˌlɪst/ *v.* [T] to put someone or something on a list of people or things that are considered bad or dangerous: *More than 200 people in the movie industry were blacklisted during the McCarthy era.* —**blacklist** *n.* [C]

ˌblack ˈmagic *n.* [U] magic that is believed to use the power of the Devil for evil purposes

black·mail /ˈblækmeɪl/ *n.* [U] the practice of making someone do what you want by threatening to tell secrets about him/her —**blackmail** *v.* [T] —**blackmailer** *n.* [C]

ˌblack ˈmarket *n.* [C] the system by which people illegally buy and sell foreign money, goods, etc. that are difficult to obtain: *The drug might be available **on the black market**.*

black·out /ˈblækaʊt/ *n.* [C] **1** a period of darkness caused by a failure of the electricity supply: *Several neighborhoods in the San Francisco area experienced blackouts last night.* **2** if someone has a blackout, s/he becomes unconscious **3 also news blackout** a situation in which particular pieces of news or information are not allowed to be reported

ˌblack ˈsheep *n.* [C usually singular] someone who is regarded by other members of his/her family as a failure or embarrassment: *My sister's **the black sheep of the family**.*

black·smith /ˈblæksmɪθ/ *n.* [C] someone who makes and repairs things made of iron

ˌblack-ˈtie *adj.* a party or social event that is black-tie is one at which you have to wear formal clothes

black·top /ˈblæktɑp/ *n.* [C,U] the thick black substance used for covering roads

blad·der /ˈblædɚ/ *n.* [C] the part of your body that holds URINE until it is passed out of your body ➔ see picture on page A3

B

blade /bleɪd/ *n.* [C] **1** the flat cutting part of a knife, tool, or weapon: *The blade is sharp.* | *razor blades* **2** a leaf of grass or a similar plant **3** the flat wide part of an OAR, PROPELLER etc.

blah¹ /blɑ/ *adj. spoken* **1** not very interesting or exciting: *The color of the walls is kind of blah.* **2** slightly sick or unhappy: *I feel really blah today.*

blah² *n.* **blah, blah, blah** *spoken* said when you do not want to say or repeat something because it is boring: *Oh, you know Michelle; it's blah, blah, blah about her kids all the time.*

blame¹ /bleɪm/ *v.* [T] **1** to say or think that someone is responsible for something bad: *Don't blame me – it's not my fault.* | *Mom **blamed** herself **for** Keith's problems.* | *The accident was **blamed on** pilot error.* | *More than one person may be **to blame** for the fire.* **2 I don't blame you/them etc.** *spoken* said when you think it was right or reasonable for someone to do what s/he did: *I don't blame her for not letting her kids see that movie!*

blame² *n.* [U] responsibility for a mistake or for something bad: *Because she's the older child, she usually **gets the blame**.* | *You can't expect Terry to **take** all **the blame**.* | *Fans often **place/put/lay the blame on*** (=say that something is someone's fault, often when this is not true) *the coach when the team fails to win.*

blame·less /ˈbleɪmlɪs/ *adj.* not guilty of anything bad: *blameless behavior*

blanch /blæntʃ/ *v.* [I] *literary* to become pale because you are afraid or shocked

bland /blænd/ *adj.* **1** without any excitement, strong opinions, or special character: *bland TV shows*

> **THESAURUS**
>
> **delicious**, **disgusting**, **horrible**, **awful**, **sweet**, **tasty**, **sour**, **salty**, **hot**, **spicy**
> ➔ see Thesaurus box at TASTE¹

2 bland food has very little taste: *bland cheese*

blank¹ /blæŋk/ *adj.* **1** without any writing, print, or recorded sound: *a blank sheet of paper* | *Are there any blank tapes?* **2 go blank a)** to be suddenly unable to remember something: *My mind went blank as I stood up to speak.* **b)** to stop showing any images, writing, etc.: *The screen suddenly went blank.* **3** showing no expression, understanding, or interest: *I said hello, and she gave me a blank look*

blank² *n.* [C] **1** an empty space on a piece of paper, where you are supposed to write a word or letter: ***Fill in the blanks** on the application form.* **2** a CARTRIDGE (=container for a bullet in a gun) that has an explosive but no bullet: *The police were only firing blanks.* —**blankness** *n.* [U]

ˌblank ˈcheck *n.* [singular] **1** a check that has been signed but has not had the amount written on it **2** *informal* the authority to do whatever you want, without any limits: *Congress **gave** President Johnson **a blank check** to wage war in Vietnam.*

blan·ket¹ /ˈblæŋkɪt/ *n.* **1** [C] a heavy cover that keeps you warm in bed **2** [singular] *literary* a thick covering of something: *a **blanket of snow** on the mountains*

blanket² *adj.* **a blanket statement/rule/ban etc.** a statement, rule, etc. that affects everyone or includes all possible cases: *You shouldn't make blanket statements about all single parents.*

blanket³ *v.* [T] to cover something with a thick layer: *The mountains were **blanketed in** snow.*

blank·ly /ˈblæŋkli/ *adv.* in a way that shows no expression, understanding, or interest: *He was staring blankly at the wall.*

blare /blɛr/ *v.* [I,T] to make a very loud unpleasant noise: *blaring horns* | *a radio **blaring out** music* —**blare** *n.* [singular]

bla·sé /blɑˈzeɪ/ *adj.* not worried or excited about things that most people think are important, impressive, etc.: *He's very blasé about money now that he's got that job.*

blas·phe·mous /ˈblæsfəməs/ *adj.* showing disrespect for God or people's religious beliefs: *a blasphemous book*

blas·phe·my /ˈblæsfəmi/ *n.* [U] something you say or do that is insulting to God or to people's religious beliefs —**blaspheme** /blæsˈfim, ˈblæsfim/ *v.* [I,T]

blast¹ /blæst/ *n.* [C] **1** a sudden strong movement of wind or air: *a **blast of** icy air* **2** an explosion: *The blast was heard three miles away.* | *a bomb blast* **3 a blast** *spoken* an enjoyable and exciting experience: *We **had a blast** at Mitch's party.* **4 full blast** as strongly, loudly, or fast as possible: *She had the TV on full blast.* **5** a sudden very loud noise: *a trumpet blast*

blast² *v.* **1** [I,T] to break something into pieces using explosives: *They **blasted** a tunnel **through** the side of the mountain.* **2** [I,T] **also blast out** to produce a lot of loud noise, especially music: *Dance music blasted out from the stereo.* **3** [T] to attack a place or person with bombs or large guns: *Two gunmen **blasted** their way **into** the building.* **4** [T] to criticize something very strongly: *The President's remarks were quickly blasted by Democratic leaders.*

blast off *phr. v.* if a SPACECRAFT blasts off, it leaves the ground

'blast-off *n.* [U] the moment when a SPACECRAFT leaves the ground

bla·tant /'bleɪt̚nt/ *adj.* very noticeable and offensive: *blatant discrimination* —**blatantly** *adv.*

blaze¹ /bleɪz/ *v.* [I] to burn or shine very brightly and strongly: *a fire blazing in the fireplace*

blaze² *n.* [singular] **1** the strong, bright flames of a fire: *Several firefighters were injured in the blaze.*

> **THESAURUS**
> **fire, flames, inferno, bonfire, campfire**
> ➔ see Thesaurus box at FIRE¹

2 a very bright light or color: *a* ***blaze of*** *sunshine* **3 (in a) blaze of glory/publicity** receiving a lot of praise or public attention: *He launched the new paper in a blaze of publicity.*

blaz·er /'bleɪzɚ/ *n.* [C] a suit JACKET (=piece of clothing like a short coat) without matching pants: *a wool blazer*

blaz·ing /'bleɪzɪŋ/ *adj.* **1** extremely hot: *a blazing summer day* **2** burning strongly: *a* ***blazing fire*** **3** full of strong emotions, especially anger: *blazing eyes*

bleach¹ /blitʃ/ *n.* [U] a chemical used in order to make things white or to kill GERMS

bleach² *v.* [T] to make something white or lighter by using chemicals or the light of the sun: *bleached hair*

bleach·ers /'blitʃɚz/ *n.* [plural] rows of seats where people sit to watch sports

bleak /blik/ *adj.* **1** without anything to make you feel happy or hopeful: *Without a job, the future can seem bleak.* **2** cold and unpleasant: *a bleak November day* —**bleakness** *n.* [U]

blear·y /'blɪri/ *adj.* unable to see clearly because you are tired or have been crying: *Sam woke up looking* ***bleary-eyed.*** —**blearily** *adv.*

bleat /blit/ *v.* [I] to make the sound that a sheep or goat makes —**bleat** *n.* [C]

bleed /blid/ *v.* past tense and past participle **bled** /blɛd/ [I] to lose blood, especially from an injury: *Your nose is bleeding.* | *He* ***bled to death*** *after being shot in the stomach.* —**bleeding** *n.* [U] *The bleeding had almost stopped.*

bleed

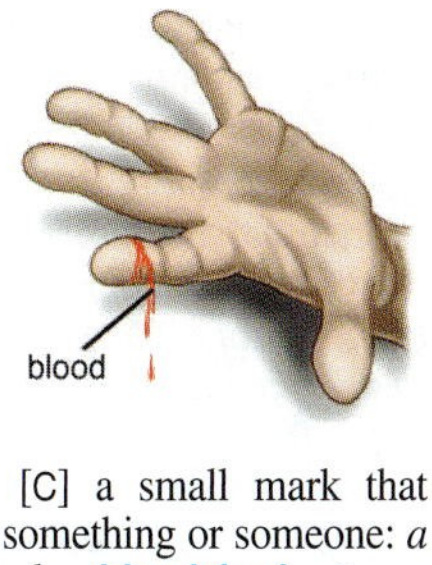

blem·ish /'blɛmɪʃ/ *n.* [C] a small mark that spoils the appearance of something or someone: *a small blemish on her cheek* —**blemished** *adj.*

> **THESAURUS**
> **mark, bruise, scar, pimple, zit, wart, blister, freckle, mole**
> ➔ see Thesaurus box at MARK²

blend¹ /blɛnd/ *v.* [I,T] **1** to mix together soft or liquid substances to form a single smooth substance: ***Blend*** *the eggs* ***with*** *the sugar.* | *Stir in the sauce and* ***blend well.***

> **THESAURUS**
> **mix, combine, stir, beat**
> ➔ see Thesaurus box at MIX¹

2 to combine different things in a way that is attractive or effective: *a story that blends fact and fiction*

blend in *phr. v.* if something blends in with the things around it, it looks similar and you do not notice it: *curtains that* ***blend in with*** *the wallpaper*

blend² *n.* [C] a mixture of two or more things: *the right* ***blend of*** *sunshine and soil for growing grapes*

> **THESAURUS**
> **mixture, combination, compound, solution**
> ➔ see Thesaurus box at MIXTURE

blend·er /'blɛndɚ/ *n.* [C] a small electric machine that you use to mix liquids together, or to make soft foods more liquid

bless /blɛs/ *v.* [T] **1 bless you** *spoken* said when someone SNEEZES **2** to ask God to protect someone or something: *May God bless you and keep you safe from harm.* **3** to make something holy: *The priest blessed the bread and wine.* **4 be blessed with sth** to have a special ability, good quality, etc.: *I'm blessed with good eyesight.* **5 bless him/her etc.** *spoken old-fashioned* said in order to show that you like someone or are pleased by something s/he has done

bless·ed /'blɛsɪd/ *adj.* **1** [only before noun] enjoyable or desirable: *a moment of blessed silence* **2** *formal* holy and loved by God: *the Blessed Virgin Mary*

bless·ing /'blɛsɪŋ/ *n.* **1** [C] something good that improves your life and makes you happy: *The rain was a real blessing after all that heat.* **2** [U] someone's approval or encouragement for a plan, activity, etc.: *She left home* ***with*** *her parents'* ***blessing.*** **3 a mixed blessing** something that is both good and bad: *Living close to the office was a mixed blessing.* **4 a blessing in disguise** something that seems to be bad but that you later realize is good: *The lack of tourism on the island could be a blessing in disguise.* **5** [singular, U] protection and help from God, or the prayer in which you ask for this: *The priest gave the blessing.*

blew /blu/ *v.* the past tense of BLOW

blight /blaɪt/ *n.* [singular, U] something that damages or spoils something else, or the condition of being damaged or spoiled: *an area suffering from* ***urban blight*** (=severe problems that only a city has) —**blight** *v.* [T]

blight·ed /ˈblaɪt̬ɪd/ *adj.* damaged or spoiled: *the blighted downtown area*

blimp /blɪmp/ *n.* [C] an aircraft without wings that looks like a very large BALLOON

blind[1] /blaɪnd/ *adj.* **1** unable to see: *My grandmother is almost **totally blind**. | People with the disease often **go blind*** (=become blind). **2 the blind** people who cannot see: *special facilities for the blind* **3 blind faith/loyalty/hate etc.** *disapproving* strong feelings that you have without thinking about why you have them: *a blind loyalty to the Communist Party* **4 be blind to sth** to completely fail to notice or realize something: *He was blind to the faults of his own children.* **5 turn a blind eye (to sth)** to ignore something that you know should not be happening: *Teachers were turning a blind eye to smoking in the school.* **6 blind corner/bend/curve** a corner, bend, etc. that you cannot see around when you are driving —**blindness** *n.* [U]

B

blind[2] *v.* [T] **1** to make someone unable to see, either permanently or for a short time: *The deer was blinded by our headlights.* **2** to make someone unable to notice or realize the truth about something: *Being in love **blinded** me **to** his faults.*

blind[3] *n.* [C] a piece of cloth or other material that you pull down to cover a window [➡ **Venetian blind**]

ˌ**blind ˈdate** *n.* [C] a DATE (=romantic meeting) arranged between a man and a woman who have not met each other before

blind·fold /ˈblaɪndfoʊld/ *n.* [C] a piece of cloth that you use to cover someone's eyes so that s/he cannot see —**blindfold** *v.* [T]

blind·ing /ˈblaɪndɪŋ/ *adj.* [usually before noun] **a blinding light/flash etc.** a very bright light that makes you unable to see for a short time

> **THESAURUS**
> **bright, strong, dazzling**
> ➔ see Thesaurus box at BRIGHT

blind·ly /ˈblaɪndli/ *adv.* **1** *disapproving* not thinking about something or trying to understand it: *Don't just blindly accept what you are told.* **2** not seeing or noticing what is around you: *She sat **staring blindly** out the window.*

blind·side /ˈblaɪndsaɪd/ *v.* [T] *informal* to hit the side of a car with your car in an accident

ˈ**blind spot** *n.* [C] **1** something that you are unable or unwilling to understand: *He **has a blind spot** when it comes to his daughter's problems.* **2** the part of the road that you cannot see in front of you or in your mirrors when you are driving a car: *The other car was right **in** my **blind spot**.*

bling bling /blɪŋ ˈblɪŋ/ *n.* [U] *informal* expensive things such as jewelry that are worn to be noticed

blink[1] /blɪŋk/ *v.* **1** [I,T] to close and open your eyes quickly: *He blinked as he stepped out into the sunlight.* **2** [I] if a light blinks, it goes on and off continuously: *The answering machine light was blinking.*

blink[2] *n.* **1 in the blink of an eye** very quickly: *With email, we can send messages across the globe in the blink of an eye.* **2 on the blink** *informal* not working correctly: *The radio's on the blink again.*

blink·ers /ˈblɪŋkɚz/ *n.* [plural] the small lights on a car that flash to show which direction you are turning

blip /blɪp/ *n.* [C] **1** a flashing light on the screen of a piece of electronic equipment **2** *informal* a sudden and temporary change from the way something normally happens: *This month's rise in prices could be just a blip.*

bliss /blɪs/ *n.* [U] perfect happiness —**blissful** *adj.* —**blissfully** *adv.* ➔ **ignorance is bliss** at IGNORANCE

blis·ter /ˈblɪstɚ/ *n.* [C] a painful swollen area on the skin containing a clear liquid, caused by a burn or by being rubbed too much: *New shoes always give me blisters.* —**blister** *v.* [I,T]

> **THESAURUS**
> **mark, blemish, bruise, scar, pimple, zit, wart, freckle, mole**
> ➔ see Thesaurus box at MARK[2]

blis·ter·ing /ˈblɪstərɪŋ/ *adj.* **1** extremely hot: *blistering summer days* **2 blistering attack/criticism etc.** very angry and disapproving remarks

blithe /blaɪð, blaɪθ/ *adj.* seeming not to care or worry about the effects of what you do: *the blithe assumption that he would always have a job* —**blithely** *adv.*: *They blithely ignored the danger.*

blitz /blɪts/ *n.* [C] **1** a situation when you use a lot of effort to achieve something, often in a short time: *an advertising blitz* **2** a sudden military attack, especially from the air —**blitz** *v.* [T]

bliz·zard /ˈblɪzɚd/ *n.* [C] a long heavy storm with a lot of wind and snow

> **THESAURUS**
> **snow, snowflakes, sleet, slush, frost, hail, rain, hailstones**
> ➔ see Thesaurus box at SNOW[1]

bloat·ed /ˈbloʊt̬ɪd/ *adj.* looking or feeling larger than usual because of being too full of water, food, gas, etc.: *I feel bloated after that meal.*

blob /blɑb/ *n.* [C] a small drop of a thick liquid: *a **blob of** paint*

bloc /blɑk/ *n.* [C] a large group of people or countries with the same political aims, working together: *the liberal bloc in Congress*

block[1] /blɑk/ *n.*

1 STREETS/AREA [C] **a)** the distance along a city street from where one street crosses it to the next: *We're just two blocks from the bus stop.* **b)** a square area of houses or buildings formed by four streets: *Let's walk around the block. | We* *were the first family* ***on*** *our* ***block*** *to get a swimming pool.*

2 SOLID MATERIAL [C] a solid piece of wood, stone, etc.: *a* ***block of*** *concrete* | *The baby was playing with wooden blocks.*

3 RELATED GROUP [C] a group of things of the same kind or an amount of something, considered as a single unit: *We were given a* ***block of*** *shares in the company.* | *Jason says he can get a* ***block of seats*** (=seats next to each other) *for the concert.*

4 a block of time a length of time that is not interrupted by anything: *Set aside a block of time to do your homework.*

5 UNABLE TO THINK [singular] the temporary loss of your normal ability to think, learn, write, etc.: *I can never remember his name – I must have a* ***mental block****.* | *After her first novel, she had* ***writer's block*** (=she could not write anything).

6 STOPPING MOVEMENT [C] something that makes it difficult to move or progress [➡ **roadblock**]: *The incident could be a* ***block to*** *the peace process.*

7 SPORTS [C] a movement in sports that stops an opponent going forward or moving the ball forward

block² *v.* [T] **1** to prevent people or things from moving through or along a space: *A fallen tree was blocking the road.* | *It looks like the sink is blocked.* | *I tried to get through, but there were too many people* ***blocking*** *my* ***way****.* | *blocked arteries* **2** to be in front of someone so that s/he cannot see something: *A tall man in front of me was* ***blocking*** *my* ***view****.* **3** to stop something happening, developing, or succeeding: *Why did the council block the plan?* **4** to stop a ball, a blow, etc. from getting to where your opponent wants it to go: *He also* ***blocked*** *4* ***shots*** *and scored 6 rebounds*

block sth ⇔ **off** *phr. v.* to close a road or path so that people cannot use it: *The freeway exit has been blocked off.*

block sth ⇔ **out** *phr. v.* **1** to stop light from reaching a place: *Heavy curtains blocked out the light.* **2** to stop yourself from thinking about or remembering something: *Carrie hears what she wants to hear and blocks out the rest.* **3** to decide that you will use a particular time only for a particular purpose: *I try to block out four hours a week for research.*

block·ade /blɑˈkeɪd/ *n.* [C] the action of surrounding an area with soldiers or ships to stop people or supplies leaving or entering a place: *a naval blockade* —**blockade** *v.* [T]

block·age /ˈblɑkɪdʒ/ *n.* [C] something that is blocking a pipe, tube, etc.: *a blockage in the drain*

block·bust·er /ˈblɑkˌbʌstɚ/ *n. informal* [C] a book or movie that is very successful: *Spielberg's new blockbuster*

THESAURUS

bestseller, hit, craze, fad, cult
➔ see Thesaurus box at POPULAR

ˈblock ˌparty *n.* [C] a party that is held in the street for all the people living in the area

blog /blɑg/ *n.* [C] a website that is made up of information about a particular subject, in which the newest information is always at the top of the page

blonde¹, blond /blɑnd/ *adj.* **1** blonde hair is pale or yellow **2** someone who is blond has pale or yellow hair

blonde² *n.* [C] *informal* a woman who has pale or yellow hair: *a good-looking blonde*

blood /blʌd/ *n.* [U] **1** the red liquid that your heart pumps through your body: *She* ***lost*** *a lot of* ***blood*** *in the accident.* | *The Red Cross is asking people to* ***give/donate blood*** (=have blood taken from them for the medical treatment of other people). ➔ see picture at BLEED **2 in cold blood** in a cruel and deliberate way: *He murdered the old man in cold blood.* **3** the family or group to which you belong from the time you are born: *There's French blood on his mother's side.* | *a* ***blood relative*** (=related by birth, not by marriage) **4 new blood** new members in a group or organization who bring new ideas and energy: *We need some new blood in the department.* **5 be/run in sb's blood** to be a strong and natural part of someone's character: *A love of politics was in his blood.* **6 bad blood** feelings of anger and hate between people: *There's been* ***bad blood between*** *them for years.* **7 -blooded** having a particular type of blood: *Fish are cold-blooded.*

ˌblood-and-ˈguts *adj. informal* full of action and violence: *a blood-and-guts horror movie*

ˈblood bank *n.* [C] a place where human blood is kept to be used in hospital treatment

blood·bath /ˈblʌdbæθ/ *n.* [singular] the violent killing of many people at the same time

blood·cur·dling /ˈblʌdˌkɚdl-ɪŋ/ *adj.* extremely frightening: *a bloodcurdling scream*

blood·hound /ˈblʌdhaʊnd/ *n.* [C] a large dog with a very good sense of smell

blood·less /ˈblʌdlɪs/ *adj.* **1** without killing or violence: *a bloodless revolution* **2** extremely pale: *bloodless cheeks*

ˈblood ˌpressure *n.* [U] the force with which blood moves around your body: *a special diet for people with* ***high/low blood pressure***

blood·shed /ˈblʌdʃɛd/ *n.* [U] the killing of people in fighting or a war

blood·shot /ˈblʌdʃɑt/ *adj.* bloodshot eyes look slightly red

blood·stain /ˈblʌdsteɪn/ *n.* [C] a mark or spot of blood —**bloodstained** *adj.*

blood·stream /ˈblʌdstrim/ *n.* [singular] blood as it flows around the body: *Drugs were found* ***in*** *her* ***bloodstream****.*

blood·thirst·y /ˈblʌdˌθɚsti/ *adj.* eager to kill and wound, or enjoying killing and violence: *bloodthirsty attacks*

ˈblood type *n.* [C] one of the groups into which human blood is divided, including A, B, AB, and O

ˈblood ˌvessel *n.* [C] one of the tubes through which blood flows in your body

blood·y /ˈblʌdi/ *adj.* **1** covered in blood, or losing blood: *a bloody nose* **2** with a lot of injuries or killing: *a bloody civil war*

bloom¹ /blum/ *n.* [C,U] a flower or flowers: *lovely yellow blooms* | *roses* ***in bloom*** (=with flowers completely open)

B

bloom² *v.* [I] **1** if a plant or flower blooms, its flowers appear or open **2** to look happy and healthy or successful: *Sheila bloomed like a woman in love.*

bloom·er /ˈblumɚ/ *n.* **late bloomer** *informal* someone who grows or becomes successful at a later age than most people

bloop·er /ˈblupɚ/ *n.* [C] *informal* an embarrassing mistake made in front of other people

blos·som¹ /ˈblɑsəm/ *n.* [C,U] a flower, or all the flowers on trees or bushes: *peach blossoms* ➔ see picture at PLANT¹

blossom² *v.* [I] **1** if trees blossom, they produce flowers: *a blossoming plum tree* **2** to become happier, more beautiful, or successful: *By the end of the year she had* ***blossomed into*** *an excellent teacher.*

blot¹ /blɑt/ *v.* past tense and past participle **blotted**, present participle **blotting** [T] to dry a wet surface by pressing soft paper or cloth on it

blot sth ⇔ **out** *phr. v.* **1** to cover or hide something completely: *Black clouds blotted out the sun.* **2** to forget something, often deliberately: *He tried to blot out the memory of that night.*

blot² *n.* [C] a mark or spot that spoils something or makes it dirty: *ink blots*

blotch /blɑtʃ/ *n.* [C] a pink or red mark on the skin, or a colored mark on something —**blotchy** *adj.*

ˈblotting ˌpaper *n.* [U] soft paper used for drying wet ink on a page

blouse /blaʊs/ *n.* [C] a shirt for a woman or girl: *a summer blouse*

blow¹ /bloʊ/ *v.* past tense **blew** /blu/ past participle **blown** /bloʊn/

1 WIND MOVING [I] if wind or air blows, it moves: *A cold wind was blowing from the east.*

2 WIND MOVING STH [I, T] to move in the wind, or to make something move somewhere in the wind: *Her hair was* ***blowing in*** *the breeze.* | *My ticket* ***blew away***. | *Hundreds of trees were* ***blown down*** *in the storm.* | *The wind must have* ***blown*** *the door* ***shut/open***.

3 USING YOUR MOUTH [I, T] to push air through your mouth: *Renée* ***blew on*** *her soup to cool it a little.* | *I hate people who blow smoke in your face.*

4 VIOLENCE [T] to damage or destroy something violently with an explosion or by shooting: *Part of his leg had been* ***blown off***. | *A bomb like that would* ***blow*** *the building* ***to bits/pieces***.

5 blow your nose to clear your nose by forcing air through it into a cloth or TISSUE (=piece of soft paper)

6 blow sth (up) out of (all) proportion to make something seem much more serious or important than it is: *The health risks had been blown out of proportion.*

7 MAKE A SOUND [I, T] to make a sound by pushing air into a whistle, horn, or musical instrument: *I could hear the train whistle blowing.*

8 ELECTRICITY STOPS [I, T] if an electrical FUSE blows, or a piece of electrical equipment blows a FUSE, the electricity suddenly stops working

9 blow the whistle (on sb) *informal* to tell the public or someone in authority about something wrong that is happening: *He blew the whistle on his colleagues.*

SPOKEN PHRASES

10 LOSE AN OPPORTUNITY [T] *informal* to lose a good opportunity, by making a mistake or being careless: *I* ***blew it*** *by talking too much in the interview.* | *We've* ***blown*** *our* ***chances*** *of getting that contract.*

11 LEAVE [T] *spoken* to leave a place quickly: *Let's* ***blow this joint*** (=leave this place).

12 SPEND MONEY [T] *informal* to spend a lot of money at one time in a careless way: *I blew all the money I won on a trip to Hawaii.*

13 sth blows your mind *informal* to make you feel very surprised and excited about something: *Seeing her again really blew my mind.*

blow sb ⇔ **away** *phr. v. spoken* **1** to completely surprise someone: *It just blows me away how friendly everyone here is.* **2** to kill someone by shooting him/her with a gun: *One move and I'll blow you away!* **3** to defeat someone completely, especially in a game: *Nancy blew away the rest of the skaters.*

blow in *phr. v.* **1 also blow into sth** *informal* to arrive in a place, especially suddenly: *Guess who's just* ***blown into town****?* **2** if a storm or bad weather blows in, it arrives and begins to affect an area

blow sb/sth ⇔ **off** *phr. v. spoken* to treat someone or something as unimportant, for example by not meeting someone or not going to an event: *I blew off my 8 a.m. class again.* | *She blew us off and went out with Jim instead.*

blow sth ⇔ **out** *phr. v.* **1** to blow air on a flame and make it stop burning: *Blow out all the candles.* **2** if a tire blows out, it bursts

blow over *phr. v.* **1** if an argument or a bad situation blows over, it does not seem important anymore or is forgotten: *Many people expected the scandal to blow over in a few days.* **2** if a storm blows over, it comes to an end

blow up *phr. v.* **1 blow** (sth ⇔) **up** to destroy something, or to be destroyed, by an explosion: *A car was blown up near the embassy.* | *Their plane* *blew up in mid-air.* **2 blow** sth ⇔ **up** to fill something with air or gas: *Come and help me blow up the balloons.* **3** to shout angrily at someone: *She **blew up at** me for no reason.* **4 blow** sth ⇔ **up** if you blow up a photograph, you make it larger: *I'd like to have this picture blown up.*

blow² *n.* [C] **1** something very sad and disappointing that happens to you: *Not getting the job was a **blow to** Kate's confidence.* | *The death of their father was **a terrible blow**.* **2** a hard hit with a hand, tool, or weapon: *The victim suffered several **blows to** the head.* **3** the act of blowing air out of your mouth: *One blow and the candles were out.* **4 come to blows** if two people come to blows, they start hitting each other: *They almost **came to blows over** the money.*

ˌblow-by-ˈblow *adj.* **a blow-by-blow account/description etc.** a description of an event that gives all the details exactly as they happened

ˈblow dry *v.* third person singular **blow-dries**, past tense and past participle **blow-dried** [T] to dry hair and give it shape by using a blow dryer

ˈblow ˌdryer *n.* [C] a small electric machine that you hold and use to blow hot air onto your hair in order to dry it

blown /bloʊn/ *v.* the past participle of BLOW

blow·out /ˈbloʊaʊt/ *n.* [C] *informal* **1** an occasion when a TIRE bursts suddenly as a vehicle is moving **2** a big expensive meal or a large party

blow·torch /ˈbloʊˌtɔrtʃ/ *n.* [C] a piece of equipment that produces a small very hot flame, used especially to remove paint

ˈblow-up *n.* [C] **1** a photograph, or part of a photograph, that has been made larger **2** *informal* a sudden loud argument

BLT *n.* [C] **bacon, lettuce, and tomato** the name of a sandwich that contains these foods

blub·ber¹ /ˈblʌbɚ/ *n.* [U] the fat of sea animals, especially WHALES

blubber² *v.* [I] *informal* to cry loudly, especially in a way that annoys people

blud·geon /ˈblʌdʒən/ *v.* [T] to hit someone many times with a heavy object: *He was **bludgeoned to death** with a hammer.*

blue¹ /blu/ *adj.* **1** having the same color as a clear sky during the day: *the blue lake water* | *a **dark/light** blue dress* **2** [not before noun] *informal* sad: *I've been **feeling** kind of **blue** lately.* **3 do sth till you're blue in the face** *informal* to do something a lot but without achieving what you want: *You can argue till you're blue in the face, but I won't change my mind.* ➔ **once in a blue moon** at ONCE¹

blue² *n.* [U] **1** the color of the sky on a clear day: *Carolyn's the one dressed in blue.* | *I like the rich greens and blues of the painting.* **2 blues also the blues** [plural] a slow and sad style of music that came from the African-American culture in the southern U.S.: *a blues singer* **3 out of the blue** *informal* suddenly and without warning: *The letter came completely out of the blue.* **4 have/get the blues** *informal* to feel sad

blue·bell /ˈblubɛl/ *n.* [C] a small plant with blue flowers that grows in the forest

blue·ber·ry /ˈbluˌbɛri/ *n.* plural **blueberries** [C] a small dark blue round BERRY: *blueberry muffins*

blue·bird /ˈbluˌbɚd/ *n.* [C] a small North American wild bird that sings and has a blue back and wings

ˌblue-ˈblooded *adj.* belonging to a royal or NOBLE family —**blue-blood** *n.* [U]

ˈblue book *n.* [C] **1** a book with a blue cover that is used in colleges for writing answers to test questions **2** a book with a list of prices that you should expect to pay for any used car

ˌblue ˈcheese *n.* [C,U] a strong-tasting pale cheese with blue spots in it

ˈblue chip *adj.* **blue chip companies/shares etc.** companies or SHARES that are very unlikely to lose money

ˌblue-ˈcollar *adj.* [only before noun] blue-collar workers do physical work, rather than working in offices [➡ **white-collar**]

blue·grass /ˈblugræs/ *n.* [U] a type of COUNTRY MUSIC from the southern and western U.S., using string instruments such as the VIOLIN or BANJO

blue·jay /ˈbludʒeɪ/ *n.* [C] a common North American wild bird that has blue, black, and white feathers

ˈblue law *n.* [C] *informal* a law that controls activities that are considered immoral, such as drinking alcohol, working on Sundays, etc.

ˌblue ˈmovie *n.* [C] a movie that shows a lot of sexual activity

blue·print /ˈbluˌprɪnt/ *n.* [C] **1** a plan for achieving something: *a **blueprint for** health care reform* **2** a photographic print of a plan for a building, machine, etc. on blue paper

ˌblue ˈribbon *n.* [C] a small piece of blue material given to someone who wins a competition

bluff¹ /blʌf/ *v.* [I,T] to pretend that you are going to do something or that you know something, in order to get what you want: *I don't believe you – I think you're bluffing!*

bluff² *n.* **1** [C,U] an attempt to make someone believe that you are going to do something when you do not really intend to: *He threatened to resign, but I'm sure it's a bluff.* **2 call sb's bluff** to tell someone to do what s/he threatens because you believe s/he has no intention of doing it **3** [C] a very steep cliff or slope: *Pine Bluff, Arkansas.*

blun·der¹ /ˈblʌndɚ/ *n.* [C] a careless or stupid mistake: *a terrible political blunder*

blunder² *v.* [I] **1** to make a careless or stupid mistake: *Police admitted that they blundered when they let Wylie go.* **2** to move forward in an unsteady way, as if you cannot see well

blunt¹ /blʌnt/ *adj.* **1** speaking in an honest way

B

even if it upsets people [➡ **bluntly**]: *Did you have to be so blunt?*

THESAURUS

honest, frank, candid, direct, straightforward, forthright
→ see Thesaurus box at HONEST

2 not sharp or pointed [≠ **sharp**]: *a blunt knife* → see picture at SHARP[1] —**bluntness** *n.* [U]

B

blunt² *v.* [T] to make something less strong: *attempts to try to blunt the impact of anti-smoking laws*

blunt·ly /ˈblʌntˀli/ *adv.* speaking in a direct, honest way that sometimes upsets people: ***To put it bluntly****, you're failing the class.*

blur¹ /blɚ/ *n.* [singular] something that you cannot see clearly or cannot remember clearly: *a blur of horses running past* | *The days following the accident were* ***all a blur****.*

blur² *v.* past tense and past participle **blurred**, present participle **blurring** [I,T] **1** to become difficult to see, or to make something difficult to see, because the edges are not clear: *Tears blurred my vision.* **2** to make the difference between two ideas, subjects, etc. less clear: *Computers have* ***blurred the distinction between*** *learning and play.* —**blurry** *adj.*: *blurry photos*

blurb /blɚb/ *n.* [C] a short description giving information about a book, new product, etc.

blurred /blɚd/ *adj.* **1** not clear in shape, or making it difficult to see shapes: *a blurred image* **2** difficult to understand or remember clearly: *blurred memories*

blurt /blɚt/ *v.* [T] also **blurt out** to say something suddenly and without thinking, usually because you are nervous or excited: *Another student blurted out the answer.*

blush¹ /blʌʃ/ *v.* [I] to become red in the face, usually because you are embarrassed: *Carlos blushes every time he talks to her.*

blush² *n.* **1** [C] the red color on your face that appears when you are embarrassed, confused, or ashamed **2 also blusher** [U] cream or powder used for making your cheeks slightly red or pink

blus·ter¹ /ˈblʌstɚ/ *v.* [I] to talk loudly and behave as if what you are doing is extremely important

bluster² *n.* [U] noisy, proud talk

blus·ter·y /ˈblʌstəri/ *adj.* blustery weather is very windy: *a blustery winter day*

Blvd. the written abbreviation of **boulevard**

B-mov·ie /ˈbi ˌmuvi/ *n.* [C] a cheaply-made movie of low quality

BO, B.O. *n.* [U] *spoken* **body odor** a bad smell from someone's body caused by SWEAT

bo·a con·strict·or /ˈboʊə kənˌstrɪktɚ/ *n.* [C] a large snake that is not poisonous, but kills animals by crushing them

boar /bɔr/ *n.* [C] **1** a male pig **2** a wild pig

board¹ /bɔrd/ *n.*

1 FOR INFORMATION [C] a flat wide piece of wood, plastic, etc. where information is written or shown [➡ **blackboard, bulletin board**]: *The teacher wrote a list of words* ***on the board****.* | *Remember to check the board for dates and times.*

2 FOR PUTTING THINGS ON [C] a flat piece of wood, plastic, etc. that you use for a particular purpose: *a cutting board* | *Where's the chessboard?*

3 GROUP OF PEOPLE [C] a group of people in an organization who make the rules and important decisions: *the local* ***school board*** | *a board meeting* | *a* ***board of*** *directors*

4 FOR BUILDING [C] a long thin flat piece of wood used for making floors, walls, fences, etc.

5 on board on an airplane, ship, etc.: *There were over 1,000 passengers on board.*

6 take sth on board to accept a suggestion, idea, etc. and do something about it: *We'll try to take some of your points on board.*

7 across the board affecting everyone or everything: *Prices have been reduced across the board.*

8 MEALS [U] the meals that are provided for you when you pay to stay somewhere: ***Room and board*** *at the college is $3,000 per semester.*

board² *v.* [I,T] **1** to get on an airplane, ship, train, etc. in order to travel somewhere: *We invite our first class passengers to board the plane now.* **2 be boarding** if an airplane or ship is boarding, passengers are getting on it: *Flight 503 for Toronto is now boarding.*

board sth ⇔ **up** *phr. v.* to cover a window or door with wooden boards: *The house next door has been boarded up for months.*

board·er /ˈbɔrdɚ/ *n.* [C] someone who pays to live in another person's house with some or all of his/her meals provided

ˈboard game *n.* [C] any indoor game in which pieces are moved around a specially designed board made of thick CARDBOARD or wood

'boarding house *n.* [C] a private house where you pay to sleep and eat

'boarding pass *n.* [C] a card that you must show before you get on an airplane or a ship

'boarding school *n.* [C] a school where students live as well as study

board·room /ˈbɔrdrum/ *n.* [C] a room where the important people in a company have meetings

board·walk /ˈbɔrdwɔk/ *n.* [C] a raised path made of wood, usually built next to the ocean

boast¹ /boʊst/ *v.* **1** [I] to talk too much about your own abilities and achievements in a way that annoys other people [= **brag**]: *Scott was **boasting about** winning the game.* **2** [T] if a place boasts something good, the place has it: *The new athletic center boasts an Olympic-sized swimming pool.*

boast² *n.* [C] something you like telling people because you are very proud of it

boast·ful /ˈboʊstfəl/ *adj.* talking too much about your own abilities and achievements —**boastfully** *adv.*

boat /boʊt/ *n.* [C] **1** a vehicle that travels across water [➡ **ship**]: *fishing boats | You can only get to the island **by boat**.* **2 be in the same boat (as sb)** to be in the same unpleasant situation as someone else: *We're all in the same boat, so stop complaining.* ➔ **miss the boat** at MISS¹ ➔ **rock the boat** at ROCK²

'boat ˌpeople *n.* [plural] people who escape from bad conditions in their country in small boats

bob¹ /bɑb/ *v.* past tense and past participle **bobbed**, present participle **bobbing** [I] to move up and down on water: *a boat **bobbing up and down** on the water*

bob² *n.* [C] a way of cutting straight hair so that it hangs to the level of your chin and is the same length all the way around your head ➔ see picture at HAIR

bob·bin /ˈbɑbɪn/ *n.* [C] a small round object that you wind thread onto

'bobby pin *n.* [C] a thin piece of metal that you use to hold your hair in place

bob·cat /ˈbɑbkæt/ *n.* [C] a North American wild cat that has no tail

bob·sled /ˈbɑbslɛd/ *n.* [C] a small vehicle with two long thin metal blades that is used for racing down a special ice track —**bobsled** *v.* [I]

bode /boʊd/ *v.* **bode well/ill** *literary* to be a good or bad sign for the future

bod·ice /ˈbɑdɪs/ *n.* [C] the part of a woman's dress above her waist

bod·i·ly¹ /ˈbɑdl-i/ *adj.* [only before noun] relating to the human body: ***bodily functions*** (=things your body does, especially going to the toilet) | *He did not suffer any **bodily harm**.*

bodily² *adv.* by moving all of your body or someone else's body: *She had to be carried bodily to bed.*

bod·y /ˈbɑdi/ *n.* plural **bodies**
1 PHYSICAL BODY [C] **a)** the physical structure of a person or animal: *a strong healthy body | Your body temperature is higher in the daytime than at night.* **b)** the central part of a person or animal's body, not including the head, arms, legs or wings: *a short body and long legs* **c)** the body of a dead person: *The **body of** a girl had been found in the river.*
2 GROUP OF PEOPLE [C] a group of people who work together for a particular purpose: *the **governing body** of a university | the president of the **student body*** (=all the students in a school or college)
3 body of sth **a)** a large amount of information, knowledge, etc.: *a body of literature | A growing **body of evidence** suggests that the girl committed suicide.* **b)** the main part of something: *The arguments are explained in **the body of the text**.*
4 [U] if your hair has body, it is thick and healthy
5 -bodied **a)** having a particular type of body: *thick-bodied men* **b)** having a particular amount of taste: *full-bodied red wine*
6 VEHICLE [C] the main structure of a vehicle, not including the engine, wheels, etc.: *The body of the airplane was not damaged.*

body building

'body ˌbuilding *n.* [U] an activity in which you do hard physical exercise in order to develop big muscles —**body builder** *n.* [C]

bodyguard

bod·y·guard /ˈbɑdiˌgɑrd/ *n.* [C] a person whose job is to protect an important person

'body ˌlanguage *n.* [U] movements that you make without thinking that show what you are feeling or thinking: *I could tell from his body language that he was nervous.*

'body ˌodor *n.* [C] BO

bod·y·work /ˈbɑdiˌwɚk/ *n.* [U] the frame of a vehicle, not including the engine, wheels, etc.

bog¹ /bɑg, bɔg/ *n.* [C,U] an area of wet, muddy ground

bog² *v.* past tense and past participle **bogged**, present participle **bogging get/be bogged down (in sth)** to become too involved in thinking about or dealing with one particular thing, so that you are not able to make any progress: *Let's not get bogged down in minor details.*

B

bo·gey·man /ˈbʊgiˌmæn/ *n.* [C] ➔ BOOGIE MAN

bog·gle /ˈbɑgəl/ *v.* **the mind boggles/sth boggles the mind** *informal* used in order to say that something is difficult to believe or very confusing: *The paperwork you have to fill out just boggles the mind.*

bo·gus /ˈboʊgəs/ *adj. informal* not true or real, although someone tries to make you think it is; [= **fake**]: *a bogus insurance claim*

bo·he·mi·an /boʊˈhimiən/ *adj.* living in a very informal or relaxed way and not accepting society's rules or behavior: *a bohemian lifestyle* —**bohemian** *n.* [C]

boil¹ /bɔɪl/ *v.* [I,T] **1** if a liquid boils, or if you boil a liquid, it is hot enough for BUBBLES to rise to the surface and for the liquid to change to steam: *Drop the noodles into boiling salted water.* | *Water* ***boils at*** *100 degrees centigrade.* **2** to cook food in boiling water: *Boil the vegetables for 10 minutes.*

> **THESAURUS**
>
> **cook, bake, fry, roast, broil, grill, sauté, steam, deep fry**
> ➔ see Thesaurus box at COOK¹

3 to clean something using boiling water: *Boil the baby's bottles before using them.*

boil down to sth *phr. v.* if a long statement, argument, etc. boils down to a single statement, that statement is the main point or cause: *Think of the money you can make – that's what it all boils down to.*

boil over *phr. v.* **1** to boil and flow over the sides of a pan **2** if a situation or emotion boils over, people begin to get angry

boil² *n.* **1** [singular] the act or state of boiling: ***Bring*** *the soup* ***to a boil*** *and cook for 5 minutes.* | *Wait until the water* ***comes to a boil.*** **2** [C] a painful infected swelling under the skin

boil·er /ˈbɔɪlɚ/ *n.* [C] a container for boiling water that provides heat and hot water in a house or steam in an engine

boil·ing /ˈbɔɪlɪŋ/ **also** **ˌboiling ˈhot** *adj.* extremely hot: *It's* ***boiling hot*** *in here.*

> **THESAURUS**
>
> **hot, scalding, warm, lukewarm**
> ➔ see Thesaurus box at HOT

ˈboiling point *n.* [C] the temperature at which a liquid boils

bois·ter·ous /ˈbɔɪstərəs, ˈbɔɪstrəs/ *adj.* noisy and full of energy: *boisterous children*

bold /boʊld/ *adj.* **1** confident and willing to take risks: *Yamamoto's plan was bold and original.*

> **THESAURUS**
>
> **brave, courageous, daring**
> ➔ see Thesaurus box at BRAVE¹

2 very clear and strong or bright: *wallpaper with bold stripes* **3 in bold (type/print/letters)** printed in letters that are darker and thicker than ordinary printed letters: *All the headings are in bold.* —**boldly** *adv.* —**boldness** *n.* [U]

bo·lo·gna /bəˈloʊni/ *n.* [C] a type of cooked meat often eaten in SANDWICHES

bol·ster /ˈboʊlstɚ/ **also bolster up** *v.* [T] to improve something by giving support and confidence: *She tried to bolster his confidence.*

bolt¹ /boʊlt/ *n.* [C] **1** a piece of metal that you slide across a door or window to close or lock it **2** a screw with a flat head and no point, used with a NUT for fastening two pieces of metal together **3 bolt of lightning** LIGHTNING that appears as a white line in the sky **4** a large long roll of cloth

bolt² *v.* **1** [I] to run away suddenly: *A gun fired, and the horse bolted.* **2** [I,T] to close or lock a door or window with a bolt: *Jason bolted the door and closed the curtains.* **3** [I,T] to fasten two things together using a bolt: *The bench is bolted to the sidewalk.*

bolt³ *adv.* **sit/stand bolt upright** to sit or stand with your back very straight: *Suddenly Dennis sat bolt upright in bed.*

bomb¹ /bɑm/ *n.* [C] **1** a weapon made of material that will explode: ***Bombs*** *were* ***dropped*** *on the city.* | *The* ***bomb went off/exploded*** *near the airport.* **2** *informal* a play, movie, etc. that is not successful **3 the bomb** the ATOMIC BOMB or any NUCLEAR WEAPON **4** a container in which insect poison, paint, etc. is kept under pressure: *a flea bomb* (=used for killing FLEAS)

bomb² *v.* **1** [T] to attack a place with bombs: *Terrorists threatened to bomb the building.* **2** [I,T] *spoken* to fail a test very badly: *I bombed my history test.* **3** [I] if a play, movie, or joke bombs, it is not successful

bom·bard /bɑmˈbɑrd/ *v.* [T] **1** to attack a place for a long time with guns and bombs: *The town was bombarded from all sides.* **2** to ask a lot of questions or give a lot of information or criticism, so that is is difficult for someone to deal with: *Viewers* ***bombarded*** *the TV station* ***with*** *complaints.* —**bombardment** *n.* [C]

bom·bas·tic /bɑmˈbæstɪk/ *adj. disapproving* bombastic language contains long words that sound important but have no real meaning

bomb·er /ˈbɑmɚ/ *n.* [C] **1** an airplane that carries and drops bombs **2** someone who puts a bomb somewhere: *a* ***suicide bomber*** (=someone who carries a bomb and allows himself or herself to be killed when the bomb explodes)

bomb·shell /'bɑmʃɛl/ *n.* [C] *informal* a shocking piece of news: *Last night she* ***dropped the bombshell*** *and told him she wouldn't marry him.*

bo·na fide /'boʊnə ˌfaɪd, 'bɑnə-/ *adj.* real, true, and not pretending to be something else: *a bona fide job offer*

bo·nan·za /bə'nænzə, boʊ-/ *n.* [C] a lucky or successful situation in which people can make a lot of money: *The discovery could represent an amazing cash bonanza.*

bond[1] /bɑnd/ *n.* **1** [C] a shared feeling or interest that unites people: *a strong* ***bond*** *of affection* ***between*** *the two women | Marilyn's* ***bond with*** *her mother was unusually strong.* **2** [C] an official document promising that a government or company will pay back money that it has borrowed, often with INTEREST: *U.S. savings bonds* **3** [C, U] money given to a court of law so that someone can be let out of prison while s/he waits for his/her TRIAL [**= bail**]: *His lawyers* ***posted*** *the $100,000* ***bond****, and he was released.*

bond[2] *v.* [I] **1** to develop a special relationship with someone: *It takes a few months for new mothers to* ***bond with*** *their babies.* **2** if two things bond to each other, they become firmly stuck together

bond·age /'bɑndɪdʒ/ *n.* [U] a situation in which people have no freedom [➡ **slavery**]

bond·ing /'bɑndɪŋ/ *n.* [U] a process by which a special close relationship develops between people: ***male bonding*** *|* ***female bonding***

bone[1] /boʊn/ *n.* [C] **1** one of the hard parts that form the frame of a human or animal body: *She* ***broke*** *two* ***bones*** *in her arm. | the thigh bone* **2 make no bones about (doing) sth** to not feel nervous or ashamed about doing or saying something: *She makes no bones about her religious beliefs.* **3 be chilled/frozen to the bone** to be extremely cold **4 a bone of contention** something that causes arguments between people

bone[2] *v.* [T] to remove the bones from fish or meat

bone up on sth *phr. v. informal* to study something a lot for an examination: *I should bone up on grammar before the test.*

ˌbone 'dry *adj.* completely dry

'bone ˌmarrow *n.* [U] the soft substance in the hollow center of bones: *a bone marrow transplant*

bon·fire /'bɑnˌfaɪɚ/ *n.* [C] a large outdoor fire

> **THESAURUS**
>
> **fire, flames, blaze, inferno, campfire**
> ➔ see Thesaurus box at FIRE[1]

bon·gos /'bɑŋgoʊz/ **also 'bongo ˌdrums** *n.* [plural] a pair of small drums that you play with your hands

bon·kers /'bɑŋkɚz/ *adj.* [not before noun] slightly crazy: *I'd* ***go bonkers*** *if I had to stay at home with the kids all day.*

bon·net /'bɑnɪt/ *n.* [C] a hat that ties under the chin, worn by babies and by women in the past

bo·nus /'boʊnəs/ *n.* [C] **1** money added to someone's pay, especially as a reward for good work: *a Christmas bonus | a $2,000 bonus* **2** something good that you did not expect in a situation: *The fact that our house is so close to the school is a bonus.*

bon·y /'boʊni/ *adj.* **1** very thin: *a bony hand* **2** full of bones: *bony fish*

B

boo[1] /bu/ *v.* [I,T] to shout BOO to show that you do not like a person, performance, etc.

boo[2] *n.* [C] a noise made by people who do not like a person, performance, etc.

boo[3] *interjection* a word you shout suddenly to someone to try to frighten him/her as a joke

boob /bub/ *n.* [C] *slang* a woman's breast

'boo-boo *n.* [C] a silly mistake

'boob tube *n.* **the boob tube** *disapproving* television

'booby prize *n.* [C] a prize given as a joke to the person who is last in a competition

'booby trap *n.* [C] a hidden bomb that explodes when you touch something else that is connected to it —**booby-trapped** *adj.*

boog·ie man /'bʊgi ˌmæn/ *n.* [C] an imaginary man who frightens children

book[1] /bʊk/ *n.* [C] **1** a set of printed pages held together in a cover so that you can read them: *I'm* ***reading*** *a good* ***book****. | a* ***book by*** *William Faulkner | a* ***book about*** *photography*

> **THESAURUS**
>
> **Types of books**
> **nonfiction** – books which describe real things or events
> **fiction** – books which describe imaginary events
> **literature** – fiction that people think is important
> **reference book** – a book such as a dictionary or encyclopedia that you look at to find specific information
> **text book** – a book that is used in the classroom
> **hardcover/hardback** – a book which has a hard stiff cover
> **paperback** – a book which has a soft cover
> **novel** – a book about imaginary events
> **science fiction** – a book about imaginary events in the future or space travel
> **biography** – a book about a real person's life, written by another person
> **autobiography** – a book about someone's life, written by that person himself or herself

2 a set of sheets of paper held together in a cover so that you can write on them: *an* ***address book*** **3** a set of things such as stamps, tickets, etc. held together inside a paper cover: *a* ***book of*** *matches* **4 books** [plural] written records of the financial accounts of a business **5 by the book** exactly according to rules or instructions: *They do everything **strictly by the book**.* → **throw the book at sb** at THROW

book² *v.* **1** [T] to arrange for someone such as a speaker or singer to perform on a particular date: *They have a speaker booked for next Tuesday.* **2** [I,T] to arrange to stay at a hotel, fly on an airplane, etc. at a particular time in the future: *I've **booked a room** for us at the Hilton.* | *The flight is **fully-booked*** (=has no seats left). **3** [T] to put someone's name officially in police records, with the charge made against him/her: *Ramey was booked on suspicion of murder.*

B

book·case /ˈbʊk-keɪs/ *n.* [C] a piece of furniture with shelves to hold books

book·end /ˈbʊkɛnd/ *n.* [C] one of a pair of objects that you put at each end of a row of books to prevent them from falling

book·ie /ˈbʊki/ *n.* [C] *informal* someone whose job is to collect money that people BET on a race, sport, etc. and who pays them if they win

book·ing /ˈbʊkɪŋ/ *n.* [C] an arrangement in which a hotel, theater, etc. agrees to let you have a particular room, seat, etc. at a future time: *Cheaper prices are available on early bookings.*

book·keep·ing /ˈbʊkˌkipɪŋ/ *n.* [U] the job or activity of recording the financial accounts of an organization —**bookkeeper** *n.* [C]

book·let /ˈbʊklɪt/ *n.* [C] a very short book that contains information: *a booklet on AIDS*

book·mark /ˈbʊkmɑrk/ *n.* [C] **1** a piece of paper that you put in a book to show you the last page you have read **2** a way of saving the address of a page on the Internet so that you can find it easily

book·shelf /ˈbʊkʃɛlf/ *n.* plural **bookshelves** /-ʃɛlvz/ [C] a shelf on a wall or a piece of furniture with shelves, used for holding books

book·store /ˈbʊkstɔr/ *n.* [C] a store that sells books

book·worm /ˈbʊkwɚm/ *n.* [C] *informal disapproving* someone who likes to read very much

boom¹ /bum/ *n.* [C] **1** a sudden increase in business activity or the popularity of something [≠ **slump**]: *a boom in sales* | *the economic boom of the 1950s* **2** a loud deep sound that you can hear for several seconds after it begins: *the boom of guns in the distance*

boom² *v.* **1** [I] if business or the economy is booming, it is very successful and growing quickly: *We're happy to report that business is booming this year.* **2** [I] to make a loud deep sound —**booming** *adj.*: *a booming economy* → BABY BOOM

ˈboom box *n.* [C] *informal* a piece of electronic equipment which has a radio, CD player, TAPE RECORDER, etc. and which you carry with you so that you can listen to music

boo·mer·ang /ˈbuməˌræŋ/ *n.* [C] a curved stick that comes back to you when you throw it

ˈboom town *n.* [C] *informal* a city that suddenly becomes very successful because of new industry

boon /bun/ *n.* [C] *literary* something that is very useful and makes your life a lot easier: *websites that are a **boon for** busy students*

boon·docks /ˈbundɑks/ **also boo·nies** /ˈbuniz/ *n. informal* **the boondocks/boonies** [plural] a place that is a long way from any town

boor /bʊr/ *n.* [C] someone who behaves in an unacceptable way in social situations —**boorish** *adj.*

boost¹ /bust/ *n.* **1** [singular] something that helps someone be more successful and confident, or that helps something increase or improve: *Immigrants provide a **boost to** the U.S. economy.* | *a good publicity **boost for** his campaign* | *a **boost from** extra vitamins* **2 give sb a boost** to lift or push someone so s/he can get over or onto something high or tall

boost² *v.* [T] **1** to increase or improve something and make it more successful: *The new facility will help boost oil production.* | *The win **boosted** the team's **confidence**.* **2** to help someone get over or onto something high or tall by lifting or pushing him/her up

boost·er /ˈbustɚ/ *n.* [C] **1** a small quantity of a drug that increases the effect of one that was given before: *a measles booster shot* **2 confidence/morale/ego etc. booster** something that increases or improves someone's confidence, etc.: *Letters from home are a great **morale booster** for the soldiers.* **3** someone who gives a lot of support to a person, organization, or idea: *fund raisers organized by the school's booster club* **4** a ROCKET that provides more power for a SPACECRAFT

boot¹ /but/ *n.* [C] **1** a type of shoe that covers your whole foot and the lower part of your leg: *hiking boots* → see picture at SHOE¹ **2 to boot** *spoken* used at the end of a list of remarks to emphasize the last one: *Jack's tall, handsome, and rich to boot.*

boot² *v.* **1** [I,T] **also boot up** to make a computer ready to be used by putting in its instructions **2** [T] *informal* to force someone to leave a place, job, or organization: *Offenders are **booted out of/from** the dorms.*

ˈboot camp *n.* [C] a training camp for people who have joined the Army, Navy, or Marines

boot·ee /ˈbuṭi/ *n.* [C] a sock that a baby wears instead of a shoe

booth /buθ/ *n.* [C] **1** a small, partly enclosed place where one person can do something privately: *a phone booth* | *a voting booth* **2** a partly enclosed place in a restaurant with a table between two long seats **3** a place at a market or FAIR where you can buy things, play games, or find information

boot·leg /ˈbut˥lɛg/ *adj.* bootleg products are made and sold illegally —**bootlegging** *n.* [U] —**bootlegger** *n.* [C]

boot·straps /ˈbutˌstræps/ *n.* **pull yourself up by your bootstraps** to get out of a difficult situation by your own effort

boo·ty /ˈbuṭi/ *n.* [U] *literary* valuable things taken or won by the winners in a war, competition, etc.

booze[1] /buz/ *n.* [U] *informal* alcoholic drinks

booze[2] *v.* [I] *informal* to drink a lot of alcohol —**boozer** *n.* [C]

bop[1] /bɑp/ *v.* past tense and past participle **bopped**, present participle **bopping** [I] to hit someone gently

bop[2] *n.* [C] **1** a gentle hit **2** ➔ BEBOP

bor·der[1] /ˈbɔrdɚ/ *n.* [C] **1** the official line that separates two countries, states, or areas: *the* ***border between*** *the U.S. and Mexico | the smuggling of drugs* ***across the border*** *| Mexico's* ***border with*** *Guatemala* **2** a band along the edge of something such as a picture or piece of material: *a skirt with a red border*

THESAURUS

edge, rim, margin
➔ see Thesaurus box at EDGE[1]

border[2] *v.* [T] **1** to share a border with another country: *Spain borders Portugal.* **2** to form a line around the edge of something: *willow trees bordering the river*

border on sth *phr. v.* to be very close to reaching an extreme feeling or quality: *She stared at him with a fear bordering on terror.*

bor·der·line[1] /ˈbɔrdɚˌlaɪn/ *adj.* very close to being unacceptable: *His grades are borderline.*

borderline[2] *n.* **1** [singular] the point at which one quality, condition, etc. ends and another begins: *The stories are on the borderline between romance and pornography.* **2** [C] a border between two countries

bore[1] /bɔr/ *v.* the past tense of BEAR

bore[2] *v.* **1** [T] to make someone feel bored: *The classes bored me.* **2** [I,T] to make a deep round hole in a hard surface: *To build the tunnel they had to* ***bore through*** *solid rock.*

THESAURUS

pierce, make a hole in, prick, punch, drill
➔ see Thesaurus box at PIERCE

3 [I] if someone's eyes bore into you or through you, s/he looks at you in a way that makes you feel nervous or afraid

bore[3] *n.* **1** [C] someone who talks too much about the same things: *Ralph is such a bore!* **2** [singular] something you have to do but do not like: *Ironing is a real bore.*

bored /bɔrd/ *adj.* tired and impatient because you do not think something is interesting, or because you have nothing to do: *I ignored him, hoping he'd* ***get bored*** *and leave. | I was* ***bored with*** *school. | I'm so bored!* ▶ Don't say "I'm so boring." ◀

bore·dom /ˈbɔrdəm/ *n.* [U] the feeling you have when you are bored

bor·ing /ˈbɔrɪŋ/ *adj.* not interesting in any way: *a boring book*

THESAURUS

dull – not interesting or exciting: *a dull lecture*
tedious – boring, and continuing for a long time: *Removing the wallpaper was a long, tedious task.*
not (very/that/all that) interesting: *The book wasn't all that interesting.*
monotonous – boring and always the same: *Every song on the album is monotonous.*
➔ INTERESTING

born /bɔrn/ *adj.* **1 be born** when a person or animal is born, it comes out of its mother's body or out of an egg: *We saw a lamb being born. | I was* ***born in*** *the South. | Lincoln was* ***born on*** *February 12.* **2 be born to do/be sth** to be very good at doing a particular job, activity, etc.: *Mantle was born to play baseball.* **3 born leader/teacher etc.** someone who has a natural ability to lead, teach, etc. **4** something that is born starts to exist: *Unions were* ***born out of*** (=started because of) *a need for better working conditions.*

ˈborn-again *adj.* **born-again Christian** someone who has become an EVANGELICAL Christian after having an important religious experience

borne /bɔrn/ *v.* the past participle of BEAR

bor·ough /ˈbɚoʊ, ˈbʌroʊ/ *n.* [C] a town or part of a large city that is responsible for managing its own schools, hospitals, roads, etc.

bor·row /ˈbɑroʊ, ˈbɔroʊ/ *v.* [I,T] **1** to use something that belongs to someone else and give it back to him/her later [➡ **lend**]: *Can I borrow your bike? | Wallace* ***borrowed*** *money* ***from*** *his father to start a business. | They* ***borrowed heavily*** (=borrowed a lot of money) *to cover their losses.*

USAGE

If you **lend** something to someone, you give it to him/her so that s/he can use it for a short time: *I lent that DVD to Rick. | Could you lend me some money?* You cannot say "Could you borrow me some money?"
If you **borrow** something from someone, you take something that belongs to him/her for a short time, with his/her permission, and then give it back: *Can I borrow your dictionary?* You cannot say "Can I lend your dictionary?"

2 to take or copy ideas or words: *English has* ***borrowed*** *many words* ***from*** *French.* —**borrower** *n.* [C]

bor·row·ings /ˈbɑroʊɪŋz, ˈbɔ-/ *n.* [plural] the total amount of money that a person, company, or organization has borrowed, usually from a bank

bos·om /ˈbʊzəm/ *n.* [C] **1** *written* a woman's

chest **2 bosom buddy** *informal* a very close friend

boss[1] /bɔs/ *n.* **1** [C] the person who employs you or who is in charge of your work: *The boss let us leave early today.* **2** [singular, U] the person who is the strongest in a relationship, who controls a situation, etc.: *You have to **let** the dog **know who's boss*** (=show that you are in control).

boss[2] *v.* [T] **also boss around** to tell people to do things, give them orders, etc., especially when you have no authority to do it: *She's always bossing her brother around.*

B

boss·y /ˈbɔsi/ *adj.* always telling other people what to do, in a way that is annoying: *her bossy older sister*

bot·a·ny /ˈbɑt˺n-i/ *n.* [U] the scientific study of plants —**botanist** *n.* [C] —**botanical** /bəˈtænɪkəl/ *adj.*: *botanical gardens*

botch /bɑtʃ/ **also botch up** *v.* [T] *informal* to do something badly because you were careless or did not have the skill to do it well: *The police botched the investigation.*

both /boʊθ/ *quantifier, pron.* **1** used in order to talk about two people or things together: *They both have good jobs.* | *Hold it in both hands.* | ***Both of** my grandfathers are farmers.* **2 both ... and ...** used in order to emphasize that something is true of two people, things, situations, etc.: *Dan plays both football and basketball.* **3 have it both ways** *disapproving* used when someone wants the advantages from two situations that cannot exist together

GRAMMAR

both, both of

Do not say "The both men were killed." Say *Both of the men were killed*, *Both men were killed*, or *Both the men were killed.*

Do not say "his both sisters." Say *both of his sisters* or *both his sisters.*

both·er[1] /ˈbɑðɚ/ *v.* **1** [I,T] to annoy someone, especially by interrupting what s/he is doing: *Don't bother your dad; he's working.* **2** [I,T] to make someone feel slightly worried, upset, or frightened: *Being in a crowd really bothers me.* | *It **bothered** her **that** he'd forgotten her birthday.* **3** [I,T] to make the effort to do something: *He hadn't bothered unpacking.* | *I'll never get the job, so **why bother** applying?* | *Only 58% of Americans even **bothered to** vote.* **4 sorry to bother you** *spoken* said in order to politely interrupt what someone is doing: *Sorry to bother you, but I have a question.* **5** [T] if a part of your body bothers you, it is slightly painful

bother[2] *n.* [U] someone or something that slightly annoys or upsets you: *"Thanks for your help." "That's okay; **it's no bother**"* (=used in order to say you were happy to help)." —**bothersome** *adj.*

bot·tle[1] /ˈbɑtl̩/ *n.* [C] **1** a container with a narrow top for keeping liquids in, usually made of glass or plastic: *a wine bottle* | *a baby's bottle* **2** the amount of liquid that a bottle contains: *We drank the entire bottle.* **3 hit the bottle** to start drinking a lot of alcohol regularly

bottle[2] *v.* [T] to put a liquid into a bottle after you have made it: *wine bottled in California*

bottle sth ⇔ **up** *phr. v.* to not allow yourself to show strong feelings or emotions: *He keeps his rage and frustration bottled up.*

bottled /ˈbɑtl̩d/ *adj.* **bottled water/beer etc.** water, beer, etc. that is sold in a bottle

bot·tle·neck /ˈbɑtl̩ˌnɛk/ *n.* [C] **1** a place in a road where the traffic cannot pass easily, so that cars are delayed **2** a delay in part of a process that makes the whole process take longer: *Phillips didn't return calls, causing a bottleneck in the negotiations.*

bot·tom[1] /ˈbɑt̬əm/ *n.* [C] **1** the lowest part of something [≠ **top**]: *the **bottom of** the hill* | *The fruit **at the bottom of** the basket was spoiled.* **2** the flat surface on the lowest side of an object: *What's **on the bottom of** your shoe?* **3** the lowest position in an organization or company, or on a list, etc. [≠ **top**]: *He started **at the bottom**, and now he manages the store.* | *Tony is **at the bottom of** the class in reading.* **4** *informal* a word meaning the part of your body that you sit on, used especially when talking to children **5** the ground under an ocean, river, etc., or the flat land in a valley: *The **bottom of** the river is rocky.* | *a ship **on/at the bottom of** the bay* **6 also bottoms** the part of a set of clothes that you wear on the lower part of your body: *pajama bottoms* **7 get to the bottom of sth** *informal* to find the cause of a problem or situation: *We will get to the bottom of this and find out who was responsible.* → ROCK BOTTOM

bottom[2] *adj.* in the lowest place or position: *the bottom drawer*

bottom[3] *v.*

bottom out *phr. v.* if a situation, price, etc. bottoms out, it stops getting worse or lower, usually before it starts improving again: *The recession seems to have bottomed out.*

bot·tom·less /ˈbɑt̬əmlɪs/ *adj.* **1** extremely deep **2** seeming to have no end: *a bottomless supply of money*

ˌbottom ˈline *n.* **the bottom line a)** the main fact about a situation, or the most important thing to consider: ***The bottom line is** that we have to win this game.* **b)** the profit or the amount of money that a business makes or loses

bough /baʊ/ *n.* [C] *literary* a main branch on a tree

bought /bɔt/ *v.* the past tense and past participle of BUY

boul·der /ˈboʊldɚ/ *n.* [C] a large stone or piece of rock

bou·le·vard /ˈbʊləvɑrd, ˈbu-/ *n.* [C] a wide road in a town or city

bounce[1] /baʊns/ *v.* **1** [I,T] if a ball or other object bounces, or you bounce it, it hits a surface and then immediately moves away from it: *The ball **bounced off** the rim.* | *The molecules start **bouncing around** when the solution is heated.* | *In basketball, you have to bounce the ball while you run.* **2** [I] to move up and down, especially because you are walking or jumping on a surface that is made of rubber, has springs, etc.: *Stop **bouncing on** the bed!* ➔ see picture at JUMP[1] **3** [I,T] if a check bounces, or a bank bounces a check, the bank will not pay any money because there is not enough money in the account of the person who wrote it **4** [I] to walk quickly and with a lot of energy: *The kids came bouncing down the stairs.* **5** [I,T] if an email that you send bounces or is bounced, it is returned to you and the other person does not receive it **6 bounce ideas off sb** to ask someone for his/her opinion about an idea, plan, etc. before you decide something

bounce around (sth) *phr. v.* to move quickly from one place to another: *Davidson bounced around the league.* | *They bounced around quite a bit before ending up here.*

bounce back *phr. v.* to feel better quickly, or to become successful again after having a lot of problems: *Experts expect the economy to bounce back.*

bounce[2] *n.* **1** [C] an act of bouncing: *Catch the ball on the first bounce.* **2** [U] the ability to bounce

bounc·er /ˈbaʊnsɚ/ *n.* [C] someone whose job is to make people who behave badly leave a club, BAR, etc.

bounc·ing /ˈbaʊnsɪŋ/ *adj.* healthy and active – used especially about babies: *a bouncing baby boy*

bounc·y /ˈbaʊnsi/ *adj.* **1** able to bounce or be bounced easily: *a bouncy ball* **2** happy and full of energy

bound[1] /baʊnd/ *v.* the past tense and past participle of BIND

bound[2] *adj.* **1 be bound to do sth** to be certain to do something: *People are bound to spell your name wrong.* **2** having a legal or moral duty to do something: *The company is **bound by** law to provide safety equipment.* | *He felt **duty bound** to help his parents.* **3 fog-bound/wheelchair-bound/tradition-bound etc.** controlled or limited by something, so that you cannot do what you want: *a fog-bound airport* **4** intending to go in a particular direction or to a particular place: *a plane **bound for** Peru* | *homeward bound* **5 bound and determined** determined to do or achieve something, even if it is difficult: *Klein is bound and determined to win at least five races this year.*

bound[3] *v.* **1 be bounded by sth** if a place is bounded by something such as a wall, river, road, etc., it has the wall, etc. at its edge: *a valley bounded by high mountains* **2** [I] to move quickly and with a lot of energy: *George came **bounding down** the stairs.*

bound[4] *n.* **1 bounds** [plural] legal or social limits or rules: *His imagination **knows no bounds*** (=has no limits). | *The police acted **within/beyond the bounds** of the law* (=they acted legally or illegally). **2 out of bounds a)** if a subject is out of bounds, you are not allowed to talk about it: *Questions about his personal life will be out of bounds.* **b)** if a place is out of bounds, you are not allowed to go there **3 in bounds/out of bounds** inside or outside the legal playing area in some sports **4** [C] a long or high jump made with a lot of energy

bound·a·ry /ˈbaʊndəri, -dri/ *n.* plural **boundaries** [C] **1** the line that marks the edge of a surface, space, or area of land inside a country [➡ **border**]: *The Mississippi forms a natural **boundary between** Tennessee and Arkansas.* **2** the limit of what is acceptable or thought to be possible: *the **boundaries of** human knowledge*

bound·less /ˈbaʊndlɪs/ *adj.* without any limits or end: *boundless optimism*

boun·ty /ˈbaʊnti/ *n.* **1** [U] *literary* a generous amount of something, especially food **2** [C] money that is given as a reward for catching a criminal —**bountiful** *adj.*: *a bountiful harvest*

bouquet

a bouquet of flowers

bou·quet /boʊˈkeɪ, bu-/ *n.* **1** [C] a group of flowers given to someone as a present or carried at a formal occasion **2** [C,U] the smell of a wine: *a rich bouquet*

bour·bon /ˈbɚbən/ *n.* [U] a type of American WHISKEY made from corn

bour·geois /bʊrˈʒwɑ, ˈbʊrʒwɑ/ *adj. disapproving* too interested in having a lot of possessions and a high position in society

bour·geoi·sie /ˌbʊrʒwɑˈzi/ *n.* **the bourgeoisie** the MIDDLE CLASS

bout /baʊt/ *n.* [C] **1** a short period of time during which you do something a lot or suffer from a particular illness: *a drinking bout* | *a **bout of** the flu* **2** a BOXING or WRESTLING competition

bou·tique /buˈtik/ *n.* [C] a small store that sells very fashionable clothes or decorations

THESAURUS

store, bookstore, clothes store, record store, grocery store, supermarket, bakery, delicatessen, deli, liquor store, drugstore, hardware store, nursery, garden center, newsstand, convenience store, department store, chain store, superstore, outlet store, warehouse store

➔ see Thesaurus box at STORE[1]

B

bo·vine /ˈboʊvaɪn/ *adj. technical* relating to cows, or like a cow

bow¹ /baʊ/ *v.* [I,T] to bend your head or the top part of your body forward, as a sign of respect or as a way of thanking an AUDIENCE after you perform: *He bowed, then began to play.* | *David* ***bowed*** *his* ***head*** *in prayer.*

bow down *phr. v.* to bend forward from your waist, especially when you are already kneeling, in order to pray: *Old women bowed down before the statue of Mary.*

bow out *phr. v.* to decide not to take part in something any longer: *Two more Republicans have* ***bowed out of*** *the race.*

bow to sb/sth *phr. v.* to finally agree to do something that other people want you to do, even though you do not want to: *Congress may bow to public pressure and reduce the gas tax.*

bow² /boʊ/ *n.* [C] **1** a knot of cloth or string with a curved part on each side: *a girl with a red bow in her hair* **2** a tool used for shooting ARROWS, made of a piece of wood held in a curve by a tight string **3** a long thin piece of wood with hair stretched tightly from one end to the other, used for playing STRING instruments

bow³ /baʊ/ *n.* [C] **1** the act of bending the top part of your body forward, as a sign of respect or to thank an AUDIENCE: *The actors* ***took a bow*** (=bowed) *and the curtain came down.* **2** the front part of a ship

bow⁴ /boʊ/ *v.* [I] to bend or curve

bow·el /ˈbaʊəl/ *n.* [C usually plural] the part of the body below the stomach where food is made into solid waste material

bowl¹ /boʊl/ *n.* [C] **1** a wide round container that is open at the top, used for holding liquids, food, etc.: *Mix the eggs and butter in a large bowl.* | *a soup bowl* **2 also bowlful** the amount that a bowl will hold: *a* ***bowlful of*** *rice* **3** a part of an object that is shaped like a bowl: *a toilet bowl* **4 also Bowl** a special game played by two of the best football teams after the normal playing season: *the Rose Bowl*

bowl² *v.* [I,T] to play the game of BOWLING

bowl sb ⇔ **over** *phr. v.* to surprise, please, or excite someone very much: *She was bowled over by her visit to the campus.*

bow-leg·ged /ˈboʊˌlɛgɪd, -ˌlɛgd/ *adj.* having legs that curve out at the knee

bowl·ing /ˈboʊlɪŋ/ *n.* [U] an indoor game in which you roll a heavy ball to try to knock down a group of objects shaped like bottles: *Let's* ***go bowling!***

ˈbowling ˌalley *n.* [C] a building where you can go bowling

bow tie /ˈboʊ taɪ/ *n.* [C] a short piece of cloth tied in the shape of a BOW, which men wear around their necks

box¹ /bɑks/ *n.* [C] **1** a container for putting things in, especially one with four stiff, straight sides: *a cardboard box* | *I put all her things* ***in a box.*** **2** the amount that a box can hold: *a* ***box of*** *candy* **3** a small area in a larger space such as a theater or court: *the jury box* **4** a small area on an official form for people to write information in: *Write your name in the box at the top.* **5** a P.O. BOX

box² *v.* **1** [I,T] to fight someone as a sport while wearing big leather GLOVES **2** [T] to put things in a box or in boxes: *a boxed set of Sinatra's recordings*

box sb/sth ⇔ **in** *phr. v.* to enclose someone or something in a small space where it is not possible to move freely: *A Honda was parked behind me, boxing me in.*

box·car /ˈbɑkskɑr/ *n.* [C] a railroad car with high sides and a roof, that is used for carrying goods

box·er /ˈbɑksɚ/ *n.* [C] **1** someone who boxes, especially as a job: *a heavyweight boxer* **2** a dog with short light brown hair and a flat nose

ˈboxer ˌshorts *n.* [plural] loose underwear for men ➔ see picture at CLOTHES

box·ing /ˈbɑksɪŋ/ *n.* [U] the sport of fighting while wearing big leather GLOVES

ˈbox ˌoffice *n.* [C] a place in a theater, concert hall, etc. where tickets are sold

TOPIC

theater, go to the theater, see a play/musical/opera/ballet, reserve tickets, seat, the floor, balcony, program, audience, orchestra, stage, intermission
➔ see Topic box at THEATER

ˈbox spring *n.* [C] a base containing metal springs that you put under a MATTRESS to make a bed

boy¹ /bɔɪ/ *n.* [C] **1** a male child or young man: *a club for both boys and girls* | *Some* ***little boys*** (=young boys) *were playing with a ball.* | *One of the* ***big boys*** (=older boys) *was picking on Sam.*

THESAURUS

man, guy, gentleman, youth
➔ see Thesaurus box at MAN¹

2 someone's son, especially a young one: *How old is your* ***little boy?*** **3 paper/delivery etc. boy** a young man who does a particular job **4 city/local etc. boy** *informal* a man of any age from a particular place or social group **5 the boys** *informal* a group of men who are friends and often go out together: *playing cards with the boys* **6** *spoken* used when speaking to a male animal, such as a horse or a dog: *Good boy, Patches!*

boy² also **oh ˈboy** *interjection* said in order to emphasize a statement: *Boy, is he mad!*

boy·cott /ˈbɔɪkɑt/ *v.* [T] to refuse to buy something, use something, or take part in something as a way of protesting: *We boycott all products tested on animals.* —**boycott** *n.* [C]

THESAURUS

protest, march, demonstrate, riot, hold/stage a sit-in, go on a hunger strike
➔ see Thesaurus box at PROTEST[2]

boy·friend /ˈbɔɪfrɛnd/ *n.* [C] a boy or man with whom you have a romantic relationship: *Have you met Leah's boyfriend?*

boy·hood /ˈbɔɪhʊd/ *n.* [U] *literary* the time in a man's life when he is very young

boy·ish /ˈbɔɪ-ɪʃ/ *adj.* looking or behaving like a boy: *his boyish laughter*

ˈBoy Scouts *n.* [plural] an organization for boys that teaches them practical skills and helps develop their character [➡ **Girl Scouts**]

bo·zo /ˈboʊzoʊ/ *n.* [C] *informal* someone who you think is stupid or silly

bps, BPS /ˌbi pi ˈɛs/ *technical* **bits per second** a measurement of how fast a computer or MODEM can send or receive information

bra /brɑ/ *n.* [C] a piece of underwear that a woman wears to support her breasts ➔ see picture at CLOTHES

brace[1] /breɪs/ *v.* [T] **1** to prepare for something unpleasant that is going to happen: *Hospitals are* ***bracing themselves for*** *a flu epidemic this winter.* **2** to prevent something from falling or moving by supporting it: *His feet were braced against the wall.*

brace[2] *n.* **1 braces** [plural] a connected set of wires that people, especially children, wear on their teeth to make them straight **2** [C] something used or worn in order to support something: *a neck brace*

brace·let /ˈbreɪslɪt/ *n.* [C] a band or chain that you wear around your wrist or arm as a decoration ➔ see picture at JEWELRY

brac·ing /ˈbreɪsɪŋ/ *adj.* **1** bracing air or weather is cold and makes you feel very awake and healthy **2** making you feel excited and interested: *a bracing selection of literary fiction*

brack·et /ˈbrækɪt/ *n.* [C] **1 income/tax/age etc. bracket** an income, tax, etc. that is inside a particular range: *the highest tax bracket* **2** one of the pair of marks [ ] put around extra information: *All grammar information is given* ***in brackets.*** **3** a piece of metal, wood, or plastic put in or on a wall to support something such as a shelf

brack·ish /ˈbrækɪʃ/ *adj.* brackish water is not pure because it is slightly salty

brag /bræg/ *v.* past tense and past participle **bragged**, present participle **bragging** [I,T] *disapproving* to talk too proudly about what you have done, what you own, etc.: *Todd was* ***bragging about*** *his grades.*

brag·gart /ˈbrægɚt/ *n.* [C] someone who brags

braid[1] /breɪd/ *n.* [C,U] a length of hair or a narrow band of material that has been separated into three parts and then woven together: *a girl with her hair* ***in braids*** —**braided** *adj.* ➔ see picture at HAIR

braid[2] *v.* [T] to make a braid

braille /breɪl/ *n.* [U] a form of printing that makes raised round marks on the paper that blind people can read by touching

brain[1] /breɪn/ *n.* **1** [C,U] the organ inside your head that controls how you think, feel, and move: *brain damage | the part of the brain that controls movement* ➔ see picture on page A3 **2** [C usually plural, U] the ability to think clearly and learn quickly: *The kid's definitely got brains.* **3** [C] *informal* someone who is very intelligent: *Some of the best brains in the country are here tonight.* **4 be the brains behind sth** to be the person who thought of and developed a particular plan, system, organization, etc. ➔ NO-BRAINER ➔ **pick sb's brain(s)** at PICK[1] ➔ **rack your brain(s)** at RACK[2]

brain[2] *v.* [T] *old-fashioned* to hit someone on the head very hard

brain·child /ˈbreɪntʃaɪld/ *n.* [singular] *informal* an idea, organization, etc. that someone has thought of without any help from anyone else: *The project was the* ***brainchild of*** *photographer Rick Smolan.*

brain·less /ˈbreɪnlɪs/ *adj. informal* silly and stupid: *a brainless movie*

brain·pow·er /ˈbreɪnˌpaʊɚ/ *n.* [U] intelligence, or the ability to think: *an industry that relies on brainpower*

brain·storm[1] /ˈbreɪnstɔrm/ *v.* [I,T] to think of many different ways of doing something, developing ideas, or solving a problem, especially in a group: *The students* ***brainstormed about*** *getting more people to participate.* —**brainstorming** *n.* [U]

brainstorm[2] *n.* [singular] *informal* a sudden intelligent idea

brain·wash /ˈbreɪnwɑʃ, -wɔʃ/ *v.* [T] to make someone believe something that is not true, by using force, confusing him/her, or continuously repeating it over a long period of time: *Two former members of the Church claim they were brainwashed into joining.* —**brainwashing** *n.* [U]

brain·y /ˈbreɪni/ *adj. informal* able to think clearly and learn quickly: *a brainy kid*

braise /breɪz/ *v.* [T] to cook meat or vegetables slowly in a small amount of liquid in a closed container

brake[1] /breɪk/ *n.* [C] **1** a piece of equipment that makes a vehicle go more slowly or stop: *Maria* ***hit the brakes/slammed on the brakes*** (=made the car stop quickly). **2 put the brakes on sth** to stop something that is happening: *efforts to put the brakes on rising prices*

brake[2] *v.* [I] to make a vehicle go more slowly or stop by using its brake: *Miguel braked suddenly.*

bran /bræn/ *n.* [U] the crushed outer skin of wheat or a similar grain

branch[1] /bræntʃ/ *n.* [C] **1** part of a tree that grows out from the TRUNK (=main stem) and has leaves, fruit, or smaller branches growing from it ➔ see picture at PLANT¹ **2** a local business, store, etc. that is part of a larger business, etc.: *The bank has branches all over the country.* **3** one part of a large subject of study or knowledge: *a branch of medicine* **4** a part of a government or other organization that deals with one particular part of its work: *the executive branch of the U.S. government* **5** a smaller, less important part of a river, road, etc. that leads away from the larger, more important part of it: *a branch of the Missouri River* **6** a group of members of a family who all have the same ANCESTORS

B

branch² **also branch off** *v.* [I] to divide into two or more smaller, narrower, or less important parts: *Turn off where the road branches to the right.*

branch out *phr. v.* to do something new in addition to what you usually do: *The bookstore has **branched out into** renting movies.*

brand¹ /brænd/ *n.* [C] **1** a type of product made by a particular company: *different **brands of** soap*

THESAURUS

type, kind, sort, category, make, model, genre
➔ see Thesaurus box at TYPE¹

2 brand of humor/politics/religion etc. a particular type of humor, politics, etc.: *his conservative brand of politics* **3** a mark burned into an animal's skin that shows whom it belongs to

brand² *v.* [T] **1** to burn a mark on an animal, in order to show whom it belongs to **2** to consider someone as a very bad type of person, often unfairly: *Republicans have been **branded as** anti-environmentalists.*

THESAURUS

call, describe, label, characterize, portray
➔ see Thesaurus box at CALL¹

brand·ing /ˈbrændɪŋ/ *n.* [U] a practice in which a company gives a product a name and tries to make that name well-known: *the global branding of Coca-Cola*

bran·dish /ˈbrændɪʃ/ *v.* [T] to wave something around in a dangerous and threatening way: *He burst into the store brandishing a knife.*

ˈbrand ˌname *n.* [C] the name a company gives to the goods it has produced: *brand names such as Jell-O and Coca-Cola*

ˌbrand-ˈnew *adj.* new and not used: *a brand-new car*

bran·dy /ˈbrændi/ *n.* plural **brandies** [C,U] a strong alcoholic drink made from wine, or a glass of this drink

brash /bræʃ/ *adj.* *disapproving* behaving and talking very confidently: *a brash young man*

brass /bræs/ *n.* **1** [U] a very hard bright yellow metal that is a mixture of COPPER and ZINC **2 the brass (section)** the people in an ORCHESTRA or band who play musical instruments such as the TRUMPET or horn

bras·siere /brəˈzɪr/ *n.* [C] a BRA

ˌbrass ˈknuckles *n.* [plural] a set of metal rings worn over your KNUCKLES, used as a weapon

brass·y /ˈbræsi/ *adj.* **1** sounding loud and unpleasant **2** *disapproving* a woman who is brassy talks loudly and behaves in a way that is too confident

brat /bræt/ *n.* [C] **1** *informal* a badly behaved child: *Stop acting like a **spoiled brat**.* **2 an Army/Air Force/military etc. brat** a child whose family moves often because one or both parents works for the army, etc.

bra·va·do /brəˈvɑdoʊ/ *n.* [U] behavior that is intended to show how brave you are, but is often unnecessary

brave¹ /breɪv/ *adj.* dealing with danger, pain, or difficult situations with courage [≠ **cowardly**]: *brave soldiers* | *her brave fight against cancer* —**bravely** *adv.*

THESAURUS

courageous – someone who is courageous behaves very bravely: *an honest and courageous leader*
daring – willing to do dangerous things: *the daring young men who flew the first airplanes*
bold – confident and willing to take risks: *Rebecca was a bold woman, willing to say what she thought.*

brave² *v.* [T] to deal with a difficult, dangerous, or unpleasant situation: *15,000 people braved the hot sun to see Mandela.*

brave³ *n.* [C] a young fighting man from a Native American tribe

brav·er·y /ˈbreɪvəri/ *n.* [U] brave behavior [= **courage**; ≠ **cowardice**]: *an act of great bravery*

THESAURUS

courage, guts
➔ see Thesaurus box at COURAGE

bra·vo /ˈbrɑvoʊ, brɑˈvoʊ/ *interjection* said in order to show your approval when someone, especially a performer, has done well

brawl¹ /brɔl/ *n.* [C] a noisy fight, especially in a public place: *a drunken brawl*

THESAURUS

fight, free-for-all, scuffle, scrap
➔ see Thesaurus box at FIGHT²

brawl² *v.* [I] to fight in a noisy way, especially in a public place: *youths brawling in the street*

brawn /brɔn/ *n.* [U] physical strength: *Today's economy depends more on brains than brawn.* —**brawny** *adj.*: *brawny arms*

bray /breɪ/ *v.* [I] if a DONKEY brays, it makes a loud sound

bra·zen /ˈbreɪzən/ *adj.* showing that you do not feel ashamed about behavior that most people think is wrong or immoral: *a brazen lie* —**brazenly** *adv.*

breach /britʃ/ *n.* **1** [C,U] an act of breaking a law, rule, agreement, etc.: *You are **in breach of** your contract.* **2** [C] a serious disagreement between people, groups, or countries: *a **breach between** the allies over the issue of sanctions* **3** [C] a hole or broken place in a wall or a similar structure, especially one made during a military attack —**breach** *v.* [T]

bread

bread /brɛd/ *n.* [U] **1** a common food made from flour, water, and YEAST: *We need **a loaf of bread**.* | *a **slice/piece of bread** with butter* | ***white/wheat/rye/French bread*** | *fresh-baked bread* **2 sb's bread and butter** *informal* the work that someone gets most of his/her income from: *Tourists are our bread and butter.*

bread·bas·ket /ˈbrɛdˌbæskɪt/ *n.* **1** [singular] *informal* the part of a country or other large area that provides most of the food: *The midwest is **the breadbasket of** America.* **2** [C] a basket for holding or serving bread

bread·crumbs /ˈbrɛdkrʌmz/ *n.* [plural] very small pieces of bread used in cooking

bread·ed /ˈbrɛdɪd/ *adj.* covered in breadcrumbs, then cooked: *breaded veal*

breadth /brɛdθ, brɛtθ/ *n.* [U] **1** the distance from one side of something to the other, especially something very wide [= **width**]: *the **breadth of** the canyon* **2** a wide range or variety: *Brennan's **breadth of** knowledge* | *Older workers have a greater **breadth of** experience.*

bread·win·ner /ˈbrɛdˌwɪnɚ/ *n.* [C] the member of a family who earns the money to support the others

break[1] /breɪk/ *v.* past tense **broke** /broʊk/ past participle **broken** /ˈbroʊkən/

1 IN PIECES [T] if something breaks or someone breaks it, it separates into two or more pieces, especially because it has been hit or dropped: *Be careful or it'll break.* | *I **broke off** a handful of basil to put in the sauce.* | *They had to break the window to get into the house.*

THESAURUS

smash – used when a plate, glass, etc. breaks or is broken with a lot of force: *Angry crowds smashed windows downtown.*
shatter – used when a plate, glass, etc. breaks into a lot of small pieces: *The glass hit the floor, shattering everywhere.*
crack – used when a plate, glass, etc. is damaged so that there is a line between two parts of it: *One of the windows was cracked.*
tear – used about paper or cloth: *I tore the letter to pieces.*
snap – used about something that breaks into two pieces, making a loud noise: *The stick snapped in two.*
burst – used when a pipe with liquid inside it breaks: *Our pipes had burst in the freezing weather.*
pop – used when a bubble or balloon breaks: *The wind was so strong some of the balloons popped.*

2 BODY PART [T] if you break a part of your body, the bone splits into two or more pieces: *Sharon broke her leg skiing.*

3 END STH [I,T] to not continue, or to end something: *Annie finally broke the silence.* | *I don't smoke anymore, but it was hard to **break the habit**.*

4 NOT WORK [I,T] if something such as a machine breaks, or you break it, it is damaged and does not work: *One of the kids poked something into the VCR and broke it.* | *My camera broke.*

5 SURFACE/SKIN [T] to damage the surface of something so that it splits or has a hole in it: *Do not use this product if the seal has been broken.*

6 break free a) to escape from someone who is trying to hold you: *I broke free and ran.* **b)** to get out of a bad situation, or out of a situation that limits what you can do: *I desperately wanted to **break free from** my parents.*

7 RULES/LAWS [T] to disobey a law or rule: *Sometimes breaking the rules is the only way to get things done.*

8 PROMISE/AGREEMENT [T] to not do what you promised to do: *politicians who break their election promises*

9 break your neck *informal* to hurt yourself very badly: *Don't run; you'll slip and break your neck.*

10 break for lunch/coffee etc. to stop working in order to eat or drink something

11 break a record to do something faster or better than it has ever been done before: *Beamon **broke the world record** in the long jump by nearly two feet.*

12 break sth to sb to tell someone about something bad that has happened: *Ellie called us to **break the news** personally.*

13 NEWS/EVENT [I] if news about an important event breaks, it becomes known by everyone after having been secret: *The next morning, the news broke that Monroe was dead.*
14 break even to neither make a profit nor lose money: *We broke even in our first year of business.*
15 break sb's heart to make someone very unhappy, by ending a relationship with him/her or doing something that upsets him/her
16 DAY [I] if day breaks, light begins to show in the sky as the sun rises
17 VOICE [I] **a)** if a boy's voice breaks, it becomes lower as he gets older **b)** if someone's voice breaks, it does not sound smooth because s/he is feeling strong emotions
18 WAVE [I] if a wave breaks, it begins to look white on top because it is coming close to the shore ➔ **break the ice** at ICE[1]

break away *phr. v.* **1** to escape from someone who is holding you: *Nelson **broke away from** the policemen.* **2** to leave your family, a group, a political party, etc. and become separate from them: *The three Baltic states were the first to **break away from** the Soviet Union.*

break down *phr. v.* **1** if a large machine breaks down, it stops working: *A truck had broken down in the intersection.* **2** to fail or stop working in a successful way: *The talks broke down completely in June 2002.* **3 break** sth ⇔ **down** to change or remove something that prevents people from working together or having a good relationship: *attempts to break down prejudice* **4 break** sth ⇔ **down** to hit something, such as a door, so hard that it falls down **5 break** (sth ⇔) **down** if a substance breaks down, or something breaks it down, it changes as a result of a chemical process: *Bacteria breaks down the raw sewage.* | *The waste products **break down into** ammonia.* **6** to be unable to stop yourself from crying: *She broke down during the funeral.* **7 break** sth ⇔ **down** to separate something into smaller parts so that it is easier to do or understand: *She showed us the dance, then broke it down to teach it to us.*

break in *phr. v.* **1** to enter a building using force, in order to steal something **2 break** sb/sth ⇔ **in** to make a person or animal become used to the work she, he, or it has to do: *a training camp for breaking in new soldiers* **3** to interrupt someone when s/he is speaking: *She broke in, saying "You know that's not true!"* **4 break** sth ⇔ **in** to make new shoes or boots less stiff and more comfortable by wearing them

break into sth *phr. v.* **1** to enter a building or vehicle using force, in order to steal something: *They broke into the house through the back window.* **2 break into a run** to suddenly begin running **3** to become involved in a new activity, especially a business activity: *companies trying to break into the East European markets*

break off *phr. v.* **1 break** sth ⇔ **off** to end a relationship, especially a political or romantic one: *They've **broken off** their **engagement**.* **2 break** (sth ⇔) **off** to suddenly stop talking: *She broke off, tears in her eyes.* | *Suddenly they saw me and **broke off** their **conversation**.*

break out *phr. v.* **1** if something bad such as a disease, fire, or war breaks out, it begins to happen: *Last night a **fire broke out** in the 12th Street warehouse.* **2** to change the way you live or behave: *Rose was determined to **break out of** the cycle of poverty.* **3** to suddenly begin to have red spots on your skin, especially on your face: *Chocolate makes me break out.* **4 break out in a sweat** to start SWEATing **5** to escape from prison

break through *phr. v.* **1** to manage to do something successfully: *Henderson broke through in 1991, winning a Grammy Award.* **2 break through** (sth) if the sun breaks through, you can see it through the clouds

break up *phr. v.* **1 break** sth ⇔ **up** to separate something into smaller parts: *The phone company was broken up to encourage competition.* **2** to end a marriage or romantic relationship, or to stop being together as a group: *Troy and I broke up last month.* | *When did the Beatles break up?* **3 break** sth ⇔ **up** to stop a fight or stop a group of people doing something: *The FBI broke up a crack ring.* **4** if a crowd or meeting breaks up, people start to leave **5 break** (sth ⇔) **up** to break into small pieces, or to break something into small pieces: *The plane hit the water and broke up.* | *We used shovels to break up the soil.*

break with sb/sth *phr. v.* **1** to leave a group or organization because you have had a disagreement with them: *Lewis broke with the Administration on this issue.* **2 break with tradition/the past etc.** to do something in a completely new way

break[2] *n.*
1 A REST [C] a period of time when you stop working or doing something: *Matthews spoke for three hours without **taking a break**.* | *She took a two-year **break from** competitive running.* | *Harris is on his **lunch/coffee break**.* | *We needed a break, so we went up to the mountains.* | ***Spring break*** (=spring vacation from college) *is at the end of March.*

> **THESAURUS**
> **vacation, holiday, leave**
> ➔ see Thesaurus box at VACATION

2 STH STOPS [C] a period of time when something stops for a while and then starts again: *There was a break of two years between his last book and this one.* | *a break in the conversation*
3 give sb a break *spoken* to stop annoying, criticizing, or being unkind to someone: *Give me a break! I can't do it that fast.*
4 A CHANCE [C] a chance to do something that allows you to become successful: *The band's **big break** came when they sang on a local TV show.*
5 END STH [singular] a time when you stop doing

something, or end a relationship with someone: *a break in relations between the two countries | She finally **made the break** and left him. | In a **break with tradition**, the parade was canceled.*

6 A SPACE [C] a space or hole in something: *a **break in** the clouds*

7 TV/RADIO [C] a pause for advertisements during a television or radio program: *the scene just before the **commercial break***

8 BROKEN PLACE [C] a place where something is broken: *a bad break in his leg*

break·a·ble /ˈbreɪkəbəl/ *adj.* made of material that breaks easily

break·age /ˈbreɪkɪdʒ/ *n.* [C] *formal* something that has been broken: *All breakages must be paid for.*

break·a·way /ˈbreɪkəˌweɪ/ *adj.* **breakaway group/party/movement etc.** a group, etc. that has been formed by people who left another group because of a disagreement: *a breakaway group of Catholics*

break·down /ˈbreɪkdaʊn/ *n.* **1** [C,U] the failure of a system or relationship: *a **breakdown in** the peace talks | the consequences of **family/marital/social, etc. breakdown*** **2** [C] a NERVOUS BREAKDOWN **3** [C] a statement or list that separates something into parts: *a **breakdown of** how government agencies will be affected by the cuts* **4** [C] an occasion when a car or a piece of machinery stops working

break·er /ˈbreɪkɚ/ *n.* [C] a large wave with a white top that rolls onto the shore

break·fast /ˈbrɛkfəst/ *n.* [C,U] the meal you have in the morning: *I **had** bacon and eggs **for breakfast**. | Make time to **eat breakfast**.*

THESAURUS

meal, **lunch**, **brunch**, **dinner**, **supper**, **picnic**, **barbecue**

➔ see Thesaurus box at MEAL

ˈbreak-in *n.* [C] an act of entering a building illegally using force

ˈbreaking ˌpoint *n.* [U] the point at which someone or something is no longer able to work well or deal with problems: *Some of them are tired, almost **to the breaking point**.*

break·neck /ˈbreɪknɛk/ *adj.* extremely and often dangerously fast: *She drove home **at breakneck speed**.*

break·out¹ /ˈbreɪkaʊt/ *adj.* successful, and making someone or something famous or popular: *a breakout performance by Williamson*

breakout² *n.* [C] an escape from a prison

break·through /ˈbreɪkθru/ *n.* [C] an important new discovery in something you have been studying: *Scientists have **made an** important **breakthrough** in the treatment of heart disease.*

break·up /ˈbreɪkʌp/ *n.* [C,U] **1** the act of ending a marriage or other relationship **2** the separation of an organization, country, etc. into smaller parts: *the **breakup of** Yugoslavia*

breast /brɛst/ *n.* **1** [C] one of the two round raised parts on a woman's chest that produce milk when she has a baby: *breast cancer* **2** [C] the part of the body between the neck and the stomach: *He cradled his injured arm against his breast.* **3** [C,U] the front part of a bird's body, or the meat from this part: *turkey breast* ➔ see picture on page A2

ˈbreast-feed *v.* [I,T] if a woman breast-feeds, she feeds a baby with milk from her breasts

breast·stroke /ˈbrɛstˌstroʊk/ *n.* [U] a way of swimming in which you push your arms out from your chest and then bring them back in a circle to your sides, while on your stomach in the water ➔ see picture at SWIM¹

breath /brɛθ/ *n.* **1** [C,U] the air that goes in or comes out of your lungs when you breathe, or the action of breathing air into or out of your lungs: *Officers could smell alcohol on his breath. | The cat has **bad breath*** (=it smells bad). *| **Take a deep breath*** (=breathe in a lot of air once) *and relax. | I was hot and sweaty and **out of breath*** (=having difficulty breathing because I had just been exercising). *| One of the symptoms is **shortness of breath*** (=being unable to breathe easily). *| My heart was pounding and I was **gasping for breath*** (=trying hard to get enough air to breathe). **2 hold your breath a)** to breathe in and keep the air in your lungs: *I couldn't hold my breath anymore.* **b)** to wait anxiously to see what is going to happen: *Patrice held her breath, waiting for Dan's reply.* **3 catch your breath** to begin breathing normally again after you have been running or exercising: *I had to sit down to catch my breath.* **4 a breath of fresh air a)** a short time when you breathe air outside a building, after being inside: *I stepped outside for a breath of fresh air.* **b)** something that is different, exciting, and enjoyable: *These books bring a breath of fresh air into the classroom.* **5 under your breath** in a quiet voice: *"I hate you," he muttered under his breath.* **6 (don't) waste your breath** *spoken* used in order to tell someone that it is not worth saying something: *You're wasting your breath; he won't change his mind.* **7 don't hold your breath** used in order to say that something is not going to happen soon **8 take your breath away** to be extremely beautiful or exciting: *a view that will take your breath away*

breath·a·ble /ˈbriðəbəl/ *adj.* **1** clothing that is breathable allows air to pass through it easily **2** able to be breathed: *The air was thin but breathable.*

Breath·a·lyz·er /ˈbrɛθəˌlaɪzɚ/ *n.* [C] *trademark* a piece of equipment used by the police to see if a car driver has drunk too much alcohol: *a **Breathalyzer** test* —**breathalyze** *v.* [T]

breathe /brið/ *v.* **1** [I,T] to take air into your lungs and send it out again: *the quality of the air* *we breathe* | *Relax and* ***breathe deeply*** (=take in a lot of air). | *He was sweating and* ***breathing hard*** (=breathing deeply and quickly).

THESAURUS

pant – to breathe quickly with short breaths, especially after exercising: *I ran to the station and arrived sweaty and panting.*
wheeze – to breathe with difficulty, making a noise in your throat and chest, usually because you are sick: *I woke up coughing and wheezing.*
be short of breath also **be out of breath** – to have difficulty breathing, often after physical activity such as running, or because of sickness: *Patients quickly become short of breath and unable to stand.*
gasp for breath – to breathe quickly and loudly, because you are having difficulty breathing either from exercising or because you are sick: *He was gasping for breath and his heart was pounding fiercely.*
gasp for air – to be unable to breathe because there is not enough air: *The massive fire sucked up all the oxygen and left firefighters gasping for air.*

2 [I,T] to blow air, smoke, or smells out of your mouth: *Roy breathed on his hands to warm them.* **3 breathe a sigh of relief** to stop being worried about something: *We all breathed a sigh of relief as he climbed off the roof.* **4 breathe down sb's neck** *informal* to watch what someone is doing so carefully that it makes him/her feel nervous or annoyed: *I can't work with you breathing down my neck.* **5 not breathe a word** to not tell anyone about a secret

breathe (sth ⇔) **in** *phr. v.* to take air into your lungs: *She breathed in deeply.* | *Wyatt breathed in the fresh sea air.*

breathe (sth ⇔) **out** *phr. v.* to send air out from your lungs: *OK, now breathe out slowly.* | *He breathed out a sigh of relief.*

breath·er /'briðɚ/ *n.* [C] *informal* a short period of rest from an activity: *OK, everybody,* ***take a breather.***

breath·ing /'briðɪŋ/ *n.* [U] the process of breathing air in and out: *his deep, regular breathing*

breath·less /'brɛθlɪs/ *adj.* having difficulty breathing in a normal way —**breathlessly** *adv.*

breath·tak·ing /'brɛθˌteɪkɪŋ/ *adj.* extremely impressive, exciting, or surprising: *breathtaking scenery*

THESAURUS

impressive, imposing, dazzling, awe-inspiring, majestic
➔ see Thesaurus box at IMPRESSIVE

breath·y /'brɛθi/ *adj.* if someone's voice is breathy, you can hear his/her breath when s/he speaks

breed¹ /brid/ *v.* past tense and past participle **bred** /brɛd/ **1** [I] if animals breed, they have babies **2** [T] to keep animals or plants in order to produce babies, or to develop new animals or plants: *He breeds horses.* **3** [T] to cause a particular feeling or condition: *The crowded living conditions bred disease and crime.*

breed² *n.* [C] **1** a type of animal, especially one that people have kept to breed: *Labradors and other breeds of dog* **2** a particular type of person or type of thing: *the first in a* ***new breed*** *of home computers*

breed·er /'bridɚ/ *n.* [C] someone who breeds animals or plants

breed·ing /'bridɪŋ/ *n.* [U] **1** the act or process of animals producing babies: *the* ***breeding season*** **2** the activity of keeping animals or plants in order to produce babies, or to develop new types **3** *old-fashioned* polite social behavior

'breeding ˌground *n.* [C] a place or situation where something grows or develops: *Universities were a* ***breeding ground for*** *protests against the war.*

breeze¹ /briz/ *n.* [C] **1** a light gentle wind

THESAURUS

wind, gust, gale, storm, hurricane, tornado, typhoon
➔ see Thesaurus box at WIND¹

2 be a breeze *spoken* to be very easy to do ➔ **shoot the breeze** at SHOOT¹

breeze² *v.* [I] *informal* to walk somewhere in a quick confident way: *She* ***breezed into*** *my office and sat down.*

breeze through sth *phr. v. informal* to finish a piece of work or pass a test very easily: *Sherry breezed through her final exams.*

breez·y /'brizi/ *adj.* **1** confident and relaxed: *his breezy way of speaking* **2** breezy weather is when the wind blows in a fairly strong way

breth·ren /'brɛðrən/ *n.* [plural] *old-fashioned* **or** *written* male members of an organization, especially a religious group

brev·i·ty /'brɛvət̬i/ *n.* [U] *formal* **1** the quality of expressing something in very few words: *the brevity of the poem* **2** the quality of continuing for only a short time: *the brevity of the meeting*

brew¹ /bru/ *v.* **1** [I,T] if tea or coffee brews or you brew it, you make it with boiling water and leave it to get a stronger taste **2** [I] if something unpleasant is brewing, it will happen soon: *There's a storm brewing.* **3** [T] to make beer

brew² *n.* [C,U] beer, or a can or glass of beer

brew·er /'bruɚ/ *n.* [C] a person or company that makes beer

brew·er·y /'bruəri/ *n.* plural **breweries** [C] a place where beer is made, or a company that makes beer

'brew pub *n.* [C] a bar or restaurant that serves beer that is made locally, rather than by large companies

bribe[1] /braɪb/ *n.* [C] money or gifts that you use to persuade someone to do something, usually something dishonest: *a judge accused of **taking bribes** | The officials said that they had been **offered bribes** before an important game.*

bribe[2] *v.* [T] to give someone a bribe: *Customs officials were **bribed to** let the trucks through.*

brib·er·y /ˈbraɪbəri/ *n.* [U] the act of giving or taking bribes

bric-a-brac /ˈbrɪk ə ˌbræk/ *n.* [U] small objects that are used for decoration in a house

brick /brɪk/ *n.* [C,U] a hard block of baked clay used for building walls, houses, etc.

brick·lay·er /ˈbrɪkˌleɪɚ/ *n.* [C] someone whose job is to build things with bricks —**bricklaying** *n.* [U]

bri·dal /ˈbraɪdl/ *adj.* relating to a BRIDE or a wedding: *a bridal gown*

bride /braɪd/ *n.* [C] a woman at the time she gets married or just after she is married: *You may kiss the bride.*

TOPIC

wedding, wedding ceremony/service, groom, best man, maid of honor, bridesmaids, reception, go on a honeymoon
➔ see Topic box at WEDDING

bride·groom /ˈbraɪdgrum/ *n.* [C] ➔ GROOM[2]

brides·maid /ˈbraɪdzmeɪd/ *n.* [C] a woman who helps the bride and stands beside her during her wedding

bridge

bridge[1] /brɪdʒ/ *n.* **1** [C] a structure built over a river, road, etc. that allows people or vehicles to cross from one side to the other: *the Brooklyn Bridge* **2** [C] something that provides a connection between two ideas, subjects, groups, or situations: *His new book acts as a **bridge between** art and science.* **3 the bridge** the raised part of a ship from which it can be controlled **4** [U] a card game for four players who play in pairs **5 the bridge of your nose** the upper part of your nose between your eyes **6** [C] a piece of metal for keeping a false tooth in place

bridge[2] *v.* [T] **1** to reduce the difference between two things: *attempting to **bridge the gap between** rich and poor* **2** to build or form a bridge over something: *a log bridging the stream*

bri·dle[1] /ˈbraɪdl/ *n.* [C] a set of leather bands put on a horse's head and used to control its movements

bridle[2] *v.* **1** [T] to put a BRIDLE on a horse **2** [I,T] to become angry or offended: *Amy **bridled at** the restrictions put on her.*

brief[1] /brif/ *adj.* **1** continuing for a short time: *a brief period of silence* **2** using only a few words and not describing things in detail: *I'll try to **be brief**. | a brief letter | **In brief**, he does not believe this to be true.* —**briefly** *adv.*

brief[2] *n.* [C] **1** a short statement giving facts about a law case: *a legal brief* **2** a short report: *Lynne took a look at the marketing briefs.* **3 briefs** [plural] men's or women's underwear worn on the lower part of the body

brief[3] *v.* [T] to give someone all the information about a situation that s/he will need: *Senate staff were **briefed on** the new law.* —**briefing** *n.* [C,U]

brief·case /ˈbrifkeɪs/ *n.* [C] a special flat bag used for carrying papers or documents ➔ see picture at CASE ➔ see picture on page A11

bri·gade /brɪˈgeɪd/ *n.* [C] **1** a large group of soldiers forming part of an army **2** *often humorous* a group of people who have similar qualities or beliefs: *the environmentalist brigade*

brig·a·dier gen·er·al, **Brigadier General** /ˌbrɪgədɪr ˈdʒɛnərəl/ *n.* [C] an officer who has a high rank in the Army, Air Force, or Marines

bright /braɪt/ *adj.* **1** shining strongly, or with plenty of light: *a bright sunny day | bright lights*

THESAURUS

strong – a strong light is very bright: *Diana squinted in the strong sunlight.*
dazzling – a dazzling light is so bright that you cannot see for a short time after you look at it: *Under the sun, the white of the snow is dazzling.*
blinding – a blinding light is very bright and makes you unable to see for a short time: *There was a blinding flash, then the noise of an explosion.*

2 intelligent: *Vicky is a very bright child. | a bright idea*

THESAURUS

intelligent, smart, brilliant, wise, clever, cunning, crafty, intellectual, gifted
➔ see Thesaurus box at INTELLIGENT

3 bright colors are strong and easy to see: *a bright red sweater* **4** happy and full of energy: *a bright smile* **5** likely to be successful: *You have a **bright future** ahead of you!* **6 bright and early** *spoken* very early in the morning: *I'll be here bright and early to pick you up.* **7 the bright side** the good things about something that is bad in other ways: ***Look on the bright side** – at least you didn't lose your job.* —**brightly** *adv.* —**brightness** *n.* [U] ➔ BRIGHTS

bright·en /ˈbraɪtˀn/ **also brighten up** *v.* **1** [I,T] to become brighter or lighter, or to make something do this: *The weather should brighten in the afternoon.* **2** [T] to make something more pleasant or attractive: *Flowers would brighten up this room.* **3** [I,T] to become happier, or to make someone else feel like this: *She brightened up when she saw us coming.*

brights /braɪts/ *n.* [plural] car HEADLIGHTS when they are on as brightly as possible

bril·liant /ˈbrɪlyənt/ *adj.* **1** brilliant light or color is very bright and strong: *brilliant sunshine* **2** extremely intelligent: *a brilliant scientist* —**brilliance** *n.* [U] —**brilliantly** *adv.*

B

THESAURUS

intelligent, smart, bright, wise, clever, cunning, crafty, intellectual, gifted
➔ see Thesaurus box at INTELLIGENT

brim¹ /brɪm/ *n.* [C] **1** the part of a hat that sticks out to protect you from sun and rain **2 the brim** the top of a container, such as a glass: *The glass was **filled to the brim**.*

brim² *v.* past tense and past participle **brimmed**, present participle **brimming** [I] **1** to start to cry: *His eyes **brimmed with** tears.* **2 be brimming (over) with sth** to be full of a particular thing, quality, or emotion

brine /braɪn/ *n.* [U] water that contains a lot of salt —**briny** *adj.*

bring /brɪŋ/ *v.* past tense and past participle **brought** /brɔt/ [T] **1** to take someone or something with you to a place or person: *I brought these pictures for you.* | *Will you bring me a glass of water?* | *Can I **bring** a friend **to** the party?* | *Dave **brought** a friend home **with** him.* | *She **brought** her daughter **along*** (=with her).

USAGE

bring – to take something or someone to a place: *We should bring a bottle of wine.* | *I bought the truck in Texas and brought it back to Mexico.*
take – to move something from one place to another, or help someone go from one place to another: *Don't forget to take your umbrella.* | *I can take you home after the concert.*
get – to go to another place and come back with something or someone: *Just a minute while I get my jacket.*

2 to cause a particular type of result or reaction: *The article brought angry letters from readers.* | *The fishing industry brings lots of money into the area.* | *efforts to bring peace to the region* **3** to make someone or something come to a place: *The project has brought inner city children new opportunities.* | ***"What brings you here?"*** *"I need to talk to Mike."* **4** to move something in a particular direction: *Bring your arm up level with your shoulder.* | *He brought the axe down with a thud.* **5** to begin a legal case against someone: *Criminal charges were **brought against** 14 officials.* **6 bring the total/number/score etc. to sth** used in order to say what the new total is, etc.: *165 agents are being hired, bringing the total to 2,313.* **7 not bring yourself to do sth** to not be able to do something, especially because you know it will upset or harm someone: *Brenda couldn't bring herself to tell him that Helen was dead.* **8** to cause someone or something to reach a particular state or condition: *Bring the mixture to a full boil.* | *The demonstration was **brought to** a peaceful **conclusion/end**.* **9 bring sth to sb's attention** a phrase used especially in formal writing that means to tell someone something: *Thank you for bringing the problem to our attention.* **10 bring sth to bear (on)** to use something in order to get the result you want: *Pressure was brought to bear by women's rights groups, and the club began admitting women.*

bring sth ⇔ **about** *phr. v.* to make something happen: *Lewis promised to bring about the needed changes.*

bring sb/sth **around** *phr. v.* **1** to change the subject of a conversation gradually to something new: *They keep **bringing the conversation/subject around** to their son.* **2** to make someone become conscious again

bring back *phr. v.* **1 bring** sth ⇔ **back** to start using something again that had been used in the past: *Some states have brought back the death penalty.* **2 bring back** sth to make you remember something: *The smell of suntan lotion brought back memories of the summer.*

bring sb/sth **down** *phr. v.* **1** to reduce something to a lower level: *The changes have brought costs down.* **2** to make something fall or come down: *A missile brought the plane down.* **3 bring down a government/president etc.** to force a government, etc. to stop being in control of a country

bring sth ⇔ **forth** *phr. v. formal* to make something happen, appear, or become available: *No evidence has been brought forth against Mr. Keele.*

bring sth ⇔ **forward** *phr. v.* **1** to change an arrangement so that something happens sooner: *They had to bring the wedding forward because Lynn got a new job.* **2** to introduce or suggest a new plan or idea: *Many arguments were brought forward supporting the changes.*

bring sb/sth ⇔ **in** *phr. v.* **1** to ask or persuade someone to become involved in a discussion, help with a problem, etc.: *The FBI were brought in to investigate.* **2** to earn or produce a particular amount of money: *The painting should bring in at least a million dollars.* **3 bring in a verdict** if a court or JURY brings in a verdict, it says whether someone is guilty or not

bring sth **off** *phr. v.* to succeed in doing something that is very difficult: *She'll get a promotion if she brings off the deal.*

bring sth ⇔ **on** *phr. v.* to make something bad or unpleasant happen or begin: *Stress can bring on an asthma attack.*

bring sth ⇔ **out** *phr. v.* **1** to make something become easier to notice, see, taste, etc.: *That shirt brings out the green in her eyes.* **2 bring out the best/worst in sb** to emphasize someone's best or worst qualities: *Becoming a father has brought out the best in Dan.* **3** to produce and begin to sell a new product, book, record, etc.: *The band is bringing out a new CD in September.*

bring sb ⇔ **together** *phr. v.* if an event brings a group of people together, it makes them care about each other more: *Stuart's death really brought the family together.*

bring sb/sth ⇔ **up** *phr. v.* **1** to start to talk about a particular subject or person: *The issue was brought up during the last election.* **2** to educate and care for a child until s/he is old enough to be independent: *She brought up three children by herself.* | *I was* ***brought up a Catholic/Muslim etc.*** (=taught to believe a particular religion). **3** to make something appear on a computer screen: *He brought up an airplane modeling website.*

brink /brɪŋk/ *n.* **the brink (of sth)** a situation in which you may soon begin a new or different situation: *Scientists say they're* ***on the brink of*** *a major discovery.*

brisk /brɪsk/ *adj.* **1** quick and full of energy: *a brisk walk* **2** trade or business that is brisk is very busy **3** weather that is brisk is cold and clear —**briskly** *adv.*

bris·tle[1] /ˈbrɪsəl/ *n.* [C,U] short stiff hair, wire, etc.: *a brush with short bristles*

bristle[2] *v.* [I] **1** to behave in a way that shows you are very angry or annoyed: *He* ***bristled at*** *my suggestion.* **2** if an animal's hair bristles, it stands up stiffly because the animal is afraid or angry

bristle with sth *phr. v.* to have a lot of something that sticks out: *Her hair bristled with curlers.*

bris·tly /ˈbrɪsəli, -sli/ *adj.* **1** bristly hair is short and stiff **2** having short stiff hairs on it: *a bristly face*

britch·es /ˈbrɪtʃɪz/ *n.* [plural] *informal* **1 too big for your britches** very confident, in a way that annoys other people **2** *humorous* **or** *old-fashioned* pants

Brit·ish[1] /ˈbrɪṭɪʃ/ *adj.* relating to or coming from Great Britain: *the British government*

British[2] *n.* **the British** the people of Great Britain

Brit·on /ˈbrɪtˀn/ *n.* [C] someone from Great Britain

brit·tle /ˈbrɪṭl/ *adj.* **1** hard but easily broken: *The paper was old and brittle.* **2** a system, relationship, feeling, etc. that is brittle is easily damaged or destroyed: *a brittle friendship* **3** showing no kind feelings: *a brittle laugh*

bro /broʊ/ *n.* [C] *slang* ➔ BROTHER[1]

broach /broʊtʃ/ *v.* **broach the subject/question etc.** to mention a subject that may be embarrassing or cause an argument: *It's often difficult to broach the subject of sex.*

broad[1] /brɔd/ *adj.* **1** very wide: *broad shoulders* | *He gave a broad smile.* | *The river is broad at this point.* **2** including many different kinds of things or people: *a movie that appeals to a* ***broad range*** *of people* | *The measure has broad support.* **3** concerning only the main ideas or parts of something: *a broad outline of the proposal* **4 in broad daylight** during the day when it is light: *He got stabbed in the street in broad daylight.*

broad[2] *n.* [C] *spoken offensive* a woman

broad·band /ˈbrɔdbænd/ *n.* [U] a system in which computers are connected to the Internet and can receive information at very high speed

> **TOPIC**
>
> **Internet, connect, modem, search engine, address, website, surfing the net, chat rooms, newsgroups, blogs, e-mail, work online**
>
> ➔ see Topic box at INTERNET

broad·cast[1] /ˈbrɔdkæst/ *n.* [C] a program on the radio or television: *a news broadcast*

broadcast[2] *v.* past tense and past participle **broadcast** [I,T] to send out a radio or television program: *Channel 5 will broadcast the game at 6 o'clock.*

broad·cast·er /ˈbrɔdˌkæstɚ/ *n.* [C] **1** someone who speaks on radio and television programs [➡ **newscaster**] **2** a company which sends out television or radio programs

broad·cast·ing /ˈbrɔdˌkæstɪŋ/ *n.* [U] the business of making radio and television programs

broad·en /ˈbrɔdn/ *v.* **1** [T] to increase something such as your knowledge, experience, or number of activities: *The class will broaden your knowledge of wine.* | *Travel* ***broadens the mind*** (=helps you understand and accept other people's beliefs, customs, etc.). **2** [T] to make something affect or include more people or things: *The industry has broadened the appeal of cruise ship vacations.* **3** [I,T] **also broaden out** to make something wider, or to become wider: *The river broadens out here.*

broad·ly /ˈbrɔdli/ *adv.* **1** in a general way: *I know broadly what to expect.* **2 smile/grin broadly** to have a big smile on your face **3** including a range of people, things, subjects, etc.: *The policy is broadly supported.*

broad·mind·ed /ˌbrɔdˈmaɪndɪd◂/ *adj.* willing to respect opinions or behavior that are very different from your own

broad·sheet /ˈbrɔdʃit/ *n.* [C] a serious newspaper printed on large sheets of paper

> **TOPIC**
>
> **newspaper, the papers, the press, the media, tabloid, front page, sports/entertainment/food etc. section, the comics page, the funnies, editorial page, headlines, article,**

story, **column**, **editor**, **reporter**, **journalist**, **correspondent**, **columnist**
➔ see Topic box at NEWSPAPER

broad·side¹ /ˈbrɔdˌsaɪd/ *adv.* with the longest side facing you: *He hit the car broadside.*

broadside² *v.* [T] to crash into the side of another vehicle

Broad·way /ˈbrɔdweɪ/ *n.* a street in New York that is known as the center of American theater

B

bro·cade /broʊˈkeɪd/ *n.* [U] thick heavy cloth that has a pattern of gold and silver threads

broc·co·li /ˈbrɑkəli/ *n.* [U] a green vegetable with thick groups of small dark green flower-like parts ➔ see picture at VEGETABLE

bro·chure /broʊˈʃʊr/ *n.* [C] a thin book that gives information or advertises something: *a travel brochure*

brogue /broʊg/ *n.* [C] **1** a strong leather shoe, especially one with a pattern in the leather **2** an ACCENT, especially an Irish or Scottish one

broil /brɔɪl/ *v.* [I,T] if you broil something, or if something broils, you cook it under or over direct heat: *broiled chicken*

THESAURUS

cook, **bake**, **fry**, **roast**, **grill**, **sauté**, **boil**, **steam**, **deep fry**
➔ see Thesaurus box at COOK¹

broil·er /ˈbrɔɪlɚ/ *n.* [C] a special area of a STOVE used for cooking food under direct heat

broke¹ /broʊk/ *v.* the past tense of BREAK

broke² *adj.* **1** completely without money: *I'm **flat broke**.*

THESAURUS

poor, **needy**, **destitute**, **impoverished**, **disadvantaged**, **underprivileged**, **deprived**
➔ see Thesaurus box at POOR

2 go broke if a company or business goes broke, it can no longer operate because it has no money: *The record store went broke last year.* **3 go for broke** *informal* to take big risks trying to achieve something

bro·ken¹ /ˈbroʊkən/ *v.* the past participle of BREAK

broken² *adj.* **1** not working correctly: *a broken clock | How did the lawn mower **get broken**?* **2** cracked or in pieces because of being hit, dropped, etc.: *a broken leg | There was broken glass everywhere.* **3** not continuous: *a broken white line | broken sleep* **4** a broken relationship is one that has ended because the husband and wife have separated: *a broken marriage | children from **broken homes*** (=their parents are divorced) **5** extremely mentally or physically weak after suffering a lot: *a broken man* **6 broken agreement/promise etc.** a situation in which someone did not do what s/he promised to **7 a broken heart** a feeling of extreme sadness because someone you love has died or left you **8 broken English/French etc.** if someone speaks broken English, French, etc., s/he speaks very slowly, with a lot of mistakes, because s/he does not know the language well

ˌbroken-ˈdown *adj.* broken, old, and needing a lot of repair: *a broken-down sofa*

ˌbroken-ˈhearted *adj.* very sad, especially because someone you love has died or left you

bro·ker¹ /ˈbroʊkɚ/ *n.* [C] someone whose job is to buy and sell property, insurance, etc. for someone else: *a real-estate broker* ➔ STOCKBROKER

broker² *v.* [T] to arrange the details of a deal, plan, etc. so that everyone can agree to it: *an agreement brokered by the UN*

bro·ker·age /ˈbroʊkərɪdʒ/ *n.* [U] the business of being a BROKER

bron·chi·tis /brɑŋˈkaɪt̬ɪs/ *n.* [U] an illness that affects your breathing and makes you cough —**bronchitic** /brɑŋˈkɪt̬ɪk/ *adj.*

bron·co /ˈbrɑŋkoʊ/ *n.* [C] a wild horse

bron·to·sau·rus /ˌbrɑntəˈsɔrəs/ *n.* [C] a large DINOSAUR with a very long neck and body

bronze¹ /brɑnz/ *n.* **1** [U] a hard metal that is a mixture of COPPER and TIN **2** [U] a dull red-brown color **3** [C] a work of art made of bronze: *a bronze by Henry Moore*

bronze² *adj.* **1** made of BRONZE: *a bronze statue* **2** having the red-brown color of bronze

ˌbronze ˈmedal *n.* [C] a prize that is given to the person who finishes third in a race, competition, etc., usually made of BRONZE

brooch /broʊtʃ, brutʃ/ *n.* [C] a piece of jewelry that you fasten to your clothes

brood¹ /brud/ *v.* [I] to think for a long time about something that you are worried, angry, or sad about: *Louise was **brooding about/over** what had happened at work.*

brood² *n.* [C] **1** a family of young birds **2** *humorous* someone's children

brook /brʊk/ *n.* [C] a small stream

broom /brum, brʊm/ *n.* [C] a large brush with a long handle, used for sweeping floors

broom·stick /ˈbrumˌstɪk, ˈbrʊm-/ *n.* [C] the long thin handle of a broom. In stories, WITCHES fly on broomsticks

broth /brɔθ/ *n.* [U] a soup made by cooking meat or vegetables in water and then removing them: *beef broth*

broth·el /ˈbrɑθəl, ˈbrɔ-, -ðəl/ *n.* [C] a house where men pay to have sex with PROSTITUTES

broth·er¹ /ˈbrʌðɚ/ *n.* [C] **1** a boy or man who has the same parents as you [➡ **sister**]: *Isn't that your **big/little brother*** (=older or younger brother)*?*

THESAURUS

relative, **parents**, **father**, **mother**, **dad**, **daddy**, **mom**, **mommy**, **sister**, **grandparents**, **grandfather**, **grandmother**, **grandpa**,

grandma, **great-grandparents**, **uncle**, **aunt**, **nephew**, **niece**, **cousin**
→ see Thesaurus box at RELATIVE[1]

2 *spoken* a male friend – used especially by African Americans **3** a man who belongs to the same race, religion, organization, etc. as you **4** a MONK: *Brother Francis* —**brotherly** *adv.*

brother² *interjection* **Oh brother!** said when you are annoyed or surprised

broth·er·hood /ˈbrʌðɚˌhʊd/ *n. old-fashioned* **1** [U] a feeling of friendship between people: *peace and brotherhood* **2** [C] a men's organization formed for a particular purpose

ˈbrother-in-law *n.* [C] **1** the brother of your husband or wife **2** the husband of your sister

broth·er·ly /ˈbrʌðɚli/ *adj.* showing feelings of kindness, loyalty, etc. that you would expect a brother to show: *brotherly love*

brought /brɔt/ *v.* the past tense and past participle of BRING

brou·ha·ha /ˈbruhɑhɑ/ *n.* [U] *informal* unnecessary noise and activity [= **commotion**]

brow /braʊ/ *n.* [C] **1** a FOREHEAD **2** an EYEBROW

brow·beat /ˈbraʊbit/ *v.* past tense **browbeat**, past participle **browbeaten** /-bitˀn/ [T] to make someone do something by continuously asking him/her to do it, especially in a threatening way

brown¹ /braʊn/ *adj.* having the same color as earth, wood, or coffee: *brown shoes* —**brown** *n.* [C,U]

brown² *v.* [I,T] to become brown, or to make food do this: *Brown the meat in hot oil.*

brown·ie /ˈbraʊni/ *n.* [C] **1** a thick flat piece of chocolate cake **2 get/earn brownie points** *informal* if you do something to get brownie points, you do it to get praise

Brown·ies /ˈbraʊniz/ *n.* [plural] the part of the GIRL SCOUTS that is for younger girls

ˈbrown-nose *v.* [I,T] *informal disapproving* to try to make someone in authority like you by being very nice to him/her —**brown-noser** *n.* [C]

brown·stone /ˈbraʊnstoʊn/ *n.* **1** [U] a type of red-brown stone, often used for building in the eastern U.S. **2** [C] a house with a front made of this stone

browse /braʊz/ *v.* **1** [I] to look at the goods in a store without wanting to buy a particular thing: *"Can I help you?" "No thanks. I'm just browsing."* **2** [I] to look through the pages of a book, magazine, etc. without a particular purpose, reading only the most interesting parts: *I was* ***browsing through*** *the catalog, and I found this.* **3** [I,T] to search for information on a computer or on the Internet: *software for browsing the Internet*

brows·er /ˈbraʊzɚ/ *n.* [C] a computer program that lets you find and use information on the INTERNET: *a Web browser*

bruise¹ /bruz/ *n.* [C] a mark on the skin of a person or piece of fruit where it has been damaged by a hit or a fall: *She was covered in cuts and bruises.*

THESAURUS

mark, **blemish**, **scar**, **pimple**, **zit**, **wart**, **blister**, **freckle**, **mole**
→ see Thesaurus box at MARK[2]
injury, **wound**, **cut**, **scrape**, **sprain**, **bump**
→ see Thesaurus box at INJURY

bruise² *v.* [I,T] to bruise a person or piece of fruit, or to get a bruise: *He fell and bruised his knee.* | *a bruised apple* —**bruising** *n.* [U]

brunch /brʌntʃ/ *n.* [C,U] a meal eaten in the late morning, as a combination of breakfast and LUNCH

THESAURUS

meal, **breakfast**, **lunch**, **dinner**, **supper**, **picnic**, **barbecue**
→ see Thesaurus box at MEAL

bru·nette /bruˈnɛt/ *n.* [C] a woman with dark brown hair

brunt /brʌnt/ *n.* **bear/take the brunt of sth** to have to deal with the worst part of something bad: *Women usually bear the brunt of caring for the sick.*

brushes

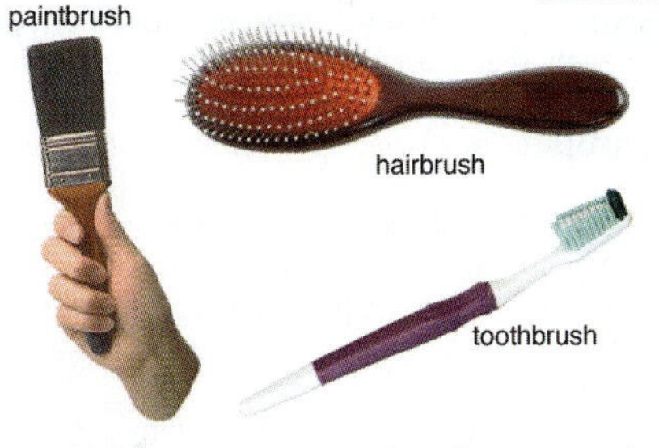

brush¹ /brʌʃ/ *n.* **1** [C] an object that you use for cleaning, painting, making your hair neat, etc., consisting of a handle with BRISTLES or thin pieces of plastic attached to it → HAIRBRUSH, PAINTBRUSH, TOOTHBRUSH **2** [U] small bushes and trees covering an open area of land: *a brush fire* **3** [C] a short time when you are in an unpleasant situation or argument: *the boy's first* ***brush with the law*** (=when he was stopped by police)

brush² *v.* **1** [T] to use a brush to clean something or to make it look smooth and neat: *Go brush your teeth.* | *He hadn't brushed his hair.* **2** [T] to remove something with a brush or your hand: *She* ***brushed*** *the crumbs* ***off*** *her lap.* **3** [I,T] to touch someone or something lightly as you pass by: *Her hair* ***brushed against*** *my arm.*

THESAURUS

touch, **feel**, **stroke**, **rub**, **scratch**, **pat**, **caress**, **fondle**, **tickle**, **grope**
→ see Thesaurus box at TOUCH[1]

brush sb/sth ⇔ **aside** *phr. v.* to refuse to listen

to someone or consider someone's opinion: *He brushed her objections aside.*

brush sth ⇔ **off** *phr. v.* to refuse to talk about something: *The President calmly brushed off their questions about his health.*

brush up (on) sth *phr. v.* to quickly practice and improve your skills or knowledge of a subject: *I have to brush up on my French before I go to Paris.*

'brush-off *n.* [singular] *informal* rude or unfriendly behavior that shows you are not interested in someone: *I thought she really liked me, but she **gave me the brush-off**.*

B

brusque /brʌsk/ *adj.* using very few words in a way that seems impolite: *a brusque manner*

brus·sels sprout /'brʌsəl ˌspraʊt/ *n.* [C] a small round green vegetable that has a slightly bitter taste ➔ see picture at VEGETABLE

bru·tal /'brutl/ *adj.* **1** very cruel and violent: *a brutal attack* **2** not sensitive to people's feelings: *the brutal truth* —**brutally** *adv.* —**brutality** /bru'tæləti/ *n.* [C,U]

bru·tal·ize /'brutlˌaɪz/ *v.* [T] to treat someone in a cruel and violent way

brute¹ /brut/ *n.* [C] **1** a man who is rough, cruel, and not sensitive **2** an animal, especially a large one

brute² *adj.* **brute force/strength** physical strength that is used rather than thought or intelligence

brut·ish /'brutɪʃ/ *adj.* very cruel: *brutish behavior*

B.S. *n.* [C] **Bachelor of Science** a university degree in a science subject [➡ **B.A.**]

bub·ble¹ /'bʌbəl/ *n.* [C] a ball of air in a liquid or solid substance: *soap bubbles | the bubbles in a glass of soda*

bubble² *v.* [I] **1** to produce bubbles: *Heat the sauce until it starts to bubble.* **2 also bubble over** to be full of a particular emotion, activity, etc.: *The kids were **bubbling over with** excitement.*

'bubble gum *n.* [U] a type of CHEWING GUM that you can blow into a bubble

bub·bly¹ /'bʌbli/ *adj.* **1** full of BUBBLES **2** happy and friendly: *a bubbly personality*

bubbly² *n.* [U] *informal* CHAMPAGNE

buck¹ /bʌk/ *n.* [C] **1** *spoken* a dollar: *Could you lend me 20 bucks?* **2** the fact of being responsible for something: *It's a way for the politicians to **pass the buck** to voters. | I'm paid to make the decisions; **the buck stops here*** (=I am responsible). **3** the male of some animals, such as DEER, rabbits, etc.

buck² *v.* **1** [I] if a horse bucks, it kicks its back feet up in the air **2** [T] if a horse bucks someone off, it throws the person riding off its back by bucking **3** [T] *informal* to oppose something, or do the opposite of something: *Fortson **bucked the trend**, deciding to stay in college rather than join the NBA.*

buck·et /'bʌkɪt/ *n.* [C] **1** an open container with a handle, used for carrying and holding things, especially liquids **2** the amount that a bucket will hold: *a **bucket of** water* ➔ **a drop in the bucket** at DROP² ➔ **kick the bucket** at KICK¹

buck·le¹ /'bʌkəl/ *v.* **1** [I,T] to fasten a buckle, or be fastened with a buckle: *The strap buckles at the side.* **2** [I] to do something that you do not want to do because of a difficult situation: ***Buckling under** the **pressure** from my parents, I broke off my engagement.* **3** [I] if your knees buckle, they become weak and bend **4** [I,T] to bend because of heat or pressure, or to make something do this

buckle down *phr. v. informal* to start working seriously: *Sanders buckled down, and his grade-point average improved.*

buckle (sth ⇔) **up** *phr. v.* to fasten your SEAT BELT in a car, aircraft, etc.

buckle² *n.* [C] a piece of metal used for fastening the two ends of a belt, or for fastening a shoe, bag, etc. ➔ see picture at WATCH²

ˌbuck 'teeth *n.* [plural] teeth that stick forward out of your mouth —**buck-toothed** *adj.*

bud¹ /bʌd/ *n.* [C] **1** *spoken* ➔ BUDDY **2** a young flower or leaf that is still tightly rolled up ➔ see picture at PLANT¹ ➔ **nip sth in the bud** at NIP¹

bud² *v.* past tense and past participle **budded**, present participle **budding** [I] to produce buds

Bud·dhis·m /'budɪzəm, 'bʊ-/ *n.* [U] a religion of east and central Asia, based on the teaching of Buddha —**Buddhist** *n.* [C] —**Buddhist** *adj.*

bud·ding /'bʌdɪŋ/ *adj.* beginning to develop: *a budding poet*

bud·dy /'bʌdi/ *n.* plural **buddies** [C] **1** *informal* a friend: *We're good buddies.* **2** *spoken* used in order to speak to a man or boy: *Hey, buddy! Leave her alone! | Thanks, buddy!*

budge /bʌdʒ/ *v.* [I,T] **1** to move, or to make someone or something move: *I pulled, but the dog wouldn't budge. | Marshal refused to **budge from** his seat.* **2** to change your opinion, or to make someone change his/her opinion: *The Union wouldn't **budge from** their demands.*

budg·et¹ /'bʌdʒɪt/ *n.* [C] a plan of how to spend the money that is available in a particular period in time, or the money itself: *a **budget of** $2 million for the project | the **budget for** the new library system | **Budget cuts*** (=a decrease in the amount of money spent) *have meant job losses. | He wants to **balance the budget*** (=make the money that is spent equal to the money coming in) *and cut taxes.* —**budgetary** /'bʌdʒəˌtɛri/ *adj.*: *budgetary limits*

budget² *v.* [I] to carefully plan and control how much you will spend: *$150,000 has been **budgeted for** the after-school program.*

budget³ *adj.* very low in price: *a budget flight*

buff[1] /bʌf/ *n.* **1 movie/jazz/computer etc. buff** someone who is interested in and knows a lot about movies, jazz, etc. **2** [U] a pale yellow-brown color

buff[2] *v.* [T] to make a surface shine by POLISHing it with something soft

buff[3] *adj. informal* having an attractive body

buf·fa·lo /ˈbʌfəˌloʊ/ *n.* plural **buffaloes** or **buffalo** [C] **1** a large animal like a cow with a very large head and thick hair on its neck and shoulders [= **bison**] **2** an animal like a large black cow with long curved horns that lives in Africa and Asia

buff·er /ˈbʌfɚ/ *n.* [C] **1** something that protects one thing from being affected by another thing: *The walls are a **buffer against** noise from the airport.* | *Use your commuting time as a **buffer between** work and home.* **2 buffer zone** a safe or quiet area where fighting or dangerous activity is not allowed to happen **3** a place in a computer's memory for storing information for a short time

buf·fet[1] /bəˈfeɪ, bʊ-/ *n.* [C] a meal in which people serve themselves at a table and then sit down somewhere else to eat: *a breakfast buffet*

buf·fet[2] /ˈbʌfɪt/ *v.* [T] to make someone or something move by hitting him, her, or it again and again: *boats buffeted by the wind and the rain*

buf·foon /bəˈfun/ *n.* [C] someone who does silly things that make you laugh —**buffoonery** *n.* [U]

bug[1] /bʌg/ *n.* [C] **1** *informal* any small insect: *a little green bug* **2** *informal* a GERM (=very small creature) that causes an illness that is not very serious: *a stomach bug* **3** a small mistake in a computer program that stops it from working correctly

THESAURUS

defect, problem, flaw, fault
→ see Thesaurus box at DEFECT[1]

4 the travel/skiing/writing etc. bug *informal* a sudden strong interest in doing something that usually only continues for a short time: *I'd been **bitten by the** travel **bug**.* **5** a small piece of electronic equipment for listening secretly to other people's conversations

bug[2] *v.* past tense and past participle **bugged**, present participle **bugging** [T] **1** *informal* to annoy someone: *It bugs me that he doesn't listen.* **2** to use a bug in order to listen secretly to other people's conversations: *Are you sure this room isn't bugged?*

bug·gy /ˈbʌgi/ *n.* plural **buggies** [C] a light carriage pulled by a horse

bu·gle /ˈbyugəl/ *n.* [C] a musical instrument like a TRUMPET, which is used in the army to call soldiers

build

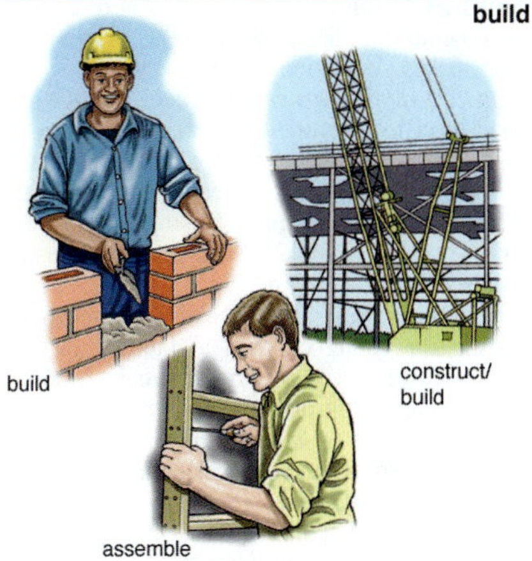

build[1] /bɪld/ *v.* past tense and past participle **built** /bɪlt/ **1** [I,T] to make a structure such as a house, factory, ship, etc.: *the money to build a new bridge* | *More homes are being built near the lake.* | *houses **built of** bamboo*

THESAURUS

construct – to build something large such as a building, bridge, etc: *There are plans to construct a new library.*
put up – to build something such as a wall or building: *It took five years to put up the skyscraper.*
erect formal – to build something: *plans to erect a memorial at the site of the World Trade Center*

2 [T] **also build up** to make something develop or form: *We're working to build a more peaceful world.* | *He'd been working 14-hour days to build up the business.* **3** [I,T] **also build up** to increase, or to make something increase: *The tension between them was building.* | *In diabetes, sugar builds up in the bloodstream and causes damage.* | *a confidence-building pregame talk*

build sth ⇔ **into** sth *phr. v.* **1** to make something a permanent part of a system, agreement, etc.: *A completion date was built into the contract.* **2** to make something so that it is a permanent part of a structure, machine, etc.: *a cash machine built into the wall*

build on *phr. v.* **1 build on** sth to use your achievements in order to develop something further: *The soccer league hopes to build on the popularity of the game among young people.* **2 build** sth **on** sth to base something on an idea or thing: *a relationship built on loyalty and trust*

build up *phr. v.* **build up sb's hopes** to unfairly make someone think that s/he will get what s/he is hoping for: *Don't build her hopes up.*

build up to sth *phr. v.* to gradually prepare for something: *I had built up to swimming 50 lengths.*

build[2] *n.* [singular, U] the shape and size of someone's body: *She has black hair and a slim build.*

B

build·er /ˈbɪldɚ/ *n.* [C] **1** a person or company that builds buildings **2** someone or something that makes something develop or form: *The win was a real confidence-builder.* | *her role as a bridge builder between the communities*

build·ing /ˈbɪldɪŋ/ *n.* **1** [C] a structure such as a house, church, or factory, that has a roof and walls: *Tall buildings lined the street.* ▶ Don't say "high buildings." ◀ **2** [U] the process or business of building things

B

ˈbuilding ˌblock *n.* **1** [C] a block of wood or plastic for young children to build things with **2** [plural] the pieces or parts that make it possible for something big or important to exist: *Reading and writing are the building blocks of education.*

build·up /ˈbɪldʌp/ *n.* **1** [singular, U] a gradual increase: *a **buildup of** greenhouse gases in the atmosphere* **2** [C] the length of time spent preparing for an event: *the **buildup to** the war*

built[1] /bɪlt/ the past tense and past participle of BUILD

built[2] *adj.* used to describe someone's size or shape: *a man who is **built like** a tank*

ˌbuilt-ˈin *adj.* forming a part of something that cannot be separated from it: *built-in cupboards*

bulb /bʌlb/ *n.* [C] **1** the glass part of an electric light that the light shines from: *a 40 watt bulb* **2** a root shaped like a ball that grows into a plant: *tulip bulbs* → see picture at PLANT[1]

bul·bous /ˈbʌlbəs/ *adj.* fat and round: *a bulbous nose*

bulge[1] /bʌldʒ/ *n.* [C] **1** a curved place on the surface of something, caused by something under or inside it: *The gun made a bulge under his jacket.* **2** an increase in the amount or level of something: *a population bulge*

bulge[2] *v.* [I] to stick out in a rounded shape: *bags **bulging with** shopping*

bu·li·mia /bəˈlimiə, bu-/ *n.* [U] a mental illness in which someone eats too much and then VOMITS because s/he is afraid of gaining weight —**bulimic** /bəˈlimɪk/ *adj.*

bulk /bʌlk/ *n.* **1 the bulk (of sth)** the main or largest part of something: *The bulk of the work has already been done.* **2** [C,U] the large size of something or someone: *the bulk of his bodyguards* **3 in bulk** in large quantities: *Businesses buy paper in bulk.*

bulk·y /ˈbʌlki/ *adj.* big and heavy: *a bulky package*

bull /bʊl/ *n.* **1** [C] a male cow, or the male of some other large animals, such as an ELEPHANT or WHALE **2** [U] *informal* something someone says that is stupid or not true: *That's bull. I never saw him before.* **3 take the bull by the horns** *informal* to bravely or confidently deal with a difficult, dangerous, or unpleasant problem

bull·dog /ˈbʊldɔg/ *n.* [C] a dog with a large head, a flat nose, a short neck, and short, thick legs

bull·doze /ˈbʊldoʊz/ *v.* [T] to move dirt and rocks, destroy buildings, etc. with a bulldozer

bull·doz·er /ˈbʊlˌdoʊzɚ/ *n.* [C] a powerful vehicle with a broad metal blade, used for moving dirt and rocks, destroying buildings, etc.

bul·let /ˈbʊlɪt/ *n.* [C] a small round piece of metal that is fired from a gun

bul·le·tin /ˈbʊlətˀn, ˈbʊlət̬ɪn/ *n.* [C] **1** a short official news report or announcement that is made to tell people about something important: *a news bulletin* **2** a letter or printed statement that a group or organization produces to tell people its news

ˈbulletin ˌboard *n.* [C] **1** a board on a wall that you put information or pictures on **2** a place in a system of computers where you can read or leave messages

bull·fight /ˈbʊlfaɪt/ *n.* [C] a type of entertainment in some countries in which a man fights and kills a BULL —**bullfighter** *n.* [C] —**bullfighting** *n.* [U]

bull·horn /ˈbʊlhɔrn/ *n.* [C] a piece of equipment that you hold up to your mouth when you talk, to make your voice louder

bul·lion /ˈbʊlyən/ *n.* [U] blocks of gold or silver

bull·ish /ˈbʊlɪʃ/ *adj.* relating to an increase in prices in the STOCK MARKET [≠ **bearish**]

ˈbull ˌmarket *n.* [C] a situation in which the value of SHARES in business increases [≠ **bear market**]

bull·pen /ˈbʊlpɛn/ *n.* [C] the area in a baseball field in which PITCHERS practice throwing

ˈbull's-eye *n.* [C] the center of a TARGET that you try to hit when shooting

bul·ly /ˈbʊli/ *v.* past tense and past participle **bullied**, third person singular **bullies** [T] to threaten to hurt someone or frighten him/her, especially someone weaker or smaller than you: *Don't let them **bully** you **into** working on Saturdays.* —**bully** *n.* [C]

bum[1] /bʌm/ *n.* [C] *informal* **1** *disapproving* a man who has no home or job, and who asks people on the street for money **2** someone who is very lazy: *Get up, you lazy bum!* **3 beach/ski etc. bum** someone who spends all of his/her time on the beach, SKIing, etc.

bum[2] *v.* past tense and past participle **bummed**, present participle **bumming** [T] *slang* to ask someone if you can borrow or have something small: *He bummed a cigarette from her.*

bum around *phr. v. slang* **1** to spend time doing nothing, or in a very lazy way **2 bum around** sth to travel around, living very cheaply, without having any plans: *He spent a year bumming around Europe.*

bum[3] *adj. informal* **1** bad and useless: *He got a bum deal.* **2** injured: *a bum leg*

bum·ble·bee /ˈbʌmbəlˌbi/ *n.* [C] a large hairy BEE

bum·bling /ˈbʌmblɪŋ/ *adj.* behaving in a careless way and making a lot of mistakes

bummed /bʌmd/ **also ˌbummed ˈout** *adj. spoken* feeling disappointed: *I'm really bummed that we can't go!*

bum·mer /ˈbʌmɚ/ *n.* [singular] *spoken* a situation that is disappointing: *You can't go? What **a bummer**.*

bump¹ /bʌmp/ *v.* **1** [I,T] to hit or knock against something, especially by accident: *It was so dark I **bumped into** a tree.* | *Don't bump your head!*

> **THESAURUS**
> **hit, knock, bang, collide, strike**
> ➔ see Thesaurus box at HIT¹

2 [I] to move up and down as you move forward in a vehicle: *We **bumped along** the dirt road.*

bump into sb *phr. v. informal* to meet someone you know when you were not expecting to: *Guess who I bumped into this morning?*

bump sb ⇔ **off** *phr. v. informal* to kill someone

bump² *n.* [C] **1** an area of skin that is swollen because you have hit it on something: *a **bump on** his head*

> **THESAURUS**
> **injury, wound, bruise, cut, scrape, sprain**
> ➔ see Thesaurus box at INJURY

2 a small raised area on a surface: *a **bump in** the road* **3** a movement in which one thing hits against another thing, or the sound that this makes: *The elevator stopped **with a bump**.*

bump·er¹ /ˈbʌmpɚ/ *n.* [C] **1** the part at the front and back of a car that protects it if it hits anything ➔ see picture on page A12 **2 bumper-to-bumper** bumper-to-bumper traffic is very close together and moving slowly

bumper² *adj.* very large: *a bumper crop*

ˈbumper ˌsticker *n.* [C] a small sign with a message on it on the bumper of a car

bumpy

bump·y /ˈbʌmpi/ *adj.* **1** a bumpy surface has a lot of raised parts on it: *a bumpy road* **2** a bumpy trip by car or airplane is uncomfortable because of bad road or weather conditions

bun /bʌn/ *n.* [C] **1** a type of bread that is small and round: *a hamburger bun* **2** if a woman has her hair in a bun, she fastens her hair in a small round shape at the back of her head **3 buns** [plural] *informal* the two round parts of a person's bottom [= **buttocks**]

bunch¹ /bʌntʃ/ *n.* [singular] a group or number of similar people or things, or a large amount of something: *The doctor asked me **a bunch of** questions.* | *a bunch of grapes* | *There are **a whole bunch of** little restaurants by the beach.* | *This beer is **the best of the bunch**.*

> **THESAURUS**
> **group, crowd, team, crew, gang, mob, mass, party, bundle**
> ➔ see Thesaurus box at GROUP¹

bunch² *v.* [I,T] **1 also bunch together** to stay close together in a group, or to form a group: *The runners were bunched together.* **2 also bunch up** to pull material together tightly in folds: *Her socks were bunched up around her ankles.*

bun·dle¹ /ˈbʌndl/ *n.* **1** [C] a group of things such as papers, clothes, or sticks that are fastened or tied together: *a **bundle of** newspapers* **2** [C] SOFTWARE that is included with the computer you buy **3** [singular] *informal* a lot of money: *That car must have **cost a bundle**.* **4 be a bundle of nerves/laughs etc.** *informal* to be very nervous, a lot of fun, etc.

bundle² *v.* **1** [I,T] **also bundle up** to make a bundle: *Dave bundled up the newspapers.* **2** [I,T] **also bundle up** to dress in a lot of warm clothes because it is cold: *Fans were **bundled up against** the cold.* **3** [T] to make someone move quickly into a particular place: *The police **bundled** him **into** a car.* **4** [T] to include computer software or other services when you sell a new computer

bun·ga·low /ˈbʌŋgəˌloʊ/ *n.* [C] a small house that usually has only one level

> **THESAURUS**
> **house, ranch house, ranch, cottage, row house, mansion, duplex, apartment, condominium, condo, townhouse, mobile home, trailer**
> ➔ see Thesaurus box at HOUSE¹

bun·gee jump·ing /ˈbʌndʒi ˌdʒʌmpɪŋ/ *n.* [U] a sport in which you jump off something very high while you are attached to a long length of special rope that stretches —**bungee jump** *n.* [C] —**bungee jumper** *n.* [C]

bun·gle /ˈbʌŋgəl/ *v.* [T] to do something badly: *They bungled the job completely.* —**bungler** *n.* [C] —**bungling** *adj.*

bun·ion /ˈbʌnyən/ *n.* [C] a painful sore on your big toe

bunk /bʌŋk/ *n.* **1** [C] a narrow bed that is attached to the wall, for example on a train or a ship **2** [C] one of the two beds that form bunk beds ➔ see picture at BED¹ **3** [U] *informal* something that is not true or that does not mean anything

ˈbunk beds *n.* [plural] two beds that are attached together, one on top of the other

bun·ker /ˈbʌŋkɚ/ *n.* [C] a strongly built shelter for soldiers, usually under the ground

B

bun·ny /'bʌni/ **also 'bunny ˌrabbit** *n.* [C] plural **bunnies** a rabbit – a word used especially by or to children

buoy¹ /'bui, bɔɪ/ *n.* [C] an object that floats on the water, used for showing boats which parts of the water are safe or dangerous

buoy² **also buoy up** *v.* [T] **1** to make someone feel happier, more confident, etc.: *The team was buoyed by their win against Stanford.* **2** to keep profits, prices, etc. at a high level

B

buoy·ant /'bɔɪənt/ *adj.* **1** happy and confident: *a buoyant mood* **2** buoyant prices, etc. tend not to fall **3** able to float —**buoyancy** *n.* [U] —**buoyantly** *adv.*

bur·den¹ /'bɚdn/ *n.* [C] *formal* **1** something that is difficult or worrying that you are responsible for: *I don't want to* ***be a burden on*** *my children when I'm old.* **2 the burden of proof** the duty to prove that something is true **3** *literary* something heavy that you have to carry

burden² *v.* [T] **1** to make someone worry or cause problems for him/her: *families* ***burdened with*** *debt* **2** to make someone carry something heavy

bu·reau /'byʊroʊ/ *n.* [C] **1** a government department or part of a government department: *the Federal Bureau of Investigation* **2** an office or organization that collects or provides information: *an employment bureau* **3** a CHEST OF DRAWERS

bu·reauc·ra·cy /byʊ'rɑkrəsi/ *n.* **1** [U] an official system that is annoying or confusing because it has a lot of rules, processes, etc. **2** [C,U] the officials in a government or business who are employed rather than elected

bu·reau·crat /'byʊrəˌkræt/ *n.* [C] someone who works in a bureaucracy and follows official rules very carefully

bu·reau·crat·ic /ˌbyʊrə'kræṭɪk/ *adj.* involving a lot of complicated official rules and processes

bur·geon·ing /'bɚdʒənɪŋ/ *adj.* growing, increasing, or developing very quickly: *the city's burgeoning population*

burger

burg·er /'bɚgɚ/ *n.* [C] *informal* a HAMBURGER: *a burger and fries*

bur·glar /'bɚglɚ/ *n.* [C] someone who goes into buildings, cars, etc. in order to steal things

THESAURUS

criminal, offender, thief, robber, shoplifter, pickpocket, attacker, mugger, murderer, rapist
→ see Thesaurus box at CRIMINAL²

bur·glar·ize /'bɚgləˌraɪz/ *v.* [T] to go into a building, car, etc. and steal things from it

THESAURUS

steal, rob, mug, shoplift, rip off
→ see Thesaurus box at STEAL¹

bur·gla·ry /'bɚgləri/ *n.* plural **burglaries** [C,U] the crime of going into a building, car, etc. to steal things

THESAURUS

crime, theft, robbery, shoplifting, assault, mugging, murder, rape
→ see Thesaurus box at CRIME

bur·gun·dy /'bɚgəndi/ *n.* plural **burgundies** **1** [C,U] red or white wine from the Burgundy area of France **2** [U] a dark red color —**burgundy** *adj.*

bur·i·al /'bɛriəl/ *n.* [C,U] the act or ceremony of putting a dead body into a GRAVE

bur·lap /'bɚlæp/ *n.* [U] a type of thick rough cloth

bur·ly /'bɚli/ *adj.* a burly man is big and strong

burn¹ /bɚn/ *v.* past tense and past participle **burned** or **burnt** /bɚnt/

1 DESTROY/INJURE WITH FIRE [I,T] to damage something or hurt someone with fire, heat, or the sun, or to be hurt or damaged in this way: *Ricky* ***burned*** *his hand* ***on*** *the stove.* | *Parts of the building are still burning.* | *I burned the toast.* | *You can still get burned at the beach even if it's cloudy.*

2 PRODUCE FLAMES [I] to produce heat and flames: *a fire burning in the fireplace*

3 get burned *spoken* **a)** to be emotionally hurt by someone or something: *I don't want to get burned again.* **b)** to lose a lot of money, especially in a business deal

4 FUEL [I,T] if you burn a FUEL, or if it burns, it is used for producing power, heat, light, etc.: *Cars burn gasoline.*

5 FACE/CHEEKS [I] if your face or cheeks are burning, you feel hot because you are embarrassed or upset

6 FAT/ENERGY [T] if you burn fat or CALORIES, you use up energy stored in your body by being physically active: *a fat-burning exercise*

7 CD/DVD [T] if you burn a CD or DVD, you record information onto it using special computer equipment

8 LIGHT [I] *literary* if a light or lamp burns, it shines or produces light —**burned** *adj.* —**burnt** *adj.*

burn sth ⇔ **down** *phr. v.* if a building burns down or is burned down, it is destroyed by fire

burn sth ⇔ **off** *phr. v.* **burn off energy/fat/calories** to use energy that is stored in your body by doing physical exercise

burn out *phr. v.* **1 burn** (sth ⇔) **out** if a fire burns out or burns itself out, it stops burning because there is no coal, wood, etc. left **2 burn** (sth ⇔) **out** if an engine or electric wire burns out or is burned out, it stops working because it has become too hot **3 be burned out** if a building, car, etc. is burned out, the inside of it is destroyed by fire **4 burn** (sb) **out** to work so hard over a period of time that you become very tired and do not want to continue: *After three years of 14-hour days, he was burned out.*

burn up *phr. v.* **1 burn** sth ⇔ **up** if something burns up or is burned up, it is completely destroyed by fire or great heat **2 burn** sb **up** *informal* to make someone angry: *The way she treats him really burns me up.*

burn² *n.* [C] an injury or mark caused by fire or heat: *a burn on her arm*

burn·er /ˈbɚnɚ/ *n.* [C] **1** the part of a STOVE that produces heat or a flame **2 put sth on the back burner** *informal* to delay dealing with something until a later time

burn·ing /ˈbɚnɪŋ/ *adj.* **1** on fire: *a burning house* **2** feeling very hot: *a burning fever* **3 burning ambition/need etc.** a very strong need, etc. **4 burning question/issue** a very important or urgent question, etc. —**burning** *adv.*

bur·nish /ˈbɚnɪʃ/ *v.* [T] to POLISH metal until it shines —**burnished** *adj.*

burnt /bɚnt/ *v.* a past tense and past participle of BURN

burp /bɚp/ *v. informal* **1** [I] if you burp, gas comes up from your stomach through your mouth and makes a noise **2** [T] to help a baby get rid of stomach gas, especially by rubbing his/her back —**burp** *n.* [C]

bur·ri·to /bəˈritoʊ/ *n.* [C] a Mexican food made from a TORTILLA folded around meat or beans

bur·ro /ˈbɚoʊ, ˈbʊroʊ/ *n.* plural **burros** [C] a small DONKEY

bur·row¹ /ˈbɚoʊ, ˈbʌroʊ/ *v.* [T] to make a hole or passage in the ground: *Gophers had **burrowed under** the wall.*

burrow² *n.* [C] a passage in the ground made by an animal such as a rabbit or a FOX for it to live in

burst¹ /bɚst/ *v.* past tense and past participle **burst** **1** [I,T] to break open or apart suddenly and violently, or to make something do this: *a game in which kids sit on balloons to try to burst them*

> **THESAURUS**
>
> **break**, **smash**, **shatter**, **crack**, **tear**, **snap**, **pop**
> ➔ see Thesaurus box at BREAK¹

2 be bursting to be very full of something: *This town **is bursting with** tourists.* | *School classrooms **are bursting at the seams*** (=are too full of students). **3** [I] to move suddenly, quickly, and often violently: *She **burst through** the door of my room.* **4 be bursting with pride/confidence/energy etc.** to be very proud, confident, etc.

burst in on sb/sth *phr. v.* to interrupt something suddenly by entering a room: *I burst in on Polly and Jack in the kitchen.*

burst into sth *phr. v.* to suddenly start to do something: *Ellen **burst into tears*** (=began crying). | *The car hit a tree and **burst into flames*** (=began burning).

burst out *phr. v.* **1 burst out laughing/crying etc.** to suddenly start to laugh, cry, etc. **2** to suddenly say something in a strong way: *"I don't believe it!" she burst out angrily.*

burst² *n.* **a burst of sth** a short sudden period of increased activity, loud noise, or strong feeling: *a sudden **burst of** laughter* | *a **burst of** machine gun fire*

bur·y /ˈbɛri/ *v.* past tense and past participle **buried**, third person singular **buries** [T] **1** to put a dead body into a GRAVE: *Aunt Betty was **buried in** Woodlawn Cemetery.* **2** to cover something with something else so that it cannot be seen: *a dog burying a bone* | *She **buried** her face **in** her hands.* | *His glasses were **buried under** a pile of papers.* **3** to ignore a feeling or memory and pretend that it does not exist **4 bury the hatchet/bury your differences** to end a disagreement about something and become friends again

bus¹ /bʌs/ *n.* plural **buses** [C] a large vehicle that people pay to travel on: *Are you going to drive or go **by bus**?* | *Five people **got on the bus**.* ▶ Don't say "...get in the bus." ◀ *They **ride/take the bus** to school.* | *I **caught the bus** at 6th Street.* ➔ see picture at TRANSPORTATION

bus² *v.* [T] **1** to take a group of people somewhere in a bus: *Many children are being **bused to** schools in other areas.* **2** to take away dirty dishes from the tables in a restaurant: *a job **busing tables***

bus·boy /ˈbʌsbɔɪ/ *n.* [C] a man whose job is to take away dirty dishes from the tables in a restaurant

bush /bʊʃ/ *n.* [C] **1** a plant with many thin branches growing up from the ground **2 the bush** wild country that has not been cleared in Australia or Africa ➔ **beat around the bush** at BEAT¹

bushed /bʊʃt/ *adj. informal* very tired: *I'm bushed.*

bush·el /ˈbʊʃəl/ *n.* [C] a unit for measuring dry food, equal to 8 gallons or 36.4 liters

bush·y /ˈbʊʃi/ *adj.* bushy hair or fur grows thickly: *a bushy tail*

bus·i·ly /ˈbɪzəli/ *adv.* in a busy way

busi·ness /ˈbɪznɪs/ *n.*

1 WORK DONE BY COMPANIES [U] the activity of buying or selling goods or services: *We **do** a lot **of business with** a company in Texas.* | *jobs in the **music/advertising/publishing business***

> **THESAURUS**
>
> **commerce** – the buying and selling of goods and services: *laws that regulate commerce between nations*
> **industry** – the production of goods, especially in factories: *a decline in manufacturing industry*

B

trade – the business of buying and selling things, especially between countries: *restrictions on trade*
private enterprise – the economic system in which private businesses can compete, and the government does not control industry

2 A COMPANY [C] an organization that produces or sells goods or services: *a real-estate business* | *He* ***runs a*** *printing* ***business***. | *the owner of a* ***small business***

B

THESAURUS

company, firm, corporation, multinational, subsidiary
→ see Thesaurus box at COMPANY

3 YOUR JOB [U] work that you do as part of your job: *Al's gone to Japan* ***on business***. | ***a business trip*** **4 AMOUNT OF WORK** [U] the amount of work a company does, or the amount of money it makes: ***Business is good/bad/slow*** *during the winter.*
5 be in business to be operating as a company: *He's in business for himself* (=he owns a small company).
6 go into business/go out of business to begin or stop operating as a company: *Many small companies have recently gone out of business.*
7 big business a) large and powerful companies in general: *the Republican's links with big business* **b)** something that makes a lot of profit: *Toys are big business.*
8 PERSONAL LIFE [U] if something is not your business, you should not be involved in it or ask about it: *It's* ***none of your business*** *how much I earn.* | *Why don't you just* ***mind your own business*** (=used in order to tell someone rudely that you do not want his/her advice, help, etc.)*!*
9 SUBJECT/ACTIVITY [singular] a subject, event, or activity, especially one that you have a particular opinion of: *Rock climbing can be a risky business.*
10 get down to business to start dealing with an important subject
11 business as usual if a situation is business as usual, things are happening as they usually do, even though there is a reason why you might expect them not to happen normally: *The owners have changed, but it's business as usual for the popular restaurant.*
12 mean business *informal* to be determined to do something: *The border is being guarded by troops who mean business.*
13 have no business doing sth if someone has no business doing something, he or she should not do it: *He was drunk and had no business driving.*
→ BIG BUSINESS

'business ˌcard *n.* [C] a card that shows your name, the name of your company, the company's address, etc.

busi·ness·like /'bɪznɪsˌlaɪk/ *adj.* effective and practical in the way you do things: *a businesslike attitude*

THESAURUS

organized, efficient, well-run
→ see Thesaurus box at ORGANIZED

busi·ness·man /'bɪznɪsˌmæn/, **busi·ness·wom·an** /'bɪznɪsˌwʊmən/ *n.* plural **businessmen** /-ˌmɛn/, **businesswomen** /-ˌwɪmɪn/ [C] someone who works at a fairly high level in a company or who owns a business

'business ˌsuit *n.* [C] a suit that a man wears during the day at work

bus·ing /'bʌsɪŋ/ *n.* [U] a system in which students ride buses to schools that are far from where they live, so that a school has students of different races

'bus lane *n.* [C] a part of a wide street that only buses can use

'bus ˌstation *n.* [C] a place where buses start and finish their trips

'bus stop *n.* [C] a place at the side of a road, marked with a sign, where buses stop for passengers

bust¹ /bʌst/ *v.* [T] **1** *nonstandard* to break something: *I busted my watch.* **2 bust sb (for sth)** *informal* if the police bust someone, they catch someone who has done something illegal **3** *informal* to use too much money: *A new car would bust our budget.* **4 bust in/out/through etc.** to go into, out of, etc. a place quickly and violently: *He came busting in here with a shotgun.* **5 crime-busting/union-busting/budget-busting etc.** *informal* used with nouns to show that a situation is being ended or an activity is being stopped

bust² *n.* [C] **1** a woman's breasts, or the measurement around a woman's breasts and back: *a 34-inch bust* **2** *informal* a situation in which the police go into a place in order to catch people doing something illegal: *a drug bust* **3** a model of someone's head, shoulders, and upper chest: *a* ***bust of*** *Beethoven*

bust³ *adj.* **go bust** a business that goes bust stops operating because it does not have enough money

bust·er /'bʌstɚ/ *n.* [C] **1** *informal* something that ends a situation, or that stops a particular activity: *The storm should be a drought-buster.* **2** *spoken* used when speaking to a man who is annoying you, or whom you do not respect

bus·tle¹ /'bʌsəl/ *n.* [singular] busy and usually noisy activity: *the* ***bustle of*** *the big city*
—**bustling** *adj.*

bustle² *v.* [I] to move around quickly, looking very busy: *Linda* ***bustled around*** *the kitchen.*

bus·y¹ /'bɪzi/ *adj.* comparative **busier**, superlative **busiest** **1** a busy person is working hard and has a lot of things to do: *Hawkins is* ***busy with*** *a customer.* | *He's busy studying for his finals.* | *a busy mother* | *I found some paper and crayons to* ***keep them busy***. **2** a busy time is full of work or other activities: *a very busy day* **3** a busy place is full of people or vehicles, or has a lot happening in it: *a busy airport* **4** a telephone that is busy is being used: *I keep getting a* ***busy signal****.*

TOPIC

telephone, make a phone call, call, phone, lift/pick up the receiver, dial a number, answer the telephone, get through, leave a message, get the wrong number, hang up
➔ see Topic box at PHONE[1]

5 *disapproving* a pattern or design that is busy is full of details

busy² *v.* past tense and past participle **busied**, third person singular **busies** **busy yourself with sth** to do something in order to make time seem to go faster: *He busied himself with cleaning.*

bus·y·bod·y /ˈbɪziˌbɑdi, -ˌbʌdi/ *n.* plural **busybodies** [C] someone who is too interested in other people's private activities

but¹ /bət; *strong* bʌt/ *conjunction* **1** used in order to connect two statements or phrases, when the second statement adds something different or seems surprising after the first one: *It's an old car, but it's reliable.* | *an expensive but useful book* **2** used before you give the reason why something did not happen or is not true or possible: *I'd like to go, but I'm awfully busy.* **3** used in order to show surprise at what has just been said: *"I have to leave tomorrow." "But you only got here this morning!"* **4** except: *I had no choice but to leave.*

SPOKEN PHRASES

5 used in order to introduce a new subject: *That's why I've been so busy this week. But, how are you anyway?* **6 but then (again)...** used in order to show that what you have just said is not as surprising as it seems: *He doesn't have a strong accent,* ***but then*** *he has lived here for 35 years.* **7** used after phrases such as "excuse me" and "I'm sorry": *I'm sorry, but you're not allowed to go in there.*

but² *prep.* except for: *Joe can come any day but Monday.* | *There's nobody here but me.*

butch·er¹ /ˈbʊtʃɚ/ *n.* [C] someone who owns or works in a store that sells meat

butcher² *v.* [T] **1** to kill animals and prepare them to be used as meat **2** to kill people in a cruel way —**butchery** *n.* [U]

but·ler /ˈbʌtˀlɚ/ *n.* [C] the main male servant of a house

butt¹ /bʌt/ *n.* [C] **1** *informal* the part of your body that you sit on [= **buttocks**] **2** the end of a cigarette after most of it has been smoked **3** the end of the handle of a gun **4 be the butt of sth** to be the person or thing that other people often make jokes about

butt² *v.* [I,T] if a person or animal butts something or someone, it hits or pushes him, her, or it with its head

butt in *phr. v.* to become involved in someone else's private situation or conversation

butt out *phr. v. informal* used in order to tell someone to stop being involved in something private: *This has nothing to do with you, so just butt out!*

butte /byut/ *n.* [C] a large hill with steep sides and a flat top

but·ter¹ /ˈbʌt̬ɚ/ *n.* [U] a yellow food made from milk or cream that you spread on bread or use in cooking —**buttery** *adj.*

butter² *v.* [T] to spread butter on something

butter sb ⇔ **up** *phr. v. informal* to say nice things to someone so that s/he will do what you want

but·ter·cup /ˈbʌt̬ɚˌkʌp/ *n.* [C] a small shiny yellow wild flower

but·ter·fin·gers /ˈbʌt̬ɚˌfɪŋgɚz/ *n.* [singular] *informal* someone who often drops things

but·ter·fly /ˈbʌt̬ɚˌflaɪ/ *n.* plural **butterflies** [C] **1** an insect with large and usually colored wings **2 have butterflies (in your stomach)** *informal* to feel very nervous

butterfly

but·ter·milk /ˈbʌt̬ɚˌmɪlk/ *n.* [U] the liquid that remains after butter has been made, used for drinking or cooking

THESAURUS

milk, skim milk, low-fat/2% milk, whole milk, half-and-half
➔ see Thesaurus box at MILK[1]

but·ter·scotch /ˈbʌt̬ɚˌskɑtʃ/ *n.* [C,U] a type of candy made from butter and sugar boiled together

but·tock /ˈbʌt̬ək/ *n.* [C usually plural] *formal* one of the soft parts of your body that you sit on

but·ton¹ /ˈbʌtˀn/ *n.* [C] **1** a small round flat object on your shirt, coat, etc. that you pass through a hole to fasten it: *He left the top* ***button undone****.* **2** a small object on a machine that you press to make it work: ***Push*** *the play* ***button****.* **3** a small metal or plastic pin with a message or picture on it **4 on the button** *informal* exactly right or at exactly the right time: *The weather forecast for the weekend was right on the button.* | *She got here at two, on the button.*

button² also **button up** *v.* [I,T] to fasten something with buttons, or to be fastened with buttons: *Button up your coat.*

ˈbutton-ˌdown *adj.* a button-down shirt or collar has the ends of the collar fastened to the shirt with buttons

but·ton·hole /ˈbʌtˀnˌhoʊl/ *n.* [C] a hole for a button to be put through to fasten a shirt, coat, etc.

but·tress¹ /ˈbʌtrɪs/ *v.* [T] *formal* to do something to support a system, idea, argument, etc.: *evidence that buttresses their argument*

B

buttress[2] *n.* [C] a structure built to support a wall

bux·om /ˈbʌksəm/ *adj.* a woman who is buxom has large breasts

buy[1] /baɪ/ *v.* past tense and past participle **bought** /bɔt/ **1** [I,T] to get something by paying money for it: *Let me buy you a drink.* | *It's best to **buy** plants **from** a good nursery.* | *The money will be used to **buy** equipment **for** the school.*

THESAURUS

purchase formal – to buy something: *Tickets for the performance can be purchased by phone.*
acquire – to buy a company or property: *They want to acquire valuable works of art as cheaply as possible.*
get – to buy or obtain something: *I never know what to get Dad for his birthday.*
snap sth up – to buy something immediately, especially because it is very cheap: *Real estate in the area is being snapped up by developers.*
pick sth up – to buy something: *Could you pick up some milk on your way home?*
stock up – to buy a lot of something that you intend to use later: *Before the blizzard, we stocked up on food.*

2 [T] *informal* to believe an explanation or reason for something: *If we tell the police it was an accident, do you think they'll buy it?*

THESAURUS

believe, **accept**, **take sb's word**, **swallow**, **fall for**
→ see Thesaurus box at BELIEVE

3 buy time *informal* to do something that will get you more time to finish something **4** [T] **also buy off** *informal* to pay money to someone in order to persuade him/her to do something dishonest [= **bribe**]: *They say the judge was bought.*

buy into sth *phr. v.* **1** to accept that an idea is right and allow it to influence you: *women who buy into the idea of having a "perfect body"* **2** to buy part of a business or organization: *How much does it cost to buy into a hamburger franchise?*

buy sb/sth ⇔ **out** *phr. v.* to buy someone's share of a business or property that you previously owned together, so that you gain control

buy sth ⇔ **up** *phr. v.* to quickly buy as much as you can of something: *Even small local papers have been bought up by the national newspaper chains.*

buy[2] *n.* **be a good/bad buy** to be worth or not worth the price you paid: *These shoes were a good buy.*

buy·er /ˈbaɪɚ/ *n.* [C] **1** someone who is buying or has bought something: *a first-time home buyer*

THESAURUS

customer, **client**, **shopper**, **consumer**
→ see Thesaurus box at CUSTOMER

2 someone whose job is to choose and buy the goods that a store or company will sell

buy·out /ˈbaɪaʊt/ *n.* [C] a situation in which someone gains control of a company by buying all of its SHARES: *a management buyout*

buzz[1] /bʌz/ *v.* **1** [I] to make a continuous noise like the sound of a BEE: *What's making that buzzing noise?* **2** [I] if a group of people or a place is buzzing, people are making a lot of noise because they are excited: *The room **buzzed with** excitement.* **3** [I,T] to call someone by pressing a buzzer: *Tina **buzzed for** her secretary.*

buzz off *phr. v. informal* used in order to tell someone to go away in an impolite way

buzz[2] *n.* **1** [C] a continuous noise like the sound of a BEE: *the buzz of traffic* → see picture on page A7 **2** [singular] *informal* a strong feeling of excitement, pleasure, or success, especially one you get from alcohol or drugs: *I **get a buzz** from just one beer.*

buz·zard /ˈbʌzɚd/ *n.* [C] a large wild bird that eats dead animals

buzz·er /ˈbʌzɚ/ *n.* [C] a small thing like a button that makes a buzzing sound when you press it: ***Press** the **buzzer** if you know the answer.*

buzz·word /ˈbʌzˌwɚd/ *n.* [C] a word or phrase relating to a particular subject that is suddenly very popular

by[1] /baɪ/ *prep.* **1** used with PASSIVE forms of verbs to show who did something or what caused something: *a play by Shakespeare* | *a film made by Steven Spielberg* | *Her money is controlled by her family.* **2** near or beside: *He was standing by the window.* **3** past: *Two dogs ran by me.* **4** used in order to say what means or method someone uses to do something: *Send the letter by airmail.* | *Carolyn earns extra money by babysitting.* | *We went from New York to Philadelphia **by car/plane/train/bus**.* **5** no later than a particular time: *This report has to be done by 5:00.* **6 by mistake/accident** without intending to do something: *She locked the door by mistake.* **7** according to a particular way of doing things: *By law, cars cannot pass a school bus that has stopped.* **8** used in order to show which part of something that someone holds: *I picked up the pot by the handle.* | *She grabbed him by the arm.* **9** used in order to show a distance, amount, or rate: *The room is 24 feet by 36 feet.* | *Are you paid by the hour?* **10 by the way** *spoken* used in order to begin talking about a subject that is not related to the one you were talking about: *Oh, by the way, Vicky called while you were out.* **11 (all) by yourself** completely alone: *They left the boy by himself for two days!* **12 day by day/little by little etc.** used in order to show that something happens gradually: *Little by little he began to understand the language.*

by[2] *adv.* **1** past: *One or two cars went by.* | *Three hours went by before we heard any news.* **2 come/stop/go by** to visit or go to a place for a short time when you intend to go somewhere else afterward: *Come by* (=come to my house, office, etc.) *any time tomorrow.* | *I had to stop by the supermarket on the way home.* **3 by and large** used when talking generally about something: *By and large, the new arrangements are working well.*

bye /baɪ/ **also ˌbye-ˈbye** *interjection spoken* goodbye: *Bye, Sandy!*

by·gone /ˈbaɪgɔn, -gɑn/ *adj.* **bygone days/age/era etc.** a period in the past

by·gones /ˈbaɪgɔnz, -gɑnz/ *n.* **let bygones be bygones** *informal* to forgive someone for something bad that s/he has done to you

by·law /ˈbaɪˌlɔ/ *n.* [C] a rule made by an organization

ˈby-line *n.* [C] a line at the beginning of a newspaper or magazine article that gives the writer's name

BYOB *adj.* **bring your own bottle** used in order to describe a party or event that you bring your own alcoholic drinks to

by·pass¹ /ˈbaɪpæs/ *n.* [C] **1** a medical operation that repairs the system of arteries (ARTERY) around the heart: *a triple heart bypass operation* **2** a road that goes around a town or other busy place rather than through it

bypass² *v.* [T] **1** to avoid a place by going around it: *If we bypass the town, we'll save time.* **2** to avoid obeying a rule, system, or someone in an official position: *He bypassed the complaints procedure and wrote straight to the chairman.*

ˈby-ˌproduct *n.* [C] **1** a substance that is produced during the process of making something else: *Whey is a* ***by-product of*** *milk.* **2** an unexpected result of an event or of something you do: *Job losses are a* ***by-product of*** *the economic slowdown.*

by·stand·er /ˈbaɪˌstændɚ/ *n.* [C] someone who watches what is happening without taking part: *Several* ***innocent bystanders*** *were killed.*

byte /baɪt/ *n.* [C] a unit for measuring the amount of information a computer can use, equal to 8 BITS

by·way /ˈbaɪˌweɪ/ *n.* [C] a small road or path that is not used very much

by·word /ˈbaɪˌwɚd/ *n.* [C] the name of someone or something that has become so well known for a particular quality that it represents that quality: *The housing projects have become a* ***byword for*** *poverty.*

C, c

C, c /si/ **1** the third letter of the English alphabet **2** the number 100 in the system of ROMAN NUMERALS

C¹ /si/ **1** [C] a GRADE given to a student's work to show that it is of average quality: *Terry* ***got a C*** *on the final exam.* **2** [C,U] the first note in the musical SCALE of C MAJOR, or the musical KEY based on this note

C² the written abbreviation of **celsius** or **centigrade**

c. the written abbreviation of **circa**

CA the written abbreviation of **California**

cab /kæb/ *n.* [C] **1** a car with a driver whom you pay to drive you somewhere [= **taxi**]: *We'll just* ***take a cab*** *home.*

COLLOCATIONS

call a cab – to telephone and ask a cab to come to where you are
call sb a cab – to telephone and ask for a cab for someone else
hail a cab – to stand outside and raise your arm so that a cab will stop for you

2 the part of a truck or train where the driver sits

cab·a·ret /ˌkæbəˈreɪ/ *n.* [C,U] entertainment such as music and dancing performed in a restaurant while customers eat and drink

cab·bage /ˈkæbɪdʒ/ *n.* [C,U] a large round vegetable with thick green or purple leaves that can be cooked or eaten raw ➔ see picture at VEGETABLE

cab·bie, cabby /ˈkæbi/ *n.* [C] *informal* someone who drives a CAB

cab·in /ˈkæbɪn/ *n.* [C] **1** a small house made of wood, usually in a forest or the mountains: *a log cabin* **2** a small room in which you sleep on a ship **3** the area inside an airplane where the passengers sit ➔ see picture at AIRPLANE

ˈcabin crew *n.* [C] the people who take care of the passengers and serve meals on an airplane

cab·i·net /ˈkæbənɪt/ *n.* [C] **1** a piece of furniture with doors and shelves or drawers, used for storing or showing things: *a filing cabinet* | *the kitchen cabinets* **2** an important group of politicians who make decisions or advise the leader of a government: *cabinet members*

ca·ble¹ /ˈkeɪbəl/ *n.* **1** [C,U] a plastic or rubber tube containing wires that carry electronic signals, telephone messages, etc.: *an underground telephone cable* **2** [U] a system of broadcasting television by using cables, paid for by the person watching it: *I'll wait for the movie to come out* ***on cable***. | *the growth of* ***cable television*** **3** [C,U] a thick strong metal rope used on ships, to support bridges, etc. **4** [C] a TELEGRAM

C

cable² *v.* [I,T] to send a TELEGRAM

cable car

'cable car *n.* [C] **1** a vehicle that is pulled by a CABLE along the road, used like a bus by people in a city **2** a vehicle that hangs from a CABLE and carries people up mountains

ca·boose /kə'bus/ *n.* [C] a small railroad car at the end of a train

cache /kæʃ/ *n.* [C] **1** a group of things that are hidden, or the place where they are hidden: *a **cache of** weapons* **2** *technical* a special part of a computer's MEMORY that helps it work faster by storing information for a short time —**cache** *v.* [T]

ca·chet /kæ'ʃeɪ/ *n.* [U] a quality that is good or desirable: *It's a great college, but it lacks the cachet of Harvard.*

cack·le /'kækəl/ *v.* [I] **1** to make the loud noise a chicken makes **2** to laugh or talk in a loud rough voice —**cackle** *n.* [C]

THESAURUS

laugh, **giggle**, **chuckle**, **snicker**, **guffaw**, **(be) in stitches**
→ see Thesaurus box at LAUGH¹

cac·tus /'kæktəs/ *n.* plural **cacti** /'kæktaɪ/ or **cactuses** [C] a desert plant with thick stems and sharp points

ca·dav·er /kə'dævɚ/ *n.* [C] *formal* a dead human body

cad·dy /'kædi/ *n.* plural **caddies** [C] someone who carries the equipment for someone who is playing GOLF —**caddy** *v.* [I]

ca·dence /'keɪdns/ *n.* [C] **1** the way someone's voice rises and falls **2** a regular repeated pattern of sounds

ca·det /kə'dɛt/ *n.* [C] someone who is studying to become an officer in the military or the police

ca·dre /'kædri, 'kɑ-, -dreɪ/ *n.* [C] *formal* a small group of specially trained people in a profession, political party, or military force: *a cadre of highly trained scientists*

cae·sar·e·an /sɪ'zɛriən/ *n.* [C] another spelling of CESAREAN

ca·fe, **café** /kæ'feɪ, kə-/ *n.* [C] a small restaurant

caf·e·te·ri·a /ˌkæfə'tɪriə/ *n.* [C] a restaurant where people get their own food at a COUNTER and take it to a table themselves: *the school cafeteria*

THESAURUS

restaurant, **cafe**, **coffee shop**, **fast food restaurant**, **diner**
→ see Thesaurus box at RESTAURANT

caf·feine /kæ'fin, 'kæfin/ *n.* [U] a chemical substance in coffee, tea, and some other drinks that makes people feel more active: *caffeine-free beverages*

cage¹ /keɪdʒ/ *n.* [C] a structure made of wires or BARS in which birds or animals can be kept: *a hamster cage*

cage² *v.* [T] to put an animal or bird in a cage

cag·ey /'keɪdʒi/ *adj. informal* not willing to talk about your plans or intentions: *The White House is being very **cagey about** the contents of the report.*

ca·hoots /kə'huts/ *n.* **be in cahoots (with sb)** *informal* to be working secretly with others, usually to do something that is not honest

ca·jole /kə'dʒoʊl/ *v.* [T] to persuade someone to do something by praising him/her or making promises to him/her: *She **cajoled** him **into** helping.*

THESAURUS

persuade, **talk into**, **encourage**, **influence**, **convince**, **coax**
→ see Thesaurus box at PERSUADE

Ca·jun /'keɪdʒən/ *n.* [C] a member of a group of people in southern Louisiana whose family originally came from the French-speaking part of Canada —**Cajun** *adj.*

cake¹ /keɪk/ *n.* **1** [C,U] a sweet food made by baking a mixture of flour, fat, sugar, and eggs: *chocolate cake* | *a **birthday cake*** | *Do you want a **piece of cake**?* **2** [C] a small piece of something, made into a flat shape: *a cake of soap* **3 salmon/rice/potato etc. cake** fish, rice, etc. that has been formed into a flat round shape and cooked **4 be a piece of cake** *informal* to be very easy: *We looked at the other team and thought, "piece of cake!"* **5 take the cake** *informal* to be worse than anything else you can imagine: *Of all the stupid things you've done, this takes the cake.* **6 have your cake and eat it too** *informal* to have all the advantages of something without any of the disadvantages

cake² *v.* **be caked in/with sth** to be covered with a thick layer of something: *Irene's boots were caked with mud.*

ca·lam·i·ty /kə'læməţi/ *n.* plural **calamities** [C] a very bad, unexpected event that causes a lot of damage or suffering: *If the crops fail again, it will be a calamity for the country.* —**calamitous** *adj.*

cal·ci·um /'kælsiəm/ *n.* [U] a silver-white metal that is an ELEMENT and that helps form teeth, bones, and CHALK

cal·cu·late /'kælkyəˌleɪt/ *v.* [I,T] **1** to find out something or measure something using numbers: *These instruments calculate distances precisely.* |

*Researchers **calculated that** the chances of having an accident rose 4.3%.*

THESAURUS

figure out – a less formal word for calculate: *Let's try to figure out how much this will cost.*
add sth and sth – to put two or more numbers together to find the total: *Add 7 and 5 to make 12.*
subtract sth from sth also **take sth away from sth** – to reduce one number by another number: *If you subtract 12 from 15, you get 3. | 8 take away 2 is 6.*
multiply – to add a number to itself a particular number of times: *4 multiplied by 10 is 40.*
divide – to calculate how many times one number contains another number: *10 divided by 2 equals 5.*
plus spoken – used between numbers to show that you are adding them together: *Two plus two equals four.*
minus spoken – used between numbers to show that you are taking one away from the other: *Six minus five is one.*

2 be calculated to do sth to be intended to have a particular effect: *The ads are calculated to attract Hispanic buyers.*

cal·cu·lat·ed /ˈkælkyəˌleɪt̬ɪd/ *adj.* **1 calculated risk/gamble** something you do after thinking carefully, although you know it may have bad results **2** deliberately and carefully planned to have a particular effect: *a calculated attempt to deceive the public*

cal·cu·lat·ing /ˈkælkyəˌleɪt̬ɪŋ/ *adj. disapproving* someone who is calculating makes careful plans to get what s/he wants, without caring about how it affects other people

cal·cu·la·tion /ˌkælkyəˈleɪʃən/ *n.* [C usually plural, U] the act of adding, multiplying, or dividing numbers to find out an amount, price, etc.: ***I made** a few quick **calculations**. | an approximate **calculation of** the cost | **By** their **calculations**, the debt will be paid off in four years.*

cal·cu·la·tor /ˈkælkyəˌleɪt̬ɚ/ *n.* [C] a small machine that can add, multiply, divide, etc. numbers ➔ see picture on page A11

cal·cu·lus /ˈkælkyələs/ *n.* [U] the part of mathematics that studies changing quantities, such as the speed of a falling stone or the slope of a curved line

cal·en·dar /ˈkæləndɚ/ *n.* [C] **1** a set of pages that show the days, weeks, and months of a year that you usually hang on the wall **2** all the things that you plan to do in the following days, months, etc.: *My calendar is full this week.* **3** a system that divides and measures time in a particular way: *the Jewish calendar* **4 calendar year/month** a period of time that continues from the first day of the month or year until the last day of the month or year

calf /kæf/ *n.* plural **calves** /kævz/ [C] **1** the part at the back of your leg between your knee and foot **2** the baby of a cow, or of some other large animals such as the ELEPHANT

cal·i·ber /ˈkæləbɚ/ *n.* [C] **1** the level of quality or ability that someone or something has achieved: *musicians **of** the highest **caliber*** **2** the width of a bullet or the inside part of a gun

cal·i·brate /ˈkæləˌbreɪt/ *v.* [T] *technical* to mark an instrument or tool so you can use it for measuring —**calibration** /ˌkæləˈbreɪʃən/ *n.* [C,U]

cal·i·co /ˈkælɪˌkoʊ/ *n.* [U] a light cotton cloth with a small pattern on it

call[1] /kɔl/ *v.*

1 TELEPHONE [I,T] to telephone someone: *I called about six o'clock. | He said he'd call me tomorrow.*

TOPIC

make a phone call, phone, lift/pick up the receiver, dial the number, answer the phone, leave a message, get the wrong number, hang up
➔ see Topic box at PHONE[1]

2 DESCRIBE [T] to describe someone or something in a particular way, or to say that s/he has a particular quality: *News reports have called it the worst disaster of this century. | Are you calling me a liar?*

THESAURUS

describe – to say what someone or something is like by giving details: *The suspect has been described as a young white man.*
characterize – describe the character of someone or something in a particular way: *Psychologists characterized her as mentally unstable.*
label – to use a particular word or phrase in order to describe someone: *He labeled their comments "ridiculous."*
brand – to consider someone as a very bad type of person, often unfairly: *You've branded him a bad guy without even knowing him.*
portray – to describe or show someone or something in a particular way: *a politician who portrayed himself as an opponent of big business*

3 ASK/ORDER [T] to ask or order someone to come to you: *Somebody call an ambulance! | I can hear Mom calling me.*
4 ARRANGE [T] to arrange for something to happen at a particular time: *A meeting was called for 3 p.m. Wednesday.*
5 SAY/SHOUT [I,T] to say or shout something so that someone can hear you: *"I'm coming!" Paula called.*
6 NAME [T] to give a person or pet a name: *What are you going to call the dog? | What **was** that movie **called** again* (=what was its name)*?*

C

7 READ NAMES [T] **also call out** to read names or numbers in a loud voice in order to get someone's attention: *When I call your name, go stand at the front.*
8 call the shots *informal* to be the person who decides what to do in a situation: *It's my business; I get to call the shots.*
9 call it a day *spoken* said when you want to stop working, either because you are tired or because you have done enough: *Come on, guys, let's call it a day.*
call (sb) **back** *phr. v.* to telephone someone again, or to telephone someone who tried to telephone you earlier: *Okay, I'll call back around three.* | *Can I call you back later?*
call for sth *phr. v.* **1** to ask publicly for something to be done: *Parents are calling for a return to basics in education.* **2** to need or deserve a particular type of behavior or treatment: *a situation that calls for immediate action* **3** to say that a particular type of weather is likely to happen: *The forecast calls for more rain.*
call in *phr. v.* **1 call** sb ⇔ **in** to ask or order someone to come and help you with a difficult situation: *The governor called in the National Guard to deal with the riots.* **2** to telephone the place where you work, especially to report something: *Jan* ***called in sick*** *this morning.* **3** to telephone a radio or television show to give your opinion or ask a question
call sb/sth ⇔ **off** *phr. v.* **1** to decide that a planned event will not happen or will not continue: *The game had to be called off due to bad weather.* **2** to order a dog or person to stop attacking someone: *Call off your dog!*
call on sb/sth *phr. v.* **1** to formally ask someone to do something: *The UN has called on both sides to observe the ceasefire.* **2** to visit someone for a short time: *a salesman calling on customers*
call out *phr. v.* **1 call** (sth ⇔) **out** to say something loudly: *"Phone for you," Rosie called out.* **2 call** sb/sth ⇔ **out** to ask or order someone to come and help you with a difficult situation: *The Army has been called out to help fight the fires.*
call up *phr. v.* **1 call** (sb ⇔) **up** to telephone someone: *Dave called me up to tell me about it.* **2 call** sth ⇔ **up** to make information appear on a computer screen
call[2] *n.* [C] **1** an action of talking to someone by telephone: *Were there any* ***phone calls*** *for me?* | *I* ***got a call*** *yesterday from Teresa.* | *Just* ***give me a call*** *from the airport.* | *I have to* ***make*** *a telephone* ***call.*** | *Why haven't you* ***returned*** *my* ***call*** (=telephoned me back)*?* | *a* ***local/long-distance call***
2 be on call ready to go to work if you are needed: *Heart surgeons are on call 24 hours a day.* **3** a shout or cry: *a call for help* **4** the sound that a bird or animal makes **5** a request or demand for someone to do something: *There have been* ***calls for*** *him to resign.* **6 no call for sth/no call to do sth** *spoken* used in order to tell someone that his/her behavior is wrong or that something is unnecessary: *She had no call to talk to you like that.* **7** a decision made by the REFEREE in a sports game: *All the calls went against us.* **8** a message or announcement: *the last call for flight 134* **9** a short visit to someone
'call ˌcenter *n.* [C] an office where a lot of people are employed to deal with customers who telephone them with questions, orders for goods, etc.
call·er /ˈkɔlɚ/ *n.* [C] someone who is making a telephone call
'call girl *n.* [C] a PROSTITUTE
cal·lig·ra·phy /kəˈlɪgrəfi/ *n.* [U] the art of writing using special pens or brushes, or the beautiful writing produced in this way
call·ing /ˈkɔlɪŋ/ *n.* [C] a strong desire or feeling of duty to do a particular type of work, especially work that helps other people: *a calling to the ministry*
'call-in ˌshow *n.* [C] a radio or television program in which people telephone to give their opinions or ask questions
cal·lous /ˈkæləs/ *adj.* unkind and not caring that other people are suffering —**callousness** *n.* [U] —**callously** *adv.*
cal·lus /ˈkæləs/ *n.* [C] an area of hard rough skin: *calluses on his feet* —**callused** *adj.*
ˌcall 'waiting *n.* [U] a telephone service that allows you to receive another call without ending the call you are already making
calm[1] /kɑm/ **also calm down** *v.* [I,T] to become quiet after you have been angry, excited, or upset, or to make someone become quiet: *Calm down and tell me what happened.* | *It took a while to calm the kids down.*
calm[2] *adj.* **1** relaxed and not angry or upset: *Glen was calm and composed at the funeral.* | *Please, everyone, try to* ***keep/stay calm!***

THESAURUS

relaxed – calm and not worried or angry: *He seemed relaxed and confident.*
laid-back – relaxed and not seeming to worry about anything: *My dad's pretty laid-back, but my mother's always nagging.*
mellow – friendly, relaxed, and calm: *Annie's family is pretty mellow, and they liked me.*
cool – calm, and not nervous or excited: *Try to stay cool during the interview.*

2 if a situation or place is calm, there is not a lot of activity or trouble: *The streets are calm again after last week's riots.*

THESAURUS

quiet, **peaceful**, **tranquil**, **sleepy**
→ see Thesaurus box at QUIET[1]

3 completely still, or not moving very much: *the calm water of the lake* → see picture at CHOPPY **4** not windy: *a calm day* —**calmly** *adv.*
calm[3] *n.* **1** [singular, U] a time that is quiet and

peaceful: *the calm of the evening* **2 the calm before the storm** a peaceful situation just before a big problem or argument

cal·o·rie /ˈkæləri/ *n.* [C] **1** a unit for measuring the amount of ENERGY a particular food can produce: *An average potato has about 90 calories.* | *a **low-calorie** snack* **2 count calories** to try to control your weight by calculating the number of calories you eat **3** *technical* a unit for measuring heat

calves /kævz/ *n.* the plural of CALF

ca·ma·ra·der·ie /kæmˈrɑdəri, kɑm-/ *n.* [U] a feeling of friendship that the people in a group have, especially when they work together: *the camaraderie of firefighters*

cam·cord·er /ˈkæmˌkɔrdɚ/ *n.* [C] a small piece of equipment like a camera that you can hold in one hand to record pictures and sound on a VIDEO

came /keɪm/ *v.* the past tense of COME

cam·el /ˈkæməl/ *n.* [C] a large animal with a long neck and one or two HUMPS (=large raised parts) on its back that lives in the desert and carries goods or people

cam·e·o /ˈkæmioʊ/ *n.* [C] **1** a small part in a movie or play acted by a famous actor: *Whoopi Goldberg makes a **cameo appearance** in the show.* **2** a piece of jewelry with a raised shape, usually of a person's face, on a dark background: *a cameo brooch*

cam·er·a /ˈkæmrə, -ərə/ *n.* [C] a piece of equipment used for taking photographs, or for making movies or television programs

TOPIC

Before you can **take** any **pictures**, you need to **load film into** the **camera**.
Digital cameras do not need film because the pictures you take are stored in the camera until you **download** them onto a computer.
When you take pictures, you need to **focus**, so the people or things in your picture will be clear.
If you are taking a picture indoors or at night, you might need to use a **flash**.
After you have taken pictures, you take the **film** to be **developed** and **printed**. The printed **photographs** are also called **prints**. When you get the prints, you also get the **negatives** which you can use in the future to get more copies of your photographs.

cam·er·a·man /ˈkæmrəˌmæn, -mən/, **cam·er·a·wom·an** /ˈkæmrəˌwʊmən/ *n.* plural **cameramen** /-ˌmɛn, -mən/, **camerawomen** /-ˌwɪmɪn/ [C] someone who operates a camera for a television or film company [➡ **photographer**]

ca·mi·sole /ˈkæmɪˌsoʊl/ *n.* [C] a light piece of clothing that women wear on the top half of their bodies under other clothes

cam·o·mile /ˈkæməˌmil/ *n.* [C,U] a plant with small white and yellow flowers, often used for making tea

cam·ou·flage /ˈkæməˌflɑʒ, -ˌflɑdʒ/ *n.* [C,U] the act of hiding something by making it look the same as the things around it, or the things you use to do this: *a soldier **in camouflage*** | *The Arctic fox's white fur is an excellent winter camouflage.* —**camouflage** *v.* [T]

camp[1] /kæmp/ *n.* [C,U] **1** a place where people stay in tents in the mountains, forest, etc. for a short time: *We got back to camp at sunset.* | *The **base camp** (=main camp) was 6,000 feet below the summit.* | *a **mining/logging camp*** (=one where people stay when they are doing those jobs) **2** a place where children go to do special activities during their vacation, often staying there for a week or more: *a **summer camp** for girls only* **3** a place where people are kept for a particular reason, when they do not want to be there: *a refugee camp* **4** a group of people who support the same ideas or principles, especially in politics: *the Kennedy camp* ➔ CONCENTRATION CAMP ➔ DAY CAMP

camp

camp[2] *v.* [I] to set up a tent or shelter in a place and stay there for a short time —**camping** *n.* [U] *We **went camping** in Yellowstone Park.*

camp out *phr. v.* to sleep outdoors, usually in a tent: *The kids camped out in the backyard.*

cam·paign[1] /kæmˈpeɪn/ *n.* [C] a series of actions that are intended to achieve a particular result, especially in business, politics, or war: *a presidential campaign* | *a military campaign* | *a **campaign for/against** a constitutional amendment*

THESAURUS

fight, battle, struggle
➔ see Thesaurus box at FIGHT[2]

campaign[2] *v.* [I] to take part in a public series of actions to try to achieve a particular result, especially in business or politics: *a group **campaigning for/against** gun control*

camp·er /ˈkæmpɚ/ *n.* [C] **1** someone who is staying in a tent or shelter for a short time **2** a vehicle that has beds and cooking equipment so that you can stay in it while you are on vacation

Camp·fire /ˈkæmpfaɪɚ/ *n.* an organization for girls and boys that teaches them practical skills and helps develop their character

camp·ground /ˈkæmpgraʊnd/ *n.* [C] a place

where people who are on vacation can stay in tents, CAMPERS etc.

THESAURUS

hotel, motel, inn, bed and breakfast (B&B)
➔ see Thesaurus box at HOTEL

camp·site /ˈkæmpsaɪt/ *n.* [C] a place where you can camp: *a lakeside campsite*

cam·pus /ˈkæmpəs/ *n.* [C] the land or buildings of a college: *the campus bookstore* | *Many students live **on campus**.*

C

can¹ /kən; *strong* kæn/ *modal verb* **1** to be able to do something or know how to do something: *I can't* (=cannot) *swim!* | *Jean can speak French.* | *Even a small computer can store immense amounts of information.*

USAGE

Use **can** and **be able to** to say that someone has the ability to do something. **Be able to** is more formal: *Can you swim?* | *He isn't able to run very fast.*
Use **could** to say that someone has the ability to do something, but does not do it: *He could do a lot better.*
Could is also the past form of **can**. Use **could** or a past form of **be able to** to say that someone had the ability to do something in the past: *She could ride a bike when she was three.* | *He was able to walk with a cane.*
Use **will be able to** to talk about future ability: *After only a few lessons, you will be able to understand basic Spanish.*

2 to be allowed to do something: *You can go out when you've finished your homework.* | *In soccer, you can't touch the ball with your hands* (=it is against the rules). **3** *spoken* used in order to ask someone to do something or give you something, or when you offer or suggest something: *Can I have a cookie?* | *Can I give you a hand?* **4** used in order to show what is possible or likely: *It can't be Steve; he's in New York right now.* | *I still think the problem can be solved.* **5** used with the verbs "see," "hear," "feel," "smell," and "taste," and with verbs relating to thinking, to show that an action is happening: *Nancy can't understand why I'm so upset.* | *I can see Ralph coming now.* **6** used in order to show what often happens or how someone often behaves: *It can get pretty cold here at night.* **7** used in order to express surprise or anger: *You can't be serious!* | *How can you be so stupid!* **8** [in questions and negatives] used in order to say that you do not believe something is true or right: *This can't be the right road.* | *It can't be easy living with him.* **9** [in questions and negatives] used in order to say that someone should not or must not do something: *You can't expect him to change.* ➔ COULD

can² /kæn/ *n.* [C] **1** a metal container in which food or liquid is kept without air, or the amount the can holds: *a soft drink can* | *Add two **cans of** kidney beans.* | *a large can of paint* **2 a (whole) can of worms** a complicated situation that causes a lot of problems when you start to deal with it

can³ /kæn/ *v.* [T] **1** to preserve food by putting it in a closed container without air: *We canned the vegetables we'd grown.* **2** *spoken* to dismiss someone from his/her job ➔ CANNED

Ca·na·di·an¹ /kəˈneɪdiən/ *adj.* relating to or coming from Canada

Canadian² *n.* [C] someone from Canada

ca·nal /kəˈnæl/ *n.* [C] a long passage dug into the ground and filled with water, either for boats to travel along, or to bring water from somewhere: *the Panama Canal* ➔ see picture at RIVER

ca·nar·y /kəˈnɛri/ *n.* plural **canaries** [C] a small yellow bird that sings and is often kept as a pet

can·cel /ˈkænsəl/ *v.* [T] **1** to decide that something you have planned will not happen: *I had to cancel my trip.* **2** to end an agreement or arrangement, especially because you no longer want something: *We're canceling our subscription to the magazine.*

cancel sth ⇔ **out** *phr. v.* to have an equal but opposite effect on something, so that a situation does not change: *The losses canceled out the profits made the previous year.*

can·cel·la·tion /ˌkænsəˈleɪʃən/ *n.* [C,U] **1** a decision that something you have planned will not happen: *The show's low ratings led to cancellation.* **2** a decision to end an agreement or arrangement: *the cancellation of an employment contract*

Can·cer /ˈkænsɚ/ *n.* **1** [U] the fourth sign of the ZODIAC, represented by a CRAB **2** [C] someone born between June 22 and July 22

cancer *n.* [C,U] a serious disease in which cells in one part of the body start to grow in a way that is not normal: *the incidence of **breast/lung/bowel, etc. cancer*** | *She **has cancer**.* | *He died of cancer at the age of 63.* —**cancerous** *adj.*

can·did /ˈkændɪd/ *adj.* telling the truth, even when the truth may be unpleasant or embarrassing: *He was surprisingly **candid about** his past drug addiction.* —**candidly** *adv.*

THESAURUS

honest, frank, direct, straightforward, blunt, forthright
➔ see Thesaurus box at HONEST

can·di·da·cy /ˈkændədəsi/ *n.* plural **candidacies** [C,U] the fact of being a candidate, usually for a political position: *She announced her **candidacy for** the Senate.*

can·di·date /ˈkændəˌdeɪt, -dɪt/ *n.* [C] **1** someone who is competing in an election or who is being considered for a job: *a presidential candidate* | *Sara seems to be a likely **candidate for** the job.* **2** someone or something that may be chosen for something: *Which patients are good* ***candidates for*** *the new treatment? | The book is a strong* ***candidate to*** *win the award.*

can·died /'kændid/ *adj.* cooked in or covered with sugar: *candied fruit*

can·dle /'kændl/ *n.* [C] a round stick of WAX with a piece of string through the middle that you burn to produce light: *She sat down and* ***lit*** *the* ***candle****.* → see picture at LIGHT[1]

can·dle·stick /'kændl,stɪk/ *n.* [C] a specially shaped metal or wooden object used for holding candles

can·dor /'kændə/ *n.* [U] the quality of being honest and telling the truth [➡ **candid**]: *She spoke with candor about the affair.*

can·dy /'kændi/ *n.* plural **candies** **1** [C,U] a sweet food made of sugar or chocolate, or a piece of this: *a* ***box of candy*** *| I gave her a* ***piece of candy****.* **2 mind/brain/eye etc. candy** *informal* something that is entertaining or pleasant to look at, but that does not make you think

'candy bar *n.* [C] a long narrow BAR of candy, usually covered with chocolate

'candy cane *n.* [C] a stick of hard sugar with a curved shape, colored red and white

cane /keɪn/ *n.* [C] a long thin stick, usually with a curved handle, used for helping you walk: *She* ***walks with a cane*** *because of her arthritis.*

ca·nine /'keɪnaɪn/ *adj.* relating to dogs

can·is·ter /'kænəstə/ *n.* [C] a metal container with a lid used for storing dry food or a gas: *a* ***flour/sugar/salt canister***

can·ker /'kæŋkə/ **also 'canker sore** *n.* [U] a sore area on the flesh of people or animals or on the wood of trees, caused by illness or a disease

can·na·bis /'kænəbɪs/ *n.* [U] MARIJUANA

canned /kænd/ *adj.* **1** preserved without air in a container: *canned tomatoes* **2 canned music/laughter/applause** music, etc. that has been recorded and is used on television or radio programs

can·ner·y /'kænəri/ *n.* plural **canneries** [C] a factory where food is put into cans

can·ni·bal /'kænəbəl/ *n.* [C] someone who eats human flesh —**cannibalism** *n.* [U] —**cannibalistic** /,kænəbə'lɪstɪk/ *adj.*

can·non /'kænən/ *n.* [C] a large gun, fixed to the ground or on wheels, used in past times

can·not /'kænɑt, kə'nɑt, kæ-/ *modal verb* the negative form of CAN: *I cannot accept your offer.*

can·ny /'kæni/ *adj.* smart, careful, and showing that you understand a situation very well

ca·noe /kə'nu/ *n.* [C] a long light narrow boat that is pointed at both ends, which you move using a PADDLE —**canoe** *v.* [I] —**canoeing** *n.* [U]

can·on /'kænən/ *n.* [C] **1** *formal* a generally accepted rule or standard for behaving or thinking **2** the books, pieces of music, etc. that are recognized as being the most important: *the literary canon* **3** an established law of the Christian church

'can ,opener *n.* [C] a tool used for opening cans of food

can·o·py /'kænəpi/ *n.* plural **canopies** [C] a cover attached above a bed or seat, used as a decoration or as a shelter —**canopied** *adj.*

can't /kænt/ *modal verb* the short form of "cannot": *I can't go with you today.*

can·ta·loupe /'kæntəl,oʊp/ *n.* [C,U] a type of MELON with a hard skin and sweet orange flesh

can·tan·ker·ous /kæn'tæŋkərəs/ *adj.* easily annoyed and complaining a lot: *a cantankerous old man*

THESAURUS

grumpy, cranky, crabby, grouchy, irritable, touchy

→ see Thesaurus box at GRUMPY

can·teen /kæn'tin/ *n.* [C] **1** a small container for carrying water or other drinks **2** a store or place where people in the military can buy things or go to be entertained

can·ter /'kæntə/ *v.* [I,T] when a horse canters, it runs fast, but not as fast as possible —**canter** *n.* [C]

Can·to·nese /,kæntən'iz◂/ *n.* [U] a language used in Hong Kong and parts of southern China

can·vas /'kænvəs/ *n.* **1** [U] a type of strong cloth that is used for making tents, sails, bags, etc.: *a canvas bag* **2** [C] a piece of canvas on which a picture is painted

can·vass /'kænvəs/ *v.* [I,T] **1** to try to persuade people to support a political party, politician, plan, etc. by going from place to place and talking to people: *Supporters were canvassing door to door.* **2** to ask people about something in order to get information: *Residents were canvassed about community needs.*

can·yon /'kænyən/ *n.* [C] a deep valley with very steep sides: *the Grand Canyon*

cap[1] /kæp/ *n.* [C] **1 a)** a soft hat with a curved part sticking out at the front: *a baseball cap* **b)** a hat that fits closely over your head: *a shower cap* **2** something that covers and protects the end or top of an object: *a bottle cap | a pen cap* **3** a limit on the amount of money that someone can earn or spend: *a* ***cap on*** *campaign spending* → ICE CAP → KNEECAP

cap[2] *v.* [T] **1** to be the last and usually best thing that happens in a game, situation, etc.: *Wilkes capped a perfect season by winning the 100 meter sprint.* **2** to cover the top of something: *the* ***snow-capped*** *peaks of the Rocky Mountains | a tower* ***capped with*** *a golden dome* **3** to cover a tooth with a special hard white substance: *Her front teeth had to be capped.* **4** to limit the amount of something, especially money, that can be used or spent: *The law caps the amount of interest that credit card companies can charge.*

ca·pa·bil·i·ty /,keɪpə'bɪləti/ *n.* plural **capabilities** [C] the ability of a machine, person, or organization to do something, especially something difficult: *The country has the **capability to** produce nuclear weapons.* | *the computer's graphics capability*

ca·pa·ble /'keɪpəbəl/ *adj.* [C,U] **1** having the power, skill, or other qualities that are needed to do something: *He is not **capable of** making these decisions by himself.* **2** able to do things well: *Mary Beth is a capable lawyer.*

ca·pac·i·ty /kə'pæsəṭi/ *n.* plural **capacities** **1** [singular, U] the amount that something can hold, produce, or carry: *The computer has a **capacity of** 400 megabytes.* | *The theater was **filled to capacity*** (=completely full). **2** [C,U] the ability to do or produce something: *a child's **capacity for** learning* | *The groups **have the capacity to** influence Congress.* | *The factory is not yet working **at full capacity**.* **3** [singular] someone's job, position, or duty: *She has traveled a lot **in her capacity as** a photojournalist.*

C

cape /keɪp/ *n.* [C] **1** a long loose piece of clothing without SLEEVES that fastens around your neck and hangs from your shoulders: *Batman's black cape* **2** a large piece of land surrounded on three sides by water: *Cape Cod*

ca·per¹ /'keɪpɚ/ *n.* [C] **1** a small dark green part of a flower that is used in cooking to give a sour taste to food **2** a planned activity, especially an illegal or dangerous one

caper² *v.* [T] to jump around and play in a happy excited way

cap·il·lar·y /'kæpəˌlɛri/ *n.* plural **capillaries** [C] a very small narrow tube that carries blood around your body [➡ **artery**, **vein**]

cap·i·tal¹ /'kæpəṭl/ *n.* **1** [C] the city where a country or state's main government is [➡ **capitol**]: *The New York state capital is Albany.* | *What's the **capital of** Sweden?* **2** [singular, U] money or property you use to start a business or to make more money: *Investors lent him the capital to start the business.* **3** [C] a letter of the alphabet written in its large form, for example at the beginning of someone's name: *Please write your name **in capitals**.* | *a capital "T"* **4** [C] a place that is important for a particular activity: *Hollywood is the **capital of** the movie industry.*

capital² *adj.* **1** relating to money that you use to start a business, make more money, improve things, etc.: *a capital investment to improve our schools* **2 capital letter** a letter of the alphabet that is printed in its large form, for example at the beginning of someone's name **3 capital offense/crime** a crime that may be punished by death

cap·i·tal·ism /'kæpəṭlˌɪzəm/ *n.* [U] an economic and political system in which businesses belong mostly to private owners, not to the government [➡ **communism**, **socialism**]

cap·i·tal·ist /'kæpəṭl-ɪst/ *adj.* relating to a system or person who supports or takes part in capitalism —**capitalist** *n.* [C]

cap·i·tal·ize /'kæpəṭlˌaɪz/ *v.* [T] **1** to write a letter of the alphabet using a CAPITAL letter **2** to supply a business with money so that it can operate **3** to calculate the value of a business based on the value of its SHARES —**capitalization** /ˌkæpəṭlə'zeɪʃən/ *n.* [U]

capitalize on sth *phr. v.* to use something in order to gain an advantage: *The company is trying to capitalize on the popularity of fruit-based drinks.*

ˌcapital 'punishment *n.* [U] the punishment of legally killing someone for a crime s/he has done ➔ DEATH PENALTY

THESAURUS

punishment, **sentence**, **penalty**, **fine**, **community service**, **corporal punishment**
➔ see Thesaurus box at PUNISHMENT

Cap·i·tol /'kæpəṭl/ *n.* [C] **1 the Capitol** the building in Washington D.C. where the U.S. Congress meets **2** the building in each U.S. state where the people who make laws for that state meet

ˌCapitol 'Hill *n.* [singular] the U.S. Congress

ca·pit·u·late /kə'pɪtʃəˌleɪt/ *v.* [I] to stop fighting someone and accept his/her conditions or demands —**capitulation** /kəˌpɪtʃə'leɪʃən/ *n.* [C,U]

cap·puc·ci·no /ˌkæpə'tʃinoʊ, ˌkɑ-/ *n.* plural **cappuccinos** [C,U] a type of Italian coffee made with hot milk

ca·price /kə'pris/ *n.* [C,U] a sudden and unreasonable change in someone's opinion or behavior

ca·pri·cious /kə'priʃəs/ *adj.* likely to change very suddenly: *capricious spring weather*

Cap·ri·corn /'kæprɪˌkɔrn/ *n.* **1** [U] the tenth sign of the ZODIAC, represented by a GOAT **2** [C] someone born between December 22 and January 19

capsize

cap·size /'kæpsaɪz, kæp'saɪz/ *v.* [I,T] if a boat capsizes, or if you capsize it, it turns over in the water

cap·sule /'kæpsəl/ *n.* [C] **1** a very small object with medicine inside that you swallow whole

THESAURUS

medicine, **pill**, **tablet**, **eye/ear drops**, **drug**, **dosage**
➔ see Thesaurus box at MEDICINE

2 the part of a space vehicle in which people live and work

cap·tain[1] /ˈkæptən/ *n.* [C] **1** someone who is in charge of a ship or plane **2** a fairly high rank in the Army, Air Force, Marines, police force, etc., or an officer who has this rank **3** someone who leads a team or group: *the **captain of** the football team*

captain[2] *v.* [T] to be the captain of a team, ship, or airplane

cap·tion /ˈkæpʃən/ *n.* [C] words written above or below a picture that explain what the picture is about

cap·ti·vate /ˈkæptəˌveɪt/ *v.* [T] to attract and interest someone very much: *Alex was captivated by her beauty.* —**captivating** *adj.*: *a particularly captivating story*

cap·tive[1] /ˈkæptɪv/ *adj.* **1** kept in prison or in a place that you are not allowed to leave: *captive animals* | *His son had been **taken captive*** (=taken and kept as a prisoner). **2 captive audience** people who listen to or watch someone or something because they have to, not because they want to

captive[2] *n.* [C] someone who is kept as a prisoner, especially in a war

THESAURUS

prisoner, **hostage**
➔ see Thesaurus box at PRISONER

cap·tiv·i·ty /kæpˈtɪvət̬i/ *n.* [U] the state of being kept as a prisoner or in a small space: *Many animals won't breed **in captivity**.*

cap·tor /ˈkæptɚ/ *n. formal* [C] someone who is keeping another person as a prisoner

cap·ture[1] /ˈkæptʃɚ/ *v.* [T] **1** to catch someone in order to keep him/her as a prisoner: *40 French soldiers were captured.*

THESAURUS

catch, **arrest**, **corner**, **trap**
➔ see Thesaurus box at CATCH[1]

2 to get control of a place that previously belonged to an enemy, during a war: *The town was captured by enemy troops.* **3 capture sb's imagination/attention etc.** to make someone feel very interested in something **4** to succeed in showing or describing something, using words or pictures: *The book really **captures the essence/spirit of** what the 1920s were like.* **5** to get something that you are competing with others for, especially in business or politics: *Mayor Agnos captured 30% of the vote.* **6** to catch an animal without killing it

capture[2] *n.* [U] **1** the act of catching someone in order to keep him/her as a prisoner: *The two soldiers somehow managed to **avoid capture**.* **2** the act of getting control of something: *the **capture of** the village*

car /kɑr/ *n.* [C] **1** a vehicle with four wheels and an engine, used by a small number of people for traveling from one place to another: *Joe **got in the car** and buckled his seatbelt.* | *She **got out of the car**.* | *You can't **park** your **car** here.* **2** one of the connected parts of a train: *I'll meet you in the **dining/sleeping car**.*

ca·rafe /kəˈræf/ *n.* [C] a glass bottle with a wide top, used for serving wine or water at meals

car·a·mel /ˈkærəməl, -ˌmɛl, ˈkɑrməl/ *n.* [C,U] candy made of cooked sugar, butter, and milk

car·at, **karat** /ˈkærət/ *n.* [C] a unit for measuring how pure gold is, or how heavy jewels are: *Pure gold is 24 carats.*

car·a·van /ˈkærəˌvæn/ *n.* [C] a group of people with animals or vehicles, who travel together

car·bo·hy·drate /ˌkɑrboʊˈhaɪdreɪt, -drɪt, -bə-/ *n.* [C,U] a substance in foods such as rice, bread, and potatoes that provides your body with heat and energy

car·bon /ˈkɑrbən/ *n.* [U] a chemical that is an ELEMENT and that forms into DIAMONDS, and is in gas, coal, etc.

car·bon·at·ed /ˈkɑrbəˌneɪt̬ɪd/ *adj.* carbonated drinks have a lot of BUBBLES in them

ˌcarbon ˈcopy *n.* [C] someone or something that is very similar to another person or thing

ˌcarbon diˈoxide *n.* [U] the gas produced when people and animals breathe out

ˌcarbon moˈnoxide *n.* [U] a poisonous gas produced when engines burn gasoline

ˈcarbon ˌpaper *n.* [C,U] special paper with a blue or black substance on one side, used especially in the past to make a copy of documents written on a TYPEWRITER

car·bu·re·tor /ˈkɑrbəˌreɪt̬ɚ/ *n.* [C] the part of an engine that mixes the air and GASOLINE to provide power

car·cass /ˈkɑrkəs/ *n.* [C] the body of a dead animal

car·cin·o·gen /kɑrˈsɪnədʒən/ *n.* [C] *technical* a substance that can cause CANCER —**carcinogenic** /ˌkɑrsɪnəˈdʒɛnɪk/ *adj.*

card[1] /kɑrd/ *n.* [C] **1** a small piece of plastic or stiff paper that shows information about someone or something: *a library card* | *an employee ID card* | *Here's my **business card**.* **2** a small piece of plastic which you use to pay for goods or to get money [➡ **credit card**, **debit card**]: *I'll use my card.* **3** a piece of folded stiff paper, usually with a picture on the front, that you send to people on special occasions: *a **birthday card*** **4** one of a set of 52 small pieces of stiff paper with pictures or numbers on them that are used for playing games: *Let's **play cards*** (=play a game using cards). | *a **deck of cards*** **5** a POSTCARD **6 baseball/sports etc. card** a small piece of thick stiff paper with a picture on one side that is part of a set which people collect **7** a small piece of thick stiff paper that information can be written or printed on [➡ **index card**]: *a set of recipe cards* **8** the thing inside a computer that the CHIPS are attached to that allows the computer to do specific things: *a*

C

sound card **9 be in the cards** to seem likely to happen: *The increase in price has been in the cards for a long time.* **10 play your cards right** *informal* to do the things that make you succeed in getting what you want **11 put/lay your cards on the table** *informal* to be completely honest about what your plans and intentions are

card² *v.* [T] to ask someone to show a card proving that s/he is old enough to be in a particular place or to buy alcohol or cigarettes: *I can't believe I still get carded.*

card·board /ˈkɑrdbɔrd/ *n.* [U] a thick material like stiff paper, used especially for making boxes

C

ˈcard ˌcatalog *n.* [C] a set of cards that contain information about something, especially books in a library, and are arranged in a particular order

car·di·ac /ˈkɑrdiˌæk/ *adj.* [only before noun] *technical* relating to the heart or to heart disease

ˌcardiac arˈrest *n.* [C] *technical* a HEART ATTACK

car·di·gan /ˈkɑrdəgən/ *n.* [C] a SWEATER that is fastened at the front

car·di·nal¹ /ˈkɑrdn-əl, -nəl/ *adj.* [only before noun] very important or basic: *a **cardinal rule***

cardinal² *n.* [C] **1** a priest of high rank in the Roman Catholic Church **2** a common North American wild bird that is a bright red color

cardinal

ˌcardinal ˈnumber *n.* [C] any of the numbers 1, 2, 3, etc. that show the quantity of something [➡ **ordinal number**]

car·di·ol·o·gy /ˌkɑrdiˈɑlədʒi/ *n.* [U] the study or science of medical treatment of the heart

care¹ /kɛr/ *v.* **1** [I, T] to be concerned about or interested in someone or something: *He doesn't **care about** anybody but himself.* | *I don't **care what** you do.* **2** [I] to like or love someone: *He really **cared for** you.*

SPOKEN PHRASES

3 who cares? used in order to say that something does not worry or upset you because you think it is not important **4 I/he/they etc. couldn't care less** used in order to say that someone is not at all concerned about or interested in something: *I couldn't care less about the Super Bowl.* **5 what do I/you/they etc. care?** used in order to say that someone does not care at all about something: *What does he care? He'll get his money whatever happens.* **6 would you care to do sth?/would you care for sth?** *formal* used in order to ask someone if s/he wants to do something: *Would you care to meet us after the show?* | *Would you care for a drink?*

care for sb/sth *phr. v.* **1** to do things for someone who is old, sick, weak, etc. and not able to do things for himself/herself [= **look after**]: *Angie cared for her mother after her stroke.* **2 not care for sb/sth** to not like someone or something: *I don't care for his brother.*

care² *n.*

1 HELP [U] the process of doing things for someone because s/he is old, sick, weak, etc.: *Your father will need constant **medical care**.* | *They shared **the care of** their children.*

2 KEEPING STH IN GOOD CONDITION [U] the process of keeping something in good condition or working correctly: *skin care* | *With proper care, your washing machine should last years.*

3 take care of sb/sth a) to watch and help someone and be responsible for him/her: *Who's taking care of the baby?* **b)** to keep something in good condition or working correctly: *Karl will take care of the house while we're on vacation.* **c)** to do the work or make the arrangements that are necessary for something to happen: *I'll take care of making the reservations.* **d)** to pay for something: *Don't worry about the bill – it's taken care of.*

4 take care a) *spoken* used when saying goodbye to family or friends **b)** to be careful: *It's very icy, so take care driving home.*

5 CAREFULNESS [U] carefulness to avoid damage, mistakes, etc.: *You need to **put** more **care into** your work.* | ***Handle** the package **with care**.*

6 WORRY [C, U] something that causes problems and makes you anxious or sad: *Eddie **doesn't have a care in the world*** (=does not have any problems or worries).

7 in care of sb c/o used when sending letters to someone at someone else's address: *Send me the package in care of my cousin.*

ca·reen /kəˈrin/ *v.* [I] to move quickly forward in an uncontrolled way, making sudden sideways movements: *Morillo's truck **careened down** the hillside and burst into flames.*

ca·reer /kəˈrɪr/ *n.* [C] **1** a job or profession that you have been trained for and intend to do for a long time: *a **career in** law* | *She's considering making a **career change**.*

THESAURUS

job, work, position, occupation, profession, vocation
➔ see Thesaurus box at JOB

2 the period of time in your life that you spend working: *Will spent most of his career as a teacher.* **3 career soldier/teacher etc.** someone who intends to be a soldier, teacher, etc. for most of his/her life, not just for a particular period of time: *a career diplomat*

care·free /ˈkɛrfri/ *adj.* without any problems or worries: *a carefree summer vacation*

care·ful /ˈkɛrfəl/ *adj.* **1** trying very hard not to

make mistakes, damage something, or cause problems [≠ **careless**]: *a careful driver* | *Anna was* ***careful*** *not* ***to*** *upset Steven.*

THESAURUS

methodical – done in a careful and well organized way, or always doing things this way: *a methodical approach to the problem*
thorough – careful to do everything that you should and avoid mistakes: *The police conducted a thorough investigation of the affair.*
meticulous – very careful about details, and always trying to do things correctly: *She keeps meticulous records.*
systematic – organized carefully and done thoroughly: *We need a systematic way to evaluate employees.*
painstaking – very careful and thorough

2 (be) careful! *spoken* used in order to tell someone to think about what s/he is doing so that something bad does not happen: *Be careful – there's broken glass on the sidewalk.* **3** paying a lot of attention to detail: *careful planning* —**carefully** *adv.*: *Please listen carefully.*

care·giv·er /ˈkɛrˌgɪvɚ/ *n.* [C] someone who takes care of a child or of someone who is old or sick

care·less /ˈkɛrlɪs/ *adj.* not paying enough attention to what you are doing, so that you make mistakes, damage things, cause problems, etc. [≠ **careful**]: *a careless mistake* | *It was very* ***careless of*** *you to leave your keys in the car.* —**carelessly** *adv.* —**carelessness** *n.* [U]

ˈcare ˌpackage *n.* [C] a package of food, candy, etc. that is sent to someone living away from home, especially a student at college

ca·ress /kəˈrɛs/ *v.* [T] to gently touch or kiss someone in a way that shows you love him/her —**caress** *n.* [C]

THESAURUS

touch, feel, stroke, rub, scratch, pat, brush, fondle, tickle, grope
➔ see Thesaurus box at TOUCH[1]

care·tak·er /ˈkɛrˌteɪkɚ/ *n.* [C] **1** someone whose job is to take care of a building or land when the person who owns it is not there **2** someone such as a nurse who takes care of other people

car·go /ˈkɑrgoʊ/ *n.* plural **cargoes** [C,U] the goods that are being carried in a ship, airplane, TRUCK, etc.: *The ship was carrying a* ***cargo of*** *oil.*

Car·ib·be·an /ˌkærəˈbiən, kəˈrɪbiən/ *adj.* from or relating to the islands in the Caribbean Sea, such as the Bahamas and Jamaica —**Caribbean** *n.* [C]

ca·ri·bou /ˈkærəbu/ *n.* [C] a North American REINDEER

car·i·ca·ture /ˈkærəkətʃɚ, -ˌtʃʊr/ *n.* [C,U] a funny drawing or description of someone that makes him/her seem silly —**caricature** *v.* [T]

THESAURUS

picture, sketch, snapshot, portrait, cartoon, illustration, poster
➔ see Thesaurus box at PICTURE[1]

car·ing /ˈkɛrɪŋ/ *adj.* someone who is caring is kind to other people and tries to help them: *a warm and caring person*

THESAURUS

kind, nice, considerate, thoughtful
➔ see Thesaurus box at KIND[2]

car·jack·ing /ˈkɑrˌdʒækɪŋ/ *n.* [C,U] the crime of using a weapon to force the driver of a car to drive you somewhere or give you his/her car —**carjacker** *n.* [C]

car·nage /ˈkɑrnɪdʒ/ *n.* [U] *formal* the killing and wounding of a lot of people, especially in a war

car·nal /ˈkɑrnl/ *adj. formal* relating to sex: *carnal desires*

car·na·tion /kɑrˈneɪʃən/ *n.* [C] a white, pink, or red flower that smells nice

car·ni·val /ˈkɑrnəvəl/ *n.* **1** [C] a noisy outdoor event where you can ride on special machines and play games for prizes [= **fair**] **2** [C,U] a public event at which people play music, wear special clothes, and dance in the streets: *carnival time in Rio*

car·ni·vore /ˈkɑrnəˌvɔr/ *n.* [C] an animal that eats meat —**carnivorous** /kɑrˈnɪvərəs/ *adj.*

car·ol /ˈkærəl/ *n.* [C] a CHRISTMAS CAROL

ca·rouse /kəˈraʊz/ *v.* [I] *literary* to drink a lot, be noisy, and have fun

car·ou·sel, **carrousel** /ˌkærəˈsɛl/ *n.* [C] **1** a machine with painted wooden horses on it that turns around, which people can ride on for fun **2** the circular moving belt that you collect your bags and SUITCASES from at an airport

carp[1] /kɑrp/ *n.* plural **carp** [C,U] a large fish that lives in lakes or rivers and can be eaten

carp[2] *v.* [I] to complain about something in an annoying way or to criticize someone all the time

car·pen·ter /ˈkɑrpəntɚ/ *n.* [C] someone whose job is making and repairing wooden objects

car·pen·try /ˈkɑrpəntri/ *n.* [U] the art or work of a carpenter

car·pet[1] /ˈkɑrpɪt/ *n.* [C,U] a heavy woven material for covering all of a floor and stairs, or a piece of this material [➡ **rug**]: *I'd like red carpet in the hall.* ➔ see picture at RUG

carpet[2] *v.* [T] to cover something with a carpet

car·pet·ing /ˈkɑrpət̬ɪŋ/ *n.* [U] carpets in general, or heavy woven material used for making carpets

ˈcar pool *n.* [C] a group of people who travel together to work, school, etc. in one car and share the costs —**carpool** *v.* [I]

car·port /ˈkɑrpɔrt/ *n.* [C] a shelter for a car that has a roof and is often built against the side of a house [➡ **garage**]

car·riage /ˈkærɪdʒ/ *n.* [C] **1** a vehicle with wheels that is pulled by a horse, used in past times **2** a BABY CARRIAGE

car·ri·er /ˈkæriɚ/ *n.* [C] **1** a company that moves goods or passengers from one place to another, especially by airplane **2** *technical* someone who passes a disease to other people without having it himself/herself **3** a telephone or insurance company: *the long-distance phone carrier MCI*

car·rot /ˈkærət/ *n.* [C] a long orange vegetable that grows under the ground → see picture at VEGETABLE

C

car·ry /ˈkæri/ *v.* past tense and past participle **carried**, third person singular **carries**

1 LIFT AND TAKE [T] to hold something in your hands or arms, or on your back, as you take it somewhere: *Can you carry that suitcase for me?* | *Angela was **carrying** the baby **in** her arms.* → see picture on page A9

THESAURUS

tote informal – to carry something: *guards toting machine guns*
lug informal – to pull or carry something that is very heavy: *We lugged our bags and chairs to the beach.*
cart – to carry or take something large and heavy somewhere: *Workers carted away several tons of trash.*
haul – to carry or pull something heavy: *Contractors have begun hauling away the debris.*
schlep informal – to carry or pull something heavy
bear formal – to bring or carry something: *They arrived bearing gifts.*

2 VEHICLE/SHIP/PLANE [T] to take people or things from one place to another: *The bus was carrying 25 passengers.* | *Pipes **carry** the water **across** the desert.*

3 HAVE WITH YOU [T] to have something with you in your pocket, on your belt, in your bag, etc. as you move from place to place: *The security guard usually carries a gun.* | *I never carry much cash.*

4 STORE [T] if a store carries goods, it has a supply of them for sale: *I'm sorry, we don't carry that brand anymore.*

5 INFORMATION/NEWS ETC. [T] to contain a particular piece of information or news: *The morning paper **carried** a **story** about the demonstration in New York.*

6 HAVE A QUALITY [T] to have a particular quality: *The job **carries** certain **risks**.* | *Lee's opinions usually **carry** a lot of **weight*** (=have influence) *with the boss.* | *Matthew's voice did not **carry** much **conviction*** (=he did not sound certain).

7 be/get carried away to be or become so excited that you are no longer in control of what you do or say

8 carry insurance/a guarantee/etc. to have insurance, etc.: *All our products carry a 12-month guarantee.*

9 DISEASE [T] to have a disease and pass it to others: *Many diseases are carried by insects.*

10 carry yourself to stand and move in a particular way: *It was obvious by the way they carried themselves that they were soldiers.*

11 CRIME/PUNISHMENT [T] if a crime carries a particular punishment, that is the usual punishment for the crime: *Murder carries a life sentence in this state.*

12 carry sth too far to do or say too much about something: *It was funny at first, but you've **carried the joke too far**.*

13 ELECTION [T] to win an election in a state or particular area: *Reagan carried California in 1980.*

14 SUPPORT [T] to support the weight of something else: *Those columns carry the whole roof.*

15 SOUND/SMELL [I] to be able to go as far as a particular place or a particular distance: *The sound of their laughter carried as far as the lake.*

16 carry a tune to sing the notes of a song correctly

17 MATHEMATICS [T] **also carry over** to move a total to the next row of figures for adding to other numbers

carry sth ⇔ **off** *phr. v.* to do something difficult successfully: *No one believed he could carry the plan off.*

carry on *phr. v.* **1** to continue doing something: *Jane plans to carry on and finish writing the book.* **2** *spoken* to behave in a silly or excited way: *We won't get anything done if you two don't stop carrying on!*

carry sth ⇔ **out** *phr. v.* **1** to do something that has to be organized and planned: *The police department will carry out a thorough investigation.* **2** to do something that you have said you will do: *The bombers have threatened to carry out more attacks.*

carry sth ⇔ **over** *phr. v.* to make an amount of something available to be used at a later time: *Can I carry over my vacation time to next year?*

carry sth ⇔ **through** *phr. v.* to complete or finish something successfully: *Once he starts a project, he always carries it through.*

ˈcarry-on *adj.* a carry-on bag is one that you can take with you onto an airplane

car·ry·out /ˈkæri,aʊt/ *n.* [C] TAKEOUT

ˈcar seat *n.* [C] a special seat for babies or young children that you attach to the seat of a car

car·sick /ˈkɑr,sɪk/ *adj.* feeling sick because of the movement of traveling in a car —**carsickness** *n.* [U]

cart[1] /kɑrt/ *n.* [C] **1 also shopping cart** a large wire basket on wheels that you use when shopping in a SUPERMARKET **2** a vehicle with two or four wheels that is pulled by a horse, used for carrying heavy things **3** a small table on wheels, used for moving and serving food: *The waiter wheeled the dessert cart over to our table.*

cart[2] *v.* [I,T] to carry or take something large and heavy somewhere: *Workers **carted away** several tons of trash.*

> **THESAURUS**
> **carry, tote, lug, haul, schlep, bear**
> ➔ see Thesaurus box at CARRY

carte blanche /ˌkɑrt 'blɑnʃ/ *n.* [U] permission or freedom to do whatever you want: *He was **given carte blanche** to pick the team he wanted.*

car·tel /kɑr'tɛl/ *n.* [C] a group of companies who all agree to charge the same amount for something they produce or sell, limiting competition in an unfair way

car·ti·lage /'kɑrtl̩-ɪdʒ/ *n.* [C,U] a strong substance that can bend and stretch, which is around the joints in your body

car·tog·ra·phy /kɑr'tɑgrəfi/ *n.* [U] the skill or practice of making maps —**cartographer** *n.* [C]

car·ton /'kɑrt̚n/ *n.* [C] a box made of CARDBOARD that contains food or a drink: *a milk carton | a **carton of** juice*

car·toon /kɑr'tun/ *n.* [C] **1** a movie or television program made with characters that are drawn and not real: *a Bugs Bunny cartoon*

> **THESAURUS**
> **television, movie, film, soap opera, sitcom, game show, talk show, drama series, documentary, the news**
> ➔ see Thesaurus box at TELEVISION

2 a funny drawing in a newspaper, usually about someone or something that is in the news [➥ **comic strip**]

> **THESAURUS**
> **drawing, picture, sketch, comic strip, portrait, caricature, illustration**
> ➔ see Thesaurus box at DRAWING, PICTURE[1]

car·toon·ist /kɑr'tunɪst/ *n.* [C] someone who draws cartoons

car·tridge /'kɑrtrɪdʒ/ *n.* [C] **1** a small piece of equipment that you put inside something to make it work: *The printer needs a new **ink cartridge**.* **2** a tube containing explosive material and a bullet for a gun

cart·wheel /'kɑrt̚wil/ *n.* [C] a movement in which you throw your body sideways onto your hands and bring your legs over your head —**cartwheel** *v.* [I]

carve /kɑrv/ *v.* **1** [T] to make an object by cutting it from a piece of wood or stone: *The statue was **carved from** a single block of marble.* **2** [T] to cut a pattern or letter on the surface of something: *Someone had **carved** their initials **on** the tree.* **3** [I,T] to cut a large piece of cooked meat into smaller pieces with a large knife: *Dad always carves the turkey.* ➔ see picture at CUT[1]

> **THESAURUS**
> **cut, chop (up), slice, dice, peel, shred, grate**
> ➔ see Thesaurus box at CUT[1]

carve sth ⇔ **out** *phr. v.* **carve out a career/niche/reputation etc.** to become successful and be respected

carve sth ⇔ **up** *phr. v. disapproving* to divide land, a company, etc. into smaller parts: *The country was carved up after the war.*

carv·ing /'kɑrvɪŋ/ *n.* **1** [C] an object that has been cut from wood, stone, etc. **2** [U] the activity of cutting objects from wood, stone, etc., or cutting patterns into wood, stone, etc.

'car wash *n.* [C] a place where you can take your car to be washed with special equipment

cas·cade /kæ'skeɪd/ *n.* [C] **1** a small steep WATERFALL **2** *literary* something that seems to flow or hang down: *Her hair fell in a **cascade of** soft curls.* —**cascade** *v.* [I]

cases

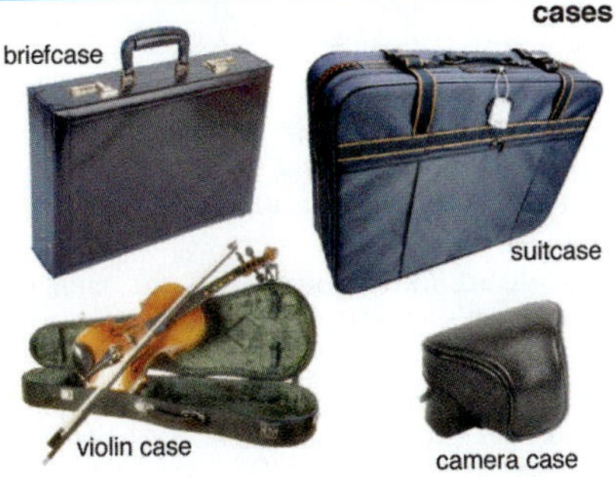

case[1] /keɪs/ *n.*

1 SITUATION/EXAMPLE [C] a particular situation, or an example of that situation: ***In some cases** snoring indicates a real medical problem. | Miller's actions were a clear **case of** sexual harassment. | We live far apart now, but that won't always **be the case**. | Many western cities are growing. Las Vegas is **a case in point*** (=a clear example).

2 (just) in case a) as a way of being prepared for something that might happen: *Take your umbrella in case it rains.* **b)** if: *In case my train is late, start the meeting without me.*

3 COURT [C] a legal matter or question that must be decided in a court of law: *a **court case** | Watson is expected to **win/lose** the **case**.*

4 POLICE [C] a crime or set of events that the police are trying to find out the truth about: *Sturgis is investigating a murder case.*

5 ARGUMENT [C] all the facts or reasons that support one side of an argument: *The prosecution's **case against** him is very strong. | There is a good **case for** changing the rule.*

6 CONTAINER [C] a container for storing something: *a jewelry case | a **case of** wine*

7 in case of sth if or when something happens: *In case of fire, break the glass and push the alarm button.*
8 DISEASE/ILLNESS [C] an example of a disease or illness, or the person suffering from this disease or illness: *There have been ten **cases of** malaria in the village recently.*
9 in that case *spoken* used in order to say what you will do or what will happen in a particular situation: *"I'll be home late tonight." "Well, in that case, I won't cook dinner."*
10 in any case used in order to give the reason why you will do something, or to say that you are determined to do it: *Sure we'll take you home – we're going that way in any case.*
11 be on sb's case *spoken* to be criticizing someone a lot: *Dad's always on my case about something.*
12 get off my case *spoken* used in order to tell someone to stop criticizing you: *OK, OK, just get off my case, will you?*
13 GRAMMAR [C,U] *technical* the form of a word, usually a noun, or the way the form changes, showing its relationship to other words in a sentence ➔ LOWERCASE ➔ UPPERCASE

case² *v.* **1 be cased in sth** to be surrounded by a substance: *The reactor will be cased in metal.* **2 case the joint** *informal* to look around a place that you intend to steal from in order to find out information

case·load /ˈkeɪsloʊd/ *n.* [C] the number of people a doctor, SOCIAL WORKER, etc. has to deal with

ˈcase ˌstudy *n.* [C] a detailed study of a particular person, group, or situation over a long period of time

case·work /ˈkeɪswɚk/ *n.* [U] work done to help particular people or families with their social problems —**caseworker** *n.* [C]

cash¹ /kæʃ/ *n.* [U] **1** money in the form of coins and bills: *There's a small discount if you **pay cash**.* | *He had about $200 **in cash** in his wallet.*

THESAURUS
money, **bill**, **coin**, **penny**, **nickel**, **dime**, **quarter**, **change**, **currency**
➔ see Thesaurus box at MONEY

2 *informal* money in any form: *I'm kind of short of cash at the moment.* | *The company had problems **raising cash** for the deal.* **3 cash on delivery C.O.D.** used when the customer must pay the person who delivers goods to them

cash² *v.* **cash a check/money order/etc.** to exchange a check for money: *Can I get this check cashed here?*

cash in *phr. v.* **1** to gain money or advantages from a situation: *Brooks is **cashing in on** his new popularity.* **2 cash** sth ⇔ **in** to exchange something for its value in money: *We decided to cash in our insurance policy early.*

ˈcash cow *n.* [C] *informal* a business or product you can always depend on to make a profit

ˈcash crop *n.* [C] a crop that is grown to be sold rather than to be used by the people growing it

cash·ew /ˈkæʃu, kæˈʃu/ *n.* [C] a small curved nut that you can eat, or the tropical American tree on which these nuts grow

ˈcash flow *n.* [singular, U] the movement of money into and out of a business or someone's bank account: *They're having **cash flow problems** and might be going out of business.*

cash·ier /kæˈʃɪr/ *n.* [C] someone whose job is to receive and pay out money in a store

THESAURUS
sales assistant, **clerk**
➔ see Thesaurus box at STORE¹

cash·less /ˈkæʃləs/ *adj.* done or working without using coins or paper money

ˈcash maˌchine *n.* [C] a machine from which you can get money by using a special plastic card [= **ATM**]

cash·mere /ˈkæʒmɪr, ˈkæʃ-/ *n.* [U] a type of fine soft wool: *a cashmere sweater*

ˈcash ˌregister *n.* [C] a machine used in stores to keep money in and to show how much customers have to pay

cas·ing /ˈkeɪsɪŋ/ *n.* [C] an outer layer of rubber, metal, etc. that covers and protects something, for example a wire

ca·si·no /kəˈsinoʊ/ *n.* plural **casinos** [C] a place where people try to win money by playing games

cask /kæsk/ *n.* [C] a round wooden container used for holding alcohol, or the amount contained in this

cas·ket /ˈkæskɪt/ *n.* [C] ➔ COFFIN

cas·se·role /ˈkæsəˌroʊl/ *n.* [C,U] food that is cooked slowly in liquid in a covered dish in the OVEN

cas·sette /kəˈsɛt/ *n.* [C] a small flat plastic case containing tape inside that can be used for playing or recording sound or pictures [= **tape**]: *an **audio/video cassette***

cast¹ /kæst/ *v.* past tense and past participle **cast** [T]
1 ACTORS to choose a particular actor for a part in a movie, play, etc.: *Coppola **cast** Gary Oldman **as** Dracula.*
2 cast doubt/suspicion on sth to make people feel less certain about something: *Recent information has cast doubt on the evidence.*
3 cast a vote to vote in an election: *I'd like to know more about the candidates before I cast my vote.*
4 cast a spell on/over sb/sth a) to make someone feel very strongly attracted to something and keep his/her attention completely: *Within minutes, Sinatra's voice had cast its spell on the audience.* **b)** to say magic words to make something happen

5 cast a shadow **a)** to make people feel less happy or hopeful about something: *Her father's illness **cast a shadow over** the wedding celebrations.* **b)** *literary* to make a shadow appear on something: *trees casting a shadow across the lawn*
6 cast light on/onto sth **a)** to explain or give new information about something: *His research has cast light on the origin of the universe.* **b)** *literary* to send light onto a surface
7 cast a look/glance (at sb/sth) *literary* to look at someone or something: *She cast an anxious glance at Guy.*
8 ART to make something by pouring metal or plastic into a specially shaped container: *a statue of Lincoln **cast in** bronze*
9 THROW to throw something somewhere: *fishermen casting their nets into the sea*
cast sb/sth ⇔ **aside** *phr. v.* to get rid of something or someone: *It's time to cast aside the past and make a new start.*
cast off *phr. v.* **1** to untie the rope that keeps a boat on shore so that it can sail away **2 cast** sb/sth ⇔ **off** *literary* to get rid of something or someone
cast sb/sth ⇔ **out** *phr. v. literary* to force someone or something to go away
cast² *n.* [C] **1** all of the actors in a movie, play, etc.: *an **all-star cast*** (=all the actors are famous) **2** a hard cover for a part of your body that supports a broken bone while it gets better: *a leg cast* **3** a MOLD (=specially shaped container) into which you pour metal or plastic in order to make an object of a particular shape
cast·a·way /ˈkæstəˌweɪ/ *n.* [C] someone who is alone on an island after his/her ship has sunk
caste /kæst/ *n.* [C,U] one of the social classes in India into which people are born that cannot be changed
cast·er /ˈkæstɚ/ *n.* [C] a small wheel fixed to the bottom of a piece of furniture so it can be moved easily
cas·ti·gate /ˈkæstəˌgeɪt/ *v.* [T] *formal* to criticize or punish someone in a severe way —**castigation** /ˌkæstəˈgeɪʃən/ *n.* [U]
cast·ing /ˈkæstɪŋ/ *n.* [U] the act of choosing actors for a movie, play, etc.: *a casting director*
ˌcast ˈiron *n.* [U] a type of iron that is very hard
ˌcast-ˈiron *adj.* **1** made of cast iron: *a cast-iron skillet* **2 cast-iron excuse/alibi/guarantee etc.** an excuse, etc. that is very certain and cannot fail
cas·tle /ˈkæsəl/ *n.* [C] a very large strong building built in past times to protect the people inside from attack
cast·offs /ˈkæstɔfs/ *n.* [plural] clothes or other things that someone does not want anymore and gives or throws away
cas·trate /ˈkæstreɪt/ *v.* [T] to remove the sexual organs of a male animal or a man —**castration** /kæˈstreɪʃən/ *n.* [C,U]
cas·u·al /ˈkæʒuəl, -ʒəl/ *adj.* **1** casual clothes are comfortable and not worn on formal occasions: *Many companies allow **casual dress** on Fridays.* | *the **casual look*** **2** relaxed and not worried about things: *The restaurant has a **casual atmosphere**.* | *Sex is talked about a lot in **casual conversation**.* | *His **casual attitude** toward work really irritates me.* **3** [only before noun] without any serious interest or attention: *Most **casual observers** won't notice anything different.* **4** knowing someone without wanting a close relationship with him/her: *a **casual acquaintance*** | *He just wanted **casual sex**.* —**casually** *adv.*: *He was casually dressed.*
cas·u·al·ty /ˈkæʒəlti, -ʒuəlti/ *n.* plural **casualties** [C] **1** someone who is hurt or killed in an accident or war: *The army suffered **heavy casualties*** (=a lot of people were hurt or killed). **2 be a casualty of sth** to suffer because of a particular event or situation: *The city library is the latest casualty of the cutbacks.*

C

cat /kæt/ *n.* [C] **1** a small animal that is often kept as a pet or is used for catching mice ➔ see picture at PET¹ **2** a large wild animal that is related to cats, such as a lion **3 let the cat out of the bag** *informal* to tell a secret without intending to
cat·a·clysm /ˈkæt̬əˌklɪzəm/ *n.* [C] *literary* a sudden violent event or change, such as a big flood or EARTHQUAKE —**cataclysmic** /ˌkæt̬əˈklɪzmɪk/ *adj.*
cat·a·log¹, **catalogue** /ˈkæt̬lˌɔg, -ˌɑg/ *n.* [C] **1** a book with pictures and information about goods or services that you can buy: *a mail order catalog* **2** a list of the objects, paintings, books, etc. in a place such as a MUSEUM or library
catalog² *v.* [T] to make a complete list of something
cat·a·lyst /ˈkæt̬l-ɪst/ *n.* [C] **1** someone or something that makes an important event or change happen: *The women's movement became a **catalyst for** change in the workplace.* **2** a substance that makes a chemical reaction happen more quickly, without being changed itself
cat·a·ma·ran /ˈkæt̬əməˌræn/ *n.* [C] a type of small boat with sails and two separate HULLS (=part that goes in the water)
cat·a·pult¹ /ˈkæt̬əˌpʌlt, -ˌpʊlt/ *v.* [T] **1** to push or throw something very hard so that it moves through the air very quickly: *Two cars were catapulted into the air by the force of the blast.* **2 catapult sb to stardom/fame etc.** to suddenly make someone very famous or successful
catapult² *n.* [C] a large weapon used in former times to throw heavy stones, iron balls, etc.
cat·a·ract /ˈkæt̬əˌrækt/ *n.* [C] a medical condition that affects the eye and makes you slowly lose your sight
ca·tas·tro·phe /kəˈtæstrəfi/ *n.* [C,U] a terrible event that causes a lot of destruction or suffering: *The oil spill will be an ecological catastrophe.* —**catastrophic** /ˌkæt̬əˈstrɑfɪk◂/ *adj.*: *catastrophic floods* ➔ see Thesaurus box at ACCIDENT
catch¹ /kætʃ/ *v.* past tense and past participle **caught** /kɔt/
1 HOLD [I, T] to get hold of and stop something that is moving through the air [≠ **drop**]: *He*

***caught the ball** and started to run.* → see picture on page A9
2 FIND SB/STH [T] **a)** to stop a person or animal that is running away: *"You can't catch me!" she yelled over her shoulder.* **b)** to find a criminal and put him/her somewhere so that s/he cannot escape: *The police have caught the man suspected of the murder.* **c)** to get a fish or animal by using a trap, net, or hook: *Did you **catch** any **fish**?*

THESAURUS

capture – to catch someone in order to keep him/her as a prisoner: *A French soldier was captured in the battle.*
arrest – if the police **arrest** someone, the person is taken away because the police think s/he has done something illegal: *He was arrested and charged with murder.*
corner – to move closer to a person or an animal so that he, she, or it cannot escape: *Once the dog was cornered, he began to growl.*
trap – to prevent someone from escaping from somewhere, especially a dangerous place: *20 miners were trapped underground.*

C

3 SEE SB DOING STH [T] to see someone doing something wrong or illegal: *I caught him looking through my letters.* | *A store detective **caught** him **red-handed*** (=saw him stealing).
4 GET SICK [T] to get an illness: *Put your coat on or you'll **catch a cold**.*
5 catch a train/plane/bus to get on a train, etc. in order to travel somewhere: *I should be able to catch the 12:05 train.*
6 NOT BE TOO LATE [T] to not be too late to do something, talk to someone, etc. [≠ **miss**]: *If you hurry you might catch her before she leaves.*
7 GET STUCK [I, T] to become stuck on or in something by mistake: *His shirt caught on the fence and tore.*
8 catch sb by surprise/catch sb off guard to do something or happen in an unexpected way, so that someone is not ready to deal with it
9 SEE/SMELL [T] to see or smell something for a moment: *I suddenly **caught sight of** Luisa in the crowd.* | *Yuck – did you **catch a whiff*** (=did you smell it?) *of his aftershave?*
10 catch sb's eye a) to attract someone's attention and make him/her look at something: *A photograph on his desk caught my eye.* **b)** to look at someone at the same moment that s/he is looking at you: *Every time she caught his eye, she would look away embarrassed.*
11 be caught in/without etc. sth to be in a situation that is difficult because you cannot easily get out of it, or because you do not have what you need: *We got caught in the storm.*
12 catch (on) fire to start burning, especially accidentally
13 catch your breath to begin breathing normally again after you have been running or exercising
14 catch sb's attention/interest/imagination to make someone feel interested in something: *a story that will catch children's imaginations*
15 STOP PROBLEM/DISEASE [T] to discover a problem, especially a disease, and stop it from developing: *It's a type of cancer that can be cured, if it is caught early.*

SPOKEN PHRASES

16 not catch sth to not hear or understand something clearly: *I'm sorry, I didn't catch your name.*
17 you won't catch me doing sth used in order to say you would never do something: *You won't catch me ironing his shirts.*
18 Catch you later! used in order to say goodbye

catch on *phr. v.* **1** to begin to understand something: *It may take time for some of the children to catch on.* **2** to become popular: *The idea never caught on in this country.*
catch up *phr. v.* **1** to reach a person or vehicle that was in front of you by going faster than him, her, or it: *I had to run to **catch up with** her.* **2** to reach the same standard or level as other people: *If you miss class, it can be difficult to catch up.* **3 be/get caught up in sth** to become involved in something, especially without wanting to: *young people who get caught up in crime*
catch up on sth *phr. v.* to do something that needs to be done that you have not had time to do in the past: *I need to catch up on some work.*
catch² *n.* **1** [C] the act of catching something that has been thrown or hit: *That was a great catch!* **2** [U] a game in which two or more people throw a ball to each other: *Let's play catch.* **3** [C] *informal* a hidden problem or difficulty: *The rent is so low there must be a catch.* **4** [C] a hook for fastening something and holding it shut: *the catch on my necklace*
Catch-22 /ˌkætʃ ˌtwɛnti ˈtu/ *n.* [singular, U] a situation in which, whatever you do, you are prevented from achieving what you want: *You can't get a job without experience, and you can't get experience without a job. It's a Catch-22.*
catch·er /ˈkætʃɚ/ *n.* [C] the baseball player who SQUATS behind the BATTER in order to catch balls that are not hit
catch·ing /ˈkætʃɪŋ/ *adj.* [not before noun] *informal* a disease or illness that is catching spreads easily from one person to another
ˈcatch phrase *n.* [C] a word or phrase that is easy to remember and is repeated by a political party, newspaper, etc.
catch·y /ˈkætʃi/ *adj.* a CATCHY tune or phrase is easy to remember: *catchy advertising slogans*
cat·e·chism /ˈkæt̬əˌkɪzəm/ *n.* [C] a set of questions and answers about the Christian religion that people learn before becoming members of the church
cat·e·gor·i·cal /ˌkæt̬əˈgɔrɪkəl, -ˈgɑr-/ *adj.* clearly stating that something is true: *Weber's agent issued a **categorical denial** that the incident*

had ever happened. —**categorically** *adv.*: *James categorically denied the charges.*

cat·e·go·rize /ˈkætəgəˌraɪz/ *v.* [T] to put people or things into groups according to what type, level, etc. they are: *We've **categorized** the wines **by** region.*

cat·e·go·ry /ˈkætəˌgɔri/ *n.* plural **categories** [C] a group of people or things that are all of the same type: *There are several **categories of** patients.* | *Voters **fall into** (=belong to) one of three **categories**.*

THESAURUS

type, kind, sort, brand, make, model, genre
→ see Thesaurus box at TYPE[1]

ca·ter /ˈkeɪtə/ *v.* [I,T] to provide and serve food and drinks at a party, meeting, etc., usually as a business: *Who's catering your daughter's wedding?* —**caterer** *n.* [C]

cater to sb *phr. v.* to provide a particular group of people with something that they need or want: *newspapers that cater to business people*

ca·ter·ing /ˈkeɪtərɪŋ/ *n.* [U] the job of providing and serving food and drinks at parties, meetings, etc.

cat·er·pil·lar /ˈkætəˌpɪlə, ˈkætə-/ *n.* [C] a small creature with a long rounded body and many legs that develops into a BUTTERFLY or MOTH → see picture on page A2

cat·fish /ˈkætˀfɪʃ/ *n.* [C,U] a common fish with long hairs around its mouth that lives mainly in rivers and lakes, or the meat from this fish

ca·thar·tic /kəˈθɑrtɪk/ *adj.* helping you to deal with difficult emotions and get rid of them —**catharsis** /kəˈθɑrsɪs/ *n.* [U]

ca·the·dral /kəˈθidrəl/ *n.* [C] the main church in a particular area

Cath·o·lic /ˈkæθlɪk, -θəlɪk/ *adj.* relating to the part of the Christian religion whose leader is the Pope —**Catholic** *n.* [C] —**Catholicism** /kəˈθɑləˌsɪzəm/ *n.* [U]

catholic *adj. formal* including a great variety of things: *Susan has **catholic tastes** in music.*

cat·nap /ˈkætˀnæp/ *n.* [C] *informal* a short sleep during the day

cat·nip /ˈkætˀnɪp/ *n.* [U] a type of grass with a pleasant smell that cats are attracted to

CAT scan /ˈkæt skæn/ also **CT scan** /si ˈti skæn/ *n.* [C] an image of the inside of someone's body produced by a special piece of hospital equipment called a SCANNER

cat·sup /ˈkɛtʃəp, ˈkæ-/ *n.* [U] another spelling of KETCHUP

cat·tle /ˈkætl/ *n.* [plural] cows and BULLS kept on a farm

cat·ty /ˈkæti/ *adj. informal* deliberately unkind in what you say about someone —**cattiness** *n.* [U]

ˈcatty-ˈcornered *adv.* KITTY-CORNER

cat·walk /ˈkætˀwɔk/ *n.* [C] **1** a long raised path that MODELS walk on in a fashion show **2** a narrow structure high up in a building or above something such as a bridge, built for people to walk on while they are working

Cau·ca·sian /kɔˈkeɪʒən/ *adj.* someone who is Caucasian belongs to the race that has pale skin —**Caucasian** *n.* [C]

cau·cus /ˈkɔkəs/ *n.* [C] a group of people in a political party, who meet to discuss and decide on political plans

caught /kɔt/ *v.* the past tense and past participle of CATCH

caul·dron /ˈkɔldrən/ *n.* [C] a large round metal pot for boiling liquids over a fire

cau·li·flow·er /ˈkɔlɪˌflaʊə, ˈkɑ-/ *n.* [C,U] a white vegetable with short firm stems and thick groups of small round flower-like parts → see picture at VEGETABLE

cause[1] /kɔz/ *n.* **1** [C] a person, event, or thing that makes something happen: *What was the **cause of** the accident.* **2** [C,U] a reason for doing something or having a particular feeling: *There is **no cause for concern/alarm**.* **3** [C] a principle or aim that a group of people support or fight for: *I don't mind giving money if it's **for a good cause**.*

cause[2] *v.* [T] to make something happen, especially something bad: *Heavy traffic is causing long delays.* | *We still don't know what **caused** the computer **to** crash.*

THESAURUS

make – to cause a particular state or situation to happen: *I'm sorry, I didn't mean to make you cry.*
be responsible for sth – if you are responsible for something bad, it is your fault that it happened: *The jury found him responsible for the deaths of his wife and child.*
bring about sth – to make something happen: *Working together, the community brought about significant changes in the local area.*
result in sth – if an action or event results in something, it makes that thing happen: *The fire resulted in the deaths of two children.*
lead to sth – if one thing leads to something else, the first thing causes the second thing to happen or exist at a later time: *The information led to several arrests.*
trigger – if one event triggers another, it makes the second event happen: *The incident triggered a wave of violence.*

caus·tic /ˈkɔstɪk/ *adj.* **1 caustic remark/comment etc.** something you say that is extremely unkind or full of criticism **2** a caustic substance can burn through things by chemical action

cau·tion[1] /ˈkɔʃən/ *n.* [U] **1** the quality of doing something carefully, not taking risks, and avoiding danger: *The animals should be handled **with caution**.* | *Travelers in the area should **use** extreme **caution**.* **2 word/note of caution** a warning to be careful: *A word of caution – be sure to make copies of all files.*

caution² *v.* [T] *formal* to warn someone that something might be dangerous or difficult: *The children were **cautioned against** talking to strangers.*

cau·tion·ar·y /ˈkɔʃəˌnɛri/ *adj.* giving a warning: *a **cautionary tale*** (=a story that is used to warn people)

cau·tious /ˈkɔʃəs/ *adj.* careful to avoid danger: *a cautious driver* | *He was **cautious about** making any predictions.* —**cautiously** *adv.*

cav·a·lier /ˌkævəˈlɪr/ *adj.* not caring or thinking enough about other people or how serious a situation might be: ***a cavalier attitude***

cav·al·ry /ˈkævəlri/ *n.* [U] soldiers who fight while riding on horses

C

cave¹ /keɪv/ *n.* [C] a large natural hole in the side of a cliff or under the ground

cave² *v.*

cave in *phr. v.* **1** if the top or sides of something cave in, they fall down or inward: *The roof of the old house had caved in.* **2** to stop opposing something because you have been persuaded or threatened

cave·man /ˈkeɪvmæn/ *n.* plural **cavemen** /-mɛn/ [C] someone who lived in a CAVE many thousands of years ago

cav·ern /ˈkævən/ *n.* [C] a large deep CAVE —**cavernous** *adj.*

cav·i·ar /ˈkæviˌɑr/ *n.* [U] fish eggs, eaten as a special expensive food

cav·i·ty /ˈkævəti/ *n.* plural **cavities** [C] **1** a hole in a tooth made by decay: *The dentist told me that **I have a cavity**.* **2** a hole or space inside something solid

ca·vort /kəˈvɔrt/ *v.* [I] to jump or dance in an excited or sexual way

CB *n.* [C,U] **Citizens Band** a radio on which people can speak to each other over short distances

CBS *n.* [singular] **Columbia Broadcasting System** one of the national companies that broadcasts television and radio programs in the U.S.

cc **1 cubic centimeter**: *a 2,000 cc engine* **2 carbon copy** used in business letters and emails to show that you are sending a copy to someone else

CD *n.* [C] **1 compact disc** a small circular piece of hard plastic on which music or computer information is recorded **2** CERTIFICATE OF DEPOSIT

CˈD ˌplayer *n.* [C] a piece of equipment used for playing music CDS

CD-ROM /ˌsi di ˈrɑm/ *n.* [C,U] **compact disc read-only memory** a CD on which a large amount of computer information is stored

cease /sis/ *v.* [I,T] *formal* to stop doing something or to make an activity stop happening: *By noon the rain had ceased.* | *He never **ceases to amaze me*** (=I am always surprised by what he does).

cease·fire /ˌsisˈfaɪə, ˈsisfaɪə/ *n.* [C] an agreement for both sides in a war to stop fighting for a period of time

cease·less /ˈsislɪs/ *adj. formal* continuing for a long time without stopping —**ceaselessly** *adv.*

ce·dar /ˈsidə/ *n.* [C,U] a tall EVERGREEN tree with leaves shaped like needles, or the red sweet-smelling wood of this tree

cede /sid/ *v.* [T] *formal* to give land, power, etc. to another country or person

ceil·ing /ˈsilɪŋ/ *n.* [C] **1** the inside surface of the top part of a room [➡ **roof**]: *an apartment with **high ceilings*** **2** the largest number or amount of something that is officially allowed: *They have put **a ceiling of** $2 million **on** the project*

cel·e·brate /ˈsɛləˌbreɪt/ *v.* [I,T] to do something special because of a particular event or special occasion: *It's our anniversary, and we're going out to dinner to celebrate.* | *How do you want to celebrate your birthday?*

cel·e·brat·ed /ˈsɛləˌbreɪtɪd/ *adj.* famous or talked about a lot: *Chicago is **celebrated for** its architecture.*

cel·e·bra·tion /ˌsɛləˈbreɪʃən/ *n.* [C] **1** an occasion or party when you celebrate something: *New Year's celebrations* ➔ see Thesaurus box at PARTY¹ **2** the act of celebrating: *There'll be a party **in celebration of** his promotion.*

ce·leb·ri·ty /səˈlɛbrəti/ *n.* plural **celebrities** [C] a famous person, especially someone in the entertainment business: *Hollywood celebrities*

cel·er·y /ˈsɛləri/ *n.* [U] a vegetable with long firm pale green stems, often eaten raw ➔ see picture at VEGETABLE

ce·les·tial /səˈlɛstʃəl/ *adj.* relating to the sky or heaven

cel·i·bate /ˈsɛləbɪt/ *adj.* someone who is celibate does not have sex —**celibacy** /ˈsɛləbəsi/ *n.* [U]

cell /sɛl/ *n.* [C] **1** the smallest part of a living thing: *red blood cells* **2** a small room where prisoners are kept: *a jail cell*

cel·lar /ˈsɛlə/ *n.* [C] a room under a house or other building, often used for storing things

cel·list /ˈtʃɛlɪst/ *n.* [C] someone who plays the cello

> **TOPIC**
>
> **conductor**, **flutist**, **violinist**, **percussionist**
> ➔ see Topic box at ORCHESTRA

cel·lo /ˈtʃɛloʊ/ *n.* [C] a large wooden musical instrument that you hold between your knees and play by pulling a BOW (=special stick) across the strings ➔ see picture on page A6

Cel·lo·phane /ˈsɛləˌfeɪn/ *n.* [U] *trademark* a thin transparent material used for wrapping things

cell phone

ˈcell phone also **ˈcel·lular ˌphone** *n.* [C] a telephone that you carry with you

TOPIC

To use a cell phone, you first **switch it on**. Then you can either **call** someone or **listen to messages** that people have left you on your **voice mail**. You can also read **text messages** (=written messages) or **text** someone (=send him/her a text message).

cel·lu·lar /ˈsɛlyələ˞/ *adj.* **1** relating to cellular phones: *a cellular network* **2** relating to the cells in a plant or animal

ˈcellular ˌphone *n.* [C] a CELL PHONE

cel·lu·lite /ˈsɛlyəˌlaɪt/ *n.* [U] fat just below someone's skin that makes it look uneven and unattractive

cel·lu·loid /ˈsɛlyəˌlɔɪd/ *n.* [C] *trademark* a substance like plastic, used in the past to make film

cel·lu·lose /ˈsɛlyəˌloʊs/ *n.* [U] a substance that forms the walls of plant cells

Cel·si·us /ˈsɛlsiəs, -ʃəs/ *n.* [U] *written abbreviation* **C** a temperature scale in which water freezes at 0° and boils at 100° [= **Centigrade**; ➡ **Fahrenheit**]

ce·ment¹ /sɪˈmɛnt/ *n.* [U] a gray powder used in building that is mixed with sand and water and allowed to dry and become hard

cement² *v.* [T] **1** to make a relationship, position, etc. stronger: *China has cemented its trade connections with the U.S.* **2** to cover something with cement

cem·e·ter·y /ˈsɛməˌtɛri/ *n.* plural **cemeteries** [C] a place where dead people are buried

cen·sor¹ /ˈsɛnsə˞/ *v.* [T] to examine books, movies, etc. and remove anything that is offensive, politically dangerous, etc. —**censorship** *n.* [U]

censor² *n.* [C] someone whose job is to censor books, movies, etc.

cen·sure /ˈsɛnʃə˞/ *v.* [T] *formal* to officially criticize someone —**censure** *n.* [U]

cen·sus /ˈsɛnsəs/ *n.* plural **censuses** [C] an occasion when a government collects information about the number of people in a country, their ages, jobs, etc.: *When was the first U.S.* ***census taken****?*

cent /sɛnt/ *n.* [C] **1** a unit of money that is worth 1/100 of a dollar. Its sign is ¢. **2 put in/add/say your two cents' worth** *informal* to give your opinion about something, when no one has asked to hear it

cen·ten·ni·al /sɛnˈtɛniəl/ **also cen·ten·a·ry** /sɛnˈtɛnəri/ *n.* [C] the day or year exactly 100 years after an important event: *This year marked the* ***centennial of*** *the composer's death.*

cen·ter¹ /ˈsɛntə˞/ *n.* [C] **1** the middle part or point of something: *We moved the table to* ***the center of*** *the room.* | *an old hotel* ***in the center of*** *town* **2** a building used for a particular purpose: *a shopping center* | *the Kennedy Space Center* **3** a place where there is a lot of a particular type of business or activity: *a major banking center* | *the* ***center of*** *the country's music industry* **4 be at the center of sth** to be the main cause of something bad, or having a very important part in it: *The senator* ***is at the center of a controversy*** *over political donations.* **5 be the center of attention** to be the person that everyone is giving attention to **6 the center** a political position which does not support extreme views **7** in basketball, the player who usually plays near the basket **8** in football, the player who starts the ball moving in each PLAY

center² *v.* [T] to move something to a position at the center of something else: *Is this painting centered?*

center on/around sth *phr. v.* if something centers on a particular thing, that is the most important thing in it or what it mainly concerns: *Their whole life centers around their children.* | *The discussion centered on gun control.*

ˈcenter field *n.* [singular] the area in baseball in the center of the OUTFIELD —**centerfielder** *n.* [C]

ˌcenter of ˈgravity *n.* [singular] the point on an object at which it can balance

cen·ter·piece /ˈsɛntə˞ˌpis/ *n.* **1** [singular] the most important, attractive, or noticeable part of something: *the* ***centerpiece of*** *Canada's foreign policy* **2** [C] a decoration in the middle of a table, usually made of flowers

Cen·ti·grade /ˈsɛntəˌgreɪd/ *n.* [U] CELSIUS

cen·ti·me·ter /ˈsɛntəˌmitə˞/ *n.* [C] *written abbreviation* **cm** a unit for measuring length, equal to 1/100 of a meter or 0.39 inches

cen·ti·pede /ˈsɛntəˌpid/ *n.* [C] a very small creature with a long thin body and many legs

cen·tral /ˈsɛntrəl/ *adj.* **1** [only before noun] in the middle of an object or area: *Central Asia* | *the central part of the island* **2** [only before noun] having control over the rest of a system, organization, etc.: *The computers are linked to a central database.* **3** more important than anything else: *Owen* ***played a central role in*** *the negotiations.* | *Tax cuts were* ***central to*** *the President's re-election campaign.*

THESAURUS

basic, fundamental, essential
→ see Thesaurus box at BASIC

4 a place that is central is near the center of a town: *I want a hotel that's central.* —**centrally** *adv.*

ˌcentral ˈair conˌditioning *n.* [U] a system of cooling buildings in which cool air is produced in one place and taken to the rest of the building by pipes

ˌcentral ˈheating *n.* [U] a system of heating buildings in which heat is produced in one place and taken to the rest of the building by pipes

ˌCentral Inˈtelligence ˌAgency *n.* [singular] CIA

C

cen·tral·ize /ˈsɛntrəˌlaɪz/ *v.* [T] to control a country, organization, or system from one place

cen·tu·ry /ˈsɛntʃəri/ *n.* plural **centuries** [C] **1** one of the 100-year periods measured from before or after the year of Christ's birth: ***the 6th/11th/21st, etc. century*** | *My grandparents moved west* ***at the turn of the century*** (=at the beginning of the century). **2** a period of 100 years

CEO *n.* [C] **Chief Executive Officer** the person with the most authority in a large company

ce·ram·ics /səˈræmɪks/ *n.* [plural, U] pots, plates, etc. made from clay, or the art of making them —**ceramic** *adj.*

C

THESAURUS

art, painting, drawing, photography, sculpture, pottery
➔ see Thesaurus box at ART

ce·re·al /ˈsɪriəl/ *n.* **1** [C,U] breakfast food made from grain and usually eaten with milk: *a* ***bowl of cereal*** **2** [C] a plant grown to produce grain for foods, such as wheat, rice, etc.

ce·re·bral /səˈribrəl, ˈsɛrə-/ *adj. technical* relating to the brain

ceˌrebral ˈpalsy *n.* [U] a medical condition that affects someone's ability to move or speak, caused by damage to the brain at birth

cer·e·mo·ni·al /ˌsɛrəˈmoʊniəl/ *adj.* used in a ceremony, or done as part of a ceremony: *Native American ceremonial pipes*

cer·e·mo·ny /ˈsɛrəˌmoʊni/ *n.* plural **ceremonies** **1** [C] a formal event that happens in public on special occasions: *a wedding ceremony* | *a graduation ceremony* | *The treaty was signed during a ceremony at the White House.* **2** [U] the formal actions and words always used on particular occasions: ***With*** *great* ***ceremony****, the Mayor opened the new concert hall.*

cer·tain /ˈsɚtⁿn/ *adj.* **1** completely sure: ***I'm not certain (that)*** *he's telling me the truth.* | *She was* ***absolutely certain*** *he was the killer.* | *No one was* ***certain what*** *to expect.* | *Are you* ***certain about*** *that?* **2** sure to happen or be true: ***It's*** *almost* ***certain that*** *the enemy will attack from the north.* | ***It seems certain*** *that the case will not end for months.* | *He's* ***certain to*** *be offered the job.* **3** [only before noun] a certain thing, person, idea, etc. is a particular thing, person, etc. that you are not naming or describing exactly: *The plant grows in certain conditions.* | *There are certain things I just can't talk about with her.* | *The poison causes* ***certain death.*** **4 make certain a)** to check that something is correct or true: *We need to make certain that it's going to fit first.* **b)** to do something in order to be sure something will happen: *Employers are required to make certain that all employees are treated fairly.* **5 a certain a)** some, but not a lot: *I had to spend* ***a certain amount of*** *time practicing, but it wasn't hard.* | *I agree with you* ***to a certain extent*** (=partly but not completely). **b)** difficult to describe exactly: *The restaurant has a certain charm.* **6 for certain** without any doubt: *I can't* ***say for certain*** *when her plane will arrive.*

cer·tain·ly /ˈsɚtⁿnli/ *adv.* without any doubt [= **definitely**]: *Diana certainly spends a lot of money on clothes.* | *His lawyers will* ***almost certainly*** *appeal.* | *"Can I borrow your notes?" "Certainly* (=yes, of course)."

cer·tain·ty /ˈsɚtⁿnti/ *n.* plural **certainties** **1** [U] the state of being completely sure about something: *We cannot say* ***with complete certainty*** *whether your wife will be all right.* **2** [C] something that is definitely true or will definitely happen: *Winning the title is almost a certainty. There's no doubt about it.*

cer·ti·fi·a·ble /ˌsɚt̬əˈfaɪəbəl/ *adj. informal* crazy

cer·tif·i·cate /sɚˈtɪfəkɪt/ *n.* [C] an official document that states the facts about something or someone: *a* ***birth/marriage/death certificate*** (=giving details of someone's birth, etc.) ➔ GIFT CERTIFICATE

cerˌtificate of deˈposit *n.* [C] *technical* a bank account that you must leave a particular amount of money in for a particular amount of time in order to get INTEREST

cer·ti·fi·ca·tion /ˌsɚt̬əfəˈkeɪʃən/ *n.* [C,U] an official document that says that someone is allowed to do a certain job, that something is of good quality, etc., or the process of doing this

ˌcertified ˈcheck *n.* [C] a check that you get from a bank for a particular amount of money that the bank promises to pay

ˌcertified ˈmail *n.* [U] a method of sending mail in which a written record is kept of when it is sent and when it is received

ˌcertified ˌpublic acˈcountant *n.* [C] CPA

cer·ti·fy /ˈsɚt̬əˌfaɪ/ *v.* past tense and past participle **certified**, third person singular **certifies** [T] **1** to officially state that something is correct or true: *Two doctors* ***certified that*** *the patient was dead.* **2** to give someone an official document that states that s/he has completed a course of training: *He has been certified as a mechanic.* | *a certified nurse*

cer·vix /ˈsɚvɪks/ *n.* [C] *technical* the narrow opening into a woman's UTERUS —**cervical** /ˈsɚvɪkəl/ *adj.*

ce·sar·e·an /sɪˈzɛriən/ **also ceˌsarean ˈsection** *n.* [C] an operation in which a woman's body is cut open to take a baby out

ces·sa·tion /sɛˈseɪʃən/ *n.* [C] *formal* a pause or stop: *the* ***cessation of*** *nuclear tests*

cess·pool /ˈsɛspul/ *n.* [C] a large hole or container under the ground for collecting waste water from a building

CFC *n.* [C] **chlorofluorocarbon** a gas used in AEROSOLS and REFRIGERATORS which causes damage to the OZONE LAYER

chafe /tʃeɪf/ *v.* [I,T] if a part of your body chafes,

or if something chafes it, your skin becomes sore because something is rubbing against it

cha·grin /ʃəˈgrɪn/ *n.* [U] *formal* a feeling of being disappointed and annoyed: ***To** the surfers' **cha-grin**, the beach was closed.*

chain¹ /tʃeɪn/ *n.* **1** [C,U] a series of metal rings connected together: *a delicate gold chain* | *a **bicycle chain*** (=that makes the wheels turn) ➔ see picture at BICYCLE **2** [C] a group of stores, hotels, etc. that is owned by the same person or company: *a **chain of** restaurants* | *a hotel chain* **3 chain of events** a series of related events or actions: *the chain of events that caused World War I* **4** [C] a series of similar things in a line: *a mountain chain* | *a **chain of** islands* **5 in chains** prisoners in chains have heavy chains fastened around their legs or arms, to prevent them from escaping

chain² *v.* [T] to use a chain to fasten one thing or person to another: *a bicycle **chained to** a fence*

ˈchain ˌletter *n.* [C] a letter that is sent to several people who send copies to more people

ˌchain of comˈmand *n.* [C] a system in an organization by which decisions are made and passed from people at the top of the organization to people lower down

ˌchain reˈaction *n.* [C] a series of related events or chemical changes that happen quickly, with each one causing the next

chain·saw /ˈtʃeɪnsɔ/ *n.* [U] a tool used for cutting wood, consisting of a circular chain with sharp edges that is moved by a motor

ˈchain-smoke *v.* [I,T] to smoke cigarettes one after the other —**chain-smoker** *n.* [C]

ˈchain store *n.* [C] one of a group of shops owned by the same company

THESAURUS

store, bookstore, clothes store, record store, grocery store, supermarket, bakery, delicatessen, deli, liquor store, drugstore, hardware store, nursery, garden center, newsstand, boutique, convenience store, department store, superstore, outlet store, warehouse store
➔ see Thesaurus box at STORE¹

chair¹ /tʃɛr/ *n.* **1** [C] a piece of furniture for one person to sit on: *He sat in a chair next to the fireplace.* ➔ see picture at SEAT¹ **2** [C] someone who is in charge of a meeting, a committee, or a university department: *She was named **chair of** the Public Safety Committee.* **3 the chair** the position of being in charge of a meeting or committee

chair² *v.* [T] to be the person in charge of a meeting or committee

chair·man /ˈtʃɛrmən/ plural **chairmen** /-mən/ *n.* [C] **1** someone, especially a man, who is in charge of a meeting or committee **2** someone, especially a man, who is in charge of a large company or organization —**chairmanship** *n.* [U]

USAGE

Chairman can be used for both men and women, though some women prefer to be called a **chairwoman.** Many people prefer to use **chairperson,** especially if the sex of the person is not known.

chair·per·son /ˈtʃɛrˌpɚsən/ *n.* plural **chairper·sons** [C] someone who is in charge of a meeting or directs the work of a committee or organization

chair·wom·an /ˈtʃɛrˌwʊmən/ *n.* plural **chairwomen** /-ˌwɪmɪn/ [C] a woman who is a chairperson

chalet

cha·let /ʃæˈleɪ, ˈʃæleɪ/ *n.* [C] a wooden house, especially one in a mountain area

chalk¹ /tʃɔk/ *n.* **1** [U] soft white rock **2** [C,U] small sticks of this substance, used for writing or drawing: *a **piece of chalk***

chalk² *v.*
chalk sth ⇔ **up** *phr. v. informal* to succeed in winning or getting something: *Boston chalked up another win over Detroit last night.*

chalk·board /ˈtʃɔkbɔrd/ *n.* [C] a BLACKBOARD

chalk·y /ˈtʃɔki/ *adj.* similar to chalk or containing chalk

chal·lenge¹ /ˈtʃæləndʒ/ *n.* **1** [C,U] something that tests your skill or ability, especially in a way that is interesting: *the **challenge of** a new job* | *Together we can **meet*** (=deal with) *this **challenge.*** | *The President **faces a** serious **challenge to** his leadership.* | *The trial will **pose a*** (=be a) *difficult **challenge** for the defense.* **2** [C] the act of questioning whether something is right, fair, or legal: *If I make any decisions myself, my boss thinks it's a direct **challenge to** her authority.* **3** [C] an invitation from someone to try to beat him/her in a fight, game, argument, etc.: *The mayor has **accepted the challenge** for a debate.*

challenge² *v.* [T] **1** to question whether something is right, fair, or legal: *They plan to **challenge the** court's **decision.*** **2** to invite someone to compete or fight against you: *They **challenged** us **to** a game of tennis.* **3** to test the skills or abilities of someone or something: *Teachers need to make sure they challenge their students.* —**challenger** *n.* [C]

chal·lenged /ˈtʃæləndʒd/ *adj.* **visually/mentally/physically challenged** an expression for describing someone who has difficulty doing things because s/he is blind, etc., used in order to be polite

chal·leng·ing /ˈtʃæləndʒɪŋ/ *adj.* difficult in an interesting way: *a challenging new job*

cham·ber /ˈtʃeɪmbɚ/ *n.* **1** [C] a room used for a special purpose: *a gas/torture chamber* (=used for killing people by gas or for hurting them) | *the council's chamber in the Town Hall* **2** [C] an enclosed space inside something, such as your body or a machine: *a gun with six chambers* | *the four chambers of the heart* **3** [C] one of the two parts of a PARLIAMENT or LEGISLATURE (=institutions that have the power to make or change laws): *the **upper/lower** chamber of parliament* **4 chambers** [plural] the offices used by judges

C

cham·ber·maid /ˈtʃeɪmbɚˌmeɪd/ *n.* [C] a woman whose job is to clean hotel BEDROOMS

ˈchamber ˌmusic *n.* [U] CLASSICAL MUSIC performed by a small group of musicians

ˌChamber of ˈCommerce *n.* [C] an organization of business people in a town or city whose aim is to encourage business

cha·me·leon /kəˈmilyən, kəˈmiliən/ *n.* [C] a small LIZARD (=type of animal) that can make its skin the color of the things around it

cham·o·mile, **camomile** /ˈkæməˌmil/ *n.* [C,U] a plant with small white and yellow flowers, often used for making tea

champ /tʃæmp/ *n.* [C] *informal* CHAMPION

cham·pagne /ʃæmˈpeɪn/ *n.* [U] a French white wine with a lot of BUBBLES, often drunk on special occasions

cham·pi·on[1] /ˈtʃæmpiən/ *n.* [C] **1** a person, team, etc. that has won a competition, especially in sports: *the **world** heavyweight boxing **champion*** | *the **defending/reigning** national soccer **champions*** (=the champions right now) **2 champion of sb/sth** someone who fights for and defends an aim or idea: *a champion of civil rights*

champion[2] *v.* [T] to publicly fight for and defend an aim or idea: *She consistently **championed the cause of** working mothers.*

cham·pi·on·ship /ˈtʃæmpiənˌʃɪp/ *n.* **1** [C] **also championships** [plural] a competition to find the best player or team in a particular sport: *the women's figure skating championships*

THESAURUS

competition, **tournament**, **contest**, **playoff**
→ see Thesaurus box at COMPETITION

2 [singular] the position or period of being a champion: *Can she win the championship again?*

chance[1] /tʃæns/ *n.* **1** [C] an opportunity to do something that you want to do: *Now I'll **have/get a chance to** find out what her husband looks like.* | *If you'll just **give me a chance**, I'll tell you what happened.* | *You should **take the chance*** (=use the opportunity) *to travel while you're young.* | *He deserves a **second chance*** (=another chance). | *Friday is our **last chance** to see the show.* **2** [C,U] a possibility that something will happen: *What are Deirdre's **chances of** getting the job?* | *Davis **has no chance** of playing on Sunday.* | ***There's a chance (that)** she left her keys in the office.* | ***Chances are*** (=it is likely) *they're stuck in traffic.* **3 by any chance** *spoken* used in order to ask politely whether something is true or possible: *Are you Ms. Hughes' daughter, by any chance?* **4 fat chance/not a chance/no chance** *spoken* used in order to emphasize that you do not think something will happen: *"Do you think Mark would let me borrow his car?" "Not a chance!"* **5 take a chance** to do something that involves risk: *The team **took a chance on** a young manager with no experience.* | *I'm **not taking any chances**.* **6** [U] the way things happen without being planned or caused: *We met **by chance** at a friend's party.* | *He supervises every detail of the business and **leaves nothing to chance**.*
→ **stand a chance (of doing sth)** at STAND[1]

chance[2] *v.* [T] *informal* to do something that involves a risk: *The bus might get me there on time but I don't want to **chance it**.*

chance[3] *adj.* not planned or expected: *a **chance encounter/meeting***

chan·cel·lor /ˈtʃænsələ/ *n.* [C] **1** the person in charge of some universities **2** the leader of the government in some countries

chanc·y /ˈtʃænsi/ *adj. informal* uncertain or involving risks: *The weather there can be chancy in the spring.*

chan·de·lier /ˌʃændəˈlɪr/ *n.* [C] a frame that holds lights or CANDLES, hangs from the ceiling, and is decorated with small pieces of glass

change[1] /tʃeɪndʒ/ *v.* **1** [I,T] to become different, or to make someone or something become different: *Ed changed after Ricky died.* | *There are plans to change the voting system.* | *In the fall, its leaves **change from** green **to** gold.* | *The water on the bridge had **changed to** ice during the night.*

THESAURUS

alter – to change something or to make something change: *Can we alter the date of the meeting?* | *Computers have radically altered* (=made big changes to) *the way we work.*

adapt/adjust/modify – to change something slightly: *The group is pressuring Congress to modify the plan.* | *His doctor has adjusted the dosage of his medication.*

reform/reorganize/restructure – to change a system or organization: *plans to reform the tax system* | *The company has been restructured from top to bottom.*

transform/revolutionize – to change something completely: *They've completely transformed the downtown area.* | *Computers have revolutionized the way we work.*

twist/distort/misrepresent – to deliberately change facts, information, someone's words, etc. in a way that is not completely true or correct: *He accused reporters of twisting his words.*

2 [I,T] to stop doing or using one thing, and start doing or using something else: *I'm thinking about changing jobs.* | *The company has* ***changed*** *its name* ***to*** *Cortlandt Capital.* | *I think we'd better* ***change the subject*** (=talk about something else). **3 change your mind** to change your decision or opinion about something: *I've* ***changed my mind about*** *selling the house.* **4** [I,T] to take off your clothes and put on different ones: *I went upstairs to change my shirt.* | *Go upstairs and* ***change into*** *your play clothes.* | *Eric went to* ***get changed.*** **5** [T] to put something new or different in place of something else: *We had to get out and change the tire.* | *She cleaned the room and* ***changed the sheets*** (=put clean sheets on a bed). | *Do you mind* ***changing the baby*** (=putting a clean DIAPER on a baby)? **6** [T] if you change money, you give it to someone and they give it back to you in smaller amounts, or in money from a different country: ***Can you change a $10 bill?*** | *I want to* ***change*** *my dollars* ***into*** *pesos.* **7** [I,T] to get out of one train, bus, or aircraft and into another in order to continue your journey: *We had to change planes in Chicago.* **8 change hands** to become someone else's property: *The house has changed hands twice in the last ten years.*

change sth ⇔ **around** *phr. v.* to move things into different positions: *The room looks bigger since we changed the furniture around.*

change over *phr. v.* to stop doing or using one thing and start doing or using something different: *We're* ***changing over to*** *the new software next month.*

change² *n.* **1** [C,U] the process or result of something or someone becoming different: *Many people find it hard to accept change.* | *a* ***change in*** *diet* | *a* ***change of*** *temperature* | *Grandpa's health has* ***taken a change for the worse*** (=become worse). **2** [C] an action or event that involves replacing one thing with another: *The car needs an oil change.* | *a* ***change of*** *leadership* | *the* ***change from*** *communism* ***to*** *democracy* **3** [singular] something that is interesting or enjoyable because it is different from what is usual: *Why don't we go out* ***for a change?*** | *I* ***need a change.*** **4** [U] **a)** the money you get back when you pay more money than something costs: *Here's your change, ma'am.* **b)** money in the form of coins: *I have about a dollar* ***in change.*** **c)** coins or paper money that add up to the same value as a larger unit of money: *Do you have* ***change for*** *a dollar?*

THESAURUS

money, **bill**, **coin**, **penny**, **nickel**, **dime**, **quarter**, **cash**, **currency**
➔ see Thesaurus box at MONEY

5 change of clothes/underwear etc. another set of clothes that you can use if necessary: *Bring a change of clothes just in case.*

change·a·ble /ˈtʃeɪndʒəbəl/ *adj.* likely to change, or changing often: *Kids' tastes are very changeable.*

change·o·ver /ˈtʃeɪndʒˌoʊvɚ/ *n.* [C] a change from one activity or system to another: *the* ***changeover from*** *military* ***to*** *civilian rule*

chan·nel¹ /ˈtʃænl/ *n.* [C] **1** a television station: *What's on channel 2?* | *Do you mind if I* ***change the channel?*** **2** [usually plural] a way of sending or obtaining information, ideas, etc.: *You'll have to* ***go through*** *official* ***channels*** *for help.* | ***channels of communication*** **3** a long passage dug into the earth that water or other liquids flow along **4 a)** water that connects two larger areas of water: *the English Channel* **b)** the deepest part of a river, sea, etc. that ships can sail through **5 channel surf** *informal* to change quickly from one television channel to another many times

channel² *v.* [T] to direct something toward a particular purpose, place, or situation: *Wayne needs to* ***channel*** *his creativity* ***into*** *something useful.* | *Profits are channeled to conservation groups.*

chant¹ /tʃænt/ *v.* [I,T] **1** to repeat a word or phrase many times: *Crowds of chanting supporters filled the streets.* **2** to sing a religious song or prayer using only one or two notes

chant² *n.* [C] **1** words or phrases that are repeated many times: *The crowd responded with* ***chants of*** *"Resign! Resign!"* **2** a religious song or prayer that is sung using only one or two notes

Cha·nu·kah /ˈhɑnəkə/ *n.* [U] HANUKKAH

cha·os /ˈkeɪɑs/ *n.* [U] a situation in which everything is confused and nothing is happening in an organized way: *After the earthquake, the city was* ***in chaos.*** | *There was* ***total chaos*** *on the roads.*

cha·ot·ic /keɪˈɑt̬ɪk/ *adj.* confused and without any order: *a chaotic scene at the site of the accident*

chap·el /ˈtʃæpəl/ *n.* [C] a small church or a room where Christians have religious services

chap·e·rone¹ /ˈʃæpəˌroʊn/ *n.* [C] an older person who is responsible for young people on social occasions

chaperone² *v.* [T] to go somewhere with someone as a chaperone

chap·lain /ˈtʃæplɪn/ *n.* [C] a minister who works for the army, a hospital, a university, etc.

chapped /tʃæpt/ *adj.* chapped lips or hands are sore, dry, and cracked

chap·ter /ˈtʃæptɚ/ *n.* [C] **1** one of the parts into which a book is divided: *Chapter 6*

THESAURUS

part, **piece**, **section**, **scene**
➔ see Thesaurus box at PART¹

2 a particular period in someone's life or in history: *a sad* ***chapter in*** *our country's history* | *one of the most shameful* ***chapters of*** *French history* **3** the local members of a large organization or club: *the Boise chapter of the Sierra Club*

C

char·ac·ter /ˈkærɪktɚ/ *n.* **1** [C,U] the qualities that make a person, place, or thing different from any other: *There's a very serious side to her character.* | *All these new buildings have really changed the **character of** this town.* | *He swore, which was completely **out of character*** (=not typical of the way he usually behaves). **2** [C] a person in a book, play, movie, etc.: *I don't like the **main character** in the book.* **3** [U] qualities that make someone or something special or interesting: *an old house with a lot of character* **4** [U] good qualities such as courage, loyalty, and honesty that people admire: *a woman of great moral character* **5** [C] a particular kind of person: *Dan's a strange character.* **6** [C] an unusual and humorous person: *Charlie's such a character!* **7** [C] a letter, mark, or sign used in writing, printing, or on a computer: *Chinese characters*

C

char·ac·ter·is·tic[1] /ˌkærɪktəˈrɪstɪk/ *n.* [C] a special quality or feature that someone or something has, and that makes that person or thing different from others: *Each wine has particular characteristics.* | *the **characteristics of** a good manager*

THESAURUS

feature – an important, interesting, or typical part of something: *An important feature of Van Gogh's paintings is their bright color.*
quality – something that someone has as part of their character, especially good things: *Tina has a lot of good qualities.*
property – a natural quality of something: *an herb with healing properties*
attribute – a good or useful quality: *What attributes should a good manager possess?*

characteristic[2] *adj.* typical of a particular thing or person: *The vase is **characteristic of** 16th century Chinese art.* | *Mark, with characteristic kindness, offered to help.* —**characteristically** *adv.*

char·ac·ter·ize /ˈkærɪktəˌraɪz/ *v.* [T] **1** to be typical of someone or something: *Alzheimer's disease is characterized by memory loss.* **2** to describe the character of someone or something in a particular way: *His book **characterizes** Eisenhower **as** a natural leader.* —**characterization** /ˌkærɪktərəˈzeɪʃən/ *n.* [C,U]

THESAURUS

call, **describe**, **label**, **brand**, **portray**
➔ see Thesaurus box at CALL[1]

cha·rade /ʃəˈreɪd/ *n.* **1** [C] a situation in which people pretend to think, feel, etc. something, although they clearly do not: *Their happy marriage is just a charade.* **2 charades** [U] a game in which one person uses actions and no words to show the meaning of a word or phrase, and other people have to guess what it is

char·coal /ˈtʃɑrkoʊl/ *n.* [U] a black substance made of burned wood, used as FUEL or for drawing

charge[1] /tʃɑrdʒ/ *n.*
1 MONEY [C,U] the amount of money you have to pay for something: *an admission **charge of** $5* | *There's a $70 **charge for** every extra piece of luggage.* | *We deliver **free of charge*** (=at no cost).

THESAURUS

cost, **expense**, **price**, **fee**, **fare**, **rent**
➔ see Thesaurus box at COST[1]

2 CONTROL [U] the position of having control over or responsibility for something or someone: *Who **is in charge of** the department?* | *Diane **took charge of** the business when her husband died.*
3 CRIME [C] a statement that says that someone has done something illegal or bad: *He's in court **on charges of** murder.* | *He denied **charges that** he used illegal drugs.* | *The **charge against** her was shoplifting.* | *They decided not to **bring/press charges*** (=to officially say that they think someone is guilty of a crime). | *The police agreed to **drop the charges*** (=decide to stop making charges) *against him.*

THESAURUS

accusation, **allegation**, **indictment**
➔ see Thesaurus box at ACCUSATION

4 ELECTRICITY [U] electricity that is put into a piece of electrical equipment such as a BATTERY
5 ATTACK [C] an attack in which people or animals move forward quickly

charge[2] *v.* **1 a)** [I,T] to ask for a particular amount of money for something you are selling: *How much do you **charge for** your eggs?* | *They **charged** me $2 **for** a candy bar.* **b)** [T] to record the cost of something that someone buys or uses, so that s/he can pay for it later: ***Charge** the room **to** my account.* | *"Would you like to pay cash?" "No, I'll **charge it*** (=pay with a CREDIT CARD)." **2** [T] to state officially that someone might be guilty of a crime: *Ron's been **charged with** assault.*

THESAURUS

accuse, **allege**, **indict**
➔ see Thesaurus box at ACCUSE

3 [I,T] if a BATTERY charges, or if you charge it, it takes in and stores electricity **4** [I,T] to move quickly forward, especially in a threatening way: *The bear charged toward her at full speed.*

THESAURUS

rush, **race**, **dash**, **speed**
➔ see Thesaurus box at RUSH[1]

ˈcharge card *n.* [C] a CREDIT CARD that you can use in a particular store

char·i·ot /ˈtʃæriət/ *n.* [C] a vehicle with two wheels pulled by a horse, used in ancient times in battles and races

cha·ris·ma /kəˈrɪzmə/ *n.* [U] the natural ability

to attract other people and make them admire you: *He **has** a lot of **charisma**.* —**charismatic** /ˌkærɪzˈmæt̬ɪk◂ / *adj.*

char·i·ta·ble /ˈtʃærət̬əbəl/ *adj.* **1** relating to charities and their work: *The money went to a charitable group.* **2** kind, generous, and sympathetic —**charitably** *adv.*

char·i·ty /ˈtʃærət̬i/ *n.* plural **charities** **1** [C] an organization that gives money, goods, or help to people who need it: *Several charities sent aid to the flood victims.* | *a **charity event*** **2** [U] charity organizations in general: *He's donated over $200,000 **to charity**.* | *The auction raised more than $75,000 **for charity**.* **3** [U] money or gifts given to people who need help: *She's too proud to accept charity.* **4** [U] *formal* kindness or sympathy towards other people

char·la·tan /ˈʃɑrlətən/ *n.* [C] *disapproving* someone who pretends to have special skills or knowledge

charm¹ /tʃɑrm/ *n.* **1** [C,U] the special quality someone or something has that makes people like him, her, or it: *Lee's boyish charm* | *This town has a charm you couldn't find in a big city.* **2** [C] something you wear, have, etc. because you believe it brings you good luck: *a **lucky charm***

charm² *v.* [T] to attract or please someone: *Grant has been charming audiences for years.* —**charmer** *n.* [C]

charmed /tʃɑrmd/ *adj.* **lead/live/have a charmed life** to be lucky all the time, especially by succeeding in avoiding danger, injury, etc.

charm·ing /ˈtʃɑrmɪŋ/ *adj.* very pleasing or attractive: *What a charming house!* —**charmingly** *adv.*

charred /tʃɑrd/ *adj.* something that is charred is so burned that it has become black

chart¹ /tʃɑrt/ *n.* [C] **1** a drawing, set of numbers, GRAPH etc. that shows information: *medical charts* | *The **chart shows** last year's sales.* **2 the charts** [plural] the official list of the most popular songs and records, produced each week: *Her new album went to **the top of the charts**.* **3** a map, especially of the sea or stars

chart² *v.* [T] **1** to record information about something over a period of time: *Scientists have been charting temperature changes in the oceans.* | *a book that charts the history of the city* **2** to make a plan of what should be done in order to achieve something: *She needs to **chart a course** for her future.* **3** to make a map of an area

char·ter¹ /ˈtʃɑrt̬ɚ/ *n.* **1** [C] a written statement of the principles, duties, and purposes of an organization: *the UN charter* **2** [C,U] the practice of renting a boat, aircraft, etc. from a company, usually for a short time, or the boat, etc. that is used in this way: *a charter service* | *fishing boats **for charter***

charter² *v.* [T] to rent a boat, aircraft, etc. from a company: *We'll have to charter a bus.*

ˈcharter flight *n.* [C] an airplane trip that is arranged for a particular group or for a particular purpose

ˌcharter ˈmember *n.* [C] an original member of a club or organization

ˈcharter ˌschool *n.* [C] a school that is run by parents, companies, etc. rather than by the public school system, but which the state government provides money for

chase¹ /tʃeɪs/ *v.* **1** [I,T] to quickly follow someone or something in order to catch him, her, or it: *Cops **chased** the mugger **down** the street.* | *a cat **chasing after** a mouse*

THESAURUS

follow, pursue, run after, tail, stalk

➔ see Thesaurus box at FOLLOW

2 [T] to make someone or something leave a place by running after them: *There was a racoon in the yard, but the dog **chased** it **away**.* **3** [I,T] to try very hard to get something: *reporters **chasing after** a story*

chase² *n.* [C] an act of following someone or something quickly to catch him/her or it: *a **car chase*** | *Police spotted the speeding car and **gave chase*** (=chased it).

chasm /ˈkæzəm/ *n.* **1** [singular] a big difference between ideas or groups of people: *the **chasm between** rich and poor* **2** [C] a very deep space between two areas of rock or ice

chas·sis /ˈtʃæsi, ˈʃæ-/ *n.* plural **chassis** /-siz/ [C] the frame on which the body, engine, etc. of a vehicle is built

chaste /tʃeɪst/ *adj.* *old-fashioned* not having sex, or not showing sexual feelings

chas·ten /ˈtʃeɪsən/ *v.* [T] *formal* to make someone realize that his/her behavior is wrong

chas·tise /tʃæˈstaɪz, ˈtʃæstaɪz/ *v.* [T] *formal* to criticize or punish someone

chas·ti·ty /ˈtʃæstət̬i/ *n.* [U] the principle or state of not having sex with anyone except your husband or wife

chat¹ /tʃæt/ *v.* past tense and past participle **chatted**, present participle **chatting** [I] to talk in a friendly and informal way, especially about unimportant things: *We were **chatting about** the weather.*

chat² *n.* [C,U] a friendly informal conversation: *I **had a** long **chat with** Rick.*

cha·teau /ʃæˈtoʊ/ *n.* plural **chateaux** /-ˈtoʊz/ or **chateaus** [C] a castle or large country house in France

ˈchat room *n.* [C] a place on the Internet where you can have a conversation with people by writing messages to them and immediately receiving their reply

chat·ter /ˈtʃæt̬ɚ/ *v.* [I] **1** to talk a lot in a quick and friendly way about unimportant things **2** if your teeth chatter, they knock together because you are cold or afraid —**chatter** *n.* [U]

chat·ty /ˈtʃæt̬i/ *adj.* *informal* **1** liking to talk a lot in a friendly way **2** having a friendly informal style: *a chatty letter*

chauf·feur /ˈʃoʊfɚ, ʃoʊˈfɚ/ *n.* [C] someone whose job is to drive a car for someone else —**chauffeur** *v.* [T] *I spent all day chauffeuring my kids everywhere.*

chau·vin·ist /ˈʃoʊvənɪst/ *n.* [C] *disapproving* **1** a man who thinks that men are better than women: *He's a **male chauvinist pig**.* **2** someone who believes that his/her country or race is better than any other —**chauvinism** *n.* [U] —**chauvinistic** /ˌʃoʊvəˈnɪstɪk/ *adj.*

cheap¹ /tʃip/ *adj.* **1** not expensive, or lower in price than you expected [≠ **expensive**]: *Back then, gas was really cheap.* | *I bought the cheapest computer I could find.* | *Their jeans are **dirt cheap*** (=very low in price)*!*

THESAURUS

If something is **inexpensive**, it is not expensive and is usually of good quality.
If something is **reasonable**, it is not too expensive and seems fair: *The restaurant serves good food at reasonable prices.*
If something is a **good/great/excellent deal** or **good/great/excellent value**, it is worth the price you pay for it: *At $3, it's a good deal.* | *The hotel offers great value for your money.*
If you think that something is worth more money than you paid for it, you can say that it is a **bargain**: *You can get some real bargains at the market.* | *bargain prices*
➔ EXPENSIVE

2 *disapproving* low in price and quality: *cheap wine* **3** *disapproving* not liking to spend money: *He's so cheap we didn't even go out on my birthday.* **4 cheap shot** an unkind and unfair criticism —**cheaply** *adv.* —**cheapness** *n.* [U]

cheap² *adv.* at a low price: *I was lucky to **get** it so **cheap**.* | *Cars like that **don't come cheap*** (=are expensive).

cheap·en /ˈtʃipən/ *v.* **1** [T] to make someone or something seem to have or deserve to have less respect: *As an actress, I'd be **cheapening myself by** doing TV commercials.* **2** [I,T] to become lower in price or value, or to make something do this: *The dollar's rise in value has cheapened imports.*

cheap·skate /ˈtʃipskeɪt/ *n.* [C] *informal disapproving* someone who does not like spending money

cheat¹ /tʃit/ *v.* **1** [I] to behave in a dishonest way in order to win or get an advantage: *He always **cheats at** cards.* | *She was caught **cheating on** the history **test**.* **2** [T] to trick or deceive someone: *The salesman **cheated** me **out of** $100.* | *The band's 30-minute show left fans **feeling cheated*** (=feeling that they had been treated unfairly). —**cheating** *n.* [U]

cheat on sb *phr. v.* to be unfaithful to your husband, wife, or sexual partner by secretly having sex with someone else: *I think Dan's cheating on Debbie again.*

cheat² **also cheat·er** /ˈtʃit̬ɚ/ *n.* [C] someone who cheats

check¹ /tʃɛk/ *v.* **1** [I,T] to look at or test something carefully in order to be sure that it is correct, in good condition, safe, etc.: *"Did Barry lock the back door?" "I don't know — I'll check."* | *I need to check the mailbox; I'm expecting a letter.* | *It's a good idea to **check for** ticks after being out in the woods.* | *Make sure you **double-check*** (=check them twice) *the spellings of these names.*

THESAURUS

make sure – to find out if a fact, statement, etc. is correct or true: *I think we're open on Sunday, but let me ask the manager to make sure.*
double-check – to check something again to find out if it is safe, ready, correct, etc.: *Double-check your answers before turning the test in.*
confirm – to say or prove that something is definitely true: *Anderson confirmed that he will step down at the end of this year.*
check out – to make sure that something is actually true, correct, or acceptable: *We thought we'd check out this new restaurant that Jim says is so good.*

2 [I] to ask someone about something: ***Check with** Jim to see if you can leave early.* | *Can you **check whether** we're still having a meeting?* | *We'd better **check that** he received your message.* **3** [T] to leave your bags, coat, etc. in a special place where they can be kept safe or put on an airplane, bus, etc., or to take someone's bags in order to do this: *Can I check that bag for you, sir?* **4** [T] to suddenly stop yourself from saying or doing something: *I had to check the urge to laugh out loud.* **5** [T] to stop something bad from getting worse: *The treatment checks the spread of the cancer.*

check in *phr. v.* to go to the desk at a hotel, airport, etc. to say that you have arrived: *Please check in at gate number 5.*

check sth ⇔ **off** *phr. v.* to put a mark (✓) next to something on a list to show that you have dealt with it: *Check their names off the list as they arrive.*

check on sb/sth *phr. v.* to make sure that someone or something is all right or is doing what he, she, or it is supposed to be doing: *I have to go check on the roast.*

check out *phr. v.* **1 a) check** sth ⇔ **out** to make sure that something is actually true, correct, or acceptable: *The police **checked out** his story **with** the other suspects.* | *We thought we'd check out this new restaurant Jim says is so good.* **b)** if something checks out, it is proven to be true, correct, or acceptable: *If your references check* *out, you can start the job on Monday.* **2 check** sb/sth ⇔ **out** *spoken* to look at someone or something because he, she, or it is interesting or attractive: *Hey, check out that car!* **3** to pay the bill and leave a hotel: *You must check out before 12 o'clock.* **4 check** sth ⇔ **out** to borrow a book from a library: *You can only check out 5 books at a time.*

check sth ⇔ **over** *phr. v.* **1** to look closely at something to make sure it is correct or acceptable: *Can you check over my paper for spelling mistakes?* **2** to examine someone to make sure s/he is healthy: *The doctor checked her over and couldn't find anything wrong.*

check up on sb/sth *phr. v.* to try to find out if someone is doing what s/he is supposed to be doing: *She was calling every ten minutes to check up on me.*

check

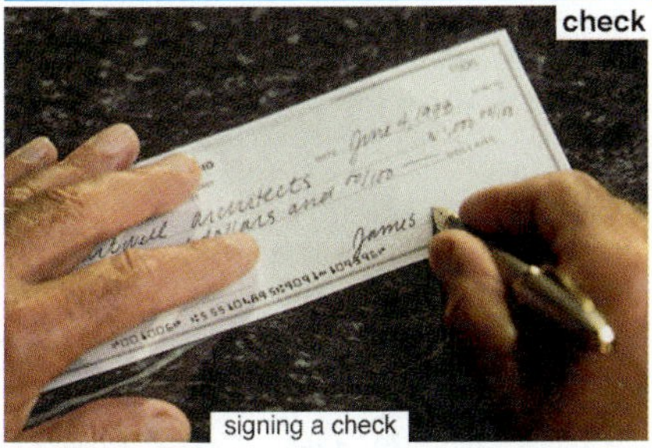

signing a check

check² *n.*

1 MONEY [C] one of a set of printed pieces of paper that you can sign and use to pay for things: *a **check for** $50 | Can I **pay by check**? | I **wrote** her **a check** for $300. | Did you **cash the check*** (=get cash in exchange for the check)*?*

2 EXAMINATION [C] a careful look at or test of something, to see if it is safe, correct, in good condition, etc.: *a **security check** | The building inspector must first do a **safety check**. | I want a **check on** the quality of all goods leaving the factory. | I want you to **do/run a check on*** (=find out information about) *this blood sample.*

3 CONTROL [C usually singular] something that controls something else and stops it from increasing: *The policy should act as a **check on** inflation. | We've **kept/held** the disease **in check*** (=kept it under control) *for over a year now.*

4 BILL [C] a list you are given in a restaurant showing what you have eaten and how much you must pay [= **bill**]: *Can I have the check, please?*

COLLOCATIONS

If you have eaten in a restaurant and are ready to pay, you **ask for the check.**
If someone who eats with other people pays for the whole meal, they **pick up the check.**
If people share the cost of the meal between them, they **split the check.**
→ see Topic box at RESTAURANT

THESAURUS

bill, invoice, tab
→ see Thesaurus box at BILL¹

5 MARK [C] a mark (√) that you put next to an answer to show that it is incorrect or next to something on a list to show that you have dealt with it

6 SQUARES [C] a pattern of squares on something: *a tablecloth with red and white checks*

check·book /ˈtʃɛkbʊk/ *n.* [C] a book of checks

checked /tʃɛkt/ *adj.* having a regular pattern of different colored squares: *a checked skirt*

check·ered /ˈtʃɛkɚd/ *adj.* **1** marked with squares of two different colors: *a checkered flag* **2 checkered past/history etc.** periods of failure as well as success in someone's or something's past: *a cop with a checkered past*

check·ers /ˈtʃɛkɚz/ *n.* [U] a game for two players, using 12 flat round pieces each and a special board with 64 squares

ˈcheck-in *n.* **1** [U] the process of reporting your arrival at a hotel, airport, hospital, etc.: *Passengers should arrive early for check-in.* **2** [singular] a place where you report your arrival at an airport, hotel, etc.: *Be at the check-in counter at least two hours before your flight.* → **check in** at CHECK¹

ˈchecking acˌcount *n.* [C] a bank account that you can take money out of at any time

THESAURUS

account, savings account, joint account, online account
→ see Thesaurus box at ACCOUNT¹

check·list /ˈtʃɛkˌlɪst/ *n.* [C] a list of things you have to do for a particular job or activity

THESAURUS

list, grocery list, shopping list, mailing list, price list, waiting list, guest list
→ see Thesaurus box at LIST¹

check·mate /ˈtʃɛkmeɪt/ *n.* [U] the position in a game of CHESS when the KING cannot escape and the game has ended

check·out coun·ter /ˈtʃɛk-aʊt ˌkaʊntɚ/ **also checkout** *n.* [C] the place in a SUPERMARKET where you pay for things

check·point /ˈtʃɛkpɔɪnt/ *n.* [C] a place, especially at a border between countries, where an official person stops people and vehicles to examine them

check·up, check-up /ˈtʃɛk-ʌp/ *n.* [C] an occasion when a doctor or DENTIST examines you to see if you are healthy: *Dentists recommend regular check-ups.*

ched·dar /ˈtʃɛdɚ/ *n.* [U] a firm smooth yellow or orange cheese

cheek /tʃik/ *n.* [C] the soft round part of your face below each of your eyes: *He kissed her lightly on the cheek.* ➔ see picture on page A3

cheek·bone /ˈtʃikboʊn/ *n.* [C] the bone just below your eye: *She had **high cheekbones** and green eyes.* ➔ see picture on page A3

cheep /tʃip/ *v.* [I] if a young bird cheeps, it makes a weak, high noise —**cheep** *n.* [C]

cheer[1] /tʃɪr/ *v.* [I,T] to shout approval, encouragement, etc.: *The audience cheered as the band began to play.*

THESAURUS

shout, call (out), scream, yell, cry out, raise your voice, bellow, holler
➔ see Thesaurus box at SHOUT[1]

cheer sb **on** *phr. v.* to encourage someone by cheering for him/her: *Hansen's family was there cheering him on.*

cheer up *phr. v.* **1 cheer** sb **up** to make someone feel happier: *I tried to cheer her up by taking her out to dinner.* **2** to become happier: *Cheer up, Connie!*

cheer[2] *n.* [C] a shout of approval and happiness: *The team was greeted with applause and cheers.*

cheer·ful /ˈtʃɪrfəl/ *adj.* **1** happy, or behaving in a way that shows you are happy: *a cheerful and easygoing guy* | *a **cheerful voice/smile*** **2** bright, pleasant, and making you feel happy: *a cheerful kitchen* —**cheerfully** *adv.* —**cheerfulness** *n.* [U]

cheer·lead·er /ˈtʃɪrˌlidɚ/ *n.* [C] a member of a team of young women who encourage a crowd to cheer at sports events

cheer·y /ˈtʃɪri/ *adj.* happy or making you feel happy: *Sullivan was in a cheery mood.*

cheese /tʃiz/ *n.* [C,U] a solid food made from milk that is usually white or yellow: *a **grilled cheese sandwich*** | *a **piece/slice/wedge of cheese*** | *I'd like a bagel with **cream cheese**.*

cheese·burg·er /ˈtʃizˌbɚgɚ/ *n.* [C] a HAMBURGER cooked with a piece of cheese on top of the meat

cheese·cake /ˈtʃizkeɪk/ *n.* [C,U] a sweet cake made with soft white cheese

cheese·cloth /ˈtʃizklɔθ/ *n.* [U] a type of very thin cotton cloth, used especially for wrapping food

chees·y /ˈtʃizi/ *adj. informal* not sincere or of good quality: *a really cheesy movie* | *a cheesy grin*

chee·tah /ˈtʃit̬ə/ *n.* [C] an African wild cat that has black spots and is able to run very fast

chef /ʃɛf/ *n.* [C] a skilled cook, especially the main cook in a restaurant

chem·i·cal[1] /ˈkɛmɪkəl/ *adj.* relating to substances used in chemistry, or involving the changes that happen when two substances combine: *a chemical reaction* —**chemically** *adv.*

chemical[2] *n.* [C] a substance used in CHEMISTRY or produced by a chemical process: ***toxic*** (=poisonous) ***chemicals***

chem·ist /ˈkɛmɪst/ *n.* [C] a scientist who does work related to chemistry

chem·is·try /ˈkɛməstri/ *n.* [U] **1** the science of studying substances and the way that they change or combine with each other **2** the way substances combine in a process, thing, person, etc.: *This drug causes changes to the body's chemistry.* **3** if there is chemistry between two people, they like each other or work well together

che·mo·ther·a·py /ˌkimoʊˈθɛrəpi/ *n.* [U] the treatment of CANCER using special drugs

cher·ish /ˈtʃɛrɪʃ/ *v.* [T] **1** if you cherish something, it is very important to you: *He cherishes his privacy.* **2** to take care of someone or something you love very much

cher·ry /ˈtʃɛri/ *n.* plural **cherries** **1** [C] a small round soft red fruit with a large seed: *a bowl of cherries* | *cherry pie* ➔ see picture at FRUIT **2** [C,U] a tree that produces cherries, or the wood of this tree

cher·ub /ˈtʃɛrəb/ *n.* [C] an ANGEL shown in paintings as a small child with wings

chess /tʃɛs/ *n.* [U] a game for two players in which you must trap your opponent's KING in order to win: *Do you know how to **play chess**?* ➔ see picture at BOARD[1]

chest /tʃɛst/ *n.* [C] **1** the front part of your body between your neck and stomach: *a man with a hairy chest* | *chest pains* ➔ see picture on page A3 **2** a large strong box with a lid that you use to keep things in: *a large wooden chest* **3 get sth off your chest** *informal* to tell someone about something that has worried or annoyed you for a long time

chest·nut /ˈtʃɛsnʌt/ *n.* **1** [C] a smooth red-brown nut you can eat **2** [C,U] the tree on which these nuts grow, or the wood of this tree **3** [U] a dark red-brown color —**chestnut** *adj.*

ˌchest of ˈdrawers *n.* plural **chests of drawers** [C] a piece of furniture with drawers that clothes can be kept in

chew /tʃu/ *v.* [I,T] **1** to bite food several times before swallowing it: *The meat's so tough I can hardly chew it.* | *We gave the dog a bone to **chew on**.* **2** to bite something several times without eating it: *Students are not allowed to **chew gum** in the classroom.*

chew sb **out** *phr. v. informal* to speak angrily to someone who has done something wrong: *Mom chewed me out for coming home late.*

chew sth ⇔ **over** *phr. v.* to think about something carefully for a period of time: *Let me chew it over for a few days, and then I'll let you have my answer.*

ˈchewing gum *n.* [U] GUM

chew·y /ˈtʃui/ *adj.* needing to be chewed a lot before it can be swallowed: *moist chewy brownies*

chic /ʃik/ *adj.* fashionable and showing good judgment about style: *a chic clothes store*

Chi·ca·no /tʃɪˈkɑnoʊ/ *n.* [C] a U.S. citizen who was born in Mexico or whose family came from Mexico

chick /tʃɪk/ *n.* [C] **1** a baby bird, especially a baby chicken **2** *informal* a word meaning a young woman that many women think is offensive

chick·a·dee /ˈtʃɪkəˌdi/ *n.* [C] a small North American wild bird with a black head

chick·en¹ /ˈtʃɪkən/ *n.* **1** [C] a farm bird that is kept for its meat and eggs ➔ see picture at FARM¹ **2** [U] the meat from this bird: *fried chicken* **3** [C] *informal* someone who lacks courage: *Don't be such a chicken!*

chicken² *adj. informal* not brave enough to do something: *Dave's too chicken to ask her out.*

chicken³ *v.*
chicken out *phr. v. informal* to decide at the last moment not to do something because you are afraid: *I was going to ask for a raise but I chickened out.*

chicken pox, **chick·en·pox** /ˈtʃɪkənˌpɑks/ *n.* [U] a disease that children often get that causes ITCHY spots on the skin and a fever

chide /tʃaɪd/ *v.* [I,T] *written* to speak in an angry way to someone who has done something wrong

chief¹ /tʃif/ *n.* [C] **1** the leader of a group or organization: *the **chief of** police* **2** the leader of a tribe: *Native American **tribal chiefs***

chief² *adj.* [only before noun] **1** most important: *Safety is our **chief concern**.* **2** highest in rank: *the company's chief financial officer*

> **THESAURUS**
>
> **senior**, **high-ranking**, **top**, **junior**, **assistant**
> ➔ see Thesaurus box at POSITION¹

ˌChief Exˈecutive *n.* **the Chief Executive Officer** the President of the United States

ˌchief exˈecutive ˌofficer *n.* [C] CEO

ˌchief ˈjustice *n.* [C] the most important judge in a court of law, especially in the U.S. Supreme Court

chief·ly /ˈtʃifli/ *adv.* mainly: *The agency deals chiefly with recent immigrants.*

> **THESAURUS**
>
> **mainly**, **principally**, **largely**, **primarily**
> ➔ see Thesaurus box at MAINLY

ˌchief of ˈstaff *n.* plural **chiefs of staff** [C] an official of high rank who advises the person in charge of an organization or government: *the White House chief of staff*

chief·tain /ˈtʃiftən/ *n.* [C] the leader of a tribe

chif·fon /ʃɪˈfɑn/ *n.* [U] a soft thin silk or NYLON material that you can see through: *a chiffon scarf*

chi·hua·hua /tʃɪˈwɑwə/ *n.* [C] a very small dog from Mexico with smooth short hair

child /tʃaɪld/ *n.* plural **children** /ˈtʃɪldrən/ [C] **1** a young person who is not yet fully grown: *Admission is free for children under 8.* | *I was very happy **as a child*** (=when I was a child).

> **THESAURUS**
>
> Child is a word that you can use to talk about **young children** and **teenagers**. You do not normally use child to refer to **babies**.
> You are a **baby** when you are first born.
> You are a **toddler** when you have just learned to walk.
> You are a **teenager** between 13 and 19.
> **Kid** is an informal word for a **child**.
> ➔ see Topic box at BABY

2 a son or daughter: *How many **children** does Jane **have**?* | *Alex is an **only child*** (=he has no brothers or sisters).

child·bear·ing /ˈtʃaɪldˌbɛrɪŋ/ *n.* **1** [U] the process of being PREGNANT and then giving birth **2 childbearing age** the period of a woman's life during which she is able to have babies: *women **of childbearing age***

child·birth /ˈtʃaɪldbɚθ/ *n.* [U] the act of giving birth: *His wife had died **in childbirth**.*

child·care /ˈtʃaɪldkɛr/ *n.* [U] an arrangement in which someone takes care of children while their parents are at work

child·hood /ˈtʃaɪldhʊd/ *n.* [C,U] the time when you are a child: *Sara had a very happy childhood.* | *We've been friends **since childhood**.*

child·ish /ˈtʃaɪldɪʃ/ *adj.* **1** *disapproving* behaving in a silly way that makes you seem younger than you really are [= **immature**]: *Stop being so childish.* **2** relating to or typical of a child: *a childish game* —**childishly** *adv.*

child·less /ˈtʃaɪldlɪs/ *adj.* having no children: *childless couples*

child·like /ˈtʃaɪldlaɪk/ *adj. approving* having the good qualities of a child, such as natural or trusting behavior: *childlike innocence*

child·proof /ˈtʃaɪldpruf/ *adj.* designed to prevent a child from being hurt: *Most medicine bottles have a childproof cap.*

chil·dren /ˈtʃɪldrən/ *n.* the plural of CHILD

ˈchild supˌport *n.* [U] money that someone pays regularly to his/her former husband or wife in order to help support his/her children

chil·i /ˈtʃɪli/ *n.* plural **chilies** **1** [C,U] **also ˈchili ˌpepper** a small thin type of red or green pepper with a very hot taste **2** [U] a dish made with beans and usually meat cooked with chilies ➔ see picture on page A5

chill¹ /tʃɪl/ *v.* **1** [I,T] to make something or someone very cold: *This wine should be chilled before serving.* **2** [I] *informal* **also chill out** to

C

relax instead of feeling angry or nervous: *Chill out, Dave, it doesn't matter.*

chill² *n.* **1** [singular] a feeling of coldness: *There was a slight **chill in the air**.* **2** [C] a slight feeling of fear: *His laugh **sent a chill down** her **spine*** (=made her feel very frightened). **3 chills** a feeling of being cold, caused by being sick: *First I had chills and then a fever.*

chil·ling /ˈtʃɪlɪŋ/ *adj.* making you feel frightened because something is cruel, violent, or dangerous: *a chilling report on child abuse*

chill·y /ˈtʃɪli/ *adj.* **1** cold enough to make you feel uncomfortable: *a chilly November morning* | *It's a little bit chilly in here.*

C

THESAURUS

cold, **cool**, **frosty**, **freezing (cold)**, **icy (cold)**, **bitter (cold)**
→ see Thesaurus box at COLD¹

2 unfriendly: *The speech met with a **chilly reception**.*

chime¹ /tʃaɪm/ *n.* **1 chimes** [plural] a set of bells or other objects that produce musical sounds: ***wind chimes*** **2** [C] the RINGing sound of a bell or clock: *the chime of the doorbell*

chime² *v.* [I,T] if a clock or bell chimes, it makes a ringing sound: *The clock chimed six.*
chime in *phr. v.* to say something in order to add your opinion to a conversation: *"The kids could go too," Maria chimed in.*

chim·ney /ˈtʃɪmni/ *n.* [C] a pipe inside a building for smoke from a fire to go out through the roof

chimpanzee

chim·pan·zee /ˌtʃɪmpænˈzi/ **also chimp** /tʃɪmp/ *n.* [C] an African animal that is like a monkey without a tail

chin /tʃɪn/ *n.* [C] the front part of your face below your mouth: *She tied the scarf under her chin.* → see picture on page A3

chi·na /ˈtʃaɪnə/ *n.* [U] plates, cups, etc. that are made from white clay of good quality

Chi·na·town /ˈtʃaɪnəˌtaʊn/ *n.* [C usually singular, U] an area in a city where there are Chinese restaurants and stores, and where a lot of Chinese people live

Chi·nese¹ /ˌtʃaɪˈniz◂/ *adj.* **1** relating to or coming from China **2** relating to a Chinese language

Chi·nese² /tʃaɪˈniz/ *n.* **1** [U] any of the languages that come from China, such as Mandarin or Cantonese **2 the Chinese** the people of China

chink /tʃɪŋk/ *n.* [C] a narrow crack or hole in something that lets light or air through: *I could see light through a chink in the wall.*

chi·nos /ˈtʃinoʊz/ *n.* [plural] loose pants made from heavy cotton

chintz /tʃɪnts/ *n.* [U] smooth cotton cloth with brightly colored patterns on it: *chintz covers on the chairs*

chintz·y /ˈtʃɪntsi/ *adj. informal* **1** cheap and badly made: *a chintzy chest of drawers* **2** unwilling to give people things or spend money

ˈchin-up *n.* [C] an exercise in which you hang on a BAR and pull yourself up until your chin is above the bar

chip¹ /tʃɪp/ *n.* [C]
1 FOOD a thin dry flat piece of potato or TORTILLA cooked in very hot oil and eaten cold: *chips and salsa* | *a bag of **potato chips***
2 COMPUTER a small piece of SILICON with electronic parts on it that is used in computers: *a **silicon chip***
3 PIECE a small piece of wood, stone, etc. that has broken off something: *Wood chips covered the floor of the workshop.*
4 MARK a small hole or crack or mark on a plate, cup, etc. where a piece has broken off: *This plate has a **chip in** it.*
5 have a chip on your shoulder *informal* to have an angry attitude to life because you think you have been treated unfairly in the past: *He's always had a chip on his shoulder about not going to college.*
6 GAME a small flat colored piece of plastic used in games to represent money: *a gambling chip*
7 be a chip off the old block *informal* to be like one of your parents in the way you look or behave
8 when the chips are down *spoken* in a serious or difficult situation: *When the chips are down, you've only got yourself to depend on.* → BARGAINING CHIP, BLUE CHIP

chip² *v.* past tense and past participle **chipped**, present participle **chipping** [I,T] **1** to break a small piece off something accidentally: *She fell and chipped a tooth.* **2** to remove something by breaking it off in small pieces: *She tried to chip the ice off the windshield.* —**chipped** *adj.*: *chipped fingernail polish*
chip away at sth *phr. v.* to gradually make something weaker or less effective: *His comments were starting to chip away at my self-esteem.*
chip in *phr. v.* if each person in a group chips in, they each give a small amount of money so that they can buy something: *We all chipped in to buy Amy a graduation present.*

chip·munk /ˈtʃɪpmʌŋk/ *n.* [C] a small brown North American animal similar to a SQUIRREL that has black and white lines on its fur

chip·per /ˈtʃɪpɚ/ *adj. informal* happy and healthy

chi·ro·prac·tor /ˈkaɪrəˌpræktɚ/ *n.* [C] someone who treats medical problems such as back pain by moving and pressing the muscles and bones

chirp /tʃɚp/ *v.* [I] if a bird or insect chirps, it makes short high sounds —**chirp** *n.* [C]

chis·el[1] /ˈtʃɪzəl/ *n.* [C] a metal tool with a sharp edge, used to cut wood or stone

chisel[2] *v.* [T] to use a chisel to cut wood or stone, especially into a particular shape

ˈchit-chat *n.* [U] *informal* informal conversation about unimportant things

chiv·al·rous /ˈʃɪvəlrəs/ *adj. formal* a man who is chivalrous behaves in a polite and honorable way to women —**chivalry** /ˈʃɪvəlri/ *n.* [U]

chive /tʃaɪv/ *n.* [C usually plural] a long thin green plant that looks and tastes like an onion and is used in cooking

chlo·ri·nat·ed /ˈklɔrəˌneɪt̬ɪd/ *adj.* chlorinated water has had chlorine added to it in order to kill BACTERIA

chlo·rine /ˈklɔrin, klɔˈrin/ *n.* [U] a yellow-green gas that is used to keep swimming pools clean

chlo·ro·fluo·ro·car·bon /ˌklɔrəˌflʊroʊˈkɑrbən/ *n.* [C] *technical* CFC

chlo·ro·form /ˈklɔrəˌfɔrm/ *n.* [U] a liquid that makes you unconscious if you breathe it

chlo·ro·phyll /ˈklɔrəˌfɪl/ *n.* [U] the green substance in plants

chock-full /ˌtʃɑk ˈfʊl/ *adj.* [not before noun] *informal* completely full: *The bus was **chock-full of** people.*

choco·late /ˈtʃɑklɪt/ *n.* **1** [U] a sweet brown food that is eaten as candy or is used in cooking: *a chocolate bar | chocolate cake* **2** [C] a small candy that consists of something such as a nut or CARAMEL covered with chocolate: *a box of chocolates*

ˌchocolate ˈchip *n.* [C usually plural] a small piece of chocolate put in foods such as cookies and cakes

choice[1] /tʃɔɪs/ *n.* **1** [C,U] the right to choose or the chance to choose between two or more things: *a **choice between** three candidates. | You **have a choice** – you can take French or Spanish. | He **had no choice** but to move back into his parents' house. | We were **given a choice of** morning or afternoon flights. | You **get a choice of** soup or salad.* **2** [C] the act of choosing someone or something: *career choices | I think I **made** the right **choice**.* **3** [C usually singular] the range of people or things that you can choose from: *We had **little choice** in the matter. | The bookstore has a wide **choice of** magazines.* **4** [C usually singular] the person or thing that someone has chosen: *Salad is a **good choice** for a snack. | Her **first choice** of college was Stanford.* **5 the sth of your choice** the person or thing of your choice is the one you would most like to choose: *Many children are not able to go to the school of their choice.* **6 the sth of choice** the thing of choice is the one that people prefer to use: *It is the treatment of choice for this particular disease.* **7 by choice** if you do something by choice, you do it because you want to: *She lives alone by choice.*

choice[2] *adj.* having a high quality or standard: *choice apples*

choir /kwaɪɚ/ *n.* [C] a group of people who sing together, especially in a church or school: *Amelia **sings in the choir**.*

choke[1] /tʃoʊk/ *v.* **1** [I,T] to have difficulty breathing because something is in your throat or there is not enough air: *The fumes were choking me. | He **choked on** a piece of bread.* **2** [T] to put your hands around someone's throat and press on it so s/he cannot breathe: *He choked me so I couldn't talk or breathe.* **3** [I,T] to be almost unable to talk because of strong emotion: *Her voice was **choked with** rage.* **4** [T] to fill a space or passage so that things cannot move through it: *The roads were **choked with** traffic.* **5** [I] *spoken* to fail at doing something that you have prepared for because there is a lot of pressure on you

choke sth ⇔ **back** *phr. v.* to control a strong feeling so that you do not show it: *Anna **choked back tears** as she tried to explain.*

choke up *phr. v.* **be/get choked up** to feel such strong emotions about something that you are almost crying

choke[2] *n.* [C] **1** the act of choking or the sound someone makes when s/he is choking **2** a piece of equipment that controls the amount of air going into a car engine

chok·er /ˈtʃoʊkɚ/ *n.* [C] a piece of jewelry or narrow cloth that fits closely around your neck

chol·er·a /ˈkɑlərə/ *n.* [U] a serious infectious disease that attacks the stomach and BOWELS

cho·les·ter·ol /kəˈlɛstəˌrɔl, -ˌroʊl/ *n.* [U] a substance in your body which doctors think may cause heart disease: *She's had* ***high cholesterol*** *for many years.*

choose /tʃuz/ *v.* past tense **chose** /tʃoʊz/ past participle **chosen** /ˈtʃoʊzən/ present participle **choosing** [I,T] **1** to decide which one of a number of things, possibilities, people, etc. that you want [➡ **choice**]: *A panel of six judges will choose the winner.* | *They* ***chose*** *Roy* ***to*** *be the team captain.* | *You can* ***choose between*** *two types of fabric.* | *There are so many movies to* ***choose from****.* | *Why did they* ***choose*** *her* ***for*** *the job?*

THESAURUS

pick – to choose something or someone from a group of people or things: *Pick any number from one to ten.*
select formal – to choose something or someone by thinking carefully about which is the best, most appropriate, etc.: *All our wines have been carefully selected.*
opt for sth – to choose one thing instead of another: *Many drivers opt for Japanese cars.*
decide on sth – to choose one thing from many possible choices: *Have you decided on a name for the baby?*

2 to decide to do something: *Donna* ***chose to*** *quit her job after she had the baby.*

THESAURUS

decide, **make up your mind**, **resolve**
➔ see Thesaurus box at DECIDE

choos·y /ˈtʃuzi/ *adj.* difficult to please: *Jean's very* ***choosy about*** *what she eats.*

chop¹ /tʃɑp/ *v.* past tense and past participle **chopped**, present participle **chopping** **1** [T] **also chop** sth ⇔ **up** to cut something, especially food, into smaller pieces: *Can you chop up some onions for me?* | ***Chop*** *the tomatoes* ***into*** *fairly large* ***pieces****.* ➔ see picture at CUT¹ **2** [I,T] to cut something by hitting it many times with a heavy sharp tool such as an AX: *She was outside chopping wood for the fire.*
chop sth ⇔ **down** *phr. v.* to make a tree fall down by cutting it with a heavy sharp tool such as an AX: *A couple of the older trees will have to be chopped down.*
chop sth ⇔ **off** *phr. v.* to remove something by cutting it with a sharp tool: *The branch had been chopped off.*

chop² *n.* [C] **1** a small flat piece of meat on a bone: *a pork chop* ➔ see picture on page A5 **2** a quick hard hit with the side of your hand or with a heavy sharp tool: *a karate chop*

chop·per /ˈtʃɑpɚ/ *n.* [C] *informal* a HELICOPTER

choppy

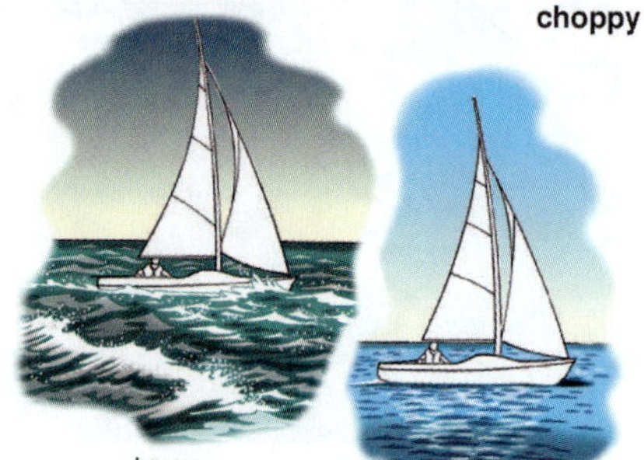

choppy calm

chop·py /ˈtʃɑpi/ *adj.* choppy water has many small waves

chop·sticks /ˈtʃɑpstɪks/ *n.* [plural] a pair of thin sticks used for eating food, especially by people in Asia

cho·ral /ˈkɔrəl/ *adj.* related to music that is sung by a large group of people [➡ **chorus**]: *choral music*

chord /kɔrd/ *n.* [C] **1** a combination of two or more musical notes played at the same time **2 strike/touch a chord** to say or do something that people feel is true or familiar to them: *Many of her experiences will* ***strike a chord with*** *other young women.*

chore /tʃɔr/ *n.* [C] a job that you have to do, especially a boring one: *household chores*

cho·re·og·ra·phy /ˌkɔriˈɑgrəfi/ *n.* [U] the art of arranging how dancers should move during a performance —**choreographer** *n.* [C] —**choreograph** /ˈkɔriəˌgræf/ *v.* [I]

chor·tle /ˈtʃɔrtl̩/ *v.* [I] *formal* to laugh because something is funny or pleases you —**chortle** *n.* [C]

cho·rus /ˈkɔrəs/ *n.* [C] **1** the part of a song that is repeated after each VERSE **2** a large group of people who sing together **3** a group of singers, dancers, or actors who perform together in a show but do not have the main parts **4 a chorus of thanks/disapproval/protest etc.** something expressed by a lot of people at the same time

chose /tʃoʊz/ *v.* the past tense of CHOOSE

cho·sen /ˈtʃoʊzən/ *v.* the past participle of CHOOSE

chow¹ /tʃaʊ/ *n.* [U] *slang* food

chow² *v.*
chow down *phr. v. spoken* to eat, especially in a noisy way or in a way that shows you are very hungry

chow·der /ˈtʃaʊdɚ/ *n.* [U] a thick soup made with milk, vegetables, and usually fish: *clam chowder*

Christ /kraɪst/ **also Jesus Christ** *n.* the man who is worshiped by Christians as the son of God

chris·ten /ˈkrɪsən/ *v.* [T] **1** to officially give a child its name at a Christian religious ceremony

[➡ **baptize**]: *She was christened Elizabeth Ann.* **2** to give something or someone a name

chris·ten·ing /ˈkrɪsənɪŋ/ *n.* [C,U] a Christian ceremony in which a baby is officially given a name and becomes a member of a Christian church [➡ **baptism**]

Chris·tian /ˈkrɪstʃən, ˈkrɪʃtʃən/ *adj.* relating to Christianity: *Christian ministers* | *Christian beliefs* —**Christian** *n.* [C]

Chris·ti·an·i·ty /ˌkrɪstʃiˈænət̬i/ *n.* [U] the religion that is based on the life and teaching of Jesus Christ

ˌChristian ˈScience *n.* [U] a religion whose members believe they can cure their own illnesses using their minds rather than with medical help —**Christian Scientist** *n.* [C]

Christ·mas /ˈkrɪsməs/ *n.* [C,U] **1** December 25, the day when Christians celebrate the birth of Jesus Christ: *Are you going home **for Christmas**?* | *a **Christmas present*** **2** the period of time just before and after this day: *We spent Christmas in Colorado.*

ˌChristmas ˈcarol *n.* [C] a Christian song that people sing at Christmas

ˌChristmas ˈDay *n.* [C,U] December 25, the day when Christians celebrate the birth of Jesus Christ

ˌChristmas ˈEve *n.* [C,U] December 24, the day before Christmas

ˈChristmas tree *n.* [C] a tree that people put inside their house and decorate for Christmas

chrome /kroʊm/ **also chro·mi·um** /ˈkroʊmiəm/ *n.* [U] a hard metal substance used for covering objects with a shiny protective surface: *the car's chrome hubcaps*

chro·mo·some /ˈkroʊməˌsoʊm, -ˌzoʊm/ *n.* [C] *technical* a part of every living cell, which contains the GENES that control the size, shape, etc. that a plant or animal has

chron·ic /ˈkrɑnɪk/ *adj.* **1** a chronic disease or illness is one that continues for a long time and cannot be cured [≠ **acute**]: *chronic back pain* **2** a chronic problem is one that continues for a long time and cannot easily be solved: *California is trying to cope with chronic water shortages.* —**chronically** *adv.*: *patients who are chronically ill*

chron·i·cle /ˈkrɑnɪkəl/ *n.* [C] a written record of historical events, arranged in the order in which they happened —**chronicle** *v.* [T]

chron·o·log·i·cal /ˌkrɑnlˈɑdʒɪkəl/ *adj.* arranged according to when something happened: *a list of World Series champions **in chronological order*** —**chronologically** *adv.*

chro·nol·o·gy /krəˈnɑlədʒi/ *n.* plural **chronologies** [C] a list of events arranged according to when they happened: *a chronology of events in the Balkans*

chrys·a·lis /ˈkrɪsəlɪs/ *n.* [C] a MOTH or BUTTERFLY at the stage of development when it has a hard outer shell, before becoming a LARVA and then an adult [➡ **cocoon**] ➔ see picture on page A2

chry·san·the·mum /krɪˈsænθəməm/ *n.* [C] a garden plant with large brightly colored flowers

chub·by /ˈtʃʌbi/ *adj.* slightly fat, used especially about children —**chubbiness** *n.* [U]

> **THESAURUS**
> **fat, overweight, big, heavy, large, obese, plump**
> ➔ see Thesaurus box at FAT[1]

chuck /tʃʌk/ *v.* [T] *informal* **1** to throw something in a careless or relaxed way: *Chuck that magazine over here, would you?*

> **THESAURUS**
> **throw, toss, hurl, fling, pass, pitch**
> ➔ see Thesaurus box at THROW[1]

2 also chuck sth ⇔ **away/out** to throw something away: *Just go ahead and chuck out the old batteries.*

chuck·le /ˈtʃʌkəl/ *v.* [I,T] to laugh quietly: *Terry chuckled to himself as he read his book.* | *"You're wearing a wig," Mario chuckled.* —**chuckle** *n.* [C]

> **THESAURUS**
> **laugh, giggle, cackle, snicker, guffaw, (be) in stitches**
> ➔ see Thesaurus box at LAUGH[1]

chug /tʃʌg/ *v.* past tense and past participle **chugged**, present participle **chugging** **1** [I] if a car, boat, or train chugs somewhere, it moves there slowly, with the engine making a repeated low sound: *The little boat **chugged along** the canal.* **2** [T] *informal* to drink all of something without stopping: *Chug that beer and let's go.* —**chug** *n.* [C usually singular]

chum /tʃʌm/ *n.* [C] *old-fashioned* a good friend

chump /tʃʌmp/ *n.* [C] *informal* **1** someone who is silly or stupid, and who can be easily deceived **2 chump change** *informal* a very small amount of money: *That sort of investment is mere chump change for a multi-billion dollar company.*

chunk /tʃʌŋk/ *n.* [C] **1** a large thick piece of something that does not have an even shape: *a **chunk of** cheese*

> **THESAURUS**
> **piece, scrap, lump, fragment, crumb, slice**
> ➔ see Thesaurus box at PIECE[1]

2 a large part or amount of something: *The rent **takes** a large **chunk out of** my monthly salary.*

chunk·y /ˈtʃʌŋki/ *adj.* **1** thick and heavy: *chunky jewelry* **2** someone who is chunky has a broad heavy body

church /tʃɚtʃ/ *n.* **1** [C] a building where Christians go to have religious services **2** [U] the religious services in a church: *Come over after church.* | *She **goes to church** every Sunday.*

3 [C] **also Church** one of the separate groups within the Christian religion: *the Catholic Church*

THESAURUS

denomination – a religious group that has slightly different beliefs from other groups who belong to the same religion: *Roman Catholicism is the largest religious denomination in the nation.*
sect – a group of people who have their own set of beliefs or religious habits, especially a group that has separated from a larger group: *He is a leader in the powerful Ansar Sunni Muslim sect.*
cult – an extreme religious group that is not part of an established religion: *Members of the cult all committed suicide on the same day.*

GRAMMAR

Do not use "a" or "the" before **church** when you are talking about a religious ceremony: *I didn't see him* ***in church*** *this morning.* | *She used* ***to go to church*** *every Sunday.*

churl·ish /ˈtʃɚlɪʃ/ *adj. formal* not polite or friendly

churn¹ /tʃɚn/ *n.* [C] a container in which milk is shaken until it forms butter

churn² *v.* **1** [I] if your stomach churns, you feel sick because you are frightened or nervous: *Thinking about the exam* ***made*** *my* ***stomach churn.*** **2** [T] to make butter using a churn **3** [I,T] **also churn up** if water, mud, etc. churns, or if something churns it, it moves around violently

churn sth ⇔ **out** *phr. v.* to produce large quantities of something quickly, especially without caring about quality: *She keeps churning out novels.*

chute /ʃut/ *n.* [C] **1** a long narrow structure that slopes down, so that things or people can slide down it from one place to another: *a mail chute* **2** *informal* a PARACHUTE

chutz·pah /ˈhʊtspə/ *n.* [U] *informal approving* if someone has chutzpah, s/he has a lot of confidence and says rude or shocking things without feeling embarrassed

CIA *n.* [C] **Central Intelligence Agency** the department of the U.S. government that collects secret information about other countries

ci·der /ˈsaɪdɚ/ **also apple cider** *n.* [C,U] a drink made from apples

ci·gar /sɪˈgɑr/ *n.* [C] a thick tube-shaped thing that people smoke, and which is made from tobacco leaves that have been rolled up

cig·a·rette /ˌsɪgəˈrɛt, ˈsɪgəˌrɛt/ *n.* [C] a thin tube-shaped thing that people smoke, that is made from finely cut tobacco leaves that have been rolled into a tube of paper: *a* ***pack of cigarettes***

cinch¹ /sɪntʃ/ *n.* **be a cinch** *informal* **a)** to be almost certain to happen: *The Cubs are a cinch to win the National League East.* **b)** to be very easy to do: *The test was a cinch.*

cinch² *v.* [T] to pull a belt, STRAP, etc. tightly around something

cin·der /ˈsɪndɚ/ *n.* [C] a very small piece of burned wood, coal, etc.

ˈcinder block *n.* [C] a large, gray brick used to build houses, etc., made from CEMENT and cinders

cin·e·ma /ˈsɪnəmə/ *n.* **1** [U] the art or business of making movies: *an important director in German cinema* **2** [C] *old-fashioned* a MOVIE THEATER

cin·e·ma·tog·ra·phy /ˌsɪnəməˈtɑgrəfi/ *n.* [U] *technical* the skill or art of movie photography —**cinematographer** *n.* [C]

cin·na·mon /ˈsɪnəmən/ *n.* [U] a sweet-smelling brown SPICE used especially in baking cakes and cookies

ci·pher /ˈsaɪfɚ/ *n.* [C] a system of secret writing [= **code**]

cir·ca /ˈsɚkə/ *prep. formal* **c.** used before a date to show that something happened close to that time, but you do not know exactly when: *He was born circa 1100.*

cir·cle¹ /ˈsɚkəl/ *n.* [C] **1** a round shape like the letter O: *Draw a circle around the right answer.* ➔ see picture at SHAPE¹

THESAURUS

shape, **square**, **semicircle**, **triangle**, **rectangle**, **oval**, **cylinder**, **square**
➔ see Thesaurus box at SHAPE¹

2 a group of people or things forming the shape of a circle: *The women sat* ***in a circle.*** **3** a group of people who know each other or have a common interest: *a large* ***circle of*** *friends* | *She is very well-known* ***in political/legal/medical etc. circles*** (=the group of people who work in a particular profession or industry). **4 come/go full circle** to end in the same situation in which you began, even though there have been changes during the time in between: *After the experiments of the 1960s, education has come full circle in its methods of teaching reading.* **5 go/run around in circles** to think or argue about something a lot without deciding anything or making any progress

circle² *v.* **1** [T] to draw a circle around something: *Circle the correct answer.* **2** [I,T] to move in a circle around something: *a plane circling an airport before landing.*

cir·cuit /ˈsɚkɪt/ *n.* **1 the talk show/golf/lecture etc. circuit** all the places that are usually visited by someone who is doing a particular activity: *Vesey returned to the nightclub circuit as a singer.* **2** [C] the complete circle that an electric current travels

ˈcircuit board *n.* [C] a set of connections between points on a piece of electrical equipment that uses a thin line of metal to CONDUCT (=carry) the electricity

ˈcircuit ˌbreaker *n.* [C] a piece of equipment that stops an electric current if it becomes dangerous

ˈcircuit ˌcourt *n.* [C] a court of law in a U.S. state that meets in different places within the area it is responsible for

cir·cu·i·tous /sɚˈkyuət̬əs/ *adj. formal* going from one place to another in a way that is longer than the most direct way: *the river's circuitous course*

cir·cuit·ry /ˈsɚkətri/ *n.* [U] a system of electric CIRCUITS

cir·cu·lar¹ /ˈsɚkyəlɚ/ *adj.* **1** shaped like a circle: *a circular table* **2** moving around in a circle: *a circular journey* **3 circular argument/discussion/logic etc.** an argument, etc. that is not helpful because it always returns to the same statements or ideas that were expressed at the beginning —**circularity** /ˌsɚkyəˈlærət̬i/ *n.* [U]

THESAURUS

semicircular, **triangular**, **rectangular**, **oval**, **cylindrical**, **round**
→ see Thesaurus box at SHAPE¹

circular² *n.* [C] a printed advertisement or notice that is sent to a lot of people at the same time

cir·cu·late /ˈsɚkyəˌleɪt/ *v.* **1** [I,T] to move around within a system, or to make something do this: *Blood circulates around the body.* **2** [I] if information, facts, or ideas circulate, they become known by many people: ***Rumors** are **circulating** that the mayor's health is getting worse.* **3** [T] to send or give information, facts, goods, etc. to a group of people: *I'll circulate the report at the meeting.* —**circulatory** /ˈsɚkyələˌtɔri/ *adj.*

cir·cu·la·tion /ˌsɚkyəˈleɪʃən/ *n.* **1** [singular, U] the movement of blood around your body: *I feel like these tight shoes are **cutting off** my **circulation**.* **2** [singular] the average number of copies of a newspaper, magazine, or book that are usually sold over a particular period of time: *The newspaper has a daily **circulation of** 400,000* **3 in/out of circulation** if something is in circulation, it is being used by people in a society and passing from one person to another: *The government has reduced the number of $100 bills in circulation.* **4** [singular, U] the movement of liquid, air, etc. in a system: *Open a window and get some circulation in here.*

cir·cum·cise /ˈsɚkəmˌsaɪz/ *v.* [T] **1** to cut off the skin at the end of the PENIS (=male sex organ) **2** to cut off a woman's CLITORIS (=part of her sex organs) —**circumcision** /ˌsɚkəmˈsɪʒən/ *n.* [C,U]

cir·cum·ference /sɚˈkʌmfrəns/ *n.* [C,U] the distance around the outside of a circle or a round object: *the **circumference of** the Earth* | *The island is only nine miles **in circumference**.*

cir·cum·spect /ˈsɚkəmˌspɛkt/ *adj. formal* thinking carefully about things before doing them [= **cautious**]: *In politics you have to be more circumspect about what you say in public.*

cir·cum·stance /ˈsɚkəmˌstæns/ *n.* **1** [C usually plural] the facts or conditions that affect a situation, action, event, etc.: *You shouldn't judge him until you know the circumstances.* | *There are plenty of people **in** similar **circumstances**.* | *Prisoners can leave their cells only **under** certain **circumstances**.* **2 under the circumstances also given the circumstances** used in order to say that a particular situation makes an action, decision, etc. necessary, acceptable, or true when it would not normally be: *Under the circumstances, she did the best job she could.* **3 under no circumstances** used in order to emphasize that something must definitely not happen: *Under no circumstances are you to leave the house.* **4** [U] *formal* the combination of facts, events, and luck that influences your life, that you cannot control: *Circumstance played a large part in her getting the job.*

cir·cum·stan·tial /ˌsɚkəmˈstænʃəl◂/ *adj.* based on something that appears to be true but is not proven: *The case against McCarthy is based largely on **circumstantial evidence**.*

cir·cum·vent /ˌsɚkəmˈvɛnt, ˈsɚkəmˌvɛnt/ *v.* [T] *formal* to avoid having to obey a rule or law, especially in a dishonest way: *The company has opened an office abroad in order to circumvent the tax laws.* —**circumvention** /ˌsɚkəmˈvɛnʃən/ *n.* [U]

cir·cus /ˈsɚkəs/ *n.* [C] a group of performers and animals that travel to different places doing tricks and other kinds of entertainment: *circus acts*

cir·rho·sis /sɪˈroʊsɪs/ *n.* [U] a serious disease of the LIVER, often caused by drinking too much alcohol

cis·tern /ˈsɪstɚn/ *n.* [C] a large container that water is stored in

cit·a·del /ˈsɪt̬ədəl, -ˌdɛl/ *n.* [C] a strong FORT built in past times as a place where people could go for safety if their city was attacked

ci·ta·tion /saɪˈteɪʃən/ *n.* [C] **1** an official order for someone to appear in court or pay a FINE for doing something illegal: *Turner was issued a traffic **citation for** reckless driving.* **2** an official statement publicly praising someone's actions or achievements: *a **citation for** bravery* **3** a line taken from a book, speech, etc. [= **quotation**]

cite /saɪt/ *v.* [T] **1** to mention something as an example or proof of something else: *The mayor **cited** the latest crime figures **as** proof of the need for more police.*

THESAURUS

mention, **refer to**, **raise**, **allude to**, **bring up**
→ see Thesaurus box at MENTION¹

2 *law* to order someone to appear before a court of law: *He has been **cited for** speeding.*

cit·i·zen /ˈsɪt̬əzən/ *n.* [C] **1** someone who lives in a particular town, state, or country: *The mayor urged citizens to begin preparing for a major storm.* **2** someone who has the legal right to live and work in a particular country: *a Brazilian* *citizen* **3 second class citizen** someone who is not as important as other people in a society and who is treated badly

cit·i·zen·ship /ˈsɪṭəzənˌʃɪp/ *n.* [U] the legal right of belonging to a particular country: *She has applied for U.S. citizenship.*

cit·rus /ˈsɪtrəs/ **also ˈcitrus ˌfruit** *n.* [C] a fruit such as an orange or a LEMON

city

cit·y /ˈsɪṭi/ *n.* plural **cities** [C] **1** a large, important town: *New York City | I've always lived in **big cities**.* **2** the people who live in a city: *The city has been living in fear since last week's earthquake.*

ˌcity ˈcouncil *n.* [C] the group of elected officials who are responsible for making a city's laws

ˌcity ˈhall *n.* [C,U] the local government of a city, or the building it uses as its offices

civ·ic /ˈsɪvɪk/ *adj.* relating to a city or the people who live in it: *an important civic and business leader | It's your **civic duty** to vote.*

civ·ics /ˈsɪvɪks/ *n.* [U] a school subject dealing with the rights and duties of citizens and the way government works

civ·il /ˈsɪvəl/ *adj.* **1** not related to military or religious organizations: *We were married in a civil ceremony, not in church.* **2** related to laws concerning the private affairs of citizens, such as laws about business or property, rather than with crime: *a civil lawsuit* **3 civil unrest/disorder etc.** violence involving different groups within a country **4** polite but not very friendly: *Please try to be civil.* —**civilly** *adv.*

THESAURUS

polite, have good manners, well-behaved, courteous
→ see Thesaurus box at POLITE

ˌcivil disoˈbedience *n.* [U] actions done by a large group of people in order to protest against the government, but without being violent

ˌcivil engiˈneering *n.* [U] the planning, building, and repair of roads, bridges, large buildings, etc.

ci·vil·ian /səˈvɪlyən/ *n.* [C] anyone who is not a member of the military or the police: *Many innocent civilians were killed in the attack.* —**civilian** *adj.*

civ·i·li·za·tion /ˌsɪvələˈzeɪʃən/ *n.* **1** [C,U] a society that is well organized and developed: *modern American civilization | the ancient **civilizations of** Greece and Rome* **2** [U] all the societies in the world considered as a whole: *The book looks at the relationship between religion and civilization.*

civ·i·lize /ˈsɪvəˌlaɪz/ *v.* [T] *old-fashioned* to improve a society so that it is more organized and developed

civ·i·lized /ˈsɪvəˌlaɪzd/ *adj.* **1** a civilized society is one that has laws and CUSTOMS and a well developed social system: *Care for the elderly is essential in a civilized society.* **2** behaving in a polite and sensible way: *Let's discuss this in a civilized way.*

ˌcivil ˈliberty *n.* plural **civil liberties** [C,U] the right of all citizens to be free to do whatever they want while obeying the law and respecting the rights of other people

ˌcivil ˈrights *n.* [plural] the legal rights that every person in a particular country has. In the U.S., these include the right to have the same treatment whatever your race or religion is

ˌcivil ˈservant *n.* [C] someone who works in the civil service

ˌcivil ˈservice *n.* **the civil service** the government departments that deal with all the work of the government except the military

ˌcivil ˈwar *n.* [C,U] a war in which opposing groups of people from the same country fight each other

clack /klæk/ *v.* [I,T] to make a continuous short hard sound: *the sound of high heels clacking across the courtyard* —**clack** *n.* [singular]

clad /klæd/ *adj. literary* wearing or covered in a particular thing: *The model was **clad in** silk and lace*

claim¹ /kleɪm/ *v.* **1** [T] to state that something is true even though it might not be: *The company **claims that** their products will help you lose weight. | George **claims to** remember exactly what the gunman looked like.* **2** [I,T] to officially ask for money that you have a right to receive: *Congress intends to make welfare harder to claim.* ► Don't say "harder to demand." ◄ **3** [T] to state that you have a right to something, or to take something that belongs to you: *Lost items can be claimed between 10 a.m. and 4 p.m.* **4** [T] *formal* if a war, accident, etc. claims lives, people die because of it: *Officials say the violence has claimed 21 lives.*

claim² *n.* **1** [C] a statement that something is true even though it might not be: *Cardoza denied **claims that** he was involved in drug smuggling.* **2** [C,U] an act of officially saying that you have a right to receive or own something, or the state of having this right: *The contract proves he has no **claim on** the house. | insurance claims* **3** [C] an official request for money that you think you have a right to: *insurance claims | She is filing a **claim for** unpaid child support.* **4** [C] a right to have or do something: *Both groups believe they **have a claim to** the land.* **5 claim to fame** the most important or interesting thing about a person or a place: *Her main claim to fame is the men she married.*

clair·voy·ant /klɛrˈvɔɪənt/ *n.* [C] someone who says s/he can see what will happen in the future —**clairvoyance** *n.* [U] —**clairvoyant** *adj.*

clam¹ /klæm/ *n.* [C,U] a small sea animal that has a shell and lives in sand and mud, or the meat from this animal

clam² *v.* past tense and past participle **clammed**, present participle **clamming**

clam up *phr. v. informal* to suddenly stop talking: *Lou always clams up if you ask him too many questions about his past.*

clam·ber /ˈklæmbɚ, ˈklæmɚ/ *v.* [I] to climb something that is difficult to climb, using your hands and feet: *Jenny and I **clambered up** the side of the hill.*

clam·my /ˈklæmi/ *adj.* wet, cold, and sticky in a way that is unpleasant: *clammy hands*

clam·or¹ /ˈklæmɚ/ *n.* [singular, U] **1** a complaint or a demand for something: *a public **clamor for** better schools* **2** a very loud continuous noise: *a **clamor of** voices in the next room* —**clamorous** *adj.*

clamor² *v.* [I] to demand something loudly: *All the kids were **clamoring for** attention at once.* | *The children were **clamoring to** have their photo taken with Santa.*

clamp¹ /klæmp/ *v.* [T] **1** to hold something tightly so that it does not move: *He **clamped** his hand **over** her mouth.* **2** to fasten or hold two things together with a CLAMP: ***Clamp** the boards **together** until the glue dries.*

clamp down *phr. v.* to become very strict in order to stop people from doing something: *The police are **clamping down on** drunk drivers.*

clamp² *n.* [C] a tool used for fastening or holding things together tightly

clamp·down /ˈklæmpdaʊn/ *n.* [C] a sudden action by the government, police, etc. to stop a particular activity: *a **clampdown on** illegal immigration*

clan /klæn/ *n.* [C] *informal* a large family: *The whole clan will be coming over for Thanksgiving.*

clan·des·tine /klænˈdɛstɪn/ *adj.* secret: *a clandestine meeting*

clang /klæŋ/ *v.* [I,T] to make a loud sound like metal being hit: *The gate clanged shut behind him.* —**clang** *n.* [C]

clank /klæŋk/ *v.* [I] to make a short, loud sound like metal objects hitting each other: *clanking chains* —**clank** *n.* [C]

clap¹ /klæp/ *v.* past tense and past participle **clapped**, present participle **clapping** **1** [I,T] to hit your hands together loudly and continuously to show that you approve of something, or want to attract someone's attention: *The audience was clapping and cheering.* | *The coach **clapped** his **hands** and yelled, "OK, listen!"* → see picture on page A8 **2 clap sb on the back/shoulder** to hit someone on the back or shoulder with your hand in a friendly way —**clapping** *n.* [U]

clap² *n.* [C] **1 a clap of thunder** a very loud sound made by THUNDER **2** the sound that you make when you hit your hands together

clap·board /ˈklæbɚd, ˈklæpbɔrd/ *n.* [C,U] a set of boards that cover the outside walls of a building, or one of these boards: *a clapboard house*

clar·i·fy /ˈklærəˌfaɪ/ *v.* past tense and past participle **clarified**, third person singular **clarifies** [I,T] to make something easier to understand by explaining it in more detail: *I need you to clarify a few points.* | *Could you **clarify what** you mean?* —**clarification** /ˌklærəfəˈkeɪʃən/ *n.* [C,U]

clar·i·net /ˌklærəˈnɛt/ *n.* [C] a wooden musical instrument shaped like a long black tube that you play by blowing into it —**clarinetist** *n.* [C] → see picture on page A6

clar·i·ty /ˈklærət̮i/ *n.* [U] the quality of speaking, writing, or thinking in a clear way: *the **clarity of** Irving's writing style*

clash¹ /klæʃ/ *v.* **1** [I] to fight or argue with someone: *Soldiers **clashed with** rebels near the border.* **2** [I] if two colors or patterns clash, they do not look nice together: *That red tie **clashes with** your jacket.* **3** [I,T] to make a loud sound by hitting two metal objects together

clash² *n.* [C] **1** a fight or argument between two people, groups, or armies: *a **clash between** Democrats and Republicans in the Senate* | *a **culture/personality clash*** (=a situation in which different types or groups of people do not like each other) **2** a loud sound made by two metal objects hitting together: *the clash of the cymbals*

clasp¹ /klæsp/ *n.* **1** [C] a small metal object used for fastening a bag, belt, piece of jewelry, etc. **2** [singular] a tight firm hold; [= **grip**]: *the firm clasp of her father's hand*

clasp² *v.* [T] to hold someone or something tightly: *Lie down with your **hands clasped** behind your head.*

class¹ /klæs/ *n.*

1 GROUP OF STUDENTS [C] **a)** a group of students who are taught together: *a small class of ten people* **b)** a group of students who finish college or HIGH SCHOOL in the same year: *Our class had its 30th reunion this year.* | *Howard was a member of the **class of '88*** (=the group of students who finished in 1988).

2 TEACHING PERIOD [C,U] a period of time during which students are taught: *When's your next class?* | *Bob wasn't **in class** today.*

3 SUBJECT [C] a set of lessons in which you study a particular subject: *a **class in** computer design* | *She's **taking** a yoga **class**.* | *a **Spanish/math/science class***

4 IN SOCIETY **a)** [C] a group of people in a society that earn a similar amount of money, have similar types of jobs, etc. [➡ **lower class**, **middle**

class, upper class]: *The Republicans are promising tax cuts for the middle class.* **b)** [U] the system in which people are divided into such groups: *People were excluded from education based on class and race.*
5 QUALITY [C] a group into which people or things are divided according to how good they are: *We can't afford to travel* ***first class*** (=the most expensive way) *on the plane.* | *As a tennis player, she's* ***not in the same class*** (=not as good as) *as Williams.* | *The car is* ***in a class of its own*** (=very good quality).
6 STYLE/SKILL [U] a particular style, skill, or way of doing something that makes people admire you: *Margaret really* ***has class.***
7 PLANTS/ANIMALS [C] a group of plants, animals, words, etc. that can be studied together because they are similar

C

class² *v.* [T] to decide that someone or something belongs in a particular group: *Heroin and cocaine are* ***classed as*** *hard drugs.*

ˌclass-ˈaction *adj.* a class-action LAWSUIT is one that a group of people bring to a court of law for themselves and all other people with the same problem —**class action** *n.* [C,U]

clas·sic¹ /ˈklæsɪk/ *adj.* [usually before noun] **1** a classic book, movie, etc. is considered to be very good and has been popular for a long time: *The Coca-Cola bottle is one of the classic designs of the last century.* | *Orson Welles directed the classic film "Citizen Kane."*

THESAURUS
old, **ancient**, **antique**, **vintage**
→ see Thesaurus box at OLD

2 a classic example/case etc. a typical or very good example, etc.: *Forgetting to release the emergency brake is a classic mistake that many new drivers make.* **3** a classic style of dressing, art, etc. is attractive in a simple or traditional way: *a classic blue suit*

classic² *n.* [C] **1** a book, movie, etc. that is considered to be very good and has been popular for a long time: *"Moby Dick" is a classic of American literature.* **2** something that is very good and one of the best examples of its kind: *The '65 Ford Mustang is a classic.* **3 classics** [plural] the study of the languages, literature, and history of ancient Greece and Rome

clas·si·cal /ˈklæsɪkəl/ *adj.* **1** based on a traditional style or set of ideas: *classical Indian dance* **2** relating to classical music: *a classical pianist* **3** belonging to the language, literature, history, etc. of ancient Greece and Rome: *classical architecture*

ˌclassical ˈmusic *n.* [U] a type of music, originally from Europe, that includes OPERAS and symphonies (SYMPHONY), is played mainly on instruments such as the VIOLIN and piano, and is considered to have serious artistic value

THESAURUS
pop (music), **rock (music)**, **rock'n'roll**, **heavy metal**, **reggae**, **house (music)**, **hip-hop**, **rap (music)**, **jazz**, **country (music)**, **folk (music)**
→ see Thesaurus box at MUSIC

clas·si·fi·ca·tion /ˌklæsəfəˈkeɪʃən/ *n.* [C,U] the process of putting people or things into groups according to their age, type, etc., or one of these groups: *the* ***classification of*** *wines according to their region* | *my job classification*

clas·si·fied /ˈklæsəˌfaɪd/ *adj.* classified information, documents, etc. are kept secret by the government or an organization

ˌclassified ˈad *n.* [C] a small advertisement that you put in a newspaper if you want to buy or sell something

clas·si·fy /ˈklæsəˌfaɪ/ *v.* past tense and past participle **classified**, third person singular **classifies** [T] to put things into groups according to their age, type, etc.: *Whales are* ***classified as*** *mammals rather than fish.*

class·less /ˈklæslɪs/ *adj.* a society is one in which people are not divided into different social classes

class·mate /ˈklæsmeɪt/ *n.* [C] someone who is in the same class as you at school or college: *I'm younger than most of my classmates.*

class·room /ˈklæsrum, -rʊm/ *n.* [C] **1** a room in a school where students are taught: *classroom materials* **2 in the classroom** in schools or classes in general: *the use of computers in the classroom*

class·work /ˈklæswɚk/ *n.* [U] work that students do in class, not at home [➡ **homework**]

class·y /ˈklæsi/ *adj.* comparative **classier**, superlative **classiest** *informal* expensive and fashionable: *a classy restaurant*

clat·ter /ˈklæt̬ɚ/ *v.* [I,T] if something clatters, it makes a loud noise when it hits something: *The pots clattered to the floor.* —**clatter** *n.* [singular, U]

clause /klɔz/ *n.* [C] **1** a part of a written law or legal document: *A clause in the contract states when payment must be made.* **2** *technical* in grammar, a group of words that is part of a sentence [➡ **phrase**]

claus·tro·pho·bi·a /ˌklɔstrəˈfoʊbiə/ *n.* [U] a strong fear of being in a small enclosed place or in a crowd of people —**claustrophobic** /ˌklɔstrəˈfoʊbɪk/ *adj.*: *I began to feel a little claustrophobic in the elevator.*

clavicle /ˈklævɪkəl/ *n.* [C] → COLLARBONE

claw¹ /klɔ/ *n.* [C] a sharp curved nail on an animal, bird, or some insects: *lobster claws* → see picture on page A2

claw² *v.* [I,T] to tear or pull at something using your fingers or claws: *The cat keeps* ***clawing at*** *the rug.*

clay /kleɪ/ *n.* [U] a type of heavy wet soil that is used to make pots or bricks: *a clay pot*

clean[1] /klin/ *adj.* **1 a)** not dirty or messy [≠ **dirty**; ➡ **cleanliness**]: *Are your hands clean?* | *clean sheets* | *I want you to **keep** this room **clean**.* | *a **squeaky clean** (=very clean) floor* **b)** not containing or producing anything harmful or dirty [≠ **polluted**]: *clean water/air* **2** not rude or offensive, or not about sex: *good clean fun* **3** honest or legal and showing that you have not broken any rules or laws: *I've had a **clean record** (=no official record of having broken the law) for five years now.* | *a clean driving record* **4** having a simple and attractive style or design: *a shape that emphasizes the furniture's **clean lines*** **5 come clean** *informal* to finally tell the truth about something you have been hiding: *Josh finally **came clean about** denting the car.* **6 a clean break** a complete and sudden separation from a person, organization, or situation: *She wanted to **make a clean break** with the past.* **7 a clean sweep** a very impressive victory in a competition, election, etc.: *It was looking like **a clean sweep for** the Democrats.* **8 a clean slate** a new situation in which there is no record of you ever breaking any rules or behaving badly, even if you have broken rules or behaved badly in the past: *He will start his school life here **with a clean slate**.* **9 a clean bill of health** a report saying that a person is healthy or that a machine or building is safe

clean[2] *v.* [I,T] **1** to remove dirt from somewhere or something: *I need to clean the bathtub.* | *She's busy cleaning.* | *We've hired a maid to clean our house.*

THESAURUS

do/wash the dishes – to wash plates and pans after a meal
scour/scrub – to wash dirty pots and pans with a rough cloth
dry – to dry plates, dishes, etc. that have been washed
do the housework – to clean the house
dust/polish – to clean furniture
vacuum – to clean carpets with a special machine
sweep (up) – to clean the dirt from the floor or ground using a broom (=brush with a long handle)
scrub – to clean the floor by rubbing it with a hard brush
mop – to clean the floor with water and a mop (=soft brush on a long handle)
do the laundry – to wash clothes
handwash clothes/wash clothes by hand
dry-clean clothes – to clean clothes with chemicals instead of water

2 to make something look neat by putting things in their correct places [= **clear**]: *Pam began to clean her desk.*

clean out *phr. v.* **1 clean** sth ⇔ **out** to make the inside of a car, room, house, etc. clean, especially by removing things from it: *We cleaned out the garage last Sunday.* **2 clean** sb/sth ⇔ **out** *informal* to steal everything from a place or from someone: *Two armed men cleaned out the computer store.* **3 clean** sb **out** if buying something cleans you out, it is so expensive you have no money left: *The new refrigerator really cleaned me out.*

clean up *phr. v.* **1 clean** sb/sth **up** to make something or someone clean and neat: *Clean up your room – it's a mess!* | *I need to go upstairs and **get cleaned up**.* **2 clean** sth ⇔ **up** to remove crime, bad behavior, etc. from a place or organization: *We need someone to clean up City Hall.* **3 clean up your act** *informal* to begin to behave in a responsible way: *You'll have to clean up your act if you want to impress Diane's parents.* —**cleaning** *n.* [U] *A woman comes twice a week to **do** the **cleaning**.*

clean[3] *adv. informal* completely: *I'm sorry, I **clean forgot** your birthday.*

ˌclean-ˈcut *adj. approving* a man who is clean-cut is clean and neat in his appearance

clean·er /ˈklinɚ/ *n.* **1** [C] a machine or substance used to clean things: *a vacuum cleaner* **2** [C] someone whose job is to clean something: *a street cleaner* **3 the cleaners** [plural] DRY CLEANERS **4 take sb to the cleaners** *informal* to get all of someone's money in a way that is not honest: *Juanita threatened to take her former husband to the cleaners.* ➔ DRY CLEANERS

clean·li·ness /ˈklɛnlinɪs/ *n.* [U] the practice of keeping yourself or the things around you clean

clean·ly /ˈklinli/ *adv.* done quickly, smoothly, and neatly: *The doctor cut cleanly through the skin.*

cleanse /klɛnz/ *v.* [T] to make something completely clean: *Cleanse the wound with alcohol.*

cleans·er /ˈklɛnzɚ/ *n.* [C,U] **1** a substance used for cleaning your skin **2** a substance used for cleaning surfaces in a house, office, etc.

clean-shaven

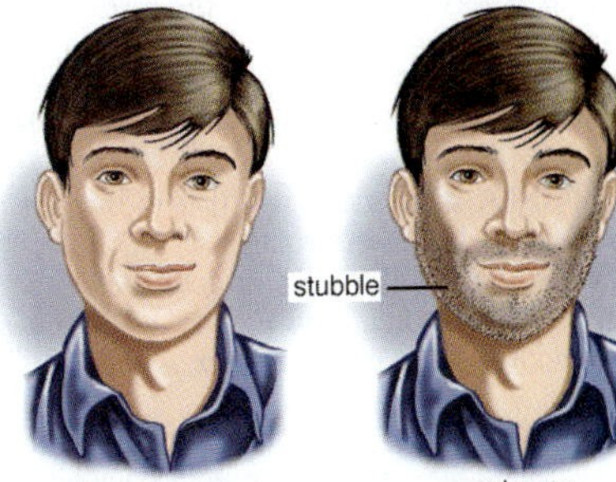

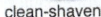

ˌclean-ˈshaven *adj.* a man who is clean-shaven does not have a BEARD or MUSTACHE (=hair on his face)

clean·up /ˈklinʌp/ *n.* [C usually singular] a process in which you clean something thoroughly: *The* *cleanup of the oil spill took months.* —**cleanup** *adj.*

clear[1] /klɪr/ *adj.*

1 SIMPLE/EASY easy to understand, hear, read, or see: *clear instructions* | *The law is quite* ***clear on*** *this issue.* | *Smith was very* ***clear about*** *the school's policies on the matter.* | *It is* ***clear to*** *me that the company will have to make further job cuts.* | *Have I* ***made myself clear****?* | *Hugh had* ***made it*** *perfectly* ***clear (that)*** *he wasn't interested.* | *We must send out a* ***clear message/signal*** *to voters.*

THESAURUS

noticeable, obvious, conspicuous, striking, eye-catching
➔ see Thesaurus box at NOTICEABLE

2 CERTAIN impossible to doubt: *clear evidence* | *It's not* ***clear how*** *it happened.* | *It became* ***clear that*** *he would soon die.* | *a* ***clear case/example of*** *fraud* | *In this situation, there is no* ***clear winner****.*
3 SURE ABOUT STH [not before noun] feeling sure that you understand something [≠ **confused**]: *I'm not* ***clear about*** *what you want me to do.*
4 SEE THROUGH easy to see through: *clear glass bottles* | *a clear mountain lake*
5 WEATHER weather that is clear is bright with no rain or clouds: *a clear sky*
6 NOT BLOCKED not blocked, hidden, or covered by anything: *a clear view of the harbor* | *smooth clear skin*
7 a clear conscience the knowledge that you have done the right thing and should not feel guilty

clear[2] *v.*

1 MAKE NEAT [T] to make a place neat by removing things from it: *Snowplows quickly* ***cleared*** *the streets* ***of*** *snow.* | *They spent the morning* ***clearing*** *garbage* ***from*** *the front yard.* | *If you* ***clear the table*** (=take away the dishes, forks, etc.)*, I'll make the coffee.* | *Can you* ***clear a space*** *for my books?*
2 REMOVE [T] to make people, cars, etc. leave a place: *Within minutes, police had cleared the area.* | *Trucks have just finished* ***clearing*** *the wreck* ***from*** *the road.*
3 LEGAL CHARGE [T] to prove that someone is not guilty of something: *The jury* ***cleared*** *Johnson* ***of*** *the murder charge.*
4 WEATHER also clear up [I] if the weather or sky clears, it becomes brighter
5 PERMISSION [T] to give or get official permission to do something: *Has the plane been* ***cleared for*** *landing?* | *I'll have to* ***clear*** *it* ***with*** *my boss first.*
6 CHECK [I,T] if a check that is made out to you clears, the money is paid into your bank account
7 clear your throat to cough a little so that you can speak clearly
8 clear the air to talk about a problem in order to solve a disagreement: *The White House hopes that the investigation will clear the air.*
9 GO OVER [T] to go over a fence, wall, etc. without touching it: *The plane barely cleared the fence as it came down.*
10 clear a debt/loan [T] to get rid of a debt by paying what you owe

clear sth ⇔ **away** *phr. v.* to make a place look neat by removing things or putting them where they belong: *Clear all these toys away before you go to bed.*

clear out *phr. v.* **1 clear** sth ⇔ **out** to make a place neat by removing things from it: *I need to clear out that closet.* **2** *informal* used in order to angrily tell someone to leave a place: *The campers were told to clear out by 9:00.*

clear up *phr. v.* **1 clear** sth ⇔ **up** to explain or solve something, or make it clearer: *We need to clear up a few points before the meeting begins.* **2** if an infection clears up, it gets better

clear[3] *adv.* **1** away from someone or something: *Firemen pulled the driver* ***clear of*** *the wreckage.* **2 steer/stay/keep clear (of sb/sth)** to avoid someone or something because of possible danger or trouble: *She told us to stay clear of bars near the docks.* **3** all the way: *You can see* ***clear to*** *the Rockies today.*

clear[4] *n.* **in the clear a)** not having difficulties because of something: *The debt is being paid off, but we're not in the clear yet.* **b)** not guilty of something

clear·ance /ˈklɪrəns/ *n.* [C,U] **1** official permission to do something: *Kameny was denied a* ***security clearance****.* **2** the distance between two objects that is needed to stop them touching: *We need twelve feet of overhead clearance for the truck.*

ˈclearance sale *n.* [C] an occasion when goods in a shop are sold cheaply in order to get rid of them

ˈclear-cut *adj.* certain or definite: *a clear-cut decision*

ˌclear-ˈheaded *adj.* able to think clearly and sensibly

clear·ing /ˈklɪrɪŋ/ *n.* [C] a small area in a forest where there are no trees

clear·ly /ˈklɪrli/ *adv.* **1** without any doubt: *Clearly, he felt he was to blame.* | *Leslie was clearly annoyed.* **2** in a way that is easy to see, understand, hear, etc.: *Slow down and speak clearly.* | *Prices were clearly marked.* **3** if you cannot think clearly, you are confused

cleat /klit/ *n.* [C] **1** one of a set of short pieces of rubber, metal, etc. attached to the bottom of a sports shoe **2 cleats** [plural] a pair of shoes with cleats attached to them

cleav·age /ˈklivɪdʒ/ *n.* [C,U] the space between a woman's breasts

clea·ver /ˈklivɚ/ *n.* [C] a knife with a large square blade: *a meat cleaver*

clef /klɛf/ *n.* [C] a sign used in written music to show the PITCH of the notes

cleft[1] /klɛft/ *n.* [C] a natural crack in the ground or in rocks

cleft² *adj.* partly split or divided: *a cleft chin*

clem·en·cy /'klɛmənsi/ *n.* [U] *formal* the act of forgiving someone for a crime and making his/her punishment less severe: *His appeal for clemency has been denied.*

clench /klɛntʃ/ *v.* [T] to close your hands, mouth, etc. tightly: *He **clenched** his **fist** and pounded it into his palm.* | *He had a cigar **clenched between** his teeth.*

cler·gy /'klɚdʒi/ *n.* **the clergy** [plural] the official leaders of organized religions

cler·gy·man /'klɚdʒimən/, **cler·gy·wom·an** /'klɚdʒi,wʊmən/ *n.* plural **clergymen** /-mən/, **clergywomen** /-,wɪmɪn/ [C] a male or female member of the clergy

cler·ic /'klɛrɪk/ *n.* [C] a member of the clergy

cler·i·cal /'klɛrɪkəl/ *adj.* **1** relating to office work: *a clerical worker* **2** relating to the clergy

clerk /klɚk/ *n.* [C] **1** someone who deals with people arriving at a hotel: *Please return your keys to the desk clerk.*

> **THESAURUS**
>
> **sales assistant**, **cashier**
> ➔ see Thesaurus box at STORE¹

2 someone whose job is to help people in a store **3** someone whose job is to keep records, accounts, etc. in an office ➔ SALES CLERK

clev·er /'klɛvɚ/ *adj.* **1** able to use your intelligence to do something, especially in a slightly dishonest way: *a lawyer's clever tricks* **2** able to learn things quickly: *a clever child*

> **THESAURUS**
>
> **intelligent**, **smart**, **bright**, **brilliant**, **wise**, **intellectual**, **gifted**
> ➔ see Thesaurus box at INTELLIGENT

3 showing ability, skill, or imagination: *a clever idea* —**cleverly** *adv.* —**cleverness** *n.* [U]

cli·ché /kli'ʃeɪ/ *n.* an idea or phrase that has been used so much that it is no longer effective or does not have any meaning any longer: *The movie avoids most of the usual clichés.*

click¹ /klɪk/ *v.* **1** [I,T] to make a short hard sound, or to make something produce this sound: *The door clicked shut.* | *He **clicked** his **heels*** (=hit the heels of his shoes together) *and jumped into the air.* **2** [I] *informal* to suddenly understand or realize something: *I was having a lot of trouble with algebra until one day **it** just **clicked**.* **3** [I] *informal* if two people click, they immediately like each other **4** [I,T] to press a button on a computer MOUSE to make the computer do something [➡ **double-click**]: ***Click on** the icon at the bottom of the screen.* ➔ see picture on page A7

click² *n.* [C] a short hard sound: *I heard a click, and the phone went dead.*

cli·ent /'klaɪənt/ *n.* [C] someone who pays a person or organization for a service: *important clients*

> **THESAURUS**
>
> **customer**, **shopper**, **consumer**, **buyer**
> ➔ see Thesaurus box at CUSTOMER

cli·en·tele /,klaɪən'tɛl, ,kliɑn-/ *n.* [singular] the people who regularly go to a store, restaurant, etc.: *The bar attracts a mostly male clientele.*

cliff /klɪf/ *n.* [C] a large area of rock with steep sides

cliff·hang·er /'klɪf,hæŋɚ/ *n.* [C] *informal* a situation in a story that excites you because you do not know what will happen next

cli·mac·tic /klaɪ'mæktɪk/ *adj.* forming an exciting or important part at the end of a story or event: *the final climactic scene of the play*

cli·mate /'klaɪmɪt/ *n.* **1** [C] the typical weather conditions in an area: *a hot and humid climate* **2** [singular] the general feelings in a situation at a particular time: *in the current **climate of** uncertainty* | *a **climate of fear/violence/hostility etc.*** | *the **economic/political, etc. climate*** —**climatic** /klaɪ'mæṭɪk/ *adj.*

cli·max¹ /'klaɪmæks/ *n.* [C] the most important or exciting things that come near the end of a story or experience: *Winning the gold medal was the **climax of** his sports career.* | *The crisis **reached** a **climax** last week, when two senators resigned.*

climax² *v.* [I,T] to reach the most important or exciting part of something: *The tournament **climaxes with** the championship game on March 31.*

climb¹ /klaɪm/ *v.* **1** [I,T] to move toward the top of something: *kids climbing a tree* | *the first man to climb Mount Everest* | *We watched as the plane **climbed into** the sky.* | *I slowly climbed three flights of stairs.* ➔ see picture on page A9 **2** [I] to move somewhere with difficulty, using your hands and feet: *Ford **climbed into** a waiting limousine.* **3** [I] to increase in number, amount, or level: *The temperature was climbing steadily.* **4** [I,T] to move to a better position in your social or professional life: *women trying to **climb the** corporate **ladder*** (=become more successful) **5 be climbing the walls** *spoken* to become extremely anxious, annoyed, or impatient: *When he hadn't gotten back by midnight, I was climbing the walls.*

climb² *n.* [C usually singular] **1** a process in which you move up toward a place while using a lot of effort: *a tough **climb to** the top* **2** an increase in value or amount: *a steady **climb in** house prices* **3** the process of improving your professional or social position: *a politician's **climb to** power*

climb·er /'klaɪmɚ/ *n.* [C] someone who climbs rocks, mountains, etc. as a sport ➔ SOCIAL CLIMBER

climb·ing /'klaɪmɪŋ/ *n.* [U] the sport of climbing mountains or rocks: *Let's **go climbing** this weekend.* ➔ see picture on page A10

clinch /klɪntʃ/ *v.* [T] *informal* to manage to win or

C

get something after trying hard: *I think I know how we can* ***clinch*** *this* ***deal***.

clinch·er /ˈklɪntʃɚ/ *n.* [C] *informal* a fact or action that finally persuades someone to do something, or that ends an argument or competition: *The real clincher was her threat to sue the city.*

cling /klɪŋ/ *v.* past tense and past participle **clung** /klʌŋ/ [I] **1** to hold onto someone or something tightly because you do not feel safe: *a climber* ***clinging onto*** *a rock* | *They* ***clung to*** *each other and cried.* **2** to stick to something: *The wet shirt* ***clung to*** *his body.*

cling to sth *phr. v.* to continue to believe or do something, even though it may no longer be true or useful: *The villagers still clung to their traditions.*

cling·y /ˈklɪŋi/ *adj.* **1** *disapproving* someone who is clingy is too dependent on another person: *a shy, clingy child* **2** clingy clothing or material sticks tightly to your body and shows its shape: *a clingy dress*

clin·ic /ˈklɪnɪk/ *n.* [C] **1** a place where medical treatment is given to people who do not need to stay in a hospital: *a dental clinic* **2** a group of doctors who share the same offices **3** a meeting during which a professional person gives advice or help to people: *a marriage clinic*

clin·i·cal /ˈklɪnɪkəl/ *adj.* **1** relating to treating or testing people who are sick: *The drug has undergone a number of* ***clinical trials/tests***. **2** *disapproving* not influenced by personal feelings: *a cold clinical attitude* —**clinically** *adv.*

clin·i·cian /klɪˈnɪʃən/ *n.* [C] a doctor who examines and treats people who are sick rather than studying disease

clink /klɪŋk/ *v.* [I,T] if glass or metal objects clink, or if you clink them, they make a short ringing sound when they touch —**clink** *n.* [singular]

clip¹ /klɪp/ *n.* [C] **1** a small metal or plastic object for holding things together: *a paper clip* **2** a short part of a movie or television program that is shown by itself, especially as an advertisement: ***clips from*** *Fox's new movie* **3 at a good/rapid/fast clip** quickly: *Witnesses say the car was moving at a rapid clip.*

clip² *v.* past tense and past participle **clipped**, present participle **clipping** **1** [I,T] to put a clip on things to hold them together: *She'd* ***clipped*** *her business card* ***to*** *the letter.*

THESAURUS

fasten, attach, join, glue, tape, staple, tie, button (up), zip (up)
➔ see Thesaurus box at FASTEN

2 [T] to cut something out of a newspaper, magazine, etc.: *Tara showed him an ad she'd* ***clipped out of*** *the Sunday paper.* **3** [T] to cut small amounts from something to make it look neater: *He went out in the yard to clip the hedges.*

clip·board /ˈklɪpbɔrd/ *n.* [C] **1** a small flat board with a clip that holds paper onto it ➔ see picture on page A12 **2** part of a computer MEMORY that stores information when you cut, copy, or move it

ˈclip-on *adj.* attached to something using a clip: *clip-on earrings*

clip·pers /ˈklɪpɚz/ *n.* [plural] a tool for cutting small pieces off something: *nail clippers*

clip·ping /ˈklɪpɪŋ/ *n.* **1** [C] an article, picture, etc. that you cut out of a newspaper or magazine **2** [C usually plural] a small piece cut from something bigger: *grass clippings*

clique /klik, klɪk/ *n.* [C] *disapproving* a small group of people who do not want others to join their group: *The girls have their own little clique.* —**cliquish** *adj.*

clit·o·ris /ˈklɪt̬ərɪs/ *n.* [C] a small part of a woman's outer sex organs where she can feel sexual pleasure

cloak¹ /kloʊk/ *n.* [C] a warm piece of clothing like a coat without sleeves

cloak² *v.* [T] *written* to deliberately cover or hide something: *The early stages of the negotiations were* ***cloaked in secrecy***.

ˌcloak-and-ˈdagger *adj.* very secret and mysterious: *a cloak-and-dagger operation*

cloak·room /ˈkloʊk-rum, -rʊm/ *n.* [C] a small room where you can leave your coat, bag, etc.

clob·ber /ˈklɑbɚ/ *v.* [T] *informal* **1** to hit someone hard **2** to affect someone or something badly, especially by making him/her or it lose money: *The project was clobbered by rising interest rates.* **3** to defeat someone easily: *Boston clobbered New York 11–1.*

THESAURUS

beat, defeat, trounce
➔ see Thesaurus box at BEAT³

clock¹ /klɑk/ *n.* [C] **1** an instrument in a room or building that shows the time [➥ **watch**]: *What* ***time*** *does that* ***clock say***? | *The* ***clock*** *had* ***stopped***. | *The* ***clock struck*** *three* (=made three loud noises to show it was three o'clock). | *Mary* ***set*** *her alarm* ***clock*** *for 7:00 a.m* (=adjusted it so that it would ring at 7:00 a.m.) | *The kitchen* ***clock is*** *five minutes* ***slow/fast*** (=shows a time that is five minutes less or more

clock

alarm clock

than the right time). **2 turn/set the clock back** *disapproving* to make a situation the same as it was in the past: *Women's groups warned that the law would turn the clock back fifty years.* **3 set the clock(s) back/ahead/forward** to change the time shown on the clock to one hour earlier or later, when the time officially changes **4 around the clock** all day and all night without stopping: *We've been **working around the clock** to get done on time.* **5 race/work against the clock** to work quickly in order to finish something because you do not have much time: *"The harvest is a race against the clock to beat the winter rains," Johnson says.* → O'CLOCK → **punch a clock** at PUNCH¹ → **watch the clock** at WATCH¹

clock² *v.* [T] **1** to measure the speed at which someone or something is moving: *The police clocked her at 86 miles per hour.* **2** to travel a particular distance in a particular time: *She clocked her best time in the 200-meter sprint.*

clock in/out *phr. v.* to record on a special card the time when you begin or stop working: *I clocked in at 8:00 this morning.*

ˌclock ˈradio *n.* [C] a clock that you can set so that it turns on a radio to wake you up

clock·wise /ˈklɑk-waɪz/ *adj., adv.* in the same direction in which the HANDS (=parts that point to the time) of a clock move [≠ **counterclockwise**]: *Turn the dial clockwise.*

clock·work /ˈklɑk-wɚk/ *n.* **like clockwork a)** *informal* happening in exactly the way you planned: *Fortunately, production has been **going like clockwork**.* **b)** happening at the same time and in the same way every time: *At 6:30 every evening, like clockwork, Ari would milk the cows.*

clod /klɑd/ *n.* [C] **1** a lump of mud or earth **2** *informal* someone who is not graceful and behaves in a stupid way

clog¹ /klɑg/ *v.* past tense and past participle **clogged**, present participle **clogging** [I,T] **also clog up** to block something, or to become blocked: *Potato peelings **clogged up** the drain.* | *freeways **clogged with** heavy traffic*

clog² *n.* [C] a shoe made of wood → see picture at SHOE¹

clone¹ /kloʊn/ *n.* [C] *technical* **1** an exact copy of a plant or animal that scientists produce from one of its cells **2** a computer that is built as an exact copy of a more famous computer: *an IBM clone*

clone² *v.* [T] to produce a plant or an animal that is a clone

close¹ /kloʊz/ *v.* [I,T] **1** to shut something, or to become shut [= **shut**; ≠ **open**]: *Rita walked over and closed the curtains.* | *The hinges creaked slightly as the door closed.* | ***Close** your **eyes** and go to sleep.*

USAGE

Do not use **open** and **close** to talk about things that use electricity or things that provide water or gas. Use **turn on/off** instead: *Can you turn off the stove?* | *I turned on the TV.*

For things that use electricity, you can also use **switch on/off**: *Don't forget to switch off the lights.*

2 if a store or building closes, or if someone closes it, it stops being open to the public for a period of time: *What time does the mall close tonight?* | *Prentice Street has been **closed to** traffic.* **3** to end something, or to end: *Professor Schmidt **closed** his speech **with** a quote from Tolstoy.* **4** to stop existing or operating, or to stop something from existing or operating: *Hundreds of timber mills have **closed down** since World War II.* | *I've closed my bank account.* **5 close a deal/sale/contract** to successfully arrange a business deal, sale, etc.

close in *phr. v.* to move closer in order to catch someone or something: *a tiger closing in for the kill*

close sth ⇔ **off** *phr. v.* if a road or area is closed off, people cannot go into it

close² /kloʊs/ *adj.*

1 NEAR STH not far from someone or something: *The closest gas station is 20 miles away.* | *We live **close to** the school.* | *The victim was shot **at close range*** (=from a short distance).

2 NEAR IN TIME near to something in time: *By the time we left it was **close to** midnight.*

3 NEAR TO A NUMBER/AMOUNT near to a number: *Inflation is now **close to** 6%.*

4 LIKELY TO HAPPEN SOON if you are close to something, you are likely to experience it soon: *They haven't reached an agreement yet, but they're close.* | *Erickson was **close to tears** as he described the accident.* | *A few of the hostages were **close to death**.*

5 SIMILAR very similar to each other: *Do you have any shoes that are **closer** in color **to** this scarf?* | *A dirt road was **the closest thing to** a highway in the area.*

6 CAREFUL giving careful attention to details: ***Take a closer look** at the facts.* | *Scientists are **keeping a close watch/eye on** the volcano.* | *The jury **paid** very **close attention to** the evidence.*

7 LIKE/LOVE SB if people are close, they like or love each other very much: *Are you very **close to** your sister?* | *We were **close friends** in high school.*

8 AT WORK relating to a situation in which people work or talk well together: *The school encourages close partnerships between teachers and parents.* | *Our job required **close contact** with the general manager.*

9 COMPETITION a close competition or game is won or lost by only a few points: *Right now it's **too close to call*** (=no one can say who the winner will be).

10 ALMOST BAD *informal* used when you just manage to avoid something bad happening: ***That was close!*** *You almost hit that car!* | *I had a couple of* ***close calls****, but they weren't my fault.* **11 too close for comfort** if something bad is too close for comfort, it is near you or happens near to you, making you feel nervous or afraid: *The terrible storm was too close for comfort.* **12 close relative** a family member, such as a parent, brother, or sister —**closeness** *n.* [U]

close³ /kloʊs/ *adv.* **1** very near: *The grocery store is* ***close by****.* | *You're planting your tomatoes too* ***close together****.* | *Dockery walked out of the room with Shane following* ***close behind****.* | *The woman* ***held*** *her baby* ***close****.*

C

USAGE

Near and **close** are both used to talk about short distances between things.
Near can be followed directly by a noun.: *Is the hotel near the beach?*
Close cannot be followed directly by a noun.
Close must be followed by the preposition "to" and then a noun.: *They live close to the park.*

2 come close to (doing) sth to almost do something: *I was so angry I came close to hitting him.* **3 close up/up close** from only a short distance away: *When I saw her close up, I realized she wasn't Jane.*

close⁴ /kloʊz/ *n.* [singular] the end of an activity or period of time: *The police* ***brought*** *the investigation* ***to a close****.* | *The summer was* ***drawing to a close****.*

closed /kloʊzd/ *adj.* **1** not open [**= shut**]: *Make sure all the windows are closed.* **2** if a store or public building is closed, it is not open and people cannot go into it or use it [**= shut**]: *Sorry, the store's closed on Sundays.* **3** restricted to a particular group of people or things [**≠ open**]: *a closed meeting between the mayor and community leaders* **4** not willing to accept new ideas or influences [**≠ open**]: *Don't go with a* ***closed mind****.* **5 behind closed doors** privately, without involving other people: *The deal was made behind closed doors.*

ˌclosed ˌcircuit ˈtelevision *n.* [C,U] cameras which are used in public places in order to help prevent crime

close-knit /ˌkloʊs ˈnɪt◂ / *adj.* a close-knit family or group of people know each other well and help each other a lot

close·ly /ˈkloʊsli/ *adv.* **1** very carefully: *The police were* ***watching*** *him* ***closely****.* | *a* ***closely guarded*** *secret* **2** if you work closely with someone, you work with and help him/her **3 closely related/linked/tied etc.** having a strong connection: *Diet and health are closely connected.* **4** in a way that is close to other things in time or space: *a flash of lightning,* ***followed closely*** *by thunder*

close-set /ˌkloʊs ˈsɛt◂ / *adj.* close-set eyes are very near to each other

clos·et¹ /ˈklɑzɪt/ *n.* [C] **1** an area that you keep clothes and other things in, built with a door behind the wall of a room: *Let me hang your coat up in the closet.* **2 come out of the closet** *informal* to say openly and publicly that you are HOMOSEXUAL after keeping it a secret

closet² *adj.* **closet liberal/homosexual etc.** someone who does not admit in public what s/he thinks or does in private

close-up /ˈkloʊs ʌp/ *n.* [C] a photograph of someone or something that is taken from very near to him, her, or it: *a* ***close-up of*** *the children*

clo·sure /ˈkloʊʒɚ/ *n.* [C,U] **1** the act of permanently closing a building, factory, school, etc.: *Several military bases are* ***threatened with closure****.* **2** an occasion in which a bad situation has ended and you can finally stop thinking about it: *Funerals help give people a sense of closure.*

clot¹ /klɑt/ *n.* [C] a mass of blood or another liquid which has become almost solid: *a* ***blood clot*** *in his leg*

clot² *v.* past tense and past participle **clotted**, present participle **clotting** [I,T] if a liquid such as blood clots or if something clots it, it becomes thicker and more solid

cloth /klɔθ/ *n.* **1** [U] material used for making things such as clothes [**➡ fabric**]: *These pants are made with the finest wool cloth.*

USAGE

Do not use **cloth** or **cloths** to mean "things that you wear." Use **clothes**: *My favorite clothes are jeans and a T-shirt.* | *a clothes store*

2 [C] a piece of cloth used for a particular purpose: *Cover the bowl with a damp cloth.*

clothe /kloʊð/ *v.* [T] to provide clothes for someone: *He could barely afford to feed and clothe his family.*

clothed /kloʊðd/ *adj. formal* dressed: *The kids were fast asleep, still* ***fully clothed****.*

clothes /kloʊz, kloʊðz/ *n.* [plural] the things that people wear to cover their bodies or keep warm: *Go to your room and* ***put on*** *some clean* ***clothes****.* | *Pete* ***took*** *his* ***clothes off*** *and went to bed.* | *What sort of* ***clothes*** *was he* ***wearing****?* | *The kids ran upstairs to* ***change into*** *dry* ***clothes****.*

COLLOCATIONS

tight: *tight jeans*
loose/baggy: *a baggy t-shirt*
fashionable/stylish: *fashionable clothes*
casual – comfortable and informal: *a casual top*
formal – appropriate for an official or serious situation: *Everyone was dressed in formal wear.*
dressy – fairly formal and appropriate for wearing to work: *a pair of dressy pants*
➔ CLOTH

clothes

TOPIC

You **look at clothes** in a store and then **try** them **on**. You want to be sure that they **fit** you (=are the right size), and also that they **look good on** you. At home you **fold** them and put them in a drawer, or you **hang** them **up** in a **closet**. If clothes are **wrinkled** (=have lines in the material), you can **iron** them.

GRAMMAR

There is no singular form of **clothes**. You have to say **a piece of clothing**, **an article of clothing** *formal*, or **an item of clothing** *formal*: *She picked up each piece of clothing and folded it carefully.*

clothes·line /ˈkloʊzlaɪn/ *n.* [C] a rope that you hang clothes on so that they will dry

clothes·pin /ˈkloʊzpɪn/ *n.* [C] a small object that you use to fasten clothes to a clothesline

cloth·ing /ˈkloʊðɪŋ/ *n.* [U] *formal* clothes: *The refugees needed **food and clothing**.* | ***Protective clothing** should be worn in the lab.*

clouds

cloud[1] /klaʊd/ *n.* **1** [C,U] a white or gray MASS in the sky, from which rain falls: *There wasn't a cloud in the sky.* | ***Storm/Dark clouds** moved overhead.* **2** [C] a mass of smoke, dust, or gas: *a **cloud of dust*** **3** [C] something that makes you feel worried or afraid: *Ryder resigned **under a cloud of** suspicion.* | *Marshall's injury **cast a cloud over** the rest of the game.* **4 on cloud nine** *informal* very happy: *When Caitlin was born, Adam was on cloud nine.*

cloud[2] *v.* **1** [T] to make something more difficult to understand or deal with: *These unnecessary* *details are only* ***clouding*** *the* ***issue****.* | *Don't allow personal feelings to* ***cloud*** *your* ***judgment****.* **2** [I,T] **also cloud up** to become difficult to see through, or to make this happen: *Steam clouded up the windows.*

cloud over *phr. v.* if the sky clouds over, it becomes darker and full of clouds

cloud·burst /ˈklaʊdbɚst/ *n.* [C] a sudden storm of rain

cloud·y /ˈklaʊdi/ *adj.* **1** dark and full of clouds: *a cloudy day* **2** cloudy liquids are not clear

clout /klaʊt/ *n.* [U] *informal* power or the ability to influence important people: ***political/economic/financial, etc. clout***

C

clove /kloʊv/ *n.* [C] **1** a piece of GARLIC: *a* ***clove of garlic*** **2** a strong sweet spice with a pointed stem

clo·ver /ˈkloʊvɚ/ *n.* [C] a small plant with three round leaves on each stem

clown[1] /klaʊn/ *n.* [C] a performer who wears MAKEUP and funny clothes and tries to make people laugh, especially in a CIRCUS

clown[2] *v.* [I] to behave in a silly or funny way: *a couple of boys* ***clowning around***

club[1] /klʌb/ *n.* [C] **1** an organization for people who share an interest or who enjoy similar activities: *a* ***member of*** *the drama* ***club*** | *I just* ***joined a*** *health* ***club****.* | *He* ***belongs to*** *the chess* ***club****.*

THESAURUS

organization, **institution**, **association**, **(political) party**, **society**, **union**
➔ see Thesaurus box at ORGANIZATION

2 NIGHTCLUB **3** the building used by a club: *The restaurant is located next to the fitness club.* **4** a specially shaped stick for hitting the ball in golf [= **golf club**] **5 clubs** [plural] in card games, the cards with black symbols with three round parts: *the five of clubs* ➔ see picture at PLAYING CARD **6** a heavy stick used as a weapon

club[2] *v.* past tense and past participle **clubbed**, present participle **clubbing** [T] to hit someone with a club

club·house /ˈklʌbhaʊs/ *n.* [C] a building used by a club, especially a sports club

ˌclub ˈsandwich *n.* [C] a sandwich consisting of three pieces of bread with meat and cheese between them

ˌclub ˈsoda *n.* [C,U] water filled with BUBBLES that is often mixed with other drinks

cluck /klʌk/ *v.* [I] to make a noise like a HEN —**cluck** *n.* [C]

clue[1] /klu/ *n.* [C] **1** a piece of information or an object that helps to solve a crime or mystery: *The police are still* ***searching for clues****.* | *No one seems to* ***have a clue as to*** *the bomber's identity.* **2 not have a clue** *informal* to definitely not know or understand something: *I don't have a clue what you're talking about.* | *"Where's Jamie?" "I don't have a clue."*

clue[2]
clue sb ⇔ **in** *phr. v. informal* to give someone information about something: *He* ***clued*** *me* ***in on*** *how the washing machine works.*

clue·less /ˈklulɪs/ *adj. disapproving* having no understanding or knowledge of something: *Jason is clueless when it comes to women.*

clump[1] /klʌmp/ *n.* [C] a group of trees or plants growing together

clump[2] *v.* [I] to walk with slow noisy steps: *I could hear Grandpa* ***clumping around*** *in the basement.*

clum·sy /ˈklʌmzi/ *adj.* **1** moving in an awkward way and tending to knock things over: *She was clumsy and shy.*

THESAURUS

awkward – moving or behaving in a way that does not seem relaxed or comfortable: *an awkward hug*
gawky – awkward in the way you move: *a gawky teenager*
inelegant *formal* – not graceful or well done: *an inelegant style of writing*

2 a clumsy object is large, heavy, and difficult to use **3** if you say or do something in a clumsy way, you do it in a careless way, without considering other people's feelings: *a clumsy attempt to apologize* —**clumsily** *adv.* —**clumsiness** *n.* [U]

clung /klʌŋ/ *v.* the past tense and past participle of CLING

clunk /klʌŋk/ *v.* [I,T] to make the loud sound of two heavy objects hitting each other —**clunk** *n.* [C]

clunk·er /ˈklʌŋkɚ/ *n.* [C] *informal* **1** an old car or other machine that does not work very well **2** something that is completely unsuccessful because people think it is bad or stupid

clus·ter[1] /ˈklʌstɚ/ *n.* [C] a group of things that are close together: *a* ***cluster of*** *grapes*

cluster[2] *v.* [I,T] to form a group of people or things: *The tulips were* ***clustered around*** *the fence.*

clutch[1] /klʌtʃ/ *v.* [T] to hold something tightly: *Jamie stood there, clutching her purse.*

THESAURUS

hold, **grip**, **catch/take/keep/get (a) hold of**, **grab (hold of)**, **seize**
➔ see Thesaurus box at HOLD[1]

clutch[2] *n.* [C] **1** the part of a car that you press with your foot to change GEARS ➔ see picture on page A12 **2 sb's clutches** if you are in someone's clutches, s/he controls you **3 in the clutch** *informal* in an important or difficult situation

clut·ter[1] /ˈklʌt̬ɚ/ *v.* [T] to make something messy by covering or filling it with things: *His desk is always* ***cluttered with*** *paper.*

clutter² *n.* [U] a lot of things scattered in a messy way

cm the written abbreviation of **centimeter**

CNN *n.* **Cable News Network** an organization that broadcasts television news programs all over the world

CO the written abbreviation of **Colorado**

Co. /koʊ/ **1** the written abbreviation of **company**: *E.F. Hutton & Co.* **2** the written abbreviation of **county**

c/o /ˌsi ˈoʊ◂/ the written abbreviation of **in care of**, used when you are sending a letter for someone to another person who will keep it for him/her: *Send the letter to me c/o Anne Miller, 8 Brown St., Peoria, IL*

coach¹ /koʊtʃ/ *n.* [C] **1** someone who trains a person or team in a sport: *a basketball/football etc. coach*

THESAURUS

teacher, professor, lecturer, instructor
➔ see Thesaurus box at TEACHER

2 the cheapest type of seats on an airplane or a train: *We* ***flew coach*** *to Seattle.* **3** someone who gives private lessons in singing, acting, etc.

coach² *v.* [I,T] **1** to train a person or team in a sport: *He coaches our tennis team.* **2** to give someone private lessons in singing, acting, etc.

co·ag·u·late /koʊˈægyəˌleɪt/ *v.* [I,T] to change from a liquid into a thicker substance or a solid: *Blood had coagulated around the wound.* —**coagulation** /koʊˌægyəˈleɪʃən/ *n.* [U]

coal /koʊl/ *n.* **1** [U] a black mineral that is dug from the earth and is burned for heat: *a lump of coal* | *coal miners* **2 coals** [plural] pieces of coal that are burning ➔ CHARCOAL ➔ **rake sb over the coals** at RAKE²

co·a·lesce /ˌkoʊəˈlɛs/ *v.* [I] *formal* to combine or grow together to form one single group

co·a·li·tion /ˌkoʊəˈlɪʃən/ *n.* [C] a union of separate political parties or people for a special purpose, usually for a short time: *Italy's* ***coalition government*** | *The two parties have decided to* ***form a coalition***.

coarse /kɔrs/ *adj.* **1** rough and thick, not smooth or fine: *a coarse cloth* **2** rude and offensive: *coarse language* —**coarsely** *adv.* —**coarseness** *n.* [U]

coast¹ /koʊst/ *n.* [C] **1** the land next to the ocean: *the Pacific coast* | *the west* ***coast of*** *Scotland* | *an island* ***off the coast*** (=in the water near the land) *of Turkey* | *a small cottage* ***on the coast***

THESAURUS

shore, beach, seashore, bank
➔ see Thesaurus box at SHORE¹

2 the coast is clear *informal* if the coast is clear, it is safe for you to do something without being seen or caught: *Let's leave now while the coast is clear!* —**coastal** *adj.*

coast² *v.* [I] **1** to continue to move forward in a car without using the engine or on a bicycle without turning the PEDALS **2** to succeed without using any effort: *Wilson* ***coasted to*** *victory in the election.*

coast·er /ˈkoʊstɚ/ *n.* [C] a small round object you put under a glass, bottle, etc. to protect a table

ˈcoast guard *n.* **the Coast Guard** the military organization whose job is to watch for ships in danger and prevent illegal activity in the ocean

coast·line /ˈkoʊstlaɪn/ *n.* [C,U] the land on the edge of the coast: *the California coastline*

coat¹ /koʊt/ *n.* [C] **1** a piece of clothing that you wear over other clothes to keep you warm when you go outside: ***Put*** *your* ***coat on****, it's cold outside!* | *He* ***took off*** *his* ***coat*** *and dropped it on the bed.* ➔ see picture at CLOTHES **2** a jacket that you wear as part of a suit **3** a thin layer of something that covers a surface: *a* ***coat of*** *paint* **4** an animal's fur: *a dog with a black and brown coat* **5** a light piece of clothing that a doctor, etc. wears over other clothes: *a lab coat*

coat² *v.* [T] to cover a surface with a layer of something: *The books were thickly* ***coated with*** *dust.*

ˈcoat ˌhanger *n.* [C] HANGER

coax /koʊks/ *v.* [T] to persuade someone to do something by talking gently and kindly: *See if you can* ***coax*** *him* ***into*** *giving us a ride home.* | *Firefighters* ***coaxed*** *the man* ***down***.

THESAURUS

persuade, talk into, get sb to do sth, encourage, influence, convince, cajole
➔ see Thesaurus box at PERSUADE

cob /kɑb/ *n.* [C] the long hard middle part of the corn plant: *corn on the cob*

cob·bled /ˈkɑbəld/ *adj.* covered with round flat stones: *a cobbled street*

cob·bler /ˈkɑblɚ/ *n.* **1** [C,U] cooked fruit covered with a sweet, bread-like mixture: *peach cobbler* **2** [C] *old-fashioned* someone who makes or repairs shoes

cob·ble·stone /ˈkɑbəlˌstoʊn/ *n.* [C] a small round stone set in the ground, especially in past times, to make a hard surface for a road

co·bra /ˈkoʊbrə/ *n.* [C] an African or Asian poisonous snake

cob·web /ˈkɑbwɛb/ *n.* [C] a very fine structure of sticky threads made by a SPIDER

Co·ca-Co·la /ˌkoʊkə ˈkoʊlə/ *n.* [C,U] *trademark* a sweet brown SOFT DRINK, or a glass of this drink [= **Coke**]

co·caine /koʊˈkeɪn, ˈkoʊkeɪn/ *n.* [U] an illegal drug, usually in the form of a white powder

cock¹ /kɑk/ *n.* [C] *old-fashioned* ROOSTER

cock² *v.* [T] **1** to raise or move part of your head or face: *Jeremy* ***cocked*** *his* ***head*** *to one side and* *smiled.* **2** to pull back the part of a gun that hits the back of a bullet, so that you are ready to shoot

cock-a-doo·dle-doo /ˌkɑk ə ˌdudl 'du/ *n.* [C] the loud sound make by a ROOSTER

cock·eyed /'kɑkaɪd/ *adj. informal* **1** not sensible or practical: *a cockeyed idea* **2** not straight or level: *His hat was on cockeyed.*

cock·pit /'kɑkˌpɪt/ *n.* [C] the part of an airplane or racing car where the pilot or driver sits → see picture at AIRPLANE

cock·roach /'kɑk-routʃ/ *n.* [C] a large insect that often lives where food is kept

C

cock·tail /'kɑkteɪl/ *n.* [C] **1** an alcoholic drink made from a mixture of different drinks **2** a dish of small pieces of food, usually eaten at the start of a meal: *a shrimp cocktail | fruit cocktail*

'cocktail ˌlounge *n.* [C] a public room in a hotel, restaurant, etc. where people can buy alcoholic drinks

'cocktail ˌparty *n.* [C] a formal party where alcoholic drinks are served

THESAURUS

party, get-together, bash, dinner party, birthday party, house-warming party, bachelor party, baby/wedding/bridal shower, reception, celebration
→ see Thesaurus box at PARTY[1]

cock·y /'kɑki/ *adj. informal* too confident, in a way which people do not like: *Howitt was young and cocky.* —**cockiness** *n.* [U]

co·coa /'koʊkoʊ/ *n.* [U] **1** a dark brown powder that tastes like chocolate and is used in cooking **2** a hot chocolate drink: *a cup of cocoa*

co·co·nut /'koʊkəˌnʌt/ *n.* [C,U] a very large brown nut which is white inside and has liquid in the middle → see picture at FRUIT

co·coon /kə'kun/ *n.* [C] **1** a silk cover that some insects make to protect themselves while they are growing **2** a place or situation in which you feel comfortable and safe: *the comfortable **cocoon of** college life* —**cocoon** *v.* [T]

C.O.D. *adv.* **cash on delivery** a system in which you pay for something when it is delivered: *Send the equipment C.O.D.*

cod /kɑd/ *n.* plural **cod** [C,U] a large ocean fish that you can eat

code[1] /koʊd/ *n.* **1** [C] a set of rules, laws, or principles that tells people how to behave: *a strong **moral code** | the company's employee **code of conduct** | The school has a **dress code*** (=rules about what to wear). **2** [C,U] a system of words, letters, or symbols used instead of ordinary writing to keep something secret: *Important reports were sent **in code**. | Agents spent years trying to **break/crack** the enemy's **code**.* **3** [C] a set of numbers, letters, or symbols that give you information about something: *Goods that you order must have a product code.* → AREA CODE, BAR CODE, ZIP CODE

code[2] *v.* [T] to put a message into code —**coded** *adj.*

co-ed /koʊ 'ɛd/ *adj.* using a system in which students of both sexes study or live together: *co-ed dormitories*

co·erce /koʊ'ɚs/ *v.* [T] *formal* to force someone to do something by threatening him/her: *The women were **coerced into** hiding the drugs.* —**coercion** /koʊ'ɚʃən, -ʒən/ *n.* [U] *torture and other extreme forms of coercion*

THESAURUS

force, make, compel, pressure
→ see Thesaurus box at FORCE[2]

co·ex·ist /ˌkoʊɪg'zɪst/ *v.* [I] to exist together: *Can the two countries coexist after the war?* —**coexistence** *n.* [U]

cof·fee /'kɔfi, 'kɑ-/ *n.* **1** [U] a hot dark brown drink that has a slightly bitter taste: *a **cup of coffee*** **2** [C] a cup of this drink: *Two **black coffees*** (=coffee with no milk added), *please.* **3** [U] whole coffee beans, crushed coffee beans, or a powder from which you make coffee: *a pound of coffee | **instant coffee*** (=powdered coffee)

'coffee cake *n.* [C,U] a sweet heavy cake, usually eaten along with coffee

'coffee house *n.* [C] a small restaurant where people go to talk and drink coffee

'coffee maˌchine *n.* [C] a machine that gives you a cup of coffee, tea, etc. when you put money in it

cof·fee·mak·er /'kɔfiˌmeɪkɚ, 'kɑ-/ *n.* [C] an electric machine that makes a pot of coffee

'coffee shop *n.* [C] a small restaurant that serves cheap meals

'coffee ˌtable *n.* [C] a low table in a LIVING ROOM

cof·fers /'kɔfɚz, 'kɑ-/ *n.* [plural] the money that an organization has: *The tax would add an estimated $500,000 to the city's coffers.*

cof·fin /'kɔfɪn/ *n.* [C] the box in which a dead person is buried

cog /kɑg/ *n.* [C] **1** a wheel in a machine with small parts on its edge that fit together with the parts of another wheel as they turn **2 a cog in the machine/wheel** an unimportant worker in a large organization

co·gent /'koʊdʒənt/ *adj. formal* if a reason, argument, etc. is cogent, it seems reasonable and correct

co·gnac /'kɑnyæk, 'kɔn-, 'koʊn-/ *n.* [C,U] a type of BRANDY (=strong alcoholic drink) from France, or a glass of this drink

co·hab·it /ˌkoʊ'hæbɪt/ *v.* [I] *formal* to live as husband and wife, without being married —**cohabitation** /koʊˌhæbə'teɪʃən/ *n.* [U]

co·her·ent /koʊ'hɪrənt/ *adj.* clear and easy to understand [≠ **incoherent**]: *a coherent message |*

He was slightly drunk, and not very coherent. —**coherently** *adv.* —**coherence** *n.* [U]

co·he·sion /koʊ'hiʒən/ *n.* [U] the ability to fit together or stay together well: *social cohesion*

coil[1] /kɔɪl/ **also coil up** *v.* [I,T] to wind or twist into a round shape, or to make something do this: *Dad coiled up the hose.* | *The snake coiled around the branch.*

coil[2] *n.* [C] a piece of wire or rope that has been wound into a circular shape

coin[1] /kɔɪn/ *n.* [C] **1** a round piece of money made of metal [➡ **bill**]: *Uncle Henry collects foreign coins.*

THESAURUS

money, **bill**, **penny**, **nickel**, **dime**, **quarter**, **cash**, **change**, **currency**
➔ see Thesaurus box at MONEY

2 toss/flip a coin to choose or decide something by throwing a coin into the air and guessing which side will show when it falls **3 the other side of the coin** a different fact or way of thinking about something

coin[2] *v.* [T] to invent a new word or phrase that many people start to use: *Who coined the word "cyberpunk"?*

co·in·cide /ˌkoʊɪn'saɪd/ *v.* [I] to happen at the same time as something else: *Their wedding anniversary* ***coincides with*** *Thanksgiving.*

co·in·ci·dence /koʊ'ɪnsədəns/ *n.* [C,U] a situation in which two things happen together by chance, in a surprising way: ***By coincidence****, my husband and my father went to the same high school.* | *It's* ***no coincidence that*** *veterans are more likely to smoke than other people.* | *By* ***sheer/pure coincidence****, he was seated next to his ex-wife.* —**coincidental** /koʊˌɪnsə'dɛntl/ *adj.* —**coincidentally** *adv.*

coke /koʊk/ *n.* **1 Coke** [C,U] *trademark* COCA-COLA **2** [U] *informal* COCAINE

co·la /'koʊlə/ *n.* [C,U] a sweet brown SOFT DRINK, or a bottle, can, or glass of this drink

col·an·der /'kɑləndɚ, 'kʌ-/ *n.* [C] a metal or plastic bowl with a lot of small holes in the bottom and sides, used for separating liquid from food

cold[1] /koʊld/ *adj.* **1** having a low temperature [≠ **hot**, **warm**]: *a cold winter morning* | *It was* ***freezing cold*** (=very cold) *in the car.* | *Let's go inside – I'm cold.* | ***bitterly cold*** *weather* | *Your coffee's* ***getting cold*** (=becoming cold). ➔ ICE-COLD

THESAURUS

cool – cold in a pleasant way, especially after it has been hot: *It's very hot during the day, but cooler at night.*
chilly – cold, but not very cold: *a chilly fall day*
frosty – very cold, with the ground covered in frost (=ice that is white and powdery and covers things when the temperature is very cold): *a bright frosty morning*
freezing (cold) – extremely cold, so that water outside becomes ice: *It was freezing cold last night.*
icy (cold) – extremely cold: *an icy wind*
bitter (cold) – very cold in a way that feels very unpleasant: *The troops have had to endure bitter cold temperatures.*
➔ HOT[1], WEATHER[1]

2 cold food has been cooked, but is not eaten while it is warm: *cold chicken* **3** without friendly feelings: *a polite but cold greeting*

THESAURUS

matter-of-fact, **detached**, **impassive**
➔ see Thesaurus box at MATTER-OF-FACT

4 leave sb cold *informal* to not interest someone at all: *Ballet just leaves me cold.* **5 get/have cold feet** *informal* to suddenly feel that you are not brave enough to do something: *She was getting cold feet about getting married.* **6 cold snap** a sudden short period of very cold weather **7 give sb the cold shoulder** to deliberately ignore someone or be unfriendly to him/her **8 in cold blood** in a cruel and deliberate way: *They shot him in cold blood.* —**coldness** *n.* [U]

cold[2] *n.* **1** [C] a common illness that makes it difficult to breathe through your nose: *You sound like you* ***have a cold****.* | *Did you* ***catch a cold*** (=get a cold)*?* **2 the cold** a low temperature or cold weather: *Don't go out in the cold without your coat.*

cold[3] *adv.* **1** suddenly and completely: *In the middle of his speech, he stopped cold.* **2 out cold** *informal* unconscious, especially because of being hit on the head

ˌcold-'blooded *adj.* **1** cruel and showing no feelings: *a* ***cold-blooded killer*** **2** a cold-blooded animal, such as a snake, has a body temperature that changes with the air or ground around it [➡ **warm-blooded**]

'cold cuts *n.* [plural] thin pieces of different kinds of cooked meat eaten cold

ˌcold-'hearted *adj.* without sympathy or pity: *a cold-hearted man*

cold·ly /'koʊldli/ *adv.* in an unfriendly way: *"I'm busy," said Sarah coldly.*

'cold sore *n.* [C] a painful spot on the inside or outside of your mouth that you sometimes get when you are sick

ˌcold 'turkey *n.* **go cold turkey** *informal* to suddenly stop taking a drug that you are ADDICTED to, and to feel sick because of this: *The only way to quit smoking is to go cold turkey.*

ˌcold 'war *n.* [C] **1** an unfriendly political relationship between two countries that do not actually fight with each other **2 the Cold War** this type of relationship between the U.S. and the Soviet Union, after World War II

cole slaw /ˈkoʊl slɔ/ *n.* [U] a SALAD made with thinly cut raw CABBAGE and CARROTS

col·ic /ˈkɑlɪk/ *n.* [U] pain in the stomach that babies often get

col·lab·o·rate /kəˈlæbəˌreɪt/ *v.* [I] **1** to work together with another person or group in order to achieve or produce something: *The author and illustrator wanted to* ***collaborate on*** *a book for children.* **2** to help a country that your country is at war with: *He was accused of* ***collaborating with*** *the Nazis.* —**collaborator** *n.* [C]

col·lab·o·ra·tion /kəˌlæbəˈreɪʃən/ *n.* [U] **1** the act of working with another person or group in order to achieve or produce something: *Our departments worked* ***in close collaboration*** *on the project.* | *The project has involved* ***collaboration with*** *the geography department.* **2** the act of helping an enemy during a war

C

col·lab·o·ra·tive /kəˈlæbrət̬ɪv/ *adj.* **collaborative project/effort/work etc.** a project, effort, etc. that involves two or more people working together to achieve something

col·lage /kəˈlɑʒ, koʊ-/ *n.* **1** [C] a picture made by sticking pictures, photographs, cloth, etc. onto a surface **2** [U] the art of making pictures in this way

col·lapse[1] /kəˈlæps/ *v.* [I] **1** to fall down or inward suddenly: *Many buildings collapsed during the earthquake.* **2** to suddenly fall down or become unconscious because you are sick or very weak: *He looked like he was going to collapse.* **3** to fail suddenly and completely: *We sold the property just before the real estate market collapsed.*

collapse[2] *n.* **1** [singular, U] a sudden failure in the way something works, so that it cannot continue: ***the collapse of*** *communism in Eastern Europe* | *The industry faces* ***economic collapse.*** **2** [U] the act of falling down or inward: *Floods caused* ***the collapse of*** *the bridge.* **3** [singular, U] an occasion when someone falls down or becomes unconscious because of a sickness

col·laps·i·ble /kəˈlæpsəbəl/ *adj.* something that is COLLAPSIBLE can be folded up into a smaller size: *collapsible chairs*

col·lar[1] /ˈkɑlɚ/ *n.* [C] **1** the part of a shirt, coat, dress, etc. that fits around your neck **2 open-collared/fur-collared etc.** having a particular type of collar: *a white-collared shirt* **3** a narrow band of leather or plastic put around the neck of a dog or cat

collar[2] *v.* [T] *informal* to catch and hold someone: *Two policemen collared the suspect near the scene.*

col·lar·bone /ˈkɑlɚˌboʊn/ *n.* [C] one of a pair of bones that go from the base of your neck to your shoulders → see picture on page A3

col·late /kəˈleɪt, kɑ-, ˈkoʊleɪt, ˈkɑ-/ *v.* [T] **1** to arrange things such as papers in the right order **2** to gather information together in order to examine it and compare it: *The system allows us to collate data from all over the country.*

col·lat·er·al /kəˈlæt̬ərəl/ *n.* [U] property or money that you promise to give to someone if you cannot pay back a debt: *They* ***put up*** *their house* ***as collateral*** *in order to raise the money.*

col·league /ˈkɑlig/ *n.* [C] someone you work with, especially in a profession

TOPIC

employer, employee, staff, co-worker
→ see Topic box at WORK[1]

col·lect[1] /kəˈlɛkt/ *v.* **1** [T] to get things and bring them together: *I'll collect everyone's tests at the end of class.* **2** [T] to get and keep objects of the same type because you think they are attractive or interesting: *She collects stamps.*

THESAURUS

keep, store, save, reserve, file
→ see Thesaurus box at KEEP[1]

3 [I,T] to get money from people: *We're* ***collecting for*** *charity.* | *The landlord was at the door, trying to collect the rent.* **4** [I] to come or gather together: *Dust had collected in the corners of the room.* **5 collect yourself/collect your thoughts** to make yourself calmer and able to think more clearly: *I had a few minutes to collect my thoughts before the meeting began.*

collect[2] *adj., adv.* **1 call sb collect** if you call someone collect, the person who gets the telephone call pays for it **2 collect call** a telephone call that is paid for by the person who gets it

col·lect·ed /kəˈlɛktɪd/ *adj.* **1 collected works/poems/stories etc.** all of the poems, stories, etc. of a particular writer included together in one book: *the collected works of Emily Dickinson* **2** in control of yourself and your thoughts, feelings, etc.: *Jason seemed* ***calm and collected.***

col·lect·i·ble /kəˈlɛktəbəl/ *n.* [C] an object that you keep as part of a group of similar things: *a store that sells antiques and collectibles*

collection

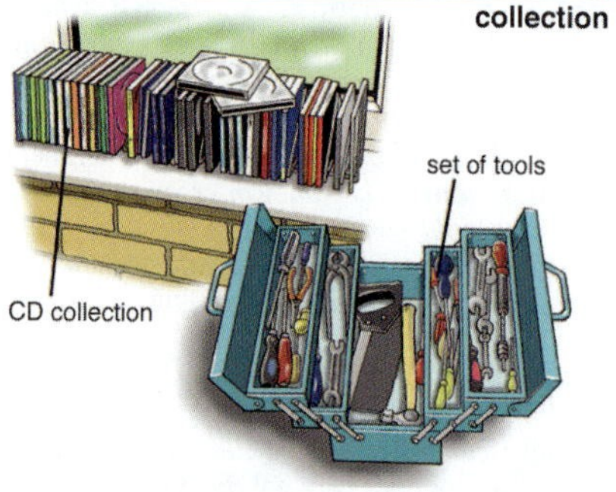

col·lec·tion /kəˈlɛkʃən/ *n.* **1** [C] a set of similar things that you keep or put together: *a coin collection* | *a* ***collection of*** *toy soldiers* **2** [U] the act of bringing together things of the same type from different places: *different methods of data collection* **3** [C] several stories, poems, pieces of music, etc. that are put together: *a **collection of** fairy tales* **4** [C,U] the act of taking something away from a place: *Garbage collection is on Fridays.* **5** [C,U] the act of asking people for money: *tax collection* | *We're planning to **have a collection for** UNICEF*

col·lec·tive[1] /kə'lɛktɪv/ *adj.* [only before noun] shared or done by all the members of a group together: *We had made a collective decision.* | *collective farms* —**collectively** *adv.*

collective[2] *n.* [C] a business or farm that is owned and operated by a group of workers who share the profits equally

col,lective 'bargaining *n.* [U] discussions between employers and unions about pay, working conditions, etc.

col·lec·tor /kə'lɛktɚ/ *n.* [C] **1** someone whose job is to collect taxes, tickets, debts, etc.: *a tax collector* **2** someone who collects things that are interesting or attractive: *a stamp collector*

col·lege /'kɑlɪdʒ/ *n.* **1** [C, U] a large school where you can study after high school [➡ **university**]: *My oldest son is **in college*** (=is a student at a college). | *I'm planning to **go to college**.* **2** [C] the part of a university that teaches a particular subject: *the College of Engineering*

GRAMMAR

Do not use "a" or "the" before **college** when you are talking about the time when someone is studying there: *They met when they were in college.*

col·le·giate /kə'lidʒət/ *adj.* relating to college or a college: *collegiate sports*

col·lide /kə'laɪd/ *v.* [I] to crash violently into something or someone: *His car **collided with** a bus.*

THESAURUS

hit, **bump**, **knock**, **bang**, **strike**
➔ see Thesaurus box at HIT[1]

col·li·sion /kə'lɪʒən/ *n.* **1** [C,U] a violent crash in which one vehicle hits another: *a **midair collision*** (=one involving two planes)

THESAURUS

accident, **crash**, **wreck**, **pile-up**, **fender-bender**
➔ see Thesaurus box at ACCIDENT

2 be on a collision course to be likely to have trouble because your aims are very different from someone else's: *The two nations are on a collision course that could lead to war.*

col·lo·qui·al /kə'loʊkwiəl/ *adj.* colloquial language is the kind of language that is used in informal conversations: *colloquial expressions* —**colloquially** *adv.* —**colloquialism** *n.* [C]

col·lu·sion /kə'luʒən/ *n.* [U] *formal* the act of agreeing secretly with someone else to do something dishonest or illegal —**collude** *v.* [I] *The companies colluded to keep prices high.*

co·logne /kə'loʊn/ *n.* [U] a liquid with a pleasant smell, which you put on your skin

co·lon /'koʊlən/ *n.* [C] **1** the mark (:) used in writing to introduce a list, examples, etc. **2** the lower part of the INTESTINES, in which food is changed into waste matter

colo·nel /'kɚnl/ *n.* [C] a high rank in the Army, Air Force, or Marines, or an officer who has this rank

co·lo·ni·al /kə'loʊniəl/ *adj.* **1** relating to the control of countries by a more powerful distant country: *the end of colonial rule in India* **2 also Colonial** relating to the time when the U.S. was a COLONY of England: *a Colonial-style brick house* —**colonialism** *n.* [U] —**colonialist** *n.* [C]

C

col·o·nize /'kɑlə,naɪz/ *v.* [I,T] to control a country or area and send your own people to live there: *Argentina was colonized by Spain.* —**colonist** *n.* [C] —**colonization** /,kɑlənə'zeɪʃən/ *n.* [U]

col·o·ny /'kɑləni/ *n.* plural **colonies** [C] **1** a country or area that is ruled by a more powerful country, usually one that is far away: *Algeria was formerly a French colony.* **2** a group of people with the same interests who live together: *an artists' colony* **3** a group of the same kind of animals living together

col·or[1] /'kʌlɚ/ *n.* **1** [C] red, blue, yellow, etc.: *"What color is your new car?" "Blue."* ▶ Don't say "What color does your new car have?" ◀ *the **color of** his eyes* | *I love wearing **bright colors**.* | *The leaves were pale green **in color**.* **2** [U] the quality of having colors: *Flowers can add color to a patio or backyard.* **3** [C,U] a substance such as paint or DYE that makes something red, blue, etc.: *He mixed the colors with his paintbrush.* **4** [C,U] how dark or light someone's skin is, which shows which race s/he belongs to: *They are trying to bring together people of all colors and religions.* | *The awards will be given without discrimination based on color, religion, or sex.* **5 people/men/women etc. of color** people who are not white: *We need to get more women and people of color into elected office.* **6** [U] showing all the different colors such as red, green, and blue rather than just black and white [≠ **black and white**]: *The book includes 200 **color photographs/pictures**.* | *"The Wizard of Oz" was the first film shot **in color**.* **7** [U] if you have some color in your face, your face is pink or red, usually because you are healthy or embarrassed: *He felt the color rise to his face.*

color[2] *v.* **1** [T] to give color to something: *Do you color your hair?* **2** [I,T] to put color onto a drawing or picture, or to draw a picture using colored pencils or pens: *Give Grandma the picture you colored, Jenny.* **3 color sb's judgment/opinions/attitudes etc.** to influence the way that someone thinks about something, especially so that s/he becomes less fair or reasonable: *Personal feelings colored his judgment.*

col·or·blind /ˈkʌlɚˌblaɪnd/ *adj.* **1** not able to see the difference between particular colors **2** treating all races of people fairly: *In this court, justice is colorblind.*

ˌcolor-coˈordinated *adj.* clothes or decorations that are color-coordinated have colors that look good together

col·ored /ˈkʌlɚd/ *adj.* **1** having a color such as red, blue, yellow, etc. rather than being black, white, or plain: *brightly colored tropical birds* **2** *old-fashioned* a word used for describing a person who has dark or black skin, now considered offensive

C

col·or·fast /ˈkʌlɚˌfæst/ *adj.* colorfast clothing has a color that will not become lighter when you wash or wear it

col·or·ful /ˈkʌlɚfəl/ *adj.* **1** having a lot of bright colors: *a colorful stained-glass window* **2** interesting and full of variety: *a colorful career* —**colorfully** *adj.*

col·or·ing /ˈkʌlərɪŋ/ *n.* **1** [U] the color of something, especially someone's hair, skin, eyes, etc.: *Mandy had her mother's dark coloring.* **2** [C,U] a substance used for giving a particular color to something, especially food: *They had added yellow* ***food coloring*** *to the rice.*

ˈcoloring book *n.* [C] a book full of pictures that are drawn without color so that a child can color them in

col·or·less /ˈkʌlɚlɪs/ *adj.* **1** not having any color: *a colorless gas* **2** not interesting or exciting

co·los·sal /kəˈlɑsəl/ *adj.* very large: *They've run up colossal debts.*

> **THESAURUS**
> **big, large, huge, enormous, vast, gigantic, massive, immense, substantial**
> ➔ see Thesaurus box at BIG

co·los·sus /kəˈlɑsəs/ *n.* [C usually singular] someone or something that is very large or very important

colt /koʊlt/ *n.* [C] a young male horse

col·umn /ˈkɑləm/ *n.* [C] **1** a tall solid round upright stone post used to support a building or as a decoration

> **TOPIC**
> **front page, sports/entertainment/food etc. section, the comics page, the funnies, editorial page, headlines, article, story**
> ➔ see Topic box at NEWSPAPER

2 an article by a particular writer that appears regularly in a newspaper or magazine: *an advice column* **3** something with a long narrow shape: *a* ***column of*** *smoke* **4** one of two or more areas of print that go down the page of a newspaper or book and that are separated from each other by a narrow space: *Let's look at the second column of table 8.5.* **5** a long moving line of people, vehicles, etc.: *A* ***column of*** *soldiers marched through the streets.*

col·um·nist /ˈkɑləmnɪst, ˈkɑləmɪst/ *n.* [C] someone who regularly writes an article for a newspaper or magazine: *a sports columnist*

> **TOPIC**
> **editor, reporter, journalist, correspondent**
> ➔ see Thesaurus box at NEWSPAPER

com /kɑm/ **commercial organization** – used in Internet addresses

co·ma /ˈkoʊmə/ *n.* [C] a state in which someone is not conscious for a long time, usually after an accident or illness: *Ben was* ***in a coma*** *for six days.*

co·ma·tose /ˈkoʊməˌtoʊs, ˈkɑ-/ *adj. technical* in a coma

comb[1] /koʊm/ *n.* [C] a flat piece of plastic or metal with a row of thin parts like teeth on one side that you use to make your hair neat [➡ **brush**]

comb[2] *v.* [T] **1** to make your hair neat with a comb: *Go comb your hair.* **2** to search a place thoroughly: *Police* ***combed*** *the woods* ***for*** *the missing boy.*

com·bat[1] /ˈkɑmbæt/ *n.* [U] fighting during a war: *Her husband was killed* ***in combat.*** —**combat** *adj.*

> **THESAURUS**
> **war, warfare, fighting, conflict**
> ➔ see Thesaurus box at WAR

com·bat[2] /kəmˈbæt, ˈkɑmbæt/ *v.* past tense and past participle **combated** [T] to try to stop something bad from happening or getting worse: *efforts to combat terrorism*

com·bat·ant /kəmˈbætˀnt/ *n.* [C] someone who fights in a war

com·ba·tive /kəmˈbæṭɪv/ *adj.* ready to fight or argue: *Paul was in a combative mood.*

com·bi·na·tion /ˌkɑmbəˈneɪʃən/ *n.* **1** [C,U] two or more different things, substances, etc. that are used or put together: *A* ***combination of*** *factors led to the decision.* | *The medication should be taken* ***in combination with*** *vitamin C.*

> **THESAURUS**
> **mixture, blend, compound, solution**
> ➔ see Thesaurus box at MIXTURE

2 [C] a series of numbers or letters you need to open a combination lock: *I forgot the combination on my lock.*

ˌcombiˈnation lock *n.* [C] a lock that is opened by using a special series of numbers or letters

com·bine[1] /kəmˈbaɪn/ *v.* **1** [I,T] to be joined together with another thing, or to join two or more things together: *The two chemicals* ***combine to***

form a powerful explosive. | *The heat* ***combined with*** *the loud music was beginning to make her feel sick.*

THESAURUS

mix, **stir**, **blend**, **beat**
→ see Thesaurus box at MIX[1]

2 [T] to do two different activities at the same time: *It's hard to* ***combine*** *family life* ***with*** *a career.*

com·bine² /ˈkɑmbaɪn/ *n.* [C] **1 also ˌcombine ˈharvester** a large machine used on a farm to cut a crop and separate the grain at the same time **2** a group of people, businesses, etc. that work together

com·bo /ˈkɑmboʊ/ *n.* plural **combos** [C] *informal* **1** a small group of musicians who play dance music: *a jazz combo* **2** a combination of things, especially food at a restaurant: *I'll have the fish combo and a beer.*

com·bus·ti·ble /kəmˈbʌstəbəl/ *adj.* able to catch fire and burn easily: *Gasoline is* ***highly combustible.*** —**combustible** *n.* [C]

com·bus·tion /kəmˈbʌstʃən/ *n.* [U] the process of burning

come /kʌm/ *v.* past tense **came** /keɪm/ past participle **come** [I]

1 MOVE TOWARD SB/STH to move toward you or arrive at the place where you are [➡ **go**]: ***Come here*** *right now!* | *A young woman* ***came into*** *the room.* | *There were no cars coming the opposite way.* | *What time will you be* ***coming home****?*

2 GO WITH SB if someone comes with you, s/he goes to a place with you: *I asked Rosie if she'd like to* ***come with*** *us.* | *Do you want to* ***come along****?*

3 TRAVEL TO A PLACE to travel to or reach a place: *He had* ***come a long way*** *to see us.* | *Will you be* ***coming by*** *bus?*

THESAURUS

arrive, **get to**, **reach**, **turn up**, **show up**, **get in**, **come in**, **land**
→ see Thesaurus box at ARRIVE

4 MAIL if a letter, etc. comes, it is delivered to you in the mail: *The phone bill hasn't come yet.*

5 HAPPEN if a time or event comes, it arrives or starts to happen: *Spring came early that year.*

6 LIST/COMPETITION ETC. to have a particular position in the order of something: *Jason* ***came first/last*** *in the 10 mile race.* | *P* ***comes before*** *Q in the alphabet.*

7 come open/loose/undone etc. to become open, loose, etc.: *The buttons had come undone.*

8 BE PRODUCED/SOLD to be produced or sold with particular features: *This shoe doesn't* ***come in*** *size 11.*

9 come as a surprise/relief/shock etc. (to sb) to make someone feel surprised, RELIEVED, etc.: *His decision to retire came as a surprise.*

10 sb/sth has come a long way to have made a lot of progress: *Computer technology has come a long way since the 1970s*

11 REACH A LENGTH/HEIGHT to reach a particular height or length: *The grass* ***came up to*** *our knees.*

12 come naturally/easily (to sb) to be easy for someone to do: *Acting came naturally to Rae.*

13 in the years/days to come in the future: *I think you might regret this decision in the years to come.*

14 come of age **a)** to reach the age, usually 18 or 21, when you are legally considered to be an adult **b)** to develop into a successful form, or to reach the time when this happens: *The sport has finally come of age.*

15 come and go to be allowed to go into and leave a place whenever you want

SPOKEN PHRASES

16 how come? used in order to ask someone why something happened or is true: *"She's moving to Alaska." "How come?"* | *So, how come we haven't met your boyfriend yet?*

17 here comes sb said when someone is about to arrive at the place where you are: *Here comes Karen now.*

18 come to think of it said when you have just realized or remembered something: *Come to think of it, Cooper did mention it to me.*

19 take sth as it comes to accept something as it happens, without trying to plan for it or change it: *I'm not going to worry about it. I'll just* ***take each day as it comes.***

20 have it coming to deserve to be punished or to have something bad happen to you: *I don't feel sorry for Brad – he had it coming.*

come about *phr. v.* to happen or develop: ***How*** *did this change* ***come about****?*

come across *phr. v.* **1 come across sb/sth** to meet, find, or discover someone or something by chance: *I came across this photograph among some old newspapers.* **2** if someone comes across in a particular way, s/he seems to have certain qualities: *She* ***comes across as*** *a really happy person.*

come along *phr. v.* **1** to appear or arrive: *Jobs like this don't come along very often!* **2** to develop or improve: *Terry's work has really come along this year.*

come apart *phr. v.* **1** to split or separate easily into pieces: *The book just came apart in my hands.* **2** to begin to fail: *Their marriage was coming apart.*

come around *phr. v.* **1** to visit someone: *What's a good time to come around and drop off his present?* **2** if someone comes around, s/he decides to agree with you after disagreeing with you: *I know he'll come around.* **3** if a regular event comes around, it happens as usual: *I can't believe his birthday is coming around already.*

C

come at sb *phr. v.* to move toward someone in a threatening way: *She came at him with a knife.*
come away *phr. v.* to leave a place with a particular feeling or idea: *I came away with a good impression.*
come back **1** to return from a place: *When is your sister coming back from Europe?* **2 come back to sb** to be remembered, especially suddenly: *Then, everything Williams had said came back to me.* **3** to become fashionable or popular again: *The styles of the seventies are coming back.* → COMEBACK
come between sb/sth *phr. v.* **1** to cause trouble between two or more people: *Don't let money come between you and David.* **2** to prevent someone from giving enough attention to something: *She never let anything come between her and her work.*
come by *phr. v.* **1 come by (sth)** to visit someone for a short time before going somewhere else: *I'll come by later to pick up Katrina.* **2 come by sth** to get something that is difficult to get: *Good jobs are **hard to come by** right now.*
come down *phr. v.* **1 a)** to become lower in price, level, etc.: *Wait until interest rates come down before you buy a house.* **b)** to offer or accept a lower price: *They refused to **come down on** the price.* **2** to fall to the ground: *A lot of trees came down in the storm.* **3** if someone comes down to a place, s/he travels south to the place where you are: *Why don't you come down for the weekend sometime?*
come down on sb/sth *phr. v.* **1** to punish someone severely: *The school **came down hard on** the students who were caught drinking.* **2 come down on the side of sth** to decide to support something or someone: *The court came down on the side of the boy's father.*
come down to sth *phr. v.* if a difficult or confusing situation comes down to something, that is the single most important thing: *It all comes down to money in the end.*
come down with sth *phr. v.* to get an illness: *I think I'm coming down with the flu.*
come forward *phr. v.* to offer to help: *Several witnesses have came forward with information.*
come from sth *phr. v.* **1** to have been born in a particular place: ***"Where do you come from?"** "Texas."* **2** to have first existed, been made, or produced in a particular place, thing, or time: *A lot of drugs come from quite common plants.* | *The lines she read come from a Rilke poem.* **3** if a sound comes from a place, it begins there: *I heard a weird sound coming from the closet.*
come in *phr. v.* **1** to enter a room or house: *Come in and sit down.* **2** to arrive or be received: *Reports were coming in of an earthquake in Mexico.* **3 come in first/second etc.** to finish first, second, etc. in a race or competition **4** to be involved in a plan, deal, etc.: *I need somebody to help and that's **where** you **come in**.* **5 come in useful/handy** to be useful: *Bring the rope – it might come in handy.* **6** when the TIDE comes in, it moves toward the land [≠ **go out**]
come in for sth *phr. v.* **come in for criticism/blame** to be criticized or blamed: *After the riots, the police came in for a lot of criticism.*
come into sth *phr. v.* **1** to begin to be in a particular state or position: *As we turned the corner, the town **came into view**.* | *The new law **comes into effect** tomorrow.* **2** to be involved in something or to influence it: *Where do I come into all this?* **3 come into money** to receive money because someone has died and given it to you
come of sth *phr. v.* to result from something: *What good can come of getting so angry?*
come off *phr. v.* **1 come off sth** to no longer be on something, connected to it, or fastened to it: *A button had come off my coat.* **2** to seem like you have a particular attitude or quality because of something you say or do: *She **came off as** a phoney.* **3** to happen in a particular way: *The wedding came off as planned.* **4 come off it!** *spoken* said when you think someone is being stupid or unreasonable
come on *phr. v.* **1** if a light or machine comes on, it starts working: *The lights suddenly came on in the theater.* **2** if a television or radio program comes on, it starts: *What time does the show come on?* **3** if an illness comes on, you start to have it: *I can feel a headache coming on.* **4 come on!** *spoken* **a)** used in order to tell someone to hurry, or to come with you **b)** said in order to encourage someone to do something: *Come on, it's not that hard.* **c)** used in order to tell someone that you know that what s/he said was not true or right: *Oh, come on, don't lie to me!*
come on to sb *phr. v. spoken* to do or say something that makes it clear that you are sexually interested in someone
come out *phr. v.* **1** to become known, especially after being hidden: *The truth will come out eventually.* **2** if something you say comes out in a particular way, you say it in that way or it is understood by someone in that way: *When I try to explain, it **comes out all wrong**, and she gets mad.* **3** to say something publicly or directly: *Senator Peters has **come out against** abortion.* | *Why don't you just **come out and say** what you think?* **4** if a book, movie, etc. comes out, it is available for people to buy or see **5** if dirt or a mark comes out of cloth, it can be washed out **6 come out well/badly/ahead etc.** to finish an action or process in a particular way: *I can never get cakes to come out right.* **7** if a photograph comes out, it looks the way it is supposed to: *Some of our wedding photos didn't come out.* **8** when the sun, moon, or stars come out, they appear in the sky
come out with sth *phr. v.* if a company comes out with a new product, it makes it available to be bought: *Ford has come out with a new sports truck.*

come over *phr. v.* **1** to visit someone at his/her house: *Do you want to come over on Friday night?* **2** to move to the country where you are now: *Her dad came over from Italy in the 1960s.* **3 come over sb** if a feeling comes over someone, s/he begins to feel it: *A wave of sleepiness came over her.*

come through *phr. v.* **1 come through sth** to continue to live, exist, be strong, or succeed after a difficult or dangerous time [= **survive**]: *Bill came through the operation all right.* **2** to be made official, especially by having the correct documents officially approved: *She's still waiting for her visa to come through.*

come to *phr. v.* **1 come to do sth** to begin to have a feeling or opinion: *She had come to think of New York as her home.* **2 come to sb** if an idea or memory comes to you, you suddenly realize or remember it: *Later that afternoon, the answer came to him.* **3 come to $20/$3 etc.** to add up to a total of $20, $3, etc.: *That comes to $24.67, ma'am.* **4 when it comes to sth** relating to a particular subject: *She's hopeless when it comes to money.* **5** to become conscious again after having been unconscious: *When I came to, I was lying on the grass.*

come under sth *phr. v.* **1 come under attack/fire/pressure etc.** to be attacked, criticized, threatened, etc.: *The president has come under fire from Democrats in Congress.* **2** to be controlled or influenced by something such as a set of rules: *All doctors come under the same rules of professional conduct.*

come up *phr. v.* **1** if someone comes up to you, s/he comes close to you, especially in order to speak to you **2** if someone comes up to a place, s/he travels north to the place where you are: *Why don't you come up to Chicago for the weekend?* **3** to be mentioned or suggested: *The subject didn't come up at the meeting.* **4 be coming up** to be happening soon: *Isn't your anniversary coming up?* **5** when the sun or moon comes up, it appears in the sky and starts to rise **6** if something, especially a problem, comes up, it suddenly happens: *Something's come up, so I won't be able to go with you Thursday.*

come up against sb/sth *phr. v.* to have to deal with difficult problems or people: *He came up against fierce resistance.*

come upon sb/sth *phr. v. literary* to find or discover something by chance

come up with sth *phr. v.* **1** to think of an idea, plan, reply, etc.: *They still haven't come up with a name for the baby.* **2** to be able to produce a particular amount of money: *I'll never be able to come up with $2,000.*

come·back /ˈkʌmbæk/ *n.* [C] **1** to become popular or successful again: *Platform shoes are **making a** big **comeback**.* **2** a quick reply that is smart or funny: *I can never think of a good comeback when I need one.*

co·me·di·an /kəˈmidiən/ *n.* [C] someone whose job is to tell jokes and make people laugh [= **comic**]: *a stand-up comedian*

com·e·dy /ˈkɑmədi/ *n.* plural **comedies** **1** [C,U] a funny movie, play, television program, etc. that makes people laugh, or this type of entertainment: *a TV comedy* | *stand-up comedy* ➔ see Thesaurus box at MOVIE **2** [U] the quality in something such as a book or movie that makes you laugh [= **humor**]

ˈcome-on *n.* [C] *informal* something that someone does to try to make someone else sexually interested in him/her: *Rick seems to think every smile is a come-on.*

com·et /ˈkɑmɪt/ *n.* [C] an object in the sky like a very bright ball with a tail, that moves through SPACE (=the area beyond the Earth where the stars are)

TOPIC

space, **meteor**, **asteroid**, **moon**, **planet**, **star**, **sun**, **constellation**, **galaxy**, **black hole**, **spacecraft**, **spaceship**, **rocket**, **(space) shuttle**, **satellite**, **probe**, **astronaut**
➔ see Topic box at SPACE[1]

come·up·pance /kʌmˈʌpəns/ *n.* [singular] *informal* a punishment or something bad that happens to you, that you deserve: *the story of a crook who finally **gets** his **comeuppance***

com·fort¹ /ˈkʌmfɚt/ *n.* **1** [U] a feeling of being physically relaxed and satisfied, so that nothing is hurting you, making you feel too hot or cold, etc. [≠ **discomfort**]: *the air-conditioned **comfort of** his car* | *We slept there **in comfort** until the dawn appeared.* **2** [U] if someone or something gives you comfort, he, she, or it makes you feel happier when you are upset or worried: *I **took comfort from** the fact that I had done my best.* | *She turned to her church **for comfort**.* **3 (be) a comfort to sb** to help someone feel happier or less worried: *Her children were a **great comfort** to her.* **4** [U] a way of living in which you have everything you need to be happy: *They had enough money to live **in comfort**.* **5 comforts** [plural] all the things that make your life easier and more comfortable: *The beach cabin has all **the comforts of home**.* ➔ **too close for comfort** at CLOSE²

com·fort² *v.* [T] to make someone feel less worried or unhappy, for example by saying kind things to him/her —**comforting** *adj.* —**comfortingly** *adv.*

com·fort·a·ble /ˈkʌmftəbəl, ˈkʌmfɚt̬əbəl/ *adj.* **1** something that is comfortable makes you feel physically relaxed: *Remember to wear comfortable shoes.* | *a **comfortable chair/bed/sofa*** **2** if you are comfortable, you feel physically relaxed: *Come in and **make yourself comfortable**.* **3** not worried about what someone will do or about what will happen: *I **feel** very **comfortable***

with him. **4** having enough money to live on without worrying: *We're not rich, but we are comfortable.* —**comfortably** *adv.*

com·fort·er /ˈkʌmfɚt̬ɚ/ *n.* [C] a thick cover for a bed ➔ see picture at BED[1]

com·fy /ˈkʌmfi/ *adj. spoken* COMFORTABLE

com·ic[1] /ˈkɑmɪk/ *adj.* funny or amusing: *a comic actress | At least Marlene was there to give us* ***comic relief*** (=make us laugh in a serious situation).

comic[2] *n.* [C] **1** a COMEDIAN **2** a COMIC BOOK **3 the comics** [plural] the part of a newspaper that has COMIC STRIPS

com·i·cal /ˈkɑmɪkəl/ *adj.* funny, especially in a strange or unexpected way —**comically** *adv.*

C

ˈcomic book *n.* [C] a magazine that tells a story using pictures that are drawn like comic strips

ˈcomic strip *n.* [C] a series of pictures that are drawn inside boxes and tell a story

THESAURUS

drawing, picture, sketch, cartoon
➔ see Thesaurus box at DRAWING

com·ing[1] /ˈkʌmɪŋ/ *n.* **1 the coming of sth/sb** the time when something or someone arrives or begins: *With the coming of the railroad, the town changed considerably.* **2 comings and goings** the movements of people as they arrive and leave places

coming[2] *adj.* [only before noun] happening soon: *the coming winter*

com·ma /ˈkɑmə/ *n.* [C] the mark (,) used in writing to show a short pause

com·mand[1] /kəˈmænd/ *n.* **1** [U] the control of a group of people or a situation: *How many officers are* ***under*** *your* ***command****? | Who is* ***in command*** *here?* **2** [C] an order that must be obeyed: *Shoot when I* ***give*** *the* ***command****.* **3 command of sth** knowledge of something, especially a language, or the ability to use something: *Fukiko* ***has a good command of*** *English.* **4** [C] an instruction to a computer to do something

command[2] *v.* **1** [I,T] to tell someone officially to do something, especially if you are a military leader, king, etc.: *The captain* ***commanded*** *the crew* ***to*** *remain on the main deck.* **2** [T] to get attention, respect, etc. because you are important or popular: *He commands one of the highest fees in Hollywood.*

com·man·dant /ˈkɑmən,dɑnt/ *n.* [C] the chief officer in charge of a military organization

com·man·deer /,kɑmənˈdɪr/ *v.* [T] to officially take someone's property for military use: *The hotel was commandeered for use as a war hospital.*

com·mand·er, Commander /kəˈmændɚ/ *n.* [C] **1** an officer in charge of a military organization or group **2** an officer who has a middle rank in the Navy

com·mand·ing /kəˈmændɪŋ/ *adj.* [only before noun] **1** having authority or confidence which makes people respect and obey you: *his* ***commanding presence*** **2** being in a position from which you are likely to win a race or competition easily: *Stevens has a* ***commanding lead*** *in the polls.*

com·mand·ment /kəˈmændmənt/ *n.* [C] one of ten rules given by God in the Bible that tell people how they should behave

com·man·do /kəˈmændoʊ/ *n.* plural **commandos** [C] a soldier who is specially trained to make quick attacks into enemy areas

com·mem·o·rate /kəˈmɛmə,reɪt/ *v.* [T] to remember someone or something by a special action, ceremony, object, etc.: *The monument commemorates those who died during the war.* —**commemoration** /kə,mɛməˈreɪʃən/ *n.* [U] —**commemorative** /kəˈmɛmərət̬ɪv/ *adj.*

com·mence /kəˈmɛns/ *v.* [I,T] *formal* to begin: *Work on the building will commence soon.*

com·mence·ment /kəˈmɛnsmənt/ *n.* **1** [C,U] a ceremony at which COLLEGE or HIGH SCHOOL students receive their DIPLOMAS [= **graduation**] **2** [U] *formal* the beginning of something

com·mend /kəˈmɛnd/ *v.* [T] *formal* to praise someone or something publicly or formally: *The three firefighters were* ***commended for*** *their bravery.*

com·mend·a·ble /kəˈmɛndəbəl/ *adj. formal* deserving praise: *Baldwin answered with commendable honesty.* —**commendably** *adv.*

com·men·da·tion /,kɑmənˈdeɪʃən/ *n.* [C] *formal* an honor or prize given to someone for being brave or successful

com·men·su·rate /kəˈmɛnsərɪt, -ʃərɪt/ *adj. formal* matching something else in size, quality, or length of time: *The salary is* ***commensurate with*** *experience* (=the salary for the job is higher if you have experience).

com·ment[1] /ˈkɑmɛnt/ *n.* **1** [C,U] an opinion that you give about someone or something: *Does anyone have any questions or comments? | He* ***made*** *rude* ***comments about*** *her.* **2 no comment** *spoken* said when you do not want to answer a question, especially in public

comment[2] *v.* [I,T] to give an opinion about someone or something: *The police have refused to* ***comment on*** *the case.*

com·men·tar·y /ˈkɑmən,tɛri/ *n.* plural **commentaries** [C,U] **1** a spoken description of an event, given while the event is happening, especially on the television or radio: *the* ***commentary on*** *the World Series* **2** a book or article that explains or discusses something, or the explanation itself: *political commentary* **3 be a sad commentary on sth** to be a sign or example of how bad a situation is: *It's a sad commentary on our culture that we need constant entertainment.*

com·men·ta·tor /ˈkɑmən,teɪt̬ɚ/ *n.* [C]

1 someone on television or radio who describes an event as it is happening: *a **sports commentator*** **2** someone who knows a lot about a subject, and who writes about it or discusses it on the television or radio: *political commentators*

com·merce /ˈkɑmɚs/ *n.* [U] the buying and selling of goods and services [= **trade**]: ***interstate commerce*** (=among U.S. states)

THESAURUS

business, industry, trade, private enterprise
➔ see Thesaurus box at BUSINESS

com·mer·cial[1] /kəˈmɚʃəl/ *adj.* **1** relating to business and the buying and selling of things: *commercial activity* **2** relating to making money or a profit: *The movie was **a commercial success/failure**.* —**commercially** *adv.*

commercial[2] *n.* [C] an advertisement on television or radio: *TV commercials*

THESAURUS

advertisement, billboard, poster, want ads, classified ads, flier, junk mail, spam
➔ see Thesaurus box at ADVERTISEMENT

com·mer·cial·is·m /kəˈmɚʃəˌlɪzəm/ *n.* [U] *disapproving* the practice of being more concerned with making money than with the quality of what you sell

com·mer·cial·ize /kəˈmɚʃəˌlaɪz/ *v.* [T] *disapproving* to be more concerned with making money from something than about its quality: *Christmas is getting so commercialized!* —**commercialization** /kəˌmɚʃələˈzeɪʃən/ *n.* [U]

com·mis·e·rate /kəˈmɪzəˌreɪt/ *v.* [I] *formal* to express your sympathy for someone who is unhappy: *We spent several hours **commiserating with** the dead child's parents.* —**commiseration** /kəˌmɪzəˈreɪʃən/ *n.* [U]

com·mis·sion[1] /kəˈmɪʃən/ *n.* **1** [C] a group of people who have been given the official job of finding out about something or controlling something: *the U.N. Commission on Human Rights* **2** [C,U] an amount of money paid to someone for selling something: *Salespeople earn a 30% **commission on** each new car.* **3** [C] a piece of work that someone, especially an artist or a musician, is asked to do: *a commission for a new sculpture* **4 out of commission a)** not working correctly, or not able to be used: *The toilets are out of commission.* **b)** *informal* sick or injured

commission[2] *v.* [T] to ask someone to do a piece of work for you: *He has been **commissioned to** design a bridge.*

com·mis·sion·er /kəˈmɪʃənɚ/ *n.* [C] someone who is officially in charge of an organization: *a police commissioner*

com·mit /kəˈmɪt/ *v.* past tense and past participle **committed**, present participle **committing** [T] **1** to do something wrong or illegal: *Police still don't know who **committed** the **crime**.* **2 commit suicide** to kill yourself deliberately **3 commit adultery** if a married person commits adultery, s/he has sex with someone who is not his/her husband or wife **4** to say that you will definitely do something: *Going to the interview doesn't **commit** you **to** anything.* | *I had **committed myself** and there was no turning back.* **5** to decide to use money, time, effort, etc. for a particular purpose: *A lot of money has been **committed to** the project.*

com·mit·ment /kəˈmɪt˺mənt/ *n.* **1** [C] a promise to do something or behave in a particular way: *Volunteers must be able to **make a commitment** of four hours a week.* | *Our company has a **commitment to** customer service.* **2** [U] the hard work and loyalty that someone gives to an organization, activity, etc.: *Sara's **commitment to** her work* **3** [C] *formal* something that you have promised you will do or that you have to do: *He had other commitments and could not attend.*

com·mit·ted /kəˈmɪt̬ɪd/ *adj.* believing that an organization, activity, etc. is right or important and willing to work hard for it: *Her parents are both committed liberals.*

com·mit·tee /kəˈmɪt̬i/ *n.* [C] a group of people chosen to do a particular job, make decisions, etc.: *I'm **on** the finance **committee**.*

com·mod·i·ty /kəˈmɑdət̬i/ *n.* plural **commodities** [C] a product that is bought and sold: *agricultural commodities*

com·mo·dore, **Commodore** /ˈkɑməˌdɔr/ *n.* [C] an officer who has a high rank in the Navy

com·mon[1] /ˈkɑmən/ *adj.* **1** something that is common is often seen or often happens [≠ **rare**]: *"Smith" is a common last name.* | *Heart disease is **common among** smokers.* | *It's **common for** new fathers **to** feel jealous of their babies.* ▶ Don't say "It is common that." ◀ **2** belonging to, or shared by two or more people or things: *We are all working towards a **common goal**.* | *a theme that is **common to** all her novels* **3 common ground** facts, opinions, and beliefs that a group of people can agree on, in a situation in which they are arguing about something: *Let's see if we can establish some common ground.* **4 the common good** what is best for everyone in a society: *They truly believed they were acting for the common good.* **5 common knowledge** something that everyone knows: ***It's common knowledge** that he's an alcoholic.* **6** ordinary and not special in any way: *The song is a tribute to **the common man*** (=ordinary people).

common[2] *n.* [C] **1 have sth in common (with sb/sth)** to have the same interests, attitudes, etc. as someone else: *Terry and I **have a lot in common**.* **2 have sth in common (with sth)** if objects or ideas have something in common, they share the same features: *The two games **have much/little in common**.* **3** a word meaning a public park, used mostly in names: *Boston Common*

ˌcommon ˈcold *n.* [C] a slight illness in which

C

your throat hurts and it is difficult to breathe normally [= **cold**]

'common-law *adj.* **common-law husband/wife** someone you have lived with for a long time as if s/he was your husband or wife

com·mon·ly /'kamənli/ *adv.* often or usually: *the most commonly used computer*

com·mon·place /'kamən,pleɪs/ *adj.* very common or not unusual: *Divorce has become commonplace.*

,common 'sense *n.* [U] the ability to behave in a sensible way and make practical decisions: ***Use** your **common sense**.*

C

com·mon·wealth /'kamən,wɛlθ/ *n.* [C] *formal* **1** a group of countries that are related politically or economically, for example the group of countries that have a strong relationship with Great Britain **2** the official legal title of some U.S. states: *The Commonwealth of Virginia* **3** the official legal title of some places, such as Puerto Rico, that are governed by the U.S. but are not states

com·mo·tion /kə'moʊʃən/ *n.* [singular, U] sudden noisy activity or arguing: *Everyone looked to see what was **causing** the **commotion**.*

com·mu·nal /kə'myunl/ *adj.* shared by a group of people: *a communal bathroom*

com·mune¹ /'kamyun/ *n.* [C] a group of people who live and work together and share their possessions

com·mune² /kə'myun/ *v.*

commune with sth/sb *phr. v. formal* **1** to communicate with a person, god, or animal, especially in a mysterious way **2 commune with nature** to spend time in the COUNTRYSIDE, enjoying it in a quiet peaceful way

com·mu·ni·ca·ble /kə'myunɪkəbəl/ *adj.* a communicable disease is one that can be passed on to other people [= **infectious**]

com·mu·ni·cate /kə'myunə,keɪt/ *v.* **1** [I] to exchange information or conversation with other people, using words, signs, writing, etc.: *We communicate mostly by email.* | *It's difficult to **communicate with** people if you don't speak their language.* **2** [I,T] to express your thoughts or feelings clearly, so that other people understand them: *A baby communicates its needs by crying.*

com·mu·ni·ca·tion /kə,myunə'keɪʃən/ *n.* **1** [U] the process of speaking, writing, etc. by which people exchange information or express their thoughts and feelings: ***communication between** parents and teachers* | *We've stayed **in** constant **communication** with each other.* | *Radio was the pilot's only **means of communication**.* **2 communications** [plural] **a)** ways of sending and receiving information using computers, telephones, radios, etc.: *Modern communications enable people to work from home.* **b)** the study of using radio, television, movies, etc. to communicate **3** [C] *formal* a letter, message, or telephone call

com·mu·ni·ca·tive /kə'myunəkət̬ɪv, -,keɪt̬ɪv/ *adj.* willing or able to talk or give information: *My son isn't very communicative.*

com·mun·ion /kə'myunyən/ *n.* **Communion also Holy Communion** the Christian ceremony in which people eat bread and drink wine as signs of Christ's body and blood

com·mu·ni·qué /kə'myunə,keɪ, kə,myunə'keɪ/ *n.* [C] an official report or announcement

com·mu·nism /'kamyə,nɪzəm/ *n.* [U] a political system in which the government controls all the production of food and goods and there is no privately owned property

com·mu·nist /'kamyənɪst/ *n.* [C] someone who is a member of a political party that supports communism, or who believes in communism —**communist** *adj.*: *the Communist Party*

com·mu·ni·ty /kə'myunət̬i/ *n.* plural **communities** [C] **1** a group of people who live in the same town or area: *The library serves the whole community.* **2** a group of people who have the same interests, religion, race, etc.: *Miami has a large Cuban community.* | *politicians who have close ties to the business community* **3 sense of community** the feeling that you belong to a group in which people work together and help each other: *Teachers are working to build a sense of community in the school.*

com'munity ,college *n.* [C] a college that people can go to, usually for two years, in order to learn a skill or to prepare to go to another college or university

com,munity 'service *n.* [U] work that someone does to help other people without being paid, especially as punishment for a crime

THESAURUS

punishment, sentence, penalty, fine, corporal punishment, capital punishment

➔ see Thesaurus box at PUNISHMENT

com·mute¹ /kə'myut/ *v.* **1** [I] to travel regularly in order to get to work: *Jerry **commutes from** Scarsdale **to** New York every day.* **2** [T] *formal* to change the punishment given to a criminal to one that is less severe: *Her sentence was **commuted** from death **to** life imprisonment.*

commute² *n.* [C usually singular] the trip made to work every day: *My morning commute takes 45 minutes.*

com·mut·er /kə'myut̬ɚ/ *n.* [C] someone who travels a long distance to work every day ➔ see Thesaurus box at TRAVEL¹

com·pact¹ /'kampækt, kəm'pækt/ *adj.* small but arranged so that everything fits neatly into the available space: *a compact car*

com·pact² /'kampækt/ *n.* [C] **1** a small flat container with a mirror, containing powder for a woman's face **2** a small car **3** *formal* an agreement between two or more people, countries, etc.

com·pact[3] /kəm'pækt/ *v.* [T] to press something together so that it becomes smaller or more solid —**compacted** *adj.*

ˌcompact 'disc *n.* [C] a CD

com·pan·ion /kəm'pænyən/ *n.* [C] **1** someone you spend a lot of time with, especially a friend: *For ten years, he had been her* ***constant companion.*** | *my* ***traveling companions*** **2** one of a pair of things that go together or can be used together: *This book is a* ***companion to*** *Professor Farrer's first work.*

com·pan·ion·a·ble /kəm'pænyənəbəl/ *adj.* pleasantly friendly: *They sat in a companionable silence.*

com·pan·ion·ship /kəm'pænyənˌʃɪp/ *n.* [U] the state of being with someone, so that you have someone to talk to and do not feel lonely: *the need for companionship*

com·pa·ny /'kʌmpəni/ *n.* plural **companies** **1** [C] a business that makes or sells things or provides a service: *What company do you work for?* | *an* ***insurance/software/phone company***

THESAURUS

firm – a company that usually provides a service rather than producing goods: *a law firm*
business – a company that often employs only a small number of people: *She set up her own catering business.* | *small businesses*
corporation – a large company that often includes several smaller companies
multinational – a very large company with offices in many different countries
subsidiary – a company that is owned by a larger company

2 [U] the state of being with someone so that s/he does not feel lonely: *Why don't you come with me? I could use the company.* | *Tim is* ***good company*** (=someone you enjoy being with). | *I'll stay here to* ***keep*** *you* ***company*** (=be with you so you are not alone). **3** [U] one or more guests, or someone who is coming to see you: *We're* ***having company*** *tonight, so be back home by five.* **4** [singular, U] the group of people that you are friends with or spend time with: *I don't like* ***the company*** *she* ***keeps.*** **5** [C] a group of actors, dancers, or singers who work together: *a ballet company*

com·pa·ra·ble /'kɑmpərəbəl/ *adj. formal* similar to something else in size, number, quality, etc.: *Is the pay rate* ***comparable to*** *that of other companies?*

com·par·a·tive[1] /kəm'pærət̬ɪv/ *adj.* **1** showing what is different and similar between things of the same kind: *a* ***comparative study*** *of European languages* **2 comparative comfort/freedom/wealth etc.** comfort, freedom, etc. that is fairly good when measured or judged against something else, or against what the situation was before [= **relative**]: *After a lifetime of poverty, his last few years were spent in comparative comfort.*

comparative[2] *n.* **the comparative** *technical* in grammar, the form of an adjective or adverb that shows an increase in quality, quantity, degree, etc. For example, "better" is the comparative of "good."

com·par·a·tive·ly /kəm'pærət̬ɪvli/ *adv.* as compared to something else or to a previous state: *The disease is comparatively rare.*

com·pare[1] /kəm'pɛr/ *v.* **1** [T] to examine or judge two or more things in order to show how they are similar to or different from each other: *We went to a few different stores to compare prices.* | ***Compared to*** *me, Al is tall.* | *The police* ***compared*** *the suspect's fingerprints* ***with*** *those found at the crime scene.* **2** [I,T] to say that something or someone is similar to someone or something else: *Critics have* ***compared*** *him* ***to*** *Robert De Niro.* | *The oranges out here* ***don't compare with*** (=are not as good as) *the Florida ones.* **3 compare notes (with sb)** *informal* to talk with someone in order to find out if his/her experience is the same as yours

compare[2] *n.* **beyond/without compare** *literary* a quality that is beyond compare is the best of its kind: *beauty beyond compare*

com·par·i·son /kəm'pærəsən/ *n.* **1** [U] the process of comparing two people or things: ***In comparison with/to*** *his brother, he's really shy.* | *My last job was so boring that this one seems great* ***by comparison.*** **2** [C] a statement or examination of how similar or different two people or things are: *a* ***comparison of*** *crime figures in Chicago and Detroit* **3** [C] a statement that someone or something is like someone or something else: *The writer* ***draws comparisons between*** *the two presidents.* | *You can't* ***make a comparison between*** *American and Japanese schools – they're too different.* **4 there's no comparison** used when you think that someone or something is much better than someone or something else: ***There's*** *just* ***no comparison between*** *canned vegetables and fresh ones.*

com·part·ment /kəm'pɑrt˺mənt/ *n.* [C] a smaller enclosed space inside something larger: *the overhead compartment on a plane*

com·part·men·tal·ize /kəmˌpɑrt˺'mɛntəlˌaɪz/ *v.* [T] to divide things into separate groups

compass

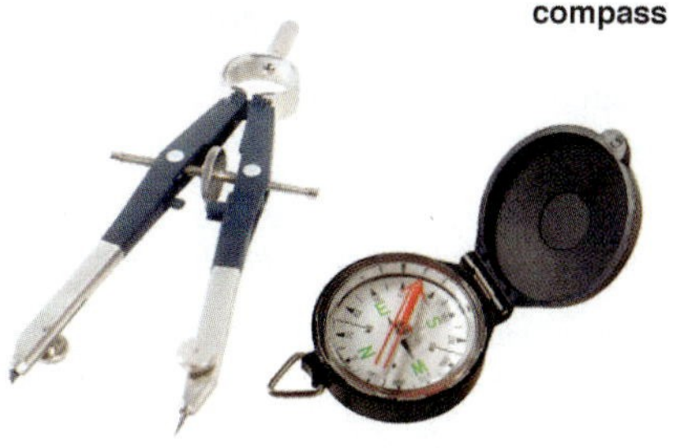

com·pass /'kʌmpəs/ *n.* [C] **1** an instrument

that shows the direction you are traveling in, with an ARROW that always points north **2** an instrument with a sharp point, used for drawing circles or measuring distances on maps

com·pas·sion /kəm'pæʃən/ *n.* [U] sympathy for someone who is suffering: *her* ***compassion for*** *the poor* | *We should* ***have compassion*** *for others.*

com·pas·sion·ate /kəm'pæʃənɪt/ *adj.* feeling sympathy for people who are suffering: *a compassionate man*

com·pat·i·ble /kəm'pæt̬əbəl/ *adj.* **1** two people who are compatible are able to have a good relationship because they share interests, ideas, etc. **2** two things that are compatible are able to exist or be used together without problems: *Is the software* ***compatible with*** *your PC?* —**compatibility** /kəm,pæt̬ə'bɪləti/ *n.* [U]

C

com·pa·tri·ot /kəm'peɪtriət/ *n.* [C] someone who is from the same country as you: *Schmidt defeated his compatriot Hausmann in the quarter final.*

com·pel /kəm'pɛl/ *v.* past tense and past participle **compelled**, present participle **compelling** [T] to force someone to do something: *He* ***felt compelled to*** *resign because of the scandal.*

THESAURUS

force, **make**, **coerce**, **pressure**
➔ see Thesaurus box at FORCE[2]

com·pel·ling /kəm'pɛlɪŋ/ *adj.* **1** very interesting or exciting: *a compelling story*

THESAURUS

interesting, **fascinating**, **intriguing**, **absorbing**
➔ see Thesaurus box at INTERESTING

2 a compelling argument, reason, etc. seems very good or strong: *The jury was presented with* ***compelling evidence***.

com·pen·di·um /kəm'pɛndiəm/ *n.* [C] *formal* a book that contains a complete collection of facts, drawings, etc. on a particular subject: *a baseball compendium*

com·pen·sate /'kɑmpən,seɪt/ *v.* **1** [I] to do something so that something bad has a smaller effect: *Her intelligence more than* ***compensates for*** *her lack of experience.* **2** [T] to pay someone money because s/he has suffered injury, loss, or damage: *The firm will* ***compensate*** *workers* ***for*** *their loss of earnings.* —**compensatory** /kəm'pɛnsə,tɔri/ *adj.*

com·pen·sa·tion /,kɑmpən'seɪʃən/ *n.* **1** [U] money that someone is given because s/he has suffered injury, loss, or damage: *The fishermen have demanded* ***compensation for*** *the damage.* | *The jury awarded Tyler $1 million* ***in compensation***. **2** [C,U] something that makes a bad situation seem better: *One of the few compensations of losing my job was seeing more of my family.*

com·pete /kəm'pit/ *v.* [I] to try to win or gain something, or try to be better or more successful than someone else: *How many runners will be* ***competing in*** *the race?* | *We just* ***can't compete with/against*** *big companies like theirs.* | *The stores are* ***competing for*** *customers.*

com·pe·tent /'kɑmpət̬ənt/ *adj.* having enough skill or knowledge to do something to a satisfactory standard: *A competent mechanic should be able to fix the problem quickly.* —**competence** *n.* [U] —**competently** *adv.*

com·pet·ing /kəm'pit̬ɪŋ/ *adj.* **1 competing interests/demands/claims etc.** two or more interests, claims, etc. that cannot both be right **2 competing products** products, etc. that are trying to be more successful than each other

com·pe·ti·tion /,kɑmpə'tɪʃən/ *n.* **1** [singular, U] a situation in which people or organizations compete with each other: *The* ***competition between*** *the two sisters is obvious.* | ***Competition for*** *the job was intense.* | *Prices have gone down due to* ***competition among*** *the airlines.* **2** [singular, U] the people or groups that are competing against you, especially in business: *You'll have* ***no competition***. | *Our aim is to be better than* ***the competition***. **3** [C] an organized event in which people or teams compete against each other: *a dancing competition* | *He decided to* ***enter*** *the* ***competition***. | *Who* ***won*** *the* ***competition***?

THESAURUS

championship – a competition to find the best player or team in a particular sport: *the Iowa State Girls' Basketball Championships*
tournament – a competition in which many players or teams compete against each other until there is one winner: *a local volleyball tournament at Sunset Park*
contest – a competition in which a judge or group of judges decides the winner: *the school's essay contest*
playoff – a game or series of games played by the best teams or players in a sports competition, in order to decide the final winner: *The Yankees make the playoffs nearly every year.* | *the divisional playoff game against San Francisco*

com·pet·i·tive /kəm'pɛt̬ət̬ɪv/ *adj.* **1** determined to be more successful than other people or companies: *Steve's very competitive.* | *What can we do to maintain our* ***competitive edge*** (=ability to be more successful)? **2** relating to competition: *competitive sports* | *Advertising is a* ***highly competitive*** *industry.* **3** competitive prices or products are cheaper than others but still of good quality: *Last year they sold twice as many computers as their* ***main competitor***. —**competitiveness** *n.* [U]

com·pet·i·tor /kəm'pɛt̬ət̬ɚ/ *n.* [C] a person, team, company, etc. that is competing with another one

com·pi·la·tion /,kɑmpə'leɪʃən/ *n.* [C] a book,

list, record, etc. which consists of different pieces of information, music, etc.: *a **compilation of** love songs*

com·pile /kəm'paɪl/ *v.* [T] to make a book, list, record, etc. using different pieces of information, music, etc.: *The report is **compiled from** a survey of 5,000 households.*

com·pla·cent /kəm'pleɪsənt/ *adj.* pleased with what you have achieved so that you stop trying to improve or change things: *We've been winning, but we're not going to get complacent.* —**complacency** *n.* [U]

com·plain /kəm'pleɪn/ *v.* [I,T] **1** to say that you are annoyed, not satisfied, or unhappy about something or someone: *Fred's always **complaining about** something.* | *Teachers **complain that** they do not get enough support from parents.* | *She **complained to** the manager.* **2 I can't complain** *spoken* said when you think a situation is satisfactory even though there may be a few problems: *I still don't feel too great, but I can't complain.*

complain of sth *phr. v.* to say that you feel sick or have a pain in a part of your body: *He complained of stomach pains.*

com·plaint /kəm'pleɪnt/ *n.* **1** [C,U] a statement in which someone complains about something: *We've **received** a large number of **complaints** from customers.* | *There have been **complaints about** the quality of her work.* | ***complaints against** the police* **2** [C] a formal statement saying that someone is guilty of a crime: *She has **filed** a formal **complaint** against her employer, alleging sexual harassment.* **3** [C] something that you complain about: *My only complaint is the high prices they charge.* **4** [C] a sickness that affects a part of your body

com·ple·ment¹ /'kɑmpləmənt/ *n.* [C] **1** someone or something that combines well with another thing, and brings out the good qualities in it: *The wine was the perfect **complement to** the meal.* **2** the number or quantity needed to make a group complete: *The school has its **full complement** of teachers.* **3** *technical* in grammar, a word or phrase that follows a verb and describes the subject of the verb. In the sentence "You look angry," "angry" is a complement.

com·ple·ment² /'kɑmplə,mɛnt/ *v.* [T] to combine well with another thing, and bring out the good qualities in it: *The colors really complement each other.* —**complementary** /,kɑmplə'mɛntri, -'mɛntəri/ *adj.*: *complementary colors*

com·plete¹ /kəm'plit/ *adj.* **1** something that is complete has all the parts it should have: *a complete set of china* | *the **complete works** of Shakespeare* | *The list of guests is not complete.* **2** [only before noun] *informal* used in order to emphasize that a quality or situation is as great as it could possibly be: *I made a **complete fool** of myself.* | *The meeting was a **complete waste of time**.* | *The news came as a **complete surprise**.* **3** finished: *Our research is nearly complete.*

THESAURUS

done, finished, over, through
→ see Thesaurus box at DONE²

4 complete with sth having particular equipment or features: *The house **comes complete with** a swimming pool.* —**completeness** *n.* [U]

complete² *v.* [T] **1** to finish doing or making something: *The book took five years to complete.* **2** to make something whole or perfect by adding what is missing: *I need one more stamp to complete my collection.* **3** to write the information that is needed on a form: *65 people completed the questionnaire.*

com·plete·ly /kəm'plit˺li/ *adv.* in every way – used for emphasis: *I completely forgot about her birthday.*

THESAURUS

absolutely – used especially to emphasize something, or to show that you strongly agree with something: *I was absolutely exhausted.* | *He's absolutely right.*
totally – used especially to show that you are annoyed about something or strongly disagree with something: *She totally ignored me.* | *The price was totally ridiculous.*
entirely – used especially in negative sentences or after "almost": *I'm not entirely sure.* | *The class was almost entirely girls.*
utterly *formal* – used to emphasize something, especially a negative quality: *The game seemed utterly pointless.*

com·ple·tion /kəm'pliʃən/ *n.* [U] the state of being finished, or the act of finishing something: *The construction is **nearing completion**.* | *the **completion of** the $80 million project*

com·plex¹ /kəm'plɛks, kɑm-, 'kɑmplɛks/ *adj.* something that is complex has a lot of different parts and is difficult to understand or deal with: ***complex systems** of irrigation* | *a **complex issue*** —**complexity** /kəm'plɛksəṭi/ *n.* [U]

com·plex² /'kɑmplɛks/ *n.* [C] **1** a group of buildings or one large building used for a particular purpose: *a new shopping complex* **2** an emotional problem in which someone is too anxious about something or thinks too much about it: *Linda has a **complex about** her appearance.*

com·plex·ion /kəm'plɛkʃən/ *n.* [C] the natural color and appearance of the skin on your face: *a young woman with a **pale/dark complexion***

com·pli·ance /kəm'plaɪəns/ *n.* [U] *formal* the act of obeying a rule or law: ***Compliance with** the law is expected of everyone.*

com·pli·ant /kəm'plaɪənt/ *adj.* willing to obey or agree to other people's wishes and demands

com·pli·cate /'kɑmplə,keɪt/ *v.* [T] to make a problem or situation more difficult [≠ **simplify**]: *There may be other factors, but let's not **complicate matters** right now.*

com·pli·cat·ed /ˈkɑmpləˌkeɪt̬ɪd/ *adj.* difficult to understand or deal with [≠ **simple**]: *The instructions are much too complicated.* | *an extremely complicated process*

com·pli·ca·tion /ˌkɑmpləˈkeɪʃən/ *n.* **1** [C usually plural] a medical problem or illness that happens while someone is already sick: *There were no complications following surgery.* **2** [C,U] a problem or situation that makes something more difficult to understand or deal with: *The drop in student numbers added further complications.*

com·plic·i·ty /kəmˈplɪsət̬i/ *n.* [U] *formal* the act of being involved in a crime with other people

C

com·pli·ment¹ /ˈkɑmpləmənt/ *n.* **1** [C] something you say that shows you admire someone or something: *"You look great." "Thanks for the compliment."* | *I was trying to **pay** her **a compliment*** (=give her a compliment). | *I wasn't sure exactly what they meant, but I **took it as a compliment*** (=accepted what was said as a compliment rather than an insult). **2 with the compliments of sb/with sb's compliments** *formal* used by a person or company when he, she, or it sends or gives something to you: *Please accept these tickets with our compliments.*

com·pli·ment² /ˈkɑmpləˌmɛnt/ *v.* [T] to say something nice to someone in order to praise him/her: *They **complimented** John **on** his excellent French.*

THESAURUS

praise, **congratulate**, **flatter**, **pay sb a compliment**
➔ see Thesaurus box at PRAISE¹

com·pli·men·ta·ry /ˌkɑmpləˈmɛntri, -ˈmɛntəri/ *adj.* **1** saying that you admire or respect someone or something: *He was very **complimentary about** your work.* **2** given free to someone: *complimentary tickets*

com·ply /kəmˈplaɪ/ *v.* past tense and past participle **complied**, third person singular **complies** [I] *formal* to do what you are asked to do or what a law or rule tells you to do: *Those who fail to **comply with** the law will be fined.*

com·po·nent /kəmˈpoʊnənt/ *n.* [C] one of several parts that make up a whole machine or system: *stereo components*

com·pose /kəmˈpoʊz/ *v.* **1 be composed of sth** to be formed from a number of substances, parts, or people: *Water is composed of hydrogen and oxygen.* **2** [T] to write a piece of music: *Schumann was better at composing music than playing it.* **3 compose yourself** to become calm after feeling angry, upset, or excited: *Lynn took a deep breath and tried to compose herself.* **4 compose a letter/poem/speech etc.** to write a letter, poem, etc., thinking very carefully about it as you write it

com·posed /kəmˈpoʊzd/ *adj.* calm, rather than upset or angry

com·pos·er /kəmˈpoʊzɚ/ *n.* [C] someone who writes music

com·pos·ite /kəmˈpɑzɪt/ *adj.* made up of different parts or materials: *a composite drawing* —**composite** *n.* [C]

com·po·si·tion /ˌkɑmpəˈzɪʃən/ *n.* **1** [U] the way in which something is made up of different parts, things, or people: *the chemical **composition of** soil* **2 a)** [U] the art or process of writing music, a poem, or an ESSAY, etc. **b)** [C] a piece of music, or art, or a poem: *one of Beethoven's early compositions*

THESAURUS

music, **tune**, **melody**, **song**, **arrangement**, **number**
➔ see Thesaurus box at MUSIC

3 [U] the way in which the different parts of a painting or photograph are arranged **4** [C,U] a short piece of writing about a particular subject that is done by a student [= **essay**]

com·post /ˈkɑmpoʊst/ *n.* [U] a mixture of decayed leaves, plants, etc. used for improving the quality of soil

com·po·sure /kəmˈpoʊʒɚ/ *n.* [singular, U] a calm feeling that you have when you feel confident about dealing with a situation: *She stopped crying and **regained** her **composure**.*

com·pound¹ /ˈkɑmpaʊnd/ *n.* [C] **1** a chemical compound is a substance that consists of two or more different substances

THESAURUS

mixture, **combination**, **blend**, **solution**
➔ see Thesaurus box at MIXTURE

2 an area that contains a group of buildings and is surrounded by a fence or wall: *a prison compound* **3** *technical* **also compound noun/adjective/verb** two or more words that are used together as a noun, adjective, or verb. For example, the noun "ice cream" is a compound

com·pound² /kəmˈpaʊnd/ *v.* [T] to make a difficult situation worse by adding more problems: *Our difficulties were **compounded by** other people's mistakes.*

ˌcompound ˈinterest *n.* [U] INTEREST that is calculated on both the sum of money lent or borrowed and on the unpaid interest already earned or charged [➡ **simple interest**]

com·pre·hend /ˌkɑmprɪˈhɛnd/ *v.* [I,T] *formal* to understand something: *I did not **fully comprehend** what had happened.*

com·pre·hen·si·ble /ˌkɑmprɪˈhɛnsəbəl/ *adj.* easy to understand [≠ **incomprehensible**]: *language that is **comprehensible to** the average reader*

com·pre·hen·sion /ˌkɑmprɪˈhɛnʃən/ *n.* [U] the ability to understand something, or knowledge about something: *The whole situation is **beyond** my **comprehension*** (=impossible for me to understand). | *a test of **reading/listening comprehension*** (=a student's ability to understand written or spoken language)

com·pre·hen·sive /ˌkɑmprɪˈhɛnsɪv◂/ *adj.* including everything that is necessary: *comprehensive health insurance*

com·press /kəmˈprɛs/ *v.* **1** [I,T] to press something or make it smaller so that it takes up less space: *This program compresses computer files so they can be easily sent by email.* **2** [T] to reduce the amount of time it takes for something to happen or be done —**compression** /kəmˈprɛʃən/ *n.* [U]

com·prise /kəmˈpraɪz/ *v. formal* **1** [linking verb] to consist of particular parts: *The World Trade Organization comprises more than 100 nations.* | *The committee **is comprised of** eight members.*

THESAURUS

Comprise, **be composed of**, and **consist of** can each be used in order to talk about the parts that things are made of, or the things that something contains. Comprise is the more formal word.
Each of the following sentences means the same thing, but the patterns are different: *The United States comprises 50 states.* | *The United States is composed of 50 states.* | *The United States consists of 50 states.*

2 [T] to form part of a larger group: *Women comprise over 75% of our staff.*

com·pro·mise¹ /ˈkɑmprəˌmaɪz/ *n.* [C,U] an agreement that is achieved after everyone involved accepts less than what s/he wanted at first: *The President and Congress are attempting to **reach a compromise**.* | *Neither of them was willing to **make compromises**.*

compromise² *v.* **1** [I] to end an argument by making an agreement in which everyone involved accepts less than what s/he wanted at first: *The President is not willing to **compromise on** the issue.* **2** [T] to risk harming or damaging something that is important: *The safety of employees had been compromised.*

com·pro·mis·ing /ˈkɑmprəˌmaɪzɪŋ/ *adj.* making it seem that someone has done something dishonest or wrong: *a compromising photograph*

comp time /ˈkɑmp ˌtaɪm/ *n.* [U] vacation time that you are given instead of money because you have worked more hours than you should have

com·pul·sion /kəmˈpʌlʃən/ *n.* **1** [C] a strong desire to do something that is wrong: *Drinking is a compulsion with her.* **2** [singular, U] the act of forcing or influencing someone to do something that s/he does not want to do: *You are **under** no **compulsion to** sign the agreement.*

com·pul·sive /kəmˈpʌlsɪv/ *adj.* **1** compulsive behavior is very difficult to stop or control: *compulsive eating* **2 compulsive liar/gambler etc.** someone who has a strong desire to lie, GAMBLE, etc. which s/he cannot control —**compulsively** *adv.*

com·pul·so·ry /kəmˈpʌlsəri/ *adj.* if something is compulsory, it must be done because of a rule or law [≠ **voluntary**]: *compulsory military service*

THESAURUS

necessary, **essential**, **vital**, **mandatory**
➔ see Thesaurus box at NECESSARY

com·punc·tion /kəmˈpʌŋkʃən/ *n.* **have/feel no compunction about (doing) sth** *formal* to not feel guilty or sorry about something although other people may think that it is wrong: *He seemed to feel no compunction about lying to us.*

C

com·pute /kəmˈpyut/ *v.* [I,T] *formal* to calculate an answer, total, result, etc.: *The machine can compute the time it takes a sound wave to bounce back.* —**computation** /ˌkɑmpyəˈteɪʃən/ *n.* [C,U]

com·put·er /kəmˈpyuṭɚ/ *n.* [C] an electronic machine that stores information and uses programs to help you find, organize, or change the information [➡ **laptop, PC**]: *We do all our work **on computer**.* | *Our office has switched to a different **computer system**.* | *the latest **computer software***

TOPIC

You **start up/boot up a computer** and **log in/on** in order to start using it.
People use computers to do a lot of different things, such as send and receive **e-mails**, look for information on **the Internet**, and work on **files** or other **documents**.
You need to **open a file** before you can work on it. When you have finished, you **save** your **work/file**, **close** the **document** or **file** that you were working on, and **shut down** the computer.
If your computer **crashes**, it suddenly stops working. You have to **reboot** or **restart** the computer to make it start working again.
➔ see Topic box at OFFICE

➔ see picture on page A11

com·put·er·ize /kəmˈpyuṭəˌraɪz/ *v.* [T] to use a computer to control the way something is done, to store information, etc.: *plans to computerize all our financial records* —**computerization** /kəmˌpyuṭərəˈzeɪʃən/ *n.* [U]

comˌputer ˈliterate *adj.* able to use a computer —**computer literacy** *n.* [U]

com·put·ing /kəmˈpyuṭɪŋ/ *n.* [U] the use of computers as a job, in a business, etc.: *personal computing*

com·rade /ˈkɑmræd/ *n.* [C] *formal* a friend, especially someone who is in the same army as you or who shares the same political aims as you —**comradeship** *n.* [U]

con¹ /kɑn/ *v.* past tense and past participle **conned**, present participle **conning** [T] *informal* to trick someone, either to take his/her money or to get him/her to do something: *That guy tried to* ***con*** *me* ***out of*** *$20.*

con² *n.* [C] **1** *informal* a trick to get someone's money or make someone do something: *The ads you see in the paper are just a con.* **2** *slang* a CONVICT → **pros and cons** at PRO

'con ˌartist *n.* [C] *informal* someone who tricks people in order to get money from them

con·cave /ˌkɑn'keɪv◂/ *adj. technical* curved inward like a bowl [≠ **convex**]: *a concave lens*

con·ceal /kən'sil/ *v.* [T] *formal* to hide something carefully: *She tried to* ***conceal*** *her emotions* ***from*** *Ted.* | *He was carrying a* ***concealed weapon.*** —**concealment** *n.* [U]

C

THESAURUS

hide, cover, cover up, disguise
→ see Thesaurus box at HIDE¹

con·cede /kən'sid/ *v.* **1** [T] to admit that something is true although you do not want to: *She reluctantly* ***conceded that*** *I was right.* **2** [I,T] to admit that you are not going to win a game, argument, battle, etc.: *Hawkins* ***conceded defeat*** *in the election.*

THESAURUS

surrender, give in, admit/accept defeat
→ see Thesaurus box at SURRENDER

3 [T] to let someone have something although you do not want to: *They have refused to* ***concede*** *any territory* ***to*** *the rebels.*

con·ceit /kən'sit/ *n.* [U] an attitude that shows that you are too proud of what you can do, how you look, etc.

con·ceit·ed /kən'siṭɪd/ *adj. disapproving* behaving in a way that shows that you are too proud of what you can do, how you look, etc.: *I don't want to seem conceited, but I know I'll win.*

THESAURUS

proud, big-headed, vain, arrogant
→ see Thesaurus box at PROUD

con·ceiv·a·ble /kən'sivəbəl/ *adj.* able to be believed or imagined [≠ **inconceivable**]: ***It is conceivable that*** *the experts could be wrong.* —**conceivably** *adv.*

con·ceive /kən'siv/ *v.* **1** [I,T] to imagine a situation or what something is like: *It is impossible to* ***conceive of*** *the size of the universe.* **2** [T] to think of a new idea or plan: *It was Dr. Salk who conceived the idea of a polio vaccine.* **3** [I,T] to become PREGNANT [➡ **conception**]: *Ben and Tracy are hoping to conceive a second child soon.*

con·cen·trate¹ /'kɑnsənˌtreɪt/ *v.* **1** [I] to think very carefully about something you are doing: *With all this noise, it's hard to concentrate.* **2 be concentrated in/on/at etc. sth** to be present in large numbers or amounts in a particular place: *Most of New Zealand's population is concentrated in the north island.*

concentrate on sth *phr. v.* to give most of your attention to one thing: *I want to concentrate on my career for a while before I have kids.*

concentrate² *n.* [C,U] a substance or liquid that has been made stronger by removing most of the water from it: *orange juice concentrate*

con·cen·trat·ed /'kɑnsənˌtreɪṭɪd/ *adj.* **1** showing a lot of determination or effort: *He made a concentrated effort to raise his grades.* **2** a substance that is concentrated has been made stronger by removing most of the water from it: *a concentrated detergent*

con·cen·tra·tion /ˌkɑnsən'treɪʃən/ *n.* **1** [U] the act of thinking very carefully about something that you are doing: *The children got tired and* ***lost*** *their* ***concentration.*** **2** [U] a process in which you put a lot of attention, energy, etc. into a particular activity: *There was too much* ***concentration on*** *one type of industry.* **3** [C,U] a large amount of something in a particular place: ***concentrations of*** *minerals in the water.*

ˌconcen'tration ˌcamp *n.* [C] a prison where large numbers of people are kept in very bad conditions, usually during a war

concentric

concentric circles

con·cen·tric /kən'sɛntrɪk/ *adj. technical* concentric circles are of different sizes and have the same center

con·cept /'kɑnsɛpt/ *n.* [C] an idea of how something is, or how something should be done: *the* ***concept of*** *universal human rights*

con·cep·tion /kən'sɛpʃən/ *n.* **1** [C] a general idea about what something is like, or a way of understanding what something is like: *One common* ***conception of*** *democracy is that it means "government by the people."* **2** [U] the process by which a woman or female animal becomes PREGNANT, or the time when this happens [➡ **conceive**]

con·cep·tu·al /kən'sɛptʃuəl/ *adj. formal* relating to CONCEPTS or based on them: *plans that are in the conceptual stage* —**conceptually** *adv.*

con·cern¹ /kən'sɚn/ *n.* **1** [C,U] a feeling of worry about something important, or the thing that worries you: *There is growing* ***concern about/over*** *ocean pollution.* | *There is* ***concern that*** *the war could continue for a long time.* | *The police officer said that there was* ***no cause for concern.*** **2** [C,U] something important that worries you or involves you: *The destruction of the rainforest is* ***of concern to*** *us all.* | *Our* ***main/primary/major concern*** *is safety.*

concern² *v.* [T] **1** to affect someone or involve him/her: *What we're planning doesn't concern you.* **2** to make someone feel worried or upset: *My daughter's problems at school concern me greatly.* **3** to be about something or someone: *Many of Woody Allen's movies concern life in New York.* **4 concern yourself (with sth)** to become involved in something that interests or worries you: *You don't need to concern yourself with this, Jan.*

con·cerned /kən'sɚnd/ *adj.* **1** [not before noun] involved in something or affected by it: *It was a shock for* ***all concerned*** (=everyone involved). | *Everyone* ***concerned with*** *the car industry will be interested.* **2** worried about something important: *We're* ***concerned about*** *the results of the test.* | *letters from concerned parents*

THESAURUS

worried, anxious, nervous, uneasy, stressed (out)
→ see Thesaurus box at WORRIED

3 believing that something is important: *They seem to be only* ***concerned with*** *making money.* **4 as far as sth is concerned** used in order to show which subject or thing you are talking about: *As far as money is concerned, the club is doing fairly well.* **5 as far as sb is concerned** used in order to show what someone's opinion on a subject is: *As far as I'm concerned, the whole idea is crazy.*

con·cern·ing /kən'sɚnɪŋ/ *prep. formal* about or relating to something: *We have questions concerning the report.*

THESAURUS

about, on, regarding, re
→ see Thesaurus box at ABOUT¹

con·cert /'kɑnsɚt/ *n.* [C] **1** a performance given by musicians or singers: *a rock concert* | *We* ***went to*** *a* ***concert*** *last night.* **2 in concert a)** playing or singing at a concert **b)** *formal* done together with someone else: *Police are working* ***in concert with*** *local authorities.*

con·cert·ed /kən'sɚtɪd/ *adj.* **a concerted effort/action/attempt etc.** something that is done by people working together in a determined way: *Libraries have* ***made*** *a* ***concerted effort*** *to attract young people.*

con·cer·to /kən'tʃɛrtoʊ/ *n.* plural **concertos** [C] a piece of CLASSICAL MUSIC, usually for one instrument and an ORCHESTRA

con·ces·sion /kən'sɛʃən/ *n.* [C] **1** something that you do in order to end an argument: *Neither side is willing to* ***make concessions*** *on the issue of pay.* **2** a special right given to someone by the government, an employer, etc.: *tax concessions for married people* **3** the right to have a business in a particular place, especially in a place owned by someone else

con'cession ˌstand *n.* [C] a small business that sells food, drinks, and other things at sports events, theaters, etc.

con·cierge /kɔn'syɛrʒ/ *n.* [C] someone in a hotel whose job is to help guests with problems, give advice about local places to go, etc.

con·cil·i·a·tion /kənˌsɪli'eɪʃən/ *n.* [U] *formal* the process of trying to end an argument between people

con·cil·i·a·to·ry /kən'sɪliəˌtɔri/ *adj. formal* intended to make someone stop being angry with you or with someone else: *a conciliatory remark*

con·cise /kən'saɪs/ *adj.* short and clear, without using too many words: *a concise answer* —**concisely** *adv.* —**conciseness** *n.* [U]

con·clude /kən'klud/ *v.* **1** [T] to decide something after considering all the information you have: *Doctors have* ***concluded that*** *sunburn can lead to skin cancer.* **2** [T] *formal* to complete something that you have been doing: *The study was concluded last month.* **3** [I,T] to end a meeting, speech, event, etc. by doing or saying one final thing, or to end in this way: *The carnival* ***concluded with*** *a fireworks display.* —**concluding** *adj.*: *concluding remarks*

con·clu·sion /kən'kluʒən/ *n.* [C] **1** something that you decide after considering all the information you have: *I've* ***come to*** *the* ***conclusion*** *that she's lying.* | *The appeal court* ***reached*** *the same* ***conclusion.*** | *It's hard to* ***draw*** *any* ***conclusions*** (=decide whether something is true) *without more data.* | *Megan, you're* ***jumping to conclusions*** (=deciding something is true without knowing all the facts). **2** the end or final part of something: *the* ***conclusion of*** *his essay* **3 in conclusion** *formal* used in speech or a piece of writing to show that you are about to finish: *In conclusion, I want to thank everyone who came out today.*

con·clu·sive /kən'klusɪv/ *adj.* proving that something is true: *There is no* ***conclusive evidence*** *connecting him with the crime.* —**conclusively** *adv.*

con·coct /kən'kɑkt/ *v.* [T] **1** to invent a false explanation or illegal plan: *She* ***concocted*** *a* ***story*** *about her mother being sick.* | *He* ***concocted*** *a* ***scheme*** *to rob the bank.* **2** to make something unusual by mixing different things together —**concoction** /kən'kɑkʃən/ *n.* [C]

con·course /'kɑŋkɔrs/ *n.* [C] a large hall or open place in an airport, train station, etc.

C

con·crete[1] /ˈkɑŋkrit/ *n.* [U] a substance used for building that is made by mixing sand, water, small stones, and CEMENT

con·crete[2] /kɑnˈkrit, ˈkɑŋkrit/ *adj.* **1** made of concrete: *a concrete floor* ➔ see picture at MATERIAL[1] **2** clearly based on facts, not on beliefs or guesses: *We need* ***concrete evidence*** *to prove that he did it.* —**concretely** *adv.*

con·cur /kənˈkɚ/ *v.* past tense and past participle **concurred**, present participle **concurring** [I] *formal* to agree with someone or have the same opinion: *Dr. Hastings* ***concurs with*** *the decision of the medical board.* —**concurrence** /kənˈkɚəns, -ˈkʌrəns/ *n.* [U]

C

con·cur·rent /kənˈkɚənt, -ˈkʌrənt/ *adj. formal* **1** existing or happening at the same time: *His work is being displayed in three concurrent art exhibitions.* **2** *formal* in agreement: *concurrent opinions* —**concurrently** *adv.*

con·cus·sion /kənˈkʌʃən/ *n.* [C,U] a small amount of damage to the brain that makes you become unconscious or feel sick, caused by hitting your head

con·demn /kənˈdɛm/ *v.* [T] **1** to say very strongly that you do not approve of someone or something: *Politicians were quick to condemn the bombing.* **2** to give a severe punishment to someone who is guilty of a crime: *The murderer was* ***condemned to death.*** **3** to force someone to live in an unpleasant way or to suffer: *families who are* ***condemned to*** *a life of poverty* **4** to say officially that a building is not safe enough to be lived in or used

con·dem·na·tion /ˌkɑndəmˈneɪʃən/ *n.* [C,U] an expression of very strong disapproval: *international* ***condemnation of*** *the war*

con·den·sa·tion /ˌkɑndənˈseɪʃən/ *n.* [U] small drops of water that appear when steam or hot air touches something that is cool, such as a window

con·dense /kənˈdɛns/ *v.* **1** [I,T] if gas or hot air condenses, it becomes a liquid as it becomes cooler **2** [T] to make a speech or piece of writing shorter by using fewer words to say the same thing **3** [T] to make a liquid thicker by removing some of the water from it: *condensed soup*

con·de·scend /ˌkɑndɪˈsɛnd/ *v.* [I] *disapproving* to behave as if you are better or more important than other people —**condescension** /ˌkɑndɪˈsɛnʃən/ *n.* [U]

con·de·scend·ing /ˌkɑndɪˈsɛndɪŋ◂/ *adj.* showing that you think you are better or more important than other people: *He gave us a condescending smile.*

con·di·ment /ˈkɑndəmənt/ *n.* [C] *formal* something such as KETCHUP or MUSTARD that you add to food when you are eating it in order to make it taste better

con·di·tion[1] /kənˈdɪʃən/ *n.* **1** [singular, U] the particular state that someone or something is in: *the miserable* ***condition of*** *the roads* | *The car is still* ***in*** *excellent* ***condition.*** | *He remained in* ***critical condition*** (=very sick or very badly injured) *at Emory University Hospital.* **2 conditions** [plural] the situation or environment in which someone lives or something happens: *Poor* ***working/living conditions*** *are part of their daily lives.* | ***Under*** *these* ***conditions*** *the plant will grow rapidly.* | *Schools closed early because of the bad* ***weather conditions.*** **3 be in no condition to do sth** to be too sick, drunk, or upset to be able to do something: *He is* ***in no condition to*** *drive.* **4** [C] an illness or health problem that affects you permanently or for a very long time: *She has a serious* ***heart condition.*** **5** [C] something that you must agree to or must happen before something else can happen: *The bank sets strict* ***conditions for*** *new loans.* | *Two employees agreed to speak* ***on condition that*** *they not be named.*

condition[2] *v.* [T] **1** to make a person or animal behave in a particular way by training him, her, or it over a period of time: *Pavlov* ***conditioned*** *the dogs* ***to*** *expect food at the sound of a bell.* **2** to put CONDITIONER on your hair when you wash it

con·di·tion·al /kənˈdɪʃənəl/ *adj.* **1** if an offer, agreement, etc. is conditional, it will only be done if something else happens: *Our buying the house is* ***conditional on*** *our loan approval.* **2** *technical* a conditional sentence is one that usually begins with "if" or "unless," and states something that must be true or must happen before something else can be true or happen

con·di·tion·er /kənˈdɪʃənɚ/ *n.* [C] a liquid that you put on your hair when you wash it in order to make it healthy and easy to comb

con·di·tion·ing /kənˈdɪʃənɪŋ/ *n.* [U] the process by which people or animals learn to behave in a particular way: *social conditioning*

con·do /ˈkɑndoʊ/ *n.* plural **condos** [C] *informal* a CONDOMINIUM ➔ see Thesaurus box at HOUSE[1]

con·do·lence /kənˈdoʊləns/ *n.* [C usually plural, U] sympathy for someone when someone s/he loves has died: *Please* ***offer*** *my* ***condolences*** *to your mother.*

con·dom /ˈkɑndəm/ *n.* [C] a thin piece of rubber that a man wears over his PENIS during sex to prevent a woman from becoming PREGNANT, or to protect against disease

con·do·min·i·um /ˌkɑndəˈmɪniəm/ *n.* [C] a building that consists of separate apartments, each of which is owned by the people living in it, or one of these apartments

THESAURUS

house, ranch house/ranch, cottage, row house, mansion, bungalow, duplex, apartment, condo, townhouse, mobile home/trailer

➔ see Thesaurus box at HOUSE[1]

con·done /kən'doʊn/ *v.* [T] to accept or allow behavior that most people think is wrong: *I cannot condone the use of violence.*

con·du·cive /kən'dusɪv/ *adj.* **be conducive to sth** *formal* to provide conditions that make it easier to do something: *The sunny climate is conducive to outdoor activities.*

con·duct¹ /kən'dʌkt/ *v.* **1** [T] to do something in an organized way, especially in order to get information or prove facts: *The District Attorney's office is* ***conducting*** *the* ***investigation****.* | *I don't think it's right to* ***conduct experiments/tests*** *on animals.* **2** [I,T] to stand in front of a group of musicians or singers and direct their playing or singing: *the Boston Pops Orchestra,* ***conducted by*** *John Williams.* **3** [T] if something conducts electricity or heat, it allows the electricity or heat to travel along or through it **4 conduct yourself** *formal* to behave in a particular way: *He conducted himself well in the job interview.*

con·duct² /'kɑndʌkt, -dəkt/ *n.* [U] *formal* **1** the way someone behaves: *standards of professional conduct*

> **THESAURUS**
> **behavior, manner, demeanor**
> → see Thesaurus box at BEHAVIOR

2 the way a business or activity is organized and done

con·duc·tor /kən'dʌktɚ/ *n.* [C] **1** someone who CONDUCTS a group of musicians or singers → see Topic box at ORCHESTRA **2** someone who is in charge of a train or the workers on it

cone /koʊn/ *n.* [C] **1** a hollow or solid object with a round base and a point at the top: *an orange traffic cone* **2** → ICE CREAM CONE **3** the hard brown woody fruit of a PINE or FIR tree → see picture at PLANT¹

con·fed·er·a·cy /kən'fɛdərəsi/ *n.* plural **confederacies** [C] **1 the Confederacy** the southern states that fought against northern states in the American Civil War **2** a confederation —**confederate** /kən'fɛdərɪt/ *adj.*

con·fed·er·ate /kən'fɛdərɪt/ *n.* [C] a soldier in the Confederacy

con·fed·e·ra·tion /kən,fɛdə'reɪʃən/ *n.* [C] a group of people, political parties, or organizations that have united in order to achieve an aim

con·fer /kən'fɚ/ *v.* past tense and past participle **conferred**, present participle **conferring** **1** [I] to discuss something with other people so everyone can give his/her opinion: *You may want to* ***confer with*** *the other team members.* **2 confer a degree/honor etc. on sb** to officially give someone a degree, etc.

con·ference /'kɑnfrəns/ *n.* [C,U] **1** a private meeting in which a few people discuss something: *We're* ***having*** *parent-teacher* ***conferences*** *at my kids' school this week.* | *The meeting will be held in the second floor* ***conference room****.* **2** a large formal meeting, often lasting for several days, at which members of an organization, profession, etc. discuss things related to their work: *a sales conference* | *The American Medical Association is sponsoring a* ***conference on*** *men's health.*

> **THESAURUS**
> **discussion, negotiations, debate, talks**
> → see Thesaurus box at DISCUSSION

3 a group of teams that play against each other in a LEAGUE

'conference ,call *n.* [C] a telephone conversation in which several people in different places can all talk to each other

C

con·fess /kən'fɛs/ *v.* [I,T] **1** to admit that you have done something wrong or illegal: *It didn't take long for her to confess.* | *He has* ***confessed to*** *the crime.* **2** to admit something that you feel embarrassed about: *I* ***confessed that*** *I hadn't understood.* **3** to tell a priest or God about the bad things you have done —**confessed** *adj.*

con·fes·sion /kən'fɛʃən/ *n.* **1** [C] a statement that you have done something wrong or illegal: *He* ***made a*** *full* ***confession*** *at the police station.* **2** [C,U] the act of telling a priest or God about the bad things you have done

con·fet·ti /kən'fɛti/ *n.* [U] small pieces of colored paper thrown into the air at a wedding, party, etc.

confetti

con·fi·dant /'kɑnfə,dɑnt/ *n.* [C] someone to whom you tell secrets or personal information

con·fi·dante /'kɑnfə,dɑnt/ *n.* [C] a woman to whom you tell secrets or personal information

con·fide /kən'faɪd/ *v.* [T] to tell someone about personal things that you do not want other people to know: *He had* ***confided to*** *friends that he was unhappy.*

confide in sb *phr. v.* to tell someone about something that is very private or secret because you feel you can trust him or her: *I've never been able to confide in my sister.*

con·fi·dence /'kɑnfədəns/ *n.* **1** [U] the feeling that you can trust someone or something to be good or successful: *Public* ***confidence in*** *the economy is at an all-time low.* | *We* ***have*** *complete* ***confidence*** *in your ability to handle the situation.* | *Employees are* ***losing confidence*** *in the company.* **2** [U] belief in your ability to do things well: *I didn't* ***have*** *any* ***confidence in*** *myself.* | *Her* ***lack of confidence*** *showed.* | *Living in another country* ***gave*** *me more* ***confidence****.*

3 gain/win/earn sb's confidence if you gain someone's confidence, s/he begins to trust you: *Gradually, the new manager began to win the employees' confidence.* **4** [U] the feeling that something is definite or true: *I **have confidence (that)** the dispute will be settled before long.* **5 in confidence** if you say something in confidence, you tell someone something and trust him or her not to tell anyone else **6** [C] a secret, or a piece of information that is private or personal

con·fi·dent /'kɑnfədənt/ *adj.* **1** sure that you have the ability to do things well or deal with situations successfully [≠ **insecure**]: *She **feels** very **confident about** her ability to do the work.* | *a **confident voice/smile/manner*** **2** [not before noun] sure that something will happen in the way you want or expect: *I'm **confident (that)** he'll help us out.* | *He was **confident of** winning the election.* —**confidently** *adv.*

C

con·fi·den·tial /ˌkɑnfə'dɛnʃəl/ *adj.* secret and not intended to be shown or told to other people: *confidential information* —**confidentially** *adv.* —**confidentiality** /ˌkɑnfədɛnʃi'æləṭi/ *n.* [U]

con·fig·u·ra·tion /kənˌfɪgyə'reɪʃən/ *n.* [C] the way in which parts of something are arranged or formed into a particular shape: *a star-shaped configuration*

con·fine /kən'faɪn/ *v.* [T] **1** to stop something bad from spreading to another place: *The fire was **confined to** one building.* **2** to have to stay in a place, especially because you are sick: *Rachel is **confined to bed**.* **3** to keep someone or something within the limits of a particular subject or activity: *Try to **confine yourself to** spending $120 a week.* | *We **confined** our research **to** young people.* **4** to keep someone in a place s/he cannot leave, such as a prison

con·fined /kən'faɪnd/ *adj.* a confined space or area is very small: *It wasn't easy to sleep in such a confined space.*

con·fine·ment /kən'faɪnmənt/ *n.* [U] the act of forcing someone to stay in a room, prison, etc., or the state of being there [➡ **solitary confinement**]

con·fines /'kɑnfaɪnz/ *n.* [plural] the walls, limits, or borders of something: *His son has only seen him **within the confines of** the prison.*

con·firm /kən'fɚm/ *v.* [T] **1** to say or prove that something is definitely true: *Blood tests confirmed the diagnosis.* | *Can you **confirm that** she really was there?* | *The article **confirms what** many experts have been saying for years.*

> **THESAURUS**
> **check, make sure, double-check, check out**
> ➔ see Thesaurus box at CHECK[1]

2 to tell someone that a possible plan, arrangement, etc. is now definite: *Please confirm your reservations 72 hours in advance.*

con·fir·ma·tion /ˌkɑnfɚ'meɪʃən/ *n.* [C,U] a statement or letter that says that something is definitely true, or the act of stating this: *We're waiting for **confirmation of** the report.*

con·firmed /kən'fɚmd/ *adj.* **a confirmed bachelor/alcoholic etc.** someone who seems unlikely to change the way of life s/he has chosen

con·fis·cate /'kɑnfəˌskeɪt/ *v.* [T] to officially take something away from someone: *Customs officers confiscated his passport.* —**confiscation** /ˌkɑnfə'skeɪʃən/ *n.* [C,U]

con·flict[1] /'kɑnˌflɪkt/ *n.* **1** [C,U] angry disagreement between people, groups, countries, etc.: *a **conflict between** father and son* | ***conflicts over** land* | *The two groups have been **in conflict with** each other for years.* **2** [C,U] fighting or a war: ***Armed conflict** might be unavoidable.* | *efforts to **resolve** the **conflict***

> **THESAURUS**
> **war, warfare, fighting, combat, action, hostilities**
> ➔ see Thesaurus box at WAR

3 [C,U] a situation in which you have to choose between opposing things: *a **conflict between** the demands of one's work and one's family* **4** [C] something that you have to do at the same time that someone wants you to do something else: *Sorry – I **have a conflict** Friday. Can we do it on Monday?* **5 conflict of interest(s)** a situation in which you cannot do your job fairly because you are personally affected by the decisions you make: *She sold her shares in the company to avoid any conflict of interest.*

con·flict[2] /kən'flɪkt/ *v.* [I] if two ideas, beliefs, opinions, etc. conflict, they cannot both be true: *That **conflicts with** what she said yesterday.* | *We have heard many **conflicting opinions** on the subject.*

con·form /kən'fɔrm/ *v.* [I] **1** to behave in the way that most people behave: *There's always pressure on kids to conform.* **2** to obey a law, rule, etc.: *Seatbelts must **conform to** safety standards.* —**conformity** /kən'fɔrməṭi/ *n.* [U]

con·form·ist /kən'fɔrmɪst/ *n.* [C] someone who behaves or thinks like everyone else because s/he does not want to be different [≠ **nonconformist**]

con·found /kən'faʊnd/ *v.* [T] to confuse and surprise people by not being what they expected: *Her amazing recovery has confounded doctors.*

con·front /kən'frʌnt/ *v.* [T] **1** if you are confronted with a problem, difficulty, etc., it appears and needs to be dealt with: *The new government has been confronted with numerous problems.* **2** to try to make someone admit s/he has done something wrong, especially by showing him/her proof: *I'm afraid to **confront** her **about** her* *drinking.* **3** to deal with something difficult or bad in a brave and determined way: *Sooner or later you'll have to* ***confront*** *your* ***problems.*** **4** to stand in front of someone, as though you are going to attack him/her: *She was confronted by two men.*

con·fron·ta·tion /ˌkɑnfrən'teɪʃən/ *n.* [C,U] an argument or fight: ***confrontations between*** *police and protesters*

con·fuse /kən'fyuz/ *v.* [T] **1** to make someone feel that s/he is unable to think clearly or understand something: *His directions really confused me.* **2** to think wrongly that a person or thing is someone or something else: *It's easy to* ***confuse*** *Sue* ***with*** *her sister.* **3** to make something more complicated or difficult to understand: *His questions were just* ***confusing*** *the* ***issue.***

con·fused /kən'fyuzd/ *adj.* **1** unable to understand clearly what someone is saying or what is happening: *I'm totally confused.* | *I'm still* ***confused about*** *what happened.* **2** complicated and difficult to understand: *confused feelings*

con·fus·ing /kən'fyuzɪŋ/ *adj.* difficult to understand: *The diagram is really confusing.*

con·fu·sion /kən'fyuʒən/ *n.* **1** [U] a state of not understanding what is happening or what something means: *There's a lot of* ***confusion about/over*** *the new rules.* | *The changes in the schedule have* ***created confusion.*** **2** [U] a situation in which you wrongly think that a person or thing is someone or something else: *To* ***avoid confusion****, the teams wore different colors.* **3** [singular, U] a very confusing situation, usually with a lot of noise and action: *With all* ***the confusion*** *nobody noticed the two boys leave.* | *The country is in a* ***state of confusion.***

con·geal /kən'dʒil/ *v.* [I] if a liquid such as blood congeals, it becomes thick or solid

con·ge·nial /kən'dʒinyəl/ *adj. formal* pleasant in a way that makes you feel comfortable and relaxed: *a congenial atmosphere*

con·gen·i·tal /kən'dʒɛnətl/ *adj. technical* **1** a congenital medical condition or disease affects someone from the time s/he is born: *a congenital heart problem* **2** [only before noun] a congenital quality is one that has always been part of your character and is unlikely to change: *He's a* ***congenital liar.***

con·gest·ed /kən'dʒɛstɪd/ *adj.* **1** too full or blocked because of too many vehicles or people: *congested freeways* **2** a congested nose, chest, etc. is filled with thick liquid that does not flow easily —**congestion** /kən'dʒɛstʃən/ *n.* [U]

con·glom·er·ate /kən'glɑmərɪt/ *n.* [C] a large company made up of many different smaller companies

con·glom·er·a·tion /kənˌglɑmə'reɪʃən/ *n.* [C] *formal* a group of many different things or people gathered together

con·grat·u·late /kən'grætʃəˌleɪt/ *v.* [T] to tell someone that you are happy because s/he has achieved something, or because something good has happened to him/her: *I want to* ***congratulate*** *you* ***on*** *a fine achievement.* —**congratulatory** /kən'grætʃələˌtɔri/ *adj.*

> **THESAURUS**
>
> **praise**, **flatter**, **compliment**, **pay sb a compliment**
>
> ➔ see Thesaurus box at PRAISE[1]

con·grat·u·la·tions /kənˌgrætʃə'leɪʃənz/ *n.* [plural] used in order to CONGRATULATE someone: *You won? Congratulations!* | ***Congratulations on*** *your engagement!* | ***Congratulations to*** *all the winners.*

con·gre·gate /'kɑŋgrəˌgeɪt/ *v.* [I] to come together in a group: *A group of protesters had congregated outside.*

con·gre·ga·tion /ˌkɑŋgrə'geɪʃən/ *n.* [C] a group of people gathered in a church for a religious service, or the people who usually go to a particular church

con·gress /'kɑŋgrɪs/ *n.* [C] **1 Congress** the group of people elected to make laws for the U.S., consisting of the Senate and the House of Representatives: *The bill has been approved by both houses of Congress.* | *an act of Congress* **2** a formal meeting in which representatives of different groups, countries, etc. exchange information and make decisions —**congressional** /kəŋ'grɛʃənəl/ *adj.*

con·gress·man /'kɑŋgrɪsmən/ *n.* plural **congressmen** /-mən/ [C] a man who is elected to be in Congress

> **THESAURUS**
>
> **politician**, **president**, **congresswoman**, **senator**, **governor**, **mayor**
>
> ➔ see Thesaurus box at POLITICIAN

con·gress·wom·an /'kɑŋgrɪsˌwʊmən/ *n.* plural **congresswomen** /-ˌwɪmɪn/ [C] a woman who is elected to be in Congress

con·i·cal /'kɑnɪkəl/ *adj.* shaped like a CONE, or relating to cones

con·i·fer /'kɑnəfə/ *n.* [C] a tree that keeps its leaves in winter and has CONES containing its seeds —**coniferous** /kə'nɪfərəs, koʊ-/ *adj.*

con·jec·ture /kən'dʒɛktʃə/ *n.* [C,U] *formal* the act of forming ideas about something when you do not have enough information to base them on: *The report is based purely on conjecture.* —**conjecture** *v.* [I,T]

con·ju·gal /'kɑndʒəgəl/ *adj. formal* [only before noun] relating to marriage or married people

con·ju·gate /'kɑndʒəˌgeɪt/ *v.* [T] *technical* to state the different forms that a verb can have —**conjugation** /ˌkɑndʒə'geɪʃən/ *n.* [C,U]

con·junc·tion /kən'dʒʌŋkʃən/ *n.* [C] **1 in conjunction with sb/sth** working, happening, or being used with someone or something else: *The* *worksheets should be used in conjunction with the video.* **2** *technical* a word such as "but," "and," or "while" that connects parts of sentences, phrases, or CLAUSES

con·jure /ˈkɑndʒɚ/ *v.* [I,T] to perform tricks in which you seem to make things appear, disappear, or change as if by magic —**conjurer, conjuror** *n.* [C]

conjure sth ⇔ **up** *phr. v.* **1** make an image, idea, memory, etc. very clear and strong in someone's mind: *Smells can often conjure up memories.* **2** to make, get, or achieve something, as if by magic

C

con·man /ˈkɑnˌmæn/ *n.* plural **conmen** /-ˌmɛn/ [C] *informal* someone who gets money or valuable things from people by tricking them

con·nect /kəˈnɛkt/ *v.* **1** [T] to join two or more things together [≠ **disconnect**]: ***Connect** the speakers **to** the stereo.* **2** [T] to realize or show that a fact, event, person, etc. is related to or involved in something: *There is little evidence to **connect** him **with** the crime.* **3** [T] to attach something to a supply of electricity, gas, or water, or to a computer or telephone network [≠ **disconnect**]: *Has the phone been connected yet?* | *Click here to **connect to** the Internet.* ➔ see Topic box at INTERNET **4** [I] if an airplane, train, etc. connects with another one, it arrives just before the other one leaves so you can change from one to the other: *a **connecting flight** to Omaha* **5** [I] *informal* if people connect, they feel that they like and understand each other: *I really felt I **connected with** Jim's parents.*

con·nect·ed /kəˈnɛktɪd/ *adj.* **1** if two facts, events, people, etc. are connected, there is some kind of relationship between them: *problems **connected with** drug abuse* **2** joined to something else: *The computer is **connected to** a printer* **3 well-connected** having important or powerful friends or relatives: *a wealthy and well-connected lawyer*

con·nec·tion /kəˈnɛkʃən/ *n.* **1** [C,U] a relationship between things, people, ideas, etc.: *the **connection between** smoking and lung disease* | *Does this have any **connection with/to** our project?* **2** [C] a piece of wire or metal joining two parts of a machine together or to an electrical system: *There must be a **loose connection** – I'm not getting any power.* **3** [C,U] the process of joining together two or more things: *free Internet connection* **4** [C] an airplane, bus, or train that leaves at a time that allows passengers from an earlier airplane, bus, or train to use it to continue their trip: *I **missed** my **connection**.* **5 in connection with sth** concerning something: *Police are questioning a man in connection with the crime.* **6 connections** [plural] people you know who can help you, especially because they are in positions of power: *He has connections in high places.*

con·nive /kəˈnaɪv/ *v.* [I] to plan something secretly, especially something that is wrong or illegal: *Together, they **connived to** deceive her.* —**connivance** *n.* [C,U]

con·nois·seur /ˌkɑnəˈsɚ, -ˈsʊr/ *n.* [C] someone who knows a lot about something such as art, food, or music: *a **connoisseur of** fine wines*

> **THESAURUS**
>
> **expert, specialist, authority**
> ➔ see Thesaurus box at EXPERT

con·no·ta·tion /ˌkɑnəˈteɪʃən/ *n.* [C] an idea or a feeling that a word makes you think of, in addition to its basic meaning: *The word "liberal" has **negative connotations** these days.* —**connote** /kəˈnoʊt/ *v.* [T]

con·quer /ˈkɑŋkɚ/ *v.* **1** [I,T] to get control of land or people by force: *Egypt was conquered by the Ottoman Empire in 1517.* **2** [T] to succeed in controlling a strong feeling or solving a serious problem that you have: *I didn't think I'd ever conquer my fear of heights.* —**conqueror** *n.* [C]

con·quest /ˈkɑŋkwɛst/ *n.* [singular, U] the act of getting control of land or people by force: *the Spanish **conquest of** Central America*

con·science /ˈkɑnʃəns/ *n.* [U] **1** the set of feelings that tell you whether what you are doing is morally right or wrong: *He had a **guilty conscience*** (=feeling of guilt). | *At least my **conscience is clear*** (=I know I have done nothing wrong).

> **THESAURUS**
>
> **guilt, shame, remorse**
> ➔ see Thesaurus box at GUILT

2 on sb's conscience making you feel guilty: *I lied and it's always going to be on my conscience.*

con·sci·en·tious /ˌkɑnʃiˈɛnʃəs◂/ *adj.* careful to do everything that it is your job or duty to do: *a conscientious teacher*

ˌconscientious obˈjector *n.* [C] someone who refuses to fight in a war because of his/her moral beliefs

con·scious /ˈkɑnʃəs/ *adj.* **1** [not before noun] noticing or realizing something [= **aware**]: *I became **conscious of** the fact that someone was watching me.* **2** awake and able to understand what is happening [≠ **unconscious**]: *Owen was still conscious when they arrived at the hospital.* **3 conscious effort/decision/attempt etc.** a deliberate effort, decision, etc.: *Vivian had made a conscious effort to be friendly.* **4** thinking that something is very important: *fashion-conscious teenagers* | *She's very **conscious of** safety.* —**consciously** *adv.*

con·scious·ness /ˈkɑnʃəsnɪs/ *n.* [U] **1** the condition of being awake and understanding what is happening: *Charlie fell down the stairs and **lost consciousness**.* | *It was two weeks before he **regained consciousness**.* **2** [U] someone's mind, thoughts, and ideas: *research into human* *consciousness* **3** the state of knowing that something exists or is true [= **awareness**]: *The march is intended to* ***raise*** *people's* ***consciousness*** *about women's health issues.*

con·script /kən'skrɪpt/ *v.* [T] *formal* to make someone join the army, navy, etc. —**conscription** /kən'skrɪpʃən/ *n.* [U]

con·se·crate /'kɑnsəˌkreɪt/ *v.* [T] to make something holy by performing a religious ceremony —**consecration** /ˌkɑnsə'kreɪʃən/ *n.* [U]

con·sec·u·tive /kən'sɛkyət̬ɪv/ *adj.* consecutive numbers or periods of time happen one after the other: *It rained for three consecutive days.* —**consecutively** *adv.*

con·sen·su·al /kən'sɛnʃuəl/ *adj.* giving your permission for something or agreeing to something

con·sen·sus /kən'sɛnsəs/ *n.* [singular, U] an agreement that everyone in a group reaches: *We failed to* ***reach a consensus*** *on the issue.*

con·sent[1] /kən'sɛnt/ *n.* [U] permission to do something: *parental consent* | *He took the car* ***without*** *my* ***consent***.

consent[2] *v.* [I] *formal* to give your permission for something to happen: *He had not* ***consented to*** *medical treatment.*

con·se·quence /'kɑnsəˌkwɛns, -kwəns/ *n.* [C] **1** something that happens as a result of a particular action: *She never thinks about the* ***consequences of*** *her actions.* | *He broke the law, and now he must* ***face the consequences*** (=accept the bad results of his actions). | *He died* ***as a consequence of*** *injuries he received in the accident.* **2 of little/no consequence** *formal* not important: *a matter of little consequence*

con·se·quent /'kɑnsəˌkwɛnt, -kwənt/ *adj.* [only before noun] *formal* happening as a result of something: *racial prejudice and its consequent violence*

con·se·quent·ly /'kɑnsəˌkwɛntli, -kwənt-/ *adv.* as a result: *He did no work and consequently failed the exam.*

con·ser·va·tion /ˌkɑnsɚ'veɪʃən/ *n.* [U] **1** the protection of natural things such as animals, plants, forests, etc.: *the* ***conservation of*** *wildlife* **2** the controlled use of a limited amount of water, gas, electricity, etc. to prevent the supply from being wasted —**conservationist** *n.* [C]

con·serv·a·tism /kən'sɚvəˌtɪzəm/ *n.* [U] the belief that any changes to the way things are done must happen slowly and have very good reasons: *political conservatism*

con·serv·a·tive /kən'sɚvət̬ɪv/ *adj.* **1** preferring to continue doing things the way they are being done or have been proven to work, rather than risking changes: *a very conservative attitude to education* | *a politically conservative family* **2** not very modern in style, taste, etc.: *a conservative business suit* **3 a conservative estimate** a guess that is deliberately lower than the real amount probably is —**conservatively** *adv.* —**conservative** *n.* [C]

con·serv·a·to·ry /kən'sɚvəˌtɔri/ *n.* plural **conservatories** [C] **1** a school where students are trained in music or acting **2** a GREENHOUSE

con·serve /kən'sɚv/ *v.* [T] to prevent something from being wasted, damaged, or destroyed: *efforts to conserve water* | *Try and rest frequently to conserve your energy.*

con·sid·er /kən'sɪdɚ/ *v.* **1** [I,T] to think about something very carefully, especially before making a decision: *I considered resigning.* | *He was considering whether to apply for the job.* | *You should* ***consider the possibility*** *of moving there permanently.* ➔ see Thesaurus box at THINK **2** [T] to think of someone or something in a particular way or have a particular opinion: *Mrs. Greenwood was* ***considered to be*** *an excellent teacher.* | *We* ***consider it important*** *to get the Director's advice on this.* | *Greg should* ***consider*** *himself* ***lucky*** (=be glad) *he wasn't badly hurt.* **3** [T] to think about someone or his/her feelings, and try to avoid upsetting him/her: *It's all right for you, but have you considered the children?*

con·sid·er·a·ble /kən'sɪdərəbəl/ *adj.* large enough to be important or have an effect: *a* ***considerable amount*** *of money* —**considerably** *adv.*: *It's considerably colder tonight.*

con·sid·er·ate /kən'sɪdərɪt/ *adj.* thinking and caring about other people's feelings, wants, or needs [≠ **inconsiderate**]: *He was always kind and considerate.* —**considerately** *adj.*

THESAURUS

kind, nice, thoughtful, caring
➔ see Thesaurus box at KIND[2]

con·sid·er·a·tion /kənˌsɪdə'reɪʃən/ *n.* **1** [U] *formal* careful thought and attention: *Several plans are* ***under consideration***. | *We will* ***give*** *careful* ***consideration*** *to your proposal.* **2** [C] a fact or detail that you think about when making a decision: *financial considerations* **3 take sth into consideration** to think about something when making a decision: *We'll take into consideration the fact that you were sick.* **4** [U] the quality of thinking and caring about other people's feelings, wants, or needs: *He* ***shows*** *no* ***consideration*** *for others.*

con·sid·ered /kən'sɪdɚd/ *adj.* **1 considered opinion/judgment** an opinion based on careful thought **2 all things considered** after thinking about all the facts: *All things considered, I think the meeting went pretty well.*

con·sid·er·ing /kən'sɪdərɪŋ/ *prep., conjunction* used to say that you are thinking about a particular fact when giving your opinion: *She did very well* ***considering (that)*** *it was her first attempt.*

con·sign /kən'saɪn/ *v.* [T] *formal*

consign sb/sth **to** sth *phr. v.* **1** to cause someone or something to be in a bad situation: *a decision that consigned him to political obscurity* **2** to put something somewhere, especially in order to get rid of it

con·sign·ment /kən'saɪnmənt/ *n.* [C] **1** a

C

quantity of goods that is sent to someone in order to be sold **2 on consignment** goods that are on consignment are being sold by a store owner for someone else, for a share of the profit

con·sist /kən'sɪst/ *v.*

consist of sth *phr. v.* to be made of or contain particular things or people: *The audience **consists largely of** teenagers.*

con·sist·en·cy /kən'sɪstənsi/ *n.* plural **consistencies** **1** [U] *approving* the quality of always being the same, or of always behaving in an expected way [≠ **inconsistency**]: *There's no **consistency in** the way they apply the rules.* **2** [C,U] how thick, smooth, etc. a substance is: *a dessert with a nice creamy consistency*

C

con·sist·ent /kən'sɪstənt/ *adj.* **1** *approving* always happening in the same way or having the same attitudes, quality, etc. [≠ **inconsistent**]: *I've tried to be **consistent in** applying the rules.* **2** containing facts, ideas, etc. that agree with other facts, etc.: *His story is not **consistent with** the facts.* —**consistently** *adv.*: *consistently good grades*

con·so·la·tion /ˌkɑnsə'leɪʃən/ *n.* [C,U] something that makes you feel better when you are sad or disappointed: *If it's any **consolation to** you, I think that you're improving.*

ˌconso'lation prize *n.* [C] a prize that is given to someone who has not won a competition

con·sole /kən'soʊl/ *v.* [T] to help someone who is sad or disappointed to feel better: *No one could console her when her dog died.* | *Danny **consoled himself with** the thought that he had done his best.*

con·sol·i·date /kən'sɑləˌdeɪt/ *v.* [I,T] **1** to make something stronger or more successful: *The company has consolidated its position in the Japanese market.* **2** to combine things so that they are more effective or easier to manage: *a loan to consolidate debts* —**consolidation** /kənˌsɑlə'deɪʃən/ *n.* [C,U]

con·so·nant /'kɑnsənənt/ *n.* [C] *technical* any letter of the English alphabet except a, e, i, o, and u [➡ **vowel**]

con·sort /kən'sɔrt/ *v. formal*

consort with sb *phr. v.* to spend time with someone who other people do not approve of

con·sor·ti·um /kən'sɔrʃiəm, -t̬iəm/ *n.* plural **consortia** /-ʃiə, -t̬iə/ or **consortiums** [C] a combination of several companies, organizations, etc. working together: *a **consortium of** banks*

con·spic·u·ous /kən'spɪkyuəs/ *adj.* very easy to notice [≠ **inconspicuous**]: *The notice must be displayed in a conspicuous place.* —**conspicuously** *adv.*

> **THESAURUS**
>
> **noticeable**, **clear**, **obvious**, **striking**, **eye-catching**
> ➔ see Thesaurus box at NOTICEABLE

conˌspicuous con'sumption *n.* [U] *disapproving* the act of buying a lot of expensive things, so that other people will see how rich you are

con·spir·a·cy /kən'spɪrəsi/ *n.* plural **conspiracies** [C,U] a secret plan made by two or more people to do something bad or illegal: *a **conspiracy to** distribute drugs*

> **THESAURUS**
>
> **plan**, **plot**, **scheme**, **strategy**
> ➔ see Thesaurus box at PLAN[1]

con·spir·a·tor /kən'spɪrət̬ɚ/ *n.* [C] someone who is part of a group that secretly plans something bad or illegal —**conspiratorial** /kənˌspɪrə'tɔriəl/ *adj.*

con·spire /kən'spaɪɚ/ *v.* [I] **1** to secretly plan with other people to do something bad or illegal: *The company was accused of **conspiring with** local stores to fix prices.* **2** *formal* if events conspire to make something happen, they happen at the same time and have a bad result

con·stant /'kɑnstənt/ *adj.* **1** happening regularly or all the time: *There was a **constant stream** of visitors to the house.* | *He's under constant pressure.* **2** staying at the same level for a long period of time: *driving at a constant speed* —**constancy** *n.* [singular, U]

con·stant·ly /'kɑnstəntˀli/ *adv.* always or regularly: *The English language is constantly changing.*

> **THESAURUS**
>
> **often**, **frequently**, **regularly**, **repeatedly**, **continuously**
> ➔ see Thesaurus box at OFTEN

con·stel·la·tion /ˌkɑnstə'leɪʃən/ *n.* [C] a group of stars that forms a particular pattern and has a name

> **TOPIC**
>
> **space**, **meteor**, **asteroid**, **comet**, **moon**, **planet**, **star**, **sun**, **galaxy**, **black hole**, **spacecraft**, **spaceship**, **rocket**, **(space) shuttle**, **satellite**, **probe**, **astronaut**
> ➔ see Topic box at SPACE[1]

con·ster·na·tion /ˌkɑnstɚ'neɪʃən/ *n.* [U] a feeling of shock or worry

con·sti·pa·tion /ˌkɑnstə'peɪʃən/ *n.* [U] a condition in which someone is unable to get rid of solid waste from his/her body —**constipated** /'kɑnstəˌpeɪt̬ɪd/ *adj.*

con·stit·u·en·cy /kən'stɪtʃuənsi/ *n.* plural **constituencies** [C] the people who live and vote in a particular area

con·stit·u·ent /kən'stɪtʃuənt/ *n.* [C] **1** someone who votes in a particular area **2** one of the parts that combine to form something: *Sodium is one of the **constituents of** salt.* —**constituent** *adj.*

con·sti·tute /'kɑnstəˌtut/ *v.* [linking verb] *formal* **1** if several parts constitute something, they form it together: *the 50 states that constitute the USA* **2** to be considered to be something: *The rise in crime constitutes a threat to society.*

con·sti·tu·tion /ˌkɑnstəˈtuʃən/ *n.* **1** [C] **also Constitution** a set of laws and principles that a country or organization is governed by: *the Constitution of the United States* **2** [singular] your general health and your body's ability to fight disease and illness: *a boy with a **strong/weak constitution***

con·sti·tu·tion·al /ˌkɑnstəˈtuʃənəl/ *adj.* **1** officially allowed or restricted by the constitution of a country or organization: *a **constitutional right** to privacy* **2** relating to the constitution of a country or organization: *a constitutional reform*

con·strain /kənˈstreɪn/ *v.* [T] *formal* to limit someone's freedom to do what s/he wants to do: *Our research was **constrained by** a lack of funds.*

con·straint /kənˈstreɪnt/ *n.* [C] something that restricts what you are doing: ***constraints on** government spending* | *We did the best we could given the **time/budget constraints**.*

con·strict /kənˈstrɪkt/ *v.* [T] to become smaller, narrower, or tighter, or to make something do this: *Her throat constricted.* —**constriction** /kənˈstrɪkʃən/ *n.* [C,U]: *constriction of the arteries*

con·struct /kənˈstrʌkt/ *v.* [T] **1** to build something large such as a building, bridge, etc.: *The Empire State Building was constructed in 1931.* ➔ see picture at BUILD[1]

> **THESAURUS**
>
> **build, put up, erect**
> ➔ see Thesaurus box at BUILD[1]

2 to form something such as a sentence or argument by joining words, ideas, etc. together

con·struc·tion /kənˈstrʌkʃən/ *n.* **1** [U] the process or method of building something large such as a house, road, etc.: *the **construction of** a new airport* | *The hotel is **under construction*** (=being built). | *a construction worker* **2** [C] the way in which words are put together in a sentence: *difficult **grammatical constructions***

conˈstruction ˌpaper *n.* [U] a thick colored paper that is used especially by children at school

con·struc·tive /kənˈstrʌktɪv/ *adj.* useful and helpful, or likely to produce good results: ***constructive criticism** of students' essays*

con·strue /kənˈstru/ *v.* [T] to understand something in a particular way [≠ **misconstrue**]: *It might be **construed as** a threat.*

con·sul /ˈkɑnsəl/ *n.* [C] an official who lives in a foreign city and whose job is to help citizens of his/her own country who also live or work there [➡ **ambassador**] —**consular** *adj.*

con·sul·ate /ˈkɑnsəlɪt/ *n.* [C] the official building where a consul lives and works [➡ **embassy**]: *the Danish Consulate*

con·sult /kənˈsʌlt/ *v.* [I,T] **1** to ask or look for advice, information, etc. from someone or something that should have the answers: *Consult your physician.* | *Don't do anything without **consulting with** your lawyer.* **2** to discuss something with someone so that you can make a decision together: *I'd better consult my wife first.*

con·sul·tan·cy /kənˈsʌltənsi/ *n.* plural **consultancies** [C] a company that gives advice and training in a particular area of business to people in other companies

con·sult·ant /kənˈsʌltənt/ *n.* [C] someone with a lot of experience in a particular area of business whose job is to give advice about it: *a marketing consultant*

con·sul·ta·tion /ˌkɑnsəlˈteɪʃən/ *n.* [C,U] **1** a discussion in which people who are affected by a decision can say what they think should be done: *The changes were made **in consultation with** community groups.* **2** a meeting in which you get advice from a professional, or the process of getting this advice: *a **consultation with** the school counselor*

con·sume /kənˈsum/ *v.* [T] **1** to completely use time, energy, goods, etc.: *Smaller cars consume less fuel.* **2** to eat or drink something: *the amount of alcohol consumed in an hour* **3 be consumed with passion/guilt/rage etc.** to have a very strong feeling that you cannot ignore **4** if a fire consumes something, it completely destroys it ➔ TIME-CONSUMING

con·sum·er /kənˈsumɚ/ *n.* [C] someone who buys or uses goods and services [➡ **customer**]: *Consumers will soon be paying higher airfares.* | *advertisements for **consumer goods*** (=things that people buy for their own use, rather than things bought by businesses)

> **THESAURUS**
>
> **customer, client, shopper, buyer**
> ➔ see Thesaurus box at CUSTOMER

con·sum·er·is·m /kənˈsuməˌrɪzəm/ *n.* [U] *disapproving* the belief that it is good to buy and use a lot of goods and services

con·sum·mate¹ /ˈkɑnsəmɪt/ *adj.* very skillful: *a consummate politician*

con·sum·mate² /ˈkɑnsəˌmeɪt/ *v.* [T] *formal* **1** to make a marriage or a relationship complete by having sex **2** to make something such as an agreement complete —**consummation** /ˌkɑnsəˈmeɪʃən/ *n.* [U]

con·sump·tion /kənˈsʌmpʃən/ *n.* [U] **1** the amount of electricity, gas, etc. that is used: *the aircraft's fuel consumption* **2** *formal* the act of eating or drinking: *The consumption of alcohol is not permitted on these premises.*

con·tact¹ /ˈkɑntækt/ *n.* **1** [C,U] communication with a person, organization, country, etc.: *Have you **kept/stayed in contact with** any of your school friends?* | *The soldiers **had** little **contact with** citizens of the country.* | *the establishment of diplomatic contacts* **2** [U] the state of touching or

C

being close to someone or something: *What happens when different cultures **come in contact with** each other? | The disease spreads by **sexual contact**.* **3** [C] someone you know who may be able to help you or give you advice: *He **has** a few **contacts** in the movie industry.* **4** [C] a CONTACT LENS **5** [C] an electrical part that completes a CIRCUIT when it touches another part

contact[2] *v.* [T] to telephone or write to someone: *I've been trying to contact you for the past three days!* ▶ Don't say "I've been trying to contact with you." ◀

'contact ˌlens *n.* [C] a small round piece of plastic you put on your eye to help you see clearly

contact lens

con·ta·gious /kənˈteɪdʒəs/ *adj.* **1** a disease that is contagious can be passed from person to person by touch or through the air **2** a person who is contagious has a disease like this **3** a feeling, attitude, action, etc. that is contagious is quickly felt or done by other people: *Jeannie's laughter was contagious.*

con·tain /kənˈteɪn/ *v.* [T] **1** to have something inside: *a wallet containing $50* **2** to be included in something or be part of something: *The report contained some shocking information. | products that contain nuts* **3** to control the emotions you feel: *Greg was so excited he could hardly **contain himself**.*

con·tain·er /kənˈteɪnɚ/ *n.* [C] something such as a box, a bowl, a bottle, etc. that can be filled with something: *an eight-gallon container*

con·tain·ment /kənˈteɪnmənt/ *n.* [U] the act of controlling something, such as the cost of a plan or the power of an unfriendly country

con·tam·i·nate /kənˈtæməˌneɪt/ *v.* [T] **1** to spoil something by adding a dangerous or poisonous substance to it: *These areas of the ocean are **contaminated with/by** oil.* **2** to influence someone or something in a way that has a bad effect: *Lack of trust will contaminate your whole relationship.* —**contaminated** *adj.* —**contamination** /kənˌtæməˈneɪʃən/ *n.* [U]

contd. the written abbreviation of **continued**

con·tem·plate /ˈkɑntəmˌpleɪt/ *v.* [T] to think seriously for a long time about something you intend to do, or something you want to understand: *The group is contemplating legal action.* —**contemplation** /ˌkɑntəmˈpleɪʃən/ *n.* [U]

con·tem·pla·tive /kənˈtɛmplət̬ɪv/ *adj.* spending a lot of time thinking seriously and quietly

con·tem·po·rar·y[1] /kənˈtɛmpəˌrɛri/ *adj.* **1** belonging to the present time [= **modern**]: *a museum of contemporary art* **2** happening or existing in the same period of time: *letters **contemporary with** his earliest compositions*

contemporary[2] *n.* [C] someone who lives in the same period of time as a particular person or event: *Mozart's contemporaries*

con·tempt /kənˈtɛmpt/ *n.* [U] **1** a feeling that someone or something does not deserve any respect: *actions that show **contempt for** women* **2 contempt of court** not doing what a judge or court of law has told you to: *Cooper was fined $100 for contempt of court.*

con·tempt·i·ble /kənˈtɛmptəbəl/ *adj.* not deserving any respect: *contemptible behavior* —**contemptibly** *adv.*

con·temp·tu·ous /kənˈtɛmptʃuəs/ *adj.* showing that you believe someone or something does not deserve any respect: *young people who are contemptuous of authority*

con·tend /kənˈtɛnd/ *v.* [I] **1** to argue or say that something is true: *Opponents **contend that** the changes will create even more problems.* **2** to compete for something: *Twelve teams are **contending for** the title.*

contend with sth *phr. v.* to deal with a problem or difficult situation: *The police would then have less paperwork to contend with.*

con·tend·er /kənˈtɛndɚ/ *n.* [C] someone who is involved in a competition: *a **contender for** the Democratic nomination*

con·tent[1] /ˈkɑntɛnt/ *n.* **1 contents** [plural] **a)** the things that are in a box, bag, room, etc.: *Officers searched through the **contents of** the desk.* **b)** the words or ideas that are written in a book, letter, etc.: *The contents of the document are still unknown. | the **table of contents*** (=a list at the beginning of a book that tells you what is in it) **2** [singular] the ideas, information, or opinions that are expressed in a speech, book, etc.: *At first, concentrate on the content of your essay, not its appearance.* **3** [singular] the amount of a substance that something contains: *Peanut butter has a high fat content.*

con·tent[2] /kənˈtɛnt/ *adj.* happy or satisfied, or willing to do or accept something: *She seemed **content to** sit and wait. | I'd say she's pretty **content with** her life.* —**contentment** *n.* [U]

THESAURUS

happy, **glad**, **pleased**
→ see Thesaurus box at HAPPY

content[3] *v.* **content yourself with sth** to do or have something that is not what you really want, but is still satisfactory: *Jack's driving, so he'll have to content himself with a soft drink.*

content[4] *n.* **do sth to your heart's content** to do something as much as you want

con·tent·ed /kənˈtɛnt̬ɪd/ *adj.* satisfied or happy [≠ **discontented**]: *a contented cat*

con·ten·tion /kənˈtɛnʃən/ *n.* **1** [C] a belief or opinion that someone expresses: *It was the* *defense's* ***contention that*** *their client was wrongly arrested.* **2** [U] a situation in which people or groups are competing: *Oregon remains* ***in contention for*** *the playoffs.* **3** [U] arguments and disagreement between people: *City planning has been a* ***bone of contention*** (=subject that people argue about) *for a long time.*

con·ten·tious /kən'tɛnʃəs/ *adj.* likely to cause a lot of argument —**contentiously** *adv.*

con·test¹ /'kɑntɛst/ *n.* [C] **1** a competition, usually a small one: *a contest to see who can run the fastest* | *The deadline for* ***entering the contest*** *is May 1.* | *Who* ***won/lost the contest****?*

> **THESAURUS**
>
> **competition**, **championship**, **tournament**, **playoff**
> → see Thesaurus box at COMPETITION

2 a struggle to win control or power: *the 1960 presidential* ***contest between*** *Kennedy and Nixon* **3 no contest** *informal* if a victory is no contest, it is very easy to achieve: *In the end, it was no contest, with the Dolphins beating the Bengals 37–13.* **4 plead no contest** to state that you will not give a defense in a court of law for something wrong you have done

con·test² /kən'tɛst/ *v.* [T] **1** to say formally that you do not think something is right or fair: *We intend to contest the judge's decision.* **2** to compete for something: *a* ***hotly contested*** (=competed for very strongly) *election*

con·test·ant /kən'tɛstənt/ *n.* [C] someone who competes in a contest

con·text /'kɑntɛkst/ *n.* [C] **1** the situation, events, or information that are related to something, and that help you to understand it: *The events have to be considered in their* ***historical/social/political context.*** | *Can students apply the skills learned in school* ***in a different context****, such as the workplace?* **2** the words and sentences that come before and after a word and that help you understand its meaning: *"Smart" can mean "intelligent" or "sarcastic," depending on the context.* **3 take sth out of context** to repeat a sentence or phrase without describing the situation in which it was said, so that its meaning seems different from what was intended: *Journalists had taken his comments completely out of context.*

con·tig·u·ous /kən'tɪgyuəs/ *adj. formal* next to something, or sharing the same border: *the 48 contiguous States*

con·ti·nent /'kɑntənənt, 'kɑnt˺n-ənt/ *n.* [C] one of the main areas of land on the earth: *the continent of Africa*

con·ti·nen·tal /ˌkɑntən'ɛntl◂/ *adj.* relating to a continent: *flights across the continental U.S.*

ˌcontinental 'breakfast *n.* [C] a breakfast consisting of coffee, juice, and a sweet ROLL (=type of bread)

con·tin·gen·cy /kən'tɪndʒənsi/ *n.* plural **contingencies** [C] an event or situation that might happen and could cause problems: *a* ***contingency plan*** *to cope with any computer failures*

con·tin·gent¹ /kən'tɪndʒənt/ *adj. formal* dependent on something that may or may not happen in the future: *The purchase of the house is* ***contingent on/upon*** *a satisfactory inspection.*

contingent² *n.* [C] a group of people who have the same aims or are from the same area, and who are part of a larger group: *By late summer, a* ***contingent of*** *scientists had arrived.*

con·tin·u·al /kən'tɪnyuəl/ *adj.* repeated often over a long period of time: *Their continual arguing really upset me.* —**continually** *adv.*

> **USAGE**
>
> **Continual** and **continuous** can be used in a very similar way: *a continual/continuous process*
> **Continual** is also used when something happens many times, especially something annoying: *There were continual interruptions all day.*
> **Continuous** is used in order to emphasize that there is no pause or break between things: *six continuous hours of meetings* | *a continuous line of trees*

con·tin·u·a·tion /kənˌtɪnyu'eɪʃən/ *n.* **1** [U] the act or state of continuing for a long time without stopping: *the continuation of family traditions* **2** [C] something that follows after or is joined to something else and seems a part of it: *Community colleges offer students a continuation of their education.*

con·tin·ue /kən'tɪnyu/ *v.* **1** [I,T] to keep happening, existing, or doing something without stopping: *She will continue her work at UCSD.* | *The city's population will* ***continue to*** *grow.* | ***Continuing with*** *the peace process is very important.* **2** [I,T] to start doing something again after a pause: *Rescuers will continue the search tomorrow.* | *After a brief ceasefire, fighting continued.* **3** [I] to go further in the same direction: *Route 66* ***continues on*** *to Texas from here.*

conˌtinuing edu'cation *n.* [U] classes for adults, often on subjects that relate to their jobs

con·ti·nu·i·ty /ˌkɑntə'nuət̬i/ *n.* [U] the state of continuing over a long period of time without being interrupted or changing: *Changing doctors can affect the* ***continuity of*** *your treatment.*

con·tin·u·ous¹ /kən'tɪnyuəs/ *adj.* **1** continuing to happen or exist without stopping or pausing: *The church has been in continuous use since 1732.* → see Usage box at CONTINUAL **2** without any spaces or holes in it: *a continuous line of cars* —**continuously** *adv.*

continuous² *n.* **the continuous** *technical* in grammar, the form of a verb that shows that an action or activity is continuing to happen, and that is formed with "be" and the PRESENT PARTICIPLE. In the sentence "She is watching TV," "is watching" is in the continuous form

con·tin·u·um /kən'tɪnyuəm/ *n.* plural **continuums** or **continua** /-nyuə/ [C] *formal* a scale of related things, on which each one is only slightly different from the one before: *Depression exists **on a continuum**, with mild sadness at one end to suicide at the other.*

con·tort /kən'tɔrt/ *v.* [I,T] to twist your face or body so that it does not have its normal shape —**contortion** /kən'tɔrʃən/ *n.* [C,U]

con·tour /'kɑntʊr/ *n.* [C] the shape of the outer edges of something such as an area of land or someone's body

C

con·tra·band /'kɑntrəˌbænd/ *n.* [U] goods that are brought into or taken out of a country illegally —**contraband** *adj.*

con·tra·cep·tion /ˌkɑntrə'sɛpʃən/ *n.* [U] the practice or methods of preventing a woman from becoming PREGNANT when she has sex [= **birth control**]

con·tra·cep·tive /ˌkɑntrə'sɛptɪv/ *n.* [U] a drug, object, or method used so that a woman does not become PREGNANT when she has sex —**contraceptive** *adj.*

con·tract¹ /'kɑntrækt/ *n.* [C] **1** a legal written agreement between two people, companies, etc. that says what each will do: *Stacy **signed** a three-year **contract**. | a **contract with** the Forest Service | a **contract to** build seven ships* **2** *informal* an agreement to kill someone for money

con·tract² /kən'trækt/ *v.* **1** [T] to get a CONTAGIOUS illness: *He contracted polio.* **2** [I] to become smaller or tighter [≠ **expand**]: *Scientists say the universe will begin to contract.*

con·tract³ /'kɑntrækt/ *v.* [I,T] to sign a contract to do something: *The city has **contracted with** a private company **to** remove garbage.*

contract sth ⇔ **out** *phr. v.* to arrange to have a job done by a person or company outside your own organization: *The city has contracted its garbage collection out to an independent company.*

con·trac·tion /kən'trækʃən/ *n.* **1** [C] a very strong and painful movement of a muscle in which it suddenly becomes tight, used especially about the muscles that become tight when a woman is going to give birth **2** [U] the process of becoming smaller or shorter **3** [C] a short form of a word or words, such as "don't" for "do not"

con·trac·tor /'kɑnˌtræktɚ, kən'træk-/ *n.* [C] a person or company that does work or supplies material for other companies

con·trac·tu·al /kən'træktʃuəl/ *adj.* agreed in a contract: *contractual obligations*

con·tra·dict /ˌkɑntrə'dɪkt/ *v.* **1** [T] if a statement, story, etc. contradicts another one, the facts in it are so different that both statements cannot be true: *The witnesses' reports contradicted each other.* **2** [I,T] to say that what someone else has just said is wrong or not true: *You shouldn't contradict me in front of the kids.* **3 contradict yourself** to say something that is the opposite of what you have said before —**contradictory** /ˌkɑntrə'dɪktəri/ *adj.*

con·tra·dic·tion /ˌkɑntrə'dɪkʃən/ *n.* **1** [C] a difference between two stories, facts, etc. that means they cannot both be true: *There were **contradictions between** the testimony of the two men.* **2** [U] the act of saying that what someone has just said is wrong or not true **3 contradiction in terms** a combination of words that seem to be the opposite of each other, so that the phrase does not have a clear meaning

con·trap·tion /kən'træpʃən/ *n.* [C] *informal* a piece of equipment that looks strange

con·trar·y¹ /'kɑnˌtrɛri/ *n. formal* **1 on the contrary** used in order to show that the opposite of what has just been said is actually true: *We didn't start the fire. On the contrary, we helped put it out.* **2 to the contrary** showing or saying the opposite: *In spite of rumors to the contrary, their marriage is fine.*

contrary² *adj.* **1** completely different or opposite: *This idea is **contrary to** Catholic teaching.* **2 contrary to popular belief** used in order to show that something is true even though people may think the opposite: *Contrary to popular belief, gorillas are shy and gentle.*

con·trar·y³ /kən'trɛri/ *adj.* deliberately doing or saying the opposite of what someone else wants: *an extremely contrary child*

con·trast¹ /'kɑntræst/ *n.* **1** [C,U] a difference between two people, situations, ideas, etc. that are being compared: *the **contrast between** the rich and poor in America | Claire is tall and dark, **in contrast to** her mother, who is short and fair. | At that time, the life of West Berlin stood **in sharp/stark/marked contrast to** East Berlin.* **2** [U] the differences in color or in light and darkness on photographs, a television picture, etc.

con·trast² /kən'træst/ *v.* **1** [T] to compare two people, ideas, objects, etc. to show how they are different from each other: *In another passage, Melville again **contrasts** the land **with** the sea.* **2** [I] if two things contrast, they are very different from each other: *His thick, bulky body **contrasted with** Len's tall lankiness.* —**contrasting** *adj.*

con·tra·vene /ˌkɑntrə'vin/ *v.* [T] *formal* to do something that is not allowed by a law or a rule —**contravention** /ˌkɑntrə'vɛnʃən/ *n.* [C,U]

con·trib·ute /kən'trɪbyut, -yət/ *v.* **1** [I,T] to give money, help, or ideas to something that other people are also giving to: *Large companies **contribute** money **to** both parties.* **2** [I] to help make something happen: *An electrical problem may have **contributed to** the crash.* **3** [I,T] to write something for a newspaper or magazine: *Several hundred people contributed articles, photographs, and cartoons.* —**contributor** *n.* [C] —**contributory** /kən'trɪbyəˌtɔri/ *adj.*

con·tri·bu·tion /ˌkɑntrə'byuʃən/ *n.* [C]

1 something that is given or done to help something else be successful: *The Mayo Clinic has* ***made*** *important* ***contributions to*** *cancer research.* | *Einstein's* ***significant/important/ valuable contributions to*** *physics* **2** an amount of money that is given to help pay for something: *Would you like to* ***make a contribution to*** *the Red Cross?* | *a* ***contribution of*** *$25* **3** a piece of writing that is printed in a newspaper or magazine

con·trite /kən'traɪt/ *adj.* feeling guilty and sorry for something bad that you have done: *a contrite apology* —**contrition** /kən'trɪʃən/ *n.* [U]

con·trive /kən'traɪv/ *v.* [T] to manage to do something difficult or to invent something by being very smart or dishonest: *Schindler* ***contrived to*** *save more than 1,000 Polish Jews from the Nazis.*

con·trived /kən'traɪvd/ *adj.* seeming false and not natural: *The plot was contrived.*

con·trol¹ /kən'troʊl/ *n.* **1** [U] the power or ability to make someone or something do what you want: *They don't* ***have*** *any* ***control over*** *their son.* | *Newborn babies have little* ***control of/over*** *their movements.* | *The car went* ***out of control*** *and hit a tree.* | *The situation is now* ***under control.*** | *These events are* ***beyond our control*** (=not possible for us to control). **2** [U] the power to rule or govern a place, organization, or company: *Rioters* ***took control of*** *the prison.* | *The airport is now* ***under the control of*** *UN troops.* | *The government is no longer* ***in control*** *of the country.* **3** [C,U] an action, method, or law that limits the amount or growth of something: *an agreement on arms control* | *Firefighters* ***brought*** *the fire* ***under control*** (=stopped it from getting worse). **4** [U] the ability to remain calm even when you are angry or excited: *I just* ***lost control*** *and punched him!* **5** [C] something that you use to make a television, machine, vehicle, etc. work: *the volume control* | *the controls of the airplane* **6** [singular] **also control key** a button on a computer that allows you to do particular things: *Press control and S to save the document.* —**controlled** *adj.*

control² *v.* past tense and past participle **controlled**, present participle **controlling** [T] **1** to make someone or something do what you want or work in a particular way: *If you can't control your dog, you should put it on a leash.* **2** to limit the amount or growth of something: *a chemical used to control weeds* **3** to rule or govern a place, organization, or company, or to have more power than someone else: *Rebels control all the roads into the capital.* **4** to make yourself behave calmly, even if you feel angry, excited, or upset: *I was furious, but I managed to* ***control myself.***

con'trol ˌfreak *n.* [C] *informal disapproving* someone who is very concerned about controlling all the details in every situation s/he is involved in

con·trol·ler /kən'troʊlɚ/ *n.* [C] *technical* someone whose job is to collect and pay money for a government or company department: *the state controller*

con'trol ˌtower *n.* [C] a building at an airport from which people direct the movements of airplanes on the ground and in the air

con·tro·ver·sial /ˌkɑntrə'vɚʃəl◂/ *adj.* something that is controversial causes a lot of disagreement because many people have strong opinions about it: *the controversial subject of abortion* | *He is a* ***controversial figure*** (=person who does controversial things) *in the art world.* —**controversially** *adv.*

con·tro·ver·sy /'kɑntrəˌvɚsi/ *n.* plural **controversies** [C,U] a serious disagreement among many people over a plan, decision, etc., over a long period of time: *There is* ***controversy over*** *the proposed development.*

con·va·lesce /ˌkɑnvə'lɛs/ *v.* [I] to spend time getting well after a serious illness —**convalescence** *n.* [singular] —**convalescent** *n.* [C]

con·va·les·cent /ˌkɑnvə'lɛsənt/ *adj.* **convalescent home/hospital etc.** a place where people stay when they need care from doctors and nurses but are not sick enough to be in a hospital

con·vene /kən'vin/ *v.* [I,T] *formal* if a group of people convenes, or if someone convenes them, they come together for a formal meeting: *A board was convened to judge the design competition.*

con·ven·ience /kən'vinyəns/ *n.* **1** [U] the quality of being good or useful for a particular purpose, especially because it makes something easier [≠ **inconvenience**]: *Most people like the* ***convenience of*** *using a credit card.* **2** [U] what is easiest and best for someone [≠ **inconvenience**]: *The package can be delivered* ***at your convenience.*** **3** [C] a service, piece of equipment, etc. that is useful because it saves you time or work: *modern conveniences such as washing machines*

con'venience ˌfood *n.* [C,U] food that is partly or completely prepared already

con'venience ˌstore *n.* [C] a store where you can buy food, newspapers, etc. and that is often open 24 hours each day

THESAURUS

store, bookstore, clothes store, record store, grocery store, supermarket, bakery, delicatessen, deli, liquor store, drugstore, hardware store, nursery, garden center, newsstand, boutique, department store, chain store, superstore, outlet store, warehouse store

➔ see Thesaurus box at STORE¹

con·ven·ient /kən'vinyənt/ *adj.* **1** useful to you because it makes something easier or saves you time [≠ **inconvenient**]: *Catalogs are a convenient way to shop.* | *What time would be* ***convenient for*** *you?* **2** near and easy to get to

C

[≠ **inconvenient**]: *a restaurant in a convenient location* —**conveniently** *adv.*

con·vent /ˈkɑnvɛnt, -vənt/ *n.* [C] a place where NUNS live and work

con·ven·tion /kənˈvɛnʃən/ *n.* **1** [C] a large, formal meeting of people who belong to the same profession, organization, etc., or who have the same interests: *the Democratic National Convention* | *a convention of science fiction fans* **2** [C,U] behavior and attitudes that most people in society think are normal and right: *He defied* ***social conventions*** *to follow his own path.* **3** [C] a formal agreement between countries: *the Geneva convention on human rights*

C

con·ven·tion·al /kənˈvɛnʃənəl/ *adj.* **1** used or existing for a long time, and considered usual: *Acupuncture is one alternative to conventional medicine.*

THESAURUS

normal, **ordinary**, **average**, **standard**, **routine**
→ see Thesaurus box at NORMAL[1]

2 always following the behavior and attitudes that most people in society think are normal and right, so that you seem boring: *a strongly conventional young man* **3 conventional wisdom** the opinion that most people consider to be normal and right **4** conventional weapons and wars do not use NUCLEAR explosives —**conventionally** *adv.*

con·verge /kənˈvɚdʒ/ *v.* [I] to move or come together from different directions to meet at the same point [≠ **diverge**]: *Thousands of fans* ***converged on*** *the stadium.* —**convergence** *n.* [C,U]

con·ver·sant /kənˈvɚsənt/ *adj. formal* having knowledge or experience of something: *Staff members are* ***conversant with*** *the issues.*

con·ver·sa·tion /ˌkɑnvɚˈseɪʃən/ *n.* [C,U] **1** a talk between two or more people in which people ask questions, exchange news, etc.: *They* ***had a*** *pleasant* ***conversation*** *during dinner.* | *a short* ***conversation with*** *his mother* | *a* ***conversation about*** *the tensions between work and family life* | *The two women were deep* ***in conversation*** (=they were concentrating on their conversation). **2 make conversation** to talk to someone to be polite, not because you really want to: *"Nice weather we're having," he said, trying to make conversation* —**conversational** *adj.* —**conversationally** *adv.*

con·verse[1] /kənˈvɚs/ *v.* [I] *formal* to have a conversation with someone: *She enjoyed the chance to* ***converse with*** *someone who spoke her language.*

THESAURUS

talk, **have a conversation**, **chat (with/to)**, **have a chat**, **visit with**
→ see Thesaurus box at TALK[1]

con·verse[2] /ˈkɑnvɚs/ *n. formal* **the converse** the opposite of something: *The converse can also be true in some cases.* —**converse** /kənˈvɚs, ˈkɑnvɚs/ *adj.* —**conversely** *adv.*

con·ver·sion /kənˈvɚʒən, -ʃən/ *n.* [C,U] **1** the act or process of changing something from one form, system, or purpose to another: *Canada's* ***conversion to*** *the metric system* **2** a change in which someone accepts a completely new religion, belief, etc.: *his* ***conversion to*** *Islam*

con·vert[1] /kənˈvɚt/ *v.* [I,T] **1** to change, or to make something change, from one form, system, or purpose to another: *We're going to* ***convert*** *the garage* ***into*** *a workshop.* **2** to change your opinions, beliefs, or habits, or to make someone do this: *She* ***converted to*** *Christianity.*

con·vert[2] /ˈkɑnvɚt/ *n.* [C] someone who has accepted a completely new religion, belief, etc.

con·vert·i·ble[1] /kənˈvɚṭəbəl/ *adj.* **1** an object that is convertible can be folded or arranged in a different way, so that it can be used as something else: *a convertible couch* (=one that unfolds to become a bed) **2** *technical* able to be exchanged for the money of another country, for STOCKS, etc.

convertible[2] *n.* [C] a car with a roof that you can fold back or remove

con·vex /ˌkɑnˈvɛks◂, kən-/ *adj. technical* curved toward the outside like the surface of the eye [≠ **concave**]: *a convex lens*

con·vey /kənˈveɪ/ *v.* [T] *formal* to communicate a message or information, with or without using words: *Please* ***convey*** *my thanks* ***to*** *her.*

con'veyor belt *n.* [C] a long continuous moving band of rubber or metal, used in a place such as a factory or airport to move things from one place to another

con·vict[1] /kənˈvɪkt/ *v.* [T] to prove or announce that someone is guilty of a crime after a TRIAL in a court of law [≠ **acquit**]: *Both men were* ***convicted of*** *fraud.*

con·vict[2] /ˈkɑnvɪkt/ *n.* [C] someone who has been proved to be guilty of a crime and sent to prison

THESAURUS

prisoner, **captive**, **hostage**
→ see Thesaurus box at PRISONER

con·vic·tion /kənˈvɪkʃən/ *n.* [C,U] **1** a very strong belief or opinion: *his religious convictions* | *He argued* ***with conviction*** *that the economy was growing.* **2** an official announcement in a court of law that someone is guilty of a crime [≠ **acquittal**]: *his third* ***conviction for*** *theft*

con·vince /kənˈvɪns/ *v.* [T] **1** to make someone feel certain that something is true: *His lawyers* ***convinced*** *the jury* ***that*** *Booth was innocent.* **2** to persuade someone to do something: *I* ***convinced*** *him* ***to*** *stay.*

THESAURUS

persuade, **talk into**, **get sb to do sth**, **encourage**, **influence**, **coax**, **cajole**
➔ see Thesaurus box at PERSUADE

con·vinced /kənˈvɪnst/ *adj.* **be convinced** to feel certain that something is true: *Her family became* ***convinced (that)*** *she was taking drugs.*

con·vinc·ing /kənˈvɪnsɪŋ/ *adj.* making you believe that something is true or right: *a convincing argument* —**convincingly** *adv.*

con·viv·i·al /kənˈvɪviəl/ *adj. formal* friendly and pleasant: *a convivial atmosphere* —**conviviality** /kənˌvɪviˈæləṭi/ *n.* [U]

con·vo·lut·ed /ˈkɑnvəˌluṭɪd/ *adj. formal* complicated and difficult to understand: *a convoluted plot*

con·voy /ˈkɑnvɔɪ/ *n.* [C,U] a group of vehicles or ships traveling together

con·vul·sion /kənˈvʌlʃən/ *n.* [C] **1** an occasion when someone cannot control the violent movements of his/her body because s/he is sick **2** [usually plural] a great change that affects a country: *the political convulsions in Eastern Europe*

coo /ku/ *v.* **1** [I] to make a sound like the low cry of a DOVE or a PIGEON **2** [I,T] to make soft loving noises: *a mother cooing to her baby*

cook¹ /kʊk/ *v.* **1** [I,T] to prepare food for eating by using heat: *Whoever gets home first* ***cooks dinner/supper****.* | *Alice said she'd cook tonight.* | *Cook the pasta for 10–12 minutes.*

THESAURUS

bake – to cook food such as bread in the oven
fry – to cook food in oil on the top part of the stove
roast – to cook meat or vegetables in an oven
broil – to cook food by placing it near to strong heat from above
grill – to cook food over strong heat, especially over flames: *a grilled steak*
sauté – to fry vegetables for a short time in a small amount of oil
boil – to cook vegetables in very hot water on the top part of the oven
steam – to cook vegetables by placing them in a container over very hot water, so that the steam from the hot water cooks them
deep fry – to fry food in a pan containing a lot of hot oil

2 [I] to be prepared for eating by using heat: *How long does it take the stew to cook?* **3 be cooking (with gas)** *spoken* to be doing something very well, or in the correct way: *The band is really cooking tonight.*

cook sth ⇔ **up** *phr. v.* **1** *informal* to invent an excuse, reason, plan, etc. that is slightly dishonest or will not work: *the plan that Larry and Jim had cooked up between them* **2** to prepare food, especially quickly: *She cooked up some beans and cornbread.*

cook² *n.* [C] someone who cooks and prepares food: *Kevin works as a cook.* | *My cousin's a* ***wonderful/good/terrible cook.***

cook·book /ˈkʊkbʊk/ *n.* [C] a book that tells you how to prepare and cook food

cooked /kʊkt/ *adj.* ready for eating and not raw: *cooked vegetables*

cook·ie /ˈkʊki/ *n.* [C] a small flat sweet cake: *chocolate chip cookies* ➔ see picture on page A5

ˈcookie ˌcutter¹ *n.* [C] an instrument that cuts cookies into special shapes before you bake them

cookie cutter² *adj.* [only before noun] almost exactly the same as other things of the same type, and not very interesting: *cookie cutter houses*

ˈcookie sheet *n.* [C] a flat metal pan that you bake food on

cook·ing¹ /ˈkʊkɪŋ/ *n.* [U] **1** the act of making food and cooking it: *I* ***do*** *most of* ***the cooking****.* **2** food made in a particular way or by a particular person: *Italian cooking*

cooking² *adj.* used for cooking: *cooking oil* | *a cooking pot*

cool¹ /kul/ *adj.* **1** low in temperature but not cold: *a cool summer evening* | *a nice cool drink*

THESAURUS

cold, **chilly**, **frosty**, **freezing (cold)**, **icy (cold)**, **bitter (cold)**
➔ see Thesaurus box at COLD¹

2 *spoken* said in order to show that you agree with something, that you understand it, or that it does not annoy you: *"Do you mind if I bring my sister?" "No,* ***that's cool****."* **3** *spoken approving* fashionable, attractive, interesting, etc. in a way that people admire: *He's a really cool guy.* | *That's such a cool car.* **4** calm and not nervous or excited: ***Stay cool****; don't let him get to you.*

THESAURUS

calm, **relaxed**, **laid-back**, **mellow**
➔ see Thesaurus box at CALM²

5 unfriendly: *a cool welcome* —**coolness** *n.* [U] —**coolly** /ˈkul-li/ *adv.*

cool² *v.* **1** [I,T] **also cool down** to make something slightly colder, or to become slightly colder: *Allow the cake to cool before cutting it.* **2** [I] feelings or relationships that cool become less strong or friendly: *Relations between the two countries have cooled considerably.* **3 cool it** *spoken* used in order to tell someone to stop being angry: *Jeez, Jim, just cool it, will you?*

cool down *phr. v.* **1** to become calm after being angry: *The long walk home helped me cool down.* **2** to do gentle physical exercises after doing more difficult exercises, so that you do not get injuries

cool off *phr. v.* **1** to return to a normal tempera-

C

ture after being hot: *They went for a swim to cool off.* **2** to become calm after being angry: *Give him some time to cool off first.*

cool[3] *n.* [U] **1 the cool** a temperature that is cool: *the cool of a spring morning* **2 keep your cool** to stay calm in a difficult situation: *The players kept their cool and started scoring.* **3 lose your cool** to stop being calm in a difficult situation: *The waiter never lost his cool.*

cool·er /'kulɚ/ *n.* [C] a small box in which you can keep food or drinks cool

coop /kup/ *n.* [C] a cage for chickens

ˌcooped 'up *adj.* [not before noun] having to stay indoors or in a place that is too small for a long period of time: *I've been cooped up in this apartment all day.*

C

co·op·er·ate /koʊ'ɑpəˌreɪt/ *v.* [I] **1** to work with someone else to achieve something that you both want: *The local police are* ***cooperating with*** *the FBI.* **2** to do what someone asks you to do: *Some of the kids refuse to* ***cooperate with*** *the teacher.*

co·op·er·a·tion /koʊˌɑpə'reɪʃən/ *n.* [U] **1** the act of working with someone else to achieve what you both want: *The sales team will be working* ***in cooperation with*** *other departments.* | *the* ***cooperation between*** *Congress and the White House* **2** willingness to work with other people, or to do what they ask you to do: *Thank you for your cooperation.*

co·op·era·tive[1] /koʊ'ɑprət̬ɪv/ *adj.* **1** willing to help or willing to do what you ask: *a happy and cooperative child* **2** made, done, or owned by people working together: *a cooperative farm* —**cooperatively** *adv.*

cooperative[2] *n.* [C] a company, farm, etc. that is owned and operated by people working together: *They turned their business into a cooperative.*

co-opt /koʊ'ɑpt/ *v.* [T] *disapproving* to use something that was not originally yours to help you do something, or to persuade someone to help you: *He saw his best ideas co-opted by his rivals.*

co·or·di·nate /koʊ'ɔrdnˌeɪt/ *v.* [T] to organize people or things so that they work together well: *The group is coordinating medical and food aid to the area.*

co·or·di·nat·ed /koʊ'ɔrdnˌeɪt̬ɪd/ *adj.* **1** able to control your body and make it move smoothly: *a well-coordinated young boy* **2** organized so that people or things work together well: *a coordinated effort to get the law changed*

co·or·di·na·tion /koʊˌɔrdn'eɪʃən/ *n.* [U] **1** the organization of people or things so that they work together well: *More* ***coordination between*** *departments is needed.* **2** the way that the parts of your body work together to do something: *Alcohol affects your coordination.*

co·or·di·na·tor /koʊ'ɔrdnˌeɪt̬ɚ/ *n.* [C] someone who organizes the way people work together

coo·ties /'kut̬iz/ *n.* [plural] LICE (=small insects that live in your hair) – used by children as an insult when they do not want to play with or sit with another child: *Jenny* ***has cooties.***

cop /kɑp/ *n.* [C] *informal* a police officer

> **THESAURUS**
>
> **police officer, policeman, policewoman, detective, plain-clothes police officer**
> → see Thesaurus box at POLICE[1]

cope /koʊp/ *v.* [I] to succeed in dealing with a difficult problem or situation: *The country is trying to* ***cope with*** *high levels of unemployment.* | *children who have trouble* ***coping with*** *change*

cop·i·er /'kɑpiɚ/ *n.* [C] a machine that quickly copies documents onto paper by photographing them

co·pi·lot /'koʊˌpaɪlət/ *n.* [C] a pilot who helps the main pilot fly an airplane

co·pi·ous /'koʊpiəs/ *adj.* produced in large amounts: *He took copious notes.* —**copiously** *adv.*

'cop-out *n.* [C] *informal* something you do or say in order to avoid doing something: *Blaming failing grades on TV is a cop-out.* —**cop out** *v.*

cop·per /'kɑpɚ/ *n.* [U] an orange-brown metal that is an ELEMENT and is often used to make wire —**copper** *adj.*

cop·ter /'kɑptɚ/ *n.* [C] *informal* a HELICOPTER

cop·u·late /'kɑpyəˌleɪt/ *v.* [I] *formal* to have sex —**copulation** /ˌkɑpyə'leɪʃən/ *n.* [U]

cop·y[1] /'kɑpi/ *n.* plural **copies** **1** [C] something that is made to look exactly like something else: *Please* ***make*** *me a* ***copy*** *of the report.* | *a good* ***copy of*** *Van Gogh's famous painting* **2** [C] one of many books, magazines, etc. that are exactly the same: *a copy of Irving's new novel* **3** [U] *technical* something written to be printed, especially for an advertisement: *We need someone who can write good copy.*

copy[2] *v.* past tense and past participle **copied**, third person singular **copies** **1** [T] to make a thing that is exactly like something else: *I copied a tape for him.* | *To copy a file, press F3.*

> **THESAURUS**
>
> **photocopy** – to copy a piece of paper with writing or pictures on it, using a special machine
> **forge** – to illegally copy something written or printed: *He forged my signature.* | *forged documents*
> **pirate** – to illegally copy and sell a film, book, CD, or DVD that was made by another company: *pirated videos*

2 [T] **also copy down** to write something down exactly as it was said or written: *She copied down the homework assignment.* **3** [T] to do something that someone else has done, or behave like someone else: *The system has been copied by other organizations, and has worked well.* **4** [I,T] to cheat by looking at someone else's work and writing what s/he has written as an answer: *Several students were punished for copying.* **5** [T] to copy writing, etc. from a computer document in order to put it in another place or document [➡ **cut**, **paste**]

copy sb ⇔ **in** *phr. v.* to send someone a copy of an E-MAIL message you are sending to someone else

cop·y·cat /ˈkɑpiˌkæt/ *n.* [C] *informal* **1** *disapproving* someone who copies other people's clothes, behavior, etc. – used especially by children **2 copycat crime/murder etc.** a crime, murder, etc. that is similar to a crime that someone else has done

cop·y·right /ˈkɑpiˌraɪt/ *n.* [C,U] the legal right to produce and sell a book, play, movie, or record

cor·al /ˈkɔrəl, ˈkɑrəl/ *n.* [U] a hard colored substance formed in warm sea water from the bones of very small creatures

cord /kɔrd/ *n.* [C,U] **1** a piece of wire covered with plastic, used especially for connecting electrical equipment to the supply of electricity: *an extension cord* | *a long phone cord* ➔ see picture at ACOUSTIC **2** a piece of thick string or thin rope **3 cords** [plural] CORDUROY pants

cor·dial /ˈkɔrdʒəl/ *adj.* friendly and polite but formal: *a cordial greeting* —**cordially** *adv.* —**cordiality** /ˌkɔrdʒiˈæləṭi/ *n.* [U]

THESAURUS

friendly, **warm**, **welcoming**, **hospitable**
➔ see Thesaurus box at FRIENDLY

cord·less /ˈkɔrdlɪs/ *adj.* a cordless piece of equipment uses a BATTERY instead of an electrical CORD: *a cordless telephone*

cor·don¹ /ˈkɔrdn/ *n.* [C] a line of police, soldiers, or vehicles that is put around an area to protect or enclose it

cordon² *v.*
cordon sth ⇔ **off** *phr. v.* to surround and protect an area with police officers, soldiers, or vehicles: *Police have cordoned off the building.*

cor·du·roy /ˈkɔrdəˌrɔɪ/ *n.* [U] thick strong cotton cloth with raised lines on one side: *a corduroy jacket*

core¹ /kɔr/ *n.* [C] **1** the central or most important part of something: *The **core of** the proposal is a tax credit.* | *the company's core customers* | *The department has a small core of experienced staff.* **2** the hard central part of an apple or PEAR ➔ see picture at FRUIT **3** the central part of the earth or any other PLANET **4** the central part of a NUCLEAR REACTOR ➔ HARDCORE

core² *v.* [T] to remove the hard center of a piece of fruit

cork¹ /kɔrk/ *n.* **1** [U] the light outer part of a particular type of tree that is used for making things: *cork mats* **2** [C] a round piece of this material that is put into the top of a bottle to keep liquid inside

cork² *v.* [T] to close a bottle tightly by putting a cork in it

cork·screw /ˈkɔrkskru/ *n.* [C] a tool used for pulling corks out of bottles

corn /kɔrn/ *n.* [U] **1** a tall plant with yellow seeds that are cooked and eaten as a vegetable: *an **ear of corn*** (=the top part of a corn plant on which these yellow seeds grow) | *steak and **corn on the cob*** (=an ear of corn that is cooked and eaten) ➔ see picture at VEGETABLE **2** a thick, hard, and painful area of skin on your foot

corn·bread /ˈkɔrnbrɛd/ *n.* [U] bread that is made from CORNMEAL

cor·ne·a /ˈkɔrniə/ *n.* [C] the strong transparent covering on the outer surface of your eye —**corneal** *adj.*

corned beef /ˌkɔrnd ˈbif◂ / *n.* [U] BEEF that has been preserved in salt water and SPICES

cor·ner¹ /ˈkɔrnɚ/ *n.* [C] **1** the point at which two lines, surfaces, or edges meet: *a table **in the corner** of the room* | *Jess sat **on the corner** of the bed.* **2** the place where two roads, streets, or paths meet: *Meet me **on the corner** of 72nd and Central Park.* | *We went to a place **around the corner** for coffee.* | *Some kids were standing **at the corner**.* | *When you **turn the corner*** (=go around the corner) *you'll see a video store.* **3** a particular part of an area, especially one that is far away or quiet: *a remote corner of the country* | *a sunny corner of the yard* **4** the sides of your mouth or eye **5 see sth out of the corner of your eye** to notice something without turning your head **6 be just around the corner** to be going to happen very soon: *Victory seemed to be just around the corner.* ➔ **cut corners** at CUT¹

corner² *v.* [T] **1** to move closer to a person or an animal so that he, she, or it cannot escape: *Gibbs cornered Cassetti after the meeting.* ➔ see Thesaurus box at CATCH¹ **2 corner the market** to sell or produce all of a particular type of goods

cor·ner·stone /ˈkɔrnɚˌstoʊn/ *n.* [C] **1** a stone set at one of the bottom corners of a building, often as part of a special ceremony **2** something that is very important because everything else depends on it: *Free speech is **the cornerstone of** democracy.*

cor·net /kɔrˈnɛt/ *n.* [C] a small musical instrument like a TRUMPET

corn·flakes /ˈkɔrnfleɪks/ *n.* [plural] a type of breakfast food made from corn

corn·meal /ˈkɔrnmil/ *n.* [U] a rough type of flour made from crushed dried corn

corn·starch /ˈkɔrnstɑrtʃ/ *n.* [U] a fine white flour made from corn, used in cooking to make liquids thicker

ˈcorn ˌsyrup *n.* [U] a very sweet thick liquid made from corn, used in cooking

corn·y /ˈkɔrni/ *adj. informal* old, silly, and very familiar: *a corny song from the '40s* ➔ see Thesaurus box at FUNNY¹

cor·o·na·ry[1] /ˈkɔrəˌnɛri/ *adj.* relating to the heart: *coronary disease*

coronary[2] *n.* [C] a HEART ATTACK

cor·o·na·tion /ˌkɔrəˈneɪʃən/ *n.* [C] a ceremony in which someone officially becomes a king or queen

cor·o·ner /ˈkɔrənɚ/ *n.* [C] an official whose job is to discover the cause of someone's death, if it is sudden or unexpected, by examining his/her body

cor·po·ral /ˈkɔrpərəl/ *n.* [C] a low rank in the Army or Marines, or an officer who has this rank

ˌcorporal ˈpunishment *n.* [U] punishment that involves hitting someone

C

THESAURUS

punishment, **sentence**, **penalty**, **fine**, **community service**, **capital punishment**
➔ see Thesaurus box at PUNISHMENT

cor·po·rate /ˈkɔrpərɪt/ *adj.* belonging to or relating to a corporation: *corporate headquarters* —**corporately** *adv.*

cor·po·ra·tion /ˌkɔrpəˈreɪʃən/ *n.* [C] a large business organization that is owned by SHAREHOLDERS: *a large corporation*

THESAURUS

company, **firm**, **business**, **multinational**, **subsidiary**
➔ see Thesaurus box at COMPANY

corps /kɔr/ *n.* [singular] *technical* **1** a trained group of people with special duties in the military: *the Naval Air Corps* **2** a group of people who do a particular job: *the press corps*

corpse /kɔrps/ *n.* [C] a dead body

cor·pu·lent /ˈkɔrpyələnt/ *adj. formal* very fat

cor·pus·cle /ˈkɔrˌpʌsəl/ *n.* [C] a red or white blood cell in your body

cor·ral[1] /kəˈræl/ *n.* [C] an enclosed area where cattle, horses, etc. are kept

corral[2] *v.* [T] to put animals into a corral

cor·rect[1] /kəˈrɛkt/ *adj.* **1** right or without any mistakes [≠ **incorrect**]: *the correct answers* | *"Your name is Ives?" "Yes, that's correct."*

THESAURUS

right, **accurate**
➔ see Thesaurus box at RIGHT[1]

2 right for a particular occasion or use: *the correct way to lift a heavy weight* —**correctly** *adv.* —**correctness** *n.* [U]

correct[2] *v.* [T] **1** to make something right or better: *Your eyesight can be corrected with glasses.* | *Paola corrected his pronunciation.* **2** if a teacher corrects a student's written work, s/he shows where the mistakes are and what the right answer is

cor·rec·tion /kəˈrɛkʃən/ *n.* [C] a change in something that makes it right or better: *Johnson **made** a few **corrections** to the article.*

cor·rec·tive /kəˈrɛktɪv/ *adj. formal* intended to make something right or better: *corrective lenses for the eyes*

cor·re·la·tion /ˌkɔrəˈleɪʃən, ˌkɑr-/ *n.* [C,U] a relationship between two ideas, facts, etc., especially when one may be the cause of the other: *There's a strong **correlation between** poverty and poor health.* —**correlate** /ˈkɔrəˌleɪt/ *v.* [I,T]

cor·re·spond /ˌkɔrəˈspɑnd, ˌkɑr-/ *v.* [I] **1** if two things correspond, they are similar to each other or relate to each other: *The name on the envelope doesn't **correspond with** the one on the letter.* | *The test gives you a qualification that **corresponds to** a high school diploma.* **2** if two people correspond, they write letters to each other: *They've been corresponding for years.*

cor·re·spond·ence /ˌkɔrəˈspɑndəns, ˌkɑr-/ *n.* [U] **1** letters that people send and receive: *Her secretary deals with her correspondence.* **2** the activity of writing letters: *His **correspondence with** Hemingway continued until his death.* **3** a relationship or connection between two things: *the correspondence between a letter and the sound it represents*

correˈspondence ˌcourse *n.* [C] a course of lessons that you receive by mail and do at home

cor·re·spond·ent /ˌkɔrəˈspɑndənt, ˌkɑr-/ *n.* [C] **1** someone whose job is to report news from a distant area, or about a particular subject, for a newspaper or television: *the White House correspondent*

TOPIC

editor, **reporter**, **journalist**, **columnist**
➔ see Topic box at NEWSPAPER

2 someone who writes to another person regularly

cor·re·spond·ing /ˌkɔrəˈspɑndɪŋ, ˌkɑr-/ *adj.* relating or similar to something: *a promotion and a corresponding increase in salary* —**correspondingly** *adv.*

cor·ri·dor /ˈkɔrədɚ, -ˌdɔr, ˈkɑr-/ *n.* [C] **1** a passage between two rows of rooms: *The bathroom is **down the corridor** to your right.* | *Please wait **in the corridor**.* **2** a narrow area of land between cities or countries, especially one used for traveling from one place to another: *the New York-Washington DC corridor*

cor·rob·o·rate /kəˈrɑbəˌreɪt/ *v.* [T] *formal* to support an opinion or claim with new information or proof: *Several witnesses corroborated McDougal's story.* —**corroboration** /kəˌrɑbəˈreɪʃən/ *n.* [U] —**corroborative** /kəˈrɑbərət̬ɪv/ *adj.*

cor·rode /kəˈroʊd/ *v.* [I,T] if metal corrodes, or if something corrodes it, it is slowly destroyed by water, chemicals, etc.

cor·ro·sion /kəˈroʊʒən/ *n.* [U] the gradual process of being destroyed by the effects of water, chemicals, etc., or a substance such as RUST that is produced by this process —**corrosive** /kəˈroʊsɪv/ *adj.*

cor·ru·gat·ed /ˈkɔrəˌgeɪt̬ɪd, ˈkɑr-/ *adj.* formed in rows of folds that look like waves: *corrugated cardboard*

cor·rupt¹ /kəˈrʌpt/ *adj.* **1** dishonest and ready to do things that will give you an advantage: *a corrupt judge who took a bribe* **2** very bad morally: *a corrupt society* —**corruptly** *adv.*

corrupt² *v.* [T] **1** to make someone dishonest or immoral: *The judicial process had been corrupted by drug money.* **2** to change or spoil something so that it is not as good: *a traditional culture corrupted by outside influences* **3** to change the information in a computer, so that the information is wrong and the computer does not work correctly: *The data had been corrupted.* —**corruptible** *adj.*

cor·rup·tion /kəˈrʌpʃən/ *n.* [U] **1** dishonest or immoral behavior: *corruption in city politics* **2** the act or process of making someone dishonest or immoral: *the corruption of today's youth by drugs*

cor·sage /kɔrˈsɑʒ/ *n.* [C] a small BUNCH (=group) of flowers that a woman wears on her dress for special occasions

cor·set /ˈkɔrsɪt/ *n.* [C] a type of underwear that fits very tightly, that women in past times wore in order to look thinner

cor·tege /kɔrˈtɛʒ/ *n.* [C] *formal* a line of people, cars, etc. that move slowly in a funeral

cor·tex /ˈkɔrtɛks/ *n.* [C] the outer layer of an organ in the body, especially the brain

cos·met·ic /kɑzˈmɛt̬ɪk/ *adj.* **1** intended to make your skin or body more beautiful: *cosmetic surgery* **2** dealing only with the appearance of something: *cosmetic changes to the policy* —**cosmetically** *adv.*

cos·met·ics /kɑzˈmɛt̬ɪks/ *n.* [plural] creams, powders, etc. that you use to make your face and body more attractive [➡ **makeup**]

cos·mic /ˈkɑzmɪk/ *adj.* relating to space or the universe: *a cosmic explosion* —**cosmically** *adv.*

cos·mo·naut /ˈkɑzməˌnɔt/ *n.* [C] an ASTRONAUT from the former Soviet Union

cos·mo·pol·i·tan /ˌkɑzməˈpɑlətən, -lət̚n/ *adj. approving* **1** a cosmopolitan place has people from many different parts of the world: *a cosmopolitan city* **2** a cosmopolitan person, attitude, etc. shows a lot of experience of different people and places: *Peyroux has a cosmopolitan view of the world.*

cos·mos /ˈkɑzmoʊs, -məs/ *n.* **the cosmos** the universe considered as a whole system

cost¹ /kɔst/ *n.* **1** [C,U] the amount of money you must pay in order to buy, do, or produce something: *the **cost of** a college education* | *Will $100 **cover the cost** of books* (=be enough to pay for them)? | *the **high cost** of car insurance* | *Legal services were provided at a **low cost**.* | *The software is available **at a cost of** $30.* | *Glasses were offered **at no extra cost**.*

THESAURUS

expense – a very large amount of money that you spend on something: *the expense of buying a computer*
price – the amount of money you must pay for something: *House prices keep going up.* | *the price of oil*
charge – the amount that you have to pay for a particular service or to use something: *There's no additional charge for the service.* | *telephone charges*
fee – the amount you have to pay to enter or join something, or that you pay to a lawyer, doctor, etc.: *There is no entrance fee to the museum.* | *The membership fee is $125 a year.* | *legal fees*
fare – the amount you have to pay to travel somewhere by bus, airplane, train, etc.: *the bus fare*
rent – the amount you have to pay to live in or use a place that you do not own: *My rent is $900 a month.*

2 costs [plural] **a)** the money that you must regularly spend in order to run a business, your home, car, etc.: *the university's annual **operating costs*** | *high **labor costs*** | *We're trying to **cut/reduce/lower costs*** (=spend less money) *by driving a smaller car.* **b)** the money that you must pay to lawyers if you are involved in a legal case: *Burdell lost the case and was ordered to pay the defense's costs.* **3** [C,U] something that you must give or lose in order to get something else: *War is never worth its cost in human life.* | *He saved his family, **at the cost of** his own life.* | *He intends to hold onto power, **whatever the cost**.* **4 at all costs/at any cost** whatever happens, or whatever effort is needed: *We need to get that contract, at any cost.* **5 at cost** for the same price that you paid: *We had to sell the van at cost.*

cost² *v.* past tense and past participle **cost** **1** [linking verb] to have a particular price: *This dress cost $75.* | *How much did your watch cost?* | *The wedding ended up costing them $50,000.* | *It'll **cost** thousands of dollars **to** fix this place up.* | *I love these boots, but they **cost an arm and a leg/cost a fortune*** (=are extremely expensive). **2** [T] to make someone lose something important: *Your mistake cost us the deal.* **3** [T] past tense and past participle **costed** to calculate how much money is needed to pay for something: *The options are being costed and analyzed.*

co-star /ˈkoʊ stɑr/ *n.* [C] one of two or more famous actors who work together in a movie or play —**co-star** *v.* [I,T] *He co-starred with Bruce Willis in the movie "Die Hard."*

C

'cost-ˌcutting *n.* [U] the things that a company or organization does in order to reduce its costs: *Cost-cutting efforts included the elimination of 4,000 jobs.*

'cost-efˌfective *adj.* producing the best profits or advantages at the lowest cost: *a cost-effective way to reduce pollution*

cost·ly /'kɔstli/ *adj.* **1** costing a lot of money [= **expensive**]: *costly repairs* **2** causing a lot of problems: *The delay* ***proved costly***.

ˌcost of 'living *n.* [singular] the amount of money you need to spend in order to buy the food, clothes, etc. that you need to live: *The cost of living is much higher in California than in Iowa.*

C

cos·tume /'kɑstum/ *n.* [C,U] **1** clothes worn to make you look like a particular type of person, animal, etc.: *a prize for the best* ***Halloween costume*** | *The actors put on their costumes and makeup.* **2** clothes that are typical of a particular country or time in the past: *We took a tour given by volunteers* ***in period costume*** (=the clothes of a period of history).

'costume ˌjewelry *n.* [U] cheap jewelry that looks expensive

cot /kɑt/ *n.* [C] a light narrow bed that folds up → see picture at BED[1]

cot·tage /'kɑt̮ɪdʒ/ *n.* [C] a small house in the country, especially an old one

THESAURUS

house, **ranch house/ranch**, **row house**, **mansion**, **bungalow**, **duplex**, **apartment**, **condominium**, **condo**, **townhouse**, **mobile home/trailer**
→ see Thesaurus box at HOUSE[1]

ˌcottage 'cheese *n.* [U] a soft wet white cheese

cot·ton /'kɑt˺n/ *n.* [U] **1** cloth or thread made from the cotton plant: *a cotton shirt* **2** a plant with white hairs used for making cotton cloth and thread **3** a soft mass of cotton, used especially for cleaning your skin

'cotton ball *n.* [C] a small soft ball made from cotton, used for cleaning skin

'cotton ˌcandy *n.* [U] a type of sticky pink candy that looks like cotton

cot·ton·wood /'kɑt˺nˌwʊd/ *n.* [C] a North American tree with seeds that look like cotton

couch[1] /kaʊtʃ/ *n.* [C] a long, comfortable piece of furniture on which you can sit or lie [= **sofa**]: *Tom offered to sleep on the couch.*

couch[2] *v.* **be couched in sth** *formal* to be expressed in a particular way: *His refusal was couched in polite terms.*

'couch poˌtato *n.* [C] *informal* someone who spends a lot of time sitting and watching television

cou·gar /'kugɚ/ *n.* [C] a large brown wild cat from the mountains of western North and South America

cougar

cough[1] /kɔf/ *v.* [I] if you cough, air suddenly comes out of your throat with a short loud sound, especially because you are sick: *He's been coughing and sneezing all day.*

cough up *phr. v.* **1 cough** sth ⇔ **up** *informal* to give someone money, information, etc. when you do not really want to: *I'm trying to get my dad to cough up some money for a motorcycle.* **2 cough up** sth if you cough up a substance such as blood, it comes from your lungs or throat into your mouth when you cough: *We rushed her to the hospital when she started coughing up blood.*

cough[2] *n.* [C] **1** the action of coughing, or the sound made when you cough: *She gave a nervous cough before speaking.* **2** an illness that makes you cough a lot: *He* ***had a*** *terrible* ***cough***.

'cough drop *n.* [C] a type of medicine like a piece of candy that you suck to help you stop coughing

'cough ˌsyrup *n.* [U] a thick liquid medicine that you take to help you stop coughing

could /kəd; *strong* kʊd/ *modal verb* **1** used as the past tense of "can" to say what someone was able to do or was allowed to do in the past: *I looked everywhere, but I couldn't* (=could not) *find it.* | *I could hear children playing.* | *When I was young, you could buy a concert ticket for $5.* | *He said we could smoke if we wanted.*

USAGE

Use **can** and **be able to** to say that someone has the ability to do something. **Be able to** is more formal: *Can you swim?* | *He isn't able to run very fast.*
Use **could** to say that someone has the ability to do something, but does not do it: *He could do a lot better.*
Could is also the past form of **can**. Use **could** or a past form of **be able to** to say that someone had the ability to do something in the past: *She could ride a bike when she was three.* | *He was able to walk with a cane.*
Use **will be able to** to talk about future ability: *After only a few lessons, you will be able to understand basic Spanish.*

2 used in order to say that something is possible or might happen: *Most accidents in the home could easily be prevented.* | *It could be weeks before they're finished.* **3 could have** used in order to say that something was possible in the past, but did not actually happen: *She could have* *been killed.* **4** *spoken* used in order to make a polite request: *Could I ask you a couple of questions?* | *Could you deposit this check at the bank for me?* **5** *spoken* said when you are annoyed about someone's behavior: *You could have told me you were going to be late!* | *How could you be so stupid!* **6** *spoken* used in order to emphasize how angry, happy, etc. you are by saying how you want to express your feelings: *I could have murdered Kerry for telling Jason that!* | *I'm so happy I could scream.* **7** *spoken* used in order to suggest doing something: *We could always stop and ask directions.* **8 I couldn't care less** *spoken* used in order to say that you are not interested at all in something: *I couldn't care less what the neighbors say.*

could·n't /'kʊdnt/ *modal verb* the short form of "could not": *We couldn't stop laughing.*

coun·cil /'kaʊnsəl/ *n.* [C] **1** a group of people who are elected as part of a town or city government: *Millard is running for city council.* | *council members* **2** a group of people who make decisions for a church, organization, etc., or who give advice: *the UN Security Council*

coun·cil·man /'kaʊnsəlmən/ *n.* plural **councilmen** /-mən/ [C] a male COUNCILOR

coun·cil·or /'kaʊnsələ/ *n.* [C] a member of a council

coun·cil·wom·an /'kaʊnsəlˌwʊmən/ *n.* plural **councilwomen** /-ˌwɪmɪn/ [C] a female COUNCILOR

coun·sel[1] /'kaʊnsəl/ *v.* [T] *formal* to advise or support someone who has problems: *Tyrone got a job counseling teenagers about drugs.*

counsel[2] *n.* **1** [C] *law* a lawyer who speaks for someone in a court of law: *The counsel for the defense gave her opening statement.* **2** [U] *formal* advice

coun·sel·ing /'kaʊnsəlɪŋ/ *n.* [U] advice given by a counselor to people about their personal problems or difficult decisions: *family/career counseling*

coun·sel·or /'kaʊnsələ/ *n.* [C] **1** someone whose job is to help and support people with problems: *a* ***marriage counselor*** **2** someone who takes care of a group of children at a camp

count[1] /kaʊnt/ *v.* **1** [T] **also count up** to calculate the total number of things or people in a group: *The nurses counted the bottles of medicine as they put them away.* **2** [I] to say numbers in the correct order: *My daughter is learning to count in French.* | *He's only three, but he can* ***count to*** *ten.* **3** [I] to be allowed or accepted: *"I won!" "You cheated, so it doesn't count."* | *Your sculpture class* ***counts as*** *a Humanities credit.* **4** [T] to include someone or something in a total: *There are five in our family, counting me.* **5** [T] to think of something or someone in a particular way: *I* ***count*** *her* ***as*** *one of my best friends.* | *You should* ***count yourself lucky*** *that you weren't hurt.* **6** [I] to be important or valuable: *I felt my opinion didn't* ***count for*** *much.* **7 I/you can count sth on one hand** *spoken* used in order to emphasize how small the number of something is: *I can count on one hand the number of times he's come to visit me.*

count sth ⇔ **down** *phr. v.* to count the number of days, minutes, etc. until a particular moment or event: *She's counting down the days until Nathan arrives.*

count sb **in** *phr. v. informal* to include someone or something in an activity: *If you're going dancing, count me in.*

count on sb/sth *phr. v.* **1** to depend on someone or something: *You can always count on him to help.* **2** to expect something: *We didn't count on this many people coming.*

count out *phr. v.* **1 count** sb **out** *informal* to not include someone or something in an activity: *If you're looking for a fight, count me out.* **2 count out** sth to put things down one by one as you count them: *He counted out ten $50 bills.*

count[2] *n.* [C] **1** the process of counting, or the total that you get when you count things: *The final count showed that Gary had won by 110 votes to 86.* | ***At last count*** (=the last and most recent time you counted), *46 students were interested in the trip.* **2** a measurement of how much of a substance is present in a place, area, etc.: *The* ***pollen count*** *is high today.* **3 keep count** to keep a record of the changing total of something over a period of time: *Are you* ***keeping count of*** *the people you've invited?* **4 lose count** to forget how many there are of something: *I've* ***lost count of*** *how many times she's been married.* **5** *law* one of the crimes that the police say someone has done: *He's guilty on two* ***counts of*** *robbery.*

count·a·ble /'kaʊntəbəl/ *adj.* a countable noun has both a singular and a plural form [≠ **uncountable**]

count·down /'kaʊnt˺daʊn/ *n.* [C] **1** the act of counting backward to zero before something happens, especially before a spacecraft is sent into the sky **2** the period before an important event happens, when it gets closer and closer: *the* ***countdown to*** *Christmas*

coun·te·nance[1] /'kaʊntənəns/ *n.* [C] *literary* your face or your expression

countenance[2] *v.* [T] *formal* to accept, support, or approve of something: *We cannot countenance violent behavior.*

coun·ter[1] /'kaʊntə/ *n.* [C] **1** a flat surface in the kitchen where you prepare food **2** the place where you pay or are served in a shop, bank, restaurant, etc.: *He started chatting with the woman* ***behind the counter***. **3 over the counter** over the counter medicines can be bought without a PRESCRIPTION from your doctor **4 under the counter** secretly and not legally: *She gets paid under the counter.*

counter[2] *v.* [I,T] **1** to do something in order to prevent something bad from happening or to reduce its bad effects: *Hospitals must offer better*

C

salaries to counter the shortage of nurses. **2** to say something to show that what someone has just said is not true: *"I could ask you the same question," she countered.*

counter[3] *adv. formal* in a way that is opposite to something: *Bradley's life has always* ***run counter to*** *expectations.* —**counter** *adj.*

coun·ter·act /ˌkaʊntɚˈækt/ *v.* [T] to reduce or prevent the bad effect of something, by doing something that has the opposite effect: *a drug to counteract the poison*

coun·ter·at·tack /ˈkaʊntɚəˌtæk/ *n.* [C] an attack that you make against someone who has attacked you, in a sport, war, or argument

C

THESAURUS

attack, **invasion**, **raid**, **assault**, **ambush**, **assault**
➔ see Thesaurus box at ATTACK[1]

—**counterattack** *v.* [I]

coun·ter·bal·ance /ˈkaʊntɚˌbæləns/ *v.* [T] to have an equal and opposite effect to something else: *Good sales in Europe have counterbalanced the weak sales in the U.S.* —**counterbalance** *n.* [C]

coun·ter·clock·wise /ˌkaʊntɚˈklɑk-waɪz/ *adj., adv.* in the opposite direction to the way the HANDS (=parts that point to the time) of a clock move [≠ **clockwise**]: *Turn the lid counterclockwise.*

coun·ter·feit /ˈkaʊntɚfɪt/ *adj.* made to look exactly like something else in order to deceive people: *counterfeit money*

THESAURUS

fake, **false**, **imitation**, **phony**, **forged**
➔ see Thesaurus box at FAKE[2]

—**counterfeit** *v.* [T] —**counterfeiter** *n.* [C]

coun·ter·part /ˈkaʊntɚˌpɑrt/ *n.* [C] a person or thing that has the same job or purpose as someone or something else in a different place: *a meeting between the U.S. president and his French counterpart*

coun·ter·pro·duc·tive /ˌkaʊntɚprəˈdʌktɪv/ *adj.* achieving the opposite result to the one you want: *Punishing children too harshly can be counterproductive.*

coun·ter·sign /ˈkaʊntɚˌsaɪn/ *v.* [T] to sign a paper that someone else has already signed: *My boss will countersign the check.*

count·less /ˈkaʊntˀlɪs/ *adj.* [only before noun] very many: *She spent countless hours making that clock.*

coun·try[1] /ˈkʌntri/ *n.* plural **countries** **1** [C] an area of land that is controlled by its own government, president, king, etc.: *Bahrain became an independent country in 1971.* | *I've always wanted to live in a* ***foreign country***. | ***developing countries*** (=countries that are poor but are trying to increase trade and industry)

THESAURUS

nation – a country and its people, used especially when considering its political and economic structures: *the major industrialized nations*
state – a country and its people, used especially when considering its political and economic structures: *state-owned industries*
power – a country that is very strong and important: *Germany is a major industrial power in Europe.*
land literary – a country or place: *Lessing's memoirs describe her many journeys to foreign lands.*

2 the country **a)** land that is away from towns and cities: *We went for a drive in the country.* **b)** all the people who live in a country: *The President has the support of over 50 per cent of the country.* **3** [U] a type of land: *farming country* **4** [U] COUNTRY MUSIC

country[2] *adj.* in the area outside cities, or relating to this area: *clean country air* | *country roads*

ˈcountry ˌclub *n.* [C] a sports and social club, especially one for rich people

coun·try·man /ˈkʌntrimən/ *n.* plural **countrymen** /-mən/ [C] *old-fashioned* someone from your own country

ˈcountry ˌmusic also **ˌcountry and ˈwestern** *n.* [U] popular music in the style of music from the southern and western U.S.

THESAURUS

pop (music), **rock (music)**, **rock'n'roll**, **heavy metal**, **reggae**, **house (music)**, **hip-hop**, **rap (music)**, **jazz**, **classical (music)**, **fold (music)**
➔ see Thesaurus Box at MUSIC

coun·try·side /ˈkʌntriˌsaɪd/ *n.* [U] land that is outside cities and towns [➥ **country**]: *the English countryside*

coun·ty /ˈkaʊnti/ *n.* plural **counties** [C] an area of land within a state or country that has its own local government: *Orange County, California*

ˌcounty ˈfair *n.* [C] an event that happens each year in a particular county, with games and competitions for the best farm animals, for the best cooking, etc.

coup /ku/ *n.* [C] **1 also coup d'état** /ˌku deɪˈtɑ/ an act in which citizens or the army suddenly take control of the government by force: *a military coup*

THESAURUS

revolution, **rebellion**, **revolt**, **uprising**
➔ see Thesaurus box at REVOLUTION

2 [usually singular] an impressive achievement: *Getting that job was quite a coup.*

cou·ple[1] /ˈkʌpəl/ *n.* [C] **1 a couple** *informal* **a)** two things or people of the same kind: *He's got* ***a couple of*** *kids.* **b)** a few: *I need to make* ***a couple***

(of) phone calls. **2** two people who are married or have a romantic relationship: *the young couple next door*

couple² *v. formal* [T] to join two things together

couple sth **with** sth *phr. v.* if one thing is coupled with another, the two things happen or exist together and produce a particular result: *Technology coupled with better health care mean people live longer.*

cou·pon /'kupɑn, 'kyu-/ *n.* [C] **1** a small piece of paper that allows you to pay less money for something or get it free: *a coupon for fifty cents off a jar of coffee* **2** a printed form, used when you order something, enter a competition, etc.

cour·age /'kɚɪdʒ, 'kʌr-/ *n.* [U] the quality of being brave when you are in danger, a difficult situation, etc. [= **bravery**]: *He didn't* ***have the courage to*** *face the media.* | *It must have* ***taken*** *a lot of* ***courage*** *for him to drive again after the accident.* —**courageous** /kə'reɪdʒəs/ *adj.*: *a courageous decision* —**courageously** *adv.*

THESAURUS

bravery – brave behavior in a dangerous or frightening situation: *Troops on both sides fought with bravery.*
guts informal – the courage and determination that you need to do something difficult, dangerous, or unpleasant: *He didn't even have the guts to tell me himself.*

cou·ri·er /'kʊriɚ, 'kɚ-/ *n.* [C] someone whose job is to deliver documents and packages

course /kɔrs/ *n.*

1 of course a) used when what you or someone else has just said is not surprising: *The insurance has to be renewed every year, of course.* **b)** *spoken* used in order to say yes very strongly or to give permission politely: *"Can I borrow your notes?" "Of course you can."* **c)** *spoken* said in order to emphasize that what you are saying is true or correct: *"You'll tell her?" "Of course!"*

2 of course not *spoken* used to say no strongly: *"Do you mind if I'm a little late?" "Of course not."*

3 SCHOOL [C] a class in a particular subject: *a computer course* | *a three-month* ***course in*** *English literature*

4 SPORTS [C] an area of land or water where races are held, or an area of land designed for playing golf: *a race course* | *a 9-hole golf course*

5 MEAL [C] one of the parts of a meal: *the* ***main course*** | *a four-course dinner*

6 ACTION [C] something you can do to deal with a situation: *The best* ***course of action*** *is to speak to her alone.*

7 DIRECTION [C,U] the planned direction taken by a boat or airplane to reach a place: *During the flight we had to* ***change course.*** | *The ship was blown* ***off course*** (=in the wrong direction).

8 in/during/over the course of sth *formal* during a period of time or a process: *During the course of our conversation, I found out that he had worked in France.*

9 be on course (for sth/to do sth) to be likely to achieve something because you have already had some success: *Hodson is on course to break the world record.*

10 WAY STH DEVELOPS [singular] the way that something changes or develops: *a major event that changed* ***the course of history*** | *The boom in World Music has* ***run its course.***

11 PLAN [singular, U] a general plan to achieve something or the general way something is happening: *The President spelt out how he would get the economy back* ***on course.***

C

court¹ /kɔrt/ *n.* **1** [C,U] the people who make a legal judgment, for example about whether someone is guilty of a crime, or the place where these judgments are made: *A crowd of reporters had gathered outside the court.* | *Please tell* ***the court*** *where you were on the night of the 15th.* | *a* ***court of law*** | *He had to appear* ***in court*** *as a witness.* | *We decided to* ***take*** *them* ***to court*** (=make them be judged in a court) *to get our money back.* | *The case should* ***go to court*** (=start being judged in a court) *in August.* | *The insurance company* ***settled out of court*** (=they made an agreement without going to court).

TOPIC

In court, the person who is said to have committed a crime is called the **defendant**. The defendant's lawyers, who are called **the defense**, try to prove that the defendant is **not guilty**. The **prosecution** tries to prove that the defendant is **guilty**. The **judge** and a **jury** listen to **testimony** and examine **evidence** in order to decide if the defendant is guilty or not guilty. Their decision is called the **verdict**.

2 [C] an area made for playing games such as tennis: *a volleyball court*

THESAURUS

sport, **field**, **stadium**, **diamond**, **track**, **gym**, **(swimming) pool**, **health club**
→ see Thesaurus box at SPORT¹

3 a) [C,U] the place where a king or queen lives and works **b)** [singular] the king or queen, their family, and their friends, advisers, etc.: *Court officials denied the rumors.*

court² *v.* **1** [T] to try to please someone so that s/he will support you: *Politicians are courting voters before the election.* **2 court disaster/danger etc.** to do something that is likely to have very bad results: *To cut taxes now would be courting disaster.* **3** [I,T] *old-fashioned* to have a romantic relationship with someone, especially someone you are likely to marry

cour·te·ous /'kɚt̬iəs/ *adj. formal* polite and respectful: *a courteous reply*—**courteously** *adv.*

THESAURUS

polite, **well-behaved**, **civil**
➔ see Thesaurus box at POLITE

cour·te·sy /ˈkɚt̬əsi/ *n.* plural **courtesies** **1** [U] polite behavior: *She didn't* ***have the courtesy*** *to apologize.* **2** [C] something you do or say to be polite: ***As a courtesy to*** *other diners, please switch off your cell phone.* **3 courtesy of sb** used in order to say in a grateful way who provided or did something for you: *We were put up in a fancy hotel, courtesy of the airline.*

court·house /ˈkɔrthaʊs/ *n.* [C] a building containing courts of law and government offices

C

ˌcourt-ˈmartial *n.* [C] a military court, or an occasion when a soldier is judged by a military court —**court-martial** *v.* [T]

court·room /ˈkɔrt˺rum, -rʊm/ *n.* [C] the room where a CASE is judged by a court of law

court·ship /ˈkɔrt˺ʃɪp/ *n.* [C,U] *old-fashioned* the time when a man and a woman have a romantic relationship before getting married

court·yard /ˈkɔrt˺yɑrd/ *n.* [C] an open space surrounded by walls or buildings

cous·in /ˈkʌzən/ *n.* [C] a child of your aunt or uncle: *Bill and I are cousins.*

THESAURUS

relative, **parents**, **father**, **mother**, **dad**, **daddy**, **mom**, **mommy**, **brother**, **sister**, **grandparents**, **grandfather**, **grandmother**, **grandpa**, **grandma**, **great-grandparents**, **uncle**, **aunt**, **nephew**, **niece**
➔ see Thesaurus box at RELATIVE[1]

cove /koʊv/ *n.* [C] a small area on the coast that is partly surrounded by land and is protected from the wind

cov·e·nant /ˈkʌvənənt/ *n.* [C] a formal agreement between two or more people or groups

cov·er[1] /ˈkʌvɚ/ *v.* [T]

1 PUT STH OVER STH also cover up to put something over the top of something else in order to hide, protect, or close it: *Cover the pan and simmer the beans for two hours.* | *We* ***covered*** *the sofa* ***with*** *a large blanket.* | *Dan covered his face with his hands.*

2 BE OVER STH to be on top of something or spread over something: *His bedroom walls are* ***covered with*** *posters.* | ***snow-covered*** *mountains*

3 INCLUDE to include or deal with something: *The class covers twentieth century American poetry.*

4 NEWS to report the details of an event for a newspaper or a television or radio program: *As a young reporter, he covered the war in Vietnam.*

5 PAY FOR STH to be enough money to pay for something: *The award should be enough to cover her college fees.* | *His family will* ***cover*** *the* ***cost*** *of the funeral.*

6 INSURANCE if your insurance covers you or your possessions, it promises to pay you money if you have an accident, something is stolen, etc.: *a policy that covers medical expenses*

7 DISTANCE to travel a particular distance: *We should cover another 50 miles before lunch.* | *A leopard can* ***cover*** *a lot of* ***ground*** *very quickly.*

8 cover your tracks to try to hide something you have done so that other people do not find out

9 GUN to aim a gun somewhere to protect someone from being attacked or to prevent someone from escaping: *We'll cover you while you run for it.* | *The police covered the back entrance.*

10 cover (all) the bases *informal* to make sure that you can deal with any situation or problem

cover for sb *phr. v.* **1** to do someone's work because s/he is sick or is somewhere else: *I'll be covering for Sandra next week.* **2** to prevent someone from getting into trouble by lying about where s/he is or what s/he is doing: *Can you cover for me? Just say I had an appointment.*

cover sth ⇔ **up** *phr. v.* to prevent people from discovering a mistake or an unfavorable fact: *A lot of people tried to cover up the Watergate affair.*

cover up for sb *phr. v.* to protect someone by hiding unfavorable facts about him/her: *The mayor's friends tried to cover up for him.*

cover[2] *n.* **1** [C] something that protects something else by covering it: *a plastic cover*

THESAURUS

lid – a cover for a container
top – the lid or cover for a container or a pen
wrapper – paper or plastic that is around something you buy
wrapping – cloth, paper, etc. that is put around something to protect it

2 [C] the outer front or back part of a book, magazine, etc.: *The Pope was* ***on the cover*** *of Time magazine.* | *I* ***read*** *the book* ***from cover to cover*** (=all of it). **3** [U] protection from bad weather or attack: *The soldiers* ***ran for cover*** *when the shooting started.* | *We* ***took cover*** *under a tree.* **4 covers** [plural] BLANKETS, SHEETS etc. that cover you in bed **5 a cover (for sth)** something a criminal uses to hide his/her activities or keep them secret: *The company is just a cover for the Mafia.* **6 under cover** pretending to be someone else in order to do something secretly: *Policemen* ***working under cover*** *arrested several drug dealers.*

cov·er·age /ˈkʌvrɪdʒ, -vərɪdʒ/ *n.* [U] **1** the amount of attention that is given to a particular subject or event on television, radio or in newspapers, or the way in which the subject is reported: *excellent news coverage of the elections* | *Most of the* ***media/press coverage*** *has been negative.* **2** the protection your insurance gives you, for example paying you money if you are injured or something is stolen: *Millions of people have no formal health care coverage.*

cov·er·alls /ˈkʌvɚˌɔlz/ *n.* [plural] a piece of

clothing that you wear over all your clothes to protect them

'cover charge *n.* [C] money that you have to pay in a restaurant in addition to the cost of food and drinks, especially when there is a band or dancing

cov·er·ing /'kʌvrɪŋ, -vərɪŋ/ *n.* **1** [singular] something that covers something: *a light* ***covering of*** *snow* **2** [C] something that covers part of a wall or floor: *silk* ***wall coverings***

'cover ˌletter *n.* [C] a letter that you send with a document or package, which gives more information about it: *Never send a résumé without a cover letter.* ➔ see Topic box at JOB

co·vert /'koʊvət, 'kʌ-, koʊ'vət/ *adj.* secret or hidden: *a covert operation* —**covertly** *adv.*

'cover-up *n.* [C] an attempt to prevent the public from discovering the truth about something: *CIA officials denied there had been a cover-up.*

cov·et /'kʌvɪt/ *v.* [T] *literary* to want something that someone else has: *The Michelin Awards are coveted by restaurants all over the world.* —**coveted** *adj.*

cow[1] /kaʊ/ *n.* [C] **1** a large female animal that is kept on farms and used to produce milk or meat [➡ **bull**] ➔ see picture at FARM[1] **2** the female of some large animals, such as the ELEPHANT or the WHALE

cow[2] *v.* [T] to frighten someone in order to make him/her do something: *The children were* ***cowed into*** *obedience.*

cow·ard /'kaʊəd/ *n.* [C] someone who is not brave at all —**cowardly** *adj.*: *a cowardly act*

cow·ard·ice /'kaʊədɪs/ *n.* [U] a lack of courage [≠ **bravery**]

cow·boy /'kaʊbɔɪ/ *n.* [C] a man whose job is to take care of cattle

cow·er /'kaʊə/ *v.* [I] to bend low and move back because you are afraid: *The hostages were cowering in a corner.*

cow·girl /'kaʊgəl/ *n.* [C] a woman whose job is to take care of cattle

co-work·er /'koʊˌwəkə/ *n.* [C] someone who works with you

TOPIC

employer, employee, staff, colleague
➔ see Topic Box at WORK[1]

coy /kɔɪ/ *adj.* **1** pretending to be shy in order to attract people's interest: *a coy smile* **2** not wanting to tell people about something: *Bourne was* ***coy about*** *his plans.* —**coyly** *adv.*

coy·o·te /kaɪ'oʊṭi, 'kaɪ-oʊt/ *n.* [C] a small wild dog that lives in western North America and Mexico

co·zy /'koʊzi/ *adj.* small, comfortable, and warm: *a cozy cabin in the woods* —**cozily** *adv.* —**coziness** *n.* [U]

CPA *n.* [C] **Certified Public Accountant** an ACCOUNTANT who has passed all of his/her examinations

CPR *n.* [U] **cardiopulmonary resuscitation** a set of actions that you do to help someone who has stopped breathing or whose heart has stopped beating

CPU *n.* [C] **Central Processing Unit** the part of a computer that controls what it does

crab /kræb/ *n.* [C,U] a sea animal with a round flat shell and two large CLAWS on its front legs, or the meat from this animal

crab·by /'kræbi/ *adj.* easily annoyed or upset: *She's been crabby all day.*

THESAURUS

grumpy, cranky, grouchy, cantankerous, irritable, touchy
➔ see Thesaurus box at GRUMPY

crack[1] /kræk/ *v.*

1 BREAK [I,T] if something cracks or is cracked, it breaks so that it gets a line on its surface, and may then break into pieces: *I just cracked my favorite coffee mug.* | *The ice was starting to crack.* | *He cracked three eggs into a bowl.*

THESAURUS

break, smash, shatter, tear, snap, burst, pop
➔ see Thesaurus box at BREAK[1]

2 NOISE OF BREAKING [I,T] to make a loud sudden noise like the sound of something breaking, or to make something do this: *A stick cracked under his foot.* | *He* ***cracked*** *his* ***knuckles***.

3 HIT STH [T] to accidentally hit something very hard: *Carly tripped and* ***cracked*** *her head* ***on*** *the sidewalk.*

4 LOSE CONTROL [I] to lose control of your emotions and become unable to deal with a situation because there is too much pressure on you: *a spy who never* ***cracked under*** *questioning*

5 VOICE [I] if your voice cracks, it changes from one level to another suddenly, especially because of strong emotions

6 SOLVE [T] to solve a difficult problem or a CODE: *Detectives believe they've finally* ***cracked*** *the* ***case***. | *It took them nearly two months to* ***crack*** *the* ***code***.

7 crack a joke *informal* to tell a joke: *John keeps* ***cracking jokes about*** *my hair.*

8 not be all sth is cracked up to be *informal* not as good as people say it is: *The movie was OK, but it's not all it's cracked up to be.*

crack down *phr. v.* to become more strict in dealing with a problem and punishing the people involved [➡ **crackdown**]: *Police are* ***cracking down on*** *drunk drivers.*

crack up *phr. v. informal* **1 crack** (sb) **up** to laugh a lot at something, or to make someone laugh a lot: *I'll try to tell the story without cracking up.* | *Sue just cracks me up!* **2** to become mentally ill because you have too many problems or too much work

crack[2] *n.* **1** [C] a very narrow space between

two things or two parts of something: *He could see them through a **crack in** the door.* | *Can you **open** the window **a crack**?*

THESAURUS

hole, **space**, **gap**, **leak**
→ see Thesaurus box at HOLE[1]

2 [C] a thin line on the surface of something when it is broken but has not actually come apart: *cracks on the wall* **3** [C] a weakness or fault in an idea, system, or organization: *The **cracks in** their relationship were starting to show.* **4** [C] *informal* an attempt to do something: *Okay, Dave, let's **take a crack** at fixing this bike.* **5** [C] a sudden loud noise that sounds like a stick breaking: *There was a loud crack of thunder as the storm began.* **6** [C] *informal* a cruel joke or remark: *Stop **making cracks about** my sister!* **7** [U] an illegal drug that is a pure form of the drug COCAINE **8 at the crack of dawn** very early in the morning: *We were up at the crack of dawn.*

crack³ *adj.* having a lot of experience and skill: *a **crack shot*** (=someone who is very good at shooting)

crack·down /ˈkrækdaʊn/ *n.* [C] an effort to stop bad or illegal behavior by being more strict: *a national **crackdown on** illegal immigrants*

cracked /krækt/ *adj.* something that is cracked has lines on the surface because it is damaged but not completely broken: *a cracked mirror*

crack·er /ˈkrækɚ/ *n.* [C] a type of hard dry bread that is thin and flat

crack·le /ˈkrækəl/ *v.* [I] to make a lot of short sharp noises: *a log fire crackling in the fireplace* —**crackle** *n.* [C] → see picture on page A7

crack·pot /ˈkrækpɑt/ *adj.* slightly crazy: *a crackpot idea*

cra·dle¹ /ˈkreɪdl/ *n.* [C] **1** a small bed for a baby that can swing gently from side to side **2 the cradle of sth** the place where something important began: *Some say Athens was the cradle of democracy.*

cradle² *v.* [T] to hold someone or something gently in your arms: *Tony cradled the baby in his arms.*

craft¹ /kræft/ *n.* [C] **1** plural **crafts** a skilled activity in which you make something using your hands: *a craft such as knitting* **2** plural **craft** a boat, ship, or airplane

craft² *v.* [T] **1** *journalism* to write a book, speech, etc. with great skill and care **2** to make something with your hands, using a special skill

crafts·man /ˈkræftsmən/ *n.* plural **craftsmen** /-mən/ [C] someone who is very skilled at making things with his/her hands: *furniture made by the finest craftsmen* —**craftsmanship** *n.* [U]

craft·y /ˈkræfti/ *adj.* good at getting what you want by deceiving people —**craftily** *adv.*

THESAURUS

clever, **cunning**
→ see Thesaurus box at INTELLIGENT

crag·gy /ˈkrægi/ *adj.* a craggy mountain or cliff is very steep and covered with large rocks

cram /kræm/ *v.* past tense and past participle **crammed**, present participle **cramming** **1** [T] to force a lot of people or things into a small space: *I managed to **cram** all my stuff **into** the closet.* **2 be crammed with sth** to be full of people or things: *The mall was crammed with shoppers.* **3** [I] to prepare yourself for a test by studying a lot of information very quickly: *Julia stayed up all night **cramming for** her math final.* —**crammed** *adj.*: *crammed sidewalks*

cramp /kræmp/ *n.* [C] **1** a severe pain that you get when a muscle becomes very tight: *I **have a cramp** in my wrist from writing all day.* **2 cramps** [plural] a severe pain in the stomach that women get when they MENSTRUATE

cramped /kræmpt/ *adj.* a cramped room or building does not have enough space for the people or things in it: *a cramped apartment*

THESAURUS

small, **little**, **tiny**
→ see Thesaurus box at SMALL

cran·ber·ry /ˈkrænˌbɛri/ *n.* plural **cranberries** [C] a small sour red BERRY: *cranberry sauce*

crane¹ /kreɪn/ *n.* [C] **1** a tall machine with a long metal arm for lifting heavy things **2** a water bird with very long legs

crane² *v.* [I,T] to look around or over something by stretching or leaning: *All the kids **craned their necks** to see who Mrs. Miller was talking to.*

cra·ni·um /ˈkreɪniəm/ *n.* [C] *technical* the part of your head that is made of bone and covers your brain [**= skull**]

crank¹ /kræŋk/ *n.* [C] **1 crank (telephone) call/letter** *informal* a telephone call or letter that is intended to frighten, annoy, or upset someone **2** *informal* someone who easily becomes angry or annoyed **3** a handle that you turn in order to make a machine work

crank² *v. informal*

crank sth **out** *phr. v.* to produce a lot of something very quickly without caring about quality: *He cranks out two novels a year.*

crank sth ⇔ **up** *phr. v.* to make the sound from a radio, etc. a lot louder: *Hey, Vince, crank up the stereo!*

crank·y /ˈkræŋki/ *adj.* very easily annoyed or made angry, especially because you are tired: *Steve woke up cranky this morning.*

THESAURUS

grumpy, **crabby**, **grouchy**, **cantankerous**, **irritable**, **touchy**
→ see Thesaurus box at GRUMPY

craps /kræps/ *n.* [U] a game played for money, using two DICE

crash¹ /kræʃ/ *v.* **1** [I,T] to have an accident in which a car, airplane, etc. hits something: *The jet crashed shortly after takeoff.* | *We* ***crashed*** *straight* ***into*** *the car ahead of us.* **2** [I,T] to hit something hard, causing a lot of damage or making a loud noise: *A baseball* ***crashed into/through*** *our living room window.* | *the sound of waves* ***crashing against*** *the rocks* **3** [I,T] if a computer crashes, or if you crash it, it suddenly stops working: *Electrical problems caused our computers to crash.* **4** [I] *spoken* **a) also crash out** to go to bed, or to go to sleep very quickly because you are very tired: *I crashed out on the sofa watching TV.* **b)** to stay at someone's house for the night: *You can crash at our place tonight.* **5** [I] if a STOCK MARKET crashes, the value of STOCKS falls suddenly and by a large amount **6** [T] *informal* if you crash a party or event, you go to it although you have not been invited

crash² *n.* [C] **1** an accident in which a vehicle hits something else: *The driver was killed in the crash.* | *a* ***plane/car/bus, etc. crash***

> **THESAURUS**
>
> **accident**, **collision**, **wreck**, **pile-up**, **fender-bender**
> ➔ see Thesaurus box at ACCIDENT

2 a sudden loud noise made by something falling, breaking, etc.: *I heard a crash coming from the kitchen.* | *The tree fell over* ***with a crash.*** ➔ see picture on page A7 **3** an occasion when a computer suddenly stops working **4** an occasion when the value of STOCKS on a STOCK MARKET falls suddenly and by a large amount: *a stock market crash*

> **THESAURUS**
>
> **recession**, **depression**, **slump**
> ➔ see Thesaurus box at RECESSION

ˈcrash course *n.* [C] a short course in which you study a subject very quickly

ˈcrash ˌdiet *n.* [C] an attempt to make yourself thinner quickly by strictly limiting how much you eat

ˈcrash ˌhelmet *n.* [C] a hard hat worn by people who drive race cars, MOTORCYCLES, etc. to protect their heads

ˌcrash ˈlanding *n.* [C] an occasion when a pilot has to bring an airplane down to the ground in a more dangerous way than usual because the airplane has a problem: *He was forced to* ***make a crash landing*** *in the middle of the desert.*

crass /kræs/ *adj.* offensive and stupid: *a crass remark*

crate /kreɪt/ *n.* [C] a large box used for carrying fruit, bottles, etc.: *a crate of wine*

crater

cra·ter /ˈkreɪt̬ɚ/ *n.* [C] **1** a round hole in the ground made by something that has fallen on it or exploded on it: *a bomb crater* **2** the round open top of a VOLCANO

crave /kreɪv/ *v.* [T] to want something very much: *Most little kids crave attention.*

crav·ing /ˈkreɪvɪŋ/ *n.* [C] a very strong desire for something: *a* ***craving for*** *chocolate*

craw·fish /ˈkrɔˌfɪʃ/ *n.* plural **crawfish** [C] CRAYFISH

crawl¹ /krɔl/ *v.* [I] **1** to move on your hands and knees or with your body close to the ground: *They had to* ***crawl through*** *a tunnel to escape.* | *The baby* ***crawled across*** *the floor.* ➔ see Topic box at BABY ➔ see picture on page A9 **2** if a vehicle crawls, it moves very slowly: *We got stuck behind a truck crawling along at 25 mph.* **3 be crawling with sth** to be completely covered with insects or people: *The food was crawling with ants.* **4** if an insect crawls somewhere, it moves there

crawl² *n.* **1** [singular] a very slow speed: *Traffic has slowed to a crawl.* **2 the crawl** a way of swimming in which you lie on your stomach and move one arm, and then the other, over your head ➔ see picture at SWIM¹

cray·fish /ˈkreɪˌfɪʃ/ *n.* plural **crayfish** [C,U] a small animal like a LOBSTER that lives in rivers and streams, or the meat from this animal

cray·on /ˈkreɪɑn, -ən/ *n.* [C] a stick of colored WAX that children use to draw pictures

craze /kreɪz/ *n.* [C] a fashion, game, type of music, etc. that is very popular for a short time: *the latest teenage craze*

> **THESAURUS**
>
> **fad**, **cult**
> ➔ see Thesaurus box at POPULAR

crazed /kreɪzd/ *adj.* a crazed person behaves in a wild and uncontrolled way, as if he/she is mentally ill: *a crazed gunman*

cra·zy /ˈkreɪzi/ *adj.* comparative **crazier**, superlative **craziest** *informal* **1** very strange or not sensible: *You must be crazy to drive in that snow!* | *Whose* ***crazy idea*** *was it to go hiking in November?* **2 be crazy about sb/sth** to like someone or something very much: *John's crazy about skiing.* **3** angry or annoyed [**= mad**]: *Shut* up! You're ***driving*** *me* ***crazy*** (=really annoying me)*! | Dad's going to* ***go crazy*** (=be very angry) *when he hears that I flunked math.* **4 like crazy** very much or very quickly: *These mosquito bites on my leg are itching like crazy.* **5** mentally ill: *Sometimes I think I'm* ***going crazy***.—**crazily** *adv.* —**craziness** *n.* [U]

THESAURUS

mentally ill – having an illness of the mind that affects the way you behave: *Her father had been mentally ill.*
insane – permanently and seriously mentally ill: *A psychiatrist said that he was insane at the time of the crime.*
disturbed – not behaving in a normal way because of mental or emotional problems: *emotionally disturbed children*
nuts informal – crazy: *He looked at me like I was nuts.*
loony informal – crazy: *De Niro plays a loony baseball fan stalking his favorite player.*

C

creak /krik/ *v.* [I] if something such as a door or wooden floor creaks, it makes a long high noise when it moves: *The door creaked shut behind him.* —**creak** *n.* [C] —**creaky** *adj.* ➔ see picture on page A7

cream¹ /krim/ *n.* **1** [U] a thick white liquid that comes from milk: *Do you take cream and sugar in your coffee?* **2** [U] a pale yellow-white color **3** [C,U] used in the names of foods containing cream or something similar to it: *banana cream pie | cream of mushroom soup* **4** [C,U] a thick smooth substance that you put on your skin to make it feel soft, treat a medical condition, etc.: *The doctor gave me a cream to put on my sunburn.* **5 the cream of the crop** the best people or things in a group: *These students represent the cream of the academic crop.* —**cream** *adj.* —**creamy** *adj.*

cream² *v.* [T] **1** to mix foods together until they become a thick smooth mixture: *Next, cream the butter and sugar.* **2 cream sb** *informal* to hit someone very hard or easily defeat someone in a game, competition, etc.: *The Yankees creamed the Red Sox 16–1.*

ˌcream ˈcheese *n.* [U] a type of soft white cheese

cream·er /ˈkrimɚ/ *n.* [U] a white substance you can use instead of milk or cream in coffee or tea

crease¹ /kris/ *n.* [C] **1** a line on a piece of cloth, paper, etc. where it has been folded, crushed, or IRONed: *She smoothed the creases from her skirt.* **2** a fold in someone's skin

crease² *v.* [T] to become marked with a line or lines, or to make a line appear on cloth, paper, etc. by folding or crushing it: *Try not to crease your jacket.* —**creased** *adj.*

cre·ate /kriˈeɪt/ *v.* [T] **1** to make something new exist or happen: *Scientists believe the universe was created by a big explosion. | Why do you want to create problems for everyone?* **2** to invent or design something: *Janet created a wonderful chocolate dessert for the party.*

THESAURUS

invent, **think up**, **come up with**, **devise**, **make up**, **dream up**
➔ see Thesaurus box at INVENT

cre·a·tion /kriˈeɪʃən/ *n.* **1** [U] the act of creating something: *the* ***creation of*** *300 new jobs* **2** [C] something that has been created: *the artist's latest creation* **3 the Creation** according to many religions, the time when the universe and everything in it was made by God

cre·a·tive /kriˈeɪt̬ɪv/ *adj.* **1** good at thinking of new ideas: *I try to surround myself with creative people.* **2** involving the use of imagination to produce new ideas or things: *a creative solution to our problems* —**creatively** *adv.* —**creativity** *n.* [U]

cre·a·tor /kriˈeɪt̬ɚ/ *n.* [C] **1** someone who made or invented a particular thing: *Walt Disney, the creator of Mickey Mouse* **2 the Creator** God

crea·ture /ˈkritʃɚ/ *n.* [C] **1** an animal, fish, or insect: *Native Americans believe that all* ***living creatures*** *should be respected.* **2** an imaginary animal or person, or one that is very strange and frightening: *creatures from outer space* **3 creature comforts** all the things that make life comfortable and enjoyable **4 a creature of habit** someone who always does things in the same way or at the same time

cre·dence /ˈkridns/ *n.* [U] *formal* the acceptance of something as true: *His ideas quickly* ***gained credence*** (=started to be believed) *among economists.*

cre·den·tials /krəˈdɛnʃəlz/ *n.* [plural] **1** someone's education, achievements, experience, etc. that prove that s/he has the ability to do something: *a woman with* ***impressive credentials*** **2** a document which proves who you are: *May I see your credentials?*

cred·i·bil·i·ty /ˌkrɛdəˈbɪlət̬i/ *n.* [U] the quality of deserving to be believed and trusted: *The scandal has ruined his credibility as a leader.*

cred·i·ble /ˈkrɛdəbəl/ *adj.* deserving or able to be believed or trusted: *a credible witness* —**credibly** *adv.*

cred·it¹ /ˈkrɛdɪt/ *n.* **1** [U] an arrangement with a bank, store, etc. that allows you to buy something and pay for it later: *We bought a new stove* ***on credit***. **2** [U] praise given to someone for doing something: *They never* ***give*** *Jess any* ***credit for*** *all the extra work he does. | I can't* ***take all the credit***; *Nicky helped a lot too. | The team* ***deserves credit*** *for playing hard until the end. | Much* ***to*** *Todd's* ***credit***, *the dance was a great success.* **3 be a credit to sb/sth** to be so successful or good that the people around you can be proud of you: *Jo's a* *credit to her family.* **4 be in credit** to have money in your bank account **5** [C] a successfully completed part of a course at a university or college: *She needs 30 more credits to graduate.* **6 have sth to your credit** to have achieved something: *She already has two best-selling novels to her credit.* **7 the credits** [plural] a list of all the people involved in making a television program or movie

credit² *v.* [T] **1** to add money to a bank account [≠ **debit**]: *The check has been **credited to** your account.* | *For some reason the bank has **credited** my account **with** an extra $237.* **2 be credited to sb/sth** if something is credited to someone or something, s/he or it is said to have achieved it or be the reason for it: *The revolutionary new drug is widely credited to Arthur Kessler.* **3 credit sb with (doing) sth** to believe that someone has a good quality or has done something good: *I wouldn't have credited him with that much intelligence.*

cred·it·a·ble /ˈkrɛdɪṭəbəl/ *adj.* deserving praise or approval: *a creditable piece of scientific research*

ˈcredit card *n.* [C] a small plastic card that you use to buy goods or services and pay for them later: *Can I **pay by credit card**?*

ˈcredit ˌlimit *n.* [C] the amount of money that you are allowed to borrow or spend using your credit card

cred·i·tor /ˈkrɛdəṭɚ/ *n.* [C] a person or organization that you owe money to [➡ **debtor**]

ˈcredit ˌrating *n.* [C] a judgment made by a bank or other company about how likely a person or a business is to pay their debts

cre·do /ˈkridoʊ/ *n.* plural **credos** [C] a short statement that expresses a belief or rule

creed /krid/ *n.* [C] a set of beliefs or principles: *people of every creed, color, and nationality*

> **THESAURUS**
>
> **faith, religion, belief**
> ➔ see Thesaurus box at FAITH

creek /krik, krɪk/ *n.* [C] **1** a small narrow stream or river **2 be up the creek (without a paddle)** *spoken* to be in a difficult situation: *I'll really be up the creek if I don't pay my bills by Friday.*

creep¹ /krip/ *v.* past tense and past participle **crept** /krɛpt/ [I] **1** to move very carefully and quietly so that no one will notice you: *She **crept down** the hall, trying not to wake up her mom.*

> **THESAURUS**
>
> **walk, march, stride, stroll, amble, wander, sneak, trudge, limp, wade, hike**
> ➔ see Thesaurus box at WALK¹

2 to move somewhere very slowly: *a tractor creeping along the road at 15 mph* **3** to gradually begin to appear: *Bitterness **crept into** his voice.* **4** to gradually increase: *The total number of people out of work **crept up** to five million.*

creep² *n.* [C] *informal* **1** someone who you dislike a lot: *Get lost, you little creep!* **2 give sb the creeps** to make you feel nervous and frightened: *That house gives me the creeps.*

creep·y /ˈkripi/ *adj.* making you feel nervous and slightly frightened: *a really creepy movie*

cre·mate /ˈkrimeɪt, krɪˈmeɪt/ *v.* [T] to burn the body of a dead person at a funeral ceremony —**cremation** /krɪˈmeɪʃən/ *n.* [C,U]

cre·ma·to·ri·um /ˌkriməˈtɔriəm/ *n.* plural **crematoriums, crematoria** /-riə/ [C] a building in which the bodies of dead people are cremated

cre·ole /ˈkrioʊl/ *n.* **1** [C,U] a language that is a combination of a European language and one or more others **2** [C] **Creole a)** someone whose family was originally from both Europe and Africa **b)** someone whose family were originally French SETTLERS in the southern U.S. —**creole** *adj.*

crepe, crêpe /kreɪp/ *n.* **1** [C] a very thin PANCAKE **2** [U] thin light cloth with very small folded lines on its surface, made from cotton, silk, wool, etc.

ˌcrepe ˈpaper *n.* [U] thin brightly colored paper with small folded lines on its surface, used for making decorations

crept /krɛpt/ *v.* the past tense and past participle of CREEP

cre·scen·do /krəˈʃɛndoʊ/ *n.* plural **crescendos** [C] a gradual increase in the loudness of a piece of music until it becomes very loud

cres·cent /ˈkrɛsənt/ *n.* [C] a curved shape that is wider in the middle and pointed on the ends: *a crescent moon* ➔ see picture at SHAPE¹

crest /krɛst/ *n.* [C] **1** [usually singular] the top of a hill or wave: *It took us over an hour to reach the **crest of** the hill.* **2** a pointed group of feathers on top of a bird's head

crest·fall·en /ˈkrɛstˌfɔlən/ *adj. formal* disappointed and sad: *Thomas was crestfallen when he heard the judge's decision.*

cre·vasse /krəˈvæs/ *n.* [C] a deep wide crack, especially in thick ice

crev·ice /ˈkrɛvɪs/ *n.* [C] a narrow crack, especially in rock

crew /kru/ *n.* [C] **1** all the people that work together on a ship, airplane, etc.: *the **crew of** the space shuttle*

> **THESAURUS**
>
> **group, crowd, team, gang, mob, bunch, mass, party**
> ➔ see Thesaurus box at GROUP¹

2 a group of people who work together on something: *the movie's cast and crew*

ˈcrew cut *n.* [C] a very short hairstyle for men

C

crib /krɪb/ *n.* [C] a baby's bed with BARS around the sides → see Topic box at BABY → see picture at BED[1]

'crib death *n.* [C] the sudden and unexpected death of a healthy baby while s/he is asleep

'crib sheet also 'crib note *n.* [C] *informal* something on which answers to questions are written, usually used in order to cheat on a test

crick /krɪk/ *n.* [C] a sudden stiff and painful feeling in a muscle in your neck or back

crick·et /'krɪkɪt/ *n.* **1** [C] a small brown insect that can jump and makes a short loud noise by rubbing its wings together **2** [U] a game in which two teams try to get points by hitting a ball and running between two sets of sticks

C

crime /kraɪm/ *n.* **1** [U] illegal activities in general: *There's very little crime in this neighborhood.* | *Women are less likely to **commit crime**.* | *methods of **crime prevention*** | *The **crime rate** has gone down in the last few years.* | ***Violent crime** is up by 8%.*

THESAURUS

Crimes that involve stealing things
theft – the crime of stealing things: *car theft*
robbery – the crime of stealing money or valuable things from a bank, store, etc.: *armed robbery*
burglary – the crime of going into someone's home in order to steal money or valuable things
shoplifting – the crime of taking things from a store without paying for them

crimes that involve attacking people
assault – a crime in which someone is physically attacked
mugging – a crime in which someone is attacked and robbed in a public place
murder – a crime in which someone is deliberately killed
rape – a crime in which someone is forced to have sex
→ ATTACK, CRIMINAL, STEAL

2 [C] an illegal action that can be punished by law: *She **committed** a number of **crimes** in the area.* ▶ Don't say "Do a crime." ◀ ***crimes against** the elderly* | *Rape is a very **serious crime**.* **3 it's a crime (to do sth)** *spoken* said when you think something is morally wrong: *It's a crime to throw away all that food.*

crim·i·nal[1] /'krɪmənəl/ *adj.* **1** relating to crime: *a **criminal record*** (=an official record of crimes someone has committed) | *street gangs involved in **criminal activity*** | *Drinking and driving is a **criminal offense*** (=a crime). **2** *informal* wrong but not illegal: *It's criminal to charge so much to go to a movie.* —**criminally** *adv.*

criminal[2] *n.* [C] someone who has done something wrong or illegal: *Police have described the man as a violent and dangerous criminal.*

THESAURUS

Types of criminals
offender – someone who is guilty of a crime
thief – someone who steals things
robber – someone who steals things, especially from stores or banks
burglar – someone who goes into buildings to steal things
shoplifter – someone who takes things from stores without paying for them
pickpocket – someone who steals things from people's pockets
attacker – someone who uses violence to hurt someone
mugger – someone who attacks and steals from another person in a public place
murderer – someone who deliberately kills another person
rapist – someone who forces another person to have sex
→ CRIME

crimp[1] /krɪmp/ *n.* **put a crimp in/on sth** to reduce or restrict something, so that it is difficult to do something else: *Falling wheat prices have put a crimp on farm incomes.*

crimp[2] *v.* [T] to restrict the development, use, or growth of something: *The lack of effective advertising has crimped sales.*

crim·son /'krɪmzən/ *n.* [U] a dark slightly purple red color —**crimson** *adj.*

cringe /krɪndʒ/ *v.* [I] **1** to move away from someone or something because you are afraid: *a dog cringing in the corner* **2** to feel embarrassed by something: *Paul **cringed at the thought** of having to speak in public.* —**cringe** *n.* [C]

crin·kle /'krɪŋkəl/ **also crinkle up** *v.* [I,T] to become covered with small folds, or make something do this: *Mandy crinkled her nose in disgust.* —**crinkled** *adj.* —**crinkly** *adv.*

crip·ple[1] /'krɪpəl/ *n.* [C] *offensive* someone who has difficulty walking because his/her legs are damaged or injured

cripple[2] *v.* [T] **1** to injure someone so s/he can no longer walk: *He was crippled in a car accident.* **2** to make something very weak or damage it: *The country's economy has been crippled by drought.* —**crippled** *adj.* —**crippling** *adj.*

cri·sis /'kraɪsɪs/ *n.* plural **crises** /'kraɪsiz/ [C,U] a time when a situation is very bad or dangerous: *an **economic/budget/financial, etc. crisis*** | *The president faces a **political crisis.*** | *In times of crisis you find out who your real friends are.* | *The stock market is suffering from a crisis of confidence.*

crisp /krɪsp/ *adj.* **1** pleasantly dry and hard enough to be broken easily: *He stepped carefully through the crisp, deep snow.* **2** food that is crisp is pleasantly hard or firm when you bite it: *a nice crisp salad* **3** paper or clothes that are crisp are fresh, clean, and new: *a crisp $20 bill* **4** weather that is crisp is cold and dry: *a crisp winter morning* —**crispy** *adv.*

crisp·y /ˈkrɪspi/ *adj.* crispy food is pleasantly hard: *crispy bacon*

criss·cross /ˈkrɪskrɔs/ *v.* [I,T] **1** to travel many times from one side of an area to the other: *crisscrossing the country by plane* **2** to make a pattern of straight lines that cross over each other

criteria /kraɪˈtɪriə/ *n.* [plural] singular **criteria** /-riən/ [C usually plural] facts or standards used in order to help you judge or decide something: *What are the main **criteria for** awarding the prize?*

crit·ic /ˈkrɪṭɪk/ *n.* [C] **1** someone whose job is to give his/her judgment about whether a movie, book, etc. is good or bad: *a literary critic for The Times* **2** someone who says that a person, organization, or idea is bad or wrong: *a **critic of** the tobacco industry*

crit·i·cal /ˈkrɪṭɪkəl/ *adj.* **1** if you are critical, you say that you think someone or something is bad or wrong: *Darren was **critical of** the plan.* | *a **highly critical** report* **2** very important: *Newspapers play a critical role in our society.* | *This next phase is **critical to** the project's success.* **3** very serious or dangerous: *The victim remains **in critical condition*** (=seriously ill or injured). **4** [only before noun] making a careful judgment about whether someone or something is good or bad: *a **critical analysis** of the play* —**critically** *adv.*

crit·i·cism /ˈkrɪṭəˌsɪzəm/ *n.* [C,U] **1** remarks that show what you think is bad about someone or something [≠ **praise**]: *I don't think his **criticisms of** the project are justified.* | *The movie **drew criticism** from religious groups.* | *U.S. officials have come under **harsh/sharp/fierce, etc. criticism** for their handling of the war.* | *Kate doesn't **take/accept criticism** well* (=accept that it may be true). | *We try to give students **constructive criticism*** (=helpful advice). **2** the activity of giving a professional judgment of a movie, play, book, etc., or the writing that expresses this judgment: *literary criticism*

crit·i·cize /ˈkrɪṭəˌsaɪz/ *v.* [I,T] to say what faults you think someone or something has [≠ **praise**]: *Journalists **criticized** the White House **for** cutting the Social Security budget.* | *The government's policies have been **sharply/harshly/severely, etc. criticized**.* | *a **widely criticized*** (=criticized by a lot of people) *ad campaign*

cri·tique[1] /krɪˈtik/ *n.* [C] a piece of writing describing the good and bad qualities of a play, film, book, etc.: *a **critique of** John Updike's latest novel*

critique[2] *v.* [T] to judge whether someone or something is good or bad: *a group of artists meeting to critique each other's work*

crit·ter /ˈkrɪṭɚ/ *n.* [C] *spoken* a creature, especially an animal

croak /kroʊk/ *v.* **1** [I] to make a deep low sound like the sound a FROG makes **2** [I,T] to speak in a low rough voice **3** [I] *slang* to die —**croak** *n.* [C]

cro·chet /kroʊˈʃeɪ/ *v.* [I,T] to make clothes, hats, etc. from YARN, using a special needle with a hook at one end

croc·o·dile /ˈkrɑkəˌdaɪl/ *n.* [C] a large REPTILE with a long body and a long mouth with sharp teeth that lives in rivers and lakes in hot countries

cro·cus /ˈkroʊkəs/ *n.* [C] a small purple, yellow, or white flower that appears in spring

crois·sant /krwɑˈsɑnt/ *n.* [C] a curved piece of soft bread, usually eaten for breakfast → see picture at BREAD

cro·ny /ˈkroʊni/ *n.* plural **cronies** [C] *informal disapproving* one of a group of friends who use their power or influence to help each other: *one of his **political cronies***

crook /krʊk/ *n.* [C] **1** *informal* a criminal or dishonest person: *a bunch of crooks* **2 the crook of your arm** the inside part of your arm, where it bends

crook·ed /ˈkrʊkɪd/ *adj.* **1** not straight: *crooked teeth*

THESAURUS

bent, twisted, curved, warped, wavy
→ see Thesaurus box at BENT[2]

2 *informal* not honest: *a crooked cop*

croon /krun/ *v.* [I,T] to sing or speak softly about love —**crooner** *n.* [C]

crop[1] /krɑp/ *n.* [C] **1** a plant such as corn, wheat, etc. that farmers grow and sell: *Most of the land is used for **growing crops**.* **2** the amount of corn, wheat, etc. that is produced in a single season: *a **bumper crop*** (=a very large amount) *of barley* **3 a crop of sb/sth** *informal* a group of people, problems, etc. that arrive at the same time: *this year's crop of college freshmen*

crop[2] *v.* past tense and past participle **cropped**, present participle **cropping** [T] to make something shorter by cutting it: *Her hair was **closely cropped**.*

crop up *phr. v.* to suddenly happen or appear: *Several problems cropped up soon after we bought the car.*

cro·quet /kroʊˈkeɪ/ *n.* [U] an outdoor game in which you hit heavy balls under curved wires using a wooden hammer

cross[1] /krɔs/ *v.* **1** [I,T] to go from one side of a road, river, place, etc. to the other: *Look both ways before **crossing the street**!* | *the first ship to cross the Pacific* | *Thousands of people **cross the border** from Mexico to the U.S. each year.* | *Thugwane was the first runner to cross the finish line.* **2** [I,T] if two or more roads, lines, etc. cross, or if one crosses another, they go across each other: *There's a post office where Main Street crosses Elm.* **3** [T] if you cross your arms, legs, or ANKLES, you put one on top of the other: *She sat down and crossed her legs.* **4 cross your mind** if something crosses your mind, you suddenly think about it: ***It** never **crossed** my **mind that** she might be sick.* **5** [T] to make someone angry by refusing to

C

do what s/he wants: *I wouldn't cross her if I were you.* **6 cross the line** to go beyond the limits of appropriate behavior and begin acting in an unacceptable way: *The officers crossed the line when they began beating the suspect.* **7** [T] to mix two different types of animal or plant to produce young animals or plants: *Wolves can be* ***crossed with*** *domestic dogs.* **8 cross my heart (and hope to die)** *spoken* used to say that you promise that you will do something or that what you are saying is true **9 cross your fingers/fingers crossed** used to say that you hope something will happen: *People vote, cross their fingers, and hope for the best.*

C

cross sth ⇔ **off** *phr. v.* to draw a line through something on a list to show that you have dealt with it: *Cross off their names as they arrive.*

cross sth ⇔ **out** *phr. v.* to draw a line through something that you have written because it is not correct: *The salesman crossed out $222 and wrote $225.*

cross² *n.* [C] **1** an upright wooden post with another post crossing it near the top. In the past, people were punished by being fastened to the post and left to die: ***the cross*** (=the cross that Jesus Christ died on) **2** an object, sign, etc. in the shape of a cross that is used to represent the Christian faith: *She wore a tiny gold cross around her neck.* **3** a mixture of two things: *His dog is a* ***cross between*** *a retriever and a collie.*

cross³ *adj. old-fashioned* annoyed and angry

cross·bow /ˈkrɔsboʊ/ *n.* [C] a weapon used in order to shoot ARROWS

cross·check /ˌkrɔsˈtʃɛk, ˈkrɔsttʃɛk/ *v.* [T] to make sure that something is correct by using a different method to check it again

ˌcross-ˈcountry *adj.* [only before noun] **1** across fields and not along roads: *cross-country running* | *cross-country skiers* **2** from one side of a country to the other side: *a cross-country flight*

ˌcross-ˈcultural *adj.* belonging to or involving two or more societies, countries, or cultures: *cross-cultural trade*

ˌcross-ˈdressing *n.* [U] the practice of wearing the clothes of the opposite sex, especially for sexual pleasure —**cross-dress** *v.* [I] —**cross-dresser** *n.* [C]

ˌcross-exˈamine *v.* [T] to ask someone questions to discover whether s/he has been telling the truth, especially in a court of law —**ˌcross-examiˈnation** *n.* [C,U]

ˌcross-ˈeyed *adj.* having eyes that both look inward toward each other

cross·fire /ˈkrɔsfaɪɚ/ *n.* [U] **1** a situation in which you are badly affected by an argument, even though it does not involve you: *During a divorce, kids often get* ***caught in the crossfire.*** **2** bullets traveling toward each other from different directions: *A few reporters were* ***caught in the crossfire.***

cross·ing /ˈkrɔsɪŋ/ *n.* [C] **1** a marked place where you can safely cross a road, railroad, river, etc. **2** a place where two roads, lines, etc. cross **3** a trip across the ocean, a lake, a river, etc.

cross-leg·ged /ˈkrɔs ˌlɛgɪd, -lɛgd/ *adj., adv.* in a sitting position with your knees apart and one foot over the opposite leg: *We* ***sat cross-legged*** *on the floor*

cross·o·ver /ˈkrɔsˌoʊvɚ/ *n.* [C,U] a situation in which something or someone is popular or successful in different areas or is liked by different types of people, for example when a popular song is liked by people who usually only like serious music: *The song became a crossover hit.*

ˌcross-ˈpurposes *n.* **at cross-purposes** if two people are at cross-purposes, they become confused because they think they are talking about the same thing, although they are not

ˌcross-ˈreference *n.* [C] a note in a book telling you to look on a different page for more information

cross·roads /ˈkrɔsroʊdz/ *n.* plural **crossroads** [C] **1** a place where two roads cross each other **2** a time when you have to make an important decision about your future: *Neale's career was* ***at a crossroads.***

ˌcross ˈsection, cross-section *n.* [C] **1** a group of people or things that is typical of a larger group: *a* ***cross-section of*** *the American public* **2** something that has been cut in half so that you can look at the inside, or a drawing of this: *a* ***cross section of*** *the brain*

ˈcross street *n.* [C] a street that crosses another street: *The nearest cross street is Victory Boulevard.*

ˌcross-ˈtrainer *n.* [C usually plural] a type of shoe that can be worn for playing different types of sports

ˌcross-ˈtraining *n.* [U] the activity of training for more than one sport at the same time

cross·walk /ˈkrɔswɔk/ *n.* [C] a marked place where people can cross a road safely [➡ **crossing**]

cross·word puz·zle /ˈkrɔswɚd ˌpʌzəl/ **also crossword** *n.* [C] a word game in which you write the answers to CLUES (=questions) in a pattern of numbered boxes ➔ see picture at PUZZLE¹

crotch /krɑtʃ/ *n.* [C] the place where your legs join at the top, or the part of a piece of clothing that covers this

crotch·et·y /ˈkrɑtʃət̬i/ *adj. informal* easily annoyed or made angry: *a crotchety old man*

crouch /kraʊtʃ/ **also crouch down** *v.* [I] to lower your body close to the ground by bending your knees and back: *We crouched down behind the wall to hide.* ➔ see picture on page A9

crow¹ /kroʊ/ *n.* [C] **1** a large black bird that makes a loud sound **2 as the crow flies** used to describe the distance between two places when measured in a straight line: *My house is ten miles from here as the crow flies.*

crow² *v.* [I] **1** to make the loud sound of a ROOSTER **2** to talk very proudly about yourself or your achievements: *His supporters are still crowing about the court's decision.*

crow·bar /'kroʊbɑr/ *n.* [C] a strong iron BAR with a curved end, used for forcing things open

crowd[1] /kraʊd/ *n.* **1** [C] a large group of people in one place: *a* ***crowd of*** *reporters* | *A* ***crowd gathered*** *to watch the parade.* | *Shop early and* ***avoid the crowds***. | ***The crowd*** (=audience at an event) *roared for more.*

THESAURUS

group, team, crew, gang, mob, bunch, mass, party
➔ see Thesaurus box at GROUP[1]

2 [singular] ordinary people: *He likes to* ***stand out from the crowd*** (=be different from ordinary people). **3** [singular] *informal* a group of people who know each other well: *I guess* ***the usual crowd*** *will be at the party.*

crowd[2] *v.* [I,T] if people crowd somewhere, they are there in large numbers: *People* ***crowded around*** *the scene of the accident.* | *The prisoners were all* ***crowded together*** *in a small cell.* | *Shoppers crowded the malls in the week before Christmas.*

crowd sb/sth ⇔ **out** *phr. v.* to force someone or something to leave a place: *Big supermarkets have been crowding out small grocery stores for years.*

crowd·ed /'kraʊdɪd/ *adj.* very full of people or things: *a crowded room* | *The streets were* ***crowded with*** *tourists.*

crown[1] /kraʊn/ *n.* [C] **1** a circle made of gold and jewels that a king or queen wears on his or her head **2** an artificial top for a damaged tooth **3** the position you have if you have won a sports competition: *He lost the heavyweight boxing crown in 1972.* **4** the top part of a hat, head, or hill: *a hat with a high crown*

crown[2] *v.* [T] **1** to put a crown on someone's head, so that s/he officially becomes king or queen: *He was crowned at the age of six.* **2** to make something complete or perfect by adding to it: *His career was crowned by the best actor award.*

crown·ing /'kraʊnɪŋ/ *adj.* [only before noun] better, more important, etc. than anything else: *Winning a fourth championship was her* ***crowning achievement***.

cru·cial /'kruʃəl/ *adj.* very important: *This election is* ***crucial to*** *Israel's future.* | *Sunday's game is* ***crucial for*** *the Giants.* | *Two witnesses* ***played a crucial role*** *in tracking down the killer.*—**crucially** *adv.*

THESAURUS

important, vital, essential, major, significant, key
➔ see Thesaurus box at IMPORTANT

cru·ci·fix /'krusəˌfɪks/ *n.* [C] a CROSS with a figure of Christ on it

cru·ci·fix·ion /ˌkrusə'fɪkʃən/ *n.* **1** [C,U] the act of killing someone by fastening him/her to a cross **2 the Crucifixion** the death of Christ in this way, or a picture or object that represents it

cru·ci·fy /'krusəˌfaɪ/ *v.* past tense and past participle **crucified**, third person singular **crucifies** [T] **1** to kill someone by fastening him/her to a cross **2** *informal* to criticize someone severely and cruelly: *If the newspapers find out, you'll be crucified.*

crud /krʌd/ *n.* [U] *informal* something that is bad or disgusting to look at, taste, smell, etc.: *I can't get this crud off my shoe.* —**cruddy** *adj.*

crude /krud/ *adj.* **1** offensive or rude, especially by referring to sex in an unacceptable way [➡ **vulgar**]: *crude language* **2** in a natural or raw condition: *crude oil* **3** not developed to a high standard: *a crude shelter in the forest* —**crudely** *adv.*

cru·el /'kruəl/ *adj.* **1** deliberately hurting people or animals: *Children can be very* ***cruel to*** *each other.* | *Keeping animals in cages seems cruel.*

THESAURUS

mean, unkind, nasty, thoughtless
➔ see Thesaurus box at MEAN[2]

2 making someone suffer or feel unhappy: *Her father's death was* ***a cruel blow***. | *Show business can be cruel.* —**cruelly** *adv.*

cru·el·ty /'kruəlti/ *n.* plural **cruelties** [C,U] behavior or actions that are cruel: ***cruelty to*** *animals* | *the cruelties of war*

cruise[1] /kruz/ *v.* **1** [I] to move at a steady speed in a car, airplane, boat, etc.: *We cruised along at 65 miles per hour.* **2** [I,T] *informal* to drive a car without going to any particular place: *Kids were cruising up and down Main Street.* **3** [I,T] to sail somewhere for pleasure: *We will cruise the Caribbean.* **4** [I] to win something easily: *Blair* ***cruised to victory*** *by a little over two minutes.*

cruise[2] *n.* [C] a vacation on a large boat: *a Caribbean cruise*

cruis·er /'kruzɚ/ *n.* [C] **1** a large fast ship used by the navy **2** a police car **3** a boat used for pleasure

'cruise ship *n.* [C] a large ship with restaurants, BARS, etc. that people travel on for a vacation

THESAURUS

ship, liner, ferry, freighter, tanker, barge, aircraft carrier, battleship, cruiser, submarine, warship
➔ see Thesaurus box at SHIP[1]

crumb /krʌm/ *n.* [C] **1** a very small piece of bread, cake, etc.

THESAURUS

piece, scrap, chunk, lump, fragment, slice
➔ see Thesaurus box at PIECE[1]

2 a very small amount: *a few* ***crumbs of*** *information*

crum·ble /ˈkrʌmbəl/ *v.* **1** [I,T] to break into small pieces, or to make something do this: *an old stone wall, crumbling with age* | *Crumble the cheese on top.* **2** [I] to lose power, become weak, or fail: *the crumbling peace process*

crum·my /ˈkrʌmi/ *adj. spoken* bad or of bad quality: *a crummy movie*

crum·ple /ˈkrʌmpəl/ *v.* [I,T] to crush paper or cloth, or to be crushed in this way: *Dan tore the page out, crumpled it, and threw it in the wastepaper basket.* —**crumpled** *adj.*

C

crunch¹ /krʌntʃ/ *v.* **1** [I] to make a sound like something being crushed: *Our feet* ***crunched on*** *the frozen snow.* **2** [I,T] to eat hard food in a way that makes a noise: *The dog was* ***crunching on*** *a bone.* —**crunchy** *adj.*

crunch² *n.* **1** [singular] a noise like the sound of something being crushed: *the* ***crunch of*** *footsteps on gravel* ➔ see picture on page A7 **2** [singular] a difficult situation caused by a lack of something, especially money or time: *the hospital's* ***budget crunch*** **3 also crunch time** [singular] the moment in a situation when you must make an important decision: *Crunch time is approaching for college applicants.*

cru·sade /kruˈseɪd/ *n.* [C] a determined attempt to change something because you think you are morally right: *a* ***crusade for*** *better schools* —**crusade** *v.* [I] *students crusading against nuclear weapons*

crush¹ /krʌʃ/ *v.* [T] **1** to press something so hard that it breaks or is damaged: *Crush two cloves of garlic.* | *a car crushed by falling rocks* | *Two workers were* ***crushed to death*** *when a building collapsed.* ➔ see picture on page A4

THESAURUS

press, **squash**, **mash**, **grind**, **squeeze**
➔ see Thesaurus box at PRESS¹

2 to completely defeat someone or something, using severe methods: *The uprising was crushed by the military.* **3 crush sb's hopes/enthusiasm/confidence etc.** to make someone lose all hope, confidence, etc.

crush² *n.* **1** [C] *informal* a strong feeling of love for someone that continues only for a short time: *Ben* ***has a crush on*** *his teacher.* **2** [singular] a crowd of people in a very small space

crush·ing /ˈkrʌʃɪŋ/ *n.* [U] **1** very hard to deal with, and making you lose hope and confidence: *The army suffered a* ***crushing defeat.*** **2** a crushing remark, reply, etc. contains a very strong criticism

crust /krʌst/ *n.* [C,U] **1** the baked outside part of bread, a PIE etc. **2** a hard covering on the surface of something: *the earth's crust*

crus·ta·cean /krʌˈsteɪʃən/ *n.* [C] *technical* an animal such as a LOBSTER or a CRAB that has a hard outer shell and several pairs of legs, and usually lives in water —**crustacean** *adj.*

crust·y /ˈkrʌsti/ *adj.* having a hard crust: *crusty bread*

crutch /krʌtʃ/ *n.* [C] **1** [usually plural] one of a pair of sticks that you lean on to help you walk: *He was* ***on crutches*** *after breaking his leg.* **2** *disapproving* something that gives someone support or help, especially when this is not good for him/her: *Tom* ***uses*** *those pills* ***as a crutch.***

crux /krʌks/ *n.* **the crux** the most important part of a problem, question, argument, etc.: *The budget plan is* ***the crux of*** *the dispute between the White House and Congress*

cry¹ /kraɪ/ *v.* past tense and past participle **cried**, third person singular **cries** **1** [I] to produce tears from your eyes, usually because you are unhappy or hurt: *What are you* ***crying about****?* | *Sydney* ***cried for*** *her mother.* | *a woman* ***crying over*** *the death of her son* | *Sad movies always* ***make*** *me* ***cry.***

THESAURUS

If someone **weeps**, s/he cries a lot because s/he feels very sad.
If someone **sobs**, s/he cries a lot in a noisy way.
If someone **is in tears**, s/he is crying.
If someone **bursts into tears**, s/he suddenly starts crying.

2 [I,T] to say something loudly: *"Stop!" she cried.* | *He* ***cried for help.*** | *The crowd cried his name.* **3 for crying out loud** *spoken* said when you feel annoyed with someone: *For crying out loud, will you shut up!* **4 cry over spilled milk** *informal* to waste time worrying about something that cannot be changed **5** [I] if an animal or bird cries, it makes a loud, high sound **6 cry wolf** to often ask for help when you do not need it, so that people do not believe you when you really need help

cry out *phr. v.* **1** to make a loud sound of fear, shock, pain, etc.: *He* ***cried out in*** *pain.* **2 be crying out for sth** to need something urgently: *The health care system is crying out for reform.*

cry² *n.* plural **cries** [C] **1** a loud sound showing fear, pain, shock, etc.: *a baby's cry* | *a* ***cry of pain/joy/alarm etc.*** **2** a loud shout: *Miller heard a cry of "Stop, thief!"* **3** a sound made by a particular animal or bird: *the cries of seagulls* **4** a phrase used in order to unite people in support of a particular action or idea: *a war/battle cry* **5 a cry for help** something someone does that shows s/he is unhappy and needs help: *A suicide attempt is a cry for help.*

cry·ba·by /'kraɪˌbeɪbi/ *n.* plural **crybabies** [C] *informal disapproving* someone who cries or complains too much

cry·ing /'kraɪ-ɪŋ/ *adj.* **1 a crying need for sth** a serious need for something: ***There's a crying need for*** *better housing.* **2 it's a crying shame** *spoken* used in order to say that something is very sad or upsetting: *It would be a crying shame if the school had to close down.*

crypt /krɪpt/ *n.* [C] a room under a church, used in past times for burying people

cryp·tic /'krɪptɪk/ *adj.* having a meaning that is hard to understand: *a cryptic message* —**cryptically** *adv.*

crys·tal /'krɪstəl/ *n.* **1** [U] high quality clear glass: *crystal wine glasses* **2** [C,U] rock that is clear, or a piece of this **3** [C] a small evenly shaped object that forms naturally when a liquid becomes solid: *ice crystals*

ˌcrystal 'ball *n.* [C] a glass ball that you look into, that some people believe can show the future

ˌcrystal 'clear *adj.* **1** clearly stated and easy to understand: *I made it crystal clear that you weren't allowed to go!* **2** completely clean and clear: *The lake was crystal clear.*

crys·tal·lize /'krɪstəˌlaɪz/ *v.* [I,T] **1** if a liquid crystallizes, it forms crystals **2** if an idea or plan crystallizes, it becomes clear in your mind: *The recent events really crystallized my opposition to war.*

c-sec·tion /'si ˌsɛkʃən/ *n.* [C] CESAREAN

CT the written abbreviation of **Connecticut**

cub /kʌb/ *n.* [C] the baby of a lion, bear, etc.

cub·by·hole /'kʌbi ˌhoʊl/ *n.* [C] a small space or room, used for storing things

cube[1] /kyub/ *n.* [C] **1** a solid square object with six equal sides: *a sugar cube | ice cubes* → see picture at SHAPE[1] **2 the cube of sth** the number you get when you multiply a number by itself twice: *The cube of 3 is 27.*

cube[2] *v.* [T] **1** to multiply a number by itself twice: *2 cubed is 8.* **2** to cut something into cubes

cu·bic /'kyubɪk/ *adj.* **cubic inch/centimeter/yard etc.** a measurement of space which is calculated by multiplying the length of something by its width and height

cu·bi·cle /'kyubɪkəl/ *n.* [C] a small partly enclosed part of a room: *office cubicles*

'Cub Scouts *n.* [plural] the part of the BOY SCOUTS that is for younger boys

cuck·oo /'kuku/ *n.* plural **cuckoos** [C] a gray European bird that puts its eggs in other birds' NESTS and that has a call that sounds like its name

cu·cum·ber /'kyuˌkʌmbɚ/ *n.* [C] a long thin green vegetable, usually eaten raw → see picture at VEGETABLE

cud·dle /'kʌdl/ *v.* [I,T] to put your arms around someone or something as a sign of love: *Chris cuddled her new puppy.* —**cuddle** *n.* [C usually singular]

cuddle

THESAURUS

hug, embrace, hold
→ see Thesaurus box at HUG[1]

cuddle up *phr. v.* to lie or sit very close to someone or something: *The children* ***cuddled up to*** *each other in the dark.*

cud·dly /'kʌdli/ *adj.* soft, warm, and nice to hold: *a cuddly stuffed animal*

cue /kyu/ *n.* [C] **1** an action or event that is a signal for something else to happen: *That was a* ***cue for*** *me to leave.* **2** a word or action that is a signal for someone to speak or act in a play, movie, etc.: *Tony stood by the stage, waiting for his cue.* **3 (right/as if) on cue** happening or done at exactly the right moment: *Then Bart walked in, right on cue.* **4 take a/your cue from sb** to copy what someone else does because s/he does it correctly **5** a long straight wooden stick used for hitting the ball in games such as POOL

cuff[1] /kʌf/ *n.* [C] **1** the end of a SLEEVE (=the arm of a shirt, dress, etc.) **2** a narrow piece of cloth turned up at the bottom of your pants **3 off-the-cuff** without previous thought or preparation: *an* ***off-the-cuff remark*** **4 cuffs** [plural] *informal* HANDCUFFS

cuff[2] *v.* [T] *informal* to put HANDCUFFS on someone

'cuff link *n.* [C] a small piece of jewelry that a man can use to fasten his shirtsleeves

cui·sine /kwɪ'zin/ *n.* [U] a particular style of cooking: *French cuisine*

cul-de-sac /ˌkʌl də 'sæk, ˌkʊl-/ *n.* [C] a street with only one way in and out

cul·i·nar·y /'kʌləˌnɛri, 'kyu-/ *adj. formal* relating to cooking: *a culinary magazine*

cull /kʌl/ *v.* **1** [T] *formal* to collect information from different places: *data* ***culled from*** *various sources* **2** [I,T] to kill some of the animals in a group so that the size of the group does not increase too much —**cull** *n.* [C]

cul·mi·nate /'kʌlməˌneɪt/ *v.*
culminate in/with sth *phr. v.* to end with a particular event, especially a big or important one: *a series of arguments that culminated in divorce*

cul·mi·na·tion /ˌkʌlməˈneɪʃən/ *n.* **the culmination of sth** something important that happens after a period of development: *That discovery was the culmination of his life's work.*

cul·pa·ble /ˈkʌlpəbəl/ *adj. formal* deserving blame: *Both sides were equally culpable.* —**culpability** /ˌkʌlpəˈbɪləṭi/ *n.* [U]

cul·prit /ˈkʌlprɪt/ *n.* [C] **1** someone who has done something wrong: *Police are still looking for the culprit.* **2** the reason for a particular problem or difficulty: *High labor costs are* ***the main culprit*** *for the rise in prices.*

cult¹ /kʌlt/ *n.* [C] **1** an extreme religious group that is not part of an established religion: *a* ***religious cult***

C

THESAURUS

church, denomination, sect
→ see Thesaurus box at CHURCH

2 a fashionable or popular belief, idea, or attitude: *The whole movie industry is built on the* ***cult of*** *personality.*

cult² *adj.* [only before noun] a cult movie, person, group, etc. is one that is very popular but only among a particular group of people: *The band has developed a* ***cult following****.*

cul·ti·vate /ˈkʌltəˌveɪt/ *v.* [T] **1** to prepare and use land for growing crops and plants **2** to work hard to develop a particular skill, quality, or attitude: *He's spent years cultivating a knowledge of art.* **3** to try to develop a friendship with someone who can help you: *She worked hard to cultivate friendships with local government leaders.* —**cultivation** /ˌkʌltəˈveɪʃən/ *n.* [U]

cul·ti·vat·ed /ˈkʌltəˌveɪṭɪd/ *adj.* **1** intelligent and knowing a lot about music, art, literature, etc.: *a cultivated gentleman* **2** cultivated land is used for growing crops or plants

cul·tur·al /ˈkʌltʃərəl/ *adj.* **1** relating to a particular society and its way of life: *England has a rich cultural heritage.* | *cultural differences* **2** relating to art, literature, music, etc.: *a guide to* ***cultural events*** *in London* | *The museum is a welcome addition to the city's* ***cultural life****.* —**culturally** *adv.*

cul·ture /ˈkʌltʃɚ/ *n.* **1** [C,U] the art, beliefs, behavior, ideas, etc. of a particular society: *the culture of ancient Greece* | *I love working abroad and meeting people from different cultures.* | ***American/Western/Hispanic etc. culture*** ► Don't say "The American culture." ◄ **2** [U] art, literature, music, etc.: *Boston is a good place for anyone who is interested in culture.* | ***popular culture*** (=the music, movies, etc. that are liked by a lot of people) **3** [C,U] the process of growing BACTERIA for scientific use, or the bacteria or cells produced by this

cul·tured /ˈkʌltʃɚd/ *adj.* intelligent, polite, and interested in art, music, etc.

ˈculture ˌshock *n.* [singular, U] a feeling of being confused or anxious when you visit a foreign country for the first time

cum·ber·some /ˈkʌmbɚsəm/ *adj.* **1** a cumbersome process is slow and difficult: *Getting a passport can be a cumbersome process.* **2** heavy and difficult to move or use: *cumbersome equipment*

cu·mu·la·tive /ˈkyumyələṭɪv, -ˌleɪ-/ *adj.* increasing gradually: *the* ***cumulative effect of*** *air pollution* —**cumulatively** *adv.*

cun·ning /ˈkʌnɪŋ/ *adj.* intelligent in a dishonest way: *a cunning criminal* | *a cunning plan* —**cunning** *n.* [U] —**cunningly** *adv.*

THESAURUS

clever, crafty
→ see Thesaurus box at INTELLIGENT

cup¹ /kʌp/ *n.* [C] **1** a small, round container, usually with a handle, that you use to drink tea, coffee, etc., or the drink it contains [➡ **saucer**]: *a cup and saucer* | *a* ***cup of*** *coffee* | *a* ***paper/plastic cup*** **2** a unit for measuring liquid or food in cooking, equal to eight FLUID OUNCES or 237 milliliters: *Stir in a* ***cup of*** *flour.* **3** a specially shaped container that is given as a prize in a competition [➡ **trophy**]

cup² *v.* past tense and past participle **cupped**, present participle **cupping** [T] to form your hands into the shape of a cup: *Greta* ***cupped*** *her hands* ***around*** *the mug.*

cup·board /ˈkʌbɚd/ *n.* [C] a piece of furniture with doors and shelves, used for storing clothes, plates, food, etc.

cup·cake /ˈkʌpkeɪk/ *n.* [C] a small round cake

cur·a·ble /ˈkyʊrəbəl/ *adj.* able to be cured [≠ **incurable**]: *a curable disease*

cu·ra·tor /ˈkyʊˌreɪṭɚ, -rəṭɚ, kyʊˈreɪṭɚ/ *n.* [C] someone who is in charge of a MUSEUM

curb¹ /kɚb/ *n.* [C] the edge of a SIDEWALK, where it joins the road

curb² *v.* [T] to control or limit something: *Doctors are trying to curb the spread of the disease.*

curd /kɚd/ *n.* [C,U] the thick substance that forms in milk when it becomes sour

cur·dle /ˈkɚdl/ *v.* [I,T] if a liquid curdles, it becomes unpleasantly thick: *Do not let the sauce boil or it will curdle.*

cure¹ /kyʊr/ *v.* [T] **1** to make an injury or illness better, so that the person who was sick is well [➡ **heal**]: *Many types of cancer can now be cured.* | *Penicillin will cure most infections.* **2** to solve a problem, or improve a bad situation: *No one can completely cure unemployment.* **3** to preserve food, leather, etc. by drying it, hanging it in smoke, or covering it with salt: *cured ham*

cure² *n.* [C] **1** a medicine or medical treatment that can cure an illness or disease: *a* ***cure for*** *cancer* **2** something that solves a problem: *There's no easy* ***cure for*** *poverty.*

cur·few /ˈkɚfyu/ *n.* [C] a law that forces people to stay indoors after a particular time at night: *The* *government* ***imposed*** *a* ***curfew*** *from sunset to sunrise.*

cu·ri·o /ˈkyʊriˌoʊ/ *n.* plural **curios** [C] a small object that is interesting because it is old, beautiful, or rare

cu·ri·os·i·ty /ˌkyʊriˈɑsəṭi/ *n.* [singular, U] the desire to know about something: *Children have a natural* ***curiosity about*** *the world around them.* | *Just* ***out of curiosity*** (=because of curiosity), *how old are you?* | *I just had to* ***satisfy*** *my* ***curiosity****, so I opened the box.*

cu·ri·ous /ˈkyʊriəs/ *adj.* **1** wanting to know or learn about something: *We were* ***curious about*** *what was going on next door.* | *I was* ***curious to*** *see how it worked.* **2** strange or unusual: *a curious noise* | ***It's curious that*** *she left without saying goodbye.* —**curiously** *adv.*

curl¹ /kɚl/ *n.* [C] **1** a piece of hair that hangs in a curved shape: *a little girl with blonde curls* ➔ see picture at HAIR **2** something that forms a curved shape: *a* ***curl of*** *smoke* —**curly** *adj.*

curl² *v.* [I,T] to form a curved shape, or to make something do this: *I don't know if I should curl my hair or leave it straight.* | *Thick smoke curled from the chimney.* | *The phone cord was* ***curled around*** *her hand.*

curl up *phr. v.* **1** to lie or sit comfortably with your arms and legs bent close to your body: *Pepe curled up on the couch to watch TV.* **2** if paper, leaves, etc. curl up, their edges become curved and point up

curl·er /ˈkɚlɚ/ *n.* [C usually plural] a small metal or plastic tube for making hair curl

ˈcurling ˌiron *n.* [C] a piece of electrical equipment that you heat and use to curl your hair

cur·rant /ˈkɚənt, ˈkʌr-/ *n.* [C] a small, round, red or black BERRY, usually dried

cur·ren·cy /ˈkɚənsi, ˈkʌr-/ *n.* plural **currencies** **1** [C,U] the type of money that a country uses: *Japanese currency* | ***foreign currency*** ➔ see Thesaurus box at MONEY **2** [U] the state of being accepted or used by a lot of people: *During the 1880s, Marxism began to* ***gain currency****.*

cur·rent¹ /ˈkɚənt, ˈkʌr-/ *adj.* happening, existing, or being used now: *Sales for the current year are low.* | *the current edition of Newsweek*

THESAURUS

present, existing
➔ see Thesaurus box at PRESENT¹

current² *n.* [C] **1** a continuous movement of water or air in a particular direction: *We were swimming against a* ***strong current****.* **2** a flow of electricity through a wire: *an* ***electrical current***

ˌcurrent afˈfairs *n.* [U] important political or social events that are happening now

cur·rent·ly /ˈkɚəntli, ˈkʌr-/ *adv.* at the present time: *She's currently studying in Japan.* | *These are the most effective drugs currently available.*

THESAURUS

now, at the moment, for the moment, at present, at the present time, presently
➔ see Thesaurus box at NOW¹

cur·ric·u·lum /kəˈrɪkyələm/ *n.* plural **curricula** /-kyələ/ or **curriculums** [C] all of the subjects that are taught at a school, college, etc.

cur·ry /ˈkɚi, ˈkʌri/ *n.* plural **curries** [C,U] meat or vegetables cooked in a spicy sauce

curse¹ /kɚs/ *v.* **1** [I] to swear: *He* ***cursed at*** *the lawn mower when it didn't start.* **2** [T] to say or think bad things about someone or something that has made you angry: *I* ***cursed*** *myself* ***for*** *not buying the car insurance sooner.* **3** [T] to ask God or a magical power to harm someone

curse² *n.* [C] **1** a swear word, or words, that you say when you are angry **2** magic words that bring someone bad luck: *It feels like someone has* ***put a curse on*** *my career.*

THESAURUS

witchcraft, spell, the occult
➔ see Thesaurus box at MAGIC¹

3 something that causes trouble or harm: *Being a war hero has been both a blessing and a curse.*

cursed /kɚst/ *adj.* **be cursed with sth** to be affected by something bad: *All his life he's been cursed with bad luck.*

cur·sor /ˈkɚsɚ/ *n.* [C] a shape on a computer screen that moves to show where you are writing

cur·so·ry /ˈkɚsəri/ *adj.* done quickly without much attention to detail: *After a* ***cursory glance/look*** *at the menu, Grant ordered coffee.*

curt /kɚt/ *adj.* using very few words in a way that seems rude: *a curt response* —**curtly** *adv.*

cur·tail /kɚˈteɪl/ *v.* [T] *formal* to reduce or limit something: *new laws to curtail immigration* —**curtailment** *n.* [C,U]

cur·tain /ˈkɚtˀn/ *n.* [C] a piece of hanging cloth that can be pulled across to cover a window, divide a room, etc.: *a shower curtain* | *a new* ***pair of curtains*** | *Can you* ***close/draw/pull the curtains*** *for me?*

curt·sy, **curtsey** /ˈkɚtsi/ *v.* past tense and past participle **curtsied**, third person singular **curtsies** [I] if a woman curtsies, she bends her knees with one foot in front of the other as a sign of respect for an important person —**curtsy** *n.* [C]

curve¹ /kɚv/ *n.* [C] **1** a line or shape that bends like part of circle: *a sharp curve in the road* ➔ see picture at BENT² **2** a method of giving GRADES based on how a student's work compares with other students' work: *The test will be graded* ***on a curve****.*

curve² *v.* [I,T] to bend or move in the shape of a curve, or to make something do this: *a golf ball curving through the air* —**curved** *adj.* —**curvy** *adj.*

cush·ion¹ /ˈkʊʃən/ *n.* [C] **1** a bag filled with soft material that you put on a chair or the floor to

C

make it more comfortable [➡ **pillow**] **2** something, especially money, that prevents you from being immediately affected by a bad situation: *Savings can act as a* ***cushion against*** *unemployment.*

cushion² *v.* [T] to reduce the effects of something bad: *The law will* ***cushion the blow*** *for homeowners by gradually phasing in the tax increases.*

cusp /kʌsp/ *n.* **on/at the cusp** at the time when a situation or state is going to change: *They were young people on the cusp of adulthood.*

cuss /kʌs/ *v.* [I] *informal* to use offensive language [= **swear, curse**]

cuss sb **out** *phr. v. informal* to swear and shout at someone because you are angry

cus·tard /ˈkʌstɚd/ *n.* [C,U] a soft baked mixture of milk, eggs, and sugar

cus·to·di·an /kəˈstoʊdiən/ *n.* [C] someone who takes care of a public building or something valuable

cus·to·dy /ˈkʌstədi/ *n.* [U] **1** the legal right to take care of a child: *My ex-wife* ***has custody of*** *the kids.* | *The judge awarded us* ***joint custody*** (=both parents will have custody) *of the children.* **2 in custody** being kept in prison until going to court: *Two robbery suspects are being* ***held/kept in custody.*** —**custodial** /kəˈstoʊdiəl/ *adj.*

cus·tom /ˈkʌstəm/ *n.* **1** [C,U] something that people in a particular society do because it is traditional: *the* ***custom of*** *throwing rice at weddings* | ***It's the custom for*** *the bride's parents* ***to*** *pay for the wedding.* | *Chinese customs and culture*

THESAURUS

habit, tradition
➔ see Thesaurus box at HABIT

2 customs [plural] the place where your bags are checked for illegal goods when you go into a country: *It took forever to* ***go through customs.***

cus·tom·ar·y /ˈkʌstəˌmɛri/ *adj.* usual or normal: ***It is customary for*** *a local band* ***to*** *lead the parade.* —**customarily** /ˌkʌstəˈmɛrəli/ *adv.*

ˈcustom-built *adj.* a custom-built car, machine, etc. is built specially for a particular person

cus·tom·er /ˈkʌstəmɚ/ *n.* [C] someone who buys things from a store or company: *Dow is one of our* ***biggest customers.*** | *Foster was a* ***regular customer*** *at Brennan's Restaurant.* | *efforts to improve* ***customer service***

THESAURUS

client – someone who pays for a service: *a business meeting with clients*
shopper – someone who goes to a store looking for things to buy: *streets full of Christmas shoppers*
consumer – anyone who buys goods or uses services: *the rights of consumers*
buyer – someone who buys something very expensive, such as a car or a house: *first-time home buyers*
➔ see Thesaurus box at STORE¹

cus·tom·ize /ˈkʌstəˌmaɪz/ *v.* [T] to change something to make it more appropriate for a particular person or purpose: *a customized software package*

ˈcustom-made *adj.* a custom-made shirt, pair of shoes, etc. is made specially for a particular person

cut

cut¹ /kʌt/ *v.* past tense and past participle **cut**, present participle **cutting**

1 USE KNIFE/SCISSORS [I, T] to divide something into two or more pieces using a knife or scissors: *Do you want me to cut the cake?* | *Abby, go* ***cut*** *Grandpa* ***a piece*** *of pie.* | ***Cut*** *the cheese* ***into*** *cubes.* | *He* ***cut*** *the tomato* ***in half/two.*** | ***Cut along*** *the dotted line.*

THESAURUS

chop (up) – to cut meat, vegetables, or wood into pieces
slice – to cut bread, meat, or vegetables into thin pieces
dice – to cut vegetables or meat into small square pieces

peel – to cut the outside part off an apple, potato, etc.
carve – to cut pieces from a large piece of meat
shred – to cut vegetables into small thin pieces
grate – to cut cheese, vegetables, etc. into small pieces using a grater

2 MAKE SHORTER [T] to make something shorter using a knife, scissors, etc.: *We **cut** the **grass** once a week.* | *Did you **get** your **hair cut**?*

THESAURUS

saw – to **cut** wood, using a saw (=a tool with a row of sharp points)
chop down – to make a tree fall down by **cutting** it
mow – to **cut** grass using a special machine: *I need to mow the lawn.*
trim – to **cut** off a small amount of something to make it look neater, for example hair or a bush
snip – to **cut** something quickly, using scissors

3 REDUCE [T] to reduce the amount of something: *You need to cut the amount of fat in your diet.* | *The company had to close several factories to **cut costs**.* | *The number of soldiers had to be **cut in half**.*

THESAURUS

reduce, lower, decrease, slash, relieve, ease, lessen
➔ see Thesaurus box at REDUCE

4 INJURE [T] to injure yourself or someone else with a knife or something else that is sharp: *He **cut** his finger **on** a piece of broken glass.* | *She fell and **cut** her head **open**.*
5 cut sb free/loose to cut something such as a rope or metal in order to let someone escape: *Firemen were carefully cutting the driver free from the wreckage.*
6 MAKE A HOLE/MARK [T] to make a mark in the surface of something, open something, etc. using a sharp tool: *She used a saw to **cut** a **hole in** the ice.* | *Strange letters had been **cut into** the stone.*
7 GO A QUICK WAY [I] to go somewhere by a quicker and more direct way than usual: *We **cut through/across** our neighbor's yard.*
8 ON COMPUTER [T] to remove writing, a picture, etc. from a computer document: ***Cut and paste** the picture into a new file* (=remove it and move it to another place).
9 REMOVE PARTS FROM A MOVIE, ETC. [T] to remove parts from a movie, book, speech, etc.: *The original version was cut by more than 30 minutes.*
10 cut corners to do something less well than you should, in order to save time, effort, or money: *Parents are worried that the city is cutting corners in education.*
11 cut class/school to deliberately not go to class or school
12 cut your losses to stop doing something that is failing so that you do not waste any more money, time, or effort: *He decided to cut his losses and sell the business.*
13 cut sth short to end something earlier than you had planned: *His career was cut short by a back injury.*

SPOKEN PHRASES

14 not cut it to not be good enough to do something: *Barry's just not cutting it as a journalist.*
15 cut it close to leave yourself just enough time or money to do something: *He cut it pretty close but he made it to the airport all right.*

➔ **cut/give sb some slack** at SLACK

cut across sth *phr. v.* if a problem or feeling cuts across different groups of people, they are all affected by it: *Johnson's popularity cuts across racial lines.*

cut sth ⇔ **back** *phr. v.* to reduce the amount, size, cost, etc. of something: *Education spending cannot be cut back any further.* | *The company is attempting to **cut back on** expenses.*

cut down *phr. v.* **1** to eat, drink, or use less of something, especially in order to improve your health: *I've always smoked, but I'm trying to cut down.* | *I'm trying to **cut down on** my drinking.* **2 cut** sth ⇔ **down** to reduce the amount of something: *Email cuts down the amount of paper passed between staff.* | *By getting the design right, you can **cut down on** accidents.* **3 cut** sth ⇔ **down** to cut a tree so that the whole of it falls to the ground: *Beautiful old oaks had been cut down to build houses.*

cut in *phr. v.* **cut in front/cut in line** to unfairly go in front of other people who are waiting to do something: *Some idiot cut in front of me on the freeway and almost caused an accident.*

cut off *phr. v.* **1 cut** sth ⇔ **off** to separate something by cutting it away from the main part: *Cut the top off a large ripe pineapple.* | *His finger was cut off in the accident.* **2 cut** sth ⇔ **off** to stop the supply of something: *They're going to cut off our electricity if you don't pay that bill.* **3 be/get cut off** to be unable to finish talking to someone because something is wrong with the telephone connection **4 be cut off** if a place is cut off, it is difficult or impossible to get to or leave: *The resort town was cut off by a heavy snowfall.* **5 cut** sb **off** to interrupt someone: *He cut her off in mid-sentence.*

cut out *phr. v.* **1 cut** sth ⇔ **out** to remove something by cutting it with a knife or scissors: *The children can cut star shapes out of colored paper.* **2 cut it/that out!** *spoken* used in order to tell someone to stop doing something that is annoying you: *Cut that out, you two, or you'll go to your rooms.* **3 not be cut out for sth/to be sth** to not have the qualities that you need for a particular job or activity: *I decided I wasn't really cut out to be a teacher.*

cut sth ⇔ **up** *phr. v.* to cut something into

C

smaller pieces: *Cut up two carrots and three potatoes.*

cut² *n.* [C] **1** a reduction in the size, number, or amount of something: ***a cut in** government spending* | ***tax/job/budget, etc. cuts*** **2** a wound that you get if a sharp object cuts your skin: *Luckily, I only got a few cuts and bruises.*

THESAURUS

injury, **wound**, **bruise**, **scrape**, **sprain**, **bump**
➔ see Thesaurus box at INJURY

3 a hole or mark in a surface made by something sharp: *Make a **cut in** the paper.* **4** [usually singular] *informal* HAIRCUT **5** [usually singular] a share of something: *Everyone's taking a **cut of** the profits.* **6** a piece of meat that is cut so you can cook it: *tender cuts of beef* **7 be a cut above sb/sth** to be better than someone or something else: *The Yankees are clearly **a cut above the rest** of baseball.*

,cut and 'dried *adj.* a situation, decision, or result that is cut and dried cannot be changed

cut·back /ˈkʌtbæk/ *n.* [C] a reduction in something, especially to save money: *a number of **cutbacks in** funding for public libraries*

cute /kyut/ *adj.* **1** attractive: *What a cute little baby!* | *a cute skirt* | *Tim is so cute.*

THESAURUS

attractive, **good-looking**, **pretty**, **beautiful**, **handsome**, **gorgeous**, **stunning**, **nice-looking**, **hot**
➔ see Thesaurus box at ATTRACTIVE

2 smart in a way that can seem rude: *Ignore him; he's just trying to be cute.* —**cutely** *adv.* —**cuteness** *n.* [U]

cu·ti·cle /ˈkyut̬ɪkəl/ *n.* [C] the hard thin skin at the bottom of your FINGERNAILS

cut·ler·y /ˈkʌtˀləri/ *n.* [U] knives, forks, and spoons [= **silverware**]

cut·let /ˈkʌtˀlɪt/ *n.* [C] a small flat piece of meat: *veal cutlets*

cut·off /ˈkʌt̬ɔf/ *n.* [C] **1** a time or level at which something stops: *The **cutoff date** for applying was June 3rd.* **2 cutoffs** [plural] a pair of SHORTS that you make by cutting off the bottom part of a pair of pants

'cut-rate also 'cut-price *adj.* cheaper than normal: *cut-rate insurance*

cut·ter /ˈkʌt̬ɚ/ *n.* [C] a tool that cuts things: *wire cutters* | *a cookie cutter*

cut·throat /ˈkʌtˀθroʊt/ *adj.* a cutthroat activity or business involves people competing with each other in an unpleasant way: *cutthroat competition*

cut·ting /ˈkʌt̬ɪŋ/ *adj.* unkind and intended to upset someone: *a cutting remark*

'cutting board *n.* [C] a piece of wood or plastic that you cut food on when you are cooking

,cutting 'edge *n.* **the cutting edge (of sth)** the newest design or the most advanced way of doing something: *artists **on the cutting edge of** computer animation* —**cutting-edge** *adj.*: *cutting-edge technology*

cy·a·nide /ˈsaɪəˌnaɪd/ *n.* [U] a very strong poison

cy·ber·ca·fé /ˈsaɪbɚkæˌfeɪ/ *n.* [C] a CAFE where you can use computers connected to the Internet

cy·ber·space /ˈsaɪbɚˌspeɪs/ *n.* [U] the imaginary place that electronic messages go through when they travel from one computer to another

cy·cle¹ /ˈsaɪkəl/ *n.* [C] a number of related events that happen again and again in the same order: *the life **cycle of** flowering plants*

cycle² *v.* [I] to ride a bicycle [= **bike**]: *I cycled to the store.* —**cyclist** *n.* [C]

cy·cli·cal /ˈsaɪklɪkəl, ˈsɪ-/ **also cy·clic** /ˈsaɪklɪk, ˈsɪ-/ *adj.* happening again and again in a regular pattern: *the cyclical nature of fashion* —**cyclically** *adv.*

cy·clone /ˈsaɪkloʊn/ *n.* [C] a TORNADO

cyl·in·der /ˈsɪləndɚ/ *n.* [C] **1** a shape, object, or container with circular ends and long straight sides ➔ see picture at SHAPE¹

THESAURUS

shape, **square**, **circle**, **semicircle**, **triangle**, **rectangle**, **oval**
➔ see Thesaurus box at SHAPE¹

2 the part of an engine that is shaped like a tube, where the PISTON moves up and down: *a six-cylinder engine*

cy·lin·dri·cal /səˈlɪndrɪkəl/ *adj.* in the shape of a cylinder

THESAURUS

square, **round**, **circular**, **semicircular**, **triangular**, **rectangular**, **oval**
➔ see Thesaurus box at SHAPE¹

cym·bal /ˈsɪmbəl/ *n.* [C] a thin round metal plate that you hit to make a musical sound

cyn·ic /ˈsɪnɪk/ *n.* [C] a cynical person —**cynicism** /ˈsɪnəˌsɪzəm/ *n.* [U]

cyn·i·cal /ˈsɪnɪkəl/ *adj.* unwilling to believe that people have good, honest, or sincere reasons for doing something: *Since her divorce she's become very **cynical about** men.* —**cynically** *adv.*

cy·pher /ˈsaɪfɚ/ *n.* [C] another spelling of CIPHER

cyst /sɪst/ *n.* [C] a small LUMP containing liquid that grows in your body or under your skin

czar /zɑr/ *n.* [C] **1** *informal* someone who is very powerful in a particular job or activity: *the President's drug czar* **2** a male ruler of Russia before 1917

D, d

D, d /di/ **1** the fourth letter of the English alphabet **2** the number 500 in the system of ROMAN NUMERALS

D /di/ *n.* **1** [C] a GRADE that a teacher gives to a student's work, showing that it is not very good: *I **got a D** on the history test.* **2** [C,U] the second note in the musical SCALE of C, or the musical KEY based on this note

d. the written abbreviation of **died**: *d. 1937*

'd /d/ **1** the short form of "would": *I asked him if he'd be willing to help.* **2** the short form of "had": *We didn't know where she'd gone.*

D.A. *n.* [C] **district attorney**

dab¹ /dæb/ *n.* [C] a small amount of something: *a **dab of** butter*

dab² *v.* past tense and past participle **dabbed**, present participle **dabbing** **1** [I,T] to lightly touch something several times, usually with a cloth: *Emily **dabbed at** her eyes **with** a handkerchief.* **2** [T] to quickly put a small amount of a substance onto something: *She **dabbed** some suntan lotion **onto** her cheeks.*

dab·ble /ˈdæbəl/ *v.* [I] to do something or be involved in something in a way that is not very serious: *He **dabbles in** art.*

dachs·hund /ˈdɑkshʊnt, -hʊnd/ *n.* [C] a small dog with short legs and a long body

dad /dæd/ **also dad·dy** /ˈdædi/ *n.* [C] *informal* FATHER: *I'm having dinner with my mom and dad.* | *Dad, can I borrow $20?*

THESAURUS

relative, **parents**, **father**, **mother**, **daddy**, **mom**, **mommy**, **brother**, **sister**, **grandparents**, **grandfather**, **grandmother**, **grandpa**, **grandma**, **great-grandparents**, **uncle**, **aunt**, **nephew**, **niece**, **cousin**

→ see Thesaurus box at RELATIVE[1]

daf·fo·dil /ˈdæfəˌdɪl/ *n.* [C] a tall yellow flower that appears in early spring

daft /ˈdæft/ *adj. informal* silly or crazy

dag·ger /ˈdægɚ/ *n.* [C] a short pointed knife used as a weapon

dai·ly¹ /ˈdeɪli/ *adj.* **1** happening, done, or produced every day: *daily flights to Miami* | *a daily newspaper*

THESAURUS

regular, **hourly**, **weekly**, **monthly**, **yearly**, **annual**, **annually**

→ see Thesaurus box at REGULAR[1]

2 relating to a single day: *a daily rate of pay* **3 daily life** the ordinary things that you usually do

daily² *adv.* every day: *The zoo is open daily.*

dain·ty /ˈdeɪnti/ *adj.* small, pretty, and delicate: *dainty white gloves*

dai·qui·ri /ˈdaɪkəri, ˈdæk-/ *n.* [C] a sweet alcoholic drink made with RUM and fruit juice

dair·y¹ /ˈdɛri/ *n.* plural **dairies** [C] **1** a place on a farm where milk is kept and butter and cheese are made **2** a company that sells milk and makes cheese, butter, etc.

dairy² *adj.* [only before noun] **1** made from milk: *dairy products* **2** relating to the production of milk: *a dairy farm*

da·is /ˈdeɪəs/ *n.* [C] a low stage in a room that you stand or sit on when you are making a speech, etc., so that people can see and hear you

dai·sy /ˈdeɪzi/ *n.* plural **daisies** [C] a white flower with a bright yellow center

dal·ly /ˈdæli/ *v.* past tense and past participle **dallied**, third person singular **dallies** [I] *old-fashioned* to move slowly or waste time: *children dallying on their way to school*

Dal·ma·tian, dalmatian /dælˈmeɪʃən/ *n.* [C] a dog with white fur and small black or brown spots

dam

dam¹ /dæm/ *n.* [C] a wall built across a river in order to stop the water and make a lake

dam² *v.* past tense and past participle **dammed**, present participle **damming** [T] to build a dam across a river

dam·age¹ /ˈdæmɪdʒ/ *n.* [U] **1** physical harm that is done to something, so that it is broken or injured: *Was there any **damage to** your car?* | *The earthquake **caused/did** serious **damage**.* | ***brain damage*** **2** a bad effect on someone or something: *The closure of the factory will cause severe **damage to** the local economy.* **3 damages** [plural] *law* money that a court orders someone to pay someone else for harming that person or his/her property: *The court ordered her to pay $2,000 **in damages**.*

damage² *v.* [T] **1** to physically harm someone or something: *The storm damaged the tobacco crop.* **2** to have a bad effect on someone or something: *She didn't want to do anything that would damage her reputation.* —**damaging** *adj.*: *Poor weather has had a damaging effect on business.*

dame /deɪm/ *n.* [C] *old-fashioned* a woman

dam·na·tion /dæmˈneɪʃən/ *n.* [U] the act of punishing someone after he or she dies by sending them to HELL forever, or the state of being in hell forever

damned /dæmdd/ *adj.* **be damned** to be punished by God after your death by being sent to HELL

damned·est /ˈdæmdɪst/ *adj. spoken* **1** said in order to emphasize that something is very surprising or strange: *It was the* ***damnedest thing*** *I ever saw!* **2 do your damnedest** to try very hard to do something

damn·ing /ˈdæmɪŋ/ *adj.* showing that someone has done something very bad or wrong: *damning evidence*

damp /dæmp/ *adj.* slightly wet, usually in a cold and unpleasant way: *The house was cold and damp.* | *a damp sponge* | *damp weather* —**dampness** *n.* [U]

D

THESAURUS

humid – used to say that the weather, especially hot weather, is slightly wet and makes you uncomfortable: *humid weather/climate* | *It's unbearably humid.*
moist – used to say that something, especially food, is slightly wet, especially in a way that seems nice: *The turkey was moist and tender.* | *moist cake*

damp·en /ˈdæmpən/ *v.* [T] **1** to make something slightly wet **2** to make something such as a feeling or activity less strong: *The rainy weather didn't* ***dampen*** *our* ***enthusiasm****.*

damp·er /ˈdæmpɚ/ *n.* [C] **1 put a damper on sth** to stop something from being enjoyable: *The sad news put a damper on our celebrations.* **2** a small metal door in a FIREPLACE that is opened in order to control how strongly a fire burns

dam·sel /ˈdæmzəl/ *n.* **damsel in distress** *humorous* a young woman who needs help

dance¹ /dæns/ *v.* **1** [I] to move your body to match the style and speed of music: *Would you like to dance?* | *Jack* ***danced with*** *his wife.* | *The children* ***danced to*** *the radio.* **2 dance the waltz/tango etc.** to do a particular type of dance **3** [I] to move up, down and around in a way that looks like dancing: *The red and white balloons danced in the wind.* —**dancer** *n.* [C] —**dancing** *n.* [U] *We* ***go dancing*** *every Friday night.*

dance² *n.* **1** [C] an act of dancing: *May I have this dance* (=will you dance with me)*?* **2** [C] a particular set of movements that you perform with music: *The only dance I know is the tango.* **3** [C] a social event or party where you dance: *a school dance*

THESAURUS

ball – a large formal occasion where people dance
prom – a formal dance party for high school students, usually held at the end of a school year

4 [U] the art or activity of dancing: *dance lessons* | *modern dance*

ˈdance floor *n.* [C] a special floor in a restaurant, club, hotel, etc. for people to dance on: *couples on the dance floor*

dan·de·li·on /ˈdændəˌlaɪən/ *n.* [C] a small bright yellow wild flower

dan·druff /ˈdændrəf/ *n.* [U] small white pieces of dead skin from your head

dan·dy /ˈdændi/ *adj. humorous* very good: *This gadget makes a dandy present for a cook.*

dan·ger /ˈdeɪndʒɚ/ *n.* **1** [C,U] the possibility that someone or something will be harmed, or that something bad will happen: *Is there any* ***danger of*** *infection?* | *The UN wants to move civilians who are* ***in danger*** (=in a dangerous situation). | *Margie is* ***in danger of*** *losing her job.* | *There is a* ***danger that*** *museums will attempt to entertain rather than educate.*

THESAURUS

risk – the chance that something bad may happen: *Smoking greatly increases the risk of lung cancer.*
threat – the possibility that something bad will happen: *At that time, there seemed a constant threat of nuclear war.*
hazard – something that may be dangerous or cause accidents, problems, etc.: *Lighting fires in the park is a safety hazard.*

2 [C] something or someone that may harm you: *the* ***dangers of*** *scuba diving* | *He's a* ***danger to*** *the community.*

dan·ger·ous /ˈdeɪndʒərəs/ *adj.* **1** able or likely to harm you: *a dangerous criminal* | *Cigarette smoking is* ***dangerous to*** *your health.* | *It's* ***dangerous for*** *women* ***to*** *walk alone at night.* | *Even tiny amounts of the gas are* ***extremely/highly, etc. dangerous****.* **2** likely to cause problems, or involving a lot of risk: *The company is in a dangerous financial position.* —**dangerously** *adv.*

dan·gle /ˈdæŋgəl/ *v.* [I,T] to hang or swing loosely, or to make something do this: *keys* ***dangling from*** *a chain*

da·nish /ˈdeɪnɪʃ/ *n.* [C] a small, sweet type of cake, often with fruit inside

dank /dæŋk/ *adj.* wet and cold, in a way that does not feel nice

dap·per /ˈdæpɚ/ *adj.* a dapper man is neatly dressed

dap·pled /ˈdæpəld/ *adj. literary* marked with spots of colour, light, or shade: *the dappled light of the forest*

dare¹ /dɛr/ *v.* **1** [T] to try to persuade someone to do something dangerous: *I* ***dare*** *you* ***to*** *jump!* **2** [I] to be brave enough to do something, used especially in negative sentences: *Susan wouldn't dare tell the boss he was wrong.* **3 don't you**

dare *spoken* said in order to warn someone not to do something because it makes you angry: *Don't you dare be late!* **4 how dare you/he etc.** *spoken* said when you are very upset about what someone has said or done: *How dare you lie to me!*

dare² *n.* [C] something dangerous that you have dared someone to do: *He swam across the river* ***on a dare.***

dare·dev·il /ˈdɛrˌdɛvəl/ *n.* [C] someone who likes doing dangerous things —**daredevil** *adj.*

dar·ing¹ /ˈdɛrɪŋ/ *adj.* **1** willing to do dangerous things: *a daring escape*

THESAURUS

brave, courageous, bold
→ see Thesaurus box at BRAVE¹

2 new or unusual in a way that may shock some people: *a daring movie*

daring² *n.* [U] courage that makes you willing to take risks

dark¹ /dɑrk/ *adj.* **1** with very little or no light [≠ **light**]: *a dark room* | *Turn on the light; it's dark in here.* | *We'd better go home:* ***it's getting dark*** (=it is becoming night). | *Suddenly the room* ***went dark*** (=became dark). **2** closer to black than to white in color [➡ **light**]: *a dark blue tie* | *dark hair* **3** a dark person has black hair, brown skin, or brown eyes [≠ **fair**]: *a small dark woman* **4** threatening, mysterious, or frightening: *a dark side to his character* **5** unhappy or without hope: *the dark days of the war*

dark² *n.* **1 the dark** a situation in which there is no light: *My son is afraid of the dark.* **2 after/before dark** at night or before night begins: *Don't go out after dark.* **3 in the dark** *informal* not knowing about something important because no one has told you about it: *Employees were* ***kept in the dark*** *about the possible layoffs.*

dark·en /ˈdɑrkən/ *v.* [I,T] to make something dark, or to become dark: *The sky darkened before the storm.* | *a darkened room*

ˌdark ˈhorse *n.* [C] someone who is not well known and who surprises people by winning a competition

dark·ly /ˈdɑrkli/ *adv.* in a sad, angry, or threatening way: *scientists speaking darkly about the future*

dark·ness /ˈdɑrknɪs/ *n.* [U] a place or time when there is no light: *The whole room was* ***in darkness.*** | *We made it home just as* ***darkness fell*** (=it became night).

dark·room /ˈdɑrkrum/ *n.* [C] a special room with a red light or no light, where film from a camera is made into photographs

dar·ling¹ /ˈdɑrlɪŋ/ *n.* [C] *spoken* used when speaking to someone you love: *Come here, darling.*

darling² *adj.* [only before noun] much loved: *my darling child*

darn¹ /dɑrn/ *v.* **1 darn it!** *spoken* said when you are annoyed about something: *Darn it! I broke my shoelace.* **2** [T] to repair a hole in clothes by sewing thread through it many times

darn² **also darned** *adj., adv. spoken* said in order to emphasize what you are saying: *a darned good movie* | *The darn fool got lost.*

darned /dɑrnd/ *adj.* **I'll be darned** *spoken* said when you are surprised about something: *You went to Rutgers, too? Well, I'll be darned.*

darts

dart¹ /dɑrt/ *n.* [C] **1** a small pointed object that is thrown in a game of darts or used as a weapon **2 darts** [U] a game in which you throw darts at a circular board: *A couple of men were* ***playing darts.***

dart² *v.* [I] to move suddenly and quickly in a particular direction: *The dog* ***darted into*** *the street.*

dash¹ /dæʃ/ *v.* **1** [I] to go somewhere very quickly: *She* ***dashed into*** *the room just before the boss arrived.*

THESAURUS

run, sprint, tear, jog, go jogging, race, rush, charge, speed
→ see Thesaurus box at RUN¹, RUSH¹

2 dash sb's hopes to ruin someone's hopes completely: *Her hopes of running in the Olympics were dashed after the accident.* **3** [T] to make something hit violently against something else: *The ship was* ***dashed against*** *the rocks.*

dash off *phr. v.* **1 dash** sth ⇔ **off** to write or draw something very quickly **2** to leave somewhere very quickly

dash² *n.* **1 make a dash for sth** to run very quickly toward something: *I made a dash for the house to get my umbrella.* **2** [singular] a small amount of a liquid: *a* ***dash of*** *lemon* **3** [C] a mark (–) used in writing to separate parts of a sentence **4** [C] DASHBOARD

dash·board /ˈdæʃbɔrd/ *n.* [C] the board in front of the driver in a car that has the controls on it → see picture on page A12

DAT /dæt/ *n.* [U] **digital audio tape** tape for recording music, sound, or information in DIGITAL form

da·ta /ˈdeɪtə, ˈdætə/ *n.* [U, plural] information or facts: *He's collecting data for his report.*

da·ta·base /ˈdeɪṭəˌbeɪs/ *n.* [C] a large amount of data stored in a computer system

ˌdata ˈprocessing *n.* [U] the use of computers to store and organize information

date¹ /deɪt/ *n.* [C] **1** a particular day of the month or of the year, shown by a number: *"What's today's date?" "It's August 11th."* | *Have you* ***set a date*** (=chosen a day) *for the wedding?* | *She refused to give her* ***date of birth/birth date*** (=the day she was born). **2** an arrangement to meet someone, especially someone you like in a romantic way: *Mike's* ***going (out) on a date*** *on Friday.* | *I've* ***got a date with*** *Andrea tomorrow night.* | *Let's* ***make a date*** (=arrange a time) *to see that new movie.* **3** someone you go on a date with: *My date's taking me out to dinner.* **4 to date** up to now: *This is the best research on the subject to date.* **5 at a later date** at some time in the future **6** a small sweet sticky brown fruit with a single long seed → OUT-OF-DATE → UP-TO-DATE

D

date² *v.* **1** [I,T] to have a romantic relationship with someone: *How long have you been dating Mona?* **2** [T] to write the date on something: *a letter dated May 1, 2004* **3** [T] to find out the age of something that is very old: *Scientists have not yet dated the human remains.*

date from sth **also date back to** sth *phr. v.* to have existed since a particular time: *Independence Hall dates from the 17th century.*

dat·ed /ˈdeɪṭɪd/ *adj.* no longer fashionable: *These shoes are really dated.*

THESAURUS

old-fashioned, outdated, out-of-date
→ see Thesaurus box at OLD-FASHIONED

ˈdate rape *n.* [C,U] a RAPE that happens during a date

daub /dɔb/ *v.* [T] to put paint or a soft substance on a surface in a careless way

daugh·ter /ˈdɔṭɚ/ *n.* [C] someone's female child [➡ **son**]: *the* ***daughter of*** *a local farmer*

ˈdaughter-in-law *n.* plural **daughters-in-law** [C] the wife of your son

daunt·ed /ˈdɔntɪd/ *adj.* [not before noun] feeling afraid or worried: *Cooper is feeling* ***daunted by*** *his new responsibilities.*

daunt·ing /ˈdɔntɪŋ/ *adj.* frightening or worrying: *a daunting task*

daw·dle /ˈdɔdl/ *v.* [I] to take a long time to do something or go somewhere: *Stop dawdling; we'll be late.*

dawn¹ /dɔn/ *n.* [C,U] **1** the time of day when light first appears: *We talked until dawn.* | *I got up* ***at dawn*** *to milk the cows.* | *As* ***dawn broke*** (=it started to get light), *the fire was under control.* | *The boat left* ***at the crack of dawn*** (=very early in the morning). **2 the dawn of sth** the time when something began or first appeared: *the dawn of civilization*

dawn² *v.* [I] if a day or morning dawns, it begins: *The morning dawned cool and clear.*

dawn on sb *phr. v.* to realize something for the first time: *It suddenly* ***dawned on*** *me* ***that*** *he was right.*

day /deɪ/ *n.*

1 24 HOURS [C] a period of time equal to 24 hours [➡ **daily**]: *I'll be back in ten days.* | *The letter arrived two days ago.* | *"What day is it today?" "Tuesday."* | *The* ***next/following day****, Hayes was fired.* | *I got a phone call from Eve* ***the other day*** (=a few days ago). | *We're leaving for Arizona* ***the day after tomorrow****.* | *I saw Margo* ***the day before yesterday****.* ▶ Don't say "We're leaving for Arizona after tomorrow" or "I saw Margo before yesterday." ◀

2 MORNING UNTIL NIGHT [C, U] the period of time between when it becomes light in the morning and when it becomes dark in the evening [≠ **night**]: *The days begin to get longer in the spring.* | *a beautiful summer day*

3 WHEN YOU ARE AWAKE [C usually singular] the time during the day when you are usually awake: *He started his day with a 3-mile run.* | *It's been a* ***long day*** (=a day when you had to get up early and were busy all day). | *Jan's been studying* ***all day*** (=for the whole day).

4 WORK [C] the hours you work in a day: *I work an eight-hour day.* | *Did you have a* ***good day*** *at work?* | *I need a* ***day off*** (=a day when you do not have to work).

5 PAST [C] used in order to talk about a time in the past: ***One day*** (=on a day in the past) *the police came and took her away.* | *Things were different* ***in my day*** (=when I was young). | *I didn't like him* ***from day one*** (=from the beginning). | *Grandpa was telling stories about* ***the good old days*** (=a time in the past when things seemed better than now).

6 NOW [C] used in order to talk about the situation that exists now: *It's not safe to walk the streets* ***these days*** (=now). | ***To this day*** (=until and including now) *we haven't heard the whole story.*

7 FUTURE [C] used in order to talk about a time in the future: *We'll buy our dream home* ***one/some day*** (=at some time in the future). | ***One of these days*** (=some time soon) *he's going to end up in jail.* | *Kelly's expecting the baby* ***any day now*** (=very soon).

8 make someone's day *informal* to make someone very happy: *That card made my day.*

9 has had its day to no longer be popular or successful: *The old steam trains have had their day.*

10 those were the days *spoken* used in order to say that a time in the past was better than the present time

11 day after day/day in day out used in order to emphasize that something bad or boring continues to happen: *I drive the same route to work day in day out.*

12 from day to day/from one day to the next if a situation changes from day to day or from one

day to the next, it changes often: *My job changes from day to day.*
13 day by day slowly and gradually: *She was getting stronger day by day.*
14 sb's days *literary* the time when someone is alive: *He began his days in a small town.*
15 be working days/be on days to work during the day at a job you sometimes have to do at night
➔ DAILY[1] ➔ **call it a day** at CALL[1]

GRAMMAR

Use **on** to talk about a particular day of the week: *I'm going to a party on Saturday.*
Use **next** to talk about a day after the present one: *I'll meet you next Tuesday.*
Use **last** to talk about a day before the present one: *He died last Friday.*
➔ TODAY, TOMORROW, YESTERDAY

day·break /ˈdeɪbreɪk/ *n.* [U] the time of day when light first appears [= **dawn**]: *We broke camp **at daybreak**.*

ˈday camp *n.* [C] a place where children go during the day to do activities, sports, art, etc. on their summer vacation from school

day·care /ˈdeɪkɛr/ *n.* [U] care of young children, or of sick or old people, during the day: *a daycare center* | *My youngest is **in daycare**.*

day·dream /ˈdeɪdrim/ *v.* [I] to think about nice things so that you forget what you should be doing: *Joan sat at her desk, **daydreaming about** Tom.* —**daydream** *n.* [C] —**daydreamer** *n.* [C]

THESAURUS

imagine, **visualize**, **picture**, **conceive of sth**, **fantasize**
➔ see Thesaurus box at IMAGINE

Day-Glo /ˈdeɪ gloʊ/ *adj. trademark* having a very bright orange, green, yellow, or pink color

day·light /ˈdeɪlaɪt/ *n.* [U] **1** the light produced by the sun during the day: *The market is crowded during **daylight hours**.* | *She was attacked **in broad daylight*** (=during the day when it is light). **2 scare/frighten the (living) daylights out of sb** *informal* to frighten someone a lot **3 beat the (living) daylights out of sb** *informal* to hit someone many times and hurt him/her badly

ˌdaylight ˈsaving time also **ˌdaylight ˈsavings** *n.* [U] the time in the spring when clocks are set one hour ahead of standard time

day·time /ˈdeɪtaɪm/ *n.* [U] the time between when it gets light in the morning and when it gets dark in the evening [≠ **nighttime**]: *I've never been here **in/during the daytime**.* | *daytime talk shows*

ˌday-to-ˈday *adj.* happening every day as a regular part of life: *our day-to-day routine at work*

daze /deɪz/ *n.* **in a daze** unable to think clearly

dazed /deɪzd/ *adj.* unable to think clearly, usually because you are shocked, have been hurt, etc.: *dazed victims of the bombing*

daz·zle /ˈdæzəl/ *v.* [T] **1** if a very bright light dazzles you, you are unable to see for a short time **2** to make someone admire someone or something a lot: *We were all dazzled by her talent and charm.*

daz·zling /ˈdæzlɪŋ/ *adj.* **1** very impressive, exciting, or interesting: *a dazzling performance*

THESAURUS

impressive, **imposing**, **awe-inspiring**, **breathtaking**, **majestic**
➔ see Thesaurus box at IMPRESSIVE

2 a dazzling light is so bright that you cannot see for a short time after you look at it

THESAURUS

bright, **strong**, **blinding**
➔ see Thesaurus box at BRIGHT

DC *n.* [U] **direct current** the type of electric current that comes from batteries (BATTERY) [➡ **AC**]

D.C. **District of Columbia** the area containing the city of Washington, the CAPITAL of the U.S.

DDT *n.* [U] a chemical used in order to kill insects that harm crops, which is now illegal

DE the written abbreviation of **Delaware**

dea·con /ˈdikən/, **dea·con·ess** /ˈdikəˌnɛs/ *n.* [C] a religious official in some Christian churches

de·ac·ti·vate /diˈæktəˌveɪt/ *v.* [T] to SWITCH a piece of equipment off, or to stop it from working

dead[1] /dɛd/ *adj.*
1 NOT ALIVE no longer alive: *Her mom's been dead for two years.* | *I think that plant is dead.* | *She found a **dead body*** (=a dead person) *in the woods.*

THESAURUS

lifeless literary – dead or seeming to be dead: *dull, lifeless eyes*
late/deceased formal – dead: *Mrs. Lombard's late husband* | *their recently deceased grandmother*

USAGE

Dead is an adjective used to describe people or things that are no longer alive: *a dead fish*
Died is the past tense and past participle of the verb "to die," used to talk about how and when someone died: *He died of a heart attack in 1992.*

2 NOT WORKING not working, especially because there is no power: *Is the **battery dead**?* | *The phones **went dead** during the storm.*
3 PLACE [not before noun] a place that is dead is boring because nothing interesting happens there: *The bar is usually dead until around 10:00.*
4 NOT USED no longer active or being used: *He says the peace plan is dead.* | *a dead language*
5 COMPLETE [only before noun] complete or exact: *For about five minutes there was **dead***

silence. | *Hit the* **dead center** *of the nail so it doesn't bend.* | *The train came to a* **dead stop**.
6 TIRED [not before noun] *informal* very tired: *I think I'll go to bed early; I'm absolutely dead.*
7 PART OF BODY a part of your body that is dead has no feeling in it for a short time: *I'd been sitting so long my legs* **went dead**.
8 over my dead body *spoken* used when you are determined not to allow something to happen: *You'll marry him over my dead body!*
9 IN TROUBLE *spoken* **also dead meat** in serious trouble: *If anything happens to the car, you're dead!*
10 sb wouldn't be caught/seen dead in sth *spoken* used to say that someone would never wear particular clothes, go to particular places, or do particular things because they would feel embarrassed: *I wouldn't be caught dead in a dress like that!*

D

dead² *adv. informal* completely or exactly: *Paula* **stopped dead** *when she saw us.* | *I'm* **dead tired**. | *You can't miss it; it's* **dead ahead**.

dead³ *n.* **1 in the dead of winter/night** in the middle of winter or in the middle of the night **2 the dead** all the people who have died [≠ **the living**]

dead·beat /ˈdɛdbiːt/ *n.* [C] someone who does not pay his/her debts

dead·en /ˈdɛdn/ *v.* [T] to make a feeling or sound less strong: *a drug to deaden the pain*

ˌdead ˈend *n.* [C] **1** a street with no way out at one end **2** a situation from which no progress is possible

dead·line /ˈdɛdlaɪn/ *n.* [C] a time by which you must finish something: *The* **deadline for** *applications is May 27th.* | *Can you* **meet** *the* **deadline?**

dead·lock /ˈdɛdlɑk/ *n.* [C,U] a situation in which a disagreement cannot be settled: *the UN's attempt to* **break the deadlock** (=end it) *in the region.*

dead·ly /ˈdɛdli/ *adj.* very dangerous and likely to cause death: *a deadly virus*

dead·pan /ˈdɛdpæn/ *adj.* sounding and looking completely serious when you are not: *a deadpan sense of humor*

deaf /dɛf/ *adj.* **1** physically unable to hear, or unable to hear well [➡ **hearing impaired**]: *I'm deaf in my right ear.*

THESAURUS

hard of hearing, hearing impaired
➔ see Thesaurus box at HEAR

2 the deaf [plural] people who are deaf **3 be deaf to sth** unwilling to listen to something: *The guards were deaf to the prisoners' complaints.* **4 fall on deaf ears** if something you say falls on deaf ears, everyone ignores it —**deafness** *n.* [U]

deaf·en·ing /ˈdɛfənɪŋ/ *adj.* **1** noise or music that is deafening is very loud

THESAURUS

loud, thunderous, ear-splitting
➔ see Thesaurus box at LOUD¹

2 deafening silence complete silence, used especially when this is uncomfortable or unusual —**deafen** *v.*

deal¹ /dil/ *n.* **1** [C] an agreement or arrangement, especially in business or politics: *She has just signed a new book deal with a different publisher.* | *Diaz tried to* **cut/make/strike a deal** *with the government.* | *You can* **get** *some* **good deals** (=buy something at a good price) *at the new travel agency.* | *"I'll give you $100 for your TV." "OK,* **it's a deal**.*"* **2 a great/good deal** a large quantity of something: *The new exhibit has gotten* **a good deal of** *attention.* | *He knows a great deal more* (=a lot more) *than I do about computers.* **3** [C usually singular] the way someone is treated in a situation: *This new law is* **a fair deal** *for the American taxpayer.* | *Women often get* **a raw deal** (=unfair treatment) *from their employers.* **4 what's the deal?** *spoken* used when you want to know what is happening in a situation: *So what's the deal? Why is he so mad?* **5** [singular] the process of giving out cards to players in a card game: *It's your deal.* ➔ BIG DEAL

deal² *v.* past tense and past participle **dealt** /dɛlt/ [I,T] **1 also deal out** to give out playing cards to players in a game: *It's my* **turn to deal**? **2** to buy and sell illegal drugs: *He was arrested for dealing heroin.* **3 deal a blow (to sb/sth)** to harm someone or something: *The ban dealt a severe blow to local tourism.*

deal in sth *phr. v.* to buy and sell a particular product: *a business dealing in medical equipment*

deal with sb/sth *phr. v.* **1** to do what is necessary, especially in order to solve a problem: *Who's dealing with the new account?*

THESAURUS

handle – to deal with someone or something: *He's finding it hard to handle the pressure at work.*
tackle – to try to deal with a difficult problem: *There are still a number of problems which we need to tackle.*
attend to sth – to give attention to someone or something: *I have some business to attend to.*
take care of sth – do the work or make the arrangements that are necessary for something to happen: *I'll take care of making the reservations.*

2 to succeed in controlling your feelings and being patient in a difficult situation: *I can't deal with any more crying children today.* **3** to do business with someone: *We've been dealing with their company for ten years.* **4** to be about a particular subject: *a book dealing with 20th century art*

deal·er /ˈdilɚ/ *n.* [C] **1** someone who buys and

sells a particular product: *a car dealer* **2** someone who buys and sells illegal drugs **3** someone who gives out the playing cards in a game

deal·er·ship /ˈdilɚˌʃɪp/ *n.* [C] a business that sells a particular company's product, especially cars

deal·ing /ˈdilɪŋ/ *n.* **1** [U] the buying and selling of things: *penalties for drug dealing* **2 dealings** [plural] personal or business relations with someone: *Have you had any **dealings with** IBM?*

dealt /dɛlt/ *v.* the past participle of DEAL

dean /din/ *n.* [C] a university official with a high rank: *the dean of admissions*

ˈdean's list *n.* [C] a list of the best students at a university

dear¹ /dɪr/ *interjection* said when you are surprised, annoyed, or upset: ***Oh dear!** I forgot to phone Jill.*

dear² *n.* [C] *spoken* used when speaking to someone you like or love: *How was your day, dear?*

dear³ *adj.* **1** used before a name at the beginning of a letter: *Dear Sue, ... | Dear Dr. Ward, ...* **2** much loved and very important to you: *She's a **dear friend**.*

dear·ly /ˈdɪrli/ *adv.* very much: *Sam **loved** her **dearly**.*

dearth /dɚθ/ *n.* [singular] *formal* a lack of something: *a **dearth of** original ideas*

death /dɛθ/ *n.* **1** [C,U] the end of a person or animal's life [≠ **birth**]: *Maretti lived in Miami until his death. | Heart disease is the number one **cause of death** in the U.S. | The number of **deaths from** AIDS is increasing. | He choked **to death*** (=choked until he died) *on a fish bone. | The horse was so badly injured it had to be **put to death*** (=killed). **2 be bored/scared etc. to death** *informal* to be very bored, afraid, etc. **3 the death of sth** the permanent end of something: *the death of Communism* ➔ **be sick (and tired) of/be sick to death of** at SICK

death·bed /ˈdɛθbɛd/ *n.* **sb's deathbed** the point in time when someone is dying and will be dead very soon: *Marquez flew home to be with his mother, who was **on her deathbed**.*

ˈdeath ˌpenalty *n.* [singular] the legal punishment of being killed for a serious crime: *Gilmore was **given the death penalty** for murder.* ➔ CAPITAL PUNISHMENT

ˌdeath ˈrow *n.* [U] the part of a prison where prisoners are kept before they are killed as a punishment: *a murderer **on death row***

ˈdeath toll *n.* [C usually singular] the total number of people who die in an accident, war, etc.

ˈdeath trap *n.* [C] *informal* a vehicle, building, etc. that is in such bad condition that it might injure or kill someone

de·base /dɪˈbeɪs/ *v.* [T] *formal* to make someone or something lose its value or people's respect —**debasement** *n.* [C,U]

de·bat·a·ble /dɪˈbeɪt̬əbəl/ *adj.* an idea, fact, or decision that is debatable may be right but it could easily be wrong

de·bate¹ /dɪˈbeɪt/ *n.* [C,U] **1** a discussion or argument on a subject in which people express different opinions: *a **debate about/over/on** equal pay | a **heated/fierce/intense, etc. debate***

THESAURUS

discussion, negotiations, talks, conference
➔ see Thesaurus box at DISCUSSION

2 a formal discussion of a subject in which people express different opinions, and sometimes vote: *After much debate, the committee decided to raise the fees. | a **debate on/about** welfare reform*

debate² *v.* **1** [I,T] to discuss a subject formally so that you can make a decision or solve a problem: *The Senate is debating the future of health care. | We were **debating which** person to hire.* **2** [T] to think about something carefully before making a decision: *I was **debating whether** to go to work.*

de·bauch·e·ry /dɪˈbɔtʃəri/ *n.* [U] immoral behavior involving drugs, alcohol, sex, etc. —**debauched** *adj.*

de·bil·i·tat·ing /dɪˈbɪləˌteɪt̬ɪŋ/ *adj.* a debilitating disease or condition makes your body or mind weak: *a debilitating illness* —**debility** /dɪˈbɪlət̬i/ *n.* [C,U]

deb·it¹ /ˈdɛbɪt/ *n.* [C] an amount of money that has been taken out of your bank account [≠ **credit**]

debit² *v.* [T] to take money out of a bank account [≠ **credit**]: *Fifty dollars has been **debited from** your account.*

ˈdebit card *n.* [C] a plastic card that you can use to buy goods or services. The money is taken directly from your bank account

deb·o·nair /ˌdɛbəˈnɛr/ *adj.* a man who is debonair is fashionable and confident

de·brief /diˈbrif/ *v.* [T] to officially ask someone such as a soldier to give a report of a job that s/he has just done —**debriefing** *n.* [C,U]

de·bris /dɪˈbri/ *n.* [U] the pieces remaining from something that has been destroyed: *The street was full of debris after the explosion.*

debt /dɛt/ *n.* **1** [C,U] money that you owe to someone: *Al can finally **pay off** his **debts**. | **debts of** $25 million | a company **heavily in debt*** (=owing a lot of money) *| He lost his job and **fell/went/got into debt**.* **2** [singular] the degree to which you have been influenced by, or helped by, someone or something: *Our club **owes a** great **debt of gratitude** to Martha Graham. | She **is** forever **in** his **debt*** (=thankful for something someone has done for her).

debt·or /ˈdɛt̬ɚ/ *n.* [C] someone who owes money

de·bug /diˈbʌg/ *v.* [T] to take the mistakes out of a computer PROGRAM

de·bunk /di'bʌŋk/ *v.* [T] to show that an idea or belief is false

de·but /deɪ'byu, 'deɪbyu/ *n.* [C] the first time that a performer or sports player performs in public: *her debut album* | *his Broadway debut* | *Foster **made** her **debut** in movies at a young age.* —**debut** *v.* [I]

dec·ade /'dɛkeɪd/ *n.* [C] a period of ten years

dec·a·dent /'dɛkədənt/ *adj.* having low moral standards and interested only in pleasure: *a decadent lifestyle* —**decadence** *n.* [U]

de·caf /'dikæf/ *n.* [U] decaffeinated coffee

de·caf·fein·at·ed /di'kæfəˌneɪtɪd/ *adj.* decaffeinated drinks have had the CAFFEINE removed: *decaffeinated coffee*

de·cal /'dikæl/ *n.* [C] a piece of paper with a pattern or picture on it that you stick onto a surface

D

de·cant·er /dɪ'kæntɚ/ *n.* [C] a container used for serving alcoholic drinks

de·cap·i·tate /dɪ'kæpəˌteɪt/ *v.* [T] to cut off someone's head: *a decapitated body* —**decapitation** /dɪˌkæpə'teɪʃən/ *n.* [C,U]

dec·ath·lon /dɪ'kæθlɑn, -lən/ *n.* [singular] a sports competition with ten different events

de·cay[1] /dɪ'keɪ/ *v.* **1** [I,T] to be slowly destroyed by a natural chemical process, or to destroy something in this way: *The dead animal started to decay.* | *Sugar decays teeth.*

THESAURUS

rot – to decay by a gradual natural process, or to make something do this: *Old food was rotting on the table.*
decompose – to decay or to make something decay: *a decomposed body*

2 [I] if buildings decay, they are slowly destroyed because no one takes care of them: *the decaying downtown area*

decay[2] *n.* [U] the process, state, or result of decaying: ***tooth decay*** | *The building has **fallen into decay**.*

de·ceased /dɪ'sist/ *n.* **the deceased** *formal* someone who has recently died —**deceased** *adj.*

de·ceit /dɪ'sit/ *n.* [U] behavior that is intended to make someone believe something that is not true: *lies and deceit* —**deceitful** *adj.*

de·ceive /dɪ'siv/ *v.* [T] **1** to make someone believe something that is not true: *Owen tried to deceive the police.* | *Customers were **deceived into** paying more than they should have.*

THESAURUS

lie, mislead
➔ see Thesaurus box at LIE[2]

2 deceive yourself to pretend to yourself that something is not true because you do not want to accept the truth

De·cem·ber /dɪ'sɛmbɚ/ *n.* *written abbreviation* **Dec.** [C,U] the TWELFTH month of the year: *Franny's birthday is **on December 6th**.* | *We mailed the invitations **in December**.* | *Kevin was promoted **last December**.* | *We're going to Florida **next December**.*

de·cen·cy /'disənsi/ *n.* [U] morally correct behavior: *At least **have the decency to** call if you'll be late.*

de·cent /'disənt/ *adj.* **1** acceptable and good enough: *a decent living* | *a decent job* | *a decent education* **2** honest and good: *Dr. Green was a decent man.* **3** wearing enough clothes, so that you are not showing too much of your body: *Don't come in, I'm not decent.* —**decently** *adv.*

de·cen·tral·ize /di'sɛntrəˌlaɪz/ *v.* [T] to change a government or organization so that decisions are made in local areas rather than in one place —**decentralization** /diˌsɛntrələ'zeɪʃən, ˌdisɛn-/ *n.* [U]

de·cep·tion /dɪ'sɛpʃən/ *n.* [C,U] the act of deliberately making someone believe something that is not true: *People were outraged when they learned of the deception.*

de·cep·tive /dɪ'sɛptɪv/ *adj.* **1** something that is deceptive seems very different from how it really is: *Clark has deceptive speed* (=moves faster than you think or expect). **2** deliberately intended to make someone believe something that is not true: *deceptive advertising* —**deceptively** *adj.*

dec·i·bel /'dɛsəˌbɛl, -bəl/ *n.* [C] *technical* a unit for measuring how loud a sound is

de·cide /dɪ'saɪd/ *v.* **1** [I,T] to make a choice or judgment about something [➡ **decision**]: *I've **decided to** stay home.* | *Jane **decided against** going* (=decided not to go) *to Washington on vacation.* | *Ted **decided (that)** the car would cost too much.* | *I can't **decide whether/if** I want fish or chicken.*

THESAURUS

make up your mind – to decide something, especially after thinking about it for a long time: *Henry made up his mind to go to college in the spring.*
choose – to decide which of a number of things, possibilities, etc. that you want: *I let the kids choose their own clothes.*
resolve – to make a definite decision to do something: *She had resolved to work hard and not disappoint her parents.*

2 deciding factor a very strong reason for making a particular decision: *Zimmer's testimony was the deciding factor in the case.* **3** [T] to be the reason why something has a particular result: *One punch decided the fight.*

decide on sth *phr. v.* to choose one thing from many possible choices: *Have you decided on a name for the baby?*

de·cid·ed /dɪ'saɪdɪd/ *adj.* [only before noun] definite and easy to notice: *The new color is a decided improvement.* —**decidedly** *adv.*

de·cid·u·ous /dɪˈsɪdʒuəs/ *adj.* deciduous trees lose their leaves in winter [➡ **evergreen**]

dec·i·mal¹ /ˈdɛsəməl/ *adj.* a decimal system is based on the number ten

decimal² *n.* [C] a number less than one that is shown by a mark (.) followed by the number of TENTHS, then the number of HUNDREDTHS, etc., for example 0.8 or 0.25

ˌdecimal ˈpoint *n.* [C] the mark (.) in a decimal

dec·i·mate /ˈdɛsəˌmeɪt/ *v.* [T] to destroy a large part of something: *a nation decimated by war*

de·ci·pher /dɪˈsaɪfɚ/ *v.* [T] to find the meaning of something that is difficult to read or understand: *I can't decipher his handwriting.*

de·ci·sion /dɪˈsɪʒən/ *n.* **1** [C] a choice or judgment that you make: *We'll **make a decision** by Friday.* | *Gina's **decision to** go to college* | *Do you expect to **reach a decision** soon?* | ***Decisions about** medical treatment should not be based on cost.* **2** [U] the ability to make choices or judgments quickly: *This job requires the ability to act with speed and decision.*

deˈcision-ˌmaking *n.* [U] the process of deciding on something —**decision-maker** *n.* [C]

de·ci·sive /dɪˈsaɪsɪv/ *adj.* **1** having an important effect on the result of something: *a decisive moment in his career* | *The U.N. **played a decisive role** in peace-making.* **2** good at making decisions quickly: *a decisive leader* **3** definite and clear: *a decisive advantage* —**decisively** *adv.*: *The President was criticized for failing to **act decisively**.*

deck

deck¹ /dɛk/ *n.* [C] **1** a wooden floor built out from the back of a house, where you can sit outdoors **2** a set of playing cards: *a **deck of** cards* **3 a)** the flat top part of a ship that you can walk on: *Let's go up **on deck**.* **b)** one of the levels on a ship, airplane, or bus: *the lower deck*

deck² *v.* [T] **1 also deck** sb/sth ⇔ **out** to decorate something with flowers, flags, etc.: *The street was **decked out with** flags for the big parade.* **2** *slang* to hit someone so hard that s/he falls over

deck sb ⇔ **out** *phr. v.* to dress in fashionable clothes or to dress in a certain style of clothes for a special occasion: *He was **decked out in** a suit and tie.*

dec·la·ra·tion /ˌdɛkləˈreɪʃən/ *n.* [C,U] an official or important statement about something: *a **declaration of** war*

de·clare /dɪˈklɛr/ *v.* [T] **1** to state officially and publicly that something is happening or that something is true: *The bridge has been declared unsafe.* | *Jones was declared the winner.* | *The U.S. **declared war on** England in 1812.* | *The doctor **declared that** she was dead.* **2** to say something in a clear firm way: *Parson **declared (that)** he would never go back there.* **3** to officially state the value of things that you have bought or own, or the amount of money you have earned, because you may have to pay taxes on them: *You must declare your full income.*

D

de·cline¹ /dɪˈklaɪn/ *v.* **1** [I] to decrease in quality, quantity or importance: *As his health has declined, so has his influence.* | *Car sales have declined.*

> **THESAURUS**
>
> **decrease, go down, drop, fall, plummet, diminish**
>
> ➔ see Thesaurus box at DECREASE¹

2 [I,T] *formal* to say no to something, usually politely: *We asked them to come, but they **declined** our **invitation**.* | *The senator **declined to** make a statement.*

> **THESAURUS**
>
> **reject, refuse, turn down, say no**
>
> ➔ see Thesaurus box at REJECT¹

decline² *n.* [C usually singular, U] a decrease in the quality, quantity, or importance of something: *a **decline in** profits* | *During the last ten years, the construction industry has been **in decline**.*

de·code /diˈkoʊd/ *v.* [T] to discover the meaning of a secret or complicated message

de·com·pose /ˌdikəmˈpoʊz/ *v.* [I,T] to decay or to make something decay: *a partially decomposed body* —**decomposition** /ˌdikɑmpəˈzɪʃən/ *n.* [U]

> **THESAURUS**
>
> **decay, rot**
>
> ➔ see Thesaurus box at DECAY¹

de·cor /ˈdeɪkɔr, deɪˈkɔr/ *n.* [C,U] the way that the inside of a building is decorated

dec·o·rate /ˈdɛkəˌreɪt/ *v.* [T] **1** to make something look more attractive by adding pretty things to it: *We **decorated** the Christmas tree **with** big red bows.* **2** to give someone an official sign of honor, such as a MEDAL: *soldiers **decorated for** bravery*

dec·o·ra·tion /ˌdɛkəˈreɪʃən/ *n.* **1** [C] something pretty that you add to something in order to make it look more attractive: *Christmas decorations* **2** [U] the style in which something is decorated **3** [C] an official sign of honor, such as a MEDAL, that is given to someone

dec·o·ra·tive /ˈdɛkərət̬ɪv/ *adj.* pretty and used as a decoration: *a decorative pot*

de·cor·um /dɪˈkɔrəm/ *n.* [U] *formal* behavior that is respectful and correct for a formal or serious situation

de·coy /ˈdikɔɪ/ *n.* [C] a person or object that is used to trick a person or animal into going somewhere or doing something —**decoy** /diˈkɔɪ/ *v.* [T]

de·crease¹ /dɪˈkris, ˈdikris/ *v.* [I,T] to become less, or to make something do this [≠ **increase**]: *The company's profits decreased in 1992.* | *the need to decrease costs* | *By 1881, the population had* ***decreased to*** *5.2 million.*

THESAURUS

go down – to become lower or less in level, amount, size, quality, etc.: *The income of ordinary workers has been going down.*
drop – to decrease to a lower level or amount, or to make something decrease: *Sales have dropped 15% this year.*
fall – to decrease to a lower level or amount: *Temperatures fell below zero last night.*
plummet – to suddenly and quickly decrease in value: *The show's ratings have plummeted.*
diminish – to become smaller or less important: *Union membership diminished from 30,000 at its height to just 20 today.*
decline – to decrease in quality, quantity, or importance: *The company's earnings declined 17% last year.*
➔ see Thesaurus box at REDUCE

de·crease² /ˈdikris, dɪˈkris/ *n.* [C,U] the process of reducing something, or the amount by which it is reduced [≠ **increase**]: *a* ***decrease in*** *sales*

de·cree /dɪˈkri/ *n.* [C] an official order or decision —**decree** *v.* [T]

de·crep·it /dɪˈkrɛpɪt/ *adj.* old and in bad condition

de·crim·i·nal·ize /diˈkrɪmənəˌlaɪz/ *v.* [T] to state officially that something is no longer illegal —**decriminalization** /diˌkrɪmɪnələˈzeɪʃən/ *n.* [U]

ded·i·cate /ˈdɛdəˌkeɪt/ *v.* [T] **1** to say that a book, movie, song, etc. has been written, made, or sung in honor of someone: *The book is* ***dedicated to*** *his mother.* **2 dedicate yourself/your life to (doing) sth** to give all your attention and effort to one thing: *I've* ***dedicated my life to*** *my work.*

ded·i·cat·ed /ˈdɛdəˌkeɪt̬ɪd/ *adj.* working very hard at something because you think it is important: *a* ***dedicated*** *teacher*

ded·i·ca·tion /ˌdɛdəˈkeɪʃən/ *n.* **1** [U] hard work or effort that you put into a particular activity because you think it is important: *He shows great* ***dedication to*** *his work.* **2** [C] the act or ceremony of dedicating something to someone **3** [C] the words used in dedicating a book, movie, song, etc. to someone

de·duce /dɪˈdus/ *v.* [T] *formal* to make a judgment based on the information that you have

de·duct /dɪˈdʌkt/ *v.* [T] to take away an amount from a total: *Taxes are* ***deducted from*** *your pay.* —**deductible** *adj.*

de·duct·i·ble /dɪˈdʌktəbəl/ *n.* [C] the part of a bill you must pay before the insurance company will pay the rest

de·duc·tion /dɪˈdʌkʃən/ *n.* [C,U] **1** the process of taking away an amount from a total, or the amount that is taken away: *I earn about $2,000 a month, after deductions.* **2** the process of making a judgment about something, based on the information that you have: *a game that teaches logic and deduction*

deed /did/ *n.* [C] **1** *literary* an action: *good deeds* **2** *law* an official paper that is a record of an agreement, especially one that says who owns property

deem /dim/ *v.* [T] *formal* to say that something has a particular quality [= **consider**]: *The judge deemed the question inappropriate.*

deep¹ /dip/ *adj.*
1 GO FAR DOWN going far down from the top or from the surface [≠ **shallow**; ➡ **depth**]: *The path was covered in deep snow.* | *The water's about* ***10 feet/6 inches, etc. deep.*** ➔ see picture at SHALLOW
2 GO FAR IN going far in from the outside or from the front: *Terry had a deep cut in his forehead.* | *a shelf 3 feet long and 8 inches deep*
3 FEELING/BELIEF a deep feeling or belief is very strong and sincere: *deep feelings of hatred*
4 SOUND a deep sound is very low: *a deep voice*
5 COLOR a deep color is dark and strong [≠ **light, pale**]: *a plant with deep green leaves*
6 SERIOUS serious and often difficult to understand: *a deep conversation about the meaning of life*
7 deep sleep if someone is in a deep sleep, it is difficult to wake him/her
8 a deep breath a deep breath is one in which you breathe a lot of air in, especially because you are upset or nervous: *I* ***took a deep breath*** *and jumped into the water.*
9 be in deep trouble *informal* to be in serious trouble or in an extremely difficult situation: *Many smaller companies are in deep trouble.*
10 deep in thought/conversation etc. thinking so hard or talking so much that you do not notice anything else: *Martin sat at his desk, deep in thought.*

deep² *adv.* **1** far into something: *He stepped* ***deep into*** *the mud.* **2 deep down a)** if you feel or know something deep down, that is what you really feel or know even though you may not admit it: *Deep down, I knew she was right.* **b)** if someone is good, evil, etc. deep down, that is what s/he is really like even though s/he usually hides it: *He seems mean, but deep down he's* *really nice.* **3 two/three etc. deep** in two, three, etc. rows or layers

deep·en /ˈdipən/ *v.* [I,T] to make something deeper, or to become deeper

ˌdeep ˈfreeze *n.* [C] FREEZER

ˈdeep fried *adj.* cooked in a lot of hot oil —**deep fry** *v.* [T]

deep·ly /ˈdipli/ *adv.* **1** extremely or very much: *Wood is a deeply religious man.* | *They knew Frank was deeply involved in criminal activities.* **2** a long way into something: *Just sit down and **breathe deeply**.* | *We started sinking even more deeply into the mud.*

ˌdeep-ˈseated also ˌdeep-ˈrooted *adj.* a deep-seated feeling or idea is strong and very difficult to change

deer /dɪr/ *n.* plural **deer** [C] a large wild animal that lives in forests. The male has long horns that look like tree branches

de·face /dɪˈfeɪs/ *v.* [T] *formal* to damage the appearance of something, especially by writing or making marks on it: *walls defaced by graffiti*

def·a·ma·tion /ˌdɛfəˈmeɪʃən/ *n.* [U] *formal* **or** *law* writing or saying something that makes people have a bad opinion of someone or something —**defamatory** /dɪˈfæməˌtɔri/ *adj.*

de·fault¹ /dɪˈfɔlt/ *v.* [I] to not do something that you are legally supposed to: *He **defaulted on** his loan payments.*

default² *n.* **1** [U] failure to do something that you are supposed to do: *We won the first game **by default*** (=because the other team failed to arrive). | *The loan is **in default*** (=it has not been paid back on time). **2** [C usually singular] the standard way in which things are arranged on a computer screen or in a program unless you change them

de·feat¹ /dɪˈfit/ *n.* **1** [C,U] failure to win or succeed: *Miami's first defeat* | *an **embarrassing defeat*** | *He'll never **admit defeat*** (=admit that he has failed). **2** [singular] victory over someone or something: *the **defeat of** the President's tax plan*

defeat² *v.* [T] **1** to win a victory over someone: *Davis easily defeated his opponent in the election.*

THESAURUS

beat, trounce, clobber
➔ see Thesaurus box at BEAT³

2 to make something fail: *The plan was defeated by a lack of money.*

def·e·cate /ˈdɛfəˌkeɪt/ *v.* [I] *formal* to get rid of waste matter from your BOWELS —**defecation** /ˌdɛfəˈkeɪʃən/ *n.* [U]

de·fect¹ /ˈdifɛkt, dɪˈfɛkt/ *n.* [C] a fault or a lack of something that makes something not perfect: *The cars are tested for defects before being sold.* | *a **birth defect*** (=a physical problem that a baby was born with)

THESAURUS

problem – a difficult situation that needs to be dealt with: *There's a problem with the brakes.*
flaw – a mark or weakness that makes something not perfect: *a flaw in its construction*
bug – a defect in a computer program: *The program had some minor bugs.*
fault – something that is wrong with a machine, design, etc., which prevents it from working correctly: *a fault in the power unit*

de·fect² /dɪˈfɛkt/ *v.* [I] to leave your own country or a group and join or go to an opposing one: *a baseball player who **defected to** the United States* —**defector** *n.* [C] —**defection** /dɪˈfɛkʃən/ *n.* [C,U]

de·fec·tive /dɪˈfɛktɪv/ *adj.* not made correctly or not working correctly: *defective products*

de·fend /dɪˈfɛnd/ *v.* **1** [T] to protect someone or something from being attacked [➡ **defense**]: *You should learn to **defend yourself**.* | *Soldiers **defended** the fort **from** attack.* **2** [T] to use arguments to protect something or someone from criticism: *The mayor defended his plan to raise taxes.* | *He had to **defend himself against** their charges.* **3** [I,T] to try to prevent your opponents from getting points in a sports game **4** [T] to be a lawyer for someone who is said to be guilty of a crime —**defender** *n.* [C] —**defensible** /dɪˈfɛnsəbəl/ *adj.*

de·fend·ant /dɪˈfɛndənt/ *n.* [C] *law* the person in a court of law who has been ACCUSEd of doing something illegal [➡ **plaintiff**] ➔ see Topic box at COURT¹

de·fense¹ /dɪˈfɛns/ *n.* **1** [U] the act of protecting someone or something from attack or criticism: *Senator Stevens spoke **in defense of** a bill to make handguns illegal.* **2** [U] the weapons, people, systems, etc. that a country uses to protect itself from attack: *the Department of Defense* | *Defense spending* (=money spent on weapons, etc.) *has increased.* **3** [C] something that is used for protection against something else: *Vitamin C is my **defense against** colds.* **4 a)** [C,U] the things that are said in a court of law to prove that someone is not guilty of a crime: *His defense is that he didn't remember the incident.* **b) the defense** the people in a court of law who are trying to show that someone is not guilty of a crime [➡ **prosecution**]: *Is the defense ready to call their first witness?*

de·fense² /ˈdifɛns/ *n.* [U] the players on a sports team whose job is to try to prevent the other team from scoring points [➡ **offense**]

de·fense·less /dɪˈfɛnslɪs/ *adj.* unable to protect yourself from being hurt or criticized: *a defenseless old woman*

deˈfense ˌmechanism *n.* [C] **1** a process in your brain that makes you forget things that are painful to think about **2** a reaction in your body that protects you from an illness or danger

D

de·fen·sive[1] /dɪˈfɛnsɪv/ *adj.* **1** used or intended for protection against attack [➡ **offensive**]: *defensive weapons* **2** behaving in a way that shows you think someone is criticizing you even if s/he is not: *She **got** really **defensive** when I asked her why she was late.* **3** relating to stopping the other team from getting points in a game [➡ **offensive**]: *a defensive play* —**defensively** *adv.* —**defensiveness** *n.* [U]

defensive[2] *n.* **on the defensive** protecting yourself because someone is criticizing you: *Her boss's comment **put** her **on the defensive**.*

de·fer /dɪˈfɚ/ *v.* past tense and past participle **deferred**, present participle **deferring** [T] to delay something until a later date: *His military service was deferred until he finished college.*

defer to sb/sth *phr. v. formal* to accept someone's opinion or decision because you have respect for that person or because s/he has power over you: *I usually defer to my wife when it comes to shopping.*

def·er·ence /ˈdɛfərəns/ *n.* [U] *formal* behavior that shows you respect someone and are willing to accept his/her opinions or judgment: ***In deference to** Saudi custom, we cover our arms and wear longer skirts.* —**deferential** /ˌdɛfəˈrɛnʃəl/ *adj.*

de·fi·ant /dɪˈfaɪənt/ *adj.* refusing to do what someone tells you to do because you do not respect him/her —**defiance** *n.* [U] —**defiantly** *adv.*

de·fi·cien·cy /dɪˈfɪʃənsi/ *n.* plural **deficiencies** [C,U] **1** a lack of something that is needed: *a vitamin deficiency* **2** a weakness or fault in something: *The computer system has serious deficiencies.*

de·fi·cient /dɪˈfɪʃənt/ *adj.* **1** not having or containing enough of something: *food **deficient in** iron* **2** not good enough

def·i·cit /ˈdɛfəsɪt/ *n.* [C] the difference between the amount of money that you have and the higher amount that you need: *a **deficit of** $2.5 million* | *a **budget deficit***

de·file /dɪˈfaɪl/ *v.* [T] *formal* to make something less pure, good, or holy: *graves defiled by Nazi symbols*

de·fine /dɪˈfaɪn/ *v.* [T] **1** to explain the exact meaning of a particular word or idea [➡ **definition**]: *Please define what you mean by "democracy."* | *A lie is **defined as** saying something in order to deceive someone.* **2** to describe something correctly and show what qualities it has that make it different from other things: *Teachers need to give students rules that are **clearly defined**.* —**definable** *adj.*

def·i·nite /ˈdɛfənɪt/ *adj.* **1** certain and not likely to change: *I'll give you a **definite answer** by tomorrow.* **2** clear and noticeable [≠ **indefinite**]: *The team has shown definite improvement in the last few games.*

ˌdefinite ˈarticle *n.* [C] the word "the" in English, or a word in another language that is like "the" [➡ **article**]

def·i·nite·ly /ˈdɛfənɪtli/ *adv.* without any doubt: *That was definitely the best movie I've seen all year.* | *"Are you going to be there tomorrow?" "Definitely."* | *It's **definitely not** the right time to tell her.*

ˌdef·i·ni·tion /ˌdɛfəˈnɪʃən/ *n.* **1** [C] a phrase or sentence that says exactly what a word, phrase, or idea means: *What's the **definition of** "palimpsest?"* | *a **dictionary definition*** **2** [U] the clearness of something such as a picture or sound: *The photograph **lacks definition**.*

de·fin·i·tive /dɪˈfɪnət̬ɪv/ *adj.* [only before noun] **1** the definitive book, description, etc. is considered to be the best of its type and cannot be improved: ***the definitive** biography of Charlie Chaplin* **2** a definitive statement, answer, etc. cannot be doubted or changed: *The group has taken a definitive stand against pornography.* —**definitively** *adv.*

de·flate /dɪˈfleɪt, di-/ *v.* **1** [I,T] if a tire, ball, etc. deflates, or if you deflate it, it becomes smaller because the air or gas inside it comes out [≠ **inflate**] **2** [T] to make someone feel less important or confident **3** [T] *technical* to change the economic rules or conditions in a country so that prices become lower or stop rising —**deflation** /dɪˈfleɪʃən/ *n.* [U]

de·flect /dɪˈflɛkt/ *v.* **1** [I,T] to hit something that is already moving and make it move in a different direction: *The ball was deflected into the crowd.* **2 deflect attention/criticism/anger etc.** to stop people from noticing something, criticizing it, etc.: *attempts to deflect attention away from his private life* —**deflection** /dɪˈflɛkʃən/ *n.* [C,U]

de·formed /dɪˈfɔrmd/ *adj.* something that is deformed has the wrong shape, especially because it has grown or developed wrongly: *a deformed foot* —**deform** *v.* [T] —**deformation** /ˌdifɔrˈmeɪʃən/ *n.* [C,U]

de·form·i·ty /dɪˈfɔrmət̬i/ *n.* plural **deformities** [C,U] a condition in which part of someone's body is not the normal shape

de·fraud /dɪˈfrɔd/ *v.* [T] to trick a person or organization in order to get money from them: *He **defrauded** his clients **of** over $5 million.*

de·frost /dɪˈfrɔst/ *v.* **1** [I,T] if frozen food defrosts, or if you defrost it, it gets warmer until it is not frozen anymore **2** [I,T] if a FREEZER or REFRIGERATOR defrosts, or if you defrost it, it is turned off so that the ice inside it melts **3** [T] to remove ice from the windows of a car by blowing warm air onto them

deft /dɛft/ *adj.* quick and skillful: *a deft catch* —**deftly** *adv.*

de·funct /dɪˈfʌŋkt/ *adj.* no longer existing or useful

de·fuse /diˈfyuz/ *v.* [T] **1** to remove or disconnect part of a bomb so that the bomb does not explode **2** to improve a difficult situation by making someone less angry: *Tim tried to **defuse** the **tension/situation**.*

de·fy /dɪ'faɪ/ *v.* [T] third person singular **defies**, past tense and past participle **defied** **1** to refuse to obey someone or something: *He defied his father's wishes and joined the army.*

THESAURUS

disobey, **rebel**
➔ see Thesaurus box at DISOBEY

2 defy description/explanation/imagination etc. to be almost impossible to describe, understand, etc.: *Her outfit defied description.*

de·gen·er·ate¹ /dɪ'dʒɛnə,reɪt/ *v.* [I] to become worse: *The party **degenerated into** a drunken fight.* —**degeneration** /dɪdʒɛnə'reɪʃən/ *n.* [U]

de·gen·e·rate² /dɪ'dʒɛnərɪt/ *adj.* **1** worse than before in quality **2** having very low moral standards —**degenerate** *n.* [C]

de·grade /dɪ'greɪd, di-/ *v.* [T] **1** to treat someone without respect and make him/her lose respect for himself or herself: *Pornography degrades women.* **2** *formal* to make a situation or condition worse: *The proposed law could degrade safety standards.* —**degradation** /,dɛgrə'deɪʃən/ *n.* [U]

de·grad·ing /dɪ'greɪdɪŋ/ *adj.* showing no respect for someone or making him/her feel very ashamed: *It was degrading to have to ask strangers for money.*

de·gree /dɪ'gri/ *n.* **1** [C] a unit for measuring temperature: *It got up to 86 degrees today.* **2** [C] a unit for measuring the size of an angle: *The plane was climbing at an angle of 20 degrees.* **3** [C,U] the level or amount of something: *students with different **degrees of** ability* | ***To what degree** is his smoking contributing to his health problems?* **4** [C] something that you get from a college or university, which officially shows that you have successfully completed a program of study: *a law degree* | *Ryan **has a degree in** chemistry.* | *You need a **college degree** for most of these jobs.*

de·hy·drat·ed /di'haɪ,dreɪṭɪd/ *adj.* people or things that are dehydrated do not have enough water inside them: *dehydrated potatoes* | *Be careful you don't get dehydrated outside in this heat.* —**dehydration** /,dihaɪ'dreɪʃən/ *n.* [U] *Several runners were suffering from dehydration.*

deign /deɪn/ *v.* **deign to do sth** *humorous* to agree to do something that you think you are too important to do: *She finally deigned to join us for lunch.*

de·i·ty /'diəṭi, 'deɪ-/ *n.* plural **deities** [C] a god or GODDESS

THESAURUS

god, **divinity**, **idol**
➔ see Thesaurus box at GOD

dé·jà vu /,deɪʒɑ 'vu/ *n.* [U] the feeling that what is happening now has happened before in exactly the same way

de·ject·ed /dɪ'dʒɛktɪd/ *adj.* sad and disappointed: *The players looked dejected after the game.* —**dejectedly** *adv.* —**dejection** /dɪ'dʒɛkʃən/ *n.* [U]

de·lay¹ /dɪ'leɪ/ *v.* past tense and past participle **delayed**, third person singular **delays** **1** [I,T] to wait until a later time to do something: *We cannot delay any longer.* | *We've decided to **delay** the trip **until** next month.*

THESAURUS

postpone – to change an event to a later time or date: *The meeting was postponed.*
put off – to delay something, or delay doing something, especially something that you do not want to do: *Regular checkups are important – don't put off visits to the dentist!*
procrastinate – to delay doing something that you ought to do: *A lot of people procrastinate when it comes to doing paperwork.*

2 [T] to make someone or something late: *Our flight was delayed by bad weather.* —**delayed** *adj.*

delay² *n.* plural **delays** [C,U] a situation in which someone or something is made to wait, or the length of the waiting time: ***Delays of** two hours or more are common.* | *There are **severe delays** on Route 95.* | *The President urged Congress to pass the bill **without delay**.*

de·lec·ta·ble /dɪ'lɛktəbəl/ *adj. formal* very good to taste or smell

del·e·gate¹ /'dɛləgɪt/ *n.* [C] someone who is chosen to speak, vote, and make decisions for a group: *Delegates from 50 colleges met to discuss the issue.*

del·e·gate² /'dɛlə,geɪt/ *v.* [I,T] to give part of your work or responsibilities to someone who is in a lower position than you in your organization: *Smaller jobs should be **delegated to** your assistant.*

del·e·ga·tion /,dɛlə'geɪʃən/ *n.* **1** [C] a group of people who represent a company, organization, etc.: *A UN delegation was sent to the peace talks.* **2** [U] the process of giving power to someone else and making that person responsible for some of your work: *the **delegation of** authority*

de·lete /dɪ'lit/ *v.* [T] **1** to remove a letter, word, etc. from a piece of writing **2** to remove a document, FILE, etc. from a computer's MEMORY: *The data has been **deleted from** the file.* —**deletion** /dɪ'liʃən/ *n.* [C,U]

del·i /'dɛli/ *n.* [C] a small store that sells cheese, cooked meat, bread, etc.

THESAURUS

store, **bookstore**, **clothes store**, **record store**, **grocery store**, **supermarket**, **bakery**, **delicatessen**, **liquor store**, **drugstore**, **hardware store**, **nursery**, **garden center**,

newsstand, boutique, convenience store, department store, chain store, superstore, outlet store, warehouse store
➔ see Thesaurus box at STORE[1]

de·lib·er·ate[1] /dɪˈlɪbrɪt, -bərɪt/ *adj.* **1** intended or planned: *I'm sure her story was a* ***deliberate attempt*** *to confuse us.* **2** deliberate speech, thought, or movement is slow and careful

de·lib·e·rate[2] /dɪˈlɪbəˌreɪt/ *v.* [I,T] to think about something very carefully: *The jury deliberated for three days before finding him guilty.*

de·lib·er·ate·ly /dɪˈlɪbrɪt˺li/ *adv.* done in a way that is intended [= **on purpose**]: *Someone had set the fire deliberately.*

THESAURUS

on purpose especially spoken – deliberately, especially in order to annoy someone or get an advantage for yourself: *He told the teacher I'd pushed him on purpose.*
intentionally – deliberately, especially in order to have a particular result or effect: *Very few teenagers become pregnant intentionally.*

D

de·lib·er·a·tion /dɪˌlɪbəˈreɪʃən/ *n.* [C,U] careful thought or discussion about a problem: *The committee will finish its deliberations today.*

del·i·ca·cy /ˈdɛlɪkəsi/ *n.* plural **delicacies** **1** [C] something good to eat that is expensive or rare: *In France, snails are considered a delicacy.* **2** [U] a careful way of speaking or behaving so that you do not upset anyone: *We need to handle this business with great delicacy.* **3** [U] the quality of being easy to harm or damage: *the delicacy of the clock's machinery*

del·i·cate /ˈdɛlɪkɪt/ *adj.* **1** easily damaged or broken: *a delicate porcelain cup* **2** needing to be done very carefully in order to avoid causing problems: *delicate surgery* **3** a part of the body that is delicate is attractive, thin, and graceful: *long delicate fingers* —**delicately** *adv.*

del·i·ca·tes·sen /ˌdɛlɪkəˈtɛsən/ *n.* [C] a DELI
➔ see Thesaurus box at STORE[1]

de·li·cious /dɪˈlɪʃəs/ *adj.* having a very enjoyable taste or smell: *a delicious meal* | *The soup* ***smelled/tasted delicious.*** ➔ see Thesaurus box at TASTE[1]

de·light[1] /dɪˈlaɪt/ *n.* **1** [U] a feeling of great pleasure and satisfaction: *Krystal laughed* ***with delight.*** **2** [C] something that makes you feel very happy or satisfied: ***the delights of*** *traveling*

delight[2] *v.* [T] to give someone a feeling of satisfaction and enjoyment: *This movie classic will delight the whole family.*

delight in sth *phr. v.* to enjoy something very much, especially something that annoys someone else: *little boys who delight in scaring people*

de·light·ed /dɪˈlaɪt̬ɪd/ *adj.* very happy or pleased: *We were* ***delighted to*** *hear their good news.* | *They were* ***delighted with*** *the results of the recent election.*

THESAURUS

happy, **glad**, **pleased**, **content**, **ecstatic**
➔ see Thesaurus box at HAPPY

de·light·ful /dɪˈlaɪt˺fəl/ *adj.* very nice, pleasant, and enjoyable: *a delightful story for younger children* —**delightfully** *adv.*

de·lin·e·ate /dɪˈlɪniˌeɪt/ *v.* [T] *formal* to make something very clear by describing it or drawing it in great detail

de·lin·quen·cy /dɪˈlɪŋkwənsi/ *n.* [U] illegal or socially unacceptable behavior, especially by young people: *the problem of* ***juvenile delinquency*** (=crime done by young people)

de·lin·quent /dɪˈlɪŋkwənt/ *adj.* **1** late in paying the money you owe: *delinquent loans* **2** behaving in a way that is illegal or that society does not approve of [➡ **juvenile delinquent**] —**delinquent** *n.* [C]

de·lir·i·ous /dɪˈlɪriəs/ *adj.* **1** confused, anxious, and excited because you are very sick **2** extremely happy and excited: *people* ***delirious with joy*** —**delirium** /dəˈlɪriəm/ *n.* [C,U]

de·liv·er /dɪˈlɪvɚ/ *v.* **1** [I,T] to take a letter, package, goods, etc. to a particular place or person: *I delivered newspapers when I was a kid.* | *I'm having some furniture delivered to the apartment.* **2** [T] to make a speech to a lot of people: *Rev. Whitman delivered a powerful sermon.* **3** [I,T] to do the things that you have promised: *Voters are angry that politicians haven't* ***delivered on their promises.*** **4 deliver a baby** to give birth to a baby, or to help a woman give birth to a baby **5** [T] to get votes or support from a particular group of people: *We're expecting Rigby to deliver the blue collar vote.*

de·liv·er·y /dɪˈlɪvəri/ *n.* plural **deliveries** **1** [C,U] the act of bringing something to someone or somewhere: *Pizza Mondo offers free delivery for any pizza over $10.* **2** [C] something that is delivered: *All deliveries should be taken to the rear entrance.* **3** [C] the process of a baby being born: *Mrs. Haims was rushed into the* ***delivery room*** (=hospital room where babies are born) *at 7:42.* **4** [singular, U] the way that someone speaks or performs in public: *I liked his jokes, but his delivery needs work.*

del·ta /ˈdɛltə/ *n.* [C] a low area of land where a river separates into many smaller rivers flowing toward an ocean: *the Mississippi Delta*

de·lude /dɪˈlud/ *v.* [T] to make someone believe something that is not true [= **deceive**]: *He's* ***deluding himself*** *if he thinks he can eat what he wants and lose weight.* —**deluded** *adj.*

del·uge[1] /ˈdɛlyudʒ/ *n.* [C] **1** a period of time when it rains continuously **2** a large amount of something such as letters, questions, etc. that someone gets at the same time

deluge[2] *v.* [T] **1** to send a lot of letters, questions, etc. to someone at the same time: *The radio* *station was* ***deluged with*** *complaints.* **2** *literary* to completely cover something with water

de·lu·sion /dɪˈluʒən/ *n.* [C,U] a false belief about something: *Walter's still* ***under the delusion that*** (=wrongly believes that) *his wife loves him.*

de·luxe /dɪˈlʌks/ *adj.* of better quality and more expensive than other similar things: *a deluxe resort*

delve /dɛlv/ *v.*
delve into sth *phr. v.* to search for more information about someone or something: *Reporters are always delving into actors' personal lives.*

dem·a·gogue /ˈdɛməˌgɑg/ *n.* [C] *disapproving* a political leader who tries to make people feel strong emotions in order to influence their opinions

de·mand¹ /dɪˈmænd/ *n.* **1** [singular, U] the desire that people have for particular goods or services: *There isn't any* ***demand for*** *leaded gas anymore.* | *Nurses are* ***in*** *great* ***demand*** (=wanted by a lot of people) *these days.* **2** [C] a strong request that shows you believe you have the right to get what you ask for: *Union members will strike until the company agrees to their demands.* **3 demands** [plural] the difficult or annoying things that you need to do: *women dealing with* ***the demands of*** *family and career* | *The school* ***makes*** *heavy* ***demands on*** *its teachers.*

demand² *v.* **1** [T] to ask strongly for something, especially because you think you have a right to do this: *The President demanded the release of the hostages.* | *Hughes* ***demanded that*** *he get his money back.*

THESAURUS
ask, **order**, **request**
➔ see Thesaurus box at ASK

2 [I,T] to order someone to tell you something or do something: *"What are you doing here?" she demanded.* **3** [T] if something demands your time, skill, attention, etc., it makes you use a lot of your time, skill, etc.: *The baby demands most of her time.*

de·mand·ing /dɪˈmændɪŋ/ *adj.* **1** making you use a lot of your time, skill, attention, etc.: *a demanding job* **2** expecting a lot of attention or expecting to have things exactly the way you want them, especially in a way that is not fair: *a demanding boss*

de·mean /dɪˈmin/ *v.* [T] to make someone or something less respectable

de·mean·ing /dɪˈminɪŋ/ *adj.* not showing respect for someone and making him/her feel ashamed: *demeaning comments*

de·mean·or /dɪˈminɚ/ *n.* [singular, U] *formal* the way someone behaves, dresses, speaks, etc., that shows what his/her character is like

THESAURUS
behavior, **conduct**, **manner**
➔ see Thesaurus box at BEHAVIOR

de·ment·ed /dɪˈmɛntɪd/ *adj.* crazy or very strange

de·mer·it /dɪˈmɛrɪt/ *n.* [C] a warning or a written symbol showing this warning that is given to a student or a soldier to tell him/her not to do something wrong again

de·mise /dɪˈmaɪz/ *n.* [singular] *formal* **1** the end of something that used to exist: *the* ***demise of*** *the steel industry* **2** death

dem·o /ˈdɛmoʊ/ *n.* plural **demos** [C] *informal* **1** a recording containing an example of someone's music: *a demo tape* **2** a computer program that shows what a new piece of software will be able to do when it is ready to be sold

de·moc·ra·cy /dɪˈmɑkrəsi/ *n.* plural **democracies** **1** [U] a system of government in which citizens in a country can vote to elect its leaders

THESAURUS
republic, **monarchy**, **regime**, **dictatorship**, **totalitarian country/state**, **police state**
➔ see Thesaurus box at GOVERNMENT

2 [C] a country that allows its people to elect government officials

dem·o·crat /ˈdɛməˌkræt/ *n.* [C] **1 Democrat** a member or supporter of the Democratic Party of the U.S. [➡ **republican**] **2** someone who believes in or works to achieve democracy

dem·o·crat·ic /ˌdɛməˈkræt̬ɪk/ *adj.* **1 Democratic** relating to or supporting the Democratic Party of the U.S. [➡ **republican**]: *the Democratic senator from Hawaii* **2** organized by a system in which everyone has the same right to vote, speak, etc.: *a democratic way of making decisions* **3** controlled by leaders who are elected by the people of a country: *a democratic government*

Demo'cratic ˌParty *n.* **the Democratic Party** one of the two main political parties of the U.S. [➡ **Republican Party**]

dem·o·graph·ics /ˌdɛməˈgræfɪks/ *n.* [plural] information about the people who live in a particular area, such as how many people there are or what types of people there are

de·mol·ish /dɪˈmɑlɪʃ/ *v.* [T] **1** to completely destroy a building or other structure: *Several houses were demolished to make space for a new park.* **2** to prove that an idea or opinion is completely wrong: *Each of his arguments was demolished by the defense lawyer.* —**demolition** /ˌdɛməˈlɪʃən/ *n.* [C,U]

de·mon /ˈdimən/ *n.* [C] an evil spirit —**demonic** /dɪˈmɑnɪk/ *adj.*

dem·on·strate /ˈdɛmənˌstreɪt/ *v.* **1** [T] to prove something clearly: *His lawyer will try to*

D

demonstrate that *Lee was out of town on the night of the murder.*

THESAURUS

show – to make it clear that something is true or exists by providing facts or information: *The case shows that women still face discrimination at work.*
mean – to be a clear sign that something has happened, or is true: *The lights are on – that means he's still up.*
indicate formal – if scientific facts, tests, official figures, etc. indicate something, they show that something exists or is likely to be true: *Research indicates that the drug may be linked to birth defects.*
suggest – to show that something is probably true, even though there is no proof: *There was nothing in the letter to suggest that he was thinking of suicide.*
prove – to show that something is definitely true: *Researchers have not been able to prove there is a link between living near a power line and getting cancer.*

D

2 [T] to show or describe how to use or do something: *Instructors should demonstrate how to use the equipment.*

THESAURUS

explain, **tell**, **show**, **go through**
➔ see Thesaurus box at EXPLAIN

3 [T] to show that you have a particular skill, quality, or ability: *The contest gave her a chance to demonstrate her ability.* **4** [I] to protest or support something in public with a lot of other people: *Thousands came to* ***demonstrate against*** *the war.*

THESAURUS

protest, **march**, **riot**, **hold/stage a sit-in**, **go on a hunger strike**, **boycott**
➔ see Thesaurus box at PROTEST[2]

dem·on·stra·tion /ˌdɛmənˈstreɪʃən/ *n.* **1** [C] an event at which a lot of people meet to protest or support something in public: *Students* ***staged/held a demonstration against*** *gun violence.* **2** [C,U] the act of showing and explaining how to do something: *Pam* ***gave a demonstration*** *on how to use the new computer system.* | *Make sure you get a* ***demonstration of*** *the software before you buy it.* **3** [C] an action, fact, etc. that proves that someone or something has a particular quality, ability, emotion, etc.: *People gathered in a* ***demonstration of support*** *for the missing children.*

de·mon·stra·tive /dɪˈmɑnstrət̬ɪv/ *adj.* willing to show how much you care about someone: *He loves me, but he's not very demonstrative.*

dem·on·strat·or /ˈdɛmənˌstreɪt̬ɚ/ *n.* [C] **1** someone who takes part in a public demonstration **2** someone who shows people how to do something or how something works

de·mor·al·ize /dɪˈmɔrəˌlaɪz, di-, -ˈmɑr-/ *v.* [T] to make someone lose his or her confidence or courage: *Too many changes can demoralize your employees.* —**demoralizing** *adj.*

de·mote /dɪˈmoʊt, di-/ *v.* [T] to make someone have a lower rank or less important position [≠ **promote**] —**demotion** /dɪˈmoʊʃən/ *n.* [C,U]

de·mure /dɪˈmyʊr/ *adj.* a girl or woman who is demure is shy, quiet, and always behaves well

den /dɛn/ *n.* [C] **1** a room in a house where people relax, read, watch television, etc. **2** the home of some types of animals such as lions and FOXES

de·ni·al /dɪˈnaɪəl/ *n.* **1** [C,U] a statement saying that something is not true [➡ **deny**]: *Diaz made a public* ***denial of*** *the rumor.* **2** [U] a situation or condition in which you refuse to admit or believe that something bad exists or has happened: *I think Becky's* ***in denial*** *about her drinking problem.* **3** [C] *formal* the act of refusing to allow someone to have or do something [➡ **deny**]: *the* ***denial of*** *basic human rights*

den·i·grate /ˈdɛnɪˌgreɪt/ *v.* [T] *formal* to do or say things to make someone or something seem less important or good

den·im /ˈdɛnəm/ *n.* [U] a type of strong cotton cloth used for making JEANS

de·nom·i·na·tion /dɪˌnɑməˈneɪʃən/ *n.* [C] **1** a religious group that has slightly different beliefs from other groups who belong to the same religion

THESAURUS

church, **sect**, **cult**
➔ see Thesaurus box at CHURCH

2 the value of a coin, paper money, or a stamp: *The robbers escaped with $12,000* ***in small/large denominations.***

de·note /dɪˈnoʊt/ *v.* [T] *written* to represent or mean something: *Each X on the map denotes 500 people.*

de·nounce /dɪˈnaʊns/ *v.* [T] to publicly express disapproval of someone or something: *The bishop* ***denounced*** *the film* ***as*** *immoral.*

dense /dɛns/ *adj.* **1** made of or containing a lot of things or people that are very close together: *the city's dense population* | *the dense jungles of northern Vietnam* **2** difficult to see through or breathe in: *a dense fog* **3** *informal* stupid —**densely** *adv.*

den·si·ty /ˈdɛnsət̬i/ *n.* [U] **1** how crowded something is: *a high density* (=very crowded) *neighborhood* **2** *technical* the relationship between an object's weight and the amount of space it fills

dent[1] /dɛnt/ *n.* [C] **1** a mark made when you hit or press something so that its surface is bent: *a big* ***dent in*** *the car* **2** a reduction in the amount of something: *I haven't **made a dent in** the money I have to pay back on my loan.*

dent² *v.* [T] to hit or press something so that its surface is bent and marked: *Some idiot dented my car door.*

den·tal /ˈdɛntəl/ *adj.* relating to your teeth: *dental care*

ˌdental ˈfloss *n.* [U] thin string that you use to clean between your teeth

dentist

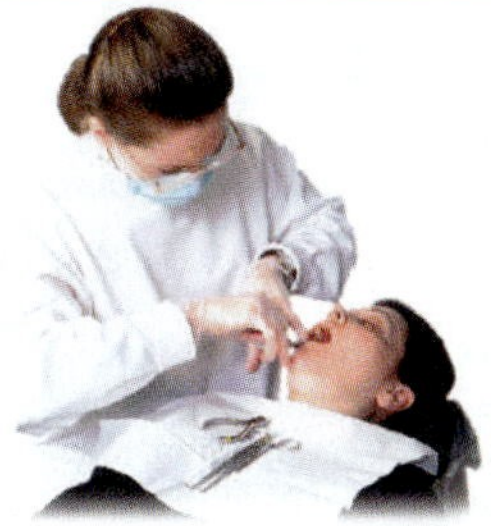

den·tist /ˈdɛntɪst/ *n.* [C] someone whose job is to treat people's teeth: *I **go to the dentist** twice a year.*

THESAURUS

doctor, physician, surgeon, specialist, psychiatrist, pediatrician
→ see Thesaurus box at DOCTOR¹

den·tures /ˈdɛntʃɚz/ *n.* [plural] artificial teeth worn to replace the natural ones that someone has lost [= **false teeth**]

de·nun·ci·a·tion /dɪˌnʌnsiˈeɪʃən/ *n.* [C,U] a public statement in which you criticize someone or something

de·ny /dɪˈnaɪ/ *v.* [T] present participle **denies**, past tense and past participle **denied** **1** to say that something is not true [➡ **denial**]: *Simmons **denied that** he had murdered his wife.* **2** to refuse to allow someone to have or do something [➡ **denial**]: *The judge denied a request to close down the school immediately.*

de·o·dor·ant /diˈoʊdərənt/ *n.* [C,U] a substance that you put on the skin under your arms to stop you from smelling bad

de·part /dɪˈpɑrt/ *v.* [I] *formal* to leave [≠ **arrive**]: *All passengers **departing for** New York on flight UA179 should go to Gate 7.* | *The train will **depart from** track 9.*

depart from sth *phr. v. formal* to start to use new ideas or do something in an unusual or unexpected way: *Parker's approach departs from the usual classroom routine.*

de·part·ment /dɪˈpɑrtˀmənt/ *n.* [C] **1** any of the groups of people working together that form part of a large organization such as a college, government, or business: *a typical university music department* | *the Department of Energy* **2** an area in a large store where particular types of product are sold: *the men's department* (=where clothes for men are sold) → see Thesaurus box at PART¹

deˈpartment ˌstore *n.* [C] a large store that sells many different products such as clothes, kitchen equipment, etc.

THESAURUS

store, bookstore, clothes store, record store, grocery store, supermarket, bakery, delicatessen, deli, liquor store, drugstore, hardware store, nursery, garden center, newsstand, boutique, convenience store, chain store, superstore, outlet store, warehouse store
→ see Thesaurus box at STORE¹

de·par·ture /dɪˈpɑrtʃɚ/ *n.* **1** [C,U] the action of leaving a place, especially to travel in an airplane, car, etc. [≠ **arrival**]: *Check in at the airport an hour before departure.* | *her **departure for** Japan* **2** [C] a change from what is usual or expected: *Their new designs represent a **departure from** their usual style.*

de·pend /dɪˈpɛnd/ *v.* **it/that depends** *spoken* used to say that you are not sure about something because you do not know what will happen: *"Are you coming to my house later?" "It depends. I might have to work."*

THESAURUS

rely on/upon – to trust or depend on someone or something: *I knew I could rely on David.*
trust – to believe that someone is honest and will not do anything bad or wrong: *I wouldn't trust him if I were you.*
count on – to depend on someone or something: *You can always count on me.*

depend on/upon sb/sth *phr. v.* **1** to need the help or support of someone or something else: *Charles **depends on** money from his parents **to** pay his rent.* **2** to be directly affected by something else: *The amount you spend depends on where you live.* **3** to trust someone or something: *Sometimes I think you're the only person I can depend on.*

de·pend·a·ble /dɪˈpɛndəbəl/ *adj.* someone or something that is dependable will always do what you need or expect him, her, or it to do: *a highly dependable employee* | *a dependable car*

de·pend·ent¹ /dɪˈpɛndənt/ *adj.* **1** needing someone or something else in order to exist, be successful, etc. [≠ **independent**]: *dependent children* | *Jan's mother was **dependent on** her **for** physical care.* **2 be dependent on/upon sth** to be directly affected by something else: *Your success is dependent on how hard you work.* —**dependence** *n.* [U]

dependent² *n.* [C] someone, especially a child, who depends on someone else for food, money, clothing, etc.

de·pict /dɪˈpɪkt/ *v.* [T] to describe or show a character, situation, or event in writing or by using pictures: *the people depicted in the movie | The god is **depicted as** a bird with a human head.*

de·plete /dɪˈplit/ *v.* [T] *formal* to reduce the amount of something: *Many of our forests have been depleted by the paper industry.*

de·plor·a·ble /dɪˈplɔrəbəl/ *adj. formal* very bad, shocking, and deserving strong disapproval: *deplorable prison conditions*

de·plore /dɪˈplɔr/ *v.* [T] *formal* to severely criticize something that you disapprove of: *a statement deploring the use of chemical weapons*

de·ploy /dɪˈplɔɪ/ *v.* past tense and past participle **deployed**, third person singular **deploys** [T] to move soldiers and military equipment to a place so that they can be used if necessary: *Nuclear missiles were being deployed in Europe.*

D

de·port /dɪˈpɔrt/ *v.* [T] to make a person from a foreign country return to the country they came from —**deportation** /ˌdipɔrˈteɪʃən/ *n.* [C,U]

de·pos·it[1] /dɪˈpɑzɪt/ *n.* [C] **1** a part of the cost of something that you pay before paying the total amount later: *We **put down a deposit on** the house yesterday.* **2** an amount of money that is put into someone's bank account [≠ **withdrawal**]: *I'd like to **make a deposit** into my savings account.* **3** money that you pay when you rent something such as an apartment or car, which will be given back if you do not damage it **4** an amount or layer of a substance in a particular place: *oil deposits*

deposit[2] *v.* [T] **1** to put money into a bank account [≠ **withdraw**]: *I'd like to deposit this in my checking account.* **2** to put something down, especially in a particular place

de·pot /ˈdipoʊ/ *n.* [C] **1** a small train or bus station **2** a place where goods are stored

de·praved /dɪˈpreɪvd/ *adj.* morally unacceptable and evil: *a depraved murderer* —**depravity** /dɪˈprævəti/ *n.* [U]

de·pre·ci·ate /dɪˈpriʃiˌeɪt/ *v.* [I] to decrease in value or price [≠ **appreciate**]: *A new car depreciates as soon as it is driven.* —**depreciation** /dɪˌpriʃiˈeɪʃən/ *n.* [U]

de·press /dɪˈprɛs/ *v.* [T] **1** to make someone feel very sad [➡ **depression**]: *All this rain is depressing me.* **2** to reduce the amount or value of something [➡ **depression**]: *The value of the peso fell, depressing the nation's economy.*

de·pressed /dɪˈprɛst/ *adj.* **1** very sad [➡ **depression**]: *I started feeling **depressed about** my mother's illness.*

THESAURUS

sad, **unhappy**, **miserable**, **down**, **low**, **gloomy**, **glum**
→ see Thesaurus box at SAD

2 not having enough jobs or business activity to make an area, industry, etc. successful [➡ **depression**]: *a depressed economy*

de·press·ing /dɪˈprɛsɪŋ/ *adj.* making you feel sad: *a depressing movie*

de·pres·sion /dɪˈprɛʃən/ *n.* **1** [C,U] **a)** a feeling of sadness and a loss of hope [➡ **depressed**]: *After her son died she **went into** a long period of **depression**.* **b)** a medical condition that makes you feel extremely unhappy, so that you cannot live a normal life [➡ **depressed**]: *The patient is suffering from depression.* **2** [C,U] a long period when businesses do not buy, sell, or produce very much and many people do not have jobs [➡ **recession**]: *the Great Depression of the 1930s*

THESAURUS

recession, **slump**, **crash**
→ see Thesaurus box at RECESSION

3 [C] an area of a surface that is lower than the other parts

de·prive /dɪˈpraɪv/ *v.*

deprive sb **of** sth *phr. v.* to take something that someone needs away from him/her: *The troops had been deprived of food and water.*

de·prived /dɪˈpraɪvd/ *adj.* not having the things that are considered to be necessary for a comfortable or happy life: *a deprived childhood*

THESAURUS

poor, **needy**, **destitute**, **impoverished**, **disadvantaged**, **underprivileged**
→ see Thesaurus box at POOR

dept. the written abbreviation of **department**

depth /dɛpθ/ *n.* **1** [C usually singular] **a)** the distance from the top of something to the bottom of it [➡ **deep**]: *The water rose to a **depth of** 12 feet.* **b)** the distance from the front of an object to the back of it [➡ **deep**]: *the **depth of** the shelves* **2** [U] how strong an emotion is or how serious a situation is: *the depth of their friendship* **3 in depth** including all the details [➡ **in-depth**]: *In her new book, she analyzes the problem in depth.*

dep·u·ty /ˈdɛpyəti/ *n.* plural **deputies** [C] **1** someone who is directly below someone else in rank, and who is officially in charge when that person is not there: *the deputy director of the Foundation* **2** someone whose job is to help a SHERIFF

de·rail /dɪˈreɪl, di-/ *v.* [I,T] to make a train go off the railroad tracks, or to go off the tracks

de·ranged /dɪˈreɪndʒd/ *adj.* behaving in a crazy or dangerous way: *a deranged criminal*

der·by /ˈdɚbi/ *n.* plural **derbies** [C] **1** a type of horse race: *the Kentucky Derby* **2** a stiff round hat for men, worn in past times

der·e·lict[1] /ˈdɛrəˌlɪkt/ *adj.* a building or piece of land that is derelict is in bad condition because no one has used it in a long time

derelict[2] *n.* [C] *disapproving* someone who has no home or money, and is very dirty

de·ride /dɪˈraɪd/ *v.* [T] *formal* to say something that shows you have no respect for someone or something —**derision** /dɪˈrɪʒən/ *n.* [U]

de·ri·so·ry /dɪˈraɪsəri/ *adj.* a derisory amount of

money is very small and is not worth considering seriously

der·i·va·tion /ˌdɛrəˈveɪʃən/ *n.* [C,U] the act or process of coming from something else, such as when a new word develops from another word

de·riv·a·tive[1] /dɪˈrɪvət̬ɪv/ *n.* [C] something that has developed or been produced from something else: *The drug is a* ***derivative of*** *Vitamin A.*

derivative[2] *adj. disapproving* copied or taken from something else: *I find his painting style very derivative.*

de·rive /dɪˈraɪv/ *v.* **1** [T] to get something such as happiness, strength, or satisfaction from someone or something: *He* ***derives*** *pleasure* ***from*** *helping others.* **2** [I,T] to develop or come from something else: *The word "benefit" is* ***derived from*** *Latin.*

der·ma·tol·o·gy /ˌdɚməˈtɑlədʒi/ *n.* [U] the part of medical science that deals with the skin, its diseases, and their treatment —**dermatologist** *n.* [C]

de·rog·a·to·ry /dɪˈrɑgəˌtɔri/ *adj.* insulting and disapproving: *He was expelled for making* ***derogatory remarks*** *about the principal.*

der·rick /ˈdɛrɪk/ *n.* [C] the tall tower over an oil well that holds the DRILL

de·scend /dɪˈsɛnd/ *v.* [I,T] *formal* to move from a higher level to a lower one [≠ **ascend**]: *She began to descend the stairs.*

descend from sb *phr. v.* **be descended from sb** to be related to someone who lived a long time ago: *My father's family is descended from the Pilgrims.*

descend on/upon sth *phr. v.* if a lot of people descend on a place, they arrive there at the same time: *A large troop of soldiers descended on the village.*

de·scend·ant /dɪˈsɛndənt/ *n.* [C] someone who is related to a person who lived a long time ago [➡ **ancestor**]: *She was a* ***direct descendant of*** *Queen Victoria.*

de·scent /dɪˈsɛnt/ *n.* **1** [C,U] *formal* the process of going down [≠ **ascent**]: *The plane began its descent.* **2** [U] your family origins, especially in relation to the country where your family came from: *We're* ***of*** *Italian* ***descent.***

de·scribe /dɪˈskraɪb/ *v.* [T] to say what someone or something is like by giving details [➡ **description**]: *Can you describe the man who took your purse?* | *It's hard to* ***describe how*** *I feel.* | *Lebanon was* ***described as*** *the "Switzerland of the Middle East."*

THESAURUS

characterize, portray
➔ see Thesaurus box at CALL[1]

de·scrip·tion /dɪˈskrɪpʃən/ *n.* [C,U] a piece of writing or speech that gives details about what someone or something is like [➡ **describe**]: *Kate* ***gave*** *us* ***a description of*** *her new house.* | *Police have a* ***detailed description*** *of the missing child.* | *You* ***fit the description of*** (=look like) *a man seen running from the scene.*

de·scrip·tive /dɪˈskrɪptɪv/ *adj.* giving a description of something in words or pictures

des·e·crate /ˈdɛsəˌkreɪt/ *v.* [T] to damage something holy or respected —**desecration** /ˌdɛsəˈkreɪʃən/ *n.* [U]

de·seg·re·gate /diˈsɛgrəˌgeɪt/ *v.* [T] to end a system in which people of different races are kept separate [≠ **segregate**]: *an attempt to desegregate the schools* —**desegregated** *adj.* —**desegregation** /diˌsɛgrəˈgeɪʃən/ *n.* [U]

desert

des·ert[1] /ˈdɛzɚt/ *n.* [C,U] a large area of land where it is always hot and dry and there is a lot of sand: *the Sahara desert*

de·sert[2] /dɪˈzɚt/ *v.* **1** [T] to leave someone alone and not help him/her anymore: *My boyfriend deserted me when I got pregnant.* **2** [I] to leave the military without permission **3** [T] to leave a place so that it is empty: *Everyone deserted the village and fled to the hills.* —**desertion** /dɪˈzɚʃən/ *n.* [C,U]

de·sert·ed /dɪˈzɚt̬ɪd/ *adj.* empty and quiet because the people who are usually there have left: *At night, the streets are deserted.*

THESAURUS

empty, bare, uninhabited
➔ see Thesaurus box at EMPTY[1]

de·sert·er /dɪˈzɚt̬ɚ/ *n.* [C] a soldier who leaves the military without permission

de·serve /dɪˈzɚv/ *v.* [T] if someone deserves something, s/he should get it because of the way s/he has behaved: *After all that work, you deserve a rest.* | *Migrant workers* ***deserve to*** *make more than $3 an hour.* | *People who go to jail for abusing children* ***get what they deserve*** (=receive the right punishment). —**deserved** *adj.*

de·sign[1] /dɪˈzaɪn/ *n.* **1** [U] the way that something has been planned or made: *We're working to improve the* ***design of*** *the computer.* **2** [C] a pattern used for decorating something: *curtains with a floral design*

THESAURUS

pattern, markings, motif
➔ see Thesaurus box at PATTERN

3 [C] a drawing that shows how something will be made or what it will look like: *We're working on **designs for** a new office building downtown.* 4 [U] the art or process of making drawings or plans for something: *Vicky studied graphic design at college.* **5 have designs on sth** to want something and be planning a way to get it

design[2] *v.* 1 [I,T] to make a drawing or plan of something that will be made or built: *Armani is designing some exciting new suits for fall.* 2 [T] to plan or develop something for a particular purpose: *an exercise **designed to** strengthen your legs | a video game **designed for** children*

des·ig·nate /ˈdɛzɪɡˌneɪt/ *v.* [T] to choose someone or something for a particular job or purpose: *$200 million was **designated for** new schools. | She has been **designated to** take over the position of treasurer.*

D

ˌdesignated ˈdriver *n.* [C] someone who does not drink alcohol at a party, bar, etc. so that s/he can drive his/her friends home

des·ig·na·tion /ˌdɛzɪɡˈneɪʃən/ *n.* [C,U] 1 the act of choosing someone or something for a particular purpose, or giving him/her, or it a particular description: *the **designation of** 100 acres around the lake as a protected area for wildlife* 2 the description or title that someone or something is given: *Any beef with the designation "extra lean" must only have 5% of its weight in fat.*

de·sign·er /dɪˈzaɪnɚ/ *n.* [C] someone whose job is to make plans or patterns for clothes, jewelry, etc.: ***designer sunglasses*** (=from a well-known designer) ➔ see Thesaurus box at FASHIONABLE

de·sir·a·ble /dɪˈzaɪrəbəl/ *adj. formal* 1 worth having or doing because it is useful, popular, or good: *a desirable job with a big law firm* 2 someone who is desirable is sexually attractive —**desirability** /dɪˌzaɪrəˈbɪləṭi/ *n.* [U]

de·sire[1] /dɪˈzaɪɚ/ *n.* [C] 1 a strong hope or wish: *the country's **desire for** peace | I have no **desire to** meet her.* 2 *formal* a strong wish to have sex with someone

desire[2] *v.* [T] **1 sth leaves a lot to be desired** said when something is not as good as it should be: *This coffee leaves a lot to be desired.* 2 *formal* to want or hope for something very much [= **want**]: *Cooper never **desired to** return to the United States.* 3 *formal* to want to have sex with someone

de·sist /dɪˈzɪst, dɪˈsɪst/ *v.* [I] *formal* to stop doing something

desk /dɛsk/ *n.* [C] 1 a piece of furniture like a table that you sit at to write and work: *Marie was sitting **at** her **desk**.* ➔ see Topic box at OFFICE ➔ see picture on page A11 2 a place where you can get information at a hotel, airport, etc.: *Check in at the **front desk**.*

desk·top computer /ˌdɛsktɑp kəmˈpyuṭɚ/ *n.* [C] a computer that is designed to be used on a desk [➡ **laptop**]

ˌdesktop ˈpublishing *n.* [U] the work of producing magazines, books, etc. with a desktop computer

des·o·late /ˈdɛsəlɪt/ *adj.* 1 a place that is desolate is empty and looks sad because there are no people there and not much activity: *a desolate stretch of highway* 2 feeling very sad and lonely —**desolation** /ˌdɛsəˈleɪʃən/ *n.* [U]

de·spair[1] /dɪˈspɛr/ *n.* [U] a feeling that you have no hope at all: *Nancy's suicide left him **in deep despair**.*

despair[2] *v.* [I] *formal* to feel that there is no hope at all: *Margaret **despaired of** ever finding a husband.*

des·per·ate /ˈdɛsprɪt, -pərɪt/ *adj.* 1 willing to do anything to change a very bad situation, and not caring about danger: *I hadn't eaten for days and was **getting desperate**.* 2 needing or wanting something very much: *By then I was so broke I was **desperate for** a job. | After a week in the hospital he was **desperate to** go home.* 3 a desperate situation is very bad or serious: *a **desperate shortage** of food* —**desperately** *adv.*: *The doctors tried desperately to save her life.*

des·per·a·tion /ˌdɛspəˈreɪʃən/ *n.* [U] a strong feeling that you will do anything to change a very bad situation: *The drowning man grabbed at the life raft **in desperation**.*

de·spic·a·ble /dɪˈspɪkəbəl/ *adj.* extremely bad or cruel

de·spise /dɪˈspaɪz/ *v.* [T] *formal* to dislike someone or something very much [= **hate**]: *He despised her from the moment they met.*

THESAURUS

hate, can't stand, detest, loathe, abhor
➔ see Thesaurus box at HATE[1]

de·spite /dɪˈspaɪt/ *prep.* without being prevented or affected by something [= **in spite of**]: *Despite the doctors' efforts, the patient died.*

de·spond·ent /dɪˈspɑndənt/ *adj.* unhappy and without hope —**despondency** *n.* [U] —**despondently** *adv.*

des·pot /ˈdɛspət, -pɑt/ *n.* [C] someone, especially the ruler of a country, who uses power in a cruel and unfair way —**despotic** /dɛˈspɑṭɪk/ *adj.*

des·sert /dɪˈzɚt/ *n.* [C,U] sweet food served after the main part of a meal: *What's **for dessert**?*

des·ti·na·tion /ˌdɛstəˈneɪʃən/ *n.* [C] the place that someone or something is going to: *The Alamo is a popular **tourist destination** in Texas. | We have just enough gas to **reach** our **destination**.*

des·tined /ˈdɛstənd/ *adj.* seeming certain to happen or do something at some time in the future: *The album is **destined to** become a classic.*

des·ti·ny /ˈdɛstəni/ *n.* [C,U] plural **destinies** the things that will happen to someone in the future, or the power that controls this [= **fate**]: *a nation fighting to **control** its **destiny***

des·ti·tute /ˈdɛstəˌtut/ *adj.* having no money, no place to live, no food, etc.: *The floods left* *thousands of people destitute.* —**destitution** /ˌdɛstəˈtuʃən/ *n.* [U]

THESAURUS

poor, **needy**, **impoverished**, **disadvantaged**, **underprivileged**
➔ see Thesaurus box at POOR

de·stroy /dɪˈstrɔɪ/ *v.* past tense and past participle **destroyed**, third person singular **destroys** [T] to damage something so badly that it cannot be used or no longer exists [➡ **destruction**]: *Two houses were destroyed in the fire.*

de·stroy·er /dɪˈstrɔɪɚ/ *n.* [C] **1** a small fast military ship with guns **2** someone or something that destroys things or people

de·struc·tion /dɪˈstrʌkʃən/ *n.* [U] the act or process of destroying something or of being destroyed: *the **destruction of** the rain forests* —**destructive** /dɪˈstrʌktɪv/ *adj.*

de·tach /dɪˈtætʃ/ *v.* [T] to remove something from something that it is attached to —**detachable** *adj.*

de·tached /dɪˈtætʃt/ *adj.* not reacting to something in an emotional way: *My father was always **emotionally detached from** the rest of us.* —**detachment** *n.* [U]

THESAURUS

matter-of-fact, **impassive**, **cold**
➔ see Thesaurus box at MATTER-OF-FACT

de·tail[1] /ˈditeɪl, dɪˈteɪl/ *n.* [C,U] a single fact or piece of information about something: *Dad planned our vacation **down to the smallest/last detail**.* | *The judge refused to discuss the case **in detail*** (=using lots of details). | *There's no need to **go into detail*** (=give a lot of details) *about the contract at this early stage.*

detail[2] *v.* [T] to list things or give all the facts or information about something: *Wooley detailed the dangers of dieting.*

de·tailed /dɪˈteɪld, ˈditeɪld/ *adj.* containing or using a lot of information or facts: *a detailed examination of the body*

de·tain /dɪˈteɪn/ *v.* [T] to officially stop someone from leaving a place: *Police detained two suspects for questioning.*

de·tect /dɪˈtɛkt/ *v.* [T] to notice or discover something, especially something that is not easy to see, hear, etc.: *I detected the faint smell of perfume.* —**detectable** *adj.* —**detection** /dɪˈtɛkʃən/ *n.* [U]

de·tec·tive /dɪˈtɛktɪv/ *n.* [C] a police officer whose job is to discover information about crimes and catch criminals

THESAURUS

police officer, **policeman**, **policewoman**, **plain-clothes police officer**, **cop**
➔ see Thesaurus box at POLICE[1]

de·tect·or /dɪˈtɛktɚ/ *n.* [C] a machine or piece of equipment that finds or measures something: *Students must pass through **metal detectors** when entering the school.*

dé·tente /deɪˈtɑnt/ *n.* [C, U] *formal* a time or situation in which two countries that are not friendly toward each other agree to behave in a more friendly way

de·ten·tion /dɪˈtɛnʃən/ *n.* **1** [U] the state of being kept in prison: *The suspect was held **in detention** for three days.* **2** [C,U] a punishment in which students who have behaved badly must stay at school for a short time after other students have left

de·ter /dɪˈtɚ/ *v.* past tense and past participle **deterred**, present participle **deterring** [T] to stop someone from doing something by making it difficult or threatening him/her with punishment: *The high cost of cigarettes has deterred many smokers.* | *The security camera was installed to **deter** people **from** stealing.*

de·ter·gent /dɪˈtɚdʒənt/ *n.* [C,U] a liquid or powder containing soap, used for washing clothes, dishes, etc.

de·te·ri·o·rate /dɪˈtɪriəˌreɪt/ *v.* [I] to become worse: *Her health is deteriorating quickly.* —**deterioration** /dɪˌtɪriəˈreɪʃən/ *n.* [U]

de·ter·mi·na·tion /dɪˌtɚməˈneɪʃən/ *n.* [U] the quality of trying to do something even when it is difficult: *Marco **shows** great **determination to** learn English.*

de·ter·mine /dɪˈtɚmɪn/ *v.* [T] **1** *formal* to find out the facts about something: *Using sonar, they determined exactly where the ship had sunk.* **2** to decide something, or to influence a decision about something: *The number of incoming students will determine the size of the classes.*

de·ter·mined /dɪˈtɚmɪnd/ *adj.* having a strong desire to do something even when it is difficult: *a determined opponent* | *Beth was **determined to** make her marriage work.*

de·ter·min·er /dɪˈtɚmənɚ/ *n.* [C] *technical* in grammar, a word that is used before a noun in order to show which thing you mean. In the phrases "the car" and "some cars," "the" and "some" are determiners

de·ter·rent /dɪˈtɚənt/ *n.* [C] something that makes someone not want to do something: *Car alarms can be an effective **deterrent to** burglars.* —**deterrence** *n.* [U]

de·test /dɪˈtɛst/ *v.* [T] to hate someone or something very much: *I detest cigarettes.*

THESAURUS

hate, **can't stand**, **loathe**, **despise**, **abhor**
➔ see Thesaurus box at HATE[1]

det·o·nate /ˈdɛtˀnˌeɪt, -ṭəˌneɪt/ *v.* [I,T] to explode, or to make something do this: *Nuclear bombs were detonated in tests in the desert.* —**detonation** /ˌdɛtˀnˈeɪʃən/ *n.* [C,U]

D

det·o·na·tor /ˈdɛtˀnˌeɪt̬ɚ, -t̬əˌneɪt̬ɚ/ *n.* [C] a small object that is used to make a bomb explode

de·tour¹ /ˈditʊr/ *n.* [C] a way of going from one place to another that is longer than the usual way because you want to avoid traffic, go somewhere special, etc.: *We* ***made/took a detour*** *to avoid the street repairs.*

detour² *v.* [I,T] to make a detour

de·tox /ˈditɑks/ *n.* [U] *informal* a special treatment to help people stop drinking alcohol or taking drugs

de·tract /dɪˈtrækt/ *v.*

detract from sth *phr. v.* to make something seem less good than it really is: *The rain did not detract from our vacation.*

det·ri·ment /ˈdɛtrəmənt/ *n.* [U] *formal* harm or damage that is done to something: *He works long hours,* ***to the detriment of*** *his marriage.* —**detrimental** /ˌdɛtrəˈmɛntl/ *adj.*

de·val·ue /diˈvælyu/ *v.* **1** [I,T] *technical* to reduce the value of a country's money, especially in relation to the value of another country's money **2** [T] to make someone or something seem less important or valuable —**devaluation** /diˌvælyuˈeɪʃən/ *n.* [C,U]

dev·as·tate /ˈdɛvəˌsteɪt/ *v.* [T] **1** to make someone feel extremely sad or shocked: *Mike was devastated by his parents' divorce.* **2** to damage something, or to destroy something completely: *Bombing raids devastated the city of Dresden.* —**devastation** /ˌdɛvəˈsteɪʃən/ *n.* [U]

dev·as·tat·ing /ˈdɛvəˌsteɪt̬ɪŋ/ *adj.* **1** badly damaging or destroying something: *Heavy rains caused devastating floods in the region.* **2** making someone feel extremely sad or shocked: *the devastating news of her sister's death*

de·vel·op /dɪˈvɛləp/ *v.* **1** [I,T] to grow or change into something bigger or more advanced, or to make someone or something do this: *It's amazing that a tree can* ***develop from*** *a small seed.* | *Chicago* ***developed into*** *a big city in the late 1800s.* | *plans to develop the local economy* **2** [T] to work on a new idea or product to make it successful: *The mayor is developing a plan to fight crime.* **3** [T] to begin to have a quality or illness: *Her baby developed a fever during the night.* **4** [I] to begin to happen, exist, or be noticed: *Clouds are developing over the mountains.* **5** [T] to use land to build things that people need: *This area will be developed over the next five years.* **6** [T] to make pictures out of film from a camera

de·vel·oped /dɪˈvɛləpt/ *adj.* **1** larger, stronger, or more advanced: *a child with* ***fully developed*** *social skills* | ***well-developed*** *muscles* **2 developed countries/nations** rich countries that have many industries, comfortable living for most people, and usually elected governments

de·vel·op·er /dɪˈvɛləpɚ/ *n.* [C] someone who makes money by buying land and then building houses, factories, etc. on it

de·vel·op·ing /dɪˈvɛləpɪŋ/ *adj.* **1** growing or changing: *a developing child* **2 developing countries/nations** poor countries that are trying to increase their industry and trade and improve life for their people

de·vel·op·ment /dɪˈvɛləpmənt/ *n.* **1** [U] the process of becoming bigger, stronger, or more advanced: *A healthy diet can prevent the* ***development of*** *heart disease.* | ***economic/industrial development*** **2** [C] a new event that changes a situation: *Our reporter in Denver has the latest developments.* **3** [C] a change that makes a product, plan, idea, etc. better: *new* ***developments in*** *computer technology* **4** [U] the process of planning and building new streets, buildings, etc. on land: *100 acres ready for development* **5** [C] a group of new buildings that have all been planned and built together on the same piece of land: *a housing development*

de·vi·ant /ˈdiviənt/ **also de·vi·ate** /ˈdivi-ɪt/ *adj. formal* different, in a bad way, from what is normal: *deviant behavior* —**deviant** *n.* [C]

de·vi·ate /ˈdiviˌeɪt/ *v.* [I] *formal* to be or become different from what is normal or acceptable: *The weather rarely* ***deviates from*** *70 degrees.*

de·vi·a·tion /ˌdiviˈeɪʃən/ *n.* [C,U] *formal* a noticeable difference from what is expected or normal: *Any* ***deviation from*** *procedures will not be tolerated.*

de·vice /dɪˈvaɪs/ *n.* [C] **1** a machine or other small object that does a special job: *a* ***device for*** *sorting mail*

> **THESAURUS**
>
> **machine, appliance, gadget**
>
> → see Thesaurus box at MACHINE¹

2 a way of achieving a particular purpose: *A contest could be a good device for raising money.*

dev·il /ˈdɛvəl/ *n.* **1 the Devil** the most powerful evil spirit in some religions, such as Christianity [= **Satan**] **2** [C] any evil spirit

dev·il·ish /ˈdɛvəlɪʃ/ *adj. old-fashioned* very bad, difficult, or evil —**devilishly** *adv.*

ˌdevil's ˈadvocate *n.* [C] someone who pretends to disagree with you in order to have a good discussion about something: *I've always enjoyed* ***playing devil's advocate.***

de·vi·ous /ˈdiviəs/ *adj.* using tricks or lies to get what you want: *a devious plan*

de·vise /dɪˈvaɪz/ *v.* [T] to plan or invent a way of doing something: *A teacher devised the game as a way of making math fun.* | *He finally* ***devised a way to*** *divide the money fairly.*

> **THESAURUS**
>
> **invent, create, think up, come up with, make up, dream up**
>
> → see Thesaurus box at INVENT

de·void /dɪˈvɔɪd/ *adj.* **be devoid of sth** to not have a particular quality at all: *The food is* ***completely devoid of*** *taste.*

de·vote /dɪˈvoʊt/ *v.* [T] **1 devote time/money/attention etc. to sb/sth** to give your time, money, etc. to someone or something: *She devotes much of her time to her family.* **2 devote yourself to sth** to do everything that you can to achieve something or help someone: *McCarthy devoted himself to ending the war.*

de·vot·ed /dɪˈvoʊt̬ɪd/ *adj.* giving someone or something a lot of love, concern, and attention: *a* ***devoted wife/father*** —**devotedly** *adv.*

THESAURUS
faithful, **loyal**, **staunch**
➔ see Thesaurus box at FAITHFUL

dev·o·tee /ˌdɛvəˈti, -ˈteɪ, -voʊ-/ *n.* [C] someone who enjoys or admires someone or something very much: ***devotees of*** *Italian wine*

de·vo·tion /dɪˈvoʊʃən/ *n.* [U] **1** a strong feeling of love that you show by paying a lot of attention to someone or something: *a father's* ***devotion to*** *his family* **2** the act of spending a lot of time and energy on something: *The actress is famous for her* ***devotion to*** *animal rights.* **3** strong religious feeling

de·vour /dɪˈvaʊɚ/ *v.* [T] **1** to eat something quickly because you are very hungry

THESAURUS
eat, **gobble up**, **wolf down**
➔ see Thesaurus box at EAT

2 if you devour information, books, etc. you read a lot very quickly

de·vout /dɪˈvaʊt/ *adj.* having very strong beliefs, especially religious ones: *a devout Catholic*

THESAURUS
religious, **practicing**
➔ see Thesaurus box at RELIGIOUS

—**devoutly** *adv.*

dew /du/ *n.* [U] the small drops of water that form on outdoor surfaces during the night

dex·ter·i·ty /dɛkˈstɛrət̬i/ *n.* [U] skill in using your hands to do things —**dexterous**, **dextrous** /ˈdɛkstrəs/ *adj.*

di·a·be·tes /ˌdaɪəˈbit̬iz, -ˈbit̬ɪs/ *n.* [U] a disease in which there is too much sugar in the blood

di·a·bet·ic /ˌdaɪəˈbɛt̬ɪk/ *n.* [C] someone who has diabetes —**diabetic** *adj.*

di·a·bol·i·cal /ˌdaɪəˈbɑlɪkəl/ *adj.* very bad, evil, or cruel: *a diabolical killer*

di·ag·nose /ˌdaɪəgˈnoʊs, ˈdaɪəgˌnoʊs/ *v.* [T] to find out what illness a person has or what is wrong with something: *A technician diagnosed a bad pump in the engine.* | *He was* ***diagnosed with*** *hepatitis.*

di·ag·no·sis /ˌdaɪəgˈnoʊsɪs/ *n.* plural **diagnoses** /-ˈnoʊsiz/ [C,U] the result of diagnosing someone or something [➡ **prognosis**]: *The doctor will* ***make a diagnosis*** *and recommend treatment.* —**diagnostic** /ˌdaɪəgˈnɑstɪk/ *adj.*

di·ag·o·nal /daɪˈægənəl/ *adj.* **1** a diagonal line joins two opposite corners of a square shape [➡ **horizontal**, **vertical**] **2** following a sloping angle: *diagonal parking spaces* —**diagonal** *n.* [C] —**diagonally** *adv.*

di·a·gram /ˈdaɪəˌgræm/ *n.* [C] a drawing that shows how something works, where something is, what something looks like, etc.: *a* ***diagram of*** *a car engine*

dial

di·al[1] /ˈdaɪəl/ *v.* [I,T] to press the buttons or turn the dial on a telephone in order to make a telephone call: *Dial 911 – there's been an accident.* | *I think I dialed the wrong number.* ➔ see Topic box at TELEPHONE[1]

dial[2] *n.* [C] **1** the round part of a clock, watch, machine, etc. that has numbers that show you the time or a measurement **2** the part of a piece of equipment, such as a radio or THERMOSTAT, that you turn in order to do something, such as find a different station or set the temperature **3** the wheel with holes for fingers on some telephones

di·a·lect /ˈdaɪəˌlɛkt/ *n.* [C,U] a form of a language that is spoken in one area which is different from the way it is spoken in other areas: *a dialect of Arabic* | *literature written* ***in*** *native* ***dialects***

THESAURUS
language, **tongue**
➔ see Thesaurus box at LANGUAGE

di·a·logue, **dialog** /ˈdaɪəˌlɔg, -ˌlɑg/ *n.* [C,U] **1** a conversation in a book, play, or movie [➡ **monologue**] **2** a formal discussion between countries or groups in order to solve problems: *an opportunity for* ***dialogue between*** *the fighting countries* | *a* ***dialogue on*** *human rights*

ˈdial tone *n.* [C] the sound you hear when you pick up a telephone that lets you know that you can make a call

di·am·e·ter /daɪˈæmət̬ɚ/ *n.* [C,U] a line or measurement from one side of a circle to the other that passes through the center: *a wheel two feet* ***in diameter***

di·a·met·ri·cally /ˌdaɪəˈmɛtrɪkli/ *adv.* **diametrically opposed/opposite** completely different or opposite: *We have diametrically opposed views on raising children.*

di·a·mond /ˈdaɪmənd, ˈdaɪə-/ *n.* **1** [C,U] a clear, very hard, valuable stone, used in jewelry and in industry: *a diamond ring* **2** [C] a shape with four straight sides of equal length that stands on one of its points ➔ see picture at PLAYING CARD **3** [C] a playing card with red diamond shapes on it **4** [C] **a)** the area in a baseball field that is within the shape formed by the four BASES **b)** the whole playing field used in baseball

THESAURUS

field, stadium, court, track
➔ see Thesaurus box at SPORT¹

di·a·per /ˈdaɪpɚ, ˈdaɪə-/ *n.* [C] a piece of material that is put between a baby's legs and fastened around its waist to hold its body wastes: *I think we need to* ***change*** *the baby's* ***diaper*** (=put on a new one).

di·a·phragm /ˈdaɪəˌfræm/ *n.* [C] **1** the muscle between your lungs and your stomach that controls your breathing **2** a small round rubber object that a woman can put inside her VAGINA to stop her from getting PREGNANT

di·ar·rhe·a /ˌdaɪəˈriə/ *n.* [U] an illness in which waste from the BOWELS is watery and comes out often

di·a·ry /ˈdaɪəri/ *n.* plural **diaries** [C] a book in which you write down important or interesting things that happen to you each day: ***I kept a diary*** (=wrote in it regularly) *when I was in the army.*

THESAURUS

record, journal, file, log (book)
➔ see Thesaurus box at RECORD¹

dice¹ /daɪs/ *n.* [C] **1** the plural form of DIE: *Jeanie* ***rolled the dice.*** **2 no dice** *spoken* said when you refuse to do something: *I asked if I could borrow the car, but she said no dice.*

dice² *v.* [T] to cut food into small square pieces: *Dice the carrots.*

THESAURUS

cut, chop (up), slice, peel, carve, shred, grate
➔ see Thesaurus box at CUT¹

➔ see picture at CUT¹

dic·ey /ˈdaɪsi/ *adj. informal* risky and possibly dangerous: *a dicey situation*

dic·tate /ˈdɪkteɪt, dɪkˈteɪt/ *v.* **1** [I,T] to say words for someone else to write down: *She* ***dictated*** *a letter* ***to*** *her secretary.* **2** [I,T] to tell someone exactly what s/he must do: *You can't* ***dictate how*** *I should live my life!* **3** [T] to influence or control something: *Where I go on vacation will be dictated by the amount of money I've saved.*

dic·ta·tion /dɪkˈteɪʃən/ *n.* **1** [U] the act of saying words for someone to write down **2** [C] sentences that a teacher reads out to test your ability to hear and write the words correctly: *Dictations are the hardest part of learning French.*

dic·ta·tor /ˈdɪkteɪt̬ɚ/ *n.* [C] a leader of a country who controls everything, and who usually has gained power by force —**dictatorial** /ˌdɪktəˈtɔriəl/ *adj.*

dic·ta·tor·ship /dɪkˈteɪt̬ɚˌʃɪp, ˈdɪkteɪt̬ɚ-/ *n.* **1** [U] government by a dictator

THESAURUS

democracy, republic, monarchy, regime, totalitarian country/state
➔ see Thesaurus box at GOVERNMENT

2 [C] a country ruled by a dictator

dic·tion /ˈdɪkʃən/ *n.* [U] **1** the way in which someone pronounces words **2** *technical* the choice and use of words and phrases to express meaning, especially in literature or poetry

dic·tion·ar·y /ˈdɪkʃəˌnɛri/ *n.* plural **dictionaries** [C] a book that gives a list of words in ALPHABETICAL order, and explains their meanings in the same or another language: *a Spanish-English dictionary*

did /dɪd/ *v.* the past tense of DO

di·dac·tic /daɪˈdæktɪk/ *adj. formal* speech or writing that is didactic is intended to teach people a lesson

did·n't /ˈdɪdnt/ *v.* the short form of "did not": *She didn't have enough money.*

die¹ /daɪ/ *v.* past tense and past participle **died**, present participle **dying** [I] **1** to stop living [➡ **dead, death**]: *She was afraid her son would die.* | *Mrs. Chen* ***died of/from*** (=because of) *heart disease.* | *Mary* ***died*** *peacefully* ***in*** *her* ***sleep.*** **2** to disappear or stop existing: *The hope that her husband would return never died.* **3** *informal* if a machine or motor dies, it stops working: *I was going down a hill when my car died.*

SPOKEN PHRASES

4 be dying to do something to want to do something very much: *I'm dying to meet her brother.* **5 be to die for** if something is to die for, it is extremely good: *Max's chocolate cake is to die for!* **6 die laughing** to laugh a lot: *When Alex fell off the stage I almost died laughing.* **7 I could have died also I almost died** said when you are very surprised or embarrassed: *I could've died when Ed said that!*

die away *phr. v.* if a sound dies away, it becomes weaker and then stops

die down *phr. v.* to become less strong or violent: *The wind finally died down this morning.*

die off *phr. v.* to die one at a time until none is left: *All the elm trees are dying off.*

die out *phr. v.* to disappear or stop existing completely: *The last bears in this area died out 100 years ago.*

die² *n.* plural **dice** /daɪs/ [C] one of two or more

small blocks of wood, plastic, etc. with a different number of spots on each side, used in games

die·hard /ˈdaɪhɑrd/ *adj. informal* **1** opposing change and refusing to accept new ideas: *a die-hard opponent of free speech* **2 die-hard fan/communist/supporter etc.** someone who is very loyal to a team, political party, person, etc.: *a diehard Dodgers fan*

die·sel /ˈdizəl/ **also ˌdiesel ˈfuel** *n.* [U] a type of FUEL used instead of gas in a special type of engine

di·et[1] /ˈdaɪət/ *n.* **1** [C,U] the type of food that you eat each day: *Many kids don't get enough fruit in their diet.* | *The animals live on a* ***diet of*** *fruit and insects.* **2** [C] a plan to eat only particular kinds or amounts of food, especially because you want to get thinner or because you have a health problem: *a low-fat diet* | *No dessert for me – I'm* ***on a diet****.*

diet[2] *v.* [I] to eat less or eat only particular foods in order to lose weight: *Jill's always dieting.*

dif·fer /ˈdɪfɚ/ *v.* [I] **1** to be different: *How does the film* ***differ from*** *the book?* **2** *formal* to have different opinions: *The two groups* ***differ on/about/over*** *where to have the meeting.*

dif·ference /ˈdɪfrəns/ *n.* **1** [C] a way in which two or more things or people are not like each other: *the* ***differences between*** *England and America* | *Can you* ***tell the difference*** *between the twins* (=recognize that they are different)*?* **2** [singular, U] the fact of not being the same as something else, or an amount by which one thing is not the same as another: *What's the* ***difference in*** *price?* | *There's an age* ***difference*** *of 4 years* ***between*** *the two children.* **3 make a difference/make all the difference** to have a good effect on a situation or person: *Swimming twice a week can* ***make a big difference*** *in the way you feel.* **4 make no difference** to be unimportant or to have no effect: *It* ***makes no difference to*** *me whether we win by one goal or ten.* **5 have your differences** to have disagreements with someone: *My sister and I have always had our differences.* **6 difference of opinion** a disagreement: *Perkins left his job because of a* ***difference of opinion with*** *his boss.*

dif·ferent /ˈdɪfrənt/ *adj.* **1** not like something or someone else, or not the same as before: *Did you get a haircut? You look different.* | *Anna is* ***different from*** *most kids at her school.* | *Writing for films is* ***different than*** *writing plays.* **2** separate: *The bookstore has a lot of different books about Kennedy.* **3** *spoken* unusual, often in a way that you do not like: *"How do you like my shirt?" "Well, it's different."* —**differently** *adv.*

GRAMMAR

different from, different than

You can use **different from** or **different than** to talk about two things that are not the same. However, most teachers prefer **different from**.

dif·fer·en·ti·ate /ˌdɪfəˈrɛnʃiˌeɪt/ *v.* **1** [I,T] to recognize or express the difference between things or people: *It was difficult for him to* ***differentiate between*** *light and dark.* **2** [T] to make one thing different from another: *Our company tries to* ***differentiate*** *its products* ***from*** *the competitors.* —**differentiation** /ˌdɪfəˌrɛnʃiˈeɪʃən/ *n.* [U]

dif·fi·cult /ˈdɪfəˌkʌlt/ *adj.* **1** not easy to do or understand: *a difficult question* | *She* ***finds*** *math* ***difficult****.* **2** involving a lot of problems and causing trouble: *This past year has been a very difficult time in my life.* | *The bus strike is* ***making life/things difficult for*** *commuters.* **3** someone who is difficult is never satisfied, friendly, or pleased

dif·fi·cul·ty /ˈdɪfɪˌkʌlti/ *n.* **1** [C usually plural, U] a problem or something that causes trouble: *Peter's* ***having difficulty in*** *finding a job.* | *She walks* ***with*** *great* ***difficulty****.* | *Their business is* ***in*** *financial* ***difficulty****.* | *We* ***ran into difficulties*** (=had trouble) *buying the house.* **2** [U] the state of being hard to do or understand: *The books vary in* ***level of difficulty****.*

dif·fuse[1] /dɪˈfyus/ *adj.* spread over a large area or in many places: *a large and diffuse organization*

dif·fuse[2] /dɪˈfyuz/ *v.* [I,T] *formal* **1** to make a bad feeling less strong: *Mara told jokes to diffuse the tension.* **2** to make ideas, information, etc. available to many people: *The language was diffused throughout the Balkans and into central Europe.* **3** to make heat, light, liquid, etc. spread through something, or to spread like this: *Smoke diffused into the living room and got into the carpet.*

dig[1] /dɪg/ *v.* past tense and past participle **dug** /dʌg/ present participle **digging** **1** [I,T] to break up and move earth, stone, snow, etc. with a tool, your hands, or a machine: *The kids enjoyed digging in the sand.* | *She dug a hole and threw some seeds in it.* | *The company began* ***digging for*** *minerals many years ago.* **2** [I] to move many things such as papers, boxes, rocks, or clothing in order to find something: *She* ***dug through*** *her purse, looking for her keys.* **3 dig yourself (into) a hole** to do or say something that makes a problem or situation so bad that it is difficult to make it better: *The mayor dug himself into a hole when he promised 3,000 new jobs.* **4** [T] *spoken* to like something or someone: *You really dig her, don't you?*

dig in *phr. v. spoken* to start eating food that is in front of you: *Come on, everyone – dig in!*

dig (sth) **into** sth *phr. v.* to push hard into something, or to make something do this: *She dug her fingernails into my arm.*

dig sth ⇔ **out** *phr. v.* **1** to get someone or something out of a place using a tool, your hands, or a machine: *We had to dig our car out after the blizzard.* **2** to find something that you have not

D

seen for a long time, or that is not easy to find: *Mom dug out her wedding dress and showed it to us.*

dig sth ⇔ **up** *phr. v.* **1** to remove something from under the ground with a tool, your hands, or a machine: *Police dug up the missing man's body from the yard.* **2** *informal* to find hidden or forgotten information by careful searching: *See what you can dig up on this guy Stark.*

dig² *n.* [C] **1** an unkind thing you say to annoy someone: *Greene's remark was meant to be a* ***dig at*** *his opponent.* **2** a small quick push that you give someone with your finger or elbow: *a dig in the ribs* **3** the process of digging in a place in order to find ancient objects to study

di·gest¹ /daɪˈdʒɛst, dɪ-/ *v.* [I,T] **1** if food digests or if you digest it, it changes in the stomach into a form your body can use: *Some babies can't digest cow's milk.* **2** to understand something after thinking about it carefully: *He'll need some time to digest the news.*

D

di·gest² /ˈdaɪdʒɛst/ *n.* [C] a short piece of writing that gives the most important facts from a book, report, etc.

di·ges·tion /daɪˈdʒɛstʃən, dɪ-/ *n.* [C,U] the process or ability to digest food —**digestive** *adj.*: *digestive problems*

dig·it /ˈdɪdʒɪt/ *n.* [C] **1** a written sign that represents any of the numbers from 0 to 9: *a seven-digit phone number* **2** *technical* a finger or toe

dig·i·tal /ˈdɪdʒɪtl/ *adj.* **1** giving information in the form of numbers: *a digital clock* **2** using a system in which information is represented in the form of numbers: *a digital camera* —**digitally** *adv.*

dig·ni·fied /ˈdɪgnəˌfaɪd/ *adj.* calm, serious, and making people feel respect: *a dignified leader*

dig·ni·tar·y /ˈdɪgnəˌtɛri/ *n.* plural **dignitaries** [C] someone who has an important official position: *foreign dignitaries*

dig·ni·ty /ˈdɪgnəti/ *n.* [U] **1** calm serious behavior, even in difficult situations, that makes people respect you: *a woman of compassion and dignity* | *She spoke* ***with*** *courage and* ***dignity***. **2** the quality of being serious and formal: *Lawyers must respect the dignity of the court.*

di·gress /daɪˈgrɛs, dɪ-/ *v.* [I] *formal* to begin talking about something that is not related to the subject you were talking about —**digression** /daɪˈgrɛʃən/ *n.* [C,U]

di·lap·i·dat·ed /dəˈlæpəˌdeɪtɪd/ *adj.* old, broken, and in very bad condition: *a dilapidated church* —**dilapidation** /dɪˌlæpəˈdeɪʃən/ *n.* [U]

di·late /daɪˈleɪt, ˈdaɪleɪt/ *v.* [I,T] to become wider or more open, or to cause something to do this: *Her eyes were dilated and her face was red.* —**dilation** /daɪˈleɪʃən/ *n.* [U]

di·lem·ma /dəˈlɛmə/ *n.* [C] a situation in which you have to make a difficult choice between two or more actions: *We're* ***in a dilemma*** *about whether to move or not.* | *a* ***moral dilemma***

dil·i·gent /ˈdɪlədʒənt/ *adj.* **1** someone who is diligent always works hard and carefully: *a diligent student* **2** done in a careful and thorough way: *diligent research* —**diligence** *n.* [U] —**diligently** *adv.*

dill /dɪl/ *n.* [U] a plant whose seeds and leaves are used in cooking

di·lute /dɪˈlut, daɪ-/ *v.* [T] to make a liquid weaker by adding water or another liquid: ***Dilute*** *the paint* ***with*** *oil.* —**diluted** *adj.* —**dilution** /daɪˈluʃən, dɪ-/ *n.* [C,U]

dim¹ /dɪm/ *adj.* comparative **dimmer**, superlative **dimmest** **1** not bright or easy to see well: *a dim hallway* | *The curtains were closed and the light was dim.* | *the dim outline of a building* **2 a dim recollection/awareness etc.** something that is difficult for someone to remember, understand, etc.: *She only has a dim memory of her parents.* **3 take a dim view of sth** to disapprove of something —**dimly** *adv.*

dim² *v.* past tense and past participle **dimmed**, present participle **dimming** [I,T] **1** if a light dims, or if you dim it, it becomes less bright: *Can you dim the lights?* **2** if a feeling or quality dims, or if something dims it, it grows weaker: *The painful memory began to dim.*

dime /daɪm/ *n.* [C] **1** a coin worth 10 cents (=1/10 of a dollar), used in the U.S. and Canada

THESAURUS

penny, **nickel**, **quarter**
→ see Thesaurus box at MONEY

2 a dime a dozen *informal* very common and not valuable: *Jobs like his are a dime a dozen.* **3 stop/park/turn on a dime** to stop, park, etc. within a small area

di·men·sion /dɪˈmɛnʃən, daɪ-/ *n.* [C] **1** a part of a situation that affects the way you think about it: *The baby added* ***a new dimension*** *to our life.* **2** a measurement of something in length, height, or width **3 dimensions** [plural] **a)** the measurement or size of something: *What are the* ***dimensions of*** *the room?* **b)** how great or serious a problem is: *The government needs to recognize the full* ***dimensions of*** *the problem.*

ˈdime store *n.* [C] a store that sells different types of cheap things, especially for the house

di·min·ish /dɪˈmɪnɪʃ/ *v.* [I,T] to become smaller or less important, or to make something do this: *The show's audience has slowly diminished.*

THESAURUS

decrease, **go down**, **drop**, **fall**, **plummet**, **decline**
→ see Thesaurus box at DECREASE¹

di·min·u·tive /dɪˈmɪnyətɪv/ *adj.* *formal* very small: *a diminutive man*

dim·ple /ˈdɪmpəl/ *n.* [C] a small hollow place on

your cheek or chin, especially one that forms when you smile —**dimpled** *adj.*

din /dɪn/ *n.* [singular, U] *literary* a loud, continuous, and annoying noise

dine

dine /daɪn/ *v.* [I] *formal* to eat dinner

dine on sth *phr. v. formal* to eat a particular type of food for dinner, especially expensive food: *We dined on shrimp and pasta.*

dine out *phr. v. formal* to eat in a restaurant

din·er /ˈdaɪnɚ/ *n.* [C] **1** a small restaurant that serves cheap meals

THESAURUS

restaurant, **cafe**, **coffee shop**, **fast food restaurant**, **cafeteria**
➔ see Thesaurus box at RESTAURANT

2 someone who is eating in a restaurant

ding-dong /ˈdɪŋ dɔŋ, -dɑŋ/ *n.* [U] the noise made by a bell

din·gy /ˈdɪndʒi/ *adj.* a dingy room, street, or place is dirty and in bad condition: *dingy offices*

ˈdining room *n.* [C] a room where you eat meals in a house

din·ner /ˈdɪnɚ/ *n.* **1** [C,U] the main meal of the day, usually eaten in the evening: *We had fish **for dinner**.* | *My aunt invited me for Thanksgiving dinner.*

THESAURUS

breakfast, **lunch**, **brunch**, **supper**
➔ see Thesaurus box at MEAL

2 [C] a formal occasion when an evening meal is eaten, often to celebrate something: *There was a dinner in honor of his retirement.*

din·ner·time /ˈdɪnɚˌtaɪm/ *n.* [U] the time when most people eat dinner, usually between 5 p.m. and 7 p.m.

di·no·saur /ˈdaɪnəˌsɔr/ *n.* [C] a very large animal that lived millions of years ago and no longer exists

dip[1] /dɪp/ past tense and past participle **dipped**, present participle **dipping** *v.* **1** [T] to put something into a liquid and quickly lift it out again: *Janet **dipped** her feet **into** the water.* | *strawberries **dipped in** chocolate* **2** [I] *informal* to go down or become lower: *The temperature could dip down to the 20s tonight.*

dip into sth *phr. v.* to use some of an amount of money that you have: *Medical bills forced her to dip into her savings.*

dip[2] *n.* **1** [C,U] a thick mixture that you can dip food into before you eat it: *a cheese dip* **2** [C] an occasion when the level or amount of something becomes lower: *a **dip in** prices* **3** [C] a place where the surface of something goes down suddenly, and then goes up again: *a dip in the road* **4** [C] *informal* a quick swim: *Is there time for a dip in the pool before lunch?*

diph·the·ri·a /dɪfˈθɪriə, dɪp-/ *n.* [U] a serious infectious throat disease that makes breathing difficult

di·plo·ma /dɪˈploʊmə/ *n.* [C] an official paper showing that someone has successfully finished his/her HIGH SCHOOL or college education: *a high school diploma*

di·plo·ma·cy /dɪˈploʊməsi/ *n.* [U] **1** the management of political relations between countries: *an expert at international diplomacy* **2** skill in dealing with people and difficult situations successfully: *I would have handled the situation with a little more diplomacy.*

dip·lo·mat /ˈdɪpləˌmæt/ *n.* [C] someone who officially represents his/her government in a foreign country

dip·lo·mat·ic /ˌdɪpləˈmæt̬ɪk◂/ *adj.* **1** relating to the work of diplomats: *Feingold plans to join the diplomatic service.* **2** good at dealing with people politely and skillfully without upsetting them: *She tried to be diplomatic, but I could tell she was upset.* —**diplomatically** *adv.*

dip·stick /ˈdɪpstɪk/ *n.* [C] a stick used for measuring the amount of liquid in a container, such as oil in a car's engine

dire /daɪɚ/ *adj.* **1** extremely serious or terrible: *Officials say the situation is not as dire as they first thought.* | *The country is **in dire need of** food aid.* **2 be in dire straits** to be in an extremely difficult or serious situation

di·rect[1] /dəˈrɛkt, daɪ-/ *adj.* **1** done without involving other people, actions, processes, etc. [≠ **indirect**]: *He has direct access to the president.* **2** going straight from one place to another, without stopping or changing direction: *What's the most direct route to the airport?* **3** saying exactly what you mean in an honest and clear way [≠ **indirect**]: *The senator avoided giving **direct answers** to reporters' questions.*

THESAURUS

honest, **frank**, **candid**, **straightforward**, **blunt**, **forthright**
➔ see Thesaurus box at HONEST

4 likely to change something immediately [≠ **indirect**]: *This job allows me to have a direct*

D

impact on people's lives. **5** exact or total: *a direct translation from French* —**directness** *n.* [U]

direct² *v.* [T] **1** to aim something in a particular direction or at a particular person, group, etc.: *My remark was* ***directed at*** *Tom, not you.* | *He* ***directed*** *the light* ***towards*** *the house.* **2** to be in charge of something: *Hanley was asked to direct the investigation.* **3** to give actors in a play, movie, etc. instructions about what to do: *In 1977, Scott directed his first movie.* **4** *formal* to tell someone the way to a place: *He directed me to the airport.*

THESAURUS

lead, **guide**, **point**
→ see Thesaurus box at LEAD¹

direct³ *adv.* **1** without stopping or changing direction: *You can fly direct from London to Nashville.* **2** without dealing with anyone else first: *You'll have to contact the manager direct.*

di,rect de'posit *n.* [U] a method of paying someone's salary directly into his/her bank account —**direct deposit** *v.* [T]

di·rec·tion /dəˈrɛkʃən, daɪ-/ *n.* **1** [C] the way someone or something is moving, facing, or aimed: *Brian drove off* ***in the direction of*** (=toward) *the party.* | *As she walked along the trail, she saw a large man coming* ***in the opposite direction.*** **2** [C] the general way in which someone or something changes or develops: *Suddenly the conversation changed direction.* **3 directions** [plural] instructions about how to go from one place to another, or about how to do something: *Could you* ***give*** *me* ***directions to*** *the airport?* | *Read the directions at the top of the page.* **4** [U] control, guidance, or advice: *The company's been successful* ***under*** *Martini's* ***direction.*** **5** [U] a general purpose or aim: *Sometimes I feel that my life lacks direction.* **6 sense of direction** the ability to know which way to go in a place you do not know well **7** [U] the instructions given to actors and other people in a play, movie, etc.

di·rec·tive /dəˈrɛktɪv/ *n.* [C] an official order or instruction to do something

di·rect·ly /dəˈrɛktli, daɪ-/ *adv.* **1** with no other person, action, process, etc. involved: *McNealy will report directly to the new sales manager.* **2** exactly: *Lucas sat directly behind us.*

,direct 'object *n.* *technical* in grammar, the person or thing that is affected by the action of the verb in a sentence. In the sentence "Sheila closed the door," "door" is the object. [➡ **indirect object**]

di·rec·tor /dəˈrɛktɚ, daɪ-/ *n.* [C] **1** someone who gives instructions to actors and other people in a movie or play

TOPIC

actor, **actress**, **star**, **producer**, **film/movie crew**
→ see Topic box at MOVIE

2 someone who controls or manages a company, organization, or activity: *Her new job is marketing director of Sun Life.*

di·rec·to·ry /dəˈrɛktəri, daɪ-/ *n.* plural **directories** [C] **1** a book or list of names, facts, events, etc., usually arranged in ALPHABETICAL order: *the telephone directory* **2** a place in a computer where FILES or programs are organized

dirt /dɚt/ *n.* [U] **1** earth or soil: *a dirt road* **2** any substance, such as dust or mud, that makes things not clean [➡ **dirty**]: *The floor was covered with dirt!* **3** *informal* information about someone's private life or activities that might give people a bad opinion about him/her

,dirt 'cheap *adj., adv. informal* extremely cheap: *We bought this house when it was dirt cheap.*

dirt·y¹ /ˈdɚṭi/ *adj.* comparative **dirtier**, superlative **dirtiest** **1** not clean, or covered in dirt: *dirty dishes in the sink* | *How did your shoes get so dirty?*

THESAURUS

filthy – very dirty: *The carpet was filthy.*
dusty – covered with dust: *piles of dusty books*
muddy – covered in mud: *muddy hiking boots*
greasy – covered with a lot of oil or grease (=an oily substance): *greasy fingermarks on the table*

2 relating to sex, in a way that is considered bad or immoral: *dirty jokes* | *students who use* ***dirty words*** *in class* **3** unfair or dishonest and intended to harm someone: *a dirty fighter* **4 do sb's dirty work** to do a bad or dishonest job for someone so that s/he does not have to do it himself or herself: *I told them to do their own dirty work.*

dirty² *v.* third person singular **dirties**, past tense **dirtied** [T] to make something dirty

dis /dɪs/ *v.* past tense and past participle **dissed**, present participle **dissing** [T] *slang* to make unfair and unkind remarks about someone

dis·a·bil·i·ty /ˌdɪsəˈbɪləṭi/ *n.* plural **disabilities** [C,U] a physical or mental condition that makes it difficult for someone to do the things most people are able to do: *Her disability prevented her from getting a driver's license.* | *learning to live with disability*

dis·a·bled /dɪsˈeɪbəld/ *adj.* **1** someone who is disabled cannot use a part of his/her body in a way that most people can: *a disabled worker* **2 the disabled** people who are disabled: *The bank has an entrance for the disabled.*

dis·ad·van·tage /ˌdɪsədˈvæntɪdʒ/ *n.* [C] **1** something that may make someone less successful than other people [➡ **advantage**]: *Your main disadvantage is lack of experience.* | *I was* ***at a disadvantage*** *because I didn't speak Spanish.* **2** something that is not good or causes problems: *The only* ***disadvantage of*** *the job is the traveling.*

dis·ad·van·taged /ˌdɪsədˈvæntɪdʒd/ *adj.* someone who is disadvantaged has social problems, such as a lack of money or education, that make it difficult for him/her to succeed: *a program for disadvantaged students*

THESAURUS

poor, **needy**, **destitute**, **impoverished**, **underprivileged**, **deprived**
➔ see Thesaurus box at POOR

dis·af·fect·ed /ˌdɪsəˈfɛktɪd◂/ *adj.* no longer loyal because you are not satisfied with your leader, ruler, etc.: *Candidates are trying to attract disaffected voters.* —**disaffection** /ˌdɪsəˈfɛkʃən/ *n.* [U]

dis·a·gree /ˌdɪsəˈgri/ *v.* [I] **1** to have or express a different opinion from someone else: *Roth doesn't like anybody who* ***disagrees with*** *him.* | *We* ***disagree about*** *the best way to solve the problem.* | *Doctors* ***disagree on*** *the best way to treat the disease.* **2** if statements or reports about the same thing disagree, they are different from each other
disagree with sb *phr. v.* if food disagrees with you, it makes you feel sick

dis·a·gree·a·ble /ˌdɪsəˈgriəbəl/ *adj.* **1** not enjoyable or pleasant: *a disagreeable incident* **2** unfriendly and in a bad mood: *a disagreeable person*

dis·a·gree·ment /ˌdɪsəˈgrimənt/ *n.* **1** [C,U] a situation in which people express different opinions about something and sometimes argue: *We* ***had a disagreement with*** *our neighbors.* | *a* ***disagreement between*** *the two countries* | *There was a slight* ***disagreement over*** *who should pay the bill.* **2** [U] differences between two statements, reports, etc. that should be similar: *There was major* ***disagreement between*** *the witnesses' statements.*

dis·al·low /ˌdɪsəˈlaʊ/ *v.* [T] *formal* to officially refuse to allow something because a rule has been broken: *The touchdown was disallowed because of a penalty.*

dis·ap·pear /ˌdɪsəˈpɪr/ *v.* [I] **1** to become impossible to see anymore: *The scars will disappear in a year or two.* | *The cat had* ***disappeared under*** *the couch.* **2** to become impossible to find or to be lost: *The plane mysteriously disappeared while flying over the Atlantic.* **3** to stop existing: *Many species of plants and animals disappear every year.* —**disappearance** *n.* [C,U]

dis·ap·point /ˌdɪsəˈpɔɪnt/ *v.* [T] to make someone unhappy because something s/he hoped for does not happen or is not as good as s/he expected: *I'm sorry to disappoint you, but the trip is canceled.*

dis·ap·point·ed /ˌdɪsəˈpɔɪntɪd/ *adj.* unhappy because something you hoped for did not happen, or because something or someone was not as good as you expected: *We're* ***disappointed (that)*** *the director is unable to attend.* | *She was* ***disappointed with*** *the election results.* | *I've been* ***disappointed in*** *his work.*

dis·ap·point·ing /ˌdɪsəˈpɔɪntɪŋ/ *adj.* not as good as you expected or hoped something would be: *disappointing sales* —**disappointingly** *adv.*

dis·ap·point·ment /ˌdɪsəˈpɔɪntˀmənt/ *n.* **1** [U] a feeling of sadness because something is not as good as you expected or has not happened: *his* ***disappointment at*** *not being chosen for the job* | *Labor unions expressed their* ***disappointment with*** *the president's proposal.* | *She tried to* ***hide*** *her* ***disappointment.*** **2** [C] someone or something that is not as good as you hoped or expected: *Her new book was* ***a big/major/real disappointment.*** | *Kate feels like she's* ***a disappointment to*** *her family.*

dis·ap·prov·al /ˌdɪsəˈpruvəl/ *n.* [U] a feeling or opinion that someone is behaving badly or that something is bad: *public* ***disapproval of*** *the war* | *Marion shook her head* ***in disapproval.***

dis·ap·prove /ˌdɪsəˈpruv/ *v.* [I] to think that something or someone is bad, wrong, etc.: *Her parents* ***disapproved of*** *her boyfriend.*

dis·arm /dɪsˈɑrm/ *v.* **1** [I] to reduce the size of your army, navy, etc. and the number of weapons: *Both sides must disarm before the peace talks.* **2** [T] to take away someone's weapons: *Benson disarmed the man as he tried to rob a liquor store.* **3** [T] to make someone less angry and more friendly: *She uses humor to disarm people.*

dis·ar·ma·ment /dɪsˈɑrməmənt/ *n.* [U] the reduction in numbers or size of a country's weapons, army, navy, etc.: *plans for* ***nuclear disarmament***

dis·arm·ing /dɪsˈɑrmɪŋ/ *adj.* making you feel less angry and more friendly or trusting: *a* ***disarming smile***

dis·ar·ray /ˌdɪsəˈreɪ/ *n.* [U] *formal* the state of being messy or not organized: *papers* ***in disarray*** *on the desk*

dis·as·so·ci·ate /ˌdɪsəˈsoʊʃiˌeɪt, -siˌeɪt/ *v.* [T] DISSOCIATE

dis·as·ter /dɪˈzæstɚ/ *n.* [C,U] **1** a sudden event such as an accident, flood, or storm that causes great harm or damage: *The 1889 flood was the most spectacular* ***natural disaster*** *the state had ever seen.* | ***Disaster struck*** *when one rider was hit by a car while cycling.* | *The town was* ***declared a disaster area*** *after the floods.*

THESAURUS

accident, **crash**, **collision**, **catastrophe**, **wreck**, **pile-up**, **mishap**
➔ see Thesaurus box at ACCIDENT

2 a complete failure: *The party was a total disaster.*

dis·as·trous /dɪˈzæstrəs/ *adj.* very bad, or ending in failure: *a disastrous marriage* —**disastrously** *adv.*

dis·a·vow /ˌdɪsəˈvaʊ/ *v.* [T] *formal* to say that you are not responsible for something, or that you do not know about it: *The President has disavowed any knowledge of the affair.* —**disavowal** *n.* [C,U]

dis·band /dɪsˈbænd/ *v.* [I,T] *formal* to stop existing as an organization, or to make something do this

dis·be·lief /ˌdɪsbəˈlif/ *n.* [U] a feeling that something is not true or does not exist: *Linder shook his head **in disbelief**.* —**disbelieving** *adj.*

disc /dɪsk/ *n.* [C] DISK

dis·card /dɪˈskɑrd/ *v.* [T] to get rid of something: *discarding old clothes*

dis·cern /dɪˈsɚn, dɪˈzɚn/ *v.* [T] *formal* to see, notice, or understand something by looking at it or thinking about it carefully: *Walters couldn't discern any difference between the two plants.* —**discernible** *adj.* —**discernibly** *adv.*

D

dis·cern·ing /dɪˈsɚnɪŋ, -ˈzɚ-/ *adj.* able to make good judgments about people, styles, and things: *the discerning traveler's guide to the Southeast*

dis·charge[1] /dɪsˈtʃɑrdʒ/ *v.* **1** [T] to officially allow someone to go or to send him/her away from a place: *Blanton was **discharged from** the hospital last night.* **2** [I,T] to send, pour, or let out a substance: *Chemicals were being **discharged into** a nearby river.* **3** [I,T] *formal* if you discharge a gun, or if it discharges, it shoots a bullet

dis·charge[2] /ˈdɪstʃɑrdʒ/ *n.* [U] **1** the official action of sending someone or something away, especially from a hospital or the military: *After his **discharge from** the army, he got married.* **2** a substance that comes out of something, especially a wound or part of your body

dis·ci·ple /dɪˈsaɪpəl/ *n.* [C] **1** a follower of a religious teacher, especially one of the 12 original followers of Jesus Christ **2** a follower of any great leader or teacher: *a **disciple of** Gandhi*

dis·ci·pli·nar·i·an /ˌdɪsəpləˈnɛriən/ *n.* [C] someone who believes that people should obey rules, and who makes them do this: *Sam's father is a **strict disciplinarian**.*

dis·ci·plin·a·ry /ˈdɪsəpləˌnɛri/ *adj.* relating to trying to make someone obey rules, or to the punishment of someone who has not obeyed rules: *disciplinary problems*

dis·ci·pline[1] /ˈdɪsəplɪn/ *n.* **1** [U] controlled behavior in which people obey rules and orders: *maintaining discipline in the classroom* | *military discipline* | *serious **discipline problems** on the police force* **2** [U] the ability to control your own behavior and way of working: *Writing requires discipline.* | *It takes a lot of **self-discipline** to work from home.* **3** [U] punishment for not obeying rules: *Employees who joined the strike face discipline.* **4** [C] *formal* an area of knowledge or teaching

discipline[2] *v.* [T] **1** to punish someone: *The staff members were disciplined for their carelessness.* **2** to train someone to obey rules and control his/her own behavior: *Working in a bakery has **disciplined** Joe **to** get up early.*

dis·claim·er /dɪsˈkleɪmɚ/ *n.* [C] *formal* a statement that you are not responsible for or do not know about something, often used in advertising

dis·close /dɪsˈkloʊz/ *v.* [T] to make something known publicly: *GM did not disclose details of the agreement.*

dis·clo·sure /dɪsˈkloʊʒɚ/ *n.* [C,U] a secret that someone tells people, or the act of telling this secret: *the **disclosure of** state secrets*

dis·co /ˈdɪskoʊ/ *n.* plural **discos** **1** [U] a type of dance music with a strong repeating beat that was first popular in the 1970s **2** [C] a place where people dance to recorded popular music

dis·col·or /dɪsˈkʌlɚ/ *v.* [I,T] to change color, or to make something change color, so that it looks unattractive: *His teeth were discolored from smoking.* —**discoloration** /dɪsˌkʌləˈreɪʃən/ *n.* [C,U]

dis·com·fort /dɪsˈkʌmfɚt/ *n.* **1** [U] slight pain or a bad feeling: *We need to treat the disease without increasing the discomfort of the patient.* **2** [C] something that makes you uncomfortable: *the **discomforts of** long-distance travel* **3** [U] a feeling of embarrassment, shame, or worry: *She could sense his **discomfort at** having to speak in front of a large group.*

dis·con·cert·ing /ˌdɪskənˈsɚt̬ɪŋ/ *adj.* making you feel slightly embarrassed, confused, or worried: *It was disconcerting to be watched while I worked.* —**disconcert** *v.* [T] —**disconcerted** *adj.*

dis·con·nect /ˌdɪskəˈnɛkt/ *v.* **1** [I,T] to separate something from the thing it is connected to, or to become separated: *Disconnect the cables before you move the computer.* **2** [T] to remove the supply of power to something such as a telephone line, building, or machine: *I tried to call, but the phone had been disconnected.* —**disconnection** /ˌdɪskəˈnɛkʃən/ *n.* [C,U]

dis·con·tent /ˌdɪskənˈtɛnt/ *n.* [U] a feeling of not being happy or satisfied —**discontented** *adj.*

dis·con·tin·ue /ˌdɪskənˈtɪnyu/ *v.* [T] to stop doing or providing something: *Five bus routes will be discontinued.* —**discontinuation** /ˌdɪskənˌtɪnyuˈeɪʃən/ *n.* [U]

dis·cord /ˈdɪskɔrd/ *n.* [U] *formal* disagreement between people: *marital discord* —**discordant** /dɪsˈkɔrdnt/ *adj.*

dis·count[1] /ˈdɪskaʊnt/ *n.* [C] a reduction in the usual price of something: *He says he can get me a **discount on** a new computer.* | *a **discount of** 25%* | *I saved $20 with my **employee discount**.* | *a **discount store***

dis·count[2] /dɪsˈkaʊnt/ *v.* [T] **1** to reduce the price of something: *Flights to Florida have been deeply discounted.* **2** to regard something as unlikely to be true or important: *Scientists discounted his method of predicting earthquakes.*

dis·cour·age /dɪˈskɚɪdʒ, -ˈskʌr-/ *v.* [T] **1** to persuade someone not to do something, especially by making it seem difficult or bad [≠ **encourage**]: *Keith's mother tried to **discourage** him **from** joining the navy.* **2** to make someone less confident or less willing to do something [≠ **encourage**]: *His failure to find a job did not discourage him.* **3** to make something become less likely to happen [≠ **encourage**]: *Put the plant in a cold room to discourage growth.*

dis·cour·aged /dɪˈskɚɪdʒd, -ˈskʌr-/ *adj.* no longer having the confidence you need to continue doing something: *Children may* ***get discouraged*** *if they are criticized too often.*

dis·cour·age·ment /dɪˈskɚɪdʒmənt, -ˈskʌr-/ *n.* **1** [C,U] a feeling of being discouraged **2** [U] the act of trying to discourage someone from doing something

dis·cour·a·ging /dɪˈskɚɪdʒɪŋ, -ˈskʌr-/ *adj.* making you lose the confidence you need to continue doing something: *It was very discouraging to see my sister do it so easily.*

dis·course /ˈdɪskɔrs/ *n.* [U] serious conversation between people: *a chance for meaningful discourse between the two leaders*

dis·cour·te·ous /dɪsˈkɚt̬iəs/ *adj. formal* not polite or respectful —**discourtesy** /dɪsˈkɚt̬əsi/ *n.* [C,U]

dis·cov·er /dɪˈskʌvɚ/ *v.* [T] **1** to find something that was hidden or that people did not know about before: *The Vikings may have discovered America long before Columbus.*

> **THESAURUS**
>
> **find**, **trace**, **locate**, **track down**, **turn up**, **unearth**
>
> → see Thesaurus box at FIND[1]

2 to find out something that is a fact, or the answer to a question: *Doctors* ***discovered that*** *her left wrist was broken.* | *Did you ever* ***discover who*** *sent you the flowers?* —**discoverer** *n.* [C]

dis·cov·er·y /dɪˈskʌvri, -vəri/ *n.* plural **discoveries** **1** [C] a fact, thing, or answer to a question that someone discovers: *Einstein* ***made an*** *important scientific* ***discovery****.* | *the* ***discovery that*** *bees can communicate with each other* **2** [U] the act of finding something that was hidden or not known before: *the* ***discovery of*** *gold in 1848*

dis·cred·it /dɪsˈkrɛdɪt/ *v.* [T] to make people stop trusting or having respect for someone or something: *The defense lawyer will try to discredit our witnesses.*

dis·creet /dɪˈskrit/ *adj.* careful about what you say or do so that you do not upset or embarrass people: *Can you please* ***be discreet*** *about this?* —**discreetly** *adv.*

dis·crep·an·cy /dɪˈskrɛpənsi/ *n.* plural **discrepancies** [C,U] a difference between two amounts, details, etc. that should be the same: *There were* ***discrepancies in*** *the expense accounts.*

dis·cre·tion /dɪˈskrɛʃən/ *n.* [U] **1** the ability to be careful about what you say or do in a particular situation, so that you do not upset or embarrass people: *This situation must be handled with discretion.* | *Prisoners are released* ***at the discretion of*** *the parole board.* **2** the ability and right to decide what should be done in a particular situation: *Pay raises are* ***left to the discretion of*** *the manager.* —**discretionary** *adj.*

dis·crim·i·nate /dɪˈskrɪməˌneɪt/ *v.* **1** [I] to treat one person or group differently from another in an unfair way: *a law that* ***discriminates against*** *immigrants* **2** [I,T] to recognize a difference between things [= **differentiate**]: *You must learn to* ***discriminate between*** *facts and opinions.*

dis·crim·i·nat·ing /dɪˈskrɪməˌneɪt̬ɪŋ/ *adj.* able to judge whether or not something is good quality: *customers with discriminating tastes*

dis·crim·i·na·tion /dɪˌskrɪməˈneɪʃən/ *n.* [U] **1** the practice of treating one group of people differently from another in an unfair way: *The company has been accused of* ***racial/age/sex discrimination****.* | *The law prohibits* ***discrimination against*** *handicapped persons.*

> **THESAURUS**
>
> **racism**, **prejudice**, **intolerance**, **anti-Semitism**
>
> → see Thesaurus box at PREJUDICE

2 the ability to judge whether or not something is good quality

dis·cus /ˈdɪskəs/ *n.* [C] **1** a heavy flat circular object which people throw as far as possible as a sport **2 the discus** the sport of throwing this object

dis·cuss /dɪˈskʌs/ *v.* [T] **1** to talk about something with someone in order to exchange ideas or decide something: *I wanted to* ***discuss*** *my plans* ***with*** *my father.* | *We need to* ***discuss how*** *to raise money for the project.*

> **THESAURUS**
>
> **talk**, **have a conversation**, **chat (with/to)**, **have a chat**, **converse**, **visit with**
>
> → see Thesaurus box at TALK[1]

2 to talk or write about a subject in detail: *The Roman Empire will be discussed in the next chapter.*

dis·cus·sion /dɪˈskʌʃən/ *n.* [C,U] **1** the act of discussing something, or a conversation in which people discuss something: *We need to* ***have a discussion about*** *your behavior in class.* | *The proposal is still* ***under discussion*** (=being discussed).

> **THESAURUS**
>
> **negotiations** – official discussions between two groups who are trying to agree on something: *Contract negotiations are continuing between the union and Amtrak.*
>
> **debate** – a formal discussion of a subject, during which people express different opinions: *the debate between the presidential candidates*

D

talks – formal discussions between governments, organizations, etc.: *The peace talks have been suspended after the latest bombing.*
conference – a large formal meeting at which members of an organization, profession, etc. discuss things related to their work: *an annual conference for software developers*

2 a piece of writing about a subject that considers different ideas or opinions about it: *The report includes a **discussion of** global warming.*

dis·dain /dɪs'deɪn/ *n.* [U] *formal* a lack of respect for someone or something because you think he, she, or it is not important or not good enough: *Mason's **disdain for** people without education* —**disdainful** *adj.*

D

dis·ease /dɪ'ziz/ *n.* [C,U] an illness that affects a person, animal, or plant, with specific SYMPTOMS (=things wrong with your body which show that you have a particular illness): *My uncle has **heart disease**.* | *Tina **suffers from a** rare brain **disease**.* | ***infectious diseases** such as tuberculosis* —**diseased** *adj.*

THESAURUS

People often use **disease** and **illness** to mean the same thing, but it is a **disease** that actually makes you sick: *He suffers from heart disease.*
Illness is the state of being sick: *Janey missed a lot of school because of illness.*
Sickness is a particular type of illness: *radiation sickness* | *motion sickness*

dis·em·bark /ˌdɪsɪm'bɑrk/ *v.* [I] to get off a ship or airplane —**disembarkation** /ˌdɪsɛmbɑr'keɪʃən/ *n.* [U]

dis·em·bod·ied /ˌdɪsɪm'bɑdid/ *adj.* a disembodied sound or voice comes from someone who cannot be seen

dis·en·chant·ed /ˌdɪsɪn'tʃæntɪd/ *adj.* disappointed with someone or something, and no longer liking or believing in the value of that person or thing: *She was becoming **disenchanted with** her marriage.* —**disenchantment** *n.* [U]

dis·en·fran·chised /ˌdɪsɪn'fræntʃaɪzd/ *adj.* not having any rights, especially the right to vote, and not feeling part of society —**disenfranchise** *v.* [T]

dis·en·gage /ˌdɪsɪn'geɪdʒ/ *v.* **1** [I,T] to move a part of a machine away from another part that it was connected to: *Disengage the gears when you park the car.* **2** [I] be no longer involved or interested in something: *The Senator feels that America should **disengage from** the United Nations.* —**disengagement** *n.* [U]

dis·en·tan·gle /ˌdɪsɪn'tæŋgəl/ *v.* [T] **1 disentangle yourself (from sth)** to escape from a difficult situation that you are involved in **2** to separate different ideas or pieces of information that have become confused together: *It's very difficult to disentangle fact from fiction in what she's saying.*

dis·fa·vor /dɪs'feɪvɚ/ *n.* [U] *formal* a feeling of dislike or disapproval

dis·fig·ure /dɪs'fɪgyɚ/ *v.* [T] to spoil the appearance of someone or something: *His face was badly disfigured in the accident.* —**disfigurement** *n.* [C,U]

dis·grace¹ /dɪs'greɪs/ *n.* [U] **1 sth is a disgrace** used in order to say that someone or something is very bad or unacceptable: *The public schools in the area are a disgrace.* | *He was a **disgrace to** the legal profession.* **2** the loss of other people's respect because you have done something they strongly disapprove of: *Harry left the school **in disgrace**.* | *There's **no disgrace** in trying.*

disgrace² *v.* [T] to do something so bad that people lose respect for your family or for the group you belong to: *How could you disgrace us like that?*

dis·grace·ful /dɪs'greɪsfəl/ *adj.* very bad, embarrassing, or unacceptable: *Their behavior was absolutely disgraceful.*

dis·grun·tled /dɪs'grʌntəld/ *adj.* annoyed, disappointed, and not satisfied: *disgruntled employees*

dis·guise¹ /dɪs'gaɪz/ *v.* [T] **1** to change your appearance or voice so that people cannot recognize you: *She **disguised** herself **as** a man.*

THESAURUS

hide, conceal, cover, cover up
→ see Thesaurus box at HIDE¹

2 to hide a fact or feeling so that people will not notice it: *We can't **disguise the fact that** the business is losing money.*

disguise² *n.* [C,U] something that you wear to change your appearance and hide who you really are, or the act of wearing this: *She went out **in disguise** to avoid reporters.*

dis·gust¹ /dɪs'gʌst/ *n.* [U] a strong feeling of dislike and disapproval: *Everyone was looking at him **with disgust**.* | *He walked out of the meeting **in disgust**.*

disgust² *v.* [T] to make someone feel very annoyed or upset about something that is not acceptable —**disgusted** *adj.*: *We **felt disgusted** by the way we'd been treated.*

dis·gust·ing /dɪs'gʌstɪŋ/ *adj.* **1** shocking and unacceptable: *The way he treats her is disgusting.*

THESAURUS

horrible, terrible, awful, dreadful
→ see Thesaurus box at HORRIBLE

2 extremely unpleasant and making you feel sick: *a disgusting smell* —**disgustingly** *adv.*

THESAURUS

horrible, awful, revolting, foul
➔ see Thesaurus box at HORRIBLE, TASTE[1]

dish[1] /dɪʃ/ *n.* [C] **1** a round container with low sides, used for holding food [➡ **plate, bowl**]: *a serving dish* **2 dishes** [plural] all the plates, cups, bowls, etc. that are used during a meal: *Who's going to **do/wash the dishes**?* **3** food cooked or prepared in a particular way: *a wonderful pasta dish* | *You can serve this soup as a **main dish*** (=the biggest part of a meal)

dish[2] *v.*

dish sth ⇔ **out** *phr. v. informal* to give something to people: *He's always dishing out unwanted advice.*

dish sth ⇔ **up** *phr. v. informal* to put food for a meal into dishes, ready to be eaten

dis·heart·ened /dɪsˈhɑrtˀnd/ *adj.* disappointed because you no longer feel that you are able to do or achieve something —**dishearten** *v.* [T]

dis·heart·en·ing /dɪsˈhɑrtˀn-ɪŋ/ *adj.* making you lose hope and confidence: ***It** was **disheartening to** see that the changes we made didn't help.* —**dishearteningly** *adv.*

di·shev·eled /dɪˈʃɛvəld/ *adj.* very messy: *She looked tired and disheveled.*

dis·hon·est /dɪsˈɑnɪst/ *adj.* not honest: *a dishonest politician* —**dishonesty** *n.* [U] —**dishonestly** *adv.*

dis·hon·or /dɪsˈɑnɚ/ *n.* [U] *formal* a state in which people no longer respect you or approve of you because you have done something dishonest or immoral: *His behavior **brought dishonor on** the family.* —**dishonor** *v.* [T] —**dishonorable** *adj.*

ˈdish rack *n.* [C] an object that holds dishes while they dry that is usually kept next to the kitchen SINK

dish·tow·el /ˈdɪʃˌtaʊəl/ *n.* [C] a cloth used for drying dishes

dish·wash·er /ˈdɪʃˌwɑʃɚ/ *n.* [C] **1** a machine that washes dishes **2** someone whose job is to wash dirty dishes in a restaurant

ˈdishwashing ˌliquid *n.* [U] liquid soap used to wash dishes

dis·il·lu·sion /ˌdɪsəˈluʒən/ *v.* [T] to make someone realize that something s/he thought was true or good is not —**disillusionment** *n.* [U]

dis·il·lu·sioned /ˌdɪsəˈluʒənd/ *adj.* unhappy because you have lost your belief that someone or something is true or good: *I have become increasingly **disillusioned with** politics.*

dis·in·cen·tive /ˌdɪsɪnˈsɛntɪv/ *n.* [C] something that makes people less willing to do something [≠ **incentive**]: *Higher taxes may act as a **disincentive to** business.*

dis·in·fect /ˌdɪsɪnˈfɛkt/ *v.* [T] to clean something with a chemical that destroys BACTERIA

dis·in·fect·ant /ˌdɪsɪnˈfɛktənt/ *n.* [C,U] a chemical that destroys BACTERIA, used for cleaning something

dis·in·her·it /ˌdɪsɪnˈhɛrɪt/ *v.* [T] to prevent someone from receiving any of your money or property after your death

dis·in·te·grate /dɪsˈɪntəˌgreɪt/ *v.* [I] **1** to break up into small pieces: *They saw the space shuttle disintegrate in the sky.* **2** to become weaker and be gradually destroyed: *Their marriage was disintegrating.* —**disintegration** /dɪsˌɪntəˈgreɪʃən/ *n.* [U]

dis·in·terest·ed /dɪsˈɪntrɪstɪd, -ˈɪntəˌrɛstɪd/ *adj.* able to judge a situation fairly because you will not gain an advantage from it [= **objective**]: *a disinterested observer of the voting process* —**disinterest** *n.* [U]

USAGE

In spoken English, many people use **disinterested** to mean "not interested." However, many teachers think that this is not correct. If you want to say that someone is "not interested," use **uninterested**: *She seemed uninterested in how it works.*

dis·joint·ed /dɪsˈdʒɔɪntɪd/ *adj.* disjointed words or images are not easy to understand because they are not arranged in a clear order

disk /dɪsk/ *n.* [C] **1** a small flat piece of plastic or metal used for storing information in a computer [➡ **hard disk, floppy disk, compact disk**] **2** something that is flat and round, or that looks this way **3** a flat piece of CARTILAGE (=a strong substance that stretches) between the bones of your back

ˈdisk drive *n.* [C] a piece of equipment in a computer that is used in order to get information from a disk or to store information on it

disk·ette /dɪˈskɛt/ *n.* [C] a FLOPPY DISK

ˈdisk ˌjockey *n.* [C] a DJ

dis·like[1] /dɪsˈlaɪk/ *v.* [T] to not like someone or something: *Many men dislike shopping.*

dislike[2] *n.* [C,U] a feeling of not liking someone or something: *She shared her mother's **dislike of** housework.*

dis·lo·cate /dɪsˈloʊkeɪt, ˈdɪsloʊˌkeɪt/ *v.* [T] to make a bone move out of its normal position in a joint, usually in an accident: *I dislocated my shoulder playing football.* —**dislocation** /ˌdɪsloʊˈkeɪʃən/ *n.* [C,U]

dis·lodge /dɪsˈlɑdʒ/ *v.* [T] to force or knock something out of its position: *Lee dislodged a few stones as he climbed over the old wall.*

dis·loy·al /dɪsˈlɔɪəl/ *adj.* doing or saying things that do not support your friends, your country, or the group you belong to: *He felt he had been **disloyal to** his friends.* —**disloyalty** /dɪsˈlɔɪəlti/ *n.* [C,U]

dis·mal /ˈdɪzməl/ *adj.* making you feel unhappy and without hope: *dismal weather* | *the team's dismal record in the past month* —**dismally** *adv.*

D

dis·man·tle /dɪs'mæntəl/ *v.* [I,T] **1** to take something apart so that it is in separate pieces: *I'll have to dismantle the engine.* **2** to gradually get rid of a system or organization: *plans to dismantle the existing tax laws*

dis·may[1] /dɪs'meɪ/ *n.* [U] a strong feeling of disappointment and worry: *He realized **to his dismay** that he had left the money behind.*

dismay[2] *v.* [T] to make someone feel worried, disappointed, or upset: *I was **dismayed to** see how thin she had become.*

dis·mem·ber /dɪs'mɛmbɚ/ *v.* [T] *formal* to cut or tear a body into pieces

dis·miss /dɪs'mɪs/ *v.* [T] **1** to refuse to consider someone's idea or opinion because you think it is not serious, true, or important: *He **dismissed** the idea **as** impossible.* **2** if a court CASE is dismissed, a judge decides that it should not continue **3** *formal* to make someone leave his/her job [= **fire**]: *The teacher was **dismissed for** incompetence.* **4** to send someone away or allow him/her to go: *Class is dismissed.* —**dismissal** *n.* [C,U]

dis·mis·sive /dɪs'mɪsɪv/ *adj.* refusing to consider someone or something seriously: *Her doctor was **dismissive of** her concerns.*

dis·mount /dɪs'maʊnt/ *v.* [I] to get off a horse, bicycle, or MOTORCYCLE

dis·o·be·di·ent /ˌdɪsə'bidiənt/ *adj.* deliberately not doing what you are told to do by someone in authority such as your parents, teacher, employer, etc.: *a disobedient child* —**disobedience** *n.* [U]

dis·o·bey /ˌdɪsə'beɪ/ *v.* [I,T] to refuse to do what someone in authority tells you to do, or to refuse to obey a rule or law: *She would never disobey her parents.*

THESAURUS

break a rule/law – to disobey a rule or law: *What happens if you break the rules?*
rebel – to oppose or fight against someone who is in authority: *Hannah eventually rebelled against her mother's control.*
defy – to refuse to obey someone or something: *Several teenagers were caught defying the curfew.*
violate – to disobey or do something against a law, rule, agreement, etc.: *Using the money in this way clearly violates the tax laws.*

dis·or·der /dɪs'ɔrdɚ/ *n.* **1** [U] a situation in which things or people are very messy or not organized **2** [C] a disease or illness that prevents part of your body from working correctly: *a mental disorder* **3** [U] a situation in which a lot of people behave in an uncontrolled, noisy, or violent way in public: *The nation is in a state of **civil disorder**.*

dis·or·der·ly /dɪs'ɔrdɚli/ *adj.* **1** messy: *clothes left in a disorderly heap* **2** behaving in a noisy or violent way in public: *He was arrested for **disorderly conduct**.*

dis·or·ga·nized /dɪs'ɔrgəˌnaɪzd/ *adj.* not arranged or planned very well: *The meeting was completely disorganized.* —**disorganization** /dɪsˌɔrgənə'zeɪʃən/ *n.* [U]

dis·o·ri·ent·ed /dɪs'ɔriˌɛntɪd/ *adj.* confused and not really able to understand what is happening or where you are —**disorienting** *adj.* —**disorientation** /dɪsˌɔriən'teɪʃən/ *n.* [U]

dis·own /dɪs'oʊn/ *v.* [T] if your parents disown you, they decide that they no longer want to have any connection with you, usually because you have done something very bad

dis·par·age /dɪ'spærɪdʒ/ *v.* [T] *formal* to criticize someone or something in a way that shows you do not think he, she, or it is very good or important

dis·par·a·ging /dɪ'spærədʒɪŋ/ *adj.* showing that you think someone or something is not very good or important: *She **made** some **disparaging comments** about his work.*

dis·par·ate /'dɪspərɪt/ *adj. formal* very different and not related to each other

dis·par·i·ty /dɪ'spærəṭi/ *n.* plural **disparities** [C,U] a difference between things, especially an unfair difference: *the **disparities between** rich and poor*

dis·pas·sion·ate /dɪs'pæʃənɪt/ *adj.* not easily influenced by personal feelings: *a dispassionate opinion* —**dispassionately** *adv.*

dis·patch[1] /dɪ'spætʃ/ *v.* [T] to send someone or something somewhere

dispatch[2] *n.* **1** [C] a message sent between government or military officials **2** [C] a report sent to a newspaper from one of its writers who is in another town or country **3** [singular] the act of sending people or things to a particular place: *the **dispatch of** troops to the area*

dis·pel /dɪ'spɛl/ *v.* past tense and past participle **dispelled**, present participle **dispelling** [T] *formal* to stop someone from believing or feeling something, especially because it is harmful or not correct: *Mark's calm words dispelled our fears.*

dis·pen·sa·ry /dɪ'spɛnsəri/ *n.* plural **dispensaries** [C] a place where medicines are prepared and given out

dis·pen·sa·tion /ˌdɪspən'seɪʃən, -pɛn-/ *n.* [C,U] special permission from someone in authority, especially a religious leader, to do something that is not usually allowed

dis·pense /dɪ'spɛns/ *v.* [T] *formal* **1** to give or provide something to people, especially as part of an official activity: *Volunteers helped dispense food and blankets.* **2** to officially provide medicine to people

dispense with sth *phr. v.* to not use or do something that people usually use or do because it is not necessary

dis·pens·er /dɪ'spɛnsɚ/ *n.* [C] a machine from which you can get things such as drinks or money when you press a button

dis·perse /dɪ'spɚs/ *v.* [I,T] to scatter in different directions, or to make something do this: *The* *police used tear gas to disperse the crowd.* —**dispersal** *n.* [U]

dis·pir·it·ed /dɪ'spɪrɪt̬ɪd/ *adj. literary* sad and without hope

dis·place /dɪs'pleɪs/ *v.* [T] **1** to take the place of someone or something by becoming more important or useful [= **replace**]: *Coal has been displaced by natural gas as a major source of energy.* **2** to make a group of people leave the place where they normally live —**displacement** *n.* [U] —**displaced** *adj.*

dis·play¹ /dɪ'spleɪ/ *n.* plural **displays** **1** [C,U] an arrangement of objects for people to look at: *a **display of** African masks | The pictures are **on display** in the lobby.* **2** [C] a public performance or something that is intended to entertain people: *a fireworks display* **3 a display of anger/affection etc.** an occasion when someone clearly shows a particular attitude, feeling, or quality **4** [C] the part of a piece of equipment that shows information, for example a computer screen: *A light flashed on the display.*

display² *v.* [T] **1** to put things in a place where people can see them easily: *a row of tables displaying pottery* **2** to clearly show a feeling or quality: *He displayed no emotion at the funeral.* **3** if a computer displays information, it shows it: *An error message was displayed.*

dis·pleased /dɪs'plizd/ *adj. formal* annoyed and not satisfied: *Many employees were **displeased with** the decision.* —**displease** *v.* [T] —**displeasure** /dɪs'plɛʒɚ/ *n.* [U]

dis·pos·a·ble /dɪ'spoʊzəbəl/ *adj.* intended to be used once or for a short time and then thrown away: *disposable razors*

dis,posable 'income *n.* [C] the amount of money that you have available to spend each month after you have paid for rent, food, etc.

dis·pos·al /dɪ'spoʊzəl/ *n.* **1** [U] the act of getting rid of something: *the safe **disposal of** radioactive waste* **2 at sb's disposal** available for someone to use: *He had a lot of cash at his disposal.* **3** [C] a GARBAGE DISPOSAL

dis·pose /dɪ'spoʊz/ *v.*

dispose of sth *phr. v.* to get rid of something: *a facility that disposes of industrial waste*

dis·posed /dɪ'spoʊzd/ *adj. formal* **1 be/feel disposed to do sth** to be willing to do something or behave in a particular way: *I don't feel disposed to interfere.* **2 well/favorably disposed to sb/sth** liking someone or something

dis·po·si·tion /,dɪspə'zɪʃən/ *n.* [C] *formal* the way someone tends to behave: *Jenny has such a sweet disposition.*

dis·pos·sess /,dɪspə'zɛs/ *v.* [T] *formal* to take property or land away from someone —**dispossession** /,dɪspə'zɛʃən/ *n.* [U]

dis·pro·por·tion·ate /,dɪsprə'pɔrʃənɪt/ *adj.* too much or too little in relation to something else, used when comparing two things: *The project consumed a disproportionate amount of time.* —**disproportionately** *adv.*

dis·prove /dɪs'pruv/ *v.* [T] to show that something is definitely wrong or not true

dis·pute¹ /dɪ'spyut/ *n.* [C,U] **1** a serious argument or disagreement: *The two men got into a **dispute over** money. | He was involved in a legal **dispute with** his neighbor. | The facts of the case are still **in dispute*** (=being argued about). **2 be beyond dispute** to clearly be true, so that no one can question it or argue about it: *Mitchell's guilt is beyond dispute.*

dispute² *v.* [T] to say that something such as a fact or idea is not correct or true: *The facts of the book have never been disputed.*

dis·qual·i·fy /dɪs'kwɑlə,faɪ/ *v.* past tense and past participle **disqualified**, third person singular **disqualifies** [T] to stop someone from taking part in an activity or competition, usually because s/he has done something wrong: *Dennis was **disqualified from** the race.* —**disqualification** /dɪs,kwɑləfə'keɪʃən/ *n.* [C,U]

dis·re·gard¹ /,dɪsrɪ'gɑrd/ *v.* [T] to ignore something, or to not treat something as important or serious: *The judge told the jury to disregard that statement.*

disregard² *n.* [U] the act of ignoring something, especially something important or serious: *Thomas' actions show a total **disregard for** the law.*

dis·re·pair /,dɪsrɪ'pɛr/ *n.* [U] buildings, roads, etc. that are in disrepair are in bad condition because they have not been cared for: *The old house had **fallen into disrepair**.*

dis·rep·u·ta·ble /dɪs'rɛpyət̬əbəl/ *adj.* not good or respected, and often thought to be involved in dishonest or illegal activities

dis·re·pute /,dɪsrə'pyut/ *n.* [U] *formal* a situation in which people no longer trust or respect a person or an idea: *His reputation has **fallen into disrepute**.*

dis·re·spect /,dɪsrɪ'spɛkt/ *n.* [U] lack of respect for someone or something: *his **disrespect for** the law* —**disrespectful** *adj.*

dis·rupt /dɪs'rʌpt/ *v.* [T] to prevent something from continuing in its usual way by causing problems: *The blizzard disrupted transportation into the city. | We cannot allow terrorists to **disrupt** our **lives**.* —**disruption** /dɪs'rʌpʃən/ *n.* [C,U] —**disruptive** /dɪs'rʌptɪv/ *adj.*: *disruptive students*

dis·sat·is·fac·tion /dɪ,sæt̬ɪs'fækʃən, dɪs,sæ-/ *n.* [U] a feeling of not being satisfied because something is not as good as you had expected: *She expressed her **dissatisfaction with** the service.*

dis·sat·is·fied /dɪ'sæt̬ɪs,faɪd/ *adj.* not satisfied because something is not as good as you had expected: *Katie is **dissatisfied with** her job.*

dis·sect /dɪ'sɛkt, daɪ-/ *v.* [T] to cut up the body of a plant or animal in order to study it —**dissection** /dɪ'sɛkʃən/ *n.* [C,U]

dis·sem·i·nate /dɪ'sɛmə,neɪt/ *v.* [T] *formal* to

spread information, ideas, etc. to as many people as possible: *The rumor has been widely disseminated on the Internet.* —**dissemination** /dɪˌsɛmə'neɪʃən/ *n.* [U]

dis·sent /dɪ'sɛnt/ *n.* [U] refusal to accept an opinion or decision that most people accept: *political dissent* —**dissent** *v.* [I] *Two of the court's nine judges dissented from the majority decision.* —**dissenter** *n.* [C]

dis·ser·ta·tion /ˌdɪsɚ'teɪʃən/ *n.* [C] a long piece of writing about a subject that you write to get a PH.D.

dis·serv·ice /dɪ'sɚvɪs, dɪs'sɚ-/ *n.* **do sb/sth a disservice** to do something that makes people have a bad opinion of someone or something, especially when this is unfair: *The players' actions have **done a** great **disservice to** the game.*

D

dis·si·dent /'dɪsədənt/ *n.* [C] someone who publicly criticizes the government in his/her country, when doing this is a crime in that country —**dissidence** *n.* [U] —**dissident** *adj.*

dis·sim·i·lar /dɪ'sɪmələ˞, dɪs'sɪ-/ *adj.* not the same: *countries with dissimilar legal systems* —**dissimilarity** /dɪˌsɪmə'lærət̬i/ *n.* [C,U]

dis·si·pate /'dɪsəˌpeɪt/ *v. formal* [I,T] to gradually get weaker and then disappear completely, or to make something do this

dis·so·ci·ate /dɪ'soʊʃiˌeɪt, -siˌeɪt/ **also disassociate** *v.* [T] *formal* to do or say something to show that you do not agree with the views or actions of someone with whom you had a connection: *He tried to **disassociate** himself **from** the chairman's remarks.* —**dissociation** /dɪˌsoʊsi'eɪʃən, -ˌsoʊʃi-/ *n.* [U]

dis·so·lute /'dɪsəˌlut/ *adj. written* having an immoral way of life: *a dissolute life*

dis·so·lu·tion /ˌdɪsə'luʃən/ *n.* [U] *formal* the act of officially ending a marriage, business arrangement, etc.

dis·solve /dɪ'zɑlv/ *v.* **1** [I,T] if a solid dissolves, or if you dissolve it, it mixes with a liquid and becomes liquid itself: *Stir the mixture until the sugar dissolves.* | ***Dissolve** the tablets **in** warm water.* **2** [T] to officially end a marriage, business arrangement, etc. **3 dissolve into tears/laughter etc.** to start crying or laughing a lot

dis·suade /dɪ'sweɪd/ *v.* [T] *formal* to persuade someone not to do something: *efforts to **dissuade** teenagers **from** drinking*

dis·tance[1] /'dɪstəns/ *n.* **1** [C,U] the amount of space between two places or things: *What's the **distance from** Louisville **to** Memphis?* | *the **distance between** the moon and the sun* | *We had gone a **long/short distance**.* | *The subway is within **walking distance** (=near enough to walk to) of my house.* **2** [singular] a point or place that is far away, but close enough to be seen or heard: *The ruins look very impressive **from a distance**.* | *We could see the Sears Tower **in the distance**.* **3 keep your distance a)** to stay far away from someone or something: *The dogs looked fierce, so I kept my distance.* **b) also keep sb at a distance** to avoid becoming too friendly with someone: *He tends to keep his distance from employees.*

distance[2] *v.* **distance yourself (from sth)** to say that you are not involved with someone or something: *The party is distancing itself from its violent past.*

dis·tant /'dɪstənt/ *adj.* **1** far away in space or time: *the sound of distant laughter* | *The building is a relic of **the distant past**.* **2** not friendly or not interested: *She seemed cold and distant.* **3** [only before noun] not closely related to you [≠ **close**]: *a distant cousin* —**distantly** *adv.*

dis·taste /dɪs'teɪst/ *n.* [singular, U] a feeling of dislike for someone or something that you think is annoying or offensive: *her **distaste for** modern art*

dis·taste·ful /dɪs'teɪstfəl/ *adj.* unpleasant or offensive

dis·till /dɪ'stɪl/ *v.* [T] to make a liquid more pure by heating it until it becomes gas and then letting it cool: *distilled water* —**distillation** /ˌdɪstə'leɪʃən/ *n.* [C,U]

dis·till·er·y /dɪ'stɪləri/ *n.* plural **distilleries** [C] a factory where strong alcoholic drinks are produced by distilling

dis·tinct /dɪ'stɪŋkt/ *adj.* **1** clearly different or separate: *African and Asian elephants are distinct species.* **2 as distinct from sth** used in order to emphasize that you are talking about one thing and not another: *I am talking about childhood as distinct from adolescence.* **3** a distinct possibility, feeling, quality, etc. definitely exists and cannot be ignored: *There's a **distinct possibility** that we'll all lose our jobs.* | *I had the **distinct impression** that she didn't like me.* **4** clearly seen, heard, smelt, etc.: *the distinct smell of cigarette smoke* —**distinctly** *adv.*: *I distinctly remember his words.*

dis·tinc·tion /dɪ'stɪŋkʃən/ *n.* **1** [C] a clear difference between things: *The law makes/draws a **distinction between** children and adults.* **2** [U] the quality of being very good, important, or special: *a poet of distinction* | *Neil Armstrong **had the distinction of** being the first man on the moon.*

dis·tinc·tive /dɪ'stɪŋktɪv/ *adj.* different from other people or things and very easy to recognize: *Chris has a very distinctive laugh.* —**distinctively** *adv.* —**distinctiveness** *n.* [U]

dis·tin·guish /dɪ'stɪŋgwɪʃ/ *v.* **1** [I,T] to recognize or understand the difference between things or people: *Young children often can't **distinguish between** TV programs and commercials.* **2** [T] to be the thing that makes someone or something different from other people or things: *The bright feathers **distinguish** the male peacock **from** the female.* **3** [T] to be able to see, hear, smell, etc. something, even if it is difficult: *It was too dark for me to distinguish anything clearly* **4 distinguish yourself** to do something so well that people notice you, praise you, or remember you:

Eastwood distinguished himself as an actor before becoming a director. —**distinguishable** *adj.*

dis·tin·guished /dɪˈstɪŋgwɪʃt/ *adj.* **1** successful and respected: *a distinguished scientist* | *his distinguished career* **2** looking important and successful

dis·tort /dɪˈstɔrt/ *v.* [T] **1** to report something in a way that is not completely correct, so that the true meaning is changed: *a reporter accused of distorting the facts*

THESAURUS
twist, **misrepresent**
➔ see Thesaurus box at CHANGE[1]

2 to change the shape or sound of something so it is strange or difficult to recognize —**distorted** *adj.* —**distortion** /dɪˈstɔrʃən/ *n.* [C,U]

dis·tract /dɪˈstrækt/ *v.* [T] to do something that takes someone's attention away from what s/he is doing: *Don't distract me while I'm driving!* | *The government is trying to* ***distract attention*** *from its failures.*

dis·tract·ed /dɪˈstræktɪd/ *adj.* anxious and not able to think clearly

dis·trac·tion /dɪˈstrækʃən/ *n.* [C,U] something that takes your attention away from what you are doing: *I can't study at home – there are too many distractions.*

dis·traught /dɪˈstrɔt/ *adj.* extremely anxious or upset: *Friends comforted his distraught mother.*

dis·tress[1] /dɪˈstrɛs/ *n.* [U] **1** a feeling of extreme worry and sadness: *Children suffer emotional distress when their parents divorce.* **2** a situation in which someone suffers because s/he does not have any money, food, etc.: *charities that help families* ***in distress*** **3 be in distress** if a ship, airplane, etc. is in distress, it is in danger of sinking or crashing —**distressed** *adj.*

distress[2] *v.* [T] to make someone feel very worried or upset: *We were distressed to learn of Thomas's death.*

dis·tress·ing /dɪˈstrɛsɪŋ/ *adj.* making someone feel very worried or upset

dis·trib·ute /dɪˈstrɪbyət/ *v.* [T] **1** to give something such as food or medicine to each person in a large group: *The Red Cross is* ***distributing*** *food and clothing* ***to*** *the refugees.*

THESAURUS
give out, **pass**, **hand**, **hand out**, **pass out**
➔ see Thesaurus box at GIVE OUT

2 to supply goods to stores and companies in a particular area so that they can be sold: *The tape costs $19.95 and is distributed by American Video.*

dis·tri·bu·tion /ˌdɪstrəˈbyuʃən/ *n.* **1** [U] the act of giving something to each person in a large group: *the* ***distribution of*** *food to disaster victims* **2** [C,U] the way in which people or things are spread over an area: *The* ***distribution of*** *wealth has become more unequal.* **3** [U] the act of supplying goods to stores, companies, etc. in a particular area so that they can be sold: *the production and* ***distribution of*** *goods*

dis·tri·bu·tor /dɪˈstrɪbyət̬ɚ/ *n.* [C] a company or person that supplies goods to stores or companies: *a beer distributor*

dis·trict /ˈdɪstrɪkt/ *n.* [C] a particular area of a city, country, etc., especially an area officially divided from others: *Ken works in the* ***financial district.*** | *Many* ***school districts*** *are cutting music programs.*

THESAURUS
area, **region**, **zone**, **neighborhood**
➔ see Thesaurus box at AREA

ˌdistrict atˈtorney, **D.A.** *n.* [C] a lawyer who works for the government in a particular district and brings criminals to court

ˌdistrict ˈcourt *n.* [C] a U.S. court of law where people are judged in cases involving national rather than state law

dis·trust /dɪsˈtrʌst/ *n.* [U] a feeling that you cannot trust someone: *He has a deep* ***distrust of*** *politicians.* —**distrust** *v.* [T] —**distrustful** *adj.*

dis·turb /dɪˈstɚb/ *v.* [T] **1** to annoy someone or interrupt what someone is doing by making a noise, asking a question, etc.: *Keep your voices low, so you don't disturb the others.* | ***Do Not Disturb*** (=a sign that you put on a door so that people will not interrupt you) **2** to make someone feel worried or upset: *Something about the situation disturbed him.* **3** *formal* to move something: *The detectives were careful not to disturb anything.*

dis·turb·ance /dɪˈstɚbəns/ *n.* **1** [C] a situation in which people fight or behave violently in public: *The police arrested three men for* ***causing/creating a disturbance*** *at the bar.* **2** [C,U] something that interrupts you so that you cannot continue what you are doing

dis·turbed /dɪˈstɚbd/ *adj.* **1** not behaving in a normal way because of mental or emotional problems: *an* ***emotionally disturbed*** *child*

THESAURUS
crazy, **mentally ill**, **insane**, **nuts**, **loony**
➔ see Thesaurus box at CRAZY

2 very worried or upset

dis·tur·bing /dɪˈstɚbɪŋ/ *adj.* worrying or upsetting: *a disturbing increase in crime*

ditch[1] /dɪtʃ/ *n.* [C] a long narrow hole in the ground for water to flow through, usually at the side of a field, road, etc.

ditch[2] *v.* [T] *informal* to get rid of something or someone because you do not like or need him, her, or it: *The bank robbers ditched the stolen car as soon as they could.*

dith·er /ˈdɪðɚ/ *v.* [I] to be unable to make a decision: *He's been* ***dithering about*** *what to do.*

dit·to /ˈdɪt̬oʊ/ *interjection informal* used in order to say that you have exactly the same opinion as someone else about something, or that something is also true for you: *"I hated school." "Ditto."*

dit·ty /ˈdɪt̬i/ *n.* plural **ditties** [C] *humorous* a short simple song or poem

di·va /ˈdivə/ *n.* [C] a very successful and famous female singer

dive

dive¹ /daɪv/ *v.* past tense **dived** or **dove** /doʊv/ past participle **dived** [I] **1** to jump into the water with your head and arms going in first: *Harry **dived into** the swimming pool.*

THESAURUS

plunge – to move, fall, or be thrown or pushed suddenly forward or downward: *The car swerved and plunged off the cliff.*
submerge – to put something completely under the surface of the water: *The tunnel entrance was submerged by the rising water.*
sink – to go down below the surface of water, mud, etc., or to make something do this: *The coin sank to the bottom of the pool.*
→ see Thesaurus box at JUMP¹

2 to swim underwater using special equipment to help you breathe **3** to travel straight down through the air or water: *The birds were **diving for** fish.* **4** to move or jump quickly: *They dove into the bushes to avoid the enemy.*

dive² *n.* [C] **1** a jump into water with your head and arms going in first **2** a sudden movement in a particular direction: *He **made a dive for** the ball.* **3** a sudden drop in the amount or value of something: *Share prices **took a dive**.* **4** a movement straight down through air or water: *The plane suddenly **went into a dive**.* **5** *informal* a place such as a BAR or a hotel that is cheap and dirty: *We ate at a dive out by the airport.*

div·er /ˈdaɪvɚ/ *n.* [C] **1** someone who swims underwater using special equipment to help him/her breathe: *a scuba diver* **2** someone who jumps into water with his/her head and arms first

di·verge /dəˈvɚdʒ, daɪ-/ *v.* [I] to be different or to develop in a different way: *At this point, his version of events **diverges from** hers.* —**divergence** *n.* [C,U] —**divergent** *adj.*: *divergent views*

di·verse /dəˈvɚs, daɪ-/ *adj.* very different from each other: *The U.S. is a **culturally diverse** nation.*

di·ver·si·fy /dəˈvɚsəˌfaɪ, daɪ-/ *v.* past tense and past participle **diversified**, third person singular **diversifies** [I,T] if a company diversifies, it begins to make new products or to become involved in new types of business in addition to what it already does: *They started as a cosmetics company and then **diversified into** clothing.* —**diversification** /dəˌvɚsəfəˈkeɪʃən/ *n.* [U]

di·ver·sion /dəˈvɚʒən, daɪ-/ *n.* **1** [C,U] a change in the direction or purpose of something: *the illegal **diversion of** money from the project* **2** [C] something that takes your attention away from something else: *One man **creates a diversion** while the other steals your purse.* **3** [C] *formal* an activity that you do for pleasure or amusement: *Fishing is a pleasant diversion.*

di·ver·si·ty /dəˈvɚsət̬i, daɪ-/ *n.* [singular, U] a range of different people or things [= **variety**]: *The school prides itself on its **ethnic/cultural diversity**.* | *a **diversity of** opinions*

di·vert /dəˈvɚt, daɪ-/ *v.* [T] **1** to change the direction in which something travels: *Traffic is being diverted to avoid the accident.* **2** to use something for a different purpose: *They plan to **divert** money **from** production **to** design.* **3 divert (sb's) attention from sth** to stop someone from paying attention to something: *The war will divert attention from the country's economic problems.*

di·vest /dɪˈvɛst, daɪ-/ *v.*
divest sb ⇔ **of** sth *phr. v. formal* to take something away from someone

di·vide /dəˈvaɪd/ *v.* **1** [I,T] to separate something into two or more parts, groups, etc., or to become separated in this way: *The teacher **divided** the class **into** groups.* | *Brenda's trying to **divide** her time **between** work and school.*

THESAURUS

separate, **split**, **break up**, **segregate**
→ see Thesaurus box at SEPARATE²

2 [T] to keep two areas separate from each other: *A river divides the north and south sides of the city.* | *A curtain **divided** his sleeping area **from** ours.* **3** [T] **also divide up** to separate something into two or more parts and share it among two or more people, groups, places, etc.: *The money will be **divided** equally **among** his children.* | *She **divides** her time **between** Atlanta and Houston.* **4** [I,T] to calculate how many times one number is contained in a larger number: *15 **divided by** 3 is 5.*

THESAURUS

add, **subtract**, **take away**, **multiply**
→ see Thesaurus box at CALCULATE

5 [T] to make people disagree and form groups with different opinions: *Experts are **divided over** the question.*

div·i·dend /ˈdɪvəˌdɛnd, -dənd/ *n.* [C] a part of a

company's profit that is paid to people who have SHARES in the company

di·vid·er /də'vaɪdɚ/ *n.* [C] something such as a wall or SCREEN that divides something else into two or more parts: *the center divider on a road*

di·vine /də'vaɪn/ *adj.* having the qualities of God, or coming from God: *a divine plan*

div·ing /'daɪvɪŋ/ *n.* [U] **1** the sport of swimming underwater using breathing equipment **2** the activity of jumping into water with your head and arms first

'diving board *n.* [C] a board above a SWIMMING POOL from which you can jump into the water

di·vin·i·ty /də'vɪnət̬i/ *n.* plural **divinities** **1** [U] the study of God and religious beliefs [= **theology**] **2** [U] the quality of being like God **3** [C] a male or female god

THESAURUS

god, **deity**, **idol**
→ see Thesaurus box at GOD

di·vis·i·ble /də'vɪzəbəl/ *adj.* able to be divided by another number: *15 is **divisible by** 3 and 5.*

di·vi·sion /də'vɪʒən/ *n.* **1** [C,U] the act of separating something into two or more parts or groups, or the way that these parts are separated: *the **division of** words **into** syllables* | *the **division of** the money **between** the government departments* **2** [C,U] a disagreement among members of a group: *There are **deep divisions** within the Republican party.* **3** [U] the process of calculating how many times a small number will go into a larger number [➡ **multiplication**] **4** [C] a group within a large company, army, organization, etc.: *the finance **division of** the company* **5** [C] a group of teams that a sports LEAGUE is divided into: *the NFC central division*

di·vi·sion·al /də'vɪʒənəl/ *adj.* [only before noun] relating to a sports division: *the **divisional playoffs*** (=games to decide who wins a division)

di·vi·sive /də'vaɪsɪv, -'vɪs-/ *adj.* causing a lot of disagreement among people: *a divisive issue*

di·vorce¹ /də'vɔrs/ *n.* [C,U] the legal ending of a marriage: *She wants to **get a divorce**.* | *Their marriage **ended in divorce**.*

divorce² *v.* **1** [I,T] to legally end a marriage: *His parents divorced when he was six.* | *They decided to **get divorced**.* | *My father threatened to divorce her.*

THESAURUS

separate – to start to live apart from your husband or wife: *They separated six months ago.*
split up/break up – to end a marriage or a long romantic relationship: *When Andy was nine, his parents split up.* | *What would it do to the kids if he and Judy broke up?*
leave sb – to stop living with your husband, wife, or partner: *Her husband left her after 27 years of marriage.*

2 [T] *formal* to separate two ideas, values, organizations, etc.: *It is difficult to **divorce** religion **from** politics.* —**divorced** *adj.*: *a divorced woman*

di·vor·cee /də,vɔr'si, -'seɪ/ *n.* [C] a woman who is divorced

di·vulge /də'vʌldʒ, daɪ-/ *v.* [T] to give someone information, especially about something that was secret: *Doctors cannot divulge information about their patients.*

Dix·ie /'dɪksi/ *n. informal* the southern states of the U.S. that fought against the North in the U.S. Civil War

diz·zy /'dɪzi/ *adj.* **1** having a feeling of not being able to balance yourself, especially after spinning around or because you feel sick: *She felt dizzy when she stood up.* **2** *informal* someone who is dizzy is silly or stupid —**dizziness** *n.* [U]

DJ /'di dʒeɪ/ *n.* [C] **disk jockey** someone whose job is to play the music on the radio or in a club where you can dance

DNA *n.* [U] a substance that carries GENETIC information in a cell

do¹ /də; *strong* du/ past tense **did** /dɪd/ past participle **done** /dʌn/ third person singular **does** /dəz; *strong* dʌz/ *auxiliary verb* **1** used with another verb to form questions or negatives: *Do you like pasta?* | *What time does Linda usually go to bed?* | *I don't think I'll be able to come.* **2** *spoken* used at the end of a sentence to make a question or to ask someone to agree with it: *You know Tom, don't you?* | *She didn't understand, did she?* **3** used in order to emphasize the main verb: *He hasn't been here in a while, but he does come to visit us most weekends.* **4** used in order to avoid repeating another verb: *"Go clean up your room." "I already did!"* | *"Craig really likes Thai food." **"So do I."*** | *"I didn't like the movie." **"Neither did I."*** | *Emilio speaks much better English than he did a year ago.*

do² /du/ *v.* past tense **did**, past participle **done**, third person singular **does** **1** [T] to perform an action or activity: *Have you done your homework yet?* | *It's Jim's turn to **do the dishes/laundry**.* | *"What are you doing?" "Making cookies."* | *It's a pleasure **doing business** with you.* **2** [I] used in order to talk about how successful someone is: *How is Jayne doing in her new job?* | *He **did well/badly** at school.* **3** [T] to have a particular effect on something or someone: *The new car factory has **done a lot for*** (=had a good effect on) *the local economy.* | *Let's take a break. Come on, it will **do you good*** (=make you feel better). **4** [T] to have a particular job: ***What do** you **do for a living**?* | *She doesn't know what she wants to do.* **5 what is sb/sth doing?** used when you are surprised or annoyed that someone or something is in a particular place or doing a particular thing: *What is my jacket doing on the floor?* | *What are you doing with my purse?* **6 do your hair/nails/makeup etc.** to spend time making your hair, nails, etc. look good **7** [T] to travel at a particular speed or to travel a particular distance: *He was doing over 90 miles per hour.* **8 do lunch/a meeting/a movie etc.** *informal* to have lunch, have a meeting, see a movie, etc. with someone else: *Let's do lunch next week.* **9** [I, T] used in order to say that something is acceptable or enough: *The recipe calls for butter, but oil will do.* | *My old black shoes* ***will have to do.*** **10** [T] to provide a service or sell a product: *They do home deliveries.* ➔ **How are you?/How's it going?/How are you doing?** at HOW ➔ **how do you do?** at HOW

do away with *phr. v. informal* **1 do away with** sth to get rid of something: *We should do away with those old customs.* **2 do away with** sb to kill someone

do sb **in** *phr. v. informal* **1** to make someone feel very tired: *That long walk did me in.* **2** to kill someone

do sth **over** *phr. v.* to do something again, especially because you did it wrong the first time: *If there are mistakes, the teacher makes you do it over.*

do with sb/sth *phr. v.* **1 have/be to do with sb/sth** to be related to or involved with something or someone: *The book has to do with new theories in physics.* | *Diane wanted* ***nothing to do with*** *the party for Sara* (=she did not want to be involved at all). | *Jack's job is* ***something to do with*** *marketing* (=related to marketing, but you are not sure exactly how).

SPOKEN PHRASES

2 what has sb done with sth? used in order to ask where someone has put something: *What have you done with the scissors?* **3 I can/could do with sth** used in order to say that you need or want something: *I could do with some help.* **4 what sb does with himself/herself** the activities that someone does as a regular part of his/her life: *What is your dad doing with himself since he retired?*

➔ **make do** at MAKE[1]

do without sth *phr. v.* **1** to manage to continue living or doing something without having a particular thing: *It's almost impossible to do without a car in Los Angeles.* **2 I can/could do without sth** *spoken* used in order to say that something is annoying you or causing problems: *I could do without his stupid comments.*

do[3] *n.* **dos and don'ts** things that you should or should not do in a particular situation: *I'm still learning all the dos and don'ts of the job.*

d.o.b. the written abbreviation of **date of birth**

do·ber·man pin·scher /ˌdoʊbɚmən ˈpɪntʃɚ/ **also doberman** *n.* [C] a large black and brown dog with very short hair, often used in order to guard property

doc /dɑk/ *n.* [C] *spoken* a DOCTOR

doc·ile /ˈdɑsəl/ *adj.* quiet and easy to control: *a docile animal*

dock[1] /dɑk/ *n.* [C] a place where goods are put onto or taken off ships

dock[2] *v.* [I,T] **1** if a ship docks, it sails into a dock **2 dock sb's pay** to take money from someone's pay, as a punishment: *If you come in late one more time, we'll have to dock your pay.*

dock·et /ˈdɑkɪt/ *n.* [C] *law* a list of legal cases that will take place in a particular court

doc·tor[1] /ˈdɑktɚ/ *n.* [C] **1** someone whose job is to treat people who are sick: *You really should* ***see a doctor*** *about that cough.* | *He very rarely* ***goes to the doctor.*** | *I have a* ***doctor's appointment*** *tomorrow.*

THESAURUS

physician formal – a doctor: *our family physician*
surgeon – a doctor who does operations in a hospital: *a brain surgeon*
specialist – a doctor who knows a lot about a particular area of medicine: *He's one of the world's leading heart specialists.*
psychiatrist – a doctor who treats mental illness
dentist – someone whose job is to take care of people's teeth
pediatrician – a doctor who treats children who are sick

2 someone who has the highest level of degree given by a university: *a Doctor of Philosophy*

doctor[2] *v.* [T] to change something, especially in a way that is not honest: *The police may have doctored the evidence.*

doc·tor·ate /ˈdɑktərɪt/ *n.* [C] a university degree at the highest level

doc·trine /ˈdɑktrɪn/ *n.* [C,U] a set of religious or political beliefs: *Catholic doctrine* —**doctrinal** *adj.*

doc·u·ment[1] /ˈdɑkyəmənt/ *n.* [C] **1** a piece of paper that has official information written on it: *a legal document* | *historical documents* **2** a piece of work that you write and keep on a computer: *Click on the document you want to open.* ➔ see Topic box at COMPUTER

doc·u·ment[2] /ˈdɑkyəˌmɛnt/ *v.* [T] to record information about something by writing about it, photographing it, etc.: *The program documents the daily life of a teenager.*

doc·u·men·ta·ry /ˌdɑkyəˈmɛntri, -ˈmɛntəri/ *n.* plural **documentaries** [C] a movie or television program that gives facts and information on something: *He made a* ***documentary about*** *a farming community in Iowa.* ➔ see Thesaurus box at TELEVISION

doc·u·men·ta·tion /ˌdɑkyəmənˈteɪʃən/ *n.* [U] official documents that are used in order to prove that something is true or correct

dodge /dɑdʒ/ *v.* **1** [I,T] to move quickly in order to avoid someone or something: *We had to* ***dodge the bullets.*** **2** [T] to avoid talking about something or doing something that you do not want to do: *The senator dodged the reporter's question.* —**dodge** *n.* [C]

doe /doʊ/ *n.* [C] a female DEER

does /dəz; *strong* dʌz/ *v.* the third person singular of the present tense of DO

does·n't /ˈdʌzənt/ *v.* the short form of "does not"

dog[1] /dɔg/ *n.* [C] a very common animal with four legs that is often kept as a pet or used for guarding buildings: *I could hear a **dog barking**. | I'm going out to **walk** the **dog**.*

dog[2] *v.* past tense and past participle **dogged**, present participle **dogging** [T] if a problem or bad luck dogs you, it causes trouble for a long time

ˈdog-eared *adj.* dog-eared books have been used so much that the corners of their pages are folded or torn

dog·ged /ˈdɔgɪd/ *adj.* determined to do something even though it is difficult: ***a dogged determination** to succeed* —**doggedly** *adv.*

dog·gone /ˌdɔˈgɔn◂ / **also dog'gone it** *interjection old-fashioned* said when you are annoyed: *Doggone it, I said leave that alone!* —**doggone** *adj.*: *It's a doggone shame.*

dog·gy, doggie /ˈdɔgi/ *n.* plural **doggies** [C] a dog – used by or when speaking to young children

ˈdoggy bag *n.* [C] a small bag for taking home the food you did not eat from a meal at a restaurant

dog·house /ˈdɔghaʊs/ *n.* [C] **1 be in the doghouse** *informal* to be in a situation in which someone is angry or annoyed with you **2** a little building for a dog to sleep in

dog·ma /ˈdɔgmə, ˈdɑgmə/ *n.* [C,U] an important belief or set of beliefs that people are supposed to accept as true without asking for any explanation: *church dogma*

dog·mat·ic /dɔgˈmæt̬ɪk, dɑg-/ *adj.* someone who is dogmatic is completely certain about his/her beliefs and expects other people to accept them without arguing —**dogmatically** *adv.*

do-good·er /ˈdu ˌgʊdɚ/ *n.* [C] *informal* someone who does things to help other people, but who often gets involved when his/her help is not wanted or needed

ˈdog ˌpaddle *n.* [singular] *informal* a simple way of swimming that you do by moving your arms and legs like a swimming dog

dog·wood /ˈdɔgwʊd/ *n.* [C] an eastern North American tree or bush with flat white or pink flowers

do·ing /ˈduɪŋ/ *n.* **1 be sb's (own) doing** to be someone's fault: *His bad luck was all his own doing.* **2 take some doing** *informal* to be hard work: *Getting this old car to run is going to take some doing.*

dol·drums /ˈdoʊldrəmz, ˈdɑl-/ *n.* [plural] *informal* **1** a state in which something is not improving or developing: *The stock market has been **in the doldrums** for most of this year.* **2** a state in which you feel sad [= **depression**]

dole /doʊl/ *v.*

dole sth ⇔ **out** *phr. v.* to give something such as money, food, advice, etc. in small amounts to a lot of people: *Vera was **doling out** candy **to** the kids.*

dole·ful /ˈdoʊlfəl/ *adj.* very sad: *a doleful song*

doll /dɑl/ *n.* [C] a toy that looks like a small person or baby: *a small wooden doll*

dol·lar /ˈdɑlɚ/ *n.* [C] **1** the standard of money used in the U.S., Canada, Australia, New Zealand, and other countries. Its sign is $ and it is worth 100 cents: *These pants cost $40. | That will be three dollars, please.* **2** a piece of paper money or a coin of this value: *dollar bills* **3 the dollar** the value of U.S. money in relation to the money of other countries: *The peso has dropped almost 1 percent **against the dollar**.*

dol·lop /ˈdɑləp/ *n.* [C] a small amount of soft food, usually dropped from a spoon: *a **dollop of** whipped cream*

dol·phin /ˈdɑlfɪn, ˈdɔl-/ *n.* [C] a very intelligent sea animal with a long gray pointed nose

do·main /doʊˈmeɪn, də-/ *n.* [C] *formal* a particular activity that is controlled by one person, group, organization, etc.: *In the past, politics was exclusively **a male domain**. | This problem is **outside the domain of** medical science.*

doˈmain ˌname *n.* [C] a part of an Internet website's address that tells you the name of the website

dome /doʊm/ *n.* [C] a round curved roof on a building or room —**domed** *adj.*

do·mes·tic /dəˈmɛstɪk/ *adj.* **1** happening within one country and not involving any other countries: *U.S. foreign and **domestic policy** | **Domestic flights*** (=flights that stay inside a particular country) *leave from Terminal C.* **2** [only before noun] relating to family relationships and life at home: *We share the **domestic chores**. | a victim of **domestic violence*** (=violence between husband and wife) **3** someone who is domestic enjoys spending time at home doing things such as cooking, cleaning, etc. **4 domestic animal** an animal that lives in someone's house or on a farm [≠ **wild**]

do·mes·ti·cat·ed /dəˈmɛstɪˌkeɪt̬ɪd/ *adj.* domesticated animals live with people as pets or

D

work for them on a farm —**domesticate** *v.* [T] —**domestication** /də,mɛstɪ'keɪʃən/ *n.* [U]

do·mes·tic·i·ty /,doʊmɛ'stɪsət̬i/ *n.* [U] life at home with your family and the activities that relate to this

do,mestic 'partner *n.* [C] someone who you live with and have a sexual relationship with, but who you are not married to

dom·i·nance /'dɑmənəns/ *n.* [U] a situation in which someone is more powerful, more important, or more noticeable than other people or things: *the **dominance of** youth culture in the U.S.*

dom·i·nant /'dɑmənənt/ *adj.* **1** strongest, most important, or most noticeable: *America's **dominant role** in international business*

> **THESAURUS**
>
> **powerful, influential, strong**
> → see Thesaurus box at POWERFUL

2 controlling other people or things, or wanting to do this: *her husband's dominant behavior*

dom·i·nate /'dɑmə,neɪt/ *v.* [I,T] **1** to have power and control over someone or something: *Five large companies dominate the auto industry.* **2** to be the strongest, most important, or most noticeable feature of something: *The murder trial has been dominating the news this week.* —**domination** /,dɑmə'neɪʃən/ *n.* [U]

dom·i·neer·ing /,dɑmə'nɪrɪŋ/ *adj. disapproving* trying to control other people without considering how they feel or what they want: *his domineering father*

do·min·ion /də'mɪnyən/ *n.* [U] *literary* the power or right to rule people

dom·i·no /'dɑmə,noʊ/ *n.* plural **dominoes** [C] **1** a small piece of wood, plastic, etc. with a different number of spots on each half of its top side, used in playing a game **2 dominoes** [U] the game that you play using dominoes **3 domino effect** a situation in which one event or action causes several other things to happen one after the other: *The weakness of the dollar had a domino effect, hurting stocks and bonds.*

do·nate /'doʊneɪt, doʊ'neɪt/ *v.* [I,T] **1** to give something, especially money, to a person or organization that needs help: *Our school **donated** $500 **to** the Red Cross.*

> **THESAURUS**
>
> **give, leave, award**
> → see Thesaurus box at GIVE[1]

2 donate blood/an organ/a kidney etc. to allow some of your blood or a part of your body to be used to help someone who is sick or injured

do·na·tion /doʊ'neɪʃən/ *n.* [C,U] something, especially money, that you give to help a person or organization: *Please **make a donation to** UNICEF.*

done[1] /dʌn/ *v.* the past participle of DO

done[2] *adj.* **1** finished or completed: *The job's almost done.* | *Are you **done with** this magazine?*

> **THESAURUS**
>
> **finished** done, and dealt with in the way you wanted: *She showed him the finished drawing.*
> **complete** – finished, and having all the necessary parts: *The project is almost complete.*
> **over** – if an event, activity, or period of time is over, it is finished: *The game was over by 10 o'clock.*
> **through** – if you are through with something, you have finished using it or doing it: *Are you through with those scissors?*

2 cooked enough to be eaten: *I think the hamburgers are done.* **3 it's a done deal** *spoken* used in order to mean that an agreement has been made and it cannot be changed **4 be done in** *spoken* to be extremely tired: *I've got to sit down – I'm done in.*

done[3] *interjection* used in order to accept a deal that someone offers you: *"How about I give you $25 for it?" "Done!"*

don·key /'dɑŋki, 'dʌŋ-, 'dɔŋ-/ *n.* [C] a gray or brown animal like a horse, but smaller and with longer ears

do·nor /'doʊnɚ/ *n.* [C] **1** someone who gives something, especially money, to an organization in order to help people: *The Museum received $10,000 from an **anonymous donor**.* **2** someone who gives blood or a part of his/her body so that it can be used to help someone who is sick or injured: *an **organ donor***

don't /doʊnt/ *v.* the short form of "do not": *I don't know.*

donut

do·nut /'doʊnʌt/ *n.* [C] another spelling of DOUGHNUT

doo·dad /'dudæd/ **also doo·hick·ey** /'du,hɪki/ *n.* [C] *informal* a small object whose name you have forgotten or do not know: *What's this doodad for?*

doo·dle /'dudl/ *v.* [I,T] to draw shapes or patterns without really thinking about what you are doing: *Stein was doodling on a napkin.* —**doodle** *n.* [C]

> **THESAURUS**
>
> **draw, sketch, scribble, trace**
> → see Thesaurus box at DRAW[1]

doom[1] /dum/ *n.* [U] **1** destruction, death, or failure that is certain to happen: *a sense of **impending doom*** (=a feeling that something bad will happen soon). **2 doom and gloom** a feeling that there is no hope for the future

doom[2] *v.* [T] to make someone or something certain to fail, be destroyed, or die: *The program* *was* ***doomed to failure*** *from the start.* —**doomed** *adj.*

dooms·day /ˈdumzdeɪ/ *n.* [singular] JUDGEMENT DAY

door /dɔr/ *n.* [C] **1** a large tall flat piece of wood, glass, etc. that you push or pull in order to go into a building, room, car, etc.: *Could someone please* ***open/close/shut the door****?* | *Don't forget to lock the* ***front/back/side door****.* | *She ran into her bedroom and* ***slammed the door*** (=shut it very hard). | *Did you hear someone* ***knock on/at the door****?* | *Marie, can you* ***get/answer the door*** (=open it after someone has knocked)*?* **2** the space made by an open door: *You just* ***go out/through*** *this* ***door*** *and turn right.* **3 next door** in the room, house, etc. next to where you are: *the people who live next door* **4 at the door** if someone is at the door, s/he is waiting for you to open it **5 two/three etc. doors down** a particular number of rooms, houses, etc. away from where you are: *Her office is just two doors down.* **6 (from) door to door a)** between one place and another: *If you drive it should only take you 20 minutes door to door.* **b)** going to each house on a street to sell something, collect money, etc.: *We went door to door asking people to sponsor us in the race.* **7 show/see sb to the door** to walk with someone to the main door of a building

door·bell /ˈdɔrbɛl/ *n.* [C] a button by the door of a house that you press to make a sound that lets the people inside know you are there

door·knob /ˈdɔrnɑb/ *n.* [C] a round handle that you turn to open a door

door·man /ˈdɔrmæn, -mən/ *n.* plural **doormen** /-mɛn, -mən/ [C] a man who works at the door of a hotel or theater, helping people who are coming in or out

door·mat /ˈdɔrmæt/ *n.* [C] **1** a thick piece of material just outside a door for you to clean your shoes on **2** *informal* someone who lets other people treat him/her badly and never complains

door·step /ˈdɔrstɛp/ *n.* [C] **1** a step just outside a door to a building **2 on your doorstep** very near to where you live or are staying: *Wow! You have the beach right on your doorstep!*

door·way /ˈdɔrweɪ/ *n.* [C] the space where a door opens into a room or building: *Cindy stood* ***in the doorway****.*

dope[1] /doʊp/ *n. informal* **1** [U] an illegal drug, especially MARIJUANA **2** [C] a stupid person

dope[2] **also dope up** *v.* [T] *informal* **1** to give a drug to a person or animal in order to make him, her, or it unconscious **2** to give a drug to a person or animal in order to make him, her, or it perform better in a race —**doping** *n.* [U]

dork /dɔrk/ *n.* [C] *informal* someone who you think is silly or stupid because s/he behaves strangely or wears strange clothes: *I look like such a dork in that picture.* —**dorky** *adj.*

dorm /dɔrm/ *n.* [C] *informal* a DORMITORY

dor·mant /ˈdɔrmənt/ *adj.* not active now, but able to be active at a later time: *a dormant volcano* —**dormancy** /ˈdɔrmənsi/ *n.* [U]

dor·mi·to·ry /ˈdɔrməˌtɔri/ *n.* plural **dormitories** [C] a large building at a college or university where students live

dor·sal /ˈdɔrsəl/ *adj. technical* on or relating to the back of a fish or animal: *a whale's dorsal fin*

dos·age /ˈdoʊsɪdʒ/ *n.* [C] the amount of medicine that you should take at any one time ➔ see Thesaurus box at MEDICINE

dose /doʊs/ *n.* [C] **1** a measured amount of medicine: *She was injected with a* ***dose of*** *insulin.* **2** an amount of something that you experience at one time: *I can only handle Jason* ***in small doses*** (=for short amounts of time).

dos·si·er /ˈdɑsiˌeɪ, ˈdɔ-/ *n.* [C] a set of papers that include detailed information about someone or something: *The police keep* ***dossiers on*** *all their prisoners.*

dot[1] /dɑt/ *n.* [C] **1** a small round mark or spot: *a pattern of dots on the screen* **2 on the dot** *informal* exactly at a particular time: *He arrived at nine o'clock on the dot.*

dot[2] *v.* past tense and past participle **dotted**, present participle **dotting** [T] **1** to mark something by putting a dot on it or above it: *She never dots her "i's."* **2** to spread things out within an area: *We have over 20 stores* ***dotted around*** *the state.*

ˌdot-ˈcom, **dot.com**, **dot com** *adj.* [only before noun] *informal* relating to a person or company that sells a product or service on the Internet: *a dot-com company* —**dot-com** *n.* [C]

dote /doʊt/ *v.*

dote on sb *phr. v.* to love someone very much and to show this by your actions: *They dote on their grandson.* —**doting** *adj.*: *doting parents*

ˌdotted ˈline *n.* [C] **1** a series of printed DOTS that form a line **2 sign on the dotted line** to officially agree to something by signing a contract

dou·ble[1] /ˈdʌbəl/ *adj.* **1** having two parts that are similar or exactly the same: *a double sink* | *the* ***double doors*** *of the cathedral* **2** twice the usual amount, size, or number: *a double whiskey* | *They have asked me to work* ***double shifts****.* **3** intended to be used by two people [➥ **single**]: *a* ***double bed*** ➔ see picture at BED[1] **4** combining or involving two things of the same type: *a double major in English and French* | *Her husband was secretly* ***leading a double life*** (=has two separate and different lives, each one secret from the other).

double[2] *v.* [I,T] to become twice as large or twice as much, or to make something do this: *Our house has* ***doubled in value*** *since we bought it.* | *The mayor wants to double the number of police officers on the street.* | *The church has doubled its membership.*

THESAURUS

increase, go up, rise, grow, shoot up
➔ see Thesaurus box at INCREASE[1]

double as sb/sth *phr. v.* to have a second use, job, or purpose: *The sofa doubles as a bed.*
double back *phr. v.* to turn around and go back in the direction you just came from: *I doubled back and headed south.*
double up, double over *phr. v.* **be doubled up/over with pain/laughter etc.** to bend at the waist because you are in pain or laughing a lot: *Both the girls were doubled up with laughter.*

double[3] *n.* **1** [C,U] something that is twice as big or twice as much as usual: *Scotch and water, please – make it a double.* **2 sb's double** someone who looks very similar to someone else: *She's her mother's double.* **3** [C] a room or bed for two people [➡ **single**] **4 on the double** *informal* very soon or immediately: *I want that report here on the double!* **5 doubles** [plural] a tennis game played by two pairs of players

D

double[4] *adv.* **see double** to have a problem with your eyes so that you see two things instead of one

double[5] *determiner* twice as much or twice as many: *The car is worth* ***double the amount*** *we paid for it.*

double bass /ˌdʌbəl ˈbeɪs/ *n.* [C] a very large wooden musical instrument, shaped like a VIOLIN, that you play while standing up ➔ see picture on page A6

ˌdouble ˈboiler *n.* [C] a pot for cooking food, made of one pot resting on top of another pot that has hot water in it

ˌdouble-ˈbreasted *adj.* a double-breasted jacket or coat has two rows of buttons on the front

ˌdouble-ˈcheck *v.* [T] to check something again to find out if it is safe, ready, correct, etc.: *I think I turned off the oven, but let me go double-check.*

THESAURUS

check, make sure, confirm
➔ see Thesaurus box at CHECK[1]

ˌdouble ˈchin *n.* [C] an additional fold of skin under someone's chin that looks like a second chin

ˌdouble-ˌclick *v.* [I] to press a button on a computer MOUSE twice in order to make the computer do something: ***Double-click on*** *the Printer icon.* —**double click** *n.* [C]

ˌdouble-ˈcross *v.* [T] to cheat someone when you are involved in something dishonest together —**double cross** *n.* [C]

ˌdouble ˈdate *n.* [C] an occasion in which two COUPLES meet to go to a movie, restaurant, etc. together

ˌdouble-ˈdigit *adj.* [only before noun] relating to the numbers 10 to 99: *double-digit unemployment rates*

ˌdouble ˈdigits *n.* [plural] the numbers from 10 to 99: *Three of the team's players scored* ***in double digits.***

ˌdouble ˈduty *n.* **do double duty** to do more than one job or be used for more than one purpose at the same time: *The lids on the pots do double duty as plates when we're camping.*

ˌdouble ˈfigures *n.* [plural] DOUBLE DIGITS

ˌdouble-ˈheader *n.* [C] two baseball games that are played one after the other

ˌdouble-ˈjointed *adj.* able to move the joints in your arms, fingers, etc. backward as well as forward

ˌdouble ˈnegative *n.* [C] two negative words used in one sentence when you should use only one in correct English grammar, for example in the sentence "I don't want nobody to help me!"

ˌdouble-ˈpark *v.* [I,T] to leave a car on the road beside another car that is already parked there: *I got a ticket for double-parking.*

ˌdouble ˈplay *n.* [C] in the game of baseball, the action of making two players who are running between the BASES have to leave the field by throwing the ball quickly from one base to the other before each runner gets there

ˌdouble ˈstandard *n.* [C] a rule or principle that is unfair because it treats one group or type of people more severely than another in the same situation

ˌdouble ˈtake *n.* **do a double take** to suddenly look at someone or something again because you are surprised by what you originally saw or heard

ˈdouble-talk *n.* [U] *disapproving* speech that is complicated, and is intended to deceive or confuse people

ˌdouble ˈvision *n.* [U] a medical condition in which you see two of everything

ˌdouble ˈwhammy *n.* plural **double whammies** [C] *informal* two bad things that happen at the same time or one after the other

dou·bly /ˈdʌbli/ *adv.* **1** much more than usual: *Be doubly careful when driving in fog.* **2** in two ways or for two reasons: *You are doubly mistaken.*

doubt[1] /daʊt/ *n.* [C,U] **1** a feeling of not being certain whether something is true or possible: *I began to* ***have*** *serious* ***doubts about*** *his ability to do the job.* | ***There is no doubt that*** *one day a cure will be found.* | ***Without a doubt,*** *Kevin is the best player on the team.* **2 no doubt** used when emphasizing that you think something is probably true: *No doubt they'll win.* | *She was a top student,* ***no doubt about it.*** **3 be in doubt** if something is in doubt, it may not happen, continue, exist, or be true: *The future of the peace talks is in doubt.* **4 beyond doubt** if something is beyond doubt, it is completely certain: *The state must* ***prove beyond*** *reasonable* ***doubt*** *that he is guilty.*

doubt[2] *v.* [T] **1** to think that something may not be true or that it is unlikely: ***I doubt that*** *we will ever see her again.* | *He might come, but I* ***doubt it.***

2 to not trust or believe in someone or something: *Nobody doubts his ability to stay calm in a crisis.*

Grammar

doubt that, doubt if, doubt whether

When you use the verb **doubt** in a simple statement, it can be followed by "that," "if," or "whether": *I **doubt that** the mail has arrived.* | *I **doubt if/whether** he's coming.*

However, if the statement is negative, **doubt** can only be followed by "that": *We don't **doubt that** she can finish on time* (=we know that she can do it).

When you use the noun **doubt** after "no" or "not," it is always followed by "that": *There is no **doubt that** she is guilty.*

doubt·ful /ˈdaʊt˺fəl/ *adj.* **1** probably not true or not likely to happen: *It's **doubtful that** voters will approve the bill.* **2** not certain about something: *I could see that he still looked doubtful.* —**doubtfully** *adv.*

doubt·less /ˈdaʊt˺lɪs/ *adv.* used when saying that something is very likely to happen or be true: *Readers will doubtless be disappointed by her new novel.*

dough /doʊ/ *n.* [U] **1** a mixture of flour and water ready to be baked into bread, cookies, etc. **2** *informal* money

dough·nut /ˈdoʊnʌt/ *n.* [C] a small round cake that is usually shaped like a ring

dour /ˈdaʊɚ, dʊɚ/ *adj.* very severe and not smiling: *a dour expression*

douse /daʊs/ *v.* [T] **1** to stop a fire from burning by throwing water on it: *Firefighters quickly doused the blaze.* **2** to cover something in water or other liquid

dove[1] /dʌv/ *n.* [C] a type of small white bird often used as a sign of peace

dove[2] /doʊv/ *v.* a past tense of DIVE

dow·dy /ˈdaʊdi/ *adj.* unattractive or unfashionable

down[1] /daʊn/ *adv., prep.* **1** toward a lower place or position [≠ **up**]: *She looked down at the street from her window.* | *David bent down to tie his shoelace.* **2** into a sitting or lying position: *Come in and sit down.* | *trees blown down by the big storm* **3** in a lower place or position [≠ **up**]: *The cows are down in the valley.* | *The bathroom is down those stairs.* **4** toward or in the south [≠ **up**]: *Gail drove down to North Carolina to see her brother.* | *We moved down south when I was a baby.* **5** at or to a place that is further along a path, road, etc.: *Could you go down to the store and get some bread?* **6** decreasing in loudness, strength, heat, activity, etc. [≠ **up**]: *Can you turn the TV down a little?* | *House prices have come down in recent months.* **7 write/note/take etc. sth down** to write something on paper: *I'll write down the address for you.* **8** *informal* paid to someone immediately [➡ **down payment**]: *The landlord wants a lot of money down.* **9** from an earlier time to a later time: *The story was **handed down** in the family from father to son.* | *traditions that have come **come down to** us from medieval times* ➔ **come down with** at COME

down[2] *adj.* [not before noun] **1** sad: *I've never seen Bret looking so down.*

THESAURUS

sad, unhappy, miserable, upset, depressed, low, homesick, gloomy, glum

➔ see Thesaurus box at SAD

2 losing to an opponent by a certain number of points [≠ **up**]: *We were down by 6 points at half-time.* **3** a computer system that is down is not working [≠ **up**] **4** a level, number, or amount that is down is lower than before [≠ **up**]: *At lunchtime, the stock market was down 77 points.* **5** *spoken* used in order to say that a particular number of things have been finished, when there are more things left to do: *That's two down. Only two more to do.* **6 be down on sb/sth** *spoken* to have a bad opinion of someone or something: *Why is Jerome so down on work?*

down[3] *prep.* **1** toward the ground or a lower point, or in a lower position: *The bathroom is down those stairs.* **2** along or toward the far end of something: *We walked down the beach as the sun rose.* | *They live down the road from us.* **3 down the road/line** *informal* at some time in the future: *We'd like to have children sometime down the line.*

down[4] *v.* [T] *informal* to drink something very quickly: *Matt downed his coffee and left for work.*

THESAURUS

sip, take a sip, slurp, gulp down, knock back, swig, take/have a swig

➔ see Thesaurus box at DRINK

down[5] *n.* **1** [U] thin soft feathers or hair: *a down pillow* **2** [C] one of the four chances that a football team has to move forward ten yards with the ball: ***first/second, etc. down***

ˌdown-and-ˈout *adj. informal* having no luck or money: *a down-and-out actor*

down·cast /ˈdaʊnkæst/ *adj.* sad or upset because something bad has happened

down·er /ˈdaʊnɚ/ *n.* [singular] *spoken* someone or something that makes you feel unhappy: *The movie was a real downer.*

down·fall /ˈdaʊnfɔl/ *n.* [C] a sudden loss of money, power, social position, etc., or something that leads to this: *Greed will be his downfall.*

down·grade /ˈdaʊngreɪd/ *v.* [T] to state that something is not as good or as valuable as it was before: *Several analysts have downgraded the stock.*

down·heart·ed /ˌdaʊnˈhɑrt̬ɪd◂/ *adj.* **be downhearted** to feel sad about something

down·hill[1] /ˌdaʊnˈhɪl/ *adv.* **1** toward the bottom of a hill or toward lower land [≠ **uphill**]: *The* *truck's brakes failed, and it rolled downhill.* **2 go downhill** to become worse: *After he lost his job, things went downhill.*

down·hill² /ˈdaʊnhɪl/ *adj.* **1** on a slope that goes down to a lower point: *downhill skiing* **2 be (all) downhill** to become worse: *We got three runs in the first inning, but* ***it was all downhill from there.***

down·load /ˈdaʊnloʊd/ *v.* [T] to move information or programs from a computer network to your computer: *The software can be downloaded from the Internet*

ˌdown ˈpayment *n.* [C] the first payment you make on something expensive that you will pay for over a longer period: *a* ***down payment on*** *a car*

down·play /ˈdaʊnpleɪ/ *v.* [T] to make something seem less important than it really is: *Fred downplayed the seriousness of his illness.*

D

down·pour /ˈdaʊnpɔr/ *n.* [C usually singular] a lot of rain that falls in a short time

THESAURUS

rain, drizzle, shower, storm, hail, hailstones, sleet
➔ see Thesaurus box at RAIN¹

down·right /ˈdaʊnraɪt/ *adv. informal* thoroughly and completely: *You're just downright lazy.*

down·riv·er /ˌdaʊnˈrɪvɚ/ *adv.* in the direction that the water in a river is flowing [≠ **upriver**]

down·shift /ˈdaʊnʃɪft/ *v.* [I] **1** to put the engine of a vehicle into a lower GEAR in order to go slower **2** if someone downshifts, s/he chooses to work less so that s/he has more time to enjoy life

down·side /ˈdaʊnsaɪd/ *n.* [singular] a disadvantage to something: *The* ***downside of*** *the plan is the cost.*

down·size /ˈdaʊnsaɪz/ *v.* [I,T] to reduce the number of people who work for a company in order to cut costs —**downsizing** *n.* [U]

ˈDown's ˌSyndrome *n.* [U] a condition that someone is born with that stops him/her from developing normally both mentally and physically

down·stairs /ˌdaʊnˈstɛrz/ *adv.* **1** on or going toward a lower floor of a building, especially a house [≠ **upstairs**]: *He* ***went downstairs*** *to make coffee.* | ***Run downstairs*** *and answer the door.* **2 the downstairs** the rooms on the first floor of a house [≠ **upstairs**]: *Let's paint the downstairs blue.* —**downstairs** /ˈdaʊnstɛrz/ *adj.*: *the downstairs rooms*

down·state /ˌdaʊnˈsteɪt◂/ *adj., adv.* in or toward the southern part of a state [≠ **upstate**]: *He lives downstate, near the city.*

down·stream /ˌdaʊnˈstrim/ *adv.* in the direction the water in a river or stream flows [≠ **upstream**]

down·time /ˈdaʊntaɪm/ *n.* [U] **1** the time when a computer is not working **2** *informal* time spent relaxing

ˌdown-to-ˈearth *adj.* practical and honest: *She's a friendly, down-to-earth person.*

down·town¹ /ˈdaʊntaʊn/ *n.* [U] the business center of a city or town: *efforts to revitalize the city's downtown*

down·town² /ˌdaʊnˈtaʊn◂/ *adv., adj.* to or in the business center of a city or town [➡ **uptown**]: *Do you work downtown?* | *downtown Atlanta* | *I need to* ***go downtown*** *later.*

down·trod·den /ˈdaʊnˌtrɑdn/ *adj. literary* treated badly by people who have power over you

down·turn /ˈdaʊntɚn/ *n.* [C usually singular] a time during which business activity is reduced and conditions become worse: *a* ***downturn in*** *the economy*

down·ward¹ /ˈdaʊnwɚd/ **also downwards** *adv.* from a higher place or position to a lower one [≠ **upward**]: *The balloon drifted slowly downward.*

downward² *adj.* going or moving down to a lower level or place [≠ **upward**]: *Stock prices continued their downward trend.*

down·wind /ˌdaʊnˈwɪnd◂/ *adj., adv.* in the same direction that the wind is moving

down·y /ˈdaʊni/ *adj.* having thin, soft feathers or hair: *the baby's downy head*

dow·ry /ˈdaʊri/ *n.* plural **dowries** [C] money or property that a woman gives to her husband when they marry in some societies

doze /doʊz/ *v.* [I] to sleep lightly for a short time

THESAURUS

sleep, take a nap
➔ see Thesaurus box at SLEEP¹

doze off to fall asleep, especially when you did not intend to: *He dozed off watching TV.*

doz·en /ˈdʌzən/ *number* **1** a group of 12 things: ***a dozen*** *eggs* **2** *informal* a lot: *I've heard this story* ***dozens of*** *times.*

Dr. /ˈdɑktɚ/ the written abbreviation of **Doctor**

drab /dræb/ *adj.* not colorful or interesting: *a drab office building*

dra·co·ni·an /dræˈkoʊniən/ *adj. formal* very strict and severe: *draconian laws*

draft¹ /dræft/ *n.* [C] **1** a piece of writing, a drawing, or a plan that is not yet in its finished form: *the* ***rough draft*** *of his essay* | *I read the* ***first draft*** *and thought it was very good.* | *She still has to review the* ***final draft*** (=final form). **2 the draft** a system in which people must join the military, especially when there is a war **3** cold air that moves through a room and that you can feel: *Is the window closed all the way? I feel a draft in here.* **4 on draft** beer that is on draft is served from a large container, rather than from a bottle or can

draft² *v.* [T] **1** to write a plan, letter, report, etc. that you will need to change before it is finished: *The House plans to draft a bill on education.* **2** to order someone to fight for his/her country during a war: *Jim* ***was drafted into*** *the army.*

'draft ˌdodger *n.* [C] someone who illegally avoids joining the military, even though s/he has been ordered to join

drafts·man /'dræftsmən/ *n.* plural **draftsmen** /-mən/ [C] someone whose job is to make detailed drawings of a building, machine, etc. that is being planned

draft·y /'dræfti/ *adj.* a drafty room is uncomfortable because cold air is blowing through it

drag[1] /dræg/ *v.* past tense and past participle **dragged**, present participle **dragging**

1 PULL STH [T] to pull something along the ground, often because it is too heavy to carry: *Ben **dragged** his sled **through** the snow.* ➔ see picture at PULL[1] ➔ see picture on page A9

THESAURUS

pull, tug, haul, tow, heave

➔ see Thesaurus box at PULL[1]

2 PULL SB [T] to pull someone in a strong or violent way when s/he does not want to go with you: *He grabbed her arm and dragged her into the room.*

3 drag yourself up/over/along etc. *informal* to move somewhere when it is difficult: *I dragged myself out of bed to call the doctor.*

4 GO SOMEWHERE [T] *informal* to make someone go somewhere that s/he does not want to go: *Mom **dragged** us **to** a concert last night.*

5 drag yourself away (from) *informal* to stop doing something, although you do not want to: *Can you drag yourself away from the TV for 5 minutes?*

6 BORING [I] if time or an event drags, it is boring and seems to go very slowly: *The last hour of the play really dragged.*

7 COMPUTER [T] to move words, images, etc. on a computer screen by pulling them along with the MOUSE

8 TOUCHING GROUND [I] if something is dragging along the ground, part of it is touching the ground as you move: *Kay's scarf **dragged along** the sidewalk as she walked.*

9 drag your feet *informal* to take too much time to do something because you do not want to do it: *The police are being accused of dragging their feet on this case.*

drag sb/sth **into** sth *phr. v.* to make someone get involved in a situation even though s/he does not want to: *I'm sorry to drag you into this mess.*

drag on *phr. v.* to continue for too long: *The meeting dragged on all afternoon.*

drag sth ⇔ **out** *phr. v.* to make a situation or event last longer than necessary: *How long are you going to drag this discussion out?*

drag sth ⇔ **out of** sb *phr. v.* to force someone to tell you something when s/he had not intended to or was not supposed to do so

drag[2] *n.* [C] **1 a drag** *informal* something or someone that is boring or annoying: *"I have to stay home tonight." **"What a drag."*** **2 the main drag** *informal* the biggest or longest street that goes through a town, especially the middle of a town: *There are a lot of restaurants along the main drag.* **3** the act of breathing in smoke from a cigarette: *Al **took a drag on** his cigarette.* **4 in drag** *informal* wearing clothes that are intended for people of the opposite sex, especially for fun or entertainment

drag·on /'drægən/ *n.* [C] a large imaginary animal that has wings, a long tail, and can breathe out fire

drag·on·fly /'drægənˌflaɪ/ *n.* plural **dragonflies** [C] a flying insect with a long brightly colored body

'drag race *n.* [C] a car race over a short distance

drain[1] /dreɪn/ *v.* **1 a)** [T] to make the water or liquid in something flow away: *The swimming pool is drained and cleaned every winter.* | *Brad **drained** all the oil **from** the engine.* **b)** [I] if something drains, the liquid in it or on it flows away: *Let the pasta drain well.* **c)** [I] if a liquid drains, it flows away: *The bath water slowly **drained away**.* **2** [T] to use up all of your energy, making you feel very tired: *Working with children all day really drains you.* **3** [I] if the color drains from your face, you suddenly become pale **4** [T] to drink all the liquid in a glass, cup, etc.: *Lori quickly drained her cup.*

drain[2] *n.* [C] **1** a pipe or hole that dirty water or other waste liquids flow into: *The drain in the sink is blocked.* **2 a drain on sth** something that uses a lot of something, such as time, money, or strength: *Doing a graduate degree has been a drain on Fran's savings.* **3 down the drain** *informal* wasted or having no result: *There's another $50 down the drain.*

drain·age /'dreɪnɪdʒ/ *n.* [U] the system or process by which water or waste liquids can flow away from a place

drained /dreɪnd/ *adj.* very tired: *I felt completely drained after they had all gone home.*

dra·ma /'drɑmə, 'dræmə/ *n.* **1** [C,U] a play for the theater, television, radio, etc., usually a serious one, or plays in general **2** [U] the study of acting and plays: *drama school* **3** [C,U] an exciting and unusual situation or event: *a life full of drama*

dra·mat·ic /drə'mæṭɪk/ *adj.* **1** sudden and surprising: *His work has shown **dramatic improvement**.* | *a **dramatic change** in temperature* **2** exciting and impressive: *a dramatic speech* **3** related to the theater or plays: *Miller's dramatic works* **4** showing your feelings in a way that makes other people notice you: *Don't be so dramatic.* —**dramatically** *adv.*: *Output has increased dramatically.*

dra·mat·ics /drə'mæṭɪks/ *n.* [plural] behavior that is intended to get attention and is not sincere: *I'm really tired of your dramatics.*

dram·a·tist /'dræməṭɪst, 'drɑ-/ *n.* [C] someone who writes plays, especially serious ones

dram·a·tize /'dræməˌtaɪz, 'drɑ-/ *v.* [T] **1** to make a book or event into a play, movie, television

D

program, etc.: *a novel dramatized for TV* **2** to make an event seem more exciting than it really is: *Do you always have to dramatize everything?* —**dramatization** /ˌdræmət̬əˈzeɪʃən/ *n.* [C,U]

drank /dræŋk/ *v.* the past tense of DRINK

drape /dreɪp/ *v.* [T] to put cloth, clothing, etc. loosely over or around something: *Mina's scarf was* ***draped over*** *her shoulders.*

drap·er·y /ˈdreɪpəri/ *n.* plural **draperies** [C,U] cloth or clothing that is arranged in folds over something

drapes /dreɪps/ *n.* [plural] heavy curtains

dras·tic /ˈdræstɪk/ *adj.* extreme and sudden: *Don't make any* ***drastic changes*** *just yet.* —**drastically** *adv.*

D

draw[1] /drɔ/ *v.* past tense **drew** /dru/ past participle **drawn** /drɔn/

1 PICTURE [I,T] to make a picture of something with a pencil or a pen: *Could you draw me a map?* | *He drew an elephant on the paper.* | *She was* ***drawing*** *a* ***picture of*** *a tree.*

THESAURUS

sketch – to draw something quickly and without a lot of detail: *He sketched a rough street plan of Moscow.*
doodle – to draw shapes or patterns without really thinking about what you are doing: *He was doodling on a sheet of paper.*
scribble – to draw or write something quickly in a messy way: *She scribbled her name and phone number on the back of the card.*
trace – to copy a picture by putting a piece of thin paper over it and drawing the lines that you can see through the paper: *The kids were tracing designs on the paper.*

2 draw (sb's) attention to sth to make someone notice something: *I'd like to draw your attention to the six exit doors in the plane.*
3 draw a conclusion to decide that something is true based on facts that you have: *Other people might easily draw a different conclusion.*
4 draw a distinction/comparison etc. to make someone understand that two things are different from or similar to each other: *It's important to* ***draw a distinction between*** *business and non-business expenses.*
5 PULL SB/STH [T] to move someone or something by pulling him, her, or it gently: *Grant* ***drew*** *me* ***aside*** *to tell me the news.*
6 MOVE [I] to move in a particular direction: *She drew away, but he pulled her close again.* | *A police car drew up behind me.*
7 ATTRACT/INTEREST [T] to attract or interest someone: *The movie* ***drew*** *large* ***crowds*** *on the first day.* | *What first* ***drew*** *you* ***to*** *him?*
8 GET A REACTION [T] to get a particular kind of reaction from someone: *His remarks drew an angry response from Democrats.* | *Her idea* ***drew praise/criticism*** *from the others.*
9 PLAYING CARD/TICKET [I,T] to choose a car, ticket, etc. by chance: *The winning lottery numbers will be drawn on Saturday.*
10 draw the line (at sth) to refuse to do something because you do not approve of it, although you are willing to do other things: *I don't mind helping you, but I draw the line at telling lies.*
11 draw a blank *informal* to be unable to think or remember something: *I drew a blank when I tried to remember the number.*
12 draw a gun/knife/sword etc. to take a weapon from its container or from your pocket: *He had drawn a knife and was pointing it at me.*
13 draw the curtains to open or close the curtains
14 draw to a close/an end *formal* to gradually stop or finish: *Our vacation in Europe was drawing to a close.*
15 draw comfort/strength etc. (from sth) [T] to get something such as comfort or strength from someone or something: *I drew a lot of comfort from her kind words.*
16 draw blood **a)** to take blood from someone at a hospital **b)** to make someone bleed: *The dog bit her so hard that it drew blood.*
17 draw near/close *literary* to move closer in time or space: *Summer vacation is drawing near.*
18 PULL A VEHICLE [T] to pull a vehicle using an animal: *a carriage drawn by six horses*

draw back *phr. v.* to move back from something: *The crowd drew back to let the police by.*

draw sb ⇔ **into** sth *phr. v.* to make someone become involved in something when s/he does not want to be: *Keith refused to be drawn into our argument.*

draw on sth *phr. v.* to use your money, experiences, etc. to help you do something: *A good writer draws on his or her own experience.*

draw sb/sth ⇔ **out** *phr. v.* **1** to make someone feel less nervous and more willing to talk: *She just needed someone to draw her out and take an interest in her.* **2** to make an event last longer than usual

draw sth ⇔ **up** *phr. v.* to prepare a written document: *We drew up some guidelines for the new committee.*

draw[2] *n.* [C] **1** an occasion when someone or something is chosen by chance, especially the winning ticket in a LOTTERY **2** something or someone that a lot of people are willing to pay to see: *The Lakers are always a* ***big draw***. **3** a game that ends with both teams or players having the same number of points [= **tie**]

draw·back /ˈdrɔbæk/ *n.* [C] something that might be a problem or disadvantage: *The main drawback to the job is that the hours wouldn't be regular.*

draw·bridge /ˈdrɔbrɪdʒ/ *n.* [C] a bridge that can be pulled up to let ships go under it

drawer /drɔr/ *n.* [C] a part of a piece of furniture that slides in and out and is used for keeping things in: *The pens are in the **bottom/top drawer** of my desk.* | *Put it in the **desk drawer**.* ➔ see picture on page A11

draw·ing /ˈdrɔ-ɪŋ/ *n.* **1** [C] a picture you make with a pen or pencil: *She showed us a **drawing of** the house.*

THESAURUS

picture – a drawing, painting, or photograph: *On the refrigerator were pictures the kids had drawn.*
sketch – a drawing that you do quickly and without a lot of details: *Andrew did a quick sketch of the harbor.*
comic strip – a series of pictures that are drawn inside boxes and tell a story: *The Doonesbury comic strip comments on political and social events.*
cartoon – a funny drawing in a newspaper, usually about someone or something that is in the news: *An editorial cartoon showed him as a baby throwing a tantrum.*

2 [U] the art or skill of making pictures with a pen or pencil: *I've never been good at drawing.*

THESAURUS

painting, photography, sculpture, pottery, ceramics
➔ see Thesaurus box at ART

ˈdrawing board *n.* **back to the drawing board** to start working on a new plan or idea after an idea you have tried has failed: *They rejected our proposal, so it's back to the drawing board.*

drawl /drɔl/ *n.* [singular] a way of speaking in which vowels are longer than usual: *a Southern drawl* —**drawl** *v.* [I,T]

drawn[1] /drɔn/ *v.* the past participle of DRAW

drawn[2] *adj.* someone who is drawn has a thin pale face because s/he is sick, tired, or worried

ˌdrawn-ˈout *adj.* seeming to continue for a very long time: *a **long drawn-out** process*

draw·string /ˈdrɔstrɪŋ/ *n.* [C] a string through the top of a bag, piece of clothing, etc. that you can pull tight or make loose

dread[1] /drɛd/ *v.* [T] to feel very worried about something that is going to happen or may happen: *I've got an interview tomorrow and I'm dreading it.*

dread[2] *n.* [singular, U] a strong fear of something that is going to happen or may happen: *The thought filled me **with dread**.*

dread·ful /ˈdrɛdfəl/ *adj.* very bad: *a dreadful movie* —**dreadfully** *adv.*

THESAURUS

horrible, awful, terrible, awful
➔ see Thesaurus box at HORRIBLE

dread·locks /ˈdrɛdlɑks/ *n.* [plural] a way of arranging your hair in which it hangs in lots of thick pieces that look like rope

dream[1] /drim/ *n.* [C] **1** a series of thoughts, images, and experiences that come into your mind when you are asleep: *I **had a** funny **dream** last night.* | *a **bad dream*** (=a frightening or unpleasant dream) **2** something that you hope will happen: *Her dream was to become an opera singer.* **3 beyond your wildest dreams** better than anything you imagined or hoped for **4 a dream come true** something that you have wanted to happen for a long time: *Owning this boat is a dream come true.*

dream[2] *v.* past tense and past participle **dreamed** or **dreamt** /drɛmt/ **1** [I,T] to have a dream while you are asleep: *I often **dream that** I'm falling.* **2** [I,T] to think about something that you would like to happen: *She **dreamed of** becoming a pilot.* | *He **never dreamed that** he would make it to the finals* (=never thought that it would happen). | *I've been **dreaming about** this moment all my life.* **3 sb wouldn't dream of (doing) sth** *spoken* used in order to say that you would never do something: *I wouldn't dream of letting you walk home alone.* **4 dream on** *spoken* said when you think that what someone is hoping for will not happen: *You really believe we'll win? Dream on!*

dream sth ⇔ **up** *phr. v.* to think of a plan or idea, especially an unusual one: *Who dreams up these TV commercials?*

dream[3] *adj.* **dream car/house/team etc.** the best car, house, etc. that you can imagine: *A Porsche is my dream car.*

dream·er /ˈdrimə/ *n.* [C] someone who has plans that are not practical

dream·y /ˈdrimi/ *adj.* **1** looking like you are thinking about something pleasant rather than what is happening around you: *a dreamy smile* **2** someone who is dreamy has a good imagination but is not very practical **3** pleasant, peaceful, and relaxing: *dreamy music* —**dreamily** *adv.*

drear·y /ˈdrɪri/ *adj.* dull and uninteresting: *a wet and dreary afternoon* —**drearily** *adv.* —**dreariness** *n.* [U]

dredge /drɛdʒ/ *v.* [I,T] to remove mud or sand from the bottom of a river, or to search the bottom of a river or lake for something

dredge sth ⇔ **up** *phr. v. informal* to start talking about something bad or unpleasant that happened a long time ago: *Why do the papers have to dredge up that old story?*

dregs /drɛgz/ *n.* [plural] small solid pieces in a liquid such as wine or coffee that sink to the bottom of the cup, bottle, etc.

drench /drɛntʃ/ *v.* [T] to make something completely wet: *I forgot my umbrella and got drenched.*

dress[1] /drɛs/ *v.* **1** [I,T] to put clothes on someone or yourself: *Can you dress the kids while I make breakfast?* | *Hurry up and **get dressed**!* **2 be dressed** to be wearing clothes: *Are you dressed* *yet?* | *She* ***was dressed in*** *a simple black dress.* | *a* ***well-dressed*** *gentleman* **3** [I] to wear a particular type of clothes: *Dress warmly – it's cold out.* | *You can* ***dress casually*** *at our office.* **4 dress a wound/cut etc.** to clean and cover a wound in order to protect it

dress down *phr. v.* to wear clothes that are less formal than the ones you usually wear

dress up *phr. v.* **1** to wear clothes that are more formal than the ones you usually wear: *It's only a small party. You don't need to dress up.* **2** to wear special clothes for fun: *She* ***dressed up as*** *a witch for Halloween.*

dress² *n.* **1** [C] a piece of clothing worn by a woman or girl that covers the top of her body and some or all of her legs: *a summer dress* | *She was* ***wearing*** *a red* ***dress.*** ➔ see picture at CLOTHES **2** [U] clothes for men or women of a particular type or for a particular occasion: ***casual dress*** *in the workplace* | *He was wearing* ***evening dress*** (=formal clothes worn at important social events). **3 dress shirt/dress shoes** a shirt or shoes that you wear with formal clothes such as a SUIT

ˈdress code *n.* [C] a standard of what you should wear for a particular situation

dress·er /ˈdrɛsɚ/ *n.* [C] a piece of furniture with drawers for storing clothes, sometimes with a mirror on top

dress·ing /ˈdrɛsɪŋ/ *n.* **1** [C,U] a mixture of oil and other things that you pour over SALAD: *salad dressing* **2** [C,U] ➔ STUFFING **3** [C] a special piece of material used for covering and protecting a wound: *a clean dressing for the cut*

ˈdressing room *n.* [C] **1** a room or area in a store where you can try on clothes **2** a room where an actor, performer, etc. gets ready before going on stage, appearing on television, etc.

ˈdress reˌhearsal *n.* [C] the last time actors practice a play, using all the clothes, objects, etc. that will be used in the real performance

dress·y /ˈdrɛsi/ *adj.* dressy clothes are appropriate for formal occasions

drew /dru/ *v.* the past tense of DRAW

drib·ble /ˈdrɪbəl/ *v.* **1** [I,T] to flow slowly in irregular drops, or to make a liquid flow in this way: *Blood was* ***dribbling from*** *his cut lip.* **2** [T] to move forward with a ball by bouncing (BOUNCE) or kicking it again and again —**dribble** *n.* [C]

dribs and drabs /ˌdrɪbz ən ˈdræbz/ *n.* **in dribs and drabs** in small amounts: *People arrived in dribs and drabs.*

dried¹ /draɪd/ *v.* the past tense and past participle of DRY

dried² *adj.* dried food or flowers have had all the water removed from them

drift¹ /drɪft/ *v.* [I] **1** to move very slowly on water or in the air: *Gray clouds were drifting over from the north.* **2** to move or go somewhere without any plan or purpose: *Julie drifted towards the window.* | *Her thoughts drifted away.* **3** to gradually change from being in one condition, situation, etc. into another: *During the ambulance ride he drifted in and out of consciousness.* **4** snow or sand that drifts is blown into a large pile by the wind

drift apart *phr. v.* if people drift apart, they gradually stop having a relationship: *Over the years my college friends and I have drifted apart.*

drift off *phr. v.* to gradually fall asleep: *After a while I* ***drifted off to sleep.***

drift² *n.* [C] **1** a large pile of snow, sand, etc. that has been blown by the wind: *snow drifts* **2 catch/get sb's drift** to understand the general meaning of what someone says: *I don't speak much Spanish, but I got her drift.* **3** a gradual change or development in a situation, people's opinion, etc.: *a long downward drift in the birth rate* **4** a very slow movement: *continental drift*

drift·er /ˈdrɪftɚ/ *n.* [C] someone who is always moving to a different place or doing different jobs

drift·wood /ˈdrɪftwʊd/ *n.* [U] wood floating in the ocean or left on the shore

drill

drill¹ /drɪl/ *n.* **1** [C] a tool or machine used for making holes in something hard: *an electric drill* | *a dentist's drill* **2** [C,U] a method of teaching something by making people repeat the same lesson, exercise, etc. many times: *a spelling drill* **3 fire/emergency etc. drill** an occasion when you practice what you should do during a dangerous situation

drill² *v.* **1** [I,T] to make a hole with a drill: *Drill a hole for the screw in each corner.* | ***drilling for*** *oil*

THESAURUS

pierce, **make a hole in**, **prick**, **punch**, **bore**
➔ see Thesaurus box at PIERCE

2 [T] to teach people something by making them repeat the same exercise, lesson, etc. many times

THESAURUS

practice, **rehearse**, **work on**, **train**
➔ see Thesaurus box at PRACTICE²

drill sth **into** sb *phr. v.* to tell something to someone many times, until s/he knows it very well: *Mom drilled it into us that we shouldn't talk to strangers.*

dri·ly /ˈdraɪli/ *adv.* another spelling of DRYLY

drink¹ /drɪŋk/ *n.* **1** [C,U] liquid that you can drink, or an amount of liquid that you drink: *Here,* ***have a drink*** *of water.* | *a* ***drink of*** *coffee* | *soft drinks* | *food and drink* **2** [C] an alcoholic drink: *How about a drink later?*

drink² *v.* past tense **drank** /dræŋk/ past participle

drunk /drʌŋk/ **1** [I,T] to pour a liquid into your mouth and swallow it: *Let me get you **something to drink**. | Charlie drinks way too much coffee.*

THESAURUS

sip/take a sip – to drink something very slowly
slurp informal – to drink something in a noisy way
gulp sth down also **down sth** informal – to drink all of something very quickly: *I downed my beer and left.*
knock sth back informal – to drink all of an alcoholic drink very quickly
swig informal also **take/have a swig** informal – to drink something quickly by taking large amounts into your mouth, especially from a bottle: *He ate a few peanuts and took a swig of his beer.*
→ EAT

2 [I] to drink alcohol, especially too much or too often: *I **don't drink**. | His father began **drinking heavily*** (=a lot).
drink sth ⇔ **in** *phr. v.* to listen, look at, feel, or smell something in order to enjoy it: *We spent the day drinking in the sights and sounds of Paris.*
drink to sth *phr. v.* to wish someone success, good health, etc. before having an alcoholic drink: *Let's all drink to their happiness!*
drink (sth ⇔) **up** *phr. v.* to drink all of something: *Drink up your milk. | Come on, drink up!*

drink·er /ˈdrɪŋkɚ/ *n.* [C] someone who often drinks alcohol: *Greg's a **heavy drinker*** (=he drinks a lot).

ˈdrinking ˌfountain *n.* [C] a piece of equipment in a public place that produces a stream of water for you to drink from

ˈdrinking ˌproblem *n.* [singular] someone who has a drinking problem drinks too much alcohol

drip[1] /drɪp/ *v.* past tense and past participle **dripped**, present participle **dripping** **1** [I,T] to produce small drops of liquid: *The faucet sounds like it's dripping. | His finger was dripping blood. | They were both **dripping with sweat**.*

THESAURUS

pour, **flow**, **leak**, **ooze**, **gush**, **spurt**, **run**, **come out**
→ see Thesaurus box at POUR

2 [I] to fall in drops: *Rain dripped off the trees.*

drip[2] *n.* **1** [C] one of the small drops of liquid that falls from something **2** [singular, U] the action or sound of a liquid falling in small drops: *the drip of rain from the roof* **3** [C] *informal* someone who is boring and annoying

drive[1] /draɪv/ *v.* past tense **drove** /droʊv/ past participle **driven** /ˈdrɪvən/ present participle **driving** **1** [I,T] to make a car, bus, etc. move and control where it goes: *teenagers learning to drive | He drives a red Porsche.*

TOPIC

When you get into a car, you **buckle/fasten your seatbelt**, then put the key in the **ignition** and turn it to **start the engine**.
You **release** the **parking/emergency brake**, and put the car in **drive**. You **check your mirrors** (=look into them) before driving onto the street. You press the **gas pedal** with your foot to make the car **accelerate** (=go faster).
When you turn right or left, you must **indicate/put on your turn signals**. When you want to slow down, you press the **brake (pedal)** with your foot.
When you **park** your car, you put the car **in park** and **set/put on the parking brake**.

2 [I,T] to travel in a car or take someone somewhere by car: *We're **driving up/down** to Washington this weekend. | Would you mind **driving** me **to** the airport? | After the party, he **drove** her **home**.* → see Thesaurus box at TRAVEL[1] **3** [I,T] to make people, animals, or an activity move somewhere: *We were driven indoors by the rain. | Large grocery chains **drove out** the small family-owned stores.* **4** [T] to strongly influence someone to do something: *What drove him to suicide?* **5 drive sb crazy/nuts/insane etc. also drive sb up the wall** to make someone feel very annoyed and angry: *The kids are driving me crazy!* **6** [T] to hit something very hard: *Barry drove the ball into left field.* **7** [T] to provide the power for a vehicle or machine: *the motor that drives the propeller*
drive sb ⇔ **away** *phr. v.* to behave in a way that makes someone want to leave you: *If you keep on drinking, I guarantee you'll drive her away.*
drive sth ⇔ **down** *phr. v.* to make prices, costs, etc. fall quickly
drive off *phr. v.* **1** if a driver or a car drives off, he, she, or it leaves **2 drive** sb ⇔ **off** to force someone or something to go away from you: *Police used tear gas to drive off the rioters.*
drive sth ⇔ **up** *phr. v.* to make prices, costs, etc. increase

drive[2] *n.* **1** [C] a trip in a car: *Let's **go for a drive**. | It's a twenty-minute drive from the city.* **2** [C] a strong natural need or desire: *the male **sex drive*** **3** [C] a planned effort by an organization to achieve a particular result: *the senator's reelection drive | a drive to raise money for starving children* **4** [C] a piece of equipment in a computer that is used to get information from a DISK or to store information on it: *the C drive* **5** [C] an act of hitting a ball hard: *a line drive to right field* **6** [U] a determination to succeed: *He has considerable drive.* **7** [C] the power from an engine that makes the wheels of a car, bus, etc. turn: *a four-wheel drive pickup*

ˈdrive-by *adj.* **drive-by shooting/killing** the act of shooting someone from a moving car

ˈdrive-in[1] *n.* [C] a place where you can watch movies outdoors while sitting in your car

'drive-in² *adj.* **drive-in restaurant/movie** a restaurant, theater, etc. where you stay in your car to eat, watch the movie, etc.

driv·el /'drɪvəl/ *n.* [U] something written or said that is silly or does not mean anything

driv·en /'drɪvən/ the past participle of DRIVE

driv·er /'draɪvɚ/ *n.* [C] **1** someone who drives: *a **truck/cab/bus driver** | Joyce is a **good/bad driver**.* **2** *technical* a piece of software that makes a computer work with another piece of equipment such as a PRINTER or a MOUSE

'driver's ˌlicense *n.* [C] an official card with your name, picture, etc. on it that says you are legally allowed to drive

'drive-through *adj.* a drive-through restaurant, bank, etc. can be used without getting out of your car

D

drive·way /'draɪvweɪ/ *n.* [C] the road or area for cars between a house and the street: *Park your car **in the driveway**.*

driz·zle¹ /'drɪzəl/ *n.* [singular, U] weather that is a combination of mist and light rain

THESAURUS

rain, **shower**, **downpour**, **storm**, **hail**, **hailstones**, **sleet**
→ see Thesaurus box at RAIN[1]

drizzle² *v.* **1 it drizzles** if it drizzles, mist and light rain come out of the sky: *It started to drizzle.* **2** [T] to pour a liquid over food in small drops or a thin stream

droll /droʊl/ *adj. old-fashioned* unusual and slightly funny

drone¹ /droʊn/ *v.* [I] to make a continuous low noise: *An airplane droned overhead.*

drone² *n.* **1** [singular] a low continuous noise: *the drone of the lawnmower* **2** [C] an aircraft that does not have a pilot, but is operated by radio

drool /drul/ *v.* [I] **1** to have SALIVA (=the liquid in your mouth) flow from your mouth: *The dog began to drool.* **2** to show in a silly way that you like or want someone or something a lot: *The thought of all that money made us drool.* —**drool** *n.* [U]

droop /drup/ *v.* [I] to hang or bend down: *Her shoulders drooped with tiredness.*

drop¹ /drɑp/ *v.* past tense and past participle **dropped**, present participle **dropping**

1 LET GO [T] to stop holding or carrying something, so that it falls: *One of the waiters tripped and dropped a tray full of food. | With this technology, planes are able to drop bombs accurately.* → see picture on page A9

2 FALL [I] to fall: *The bottle rolled off the table and **dropped onto** the floor. | He **dropped into** his chair with a sigh.*

3 TAKE IN A CAR [T] **also drop off** to take someone or something to a place in a car, when you are going on to somewhere else: *I'll drop you at the corner, okay? | She drops the kids off at school on her way to work.*

4 DECREASE [I,T] to decrease to a lower level or amount, or to make something decrease: *Crime on the buses has dropped 25%. | The store has dropped its prices.*

THESAURUS

decrease, **go down**, **fall**, **plummet**, **diminish**, **decline**
→ see Thesaurus box at DECREASE[1]

5 STOP DOING STH [T] to stop doing something or stop planning to do something: *The charges against him have been dropped. | He expects me to just **drop everything*** (=stop everything I am doing) *and go with him. | I wasn't doing very well, so I dropped French* (=stopped studying French). | ***Drop it*** (=stop talking about it), *Ted, it's just a rumor.*

6 STOP INCLUDING [T] to decide not to include someone or something: *Morris has been **dropped from** the team.*

7 STOP A RELATIONSHIP [T] to stop having a relationship with someone, especially suddenly: *She found out he was seeing someone else, so she dropped him.*

8 drop dead a) to die suddenly **b)** *spoken* used when you are very angry with someone

9 drop the ball to stop doing something, when people expected you to continue doing it

10 work/run etc. until you drop *informal* to do something until you are extremely tired

11 drop sb a line *informal* to write to someone: *Drop us a line sometime.*

drop by also drop in *phr. v.* to visit someone when you have not arranged to come at a particular time: *Doris and Ed dropped by on Saturday.*

drop off *phr. v.* **1** to begin to sleep: *The baby dropped off to sleep in the car.* **2** to become less in level or amount: *The demand for leaded fuel dropped off in the late 1970s.*

drop out *phr. v.* to stop going to school or stop an activity before you have finished it: *teenagers **dropping out of** high school | The injury forced him to **drop out of** the race.*

drop² *n.* **1** [C] a very small amount of liquid that falls in a round shape: *big **drops of** rain | a tear drop* **2** [C] a small amount of a liquid: *Add a couple **drops of** lemon juice.* **3** [singular] a distance from something down to the ground: *It's a twenty-five foot drop from this cliff.* **4** [singular] a decrease in the amount, level, or number of something: *a **steep/sharp drop**, from 72% to 34% | a **drop in** temperature* **5 eye/ear/nose drops** medicine that you put in your eye, etc. one drop at a time **6 a drop in the bucket** an amount of something that is too small to have any effect **7 at the drop of a hat** immediately: *He could fall asleep at the drop of a hat.*

drop·let /ˈdrɑplɪt/ *n.* [C] a very small drop of liquid

drop·out /ˈdrɑp-aʊt/ *n.* [C] someone who leaves school or college without finishing it

drop·per /ˈdrɑpɚ/ *n.* [C] a short glass tube with a hollow rubber part at one end, used for measuring liquid in drops

drop·pings /ˈdrɑpɪŋz/ *n.* [plural] solid waste from animals or birds

drought /draʊt/ *n.* [C] a long period of dry weather when there is not enough water: *a **severe drought***

drove¹ /droʊv/ the past tense of DRIVE

drove² *n.* [C] a large group of animals or people that move or are moved together: *Tourists **come in droves** to see the White House.*

drown /draʊn/ *v.* **1** [I,T] to die from being underwater too long, or to kill someone in this way: *Many people drowned when the boat overturned.* | *Five people **drowned in** the flood.* | *She **drowned herself** in the river.* **2** [T] **also drown out** if a loud noise drowns out another sound, it prevents it from being heard: *The president's words were drowned out by cheers.* **3** [T] to completely cover something with liquid: *Dad always **drowns** his pancakes **in/with** maple syrup.* **4 drown your sorrows** to drink a lot of alcohol in order to forget your problems

drown·ing /ˈdraʊnɪŋ/ *n.* [C,U] death caused by staying underwater too long

drows·y /ˈdraʊzi/ *adj.* tired and almost asleep [**= sleepy**]: *The medicine can make you drowsy.* —**drowsiness** *n.* [U]

drudge /drʌdʒ/ *n.* [C] someone who does difficult boring work —**drudge** *v.* [I]

drudg·er·y /ˈdrʌdʒəri/ *n.* [U] difficult boring work

drug¹ /drʌg/ *n.* [C] **1** an illegal substance that people smoke, INJECT etc. for pleasure: *Bill was accused of **taking/using drugs**.* | *Her parents are afraid she's **on drugs**.* | *Dave's been **doing drugs*** (=using drugs regularly) *since he was thirteen.* | *the problem of **drug abuse*** (=the use of illegal drugs) | ***drug dealing*** (=selling illegal drugs) *in the neighborhood* | *He was sent to prison for selling **hard drugs*** (=dangerous illegal drugs such as HEROIN and COCAINE). **2** a medicine or a substance for making medicines: *a **drug** used **for** depression* ➔ see Thesaurus box at MEDICINE

drug² *v.* past tense and past participle **drugged**, present participle **drugging** [T] to give a person or animal a drug, especially to make him/her feel tired or go to sleep or to get rid of pain: *Several women reported being drugged and raped.*

drug·store /ˈdrʌgstɔr/ *n.* [C] a store where you can buy medicines, beauty products, etc. [**= pharmacy**]

THESAURUS

store, bookstore, clothes store, record store, grocery store, supermarket, bakery, delicatessen, deli, liquor store, hardware store, nursery, garden center, newsstand, boutique, convenience store, department store, chain store, superstore, outlet store, warehouse store

➔ see Thesaurus box at STORE¹

drum¹ /drʌm/ *n.* [C] **1** a musical instrument made of skin stretched over a circular frame, which you play by hitting it with your hand or a stick: *a bass drum* | *Johnny **plays the drums** in a band.* ➔ see picture on page A6 **2** something that looks like a drum, especially part of a machine **3** a large round container for storing liquids such as oil, chemicals, etc.

drum² *v.* past tense and past participle **drummed**, present participle **drumming** **1** [I,T] to hit the surface of something again and again in a way that sounds like drums: *He **drummed** his **fingers** on the table.* | *rain drumming on the roof* **2** [I] to play a drum

drum sth **into** sb *phr. v.* to say something to someone so often that s/he cannot forget it: *Safety rules are drummed into the workers.*

drum sth ⇔ **up** *phr. v.* to obtain help, money, etc. by asking a lot of people: *The group drummed up corporate sponsors for the event.*

drum·mer /ˈdrʌmɚ/ *n.* [C] someone who plays the drums

drum·stick /ˈdrʌmˌstɪk/ *n.* [C] **1** the leg of a chicken, TURKEY etc. cooked as food **2** a stick that you use to hit a drum

drunk¹ /drʌŋk/ *adj.* unable to control your behavior, speech, etc. because you have drunk too much alcohol: *college students **getting drunk** at parties* | *He was too drunk to drive.*

drunk² the past participle of DRINK

drunk³ also drunk·ard /ˈdrʌŋkɚd/ *n.* [C] *disapproving* someone who is drunk or often gets drunk

ˌdrunk ˈdriving *n.* [U] the illegal act of driving a car after having drunk too much alcohol

drunk·en /ˈdrʌŋkən/ *adj.* **1** drunk: *a drunken crowd* **2** resulting from or related to drinking too much alcohol: *drunken shouting* —**drunkenness** *n.* [U] —**drunkenly** *adv.*

dry¹ /draɪ/ *adj.* **1** having no water or other liquid inside or on the surface [**≠ wet**]: *I changed into dry clothes.* | *Store in a cool, dry place.* | *Is the paint dry yet?* **2** dry weather does not have much rain or MOISTURE [**≠ wet**]: *The weather was hot and dry.* | *the beginning of the **dry season*** **3** if your mouth, throat, or skin is dry, it does not have enough of the natural liquid that is usually in it: *My skin has been so dry lately.* | *Ted's mouth was dry and his heart pounded.* **4 dry wine/champagne etc.** wine, etc. that is not sweet: *a glass of dry white wine* **5** someone with a dry WIT or humor, or who says things in a dry voice, says

D

funny things in a serious way **6** boring and very serious: *a dry subject*

dry² *v.* past tense and past participle **dried**, third person singular **dries** [I,T] to become dry, or to make something dry: *It'll only take me a few minutes to dry my hair.* | *Mae hung the washing out to dry.* ➔ DRIED²

dry (sth ⇔) **off** *phr. v.* to become dry, or to make the surface of something dry: *We swam, then dried off in the sun.* | *She began to dry herself off.*

dry (sth ⇔) **out** *phr. v.* to dry completely, or to dry something completely: *Keep the dough covered so that it doesn't dry out.*

dry up *phr. v.* **1 dry** (sth ⇔) **up** a river, lake, or area of land that dries up has no more water in it: *Water holes and wells have dried up across the state.* **2** if a supply of something dries up, there is no more of it: *Companies get rid of employees when the work dries up.*

D

ˈdry clean *v.* [T] to clean clothes with chemicals instead of water

ˌdry ˈcleaners *n.* [C] a place where you take clothes to be dry cleaned

dry·er /ˈdraɪɚ/ *n.* [C] a machine that dries things, especially clothes or hair

ˌdry ˈice *n.* [U] CARBON DIOXIDE in a solid state, often used for keeping food and other things cold

dry·ly /ˈdraɪli/ *adv.* speaking in a serious way, although you are actually joking

ˌdry ˈrun *n.* [C] an occasion when you practice for an important event

ˌdry ˈwall *n.* [U] a type of board made of two large sheets of CARDBOARD with PLASTER between them, used to cover walls and ceilings —**ˈdry-wall** *v.* [I,T]

du·al /ˈduəl/ *adj.* having two of something, or two parts: *My wife has **dual nationality/citizenship** – American and Brazilian.*

dub /dʌb/ *v.* past tense and past participle **dubbed**, present participle **dubbing** [T] **1** to give someone or something a name that describes him, her, or it in some way: *The area was dubbed "Tornado Alley" because of its strong winds.* **2** to replace the original spoken language of a film, television show, etc. with a recording of a different language: *an Italian movie that's been **dubbed into** English*

du·bi·ous /ˈdubiəs/ *adj.* **1** not sure whether something is good, true, etc.: *Employees are **dubious about** the proposed changes.* **2** not seeming honest, safe, valuable, etc.: *an idea based on dubious research* | *The state has the **dubious distinction** of being in the worst financial situation.*

duch·ess /ˈdʌtʃɪs/ *n.* [C] a woman with the highest social rank below a PRINCESS, or the wife of a DUKE

duck¹ /dʌk/ *n.* **1** [C] a common water bird with short legs and a wide beak that is used for its meat, eggs, and soft feathers **2** [U] the meat from this bird: *roast duck*

duck² *v.* **1** [I,T] to lower your body or head very quickly, or move away very quickly, especially to avoid being hit or seen: *She **ducked** her **head** to get through the doorway.* | *Tom **ducked into** an alley.* **2** [T] *informal* to avoid something that is difficult or unpleasant: *His campaign speech ducked all the major issues.*

duck·ling /ˈdʌklɪŋ/ *n.* [C] a young duck

duct /dʌkt/ *n.* [C] **1** a pipe or tube in a building that liquid, air, electric CABLES, etc. go through **2** a thin narrow tube inside your body, a plant, etc. that liquid, air, etc. goes through: *a tear duct*

dud /dʌd/ *n.* [C] *informal* **1** something that does not work or is useless: *This battery's a dud.* **2 duds** [plural] *humorous* clothes —**dud** *adj.*

dude /dud/ *n.* [C] *slang* a man: *Hey, dudes, how's it going?*

ˈdude ranch *n.* [C] a vacation place where you can ride horses and live like a COWBOY

due¹ /du/ *adj.* **1 be due** to be expected to happen or arrive at a particular time: *The flight from Chicago is **due at** 7:48 p.m.* | *The baby is **due in** March.* | *What's the baby's **due date** (=the day it is expected to be born)?* | *My library books are **due back** tomorrow.* | *The book is **due out** in the spring.* | *The new museum is **due to** open next year.* | *I feel I'm **due for** a raise.* **2 due to** because of: *The program was canceled, due to lack of funds.* | *She was absent due to illness.* **3** needing to be paid: *The first installment of $250 is now due.* **4** deserved by someone or owed to someone: *He never got the recognition he was due.* | *Much of the credit **is due to** our backup team.* **5 in due course/time** at a more appropriate time in the future: *The committee will answer your complaints in due course.* **6 with (all) due respect** *spoken* used when you disagree with someone or criticize him/her in a polite way

due² *adv.* **due north/south/east/west** directly or exactly north, etc.

due³ *n.* **1 dues** [plural] the money that you pay to be a member of an organization: *union dues* **2 give sb his/her due** to admit that someone has good qualities, even though you are criticizing him/her: *To give him his due, he tries very hard.*

du·el /ˈduəl/ *n.* [C] **1** a situation in which two people or groups are involved in a competition or disagreement: *a duel for the 100-meter record* **2** a fight in past times between two people with guns or swords —**duel** *v.* [I]

due ˈprocess **also** **due ˌprocess of ˈlaw** *n.* [U] *law* the correct process that should be followed by law and that is designed to protect someone's legal rights

du·et /duˈɛt/ *n.* [C] a piece of music written for two performers

duf·fel bag /ˈdʌfəl ˌbæg/ *n.* [C] a cloth bag with a round bottom and a string around the top to tie it closed

dug /dʌg/ *v.* the past tense and past participle of DIG

dug·out /ˈdʌgaʊt/ *n.* [C] a low shelter at the side of a baseball field, where players and team officials sit

duh /dʌ/ *interjection spoken* used in order to say that what someone else has just said is stupid

duke /duk/ *n.* [C] a man with the highest social rank below a PRINCE

dull[1] /dʌl/ *adj.* **1** not interesting or exciting: *a dull book*

THESAURUS

boring, tedious, not (very/that/all that) interesting, monotonous

→ see Thesaurus box at BORING

2 a dull sound is not clear or loud: *I heard a dull thud from upstairs.* **3** a dull pain is not severe but does not stop: *a dull ache in my shoulder* **4** not bright or shiny: *dull brown walls* **5** not sharp [= **blunt**]: *a dull knife* → see picture at SHARP[1] —**dully** *adv.* —**dullness** *n.* [U]

dull[2] *v.* [T] to make something become less sharp, less clear, etc.: *a drug to dull the pain*

du·ly /ˈduli/ *adv. formal* at the correct time or in the correct way: *Your suggestion has been duly noted.*

dumb[1] /dʌm/ *adj.* **1** *informal* stupid: *a dumb movie* | *How could you be so dumb?* **2** *old-fashioned* unable to speak [= **mute**]

dumb[2] *v. informal*

dumb sth ⇔ **down** *phr. v.* to make something such as news or information less detailed and present it in an attractive way, so that more people can understand it very easily: *Textbooks have been dumbed down.*

dumb·bell /ˈdʌmbɛl/ *n.* [C] **1** two weights connected by a short piece of metal that you lift for exercise **2** *informal* someone who is stupid

dumb·found·ed /ˈdʌmˌfaʊndɪd/ *adj.* so surprised that you cannot speak

THESAURUS

surprised, amazed, shocked, astonished, astounded, flabbergasted, stunned, nonplussed

→ see Thesaurus box at SURPRISED

dum·my[1] /ˈdʌmi/ *n.* plural **dummies** [C] **1** *informal* someone who is stupid **2** a figure made to look like a person

dummy[2] *adj.* a dummy tool, weapon, etc. looks like a real one but does not work: *a dummy rifle*

dump[1] /dʌmp/ *v.* [T] **1** to drop or put something somewhere in a careless way, sometimes in order to get rid of it: *illegal chemicals **dumped in** the river* | *They **dumped** their bags **on** the floor and left.*

THESAURUS

shove, stick, thrust

→ see Thesaurus box at SHOVE

2 to suddenly end a relationship: *Tammy dumped her boyfriend.*

dump on *phr. v. informal* **1 dump on** sb to criticize someone or complain to someone: *reporters dumping on the White House* **2 dump** sth **on** sb to unfairly give someone an unwanted job, duty, or problem to deal with: *Don't just dump the extra work on me.*

dump[2] *n.* [C] **1** a place where unwanted waste is taken and left: *the town's **garbage dump*** | *a toxic waste dump* **2** a place where military supplies are stored, or the supplies themselves: *an ammunition dump* **3** *informal* a place that is unpleasant because it is dirty, ugly, or boring: *This place is such a dump.* **4 be down in the dumps** *informal* to feel very sad

Dump·ster /ˈdʌmpstɚ/ *n.* [C] *trademark* a large metal container used for holding waste

ˈdump truck *n.* [C] a vehicle with a large open container at the back that can pour sand, soil, etc. onto the ground

dump·y /ˈdʌmpi/ *adj. informal* short and fat: *a dumpy little man*

dunce /dʌns/ *n.* [C] *informal offensive* someone who is slow at learning things

dune /dun/ *n.* [C] a hill made of sand near the ocean or in the desert

dung /dʌŋ/ *n.* [U] solid waste from animals, especially large ones

dun·geon /ˈdʌndʒən/ *n.* [C] a prison under the ground, used in past times

dunk /dʌŋk/ *v.* [T] **1** to quickly put something that you are eating into coffee, milk, etc., and take it out again **2** to push someone underwater for a short time as a joke **3** to jump up toward the basket in a game of basketball and throw the ball down into it —**dunk** *n.* [C]

dun·no /dəˈnoʊ/ **I dunno** a short form of "I do not know", used in writing to show how people sound when they speak

du·o /ˈduoʊ/ *n.* [C] two people who do something together, especially play music or sing

dupe /dup/ *v.* [T] to trick or deceive someone: *People were **duped into** buying worthless insurance.* —**dupe** *n.* [C]

du·plex /ˈdupleks/ *n.* [C] a type of house that is divided so that it has two separate homes in it

> **THESAURUS**
>
> **house, ranch house/ranch, cottage, row house, mansion, bungalow, apartment, condominium, condo, townhouse, mobile home/trailer**
> → see Thesaurus box at HOUSE[1]

du·pli·cate[1] /ˈdupləkɪt/ *n.* [C] an exact copy of something that you can use in the same way: *a duplicate of the front door key* —**duplicate** *adj.*: *a duplicate key*

du·pli·cate[2] /ˈdupləˌkeɪt/ *v.* [T] **1** to copy something exactly: *Duplicate the letter, just changing the addresses.* **2** to have a situation in which something is done twice, in a way that is not necessary: *The company plans on closing a nearby hospital which duplicates the bigger hospital's services.* —**duplication** /ˌdupləˈkeɪʃən/ *n.* [U]

du·plic·i·ty /duˈplɪsət̬i/ *n.* [U] *formal* dishonest behavior that is intended to deceive someone

dur·a·ble /ˈdʊrəbəl/ *adj.* **1** staying in good condition for a long time: *durable materials* **2** *formal* continuing for a long time: *a durable peace* —**durability** /ˌdʊrəˈbɪlət̬i/ *n.* [U]

du·ra·tion /dʊˈreɪʃən/ *n.* [U] *formal* the length of time that something continues: *Food was rationed **for the duration of** the war.*

du·ress /dʊˈrɛs/ *n. formal* **under duress** as a result of using illegal or unfair threats: *Her confession was made under duress.*

dur·ing /ˈdʊrɪŋ/ *prep.* **1** all through a particular period of time: *These animals sleep during the day.*

> **USAGE**
>
> **During** is followed by a particular period of time and is used to say when something happens: *During the summer, she worked as a lifeguard.*
> **For** is followed by words describing a length of time and is used to say how long something continues: *She was in the hospital for two weeks.*

2 at some point in a period of time: *Henry died during the night.*

dusk /dʌsk/ *n.* [U] the time before it gets dark when the sky is becoming less bright

dust[1] /dʌst/ *n.* [U] dry powder that consists of extremely small pieces of dirt, sand, etc.: *The truck drove off in a **cloud of dust**. | The piano was covered **with/in dust**.*

dust[2] *v.* **1** [I,T] to clean the dust from something: *I just dusted the living room. | He got to his feet and **dusted himself off**.* → see Thesaurus box at CLEAN[2] **2** [T] to cover something with a fine powder: *Lightly dust the cakes with sugar.*

dust sth ⇔ **off** *phr. v.* to remove something such as dust or dirt from a surface, using a dry cloth or your hand

ˈdust ˌjacket *n.* [C] a paper cover that fits over the hard cover of a book

dust·pan /ˈdʌstpæn/ *n.* [C] a flat container with a handle that you use with a brush to remove dust and waste from the floor

dust·y /ˈdʌsti/ *adj.* covered or filled with dust: *a dusty room*

> **THESAURUS**
>
> **dirty, filthy, muddy, greasy**
> → see Thesaurus box at DIRTY[1]

Dutch[1] /dʌtʃ/ *adj.* **1** relating to or coming from the Netherlands **2** relating to the Dutch language

Dutch[2] *n.* **1** [U] the language used in the Netherlands **2 the Dutch** the people of the Netherlands

du·ti·ful /ˈdut̬ɪfəl/ *adj.* doing what you are expected to do and behaving in a loyal way: *a dutiful son* —**dutifully** *adv.*

du·ty /ˈdut̬i/ *n.* plural **duties** **1** [C,U] something that you have to do because it is morally or legally right: ***It is** our **duty to** speak out against injustice. | Parents **have a duty to** protect their children. | jury duty* **2** [C,U] something that you have to do because it is part of your job: *Soldiers are expected to **do their duty**. | Please **report for duty** tomorrow morning. | his duties at the airport* **3 be on/off duty** to be working or not working at a particular time: *Which nurse was on duty last night?* **4** [C] a tax you pay on something, especially on goods you bought in another country

ˌduty-ˈfree *adj.* duty-free goods can be brought into a country without paying tax on them —**duty-free** *adv.*

DVD *n.* [C] **digital versatile disc or digital video disc** a type of CD that can store large amounts of sound, VIDEO, and information

dwarf[1] /dwɔrf/ *n.* [C] **1** an imaginary creature that looks like a small man: *Snow White and the Seven Dwarfs* **2** a person, animal, or plant that does not grow to the normal height

dwarf[2] *v.* [T] to be so big that other things seem very small: *The church is dwarfed by the surrounding buildings.*

dweeb /dwib/ *n.* [C] *slang* a weak, slightly strange person who is not popular or fashionable

dwell /dwɛl/ *v.* past tense and past participle **dwelled** or **dwelt** /dwɛlt/ [I] *literary* to live in a particular place

dwell on/upon sth *phr. v.* to think or talk for too long about something, especially something unpleasant: *Quit dwelling on the past.*

dwell·er /ˈdwɛlɚ/ *n.* **city/town/cave dweller etc.** a person or animal that lives in a city, town, etc.

dwell·ing /ˈdwɛlɪŋ/ *n.* [C] *formal* a house, apartment, etc. where people live

dwelt /dwɛlt/ *v.* a past tense and past participle of DWELL

dwin·dle /ˈdwɪndl/ *v.* [I] to gradually become fewer or smaller: *Their ten-point lead has **dwindled** now **to** only four points.* —**dwindling** *adj.*

dye¹ /daɪ/ *n.* [C,U] a substance you use to change the color of your hair, clothes, etc.

dye² *v.* [T] to give something a different color using a DYE: *Brian dyed his hair green.*

ˌdyed-in-the-ˈwool *adj.* having strong beliefs or opinions that will never change: *a dyed-in-the-wool Republican*

dy·ing /ˈdaɪ-ɪŋ/ *v.* the present participle of DIE

dy·nam·ic /daɪˈnæmɪk/ *adj.* **1** interesting, exciting, and full of energy and determination to succeed: *a dynamic young man*

THESAURUS

energetic, **vigorous**, **tireless**
➔ see Thesaurus box at ENERGETIC

2 continuously moving or changing: *a dynamic process* **3** *technical* relating to a force or power that causes movement: *dynamic energy*

dy·nam·ics /daɪˈnæmɪks/ *n.* [U] **1** the way in which systems or people behave, react, and affect each other: *family dynamics* | *the **dynamics of** power in large businesses* **2** the science concerned with the movement of objects and with the forces related to movement

dy·na·mism /ˈdaɪnəˌmɪzəm/ *n.* [U] energy and determination to succeed

dy·na·mite¹ /ˈdaɪnəˌmaɪt/ *n.* [U] a powerful explosive

dynamite² *v.* [T] to damage or destroy something with dynamite

dy·na·mo /ˈdaɪnəˌmoʊ/ *n.* [C] **1** *informal* someone who has a lot of energy and is very excited about what s/he does **2** a machine that changes some other form of power into electricity

dy·nas·ty /ˈdaɪnəsti/ *n.* plural **dynasties** [C] a family of kings or other rulers who have ruled a country for a long time, or the period of time during which this family rules: *the Ming dynasty* —**dynastic** /daɪˈnæstɪk/ *adj.*

dys·en·ter·y /ˈdɪsənˌtɛri/ *n.* [U] a serious disease of the BOWELS that makes someone pass much more waste than usual

dys·func·tion·al /dɪsˈfʌŋkʃənəl/ *adj.* not working normally or not showing normal social behavior: *dysfunctional relationships within the family*

dys·lex·i·a /dɪsˈlɛksiə/ *n.* [U] a condition that makes it difficult for someone to read —**dyslexic** /dɪsˈlɛksɪk/ *adj.*

E, e

E¹, e /i/ *n.* [C,U] **1** the fifth letter of the English alphabet **2** the third note in the musical SCALE of C, or the musical KEY based on this note **3** *slang* the abbreviation of Ecstasy, an illegal drug

E² the written abbreviation of **east** or **eastern**

each¹ /itʃ/ *determiner, pron.* **1** every one of two or more things or people, considered separately: *Each student will be given a book.* | *We watched as **each of** the children performed a dance.*

USAGE

Each, **every**, and **all** are all used to talk about every person or thing in a group.
When you are considering them separately, use **each** or **every** with a singular noun: *Each/Every child at the party was given a balloon.*
When you are considering them together, use **all** with a plural noun: *All the children enjoyed the trip.*

2 each and every used in order to emphasize that you are talking about every person or thing in a group: *This will affect each and every one of us.*

each² *adv.* for or to every one: *The tickets are $5 each.* | *You can have two cookies each.*

each ˈother *pron.* used in order to show that each of two or more people does something to the other or others: *Susan and Robert kissed each other.* | *They played with each other all morning.* | *It's normal for people to ignore each other in an elevator.*

ea·ger /ˈigɚ/ *adj.* **1** having a strong desire to do something or a strong interest in something: *I've been **eager to** meet you.* | *a young woman **eager for** success* | *hundreds of eager fans* **2 eager to please** willing to do what people want —**eagerly** *adv.* —**eagerness** *n.* [U]

eagle

ea·gle /ˈigəl/ *n.* [C] a large wild bird, with a beak like a hook, that eats small animals, birds, etc.

ear /ɪr/ *n.* **1** [C] one of the two parts of your body that you hear with: *She got her ears pierced.* | *Mark whispered something in her ear.* ➔ see picture on page A3 **2** [U] the ability to hear, recognize, or copy sounds, especially in music

E

and languages: *Joel* ***has a good ear for*** *music.* **3** [C] the top part of plants that produce grain: *an ear of corn* **4 go in one ear and out the other** *informal* to be heard and then forgotten immediately **5 be all ears** *informal* to be very interested in listening to someone: *Go ahead, I'm all ears.* **6 be up to your ears in sth** *informal* to be very busy with something: *I'm up to my ears in work.* **7 smile/grin from ear to ear** to smile in a very happy way → **play it by ear** at PLAY[1] → **play sth by ear** at PLAY[1] → **wet behind the ears** at WET[1]

ear·drum /ˈɪrdrʌm/ *n.* [C] a tight thin MEMBRANE (=layer like skin) over the inside of your ear that allows you to hear sound

ear·lobe /ˈɪrloʊb/ *n.* [C] the soft piece of flesh at the bottom of your ear

ear·ly[1] /ˈɚli/ *adj.* **1** in the first part of a period of time, event, or process [≠ **late**]: *She woke in the early morning.* | *a man in his early twenties* | *Gershwin's early work* **2** before the usual or expected time [≠ **late**]: *The train was ten minutes early.* | *I was a few minutes* ***early for*** *my appointment.* **3** existing before other people, events, machines, etc. of the same kind [≠ **late**]: *early settlers in New England* **4 the early days** the time when something had just started to be done or to exist: *the early days of television* | *the early days of Bush's presidency* **5 at an early age** when someone is very young: *He was orphaned at an early age.* **6 at the earliest** used in order to say that a particular time is the soonest that something can happen: *He'll arrive on Monday at the earliest.* **7 the early hours** the time between MIDNIGHT and morning **8 early bird** someone who gets up early or arrives early

early[2] *adv.* **1** before the usual, arranged, or expected time [≠ **late**]: *Arrive early if you want a good seat.* **2** near the beginning of a period of time, an event, a process, etc. [≠ **late**]: *These flowers were planted early in the spring.* | *I'll have to leave early.* **3 early on** near the beginning of an event, relationship, process, etc.: *I realized* ***early on*** *that it wasn't going to work.*

ear·mark /ˈɪrmɑrk/ *v.* [T] to decide that something will be used for a particular purpose: *funds that are* ***earmarked for*** *high repairs*

ear·muffs /ˈɪrmʌfs/ *n.* [plural] two pieces of material attached to the ends of a band that you wear to keep your ears warm

earn /ɚn/ *v.* [T] **1** to get money for the work you do: *Alan earns $30,000 a year.* | *I'd like to* ***earn*** *some extra* ***money.*** | *She* ***earns a living*** (=gets the money for the things she needs) *as a teacher.*

> **THESAURUS**
>
> **make** – to earn or get money: *Debbie makes a little money by babysitting.*
> **get** – to receive money for doing work or selling something: *How much do you get an hour?*
> **be/get paid** – to be given money for doing a job: *I get paid monthly.*

2 to make a profit from business, or from putting money in a bank, lending it, etc.: *The movie earned $7 million during the opening weekend.* | *I* ***earned*** *$5,000* ***from*** *my investments last year.* **3** to get something that you deserve or have worked for: *Earhart had earned the respect of the male pilots.* | *He earned a degree in history at Columbia.*

ear·nest[1] /ˈɚnɪst/ *adj.* serious and sincere —**earnestly** *adv.* —**earnestness** *n.* [U]

earnest[2] *n.* **1 in earnest** happening more seriously or with greater effort than before: *Training begins in earnest on Monday.* **2 be in earnest** to be serious about what you are saying: *Are you sure he was in earnest?*

earn·ings /ˈɚnɪŋz/ *n.* [plural] **1** the money that you earn by working

> **THESAURUS**
>
> **pay, income, salary, wages**
> → see Thesaurus box at PAY[2]

2 the profit that a company makes

ear·phones /ˈɪrfoʊnz/ *n.* [plural] electrical equipment that you put over or into your ears to listen to a radio, CD player, etc.

ear·plug /ˈɪrplʌg/ *n.* [C usually plural] a small piece of rubber that you put into your ear to keep out noise or water

ear·ring /ˈɪrɪŋ/ *n.* [C usually plural] a piece of jewelry that you fasten to your ear → see picture at JEWELRY

ear·shot /ˈɪrʃɑt/ *n.* **within earshot/out of earshot** near enough or not near enough to hear what someone is saying

ˈear-ˌsplitting *adj.* very loud: *an ear-splitting scream*

> **THESAURUS**
>
> **loud, thunderous, deafening**
> → see Thesaurus box at LOUD[1]

earth /ɚθ/ *n.* **1 also Earth** the PLANET that we live on, which is third from the sun [➡ **world**]: ***The Earth*** *moves around the sun.* | *the return to Earth after landing on the moon* | *water below the earth's surface* | *the most beautiful woman* ***on earth***

> **THESAURUS**
>
> **earth** – the planet we live on: *The earth moves around the sun.*
> **world** – the planet we live on, considered as a place where there are people and countries, mountains and oceans, etc.: *It's one of the largest countries in the world.*
> You can use **earth** to mean "the world": *It's the highest mountain on earth.* | *It's the highest mountain in the world.*
> When you compare the earth's surface to the ocean, use **land**: *After weeks at sea, the sailors saw land.*

When you compare the earth's surface to the sky, use **earth**: *The space shuttle returned to earth safely.*

2 [U] the substance that plants, trees, etc. grow in [= **dirt, soil**]: *footprints in the wet earth* **3 what/why/how etc. on earth...?** *spoken* said when you are asking a question when you are very surprised or annoyed: *What on earth did you do to your hair?* ➔ DOWN-TO-EARTH

earth·ly /'ɚθli/ *adj.* **1** *literary* relating to life on Earth rather than in heaven: *all my earthly possessions* **2 no earthly reason/use/chance etc.** no reason, use, etc. at all

earth·quake /'ɚθkweɪk/ *n.* [C] a sudden shaking of the earth's surface that often causes a lot of damage

'earth-ˌshattering also **'earth-ˌshaking** *adj.* surprising or shocking and very important

earth·worm /'ɚθwɚm/ *n.* [C] a WORM

earth·y /'ɚθi/ *adj.* **1** talking about life, sex, and the human body in an honest and direct way: *an earthy sense of humor* **2** tasting, smelling, or looking like earth or soil: *mushrooms with an earthy flavor* —**earthiness** *n.* [U]

ease¹ /iz/ *n.* [U] **1 with ease** if you do something with ease, it is very easy for you to do it: *They won with ease.* **2 at ease a)** feeling comfortable and confident: *She tried to make the new students* ***feel at ease.*** | *She felt completely* ***at ease with*** *Barry.* | *You always look* ***ill at ease*** (=not relaxed) *in a suit.* | *Miguel's smile* ***put*** *her* ***at ease.*** **b)** *spoken* used in order to tell soldiers to stand in a relaxed way with their feet apart **3 ease of use/access/repair etc.** *written* the quality of being easy to use, etc.: *The computer's ease of use is an important selling point.* **4** the ability to feel or behave in a natural or relaxed way: *He had a natural ease which made him very popular.*

ease² *v.* **1** [I,T] to make something less severe or difficult, or to become less severe or difficult: *He was given drugs to ease the pain.* | *Tensions in the region have eased slightly.*

THESAURUS

reduce, relieve, lessen, alleviate
➔ see Thesaurus box at REDUCE

2 [T] to move something or someone slowly and carefully into another place: ***Ease*** *the patient* ***onto/out of*** *the bed.*

ease up *phr. v.* **1 also ease off** if something, especially something that annoys you, eases off or eases up, it becomes less or gets better: *The rain is starting to ease up.* **2** to work less hard or do something less often than before: *Stanford's defense seemed to be easing up.*

ea·sel /'izəl/ *n.* [C] a frame that you put a painting on while you paint it

eas·i·ly /'izəli/ *adv.* **1** without difficulty: *They won easily.* | *The instructions can be easily understood.* **2** without doubt [= **easily**]: *She is easily the most intelligent girl in the class.* **3** used in order to say that something is possible or very likely: *The first signs of the disease can easily be overlooked.*

east¹, **East** /ist/ *n.* [singular, U] **1** the direction from which the sun rises: *Which way is east?* ➔ see picture at NORTH¹ **2 the east** the eastern part of a country, state, etc.: *Rain will spread* ***to the east*** *later today.* | *the* ***east of*** *Texas* **3 the East a)** the countries in Asia, especially China, Japan, and Korea **b)** the countries in the eastern part of Europe, especially the ones that had Communist governments **c)** the part of the U.S. east of the Mississippi River, especially the states north of Washington, D.C.: *He went to college* ***back East*** (=in the East).

USAGE

Use **north/south etc. of sth** in order to describe where a place is in relation to another place: *Chicago is south of Milwaukee.*
Use **in the north/south etc. of sth** in order to say which part of a place you are talking about: *The mountains are in the west of the province.*
Use **northern**, **southern,** etc. with the name of a place: *They have a cabin in northern Ontario.* Don't say "in the north of Ontario."

east² *adj.* **1** in, to, or facing east: *12 miles* ***east of*** *Portland* | *the east coast of the island* **2 east wind** a wind coming from the east

east³ *adv.* toward the east: *Go east on I-80 to Omaha.* | *The window faces east.*

east·bound /'istbaʊnd/ *adj.* traveling or leading toward the east: *eastbound traffic* | *the eastbound lanes of the freeway*

ˌEast 'Coast *n.* **the East Coast** the part of the U.S. that is next to the Atlantic Ocean, especially the states north of Washington, D.C.

Eas·ter /'istɚ/ *n.* [C,U] **1** a holiday on a Sunday in March or April when Christians celebrate the death of Christ and his return to life: *Easter Sunday* **2** the period of time just before and after this day: *We went skiing in Vermont* ***at Easter.***

ˌEaster 'Bunny *n.* **the Easter Bunny** an imaginary rabbit that children believe brings colored eggs and chocolate at Easter

'Easter egg *n.* [C] an egg that has been colored and decorated

east·er·ly /'istɚli/ *adj.* **1** in or toward the east: *sailing in an easterly direction* **2** easterly winds come from the east

east·ern /'istɚn/ *adj.* **1** in or from the east part of an area, country, state, etc.: *eastern Oregon* **2 Eastern** in or from the countries in Asia, especially China, Japan, and Korea: *Eastern religions* **3** in or from the countries in the eastern part of Europe, especially the ones that used to have Communist governments ➔ see Usage box at EAST¹

E

east·ern·er, **Easterner** /ˈistɚnɚ/ *n.* [C] someone who comes from the eastern part of a country or the eastern HEMISPHERE

ˌEastern ˈEurope *n.* the eastern part of Europe, including places such as Poland and part of Russia —**Eastern European** *adj.*

east·ern·most /ˈistɚnˌmoʊst/ *adj.* farthest east: *the easternmost part of the island*

east·ward /ˈistwɚd/ *adj., adv.* toward the east

eas·y¹ /ˈizi/ *adj.* **1** not difficult: *Making brownies is easy.* | *I want a book that's* ***easy to*** *read.* | *There must be an easier way to do this.* | *The programs are* ***easy for*** *teachers to use in the classroom.* | *Having a computer will definitely* ***make things*** *a lot* ***easier****.*

THESAURUS

simple, **straightforward**
➔ see Thesaurus box at SIMPLE

2 comfortable and not feeling worried or anxious: *I have a pretty easy life.* **3 easy way out** a way of doing something that ends a difficult situation, but that is not the best way **4 I'm easy** *spoken* used in order to show that you do not mind what choice is made: *"Do you want to go to the movies or out to eat?" "Oh, I'm easy."* **5 easy money** *informal* money that you do not have to work hard to get **6** *informal disapproving* someone who is easy has a lot of sexual partners **7 eggs over easy** eggs cooked on a hot surface and turned over quickly before serving, so that the YOLKS (=yellow part) are not completely cooked

easy² *adv.* **1 take it easy a)** to relax and not do very much: *The doctor told him to take it easy when he got home.* **b)** *spoken* used in order to tell someone to become less upset or angry **2 go easy on/with sth** *informal* to not use too much of something: *Go easy on the salt; it's not good for you.* **3 go easy on sb** *informal* to be more gentle and less strict or angry with someone: *Go easy on Peter – he's having a hard time at school.* **4 rest/sleep easy** to be able to relax because you are not worried or anxious: *I won't rest easy until I know she's safe.* **5 easier said than done** *spoken* used when it would be difficult to actually do what someone has suggested: *I should just tell her to go away, but that's easier said than done.* **6 easy does it** *spoken* used in order to tell someone to be careful, especially when s/he is moving something

ˈeasy chair *n.* [C] a large comfortable chair

eas·y·go·ing /ˌiziˈgoʊɪŋ◂/ *adj.* not easily worried or annoyed: *Phil's pretty easygoing.*

ˌeasy ˈlistening *n.* [U] music that is relaxing to listen to

eat /it/ *v.* past tense **ate** /eɪt/ past participle **eaten** /ˈitˀn/ **1** [I,T] to put food in your mouth and swallow it: *Paula ate a sandwich.* | *Jimmy chatted happily as he ate.* | *Do you want* ***something to eat****?* | *Tom sat at the table,* ***eating breakfast/lunch/dinner****.* | *You need to exercise,* ***eat right*** (=eat healthy food), *and get plenty of rest.* | *I haven't had a* ***bite to eat*** (=some food) *all day!*

THESAURUS

If you eat something very quickly, you **devour** it, **gobble** it **up** informal, or **wolf** it **down** informal: *He devoured the rest of the cake.*
If you **nibble (on)** something, you take small bites and eat only a little bit of it: *Sarah nibbled on a cookie and sipped her coffee.*
If you **pick at** your food, you eat only a little bit of it because you are not hungry.
If you are **dieting**, or if you go **on a diet**, you eat less than normal in order to become thinner.
If you are **fasting**, you do not eat for a period of time, often for religious reasons: *Muslims fast during the holy month of Ramadan.*
➔ DRINK

2 [I] to have a meal: *What time do we eat?* | *We can't afford to eat at restaurants very often.* **3 eat your words** *informal* to admit that what you said was wrong **4** [T] **also eat up** *spoken* to use all of something until it is gone: *That car of mine just eats up money.*

eat sth ⇔ **away**, **eat away at** sth *phr. v.* to gradually remove, reduce, or destroy something: *Rust had eaten away at the metal frame.*

eat into sth *phr. v.* **1** to gradually reduce the amount of time, money, etc. that is available: *All these car expenses are really eating into our savings.* **2** to damage or destroy something: *This acid will eat into the surface of the metal.*

eat out *phr. v.* to eat in a restaurant: *Do you eat out a lot?*

eat (sth ⇔) **up** *phr. v.* *spoken* to eat all of something: *Come on, Kaylee, eat up!* | *I told her to eat up her breakfast.*

eat·er /ˈit̬ɚ/ *n.* **big/light/fussy etc. eater** someone who eats a lot, not much, only particular things, etc.

eat·er·y /ˈit̬əri/ *n.* plural **eateries** [C] a restaurant, especially an informal one

ˈeating disˌorder *n.* [C] a medical condition in which you do not eat normal amounts of food or do not eat regularly ➔ ANOREXIA, BULIMIA

eaves /ivz/ *n.* [plural] the edges of a roof that stick out beyond the walls

eaves·drop /ˈivzdrɑp/ *v.* past tense and past participle **eavesdropped**, present participle **eavesdropping** [I] to listen secretly to other people's conversations [➡ **overhear**]: *The FBI had been* ***eavesdropping on*** *Martin's phone conversations.* —**eavesdropper** *n.* [C]

ebb¹ /ɛb/ *n.* **1 ebb and flow** a situation or state in which something increases and decreases in a type of pattern: *the ebb and flow of his popularity* **2 be at a low ebb** to be in a bad state or condition: *By March 1933, the economy was at its* *lowest ebb.* **3 also ebb tide** [singular, U] the flow of the sea away from the shore, when the TIDE goes out

ebb² *v.* [I] **1 also ebb away** *literary* to gradually decrease: *His courage slowly ebbed away.* **2** if the TIDE ebbs, it flows away from the shore

eb·o·ny /'ɛbəni/ *n.* **1** [C,U] a tree with dark hard wood, or the wood itself **2** [U] *literary* a black color —**ebony** *adj.*

e·bul·lient /ɪ'bʌlyənt, ɪ'bʊl-/ *adj. formal* very happy and excited: *an ebullient live performance* —**ebullience** *n.* [U]

ec·cen·tric¹ /ɪk'sɛntrɪk/ *adj.* behaving in a way that is unusual and different from most people: *an eccentric professor* —**eccentricity** /ˌɛksɛn'trɪsət̬i/ *n.* [C,U]

THESAURUS

strange, funny, peculiar, odd, weird
→ see Thesaurus box at STRANGE¹

eccentric² *n.* [C] someone who behaves in a way that is different from what is usual or socially accepted

ec·cle·si·as·ti·cal /ɪˌklizi'æstɪkəl/ *adj.* relating to the Christian church

ech·e·lon /'ɛʃəˌlɑn/ *n.* [C] a rank or level of authority in an organization, business, etc., or the people at that level

ech·o¹ /'ɛkoʊ/ *v.* past tense and past participle **echoed** **1** [I] if a sound echoes, it is heard again because it was made near something such as a wall or a hill: *voices echoing around the cave* **2** [I] if a place echoes, it is full of a sound: *The theater **echoed with** laughter.* **3** [T] to repeat what someone else has said, an idea, or an opinion: *This man's words echo the feelings of soldiers throughout history.*

ech·o² /'ɛkoʊ/ *n.* plural **echoes** [C] **1** a sound that you hear again because it was made near something such as a wall or a hill **2** something that is very similar to something that has happened or been said before: *the play has **echoes of** Chekhov*

e·clec·tic /ɪ'klɛktɪk/ *adj.* including a mixture of many different things or people

e·clipse¹ /ɪ'klɪps/ *n.* [C] an occasion when you cannot see the sun because the moon is in front of it, or when you cannot see the moon because it is covered by the earth's shadow: *an **eclipse of** the moon*

eclipse² *v.* [T] **1** to become more powerful, famous, important, etc. than someone or something else, so that he, she, or it is no longer noticed: *The state of the economy has eclipsed every other issue in this election year.* **2** to make the sun or moon disappear in an eclipse

e·co·log·i·cal /ˌikə'lɑdʒɪkəl, ˌɛ-/ *adj.* **1** relating to the way that plants, animals, and people are related to each other and to their environment: *ecological problems caused by the oil spill* **2** relating to making or keeping the environment healthy: *an ecological study* —**ecologically** *adv.*

e·col·o·gy /ɪ'kɑlədʒi/ *n.* [singular, U] the way in which plants, animals, and people are related to each other and to their environment, or the study of this —**ecologist** *n.* [C]

e-com·merce /'i ˌkɑmɚs/ **also e-busi·ness** /'i ˌbɪznɪs/ *n.* [U] the practice of buying and selling things using the Internet

ec·o·nom·ic /ˌɛkə'nɑmɪk◂, ˌi-/ *adj.* relating to business, industry, and managing money: *Economic growth has been slow.* | *the country's economic system* —**economically** *adv.*

ec·o·nom·i·cal /ˌɛkə'nɑmɪkəl, ˌi-/ *adj.* using time, money, products, etc. without wasting any: *an economical way to produce energy* —**economically** *adv.*: *economically developed countries*

ec·o·nom·ics /ˌɛkə'nɑmɪks, ˌi-/ *n.* [U] the study of the way in which money, goods, and services are produced and used

e·con·o·mist /ɪ'kɑnəmɪst/ *n.* [C] someone who studies economics

e·con·o·mize /ɪ'kɑnəˌmaɪz/ *v.* [I] to reduce the amount of money, time, goods, etc. that you use

e·con·o·my¹ /ɪ'kɑnəmi/ *n.* **1** [C] the way that money, businesses, and products are organized in a particular country, area, etc.: *the growing economies of southeast Asia* | *The project will add 600 jobs to the **local economy*** (=in a particular town or city). | *the **global/world economy*** **2** [U] the careful use of money, time, products, etc. so that nothing is wasted

economy² *adj.* **economy size/package etc.** the biggest container that a product is sold in

e'conomy ˌclass also economy *n.* [U] the cheapest way to travel on an airplane

e·co·sys·tem /'ikoʊˌsɪstəm/ *n.* [C] all the animals and plants in a particular area, and the way in which they are related to each other and to their environment

e·co·tour·ism /ˌikoʊ'tʊrɪzəm/ *n.* [U] the business of organizing vacations to areas where people can see the beauty of nature in a way that will not hurt the environment

ec·sta·sy /'ɛkstəsi/ *n.* **1** [C,U] a feeling of extreme happiness: *I laughed **in pure ecstasy**.* **2 Ecstasy** [U] an illegal drug used especially by young people to give a feeling of happiness and energy

ec·stat·ic /ɪk'stæt̬ɪk, ɛk-/ *adj.* feeling extremely happy and excited: *Luke is **ecstatic about** being accepted at Harvard.*

THESAURUS

happy, glad, pleased, delighted
→ see Thesaurus box at HAPPY

ec·u·men·i·cal /ˌɛkyə'mɛnɪkəl/ *adj.* bringing together different Christian churches, or supporting this

E

ec·ze·ma /ˈɛksəmə, ˈɛgzəmə, ɪgˈzimə/ *n.* [U] a condition in which skin becomes dry and red, and begins to ITCH

ed. *n.* the written abbreviation of **education**

ed·dy /ˈɛdi/ *n.* plural **eddies** [C] a circular movement of water, wind, dust, etc. —**eddy** *v.* [I]

edge[1] /ɛdʒ/ *n.* [C] **1** the part of something that is farthest from the center: *the **edge of** the table* | *Bill sat **on the edge** of the bed.* | *cars parked **at the edge** of the street*

THESAURUS

border – the official line that separates two countries, states, or areas: *the border between Mexico and the United States*
rim – the outside edge of something, especially something circular such as a glass: *There was a lipstick stain on the rim of the cup.*
margin – the empty space at the side of a printed page: *I wrote some notes in the margins.*

2 the area beside a steep slope: *the edge of a cliff* **3** the thin sharp part of a tool used for cutting **4** an advantage in a competition, game, or fight: *Good service **gives** our company **an edge**.* | *American companies **have an edge over/on** their competition in this technology.* **5 be on edge** to feel nervous because you are expecting something bad to happen: *Rudy was on edge all night.* **6** a quality in someone's voice that makes it sound angry or not sympathetic **7 on the edge of sth** close to the point at which something different, especially something bad, will happen: *an economy on the edge of collapse* **8 on the edge of your seat** excited and interested: *a thriller that will keep you on the edge of your seat* ➔ CUTTING EDGE

edge[2] *v.* **1** [I,T] to move slowly and gradually, or to make something do this: *Robert **edged toward** the door.* | *We edged closer, trying to see.* **2** [I,T] to develop or increase slowly and gradually, or to make something do this: *The price of gasoline is **edging up**.* **3** [T] to put something on the edge or border of something else: *a tablecloth **edged with** lace*

edge sb ⇔ **out** *phr. v.* to beat someone in an election, competition, etc. by a small amount: *He edged out Sorenson by fewer than 200 votes.*

edge·wise /ˈɛdʒwaɪz/ *adv.* **1 not get a word in edgewise** to not be able to say something in a conversation because someone else is talking too much **2** with the edge or thinnest part forward: *Slide the table in edgewise.*

edg·y /ˈɛdʒi/ *adj.* nervous and easy to upset

ed·i·ble /ˈɛdəbəl/ *adj.* something that is edible is safe or acceptable to eat [≠ **inedible**]

e·dict /ˈidɪkt/ *n.* [C] *formal* an official public order made by someone in a position of power

ed·i·fice /ˈɛdəfɪs/ *n.* [C] *formal* a large building

ed·it /ˈɛdɪt/ *v.* [T] to prepare a book, movie, article, etc. for printing or broadcasting by removing mistakes, deciding what to include, etc.

e·di·tion /ɪˈdɪʃən/ *n.* [C] **1** the form that a book is printed in: *the new edition of this dictionary* **2** the copies of a book, newspaper, etc. that are produced and printed at the same time: *a limited edition of 2,000 copies* | *The **first edition** of the book was published in 1836.*

ed·i·tor /ˈɛdət̬ɚ/ *n.* [C] **1** the person who decides what should be included in a newspaper, magazine, etc.

TOPIC

reporter, **journalist**, **correspondent**, **columnist**
➔ see Topic box at NEWSPAPER

2 someone who prepares a book, movie, etc. for printing or broadcasting by deciding what to include and checking for any mistakes **3** a computer program that allows you to write and make changes to saved information —**editorial** /ˌɛdəˈtɔriəl/ *adj.*

ed·i·to·ri·al /ˌɛdəˈtɔriəl/ *n.* [C] a piece of writing in a newspaper that gives the opinion of the writer rather than reporting facts: *an **editorial on*** (=about) *gun control laws*

ed·u·cate /ˈɛdʒəˌkeɪt/ *v.* [T] to teach someone, especially in a school or college: *Most Americans are **educated in** public schools.* | *He was **educated at** Harvard.* | *a program to **educate** teenagers **about** contraception* —**educator** *n.* [C]

ed·u·cat·ed /ˈɛdʒəˌkeɪt̬ɪd/ *adj.* **1** having knowledge as a result of studying or being taught: ***well-educated** women* **2 educated guess** a guess that is likely to be correct because you know something about the subject

ed·u·ca·tion /ˌɛdʒəˈkeɪʃən/ *n.* **1** [singular, U] the process of learning in a school or other program of study: *They wanted their children to **get a good education**.* | *parents saving for their kids' **college education*** **2** [U] the institutions and people involved with teaching: *careers in education* | *funding for schools and **higher education*** (=colleges)

ed·u·ca·tion·al /ˌɛdʒəˈkeɪʃənəl/ *adj.* **1** relating to teaching and learning: *educational systems* **2** teaching you something that you did not know: *educational television* | *The games are educational.* —**educationally** *adv.*

ed·u·tain·ment /ˌɛdʒuˈteɪnmənt/ *n.* [U] movies, television programs, or computer SOFTWARE that both educate and entertain children

eel /il/ *n.* [C] a long thin fish that looks like a snake

ee·rie /ˈɪri/ *adj.* strange and frightening: *an eerie light* —**eerily** *adv.*

ef·fect[1] /ɪˈfɛkt/ *n.* **1** [C,U] the way in which an event, action, or person changes someone or something [➡ **affect**]: *the **effects of** a long illness* | *Her parents' divorce **had** a big **effect on** her.* | *One **side effect*** (=additional effect) *of the* *drug is drowsiness.* | *What parents do has a* ***profound/lasting/major effect*** *on children's lives.*

THESAURUS

result, consequences, outcome, upshot
➔ see Thesaurus box at RESULT[1]

2 put sth into effect to make a plan or idea happen: *The policy was put into effect in 1994.* **3 come/go into effect** to start officially: *The new tax laws come into effect January 1st.* **4 be in effect** to be being used: *The ban is already in effect.* **5 take effect** to start to have results, or to start being used: *The drug should take effect in about ten minutes.* **6 in effect** used when you are describing what the real situation is, instead of what it seems to be: *In effect, I'll be earning less than last year.* **7 effects** [plural] *formal* the things that someone owns [= **belongings**] ➔ SPECIAL EFFECTS

effect[2] *v.* [T] *formal* to make something happen

USAGE

Use **affect** to talk about making changes, and use **effect** to talk about the results of those changes: *Do you think the changes in the law will affect us?* | *I don't know what effect they will have.*
Effect can be used as a verb to mean "to make something happen." This use is formal and not very common: *No law is going to effect change in a parent who does not take his or her role seriously.*

ef·fec·tive /ɪ'fɛktɪv/ *adj.* **1** producing the result that was wanted or intended [≠ **ineffective**]: *an effective medicine for headaches* | *an effective way to teach reading* | *Bicycle helmets are* ***effective in*** *preventing some types of injuries.* **2 be/become effective** to be in use, or to start to be in use officially: *These prices* ***are effective from*** *April 1.* —**effectiveness** *n.* [U]

ef·fec·tive·ly /ɪ'fɛktɪvli/ *adv.* **1** in a way that produces the result you wanted: *Even young children can use the computer effectively.* **2** used in order to describe the real facts of a situation [= **actually**]: *Many of these students are effectively not receiving an education.*

ef·fem·i·nate /ɪ'fɛmənɪt/ *adj.* a man or boy who is effeminate behaves like a woman or girl

ef·fer·ves·cent /ˌɛfɚ'vɛsənt/ *adj.* **1** *technical* a liquid that is effervescent has BUBBLES of gas rising in it **2** someone who is effervescent is very active and happy —**effervescence** *n.* [U]

ef·fi·cient /ɪ'fɪʃənt/ *adj.* working well, quickly, and without wasting time, energy, or effort [≠ **inefficient**]: *an efficient use of space* | *She's very efficient.*

THESAURUS

organized, well-run, businesslike
➔ see Thesaurus box at ORGANIZED

—**efficiency** *n.* [U] *The company needs to improve the efficiency of its factories.* —**efficiently** *adv.*

ef·fi·gy /'ɛfədʒi/ *n.* plural **effigies** [C] a model of someone, especially one that is burned as a protest

ef·flu·ent /'ɛfluənt/ *n.* [C,U] *formal* liquid waste

ef·fort /'ɛfɚt/ *n.* **1** [U] the physical or mental energy needed to do something: *Kenny* ***put*** *a lot of* ***effort into*** *his report.* | *It* ***takes*** *very little* ***effort*** *to watch TV.* | *This dish takes time to prepare, but it's* ***worth the effort.*** **2** [C,U] an attempt to do something, especially something difficult: *The area has been restored* ***in an effort to*** *attract tourists.* | *Ken* ***made a*** *conscious* ***effort*** (=deliberate effort) *to avoid the same mistakes.* | *a famine relief effort*

ef·fort·less /'ɛfɚt˺lɪs/ *adj.* done in a skillful way that seems easy: *Brad's effortless skiing* —**effortlessly** *adv.*

ef·fu·sive /ɪ'fyusɪv/ *adj.* showing strong, excited feelings: *effusive greetings* —**effusively** *adv.*

EFL *n.* [U] **English as a Foreign Language** the methods used for teaching English to people whose first language is not English, and who do not live in an English-speaking country

e.g. /ˌi 'dʒi/ a written abbreviation that means **for example**: *the Gulf States, e.g. Texas, Louisiana, and Mississippi*

e·gal·i·tar·i·an /ɪˌgælə'tɛriən/ *adj.* believing that everyone should have the same rights and opportunities —**egalitarianism** *n.* [U]

egg[1] /ɛg/ *n.* [C] **1** a round object with a hard surface that contains a baby bird, insect, snake, etc.: *a turtle* ***laying eggs*** *in the sand* | *Some of the* ***eggs*** *were* ***hatching*** (=breaking open to allow the baby out). **2** an egg, especially from a chicken, used as food: *fried eggs* | *Joe dipped his toast in his* ***egg yolk*** (=the yellow part). | *Whisk the* ***egg whites*** (=white part) *until stiff.* **3** a cell produced inside a female that can combine with a SPERM (=male cell) to make a baby animal or person

egg[2] *v.*

egg sb ⇔ **on** *phr. v.* to encourage someone to do something, especially something s/he does not want to do or should not do

egg·plant /'ɛgplænt/ *n.* [C,U] a large shiny dark purple fruit that is cooked and eaten as a vegetable ➔ see picture at VEGETABLE

egg·shell /'ɛgʃɛl/ *n.* [C,U] the hard outside part of a bird or REPTILE's egg

e·go /'igoʊ/ *n.* [C] **1** the opinion that you have about yourself: *a player with a* ***big ego*** (=he thinks he is very good) **2 ego trip** *informal disapproving* something that someone does for himself/herself because it makes him/her feel good or important

e·go·tism /'igəˌtɪzəm/ **also e·go·ism** /'igoʊˌɪzəm/ *n.* [U] the belief that you are more interesting or important than other people —**egotist** *n.* [C] —**egotistical** /ˌigə'tɪstɪkəl/ *adj.*

e·gre·gious /ɪ'gridʒəs/ *adj. formal* an egregious

ERROR (=mistake), failure, etc. is extremely bad and noticeable —**egregiously** *adv.*

eight /eɪt/ *number* **1** 8 **2** eight O'CLOCK: *Dinner will be at eight.*

eight·een /ˌeɪ'tin◂/ *number* 18 —**eighteenth** *number*

eighth /eɪtθ/ *number* **1** 8th **2** 1/8

eight·y /'eɪṭi/ *number* **1** 80 **2 the eighties a)** the years between 1980 and 1989 **b)** the numbers between 80 and 89, especially when used in measuring temperature **3 be in your eighties** to be between 80 and 89 years old: *He's **in** his **early/mid/late eighties**.* —**eightieth** /'eɪṭiɪθ/ *number*

ei·ther[1] /'iðɚ, 'aɪ-/ *conjunction* used in order to begin a list of possibilities separated by "or": *There's either coffee or tea to drink.* | *Either she leaves, or I do!*

either[2] *determiner, pron.* **1** one or the other of two people or things: *Do you know **either of** these two women?* | *There's chocolate or vanilla – you can have either.* **2** used in order to show that a negative statement is true about both of two things or people: *I've lived in New York and Chicago, but I don't like either city very much.* **3 either side/end/hand etc.** both sides, ends, etc.: *He was standing there with a policeman **on either side** of him.* **4 either way** used to show that both of two things are true, possible, or likely: *You can go by train or plane, but either way it's expensive.* | *The vote could **go either way*** (=both results are possible).

E

GRAMMAR

either, either of

Either is used with a singular noun form and a singular verb: *I can meet you on Wednesday or Thursday – either day is good for me.*

Either of is used with a plural noun form or pronoun. In formal speech and writing, use a singular verb: *Has either of them called yet?* In informal speech and writing, you can use a plural verb: *Have either of them called yet?*

either ... or, neither ... nor

When you use these phrases in formal speech or writing, use a singular verb if the second noun is singular: *If either Doris or Meg calls, please take a message.* | *Neither Ted nor Gary is very tall.*

If the second noun is plural, use a plural verb: *If either my sister or my parents come, please let them in.* In informal speech, the verb is usually plural.

either[3] *adv.* **1** used in negative sentences to mean "also": *"I can't swim." "I can't either."*

USAGE

In negative sentences, use **either** rather than **also** or **too**. Do not say "Tom was also not hungry" or "Tom was not hungry too." Say "Tom was not hungry either."

2 me either *spoken nonstandard* used in order to say that a negative statement is also true about you: *"I don't like broccoli." "Me either."*

e·jac·u·late /ɪ'dʒækyəˌleɪt/ *v.* [I,T] when a male ejaculates, SPERM comes out of his PENIS —**ejaculation** /ɪˌdʒækyə'leɪʃən/ *n.* [C,U]

e·ject /ɪ'dʒɛkt/ *v.* **1** [T] to make something come out of a machine by pressing a button: *Rewind and eject the tape.* **2** [T] to push or throw out with force: *the lava and ash ejected by the volcano* **3** [T] to make someone leave a place: *Both players were ejected from the game.* **4** [I] to jump out of an airplane that is going to crash —**ejection** /ɪ'dʒɛkʃən/ *n.* [C,U]

eke /ik/ *v.*

eke sth ⇔ **out** *phr. v.* **1** to make something such as food or money last a long time by carefully using only small amounts of it **2 eke out a living/existence** to get just enough food or money to live on

e·lab·o·rate[1] /ɪ'læbrɪt/ *adj.* having a lot of small details or parts that are connected together in a complicated way: *elaborate plans for the wedding* | *an elaborate design* —**elaborately** *adv.*

e·lab·o·rate[2] /ɪ'læbəˌreɪt/ *v.* [I,T] to give more details about something you have said or written: *The spokesman would not **elaborate on** the investigation.* —**elaboration** /ɪˌlæbə'reɪʃən/ *n.* [U]

e·lapse /ɪ'læps/ *v.* [I] *formal* if a period of time elapses, it passes

e·las·tic /ɪ'læstɪk/ *adj.* able to stretch and then go back to its usual shape or size: *an elastic waistband* —**elastic** *n.* [U] —**elasticity** /ɪˌlæs'tɪsəṭi/ *n.* [U]

e·lat·ed /ɪ'leɪṭɪd/ *adj.* [not before noun] extremely happy and excited —**elation** /ɪ'leɪʃən/ *n.* [U]

el·bow[1] /'ɛlboʊ/ *n.* [C] **1** the joint where your arm bends ➔ see picture on page A3 **2 elbow room** *informal* enough space, so that you can move easily **3 elbow grease** *informal* hard physical effort, especially when cleaning something

elbow[2] *v.* [T] to push someone with your elbows, especially in order to move past him/her: *She **elbowed her way through** the crowd.*

THESAURUS

push, **roll**, **poke**, **shove**, **nudge**
➔ see Thesaurus box at PUSH[1]

el·der[1] /'ɛldɚ/ *adj.* the elder of two people, especially brothers and sisters, is the one who was born first: *My elder sister is a nurse.*

USAGE

Use **elder** to talk about the members of a family: *Nick is my elder brother.*
Use **older** to compare the age of people or things: *My sister is two years older than I am.*

elder[2] *n.* **1** [C usually plural] someone who is older than you are: *Young people should have* *respect for their elders.* **2** [C] an older person who is important and respected: *the town elders*

el·der·ly /ˈɛldəli/ *adj.* **1** old – used in order to be polite: *an elderly woman with white hair* **2 the elderly** people who are old

el·dest /ˈɛldɪst/ *adj.* the eldest of a group of people, especially brothers and sisters, is the one who was born first: *My eldest daughter is 17.*

e·lect[1] /ɪˈlɛkt/ *v.* [T] **1** to choose someone for an official position by voting: *She was first* ***elected to*** *Congress in 1988.* | *What are the chances that a Democrat will be* ***elected president/governor/mayor****?* **2 elect to do sth** *formal* to choose to do something: *Hanley elected to take early retirement.*

elect[2] *adj.* **president-elect/senator-elect etc.** the person who has been elected but has not officially started his/her job

e·lec·tion /ɪˈlɛkʃən/ *n.* [C] an occasion when you vote in order to choose someone for an official position: *The election results are still coming in.* | *She* ***won*** *the* ***election*** *by a large margin.* | *the* ***national/local elections*** *on Tuesday* | *More people voted* ***in*** *this* ***election*** *than in previous years.* —**electoral** /ɪˈlɛktərəl/ *adj.* → GENERAL ELECTION

e·lec·tive[1] /ɪˈlɛktɪv/ *n.* [C] a subject that a student chooses to study, that is not one of the classes s/he must take

elective[2] *adj.* **1** an elective office, position, etc. is one for which there is an election **2** elective medical treatment is treatment that you choose to have

e,lectoral ˈcollege *n.* [singular] a group of people chosen by the votes of the people in each U.S. state, who come together to elect the president

e·lec·tor·ate /ɪˈlɛktərɪt/ *n.* [singular] all the people who are allowed to vote in an election

e·lec·tric /ɪˈlɛktrɪk/ *adj.* **1** needing electricity in order to work: *an electric oven* | *an electric guitar*

USAGE

Use **electric** before the names of things that need electricity in order to work: *an electric clock* | *electric lights*
Use **electrical** to talk about things that use or produce electricity, or to refer to someone who works with electricity: *electrical goods* | *an electrical engineer*

2 making people feel very excited: *The atmosphere at the concert was electric.*

THESAURUS

exciting, thrilling, gripping, exhilarating
→ see Thesaurus box at EXCITING

e·lec·tri·cal /ɪˈlɛktrɪkəl/ *adj.* relating to or using electricity: *Solar panels change sunlight into electrical power.* | *electrical goods* → see Usage box at ELECTRIC

e,lectric ˈchair *n.* **the electric chair** a chair in which criminals are killed using electricity

e·lec·tri·cian /ɪ,lɛkˈtrɪʃən, i-/ *n.* [C] someone whose job is to fit and repair electrical equipment

e·lec·tric·i·ty /ɪ,lɛkˈtrɪsəṭi, i-/ *n.* [U] **1** the power that is carried by wires and used in order to provide heat or light, to make machines work, etc.: *houses that lack electricity or running water* | *Wind power is used to* ***generate electricity*** (=make electricity). **2** a feeling of excitement

e·lec·tri·fy /ɪˈlɛktrə,faɪ/ *v.* past tense and past participle **electrified**, third person singular **electrifies** [T] **1** to make people feel very excited or interested: *His speech electrified the Democratic Convention.* **2** to make electricity available in a particular area —**electrified** *adj.* —**electrifying** *adj.*

e·lec·tro·cute /ɪˈlɛktrə,kyut/ *v.* [T] to kill someone by passing electricity through his/her body —**electrocution** /ɪ,lɛktrəˈkyuʃən/ *n.* [U]

e·lec·trode /ɪˈlɛktroʊd/ *n.* [C] the point at which electricity enters or leaves something such as a BATTERY

e·lec·trol·y·sis /ɪ,lɛkˈtrɑləsɪs/ *n.* [U] the process of using electricity to remove hair from your face, legs, etc.

e·lec·tron /ɪˈlɛktrɑn/ *n.* [C] a very small piece of matter that moves around the NUCLEUS (=central part) of an atom [➡ **neutron, proton**]

e·lec·tron·ic /ɪ,lɛkˈtrɑnɪk/ *adj.* **1** electronic equipment, such as computers or televisions, uses electricity that has passed through computer CHIPS, TRANSISTORS, etc. **2** using electronic equipment: *electronic banking* —**electronically** *adv.*

e·lec·tron·ics /ɪ,lɛkˈtrɑnɪks/ *n.* [U] the study or industry of making electronic equipment, such as computers or televisions

el·e·gant /ˈɛləgənt/ *adj.* very beautiful and graceful: *a tall elegant woman* —**elegance** *n.* [U] —**elegantly** *adv.*

el·e·gy /ˈɛlədʒi/ *n.* plural **elegies** [C] a sad poem or song, especially about someone who has died

el·e·ment /ˈɛləmənt/ *n.* [C] **1** one part of a plan, system, piece of writing, etc.: *the two main* ***elements of*** *the bill* | *a* ***key/major/basic element*** *of his campaign* | *The trial is a central* ***element in*** *the novel.* **2 an element of danger/truth/risk etc.** a small amount of danger, truth, risk, etc.: *The movie is a fantasy, but there is still an element of truth in it.* **3** a simple chemical substance such as oxygen or gold that is made of only one type of atom [➡ **compound**] **4 be in your element, be out of your element** to be in a situation that you enjoy a lot, or to be in a situation that makes you uncomfortable or unhappy: *I felt out of my element among this group of scientists.* **5 the elements** [plural] weather, especially bad weather: *A tent provided shelter from the elements.*

E

el·e·men·tal /ˌɛləˈmɛntəl/ *adj.* an elemental feeling is simple, basic, and strong

el·e·men·ta·ry /ˌɛləˈmɛntri, -ˈmɛntəri/ *adj.* **1** relating to the first and easiest part of a subject: *elementary piano exercises* **2** simple or basic: *the elementary human need for food* **3** relating to an elementary school

eleˈmentary ˌschool *n.* [C] a school in the U.S. for the first six or eight years of a child's education [= **grade school**]

el·e·phant /ˈɛləfənt/ *n.* [C] a very large gray animal with two TUSKS (=long curved teeth), big ears, and a TRUNK (=a long nose) that it can use to pick things up

elephant

el·e·vate /ˈɛləˌveɪt/ *v.* [T] *formal* **1** to make someone more important, or to make something better: *Sloane was **elevated to** captain.* **2** to raise someone or something to a higher position or level: *This drug tends to elevate body temperature.*

el·e·va·tion /ˌɛləˈveɪʃən/ *n.* **1** [C] a height above the level of the sea: *an **elevation of** 7,000 feet* **2** [U] *formal* the act of moving someone to a more important rank or position: *the judge's **elevation to** the Supreme Court* **3** [C,U] *formal* an increase in the quantity or level of something: *Elevation of blood pressure can cause headaches.*

el·e·va·tor /ˈɛləˌveɪtə/ *n.* [C] a machine in a building that takes people from one level to another: *I decided to **take** the **elevator**.*

e·lev·en /ɪˈlɛvən/ *number* **1** 11 **2** 11 O'CLOCK: *an appointment at eleven* **3** 11 years old: *My son is eleven.*

e·lev·enth /ɪˈlɛvənθ/ *number* **1** 11th **2** 1/11

elf /ɛlf/ *n.* plural **elves** /ɛlvz/ [C] a small imaginary person with pointed ears —**elfin** /ˈɛlfɪn/ *adj.*

e·lic·it /ɪˈlɪsɪt/ *v.* [T] *formal* to get information, a reaction, etc. from someone, when this is difficult: *Short questions are more likely to **elicit a response**.*

el·i·gi·ble /ˈɛlədʒəbəl/ *adj.* **1** able or allowed to do something: *You are **eligible to** vote at the age of 18.* | *Are you **eligible for** a loan?* **2** an eligible man or woman would be good to marry because s/he is rich, attractive, etc.: *an **eligible bachelor*** —**eligibility** /ˌɛlədʒəˈbɪləti/ *n.* [U]

e·lim·i·nate /ɪˈlɪməˌneɪt/ *v.* [T] **1** to get rid of something completely: *a plan to eliminate all nuclear weapons* **2 be eliminated** to be defeated in a sports competition, so that you can no longer take part in it

e·lim·i·na·tion /ɪˌlɪməˈneɪʃən/ *n.* [U] **1** the removal or destruction of something: *the **elimination of** 250 jobs* **2 process of elimination** a way of finding out the answer to something by getting rid of other answers that are not correct until only one is left

e·lite /eɪˈlit, ɪ-/ *n.* [C] a small group of people who are powerful or important because they have money, knowledge, special skills, etc.: *The competition is only open to an elite group of athletes.*

e·lit·ist /eɪˈlitɪst, ɪ-/ *adj. disapproving* an elitist system, government, etc. is one in which a small group of people have much more power than other people —**elitism** *n.* [U]

elk /ɛlk/ *n.* [C] a large DEER with a lot of hair around its neck

el·lip·ti·cal /ɪˈlɪptɪkəl/ **also el·lip·tic** /ɪˈlɪptɪk/ *adj.* shaped like a circle but with slightly flat sides [= **oval**]: *the elliptical orbit of the planets* —**ellipse** *n.* [C]

elm /ɛlm/ *n.* [C,U] a large tall tree with broad leaves, or the wood of this tree

e·lon·gat·ed /ɪˈlɔŋˌgeɪtɪd/ *adj.* long and thin: *elongated shadows* —**elongate** *v.* [I,T]

e·lope /ɪˈloʊp/ *v.* [I] to go away secretly with someone to get married —**elopement** *n.* [C,U]

el·o·quent /ˈɛləkwənt/ *adj.* able to express ideas, opinions, or feelings clearly, in a way that influences other people: *Brennan's eloquent response* —**eloquently** *adv.* —**eloquence** *n.* [U]

else /ɛls/ *adv.* **1** in addition – used after words beginning with "any-," "no-," "some-," and after question words: *Clayton needs someone else to help him.* | *There's nothing else we can do.* | *What else can I get you?* **2** different – used after words beginning with "any-," "no-," "some-," and after question words: *Is there anything else to eat?* | *She was wearing someone else's coat* (=not her own coat). | *Well, what else can I do?* **3 or else** used when saying that there will be a bad result if someone does not do something: *Hurry up, or else you'll be late for school!* **4 if nothing else** used in order to say that there is one good quality or feature of something, even if there are no others: *If nothing else, the report shows that better facilities are needed.*

else·where /ˈɛlswɛr/ *adv.* in or to another place: *Most of the city's residents were born elsewhere.*

e·lu·ci·date /ɪˈlusəˌdeɪt/ *v.* [I,T] *formal* to explain very clearly something that is difficult to understand

e·lude /ɪˈlud/ *v.* [T] **1** to avoid being found or caught by someone, especially by tricking him/her: *Jones eluded the police for six weeks.* **2** if something that you want eludes you, you do not find it or achieve it: *Success has eluded him so far.* **3** if a fact, someone's name, etc. eludes you, you cannot remember it

e·lu·sive /ɪˈlusɪv/ *adj.* **1** difficult to find: *an elusive animal* **2** difficult to achieve or understand: *Success has been elusive.* | *the poem's elusive meaning*

elves /ɛlvz/ *n.* [C] the plural of ELF

e·ma·ci·at·ed /ɪˈmeɪʃiˌeɪt̬ɪd/ *adj.* extremely thin because of illness or lack of food

THESAURUS

thin, slim, slender, skinny, lean, underweight
➔ see Thesaurus box at THIN[1]

e-mail, email /ˈi meɪl/ *n.* **1** [U] **electronic mail** a system that allows you to send and receive messages by computer: *What's your **e-mail address**? | A confirmation of your order will be sent **by/via email**.* ➔ see picture on page A11 **2** [C,U] a message that is sent using this system: *I got an email from her yesterday. | I haven't **checked** my **e-mail** yet.* —**e-mail, email** *v.* [T]

COLLOCATIONS

You can **read, write, send,** and **receive** an **e-mail**.
If you **check** your **e-mail**, you look on your computer to see if you have received any.
If you **reply to** an **e-mail**, you write an e-mail to someone who has sent one to you.
If you get a **reply**, you receive an e-mail from someone you have written an e-mail to.
If you **forward** an **e-mail**, you send an e-mail that you have received to another person.
If you **send an attachment**, you send someone a document which can be opened and read when s/he receives your **e-mail message**.
If an e-mail **bounces back**, it is sent back to the person who sent it, usually because the address is wrong.
➔ see Topic box at INTERNET, COMPUTER, LETTER

em·a·nate /ˈɛməˌneɪt/ *v.*
emanate from sth *phr. v.* to come from or out of something: *Wonderful smells were emanating from the kitchen.*

e·man·ci·pate /ɪˈmænsəˌpeɪt/ *v.* [T] *formal* to make someone free from social, political, or legal rules that limit what s/he can do —**emancipated** *adj.* —**emancipation** /ɪˌmænsəˈpeɪʃən/ *n.* [U]

em·balm /ɪmˈbɑm/ *v.* [T] to use chemicals to prevent a dead body from decaying

em·bank·ment /ɪmˈbæŋkmənt/ *n.* [C] a wide wall of earth or stones built to stop water from flooding an area, or to support a road or railroad

em·bar·go[1] /ɪmˈbɑrgoʊ/ *n.* plural **embargoes** [C] an official order to stop trade with another country: *The UN **imposed an** arms **embargo on** the country.*

embargo[2] *v.* past tense and past participle **embargoed** [T] to officially stop particular goods from being traded with another country

em·bark /ɪmˈbɑrk/ *v.* [I] to go onto a ship or airplane [≠ **disembark**]
embark on/upon sth *phr. v.* to start something new, difficult, or exciting: *Terry then embarked on a new career as a teacher.*

em·bar·rass /ɪmˈbærəs/ *v.* [T] to make someone feel embarrassed: *I didn't want to embarrass her in front of Paul.*

em·bar·rassed /ɪmˈbærəst/ *adj.* ashamed, nervous, or uncomfortable, especially in front of other people: *I could see he **felt embarrassed**, so I changed the subject. | I was **embarrassed about** how messy my house was. | He was too **embarrassed to** talk about it. | an embarrassed silence*

THESAURUS

guilty, ashamed
➔ see Thesaurus box at GUILTY

em·bar·ras·sing /ɪmˈbærəsɪŋ/ *adj.* making you feel embarrassed: *a lot of embarrassing questions*

em·bar·rass·ment /ɪmˈbærəsmənt/ *n.* [U] **1** the feeling that you have when you are embarrassed: *Jody squirmed **with embarrassment**.* **2** [C] something that causes problems and makes someone look stupid: *The matter has been an **embarrassment to** the White House.*

em·bas·sy /ˈɛmbəsi/ *n.* plural **embassies** [C] a group of officials who represent their country in a foreign country, or the building they work in: *the Peruvian Embassy*

E

em·bat·tled /ɪmˈbæt̬ld/ *adj. formal* **1** surrounded by enemies, especially in a war: *the embattled city* **2** an embattled person, company, etc. has many problems or difficulties

em·bed /ɪmˈbɛd/ *v.* past tense and past participle **embedded**, present participle **embedding** [T] **1** to put something firmly and deeply into something else: *a spider **embedded in** a glass paperweight* **2** if your ideas, feelings, or attitudes are embedded, you believe them very strongly: *The idea of freedom is **deeply embedded in** America's values.*

em·bel·lish /ɪmˈbɛlɪʃ/ *v.* [T] **1** to make something more beautiful by adding decorations to it: *a crown **embellished with** jewels* **2** to make a story or statement more interesting by adding details to it that are not true: *Larry couldn't help embellishing his story.* —**embellishment** *n.* [C,U]

em·ber /ˈɛmbɚ/ *n.* [C] a piece of wood or coal that stays red and very hot after a fire has stopped burning

em·bez·zle /ɪmˈbɛzəl/ *v.* [I,T] to steal money from the place where you work —**embezzlement** *n.* [U] —**embezzler** *n.* [C]

em·bit·tered /ɪmˈbɪt̬ɚd/ *adj.* angry, sad, or full of hate because of bad or unfair things that have happened to you —**embitter** *v.* [T]

em·bla·zoned /ɪmˈbleɪzənd/ *adj.* showing a name, design, etc.: *a t-shirt **emblazoned with** the group's name*

em·blem /ˈɛmbləm/ *n.* [C] a picture, shape, or object that represents a country, company, idea, etc.: *The national **emblem of** Canada is the maple leaf.*

em·bod·y /ɪmˈbɑdi/ *v.* [T] to be the best example

of an idea or quality: *Mrs. Miller embodies everything I admire in a teacher.* —**embodiment** *n.* [U]

em·boss /ɪm'bɔs, ɪm'bɑs/ *v.* [T] to decorate the surface of metal, leather, paper, etc. with a raised pattern —**embossed** *adj.*: *embossed stationery*

em·brace /ɪm'breɪs/ *v.* [T] **1** to put your arms around someone and hold him/her in a caring way [= **hug**]: *Rob reached out to embrace her.*

> **THESAURUS**
>
> **hug, cuddle, hold**
> → see Thesaurus box at HUG[1]

2 *formal* to eagerly accept ideas, opinions, religions, etc.: *young men who are embracing Islam* —**embrace** *n.* [C]

em·broi·der /ɪm'brɔɪdɚ/ *v.* **1** [I,T] to decorate cloth by sewing a picture or pattern on it with colored threads **2** [T] to add details that are not true to a story to make it more interesting or exciting —**embroidery** *n.* [U]

E

em·broil /ɪm'brɔɪl/ *v.* [T] to involve someone in a difficult situation: *Soon the whole group was **embroiled in** a fierce argument.*

em·bry·o /'ɛmbri,oʊ/ *n.* [C] an animal or human that has not yet been born and has just begun to develop [➡ **fetus**]

em·bry·o·nic /,ɛmbri'ɑnɪk/ *adj.* not fully developed: *the country's embryonic nuclear weapons program*

em·cee /,ɛm'si/ *n.* [C] **master of ceremonies** someone who introduces the performers on a television program or at a social event —**emcee** *v.* [I,T]

em·er·ald /'ɛmərəld/ *n.* [C] a valuable bright green jewel

e·merge /ɪ'mɚdʒ/ *v.* [I] **1** to appear after being hidden: *The sun **emerged from** behind the clouds.* | *New evidence has emerged during the trial.* **2** to have a particular quality or position after experiencing a difficult situation: *She **emerged from** the divorce a stronger person.* —**emergence** *n.* [U] *the emergence of a rare political talent*

e·mer·gen·cy /ɪ'mɚdʒənsi/ *n.* plural **emergencies** [C] an unexpected and dangerous situation that you must deal with immediately: *Call an ambulance! This is an emergency!* —**emergency** *adj.*: *an emergency exit*

e'mergency ,room *n.* [C] the part of a hospital that immediately treats people who have been hurt in a serious accident

e·mer·gent /ɪ'mɚdʒənt/ *adj.* beginning to develop and be noticeable: *the emergent nations of Eastern Europe and Africa*

e·mer·i·tus /ɪ'mɛrəţəs/ *adj.* a PROFESSOR emeritus is no longer working but still has an official title

em·er·y board /'ɛməri bɔrd/ *n.* [C] a NAIL FILE made from thick card covered with a mineral powder

em·i·grant /'ɛməgrənt/ *n.* [C] someone who leaves his/her own country to live in another: *an **emigrant to** the United States* → —compare IMMIGRANT

em·i·grate /'ɛmə,greɪt/ *v.* [I] to leave your own country in order to live in another: *Maria **emigrated from** Canada three years ago.* —**emigration** /,ɛmə'greɪʃən/ *n.* [C,U] → —compare IMMIGRATION

> **THESAURUS**
>
> **immigrate, migrate**
> → see Thesaurus box at IMMIGRATE

em·i·nent /'ɛmənənt/ *adj.* famous and admired by many people: *an eminent professor of medicine*

,eminent do'main *n.* [C] *law* the right of the U.S. government to pay for and take someone's private land so it can be used for a public purpose

em·i·nent·ly /'ɛmənənt˺li/ *adv. formal* completely, and without any doubt: *He's eminently qualified to do the job.*

e·mir /ɛ'mɪr, i-/ *n.* [C] a Muslim ruler, especially in Asia and parts of Africa

e·mir·ate /'ɛmərɪt/ *n.* [C] the country ruled by an EMIR

em·is·sar·y /'ɛmə,sɛri/ *n.* plural **emissaries** [C] someone who is sent with an official message, or who must do other official work: *an emissary from the Italian government*

e·mis·sion /ɪ'mɪʃən/ *n.* [C,U] the sending out of gas, heat, light, sound, etc., or the gas, etc. that is sent out: *an emissions test* (=a test to make sure the gases your car sends out are at the right level)

e·mit /ɪ'mɪt/ *v.* past tense **-tted**, past participle **-tting** [T] *formal* to send out gas, heat, light, sound, etc.: *The kettle emitted a shrill whistle.*

Em·my /'ɛmi/ *n.* plural **Emmies** [C] a prize given every year to the best program, actor, etc. on U.S. television

e·mo·tion /ɪ'moʊʃən/ *n.* [C,U] a strong human feeling such as love or hate: *David doesn't usually **show** his true **emotions**.* | *Her voice was **full of emotion**.* | *She trembled **with emotion**.*

e·mo·tion·al /ɪ'moʊʃənəl/ *adj.* **1** making people have strong feelings: *The end of the movie was really emotional.*

> **THESAURUS**
>
> **moving** – making you feel strong emotions, especially sadness or sympathy: *Kelly's book about her illness is deeply moving.*
> **touching** – making you feel sympathy or sadness: *a touching tribute to the victims of the attack*
> **poignant** – making you feel sad or full of pity: *poignant memories*
> **sentimental** and **schmalzy** informal – showing emotions such as love, pity, and sadness too strongly: *a sentimental love song*

2 showing your emotions to other people, especially by crying: *Please don't **get all emotional**.*

3 relating to your feelings or how they are controlled: *the emotional development of children* | *Ann suffered from a number of **emotional problems**.* **4** influenced by what you feel rather than what you know: *an emotional response to the problem* —**emotionally** *adv.*: *Family members reacted emotionally to the verdict.*

e·mo·tive /ɪ'moʊt̬ɪv/ *adj.* making people have strong feelings: *an emotive speech about the effects of war*

em·pa·thy /'ɛmpəθi/ *n.* [U] the ability to understand someone else's feelings and problems —**empathize** *v.* [I] → —compare SYMPATHY

em·per·or /'ɛmpərə·/ *n.* [C] the ruler of an EMPIRE

THESAURUS

king, **queen**, **monarch**, **ruler**, **sovereign**
→ see Thesaurus box at KING

em·pha·sis /'ɛmfəsɪs/ *n.* plural **emphases** /-fəsiz/ [C,U] special importance: *Jamieson's report **puts/places an emphasis on** the need for better working conditions.*

em·pha·size /'ɛmfə,saɪz/ *v.* [T] to show that an opinion, idea, quality, etc. is important: *My teacher emphasized the importance of grammar.* ▶ Don't say "...emphasize on." ◀

THESAURUS

stress – to emphasize a statement, fact, or idea: *Mother always stressed the importance of good manners.*
highlight – to make a problem, subject, etc. easy to notice so people will pay attention to it: *Your résumé should highlight your skills and experience.*
underline – to show that something is important: *The tragic incident underlines the need for improved safety standards.*
accentuate – to make something easier to notice: *Let's try to accentuate the positive.*
underscore – to emphasize that something is important: *The president's speech repeatedly underscored the progress that has been made.*

em·phat·ic /ɪm'fæt̬ɪk/ *adj.* done or said in a way that shows something is important or should be believed: *Dale's answer was an emphatic "No!"* —**emphatically** *adv.*

em·phy·se·ma /,ɛmfə'zimə, -'si-/ *n.* [U] a serious disease that affects the lungs, making it difficult to breathe

em·pire /'ɛmpaɪə·/ *n.* [C] **1** a group of countries that are all controlled by one ruler or government: *the Roman Empire* **2** a group of organizations that are all controlled by one person or company: *a media empire*

em·pir·i·cal /ɪm'pɪrɪkəl, ɛm-/ *adj.* based on practical experience rather than on ideas: *an empirical approach to studying sociology*

em·ploy /ɪm'plɔɪ/ *v.* [T] **1** to pay someone to work for you: *The factory employs over 2,000 people.* **2** to use a particular object, method, or skill in order to achieve something: *research methods employed by scientists*

em·ploy·ee /ɪm'plɔɪ-i, ,ɪmplɔɪ'i, ,ɛm-/ *n.* [C] someone who is paid to work for a person, organization, or company: *a government employee* → see Topic box at WORK[1]

TOPIC

employer, **staff**, **colleague**, **co-worker**
→ see Topic box at WORK[1]

em·ploy·er /ɪm'plɔɪə·/ *n.* [C] a person, company, or organization that employs people: *The shoe factory is the largest employer in this area.* → see Topic box at WORK[1]

em·ploy·ment /ɪm'plɔɪmənt/ *n.* [U] **1** work that you do to earn money: *Steve's still looking for employment.* **2** the use of an object, method, skill, etc. to achieve something: *the employment of weapons to gain control of the area* → —compare UNEMPLOYMENT

em·po·ri·um /ɪm'pɔriəm/ *n.* [C] a word meaning a large store, used in the names of stores

em·pow·er /ɪm'paʊə·/ *v.* [T] to give someone the confidence, power, or right to do something: *Our aim is to **empower** women **to** defend themselves.*

em·press /'ɛmprɪs/ *n.* [C] the female ruler of an EMPIRE, or the wife of an EMPEROR

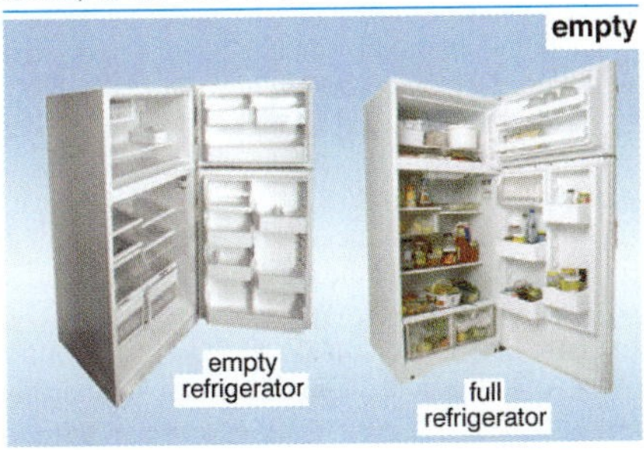

emp·ty[1] /'ɛmpti/ *adj.* **1** having nothing inside: *Your glass is empty – would you like some more wine?* | *an empty box*

THESAURUS

bare – used about a room or area that has very little in it: *Apart from a bed, the room was bare.*
deserted – used about a place or building that is empty and quiet because no people are there: *a deserted beach* | *By now, the streets were deserted.*
uninhabited – used about a place that has no people living in it: *an uninhabited island*
free – used about a seat, space, or room that no one is using: *Is this seat free?*
hollow – used about something that has an empty space inside: *The water flows through a hollow tube and into the drain.*

E

2 not filled with people, or not being used by anyone: *Is this seat empty? | an empty restaurant* **3** unhappy because nothing seems interesting, important, or worth doing: *After the divorce, my life felt empty.* **4 empty words/promises/gestures etc.** words, etc. that are not sincere and therefore have no meaning **5 on an empty stomach** without having eaten anything first: *You shouldn't go to school on an empty stomach.* **6 empty nest (syndrome)** a situation in which parents become sad because their children have grown up and left home

empty² *v.* past tense and past participle **emptied**, third person singular **empties** **1** [T] **also empty out** to remove everything that is inside of something else: *I found your umbrella when I was emptying out the closet. | Troy, please empty the dishwasher.* **2** [T] to pour the things that are in a container into or onto something else: ***Empty** the contents of one pudding package **into** a large bowl.* **3** [I,T] to leave a place, vehicle, etc., or to make someone do this: *Judge Sinclair ordered the courtroom to be emptied.* **4** [I] to flow into a large area of water: *the place where Waddell Creek **empties into** the ocean*

E

ˌempty-ˈhanded *adj.* without gaining or getting anything: *The thieves fled the building empty-handed.*

em·u·late /ˈɛmyəˌleɪt/ *v.* [T] *formal* to try to do something or behave in the same way as someone; copy: *Children emulate their parents' behavior.*

en·a·ble /ɪˈneɪbəl/ *v.* [T] to make someone or something able to do something: *The new plastic enables us to make our products more cheaply.*

en·act /ɪˈnækt/ *v.* [T] to make something a law: *The measure was enacted to prevent tax abuses.*

en·am·el /ɪˈnæməl/ *n.* [U] **1** a substance like glass that is put on metal, clay, etc. for decoration or for protection **2** the hard smooth outer surface of your teeth

en·am·ored /ɪˈnæmɚd/ *adj. formal* **be enamored of** to like and admire someone or something very much: *Not everyone in town is quite so enamored of the new building.*

en·case /ɪnˈkeɪs/ *v.* [T] to cover or surround something completely: *art objects **encased in** a glass box*

en·chant·ed /ɪnˈtʃæntɪd/ *adj.* something that is enchanted has been changed by magic so that it has special powers: *an enchanted forest*

en·chant·ing /ɪnˈtʃæntɪŋ/ *adj.* very pleasant in a way that makes you feel very interested, happy, or excited: *an enchanting movie about young love*

en·chi·la·da /ˌɛntʃəˈlɑdə/ *n.* [C] a Mexican food made from a corn TORTILLA rolled around meat or beans and covered with a hot-tasting liquid

en·clave /ˈɛnkleɪv, ˈɑŋ-/ *n.* [C] a place or group of people that is surrounded by areas or groups of people that are different from it: *the Italian-American enclave in New York*

en·close /ɪnˈkloʊz/ *v.* [T] **1** to put something inside an envelope with a letter: *A copy of the article is enclosed.* **2** to surround an area, especially with a fence or wall: *A high wall enclosed the yard.* —**enclosed** *adj.*

en·clo·sure /ɪnˈkloʊʒɚ/ *n.* [C] **1** an area that is surrounded by something such as a wall or fence: *The animals are kept in a large enclosure.* **2** things such as documents, photographs, money, etc. that you send with a letter

en·com·pass /ɪnˈkʌmpəs/ *v.* [T] **1** to include a range of ideas, subjects, etc.: *Crosby's career encompassed radio, records, TV, and movies.* **2** to completely cover or surround an area: *a national park encompassing 400 square miles*

en·core /ˈɑŋkɔr/ *n.* [C] an additional piece of music a performer plays because the people listening want to hear more

en·coun·ter¹ /ɪnˈkaʊntɚ/ *n.* [C] **1** an occasion when you meet or experience something: *It was my first **encounter with** blatant racism.* **2** an occasion when you meet someone without planning to: *a chance **encounter with** Graham*

encounter² *v.* [T] **1** to experience something bad that you have to deal with: *She encountered a lot of difficulties trying to get her article published. | The president **encountered resistance** to his plans.* **2** *formal* to see or meet someone or something without planning to

en·cour·age /ɪnˈkɚɪdʒ, -ˈkʌr-/ *v.* [T] **1** to persuade someone to do something [≠ **discourage**]: *a program to **encourage** children **to** wear bicycle helmets*

THESAURUS

persuade, talk into, get sb to do sth, influence, convince, coax, cajole
→ see Thesaurus box at PERSUADE

2 to help someone become confident or brave enough to do something [≠ **discourage**]: *Cooder's father **encouraged** him **to** play the guitar.* **3** to make something more likely to happen [≠ **discourage**]: *a plant food that encourages growth* —**encouragement** *n.* [C,U] *words of encouragement*

en·cour·ag·ing /ɪnˈkɚɪdʒɪŋ, -ˈkʌr-/ *adj.* giving you hope and confidence: *This is encouraging news.* —**encouragingly** *adv.*

en·croach /ɪnˈkroʊtʃ/ *v.* [T] **1** to gradually cover more and more land: *Housing developments are **encroaching on** the habitats of wild animals.* **2** to gradually take away more and more of someone's time, rights, etc.: *new laws that **encroach on** civil liberties*

en·crust·ed /ɪnˈkrʌstɪd/ *adj.* covered with something hard and sharp, such as jewels, ice, or dried mud

en·cum·ber /ɪnˈkʌmbɚ/ *v.* [T] *formal* to make it more difficult for someone to do something, or for something to happen —**encumbrance** /ɪn'kʌmbrəns/ *n.* [C]

en·cy·clo·pe·di·a /ɪnˌsaɪklə'pidiə/ *n.* [C] a book, set of books, or CD that contains facts about many subjects or about one particular subject

end[1] /ɛnd/ *n.*

1 LAST PART [singular] the last part of a period of time, activity, book, movie, etc. [≠ **beginning**]: *There are study questions **at the end of** each chapter.* | *I'll know **by the end of** the week.*

2 FARTHEST POINT [C] the part of a place or long object that is furthest from its beginning or center: *the **ends of** his fingers* | *I went to the **end of** the line.* | *the **far end** of the room* | *The two teams pull at **opposite ends** of the rope.*

THESAURUS

point – the sharp end of something: *the point of a needle*
tip – the end of something, especially something pointed: *the tip of your nose*

3 OF A SITUATION [singular] a situation in which something is finished or no longer exists: *The conversation seemed to have **come to an end**.* | *the UN's latest plan to **put an end to*** (=stop) *the war* | *My month of freedom was **at an end**.*

4 in the end after a lot of thinking or discussion [= **finally**]: *In the end, we decided to go to Florida.*

5 for days/weeks etc. on end for many days, weeks, etc. without stopping

6 at the end of the day *spoken* used in order to say what the most important point is: *At the end of the day, it's up to Jim to make the changes.*

7 make ends meet to have just enough money to buy what you need

8 it's not the end of the world *spoken* used in order to say that a problem is not too serious or bad

9 RESULT [C] *formal* the aim or purpose of something, or the result that you hope to achieve: *Learning can be both **an end in itself*** (=a good goal), *and a means to success.* | *Stalin wanted a weak China, and worked **to that end*** (=to achieve that result).

10 no end a lot: *He was enjoying himself no end.* | *The changes caused **no end of** trouble.*

11 PART OF AN ACTIVITY [singular] *informal* the part of a job, activity, or situation that involves a person or group: *She works in the sales end of things.*

12 SCALE [C usually singular] one of the two points that begin or end a scale or range: *a politician at the liberal **end of the** political **spectrum***

13 end to end with the end of something next to the end of something else: *cars parked end to end*

14 IN SPORTS [C] in football, one of two players who play on the outside of the TACKLES and try to catch the ball ➔ DEAD END

end[2] *v.* [I,T] to finish or stop, or to make something do this [≠ **begin**]: *World War II ended in 1945.* | *Janet finally ended the relationship.* | *The concert **ended with** fireworks.*

end in sth *phr. v.* to have a particular result or to finish in a particular way: *One in three marriages ends in divorce.*

end up *phr. v.* to be in a place, situation, or condition after a series of events, usually when you did not plan it: *I always end up paying the bill.*

en·dan·ger /ɪn'deɪndʒɚ/ *v.* [T] to put someone or something in a dangerous or harmful situation: *Smoking seriously endangers your health.* —**endangered** *adj.* —**endangerment** *n.* [U]

enˌdangered 'species *n.* [C] a type of animal or plant that soon might not exist

en·dear /ɪn'dɪr/ *v.*

endear sb **to** sb *phr. v.* to make someone be liked by other people: *The proposals are meant to endear him to the voters.*

en·dear·ing /ɪn'dɪrɪŋ/ *adj.* making someone like or love you: *an endearing smile*

en·dear·ment /ɪn'dɪrmənt/ *n.* [C,U] something you say that shows your love for someone

en·deav·or[1] /ɪn'dɛvɚ/ *n.* [C,U] an attempt or effort to do something new or difficult: ***an endeavor to** create a lasting peace*

endeavor[2] *v.* [I] *formal* to try very hard to do something: *One must always **endeavor to** do one's best.*

THESAURUS

try, **attempt**, **see if you can do sth**, **do your best**, **make an effort to do sth**
➔ see Thesaurus box at TRY[1]

en·dem·ic /ɛn'dɛmɪk, ɪn-/ *adj.* regularly happening in a particular place or among a particular group of people: *Violent crime is now endemic in parts of the city.*

end·ing /'ɛndɪŋ/ *n.* **1** [C] the end of a story, movie, play, etc.: *a happy ending* **2** [U] the act of finishing or stopping a process: *the ending of travel restrictions*

en·dive /'ɛndaɪv/ *n.* [C,U] a vegetable with bitter-tasting leaves that are eaten raw in SALADS

end·less /'ɛndlɪs/ *adj.* continuing for a very long time, especially in a way that is annoying: *the endless hours of practice* | *The **possibilities** are **endless**.*

en·dorse /ɪn'dɔrs/ *v.* [T] **1** to officially say that you support or approve of someone or something: *Several European countries have endorsed the idea.* | *The mayor has decided not to endorse a candidate in the presidential election this year.* **2** to sign your name on the back of a check —**endorsement** *n.* [C,U]

en·dow /ɪn'daʊ/ *v.* [T] **1** to give an endowment to a college, hospital, etc. **2 be endowed with talent/resources/rights etc.** *formal* to have or be given a good quality, feature, or ability

E

en·dow·ment /ɪn'daʊmənt/ *n.* [C,U] a large amount of money or property that is given to a college, hospital, etc. so that it has an income

en·dur·ance /ɪn'dʊrəns/ *n.* [U] the ability to continue doing something difficult or painful over a long period of time: *Jogging will help increase your endurance.*

en·dure /ɪn'dʊr/ *v.* **1** [T] to suffer pain or deal with a very difficult situation for a long time: *People have endured months of fighting.* **2** [I] to continue for a long time: *a marriage that has endured for fifty years*

en·dur·ing /ɪn'dʊrɪŋ/ *adj.* continuing to exist in spite of difficulties: *an enduring peace*

'end zone *n.* [C] the end of a football field to which you carry or catch a ball to win points

en·e·my /'ɛnəmi/ *n.* plural **enemies** [C] **1** someone who hates you and wants to harm you or prevent you from being successful: *Judge Lonza has* ***made a lot of enemies*** *during her career.* **2** the person or group of people that you are fighting in a war: ***The enemy*** *had at least 50 large aircraft in good condition.* | *an attack on an* ***enemy submarine/ship/soldier etc.*** **3** something that people think is harmful or damaging: *This policy was declared an enemy of economic growth.*

E

en·er·get·ic /ˌɛnɚ'dʒɛt̬ɪk/ *adj.* very active: *a cast of young and energetic actors* —**energetically** *adv.*

> **THESAURUS**
>
> **vigorous** – using a lot of energy and strength or determination: *a vigorous opponent of capital punishment*
> **full of energy** – having a lot of energy: *Katie is fun and full of energy.*
> **dynamic** – interesting, exciting, and full of energy and determination to succeed: *a dynamic new candidate*
> **hyperactive** – too active, and not able to keep still or quiet for very long: *a hyperactive child*
> **tireless** – working very hard in a determined way: *a tireless defender of human rights*

en·er·gize /'ɛnɚˌdʒaɪz/ *v.* [T] to make someone feel more determined and full of energy

en·er·gy /'ɛnɚdʒi/ *n.* plural **energies** [C,U] **1** the physical and mental strength that makes you able to do things: *Younger people generally* ***have*** *more* ***energy***. | *She's usually* ***full of energy***. | *She had* ***put*** *a good deal of time and* ***energy into*** *the project.* **2** power that is used to produce heat, make machines work, etc.: *atomic energy* | *the world's energy resources*

en·force /ɪn'fɔrs/ *v.* [T] to make people obey a rule or law: *It's our responsibility to* ***enforce*** *the* ***law***. | *The speed limit is* ***strictly enforced***. —**enforcement** *n.* [U] —**enforceable** *adj.*

en·fran·chise /ɪn'frænˌtʃaɪz/ *v.* [T] *formal* to give a group of people rights, especially the right to vote [≠ **disenfranchise**]

en·gage /ɪn'geɪdʒ/ *v.* [T] *formal* **1** to make someone remain interested in something: *a storyteller able to engage the children's imaginations* **2 engage sb in (a) conversation** to begin talking to someone **3** to employ someone

engage in sth *phr. v.* to be doing or become involved in an activity: *Only 10% of Americans engage in regular exercise.*

en·gaged /ɪn'geɪdʒd/ *adj.* two people who are engaged have agreed to marry each other: *Viv and Tyrell* ***got engaged*** *last month.* | *Sheri's* ***engaged to*** *a guy in the Army.* ▶ Don't say "engaged with someone." ◀

> **THESAURUS**
>
> **married**, **single**, **separated**, **divorced**, **living together**, **widowed**
> → see Thesaurus box at MARRIED

en·gage·ment /ɪn'geɪdʒmənt/ *n.* **1** [C] an agreement to marry someone: *Charlene and I have* ***broken off*** *our* ***engagement*** (=decided to end it). | *an* ***engagement ring*** (=a ring that a man gives a woman to show that they are engaged) **2** [C] *formal* an arrangement to do something or meet someone: *Professor Campbell is in Fort Worth for a speaking engagement.* **3** [U] the process of being involved with someone or something: *a strategy of engagement and cooperation with China* **4** [C,U] fighting between people or armies: *military* ***rules of engagement*** (=rules that say when you should fight)

en·gag·ing /ɪn'geɪdʒɪŋ/ *adj.* attracting people's attention and interest: *an engaging personality*

en·gen·der /ɪn'dʒɛndɚ/ *v.* [T] *formal* to be the cause of something such as a situation, action, or emotion: *the excitement engendered by the Pope's visit*

en·gine /'ɛndʒɪn/ *n.* [C] **1** the part of a vehicle or machine that produces power to make it move: *the engine of a car* | *I waited with the* ***engine running*** (=with the engine on). **2** the part of a train that pulls the other CARS along a railroad

en·gi·neer¹ /ˌɛndʒə'nɪr/ *n.* [C] **1** someone whose job is to design, build, and repair roads, bridges, machines, etc. **2** someone who controls the engines on a ship, airplane, or train

engineer² *v.* [T] **1** to arrange something, especially secretly: *He engineered a cover-up.* **2** to design, plan, and make something new: ***genetically engineered*** *corn* (=in which the GENES have been changed)

en·gi·neer·ing /ˌɛndʒə'nɪrɪŋ/ *n.* [U] the profession or activity of designing, building, and repairing roads, bridges, machines, etc.

En·glish¹ /'ɪŋglɪʃ/ *n.* **1** [U] the language used in places such as the U.S., Canada, and Great Britain **2 the English** [plural] the people of England

English² *adj.* **1** relating to the English language **2** relating to or coming from England

en·grave /ɪn'greɪv/ *v.* [T] to cut words or pictures onto the surface of metal, wood, glass, etc. —**engraver** *n.* [C]

en·grav·ing /ɪn'greɪvɪŋ/ *n.* [C] a picture printed from an ENGRAVED piece of metal or wood

en·grossed /ɪn'groʊst/ *adj.* so interested in something that you do not notice anything else: *Kit was **engrossed in** a book.*

en·gross·ing /ɪn'groʊsɪŋ/ *adj.* so interesting that you do not notice anything else: *an engrossing story*

en·gulf /ɪn'gʌlf/ *v.* [T] **1** if a bad feeling engulfs you, you feel it very strongly: *Fear suddenly engulfed him.* **2** to completely surround or cover something: *a home **engulfed in** flames*

en·hance /ɪn'hæns/ *v.* [T] to improve something: *Adding lemon juice will enhance the flavor.* —**enhancement** *n.* [C,U]

e·nig·ma /ɪ'nɪgmə/ *n.* [C] a person, thing, or event that is strange, mysterious, and difficult to understand —**enigmatic** /ˌɛnɪg'mæt̮ɪk◂/ *adj.*

en·joy /ɪn'dʒɔɪ/ *v.* [T] **1** if you enjoy something, it gives you pleasure: *Did you enjoy the movie?* | *I really enjoy walking the dog.* ▶ Don't say "I enjoy to walk the dog." ◀

THESAURUS

like – to enjoy something, or think that it is nice or good: *Do you like Mexican food?*
love – to like something very much, or enjoy doing something very much: *My daughter loves to read.*
have a good/great time – to have experiences that you enjoy: *Did you have a good time at the party?*
have fun – to enjoy doing something: *I had a lot of fun in class today.*

2 enjoy yourself to be happy and have fun in a particular situation: *I missed Ted, but I was starting to enjoy myself.* **3** to have a particular ability, advantage, or success: *The team has enjoyed some success this season.* —**enjoyment** *n.* [U]

en·joy·a·ble /ɪn'dʒɔɪəbəl/ *adj.* giving you pleasure: *an enjoyable afternoon*

THESAURUS

great, **pleasant**, **fantastic**, **wonderful**
➔ see Thesaurus box at NICE

en·large /ɪn'lɑrdʒ/ *v.* [T] to become bigger, or to make something become bigger: *I'm going to get some of these pictures enlarged.*

en·large·ment /ɪn'lɑrdʒmənt/ *n.* [C] a photograph that has been printed again in a larger size

en·light·en /ɪn'laɪt̚n/ *v.* [T] *formal* to explain something to someone —**enlightening** *adj.*: *an enlightening experience*

en·light·ened /ɪn'laɪt̚nd/ *adj.* having sensible modern attitudes and treating people fairly and kindly: *an enlightened company that treats its employees well*

en·light·en·ment /ɪn'laɪt̚nmənt/ *n.* [U] the process of understanding something clearly, or when you help someone do this

en·list /ɪn'lɪst/ *v.* **1** [T] to persuade someone to help you, support you, etc.: *Children who are doing well are **enlisted to help** children who are struggling.* **2** [I] to join the army, navy, etc.: *I've **enlisted in** the Marines.* —**enlistment** *n.* [C,U]

TOPIC

join up, **be drafted**
➔ see Topic box at ARMY

en·list·ed /ɪn'lɪstɪd/ *adj.* **enlisted man/woman/personnel etc.** someone in the army, navy, etc. whose rank is below that of an officer

en·liv·en /ɪn'laɪvən/ *v.* [T] to make something more interesting or exciting

en masse /ɑn 'mæs, -'mɑs, ɛn-/ *adv.* together as one group: *City councilors threatened to resign en masse.*

en·mi·ty /'ɛnməṯi/ *n.* [U] feelings of hatred and anger

e·nor·mi·ty /ɪ'nɔrməṯi/ *n.* [singular, U] the fact of being very large or serious: *the enormity of the crime*

e·nor·mous /ɪ'nɔrməs/ *adj.* extremely large in size or amount [= **huge**]: *You should see their house – it's enormous!* | *an enormous amount of work* —**enormously** *adv.*

THESAURUS

huge, **vast**, **gigantic**, **massive**, **immense**, **colossal**, **substantial**
➔ see Thesaurus box at BIG

e·nough /ɪ'nʌf/ *adv., determiner, pron.* **1** as big, as many, as far, as much, etc. as necessary: *This bag isn't big **enough to** hold all my stuff.* | *He doesn't even earn **enough to** pay the rent.* | *Is he old **enough for** school?* | *Do we have **enough** food **for** everybody?* | *The coach thinks she's not trying hard enough.* | *Do you have enough money?* | *I think we've done enough.*

THESAURUS

plenty – a large amount that is enough or more than enough: *Try to eat plenty of fruits and vegetables.*
sufficient – as much as you need for a particular purpose: *His wages are barely sufficient to pay for his family's rent and food.*
adequate – enough in quantity or good enough in quality for a particular purpose: *If we are given adequate resources, we can finish the job on time.*

2 *spoken* used in order to say that you are tired or angry about a situation and want it to stop: ***I have***

E

***had enough** of your lies!* | ***That's enough**, you two. Stop yelling!* | *Finally my mother said **enough is enough** and kicked him out of the house.* **3** *spoken* said when a situation is already bad and you do not want it to get worse: *It's **bad enough** that you lied to me, without lying to Mother too.* | *I have **enough trouble/problems**; don't you go making it worse!* **4** not very, but in an acceptable way: *She's nice enough, but we don't have much in common.* **5 strangely/oddly/funnily enough** *spoken* used in order to say that a fact or something that happens is strange or surprising: *Funnily enough, I met him today after not having seen him for months.* ➔ **sure enough** at SURE[2]

GRAMMAR

Use **enough** after adjectives or adverbs, or before nouns: *These jeans aren't big enough.* | *There isn't enough space in this office.*

E

en·rage /ɪn'reɪdʒ/ *v.* [T] to make someone very angry —**enraged** *adj.*

en·rich /ɪn'rɪtʃ/ *v.* [T] to improve the quality of something: *vitamin-enriched flour* —**enrichment** *n.* [U]

en·roll, **enrol** /ɪn'roʊl/ *v.* [I,T] to officially join a school, university, etc., or to arrange for someone else to do this.: *the students **enrolled in** honors classes* | *Nathan **enrolled at** City College.*

en·roll·ment /ɪn'roʊlmənt/ *n.* [C,U] the number of students who are enrolled in a school or class, or the process of enrolling them: *Enrollment was high this year.*

en route /ɑn 'rut, ɛn-/ *adv.* on the way: *Dinner will be served **en route to** Dallas.*

en·sconce /ɪn'skɑns/ *v.* [T] *formal* to put someone in a safe and comfortable place: *Martha was **ensconced in** the biggest chair.*

en·sem·ble /ɑn'sɑmbəl/ *n.* [C] a small group of musicians who play together regularly

en·shrine /ɪn'ʃraɪn/ *v.* [T] *formal* to put something in a special place so that people can see it and remember it: *civil rights **enshrined in** the Constitution*

en·sign /'ɛnsən/ *n.* [C] a low rank in the Navy, or an officer who has this rank

en·slave /ɪn'sleɪv/ *v.* [T] *formal* **1** if something enslaves you, it completely controls your life and your actions **2** to make someone a SLAVE

en·sue /ɪn'su/ *v.* [I] *formal* to happen after something, often as a result of it: *A heated discussion ensued.* —**ensuing** *adj.*

en·sure /ɪn'ʃʊr/ *v.* [T] to do something to be certain of a particular result: *The troops will **ensure that** food aid goes where it is most needed.*

en·tail /ɪn'teɪl/ *v.* [T] to make something necessary, or have something as a necessary part: *Does your job entail much traveling?*

en·tan·gle /ɪn'tæŋgəl/ *v.* [T] **1 be entangled in/with** to make someone be involved with someone or something bad: *fears that the U.S. will get **entangled in** another war* **2** to make something be twisted or caught in a rope, net, etc.: *a fish **entangled in** the net* —**entanglement** *n.* [C,U]

en·ter[1] /'ɛntɚ/ *v.* **1** [I,T] to go or come into a place: *A nurse entered.* | *Army tanks entered the capital.*

THESAURUS

go in – to move into a particular place: *Frank opened the door, and we went in.*
come in – to enter a room or house: *Come in and sit down.*
barge in – to interrupt someone or go into a place when you were not invited: *He just barged in.*
sneak in – to go somewhere quietly and secretly: *After the movie had already started, we snuck in.*
get in – to be allowed or able to enter a place: *You can't get in without ID.*
trespass – to go onto someone's land without permission: *The sign said "No Trespassing."*

2 [T] to go inside something: *The virus enters the body through the lungs.* **3** [T] to start working in a particular profession, or studying at a particular university, school, etc.: *Both boys entered the Navy.* | *Many older students are now entering university.* **4** [T] to start to take part in an activity: *The U.S. entered the war in 1941.* | *More women began entering the workforce.* **5** [I,T] to take part in something such as a competition, or to arrange for someone else to do this: *Powell announced he would not enter the presidential race.* | *The school **entered** three candidates **in** the spelling bee.* **6** [T] to put information into a computer by pressing the keys, or to write information on a form, document, etc.: *Enter your name in block capitals.* **7** [T] to begin a period of time: *The economy is entering a period of growth.*

enter into sth *phr. v.* **1** to start doing something, discussing something, etc.: *Both sides must enter into negotiations.* **2** to be considered as a reason for something: *Money didn't enter into my decision to leave.* **3 enter into an agreement/contract etc.** *formal* to officially make an agreement

enter[2], **Enter** *n.* [singular] the key on a computer that you press to put information into a document, give an instruction, etc.: *Make a selection from the menu, then press Enter.*

en·ter·prise /'ɛntɚˌpraɪz/ *n.* **1** [C] a company, organization, or business: *The store is a family enterprise* (=owned by one family). **2** [U] the activity of starting and running businesses: *private enterprise* **3** [C] a large and complicated plan or process that you work on with other people: *The show is a huge enterprise.* **4** [U] the ability to work hard and think of new ideas, especially in business: *his enterprise and creativity* ➔ FREE ENTERPRISE

en·ter·pris·ing /ˈɛntɚˌpraɪzɪŋ/ *adj.* able and willing to do things that are new or difficult: *an enterprising law student*

en·ter·tain /ˌɛntɚˈteɪn/ *v.* **1** [I,T] to do something that interests and amuses people: *She **entertained** the children **with** stories and songs.* | *A museum should aim to entertain as well as educate.* **2** [I,T] to treat someone as a guest by providing food and drink for him/her: *Mike's entertaining clients tonight.* **3** [T] *formal* to consider or think about an idea, doubt, suggestion, etc.

en·ter·tain·er /ˌɛntɚˈteɪnɚ/ *n.* [C] someone whose job is to tell jokes, sing, etc.

en·ter·tain·ing /ˌɛntɚˈteɪnɪŋ/ *adj.* amusing and interesting: *an entertaining movie*

en·ter·tain·ment /ˌɛntɚˈteɪnmənt/ *n.* [U] things such as television, movies, etc. that amuse or interest people: *the entertainment industry* | *a bar with **live entertainment*** (=people who perform)

en·thrall /ɪnˈθrɔl/ *v.* [T] to completely hold someone's attention and interest —**enthralling** *adj.*

en·thuse /ɪnˈθuz/ *v.* [I] to talk about something with excitement and admiration

en·thu·si·as·m /ɪnˈθuziˌæzəm/ *n.* [U] a strong feeling of interest and enjoyment: *He sang **with enthusiasm**.* | *a teacher who shared my **enthusiasm for** history* | *The new students were **full of enthusiasm*** (=very enthusiastic). —**enthusiast** /ɪnˈθuziəst/ *n.* [C]

en·thu·si·as·tic /ɪnˌθuziˈæstɪk/ *adj.* showing a lot of interest and excitement about something: *a program that makes kids **enthusiastic about** learning* | *an enthusiastic crowd* —**enthusiastically** *adv.*

en·tice /ɪnˈtaɪs/ *v.* [T] to persuade someone to do something by offering him/her something nice: *The tax break is meant to **entice** businesses **to** locate in the city.* —**enticing** *adj.* —**enticement** *n.* [C,U]

en·tire /ɪnˈtaɪɚ/ *adj.* whole or complete – used in order to emphasize what you are saying: *I've spent the entire day cooking.*

en·tire·ly /ɪnˈtaɪɚli/ *adv.* completely: *Things are entirely different now.*

THESAURUS

completely, absolutely, totally, utterly
➔ see Thesaurus box at COMPLETELY

en·tire·ty /ɪnˈtaɪɚṭi/ *n.* **in sth's entirety** including all of something: *The speech is published in its entirety.*

en·ti·tle /ɪnˈtaɪṭl/ *v.* [T] **1** to give someone the right to have or do something: *Full-time employees are **entitled to** receive health insurance.* | *Membership **entitles** you **to** the full use of our fitness facilities.* **2** to give a title to a book, play, etc., or to have a particular title: *a book entitled "The Stone Diaries"*

en·ti·tle·ment /ɪnˈtaɪṭlmənt/ *n.* [C,U] the official right to have or receive something, or the amount you receive: *an employee's **entitlement to** free medical care*

en·ti·ty /ˈɛntəṭi/ *n.* plural **entities** [C] *formal* something that exists as a single and complete unit

en·to·mol·o·gy /ˌɛntəˈmɑlədʒi/ *n.* [U] the scientific study of insects —**entomologist** *n.* [C]

en·tou·rage /ˌɑntʊˈrɑʒ/ *n.* [C] a group of people who travel with an important person: *the President's entourage*

en·trails /ˈɛntreɪlz/ *n.* [plural] the inside parts of a person or animal, especially the BOWELS

entrance

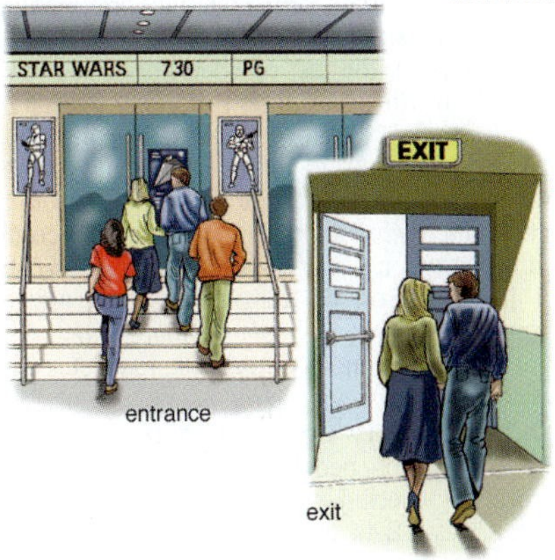

en·trance¹ /ˈɛntrəns/ *n.* **1** [C] a door, gate, or other opening that you go through to enter a place [≠ **exit**]: *the main **entrance to** the school* | *the **back/front/side entrance** of the hotel* **2** [U] the right or opportunity to enter a place: *Entrance will be denied to those without tickets.* | *an **entrance fee** for the museum* | ***Entrance to** the park is free.* **3** [U] permission to become a member of or become involved in a profession, a university, etc.: *the requirements for college entrance* **4 make an entrance** to come into a place in a way that makes people notice you ➔ —compare ENTRY

en·trance² /ɪnˈtræns/ *v.* [T usually passive] to make someone feel very interested in and pleased with something: *We were entranced by the brilliant colors.* —**entranced** *adj.*: *his entranced listeners* —**entrancing** *adj.*: *entrancing stories*

en·trant /ˈɛntrənt/ *n.* [C] *formal* someone who enters a competition

en·trap /ɪnˈtræp/ *v.* past tense and past participle **entrapped**, present participle **entrapping** [T] *formal* to trick someone so that s/he is caught doing something illegal —**entrapment** *n.* [U]

en·treat /ɪnˈtrit/ *v.* [T] *formal* to ask someone, with a lot of emotion, to do something —**entreaty** *n.* [C,U]

en·trée /ˈɑntreɪ/ *n.* [C] the main dish of a meal

en·trenched /ɪnˈtrɛntʃt/ *adj.* strongly estab-

E

lished and not likely to change: *entrenched attitudes*

en·tre·pre·neur /ˌɑntrəprəˈnɚ, -ˈnʊr/ *n.* [C] someone who starts a company, arranges business deals, and takes risks in order to make a profit —**entrepreneurial** /ˌɑntrəprəˈnʊriəl/ *adj.*

en·trust /ɪnˈtrʌst/ *v.* [T] to give someone something to be responsible for: *Bergen was* ***entrusted with*** *delivering the documents.*

en·try /ˈɛntri/ *n.* **1** [C,U] the act of going into a place, or the right or opportunity to enter a place [≠ **exit**]: *The papers granted him* ***entry into*** *the American Embassy.* | *There were no signs of* ***forced entry*** *into the house.* | *They were refused entry at the border.* **2** [U] the right or opportunity to become a member of a group or take part in something, or the fact of doing this: *the* ***entry of*** *new firms* ***into*** *the market* | *America's* ***entry into*** *the war* **3** [C] **also entryway** a door, gate, or passage that you go through to go into a place **4** [C] something written or printed in a book, list, etc.: *a dictionary entry* **5** [U] the act of recording information on paper or in a computer: *data entry* **6** [C] a person or thing that takes part in a competition, race, etc.: *the winning entry* **7** [U] the act of entering a competition, race, etc.: *Entry is open to anyone over 18.*

en·twine /ɪnˈtwaɪn/ *v.* [T] **1 be entwined** if two things or people are entwined, they are closely connected with each other in a complicated way **2** to twist something around something else: *flowers* ***entwined in*** *her hair*

e·nu·mer·ate /ɪˈnuməˌreɪt/ *v.* [T] *formal* to name a list of things, one by one

e·nun·ci·ate /ɪˈnʌnsiˌeɪt/ *v. formal* **1** [I,T] to pronounce words or sounds clearly **2** [T] to express ideas or principles clearly and firmly —**enunciation** /ɪˌnʌnsiˈeɪʃən/ *n.* [C,U]

en·vel·op /ɪnˈvɛləp/ *v.* [T] to cover something completely: *a building* ***enveloped in*** *flames* —**enveloping** *adj.*

en·ve·lope /ˈɛnvəˌloʊp, ˈɑn-/ *n.* [C] the paper cover in which you put a letter

en·vi·a·ble /ˈɛnviəbəl/ *adj.* an enviable quality, position, or possession is good and other people would like to have it: *an enviable position in the company* —**enviably** *adv.*

en·vi·ous /ˈɛnviəs/ *adj.* wishing that you had someone else's qualities or things: *Jackie was* ***envious of*** *Sylvia's success.* —**enviously** *adv.*

THESAURUS

jealous – angry or unhappy because you do not have something that someone else has: *Bill was jealous of his brother's success.*
envious – wishing that you had the qualities or things that someone else has: *I've been envious of all his free time.*

en·vi·ron·ment /ɪnˈvaɪrənmənt/ *n.* **1 the environment** the land, water, and air in which people, animals, and plants live: *laws to protect the environment*

TOPIC

things that are harmful to the environment
pollution – damage caused to air, water, soil, etc. by harmful chemicals and waste
the greenhouse effect – the warming of the air around the Earth as a result of the sun's heat being trapped by pollution
global warming – an increase in world temperatures, caused by pollution in the air
acid rain – rain that contains acid chemicals from factory smoke and cars, etc.
deforestation – when all the trees in an area are cut down or destroyed

describing things that are good for the environment
environmentally friendly/eco-friendly – products that are environmentally friendly or eco-friendly are not harmful to the environment
recycle – if materials such as glass or paper are recycled, they are put through a special process so that they can be used again
biodegradable – a material that is biodegradable can be destroyed by natural processes, in a way that does not harm the environment
organic – organic food or organic farming does not use chemicals that are harmful to the environment

2 [C,U] the situations, things, people, etc. that affect the way in which people live and work: *a pleasant work environment* **3** [C] the natural features of a place, for example its weather, the type of plants that grow there, etc.: *a forest environment*

en·vi·ron·men·tal /ɪnˌvaɪrənˈmɛntl/ *adj.* relating to or affecting the air, land, or water on Earth: *environmental damage caused by oil spills* —**environmentally** *adv.*

en·vi·ron·men·tal·ist /ɪnˌvaɪrənˈmɛntl-ɪst/ *n.* [C] someone who is concerned about protecting the environment

en·vi·rons /ɪnˈvaɪrənz, ɛn-/ *n.* [plural] *formal* the area surrounding a place

en·vi·sion /ɪnˈvɪʒən/ **also en·vis·age** /ɪnˈvɪzɪdʒ/ *v.* [T] to imagine something as a future possibility: *Eve had envisioned a career as a diplomat.*

en·voy /ˈɛnvɔɪ, ˈɑn-/ *n.* [C] someone who is sent to another country as an official representative

en·vy¹ /ˈɛnvi/ *n.* [U] **1** the feeling of wanting to have the qualities or things that someone else has: *She watched the other girls* ***with envy.*** **2 be the envy of sb** to be something that other people admire and want: *an education system that is the envy of the world*

envy² *v.* past tense and past participle **envied**, third person singular **envies** [T] to wish you had

E

the qualities or things that someone else has: *I really envy you and Meg; you seem so happy together.* | *I envied John his freedom.*

en·zyme /ˈɛnzaɪm/ *n.* [C] *technical* a chemical substance produced by living cells in plants and animals that causes changes in other chemical substances

e·on /ˈiɑn/ *n.* [C] an extremely long period of time

ep·au·let /ˌɛpəˈlɛt, ˈɛpəˌlɛt/ *n.* [C] a shoulder decoration on a military uniform

e·phem·er·al /ɪˈfɛmərəl/ *adj.* existing only for a short time

ep·ic[1] /ˈɛpɪk/ *adj.* **1** full of brave action and excitement: *an epic journey* **2** very big, long, or impressive: *an epic movie*

epic[2] *n.* [C] **1** a book or movie that tells a long story **2** a long poem about what gods or important people did in past times: *Homer's epic "The Odyssey"*

ep·i·cen·ter /ˈɛpəˌsɛntɚ/ *n.* [C] *technical* the place on the Earth's surface above the point where an EARTHQUAKE begins

ep·i·dem·ic /ˌɛpəˈdɛmɪk/ *n.* [C] **1** a large number of cases of a particular infectious disease happening at the same time: *a typhoid epidemic* **2** something bad that develops and spreads quickly: *an epidemic of crime* —**epidemic** *adj.*

ep·i·gram /ˈɛpəˌgræm/ *n.* [C] a short amusing poem or saying that expresses a wise idea

ep·i·lep·sy /ˈɛpəˌlɛpsi/ *n.* [U] a medical condition in the brain that can make someone become unconscious or unable to control his/her movements for a short time

ep·i·lep·tic /ˌɛpəˈlɛptɪk◂ / *n.* [C] someone who has EPILEPSY —**epileptic** *adj.*

ep·i·logue /ˈɛpəˌlɔg, -ˌlɑg/ *n.* [C] a speech or piece of writing added to the end of a book, movie, or play

E·pis·co·pal /ɪˈpɪskəpəl/ *adj.* relating to the Protestant church in America that developed from the Church of England —**Episcopalian** /ɪˌpɪskəˈpeɪliən/ *adj.*

ep·i·sode /ˈɛpəˌsoʊd/ *n.* [C] **1** a television or radio program that is one of a series of programs that tell a story: *It's my favorite episode of "I Love Lucy."* **2** an event, or a short time that is different from the time around it: *several episodes of depression* —**episodic** /ˌɛpəˈsɑdɪk/ *adj.*

e·pis·tle /ɪˈpɪsəl/ *n.* [C] *formal* **1** a long and important letter **2 Epistle** one of the letters written by the first Christians, which are in the New Testament of the Bible

ep·i·taph /ˈɛpəˌtæf/ *n.* [C] a statement about a dead person, on the stone over his/her grave

ep·i·thet /ˈɛpəˌθɛt/ *n.* [C] an adjective or short phrase used for describing someone

e·pit·o·me /ɪˈpɪt̬əmi/ *n.* **the epitome of sth** the perfect example of something: *Hitler is considered the epitome of evil.*

e·pit·o·mize /ɪˈpɪt̬əˌmaɪz/ *v.* [T] to be the perfect or most typical example of something: *Chicago's busy liveliness seemed to epitomize the U.S.*

ep·och /ˈɛpək/ *n.* [C] a period in history during which important events or developments happened

e·qual[1] /ˈikwəl/ *adj.* **1** the same in size, value, amount, etc.: *Divide the dough into three equal parts.* | *Both candidates received an* ***equal number*** *of votes.* | *Population growth is* ***equal to*** *2% a year.* | *two areas* ***of equal*** *size* **2** having the same rights, chances, etc. as everyone else.: *The Constitution says that all people are created equal.* | *equal partners in the business* | *equal rights for women* | *an equal opportunity employer* **3 be equal to the task/challenge etc.** to have the ability to deal with something successfully **4 on (an) equal footing also on equal terms** with neither side having any advantages over the other

equal[2] *v.* past tense and past participle **equaled** or **equalled** present participle **equaling** or **equalling** **1** [linking verb] to be the same as something else in size, number, amount, etc.: *Four plus four equals eight.* **2** [T] to be as good as something or someone else: *He has equalled the Olympic record!*

equal[3] *n.* [C] someone who is as important, intelligent, etc. as you are, or who has the same rights and opportunities as you do: *My boss treats her employees as equals.* | *Rembrandt was an artist* ***without equal*** (=no one was as good as he).

e·qual·i·ty /ɪˈkwɑlət̬i/ *n.* [U] the state of having the same conditions, opportunities, and rights as everyone else [≠ **inequality**]: *Women haven't achieved equality in the work force.* | ***equality of*** *opportunity* | *the struggle for* ***racial equality***

e·qual·ize /ˈikwəˌlaɪz/ *v.* [T] to make two or more things equal in size, value, etc.: *The funds given to all schools should be equalized.*

e·qual·ly /ˈikwəli/ *adv.* **1** to the same degree or limit: *The candidates are equally qualified for the job.* **2** in parts that are the same size: *We'll divide the work equally.*

ˈequal sign *n.* [C] the sign (=), used in mathematics to show that two amounts or numbers are the same

e·qua·nim·i·ty /ˌikwəˈnɪmət̬i, ˌɛk-/ *n.* [U] *formal* calmness in a difficult situation

e·quate /ɪˈkweɪt/ *v.* [T] *formal* to consider that one thing is the same as something else: *Don't* ***equate*** *criticism* ***with*** *blame.*

e·qua·tion /ɪˈkweɪʒən/ *n.* [C] a statement in mathematics showing that two quantities are equal, for example 2 x 3 + 4 = 10

e·qua·tor /ɪˈkweɪt̬ɚ/ *n.* **the equator** an imaginary circle around the Earth, that divides it equally into its northern and southern halves —**equatorial** /ˌɛkwəˈtɔriəl◂ / *adj.* ➔ see picture at GLOBE

e·ques·tri·an /ɪˈkwɛstriən/ *adj.* relating to horse riding

e·qui·lat·er·al /ˌikwəˈlæt̬ərəl/ *adj.* having all sides equal: *an equilateral triangle*

e·qui·lib·ri·um /ˌikwəˈlɪbriəm/ *n.* [U] **1** a balance between opposing forces, influences, etc.: *The supply and the demand for money must be kept **in equilibrium**.* **2** a calm emotional state

e·qui·nox /ˈikwəˌnɑks, ˈɛ-/ *n.* [C] one of the two times each year when day and night are equal in length everywhere

e·quip /ɪˈkwɪp/ *v.* past tense and past participle **equipped**, present participle **equipping** [T] **1** to provide a person, group, building, etc. with the things that are needed for a particular purpose: *The new school will be **equipped with** computers.* **2** to prepare someone for a particular purpose: *The program **equips** youngsters **with** technical skills.* | *a problem we weren't **equipped to** handle* —**equipped** *adj.*

e·quip·ment /ɪˈkwɪpmənt/ *n.* [U] the tools, machines, etc. that you need for a particular activity: *camera equipment* | *new **pieces of equipment** for the chemistry lab*

GRAMMAR

Equipment does not have a plural form. You can say **some equipment**, **any equipment**, or **pieces of equipment**: *We need to buy some extra equipment.*

E

eq·ui·ta·ble /ˈɛkwət̬əbəl/ *adj. formal* fair and equal to everyone involved: *an equitable solution*

THESAURUS

fair, **just**, **reasonable**, **balanced**, **even-handed**
➔ see Thesaurus box at FAIR[1]

eq·ui·ty /ˈɛkwət̬i/ *n.* [U] **1** *formal* a situation in which everyone is fairly treated **2** *technical* the value of something you own, such as a house or SHARES, after you have taken away the amount of money you still owe on it

e·quiv·a·lent[1] /ɪˈkwɪvələnt/ *adj.* equal in value, purpose, rank, etc. to something or someone else: *The atomic bomb has power **equivalent to** 10,000 tons of dynamite.*

equivalent[2] *n.* [C] something that has the same value, size, etc. as something else: *Some French words have no equivalents in English.* | *He had drunk the **equivalent of** two bottles of wine.*

e·quiv·o·cal /ɪˈkwɪvəkəl/ *adj.* **1** deliberately not clear or definite in meaning: *an equivocal answer* **2** difficult to understand or explain: *The results of the test were equivocal.*

ER *n.* [C] **emergency room**

e·ra /ˈɪrə, ˈɛrə/ *n.* [C] a long period of time that begins with a particular date or event: *the colonial era*

e·rad·i·cate /ɪˈrædəˌkeɪt/ *v.* [T] to completely destroy something: *Smallpox has been eradicated.* —**eradication** /ɪˌrædəˈkeɪʃən/ *n.* [U]

e·rase /ɪˈreɪs/ *v.* [T] **1** to completely remove written or recorded information so that it cannot be seen or heard: *I erased the answer.* | *Ben erased one of my favorite tapes.* **2** to get rid of something so that it is gone completely: *I could not erase the memories from that time.*

e·ras·er /ɪˈreɪsɚ/ *n.* [C] **1** a piece of rubber used for erasing pencil marks from paper **2** an object used for cleaning marks from a BLACKBOARD

e·rect[1] /ɪˈrɛkt/ *adj.* in a straight upright position: *He stood erect.*

erect[2] *v.* [T] **1** *formal* to build something: *Officials plan to erect a monument in Lindbergh's honor.*

THESAURUS

build, **construct**, **put up**
➔ see Thesaurus box at BUILD[1]

2 to put something in an upright position: *The tents for the fair were erected overnight.*

e·rec·tion /ɪˈrɛkʃən/ *n.* **1** [C] the swelling of a man's PENIS during sexual excitement **2** [U] the act of building something: *the erection of a new church*

The ocean has eroded the coastline.

e·rode /ɪˈroʊd/ *v.* **1** [I,T] to destroy something gradually by the action of wind, rain, or acid, or to be destroyed in this way: *The cliffs had been eroded by the sea.* **2** [T] to gradually reduce someone's power, authority, etc.

e·ro·sion /ɪˈroʊʒən/ *n.* [U] the process of eroding something: *soil erosion* | *the **erosion of** society's values*

e·rot·ic /ɪˈrɑt̬ɪk/ *adj.* relating to sexual love and desire: *erotic pictures* —**erotically** *adv.* —**eroticism** /ɪˈrɑt̬əˌsɪzəm/ *n.* [U]

err /ɛr, ɚ/ *v.* [I] **1 err on the side of caution/mercy etc.** to be very careful, very kind, etc. rather than risk making mistakes **2** *formal* to make a mistake

er·rand /ˈɛrənd/ *n.* [C] a short trip that you make to take a message or buy something: *I **have** some **errands** to do downtown.* | *Could you **run an errand** for Grandma?*

er·rant /ˈɛrənt/ *adj. formal* **1** behaving badly: *an errant husband* **2** going in the wrong direction: *Rainer caught the errant pass.*

er·rat·ic /ɪˈræt̬ɪk/ *adj.* changing often or moving in an irregular way, without any reason: *erratic behavior* —**erratically** *adv.*

er·ro·ne·ous /ɪˈroʊniəs/ *adj. formal* not correct: *erroneous statements* —**erroneously** *adv.*

er·ror /ˈɛrɚ/ *n.* [C,U] a mistake: *They had **made***

several ***errors***. | *an accident caused by* ***human error*** (=by a person rather than a machine) | *The company admitted it* ***was in error*** (=made a mistake). | *Kovitz apologized yesterday for his* ***error in/of judgment*** (=a decision that was a mistake).

THESAURUS

A **mistake** is something that you do by accident, or that is the result of a bad judgment: *I took Larry's coat by mistake.* | *We made a mistake in buying this car.*
An **error** is a mistake that you do not realize you are making, and that can cause problems: *He made several errors when adding up the bill.*

er·u·dite /ˈɛryəˌdaɪt, ˈɛrə-/ *adj. formal* showing a lot of knowledge —**erudition** /ˌɛryəˈdɪʃən/ *n.* [U]

e·rupt /ɪˈrʌpt/ *v.* [I] **1** to happen suddenly: *the bloody war that erupted in Rwanda* **2** if a VOLCANO erupts, it sends out smoke, fire, and rock into the sky **3** if a place erupts, the people there suddenly become very angry or excited: *The crowd erupted into applause.* —**eruption** /ɪˈrʌpʃən/ *n.* [C,U] *a volcanic eruption*

es·ca·late /ˈɛskəˌleɪt/ *v.* **1** [I,T] if violence or a war escalates, or if someone escalates it, it becomes much worse: *Fighting has escalated in several areas.* | *a dispute which has* ***escalated into*** *violence* **2** [I] to become higher or increase: *Housing prices escalated recently.* —**escalation** /ˌɛskəˈleɪʃən/ *n.* [C,U]

es·ca·la·tor /ˈɛskəˌleɪtə/ *n.* [C] a set of stairs that move and carry people from one level of a building to another

es·ca·pade /ˈɛskəˌpeɪd/ *n.* [C] an exciting adventure or series of events that may be dangerous

es·cape[1] /ɪˈskeɪp/ *v.* **1** [I,T] to succeed in going away from a place where you do no want to be, or from a dangerous situation: *He* ***escaped from*** *a maximum security prison.* | *The girl climbed through a window to escape the fire.*

THESAURUS

get away – to escape from someone who is chasing you: *In the dream a man with a knife is chasing me, and I can't get away.*
flee – to leave somewhere very quickly in order to escape from danger: *refugees who were forced to flee their country*
get out – to escape from a place
break out – to escape from prison: *Several inmates have broken out of the state penitentiary.*
break free/break away – to escape from someone who is trying to hold you: *She broke free and started running.*

2 [I,T] to avoid something bad: *The two boys managed to escape punishment.* | *The driver narrowly escaped death. She escaped with minor* ***injuries*** (=she avoided being seriously hurt) **3** [I] if gas, liquid, light, etc. escapes from somewhere, it comes out **4 escape sb's notice/attention** to not notice something —**escaped** *adj.*: *escaped prisoners*

escape[2] *n.* **1** [C,U] the act of escaping: *There was no chance of escape.* | *He crouched down, ready to* ***make*** *his* ***escape***. | *Passengers talked about their* ***escape from*** *the wreckage.* **2** [U] a way to forget about an unpleasant situation: *Books are a good form of escape.*

es·cap·ism /ɪˈskeɪpˌɪzəm/ *n.* [U] a way of forgetting about an unpleasant situation and thinking of pleasant things: *the escapism of the movies* —**escapist** *adj.*

es·chew /ɛsˈtʃu/ *v.* [T] *formal* to deliberately avoid doing, using, or having something

es·cort[1] /ɪˈskɔrt, ˈɛskɔrt/ *v.* [T] **1** to go somewhere with someone, especially in order to protect him/her: *Armed guards escorted the prisoners.* | *I escorted her to the door.* **2** to go with someone of the opposite sex to a social event: *The princess was escorted by her cousin.*

es·cort[2] /ˈɛskɔrt/ *n.* [C] the person or people who escort someone: *The Governor travels with a* ***police escort***. | *prisoners transported* ***under escort*** (=with an escort)

Es·ki·mo /ˈɛskəˌmoʊ/ *n.* [C] an Inuit. Some people now consider this word offensive.

ESL *n.* [U] **English as a Second Language** the teaching of English to people whose first language is not English, but who are living in an English-speaking country

e·soph·a·gus /ɪˈsɑfəgəs/ *n.* [C] the tube that goes from the mouth to the stomach

es·o·ter·ic /ˌɛsəˈtɛrɪk/ *adj.* known and understood only by a few people

ESP *n.* [U] **extrasensory perception** the ability to know what another person is thinking, see GHOSTS, etc.

es·pe·cial·ly /ɪˈspɛʃəli/ *adv.* **1** used in order to emphasize that something is more important than others, or that it happens more with one thing than with others: *Everyone's excited, especially Doug.* | *There may be feelings of dizziness,* ***especially when*** *walking or turning.* **2** to a particularly high degree, or more than usual: *The bread tasted especially good.* **3** for a particular purpose, reason, etc. [➡ **specially**]: *Several songs were recorded especially for the new collection.*

es·pi·o·nage /ˈɛspiəˌnɑʒ/ *n.* [U] the activity of finding out secret information and giving it to a country's enemies or a company's competitors

ESPN *n.* a CABLE television company that broadcasts sports programs in the U.S.

es·pouse /ɛˈspaʊz, ɪ-/ *v.* [T] *formal* to believe in and support an idea, especially a political one: *anti-drug policies espoused by the government*

es·pres·so /ɛˈsprɛsoʊ/ *n.* [C,U] very strong coffee that you drink in small cups

es·say /ˈɛseɪ/ *n.* [C] a short piece of writing about

a particular subject, especially as part of a course of study: *an **essay on/about** race relations*

es·sence /ˈɛsəns/ *n.* **1** [singular] the most basic and important quality of something: *Using scents to create a sense of well-being is the **essence of** aromatherapy.* | ***In essence*** (=basically), *these novels are all love stories.* **2** [U] a liquid that has a strong smell or taste and is obtained from a plant, flower, etc.: *vanilla essence*

es·sen·tial[1] /ɪˈsɛnʃəl/ *adj.* **1** important and necessary: *an essential element in the peace process* | *Good food is **essential for/to** your health.*

THESAURUS

important, crucial, vital, major, significant, key, necessary, mandatory, compulsory
➔ see Thesaurus box at IMPORTANT, NECESSARY

2 the essential parts, qualities, or features of something are the ones that are most important, typical, or easily noticed: *the **essential difference** between Democrats and Republicans*

essential[2] *n.* [C usually plural] something that is important and necessary: *the essentials of democracy* | *I packed only the **bare essentials*** (=the most necessary things).

es·sen·tial·ly /ɪˈsɛnʃəli/ *adv.* relating to the most important or basic qualities of something: *He is paid less for doing essentially the same job.*

es·tab·lish /ɪˈstæblɪʃ/ *v.* [T] **1** to start something such as a company, system, situation, etc., especially one that will exist for a long time: *The school was established in 1922.* **2** to begin a relationship, conversation, etc. with someone: *In the 1980s, the two countries began to establish trade relations.* **3** to make people accept that you can do something, or that you have a particular quality: *He's **established himself as** the most powerful man in the state.* **4** to find out facts that will prove that something is true: *Several studies have **established that** good daycare does children no harm.*

es·tab·lish·ment /ɪˈstæblɪʃmənt/ *n.* **1** [C] *formal* an institution, especially a business, store, hotel, etc.: *an educational establishment* **2 the Establishment** the organizations and people in a society who have a lot of power and who often are opposed to change or new ideas: *the **political/medical/military establishment*** **3** [U] the act of starting something such as a company, organization, system, etc.: *the establishment of new laws protecting children*

es·tate /ɪˈsteɪt/ *n.* **1** [singular] *law* all of someone's property and money, especially everything that is left after s/he dies **2** [C] a large area of land in the country, usually with one large house on it ➔ REAL ESTATE

es·teem[1] /ɪˈstim/ *n.* [U] *formal* a feeling of respect and admiration for someone: *She was **held in high esteem** by everyone on the team.* ➔ SELF-ESTEEM

esteem[2] *v.* [T] *formal* to respect and admire someone: *a **highly esteemed*** (=greatly respected) *artist*

es·thet·ic /ɛsˈθɛt̬ɪk/ *adj.* relating to beauty and the study of beauty —**esthetically** *adj.*

es·thet·ics /ɛsˈθɛt̬ɪks/ *n.* [U] the study of beauty, especially beauty in art

es·ti·mate[1] /ˈɛstəˌmeɪt/ *v.* [T] to judge the value, size, etc. of something: *We **estimate that** 75% of our customers are men.* | *Organizers **estimated** the crowd **at** 50,000 people.* | *The tree is **estimated to** be at least 700 years old.* —**estimated** *adj.*

es·ti·mate[2] /ˈɛstəmɪt/ *n.* [C] **1** a calculation or judgment of the value, size, etc. of something: ***a rough estimate*** (=a calculation that is not very exact) *of the distance* **2** a statement of how much it will probably cost to build or repair something: *Try to get three estimates.*

es·ti·ma·tion /ˌɛstəˈmeɪʃən/ *n.* [U] a judgment or opinion about someone or something: ***In** his **estimation**, they had greatly improved.*

es·tranged /ɪˈstreɪndʒd/ *adj.* **1** no longer living with your husband or wife **2** no longer having any relationship with a relative or friend: *Molly is **estranged from** her son.* —**estrangement** *n.* [C,U] *formal*

es·tro·gen /ˈɛstrədʒən/ *n.* [U] *technical* a HORMONE (=chemical substance) that is produced by a woman's body

es·tu·ar·y /ˈɛstʃuˌɛri/ *n.* plural **estuaries** [C] the wide part of a river where it goes into the ocean

ETA *n.* [U] **estimated time of arrival** the time when an airplane, train, etc. is expected to arrive

e-tail·er /ˈi ˌteɪlɚ/ *n.* [C] **electronic retailer** a business that sells products or services on the Internet

et al. /ˌɛt̬ ˈɑl, -ˈæl/ *adv. formal* used after a list of names to mean that other people, who are not named, are also involved in something

etc. /ɛt ˈsɛtrə, -t̬ərə/ *adv.* the written abbreviation of **et cetera** – used after a list to show that there are many other similar things or people that could be added

etch /ɛtʃ/ *v.* [I,T] to cut lines on a metal plate, piece of glass, stone, etc. to form a picture

e·ter·nal /ɪˈtɚnl/ *adj.* continuing for ever: *eternal life* —**eternally** *adv.*

e·ter·ni·ty /ɪˈtɚnət̬i/ *n.* **1 an eternity** a period of time that seems long because you are annoyed, anxious, etc.: *We waited for what seemed like an eternity.* **2** [U] time without any end, especially the time after death that some people believe continues for ever

e·ther /ˈiθɚ/ *n.* [U] **1** a clear liquid, used in past times to make people sleep during a medical operation **2** the air, considered as the place where computer information is

e·the·re·al /ɪ'θɪriəl/ *adj.* very delicate and light, in a way that does not seem real

eth·ic /'ɛθɪk/ *n.* [C] **1** an idea or belief that influences people's behavior and attitudes: *an ethic of fairness* **2 ethics** [plural] moral rules or principles of behavior for deciding what is right and wrong: *medical ethics*

eth·i·cal /'ɛθɪkəl/ *adj.* **1** relating to principles of what is right and wrong: *The use of animals in scientific tests raises difficult ethical questions.* **2** morally good and correct: *Is it ethical to use drugs to control behavior?* —**ethically** *adv.*

eth·nic /'ɛθnɪk/ *adj.* relating to a particular race, nation, tribe, etc.: *Bosnia's three main **ethnic groups** | students from a wide variety of **ethnic backgrounds***

ˌethnic 'cleansing *n.* [U] the use of violence in order to force people to leave an area because of their ethnic group

ˌethnic mi'nority *n.* [C] a group of people from a different ethnic group than the main group in a country

e·thos /'iθɑs/ *n.* [singular] the set of ideas and moral attitudes belonging to a person or group

e-tick·et /'i ˌtɪkɪt/ *n.* [C] **electronic ticket** a ticket, especially for an airplane, that is stored in a computer and is not given to the customer in paper form ➔ see Thesaurus box at TICKET[1]

et·i·quette /'ɛt̬ɪkɪt/ *n.* [U] the formal rules for polite behavior in society or in a particular group

et·y·mol·o·gy /ˌɛt̬ə'mɑlədʒi/ *n.* plural **etymologies** [C,U] the study of the origins, history, and meanings of words, or a description of the history of a particular word —**etymological** /ˌɛt̬əmə'lɑdʒɪkəl/ *adj.*

EU *n.* **the EU** the **European Union**

Eu·cha·rist /'yukərɪst/ *n.* **the Eucharist** the bread and wine that represent Christ's body and blood and are used during a Christian ceremony, or the ceremony itself

eu·lo·gy /'yulədʒi/ *n.* plural **eulogies** [C,U] *formal* a speech or piece of writing that praises someone or something very much, especially at a funeral

eu·phe·mism /'yufəˌmɪzəm/ *n.* [C] a polite word or expression that you use instead of a more direct one, in order to avoid shocking or upsetting someone —**euphemistic** /ˌyufə'mɪstɪk/ *adj.* —**euphemistically** *adv.*

eu·pho·ri·a /yu'fɔriə/ *n.* [U] a feeling of extreme happiness and excitement —**euphoric** /yu'fɔrɪk/ *adj.*

eu·ro /'yʊroʊ/ *n.* [C] a unit of money that is used in most countries belonging to the European Union

Eu·rope /'yʊrəp/ *n.* [C] one of the seven CONTINENTS that includes land north of the Mediterranean Sea and west of the Ural mountains

Eu·ro·pe·an[1] /ˌyʊrə'piən◂/ *adj.* relating to or coming from Europe

European[2] *n.* [C] someone from Europe

ˌEuropean 'Union *n.* a European political and economic organization

eu·tha·na·sia /ˌyuθə'neɪʒə/ *n.* [U] the act of killing in a painless way someone who is very sick, in order to stop him/her suffering —**euthanize** /'yuθəˌnaɪz/ *v.* [T]

e·vac·u·ate /ɪ'vækyuˌeɪt/ *v.* [I,T] to move people from a dangerous place to a safe place: *The police evacuated the building.* —**evacuation** /ɪˌvækyu'eɪʃən/ *n.* [C,U]

e·vac·u·ee /ɪˌvækyu'i/ *n.* [C] someone who has been evacuated

e·vade /ɪ'veɪd/ *v.* [T] **1** to avoid doing something you should do, or avoid talking about something [➡ **evasion**]: *Briggs evaded the issue.* **2** to avoid being caught by someone who is trying to catch you: *So far he has evaded capture.*

e·val·u·ate /ɪ'vælyuˌeɪt/ *v.* [T] *formal* to judge how good, useful, or successful someone or something is: *a chance for students to evaluate teachers*

THESAURUS

judge, **assess**, **appraise**, **gauge**
➔ see Thesaurus box at JUDGE[2]

e·val·u·a·tion /ɪˌvælyu'eɪʃən/ *n.* [C,U] the act of judging something or someone, or a document in which this is done: *an evaluation of new surgical techniques*

e·van·gel·i·cal /ˌivæn'dʒɛlɪkəl, ˌɛvən-/ *adj.* believing that religious ceremonies are not as important as Christian faith and studying the Bible, and trying to persuade other people to accept these beliefs

e·van·ge·list /ɪ'vændʒəlɪst/ *n.* [C] someone who travels from place to place in order to try to persuade people to become Christians —**evangelism** *n.* [U] —**evangelistic** /ɪˌvændʒə'lɪstɪk/ *adj.*

e·vap·o·rate /ɪ'væpəˌreɪt/ *v.* **1** [I,T] if a liquid evaporates, or if something evaporates it, it changes into a gas **2** [I] to slowly disappear: *Support for the idea has evaporated.* —**evaporation** /ɪˌvæpə'reɪʃən/ *n.* [U]

e·va·sion /ɪ'veɪʒən/ *n.* [C,U] **1** the act of avoiding doing something you should do: *tax evasion* **2** the act of deliberately avoiding talking about something or dealing with something: *a speech full of lies and evasions*

e·va·sive /ɪ'veɪsɪv/ *adj.* **1** not willing to answer questions directly: *an evasive answer* **2 evasive action** an action someone does to avoid being injured or harmed —**evasively** *adv.*

eve /iv/ *n.* **1** [C usually singular] the night or day before a religious day or a holiday: *a party on New Year's Eve* **2 the eve of sth** the time just before an important event: *the eve of the election*

e·ven[1] /'ivən/ *adv.* **1** used in order to emphasize that something is surprising or unexpected: *Even*

E

with the light on, it was hard to see. | *Carrie doesn't even like cookies!* **2** used in order to make a comparison stronger: *That just made me feel even worse.* | *an even bigger house* **3 even if** used in order to show that what you have just said will not change for any reason: *If you ask a question, you'll get an answer, even if it's "I don't know."* **4 even though** used in order to emphasize that although one thing happens or is true, something else also happens or is true: *He still remembers it, even though it happened more than 20 years ago.* **5 even so** used in order to say that something is true, although it is different from something you have just said: *I knew he had gone, but even so, I waited a few minutes more.*

even[2] *adj.* **1** flat, level, or smooth: *You need a flat, even surface to work on.*

> **THESAURUS**
>
> **flat, level, smooth, horizontal**
> → see Thesaurus box at FLAT[1]

E

2 an even rate, temperature, etc. does not change much: *Store the chemicals at an even temperature.* **3** separated or divided by equal amounts, spaces, etc.: *his even white teeth* | *an even distribution of wealth* **4 be even** *informal* to no longer owe someone money: *If you give me $5, we'll be even.* **5** an even number can be divided by 2 [≠ **odd**] **6 get even (with sb)** *informal* to do something bad to someone to punish him/her for something s/he did to you —**evenness** *n.* [U] → **break even** at BREAK[1]

even[3] *v.*

even (sth ⇔) **out** *phr. v.* to become equal or level, or to make something do this: *If I give you two, that'll even things out.* | *Over the year the rise and fall in share prices has tended to even out.*

even (sth ⇔) **up** *phr. v.* to become equal or the same, or to make something do this: *O'Malley hit a home run to even up the score.*

ˌeven-ˈhanded *adj.* giving fair and equal treatment to everyone

> **THESAURUS**
>
> **fair, just, reasonable, equitable, balanced**
> → see Thesaurus box at FAIR[1]

eve·ning /ˈivnɪŋ/ *n.* **1** [C,U] the end of the day and the early part of the night: *Are you doing anything tomorrow evening?* | *I have a class **on** Thursday **evenings**.* | *She does her homework **in the evening**.* **2 (Good) Evening** *spoken* said in order to greet someone when you meet him/her in the evening: *Evening, Rick.*

ˈevening gown also **ˈevening dress** *n.* [C] a dress worn by women for formal occasions in the evening

e·ven·ly /ˈivənli/ *adv.* **1** covering or affecting all parts of something equally: *Spread the paint evenly over the surface.* | *Make sure the weight is **evenly distributed**.* **2** divided in an equal way: *We split the money evenly.* **3** in a steady or regular way: *She was breathing evenly.* | *evenly spaced rows of young trees*

e·vent /ɪˈvɛnt/ *n.* [C] **1** something that happens, especially something important, interesting, or unusual: *a novel based on a historical event* | *the **sequence of events** leading up to the war*

> **THESAURUS**
>
> **occurrence** – something that happens: *a common occurrence*
> **incident** – something unusual, serious, or violent that happens: *an upsetting incident*
> **happening** – something that happens, especially a strange event: *There have been reports of strange happenings in the town.*
> **phenomenon** – something that happens or exists in society, science, or nature that is unusual or difficult to understand: *Homelessness is not a new phenomenon.*

2 a performance, sports competition, party, etc. that has been arranged for a particular date and time: *It was the **social event** of the summer.* | *Security is tight for large **sporting events**.* **3** one of the races or competitions that are part of a large sports competition: *"Which event are you entered in?" "The long jump."* **4 in any event** whatever happens or whatever situation: *My career, after this trial, is probably over in any event.* **5 in the event of rain/fire/an accident etc.** used in order to tell people what they should do or what will happen if something else happens: *Britain agreed to support the U.S. in the event of war.*

e·vent·ful /ɪˈvɛntˀfəl/ *adj.* full of interesting or important events: *an eventful meeting*

e·ven·tu·al /ɪˈvɛntʃuəl/ *adj.* happening at the end of a process: *Reading to a child is a strong factor in that child's eventual success at school.*

e·ven·tu·al·i·ty /ɪˌvɛntʃuˈæləṭi/ *n.* plural **eventualities** [C] *formal* a possible event or result, especially an unpleasant one

e·ven·tual·ly /ɪˈvɛntʃəli, -tʃuəli/ *adv.* after a long time: *He eventually became one of the top salesmen.*

> **USAGE**
>
> Use **eventually** or **finally** to say that something happens after a long time: *Eventually/Finally, we managed to get the car started.* | *She eventually/finally apologized.*
> Use **lastly** or **finally** to introduce the last point, action, or instruction in a list: *Finally/Lastly, I'd like to thank everyone for all their hard work.*
> Use **at last** to emphasize that you are glad when something happens because you have been waiting a long time for it: *Spring's here at last!*
> → FIRST

ev·er /ˈɛvɚ/ *adv.* **1** at any time – used mostly in questions, negatives, comparisons, or sentences with "if": *Nothing ever makes Paula angry.* | ***Have you ever** eaten snails?* | *If you're ever in Wilmington, give us a call.* | *That was one of the best meals I've ever had.* | *I **hardly ever*** (=almost never) *watch TV.* **2 ever since** continuously since: *He moved to Seattle after college and has lived there ever since.* **3 as good/much/long etc. as ever** as good, much, etc. as always or as usual: *The food was as good as ever.* **4 better/higher/more than ever** even better, higher, etc. than before: *People are having to work harder than ever just to pay the rent.* **5 ever-growing/ever-increasing etc.** continuously becoming longer, etc.: *the ever-growing population problem*

GRAMMAR

You use **ever** when you ask a question, but not when you answer a question: *"Have you ever been to France?" "Yes, I have been there."*

ev·er·green /ˈɛvɚˌgrin/ *adj.* evergreen trees have leaves that do not fall off in winter [➡ **deciduous**] —**evergreen** *n.* [C]

ev·er·last·ing /ˌɛvɚˈlæstɪŋ◂/ *adj.* continuing for ever: *everlasting peace*

ev·ery /ˈɛvri/ *determiner* **1** each one of a group of people or things: *Every student will receive a certificate.* | *He told Jan **every single** thing* (=all the things) *I said.* | *If you play this hard **every time*** (=each occasion), *you'll win every game.*

USAGE

Each, **every**, and **all** are all used to talk about every person or thing in a group.
When you are considering them separately, use **each** or **every** with a singular noun: *Each/Every child at the party was given a balloon.*
When you are considering them together, use **all** with a plural noun: *All the children enjoyed the trip.*

2 used in order to show how often something happens: *We get the newspaper every day.* | *Change the oil in the car every 5,000 miles.* | *He came to see us **every other day*** (=every two days). | *I still see her **every now and then/every so often*** (=sometimes but not often). **3 one in every 100/3 in every 5 etc.** used in order to show how often something affects a particular group of people or things: *One in every three couples live together without being married.* **4 every which way** *informal* in every direction: *People were running every which way.*

GRAMMAR

every, every one, everyone
These are all followed by a singular verb: *Almost every house has a computer nowadays.* | *Every one was different.* | *Everyone likes him.*
Every one is used to emphasize that you mean each person or thing in a group: *I've read every one of his books.*
Everyone means all the people in a group: *Hello, everyone, I'd like to introduce Denise, your new teacher.*
➔ ALL[1]

ev·ery·bod·y /ˈɛvriˌbɑdi, -ˌbʌdi/ *pron.* EVERYONE

ev·ery·day /ˈɛvriˌdeɪ/ *adj.* ordinary, usual, or happening every day: *Stress is just part of **everyday life**.*

ev·ery·one /ˈɛvriˌwʌn/ **also everybody** *pron.* **1** every person involved in a particular activity or in a particular place: *Is everyone ready to go?* | *They gave a small prize to everyone who played.* | *Where is everybody* (=where are the people that are usually here)*?* | *I was still awake but **everybody else*** (=all the other people) *had gone to bed.* | ***Everyone but*** (=all the people except) *Lisa went home.*

USAGE

Use **everyone** to mean all the people in a group: *Everyone is waiting for you.*
Use **every one** to mean each single person or thing in a group: *Every one of the books had a torn page.*

2 all people in general: *Everyone has a bad day now and then.*

ev·ery·place /ˈɛvriˌpleɪs/ *adv. spoken* EVERYWHERE

ev·ery·thing /ˈɛvriˌθɪŋ/ *pron.* **1** each thing or all things [➡ **nothing**]: *I think everything is ready.* | *I've forgotten everything I learned about math in school.* | *There's only bread left. They've eaten **everything else*** (=all other things). **2** used when you are talking in general about your life or about a situation [➡ **nothing**]: *Everything was going wrong.* **3 be/mean everything** to be the thing that matters most: *Money isn't everything.* **4 and everything** *spoken* and a lot of similar things: *She's at the hospital having tests and everything.*

ev·ery·where /ˈɛvriˌwɛr/ *adv.* in or to every place [➡ **nowhere**]: *I've looked everywhere for my keys.* | *People here are the same as people **everywhere else**.*

THESAURUS

all over – everywhere on a surface or in a place: *Jack's clothes were all over the floor.*
worldwide – everywhere in the world: *He has fans worldwide.*
nationwide – everywhere in a particular nation: *The company has over 350 stores nationwide.*
everyplace spoken – everywhere: *There you are. I've been looking for you everyplace.*

e·vict /ɪˈvɪkt/ *v.* [T] to legally force someone to leave the house s/he is renting from you: *Frank was **evicted from** his apartment four months ago.* ➔ see Topic box at RENT[1] —**eviction** /ɪˈvɪkʃən/ *n.* [C,U]

ev·i·dence /ˈɛvədəns/ *n.* **1** [U] facts, objects, or signs that show that something exists or is true: *The police **have evidence that** the killer was a*

E

woman. | *scientists looking for* ***evidence of*** *life on other planets* | *I had to* ***give evidence*** (=tell the facts) *in my brother's trial.* | *There was very little* ***evidence against*** *him.* | *medical/scientific evidence* ➔ see Topic box at COURT[1] **2 be in evidence** *formal* to be easily seen or noticed: *The police were very much in evidence at the march.*

GRAMMAR

Evidence does not have a plural form. You can say **some evidence**, **any evidence**, or **pieces of evidence**: *There is some evidence that foods rich in vitamin C can give protection against cancer.*

ev·i·dent /ˈɛvədənt/ *adj.* easily noticed or understood: ***It was*** *clearly* ***evident that*** *she was unhappy.* —**evidently** *adv.*

e·vil[1] /ˈivəl/ *adj.* **1** deliberately cruel or harmful: *an evil dictator* **2** morally wrong: *Slavery was evil.*

THESAURUS

bad, wicked, immoral, wrong, reprehensible
➔ see Thesaurus box at BAD[1]

3 relating to the Devil: *evil spirits*

evil[2] *n. formal* **1** [U] actions and behavior that are morally wrong and cruel: *the battle between* ***good and evil*** **2** [C] something that is very bad or harmful: *the* ***evils of*** *alcohol*

e·voc·a·tive /ɪˈvɑkət̬ɪv/ *adj.* making people remember something by reminding them of a feeling or memory: *the evocative smell of baking bread*

e·voke /ɪˈvoʊk/ *v.* [T] to produce a strong feeling or memory in someone: *Hitchcock's movies can evoke a sense of terror.* —**evocation** /ˌɛvəˈkeɪʃən, ˌivoʊ-/ *n.* [C,U]

ev·o·lu·tion /ˌɛvəˈluʃən/ *n.* [U] **1** the scientific idea that plants and animals develop gradually from simpler to more complicated forms **2** the gradual change and development of an idea, situation, or object: *the* ***evolution of*** *the home computer* —**evolutionary** *adj.*

e·volve /ɪˈvɑlv/ *v.* **1** [I] to develop and change gradually over a long period of time: *Did man* ***evolve from*** *apes?* **2** [T] to develop something gradually: *In America, we have evolved legal structures to protect people's rights.*

ewe /yu/ *n.* [C] a female sheep

ex /ɛks/ *n.* [C usually singular] *informal* someone's former wife, husband, GIRLFRIEND, or BOYFRIEND

ex·ac·er·bate /ɪgˈzæsɚˌbeɪt/ *v.* [T] *formal* to make a bad situation worse: *Higher taxes exacerbated the problem.* —**exacerbation** /ɪgˌzæsɚˈbeɪʃən/ *n.* [U]

ex·act[1] /ɪgˈzækt/ *adj.* **1** correct and including all the necessary details: *The* ***exact time*** *is 2:47.* | *What were her* ***exact words****?* | *It has been nine months,* ***to be exact.*** **2 the exact opposite** someone or something that is as different as possible from another person or thing: *Unfortunately, today the exact opposite is true.*

exact[2] *v.* [T] *formal* **1** to punish someone or have a bad effect on him/her: *the penalty exacted for breaking the rules* **2** to demand and get something from someone by using threats, force, etc.

ex·act·ing /ɪgˈzæktɪŋ/ *adj.* demanding a lot of care, effort, and attention: *an exacting piece of work*

ex·act·ly /ɪgˈzæktli/ *adv.* **1** used in order to emphasize that a particular number, amount, or piece of information is completely correct: *We got home at exactly six o'clock.* | *You're exactly right.* | *I don't know* ***exactly where*** *she lives.* | ***What exactly*** *did she say?* **2** *spoken* said in order to emphasize that something is the same in every way: *That's* ***exactly what*** *I've been trying to tell you!* | *She's* ***exactly like*** *her mother.* | *The changes have had* ***exactly the opposite*** *effect from what was intended.* **3** *spoken* said when you agree with what someone is saying: *"So we should spend more on education?" "Exactly!"* **4 not exactly** *spoken* **a)** used as a reply to show that what someone has said is not completely correct or true: *"He told you?" "Not exactly. I heard him talking to Sarah."* **b)** used in order to show that you mean the opposite: *The report isn't exactly beach reading.*

ex·ag·ger·ate /ɪgˈzædʒəˌreɪt/ *v.* [I,T] to make something seem better, larger, worse, etc. than it really is: *The danger should not be exaggerated.* —**exaggerated** *adv.* —**exaggeration** /ɪgˌzædʒəˈreɪʃən/ *n.* [C,U]

ex·alt /ɪgˈzɔlt/ *v.* [T] *formal* to praise someone

ex·al·ta·tion /ˌɛgzɔlˈteɪʃən, ˌɛksɔl-/ *n.* [C,U] *formal* a very strong feeling of happiness

ex·alt·ed /ɪgˈzɔltɪd/ *adj. formal* **1** having a very high rank and highly respected **2** filled with a feeling of great happiness

ex·am /ɪgˈzæm/ *n.* [C] **1** an official test of knowledge or ability in a particular subject: *a chemistry exam* | *When do you* ***take*** *your final* ***exams****?* | *How did you do* ***on the exam****?* **2** a set of medical tests: *an eye exam*

ex·am·i·na·tion /ɪgˌzæməˈneɪʃən/ *n.* [C] **1** the process of looking at something carefully in order to see what it is like or find out something: *a detailed* ***examination of*** *the photographs* | ***On closer examination*** *the vases were seen to be cracked.* **2** *formal* an EXAM

ex·am·ine /ɪgˈzæmɪn/ *v.* [T] **1** to look at something carefully in order to make a decision, find out something, etc.: *The doctor examined me thoroughly.* | *The study* ***examines how*** *alcohol abuse affects family relationships.* | *The police* ***examined*** *the room* ***for*** *fingerprints.* **2** *formal* to ask someone questions to get information or to test his/her knowledge about some-

examine

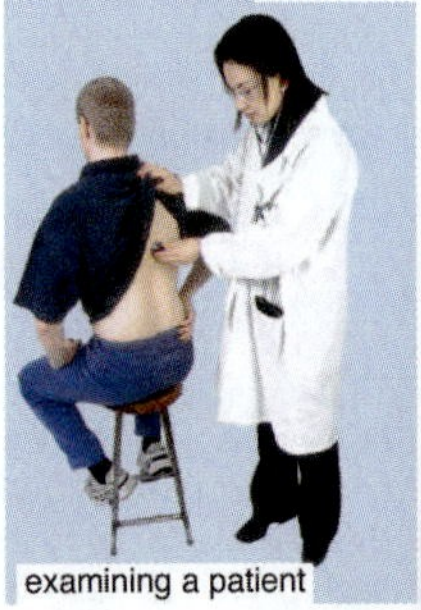

examining a patient

thing: *You will be* ***examined on*** *everything covered this semester.* —**examiner** *n.* [C]

ex·am·ple /ɪgˈzæmpəl/ *n.* [C] **1** someone or something that you mention to show what you mean, show that something is true, or show what something is like: *an* ***example of*** *students' writing* | *This church is a* ***good/typical/classic example*** *of Gothic architecture.* | *Can anyone* ***give*** *me* ***an example*** *of a transitive verb?* | *Many countries,* ***for example*** (=as an example) *Mexico and Japan, have a lot of earthquakes.* **2** someone whose behavior is very good and should be copied by other people: *Parents should* ***set an example for*** *their children* (=behave in the way they want their children to behave). | *She's an* ***example to*** *us all.* **3 make an example of sb** to punish someone so that other people are afraid to do the same thing

ex·as·per·ate /ɪgˈzæspəˌreɪt/ *v.* [T] to make someone feel very annoyed by continuing to do something that upsets him/her: *His refusal to agree has exasperated his lawyers.* —**exasperating** *adj.* —**exasperation** /ɪgˌzæspəˈreɪʃən/ *n.* [U]

ex·as·pe·rat·ed /ɪgˈzæspəˌreɪt̬ɪd/ *adj.* feeling annoyed because someone is continuing to do something that upsets you

ex·ca·vate /ˈɛkskəˌveɪt/ *v.* [I,T] **1** to dig a hole in the ground **2** to dig up the ground in order to find something that was buried there in an earlier time: *archeologists excavating an ancient city* —**excavation** /ˌɛkskəˈveɪʃən/ *n.* [C,U]

ex·ceed /ɪkˈsid/ *v.* [T] *formal* **1** to be more than a particular number or amount: *The cost must not exceed $150.* | *Sales have* ***exceeded*** *our* ***expectations****.* **2** to go beyond an official or legal limit: *a fine for exceeding the speed limit*

ex·ceed·ing·ly /ɪkˈsidɪŋli/ *adv.* *formal* extremely: *The show has done exceedingly well.*

ex·cel /ɪkˈsɛl/ *v.* past tense and past participle **excelled**, present participle **excelling** [I] *formal* to do something very well, or much better than most people: *He had* ***excelled in*** *volleyball and track.*

ex·cel·lence /ˈɛksələns/ *n.* [U] the quality of being excellent: *an honor given for academic excellence*

ex·cel·lent /ˈɛksələnt/ *adj.* **1** extremely good or of very high quality: *Jim's in excellent health.* | *The food was excellent.*

> **THESAURUS**
>
> **good, great, wonderful, fantastic, first-class, outstanding, ace**
> ➔ see Thesaurus box at GOOD[1]

2 *spoken* said when you approve of something: *"There's a party at Becky's house tonight." "Excellent!"* —**excellently** *adv.*

ex·cept[1] /ɪkˈsɛpt/ *prep.* used in order to show the things or people who are not included in a statement: *We're open every day except Monday.* | *Everyone went to the show,* ***except for*** *Scott and Danny.* | *I don't know anything about it,* ***except what*** *I've read in the newspaper.*

except[2] *conjunction* used in order to show that the statement you have just made is not true or not completely true: *It is like all the other houses,* ***except that*** *it's painted bright blue.* | *I have earrings just like those, except they're silver.* | *I'd go, except it's too far.*

except[3] *v.* [T] *formal* to not include something

ex·cept·ed /ɪkˈsɛptɪd/ *adj.* not included: *$5 per person, children excepted.*

ex·cept·ing /ɪkˈsɛptɪŋ/ *prep.* *formal* not including

ex·cep·tion /ɪkˈsɛpʃən/ *n.* [C,U] **1** someone or something that is not included in something: *It's been very cold, but today's an exception.* | *He was asked to* ***make an exception*** *to company policy* (=not include something in the policy). | *Everyone has improved,* ***with the*** *possible* ***exception of*** *Simon.* **2 be no exception** used in order to say that something is not different than before or than the other things mentioned: *March weather is usually changeable and this year was no exception.* **3 without exception** *formal* used in order to say that something is true of all the people or things in a group: *Almost without exception, teachers said that students do not work hard enough.*

ex·cep·tion·al /ɪkˈsɛpʃənəl/ *adj.* **1** unusually good: *an exceptional student*

> **THESAURUS**
>
> **good, great, excellent, wonderful, fantastic, outstanding, first-class, ace**
> ➔ see Thesaurus box at GOOD[1]

2 unusual and not likely to happen often: *The teachers were doing their best under* ***exceptional circumstances****.* —**exceptionally** *adv.*

ex·cerpt /ˈɛksɚpt/ *n.* [C] a short piece of writing or music taken from a longer book, poem, etc.: *an* ***excerpt from*** *his poem*

ex·cess[1] /ˈɛksɛs, ɪkˈsɛs/ *n.* **1** [singular, U] a larger amount of something than is needed, usual, or allowed: *There is* ***an excess of*** *alcohol in his blood.* **2 in excess of sth** more than a particular amount: *Our profits were in excess of $5 million.* **3 do sth to excess** to do something too much or too often: *He drinks to excess.* **4 excesses** [plural] actions that are socially or morally unacceptable: *the worst* ***excesses of*** *capitalism*

excess[2] *adj.* additional and more than is needed or allowed: *a charge of $75 for excess baggage*

ex·ces·sive /ɪkˈsɛsɪv/ *adj.* much more than is reasonable or necessary: *excessive fees* —**excessively** *adv.*

ex·change[1] /ɪksˈtʃeɪndʒ/ *n.* **1** [C,U] the act of giving someone something and receiving something else from him/her: *an* ***exchange of*** *political prisoners* | *The police offered him protection* ***in exchange for*** *information.* **2** [C] a short conver-

E

sation, especially an angry one **3 exchange of ideas/information etc.** an action in which people discuss or share ideas, information, etc. **4** [C] an arrangement in which a student, teacher, etc. visits another country to work or study **5** [C] → STOCK EXCHANGE

exchange² *v.* [T] **1** to give something to someone who gives you something else: *We still exchange gifts at Christmas.*

THESAURUS

trade – to exchange something that you have for something that someone else has: *He had traded milk and eggs from the farm for flour and sugar.*
swap – to give something to someone, who gives you something similar: *The two schools use the Internet to swap pictures, stories, and jokes.*
in exchange/return (for sth) – if you give something in exchange or in return for something else, you give it in order to get something else back: *Williams will plead guilty in exchange for a reduced sentence.*

2 to replace one thing with another: *This shirt is too big. Can I* ***exchange*** *it* ***for*** *a smaller one?* **3** if two people exchange words, information, looks, etc., they talk to each other, look at each other, etc. —**exchangeable** *adj.*

ex'change rate *n.* [C] the value of the money of one country compared to the money of another country

ex·cise¹ /'ɛksaɪz, -saɪs/ *n.* [C,U] the government tax on particular goods produced and used inside a country

ex·cise² /ɪk'saɪz/ *v.* [T] *formal* to remove something completely by cutting it out —**excision** /ɪk'sɪʒən/ *n.* [C,U]

ex·cit·a·ble /ɪk'saɪṭəbəl/ *adj.* easily excited

ex·cite /ɪk'saɪt/ *v.* [T] **1** to make someone feel happy, eager, or nervous: *The thought of returning to Montana excited me.* **2** to make someone have strong feelings: *The murder trial has excited public interest.*

ex·cit·ed /ɪk'saɪṭɪd/ *adj.* **1** happy, interested, or hopeful because something good has happened or will happen: *We're really* ***excited about*** *our trip to California.* | *These teachers want kids to* ***get excited*** *about learning.* **2** feeling sexual desire —**excitedly** *adv.*

ex·cite·ment /ɪk'saɪt˺mənt/ *n.* [U] the feeling of being excited: *the city's* ***excitement about/over*** *the Olympics* | *Their eyes sparkled* ***with excitement.***

ex·cit·ing /ɪk'saɪṭɪŋ/ *adj.* making you feel happy or interested in something: *an exciting story*

THESAURUS

thrilling – exciting and interesting: *a thrilling 3–2 victory*
gripping – a gripping movie, story, etc. is very exciting and interesting: *The novel is a gripping tale of power and corruption in ancient Rome.*
exhilarating – making you feel happy, excited, and full of energy: *an exhilarating ride*
electric – making you feel very excited: *There was an almost electric atmosphere in the stadium.*

ex·claim /ɪk'skleɪm/ *v.* [I,T] *written* to say something suddenly because you are surprised, excited, or angry: *"Oh!" exclaimed Stella. "What happened?"* —**exclamation** /ˌɛksklə'meɪʃən/ *n.* [C]

excla'mation ˌpoint also **excla'mation ˌmark** *n.* [C] the mark (!) used in writing after a sentence or word that expresses surprise, excitement, or anger

ex·clude /ɪk'sklud/ *v.* [T] **1** to not allow someone to enter a place, or to do something: *Women are* ***excluded from*** *the priesthood.* **2** to deliberately not include something: *Some of the data was* ***excluded from*** *the report.*

ex·clud·ing /ɪk'skludɪŋ/ *prep.* not including: *The trip costs $1,300, excluding airfare.*

ex·clu·sion /ɪk'skluʒən/ *n.* [U] **1** a situation in which someone is not allowed to do something or something is not used: *At that time, the judges upheld the* ***exclusion*** *of women* ***from*** *juries.* **2 do sth to the exclusion of sth** to do something so much that you do not do, consider, or have time for something else

ex·clu·sive¹ /ɪk'sklusɪv, -zɪv/ *adj.* **1** exclusive places, organizations, etc. are for people who have a lot of money, or who belong to a high social class: *an exclusive Manhattan hotel* **2** used by only one person or group, and not shared: *a car for the* ***exclusive use*** *of the Pope* **3 exclusive of sth** not including something: *The trip cost $450, exclusive of meals.*

exclusive² *n.* [C] an important news story that is in only one newspaper, magazine, television news program, etc.

ex·clu·sive·ly /ɪk'sklusɪvli, -zɪv-/ *adv.* only: *Businesses should not focus exclusively on profit.*

ex·com·mu·ni·cate /ˌɛkskə'myunəˌkeɪt/ *v.* [T] if a church excommunicates someone, it punishes him/her by not allowing him/her to continue to be a member —**excommunication** /ˌɛkskəˌmyunə'keɪʃən/ *n.* [C,U]

ex·cre·ment /'ɛkskrəmənt/ *n.* [U] *formal* the solid waste from a person's or animal's body

ex·crete /ɪk'skrit/ *v.* [I,T] *formal* to get rid of waste from the body through the BOWELS, or to get rid of waste liquid through the skin

ex·cru·ci·at·ing /ɪk'skruʃiˌeɪṭɪŋ/ *adj.* **1** extremely painful **2** extremely boring or embarrassing: *a story told in excruciating detail* —**excruciatingly** *adv.*

ex·cur·sion /ɪk'skɚʒən/ *n.* [C] a short trip, usually made by a group of people: *an* ***excursion to*** *Sea World*

E

ex·cus·a·ble /ɪk'skyuzəbəl/ *adj.* behavior or words that are excusable are easy to forgive [≠ **inexcusable**]

ex·cuse¹ /ɪk'skyuz/ *v.* [T] **1 excuse me** *spoken* **a)** said when you want to politely get someone's attention in order to ask a question: *Excuse me, is this the right bus for the airport?* **b)** used in order to say you are sorry when you have done something that is embarrassing or rude: *Oh, excuse me, I didn't know anyone was in here.* **c)** used in order to politely tell someone that you are leaving a place: *Excuse me, I'll be right back.* **d)** used in order to ask someone to repeat what s/he has just said: *"What time is it?" "Excuse me?" "I asked what time it is."* **e)** used in order to ask someone to move so you can go past him/her: *Excuse me, I need to get through.* **2** to forgive someone, usually for something not very serious: *Please excuse my bad handwriting.* | *Please* ***excuse*** *me* ***for*** *being so late.* **3** to not make someone do something that s/he is supposed to do: *She was* ***excused from*** *jury duty.*

ex·cuse² /ɪk'skyus/ *n.* [C] **1** a reason that you give to explain why you did something: *What's your* ***excuse for*** *being late?* | *There's* ***no excuse*** *for laziness.* | *You need to stop* ***making excuses*** *and take responsibility.* | *I was glad to* ***have an excuse*** *to put it off another day.*

THESAURUS

reason, explanation, motive
→ see Thesaurus box at REASON¹

2 a false reason that you give to explain why you are or are not doing something: *I'll* ***make an excuse*** *and leave early.* | *They were looking for any* ***excuse to*** *start a fight.*

ex·ec /ɪg'zɛk/ *n.* [C] *informal* a business EXECUTIVE

ex·e·cute /'ɛksɪˌkyut/ *v.* [T] **1** to kill someone, especially as a legal punishment for a crime **2** *formal* to do something that you have planned: *These ideas require money and materials to execute.*

ex·e·cu·tion /ˌɛksɪ'kyuʃən/ *n.* **1** [C,U] the act of killing someone, especially as a legal punishment for a crime **2** [U] *formal* a process in which you do something that you have planned to do: *the planning and* ***execution of*** *urban policy*

ex·e·cu·tion·er /ˌɛksɪ'kyuʃənɚ/ *n.* [C] someone whose job is to kill someone else as a legal punishment for a crime

ex·ec·u·tive¹ /ɪg'zɛkyət̬ɪv/ *n.* [C] a manager in an organization or company who helps make important decisions

executive² *adj.* **1** relating to making decisions, especially in a company or business: *an executive committee* **2 executive branch** the part of a government that approves decisions and laws and organizes how they will work [➡ **judiciary, legislature**]

ex·ec·u·tor /ɪg'zɛkyət̬ɚ/ *n.* [C] *law* someone who deals with the instructions in a WILL

ex·em·pla·ry /ɪg'zɛmpləri/ *adj. formal* **1** excellent and providing a good example to follow: *the students' exemplary behavior* **2** severe and used as a warning: *an exemplary punishment*

ex·em·pli·fy /ɪg'zɛmpləˌfaɪ/ *v.* past tense and past participle **exemplified**, third person singular **exemplifies** [T] *formal* **1** to be a very typical example of something: *This dish exemplifies her style of cooking.* **2** to give an example of something: *Exemplify each part of your argument.*

ex·empt¹ /ɪg'zɛmpt/ *adj.* having special permission not to do something or pay for something: *The money is* ***exempt from*** *state taxes.*

exempt² *v.* [T] to give someone special permission not to do or pay something: *Children are* ***exempted from*** *this rule.*

ex·emp·tion /ɪg'zɛmpʃən/ *n.* **1** [C] an amount of money that you do not have to pay tax on in a particular year: *a* ***tax exemption*** *for gifts to charity* **2** [C,U] permission not to do or pay something: *an* ***exemption from*** *military service*

E

ex·er·cise¹ /'ɛksɚˌsaɪz/ *n.* **1** [C,U] physical activity that you do in order to stay strong and healthy: *stretching exercises* | *I don't* ***get*** *much* ***exercise.*** | *Have you* ***done*** *your stomach* ***exercises*** *today?* **2** [C] a set of written questions that test your skill or knowledge: *For homework,* ***do exercises*** *1 and 2.* **3** [C] an activity or process that helps you practice a particular skill: *military exercises in the Pacific Ocean* | *We practiced relaxation exercises.* **4** [singular] an activity or situation that has a particular quality or result: *Trying to use public transportation to get downtown is an* ***exercise in*** *frustration.* **5** [C] *formal* the use of power or a right: *laws that protect the exercise of freedom of speech*

exercise² *v.* [I,T] **1** to do physical activities regularly so that you stay strong and healthy: *Eat right and exercise regularly.* | *Swimming exercises all the major muscle groups.*

TOPIC

People exercise so they can **stay/keep/get in shape** (=be healthy and strong). There are many different kinds of exercise, for example **jogging**, **lifting weights**, and **aerobics**. People often go to a **gym** or a **health club** to exercise. The series of exercises you do is called a **workout**. Before exercising, you **warm up** (=get your body ready) by **stretching** or jogging slowly.

2 *formal* to use power, a right, etc. to make something happen: *More young people need to exercise their right to vote.*

'exercise ˌbike *n.* [C] a bicycle that does not move and is used indoors for exercise

ex·ert /ɪg'zɚt/ *v.* [T] **1** to use your authority, power, influence, etc. to make something happen: *Powerful people* ***exerted pressure on*** *the paper* *not to run the story.* **2 exert yourself** to work very hard, using a lot of physical or mental energy

ex·er·tion /ɪg'zɚʃən/ *n.* [C,U] strong physical or mental effort

ex·hale /ɛks'heɪl, ɛk'seɪl/ *v.* [I,T] to breathe air, smoke, etc. out of your mouth [≠ **inhale**]: *Take a deep breath, then exhale slowly.*

ex·haust[1] /ɪg'zɔst/ *v.* [T] **1** to make someone very tired: *The effort exhausted her.* **2** to use all of something: *We are in danger of exhausting the world's oil supply.*

exhaust[2] *n.* **1** [U] the gas that is produced when a machine is working: *exhaust fumes* **2** [C] **also exhaust pipe** a pipe on a car or machine that exhaust comes out of

ex·haust·ed /ɪg'zɔstɪd/ *adj.* extremely tired: *He was* ***exhausted by/from*** *the long day.*

THESAURUS

tired, **worn out**, **weary**, **run-down**, **beat**
→ see Thesaurus box at TIRED

ex·haust·ing /ɪg'zɔstɪŋ/ *adj.* making you feel extremely tired: *an exhausting trip*

ex·haus·tion /ɪg'zɔstʃən/ *n.* [U] the state of being extremely tired

ex·haus·tive /ɪg'zɔstɪv/ *adj.* extremely thorough: *an exhaustive search* —**exhaustively** *adv.*

ex·hib·it[1] /ɪg'zɪbɪt/ *v.* **1** [I,T] to put something in a public place so people can see it: *The gallery will exhibit some of Dali's paintings.* **2** [T] *formal* to show a quality, sign, emotion, etc. in a way that people easily notice: *The patient exhibited symptoms of heart disease.*

exhibit[2] *n.* **1** [C] something that is put in a public place so people can see it: *the museum's interactive exhibits* **2** [C,U] an EXHIBITION: *The painting is currently* ***on exhibit*** *in the Metropolitan Museum.* **3** [C] something that is shown in a court of law to prove that someone is guilty or not guilty

ex·hi·bi·tion /ˌɛksə'bɪʃən/ *n.* **1** [C] a public show where you put something so people can see it: *an* ***exhibition of*** *historical photographs* **2** [U] the act of showing something such as a painting in a public place: *A collection of rare books is* ***on exhibition*** *at the city library.*

ex·hi·bi·tion·ism /ˌɛksə'bɪʃəˌnɪzəm/ *n.* [U] **1** behavior that makes people notice you, but that most people think is not acceptable **2** a mental problem that makes someone want to show his/her sexual organs in public places —**exhibitionist** *n.* [C]

ex·hil·a·rat·ed /ɪg'zɪləˌreɪṭɪd/ *adj.* feeling extremely happy and excited: *Rita felt exhilarated by the crashing of the waves.*

ex·hil·a·ra·ting /ɪg'zɪləˌreɪṭɪŋ/ *adj.* making you feel extremely happy and excited: *The balloon ride was exhilarating.*

THESAURUS

exciting, **thrilling**, **gripping**, **electric**
→ see Thesaurus box at EXCITING

ex·hil·a·ra·tion /ɪgˌzɪlə'reɪʃən/ *n.* [U] a feeling of being extremely happy and excited —**exhilarate** /ɪg'zɪləˌreɪt/ *v.* [T]

ex·hort /ɪg'zɔrt/ *v.* [T] *formal* to try to persuade someone to do something —**exhortation** /ˌɛksɔr'teɪʃən, ˌɛgzɔr-/ *n.* [C,U]

ex·hume /ɪg'zum, ɛks'hyum/ *v.* [T] *formal* to remove a dead body from the ground after it has been buried —**exhumation** /ˌɛksyu'meɪʃən/ *n.* [C,U]

ex·ile[1] /'ɛgzaɪl, 'ɛksaɪl/ *v.* [T] to force someone to leave his/her country and live in another country, usually for political reasons —**exiled** *adj.*

exile[2] *n.* **1** [U] a situation in which someone is exiled: *a writer who lives* ***in exile*** *in Britain* **2** [C] someone who has been exiled

ex·ist /ɪg'zɪst/ *v.* [I] **1** to happen or be present in a particular situation or place: *the gap that exists between rich and poor* **2** to be real or alive: *Do ghosts really exist?* ▶ Don't say "It is existing/they are existing." ◀ **3** to stay alive, especially in difficult conditions: *These wild birds* ***exist on*** *nuts, berries, and insects.*

ex·ist·ence /ɪg'zɪstəns/ *n.* **1** [U] the state of existing: *Do you believe in the* ***existence of*** *God?* | *laws that are already* ***in existence*** **2** [C] the type of life that someone has, especially when it is difficult: *a terrible existence*

ex·ist·ing /ɪg'zɪstɪŋ/ *adj.* present now and available to be used: *Businesses want to hold onto existing customers.*

THESAURUS

present, **current**
→ see Thesaurus box at PRESENT[1]

ex·it[1] /'ɛgzɪt, 'ɛksɪt/ *n.* [C] **1** a door through which you can leave a room, building, etc.: *There are two exits at the back of the plane.* | *the theater's* ***emergency exit*** → see picture at ENTRANCE[1] **2** the act of leaving a room, stage, etc.: *The President* ***made a*** *quick* ***exit*** *after his speech.* **3** a place where vehicles can leave a large road such as a FREEWAY or HIGHWAY, and join another road: *Take the Spring Street exit.*

exit[2] *v.* [I,T] **1** to leave a place: *The band* ***exited through*** *a door behind the stage.* **2** to stop using a computer or computer program: *Press F3 to exit.*

ex·o·dus /'ɛksədəs/ *n.* [singular] a situation in which a lot of people leave a particular place at the same time: *the **exodus** of Russian scientists **to** America*

ex·on·er·ate /ɪg'zɑnə,reɪt/ *v.* [T] *formal* to say officially that someone who has been blamed for something is not guilty: *Ross was **exonerated from** all charges of child abuse.* —**exoneration** /ɪg,zɑnə'reɪʃən/ *n.* [U]

ex·or·bi·tant /ɪg'zɔrbətənt/ *adj.* an exorbitant price, demand, etc. is much higher or greater than it should be

THESAURUS

expensive, **pricey**, **overpriced**, **extortionate**, **astronomical**
➔ see Thesaurus box at EXPENSIVE

ex·or·cize /'ɛksɔr,saɪz, -sɚ-/ *v.* [T] **1** to make yourself no longer be affected by a bad memory or experience **2** to force evil spirits to leave a place or someone's body by using special words and ceremonies —**exorcism** /'ɛksɔr,sɪzəm/ *n.* [C,U] —**exorcist** *n.* [C]

ex·ot·ic /ɪg'zɑt̬ɪk/ *adj.* unusual and exciting because of a connection with a foreign country: *an exotic flower | exotic places* —**exotically** *adv.*

ex·pand /ɪk'spænd/ *v.* [I,T] **1** to become larger in size, area, or amount, or to make something become larger [≠ **contract**]: *The population of Texas **expanded rapidly** in the '60s.* **2** to open more shops, factories, etc.: *Starbucks coffee shops are **expanding into** Europe.* —**expandable** *adj.*

expand on/upon sth *phr. v. formal* to add more details or information to something that you have already said: *Could you expand on your last comment, please?*

ex·panse /ɪk'spæns/ *n.* [C] a very large area of water, sky, land, etc.

ex·pan·sion /ɪk'spænʃən/ *n.* [U] the process of increasing in size, number, or amount: *a period of economic expansion* —**expansionist** *adj.*

ex·pan·sive /ɪk'spænsɪv/ *adj.* **1** very friendly and willing to talk a lot: *an expansive mood* **2** very large and wide in area: *expansive beaches* **3** including a lot of information: *an expansive history book*

ex·pa·tri·ate /ɛks'peɪtriɪt/ *n.* [C] someone who lives in a foreign country —**expatriate** *adj.*

ex·pect /ɪk'spɛkt/ *v.* [T] **1** to think that something will happen: *The hotel bill came to more than we expected. | I'm **expecting** her **to** arrive any day now. | Republicans **expect to** win a majority in the House. | He had a right to **expect (that)** his conversation would be private.*

USAGE

Expect can be followed directly by a noun. Use it to say that you strongly believe that something will come, happen, etc.: *I'm expecting a phone call. | The police are expecting trouble.*
Wait is never followed directly by a noun. You must say "wait for": *I'm waiting for a phone call.* Or you can say "wait to do something": *We're waiting to hear the news.*
Look forward to means to be excited and pleased about something that you know is going to happen: *I'm looking forward to seeing you all.*

2 to demand that someone should do something, because it is his/her duty: *Students are **expected to** return their homework on Friday. | Wanda's parents **expect too much of** her* (=think she can do more than she really can). **3 be expecting** if a woman is expecting, she is going to have a baby soon

ex·pect·an·cy /ɪk'spɛktənsi/ *n.* [U] the feeling that something exciting or interesting is about to happen: *a look of expectancy in her eyes* ➔ LIFE EXPECTANCY

ex·pect·ant /ɪk'spɛktənt/ *adj.* **1** hopeful that something good or exciting will happen: *An expectant crowd gathered.* **2 expectant mother/father** someone whose baby will be born soon —**expectantly** *adv.*

ex·pec·ta·tion /,ɛkspɛk'teɪʃən/ *n.* **1** [C,U] the belief or hope that something will happen: *Sales of the car have **exceeded expectations*** (=have been better than expected). *| **expectations that** the dollar will drop in value | We have a reasonable **expectation of** success.* **2** [C usually plural] a feeling or belief about the way something should be or how someone should behave: *customers' **expectations about** the quality of the products | The movie didn't **live up to** our **expectations*** (=was not as good as we thought it would be). *| Her parents **have** very **high expectations** of her* (=believe she should succeed).

ex·pe·di·en·cy /ɪk'spidiənsi/ **also ex·pe·di·ence** /ɪk'spidiəns/ *n.* plural **expediencies** [C,U] the act of doing what is useful, easy, or necessary in a particular situation, even if it is morally wrong

ex·pe·di·ent /ɪk'spidiənt/ *adj.* helpful or useful, sometimes in a way that is morally wrong: *It would be **expedient to** consult a lawyer.* —**expedient** *n.* [C]

ex·pe·dite /'ɛkspə,daɪt/ *v.* [T] to make a process, action, etc. happen more quickly

ex·pe·di·tion /,ɛkspə'dɪʃən/ *n.* [C] **1** a long and carefully organized trip, especially to a dangerous place: *an expedition to the North Pole* **2** a short trip, usually made for a particular purpose: *a shopping expedition*

ex·pel /ɪk'spɛl/ *v.* past tense and past participle **expelled**, present participle **expelling** [T] **1** to officially make someone leave a school, organization, or country: *Larry was **expelled from** school for smoking.* **2** to force air, water, or gas out of something

ex·pend /ɪk'spɛnd/ *v.* [T] *formal* to use money, time, energy, etc. to do something: *the time* ***expended on*** *meetings*

ex·pend·a·ble /ɪk'spɛndəbəl/ *adj.* not needed enough to be kept or saved: *workers who are considered expendable*

ex·pend·i·ture /ɪk'spɛndətʃɚ/ *n. formal* **1** [C,U] the total amount of money that a person or organization spends: ***Expenditure on*** *welfare programs went down by 5%.* **2** [U] the action of spending or using time, money, effort, etc.

ex·pense /ɪk'spɛns/ *n.* [C,U] **1** the amount of money you spend on something: *Sally's parents* ***spared no expense*** (=spent a lot of money) *for her wedding.* | *the $30,000 needed for* ***medical/legal expenses***

THESAURUS

cost, price, charge, fee, fare
→ see Thesaurus box at COST[1]

E

2 at the expense of sb/sth if something is done at the expense of someone or something else, it is only achieved by doing something that could harm that person or thing: *The cars were produced quickly, at the expense of safety.* **3 at sb's expense a)** if you do something at someone's expense, that person pays for you to do it: *Education is provided at the public's expense.* **b)** if you make jokes at someone's expense, you make him/her seem stupid: *He kept making jokes at his wife's expense.* **4 expenses** [plural] money that you spend on travel, hotels, meals, etc. when you are working, and that your employer gives back to you later **5 all expenses paid** having all of your costs for hotels, travel, meals, etc. paid for by someone else

ex'pense ac,count *n.* [C] money that is available to someone who works for a company so that s/he can pay for hotels, meals, etc. when traveling for work

ex·pen·sive /ɪk'spɛnsɪv/ *adj.* something that is expensive costs a lot of money [≠ **inexpensive, cheap**]: *expensive jewelry* | *The car is* ***expensive to*** *maintain.*

THESAURUS

high – used about prices or amounts that are greater than normal or usual: *Gas prices are very high right now.* | *If we want better public services, we will have to pay higher taxes.*
pricey informal – expensive: *The hotel was a little bit pricey.*
overpriced – something that is overpriced is more expensive than it should be: *overpriced running shoes*
be a ripoff informal – if something is a ripoff, it is more expensive than it should be: *$125 for a shirt. What a ripoff!*
extortionate/astronomical/exorbitant – used about things that are much too expensive: *Housing prices in New York are exorbitant.*
fancy – used about fashionable restaurants, cars, clothes, etc. that look expensive: *a fancy hotel in Manhattan*
posh informal – used about expensive hotels, restaurants, schools, etc. that are used by rich people: *a posh five-star hotel*
→ CHEAP

ex·pe·ri·ence[1] /ɪk'spɪriəns/ *n.* **1** [U] knowledge or skill that you gain from doing a job or activity: *Scott* ***has*** *a* ***lot*** *of* ***experience in*** *publishing.* | *a good way of* ***gaining/getting experience*** | *Do you have any* ***previous experience*** *in sales?* **2** [U] knowledge that you gain about life and the world by being in different situations and meeting different people: ***In my experience,*** *it is hard work, not luck, that brings success.* | *I know* ***from*** *personal* ***experience*** *that this is not easy.* **3** [C] something that happens to you and has an effect on how you feel or what you think: *Visiting Paris was a wonderful experience.* | *Other people have* ***had*** *similar* ***experiences.***

experience[2] *v.* [T] to be happening to you or affecting you: *The plane experienced engine problems.* | *Patients often experienced extreme pain.*

ex·pe·ri·enced /ɪk'spɪriənst/ *adj.* having particular skills or knowledge because you have done something often or for a long time [≠ **inexperienced**]: *an experienced pilot*

ex·per·i·ment[1] /ɪk'spɛrəmənt/ *n.* [C] **1** a scientific test done to show how something will react in a particular situation, or to prove that an idea is true: ***Experiments*** *were* ***performed/conducted/done*** *on rats to test the drug.* | ***experiments on/with*** *solar-powered vehicles* **2** a process in which you try a new idea, method, etc. in order to find out if it is effective: *St. Mary's School is an* ***experiment in*** *bilingual education.*

ex·per·i·ment[2] /ɪk'spɛrə,mɛnt/ *v.* [I] **1** to try using various ideas, methods, materials, etc. in order to find out how effective or good they are: *Many teenagers* ***experiment with*** *drugs.* **2** to do a scientific test in order to find out if a particular idea is true or to obtain more information: *Researchers* ***experimented on*** *animals when testing the treatment.* —**experimentation** /ɪk,spɛrəmən'teɪʃən/ *n.* [U]

ex·per·i·men·tal /ɪk,spɛrə'mɛntəl/ *adj.* **1** used for or related to experiments: *experimental research* **2** using or testing new ideas: *an experimental theater group* —**experimentally** *adv.*

ex·pert /'ɛkspɚt/ *n.* [C] someone with special skills or knowledge of a subject, gained as a result of training or experience: *an* ***expert on/in*** *ancient Egyptian art* —**expert** *adj.* —**expertly** *adv.*

THESAURUS

specialist – someone who knows a lot about something because s/he has studied it for a long time: *Lowe is a specialist in immigration law.*

authority – someone who is very respected because s/he knows more about a subject than other people: *She is a leading authority on modern art.*
connoisseur – someone who knows a lot about something such as art, food, or music: *a connoisseur of fine wines*

ex·per·tise /ˌɛkspɚ'tiz/ *n.* [U] a special skill or knowledge that you learn by experience or training: *her **technical/medical/legal expertise***

ex·pi·ra·tion /ˌɛkspə'reɪʃən/ *n.* [U] the end of a period of time during which an official document or agreement is allowed to be used: *the expiration of the treaty*

expi'ration ˌdate *n.* [C] the date when something stops being safe to eat or to use

ex·pire /ɪk'spaɪɚ/ *v.* [I] **1** if a document expires, you cannot legally continue to use it beyond a particular date: *My driver's license **expires in** September.* **2** *literary* to die

ex·plain /ɪk'spleɪn/ *v.* [I,T] **1** to tell someone about something in a way that it is easy to understand: *Dr. Brasco carefully explained the procedure.* | *Don **explained** the rules **to** me.* ▶ Don't say "explained me the rules." ◀ *Could you **explain how** this thing works?* ▶ Don't say "explain me how it works." ◀

THESAURUS

tell – to give someone facts or information in speech or writing: *Can you tell me how to get to the Empire State Building?*
show – to tell someone how to do something or where something is: *Ellen showed me how to work the coffee maker.*
demonstrate – to show or describe how to use or do something: *Fred will now demonstrate how easy it is to use the drill.*
go through sth – to explain something carefully, especially one step at a time: *Mrs. Riddell went through the homework assignment.*

2 to give or be the reason for something: *Brad never **explained why** he was late.* | *The doctor **explained that** he had to wait for the test results first.*
explain sth ⇔ **away** *phr. v.* to make something seem to be less important or not your fault by giving reasons for it: *Claire tried to explain away the bruises on her arm.*

ex·pla·na·tion /ˌɛksplə'neɪʃən/ *n.* **1** [C] a statement or piece of writing intended to make something easier to understand or to describe how something works: *an **explanation of** how the disease is passed to other people* **2** [C,U] the reasons you give for why something happened or why you did something: *an **explanation for** the changes in weather patterns* | *Smith refused to **give/provide an explanation for** his behavior.*

THESAURUS

reason, excuse, motive
➔ see Thesaurus box at REASON¹

ex·plan·a·to·ry /ɪk'splænəˌtɔri/ *adj.* giving information about something or describing how something works: *an explanatory booklet* ➔ SELF-EXPLANATORY

ex·ple·tive /'ɛksplət̬ɪv/ *n.* [C] *formal* a rude word that you use when you are angry or in pain

ex·pli·ca·ble /ɪk'splɪkəbəl, 'ɛksplɪ-/ *adj.* able to be easily understood or explained [≠ **inexplicable**]

ex·plic·it /ɪk'splɪsɪt/ *adj.* **1** expressed in a way that is very clear: *explicit instructions* **2** language or pictures that are explicit describe or show a lot of sex or violence —**explicitly** *adv.*

ex·plode /ɪk'sploʊd/ *v.* **1** [I,T] to burst into small pieces, making a loud noise and causing damage, or to make something do this: *The car bomb exploded at 6:16.* | *In 1949 the USSR exploded its first atomic bomb.* **2** [I] to suddenly express strong emotions, especially anger: *John **exploded with/in** rage at the news.* **3** [I] if a situation explodes, it is suddenly no longer controlled: *the violence that has exploded in the city* **4** [I] to increase a lot in number, amount, or degree: *Florida's population exploded after World War II.*

ex·ploit¹ /ɪk'splɔɪt/ *v.* [T] **1** to treat someone unfairly in order to gain what you want: *employers who exploit their workers* **2** to use something effectively and completely, or get as much as you can out of a situation: *The country must exploit its resources more effectively.* —**exploitation** /ˌɛksplɔɪ'teɪʃən/ *n.* [U]

ex·ploit² /'ɛksplɔɪt/ *n.* [C usually plural] a brave, exciting, and interesting action

ex·plo·ra·tion /ˌɛksplə'reɪʃən/ *n.* [C,U] **1** a trip to a place you have not been, or a place where you are looking for something: *exploration for oil* | *space exploration* **2** an examination or discussion about something to find out more about it: *an **exploration of** spiritual issues*

ex·plo·ra·to·ry /ɪk'splɔrəˌtɔri/ *adj.* done in order to find out more about something: *exploratory surgery*

ex·plore /ɪk'splɔr/ *v.* **1** [I,T] to travel around an area in order to find out what it is like: *We spent a week exploring the Oregon coastline.* **2** [I] to discuss or think about something carefully: *I want to make sure I've **explored** all my **options** before I decide.* | *The company is **exploring** the **possibility** of moving.*

ex·plor·er /ɪk'splɔrɚ/ *n.* [C] someone who travels to places that people have not visited before ➔ see Thesaurus box at TRAVEL¹

ex·plo·sion /ɪk'sploʊʒən/ *n.* [C] **1** an occasion when something such as a bomb explodes, or the noise it makes: *We heard a huge explosion.* | *a nuclear explosion* **2** [usually singular] a sudden

E

large increase: *the* ***population explosion*** | *an* ***explosion of*** *interest in Celtic music*

ex·plo·sive[1] /ɪk'sploʊsɪv/ *adj.* **1** able or likely to explode: *Dynamite is highly explosive.* **2** likely to make people become violent or angry: *the explosive issue of abortion* | *the* ***explosive situation*** *in the Middle East* **3** likely to suddenly become violent and angry: *a man with an explosive temper* **4** increasing suddenly or quickly: *the* ***explosive growth*** *of the Internet*

explosive[2] *n.* [C] a substance that can cause an explosion

ex·po /'ɛkspoʊ/ *n.* plural **expos** [C] an EXPOSITION[2]

ex·po·nent /ɪk'spoʊnənt, 'ɛkspoʊ-/ *n.* [C] an exponent of an idea or belief tries to persuade other people that it is good: *an* ***exponent of*** *socialism*

ex·port[1] /'ɛkspɔrt/ *n.* **1** [U] the business of selling goods to another country [➡ **import**]: *the* ***export of*** *lumber* **2** [C] a product that is sold to another country [➡ **import**]: *Wheat is one of our country's chief exports.*

ex·port[2] /ɪk'spɔrt/ *v.* [I,T] to sell goods to another country [➡ **import**]: *The company* ***exports*** *machines* ***to*** *Russia.* —**exporter** *n.* [C] —**exportation** /ˌɛkspɔr'teɪʃən/ *n.* [U]

> **THESAURUS**
>
> **sell, put up, auction, peddle**
> ➔ see Thesaurus box at SELL

ex·pose /ɪk'spoʊz/ *v.* [T] **1** to show something that is usually covered or hidden: *Her skin has never been* ***exposed to*** *the sun.* **2** to put someone in a situation or place that could be harmful or dangerous: *The test will tell you if you've been* ***exposed to*** *the virus.* **3** to make it possible for someone to experience new ideas, ways of life, etc.: *The Shinsekis* ***exposed*** *me* ***to*** *Japanese art.* **4** to tell people the truth about someone or something that is bad or dishonest: *We threatened to* ***expose*** *him* ***to*** *the police.* **5** to allow light onto a piece of film in a camera in order to produce a photograph

ex·po·sé /ˌekspoʊ'zeɪ/ *n.* [C] a story in a newspaper or on television that shows the truth about something, especially something dishonest or shocking

ex·posed /ɪk'spoʊzd/ *adj.* **1** not protected from the weather: *an exposed coastline* **2** not covered: *exposed skin*

ex·po·si·tion /ˌɛkspə'zɪʃən/ *n.* **1** [C,U] *formal* a clear and detailed explanation **2** [C] a large public event at which you show or sell products, art, etc.

ex·po·sure /ɪk'spoʊʒɚ/ *n.* **1** [C,U] the state of being put into a harmful or bad situation without any protection: *Skin cancer is often caused by too much* ***exposure to*** *the sun.* **2** [singular, U] the chance to experience new ideas, ways of life, etc.: *My first* ***exposure to*** *classical music was at college.* **3** [U] the attention that someone or something gets from newspapers, television, etc.: *The issue has* ***received*** *a lot of* ***exposure*** *in the press.* **4** [C,U] the action of showing the truth about someone or something that is bad or dishonest: *the paper's* ***exposure of*** *a scandal in the Oakland school district* **5** [U] the harmful effects of staying outside for a long time when the weather is extremely cold: *Three climbers died of exposure.* **6** [C] a length of film in a camera that is used to take one photograph: *This roll has 36 exposures.*

ex·press[1] /ɪk'sprɛs/ *v.* [T] to tell or show what you are feeling or thinking by using words, looks, or actions: *A number of people* ***expressed*** *their* ***concern.*** | *It's hard sometimes for children to* ***express themselves*** (=clearly say what they think or feel). | *None of his children have* ***expressed an interest in*** *running the company.*

> **THESAURUS**
>
> **say, mention, add, point out, suggest, imply**
> ➔ see Thesaurus box at SAY[1]

express[2] *adj.* **1** clear and definite: *It was her* ***express wish*** *that you inherit her house.* **2 express train/bus** a train or bus that does not stop at many places and can therefore travel more quickly **3** [only before noun] designed to help you move through a place more quickly: *the* ***express lane*** *on the freeway* | *the* ***express*** *line at the supermarket* (=one for people who are buying a limited number of items) **4** [only before noun] delivered more quickly than normal: *express mail*

ex·pres·sion /ɪk'sprɛʃən/ *n.* **1** [C] a word or phrase that has a particular meaning: *You use the expression "break a leg" to wish an actor good luck.*

> **THESAURUS**
>
> **phrase, idiom, cliché, saying, proverb**
> ➔ see Thesaurus box at PHRASE[1]

2 [C] a look on someone's face: *a cheerful expression* | *an* ***expression of*** *shock* **3** [C,U] something that you say, do, or write that shows what you think or feel: *I'm sending these flowers as an* ***expression of*** *my thanks.* | *Crying is a healthy expression of grief.*

ex·pres·sion·less /ɪk'sprɛʃənlɪs/ *adj.* an expressionless face or voice does not show what someone is feeling or thinking

ex·pres·sive /ɪk'sprɛsɪv/ *adj.* showing what someone is thinking or feeling: *expressive eyes*

ex·press·ly /ɪk'sprɛsli/ *adv. formal* clearly and firmly: *Mr. Samson expressly asked you to leave.*

ex·press·way /ɪk'sprɛsˌweɪ/ *n.* [C] a wide road in a city on which cars can travel fast

THESAURUS

highway, freeway, turnpike, road, street, main street, avenue, lane, main road, the main drag, toll road
➔ see Thesaurus box at ROAD

ex·pro·pri·ate /ɛks'proupri,eɪt/ *v.* [T] *formal* to take away someone's private property for public use —**expropriation** /ɛks,proupri'eɪʃən/ *n.* [C,U]

ex·pul·sion /ɪk'spʌlʃən/ *n.* [C,U] the official act of making someone leave a place: *the **expulsion of** Communists from the government*

ex·quis·ite /ɪk'skwɪzɪt, 'ɛkskwɪ-/ *adj.* beautiful and delicate: *an exquisite piece of jewelry* —**exquisitely** *adv.*

ex·tem·po·ra·ne·ous /ɪk,stɛmpə'reɪniəs, ɛk-/ *adj.* spoken or done without any preparation or practice: *an extemporaneous speech*

ex·tend /ɪk'stɛnd/ *v.* **1** [I,T] to continue for a longer period of time, or to make something last longer: *Management have agreed to extend the deadline.* | *The warm weather extended into November.* | *Immigration is extending her visa by another six months.*

THESAURUS

prolong, lengthen, drag out
➔ see Thesaurus box at PROLONG

2 [I] to cover a particular distance or area: *The river **extends** more than 200 miles **through** the Grand Canyon.* **3** [T] to make a room, building, road, etc. bigger: *The developer plans to extend Thomas Road to meet Tenth Street.* **4** [I,T] to make something include or affect more things or people: *My insurance policy can be **extended to** cover my family too.* **5** [T] *formal* to officially offer someone help, thanks, sympathy, etc.: *I'd like to **extend a** warm **welcome** to our new members.* **6** [T] to stretch out your hand, arm, or leg: *"Hi, I'm Bill," he said, extending his hand.*

ex,tended 'family *n.* [C] a family group that consists not only of parents and children but also of grandparents, AUNTS, etc. [➡ **nuclear family**]

ex·ten·sion /ɪk'stɛnʃən/ *n.* **1** [C] **a)** one of many telephone lines connected to a central system in a large building, which all have different numbers: *Hello, I'd like extension 1334, please.* | *What's your **extension number**?* **b)** one of the telephones in a house that all have the same number **2** [C usually singular] an extra period of time allowed for something: *The professor gave me a two-week extension on my paper.* **3** [C,U] the process of making something bigger or longer, or the part that is added in this process: *The city is building an **extension to** the subway line.* | *an **extension of** the museum* **4** [singular, U] the development of something so that it affects more things or people: *an **extension of** employee health care*

ex'tension ,cord *n.* [C] an additional electric CORD that you attach to another cord in order to make it longer

ex·ten·sive /ɪk'stɛnsɪv/ *adj.* **1** containing a lot of information and details: *Doctors have done extensive research into the effects of stress.* | *The networks are planning **extensive** television **coverage**.* **2** large in size, amount, or degree: *The flood caused **extensive damage** to the town.* | *the **extensive use** of pesticides*

ex·tent /ɪk'stɛnt/ *n.* **1** [U] how big, important, or serious something is: *What's the **extent of** the damage?* | *Medical tests were done to determine the extent of his injury.* **2 to ... extent** used to say how true something is: *I do agree with him **to some extent/a certain extent*** (=partly). | *Stock prices fell sharply in Asia and Europe, and **to a lesser/greater extent**, in the United States.* **3 to such an extent that/to the extent that** used to say how great an effect or change is: *The building was damaged to such an extent that it had to be knocked down.*

ex·te·ri·or[1] /ɪk'stɪriə/ *n.* [C] **1** the outside of something [≠ **interior**]: *the **exterior of** the house* **2 calm/confident etc. exterior** someone's behavior, which often does not show his/her real feelings or nature

exterior[2] *adj.* on the outside of something [≠ **interior**]: *the **exterior walls** of the church*

ex·ter·mi·nate /ɪk'stəmə,neɪt/ *v.* [T] to kill all of a particular group of animals or people —**exterminator** *n.* [C] —**extermination** /ɪk,stəmə'neɪʃən/ *n.* [C,U]

ex·ter·nal /ɪk'stənl/ *adj.* **1** relating to the outside of something [≠ **internal**]: *This medicine is **for external use only*** (=you should put it on your skin and not eat it). **2** from outside your organization, country, university, etc. [≠ **internal**]: *information from external sources*

ex·tinct /ɪk'stɪŋkt/ *adj.* an extinct plant or animal no longer exists: *Activists fear that the tiger may **become extinct**.*

ex·tinc·tion /ɪk'stɪŋkʃən/ *n.* [U] the state of being extinct: *Greenpeace believes that whales are **in danger of extinction**.*

ex·tin·guish /ɪk'stɪŋgwɪʃ/ *v.* [T] to make a fire or light stop burning or shining: *Please extinguish all cigarettes.*

ex·tin·guish·er /ɪk'stɪŋgwɪʃə/ *n.* [C] a FIRE EXTINGUISHER

ex·tol /ɪk'stoul/ *v.* past tense and past participle **extolled**, present participle **extolling** [T] *formal* to praise something very much: *Jack was **extolling the virtues of** being vegetarian.*

ex·tort /ɪk'stɔrt/ *v.* [T] to force someone to give you money by threatening him/her: *The policemen were actually **extorting** money **from** drug dealers.* —**extortion** /ɪk'stɔrʃən/ *n.* [U]

ex·tor·tion·ate /ɪk'stɔrʃənɪt/ *adj.* *disapproving* extortionate prices, demands, etc. are much bigger than they should be

E

THESAURUS

expensive, high, pricey, overpriced, astronomical, exorbitant
→ see Thesaurus box at EXPENSIVE

ex·tra[1] /ˈɛkstrə/ *adj.* **1** [only before noun] more than the usual or standard amount of something: *a large mushroom pizza with extra cheese* | *The company gives employees extra time off to take care of sick family members.*

THESAURUS

more, another, additional, further
→ see Thesaurus box at MORE[2]

2 [not before noun] if something is extra, it is not included in the price of something and you have to pay more for it: *Steaks are $9 a pound. Shipping is extra.*

extra[2] *adv.* **1** in addition to the usual things or the usual amount: *You have to pay extra if you want to travel first class.* **2** used when emphasizing an adjective or adverb: *If you're extra good, I'll buy you an ice cream.* | *Henry's been working extra hard.*

E

extra[3] *n.* [C] **1** something that can be added to a product or service and that makes it cost more: *The tour does not include extras, such as meals.*

THESAURUS

addition, additive, supplement
→ see Thesaurus box at ADDITION

2 an actor who has a small unimportant part in a movie

ex·tract[1] /ɪkˈstrækt/ *v.* [T] **1** *formal* to remove something from a place or thing: *I'm having my wisdom **teeth extracted**.* | *Olive oil is **extracted from** green olives.* **2** to make someone give you information, money, etc. that s/he does not want to give: *The police couldn't **extract** any information **from** him.*

ex·tract[2] /ˈɛkstrækt/ *n.* **1** [C] a small part taken from a story, poem, etc.: *an **extract from** the article* **2** [C,U] a substance that is removed from a plant: *vanilla extract*

ex·trac·tion /ɪkˈstrækʃən/ *n.* **1** [C,U] the process of removing something from something else: *the **extraction of** coal* **2 be of French/Irish etc. extraction** to be from a family that is originally from France, Ireland, etc., though you were not born in that country

ex·tra·cur·ric·u·lar /ˌɛkstrəkəˈrɪkyələ/ *adj.* [only before noun] extracurricular activities are those that you do for fun and are not part of the usual work you do for school

ex·tra·dite /ˈɛkstrəˌdaɪt/ *v.* [T] to send someone who may be guilty of a crime back to the country where the crime happened —**extradition** /ˌɛkstrəˈdɪʃən/ *n.* [C,U]

ex·tra·ne·ous /ɪkˈstreɪniəs/ *adj. formal* not directly related to a particular subject: *extraneous details*

ex·traor·di·nar·y /ɪkˈstrɔrdnˌɛri/ *adj.* very unusual, special, or surprising: *an extraordinary talent* | *an extraordinary event*

THESAURUS

surprising, amazing, shocking, astonishing, astounding, staggering, stunning
→ see Thesaurus box at SURPRISING

ex·trap·o·late /ɪkˈstræpəˌleɪt/ *v.* [I,T] *formal* to use facts about a current situation in order to say what might happen in another

ex·tra·ter·res·tri·al /ˌɛkstrətəˈrɛstriəl/ *adj.* in or from a place that is not the Earth: *the search for extraterrestrial life* —**extraterrestrial** *n.* [C]

ex·trav·a·gant /ɪkˈstrævəgənt/ *adj.* **1** spending or costing too much money: *extravagant parties* **2** extravagant claims, promises, etc. are not likely to be true —**extravagantly** *adv.* —**extravagance** *n.* [C,U]

ex·treme[1] /ɪkˈstrim/ *adj.* **1** very great in degree: *extreme violence* | *Mountain climbers face extreme danger.* **2** very unusual and severe or serious: *Mr. Wong uses extreme methods to discipline his students.* | ***In extreme cases**, the spider's bite can kill.* **3** extreme opinions are very strong and most people think they are unreasonable: *the party's extreme left wing* **4 extreme sport/skiing etc.** a sport that is done in a way that is more dangerous than usual

extreme[2] *n.* **1** [C] something that is much greater, more severe, etc. than usual: *the **extremes of** wealth and poverty* | *The temperature has gone **from one extreme to another*** (=from hot to cold or cold to hot). | *People were willing to **go to extremes*** (=do something to the greatest possible extent) *to prevent the prison from being built near their homes.* **2 in the extreme** extremely: *His new movie is violent in the extreme.*

ex·treme·ly /ɪkˈstrimli/ *adv.* to a very great degree: *She's extremely pretty.* | *an extremely difficult job*

ex·trem·ist /ɪkˈstrimɪst/ *n.* [C] *disapproving* someone with very strong political or religious opinions: *right-wing extremists* —**extremist** *adj.* —**extremism** *n.* [U]

ex·trem·i·ty /ɪkˈstrɛməṭi/ *n.* plural **extremities** [C] **1** the part that is furthest from the center of something: *the city's northern extremity* **2 extremities** [plural] one of the parts of your body that is furthest away from the center, for example your fingers or toes

ex·tri·cate /ˈɛkstrəˌkeɪt/ *v.* [T] to get someone out of a place or a difficult situation: *They couldn't **extricate** themselves **from** the huge crowd of people.*

ex·tro·vert·ed /ˈɛkstrəˌvəṭɪd/ *adj.* confident and

enjoying being with other people [≠ **introverted**] —**extrovert** *n.* [C]

THESAURUS

sociable, **outgoing**, **gregarious**
→ see Thesaurus box at SOCIABLE

ex·u·ber·ant /ɪgˈzubərənt/ *adj.* very happy, excited, and full of energy: *the exuberant bride* —**exuberance** *n.* [U]

ex·ude /ɪgˈzud, ɪkˈsud/ *v.* [T] to show that you have a lot of a particular feeling: *On the morning of the big game, the team exuded confidence.*

ex·ult /ɪgˈzʌlt/ *v.* [I] *formal* to show that you are very happy and proud because you have achieved something: *The people* ***exulted over*** *the defeat of their enemy.* —**exultant** *adj.* —**exultation** /ˌɛgzʌlˈteɪʃən, ˌɛksʌl-/ *n.* [U]

eye

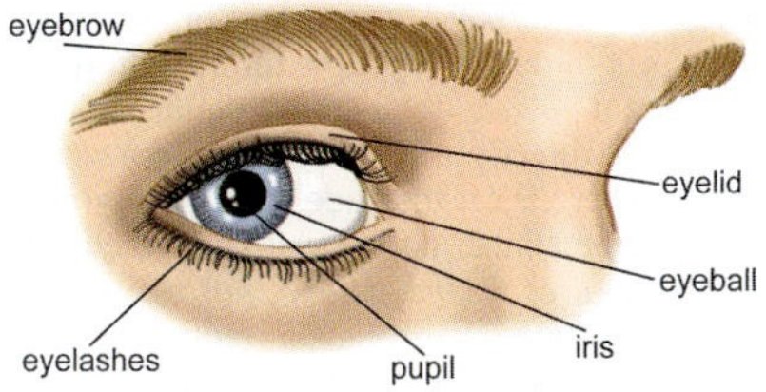

eye¹ /aɪ/ *n.* [C]
1 SEE one of the two parts of your face that you see with: *Gina has blue/brown etc. eyes.* | *My eyes are going bad; I think I need glasses.* | ***Close/shut*** *your eyes and go to sleep.* | *She* ***opened*** *her* ***eyes***. | *He spoke with* ***tears in*** *his* ***eyes***. | *Dave is* ***blind in one eye***. | ***blue-eyed/bright-eyed etc.***

COLLOCATIONS

If you **lower** your **eyes**, you look down.
Your **eyes narrow** if you are watching something carefully or thinking hard about something.
Your **eyes widen** if you are surprised, afraid, etc.
Your **eyes sparkle** if you are excited or very happy.

2 SEE/UNDERSTAND a particular way of seeing, judging, or understanding something: *The story is told* ***through the eyes of*** *a young boy.* | *a good* ***eye for*** *detail*
3 keep an eye on sb/sth *informal* to watch someone or something to make sure nothing bad happens: *Can you keep an eye on the baby while I go to the store?*
4 lay/set eyes on sb/sth *spoken* to see someone or something, especially for the first time: *The first time I laid eyes on him I knew I liked him.*
5 cannot take your eyes off sb/sth to be unable to stop looking at someone or something because s/he or it is attractive or interesting: *When I watch him play, I just can't take my eyes off him.*
6 eye contact a situation in which you look directly at someone while s/he is looking at you: *I made a point to* ***make eye contact*** *with Marcus.* | *Tina* ***avoided eye contact*** *with her mother.*
7 keep an eye out for sb/sth to be ready to notice something when it appears: *Keep an eye out for Rick's car.*
8 in the eyes of the law/world/police etc. in the opinion or judgment of the law, world, etc.: *Divorce is a sin in the eyes of the Catholic Church.*
9 have your eye on sb to notice someone that you think is attractive or interesting: *Mark really has his eye on Yvonne.*
10 have your eye on sth to want something that you think might become available: *Harris has his eye on a two-story house in Woodside.*
11 see eye to eye if two people or groups see eye to eye, they have the same opinions about something: *Baker and Quinn don't always* ***see eye to eye on*** *every issue.*
12 close/open your eyes to sth to ignore something bad that is happening, or to start to realize that something bad is happening: *The trip opened his eyes to the poverty in the countryside.*
13 NEEDLE the hole in a needle that you put thread through
14 the eye of a storm/hurricane/tornado the calm center of a big storm
15 an eye for an eye the idea that if someone does something wrong, you should punish them by doing the same thing to them → **catch sb's eye** at CATCH¹ → **look sb in the eye** at LOOK¹

eye² *v.* present participle **eyeing** or **eying** [T] to look at someone or something with great interest: *Sarah kept eyeing my boyfriend all night.*

THESAURUS

stare – to look at someone or something for a long time
glare – to look angrily at someone or something

eye·ball /ˈaɪbɔl/ *n.* [C] the whole of your eye, including the part inside your head → see picture at EYE¹

eye·brow /ˈaɪbraʊ/ *n.* [C] the line of short hairs above your eye

ˈeye-ˌcatching *adj.* unusual, attractive, or noticeable: *an eye-catching dress*

THESAURUS

noticeable, **clear**, **obvious**, **conspicuous**, **striking**
→ see Thesaurus box at NOTICEABLE

eye·lash /ˈaɪlæʃ/ *n.* [C] one of the small hairs that grow on the edge of your eyelid

eye·lid /ˈaɪˌlɪd/ *n.* [C] the piece of skin that covers your eye when it is closed → see picture at EYE¹

eye·lin·er /ˈaɪˌlaɪnɚ/ *n.* [C,U] a type of MAKEUP that you put in a thin line along the edges of your eyelids

E

'eye-ˌopener *n.* [C usually singular] an experience from which you learn something new or surprising: *Seeing inside a prison was a real eye-opener for me.*

eye·shad·ow /'aɪˌʃædoʊ/ *n.* [U] colored MAKEUP that you put on your eyelids to make them look attractive

eye·sight /'aɪsaɪt/ *n.* [U] the ability to see: *Grandma is slowly* ***losing*** *her* ***eyesight****.*

eye·sore /'aɪsɔr/ *n.* [C] something that is very ugly, especially a building surrounded by other things that are not ugly

eye·wit·ness /ˌaɪ'wɪt˺nɪs, 'aɪˌwɪt˺nɪs/ *n.* [C] someone who has seen a crime or accident: *an* ***eyewitness account*** *of the incident*

F, f

F

F, f /ɛf/ the sixth letter of the English alphabet

F¹ /ɛf/ *n.* **1** [C] a GRADE that a teacher gives to a student's work, showing that the student has failed: *Jill* ***got an F*** *in Physics.* **2** [C,U] the fourth note in the musical SCALE of C, or the musical KEY based on this note

F² **1** the written abbreviation of **Fahrenheit** **2** the written abbreviation of **female**

fa·ble /'feɪbəl/ *n.* [C] a traditional story that teaches a moral lesson

THESAURUS

story, **tale**, **myth**, **legend**, **yarn**
→ see Thesaurus box at STORY

fab·ric /'fæbrɪk/ *n.* **1** [C,U] cloth **2** [singular] the structure and CUSTOMS of a society: *Discrimination is threatening the whole* ***fabric of society****.*

fab·ri·cate /'fæbrəˌkeɪt/ *v.* [T] to make up a story, piece of information, etc. in order to deceive someone: *He later admitted that he had fabricated the whole story.* —**fabrication** /ˌfæbrə'keɪʃən/ *n.* [C,U]

fab·u·lous /'fæbyələs/ *adj.* **1** very good: *You look fabulous!* **2** unusually large in amount or size: *a fabulous sum of money* —**fabulously** *adv.*

fa·cade, **façade** /fə'sɑd/ *n.* [C] **1** [usually singular] a way of behaving that hides your real feelings or character: *Behind that cheerful facade she's really a lonely person.* **2** the front of a building

face¹ /feɪs/ *n.* [C] **1** the front of your head, where your eyes, nose, and mouth are: *Jodi has such a pretty face.* | *He had a surprised* ***look on*** *his* ***face****.* | *Keith was* ***lying face down*** (=with his face towards the ground) *on the bed.* | *a* ***round-faced*** *man* **2** an expression on someone's face: *the children's happy faces* | *Carl was* ***making faces at*** *Lisa* (=making expressions with his face to try to annoy her or make her laugh). | *I just couldn't* ***keep a straight face*** (=avoid laughing). | *When I told Garry I was quitting,* ***you should have seen*** *his* ***face*** (=used to say that someone was very angry, surprised, etc.). **3** a person: *There are a few new faces in class this year.* | *It was so nice to see a friendly face.* **4 face to face** **a)** while physically close to someone: *I've spoken to her on the phone but I've never* ***met*** *her* ***face to face****.* **b)** in a situation in which you experience something difficult and have to deal with it: *It was the first time he'd ever* ***come face to face with*** *death.* **5 in the face of sth** in a difficult or dangerous situation: *Delmore kept his composure in the face of racial threats.* **6** the front or surface of something: *a clock face* | *the north* ***face of*** *Mount Rainier* → see picture at WATCH² **7 lose/save face** to lose or avoid losing the respect of other people [➡ **face-saving**] **8 to sb's face** if you say something to someone's face, you say it directly to that person when you are with him/her **9 on the face of it** when you first consider something, before you know the details: *On the face of it, the data is not very helpful.* **10 in your face** *slang* behavior, remarks, etc. that are in your face are very direct and often shocking or surprising: *an "in your face" style of politics*

face² *v.* [T] **1 also face up to sth** to accept that a difficult situation or problem exists: *Randy refuses to* ***face the fact that*** *he needs help.* | ***Let's face it*** *— nobody wants to hire someone my age.* **2 also be faced with sth** to have to deal with a difficult situation: *She's faced with some very tough choices.* | *Jones is facing up to 20 years in jail.* **3 sb can't face (doing) sth** used in order to say that someone does not feel able to do something, especially because it upsets him/her: *I can't face going back to work again.* **4** to be looking at or pointing toward someone or something: *Dean* ***turned to face*** *me.* | *a north-facing window* | *My apartment faces the ocean.* **5** to talk to or deal with someone, when this is difficult: *You're going to* ***have to face*** *him sooner or later.* **6** to play against an opponent or team in a game or competition: *The Jets face the Dolphins in two weeks.*

face sb ⇔ **down** *phr. v.* to deal in a strong and confident way with someone who opposes you: *Frost faced down a serious challenge from his opponent.*

face off *phr. v.* to get in a position in which you are ready to fight, argue, or compete with someone: *The two candidates will face off in the election in November.*

face·less /'feɪslɪs/ *adj. disapproving* a faceless person, organization, etc. is not clearly known and seems unfriendly or not worth caring about

face·lift /ˈfeɪslɪft/ *n.* [C] **1** a medical operation to make your face look younger **2** work or repairs that make something look newer or better: *The offices were* ***given a facelift.***

ˈface-ˌsaving *adj.* [only before noun] a face-saving action or arrangement prevents you from losing other people's respect: *a face-saving agreement*

fac·et /ˈfæsɪt/ *n.* [C] one of several parts of someone's character, a situation, etc.: *You've only seen one* ***facet of*** *his personality.*

fa·ce·tious /fəˈsiʃəs/ *adj. disapproving* saying things in order to be funny, in a way that is annoying or not appropriate —**facetiously** *adv.*

ˌface-to-ˈface *adj.* [only before noun] a face-to-face meeting, conversation, etc. is one where you are with another person and talking to them: *a face-to-face interview*

ˌface ˈvalue *n.* **1 take sth at face value** to accept what you are told without thinking carefully first: *Don't take anything Burgess tells you at face value.* **2** [singular, U] the value or cost shown on a coin, ticket, etc.

fa·cial[1] /ˈfeɪʃəl/ *adj.* on or relating to the face: *facial hair*

facial[2] *n.* [C] a beauty treatment to clean the skin on your face and make it softer

fac·ile /ˈfæsəl/ *adj. disapproving* too simple and showing a lack of careful thought or understanding: *a facile solution*

fa·cil·i·tate /fəˈsɪləˌteɪt/ *v.* [T] *formal* to make it easier for something to happen: *Computers can be used to facilitate language learning.*

fa·cil·i·ty /fəˈsɪləti/ *n.* plural **facilities 1 facilities** [plural] rooms, equipment, or services that are provided for a particular purpose: *The college has excellent research facilities.* **2** [C] a place or building used for a particular purpose: *a sports facility* **3** [C usually singular] a helpful service or feature that a machine or system has: *The phone is equipped with a call-back facility.*

fac·sim·i·le /fækˈsɪməli/ *n.* [C] an exact copy of a picture, piece of writing, etc.

fact /fækt/ *n.* [C] **1** something that is true: *I cannot accept* ***the fact that*** *our marriage is over.* | ***The fact remains that*** *people are still starving.* | *What are the* ***facts of/in*** *this case?* | *interesting* ***facts about*** *plants* | ***The fact of the matter is,*** *I don't have enough money.* | ***I know for a fact that*** *he was here last night.* **2 in (actual) fact a)** used in order to add information: *I know her really well. In fact, I had dinner with her last week.* **b)** used in order to emphasize that something is true, especially when it is surprising: *It's cheaper to fly, as a matter of fact.* **3 a fact of life** something bad that people must accept: *Violent crime seems to have become a fact of life.* **4 the facts of life** the details about sex and how babies are born ➔ **as a matter of fact** at MATTER[1]

fac·tion /ˈfækʃən/ *n.* [C] a small group of people within a larger group, who have different ideas from the other members —**factional** *adj.*

fac·tor /ˈfæktɚ/ *n.* [C] **1** one of several things that influence or cause a situation: *The weather could be an important/major/key* ***factor in*** *tomorrow's game.* | *Crime is due to* ***economic/social factors.*** | *We liked both houses, but price was the* ***deciding factor*** (=most important factor). **2** *technical* a number that divides into another number exactly: *3 is a factor of 15.*

fac·to·ry /ˈfæktəri/ *n.* plural **factories** [C] a building where goods are produced in large quantities: *a shoe factory*

fac·tu·al /ˈfæktʃuəl/ *adj.* based on or relating to facts: *The movie has many* ***factual errors.*** —**factually** *adv.*

fac·ul·ty /ˈfækəlti/ *n.* plural **faculties 1** [C,U] all the teachers in a school or college, or in a particular department of a school or college: *a faculty meeting* | *the history faculty* **2** [C usually plural] a natural ability, such as the ability to see or think: *He wants to make out a will while he still has all his faculties* (=is still able to see, hear, think, etc. in the normal way).

fad /fæd/ *n.* [C] something that is very popular for a short period of time: *the newest fitness fad*

THESAURUS

craze, cult
➔ see Thesaurus box at POPULAR

fade /feɪd/ *v.* **1** [I] **also fade away** to gradually disappear: *Hopes of a peace settlement are beginning to fade.* | *Their faces have* ***faded from*** *my memory now.* **2** [I,T] to lose color or brightness, or to make something do this: *faded jeans*
fade (sth ⇔) **out** *phr. v.* to disappear slowly or become quieter, or to make a picture or sound do this: *The radio signal faded out.*

Fahr·en·heit /ˈfærənˌhaɪt/ *n.* [U] *written abbreviation* **F** a temperature scale in which water freezes at 32° and boils at 212° [➥ **Celsius**]

fail[1] /feɪl/ *v.* **1** [I] to be unsuccessful in what you are trying to do [≠ **succeed**]: *It looks likely that the peace talks will fail.* | *Doctors* ***failed to*** *save the girl's life.* | *The President* ***failed in*** *his efforts to establish a national health care system.* | *He* ***failed in*** *his* ***attempt*** *to regain the world title.* **2** [I] to not do what is expected, needed, or wanted: *Larry* ***failed to*** *present his proposal on time.* | *She felt she had* ***failed in*** *her* ***duty*** *as a parent.* **3** [I,T] if you fail a test, or if someone fails you, you do not pass it [≠ **pass**]: *I failed my math test.* | *The teacher had no choice but to fail her.* **4** [I] if a machine, a part of your body, etc. fails, it stops working: *The engine failed just after the plane took off.* | *her*

F

failing eyesight **5** [I] if a business fails, it has to stop operating because of a lack of money **6 fail sb** to not do what someone has trusted you to do: *I feel I've failed my children by not spending more time with them.* **7 I fail to see/understand** *spoken formal* used in order to show that you are annoyed by something that you do not accept or understand: *I fail to see the humor in this situation.* **8 sb's courage/nerve fails them** if your courage, etc. fails you, you suddenly do not have it when you need it —**failed** *adj.* [only before noun] *a failed marriage*

fail² *n.* **without fail** if you do something without fail, you always do it: *Barry comes over every Friday without fail.*

fail·ing¹ /ˈfeɪlɪŋ/ *n.* [C] a fault or weakness: *He loved her in spite of her failings.*

failing² *prep.* used in order to say that if one thing is not possible, there is something else you could try: *You could try to fix it yourself, or,* ***failing that****, call a plumber.*

ˈfail-safe *adj.* **1** a fail-safe machine, piece of equipment, etc. will stop working if one part of it breaks or stops working correctly **2** a fail-safe plan is certain to succeed

F

fail·ure /ˈfeɪlyɚ/ *n.* **1** [U] a lack of success in achieving or doing something [**≠ success**]: *The recession has caused the* ***failure of*** *many small businesses.* | *Are teachers to blame for students'* ***failure to*** *learn?* | *The whole project* ***ended in failure****.* **2** [C] someone or something that is not successful [**≠ success**]: *I feel like such a failure.* | *The plan to expand the company overseas was a* ***complete/total failure****.* **3** [C,U] an occasion when a machine or part of your body stops working in the correct way: *He died of heart failure.* | *A mechanical failure caused the plane to crash.* **4 failure to do sth** the fact that someone has not done something that s/he should have done: *Failure to show proof of car insurance to an officer will result in a fine.*

faint¹ /feɪnt/ *adj.* **1** difficult to see, hear, or smell: *a faint sound* **2 a faint possibility/chance etc.** a very small possibility, etc.: *There's a faint hope that they're still alive.* **3** [not before noun] feeling weak and unsteady: *He was* ***faint with*** *hunger* **4 not have the faintest idea** to not know anything at all about something: *I* ***don't have the faintest idea what*** *you're talking about.* —**faintly** *adv.*

faint² *v.* [I] to become unconscious for a short time —**faint** *n.* [C]

fair¹ /fɛr/ *adj.*

1 REASONABLE reasonable, right, and accepted by most people [**≠ unfair**]: *What do you think is the fairest solution?* | *We paid what we think is a fair price.* | ***It's fair to say that*** *both sides were happy with the agreement.* | *I felt it was* ***fair to*** *let our employees know what was going on.*

THESAURUS

just – morally right and fair: *a just ruler*
reasonable – fair and sensible: *a reasonable request*
equitable formal – fair and equal to everyone involved
balanced – fair and sensible: *balanced news coverage*
even-handed – giving fair and equal treatment to everyone: *He was very even-handed in the way he treated employees.*

2 EQUAL treating everyone equally or in the right way [**≠ unfair**]: *Why does Eric get to go and I don't?* ***It's not fair!*** | *The law isn't* ***fair to*** *women.*
3 AVERAGE neither very good nor very bad [**= average**]: *Her written work is excellent but her practical work is only fair.*
4 ACCORDING TO RULES played or done according to the rules: *free and fair elections*
5 have more than your fair share of sth to have more problems than other people, in a way that seems unfair: *Tim's had more than his fair share of bad luck this year.*
6 HAIR/SKIN light in color [**≠ dark**]
7 WEATHER sunny and pleasant
8 fair game if someone or something is fair game, it is reasonable and right to criticize him/her or it: *If you're in show business, your personal life is considered fair game.*
9 give sb/get a fair shake *informal* to treat someone, or to be treated, in a way that gives everyone the same chances as everyone else: *Women don't always get a fair shake in business.* —**fairness** *n.* [U]

fair² *adv.* **1 fair and square** in a fair and honest way: *They won fair and square.* **2 play fair** to play or behave in a fair and honest way

fair³ *n.* [C] **1** an outdoor event, at which there are large machines to ride on, games to play, and sometimes farm animals being judged and sold: *a* ***state/county fair*** **2** an event at which people or businesses show and sell their products: *a trade/book etc. fair*

fair·ground /ˈfɛrgraʊnd/ *n.* [C] an open space on which a fair takes place

fair·ly /ˈfɛrli/ *adv.* **1** more than a little, but much less than very: *She speaks English fairly well.* | *The recipe is fairly simple.*

THESAURUS

rather, **pretty**, **quite**
→ see Thesaurus box at RATHER

2 in a way that is fair and reasonable: *I felt that I hadn't been treated fairly.*

fair·way /ˈfɛrweɪ/ *n.* [C] the part of a GOLF COURSE that you hit the ball along toward the hole

fair·y /ˈfɛri/ *n.* plural **fairies** [C] an imaginary magical creature like a very small person

ˈfairy tale *n.* [C] a children's story in which magical things happen

faith /feɪθ/ *n.* **1** [U] a strong feeling of trust in someone or something: *My **faith in** his ability was justified.* | *I **have** great **faith** in her ability to succeed.* | *People seem to have **lost faith** in the justice system.* **2** [U] belief and trust in God: *a man of deep religious faith* | *his **faith in** God* **3 good faith** honest and sincere intentions: *He claimed he sold me the car **in good faith*** (=without meaning to deceive me). **4** [C] a religion: *the **Jewish/Muslim/Christian, etc. faith***

THESAURUS

religion – belief in one or more gods, or a particular system of beliefs in one or more gods: *a book about world religions*
belief – an idea or set of ideas that you think are true: *She has strong religious beliefs.*
creed – a set of beliefs or principles: *The scholarship is available to anyone, regardless of race, creed, or color.*

faith·ful /ˈfeɪθfəl/ *adj.* **1** remaining loyal and continuing to support someone or something: *a faithful friend* | *He remained **faithful to** his beliefs.*

THESAURUS

loyal – always supporting a particular person, set of beliefs, or country: *a loyal friend*
devoted – giving someone or something a lot of love, concern, and attention: *a devoted mother*
staunch very loyal: staunch supporters of the president

2 loyal to your wife, BOYFRIEND, etc. by not having a sexual relationship with anyone else [≠ **unfaithful**]: *She hasn't always been **faithful to** me, but I love her anyway.* **3** representing an event or image exactly: *The movie is **faithful to** the book.* —**faithfulness** *n.* [U]

faith·ful·ly /ˈfeɪθfəli/ *adv.* in a faithful way: *He visited his aunt faithfully.*

fake

fake¹ /feɪk/ *n.* [C] **1** a copy of a valuable object that is intended to deceive people: *We thought it was a Picasso, but it was a fake.* **2** someone who does not really have the knowledge, skills, etc. that s/he claims to have: *It turned out her doctor was a fake.*

fake² *adj.* made to look or seem like something else in order to deceive people: *fake fur* | *She used a fake name to apply for a credit card.*

THESAURUS

false/imitation – not real, but intended to look real: *false teeth* | *imitation leather*
counterfeit – counterfeit money or a counterfeit product is made to look real in order to deceive people: *counterfeit credit cards* | *counterfeit lottery tickets* | *a million dollars in counterfeit bills*
phony – not real and intended to deceive people: *a phony birth certificate*
forged – used about writing or documents that have been illegally copied in order to deceive people: *forged passports*
→ see Thesaurus box at ARTIFICIAL

fake³ *v.* **1** [T] to make something seem real in order to deceive people: *He faked his uncle's signature on the check.* **2** [I,T] to pretend to be sick, interested, pleased, etc. when you are not: *I thought he was really hurt but he was just **faking it**.*

fal·con /ˈfælkən, ˈfɔl-/ *n.* [C] a large bird that is often trained to hunt small animals

fall¹ /fɔl/ *v.* past tense **fell** /fɛl/ past participle **fallen** /ˈfɔlən/

1 MOVE DOWNWARD [I] to drop down toward the ground [➡ **plummet**]: *Snow began to fall.* | *Apples had **fallen from** the trees.* | *A large tree **fell down** during the storm.*

2 STOP STANDING/WALKING, ETC. [I] to accidentally go down onto the ground when you are standing, walking, etc.: *Don't worry, I'll catch you if you fall.* | *She **fell down** the stairs.* | *Sam tripped and **fell into** a ditch.* → see picture on page A9

THESAURUS

trip – to hit your foot against something, so that you fall or nearly fall: *Be careful not to trip on that step.*
slip – to slide on something that is wet or icy, so that you fall or nearly fall: *She slipped on the ice and broke her leg.*
stumble – to put your foot down in an awkward way, so that you nearly fall: *She stumbled backwards and hit her head on the bed.*
lose your balance – to fall, for example, when you are climbing a ladder or riding a bicycle

3 LOWER LEVEL/AMOUNT [I] to go down to a lower level or amount [≠ **rise**]: *Temperatures should fall below zero tonight.* | *The number of traffic deaths fell by 10% last year.* | *The unemployment rate **fell to** 4.8%.*

F

THESAURUS

decrease, **go down**, **drop**, **plummet**, **diminish**, **decline**
→ see Thesaurus box at DECREASE[1]

4 BECOME [I, linking verb] to begin to be in a new or different state: *I* ***fell asleep*** *at 8:30.* | *Your father and I* ***fell in love*** *during the war.* | *Everyone* ***fell silent*** *as Beth walked in.* | *The house* ***fell into*** *disrepair.*
5 GROUP [I] to be part of a particular group: *These substances* ***fall into*** *two categories.* | *The program* ***falls under*** *the authority of the Department of Education.*
6 fall into place if things fall into place, they become clear or start to happen as you want
7 HAPPEN [I] to happen on a particular day or date: *Christmas* ***falls on*** *a Monday this year.*
8 LIGHT/DARKNESS [I] if light or darkness falls, it makes something brighter or darker: ***Darkness/Night fell on*** *the city.* | *A shadow* ***fell across*** *his face.*
9 HANG DOWN [I] to hang loosely: *Maria's hair fell over her shoulders.*
10 fall short (of sth) to be less than is needed or less than you want: *Her newest book fell short of my expectations.*
11 FACE [I] if your face falls, you suddenly look sad or disappointed
12 fall flat to fail to amuse or interest people: *His attempt at humor fell flat.*
13 DIE [I] *written* to be killed in a war
14 LOSE POWER [I] to lose power: *After World War II, the British Empire fell.*

fall apart *phr. v.* **1** to separate into many pieces: *The old book fell apart in my hands.* **2** to stop being effective or successful: *The economy was falling apart.* **3** to be unable to deal with your personal or emotional problems: *When Pam left, I thought I was going to fall apart.*

fall back on sth *phr. v.* to use something or someone after other things or plans have failed: *Athletes need an education to fall back on.*

fall behind (sb/sth) *phr. v.* to make progress more slowly than other people or than you should: *The older walkers soon fell behind.* | *The manufacturers have fallen behind schedule.*

fall for sb/sth *phr. v.* **1** to be tricked into believing something that is not true: *He said he was a police officer and I almost* ***fell for it***. **2** to start to love someone: *Samantha fell for a man half her age.*

fall off *phr. v.* **1** if part of something falls off, it becomes separated from the main part: *This button keeps falling off.* **2** to decrease: *Demand for records has fallen off recently.*

fall out *phr. v.* **1** if a tooth or your hair falls out, it is no longer attached to your body **2** to argue or fight with someone: *Walker recently* ***fell out with*** *his publisher.*

fall over *phr. v.* to fall to the ground or to fall from an upright position: *She fell over and cut her knee.* | *The Christmas tree fell over.*

fall through *phr. v.* to fail to happen or be completed: *The deal fell through at the last minute.*

fall[2] *n.* **1** [C,U] the season between summer and winter, when the weather becomes cooler [**= autumn**]: *Brad's going to Georgia Tech* ***in the fall***. | *Dad's going to retire* ***this fall***. | ***last/next fall*** (=the fall before or after this one) **2** [C] a decrease in the level, quantity, price, etc. of something [**≠ rise**]: *a sudden* ***fall in*** *temperature* | *a* ***fall of*** *25% in unemployment* **3** [C] a movement down toward the ground: *He* ***had a*** *bad* ***fall*** *from a ladder.* | *He put his hand down to* ***break*** *his* ***fall*** (=prevent himself from falling too quickly and hurting himself). **4** [singular] a situation when someone or something is defeated or loses power: *the* ***fall of*** *Rome* | *the party's* ***fall from*** *power* **5 falls** [plural] a WATERFALL

fal·la·cious /fəˈleɪʃəs/ *adj. formal* containing or based on false ideas: *a fallacious statement* —**fallaciously** *adv.*

fal·la·cy /ˈfæləsi/ *n.* plural **fallacies** [C] a false idea or belief: *the fallacy that money brings happiness*

fall·en /ˈfɔlən/ *v.* the past participle of FALL

ˈfall guy *n.* [C] *informal* someone who is punished for someone else's crime or mistake

fal·li·ble /ˈfæləbəl/ *adj.* able to make a mistake [**≠ infallible**]: *Steyer's murder trial showed that the justice system is fallible.* —**fallibility** /ˌfæləˈbɪləṭi/ *n.* [U]

fall·out /ˈfɔlaʊt/ *n.* [U] **1** the bad results or effects of an event: *The* ***fallout from*** *the scandal cost him his job.* **2** the dangerous RADIOACTIVE dust that is in the air after a NUCLEAR explosion

false /fɔls/ *adj.* **1** untrue or wrong: *He gave the police false information.* | *Are these statements* ***true or false***? | *The article gave a* ***false impression*** *of the company's finances.*

THESAURUS

wrong, **incorrect**, **inaccurate**, **misleading**
→ see Thesaurus box at WRONG[1]

2 not real, but intended to seem real: *He gave a false name.* | *false eyelashes*

THESAURUS

artificial, **synthetic**, **fake**, **simulated**, **imitation**, **virtual**, **counterfeit**, **phony**, **forged**
→ see Thesaurus box at ARTIFICIAL, FAKE[2]

3 not sincere or honest: *Her smile and welcome seemed false.* **4 false alarm** a situation in which people wrongly think that something bad is going to happen **5 false start** an unsuccessful attempt to begin a process or event **6 under false pretenses** if you get something under false pretenses, you get it by deceiving people —**falsely** *adv.*: *a man falsely accused of murder*

false·hood /ˈfɔlshʊd/ *n.* [C] *formal* a statement that is untrue [= **lie**]

ˌfalse ˈteeth *n.* [plural] DENTURES

fal·set·to /fɔlˈsɛt̬oʊ/ *n.* plural **falsettos** [C] a very high male voice —**falsetto** *adv.*

fal·si·fy /ˈfɔlsəˌfaɪ/ *v.* past tense and past participle **falsified**, third person singular **falsifies** [T] to change figures, records, etc. so that they contain false information: *He was accused of falsifying the company's records.* —**falsification** /ˌfɔlsəfəˈkeɪʃən/ *n.* [C,U]

fal·ter /ˈfɔltɚ/ *v.* [I] **1** to become weaker: *The economy is faltering.* **2** to speak or move in a way that seems weak or uncertain: *She faltered for a moment.*

fame /feɪm/ *n.* [U] the state of being known about by a lot of people because of your achievements: *Elizabeth Taylor's **rise to fame** came in the movie "National Velvet."* | *Tina Louise **gained/won/achieved fame** as actress Ginger Grant on "Gilligan's Island."* ➔ **claim to fame** at CLAIM²

famed /feɪmd/ *adj. written* well-known: *mountains **famed for** their beauty*

fa·mil·iar /fəˈmɪlyɚ/ *adj.* **1** well-known to you and easy to recognize: *Your face **looks familiar** to me.* | *a room full of **familiar faces*** (=people you know) | *The details are **familiar to** anyone who has followed the case.* | *The story covers **familiar ground/territory**.* **2 be familiar with sth** to know about something: *Are you familiar with his books?* **3** *disapproving* too informal and friendly with someone you do not know very well: *The waiter was a bit too familiar.* —**familiarly** *adv.*: *Robert, familiarly known as Bob*

fa·mil·iar·i·ty /fəˌmɪlˈyærət̬i, -ˌmɪliˈær-/ *n.* [U] **1** a good knowledge of something: *her **familiarity with** this software* **2** a relaxed feeling or way of behaving because you know a person or place well: *the familiarity of home*

fa·mil·iar·ize /fəˈmɪlyəˌraɪz/ *v.* **familiarize yourself with sth** to learn about something so that you know it well: *I spent the first week familiarizing myself with my new job.* —**familiarization** /fəˌmɪlyərəˈzeɪʃən/ *n.* [U]

fam·i·ly /ˈfæmli, -məli/ *n.* plural **families** **1** [C,U] a group of people who are related to each other, especially parents and their children: *Do you know the family next door?* | *a car that will comfortably seat **a family of** five* | *I know her **whole/entire family**.* | *Heart disease **runs in** our **family*** (=is common in our family).

COLLOCATIONS

Your **immediate family** includes the people you are very closely related to, such as your parents, brothers, sisters, and children.
Your **extended family** includes all of your relatives such as aunts, uncles, cousins, and grandparents.

THESAURUS

relative – a member of your family: *Most of my relatives are in California.*
relation – a member of your family: *Hugh is a distant relation of mine.*
folks – your parents or family: *Where do your folks live?*
➔ RELATIVE⁴

2 [C] children: *Steve and Linda want to **start a family*** (=have children). | *a great place to **raise a family*** **3** [C] a group of related animals, plants, languages, etc.: *tigers and other members of the cat family*

ˈfamily ˌname *n.* [C] the name someone shares with other members of his/her family [= **last name**]

ˌfamily ˈplanning *n.* [U] the practice of controlling the number of children you have by using CONTRACEPTION

ˈfamily ˌroom *n.* [C] a room in a house where the family can play games, watch television, etc.

ˌfamily ˈtree *n.* [C] a drawing that shows the names of the members of a family over a period of time and how they are related to each other

fam·ine /ˈfæmɪn/ *n.* [C,U] a situation in which a large number of people have little or no food for a long time and many people die

fam·ished /ˈfæmɪʃt/ *adj. informal* [not before noun] very hungry: *What's for dinner? I'm famished.*

fa·mous /ˈfeɪməs/ *adj.* known about by a lot of people: *a famous actor* | *France is **famous for** its food and wine.* | *Da Vinci's **world-famous*** (=famous all over the world) *portrait of the Mona Lisa* —**famously** *adv.*

THESAURUS

If someone or something is **well-known**, a lot of people know about him, her, or it: *a well-known actor* | *He is well-known for his charity work.* | *It's a well-known fact that smoking causes cancer.*
If someone is **legendary**, s/he is very famous and has been admired for a long time: *the legendary blues guitarist, BB King*
If someone is **infamous** or **notorious**, s/he is known by a lot of people for something bad: *an infamous criminal*

fan¹ /fæn/ *n.* [C] **1** someone who likes a particular sport, type of music, etc. very much, or who admires a famous person: *a **hockey/jazz/Yankee etc. fan*** | *He was a big **fan of** Elvis Presley.* **2** a machine, or a thing that you wave with your hand, that cools you by making the air move

fan² *v.* past tense and past participle **fanned**, present participle **fanning** [T] to make air move by waving a fan, piece of paper, etc.: *She fanned her face with a newspaper.*

F

fan out *phr. v.* if a group of people fan out, they walk forward while spreading over a wide area: *Thousands of soldiers and police fanned out across the state.*

fa·nat·ic /fəˈnæt̬ɪk/ *n.* [C] **1** someone who has extreme religious or political ideas and may be dangerous: *a religious fanatic* **2** someone who likes a particular thing or activity very much: *a fitness fanatic* —**fanatical** *adj.* —**fanaticism** /fəˈnæt̬əˌsɪzəm/ *n.* [U]

fan·ci·ful /ˈfænsɪfəl/ *adj.* imagined rather than based on facts: *fanciful ideas*

ˈfan club *n.* [C] an organization for fans of a particular team, famous person, etc.

fan·cy¹ /ˈfænsi/ *adj.* comparative **fancier**, superlative **fanciest** **1** expensive and fashionable: *a fancy hotel*

> **THESAURUS**
>
> **expensive**, **pricey**, **posh**
> ➔ see Thesaurus box at EXPENSIVE

2 unusual and complicated or having a lot of decorations: *I'd just like plain brown shoes, **nothing fancy**.* **3** [only before noun] fancy food is of a very high quality

F

fancy² *n.* [singular] *old-fashioned* a feeling that you like something or someone: *Grant's **taken a fancy to** you.*

fancy³ *v.* past tense and past participle **fancied**, third person singular **fancies**, **fancy yourself sth** to believe, usually wrongly, that something is true: *Hiram fancies himself a good writer.*

fan·fare /ˈfænfɛr/ *n.* [C] a short piece of music played on a TRUMPET to introduce an important person or event

fang /fæŋ/ *n.* [C] a long sharp tooth of an animal such as a snake or dog ➔ see picture on page A2

ˈfan mail *n.* [U] letters sent to famous people by their FANS

fan·ta·size /ˈfæntəˌsaɪz/ *v.* [I,T] to think about something that is pleasant or exciting, but unlikely to happen: *I used to **fantasize about** buying a boat and sailing around the world.*

> **THESAURUS**
>
> **imagine**, **visualize**, **picture**, **conceive of**, **daydream**
> ➔ see Thesaurus box at IMAGINE

fan·tas·tic /fænˈtæstɪk/ *adj.* **1** extremely good: *You look fantastic! | He's doing a fantastic job. | "I passed my math test!" "Fantastic!"*

> **THESAURUS**
>
> **good**, **great**, **excellent**, **wonderful**
> ➔ see Thesaurus box at GOOD¹, NICE

2 very large: *She spends fantastic amounts of money on clothes.* **3** strange or unreal: *a fantastic dream* —**fantastically** *adv.*

fan·ta·sy /ˈfæntəsi, -zi/ *n.* plural **fantasies** [C,U] an experience or situation that you imagine but is not real: *When I was young, I had **fantasies about** becoming a race car driver.*

FAQ /fæk, ˌɛf eɪ ˈkjuː/ *n.* [C usually plural] **frequently asked question** a question that people often ask about something, which is shown together with its answer: *There's a section with tax FAQs.*

far¹ /fɑr/ *adv.* comparative **farther** or **further**, superlative **farthest** or **furthest**

1 DISTANCE a) a long distance: *I don't want to drive very far. | Let's see who can swim the farthest. | They found the body not too **far from** here. | His office is a little **farther down** the hallway. | The boat had moved **farther away** from the dock.* ▶ Don't say "I walked far." say "I walked a long way." ◀ **b)** used when asking the distance between two places, or when talking about the distance between two places: ***How far** is Boston from here?*

2 A LOT/VERY MUCH very much, or to a great degree: *Our new car is **far better** than the old one. | Dinner cost **far more/less** than I expected. | It would take me **far too** long to explain. | This is **by far** the best movie she's ever made.*

3 PROGRESS used in order to talk about how much progress someone makes: *We only **got as far as** the first ten minutes of the video. | Republicans claimed that the bill did not **go far enough*** (=did not have a big enough effect). | *She's a good dancer and should **go far*** (=be very successful).

4 TIME in the past or in the future: *The church dates **as far back as** the 12th century. | They worked **far into** the night. | Let's not plan too **far ahead**.*

5 so far until now: *We haven't had any problems so far.*

6 go too far to do something that is too extreme: *He's always been a little rude, but this time he went too far.*

7 go so far as to do sth to do something that seems surprising or extreme: *He even went so far as to call her a liar.*

8 far from sth used to say that something is not at all true: *The deal is far from certain.*

9 not go far if money does not go far, you cannot buy very much with it: *A dollar doesn't go far anymore.*

➔ **as far as sb's concerned** at CONCERNED

> **SPOKEN PHRASES**
>
> **10 as far as I know also as far as I can remember/tell** used to say that you think something is true, but you may be wrong: *Cole wasn't even there, as far as I can remember.*
>
> **11 so far so good** used to say that something has been successful until now: *"How's your new job?" "So far so good."*

GRAMMAR

When you are talking about distances, you can use **far** in questions and negative sentences: *How far is it to the stadium? | It's not very far.*
You can also use **far** after "too," "as," and "so": *It's too far to walk. | I ran as far as I could. | I wish he didn't live so far away.*
But do not use **far** in other kinds of sentence. For example, do not say "It's far to Boston from here." Say *"It's **a long way** to Boston from here."*

far² *adj.* comparative **farther** or, **further**, superlative **farthest** or, **furthest** **1** a long distance away [≠ **near**]: *We can walk if it's not far.* ➔ see picture at NEAR² **2 the far side/end etc.** the side, etc. most distant from where you are: *the far side of the building* **3 the far north/south etc.** the part of an area that is furthest to the north, the south, etc.: *Nguyen was born in the far south of Vietnam.* **4 the far left/right** people who have extreme political opinions **5 be a far cry from sth** to be very different from something: *Europe was a far cry from what Tom had expected.*

far·a·way /ˈfɑrəˌweɪ/ *adj.* **1** *literary* distant: *faraway lands* **2 a faraway look** an expression on your face that shows that you are not thinking about what is around you

farce /fɑrs/ *n.* **1** [singular] an event or situation that is badly organized and does not happen in the way that it should: *The trial was a total farce.* **2** [C] a humorous play or movie in which a lot of silly things happen —**farcical** *adj.*

fare¹ /fɛr/ *n.* [C] **1** the price you pay to travel by train, airplane, bus, etc.: ***Air/Bus/Train fares** are going up again.*

THESAURUS

cost, **expense**, **price**, **charge**, **fee**
➔ see Thesaurus box at COST¹

2 food, especially food served in a restaurant: *vegetarian fare*

fare² *v.* **fare well/better/badly etc.** *formal* to be successful or unsuccessful in a particular situation: *Polls suggest Kramer will fare well in the election.*

ˌFar ˈEast *n.* **the Far East** the countries in the east of Asia, such as China, Japan, Korea, etc.

fare·well /ˌfɛrˈwɛl/ *n.* [C] **1** *old-fashioned* the action of saying goodbye: *We **bid farewell to** our friends. | a farewell speech* **2 a farewell party/drink** a party or drink that you have with someone who is leaving

ˌfar-ˈfetched *adj.* unlikely to be true, and so difficult to believe: *Her story was pretty far-fetched.*

ˌfar-ˈflung *adj.* very far away: *the far-flung regions of Russia*

farm animals

farm¹ /fɑrm/ *n.* [C] an area of land used for raising animals or growing food: *farm animals | I grew up **on a farm**. | a **dairy/hog/cattle etc.** farm*

farm² *v.* [I,T] to use land for growing crops or raising animals: *Our family has farmed here for years.*

farm·er /ˈfɑrmɚ/ *n.* [C] someone who owns or manages a farm

farm·hand /ˈfɑrmhænd/ *n.* [C] someone who works on a farm

farm·ing /ˈfɑrmɪŋ/ *n.* [U] the activity of raising animals or growing crops on a farm

farm·land /ˈfɑrmlænd/ *n.* [U] land used for farming

farm·yard /ˈfɑrmyɑrd/ *n.* [C] an area with farm buildings around it

ˌfar-ˈoff *adj. literary* a long distance away or a long time ago: *a far-off land*

ˌfar-ˈout *adj. informal* unusual or strange: *far-out clothes*

ˌfar-ˈreaching *adj.* having a big influence or effect: *far-reaching tax reforms*

far·sight·ed /ˈfɑrˌsaɪṭɪd/ *adj.* **1** able to see or read things clearly only when they are far away from you [≠ **nearsighted**] **2** *approving* considering what will happen in the future: *farsighted leaders*

fart /fɑrt/ *v.* [I] *informal* an impolite word meaning to make air come out of your BOWELS —**fart** *n.* [C]

far·ther /ˈfɑrðɚ/ *adj., adv.* the comparative of FAR [➡ **further**]

USAGE

Use **farther** to talk about distance: *The restaurant's just a little farther down the street.*
Use **further** to talk about time, quantities, or degrees: *House prices will probably drop further next year. | I don't want to discuss this any further.*
Many people use **further** in spoken English to talk about distance, but many teachers think that this is not correct.

far·thest /ˈfɑrðɪst/ *adj., adv.* the superlative of FAR [➡ **furthest**]

F

fas·ci·nate /ˈfæsəˌneɪt/ *v.* [T] to interest you very much: *Mechanical things fascinate me.* | *We were* ***fascinated to learn*** *she had grown up in Kenya.*

fas·ci·nat·ing /ˈfæsəˌneɪṭɪŋ/ *adj.* extremely interesting: *a fascinating movie* | *I* ***found*** *her* ***fascinating.***

THESAURUS

interesting, intriguing, absorbing, compelling
→ see Thesaurus box at INTERESTING

fas·ci·na·tion /ˌfæsəˈneɪʃən/ *n.* [singular, U] the state of being very interested in something: *Jan* ***had a fascination with/for*** *movie stars.*

fas·cism /ˈfæʃɪzəm/ *n.* [U] an extreme RIGHT-WING political system in which people's lives are completely controlled by the state

fas·cist /ˈfæʃɪst/ *n.* [C] **1** someone who supports fascism **2** someone who is cruel and unfair **3** someone who has extreme RIGHT-WING political opinions that you do not approve of —**fascist** *adj.*

fash·ion¹ /ˈfæʃən/ *n.* **1** [C,U] something such as a style of clothes or hair that is popular at a particular time: *Hats are* ***in fashion*** *again.* | *Shoes like that* ***went out of fashion*** *years ago.* | *The martini has* ***come back into fashion.*** | *She always buys* ***the latest fashions.*** **2** [U] the business or study of making or selling clothes: ***fashion show/model/magazine etc.*** **3 in a ... fashion** *formal* in a particular way: *Please return all phone calls in a timely fashion.*

fashion² *v.* [T] *formal* to shape or make something with your hands or a few tools: *Many fans had fashioned home-made banners.*

fash·ion·a·ble /ˈfæʃənəbəl/ *adj.* popular, especially for a short time [≠ **unfashionable**]: *Long skirts are fashionable now.* | *a fashionable restaurant* | ***It's*** *become* ***fashionable to*** *wear fake fur.*

THESAURUS

trendy – modern and fashionable: *trendy restaurants*
stylish – attractive in a fashionable way: *a stylish deep blue suit*
designer – designer clothes, watches, etc. are made by someone who is famous for designing fashionable things: *a pair of designer jeans*
be in style/fashion – to be fashionable during a particular period of time: *At that time, plaid skirts were in fashion.*

ˈfashion show *n.* [C] an event at which new styles of clothes are shown to the public

fast¹ /fæst/ *adj.* **1** moving, happening, or doing something quickly [≠ **slow**]: *a fast runner* | *a fast car* | *The subway is the fastest way to get downtown.* **2** [not before noun] showing time that is later than the true time [≠ **slow**]: *I think my watch is fast.* **3 fast track** a way of achieving something more quickly than it is normally done: *young professionals* ***on the fast track*** *for promotion* **4 the fast lane a)** an exciting way of living that involves dangerous or expensive activities: *She loves* ***life in the fast lane.*** **b)** the part of a big road where people drive fastest

fast² *adv.* **1** at a great speed, or in not much time: *He likes driving fast.* | *You're learning fast.*

THESAURUS

quickly/swiftly – used especially about movement: *I ran quickly down the stairs.* | *Anna looked swiftly up at him.*
rapidly/speedily – used especially about the speed at which something happens: *Unemployment rose rapidly.* | *Police reacted speedily to the calls.*

2 fast asleep sleeping very deeply **3** firmly or tightly: *Walter* ***held fast*** *to the rope.* | *The boat's* ***stuck fast*** *in the mud.* **4 hold fast to sth** to continue to believe in or support an idea, principle, etc.: *In spite of everything, her father held fast to his religion.*

fasten

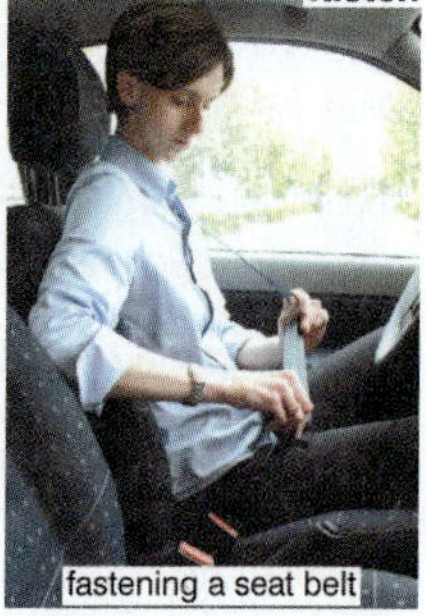

fastening a seat belt

fast³ *v.* [I] to eat little or no food for a period of time, especially for religious reasons —**fast** *n.* [C]

fas·ten /ˈfæsən/ *v.* **1** [I,T] to join together the two sides of something so that it is closed, or to become joined [≠ **unfasten, undo**]: *Fasten your seat belts.* | *The skirt fastens at the back.*

THESAURUS

attach – to fasten something firmly to another object or surface
join – to connect or fasten things together
glue – to join things together using glue
tape – to fasten something using tape
staple – to fasten something using staples (=small pieces of bent wire that go through paper)
clip – to fasten things together using a clip (=a small object that goes over paper to hold it together)
tie – to fasten a tie or shoes, etc. by making a knot: *Don't forget to tie your shoelaces.*
button (up) – to fasten the buttons on a shirt, coat, etc.: *Craig buttoned up his jacket.*
zip (up) – to fasten clothes, bags, etc. with a zipper: *I can't zip up these jeans.*

2 [T] to attach something firmly to another object or surface: *Jill* ***fastened*** *a flower* ***to/onto*** *her dress.* **3** [T] to firmly close and lock a window, gate, etc.

fas·ten·er /ˈfæsənɚ/ *n.* [C] something such as a button or pin that you use to join something together

ˈfast food *n.* [U] food such as HAMBURGERS, that is prepared and served quickly in a restaurant

THESAURUS

junk food, health food, vegetarian food
➔ see Thesaurus box at FOOD

fast ˈforward *v.* [T] to wind a tape or video forward quickly in a machine without watching it [➡ **play**] —**fast-forward** *n.* [U]

fas·tid·i·ous /fæˈstɪdiəs, fə-/ *adj.* very careful about small details: *He is fastidious about hygiene.* —**fastidiously** *adv.*

fat[1] /fæt/ *adj.* **1** weighing too much because you have too much flesh on your body [≠ **thin**]: *Chris thinks he's **getting fat**.* | *a big fat guy*

THESAURUS

You can call yourself **fat**, but it is not polite to directly tell someone else that they are fat: *I'm getting really fat.*
overweight – used as a more polite way of describing someone who is fat: *He's a little overweight.*
big, **heavy**, **large** – used as polite ways to describe someone who is big, strong, or fat: *a heavy woman in her fifties* | *He's a pretty big guy.*
obese – used about someone who is extremely fat in a way that is dangerous to their health
chubby – used about someone, especially a baby or a child, who is slightly fat
plump – used to say that someone, especially a woman or a child, is slightly fat in a pleasant way
➔ THIN

2 thick or wide [≠ **thin**]: *a fat cigar* **3** [only before noun] *informal* containing or worth a lot of money: *I should get a nice **fat check** at the end of the month.* **4 fat chance** *spoken* said when something is very unlikely to happen: *Sean said he'd be here at 5:00? Fat chance.*

fat[2] *n.* **1** [U] the substance under the skin of people and animals that helps keep them warm **2** [C,U] an oily substance in some foods: *food that is **low/high in fat*** | *a **low-fat/high-fat** diet* **3** [C,U] an oily substance taken from animals or plants and used in cooking: *Fry the potatoes in oil or melted fat.*

fa·tal /ˈfeɪṭl/ *adj.* **1** resulting in someone's death: *a **fatal crash/accident*** | *a **fatal shooting*** | *The disease **proved fatal*** (=killed someone). **2** having a very bad effect: *Her **fatal mistake** was to marry too young.* | *There's a **fatal flaw** in his argument.* —**fatally** *adv.*

fa·tal·ism /ˈfeɪṭlˌɪzəm/ *n.* [U] the belief that there is nothing you can do to prevent events from happening —**fatalistic** /ˌfeɪṭlˈɪstɪk◂ / *adj.*

fa·tal·i·ty /feɪˈtæləṭi, fə-/ *n.* plural **fatalities** [C] a death in an accident or violent attack: *traffic fatalities*

fate /feɪt/ *n.* **1** [C] the things that happen to someone, especially bad events: *No one knows what the **fate of** the refugees will be.* | *He hopes his new restaurant doesn't **suffer** the same **fate** as his last one.* **2** [U] a power that is believed to control what happens in people's lives: *Fate brought us together.* | ***By a** lucky **twist of fate*** (=completely unexpected event), *we were on the same plane.*

fat·ed /ˈfeɪṭɪd/ *adj.* **be fated to do sth** certain to happen or to do something because a mysterious force is controlling events: *We were fated to meet.*

fate·ful /ˈfeɪtfəl/ *adj.* having an important, usually bad, effect on future events: *a fateful decision*

ˌfat-ˈfree *adj.* containing no fat: *fat-free yogurt*

fa·ther[1] /ˈfɑðɚ/ *n.* [C] **1** a male parent [➡ **dad**, **stepfather**, **mother**]: *a father of four* (=a man with four children)

THESAURUS

relative, parents, mother, dad, daddy, mom, mommy, brother, sister, grandparents, grandfather, grandmother, grandpa, grandma, great-grandparents, uncle, aunt, nephew, niece, cousin
➔ see Thesaurus box at RELATIVE[1]

2 Father a priest, especially in the Roman Catholic Church: *Do you know Father Vernon?* **3 the father of sth** the man who was responsible for starting something: *George Washington is the father of our country.*

father[2] *v.* [T] to become a male parent: *Taylor denies fathering her 4-month-old son.*

ˈfather ˌfigure *n.* [C] an older man whom you trust and respect

fa·ther·hood /ˈfɑðɚˌhʊd/ *n.* [U] the state of being a father

ˈfather-in-ˌlaw *n.* plural **fathers-in-law** [C] the father of your husband or wife

fa·ther·ly /ˈfɑðɚli/ *adj.* typical of a kind or concerned father: *fatherly advice*

ˈFather's Day *n.* [C] a holiday in honor of fathers, celebrated in the U.S. and Canada on the third Sunday of June

fath·om[1] /ˈfæðəm/ *v.* [T] to understand what something means after thinking about it carefully: *I cannot fathom why it took them so long to respond.*

fathom[2] *n.* [C] a unit for measuring how deep water is, equal to 6 feet or 1.83 meters

fa·tigue /fəˈtig/ *n.* [U] **1** extreme tiredness: *They were weak with fatigue, but not hurt.* **2 fatigues** [plural] loose-fitting army clothes **3** *technical* weakness in a substance such as metal that may cause it to break —**fatigue** *v.* [T]

F

fat·ten /ˈfætˀn/ *v.* [T] to make an animal become fatter so that it is ready to eat
fatten sb/sth **up** *phr. v.* to make a thin person or animal fatter: *Grandma's always trying to fatten me up.*

fat·ten·ing /ˈfætˀn-ɪŋ/ *adj.* likely to make you fat: *I try to stay away from fattening foods.*

fat·ty /ˈfæt̬i/ *adj.* containing a lot of fat: *fatty foods*

fat·u·ous /ˈfætʃuəs/ *adj.* very silly or stupid: *a fatuous remark*

fau·cet /ˈfɔsɪt/ *n.* [C] the thing that you turn on and off to control the flow of water from a pipe

fault[1] /fɔlt/ *n.* [C]
1 BLAME responsibility for a mistake: ***It's** not my **fault (that)** we missed the bus.* | *I injured my back, but it **was** my **own fault**.* | ***It's** my **fault for** not bringing enough money.*
2 be at fault to be responsible for something bad that has happened: *It was the other driver who was at fault.*
3 PROBLEM a problem with something that stops it working correctly: *a **fault in** the electrical system*

F

THESAURUS
defect, **problem**, **flaw**, **bug**
→ see Thesaurus box at DEFECT[1]

4 find fault with sb/sth to criticize someone or something: *Why do you always have to find fault with my work?*
5 through no fault of my/his etc. own used in order to say that a bad thing that happened to someone was not caused by him/her: *Many Americans lost their job through no fault of their own.*
6 SB'S CHARACTER a bad part of someone's character: ***For all her faults*** (=in spite of her faults) *I still love her.*
7 CRACK a large crack in the rocks that form the Earth's surface: *the San Andreas fault*
8 generous/loyal/honest etc. to a fault very generous, kind, etc.

fault[2] *v.* [T] to find a mistake in something: *We couldn't fault her singing.*

fault·less /ˈfɔltlɪs/ *adj.* having no mistakes [= **perfect**]: *a faultless performance*

fault·y /ˈfɔlti/ *adj.* **1** not working correctly: *faulty wires* **2** not correct: *faulty reasoning*

fau·na /ˈfɔnə/ *n.* [U] *technical* all the animals living in a particular area [➡ **flora**]

faux pas /ˌfoʊ ˈpɑ/ *n.* [C] an embarrassing mistake in a social situation

fa·vor[1] /ˈfeɪvɚ/ *n.* **1** [C] something you do for someone to help or be kind to him/her: *Could you **do me a favor** and watch the baby for half an hour?* | *Can I **ask you a favor**?* | *She offered Willis a job **as a favor to** his mother.* **2 abandon/drop etc. sth in favor of sth** to decide not to have one thing and have something else instead: *Plans for a tunnel were rejected in favor of the bridge.* **3** [U] support, approval, or agreement for something: *All the board members were **in favor of** the idea.* **4 in sb's favor** to someone's advantage, or so that someone wins: *The vote was 60–59 in his favor.* **5 in favor/out of favor** liked and approved of, or no longer liked and approved of: *His books have gone out of favor.* **6** [C] a small gift that is given to guests at a party: *party favors*

favor[2] *v.* [T] **1** to prefer something or someone to other things or people: *Blyth favors gun control laws.* **2** to treat someone better than someone else, in way that is not fair: *tax cuts that favor the rich* | *a judicial system that **favors** men **over** women* **3** to provide the right conditions for something to happen: *wind conditions that favor sailing*

fa·vor·able /ˈfeɪvərəbəl/ *adj.* **1** making people like or approve of someone or something: *Try to **make a favorable impression**.* **2** showing that you like or approve of something or someone: *I've heard favorable reports about your work.* **3** appropriate and likely to make something happen or succeed: *a favorable economic environment* —**favorably** *adv.*

fa·vor·ite[1] /ˈfeɪvrɪt, -vərɪt/ *adj.* your favorite person or thing is the one you like most: *Who's your favorite actor?* | *My favorite sport is baseball.* ▶ Don't say "most favorite." ◀

favorite[2] *n.* [C] **1** something that you like more than others of the same kind: *I like all her books, but this one is my favorite.* **2** someone who is liked and treated better than others by a teacher or parent: *Katie was always Mom's favorite.* **3** the team, person, etc. that is expected to win a competition: *The Yankees are **favorites to** win the World Series.*

fa·vor·it·ism /ˈfeɪvrəˌtɪzəm/ *n.* [U] the act of treating one person or group better than another, in a way that is not fair

fawn[1] /fɔn/ *v.* [I] *disapproving* to praise someone and be friendly to him/her because you want something: *businessmen **fawning over** the mayor*

fawn[2] *n.* [C] a young DEER

fax /fæks/ *n.* **1** [C] a document that is sent in electronic form down a telephone line and then printed using a special machine: *Did you get my fax?* **2** [C] **also fax machine** a machine used for sending and receiving faxes: *What's your fax number?* **3** [U] the system of sending documents using a fax machine: *You can send your résumé **by fax**.* —**fax** *v.* [T] *Please fax me the contract.*

faze /feɪz/ *v.* [T] *informal* to make someone feel nervous or confused: *Nothing ever seemed to faze Rosie.* —**fazed** *adj.*

FBI *n.*, **the FBI the Federal Bureau of Investigation** the U.S. police department that is controlled by the government and is concerned with crimes that happen in more than one state

FDA *n.*, **the FDA the Food and Drug Administration** a U.S. government organization which makes sure that food and drugs are safe enough to be sold

fear[1] /fɪr/ *n.* **1** [C,U] the feeling you get when you are afraid or worried that something bad will happen: *a* ***fear of*** *heights* | *Here, refugees* ***live in fear of*** *being sent back.* | ***fears that*** *prices might continue to rise* | *parents'* ***fears for*** *their children's safety* | *Their* ***worst fears*** *became a reality.* **2 for fear of sth/for fear (that)** because you are worried that something bad will happen: *She kept quiet, for fear of saying the wrong thing.*

fear[2] *v.* **1** [I,T] to feel afraid or worried that something bad will happen: *Fearing a snowstorm, many people stayed home.* | *When they heard about Heidi's car crash, they* ***feared the worst*** (=were afraid something very bad had happened). | *They left because they* ***feared for*** *their* ***lives.*** **2** [T] to be afraid of someone: *a dictator feared by his country*

fear·ful /ˈfɪrfəl/ *adj. formal* afraid: *Even doctors are* ***fearful of*** *getting the disease.* —**fearfully** *adv.*

fear·less /ˈfɪrlɪs/ *adj.* not afraid of anything: *a fearless soldier* —**fearlessly** *adv.* —**fearlessness** *n.* [U]

fear·some /ˈfɪrsəm/ *adj.* very frightening: *his fearsome reputation* | *a fearsome weapon*

fea·si·ble /ˈfizəbəl/ *adj.* possible, and likely to work: *a feasible plan*

feast[1] /fist/ *n.* [C] a large meal for many people, especially a meal to celebrate a special occasion: *a wedding feast*

feast[2] *v.* **1 feast on sth** to eat a lot of a particular food with great enjoyment: *We feasted on chicken and roast potatoes.* **2 feast your eyes on sb/sth** to look at someone or something with great pleasure

feat /fit/ *n.* [C] an impressive achievement needing a lot of strength or skill: *an amazing* ***feat of*** *engineering* | *Getting your doctorate is* ***no mean feat*** (=difficult to do).

feath·er /ˈfɛðɚ/ *n.* [C] one of the light soft things that cover a bird's body ➔ see picture on page A2

feath·er·y /ˈfɛðəri/ *adj.* soft and light like feathers: *feathery snow*

fea·ture[1] /ˈfitʃɚ/ *n.* [C] **1** an important, interesting, or typical part of something: *Air bags are a standard feature in most new cars.* | *One of the best* ***features of*** *this camera is its size.* | *The crescent moon is a* ***common feature*** *of the flags of Islamic countries.*

> **THESAURUS**
>
> **characteristic, quality, property, attribute**
> ➔ see Thesaurus box at CHARACTERISTIC[1]

2 a piece of writing about a subject in a newspaper or a magazine, or a special report on television or on the radio: *a* ***feature on*** *Johnny Depp* **3** a part of someone's face: *her delicate* ***facial features*** | *Her eyes are her best feature.* **4** a movie: *There's a* ***double feature*** (=two movies the same evening) *playing at the mall theater.*

feature[2] *v.* **1** [T] to show a particular person or thing in a film, magazine, show, etc.: *a new movie featuring Julia Roberts* **2** [I] to be an important part of something: *Violence* ***features*** *too strongly* ***in*** *many TV shows.* **3** [T] to advertise a particular product: *The supermarket's featuring a new ice cream.*

Feb·ru·ar·y /ˈfɛbyuˌɛri, ˈfɛbruˌɛri/ *written abbreviation* **Feb.** *n.* [C,U] the second month of the year: *Rick and Allison were married* ***on February 14th.*** | *The accident was* ***in February.*** | *She retired* ***last February.*** | *The book won't be finished until* ***next February.***

fe·ces /ˈfisiz/ *n.* [plural] *formal* solid waste material from the BOWELS —**fecal** /ˈfikəl/ *adj.*

feck·less /ˈfɛklɪs/ *adj.* a feckless person is not determined, effective, or successful

Fed /fɛd/ *n.*, **the Fed** *informal* the FEDERAL RESERVE

fed *v.* the past tense and past participle of FEED

fed·er·al /ˈfɛdərəl/ *adj.* **1** relating to the central government of a country which consists of several states: *federal taxes* | *federal law* **2** consisting of a group of states that make some of their own decisions but are controlled by a central government: *the Federal Republic of Germany*

ˌFederal ˌBureau of Investiˈgation *n.* the FBI

fed·er·al·ism /ˈfɛdərəˌlɪzəm/ *n.* [U] belief in or support for a federal system of government —**federalist** *n.* [C] *adj.*

ˌFederal Reˈserve *n.* **the Federal Reserve** the group of banks in the U.S. that control the way all of the country's banks work

fed·er·a·tion /ˌfɛdəˈreɪʃən/ *n.* [C] a group of states, countries, or organizations that have joined together to form a single group: *the American Federation of Teachers*

ˌfed ˈup *adj. informal* annoyed or bored, and wanting change: *I'm really* ***fed up with*** *all these meetings.*

fee /fi/ *n.* [C] an amount of money that you pay for professional services or that you pay to do something: *medical/legal fees* | *college fees* | *State parks charge a small* ***entrance fee.***

> **THESAURUS**
>
> **cost, expense, price, charge, fare**
> ➔ see Thesaurus box at COST[1]

fee·ble /ˈfibəl/ *adj.* **1** extremely weak: *His voice sounded feeble.* **2** not good or effective: *a feeble attempt*

ˌfeeble-ˈminded *adj.* unable to think clearly and decide what to do, or showing this quality

F

feed[1] /fid/ *v.* past tense and past participle **fed** /fɛd/ **1** [T] to give food to a person or animal [➡ **well-fed**]: *Did you feed the dog?* | *She was too weak to feed herself.* | *Jimmy was* ***feeding*** *acorns* ***to*** *the squirrels.* **2** [T] to provide enough food for a group of people: *How can you feed a family on $50 a week?* **3** [I] if animals or babies feed, they eat: *Frogs feed at night.* | *Cows* ***feed on*** *grass.* **4** [T] to give a substance to a plant to help it grow: *Feed your violets once a month.* **5** [T] to put something slowly and continuously into something else: *The tube was fed into the patient's stomach.* **6** [T] to supply something in a continuous flow: *The sound is* ***fed*** *directly* ***to*** *the headphones.*

feed[2] *n.* [U] food for animals: *cattle feed*

feed·back /ˈfidbæk/ *n.* [U] advice, criticism, etc. about how successful or useful something is, given so that something can be improved: *She's been* ***giving*** *me* ***feedback on*** *my presentation.*

feed·ing /ˈfidɪŋ/ *n.* [C] one of the times when you give milk to a small baby: *It's time for her noon feeding.*

F

feel[1] /fil/ *v.* past tense and past participle **felt** /fɛlt/ **1 EMOTIONS** [linking verb, T] to experience a particular physical feeling or emotion: *Let me know if you feel any pain.* | *We felt guilty for not asking her to come with us.* | *I'm feeling a little better today.* | *"How do you feel?" "Fine."* | *They didn't make us feel very welcome.* | *I walked through the door, and I* ***felt like/as if/as though*** *I had never been away.*

2 FEEL SMOOTH/DRY ETC. [linking verb] to seem to have a particular quality when touched or experienced by someone: *The ground still* ***feels damp***. | *Her hands* ***felt cold***. | *It* ***felt great*** *to see her after so many years.* | *How does* ***it feel*** *to be graduating?* | *It was a year ago, but it still* ***feels like*** *yesterday.*

3 OPINION [I,T] to have an opinion based on your feeling rather than on facts: *How do you* ***feel about*** *your new stepfather?* | *I* ***felt (that)*** *I could've helped more.* | *I* ***feel like*** *I'm being treated unfairly.*

4 TOUCH [T] to touch something with your fingers to find out about it: *Feel my forehead. Does it seem hot?*

THESAURUS

touch, **stroke**, **rub**, **scratch**, **pat**, **brush**, **caress**, **fondle**, **tickle**, **grope**

→ see Thesaurus box at TOUCH[1]

5 NOTICE STH [T] to notice something that is touching you or happening to you: *She felt a bug crawling up her leg.* | *Just feel that fresh sea air!* | *I felt her body brush against mine.*

6 feel the effects/benefits etc. of sth to experience the good or bad results of something: *We've started to feel the effects of the recession.*

7 feel your way a) to move carefully with your hands out in front of you because you cannot see well: *He felt his way across the room.* **b)** to do things slowly and carefully because you are unsure about a new situation: *Businesses are* ***feeling*** *their* ***way toward*** *a new relationship with their employees.*

8 feel around/in sth etc. (for sth) to try to find something by using your fingers: *She felt around in her bag for a pen.*

SPOKEN PHRASES

9 feel like (doing) sth to want to have something or do something: *He didn't feel like going to work.* | *I feel like a cigarette* (=feel like having a cigarette).

10 feel free used in order to tell someone that you do not mind if s/he does something: *Feel free to come by my office.*

11 I know (just/exactly) how you feel said in order to show your sympathy with someone or with something s/he has just said: *"I can't seem to do anything right today." "I know exactly how you feel."*

feel for sb *phr. v.* to feel sympathy for someone: *All I could do was let him know that I felt for him.*

feel sb ⇔ **out** *phr. v. informal* to find out what someone's opinions or feelings are without asking him/her directly: *I'm not sure if he'll lend us the money. Let me feel him out.*

feel up to sth *phr. v. informal* to have the strength, energy, etc. to do something: *I don't really feel up to going out tonight.*

feel[2] *n.* [singular] **1** the way something feels when you touch it: *the* ***feel of*** *the sand under our feet* | *Wet soap has a greasy feel.* **2** the quality something seems to have: *The beach has a kind of lonely feel.* | *The house had a nice* ***feel about it***. **3 have/get a feel for sth** *informal* to have or develop an understanding of something or ability with something: *Pete has a real feel for music.*

feel·er /ˈfilɚ/ *n.* [C] **1 put/send out feelers** to start to try to discover what people think about something that you want to do: *Possible presidential candidates are already putting out feelers.* **2** one of the two long things on an insect's head that it uses to feel or touch things

ˈfeel-good *adj.* **feel-good movie/comedy/music etc.** a movie, etc. whose main purpose is to make you feel happy

feel·ing /ˈfilɪŋ/ *n.* **1 a)** [C,U] an emotion that you feel, such as anger or happiness: *It's always a great feeling to win a game at home.* | *Share your feelings with the class.* | *a* ***feeling of*** *confidence* **b)** [C] something that you physically feel in your body: *He has no feeling in his legs.* | *feelings of* ***dizziness*** **2 sb's feelings** [plural] someone's feelings are his/her thoughts, emotions, and attitudes: *He doesn't care about my feelings.* | *Tell me the truth. You won't* ***hurt*** *my* ***feelings***. **3** [C] a belief or opinion about something: *The President has strong* ***feelings about/on*** *abortion.* | *I* ***have a feeling (that)*** *she's lying to us.* | *Mothers sometimes have* ***mixed feelings*** (=sometimes feel happy and sometimes feel sad) *about going to work.* **4** [U] a general attitude among a group of people about a subject: *a strong anti-war feeling* | *the depth of **feeling against/in favor of** the war* **5 I know the feeling** *spoken* said when you understand how someone feels because you have had the same experience: *"I'm too tired to work today." "I know the feeling."* **6 bad/ill feeling** anger or lack of trust between people: *The divorce caused a lot of bad feeling between them.* **7 with feeling** in a way that shows you care very much about something: *She plays the violin with great feeling.*

feet /fit/ *n.* the plural of FOOT

feign /feɪn/ *v.* [T] *formal* to pretend to have a feeling, be sick, be asleep, etc.: *We feigned interest in Mr. Dixon's stamp collection.*

feint /feɪnt/ *n.* [C] a movement or an attack that is intended to deceive an opponent

feist·y /ˈfaɪsti/ *adj. approving* having a strong determined character and a lot of energy: *a feisty old man*

fe·line /ˈfilaɪn/ *n.* [C] *technical* a cat or a member of the cat family —**feline** *adj.*

fell[1] /fɛl/ *v.* the past tense of FALL

fell[2] *v.* [T] *written* **1** to cut down a tree **2** to knock someone down

fel·low[1] /ˈfɛloʊ/ *n.* [C] **1** *old-fashioned* a man: *a nice young fellow from Iowa* **2** a GRADUATE student who has a fellowship in a university **3** a member of a society in a school or university

fellow[2] *adj.* **fellow workers/students/citizens etc.** people you work with, study with, etc.

fel·low·ship /ˈfɛloʊˌʃɪp, -lə-/ *n.* **1** [C] money given to a student to allow him/her to continue his/her studies at an advanced level: *a graduate fellowship* **2** [C] a group with similar interests or beliefs, who have meetings together: *a Christian youth fellowship* **3** [U] a feeling of friendship that people have because they have the same interests or experiences

fel·on /ˈfɛlən/ *n.* [C] someone who is guilty of a serious crime: *a **convicted felon*** (=a criminal who is sent to prison)

fel·o·ny /ˈfɛləni/ *n.* plural **felonies** [C] *law* a serious crime such as murder

felt[1] /fɛlt/ *v.* the past tense and past participle of FEEL

felt[2] *n.* [U] a thick soft material made of wool, hair, or fur that has been pressed flat

ˌfelt tip ˈpen *n.* [C] a pen that has a hard piece of felt at the end that the ink comes through

fe·male[1] /ˈfimeɪl/ *n.* [C] a person or animal that belongs to the sex that can have babies or produce eggs [≠ **male**]

female[2] *adj.* **1** belonging to the sex that can have babies or produce eggs [≠ **male**; ➡ **feminine**]: *a female horse* | *female athletes* **2** a female plant or flower produces fruit [➡ **male**]

fem·i·nine /ˈfɛmənɪn/ *adj.* **1** having qualities that are considered to be typical of women [➡ **masculine**]: *feminine clothes* **2** *technical* in grammar, a feminine noun or PRONOUN has a form that means it relates to a female, such as "waitress" or "her"

fem·i·nin·i·ty /ˌfɛməˈnɪnət̬i/ *n.* [U] qualities that are thought to be typical of women [➡ **masculinity**]

fem·i·nism /ˈfɛməˌnɪzəm/ *n.* [U] the belief that women should have the same rights and opportunities as men —**feminist** *n.* [C] *adj.*: *feminist authors*

fe·mur /ˈfimɚ/ *n.* [C] *technical* the bone in the top part of your leg, above the knee

fence[1] /fɛns/ *n.* [C] **1** a structure made of wood, metal, etc. that surrounds a piece of land **2** a structure that horses jump over in a race or competition **3 sit/be on the fence** to avoid saying which side of an argument you support

fence[2] *v.* **1** [T] to put a fence around something **2** [I] to fight with a sword as a sport

fence sth ⇔ **in** *phr. v.* to surround a place with a fence —**fenced-in** /ˌfɛnst ˈɪn◂/ *adj.*

fence sth ⇔ **off** *phr. v.* to separate one area from another with a fence: *We fenced off part of the backyard.*

fencing

fenc·ing /ˈfɛnsɪŋ/ *n.* [U] **1** the sport of fighting with a long thin sword **2** fences, or the material used for making them

fend /fɛnd/ *v.* **fend for yourself** to take care of yourself without help from other people: *You'll have to fend for yourself while I'm gone.*

fend sb/sth ⇔ **off** *phr. v.* to defend yourself when you are being attacked, asked difficult questions, etc.: *Mrs. Spector tried to fend off the other mugger.*

fend·er /ˈfɛndɚ/ *n.* [C] the side part of a car that covers the wheels ➔ see picture on page A12

ˈfender-ˌbender *n.* [C] *informal* a car accident in which little damage is done

THESAURUS

accident, **crash**, **collision**, **wreck**, **pile-up**
➔ see Thesaurus box at ACCIDENT

fer·ment[1] /fɚˈmɛnt/ *v.* [I,T] if fruit, beer, or wine ferments or is fermented, the sugar in it changes to alcohol —**fermentation** /ˌfɚmənˈteɪʃən/ *n.* [U]

F

fer·ment² /ˈfɚmɛnt/ *n.* [U] excitement or trouble in a country, caused especially by political change

fern /fɚn/ *n.* [C] a plant with green leaves shaped like large feathers, but no flowers

fe·ro·cious /fəˈroʊʃəs/ *adj.* extremely violent or severe: *a ferocious dog | a ferocious storm* —**ferociously** *adv.*

fe·ro·ci·ty /fəˈrɑsət̬i/ *n.* [U] extremely violence: *Felipe was shocked by the **ferocity of** her anger.*

fer·ret¹ /ˈfɛrɪt/ *n.* [C] a small animal, used in the past for hunting rats and rabbits

ferret² *v.*

ferret sth ⇔ **out** *phr. v. informal* to succeed in finding something, especially information: *It took years of research to ferret out the truth.*

fer·ris wheel /ˈfɛrɪs ˌwil/ *n.* [C] a very large upright wheel with seats on it for people to ride on in an AMUSEMENT PARK

fer·rous /ˈfɛrəs/ *adj. technical* containing or relating to iron: *ferrous metals*

fer·ry¹ /ˈfɛri/ *n.* plural **ferries** [C] a boat that carries people, often with their cars, across a stretch of water ➔ see picture at TRANSPORTATION

F

THESAURUS

ship, **cruise ship**, **liner**, **freighter**, **tanker**, **barge**, **aircraft carrier**, **battleship**, **cruiser**, **submarine**, **warship**
➔ see Thesaurus box at SHIP¹

ferry² *v.* past tense and past participle **ferried**, third person singular **ferries** [T] to carry people or goods a short distance from one place to another: *a bus that **ferries** tourists **from** the hotel **to** the beach*

fer·tile /ˈfɚt̬l/ *adj.* **1** fertile land or soil is able to produce good crops [≠ **infertile**] **2** able to become PREGNANT or make someone pregnant [≠ **infertile**] **3 fertile imagination/mind** an imagination or mind that is able to produce a lot of unusual ideas —**fertility** /fɚˈtɪləti/ *n.* [U]

fer·til·ize /ˈfɚt̬lˌaɪz/ *v.* [T] **1** to put fertilizer on the soil to help plants grow **2** to make new animal or plant life develop: *a fertilized egg* —**fertilization** /ˌfɚt̬ləˈzeɪʃən/ *n.* [U]

fer·til·iz·er /ˈfɚt̬lˌaɪzɚ/ *n.* [C,U] a substance that is put on the soil to help plants grow

fer·vent /ˈfɚvənt/ *adj.* believing or feeling something very strongly: *Marion's a **fervent believer in** working hard.* —**fervently** *adv.*

fer·vor /ˈfɚvɚ/ *n.* [U] very strong belief or feeling: *religious fervor*

fess /fɛs/ *v.*

fess up *phr. v. informal* to admit that you have done something wrong, although it is not serious: *He later **fessed up to** his mistake.*

fest /fɛst/ *n.* **beer/song/food fest etc.** an informal occasion when a lot of people do a fun activity together

fes·ter /ˈfɛstɚ/ *v.* [I] **1** if a bad situation or a problem festers, it gets worse because is has not been dealt with: *Letting your anger fester will only make things worse.* **2** if a wound festers, it becomes infected

fes·ti·val /ˈfɛstəvəl/ *n.* [C] **1** an occasion when there are performances of many films, plays, pieces of music, etc.: *the Cannes film festival | a **festival of** Japanese culture* **2** a special occasion when people celebrate something such as a religious event: *religious festivals*

fes·tive /ˈfɛstɪv/ *adj.* happy or cheerful in a way that seems appropriate for celebrating something: *Hollie was in a **festive mood**. | the **festive season*** (=Christmas)

fes·tiv·i·ties /fɛˈstɪvət̬iz/ *n.* [plural] things that people do to celebrate, such as dancing, eating, and drinking

fes·toon /fɛˈstun/ *v.* [T] to cover something with cloth, flowers, etc. as a decoration

fe·tal /ˈfit̬l/ *adj.* relating to a FETUS: *fetal development*

ˈfetal poˌsition *n.* [singular] a body position in which your body is curled up, and your arms and legs are pulled up against your chest

fetch /fɛtʃ/ *v.* [T] **1** to be sold for a particular amount of money: *The tractor should fetch over $10,000.* **2** *old-fashioned* to go and get something and bring it back: *Rushworth went to fetch the key to the gate.*

fetch·ing /ˈfɛtʃɪŋ/ *adj. old-fashioned* attractive

fete¹ /feɪt/ *v.* [T] to honor someone by having a public celebration for him/her: *Mandela will be feted at a government banquet.*

fete² *n.* [C] a special occasion to celebrate something

fet·id /ˈfɛt̬ɪd/ *adj. formal* having a very bad smell: *the black fetid water*

fet·ish /ˈfɛt̬ɪʃ/ *n.* [C] **1** an object, thing, or activity that gives someone sexual pleasure, when this is not considered to be normal: *a **fetish for** women's underwear | a foot fetish* **2** something that someone does too much or thinks about too much

fet·ter /ˈfɛt̬ɚ/ *v.* [T] *formal* to prevent someone from doing what s/he wants to do: *managers **fettered by** rules and regulations*

fet·ters /ˈfɛt̬ɚz/ *n.* [plural] **1** things that prevent someone from doing what s/he wants to do **2** chains that were put around a prisoner's feet in past times

fe·tus /ˈfit̬əs/ *n.* [C] a baby before it is born

feud /fyud/ *n.* [C] an angry and often violent argument between two people or groups that continues for a long time: *a bitter **feud between** neighbors* —**feud** *v.* [I]

feu·dal·is·m /ˈfyudlˌɪzəm/ *n.* [U] a social system in the Middle Ages, in which people received land and protection from someone of higher rank whom they worked and fought for —**feudal** *adj.*

fe·ver /ˈfivɚ/ *n.* **1** [C,U] an illness in which you

have a very high temperature: *Andy **has a fever** and won't be coming into work today.* | *She's **running a fever*** (=has a fever). **2** [U] a situation in which people feel very excited or anxious: *Baseball fans are gripped by World Series fever.* | *When the TV crews arrived, the demonstration reached **fever pitch*** (=an extreme level of excitement or anxiety). —**fevered** *adj.* ➔ HAY FEVER, SPRING FEVER

fe·ver·ish /ˈfivərɪʃ/ *adj.* **1** suffering from a fever **2** done extremely quickly by people who are very excited or worried: *working at a feverish pace* —**feverishly** *adv.*

few /fyu/ *quantifier, pron., adj.* **1 a few/the few** a small number of things or people: *Let's wait a few minutes and see if Carrie gets here.* | *I've seen **a few of** those new cars around.* | *Don has seemed really happy these **last few** weeks.* | *You'll have to work hard over the **next few** months.* | *There are **a few more** things I'd like to talk about before we go.* **2 quite a few** a fairly large number of things or people: *Quite a few people came to the meeting.* | ***Quite a few of** the customers got sick.* **3** not many: *There are few events that are as exciting as having a baby.* | *Women are having fewer children.* | *Grant's **one of the few** people I know who can tell stories well.* | ***Very few of** these players will play professionally.* **4 be few and far between** to be rare: *Good jobs are few and far between these days.*

GRAMMAR

few, a few

Use **few** when you mean "not many" or "not enough": *Very few people came to the meeting.*

Use **a few** when you mean "some" or "a small number": *There are still a few bottles of beer left.*

Few and **a few** are always used with plural noun forms.

➔ LESS, LITTLE²

fi·an·cé /ˌfiɑnˈseɪ, fiˈɑnseɪ/ *n.* [C] the man whom a woman is going to marry

fi·an·cée /ˌfiɑnˈseɪ, fiˈɑnseɪ/ *n.* [C] the woman whom a man is going to marry

fi·as·co /fiˈæskoʊ/ *n.* plural **fiascoes** or **fiascos** [C] an event that is completely unsuccessful, in a way that is very embarrassing or disappointing: *Their attempt to compete in the software market has been a total fiasco.*

fi·at /ˈfiæt, -ɑt, -ət/ *n.* [C,U] *formal* an order that is given by someone in authority without considering what other people want: *Too often he governed **by fiat** rather than by the law.*

fib /fɪb/ *n.* [C] a small, unimportant lie: *You shouldn't **tell fibs**.* —**fib** *v.* [I] —**fibber** *n.* [C]

THESAURUS

lie, white lie, slander, libel

➔ see Thesaurus box at LIE³

fi·ber /ˈfaɪbɚ/ *n.* **1** [U] parts of plants that you eat but do not DIGEST, that help food to move through your body: *The doctor said I need more fiber in my diet.* **2** [C,U] a mass of threads used to make rope, cloth, etc. **3** [C] a thin thread, or one of the thin parts like threads that form natural materials such as wood —**fibrous** /ˈfaɪbrəs/ *adj.*

fi·ber·glass /ˈfaɪbɚˌglæs/ *n.* [U] a light material made from small glass threads pressed together

ˌfiber ˈoptics *n.* [U] the use of long thin threads of glass to carry information in the form of light, especially on telephone lines —**fiber optic** *adj.*

fick·le /ˈfɪkəl/ *adj.* **1** someone who is fickle is always changing his/her opinion about people or things: *Voters are fickle.* **2** something that is fickle, such as the weather, often changes suddenly

fic·tion /ˈfɪkʃən/ *n.* **1** [U] books and stories about imaginary people and things [≠ **nonfiction**]: *a popular writer of children's fiction* | *detective fiction* ➔ see Thesaurus box at BOOK¹ **2** [C,U] something that someone wants you to believe is true, but that is not true: *The newspaper story turned out to be a complete fiction.*

fic·tion·al /ˈfɪkʃənəl/ *adj.* fictional people or events are from a book or story, and are not real

fic·tion·al·ize /ˈfɪkʃənəˌlaɪz/ *v.* [T] to tell the story of a real event, changing some details and adding imaginary characters

fic·ti·tious /fɪkˈtɪʃəs/ *adj.* not true, or not real: *a fictitious name*

fid·dle¹ /ˈfɪdl/ *n.* [C] *informal* a VIOLIN ➔ **play second fiddle to sb/sth** at PLAY¹

fiddle² *v.*

fiddle around *phr. v.* to waste time by doing things that are not important: *Stop fiddling around or we'll be late!*

fiddle with sth *phr. v.* to keep moving and touching something, especially because you are bored or nervous: *She started fiddling with her hair.*

fid·dler /ˈfɪdlɚ/ *n.* [C] someone who plays the VIOLIN

fi·del·i·ty /fəˈdɛləṭi, faɪ-/ *n.* [U] *formal* **1** loyalty to your wife, husband, or partner by not having sex with other people [≠ **infidelity**] **2** loyalty to a person, organization, set of beliefs, etc.: *his **fidelity to** the Republican Party*

fidg·et /ˈfɪdʒɪt/ *v.* [I] to keep moving your hands or feet, especially because you are bored or nervous: *children fidgeting in their seats* —**fidgety** *adj.*

field¹ /fild/ *n.* [C] **1** an area of land in the country where crops are grown or animals feed on grass: *a corn field* | ***fields of** sunflowers* **2** an area of ground where sports are played: *a **football/baseball/soccer etc. field***

THESAURUS

stadium, court, diamond, track

➔ see Thesaurus box at SPORT¹

F

3 a subject that people study or a type of work that they are involved in: *Professor Kramer is an expert in the **field of** ancient history.* | *Sullivan's an expert **in** his **field**.* **4 the field** all the people, companies, or horses that are competing against each other: *They now **lead the field*** (=are the most successful company) *in making powerful computer chips.* **5 oil/gas/coal field** an area where there is a lot of oil, gas, or coal under the ground **6 magnetic/gravitational/force field** an area in which a strong natural force has an effect **7 field of view/vision** the whole area that you can see without turning your head

field[2] *v.* [T] **1** if you field a ball in a game of baseball, you stop it after it has been hit **2** if you field a team, an army, etc., they represent you or fight for you in a competition, election, or war: *There may not be enough healthy players to **field a team**.* **3** to answer questions, telephone calls, etc., especially when there are a lot of them or they are difficult: *Riordan left without **fielding questions** from reporters.*

'field day *n.* [C] **1 have a field day** *informal* to have the chance to do something you enjoy a lot, especially a chance to criticize someone: *Talk radio hosts **had a field day with** the story.* **2** a day when students at a school have sports competitions

field·er /'fildɚ/ *n.* [C] one of the players who tries to catch the ball in baseball

'field e,vent *n.* [C] a sports activity, such as the HIGH JUMP or the JAVELIN, that is part of an outdoor competition [➡ **track event**]

'field ,goal *n.* [C] the action of kicking the ball over the bar of the GOAL for three points in football

'field ,hockey *n.* [U] HOCKEY played on grass

'field test *n.* [C] a test of a new product or system that is done in the place where it will be used rather than in a LABORATORY —**field-test** *v.* [T]

'field trip *n.* [C] an occasion when students go somewhere to learn about a particular subject: *a field trip to the Maryland Science Center*

field·work /'fildwɚk/ *n.* [U] study which involves going somewhere, rather than working in a class or LABORATORY

fiend /find/ *n.* [C] **1** *informal* someone who likes something much more than other people normally do: *Isaac turns into a football fiend during the Super Bowl.* **2 dope/drug etc. fiend** *informal* someone who takes a lot of drugs **3** *literary* an evil spirit or person

fiend·ish /'findɪʃ/ *adj.* **1** *literary* very bad or cruel: *a fiendish temper* **2** very difficult or complicated: *a fiendish puzzle*

fierce /fɪrs/ *adj.* **1** done with a lot of energy and strong feelings: *a **fierce debate** between the political parties* | ***fierce competition** between banks* | *The two teams are in a fierce battle for first place.* **2** a fierce person or animal looks very violent or angry and ready to attack: *fierce dogs* **3** fierce heat, cold, weather, etc. is very extreme or severe —**fiercely** *adv.*

fi·er·y /'faɪəri/ *adj.* **1** full of strong or angry emotion: *a fiery speech* | *her fiery temper* **2** *written* involving fire, or on fire: *All perished* (=died) *in the fiery crash.* | *a fiery sunset*

fi·es·ta /fi'ɛstə/ *n.* [C] a religious holiday with dancing, music, etc., especially in Spain or Latin America

fif·teen /,fɪf'tin◂ / *number* 15 —**fifteenth** *number*

fifth[1] /fɪfθ/ *number* **1** 5th **2** 1/5

fifth[2] *n.* [C] an amount of alcohol equal to 1/5 of a gallon, sold in bottles: *a fifth of bourbon*

fif·ty[1] /'fɪfti/ *number* **1** 50 **2 the fifties a)** the years between 1950 and 1959 **b)** the numbers between 50 and 59, especially when used for measuring temperature **3 be in your fifties** to be aged between 50 and 59: *She's **in** her **early/mid/late fifties**.* —**fiftieth** /'fɪftiəθ/ *number*

fifty[2] *n.* plural **fifties** [C] a piece of paper money worth $50

,fifty-'fifty *adj., adv. spoken* **1** divided equally between two people: *We should divide the profits fifty-fifty.* **2 a fifty-fifty chance** an equal chance that something will happen or not happen: ***a fifty-fifty chance of** winning*

fig /fɪg/ *n.* [C] a small soft sweet fruit, often eaten dried, or the tree on which this grows

fig. the written abbreviation of **figure**

fight[1] /faɪt/ *v.* past tense and past participle **fought** /fɔt/ **1** [I,T] to take part in a war or battle: *The country **fought** a three-year civil **war**.* | *Did your uncle **fight in** the war?* | *rebel forces **fighting against** the Russians* | *They **fought over/for** a small piece of land.* **2** [I,T] if people or animals fight, they use violence against each other: *Police **fought with** protesters in the streets.* | *dogs **fighting over** a bone* **3** [I] to argue: *Are the kids fighting again?* | *He was always **fighting with** his girlfriend.* | *They **fought over** custody of the children.*

THESAURUS

argue, **have an argument**, **have a fight**, **quarrel**, **have a quarrel**, **squabble**, **bicker**

→ see Thesaurus box at ARGUE

4 [I] to try hard to do or get something: *The union **fought for** a better health care package.* | *Parents are **fighting to** save the school.* | *Perkins was lying in bed, **fighting for** his **life**.* **5** [I,T] to try hard to prevent something or to get rid of something: *Senator Redkin is fighting the proposal.* | *She spent her life **fighting against** poverty and injustice.* **6** [I,T] to take part in a BOXING match: *Ali fought Foreman for the heavyweight title.* **7** [T] **also fight back** to try hard not to have or show a feeling: *He fought the impulse to yell at her.* | *Benson bit his lip and **fought back tears**.* **8 fight a fire/blaze etc.** to try to stop a fire from burning **9 fight your way** to move somewhere with difficulty: *We had to **fight** our **way through** the crowd.* **10 have a fighting chance** to have a chance to achieve something if you work very hard: *Davis believes he still has a fighting chance of winning the election.* **11 fight it out** to fight, argue, or compete until one person wins: *We left them alone to fight it out.*

fight back *phr. v.* **1** to work hard to achieve or oppose something, especially in a situation where you are losing: *Lewis fought back to win the match.* **2** to use violence or arguments against someone who has attacked you or criticized you: *The rebels are fighting back.*

fight sb/sth ⇔ **off** *phr. v.* **1** to use violence to keep someone or something away, or to stop him/her from doing something to you: *They managed to fight off their attackers.* **2** to succeed in stopping other people from getting something, and to get it for yourself: *The president fought off a challenge from within his own party.* **3** to try hard to get rid of a feeling or illness: *I've been fighting off a cold for days.*

fight² *n.* **1** [C] an act of fighting between two people or groups: *He's always **getting into fights** at school.* | *A drunk tried to **pick/start a fight** with him.* | *a **fight between** rival gangs* | *The police were called in to **break up** (=stop) the **fight**.*

THESAURUS

brawl – a noisy fight among a lot of people
free-for-all – a fight or argument involving a lot of people
scuffle – a short fight
scrap informal – a short fight
boxing match
wrestling match

2 [C] an argument: *He's **had a fight** with his mother.* | ***fights over/about** money* **3** [singular] the process of trying very hard to achieve something or prevent something: *the union's **fight for** better working conditions.* | *the **fight against** drugs* | *the **fight to** reduce world hunger*

THESAURUS

battle – an attempt to stop something happening or to achieve something difficult: *the battle for equal rights*
campaign – a series of actions that are intended to achieve a particular result: *She helped lead the campaign against drunk driving.*
struggle – a long, hard fight for freedom, political rights, etc.: *the country's struggle for independence*

4 [C] a battle between two armies: *a **fight for** control of the islands*

fight·er /ˈfaɪt̬ɚ/ *n.* [C] **1** *approving* someone who continues to try to do something although it is difficult **2** someone who fights, especially as a sport [**= boxer**] **3 also fighter plane** a small fast military airplane that can destroy other airplanes

fight·ing /ˈfaɪt̬ɪŋ/ *n.* [U] an occasion when people or groups fight each other in a war, in the street, etc.: *seven days of **heavy fighting***

THESAURUS

war, warfare, conflict, combat, hostilities
➔ see Thesaurus box at WAR

fig·ment /ˈfɪgmənt/ *n.* **a figment of sb's imagination** something you imagine to be real, but does not exist

fig·u·ra·tive /ˈfɪgyərət̬ɪv/ *adj.* a figurative word or expression is used in a different way from its usual meaning, to give you a picture or idea in your mind. For example, in "a mountain of debt," "mountain" is used in a figurative way and means "a large amount" not "a high hill." [➡ **literal**] —**figuratively** *adv.*

fig·ure¹ /ˈfɪgyɚ/ *n.* [C] **1 a)** [usually plural] a number representing an amount, especially an official number: ***sales/crime/population, etc. figures*** **b)** a number from 0 to 9, written as a sign, not as a word: *a **six-figure** income* (=between $100,000 and $999,999) | *Five players scored in **double figures*** (=numbers between 10 and 99). | ***single figures*** (=numbers between 0 and 9) **2** a particular amount of money: *The report quoted an estimated **figure of** $200 million.* **3** [usually singular] the shape of a woman's body: *She **has a** great **figure**.* **4 a)** someone who is important or famous in some way: *an important political figure* **b)** someone with a particular type of appearance or character, especially when s/he is difficult to see: *a dark figure in the distance* **c)** a person in a picture **5 fig.** a numbered drawing in a book **6** a shape in mathematics: *a six-sided figure*

figure² *v.* **1** [I] *informal* to be included as an important part of something: *The Kennedys **figure in** her recent book.*

SPOKEN PHRASES

2 [T] to have a particular opinion after thinking about a situation: *I **figured (that)** you'd need help moving.*

THESAURUS

think, believe, suspect, consider, guess
➔ see Thesaurus box at THINK

SPOKEN PHRASES

3 that figures/(it) figures said when something happens or someone behaves in a way that you expect, but do not like: *"I forgot to bring my checkbook again." "Figures."* **4 go figure** said to show that you think something is strange or difficult to explain: *"He didn't even say goodbye!" "Go figure."*

figure on sth *phr. v. spoken* to expect something or include it in your plans: *With traffic so heavy, we'd better figure on an extra hour.*

figure sb/sth ⇔ **out** *phr. v.* to understand someone or something after thinking about him, her, or it: *Can you figure out how to open this?* | *I can't figure Betty out.*

ˌfigure 'eight *n.* [C] the pattern or shape of a number eight, for example, in a dance

fig·ure·head /ˈfɪgyɚˌhɛd/ *n.* [C] a leader who has no real power

ˌfigure of 'speech *n.* [C] a word or expression that is used in a different way from the usual one, to give you a picture in your mind: *"We died laughing" is a figure of speech.*

'figure ˌskating *n.* [U] a type of skating (SKATE) in which you move in patterns on the ice

fil·a·ment /ˈfɪləmənt/ *n.* [C] a very thin thread or wire

filch /fɪltʃ/ *v.* [T] *informal* to steal something small or not very valuable: *teenagers filching cigarettes*

file[1] /faɪl/ *n.* [C] **1** a set of papers, records, etc. that contain information about a particular person or subject: *The school* ***keeps files on*** *each student.* | *We'll keep your application* ***on file*** (=store it for later use). | *medical files*

THESAURUS

record, diary, roll, log (book)
➔ see Thesaurus box at RECORD[1]

2 a box or folded piece of heavy paper in which you keep loose papers: *He took a file down from the shelf.* **3** information on a computer that is stored under a particular name: ***open/close*** *a file* | ***save/delete/copy/create*** *a file* ➔ see Topic box at COMPUTER **4** a metal tool with a rough surface that you rub on something to make it smooth [➡ **nail file**] **5 in single file** moving in a line, with one person behind another

file[2] *v.* **1** [T] to store papers or information in a particular order or a particular place: ***File*** *the contracts* ***alphabetically***.

THESAURUS

keep, store
➔ see Thesaurus box at KEEP[1]

2 [I,T] *law* to give a document to a court or other organization so that it can be officially recorded and dealt with: *Some employees are* ***filing a claim*** *against the department.* **3** [I] to walk somewhere in a line of people, one behind the other: *The jury* ***filed into/filed out of*** *the courtroom.* **4** [T] to rub something with a metal tool to make it smooth or cut it: *I need to* ***file*** *my* ***nails***.

'file ˌcabinet *n.* [C] a piece of office furniture with drawers for storing important papers ➔ see picture on page A11

fil·et /fɪˈleɪ/ *n.* [C,U] FILLET[1]

fil·i·bus·ter /ˈfɪləˌbʌstɚ/ *v.* [I,T] to try to delay action in Congress by making very long speeches —**filibuster** *n.* [C]

fil·i·gree /ˈfɪləˌgri/ *n.* [U] delicate decoration made of gold or silver wire

'filing ˌcabinet *n.* [C] FILE CABINET

fil·ings /ˈfaɪlɪŋz/ *n.* [plural] very small pieces that come off a piece of metal when it is cut or FILED

fill[1] /fɪl/ *v.* **1 also fill up a)** [I,T] to become full of something, or to make something full: *He turned on the faucet and filled the bucket.* | *She kept filling up our glasses.* | *The kids* ***filled*** *their bags* ***with*** *candy.* **b)** [T] if something fills up a place, it takes up all of the space in that place: *The audience soon filled the theater.* | *The bedroom was* ***filled with*** *smoke.* **2** [T] **also fill in** to put something in a hole or crack in order to make a smooth surface: *Fill any cracks in the wall before you paint.* **3** [T] if a sound, smell, or light fills a place or space, you notice it because it is loud or strong: *The smell of fresh bread filled the kitchen.* **4** [T] to provide something that is needed or wanted: *Daycare centers* ***fill a need*** *for working parents.* | *The company is* ***filling a gap*** *in the market.* **5** [T] to do a particular job, or to find someone to do a job: *Anderson says he hopes to* ***fill the position*** *by spring.* | *Sorry, but the post has already been filled.* **6** [T] if you are filled with an emotion, you feel it strongly: *She was* ***filled with*** *excitement.* | *Her achievements* ***filled*** *him* ***with*** *pride.* **7** [T] if you fill a period of time with a particular activity, you spend that time doing it: *He filled his days playing golf and tennis.*

fill in *phr. v.* **1 fill** sth ⇔ **in** to write all the necessary information on a document: *You'll have to fill in an application form.* **2 fill** sb ⇔ **in** to tell someone about things that have happened recently: *I'll* ***fill*** *you* ***in on*** *all the news later.* **3** to do someone's job because s/he is not there: *Could you* ***fill in for*** *Bob while he's sick?*

fill out *phr. v.* **1 fill** sth ⇔ **out** to write all the necessary information on a document **2** to get fatter or larger in a way that is considered attractive: *At puberty, a girl's body begins to fill out.*

fill[2] *n.* **your fill** as much of something as you want, or can deal with: *I've* ***had*** *my* ***fill of*** *screaming kids today!*

fil·let[1], **filet** /fɪˈleɪ/ *n.* [C,U] a piece of meat or fish without bones: *a* ***fillet of*** *cod*

fillet[2] *v.* [T] to remove the bones from a piece of meat or fish

fill·ing[1] /ˈfɪlɪŋ/ *n.* **1** [C] a small amount of metal that is put into a hole in your tooth **2** [C,U] the food that is put inside a PIE, SANDWICH, etc.: *apple pie filling*

filling[2] *adj.* food that is filling makes your stomach feel full

fil·ly /ˈfɪli/ *n.* plural **fillies** [C] a young female horse

film[1] /fɪlm/ *n.* **1** [U] the material used in a camera for taking photographs or recording moving pictures: *a* ***roll of film*** | *The coach has the game* ***on film***. ➔ see Topic box at CAMERA **2** [C] a MOVIE: *the Sundance Film Festival* | *We like to go see* ***foreign films***. ➔ see Thesaurus box at MOVIE **3** [U] the art or business of making movies: *the* *film industry* **4** [singular] a very thin layer of liquid, powder, etc. on the surface of something

film² *v.* [I,T] to use a camera to make a movie or a television program: *The movie was filmed in China.* —**filming** *n.* [U] *The filming was completed in six weeks.*

film·mak·er /ˈfɪlmˌmeɪkɚ/ *n.* [C] someone who makes movies

film·strip /ˈfɪlmˌstrɪp/ *n.* [C] a short film that shows photographs, pictures, etc. one at a time, not as moving pictures

fil·ter¹ /ˈfɪltɚ/ *n.* [C] a piece of equipment that you put gas or liquid through in order to remove solid substances that are not wanted: *a water filter*

filter² *v.* **1** [T] to clean a liquid or gas using a filter: *filtered drinking water* **2** [I] if people filter somewhere, they gradually move in that direction: *The audience began to* ***filter into*** *the hall.* **3** [I] if information filters out to people, people gradually hear about it: *The news slowly* ***filtered through to*** *everyone in the office.* | *Eventually* ***word filtered out to*** *the guests that something was wrong.* **4** [I] if light or sound filters into a place, it can be seen or heard only slightly: *Hazy sunshine* ***filtered through*** *the curtains.*

filth /fɪlθ/ *n.* [U] **1** an extremely dirty substance: *Wash that filth off your shoes.* **2** very rude or offensive language, stories, or pictures about sex

filth·y¹ /ˈfɪlθi/ *adj.* comparative **filthier**, superlative **filthiest** **1** extremely dirty: *Doesn't he ever wash that jacket? It's filthy.*

> **THESAURUS**
>
> **dirty**, **dusty**, **muddy**
> ➔ see Thesaurus box at DIRTY¹

2 showing or describing sexual acts in a very rude or offensive way: *filthy language*

filthy² *adv.* **filthy rich** *informal* extremely rich

fin /fɪn/ *n.* [C] one of the thin body parts that a fish uses to swim ➔ see picture on page A2

fi·na·gle /fəˈneɪgəl/ *v.* [T] *informal* to get something that is difficult to get by using unusual or unfair methods

fi·nal¹ /ˈfaɪnl/ *adj.* **1** [only before noun] last in a series of actions, events, parts of a story, etc.: *the final chapter of the book* **2** if a decision, offer, or agreement is final, it cannot be changed: *I don't think the* ***final decision*** *has been made.* | *You can't go,* ***and that's final.*** **3** [only before noun] being the result at the end of a process: *What was the* ***final score****?*

final² *n.* [C] **1** the last and most important game, race, etc. in a competition: *She skated very well in the final.* | *the NBA Finals* **2** an important test that students take at the end of each class in HIGH SCHOOL or college: *How did your finals go?*

fi·nal·e /fɪˈnæli, -ˈnɑ-/ *n.* [C] the last part of a piece of music or a performance, which is often the most exciting part: *the* ***grand finale*** *of a Broadway musical*

fi·nal·ist /ˈfaɪnl-ɪst/ *n.* [C] one of the people or teams that reaches the last part of a competition

fi·nal·i·ty /faɪˈnæləṭi, fə-/ *n.* [U] the feeling or idea that something is finished and cannot be changed: *the finality of death*

fi·nal·ize /ˈfaɪnlˌaɪz/ *v.* [T] to finish the last details or part of a plan, business deal, etc.: *Can we finalize the details tomorrow?*

fi·nal·ly /ˈfaɪnl-i/ *adv.* **1** after a long time: *After several delays, the plane finally took off at 6:00.*

> **USAGE**
>
> Use **lastly** or **finally** to introduce the last point, action, or instruction in a list: *Finally/Lastly, I'd like to thank everyone for all their hard work.*
> Use **finally** or **eventually** to say that something happens after a long time: *Eventually/Finally, we managed to get the car started.* | *She eventually/finally apologized.*
> Use **at last** to emphasize that you are glad when something happens because you have been waiting a long time for it: *Spring's here at last!*
> ➔ FIRST

2 as the last of a series of things: *And finally, I'd like to thank my teachers.* **3** in a way that does not allow further change: *It's not finally settled yet.*

fi·nance¹ /fəˈnæns, ˈfaɪnæns/ *n.* [U] **1** the control of how money is spent, especially for a company or a government: *She's an accountant in the Finance Department.* **2 finances** [plural] the money that a person, company, organization, etc. has available, or the control of how this money is spent: *My finances are a mess.* | *The school's finances are limited.*

finance² *v.* [T] to provide money, especially a large amount of money, to pay for something: *The program is financed by the government.*

fi·nan·cial /fəˈnænʃəl, faɪ-/ *adj.* relating to money or the management of money: *a company that provides* ***financial services*** | *He had no* ***financial support*** *from his parents.* | *the company's* ***financial assets*** —**financially** *adv.*

fiˌnancial ˈaid *n.* [U] money that is given or lent to students at college to pay for their education

fin·an·cier /ˌfaɪnænˈsɪr, fəˌnæn-, ˌfɪnən-/ *n.* [C] someone who controls or lends large sums of money

fi·nanc·ing /ˈfaɪnænsɪŋ/ *n.* [U] money that you borrow to start a business, buy something, etc., and which you pay back over an agreed period of time

finch /fɪntʃ/ *n.* [C] a small wild bird with a short beak

find¹ /faɪnd/ *v.* past tense and past participle **found** /faʊnd/ [T]

1 GET BY SEARCHING to discover and get something that you have been looking for: *I can't find* *my keys.* | *He's having a hard time finding a job.* | *Can you find the kids something clean to wear?*

THESAURUS

discover – to find something that was hidden or that people did not know about before: *They never discovered the truth about his past.*
trace – to find someone or something that has disappeared: *She had given up all hope of tracing her missing daughter.*
locate – to find the exact position of something: *We couldn't locate the source of the radio signal.*
track sb/sth down – to find someone or something after searching in different places: *Detectives finally tracked her down in California.*
turn sth up – to find something by searching for it thoroughly: *The investigation hasn't turned up any new evidence.*
unearth – to find out information or the truth about something: *It was years before the full story was unearthed.*

2 SEE BY CHANCE to discover something by chance: *She found a purse in the street.* | *We found a good restaurant near the hotel.* **3 LEARN STH** to discover or learn new information: *Researchers have **found that** girls tend to speak earlier than boys.* | *We got there early **only to find that** the tickets had all been sold.* | *Scientists are trying to find a cure for AIDS.* **4 OPINION** to have an opinion or feeling about someone or something: *Do you find him attractive?* | *I **found it difficult/easy to** understand her.* **5 EXPERIENCE** to learn or know something by experience: *I tried using oil, but I've **found that** butter works best.* **6 TIME/MONEY/ENERGY** to have enough of something to be able to do what you want to do: *When do you find the time to read?* **7 be found** to live or exist somewhere: *This type of grass is found only in the swamp.* **8 find yourself somewhere** to be in a place although you did not plan to be there: *Suddenly I found myself back at the hotel.* **9 find your way (somewhere)** to arrive at a place by discovering the way to get there: *Can you find your way, or do you need a map?* **10 find sb guilty/not guilty (of sth)** *law* to officially decide that someone is guilty or not guilty of a crime: *He was found guilty of murder.*

find out *phr. v.* **1 find** (sth) **out** to learn information after trying to discover it or by chance: *If Dad ever **finds out about** this, he'll be furious.* | *He hurried off to **find out what** the problem was.* | *We need to find out everything we can about the disease.* **2 find** sb **out** *informal* to discover that someone has been doing something dishonest or illegal [**= caught**]: *What happens if we **get found out**?*

find² *n.* [C] something very good or valuable that you discover by chance: *That little Greek restaurant was **a real find**.*

find·ing /ˈfaɪndɪŋ/ *n.* [C usually plural] information that someone has learned as a result of studies, work, etc.: *the newest research findings*

fine¹ /faɪn/ *adj.* **1** good enough or acceptable [**= all right**]: *"What do you want for lunch?" "A sandwich is fine."* | *"More coffee?" "No, **I'm fine**, thanks."* | *"How about seeing a movie?" "That's **fine by me**."* **2** healthy and well: *"How are you?" "Fine, thanks."*

THESAURUS

healthy, well, better
→ see Thesaurus box at HEALTHY

3 very good: *a fine performance by William Hurt* | *a selection of **fine wines*** **4** very thin or narrow, or made of very small pieces: *fine hair* | *a fine layer of dust* **5** fine differences, changes, or details are small or exact and difficult to see: *I didn't understand some of the **finer points** of his argument.* **6 a fine line** if you say that there is a fine line between two different things, you mean that they are so similar that one can easily become the other: *There's **a fine line between** genius and madness.*

fine² *adv. spoken* in a way that is satisfactory or acceptable [**= well**]: *"How's everything going?" "Fine."* | *The washer's working fine now.* | *"I can't paint." "Come on, you're **doing fine**."*

fine³ *n.* [C] money that you have to pay as a punishment for breaking a law or rule: *a parking fine*

THESAURUS

punishment, sentence, penalty, community service
→ see Thesaurus box at PUNISHMENT

fine⁴ *v.* [T] to make someone pay money as a punishment: *He was **fined** $50 **for** speeding.*

ˌfine ˈarts *n.* **the fine arts** activities such as painting, music, etc. that are concerned with making beautiful things

fine·ly /ˈfaɪnli/ *adv.* **1** in very thin or small pieces: *finely chopped onion* **2** to a very exact degree: *finely tuned instruments*

ˌfine ˈprint *n.* [U] the part of a contract or other document that has important information, often written in small print: *Before signing the contract, make sure you **read the fine print**.*

fi·nesse /fɪˈnɛs/ *n.* [U] if you do something with finesse, you do it with a lot of skill and style

ˌfine-ˈtune *v.* [T] to make small changes to something in order to make it as good as possible: *The team is still fine-tuning its game plan.*

fin·ger¹ /ˈfɪŋgɚ/ *n.* [C] **1** one of the four long thin parts at the end of your hand, not including your thumb: *Hold the thread **between** your **fingers**.* | *The woman had a ring **on** her **finger**, so I assumed she was married.* → INDEX FINGER,

MIDDLE FINGER, LITTLE FINGER ➔ see picture on page A3 **2 not lift a finger** to not make any effort to help someone: *I do all the work – Frank never lifts a finger.* **3 keep/have your fingers crossed** *spoken* said when you hope that something will happen the way you want: *I had a job interview today. Keep your fingers crossed!* **4 put your finger on sth** *informal* to realize exactly what is wrong, different, or unusual about something: *There's something strange about him, but I can't put my finger on what it is.*

finger[2] *v.* [T] to touch or feel something with your fingers

fin·ger·nail /ˈfɪŋɡɚˌneɪl/ *n.* [C] the hard flat part that covers the top end of your finger ➔ see picture at HAND[1]

fingerprint

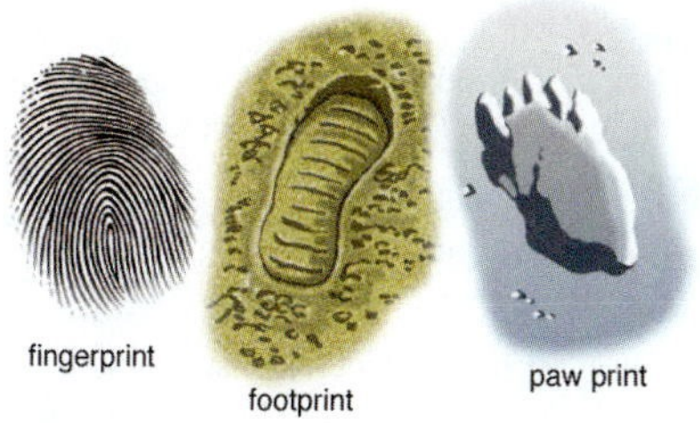

fin·ger·print /ˈfɪŋɡɚˌprɪnt/ *n.* [C] the mark made by the pattern of lines at the end of someone's finger

fin·ger·tip /ˈfɪŋɡɚˌtɪp/ *n.* [C] **1** the end of a finger **2 have something at your fingertips** to have something easily available and ready to use, especially knowledge or information

fin·ick·y /ˈfɪnɪki/ *adj.* someone who is finicky only likes a few kinds of food, clothes, music, etc. and is difficult to please: *a finicky eater*

fin·ish[1] /ˈfɪnɪʃ/ *v.* **1** [I,T] to come to the end of doing or making something, so it is complete [≠ **start**]: *Have you finished your homework?* | *Everyone applauded when she finished speaking.* **2** [T] **also finish off/up** to eat, drink, or use all the rest of something: *Finish your breakfast before it gets cold.* | *Who finished off the cake?* | *Why don't you finish up the apple pie?* **3** [I,T] to be in a particular position at the end of a race, competition, etc.: *She **finished second** in the marathon.* **4** [T] to give the surface of something a smooth appearance by painting, POLISHING, etc.

finish up sth ⇔ **up** *phr. v.* to end an event, situation, etc. by doing one final thing: *We finished up the evening with drinks in a bar downtown.*

finish with sth *phr. v.* **be finished with sth** to no longer need to use something: *Are you finished with the scissors?*

finish[2] *n.* **1** [C usually singular] the end or last part of something, especially a race: *It was **a close finish*** (=the race ended with the competitors close together)*, but Jarrett won.* **2** [C,U] the way that a surface looks after it has been painted or POLISHED: *a table with a glossy finish* | *What kind of finish did you put on the deck?*

fin·ished /ˈfɪnɪʃt/ *adj.* **1** [only before noun] completed: *the finished product*

THESAURUS

done, complete, over, through
➔ see Thesaurus box at DONE[2]

2 [not before noun] at the end of an activity: *I'm not quite finished.* **3** [not before noun] *informal* no longer able to do something successfully: *If the bank doesn't loan us the money, we're finished.*

ˈfinish line *n.* [C] the line at the end of a race that a competitor must cross first in order to win

fi·nite /ˈfaɪnaɪt/ *adj.* having an end or a limit: *the Earth's finite resources*

fir /fɚ/ *n.* [C] a tree with leaves shaped like needles that do not fall off in winter

fire[1] /faɪɚ/ *n.* **1** [C,U] uncontrolled flames and heat that destroy and damage things: *Fire destroyed part of the building.* | *a forest fire* | *Police are trying to find out who **started** the **fire**.* | *It took firefighters two days to **put out** the **fire*** (=stop it burning). | *The house **is on fire*** (=burning)! | *Some other buildings **caught fire*** (=started to burn). | *Rioters **set fire to** cars and stores* (=made them burn).

COLLOCATIONS

verbs used with fire
burn – to produce heat and flames
break out – to start burning suddenly
rage/blaze – to burn strongly for a long time over a large area
die down – to stop burning strongly
go out/die – to stop burning completely
smolder – to burn slowly with no flames and only a little smoke
extinguish/put out – to make a fire stop burning

THESAURUS

flames – the bright parts of a fire that you see burning in the air
blaze – the flames from a fire, or a large and dangerous fire: *Firemen fought to keep the blaze under control.*
inferno literary – a very large and very dangerous fire: *Soon, the house became a raging inferno.*
bonfire – a large outdoor fire: *a bonfire at the beach*
campfire – a fire that you build outdoors when you are camping

2 [C] burning wood or coal used to heat a room or provide heat: *a campfire* | *Let's **light a fire** in the fireplace.* **3** [U] shooting by guns: *Troops **opened fire on*** (=started shooting at) *the rebels.* **4 be/come under fire** to be criticized very strongly

F

fire² *v.* **1** [T] to make someone leave his/her job: *She didn't want to* ***get fired****.* | *Brian was* ***fired from*** *his job at the bank.* **2** [I,T] to shoot bullets from a gun: *Someone* ***fired*** *a* ***shot****.* | *Frank* ***fired at*** *the target.* **3 fire questions (at sb)** to ask someone a lot of questions very quickly **4 fire away** *spoken* said in order to show that you are ready to answer someone's questions

fire sth ⇔ **off** *phr. v.* **1** to quickly send an angry letter to someone: *She fired off an angry e-mail to the manager.* **2** to shoot a weapon, often so that there are no bullets, etc. left

fire sb/sth ⇔ **up** *phr. v.* **1** *informal* to start a machine or piece of equipment, especially one that burns gas: *Let's fire up the grill.* **2** to make someone very excited and eager: *The kids were all fired up for the game.*

'fire a,larm *n.* [C] a piece of equipment that makes a loud noise to warn people of a fire in a building

fire·arm /'faɪɚɑrm/ *n.* [C] *formal* a gun

fire·brand /'faɪɚbrænd/ *n.* [C] *formal* someone who tries to make people angry about a law, government, etc. so that they will try to change it

F

fire·crack·er /'faɪɚ,krækɚ/ *n.* [C] a small FIREWORK that explodes loudly

'fire de,partment *n.* [C] an organization that works to prevent fires and stop them from burning

'fire drill *n.* [C] an occasion when people practice how to leave a burning building safely

'fire ,engine *n.* [C] a special large vehicle that carries people and equipment to stop fires from burning

'fire es,cape *n.* [C] metal stairs on the outside of a building that people can use in order to escape if there is a fire

'fire ex,tinguisher *n.* [C] a metal container with water or chemicals in it, used for stopping small fires

fire·fight·er /'faɪɚ,faɪtɚ/ *n.* [C] someone whose job is to stop fires

fire·fly /'faɪɚflaɪ/ *n.* plural **fireflies** [C] an insect with a tail that shines in the dark

'fire ,hydrant *n.* [C] a water pipe in a street, used for getting water to stop fires

fire·man /'faɪɚmən/ *n.* plural **firemen** /-mən/ [C] a man whose job is to stop fires

fire·place /'faɪɚpleɪs/ *n.* [C] an open place in the wall of a room where you can make a fire

fire·proof /'faɪɚpruf/ *adj.* something that is fireproof cannot be damaged by fire —**fireproof** *v.* [T]

fire·side /'faɪɚsaɪd/ *n.* [singular] the area close to a FIREPLACE or around a small fire: *We were sitting by the fireside.*

'fire ,station *n.* [C] a building where the equipment used to stop fires from burning is kept, and where FIREFIGHTERS stay until they are needed

'fire truck *n.* [C] a FIRE ENGINE

fire·wall /'faɪɚwɔl/ *n.* [C] *technical* a system that protects a computer NETWORK from being used or looked at by people who do not have permission to do so

fire·wood /'faɪɚwʊd/ *n.* [U] wood that has been cut or collected in order to be burned on a fire

fire·work /'faɪɚwɚk/ *n.* [C usually plural] an object that burns or explodes to produce colored lights and noise in the sky: *a Fourth of July* ***fireworks display***

'firing squad *n.* [C] a group of soldiers whose duty is to shoot and kill a prisoner

firm¹ /fɚm/ *n.* [C] a business or small company: *a law firm*

THESAURUS

company, **business**, **corporation**, **multinational**, **subsidiary**

→ see Thesaurus box at COMPANY

firm² *adj.* **1** not completely hard, but not soft and not easy to bend: *a bed with a firm mattress* | *Choose the ripest firmest tomatoes.*

THESAURUS

hard, **stiff**, **solid**

→ see Thesaurus box at HARD¹

2 [only before noun] definite and not likely to change: *No firm decision has been reached.* | *I'm a* ***firm believer*** *in the value of education.* **3** strong and in control: *You need to be* ***firm with*** *children.* **4** strongly fastened or placed in position and not likely to move: *Make sure the ladder feels firm before you climb up.* **5 a firm grip/grasp/hold etc.** a tight, strong hold on something: *a firm handshake*

firm³ *v.*

firm sth ⇔ **up** *phr. v.* to make arrangements, ideas, or plans more definite and exact: *We hope to firm up the deal later this month.*

first¹ /fɚst/ *adj.* **1** coming before all the other things or people in a series: *Susan was his first girlfriend.* | ***The first time*** *I flew on a plane I was really nervous.* | *I've only read the first chapter.*

USAGE

Use **first** or **first of all** when you are giving a list of points, reasons, etc.: *There are three reasons for this. First of all...*

Use **first** or **first of all** to say what happens first in a series of actions: *First I checked my e-mail. Then I made a couple of calls.*

Use **at first** to say what happened at the beginning of a situation or time, when this changed later: *At first, we were very happy together.*

2 most important [= **main**]: *Our first priority is to maintain the quality of the product.* **3 in the first place** *spoken* used in order to talk about the beginning of a situation: *Why did you agree to meet her in the first place?* **4 at first sight/glance** the first time that you look at someone or something, before you notice any details: *At first sight, there didn't appear to be much damage.* **5 first thing** *spoken* as soon as you wake up or start work in the morning: *I'll call you first thing tomorrow, okay?* **6 first things first** *spoken* used in order to say that something is important and must be dealt with before other things ➔ **first/second/third string** at STRING[1] ➔ **in the first/second/third place** at PLACE[1]

first[2] *adv.* **1** before anything or anyone else: *Who's going first?* | ***First of all**, we'd better make sure we have everything we need.* **2** before doing anything else, or before anything else happens: *I'll join you in a minute, but first I've got to make a phone call* **3** done for the first time: *The book was first published in 1995.* **4 first come, first served** used in order to say that only the first people to arrive, ask for something, etc. will be given something: *Free movie tickets are being given away **on a first come, first served basis**.*

first[3] *number, pron.* **1 at first** in the beginning: *At first I thought he was weird, but now I really like him.* **2 a first** something that has never happened before: *"Dad actually washed the dishes tonight." **"That's a first."*** **3** the first person or thing in a series: *My uncle was **the first** in my family to go to college.* | *the 1st of June* (=first day of June)

ˌfirst ˈaid *n.* [U] basic medical treatment that is given as soon as possible to someone who is injured or who suddenly becomes sick

ˌfirst ˈbase *n.* [singular] the first of the four places in a game of baseball that a player must touch before gaining a point

ˌfirst ˈclass *n.* [U] the best and most expensive place to sit on an airplane, train, or ship: *He was sitting **in first class**.*

ˌfirst-ˈclass[2] *adj.* **1** much better than other things of the same type: *a first-class educational system*

THESAURUS

good, **great**, **excellent**, **wonderful**, **outstanding**, **exceptional**
➔ see Thesaurus box at GOOD[1]

2 using the FIRST CLASS on an airplane, train, or ship: *two first-class tickets to Hawaii* —**first class** *adv.*: *flying first class*

ˌfirst ˈfloor *n.* [C] the floor of a building that is at ground level [= **ground floor**]

first·hand /ˌfɚstˈhænd◂/ *adj.* [only before noun] firsthand knowledge is knowledge that you get or learn yourself, not from other people —**firsthand** *adv.*: *experience you have gained firsthand*

ˌfirst ˈlady *n.* **the First Lady** the wife of the President of the U.S.

first·ly /ˈfɚstli/ *adv.* used before saying the first of several things: *Firstly, I would like to thank everyone for coming.*

ˈfirst name *n.* [C] the name that, in English, comes before your family's name [➡ **last name**, **middle name**]: *Her first name is Caroline.*

ˌfirst ˈperson *n.* [singular] *technical* in grammar, a form of a verb or PRONOUN that you use to show that you are the speaker. "I," "we," "me," and "us" are all first person pronouns, and "I am" is the first person singular of the verb "to be"

ˌfirst-ˈrate *adj.* extremely good: *a first-rate performance*

fis·cal /ˈfɪskəl/ *adj. formal* connected with money, taxes, debts, etc., especially those relating to the government: *the city's social and fiscal policies* —**fiscally** *adv.*

ˌfiscal ˈyear *n.* [C] a period of 12 months, used by a government or business to calculate its accounts

fish[1] /fɪʃ/ *n.* plural **fish** or **fishes** **1** [C] an animal that lives in water and uses its FINS and tail to swim: *How many **fish** did you **catch**?* **2** [U] the flesh of a fish used as food: *We had fish for dinner.*

fish[2] *v.* **1** [I] to try to catch fish: *Dad's **fishing for** salmon.* **2** [I,T] to search for something in a bag, pocket, etc., or to bring it out when you have found it: *He **fished around in** his pocket for a quarter.* | *She finally **fished** a quarter **out of** her jeans.* **3 be fishing for compliments** to be trying to make someone say nice things about you

fish·bowl /ˈfɪʃboʊl/ *n.* [C] **1** a place or situation in which you cannot do anything without people knowing about it **2** a glass container that pet fish are kept in

fish·er·man /ˈfɪʃɚmən/ *n.* plural **fishermen** /-mən/ [C] a man who catches fish as a job or a sport

fish·er·y /ˈfɪʃəri/ *n.* plural **fisheries** [C] a part of the ocean that is used for catching fish as a business

fish·ing /ˈfɪʃɪŋ/ *n.* [U] the sport or job of catching fish: *Do you want to **go fishing**?*

ˈfishing pole also **ˈfishing rod** *n.* [C] a long thin pole with a long string and a hook tied to it, used for catching fish

fish·net /ˈfɪʃnɛt/ *n.* [U] a material with a pattern of threads and small holes like a net: *fishnet stockings*

fish·y /ˈfɪʃi/ *adj.* **1** *informal* seeming bad or dishonest: *There's something fishy about his business deals.* **2** tasting or smelling like fish

fis·sion /ˈfɪʃən/ *n.* [U] *technical* the process of splitting an atom to produce large amounts of energy or an explosion [➡ **fusion**]

fis·sure /ˈfɪʃɚ/ *n.* [C] a deep crack in rock or the ground

fist /fɪst/ *n.* [C] a hand with all the fingers bent tightly in toward the PALM: *She held the money tightly in her fist.*

fit[1] /fɪt/ past tense and past participle **fit** or **fitted**, present participle **fitting** *v.* **1** [I,T] to be the right size and shape for someone or something: *The dress **fit** her **perfectly**.* | *This lid doesn't **fit** very **well**.* ➔ see Topic box at CLOTHES **2** [I] to be the right size and shape for a particular space, and not be too big or too small: *This key doesn't seem to fit in the lock.* | *All of these pieces are supposed to* ***fit together***. **3** [I,T] if something fits into a place, there is enough space for it: *I don't think we'll be able to* ***fit*** *any more people* ***into*** *the car.* | *You can't move the table there. It won't* ***fit through*** *the door.* **4** [T] to put a piece of equipment into a place, or a new part onto a machine, so that it is ready to be used: *The windows and doors are all* ***fitted with*** *security locks.* **5** [I,T] if something fits another thing, it is similar to it or appropriate for it: *A man* ***fitting the*** *police* ***description*** (=looking like it) *was seen running from the park.* | *We wanted an experienced journalist, and Watts* ***fit the bill*** (=had the right experience).

fit in *phr. v.* **1** if someone fits in, s/he is accepted by the other people in a group: *New students often have a hard time fitting in.* **2 fit** sb/sth ⇔ **in** to manage to do something or see someone, even though you have a lot of other things to do: *Dr. Tyler can fit you in on Monday at 3:30 p.m.*

fit² *n.* [C] **1 have/throw a fit** *spoken* to become very angry and shout a lot: *Mom's going to have a fit when she sees what you've done.* **2** a short period of time when someone stops being conscious and cannot control his/her body: *an epileptic fit* **3** a very strong emotion that you cannot control: *a* ***fit of*** *rage* **4** a period during which you laugh or cough a lot: *I had a* ***coughing fit*** *during the concert.* **5 be a good/tight/perfect etc. fit** to fit a person or a particular space well, tightly, perfectly, etc.: *The skirt's* ***a perfect fit***.

F

fit³ *adj.* **1** appropriate or good enough for something [≠ **unfit**]: *This book is not* ***fit for*** *publication.* | *You're* ***in no fit state*** *to drive.* **2** healthy and strong: *He was young and* ***physically fit***. **3 see fit to do sth** *formal* to decide that it is right to do something, even though many people disagree: *The government has seen fit to start testing more nuclear weapons.* → **see fit to do something** at SEE

fit·ful /ˈfɪtfəl/ *adj.* always starting and stopping, not continuous or regular: *a* ***fitful sleep***

fit·ness /ˈfɪt˺nɪs/ *n.* [U] **1** the condition of being healthy or strong enough to do hard work or sports: *classes to improve your* ***physical fitness*** **2** the quality of being appropriate for something, especially a job: *They were unsure of his* ***fitness for*** *the job.*

fit·ted /ˈfɪt̬ɪd/ *adj.* **1** fitted clothes are designed so that they fit closely to someone's body: *a fitted jacket* **2 be fitted with sth** to have or include something as a permanent part: *The food processor is fitted with three blades.*

fit·ting¹ /ˈfɪt̬ɪŋ/ *adj. formal* right or appropriate: ***It was fitting that*** *it rained the day of his funeral.* | *The game was a* ***fitting end*** *to the season.*

fitting² *n.* [C] an occasion when you put on clothes that are being made for you to find out if they fit

ˈfitting room *n.* [C] a DRESSING ROOM

five¹ /faɪv/ *number* **1** 5 **2** five O'CLOCK: *I get off work* ***at five***.

five² *n.* [C] **1** a piece of paper money worth $5 **2 give sb five** *informal* to hit the inside of someone's hand with the inside of your hand in order to show that you are very pleased about something

fix¹ /fɪks/ *v.* [T]

1 REPAIR to repair something that is broken or not working correctly: *I've fixed your bike.* | *Do you know how to* ***fix*** *the* ***problem***?

> **THESAURUS**
>
> **repair**, **mend**, **renovate**, **restore**
> → see Thesaurus box at REPAIR²

2 PREPARE to prepare a meal or drinks: *Let me fix you a drink.* | *Mom was* ***fixing dinner***.

3 DECIDE to decide on an exact time, place, price, etc.: *Have you fixed a date for the wedding?* | *The interest rate was fixed at 6.5%*

4 HAIR/FACE to make your hair or MAKEUP look neat and attractive: *Let me fix my hair first and then we can go.*

5 RESULT to make dishonest arrangements so that an election, competition, etc. has the results that you want: *If you ask me, the game was fixed.*

fix sb/sth ⇔ **up** *phr. v.* **1** to decorate or repair a room or building: *We fixed up the guest bedroom.* **2** *informal* to find a romantic partner for someone: *Rachel keeps trying to fix me up with her brother.*

fix² *n.* **1 a quick fix** something that solves a problem quickly but is only a temporary solution **2 be in a fix** to have a problem that is difficult to solve: *We're going to be in a real fix if we miss the last bus.* **3 get a fix on sb/sth a)** to find out exactly where someone or something is **b)** to understand what someone or something is really like **4** [singular] *slang* an amount of an illegal drug that someone needs to take regularly

fix·a·tion /fɪkˈseɪʃən/ *n.* [C] a very strong interest in someone or something that is not healthy or natural: *Brian* ***has a fixation with*** *motorcycles.* —**fixated** /ˈfɪkseɪt̬ɪd/ *adj.*

fixed /fɪkst/ *adj.* **1** a fixed amount or time cannot be changed: *pensioners on a* ***fixed income*** | *fixed costs* **2** firmly fastened to something and in a particular position: *a mirror fixed to the wall* **3 have fixed ideas/opinions** *disapproving* to have opinions or ideas that will not change

fix·ed·ly /ˈfɪksɪdli/ *adv.* without looking at or thinking about anything else: *Ann* ***stared fixedly*** *at the screen.*

fix·ture /ˈfɪkstʃə/ *n.* **1** [C usually plural] a piece of equipment that is attached inside a house, such as an electric light or a FAUCET: *a bathroom with gold-plated fixtures* **2 be a (permanent) fixture** to always be present, and unlikely to move or go away: *He's been a fixture in the Senate since 1968.*

fizz /fɪz/ *n.* [singular,U] the BUBBLES of gas in some

types of drinks, or the sound they make **—fizz** *v.* [I] **—fizzy** *adj.* ➔ see picture on page A7

fiz·zle /'fɪzəl/ *v.*

fizzle out *phr. v.* to gradually end in a weak or disappointing way: *The party fizzled out before midnight.*

FL the written abbreviation of **Florida**

flab /flæb/ *n.* [U] *informal* soft loose fat on a person's body

flab·ber·gast·ed /'flæbɚˌgæstɪd/ *adj. informal* extremely shocked or surprised

THESAURUS

surprised, **amazed**, **shocked**, **astonished**, **astounded**, **stunned**, **dumbfounded**, **nonplussed**

➔ see Thesaurus box at SURPRISED

flab·by /'flæbi/ *adj. informal* having too much soft loose fat instead of strong muscles: *flabby arms*

flac·cid /'flæsɪd/ *adj. technical* soft and weak instead of firm: *flaccid muscles*

flag¹ /flæg/ *n.* [C] **1** a piece of cloth with a picture or pattern that is used to represent a particular country or organization: *The children were **waving flags**.* | *the French flag* **2** a piece of colored cloth used as a signal: *The flag went down, and the race began.*

flag² *v.* past tense and past participle **flagged**, present participle **flagging** [I] to become tired, weak, or less interested in something: *By the end of the meeting we had begun to flag.* **—flagging** *adj.*

flag sb/sth ⇔ **down** *phr. v.* to make the driver of a vehicle stop by waving at him/her: *I flagged down a cab.*

flag·pole /'flægpoʊl/ *n.* [C] a tall pole used for hanging flags

fla·grant /'fleɪgrənt/ *adj.* a flagrant action is shocking because it is done in a very noticeable way and shows no respect for the law, the truth, etc.: *The arrests are a **flagrant violation** of human rights.* **—flagrantly** *adv.*

flag·ship /'flægˌʃɪp/ *n.* [C] **1** the most important ship in a group of Navy ships, on which the ADMIRAL sails **2** [usually singular] a company's best and most important product, building, etc.

flag·stone /'flægstoʊn/ *n.* [C] a smooth flat piece of stone used for floors, paths, etc.

flail /fleɪl/ *v.* [I,T] to wave your arms and legs in a fast but uncontrolled way

flair /flɛr/ *n.* [singular, U] a natural ability to do something very well: *He **has a flair for** languages.*

flak /flæk/ *n.* [U] *informal* strong criticism: *She **got a lot of flak** for that decision.*

flake¹ /fleɪk/ *v.* [I] to break or come off in small thin pieces: *The paint on the door is starting to flake off.*

flake out *phr. v. spoken* to do something strange or to not do what you said you were going to do: *Kathy kind of flaked out on us today.*

flake² *n.* [C] **1** a small flat thin piece that breaks off of something: *The paint was coming off the door in flakes.* **2** *slang* someone who easily forgets things or who does strange things

flak·y /'fleɪki/ *adj.* **1** tending to break into small, thin pieces: *rich, flaky croissants* **2** *slang* someone who is flaky easily forgets things or does strange things

flam·boy·ant /flæm'bɔɪənt/ *adj.* **1** behaving in a loud, confident, or exciting way that makes people notice you: *flamboyant gestures* **2** noticeable because of being brightly colored, expensive, big, etc.: *a flamboyant red sequined dress* **—flamboyance** *n.* [U]

flame /fleɪm/ *n.* [C,U] **1** hot bright burning gas that you see when something is on fire: *Flames poured out of the windows.* **2 in flames** burning strongly: *By the time the firemen arrived, the house was in flames.*

fla·men·co /flə'mɛŋkoʊ/ *n.* [C,U] a very fast and exciting Spanish dance, or the music for this dance

flam·ing /'fleɪmɪŋ/ *adj.* [only before noun] **1** very bright: *flaming red hair* **2** burning strongly and brightly: *flaming torches*

flamingo

fla·min·go /flə'mɪŋgoʊ/ *n.* plural **flamingos** or **flamingoes** [C] a tall tropical water bird with long thin legs, pink feathers, and a long neck

flam·ma·ble /'flæməbəl/ *adj.* something that is flammable burns very easily [≠ **nonflammable**]

THESAURUS

Flammable and **inflammable** both describe something that burns very easily, but people usually use **flammable**. **Nonflammable** describes something that does not burn easily.

flank¹ /flæŋk/ *n.* [C] **1** the side of a person's or animal's body between the RIBS and the HIP **2** the side of an army in a battle: *The enemy attacked us on our left flank.*

flank² *v.* [T] to be on both sides of someone or something: *The President arrived, flanked by bodyguards.*

flan·nel /'flænl/ *n.* [U] soft light cotton or wool cloth that is used for making warm clothes: *a flannel shirt*

F

flap[1] /flæp/ *v.* past tense and past participle **flapped**, present participle **flapping** **1** [T] if a bird flaps its wings, it moves them up and down **2** [I] if a piece of cloth, paper, etc. flaps, it moves around quickly and makes a noise: *The ship's sails flapped in the wind.*

flap[2] *n.* [C] a thin flat piece of cloth, paper, skin, etc. that is attached by one end to a surface, which you can lift up easily: *the **flap of** the envelope*

flare[1] /flɛr/ *v.* **1** [I] **also flare up** to suddenly begin to burn very brightly: *The fire flared up again.* **2** [I] **also flare up** if strong feelings flare or flare up, people suddenly become angry, violent, etc.: ***Tempers flared** during the debate.* **3** [I] **also flare up** if a disease or illness flares up, it suddenly becomes worse: *My allergies are flaring up.* **4** [I,T] to become wider at the bottom edge, or to make something do this: *a skirt that **flares out***

flare[2] *n.* [C] a very bright light used outdoors as a signal to show people where you are, especially because you need help

'flare-up *n.* [C] **1** a situation in which someone suddenly becomes angry or violent **2** a situation in which someone suddenly has problems because of a disease or illness after not having any problems for a long time: *a flare-up of her arthritis*

F

flash[1] /flæʃ/ *v.* **1** [I,T] to suddenly shine brightly for a short time, or to make something shine in this way: *Lightning flashed overhead.* | *Why did that guy **flash** his headlights **at** me?*

THESAURUS

shine, flicker, twinkle, sparkle, shimmer
➔ see Thesaurus box at SHINE[1]

2 [I] to move very quickly: *An ambulance **flashed by/past**.* **3** [T] to show something to someone suddenly and for a short amount of time: *Sergeant Wicks flashed his badge.* **4** [I] **flash through sb's mind/head/brain** if images, thoughts, memories, etc. flash through your mind, you suddenly remember or think about them: *The possibility that he was lying flashed through my mind.* **5 flash a smile/glance/look etc.** to smile or look at someone quickly

flash[2] *n.* [C] **1** a sudden quick bright light: *a **flash of** lightning* **2** a bright light on a camera that you use when taking photographs indoors or when there is not much light: *Did the flash go off?* ➔ see Topic box at CAMERA **3 in a flash** very quickly: *Wait right here. I'll be back in a flash.* **4 a flash in the pan** someone or something that is successful only for a very short time

flash·back /ˈflæʃbæk/ *n.* **1** [C,U] part of a movie, play, book, etc. that shows something that happened earlier **2** [C] a very sudden memory of a past event

flash·card /ˈflæʃkɑrd/ *n.* [C] a card with a word or picture on it, used in teaching

flash·er /ˈflæʃɚ/ *n.* [C] *informal* someone who shows his or her sex organs in public

'flash flood *n.* [C] a sudden flood that is caused by a lot of rain falling in a short period of time

flash·light /ˈflæʃlaɪt/ *n.* [C] a small electric light that you carry in your hand ➔ see picture at LIGHT[1]

flash·y /ˈflæʃi/ *adj.* very big, bright, or expensive: *a flashy new sports car*

flask /flæsk/ *n.* [C] **1** a small flat container used for carrying alcohol in your pocket **2** a glass bottle with a narrow top used by scientists

flat[1] /flæt/ *adj.* comparative **flatter**, superlative **flattest** **1** smooth and level, with no slopes or raised parts: *The highway stays flat for the next 50 miles.* | *a flat roof*

THESAURUS

level – a surface or area that is level does not slope in any direction, so that every part of it is at the same height: *Make sure the shelves are level.*
smooth – having an even surface, without any holes or raised areas: *Sand the wood until it is smooth.*
even – flat, level, and smooth: *The paint is best applied to an even surface.*
horizontal – a horizontal line, position, or surface is straight, flat, and not sloping: *horizontal layers of rock*

2 flat rate/fee etc. an amount of money that is paid and that does not increase or decrease: *They charge a flat rate for delivery.* **3** a tire that is flat does not have enough air inside it **4** a drink that is flat does not taste fresh because it has no more BUBBLES of gas: *This Coke is completely flat.* **5 a flat refusal/denial etc.** a refusal, etc. that is definite and which someone will not change **6** a musical note that is flat is played or sung slightly lower than it should be [➡ **sharp**] **7 E flat/B flat etc.** a musical note that is slightly lower than E, B, etc. [➡ **sharp**]

flat[2] *adv.* **1** in a straight position or stretched against a flat surface: *The box can be folded flat for storage.* | *I have to **lie flat on** my **back** when I sleep.* **2 in 10 seconds/two minutes etc. flat** *informal* very quickly, in 10 seconds, two minutes, etc.: *I was out of the house in 10 minutes flat.* **3 fall flat** if a joke, story, etc. falls flat, it does not achieve the effect that is intended: *All of her jokes fell flat.* **4** if you sing or play music flat, you sing or play slightly lower than the correct note so that the sound is unpleasant [≠ **sharp**] **5 flat out** *informal* in a direct and complete way: *She **asked** him **flat out** if he was seeing another woman.*

flat[3] *n.* [C] **1** *informal* a tire that does not have enough air inside it: *The car **has a flat**.* **2** a musical note that is one half STEP lower than a particular note [➡ **sharp**] **3 flats** [plural] a type of women's shoes with very low heels

flat·ly /ˈflætli/ *adv.* **1** said in a definite way that is not likely to change: *They **flatly refused** to help me.* **2** without showing any emotion: *"It's hopeless," he said flatly.*

flat·ten /ˈflæt̚n/ *v.* [I,T] to make something flat or to become flat: *The hills **flatten out** near the coast.*

flat·ter /ˈflæt̬ɚ/ *v.* [T] **1 be/feel flattered** to be pleased because someone has shown you that s/he likes or admires you: *When they asked me to come, I felt flattered.* **2** to say nice things about someone or show that you admire him or her, sometimes when you do not really mean it: *He flattered me by praising my cooking.*

THESAURUS

praise, congratulate, compliment, pay a compliment
➔ see Thesaurus box at PRAISE[1]

3 to make someone look as attractive as s/he can: *That dress really flatters your figure.* **4 flatter yourself** to believe that your abilities or achievements are better than they really are: *"I think you like me more than you'll admit." "Don't flatter yourself."* —**flatterer** *n.* [C] —**flattering** *adj.*

flat·ter·y /ˈflæt̬əri/ *n.* [U] nice things that you say about someone or something, but which you do not really mean: *Flattery will get you nowhere!* (=will not help you get what you want)

flat·u·lence /ˈflætʃələns/ *n.* [U] *formal* the condition of having too much gas in your stomach

flaunt /flɔnt, flɑnt/ *v.* [T] to deliberately show your money, success, beauty, etc. in order to make other people notice it: *Pam was flaunting a new diamond ring.*

fla·vor[1] /ˈfleɪvɚ/ *n.* **1** [C] the particular taste of a food or a drink: *Which flavor do you want – chocolate or vanilla?* | *The wine **has** a smoky **flavor**.* | *the strong **flavor of** the cheese* **2** [U] the quality of tasting good: *The meat was cooked exactly right and full of flavor.* **3** [singular] a small amount of a particular quality that shows what the typical qualities of something are: *His book **gives** us the **flavor of** life on a midwestern farm.*

flavor[2] *v.* [T] to give something a particular taste or more taste: *The sauce is flavored with herbs.*

fla·vored /ˈfleɪvɚd/ *adj.* **strawberry-flavored/chocolate-flavored etc.** tasting like a STRAWBERRY, chocolate, etc.: *almond-flavored cookies*

fla·vor·ing /ˈfleɪvərɪŋ/ *n.* [C,U] a substance used to give food or drink a particular FLAVOR

flaw /flɔ/ *n.* [C] **1** a mark or weakness that makes something not perfect: *a **flaw in** the glass*

THESAURUS

defect, problem, bug, fault
➔ see Thesaurus box at DEFECT[1]

2 a mistake in an argument, plan, etc.: *There is a fundamental **flaw in** his argument.* **3** a bad part of someone's character

flawed /flɔd/ *adj.* spoiled by having mistakes, weaknesses, or damage: *The whole system is **deeply flawed**.*

flaw·less /ˈflɔlɪs/ *adj.* perfect, with no mistakes, marks, or weaknesses [= **perfect**]: *Lena has flawless skin.* —**flawlessly** *adv.*

flea /fli/ *n.* [C] a very small jumping insect that bites animals to drink their blood

flea·bag /ˈflibæg/ *adj. informal* cheap and dirty: *a fleabag hotel*

ˈflea ˌmarket *n.* [C] a market, usually in the street, where old or used goods are sold

fleck /flɛk/ *n.* [C] a small mark or spot: *a black beard with **flecks of** gray*

flecked /flɛkt/ *adj.* having small marks or spots: *red cloth **flecked with** white*

fledg·ling /ˈflɛdʒlɪŋ/ *adj.* a fledgling country, organization, etc. is new and still developing: *a fledgling republic*

flee /fli/ *v.* past tense and past participle **fled** /flɛd/ [I,T] to leave somewhere very quickly in order to escape from danger: *The president was forced to **flee the country**.*

THESAURUS

escape, get away, get out
➔ see Thesaurus box at ESCAPE[1]

F

fleece[1] /flis/ *n.* [C] **1** the wool of a sheep **2** an artificial soft material used for making warm coats —**fleecy** *adj.*

fleece[2] *v.* [T] *informal* to charge someone too much money for something, usually by tricking him/her

fleet /flit/ *n.* [C] **1** a group of ships, or all the ships in a navy **2** a group of vehicles that are controlled by one company: *a **fleet of** trucks*

fleet·ing /ˈflit̬ɪŋ/ *adj.* happening for only a moment: *a fleeting smile*

flesh[1] /flɛʃ/ *n.* [U] **1** the soft part of the body of a person or animal, between the skin and the bones: *a freshwater fish with firm white flesh* **2** the soft part of a fruit or vegetable that you eat ➔ see picture at FRUIT **3 (see/meet sb) in the flesh** to see someone whom you previously had only seen in a picture, on television, or in a movie: *He's more handsome in the flesh than on television.* **4 your own flesh and blood** someone who is part of your family

flesh[2] *v.*

flesh sth ⇔ **out** *phr. v.* to add more details to something: *You need to flesh out your essay with more examples.*

flesh·y /ˈflɛʃi/ *adj.* having a lot of flesh: *a round fleshy face*

flew /flu/ *v.* the past tense of FLY

flex /flɛks/ *v.* [T] to bend and move part of your body so that your muscles become tight

flex·i·ble /ˈflɛksəbəl/ *adj.* **1** able to change easily [≠ **inflexible**]: *flexible working hours* | *Teachers have to be flexible.* **2** easy to bend: *flexible plastic* —**flexibility** /ˌflɛksəˈbɪləti/ *n.* [U]

flex·time /ˈflɛksˌtaɪm/ *n.* [U] a system in which people can change the times at which they start and finish working

flick¹ /flɪk/ *v.* **1** [T] to make something move by hitting or pushing it quickly, especially with your thumb and finger: *Barry **flicked** the ash **from** his cigarette.* ➔ see picture on page A8 **2** [I,T] to move with a quick sudden movement, or to make something move in this way: *She flicked her hair back from her face.* **3** [T] to press a SWITCH to start or stop electrical equipment: *He **flicked** the light **switch** on.*

flick² *n.* [C] **1** *spoken* a movie: *That was a great flick!*

> **TOPIC**
> **movie, feature film, film, comedy, romantic comedy, thriller, western, action movie, horror movie, science fiction movie, animated movie/cartoon**
> ➔ see Topic box at MOVIE

2 a short, quick, sudden movement or hit with your hand, a whip, etc.

flick·er¹ /ˈflɪkɚ/ *v.* [I] **1** to burn or shine with an unsteady light: *flickering candles*

> **THESAURUS**
> **shine, flash, twinkle, glow, sparkle, shimmer**
> ➔ see Thesaurus box at SHINE¹

2 *written* if an emotion or expression flickers on someone's face, it appears for only a short time: *A look of anger **flickered across** Andrea's face.*

flicker² *n.* **1** [singular] an unsteady light that goes on and off quickly: *the **flicker of** the old gas lamp* **2 a flicker of interest/guilt etc.** a feeling or an expression on your face that only continues for a short time: *Not even a flicker of emotion showed on his face.*

fli·er /ˈflaɪɚ/ *n.* [C] a sheet of paper advertising something

> **THESAURUS**
> **advertisement, commerical, billboard, poster, want ads, classified ads, junk mail, spam**
> ➔ see Thesaurus box at ADVERTISEMENT

flight /flaɪt/ *n.* **1** [C] a trip in an airplane or space vehicle, or the airplane or vehicle that is making the trip: *We **caught** the next **flight** home.* | *Our **flight leaves** in 20 minutes.* | *We almost **missed** our **flight**.* | *I'm coming in on Flight 255 from Chicago.*

> **TOPIC**
> **airport, terminal, check in, check-in counter/desk, airport security, departure lounge, flight number, departure gate, boarding, take off, runway, land, baggage claim, passport, immigration, go through customs**
> ➔ see Topic box at AIRPORT

2 [U] the act of flying through the air: *a bird **in flight*** **3** [C] a set of stairs between one floor and the next: *She fell down a whole **flight of stairs**.* **4** [U] the act of avoiding a difficult situation by leaving or escaping: *The movie ends with the family's **flight from** Austria in World War II.*

ˈflight atˌtendant *n.* [C] someone who is responsible for the comfort and safety of the passengers on an airplane

ˈflight deck *n.* [C] the place where the pilot sits to control the airplane

flight·less /ˈflaɪtlɪs/ *adj.* a bird that is flightless is unable to fly

flight·y /ˈflaɪt̬i/ *adj.* someone who is flighty changes his/her ideas or activities a lot without finishing them or being serious about them

flim·sy /ˈflɪmzi/ *adj.* **1** flimsy clothing or material is thin, light, and does not cover much of the body: *a rather flimsy skirt* **2** weak and not made very well: *a flimsy table* **3** a flimsy argument, excuse, etc. does not seem very likely and people do not believe it: *The **evidence** against him is very **flimsy**.*

flinch /flɪntʃ/ *v.* [I] **1** to make a sudden small backward movement when you are hurt or afraid of something: *He raised his hand, and the child flinched.* **2** to avoid doing something because it is difficult or unpleasant: *He **never flinches from** the truth, no matter how painful.*

fling¹ /flɪŋ/ *v.* past tense and past participle **flung** /flʌŋ/ [T] to throw or move something quickly with a lot of force: *She **flung** her coat **onto** the bed and sat down.* | *Val **flung** her arms **around** my neck.*

> **THESAURUS**
> **throw, toss, chuck, hurl, pass, pitch**
> ➔ see Thesaurus box at THROW¹

fling² *n.* [C] a short and not very serious sexual relationship

flint /flɪnt/ *n.* [C,U] a type of very hard black or gray stone that makes a small flame when you strike it with steel

flip¹ /flɪp/ *v.* past tense and past participle **flipped**, present participle **flipping** **1** [I,T] to turn over quickly, or to make something turn over: *The vehicle **flipped over** several times.* | *Let's **flip a coin** to see who goes first.* **2** [T] to change the position of something: *You just **flip** a **switch** and the machine does everything for you.* **3 also flip out** [I] *informal* to suddenly become very angry or upset, or start behaving in a crazy way: *Harry flipped out when he found out that I wrecked his motorcycle.*

flip sb ⇔ **off** *phr. v. slang* to make a rude sign at someone by holding up your middle finger

flip through sth *phr. v.* to look at a book, magazine, etc. quickly

flip² *n.* [C] a movement in which you jump up and turn over in the air, so that your feet go over your head

flip³ *adj. informal* FLIPPANT

'flip chart *n.* [C] large pieces of paper which are connected at the top so that you can turn the pages over to present information to groups of people ➔ see picture on page A11

'flip-flop *n.* [C] *informal* an occasion when someone changes his/her decision —**flip-flop** *v.* [I]

flip·pant /ˈflɪpənt/ *adj.* not serious about something that other people think you should be serious about: *a flippant answer to her question*

flip·per /ˈflɪpɚ/ *n.* [C] **1** a flat part on the body of some large sea animals, used for pushing themselves through water **2** a large flat rubber shoe that you use in order to help you swim faster

'flip side *n.* [singular] *informal* the bad effects of something that also has good effects: *The flip side is that the medicine may cause hair loss.*

flirt[1] /flɚt/ *v.* [I] to behave toward someone as though you are sexually attracted to him/her, but not in a very serious way: *He's always **flirting with** the women in the office.*

flirt with sth *phr. v.* **1** to consider doing something, but not be very serious about it: *I've been flirting with the idea of moving to Greece.* **2 flirt with danger/disaster etc.** to do something that might be dangerous or have a very bad effect

flirt[2] *n.* [C] someone who flirts: *Dave is such a flirt!*

flir·ta·tion /flɚˈteɪʃən/ *n.* **1** [U] behavior that shows you are sexually attracted to someone, though not in a serious way **2** [C] a short period of time during which you are interested in someone or something

flir·ta·tious /flɚˈteɪʃəs/ *adj.* behaving as if you are sexually attracted to someone, but not in a serious way

flit /flɪt/ *v.* past tense and past participle **flitted**, present participle **flitting** [I] to move quickly from one place to another, never staying long in any one place: *birds flitting from branch to branch*

float

float[1] /floʊt/ *v.* **1 a)** [I] to stay or move on the surface of a liquid without sinking: *Leaves were **floating on** the surface of the water.* | *Their raft was **floating away**.* **b)** [T] to put something on the surface of a liquid so that it does not sink: *Children were floating small boats on the lake.* **2** [I] to stay in the air or move slowly through the air: *I watched a balloon **float up** into the sky.* **3** [T] to suggest an idea or plan, especially in order to find out what people think about it: *Bob **floated** the **idea** in a recent meeting.* **4** [T] to sell SHARES in a company or business to the public for the first time

float[2] *n.* [C] **1** a large vehicle that is decorated to be part of a PARADE **2** a SOFT DRINK that has ICE CREAM floating in it

flock[1] /flɑk/ *n.* [C] **1** a group of sheep, goats, or birds: *a **flock of** geese*

> **THESAURUS**
>
> **herd, school, shoal, pack, litter**
> ➔ see Thesaurus box at GROUP[1]

2 a large group of people of the same type

> **THESAURUS**
>
> **crowd, team, crew, gang, mob, bunch, mass, party**
> ➔ see Thesaurus box at GROUP[1]

flock[2] *v.* [I] if people flock to a place, a lot of them go there: *People are **flocking to** that new Thai restaurant.*

flog /flɑg, flɔg/ *v.* past tense and past participle **flogged**, present participle **flogging** [T] to beat a person or animal with a whip or stick as a punishment —**flogging** *n.* [C]

flood[1] /flʌd/ *v.* **1** [I,T] to make a place become covered with water, or to become covered with water: *The river floods the valley every spring.* | *The basement flooded and everything got soaked.* **2** [I,T] to arrive or go somewhere in large numbers or amounts: *Offers of help came **flooding in**.* **3 be flooded with sth** to receive so many letters, complaints, etc. that you cannot deal with them all: *After the show, the station was flooded with calls from angry viewers.* **4 flood the market** to sell something in very large quantities, so that the price goes down **5** [I] if a memory or a feeling floods back, you remember it very strongly

flood[2] *n.* [C] **1** a very large amount of water that covers an area that is usually dry: *The town was destroyed by floods.* **2** a very large number of things or people that arrive at the same time: *A **flood of lawsuits** followed the plane crash.*

flood·gate /ˈflʌdgeɪt/ *n.* **open the floodgates** to suddenly make it possible for a lot of people to do something: *The case could open the floodgates for thousands of other similar claims*

flood·ing /ˈflʌdɪŋ/ *n.* [U] a situation in which an area that is usually dry becomes covered with water: *The heavy rain has caused more flooding.*

flood·light /ˈflʌdlaɪt/ *n.* [C] a very bright light, used at night to light the outside of buildings, sports fields, etc.

flood·lit /ˈflʌdˌlɪt/ *adj.* lit by floodlights

floor[1] /flɔr/ *n.* [C] **1** the surface that you stand on when you are inside a building: *the kitchen floor* | *She found her keys **on the floor**.* ➔ see Thesaurus box at GROUND[1] **2** one of the levels in a building: *My office is **on the** third **floor**.* **3 ocean/forest**

floor the ground at the bottom of the ocean or in a forest **4 the floor a)** the part of a public or government building where people discuss things: *an argument on the Senate floor* **b)** the people attending a public meeting: *Are there any questions from the floor?* **5** an area in a room where people can dance: *couples on the* ***dance floor*** **6** an area in a building where a lot of people do their job: *the* ***factory floor***

floor² *v.* [T] **1** to surprise or shock someone so much that s/he does not know what to say or do: *I was completely floored by his question.* **2** to make a car go as fast as possible

floor·board /ˈflɔrbɔrd/ *n.* [C] **1** a board in a wooden floor **2** the floor in a car

floorboards

floor·ing /ˈflɔrɪŋ/ *n.* [U] a material used to make or cover floors

ˈfloor-length *adj.* long enough to reach the floor: *a floor-length skirt*

ˈfloor plan *n.* [C] a drawing that shows the shape of a room or rooms in a building and the positions of things in it, as seen from above

floo·zy /ˈfluzi/ *n.* plural **floozies** *informal disapproving* [C] a woman who has sexual relationships with a lot of different men, when this is considered to be immoral

flop¹ /flɑp/ *v.* past tense and past participle **flopped**, present participle **flopping** [I] **1** to sit or fall down quickly, especially because you are tired: *Jan* ***flopped down*** *on the bed.* **2** *informal* if something such as a product, play, or plan flops, it is not successful: *The musical flopped after its first week on Broadway.*

flop² *n.* [C] **1** *informal* a film, play, plan, etc. that is not successful: *Her last movie was a flop.* **2** a heavy falling movement or the noise that it makes: *He fell with a flop into the water.*

flop·house /ˈflɑphaʊs/ *n.* [C] *slang* a cheap hotel, especially one that has many beds in one room

flop·py /ˈflɑpi/ *adj.* soft and hanging loosely down: *a floppy hat*

ˌfloppy ˈdisk **also floppy** *n.* [C] a small flat piece of plastic, used for storing information from a computer

flo·ra /ˈflɔrə/ *n.* [U] *technical* all the plants that grow in a particular place [➡ **fauna**]

flo·ral /ˈflɔrəl/ *adj.* made of flowers or decorated with flowers: *fabrics with floral patterns*

flor·id /ˈflɔrɪd, ˈflɑrɪd/ *adj.* **1** florid language, writing, or music, etc. has too much decoration or detail: *florid language* **2** *literary* skin that is florid is red: *florid cheeks*

flo·rist /ˈflɔrɪst, ˈflɑr-/ *n.* [C] someone who owns or works in a store that sells flowers

floss /flɔs, flɑs/ *v.* [I,T] to clean between your teeth with DENTAL FLOSS

flo·til·la /floʊˈtɪlə/ *n.* [C] a group of small ships

flounce /flaʊns/ *v.* [I] to walk in a way that shows you are angry: *She frowned and* ***flounced out*** *of the room.*

floun·der /ˈflaʊndɚ/ *v.* [I] **1** to not know what to say or do because you feel confused or upset: *She floundered helplessly, unable to answer his question.* **2** to have a lot of problems and be likely to fail completely: *The economy is floundering.* **3** to move awkwardly or with difficulty, especially in water, mud, etc.

flour /flaʊɚ/ *n.* [U] a powder made from grain, usually wheat, that is used for making bread, cakes, etc.

flour·ish¹ /ˈflɚɪʃ, ˈflʌrɪʃ/ *v.* [I] to grow or develop well: *The plants flourished in the warm sun.* | *His business is flourishing.*

flourish² *n.* **with a flourish** with a large confident movement that makes people notice you: *He opened the door with a flourish.*

flout /flaʊt/ *v.* [T] *formal* to deliberately disobey a rule or law

flow¹ /floʊ/ *v.* [I] **1** if a liquid flows, it moves in a steady continuous stream: *The river flows past our cabin.*

THESAURUS

pour, **drip**, **leak**, **ooze**, **gush**, **spurt**, **run**, **come out**
➔ see Thesaurus box at POUR

2 to move easily, smoothly, and continuously from one place to another: *The cars flowed in a steady stream.* **3 a)** if conversation or ideas flow, people talk or have ideas without being interrupted **b)** if the ideas or words of a speech or piece of writing flow, they seem to go well together and make sense: *If I change this paragraph, do you think it will flow better?* **4** if clothing, hair, etc. flows, it hangs loosely and gracefully: *Her hair flowed down over her shoulders.*

flow² *n.* **1** [C usually singular] a smooth steady movement of liquid: *They tried to stop the* ***flow of*** *blood* **2** [C usually singular] a continuous movement of something from one place to another: *the constant* ***flow of*** *traffic in the street* **3** [U] actions, words or ideas that are produced continuously: *I had* ***interrupted the flow of*** *their conversation.* **4 go with the flow** *spoken* to do what is easiest in your situation, and not try to do something difficult ➔ CASH FLOW

ˈflow chart *n.* [C] a drawing that uses shapes and ARROWS to show how a series of actions or parts of a system are connected with each other

flow·er¹ /ˈflaʊɚ/ *n.* [C] **1** the colored part of a plant or tree that produces the seeds or fruit: *The* *tree has beautiful pink flowers in early spring.* → see picture at PLANT[1] **2** a small plant that produces beautiful flowers: *She's growing vegetables and flowers in the garden.* | *a* ***bouquet of flowers*** **3 in flower** a plant that is in flower has flowers on it

flower[2] *v.* [I] to produce flowers

flow·er·bed /ˈflaʊɚˌbɛd/ *n.* [C] an area of ground in which flowers are grown

flow·ered /ˈflaʊɚd/ *adj.* decorated with pictures of flowers: *a flowered dress*

flow·er·pot /ˈflaʊɚˌpɑt/ *n.* [C] a pot in which you grow plants

flow·er·y /ˈflaʊəri/ *adj.* **1** decorated with pictures of flowers: *a flowery pattern* **2** flowery speech or writing uses complicated and unusual words instead of simple clear language

flown /floʊn/ *v.* the past participle of FLY

flu /flu/ *n.* [U] a common disease that is like a bad cold but is more serious: *Both of us have* ***had the flu*** *recently.* | *I was in bed* ***with the flu****.* | *She fell ill with* ***flu-like symptoms*** (=felt tired, had a sore throat, was coughing, etc.). | *a* ***flu bug/virus***

flub /flʌb/ *v.* past tense **flubbed**, past participle **flubbing** [I,T] *informal* to make a mistake or do something badly: *Several of the actors flubbed their lines.*

fluc·tu·ate /ˈflʌktʃuˌeɪt/ *v.* [I] if a price or amount fluctuates, it keeps changing from a high level to a low one and back again: *Interest rates fluctuate from day to day.* —**fluctuation** /ˌflʌktʃuˈeɪʃən/ *n.* [C] *fluctuations in oil prices*

flue /flu/ *n.* [C] a pipe through which smoke or heat from a fire can pass out of a building

flu·ent /ˈfluənt/ *adj.* able to speak or write a language very well: *Ted is* ***fluent in*** *French.* | *He spoke fluent English.* —**fluently** *adv.*: *She speaks Spanish fluently.* —**fluency** *n.* [U]

fluff[1] /flʌf/ *n.* [U] **1** small light pieces of waste wool, thread, etc. **2** *disapproving* news, music, writing, work, etc. that is not serious or important: *The movie is pure romantic fluff.* **3** very soft fur or feathers, especially from a young animal or bird

fluff[2] **also fluff up/out** *v.* [T] to make something soft appear larger by shaking or brushing it: *a bird fluffing out its feathers*

fluff·y /ˈflʌfi/ *adj.* made of or covered with something soft and light: *a fluffy kitten*

flu·id[1] /ˈfluɪd/ *n.* [C,U] *technical* a liquid: *My doctor told me to rest and drink plenty of fluids.*

fluid[2] *adj.* **1** fluid movements are smooth and graceful **2** a situation that is fluid is likely to change or able to change —**fluidity** /fluˈɪdəṭi/ *n.* [U]

ˌfluid ˈounce *written abbreviation* **fl oz** *n.* [C] a unit for measuring liquid, equal to 1/16 of a PINT or 0.0296 liters

fluke /fluk/ *n.* [C] *informal* something that only happens because of chance or luck: *Their victory was a fluke.*

flung /flʌŋ/ *v.* the past tense and past participle of FLING

flunk /flʌŋk/ *v.* [I,T] *informal* to fail a test or course, or to give someone a low GRADE so s/he does this: *I flunked the history exam.* | *Mrs. Harris flunked me in English.*

flunk out *phr. v. informal* to be forced to leave a school or college because your work is not good enough: *Tim* ***flunked out of*** *Yale.*

flun·ky /ˈflʌŋki/ *n.* plural **flunkies** [C] *informal* someone who does the boring or physical work that someone else tells him or her to do

flu·o·res·cent /flʊˈrɛsənt, flɔ-/ *adj.* **1** a fluorescent light is a very bright electric light in the form of a tube **2** fluorescent colors shine very brightly

fluor·ide /ˈflɔraɪd/ *n.* [U] a chemical that helps to protect teeth against decay

flur·ry /ˈflɚi, ˈflʌri/ *n.* plural **flurries** **1** [C usually singular] an occasion when there is suddenly a lot of activity for a short time: *His arrival produced a* ***flurry of*** *excitement.* **2** [C usually plural] an occasion when it snows for a short time: ***Snow flurries*** *are expected tonight.*

flush[1] /flʌʃ/ *v.* **1** [I,T] if a toilet flushes, or if you flush it, you make water go through it to clean it **2** [I] to become red in the face, especially because you are embarrassed or angry [➡ **flushed**]: *Billy flushed and looked down.* **3** [T] **also flush out** to clean something by forcing water through it: *Drinking water helps flush out toxins from the body.*

flush[2] *n.* **1** [singular] the red color that appears on your face when you are embarrassed or angry **2 a flush of pride/embarrassment/happiness etc.** a sudden feeling of pride, embarrassment, etc.: *He felt a strong flush of pride as he watched his daughter on stage.*

flush[3] *adj.* [not before noun] **1** if two surfaces are flush, they are at exactly the same level, so that the place where they meet is flat: *Is that cupboard* ***flush with*** *the wall?* **2** *informal* if someone is flush, s/he has plenty of money: *I'll buy dinner. I'm feeling flush right now.*

flushed /flʌʃt/ *adj.* **1** red in the face: *You look a little flushed.* **2 flushed with excitement/success** excited or pleased in a way that is easy to notice: *Jill ran in, flushed with excitement.*

flus·tered /ˈflʌstɚd/ *adj.* feeling nervous and confused: *Jay got flustered and forgot what he was supposed to say.*

flute /flut/ *n.* [C] a musical instrument shaped like a pipe that you play by holding it across your lips and blowing into it → see picture on page A6

flut·ist /ˈfluṭɪst/ *n.* [C] someone who plays the flute

TOPIC

conductor, cellist, violinist, percussionist
→ see Topic box at ORCHESTRA

flut·ter /ˈflʌṭɚ/ *v.* **1** [I,T] if a bird or insect flutters, or flutters its wings, its wings move quickly and lightly up and down: *moths fluttering around the light* **2** [I] to wave or move gently in the air: *flags fluttering in the wind* **3** [I] if your heart or your stomach flutters, you feel very excited or nervous —**flutter** *n.* [singular]

flux /flʌks/ *n.* **be in (a state of) flux** to be changing a lot so that you cannot be sure what will happen: *The economy is in flux at the moment.*

fly¹ /flaɪ/ *v.* past tense **flew** /flu/ past participle **flown** /floʊn/ third person singular **flies**
1 THROUGH AIR [I,T] to move through the air, or to make something do this: *We watched the birds flying overhead.* | *He was flying a kite in the park.* | *The planes fly right over our house.*
2 TRAVEL [I] to travel by airplane: *Are you going to fly or drive?* | *Fran* ***flew to*** *Paris last week.*

TOPIC

airport, terminal, check in, check-in counter/desk, airport security, departure lounge, flight number, departure gate, boarding, take off, runway, land, baggage claim, passport, immigration, go through customs
→ see Thesaurus box at AIRPORT¹

3 AIRLINE [I,T] to use a particular AIRLINE or use a particular type of ticket when flying: *He usually flies first class.*
4 BE A PILOT [I,T] to be the pilot of an airplane: *Bill's learning to fly.*
5 SEND SB/STH BY AIRPLANE [T] to take goods or people somewhere by airplane: *Food and medicine are being* ***flown into*** *the area.*
6 MOVE [I] to suddenly move very quickly: *Timmy* ***flew down*** *the stairs and out the door.* | *The door suddenly* ***flew open****.*
7 TIME [I] *informal* if time flies, it seems to pass quickly: *Is it 5:30 already? Boy, time sure does fly!* | *Last week just* ***flew by****.*
8 fly off the handle *informal* to suddenly become angry for no good reason
9 FLAG [I,T] if a flag is flying, it is fixed to the top of a tall pole

fly² *n.* plural **flies** [C] **1** a common small flying insect with two wings: *There were flies all over the food.* **2** *informal* the part at the front of a pair of pants that you can open: *Your fly is unzipped.* **3** a hook that is made to look like a fly, used for catching fish

ˈfly-by-ˌnight *adj.* [only before noun] *informal disapproving* a fly-by-night organization cannot be trusted and is not likely to exist very long: *fly-by-night operators who take your money and run*

fly·er /ˈflaɪɚ/ *n.* [C] a FLIER

fly·ing¹ /ˈflaɪ-ɪŋ/ *n.* [U] the activity of traveling by airplane or of being a pilot: *fear of flying*

flying² *adj.* **1** able to fly: *a type of flying insect* **2 with flying colors** if you pass a test with flying colors, you are very successful on it

ˌflying ˈsaucer *n.* [C] a space vehicle shaped like a plate that some people believe carries creatures from another world [= **UFO**]

fly·swat·ter /ˈflaɪˌswɑṭɚ/ *n.* [C] a plastic square attached to a long handle, used for killing flies

FM *n.* [U] **frequency modulation** a system of broadcasting radio programs which produces a clear sound [➡ **AM**]

foal /foʊl/ *n.* [C] a very young horse

foam¹ /foʊm/ *n.* [U] **1** a lot of very small BUBBLES on the surface of something: *white foam on the tops of the waves* **2** a light solid substance filled with many very small BUBBLES of air: *foam packing material* —**foamy** *adj.*

foam² *v.* [I] **1** to produce foam **2 foam at the mouth** to be very angry

ˌfoam ˈrubber *n.* [U] soft rubber full of air BUBBLES that is used, for example, to fill PILLOWS

fo·cal point /ˈfoʊkəl ˌpɔɪnt/ *n.* [C] someone or something that you pay the most attention to: *Television has become* ***the focal point of*** *most American homes.*

fo·cus¹ /ˈfoʊkəs/ *v.* [I,T] **1** to give all your attention to a particular thing: *In his speech he* ***focused on*** *the economy.* | *She tried to* ***focus*** *her* ***attention*** *on her work.* **2** to change the position of the LENS on a camera, TELESCOPE, etc. so you can see something clearly: *He turned the camera and* ***focused on*** *Tricia's face.* → see Topic box at CAMERA **3** if you focus your eyes, or if your eyes focus, you are able to see something clearly

focus² *n.* **1** [singular] the thing, person, situation, etc. that people pay special attention to: *He is the* ***focus of*** *intense media scrutiny.* | *She loves being* ***the focus of attention****.* **2** [U] special attention that you give to a particular person or subject: *Our main* ***focus*** *is* ***on*** *helping people get back to work.* **3 in focus/out of focus** if a photograph, camera, etc. is in focus, the edges of the things you see are clear; if it is out of focus, the edges are not clear —**focused** *adj.*

fod·der /ˈfɑdɚ/ *n.* [U] food for farm animals

foe /foʊ/ *n.* [C] *literary* an enemy

fog¹ /fɑg, fɔg/ *n.* [C,U] cloudy air near to the ground that is difficult for you to see through: *I could hardly see the road through* ***thick/heavy*** *fog.*

fog² **also fog up** *v.* past tense **fogged**, past participle **fogging** [I,T] if glass fogs or becomes fogged, it becomes covered with very small drops of water so you cannot see through it: *My glasses fogged up as soon as I stepped outside.*

fo·gey, **fogy** /ˈfoʊgi/ *n.* plural **fogeys** or **fogies** [C] *informal* someone who is old-fashioned and who does not like change: *Don't be such an **old fogey**.*

fog·gy /ˈfɑgi, ˈfɔgi/ *adj.* comparative **foggier**, superlative **foggiest** **1** not clear because of FOG: *a foggy morning* **2 I don't have the foggiest (idea)** *spoken old-fashioned* said in order to emphasize that you do not know something: *I don't have the foggiest idea what his address is.*

fog·horn /ˈfɑghɔrn, ˈfɔg-/ *n.* [C] a loud horn used by ships in a FOG to warn other ships of their position

foi·ble /ˈfɔɪbəl/ *n.* [C] *formal* a habit that someone has that is slightly strange or silly

foil[1] /fɔɪl/ *n.* [U] metal sheets that are thin like paper, used for wrapping food: *Cover the pan tightly with **aluminum foil**.*

foil[2] *v.* [T] if you foil someone's plans, you stop him/her from doing something

foist /fɔɪst/ *v.*
foist sth **on/upon** sb *phr. v.* to make someone accept something that s/he does not want: *Marie is always trying to foist her religious beliefs on everyone.*

fold

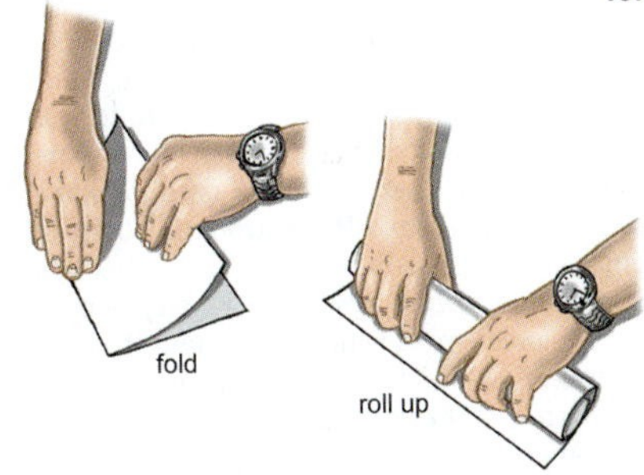

fold[1] /foʊld/ *v.* **1** [T] to bend a piece of paper, cloth, etc. so that one part covers another part: *She folded her clothes and put them on a chair.* | ***Fold** the paper **in half*** (=fold it across the middle). **2** [I,T] to make something, for example a table or chair, smaller by bending it or closing it, so that it can be stored: *Be sure to fold up the ironing board when you're finished.* **3 fold your arms** to bend your arms so they are resting across your chest: *George stood silently with his arms folded.* **4** [I] if a business folds, it fails and is not able to continue
fold sth **in** *phr. v.* to gently mix another substance into a mixture when you are preparing food

fold[2] *n.* **1** [C] a line made in paper, cloth, etc. when you fold one part of it over another: *Bend the card and cut along the fold.* **2** [C usually plural] the folds in material, skin, etc. are the loose parts that hang over other parts of it: *She adjusted the folds of her dress.* **3 the fold** the group of people you belong to or have the same beliefs as: *The church will welcome him **back to the fold**.* **4** [C] a small area where sheep are kept for safety

fold·er /ˈfoʊldɚ/ *n.* [C] **1** a large folded piece of hard paper, in which you keep loose papers → see picture on page A11 **2** a picture on a computer screen that shows you where a FILE is kept

fo·li·age /ˈfoʊliɪdʒ/ *n.* [U] the leaves of a plant

folk[1] /foʊk/ *adj.* [only before noun] folk music, art, dancing, etc. is traditional and typical of the ordinary people who live in a particular area

folk[2] *n.* **1 sb's folks** your parents or family: *I need to call my folks sometime this weekend.* **2 folks** [plural] *spoken* said when you are talking to a group of people in a friendly way: *That's all for now, folks.* **3 folks** [plural] *informal* people: *Most folks around here are very friendly.* **4** [U] FOLK MUSIC

folk·lore /ˈfoʊk-lɔr/ *n.* [U] the traditional stories, CUSTOMS, etc. of the ordinary people of a particular area

ˈfolk ˌmusic *n.* [U] traditional music that is played by the ordinary people of a particular area

THESAURUS

pop (music), **rock (music)**, **rock'n'roll**, **heavy metal**, **reggae**, **house (music)**, **hip-hop**, **rap (music)**, **jazz**, **classical (music)**, **country music**
→ see Thesaurus box at MUSIC[1]

folk·sy /ˈfoʊksi/ *adj. informal* friendly and informal: *The town has a certain folksy charm.*

fol·li·cle /ˈfɑlɪkəl/ *n.* [C] one of the small holes in the skin that hair grows from

fol·low /ˈfɑloʊ/ *v.*
1 COME BEHIND [I,T] to walk, drive, etc. behind or after someone else: *If you follow me, I'll show you to your room.* | *The president came in, **followed by** a crowd of photographers.* | *You go ahead – I'll follow later.*
2 IN ORDER TO WATCH SB [T] to go closely behind someone else in order to find out where s/he is going: *Marlowe looked over his shoulder to make sure no one was following him.*

THESAURUS

chase – to quickly follow someone or something in order to catch him, her, or it: *Police chased the thief down the street.*
pursue – to chase or follow someone or something in order to catch him, her, or it: *We ran faster, but he continued to pursue us.*
run after – to chase someone or something: *She started to leave, and Smith ran after her.*
tail informal – to secretly watch and follow someone such as a criminal: *Police have been tailing him.*

stalk – to follow a person or animal quietly in order to catch, attack, or kill him, her, or it: *a tiger stalking its prey*

3 HAPPEN AFTER [I,T] to happen or come immediately after something else: *There was a shout from the garage **followed by** a loud crash.* | *In the days that followed, Angie tried to forget about Sam.*
4 follow the instructions/rules/advice etc. to do something according to how the instructions, rules, etc. say it should be done: *Did you follow the instructions on the box?*
5 follow suit to do the same thing as someone else, after s/he has done it: *He praised Kim and encouraged others to **follow suit**.* | *When Allied Stores reduced prices, other companies were forced to **follow suit**.*
6 follow (in) sb's footsteps to do the same job that someone else did before you: *Toshi followed in his father's footsteps and started his own business.*
7 BE INTERESTED [T] to be interested in something, and watch how it progresses: *Do you follow baseball at all?*
F
8 as follows used in order to introduce a list of names, instructions, etc.: *The winners are as follows: first place, Tony Gwynn; second place, ...*
9 UNDERSTAND [I,T] *spoken* to understand something such as an explanation or story: *Sorry, I **don't follow you**.*
10 it follows that used in order to show that something must be true as a result of something else that is true: *It doesn't necessarily follow that you're going to do well academically even if you're highly intelligent.*
11 GO IN A DIRECTION [T] to continue on a road or path, or go in the same direction as a river: *The road follows the river for the next six miles.*
12 BELIEVE/OBEY [T] to believe in or obey a particular set of religious or political ideas: *They still **follow** the **teachings** of Gandhi.*

follow sb **around** *phr. v.* to keep following someone everywhere s/he goes: *My little brother is always following me around.*

follow sth ⇔ **through** *phr. v.* to do what needs to be done to complete something or make it successful: *Harry was trained as an actor, but he never followed through with it.*

follow sth ⇔ **up** *phr. v.* to find out more about something, or to do more about something: *Did Jay ever **follow up on** that job possibility in Tucson?*

fol·low·er /ˈfɑloʊɚ/ *n.* [C] someone who believes in or supports a particular leader or set of ideas: *the early **followers of** Buddha*

fol·low·ing¹ /ˈfɑloʊɪŋ/ *adj.* **the following day/year/chapter etc.** the day, year, etc. after the one you have just mentioned: *Neil arrived on Friday, and his wife came the following day.*

THESAURUS

next, **subsequent**, **succeeding**, **later**
→ see Thesaurus box at NEXT¹

following² *n.* **1** [singular] a group of people who support or admire someone such as a performer: *The band has a big following in Europe.* **2 the following** the people or things that you are going to mention next: *Typical examples of opposites include the following: small and large, cold and hot...*

following³ *prep.* immediately after: *There will be time for questions following the lecture.*

ˈfollow-up *n.* **1** [C] a book, movie, article, etc. that comes after another one that has the same subject or characters: *Spielberg says he's planning to do a follow-up next year.* | *a **follow-up to** their successful first album* **2** [C,U] something that is done to make sure that earlier actions have been successful or effective —**follow-up** *adj.* [only before noun]

fol·ly /ˈfɑli/ *n.* plural **follies** [C,U] *formal* a very stupid thing to do: ***It would be** sheer **folly to** buy another car at this point.*

fo·ment /ˈfoʊmɛnt, foʊˈmɛnt/ *v.* **foment war/revolution/trouble etc.** *formal* to do something that encourages people to cause a lot of trouble in a society

fond /fɑnd/ *adj.* **1 be fond of sb/sth** to like someone or something very much: *Mrs. Winters is very fond of her grandchildren.* **2 fond memories** memories that make you happy when you think of them: *Marie still **had fond memories of** their time together.* **3 be fond of doing sth** to enjoy doing something, and to do it often: *Dad is very fond of telling that story.* **4** [only before noun] a fond look, smile, action, etc. shows that you like someone very much: *As we left, we said a **fond farewell**.* —**fondness** *n.* [U]

fon·dle /ˈfɑndl/ *v.* [T] to gently touch and move your fingers over part of someone's body in a way that shows love or sexual desire

THESAURUS

touch, **feel**, **stroke**, **caress**, **grope**
→ see Thesaurus box at TOUCH¹

fond·ly /ˈfɑndli/ *adv.* **1** in a way that shows you like someone or something very much: *Greta smiled fondly at him from across the room.* **2 fondly remember/recall** to feel happy when you remember what you liked about a person or place: *That trip is still fondly remembered by all of us.*

font /fɑnt/ *n.* [C] **1** a set of printed letters that is a particular size and shape **2** a stone container in a church that holds the water used for the ceremony of BAPTISM

food /fud/ *n.* **1** [C,U] things that people and animals eat, such as vegetables or meat [➡ **fast food**, **junk food**, **health food**]: *I love Chinese* *food.* | *We didn't have enough food for everyone.* | *the frozen foods section of the supermarket*

COLLOCATIONS

fresh – recently picked or prepared, and not dried, put in cans, or frozen
stale – used about bread or cake that is not good any more because it has become hard and dry
sour – used about milk or cream that tastes and smells bad and is not good any more
frozen – packed and stored at very low temperatures
canned – stored and sold in cans
processed – processed food has chemicals in it to make it last longer
organic – produced without using harmful chemicals
nutritious/nourishing/wholesome – good for your health

THESAURUS

vegetarian food – food that has no meat or animal products in it
health food – food that contains only natural substances
fast food – food such as hamburgers that you can buy quickly
junk food – food that is not healthy because it contains a lot of fat or sugar
➔ TASTE

2 food for thought something that makes you think carefully about something: *The teacher's advice certainly **gave** me **food for thought**.*

'food bank *n.* [C] a place that gives food to people who need it

'food chain *n.* [singular] animals and plants considered as a group in which one animal is eaten by another animal, which is eaten by another, etc.

'food ˌpoisoning *n.* [U] an illness caused by eating food that contains harmful BACTERIA

'food ˌprocessor *n.* [C] a piece of electrical equipment for preparing food, that cuts or mixes it very quickly

'food stamp *n.* [C usually plural] an official piece of paper, given by the government to poor people, that can be used instead of money to buy food

food·stuff /'fudstʌf/ *n.* [C usually plural] food – used especially when talking about the business of producing or selling food

fool[1] /ful/ *n.* [C] **1** a stupid person: *I **felt like a fool**, locking my keys in the car like that.* **2 make a fool of yourself** to do something stupid that you feel embarrassed about later: *Sorry if I made a fool of myself last night. I was drunk.* **3 make a fool of sb** to deliberately try to make someone seem stupid: *She made a fool of me in front of all the other students.*

fool[2] *v.* **1** [T] to trick or deceive someone: *Don't **be fooled into** buying more insurance than you need.* **2 you could have fooled me** *spoken* said when you do not believe what someone has told you: *"Look, we're doing our best to fix it." "Well, you could have fooled me."* **3 be fooling yourself** to try to make yourself believe something that you know is not really true: *You're fooling yourself if you think he's going to come back to you.*

fool around *phr. v.* **1** to waste time behaving in a silly way or doing things that are not important: *Stop fooling around and start studying!* **2** to behave in a way which is careless and not responsible: *Stop **fooling around with** those scissors before someone gets hurt.* **3** to have a sexual relationship with someone else, especially when you should not: *Matt thinks his wife is **fooling around with** someone.*

fool with sb/sth *phr. v. informal* to do something that could be dangerous or could ruin something: *A hacker had been fooling with the hospital computers.*

fool·har·dy /'fulˌhɑrdi/ *adj.* taking risks that are not necessary

fool·ish /'fulɪʃ/ *adj.* not sensible or wise: *It was a very foolish thing to do.* | *a foolish woman* —**foolishly** *adv.*: *I foolishly agreed to go with them.* —**foolishness** *n.* [U]

fool·proof /'fulpruf/ *adj.* a foolproof plan, method, etc. is certain to be successful

foot[1] /fʊt/ *n.* [C]
1 BODY PART plural **feet** /fit/ the part of your body that you stand on and walk on: *Turner kicks with his **left/right foot**.* | *He always walks around **in bare feet*** (=without shoes and socks). ➔ see picture on page A3
2 MEASUREMENT plural **feet** or **foot/ft.** a unit for measuring length, equal to 12 INCHES or 0.3048 meters
3 on foot if you go somewhere on foot, you walk there: *We set out to explore the city on foot.*
4 the foot of sth the lowest part of something such as a mountain or tree, or the end of something such as a bed
5 on your feet a) to be standing for a long time without sitting down: *Waitresses are on their feet all day.* **b)** to be healthy again after being sick: *It's good to see you on your feet again!*
6 off your feet sitting or lying down, rather than standing or walking: *The doctor told me to stay off my feet for a few days.*
7 get/rise/jump etc. to your feet to stand up after you have been sitting: *The fans cheered and rose to their feet.*
8 set foot in sth to go into a place: *If that woman ever sets foot in this house, I'm leaving!*
9 put your foot down a) to say very firmly what someone must do or not do: *Brett didn't want to go to the doctor, but Dad put his foot down.* **b)** to make a car go faster
10 put your feet up to relax and rest, especially by having your feet supported on something

F

11 put your foot in your mouth to accidentally say something that embarrasses or upsets someone
12 have/keep both feet on the ground to be sensible and practical in the way you live your life
13 get your foot in the door to get your first opportunity to work in a particular organization or industry
14 have one foot in the grave *humorous* to be old
15 -footed having a particular number or type of feet: *a four-footed animal | a flat-footed man*
16 -footer being a particular number of feet in length: *Our sailboat's a twenty-footer.*

foot² *v.* **foot the bill** *informal* to pay for something: *Her father is footing the bill for flying lessons.*

foot·age /ˈfʊt̬ɪdʒ/ *n.* [U] film that shows a particular event: *black-and-white footage of the 1936 Olympics*

foot·ball /ˈfʊt˺bɔl/ *n.* **1** [U] a game in which two teams of 11 players carry, kick, or throw a ball into an area at the end of a field to win points: *a football game* **2** [C] the ball used in this game

foot·bridge /ˈfʊtˌbrɪdʒ/ *n.* [C] a narrow bridge for people to walk over

F

foot·fall /ˈfʊtfɔl/ *n. literary* [C,U] the sound of each step when someone is walking [= **footstep**]

foot·hill /ˈfʊtˌhɪl/ *n.* [C usually plural] one of the low hills at the bottom of a group of mountains: *the foothills of the Rockies*

foot·hold /ˈfʊthoʊld/ *n.* [C] **1** a position from which you can start trying to get what you want: *The Republicans* ***gained a foothold*** *during the last elections.* **2** a space where you can safely put your foot when climbing a rock

foot·ing /ˈfʊt̬ɪŋ/ *n.* [singular] **1** the conditions or arrangements under which something exists or operates: *Most of all, the city needs to get on a* ***firm*** *financial* ***footing****. | Talks were held in Geneva so that the two sides were* ***on an equal footing*** (=had the same advantages and disadvantages). **2** a firm hold with your feet on a surface: *He* ***lost*** *his* ***footing*** *and fell down the stairs.*

foot·lights /ˈfʊtlaɪts/ *n.* [plural] a row of lights along the front of the stage in a theater

ˈfoot ˌlocker *n.* [C] a large strong box that you keep your things in

foot·loose /ˈfʊtlus/ *adj.* able to do what you want and enjoy yourself because you are not responsible for anyone or anything: *No, I'm not married – still* ***footloose and fancy free****.*

foot·note /ˈfʊt˺noʊt/ *n.* [C] a note at the bottom of the page in a book that gives more information about something on that page

foot·path /ˈfʊtpæθ/ *n.* [C] a TRAIL

foot·print /ˈfʊtˌprɪnt/ *n.* [C] a mark made by a foot or shoe: *a deer's footprints in the snow* → see picture at FINGERPRINT

foot·rest /ˈfʊt˺rɛst/ *n.* [C] a part of a chair that you can raise or lower in order to support your feet when you are sitting down

foot·sie /ˈfʊtsi/ *n.* **play footsie (with sb)** *informal* to secretly touch someone's feet with your feet under a table, to show that you think s/he is sexually attractive

foot·step /ˈfʊtstɛp/ *n.* [C] the sound of each step when someone is walking: *He heard someone's footsteps in the hall.* → **follow (in) sb's footsteps** at FOLLOW

foot·stool /ˈfʊtstul/ *n.* [C] a low piece of furniture used for supporting your feet when you are sitting down

foot·wear /ˈfʊt˺wɛr/ *n.* [U] things you wear on your feet, such as shoes or boots

foot·work /ˈfʊt˺wɚk/ *n.* [U] skillful use of your feet when dancing or playing a sport: *the dancer's* ***fancy footwork***

for¹ /fɚ; *strong* fɔr/ *prep.* **1** intended to be given to or used by a particular person or group: *Save a piece of cake for Noah. | Somebody left a message for you. | We made cookies for the party.* **2** used in order to show the purpose of an object, action, etc.: *a knife for cutting bread |* ***What*** *did you* ***do*** *that* ***for****?* (=why did you do it?) | ***What's*** *this gadget* ***for****?* (=what is its purpose?) **3 for sale/rent** used in order to show that something is available to be sold or rented: *They've just put their house up for sale.* **4** in order to get or do something: *Alison is looking for a job. | We were waiting for the bus. | Let's* ***go for*** *a walk. |* ***For more information****, write to this address.* **5** used in order to show the time when something is planned to happen: *an appointment for 3:00 |* ***It's time for*** *dinner* (=we're going to have dinner now). **6** in order to help someone: *Let me lift that box for you. |* ***What can I do for you?*** (=can I help you?) **7** used in order to talk about a particular length of time: *I've known Kim for a long time. | Bake the cake for 40 minutes.*

USAGE

For is followed by words describing a length of time and is used to say how long something continues: *She was in the hospital for two weeks.*
During is followed by a particular period of time and is used to say when something happens: *During the summer, she worked as a lifeguard.*

8 because of or as a result of: *I got a ticket for going through a red light. | The award for the highest sales goes to Pete McGregor.* **9** used in order to show where a person, vehicle, etc. is going: *The plane for Las Vegas took off an hour late. | I was just leaving for church when the phone rang.* **10** used in order to express a distance: *We walked for miles.* **11** used in order to show a price or amount: *a check for $100 | an order for 200 copies | I'm not working* ***for nothing/for free*** (=without being paid). **12 for breakfast/lunch/dinner** used in order to say what you ate or will eat at breakfast, LUNCH, etc.: ***"What's for lunch?"*** *"Hamburgers." | We* ***had***

steak ***for dinner*** *last night.* **13 for sb/sth to do sth** used when discussing what is happening, what may happen, or what can happen: *It's unusual* ***for*** *it* ***to*** *be this cold in June.* | *The plan is* ***for*** *us* ***to*** *leave on Friday morning and pick up Joe.* **14** if you are happy, sad, etc. for someone, you feel happy, sad, etc. because something has happened to him or her: *I'm really happy for you.* | *He has a lot of respect for his teachers.* **15 for now** used in order to say that a situation can be changed later: *Just put the pictures in a box for now.* **16 work for/play for etc.** to play a sport on a particular team, work at a particular company, etc.: *She worked for Exxon until last year.* | *He plays for the Boston Red Sox.* **17** supporting or agreeing with someone or something: *How many people voted for Mulhoney?* | *I'm for getting a pizza, what about you?* **18 for all a)** considering how little: *For all the good I did, I shouldn't have tried to help.* **b)** in spite of: *For all his expensive education, Leo doesn't know very much.* **19 for all I know/care** *spoken* used in order to say that you really do not know or care: *He could be in Canada by now for all I know.* **20 for Christmas/for sb's birthday etc.** in order to celebrate Christmas, someone's BIRTHDAY, etc.: *What did you get for your birthday?* | *We went to my grandmother's for Thanksgiving last year.* **21** having the same meaning as another word, sign, etc.: *What's the Spanish word for oil?* **22** when you consider a particular fact: *Libby's very tall for her age.* **23 if it hadn't been for/if it weren't for sb/sth** if something had not happened, or if a situation were different: *If it weren't for Michelle's help, we'd never get this job done.*

for² *conjunction literary* because

for·age /ˈfɔrɪdʒ, ˈfɑr-/ *v.* [I] to go to a lot of places searching for food or other supplies: *animals* ***foraging for*** *food*

for·ay /ˈfɔreɪ, ˈfɑreɪ/ *n.* [C] **1** a short attempt at doing a particular job or activity: *a brief* ***foray into*** *politics* **2** a short sudden attack by a group of soldiers

for·bade /fɚˈbæd/ *v.* the past tense of FORBID

for·bear·ance /fɔrˈbɛrəns, fɚ-/ *n.* [U] *literary* the quality of being patient, having control over your emotions, and being willing to forgive someone

for·bid /fɚˈbɪd/ *v.* past tense **forbade** /-ˈbæd/ past participle **forbidden** /-ˈbɪdn/ [T] **1** to order someone not to do something [≠ **permit**]: *I* ***forbid*** *you* ***to*** *see that man again.*

THESAURUS

not allow/permit/let – to say that someone must not do something, and stop him/her doing it: *People are not allowed to sell food or drinks along the parade route.*

ban – to officially say that people must not do something or that something is not allowed: *The country's government has banned foreign journalists from the area.*

prohibit – to say officially that an action is illegal or not allowed: *In the sea near the reef, the use of anchors is prohibited.*

bar – to officially prevent someone from doing something: *During the drought, residents were barred from watering their lawns.*

2 God/Heaven forbid *spoken* said in order to emphasize that you hope that something will not happen: *God forbid you should have an accident.*

for·bid·den /fɚˈbɪdn/ *adj.* not allowed, especially because of an official rule: ***It's forbidden to*** *smoke in the hospital.* | *This area is* ***forbidden to*** *everyone but the police.*

for·bid·ding /fɚˈbɪdɪŋ/ *adj.* looking frightening, unfriendly, or dangerous: *The mountains looked more forbidding as we got closer.*

force¹ /fɔrs/ *n.*

1 TRAINED GROUP [C] a group of people who have been trained to do military or police work [➡ **armed forces, air force, police force**]: *Rebel forces are seeking to overthrow the government* | *More* ***military forces*** *are being sent to the region.*

2 VIOLENT ACTION [U] violent physical action used in order to achieve something: *The police* ***used force*** *to break up the demonstration.* | *an investigation into the excessive* ***use of force***

3 NATURAL POWER a) [U] the natural power that is used or produced when one thing moves or hits another thing: *Waves were hitting the rocks* ***with great force.*** | *The* ***force of*** *the explosion threw her backwards.* **b)** [C,U] a natural power that produces movement in another object: *the* ***force of*** *gravity*

THESAURUS

force – the natural power that something has: *The force of the wind knocked the fence down.*

power – the physical strength of something such as an explosion, or the energy produced by a natural force: *wind power* | *Their home is heated by solar power.*

strength – the physical quality that makes you strong: *I don't have the strength to lift this.*

4 SB/STH THAT INFLUENCES [C] something or someone that has a strong influence or a lot of power: *Mandela was the* ***driving force*** *behind the changes* (=the one who made them happen). | *Technology can be a* ***force for*** *good* (=it can make good things happen).

5 STRONG EFFECT [U] the powerful effect of someone or something: *The* ***force of*** *public opinion stopped the new highway project.*

6 join/combine forces to work together to do something: *Various community groups have joined forces on the project.*

7 in force a) if a law or rule is in force, it must

F

be obeyed **b)** in a large group: *The mosquitoes are going to be* ***out in force*** *tonight!*
8 by/from force of habit because you have always done a particular thing: *Ken puts salt on everything by force of habit.*

force² *v.* [T] **1** to make someone do something s/he does not want to do: *Nobody's* ***forcing*** *you* ***to*** *come, you know.* | *I had to* ***force myself*** *to get up this morning.* | *Bad health* ***forced*** *him* ***into*** *early retirement.*

THESAURUS

make – to force someone to do something: *I wish there were something I could do to make her quit smoking.*
coerce formal – to force someone to do something by threatening him/her: *They have no right to coerce you into doing anything.*
compel – to force someone to do something: *She felt compelled to resign because of the scandal.*
pressure – to try to make someone do something by using influence, arguments, threats, etc: *Don't let them pressure you into making a donation.*

F

2 to use physical strength to move something or go somewhere: *Firefighters had to* ***force open*** *the door* (=open it using force). | *The doctor* ***forced*** *his* ***way through*** *the crowd.* **3 force the issue** to do something that makes it necessary for someone to make decisions or take action: *Don't force the issue; give them time to decide.*

force sth ⇔ **on/upon** sb *phr. v.* to make someone accept something even though s/he does not want it: *They tried to force their own views on me.*

forced /fɔrst/ *adj.* **1** done because you must do something, not because of any sincere feeling: *a forced smile* **2** [only before noun] done suddenly and quickly because a situation makes it necessary: *The plane had to make a forced landing in a field.*

ˈforce-feed *v.* past tense and past participle **force-fed** [T] to force someone to eat by putting food or liquid down his/her throat

force·ful /ˈfɔrsfəl/ *adj.* powerful and strong: *a forceful personality* | *a forceful argument* —**forcefully** *adv.*

for·ceps /ˈfɔrsəps, -sɛps/ *n.* [plural] a medical tool used for picking up, holding, or pulling things

forc·i·ble /ˈfɔrsəbəl/ *adj.* done using physical force: *There aren't any signs of* ***forcible entry*** *into the building.* —**forcibly** *adv.*: *The demonstrators were forcibly removed from the embassy.*

ford¹ /fɔrd/ *n.* [C] a place in a river that is not deep, so that you can walk or drive across it

ford² *v.* [T] to walk or drive across a river at a place where it is not too deep

fore /fɔr/ *n.* **come to the fore** to become important or begin to have influence: *Environmental issues came to the fore in the 1980s.*

fore·arm /ˈfɔrɑrm/ *n.* [C] the lower part of the arm between the hand and the elbow

fore·bear /ˈfɔrbɛr/ *n.* [C usually plural] *formal* the people who were part of your family a long time ago [= **ancestor**]

fore·bod·ing /fɔrˈboʊdɪŋ/ *n.* [C,U] a feeling that something bad will happen soon: *We waited for news of the men with a* ***sense of foreboding****.*

fore·cast¹ /ˈfɔrkæst/ *n.* [C] a description of what is likely to happen in the future, based on information you have now: *the* ***weather forecast*** | *the company's* ***sales forecast***

forecast² past tense and past participle **forecast** or **forecasted** *v.* [T] to say what is likely to happen in the future, based on information you have now: *Warm weather has been forecast for this weekend.* —**forecaster** *n.* [C] *a weather forecaster* | *a stock market forecaster*

THESAURUS

predict, prophesy, foresee, have a premonition
→ see Thesaurus box at PREDICT

fore·close /fɔrˈkloʊz/ *v.* [I] *technical* to take away someone's property because s/he cannot pay back the money that s/he has borrowed to buy it —**foreclosure** /fɔrˈkloʊʒɚ/ *n.* [C,U]

fore·fa·ther /ˈfɔrˌfɑðɚz/ *n.* [C usually plural] the people who were part of your family a long time ago [= **ancestor**]

fore·fin·ger /ˈfɔrˌfɪŋgɚ/ *n.* [C] the finger next to your thumb [= **index finger**]

fore·front /ˈfɔrfrʌnt/ *n.* **in/at/to the forefront of sth** in the main or most important position: *The company has always been at the forefront of science and technology.*

fore·gone con·clu·sion /ˌfɔrgɔn kənˈkluʒən/ *n.* **be a foregone conclusion** if something is a foregone conclusion, the result of it is certain even though it has not happened yet

fore·ground /ˈfɔrgraʊnd/ *n.* **the foreground** the part of a picture, photograph, etc. nearest to you [≠ **background**]

fore·head /ˈfɔrhɛd, ˈfɔrɪd, ˈfɑrɪd/ *n.* [C] the part of the face above the eyes and below the hair: *He wiped his forehead with a handkerchief.* → see picture on page A3

for·eign /ˈfɑrɪn, ˈfɔrɪn/ *adj.* **1** not from your own country: *Can you speak a foreign language?* | *He was in a foreign country, far away from home.* **2** [only before noun] involving or dealing with other countries [≠ **domestic**]: *American* ***foreign policy*** | *The budget calls for cuts in* ***foreign aid****.* **3 foreign to sb** not familiar, or not typical: *Their way of life was* ***completely foreign*** *to her.* **4 foreign body/matter** *technical* something that has come into a place where it does not belong, especially someone's body: *foreign matter in someone's eye*

for·eign·er /ˈfɑrənɚ, ˈfɔr-/ *n.* [C] someone who is from a country that is not your own

ˌforeign exˈchange *n.* **1** [U] the system of buying and selling foreign money: *The dollar is expected to fall in the **foreign exchange markets**.* **2** [C] an arrangement in which people, especially students, travel to another country to work or study for a particular length of time: *a **foreign exchange student***

fore·leg /ˈfɔrlɛg/ *n.* [C] one of the two front legs of an animal that has four legs

fore·man /ˈfɔrmən/ *n.* plural **foremen** /-mən/ [C] **1** someone who is in charge of a group of workers, for example, in a factory **2** the leader of a JURY

fore·most /ˈfɔrmoʊst/ *adj.* [only before noun] the most famous or important: *the foremost writer of her time*

fo·ren·sic /fəˈrɛnsɪk, -zɪk/ *adj.* [only before noun] relating to methods for finding out about a crime: *the analysis of forensic evidence* —**forensics** *n.* [U]

fore·play /ˈfɔrpleɪ/ *n.* [U] sexual activity, such as touching the sexual organs and kissing, that happens before having sex

fore·run·ner /ˈfɔrˌrʌnɚ/ *n.* [C] someone or something that is an early example or a sign of something that comes later: *a race that was the **forerunner of** the Grand Prix*

fore·see /fɔrˈsi/ *v.* past tense **foresaw** /-ˈsɔ/ past participle **foreseen** /-ˈsin/ [T] *formal* to know that something will happen before it happens [= **predict**]: *No one could have foreseen such a disaster.*

THESAURUS

predict, prophesy, forecast, have a premonition
→ see Thesaurus box at PREDICT

fore·see·a·ble /fɔrˈsiəbəl/ *adj.* **1 for/in the foreseeable future** continuing for as long as you can imagine: *Leila will be staying here for the foreseeable future.* **2 in the foreseeable future** fairly soon: *There is a chance of water shortages in the foreseeable future.* **3** foreseeable difficulties, events, etc. should be planned for because they are very likely to happen in the future

fore·shad·ow /fɔrˈʃædoʊ/ *v.* [T] *literary* to be a sign of something that will happen in the future

fore·sight /ˈfɔrsaɪt/ *n.* [singular, U] the ability to imagine what might happen in the future, and to consider this in your plans: *Luckily, we'd **had** the **foresight** to get plenty of food.*

fore·skin /ˈfɔrˌskɪn/ *n.* [C] a loose fold of skin covering the end of a man's PENIS

forest

for·est /ˈfɔrɪst, ˈfɑr-/ *n.* [C,U] a very large area of land that is covered with trees: *tropical rain forests* | *a **virgin forest*** (=a forest that is still in its natural state and has not been used or changed by people)

THESAURUS

woods, woodland, rain forest, jungle
→ see Thesaurus box at TREE

fore·stall /fɔrˈstɔl/ *v.* [T] to prevent something from happening by doing something first: *The National Guard was sent in, to forestall trouble.*

ˌforest ˈranger *n.* [C] someone whose job is to protect or manage part of a public forest

for·est·ry /ˈfɔrəstri, ˈfɑr-/ *n.* [U] the science and practice of planting and taking care of forests

fore·taste /ˈfɔrteɪst/ *n.* **be a foretaste of something** to be a sign of something more important, more impressive, etc. that will happen in the future

fore·tell /fɔrˈtɛl/ *v.* past tense and past participle **foretold** /-ˈtoʊld/ [T] to say what will happen in the future, especially by using special magic powers

fore·thought /ˈfɔrθɔt/ *n.* [U] careful thought or planning before you do something

for·ev·er /fəˈrɛvɚ, fɔ-/ *adv.* **1** for all future time [= **always**]: *I wanted the holiday to **last forever**.* | *You can't avoid him forever.*

THESAURUS

always, permanently, for life, for good
→ see Thesaurus box at ALWAYS

2 *spoken* for a very long time: *Greg will probably be a student forever.* | *It'll **take forever** to drive to Helen's.* **3 go on forever** to be extremely long or large: *The roads out west seem to go on forever.*

fore·warn /fɔrˈwɔrn/ *v.* [T] **1** to warn someone about something dangerous or unpleasant that may happen **2 forewarned is forearmed** used in order to say that if you know about something before it happens, you can be prepared for it

fore·wom·an /ˈfɔrˌwʊmən/ *n.* [C] **1** a woman who is the leader of a group of workers, for

F

example in a factory **2** a woman who is the leader of a JURY

fore·word /ˈfɔrwɚd/ *n.* [C] a short piece of writing at the beginning of a book that introduces the book or the person who wrote it

for·feit¹ /ˈfɔrfɪt/ *v.* [T] to give something up or have it taken away from you because of a rule or law: *criminals who have **forfeited** their **right** to freedom.*

forfeit² *n.* [C] something that you have to give away or do as a punishment because you have broken a rule or law

for·gave /fɚˈgeɪv/ *v.* the past tense of FORGIVE

forge¹ /fɔrdʒ/ *v.* [T] **1** to illegally copy something such as a document, a painting, or money in order to make people think it is real: *The signature on the check had been forged.*

THESAURUS

copy, **pirate**
➔ see Thesaurus box at COPY²

2 to develop something new, especially a strong relationship with other people or groups: *A special alliance has been forged between the U.S. and Canada.* **3** to make something from a piece of metal by heating and shaping it

forge ahead *phr. v.* to make progress: *The organizers are **forging ahead with** a program of public events.*

forge² *n.* [C] a large piece of equipment that is used for heating and shaping metal objects, or the building where this is done

forg·er /ˈfɔrdʒɚ/ *n.* [C] someone who illegally copies documents, money, paintings, etc. and tries to make people think they are real

for·ger·y /ˈfɔrdʒəri/ *n.* plural **forgeries** **1** [C] a document, painting, or piece of paper money that has been illegally copied [**= fake**]: *An art dealer insisted that the portrait is a forgery.* **2** [U] the crime of illegally copying something

for·get /fɚˈgɛt/ *v.* past tense **forgot** /-ˈgɑt/ past participle **forgotten** /-ˈgɑt˺n/ present participle **forgetting** **1** [I,T] to be unable to remember facts, information, or something that happened: *I've forgotten her name.* ► Don't say "I am forgetting." ◄ *I know you told me, but I forgot.* | *He **forgot all about** our anniversary.* **2** [I,T] to not remember to do something that you should do: *I **forgot to** turn off my headlights.* | *David had **forgotten (that)** we had a meeting.* **3** [T] to not remember to bring something that you should have taken with you: *Oh, I forgot your book.*

USAGE

You can say "I forgot my passport." You cannot say "I forgot my passport at home."
When you want to talk about the place where you left something by mistake, you must use "leave": *I left my passport at home.*

4 [I,T] to stop thinking or worrying about someone or something: *You'll **forget (that)** you're wearing contact lenses after a while.* | *I'll never forget her.* | *I can't just **forget about** the accident.* **5** [I,T] to stop planning to do or get something because it is no longer possible: *With this injury, you can **forget about** playing this season.*

SPOKEN PHRASES

6 forget it **a)** used in order to tell someone that something is not important: *"I'm sorry I broke your mug." "Forget it."* | *"Did you say something?" "No, forget it."* **b)** used in order to tell someone to stop asking or talking about something because it is annoying you: *I'm not buying you that bike, so just forget it.* **7 don't forget** used in order to remind someone about something: *Don't forget your lunchbox!* | *Don't forget to turn off the lights.* **8 I forget** *nonstandard* said instead of "I have forgotten": *You know the guy we saw last week – I forget his name.* **9 forget it/you/that!** used in order to refuse to do something, or to say that something is impossible: *Drive to the airport in this snow? Forget it.* **10 ...and don't you forget it!** said in order to remind someone angrily about something important that should make him/her behave differently: *I'm your father, and don't you forget it!*

for·get·ful /fɚˈgɛtfəl/ *adj.* often forgetting things —**forgetfulness** *n.* [U]

for'get-me-ˌnot *n.* [C] a plant with small blue flowers

for·give /fɚˈgɪv/ *v.* past tense **forgave** /-ˈgeɪv/ past participle **forgiven** /-ˈgɪvən/ [I,T] **1** to stop being angry and blaming someone, although s/he has done something wrong: *I can't **forgive** him **for** what he did to her.* | *"I'm sorry." "That's OK – **you're forgiven** (=I forgive you)."* | *If anything happened to the kids, I'd never **forgive myself**.* | *Maybe you can **forgive and forget**, but I can't* (=forgive someone and behave as if s/he had never done anything wrong). **2 forgive me** *spoken* said when you are going to say or ask something that might seem rude or offensive: ***Forgive me for saying so**, but that's nonsense.* **3 forgive a loan/debt** if a country forgives a LOAN, it says that the country that borrowed the money does not have to pay it back

for·give·ness /fɚˈgɪvnɪs/ *n.* [U] *formal* the act of forgiving someone

for·giv·ing /fɚˈgɪvɪŋ/ *adj.* willing to forgive: *a forgiving person*

for·go /fɔrˈgoʊ/ *v.* [T] *formal* to decide not to do or have something

for·got /fɚˈgɑt/ *v.* the past tense of FORGET

for·got·ten /fɚˈgɑt˺n/ *v.* the past participle of FORGET

fork¹ /fɔrk/ *n.* [C] **1** a tool used for picking up and eating food, with a handle and three or four points: *knives, forks, and spoons* **2** a place where a road or river divides into two parts: *Turn left at* *the fork in the road.* **3** a tool with a handle and three or four points, used for digging and breaking up soil: *a gardening fork* **4** → PITCHFORK

fork² *v.* **1** [I] if a road or river forks, it divides into two parts **2** [T] to pick up, carry, or turn something over using a fork

fork sth ⇔ **over/out** *phr. v. informal* to spend a lot of money on something because you have to: *If I'm going to fork over $25 for a book, I want to be sure it's good.*

forked /fɔrkt/ *adj.* with one end divided into two or more parts: *a snake's forked tongue*

fork·lift /ˈfɔrkˌlɪft/ *n.* [C] a vehicle with special equipment on the front for lifting and moving heavy things, for example, in a factory

for·lorn /fɚˈlɔrn, fɔr-/ *adj. literary* sad and lonely: *The child looked forlorn.*

form¹ /fɔrm/ *n.* **1** [C] one type of something, that exists in many different varieties [= **kind**]: *ballet and other **forms of** dance | a severe **form of** cancer* **2** [C,U] the way in which something exists or appears: *You can get the vitamin C **in** tablet or liquid **form**. | The story is written **in the form of** a letter. | Language practice can **take the form of** drills or exercises.* **3** [C] an official document with spaces where you have to provide information: *an application form for college | Please **fill out** the **form** in black ink.* **4** [C] a shape, especially of something you cannot see clearly: *dark forms behind the trees* **5** [C] *technical* in grammar, a way of writing or saying a word that shows its number, tense, etc. For example, "was" is a past form of the verb "to be."

form² *v.* **1** [I,T] to start to exist, or to make something start to exist [= **develop**]: *Ice was already **forming on** the roads. | the cloud of dust and gas that formed the universe | Reporters had already **formed the impression** (=begun to think) that Myers was guilty.* **2** [I,T, linking verb] to come together in a particular shape or a line, or to make something have a particular shape: ***Form** the dough **into** a circle, then roll it out. | The line forms to the right. | The birch trees formed a ring around a grassy hollow.* **3** [T] to start a new organization, committee, relationship, etc.: *Students formed a protest group. | Everett seemed unable to form close friendships.* **4** [T] to make something by combining two or more parts: *One way to form nouns is to add the suffix "-ness."* **5** [linking verb] to be the thing, or one of the things, that makes up something else: *Rice forms a basic part of their diet. | The Rio Grande forms the boundary between Texas and Mexico.*

for·mal¹ /ˈfɔrməl/ *adj.* **1** formal language, behavior, or clothes are used for official or serious situations, or for when you do not know the people you are with very well [≠ **informal**]: *a formal letter | Jack won't wear a tie, even on **formal occasions**. | men's **formal wear*** (=clothes for important events, parties, etc.) **2** official or public [≠ **informal**]: *a formal announcement | The German Democratic Republic was the formal name of East Germany.* **3 formal education/training/qualifications** education in a subject or skill that you get in school rather than by practical experience: *Most priests have no formal training in counseling.* —**formally** *adv.*: *The winner will be formally announced this afternoon.*

formal² *n.* [C] **1** a dance at which you have to wear formal clothes **2** an expensive and usually long dress that women wear on formal occasions

for·mal·de·hyde /fɚˈmældəˌhaɪd, fɔr-/ *n.* [U] a strong-smelling gas that can be mixed with water and used for preserving things such as parts of a body

for·mal·i·ty /fɔrˈmæləṭi/ *n.* **1** [C usually plural] something formal or official that you must do as part of an activity or process, even though it may not have any practical importance: *I need your signature here, but it's **just a formality**.* **2** [U] careful attention to polite behavior or language in formal situations

for·mal·ize /ˈfɔrməˌlaɪz/ *v.* [T] to make a plan or decision official and describe all its details: *The contracts must be formalized within one month.*

for·mat¹ /ˈfɔrmæt/ *n.* [C] **1** the way something such as a computer document, television show, or meeting is organized or arranged: *The interview was written in a question and answer format.* **2** used when talking about what type of equipment is needed to play a video, CD, tape, etc. **3** the size, shape, design, etc. in which something such as a book or magazine is produced: *large-format books for the visually impaired*

format² *v.* past tense and past participle **formatted**, present participle **formatting** [T] **1** *technical* to organize the space on a computer DISK so that information can be stored on it **2** to arrange a book, document, page, etc. according to a particular design or plan —**formatting** *n.* [U] —**formatted** *adj.*

for·ma·tion /fɔrˈmeɪʃən/ *n.* **1** [U] the process by which something develops into a particular thing or shape: *the **formation of** the solar system* **2** [U] the process of starting a new organization or group: *the **formation of** a democratic government* **3** [C,U] something that is formed in a particular shape, or the shape in which it is formed: *rock formations | soldiers marching **in formation*** (=in a special order)

form·a·tive /ˈfɔrməṭɪv/ *adj.* having an important influence on the way someone or something develops: *a child's **formative years*** (=when his/her character develops)

for·mer¹ /ˈfɔrmɚ/ *adj.* **1** having a particular position in the past, but not now: *our former president*

THESAURUS

last, previous
→ see Thesaurus box at LAST¹

F

2 happening or existing before, but not now: *the former Soviet Union*

former² *n.* **the former** *formal* the first of two people or things that are mentioned [➥ **latter**]: *Of the two possibilities, the former seems more likely.*

for·mer·ly /ˈfɔrmɚli/ *adv.* in earlier times: *New York was formerly called New Amsterdam.*

for·mi·da·ble /ˈfɔrmədəbəl, fɔrˈmɪdə-/ *adj.* **1** very powerful or impressive: *a formidable opponent | He had a formidable lead in the polls.* **2** difficult to deal with and needing a lot of skill: *the formidable task of working out a peace plan* —**formidably** *adv.*

form·less /ˈfɔrmlɪs/ *adj.* without a definite shape

ˈform ˌletter *n.* [C] a standard letter that is sent to many people, without any personal details in it

for·mu·la /ˈfɔrmyələ/ *n.* plural **formulas** or **formulae** /ˈfɔrmyəli/ **1** [C] a method or set of principles that you use in order to solve a problem or to make sure that something is successful: *a **formula for** peace | There's no **magic formula for** a happy marriage.* **2** [C] a series of numbers or letters that represent a mathematical or scientific rule **3** [C] a list of substances used in order to make something, showing the amounts of each substance to use: *Coca Cola's secret formula* **4** [C,U] a liquid food for babies that is similar to a woman's breast milk

for·mu·late /ˈfɔrmyəˌleɪt/ *v.* [T] **1** to develop something such as a plan or set of rules, and decide all the details of how it will be done: *What role does he have in formulating foreign policy?* **2** to think carefully about what you want to say, and say it clearly: *Ricardo asked for time to formulate a reply.* —**formulation** /ˌfɔrmyəˈleɪʃən/ *n.* [C,U]

for·sake /fɚˈseɪk, fɔr-/ *v.* past tense **forsook** /-ˈsʊk/ past participle **forsaken** /-ˈseɪkən/ [T] *formal* **1** to leave someone, especially when s/he needs you **2** to leave a place or stop doing or having something: *We have forsaken our heritage.*

fort /fɔrt/ *n.* [C] a strong building or group of buildings used by soldiers or an army for defending an important place

forte /fɔrt, ˈfɔrteɪ/ *n.* **be sb's forte** to be something that someone is good at doing: *Cooking isn't my forte.*

forth /fɔrθ/ *adv.* **go forth** *literary* to go out or away from where you are ➔ **back and forth** at BACK¹ ➔ **and so on/forth** at SO¹

forth·com·ing /ˌfɔrθˈkʌmɪŋ◂/ *adj.* *formal* **1** happening or coming soon: *her forthcoming novel* **2** given or offered when needed: *If more money is not forthcoming, we'll have to close the theater.* **3** willing to give information about something: *Lassen was not very forthcoming.*

forth·right /ˈfɔrθraɪt/ *adj.* saying honestly what you think, in a way that may seem rude: *a forthright answer*

THESAURUS

honest, **frank**, **candid**, **direct**, **straightforward**, **blunt**

➔ see Thesaurus box at HONEST

for·ti·eth /ˈfɔrt̬iɪθ/ *number* 40th

for·ti·fi·ca·tion /ˌfɔrt̬əfəˈkeɪʃən/ *n.* **1** [U] the process of making something stronger **2 fortifications** [plural] towers, walls, etc. built around a place in order to protect it

for·ti·fy /ˈfɔrt̬əˌfaɪ/ *v.* past tense and past participle **fortified**, third person singular **fortifies** [T] **1** to build towers, walls, etc. around a place in order to defend it: *a fortified city* **2** *formal* **or** *humorous* to make someone feel physically or mentally stronger: *She was fortified by her friends' prayers.* **3** to make food or drinks more healthy by adding VITAMINS to them: *vitamin D fortified milk*

for·ti·tude /ˈfɔrt̬əˌtud/ *n.* [U] courage shown when you are in pain or having a lot of trouble

for·tress /ˈfɔrtrɪs/ *n.* [C] a large, strong building used for defending an important place

for·tu·i·tous /fɔrˈtuət̬əs/ *adj.* *formal* lucky and happening by chance: *a fortuitous discovery*

for·tu·nate /ˈfɔrtʃənɪt/ *adj.* **1** lucky [≠ **unfortunate**]: *We were **fortunate enough to** get tickets for the last show. | It was **fortunate that** the ambulance arrived so quickly.* **2 less fortunate** people who are less fortunate are poor: *Less fortunate children should still get a good education. | Welfare should provide a safety net for **the less fortunate*** (=poor people).

for·tu·nate·ly /ˈfɔrtʃənɪtli/ *adv.* happening because of good luck: *Fortunately, firefighters quickly put out the blaze.*

for·tune /ˈfɔrtʃən/ *n.* **1** [C] a very large amount of money: *Hunter **made a fortune*** (=earned a lot of money) *in real estate. | Julia must've **spent a fortune** on her wedding dress. | He lost a **small fortune*** (=a lot of money) *playing the stock market.* **2** [U] chance or luck: *I **had the good fortune** to have Mrs. Dawson as my instructor.* **3** [C usually plural] the good or bad things that happen in life: *The loss marked a change in the team's fortunes.* **4 tell sb's fortune** to tell someone what will happen to him/her in the future, by using special cards, or looking at his/her hand, etc.

ˈfortune ˌcookie *n.* [C] a Chinese-American cookie with a piece of paper inside it that tells you what will happen in your future

ˈfortune ˌteller *n.* [C] someone who tells you what is going to happen to you in the future

for·ty /ˈfɔrt̬i/ *number* **1** 40 **2 the forties a)** the years between 1940 and 1949 **b)** the numbers between 40 and 49, especially when used for measuring temperature **3 be in your forties** to be aged between 40 and 49: *He's in his **early/mid/late forties**.* —**fortieth** *number*

fo·rum /ˈfɔrəm/ *n.* [C] **1** an organization, meeting, report, etc. in which people have a chance to publicly discuss an important subject: *a **forum for** discussing ideas | a **forum on** neighborhood crime* **2** a group of computer users who are interested in a particular subject and discuss it using a website on the Internet

for·ward¹ /ˈfɔrwɚd/ **also forwards** *adv.* **1** toward a place or position that is in front of you [≠ **backward**]: *The crowd moved forward. | He **leaned forward** to hear what they were saying.* **2** toward more progress, improvement, or development: *NASA's space project cannot **go forward** without more money. | The business is ready to **move forward**.* **3** toward the future [≠ **backward**]: *The company must **look forward*** (=make plans for the future) *and use the newest technology.* → FAST FORWARD → **look forward to sth** at LOOK¹ → **step forward** at STEP²

forward² *adj.* **1 forward progress/planning/thinking etc.** progress, plans, ideas, etc. that are helpful in a way that prepares you for the future **2** [only before noun] closer to a person, place, etc. that is in front of you [≠ **backward**]: *Troops were moved to a forward position on the battlefield.* **3** [only before noun] at the front part of a ship, car, airplane, etc. [≠ **rear**]: *the forward cabin*

forward³ *v.* [T] to send a message or letter that you have received to the person it was intended for, usually at his/her new address: *The Post Office should be forwarding all my mail.*

forward⁴ *n.* [C] in basketball, one of two players whose main job is to SHOOT the ball at the other team's BASKET

ˈforwarding adˌdress *n.* [C] an address you give to someone when you move so that s/he can send your mail to you

ˈforward-ˌlooking also ˈforward-ˌthinking *adj.* thinking about and planning for the future in a positive way, especially by being willing to try new ideas

fossil

fos·sil /ˈfɑsəl/ *n.* [C] part of an animal or plant that lived millions of years ago, or the shape of one of these plants or animals that is now preserved in rock —**fossil** *adj.*

ˈfossil ˌfuel *n.* [C,U] a FUEL such as gas or oil that has been formed from plants and animals that lived millions of years ago

fos·sil·ize /ˈfɑsəˌlaɪz/ *v.* [I,T] to become a FOSSIL by being preserved in rock, or to make something do this

fos·ter¹ /ˈfɔstɚ, ˈfɑ-/ *v.* [T] **1** to help to develop an idea, skill, feeling, etc.: *Teachers want to foster a spirit of cooperation in their classrooms.* **2** to take care of someone else's child for a period of time without becoming his/her legal parent [➡ **adopt**]

foster² *adj.* **1 foster mother/father/parents/family** the person or people who FOSTER a child **2 foster child** a child who is fostered **3 foster home** a person's or family's home where a child is fostered

fought /fɔt/ the past tense and past participle of FIGHT

foul¹ /faʊl/ *v.* **1** [I,T] to do something in a sport that is against the rules: *Rickey fouled the first pitch* (=hit it outside the legal area). *| Sal hit two free throws after being fouled.* **2** [T] to make something very dirty: *The water had been fouled by industrial waste.*

foul (sth ⇔) **up** *phr. v. informal* to do something wrong or to ruin something by making a mistake: *Glen fouled up the seating arrangements. | You've totally fouled up this time.*

foul² *adj.* **1** very dirty or not having a pleasant smell or taste: *A foul smell filled the cell. | foul-tasting coffee*

> **THESAURUS**
>
> **horrible, disgusting, awful, revolting, terrible, dreadful**
>
> → see Thesaurus box at HORRIBLE

2 foul language rude and offensive words **3 in a foul mood/temper** likely to get angry easily **4 foul weather** bad weather, with strong winds, rain, or snow

foul³ *n.* [C] an action in a sport that is against the rules

ˌfoul ˈplay *n.* [C,U] **1** murder or illegal violence: *Cattrell may have been the victim of foul play.* **2** an activity that is dishonest and unfair

ˈfoul-up *n.* [C] *informal* a mistake: *a bureaucratic foul-up*

found¹ /faʊnd/ the past tense and past participle of FIND

found² *v.* [T] **1** to start an organization, town, or institution that is intended to continue for a long time: *The college was founded in 1701. | The Center for Auto Safety was founded by Ralph Nader.* **2 be founded on/upon sth** to base your ideas, beliefs, etc. on something: *The U.S. was founded on the idea of religious freedom.*

foun·da·tion /faʊnˈdeɪʃən/ *n.* **1** [C] an idea, fact, or system from which a religion, way of life, etc. develops: *The Constitution **provided/laid the foundation for** the American government. | The children had a **solid foundation** in reading and writing.* **2** [C] an organization that gives or collects money to be used for special purposes: *the National Foundation for the Arts* **3** [C] the solid base that is built underground to support a building: *It should take them about three weeks to **lay the foundation*** (=build it). **4** [C,U] the action of establishing an organization, city, or institution **5 without foundation** not true, reasonable, or able to be proved: *Luckily my fears were without foundation.*

found·er¹ /ˈfaʊndɚ/ *n.* [C] someone who estab-

F

lishes a business, organization, school, etc.: *the founders of Brandon College*

founder[2] *v.* [I] *formal* **1** to fail after a period of time: *His campaign foundered before the first primary.* **2** if a ship or boat founders, it fills with water and sinks

ˌfounding 'father *n.* **the Founding Fathers** the men who started the government of the U.S. by writing the Constitution and the Bill of Rights

found·ry /'faʊndri/ *n.* plural **foundries** [C] a place where metals are melted and made into new parts for machines

foun·tain /'faʊntˀn/ *n.* [C] a structure that sends water straight up into the air, built for decoration → DRINKING FOUNTAIN

four /fɔr/ *number, n.* [C] **1** 4 **2** four O'CLOCK: *I'll meet you at four.* **3** four years old: *My son is four.* **4 on all fours** on your hands and knees: *Andy was on all fours looking for something.*

ˌfour-leaf 'clover *n.* [C] a CLOVER plant with four leaves instead of the usual three, that is considered to be lucky

ˌfour-letter 'word *n.* [C] a word that is considered offensive or shocking by most people

F

four·teen /ˌfɔr'tin◂/ *number* 14 —**fourteenth** *number*

fourth /fɔrθ/ *number, n.* **1** [C] 4th **2** [C] 1/4 [= **quarter**]: *5*

ˌFourth of Ju'ly *n.* [singular] a U.S. national holiday to celebrate the beginning of the United States as an independent nation

fowl /faʊl/ *n.* [C] a bird, especially one such as a chicken that is kept for its meat and eggs

FOX /fɑks/ *n.* [C] one of the main companies that broadcasts television programs in the U.S.

fox

fox /fɑks/ *n.* [C] **1** a wild animal like a small dog with dark red fur, a pointed face, and a thick tail **2** *spoken* an attractive person: *He is such a fox!*

fox·trot /'fɑkstrɑt/ *n.* [C] a type of formal dance with quick movements, or the music for this dance

fox·y /'fɑksi/ *adj. informal* someone who is foxy is sexually attractive

foy·er /'fɔɪɚ/ *n.* [C] a room or hall at the entrance of a house, hotel, theater, etc.

fra·cas /'frækəs, 'freɪ-/ *n.* [C] a short noisy fight involving a lot of people

frac·tion /'frækʃən/ *n.* [C] **1** a very small amount of something: *For a **fraction of** a second, there was silence.* **2** a number that is smaller than 1, such as 3/4 or 1/2 —**fractional** *adj.* —**fractionally** *adv.*

frac·tious /'frækʃəs/ *adj.* someone who is fractious gets angry very easily and tends to start fights

frac·ture[1] /'fræktʃɚ/ *n.* [C] *technical* a crack or break in something hard such as a bone or rock

fracture[2] *v.* [I,T] *technical* to crack or break something hard such as a bone or rock: *He fractured his arm when he fell.*

frag·ile /'frædʒəl/ *adj.* **1** easily broken, damaged, harmed, or ruined: *a fragile china teapot* **2** weak, and likely to become worse: *the country's fragile peace | Mama's fragile health* —**fragility** /frə'dʒɪləṭi/ *n.* [U]

frag·ment /'frægmənt/ *n.* [C] **1** a part of something, or a small piece that has broken off of something: *Only **fragments of** the text have survived. | glass fragments*

THESAURUS

piece, scrap
→ see Thesaurus box at PIECE[1]

2 also sentence fragment a sentence that is not complete, often because it does not have a verb [➡ **run-on sentence**] —**fragment** /'frægˌmɛnt/ *v.* [T]

frag·ment·ed /'frægˌmɛntɪd/ *adj.* separated into many parts, groups, or events and not seeming to have a main purpose: *Our society seems to be becoming more fragmented.*

fra·grance /'freɪgrəns/ *n.* **1** [C,U] a pleasant smell: *the sweet fragrance of the flowers*

THESAURUS

smell, aroma, scent, perfume
→ see Thesaurus box at SMELL[2]

2 [C] a PERFUME

fra·grant /'freɪgrənt/ *adj.* having a pleasant smell: *a fragrant bouquet of red roses*

frail /freɪl/ *adj.* thin and weak, especially because of being old: *Grandpa looked tiny and frail in the hospital bed.*

frail·ty /'freɪlti/ *n.* plural **frailties** [C,U] *formal* a lack of physical or moral strength: *human frailties*

frame[1] /freɪm/ *n.* [C] **1** a structure made of wood, metal, etc. that holds or surrounds something such as a picture, door, or window: *I should put this graduation picture in a frame. | Wes leaned against the door frame.* **2** the main structure that supports something such as a house, piece of furniture, or vehicle: *a bicycle frame | a frame house* (=with a wooden frame) → see picture at BICYCLE **3** an area of film that contains one photograph, or one of the series of separate photographs that make up a movie or video **4** one of the areas into which a WEB PAGE is divided **5** *literary* someone's body: *her slender frame* **6 frame of mind** a particular attitude or feeling that you have: *Melissa was* ***in a good frame of mind*** *when we visited.* **7 frame of reference** all your knowledge, experiences, etc. that influence the way you think **8 frames** [plural] the metal or plastic part of a pair of glasses that surrounds each LENS ➔ TIME FRAME

frame² *v.* [T] **1** to put a picture in a frame: *a framed photo of her daughter* **2** to surround something or be surrounded by something: *Tammy's sweet face was framed by golden curls.* **3** to try to make someone seem guilty of a crime by deliberately giving false information: *His lawyers claimed he had been framed by racist police.* **4** to organize and develop something in a particular way: *The relationship between North and South Korea is framed by the agreement that ended the fighting in 1953.* | *He framed his response to the question carefully.* **5** to build or have a main structure that supports something: *iron-framed windows*

frame·work /ˈfreɪmwɚk/ *n.* [C] **1** a set of rules, beliefs, knowledge, etc. that people use when making a decision or planning something: *a* ***framework for*** *further research* | *the country's existing* ***legal/political/social framework*** **2** the main structure that supports a large thing such as a building or vehicle

fran·chise /ˈfræntʃaɪz/ *n.* [C] permission that a company gives to a person or group so that she, he, or it can sell the company's products or services: *a McDonald's franchise* —**franchise** *v.* [T]

frank /fræŋk/ *adj.* honest and direct in the way that you speak: *Jane said she would be* ***frank with*** *me.* | *Well,* ***to be frank,*** *I don't think this is going well.*

THESAURUS

honest, **candid**, **direct**, **straightforward**, **blunt**, **forthright**
➔ see Thesaurus box at HONEST

frank·fur·ter /ˈfræŋkˌfɚtɚ/ also **frank** /fræŋk/ *n.* [C] a HOT DOG

frank·ly /ˈfræŋkli/ *adv.* **1** used in order to show that you are saying what you really think about something: *Frankly, it was boring.* **2** honestly and directly: *Miller spoke frankly about teen sexuality.*

fran·tic /ˈfræntɪk/ *adj.* **1** extremely hurried and not very organized: *the frantic rush to get things ready* **2** very worried, frightened, or anxious: *His mother was* ***frantic with*** *worry.* —**frantically** *adv.*

frat¹ /fræt/ *adj. informal* belonging or relating to a FRATERNITY: *a frat house*

frat² *n.* [C] *informal* a FRATERNITY

fra·ter·nal /frəˈtɚnl/ *adj.* **1** friendly because you share the same interests with someone: *a fraternal organization* **2** relating to brothers: *fraternal love*

fra·ter·ni·ty /frəˈtɚnəṭi/ *n.* **1** [C] **also fraternity house** a club at a college or university that has only male members [➥ **sorority**] **2** [U] a feeling of friendship among people who have the same interests, job, or nationality

frat·er·nize /ˈfræṭɚˌnaɪz/ *v.* [I] to be friendly with someone who is not allowed to be your friend: *Soldiers who* ***fraternize with*** *the enemy will be shot.*

fraud /frɔd/ *n.* **1** [C,U] the crime of deceiving people in order to gain money or goods: *The police arrested him for* ***tax/credit card/insurance fraud.*** **2** [C] someone or something that is not what it is claimed to be: *He wasn't a real doctor – he was a fraud.*

fraud·u·lent /ˈfrɔdʒələnt/ *adj.* intended to deceive people: *the sale of fraudulent bonds* | *fraudulent statements* —**fraudulently** *adv.*

fraught /frɔt/ *adj.* **fraught with problems/danger/pain etc.** full of problems, danger, pain, etc.

fray¹ /freɪ/ *v.* [I] if a cloth or rope frays, its threads become loose because it is old or torn —**frayed** *adj.*

fray² *n.* **the fray** a fight or argument: *Then, two junior congressmen* ***joined/entered the fray.***

fraz·zled /ˈfræzəld/ *adj. informal* confused, tired, and worried

freak¹ /frik/ *n.* **1 bike/movie/health etc. freak** someone who is so interested in bikes, movies, etc. that other people think s/he is strange **2** someone or something that looks very strange or behaves in an unusual way: *He looked at me as if I were some kind of freak.* ➔ CONTROL FREAK

freak² *adj.* unexpected and very unusual: *Her parents were killed in a freak accident.*

freak³ **also freak out** *v.* [I,T] *spoken* to suddenly become very angry, frightened, or anxious, or to make someone do this: *When she heard the news, she just freaked.* | *Horror films always freak me out.*

freak·y /ˈfriki/ *adj. spoken* strange and slightly frightening

freck·le /ˈfrɛkəl/ *n.* [C usually plural] a small brown spot on someone's skin, especially the face: *a little girl with red hair and freckles* —**freckled** *adj.*

THESAURUS

mark, **blemish**, **bruise**, **scar**, **pimple**, **zit**, **wart**, **blister**, **mole**
➔ see Thesaurus box at MARK²

free¹ /fri/ *adj.*

1 NOT RESTRICTED allowed to live, exist, or happen without being controlled or restricted: *Students are* ***free to*** *choose the activities they want to work on.* | *The media is* ***free from*** *governmental control.* | *the right to* ***free speech***

2 NO COST not costing any money: *I won free tickets to the concert.* | *Admission is free for children.*

3 NOT CONTAINING STH not having any of a par-

F

ticular substance: *sugar-free bubble gum* | *The water is **free from** chemical pollutants.*
4 NOT BUSY not busy doing other things: *Are you **free for** lunch?* | *Hansen does volunteer work in her **free time**.*
5 NOT BEING USED not being used at this time: *Excuse me, is this seat free?* ➔ see Thesaurus box at EMPTY[1]
6 feel free *spoken* used in order to tell someone that s/he is allowed to do something: *Feel free to ask me any questions after the class.*
7 NOT A PRISONER not a prisoner or SLAVE: *Muller will be free in three years.* | *The UN demanded that the three hostages be **set free*** (=be given their freedom).
8 NOT SUFFERING not suffering or not having to deal with something bad: ***free of** danger* | *Patients undergoing the treatment are now **free from** cancer.* | *a happy and trouble-free life*
9 TAX if something is free of tax, you do not have to pay tax: *the duty-free store at the airport*
10 free hand if someone has a free hand to do something, s/he is allowed to do what s/he wants or needs to do: *The police were **given a free hand** to deal with the gang problems.*
11 a free ride something you get without paying or working for it

free² *v.* [T] **1** to allow someone to leave prison or somewhere s/he has been kept as a prisoner: *After nine months, the hostages were finally freed.* **2** to move someone or something that is trapped or stuck, or to make something loose: *Firefighters helped free two men trapped in the car.* **3** to stop someone or something from being controlled or restricted: *The farmers were **freed from** government limits on what they could plant.* **4** to stop someone suffering, or help someone by removing something bad or difficult: *The scholarship **freed** her **from** having to work while attending college.* **5 also free up** to help someone be able to do something or to make something be able to be used: *Hiring an assistant will free up your time to do other tasks.* | *I need to free up some space on the hard disk.*

free³ *adv.* **1** without having to pay any money: *Students can visit the museum **free of charge**.* | *Kyle is fixing my car **for free**.* **2** not being restricted or controlled by someone: *He created music that **broke free** of tradition.* **3** not stuck or held in a particular place or position: *He grabbed my wrist but I managed to **struggle/pull free**.*

ˌfree ˈagent *n.* [C] a professional sports player who can choose whether to sign a contract with a team

free·bie /ˈfribi/ *n.* [C] *informal* something that you are given free, especially by a business, store, etc.

free·dom /ˈfridəm/ *n.* **1** [C,U] the right to do what you want without being restricted or controlled by someone else: *The First Amendment guarantees **freedom of speech/religion etc.*** (=the legal right to say what you want, choose your own religion, etc.) | *The government must respect our basic freedoms.* | *Individual freedom is limited by social responsibilities.* **2** [U] the state of being free and allowed to do what you want: *I had a great sense of freedom when I first left home.* | *One of the benefits of working for the airline is the **freedom to** fly anywhere it goes.* **3 freedom from sth** the state of not being hurt or affected by something: *freedom from hunger*

ˈfreedom ˌfighter *n.* [C] someone who fights in a war against a dishonest government, army, etc.

free ˈenterprise *n.* [U] the freedom for companies to control their own business without being limited by the government very much

ˌfree-for-ˈall *n. informal* [C] a fight or noisy argument that a lot of people join: *The argument in the bar turned into a free-for-all.*

> **THESAURUS**
> **fight**, **brawl**, **scuffle**, **scrap**
> ➔ see Thesaurus box at FIGHT²

free·hand /ˈfrihænd/ *adj.* drawn by hand without using any special tools

free·lance /ˈfrilæns/ *adj., adv.* doing work for one or more companies, rather than being employed only by one particular company: *a freelance journalist* | *She works freelance from home.* —**freelancer** *n.* [C] —**freelance** *v.* [I]

free·load·er /ˈfriˌloʊdɚ/ *n.* [C] *informal disapproving* someone who takes food, money, or other things from other people, without giving them anything in return —**freeload** *v.* [I]

free·ly /ˈfrili/ *adv.* **1** without anyone or anything preventing or limiting something: *People can now travel freely across the border.* | *They were speaking freely, assuming we could not understand.* **2 freely admit/acknowledge** to say that something is true, even though this is difficult: *I freely admit I made a bad choice.* **3 freely available** very easy to get: *Information is freely available on the Internet.* **4** generously or in large amounts: *a company that gives freely to local charities*

ˌfree ˈmarket *n.* [singular] a situation in which prices are not controlled by the government or any other powerful group

Free·ma·son /ˈfriˌmeɪsən/ *n.* [C] a MASON

ˌfree-ˈrange *adj.* relating to a type of farming which allows animals such as chickens and pigs to move around and eat naturally, rather than being kept in cages: *free-range eggs*

ˌfree ˈspirit *n.* [C] someone who lives the way s/he wants to, rather than in the way society considers usual

ˌfree ˈthrow *n.* [C] an occasion in the game of basketball when a player is allowed to throw the ball toward the basket without anyone trying to prevent him/her because another player has FOULed him/her

free·way /ˈfriweɪ/ *n.* [C] a very wide road in a city on which cars can travel very fast

F

THESAURUS

highway, **expressway**, **turnpike**
→ see Thesaurus box at ROAD

free·wheel·ing /ˌfriˈwilɪŋ◂/ *adj. informal* not worrying about rules or what will happen in the future: *a freewheeling lifestyle*

ˌfree ˈwill *n.* **do sth of your own free will** to do something because you want to and not because someone forces you to: *She's offered to go of her own free will.*

freeze¹ /friz/ *v.* past tense **froze** /froʊz/ past participle **frozen** /ˈfroʊzən/ **1** [I,T] if a liquid or thing freezes, or if something freezes it, it becomes solid and hard because it is so cold: *The lake had frozen overnight.* | *One man got lost in the blizzard and **froze to death**.* | *The ground was **frozen solid**.* **2** [I,T] to preserve food for a long time by keeping it very cold in a FREEZER: *Do you want to freeze some of these pies?* **3 it's freezing** *spoken* said when the temperature is extremely cold **4** [I] *spoken* to feel very cold: *Put on a coat – you'll freeze.* | *I'm freezing; put on the heat.* **5** [I] to suddenly stop moving and stay very quiet and still: *Officer Greer shouted, "Freeze!"* **6** [T] to officially prevent money from being spent, or prevent prices, salaries, etc. from being increased → FROZEN

freeze sb ⇔ **out** *phr. v.* to deliberately prevent someone from being involved in something

freeze over *phr. v.* if an area of water freezes over, its surface turns into ice

freeze up *phr. v.* to suddenly be unable to speak normally because you are nervous: *He freezes up whenever she asks him a question.*

freeze² *n.* [C] **1** an occasion when something is stopped or kept at a particular level: *a **freeze on** hiring new employees* | *a pay freeze* **2** a short period of time, especially at night, when the temperature is very low

ˌfreeze-ˈdried *adj.* freeze-dried food or drinks are preserved by being frozen and then dried very quickly: *freeze-dried coffee*

freez·er /ˈfrizɚ/ *n.* [C] a large piece of electrical equipment that is usually part of a REFRIGERATOR and is used for storing food at a very low temperature for a long time

freez·ing /ˈfrizɪŋ/ *n.* **above/below freezing** above or below the temperature at which water freezes

ˈfreezing ˌpoint *n.* [C] *technical* the temperature at which a liquid freezes

freight /freɪt/ *n.* [U] goods that are carried by train, airplane, or ship

freight·er /ˈfreɪt̬ɚ/ *n.* [C] an airplane or ship that carries goods

THESAURUS

ship, **ferry**, **tanker**, **barge**
→ see Thesaurus box at SHIP¹

ˈfreight train *n.* [C] a train that carries goods

French¹ /frɛntʃ/ *adj.* **1** relating to or coming from France **2** relating to the French language

French² *n.* **1** [U] the language used in France **2 the French** [plural] the people of France

ˌFrench ˈbread *n.* [U] white bread that is shaped like a long stick

ˌFrench ˈfry *n.* plural **French fries** [C usually plural] a FRY

French fries

ˌFrench ˈtoast *n.* [U] pieces of bread that are put into a mixture of egg and milk, then cooked in hot oil

fre·ne·tic /frəˈnɛt̬ɪk/ *adj.* frenetic activity happens in a way that is fast and not very organized: *the frenetic pace of life in the city*

fren·zied /ˈfrɛnzid/ *adj.* frenzied activity is completely uncontrolled: *a frenzied attack*

fren·zy /ˈfrɛnzi/ *n.* [singular, U] **1** the state of being very anxious, excited, and unable to control your behavior: *The kids had worked themselves **into a frenzy** of anticipation.* **2** a period in which people do a lot of things very quickly: *The house was a **frenzy of activity** as we got ready for the party.* **3 feeding frenzy** an occasion when a lot of people get involved in something in an uncontrolled way: *The media went into a feeding frenzy over this story.*

fre·quen·cy /ˈfrikwənsi/ *n.* **1** [U] the number of times that something happens within a particular period, or the fact that it happens a lot: *the **frequency of** fatal road accidents* | ***high frequency** names such as Smith or Johnson* | *Arguments began taking place **with increasing frequency**.* **2** [C,U] the rate at which a sound or light WAVE pattern is repeated

fre·quent¹ /ˈfrikwənt/ *adj.* happening very often [≠ **infrequent**]: *He's **a frequent guest** on TV talk shows.* | *Her absences were becoming **more/less frequent**.*

fre·quent² /ˈfrikwənt, friˈkwɛnt/ *v.* [T] to go to a particular place very often: *a restaurant **frequented by** students*

ˌfrequent ˈflier *n.* [C] someone who travels on airplanes very often, especially using a particular AIRLINE —**frequent-flier** *adj.*

fre·quent·ly /ˈfrikwəntˀli/ *adv.* very often: *We call each other frequently.*

THESAURUS

often, **a lot**, **regularly**, **repeatedly**, **constantly**, **continuously**
→ see Thesaurus box at OFTEN

fresh /frɛʃ/ *adj.*
1 ADDED/REPLACING adding to or replacing

what was there before: *Let me make some fresh coffee.* | *fresh sheets for the bed*

2 RECENT recently done, made, or learned: *fresh tracks in the snow* | *fresh-squeezed orange juice* | *Researchers have presented fresh data.* | *Write about your trip while it's still* ***fresh in your mind****.*

THESAURUS

new, recent, modern, latest

3 NEW not done, seen, etc. before: *a new manager with fresh ideas* | *a fresh approach to teaching*

4 FOOD fresh food or flowers are in good condition because they have recently been produced, picked, or prepared: *fresh strawberries* | *bread fresh from the bakery*

5 CLEAN looking, feeling, smelling, or tasting clean, cool, and nice: *a fresh breeze* | *a fresh minty taste*

6 fresh air air from outside, especially clean air: *Let's go and* ***get some fresh air****.*

7 be fresh out of sth *spoken* **a)** used in order to say that you have just used or given away the last supply of something: *I'm sorry, we're fresh out of bagels.* **b) also be fresh from sth** to have recently finished doing something: *He's fresh out of college.*

8 WATER fresh water has no salt and comes from rivers and lakes

9 fresh start the act of starting doing something again in a new or different way, especially after being unsuccessful: *immigrants who came to America to* ***make a fresh start*** (=start a new life)

fresh·en /ˈfrɛʃən/ *v.* **1** [I] if the wind freshens, it becomes stronger **2** [T] **also freshen up** to add more liquid to a drink

freshen up *phr. v.* to wash your hands and face in order to feel comfortable: *Would you like to freshen up before dinner?*

fresh·ly /ˈfrɛʃli/ *adv.* very recently: *freshly mown grass*

THESAURUS

recently, just, newly
→ see Thesaurus box at RECENTLY

fresh·man /ˈfrɛʃmən/ *n.* [C] a student in the first year of HIGH SCHOOL or college

fresh·wa·ter /ˈfrɛʃˌwɔt̬ɚ, -ˌwɑt̬ɚ/ *adj.* relating to rivers or lakes rather than the ocean: *freshwater fish*

fret¹ /frɛt/ *v.* [I] to worry about small or unimportant things, or to make someone do this: *Don't* ***fret about*** *a thing.*

fret² *n.* [C] one of the raised lines on the long straight part of a GUITAR or similar instruments

fret·ful /ˈfrɛtfəl/ *adj. old-fashioned* worried, complaining, and unable to relax: *a fretful child*

Freud·i·an /ˈfrɔɪdiən/ *adj.* **1** relating to Sigmund Freud's ideas about the way the mind works **2 Freudian slip** something you say by mistake that shows a thought or feeling you did not mean to show, or did not know you had

fri·ar /ˈfraɪɚ/ *n.* [C] a man who belongs to a Roman Catholic group, whose members in past times traveled around teaching about religion and who were very poor

fric·tion /ˈfrɪkʃən/ *n.* [U] **1** disagreement, angry feelings, or lack of friendship between people: *the things that create* ***friction between*** *parent and child* **2** the rubbing of one surface against another: *friction between tires and the road*

Fri·day /ˈfraɪdi, -deɪ/ *n.* [C,U] *written abbreviation* **Fri.** the sixth day of the week: *Diane won't be here Friday.* | *I have class* ***on Friday****.* | ***Next Friday*** *is my birthday.* | *I talked to Jim* ***last Friday****.* | *Do you have plans for* ***Friday night****?*

fridge /frɪdʒ/ *n.* [C] *informal* a REFRIGERATOR

fried¹ /fraɪd/ *adj.* **1** cooked in hot fat: *a fried egg* **2** *slang* very tired: *My brain is fried today.*

fried² *v.* the past tense and past participle of FRY

friend /frɛnd/ *n.* [C] **1** someone whom you like very much and enjoy spending time with: *I'm meeting a friend for lunch.* | *Is she a* ***friend of yours****?* | *Tony's her* ***best friend****.* | *one of my* ***closest friends*** | *Lee's an* ***old friend****.*

COLLOCATIONS

You may have lots of **good/close friends** but your **best friend** is the one you like most.
An **old friend** is one you have known for a long time.
If you **have friends**, you know and like them already.
If you **make friends** with someone, you start to know and like them.
If **friends hang out together** informal, or if you **hang out with friends** informal, you spend time together in a relaxed way.
If **friends come over**, they visit you at home.

2 make friends (with sb) to become friendly with someone: *Kate makes friends easily.* **3 be friends (with sb)** to be someone's friend: *They've* ***been friends with*** *the Wilsons for years.* **4** someone who has the same beliefs or wants to achieve the same things: *our friends and allies around the world* **5** someone who supports a theater, MUSEUM, etc. by giving money or help **6 have friends in high places** to know important people who can help you

friend·ly /ˈfrɛndli/ *adj.* **1** showing that you like someone and are ready to talk to him/her: *Diane's* ***friendly to/with*** *everyone.* | *a friendly smile*

THESAURUS

warm – friendly: *Sonya's a very warm person.*
cordial – friendly and polite but formal: *The two nations have always maintained cordial relations.*
welcoming – making you feel happy and relaxed: *Everyone was very welcoming.*

hospitable – friendly, welcoming, and generous to visitors: *They were very kind and hospitable to us.*

THESAURUS

nice, kind, likeable, sweet, pleasant
➔ see Thesaurus box at NICE

2 user-friendly/ozone-friendly etc. a) easy for people to use or be comfortable with: *user-friendly computers* | *a kid-friendly house* **b)** not damaging or harming something: *environmentally friendly detergent* **3** not at war with you, or not your enemy or opponent: *The two countries have friendly relations.* **4 friendly fire** bombs, bullets, etc. that accidentally kill people who are fighting on the same side —**friendliness** *n.* [U]

friend·ship /ˈfrɛndʃɪp/ *n.* **1** [C] a relationship between friends: *Their friendship began in college.* | *his* ***friendship with*** *Bill* | *The two boys* ***formed/developed*** *a lasting* ***friendship***. | *a* ***close friendship*** **2** [U] the feelings that exist between friends: *I was grateful for her friendship and support.*

frieze /friz/ *n.* [C] a decoration that goes along the top of a wall

frig·ate /ˈfrɪgɪt/ *n.* [C] a small fast ship used especially for protecting other ships in a war

fright /fraɪt/ *n.* [singular, U] a sudden fear: *People screamed* ***in fright***. | *He was shaking* ***with fright***.

fright·en /ˈfraɪtˀn/ *v.* [T] to make someone feel afraid: *Libby was frightened by the thunder.* | *Don't stand so close to the edge – you're frightening me.*

frighten sb/sth ⇔ **away** *phr. v.* to make a person or animal go away by making him, her, or it afraid: *Be quiet or you'll frighten away the birds.*

frighten sb ⇔ **off** *phr. v.* to make someone so nervous or afraid that s/he goes away and does not do something s/he was going to do: *A car alarm is usually enough to frighten off a burglar.*

fright·ened /ˈfraɪtˀnd/ *adj.* feeling afraid: *a frightened child* | *He was* ***frightened of*** *losing her.* | *She was* ***frightened that*** *he might hit her.*

THESAURUS

afraid/scared – frightened because you think that you may get hurt or that something bad may happen: *I'm afraid to go out alone after dark.* | *I've always been scared of dogs.*
terrified – very frightened: *I'm terrified of heights.*
petrified – very frightened: *He's petrified of snakes.*

fright·en·ing /ˈfraɪtˀnɪŋ/ *adj.* making you feel afraid or nervous: *a frightening experience* —**frighteningly** *adv.*

frig·id /ˈfrɪdʒɪd/ *adj.* **1** a woman who is frigid does not like having sex **2** very cold **3** *literary* not friendly: *She gave me a frigid look.* —**frigidity** /frɪˈdʒɪdət̬i/ *n.* [U]

frill /frɪl/ *n.* [C] **1** a decoration on the edge of a piece of cloth, made of another piece of cloth with many small folds in it **2** additional features that are nice but not necessary: *The airline offers few frills.* ➔ NO-FRILLS

frill·y /ˈfrɪli/ *adj.* with many FRILLS: *a frilly blouse*

fringe¹ /frɪndʒ/ *n.* **1** [C] a small number of people whose ideas are more unusual or extreme than those of most other people: *the environmental fringe* **2** [C,U] an edge of hanging threads used as a decoration on a curtain, piece of clothing, etc.: *a cowboy jacket with leather fringe* **3** [C] the area that is furthest from the center of something: *the eastern fringe of Vancouver* **4 on the fringes of sth** not completely involved in or accepted by a particular group: *Cato lived on the fringes of society.*

fringe² *adj.* not representing or involving many people, and expressing unusual ideas: *a* ***fringe group*** *of political extremists*

ˈfringe ˌbenefit *n.* [C usually plural] a service or advantage that you are given with your job in addition to pay: *Fringe benefits include a company car.*

fringed /frɪndʒd/ *adj.* **1** decorated with a FRINGE: *a large fringed shawl* **2** having something on the edge: *a palm-fringed beach*

Fris·bee /ˈfrɪzbi/ *n.* [C,U] *trademark* a piece of plastic shaped like a plate that people throw and catch as a game

frisk /frɪsk/ *v.* [T] to search someone for hidden weapons, drugs, etc. by passing your hands over his/her body

frisk·y /ˈfrɪski/ *adj.* full of energy, happiness, and fun: *a frisky kitten*

frit·ter¹ /ˈfrɪt̬ɚ/ *n.* [C] a piece of fruit, vegetable, or meat covered with a mixture of eggs and flour and cooked in oil: *corn fritters*

fritter²

fritter sth ⇔ **away** *phr. v.* to waste time, money, or effort on something that is not important

fritz /frɪts/ *n. informal* **be on the fritz** if something electrical is on the fritz, it is not working correctly

fri·vol·i·ty /frɪˈvɑlət̬i/ *n.* plural **frivolities** [C,U] behavior or activities that are not serious or sensible

friv·o·lous /ˈfrɪvələs/ *adj.* **1** not sensible: *pretty, frivolous clothes* **2** not important or necessary: *a frivolous request*

frizz·y /ˈfrɪzi/ *adj.* frizzy hair is very tightly curled in an unattractive way —**frizz** *v.* [I,T]

fro /froʊ/ *adv.* ➔ TO AND FRO

frog /frɔg, frɑg/ *n.* [C] **1** a small animal with smooth skin that lives in or near water, makes a deep sound, and has long legs for jumping [➡ **toad**] **2 have a frog in your throat** *informal* to have difficulty in speaking because your throat is dry or sore

frol·ic /ˈfrɑlɪk/ *v.* [I] to play in an active, happy way —**frolic** *n.* [C]

F

from /frəm; *strong* frʌm/ *prep.*
1 WHERE SB/STH STARTS starting at a particular place, position, or condition: *He drove all the way from Colorado.* | *I liked him from the first time I met him.* | *prices ranging from $80 to $250*
2 ORIGIN a) used in order to show the origin of someone or something: *lines from a play* | *I got the idea from Scott.* | *"Where do you* ***come from****?" "I'm from Norway."* **b)** sent or given by someone: *Who is the present from?* | *I got a phone call from Ernie today.*
3 MOVED/SEPARATED used in order to show that things or people are moved, separated, or taken away: *He pulled his shoes out from under the bed.* | *I'll* ***take*** *that* ***away from*** *you!* | *She needs some time* ***away from*** *the kids* (=time when she is not with them). | *Subtract $40 from the total.*
4 DISTANCE/TIME used in order to show distance or time: *We live about 3 miles from Des Moines.* | *It'll cost $400 to fly* ***from*** *Albuquerque* ***to*** *Atlanta.* | *The morning class is* ***from*** *9:00* ***to*** *11:00.* | *One month* ***from now*** *we'll be in Mexico!*
5 from now on starting now and continuing into the future: *I decided that, from now on, I would keep a journal.*
6 from day to day/person to person/place to place etc. used in order to say that something continues or keeps changing: *The number of meteors seen* ***varies from*** *year* ***to*** *year.*
7 from time to time sometimes, but not regularly [= **occasionally**]: *We talk on the phone from time to time.*
8 POSITION used in order to show where you are when you see, watch, or do something: *There's a man watching us from behind that fence.* | *From the top of the mountain, you can see the ocean.*
9 RESULT because of, or as a result of: *the number of injuries from car accidents* | *We could tell what he was thinking from the expression on his face.*
10 STOP SOMETHING HAPPENING used in order to say what is stopped, avoided, or prevented: *The fog* ***prevented*** *planes* ***from*** *landing.*
11 COMPARING used when comparing things: *Frieda is very different from her sister.*

frond /frɑnd/ *n.* [C] a leaf of a FERN or PALM TREE

front[1] /frʌnt/ *n.* [C]
1 the front a) the part of something that is furthest forward, and closest to the direction it faces [≠ **back**]: *Good students tend to sit near the front.* | *Let's sit* ***at the front of*** *the bus.* **b)** the side or surface of something that faces or moves forward [≠ **back**]: *the large doors* ***at the front of*** *the building* | *He ran around the front of the car.* | *a sweatshirt with the college's name* ***on the front*** **c)** the most important side or surface of something, that you look at first [≠ **back**]: *a postcard with a picture of a lighthouse* ***on the front*** | *The author had signed his name* ***in the front of*** *the book* (=on one of the first pages).
2 in front of sb/sth a) further forward than or ahead of someone or something [≠ **behind**]: *A car suddenly pulled out in front of my truck.* | *two girls standing in front of me in line* **b)** facing someone or something [≠ **behind**]: *She sat in front of the mirror.* | *Mrs. Podell stood in front of the class.* **c)** near the entrance of a building [≠ **behind**]: *Drop me off in front of the theater.* | *a tree in front of their house* **d)** where someone can see or hear you: *He threatened her in front of several witnesses.* | *They won in front of 13,000 fans.*
3 in (the) front a) in the most forward or leading position [= **ahead**]: *Watch the car in front!* **b)** in the area nearest to the most forward part of something, or nearest to the entrance to a building: *The club has two bars, one in the front and one in the back.*
4 in front of the TV/computer etc. watching a television or using a computer: *They'd eaten supper in front of the TV.*
5 out front in the area near the entrance to the building that you are in: *Jim's waiting out front.*
6 in (the) front in the part of a car where the driver sits: *Can I sit in front with you?*
7 WEATHER *technical* the place where two areas of air that have different temperatures meet each other: *The weather report says a* ***warm/cold front*** *is coming.*
8 on the publicity/money/health etc. front in a particular area of activity: *new developments on the economic front*
9 up front *informal* **a)** money that is paid up front is paid before work is done or goods are supplied: *We need the money up front before we can do anything.* **b)** directly and clearly from the start: *She told him up front she wasn't interested in marriage.*
10 ON YOUR BODY *informal* someone's chest, or the part of the body that faces forward: *Oh, I've just spilled milk down my front!*
11 BEHAVIOR a way of behaving that shows what you want people to see, rather than what you may feel: *Parents should try to present a* ***united front*** (=seem to agree with each other) *to their children.* | *Celia was nervous, but she* ***put up a*** *brave* ***front****.*
12 ILLEGAL ACTIVITIES [C] a legal business that someone operates in order to hide the illegal activities s/he is involved in
13 POLITICAL PARTY used in the names of political parties or unofficial military organizations: *the Quebec Liberation Front*
14 WAR a line along which fighting takes place during a war

front[2] *adj.* [only before noun] **1** at, on, or in the front of something [≠ **back**]: *the front door* | *tickets for front row seats* | *the magazine's front cover* | *one of the front wheels* **2** legally doing business as a way of hiding a secret or illegal activity: *a front organization for drug dealing*

front[3] *v.* **1** [T] to lead something such as a musical group by being the person that the public sees most: *He's now fronting his own band.*

2 [I,T] to face something, or to be in front of something: *a building fronting Lake Michigan*

front·age /ˈfrʌntɪdʒ/ *n.* [C] the part of a building or piece of land that is along a road, river, etc.

fron·tal /ˈfrʌntəl/ *adj.* **1** toward the front of something: *a frontal attack* **2** at the front part of something: *the frontal lobe of the brain*

fron·tier /frʌnˈtɪr/ *n.* [C] **1 the frontier** the area beyond the places that people know well, especially in the western U.S. in the 19th century: *the settlement of the Oklahoma frontier* **2** the limit of what is known about something: *the frontiers of science* **3** the border of a country, or the area near the border

ˈfront man *n.* [C] **1** someone who speaks for an organization, often an illegal one, but is not the leader of it **2** the leader of a JAZZ or ROCK band

front·run·ner /ˈfrʌntˌrʌnɚ/ *n.* [C] the person or thing that is most likely to succeed in a competition: *the frontrunner for the Republican nomination*

frost[1] /frɔst/ *n.* **1** [U] ice that looks white and powdery and covers things that are outside when the temperature is very cold: *trees white with frost*

THESAURUS

snow, snowflakes, sleet, slush, blizzard, hail, rain, hailstones

➔ see Thesaurus box at SNOW[1]

2 [C,U] very cold weather, when water freezes: *an early frost*

frost[2] *v.* [T] **1** to cover a cake with FROSTING **2** to cover something with FROST, or to become covered with frost

frost·bite /ˈfrɔstbaɪt/ *n.* [U] a condition caused by extreme cold, in which your fingers, toes, etc. freeze, so that they swell, become darker, and sometimes drop off —**frostbitten** /ˈfrɔstˌbɪtn/ *adj.*

frost·ing /ˈfrɔstɪŋ/ *n.* [U] a sweet substance that you put on cakes, made from sugar and liquid: *chocolate frosting*

frost·y /ˈfrɔsti/ *adj.* **1** very cold or covered with FROST: *a frosty morning*

THESAURUS

cold, cool, chilly, freezing (cold), icy (cold), bitter (cold)

➔ see Thesaurus box at COLD[1]

2 unfriendly: *a frosty greeting*

froth[1] /frɔθ/ *n.* [singular, U] a lot of BUBBLES formed on top of a liquid

froth[2] *v.* [I] to produce FROTH

froth·y /ˈfrɔθi, -ði/ *adj.* full of FROTH or covered with froth: *frothy beer*

frown[1] /fraʊn/ *v.* [I] to make an angry or unhappy expression by moving your EYEBROWS together, so that lines appear on your FOREHEAD: *Debbie's mother **frowned at** her.*

frown on/upon sth *phr. v.* to disapprove of something: *Even though divorce is legal, it's often frowned upon.*

frown[2] *n.* [C] the expression on your face when you frown

froze /froʊz/ *v.* the past tense of FREEZE

fro·zen[1] /ˈfroʊzən/ *v.* the past participle of FREEZE

frozen[2] *adj.* **1** preserved by being kept at a very low temperature: *frozen peas* **2 be frozen (stiff)** *spoken* to feel very cold: *Can you turn up the heat? I'm frozen!* **3** made very hard or turned to ice because of the cold: *the frozen lake* ➔ see picture at MELT **4 be frozen with fear/terror/fright** to be so afraid, shocked, etc. that you cannot move

fru·gal /ˈfrugəl/ *adj.* **1** careful to only buy what is necessary: *My parents were very frugal.* **2** small in quantity and cost: *a frugal lunch of cheese and bread* —**frugally** *adv.* —**frugality** /fruˈgæləṭi/ *n.* [U]

fruit /frut/ *n.* plural **fruit** or **fruits** **1** [C,U] something that grows on a plant, tree, or bush, can be eaten as food, contains seeds, and is usually sweet: *Apples and bananas are Nancy's favorite fruits.* | *Would you like **a piece of fruit**?* **2 the fruit(s) of sth** the good results that you have from something, after you have worked hard: *the fruits of his research* ➔ **bear fruit** at BEAR[1]

fruit·cake /ˈfrutkeɪk/ *n.* **1** [C,U] a cake that has dried fruit in it **2** [C] *informal* someone who seems to be mentally ill or behaves in a strange way

ˈfruit fly *n.* [C] a small fly that eats and lays eggs on fruit

fruit·ful /ˈfrutfəl/ *adj.* producing good results: *a fruitful meeting*

fru·i·tion /fruˈɪʃən/ *n.* [U] *formal* the successful result of a plan, idea, etc.: *The community has worked hard for this plan to **come to/be brought to fruition**.*

fruit·less /ˈfrutlɪs/ *adj.* failing to produce good results, especially after much effort: *a **fruitless attempt** to end the fighting* —**fruitlessly** *adv.*

fruit·y /ˈfruṭi/ *adj.* tasting or smelling strongly of fruit: *a fruity wine*

frump·y /ˈfrʌmpi/ *adj.* someone, especially a woman, who is frumpy wears old-fashioned clothes and looks unattractive

frus·trate /ˈfrʌstreɪt/ *v.* [T] **1** if something frustrates you, it makes you feel annoyed or angry because you are unable to do what you want: *The lack of public transportation frustrates commuters.* **2** to prevent someone's plans, efforts, or attempts from succeeding: *They feel the system frustrates their attempts to improve productivity.*

frus·trat·ed /ˈfrʌˌstreɪṭɪd/ *adj.* feeling annoyed or angry because you are unable to do what you want to do: *He **gets frustrated** and angry because*

F

fruit

he feels stupid. | I was **frustrated with** the lack of progress.

frus·trat·ing /ˈfrʌˌstreɪt̬ɪŋ/ *adj.* making you feel annoyed or angry because you cannot do what you want to do: *They keep sending me the wrong forms – it's really frustrating.*

frus·tra·tion /frʌˈstreɪʃən/ *n.* [C,U] the feeling of being annoyed or angry because you are unable to do what you want to do: *A toddler was kicking the ground* ***in frustration.***

fry¹ /fraɪ/ *n.* plural **fries** [C usually plural] a long thin piece of potato that has been cooked in hot oil

fry² *v.* past tense and past participle **fried** [I,T] to cook something in hot fat or oil, or to be cooked in hot fat or oil: *I fried some bacon for breakfast.*

THESAURUS

cook, bake, roast, broil, sauté, deep fry, boil, steam

➔ see Thesaurus box at COOK¹

ˈfrying ˌpan *n.* [C] a round pan with a flat handle, used for FRYing food

ft. the written abbreviation of **foot**

fudge¹ /fʌdʒ/ *n.* [U] a soft creamy sweet food, usually made with chocolate

fudge² *v.* [I,T] to avoid giving exact figures or facts, in order to deceive people

fu·el¹ /ˈfyuəl, fyul/ *n.* [C,U] a substance such as coal, gas, or oil that can be burned to produce heat or energy

fuel² *v.* **1** [T] to make a situation worse or to make someone's feelings stronger: *The increase in property prices only fueled inflation.* **2** [I,T] **also fuel up** to take fuel into a vehicle, or to provide a vehicle with fuel

fu·gi·tive /ˈfyudʒət̬ɪv/ *n.* [C] someone who is trying to avoid being caught, especially by the police: *a* ***fugitive from*** *justice*

ful·crum /ˈfʊlkrəm, ˈfʌl-/ *n.* [C] the point on which a BAR that is being used for lifting something turns or is supported

ful·fill /fʊlˈfɪl/ *v.* [T] **1** to get, do, or achieve something you wanted, promised, or hoped for: *The president fulfilled his election promise to cut taxes.* | *Learning to fly fulfilled a childhood dream.* | *an education that will help each child* ***fulfill*** *his* ***potential*** (=be as successful as he can be) **2** to do or provide what is necessary or needed: *The firm failed to fulfill its obligations under the contract.* | *The breakfast club fulfills a need in this poor neighborhood school.* **3** to make you feel satisfied because you are doing something useful and interesting and using your skills and qualities: *She wanted work that would fulfill her.*

ful·filled /fʊlˈfɪld/ *adj.* satisfied with your life, job, etc. because you feel that it is interesting or useful and you are using all your skills

ful·fill·ing /fʊlˈfɪlɪŋ/ *adj.* making you feel happy

and satisfied because you are doing interesting, useful, or important things: *a fulfilling career*

ful·fill·ment /fʊl'fɪlmənt/ *n.* [U] **1** the feeling of being happy and satisfied with your life because you are doing interesting, useful, or important things: *Ann's work gives her a real* ***sense of fulfillment***. **2** the act or state of meeting a need, demand, or condition: *This contract offer depends upon the fulfillment of certain conditions.*

full[1] /fʊl/ *adj.*

1 CONTAINER/ROOM/PLACE ETC. holding or containing as much or as many things or people as possible [≠ **empty**]: *Don't talk with your mouth full.* | *a full glass of milk* | *The bottle was only* ***half full***. | *a box* ***full of*** *paper* ➔ see picture at EMPTY[1]

THESAURUS

filled with sth – full of something: *a shopping cart filled with groceries*
packed – extremely full of people or things: *The trial took place in front of a packed courtroom.* | *The stadium was packed with fans.*
crammed – full of people or things: *The garage was crammed with junk.*
stuffed (full of sth) – full of things: *a suitcase stuffed full of clothes*
bursting (with sth) – very full of something: *a muffin bursting with blueberries*
overflowing – a container that is overflowing is so full that the liquid or things inside it come out over the top: *an overflowing trash basket*
overloaded – if a vehicle or ship is overloaded, too many people or things have been put in it: *The helicopter was overloaded and barely got off the ground.*

2 COMPLETE [only before noun] including all parts or details: *Please write your* ***full name*** *and address in the boxes.* | *We will pay* ***the full cost*** *of repairs.*

3 HIGHEST AMOUNT/LEVEL [only before noun] the highest level or greatest amount of something that is possible: *The ship was going at* ***full speed***. | *You have our* ***full support***. | *I didn't pay* ***full price*** *for the jacket.*

4 be full of sth a) to contain many things of the same kind: *Eric's essay is full of mistakes.* | *a garden full of flowers* **b)** to feel or express a strong emotion: *Cathy woke up full of excitement.* | *He was full of praise for the children's achievement.* **c)** to think or talk about only one subject all the time: *She's full of plans for the wedding.*

5 FOOD [not before noun] having eaten so much food that you cannot eat any more: *"Would you like some more soup?" "No thanks.* ***I'm full***.*"*

6 CLOTHING a full skirt, pair of pants, etc. is made with a lot of material and fits loosely

7 BODY a full face, body, etc. is rounded or large: *clothes for the fuller figure*

8 TASTE/SOUND ETC. a full taste, sound, color, etc. is strong and pleasant: *a* ***full-bodied*** *wine*

9 RANK [only before noun] having or giving all the rights, duties, etc. that belong to a particular rank or position: *a full professor*

full[2] *n.* **1 in full** if you pay an amount of money in full, you pay the whole amount **2 to the full** in the best or most complete way: *Ronnie lived his life to the full.*

full[3] *adv. literary* directly: *The sun shone* ***full on*** *her face.*

'full-blown *adj.* fully developed: *full-blown AIDS*

ˌfull-'fledged *adj.* completely developed, trained, or established: *a full-fledged lawyer*

ˌfull-'grown *adj.* a full-grown animal, plant, or person has developed to his, her, or its full size and will not grow any bigger

ˌfull 'house *n.* [C] an occasion at a concert hall, sports field, etc. when every seat has someone sitting in it

ˌfull-'length *adj.* **1 full-length mirror/photograph etc.** a mirror, etc. that shows all of a person, from his/her head to his/her feet **2 full-length skirt/dress** a skirt, etc. that reaches the ground **3 full-length play/book etc.** a play, etc. of the normal length

ˌfull 'moon *n.* [singular] the moon when it looks completely round

full·ness /'fʊlnɪs/ *n.* **1 in the fullness of time** *formal* when the right time comes: *I'm sure he'll tell us everything in the fullness of time.* **2** [U] the condition of having eaten enough food **3** [U] the quality of being large and round: *the fullness of her breasts*

ˌfull-'scale *adj.* **1** as complete or thorough as possible: *a full-scale investigation* **2** a full-scale model, copy, picture, etc. is the same size as the thing it represents

ˌfull-'time *adj., adv.* working or studying for the number of hours that people usually work or study [➡ **part-time**]: *Andrea works full-time for an insurance company.* | *full-time students*

ful·ly /'fʊli/ *adv.* completely: *a fully trained nurse*

fum·ble /'fʌmbəl/ *v.* **1** [I] to try to hold, move, or find something with your hands in an awkward way: *Gary* ***fumbled for*** *the light switch in the dark.* **2** [I,T] to have difficulty saying something: *She* ***fumbled for*** *an appropriate response.* **3** [I,T] to drop a ball after catching it —**fumble** *n.* [C]

fume /fyum/ *v.* [I] to be very angry: *He was* ***fuming about/over/at*** *the repair costs.*

fumes /fyumz/ *n.* [plural] strong-smelling gas or smoke that is unpleasant to breathe in: *gasoline fumes*

fu·mi·gate /'fyuməˌgeɪt/ *v.* [T] to remove disease, BACTERIA, insects, etc. from somewhere using chemical smoke or gas —**fumigation** /ˌfyumə'geɪʃən/ *n.* [U]

fun[1] /fʌn/ *n.* [U] **1** pleasure, amusement, and enjoyment, or an activity that is enjoyable: *Swimming is a lot of fun.* | *Did you* ***have fun*** *at Phil's house?* | *I have to admit –* ***it's*** *more* ***fun*** *to win.* | *It's nice to have time to read something* ***for fun***. |

F

The trip would be ***no fun*** (=not fun) *with a bad back.*

USAGE

Use **fun** to talk about situations or activities that you enjoy: *Ice skating is a lot of fun.*
Use **funny** to describe someone or something that makes you laugh: *The movie was so funny we couldn't stop laughing.*

2 make fun of sb/sth to make unkind jokes about someone or something: *I thought he was making fun of me, and I started to get mad.* **3 in fun** if you make a joke or say something about someone in fun, you do not intend it to be insulting: *I'm sorry, I only said it in fun.*

fun² *adj.* **1** a fun activity or experience is enjoyable: *It was a fun day.* **2** a fun person is enjoyable to be with: *Terry is always fun to be with.*

func·tion¹ /ˈfʌŋkʃən/ *n.* [C] **1** the usual purpose of a thing, or the job that someone usually does: *What's* ***the*** *exact* ***function of*** *this program?* | *A manager has to* ***perform*** *many different* ***functions***. **2** a large party or ceremonial event, especially for an important or official occasion: *The mayor has to attend all kinds of official functions.*

F

function² *v.* [I] to work in a particular way or in the correct way: *Her kidneys had stopped functioning.*

function as sth *phr. v.* to be used or work as something: *The space station functions as a laboratory in space.*

func·tion·al /ˈfʌŋkʃənəl/ *adj.* designed to be useful rather than attractive: *functional furniture* —**functionally** *adv.*

ˈfunction key *n.* [C] *technical* a key on the KEYBOARD of a computer that tells it to do something

fund¹ /fʌnd/ *n.* [C] **1** an amount of money that is kept for a particular purpose: *candidates' campaign funds* **2 funds** [plural] the money that an organization needs or has: *The PTO helps* ***raise funds*** *for the school.* | *federal funds for welfare programs* → MUTUAL FUND

fund² *v.* [T] to provide money for an activity, organization, event, etc.: *federally funded research work*

fun·da·men·tal /ˌfʌndəˈmɛntəl◂/ *adj.* **1** relating to the most basic and important parts of something: *a* ***fundamental change*** *in society* | *the fundamental democratic principle of free speech*

THESAURUS

basic, essential, central
→ see Thesaurus box at BASIC

2 necessary for something to exist or develop: *Water is* ***fundamental to*** *life.* —**fundamentally** *adv.*: *Our political views are fundamentally different.*

fun·da·men·tal·ist /ˌfʌndəˈmɛntəlɪst/ *n.* [C] **1** someone who follows the rules of his/her religion very strictly **2** a Christian who believes that everything in the Bible is completely and actually true —**fundamentalist** *adj.* —**fundamentalism** *n.* [U]

fun·da·men·tals /ˌfʌndəˈmɛntəlz/ *n.* **the fundamentals of sth** the most important ideas, rules, etc. that something is based on: *a class in the fundamentals of computer programming*

fund·ing /ˈfʌndɪŋ/ *n.* [U] an amount of money used for a special purpose: *The university is providing* ***funding for*** *the research.*

ˈfund-ˌraising *adj.* fund-raising events collect money for a specific purpose

fu·ner·al /ˈfyunərəl/ *n.* [C] a ceremony, usually religious, for burying or burning a dead person: *The* ***funeral*** *will be* ***held*** *on Thursday at St. Patrick's church.* | *More than 150 people* ***attended the funeral***.

ˈfuneral diˌrector *n.* [C] someone whose job is to arrange funerals

ˈfuneral home also **ˈfuneral ˌparlor** *n.* [C] the place where a body is kept before a funeral and where sometimes the funeral is held

fun·gus /ˈfʌŋgəs/ *n.* plural **fungi** /ˈfʌndʒaɪ, -gaɪ/ or **funguses** [C,U] a simple plant without leaves, such as MUSHROOMS and MOLD, that grows in dark, warm, slightly wet places —**fungal** /ˈfʌŋgəl/ *adj.*

funk /fʌŋk/ *n.* [U] **1** a type of popular music with a strong beat that is based on JAZZ and African music **2 in a funk** *informal* unhappy or worried about something

funk·y /ˈfʌŋki/ *adj. informal* **1** modern, fashionable, and interesting: *funky boots* **2** funky music is simple, with a strong RHYTHM that is easy to dance to

fun·nel¹ /ˈfʌnl/ *n.* [C] a tube with a wide top and a narrow bottom, used for pouring liquids or powders into a container

funnel² *v.* **1** [I,T] if you funnel something somewhere, or if it funnels there, it goes there by passing through a narrow opening: *The crowd* ***funneled through*** *the narrow streets.* **2** [T] to send things or money from different places to a particular place or person: *a policy of* ***funneling*** *the most talented students* ***into*** *special schools*

fun·nies /ˈfʌniz/ *n.* **the funnies** a number of different CARTOONS (=funny pictures) printed together in newspapers or magazines

fun·ni·ly /ˈfʌnəli/ *adv.* → **strangely/oddly/funnily enough** at ENOUGH

funny¹ /ˈfʌni/ *adj.* **1** amusing you and making you laugh: *John gave a funny little speech.* | *What's so funny?* | *He looked really funny.*

THESAURUS

hilarious/hysterical – extremely funny
witty – using words in a funny and intelligent way: *witty remarks*

corny – corny jokes, etc. have been told many times or are so silly that they are not funny
amusing/humorous – slightly more formal ways to say that something is funny: *an amusing anecdote* (=a short, interesting, and funny story about an event or person)
➔ see also Usage box at FUN[1]

2 strange or unexpected, and difficult to understand or explain: *What's that funny noise?* | *The room smelled funny.* | *I got a funny feeling that someone was watching me.*

THESAURUS

strange, **peculiar**, **mysterious**, **odd**, **weird**, **bizarre**
➔ see Thesaurus box at STRANGE[1]

3 slightly sick: *It makes my stomach* ***feel funny***.

SPOKEN PHRASES

4 it's funny used in order to say that you do not understand something that seems strange or unexpected: *"It's funny," she said. "You seem different somehow."* | ***It's funny how*** *you can affect people and not even realize it.* **5 that's funny** said when you are surprised by something that has happened, that you cannot explain: *That's funny! She was here just a minute ago.* **6 the funny thing is** used in order to say what the strangest or most amusing part of a story or situation is: *The funny thing is, once I stopped dieting I started to lose weight.* **7 very funny!** said when someone is laughing at you or making a joke that you do not think is funny

funny[2] *adv.* in a strange or unusual way: *Judy's been acting kind of funny lately.*

funny bone *n.* [singular] the soft part of your elbow that hurts a lot when you hit it against something

fur /fɚ/ *n.* **1** [U] the thick soft hair that covers the bodies of some animals, such as dogs and cats ➔ see picture on page A2 **2** [C,U] the skin of a dead animal with the fur still attached to it, or a piece of clothing made from this: *a fur coat*

fu·ri·ous /ˈfyʊriəs/ *adj.* **1** very angry: *Jim'll be* ***furious with*** *me if I'm late.* | *Dad was* ***furious that*** *I had taken the car without asking.*

THESAURUS

angry, **annoyed**, **irritated**, **livid**, **mad**
➔ see Thesaurus box at ANGRY

2 done with a lot of uncontrolled energy or anger: *He woke up to a furious pounding at the door.* —**furiously** *adv.*

furled /fɚld/ *adj.* rolled or folded: *a furled umbrella* —**furl** *v.* [T]

fur·long /ˈfɚlɔŋ/ *n.* [C] *old-fashioned* a unit for measuring length that is used in horse racing. A furlong equals 201 meters and there are eight furlongs in a mile

fur·lough /ˈfɚloʊ/ *n.* [C] a short period of time in which someone is allowed to be away from his/her job, especially in the military: *a soldier home* ***on furlough***

fur·nace /ˈfɚnɪs/ *n.* [C] a large container with a hot fire inside it, used for producing power or heat, or to melt metals and other materials

fur·nish /ˈfɚnɪʃ/ *v.* [T] **1** to put furniture and other things into a house or room: *a room* ***furnished with*** *two beds* **2** to supply something: *Your Internet provider will* ***furnish*** *you* ***with*** *e-mail software.* —**furnished** *adj.*: *a furnished apartment*

fur·nish·ings /ˈfɚnɪʃɪŋz/ *n.* [plural] the furniture and other things in a room, such as curtains, decorations, etc.

fur·ni·ture /ˈfɚnɪtʃɚ/ *n.* [U] large objects such as chairs, tables, and beds that you use in a room, office, etc.: *The room's only* ***piece of furniture*** *was an old sofa.* | *office furniture*

GRAMMAR

Furniture does not have a plural form. You can say **some furniture**, **any furniture**, or **pieces of furniture**: *When we first got married, we didn't have any furniture at all.*

fu·ror /ˈfyʊrɔr/ *n.* [singular] a sudden expression of anger or excitement among a large group of people: *His decision to resign* ***caused/created a furor***.

fur·row[1] /ˈfɚoʊ, ˈfʌroʊ/ *n.* [C] a long deep fold or line in the surface of something such as skin or the ground: *the furrows of a plowed field*

furrow[2] *v.* [T] to make a long deep fold or line in the surface of something such as skin or the ground: *Saks furrowed his brow.* —**furrowed** *adj.*

fur·ry /ˈfɚi/ *adj.* covered with fur, or looking or feeling as if covered with fur: *furry material*

fur·ther[1] /ˈfɚðɚ/ *adv.* **1** more, or to a greater degree: *I have nothing further to say.* | *Mark went* ***further into*** *debt.* | *He was falling* ***further and further*** *behind in his schoolwork.*

USAGE

Use **further** to talk about time, quantities, or degrees: *House prices will probably drop further next year.* | *I don't want to discuss this any further.*
Use **farther** to talk about distance: *The restaurant's just a little farther down the street.*
Many people use **further** in spoken English to talk about distance, but many teachers think that this is not correct.

2 a longer way in time or space: *The records don't go any* ***further back*** *than 1960.* | *Their home is* ***further down*** *the street.* **3 take sth further** to do something at a more serious or higher level: *Hallas decided not to take the court case any further.* **4** *formal* FURTHERMORE

further[2] *adj.* additional: *Are there any further*

F

questions? | ***Further information/details*** *is available on the website.*

THESAURUS

more, another, extra, additional
➔ see Thesaurus box at MORE[2]

further[3] *v.* [T] *formal* to help something to succeed: *The training should help him further his career.*

fur·ther·more /ˈfɚðɚˌmɔr/ *adv. formal* in addition to what has already been written or said: *Jones had reason to fear for her safety. Furthermore, she could not trust anyone to protect her.*

fur·thest /ˈfɚðɪst/ *adj., adv.* **1** to the greatest degree or amount, or more than before: *Smith's book has probably* ***gone furthest*** (=done the most) *in explaining these events.* **2** at the greatest distance from a place or point in time: *the houses* ***furthest from*** *the center of town*

fur·tive /ˈfɚṭɪv/ *adj.* behaving as if you want to keep something secret: *a* ***furtive glance*** —**furtively** *adv.*

F

fu·ry /ˈfyʊri/ *n.* **1** [singular, U] a state or feeling of extreme anger: *She was filled* ***with fury***. | *Hanson left the meeting* ***in a fury***. **2 the fury of the wind/sea/storm etc.** used in order to describe very bad weather **3 a fury of sth** a state of great activity or strong feeling: *Joe went home in a fury of frustration.*

fuse[1] /fyuz/ *n.* [C] **1** a short wire inside a piece of electrical equipment that prevents damage to the equipment by melting if too much electricity tries to pass through it: *I went down to the basement and replaced a* ***blown fuse*** (=a fuse that had melted). **2** a thing such as a string that is connected to a bomb and used for making it explode **3** used in expressions relating to someone becoming angry: *Randy finally* ***blew a fuse*** (=got angry very suddenly) *and screamed at us.* | *Martina* ***has a short fuse*** (=gets angry easily) *when she's tired.*

fuse[2] *v.* [I,T] **1** to join together and become one thing, or to join two things together: *His novel fuses historical information with a romantic story.* **2** *technical* if metals, rocks, etc. fuse together, they become melted and are joined together

fuse·box /ˈfyuzbɑks/ *n.* [C] a metal box that contains the FUSES for the electrical system in a building

fu·se·lage /ˈfyusəˌlɑʒ, -lɪdʒ, -zə-/ *n.* [C] the main part of an airplane, in which people sit or goods are carried ➔ see picture at AIRPLANE

fu·sion /ˈfyuʒən/ *n.* [C,U] **1** a physical combination of separate things [➡ **fission**]: *experiments in nuclear fusion* **2** the combination of separate things, groups, or ideas: *a fusion of French and Indian cuisine*

fuss[1] /fʌs/ *n.* **1** [singular, U] attention, excitement, or activity that is not really necessary: *Hey, what's all the fuss about* (=why are people so excited, angry, busy, etc.)*?* | *They wanted a quiet wedding without any fuss.* **2 make a fuss/kick up a fuss** to complain or become angry about something that other people do not think is important: *Don't be afraid to make a fuss if you think you're not being treated right.* **3 make a fuss over sb/sth** to pay a lot of attention to someone or something that you like, in a way that is slightly silly: *His mother made a fuss over him, stroking his hair.*

fuss[2] *v.* [I] to complain or become upset: *The baby woke up and started to fuss.*

fuss over sb/sth *phr. v.* to pay a lot of attention to someone or something that you like: *The women started fussing over Kate's baby.*

fuss with sth *phr. v.* to move or touch something again and again in a nervous way: *Stop fussing with your hair!*

fuss·y /ˈfʌsi/ *adj.* comparative **fussier**, superlative **fussiest** **1** concerned or worried about things that are not very important: *Many kids are fussy eaters.* **2** a fussy baby cries a lot **3** very detailed or decorated, in a way that is unpleasant

fu·tile /ˈfyuṭl/ *adj.* having no chance of being effective or successful: *a* ***futile attempt/effort*** *to prevent the war* —**futility** /fyuˈtɪləṭi/ *n.* [U]

THESAURUS

pointless, useless
➔ see Thesaurus box at POINTLESS

fu·ton /ˈfutɑn/ *n.* [C] a soft flat MATTRESS that can be used as a bed or folded into a chair

fu·ture[1] /ˈfyutʃɚ/ *n.* **1 the future** the time that will happen after the present: *Each story has a different vision of the future.* | *a feeling of hope* ***for the future*** | *The airport has room for another runway to be built* ***in the future*** (=at some time in the future). | *Investigators hope to wrap up the case* ***in the near/immediate future*** (=soon). | *This will remain a problem* ***for the foreseeable future*** (=for as long as we can plan for). | *a story set* ***in the not too distant future*** (=not too far in the future) **2 in the future** the next time you do the same activity: *In the future I'll be sure to reserve tickets.* **3** [C] what will happen to someone or something, or what he, she, or it will do in the future: *Parents want the best for their children's futures.* | *an issue that will affect* ***the future of*** *our country* | *Businesses must* ***look to the future*** (=plan for what will happen). **4 the future** *technical* in grammar, the tense of a verb that shows that an action or state will happen or exist at a later time. It is often shown in English by the MODAL VERB "will" followed by a verb. In the sentence "We will leave tomorrow," "will leave" is in the future tense

future[2] *adj.* **1** likely to happen or exist during the time after the present: *The park will be preserved for future generations.* | *companies planning for future growth* | *I'd like you to meet my future wife* (=the person who will be your wife). **2** *technical* in grammar, being a tense of a verb that shows a future action or state: *the future tense* **3 for future reference** in order to be used again at a later time: *Can I **keep** that article **for future reference**?*

ˌfuture ˈperfect *n.* **the future perfect** *technical* in grammar, the tense of a verb that shows that an action will be completed before a particular time in the future. It is shown by the AUXILIARY VERBS "will have" followed by a past participle. In the sentence "I will have finished my finals by next Friday," "will have finished" is in the future perfect

fu·tur·is·tic /ˌfyutʃəˈrɪstɪk◂/ *adj.* futuristic ideas, books, movies, etc. describe what might happen in the future, especially because of scientific developments

fuzz /fʌz/ *n.* [U] *informal* small soft thin hairs, or a similar material, on fruit such as PEACHES

fuzz·y /ˈfʌzi/ *adj.* **1** if a sound or picture is fuzzy, it is not clear: *Unfortunately, a lot of the photos were a little fuzzy.* **2** not easy to understand or not having very clear details: *The distinction between the two is fuzzy.* **3** having a lot of very small thin hairs, fur, etc. that are very soft: *a fuzzy sweater* **4 warm and fuzzy** making you feel comfortable and happy, but often having little importance: *the warm and fuzzy messages we're getting from the governor*

fwy. the written abbreviation of **freeway**

FYI the abbreviation of **for your information**, used especially on MEMOS (=short business notes)

G, g

G¹, g /dʒi/ *n.* **1** [C,U] the seventh letter of the English alphabet **2** [C,U] the fifth note in the musical SCALE of C, or the musical KEY based on this note **3** [C] *technical* an amount of force that is equal to the Earth's GRAVITY

G² *adj.* the written abbreviation of **general audience**, used in order to show that a movie has been officially approved for people of all ages

GA the written abbreviation of **Georgia**

gab /gæb/ *v.* past tense **gabbed**, past participle **gabbing** [I] *informal* to talk continuously, usually about things that are not important

ga·ble /ˈgeɪbəl/ *n.* [C] the top part of a wall of a house where it joins with a pointed roof, making a shape like a TRIANGLE

gadg·et /ˈgædʒɪt/ *n.* [C] a small tool or machine that makes a particular job easier: *a handy kitchen gadget*

THESAURUS

machine, appliance, device
→ see Thesaurus box at MACHINE¹

gaffe /gæf/ *n.* [C] an embarrassing mistake made in a social situation

gag¹ /gæg/ *v.* past tense **gagged**, past participle **gagging** **1** [I] to be unable to swallow and feel sick in a way that makes you feel as if you are going to bring up the food from your stomach: *I **gagged on** my coffee.* **2** [T] to tie a piece of cloth over someone's mouth so that s/he cannot make any noise

gag² *n.* [C] **1** *informal* a joke or funny story

THESAURUS

joke, wisecrack, one-liner, pun, funny story
→ see Thesaurus box at JOKE¹

2 a piece of cloth used in order to GAG someone **3 gag gift** a present for someone that is meant to be funny → GAG ORDER

gagged /gægd/ *adj.* having your mouth tied with a piece of cloth so that you cannot make any noise

gag·gle /ˈgægəl/ *n.* [C] a group of GEESE, or a noisy group of people

ˈgag ˌorder *n.* [C] an order given by a court of law to prevent any public reporting of a case that is still being considered in the court

gai·e·ty /ˈgeɪət̬i/ *n.* [U] *old-fashioned* the state of having fun and being happy

gai·ly /ˈgeɪli/ *adv.* *old-fashioned* in a happy way

gain¹ /geɪn/ *v.* **1** [I,T] to get, win, or achieve something that you want or need [≠ **lose**]: *The Republicans gained control of Congress.* | *India gained independence in 1947.* | *What do you hope to **gain from** the course?*

USAGE

Gain means to get something useful or necessary: *I've gained a lot of useful experience.*
Do not use **gain** to talk about getting money for the work you do. Use **earn**: *He earns more than I do.*
Make is a less formal way of saying **earn**: *I make $20 an hour.*
Win means to get a prize in a game or competition: *The first person to get all the answers right will win $100.*

2 [I,T] to gradually get more of a quality, feeling, etc.: *The ideas quickly gained popular support.* | *a chance to gain experience in publishing* | *The show has been **gaining in** popularity.* **3** [T] to increase in weight, speed, height, or value: *Bea has **gained** a lot of **weight** since Christmas.* | *The dollar gained 4% against the yen.* **4 gain access a)** to be able to enter a room or building: *Somehow the thief had gained access to his apart-*

G

ment. **b)** to be allowed to see or use something: *Marston had difficulty gaining access to official documents.*

gain on sb/sth *phr. v.* to start getting closer to the person, car, etc. that you are chasing: *Hurry up! They're **gaining on** us!*

gain² *n.* **1** [C,U] an increase in the amount or level of something: *the program's **gain in** popularity* | *weight gain* | *the country's recent economic gains* **2** [C] an advantage or an improvement: ***gains in** medical science*

gait /geɪt/ *n.* [U] the way that someone walks

gal /gæl/ *n.* [C] *informal* a girl or woman

ga·la /ˈgælə, ˈgeɪlə/ *n.* [C] an event at which a lot of people are entertained and celebrate a special occasion —**gala** *adj.*

ga·lac·tic /gəˈlæktɪk/ *adj.* relating to the GALAXY

gal·ax·y /ˈgæləksi/ *n.* plural **galaxies** [C] one of the large groups of stars that are in the universe

TOPIC

space, **meteor**, **asteroid**, **comet**, **moon**, **planet**, **star**, **sun**, **constellation**, **black hole**, **spacecraft**, **spaceship**, **rocket**, **(space) shuttle**, **satellite**, **probe**, **astronaut**
➔ see Topic box at SPACE[1]

G

gale /geɪl/ *n.* [C] a very strong wind: *a fierce gale*

THESAURUS

gust, **storm**, **hurricane**, **tornado**, **typhoon**
➔ see Thesaurus box at WIND[1]

gall /gɔl/ *n.* **have the gall to do sth** to do something rude or unreasonable that most people would be embarrassed to do: *She had the gall to say that I looked fat!*

gal·lant /ˈgælənt/ *adj. old-fashioned* brave and kind: *a gallant soldier* —**gallantly** *adv.* —**gallantry** *n.* [U]

ˈgall ˌbladder *n.* [C] the organ in your body that stores BILE

gal·ler·y /ˈgæləri/ *n.* plural **galleries** [C] **1** a room, hall, or building where people can look at paintings or other types of art: *the National Gallery of Art in Washington* **2** a small expensive store where people can look at and buy art: ***art galleries** in Manhattan* **3** an upper floor like a BALCONY inside a hall, church, or theater, where people can sit

gal·ley /ˈgæli/ *n.* [C] **1** a kitchen on a ship or an airplane **2** a long Greek or Roman ship that was rowed by SLAVES

gall·ing /ˈgɔlɪŋ/ *adj.* annoying: *a galling defeat*

gal·lon /ˈgælən/ *n.* [C] a unit for measuring liquid, equal to 4 QUARTS or 3.785 liters: *a **gallon of** gas*

gallop

gal·lop¹ /ˈgæləp/ *v.* [I] if a horse gallops, it runs as fast as it can

gallop² *n.* [singular] the fastest speed that a horse can go, or the movement of a horse at this speed

gal·lop·ing /ˈgæləpɪŋ/ *adj.* increasing or developing very quickly: *galloping inflation*

gal·lows /ˈgæloʊz/ *n.* plural **gallows** [C] a structure that is used for killing criminals by hanging them

ga·lore /gəˈlɔr/ *adj.* in large amounts or numbers: *He had toys and clothes galore.* ▶ Don't say "He had galore clothes." ◀

ga·losh·es /gəˈlɑʃɪz/ *n.* [plural] *old-fashioned* rubber shoes you wear over your normal shoes when it rains or snows

gal·va·nize /ˈgælvəˌnaɪz/ *v.* [T] to shock someone so much that s/he realizes s/he needs to do something to solve a problem or improve the situation: *Martin Luther King's protests galvanized the nation.*

gal·va·nized /ˈgælvəˌnaɪzd/ *adj.* galvanized metal has been treated in a special way so that it does not RUST

gam·bit /ˈgæmbɪt/ *n.* [C] something you do or say in order to gain control in an argument, conversation, or meeting

gam·ble¹ /ˈgæmbəl/ *v.* **1** [I] to risk money or possessions on the result of something such as a race or card game because you might win a lot more money if the race, etc. has the result you want: *Jack won $700 gambling in Las Vegas.* | *They **gambled on** the horses.* **2** [I,T] to do something that involved risk because you hope things will happen the way you want them to: *Many investors **gambled that** the market would continue to improve.*

gamble sth ⇔ **away** *phr. v.* to lose money or possessions by gambling

gamble² *n.* [singular] an action or plan that involves risk because it might not be successful: *The coach **took a gamble** in playing Collins, who is inexperienced.*

gam·bler /ˈgæmblɚ/ *n.* [C] someone who GAMBLES, especially as a habit

gam·bling /ˈgæmblɪŋ/ *n.* [U] the activity of risking money and possessions because you might win a lot more if a card game, race, etc. has the result you want: *Gambling is legal in Nevada.*

game[1] /geɪm/ *n.* **1** [C] an activity or sport that people play for fun or in a competition: *a good* ***card/video/board game*** | *The boys are outside,* ***playing*** *some kind of* ***game****.*

THESAURUS

game – a particular competition in a sport, or a competition that involves mental skill, knowledge, or luck: *last night's football game* | *a game of cards*
sport – a physical activity in which people or teams play against each other and try to win: *Her favorite sport is basketball.*
recreation – all the activities that people do in order to relax: *the city's parks and recreation department*
hobby – an activity that you do in your free time: *Her hobbies are reading and music.*

2 [C] a particular occasion when you play a sport or activity: *Who* ***won/lost*** *the football* ***game****?* | *The Aztecs* ***play*** *only two* ***games*** *this month.* | *How about a* ***game of*** *chess?* **3 games** [plural] a large sports event, where a variety of sports are played: *the Olympic Games* **4** [C] one of the parts of a competition, such as in tennis or BRIDGE: *Williams leads, two games to one.* **5 sb's game** how well someone plays a particular game or sport: *Ramone's* ***game*** *steadily* ***improved****.* | *Abdul-Jabbar was* ***at the top of*** *his* ***game*** (=playing very well). **6 play games** to behave in a way that is not serious or that is dishonest or unfair: *Don't* ***play games with*** *me. I don't have time.* **7 be (just) a game** if something is just a game to you, you do not consider how serious or important it is: *Marriage is just a game to you, isn't it?* **8** [U] wild animals and birds that are hunted for food and as a sport

game[2] *adj.* willing to do something dangerous, new, or difficult: *I'm game if you are.*

'game plan *n.* [C] a plan for achieving success, especially in business or politics: *the Senator's political game plan*

'game show *n.* [C] a television program in which people play games or answer questions in order to win money and prizes ➔ see Thesaurus box at TELEVISION

gam·ut /'gæmət/ *n.* [singular] a complete range of possibilities: *His musical influences* ***ran the gamut from*** *Elvis* ***to*** *the Sex Pistols* (=included all the possibilities between two extremes).

gan·der /'gændɚ/ *n.* [C] **1** a male GOOSE **2 have/take a gander at sth** *informal* to look at something

gang[1] /gæŋ/ *n.* [C] **1** a group of young people who often cause trouble and fight other similar groups: *teenage* ***gang members*** | *Chicago* ***street gangs*** | *the victims of* ***gang violence***

THESAURUS

group, crowd, team, crew, mob, bunch
➔ see Thesaurus box at GROUP[1]

2 a group of criminals who work together: *a* ***gang of*** *drug dealers* **3** a group of friends: *All the old gang will be there.*

gang[2] *v.*
gang up on sb *phr. v.* to join a group in order to criticize or attack someone: *My brothers used to gang up on me.*

gang·bust·ers /'gæŋˌbʌstɚz/ *n.* **like gangbusters** *informal* very quickly and successfully: *The town is growing like gangbusters.*

gang·land /'gæŋlænd/ *adj.* **a gangland killing/shooting/murder** a violent action that happens because of organized crime

gan·gly /'gæŋgli/ **also gan·gling** /'gæŋglɪŋ/ *adj.* very tall and thin and unable to move gracefully: *a gangly teenager*

gang·plank /'gæŋplæŋk/ *n.* [C] a board you walk on between a ship and the shore, or between two ships

gan·grene /'gæŋgrin, gæŋ'grin/ *n.* [U] a medical condition in which your flesh decays on part of your body because blood has stopped flowing there as a result of an illness or injury

gang·ster /'gæŋstɚ/ *n.* [C] a member of a group of violent criminals

gang·way /'gæŋweɪ/ *n.* [C] a large GANGPLANK

gap /gæp/ *n.* [C] **1** an empty space between two things or two parts of something: *a big* ***gap between*** *her two front teeth* | *a* ***gap in*** *the fence*

THESAURUS

hole, space, leak, crack
➔ see Thesaurus box at HOLE[1]

2 a difference between two situations, groups, amounts, etc.: *a large age* ***gap between*** *Jorge and his sister* | *We should be trying to* ***bridge the gap between*** *rich and poor.* **3** something that is missing that stops something else from being good or complete: *His death left a* ***gap in*** *my life.* | *a* ***gap in*** *her memory* | *The company has* ***filled a gap in the market*** (=they produce a product or service that did not exist before). **4** a period of time in which nothing happens or nothing is said: *an uncomfortable* ***gap in*** *the conversation* **5** a low place between two higher parts of a mountain

gape /geɪp/ *v.* [I] **1** to look at something for a long time, usually with your mouth open, because you are very shocked or surprised: *She backed away from the children, who were* ***gaping at*** *her.*

THESAURUS

look, glance, peek, peer, stare, gaze
➔ see Thesaurus box at LOOK[1]

2 also gape open to come apart or open widely

G

gap·ing /ˈgeɪpɪŋ/ *adj.* a gaping hole, wound, or mouth is very wide and open

ga·rage /gəˈrɑʒ, gəˈrɑdʒ/ *n.* [C] **1** a building, usually connected or next to your house, where you keep your car: *I think my tools are out in the garage.* | *a* ***one-car/two-car garage*** **2** a place where cars are repaired: *We took the car to a garage on Fourth Street.* ➔ PARKING GARAGE

gaˈrage ˌsale *n.* [C] a sale of used clothes, furniture, toys, etc. that you no longer want, usually held in your garage

garb /gɑrb/ *n.* [U] *literary* a particular style of clothing

gar·bage /ˈgɑrbɪdʒ/ *n.* **1** [singular, U] waste material such as old food, dirty paper, and empty bags, usually considered together with the container that holds it: *The place smelled of garbage.* | *Can somebody* ***take out the garbage****?* | *We threw the paper plates* ***in the garbage****.*

THESAURUS

trash – things that you throw away, such as old food, dirty paper, etc.: *a bag stuffed with trash*
refuse formal – things that you throw away, such as old food, dirty paper, etc.: *the money spent on refuse collection*
litter – garbage, especially pieces of paper, food containers, etc., that people leave on the ground in public places: *The Scouts picked up litter in the park.*
waste – unwanted things or substances that are left after you have used something: *the safe disposal of nuclear waste*

2 [singular] *informal* something that is of very low quality: *Most of the stuff they sell is just garbage.* **3** [U] *informal* statements or ideas that are silly or wrong [= **nonsense**]: *I don't want to hear this garbage.*

ˈgarbage ˌcan *n.* [C] a large container with a lid in which you put waste materials, usually kept outside [= **trash can**]

ˈgarbage colˌlector *n.* [C] someone whose job is to remove waste from GARBAGE CANS

ˈgarbage disˌposal *n.* [C] a small machine in a kitchen SINK that cuts food waste into small pieces

ˈgarbage man *n.* [C] a GARBAGE COLLECTOR

ˈgarbage ˌtruck *n.* [C] a large vehicle used for carrying waste that is removed from people's GARBAGE CANS

gar·bled /ˈgɑrbəld/ *adj.* confusing and not giving correct information: *a garbled version of the story*

gar·den /ˈgɑrdn/ *n.* [C] **1** the part of someone's land used for growing flowers, or vegetable and fruit plants: *Jane was weeding the* ***vegetable/flower garden****.* **2 gardens** [plural] a public park where a lot of flowers and unusual plants are grown: *the Japanese Tea Gardens in Golden Gate park*

gar·den·er /ˈgɑrdnɚ/ *n.* [C] someone who does gardening as a job

gar·den·ing /ˈgɑrdn-ɪŋ/ *n.* [U] the activity or job of making a garden, yard, etc. look pretty by growing flowers, removing WEEDS etc.: *gardening tools*

gar·gan·tu·an /gɑrˈgæntʃuən/ *adj.* extremely large: *a gargantuan bed*

gar·gle /ˈgɑrgəl/ *v.* [I] to move medicine or liquid around in your throat in order to make it stop feeling sore, or to clean the inside of your mouth: *If you have a sore throat,* ***gargling with*** *salt water might help.* —**gargle** *n.* [C,U]

gar·goyle /ˈgɑrgɔɪl/ *n.* [C] a stone figure shaped like the face of a strange creature, usually on the roofs of old buildings

gar·ish /ˈgærɪʃ, ˈgɛr-/ *adj.* very brightly colored and unpleasant to look at: *the garish carpet in the hotel lobby*

gar·land /ˈgɑrlənd/ *n.* [C] a ring of flowers or leaves, worn for decoration or in special ceremonies

gar·lic /ˈgɑrlɪk/ *n.* [U] a small plant like an onion with a very strong taste, used in cooking

gar·ment /ˈgɑrmənt/ *n.* [C] *formal* a piece of clothing

gar·ner /ˈgɑrnɚ/ *v.* [T] *formal* to take or collect something, especially information or support: *Harris garnered 54% of the vote.*

gar·net /ˈgɑrnɪt/ *n.* [C] a dark red stone used in jewelry

gar·nish¹ /ˈgɑrnɪʃ/ *v.* [T] **1** to decorate food with a small piece of a fruit or vegetable: ***Garnish*** *each plate* ***with*** *a slice of lemon.* **2** *technical* **also gar·nish·ee** /ˈgɑrnəˈʃi/ to take money directly from someone's salary because s/he has not paid his/her debts

garnish² *n.* [C] a small piece of a fruit or vegetable that you use to decorate food

gar·ret /ˈgærɪt/ *n.* [C] *literary* a small room at the top of a house

gar·ri·son /ˈgærəsən/ *n.* [C] a group of soldiers who live in a particular area in order to defend it —**garrison** *v.* [T]

gar·ter /ˈgɑrt̬ɚ/ *n.* [C] a piece of ELASTIC (=material that stretches) attached to a woman's underwear and to her STOCKINGS to hold them up

gas¹ /gæs/ *n.* plural **gases** or **gasses** **1** [U] **also gasoline** a liquid that is used for producing power in the engines of cars, trucks, etc.: *How much is a gallon of gas?* | *The mechanic found a hole in the* ***gas tank*** (=container for holding gas). **2** [C,U] a substance such as air that is not liquid or solid, and usually cannot be seen: *hydrogen gas* **3** [U] a clear substance like air that is burned to give heat for cooking and heating: *a gas stove* | *I think we might have a* ***gas leak*** *in here.* **4 the gas** the GAS PEDAL on a car: ***Step on the gas*** (=push down the gas pedal and made the car go faster). **5** [U] the condition of having a lot of air in your stomach ➔ NATURAL GAS

G

gas² *v.* past tense and past participle **gassed**, present participle **gassing** [T] to attack or kill someone with poisonous gas

'gas ˌchamber *n.* [C] a large room in which people or animals are killed with poisonous gas

gash /gæʃ/ *n.* [C] a deep cut —**gash** *v.* [T]

gas·ket /'gæskɪt/ *n.* [C] a flat piece of rubber between two surfaces of a machine that prevents steam, oil, etc. from escaping

'gas mask *n.* [C] a piece of equipment that you wear over your face to protect you from breathing poisonous gases

gas·o·line /ˌgæsə'lin, 'gæsəˌlin/ *n.* [U] GAS

gasp /gæsp/ *v.* [I] **1** to breathe in suddenly and loudly because you are surprised or in pain: *The audience **gasped in/with** surprise.* **2** to quickly breathe in a lot of air because you are having difficulty breathing normally: *Kim crawled out of the pool, **gasping for air/breath**.* —**gasp** *n.* [C] *a **gasp of** disbelief*

'gas ˌpedal *n.* [C] the thing that you press with your foot to make a car go faster [= **accelerator**] ➔ see Topic box at DRIVE¹ ➔ see picture on page A12

'gas ˌstation *n.* [C] a place that sells gas for your car

gas·tric /'gæstrɪk/ *adj. technical* relating to the stomach: *gastric ulcers*

gas·tro·nom·ic /ˌgæstrə'nɑmɪk/ *adj.* [only before noun] relating to cooking and eating good food: *the **gastronomic delights** of Chinatown*

gate /geɪt/ *n.* [C] **1** a door in a fence or outside wall [➡ **door**]: *Who left the gate open? | Make sure the **front/back/rear/main gate** is locked.* **2** the place where you leave an airport building to get on the airplane: *Flight 207 to Chicago will be leaving from gate 16. | the **departure gate***

'gate-crasher, **gate·crash·er** /'geɪtˌkræʃɚ/ *n.* [C] someone who goes to a party that s/he has not been invited to —**gate-crash** *v.* [I,T]

gate·way /'geɪtˀweɪ/ *n.* [C] **1** an opening in a fence or wall that can be closed by a gate **2 the gateway to sth** a place, especially a city, that you go through in order to reach another place: *St. Louis was once the gateway to the West.* **3** *technical* a way of connecting two different computer networks that helps them to work together

gath·er /'gæðɚ/ *v.* **1** [I,T] if people gather somewhere, or if someone gathers them, they come together in the same place: *A **crowd gathered** to watch the fight. | **Gather around** and I'll tell you a story. | Jill gathered the children and lined them up. | Dozens of reporters were gathered outside the hotel.*

> **THESAURUS**
> **meet, get together, assemble, come together**
> ➔ see Thesaurus box at MEET¹

2 [T] to bring things from different places together: *I'm currently trying to gather new ideas for my next novel. | "Wait for me," said Anna, **gathering up** her books.* **3** [T] to believe that something is true based on the information you have: ***From what I can gather/As far as I can gather*** (=I think it is true that) *he never intended to sell the house. | I **gather (that)** he won't be coming.* **4 gather steam/speed/momentum/force etc.** to become faster, stronger, etc.: *The car gathered speed as it rolled down the hill.* **5 gather dust** if something useful gathers dust, it is not being used: *The report has been gathering dust for 18 years.*

gath·er·ing /'gæðərɪŋ/ *n.* [C] a meeting of a group of people: *a family gathering | a **gathering of** war veterans*

gauche /goʊʃ/ *adj.* someone who is gauche says or does things that are considered impolite because s/he does not know the right way to behave

gaud·y /'gɔdi/ *adj.* something that is gaudy is too bright and looks cheap: *gaudy jewelry*

gauge¹ /geɪdʒ/ *n.* [C] **1** an instrument that measures the amount or size of something: *a car's gas gauge* **2 a gauge of sth** something that helps you make a judgment about a person or situation: *The amount of money you make is not the only gauge of your success.* **3** a measurement of the width or thickness of something: *a 12-gauge shotgun*

gauge² *v.* [T] **1** to judge what someone is likely to do or how s/he feels: *It's difficult to **gauge** exactly **how** he's going to respond.*

> **THESAURUS**
> **judge, evaluate, assess, appraise**
> ➔ see Thesaurus box at JUDGE²

2 to calculate the size or amount of something: *The thermostat will gauge the temperature and control the heat.*

gaunt /gɔnt, gɑnt/ *adj.* very thin, pale, and unhealthy

gaunt·let /'gɔntˀlɪt, 'gɑntˀ-/ *n.* [C] **1 run the gauntlet** to be criticized or attacked by a lot of people: *There was no way to avoid running the gauntlet of media attention.* **2 throw down the gauntlet** to invite someone to fight, argue, or compete with you **3** a thick long GLOVE that you wear to protect your hand

gauze /gɔz/ *n.* [U] a very thin light cloth used for covering wounds and making clothes: *His hand was wrapped in a **gauze bandage**.*

gave /geɪv/ *v.* the past tense of GIVE

gav·el /'gævəl/ *n.* [C] a small hammer that someone in charge of a court of law, meeting, etc. hits on a table to get people's attention

gawk /gɔk/ *v.* [I] to look at someone or something for a long time, in a way that looks stupid: *Drivers slowed to **gawk at** the accident.*

gawk·y /'gɔki/ *adj.* tall and not graceful: *a tall gawky teenager*

G

THESAURUS

clumsy, awkward, inelegant
→ see Thesaurus box at CLUMSY

gay[1] /geɪ/ *adj.* **1** sexually attracted to people of the same sex [= **homosexual**; ➡ **lesbian**]: *the gay community* | *He told me she's gay.* **2** *old-fashioned* bright and attractive: *a room painted in gay colors* **3** *old-fashioned* happy and cheerful: *gay laughter*

gay[2] *n.* [C] someone, especially a man, who is sexually attracted to people of the same sex [= **homosexual**; ➡ **lesbian**]

gaze[1] /geɪz/ *v.* [I] to look at someone or something for a long time: *He sat for hours just **gazing out** the window.*

THESAURUS

look, glance, peek, peer, stare, gape
→ see Thesaurus box at LOOK[1]

gaze[2] *n.* [singular] a long steady look: *Molly felt uncomfortable under the teacher's **steady gaze**.*

ga·ze·bo /gəˈziboʊ/ *n.* [C] a small building in a garden or park that you can sit in

gazebo

ga·zelle /gəˈzɛl/ *n.* [C] an animal like a small DEER

gear[1] /gɪr/ *n.* **1** [C,U] the machinery in a vehicle such as a car, truck, or bicycle that you use to go at different speeds: *There's a weird noise every time I **change/shift gears**.* | *The car's **in first/second etc. gear**.* → see picture at BICYCLE **2** [U] special equipment, clothing, etc. that you need for a particular activity: *camping gear* **3** [U] a piece of machinery that does a particular job: *the landing gear on a plane*

gear[2] *v.* **be geared to/toward sb/sth** to be organized in order to achieve a particular purpose: *All his training was geared to winning an Olympic gold medal.* | *concerts geared toward young children*

gear up *phr. v.* to prepare for something: *Congress is **gearing up for** a debate on Social Security.*

gear·box /ˈgɪrbɑks/ *n.* [C] the system of gears in a vehicle

ˈgear shift *n.* [C] a stick that you move to change gears in a vehicle → see picture on page A12

GED *n.* **the GED** or **General Equivalency Diploma** a DIPLOMA that people who did not finish HIGH SCHOOL can get by taking a test

gee /dʒi/ *interjection spoken old-fashioned* said when you are surprised or annoyed: *Aw, gee, Mom, I don't want to go to bed.*

geek /gik/ *n.* [C] *slang* someone who is not popular because s/he wears unfashionable clothes and does not know how to behave in social situations: *a computer geek* —**geeky** *adj.*

geese /gis/ *n.* the plural of GOOSE

gee·zer /ˈgizɚ/ *n.* [C] *informal* an old man

Gei·ger count·er /ˈgaɪgɚ ˌkaʊntɚ/ *n.* [C] an instrument that finds and measures RADIOACTIVITY

gei·sha /ˈgeɪʃə, ˈgiʃə/ *n.* [C] a Japanese woman who is trained to dance, play music, and entertain men

gel[1] /dʒɛl/ *n.* [C,U] a thick liquid, used in beauty or cleaning products: *hair gel* | *shower gel*

gel[2] *v.* past tense and past participle **gelled**, present participle **gelling** [I] **1** if people gel, they begin to work together well as a group: *As yet, the team hasn't quite gelled.* **2** if an idea or plan gels, it becomes clearer or more definite: *These new trends have not yet gelled.* **3** if a liquid gels, it becomes thicker

gel·a·tin /ˈdʒɛlətən, -lət̚n/ *n.* [U] a clear substance used for making liquid food more solid and in sweet foods such as Jell-O

geld·ing /ˈgɛldɪŋ/ *n.* [C] a horse that has had its TESTICLES removed

gem /dʒɛm/ *n.* [C] **1** a valuable stone that has been cut into a particular shape: *precious gems* **2** *informal* someone or something that is very special: *a little **gem of** a movie*

Gem·i·ni /ˈdʒɛməˌnaɪ/ *n.* **1** [U] the third sign of the ZODIAC, represented by TWINS **2** [C] someone born between May 21 and June 21

gen·der /ˈdʒɛndɚ/ *n.* **1** [C,U] *formal* the fact of being male or female: *A person cannot be denied a job because of age, race, or gender.* | *traditional **gender roles*** **2** [U] the system in some languages of dividing nouns, adjectives, and PRONOUNS into MASCULINE, FEMININE, and NEUTER

gene /dʒin/ *n.* [C] a part of a cell in a living thing that controls how it develops. Parents pass genes on to their children

ge·ne·al·o·gy /ˌdʒiniˈɑlədʒi/ *n.* plural **genealogies** [C,U] the history of a family, or the study of family histories —**genealogist** *n.* [C] —**genealogical** /ˌdʒiniəˈlɑdʒɪkəl/ *adj.*

gen·er·al[1] /ˈdʒɛnərəl/ *adj.*

1 NOT DETAILED relating to the whole of something or its main features, not the details: *a general introduction to computers* | *The general standard of the students isn't very high.* | *I've got a **general idea** of how I want the room to look.* | *The mayor spoke **in general terms** about his plans for the next four years.*

2 in general **a)** usually, or in most situations: *In general, the Republicans favor tax cuts.* **b)** as a whole: *I love jazz, blues, and music in general.*

3 MOST PEOPLE including most people or situations: *How soon will the drug be available for **general use**?* | ***As a general rule**, you should call before visiting someone.* | *The service will soon become available to **the general public*** (=most ordinary people).

4 NOT LIMITED not limited to one subject, service, product, etc.: *a general education* | *Montreal General Hospital*
5 JOB used in the job title of someone who has complete responsibility for a particular area of work: *the **general manager***

general² *n.* [C] an officer with a very high rank in the Army, Air Force, or Marines

ˌgeneral anesˈthetic *n.* [C,U] a medicine that makes you unconscious during an operation so that you do not feel any pain

ˌgeneral eˈlection *n.* [C] an election in which all the voters in a country elect a government

gen·er·al·i·ty /ˌdʒɛnəˈrælət̬i/ *n.* plural **generalities** [C usually plural] a general statement that does not mention specific facts, details, etc.: *Bryant spoke **in generalities** about his plans to protect the environment.*

gen·er·al·i·za·tion /ˌdʒɛnərələˈzeɪʃən/ *n.* [C,U] *disapproving* a statement that may be true in most situations, but is not true all of the time, or the act of doing this: *Don't **make** sweeping **generalizations**.*

gen·er·al·ize /ˈdʒɛnərəˌlaɪz/ *v.* [I] **1** *disapproving* to form an opinion about something after considering only a few examples of it: *statements that **generalize about** women* **2** to make a statement about people, events, or facts without mentioning any details: *It's difficult to **generalize about** a subject as big as American history.*

gen·er·al·ly /ˈdʒɛnərəli/ *adv.* **1** considering something as a whole, rather than its details: *Her school work is generally very good.* | ***Generally speaking**, movie audiences like happy endings.* **2** by or to most people: *It's generally believed that the story is true.* | *an agreement that is generally acceptable* **3** usually: *Megan generally works late on Fridays.*

ˈgeneral ˌstore *n.* [C] a store that sells a lot of different things, especially in a small town

gen·er·ate /ˈdʒɛnəˌreɪt/ *v.* [T] **1** to produce or make something: *Our discussion generated a lot of new ideas.* | *The program will generate a lot of new jobs.* | *Reed hopes the exhibit will **generate interest** in the museum.* **2** to produce energy, power, heat, etc.

gen·er·a·tion /ˌdʒɛnəˈreɪʃən/ *n.* **1** [C] all the people in a society or family who are about the same age: *Three **generations of** Monroes have lived in this house.* | *music for the **younger/older generation*** | ***first-generation/second-generation, etc.** Americans* (=being a member of the first, second, etc. generation to be born in America) **2** [C] the average period of time between your birth and the birth of your children: *A generation ago, no one had home computers.* | *This store has been here **for generations**.* **3** [C] machines that are at the same stage of development: *the next **generation of** TV technology* **4** [U] the process of producing power or energy: *the **generation of** electricity*

ˌgeneˈration ˌgap *n.* [singular] a lack of understanding between older and younger people

ˌGeneration ˈX *n.* [U] the group of people who were born during the late 1960s and 1970s in the U.S.

gen·er·a·tor /ˈdʒɛnəˌreɪt̬ɚ/ *n.* [C] a machine that produces electricity

ge·ner·ic /dʒəˈnɛrɪk/ *adj.* **1** a generic drug or other product is an exact copy of an existing drug or product, but does not have a BRAND NAME (=the name a company gives to each of its products): *the need for cheaper **generic drugs*** **2** relating to a whole group of similar things, rather than just one of them: *Fine Arts is a **generic term** for subjects such as painting, music, and sculpture.* —**generically** *adv.*

gen·er·os·i·ty /ˌdʒɛnəˈrɑsət̬i/ *n.* [U] a generous attitude, or generous behavior: *Thank you for your generosity.* | *The company is known for its **generosity toward** employees.*

gen·er·ous /ˈdʒɛnərəs/ *adj.* **1** someone who is generous is kind and enjoys giving people things or helping them: *She's always been **generous to** the kids.* | *Carl is **generous with** his time* (=is willing to spend time helping people). | ***It is** very **generous of** you **to** help.* **2** more than the usual amount: *a generous slice of cake* —**generously** *adv.*: *Clark **gives generously** to local charities.*

gen·e·sis /ˈdʒɛnəsɪs/ *n.* [singular] *formal* the beginning of something

ge·net·ic /dʒəˈnɛt̬ɪk/ *adj.* relating to GENES or genetics: *genetic research* | *genetic defects* —**genetically** *adv.*

geˌnetically ˈmodified *adj.* genetically modified food, crops, etc. have been changed so that their GENE structure is different from the one they have naturally

geˌnetic enginˈeering *n.* [U] the science of changing the GENES of a living thing

ge·net·ics /dʒəˈnɛt̬ɪks/ *n.* [plural] the study of how GENES affect the development of living things —**geneticist** *n.* [C]

ge·nial /ˈdʒinyəl, -niəl/ *adj.* cheerful, kind, and friendly: *a genial host*

ge·nie /ˈdʒini/ *n.* [C] a magical creature in old stories who can make wishes come true

gen·i·tals /ˈdʒɛnət̬lz/ **also gen·i·ta·lia** /ˌdʒɛnəˈteɪlyə/ *n.* [plural] *technical* the outer sex organs —**genital** *adj.*

ge·nius /ˈdʒinyəs/ *n.* **1** [U] a very high level of intelligence or ability: *a man **of genius*** | *Even the movie's title was **a stroke of genius*** (=a very smart idea). **2** [C] someone who has a very high level of intelligence or ability: *a musical genius*

gen·o·cide /ˈdʒɛnəˌsaɪd/ *n.* [U] the deliberate murder of a whole race of people —**genocidal** /ˌdʒɛnəˈsaɪdl/ *adj.*

ge·nome /ˈdʒinoʊm/ *n.* [C] *technical* all the GENES in one cell of a living thing: *the human genome*

G

gen·re /ˈʒɑnrə/ *n.* [C] *formal* a type of art, music, literature, etc. that has a particular style or feature: *the science fiction genre*

THESAURUS
type, kind, sort, category
→ see Thesaurus box at TYPE[1]

gent /dʒɛnt/ *n.* [C] *informal* GENTLEMAN

gen·teel /dʒɛnˈtil/ *adj.* polite, gentle, or graceful —**gentility** /dʒɛnˈtɪləṭi/ *n.* [U]

gen·tile /ˈdʒɛntaɪl/ *n.* [C] someone who is not Jewish —**gentile** *adj.*

gen·tle /ˈdʒɛnṭəl/ *adj.* **1** kind, and careful not to hurt anyone or anything: *Be **gentle with** the baby.* | *a gentle young man* **2** not strong, extreme, or violent: *a gentle voice* | *a gentle breeze* | *gentle persuasion* | *gentle humor* **3** a gentle hill or slope is not steep —**gentleness** *n.* [U] —**gently** *adv.*: *He gently lifted the baby from the cradle.*

gen·tle·man /ˈdʒɛnṭəlmən/ *n.* plural **gentlemen** /-mən/ [C] **1** a man who is polite and behaves well: *Roland was a **perfect gentleman** last night.*

THESAURUS
man, guy, boy, youth
→ see Thesaurus box at MAN[1]

2 a polite word used for a man you do not know: *Can you show this gentleman to his seat?* | *Thank you, **ladies and gentlemen**.* —**gentlemanly** *adj.*

gen·tri·fi·ca·tion /ˌdʒɛntrəfəˈkeɪʃən/ *n.* [U] a process in which a poor area improves after people who have money move there

gen·try /ˈdʒɛntri/, **the gentry** *n.* [plural] *old-fashioned* people of a high social class

gen·u·flect /ˈdʒɛnyəˌflɛkt/ *v.* [I] to bend one knee when in a church or a holy place, as a sign of respect

gen·u·ine /ˈdʒɛnyuɪn/ *adj.* **1** a genuine feeling or desire is one that you really have, not one that you pretend to have [= **sincere**]: *He has a **genuine interest** in seeing his students succeed.* | *Mrs. Liu showed a **genuine concern** for Lisa's well-being.* **2** something that is genuine is real or true [= **real**]: *a genuine diamond* **3** someone who is genuine is honest and sincere —**genuinely** *adv.*: *She seemed genuinely surprised.*

ge·nus /ˈdʒinəs/ *n.* plural **genera** /ˈdʒɛnərə/ [C] *technical* a group of animals or plants that are closely related [➡ **species**]

ge·o·graph·i·cal /ˌdʒiəˈgræfɪkəl/ **also ge·o·graph·ic** /ˌdʒiəˈgræfɪk/ *adj.* relating to geography: *geographical maps of the area*

ge·og·ra·phy /dʒiˈɑgrəfi/ *n.* [U] the study of the countries, oceans, cities, populations, etc. of the world or of a particular area —**geographer** *n.* [C]

ge·ol·o·gy /dʒiˈɑlədʒi/ *n.* [U] the study of materials such as rocks, soil, and minerals, and how they have changed over time —**geologist** *n.* [C] —**geological** /ˌdʒiəˈlɑdʒɪkəl/ *adj.*

ge·o·met·ric /ˌdʒiəˈmɛtrɪk◂/ **also ge·o·met·ric·al** /ˌdʒiəˈmɛtrɪkəl/ *adj.* **1** having a regular pattern of shapes and lines: *geometric shapes* **2** relating to geometry

ge·om·e·try /dʒiˈɑmətri/ *n.* [U] the mathematical study of angles, shapes, lines, etc.

ge·ra·ni·um /dʒəˈreɪniəm/ *n.* [C] a common house plant with colorful flowers and large round leaves

ger·bil /ˈdʒɚbəl/ *n.* [C] a small animal with soft fur and a long tail that is often kept as a pet

ger·i·at·ric /ˌdʒɛriˈætrɪk◂/ *adj.* relating to geriatrics: *geriatric patients*

ger·i·at·rics /ˌdʒɛriˈætrɪks/ *n.* [U] the medical treatment and care of old people

germ /dʒɚm/ *n.* [C] **1** a very small living thing that can make you sick [= **bacteria**]: *Sneezing spreads germs.* **2 the germ of an idea/hope etc.** the beginning of an idea, etc. that may develop into something else

Ger·man[1] /ˈdʒɚmən/ *adj.* relating to Germany, its people, or its language

German[2] *n.* **1** [U] the language used in Germany, Austria, and parts of Switzerland **2** [C] someone from Germany

ˌGerman ˈmeasles *n.* [plural] an infectious disease that causes red spots on the body [= **rubella**]

ˌGerman ˈshepherd *n.* [C] a large dog that looks like a WOLF, often used by the police and for guarding property

ger·mi·nate /ˈdʒɚməˌneɪt/ *v.* [I,T] if a seed germinates, or if it is germinated, it begins to grow —**germination** /ˌdʒɚməˈneɪʃən/ *n.* [U]

ger·ry·man·der·ing /ˈdʒɛriˌmændərɪŋ/ *n.* [U] the practice of changing the size and borders of an area before an election, so that one person or party has an unfair advantage —**gerrymander** *v.* [I,T]

ger·und /ˈdʒɛrənd/ *n.* [C] *technical* in grammar, a noun formed from the PRESENT PARTICIPLE of a verb, such as "reading" in the sentence "He enjoys reading"

ges·ta·tion /dʒɛˈsteɪʃən/ *n.* [U] *technical* the process during which a baby grows inside its mother's body, or the period when this happens: *a nine-month **gestation period***

ges·tic·u·late /dʒɛˈstɪkyəˌleɪt/ *v.* [I] to make movements with your arms and hands while speaking, usually because you are excited or angry

ges·ture[1] /ˈdʒɛstʃɚ, ˈdʒɛʃtʃɚ/ *n.* **1** [C,U] a movement of your head, arm, or hand to express your feelings: *He **made** a rude **gesture** at us as he drove by.* | *He made a fist in a **gesture of** disgust.* **2** [C] something you do or say to show that you care about someone or something: *The flowers were a **nice gesture**.* | *a **gesture of** friendship/support*

gesture² *v.* [I] to move your head, arm, or hand in order to tell someone something: *Tom* ***gestured for*** *me* ***to*** *move out of the way.*

get /gɛt/ *v.* past tense **got** /gɑt/ past participle **gotten** /ˈgɑt˺n/ present participle **getting**
1 RECEIVE/BUY [T] to receive, buy, or obtain something: *Did you get the job? | We haven't gotten any mail for three days. | I got an A/B/C etc. in Spanish. | How much money did you* ***get from*** *Grandma? | My mom* ***got*** *these earrings* ***for*** *a dollar. | Jill knows a woman who can get the material for you.*
2 have got ➔ HAVE² *I've got a lot of work to do.*
3 BECOME [linking verb] to change from one state, feeling, etc. to another [= **become**]: *Vicky got really mad at him. | If I wear wool, my skin gets all red. | The weather had suddenly gotten cold. | I got lost on the way to the stadium. | Sean's getting married next week. | Hurry up and get dressed!*

USAGE

Become is used in both written and spoken English: *He's becoming very successful. | Canada has become popular with tourists.*
Get and **go** are less formal than **become**, and are used more often in spoken English: *I got very hungry. | Have you gone crazy?*
Become can be used in front of an adjective or a noun, but **get** and **go** are only used in front of an adjective: *The noise from the airport is becoming a problem. | It became clear that the company would lose the contract. | It's getting dark. | Beethoven went deaf when he was 40 years old.*

4 CHANGE POSITION/STATE [I,T] to change or move from one place, position, or state to another, or to make something do this: *How did the guy* ***get into*** *their house? | I can't* ***get*** *this jar* ***open****. | Everybody* ***get down*** *on the floor!*
5 REACH A PLACE [I] to reach a particular place or position: *When did you get home? | She got downstairs, and found that the room was full of smoke. | The thieves* ***got away*** (=escaped). *| You might be disappointed when you* ***get to*** *the end of the book.*
6 BRING/TAKE [T] to bring someone or something back from somewhere, or take something from somewhere: *Run upstairs and get me that book. | She* ***got*** *some money* ***out of*** *her purse. | I'm going to go* ***get*** *the kids* ***from*** *the babysitter's.*

USAGE

get – to go to another place and come back with something or someone: *Just a minute while I get my jacket.*
bring – to take something or someone to a place: *We should bring a bottle of wine. | I bought the truck in Texas and brought it back to Mexico.*
take – to move something from one place to another, or help someone go from one place to another: *Don't forget to take your umbrella. | I can take you home after the concert.*

7 MONEY [T] to receive money for doing work or selling something: *He gets $12 an hour at his job. | How much can you* ***get for*** *a house this size?*
8 get to do sth *informal* to have an opportunity to do something: *As you* ***get to know*** *the city, I'm sure you'll like it better. | I didn't* ***get to see*** *the game last night.*
9 MAKE STH HAPPEN [T] to make or arrange for someone or something to do a particular job or action: *I have to get this work done by tomorrow. | We'll have to get this room painted before they move in.*
10 ILLNESS [T] to begin to have an illness: *I got the flu when we were on vacation.*
11 REACH A STAGE [I] to reach a particular stage in a process successfully: *We didn't seem to be getting anywhere. | I started reading the book, but I didn't get very far.*
12 get sb to do sth to persuade or force someone to do something: *I tried to get Jill to come out tonight, but she was too tired.*
13 get sth to do sth to make something do something: *Bert couldn't get the light to work.*
14 get the feeling/idea etc. to start to have a feeling or an idea: *I get the feeling you don't like her.*
15 get the bus/a flight etc. to travel somewhere on a bus, airplane, etc.: *She managed to get a flight into Detroit.*
16 RECEIVE A PUNISHMENT [T] to receive a punishment: *He got ten years for robbery.*
17 RADIO/TV [T] to be able to receive a particular radio signal, television station, etc.: *Her TV doesn't get channel 24.*

SPOKEN PHRASES

18 [T] to understand something: *Tracey didn't* ***get*** *the* ***joke****. |* ***I*** *don't* ***get it****!*
19 you/we etc. get sth used in order to say that something happens or exists: *We get a lot of rain around here in the summer.*
20 get moving/going to begin moving or going somewhere: *We have to get going, or we'll be late!*
21 get the door/phone to answer the door or telephone: *Can you get the phone, please?*
22 [T] to prepare a meal: *Are you hungry? Can I get you anything?*
23 get sb to attack, hurt, or catch someone: *I want to get him before he gets me.* ➔ HAVE TO

get sth ⇔ **across** *phr. v.* to be understood, or to make someone understand something: *The message isn't getting across. | It was difficult to* ***get*** *my idea* ***across to*** *the committee.*

get ahead *phr. v.* to be successful in your job, work, etc.: *She lacks the business skills she'll need to get ahead.*

G

get along *phr. v.* **1** to have a friendly relationship with someone: *She* ***gets along with*** *Cy really well.* **2 get along without sb/sth** to be able to continue doing something without having someone or something to help: *We'll have to get along without the car until the new part arrives.*

get around *phr. v.* **1 get around** sth to avoid something that will cause problems: *There are ways of getting around the law.* **2 get around** (sth) to go to different places: *His new wheelchair lets him get around more easily.* **3** if news or information gets around, a lot of people hear about it

get around to sth *phr. v.* to do something you have been intending to do for a long time: *I meant to go to the bookstore, but I never got around to it.*

get at sth *phr. v.* **1 be getting at sth** to be trying to explain an idea: *Did you understand what he was getting at?* **2 get at the meaning/facts etc.** to discover information about something: *The judge asked a few questions to try to get at the truth.* **3** to be able to reach something: *I could see the ring stuck under there, but I couldn't get at it.*

get away *phr. v.* **1** to leave a place: *Barney had to work late, and couldn't get away until 9:00.* **2** to escape from someone who is chasing you: *The two men got away in a blue pickup truck.* **3** to go on vacation: *Are you going to be able to get away this summer?*

G

get away with sth *phr. v.* to not be noticed or punished when you have done something wrong: *He'll cheat if he thinks he can get away with it.*

get back *phr. v.* **1** to return to a place: *I didn't get back until after midnight.* | *Call me when you* ***get back to*** *Miami.* **2 get** sth ⇔ **back** to have something again after you had lost it or given it to someone: *Did you get your wallet back?* **3 get** sb **back also get back at** sb to hurt or embarrass someone who has hurt or embarrassed you: *Jerry's wants to* ***get back at*** *her* ***for*** *leaving him.*

get back to *phr. v.* **1 get back to** sth to return to a previous state, condition, or activity: *It was hard to get back to work after my vacation.* | *Life is beginning to* ***get back to normal.*** **2 get back to** sb to talk to or telephone someone later in order to answer a question or give him/her information: *I'll try to get back to you later today.*

get behind *phr. v.* if you get behind with work or a regular payment, you fail to do the work or pay the money in time: *They made people pay extra if they* ***got behind in/on*** *their rent.*

get by *phr. v.* to have only just enough of something to be able to do the things you need to do: *I know enough French to get by.* | *He* ***gets by on*** *just $800 a month.*

get down *phr. v.* **1 get** sth ⇔ **down** to quickly write something down on paper: *Let me get your number down before I forget it.* **2 get** sb **down** *informal* to make someone feel unhappy: *Don't let his criticism get you down.* **3 get** sth ⇔ **down** to be able to swallow food or drink: *I knew I'd feel better once I got some food down.*

get down to sth *phr. v.* to start doing something that needs time or energy: *It's time to* ***get down to work.***

get in *phr. v.* **1** to be allowed or able to enter a place: *The door was locked, and he couldn't get in.* | *I applied to Princeton but I didn't get in.* **2** to arrive at a particular time or in a particular place: *What time does the plane get in?* **3** to arrive home: *Steve just got in a few minutes ago.* **4 get** sth **in** to send or give something to a particular person, company, etc.: *Make sure you get your homework in by Thursday.*

get in on sth *phr. v. informal* to become involved in something that other people are doing: *The kids saw us playing and wanted to get in on the game.*

get into sth *phr. v.* **1** to be allowed to go to a school, college, or university: *Liz got into the graduate program at Berkeley.* **2** to start being involved in a situation: *He's always* ***getting into trouble.*** **3** *informal* to start being interested in something: *When I was in high school I got into rap music.* **4** *informal* to begin to have a discussion about something: *Let's not get into it right now. I'm tired.*

get off *phr. v.* **1 get off** (sth) to finish working: *What time do you* ***get off (work)****?* **2 get** (sb) **off** to get little or no punishment for a crime, or to help someone escape punishment: *I can't believe his lawyers managed to get him off.* | *He* ***got off lightly*** (=received a very small punishment). **3 where does sb get off (doing sth)?** *spoken* said when someone has done something that you think s/he does not have a right to do: *Where does he get off telling me how to raise my kids?*

get off on sth *phr. v. slang* to become excited by something, especially sexually excited

get on *phr. v.* **1 get on with sth** to continue or to make progress with a job, work, etc.: *Let's get on with the meeting, so we can go home on time.* **2 be getting on (in years)** to be old

get onto sth *phr. v.* to start talking about a particular subject: *Then, we got onto the subject of women, and Craig wouldn't shut up.*

get out *phr. v.* **1 get** (sb) ⇔ **out** to leave or escape from a place, or to help someone do this: *How did the dog* ***get out of*** *the yard?* | *We knew it was going to be difficult to get him out of the country.* **2** if secret information gets out, people find out about it: *Once* ***word gets out****, we're going to be in big trouble.*

get out of sth *phr. v.* **1** to avoid doing something that you should do: *She couldn't get out of the meeting, so she canceled our dinner.* **2 get** sth **out of** sb to persuade someone to tell or give you something: *I was determined to get the truth* *out of her.* **3 get** sth **out of** sth to enjoy an activity and feel you have gained something from it: *She gets a lot of pleasure out of acting.*

get over *phr. v.* **1 get over** sth to feel better after an illness or bad experience: *It will take a couple of weeks to get over the infection.* | *Her son died suddenly, and she never **got over it**.* **2 get** sth **over with** to finish something you do not like doing as quickly as possible: *"It should only hurt a little." "OK. Just get it over with."* **3 sb can't/couldn't get over sth** *spoken* said when you are surprised, shocked, or amused by something: *I can't get over how much weight you've lost.*

get through *phr. v.* **1 get** (sb) **through** sth to manage to deal with a difficult or bad experience until it ends: *I was so embarrassed. I don't know how I got through the rest of the dinner.* **2** to succeed in calling someone on the telephone: *When she finally got through, the department manager wasn't there.* **3 get** (sth) **through** sth if a law gets through Congress, it is officially accepted

get through to sb *phr. v.* to succeed in making someone understand you: *I tried to explain, but I couldn't get through to her.*

get to sb *phr. v. informal* to upset someone: *Don't let him get to you, honey. He's just teasing you.*

get together *phr. v.* **1** to meet with someone or with a group of people: *We should get together for a drink.* | *Every time he **got together with** Murphy they argued.* **2** to start a romantic relationship with someone **3 get yourself together/get it together** to change the way you live so that you are better organized, happier, etc.: *It took a year for me to get myself together after she left.*

get up *phr. v.* **1 get** (sb) **up** to get out of your bed after sleeping, or to make someone do this: *I have to **get up at** 6:00 tomorrow.* | *Could you **get** me **up at** 8:00?* **2** to stand up: *Corrinne got up slowly and went to the window.*

get·a·way /ˈgɛt̬əˌweɪ/ *n.* [C] an escape from a place after doing something wrong: *a **getaway car*** (=a car used by criminals to escape after a crime) | *The bank robber **made** his **getaway** in a red truck.*

ˈget-toˌgether *n.* [C] an informal meeting or party: *a small get-together with friends* → see Thesaurus box at PARTY¹

get·up /ˈgɛt̬ʌp/ *n.* [C] *informal* strange or unusual clothes that someone is wearing

gey·ser /ˈgaɪzɚ/ *n.* [C] a natural spring that sends hot water and steam suddenly into the air from a hole in the ground

ghast·ly /ˈgæstli/ *adj.* extremely bad, shocking, or upsetting: *ghastly injuries* | *a ghastly noise*

ghet·to /ˈgɛt̬oʊ/ *n.* plural **ghettos** or **ghettoes** [C] a part of a city where poor people live in bad conditions, especially people of one particular race or social class

> **THESAURUS**
>
> **neighborhood, suburb, slum**
> → see Thesaurus box at AREA

ˈghetto ˌblaster *n.* [C] *informal* a BOOM BOX

ghost /goʊst/ *n.* [C] the spirit of a dead person that some people think they can see: *They say the captain's **ghost** still **haunts** the waterfront.* —**ghostly** *adj.*

> **THESAURUS**
>
> **spirit** – a creature without a physical body, such as an angel or ghost
> **phantom/specter/apparition** literary – a ghost

ˈghost ˌstory *n.* [C] a story about ghosts that is intended to frighten people

ˈghost town *n.* [C] a town that is empty because most of its people have left

ˈghost ˌwriter, **ghost·writ·er** /ˈgoʊstˌraɪt̬ɚ/ *n.* [C] someone who is paid to write a book or story for another person, whose name then appears as the writer of the book —**ghostwrite** *v.* [T]

ghoul /gul/ *n.* [C] an evil spirit in stories that steals and eats dead bodies —**ghoulish** *adj.*

GI /ˌdʒi ˈaɪ/ *n.* [C] a soldier in the U.S. army

gi·ant¹ /ˈdʒaɪənt/ *adj.* much bigger than other things of the same type: *a **giant step** towards peace in the region* | *a giant TV screen*

giant² *n.* [C] **1** a very tall strong man in stories **2** a very successful person or company: *one of the **giants of** the music industry*

gib·ber·ish /ˈdʒɪbərɪʃ/ *n.* [U] things you say or write that have no meaning or are difficult to understand

gibe /dʒaɪb/ *n.* [C] an unkind remark intended to make someone seem silly

gib·lets /ˈdʒɪblɪts/ *n.* [plural] organs such as the heart and LIVER that you remove from a bird before cooking it

gid·dy /ˈgɪdi/ *adj.* comparative **giddier**, superlative **giddiest** **1** behaving in a silly, happy, and excited way: *We were **giddy with** excitement.* **2** feeling slightly sick and unable to stand up because everything seems to be spinning around [**= dizzy**]

gift /gɪft/ *n.* [C] **1** something that you give to someone as a present: *a **birthday/Christmas/wedding, etc.** gift* | *a **gift from** my mother* | *He sent her **gifts of** flowers and chocolate.* **2** a natural ability to do something [**= flair**]: *Ekena sure **has a gift for** making people laugh.*

ˈgift cerˌtificate *n.* [C] a special piece of paper that is worth a specific amount of money when it is exchanged at a store for goods

gift·ed /ˈgɪftɪd/ *adj.* having the natural ability to do something very well: *a gifted poet* | *a **gifted child*** (=a child who is extremely intelligent)

G

THESAURUS

intelligent, **smart**, **bright**, **brilliant**, **intellectual**
➔ see Thesaurus box at INTELLIGENT

ˈgift wrap *n.* [U] attractive colored paper used for wrapping presents in —**gift wrap** *v.* [T] *Would you like this gift wrapped?*

gig /gɪg/ *n.* [C] *informal* a concert at which musicians play popular music or JAZZ

gig·a·byte /ˈgɪgəˌbaɪt/ *n.* [C] *technical* a unit for measuring computer information, equal to 1024 MEGABYTES

gi·gan·tic /dʒaɪˈgæntɪk/ *adj.* extremely large: *a gigantic skyscraper*

THESAURUS

huge, **enormous**, **vast**, **massive**, **immense**, **colossal**
➔ see Thesaurus box at BIG

gig·gle /ˈgɪgəl/ *v.* [I] to laugh quickly in a high voice, especially because you are nervous or embarrassed: *If you can't stop giggling, you'll have to leave the room.* —**giggle** *n.* [C] *a nervous giggle*

G

THESAURUS

laugh, **chuckle**, **cackle**, **snicker**, **guffaw**
➔ see Thesaurus box at LAUGH[1]

gild /gɪld/ *v.* [T] to cover the surface of something with a thin layer of gold or gold paint

gill /gɪl/ *n.* [C] one of the organs on the side of a fish through which it breathes ➔ see picture on page A2

gilt /gɪlt/ *adj.* covered with a thin layer of gold or gold-colored paint —**gilt** *n.* [U]

gim·me /ˈgɪmi/ *spoken* a short form of "give me": *Gimme that ball back!*

gim·mick /ˈgɪmɪk/ *n.* [C] *informal disapproving* something unusual that is used to make people notice something: *advertising gimmicks* —**gimmicky** *adj.*

gin /dʒɪn/ *n.* [U] a strong clear alcoholic drink made from grain

gin·ger /ˈdʒɪndʒɚ/ *n.* [U] a hot-tasting light brown root, or the powder made from this root, used in cooking

ˌginger ˈale *n.* [U] a SOFT DRINK (=drink with no alcohol in it) with a ginger taste

gin·ger·bread /ˈdʒɪndʒɚˌbrɛd/ *n.* [U] a type of cookie or cake with ginger in it: *a **gingerbread house/man*** (=cookie in the shape of a house or person)

gin·ger·ly /ˈdʒɪndʒɚli/ *adv.* very slowly, carefully, and gently: *They gingerly loaded the patient into the ambulance.*

ging·ham /ˈgɪŋəm/ *n.* [U] cotton cloth that has a pattern of small white and colored squares on it

gi·raffe /dʒəˈræf/ *n.* [C] a tall African animal with a very long neck and legs and dark spots on its yellow-brown fur

gird·er /ˈgɚdɚ/ *n.* [C] an iron or steel beam that supports a floor, roof, or bridge

gir·dle /ˈgɚdl/ *n.* [C] a piece of women's underwear that fits tightly around her waist and HIPS

girl /gɚl/ *n.* [C] **1** a female child: *She's tall for a girl of her age.* | *a six-year-old girl* | *I've wanted to be in the movies since I was **a little girl**.* **2** a daughter [➥ **boy**]: *They have two boys and a girl.* **3** a word meaning a young woman, which is considered offensive by some women: *A nice girl like you needs a boyfriend.* **4 the girls** *informal* a woman's female friends: *I'm going out with the girls tonight.*

girl·friend /ˈgɚlfrɛnd/ *n.* [C] **1** a girl or woman with whom you have a romantic relationship **2** a woman or girl's female friend

girl·hood /ˈgɚlhʊd/ *n.* [U] the time in a woman's life when she is a girl

ˈGirl Scout *n.* **1** [C] a member of the Girl Scouts **2 the Girl Scouts** an organization for girls that teaches them practical skills and helps develop their character [➥ **Boy Scouts**]

girth /gɚθ/ *n.* [C,U] the distance around the middle of something: *the girth of the tree's trunk*

gist /dʒɪst/ *n.* **the gist** the main idea or meaning of what someone has said or written: *After a while I began to **get the gist of** his speech* (=understand the main ideas).

give[1] /gɪv/ *v.* past tense **gave** /geɪv/ past participle **given** /ˈgɪvən/

1 PROVIDE [T] to provide something for someone: *Dan gave me a ride to work.* | *She refused to give me any help.* | *They **gave** the job **to** that guy from Texas.*

THESAURUS

donate – to give money to an organization that uses it to help people: *Would you like to donate something to charity?*
leave – to give something to people after you die: *This house was left to me by my aunt.*
award – to officially **give** money or a prize to someone: *Heaney was awarded the Nobel Prize for Literature.*

2 PUT STH IN SB'S HAND [T] to put something in someone's hand: *Give me your coat.* | *He **gave** the books **to** Carl.*

3 LET SB DO STH [T] to allow or make it possible for someone to do something: *I was never **given a chance** to explain.* | *She **gave** me some **time** to finish the report.* | *Who **gave** you **permission** to come in here?* | *This bill will **give** more power **to** local authorities.*

4 PRESENT [T] to let someone have something as a present: *She gave Jen a CD for Christmas.*

5 TELL SB STH [T] to tell someone information or details about something, or tell someone to do something: *Would you give Kim a message for me?* | *Let me **give** you some **advice**.* | *The police will ask him to **give** a **description** of the man.* | *Could you **give** me **directions** to the airport* (=tell me how to get there)*?* | *Harris walked into the room and started **giving orders**.*
6 PERFORM AN ACTION [T] to perform a particular action: *The boy gave Lydia a big smile.* | *Yo Yo Ma gave a performance of pieces by Bach.* | ***Give** me a **call*** (=telephone me) *tonight.* | *Come on, give your Grandpa a hug.*
7 give sb trouble/problems etc. to make someone have problems: *The machines in the lab are giving us trouble.* | *Stop **giving** me **a hard time*** (=stop criticizing me)*!*
8 ILLNESS [T] to infect someone with the same illness that you have, or make someone feel a particular emotion or sensation: *The noise is giving me a headache.* | *My husband **gave** this cold **to** me.*
9 QUALITY [T] to make someone or something have a particular quality: *The color of the room gives it a warm cozy feeling.*
10 give (sb) an idea/feeling etc. to make someone think about something in a particular way: *She gave me the impression she wasn't interested.*
11 MONEY [T] to pay a particular amount of money for something: *I'll give you $75 for the oak desk.*
12 BEND/STRETCH [I] to bend, stretch, or break because of weight or pressure: *The leather will give slightly when you wear the boots.*
13 give or take a few minutes/a mile/a dollar etc. used in order to show that a number or amount is not exact: *The show lasts about an hour, give or take five minutes.*
14 give (sth) thought/attention/consideration etc. to spend some time thinking about something carefully
15 not give sth another/a second thought to not think or worry about something
16 BREAK/FALL [I] **also give way** to break or fall down suddenly under pressure: *The branch suddenly gave way beneath him.*

SPOKEN PHRASES

17 sb would give anything/a lot/your right arm etc. for sth said in order to emphasize that you want something very much: *I'd give my right arm for his job.*
18 don't give me that! said when someone has just said something that you know is not true: *"I'm too tired." "Oh, don't give me that. You just don't want to come."*

→ GIVE AND TAKE → **give sb a (big) hand** at HAND[1] → **give/lend sb a hand** at HAND[1]

give away *phr. v.* **1 give** sth ⇔ **away** to give someone something without asking for money: *I gave my old clothes away.* | *The store is **giving away** toasters **to** the first 50 customers.* **2 give** sb/sth ⇔ **away** to do or say something that lets someone know a secret: *They said they were English, but their New York accents gave them away* (=showed they were lying). → GIVEAWAY
give (sb) sth ⇔ **back** to return something to its owner: *Give him back his toy.* | *I gave her the book back.* | *I'll **give** the money **back to** you next week.*
give in *phr. v.* **1** to finally agree to do something that you did not want to do: *Randy asked her out for months until she finally gave in.* | *The government refused to **give in to** their demands.* **2** to accept that you have lost a fight, game, etc.: *Even when they fell behind by three goals, the team refused to give in.*
give in to sth *phr. v.* to no longer try to stop yourself from doing something you want to do: *If you feel the need for a cigarette, don't give in to it.*
give off sth *phr. v.* to produce a smell, light, heat, a sound, etc.: *The factory gives off a terrible smell.*
give out *phr. v.* **1 give** sth ⇔ **out** to give something to each person in a group: *She stood on the corner, giving out flyers.* | *He **gave out** candy **to** the kids.*

THESAURUS

pass – to take something and put it in someone's hand: *Could you pass me the salt?*
hand – to pass something to someone: *He handed me a card with his phone number on it.*
hand out/pass out – to give something to each of the people in a group: *Mr. Goodmanson handed out the test.* | *Pass those cookies around, please.*
share – to divide something into equal parts and give a part to each person: *She made a cake and shared it with the children.*
distribute – to give things to a large number of people, especially on the street: *Anti-war protesters were distributing leaflets.*

2 to stop working correctly: *My voice gave out half way through the song.*
give up *phr. v.* **1 give** (sth ⇔) **up** to stop trying to do something: *I looked everywhere for the keys – finally, I just gave up.* | *Vladimir has given up trying to teach her Russian.* **2 give** sth ⇔ **up** to stop doing something, especially something that you do regularly: *I've been trying to give up smoking.* | *She gave up her job, and started writing full time.* **3 give** yourself/sb **up** to allow yourself or someone else to be caught by the police or enemy soldiers
give up on sb *phr. v.* to stop hoping that someone or something will change or improve: *His parents finally gave up on him.*
give[2] *n.* [U] the ability of a material to bend or stretch when it is under pressure
ˌgive and ˈtake *n.* [U] if there is give and take between two people, each person agrees to do

some of the things that the other person wants: *In every successful marriage there is a certain amount of give and take.*

give·a·way /ˈgɪvəˌweɪ/ *n.* [C] **1 be a giveaway** to make it very easy to guess something: *Vince was lying. His red face* ***was a dead giveaway****.* **2** a product, prize, etc. that a store or company gives to its customers for free —**giveaway** *adj.*: *giveaway prices*

giv·en¹ /ˈgɪvən/ *adj.* **1 any/a given day/time/situation** any particular time, situation, etc., used when giving an example: *In any given year, over half of all accidents happen in the home.* **2** [only before noun] previously arranged: *Candidates will have to give a presentation on a given topic.*

given² *prep.* taking something into account: *Given the number of people we invited, I'm surprised that so few came.*

given³ *v.* the past participle of GIVE

given⁴ *n.* **a given** a basic fact that you accept as the truth: *it'll be a very difficult game – that's a given.*

ˈgiven name *n.* [C] FIRST NAME

giz·mo /ˈgɪzmoʊ/ *n.* plural **gizmos** [C] *informal* GADGET

giz·zard /ˈgɪzɚd/ *n.* [C] an organ near a bird's stomach that helps it break down food

G

gla·cial /ˈgleɪʃəl/ *adj.* relating to ice or glaciers, or formed by glaciers: *glacial streams*

gla·cier /ˈgleɪʃɚ/ *n.* [C] a large area of ice that moves slowly over an area of land

glad /glæd/ *adj.* [not before noun] **1** pleased and happy about something: *Mom's really* ***glad (that)*** *you came.* | *I'm* ***glad to*** *hear that you're feeling better.* | *I'll be* ***glad when*** *this is over.* ▶ Don't say "She's a really glad person." ◀

THESAURUS

happy, pleased, content, delighted, ecstatic
➔ see Thesaurus box at HAPPY

2 be glad to do sth to be willing to do something: *He said he'd be glad to help me.*

glade /gleɪd/ *n.* [C] *literary* a small open space inside a forest

glad·i·a·tor /ˈglædiˌeɪt̬ɚ/ *n.* [C] a man who had to fight other men or animals as entertainment in ancient Rome

glad·ly /ˈglædli/ *adv.* willingly or eagerly: *"Would you drive Jenny to school today?" "Gladly."*

glam·or·ize /ˈglæməˌraɪz/ *v.* [T] to make something seem more attractive or exciting than it really is: *Hollywood has always glamorized drinking.*

glam·or·ous /ˈglæmərəs/ *adj.* attractive, exciting, and relating to wealth and success: *a glamorous lifestyle*

glam·our, glamor /ˈglæmɚ/ *n.* [U] the attractive and exciting quality of being connected with wealth and success: *the* ***glamour of*** *Hollywood*

glance¹ /glæns/ *v.* [I] **1** to look at someone or something for a short time and then look quickly away: *He* ***glanced at*** *his watch.*

THESAURUS

look, peek, peer, stare, gaze, gape
➔ see Thesaurus box at LOOK¹

2 to read something very quickly: *Paul* ***glanced at/through*** *the menu and ordered a sandwich.*

glance² *n.* [C] **1** a quick look: *He* ***gave*** *her a* ***glance*** *as she walked by.* **2 at a glance** immediately: *I knew at a glance that something was wrong.* **3 at first glance** when you first look at or think about something: *At first glance, the place seemed completely empty.*

gland /glænd/ *n.* [C] an organ in the body that produces a substance such as SWEAT or SALIVA —**glandular** /ˈglændʒəlɚ/ *adj.*

glare¹ /glɛr/ *v.* [I] **1** to look angrily at someone or something for a long time: *They* ***glared at*** *each other across the room.*

THESAURUS

eye, stare, blink, wink, squint
➔ see Thesaurus box at EYE¹

2 to shine with a strong bright light that hurts your eyes: *Sunlight was* ***glaring off*** *the hood of the car.*

glare² *n.* **1** [singular, U] a strong bright light that hurts your eyes: *the* ***glare of*** *the sun* **2** [C] a long angry look: *a menacing glare*

glar·ing /ˈglɛrɪŋ/ *adj.* **1** too bright to look at: *a glaring white light* **2** bad and very noticeable: *glaring mistakes*

glass /glæs/ *n.* **1** [U] a hard transparent material that is used for making windows, bottles, etc.: *a glass jar* | *a piece of* ***broken glass*** | *panes of glass* | *the cathedral's* ***stained-glass windows*** ➔ see picture at MATERIAL¹ **2** [C] a container made of glass used for drinking, or the drink in it: *Did you put the wine glasses on the table?* | *a* ***glass of*** *milk* **3 glasses** [plural] two pieces of specially cut glass or plastic in a FRAME that you wear in front of your eyes in order to see better: *I need to buy a new* ***pair of glasses****.* | *He just started* ***wearing glasses****.* **4** [U] objects made of glass: *a collection of Venetian glass*

ˌglass ˈceiling *n.* [C] the fact that women or people from MINORITY groups are not given jobs at the highest level in a company

ˌglassed-ˈin *adj.* surrounded by a glass structure: *a glassed-in porch*

glass·ware /ˈglæswɛr/ *n.* [U] glass objects, especially ones used for drinking and eating

glass·y /ˈglæsi/ *adj.* **1** smooth and shiny, like glass: *the glassy surface of the lake* **2** glassy eyes do not show any expression

glaze¹ /gleɪz/ *v.* **1** [I] **also glaze over** if your eyes glaze, they show no expression because you are bored or tired: *Her eyes glazed over as if she were daydreaming.* **2** [T] to cover clay pots, bowls, etc. with a thin liquid that gives them a shiny surface **3** [T] to cover food with a liquid that gives it an attractive shiny surface **4** [T] to put glass into a window frame —**glazed** *adj.*

glaze² *n.* [C,U] **1** a liquid that is put on clay pots, bowls, etc. to give them a shiny surface **2** a liquid put on food to give it an attractive shiny surface

gleam¹ /glim/ *v.* [I] **1** to shine, especially after being cleaned: *Grandpa polished his shoes until they gleamed.* **2** if your eyes or face gleam with a feeling, they show it: *Her eyes **gleamed with** excitement.*

gleam² *n.* [C] **1** the shiny quality that something, especially something POLISHed, has when light shines on it **2** an emotion or expression that appears on someone's face for a short time: *There was a **gleam of** happiness on his face.*

glean /glin/ *v.* [T] to find out information slowly and with difficulty: *Several lessons can be **gleaned from** our experience so far.*

glee /gli/ *n.* [U] a feeling of excitement and satisfaction: *The kids shouted with glee when they saw Santa.* —**gleefully** *adv.*

glen /glɛn/ *n.* [C] a deep narrow valley in Scotland or Ireland

glib /glɪb/ *adj. disapproving* **1** said in a way that makes something sound simple, easy, or true when it is not: *The doctor made some glib comment about my headaches being "just stress."* **2** speaking easily but not sincerely: *a glib salesman* —**glibly** *adv.*

glide /glaɪd/ *v.* [I] to move smoothly and quietly, as if without effort: *We watched the sailboats **glide across** the lake.* —**glide** *n.* [C]

glid·er /ˈglaɪdɚ/ *n.* [C] a light airplane that flies without an engine ➔ see picture on page A10

glid·ing /ˈglaɪdɪŋ/ *n.* [U] the sport of flying a glider

glim·mer¹ /ˈglɪmɚ/ *n.* [C] **1 a glimmer of hope/doubt etc.** a small amount of hope, doubt, etc. **2** a light that is not very bright

glimmer² *v.* [I] to shine with a light that is not very bright

glimpse¹ /glɪmps/ *n.* [C] **1** a quick look at someone or something that does not allow you to see them clearly: *Dad only **got/caught a glimpse** of the guy who stole our car.* **2** a short experience of something that helps you to understand it: *a glimpse into the future*

glimpse² *v.* [T] to see someone or something for a moment without getting a complete view of them: *I glimpsed a figure at the window.*

glint /glɪnt/ *v.* [I] if something that is shiny or smooth glints, it flashes with a very small amount of light: *Her teeth glinted as she smiled.* —**glint** *n.* [C]

glis·ten /ˈglɪsən/ *v.* [I] to shine and look wet or oily: *His back was **glistening with** sweat.*

glitch /glɪtʃ/ *n.* [C] a small problem that prevents something from working correctly: *Company records were lost due to a computer glitch.*

glit·ter¹ /ˈglɪt̬ɚ/ *v.* [I] to shine brightly with a lot of small flashes of light: *Fresh snow glittered in the morning light.* —**glittering** *adj.*

glitter² *n.* [U] **1** brightness consisting of many flashing points of light: *the glitter of her diamond ring* **2** the attractiveness and excitement connected with rich and famous people or places: *the glitter of L.A.* **3** very small pieces of shiny plastic, metal, or paper that are used for decoration

gloat /gloʊt/ *v.* [I] to show in an annoying way that you are proud of your success, or happy about someone else's failure: *The fans are still **gloating over** the team's victory.*

glob /glɑb/ *n.* [C] *informal* a small amount of a soft substance or thick liquid, that has a round shape: *a **gob of** ketchup*

glob·al /ˈgloʊbəl/ *adj.* **1** affecting or including the whole world: *the **global economy** | **global climate change*** **2** affecting a whole computer system, program, or FILE: *a global computer network* **3** considering all the parts of a problem or a situation: *a global study on the company's weaknesses* —**globally** *adv.*

glob·al·i·za·tion /ˌgloʊbələˈzeɪʃən/ *n.* [U] the process of operating a business in a lot of countries all over the world, or the result of this

ˌglobal ˈwarming *n.* [U] an increase in the world temperatures, caused by an increase of CARBON DIOXIDE around the Earth

TOPIC

environment, pollution, the greenhouse effect, acid rain, deforestation, environmentally friendly, eco-friendly, recycle, biodegradable, organic

➔ see Topic box at ENVIRONMENT

globe

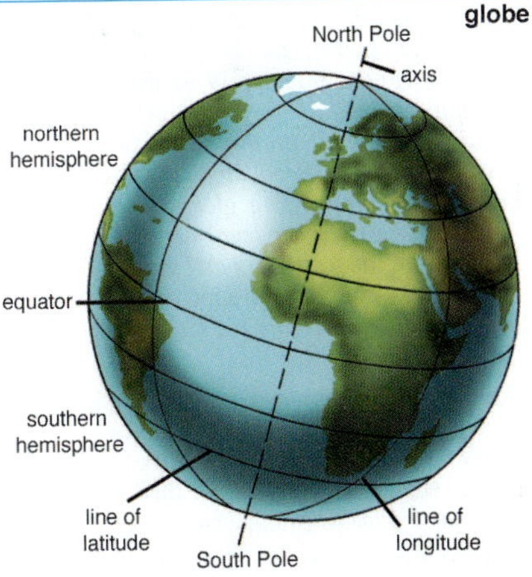

globe /gloʊb/ *n.* [C] **1** a round object that has a map of the earth painted on it **2 the globe** the world: *Our company has offices all over the globe.* **3** an object shaped like a ball

glob·u·lar /ˈglɑbyələ˞/ *adj.* shaped like a ball or a drop of liquid

glob·ule /ˈglɑbyul/ *n.* [C] a small drop of liquid or a melted substance

gloom /glum/ *n.* [singular, U] **1** *literary* darkness that you can hardly see through: *He was sitting alone in the gloom.* **2** a feeling of sadness, or having no hope ➔ **doom and gloom** at DOOM[1]

gloom·y /ˈglumi/ *adj.* comparative **gloomier**, superlative **gloomiest** **1** making you feel that a situation will not improve: *The report **paints a gloomy picture** of the economy.* **2** sad because you do not have a lot of hope: *gloomy thoughts*

> **THESAURUS**
> **sad**, **unhappy**, **miserable**, **depressed**, **down**, **low**, **glum**
> ➔ see Thesaurus box at SAD

3 dark in a way that makes you feel sad: *the cold gloomy weather* —**gloomily** *adv.*

glo·ri·fied /ˈglɔrəˌfaɪd/ *adj.* [only before noun] made to seem like something more important: *My title is "Editorial Assistant," but I'm just a glorified secretary.*

G

glo·ri·fy /ˈglɔrəˌfaɪ/ *v.* past tense and past participle **glorified**, third person singular **glorifies** [T] **1** to make someone or something seem more important or better than he, she, or it is: *movies that glorify violence* **2** to praise someone or something, especially God —**glorification** /ˌglɔrəfəˈkeɪʃən/ *n.* [U] *the glorification of war*

glo·ri·ous /ˈglɔriəs/ *adj.* **1** having or deserving praise and honor: *a glorious achievement* | *the country's **glorious past*** **2** very beautiful or impressive: *glorious views of the coast* | *a glorious fall morning* —**gloriously** *adv.*

glo·ry[1] /ˈglɔri/ *n.* plural **glories** **1** [U] the importance, praise, and honor that people give someone they admire: *At 19 he **won glory** as an Olympic champion.* **2** [C] an achievement that is greatly admired or respected, or that makes you feel proud: *Becoming a Supreme Court judge was the **crowning glory*** (=the final, most successful part) *of her legal career.* | *the **glories of** nature* | *the team's **past glories*** **3** [U] a beautiful and impressive appearance: *They spent $10 million on restoring the Grand Theater to its **former glory**.*

glory[2] *v.* past tense and past participle **gloried**, third person singular **glories**

glory in sth *phr. v.* to enjoy or be proud of the praise, attention, and success that you get: *The new mayor gloried in his victory.*

gloss[1] /glɔs, glɑs/ *n.* **1** [singular, U] a shiny attractive surface: *a hair gel that adds gloss to your hair* **2** [C] a note in a piece of writing that explains a difficult word, phrase, or idea

gloss[2] *v.* [T] to provide a note in a piece of writing which explains a difficult word, phrase, or idea

gloss over sth *phr. v.* to avoid talking about something unpleasant, or to say as little as possible about it: *She glossed over the details of her divorce.*

glos·sa·ry /ˈglɑsəri, ˈglɔ-/ *n.* plural **glossaries** [C] a list of technical or unusual words with an explanation of their meaning, printed at the end of a book

gloss·y /ˈglɔsi, ˈglɑsi/ *adj.* **1** shiny and smooth: *glossy healthy hair* **2** a glossy magazine, book, or photograph is printed on shiny, good quality paper

glove /glʌv/ *n.* [C] a piece of clothing worn on your hand, with separate parts to cover the thumb and each finger [➡ **mitten**]: *a **pair of gloves*** ➔ see picture at CLOTHES

ˈglove comˌpartment also **ˈglove box** *n.* [C] a small cupboard in a car in front of the passenger seat, where small things such as maps can be kept

glow[1] /gloʊ/ *v.* [I] **1** to shine with a soft steady light: *The red tip of his cigarette was glowing in the dark*

> **THESAURUS**
> **shine**, **flash**, **flicker**, **twinkle**, **sparkle**, **shimmer**
> ➔ see Thesaurus box at SHINE[1]

2 if your face glows, it is bright or hot because you are healthy, have been doing exercise, or are feeling a strong emotion **3 glow with happiness/pride/pleasure etc.** to show in your expression that you are very happy, proud, etc.: *Jodie was glowing with pride as she looked at the baby.*

glow[2] *n.* [singular] **1** a soft steady light: *the **glow of** candlelight* | *At sunset we could see an orange **glow from** the clouds.* **2** the bright color your face has when you are healthy, have been exercising, or are feeling a strong emotion: *the **healthy glow** in her cheeks* **3 a glow of pleasure/pride/satisfaction etc.** a strong feeling of pleasure, pride, etc.

glow·er /ˈglaʊə˞/ *v.* [I] to look at someone in an angry way: *Donna **glowered at** her husband but said nothing.* —**glowering** *adj.*

glow·ing /ˈgloʊɪŋ/ *adj.* **glowing report/review/description etc.** a report, etc. that is full of praise for someone or something: *He spoke **in glowing terms** about the concert.* —**glowingly** *adv.*

glow·worm /ˈgloʊwə˞m/ *n.* [C] an insect that gives out light from its body

glu·cose /ˈglukoʊs/ *n.* [U] a natural form of sugar that is in fruits

glue[1] /glu/ *n.* [C,U] a sticky substance used for joining things together: *Stick the ribbon on with glue.*

glue[2] *v.* [T] **1** to join things together using glue: *The two pieces of leather were **glued together**.*

THESAURUS

fasten, **attach**, **join**, **tape**, **staple**, **clip**, **tie**, **button (up)**, **zip (up)**
→ see Thesaurus box at FASTEN

2 be glued to sth to look at something with all your attention: *He was glued to the TV set again.*

glum /glʌm/ *adj.* unhappy and quiet: *Anna looked glum.*

THESAURUS

sad, **unhappy**, **miserable**, **depressed**, **down**
→ see Thesaurus box at SAD

glut[1] /glʌt/ *n.* [C] a supply of something that is more than you need: *a* ***glut of*** *new cars on the market*

glut[2] *v.* **be glutted with sth** to be supplied with too much of something: *The world market is glutted with oil.*

glut·ton /ˈglʌt˺n/ *n.* [C] **1** someone who eats too much food **2 a glutton for punishment** someone who seems to enjoy working very hard or doing something unpleasant

glut·ton·y /ˈglʌt˺n-i/ *n.* [U] *formal* the bad habit of eating and drinking too much

glyc·er·in /ˈglɪsərɪn/ *n.* [U] a sticky colorless liquid used in making soap, medicine, and EXPLOSIVES

gm. the written abbreviation of **gram**

GMAT /ˈdʒi mæt/ *n.* [C] *trademark* **Graduate Management Admission Test** an examination taken by students who have completed a first degree and want to go to GRADUATE SCHOOL to study business

GMO *n.* [C] **genetically modified organism** a plant or other living thing whose GENES have been changed by scientists in order to make it stronger, less likely to get diseases, etc. —**GMO** *adj.*

gnarled /nɑrld/ *adj.* rough and twisted: *a gnarled branch*

gnash·ing /ˈnæʃɪŋ/ *n.* **gnashing of teeth** *humorous* used in order to say that people are very angry about something and are complaining loudly

gnat /næt/ *n.* [C] a small flying insect that bites

gnaw /nɔ/ *v.* [I,T] to keep biting something: *a dog* ***gnawing on*** *a bone*

gnaw at sb *phr. v.* to make you feel worried or anxious over a long time: *Guilt had been gnawing at him all day.*

gnaw·ing /ˈnɔ-ɪŋ/ *adj.* [only before noun] worrying or painful for a long time: *gnawing doubts*

gnome /noʊm/ *n.* [C] a creature in children's stories like a little old man, who lives under the ground

GNP *n.* [singular, U] **Gross National Product** the total value of the goods and services produced in a country, including income from ABROAD

go[1] /goʊ/ *v.* past tense **went** /wɛnt/ past participle **gone** /gɔn, gɑn/ third person singular **goes** /goʊz/

1 LEAVE [I] to leave a place in order to go somewhere else [➡ **come**]: *I wanted to go, but Craig wanted to stay.* | *Let's* ***go home***. | *Are you* ***going to*** *Gloria's party?* | *It's late – we should* ***be/get going***.

2 VISIT also **been** [I] to visit a place and then leave it: *Lucia* ***has gone to*** *Paris* (=she is in Paris now). | *Lucia* ***has been to*** *Paris* (=she has visited Paris in the past).

3 TRAVEL/MOVE [I] to travel or move in a particular way or for a particular distance: *The car was going much too fast.* | *We can* ***go by bus/car/train etc.***

4 be going to do sth used in order to say that something will happen, or is supposed to happen in the future: *It looks like it's going to rain.*

5 DO A PARTICULAR ACTIVITY [I] to leave the place where you are in order to do something: *Let's* ***go for*** *a walk.* | *I'll* ***go and*** *pick up the car for you.*

6 go shopping/swimming/clubbing etc. to leave somewhere in order to shop, swim, etc.

7 REACH [I] to reach as far as a particular place, or lead to a particular place: *The roots of the tree go very deep.* | *The belt won't go around my waist.*

8 BE SENT [I] to be sent or passed on: *The email* ***went to*** *everyone in the company.*

9 USUAL POSITION [I] if something goes somewhere, that is its usual position: *"Where do the plates go?" "On the shelf."*

10 FIT [I] to be the right size, shape, or amount for a particular space: *I don't think all this will* ***go in*** *the suitcase.*

11 CHANGE [linking verb] to change in some way, especially by becoming worse than before: *The company went bankrupt last year.* | *Her hair is starting to go gray.*

USAGE

Become is used in both written and spoken English: *He's becoming very successful.* | *Canada has become popular with tourists.*
Get and **go** are less formal than **become**, and are used more often in spoken English: *I got very hungry.* | *Have you gone crazy?*
Become can be used in front of an adjective or a noun, but **get** and **go** are only used in front of an adjective: *The noise from the airport is becoming a problem.* | *It became clear that the company would lose the contract.* | *It's getting dark.* | *Beethoven went deaf when he was 40 years old.*

12 BE IN A STATE [linking verb] to be or remain in a particular state: *Many families are forced to* ***go hungry***. | *His letter* ***went unanswered*** (=nobody replied to his letter).

13 ATTEND [I] to regularly attend school, a church, etc.: *Is Brett* ***going to*** *college next year?*

14 HAPPEN [I] to happen or develop in a particular way: *How did your French test go?* | *The party* ***went well***.

G

15 START [I] to start doing something: *It's time to **get going on** the cleaning.* | *The builders are **ready to go**, but their equipment isn't here yet.*
16 GET RID OF SB/STH [I] to be bad enough to be made to leave or be thrown away: *They knew that Parker **had to go**.* | *"Do you want all these magazines?" "No, they **can go**."*
17 MONEY [I] if money goes, it is spent: *The money **goes to** local charities.*
18 TIME [I] if time goes, it passes: *I just don't know where the time goes!*
19 BE SOLD [I] to be sold: *The painting should **go for** $2,000.*
20 SOUND/SONG [T] to make a particular sound, or have particular words or music: *Do you remember how that song goes?*
21 MATCH [I] to look or taste good together: *Those colors don't **go together** very well.* | *Does red wine **go with** chicken?*
22 GET WORSE [I] to become weak and not work correctly: *He's old, and his hearing is going.*
23 to go **a)** remaining before something happens: *Only two weeks to go before we leave for South America!* **b)** food that is to go is bought from a restaurant and taken away to be eaten: *I'll have an order of fries to go, please.*

SPOKEN PHRASES

24 How's it going?/How are things going? said in order to ask someone how s/he is: *"Hey, Jimmy, how's it going?" "All right, I guess."*
25 go like this/that used in order to tell someone about what movement someone or something made: *He **went like this** and knocked the lamp over.*
26 don't (even) go there used in order to say that you do not want to think or talk about something: *"What if the two of them...?" "Don't even go there."*
27 it (just) goes to show used in order to emphasize what something proves or shows: *It just goes to show how important your first impression is.*
28 go (to the bathroom) to pass liquid or solid waste from your body: *Mommy, I **have to go**!*

go about sth *phr. v.* to do something or begin doing something: *I don't know how to go about this.* | *I didn't have the slightest idea how to go about making a movie.*
go after sb/sth *phr. v.* **1** to follow or chase someone: *Joe went after her to make sure she was okay.* **2** to try to get something: *I can't decide whether to go after the job or not.*
go against sb/sth *phr. v.* **1** if something goes against your beliefs, principles, etc., it is the opposite of what you believe in: *This goes against everything I've been brought up to believe in.* **2** to do the opposite of what someone wants or advises you to do: *She was scared to go against her father's wishes.*
go ahead *phr. v.* **1** *spoken* said in order to give someone permission to do something, or to let him/her speak before you: *You can **go ahead of** me – I'm waiting for someone.* **2** to start or continue to do something: *They've decided to **go ahead with** plans to build 50 new houses on the site.* **3 also go on ahead** to go somewhere before the other people in your group: *You can go ahead and we'll catch up with you later.*
go along *phr. v.* **1** to continue doing something: *I went along making the same mistakes for weeks.* **2** if you do something as you go along, you do it without preparing or planning it: *I just made up the story as I went along.*
go along with sb/sth *phr. v.* to agree with or support someone or something: *You'll never get Mom to go along with it.*
go around *phr. v.* **1 go around doing sth** to behave or dress in a particular way: *You can't go around lying to people all the time!* **2** if something such as an illness or news is going around, it is being passed from one person to another: *There's a rumor going around that Hugh is having an affair.* **3 enough/plenty to go around** enough for each person: *Is there enough ice cream to go around?*
go at sb/sth *phr. v.* to attack someone or start a fight: *The dogs went at each other as soon as we let go.*
go away *phr. v.* **1** to leave a place or a person: *Go away! Leave me alone!* **2** to spend some time away from home, especially on vacation: *We're going away for two weeks in June.* **3** if a problem or bad feeling goes away, it disappears: *My headache hasn't gone away.*
go back *phr. v.* **1** to return to a place that you have just come from: *I think we ought to go back now.* **2** to continue something that you were doing before: *I'll **go back to** studying after the news is over.* **3** to have been made, built, or started at some time in the past: *Their family history **goes back to** the 16th century.*
go back on sth *phr. v.* if you go back on a promise or agreement, you do not do what you promised to do: *We're not **going back on** our **word**.*
go by *phr. v.* **1** if time goes by, it passes: *Two months went by before Winton called.* **2 go by** sth to use information, rules, etc. to help you decide what to do: *Don't go by that map. It's really old.*
go down *phr. v.*
1 BECOME LESS to become lower or less in level, amount, size, quality, etc.: *The temperature **went down to** freezing last night.* | *The swelling in her knee didn't go down for days.*
2 GO FROM ONE PLACE TO ANOTHER *spoken* to go to a place for a particular purpose: *We **went down to** Hudson's to buy a camera.*
3 SUN when the sun goes down, it appears to move down until you cannot see it anymore
4 AIRPLANE if an airplane goes down, it crashes
5 SHIP if a ship goes down, it sinks
6 COMPUTER to stop working for a short time: *My computer went down an hour ago.*

7 go down well/badly etc. to get a particular reaction from someone: *Robbie's jokes didn't go down very well with her parents.*
8 BE REMEMBERED to be remembered or recorded in a particular way: *This day will* ***go down in history*** (=be remembered always).

go for sb/sth *phr. v.* **1** to try to get or win something: *a swimmer going for an Olympic record* **2 go for it** *spoken* said when you want to encourage someone to do something: *Well, if you're sure you want to, go for it!* **3 I could/would go for sth** *spoken* to want or like something: *I could really go for a taco right now.* **4** *spoken* to usually like a particular type of person or thing: *Kathy tends to go for older men.*

go into sth *phr. v.* **1** to start working in a particular profession or type of business: *Vivian wants to go into politics.* **2** to be used in order to make something work or happen: *A lot of money has gone into building this house.* **3** to describe or explain something thoroughly: *I don't want to* ***go into details*** *right now, but it was horrible.* **4** if one number goes into another, it can divide it: *12 goes into 60 five times.*

go off *phr. v.* **1** to explode: *Fireworks went off all over the city that night.* **2** to make a loud noise: *My alarm clock didn't go off.* **3** to leave a place, especially in order to do something: *He* ***went off to*** *get something to eat.* **4** if a machine or light goes off, it stops working or stops shining: *Suddenly, all the lights went off.*

go on *phr. v.* **1** to continue without stopping or changing: *We can't go on fighting like this!* | *This guy* ***went on and on*** (=talked for a long time) *about himself all night.* | *We had to* ***go on with*** *our lives.* **2** to happen: ***What's going on*** *down there? Did something break?* **3** to do something new when you have finished something else: ***Go on to*** *question number 5 when you're done.* **4** to continue talking or explaining something, after you have stopped for a while: *After a minute, she stopped crying and* ***went on with*** *the story.* **5** *spoken* said in order to encourage someone to do something: *Go on, have another drink.* **6** to base an opinion or judgment on something: *The police don't have much to go on.* **7 be going on six o'clock/25 etc.** to be nearly a time, age, number, etc.: *Aunt Tess must be going on 70 by now.* **8** if time goes on, it passes: *As time went on, he became more friendly.* **9** if a machine or light goes on, it starts working or starts shining

go out *phr. v.* **1** to leave your house, especially in order to do something you enjoy: *Are you going out tonight?* | *We* ***went out for dinner/lunch, etc.*** *on Saturday.* | *Can I* ***go out and*** *play now?* **2** to have a romantic relationship with someone: *Leah used to* ***go out with*** *Dan's brother.* **3** if the TIDE goes out, the water moves away from the land [≠ **come in**] **4** if a light or fire goes out, it stops shining or burning

go over *phr. v.* **1 go over** sth to look at or think about something carefully: *I've gone over the budget and I don't think we can afford a new computer.* **2 go over well** if something goes over well, people like it: *His comments didn't go over very well with customers.*

go through *phr. v.* **1 go through** sth to have a very upsetting or difficult experience: *She's just been through a divorce.* **2 go through** sth to use all of something: *Jeremy goes through at least a quart of milk every day!* **3** if a deal, agreement, or law goes through, it is officially accepted: *My car loan has finally gone through.* **4 go through** sth to look at, read, or explain something carefully: *She had to go through all her uncle's papers after he died.*

go through with sth *phr. v.* to do something you had planned or promised to do: *I'm not sure if I can go through with the wedding.*

go to sth *phr. v.* **1 go to a lot of trouble/go to great lengths** to use a lot of effort to get something or do something: *Suki went to a lot of trouble to get us the tickets.* **2** to begin to experience or do something, or begin to be in a particular state: *I lay down and went to sleep.*

go under *phr. v.* if a business goes under, it has serious problems and fails

go up *phr. v.* **1** to increase in number or amount: *Our rent has* ***gone up by*** *almost 20%.* **2** to be built: *All of those houses have gone up in the past six months.* **3** to explode or be destroyed by fire: *The factory* ***went up in flames*** *before the firemen got there.*

go with sb/sth *phr. v.* **1** to be included as part of something: *The car goes with the job.* **2** to accept someone's idea or plan: *Let's go with John's original proposal.*

go without sth *phr. v.* **1** to not have something you need or want: *We can go without a car in the city.* **2 it goes without saying** used in order to say that something should be clear without needing to be said: ***It goes without saying that*** *you should stay with us when you're in Boston.*

GRAMMAR

gone and been

Gone is the usual past participle of **go**: *George has gone to Denver.* (=George has traveled to Denver and is there now.)

Been is the past participle of the sense of **go** that means "visit": *George has been to Denver.* (=George has visited Denver before, but is not there now.)

go² *n.* plural **goes** [C] **1** an attempt to do something: *Don't worry about getting it right – just* ***give it a go.*** **2 on the go** *informal* very busy or working all the time: *Susan's three children really keep her on the go.*

goad /goʊd/ *v.* [T] to make someone do something by annoying him/her until s/he does it: *Kathy* ***goaded*** *him* ***into*** *confessing that he had lied.*

ˈgo-aˌhead *n.* **give sb the go-ahead** *informal* to officially give someone permission to start doing something: *The bank finally* ***gave us the go-ahead*** *to start building.*

goal /goʊl/ *n.* [C] **1** something that you hope to achieve in the future: *My* ***ultimate/long-term goal*** *is to become a doctor.* | *He will do anything it takes to* ***achieve/reach*** *his* ***goal.***

THESAURUS

purpose, aim, objective
➔ see Thesaurus box at PURPOSE

2 the action in a game or sport of making the ball go into a particular area to win a point, or the point won by doing this: *Ronaldo* ***scored*** *two* ***goals*** *for Brazil.* **3** the area into which a player tries to put the ball in order to win a point

goal·ie /ˈgoʊli/ *n.* [C] *informal* ➔ GOALKEEPER

goal·keep·er /ˈgoʊlˌkipɚ/ **also goal·tend·er** /ˈgoʊlˌtɛndɚ/ *n.* [C] the player on a sports team who tries to stop the ball from going into the GOAL

goal·post /ˈgoʊlpoʊst/ *n.* [C] one of the two upright BARS, with another bar along the top or across the middle, that form the GOAL in games like SOCCER and football

goat /goʊt/ *n.* [C] **1** a common farm animal with horns and with long hair under its chin ➔ see picture at FARM[1] **2 get sb's goat** *informal* to make someone very angry or annoyed

goat·ee /goʊˈti/ *n.* [C] a small BEARD on the end of a man's chin

gob·ble /ˈgɑbəl/ **also gobble up** *v.* [T] *informal* to eat something very quickly

THESAURUS

eat, devour, wolf down
➔ see Thesaurus box at EAT

gob·ble·dy·gook, gobbledegook /ˈgɑbəldiˌgʊk/ *n.* [U] *informal disapproving* very complicated or technical language that seems to have no meaning

ˈgo-between *n.* [C] someone who takes messages from one person or group to another because the two sides do not want to meet or cannot meet: *The lawyer will* ***act as a go-between*** *for the couple.*

gob·let /ˈgɑblɪt/ *n.* [C] a cup made of glass or metal with a base and long stem but no handles

gob·lin /ˈgɑblɪn/ *n.* [C] a small and ugly creature in children's stories who likes to trick people

gobs /gɑbz/ *n.* [plural] *informal* a large amount of something: *They must have* ***gobs of*** *money.*

ˈgo-cart *n.* [C] a small car made of an open frame on four wheels that people race for fun

god /gɑd/ *n.* **1 God** the spirit or BEING whom Christians, Jews, Muslims, etc. pray to, and who they believe created the universe: *She* ***believes in God.*** **2** [C] a male spirit or BEING who is believed by some religions to control the world or part of it, or who represents a particular quality [➡ **goddess**]: *Mars, the* ***god of*** *war*

THESAURUS

deity/divinity – a god or goddess
idol – an image or object that people pray to as a god

3 [C] someone or something that is given too much importance or respect: *Money became his god.* **4 a God-given duty/right/talent etc.** a duty, etc. received from God **5 God's gift to sb/sth** someone who thinks s/he is perfect or extremely good: *Paul thinks he's* ***God's gift to women.***

SPOKEN PHRASES

6 God/oh (my) God/good God/God almighty a phrase said in order to add force to what you are saying when you are surprised, angry, etc.: *Oh my God, I can't believe she said that!* **7 I swear/hope/wish etc. to God** said in order to emphasize that you promise, hope, etc. that something is true **8 for God's sake** used in order to emphasize something that you are saying: *For God's sake, shut up!* **9 God (only) knows** said in order to show that you are annoyed because you do not know something or understand something: *God only knows where those kids are now!* **10 what/how/where/who in God's name** said in order to add force to a question when you are surprised or angry: *Where in God's name have you been?* **11 honest to God** said in order to emphasize that you are not lying or joking: *Honest to God, I didn't tell her!*

god·child /ˈgɑdtʃaɪld/ *n.* plural **godchildren** /-ˌtʃɪldrən/ [C] a child that a GODPARENT promises to help, usually by teaching him/her Christian values

god·dess /ˈgɑdɪs/ *n.* [C] a female spirit or BEING who is believed by some religions to control the world or part of it, or who represents a particular quality [➡ **god**]: *Athena, the Greek goddess of wisdom*

god·fa·ther /ˈgɑdˌfɑðɚ/ *n.* [C] **1** a male GODPARENT **2** *slang* the leader of a criminal organization

ˈgod-ˌfearing *adj. old-fashioned* behaving according to the moral rules of a religion: *god-fearing men and women*

god·for·sak·en /ˈgɑdfɚˌseɪkən/ *adj.* a godforsaken place is far away from where people live, and does not have anything interesting or cheerful in it

god·less /ˈgɑdlɪs/ *adj.* not showing any respect for or belief in God

god·like /ˈgɑdlaɪk/ *adj.* having a quality like God or a god

god·ly /ˈgɑdli/ *adj. old-fashioned* showing that you obey God by behaving according to the moral rules of a religion

god·moth·er /ˈgɑdˌmʌðɚ/ *n.* [C] a female GODPARENT

G

god·par·ent /ˈgɑdˌpɛrənt/ *n.* [C] someone who promises to help a child, usually by teaching him/her Christian values

god·send /ˈgɑdsɛnd/ *n.* [singular] something good that happens to you at a time when you really need it: *The drug has proved a* ***godsend to*** *people with the disease.*

go·fer /ˈgoʊfɚ/ *n.* [C] *informal* someone whose job is to get and carry things for other people

ˌgo-ˈgetter *n.* [C] *informal* someone who is very determined to succeed

ˌgoggle-ˈeyed *adj. informal* with your eyes wide open and looking at something that surprises you

gog·gles /ˈgɑgəlz/ *n.* [plural] special glasses that protect your eyes, for example when you are swimming

goggles

swimming goggles

go·ing¹ /ˈgoʊɪŋ/ *n.* [U] **1** the act of leaving a place: *His going will be a great loss to the company.* **2 rough/hard/good etc. going** *informal* the speed at which you do something: *I'm getting the work done, but it's slow going.*

going² *adj.* **1 the going rate** the usual cost of a service, or the usual pay for a job **2** [not before noun] available, or able to be found: *We think we make* ***the best*** *computers* ***going****.*

ˌgoing-ˈover *n.* [singular] a thorough examination of something to make sure it is all right: *Our lawyers will* ***give*** *the contract* ***a good going-over****.*

ˌgoings-ˈon *n.* [plural] *informal* activities or events that you think are strange or interesting

gold¹ /goʊld/ *n.* **1** [U] a valuable soft yellow metal that is used to make jewelry, coins, etc.: *The locket is made of* ***pure gold****.* **2** [C,U] a bright shiny yellow color

gold² *adj.* **1** made of gold: *a gold necklace* **2** having the color of gold: *a gold dress*

ˈgold ˌdigger *n.* [C] *informal* someone who marries someone else only for his/her money

gold·en /ˈgoʊldən/ *adj.* **1** having a bright shiny yellow color: *golden hair* **2 golden age** the time when something was at its best: *the* ***golden age of*** *television* **3 a golden opportunity** a good chance to get something valuable, or to be very successful **4** *literary* made of gold: *a golden crown*

gold·fish /ˈgoʊldˌfɪʃ/ *n.* [C] a small shiny orange fish often kept as a pet

ˌgold ˈmedal *n.* [C] a prize that is given to the winner of a race or competition, and that is usually made of gold: *He* ***won*** *three* ***gold medals*** *at the Olympics.* —**gold medalist** *n.* [C]

gold·mine /ˈgoʊldmaɪn/ *n.* [C] **1** *informal* a business or activity that produces a lot of money **2** a hole under the ground from which gold is taken

golf

golf /gɑlf, gɔlf/ *n.* [U] a game in which you hit a small white ball into a hole in the ground with a golf club, using as few hits as possible: *I* ***play golf*** *every weekend.* —**golfer** *n.* [C]

ˈgolf club *n.* [C] **1** a long wooden or metal stick used for hitting the ball in golf **2** a place where a group of people pay to play golf

ˈgolf course *n.* [C] an area of land on which you play golf

gol·ly /ˈgɑli/ *interjection old-fashioned* said when you are surprised

gon·do·la /ˈgɑndələ, gɑnˈdoʊlə/ *n.* [C] a long narrow boat, used on the CANALS of Venice

gone /gɔn, gɑn/ *v.* the past participle of GO

gon·er /ˈgɔnɚ, ˈgɑ-/ *n.* **be a goner** *informal spoken* to be about to die, or in a lot of danger: *Someone hit me from behind, and I thought I was a goner.*

gong /gɔŋ, gɑŋ/ *n.* [C] a round piece of metal that hangs in a frame and is hit with a stick to make a loud sound as a signal

gon·na /ˈgɔnə, gənə/ *spoken* a short form of "going to," used when talking about the future: *I'm gonna talk to her about it tomorrow.*

gon·or·rhe·a /ˌgɑnəˈriə/ *n.* [U] a disease of the sex organs that is passed from one person to another during sex

goo /gu/ *n.* [U] a thick unpleasant sticky substance —**gooey** *adj.*: *gooey caramel*

good¹ /gʊd/ *adj.* comparative **better**, superlative **best**

1 HIGH IN QUALITY of a high standard [≠ **bad, poor**]: *The food was really good.* | *Who's the best player on the team?* | *His work just isn't* ***good enough****.*

THESAURUS

great especially spoken: *We had a really great time at camp.*
excellent: *It was an excellent concert.*
wonderful: *a wonderful place for a picnic*
fantastic: *The movie's special effects were fantastic.*
outstanding: *an outstanding achievement*
exceptional: *Ruth's an exceptional student.*
first-class: *This is a first-class wine.*
ace informal: *an ace guitarist*
➔ BAD

USAGE

Use **good** to describe the quality of something or someone: *a good teacher* | *Was the movie good?* Use **well** to talk about the way someone does something: *He plays tennis very well.*

G

2 APPROPRIATE appropriate or convenient [≠ **bad**]: *When would be* ***a good time*** *for us to meet?* | *It was a good place to rest.*
3 SUCCESSFUL likely to be successful [≠ **bad**]: *That's a* ***good idea.*** | *We stand a* ***good chance*** *of winning.*
4 SKILLFUL smart or skillful: *a good swimmer* | *Andrea is very* ***good at*** *languages.*
5 NICE enjoyable and pleasant: *good weather* | ***It's good to*** *see you again.* | *We had such* ***a good time.***
6 HEALTHY **a)** useful for your health or character: *Watching so much TV isn't* ***good for you.*** **b)** healthy: *"How do you feel today?" "Better, thanks."* | *I'm in reasonably* ***good health.***
7 ABLE TO BE USED able to be used, and not broken or damaged: *There, now the table is* ***as good as new*** (=fixed so that it looks new again). | *The guarantee on my new watch is* ***good for*** (=can be used for) *three years.*
8 WELL-BEHAVED behaving well, used especially about children: *Sit here and be a good girl.*
9 KIND kind and helpful: *It's* ***good of*** *you to come.* | *Dad was always* ***good about*** *helping me with my homework.*
10 as good as almost: *The work is as good as finished.*
11 a good deal (of sth) a lot: *I spent a good deal of time preparing for this test.*
12 RIGHT morally right: *He had always tried to lead a good life.*
13 LARGE/LONG large in amount, size, etc.: *a good-sized car* | *They've been gone* ***a good while*** (=a long time).
14 COMPLETE [only before noun] complete or thorough: *The car needs a good wash.* | ***Take a good look*** *at this picture.*
15 too good to be true/too good to last *informal* so good that you cannot believe it is real, or you expect something bad to happen: *Their relationship had always seemed too good to be true.*

SPOKEN PHRASES

16 good/oh good said when you are pleased that something has happened or has been done: *"I've finished." "Good, put your papers in the box."*
17 good luck used in order to say that you hope that someone is successful
18 good idea/question/point etc. used when someone says or suggests something interesting or important that you had not thought of before: *"But it's Sunday – the bank will be closed." "Good point."*
19 it's a good thing said when you are glad that something has happened: *It's a good thing you remembered to bring napkins.*
20 Good for sb! used in order to say that you approve of something that someone has done: *"I've decided to accept the job." "Good for you!"*
21 good God/grief/heavens etc. said in order to express anger, surprise, or other strong feelings. Saying "God" in this way is offensive to some people: *Good grief! Is it that late?*

G

good² *n.* [U] **1** something that improves a situation or gives you an advantage: *It'll* ***do you good*** (=make you feel better) *to take a vacation.* | *Take your medicine – it's* ***for your own good*** (=it will help you). **2 no good/not much good/not any good** **a)** not likely to be useful or successful: *It's no good trying to explain it to her – she won't listen.* **b)** bad: *That movie isn't any good.*
3 what's the good of...?/what good is...? used in order to say that it is not worth doing or having something in a particular situation: ***What good is*** *an expensive house* ***if*** *you're always traveling?*
4 goods [plural] things that are produced in order to be sold: *household goods* | *They were caught moving* ***stolen goods.*** **5 for good** permanently: *I'd like to stay in Colorado for good.* **6 be up to no good** *informal* to be doing or planning to do something that is wrong or bad **7 deliver the goods/come up with the goods** *informal* to do what other people need or expect **8 make good on a promise/threat/claim etc.** to do what you say you are going to do or what you should do: *They're asking for more time to make good on their debts.* **9** behavior or actions that are morally right or follow religious principles: *the battle between good and evil*

good ˌafter'noon *interjection* used in order to say hello to someone in the afternoon

good·bye /gʊd'baɪ, gəd'baɪ/ *interjection* said when you are leaving or being left by someone [➡ **hello**]: *Goodbye, Mrs. Anderson.* | *I just have to* ***say goodbye to*** *Erica.*

COMMUNICATION

Ways of saying goodbye

bye
see you informal
take it easy informal
so long informal
have a good day, have a good weekend,
have a great time
(it was) nice to meet you
have a good day – used especially by people working in stores, etc. when saying goodbye to a customer
take care
➔ HELLO

good 'evening *interjection* used in order to say hello to someone in the evening [➡ **good night**]: *Good evening, ladies and gentlemen.*

ˌgood-for-'nothing *n.* [C] *adj.* someone who is lazy or has no skills: *He's a lazy good-for-nothing.*

ˌGood 'Friday *n.* [C,U] the Friday before EASTER

ˌgood-ˌhumored *adj.* cheerful and friendly

ˌgood-'looking *adj.* someone who is good-looking is attractive

THESAURUS

attractive, pretty, beautiful, handsome, gorgeous, stunning, nice-looking, cute, hot
➔ see Thesaurus box at ATTRACTIVE

ˌgood ˈlooks *n.* [plural] if someone has good looks, s/he is attractive

good ˈmorning *interjection* used in order to say hello to someone in the morning

ˌgood-ˈnatured *adj.* naturally kind and helpful, and not easily made angry —**good-naturedly** *adv.*

good·ness /ˈgʊdnɪs/ *n.* [U] **1** *spoken* said when you are surprised or annoyed: ***My goodness**, you've lost a lot of weight!* | ***For goodness' sake**, will you be quiet!* **2** the quality of being good: *Anne believed in the basic goodness of people.*

good ˈnight *interjection* said when you are leaving or being left by someone at night, especially late at night [➡ **good evening**]

good·will /gʊdˈwɪl/ *n.* [U] kind feelings toward or between people: *Christmas should be a time of peace and goodwill.*

good·y /ˈgʊdi/ *n.* plural **goodies** [C usually plural] *informal* something that is attractive, pleasant, or desirable, especially something good to eat: *We brought lots of goodies for the picnic.*

ˈgoody-ˌgoody **also** **ˌgoody-ˈtwo-shoes** *n.* plural **goody goodies** [C] *disapproving* someone who tries too hard to be good and helpful, in a way that others think is annoying

goof[1] /guf/ *v.* [I] *informal* to make a silly mistake

goof around/off *phr. v. informal* to spend time doing silly things or not doing very much: *We spent the afternoon just goofing around at the mall.*

goof[2] *n.* [C] *informal* **1** a silly mistake **2** someone who is silly

goof·y /ˈgufi/ *adj. informal* stupid or silly: *a goofy smile*

goon /gun/ *n.* [C] *informal* **1** a violent criminal who is paid to frighten or attack people **2** a silly or stupid person

goop /gup/ *n.* [U] *informal* a thick slightly sticky substance: *What's that goop in your hair?*

goose /gus/ *n.* plural **geese** /gis/ **1** [C] a common water bird that is similar to a duck but larger, and makes loud noises **2** [U] the meat from this bird

goose·bumps /ˈgusbʌmps/ **also** **ˈgoose ˌpimples** *n.* [plural] a condition in which your skin is raised up in small points because you are cold, afraid, or excited: *I **get goosebumps** every time I think about playing in the championship.*

GOP *n.* **the GOP** Grand Old Party; another name for the Republican party in U.S. politics

go·pher /ˈgoʊfɚ/ *n.* [C] a North and Central American animal like a SQUIRREL with a short tail, that lives in holes in the ground

gore[1] /gɔr/ *v.* [T] if an animal gores someone, it wounds him/her with its horns

gore[2] *n.* [U] blood that has flowed from a wound and become thicker and darker [➡ **gory**]: *There's too much **blood and gore** (=violence and blood) in the movie.*

gorge[1] /gɔrdʒ/ *n.* [C] a deep narrow valley with steep sides

gorge[2] *v.* **gorge yourself on/with sth** to eat until you are too full: *We gorged ourselves on popcorn and hot dogs at the game.*

gor·geous /ˈgɔrdʒəs/ *adj.* very beautiful or pleasant: *What a gorgeous sunny day!* | *Liz looked gorgeous.*

> **THESAURUS**
>
> **attractive, good-looking, pretty, beautiful, handsome, stunning, nice-looking, cute, hot**
> ➔ see Thesaurus box at ATTRACTIVE

go·ril·la /gəˈrɪlə/ *n.* [C] the largest type of APE (=animal like a monkey)

gor·y /ˈgɔri/ *adj.* clearly describing or showing violence, blood, and killing: *a gory movie*

gosh /gɑʃ/ *interjection* said when you are surprised: *Gosh! I never knew that!*

gos·ling /ˈgɑzlɪŋ/ *n.* [C] a baby GOOSE

gos·pel /ˈgɑspəl/ *n.* **1** [C] **also Gospel** one of the four stories of Christ's life in the Bible **2** [U] **also gospel truth** something that is completely true: *Don't **take** what Ellen says **as gospel*** (=believe it to be completely true). **3** [U] **also ˈgospel ˌmusic** a type of Christian music, performed especially in African-American churches

gos·sip[1] /ˈgɑsəp/ *n.* **1** [U] conversation or information about other people's behavior and private lives, often including unkind or untrue remarks: *People love hearing gossip about movie stars.* **2** [C] someone who likes talking about other people's private lives

G

gossip[2] *v.* [I] to talk or write gossip about someone or something: *What are you **gossiping about**?*

> **THESAURUS**
>
> **talk, have a conversation, chat (with/to), converse**
> ➔ see Thesaurus box at TALK[1]

got /gɑt/ *v.* **1** the past tense of GET **2** a past participle of GET

got·cha /ˈgɑtʃə/ *interjection spoken* **1** a short form of "I've got you," said when you catch someone, or you have gained an advantage over him/her **2** a word meaning "I understand" or "all right": *"First put this one here, and then tie them like this, OK?" "Gotcha."*

got·ta /ˈgɑt̬ə/ *v. spoken* a short form of "got to," used alone or with "have": *I gotta go now.* | *You've gotta admit he plays really well.*

got·ten /ˈgɑt˺n/ *v.* the usual past participle of GET

gouge /gaʊdʒ/ *v.* [T] **1** to make a deep hole or cut in the surface of something **2** *informal* to charge someone too much money for something: *Hotels are ready to gouge Olympic visitors by raising their prices.* —**gouge** *n.* [C]

gouge sth ⇔ **out** *phr. v.* to make a hole in something by removing material that is on its surface

gourd /gɔrd, gʊrd/ *n.* [C] a large fruit with a hard shell that is sometimes used as a container

gour·met¹ /gʊr'meɪ, 'gʊrmeɪ/ *adj.* [only before noun] relating to very good food and drink: *a gourmet restaurant*

gourmet² *n.* [C] someone who knows a lot about good food and drink, and who enjoys them

gout /gaʊt/ *n.* [U] a disease that makes your toes, knees, and fingers hurt and swell

gov·ern /'gʌvən/ *v.* **1** [I,T] to officially control a country, state, etc. and make all the decisions about things such as taxes and laws: *The same party governed for thirty years.* **2** [T] *formal* to control the way a system or situation works: *new rules governing immigration*

gov·ern·ess /'gʌvənɪs/ *n.* [C] a woman who lives with a family and teaches the children at home, especially in past times

gov·ern·ment /'gʌvəmənt, 'gʌvənmənt/ *n.* **1** [C] **also Government** the group of people who govern a country, state, etc.: *The government will send aid to the disaster area.* | *the* ***British/German etc. government***

THESAURUS

democracy – a political system in which everyone can vote to choose the government, or a country that has this system
republic – a country that has an elected government, and does not have a king or queen
monarchy – a country that has a king or queen as the head of state, and which may or may not also have an elected government
regime – a government, especially one that was not elected fairly or that you disapprove of: *a brutal military regime*
dictatorship – a political system in which a dictator (=a leader who has complete power and who has not been elected) controls a country, or a country that has this system
totalitarian country/state etc. – a country in which the government has complete control over everything
police state – a country where the government strictly controls people's freedom, for example to travel or to talk about politics
→ POLITICIAN

2 [U] the process of governing, or the system used for governing: *Voting is essential to democratic government.* —**governmental** /ˌgʌvən'mɛntl/ *adj.*

gov·er·nor, **Governor** /'gʌvənə, -və-/ *n.* [C] the person in charge of governing a U.S. state: *the Governor of California* —**governorship** *n.* [U]

THESAURUS

president, **congressman**, **congresswoman**, **senator**, **mayor**
→ see Thesaurus box at POLITICIAN

gown /gaʊn/ *n.* [C] **1** a long dress worn by a woman on formal occasions: *a silk evening gown* **2** a long loose piece of clothing worn for a particular activity or ceremony: *a graduation gown*

GPA *n.* [C] **grade point average** the average score that a student earns based on all of his/her GRADES, in which an A is 4 points, a B is 3 points, a C is 2 points, a D is 1 point, and an F is 0 points: *Kim has a really* ***high/low GPA.*** | *He graduated with a 3.5 GPA.*

grab¹ /græb/ *v.* past tense **grabbed**, past participle **grabbing** [T] **1** to take hold of someone or something with a sudden or violent movement: *He grabbed my bag and ran off.* | *Kay* ***grabbed hold*** *of my arm to stop me from going.* **2** *informal* to eat or sleep for a very short time: *I'll just grab a sandwich for lunch.* **3** *informal* to quickly take an opportunity to do something: *Try to get there early and grab a seat.* | *You should* ***grab the chance*** *to travel while you're young.* **4 how does sth grab you?** *spoken* used in order to ask if someone would be interested in doing a particular thing: *How does the idea of a trip to Hawaii grab you?*

grab at sth *phr. v.* to quickly and suddenly put out your hand in order to take hold of something: *I grabbed at the glass just before it fell.*

grab² *n.* **1 make a grab for/at sth** to suddenly try to take hold of something: *Parker made a grab for the knife.* **2 be up for grabs** *informal* if a job, prize, opportunity, etc. is up for grabs, it is available for anyone who wants to try to get it

grace¹ /greɪs/ *n.* [U] **1** a smooth way of moving that appears natural, relaxed, and attractive: *She moved with the grace of a dancer.* **2 a)** polite and pleasant behavior: *At least he* ***had the grace to*** *admit he was wrong.* | *Kevin accepted his defeat* ***with good grace*** (=without complaining). **b) graces** [plural] the skills needed to behave in a way that is considered polite and socially acceptable: *Her parents tried to teach her all the finer* ***social graces.*** **3 also grace period** more time that is added to the period you are allowed for finishing a piece of work, paying a debt, etc.: *The bill was supposed to be paid by Friday, but they're giving me* ***a week's grace.*** **4** *formal* God's kindness that is shown to people: *Through* ***the grace of God*** *my dream became reality.* **5** a short prayer before a meal: *Who would like to* ***say grace****?*

grace² *v.* [T] **1 grace sb/sth with your presence** *humorous* said when someone arrives late, or when someone who rarely comes to meetings or events arrives: *I'm so glad you've decided to grace us with your presence!* **2** *formal* to make a place or an object look more beautiful or attractive: *His new painting now graces the wall of the dining room.*

grace·ful /'greɪsfəl/ *adj.* **1** moving in a smooth and attractive way, or having an attractive shape: *a graceful dancer* | *the car's* ***graceful curves***

2 polite and exactly right for a situation: *They urged him to take the graceful way out and resign.* —**gracefully** *adv.*

gra·cious /ˈgreɪʃəs/ *adj.* **1** behaving in a polite, kind, and generous way: *a gracious host* **2** having the type of expensive style, comfort, and beauty that only wealthy people can afford: *gracious living* **3 (goodness) gracious!** *spoken old-fashioned* used in order to express surprise or to emphasize "yes" or "no" —**graciously** *adv.*: *Valerie graciously agreed to let the group meet at her house.*

grad /græd/ *n.* [C] *spoken* ➔ GRADUATE[1]

gra·da·tion /greɪˈdeɪʃən, grə-/ *n.* [C] *formal* a small change in a set of changes: *gradations of color from dark red to pink*

grade[1] /greɪd/ *n.* **1** [C] one of the 12 years you are in school in the U.S., or the students in a particular year: *My brother is* ***in the third grade.*** | *a fifth-grade teacher* **2** [C] a number or letter that shows how well you have done at school, college, etc.: *Betsy always* ***gets good grades.*** **3** [C,U] a particular standard or level of quality that a product, material, etc. has: *Grade A beef* **4 make the grade** to succeed or reach the necessary standard: *Only a few athletes make the grade in professional sports.*

grade[2] *v.* [T] **1** to separate things, or arrange them in order according to their quality or rank: *The eggs are graded according to size.* **2** to give a grade to an examination paper or to a piece of school work: *I spent the weekend grading tests.*

ˈgrade point ˌaverage *n.* [C] ➔ GPA

-grad·er /ˈgreɪdɚ/ *n.* [C] a child in a particular grade: *a cute little first-grader*

ˈgrade ˌschool *n.* [C] ➔ ELEMENTARY SCHOOL

gra·di·ent /ˈgreɪdiənt/ *n.* [C] a slope, or a measurement of how steep a slope is, especially in a road or railroad

ˈgrad school *n.* [C] *informal* ➔ GRADUATE SCHOOL

grad·u·al /ˈgrædʒuəl/ *adj.* **1** happening, developing, or changing slowly over a long time [≠ **sudden**]: *gradual changes* **2** a gradual slope is not steep

grad·u·al·ly /ˈgrædʒuəli, -dʒəli/ *adv.* in a way that happens or develops slowly over time: *Gradually, his back got better.* | *The situation is gradually getting better.* | *Climate change happens gradually.*

grad·u·ate[1] /ˈgrædʒuɪt/ *n.* [C] someone who has successfully completed his/her studies at a school, college, or university [➡ **undergraduate**]: *high school graduates* | *a* ***graduate of*** *UCLA* —**graduate** *adj.*: *graduate students*

grad·u·ate[2] /ˈgrædʒuˌeɪt/ *v.* [I] to obtain a DIPLOMA or a degree by completing your studies at a school, college, or university: *Ruth has just* ***graduated from*** *Princeton.*

grad·u·at·ed /ˈgrædʒuˌeɪtɪd/ *adj.* divided into different levels or sizes from lower to higher amounts or degrees: *graduated rates of income tax*

ˈgraduate ˌschool *n.* [C,U] a college or university where you can study for a MASTER'S DEGREE or a PH.D., or the period of time when you do this

grad·u·a·tion /ˌgrædʒuˈeɪʃən/ *n.* **1** [U] the time when you complete a college or university degree or HIGH SCHOOL education: *After graduation, Jayne went to nursing school.* **2** [C,U] a ceremony at which you receive a degree or DIPLOMA: *We're going to Sara's graduation today.*

graffiti

graf·fi·ti /grəˈfit̬i/ *n.* [U] writing and pictures that are drawn illegally on the walls of buildings, trains, etc.

graft[1] /græft/ *n.* **1** [U] the practice of dishonestly using your position to get money or advantages: *politicians accused of graft* **2** [C] a piece of healthy skin or bone taken from someone's body and put on a damaged part of his/her body: *skin grafts* **3** [C] a piece cut from one plant and joined to another plant so that it grows where it is joined

graft[2] *v.* [I,T] **1** to put a piece of skin or bone from one part of someone's body onto another part that has been damaged: *Doctors* ***grafted*** *skin from Mike's arm* ***onto*** *his face where it was burned.* **2** to join a part of a flower, plant, or tree onto another flower, plant, or tree

grain /greɪn/ *n.* **1** [C,U] a seed or seeds of crops such as corn, wheat, or rice that are used for food, or the crops themselves: *five-grain cereal* | *fields of grain* **2** [C] a very small piece or amount of something: *a* ***grain of*** *sand* | *There's not a* ***grain of truth*** *in what she said.* **3 the grain** the lines or patterns you can see in things such as wood or rock: *Split the wood along the grain.* **4 go against the grain** if something that you must do goes against the grain, you do not like doing it because it is not what you would naturally do **5 take sth with a grain of salt** to not completely believe what someone tells you because you know that s/he often lies or is wrong

grain·y /ˈgreɪni/ *adj.* a photograph that is grainy has a rough appearance, as if the images are made up of spots

gram /græm/ *n.* [C] *written abbreviation* **gm** a unit for measuring weight, equal to 1/1000 of a kilogram or 0.035 OUNCES

gram·mar /ˈgræmɚ/ *n.* [U] the rules by which words change their form and are combined into sentences: *Check your spelling and grammar.* | *the rules of English grammar*

gram·mat·i·cal /grəˈmæt̬ɪkəl/ *adj.* **1** [only before noun] relating to the use of grammar: *gram-*

G

matical errors **2** correct according to the rules of grammar: *a grammatical sentence* —**grammatically** *adv.*: *The sentence is grammatically correct.*

Gram·my /ˈgræmi/ *n.* plural **Grammies** [C] a prize given in the U.S. every year to the best song, the best singer, etc. in the music industry

grand¹ /grænd/ *adj.* **1** higher in rank than others of the same kind: *the grand prize* **2 grand total** the final total you get when you add up several numbers or amounts **3** *old-fashioned* very good or impressive: *a grand old house* —**grandly** *adv.*

grand² *n.* plural **grand** [C] *informal* 1,000 dollars: *Bill only paid five grand for that car.*

grand·child /ˈgræntʃaɪld/ *n.* plural **grandchildren** /-ˌtʃɪldrən/ [C] the child of your son or daughter

grand·dad /ˈgrændæd/ *n.* [C] *informal* ➔ GRANDFATHER

grand·daugh·ter /ˈgrænˌdɔt̬ɚ/ *n.* [C] the daughter of your son or daughter

gran·deur /ˈgrændʒɚ, -dʒʊr/ *n.* [U] impressive beauty, power, or size: *the grandeur of the Pacific Ocean*

grand·fa·ther /ˈgrændˌfɑðɚ/ *n.* [C] the father of your mother or father

G

THESAURUS

relative, **parents**, **father**, **mother**, **dad**, **daddy**, **mom**, **mommy**, **brother**, **sister**, **grandparents**, **grandmother**, **grandpa**, **grandma**, **great-grandparents**, **uncle**, **aunt**, **nephew**, **niece**, **cousin**

➔ see Thesaurus box at RELATIVE¹

ˈgrandfather ˌclock *n.* [C] a tall clock in a wooden case that stands on the floor

gran·di·ose /ˈgrændiˌoʊs, ˌgrændiˈoʊs/ *adj.* grandiose plans sound very important but are really not practical

ˌgrand ˈjury *n.* [C] a group of people who decide whether someone who may be guilty of a crime should be judged in a court of law

grand·ma /ˈgrændmɑ, ˈgræmɑ/ *n.* [C] *informal* ➔ GRANDMOTHER

grand·moth·er /ˈgrændˌmʌðɚ/ *n.* [C] the mother of your mother or father

THESAURUS

relative, **parents**, **father**, **mother**, **dad**, **daddy**, **mom**, **mommy**, **brother**, **sister**, **grandparents**, **grandfather**, **grandpa**, **grandma**, **great-grandparents**, **uncle**, **aunt**, **nephew**, **niece**, **cousin**

➔ see Thesaurus box at RELATIVE¹

grand·pa /ˈgrændpɑ, ˈgræmpɑ/ *n.* [C] *informal* ➔ GRANDFATHER

grand·par·ent /ˈgrændˌpɛrənt/ *n.* [C] the parent of your mother or father

ˌgrand piˈano *n.* [C] the type of large piano often used at concerts

grand prix /ˌgrɑn ˈpri/ *n.* [C] one of a set of international races, especially a car race

ˌgrand ˈslam *n.* [C] **1** a hit in baseball that gets four points because it is a HOME RUN and there are players on all the bases **2** the act of winning all of a set of important sports competitions in the same year

grand·son /ˈgrændsʌn/ *n.* [C] the son of your son or daughter

grandstand

grand·stand /ˈgrændstænd/ *n.* [C] a large structure that has many rows of seats and a roof, where people sit to watch sports competitions or races [➡ **bleachers**]

gran·ite /ˈgrænɪt/ *n.* [U] a very hard gray rock, often used in buildings

gran·ny /ˈgræni/ *n.* plural **grannies** [C] *informal* GRANDMOTHER

gra·no·la /grəˈnoʊlə/ *n.* [U] a breakfast food made from nuts, OATS, and seeds

grant¹ /grænt/ *n.* [C] an amount of money given to someone by an organization for a particular purpose: *a research grant*

grant² *v.* **1 take it for granted (that)** to believe that something is true without making sure [= **assume**]: *You shouldn't take it for granted that your parents will pay for college.* **2 take sb for granted** to expect that someone will always be there when you need him/her, and never thank him/her: *He's so busy with his work that he takes his family for granted.* **3** [T] *formal* to give someone something that s/he has asked for or earned, especially official permission to do something: *Ms. Chung was granted American citizenship last year.* **4 granted (that)** used in order to say that something is true, before you say something else about it: *Granted, he didn't practice much, but he played well anyway.*

gran·u·lat·ed /ˈgrænyəˌleɪt̬ɪd/ *adj.* granulated sugar is in the form of small white grains

gran·ule /ˈgrænyul/ *n.* [C] a very small hard piece of something: *coffee granules* —**granular** /ˈgrænyəlɚ/ *adj.*

grape /greɪp/ *n.* [C] a small round green or purple fruit that grows on a VINE and is often used to make wine: *a **bunch of grapes*** ➔ see picture at FRUIT

grape·fruit /'greɪpfrut/ *n.* [C] a large yellow or pink CITRUS fruit with a thick skin, like a large orange

grape·vine /'greɪpvaɪn/ *n.* **hear sth on/through the grapevine** to hear news because it has been passed from one person to another in conversation: *Sarah had heard through the grapevine that Larry was getting the job.*

graph /græf/ *n.* [C] a drawing that shows how two or more sets of measurements are related to each other: *a graph showing population growth over 50 years*

graph·ic /'græfɪk/ *adj.* **1 a graphic account/description etc.** a very clear detailed description of an event **2** relating to drawing or printing: *graphic art* —**graphically** *adv.*: *She described the scene so graphically that we felt we were there.*

ˌgraphic de'sign *n.* [U] the art of combining pictures and words in the production of books, magazines, etc. —**graphic designer** *n.* [C]

graph·ics /'græfɪks/ *n.* [plural] pictures or images, especially those produced on a computer: *the latest **computer graphics***

graph·ite /'græfaɪt/ *n.* [U] a soft black substance that is a type of CARBON and is used in pencils

grap·ple /'græpəl/ *v.* [I] to fight or struggle with someone, holding him/her tightly: *A young man was **grappling with** the guard.*

grapple with sth *phr. v.* to try hard to understand or solve a difficult problem: *The new governor will have to grapple with the problem of unemployment.*

grasp¹ /græsp/ *v.* [T] **1** to take and hold something firmly in your hands: *I grasped his arm firmly and led him away.* **2** to completely understand a fact or an idea, especially a complicated one: *They couldn't quite grasp the significance of the problem.* ➔ **grasp at straws** at STRAW

grasp at sth *phr. v.* to eagerly try to get or hold on to something: *He was desperately grasping at some way to stay in power.*

grasp² *n.* [singular] **1** the ability to understand a complicated idea or situation: *He **has** a good **grasp of** English grammar.* | *ideas that are **beyond** my **grasp*** (=too difficult to understand) **2** the possibility of being able to achieve or gain something: *Eve felt that success was finally **within** her **grasp**.* **3** a hold on something, or your ability to hold it: *The bottle slipped out of his grasp and smashed on the floor.*

grasp·ing /'græspɪŋ/ *adj. disapproving* too eager to get money: *a grasping man*

grass /græs/ *n.* **1** [U] a very common plant with thin green leaves that grows across fields, parks, hills, and yards: *Please keep off the grass.* | *a **blade of grass*** (=a single leaf) **2** [C,U] a particular type of grass: *mountain grasses* **3** [U] *informal* MARIJUANA

grass·hop·per /'græs,hɑpɚ/ *n.* [C] an insect that jumps with its long back legs and makes short loud noises

grass·land /'græslænd/ *n.* [U] **also grasslands** [plural] a large area of land covered with wild grass

ˌgrass 'roots *n.* **the grass roots** the ordinary people in an organization rather than the leaders —**grass-roots** *adj.*: *a grass-roots campaign*

gras·sy /'græsi/ *adj.* covered with grass: *a grassy hill*

grate¹ /greɪt/ *v.* **1** [T] to rub food such as cheese, vegetables, etc. against a rough or sharp surface in order to break it into small pieces: *grated cheese* ➔ see picture at CUT¹

THESAURUS

chop (up) – to cut meat, vegetables, or wood into pieces
slice – to cut bread, meat, or vegetables into thin pieces
dice – to cut vegetables or meat into small square pieces
peel – to cut the outside part off an apple, potato, etc.
carve – to cut pieces from a large piece of meat
shred to cut vegetables into small thin pieces
➔ see Thesaurus box at CUT¹

2 [I] *informal* to annoy someone: *She's really beginning to **grate on** my **nerves**.*

grate² *n.* [C] **1** the frame and metal BARS that hold wood, coal, etc. in a FIREPLACE **2** a metal frame with bars across it that covers a hole, window, etc.: *iron grates on the windows*

grate·ful /'greɪtfəl/ *adj.* **1** feeling that you want to thank someone because of something kind that s/he has done [≠ **ungrateful**]: *I'm very **grateful for** the opportunity to study at Harvard.* | *Mona **was grateful to** Lorenzo **for** his support.* | *We're just **grateful that** you can help.* | *the thanks of a **grateful nation*** **2 I/we would be grateful if...** used in formal situations or letters to make a request: *I would be grateful if you would allow me to visit your school.* —**gratefully** *adv.*: *We gratefully accepted their offer.*

grat·er /'greɪt̬ɚ/ *n.* [C] a kitchen tool used for grating food

grat·i·fy /'græt̬ə,faɪ/ *v.* past tense and past participle **gratified**, third person singular **gratifies** [T] *formal* to make someone feel pleased and satisfied: *We were gratified by the result of the vote.* —**gratification** /ˌgræt̬əfə'keɪʃən/ *n.* [U]

grat·i·fy·ing /'græt̬ə,faɪ-ɪŋ/ *adj. formal* pleasing and satisfying: ***It's gratifying to** know that we have achieved so much.*

grat·ing¹ /'greɪt̬ɪŋ/ *n.* [C] a metal frame with BARS across it that covers a hole, window, etc.

grating² *adj.* a grating sound is unpleasant and annoying: *a grating voice*

gra·tis /'græt̬ɪs, 'grɑ-/ *adj., adv. formal* provided without payment [= **free**]

grat·i·tude /'græt̬ə,tud/ *n.* [U] the feeling of being grateful [≠ **ingratitude**]: *I would like to **express** my **gratitude** to everyone who helped us.*

gra·tu·i·tous /grə'tuət̬əs/ *adj.* said or done with-

G

out a good reason in a way that offends someone: *television programs with **gratuitous violence***

gra·tu·i·ty /grəˈtuət̬i/ *n.* plural **gratuities** [C] *formal* TIP

grave¹ /greɪv/ *n.* [C] **1** the place where a dead body is buried: *We visited my grandfather's grave.* | *They buried him in an **unmarked grave*** (=one with no name on it). **2 sb would turn/roll over in the grave** used in order to say that someone who is dead would strongly disapprove of something that is happening now **3 the grave** *literary* death: *He took the secret to the grave with him.*

grave² *adj.* **1** very serious and worrying: *I think he is making a **grave mistake**.* | *The war is a cause of **grave concern**.* **2** looking or sounding very serious: *My parents spoke quietly and **looked grave** for the rest of the day.* —**gravely** *adv.*

grav·el /ˈgrævəl/ *n.* [U] small stones used in order to make a surface for paths or roads

grav·el·ly /ˈgrævəli/ *adj.* a gravelly voice sounds low and rough

grave·side /ˈgreɪvsaɪd/ *n.* [C usually singular] the area around a grave: *Mourners stood somberly **at his graveside*** (=beside it).

grave·stone /ˈgreɪvstoʊn/ *n.* [C usually singular] a stone on a grave that shows the name of the dead person and the dates of his/her birth and death

G

grave·yard /ˈgreɪvyɑrd/ *n.* [C] an area of ground where people are buried, often near a church [➡ **cemetery**]

ˈgraveyard ˌshift *n.* [C] a period of working time that begins late at night and continues until the early morning, or the people who work during this time

grav·i·tate /ˈgrævəˌteɪt/ *v.* [I] to be attracted to something and move toward it, or become involved with it: *Students **gravitate toward** others with similar interests.*

grav·i·ta·tion /ˌgrævəˈteɪʃən/ *n.* [U] *technical* the force that makes two objects, such as PLANETS, move toward each other because of their MASS

grav·i·ta·tion·al /ˌgrævəˈteɪʃənəl/ *adj. technical* relating to gravity: *the Earth's gravitational pull*

grav·i·ty /ˈgrævət̬i/ *n.* [U] **1** *technical* the force that makes objects fall to the ground: *the laws of gravity* **2** *formal* the seriousness or importance of an event, situation, etc.: *I don't think they understand the **gravity of** the situation.*

gra·vy /ˈgreɪvi/ *n.* [U] SAUCE made from the juice of cooked meat, flour, and milk: *mashed potatoes and gravy*

ˈgravy ˌtrain *n.* [singular] *informal* an organization, activity, or business from which many people can make money without much effort

gray¹ /greɪ/ *adj.* **1** having the color of black mixed with white: *He was wearing a gray suit.* **2** having gray hair: *Ryan's black hair is **turning/going gray**.* **3** if the weather is gray, the sky is full of clouds and the sun is not bright: *a gray day* **4 gray area** a part of a subject such as law or science that is hard to deal with because the rules are not clear

gray² *n.* [U] a color made from black mixed with white: *The suit comes in gray or red.*

gray³ *v.* [I] if someone is graying, his/her hair is becoming gray

ˈgray ˌmatter *n.* [U] *informal* your intelligence, or the part of your brain that thinks

graze¹ /greɪz/ *v.* **1** [I,T] if an animal grazes, it eats grass: *cattle grazing in the field* **2** [T] to injure yourself by accidentally rubbing against something rough: *Billy grazed his knee when he fell.* **3** [T] to touch something lightly while passing it, sometimes damaging it: *The bullet grazed his arm.*

graze² *n.* [C] a wound caused by rubbing against something rough, which slightly breaks your skin: *minor cuts and grazes*

GRE *n.* [C] *trademark* **Graduate Record Examination** an examination taken by students who have completed a first degree and want to go to GRADUATE SCHOOL

grease¹ /gris/ *n.* [U] **1** a thick oily substance that is put on the moving parts of a car or machine to make it run smoothly **2** soft fat from animals or vegetables

grease² *v.* [T] to put grease on something: *Grease the pan lightly with butter.*

greas·y /ˈgrisi, -zi/ *adj.* covered in grease or oil: *greasy food* | *greasy hair*

> **THESAURUS**
>
> **dirty**, **filthy**, **dusty**, **muddy**
> → see Thesaurus box at DIRTY¹

ˌgreasy ˈspoon *n.* [C] *informal* a small cheap restaurant that mainly serves fried (FRY) food

great /greɪt/ *adj.*

1 USEFUL *informal* very useful or appropriate for something: *This stuff's **great for** getting stains out of clothes.*

2 LARGE very large in size, amount, or degree: *Willis caught a **great big** fish!* | ***A great many** people died in the earthquake.*

3 IMPORTANT very important, successful, or famous: *the great civilizations of the past* | *Ella Fitzgerald was the greatest jazz singer ever.*

4 very good [= **excellent**]: *It's great to see you again!* | *We had a great time.*

> **THESAURUS**
>
> **good**, **excellent**, **wonderful**, **fantastic**, **outstanding**, **exceptional**, **first-class**, **ace**, **enjoyable**, **nice**
> → see Thesaurus box at GOOD¹, NICE

> **SPOKEN PHRASES**
>
> **5** said when you are annoyed and think that something is not good at all: *"Your car won't be ready until next week." "Oh, great!"*

6 a great deal a lot: *He's traveled a great deal.* | *The explosion caused* ***a great deal of*** *damage.* **7 great-grandmother/great-uncle etc.** the grandmother, uncle, etc. of one of your parents **8 great-granddaughter/great-nephew etc.** the GRANDDAUGHTER, NEPHEW, etc. of your child **9 (the) Great** used in names to mean large or important: *Alexander the Great* | *the Great Lakes* **10 Greater Boston/New York etc.** used to talk about a large city, including all the outer areas: *the Greater Los Angeles area* —**greatness** *n.* [U]

great·ly /ˈgreɪt˺li/ *adv. formal* extremely or very much: *The money you lent us was greatly appreciated.* ▶ Don't say "The money was appreciated greatly." ◀

greed /grid/ *n.* [U] a strong desire for more money, power, possessions, etc. than you need

greed·y /ˈgridi/ *adj.* comparative **greedier**, superlative **greediest** always wanting more money, power, possessions, etc.: *He was being selfish and greedy.* —**greedily** *adv.* —**greediness** *n.* [U]

Greek¹ /grik/ *adj.* **1** relating to or coming from Greece **2** relating to the Greek language

Greek² *n.* **1** [U] the language used in Greece **2** [C] someone from Greece

green¹ /grin/ *adj.* **1** having the color of grass: *green eyes* | *pale/dark green leaves* **2** covered with grass, trees, bushes, etc.: *green fields* **3** fruit that is green is not yet ready to be eaten: *green bananas* **4** relating to or concerned about the environment: *green issues* **5 be green with envy** wishing very much that you had something that someone else has **6 give sb/sth the green light** to allow a project, plan, etc. to begin: *The board just* ***gave*** *us* ***the green light to*** *begin research.* **7** *informal* young and lacking experience: *The trainees are still pretty green.* **8 have a green thumb** to be good at making plants grow

green² *n.* **1** [C,U] the color of grass **2** [C] the smooth flat area of grass around a hole on a GOLF COURSE: *the 18th green* **3 greens** [plural] vegetables with large green leaves: *salad greens*

green·back /ˈgrinbæk/ *n.* [C] *informal* a dollar BILL

ˌgreen ˈbean *n.* [C] a long thin green vegetable that is picked and eaten before the beans inside it grow

ˌgreen ˈcard *n.* [C] a document that shows that a foreigner can live and work in the U.S.

green·er·y /ˈgrinəri/ *n.* [U] green leaves and plants

green·horn /ˈgrinhɔrn/ *n.* [C] *informal* someone who lacks experience in a job and can be easily deceived

green·house /ˈgrinhaʊs/ *n.* [C] a glass building in which you grow plants that need to be protected from the weather

ˈgreenhouse efˌfect *n.* **the greenhouse effect** the gradual warming of the air around the Earth as a result of the sun's heat being trapped by POLLUTION [➡ **global warming**]

ˌgreen ˈonion *n.* [C,U] a small white onion with long thin green leaves that you eat raw [= **scallion**]

greet /grit/ *v.* [T] **1** to say hello to someone or welcome him/her: *Carol's mother* ***greeted*** *her* ***with*** *hugs and kisses.* **2** to react to something in a particular way: *The first speech* ***was greeted with*** *cheers and laughter.*

greet·ing /ˈgriṭɪŋ/ *n.* [C] **1** something that you say or do when you meet someone: *The two men* ***exchanged greetings*** (=said hello to each other). | *We received a* ***warm*** (=friendly) ***greeting***. **2 holiday/birthday/Christmas etc. greetings** a message saying that you hope someone will be happy and healthy on his/her BIRTHDAY, at Christmas, etc.

ˈgreeting ˌcard *n.* [C] a card that you send to someone on his/her BIRTHDAY, at Christmas, etc.

gre·gar·i·ous /grɪˈgɛriəs/ *adj.* someone who is gregarious is friendly and enjoys being with other people [= **sociable**]

THESAURUS

sociable, outgoing, extroverted
➔ see Thesaurus box at SOCIABLE

grem·lin /ˈgrɛmlən/ *n.* [C] an imaginary evil spirit that is blamed for problems in machinery

gre·nade /grəˈneɪd/ *n.* [C] a small bomb that can be thrown by hand or fired from a gun

grew /gru/ *v.* the past tense of GROW

grey /greɪ/ *adj.* another spelling of GRAY

grey·hound /ˈgreɪhaʊnd/ *n.* [C] a thin dog with long legs that can run very fast, often used in races

grid /grɪd/ *n.* [C] **1** a pattern of straight lines that cross each other and form squares: *streets organized in a grid system* **2** the system of squares with numbers on them that are printed on a map so the exact position of any place can be found **3** a network of CABLES that supply an area with electricity

grid·dle /ˈgrɪdl/ *n.* [C] an iron plate used for cooking food on top of a STOVE

grid·i·ron /ˈgrɪdaɪɚn/ *n.* [C] *informal* a football field

grid·lock /ˈgrɪdlɑk/ *n.* [U] **1** a situation in which the streets have so many cars, etc. using them that the cars cannot move **2** a situation in which nothing can happen, usually because people disagree strongly —**gridlocked** *adj.*: *Traffic was gridlocked in the downtown area.*

grief /grif/ *n.* [U] **1** extreme sadness, especially because someone you love has died: *His grief was obvious from the way he spoke.* **2 give sb grief** *informal* to say something that annoys or causes trouble for someone: *My mom's been giving me grief about not helping with my little sister.*

griev·ance /ˈgrivəns/ *n.* [C,U] something that you complain about because you think it is unfair: *He obviously has major* ***grievances against*** *us.*

G

grieve /griv/ *v.* [I,T] to feel extremely sad, especially because someone you love has died: *We are still **grieving over** the death of our mother.* | *families **grieving for** their loved ones* | *grieving parents*

griev·ous /ˈgrivəs/ *adj. formal* very serious and likely to be harmful: *a grievous error* —**grievously** *adv.*

grift·er /ˈgrɪftɚ/ *n.* [C] *informal* someone who dishonestly obtains something, especially money

grill[1] /grɪl/ *v.* **1** [I,T] if you grill food, or if it grills, you cook it over a fire [➡ **broil**]

> **THESAURUS**
> **cook, bake, fry, roast, broil, sauté, boil, steam, deep fry**
> ➔ see Thesaurus box at COOK[1]

2 [T] *informal* to ask someone a lot of difficult questions for a long period of time: *The police **grilled** him **about** the murder.*

grill[2] *n.* [C] **1** a flat metal frame with BARS across it that can be put over a fire so that food can be cooked on it: *Let's put a few steaks **on the grill**.* **2 also grille** a frame of metal bars used for protecting something such as a window

G

grim /grɪm/ *adj.* **1** making you feel worried and unhappy: *grim news on the economy* | *We were running out of money and **things were looking** pretty **grim**.* **2** looking or sounding very serious: *a grim-faced judge* **3** a place that is grim is unattractive and unpleasant —**grimly** *adv.*

grim·ace /ˈgrɪməs/ *v.* [I] to twist your face in an ugly way because you feel pain, do not like something, or are trying to be funny: *Theo rolled around on the field **grimacing with** pain.* —**grimace** *n.* [C]

grime /graɪm/ *n.* [U] thick black dirt that forms a layer on surfaces

grim·y /ˈgraɪmi/ *adj.* covered in thick black dirt: *a grimy apartment building*

grin[1] /grɪn/ *v.* past tense **grinned**, past participle **grinning** [I] **1** to smile continuously with a very big smile: *Sally was **grinning at** Martin from across the room.*

> **THESAURUS**
> **smile, beam, smirk**
> ➔ see Thesaurus box at SMILE

2 grin and bear it *informal* to accept a difficult situation without complaining because you cannot change it: *It won't be fun, but we'll have to grin and bear it.*

grin[2] *n.* [C] a wide smile: *He looked back at me with a **big grin** on his face.*

grind[1] /graɪnd/ *v.* past tense and past participle **ground** /graʊnd/ [T] **1** to crush something such as coffee beans into small pieces or powder: *Could you grind some coffee for me?*

> **THESAURUS**
> **press, squash, crush, mash, squeeze**
> ➔ see Thesaurus box at PRESS[1]

2 to cut food such as raw meat into small pieces, using a machine **3** to press something down into a surface and rub it with a strong twisting movement: *He paused and **ground** his cigarette butt **into** the ashtray.* **4** to make something smooth or sharp by rubbing it on a hard surface or by using a machine: *a stone for grinding knives and scissors* **5 grind your teeth** to rub your upper and lower teeth together, making a noise **6 grind to a halt** if something grinds to a halt, it stops moving or making progress: *Traffic slowly ground to a halt.*

grind[2] *n.* [singular] *informal* something that is hard, boring, and tiring: *The work has become a grind to them.*

grind·er /ˈgraɪndɚ/ *n.* [C] a machine that grinds something: *a coffee grinder*

grind·ing /ˈgraɪndɪŋ/ *adj.* **grinding poverty** the state of being extremely poor

grind·stone /ˈgraɪndstoʊn/ *n.* [C] a large round stone that is turned like a wheel and is used for making tools sharp ➔ **keep your nose to the grindstone** at NOSE[1]

grip[1] /grɪp/ *n.* **1** [singular] a tight hold on something, or your ability to hold it: *Get a firm **grip on** the rope, and then pull.* **2** [singular] the control that you have over a person, a situation, or your emotions: *Come on, Dee, **get a grip on yourself*** (=try to control your emotions)*!* **3 come/get to grips with sth** to understand and deal with a difficult problem or situation: *Eric still hasn't come to grips with his drug problem.* **4 be in the grip of sth** to be experiencing a very unpleasant situation: *The economy is deep in the grip of a recession.*

grip[2] *v.* past tense **gripped**, past participle **gripping** **1** [T] to hold something very tightly: *I gripped his hand in fear.*

> **THESAURUS**
> **hold, clutch**
> ➔ see Thesaurus box at HOLD[1]

2 [T] to have a strong effect: *Unusually cold weather has gripped the northwest.* **3** [I,T] if something grips a surface, it stays on without slipping: *tires that grip the road* **4** [T] to hold all of your attention and interest: *a book that really grips you*

gripe[1] /graɪp/ *v.* [I] *informal* to complain about something continuously and in an annoying way: *Now what's Pete **griping about**?*

gripe[2] *n.* [C] something that you keep complaining about: *The students' main gripe is the dorm food.*

grip·ping /ˈgrɪpɪŋ/ *adj.* very exciting and interesting: *a gripping story*

THESAURUS

exciting, **thrilling**, **exhilarating**
➔ see Thesaurus box at EXCITING

gris·ly /ˈgrɪzli/ *adj.* extremely unpleasant because death or violence is involved: *a grisly murder*

grist /grɪst/ *n.* **grist for the mill** something that is useful in a particular situation: *The president's comments provided journalists with plenty of* ***grist for*** *their mill.*

gris·tle /ˈgrɪsəl/ *n.* [U] the part of a piece of meat that is not soft enough to eat

grit[1] /grɪt/ *n.* [U] **1** very small pieces of stone **2** *informal* determination and courage [**= guts**] **3 grits** [plural] a type of crushed grain that is cooked and eaten for breakfast, especially in the southern U.S. —**gritty** *adj.*

grit[2] *v.* **grit your teeth** to use all your determination to continue doing something in spite of pain or difficulties: *Just grit your teeth; the worst is almost over.*

griz·zly bear /ˈgrɪzli ˌbɛr/ **also grizzly** *n.* [C] a large brown bear that lives in the northwest of North America

groan /groʊn/ *v.* [I] to make a long deep sound, for example because you are in pain or are not happy about something: *Charlie was holding his arm and groaning.* —**groan** *n.* [C] *Loud groans came from the crowd.*

gro·cer /ˈgroʊsɚ, -ʃɚ/ *n.* [C] someone who owns or works in a GROCERY STORE

gro·cer·ies /ˈgroʊsəriz, ˈgroʊʃriz/ *n.* [plural] the food or other things that are sold in a GROCERY STORE or SUPERMARKET

gro·cer·y store /ˈgroʊsəri ˌstɔr, -ʃri-/, **grocery** *n.* [C] a store that sells food and other things used in the home

groceries

THESAURUS

bookstore, **clothes store**, **record store**, **supermarket**, **bakery**, **delicatessen**, **deli**, **liquor store**, **drugstore**, **hardware store**, **nursery**, **garden center**, **newsstand**, **boutique**, **convenience store**, **department store**, **chain store**, **superstore**, **outlet store**, **warehouse store**
➔ see Thesaurus box at STORE[1]

grog·gy /ˈgrɑgi/ *adj.* weak and unable to walk steadily or think clearly because you are sick or very tired

groin /grɔɪn/ *n.* [C] the place where your legs join at the front of your body

groom[1] /grum/ *v.* [T] **1** to prepare someone for an important job or position by training him/her: *Sharon's being* ***groomed to*** *take over the business.* **2** to take care of your appearance by keeping your hair and clothes clean and neat: *a* ***well-groomed*** *young man* **3** to take care of animals by cleaning and brushing them —**grooming** *n.* [U]

groom[2] *n.* [C] **1** a man at the time he gets married, or just after he is married: *a wedding photo of* ***the bride and groom***

TOPIC

bride, **best man**, **maid of honor**, **bridesmaids**
➔ see Topic box at WEDDING

2 someone whose job is to take care of horses

groove /gruv/ *n.* **1** [C] a thick line cut into a surface to hold something, or to make something move or flow where you want it to: *Plant the seeds in grooves about a foot apart.* **2** [singular] *informal* the way things should be done, so that it seems easy and natural: *It will take the players a while to* ***get back in the groove.***

grope /groʊp/ *v.* **1** [I] to try to find something you cannot see, using your hands: *She* ***groped*** *in the dark* ***for*** *the flashlight.* **2 grope your way along/across etc.** to go somewhere by feeling the way with your hands because you cannot see **3 grope for sth** to have difficulty in finding the right words to say or the right solution to a problem **4** [T] *informal* to touch someone's body in a sexual way when s/he does not want to be touched

THESAURUS

touch, **stroke**, **caress**, **fondle**
➔ see Thesaurus box at TOUCH[1]

gross[1] /groʊs/ *adj.* **1** *spoken* very unpleasant to look at or think about: *There was one really gross part in the movie.* | *Oh, gross! I hate spinach!* **2** [only before noun] a gross amount of money is the total amount before any tax or costs have been taken away [➡ **net**]: *His* ***gross profit*** *was $300,000.* **3** a gross weight is the total weight of something, including its wrapping **4** [only before noun] wrong and unacceptable: *Workers are suing the company for* ***gross negligence.*** | *That's a* ***gross exaggeration.*** —**grossly** *adv.* —**grossness** *n.* [U]

gross[2] *v.* [T] to earn an amount as a total profit or earn it as a total amount, before tax has been taken away: *The movie has already grossed over $10 million.*

gross sb ⇔ **out** *phr. v.* if something grosses you out, it is very unpleasant and almost makes you feel sick: *His dirty fingernails really gross me out.*

ˌgross ˌnational ˈproduct *n.* [singular, U] GNP

gro·tesque /groʊˈtɛsk/ *adj.* ugly or strange in a way that is unpleasant or frightening: *drawings of grotesque monsters* —**grotesquely** *adv.*: *The movie is grotesquely violent.*

grot·to /ˈgrɑt̬oʊ/ *n.* plural **grottos** or **grottoes** [C] a small CAVE

G

grouch[1] /graʊtʃ/ *n.* [C] *informal* someone who is always complaining

grouch[2] *v.* [I] *informal* to complain in a slightly angry way

grouch·y /ˈgraʊtʃi/ *adj.* feeling annoyed and complaining a lot

THESAURUS

grumpy, **cranky**, **crabby**, **cantankerous**, **irritable**, **touchy**
→ see Thesaurus box at GRUMPY

ground[1] /graʊnd/ *n.*
1 EARTH'S SURFACE [singular, U] **a)** the surface of the earth: *We were all sitting* ***on the ground****.* | *People in the area were advised to move to* ***higher ground*** *in the event of a flood.* | *The fuel is stored* ***below ground****.* | *The pipes are laid* ***above ground****.* **b)** the soil on and under the surface of the earth: *We put seeds in the ground.*

USAGE

Use **on the ground** to say where something is: *The boy's coats were on the ground.*
Use **to the ground** to show movement that goes down: *Eddie was knocked to the ground.*

THESAURUS

The **ground** is the surface under your feet when you are outside: *There was snow on the ground.*
The **floor** is the surface under your feet when you are inside a building: *the kitchen floor*
Land is an area of ground that is owned or controlled by someone: *That land belongs to the farm.*
Earth or **soil** is the substance that plants grow in: *fertile soil*

G

2 AREA OF LAND **a)** [C] a large area of land or ocean that is used for a particular purpose: *a burial ground* **b) grounds** the land or gardens around a building: *prison grounds*
3 KNOWLEDGE [U] an area of knowledge, ideas, experience, etc.: *Scientists are* ***breaking new ground*** (=discovering new ideas) *in cancer research.* | *We* ***covered*** *a lot of* ***ground*** *in class today.*
4 OPINIONS [U] the general opinions you have about something: *There has to be a way we can find some* ***common/middle ground*** (=something that everyone can agree about). | *Neither side was willing to* ***give*** *any* ***ground*** (=agree that someone else is right).
5 hold/stand your ground **a)** to refuse to move when someone threatens you, in order to show that you are not afraid **b)** to refuse to change your opinion, belief, etc., even though people are trying to make you change it: *Joanne held her ground and made no apologies.*
6 REASON **grounds** [plural] a good reason for doing, believing, or saying something: *Mental cruelty can be* ***grounds for*** *divorce.* | *The committee rejected the proposal* ***on the grounds that*** *it would be too expensive.*
7 get off the ground to start being successful: *His company hasn't really gotten off the ground yet.*
8 gain/lose ground to become more or less successful or popular: *Republicans have been gaining ground in recent months.*
9 WIRE [singular] a wire that connects a piece of electrical equipment to the ground for safety
10 SMALL PIECES **grounds** [plural] the small pieces of something such as coffee which sink to the bottom of a liquid: *coffee grounds*

ground[2] *v.* [T] **1** to stop an aircraft or pilot from flying: *All planes were grounded due to the snow.* **2 be grounded in sth** to be based on something: *His theories about education are grounded in years of research.* **3** *informal* to stop a child from going out with his/her friends as a punishment for doing something wrong: *If you stay out that late again, you'll be grounded for a week.* **4** to make a piece of electrical equipment safe by connecting it to the ground with a wire

ground[3] *adj.* **1 ground beef/turkey/pork etc.** meat that has been cut up into very small pieces **2** ground coffee, pepper, etc. has been crushed into small pieces: ***freshly ground*** *pepper*

ground[4] *v.* the past tense and past participle of GRIND

ground·break·ing /ˈgraʊndˌbreɪkɪŋ/ *adj.* groundbreaking work involves making new discoveries, using new methods, etc.: *groundbreaking research*

ˈground crew *n.* [C] the group of people who work at an airport taking care of the aircraft

ˌground ˈfloor *n.* [C] the part of a building that is on the same level as the ground

ground·hog /ˈgraʊndˌhɔg/ *n.* [C] a small North American animal that has thick brown fur and lives in holes in the ground [= **woodchuck**]

ˈGroundhog ˌDay *n.* [C] February 2; according to American stories, the first day of the year that a groundhog comes out of its hole. If it sees its shadow, there will be six more weeks of winter; if it does not, good weather will come early

ground·less /ˈgraʊndlɪs/ *adj.* not based on facts or reason: *They assured me that my fears were totally groundless.*

ˈground rule *n.* [C] a rule or principle on which future actions should be based

ground·swell /ˈgraʊndswɛl/ *n.* **a groundswell of support/enthusiasm** a sudden increase in how strongly people feel about something: *There has been a groundswell of support for change.*

ground·work /ˈgraʊndwɚk/ *n.* [U] work that needs to be done in order for an activity or plan to be successful: *Amelia is already* ***laying*** *the* ***groundwork*** *for her re-election campaign.*

ˌground ˈzero *n.* [U] the place where an explosion happens, where a lot of damage has been done and a lot of people have been killed

group¹ /grup/ *n.* [C] **1** several people or things that are all together in the same place: *a **group of** children | The teacher asked everyone to get into groups of four.*

THESAURUS

group of people
crowd – a large group of people in one place
team – a group of people who work together: *a team of doctors | a successful baseball team*
crew – a group of people who all work together, especially on a ship or airplane: *the flight crew*
gang – a group of young people, especially a group that often causes trouble and fights
mob – a large noisy group of people, especially one that is angry and violent: *an angry mob | mob violence*
bunch informal – a group of people: *They're a nice bunch of kids*
flock – a large group of people of the same type: *a flock of tourists*
mass – a large group of people all close together in one place: *As soon as the doors opened a mass of people pushed their way into the store.*
party – a group of people who have been organized to do something together: *a search party*
group of animals
herd of cows/deer/elephants
flock of sheep/birds
school/shoal of fish/dolphins/herring etc.
pack of dogs
litter of puppies/kittens (=a group of baby animals born from the same mother at the same time)
group of things
bunch of flowers/grapes/keys etc. (=several flowers, etc. tied or held together)
bundle of papers/clothes/sticks (=several papers, etc. tied or held together)

2 several people or things that are connected with each other in some way: *a **terrorist group** | There should be equal treatment of all **racial** and **ethnic groups**.* **3** musicians or singers who perform together, usually playing popular music: *a **rock group***

group² *v.* [I,T] to come together to make a group, or to arrange people or things in a group: *The visitors **grouped** themselves **around** the statue. | Birds can be **grouped into** several types.*

group·ie /ˈgrupi/ *n.* [C] *informal* someone, especially a young woman, who follows popular musicians or other famous people around, hoping to meet them

group·ing /ˈgrupɪŋ/ *n.* [C] a set of people, things, or organizations that have the same interests, qualities, or features: *social groupings*

ˌgroup ˈtherapy *n.* [U] a method of treating people with emotional or PSYCHOLOGICAL problems by bringing them together in groups to talk about their problems

grouse¹ /graʊs/ *v.* [I] *informal disapproving* to complain about something: *He's always **grousing about** the weather.*

grouse² *n.* [C,U] a small fat bird that is hunted for food and sport, or the meat from this bird

grove /groʊv/ *n.* [C] a piece of land with trees growing on it: *a lemon grove*

grov·el /ˈgrɑvəl, ˈgrʌ-/ *v.* [I] to try too hard to please someone or to keep telling him/her that you are sorry: *I hate it when people start groveling to the boss.*

grow /groʊ/ *v.* past tense **grew** /gru/ past participle **grown** /groʊn/

1 PERSON/ANIMAL [I] to develop and become bigger over a period of time: *Jamie's grown two inches this year.*

2 HAIR/NAILS [I,T] to let your hair or nails become longer: *He's growing a beard.*

3 PLANTS [I,T] if plants grow, or if you grow them, they develop and become bigger: *Not many plants can grow in the far north. | We're trying to grow roses this year.*

4 INCREASE [I] to increase in amount, size, or degree: *a growing business | The number of students **grew by** 5% last year. | A **growing number** of people are working from home.*

THESAURUS

increase, go up, rise, double, shoot up
→ see Thesaurus box at INCREASE¹

5 BECOME [linking verb] to become old, hot, worse, etc. over a period of time: *He became more conservative as he grew older.*

6 grow to like/fear/respect etc. to gradually start to like, fear, etc. someone or something: *She had grown to love the city.*

7 IMPROVE [I] to improve in ability or character: *Beth's really growing as a singer.*

8 BUSINESS [T] to make something such as a business become larger or more successful: *The president thinks cutting taxes will help **grow the economy**.*

grow apart *phr. v.* if two people grow apart, their relationship changes and they become less close

grow into sb/sth *phr. v.* **1** to develop over time and become a particular type of person or thing: *Gene's grown into a handsome young man.* **2** if a child grows into clothes, s/he becomes big enough to wear them: *The jacket's a little bit big for him now, but he'll soon grow into it.*

grow on sb *phr. v.* if someone or something grows on you, you gradually start to like him, her, or it: *I didn't like blue cheese at first, but the taste has kind of grown on me.*

grow out of sth *phr. v.* **1** if a child grows out of clothes, s/he becomes too big to wear them **2** to stop doing something as you get older: *Sarah still sucks her thumb, but she'll grow out of it.*

grow up *phr. v.* **1** to develop from being a child

G

to being an adult: *I grew up in San Diego.* **2 grow up!** *spoken* said in order to tell someone to behave more like an adult

grow·er /ˈgroʊɚ/ *n.* [C] a person or company that grows fruit, vegetables, etc. in order to sell them

ˈgrowing ˌpains *n.* [plural] problems and difficulties that start at the beginning of a new activity, for example starting a business

growl /graʊl/ *v.* **1** [I] if an animal growls, it makes a deep angry sound: *dogs* ***growling at*** *a visitor* **2** [I,T] to say something in a low angry voice: *"Go away!" he growled.* —**growl** *n.* [C]

grown¹ /groʊn/ *adj.* **grown man/woman** an adult, used especially when you think someone is not behaving as an adult should: *I've never seen a grown man act like that.*

grown² *v.* the past participle of GROW

ˈgrown-up¹ *n.* [C] an adult, used especially by children or when talking to children: *Ask a grown-up to help you.*

ˈgrown-up² *adj.* fully developed as an adult: *a grown-up son*

growth /groʊθ/ *n.* **1** [singular, U] an increase in amount, size, or degree: *rapid population growth* | *There's been tremendous* ***growth in*** *the health food industry.* | *the* ***growth of*** *modern technology* **2** [U] the increase in the physical size and strength of a person, animal, or plant over a period of time: *Vitamins are necessary for healthy growth.* **3** [U] the development of someone's character, intelligence, or emotions: *a job that provides opportunities for* ***personal growth*** **4** [C] something that grows in your body or on your skin, caused by a disease: *a cancerous growth* **5** [C,U] something that is growing: *There are signs of new growth on the tree.*

G

grub /grʌb/ *n.* [U] *informal* food

grub·by /ˈgrʌbi/ *adj.* dirty: *grubby hands*

grudge¹ /grʌdʒ/ *n.* [C] a feeling of anger or dislike you have for someone who has harmed you: *Diane doesn't* ***hold grudges*** (=stay angry with people). | *Aunt Alice* ***bore a grudge against*** *him for 25 years.*

grudge² *v.* [T] BEGRUDGE

grudg·ing /ˈgrʌdʒɪŋ/ *adj.* done in a way that shows you do not really want to do something: *Some of the staff had grudging respect for her.* —**grudgingly** *adv.*: *They grudgingly agreed.*

gru·el·ing /ˈgruəlɪŋ/ *adj.* very difficult and tiring: *a grueling entrance exam*

grue·some /ˈgrusəm/ *adj.* very unpleasant to look at, and usually involving death or injury: *a gruesome accident*

gruff /grʌf/ *adj.* unfriendly or annoyed: *a gruff answer* —**gruffly** *adj.*

grum·ble /ˈgrʌmbəl/ *v.* [I] to keep complaining in a quiet but slightly angry way: *He's always* ***grumbling about*** *how expensive everything is.*

grump·y /ˈgrʌmpi/ *adj.* comparative **grumpier**, superlative **grumpiest** easily annoyed and tending to complain: *a grumpy old man* —**grumpily** *adv.*

THESAURUS

cranky/crabby/grouchy informal – easily annoyed and complaining a lot: *I was feeling hungry and cranky.*
cantankerous – easily annoyed and complaining a lot: *a cantankerous old man*
irritable – easily annoyed or made angry: *He's been a little irritable lately.*
touchy – easily offended or annoyed: *She's touchy about her weight.*

grunge /grʌndʒ/ *n.* [U] *informal* dirt and GREASE —**grungy** *adj.*

grunt /grʌnt/ *v.* **1** [I,T] to make short sounds or say only a few words, especially because you do not want to talk: *He just grunted hello and kept walking.* **2** [I] if a pig grunts, it makes short low sounds —**grunt** *n.* [C]

G-string /ˈdʒi strɪŋ/ *n.* [C] very small underwear that does not cover the BUTTOCKS

gua·ca·mo·le /ˌgwɑkəˈmoʊleɪ/ *n.* [U] a Mexican dish made with crushed AVOCADOS

guar·an·tee¹ /ˌgærənˈti/ *v.* [T] **1** to promise that something will happen or be done: *We guarantee delivery within 48 hours.* | *Can you* ***guarantee that*** *it will arrive tomorrow?* | *It's impossible to guarantee everyone a job.*

THESAURUS

promise, swear, take/swear an oath, vow, give your word
→ see Thesaurus box at PROMISE¹

2 to make a formal written promise to repair or replace a product if it has a problem within a specific time **3** to make it certain that something will happen: *An education doesn't guarantee a good job.* **4 be guaranteed to do sth** to be certain to behave, work, or happen in a particular way: *Going out with friends is guaranteed to cheer you up.*

guarantee² *n.* [C] **1** a formal written promise that a product will please the customer or perform in a particular way for a specific length of time: *a two-year guarantee* | *The microwave comes with a* ***money-back guarantee*** (=a promise that you will get your money back if it doesn't work). **2** a formal promise that something will be done or will happen: ***There's no guarantee that*** *the books will be delivered this week* (=it is not sure to happen).

guar·an·tor /ˌgærənˈtɔr, ˈgærəntɚ/ *n.* [C] *law* someone who promises that s/he will pay for something if the person who should pay for it does not

guard¹ /gɑrd/ *n.* [C] **1** someone whose job is to guard people, places, or objects so that they are not attacked or stolen: *The guards stopped us at* *the gate.* | *a security guard* | *prison guards* **2** [U] the act of protecting a place or person, or preventing a prisoner from escape: *Soldiers are always **on guard** at the embassy.* | *The prisoners were held **under armed guard** in brutal conditions.* **3 catch/take sb off guard** to surprise someone by doing something that s/he is not ready to deal with: *The question caught the senator off guard.* **4** something that covers and protects someone or something: *a hockey player's face guard* **5 sb's guard** the state of paying careful attention to what is happening in order to avoid being tricked or getting into danger: *These men are dangerous, so you'll need to **be on** your **guard*** (=be careful). | *He never **let down** his **guard*** (=relaxed and felt comfortable with others). **6 a)** one of two players in basketball whose main job is to defend his/her BASKET **b)** one of two football players who play on either side of the CENTER

guard² *v.* [T] **1** to protect someone or something from being attacked or stolen, or to prevent a prisoner from escaping: *They have a dog to guard their house.* | *a **heavily-guarded** courtroom*

THESAURUS

protect, **shield**, **give/offer/provide protection**
➔ see Thesaurus box at PROTECT

2 to protect something such as a right or secret by preventing other people from taking it: *a **closely-guarded secret***

guard against sth *phr. v.* to try hard to prevent something from happening: *Exercise can help guard against a number of serious illnesses.*

guard·ed /ˈgɑrdɪd/ *adj.* careful not to show your emotions or give away information: *a guarded answer*

guard·i·an /ˈgɑrdiən/ *n.* [C] **1** someone who is legally responsible for a child, but who is not the child's parent: *His aunt is his **legal guardian**.* **2** *formal* a person or organization that tries to protect something —**guardianship** *n.* [U]

ˌguardian ˈangel *n.* [C] an imaginary good spirit who protects a person

guard·rail /ˈgɑrd-reɪl/ *n.* [C] a long metal BAR that keeps cars or people from falling over the edge of a road, boat, or high structure

gua·va /ˈgwɑvə/ *n.* [C] a small tropical fruit with pink flesh and many seeds inside

gu·ber·na·to·ri·al /ˌgubərnəˈtɔriəl/ *adj. formal* relating to the position of being a GOVERNOR

guer·ril·la, **guerilla** /gəˈrɪlə/ *n.* [C] a member of a military group that is fighting for political reasons: *guerrilla warfare*

guess¹ /gɛs/ *v.* **1** [I,T] **a)** to try to answer a question or form an opinion when you are not sure whether you will be correct: *I'd say he's about 40, but I'm **just guessing**.* **b)** to guess something correctly: *"Don't tell me; you got the job." "How did you guess?"* | *I never would have **guessed that** they were sisters.* **2 keep sb guessing** to not tell someone what is going to happen next: *a film that really keeps the audience guessing*

SPOKEN PHRASES

3 I guess a) said when you think that something is true or likely: *I wasn't there, but I guess Mr. Radkin yelled at Jeannie.* | *His light's on, so I guess he's still up.* **b)** said in order to show that you do not feel very strongly about what you are planning or agreeing to do: *I guess I'll stay home tonight.* ➔ see Thesaurus box at THINK **4 I guess so/not** used in order to say yes or no to a question or statement, when you are not very sure: *"She wasn't happy?" "I guess not."* **5 guess what/you'll never guess who/what etc.** said when you are about to tell someone something that will surprise him/her: *You'll never guess who I saw today.*

guess² *n.* [C] **1** an attempt to guess something: *Just **take/make a guess**.* | *I can only **hazard a guess*** (=make a guess) *on how old she is.*

COLLOCATIONS

good guess – a guess that is likely to be right
educated guess – a guess that is likely to be correct because it is based on some information
wild guess – a guess that you make when you do not have any information, and that is likely to be wrong
lucky guess – a guess that is right, and that you made without very much information
rough guess – a guess that is not exact

2 an opinion formed by guessing: ***My guess is (that)** Don won't come.* **3 be anybody's guess** to be something that no one knows: *What she's going to do with her life now is anybody's guess.* **4 your guess is as good as mine** *spoken* said in order to tell someone that you do not know any more than s/he does about something

guess·ti·mate /ˈgɛstəmɪt/ *n.* [C] *informal* an attempt to judge a quantity by guessing it —**guesstimate** /ˈgɛstəˌmeɪt/ *v.* [I,T]

guess·work /ˈgɛswək/ *n.* [U] a way of trying to find the answer to something by guessing

guest¹ /gɛst/ *n.* [C] **1** someone whom you invite to stay in your home, be at your party, etc.: *a dinner guest* | *He was a frequent **guest at** the White House.* **2** someone famous who is invited to take part in a television program, concert, etc.: *Tonight's **special guest** will be Aretha Franklin.* **3** someone who is paying to stay in a hotel: *Use of the swimming pool is free for guests.* **4 be my guest** *spoken* said when giving someone permission to do what s/he has asked to do: *"Could I use your phone?" "Be my guest."*

guest² *adj.* **1 guest speaker/artist/star etc.** someone famous who is invited to speak on a subject or take part in a performance **2** [only before noun] for guests to use: *the guest room* | *guest towels*

guf·faw /gə'fɔ/ *v.* [I] to laugh loudly —**guffaw** *n.* [C]

THESAURUS

laugh, **giggle**, **chuckle**, **cackle**, **snicker**
➔ see Thesaurus box at LAUGH[1]

guid·ance /'gaɪdns/ *n.* [U] helpful advice about work, education, etc.: *Ms. Norris has* ***given*** *me a lot of* ***guidance*** *about colleges and careers.*

THESAURUS

advice, **tip**, **recommendation**
➔ see Thesaurus box at ADVICE

'guidance ˌcounselor *n.* [C] someone who works in a school, giving advice to students about what subjects to study and helping them with personal problems

guide[1] /gaɪd/ *n.* [C] **1** someone whose job is to show a place to tourists: *a* ***tour guide*** **2** a book that provides information about a particular subject or explains how to do something: *a* ***guide for*** *new parents* **3** something that helps you decide what to do or how to do it: *A friend's experience isn't always the best guide for you.*

guide[2] *v.* [T] **1** to take someone to or through a place that you know very well, showing him/her the way: *He offered to* ***guide*** *us* ***around/through*** *the city.*

THESAURUS

lead, **direct**, **point**
➔ see Thesaurus box at LEAD[1]

2 to help someone or something to move in a particular direction: *The pilot guided the plane to a safe landing.* **3** to help someone to do something or to make a decision: *Children need parents to guide them.*

guide·book /'gaɪdbʊk/ *n.* [C] a special book about a city or country that gives details about the place and its history

guide·lines /'gaɪdlaɪnz/ *n.* [plural] rules or instructions about the best way to do something: *the* ***guidelines for*** *health and safety at work*

THESAURUS

rule, **law**, **regulation**, **restriction**, **statute**
➔ see Thesaurus box at RULE[1]

guild /gɪld/ *n.* [C] an organization of people who share the same interests, skills, or profession: *the writers' guild*

guile /gaɪl/ *n.* [U] *formal* the use of smart but dishonest methods to deceive someone

guile·less /'gaɪl-lɪs/ *adj.* behaving in an honest way, without trying to deceive people

guil·lo·tine /'gɪləˌtin, 'giə-, ˌgiə'tin/ *n.* [C] a piece of equipment that was used in past times to cut off the heads of criminals —**guillotine** *v.* [T]

guilt /gɪlt/ *n.* [U] **1** a strong feeling of shame and sadness that you have when you know or believe you have done something wrong: *Marta felt a* ***sense of guilt*** *about leaving home.* | *He used to buy them expensive presents* ***out of guilt***.

THESAURUS

shame – the feeling of being guilty or embarrassed that you have after doing something that is wrong: *He seems to have no sense of shame.*

remorse – a strong feeling of being sorry for doing something very bad: *a murderer who showed no remorse.*

conscience – the set of feelings that tell you whether what you are doing is morally right or wrong: *My conscience wouldn't allow me to lie to her.*

2 guilt trip *informal* a feeling of guilt about something, when this is unreasonable: *I wish my parents would stop* ***laying a guilt trip on*** *me* (=making me feel guilty) *about not going to college.* **3** the fact that someone has broken an official law or moral rule [≠ **innocence**]: *The jury was sure of the defendant's guilt.* **4** the state of being responsible for something bad that has happened [= **fault**]: *Ron admitted that the guilt was his.*

'guilt-ˌridden *adj.* feeling extremely guilty about something

guilt·y /'gɪlti/ *adj.* **1** ashamed and sad because you have done something that you know is wrong: ***I feel guilty about*** *not inviting her to the party.* | *I don't think of watching TV as a* ***guilty pleasure*** (=something you like doing but feel guilty about).

THESAURUS

ashamed – unhappy and disappointed with yourself because you have done something wrong or unpleasant: *You should be ashamed of yourself for lying to your mother.*

embarrassed – feeling slightly worried about what people will think of you because you have done something stupid or silly: *When something like that happens, you feel really embarrassed.* | *I'm embarrassed to say I voted for him.*

2 having broken a law or a rule [≠ **innocent**]: *I was not* ***guilty of*** *doing anything wrong.* | *The jury* ***found*** *him* ***guilty of*** *murder.* | *Her lawyers entered a* ***guilty plea***. ➔ see Topic box at COURT[1] —**guiltily** *adv.* —**guiltiness** *n.* [U]

guin·ea pig /'gɪni pɪg/ *n.* [C] **1** a small animal like a rat with fur, short ears, and no tail that is often kept as a pet **2** *informal* someone who is used in a test to see how successful or safe a new product, system, etc. is

guise /gaɪz/ *n.* [C] *formal* the way someone or something seems to be, which is meant to hide the truth: ***In/under the guise of*** *being protectors, the army took over the government.*

gui·tar /gɪ'tɑr/ *n.* [C] a musical instrument with six strings, a long neck, and a wooden body, which you play by pulling the strings —**guitarist** *n.* [C] → see picture on page A6

gulch /gʌltʃ/ *n.* [C] a narrow deep valley formed by flowing water, but usually dry

gulf /gʌlf/ *n.* [C] **1** a large area of ocean partly enclosed by land: *the Gulf of Mexico* **2** a serious and important difference between two groups of people, where neither understands or is concerned about the other: *There is a widening **gulf between** the rich and the poor.*

gull /gʌl/ *n.* [C] a SEAGULL

gul·let /ˈgʌlɪt/ *n.* [C] *informal* the tube through which food goes down your throat

gul·li·ble /ˈgʌləbəl/ *adj.* a gullible person always believes what other people say, and is therefore easy to trick —**gullibility** /ˌgʌləˈbɪləṭi/ *n.* [U]

gul·ly /ˈgʌli/ *n.* plural **gullies** [C] **1** a small narrow valley, formed by a lot of rain flowing down the side of a hill **2** a deep DITCH

gulp[1] /gʌlp/ *v.* **1** [T] **also gulp down** to swallow something quickly: *She gulped her tea and ran to catch the bus.* **2** [T] **also gulp in** to take in large breaths of air quickly: *Steve leaned on the car and gulped in the night air.* **3** [I] to swallow suddenly because you are surprised or nervous: *Shula read the test questions, and gulped.*

gulp sth ⇔ **back** *phr. v.* to stop yourself from expressing your feelings: *The boy was trying to gulp back his tears.*

gulp[2] *n.* [C] an act of swallowing something quickly: *He drank his beer **in one gulp**.*

gum /gʌm/ *n.* **1** [C] a sweet substance that you CHEW for a long time but do not swallow **2** [C usually plural] the pink part inside your mouth that holds your teeth **3** [U] a sticky substance in the stems of some trees —**gummy** *adj.*

gum·bo /ˈgʌmboʊ/ *n.* [U] a thick soup made with meat, fish, and particular vegetables

gump·tion /ˈgʌmpʃən/ *n.* [U] *informal* the ability and determination to decide what needs to be done and to do it: *At least he had the gumption to call the police.*

gun[1] /gʌn/ *n.* [C] **1** a weapon from which bullets are fired: *He was **carrying a gun**. | a **loaded gun** | I've never **fired a gun** in my life. | He **had a gun** in the car.* **2 big/top gun** *informal* someone who controls an organization, or who is the most successful person in a group **3** a tool used in order to send out a liquid by pressure: *a spray gun* → **jump the gun** at JUMP[1] → **stick to your guns** at STICK[1]

gun[2] *v.* past tense and past participle **gunned**, present participle **gunning** [T] **1** *informal* to make the engine of a car go very fast by pressing the ACCELERATOR very hard **2 be gunning for sth** *journalism* to be trying very hard to obtain something: *They're gunning for their third straight Superbowl win.* **3 be gunning for sb** *informal* be trying to find an opportunity to criticize or harm someone

gun sb ⇔ **down** *phr. v.* to shoot someone and badly injure or kill him/her: *Bobby Kennedy was gunned down in a hotel.*

gun·boat /ˈgʌnboʊt/ *n.* [C] a small military ship that carries several large guns

ˈgun conˌtrol *n.* [U] laws that restrict the possession and use of guns

gun·fire /ˈgʌnfaɪə/ *n.* [U] the repeated shooting of guns, or the noise made by this [➡ **gunshot**]: *We **heard gunfire** in the distance. | an **exchange of gunfire*** (=when people are shooting at each other for a short time)

gung-ho /ˌgʌŋˈhoʊ/ *adj. informal* very eager, or too eager to do something: *a gung-ho supporter of the president*

gunk /gʌŋk/ *n.* [U] *informal* any substance that is thick, dirty and sticky: *There's a bunch of gunk clogging the drain.*

gun·man /ˈgʌnmən/ *n.* plural **gunmen** /-mən/ [C] a criminal who uses a gun

gun·ner /ˈgʌnə/ *n.* [C] a soldier, sailor, etc. whose job is to aim or fire a large gun

gun·point /ˈgʌnpɔɪnt/ *n.* **at gunpoint** while threatening people with a gun, or being threatened with a gun: *She was robbed at gunpoint*

gun·pow·der /ˈgʌnˌpaʊdə/ *n.* [U] an explosive substance in the form of powder

gun·run·ning /ˈgʌnˌrʌnɪŋ/ *n.* [U] the activity of taking guns into a country secretly and illegally —**gunrunner** *n.* [C]

gun·shot /ˈgʌnʃɑt/ *n.* **1** [C] the action of shooting a gun, or the sound that this makes [➡ **gunfire**]: *We **heard a gunshot** and a loud scream.* **2** [U] the bullets that are shot from a gun: *a **gunshot wound***

gup·py /ˈgʌpi/ *n.* plural **guppies** [C] a small brightly colored tropical fish

gur·gle /ˈgəgəl/ *v.* [I] **1** if water gurgles, it flows along gently with a pleasant low sound **2** if a baby gurgles, it makes a happy low sound in its throat —**gurgle** *n.* [C]

gu·ru /ˈguru, ˈgʊru/ *n.* [C] **1** *informal* someone who knows a lot about a particular subject, and to whom people go for advice: *a fashion guru* **2** a Hindu religious teacher or leader

gush[1] /gʌʃ/ *v.* [I,T] **1** to flow or pour out quickly in large quantities: *water **gushing out** of a pipe | Blood was **gushing from** the wound. | His cheek was gushing blood.*

THESAURUS

pour, flow, drip, leak, ooze, spurt, run, come out

→ see Thesaurus box at POUR

2 to express your praise, pleasure, etc. in a way that other people think is too strong: *"This is so exciting," gushed Dana.*

gush[2] *n.* [C] **1** a large quantity of liquid that suddenly flows from somewhere: *a **gush of** warm water* **2 a gush of sth** a sudden feeling or emotion, or a large amount of something

G

gush·er /ˈgʌʃɚ/ *n.* [C] *informal* an oil WELL where the flow of oil is suddenly so strong that it shoots into the air

gush·ing /ˈgʌʃɪŋ/ **also gush·y** /ˈgʌʃi/ *adj.* expressing admiration, pleasure, etc. in a way that other people think is too strong: *gushing praise*

gust¹ /gʌst/ *n.* [C] a sudden strong wind that blows for a short time: *A **gust of wind** blew our tent over.* —**gusty** *adj.*

THESAURUS

wind, **gale**, **storm**, **hurricane**, **tornado**, **typhoon**
→ see Thesaurus box at WIND¹

gust² *v.* [I] if wind gusts, it blows strongly with sudden short movements: *Winds were gusting up to 70 mph.*

gus·to /ˈgʌstoʊ/ *n.* **with gusto** if you do something with gusto, you do it with a lot of eagerness and energy: *a band playing with gusto*

gut¹ /gʌt/ *n.* **1 gut reaction/feeling/instinct** *informal* a reaction or feeling that you are sure is right, although you cannot give a reason for it: *My gut reaction is that it's a bad idea.* **2 guts** [plural] *informal* the courage and determination you need to do something difficult or unpleasant: *He didn't **have the guts** to say what he really thought.* | *It **takes guts** to start a business on your own.* **3** [C] *informal* someone's stomach, especially when it is large: *He felt as if someone had just kicked him in the gut.* | *a **beer gut*** **4 a) guts** [plural] the organs inside your body **b)** [C] the tube in your body through which food passes

H

gut² *v.* past tense **gutted**, past participle **gutting** [T] **1** to completely destroy the inside of a building, especially by fire **2** to remove the organs from inside a fish or animal in order to prepare it for cooking

gut·sy /ˈgʌtsi/ *adj. informal* brave and determined: *It was a gutsy performance.*

gut·ter /ˈgʌt̬ɚ/ *n.* [C] **1** the low place along the edge of a road, where water collects and flows away **2** an open pipe at the edge of a roof for collecting and carrying away rain water **3 the gutter** the bad social conditions of the lowest and poorest people in society

gut·tur·al /ˈgʌt̬ərəl/ *adj.* a guttural sound is produced deep in the throat

guy /gaɪ/ *n.* [C] **1** *informal* a man: *He's a really nice guy.* | *There's some guy who wants to talk to you.*

THESAURUS

man, **gentleman**, **boy**, **youth**
→ see Thesaurus box at MAN¹

2 you guys/those guys *spoken* said when talking to or about two or more people, male or female [➡ **y'all**]: *We'll see you guys Sunday, okay?*

guz·zle /ˈgʌzəl/ *v.* [I,T] *informal* to drink a lot of something eagerly and quickly: *Chris has been guzzling beer all evening.*

gym /dʒɪm/ *n.* **1** [C] a special building or room that has equipment for doing physical exercise: *I **go to the gym** as often as I can.*

THESAURUS

health club, **(swimming) pool**
→ see Thesaurus box at SPORT¹, EXERCISE²

2 [U] sports and exercises done indoors, especially as a school subject: *gym class*

gym·na·si·um /dʒɪmˈneɪziəm/ *n.* [C] → GYM

gymnast

gym·nast /ˈdʒɪmnæst, -nəst/ *n.* [C] someone who does GYMNASTICS as a sport: *an Olympic gymnast*

gym·nas·tics /dʒɪmˈnæstɪks/ *n.* [plural] a sport involving physical exercises and movements that need skill and control, often performed in competitions

gy·ne·col·o·gy /ˌgaɪnəˈkɑlədʒi/ *n.* [U] the study and treatment of medical conditions that affect women —**gynecologist** *n.* [C] —**gynecological** /ˌgaɪnəkəˈlɑdʒɪkəl/ *adj.*

gyp·sy /ˈdʒɪpsi/ *n.* plural **gypsies** [C] **1** a member of a group of people who traditionally live and travel around in CARAVANS. Most gypsies prefer to be called Romanies. **2** someone who does not like to stay in the same place for a long time

gy·rate /ˈdʒaɪreɪt/ *v.* [I] to turn around fast in circles: *dancers gyrating wildly*

H,h

H, h /eɪtʃ/ the eighth letter of the English alphabet

ha /hɑ/ *interjection spoken* said when you are surprised or pleased about something: *Ha! I knew I was right.* → HA HA

hab·er·dash·er·y /ˈhæbɚˌdæʃəri/ *n.* plural **haberdasheries** [C,U] *old-fashioned* a store or part of a store that sells men's clothing, or the clothes sold there

hab·it /ˈhæbɪt/ *n.* **1** [C,U] something that you do regularly, and usually without thinking: *healthy **eating habits*** | *Jen was **in the habit of** going to lunch with them every day.* | *Try to **get in the habit***

of exercising regularly. | *After he moved out, I was still cleaning his room* ***out of habit*** (=because it was a habit).

THESAURUS

custom – something that people in a particular society do because it is traditional, or something that people think is the normal and polite thing to do: *the Japanese custom of taking off your shoes when you enter a house*
tradition – a belief, custom, or way of doing something that has existed for a long time: *In many countries it's a tradition for the bride to wear white.* | *a family tradition*

2 [C] something you do regularly that annoys other people or is bad for your health: *Biting your nails is a very* ***bad habit.*** | *He* ***has a habit of*** *being late.* | *Brad's been smoking for twenty years, and he just can't* ***break/kick*** *the* ***habit.*** | *a* ***drug/drink habit*** **3 don't make a habit of (doing) sth** used in order to tell someone who has done something bad or wrong that s/he should not do it again: *You can turn your paper in late this time, but don't make a habit of it.* **4** [C] a set of long loose clothes worn by members of some religious groups

hab·it·a·ble /ˈhæbət̬əbəl/ *adj.* good enough for people to live in

hab·i·tat /ˈhæbəˌtæt/ *n.* [C] the natural environment in which a plant or animal lives: *a chance to see the gorillas in their* ***natural habitat***

hab·i·ta·tion /ˌhæbəˈteɪʃən/ *n.* [U] *formal* the act of living in a place: *There was no sign of habitation on the island.*

ha·bit·u·al /həˈbɪtʃuəl/ *adj.* **1** happening as a habit, or often doing something because it is a habit: *a habitual smoker* **2** [only before noun] usual or typical: *James took his habitual morning walk around the park.* —**habitually** *adv.*

hack[1] /hæk/ *v.* **1** [I,T] to cut something into pieces roughly or violently, or to hurt someone badly with a weapon such as a sword: *She hacked away at the ice, trying to make a hole.* | *He was* ***hacked to death*** *by the mob.* **2** [I,T] to use a computer in order to secretly and illegally enter someone else's computer system: *Somebody* ***hacked into*** *the company's central database.* **3 sb can't hack it** *informal* used in order to say that someone cannot continue to do something because it is too difficult or boring **4** [I] to cough very loudly and painfully: *a* ***hacking cough***

hack[2] *n.* [C] someone who writes low quality books, articles, etc.

hack·er /ˈhækɚ/ *n.* [C] *informal* someone who uses a computer to secretly use or change the information in another person's computer system —**hacking** *n.* [U]

hack·neyed /ˈhæknid/ *adj.* a hackneyed phrase is boring and does not have much meaning because it has been used too often

hack·saw /ˈhæksɔ/ *n.* [C] a small SAW (=cutting tool) used especially to cut metal

had /d, əd, həd; *strong* hæd/ *v.* **1** the past tense and past participle of HAVE **2 be had** to be tricked or made to look stupid: *She had the feeling she'd been had.*

had·dock /ˈhædək/ *n.* plural **haddock** [C,U] a common fish that lives in northern oceans, or the meat from this fish

had·n't /ˈhædnt/ *v.* the short form of " had not": *We hadn't been there long.*

hag /hæg/ *n.* [C] an ugly or mean woman, especially one who is old or looks like a WITCH

hag·gard /ˈhægɚd/ *adj.* having lines on your face and dark marks around your eyes because you are tired, sick, or worried: *He was thin and haggard.*

hag·gle /ˈhægəl/ *v.* [I] to argue about the amount of money you will pay for something: *The car dealer and I were* ***haggling over*** *the price for an hour.*

hah /hɑ/ *interjection* → HA

ha ha /hɑ ˈhɑ/ *interjection* used in writing to represent laughter

H

hail[1] /heɪl/ *v.* **1** [T] to call out to someone in order to get his/her attention: *He was* ***hailing a taxi/cab*** (=waving at a taxi to make it stop). **2** [I] if it hails, frozen rain falls from the sky
hail sb/sth **as** sth *phr. v.* to publicly state how good someone or something is: *Their discovery was hailed as the most important event of the century.*
hail from sth *phr. v.* to come from a particular place: *The professor hailed from Massachusetts.*

hail[2] *n.* **1** [U] small hard drops of frozen rain that fall from the sky

THESAURUS

snow, snowflakes, sleet, slush, blizzard, frost, rain, hailstones
→ see Thesaurus box at SNOW[1]

2 a hail of bullets/stones etc. a lot of bullets, stones, etc. that are shot or thrown at someone

hail·stone /ˈheɪlstoʊn/ *n.* [C usually plural] a small drop of hard frozen rain

hail·storm /ˈheɪlstɔrm/ *n.* [C] a storm when a lot of HAIL falls

hair /hɛr/ *n.* **1** [U] the things like thin threads that grow on your head: *He has brown hair and blue eyes.* | *She was* ***brushing*** *her* ***hair.*** | *I used to* ***have/wear my hair*** *very long.*

hair

COLLOCATIONS

Describing hair
short/long hair
shoulder-length hair
blond/light hair
dark/brown/black/gray hair
red/auburn hair
straight/wavy/curly hair
frizzy hair – hair with many small curls in it
spiky hair – hair that sticks up from your head in thin stiff points
fine/thin/thick hair
white-haired/dark-haired/red-haired/long-haired/curly-haired, etc. (=used to describe someone)

Verbs you can use with hair
cut/trim your **hair**
wash/shampoo your **hair**
dry your **hair**
blow dry your **hair** – to dry your hair, using an electric hairdryer
comb/brush your **hair**
style your **hair** – to arrange your hair in a particular way
dye your **hair** – to change the color of your hair, using a dye
bleach your **hair** – to dye your hair a blond color, using chemicals
→ HEAD, SKIN

2 [C,U] the things like thin threads that grow on a person's or animal's skin [➡ **fur**]: *an old blanket covered with cat hair* **3 short-haired/dark-haired etc.** having a particular type of hair or fur: *a long-haired cat* **4 let your hair down** *informal* to stop being serious and enjoy yourself **5 a hair** a small amount: *Larson won the race by a hair.*

hair·brush /ˈhɛrbrʌʃ/ *n.* [C] a brush you use on your hair to make it look neat → see picture at BRUSH[1]

hair·cut /ˈhɛrkʌt/ *n.* [C] **1** the act of having your hair cut by someone: *I'm **getting a haircut** tomorrow.* **2** the style your hair has when it is cut: *Do you like my new haircut?*

hair·do /ˈhɛrdu/ *n.* plural **hairdos** [C] *informal* the style in which someone's hair is cut or shaped

hair·dress·er /ˈhɛrˌdrɛsɚ/ *n.* [C] someone who washes, cuts, and arranges people's hair

hair·dryer /ˈhɛrˌdraɪɚ/ *n.* [C] a machine that you sit under that blows out hot air, used for drying hair [➡ **blow dryer**]

hair·line /ˈhɛrlaɪn/ *n.* [C] **1** the area around the top of your face where your hair starts growing **2 a hairline crack/fracture** a very thin crack in something hard such as glass or bone

hair·net /ˈhɛrnɛt/ *n.* [C] a thin net worn over your hair in order to keep it in place

ˈhair-ˌraising *adj.* frightening in an exciting way: *a hair-raising adventure*

hair·split·ting /ˈhɛrˌsplɪṭɪŋ/ *n.* [U] the act of paying too much attention to unimportant details and differences

ˈhair spray *n.* [C,U] a sticky liquid that you put onto your hair in order to make it stay in place

hair·style /ˈhɛrstaɪl/ *n.* [C] the particular style your hair has when it is cut, brushed, or arranged

hair·y /ˈhɛri/ *adj.* **1** having a lot of body hair: *a **hairy chest*** **2** *informal* dangerous or frightening: *I've had a few hairy moments when sailing.*

hal·cy·on /ˈhælsiən/ *adj.* **halcyon days** *literary* a time in the past when you were very happy

hale /heɪl/ *adj.* **hale and hearty** someone, especially an old person, who is hale and hearty is very healthy and active

half[1] /hæf/ *determiner, adj.* [only before noun] **1** 1/2 of an amount, time, distance, number, etc.: *The wall is half a mile long. | Only half the guests had arrived by 7:00. | I'll wait another **half hour*** (=30 minutes), *but then I have to go.* **2 half the time/people etc.** a lot of the time, people, etc.: *I was up half the night worrying about you.* **3 be half the battle** *spoken* used in order to say that when you have done the most difficult part of an activity, the rest is easy: *Getting your children to listen to you is half the battle.* **4** if something or someone is half one thing and half something else, he, she, or it is a combination of those two things: *She's half Mexican and half German.* **5 half a dozen also a half dozen a)** six: *half a dozen eggs* **b)** a small number of people or things: *There were half a dozen other people in front of me.* **6 half a second/minute** *spoken* a very short time: *If you can wait half a second, I'll be ready to go.*

half[2] *n.* [C] plural **halves** /hævz/ **1** one of two equal parts of something [**= 1/2**]: ***Half of** 10 is 5. | Do you want the sandwich cut **in half*** (=in two equal pieces)? *| **Half of** the rooms have double beds in them.* ▶ Don't say "the half of the rooms." ◀ *Our profits increased in the second half of the year. | My son's two and a half now.* ▶ Don't say "two and one half." ◀ **2 half past one/two/three etc.** thirty minutes after the hour mentioned: *We should arrive there at half past three.* **3** one of two parts into which a sports event is divided: *The score was 21 to 10 at the end of the second half.*

half[3] *adv.* **1** partly but not completely: *I was half expecting her to say "no." | She sat up in bed, still half asleep. | There were several **half-empty** coffee cups on the table.* **2 half as good/interesting etc. (as sth)** much less good, less interesting, etc. than someone or something else: *The movie wasn't half as good as the book.* **3 not half bad** said when something that you expected to be bad is actually good: *The dinner wasn't half bad.* **4 half and half** partly one thing and partly something else: *The group was about half and half, men and women.*

ˌhalf-and-ˈhalf *n.* [U] a mixture of milk and cream, used in coffee

> **THESAURUS**
>
> **milk, skim milk, low-fat/2% milk, whole milk, buttermilk**
>
> ➔ see Thesaurus box at MILK[1]

ˌhalf-ˈbaked *adj. informal* a half-baked idea, plan, or suggestion is not sensible or intelligent enough to be successful

ˈhalf-ˌbrother *n.* [C] a brother who is the child of only one of your parents

ˌhalf-ˈhearted *adj.* a half-hearted attempt is something that you do without really trying or wanting to be successful: *a half-hearted effort*

ˈhalf-life *n.* [singular] *technical* the amount of time it takes for a RADIOACTIVE substance to lose half of its RADIOACTIVITY

ˌhalf-ˈmast *adj.* **fly/be at half-mast** if a flag flies or is at half-mast, it is lowered to the middle of its pole because someone important has died

ˈhalf-ˌsister *n.* [C] a sister who is the child of only one of your parents

half·time /ˈhæftaɪm/ *n.* [U] a period of rest between two parts of a game such as football or basketball: *Our team was in the lead **at halftime**.*

half·way /ˌhæfˈweɪ◂/ *adj., adv.* at the middle point in space or time between two things: *I fell asleep **halfway through** the concert. | a town **halfway between** Los Angeles and San Francisco | Their boat was **halfway across** the lake when it started to rain. | We had reached **the halfway mark/point** of the trail.* ➔ **meet (sb) halfway** at MEET[1]

hal·i·but /ˈhæləbət/ *n.* [C,U] a large flat sea fish, or the meat from this fish

hall /hɔl/ *n.* [C] **1** a passage in a house or building that leads to other rooms: *The bathroom's just down the hall.* **2** a public building or large room that is used for events such as meetings, concerts, and parties: *Carnegie Hall | a dance hall*

hal·le·lu·jah /ˌhæləˈluyə/ *interjection* said in order to express thanks, or praise to God

hall·mark /ˈhɔlmɑrk/ *n.* [C] **1** a quality, idea, or method that is typical of a particular person or thing: *Excellent service has always been **the hallmark of** this hotel.* **2** an official mark put on silver, gold, or PLATINUM to prove that it is real

ˌHall of ˈFame *n.* plural **Halls of Fame** [C] a list

H

of famous sports players, or a building in which the players' uniforms, sports equipment, and information about them is kept —**Hall of Famer** *n.* [C] *baseball Hall of Famer, Roger Clemens*

hal·lowed /ˈhæloʊd/ *adj.* **1** made holy: *hallowed ground* **2** respected, honored, and important: *the hallowed walls of the U.S. Supreme Court*

Hal·low·een /ˌhæləˈwin, ˌhɑ-/ *n.* [U] a holiday on the night of October 31, when children wear COSTUMES, play tricks, and walk from house to house in order to get candy [➥ **trick or treat**]

hal·lu·ci·na·tion /həˌlusəˈneɪʃən/ *n.* [C,U] something you see or hear that is not really there, or the experience of this, usually caused by a drug or mental illness —**hallucinate** /həˈlusəˌneɪt/ *v.* [I]

hal·lu·ci·no·gen·ic /həˌlusənəˈdʒɛnɪk/ *adj.* hallucinogenic drugs cause HALLUCINATIONS

hall·way /ˈhɔlweɪ/ *n.* [C] ➔ HALL

ha·lo /ˈheɪloʊ/ *n.* plural **halos** [C] a circle of light that is painted above or around the head of a holy person in a religious painting

halt¹ /hɔlt/ *v.* [I,T] to stop or make something stop: *Safety concerns have halted work on the dam.*

halt² *n.* [singular] a stop or pause: *Traffic suddenly* ***came/ground to a halt.*** | *The project was* ***brought to a halt*** (=ended) *due to lack of money.*

hal·ter /ˈhɔltɚ/ *n.* [C] **1 also halter top** a piece of women's clothing that ties behind the neck and does not cover the arms or back **2** a rope or leather band fastened around a horse's head in order to lead it

halt·ing /ˈhɔltɪŋ/ *adj.* stopping a lot when you move or speak, especially because you are nervous: *her halting voice*

halve /hæv/ *v.* [T] **1** to reduce the amount of something by half: *Food production was almost halved during the war.* **2** to cut something into two equal parts: *Wash and halve the mushrooms.*

halves /hævz/ *n.* the plural of HALF

ham¹ /hæm/ *n.* [C,U] meat from the upper part of a pig's leg that is preserved with salt or smoke: *a ham sandwich*

THESAURUS

pork, **bacon**
➔ see Thesaurus box at MEAT

ham² *v.* past tense and past participle **hammed**, present participle **hamming ham it up** *informal* to perform or behave with too much false emotion

ham·burg·er /ˈhæmˌbɚgɚ/ *n.* **1** [U] BEEF that is ground (GRIND) into very small pieces: *a pound of hamburger* **2** [C] BEEF that has been ground (GRIND) into very small pieces and is then cooked in a flat round shape and eaten between pieces of round bread [➥ **cheeseburger**]

ham·let /ˈhæmlɪt/ *n.* [C] a very small VILLAGE

ham·mer¹ /ˈhæmɚ/ *n.* [C] a tool with a heavy metal part on a straight handle, used for hitting nails into wood

hammer² *v.* **1** [I,T] to hit something with a hammer in order to force it into a particular position or shape: *You'll have to* ***hammer*** *a few nails* ***into*** *the frame.* **2** [I] to hit something again and again, making a lot of noise: *They hammered on the door until I opened it.*

THESAURUS

bang, **knock**, **tap**, **pound**, **rap**
➔ see Thesaurus box at HIT¹

hammer sth **into** sb **also hammer** sth **home** *phr. v.* to continue repeating something until people completely understand it: *The message must be hammered home that crime doesn't pay.*

hammer out sth *phr. v.* to finally agree on a solution, contract, etc. after arguing about details for a long time: *It took several days to hammer out an agreement.*

ham·mock /ˈhæmək/ *n.* [C] a large piece of material or a net you can sleep on that hangs between two trees or poles

ham·per¹ /ˈhæmpɚ/ *v.* [T] to make someone have difficulty moving, doing something, or achieving something: *The searches for the missing girl were hampered by the bad weather.*

hamper² *n.* [C] a large basket with a lid, used for holding dirty clothes until they can be washed

ham·ster /ˈhæmstɚ/ *n.* [C] a small animal with soft fur and no tail that is often kept as a pet ➔ see picture at PET¹

ham·string¹ /ˈhæmˌstrɪŋ/ *n.* [C] a TENDON behind your knee

hamstring² *v.* past tense and past participle **hamstrung** /-ˌstrʌŋ/ [T] to make a person or group have difficulty doing or achieving something: *a government hamstrung by student protests*

hand

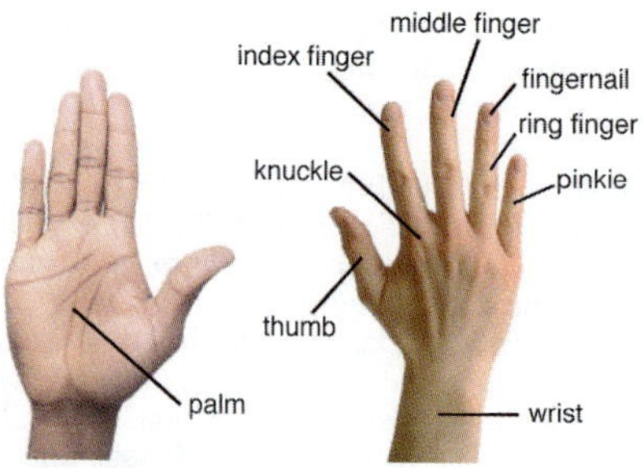

hand¹ /hænd/ *n.* [C]
1 BODY PART the body part at the end of a person's arm that includes the fingers and thumb, used for holding, etc. things: *Go wash your hands.* | *I write with my* ***right/left hand.*** | *I saw them* ***holding hands*** *and kissing.* | *Maria* ***took*** *the child* ***by the hand*** *and led him away.* | ***Raise your***

hand (=lift it up) *if you know the answer.* | *a picture of me* ***shaking hands*** (=as a greeting or sign of friendship) *with Elvis*

2 a hand help: *Can you* ***give/lend me a hand*** *with this box? It's really heavy.* | *Do you* ***need a hand*** *with the cooking?*

3 (on the one hand...) on the other hand used when comparing two different or opposite facts or ideas: *The movie was scary, but on the other hand it made me laugh.* | *On the one hand, they work slowly, but on the other hand they always finish the job.*

4 get out of hand to become impossible to control: *The demonstration seemed to be getting out of hand.*

5 in sb's hands/in the hands of sb being dealt with or cared for by someone: *The decision is in your hands.* | *Don't worry – the children are* ***in good hands.*** | *Most farmland is* ***in private hands*** (=owned or controlled by someone, not the government). | *The decision is now in the hands of the court.*

6 on hand close and ready when needed: *Our staff is always on hand to help.*

7 hand in hand a) holding each other's hands: *They strolled hand in hand through the rose garden.* **b)** if two things go hand in hand, they are closely connected: *Wealth and power* ***go hand in hand*** *in most societies.*

8 by hand a) done or made by a person, not a machine: *The rug was made by hand.* **b)** delivered from one person to another, not through the mail

9 out of sb's hands if something is out of your hands, you have no control over it: *The decision was out of her hands.*

10 get/lay your hands on sth to find or obtain something: *I read every book I could get my hands on at school.*

11 have a hand in sth to influence or be involved in something: *He scored one goal and had a hand in two others.*

12 at hand *formal* **a)** near in time or space: *Graduation day is* ***close at hand.*** **b)** needing to be dealt with now: *Let's discuss the case at hand, shall we?*

13 in hand being dealt with and controlled: *Lisa seemed to* ***have*** *things* ***in hand*** *by the time he returned.*

14 off your hands if someone or something is off your hands, you are not responsible for him, her, or it anymore: *Once this problem is off our hands we can relax.*

15 hands down easily: *He would have* ***won hands down*** *if he hadn't hurt his knee.*

16 have your hands full to be very busy or too busy: *You're going to have your hands full once you have the baby!*

17 give sb a (big) hand to CLAP loudly for a performer or speaker

18 CLOCK one of the long things that point to the numbers on a clock → see picture at WATCH²

19 CARDS the cards that you are holding in a game → FIRSTHAND → LEFT-HAND → RIGHT-HAND → SECOND-HAND → **change hands** at CHANGE¹ → **shake sb's hand/shake hands (with sb)** at SHAKE¹ → **wait on sb hand and foot** at WAIT¹

hand² *v.* [T] **1** to pass something to someone else: *Can you hand me a towel?* **2 you have to hand it to sb** *spoken* said when you are admiring something that someone has done: *I have to hand it to you, Claire: you sure know how to cook!*

hand sth ⇔ **back** *phr. v.* to give something back to the person who gave it to you: *Mr. Evans handed back our essays today.*

hand sth ⇔ **down** *phr. v.* **1** to give something to a younger relative, or to people who live after you: *The ring was* ***handed down to*** *her from her grandmother.* **2** if a court of law hands down a decision or sentence, it officially announces a decision or punishment

hand sth ⇔ **in** *phr. v.* to give something to someone in a position of authority: *Please hand in your application by September 30.*

hand sth ⇔ **out** *phr. v.* to give something to everyone in a group: *They were handing out free t-shirts at the club.*

> **THESAURUS**
>
> **give out, hand out, pass out**
> → see Thesaurus box at GIVE OUT

hand over *phr. v.* **1 hand** sth ⇔ **over** to give something to someone with your hand, especially because s/he has asked for it or should have it: *She handed the phone over to me.* **2** to give someone power or responsibility over something which you used to be in charge of: *He will be handing over the business to his son.*

hand·bag /ˈhændbæg/ *n.* [C] → PURSE¹

hand·book /ˈhændbʊk/ *n.* [C] a small book with instructions and information about a particular subject: *an employee handbook*

hand·cuff /ˈhændkʌf/ *v.* [T] to put HANDCUFFS on someone

hand·cuffs /ˈhændkʌfs/ *n.* [plural] two metal rings joined by a chain, used for holding a prisoner's wrists together: *Two people were arrested and taken away* ***in handcuffs.***

hand·ful /ˈhændfʊl/ *n.* [C] **1** an amount that you can hold in your hand: *a* ***handful of*** *nuts* **2 a handful of sth** a small number of people or things: *Only a handful of people showed up.* **3 a handful** *informal* someone, especially a child, who is difficult to control: *She's a real handful!*

hand·gun /ˈhændgʌn/ *n.* [C] a small gun you hold in one hand when you shoot

hand·held /ˈhændhɛld/ *adj.* [only before noun] a handheld machine is small enough to hold in your hand when using it: *a handheld computer* —**handheld** *n. C*

hand·i·cap¹ /ˈhændiˌkæp/ *n.* [C] **1** something permanently wrong with a person's mind or body: *a severe physical handicap* **2** something that makes it difficult for you to do or achieve something: *Not being able to speak French was a real handicap.*

handicap² *v.* past tense and past participle **handicapped**, present participle **handicapping**

H

[T] to make it difficult for someone to do something that s/he wants to do: *The charity is handicapped by a lack of funds.*

hand·i·capped /ˈhændiˌkæpt/ *adj.* **1** not able to use a part of your body or mind normally because it has been damaged. Many people think that this word is offensive [➡ **disabled, impaired**]: *schools for **mentally/physically handicapped** children* **2 the handicapped** people who are mentally or physically handicapped

hand·i·work /ˈhændiˌwɚk/ *n.* [U] something that someone does or makes: *The documentary is the handiwork of a respected director.*

hand·ker·chief /ˈhæŋkɚtʃɪf, -ˌtʃif/ *n.* [C] a piece of cloth that you use for drying your nose or eyes

han·dle¹ /ˈhændl/ *v.* [T] **1** to deal with a situation or problem: *The principal handled the situation very well.* | *The job was so stressful, he couldn't handle it any longer.*

THESAURUS

deal with, tackle, attend to, take care of
➔ see Thesaurus box at DEAL WITH

2 to organize or be in charge of something: *Ms. Lee handled all of our travel arrangements.* **3** to pick up, hold, or touch something: *Please **handle** this package **with care**.* **4** to buy, sell, or deal with particular products or services: *Upton was charged with **handling stolen goods**.*

H

handle² *n.* [C] the part of something that is used for holding or opening it: *a door handle* | *a knife with an ivory handle*

han·dle·bars /ˈhændlˌbɑrz/ *n.* [plural] the metal BARS above the front wheel of a bicycle or MOTORCYCLE that you turn to control the direction you go in ➔ see picture at BICYCLE

han·dler /ˈhændlɚ/ *n.* [C] someone whose job is to deal with or be in charge of a particular kind of thing: *baggage handlers* | *a police dog and its handler*

hand·made /ˌhændˈmeɪd◂/ *adj.* made by a person and not a machine: *handmade quilts*

ˈhand-me-ˌdown *n.* [C] a piece of clothing that has been worn by someone and then given to his/her younger relative —**hand-me-down** *adj.*

hand·out /ˈhændaʊt/ *n.* [C] **1** money or food that is given to someone, usually because s/he is poor: *We're not looking for a handout from the government.* **2** a piece of paper with printed or copied information that is given to people in a class, meeting, etc.: *Let's look at the first page of the handout.*

hand·o·ver /ˈhændoʊvɚ/ *n.* [singular] the act of formally giving someone else control of a place or business: *the **handover of** Hong Kong to China*

hand·picked /ˌhændˈpɪkt◂/ *adj.* someone who is handpicked has been carefully chosen for a particular purpose

hand·shake /ˈhændʃeɪk/ *n.* [C] the action of taking someone's right hand and shaking it, usually done when people meet or leave each other: *a **firm handshake***

hands ˈoff *interjection* said when warning someone not to touch something that is yours: *Hands off my cookies!*

ˈhands-off *adj.* **1 a hands-off approach/attitude etc.** an approach, attitude etc. taken by someone who likes to leave other people to make decisions and do all the work **2** someone who is hands-off does not like to be directly involved in a job and leaves other people to make the decisions and do all the work

hand·some /ˈhænsəm/ *adj.* **1 a)** a man who is handsome is attractive: *He was a handsome young man.* **b)** a woman who is handsome looks healthy and strong in an attractive way

THESAURUS

attractive, good-looking, pretty, beautiful, gorgeous, stunning, nice-looking, cute
➔ see Thesaurus box at ATTRACTIVE

2 a handsome gift/reward/profit a gift, etc. that is valuable or is a lot of money

ˈhands-on *adj.* **1 hands-on experience/training etc.** experience, training, etc. that you get by doing something rather than studying it **2** someone who is hands-on likes to be involved in a job and does not let other people make all the decisions and do all the work

hand·stand /ˈhændstænd/ *n.* [C] a movement in which you kick your legs up into the air so that you are upside down and supporting yourself on your hands

ˌhand to ˈmouth *adv.* with just enough money and food to live, and nothing for the future: *For years they had been **living hand to mouth**.*

hand·writ·ing /ˈhændˌraɪṭɪŋ/ *n.* [U] the way someone writes when s/he uses a pen or a pencil: *She has very **neat handwriting**.*

hand·y /ˈhændi/ *adj.* **1** useful, or simple to use: *The extra key may **come in handy*** (=be useful in the future). **2** *informal* near and easy to reach: *You should always **keep** a first aid kit **handy**.* **3 be handy with sth** to be good at using something, especially a tool: *Terry's very handy with a needle and thread.*

hand·y·man /ˈhændiˌmæn/ *n.* plural **handymen** /-ˌmɛn/ [C] someone who is good at making and repairing things

hang¹ /hæŋ/ *v.* past tense and past participle **hung** /hʌŋ/ **1** [I,T] to put something somewhere so that its top part is fixed but its bottom part is free to move, or to be in this position: *You can hang your coat in the closet.* | *paintings **hanging on** the wall* **2 hang in the balance** to be in a situation in which the result is not certain, and something bad may happen: *The whole future of the airline is hanging in the balance.* **3 leave sb/sth hanging** to fail to finish something, or tell someone your decision about something: *The investigation should not be left hanging.* **4** [I] to stay in the air in the same place for a long time: *Dark clouds hung over the valley.* **5 hang your head** to look ashamed and embarrassed: *Kevin hung his head and left the room in silence.*

SPOKEN PHRASES

6 hang in there also hang tough to remain determined to succeed in a difficult situation: *Just hang in there, Midori, things will get better.* **7 hang a right/left** said in order to tell the driver of a car to turn right or left

hang around *phr. v. informal* **1** to stay in one place without doing very much, often because you are waiting for someone: *I hung around for about an hour and then left.* **2 hang around with sb** to spend a lot of time with someone: *He's been hanging around with Rick a lot lately.*

hang back *phr. v.* to be unwilling to say or do something, often because you are shy: *Stella ran out to see what was happening, but the others hung back.*

hang on *phr. v.* **1** *informal* to hold something tightly: *Hang on, everybody, the road's pretty bumpy.* **2 hang on!** *spoken* said in order to tell someone to wait for you: *Hang on, I'll be with you in a minute!*

hang onto sb/sth *phr. v. spoken* to keep something: *I'd hang onto that letter. You might need it later.*

hang out *phr. v. informal* to spend a lot of time at a particular place or with particular people: *kids hanging out at the mall*

hang up *phr. v.* **1** to put the telephone down at the end of a conversation: *Please hang up and dial again.* | *She got mad and* ***hung up on*** *me* (=put the phone down before I was finished speaking). **2 hang** sth ⇔ **up** to put something such as clothes on a hook or HANGER

hang² *v.* past tense and past participle **hanged** [I,T] to kill someone by dropping them with a rope around his/her neck, as a punishment for a crime, or to die in this way: *Clayton* ***hanged himself*** *in his prison cell.* | *He was* ***hanged for*** *the killings.*

hang³ *n.* **get the hang of sth** *informal* to learn how to do something: *Driving a car is hard at first, but you'll get the hang of it.*

hang·ar /ˈhæŋɚ, ˈhæŋgɚ/ *n.* [C] a very large building where aircraft are kept

hang·er /ˈhæŋɚ/ *n.* [C] a thing for hanging clothes on, made of a curved piece of metal, wood, or plastic with a hook on it

ˌhanger-ˈon *n.* plural **hangers-on** [C] *disapproving* someone who tries to spend a lot of time with important people, so that s/he can get some advantage

ˈhang ˌglider *n.* [C] a large frame covered with cloth that you hold on to and fly slowly through the air on, without an engine ➔ see picture on page A10

ˈhang ˌgliding *n.* [U] the sport of flying using a hang glider

hang·ing /ˈhæŋɪŋ/ *n.* [C,U] the action of killing someone by dropping him/her with a rope around his/her neck as a punishment for a crime

hang·man /ˈhæŋmən/ *n.* plural **hangmen** /-mən/ [C] someone whose job is to kill criminals by hanging them

hang·nail /ˈhæŋneɪl/ *n.* [C] a piece of dead skin that has become loose near the bottom of your FINGERNAIL

hang·out /ˈhæŋaʊt/ *n.* [C] *informal* a place that you like to go to often, especially with friends: *Club Lucky is our* ***favorite hangout***.

hang·o·ver /ˈhæŋˌoʊvɚ/ *n.* [C] the feeling of sickness that someone has the day after s/he has drunk too much alcohol: *I* ***have*** *a really bad* ***hangover***.

hang·up /ˈhæŋʌp/ *n.* [C] *informal* something that you are worried or embarrassed about: *She* ***has*** *a lot of* ***hang-ups about*** *relationships.*

hank·er /ˈhæŋkɚ/ *v.* [I] *informal* to have a very strong desire for something over a period of time: *The voters seem to be* ***hankering for*** *change.* —**hankering** *n.* [singular]

han·kie, **hanky** /ˈhæŋki/ *n.* [C] *informal* ➔ HANDKERCHIEF

han·ky-pan·ky /ˌhæŋki ˈpæŋki/ *n.* [U] *informal humorous* sexual or criminal behavior that is not very serious

Ha·nuk·kah /ˈhɑnəkə/ *n.* [U] an eight-day Jewish holiday in December

hap·haz·ard /ˌhæpˈhæzɚd/ *adj. disapproving* happening or done in a way that is not organized or planned —**haphazardly** *adv.*

hap·less /ˈhæplɪs/ *adj. literary* unlucky

hap·pen /ˈhæpən/ *v.* [I] **1** if an event or situation happens, it exists and continues for a period of time, usually without being planned: *Did anything exciting happen while I was away?* | *We must do all we can to prevent such a disaster ever happening again.* | *We'll still be friends* ***whatever happens***.

THESAURUS

Happen is mainly used to talk about things that have not been planned: *A funny thing happened on my way to work.* | *No one knows exactly what will happen.*
Take place is mainly used to talk about events that have been planned or that have already happened: *The next meeting will take place on Thursday.*
Occur is a formal word, used especially to say that something happens in a particular place or situation: *The accident occurred around 9 pm.*

2 happen to sb/sth to affect someone or something: *Strange things have been happening to me lately.* **3** to be the result of something you do: *When I try to turn on the motor, nothing happens.* | ***What happens if*** *your parents find out?*

H

4 happen to do sth to do or to have something by chance: *I happened to see Hannah at the store today.* **5 sb/sth happens to be sth** *spoken* said when you are angry or annoyed, to add force to what you are saying: *That happens to be my foot that you just stepped on!* **6 as it happens/it (just) so happens** *spoken* used in order to say that something happens by chance, especially when this is surprising: *It just so happened that Mike and I had gone to the same school.* **7 what/whatever happened to sb?** used in order to ask where a person or thing is now: *What happened to my blue sweater?* | *Whatever happened to Jenny Beale?*

happen on/upon sb/sth *phr. v.* to find something or meet someone by chance: *We just happened on the cabin when we were hiking one day.*

hap·pen·ing¹ /ˈhæpənɪŋ/ *adj. slang* fashionable and exciting: *a happening club*

happening² *n.* [C] something that happens: *The paper has a listing of the day's happenings.*

THESAURUS

event, **occurrence**, **incident**, **phenomenon**
→ see Thesaurus box at EVENT

hap·pi·ly /ˈhæpəli/ *adv.* **1** in a happy way: *Michelle smiled happily.* | *a **happily married** couple* | *Cinderella marries the prince and they **live happily ever after*** (=for the rest of his/her life – used especially in children's stories). **2** fortunately: *Happily, no one was hurt in the fire.* **3** very willingly: *I'll happily watch the kids for you while you're gone.*

hap·pi·ness /ˈhæpinɪs/ *n.* [U] the state of being happy: *Her face was glowing with happiness.* | *They **found happiness** together at last.*

hap·py /ˈhæpi/ *adj.* comparative **happier**, superlative **happiest** **1** feeling pleased and cheerful, often because something good has happened to you [≠ **unhappy**, **sad**]: *He was a happy child.* | *I've never **felt happier** in my life.* | *I'm **happy (that)** everything worked out in the end.* | *I don't think he was too **happy about** having to stay late.* | *Congratulations! I'm so **happy for you**.*

THESAURUS

glad – pleased about a situation or something that has happened: *I'm so glad you were able to come.*
pleased – happy and satisfied with something that has happened: *Her parents were pleased that she had done so well.*
content – happy and satisfied: *We're usually content to stay at home and read or watch TV.*
delighted – extremely happy because something good has happened: *We were delighted when she had a baby girl.*
ecstatic – extremely happy and excited: *When he heard he'd gotten the job, he was ecstatic.*

2 be happy to do sth to be willing to do something, especially to help someone else: *I'll be happy to answer questions later.* **3** a happy time, place, etc. is one that makes you feel pleased or happy: *Those were the happiest years of my life.* | *They had a very happy marriage.* **4** [not before noun] satisfied or not worried: *Amy was not very **happy with** their decision.* **5 Happy Birthday/New Year etc.** used as a greeting, or to wish someone good luck on his/her BIRTHDAY or a special occasion

ˌhappy-go-ˈlucky *adj.* enjoying life and not worrying about things

ˈhappy hour *n.* [C,U] a short period of time when a BAR sells drinks at a lower price

ha·rangue /həˈræŋ/ *v.* [T] to speak in an angry way, often for a long time, to try to persuade someone that you are right —**harangue** *n.* [C]

ha·rass /həˈræs, ˈhærəs/ *v.* [T] to deliberately annoy or threaten someone, often over a long period of time: *They claim that they are being harassed by the police.*

ha·rass·ment /həˈræsmənt, ˈhærəs-/ *n.* [U] behavior that is threatening or offensive to other people: *Tina accused her boss of **sexual harassment**.*

har·bor¹ /ˈhɑrbɚ/ *n.* [C,U] an area of water next to the land, where ships can stay safely

harbor² *v.* [T] **1** to protect someone by hiding him/her from the police **2** to keep hopes, bad thoughts, or fears in your mind for a long time: *Ralph harbors no bitterness toward his ex-wife.*

hard¹ /hɑrd/ *adj.*

1 FIRM TO TOUCH firm and stiff, and difficult to cut, press down, or break [≠ **soft**]: *I can't sleep on a hard mattress.* | *hard candy* | *The plums are still too hard to eat.*

THESAURUS

firm – not completely hard, but not soft and not easy to bend: *Brownies are done when the edges are firm but the middle is still soft.*
stiff – difficult to bend or move: *a piece of stiff, brightly colored cardboard*
solid – firm and usually hard, without spaces or holes: *They blasted the tunnel through solid rock.*

2 DIFFICULT difficult to do or understand [≠ **easy**]: *Chemistry was one of the hardest classes I've ever taken.* | *The print was small and **hard to** read.* | *I **find it** extremely **hard to believe** that no one saw the accident.* | *It was **hard for** me to tell him the truth.* | *It's **hard to say*** (=difficult to know) *when Glenn will be back.*

3 A LOT OF EFFORT involving a lot of physical or mental effort: *I had a **hard day** at work.* | *Mowing the lawn is **hard work**.*

4 be hard on sb *informal* **a)** to treat someone in a way that is unfair or too strict: *Don't be too hard on the children – they were only playing.* **b)** to

H

cause someone a lot of problems: ***It's hard on** her, having her husband in the hospital.*

5 be hard on sth *informal* to have a bad effect on something: *Those pills are pretty hard on your stomach.*

6 give sb a hard time *informal* **a)** to make someone feel embarrassed or uncomfortable, often by making jokes about him/her: *The guys were giving him a hard time about missing the ball.* **b)** to criticize someone a lot

7 NOT KIND showing no kindness or sympathy: *Mr. Katz is a hard man to work for, but he's fair.*

8 PROBLEMS full of problems, especially not enough money: ***Times were hard**, and we were forced to sell our house.* | *My mother has **had a hard life**.*

9 do/learn sth the hard way to learn about something by a bad experience or by making mistakes

10 no hard feelings *spoken* used in order to tell someone that you no longer feel angry with him/her

11 WATER hard water has a lot of MINERALS in it and does not mix easily with soap [≠ **soft**] —**hardness** *n.* [U]

hard² *adv.* **1** using a lot of effort: *She has **worked hard** all her life.* | *We try hard to keep our customers happy.* **2** with a lot of force: *You need to hit the ball hard.* | *It's raining hard outside.* **3 be hard pressed/put/pushed to do sth** *informal* to have difficulty doing something: *The painters will be hard pressed to finish by 6 o'clock.* **4 take sth hard** to feel very upset about something: *I didn't know that Joe would take the news so hard.*

ˌhard-and-ˈfast *adj.* **hard-and-fast rules/regulations** rules that cannot be changed

hard·back /ˈhɑrdbæk/ *n.* [C] a book that has a strong stiff cover

> **THESAURUS**
> **hardcover, paperback**
> → see Thesaurus box at BOOK¹

hard·ball /ˈhɑrdbɔl/ *n.* **play hardball** *informal* to be very determined to get what you want, especially in business or politics

ˌhard-ˈboiled *adj.* **1** a hard-boiled egg has been boiled until it becomes solid **2** *written* not showing or influenced by your emotions [= **tough**]: *a hard-boiled policeman*

ˌhard ˈcash *n.* [U] paper money and coins, not checks or CREDIT CARDS

ˈhard ˌcopy *n.* plural **hard copies** [C,U] information from a computer that is printed onto paper, or the printed papers themselves

hard·core /ˈhɑrdkɔr/ *adj.* [only before noun] extreme, and unlikely to change: *hardcore criminals* —**hardcore** *n.* [C]

hard·cov·er /ˈhɑrdˌkʌvɚ/ *n.* [C] a book that has a strong stiff cover —**hardcover** *adj.*

> **THESAURUS**
> **hardback, paperback**
> → see Thesaurus box at BOOK¹

ˌhard ˈcurrency *n.* [C,U] money from a country that has a strong ECONOMY, that is unlikely to lose its value

ˌhard ˈdisk also **ˌhard ˈdrive** *n.* [C] a part that is fixed inside a computer, used for permanently keeping information

ˌhard ˈdrugs *n.* [plural] very strong illegal drugs such as COCAINE

hard·en /ˈhɑrdn/ *v.* [I,T] **1** to become firm or stiff, or to make something do this: *The glue takes about an hour to harden.* **2** to become less kind, less afraid, and more determined, or to make someone become this way: *Leslie's face hardened, and she turned away from him.* | *a **hardened criminal***

ˌhard ˈhat *n.* [C] a protective hat, worn by workers in places where buildings are being built → see picture at HAT

ˌhard-ˈheaded *adj.* able to make difficult decisions without being influenced by your emotions

ˌhard-ˈhearted *adj.* not caring about other people's feelings

ˌhard-ˈhitting *adj.* criticizing someone or something in a strong and effective way: *a hard-hitting TV documentary*

hard·line /ˌhɑrdˈlaɪn◂ / *adj.* unwilling to change your extreme political opinions: *hardline conservatives* —**hardliner** *n.* [C]

ˌhard ˈliquor *n.* [U] strong alcohol such as WHISKEY

hard·ly /ˈhɑrdli/ *adv.* **1** almost not or almost none: *I hardly know the people I'm working with.* | *The children were so excited they **could hardly** speak.* | ***Hardly anyone*** (=very few people) *goes to the old theater anymore.* | *Katy is **hardly ever*** (=almost never) *at home.* **2** *formal* used in order to say that something is not at all true, surprising, etc.: *It's **hardly surprising** that she won't answer his calls after the way he's treated her.* | *You **can hardly blame** Tom for not waiting.*

ˌhard-ˈnosed *adj.* not affected by emotions, and determined to get what you want: *a hard-nosed negotiator*

ˌhard of ˈhearing *adj.* [not before noun] unable to hear well

> **THESAURUS**
> **hearing impaired, deaf**
> → see Thesaurus box at HEAR

ˌhard-ˈpressed *adj.* having a lot of problems and not enough money or time: *help for hard-pressed families with young children*

ˌhard ˈrock *n.* [U] loud ROCK music

ˌhard ˈsell *n.* [singular] a way of selling in which someone tries very hard to persuade you to buy something

H

hard·ship /ˈhɑrd͵ʃɪp/ *n.* [C,U] something that makes your life difficult, especially the condition of having very little money: *Many families were **suffering** economic **hardship**.* | *the **hardships of** war*

͵hard ˈup *adj. informal* not having much money: *Scott was pretty hard up, so I gave him $20.*

hard·ware /ˈhɑrdwɛr/ *n.* [U] **1** computer machinery and equipment, as opposed to the programs that make computers work [➡ **software**] **2** equipment and tools you use in your home and yard: *a **hardware store*** (=where you can buy these things)

hard·wood /ˈhɑrdwʊd/ *n.* [C,U] strong heavy wood used for making furniture, or a type of tree that produces this kind of wood

͵hard-ˈworking *adj.* working seriously with a lot of effort, and not wasting time [≠ **lazy**]: *a hard-working student*

har·dy /ˈhɑrdi/ *adj.* strong and healthy and able to live through difficult conditions: *hardy plants*

hare /hɛr/ *n.* [C] an animal like a rabbit, but larger, with longer ears and longer back legs

hare·brained /ˈhɛrbreɪnd/ *adj.* not sensible or practical: *a **harebrained scheme***

hare·lip /ˈhɛr͵lɪp/ *n.* [singular, U] the condition of having a top lip that is divided into two parts

har·em /ˈhɛrəm, ˈhærəm/ *n.* [C] **1** the group of wives or women who lived with a rich or powerful man in some Muslim societies in past times **2** the rooms in a Muslim home where the women live

hark /hɑrk/ **also hark·en** /ˈhɑrkən/ *v.*

hark/harken back to sth *phr. v.* to remember or to remind people of something from the past: *The band's music harks back to the 1950s.*

har·lot /ˈhɑrlət/ *n.* [C] *literary* a PROSTITUTE

harm¹ /hɑrm/ *n.* [U] **1** damage, injury, or trouble caused by someone's actions or by an event: *chemicals that **cause harm to** the environment* | *A little wine won't **do** you any **harm**.* | *Trying to lose weight can **do more harm than good*** (=cause problems). **2 there's no harm in doing sth** used in order to suggest that doing something may be helpful or useful: *There's no harm in asking.* **3 not mean any harm** used in order to say that even though someone hurt or upset someone else, this was not his/her intention: *I'm sure he didn't mean any harm.* **4 no harm done** *spoken* said in order to tell someone that you are not upset by what s/he has done or said: *"I'm sorry." "That's OK; no harm done."*

harm² *v.* [T] to damage or hurt something: *Too much sun will harm your skin.*

harm·ful /ˈhɑrmfəl/ *adj.* causing harm, or likely to cause harm: *the harmful effects of pollution* | *Some pesticides are **harmful to** the environment.*

THESAURUS

poisonous/toxic – containing a substance that can kill you or make you sick if you eat it, breathe it, etc: *a poisonous snake* | *toxic fumes*
detrimental formal – harmful or damaging to something: *Fatty foods are detrimental to your health.*
damaging – having a bad effect on someone or something

harm·less /ˈhɑrmlɪs/ *adj.* **1** unable or unlikely to hurt anyone or cause damage: *harmless bacteria* **2** not likely to upset or offend anyone: *harmless fun* —**harmlessly** *adv.*

har·mon·i·ca /hɑrˈmɑnɪkə/ *n.* [C] a small musical instrument that you play by blowing into it and moving it from side to side

har·mo·nize /ˈhɑrmə͵naɪz/ *v.* [I] **1** to work well or look good together: *clothes that **harmonize with** her coloring* **2** to sing or play music in harmony

har·mo·ny /ˈhɑrməni/ *n.* **1** [U] a situation in which people are friendly and peaceful, and agree with each other: *a city that **lives/works in** racial **harmony*** **2** [C,U] combinations of musical notes that sound good together: *four-part harmony* —**harmonious** /hɑrˈmoʊniəs/ *adj.*

har·ness¹ /ˈhɑrnɪs/ *n.* **1** [C,U] a set of leather bands fastened with metal, used in order to control a horse and attach it to a vehicle that it pulls **2** [C] a set of bands that is used to hold someone in a place, or to stop him/her from falling: *a safety harness*

harness² *v.* [T] **1** to control and use the natural force or power of something: *a dam to harness the power of the river* **2** to fasten two animals together, or to fasten an animal to something using a harness

harp¹ /hɑrp/ *n.* [C] a large musical instrument with strings stretched on a frame with three corners —**harpist** *n.* [C] ➔ see picture on page A6

harp² *v.*

harp on sth *phr. v. informal disapproving* to talk about something again and again, in a way that is annoying or boring: *I wish they'd stop harping on my boyfriend's faults.*

har·poon /hɑrˈpun/ *n.* [C] a weapon used for hunting WHALES

harp·si·chord /ˈhɑrpsɪ͵kɔrd/ *n.* [C] a musical instrument like a piano, used especially in CLASSICAL MUSIC

har·row·ing /ˈhæroʊɪŋ/ *adj. formal* a harrowing sight or experience is one that frightens, shocks, or upsets you very much

harsh /hɑrʃ/ *adj.* **1** harsh conditions are difficult to live in and very uncomfortable: *harsh Canadian winters* | *the **harsh realities** of war* **2** too loud or too bright, and making you feel uncomfortable: *a harsh voice* | *the harsh street lights* **3** unkind, cruel, or strict: *harsh criticism* | *He had*

harsh words *for the way the mayor has handled the case.* —**harshly** *adv.* —**harshness** *n.* [U]

har·vest¹ /'hɑrvɪst/ *n.* **1** [C,U] the time when crops are gathered from the fields, or the act of gathering them: *It was harvest time.* | *the wheat harvest* **2** [C] the size or quality of the crops: *a good harvest*

harvest² *v.* [T] to gather crops from the fields

has /z, s, əz, həz; *strong* hæz/ *v.* the third person singular of the present tense of HAVE

'has-been *n.* [C] *informal* someone who was important or popular, but who has been forgotten

hash¹ /hæʃ/ *n.* **1** [C,U] a dish made with cooked meat and potatoes **2** [U] *informal* HASHISH

hash² *v.*
hash sth ⇔ **out** *phr. v.* to discuss something very thoroughly and carefully: *It took them a long time to hash out a compromise.*

,hash 'browns *n.* [plural] potatoes that have been cut into very small pieces, pressed together, and cooked in oil

hash·ish /'hæʃiʃ, hæ'ʃiʃ/ *n.* [U] a form of the drug MARIJUANA

has·n't /'hæzənt/ *v.* the short form of "has not": *She hasn't seen Bruce in seven years.*

has·sle¹ /'hæsəl/ *n.* **1** [C,U] something that is annoying because it causes problems, or is difficult to do: *Driving downtown is just too much hassle.* | *legal hassles*

> **THESAURUS**
> **problem, trouble**
> → see Thesaurus box at PROBLEM

2 [C] *informal* an argument: *a few hassles with the management*

hassle² *v. informal* [T] to ask someone again and again to do something, in a way that is annoying: *She just kept **hassling** me **to** get a summer job.*

haste /heɪst/ *n.* [U] **1** great speed in doing something, especially because you do not have enough time: ***In** her **haste to** get to the airport, Pam forgot the tickets.* **2 in haste** quickly or in a hurry **3 haste makes waste** used in order to say that if you do something too quickly, it will not turn out well

has·ten /'heɪsən/ *v. formal* **1** [T] to make something happen faster or sooner: *The popularity of radio **hastened the end** of silent movies.* **2 hasten to do sth** to do or say something quickly or without delay

hast·y /'heɪsti/ *adj. formal* done in a hurry, especially with bad results: *a hasty decision* —**hastily** *adv.*: *a hastily written speech*

> **THESAURUS**
> **impulsive, rash, hotheaded**
> → see Thesaurus box at IMPULSIVE

hats

hat /hæt/ *n.* [C] **1** a piece of clothing that you wear on your head: *a big straw hat* | *a cowboy hat* **2 keep sth under your hat** to keep information secret **3 throw/toss your hat into the ring** *journalism* to officially announce that you will compete or take part in a competition

hatch¹ /hætʃ/ *v.* **1** [I,T] if an egg hatches or is hatched, it breaks and a baby bird, fish, or insect is born **2** [I] **also hatch out** to break through an egg in order to be born

hatch² *n.* [C] a hole in a ship or aircraft, used for loading goods, or the door that covers it

hatch·back /'hætʃbæk/ *n.* [C] a car with a door at the back that opens up

hatch·et /'hætʃɪt/ *n.* [C] **1** a small AX with a short handle **2 do a hatchet job on sb** *informal* to criticize someone severely and often unfairly → **bury the hatchet** at BURY

hate¹ /heɪt/ *v.* [T] **1** to dislike someone or something very much: *She hated my father.* | *I really hate spinach.* | *Tony **hates it when** people are late.*

> **THESAURUS**
> **can't stand** – to hate someone or something: *I can't stand being late.*
> **detest** formal – to hate someone or something very much: *I was going out with a boy my mother detested.*
> **loathe** – to hate something or someone very much: *I loathe my job.*
> **despise** – to hate someone very much and not respect him/her at all: *She despised her neighbors.*
> **abhor** formal – to hate something because you think it is morally wrong: *He abhors violence of any kind.*
> → LOVE

2 I hate to think what/how *spoken* used when you feel sure that something would have a bad result: *I hate to think what would happen if Joe*

H

got lost. **3 hate sb's guts** *informal* to hate someone very much —**hated** *adj.*

hate² *n.* [U] an angry feeling of wanting to harm someone you dislike: *a look of hate*

'hate crime *n.* [C] a crime that is committed against someone only because s/he belongs to a particular race, religion, etc.

hate·ful /'heɪtfəl/ *adj.* very bad or unkind: *a hateful thought*

ha·tred /'heɪtrɪd/ *n.* [U] *formal* HATE: *his* ***hatred of*** *racism*

haugh·ty /'hɔṭi/ *adj. literary disapproving* proud and unfriendly —**haughtily** *adv.*

haul¹ /hɔl/ *v.* [T] to carry or pull something heavy: *trucks hauling cement*

THESAURUS

carry, **tote**, **lug**, **cart**, **schlep**, **pull**, **tug**, **drag**, **tow**, **heave**
→ see Thesaurus box at CARRY, PULL¹

haul sb **off** *phr. v. informal* to take someone somewhere s/he does not want to go: *Dave got* ***hauled off to*** *jail.*

haul² *n.* **1** [C] a large amount of illegal or stolen goods that are found by the police: *a huge drug haul* **2 the long haul** the long time that it takes to achieve something difficult: *"We're* ***in this for the long haul****," said a government source.* **3 a long haul** a long distance to travel

H

haunch /hɔntʃ, hɑntʃ/ *n.* the part of your body at the back between your waist and legs: *They squatted on their haunches playing dice.*

haunt¹ /hɔnt, hɑnt/ *v.* [T] **1** if the spirit of a dead person haunts a place, it appears there often: *a ship haunted by ghosts of sea captains* **2** if something haunts you, you keep remembering it or being affected by it, although you do not want this: *It's the kind of decision that* ***comes back to haunt*** *you later.*

haunt² *n.* [C] a place that someone likes to go to often: *Dan went back to visit his favorite old haunts.*

haunt·ed /'hɔnṭɪd, 'hɑn-/ *adj.* a place that is haunted is one where the spirits of dead people are believed to live: *a* ***haunted house***

haunt·ing /'hɔnṭɪŋ, 'hɑn-/ *adj.* sad, beautiful, and staying in your thoughts for a long time: *a haunting memory* —**hauntingly** *adv.*

have¹ /v, əv, həv; *strong* hæv/ *auxiliary verb* past tense and past participle **had**, third person singular **has** **1** used with the past participle of a verb to make the perfect tenses: *Yes, I've read the book.* | *Have you seen the new Disney movie?* | *She had lived in Peru for 30 years.* | *Rick has not been honest with us.* **2** used with some modal verbs and a past participle to make a past modal: *Carrie should have been nicer.* | *I must've left my wallet at home.* **3 had better** used in order to give advice, or to say what is the best thing to do: *You'd better take the popcorn off the stove or it'll burn.* | *I'd better not go out tonight – I'm too tired.* **4 have had it** *spoken* **a)** said when someone or something is old, broken, or not good any longer: *I think the car has had it. It wouldn't start this morning.* **b) I've had it with** said when you are so annoyed by someone or something that you do not want to deal with him, her, or it any longer: *I've had it with the noise here. I want to move!*

have² /hæv/ *v.* [T not in passive]

1 FEATURES/QUALITIES used when saying what someone or something looks like, or what qualities or features he, she, or it possesses: *Rudy has brown eyes and dark hair.* | *The stereo doesn't have a tape deck.* | *Japan has a population of over 120 million.*

2 OWN OR USE to own something, or be able to use something: *Kurt had a nice bike, but it got stolen.* | *The school doesn't* ***have room for*** *any more students.* | *We don't have enough money for a washing machine.* | *Dad, can I have the car tonight?*

3 have got used instead of "have" to mean "possess": *I've got four tickets to the opera.*

4 EAT/DRINK to eat, drink, or smoke something: *Do you want to come have a beer with us?* | *We're having steak for dinner tonight.* | *What time do you usually* ***have lunch/breakfast/dinner****?*

5 EXPERIENCE/DO to experience or do something: *I have a meeting in 15 minutes.* | *The kids will* ***have fun*** *at the circus.* | *Her secretary* ***had trouble/problems with*** *the copy machine.*

6 RECEIVE to receive something: *Jenny! You have a phone call!* | *I'm sure he had help from his father on his homework.*

7 IN A POSITION/STATE to put or keep something in a particular position or state: *He had his eyes closed.* | *Why do you always* ***have*** *the TV* ***on*** *so loud?*

8 may I have/can I have/I'll have *spoken* said when you are asking for something: *I'll have two hot dogs to go, please.* | *Could I have that pencil, please?*

9 SELL/MAKE AVAILABLE to sell something, or make it available for people to use: *Do they have lawn mowers at Sears?* | *The other pool has a water slide.*

10 FAMILY/FRIENDS ETC to know or be related to someone: *She has six brothers.* | *Chris has a friend who lives in Malta.*

11 AMOUNT OF TIME also have got to be allowed a particular amount of time to do something: *You have 30 minutes to finish the test.*

12 have time if you have time to do something, there is nothing else that you must do at that particular time: *Do you* ***have time to*** *come and have a cup of coffee with us?*

13 BE SICK/INJURED to become sick with a particular illness, or be injured in a particular way: *Sheila had the flu for a week.* | *He has a broken leg.*

14 CARRY WITH YOU to be carrying something with you: *Do you have your knife?* | *How much money do you* ***have on you****?*

15 IDEA/THOUGHT to think of something, or realize something: *Listen, I have an idea.*

16 have sth ready/done etc. to make something ready, or finish something: *They promised to have it done by Friday.*

17 GIVE BIRTH to give birth: *Sasha had twins!*

18 have your hair cut/have your house painted etc. to employ someone to cut your hair, paint your house, etc.
19 GUESTS to be with someone, or be visited by someone: *Sorry, I didn't realize you had guests.* | *Barry had an Australian guy with him.*
20 have an influence/effect etc. to influence someone or something, or cause a particular effect: *Hungarian folk songs* ***had*** *a great* ***influence on*** *Bartok's music.*
21 have nothing against used in order to say that you do not dislike someone or something: *I have nothing against hard work, but 80 hours a week is too much.* ➔ **be had** at HAD

have on *phr. v.* **1 have** sth **on** to be wearing something: *Marty had a blue shirt on.* **2 have** sth **on** sb to know about something bad someone has done: *Do the police have anything on him?*

ha·ven /ˈheɪvən/ *n.* [C,U] a place where people go to be safe: *a* ***haven for*** *refugees*

have·n't /ˈhævənt/ *v.* the short form of "have not": *We haven't tried Indian food yet.* ▶ Don't say "haven't to." ◀

have to /ˈhæftə; *strong* ˈhæftu/ **also have got to** /v ˈgɑṭə, əv-, həv-/ *modal verb* **1** to be forced to do something because someone makes you do it, or because a situation makes it necessary: *We don't have to answer their questions.* | *Susan hates having to get up early.* | *I've got to go now. I'm already late!* **2** used when saying that it is important that something happens: *You'll have to be nice to Aunt Lynn.* **3** used when telling someone how to do something: *First you have to take the wheel off.* **4** used when saying that you are sure that something will happen or is true: *He has to be stuck in traffic – he wouldn't be late otherwise.*

GRAMMAR

have to, have got to, must
have to – used when a rule, law, situation, etc. forces you to do something and you do not have a choice about it: *You have to pay tax on your income* (=because the law says it is necessary). | *We have to visit Grandma on Sunday* (=e.g. because my mother says it is necessary).
must – used especially in more formal writing when a law or person in authority forces you do to something: *All visitors must report to reception.*
must – used when you make yourself do something because you think it is a good idea or necessary: *We must visit Grandma on Sunday* (=e.g. because we haven't seen her for a long time and it would be a good idea). | *I must study for tomorrow's test* (=because I know it is a good idea if I want to do well).
have got to – used in spoken English instead of **have to** or **must** to emphasize how important it is to do something: *I've got to talk to him.*

hav·oc /ˈhævək/ *n.* [U] a situation in which there is a lot of confusion and damage: *a bus strike that* ***caused/created havoc*** *in the city's streets* | *The war will* ***wreak havoc on*** *the country's economy.*

hawk[1] /hɔk/ *v.* [T] to try to sell goods by carrying them around and talking about them —**hawker** *n.*

hawk[2] *n.* [C] a large wild bird that eats small birds and animals

hay /heɪ/ *n.* [U] a type of long grass that has been cut and dried, used as food for farm animals [➡ **straw**]

ˈhay ˌfever *n.* [U] a medical condition like a bad COLD, caused by breathing in POLLEN (=dust from plants) [➡ **allergy**]

hay·ride /ˈheɪraɪd/ *n.* [C] an organized ride in a CART filled with HAY, usually as part of a social event

hay·stack /ˈheɪstæk/ *n.* [C] a large, firmly built pile of HAY

hay·wire /ˈheɪwaɪɚ/ *adj.* **go haywire** *informal* to start working in completely the wrong way: *My computer's going haywire again.*

haz·ard[1] /ˈhæzɚd/ *n.* [C] **1** something that may be dangerous or cause accidents, problems, etc.: *a* ***health hazard*** | *the hazards of starting your own business*

THESAURUS

danger, risk, threat
➔ see Thesaurus box at DANGER

2 occupational hazard a problem or risk that cannot be avoided in the job that you do —**hazardous** *adj.*: *hazardous waste from factories*

hazard[2] *v.* [T] to say something that is only a suggestion or guess: *I don't know, but I could* ***hazard a guess.***

haze /heɪz/ *n.* [U] smoke, dust etc. in the air that is difficult to see through [➡ **hazy, fog, smog**]: *a gray haze of smoke over the mountains*

ha·zel /ˈheɪzəl/ *adj.* eyes that are hazel are greenish-brown

ha·zel·nut /ˈheɪzəlˌnʌt/ *n.* [C] a sweet round nut

haz·ing /ˈheɪzɪŋ/ *n.* [C,U] the activity of making people who want to join a club or FRATERNITY do silly or dangerous things before they can join

haz·y /ˈheɪzi/ *adj.* **1** air that is hazy is not clear because there is a lot of smoke, dust, or mist in it: *a hazy sky* **2** an idea, memory etc. that is hazy is not clear: *My memories of that night are a little hazy.*

he /i; *strong* hi/ *pron.* a male person or animal that has already been mentioned or is already known about: *"Does Matt still work here?" "No, he works in Ohio now."* | *How old is he?* | *He's* (=he is) *my brother.*

head[1] /hɛd/ *n.*
1 TOP OF BODY [C] the top part of your body that has your eyes, mouth, etc. in it: *He turned his head to kiss her.* ➔ see picture on page A3

H

COLLOCATIONS

turn your **head** to look at something.
shake your **head** (=move it from side to side) to disagree or say "no."
nod your **head** (=move it up and down) to agree or say "yes."
raise/lift your **head** to look up.
bend/lower your **head** to look down.
bow your **head** (=move it down) to show respect for someone.
hang your **head** (=lower it and keep it lowered) if you are ashamed.
scratch your **head** (=rub it with your fingers) if you are thinking hard.
➔ HAIR, EYE

2 MIND [C] your mind: *Phil has some strange ideas **in** his **head**.* | *Ann has **a good head for** math* (=she is good at doing math). | *Why don't you **use your head*** (=think carefully and sensibly) *to find a solution?* | *I wish he'd **get** it **into his head*** (=realize or understand) *that school is important.* **3 LEADER** [C] the leader or most important person in a group or organization: *the **head of** the biology department* | *the head waiter* **4 POSITION** [singular] the top or front of something, or the most important part of it: *Edgar sat proudly **at the head of the table*** (=at the end where the most important people sit). **5 ON A TOOL** [C] the widest or top part of something such as a piece of equipment or a tool: *a shower head* **6 PLANT** [C] the top part of a plant with a lot of leaves: *a head of lettuce/cabbage* **7 (from) head to toe/foot** over your whole body: *The kids were covered from head to toe in mud.* **8 put your heads together** *spoken* to discuss a difficult problem together: *If we put our heads together, we'll think of a way.* **9 be/go over sb's head a)** to be too difficult for someone to understand: *Most of the lecture was way over my head.* **b)** to ask a more important person to deal with something than the person you would normally ask **10 keep/lose your head** to behave reasonably or stupidly in a difficult situation: *I guess I just lost my head for a minute.* **11 go to sb's head a)** to make someone feel more important than s/he really is: *It's too bad Dave **let** his promotion **go to his head**.* **b)** to make someone quickly feel slightly drunk: *That beer went right to my head.* **12 come to a head** if a problem comes to a head, it becomes worse and you have to do something about it immediately: *The situation came to a head when the workers went on strike.* **13 heads up!** *spoken* used in order to warn people that something is falling from above, or that something is being thrown to them **14 keep your head above water** to barely be able to live or keep your business working when you have money problems **15 laugh/scream/shout etc. your head off** *informal* to laugh, scream etc. very much **16 head over heels (in love)** loving someone very much **17 COIN heads** the side of a coin that has a picture of a head on it [≠ **tails**] ➔ —see also BIGHEADED, REDHEAD

head² *v.* **1** [I,T] to go or make something go in a particular direction: *Where were they heading when you saw them?* | *a boat **heading toward/for** the shore* | *Roz headed the car down the hill.* **2** [T] to be in charge of a government, organization, or group: *a committee headed by Jake Wilson* | *Most single-parent families are headed by women.* **3 be heading/headed for sth** if you are heading for a situation, it is likely to happen: *They're heading for trouble.* **4 be headed** if a list, page, etc. is headed with particular words, those words are at the top: *The longest list was headed "Problems."*

head sb/sth ⇔ **off** *phr. v.* to stop someone moving in a particular direction by moving in front of him/her: *We'll try to head them off at the next intersection.*

head·ache /ˈhɛdeɪk/ *n.* [C] **1** a pain in your head: *I **have a** bad **headache**.* **2** *informal* an annoying or worrying problem: *Balancing the checkbook is always a headache.*

head·band /ˈhɛdbænd/ *n.* [C] a band that you wear around your head to keep your hair off your face

ˈhead count, **head·count** /ˈhɛdkaʊnt/ *n.* [C usually singular] the process of counting the number of people in a particular place or event, or the actual number: *Hal **did a** quick **head count** before the meeting began.*

head·dress /ˈhɛd-drɛs/ *n.* [C] something that someone wears on his/her head for decoration on a special occasion

head·first /ˌhɛdˈfɚst/ *adv.* moving or falling forward with your head going first: *He fell down the stairs headfirst.*

head·gear /ˈhɛdgɪr/ *n.* [U] hats and similar things that you wear on your head

head·hunt·er /ˈhɛdˌhʌntɚ/ *n.* [C] someone who finds people with the right skills and experience to do a particular job

head·ing /ˈhɛdɪŋ/ *n.* [C] the title written at the top of a piece or section of writing

head·land /ˈhɛdlənd, -lænd/ *n.* [C] an area of land that sticks out from the coast into the ocean

head·light /ˈhɛdlaɪt/ *n.* [C] one of the large lights at the front of a vehicle: *She **flashed** her **headlights*** (=quickly turned them on and off) *at me.* ➔ see picture on page A12

head·line /ˈhɛdlaɪn/ *n.* [C] **1** the title of a newspaper article, printed in large letters above the article **2 make (the) headlines** to do something important, shocking, or new, so that newspapers, television shows, etc. talk about you: *The attacks made headlines around the world.*

H

head·long /ˈhɛdlɔŋ, ˌhɛdˈlɔŋ◂/ *adj. adv.* **1** without thinking carefully: *They **rushed headlong into** marriage.* **2** falling or moving quickly with your head going first: *a headlong rush down the slope*

head·mas·ter /ˈhɛdˌmæstɚ/, **head·mis·tress** /ˈhɛdˌmɪstrɪs/ *n.* [C] a PRINCIPAL in a private school

ˌhead-ˈon *adv.* **1 meet/hit/crash etc. head-on** if two vehicles meet or hit head-on, the front part of one vehicle comes toward or hits the front part of the other vehicle **2** to deal with someone or something in a direct and determined way: *She intended to **face** her difficulties **head-on**.* —**head-on** *adj.*: *a head-on crash*

headphones

head·phones /ˈhɛdfoʊnz/ *n.* [plural] a piece of equipment that you wear over your ears to listen to a radio or recording [➡ **earphones**]

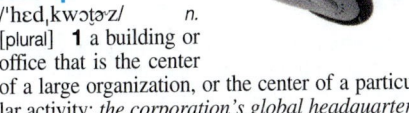

head·quar·ters /ˈhɛdˌkwɔt̬ɚz/ *n.* [plural] **1** a building or office that is the center of a large organization, or the center of a particular activity: *the corporation's global headquarters in New York* **2 also HQ** the place from which military operations are controlled

head·rest /ˈhɛd-rɛst/ *n.* [C] the top part of a chair or seat that supports the back of your head

head·room /ˈhɛd-rum, -rʊm/ *n.* [U] the amount of space above your head inside a car

ˌhead ˈstart *n.* [C] the advantage you gain in a particular activity by starting before other people: *We should **give** the younger kids **a head start** in the race.*

head·stone /ˈhɛdstoʊn/ *n.* ➔ GRAVESTONE

head·strong /ˈhɛdstrɔŋ/ *adj.* very determined to do what you want, even when other people advise you not to do it: *a headstrong child*

ˌhead-to-ˈhead *adj., adv.* directly competing with another person or group: *The new sitcom will **go head-to-head with** the top-rated show on Thursday nights.* | *head-to-head competition*

head·way /ˈhɛdweɪ/ *n.* **make headway** to make progress toward achieving something even when you have difficulties [= **make progress**]: *They have made little headway in the peace talks.*

head·wind /ˈhɛdˌwɪnd/ *n.* [C] a wind that blows directly toward you when you are moving

head·y /ˈhɛdi/ *adj. written* exciting in a way that makes you feel you can do anything: *the heady days of our youth*

heal /hil/ *v.* **1** [I] if a wound or broken bone heals, it becomes healthy again: *The scratch on her finger healed quickly.* **2** [T] to cure someone who is ill, or make a wound get better

health /hɛlθ/ *n.* [U] **1** the general condition of your body, and how healthy you are: *You should take better care of your health.* | *a 68-year-old man **in good health*** | *serious **health problems*** **2** the state of being without illness or disease: *I wish you health and happiness.* **3** how successful an ECONOMY, business, or organization is

ˈhealth care, health·care /ˈhɛlθkɛr/ *n.* [U] the service of taking care of the health of all the people in a country or area: *the high cost of health care*

ˈhealth club *n.* [C] a place where people go to exercise that you have to pay to use

> **THESAURUS**
>
> **gym, (swimming) pool**
> ➔ see Thesaurus box at SPORT[1], EXERCISE[2]

ˈhealth food *n.* [C,U] food that contains only natural substances

> **THESAURUS**
>
> **fast food, junk food, vegetarian food**
> ➔ see Thesaurus box at FOOD

health·ful /ˈhɛlθfəl/ *adj. written* likely to make you healthy

health·y /ˈhɛlθi/ *adj.* **1** physically strong and not likely to become sick: *a healthy baby girl* | *Rachel's always been **perfectly healthy**.*

> **THESAURUS**
>
> **well** – healthy, used especially when describing how someone feels or looks: *I'm not feeling very well.*
> **fine** spoken – healthy, used when someone has asked you how you feel and you are replying that you feel well: *"Hi, Tom, how are you?" "Fine, thanks."*
> **better** – less sick than you were, or no longer sick: *I'm feeling a lot better now.*
> **in (good) shape** – in a good state of health and physically strong: *Jogging keeps me in pretty good shape.*
> **physically fit** – healthy and having a strong body: *Even kids need exercise to be physically fit.*

2 good for your body or your mind: *a **healthy diet/lifestyle*** | *It's not **healthy for** her to depend on him like that.* **3** successful and likely to stay that way: *a **healthy economy/business*** **4** *informal* fairly large or noticeable: *She seems to have a **healthy appetite**.* | *a **healthy increase** in sales* | *Reed has a **healthy respect** for rattlesnakes.* **5** showing that you are healthy: *healthy skin* —**healthiness** *n.* [U]

heap[1] /hip/ *n.* [C] **1** a large messy pile of things: *a **heap of** newspapers* | *His clothes lay **in a heap** by the bed.*

> **THESAURUS**
>
> **pile, mound**
> ➔ see Thesaurus box at PILE[1]

2 *informal* an old car that is in bad condition

H

heap² *v.* [T] **1** to put a lot of things on top of each other in a messy way: *magazines heaped on the table* **2 be heaped with sth** to have a lot of things on top of something: *a plate heaped with food*

heap·ing /ˈhipɪŋ/ *adj.* a heaping measurement of food is slightly more than the tool it is being measured with can hold: *two heaping teaspoons of sugar*

hear /hɪr/ *v.* past tense and past participle **heard** /hɚd/ **1** [I,T] to know that a sound is being made, using your ears: *I love to hear the baby laugh like that.* | *Didn't you hear when I called you?*

THESAURUS

If a sound is **drowned out** by something, it prevents you from hearing the sound: *His voice was drowned out by the traffic.*
If someone cannot hear you because s/he is very far away from you, s/he is **out of earshot**: *"What are we going to do if you lose your job?" I asked John, as soon as the children were out of earshot.*
If someone is close enough to hear what you say, s/he is **within earshot**.
If someone says something **under his/her breath**, s/he makes a rude or angry statement very quietly because s/he does not want anyone to hear him/her: *"You rat," he muttered under his breath.*
If someone is **inaudible**, s/he speaks so quietly that you cannot hear him/her.
If someone is not able to hear very well because of a physical problem with his/her ears, you can say that s/he is **hard of hearing** or **hearing impaired**: *My grandmother's a little hard of hearing.*
If someone is **deaf**, s/he is not able to hear anything at all.
You **hear** a noise or something that someone says, often without trying to: *Did you hear that noise?* | *I could hear the phone ringing.*
If you **listen to** words, sounds, or music, you pay attention to them: *I enjoy watching movies and listening to music.* | *She listened carefully to his advice.*
→ SEE

2 [T] to listen to music that is being played, what someone is saying, etc.: *I heard a great song on the radio.* | *You should at least hear what she has to say.* **3** [I,T] to be told or find out a piece of information: *Have you **heard about** the new project?* | *"Mark's going to law school." **"So I've heard."*** (=said when you already know about something) **4 hear a case** to listen to what is said in a court of law, and make a decision: *The case will be heard on July 16.* **5 (do) you hear (me)?** *spoken* said when you are giving someone an order and want to be certain that s/he will obey you: *Be home by ten, you hear?*

hear from sb *phr. v.* to get news or information from someone, usually by letter: *Have you heard from Jane yet?*

hear of sb/sth *phr. v.* **have heard of sb/sth** to know that someone or something exists because you have been told about him, her, or it: *"Do you know a guy named Phil Merton?" "I've never heard of him."*

hear sb **out** *phr. v.* to listen to all of someone's explanation for something, without interrupting: *Look, I know you're mad, but at least hear me out.*

hear·ing /ˈhɪrɪŋ/ *n.* **1** [U] the sense that you use to hear sounds: *My hearing's not as good as it used to be.* **2** [C] a meeting of a court or special committee to find out the facts about a case

ˈhearing aid *n.* [C] a small thing that you put in your ear if you cannot hear well, to make sounds louder

ˈhearing imˌpaired *adj.* unable to hear well or hear at all

THESAURUS

hard of hearing, deaf
→ see Thesaurus box at HEAR

hear·say /ˈhɪrseɪ/ *n.* [U] something that you have heard about from other people, but do not know to be true [➡ **gossip**]: *Her opinions are based mainly on rumors and hearsay.*

hearse /hɚs/ *n.* [C] a large car in which a dead body in a CASKET is carried to or from a funeral

heart /hɑrt/ *n.*
1 BODY [C] the body part inside a person's or animal's chest that pumps blood through the body: *He could feel his **heart beating** faster.* | *Dad's had some **heart trouble** this year.* → see picture on page A3
2 EMOTIONS [C,U] the part of you that is able to feel strong emotions such as love: *I knew **in my heart** that I wouldn't see her again.* | *I loved her **with all my heart**.*
3 SHAPE [C] a shape used for representing love
4 the heart of sth a) the main or most important part of something: *We talked for hours before we got to **the heart of the problem/matter**.* **b)** [singular] the middle or the busiest part of an area: *a big hotel **in the heart of** the city*
5 a sth at heart if you are a particular type of person at heart, that is the type of person you really are: *Bob can seem tough, but he's really a sweet guy at heart.*
6 know/learn/recite etc. sth by heart to correctly remember or say all of something that you have been taught, without needing to read it
7 GAME [C usually plural] a playing card with one or more red heart shapes on it → see picture at PLAYING CARD
8 sb's heart sank used in order to say that someone suddenly became very sad or disappointed: *Nick's heart sank when he heard the news.*
9 do sth to your heart's content to do some-

H

thing as much as you want to: *a resort where you can go sailing to your heart's content*

10 -hearted having a particular type of character: *a kind-hearted old lady*

11 have a heart of gold to be very generous and kind

12 take/lose heart to begin to have more hope, or to stop having hope ➔ **cross my heart (and hope to die)** at CROSS[1]

heart·ache /'hartˌeɪk/ *n.* [U] a strong feeling of sadness

'heart at,tack *n.* [C] a serious medical condition in which a person's heart suddenly stops working: *Jo's dad* ***had a heart attack*** *last year.*

heart·beat /'hart˺bit/ *n.* [C usually singular] the action or the sound of a heart pumping blood through the body

heart·break /'hart˺breɪk/ *n.* [U] a strong feeling of sadness and disappointment

heart·break·ing /'hart˺ˌbreɪkɪŋ/ *adj.* making you feel very upset: *a heartbreaking story*

heart·bro·ken /'hart˺ˌbroʊkən/ *adj.* very sad because someone or something has disappointed you

heart·burn /'hart˺bɚn/ *n.* [U] a slightly painful burning feeling in your stomach or chest caused by INDIGESTION

'heart dis,ease *n.* [U] a medical condition in which a person's heart has difficulty pumping blood

heart·ened /'hart˺nd/ *adj.* feeling happier and more hopeful —**hearten** *v.* [T] ➔ —opposite DISHEARTENED

heart·en·ing /'hart˺n-ɪŋ/ *adj.* making you feel happier and full of hope: *heartening news* ➔ —opposite DISHEARTENING

'heart ,failure *n.* [U] the failure of the heart to continue working, which causes death

heart·felt /'hartfɛlt/ *adj.* felt very strongly and sincerely: *heartfelt thanks*

hearth /harθ/ *n.* [C] the part of the floor around a FIREPLACE

heart·i·ly /'hartl-i/ *adv.* **1** loudly and cheerfully: *He laughed heartily.* **2** very much or completely: *I* ***heartily agree*** *with you.*

heart·land /'hartlænd/ *n.* **the heartland** the part of a country where most of the food is produced and where people live in a way that represents the basic values of that country

heart·less /'hartlɪs/ *adj.* cruel or unkind

heart·rend·ing /'hartˌrɛndɪŋ/ *adj.* making you feel great pity: *heartrending sobs*

heart·strings /'hartˌstrɪŋz/ *n.* **tug/pull on sb's heartstrings** to make someone feel a lot of pity or love

heart·throb /'hartθrab/ *n. humorous* a famous person whom many young people feel romantic love for: *a movie heartthrob from the 1950s*

,heart-to-'heart *n.* [C usually singular] a conversation in which two people honestly express their feelings or opinions about something: *I sat down and* ***had a heart-to-heart with*** *Emily.* —**heart-to-heart** *adj.*

heart·warm·ing /'hart˺ˌwɔrmɪŋ/ *adj.* making you feel happy, calm, and hopeful: *a heartwarming story*

heart·y /'harti/ *adj.* **1** very cheerful and friendly: *a hearty laugh* **2** a hearty meal or APPETITE is very large

heat[1] /hit/ *n.* **1** [U] warmth or hotness: *heat generated by the sun* **2** [U] very hot weather: *I can't work in this heat.* | *The heat has been almost unbearable.* **3** [U] the system in a house that keeps it warm, or the warmth that comes from this system: *Can you* ***turn the heat on/off****?* | *houses with no heat or electricity* **4 the heat of the moment/argument etc.** the period in a situation, argument, etc. when you feel extremely angry or excited: ***In the heat of the moment****, I said some things I didn't mean.* **5 take the heat** to deal with difficulties in a situation, especially by saying that you are responsible for them: *Coach Brown had to* ***take the heat for*** *the team's loss in the press.* **6** [C] one of the parts of a sports competition from which the winners are chosen to go on to the next part **7 in heat** if a female animal is in heat, she is able to become PREGNANT

heat[2] **also heat up** *v.* [I,T] to become warm or hot, or to make something warm or hot: *I'll just heat some soup for dinner.* | *The oven heats up pretty quickly.*

heat up *phr. v.* if a situation, argument, etc. heats up, the people involved in it become angrier and more excited

heat·ed /'hitɪd/ *adj.* **1** kept warm by a HEATER: *a heated swimming pool* **2 heated argument/discussion etc.** an argument, etc. in which people become very angry and excited

heat·er /'hitɚ/ *n.* [C] a machine used for heating air or water

hea·then /'hiðən/ *n. old-fashioned disapproving* [C] plural **heathen** someone who does not belong to the Christian religion, or to any of the main world religions —**heathen** *adj.*

'heat wave *n.* [C] a period of unusually hot weather

heave[1] /hiv/ *v.* **1** [I,T] to pull, throw, or lift something with a lot of effort: *She heaved the box onto the back of the truck.*

THESAURUS

pull, tug, drag, haul, tug
➔ see Thesaurus box at PULL[1]

2 heave a sigh to breathe out loudly, especially because you have stopped worrying about something: *We all* ***heaved a sigh of relief*** *when it was over.* **3** [I] if your chest heaves, it moves up and down quickly because it is difficult to breathe **4** [I] *informal* VOMIT

H

heave² *n.* [C] a strong pulling, pushing, or throwing movement

heav·en /ˈhɛvən/ *n.* **1** [U] **also Heaven** the place where God or the gods are believed to live, and where good people go after they die ➔ —compare HELL **2** [U] *informal* a very good thing, situation, or place: *Give Brad a TV and a comfortable chair, and he's* ***in heaven***. **3 (Good) Heavens!** *spoken* said when you are surprised or slightly annoyed: *Good heavens! Where have you been?* **4 for heaven's sake** *spoken* said when you are annoyed or angry: *For heaven's sake, just shut up!* **5 heaven forbid** *spoken* said in order to emphasize that you hope something will not happen: *And if – heaven forbid – he has an accident, what do I do then?* **6 the heavens** *literary* the sky: *Their eyes lifted to the heavens.*

heav·en·ly /ˈhɛvənli/ *adj.* **1** relating to heaven **2** very good or pleasing: *a heavenly dessert*

ˌheavenly ˈbody *n.* [C] a star, PLANET, or moon

heav·i·ly /ˈhɛvəli/ *adv.* **1** in very large amounts: *He's been* ***drinking heavily*** *recently.* **2** very or very much: ***heavily armed*** *rebels* | *The band's sound is* ***heavily influenced*** *by early punk rock.* **3** someone who is breathing heavily is breathing very loudly and slowly

heav·y /ˈhɛvi/ *adj.*

1 THINGS weighing a lot: *Be careful lifting that box – it's really heavy.* | *The suitcase feels heavier than before.*

2 PEOPLE used in order to politely describe someone who is fat: *He's gotten very heavy since we saw him last.* | *Tom's at least twenty pounds heavier than he was last year.*

THESAURUS

fat, **overweight**, **chubby**, **plump**, **big**, **large**, **obese**
➔ see Thesaurus box at FAT¹

3 AMOUNT unusually large in amount or quantity: *Roads were closed due to* ***heavy rains/snow*** (=a large amount of rain or snow). | *Traffic is heavy on the 405 freeway.*

COLLOCATIONS

heavy losses – used especially in order to say that a company has earned a lot less money than it has spent
heavy casualties/losses – used in order to say that a lot of people have been injured or killed in a war, battle, etc.

4 BUSY very busy and full of activities: *a* ***heavy day/schedule***
5 heavy sleeper someone who does not wake up very easily
6 a heavy smoker/drinker someone who smokes a lot or drinks a lot of alcohol
7 SERIOUS very complicated or serious and involving a lot of mental effort: *a heavy discussion* | *For a comedy, that movie was* ***heavy going***.
8 heavy breathing breathing that is slow and loud
9 be heavy into sth *spoken nonstandard* to be very involved in an activity, especially one that is not good for you: *Eric was real heavy into drugs.*
10 a heavy workload/load/burden a problem or situation that is large or too difficult to deal with: *Three jobs! That's a heavy load for just one person.*
11 with a heavy heart *literary* feeling very sad —**heaviness** *n.* [U] ➔ —compare LIGHT²

ˌheavy-ˈduty *adj.* **1** strong enough to be used often or for hard work without being damaged: *heavy-duty plastic gloves* **2** *informal* said when you want to emphasize how complicated, serious, etc. someone or something is: *The movie deals with some heavy-duty issues.*

ˌheavy-ˈhanded *adj.* strict, unfair, and not considering other people's feelings: *heavy-handed demands*

ˌheavy ˈindustry *n.* [C,U] an industry that produces goods such as coal, steel, or chemicals, or large goods such as cars and machines

ˌheavy ˈmetal *n.* [U] a type of ROCK music with a strong beat that is played very loudly on electric GUITARS

THESAURUS

pop (music), **rock (music)**, **rock'n'roll**, **reggae**, **house (music)**, **hip-hop**, **rap (music)**, **jazz**, **classical (music)**, **country (music)**, **folk (music)**
➔ see Thesaurus box at MUSIC

heav·y·weight /ˈhɛviˌweɪt/ *n.* [C] **1** someone who BOXES or WRESTLES, and is in the heaviest weight group [➡ **lightweight**] **2** someone who has a lot of power and experience in a particular business or job: *political heavyweights* —**heavyweight** *adj*

He·brew /ˈhibru/ *n.* [U] the official language of Israel, also used in many other places by Jewish people —**Hebrew**, **Hebraic** /hɪˈbreɪ-ɪk/ *adj.*

heck /hɛk/ *interjection* **1** said in order to emphasize a question, or when you are annoyed: ***Who/what/where etc. the heck*** *is that?* | *Ah, heck! I've lost my glasses.* **2 a/one heck of a sth** said in order to emphasize a statement: *That was one heck of a storm!* | *We had a heck of a time finding a parking space.* **3 What the heck!** said when you do something that you should not do: *"Want another piece of pie?" "Yeah, what the heck!"*

heck·le /ˈhɛkəl/ *v.* [T] to interrupt someone who is speaking or performing in front of a group of people by making loud, rude comments —**heckler** *n.* [C] —**heckling** *n.* [U]

hec·tare /ˈhɛktɛr/ *n.* [C] a unit for measuring an

area of land, equal to 10,000 square meters or 2.471 ACRES

hec·tic /ˈhɛktɪk/ *adj.* very busy, hurried, and slightly exciting: *It's been a really hectic week.*

he'd /id; *strong* hid/ **1** the short form of "he would": *Ed said he'd be a little late.* **2** the short form of "he had": *He'd never been a good dancer.*

hedge¹ /hɛdʒ/ *n.* [C] **1** a row of bushes used as a border around a yard or between two yards **2 hedge against disaster/inflation etc.** something that helps avoid problems, losing a lot of money, etc.: *a hedge against financial risk*

hedge² *v.* **1** [I] to avoid giving a direct answer to a question: *She tried to hedge when Tom asked her age.* **2 hedge your bets** to reduce your chances of failing by trying several different possibilities instead of one: *It's a good idea to hedge your bets by applying to more than one college.*

hedge against sth *phr. v.* to protect yourself from having problems, losing a lot of money, etc.: *You could invest in bonds to hedge against sudden changes in interest rates.*

hedge·hog /ˈhɛdʒhɑg, -hɔg/ *n.* [C] a small brown European animal whose body is round and covered with sharp needle-like hairs

he·do·nism /ˈhidn,ɪzəm/ *n.* [U] the belief that pleasure is the most important thing in life —**hedonist** *n.* —**hedonistic** /ˌhidnˈɪstɪk◂/ *adj.*

heed¹ /hid/ *v.* [T] *formal* to pay attention to someone's advice or warning: *Congress has taken heed of voter dissatisfation.*

heed² *n.* [U] *formal* **take heed of sth/pay heed to sth** to pay attention to something and think about it seriously

heed·less /ˈhidlɪs/ *adj. literary* not paying attention to something important

heel¹ /hil/ *n.* **1** [C] the back part of your foot **2** [C] the back raised part of a shoe, or the back part of a sock that is under your heel: *shoes with **high/low heels*** ➔ see picture at SHOE¹ **3 heels** [plural] ➔ HIGH HEELS **4 -heeled** having a particular type of heel: *a high-heeled shoe* **5 on the heels of sth** very soon after something: *The team's loss **came on the heels of** another defeat in Dallas.* **6** the raised part of your hand near your wrist: *Use **the heel of your hand** to knead the bread dough.*

heel² *v.* **heel!** used in order to tell your dog to stay near you

heels /hilz/ *n.* [plural] ➔ HIGH HEELS

heft·y /ˈhɛfti/ *adj.* **1** big, heavy, or strong: *a hefty man* **2 a hefty price/sum etc.** a large amount of money

heif·er /ˈhɛfɚ/ *n.* [C] a young female cow that has not yet given birth to a CALF (=baby cow)

height /haɪt/ *n.* **1** [C,U] how tall someone or something is: *Sue is about the same height as her mom.* | *Sunflowers can grow to **a height of** 15 feet.* **2** [C] a particular distance above the ground: *The shelves were installed **at** the wrong **height**.* **3 the height of sth a)** the period when something is the strongest, most intense, best, etc. it can ever be: ***At the height of** the dotcom boom, web designers were in short supply.* **b)** the greatest degree or amount of something: *rich people living in the height of luxury* **4 heights** [plural] high places: *I'm **afraid of heights**.* **5 to new heights** to an increased or more successful level: *Prices jumped to new heights Wednesday.*

height·en /ˈhaɪtˀn/ *v.* [I,T] to increase or make something become increased [**= increase, intensify**]: *Recent events have **heightened** residents' **awareness** of crime.*

hei·nous /ˈheɪnəs/ *adj.* extremely bad: *a heinous crime*

heir /ɛr/ *n.* [C] someone who will legally receive all of the money, property, etc. of a person who has died: *the sole **heir to** a vast fortune*

heir·ess /ˈɛrɪs/ *n.* [C] a woman who will legally receive all the money, property, etc. after an older member of her family dies

heir·loom /ˈɛrlum/ *n.* [C] a valuable object that a family owns for many years

heist /haɪst/ *n.* [C] *journalism* a BURGLARY

held /hɛld/ the past tense and past participle of HOLD

hel·i·cop·ter /ˈhɛlə,kɑptɚ/ *n.* [C] a type of aircraft with metal blades on top of it that spin very fast ➔ see picture at TRANSPORTATION

hel·i·port /ˈhɛlə,pɔrt/ *n.* [C] an airport for HELICOPTERS

he·li·um /ˈhiliəm/ *n.* [U] **He** a gas that is an ELEMENT and that is lighter than air, often used in order to make BALLOONS float

he'll /ɪl, il, hɪl; *strong* hil/ the short form of "he will": *I'm sure he'll get here soon.*

hell /hɛl/ **also Hell** *n.* [singular] the place where bad people will be punished after they die, according to some religions

hel·lo /həˈloʊ, hɛˈloʊ, ˈhɛloʊ/ *interjection* **1** used when meeting someone or greeting someone: *Hello, my name is Betty.*

COMMUNICATION

Ways of saying hello

hi informal
hey informal – only use this with people you know very well
how are you? also **how are you doing?**
how's it going? – used especially by young people
nice/good/glad to see you
good morning/afternoon/evening
pleased/nice/good to meet you
how do you do? formal – only use this when you meet someone for the first time
➔ GOODBYE, INTRODUCE

2 said when answering the telephone or when starting a telephone conversation: *"Hello?" "Hello, is Chad there?"* **3** said when trying to

H

get someone's attention: *Hello? Is anybody here?* **4 say hello** to have a quick conversation with someone: *I'll drop by later and say hello.*

helm /hɛlm/ *n.* [C] **1 at the helm (of sth)** controlling a group or organization: *With Ms. Mathis at the helm, the company has grown by 20%.* **2** a wheel used for guiding a ship's direction

hel·met /ˈhɛlmɪt/ *n.* [C] a hard hat that covers and protects your head: *a motorcycle helmet*

help¹ /hɛlp/ *v.* **1** [I,T] if you help someone, you do something for them that makes it easier for them to do something: *Do you want me to help you move that table?* | *Mom, can you* ***help*** *me* ***with*** *my homework?* | *Is there anything I can do to help?*

THESAURUS

give sb a hand (with sth) – to help someone do something: *Can you give me a hand moving these boxes?*
need a hand – to need help doing something: *I need a hand to paint the house.*
lend a hand (with sth) – to help someone, especially when there are not enough people to do something: *I went over to see if I could lend a hand.*
assist formal – to help someone, especially when you use special skills: *Dr. Taylor assisted in the research for this article.*

H

2 [I,T] to make it possible for something to become better, easier, or more developed: *It might* ***help to*** *talk to someone about your problems.* | *Brushing your teeth helps prevent cavities.*

SPOKEN PHRASES

3 can't/couldn't help said when you are unable to stop doing something: *I just couldn't help laughing.* **4 I can't help it** said when you think something is not your fault: *I can't help it if she lost the stupid book!* **5 help yourself** used when telling someone to take as much food or drink as s/he wants: ***Help yourself to*** *anything in the fridge.* **6 help!** said when you need someone to help you, especially because you are in danger

help (sb ⇔) **out** *phr. v.* to help someone because s/he is very busy, has a lot of problems, etc.: *They did everything they could to help us out.* | *Do you need anyone to help out in the store?*

help² *n.* **1** [U] the action of helping someone: *Do you* ***need*** *any* ***help*** *washing the dishes?* | *They* ***gave*** *us some* ***help*** *filling out the forms.* | *Dave built the garage* ***with the help of*** *his brother.* **2** [singular, U] someone or something that is useful or helpful: *The instructions* ***weren't much help.*** | *Thanks a lot – you've been* ***a big help.*** **3** [U] advice, treatment, money, etc. given in order to help someone: *professional help from a psychiatrist*

help·er /ˈhɛlpɚ/ *n.* [C] someone who helps another person

help·ful /ˈhɛlpfəl/ *adj.* **1** useful [≠ **unhelpful**]: *helpful advice* | *an extremely helpful guidebook* **2** willing to help: *Everyone was so helpful and friendly.* —**helpfully** *adv.*

help·ing¹ /ˈhɛlpɪŋ/ *n.* [C] the amount of food you are given or that you take: *Teri ate two* ***helpings of*** *pie.*

helping² *adj.* **lend/give a helping hand** to help someone

ˈhelping ˌverb *n. technical* ➔ AUXILIARY VERB

help·less /ˈhɛlplɪs/ *adj.* unable to take care of yourself or protect yourself: *The man lay helpless in the street.* —**helplessness** *n.* [U] —**helplessly** *adv.*

hel·ter-skel·ter /ˌhɛltɚˈskɛltɚ/ *adj., adv.* done in a disorganized, confusing, and hurried way

hem¹ /hɛm/ *n.* [C] the folded and sewn edge of a piece of clothing

hem² *v.* past tense and past participle **hemmed**, present participle **hemming** [T] to fold and sew the edge of a piece of clothing

hem sb ⇔ **in** *v.* **1** to surround someone or something closely: *The valley is hemmed in by mountain ranges on both sides.* **2** to make someone feel that s/he is not free to do what s/he wants: *She felt hemmed in by her tight schedule.*

hem·i·sphere /ˈhɛməˌsfɪr/ *n.* [C] one of the halves of the earth, especially the northern or southern parts above and below the EQUATOR: *the* ***northern/southern hemisphere*** ➔ see picture at GLOBE

hem·line /ˈhɛmlaɪn/ *n.* [C] the bottom edge or length of a dress, skirt, or pair of pants

hem·lock /ˈhɛmlɑk/ *n.* [C,U] a very poisonous plant, or the poison of this plant

he·mo·glo·bin /ˈhiməˌgloʊbɪn/ *n.* [U] a red substance in the blood that carries oxygen and iron

he·mo·phil·i·a /ˌhiməˈfɪliə, -ˈfilyə/ *n.* [U] a serious disease that usually affects only men, in which the blood does not become thick, so that they lose too much blood after being cut or wounded —**hemophiliac** /ˌhiməˈfɪliˌæk/ *n.* [C]

hem·or·rhage /ˈhɛmərɪdʒ/ *n.* [C] a serious medical condition in which an area in someone's body loses too much blood

hem·or·rhoids /ˈhɛməˌrɔɪdz/ *n.* [plural] painfully swollen BLOOD VESSELS at the ANUS

hemp /hɛmp/ *n.* [U] a plant used for making strong rope, a rough cloth, and the drug MARIJUANA

hen /hɛn/ *n.* [C] a fully grown female bird, especially a female chicken

hence /hɛns/ *adv. formal* for this reason: *The sugar from the grapes remains in the wine, hence the sweet taste.*

hence·forth /ˈhɛnsfɔrθ, ˌhɛnsˈfɔrθ/ *adv. formal* from this time on: *Henceforth in this book, these people will be called "The Islanders."*

hench·man /ˈhɛntʃmən/ *n.* [C] someone who faithfully obeys a powerful person such as a politician or a criminal

hep·a·ti·tis /ˌhɛpəˈtaɪt̬ɪs/ *n.* [U] a serious disease of the LIVER

her[1] /ɚ; *strong* hɚ/ *adj.* **1** belonging to or relating to a female person or animal that has been mentioned or is known about: *Lori said her cat died last week.* | *Have you seen her new house?* **2** used when talking about a country, car, ship, etc. that has been mentioned: *Her top speed is 110 miles per hour.*

her[2] *pron.* **1** the object form of "she": *I gave her $20.* | *Did you see her at the concert?* **2** a country, ship, car, etc. that has been mentioned

her·ald /ˈhɛrəld/ *v.* [T] **1** to say publicly that someone or something is likely to be successful: *He was* ***heralded as*** *the poet of his generation.* **2** to be a sign that something is going to come or happen soon: *The Internet heralded a new age of communications.*

herb /ɚb/ *n.* [C] a plant used in cooking to give food more taste, or to make medicine: *herbs and spices*

herb·al /ˈɚbəl/ *adj.* relating to HERBS: *herbal tea*

herb·i·vore /ˈhɚbəˌvɔr, ˈɚbə-/ *n.* [C] *technical* an animal that only eats plants ➔ —compare CARNIVORE

herd[1] /hɚd/ *n.* [C] a group of a particular type of animal that lives together: *a* ***herd of*** *cattle*

THESAURUS

flock, school, shoal, pack, litter
➔ see Thesaurus box at GROUP[1]

herd[2] *v.* [I,T] to form a group, or to make people or animals move together as a group: *The tour guide herded us onto the bus.*

here[1] /hɪr/ *adv.* **1** in or to this place: *I'm going to stay here with Kim.* | *How long have you lived here?* | *Chuck said he's never been here before.* | *It's so dark* ***in/out here***. | *Come* ***over here*** *so I can talk to you.* **2** if a period of time is here, it has begun: *Spring is here!* **3 here and there** scattered in several different places: *There were a few magazines lying around here and there.* **4** at this point in a discussion or piece of writing: *We might as well take a break here.*

here[2] *interjection* said when you offer something to someone: *Here, use my pen.*

here·a·bouts /ˈhɪrəˌbaʊts, ˌhɪrəˈbaʊts/ *adv.* around or near the place where you are: *Everyone hereabouts thinks he's guilty.*

here·af·ter[1] /ˌhɪrˈæftɚ/ *adv. formal* from this time or in the future

hereafter[2] *n.* **the hereafter** life after you die: *Do you believe in the hereafter?*

here·by /ˌhɪrˈbaɪ, ˈhɪrbaɪ/ *adv. formal* as a result of this statement: *I hereby pronounce you man and wife.*

he·red·i·tar·y /həˈrɛdəˌtɛri/ *adj.* if a mental or physical quality, or a disease is hereditary, it is passed to a child from the GENES of his/her parents: *a hereditary condition*

he·red·i·ty /həˈrɛdət̬i/ *n.* [U] the process of passing on a mental or physical quality from a parent's GENES to a child

here·in /ˌhɪrˈɪn/ *adv. formal* in this place, situation, or piece of writing

her·e·sy /ˈhɛrəsi/ *n.* plural **heresies** [C,U] a belief that a religious, political, or social group considers to be wrong or evil

her·e·tic /ˈhɛrətɪk/ *n.* [C] someone whose beliefs are considered to be wrong or evil —**heretical** /həˈrɛt̬ɪkəl/ *adj.*

here·with /ˌhɪrˈwɪθ, -ˈwɪð/ *adv. formal* with this letter or document

her·it·age /ˈhɛrət̬ɪdʒ/ *n.* [C,U] the traditional beliefs, values, CUSTOMS, etc. of a family, group of people, or country: *Black Americans' cultural heritage*

her·met·i·cal·ly /hɚˈmɛt̬ɪkli/ *adv. technical* **hermetically sealed** very tightly closed so that no air can get in or out —**hermetic** *adj.*

her·mit /ˈhɚmɪt/ *n.* [C] someone who prefers to live far away from other people

her·ni·a /ˈhɚniə/ *n.* [C,U] a medical condition in which an organ pushes through the skin or muscle that covers it

he·ro /ˈhɪroʊ/ *n.* [C] plural **heroes** **1** someone who is admired for doing something very brave or good: *one of America's* ***national heroes*** | *It was a chance to meet my hero in person.* **2** someone, especially a man or boy, who is the main character of a book, play, or movie [➡ **heroine**]: *The* ***hero of*** *the story is a young soldier.* **3 also hero sandwich** ➔ SUB

he·ro·ic /hɪˈroʊɪk/ *adj.* **1** admired for being brave, strong, and determined: *the firefighters'* ***heroic efforts*** *to rescue people from the fire* **2** a heroic story, poem, etc. has a HERO in it

he·ro·ics /hɪˈroʊɪks/ *n.* [plural] brave or impressive actions or words that someone does in order to seem impressive to other people

her·o·in /ˈhɛroʊɪn/ *n.* [U] a strong illegal drug that people often take by putting it into their arms with a special needle

her·o·ine /ˈhɛroʊɪn/ *n.* [C] a female HERO

her·o·ism /ˈhɛroʊˌɪzəm/ *n.* [U] very great courage: *the soldiers' heroism in battle*

her·on /ˈhɛrən/ *n.* [C] a large wild bird with very long legs and a long beak that lives near water

her·pes /ˈhɚpiz/ *n.* [U] a very infectious disease that causes spots on the skin, especially on the face or sexual organs

her·ring /ˈhɛrɪŋ/ *n.* [C,U] plural **herring** or **herrings** a long thin silver sea fish, or the meat from this fish

hers /hɚz/ *pron.* the thing or things belonging to or relating to a female person or animal that has been mentioned or is known about: *That's my car. This is hers.* | *Tim is a friend of hers.* | *My boots are black. Hers are brown.*

her·self /ɚ'sɛlf; *strong* hɚ'sɛlf/ *pron.* **1** the REFLEXIVE form of "she": *Carol hurt herself.* | *She bought herself a new scarf.* **2** the strong form of "she," used in order to emphasize the subject or object of a sentence: *She installed the cabinets herself.* | *It's true! Vicky told me herself.* **3 (all) by herself a)** without help: *My daughter made dinner all by herself.* **b)** alone: *She went for a walk by herself.* **4 (all) to herself** for her own use: *Alison had the whole house to herself that night.* **5 not be herself** *spoken* if someone is not herself, she is not behaving or feeling the way she usually does because she is sick or upset: *Mom hasn't been herself lately.*

hertz /hɚts/ *written abbreviation* **Hz** *n.* [C] plural **hertz** a unit for measuring sound WAVES

he's /iz; *strong* hiz/ **1** the short form of "he is": *He's a lawyer.* **2** the short form of "he has," used when "has" is an AUXILIARY VERB: *He's been in prison.*

hes·i·tant /'hɛzət̬ənt/ *adj.* not willing to do or say something because you are uncertain or worried: *He was **hesitant to** discuss the details.*

hes·i·tate /'hɛzə,teɪt/ *v.* [I] **1** to pause before doing or saying something because you are uncertain: *She hesitated before answering his question.* **2 do not hesitate to do sth** *formal* used in order to tell someone not to worry about doing something: *Don't hesitate to call me if you need any help.*

H

hes·i·ta·tion /,hɛzə'teɪʃən/ *n.* [U] the action of hesitating: ***Without hesitation** he said, "Yes!"*

het·er·o·ge·ne·ous /,hɛt̬ərə'dʒiniəs, -nyəs/ **het·er·og·e·nous** /,hɛt̬ə'rɑdʒənəs/ *adj. formal* consisting of parts or members that are very different from each other [➡ **homogeneous**]: *a heterogeneous population* —**heterogeneity** /,hɛt̬əroʊdʒə'niət̬i/ *n.* [U]

het·er·o·sex·u·al /,hɛt̬ərə'sɛkʃuəl/ *adj. formal* sexually attracted to people of the opposite sex [= **straight**; ➡ **bisexual**, **homosexual**] —**heterosexuality** /,hɛt̬ərə,sɛkʃu'æləti/ *n.* [U]

hew /hyu/ *v.* past tense and past participle **hewed** or **hewn** /hyun/ [T] *literary* to cut something with a cutting tool

hex·a·gon /'hɛksə,gɑn/ *n.* [C] a flat shape with six sides —**hexagonal** /hɛk'sægənəl/ *adj.*

hey /heɪ/ *interjection* **1** said in order to get someone's attention, or to show someone you are surprised or annoyed: *Hey, you! Get away from my car!* **2** said in order to greet someone who you know well [= **hi**]: *Hey, Rob. How's it going?*

hey·day /'heɪdeɪ/ *n.* [C] the time when someone or something was most popular, successful, or powerful: *the **heyday of** silent movies*

HI the written abbreviation of **Hawaii**

hi /haɪ/ *interjection informal* hello: *Hi! How are you?*

hi·a·tus /haɪ'eɪt̬əs/ *n.* [C usually singular] *formal* a pause in an activity

hi·ber·nate /'haɪbɚ,neɪt/ *v.* [I] if an animal hibernates, it sleeps all the time during the winter —**hibernation** /,haɪbɚ'neɪʃən/ *n.* [U]

hic·cup[1] /'hɪkʌp/ *n.* [C usually plural] **1** a sudden repeated stopping of the breath, usually caused by eating or drinking too fast: *I **have** the **hiccups**.* **2** a small problem or delay: *There's a slight **hiccup in** the schedule for today.*

hiccup[2] *v.* past tense and past participle **-pped**, present participle **-pping** [I] to have the HICCUPS

hick /hɪk/ *n.* [C] *disapproving* someone who lives in the country and is thought to be uneducated or stupid

hick·ey /'hɪki/ *n.* plural **hickeys** [C] *informal* a slight BRUISE (=dark mark on your skin) from being kissed too hard

hick·o·ry /'hɪkəri/ *n.* [U] a North American tree that produces nuts, or the hard wood from this tree

hid /hɪd/ *v.* the past tense of HIDE

hid·den[1] /'hɪdn/ *v.* the past participle of HIDE

hidden[2] *adj.* **1** difficult to see or find: *Marcia **kept** her letters **hidden in** a box.* **2** not easy to notice or discover: *a hidden meaning*

hide

hide[1] /haɪd/ past tense **hid** /hɪd/ past participle **hidden** /'hɪdn/ *v.* **1** [T] to put something in a place where no one else can see or find it: *Jane **hid** the Christmas presents **in** the closet.*

THESAURUS

conceal formal – to hide something carefully: *She dyes her hair to conceal the gray.*
cover/cover up – to put something over the top of something else in order to hide it: *A green blanket covered the old chair.*
disguise – to change your appearance or voice so that people cannot recognize you: *In the story, the queen disguises herself as an old woman.*

2 [I] to go to or stay in a place where no one can see or find you: *I'll **hide behind/under** the bed.* **3** [T] to not show your feelings to people, or to not tell someone about something: *She could not hide her embarrassment.* **4** [T] to not tell someone about something: *The police knew Wilson was hiding something.*

hide[2] *n.* [C] an animal's skin, especially when it is removed to be used for leather

,hide-and-'seek *n.* [U] a children's game in which one child shuts his/her eyes while the other children hide, and then s/he tries to find them

hide·a·way /ˈhaɪdəˌweɪ/ *n.* plural **hideaways** [C] a place where you can go to hide or be alone

hid·e·ous /ˈhɪdiəs/ *adj.* extremely ugly or disgusting: *a hideous monster* —**hideously** *adv.*

hide·out /ˈhaɪdaʊt/ *n.* [C] a place where you can hide

hid·ing /ˈhaɪdɪŋ/ *n.* **go into hiding** to stay somewhere in secret, often because you have done something illegal or you are in danger

hi·er·ar·chy /ˈhaɪəˌrɑrki/ *n.* plural **hierarchies** **1** [C,U] a system of organization in which people have higher and lower ranks **2** [C] the most powerful members of an organization —**hierarchical** /haɪəˈrɑrkɪkəl/ *adj.*

hi·er·o·glyph·ics /ˌhaɪrəˈglɪfɪks/ *n.* [U] a system of writing that uses pictures to represent words —**hieroglyphic** *adj.*

hi-fi /ˌhaɪ ˈfaɪ/ *n.* [C] *old-fashioned* a piece of electronic equipment for playing recorded music

high[1] /haɪ/ *adj.*

1 TALL having a top that is a long distance from its bottom [≠ **low**; ➡ **tall**]: *the highest mountain in Colorado | a high wall*

2 ABOVE GROUND being a long way above the ground: *The shelf was too high for me.*

USAGE

Use **tall** to talk about the height of people and trees: *She's only five feet tall. | a road with tall trees on either side*

Use **tall** to talk about other narrow objects: *an old house with tall chimneys | the tall mast of a ship*

Use **high** to talk about mountains, walls, fences, etc.: *the highest mountain in the world | How high will the wall be?*

Use **high** to talk about how far something is from the ground: *The shelf's too high for the kids to reach.*

You can use both **tall** and **high** to talk about buildings: *one of the highest buildings in the world | a city with crowded streets and tall buildings*

3 MORE THAN USUAL a high amount, number, or level is greater than usual: *clothes selling at **high prices** | high speed | a higher level of productivity*

4 RANK/POSITION having an important or powerful position or rank: *She was elected to **high office**. | the highest levels of management*

5 GOOD very good: *Most items were of very **high quality**. | We insist on **high standards**.*

6 DRUGS under the effects of drugs: *He was **high on** drugs. | kids **getting high** on marijuana*

7 CONTAINING A LOT containing a lot of a particular substance or quality: *Candy bars are **high in** calories.*

8 SOUND/VOICE near the top of the range of sounds that humans can hear: *singing the high notes*

THESAURUS

high-pitched – higher than most sounds or voices: *a high-pitched voice*

piercing – very high and loud in a way that is not nice to listen to: *a piercing scream*

shrill – high and unpleasant: *a shrill whistle*

squeaky – making very high noises that are not loud: *squeaky floorboards*

9 knee-high/waist-high etc. having a particular height: *The grass was knee-high.*

10 high noon *old-fashioned* exactly 12 O'CLOCK in the day

high[2] *adv.* **1** at or to a level that is far above the ground: *kites flying **high in** the sky | She held her award high above her head.* **2** at or to a high value, amount, rank, etc.: *Jenkins has risen high in the company. | Ribas advised the students to "**aim high**."* (=try to be successful) **3 look/search high and low** to look everywhere for someone or something: *I searched high and low for the car keys.* **4 be left high and dry** *informal* to be left without any help in a difficult situation

high[3] *n.* [C] **1** the highest level, number, temperature, etc. that has been recorded in a particular time period: *The price of gold **reached a new high** yesterday. | a high* (=high temperature) *in the mid 90s* **2** *informal* a feeling of great excitement caused by drugs or success, enjoyment, etc.

high·brow /ˈhaɪbraʊ/ *adj.* a highbrow book, movie, etc. is very serious and may be difficult to understand

high·chair /ˈhaɪtʃɛr/ *n.* [C] a tall chair that a baby sits in to eat

ˌhigh-ˈclass *adj.* of good quality and style, and usually expensive: *a high-class restaurant*

ˌhigher eduˈcation *n.* [U] education at a college or university

ˌhigh-ˈgrade *adj.* of high quality: *high-grade motor oil*

ˌhigh ˈheels *n.* [plural] women's shoes with a high HEEL (=raised part at the back) —**high-heeled** *adj.* ➔ see picture at SHOE[1]

ˈhigh jinks *n.* [U] *old-fashioned* noisy or excited behavior when people are having fun

ˈhigh jump *n.* **the high jump** a sport in which you run and jump over a BAR that is raised higher after each successful jump —**high jumper** *n.* [C]

high·lands /ˈhaɪləndz/ *n.* [plural] an area with a lot of mountains

ˌhigh-ˈlevel *adj.* involving important people, especially in the government: *high-level peace talks*

high·light[1] /ˈhaɪlaɪt/ *v.* [T] **1** to make a problem, subject, etc. easy to notice so people will pay attention to it: *The report highlights the problem of inner-city crime.*

THESAURUS

emphasize, stress, underline, accentuate, underscore

➔ see Thesaurus box at EMPHASIZE

2 to mark written words with a pen or on a computer so you can see them more easily

highlight² *n.* [C] the most important or exciting part of a movie, sports event, etc.: *the **highlights** of our trip*

high·light·er /ˈhaɪˌlaɪtə/ *n.* [C] a special pen that you use to mark written words so that you can see them more easily ➔ see picture on page A11

high·ly /ˈhaɪli/ *adv.* **1** very: *a **highly successful** meeting* | ***highly skilled** workers* **2** to a high level or degree: *a highly paid attorney*

ˌhigh-ˈminded *adj.* having high moral standards or principles

High·ness /ˈhaɪnɪs/ *n.* **Your/His etc. Highness** a royal title used when speaking to a king, queen, etc.

ˌhigh-ˈpitched *adj.* a high-pitched song or voice is higher than most sounds or voices

THESAURUS
high, piercing, shrill, squeaky
➔ see Thesaurus box at HIGH¹

ˌhigh-ˈpowered *adj.* **1** very powerful: *a high-powered speedboat* **2** very important or successful: *a high-powered businessman*

ˌhigh-ˈpressure *adj.* **1** a high-pressure job or situation is one in which you need to work very hard to be successful **2** having or using a lot of pressure: *a high-pressure hose*

ˌhigh-ˈprofile *adj.* attracting a lot of attention from people: *a high-profile court case*

ˈhigh-rise, high·rise /ˈhaɪraɪz/ *n.* [C] a tall building —**high-rise** *adj.*: *high-rise apartment buildings*

ˌhigh ˈroller *n.* [C] *informal* someone who spends a lot of money, especially by BETting on games, races, etc.

ˈhigh school *n.* [C,U] a school in the U.S. and Canada for students over the age of 14: *Most **high school students** take three years of math.* | *Wendy and I were best friends **in high school**.*

ˈhigh-speed *adj.* [only before noun] designed to travel or operate very fast: *a high-speed train*

ˌhigh-ˈspirited *adj.* having a lot of energy and liking to have fun: *a high-spirited four-year-old boy*

ˌhigh-ˈstrung *adj.* nervous, and easily upset or excited: *a high-strung horse*

high-tech, hi-tech /ˌhaɪ ˈtɛk◂/ *adj.* using the most modern information, machines, etc.: *a new high-tech camera*

THESAURUS
advanced, sophisticated, state-of-the-art, cutting-edge
➔ see Thesaurus box at ADVANCED

ˌhigh ˈtide *n.* [C,U] the time when the sea is at its highest level ➔ see picture at TIDE¹

ˈhigh-tops, high·tops /ˈhaɪtɑps/ *n.* [plural] sports shoes that cover your ANKLES

high·way /ˈhaɪweɪ/ *n.* plural **highways** [C] a wide fast road that connects cities or towns: *There's always a lot of traffic **on** that **highway**.*

THESAURUS
freeway, expressway, turnpike
➔ see Thesaurus box at ROAD

hi·jack /ˈhaɪdʒæk/ *v.* [T] **1** to take control of an airplane, vehicle, etc. illegally: *The plane was hijacked by terrorists.* **2** to take control of something and use it for your own purposes: *The protesters tried to hijack the meeting.* —**hijacker** *n.* [C] —**hijacking** *n.* [C,U]

hike¹ /haɪk/ *n.* [C] **1** a long walk in the country, mountains, etc.: *We **went for a hike** on Sunday.* **2** *informal* a large increase in something: *a huge **tax hike*** **3 take a hike** *spoken* a rude way of telling someone to go away

hike² *v.* **1** [I,T] to take a long walk in the country, mountains, etc.

THESAURUS
march, stride, stroll, amble, wander, creep, sneak, trudge, limp, wade
➔ see Thesaurus box at WALK¹

2 [T] **also hike** sth ⇔ **up** to increase the price of something by a large amount: *The governor plans to hike gasoline tax next month.*

hik·ing /ˈhaɪkɪŋ/ *n.* [U] an outdoor activity in which you take long walks in the mountains or country: *We could **go hiking** tomorrow.*

hi·lar·i·ous /hɪˈlɛriəs, -ˈlær-/ *adj.* extremely funny: *a hilarious video* —**hilariously** *adv.* —**hilarity** /hɪˈlærəṭi/ *n.* [U]

THESAURUS
funny, hysterical, witty, amusing, humorous
➔ see Thesaurus box at FUNNY¹

hill /hɪl/ *n.* [C] **1** an area of high land, like a small mountain: *driving up a steep hill* **2 over the hill** *informal* no longer young, or too old to do a job well **3 the Hill** ➔ CAPITOL HILL —**hilly** *adj.*

hill·bil·ly /ˈhɪlˌbɪli/ *n.* plural **hillbillies** [C] someone who lives in the mountains and is thought to be uneducated or stupid

hill·side /ˈhɪlsaɪd/ *n.* [C] the side of a hill

hilt /hɪlt/ *n.* **1 to the hilt** completely or extremely: *Their house had been mortgaged to the hilt.* **2** [C] the handle of a sword or a large knife

him /ɪm; *strong* hɪm/ *pron.* the object form of "he": *Why don't you just ask him yourself?* | *The cop ordered him out of the car.*

him·self /ɪmˈsɛlf; *strong* hɪmˈsɛlf/ *pron.* **1** the REFLEXIVE form of "he": *Bill looked at himself in the mirror.* **2** the strong form of "he," used in order to emphasize the subject or object of a sentence: *It's true! He told me himself.* **3 (all) by himself a)** without help: *He tried to fix the car by himself.* **b)** alone: *Sam was all by himself on the mountain trail.* **4 (all) to himself** *spoken* for his own use: *Ben had the house to himself for a*

H

week. **5 not feel/look/seem like himself** if someone does not feel like himself, he is not behaving or feeling as he usually does, because he is sick or upset

hind /haɪnd/ *adj.* **hind legs/feet** the back legs or feet of an animal ➔ see picture on page A2

hin·der /ˈhɪndɚ/ *v.* [T] to make it difficult for someone to do something: *The bad weather is hindering rescue efforts.*

Hin·di /ˈhɪndi/ *n.* [U] a language used in India

hind·quar·ters /ˈhaɪndˌkwɔrt̬ɚz/ *n.* [plural] *formal* the back part of an animal

hin·drance /ˈhɪndrəns/ *n.* [C] someone or something that makes it difficult for you to do something: *Students' family problems can be a **hindrance to** their education.*

hind·sight /ˈhaɪndsaɪt/ *n.* [U] the ability to understand something after it has happened: ***In hindsight**, it was a terrible mistake.*

Hin·du /ˈhɪndu/ *n.* [C] someone who believes in Hinduism —**Hindu** *adj.*

Hin·du·ism /ˈhɪnduˌɪzəm/ *n.* [U] the main religion in India, which includes belief in REINCARNATION

hinge¹ /hɪndʒ/ *n.* [C] a metal part that joins two things together, such as a door and a frame, so that one part can swing open and shut —**hinged** *adj.*

hinge² *v.*
hinge on/upon sth *phr. v.* to depend on something: *His political future hinges on this election.*

hint¹ /hɪnt/ *n.* [C] **1** something that you say or do that helps someone guess what you really want: *Come on, **give** me **a hint**.* | *Sue has been **dropping hints*** (=giving hints) *about what she wants for her birthday.* **2 a hint of sth** a small amount of something: *a hint of perfume in the air* **3** a useful piece of advice on how to do something: *a book full of **hints on** gardening*

hint² *v.* [I,T] to say something that helps someone guess what you want, or what will happen: *Irene **hinted that** I might get a raise.*

hin·ter·land /ˈhɪntɚˌlænd/ *n.* **the hinterland** the inner part of a country, usually away from cities or the coast

hip¹ /hɪp/ *n.* [C] one of the two parts on either side of your body, where your legs join your body: *She stood there with her **hands on** her **hips**.* ➔ see picture on page A3

hip² *adj. informal* modern and fashionable: *a hip new comedy on NBC*

ˈhip-hop *n.* [U] **1** a type of dance music with a strong regular beat and spoken words

THESAURUS

pop (music), rock (music), rock'n'roll, heavy metal, reggae, house (music), rap (music), jazz, classical (music), country (music), folk (music)
➔ see Thesaurus box at MUSIC

2 a type of popular culture among young people in big cities which includes RAP music, dancing, and GRAFFITI art

hip·pie, hippy /ˈhɪpi/ *n.* [C] someone, especially in the 1960s and 1970s, who usually had long hair, opposed the standards of society, and took drugs for pleasure

hip·po·pot·a·mus /ˌhɪpəˈpɑt̬əməs/ **also hip·po** /ˈhɪpoʊ/ *n.* plural **hippopotamuses** [C] a large African animal with a big head, fat body, and thick gray skin, that lives in and near water

hire¹ /haɪɚ/ *v.* [T] to employ someone to work for you: *We're going to **hire** a lawyer **to** handle the case.*

hire² *n.* [C] someone who has recently been hired by a company: *All **new hires** will receive training.*

his¹ /ɪz; *strong* hɪz/ *determiner* belonging to or relating to a male person or animal that has been mentioned or is known about: *Leo hates cleaning his room.*

his² *pron.* the thing or things belonging to or relating to a male person or animal that has been mentioned or is known about: *I think he has my suitcase, and I have his.* | *Dave is a friend **of his**.* | *My boots are black. His are brown.*

His·pan·ic /hɪˈspænɪk/ *adj.* from or relating to a country where Spanish or Portuguese is spoken —**Hispanic** *n.* [C]

hiss /hɪs/ *v.* [I] to make a noise that sounds like "ssss": *steam hissing from the pipe* —**hiss** *n.* [C] ➔ see picture on page A7

his·to·ri·an /hɪˈstɔriən/ *n.* [C] someone who studies or writes about history

his·tor·ic /hɪˈstɔrɪk, -ˈstɑr-/ *adj.* a historic place or event is important as a part of history: *important **historic sites*** | *"This is a **historic moment**," he told journalists.*

his·tor·i·cal /hɪˈstɔrɪkəl, -ˈstɑr-/ *adj.* **1** relating to the study of history: *a collection of historical documents* **2** historical events, people, etc. really happened or existed in the past

his·to·ry /ˈhɪstəri/ *n.* **1** [U] all the things that happened in the past: ***Throughout history**, wars have been fought over religion.* | *Lincoln has an important place **in** American **history**.* **2** [U] the study of history, especially the political, social, or economic development of a particular country: *a class in European history* **3** [C] a book about events that happened in the past: *a **history of** the Roman empire* **4 be (ancient) history** *spoken* to not exist any more or not affect you any more: *One more losing season, and the coach will be history.* **5 have a history of sth** to have had illness, problems, etc. in the past: *Paul has a history of heart disease.* **6 make history/go down in history** to do something important that will be remembered

H

his·tri·on·ics /ˌhɪstriˈɑnɪks/ *n.* [plural] *disapproving* behavior that is very emotional but is not sincere —**histrionic** *adj.*

hit[1] /hɪt/ *v.* past tense and past participle **hit**, present participle **hitting** [T]
1 STRIKE to swing your hand, or something held in your hand, hard against someone or something: *He **hit** the boy **on the nose**. | She swung the bat and hit the ball.*

THESAURUS

punch – to hit someone hard with your closed hand, especially in a fight: *Steve punched him in the nose.*
slap – to hit someone with the flat part of your hand, especially because you are angry with them: *I felt like slapping his face.*
beat – to hit someone or something deliberately many times, or to hit against the surface of something continuously: *He had been robbed and beaten. | The wind howled and rain beat against the windows.*
smack – to hit someone or something, usually with your open hand: *Rick smacked him in the face. | Should a parent ever smack a child?*
whack informal – to hit someone or something very hard: *Edmonds whacked the ball over the fence.*
strike formal – to hit someone or something very hard: *She had been struck on the side of the head.*
knock – to hit a door or window with your closed hand in order to attract the attention of the people inside: *Someone was knocking on the door.*
bang – to make a loud noise, especially by hitting something against something hard: *A policeman was banging on the door.*
tap – to gently hit your fingers or foot against something: *I tapped him on the shoulder.*
pound – to knock very hard, making a lot of noise: *Thomas pounded on the door with his fist.*
rap – to knock quickly several times: *She rapped on his window angrily.*
hammer – to hit against something several times, making a lot of noise: *They hammered on my door until I opened up.*

2 CRASH to crash into someone or something quickly and hard: *Ann's car hit a tree. | I hit my head on the table.*

THESAURUS

bump – to hit or knock against something, especially by accident: *I bumped my head on the wall.*
collide – to crash violently into something or someone: *The two cars almost collided.*
bang – to hit a part of your body against something by accident: *I banged my toe on the dresser.*

3 BAD EFFECT to have a bad effect on someone or something: *The state's economy has been hit by budget cuts.*
4 BULLET/BOMB to wound someone or damage something with a bullet or bomb: *Over 90% of the bombs hit their intended targets.*
5 REACH STH to reach a particular level, number, position, etc.: *Unemployment has hit a new high, at 11.3%. | We'll hit the exit in three miles.*
6 hit it off (with sb) *informal* to like someone as soon as you meet him/her
7 THINK OF if an idea, thought, etc. hits you, you suddenly think of it: *It suddenly hit me that he was just lonely.*
8 hit the roof/ceiling *informal* to become very angry: *Cheryl really hit the roof when I told her.*
9 hit the road *informal* to start on a trip
10 hit the hay/sack *spoken* to go to bed
11 hit the spot *spoken* if a food or drink hits the spot, it tastes good and is exactly what you want
→ **hit the bottle** at BOTTLE[1]

hit back *phr. v.* to attack or criticize someone who is attacking or criticizing you: *Today the President **hit back at** his critics.*

hit on sb/sth *phr. v.* **1 hit on** sth to have a good idea about something, often by chance: *Turner may have hit on a solution.* **2 hit on** sb *informal* to try to talk to someone whom you are sexually interested in: *Men are always trying to hit on me at parties.*

hit sb **up for** sth *phr. v.* *spoken* to ask someone for something: *Mitch hit him up for a loan.*

hit[2] *n.* [C] **1** a movie, song, play, etc. that is very successful: *Her first novel was a **big hit**.*

THESAURUS

bestseller, **blockbuster**
→ see Thesaurus box at POPULAR

2 the action of successfully striking something you are aiming at: *The missile scored a **direct hit**.* **3 be a hit (with sb)** to be liked very much by someone: *These brownies are always a hit.* **4** a quick hard blow with your hand, or with something in your hand

ˌhit-and-ˈmiss also **ˌhit-or-ˈmiss** *adj.* *informal* done in a way that is not planned or organized well

ˌhit-and-ˈrun *adj.* a hit-and-run accident is one in which a car hits someone and then drives away without stopping to help

hitch[1] /hɪtʃ/ *v.* **1** [I,T] *informal* to travel by asking for free rides in other people's cars [= **hitchhike**]: *We **hitched a ride with** a couple from Florida.* **2** [T] to fasten something to something else: *Dad finished **hitching** the trailer **to** the car.* **3 get hitched** *informal* to get married

hitch sth ⇔ **up** *phr. v.* to pull a piece of clothing up: *Bill hitched up his pants.*

hitch[2] *n.* [C] **1** a small problem that causes a delay: *The performance **went off without a hitch*** (=happened with no problems).

THESAURUS

problem, setback, snag
➔ see Thesaurus box at PROBLEM

2 a part on a vehicle that is used to connect it to something it is pulling

hitch·hike /ˈhɪtʃhaɪk/ *v.* [I] to travel by asking for free rides in other people's cars —**hitchhiker** *n.* [C] —**hitchhiking** *n.* [U]

hi-tech *adj.* another spelling of HIGH-TECH

hith·er /ˈhɪðɚ/ *adv. literary* **1** *old-fashioned* here, to this place **2 hither and thither/yon** in many directions

hith·er·to /ˌhɪðɚˈtu, ˈhɪðɚˌtu/ *adv. formal* up until now: *a hitherto unexplored land*

ˈhit list *n.* [C usually singular] *informal* the names of people, organizations, etc. whom you would like to damage, hurt, or deal with

ˈhit man *n.* [C] *informal* a criminal whose job is to kill someone

HIV *n.* [U] **Human Immunodeficiency Virus** a type of VIRUS that enters the body through the blood or sexual activity, and can cause AIDS: *Brad tested* ***HIV positive*** (=he has HIV).

hive /haɪv/ *n.* **1** [C] **also beehive** a place where BEES live **2 hives** [plural] a condition in which someone's skin swells and becomes red, usually because s/he is ALLERGIC to something

hmm, hm /hm, hmh/ *interjection* a sound that you make to express doubt or disagreement

HMO *n.* [C] **health maintenance organization** a type of health insurance organization in which members can only go to doctors and hospitals that are part of the organization

ho *interjection* used in writing to represent a shout of laughter in a deep voice

hoard¹ /hɔrd/ **also hoard up** *v.* [T] to collect things in large amounts and keep them in a secret place: *Fearful citizens were hoarding food in case of war.*

hoard² *n.* [C] a group of valuable things that someone has hidden to keep it safe: *a* ***hoard of*** *gold*

hoarse /hɔrs/ *adj.* someone who is hoarse has a voice that sounds rough, often because of a sore throat

hoax /hoʊks/ *n.* [C] a trick that makes someone believe something that is not true: *The bomb threat turned out to be a hoax.* —**hoaxer** *n.* [C]

hob·ble /ˈhɑbəl/ *v.* [I] to walk with difficulty, taking small steps, usually because you are injured

hob·by /ˈhɑbi/ *n.* plural **hobbies** [C] an activity that you enjoy doing in your free time: *Do you* ***have a hobby****? | I started painting* ***as a hobby****.*

THESAURUS

game, sport, recreation
➔ see Thesaurus box at GAME¹

ho·bo /ˈhoʊboʊ/ *n.* plural **hoboes** or **hobos** [C] *old-fashioned* someone who travels around and has no home or regular job

hock¹ /hɑk/ *v.* [T] *informal* to PAWN something

hock² *n.* **be in hock** *informal* to be in debt

hock·ey /ˈhɑki/ *n.* [U] **also ice hockey** a sport played on ice in which players use long curved sticks to try to hit a hard flat round object into a GOAL [➡ **field hockey**]: *a* ***hockey team/player/game***

hodge·podge /ˈhɑdʒpɑdʒ/ *n.* [singular] a lot of things put together with no order or arrangement: *a* ***hodgepodge of*** *artistic styles*

hoe /hoʊ/ *n.* [C] a garden tool with a long handle, used for making the soil loose and for removing wild plants —**hoe** *v.* [I,T]

hog¹ /hɔg, hɑg/ *n.* [C] **1** a large pig that is kept for its meat **2** *informal* someone who keeps or uses all of something for himself/herself **3 go (the) whole hog** *informal* to do something thoroughly or completely

hog² *v.* past tense and past participle **hogged**, present participle **hogging** [T] *informal* to keep or use all of something for yourself in a way that is unfair: *My sister was hogging the mirror.*

ho-hum /ˌhoʊ ˈhʌm/ *adj. informal* disappointing or boring: *a ho-hum movie*

hoist¹ /hɔɪst/ *v.* [T] to raise or lift something, especially using ropes or a special machine

hoist² *n.* [C] a piece of equipment used for lifting heavy things

ho·key /ˈhoʊki/ *adj. informal disapproving* expressing emotions in a way that seems old-fashioned, silly, or too simple: *a hokey love song*

hold¹ /hoʊld/ *v.* past tense and past participle **held** /hɛld/

1 IN YOUR HANDS/ARMS [T] to have something firmly in your hands or arms: *Will you hold my purse for a minute? | Hold my hand when we cross the street. | He* ***held*** *it carefully* ***in*** *his hands. | I* ***held*** *her* ***tight****. | a couple* ***holding hands*** (=holding each other's hands) ➔ see picture on page A9

THESAURUS

grip: *I gripped the rail and tried not to look down.*
clutch: *a child clutching a bag of candy*
catch/take/keep/get (a) hold of sth – to take something in your hands and hold it tightly: *Catch hold of the rope and pull.*
grab (hold of sth)/seize – to take hold of someone or something suddenly or violently: *He grabbed the bag and ran.*
➔ see also Thesaurus box at HUG¹

2 EVENT [T] to have a meeting, party, etc., especially in a particular place or at a particular time: *a conference* ***held in*** *Las Vegas | Elections will be* ***held in*** *March. | The Senate will be* ***holding hearings*** *into the matter. | In April, the president* ***held talks*** *with Chinese leaders.*

H

3 MOVE IN YOUR HAND [T] to move your hand or something in your hand in a particular direction: *She **held** the picture **up** so we could see it.* | ***Hold out** your hand.*
4 KEEP IN POSITION [T] to make something stay in a particular position: *He **held** the door **open** for me.* | *Some tape **held** it **in place/position**.* | ***Hold still*** (=don't move) *for a minute.*
5 HAVE SPACE FOR [T] to have space for a particular amount of something: *The jug holds two gallons of liquid.*
6 KEEP/CONTAIN [T] to keep or contain something: *The files are held on computer.* | *the closet that held our winter clothes*
7 POSITION/RANK/JOB [T] to have a particular position, job, or level of achievement: *The permit allows foreign workers to hold jobs in the U.S.* | *the first woman to **hold** high **office*** | *He **holds the record** for the 10,000 meters.*
8 CONTINUE/NOT CHANGE [I,T] to continue at a particular level, rate, or number, or to make something do this: ***Hold** your speed **at** fifty.* | *Housing prices are **holding steady**.*
9 hold it! *spoken* used in order to tell someone to wait, or to stop doing something
10 TELEPHONE [I] to wait until the person you have telephoned is ready to answer: *Will you hold, please?*
11 hold sb's interest/attention to keep someone interested: *She knows how to hold her students' interest.*
12 hold sb responsible/liable/accountable etc. to think that someone is responsible for something bad that has happened: *Parents may be **held responsible for** their children's crimes.*
13 hold your own to succeed in a difficult situation, or to be good enough when compared to similar things: *The rebels held their own against the better-equipped army.*
14 HAVE A QUALITY [T] to have a particular quality: *a drug that **holds promise** for cancer sufferers*
15 CAGE/PRISONER [T] to keep a person or animal in a place that he, she, or it cannot leave: *Police are holding two suspects.* | *tigers held in cages* | *He was **held hostage/prisoner/captive** for two years.*
16 SUPPORT WEIGHT [I,T] to support the weight of something: *I wasn't sure the branch would hold him.*
17 THINK/BELIEVE [T] *formal* to think or believe something: *the **views/beliefs/opinions held** by Republican politicians* | *The theory **holds that** tax cuts help economic growth.*
18 hold true/good *formal* to be true in particular situations: *I think her statement **holds true for** older women* (=is true about them). → **hold your breath** at BREATH → **hold your horses!** at HORSE[1] → **hold sway** at SWAY → **bite/hold your tongue** at TONGUE

hold sth **against** sb *phr. v.* to blame someone for something s/he has done: *If the economy worsens, voters are likely to hold it against him.*

hold back *phr. v.* **1 hold** sth ⇔ **back** to control something or make it stay in one place: *The police couldn't hold the crowds back.* **2 hold** (sth ⇔) **back** to stop yourself from showing a particular feeling or saying something: *She struggled to hold back her tears.* **3 hold** sb/sth ⇔ **back** to prevent someone or something from developing or improving: *Your son's reading problems are holding him back.*

hold sth **down** *phr. v.* **1** to stop someone or something from moving, by pressing or holding him, her, or it: *Hold down the red button while lifting the handle.* **2** to keep something at a low level: *Insurance companies want to hold down health care costs.* **3 hold down a job** to keep your job: *It's hard to hold down a job and go to college at the same time.*

hold off *phr. v.* **1** to delay doing something: *We **held off on** making the decision.* **2 hold** sb ⇔ **off** to prevent someone from attacking or defeating you: *The Jaguars held off the Buccaneers with a late touchdown.*

hold on *phr. v.* **1** *spoken* said when you want someone to wait or stop talking for a short time: *Yeah, hold on, Mike is right here.* | ***Hold on a minute/second**. Let me put this in the car.* **2** to hold something tightly with your hand or arms: *She can hardly walk without **holding on to** something.* | *Okay, Becky, **hold on tight**!* **3** to continue to do something difficult until it gets better: *The Rangers held on to win the game in the final period.*

hold on to sth *phr. v.* to keep something, especially something that someone else wants: *People are holding on to their cars for longer.*

hold out *phr. v.* **1** to continue to defend yourself, or keep on refusing to do something: *Churchill believed the Soviet army would hold out against the Germans.* **2 hold out hope/the prospect etc.** to say that something may happen: *The doctors don't hold out much hope.* **3** if a supply of something holds out, there is still some of it left: *We talked for as long as the wine held out.*

hold out for sth *phr. v.* to refuse to accept less than you have asked for: *He hasn't signed a contract; he's holding out for more money.*

hold out on sb *phr. v.* to refuse to tell someone something s/he wants or needs to know

hold over *phr. v.* **be held over** if a concert, play, or movie is held over, it is shown for longer than was planned because it is very good: *The play has been held over for another week.*

hold sb **to** sth *phr. v.* to make someone do what s/he has promised to do: *"He said he would do it." "Well, you'd better hold him to it."*

hold together *phr. v.* **1 hold** sth ⇔ **together** if a group, family, organization, etc. holds together, or something holds it together, it stays together: *The children are the only thing holding their marriage together.* **2** to remain whole, without breaking: *I hope this bus holds together long enough to get us to Fresno.*

hold up *phr. v.* **1 hold** sb/sth ⇔ **up** to make someone or something late: *I got held up in traffic.*

2 hold up sth to try to steal money from a store, bank, etc. using a gun: *Two men held up the convenience store.* **3 hold** sth ⇔ **up** to support something: *a tin roof held up by posts* **4** to remain strong or effective: *The theory didn't hold up in practice.*

hold² *n.* **1** [singular, U] the action of holding something: *He **grabbed/took/caught hold** of my arm.* **2 get (a) hold of sth** to find someone or something for a particular purpose: *Were you able to get a hold of Mike? | See if you can get hold of an overhead projector.* **3 on hold a)** waiting on the telephone before speaking to someone: *His secretary **put** me **on hold**.* **b)** if something is on hold, it is going to be done or dealt with later: *Her own plans had to be **put on hold** while she took care of mother.* **4** [singular] control, power, or influence over something or someone: *The rebels were tightening their **hold over** the countryside.* **5 take hold** to start to have an effect on someone or something: *The ceasefire took hold in December.* **6** [C] the part of a ship where goods are stored

hold·er /ˈhoʊldɚ/ *n.* [C] **1** someone who has control of or owns a place, position, or thing: *Only **ticket holders** will be admitted.* **2** something that holds or contains something else: *a napkin holder*

hold·ing /ˈhoʊldɪŋ/ *n.* [C] something that you own or rent, especially land or part of a company

ˈholding ˌcompany *n.* [C] a company that owns a controlling number of SHARES in other companies

hold·o·ver /ˈhoʊldˌoʊvɚ/ *n.* [C] a feeling, idea, fashion, etc. from the past that has continued to the present: *styles that are a **holdover from** the '60s*

hold·up /ˈhoʊldʌp/ *n.* [C] **1** a delay, especially one caused by traffic **2** an attempt to rob someone, especially using a gun

hole¹ /hoʊl/ *n.* [C] **1** an empty or open space in something solid: *a **hole in** my sock | The dog **dug a hole** in the yard.*

THESAURUS

space – the empty area between two things, into which you can put something: *There's a space for that box on the shelf over there.*
gap – an empty space between two things or two parts of something: *A cold wind blew through the gap in the window.*
leak – a small hole that lets liquid or gas flow into or out of something: *a leak in the oil tank*
crack – a very narrow space between two things or two parts of something: *John peeked through the crack in the door.*

2 the home of a small animal: *a rabbit hole* **3** one of the small holes in the ground that you try to hit the ball into in GOLF **4** a problem or fault in an idea, plan, or story, so that it can be proven wrong or does not make sense: *The witness's testimony was **full of holes**.* **5** *informal* a bad, ugly, or dirty place: *I have to get out of this hole.* **6 be in the hole** *spoken* to owe money: *We're still $600 in the hole.*

hole² *v.*
hole up *phr. v.* to hide somewhere, or find shelter somewhere: *The rebels are **holed up in** an army building.*

hol·i·day /ˈhɑləˌdeɪ/ *n.* plural **holidays** [C] a day when you do not have to go to work, school, etc.: *July 1 is a **national holiday** in Canada.*

THESAURUS

vacation, **break**, **leave**
➔ see Thesaurus box at VACATION

ho·li·ness /ˈhoʊlinɪs/ *n.* **1** [U] the quality of being pure and holy **2 Your/His Holiness** a title used for talking to or about some religious leaders, especially the Pope

ho·lis·tic /hoʊˈlɪstɪk/ *adj.* concerning the whole of something, rather than its parts: *a doctor interested in **holistic medicine*** (=medicine that treats the whole person, not just the illness)

hol·ler /ˈhɑlɚ/ *v.* [I,T] *informal* to shout loudly: *Dad **hollered at** me to hurry up.* —**holler** *n.* [C]

THESAURUS

shout, call (out), scream, yell, cry out, raise your voice, bellow
➔ see Thesaurus box at SHOUT¹

H

hollow

hol·low¹ /ˈhɑloʊ/ *adj.* **1** having an empty space inside: *a hollow chocolate bunny* ➔ see Thesaurus box at EMPTY¹ **2** feelings or words that are hollow are not sincere: *His promises **ring hollow*** (=seem insincere). **3 hollow cheeks/eyes etc.** cheeks, eyes, etc. where the skin has sunk inward, especially because the person is sick or too thin

hollow² *n.* [C] **1** a hole in something, especially the ground, that is not very deep **2** a small valley

hollow³ *v.*
hollow sth ⇔ **out** *phr. v.* to remove the inside of something

hol·ly /ˈhɑli/ *n.* [U] a small tree with dark shiny pointed green leaves and red berries, often used as a decoration at Christmas

Hol·ly·wood /ˈhɑliˌwʊd/ *n.* a city in California

near Los Angeles, known as the center of the American movie industry

hol·o·caust /ˈhɑləˌkɔst, ˈhoʊ-/ *n.* [C] **1** an event that kills many people and destroys many things: *a nuclear holocaust* **2 the Holocaust** the killing of millions of Jews by the Nazis in Europe in World War II

hol·o·gram /ˈhoʊləˌgræm, ˈhɑ-/ *n.* [C] a special picture made with a LASER that looks as if it is not flat

hol·ster /ˈhoʊlstɚ/ *n.* [C] a leather object that you use for carrying a gun

ho·ly /ˈhoʊli/ *adj.* comparative **holier**, superlative **holiest** **1** relating to God or religion [= **sacred**]: *the holy city of Jerusalem* **2** very religious and morally pure: *a holy man* **3 holy cow/mackerel/moly** *spoken* used in order to express surprise, admiration, or fear

ˈHoly Land *n.* **the Holy Land** the parts of the Middle East where the events in the Bible happened

hom·age /ˈhɑmɪdʒ, ˈɑ-/ *n.* [singular, U] *formal* something that you say or do to show respect for an important person: *The visitors* ***paid homage to*** *the war veterans.*

home[1] /hoʊm/ *n.* **1** [C,U] the place where you usually live, especially with your family: *I decided just to stay* ***at home***. | *I've been* ***living at home*** (=living with my parents) *for the past two years.*

H

THESAURUS

place informal – the house, apartment, or room where someone lives: *Do you want to come back to my place for coffee?*
residence formal – the place where you live: *a private residence*
house – the house, apartment, or room where someone lives: *Let's go over to Dave's house.*

2 [C,U] the place where you come from or your country: *car sales* ***at home*** *and abroad* | *It even made the news* ***back home***. **3 be/feel at home** to feel comfortable somewhere, or confident doing something: *I grew up in Manhattan, and this is where I feel at home.* | *The children feel at home using the computers.* **4 the home of sth** the place where something lives or comes from: *Australia is the home of the kangaroo.* **5 make yourself at home** *spoken* said in order to tell someone who is visiting that s/he should relax **6** [C] a place where people live who cannot take care of themselves because they are very old, sick, etc.: *I could never* ***put*** *Dad* ***into*** *a* ***home***. **7** [C] **also home plate** the base that players must touch in baseball to gain a point

home[2] *adv.* **1** to or at the place where you live: *Hi, honey,* ***I'm home***. | *Come on, Andy, it's time to* ***go home***. | *kids who* ***come home*** *to an empty house* | *I should* ***get home*** *in time for dinner.* ▶ Don't say "go/get/come at home." ◀ **2 take home** to earn a particular amount of money after tax has been taken away: *I take home about $200 a week.* **3 drive/hammer sth home** to make someone understand what you mean by saying it in a very clear and determined way: *We need to hammer home the message that drugs are dangerous.* **4 hit home** if something hits home, it makes you realize or understand something more clearly: *She said I was bullying her, and that really hit home.*

home[3] *adj.* **1** relating to or belonging to your home or family, or done at home: *My* ***home town*** *is Matamata.* | *What's your* ***home address***? | *some good* ***home cooking*** (=meals cooked by your family) **2** playing on your own sports field rather than an opponent's field [≠ **away**]: *The* ***home team*** *is ahead by four runs.*

home[4] *v.*
home in on sth *phr. v.* to aim exactly at something and move directly toward it: *A rescue plane homed in on the location of the crash.*

home·boy /ˈhoʊmbɔɪ/ *n.* [C] *slang* ➔ HOMEY[2]

home·com·ing /ˈhoʊmˌkʌmɪŋ/ *n.* [C] **1** an occasion when someone comes back to his/her home after being away for a long time **2** an occasion when former students return to their school or college

home·land /ˈhoʊmlænd/ *n.* [C] the country where you were born

home·less /ˈhoʊmlɪs/ *adj.* **1 the homeless** people who do not have a place to live, and who often live in the streets **2** without a home: *The war left a lot of people homeless.* —**homelessness** *n.* [U]

home·ly /ˈhoʊmli/ *adj.* a homely person is not very attractive —**homeliness** *n.* [U]

home·made /ˌhoʊmˈmeɪd◂/ *adj.* made at home and not bought from a store: *homemade jam*

home·mak·er /ˈhoʊmˌmeɪkɚ/ *n.* [C] someone who works at home cooking and cleaning, and does not have another job

ˌhome ˈoffice *n.* [C] an office you have in your house so that you can do your job at home

ho·me·op·a·thy /ˌhoʊmiˈɑpəθi/ *n.* [U] a system of medicine in which someone who is sick is given very small amounts of a substance that has the same effects as the disease —**homeopathic** /ˌhoʊmiəˈpæθɪk/ *adj.*

ˈhome page, home·page /ˈhoʊmpeɪdʒ/ *n.* [C] the first page of a website on the Internet, which usually has LINKS to the other parts of the website

hom·er /ˈhoʊmɚ/ *n.* [C] ➔ HOME RUN —**homer** *v.* [I]

home·room /ˈhoʊmrum, -rʊm/ *n.* [C] the room where students go at the beginning of the school day, or at the beginning of each SEMESTER

ˌhome ˈrun *n.* [C] a long hit in baseball that lets the player run around all the bases and get a point

ˌhomeˈ shopping *n.* [U] shopping that you do at home by telephone, mail, or Internet, buying things that you have seen on the television or Internet

home·sick /ˈhoʊmˌsɪk/ *adj.* feeling sad because you are away from your home: *I felt **homesick** already **for** my family.* —**homesickness** *n.* [U]

THESAURUS

sad, **unhappy**, **miserable**, **upset**, **depressed**, **down**, **low**, **gloomy**, **glum**
➔ see Thesaurus box at SAD

home·stead /ˈhoʊmstɛd/ *n.* [C] a farm and the area of land and buildings around it, especially one that was originally given to someone by the government —**homestead** *v.* [I,T]

home·ward /ˈhoʊmwɚd/ *adj.* going toward home —**homeward** *adv.*

home·work /ˈhoʊmwɚk/ *n.* [U] **1** work for school that a student does at home [➡ **housework**]: *Have you **done** your **homework**? | my **math/history/English etc. homework*** **2 do (sb's) homework** to prepare for something by finding out information: *Before the interview, do some homework about the company.*

hom·ey[1] /ˈhoʊmi/ *adj.* comfortable and pleasant, like home: *The restaurant had a nice homey atmosphere.*

homey[2] *n.* [C] *slang* a friend, or someone who comes from your area or GANG

hom·i·ci·dal /ˌhɑməˈsaɪdl◂, ˌhoʊ-/ *adj.* likely to murder someone

hom·i·cide /ˈhɑməˌsaɪd, ˈhoʊ-/ *n.* [C,U] the crime of murder

ho·mo·ge·ne·ous /ˌhoʊməˈdʒiniəs, -nyəs/ also **ho·mog·e·nous** /həˈmɑdʒənəs/ *adj. formal* consisting of parts or members that are all the same [➡ **heterogeneous**] —**homogeneity** /ˌhoʊmoʊdʒəˈniət̬i, -ˈneɪət̬i/ *n.* [U]

ho·mo·ge·nize /həˈmɑdʒəˌnaɪz/ *v.* [T] *formal* to change something so that its parts become similar or the same

ho·mo·ge·nized /həˈmɑdʒəˌnaɪzd/ *adj.* homogenized milk has had its cream mixed in with the milk

hom·o·nym /ˈhɑməˌnɪm/ *n.* [C] a word that sounds the same and is spelled the same as another word, but has a different meaning. For example, the noun "bear" and the verb "bear" are homonyms.

ho·mo·pho·bi·a /ˌhoʊməˈfoʊbiə/ *n.* [U] hatred and fear of HOMOSEXUALS —**homophobic** *adj.*

hom·o·phone /ˈhɑməˌfoʊn, ˈhoʊ-/ *n.* [C] a word that sounds the same as another word, but is different in spelling or meaning. For example, "pair" and "pear" are homophones.

ho·mo·sex·u·al /ˌhoʊməˈsɛkʃuəl/ *adj. formal* sexually attracted to people of the same sex [= **gay**; ➡ **bisexual**; ≠ **heterosexual**] —**homosexual** *n.* [C] —**homosexuality** /ˌhoʊməˌsɛkʃuˈælət̬i/ *n.* [U]

hon·cho /ˈhɑntʃoʊ/ *n.* plural **honchos** [C] *informal* an important person who controls something: *Where's the **head honcho**?*

hone /hoʊn/ *v.* [T] **1** to improve a skill: *players honing their skills* **2** to make a knife, sword, etc. sharp

hon·est /ˈɑnɪst/ *adj.* **1** someone who is honest does not lie, cheat, or steal [≠ **dishonest**]: *an honest, hardworking man* **2** not hiding the truth or the facts about something: *The **honest answer** was that I didn't know. | I need you to be **honest with** me.*

THESAURUS

frank – honest and direct in the way that you speak: *To be frank, I don't like him very much.*
candid – telling the truth, even when the truth may be unpleasant or embarrassing: *It sounds like you need to have a candid talk with him.*
direct – saying exactly what you mean in an honest and clear way: *direct criticism*
straightforward – honest and not hiding what you think: *He seems like a straightforward guy.*
blunt – speaking in an honest way even if it upsets people: *She was blunt about her feelings.*
forthright – saying honestly what you think, in a way that may seem rude: *She answered the questions in a forthright manner.*

3 honest/to be honest *spoken* said to emphasize that what you are saying is true: *We didn't think of that, to be honest with you.* **4 honest mistake** a mistake you make when you did not intend to deceive anyone or be cruel

H

hon·est·ly /ˈɑnɪstli/ *adv.* **1** *spoken* said to emphasize that what you are saying is true, even though it may seem surprising: *I honestly don't know what to do. | Honestly, it doesn't matter.* **2** in an honest way [≠ **dishonestly**]: *Walters spoke honestly about her problems.*

hon·es·ty /ˈɑnəsti/ *n.* [U] **1** the quality of being honest [≠ **dishonesty**]: *He has a reputation for honesty and decency.* **2 in all honesty** *spoken* said when you tell someone what you really think: *In all honesty, we made a lot of mistakes.*

hon·ey /ˈhʌni/ *n.* [U] **1** a sweet sticky substance made by BEES, used as food **2** *spoken* a name that you call someone you love: *Have a good day, honey.*

hon·ey·comb /ˈhʌniˌkoʊm/ *n.* [C] a structure made by BEES to store HONEY in

hon·ey·moon /ˈhʌniˌmun/ *n.* [C] a vacation taken by two people who have just gotten married: *a picture of them **on** their **honeymoon*** —**honeymooner** *n.* [C]

hon·ey·suck·le /ˈhʌniˌsʌkəl/ *n.* [C,U] a climbing plant with yellow or pink flowers that smell sweet

honk /hɑŋk, hɔŋk/ *v.* [I,T] to make a loud noise like a car horn or a GOOSE: *A taxi driver **honked** his **horn** behind her.* —**honk** *n.* [C]

hon·or¹ /ˈɑnɚ/ *n.* **1** [singular] something that makes you feel proud and glad: ***It's an honor to*** *meet you.* | *Being chosen to give the speech was a **great honor**.* **2** [U] the respect that someone or something receives from other people [➡ **dishonor**]: *a statue **in honor of*** (=to show respect for) *Abraham Lincoln* **3** [C] something that is given to someone to show him/her that people respect and admire what s/he has done: *The medal is the government's **highest honor** for artists.* **4 with honors** if you finish high school or college with honors, you get one of the highest GRADES: *Sabrina **graduated with honors**.* **5** [U] strong moral beliefs and standards of behavior that make people respect and trust you: *a **man of honor*** **6 Your Honor** used when speaking to a judge

honor² *v.* [T] **1** to do something to show publicly that someone is respected and admired: *The team will be **honored with** a parade.* **2 be honored** to feel very proud and glad: ***I'm honored to** meet you.* **3 honor a contract/agreement etc.** to do what you have agreed to do in a contract, etc. **4 honor a check** to accept a check as payment

hon·or·a·ble /ˈɑnərəbəl/ *adj.* morally correct, and deserving respect and admiration [≠ **dishonorable**]: *an honorable action* —**honorably** *adv.*

hon·or·ar·y /ˈɑnəˌrɛri/ *adj.* **1** given to someone as an honor: *an honorary degree* **2** someone who has an honorary position does not receive payment for his/her work

H

ˈhonor roll *n.* [C] a list of the best students in a school: *Don **made the honor roll** for the first time.*

ˈhonor ˌstudent *n.* [C] a student whose GRADES are good enough that his/her name is included on the honor roll

hood /hʊd/ *n.* [C] **1** the metal cover over the engine of a car ➔ see picture on page A12 **2** the part of a coat that you pull up to cover your head **3** *slang* NEIGHBORHOOD **4** *informal* HOODLUM

hood·ed /ˈhʊdɪd/ *adj.* having a hood or wearing a hood: *a hooded jacket*

hood·lum /ˈhudləm, ˈhʊd-/ *n.* [C] *old-fashioned* a young person who does bad, often illegal things

hoof /huf, hʊf/ *n.* plural **hoofs** or **hooves** /huvz, hʊvz/ [C] the hard foot of an animal such as a horse ➔ see picture on page A2

hook¹ /hʊk/ *n.* [C] **1** a curved object that you hang things on: *a coat hook* **2** a curved piece of metal with a sharp point that you use for catching fish **3 let sb off the hook** to allow someone to get out of a difficult situation: *I'll let you off the hook today, but don't be late again.* **4 off the hook** if a telephone is off the hook, the part of the telephone that you speak into is not on its base, so no one can call you

hook² *v.* [T] **1** to fasten or hang something onto something else: ***Hook** the rope **over/on** the nail.* **2** to succeed in making someone interested in something or attracted to something: *ads designed to hook young people* **3** *informal* to catch a fish with a hook

hook sth ⇔ **up** *phr. v.* to connect something, especially a piece of equipment, to another piece of equipment or to an electricity supply: *Jen helped me **hook up** the printer **to** my computer.*

hook up with sb *phr. v.* to meet someone and become friendly with him/her or start a romantic relationship with him/her

hooked /hʊkt/ *adj.* **1 be/get hooked on sth** *informal* **a)** to be or become very interested in something and want to do or see it a lot: *We're trying to get kids hooked on books.* **b)** to be unable to stop taking a drug [= **addicted**] **2** shaped like a hook: *a hooked nose*

hook·er /ˈhʊkɚ/ *n.* [C] *informal* PROSTITUTE

hook·y /ˈhʊki/ *n. informal* **play hooky** to stay away from school without permission

hoo·li·gan /ˈhulɪgən/ *n.* [C] a noisy violent person who causes trouble by fighting or damaging things

hoop /hup/ *n.* [C] **1** a circular piece of wood, metal, plastic, etc.: *hoop earrings* | *a basketball hoop* (=what you throw the ball through) **2 hoops** [plural] *informal* basketball: *The guys are out **shooting hoops*** (=playing basketball).

hoo·ray /hʊˈreɪ/ *interjection* shouted when you are very excited and happy about something

hoot¹ /hut/ *n.* [C] **1** the sound made by an OWL or a ship's horn **2** a shout or laugh that shows you think something is funny, exciting, or stupid: *hoots of laughter* **3 be a hoot** *spoken* to be a lot of fun **4 not give a hoot** *spoken* to not care or be interested in something

hoot² *v.* [I,T] **1** if an OWL or a ship's horn hoots, it makes a loud clear noise **2** to shout or laugh loudly because you think something is funny or stupid

hooves /huvz, hʊvz/ *n.* the plural of HOOF

hop¹ /hɑp/ *v.* past tense and past participle **hopped**, present participle **hopping** [I] **1** to move by making short quick jumps ➔ see picture at JUMP¹

> **THESAURUS**
>
> **jump, skip, leap, dive, vault**
> ➔ see Thesaurus box at JUMP¹

2 *informal* to get into, onto, or out of something, for example a vehicle: ***Hop in** and I'll give you a ride.*

hop² *n.* [C] **1** a short jump **2 short hop** *informal* a short trip by airplane

hope¹ /hoʊp/ *v.* [I,T] to want something to happen or be true: *I **hope (that)** you feel better soon.* | *We **hope to** reduce our costs.* | *Leaders are **hoping for** a quick end to the fighting.* | *You just do what you can and **hope for the best*** (=hope a situation will end well). | *"Can I help you?" "**I hope so*** (=I hope this will happen)." | *"Do you think it's going to rain?" "**I hope not**!* (=I hope this will not happen)*"*

USAGE

Use **hope to** to talk about something that you or someone else wants to do: *Michelle hopes to go to college.*
Use **hope that** to talk about what you hope will happen: *I hope that Michelle will decide to go to college.*

hope² *n.* **1** [C usually singular, U] the feeling that good things can or will happen: *a new treatment that* ***gives/offers hope to*** *cancer patients* (=makes them have hope) | *The report expresses little* ***hope that*** *the economy will improve soon.* | *our* ***hopes for*** *peace* | *We have* ***high hopes*** (=strong feelings that something good will happen) *for this year's team.* **2** [C,U] a chance of succeeding or of something good happening: *Many of these children have no* ***hope of*** *going to college.* | *There is still a faint* ***hope that*** *the two sides will reach an agreement.* **3** [C] something that you hope will happen: *her hopes and fears* **4 in the hope that/of sth** if you do something in the hope that you will get a particular result, you do it, even though you cannot be sure of this result: *Her parents put her in a new school,* ***in the hope that*** *her work would improve.* **5 don't get your hopes up** *spoken* used in order to tell someone that something s/he is hoping for is not likely to happen

hope·ful /ˈhoʊpfəl/ *adj.* **1** believing that what you want is likely to happen: *We're* ***hopeful about*** *our chances of winning.* | *I'm* ***hopeful that*** *the situation will improve.* **2** making you feel that what you want is likely to happen: *There are* ***hopeful signs*** *that an agreement will be reached.* —**hopefulness** *n.* [U]

hope·ful·ly /ˈhoʊpfəli/ *adv.* **1** a way of saying what you hope will happen, which some people think is not correct: *Hopefully, I'll be home early.* **2** in a hopeful way: *They talked hopefully about their futures.*

hope·less /ˈhoʊp-lɪs/ *adj.* **1** without any chance of success or improvement: *the hopeless poverty of the inner cities* **2** feeling no hope, or showing this —**hopelessly** *adv.* —**hopelessness** *n.* [U]

hop·scotch /ˈhɑpskɑtʃ/ *n.* [U] a game in which children jump on squares drawn on the ground

horde /hɔrd/ *n.* [C] a large crowd moving in a noisy uncontrolled way: ***hordes of*** *tourists*

ho·ri·zon /həˈraɪzən/ *n.* **1 the horizon** the place where the land or ocean seems to meet the sky: *a ship* ***on the horizon*** **2 horizons** [plural] the limit of your ideas, knowledge, and experience: *I took an evening class to* ***broaden my horizons.*** **3 on the horizon** seeming likely to happen in the future: *a recession on the horizon*

hor·i·zon·tal /ˌhɔrəˈzɑntəl, ˌhɑr-/ *adj.* flat and level [➥ **vertical, diagonal**]: *a horizontal surface* —**horizontally** *adv.*

THESAURUS

flat, level, smooth, even
➔ see Thesaurus box at FLAT¹

hor·mone /ˈhɔrmoʊn/ *n.* [C] a substance produced by your body that influences its growth, development, and condition —**hormonal** /hɔrˈmoʊnl/ *adj.*

horn /hɔrn/ *n.* **1** [C,U] a hard pointed thing that grows in pairs on the heads of cows, goats, etc., or the substance this is made of [➥ **antlers**] ➔ see picture on page A2 **2** [C] the thing in a car, truck, etc. that you push to make a sound as a warning: *Someone was* ***honking/blowing a horn*** (=made a noise with the horn) *behind him.* **3** [C] TRUMPET

hor·net /ˈhɔrnɪt/ *n.* [C] a large black and yellow insect that can sting you

hor·o·scope /ˈhɔrəˌskoʊp, ˈhɑr-/ *n.* [C] a description of your character and things that will happen to you, based on the position of the stars and PLANETS when you were born [➥ **zodiac**]

hor·ren·dous /həˈrɛndəs, hɔ-/ *adj.* **1** frightening and terrible: *a horrendous disaster*

THESAURUS

bad, awful, terrible, horrible, appalling, horrific, lousy, atrocious, abysmal
➔ see Thesaurus box at BAD¹

2 extremely bad or difficult: *Traffic was horrendous on the freeway.*

hor·ri·ble /ˈhɔrəbəl, ˈhɑr-/ *adj.* **1** very bad, and sometimes frightening [= **terrible, awful**]: *a horrible accident* | *The weather was horrible.*

THESAURUS

Describing a horrible taste or smell
disgusting: *It tastes disgusting.*
awful: *The wine was awful.*
revolting: *What's that revolting smell?*
foul: *the foul smell of the chemicals*
Describing a horrible experience, situation, or feeling
terrible: *I feel terrible.*
awful: *an awful headache*
dreadful: *What a dreadful thing to happen.*
➔ see also Thesaurus box at BAD¹

2 not polite or not friendly [= **terrible, awful**]: *horrible manners* —**horribly** *adv.*

hor·rif·ic /hɔˈrɪfɪk, hə-/ *adj.* very bad, frightening, and upsetting: *horrific violence*

THESAURUS

bad, awful, terrible, horrible, appalling, lousy, horrendous, atrocious, abysmal
➔ see Thesaurus box at BAD¹

hor·ri·fied /ˈhɔrəˌfaɪd, ˈhɑr-/ *adj.* feeling very shocked or upset: *We were* ***horrified to hear/see/learn*** *how sick he was.* —**horrifying** *adj.* —**horrify** *v.* [T]

hor·ror /ˈhɔrɚ, ˈhɑrɚ/ *n.* **1** [U] a strong feeling of shock and fear: *I watched **in horror** as Ramsey hit her.* **2** [C] something that is very shocking or frightening: *the horrors of war*

hors d'oeu·vre /ɔr ˈdɚv/ *n.* [C] a small amount of food that is served before people sit down at the table for the main meal

horse¹ /hɔrs/ *n.* [C] **1** a large strong animal that people ride on and use for pulling heavy things [➡ **pony**]: *a girl **riding a** white **horse** | a horse race* ➔ see picture at FARM¹ **2 hold your horses!** *spoken* said when you want someone to wait or to stop doing something

horse² *v.*
horse around *phr. v. informal* to play in a rough and silly way

horse·back /ˈhɔrsbæk/ *n.* [C] **1 horseback riding** the activity of riding a horse for pleasure **2 on horseback** riding a horse: *two men on horseback*

horse·play /ˈhɔrs-pleɪ/ *n.* [U] rough noisy play

horse·pow·er /ˈhɔrsˌpaʊɚ/ *n.* plural **horsepower** [C] **hp** a unit for measuring the power of an engine

horse·shoe /ˈhɔrʃ-ʃu, ˈhɔrs-/ *n.* **1** [C] a curved piece of iron that is attached to the bottom of a horse's foot to protect it **2 horseshoes** [U] an outdoor game in which horseshoes are thrown at a post

H

hor·ti·cul·ture /ˈhɔrt̬əˌkʌltʃɚ/ *n.* [U] the practice or science of growing plants —**horticultural** /ˌhɔrt̬əˈkʌltʃərəl/ *adj.*

hose¹ /hoʊz/ *n.* **1** [C,U] a long rubber or plastic tube that can be moved and bent, used to put water onto plants, fires, etc., or to allow liquids or air to flow through an engine, etc. **2** [plural] PANTYHOSE

hose² *v.*
hose sb/sth ⇔ **down/off** *phr. v.* to wash or pour water over something or someone, using a hose: *Would you hose down the car for me?*

hos·pice /ˈhɑspɪs/ *n.* [C] a special hospital where people who are dying are cared for

hos·pi·ta·ble /hɑˈspɪt̬əbəl, ˈhɑspɪ-/ *adj.* **1** friendly, welcoming, and generous to visitors [≠ **inhospitable**; ➡ **hospitality**]: *a hospitable family*

> **THESAURUS**
>
> **friendly**, **warm**, **cordial**, **welcoming**
> ➔ see Thesaurus box at FRIENDLY

2 providing a situation in which something can succeed or happen [≠ **inhospitable**]: *Nursing was a field **hospitable to** women.*

hos·pi·tal /ˈhɑspɪtl/ *n.* [C,U] a building where sick or injured people receive medical treatment: *Rick's dad is still **in the hospital*** (=being cared for in a hospital). | *He was unconscious and had to be **taken/rushed to the hospital**.* | *His wife had been **admitted to/released from the hospital** the day before.*

hos·pi·tal·i·ty /ˌhɑspəˈtæləṭi/ *n.* [U] friendly behavior toward visitors

hos·pi·tal·ize /ˈhɑspɪtlˌaɪz/ *v.* [T] to put someone into a hospital for medical treatment: *Two people were hospitalized with stab wounds.* —**hospitalization** /ˌhɑspɪtl-əˈzeɪʃən/ *n.* [U]

host¹ /hoʊst/ *n.* [C] **1** the person at a party who invited the guests and organized the party [➡ **hostess**]: *Our host greeted us at the door.* **2** someone who introduces and talks to the guests on a television or radio show: *a game show host* **3** a country or organization that provides the space, equipment, etc. for a special event: *The bookstore will **play host to** a poetry reading.* **4 a (whole) host of sth** a large number of things: *a host of possibilities*

host² *v.* [T] to be the host of an event, television program, etc.

hos·tage /ˈhɑstɪdʒ/ *n.* [C] someone who is kept as a prisoner by an enemy, so that the other side will do what the enemy demands: *Three nurses were **taken/held hostage*** (=caught and used as hostages) *by the rebels.*

> **THESAURUS**
>
> **prisoner**, **captive**
> ➔ see Thesaurus box at PRISONER

hos·tel /ˈhɑstl/ *n.* [C] a cheap place for young people to stay when they are traveling

host·ess /ˈhoʊstɪs/ *n.* [C] **1** the woman at a party who invited the guests and organized the party **2** a woman who takes people to their seats in a restaurant

hos·tile /ˈhɑstl, ˈhɑstaɪl/ *adj.* **1** very unfriendly and ready to fight or argue with someone: *a hostile audience* **2** opposing a plan or idea very strongly: *Several unions are **hostile to** the proposals.* **3** belonging to an enemy: *hostile territory* **4** difficult to live in: *plants that survive in hostile environments* **5 hostile takeover/bid** a situation in which a company tries to buy another company which does not want to be bought

hos·til·i·ty /hɑˈstɪləṭi/ *n.* **1** [U] unfriendly and angry feelings or behavior: ***hostility toward** immigrants* **2** [U] strong opposition to a plan or idea: ***hostility to** the changes* **3 hostilities** [plural] *formal* the fighting in a war: *an end to hostilities*

hot /hɑt/ *adj.* comparative **hotter**, superlative **hottest** **1** high in temperature [≠ **cold**]: *Be careful – the soup's hot.* | *a hot shower* | ***It's hot*** (=the weather is hot) *today.* | *The Mojave Desert is the hottest place in America.* | *We were all hot and tired.* | *a **steaming/piping/boiling hot** cup of coffee* | *a **scorching/broiling/boiling hot** day in August* | *The metal became **red hot*** (=extremely hot).

THESAURUS

warm – a little hot, especially in a pleasant way: *a warm summer evening*
humid – having air that feels hot and wet rather than dry: *the humid heat of the Brazilian rainforest*
boiling/boiling hot – extremely hot: *a boiling hot weekend in August*
sweltering – hot in a very unpleasant, uncomfortable way: *the sweltering heat of the desert*
lukewarm – a liquid that is lukewarm is only slightly warm, and not as cold or hot as it should be: *a glass of lukewarm water*
scalding – a scalding liquid is extremely hot, and hot enough to burn you: *a cup of scalding coffee*
→ COLD[1], WEATHER[1]

2 food that tastes hot has a burning taste [**= spicy**; **≠ mild**]: *hot peppers*

THESAURUS

sweet, **sour**, **salty**, **bland**
→ see Thesaurus box at TASTE[1]

3 *informal* very good, popular, or exciting: *the tennis program's hot young talents* | *the hottest toy this Christmas* **4** difficult or dangerous to deal with: *Studio bosses decided her video was* ***too hot to handle*** (=too much trouble to deal with). | *Education has become the* ***hot topic/issue*** (=subject that people are arguing about) *in this election.* **5** *informal* sexually exciting or attractive: *Then this hot guy sat down at the next table.*

THESAURUS

attractive, **good-looking**, **pretty**, **beautiful**, **handsome**, **gorgeous**, **stunning**, **nice-looking**, **cute**
→ see Thesaurus box at ATTRACTIVE

6 not so hot *spoken* not very good: *I'm not feeling so hot.* **7 be in hot water** *informal* to be in trouble because you have done something wrong: *He was always in hot water at school.* **8 hot air** *informal* things that someone says to sound important, but that do not really mean anything or are not true **9** *slang* goods that are hot have been stolen **10 be hot at sth** to be very good at doing something: *I wasn't too hot at math.* **11 a hot potato** *informal* a subject or problem that no one wants to deal with because any decision would make a lot of people angry **12 be in/on the hot seat** to be forced to deal with a difficult or bad situation, especially in politics

hot-ˈair balˌloon *n.* [C] a very large BALLOON made of cloth and filled with hot air, used for carrying people in the air

hot·bed /ˈhɑt˺bɛd/ *n.* **a hotbed of sth** a place where a lot of a particular type of activity happens: *a school that was a hotbed of liberal ideas*

hot·cake /ˈhɑt˺keɪk/ *n.* [C] **1 sell/go like hotcakes** *spoken* to sell very quickly and in large amounts **2** PANCAKE

hotdog

ˈhot dog, **hot·dog** /ˈhɑtdɔg/ *n.* [C] a long SAUSAGE (=tube-shaped piece of cooked meat), eaten in a long BUN (=type of bread)

ho·tel /hoʊˈtɛl/ *n.* [C] a large building where people pay to stay for a short time: *I prefer to* ***stay in*** *a small* ***hotel.*** | *We* ***checked into*** *our* ***hotel*** *by six.*

TOPIC

In order to arrange to stay at a hotel, you can **make a reservation** or **reserve a room**.
When you arrive at the hotel, you **check in** or **check into the hotel** by going to the **reception desk** and saying that you have arrived.
In many hotels, you can eat a meal in the restaurant or **call/order room service** in order to arrange for food to be delivered to your room.
When you leave the hotel, you **check out** or **check out of the hotel** and pay the bill.
→ ACCOMMODATION

THESAURUS

motel – a hotel for people traveling by car, usually with a place for the car near each room
inn – a small hotel, especially one where you can have breakfast and that is not in a city
bed and breakfast (B&B) – a house or a small hotel where you pay to sleep and have breakfast
campground – a place where you camp in a tent

hot ˈflash *n.* [C] a sudden hot feeling that women have during MENOPAUSE

hot·head /ˈhɑthɛd/ *n.* [C] someone who gets angry or excited easily and does things too quickly, without thinking —**hotheaded** *adj.*

ˈhot key *n.* [C] one or more keys that you can press on a computer KEYBOARD to make the computer quickly do a particular set of actions

hot·line /ˈhɑt˺laɪn/ *n.* [C] a special telephone number that people can call for quick help with questions or problems: *a suicide hotline*

hot·ly /ˈhɑtli/ *adv.* **1** in an angry or excited way: *a* ***hotly debated/disputed*** *issue* **2** done with a lot of energy or effort: *the* ***hotly contested*** *race for governor*

ˈhot plate, **hot·plate** /ˈhɑtpleɪt/ *n.* [C] a small piece of equipment with a flat heated top, used for cooking food

ˈhot rod *n.* [C] *informal* a car that you have put a powerful engine into

hot·shot /ˈhɑt-ʃɑt/ *n.* [C] *informal disapproving* someone who is very successful and confident —**hotshot** *adj.*: *a hotshot lawyer*

ˈhot spot *n.* [C] **1** a place where there is likely to be fighting or a particular problem: *hot spots around the globe* **2** a place where there is a lot of heat or RADIATION **3** an area on a computer screen that you CLICK on in order to make other pictures, words, etc. appear

ˌhot-ˈtempered *adj.* tending to become angry very easily

hot tub

ˈhot tub *n.* [C] a heated bathtub that several people can sit in

hot-ˈwater ˌbottle *n.* [C] a rubber container filled with hot water, used to make a bed warm

ˈhot-wire *v.* [T] *informal* to start the engine of a vehicle without a key, by using the wires of the IGNITION system

hound¹ /haʊnd/ *v.* [T] to keep following someone and asking him/her questions in an annoying or threatening way: *celebrities hounded by reporters*

H

hound² *n.* [C] a dog used for hunting

hour /aʊɚ/ *n.* **1** [C] a unit for measuring time. There are 60 minutes in one hour: *It **takes** two **hours** to get here from the airport.* | *I'll be home **in an hour**.* | *We met **for an hour** over lunch.* | *Paul should have been here **a half hour/half an hour*** (=30 minutes) *ago.* | *A bomb exploded in the airport just hours before* (=a few hours before) *the President's arrival.* | *a ten-hour trip* (=one that is ten hours long) | *a top speed of 120 **miles per hour*** ▶ Don't say "a ten hours trip." ◀ **2** [C] the distance you can travel in an hour: *The lake is **an hour from** Hartford.* **3** [singular] a time of day when a new hour starts: *Classes begin **on the hour*** (=exactly at 1 o'clock, 2 o'clock, etc.). **4** [C] a particular period or point in time during the day or night: *I'll go to the store **on** my **lunch hour**.* | *Montana will have no speed limit during **daylight hours**.* | *I'm sorry to bother you **at this hour*** (=at this late time). **5** [C] an important time in history or in your life: *You were there **in my hour of need*** (=when I needed help). **6 hours** [plural] **a)** the period of time when a store or business is open, or when a particular activity happens: *The mall's **opening hours** are from 9 a.m. till 9 p.m.* | *Please phone during **office hours**.* | ***visiting hours*** (=the time when you can visit) *at the hospital* | *The inventory will be done **after hours*** (=when the store is closed). **b)** *informal* a long time: *She spends hours on the phone.* **7 at all hours** at any time during the day and night: *People wander through the lobby at all hours.*

hour·glass /ˈaʊɚglæs/ *n.* [C] a glass container for measuring time, in which sand moves from the top half through a narrow middle part to the bottom half in exactly one hour

hour·ly /ˈaʊɚli/ *adj., adv.* **1** happening or done every hour: *Trains from Boston arrive hourly.* | *an hourly news bulletin*

THESAURUS

regular, **daily**, **weekly**, **monthly**, **yearly**, **annual**, **annually**
→ see Thesaurus box at REGULAR¹

2 hourly pay/fees etc. the amount you earn or charge for every hour you work

house¹ /haʊs/ *n.* plural **houses** /ˈhaʊzɪz/ [C] **1** a building that you live in, especially one that is intended to be used by one family: *I'm going over to Dean's house.* | *a three-bedroom house* | *Every room **in the house** was cluttered with books.* | *You're welcome to stay **at** my **house**.*

THESAURUS

ranch house/ranch – a long narrow house built on one level
cottage – a small house in the country
row house – one of a row of houses that are joined together
mansion – a very large house
bungalow – a small house that is usually all on one level
duplex – a house that is divided into two separate homes
apartment – a set of rooms that is part of a bigger building
condominium/condo – one apartment in a building with several apartments, each of which is owned by the people living in it
townhouse a house in a group of houses that share one or more walls
mobile home/trailer – a type of house that can be pulled by a large vehicle and moved to another place
→ HOME¹

2 all the people who live in a house: *Be quiet, or you'll wake the whole house!* **3** a building used for a particular purpose or to keep a particular thing in: *the Opera House* | *a hen house* **4 a)** one of the groups of people who make the laws of a state or country: *The President will speak to both **houses of Congress** on Thursday.* **b) the House** HOUSE OF REPRESENTATIVES **5** a company, especially one involved in a particular area of business: *America's oldest publishing house* **6** the part of a theater where people sit, or the people in it: *There was a **full house*** (=every seat was full) *at Friday's performance.* **7 be on the house** *spoken* if drinks or meals in a restaurant are on the house, they are free **8 also house music** [U] a type of modern dance music

THESAURUS

pop (music), rock (music), rock'n'roll, heavy metal, reggae, hip-hop, rap (music), jazz, classical (music), country (music), folk (music)
→ see Thesaurus box at MUSIC

house[2] /haʊz/ *v.* [T] **1** to provide someone with a place to live: *More than 150,000 prisoners are* ***housed in*** *32 prisons.*

THESAURUS

home, place, residence
→ see Thesaurus box at HOME[1]

2 if a building houses something, that thing is kept there

'house ar,rest *n.* **be under house arrest** to not be allowed to leave your house by the government or police

house·bound /ˈhaʊsbaʊnd/ *adj.* not able to leave your house, especially because you are sick or old

house·bro·ken /ˈhaʊsˌbroʊkən/ *adj.* a pet animal that is housebroken has been trained not to make the house dirty with its URINE or other body waste

house·hold[1] /ˈhaʊshoʊld, ˈhaʊsoʊld/ *n.* [C] all the people who live together in one house

household[2] *adj.* **1** relating to taking care of a house and the people in it: *household chores* **2 be a household name/word** to be famous or known about by many people

house·keep·er /ˈhaʊsˌkipɚ/ *n.* [C] someone whose job is to do the cooking, cleaning, etc. in a house or hotel

house·keep·ing /ˈhaʊsˌkipɪŋ/ *n.* [U] **1** the work that needs to be done in a house, hotel, etc. to keep it clean **2** the department in a large building such as a hotel or hospital that is in charge of keeping the building clean inside

,House of Repre'sentatives *n.* [singular] the larger of the two groups of people who are part of the government and who make the laws in countries such as the U.S. and Australia [➡ **Senate**]

house·plant /ˈhaʊsplænt/ *n.* [C] a plant that is grown indoors for decoration

'house-sit *v.* [I] to take care of someone's house while s/he is away

house·wares /ˈhaʊswɛrz/ *n.* [plural] things used in the home, such as plates and lamps

house·warm·ing /ˈhaʊsˌwɔrmɪŋ/ *n.* [C] a party that you give to celebrate moving into a new house

house·wife /ˈhaʊswaɪf/ *n.* plural **housewives** /-waɪvz/ [C] a married woman who works at home doing the cooking, cleaning, etc. [➡ **homemaker**]

house·work /ˈhaʊswɚk/ *n.* [U] the work that you do to take care of a house, for example cleaning and washing clothes [➡ **homework**]

hous·ing /ˈhaʊzɪŋ/ *n.* **1** [U] the buildings that people live in: *a lack of affordable housing* **2** [U] the work of providing houses for people to live in: *a housing program* **3** [C] a protective cover for a machine: *the engine housing*

'housing de,velopment *n.* [C] a number of houses built in the same area at the same time, usually in a similar style

'housing ,project *n.* [C] a group of houses or apartments for poor families, usually built with money from the government

hov·el /ˈhʌvəl, ˈhɑ-/ *n.* [C] *literary* a small dirty place where someone lives

hov·er /ˈhʌvɚ/ *v.* [I] **1** if a bird, insect, or HELICOPTER hovers, it stays in one place in the air **2** to stay in the same place, especially because you are waiting for something: *Her family hovered at her bedside.* **3** to stay close to a particular amount: *The temperature hovered just above freezing.*

how /haʊ/ *adv., conjunction* **1** used in order to ask about or explain the way something happens or is done: *How do you spell your name?* | *Martin explained how the system worked.* | *The advisor can show you* ***how to*** *apply for the loan.* **2** used in order to ask about the amount, size, or degree of something: *How old is Debbie?* | *How long have you been here?* | *How much are the tickets?* (=what do they cost?) **3** used in order to ask about someone's health: *How is your mother these days?* **4** used in order to ask someone about his/her opinion or his/her experience of something: *"How do I look?" "Great!"* | *How was your vacation?* **5** used in order to ask what someone or something looks like, behaves like, or the way something is expressed: *How does that song go?* | *How does she act with other children?* **6** used before an adjective or adverb to emphasize it: *How odd that they didn't tell anyone they were leaving.*

SPOKEN PHRASES

7 how are you?/how's it going?/how are you doing? used when asking if someone is well and happy: *So, how's it going at work?* **8 how about ...?** used when making a suggestion about what to do: *I'm busy tonight, but how about tomorrow?* **9 how come?** used when asking why something has happened [= **why?**]: *How come you didn't tell me this before?* **10 how do you know?** used when asking why someone is sure about something: *"He's not back yet." "How do you know?"* **11 how can/could sb do sth?** said when you are very surprised by something or disapprove strongly of it: *How could you say that to her?* **12 how do you do?** *formal* said when you meet someone for the first time

how·dy /ˈhaʊdi/ *spoken informal humorous* used in order to say "hello" in an informal, usually humorous way

how·ev·er[1] /haʊˈɛvɚ/ *adv.* **1** used in order to

H

add an idea or fact that is surprising or seems very different from what you have just said: *It is a serious disease that is, however, easy to treat.* **2** used in order to say that it does not matter how big, good, serious, etc. something is because it will not change a situation in any way: *However difficult it is for you to accept, it is the truth.*

however² *conjunction* in whatever way: *However you do it, I'm sure it will be good.*

howl /haʊl/ *v.* [I] **1** to make a long loud crying sound like a dog or a WOLF [➡ **bark**] **2** if the wind howls, it makes a loud high sound as it blows **3** to make a loud shouting or crying sound: *an audience* ***howling with laughter*** —**howl** *n.* [C]

HQ *n.* the written abbreviation of **headquarters**

hr. *n.* plural **hrs.** [C] the written abbreviation of **hour**

hub /hʌb/ *n.* [C] **1** the central part of an area, system, etc. that all the other parts are connected to: *the* ***hub of*** *a transit system* **2** the central part of a wheel

hub·bub /ˈhʌbʌb/ *n.* [singular, U] *informal* **1** the noise of a lot of people all talking at the same time **2** a situation in which there is a lot of activity or excitement: *the hubbub surrounding the trial*

hub·cap /ˈhʌbkæp/ *n.* [C] a metal cover for the center of a wheel on a vehicle

hud·dle /ˈhʌdl/ *v.* **1** [I,T] **also huddle together/up** if a group of people huddle together, they gather very closely together: *a group of reporters* ***huddled around*** *the door* **2** [I always + adv/prep] to lie or sit with your arms and legs close to your body because you are cold or frightened: *Rosie huddled under the blankets.* —**huddle** *n.* [C]

hue /hyu/ *n.* [C] *literary* a color or type of color [➡ **shade**]: *a golden hue*

huff¹ /hʌf/ *n.* **in a huff** feeling angry: *Ray left in a huff.*

huff² *v. informal* **huff and puff** to breathe out in a noisy way, especially because you have been doing physical work

huff·y /ˈhʌfi/ *adj. informal* annoyed or slightly angry: *Don't* ***get huffy with*** *me.*

hug¹ /hʌg/ *v.* past tense and past participle **hugged**, present participle **hugging** [T] **1** to put your arms around someone and hold him/her tightly to show love or friendship: *Hug your children.*

> **THESAURUS**
>
> **embrace** – to put your arms around someone and hold him/her in a caring way: *Jason warmly embraced his son.*
>
> **cuddle** – to put your arms around someone or something as a sign of love: *Dawn and her boyfriend were cuddling on the sofa.*
>
> **hold** – to have something firmly in your hands or arms: *She held the baby in her arms.*

2 to move along the side, edge, top, etc. of something, staying very close to it: *a boat hugging the coast*

hug² *n.* [C] the act of hugging: ***Give me a hug.***

huge /hyudʒ/ *adj.* very big: *Their house is huge.* | *a huge problem* —**hugely** *adv.*

> **THESAURUS**
>
> **big**, **large**, **enormous**, **vast**, **gigantic**, **massive**, **immense**, **colossal**, **substantial**
>
> → see Thesaurus box at BIG

huh /hʌ/ *interjection* **1** said when you have not heard or understood a question: *"What do you think, Bob?" "Huh?"* **2** said at the end of a question to ask for agreement: *Not a bad restaurant, huh?*

hulk /hʌlk/ *n.* [C] **1** an old ship, airplane, or vehicle that is no longer used **2** a large heavy person or thing

hull /hʌl/ *n.* [C] the main outer structure or body of a ship

hul·la·ba·loo /ˈhʌləbəˌlu, ˌhʌləbəˈlu/ *n.* [singular, U] *informal* a lot of noise, excited talk, newspaper stories, etc., especially about something surprising or shocking: *the hullabaloo about the Olympics*

hum /hʌm/ *v.* past tense and past participle **hummed**, present participle **humming** **1** [I,T] to sing a tune by making a continuous sound with your lips closed: *Mrs. Garner hummed while she worked.* **2** [I] to make a low continuous sound: *Air conditioners hummed in the windows.* **3** [I] if a place is humming, it is very busy and full of activity —**hum** *n.* [singular]

hu·man¹ /ˈhyumən/ *adj.* **1** belonging to or relating to people: *human behavior* | *the different cell types in* ***the human body*** | *too small to be seen by* ***the human eye*** | *NASA said the accident was a result of* ***human error*** (=a mistake made by a person, not a machine). | *the value of* ***human life*** **2** human weaknesses, emotions, etc. are typical of ordinary people [➡ **inhuman**]: *a movie that shows us* ***human nature*** (=the good and bad qualities that are typical of people) *at its best and worst* **3 sb is only human** used in order to say that someone should not be blamed for what s/he has done **4 human interest** a quality that makes a story interesting because it is about people's lives, feelings, relationships, etc.

human² **also** ˌ**human** ˈ**being** *n.* [C] a man, woman, or child

hu·mane /hyuˈmeɪn/ *adj.* treating people or animals in a way that is kind, not cruel [≠ **inhumane**] —**humanely** *adv.*

hu·man·ism /ˈhyuməˌnɪzəm/ *n.* [U] the belief that human problems can be solved through science rather than religion —**humanist** *n.* [C] —**humanistic** /ˌhyuməˈnɪstɪk◂/ *adj.*

hu·man·i·tar·i·an /hyuˌmænəˈtɛriən/ *adj.* [only before noun] concerned with improving bad living conditions and preventing unfair treatment of people: ***Humanitarian aid/relief/assistance** is flowing into the country.* —**humanitarianism** *n.* [U] —**humanitarian** *n.* [C]

hu·man·i·ty /hyu'mænət̬i/ *n.* **1** [U] people in general [➡ **humankind**]: *the danger pollution poses to humanity* **2** [U] kindness, respect, and sympathy toward other people [≠ **inhumanity**]: *a man of great humanity* **3 the humanities** [plural] subjects you study that are related to literature, history, art, etc. rather than mathematics or science **4** [U] the state of being human

hu·man·ize /'hyuməˌnaɪz/ *v.* [T] to make a system more pleasant for people: *attempts to humanize the prison*

hu·man·kind /'hyumənˌkaɪnd/ *n.* [U] people in general [= **mankind**; ➡ **humanity**]

THESAURUS

people, **the public**, **society**, **the human race**, **mankind**, **population**
➔ see Thesaurus box at PEOPLE[1], MAN[1]

hu·man·ly /'hyumənli/ *adv.* **humanly possible** able to be done using all your skills, knowledge, time, etc.: *The doctors **did everything humanly possible** to save his life.*

ˌhuman 'race *n.* **the human race** all people, considered as a single group

ˌhuman 'resources *n.* [U] the department in a company that deals with employing, training, and helping people [= **personnel**]

ˌhuman 'rights *n.* [plural] the basic rights that every person should have to be treated in a fair, equal way without cruelty, especially by his/her government

hum·ble[1] /'hʌmbəl/ *adj.* **1** *approving* not considering yourself or your ideas to be as important as other people's [≠ **proud**; ➡ **humility**]: *a quiet, humble man* **2** relating to a low social class or position: *the senator's **humble beginnings/background** on a farm in Iowa* —**humbly** *adv.*

humble[2] *v.* [T] to make someone realize that s/he is not as important, good, kind, etc. as s/he thought: *The team was humbled by a surprise defeat.* —**humbling** *adj.*

hum·drum /'hʌmdrʌm/ *adj.* boring, ordinary, and having very little variety: *a humdrum job*

hu·mid /'hyumɪd/ *adj.* if the weather is humid, the air feels warm and wet [➡ **damp**]: *Summers here are **hot and humid**.*

THESAURUS

hot, **warm**, **boiling hot**, **sweltering**
➔ see Thesaurus box at HOT

hu·mid·i·fier /hyu'mɪdəˌfaɪɚ/ *n.* [C] a machine that makes the air in a room less dry —**humidify** *v.* [T]

hu·mid·i·ty /hyu'mɪdət̬i/ *n.* [U] the amount of water that is contained in the air: *Atlanta's heat and **high humidity** during the summer*

hu·mil·i·ate /hyu'mɪliˌeɪt/ *v.* [T] to make someone feel ashamed or stupid, especially when other people are present [➡ **embarrass**]: *Her husband abused and humiliated her.* —**humiliated** *adj.* —**humiliation** /hyuˌmɪli'eɪʃən/ *n.* [C,U]

hu·mil·i·at·ing /hyu'mɪliˌeɪt̬ɪŋ/ *adj.* making you feel ashamed or embarrassed: *a humiliating defeat at the polls*

hu·mil·i·ty /hyu'mɪlət̬i/ *n.* [U] *approving* the quality of not being too proud about yourself

hu·mor[1] /'hyumɚ/ *n.* [U] **1** the ability to laugh at things and think that they are funny, or funny things you say that show you have this ability: *She has a great **sense of humor**. | Allen's **dry/black/wry humor*** (=humor with a particular quality) **2** the quality in something that makes it funny and makes people laugh: *a novel full of humor and intelligence* **3 good humor** a happy friendly attitude to people and events

humor[2] *v.* [T] to do what someone wants so s/he will not become angry or upset: *Just humor me and listen, please.*

hu·mor·ist /'hyumərɪst/ *n.* [C] someone, especially a writer, who tells jokes and funny stories

hu·mor·less /'hyumɚlɪs/ *adj. disapproving* too serious and not able to laugh at things that are funny

hu·mor·ous /'hyumərəs/ *adj.* funny and enjoyable: *a humorous look at relationships* —**humorously** *adv.*

THESAURUS

funny, **hilarious**, **hysterical**, **witty**, **amusing**
➔ see Thesaurus box at FUNNY[1]

hump /hʌmp/ *n.* [C] **1** a raised part on the back of a person or animal: *a camel's hump* **2** a round shape that rises above a surface: *a big hump of rock sticking out of the prairie* **3 be over the hump** to have finished the most difficult part of something

hunch[1] /hʌntʃ/ *n.* [C] a feeling that something is true or that something will happen: ***My hunch is that** things will improve soon. | I **had a hunch** you'd call today.*

hunch[2] *v.* [I] to bend down and lean forward so that your back forms a curve: *employees **hunched over** their computer screens* —**hunched** *adj.*

hunch·back /'hʌntʃbæk/ *n.* [C] *offensive* someone who has a large HUMP on his/her back

hun·dred[1] /'hʌndrɪd/ *number* **1** 100: *a hundred years | two hundred miles* **2** a very large number of things or people: ***Hundreds of** people marched in protest. | You've seen that program **a hundred times**!* **3 a/one hundred percent** completely: *I agree one hundred percent.* **4 give a hundred percent** to do everything you can in order to achieve something: *Everyone on the team gave a hundred percent.* —**hundredth** /'hʌndrɪdθ/ *number*

H

hundred² *n.* [C] a piece of paper money worth $100

hun·dred·weight /ˈhʌndrɪdˌweɪt/ *n.* plural **hundredweight** [C] **cwt** a measure of weight equal to 100 pounds or 45.36 kilograms

hung /hʌŋ/ the past tense and past participle of HANG

hun·ger¹ /ˈhʌŋgɚ/ *n.* **1** [U] the feeling that you want or need to eat [➡ **hungry, thirsty**]: *He had **hunger pangs** (=feelings of being hungry) from missing lunch.* ▶ Don't say "I have hunger." Say "I am hungry." ◀ **2** [U] a severe lack of food, especially for a long period of time [= **starvation**]: *people **dying of hunger*** **3** [singular, U] a strong need or desire for something: *a **hunger for** power*

hunger² *v.*

hunger for sth *phr. v.* to want something very much

ˈ**hunger strike** *n.* [C] a situation in which someone refuses to eat, in order to protest about something

ˌ**hung ˈjury** *n.* [C usually singular] a JURY that cannot agree about whether someone is guilty of a crime

ˌ**hung ˈover** *adj.* feeling sick because you drank too much alcohol the previous day [➡ **hangover**]

hun·gry /ˈhʌŋgri/ *adj.* comparative **hungrier**, superlative **hungriest** **1** wanting to eat something [➡ **hunger, thirst**]: *When's dinner? I'm hungry.* | *If you **get hungry**, there's some turkey in the fridge.* **2 go hungry** to not have enough food to eat: *Despite our country's wealth, many poor families still go hungry.* **3 be hungry for sth** to want something very much: *a lonely child who was hungry for a friend* —**hungrily** *adv.*

ˌ**hung ˈup** *adj. informal* worrying too much about someone or something: *Let's not **get hung up on** the details here.*

hunk /hʌŋk/ *n.* [C] **1** a thick piece of something that has been taken from a bigger piece: *a **hunk of** bread* **2** *informal* an attractive man who has a strong body

hun·ker /ˈhʌŋkɚ/ *v.*

hunker down *phr. v.* **1** *informal* to not do things that may be risky, so that you are safe and protected: *People are hunkering down and waiting for the economy to get better.* **2** to bend your knees so that you are sitting on your heels, close to the ground [= **squat**]

hunt¹ /hʌnt/ *v.* [I,T] **1** to chase animals or birds in order to catch and kill them: *This isn't the season for hunting deer.* **2** to look for someone or something very carefully: *women **hunting for** the perfect wedding gown*

hunt sb/sth ⇔ **down** *phr. v.* to find an enemy or criminal after searching hard: *The agency was created to hunt down war criminals.*

hunt² *n.* [C] **1** a careful search for someone or something: *The **hunt for** the missing child continues today.* **2** an occasion when people chase animals in order to catch or kill them

hunt·er /ˈhʌntɚ/ *n.* [C] **1** a person or animal that hunts wild animals **2** someone who is looking for a particular thing: *job hunters*

hunt·ing /ˈhʌntɪŋ/ *n.* [U] **1** the act of chasing animals in order to catch or kill them: *Ed's going to **go** deer **hunting** next weekend.* **2 job-hunting/house-hunting etc.** the activity of looking for a job, a house to live in, etc. —**hunting** *adj.*

hur·dle¹ /ˈhɚdl/ *n.* [C] **1** a problem or difficulty that you must deal with before you can achieve something: *The drug has **cleared the final hurdle** for FDA approval.* **2** a type of small fence that a person or a horse jumps over during a race

hurdle² *v.* [T] to jump over something while you are running —**hurdler** *n.* [C]

hurl /hɚl/ *v.* **1** [T] to throw something using a lot of force: *He **hurled** a brick **through/out** the window.*

THESAURUS

throw, toss, chuck, fling, pass, pitch
→ see Thesaurus box at THROW¹

2 hurl insults/abuse etc. at sb to shout at someone in a loud and angry way **3** [I] *spoken humorous* to VOMIT

hur·ray /həˈreɪ, hʊˈreɪ/ **also hur·rah** /hʊˈrɑ/ *interjection* HOORAY

hur·ri·cane /ˈhɚɪˌkeɪn, ˈhʌr-/ *n.* [C] a storm that has very strong fast winds [➡ **tornado**]

THESAURUS

storm, tornado, typhoon
→ see Thesaurus box at WIND¹

hur·ried /ˈhɚid, ˈhʌrid/ *adj.* done more quickly than usual: *We ate a hurried breakfast.* —**hurriedly** *adv.*

hur·ry¹ /ˈhɚi, ˈhʌri/ *v.* past tense and past participle **hurried**, third person singular **hurries** [I,T] to do something or go somewhere more quickly than usual, or to make someone or something do this [= **rush**]: *students **hurrying across/around etc.** campus* | *The girls **hurried home** to tell their parents.* | *I spend so much time **hurrying** the kids **to/from** activities.*

> **COMMUNICATION**
>
> **Ways of telling someone to hurry**
>
> **come on** spoken: *Come on, we've got to catch the next bus.*
> **get a move on/get moving** spoken: *Let's get a move on or we'll be late.*

hurry up *phr. v.* **1** to do something or move somewhere more quickly: *I wish the bus would hurry up and get here.* | *Hurry up!* (=said when you want someone to hurry) *We're going to be late!* **2 hurry** sth/sth **up** to make someone do something more quickly, or to make something happen more quickly

hurry[2] *n.* **1 be in a hurry** to need to do something, go somewhere, etc. more quickly than usual: *Why is she in such a hurry?* | *He was* ***in a hurry to*** *get to town.* **2 (there's) no hurry** *spoken* said in order to tell someone that s/he does not have to do something quickly or soon: *Relax, there's no hurry.* **3 not be in any hurry/be in no hurry** to be able to wait because you have a lot of time in which to do something: *Take your time; I'm not in any hurry.* **4 what's (all) the hurry?** *spoken* said when you think someone is doing something too quickly

hurt[1] /hɚt/ *v.* past tense and past participle **hurt** **1** [T] to injure yourself or someone else: *She hurt her knee playing volleyball.* | *Did you hurt yourself?*

> **THESAURUS**
>
> **Hurt** and **injure** can mean the same, but **hurt** is usually used when the damage to your body is not very great: *Alex fell and hurt his knee.*
> **Injure** is used especially to say that someone has been hurt in an accident: *Three people were seriously injured in the crash.*
> **Wound** is used to say that someone has been hurt by a weapon such as a gun or knife: *The gunman killed two people and wounded six others.*

2 [I,T] to feel pain or cause pain in a part of your body: *My stomach hurts.* | *It hurts my knees to run.*

> **THESAURUS**
>
> **ache** – to feel a continuous pain: *My back was aching.*
> **throb** – if a part of your body throbs, you get a regular feeling of pain in it: *My throat was dry and my head was throbbing.*
> **sting** – to feel a sudden sharp pain in your eyes, throat, or skin, or to make someone feel this: *The antiseptic might sting a little*
> → PAINFUL

3 [I,T] to make someone feel very upset or unhappy: *I'm sorry, I didn't mean to* ***hurt*** *your* ***feelings***. **4** [T] to have a bad effect on someone or something: *The loss* ***hurts*** *the team's* ***chances*** *of getting to the playoffs.* **5 it won't/doesn't hurt to do sth** *spoken* said when you think someone should do something or something is a good idea: *It won't hurt him to clean his room.* **6 be hurting** *informal* to feel upset or unhappy about something —**hurt** *n.* [C,U]

hurt[2] *adj.* **1** suffering pain or injury: *It's okay, nobody* ***got hurt***. | *Kerry was* ***badly/seriously/ slightly hurt*** *in a skiing accident.* **2** very upset or unhappy: *Debra* ***felt hurt*** *and betrayed.* ► You say "seriously/badly/slightly hurt" about an injury, but "very hurt" when someone upsets you. ◄

hurt·ful /ˈhɚtfəl/ *adj.* making you feel upset or unhappy

hur·tle /ˈhɚtl̩/ *v.* [I] to move or fall very fast

hus·band /ˈhʌzbənd/ *n.* [C] the man that a woman is married to [➡ **wife**]: *I'd like you to meet my husband Leon.*

hush[1] /hʌʃ/ *v.* [I] *spoken* said in order to tell someone to be quiet, or to comfort a child who is crying

hush sth ⇔ **up** *phr. v.* to prevent people from knowing about something dishonest: *The senator denied that he had tried to hush up the story.*

hush[2] *n.* [singular] a peaceful silence: *A* ***hush fell*** *over the room* (=everyone suddenly became quiet).

hushed /hʌʃt/ *adj.* quiet: *They were speaking* ***in hushed tones***.

> **THESAURUS**
>
> **quiet**, **low**, **soft**, **muffled**, **subdued**
> ➔ see Thesaurus box at QUIET[1]

ˌhush-ˈhush *adj. informal* secret: *The whole project was very hush-hush.*

husk /hʌsk/ *n.* [C] the dry outer part of some grains, nuts, corn, etc.

husk·y[1] /ˈhʌski/ *adj.* **1** a husky voice is deep and sounds rough **2** a husky boy or man is big and strong

husky[2] *n.* plural **huskies** [C] a dog with thick hair, often used for pulling SLEDS over snow

hus·tle[1] /ˈhʌsəl/ *v.* **1** [T] to make someone move quickly, often by pushing him/her: *Jackson was* ***hustled into*** *his car by bodyguards.* **2** [I] to hurry in doing something or going somewhere: *Come on, you guys! Let's hustle!* **3** [I,T] *informal* to cheat someone in order to get money

hustle[2] *n.* **1 hustle and bustle** busy and noisy activity **2** [U] *informal* energy and determination in doing an activity: *She's a good worker with a lot of hustle.* **3** [C] *informal* a way of getting money that is illegal and dishonest

hus·tler /ˈhʌslɚ/ *n.* [C] someone who gets money in a way that is illegal and dishonest

hut /hʌt/ *n.* [C] a small wooden building with only one or two rooms

hutch /hʌtʃ/ *n.* [C] **1** a small wooden box in which you can keep rabbits **2** a piece of furniture used for storing and showing dishes

hwy. the written abbreviation of **highway**

hy·brid /ˈhaɪbrɪd/ *n.* [C] **1** an animal or plant that is produced from parents of different breeds or types **2** something that is a mixture of two or more things: *The book is a* ***hybrid of*** *fantasy and satire.* —**hybrid** *adj.*: *hybrid seed corn*

hy·drant /ˈhaɪdrənt/ *n.* [C] FIRE HYDRANT

hy·drau·lic /haɪˈdrɔlɪk/ *adj.* moved or operated by the pressure of water or other liquids: *hydraulic brakes* —**hydraulically** *adv.*

hy·drau·lics /haɪˈdrɔlɪks/ *n.* [U] the study of how to use water pressure to produce power

hy·dro·e·lec·tric /ˌhaɪdroʊɪˈlɛktrɪk/ *adj.* using water power to produce electricity: *a hydroelectric dam*

hy·dro·gen /ˈhaɪdrədʒən/ *n.* [U] **H** a gas that is an ELEMENT and is lighter than air, and that forms water when it combines with OXYGEN

hy·dro·plane /ˈhaɪdrəˌpleɪn/ *v.* [I] if a car hydroplanes, it slides on a wet road

hy·e·na /haɪˈinə/ *n.* [C] a wild animal like a dog that makes a loud sound like a laugh

hy·giene /ˈhaɪdʒin/ *n.* [U] the practice of keeping yourself and the things around you clean in order to prevent diseases: *The rules help to ensure* ***good hygiene*** *in school kitchens.* | *Good eating habits and* ***personal hygiene*** (=keeping your body clean) *can prevent infections.*

hy·gi·en·ic /haɪˈdʒɛnɪk, -ˈdʒinɪk/ *adj.* clean and likely to prevent diseases from spreading

hymn /hɪm/ *n.* [C] a song of praise to God

hym·nal /ˈhɪmnəl/ *n.* [C] a book of HYMNS

H

hype[1] /haɪp/ *n.* [U] attempts to make people think something is good or important by talking about it a lot on television, the radio, etc.: *the* ***media hype*** *surrounding Spielberg's new movie*

hype[2] **also hype up** *v.* [T] to try to make people think something is good or important by advertising or talking about it a lot on television, the radio, etc.: *The mayor's speech has been hyped for weeks.*

THESAURUS

advertise, promote, market, plug
➔ see Thesaurus box at ADVERTISE

ˌhyped ˈup *adj. informal* very excited or anxious about something: *They're all* ***hyped up about*** *getting into the playoffs.*

hy·per /ˈhaɪpɚ/ *adj. informal* extremely excited or nervous

hy·per·ac·tive /ˌhaɪpɚˈæktɪv/ *adj.* someone, especially a child, who is hyperactive is too active, and not able to keep still or quiet for very long —**hyperactivity** /ˌhaɪpɚækˈtɪvət̬i/ *n.* [U]

THESAURUS

energetic, vigorous, full of energy, dynamic, tireless
➔ see Thesaurus box at ENERGETIC

hy·per·bo·le /hɪˈpɚbəli/ *n.* [C,U] a way of describing something by saying that it is much bigger, smaller, heavier, etc. than it really is

hy·per·link /ˈhaɪpɚˌlɪŋk/ *n.* [C] a word or picture on a WEBSITE or computer document that will take you to another page or document if you CLICK on it [= **link**]

hy·per·sen·si·tive /ˌhaɪpɚˈsɛnsət̬ɪv/ *adj.* very easily offended or upset

hy·per·ten·sion /ˌhaɪpɚˈtɛnʃən, ˈhaɪpɚˌtɛnʃən/ *n.* [U] *technical* a medical condition in which someone's BLOOD PRESSURE is too high

hy·per·ven·ti·late /ˌhaɪpɚˈvɛntlˌeɪt/ *v.* [I] to breathe too quickly because you are very excited or upset

hy·phen /ˈhaɪfən/ *n.* [C] a mark (-) used in writing to join words or parts of words

hy·phen·ate /ˈhaɪfəˌneɪt/ *v.* [T] to join words or parts of words with a hyphen —**hyphenated** *adj.* —**hyphenation** /ˌhaɪfəˈneɪʃən/ *n.* [U]

hyp·no·sis /hɪpˈnoʊsɪs/ *n.* [U] a state similar to sleep, in which someone's thoughts and actions can be influenced by someone else [➡ **hypnotize**]: *He remembered details of the crime* ***under hypnosis.***

hyp·not·ic /hɪpˈnɑt̬ɪk/ *adj.* **1** making someone feel tired, especially because sound or movement is repeated **2** relating to hypnosis: *He was in a hypnotic trance.* —**hypnotically** *adv.*

hyp·no·tize /ˈhɪpnəˌtaɪz/ *v.* [T] to produce a sleep-like state in someone, so that you can influence his/her thoughts or actions —**hypnotism** /ˈhɪpnəˌtɪzəm/ *n.* [U] —**hypnotist** /ˈhɪpnətɪst/ *n.* [C]

hy·po·chon·dri·ac /ˌhaɪpəˈkɑndriˌæk/ *n.* [C] someone who worries all the time about his/her health, even when s/he is not sick —**hypochondriac** *adj.* —**hypochondria** /ˌhaɪpəˈkɑndriə/ *n.* [U]

hy·poc·ri·sy /hɪˈpɑkrəsi/ *n.* [U] *disapproving* the act of saying you have particular beliefs, feelings, etc., but behaving in a way that shows you do not really have these beliefs or feelings

hyp·o·crite /ˈhɪpəˌkrɪt/ *n.* [C] *disapproving* someone who pretends to believe something or behave in a good way when really s/he does not —**hypocritical** /ˌhɪpəˈkrɪt̬ɪkəl/ *adj.*

hy·po·der·mic /ˌhaɪpəˈdɚmɪk◂/ **also ˌhypodermic ˈneedle** *n.* [C] an instrument with a hollow needle used for putting drugs into someone's body through the skin [➡ **syringe**] —**hypodermic** *adj.*

hy·pot·e·nuse /haɪˈpɑtˀn-us/ *n.* [C] *technical* the longest side of a TRIANGLE that has a RIGHT ANGLE

hy·po·ther·mi·a /ˌhaɪpəˈθɚmiə/ *n.* [U] *technical* a serious medical condition in which someone's body temperature becomes very low, caused by extreme cold

hy·poth·e·sis /haɪˈpɑθəsɪs/ *n.* plural **hypotheses** /-θəsiz/ [C] an idea that is suggested as an explanation of something, but that has not yet been proven to be true [= **theory**] —**hypothesize** /haɪˈpɑθəˌsaɪz/ *v.* [T]

hy·po·thet·i·cal /ˌhaɪpəˈθɛt̬ɪkəl/ *adj.* based on a situation that is not real, but that might happen: *The question was purely hypothetical.* —**hypothetically** *adv.*

hys·ter·ec·to·my /ˌhɪstəˈrɛktəmi/ *n.* plural **hysterectomies** [C] a medical operation to remove a woman's UTERUS

hys·ter·i·a /hɪˈstɛriə, -ˈstɪriə/ *n.* [U] extreme excitement, anger, fear, etc. that you cannot control: *News stories like these could cause mass hysteria.*

hys·ter·i·cal /hɪˈstɛrɪkəl/ *adj.* **1** *informal* extremely funny: *a hysterical comedy act*

THESAURUS

funny, **hilarious**, **witty**, **corny**, **amusing**, **humorous**
→ see Thesaurus box at FUNNY[1]

2 unable to control your behavior or emotions because you are very upset, afraid, excited, etc.: *Don't tell Rob – he'll just get hysterical.* —**hysterically** *adv.*

hys·ter·ics /hɪˈstɛrɪks/ *n.* [plural] **1** a state of being unable to control your behavior or emotions because you are very upset, afraid, excited, etc.: *As soon as she saw the rat she **went into hysterics**.* **2 be in hysterics** *informal* to be unable to stop laughing: *The audience was in hysterics.*

I, i

I, i /aɪ/ **1** the ninth letter of the English alphabet **2** the ROMAN NUMERAL for 1

I /aɪ/ *pron.* used as the subject of a verb when you are the person speaking: *I saw Mike yesterday.* | *I've been playing softball.* | *I'm thirsty.* | *My boyfriend and I went to Miami.* ▶ When you write or talk about yourself and another person, you should always mention the other person first, so don't say "I and my boyfriend...". ◀

IA the written abbreviation of **Iowa**

ice[1] /aɪs/ *n.* **1** [U] water that has frozen into a solid: *Do you want some ice in your drink?* | *There's too much ice and snow on the roads.* **2 break the ice** to begin to be friendly to someone by talking to him/her: *Stan tried to break the ice by asking her where she was from.*

ice[2] *v.* [T] **1** to put ice on a part of your body that is injured **2** FROST
ice over/up *phr. v.* to become covered with ice: *The lake iced over during the night.*

ice·berg /ˈaɪsbɚg/ *n.* [C] an extremely large piece of ice floating in the ocean → **tip of the iceberg** at TIP[1]

ice·break·er /ˈaɪsˌbreɪkɚ/ *n.* [C] **1** something you say or do to make someone less nervous **2** a ship that can sail through ice

ˈice cap *n.* [C usually singular] an area of thick ice that always covers the North and South Poles

ˌice-ˈcold *adj.* extremely cold: *ice-cold drinks*

ˈice cream *n.* [U] a frozen sweet food made of milk or cream and sugar, usually with fruit, nuts, chocolate, etc. added to it: *vanilla ice cream*

ice cream cone

ˈice cream ˌcone *n.* [C] a hard thin cookie shaped like a CONE, with ice cream in it

ˈice cube *n.* [C] a small block of ice that you put in cold drinks

ˌiced ˈcoffee also **ˌice ˈcoffee** *n.* [C,U] cold coffee that is served with ice, milk, and sometimes sugar, or a glass of this drink

ˌiced ˈtea also **ˌice ˈtea** *n.* [C,U] cold tea that is served with ice and sometimes LEMON or sugar, or a glass of this drink

ˈice ˌhockey *n.* [U] HOCKEY → see picture on page A10

ˈice pack *n.* [C] a bag of ice used for keeping something cold

ˈice skate[1] *n.* [C usually plural] one of two special boots with metal blades on the bottom that let you slide quickly on ice

ˈice skate[2] *v.* [I] to move along on ice for fun wearing ice skates —**ice skater** *n.* [C] —**ice skating** *n.* [U]

icicle

i·ci·cle /ˈaɪsɪkəl/ *n.* [C] a thin pointed piece of ice that hangs down from something such as a roof

ic·ing /ˈaɪsɪŋ/ *n.* [U] **1** FROSTING **2 sth is (the) icing on the cake** used to say that something makes a good situation even better: *Coe was delighted to win the race, but breaking the world record was the icing on the cake.*

ick·y /ˈɪki/ *adj. spoken* very disgusting to look at, taste, or feel: *The soup tasted icky.*

i·con /ˈaɪkɑn/ *n.* [C] **1** a small picture on a computer screen that makes the computer do

I

something when you CLICK on it with the MOUSE **2** someone or something famous that people think represents an important idea: *The peace symbol is an icon of the sixties.* **3** a picture or figure of a holy person: *religious icons*

ic·y /ˈaɪsi/ *adj.* comparative **icier**, superlative **iciest** **1** extremely cold: *a burst of icy air* **2** covered in ice: *an icy road* **3** unfriendly and frightening: *an icy stare* —**icily** *adv.* —**iciness** *n.* [U]

I'd /aɪd/ **1** the short form of "I had": *I'd never met Kurt before today.* **2** the short form of "I would": *I'd love to come!*

ID[1] *n.* [C,U] **identification** something that shows your name, address, the date you were born, etc., usually with a photograph: *Can I see your ID?* | *Pete got into the club with a fake ID.*

ID[2] the written abbreviation of **Idaho**

i·de·a /aɪˈdiə/ *n.* **1** [C] a plan or suggestion that someone thinks of: *Braby got the **idea for** his book from some old letters.* | *That sounds like a **good/great idea**.* | *Ann thinks it's a **bad idea** to go today.* | *I **have an idea** – let's get Dad a set of golf clubs.*

THESAURUS

thought – something that you think of, think about, or remember: *Erika had a sudden thought: "Why don't you come with me?"*
inspiration – something or someone that encourages you to do or produce something good: *People like Tara are an inspiration to us all.*

2 [C,U] understanding or knowledge of something: *The book gives you a pretty good **idea of** the basic principles of law.* | *Can you **give** me **a rough idea of*** (=a not very exact description of) *how much it will cost?* | ***I had no idea*** (=did not know at all) *what they were talking about.* | ***I don't have the faintest idea*** (=I don't know at all) *what to get Rachel for her birthday.* **3** [C,U] the aim or purpose of doing something: *The **idea of** the game is to hit the ball into the holes.* **4** [C] an opinion or belief: *Bill has some strange **ideas about** religion.* | *I don't want you to **get the idea*** (=begin to believe) *that I look like this all the time.*

i·de·al[1] /aɪˈdiəl/ *adj.* **1** being the best that something could possibly be: *ideal weather conditions* | *The beaches are **ideal for** evening strolls.*

THESAURUS

perfect, **just right**
➔ see Thesaurus box at PERFECT[1]

2 perfect, but not likely to exist: *In an **ideal world**, no one would ever get sick.*

ideal[2] *n.* [C] **1** a principle or standard that you would like to achieve: *the **ideal of** perfect equality* **2** a perfect example of something: *current **ideals of** beauty*

i·de·al·ism /aɪˈdiəˌlɪzəm/ *n.* [U] the belief that you should live according to your high standards or principles, even if it is difficult

i·de·al·ist·ic /ˌaɪdiəˈlɪstɪk/ *adj. approving* believing in principles and high standards, even if they cannot be achieved in real life: *idealistic young people* —**idealist** /aɪˈdiəlɪst/ *n.* [C]

i·de·al·ize /aɪˈdiəˌlaɪz/ *v.* [T] to imagine or suggest that something is perfect or better than it really is: *The show idealizes family life.* —**idealized** *adj.*

i·de·al·ly /aɪˈdiəli/ *adv.* **1** [sentence adverb] in a way that you would like things to be, even if it is not possible: *Ideally, I'd like to work at home.* **2** perfectly: *The job is **ideally suited to** Amy's circumstances.*

i·den·ti·cal /aɪˈdɛntɪkəl, ɪ-/ *adj.* exactly the same: *The two pictures looked identical.* | *Jan's dress is **identical to** mine.* | *William and David are **identical twins*** (=two brothers or sisters who were born together and look the same). —**identically** *adv.*

THESAURUS

similar, **like**, **alike**, **matching**
➔ see Thesaurus box at SIMILAR

i·den·ti·fi·a·ble /aɪˌdɛntəˈfaɪəbəl, ɪ-/ *adj.* able to be recognized: *The male birds are **easily/readily identifiable by** their bright colors.*

i·den·ti·fi·ca·tion /aɪˌdɛntəfəˈkeɪʃən, ɪ-/ *n.* [U] **1** official documents that prove who you are: *You can use a passport as identification.* **2** the act of recognizing someone or something: *The bodies have been brought to the hospital for identification.*

i·den·ti·fy /aɪˈdɛntəˌfaɪ, ɪ-/ *v.* past tense and past participle **identified**, third person singular **identifies** [T] to recognize and name someone or something: *Can you identify the man who robbed you?*

identify with sb/sth *phr. v.* **1 identify with** sb to be able to share or understand the feelings of someone else: *It was easy to identify with the novel's main character.* **2 be identified with** sb/sth to be closely connected with an idea or organization: *She will always be identified with the musical Evita.*

i·den·ti·ty /aɪˈdɛntət̬i, ɪ-/ *n.* plural **identities** **1** [C,U] who someone is: *She refused to reveal the **identity of** the killer.* | *All passengers must provide proof of identity at check-in.* **2** [U] the qualities someone has that make him/her different from other people: *Many people's **sense of identity** comes from their job.* | *a strong sense of **national identity***

i·de·o·log·i·cal /ˌaɪdiəˈlɑdʒɪkəl, ˌɪdiə-/ *adj.* based on a particular set of beliefs or ideas —**ideologically** *adv.*

i·de·ol·o·gy /ˌaɪdiˈɑlədʒi, ˌɪdi-/ *n.* plural **ideologies** [C,U] a set of beliefs or ideas, especially political beliefs: *Communist ideology*

id·i·o·cy /ˈɪdiəsi/ *n.* [U] something that is extremely stupid [➡ **idiot**]

id·i·om /ˈɪdiəm/ *n.* [C] a group of words that have a special meaning that is very different from the ordinary meaning of the separate words —**idiomatic** /ˌɪdiəˈmæt̮ɪk◂ / *adj.*: *an idiomatic expression*

> **THESAURUS**
>
> **phrase, expression, cliché, saying, proverb**
> ➔ see Thesaurus box at PHRASE[1]

id·i·o·syn·cra·sy /ˌɪdiəˈsɪŋkrəsi/ *n.* plural **idiosyncrasies** [C] an unusual habit or way of behaving —**idiosyncratic** /ˌɪdioʊsɪnˈkræt̮ɪk/ *adj.*: *idiosyncratic behavior*

id·i·ot /ˈɪdiət/ *n.* [C] a stupid person, or someone who has done something stupid: *You idiot! What did you say that for?* —**idiotic** /ˌɪdiˈɑt̮ɪk/ *adj.*

i·dle[1] /ˈaɪdl/ *adj.* **1** not working or being used: *Many aircraft **sat idle** during the strike.* **2** *old-fashioned* lazy

> **THESAURUS**
>
> **lazy, indolent, shiftless, slack**
> ➔ see Thesaurus box at LAZY

3 having no useful purpose: *idle gossip* —**idleness** *n.* [U] —**idly** *adv.*

idle[2] *v.* [I] if an engine idles, it runs slowly because it is not doing much work

i·dol /ˈaɪdl/ *n.* [C] **1** someone or something that you admire very much: *Janet was always my idol when I was a kid.* **2** an image or object that people pray to as a god

> **THESAURUS**
>
> **god, deity, divinity**
> ➔ see Thesaurus box at GOD

i·dol·ize /ˈaɪdlˌaɪz/ *v.* [T] to admire someone so much that you think s/he is perfect: *Susan idolizes her mother.*

> **THESAURUS**
>
> **admire, respect, look up to**
> ➔ see Thesaurus box at ADMIRE

i·dyl·lic /aɪˈdɪlɪk/ *adj.* very happy and peaceful

i.e. /ˌaɪ ˈi/ a written abbreviation used when you want to explain the exact meaning of something [**= that is**]: *Transfer the text via the clipboard (i.e. cut and paste).*

if[1] /ɪf/ *conjunction* **1** used in order to talk about something that might happen or that might have happened: *If I call her now, she should still be at home.* | *If I get the job, I'll move to New York.* ***If not***, *I'll stay in Dallas.* | *The crew will work all weekend **if necessary**.* | *I want to leave by 5 o'clock **if possible**.* | *We would've canceled the game if the weather was too bad.* ▶ Don't use the future tense with "will" in a clause beginning with "if." ◀ **2** used in order to mean "whether," when you are asking or deciding something: *Do you mind if I close the door?* | *We really don't know if there's a problem with the phone line.* **3** used when you are talking about something that always happens [**= whenever**]: *If I drink milk, I get a stomachache.* **4** said when you are surprised, angry, or upset because something has happened or is true: *I'm sorry if I upset you.* **5 if I were you** used in order to give advice to someone: *If I were you, I'd call him instead of writing to him.* ➔ **even if** at EVEN[1] ➔ **as if/though** at AS ➔ **if only** at ONLY[1]

if[2] *n.* [C] **1** a condition or possibility: *There are still too many ifs to know if this will succeed.* | *Parry will start in Sunday's game if he's healthy – but **that's a big if*** (=it is unlikely). **2 no ifs, ands, or buts** if you want something done with no ifs, ands, or buts, you want it done quickly, without any arguing

if·fy /ˈɪfi/ *adj. informal* an iffy situation is one in which you do not know what will happen: *The weather looks iffy today.*

ig·loo /ˈɪglu/ *n.* plural **igloos** [C] a round house made from blocks of hard snow and ice

ig·nite /ɪgˈnaɪt/ *v. formal* **1** [T] to start a dangerous situation, angry argument, etc.: *actions that could ignite a civil war* **2** [I,T] to start burning, or to make something do this: *A spark caused fuel vapors in the tank to ignite.*

ig·ni·tion /ɪgˈnɪʃən/ *n.* **1** [singular] the electrical part of an engine in a car that makes it start working: *Put the key in the ignition.* ➔ see Topic box at DRIVE[1] ➔ see picture on page A12 **2** [U] *formal* the act of making something start to burn

ig·no·rance /ˈɪgnərəns/ *n.* [U] **1** *disapproving* lack of knowledge or information about something: *Many mistakes were caused by **ignorance of/about** the law.* | *I would have remained **in ignorance** if Shaun hadn't mentioned it.* **2 ignorance is bliss** used in order to say that if you do not know about a problem, you cannot worry about it

ig·no·rant /ˈɪgnərənt/ *adj.* *disapproving* not knowing facts or information that you should know: *students who are **ignorant of** geography* | *He was a brutal, ignorant man.*

ig·nore /ɪgˈnɔr/ *v.* [T] to not pay any attention to someone or something: *Jeannie ignored me all night!* | *The school board has ignored our complaints.*

> **USAGE**
>
> **ignore** – to know about something but deliberately not pay any attention to it: *You must not ignore other people's feelings.*
> **be ignorant of sth** – to not know about something: *We were ignorant of the dangers involved.*

i·gua·na /ɪˈgwɑnə/ *n.* [C] a large tropical American LIZARD

IL the written abbreviation of **Illinois**

I'll /aɪl/ the short form of "I will": *I'll be there in a minute.*

ill¹ /ɪl/ *adj.* **1** [not usually before noun] suffering from a disease or not feeling well [= **sick**; ➡ **illness**]: *The doctor said Patty was **seriously/critically ill*** (=extremely ill). | *patients who are **terminally ill*** (=who are going to die from their illness) | *Don's brother is **mentally ill**.*

> **THESAURUS**
> **sick**, **not very well**, **under the weather**
> ➔ see Thesaurus box at SICK

2 [only before noun] bad or harmful: *Has he suffered any **ill effects** from the treatment?* | *Anita felt no **ill will*** (=unkind feelings) *toward her ex-husband.* | *Several prisoners complained of **ill treatment**.* **3 ill at ease** nervous or embarrassed

ill² *adv. formal* **1** badly or not enough: *We were **ill-prepared** for the cold weather.* **2 sb can ill afford (to do) sth** used in order to say that you cannot or should not do something because it would make your situation more difficult: *Congress can ill afford to raise taxes so close to an election.*

ill³ *n.* [C] *formal* a bad thing, especially a problem or something that makes you worry: *the **social ills** caused by poverty*

ˌill-adˈvised *adj. formal* not sensible or not wise

il·le·gal¹ /ɪˈligəl/ *adj.* not allowed by the law [≠ **legal**]: *Did you know **it is illegal to** park your car here?* | *the number of **illegal immigrants/aliens** in the U.S.* | *illegal drugs* —**illegally** *adv.*: *Most of the software had been illegally copied.*

illegal² also **ilˌlegal ˈimmigrant/ˈalien** *n.* [C] someone who comes into a country to live or work without official permission

il·leg·i·ble /ɪˈlɛdʒəbəl/ *adj.* difficult or impossible to read: *His handwriting was completely illegible.* —**illegibly** *adv.*

il·le·git·i·mate /ˌɪləˈdʒɪt̬əmɪt/ *adj. formal* **1** born to parents who are not married to each other: *He admitted that he had an illegitimate son.* **2** not allowed by the rules or law: *an illegitimate use of public money* —**illegitimacy** /ˌɪləˈdʒɪt̬əməsi/ *n.* [U]

ˌill-eˈquipped *adj.* not having the necessary equipment or skills for something: *Many companies are **ill-equipped to** survive in today's economy.*

ˌill-ˈfated *adj.* unlucky and leading to serious problems or bad results: *an ill-fated attempt to reach the South Pole*

il·lic·it /ɪˈlɪsɪt/ *adj.* not allowed by the law, or not approved of by society, and kept secret: *an illicit love affair* | *illicit drugs* —**illicitly** *adv.*

il·lit·er·ate /ɪˈlɪt̬ərɪt/ *adj.* not able to read or write —**illiteracy** /ɪˈlɪt̬ərəsi/ *n.* [U]

ill·ness /ˈɪlnɪs/ *n.* [C,U] a disease of the body or mind, or the state of having a disease or sickness: *Mrs. Elms died Friday after a long illness.* | *the connections between homelessness and **mental illness*** | *a **serious/chronic/terminal illness***

> **THESAURUS**
> **disease**, **sickness**
> ➔ see Thesaurus box at DISEASE

il·log·i·cal /ɪˈlɑdʒɪkəl/ *adj.* not sensible or reasonable [≠ **logical**]

ˌill-ˈtreat *v.* [T] to be cruel to a person or animal

il·lu·mi·nate /ɪˈluməˌneɪt/ *v.* [T] to make a light shine on something: *Their faces were illuminated by the candle on the table.* —**illuminated** *adj.*

il·lu·mi·nat·ing /ɪˈluməˌneɪt̬ɪŋ/ *adj. formal* making something easier to understand: *an illuminating lecture*

il·lu·mi·na·tion /ɪˌluməˈneɪʃən/ *n.* [U] *formal* the light provided by a lamp, fire, etc.

il·lu·sion /ɪˈluʒən/ *n.* [C] **1** something that seems to be different from what it really is [➡ **optical illusion**]: *Large mirrors gave the room **an illusion of** space.* **2** an idea or belief that is false: *Terry **is under the illusion that*** (=wrongly believes that) *he's going to pass the test.* | *We **have no illusions about** the hard work that lies ahead* (=we know there will be a lot of hard work).

il·lu·so·ry /ɪˈlusəri, -zəri/ *adj. formal* false, but seeming to be true or real

il·lus·trate /ˈɪləˌstreɪt/ *v.* [T] **1** to explain or make something clear by giving examples: *The charts will help to illustrate this point.* | *The following examples **illustrate how** the system works.* **2** to draw, paint, etc. pictures for a book —**illustrative** /ɪˈlʌstrət̬ɪv, ˈɪləˌstreɪt̬ɪv/ *adj.*

il·lus·tra·tion /ˌɪləˈstreɪʃən/ *n.* [C] **1** a picture in a book [➡ **graphic, diagram**]: *watercolor illustrations*

> **THESAURUS**
> **picture**, **sketch**, **snapshot**, **portrait**, **cartoon**, **caricature**
> ➔ see Thesaurus box at PICTURE¹

2 an example that helps you understand something: *Saturday's game provided a vivid **illustration of** how popular soccer has become.*

il·lus·tra·tor /ˈɪləˌstreɪt̬ɚ/ *n.* [C] someone whose job is to draw pictures for books, magazines, etc.

il·lus·tri·ous /ɪˈlʌstriəs/ *adj. formal* very famous and admired by a lot of people

I'm /aɪm/ the short form of "I am": *I'm not sure where he is.* | *Hi, I'm Tim, Ann's brother.*

im·age /ˈɪmɪdʒ/ *n.* [C] **1** the opinion that people have about someone or something, especially because of the way he, she, or it is shown on television, in newspapers, etc.: *The mayor did not want to spoil his **public image** so close to the election.* | *The party is trying to **improve** its **image**.* | *We need to **project** the right **image** in our* *advertising.* | *the old* ***image of*** *New York* ***as*** *an unfriendly city* **2** a picture that you can see through a camera, on a television, in a mirror, etc.: *a baby looking at his image in the mirror* | ***images of*** *starving people on the news* **3** a picture that you have in your mind: *She had a clear* ***image of*** *how he would look in 20 years.* **4** a word, picture, or phrase that describes an idea in a poem, book, movie, etc.

im·age·ry /ˈɪmɪdʒri/ *n.* [U] the use of words, pictures, or phrases to describe ideas or actions in poems, books, movies, etc.: *video games full of violent imagery*

i·mag·i·na·ble /ɪˈmædʒənəbəl/ *adj.* able to be imagined: *I had* ***the worst/best*** *day* ***imaginable****.*

i·mag·i·nar·y /ɪˈmædʒəˌnɛri/ *adj.* not real, but imagined [➡ **imaginative**]: *Many children have* ***imaginary friends****.*

i·mag·i·na·tion /ɪˌmædʒəˈneɪʃən/ *n.* [C,U] the ability to form pictures or ideas in your mind [➡ **fantasy**]: ***Use*** *your* ***imagination*** *to come up with a new dessert.* | *Ben always had a* ***vivid/lively imagination****.* | *Sheila realized that her fears had all been* ***in*** *her* ***imagination*** (=were not true). | *It does not* ***take*** *much* ***imagination*** *to understand the depth of their grief.*

i·mag·i·na·tive /ɪˈmædʒənətɪv/ *adj.* **1** able to think of new and interesting ideas: *an imaginative writer* **2** containing new and interesting ideas: *an imaginative story* —**imaginatively** *adv.* [➡ **imaginary**]

i·mag·ine /ɪˈmædʒɪn/ *v.* [T] **1** to form pictures or ideas in your mind [➡ **imaginary, imagination**]: ***Imagine (that)*** *you're lying on a beach somewhere.* | *Just* ***imagine what*** *you could do with ten million dollars.*

THESAURUS

visualize – to form a picture of someone or something in your mind: *Evans visualized every step he would take in the 400-meter race.*
picture – to imagine something, especially by making an image in your mind: *I had pictured him as short and dark, but he was actually very tall.*
conceive of sth – to imagine a situation or what something is like: *It's difficult to conceive of any reason why he would do something like that.*
fantasize – to think about something that is pleasant or exciting, but unlikely to happen: *I fantasized about losing weight and becoming a thin person.*
daydream – to think about nice things, so that you forget what you should be doing: *Eddie used to daydream about finding treasure in the woods.*

2 to have a false or wrong idea about something: *There's no-one there – you must* ***be imagining things****.* **3** *spoken* to think that something may happen or may be true: *I imagine Kathy will be there tomorrow.*

im·ag·ing /ˈɪmɪdʒɪŋ/ *n.* [U] the process of producing images or photographs of something using technical equipment

im·bal·ance /ɪmˈbæləns/ *n.* [C,U] a lack of balance between two things, so they are not equal or correct: *a trade imbalance* —**imbalanced** *adj.*

im·be·cile /ˈɪmbəsəl/ *n.* [C] someone who is extremely stupid [= **idiot**]

im·bibe /ɪmˈbaɪb/ *v.* [I,T] *formal* or *humorous* to drink something, especially alcohol

im·bue /ɪmˈbyu/ *v.*
imbue sb/sth **with** sth *phr. v.* to make someone feel an emotion very strongly, or to make something contain a strong emotion or other quality: *The movie is imbued with a real sense of optimism.*

im·i·tate /ˈɪməˌteɪt/ *v.* [T] **1** to copy the way someone else speaks, moves, etc., especially in order to make people laugh: *Jerry started imitating his uncle, but his aunt didn't realize what he was doing.* **2** to copy something because you think it is good: *The first successful program was* ***widely imitated*** *in Latin America.* —**imitative** *adj.* —**imitator** *n.* [C]

im·i·ta·tion¹ /ˌɪməˈteɪʃən/ *n.* **1** [C,U] a copy of someone's speech, behavior, etc., or the act of copying: *Harry* ***does an*** *excellent* ***imitation of*** *Elvis.* | *Children learn* ***by imitation****.* **2** [C] a copy of something [= **reproduction**]: *It's not an antique; it's an imitation.*

imitation² *adj.* [only before noun] **imitation leather/wood/ivory etc.** something that looks real, but that is a copy [= **artificial, fake**; ≠ **genuine, real**]

THESAURUS

fake, false, counterfeit, phony, forged
➔ see Thesaurus box at FAKE², ARTIFICIAL

im·mac·u·late /ɪˈmækyəlɪt/ *adj.* **1** very clean and neat: *Barb's house is always immaculate.* **2** perfect and without any mistakes: *dancing with immaculate precision* —**immaculately** *adv.*

im·ma·te·ri·al /ˌɪməˈtɪriəl/ *adj.* not important in a particular situation [= **unimportant, irrelevant**]

im·ma·ture /ˌɪməˈtʃʊr, -ˈtʊr/ *adj.* **1** *disapproving* behaving in a way that is not sensible because it is typical of the behavior of someone much younger [= **childish**]: *I think Jim's too immature to live on his own.* **2** not fully formed or developed: *immature plants* —**immaturity** *n.* [U]

im·me·di·a·cy /ɪˈmidiəsi/ *n.* [U] the quality of seeming to be important and urgent, and directly relating to what is happening now

im·me·di·ate /ɪˈmidiɪt/ *adj.* [usually before noun] **1** happening or done with no delay: *Carla's first cafe was an immediate success.* | *Police demanded the immediate release of the hostages.* | *When we launched the new system, the results were*

I

immediate. **2** existing now, and needing to be dealt with quickly: *Our immediate concern was to stop the fire from spreading.* | *Doctors knew his life was in* ***immediate danger***. **3** near something or someone in time or place: *We have no plans to expand the business in* ***the immediate future***. | *homes located* ***in the immediate vicinity of*** (=very close to) *the sports arena* **4 sb's immediate family** someone's parents, children, brothers, and sisters

im·me·di·ate·ly /ɪ'midiɪt˺li/ *adv.* **1** with no delay [= **right away, at once**]: *Mix in the other ingredients and serve immediately.* | *She realized her mistake almost immediately.* | *The rescue team immediately went to work.* | *The victims' names were not immediately available.*

> **THESAURUS**
>
> **instantly** – immediately, used when something happens at almost the same time as something else: *Data is available instantly over the computer network.*
> **right away** especially spoken – immediately, used especially when something needs to be done urgently: *Jill called him right away.*
> **at once** – immediately or without waiting: *I realized at once I had said the wrong thing.*
> **right now** spoken – immediately, used especially when something needs to be done urgently: *I need it right now!*

2 very near to something in time or place: *Jon arrived* ***immediately before/after*** *the end of the show.*

im·mense /ɪ'mɛns/ *adj.* extremely large [= **huge**]: *an immense palace*

> **THESAURUS**
>
> **big, large, huge, enormous, vast, gigantic, massive, colossal, substantial**
> ➔ see Thesaurus box at BIG

im·mense·ly /ɪ'mɛnsli/ *adv.* very or very much: *The bikes have become* ***immensely popular*** *in cities.* | *He* ***enjoyed*** *it* ***immensely***.

im·merse /ɪ'mɚs/ *v.* [T] **1 be immersed in sth/immerse yourself in sth** to be or become completely involved in something: *Grant is completely immersed in his work.* **2** to put something completely in a liquid: *First,* ***immerse*** *the jars* ***in*** *boiling water.* —**immersion** /ɪ'mɚʒən/ *n.* [U]

im·mi·grant /'ɪməgrənt/ *n.* [C] someone who enters another country to live there [➥ **emigrant, migrant**]: *an* ***immigrant from*** *Russia* | *Chinese* ***immigrants to*** *the U.S.* | *the number of* ***legal/illegal immigrants*** *each year*

im·mi·grate /'ɪmə,greɪt/ *v.* [I] to enter another country in order to live there: *families who* ***immigrate to*** *Canada*

> **THESAURUS**
>
> **immigrate** – to enter a new country in order to live there: *Yuko immigrated to the U.S. last year.*
> **emigrate** – to leave your own country in order to live in a different one: *My grandparents emigrated from Italy.*
> **migrate** – if birds **migrate**, they go to another part of the world in the fall and in the spring

im·mi·gra·tion /,ɪmə'greɪʃən/ *n.* [U] **1** the process of entering another country in order to live there [➥ **emigration, migration**]: *a rise in* ***immigration to*** *the United States* ➔ see Topic box at AIRPORT **2** the place in an airport, at a border, etc. where officials check your documents, such as your PASSPORT

im·mi·nent /'ɪmənənt/ *adj.* likely to happen very soon: *We believe that an attack is imminent.* | *The city is not in* ***imminent danger***. —**imminently** *adv.*

im·mo·bile /ɪ'moʊbəl/ *adj.* not moving, or not able to move

im·mor·al /ɪ'mɔrəl, ɪ'mɑr-/ *adj.* morally wrong, and not accepted by society: *Their church believes that dancing is sinful and immoral.* —**immorality** /,ɪmə'rælət̬i, ,ɪmɔ-/ *n.* [U]

> **THESAURUS**
>
> **bad, evil, wicked, wrong, reprehensible**
> ➔ see Thesaurus box at BAD[1]

im·mor·tal /ɪ'mɔrt̬l/ *adj.* **1** living or continuing forever: *your immortal soul* **2** an immortal phrase, song, etc. is so famous that it will never be forgotten: *In the immortal words of James Brown, "I feel good!"* —**immortality** /,ɪmɔr'tælət̬i/ *n.* [U]

im·mov·a·ble /ɪ'muvəbəl/ *adj.* impossible to move, change, or persuade

im·mune /ɪ'myun/ *adj.* **1** not able to be affected by a disease or illness: *Young children may not be* ***immune to*** *the virus.* **2** not affected by bad things that affect people, organizations, etc. in similar situations: *The company seems to be* ***immune to*** *economic pressures.* | *The Governor is popular, but not* ***immune from*** *criticism.*

im'mune ,system *n.* [C] the system by which your body protects itself against disease

im·mun·i·ty /ɪ'myunət̬i/ *n.* [U] **1** the state or right of being protected from particular laws or punishment: *Congress* ***granted immunity*** (=gave immunity) *to both men.* **2** the state of being IMMUNE to diseases or illnesses: *babies' low* ***immunity to*** *infections*

im·mu·ni·za·tion /,ɪmyənə'zeɪʃən/ *n.* [C,U] the act of immunizing someone: *the* ***immunization*** *of babies in the U.S.* ***against*** *hepatitis B*

im·mu·nize /'ɪmyə,naɪz/ *v.* [T] to protect someone from disease by giving him/her a VACCINE: *Have you been* ***immunized against*** *cholera?*

im·pact[1] /'ɪmpækt/ *n.* **1** [C] the effect that an event or situation has on someone or something:

*Every decision at work **has** an **impact on** profit.* | *the **economic impact** of a possible strike* | *Rising fuel costs could have a **major impact** on consumers.* **2** [C,U] the force of one object hitting another: *The impact of the crash made the car turn over.* **3 on impact** at the moment when one thing hits another: *a missile that explodes on impact*

im·pact² /ɪm'pækt/ *v.* [I,T] to have an important or noticeable effect on someone or something: *The growth of the airport has impacted the city's economy.* | *Childcare is an issue that **impacts on** many women's lives.*

im·pair /ɪm'pɛr/ *v.* [T] to damage something or make it less good: *Her sight was impaired as a result of the disease.* —**impairment** *n.* [U]

im·paired /ɪm'pɛrd/ *adj.* **1** damaged, less strong, or less good: *impaired kidney function* **2 hearing/visually/physically impaired** someone who is hearing impaired or visually impaired cannot hear, see, etc. well

im·pale /ɪm'peɪl/ *v.* [T] if someone or something is impaled on something, a sharp pointed object goes through him, her, or it

im·part /ɪm'pɑrt/ *v.* [T] *formal* **1** to give a particular quality to something: *Roasted chili peppers **impart** a smoky flavor **to** the dish.* **2** to give information, knowledge, etc. to someone: *He accused the universities of failing to **impart** moral values **to** students.*

im·par·tial /ɪm'pɑrʃəl/ *adj.* not giving special attention or support to any one person or group [= **objective**; ≠ **biased**]: *impartial advice* | *Rosen said he was unable to remain impartial in the case.* —**impartially** *adv.* —**impartiality** /ɪm,pɑrʃi'æləṭi/ *n.* [U]

im·pass·a·ble /ɪm'pæsəbəl/ *adj.* impossible to travel along or through: *The road into the valley had become impassable.*

im·passe /'ɪmpæs/ *n.* [singular] a situation in which it is impossible to continue with a discussion or plan because the people involved cannot agree: *Discussions about pay have **reached an impasse**.*

im·pas·sioned /ɪm'pæʃənd/ *adj.* full of strong feelings and emotion: *an impassioned speech*

im·pas·sive /ɪm'pæsɪv/ *adj.* *formal* not showing any emotions: *His face was impassive as the judge spoke.* —**impassively** *adv.*

THESAURUS

matter-of-fact, **detached**, **cold**
➔ see Thesaurus box at MATTER-OF-FACT

im·pa·tient /ɪm'peɪʃənt/ *adj.* **1** annoyed because of delays or mistakes that make you wait: *After numerous delays in the project, some people began to **get/grow impatient**.* | *Rob's teacher seems very **impatient with** some of the slower kids.* **2** very eager for something to happen, and not wanting to wait: *Gary was **impatient to** leave.* —**impatience** *n.* [U] —**impatiently** *adv.*

im·peach /ɪm'pitʃ/ *v.* [T] *law* to say officially that a public official is guilty of a serious crime —**impeachment** *n.* [C,U]

im·pec·ca·ble /ɪm'pɛkəbəl/ *adj.* completely perfect and impossible to criticize: *She has impeccable taste in clothes.* —**impeccably** *adv.*

im·pede /ɪm'pid/ *v.* [T] *formal* to make it difficult for someone or something to make progress: *Rescue attempts were impeded by storms.*

im·ped·i·ment /ɪm'pɛdəmənt/ *n.* [C] **1** a physical problem that makes speaking, hearing, or moving difficult: *Gina **has a** slight **speech impediment**.* **2** a fact or event that makes action difficult or impossible: *The current law is a major **impediment to** trade.*

im·pel /ɪm'pɛl/ past tense and past participle **impelled**, present participle **impelling** *v.* [T] *formal* to make you feel very strongly that you must do something: *He **felt impelled to** explain his actions.*

im·pend·ing /ɪm'pɛndɪŋ/ *adj.* [only before noun] likely to happen soon: *the Johnsons' impending divorce*

im·pen·e·tra·ble /ɪm'pɛnətrəbəl/ *adj.* **1** impossible to get through, see through, or get into [➡ **penetrate**]: *impenetrable fog* **2** very difficult or impossible to understand: *impenetrable business jargon*

im·per·a·tive¹ /ɪm'pɛrəṭɪv/ *adj.* **1** *formal* extremely important and urgent: ***It is imperative that** all fees be paid in full.* **2** *technical* an imperative verb expresses a COMMAND. In the sentence "Go to your room," "go" is an imperative verb.

imperative² *n.* [C] **1** *formal* something that must be done urgently: *Reducing air pollution has become an imperative.* **2** *technical* the form of a verb that expresses a COMMAND. In the sentence "Do it now!" the verb "do" is in the imperative

im·per·cep·ti·ble /,ɪmpɚ'sɛptəbəl/ *adj.* impossible to notice: *an almost imperceptible change* —**imperceptibly** *adv.*

im·per·fect¹ /ɪm'pɚfɪkt/ *adj.* not completely perfect: *an imperfect legal system* —**imperfectly** *adv.*

imperfect² *n.* [singular] *technical* the form of a verb that shows an incomplete action in the past that is formed with "be" and the PRESENT PARTICIPLE. In the sentence "We were walking down the road," the verb phrase "were walking" is in the imperfect.

im·per·fec·tion /,ɪmpɚ'fɛkʃən/ *n.* [C,U] the state of being imperfect, or something that is imperfect: *A few **slight/small imperfections** won't spoil the overall appearance.*

im·pe·ri·al /ɪm'pɪriəl/ *adj.* relating to an EMPIRE or to the person who rules it

im·pe·ri·al·ism /ɪm'pɪriə,lɪzəm/ *n.* [U] *disapproving* a political system in which one country controls a lot of other countries —**imperialist** *n.*

I

[C] —**imperialist, imperialistic** /ɪm,pɪriə'lɪstɪk/ *adj.*

im·per·son·al /ɪm'pɚsənəl/ *adj.* not showing any feelings of sympathy, friendliness, etc.: *an impersonal letter* —**impersonally** *adv.*

im·per·so·nate /ɪm'pɚsə,neɪt/ *v.* [T] **1** to pretend to be someone else by copying his/her appearance, voice, etc. in order to deceive people: *Quinn was arrested for impersonating a police officer.* **2** to copy someone's voice and behavior in order to make people laugh: *a comedian who impersonates politicians* —**impersonator** *n.* [C] —**impersonation** /ɪm,pɚsə'neɪʃən/ *n.* [U]

im·per·vi·ous /ɪm'pɚviəs/ *adj. formal* **1 impervious to sth** not affected or influenced by something: *He seemed impervious to the noise around him.* **2 impervious to sth** not allowing anything to pass through: *The container must be impervious to water.*

im·pet·u·ous /ɪm'pɛtʃuəs/ *adj. formal* tending to do things quickly, without thinking —**impetuously** *adv.* —**impetuousness** *n.* [U]

im·pe·tus /'ɪmpət̬əs/ *n.* [U] *formal* an influence that makes something happen, or happen more quickly: *Much of the **impetus for** reform came from local activists.* | *The conference **gave** fresh **impetus to** change.*

im·pinge /ɪm'pɪndʒ/ *v.*

impinge on/upon sth *phr. v. formal* to have an unwanted or bad effect on someone or something: *International politics have impinged on decisions made in Congress.*

im·plac·a·ble /ɪm'plækəbəl/ *adj. formal* very determined to continue opposing someone or something: *an implacable enemy* —**implacably** *adv.*

im·plant¹ /ɪm'plænt/ *v.* [T] **1** to put something into someone's body in a medical operation: *Some healthy cells were **implanted in/into** the patient's brain.* **2** to influence someone so that s/he believes or feels something strongly: *the patriotism **implanted in** him by his father*

im·plant² /'ɪmplænt/ *n.* [C] something that has been put into someone's body in a medical operation: *silicone breast implants*

im·plau·si·ble /ɪm'plɔzəbəl/ *adj.* difficult to believe and not likely to be true: *an implausible excuse*

im·ple·ment¹ /'ɪmplə,mɛnt/ *v.* [T] if you implement a plan, process, etc., you begin to make it happen: *Their recommendations may be difficult to implement.* —**implementation** /,ɪmpləmən'teɪʃən/ *n.* [U]

im·ple·ment² /'ɪmpləmənt/ *n.* [C] a large tool or instrument with no motor: *farming implements*

im·pli·cate /'ɪmplɪ,keɪt/ *v.* [T] to show that someone is involved in something wrong: *The witness **implicated** two other men **in** the robbery.*

im·pli·ca·tion /,ɪmplɪ'keɪʃən/ *n.* **1** [C] a possible effect or result of a plan, action, etc.: *What are the **implications of** their research?* | *This ruling will **have implications for** many people.* **2** [C,U] something you do not say directly but that you want people to understand: *I don't like the **implication that** I was lying.* **3** [U] the act of making a statement that suggests that someone has done something wrong or illegal: *the implication of the bank president in the theft*

im·plic·it /ɪm'plɪsɪt/ *adj.* **1** suggested or understood but not stated directly [➡ **explicit**]: *There was implicit criticism in the principal's statement.* **2** complete and containing no doubts: *She has **implicit faith** in her husband.* **3 be implicit in sth** *formal* to be a central part of something, without being stated: *Risk is implicit in owning a business.* —**implicitly** *adv.*

im·plode /ɪm'ploʊd/ *v.* [I] to explode inward

im·plore /ɪm'plɔr/ *v.* [T] *formal* to ask for something in an emotional way [= **beg**]: *Joan **implored** him not **to** leave.*

im·ply /ɪm'plaɪ/ *v.* past tense and past participle **implied**, third person singular **implies** [T] to suggest that something is true without saying or showing it directly: *He **implied that** the money hadn't been lost, but was stolen.*

> **THESAURUS**
>
> **say, mention, add, express, point out, suggest**
>
> ➔ see Thesaurus box at SAY¹

im·po·lite /,ɪmpə'laɪt/ *adj.* not polite [= **rude**]: ***It would be impolite to** leave in the middle of her recital.*

> **THESAURUS**
>
> **rude, insulting, tactless, offensive**
>
> ➔ see Thesaurus box at RUDE

im·port¹ /'ɪmpɔrt/ *n.* **1** [C,U] the business of bringing products into one country from another in order to be sold, or the products that are sold [≠ **export**]: *Car imports have risen recently.* | *The government has banned the **import of** weapons.* **2** *formal* [U] importance or meaning: *a matter **of great import***

im·port² /ɪm'pɔrt/ *v.* [T] to bring something into a country from ABROAD in order to sell it [≠ **export**]: *oil imported from the Middle East* —**importer** *n.* [C]

im·por·tance /ɪm'pɔrt̚ns, -pɔrt̬ns/ *n.* [U] the quality of being important: ***the importance of** regular exercise* | *The company **attaches great importance** to employee training.* | *These issues are **of great/critical/vital importance**.*

im·por·tant /ɪm'pɔrt̚nt, -'pɔrt̬nt/ *adj.* having a big effect or influence: *a very important meeting* | *Ellen's family is more **important to** her than anything else.* | ***It's important that** you look professional at the interview.*

THESAURUS

crucial – very important: *The U.S. plays a crucial role in the region.*
vital – extremely important or necessary: *vital information*
essential – extremely important: *It's essential that you buy tickets in advance.*
major – very large or important, especially when compared to other things: *our major cities* | *a major problem*
significant – noticeable or important: *The film upset a significant number of people.*
key – very important and necessary for success or to understand something: *the team's key players* | *He plays a key role in the company.* | *The key question is whether to buy or sell.*

—**importantly** *adv.*

im·por·ta·tion /ˌɪmpɔrˈteɪʃən/ *n.* [U] the business of bringing goods from another country to sell in your country

im·pose /ɪmˈpoʊz/ *v.* **1** [T] to introduce a rule, tax, punishment, etc. and force people to accept it: *City officials have **imposed** limits **on** commercial development.* **2** [T] to force someone to have the same ideas, beliefs, etc. as you: *parents **imposing** their values **on** their children* **3** [I] to unreasonably ask or expect someone to do something: *I didn't ask you because I didn't want to impose.*

im·pos·ing /ɪmˈpoʊzɪŋ/ *adj.* large and impressive: *an imposing building*

THESAURUS

impressive, **dazzling**, **awe-inspiring**, **breathtaking**, **majestic**
➔ see Thesaurus box at IMPRESSIVE

im·po·si·tion /ˌɪmpəˈzɪʃən/ *n.* **1** [C usually singular] something that someone unreasonably expects or asks you to do for him/her: *We want you to stay with us – it's not an imposition at all.* **2** [U] the introduction of something such as a rule, tax, or punishment: *the **imposition of** taxes **on** cigarettes*

im·pos·si·ble /ɪmˈpɑsəbəl/ *adj.* **1** not able to be done or to happen: ***It was impossible for** us **to** answer all their questions.* | ***It is impossible to** predict what will happen.* | *The storm **made** driving **impossible**.* **2** extremely difficult to deal with: *an impossible situation* **3** behaving in an unreasonable and annoying way: *You're impossible!* —**impossibly** *adv.* —**impossibility** /ɪmˌpɑsəˈbɪləṭi/ *n.* [C,U]

im·pos·ter /ɪmˈpɑstɚ/ *n.* [C] someone who pretends to be someone else in order to trick people

im·po·tent /ˈɪmpəṭənt/ *adj.* **1** a man who is impotent is unable to have sex because he cannot have an ERECTION **2** unable to take effective action because you do not have enough power, strength, or control: *an impotent city government* —**impotence** *n.* [U]

im·pound /ɪmˈpaʊnd/ *v.* [T] *law* if the police or court of law impound your possessions, they take them and keep them until you go and get them

im·pov·er·ished /ɪmˈpɑvərɪʃt/ *adj.* very poor: *an impoverished country*

THESAURUS

poor, **needy**, **destitute**, **broke**, **disadvantaged**, **underprivileged**, **deprived**
➔ see Thesaurus box at POOR

im·prac·ti·cal /ɪmˈpræktɪkəl/ *adj.* **1** an impractical plan, suggestion, etc. is not sensible because it would be too expensive or difficult **2** not good at dealing with ordinary practical matters —**impractically** *adv.* —**impracticality** /ɪmˌpræktɪˈkæləṭi/ *n.* [U]

im·pre·cise /ˌɪmprɪˈsaɪs/ *adj.* not exact: *an imprecise estimate* —**imprecisely** *adv.* —**imprecision** /ˌɪmprɪˈsɪʒən/ *n.* [U]

im·preg·na·ble /ɪmˈprɛgnəbəl/ *adj.* very strong and unable to be entered: *an impregnable fort*

im·preg·nate /ɪmˈprɛgˌneɪt/ *v.* [T] *formal* **1** to make a woman or female animal PREGNANT **2** to make a substance spread completely through something, or to spread completely through something: *paper **impregnated with** perfume*

im·press /ɪmˈprɛs/ *v.* [T] **1** to make someone feel admiration and respect: *She dresses like that to impress people.* | *We were **impressed by/with** the size of his art collection.* **2** to make the importance of something clear to someone: *My parents **impressed on** me the value of an education.*

im·pres·sion /ɪmˈprɛʃən/ *n.* **1** [C,U] the opinion or feeling you have about someone or something because of the way she, he, or it seems: ***I get the impression that** something's wrong here.* | ***First impressions** can be wrong.* | *It's important to **make a** good **impression** at your interview.* **2 be under the impression (that)** to think that something is true when it is not true: *I was under the impression that Marcie was coming to dinner too.* **3** [C] the act of copying the speech or behavior of a famous person in order to make people laugh: *Eric **does** a great **impression of** Mick Jagger.* **4** [C] the mark left by pressing something into a soft surface

im·pres·sion·a·ble /ɪmˈprɛʃənəbəl/ *adj.* easy to influence: *The girls are **at an impressionable age**.*

im·pres·sion·is·tic /ɪmˌprɛʃəˈnɪstɪk/ *adj.* based on a general feeling of what something is like rather than on details: *an impressionistic account of the events*

im·pres·sive /ɪmˈprɛsɪv/ *adj.* causing admiration: *an impressive performance on the piano* | *The view was impressive.* —**impressively** *adv.*

THESAURUS

imposing – large and impressive: *The judge sat behind an imposing desk.*
dazzling – very impressive, exciting, or interesting: *a dazzling display of Christmas decorations*
awe-inspiring – so impressive that you feel awe (=a feeling of respect and admiration): *The cathedral was an awe-inspiring sight.*
breathtaking – extremely impressive, exciting, or surprising: *breathtaking views of the Rocky Mountains*
majestic – looking very big and impressive: *the majestic pyramids at Giza in Egypt*

im·print[1] /ˈɪmˌprɪnt/ *n.* [C] the mark left by an object that has been pressed into or onto something: *the **imprint of** her thumb on the clay*

im·print[2] /ɪmˈprɪnt/ *v.* **be imprinted on your mind/memory** if something is imprinted on your mind or memory, you can never forget it

im·pris·on /ɪmˈprɪzən/ *v.* [T] to put someone in prison or to keep him/her in a place s/he cannot escape from: *The opposition leaders were imprisoned and tortured.* —**imprisonment** *n.* [U]

im·prob·a·ble /ɪmˈprɑbəbəl/ *adj.* **1** not likely to happen or to be true [**= unlikely**]: ***It is highly improbable that** you will find sharks in these waters.* **2** surprising and slightly strange: *an improbable partnership* —**improbably** *adv.* —**improbability** /ɪmˌprɑbəˈbɪləṭi/ *n.* [C,U]

im·promp·tu /ɪmˈprɑmptu/ *adj.* done or said without any preparation or planning: *an impromptu speech* —**impromptu** *adv.*

im·prop·er /ɪmˈprɑpɚ/ *adj.* unacceptable according to professional, moral, or social rules of behavior: *Many cases of "stomach flu" result from improper cooking of food.* | *the improper use of funds* —**improperly** *adv.*: *The car alarm had been improperly installed.*

im·pro·pri·e·ty /ˌɪmprəˈpraɪəṭi/ *n.* [U] *formal* behavior or an action that is unacceptable according to moral, social, or professional standards

im·prove /ɪmˈpruv/ *v.* [I,T] to become better, or to make something better: *exercises to improve muscle strength* | *Your math skills have improved this year.* | *The situation **improved dramatically**.* —**improved** *adj.*

improve on/upon sth *phr. v.* to do something better than before, or to make it better: *No one's been able to improve on her Olympic record.*

im·prove·ment /ɪmˈpruvmənt/ *n.* **1** [C,U] an act of improving, or the state of being improved: *There's certainly been an **improvement in** Danny's behavior.* | *Your German is getting better, but there's still **room for improvement*** (=the possibility of more improvement). | *Jerry has **made** dramatic **improvement** since the surgery.* | *Ben's work is showing **signs of improvement**.* **2** [C] a change or addition that makes something better: ***home improvements***

im·pro·vise /ˈɪmprəˌvaɪz/ *v.* **1** [I,T] to make or do something without any preparation, using what you have: *I left my lesson plans at home, so I'll have to improvise.* **2** [I] to perform music, sing, etc. from your imagination: *Jazz musicians are good at improvising.* —**improvisation** /ɪmˌprɑvəˈzeɪʃən/ *n.* [C,U]

im·pu·dent /ˈɪmpyədənt/ *adj. formal* rude and not showing respect —**impudence** *n.* [U]

im·pulse /ˈɪmpʌls/ *n.* **1** [C,U] a sudden desire to do something without thinking about the results: *She resisted the **impulse to** hit him.* | *I bought this shirt **on impulse**, and now I don't like it.* **2** [C] *technical* a short electrical signal sent in one direction along a wire or nerve, or through the air

im·pul·sive /ɪmˈpʌlsɪv/ *adj.* tending to do things without thinking about the results, or showing this quality: *an impulsive shopper* | *an impulsive decision* —**impulsively** *adv.*

THESAURUS

rash – done too quickly without thinking carefully first, or behaving in this way: *Don't do anything rash!*
hotheaded – someone who gets angry or excited easily and does things too quickly, without thinking: *a hotheaded young man*
hasty formal – done in a hurry, especially with bad results: *He soon regretted his hasty decision.*

im·pu·ni·ty /ɪmˈpyunəṭi/ *n.* **with impunity** without risk of punishment: *We cannot let them break laws with impunity.*

im·pure /ɪmˈpyʊr/ *adj.* **1** mixed with other substances: *impure drugs* **2** *old-fashioned* morally bad, especially when relating to sex: *impure thoughts*

im·pu·ri·ty /ɪmˈpyʊrəṭi/ *n.* plural **impurities** **1** [C usually plural] a part of an almost pure substance that is of a lower quality: *minerals containing impurities* **2** [U] the state of being impure

IN the written abbreviation of **Indiana**

in[1] /ɪn/ *prep.* **1** used with the name of a container, place, or area to show where something is: *The paper is in the top drawer.* | *I was still in bed at 11:30.* | *cows standing in a field* | *He lived in Boston for 15 years.* **2** used with the names of months, years, seasons, etc. to say when something happens: *We bought our car in April.* | *In 1969 the first astronauts landed on the moon.* | *Sarah starts college in the fall.* **3** during a period of time: *We finished the whole project in a week.* **4** at the end of a period of time: *Gerry should be home in an hour.* | *I wonder if the business will still be going in a year.* **5** included as part of something: *One of the people in the story is a young doctor.* | *In the first part of the speech, he talked about the environment.* **6 sb has not done sth in years/months/weeks** if you have not done something in years, etc., you have not done it for that amount of time: *I haven't been to the circus in years!* **7** using a particular kind of voice, or a particular way of speaking or writing: *"Why?" she asked him in a whisper.* | *Their parents always talk to them in Italian.* | *Do not write in pen on this test.* **8** working at a particular kind of job: *She's in advertising.* **9** arranged in a particular way, often to form a group or shape: *Stand against the wall in a line.* | *He had made a bowl in the shape of a heart.* | *Put the words in alphabetical order.* **10** used in order to show the connection between two ideas or subjects: *I was never interested in sports as a kid.* **11** used before the bigger number when you are talking about a relationship between two numbers: *1 in 10 women* (=10% of all women) *have the disease.* **12 in shock/horror etc.** used in order to describe a strong feeling someone has when s/he does something: *She looked at me in shock as I told her how everything had gone wrong.* **13 in all** used when giving a total amount: *There were about 50 of us in all at the reunion.*

in² *adj., adv.* **1** so as to be contained inside or surrounded by something: *She pushed the box towards me so that I could put my money in.* **2** inside a building, especially the one where you live or work: *Mr. Linn should be in soon.* | *You're never in when I call.* **3** if an airplane, bus, train, or boat is in, it has arrived at the airport, station, etc.: *Her flight gets in at 5:30.* **4** given or sent to a particular place in order to be read or looked at: *Your final papers have to be in by Friday.* **5** if you write, paint, or draw something in, you write it, etc. in the correct place: *Fill in the blanks, using a number 2 pencil.* **6** if clothes, colors, etc. are in, they are fashionable: *Long hair is in again.* **7** if a ball is in during a game, it is inside the area where the game is played **8 be in for sth** if someone is in for something, something bad is about to happen to him/her: *She's in for a shock if she thinks we're going to help her pay for it.* **9 be in on sth** to be involved in doing, talking about, or planning something: *Everyone was in on the secret except Cheryl.* **10** if the TIDE comes in or is in, the ocean water is at its highest level **11 in joke** an in joke is one that is only understood by a small group of people

in·a·bil·i·ty /ˌɪnəˈbɪləṭi/ *n.* [singular, U] a lack of the ability, skill, etc. to do something: *an* ***inability to*** *remember details*

in·ac·ces·si·ble /ˌɪnəkˈsɛsəbəl/ *adj.* difficult or impossible to reach: *roads that are inaccessible in winter*

in·ac·cu·ra·cy /ɪnˈækyərəsi/ *n.* plural **inaccuracies** [C,U] a mistake, or a lack of correctness: *There were several inaccuracies in the report.*

in·ac·cu·rate /ɪnˈækyərɪt/ *adj.* not completely correct: *an inaccurate description* —**inaccurately** *adv.*

THESAURUS

wrong, incorrect, misleading, false
➔ see Thesaurus box at WRONG¹

in·ac·tion /ɪnˈækʃən/ *n.* [U] lack of action

in·ac·tive /ɪnˈæktɪv/ *adj.* not doing anything or not working: *inactive volcanoes* | *He injured his knee and was inactive for the rest of the season.* —**inactivity** /ˌɪnækˈtɪvəṭi/ *n.* [U]

in·ad·e·qua·cy /ɪnˈædəkwəsi/ *n.* plural **inadequacies** **1** [U] a feeling that you are unable to deal with situations because you are not as good as other people: *Not having a job can cause strong* ***feelings of inadequacy.*** **2** [C,U] the fact of not being good enough for a particular purpose, or something that is not good enough: *the* ***inadequacy of*** *America's health-care system*

in·ad·e·quate /ɪnˈædəkwɪt/ *adj.* not good enough, big enough, skilled enough, etc. for a particular purpose: *inadequate heating* | *She made me* ***feel*** *so* ***inadequate.*** —**inadequately** *adv.*

in·ad·mis·si·ble /ˌɪnədˈmɪsəbəl/ *adj. formal* not allowed: *Some of the evidence was inadmissible.*

in·ad·vert·ent·ly /ˌɪnədˈvɚtˀntli/ *adv.* without intending to do something: *She inadvertently hit the brakes.* —**inadvertent** *adj.*

in·al·ien·a·ble /ɪnˈeɪlyənəbəl/ *adj. formal* an inalienable right cannot be taken away from you

in·ane /ɪˈneɪn/ *adj.* extremely stupid or without much meaning: *inane jokes*

in·an·i·mate /ɪnˈænəmɪt/ *adj.* not living: *Rocks are* ***inanimate objects.***

in·ap·pro·pri·ate /ˌɪnəˈproʊpriɪt/ *adj.* not appropriate for a particular purpose or situation: *inappropriate behavior* | *The movie may be* ***inappropriate for*** *children under 14.* —**inappropriately** *adv.*

in·ar·tic·u·late /ˌɪnɑrˈtɪkyəlɪt/ *adj.* not able to express yourself or speak clearly

in·as·much as /ˌɪnəzˈmʌtʃ əz/ *conjunction formal* used in order to begin a phrase that explains the rest of your sentence by showing the limited way that it is true: *She's guilty, inasmuch as she knew what the other girls were planning to do.*

in·au·di·ble /ɪnˈɔdəbəl/ *adj.* too quiet to be heard: *Her reply was inaudible.* ➔ see Thesaurus box at HEAR —**inaudible** *adv.*

in·au·gu·rate /ɪˈnɔgyəˌreɪt/ *v.* [T] **1** to have an official ceremony in order to show that someone is beginning an important job: *The President is inaugurated in January.* **2** to open a new building or start a new service with a ceremony —**inaugural** /ɪˈnɔgyərəl/ *adj.*: *the president's inaugural speech* —**inauguration** /ɪˌnɔgyəˈreɪʃən/ *n.* [C,U]

in·aus·pi·cious /ˌɪnɔˈspɪʃəs◂/ *adj. formal* seeming to show that the future will be unlucky: *an* ***inauspicious start*** *to our trip*

ˌin-ˈbetween *adj. informal* in the middle of two points, sizes, etc.: *She's at that in-between age, neither a girl nor a woman.*

in·born /ˌɪnˈbɔrn◂/ *adj.* an inborn quality or ability is one that you have had naturally since

I

birth: *Humans have an almost inborn love of stories.*

in·bred /ˌɪnˈbrɛd◂/ *adj.* produced by the breeding of closely related members of a family, which often causes problems: *an inbred genetic defect* —**inbreeding** /ˈɪnˌbridɪŋ/ *n.* [U]

Inc. /ɪŋk, ɪnˈkɔrpəˌreɪt̬ɪd/ the written abbreviation of **Incorporated**: *General Motors Inc.*

in·cal·cu·la·ble /ɪnˈkælkyələbəl/ *adj.* too many or too great to be measured: *The scandal has done* ***incalculable damage*** *to the college's reputation.*

in·can·des·cent /ˌɪnkənˈdɛsənt/ *adj.* giving a bright light when heated —**incandescence** *n.* [U]

in·can·ta·tion /ˌɪnkænˈteɪʃən/ *n.* [C,U] a set of special words that someone uses in magic, or the act of saying these words

in·ca·pa·ble /ɪnˈkeɪpəbəl/ *adj.* unable to do something or to feel a particular emotion: *He seemed* ***incapable of*** *understanding how I felt.*

in·ca·pac·i·tate /ˌɪnkəˈpæsəˌteɪt/ *v.* [T] to make someone too sick or weak to live or work normally: *He was incapacitated for a while after the operation.*

in·ca·pac·i·ty /ˌɪnkəˈpæsət̬i/ *n.* [U] lack of ability, strength, or power to do something, especially because you are sick

in·car·cer·ate /ɪnˈkɑrsəˌreɪt/ *v.* [T] *formal* to put someone in a prison or keep him/her there —**incarceration** /ɪnˌkɑrsəˈreɪʃən/ *n.* [U]

in·car·nate /ɪnˈkɑrnɪt, -ˌneɪt/ *adj.* **evil/beauty/greed etc. incarnate** someone who is considered extremely evil, beautiful, etc.

in·car·na·tion /ˌɪnkɑrˈneɪʃən/ *n.* **1** [C] a time before or after the life you are living now when, according to some religions, you were alive in the form of a different person or animal **2 the incarnation of sth** someone who has a lot of a particular quality, or represents it: *She was the incarnation of wisdom.*

in·cen·di·ar·y /ɪnˈsɛndiˌɛri/ *adj. formal* designed to cause a fire: *an* ***incendiary device/bomb***

in·cense /ˈɪnsɛns/ *n.* [U] a substance that is burned in order to fill a room with a particular smell

in·censed /ɪnˈsɛnst/ *adj.* extremely angry

in·cen·tive /ɪnˈsɛntɪv/ *n.* [C,U] something that encourages you to work harder, start new activities, etc.: *The government* ***provides incentives for*** *new businesses.*

in·cep·tion /ɪnˈsɛpʃən/ *n.* [singular] *formal* the start of an organization or institution: *He has worked for the company* ***since its inception*** *in 1970.*

in·ces·sant /ɪnˈsɛsənt/ *adj. formal* without stopping: *the incessant traffic noise* —**incessantly** *adv.*

in·cest /ˈɪnsɛst/ *n.* [U] illegal sex between people who are closely related to each other —**incestuous** /ɪnˈsɛstʃuəs/ *adj.* —**incestuously** *adv.*

inch¹ /ɪntʃ/ *n.* plural **inches** [C] **1** *written abbreviation* **in** a unit for measuring length, equal to 1/12 of a foot or 2.54 centimeters: *The females lay eggs that are about 5 inches long.* **2 every inch** all of someone or something: ***Every inch of*** *the closet was filled with boxes.* **3 inch by inch** very slowly or by a small amount at a time: *The old buses moved inch by inch toward the pyramids.* **4 not give/budge an inch** to refuse to change your opinions at all: *At first Will refused to give an inch in the argument.*

inch² *v.* [I,T] to move very slowly and carefully, or to move something this way: *I got a glass of wine and* ***inched*** *my* ***way*** *across the crowded room.*

in·ci·dence /ˈɪnsədəns/ *n.* [singular] *formal* the number of times something happens: *Researchers found a high* ***incidence of*** *asthma in Detroit.*

in·ci·dent /ˈɪnsədənt/ *n.* [C] something unusual, serious, or violent that happens: *Any witnesses to the incident should speak to the police.* | *The plane took off* ***without incident*** (=without anything unusual or bad happening).

> **THESAURUS**
>
> **event, occurrence, happening, phenomenon**
> → see Thesaurus box at EVENT

in·ci·den·tal /ˌɪnsəˈdɛntl◂/ *adj.* happening or existing in connection with something else that is more important: *The issue that he brought up was* ***incidental to*** *the main debate.*

in·ci·den·tal·ly /ˌɪnsəˈdɛntˈli/ *adv.* used when giving additional information, or when changing the subject of a conversation: *Incidentally, Jenny's coming over tonight.*

in·cin·er·ate /ɪnˈsɪnəˌreɪt/ *v.* [T] *formal* to burn something in order to destroy it —**incineration** /ɪnˌsɪnəˈreɪʃən/ *n.* [U]

in·cin·er·a·tor /ɪnˈsɪnəˌreɪt̬ɚ/ *n.* [C] a machine that burns things at very high temperatures

in·ci·sion /ɪnˈsɪʒən/ *n. technical* [C] a cut that a doctor makes in someone's body during an operation

in·ci·sive /ɪnˈsaɪsɪv/ *adj.* incisive words, remarks, etc. are very direct and deal with the most important part of a subject

in·ci·sor /ɪnˈsaɪzɚ/ *n. technical* [C] one of your eight front teeth that has sharp edges

in·cite /ɪnˈsaɪt/ *v.* [T] to deliberately encourage people to fight, argue, etc.: *One man was jailed for* ***inciting a riot.***

in·cli·na·tion /ˌɪnkləˈneɪʃən/ *n.* **1** [C,U] the desire to do something: *I didn't have* ***the time or inclination to*** *go with them.* **2** [C,U] a tendency to think or behave in a particular way: *his* ***inclination to*** *act violently*

in·cline¹ /ɪnˈklaɪn/ *v.* [I,T] to slope at a particular angle, or make something do this

in·cline² /ˈɪnklaɪn/ *n.* [C] a slope: *a steep incline*

in·clined /ɪnˈklaɪnd/ *adj.* **1 be inclined to agree/believe/think etc.** to have a particular opinion, but not have it very strongly: *I'm inclined to agree with you, but I don't really know.* **2** wanting to do something: *My client is not **inclined to** speak with reporters.* **3** likely or tending to do something: *He's **inclined to** get upset over small things.*

in·clude /ɪnˈklud/ *v.* [T] **1** if one thing includes another, the second thing is part of the first: *The price includes your flight, hotel, and car rental.* | *Tim's job responsibilities include hiring new teachers.* | *Service is **included in** the bill.* **2** to make someone or something part of a larger group or set [≠ **exclude**]: *Homework exercises are **included in** the book.* | *You should **include** your educational background **on** your résumé.*

in·clud·ing /ɪnˈkludɪŋ/ *prep.* used in order to show that someone or something is part of a larger group or set that you are talking about [≠ **excluding**]: *There were 20 people in the room, including the teacher.* | *We only paid $12 for dinner, including the tip.*

in·clu·sion /ɪnˈkluʒən/ *n.* **1** [U] the action of including someone or something in a larger group or set, or the fact of being included in one: *I am surprised at his **inclusion in** the team.* | *Here's the list of books we're considering **for inclusion** on the reading list.* **2** [C] someone or something that is included

in·clu·sive /ɪnˈklusɪv/ *adj.* including a wide variety of people, things, etc.: *American colleges have become much more inclusive.*

in·cog·ni·to /ˌɪnkɑgˈnit̬oʊ/ *adv.* if a famous person does something incognito, s/he is hiding who s/he really is

in·co·her·ent /ˌɪnkoʊˈhɪrənt/ *adj.* **1** not clear and hard to understand: *Joey mumbled something incoherent.* | *a dull incoherent speech* **2** unable to express yourself clearly: *She was incoherent with grief.* —**incoherently** *adv.*

in·come /ˈɪnkʌm, ˈɪŋ-/ *n.* [C,U] the money that you earn from working or making INVESTMENTS: *a **good/high/low income** | She has an **annual income** of $40,000.* | *an elderly couple living on a **fixed income*** (=an income that does not change or grow)

> **THESAURUS**
>
> **pay, salary, wages, earnings**
> → see Thesaurus box at PAY²

ˈincome tax *n.* [U] tax paid on the money you earn

in·com·ing /ˈɪnˌkʌmɪŋ/ *adj.* **1 incoming call/letter/fax** a telephone call, letter, or FAX that you receive [≠ **outgoing**] **2** coming toward a place, or about to arrive [≠ **outgoing**]: *the incoming tide*

in·com·mu·ni·ca·do /ˌɪnkəˌmyunɪˈkɑdoʊ/ *adj., adv.* not allowed or not wanting to communicate with anyone

in·com·pa·ra·ble /ɪnˈkɑmpərəbəl/ *adj.* so impressive, beautiful, etc. that nothing or no one is better: *her incomparable beauty* —**incomparably** *adv.*

in·com·pat·i·ble /ˌɪnkəmˈpæt̬əbəl/ *adj.* too different to be able to work together well or have a good relationship: *The software is **incompatible with** the operating system.* | *Tony and I have always been incompatible.* —**incompatibility** /ˌɪnkəmˌpæt̬əˈbɪləti/ *n.* [U]

in·com·pe·tence /ɪnˈkɑmpət̬əns/ *n.* [U] lack of ability or skill to do your job: *Police have been accused of incompetence.*

in·com·pe·tent /ɪnˈkɑmpət̬ənt/ *adj.* not having the ability or skill to do your job: *a totally incompetent waitress* —**incompetent** *n.* [C]

in·com·plete¹ /ˌɪnkəmˈplit/ *adj.* not having all its parts or not finished yet: *an incomplete sentence* | *The report is still incomplete.*

incomplete² *n.* [C] a GRADE given to college students, which shows that they still have to finish some work for a course: ***I got an incomplete in** French.*

in·com·pre·hen·si·ble /ˌɪnkɑmpriˈhɛnsəbəl/ *adj.* impossible to understand: *His speech was incomprehensible.*

in·con·ceiv·a·ble /ˌɪnkənˈsivəbəl/ *adj.* too strange or unusual to seem real or possible: ***It was inconceivable that** such a quiet man could be violent.* —**inconceivably** *adj.*

in·con·clu·sive /ˌɪnkənˈklusɪv/ *adj.* not leading to any decision or result: *Our experiments are inconclusive.* | *inconclusive evidence* (=not proving anything) —**inconclusively** *adv.*

in·con·gru·ous /ɪnˈkɑŋgruəs/ *adj. formal* seeming to be wrong or unusual in a particular situation: *Her quiet voice seemed **incongruous with** her hard face.* —**incongruously** *adv.* —**incongruity** /ˌɪnkənˈgruəti/ *n.* [C,U]

in·con·se·quen·tial /ˌɪnkɑnsəˈkwɛnʃəl/ *adj. formal* not important [= **insignificant**]: *The issue is totally inconsequential.* —**inconsequentially** *adv.*

in·con·sid·er·ate /ˌɪnkənˈsɪdərɪt/ *adj.* not caring about other people's needs or feelings: *It was really **inconsiderate of** you not to call and say you'd be late.* —**inconsiderately** *adv.*

in·con·sist·en·cy /ˌɪnkənˈsɪstənsi/ *n.* **1** [C,U] a situation in which two statements are different and cannot both be true: *The police became suspicious because of the **inconsistencies in** her statement.* **2** [U] the quality of changing your ideas too often or of doing something differently each time, so that people do not know what to expect: *I don't see any inconsistency in my views.*

in·con·sist·ent /ˌɪnkənˈsɪstənt/ *adj.* **1** two ideas or statements that are inconsistent are different and cannot both be true: *We're getting incon-*

I

sistent results from the lab tests. | *His story was* ***inconsistent with*** *the evidence.* **2** not doing things in the same way each time, or not following an expected principle or standard: *How can she be so inconsistent?* | *What they have done is* ***inconsistent with*** *the agreement that they made with us.* —**inconsistently** *adv.*

in·con·sol·a·ble /ˌɪnkənˈsoʊləbəl/ *adj. literary* so sad that you cannot be comforted: *His widow was inconsolable.*

in·con·spic·u·ous /ˌɪnkənˈspɪkyuəs/ *adj.* not easily seen or noticed: *I sat in the corner,* ***trying to look/be inconspicuous.***

in·con·ti·nent /ɪnˈkɑntˀn-ənt, -tənənt/ *adj.* unable to control your BLADDER or BOWELS —**incontinence** *n.* [U]

in·con·tro·vert·i·ble /ˌɪnkɑntrəˈvɚṭəbəl/ *adj.* an incontrovertible fact is definitely true: *The police have* ***incontrovertible evidence*** *that he committed the crime.* —**incontrovertibly** *adv.*

in·con·ven·ience[1] /ˌɪnkənˈvinyəns/ *n.* [C,U] something that causes you problems or difficulties, or the state of having problems or difficulties: *We apologize for any inconvenience caused by the delay to the bus service.*

inconvenience[2] *v.* [T] to cause problems or difficulties for someone: *"I'll drive you home." "Are you sure? I don't want to inconvenience you."*

in·con·ven·ient /ˌɪnkənˈvinyənt/ *adj.* causing problems or difficulties, especially in an annoying way: *Is this an inconvenient time for you to talk?* —**inconveniently** *adv.*

in·cor·po·rate /ɪnˈkɔrpəˌreɪt/ *v.* [T] **1** to include something as part of a group, system, etc.: *Several safety features have been* ***incorporated into*** *the car's design.* **2** to form a CORPORATION —**incorporation** /ɪnˌkɔrpəˈreɪʃən/ *n.* [U]

In·cor·po·rat·ed /ɪnˈkɔrpəˌreɪṭɪd/ *written abbreviation* **Inc.** *adj.* used after the name of a company in the U.S. to show that it is a CORPORATION

in·cor·rect /ˌɪnkəˈrɛkt/ *adj.* not correct [= **wrong**]: *incorrect answers* —**incorrectly** *adv.*

THESAURUS

wrong, **inaccurate**, **misleading**, **false**
→ see Thesaurus box at WRONG[1]

in·cor·ri·gi·ble /ɪnˈkɔrədʒəbəl, -ˈkɑr-/ *adj.* someone who is incorrigible is bad in some way and cannot be changed: *an* ***incorrigible liar***

in·crease[1] /ɪnˈkris/ *v.* [I,T] to become larger in number, amount, or degree or make something do this [≠ **decrease**]: *The price of gas has* ***increased by*** *4%.* | *Immigration has* ***increased dramatically*** *in recent decades.* | *The waves were* ***increasing in*** *size.* | *Smoking increases your chances of getting cancer.* —**increasing** *adj.*: *increasing concern about job security*

THESAURUS

go up – to increase in number, amount, or value: *Prices have gone up 2%.*
rise – to increase in number, amount, quality, or value: *Motor vehicle thefts rose from 145 to 312 last year.*
grow – to increase in amount, size, or degree: *The number of people working from home has grown substantially.*
double – to become twice as large or twice as much, or to make something do this: *The firm has doubled in size in ten years.*
shoot up – to quickly increase in number, size, or amount: *Unemployment shot up.*

increase

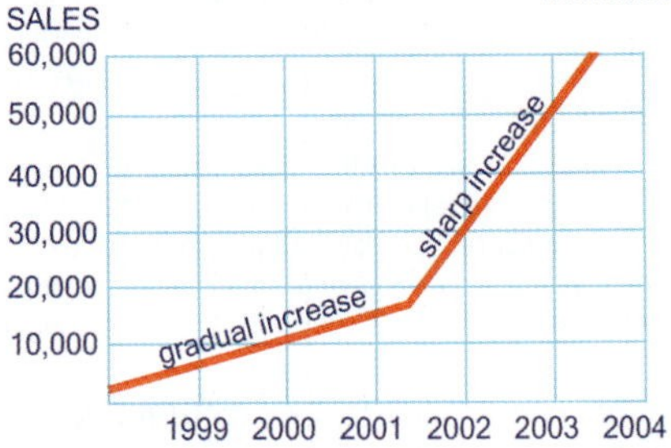

in·crease[2] /ˈɪŋkris/ *n.* [C,U] a rise in number, amount, or degree [≠ **decrease**]: *an* ***increase in*** *sales* | *People are complaining about the large* ***tax increase.*** | *There has been a* ***dramatic/significant increase*** *in housing prices.* | *Crime in the city is* ***on the increase*** (=increasing).

in·creased /ɪnˈkrist/ *adj.* larger or more than before: *an increased awareness of environmental issues*

in·creas·ing·ly /ɪnˈkrisɪŋli/ *adv.* more and more: *It's becoming increasingly difficult to find employment.*

in·cred·i·ble /ɪnˈkrɛdəbəl/ *adj.* **1** extremely good, large, or impressive: *The view from our hotel window was incredible.* | *an incredible bargain* **2** very hard to believe: ***It's incredible that*** *he survived the fall.* | ***It's incredible to think*** *they actually lost the game.*

in·cred·i·bly /ɪnˈkrɛdəbli/ *adv.* **1** extremely: *It's incredibly beautiful here in the spring.* **2** in a way that is difficult to believe: *Incredibly, he was not injured.*

in·cred·u·lous /ɪnˈkrɛdʒələs/ *adj.* showing that you are unable or unwilling to believe something: *"You sold the car?" she asked, incredulous.* —**incredulously** *adv.* —**incredulity** /ˌɪnkrɪˈduləṭi/ *n.* [U]

in·cre·ment /ˈɪnkrəmənt, ˈɪŋ-/ *n.* [C] an amount by which a value, number, or amount of money increases: *an annual salary increment of 2.9%* | *He is paying off the $5000 fine* ***in small increments.*** —**incremental** /ˌɪnkrəˈmɛntl◂/ *adj.*

in·crim·i·nate /ɪn'krɪmə,neɪt/ *v.* [T] to make someone seem guilty of a crime: *He refused to **incriminate himself** by answering questions.* —**incriminating** *adj.*: *incriminating evidence* —**incrimination** /ɪn,krɪmə'neɪʃən/ *n.* [U]

in·cu·bate /'ɪŋkyə,beɪt/ *v.* [I,T] if a bird incubates its egg or if an egg incubates, it is kept warm under a bird's body until the baby bird comes out —**incubation** /,ɪŋkyə'beɪʃən/ *n.* [U]

in·cu·ba·tor /'ɪŋkyə,beɪtə/ *n.* [C] **1** a machine used by hospitals for keeping very small or weak babies alive **2** a machine for keeping eggs warm until the young birds come out

in·cum·bent¹ /ɪn'kʌmbənt/ *n.* [C] *journalism* someone who has been elected to an official position and is now serving in that position: *The election will be tough for the incumbents on the city council.*

incumbent² *adj. formal* **1 it is incumbent on/upon sb to do sth** if it is incumbent upon you to do something, it is your duty or responsibility to do it **2 the incumbent President/Senator etc.** the president, senator, etc. who has been elected to an official position and is now serving in that position

in·cur /ɪn'kə/ *v.* past tense and past participle **incurred**, present participle **incurring** [T] to have something bad, such as a punishment or debt, happen because of something you have done: *The oil company incurred a debt of $5 million last year.*

in·cur·a·ble /ɪn'kyʊrəbəl/ *adj.* impossible to cure or change: *an incurable disease | I am an incurable optimist.* —**incurably** *adv.*

in·cur·sion /ɪn'kəʒən/ *n.* [C] *formal* a sudden attack or arrival into an area that belongs to other people: *the army's **incursion into** the northern provinces*

in·debt·ed /ɪn'dɛtɪd/ *adj.* **be indebted to sb** to be very grateful to someone for the help s/he has given you: *I am indebted to my friend Catherine, who edited my manuscript.* —**indebtedness** *n.* [U]

in·de·cent /ɪn'disənt/ *adj.* indecent behavior, clothes, or actions are likely to offend or shock people because they are against social or moral standards, or because they involve sex: *You can't wear a skirt that short – it's indecent! | indecent material on the Internet* —**indecency** *n.* [C,U]

in·de·ci·sion /,ɪndɪ'sɪʒən/ *n.* [U] the state of not being able to make decisions: *After a week of indecision, we agreed to buy the house.*

in·de·ci·sive /,ɪndɪ'saɪsɪv/ *adj.* **1** unable to make decisions: *He was criticized for being a weak, indecisive leader.* **2** not having a clear result: *an indecisive battle* —**indecisiveness** *n.* [U]

in·deed /ɪn'did/ *adv.* **1** used when adding more information to a statement: *Most people at that time were illiterate. Indeed, only 8% of the population could read.* **2** used when emphasizing a statement or a question: *Jackson is indeed the best player in the league.*

in·de·fen·si·ble /,ɪndɪ'fɛnsəbəl/ *adj.* too bad to be excused or defended: *indefensible behavior*

in·de·fin·a·ble /,ɪndɪ'faɪnəbəl/ *adj.* difficult to describe or explain: *For some indefinable reason she felt afraid.*

in·def·i·nite /ɪn'dɛfənɪt/ *adj.* **1** an indefinite action or period of time has no definite end arranged for it: *He was away in Alaska for an **indefinite period**.* **2** not clear or definite [= **vague**]: *Our plans are still indefinite.*

in,definite 'article *n.* [C] the words "a" and "an" [≠ **definite article**]

in·def·i·nite·ly /ɪn'dɛfənɪtli/ *adv.* for a period of time without an arranged end: *I'll be staying here indefinitely.*

in·del·i·ble /ɪn'dɛləbəl/ *adj.* impossible to remove or forget [= **permanent**]: *indelible ink | The movie **left an indelible impression** on her* (=she could not forget it). —**indelibly** *adv.*

in·del·i·cate /ɪn'dɛlɪkɪt/ *adj. literary* slightly impolite or offensive: *an indelicate question* —**indelicately** *adv.*

in·dem·ni·fy /ɪn'dɛmnə,faɪ/ *v.* past tense and past participle **indemnified**, third person singular **indemnifies** [T] *law* to promise to pay someone if something s/he owns becomes lost or damaged, or if s/he is injured

in·dem·ni·ty /ɪn'dɛmnəṭi/ *n. law* **1** [U] protection in the form of a promise to pay for any damage or loss **2** [C] money that is paid to someone for any damages, losses, or injury

in·dent /ɪn'dɛnt/ *v.* [T] to start a line of writing closer to the middle of the page than the other lines

in·den·ta·tion /,ɪndɛn'teɪʃən/ *n.* [C] **1** a space at the beginning of a line of writing **2** a cut or space in the edge of something

in·de·pend·ence /,ɪndɪ'pɛndəns/ *n.* [U] **1** the freedom and ability to make your own decisions and take care of yourself without having to ask other people for help, money, or permission: *old people who want to **keep/maintain** their **independence** | Staying out late is one way teenagers try to **assert** their **independence**. | Having a job gives you **financial independence**.* **2** political freedom from control by another country: *The United States **declared independence** in 1776. | Nigeria **gained independence from** Britain in 1960.*

Inde'pendence ,Day *n.* [U] a U.S. national holiday on July 4th that celebrates the beginning of the United States as an independent nation

in·de·pend·ent /,ɪndɪ'pɛndənt◂/ *adj.* **1** confident, free, and not needing to ask other people for help, money, or permission to do something: *Women have become better educated and more independent. | He helps disabled people to lead independent lives.* **2** not controlled by another government or organization: *India became an*

I

independent nation in 1947. | *a European army **independent of** NATO* **3** not influenced by other people: *an independent report on the experiment* —**independently** *adv.*

'in-depth *adj.* **in-depth study/report** a study or report that is very thorough and considers all the details

in·de·scrib·a·ble /ˌɪndɪ'skraɪbəbəl/ *adj.* too good, strange, frightening, etc. to be described: *My joy at seeing him was indescribable.*

in·de·struct·i·ble /ˌɪndɪ'strʌktəbəl/ *adj.* impossible to destroy: *The tank was built to be indestructible.*

in·de·ter·mi·nate /ˌɪndɪ'tɚmənɪt/ *adj.* impossible to find out or calculate exactly: *a woman of indeterminate age*

in·dex[1] /'ɪndɛks/ *n.* plural **indexes** or **indices** /'ɪndəˌsiz/ [C] **1** an ALPHABETICAL list at the end of a book, that lists all the names, subjects, etc. in the book and the pages where you can find them **2** a set of cards with information, or a DATABASE in ALPHABETICAL order **3** a standard or level you can use for judging or measuring something: *an index of economic growth*

index[2] *v.* [T] to make an index for something

'index card *n.* [C] a small card that you write information on

'index ˌfinger *n.* [C] the finger next to the thumb [= **forefinger**] ➔ see picture at HAND[1]

In·di·an[1] /'ɪndiən/ *adj.* **1** ➔ NATIVE AMERICAN **2** relating to or coming from India

Indian[2] *n.* [C] **1** ➔ NATIVE AMERICAN **2** someone from India

ˌIndian 'Ocean *n.* **the Indian Ocean** the ocean surrounded by Africa in the west, India in the north, and Australia in the east

ˌIndian 'summer *n.* [C,U] a period of warm weather in the fall

in·di·cate /'ɪndəˌkeɪt/ *v.* [T] **1** to show that something exists or is likely to be true: *Research **indicates that** women live longer than men.* | *Her writing indicated a deep understanding of science.*

THESAURUS

demonstrate, show, mean, suggest, prove
➔ see Thesaurus box at DEMONSTRATE

2 to point at something: *Indicating a chair, he said, "Please, sit down."* **3** to say or do something that shows what you want or intend to do: *He **indicated that** he had no desire to come with us.*

in·di·ca·tion /ˌɪndə'keɪʃən/ *n.* [C,U] a sign that something exists or is likely to be true: *Did Rick ever **give any indication that** he was unhappy?*

in·dic·a·tive /ɪn'dɪkət̬ɪv/ *adj. formal* **be indicative of sth** to show that something exists or is likely to be true: *His reaction is indicative of how frightened he is.*

in·di·ca·tor /'ɪndəˌkeɪt̬ɚ/ *n.* [C] an event, fact, etc. that shows that something exists, or shows you the way something is developing: *All the main **economic indicators** suggest that business is improving.*

in·di·ces /'ɪndəˌsiz/ *n.* [C] a plural of INDEX

in·dict /ɪn'daɪt/ *v.* [I,T] *law* to officially charge someone with a crime: *He was **indicted on charges of** perjury.* —**indictable** /ɪn'daɪt̬əbəl/ *adj.*

THESAURUS

accuse, allege, charge
➔ see Thesaurus box at ACCUSE

in·dict·ment /ɪn'daɪt˺mənt/ *n.* [C] **1** *law* an official written statement saying that someone has done something illegal

THESAURUS

accusation, allegation, charge
➔ see Thesaurus box at ACCUSATION

2 be an indictment of sth something which shows that a system, method, etc. is very bad or wrong: *Bellow's novel can be read as **an indictment of** modern society.*

in·dif·ference /ɪn'dɪfrəns/ *n.* [U] lack of interest or concern: *his **indifference to** the suffering of others*

in·dif·ferent /ɪn'dɪfrənt/ *adj.* not interested in someone or something, or not having any feelings or opinions about him, her, or it: *The industry seems **indifferent to** environmental concerns.*

in·dig·e·nous /ɪn'dɪdʒənəs/ *adj. formal* indigenous plants, animals, etc. have always lived or grown naturally in the place where they are [= **native**]: *plants **indigenous to** the Amazon region*

in·di·gest·i·ble /ˌɪndɪ'dʒɛstəbəl, -daɪ-/ *adj.* food that is indigestible cannot easily be broken down in the stomach [➡ **digest**]

in·di·ges·tion /ˌɪndə'dʒɛstʃən, -daɪ-/ *n.* [U] the pain caused by eating food that cannot easily be broken down in the stomach

in·dig·nant /ɪn'dɪgnənt/ *adj.* angry because you feel you have been insulted or unfairly treated: *Marsha was **indignant about** the poor service she had received.* —**indignantly** *adv.* —**indignation** /ˌɪndɪg'neɪʃən/ *n.* [U]

in·dig·ni·ty /ɪn'dɪgnət̬i/ *n.* plural **indignities** [C,U] a situation that makes you feel very ashamed and not respected: *Many women have **suffered the indignity of** being sexually harassed.*

in·di·rect /ˌɪndə'rɛkt◂, -daɪ-/ *adj.* **1** not directly caused by something or relating to it: *The accident was an **indirect result** of the heavy rain.* **2** not using the straightest or most direct way to get to a place: *an indirect route* **3** suggesting something without saying it directly or clearly: *He never mentioned my work, which I felt was an indirect criticism of its quality.* —**indirectly** *adv.*

ˌindirect 'object *n.* [C] *technical* in grammar, the person or thing that received something as the result of the action of the verb in a sentence. In the sentence "Pete gave me the money," "me" is the indirect object

ˌindirect 'speech *n.* [U] *technical* ➔ REPORTED SPEECH

in·dis·creet /ˌɪndɪ'skrit/ *adj.* careless about what you say or do, so that you let people know too much

in·dis·cre·tion /ˌɪndɪ'skrɛʃən/ *n.* [C,U] an action, remark, or behavior that shows bad judgment and is usually considered socially or morally unacceptable: *his embarrassing sexual indiscretions | youthful indiscretion*

in·dis·crim·i·nate /ˌɪndɪ'skrɪmənɪt/ *adj.* an indiscriminate action is done without thinking about what harm it might cause: *indiscriminate acts of violence*

in·dis·pen·sa·ble /ˌɪndɪ'spɛnsəbəl/ *adj.* someone or something that is indispensable is so important or useful that you cannot manage without him, her, or it: *The information he provided was* ***indispensable to*** *our research.*

in·dis·pu·ta·ble /ˌɪndɪ'spyut̬əbəl/ *adj.* a fact that is indisputable must be accepted because it is definitely true —**indisputably** *adv.*

in·dis·tinct /ˌɪndɪ'stɪŋkt/ *adj.* not able to be seen, heard, or remembered very clearly [= **unclear**]: *indistinct voices in the next room* —**indistinctly** *adv.*

in·dis·tin·guish·a·ble /ˌɪndɪ'stɪŋgwɪʃəbəl/ *adj.* things that are indistinguishable are so similar that you cannot see any difference between them: *This material is* ***indistinguishable from*** *real silk.*

in·di·vid·u·al¹ /ˌɪndə'vɪdʒuəl/ *adj.* **1** considered separately from other people or things in the same group: *Each individual drawing is slightly different. | We try to meet the needs of the individual customer.* **2** belonging to or intended for one person rather than a group: *Individual attention must be given to each student. | The gallery relies on both corporate and individual donations.*

individual² *n.* [C] one person, considered separately from the rest of the group or society that s/he lives in: *the rights of the individual | Effects of the drug vary from individual to individual.*

in·di·vid·u·al·ism /ˌɪndə'vɪdʒuəˌlɪzəm/ *n.* [U] the belief or practice of allowing people to do things their own way without being influenced by other people —**individualist** *n.* [C] —**individualistic** /ˌɪndəˌvɪdʒuə'lɪstɪk/ *adj.*

in·di·vid·u·al·i·ty /ˌɪndəˌvɪdʒu'ælət̬i/ *n.* [U] the quality that makes someone or something different from all others: *His individuality shows in his art work.*

in·di·vid·u·al·ly /ˌɪndə'vɪdʒuəli, -dʒəli/ *adv.* separately, not together in a group: *Mr. Wong met with each employee individually.*

in·di·vis·i·ble /ˌɪndə'vɪzəbəl/ *adj.* not able to be separated or divided into parts —**indivisibly** *adv.*

in·doc·tri·nate /ɪn'dɑktrəˌneɪt/ *v.* [T] *disapproving* to teach someone to accept a particular set of beliefs and not consider any others —**indoctrination** /ɪnˌdɑktrə'neɪʃən/ *n.* [U]

in·do·lent /'ɪndələnt/ *adj. formal* lazy —**indolently** *adv.* —**indolence** *n.* [U]

THESAURUS

lazy, idle, shiftless, slack
➔ see Thesaurus box at LAZY

in·dom·i·ta·ble /ɪn'dɑmət̬əbəl/ *adj.* **indomitable spirit/courage etc.** *formal* determination, courage, etc. that can never be defeated

indoor

indoor swimming pool

in·door /'ɪndɔr/ *adj.* [only before noun] used or happening inside a building [≠ **outdoor**]: *an indoor swimming pool*

in·doors /ˌɪn'dɔrz/ *adv.* into or inside a building [≠ **outdoors**]: *He stayed indoors all morning.*

in·duce /ɪn'dus/ *v. formal* **1** [T] to make someone decide to do something: *What* ***induced*** *you* ***to*** *spend so much money on a car?* **2** [T] to cause a particular physical condition: *This drug may induce drowsiness.* **3** [I,T] to make a woman give birth to her baby by giving her a special drug

in·duce·ment /ɪn'dusmənt/ *n.* [C,U] something that you are offered to persuade you to do something: *He was given $10,000 as an* ***inducement to*** *leave the company.*

in·duct /ɪn'dʌkt/ *v.* [T] to officially make someone a member of a group or organization: *Joni Mitchell was* ***inducted into*** *the Rock and Roll Hall of Fame.* —**inductee** /ɪnˌdʌk'ti/ *n.* [C]

in·duc·tion /ɪn'dʌkʃən/ *n.* [C,U] the act or ceremony of officially making someone a member of a group or organization

in·dulge /ɪn'dʌldʒ/ *v.* **1** [I,T] to let yourself do or have something that you enjoy, especially something that is considered bad for you: *We* ***indulged in*** *a nice bottle of wine with lunch. | Go ahead –* ***indulge yourself.*** **2** [T] to let someone do or have whatever s/he wants, even if it is bad

I

for him/her: *She did not like her children to be indulged.*

in·dul·gence /ɪnˈdʌldʒəns/ *n.* **1** [U] the habit of eating too much, drinking too much, etc.: *a life of indulgence* **2** [C] something that you do or have for pleasure, not because you need it: *Chocolate is my only indulgence.*

in·dul·gent /ɪnˈdʌldʒənt/ *adj.* allowing someone to do or have whatever s/he wants, even if it is bad for him/her: *indulgent parents* —**indulgently** *adv.*

in·dus·tri·al /ɪnˈdʌstriəl/ *adj.* **1** relating to industry or the people working in industry: *industrial waste | industrial production* **2** having many industries, or industries that are well developed: *an industrial region* —**industrially** *adv.*

in·dus·tri·al·ist /ɪnˈdʌstriəlɪst/ *n.* [C] the owner of a factory, industrial company, etc.

in·dus·tri·al·ize /ɪnˈdʌstriəˌlaɪz/ *v.* [I,T] if a country or place is industrialized or if it industrializes, it develops a lot of industry —**industrialization** /ɪnˌdʌstriələˈzeɪʃən/ *n.* [U]

inˈdustrial ˌpark *n.* [C] an area of land that has offices, businesses, small factories, etc. on it

inˌdustrial revoˈlution *n.* **the Industrial Revolution** the period in the 18th and 19th centuries in Europe, when machines and factories began to be used to produce goods in large quantities

in·dus·tri·ous /ɪnˈdʌstriəs/ *adj. formal* tending to work hard: *an industrious young woman* —**industriously** *adv.*

in·dus·try /ˈɪndəstri/ *n.* plural **industries** **1** [U] the production of goods, especially in factories [➡ **industrial**]: *The country's economy is supported by industry.*

> **THESAURUS**
>
> **business, commerce, trade, private enterprise**
> → see Thesaurus box at BUSINESS

2 [C] a particular type of trade or service that produces things: *He works in **the auto/retail/insurance industry**. | She's one of the most successful people in this industry.*

in·e·bri·at·ed /ɪˈnibriˌeɪtɪd/ *adj. formal* drunk —**inebriation** /ɪˌnibriˈeɪʃən/ *n.* [U]

in·ed·i·ble /ɪnˈɛdəbəl/ *adj.* not good enough to eat or not appropriate for eating: *inedible mushrooms*

in·ef·fec·tive /ˌɪnəˈfɛktɪv/ *adj.* something that is ineffective does not achieve what it was intended to achieve: *Critics say that gun-control laws have been ineffective.* —**ineffectiveness** *n.* [U]

in·ef·fec·tu·al /ˌɪnəˈfɛktʃuəl/ *adj.* not achieving what someone or something is trying to do: *an ineffectual leader* —**ineffectually** *adv.*

in·ef·fi·cient /ˌɪnəˈfɪʃənt/ *adj.* not working well and wasting time, money, or energy: *an inefficient use of good farm land* —**inefficiently** *adv.* —**inefficiency** *n.* [C,U]

in·el·e·gant /ɪnˈɛləgənt/ *adj. formal* not graceful or well done: *inelegant manners*

> **THESAURUS**
>
> **clumsy, awkward, gawky**
> → see Thesaurus box at CLUMSY

in·el·i·gi·ble /ɪnˈɛlədʒəbəl/ *adj.* not allowed to do or have something: *Our family is **ineligible for** state aid.* —**ineligibility** /ɪnˌɛlədʒəˈbɪləṭi/ *n.* [U]

in·ept /ɪˈnɛpt/ *adj.* having no skill: *an inept driver* —**ineptitude** /ɪˈnɛptəˌtud/ *n.* [U]

in·e·qual·i·ty /ˌɪnɪˈkwɑləṭi/ *n.* plural **inequalities** [C,U] an unfair situation, in which some groups in society have more money, opportunities, power, etc. than others [➡ **unequal**]: *There are many **inequalities in** our legal system.*

in·eq·ui·ty /ɪnˈɛkwəṭi/ *n.* plural **inequities** [C,U] *formal* lack of fairness, or something that is unfair: ***inequities in** the grading system*

in·ert /ɪˈnɚt/ *adj.* **1** *technical* not producing a chemical reaction when combined with other substances: *inert gases* **2** not moving: *He lay there, inert.*

in·er·tia /ɪˈnɚʃə/ *n.* [U] **1** a tendency for a situation to stay unchanged for a long time: *the problem of inertia in large bureaucracies* **2** a feeling that you do not want to do anything at all **3** *technical* the force that keeps an object in the same position or keeps it moving until it is moved or stopped by another force

in·es·cap·a·ble /ˌɪnəˈskeɪpəbəl/ *adj. formal* impossible to avoid or ignore: *The inescapable fact is that he has a drinking problem.* —**inescapably** *adv.*

in·es·ti·ma·ble /ɪnˈɛstəməbəl/ *adj. formal* too much or too great to be calculated —**inestimably** *adv.*

in·ev·i·ta·ble /ɪˈnɛvəṭəbəl/ *adj.* **1** certain to happen and impossible to avoid: *A lawsuit seems inevitable. | **It was inevitable that** someone would get hurt.* **2 the inevitable** something that is certain to happen: *Finally, the inevitable happened and he lost his job.* —**inevitability** /ɪˌnɛvəṭəˈbɪləṭi/ *n.* [U]

in·ev·i·ta·bly /ɪˈnɛvəṭəbli/ *adv.* as was certain to happen: *Inevitably, there were a few mistakes. | Questions will inevitably arise.*

in·ex·act /ˌɪnɪgˈzækt◂/ *adj.* not exact: *Psychology is **an inexact science*** (=you cannot measure things exactly in it).

in·ex·cus·a·ble /ˌɪnɪkˈskyuzəbəl/ *adj.* inexcusable behavior is too bad to be excused: *Being late on your first day at a job is inexcusable.* —**inexcusably** *adv.*

in·ex·haust·i·ble /ˌɪnɪgˈzɔstəbəl/ *adj.* something that is inexhaustible exists in such large amounts that it can never be used up: *Warton* *seems to have an* ***inexhaustible supply*** *of energy.* —**inexhaustibly** *adv.*

in·ex·o·ra·ble /ɪn'ɛksərəbəl/ *adj. formal* an inexorable process cannot be stopped: *the inexorable aging of the body* —**inexorably** *adv.*

in·ex·pen·sive /ˌɪnɪk'spɛnsɪv/ *adj.* low in price [= **cheap**]: *an inexpensive vacation* —**inexpensively** *adv.*

THESAURUS

cheap, reasonable, good/great/excellent value
➔ see Thesaurus box at CHEAP[1]

in·ex·pe·ri·enced /ˌɪnɪk'spɪriənst/ *adj.* not having much experience or knowledge: *an inexperienced driver* —**inexperience** *n.* [U]

in·ex·pli·ca·ble /ˌɪnɪk'splɪkəbəl/ *adj.* too unusual or strange to be explained or understood: *the inexplicable disappearance of the young man* —**inexplicably** *adv.*

in·ex·tri·ca·bly /ˌɪnɪk'strɪkəbli/ *adv. formal* things that are inextricably connected or related cannot be separated from each other: *Their political beliefs and their religion are* ***inextricably linked****.* —**inextricable** /ˌɪnɪk'strɪkəbəl, ɪn'ɛkstrɪk-/ *adj.*

in·fal·li·ble /ɪn'fæləbəl/ *adj.* **1** always right, and never making mistakes: *Many small children believe their parents are infallible.* **2** always having the intended effect: *an infallible cure for hiccups* —**infallibility** /ɪnˌfælə'bɪləṭi/ *n.* [U]

in·fa·mous /'ɪnfəməs/ *adj.* well known for being bad or evil [➡ **famous**]: *an infamous criminal*

THESAURUS

famous, well-known, legendary, notorious
➔ see Thesaurus box at FAMOUS

—**infamously** *adv.*

in·fa·my /'ɪnfəmi/ *n.* [U] the state of being evil or of being well known for evil things

in·fan·cy /'ɪnfənsi/ *n.* [U] **1** the period in a child's life before s/he can walk or talk: *Their son died* ***in infancy****.* **2 in its infancy** something that is in its infancy is just starting to be developed: *The project is still in its infancy.*

in·fant /'ɪnfənt/ *n.* [C] *formal* a baby, especially one that cannot walk yet

TOPIC

baby, newborn, toddler
➔ see Topic box at BABY

in·fan·tile /'ɪnfənˌtaɪl, -təl/ *adj.* **1** *disapproving* infantile behavior seems silly in an adult because it is typical of a child: *his infantile jokes* **2** [only before noun] affecting very small children: *infantile illnesses*

in·fan·try /'ɪnfəntri/ *n.* [U] soldiers who fight on foot

in·fat·u·at·ed /ɪn'fætʃuˌeɪṭɪd/ *adj.* having unreasonably strong feelings of love for someone: *He's* ***infatuated with*** *her.* —**infatuation** /ɪnˌfætʃu'eɪʃən/ *n.* [C,U]

in·fect /ɪn'fɛkt/ *v.* [T] **1** to give someone a disease: *People can feel well but still infect others.* | *a young man* ***infected with*** *the AIDS virus* **2** to make food, water, etc. dangerous and able to spread disease: *a bacteria that can infect fruit* **3** if a feeling that you have infects other people, it makes them begin to feel the same way: *Lucy's enthusiasm soon infected the rest of the class.* **4** if a computer VIRUS infects your computer or DISKS, it changes or destroys the information in them

in·fect·ed /ɪn'fɛktɪd/ *adj.* **1** a part of your body or a wound that is infected has harmful BACTERIA in it that prevent it from HEALing: *an infected finger* **2** food, water, etc. that is infected contains BACTERIA that spread disease: *water* ***infected with*** *cholera* **3** if a computer or DISK is infected, the information in it has been changed or destroyed by a computer VIRUS

in·fec·tion /ɪn'fɛkʃən/ *n.* [C,U] a disease or sickness in a part of your body caused by BACTERIA or a VIRUS: *Wash the cut thoroughly to protect against infection.* | *an ear infection*

in·fec·tious /ɪn'fɛkʃəs/ *adj.* **1** an infectious disease can be passed from one person to another: *Flu is* ***highly infectious****.* **2** someone who is infectious has a disease that could be passed to other people **3** infectious feelings or laughter spread quickly from one person to another

in·fer /ɪn'fɚ/ *v.* past tense and past participle **inferred**, present participle **inferring** [T] *formal* to form an opinion that something is probably true because of information that you have: *What can you* ***infer from*** *the available data?*

in·fer·ence /'ɪnfərəns/ *n.* [C,U] something that you think is true, based on information that you have: *You'll have to* ***draw*** *your own* ***inferences*** *from the evidence* (=decide what you think is true).

in·fe·ri·or[1] /ɪn'fɪriɚ/ *adj.* not good, or not as good as someone or something else [≠ **superior**]: *Larry always makes me feel inferior.* | *Her work is* ***inferior to*** *mine.* —**inferiority** /ɪnˌfɪri'ɑrəṭi, -'ɔr-/ *n.* [U]

inferior[2] *n.* [C] someone who has a lower position or rank than you in an organization [≠ **superior**]

in·fer·no /ɪn'fɚnoʊ/ *n. literary* [C] a very large and dangerous fire: *a* ***raging inferno*** (=an extremely violent fire)

THESAURUS

fire, flames, blaze, bonfire, campfire
➔ see Thesaurus box at FIRE[1]

in·fer·tile /ɪn'fɚṭl/ *adj.* **1** an infertile person or animal cannot have babies **2** infertile land or soil is not good enough to grow plants in —**infertility** /ˌɪnfɚˈtɪləti/ *n.* [U]

in·fest /ɪnˈfɛst/ *v.* [T] if insects, rats, etc. infest a place, they are there in large numbers and usually cause damage: *an old carpet* ***infested with*** *fleas* —**infestation** /ˌɪnfɛˈsteɪʃən/ *n.* [C,U]

in·fi·del /ˈɪnfədl, -ˌdɛl/ *n. old-fashioned disapproving* [C] someone who does not believe in what you consider to be the true religion

in·fi·del·i·ty /ˌɪnfəˈdɛləti/ *n.* plural **infidelities** [C,U] an act of being unfaithful to your wife or husband by having sex with someone else

in·field /ˈɪnfild/ *n.* [singular] the part of a baseball field inside the four bases —**infielder** *n.* [C]

in·fight·ing /ˈɪnˌfaɪtɪŋ/ *n.* [U] unfriendly competition and disagreement among members of the same group or organization: *political infighting*

in·fil·trate /ɪnˈfɪlˌtreɪt, ˈɪnfɪl-/ *v.* [I,T] to join an organization or enter a place, especially in order to find out secret information about it or to harm it: *The police have made several attempts to infiltrate the Mafia.* —**infiltrator** *n.* [C] —**infiltration** /ˌɪnfɪlˈtreɪʃən/ *n.* [U]

in·fi·nite /ˈɪnfənɪt/ *adj.* **1** very great: *a teacher with infinite patience* **2** without limits in space or time: *The universe is infinite.*

in·fi·nite·ly /ˈɪnfənɪtli/ *adv.* very much: *This stove is* ***infinitely better/worse*** *than the other one.*

in·fin·i·tes·i·mal /ˌɪnfɪnəˈtɛsəməl/ *adj.* extremely small: *infinitesimal changes in temperature* —**infinitesimally** *adv.*

in·fin·i·tive /ɪnˈfɪnətɪv/ *n.* [C] *technical* in grammar, the basic form of a verb, used with "to." In the sentence "I forgot to buy milk," "to buy" is an infinitive

in·fin·i·ty /ɪnˈfɪnəti/ *n.* **1** [U] a space or distance without limits or an end **2** [singular, U] a number that is larger than all others

in·firm /ɪnˈfɚm/ *adj. formal* weak or sick, especially because of being old

in·fir·ma·ry /ɪnˈfɚməri/ *n.* plural **infirmaries** [C] *formal* a place where sick people can receive medical treatment, especially in a place such as a school

in·fir·mi·ty /ɪnˈfɚməti/ *n.* plural **infirmities** [C,U] *formal* bad health or a particular illness

in·flame /ɪnˈfleɪm/ *v.* [T] *literary* to make someone have strong feelings of anger, excitement, etc.

in·flam·ma·ble /ɪnˈflæməbəl/ *adj. formal* inflammable materials or substances will start to burn very easily [= **flammable**; ≠ **nonflammable**]: *Gasoline is* ***highly inflammable.***

THESAURUS

Flammable and **inflammable** both describe something that burns very easily, but people usually use **flammable. Nonflammable** describes something that does not burn easily.

in·flam·ma·tion /ˌɪnfləˈmeɪʃən/ *n.* [C,U] swelling and soreness on or in a part of your body, which is often red and hot to touch —**inflamed** /ɪnˈfleɪmd/ *adj.*

in·flam·ma·to·ry /ɪnˈflæməˌtɔri/ *adj. formal* an inflammatory speech, piece of writing, etc. is likely to make people angry

in·flat·a·ble /ɪnˈfleɪtəbəl/ *adj.* an inflatable object has to be filled with air before you can use it: *an inflatable mattress*

in·flate /ɪnˈfleɪt/ *v.* **1** [I,T] to fill something with air or gas, so that it becomes larger, or to make something do this [≠ **deflate**]: *The machine quickly inflates the tires.* **2** [T] to make something larger in size, amount, or importance: *a policy that inflates land prices*

in·flat·ed /ɪnˈfleɪtɪd/ *adj.* **1** greater or larger than is reasonable: *He has an inflated opinion of his own importance.* **2** filled with air or gas: *an inflated balloon*

in·fla·tion /ɪnˈfleɪʃən/ *n.* [U] **1** a continuing increase in prices or the rate at which prices increase: *countries with* ***high/low inflation*** | *the* ***inflation rate*** **2** the process of filling something with air or gas

in·fla·tion·a·ry /ɪnˈfleɪʃəˌnɛri/ *adj.* relating to or causing price increases: *inflationary wage increases*

in·flex·i·ble /ɪnˈflɛksəbəl/ *adj.* **1** impossible to influence or change: *a school with inflexible rules* **2** inflexible material is stiff and will not bend —**inflexibility** /ɪnˌflɛksəˈbɪləti/ *n.* [U]

in·flict /ɪnˈflɪkt/ *v.* [T] to make someone suffer something bad: *the damage* ***inflicted on/upon*** *the enemy* —**infliction** /ɪnˈflɪkʃən/ *n.* [U]

in·flu·ence[1] /ˈɪnfluəns/ *n.* **1** [C,U] the power to have an effect on the way someone or something develops, behaves, or thinks: *Diego Rivera* ***had*** *a profound* ***influence on*** *artists of the 1930s.* | *He has a lot of* ***political influence*** *in the community.* | *Lewis* ***used his influence*** *to avoid military service.* **2** [C] someone or something that has an effect on other people or things: *Alex's parents always thought that I was* ***a good/bad influence on*** *him.* | *The country remains untouched by* ***outside influences.*** **3 under the influence** drunk or feeling the effects of a drug

influence[2] *v.* [T] to have an effect on the way someone or something develops, behaves, or thinks: *I don't want to influence your decision.* | *a singer who was influenced by gospel music*

THESAURUS

persuade, **talk into**, **get sb to do sth**, **encourage**, **convince**, **coax**, **cajole**
→ see Thesaurus box at PERSUADE

in·flu·en·tial /ˌɪnfluˈɛnʃəl/ *adj.* having a lot of influence: *an influential politician* | *Dewey was* ***influential in*** *shaping economic policy.* —**influentially** *adv.*

THESAURUS

powerful, strong, dominant
→ see Thesaurus box at POWERFUL

in·flu·en·za /ˌɪnfluˈɛnzə/ *n.* [U] *formal* FLU

in·flux /ˈɪnflʌks/ *n.* [C usually singular] the arrival of large numbers of people or things: *an **influx of** cheap imported goods*

in·fo /ˈɪnfoʊ/ *n.* [U] *informal* INFORMATION

in·fo·mer·cial /ˈɪnfoʊˌmɚʃəl/ *n.* [C] a long television advertisement that is made to seem like a regular program

in·form /ɪnˈfɔrm/ *v.* [T] to formally tell someone about something: *Please **inform** us **of** any progress.*
inform against/on sb *phr. v.* to tell the police, an enemy, etc. about what someone has done

in·for·mal /ɪnˈfɔrməl/ *adj.* **1** relaxed and friendly: *an informal meeting* **2** appropriate for ordinary situations or conversations: *an informal letter to your family* —**informally** *adv.* —**informality** /ˌɪnfɔrˈmæləṭi/ *n.* [U]

in·form·ant /ɪnˈfɔrmənt/ *n.* [C] someone who gives secret information to the police, a government department, etc.: *a CIA informant*

in·for·ma·tion /ˌɪnfɚˈmeɪʃən/ *n.* [U] **1** facts or details that tell you something about a situation, person, event, etc.: *I need some more **information about/on** this machine.* | *Goodwin was able to provide several new **pieces of information**.* | *For **further information**, call the number below.* **2** the telephone service that you can call to get someone's telephone number

GRAMMAR

Information is an uncountable noun and is never plural. Do not say "an information" or "some informations." Say **some information**, **a lot of information**, or **a piece/bit of information**: *Where can I find some information about your company?* | *That's an interesting bit of information.*

inforˈmation techˌnology, IT *n.* [U] the use of electronic processes, especially computers, for gathering information, storing it, and making it available

in·form·a·tive /ɪnˈfɔrməṭɪv/ *adj.* providing many useful facts or ideas: *a very informative book* —**informatively** *adv.*

in·formed /ɪnˈfɔrmd/ *adj.* having a lot of knowledge or information about a particular subject or situation: *well-informed voters*

in·form·er /ɪnˈfɔrmɚ/ *n.* [C] INFORMANT

in·fo·tain·ment /ˌɪnfoʊˈteɪnmənt/ *n.* [U] television programs that present news and other types of information in an entertaining way

in·frac·tion /ɪnˈfrækʃən/ *n.* [C,U] *formal* an act of breaking a rule or law

in·fra·red /ˌɪnfrəˈrɛd◂/ *adj.* infrared light produces heat but cannot be seen [➡ **ultraviolet**]

in·fra·struc·ture /ˈɪnfrəˌstrʌktʃɚ/ *n.* [C] the basic systems that a country or organization needs in order to work in the right way, for example roads, COMMUNICATIONS, and banking systems: *Japan's economic infrastructure*

in·fre·quent /ɪnˈfrikwənt/ *adj.* not happening often [= **rare**]: *one of our infrequent visits to Uncle Edwin's house* —**infrequently** *adv.*

in·fringe /ɪnˈfrɪndʒ/ *v.* [T] to do something that is against the law or someone's legal rights —**infringement** *n.* [C,U] *copyright infringement*
infringe on/upon sth *phr. v.* to limit someone's freedom in some way: *The new law infringes on our basic right to freedom of speech.*

in·fu·ri·ate /ɪnˈfyʊriˌeɪt/ *v.* [T] to make someone very angry: *He really infuriates me!*

in·fu·ri·at·ing /ɪnˈfyʊriˌeɪṭɪŋ/ *adj.* very annoying: *an infuriating delay of four hours* —**infuriatingly** *adv.*

in·fuse /ɪnˈfyuz/ *v.* **1** [T] to fill someone or something with a particular feeling or quality: *The coach has managed to **infuse** the team **with** new enthusiasm.* **2** [I,T] to put a substance such as tea in very hot water, so that its taste passes into the water —**infusion** /ɪnˈfyuʒən/ *n.* [C,U]

in·ge·nious /ɪnˈdʒinyəs/ *adj.* **1** an ingenious plan, idea, etc. works well and is the result of intelligent thinking and new ideas: *an ingenious device* **2** an ingenious person is very good at inventing things, thinking of new ideas, etc. —**ingeniously** *adv.*

in·ge·nu·i·ty /ˌɪndʒəˈnuəṭi/ *n.* [U] skill at inventing things, thinking of new ideas, etc.

in·gest /ɪnˈdʒɛst/ *v.* [T] *technical* to eat something —**ingestion** /ɪnˈdʒɛstʃən/ *n.* [U]

in·grained /ɪnˈgreɪnd, ˈɪngreɪnd/ *adj.* ingrained attitudes or behavior are firmly established and difficult to change: *A sense of duty is **deeply ingrained in** most people.*

in·gra·ti·ate /ɪnˈgreɪʃiˌeɪt/ *v.* **ingratiate yourself (with sb)** *disapproving* to try to get someone's approval by doing things to please him/her, expressing admiration, etc., especially in a way that does not seem sincere: *a politician trying to ingratiate himself with the voters* —**ingratiating** *adj.* —**ingratiatingly** *adv.*

in·grat·i·tude /ɪnˈgræṭəˌtud/ *n.* [U] the quality of not being grateful for something

in·gre·di·ent /ɪnˈgridiənt/ *n.* [C] **1** one of the things that goes into a mixture from which a type of food is made: *Combine all the ingredients in a large bowl.* | *Flour, water, and eggs are the **main ingredients**.* **2** a quality that helps to achieve something: *Jack seems to **have all the ingredients** to succeed in business.*

in·hab·it /ɪnˈhæbɪt/ *v.* [T] to live in a particular place: *a forest inhabited by bears and moose*

in·hab·it·ant /ɪnˈhæbəṭənt/ *n.* [C] one of the people who live in a particular place: *the **inhabitants of** large cities*

in·hale /ɪnˈheɪl/ *v.* [I,T] to breathe in air, smoke,

or gas: *Try not to inhale the fumes from the glue.* —**inhalation** /ˌɪnhəˈleɪʃən/ *n.* [C,U]

in·hal·er /ɪnˈheɪlɚ/ *n.* [C] a plastic tube containing medicine that someone, especially someone with ASTHMA, breathes in in order to make his/her breathing easier

in·her·ent /ɪnˈhɪrənt, -ˈhɛr-/ *adj.* a quality that is inherent in something is a natural part of it and cannot be separated from it: *a problem that is* ***inherent in*** *the system* —**inherently** *adv.*

in·her·it /ɪnˈhɛrɪt/ *v.* **1** [I,T] to receive something from someone after s/he has died: *I* ***inherited*** *the house* ***from*** *my uncle.* **2** [T] to get a quality, type of behavior, appearance, etc. from one of your parents: *Suzy inherited her mother's good looks.*

in·her·i·tance /ɪnˈhɛrɪṭəns/ *n.* [C,U] money, property, etc. that you receive from someone after s/he has died

in·hib·it /ɪnˈhɪbɪt/ *v.* [T] **1** to prevent something from growing or developing in the usual or expected way: *new treatments to inhibit the spread of the disease* **2** to make someone feel embarrassed or less confident, so s/he cannot do or say what s/he wants to: *Fear of criticism may inhibit a child's curiosity.*

in·hib·it·ed /ɪnˈhɪbɪṭɪd/ *adj.* not confident or relaxed enough to express how you really feel or do what you really want to do [≠ **uninhibited**]: *Julie's too inhibited to talk about sex.*

in·hi·bi·tion /ˌɪnhɪˈbɪʃən, ˌɪnə-/ *n.* [C,U] a feeling of worry or embarrassment that stops you from expressing how you really feel or doing what you really want to do: *She seems to* ***lose*** *her* ***inhibitions*** (=stops feeling worried or embarrassed) *after a few drinks.*

in·hos·pi·ta·ble /ˌɪnhɑˈspɪṭəbəl/ *adj. formal* **1** not friendly, welcoming, or generous to visitors **2** difficult to live or stay in because of severe weather conditions or lack of shelter: *an inhospitable climate* —**inhospitably** *adv.*

ˌin-ˈhouse *adj., adv.* within a company or organization rather than outside it: *an in-house training department*

in·hu·man /ɪnˈhyumən/ *adj.* **1** very cruel and without any normal feelings of pity: *inhuman treatment* **2** lacking any human qualities in a way that seems strange or frightening: *an inhuman scream*

in·hu·mane /ˌɪnhyuˈmeɪn/ *adj.* treating people or animals in a cruel and unacceptable way: *inhumane living conditions* —**inhumanely** *adv.* —**inhumanity** /ˌɪnhyuˈmænəṭi/ *n.* [U]

in·im·i·ta·ble /ɪˈnɪməṭəbəl/ *adj.* too good for anyone else to copy: *Jerry gave the speech in his own inimitable style.*

i·ni·tial[1] /ɪˈnɪʃəl/ *adj.* happening at the beginning [= **first**]: *the initial stages of the disease* —**initially** *adv.*: *He initially refused the offer.*

initial[2] *n.* [C] the first letter of a name: *a suitcase with the initials S.H. on it*

initial[3] *v.* [T] to write your initials on a document: *Could you initial this form for me, please?*

i·ni·ti·ate /ɪˈnɪʃiˌeɪt/ *v.* [T] **1** *formal* to arrange for something important to start: *The prison has recently initiated new security procedures.* **2** to introduce someone into an organization, club, etc., usually with a special ceremony: *students* ***initiated into*** *the school's honor society* —**initiation** /ɪˌnɪʃiˈeɪʃən/ *n.* [C,U]

i·ni·tia·tive /ɪˈnɪʃəṭɪv/ *n.* **1** [U] the ability to make decisions and take action without waiting for someone to tell you what to do: *I wish he would* ***show*** *more* ***initiative***. | *Try using* ***your own initiative*** (=doing something without being told what to do). **2** [C] a plan or process that has been started in order to achieve a particular aim or to solve a particular problem: *state* ***initiatives to*** *reduce spending* **3 take the initiative** to be the first one to take action to achieve a particular aim or solve a particular problem

in·ject /ɪnˈdʒɛkt/ *v.* [T] **1** to put a liquid, especially a drug, into your body by using a special needle: *His shoulder was* ***injected with*** *a painkiller.* **2** to improve something by adding an important thing or quality to it: *remarks that* ***injected*** *some humor* ***into*** *the situation*

in·jec·tion /ɪnˈdʒɛkʃən/ *n.* **1** [C,U] an act of putting a liquid, especially a drug, into your body by using a special needle [= **shot**]: *The nurse* ***gave*** *me an* ***injection*** *of painkillers.* **2** [C] an addition of an important thing or quality to something in order to improve it: *The business received a* ***cash injection of*** *$20,000.*

injection

in·junc·tion /ɪnˈdʒʌŋkʃən/ *n.* [C] *law* an official order given by a court that stops someone from being allowed to do something

in·jure /ˈɪndʒɚ/ *v.* [T] to hurt a person or animal: *She was* ***seriously/badly injured*** *in the accident.* | *Frank has injured his knee again.* —**injured** *adj.*

THESAURUS

hurt, **wound**

→ see Thesaurus box at HURT[1]

in·ju·ry /ˈɪndʒəri/ *n.* plural **injuries** [C,U] physical harm or damage that is caused by an accident or attack, or a particular example of this: *a knee/back/head injury* | ***serious injuries*** *to the head and neck* | *Luckily, she* ***suffered*** *only minor* ***injuries***.

THESAURUS

wound – an injury, especially a deep cut made in your skin by a knife or bullet: *He needed emergency treatment for a gunshot wound.*

bruise – a black or blue mark on your skin that

you get when you fall or get hit: *There was a dark bruise on her cheek.*
cut – the small wound you get if a sharp object cuts your skin: *a cut on her finger*
scrape – a mark or slight injury caused by rubbing your skin against a rough surface: *His legs were covered in scrapes and bruises.*
sprain – an injury to a joint in your body, caused by suddenly twisting it: *a slight ankle sprain*
bump – an area of skin that is swollen because you have hit it on something: *a bump on his forehead*

in·jus·tice /ɪn'dʒʌstɪs/ *n.* [C,U] a situation in which people are treated very unfairly: *a history of injustices against black people*

ink /ɪŋk/ *n.* [U] a colored liquid used for writing, printing, etc.

ink·ling /'ɪŋklɪŋ/ *n.* [singular] a slight idea about something: *We **had no inkling** that he was leaving.*

in·laid /'ɪnleɪd, ɪn'leɪd/ *adj.* having a thin layer of a material set into the surface for decoration: *a wooden box **inlaid with** gold*

in·land[1] /'ɪnlənd/ *adj.* an inland area, city, etc. is not near the coast

in·land[2] /ɪn'lænd, 'ɪnlænd, -lənd/ *adv.* in a direction away from the coast and toward the center of a country

'in-laws *n.* [plural] your relatives by marriage, especially the mother and father of your husband or wife: *We're spending Christmas with my in-laws.*

in·lay /'ɪnleɪ/ *n.* [C,U] a material that has been set into the surface of another material as a decoration, or the pattern made by this

in·let /'ɪnlɛt, 'ɪnlət/ *n.* [C] **1** a narrow area of water reaching from the sea or a lake into the land, or between islands **2** the part of a machine through which liquid or gas flows in

ˌin-line 'skate *n.* [C] a special boot with a single row of wheels fastened under it [= **Rollerblade**; ➡ **rollerskate**]

in·mate /'ɪnmeɪt/ *n.* [C] someone who is kept in a prison or in a hospital for people with mental illnesses

inn /ɪn/ *n.* [C] a small hotel, especially one that is not in a city

THESAURUS

hotel, motel, bed and breakfast (B&B), campground
➔ see Thesaurus box at HOTEL

in·nards /'ɪnɚdz/ *n.* [plural] *informal* the parts inside your body, especially your stomach

in·nate /ˌɪ'neɪt◂/ *adj.* an innate quality has been part of your character since you were born: *an innate sense of fun* —**innately** *adv.*

in·ner /'ɪnɚ/ *adj.* [only before noun] **1** on the inside or close to the center of something [≠ **outer**]: *the inner ear* **2** inner feelings, thoughts, meanings, etc. are secret and not expressed **3 inner circle** the few people in an organization, political party, etc. who control it or share power with its leader

ˌinner 'city *n.* [C] the part of a city that is near the middle, especially the part where the buildings are in a bad condition and the people are poor —**inner city** *adj.*: *an inner city school*

in·ner·most /'ɪnɚˌmoʊst/ *adj.* **1** your innermost feelings, desires, etc. are the ones you feel most strongly and keep private [≠ **outermost**]

THESAURUS

private, secret, personal
➔ see Thesaurus box at PRIVATE[1]

2 *formal* farthest inside

'inner tube *n.* [C] the rubber tube that is filled with air inside a tire

in·ning /'ɪnɪŋ/ *n.* [C] one of the nine playing periods in a game of baseball

inn·keep·er /'ɪnˌkipɚ/ *n.* [C] *old-fashioned* someone who owns or manages an INN

in·no·cence /'ɪnəsəns/ *n.* [U] **1** the fact of not being guilty of a crime [≠ **guilt**]: *How did they **prove her innocence**?* **2** the state of not having much experience of life, especially experience of bad or complicated things: *a child's innocence*

in·no·cent /'ɪnəsənt/ *adj.* **1** not guilty of a crime [≠ **guilty**]: *Nobody would believe that I was innocent.* | *He was **found innocent of** murder by the jury* (=they decided he was innocent). **2 innocent victims/bystanders/people etc.** people who get hurt or killed in a war or as a result of a crime, though they are not involved in it **3** not having much experience of life, especially so that you are easily deceived: *I was 13 years old and very innocent.* **4** done or said without intending to harm or offend anyone: *It was a perfectly innocent question.* —**innocently** *adv.*

in·noc·u·ous /ɪ'nɑkyuəs/ *adj.* not offensive, dangerous, or harmful: *an innocuous but boring movie* —**innocuously** *adv.*

in·no·va·tion /ˌɪnə'veɪʃən/ *n.* [C,U] the introduction of new ideas, methods, or inventions, or the idea, method, or invention itself: ***innovations in** design* | *Too many regulations can discourage innovation.* —**innovate** /'ɪnəˌveɪt/ *v.* [I] —**innovator** *n.* [C]

in·no·va·tive /'ɪnəˌveɪṭɪv/ *adj.* using new ideas, methods, or inventions: *an **innovative approach** to language teaching*

in·nu·en·do /ˌɪnyu'ɛndoʊ/ *n.* plural **innuendoes** or **innuendos** [C,U] an indirect remark about sex or about something bad that someone has done, or the act of making this type of remark: *nasty innuendos about Laurie and the boss* | *His writing is full of **sexual innuendoes**.*

in·nu·mer·a·ble /ɪ'numərəbəl/ *adj. formal* very many

I

in·oc·u·late /ɪ'nɑkyəˌleɪt/ *v.* [T] *formal* to protect someone against a disease by introducing a weak form of it into his/her body [= **immunize**, **vaccinate**]: *Children should be **inoculated against** measles.* —**inoculation** /ɪˌnɑkyə'leɪʃən/ *n.* [C,U]

in·of·fen·sive /ˌɪnə'fɛnsɪv/ *adj.* unlikely to offend anyone: *a quiet, inoffensive man*

in·op·por·tune /ɪnˌɑpɚ'tun, ˌɪnɑ-/ *adj.* *formal* not appropriate or not good for a particular situation: *They arrived at **an inopportune moment**.*

in·or·di·nate /ɪn'ɔrdn-ɪt/ *adj.* *formal* much greater than is reasonable: *an **inordinate amount** of work* —**inordinately** *adv.*

in·or·gan·ic /ˌɪnɔr'gænɪk◂ / *adj.* not consisting of anything that is living: *inorganic matter* —**inorganically** *adv.*

in·pa·tient /'ɪnˌpeɪʃənt/ *n.* [C] someone who stays and sleeps in a hospital while s/he is getting medical treatment [➡ **outpatient**]

in·put /'ɪnpʊt/ *n.* **1** [C,U] ideas, advice, money, or effort that you put into a job or activity in order to help it succeed: *I'd like to **get** your **input on** a few issues.* | *I'd like **input from** each of our employees.* **2** [U] information that is put into a computer [≠ **output**] **3** [C,U] electrical power that is put into a machine for it to use

in·quest /'ɪnkwɛst/ *n.* [C] *law* an official process to find out the cause of a sudden or unexpected death, especially if there is a possibility that the death is the result of a crime

in·quire /ɪn'kwaɪɚ/ *v.* [I,T] *formal* to ask someone for information: *I am writing to **inquire about** your advertisement in the New York Post.* | *She called to **inquire whether** her application had been received.* —**inquirer** *n.* [C]

> **THESAURUS**
>
> **ask**, **order**, **demand**, **request**, **beg**, **question**, **interrogate**, **enquire**
> ➔ see Thesaurus box at ASK

inquire into sth *phr. v.* to ask questions in order to get more information about something or to find out why something happened: *The investigation will inquire into the reasons for the disaster.*

in·quir·ing /ɪn'kwaɪərɪŋ/ *adj.* wanting to find out more about something: *Dad taught us to have **inquiring minds**.* —**inquiringly** *adv.*

in·quir·y /ɪn'kwaɪəri, 'ɪŋkwəri/ *n.* plural **inquiries** [C] **1** a question you ask in order to get information: *We're getting a lot of **inquiries about** our new train service.* **2** the official process of finding out why something happened, especially something bad

in·qui·si·tion /ˌɪnkwə'zɪʃən/ *n.* [singular] *formal* a series of questions that someone asks you in a way that seems threatening or not nice

in·quis·i·tive /ɪn'kwɪzəṭɪv/ *adj.* interested in a lot of different things and wanting to find out more about them: *a very inquisitive little boy*

in·roads /'ɪnroʊdz/ *n.* **make inroads into/on sth** to become more and more successful, powerful, or popular and so take away power, trade, votes, etc. from a competitor or enemy: *Their new soft drink is already making huge inroads into the market.*

INS *n.* **the INS the Immigration and Naturalization Service** the U.S. government department that deals with people who come to live in the U.S. from other countries

ˌins and 'outs *n.* **the ins and outs of sth** all the exact details of a complicated situation, system, problem, etc.: *I'm still learning the ins and outs of my new job.*

in·sane /ɪn'seɪn/ *adj.* **1** *informal* completely stupid or crazy, often in a way that is dangerous: *You must've been totally insane to go with him!* | *an insane idea* **2** someone who is insane is permanently and seriously mentally ill —**insanely** *adv.*

> **THESAURUS**
>
> **crazy**, **mentally ill**, **disturbed**, **nuts**, **loony**
> ➔ see Thesaurus box at CRAZY

in·san·i·ty /ɪn'sænəṭi/ *n.* [U] **1** very stupid actions that may cause you serious harm **2** the state of being seriously mentally ill: *A jury found him not guilty by reason of insanity.*

in·sa·tia·ble /ɪn'seɪʃəbəl/ *adj.* always wanting more and more of something: *an insatiable appetite*

in·scribe /ɪn'skraɪb/ *v.* [T] to cut, print, or write words on something, especially on the surface of a stone or coin: *a tree **inscribed with** the initials J.S.* —**inscription** /ɪn'skrɪpʃən/ *n.* [C]

in·scru·ta·ble /ɪn'skruṭəbəl/ *adj.* *formal* not easily understood because you cannot tell what someone is thinking or feeling: *an inscrutable smile* —**inscrutably** *adv.*

in·sect /'ɪnsɛkt/ *n.* [C] a small creature such as an ANT or a fly, with six legs and a body divided into three parts

in·sec·ti·cide /ɪn'sɛktəˌsaɪd/ *n.* [C,U] a chemical substance used for killing insects

in·se·cure /ˌɪnsɪ'kyʊr/ *adj.* **1** not feeling confident about yourself, your abilities, your relationships, etc. [≠ **confident**]: *Jane is **insecure about** her looks.*

> **THESAURUS**
>
> **unsure of yourself** – not very confident about yourself: *She's nervous and unsure of herself.*
> **lack confidence** also **be lacking in confidence** – to not believe that you have the ability to do something well: *He is completely lacking in confidence.*
> ➔ SHY[1]

2 not safe or not protected: *She feels that her position in the company is insecure* (=she may lose her job). —**insecurity** *n.* [U] —**insecurely** *adv.*

in·sem·i·na·tion /ɪnˌsɛmə'neɪʃən/ *n.* [U] the

act of putting SPERM into a female's body in order to make her have a baby: *the artificial insemination of cattle* (=done by medical treatment, not sex)

in·sen·si·tive /ɪn'sɛnsət̬ɪv/ *adj.* **1** not noticing other people's feelings, and not realizing that something that you do will upset them: *insensitive remarks* | *She's totally* ***insensitive to*** *my feelings.* **2** not affected by physical effects or changes —**insensitively** *adv.* —**insensitivity** /ɪnˌsɛnsə'tɪvət̬i/ *n.* [U]

in·sep·a·ra·ble /ɪn'sɛpərəbəl/ *adj.* **1** people who are inseparable are always together and are very friendly with each other: *When they were younger, the boys were inseparable.* **2** unable to be separated or not able to be considered separately: *The patient's mental and physical problems are inseparable.* —**inseparably** *adv.*

in·sert¹ /ɪn'sɚt/ *v.* [T] to put something inside or into something else: ***Insert*** *the key* ***in/into*** *the lock.* —**insertion** /ɪn'sɚʃən/ *n.* [C,U]

insert

in·sert² /'ɪnsɚt/ *n.* [C] **1** something that is designed to be put inside something else: *special inserts to protect your heels* **2** printed pages that are put inside a newspaper or magazine in order to advertise something

in·side¹ /ɪn'saɪd, 'ɪnsaɪd/ *adv., prep.* **1** in or into a container, room, building, etc. [≠ **outside**]: *He opened the box to find two kittens inside.* | *Go inside and get your jacket.* **2** if you have a feeling or thought inside you, you feel or think it but do not always express it: *You never know what's happening inside his head.* | *Don't keep the anger inside.* **3** used in order to emphasize that what is happening in a country or organization is known about there, but not outside it: *Sources inside the company confirmed that there will be more layoffs.* **4** in less time than: *We'll be there* ***inside of*** *an hour.*

inside² *n.* [C] **1 the inside** the inner part of something [≠ **outside**]: ***The inside of*** *the house was nicer than the outside.* | *The door had been locked* ***from the inside.*** **2 inside out** with the usual outside part on the inside: *Your shirt is on inside out.* **3 know/learn sth inside out** to know everything about a subject: *She knows the business inside out.*

inside³ *adj.* **1** on or facing the inside of something: *the inside pages of a magazine* **2 inside information/the inside story** information that is known only by people who are part of an organization, company, etc.

in·sid·er /ɪn'saɪdɚ/ *n.* [C] someone who has special knowledge of a particular organization because s/he is part of it

in·sid·i·ous /ɪn'sɪdiəs/ *adj.* happening gradually without being noticed, but causing great harm: *the insidious effects of breathing polluted air* —**insidiously** *adv.*

in·sight /'ɪnsaɪt/ *n.* [C,U] the ability to understand something clearly, or an example of this: *The article gives us a real* ***insight into*** *Chinese culture.*

in·sig·ni·a /ɪn'sɪgniə/ *n.* plural **insignia** [C] a BADGE or other object that shows what official or military rank someone has, or which group or organization s/he belongs to

in·sig·nif·i·cant /ˌɪnsɪg'nɪfəkənt/ *adj.* too small or unimportant to consider or worry about: *an insignificant change in the unemployment rate* —**insignificantly** *adv.* —**insignificance** *n.* [U]

in·sin·cere /ˌɪnsɪn'sɪr/ *adj.* pretending to be pleased, sympathetic, etc., but not really meaning what you say: *an insincere smile* —**insincerely** *adv.* —**insincerity** /ˌɪnsɪn'sɛrət̬i/ *n.* [U]

in·sin·u·ate /ɪn'sɪnyuˌeɪt/ *v.* [T] to say something that seems to mean something unpleasant, without saying it directly: *Are you* ***insinuating that*** *she didn't deserve the promotion?* —**insinuation** /ɪnˌsɪnyu'eɪʃən/ *n.* [C,U]

in·sip·id /ɪn'sɪpɪd/ *adj. disapproving* not interesting, exciting, or attractive: *the movie's insipid story* —**insipidly** *adv.*

in·sist /ɪn'sɪst/ *v.* [I] **1** to say firmly and again and again that something is true, especially when other people think it may not be true: *The boys* ***insisted that*** *that they were innocent.* **2** to demand that something happen: *I* ***insisted that*** *he leave.* | *They're* ***insisting on*** *your resignation.*

in·sist·ence /ɪn'sɪstəns/ *n.* [U] the act of insisting that something should happen: *He came, but only* ***at*** *my* ***insistence.***

in·sist·ent /ɪn'sɪstənt/ *adj.* insisting that something should happen: *She's very* ***insistent that*** *we should all be on time.* —**insistently** *adv.*

in so far as, insofar as /ˌɪnsoʊ'fɑr əz/ *conjunction formal* to the degree that something affects another thing: *Insofar as sales are concerned, the company is doing very well.*

in·so·lent /'ɪnsələnt/ *adj. formal* rude and not showing any respect: *She gave me a cold, insolent look.* —**insolence** *n.* [U] —**insolently** *adv.*

in·sol·u·ble /ɪn'sɑlyəbəl/ *adj.* **1** an insoluble substance does not DISSOLVE when you put it into a liquid **2 also insolvable** impossible to explain or solve: *a seemingly insoluble problem*

in·sol·vent /ɪn'sɑlvənt/ *adj. formal* not having enough money to pay what you owe —**insolvency** *n.* [U]

in·som·ni·a /ɪn'sɑmniə/ *n.* [U] the condition of not being able to sleep —**insomniac** /ɪn'sɑmniˌæk/ *n.* [C]

in·spect /ɪn'spɛkt/ *v.* [T] **1** to examine something carefully: *She bent down to* ***inspect*** *the plant*

I

more ***closely***. | *We* ***inspected*** *the roof of our house* ***for*** *leaks.* **2** to make an official visit to a building, organization, etc. to check that everything is satisfactory and that rules are being obeyed: *Nursing homes must be inspected once a year.*

in·spec·tion /ɪn'spɛkʃən/ *n.* [C,U] the act of carefully checking a place, thing, or organization in order to be sure that it is in good condition or that rules are being obeyed: *The ship had recently passed a safety inspection.* | *a close* ***inspection of*** *the soldiers' living areas*

in·spec·tor /ɪn'spɛktɚ/ *n.* [C] **1** an official whose job is to inspect something: *a health inspector* **2** a police officer of middle rank

in·spi·ra·tion /ˌɪnspə'reɪʃən/ *n.* [C,U] something or someone that encourages you to do or produce something good: *Dante was* ***the inspiration for*** *my book on Italy.* | *Her hard work and imagination should be* ***an inspiration to*** *everyone.* —**inspirational** *adj.*: *an inspirational speech*

in·spire /ɪn'spaɪɚ/ *v.* [T] **1** to encourage someone to do or produce something good: *The church is trying to* ***inspire*** *more young men* ***to*** *become priests.* **2** to make someone have a particular feeling: *The captain* ***inspires*** *confidence* ***in*** *his men.* —**inspiring** *adj.*: *a powerful, inspiring story*

in·spired /ɪn'spaɪɚd/ *adj.* having very exciting special qualities: *an inspired leader*

in·sta·bil·i·ty /ˌɪnstə'bɪləṭi/ *n.* [U] the state of being uncertain and likely to change suddenly [➡ **unstable**]: *political instability in the region*

in·stall /ɪn'stɔl/ *v.* [T] **1** to put a piece of equipment somewhere and connect it so that it is ready to be used: *Many residents have installed new burglar alarms.* **2** to copy computer software onto a computer so that the software is ready to be used **3** to put someone in an important job or position, especially with a ceremony: *She will be installed as president of the college next week.* —**installation** /ˌɪnstə'leɪʃən/ *n.* [C,U]

in·stall·ment /ɪn'stɔlmənt/ *n.* [C] **1** one of a series of regular payments that you make until you have paid all the money you owe: *You can pay for the computer* ***in*** *twelve monthly* ***installments***. **2** one of the parts of a story that appears as a series in a magazine, newspaper, etc.

in·stance /'ɪnstəns/ *n.* **1 for instance** for example: *There are some promising signs. For instance, high-school students' test scores have risen.* **2** [C] an example of a particular fact, event, etc.: *reports on* ***instances of*** *police brutality*

in·stant¹ /'ɪnstənt/ *adj.* **1** happening or produced immediately: *The movie was an instant success.* **2** [only before noun] instant food, coffee, etc. is in the form of powder and is made ready to eat or drink by adding liquid to it

instant² *n.* **1** [C usually singular] a moment in time: *I didn't believe her for an instant.* **2 this instant** *spoken* now, without delay [= **immediately**]: *Come here this instant!*

in·stan·ta·ne·ous /ˌɪnstən'teɪniəs/ *adj.* happening immediately: *an instantaneous reaction to the drug* —**instantaneously** *adv.*

in·stant·ly /'ɪnstəntli/ *adv.* immediately: *He was killed instantly.*

> **THESAURUS**
>
> **immediately**, **right away**, **at once**, **right now**
> ➔ see Thesaurus box at IMMEDIATELY

ˌinstant 'replay *n.* [C] the immediate repeating of an important moment in a sports game on television by showing the film or VIDEOTAPE again

in·stead /ɪn'stɛd/ *adv.* **1 instead of sb/sth** in place of someone or something: *Can I have chicken instead of beef?* | *You should do something instead of just sitting around all day.* **2** in place of someone or something that has just been mentioned: *I can't go, but Lilly could go instead.*

in·step /'ɪnstɛp/ *n.* [C usually singular] the raised part of your foot between your toes and your ANKLE, or the part of a shoe that covers this part of your foot

in·sti·gate /'ɪnstəˌgeɪt/ *v.* [T] to make something start to happen, especially something that will cause trouble: *Gang leaders were accused of instigating the riot.* —**instigator** *n.* [C] —**instigation** /ˌɪnstə'geɪʃən/ *n.* [U]

in·still /ɪn'stɪl/ *v.* [T] to teach someone a way of thinking or behaving over a long time: *Bonilla says he tries to* ***instill*** *hope* ***in*** *his students.*

in·stinct /'ɪnstɪŋkt/ *n.* [C,U] a natural tendency or ability to behave or react in a particular way, without having to learn it or think about it: *a lion's* ***instinct to*** *hunt* | *people's natural* ***instinct for*** *survival*

in·stinc·tive /ɪn'stɪŋktɪv/ *adj.* based on instinct: *an instinctive reaction* —**instinctively** *adv.*

in·sti·tute¹ /'ɪnstəˌtut/ *n.* [C] an organization that has a particular purpose, such as scientific or educational work: *research institutes*

institute² *v.* [T] *formal* to introduce or start a system, rule, legal process, etc.: *The governor is planning to institute major tax reforms.*

in·sti·tu·tion /ˌɪnstə'tuʃən/ *n.* **1** [C] a large organization that has a particular purpose, such as scientific, educational, or medical work: *financial/religious/educational, etc. institutions*

> **THESAURUS**
>
> **organization**, **association**, **(political) party**, **club**, **society**, **union**
> ➔ see Thesaurus box at ORGANIZATION

2 [C] an established system or tradition in society: *the* ***institution of*** *marriage* **3** [U] the act of introducing or starting a system, rule, legal process, etc.: *the* ***institution of*** *a new law* —**institutional** *adj.* ➔ MENTAL INSTITUTION

in·sti·tu·tion·al·ize /ˌɪnstə'tuʃənəˌlaɪz/ *v.* [T] to send someone to live in a mental hospital, a special home for old people, etc.

in·sti·tu·tion·al·ized /ˌɪnstəˈtuʃənəˌlaɪzd/ *adj.* **institutionalized violence/racism/corruption** violence, etc. that has happened for so long in an organization or society that it has become accepted as normal

in·struct /ɪnˈstrʌkt/ *v.* [T] **1** to officially tell someone what to do: *In 1991, the government **instructed** auto companies **to** install airbags in all new cars.* **2** to teach someone or show him/her how to do something: *Diane **instructs** senior citizens **in** basic computer skills.*

in·struc·tion /ɪnˈstrʌkʃən/ *n.* **1 instructions** [plural] information or advice that tells you how to do something, how to use a piece of equipment or machine, etc. [= **directions**]: ***Follow the instructions** on the back of the box.* | *Did you read the instructions first?* | *He gave us **instructions on/about how to** fix the toilet.* | *Inside you'll find **instructions for** setting up your computer.* **2** [U] teaching in a particular skill or subject: *She's never had any **formal instruction*** (=lessons or classes) *in music.* —**instructional** *adj.*

in·struc·tive /ɪnˈstrʌktɪv/ *adj. formal* giving useful information

in·struc·tor /ɪnˈstrʌktɚ/ *n.* [C] **1** someone who teaches a particular subject, sport, skill, etc.: *a ski instructor*

THESAURUS

teacher, professor, lecturer, coach
➔ see Thesaurus box at TEACHER

2 someone who teaches at a college or university and has a rank below that of PROFESSOR

in·stru·ment /ˈɪnstrəmənt/ *n.* [C] **1** an object such as a piano, TRUMPET, VIOLIN, etc., used for producing musical sounds: *Can you play any **musical instruments**?* **2** a tool used in work such as science or medicine: *medical instruments*

in·stru·men·tal /ˌɪnstrəˈmɛntl/ *adj.* **1 be instrumental in (doing) sth** to be important in making something happen: *Helen has been instrumental in organizing the festival.* **2** instrumental music is for instruments, not voices

in·sub·or·di·na·tion /ˌɪnsəˌbɔrdnˈeɪʃən/ *n.* [U] *formal* refusal to obey someone who has a higher rank

in·sub·stan·tial /ˌɪnsəbˈstænʃəl/ *adj.* not solid, large, strong, or not enough: *The evidence against him was insubstantial.*

in·suf·fi·cient /ˌɪnsəˈfɪʃənt/ *adj.* not enough: *insufficient supplies of food* —**insufficiently** *adv.* —**insufficiency** *n.* [singular, U]

in·su·lar /ˈɪnsəlɚ, ˈɪnsyə-/ *adj. formal disapproving* not interested in anything except your own group, country, way of life, etc. —**insularity** /ˌɪnsəˈlærət̬i/ *n.* [U]

in·su·late /ˈɪnsəˌleɪt/ *v.* [T] **1** to cover or protect something so that electricity, sound, heat, etc. cannot get in or out: *Insulate your garage to make it into a year-round workshop.* **2** to protect someone from bad experiences or unwanted influences: *college students **insulated from** the hardships of real life*

in·su·la·tion /ˌɪnsəˈleɪʃən/ *n.* [U] the material used in order to INSULATE something, especially a building: *Insulation can save money on heating bills.*

in·su·lin /ˈɪnsələn/ *n.* [U] a substance produced naturally by your body that allows sugar to be used for energy

in·sult¹ /ɪnˈsʌlt/ *v.* [T] to say or do something that offends someone, by showing that you do not respect him/her: *She didn't want to insult her hosts by leaving too early.* | *John would be insulted if we didn't go.* —**insulting** *adj.*

in·sult² /ˈɪnsʌlt/ *n.* [C] a rude or offensive remark or action: *Both groups screamed and shouted insults at each other.* | *The plan is an **insult to** teachers.* ➔ **add insult to injury** at ADD

in·sur·ance /ɪnˈʃʊrəns/ *n.* [U] **1** an arrangement with a company in which you pay it money regularly and the company pays the costs if anything bad happens to you or your property, such as an illness or an accident: *Do you have **insurance on/for** your car?* | *The club **took out insurance** for all its members.* | *an **insurance policy*** | ***life/health/auto insurance** companies* | *It's a good idea to **buy** travel **insurance**.* **2** protection against something bad that might happen: *We bought an alarm as **insurance against** burglary.*

in·sure /ɪnˈʃʊr/ *v.* [T] **1** to buy or provide insurance: *Is your house **insured against** flooding?* | *This painting is **insured for** $5,000.* **2** to make something certain to happen: *The board will **insure that** all schools have adequate funds.*

in·sur·gent /ɪnˈsɚdʒənt/ *n.* [C] one of a group of people fighting against the government of their own country —**insurgency** *n.* [U] —**insurgent** *adj.*

in·sur·mount·a·ble /ˌɪnsɚˈmaʊnt̬əbəl/ *adj. formal* a difficulty or problem that is insurmountable is too large or too difficult to deal with

in·sur·rec·tion /ˌɪnsəˈrɛkʃən/ *n.* [C,U] an attempt by a group of people within a country to take control using force and violence: *an armed insurrection led by the army*

in·tact /ɪnˈtækt/ *adj.* [not before noun] not broken, damaged, or spoiled: *Almost nothing was left intact by the storm.* | *The team's management system will **remain intact**.*

in·take /ˈɪnteɪk/ *n.* [singular] the amount of food, FUEL, etc. that is taken in by someone or something: *I've been told to lower my **intake of** fat and alcohol.*

in·tan·gi·ble /ɪnˈtændʒəbəl/ *adj.* an intangible quality or feeling cannot be clearly felt or described, although you know it exists —**intangibly** *adv.*

in·te·ger /ˈɪnt̬ədʒɚ/ *n.* [C] *technical* a number that is positive, negative, or zero, such as 3, -2, or 0

in·te·gral /ˈɪntəgrəl, ɪnˈtɛgrəl/ *adj.* forming a necessary part of something: *an* ***integral part*** *of the contract*

in·te·grate /ˈɪntəˌgreɪt/ *v.* **1** [I,T] to join in the life and traditions of a group or society, or to help someone do this: *It will take time for new members to* ***integrate into*** *the group.* **2** [T] to combine two or more things in order to make an effective system: *This software* ***integrates*** *moving pictures* ***with*** *sound.* **3** [I,T] to end the practice of separating people of different races in a place or institution [= **desegregate**; ≠ **segregate**]: *the Supreme Court's decision to integrate public schools* —**integrated** *adj.* —**integration** /ˌɪntəˈgreɪʃən/ *n.* [U]

in·teg·ri·ty /ɪnˈtɛgrəṭi/ *n.* [U] **1** the quality of being honest and having high moral principles: *a man* ***of integrity*** **2** *formal* the state of being united as one complete thing: *the building's structural integrity*

in·tel·lect /ˈɪntəlˌɛkt/ *n.* [C,U] the ability to understand things and think intelligently: *an artist of great intellect*

in·tel·lec·tu·al[1] /ˌɪntəlˈɛktʃuəl/ *adj.* **1** concerning the ability to think and understand ideas and information: *the intellectual development of children* **2** an intellectual person is well-educated and interested in complicated ideas and subjects such as science, literature, etc. —**intellectually** *adv.*

THESAURUS

intelligent, **smart**, **bright**, **brilliant**, **wise**, **clever**, **gifted**
→ see Thesaurus box at INTELLIGENT

intellectual[2] *n.* [C] someone who is well-educated and interested in complicated ideas and subjects such as science, literature, etc.

in·tel·li·gence /ɪnˈtɛlədʒəns/ *n.* [U] **1** the ability to learn, understand, and think about things: *a child of average intelligence* **2** information about the secret activities of other governments, or the group of people who gather this

in·tel·li·gent /ɪnˈtɛlədʒənt/ *adj.* having a high level of ability to learn, understand, and think about things [= **smart**; ≠ **stupid**] —**intelligently** *adv.*

THESAURUS

smart – intelligent: *a really smart guy*
bright – intelligent, used especially about children and young people: *a bright kid*
brilliant – extremely intelligent and good at the work you do: *a brilliant scientist*
wise – having a lot of experience and knowledge about people and the world: *a wise old man*
clever – intelligent, especially in a way that is unusual: *She's clever and creative.*
cunning/crafty – good at using your intelligence to trick people: *a cunning criminal*
intellectual – having a lot of education and interested in learning about art, science, literature, etc.
gifted – a gifted child is much more intelligent than most other children

in·tel·li·gi·ble /ɪnˈtɛlədʒəbəl/ *adj.* able to be understood [= **clear**] —**intelligibly** *adv.*

in·tend /ɪnˈtɛnd/ *v.* **1** [T] to have something in your mind as a plan or purpose [= **mean**]: *The work took longer than we intended.* | *Bob never* ***intended to*** *hurt him.* **2 be intended for sb/sth** to be provided or designed for someone or something: *a program intended for the families of deaf children* —**intended** *adj.*: *the movie's intended audience*

in·tense /ɪnˈtɛns/ *adj.* **1** very extreme or having a very strong effect: *The department's researchers have been under intense pressure.* | *We weren't prepared for the intense heat.* **2** making you do a lot of work, think hard, etc.: *intense physical exercise* **3** serious and having very strong feelings or opinions: *an intense young woman* —**intensely** *adv.*

in·ten·si·fi·er /ɪnˈtɛnsəˌfaɪɚ/ *n.* [C] *technical* in grammar, a word that changes the meaning of another word, phrase, or sentence, in order to make its meaning stronger or weaker

in·ten·si·fy /ɪnˈtɛnsəˌfaɪ/ *v.* past tense and past participle **intensified**, third person singular **intensifies** [I,T] to increase in strength, size, or amount, etc., or to make something do this: *Spices will intensify the flavor.* | *Global competition has continued to intensify.* —**intensification** /ɪnˌtɛnsəfəˈkeɪʃən/ *n.* [U]

in·ten·si·ty /ɪnˈtɛnsəṭi/ *n.* [U] the quality of being felt very strongly or of having a strong effect: *the intensity of his anger*

in·ten·sive /ɪnˈtɛnsɪv/ *adj.* involving a lot of activity, effort, or attention in order to achieve something: *an intensive English course* —**intensively** *adv.*

inˌtensive ˈcare *n.* [U] a department in a hospital that treats people who are very seriously sick or injured: *She's been* ***in intensive care*** *for two days.*

in·tent[1] /ɪnˈtɛnt/ *n.* [C] **1** *formal* what you intend to do [= **intention**]: *Our intent is to become the market leader.* **2 for all intents and purposes** almost completely, or very nearly: *For all intents and purposes, their marriage was over.*

intent[2] *adj.* **be intent on (doing) sth** to be determined to do something: *Nick is intent on going to an Ivy League college.*

in·ten·tion /ɪnˈtɛnʃən/ *n.* [C,U] something that you plan to do: *I* ***have no intention of*** *retiring anytime soon.*

in·ten·tion·al /ɪnˈtɛnʃənəl/ *adj.* done deliberately: *If he did break the rules, I'm sure it was not intentional.* —**intentionally** *adv.*

in·ter /ɪn'tɚ/ *v.* past tense and past participle **interred**, present participle **interring** [T] *formal* to bury a dead body

in·ter·act /ˌɪntə'rækt/ *v.* [I] **1** to talk to other people and work together with them: *The website allows visitors to **interact with** other users.* **2** if two or more things interact, they have an effect on each other: *How will the drug **interact with** other medicines?*

in·ter·ac·tion /ˌɪntə'rækʃən/ *n.* [C,U] the activity of talking with other people and working together with them: *social **interaction between** teenagers*

in·ter·ac·tive /ˌɪntə'ræktɪv/ *adj.* **1** involving communication between a computer, television, etc. and the person using it: *an interactive software program for children* **2** involving people talking and working together: *interactive teaching methods*

in·ter·cept /ˌɪntɚ'sɛpt/ *v.* [T] to stop someone or catch something that is going from one place to another: *O'Neill intercepted the ball.* —**interception** /ˌɪntɚ'sɛpʃən/ *n.* [C,U]

in·ter·change /'ɪntɚˌtʃeɪndʒ/ *n.* **1** [C] a place where two HIGHWAYS, FREEWAYS, or railroad tracks meet **2** [singular, U] an exchange of ideas, thoughts, etc.: *a friendly **interchange of** ideas*

in·ter·change·a·ble /ˌɪntɚ'tʃeɪndʒəbəl/ *adj.* things that are interchangeable can be used instead of each other: *a toy with interchangeable parts* —**interchangeably** *adv.*

in·ter·com /'ɪntɚˌkɑm/ *n.* [C] a communication system by which people in different parts of a building, aircraft, etc. can speak to one another: *Suddenly, the captain's voice came **over the intercom**.*

in·ter·con·ti·nen·tal /ˌɪntɚˌkɑntə'nɛntl, -ˌkɑntˀn'ɛntl/ *adj.* happening between or going from one CONTINENT to another: *an intercontinental flight*

in·ter·course /'ɪntɚˌkɔrs/ *n.* [U] *formal* the act of having sex

in·ter·de·pend·ent /ˌɪntɚdɪ'pɛndənt/ *adj.* depending on or necessary to each other: *interdependent networks of plants and animals* —**interdependence** *n.* [U]

in·terest¹ /'ɪntrɪst/ *n.* **1** [singular, U] a feeling that makes you want to pay attention to something and find out more about it: *Both girls share an **interest in** politics.* | *Kelly **lost interest*** (=stopped being interested) *halfway through the movie.*

COLLOCATIONS

have an/no/some/little interest in sth: *Many young people have no interest in politics.*
show (an/no/some/little) interest in sth: *Joe has never shown any interest in baseball.*
express (an) interest in sth – to say that you are interested in something: *The airline has expressed an interest in buying the plane.*
attract/arouse (little/some) interest – to make people interested: *His first film attracted interest from the big Hollywood studios.*
lack interest (in sth) – to not have much interest in something: *It's hard to teach students if they lack interest in the subject.*

2 [C] a subject or activity that you enjoy studying or doing: *a list of your hobbies and interests* **3** [U] **a)** money that you must pay for borrowing money: *a high/low **interest rate*** **b)** money that a bank pays you when you keep your money there **4** [U] a quality of something that attracts your attention and makes you want to know more about it: *a tourist guide to local places **of interest*** **5 be in sb's interest** to be an advantage to someone: *It would be in your interest to study the handbook carefully.*

interest² *v.* [T] to make someone want to pay attention to something and find out more about it: *I have some books that might interest you.*

in·terest·ed /'ɪntrɪstɪd, 'ɪntəˌrɛstɪd/ *adj.* **1** giving a lot of attention to something because you want to find out more about it: *Tim's really **interested in** antique cars.* | *I'd be **interested to know** what you think about it.* **2** eager to do or have something: *Jill is **interested in** studying in Europe.*

'interest ˌgroup *n.* [C] a group of people who join together to try to influence the government in order to protect their own particular rights, advantages, etc.

in·terest·ing /'ɪntrɪstɪŋ, 'ɪntəˌrɛstɪŋ/ *adj.* unusual or exciting in a way that keeps your attention: *That's an interesting idea.* | *Amy's a very interesting person.* | ***It's interesting that** so many people choose to live in remote locations.* —**interestingly** *adv.*

THESAURUS

fascinating – very interesting: *He's had a fascinating life.*
intriguing – something that is intriguing is interesting because it is unusual or mysterious, and you want to find out more: *That raises some intriguing questions.*
absorbing – interesting and keeping your attention: *The book is an absorbing read.*
compelling – very interesting or exciting: *a compelling story*
→ BORING

in·ter·face /'ɪntɚˌfeɪs/ *n.* [C] **1** the way a computer program looks on screen, or the way you type or put information into the program **2** the way two subjects, events, etc. affect each other: *the **interface between** Islam and the West*

in·ter·fere /ˌɪntɚ'fɪr/ *v.* [I] to deliberately get involved in a situation when you are not wanted or

I

needed: *It's better not to* ***interfere in*** *their arguments.*

interfere with sth *phr. v.* **1** to prevent something from succeeding or happening in the way it was planned: *Don't let sports interfere with your schoolwork.* **2** to spoil the sound or picture of a radio or television broadcast

in·ter·fer·ence /ˌɪntɚˈfɪrəns/ *n.* [U] **1** the act of interfering: *I resented his* ***interference in*** *my personal life.* **2** in sports, the act of blocking or touching another player, when you are not supposed to do this **3** unwanted noise, a spoiled picture, etc. on the radio, telephone, or television

in·ter·im¹ /ˈɪntərəm/ *adj.* [only before noun] an interim report, payment, manager, etc. is used or accepted for a short time until a final one is made or found [= **temporary**]

interim² *n.* **in the interim** in the period of time between two events: *The new stadium will not be ready until November, so games will be played at the university in the interim.*

in·te·ri·or¹ /ɪnˈtɪriɚ/ *n.* [C] the inner part or inside of something [≠ **exterior**]: *a car with a brown leather interior*

interior² *adj.* inside or indoors [≠ **exterior**]: *interior lighting*

inˌterior deˈsign *n.* [U] the job or skill of choosing and arranging furniture, colors, art, etc. for the inside of houses or buildings —**interior designer** *n.* [C]

in·ter·ject /ˌɪntɚˈdʒɛkt/ *v.* [I,T] *formal* to interrupt what someone is saying with a sudden remark

in·ter·jec·tion /ˌɪntɚˈdʒɛkʃən/ *n.* [C] in grammar, a word or phrase that is used in order to express surprise, shock, pain, etc. In the sentence "Ouch! That hurt!", "ouch" is an interjection.

in·ter·lock·ing /ˌɪntɚˈlɑkɪŋ◂/ *adj.* connected firmly together: *the Olympic symbol of interlocking circles* —**interlock** *v.* [I,T]

in·ter·lop·er /ˈɪntɚˌloʊpɚ/ *n.* [C] *formal* someone who enters a place where s/he should not be

in·ter·lude /ˈɪntɚˌlud/ *n.* [C] a period of time between activities or events: *a brief interlude of peace before the fighting began again*

in·ter·me·di·ar·y /ˌɪntɚˈmidiˌɛri/ *n.* plural **intermediaries** [C] someone who tries to help two other people or groups to agree with one another

in·ter·me·di·ate /ˌɪntɚˈmidiɪt/ *adj.* done or happening between two other stages, levels, etc. [➡ **beginning, elementary, advanced**]: *an intermediate Spanish class*

in·ter·mis·sion /ˌɪntɚˈmɪʃən/ *n.* [C,U] a short period of time between the parts of a play, concert, etc.: *We talked for a while* ***during the intermission.*** ➔ see Topic box at THEATER

in·ter·mit·tent /ˌɪntɚˈmɪt˺nt/ *adj.* happening at some times, but not regularly or continuously: *clouds and intermittent rain* —**intermittently** *adv.*

in·tern¹ /ˈɪntɚn/ *n.* [C] **1** someone, especially a student, who works for a short time in a particular job in order to gain experience [➡ **internship**] **2** someone who has almost finished training as a doctor and is working in a hospital [➡ **resident**]

in·tern² /ɪnˈtɚn/ *v.* **1** [I] to work as an intern: *Pena interned at the newspaper's Austin bureau for a year.* **2** [T] *formal* to put someone in prison, especially for political reasons [➡ **internment**]

in·ter·nal /ɪnˈtɚnl/ *adj.* **1** inside something such as your body [≠ **external**]: *internal bleeding* | *internal injuries* **2** within a particular company, organization, country, etc.: *the company's confidential internal documents* | *A major internal investigation is underway.* —**internally** *adv.*: *This product should not be taken internally.*

Inˌternal ˈRevenue ˌService *n.* **the Internal Revenue Service** IRS

in·ter·na·tion·al /ˌɪntɚˈnæʃənəl/ *adj.* relating to more than one country: *an international agreement* | *international trade* | *an international airport* —**internationally** *adv.*

in·ter·net /ˈɪntɚˌnɛt/ *n.* **the Internet** a system of connected computers that allows computer users around the world to exchange information [= **the Net, the Web**]: *I found information about the college* ***on the Internet.***

TOPIC

To use the Internet, you first have to **connect** to it, using a **modem**. Some people use a **broadband** connection so that they can get Internet information faster. On the Internet, you can look for information using a **search engine**, or you can type in the **address** of a **website**. If you spend a lot of time looking at different websites, you can say that you are **surfing the net**. Many people also visit **chat rooms** (=a site where you can have a conversation with other people) and **newsgroups** (=a site where people with a shared interest exchange messages), and some people write **blogs** (=a website that you keep adding new information to). People use **e-mail** to contact friends and family, or for work. More and more people and companies are using the Internet to send and receive work, and some people **work online**.

➔ EMAIL, COMPUTER

in·ter·nist /ˈɪntɚnɪst/ *n.* [C] a doctor who treats medical conditions of the organs inside your body by using medicines, rather than by using SURGERY [➡ **surgeon**]

in·tern·ment /ɪnˈtɚnmənt/ *n.* [C,U] the act of keeping someone in prison, especially for political reasons

in·tern·ship /ˈɪntɚnˌʃɪp/ *n.* [C] the period of time when an INTERN works, or the particular job s/he does: *an internship in a law firm*

in·ter·per·son·al /ˌɪntɚˈpɚsənl/ *adj.* involving relationships between people: *interpersonal skills*

in·ter·plan·e·tar·y /ˌɪntɚˈplænəˌtɛri/ *adj.* happening or done between the PLANETS

in·ter·play /ˈɪntɚˌpleɪ/ *n.* [U] the way that two people or things affect each other: *the* ***interplay between*** *man and nature*

in·ter·pret /ɪnˈtɚprɪt/ *v.* **1** [I,T] to change words spoken in one language into another [➡ **translate**]: *Gina spoke enough Spanish to be able to interpret for me.* **2** [T] to explain or decide on the meaning of an event, statement, etc.: *His silence was* ***interpreted as*** *guilt.* | *A judge's main role is to interpret the law.*

in·ter·pre·ta·tion /ɪnˌtɚprəˈteɪʃən/ *n.* [C,U] an explanation for an event, someone's actions, etc.: *one scientist's* ***interpretation of*** *the data*

in·ter·pret·er /ɪnˈtɚprət̬ɚ/ *n.* [C] someone who changes the spoken words of one language into another [➡ **translator**]

in·ter·ra·cial /ˌɪntɚˈreɪʃəl◂/ *adj.* between different races of people: *an interracial marriage*

in·ter·re·lat·ed /ˌɪntərɪˈleɪt̬ɪd/ *adj.* things that are interrelated all have an effect on each other

in·ter·ro·gate /ɪnˈtɛrəˌgeɪt/ *v.* [T] to ask someone a lot of questions, sometimes in a threatening way: *Police are interrogating the suspect now.* —**interrogator** *n.* [C] —**interrogation** /ɪnˌtɛrəˈgeɪʃən/ *n.* [C,U]

THESAURUS

ask, **order**, **demand**, **request**, **beg**, **question**, **inquire**, **enquire**
➔ see Thesaurus box at ASK

in·ter·rupt /ˌɪntəˈrʌpt/ *v.* **1** [I,T] to stop someone from speaking by suddenly saying or doing something: *Sorry, I didn't mean to interrupt you.* | *One guy in the front row kept interrupting during Kay's talk.* **2** [T] to stop a process or activity for a short time: *The war interrupted the supply of oil.* —**interruption** /ˌɪntɚˈrʌpʃən/ *n.* [C,U] *Work on the bridge continued* ***without interruption.*** | *several* ***interruptions in*** *the schedule*

in·ter·sect /ˌɪntɚˈsɛkt/ *v.* [I,T] if two lines, roads, etc. intersect, they meet or go across each other

in·ter·sec·tion /ˈɪntɚˌsɛkʃən, ˌɪntɚˈsɛkʃən/ *n.* [C] the place where two roads, lines, etc. meet and go across each other

in·ter·sperse /ˌɪntɚˈspɚs/ *v.* [T] to mix something together with something else: *The speeches were* ***interspersed with*** *short musical performances.*

in·ter·state¹ /ˈɪntɚˌsteɪt/ *n.* [C] a road for fast traffic that goes between states

interstate² *adj.* [only before noun] between or involving different states in the U.S.: *interstate trade*

in·ter·twined /ˌɪntɚˈtwaɪnd/ *adj.* twisted together or closely related: *several intertwined stories*

in·ter·val /ˈɪntɚvəl/ *n.* [C] **1** a period of time between two events, activities, etc.: *The Bijou Theater opened again after an interval of five years.* | *There was a brief* ***interval between*** *the battles.* **2 at daily/weekly/monthly etc. intervals** every day, week, month, etc. **3 at regular intervals** with the same amount of time or distance between each thing, activity, etc.: *Look away from your screen at regular intervals to rest your eyes.* **4 at intervals of sth** with a particular amount of time or distance between things, activities, etc.: *planes were landing at intervals of two minutes*

in·ter·vene /ˌɪntɚˈvin/ *v.* [I] **1** to do something to try to stop an argument, problem, war, etc.: *The police had to* ***intervene in*** *the march to stop the fighting.* **2** to happen between two events, especially in a way that interrupts or prevents something: *They had planned to get married, but the war intervened.* —**intervening** *adj.*: *He had aged a lot in the intervening years.*

in·ter·ven·tion /ˌɪntɚˈvɛnʃən/ *n.* [C,U] the act of intervening: *military* ***intervention in*** *troubled nations*

in·ter·view¹ /ˈɪntɚˌvyu/ *n.* **1** [C] an occasion when someone famous is asked questions about his/her life, opinions, etc.: *The former President* ***gave an interview*** *to Barbara Walters* (=he answered her questions). | *an* ***interview with*** *several sports stars* **2** [C,U] **also job interview** a formal meeting in which someone is asked questions, usually to find out if s/he is good enough for a job: *I have an* ***interview for*** *a job as a project manager tomorrow.* ➔ see Topic box at JOB

interview² *v.* [T] to ask someone questions during an interview: *Kelly was interviewed on the radio after the game.* —**interviewer** *n.* [C]

in·ter·weave /ˌɪntɚˈwiv/ *v.* past tense **interwove** /-ˈwoʊv/ past participle **interwoven** /-ˈwoʊvən/ present participle **interweaving** [T] if two or more ideas or situations are interwoven, they are too closely related to be separated easily: *The histories of the two countries are closely interwoven.*

in·tes·tine /ɪnˈtɛstɪn/ *n.* [C] the long tube that takes food from your stomach out of your body: *the* ***large/small intestine*** —**intestinal** *adj.* ➔ see picture on page A3

in·ti·ma·cy /ˈɪntəməsi/ *n.* [U] a state of having a close personal relationship with someone [➡ **intimate**]: *the intimacy of good friends*

in·ti·mate¹ /ˈɪntəmɪt/ *adj.* **1** having a very close relationship with someone: *a party for a few intimate friends* **2** *formal* relating to sex: *The virus can only be transmitted through intimate contact.* **3** relating to very private or personal matters: *intimate secrets* —**intimately** *adv.*

in·ti·mate² /ˈɪntəˌmeɪt/ *v.* [T] *formal* to make someone understand what you mean without saying it directly —**intimation** /ˌɪntəˈmeɪʃən/ *n.* [C,U]

in·tim·i·date /ɪnˈtɪməˌdeɪt/ *v.* [T] to make

someone afraid, often by using threats, so that s/he does what you want —**intimidation** /ɪnˌtɪmə'deɪʃən/ *n.* [U]

in·tim·i·dat·ed /ɪn'tɪməˌdeɪṭɪd/ *adj.* feeling worried or afraid because you are in a difficult situation: *Ben felt intimidated by the older boys.*

in·tim·i·dat·ing /ɪn'tɪməˌdeɪṭɪŋ/ *adj.* making you feel worried and less confident: *Interviews can be an intimidating experience.*

in·to /'ɪntə; *before vowels* 'ɪntʊ; *strong* 'ɪntu/ *prep.* **1** in order to be inside something or in a place: *Amy went into the next room.* | *She put the fish back into the water.* **2** involved in a situation or activity: *He decided he would try to **go into** business for himself* (=start his own business). | *Try not to **get into** trouble.* **3** in a different situation or physical form: ***Make** the bread dough **into** a ball* (=the shape of a ball). | *Poe's house has been **turned into** a museum.* **4** to a point where you hit something, usually causing damage: *Dick drove his dad's car into a tree.* **5 be into sth** *spoken* to like and be interested in something: *I was really into music in high school.* **6** in a particular direction: *Look into my eyes.* **7** at or until a particular time: *We talked long into the night.*

in·tol·er·a·ble /ɪn'tɑlərəbəl/ *adj.* too difficult, bad, or painful for you to bear: *intolerable conditions* —**intolerably** *adv.*

in·tol·er·ant /ɪn'tɑlərənt/ *adj.* not willing to accept ways of thinking and behaving that are different from your own: *He's very **intolerant of** other people's political opinions.* —**intolerance** *n.* [U]

in·to·na·tion /ˌɪntə'neɪʃən, -toʊ-/ *n.* [C,U] the rise and fall in the level of your voice

in·tox·i·cat·ed /ɪn'tɑksəˌkeɪṭɪd/ *adj. formal* **1** drunk: *He was intoxicated at the time of the accident.* **2** happy and excited because of success, love, power, etc. —**intoxicating** *adj.* —**intoxication** /ɪnˌtɑksə'keɪʃən/ *n.* [U]

in·tra·mu·ral /ˌɪntrə'myʊrəl/ *adj.* intended for the students of one school: *intramural sports*

in·tran·si·tive /ɪn'trænsəṭɪv, -zə-/ *adj. technical* in grammar, an intransitive verb has a subject but no object. In the sentence "They arrived early," "arrive" is an intransitive verb [➡ **transitive**]

in·tra·ve·nous /ˌɪntrə'vinəs◂/ *adj.* in or connected to a VEIN (=a tube that takes blood to your heart) [➡ **IV**]: *an intravenous injection* —**intravenously** *adv.*

in·trep·id /ɪn'trɛpɪd/ *adj. literary* willing to do dangerous things or go to dangerous places: *intrepid travelers*

in·tri·ca·cy /'ɪntrɪkəsi/ *n.* **1 the intricacies of sth** the complicated details of something: *You need an expert to help you with the intricacies of the tax system.* **2** [U] the state of containing a lot of parts or details: *the intricacy of the plot*

in·tri·cate /'ɪntrɪkɪt/ *adj.* containing a lot of parts or details: *an intricate pattern*

in·trigue[1] /ɪn'trig/ *v.* [T] to interest someone a lot, especially by being strange or mysterious: *I was intrigued by her story.*

in·trigue[2] /'ɪntrig, ɪn'trig/ *n.* [C,U] the practice of making secret plans to harm or deceive someone: *a book about **political intrigue***

in·tri·guing /ɪn'trigɪŋ/ *adj.* very interesting because it is strange or mysterious: *an intriguing new book* —**intriguingly** *adv.*

THESAURUS

interesting, fascinating, absorbing, compelling
➔ see Thesaurus box at INTERESTING

in·trin·sic /ɪn'trɪnzɪk, -sɪk/ *adj.* being part of the basic nature or character of someone or something: *the **intrinsic value** of good behavior* —**intrinsically** *adv.*

in·tro /'ɪntroʊ/ *n.* plural **intros** [C] *informal* INTRODUCTION

in·tro·duce /ˌɪntrə'dus/ *v.* [T] **1** if you introduce someone to another person, you tell them each other's name for the first time [➡ **introduction**]: *Al, let me **introduce** you **to** my parents.* | *Have you two been introduced yet?*

COMMUNICATION

Ways of introducing people

Alice, this is Megan
Alice, have you met Megan?
Alice, I'd like you to meet Megan
➔ HELLO

2 to make a change, plan, product, etc. happen or exist or be available for the first time [➡ **introduction**]: *Over 60 new computer models were introduced last year.* **3 introduce sb to sth** to show someone something or tell him/her about it for the first time: *My aunt introduced me to cooking when I was 12.* **4** to speak at the beginning of a television program, public speech, etc. to say what will happen next [➡ **introduction**]

in·tro·duc·tion /ˌɪntrə'dʌkʃən/ *n.* **1** [C,U] the act of making a change, plan, product, etc. happen or exist or be available for the first time [➡ **introduce**]: *the **introduction of** new drugs* **2** [C] the act of telling two people each other's names when they meet for the first time [➡ **introduce**] **3** [C] a written or spoken explanation at the beginning of a book or speech [➡ **introduce**]

in·tro·duc·to·ry /ˌɪntrə'dʌktəri/ *adj.* relating to the beginning of a book, speech, course, etc.: *the introductory chapter*

in·tro·vert·ed /'ɪntrəˌvəṭɪd/ *adj.* thinking a lot about your own problems, interests, etc. and not wanting to be with other people [= **shy**; ➡ **extroverted**] —**introvert** *n.* [C]

THESAURUS

shy, **timid**, **bashful**, **reserved**, **withdrawn**, **antisocial**, **retiring**
→ see Thesaurus box at SHY[1]

in·trude /ɪn'trud/ *v.* [I] to go into a place or get involved in a situation where you are not wanted: *newspapers that **intrude into/on** people's private lives*

in·trud·er /ɪn'trudɚ/ *n.* [C] someone who enters a building or area where s/he is not supposed to be

in·tru·sion /ɪn'truʒən/ *n.* [C,U] an unwanted person, event, etc. that interrupts or annoys you: *Some people feared the government's **intrusion into** their personal lives.* —**intrusive** /ɪn'trusɪv/ *adj.*

in·tu·i·tion /ˌɪntu'ɪʃən/ *n.* [C,U] the ability to understand or know that something is true based on your feelings rather than facts: ***Trust** your **intuition** if you feel a situation is unsafe.*

in·tu·i·tive /ɪn'tuət̬ɪv/ *adj.* based on feelings rather than facts: *an intuitive understanding of the problem* —**intuitively** *adv.*

In·u·it /'ɪnuɪt/ *n.* **the Inuit** [plural] a group of people who live in places such as northern Canada, Greenland, Alaska, and eastern Siberia —**Inuit** *adj.*

in·un·date /'ɪnənˌdeɪt/ *v.* [T] **1 be inundated with/by sth** to receive so much of something that you cannot deal with all of it: *We were inundated with requests for tickets.* **2** *formal* to flood a place —**inundation** /ˌɪnən'deɪʃən/ *n.* [C,U]

in·vade /ɪn'veɪd/ *v.* **1** [I,T] to enter a place using military force [➡ **invasion**]: *A few days later, the island was invaded.* **2** [T] to go into a place in large numbers [➡ **invasion**]: *All the neighborhood kids invaded our pool yesterday.* —**invader** *n.* [C]

in·val·id[1] /ɪn'vælɪd/ *adj.* not legally or officially acceptable [≠ **valid**]: *an invalid bus pass*

in·va·lid[2] /'ɪnvələd/ *n.* [C] someone who needs to be cared for because s/he is sick, injured, or very old —**invalid** *adj.*

in·val·i·date /ɪn'væləˌdeɪt/ *v.* [T] **1** to make a document, ticket, etc. not legally acceptable anymore [➡ **valid**] **2** to show that something such as a belief, explanation, etc. is wrong: *New research has invalidated the theory.*

in·val·u·a·ble /ɪn'vælyəbəl, -yuəbəl/ *adj.* extremely useful [= **valuable**]: *Your advice has been invaluable.*

in·var·i·a·bly /ɪn'vɛriəbli, -'vær-/ *adv. formal* always, without changing: *The disease almost invariably ends in death.* —**invariable** *adj.*

in·va·sion /ɪn'veɪʒən/ *n.* [C,U] **1** an occasion when an army enters a country using military force [➡ **invade**]: *the **invasion of** Normandy*

THESAURUS

attack, **raid**, **assault**, **ambush**, **counterattack**
→ see Thesaurus box at ATTACK[1]

2 the arrival of people or things at a place where they are not wanted [➡ **invade**]: *Ron has tried everything to get rid of the invasion of ants in his kitchen.* **3 invasion of privacy** a situation in which someone tries to find out about someone else's personal life, in a way that is upsetting and often illegal —**invasive** /ɪn'veɪsɪv/ *adj.*

in·vent /ɪn'vɛnt/ *v.* [T] **1** to make, design, or produce something for the first time [➡ **invention, inventor**]: *Who invented the light bulb?*

THESAURUS

create – to invent or design something: *a dish created by our chef*
think up – to produce an idea, plan, etc. that is completely new: *Teachers constantly have to think up new ways to keep the kids interested.*
come up with sth – to think of a new idea, plan, reply, etc.: *Carson said he came up with the idea for the book about five years ago.*
devise formal – to plan or invent a way of doing something: *The system was devised as a way of measuring students' progress.*
make up sth – to produce a new story, song, game, etc.: *Grandpa made up stories for us at bedtime.*
dream sth up – to think of a plan or idea, especially an unusual one: *The company's name was dreamed up by Harris' fifteen-year-old daughter.*

2 to think of an idea, story, etc. that is not true, usually to deceive people

THESAURUS

lie, **make sth up**
→ see Thesaurus box at LIE[2]

in·ven·tion /ɪn'vɛnʃən/ *n.* **1** [C,U] the act of inventing something, or the thing that is invented [➡ **inventor**]: *Bell exhibited his new invention in Philadelphia.* | *the **invention of** television* **2** [C] an idea, story, etc. that is not true

in·ven·tive /ɪn'vɛntɪv/ *adj.* able to think of new and interesting ideas: *an inventive cook* —**inventiveness** *n.* [U]

in·ven·tor /ɪn'vɛntɚ/ *n.* [C] someone who has invented something

in·ven·to·ry /'ɪnvənˌtɔri/ *n.* plural **inventories** **1** [U] all the goods in a store **2** [C,U] a list of all the things in a place: *The store will be closed on Friday to **take inventory*** (=make a list of its goods).

in·verse /ɪn'vɚs, 'ɪnvɚs/ *adj.* **in inverse proportion/relation etc. to sth** getting larger as something else gets smaller, or getting smaller as something else gets larger —**inversely** *adv.* —**inverse** /'ɪnvɚs, ɪn'vɚs/ *n.* [C]

in·vert /ɪn'vɚt/ *v.* [T] *formal* to put something in the opposite position, especially by turning it upside down —**inversion** /ɪn'vɚʒən/ *n.* [C,U]

in·vest /ɪn'vɛst/ *v.* **1** [I,T] to give money to a company, bank, etc., or to buy something, in order to get a profit later [➡ **investment**]: ***investing in*** *stocks and bonds* | *Greg invested his life savings in high-tech companies.* **2** [T] to use a lot of time or effort to make something succeed: *How much time are you prepared to* ***invest in*** *this project?* —**investor** *n.* [C]

in·ves·ti·gate /ɪn'vɛstəˌgeɪt/ *v.* [I,T] to try to find out the truth about a crime, accident, etc.: *Police are currently investigating the case.* | *I heard a noise and went downstairs to investigate.* —**investigator** *n.* [C]

in·ves·ti·ga·tion /ɪnˌvɛstə'geɪʃən/ *n.* [C,U] an official attempt to find out the reasons for something, such as a crime or scientific problem: *an* ***investigation into*** *the plane crash* | *The issue is still* ***under investigation*** (=being investigated). —**investigative** /ɪn'vɛstəˌgeɪt̬ɪv/ *adj.*: *investigative journalism*

in·vest·ment /ɪn'vɛstmənt/ *n.* **1** [C,U] the money that you give to a company, bank, etc. in order to get a profit later, or the act of doing this [➡ **invest**]: *a $5,000* ***investment in*** *stocks* **2** [C] something that you buy or do because it will be more valuable or useful later: *We bought the house* ***as an investment.*** | *Going back to college was a* ***good investment.***

in·vig·o·rat·ing /ɪn'vɪgəˌreɪt̬ɪŋ/ *adj.* making you feel more active and healthy: *an invigorating morning run* —**invigorate** *v.* [T] —**invigorated** *adj.*

in·vin·ci·ble /ɪn'vɪnsəbəl/ *adj.* too strong to be defeated or destroyed —**invincibly** *adv.*

in·vis·i·ble /ɪn'vɪzəbəl/ *adj.* not able to be seen: *organisms that are invisible without using a microscope* | *a plane that's* ***invisible to*** *enemy radar* —**invisibly** *adv.* —**invisibility** /ɪnˌvɪzə'bɪlət̬i/ *n.* [U]

in·vi·ta·tion /ˌɪnvə'teɪʃən/ *n.* [C] a request to someone that invites him/her to go somewhere or do something, or the card this is written on: *Mel didn't get an* ***invitation to*** *Tom's party.*

COLLOCATIONS

a party/wedding/dinner etc. invitation
send out invitations – to send them to a number of people
get/receive an invitation
accept an invitation – to say yes
turn down/refuse an invitation – to say no

in·vite¹ /ɪn'vaɪt/ *v.* [T] **1** to ask someone to come to a party, meal, wedding, etc. [➡ **invitation**]: *I* ***invited*** *the Rosens* ***to*** *dinner next Friday.* | *They've* ***invited*** *us* ***for*** *lunch.* | *"Why weren't you at Eva's party?" "I wasn't invited."* **2 invite trouble/criticism etc.** to make trouble, criticism, etc. more likely to happen to you

invite sb **along** *phr. v.* to ask someone to come with you when you go somewhere: *You can invite one of your friends along.*

invite sb **in** *phr. v.* to ask someone to come into your home, usually when s/he is standing at the door

invite sb **over** *phr. v.* to ask someone to come to your home for a party, meal, etc.: *You could* ***invite*** *the Chans* ***over for*** *dinner.*

in·vite² /'ɪnvaɪt/ *n.* [C] *informal* an invitation

in·vit·ing /ɪn'vaɪt̬ɪŋ/ *adj.* an inviting sight, smell, etc. is attractive and makes you want to do something: *The lake looked inviting* (=made me want to swim in it). —**invitingly** *adv.*

in·voice /'ɪnvɔɪs/ *n.* [C] a list that shows how much you owe for goods, work, etc. [= **bill**] —**invoice** *v.* [T] *We were* ***invoiced for*** *two parts that never arrived.*

THESAURUS

bill, **check**, **tab**
➔ see Thesaurus box at BILL¹

in·voke /ɪn'voʊk/ *v.* [T] *formal* **1** to use a law, principle, etc. to support your opinions or actions **2** *literary* to ask for help from someone, especially a god

in·vol·un·tar·y /ɪn'vɑlənˌtɛri/ *adj.* an involuntary movement, reaction, etc. is one that you make suddenly without intending to —**involuntarily** /ɪnˌvɑlən'tɛrəli/ *adv.*

in·volve /ɪn'vɑlv/ *v.* [T] **1** to include or affect someone or something: *a riot involving 45 prisoners* **2** to ask or allow someone to take part in something: *efforts to* ***involve*** *kids* ***in*** *sports activities* **3** to include something as a necessary part or result of something else: *Taking the job involves moving to Texas.*

in·volved /ɪn'vɑlvd/ *adj.* **1** taking part in an activity or event: *I don't want to* ***get involved in*** *her personal problems.* | *Parents need to be* ***involved with*** *their children's education.* **2** difficult to understand because it is complicated or has a lot of parts: *a long involved answer* **3 be involved with sb** to be having a sexual relationship with someone

in·volve·ment /ɪn'vɑlvmənt/ *n.* [U] the act of taking part in an activity or event: *Brian's earlier* ***involvement in*** *local politics*

in·vul·nerable /ɪn'vʌlnərəbəl/ *adj.* not easy to harm, hurt, or attack

in·ward¹ /'ɪnwɚd/ *adj.* [only before noun] **1** felt in your own mind, but not expressed to other people [≠ **outward**]: *inward panic* **2** on or toward the inside of something —**inwardly** *adv.*: *Ginny was inwardly disappointed that she hadn't seen him at the party.*

inward² **also inwards** *adv.* toward the inside [≠ **outward**]

i·o·dine /'aɪəˌdaɪn, -ˌdɪn/ *n.* [U] a chemical that is added to salt to prevent disease and is sometimes used as a medicine for wounds

i·on /'aɪən, 'aɪɑn/ *n.* [C] *technical* an atom that has been given a positive or negative force

i·o·ta /aɪˈoʊt̬ə/ *n.* **not one/an iota of sth** not even a small amount of something: *There's not an iota of truth in what he says.*

IOU *n.* [C] *informal* **I owe you** a note that you sign to say that you owe someone some money

IPA *n.* [singular] **International Phonetic Alphabet** a system of signs that represent the sounds made in speech

IQ *n.* [C usually singular] **intelligence quotient** the level of someone's intelligence, with 100 being the average level: *He has an IQ of 130.*

IRA /ˈaɪrə/ *n.* [C] **individual retirement account** a special bank account in which you can save money for your RETIREMENT without paying taxes on it until later

i·rate /ˌaɪˈreɪt◂/ *adj.* extremely angry: *an irate customer* —**irately** *adv.*

ir·i·des·cent /ˌɪrəˈdɛsənt/ *adj.* showing colors that seem to change in different lights —**iridescence** *n.* [U]

i·ris /ˈaɪrɪs/ *n.* [C] **1** the round colored part of your eye ➔ see picture at EYE[1] **2** a tall plant with purple, yellow, or white flowers and long thin leaves

I·rish¹ /ˈaɪrɪʃ/ *adj.* relating to or coming from Ireland

Irish² *n.* **the Irish** [plural] the people of Ireland

irk /ɚk/ *v.* [T] to annoy someone

i·ron¹ /ˈaɪɚn/ *n.* **1** [C] an object that is heated and that you push across a piece of clothing to make it smooth **2** [U] a common hard metal that is used to make steel, and is found in very small quantities in food and in blood

iron² *v.* [T] to make your clothes smooth using an iron: *Can you iron my shirt for me?*

iron sth ⇔ **out** *phr. v.* to solve a small problem: *Jim and Sharon are ironing out their differences.*

iron³ *adj.* **1** made of iron: *iron bars on the gate* **2** very firm or strict: *He **ruled** the country **with an iron fist*** (=in a very strict and powerful way).

ˌIron ˈCurtain *n.* **the Iron Curtain** a name used in past times for the border between the Communist countries of eastern Europe and the rest of Europe

i·ron·ic /aɪˈrɑnɪk/ *adj.* **1** using words that are the opposite of what you really mean in order to be amusing, or show that you are annoyed **2** an ironic situation is unusual or amusing because something strange or unexpected happens: ***It's ironic that** your car was stolen outside the police station.* —**ironically** *adv.*

i·ron·ing /ˈaɪɚnɪŋ/ *n.* [U] the activity of making clothes smooth with an iron

ˈironing ˌboard *n.* [C] a narrow board for ironing clothes ➔ see picture at BOARD[1]

i·ro·ny /ˈaɪrəni/ *n.* plural **ironies** **1** [U] the use of words that are the opposite of what you really mean in order to be amusing, or show that you are annoyed **2** [C,U] the part of a situation that is unusual or amusing because something strange happens, or the opposite of what is expected happens: ***The irony is that** the drug was supposed to save lives.*

ir·ra·tion·al /ɪˈræʃənəl/ *adj.* not based on sensible or clear reasons: *an **irrational fear of** spiders* —**irrationally** *adv.* —**irrationality** /ɪˌræʃəˈnæləti/ *n.* [U]

ir·rec·on·cil·a·ble /ɪˌrɛkənˈsaɪləbəl/ *adj.* irreconcilable opinions, positions, etc. are very different, making it impossible to reach an agreement: *They are getting divorced because of **irreconcilable differences**.* —**irreconcilably** *adv.*

ir·re·fut·a·ble /ˌɪrɪˈfyut̬əbəl/ *adj. formal* an irrefutable statement, argument, etc. cannot be proved wrong: *There was **irrefutable proof/evidence** that he had lied.*

ir·reg·u·lar /ɪˈrɛgyəlɚ/ *adj.* **1** having a shape, surface, etc. that is not even or smooth: *a face with irregular features* **2** not happening at regular times or at the usual time: *an **irregular heartbeat*** **3** not following the usual pattern in grammar: *an irregular verb* —**irregularly** *adv.* —**irregularity** /ɪˌrɛgyəˈlærət̬i/ *n.* [C,U]

ir·rel·e·vance /ɪˈrɛləvəns/ **also ir·rel·e·van·cy** /ɪˈrɛləvənsi/ *n.* [U] a lack of importance in a particular situation

ir·rel·e·vant /ɪˈrɛləvənt/ *adj.* not useful or not relating to a particular situation, and therefore not important: *His age is irrelevant if he can do the job.* —**irrelevantly** *adv.*

ir·rep·a·ra·ble /ɪˈrɛpərəbəl/ *adj.* irreparable damage, harm, etc. is so bad that it can never be repaired or made better —**irreparably** *adv.*

ir·re·place·a·ble /ˌɪrɪˈpleɪsəbəl/ *adj.* too special, valuable, or rare to be replaced by anything else: *an irreplaceable work of art*

ir·re·press·i·ble /ˌɪrɪˈprɛsəbəl/ *adj.* always full of energy, happiness, or confidence, and never letting anything affect this: *Nathan's excitement was irrepressible.*

ir·re·proach·a·ble /ˌɪrɪˈproʊtʃəbəl/ *adj. formal* so good that you cannot criticize it: *Her behavior was irreproachable.*

ir·re·sist·i·ble /ˌɪrɪˈzɪstəbəl/ *adj.* **1** so attractive or desirable that you cannot stop yourself from wanting it: *The dessert looks irresistible.* | *The offer of so much money would be **irresistible to** most people.* **2** too strong or powerful to be stopped: *an **irresistible urge** to cry* —**irresistibly** *adv.*

ir·re·spec·tive /ˌɪrɪˈspɛktɪv/ *adv.* **irrespective of sth** used in order to show that a particular fact does not affect a situation at all: *Anyone can play, irrespective of age.*

ir·re·spon·si·ble /ˌɪrɪˈspɑnsəbəl/ *adj.* doing careless things without thinking about the possible bad results: *It was **irresponsible of** John to leave the kids alone.* —**irresponsibly** *adv.* —**irresponsibility** /ˌɪrɪˌspɑnsəˈbɪlət̬i/ *n.* [U]

ir·rev·er·ent /ɪˈrɛvərənt/ *adj.* not showing respect for religion, CUSTOMS, etc.: *an irreverent* *sense of humor* —**irreverence** *n.* [U] —**irreverently** *adv.*

ir·re·ver·si·ble /ˌɪrɪˈvɚsəbəl/ *adj.* something that has irreversible damage, change, etc. cannot be changed back to how it was before: *irreversible brain damage*

ir·rev·o·ca·ble /ɪˈrɛvəkəbəl/ *adj.* not able to be changed or stopped: *an irrevocable decision* —**irrevocably** *adv.*

ir·ri·gate /ˈɪrəˌgeɪt/ *v.* [T] to supply water to land or crops —**irrigation** /ˌɪrəˈgeɪʃən/ *n.* [U] *an agricultural irrigation system*

ir·ri·ta·ble /ˈɪrət̬əbəl/ *adj.* easily annoyed or made angry: *He's always irritable in the morning.* —**irritably** *adv.* —**irritability** /ˌɪrət̬əˈbɪlət̬i/ *n.* [U]

THESAURUS

grumpy, cranky, crabby, grouchy, cantankerous, touchy
→ see Thesaurus box at GRUMPY

ir·ri·tant /ˈɪrətənt/ *n.* [C] *formal* **1** something that makes you feel angry or annoyed: *Traffic noise is a constant irritant in the city.* **2** a substance that makes part of your body painful and sore

ir·ri·tate /ˈɪrəˌteɪt/ *v.* [T] **1** to make someone angry or annoyed: *Her voice really irritates me.* **2** to make a part of your body painful and sore: *Wool **irritates** my **skin**.*

ir·ri·tat·ing /ˈɪrəˌteɪt̬ɪŋ/ *adj.* annoying: *his irritating habit of always being late* —**irritatingly** *adv.*

ir·ri·ta·tion /ˌɪrəˈteɪʃən/ *n.* **1** [C,U] the feeling of being annoyed, or something that makes you feel this way: *Tim made no secret of his **irritation with** me.* **2** [U] a painful, sore feeling on a part of your body

IRS *n.* **the IRS the Internal Revenue Service** the government organization in the U.S. that deals with taxes

is /z, s, əz; *strong* ɪz/ the third person singular of the present tense of BE

Is·lam /ˈɪzlɑm, ɪzˈlɑm, ˈɪslɑm/ *n.* [U] the Muslim religion, which was started by Muhammad and whose holy book is the Koran —**Islamic** /ɪzˈlɑmɪk, ɪs-/ *adj.*

island

is·land /ˈaɪlənd/ *n.* [C] a piece of land completely surrounded by water: *a hotel development **on the island** | the **island of** St. Kitts*

is·land·er /ˈaɪləndɚ/ *n.* [C] someone who lives on an island

isle /aɪl/ *n.* [C] an island, used in poetry or in names of islands

is·n't /ˈɪzənt/ *v.* the short form of "is not": *That isn't true.*

i·so·late /ˈaɪsəˌleɪt/ *v.* [T] to make or keep one person or thing separate from others: *The town was isolated by the floods. | Computers seem to have **isolated** us **from** one another.*

i·so·lat·ed /ˈaɪsəˌleɪt̬ɪd/ *adj.* **1** far away from other things: *an isolated farm* **2** feeling alone or unable to meet or speak to other people: *New mothers often feel isolated.* **3 an isolated case/example etc.** a case, example, etc. that happens only once: *an isolated case of the disease | The violence was an **isolated incident**.*

i·so·la·tion /ˌaɪsəˈleɪʃən/ *n.* [U] **1** the state of being separate from other places, things, or people: *the city's geographical isolation* (=its location far away from other cities) **2 in isolation** separately: *These events cannot be examined in isolation from one another.* **3** a feeling of being lonely

is·sue¹ /ˈɪʃu/ *n.* [C] **1** a subject or problem that people discuss: *We should **raise the issue*** (=begin to discuss it) *at our next meeting. | the controversial **issue of** abortion | Safety is the most **important issue**.* **2** a magazine, newspaper, etc. printed for a particular day, week, month, or year: *the April **issue of** Vogue* **3 make an issue (out) of sth** to argue about something **4 at issue** *formal* being discussed or considered: *At issue is whether the senator improperly used campaign funds.* **5 take issue with sb/sth** to disagree or argue with someone about something: *He took issue with Mayor Farrell's statement.*

issue² *v.* [T] **1** to officially make a statement or give a warning: *The president is expected to **issue** a **statement** later today.* **2** to officially provide or produce something: *Every player was **issued with** a new uniform.*

isth·mus /ˈɪsməs/ *n.* [C] a narrow piece of land with water on both sides, that connects two larger areas of land

IT *n.* [U] **information technology**

it /ɪt/ *pron.* [used as a subject or object] **1** a thing, situation, or idea that has been mentioned or is known about: *"Did you bring your umbrella?" "No, I left it at home." | "Where's the bread?" "It's* (=it is) *on the shelf." | In the summer, it must be beautiful here.* **2** the situation that someone is in now: *I can't stand it any longer. I'm resigning. | How's it going, Bob?* (=How are you?) **3** used as the subject or object of a sentence when the real subject or object is later in the sentence: *It costs less to drive than to take the bus.* **4** used with the verb "be" to talk about the weather, time, distance, etc.: *It's raining. | It's only a few miles from here* *to the beach.* **5** used in order to emphasize one piece of information in a sentence: *I don't know who took your book, but it wasn't me.* | *It was last year at this time that they went to Australia.* **6** used as the subject of the words "seem," "appear," "look," and "happen": *It seemed like she was angry.* **7 it's...** used in order to give the name of a person or thing when it is not already known: *"What's that?" "It's a pen."* | *"Who's on the phone?" "It's Jill."* **8** used in order to talk about a child or animal when you do not know what sex s/he is: *"Marilyn had a baby." "Is it a boy or girl?"* ➔ **that's it** at THAT[1]

I·tal·ian[1] /ɪ'tælyən/ *adj.* **1** relating to or coming from Italy **2** relating to the Italian language

Italian[2] *n.* **1** [U] the language used in Italy **2** [C] someone from Italy

i·tal·ics /ɪ'tælɪks, aɪ-/ *n.* [plural] a type of printed letters that lean to the right: *This example is printed **in italics**.*

itch[1] /ɪtʃ/ *v.* **1** [I,T] to have an unpleasant ITCH: *My back is itching.* **2 be itching to do sth** *informal* to want to do something very much: *Ian's been itching to try out his new bike.*

itch[2] *n.* [C] **1** an unpleasant feeling on your skin that makes you want to rub it with your nails **2** *informal* a strong desire to do or have something: *an **itch to** do something different*

itch·y /'ɪtʃi/ *adj.* comparative **itchier**, superlative **itchiest** **1** if part of your body is itchy, it feels unpleasant and you want to rub it: *My eyes are really itchy.* **2** itchy clothes make your skin feel unpleasant and you want to rub it —**itchiness** *n.* [U]

it'd /'ɪt̬əd/ **1** the short form of "it would": *It'd be easier if we both did it.* **2** the short form of "it had": *It'd been raining since Sunday.*

i·tem /'aɪt̬əm/ *n.* [C] **1** a single thing in a set, group, or list: *an **item of** clothing* | *There is one more **item on** the **agenda**.* | *household items*

THESAURUS

thing, object, article
➔ see Thesaurus box at THING

2 a piece of news in the newspaper or on television: *I saw an item about the kidnapping in the paper.*

i·tem·ize /'aɪt̬ə,maɪz/ *v.* [T] to write down all of the parts of something in a list —**itemized** *adj.*

i·tin·er·ant /aɪ'tɪnərənt/ *adj. formal* traveling from place to place: *itinerant farm workers*

i·tin·er·ar·y /aɪ'tɪnə,rɛri/ *n.* plural **itineraries** [C] a plan of a trip, usually including the places you want to see

it'll /'ɪt̬l/ the short form of "it will": *It'll be nice to see Martha again.*

it's /ɪts/ **1** the short form of "it is": *It's snowing!* **2** the short form of "it has": *It's been snowing all day.*

USAGE

Its is a possessive form and does not have the apostrophe (') before the "s": *Their dog broke its leg.*
It's with the apostrophe (') before the "s" means "it is" or "it has": *It's raining.* | *It's been raining all day.*

its /ɪts/ *determiner* belonging or relating to a thing, situation, person, or idea that has been mentioned or is known about: *The tree has lost all of its leaves.* ➔ see Usage box at IT'S

it·self /ɪt'sɛlf/ *pron.* **1** the REFLEXIVE form of "it": *The cat was licking itself.* **2 in itself** only the thing mentioned, and not anything else: *We're proud you finished the race. That in itself is an accomplishment.*

it·sy-bit·sy /,ɪtsi 'bɪtsi◂/ **also it·ty-bit·ty** /,ɪt̬i 'bɪt̬i◂/ *adj. informal* very small

IUD *n.* [C] **intrauterine device** a small plastic or metal object placed in a woman's UTERUS to prevent her from having a baby

IV *n.* [C] **intravenous** medical equipment that is used for putting liquid directly into your body

I've /aɪv/ the short form of "I have": *I've seen you somewhere before.*

i·vo·ry /'aɪvəri/ *n.* [U] **1** the hard smooth yellow-white substance from the TUSK (=long teeth) of an elephant **2** a pale yellow-white color —**ivory** *adj.*

i·vy /'aɪvi/ *n.* [U] a climbing plant with dark green shiny leaves ➔ POISON IVY

'Ivy ,League *adj.* relating to a small group of old respected colleges in the north east of the U.S.: *an Ivy League graduate* —**Ivy League** *n.* [singular]

J, j

J, j /dʒeɪ/ the tenth letter of the English alphabet

jab /dʒæb/ *v.* past tense and past participle **jabbed**, present participle **jabbing** [I,T] to quickly push something pointed into something else, or toward it: *The nurse **jabbed** a needle **into** his arm.* —**jab** *n.* [C]

jab·ber /'dʒæbɚ/ *v.* [I] to talk quickly, in an excited way, and not very clearly

jack[1] /dʒæk/ *n.* [C] **1** a piece of equipment used for lifting something heavy, such as a car, and supporting it **2** an electronic connection for a telephone or other electronic machine **3** a card used in card games which has a young man's picture on it: *the jack of clubs* ➔ see picture at PLAYING CARDS

jack[2] *v.*

jack sb/sth ⇔ **up** *phr. v.* **1** to lift something heavy using a JACK: *Dad jacked the car up so I* *could change the tire.* **2** *informal* to increase prices, sales, etc. by a large amount: *Stores have jacked up their prices since July.*

jack·al /'dʒækəl/ *n.* [C] a wild animal like a dog that lives in Africa and Asia

jack·ass /'dʒækæs/ *n.* [C] **1** *spoken* an impolite word meaning an annoying stupid person **2** a male DONKEY

jack·et /'dʒækɪt/ *n.* [C] **1** a short light coat: *a leather jacket | a rain jacket* → see picture at CLOTHES **2** the part of a SUIT that covers the top part of your body **3** a stiff piece of folded paper that fits over the cover of a book to protect it

jack·ham·mer /'dʒæk,hæmɚ/ *n.* [C] a large powerful tool used for breaking hard materials such as the surface of a road

'jack-in-the-,box *n.* [C] a toy shaped like a box from which a figure jumps out when the box's lid is lifted

'jack knife *n.* [C] → POCKET KNIFE

jack·knife /'dʒæknaɪf/ *v.* [I] if a truck or train with two or more parts jackknifes, the back part swings toward the front part

,jack-of-'all-trades *n.* [singular] someone who can do many different types of jobs

jack-o-lan·tern /'dʒæk ə ,læntɚn/ *n.* [C] a PUMPKIN with a face cut into it, usually with a light inside, made at HALLOWEEN

jack·pot /'dʒækpɑt/ *n.* [C] **1** a very large amount of money that you can win in a game **2 hit the jackpot a)** to win a lot of money **b)** to be very successful or lucky

Ja·cuz·zi /dʒə'kuzi/ *n. trademark* [C] → HOT TUB

jade /dʒeɪd/ *n.* [C] [U] a green stone used for making jewelry and ORNAMENTS

J

jad·ed /'dʒeɪdɪd/ *adj.* not interested in or excited by things, usually because you have seen them or done them too much

jag·ged /'dʒægɪd/ *adj.* having a rough uneven edge with a lot of sharp points: *jagged rocks*

jag·uar /'dʒægwɑr/ *n.* [C] a large wild cat with black spots from Central and South America

jail¹ /dʒeɪl/ *n.* [C,U] a place where someone is sent to be punished for a crime [= **prison**]: *overcrowded jails | He was* ***in jail*** *for 15 years. | a two-year* ***jail sentence***

COLLOCATIONS

go to jail: *If you commit a crime, you should go to jail.*
put sb in jail: *I hope they put him in jail and never let him out.*
send sb to jail: *He has a record of sending even petty criminals to jail.*
spend time in jail
release sb from jail: *She was released from jail and given parole.*
get out of jail: *We want to get these men out of jail and into a drug rehabilitation program.*
escape from jail: *He escaped from jail last year and has been on the run ever since.*
end up in jail: *I always said he'd end up in jail.*

jail² *v.* [T] to put someone in JAIL

jail·er, jailor /'dʒeɪlɚ/ *n.* [C] someone whose job is to guard a prison or prisoners

ja·lop·y /dʒə'lɑpi/ *n.* plural **jalopies** *informal* [C] a very old car in bad condition

jam¹ /dʒæm/ *v.* past tense and past participle **jammed**, present participle **jamming** **1** [T] to push someone or something using a lot of force, especially into a small place: *Mr. Braithe jammed the letters into his pockets and left.* **2** [I,T] **also jam up** if a machine jams up or if you jam it, it stops working because something is stuck inside it: *Every time I try to use the Xerox machine it jams.* **3** [T] to fill a place with a lot of people or things, so that nothing can move: *The roads* ***were jammed with*** *cars.* **4** [I] to play music for fun with a group of people without practicing first

jam² *n.* **1** [U] a thick sticky sweet substance made from fruit, usually eaten on bread: *strawberry jam* **2 be in a jam/get into a jam** *informal* to be or become involved in a difficult or bad situation: *Sarah, I'm in a jam — could you do me a favor?* **3** [C] a situation in which something is stuck somewhere: *a jam in the fax machine* → TRAFFIC JAM

jamb /dʒæm/ *n.* [C] the side post of a door or window

jam·bo·ree /,dʒæmbə'ri/ *n.* [C] a big noisy party or celebration

jammed /dʒæmd/ *adj.* impossible to move because of being stuck: *The stupid door's jammed again.*

,jam-'packed *adj. informal* completely full of people or things: *a cereal* ***jam-packed with*** *vitamins*

'jam ,session *n.* [C] an occasion when people meet to play music together for fun

Jane Doe /,dʒeɪn 'doʊ/ *n.* [C,U] a name used in legal forms, documents, etc. when a woman's name is not known

jan·gle /'dʒæŋgəl/ *v.* [I,T] to make a noise that sounds like metal objects hitting against each other: *His keys were jangling in his pocket.*

jan·i·tor /'dʒænəṭɚ/ *n.* [C] someone whose job is to clean and take care of a large building: *the school janitor*

Jan·u·ar·y /'dʒænyu,ɛri/ *n.* [C,U] *written abbreviation* **Jan.** the first month of the year

Jap·a·nese¹ /,dʒæpə'niz◂ / *adj.* **1** relating to or coming from Japan **2** relating to the Japanese language

Japanese² *n.* **1** [U] the language used in Japan **2 the Japanese** [plural] the people of Japan

jar¹ /dʒɑr/ *n.* [C] **1** a round glass container with a lid, used for storing food **2** the amount of food contained in a jar: *half a* ***jar of*** *peanut butter*

jar² *v.* past tense and past participle **jarred**, present participle **jarring** [I,T] **1** to shock someone, especially by making an unpleasant noise: *The alarm jarred her awake.* **2** to shake or hit something with enough force to damage it or make it become loose: *Alice jarred her knee when she jumped off the wall.*

jar·gon /ˈdʒɑrgən/ *n.* [U] technical words and phrases used by people in a particular profession that are difficult for other people to understand: *medical/legal/technical jargon*

THESAURUS

language, slang, terminology
➔ see Thesaurus box at LANGUAGE

jaun·dice /ˈdʒɔndɪs, ˈdʒɑn-/ *n.* [U] a medical condition in which your skin and the white part of your eyes become yellow

jaun·diced /ˈdʒɔndɪst, ˈdʒɑn-/ *adj.* **1** tending to judge people, things, or situations in a negative way, often because of your own bad experiences in the past: *a jaundiced view of the world* **2** suffering from JAUNDICE

jaunt /dʒɔnt, dʒɑnt/ *n.* [C] a short trip for pleasure

jaun·ty /ˈdʒɔnti, ˈdʒɑnti/ *adj.* showing that you feel confident and cheerful —**jauntily** *adv.*

jav·e·lin /ˈdʒævəlɪn, -vlɪn/ *n.* **1** [U] a sport in which you throw a SPEAR (=a long pointed stick) as far as you can **2** [C] the stick used in this sport

jaw /dʒɔ/ *n.* [C] **1** one of the two bones that form your mouth and that have all your teeth: *a broken jaw* ➔ see picture on page A3 **2 sb's jaw dropped** used in order to say that someone looked very surprised or shocked: *Sam's jaw dropped when Katy walked into the room.* **3 jaws** [plural] the mouth of a person or animal, especially a dangerous animal

jay·walk·ing /ˈdʒeɪˌwɔkɪŋ/ *n.* [U] the action of walking across a street in an area that is not marked for walking —**jaywalker** *n.* [C]

jazz¹ /dʒæz/ *n.* [U] **1** a type of popular music that usually has a strong beat and parts for performers to play alone

THESAURUS

pop (music), rock (music), rock'n'roll, heavy metal, reggae, house (music), hip-hop, rap (music), classical (music), country (music), folk (music)
➔ see Thesaurus box at MUSIC

2 and all that jazz *spoken* and things like that: *I'm sick of rules, responsibilities, and all that jazz.*

jazz² *v.*

jazz sth ⇔ **up** *phr. v. informal* to make something more exciting and interesting: *You could jazz up that shirt with some accessories.*

jazzed /dʒæzd/ *adj. spoken* excited

jazz·y /ˈdʒæzi/ *adj.* comparative **jazzier**, superlative **jazziest** **1** bright, colorful, and easily noticed: *a jazzy tie* **2** similar to the style of JAZZ music

jeal·ous /ˈdʒɛləs/ *adj.* **1** feeling angry or unhappy because someone else has a quality, thing, or ability that you wish you had: *Diane was **jealous of** me because I got better grades.*

THESAURUS

jealous – angry or unhappy because you do not have something that someone else has: *Bill was jealous of his brother's success.*
envious – wishing that you had the qualities or things that someone else has: *I've been envious of all his free time.*

2 feeling angry or unhappy because someone you love is paying attention to another person, or because another person is showing too much interest in someone you love: *It used to **make** me **jealous** when he danced with other women.* | *a jealous husband*

jeal·ous·y /ˈdʒɛləsi/ *n.* [U] the feeling of being JEALOUS

jeans /dʒinz/ *n.* [plural] a popular type of pants made from DENIM: *a pair of jeans* ➔ see picture at CLOTHES

Jeep /dʒip/ *n.* [C] *trademark* a type of car made to travel over rough ground

jeer /dʒɪr/ *v.* [I,T] to shout, speak, or laugh in order to annoy or frighten someone you dislike: *The crowd **jeered at** the speaker.* —**jeer** *n.* [C]

jeez /dʒiz/ *interjection* said in order to express sudden feelings such as surprise, anger, or shock

Je·ho·vah's Wit·ness /dʒɪˌhoʊvəz ˈwɪtnɪs/ *n.* [C] a member of a religious organization that believes the end of the world will happen soon and sends its members to people's houses to try to persuade them to join

jell /dʒɛl/ *v.* [I] another spelling of GEL²

Jell-O, jello /ˈdʒɛloʊ/ *n.* [U] *trademark* a soft solid substance made from GELATIN and sweet fruit juice

jel·ly /ˈdʒɛli/ *n.* [U] a thick sticky sweet substance made from fruit but having no pieces of fruit in it, usually eaten on bread: *a peanut butter and jelly sandwich*

jel·ly·fish /ˈdʒɛliˌfɪʃ/ *n.* [C] a round transparent sea animal with long things that hang down from its body

jeop·ard·ize /ˈdʒɛpɚˌdaɪz/ *v.* [T] to risk losing or destroying something that is valuable or important: *Junot was too worried about jeopardizing his career to say anything.*

jeop·ard·y /ˈdʒɛpɚdi/ *n.* **in jeopardy** in danger of being lost or destroyed: *My job is in jeopardy.*

jerk¹ /dʒɚk/ *v.* **1** [I,T] to move with a quick movement, or to make something move this way: *He jerked his head around to see her.* **2** [I,T] to pull something suddenly and quickly: *Tom **jerked open** the door.*

jerk sb **around** *phr. v. informal* to waste someone's time or deliberately make things difficult for him/her: *Don't jerk me around.*

jerk² *n.* [C] **1** *informal* someone, especially a man, who is stupid or who does things that annoy or hurt other people: *What a jerk!* **2** a quick movement, especially a pulling movement: *He pulled the cord **with a jerk**.* —**jerky** *adj.*

jerk·y /ˈdʒɚki/ *n.* [U] pieces of dried meat, usually with a salty or SPICY taste

jer·sey /ˈdʒɚzi/ *n.* plural **jerseys** [C] a shirt worn as part of a sports uniform

jest /dʒɛst/ *n.* **in jest** intending to be funny: *The criticisms were said in jest.*

jest·er /ˈdʒɛstɚ/ *n.* [C] a man employed in past times to entertain important people with jokes, stories, etc.

Je·sus /ˈdʒizəs/ **also** **ˌJesus ˈChrist** the person who Christians believe was the son of God, and whose life and TEACHINGS Christianity is based on

jet[1] /dʒɛt/ *n.* [C] **1** a fast airplane with a jet engine **2** a narrow stream of liquid or gas that comes quickly out of a small hole, or the hole itself: *a strong **jet of** water*

jet[2] *v.* past tense and past participle **jetted**, present participle **jetting** [I] *informal* to travel in a JET: *He **jetted off to** Paris yesterday.*

ˌjet ˈengine *n.* [C] an engine that forces out a stream of hot air and gases, used in planes

ˈjet lag *n.* [U] the feeling of being very tired after traveling a long distance in an airplane —**jet-lagged** *adj.*

ˌjet-proˈpelled *adj.* using a JET ENGINE for power —**jet propulsion** *n.* [U]

ˈjet set *n.* [singular] rich and fashionable people who travel a lot —**jet setter** *n.* [C]

jet·ti·son /ˈdʒɛtəsən, -zən/ *v.* [T] **1** to get rid of someone or something or decide not to use him/her anymore: *The state is prepared to jettison incompetent teachers.* **2** to throw things away, especially from a moving airplane or ship

jet·ty /ˈdʒɛti/ *n.* plural **jetties** [C] **1** a wide wall built out into the water, as protection against large waves **2** → WHARF

jew·el /ˈdʒuəl/ *n.* **1** [C] a small valuable stone, such as a DIAMOND **2** **jewels** [plural] jewelry

jew·eled /ˈdʒuəld/ *adj.* decorated with valuable stones

jew·el·er /ˈdʒuəlɚ/ *n.* [C] someone who buys, sells, makes, or repairs jewelry

jewelry

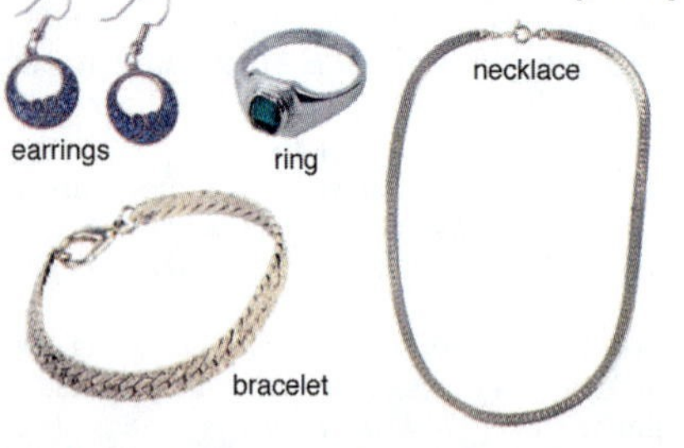

jew·el·ry /ˈdʒuəlri/ *n.* [U] small decorations you wear that are usually made from gold, silver, and jewels, such as rings and NECKLACES

Jew·ish /ˈdʒuɪʃ/ *adj.* relating to Judaism —**Jew** *n.* [C]

jibe[1] /dʒaɪb/ *n.* [C] → GIBE

jibe[2] *v.* [I] if two statements, actions, etc. jibe with each other, they agree or make sense together: *Your statement to the police does not **jibe with** the facts.*

jif·fy /ˈdʒɪfi/ *n. spoken* **in a jiffy** very soon: *I'll be back in a jiffy.*

jig /dʒɪg/ *n.* [C] a type of quick dance, or the music for this dance

jig·ger /ˈdʒɪgɚ/ *n.* [C] a unit for measuring alcohol, equal to 1.5 OUNCES

jig·gle /ˈdʒɪgəl/ *v.* past tense and past participle **jiggled**, present participle **jiggling** [I,T] to move from side to side with short quick movements, or to make something do this

jig·saw puz·zle /ˈdʒɪgsɔ ˌpʌzəl/ *n.* [C] a picture cut up into many small pieces that you try to fit together for fun

jilt /dʒɪlt/ *v.* [T] to suddenly end a relationship with someone: *His girlfriend jilted him.* —**jilted** *adj.*

jin·gle[1] /ˈdʒɪŋgəl/ *v.* [I,T] to shake small metal objects together so that they produce a noise, or to make this noise: *He jingled his keys in his pocket.*

jingle[2] *n.* **1** [C] a short song used in television and radio advertisements **2** [singular] the sound made by metal objects touching together

jinx[1] /dʒɪŋks/ *n.* [singular] someone or something that brings bad luck, or a period of bad luck that results from this

jinx[2] /dʒɪŋkst/ *v.* [I,T] to make someone have bad luck: *I don't want to talk about winning – I'm afraid I'll jinx myself.* —**jinxed** *adj.*

jit·ters /ˈdʒɪtɚz/ *n.* **the jitters** the feeling of being nervous and anxious, especially before an important event: *I always **get the jitters** before I go on stage.*

jit·ter·y /ˈdʒɪtəri/ *adj.* worried and nervous: *The recession has made consumers jittery.*

jive[1] /dʒaɪv/ *v.* **1** **sth doesn't jive (with sth)** *informal* to seem so strange or unusual that something does not make sense: *The newspaper report doesn't jive with the story on TV.* **2** [T] *slang* to try to make someone believe something that is not true: *You're jiving me!*

jive[2] *n.* **1** [C,U] a very fast type of dance, often performed to fast JAZZ music **2** [U] *slang* statements that you do not believe are true: *Don't you go giving me any of that jive!*

job /dʒɑb/ *n.* [C]

1 WORK work that you do regularly in order to earn money: *She **applied for a job** at the bank.* | *a **part-time/full-time job*** | *Suzy **got a job as** a legal secretary.* | *He **quit/left his job** so he could go back to school.* | *I **lost my job** last week.*

THESAURUS

Your **job** is the particular work you do regularly to earn money.
Work is used in a more general way to talk about employment or the activities involved in it: *I started work when I was 18.*
Position is a more formal word for a job in a particular organization: *How long have you been in your current position?*
Occupation is used mainly on official forms to mean your **job**: *Please give your name, age, and occupation.*
A **profession** is a job for which you need special education and training: *the legal profession*
Your **career** is the work you do for most of your life: *I'm interested in a career in journalism.*
A **vocation** is a feeling that the purpose of your life is to do a particular job, or the job itself: *I accepted that nursing was both my job and my vocation.*
➔ WORK

USAGE

Do not say "What is your job?" or "What is your work?" Say **"What do you do?"** or **"What kind of work do you do?"**

TOPIC

You can find jobs by looking at the **job listings** in newspapers, magazines, etc. Stores, restaurants, etc. also put **Help Wanted** signs in windows when they need to hire someone.
When you **apply for a job**, you **fill out** an **application form**. You may have to send your **résumé** (=a list describing your education, previous jobs, etc.), with a **cover letter**. You will need to give **references** (=names, phone numbers, and addresses of people who can describe your experience and say whether you would be a good employee).
If an employer is interested in you, s/he will **invite** you **to** an **interview**. If you are chosen, you will be **offered** the **job**.
If you **get promoted** or receive a **promotion**, you move to a better, more responsible position at work, for which you are given an **increase in salary**.
When you are going to leave your job, you **give notice** or **hand in** your **notice**, usually in writing, telling your employer that you will be leaving soon. If you **get fired**, your employer makes you leave your job. If you **retire**, you leave your job at the end of your working life.

2 on the job while doing work or at work: *Our reporters are on the job now.* | *All our employees get on-the-job training.*
3 DUTY a particular duty or responsibility that you have: ***It's my job to** take care of my little brother.*
4 IMPROVE STH something you do to fix or improve something: *The car needs a paint job.* | *a nose job* (=an operation to change the shape of your nose)
5 STH YOU MUST DO a piece of work you must do, usually without being paid: *I have a lot of **odd jobs*** (=different things) *to do on Saturday.*
6 do a good/great/bad etc. job to do something well or badly
7 Good job! *spoken* used to tell someone that they have done something well
8 KIND OF THING also jobby *spoken* used in order to say that something is of a particular type: *His new computer's one of those little portable jobs.*
9 do the job *informal* to make something have the result that you want or need: *A little more glue should do the job.*
10 CRIME *informal* a crime such as robbing a bank

jock /dʒɑk/ *n.* [C] *informal* a student who plays a lot of sports

jock·ey[1] /ˈdʒɑki/ *n.* [C] someone who rides horses in races

jockey[2] *v.* **jockey for position** to try to be in the best position or situation

jock·strap /ˈdʒɑkstræp/ *n.* [C] underwear that men wear to support their sex organs when playing sports

joc·u·lar /ˈdʒɑkyələ˞/ *adj. formal* joking or humorous —**jocularity** /ˌdʒɑkyəˈlærəṭi/ *n.* [U]

jog[1] /dʒɑg/ *v.* past tense and past participle **jogged**, present participle **jogging** **1** [I] to run slowly and in a steady way, especially for exercise: *Julie jogs every morning.* ➔ see picture on page A9 **2 jog sb's memory** to make someone remember something: *This picture might jog your memory.* **3** [T] to knock or push something lightly by mistake: *Someone jogged my elbow and I dropped the plate.*

jog[2] *n.* [singular] a slow steady run, especially for exercise: *Let's **go for a jog**.*

jog·ging /ˈdʒɑgɪŋ/ *n.* [U] the activity of running as a way of exercising: *We **went jogging** in Central Park.* ➔ see Topic box at EXERCISE[2] —**jogger** *n.* [C]

john /dʒɑn/ *n.* [C] *spoken informal* a toilet

ˌJohn ˈDoe *n.* [C,U] a name used in legal forms, documents, etc. when a man's name is not known

join /dʒɔɪn/ *v.* **1** [I,T] to become a member of an organization, society, or group: *Mary joined the gym last month.* | *It doesn't cost anything to join.* **2** [T] **also join in** to begin to take part in an activity that other people are involved in: *joining a political campaign* **3** [T] to do something together with someone else: *Why don't you **join** us **for** dinner?* | *Please **join with** me **in** welcoming tonight's speaker.* **4** [I,T] to connect or fasten things together, or to be connected: *the place where the two roads join*

THESAURUS

fasten, attach, glue, tape, staple, clip, tie, button (up), zip (up)
➔ see Thesaurus box at FASTEN

J

5 join hands if two or more people join hands, they hold each other's hands

joint[1] /dʒɔɪnt/ *adj.* **1** involving two or more people, or owned or shared by them: *They have to reach a joint decision.* | *a joint bank account* | *"Who cooked dinner?" "It was a* ***joint effort*** (=we did it together)." **2 joint resolution** *law* a decision or law agreed by both houses of the U.S. Congress and signed by the President —**jointly** *adv.*: *The company is* ***jointly owned*** *by Time Warner and Disney.*

joint[2] *n.* [C] **1** a part of the body where two bones meet, that can bend: *the knee joint* **2** *slang* a place, especially a BAR, club, or restaurant: *a fast-food joint* **3** *slang* a MARIJUANA cigarette **4** a place where two things or parts of an object are joined together: *One of the pipe joints was leaking.* **5 out of joint** a bone that is out of joint has been pushed out of its correct position

ˌjoint ˈventure *n.* [C] a business arrangement in which two or more companies work together to achieve something

joke[1] /dʒoʊk/ *n.* [C] **1** something funny that you say or do to make people laugh: *Let me* ***tell*** *you a* ***joke****.*

COLLOCATIONS

inside joke – a joke that only a few people with knowledge about a particular subject or event will understand
running joke – a joke that continues or is repeated over a long period of time
practical joke – a trick that is intended to surprise someone or make other people laugh at him/her
dirty joke – a joke that is about sex
sick joke – a joke that is very cruel or disgusting

THESAURUS

gag – a short joke, especially one told by a professional entertainer: *His first job was writing gags for radio comedians.*
wisecrack – a quick, funny, and often slightly unkind remark: *She made the other kids laugh with her jokes and wisecracks.*
one-liner – a very short joke: *The play is full of hilarious one-liners.*
pun – an amusing use of a word or phrase that has two meanings, or of words with the same sound but different meanings: *The band is called Esso Es, a pun that to English-speakers sounds like a call for help, but in Spanish means "That's what it is."*
funny story – a short story that is told to make people laugh: *He was telling funny stories about his college days.*

2 *informal* a situation that is so silly or unreasonable that it makes you angry: *What a joke that meeting was.* **3 take a joke** to be able to laugh at a joke about yourself: *Come on – can't you take a joke?*

J

joke[2] *v.* [I] to say things that are intended to be funny: *Owen's always* ***joking about*** *something.* | *Davis was* ***joking with*** *reporters.* —**jokingly** *adv.*

jok·er /ˈdʒoʊkɚ/ *n.* [C] someone who makes a lot of jokes

jol·ly /ˈdʒɑli/ *adj.* comparative **jollier**, superlative **jolliest** happy and cheerful

jolt[1] /dʒoʊlt/ *n.* [C] **1** a sudden shock: *a* ***jolt of*** *electricity* | *Being fired came as quite a* ***jolt to*** *her.* **2** a sudden rough or violent movement: *We felt a big jolt, and then things started shaking.*

jolt[2] *v.* **1** [I,T] to move suddenly and roughly, or to make someone or something do this: *The earthquake jolted southern California.* **2** [T] to give someone a sudden shock: *companies jolted by the tax changes*

jos·tle /ˈdʒɑsəl/ *v.* [I,T] to push or knock against someone in a crowd: *Spectators* ***jostled for*** *a better view.*

jot /dʒɑt/ *v.* past tense and past participle **jotted**, present participle **jotting**

jot sth ⇔ **down** *phr. v.* to write something quickly: *She jotted down some ideas for her essay.*

jour·nal /ˈdʒɚnl/ *n.* [C] **1** a written record that you make of the things that happen to you each day

THESAURUS

record, **diary**, **log (book)**
→ see Thesaurus box at RECORD[1]

2 a magazine or newspaper for people who are interested in a particular subject: *The Wall Street Journal* | *a medical journal*

jour·nal·is·m /ˈdʒɚnlˌɪzəm/ *n.* [U] the job or activity of writing reports for newspapers, magazines, television, or radio

jour·nal·ist /ˈdʒɚnl-ɪst/ *n.* [C] someone who writes reports for newspapers, magazines, television, or radio

TOPIC

reporter, **correspondent**, **columnist**, **editor**
→ see Topic box at NEWSPAPER

jour·ney /ˈdʒɚni/ *n.* [C] a trip from one place to another, especially over a long distance: *a two-month* ***journey to*** *Morocco* | *our* ***journey across*** *the United States*

THESAURUS

travel, **trip**, **voyage**
→ see Thesaurus box at TRAVEL[2]

jo·vi·al /ˈdʒoʊviəl/ *adj.* friendly and cheerful: *a jovial face*

jowls /dʒaʊlz/ *n.* [plural] loose skin on someone's lower jaw

joy /dʒɔɪ/ *n.* [C,U] great happiness and pleasure, or something that gives you this feeling: *She laughed* ***with joy*** *at the news.* | *I almost* ***jumped for joy*** (=I was very happy).

joy·ful /ˈdʒɔɪfəl/ *adj.* very happy, or likely to make people very happy: *joyful laughter* —**joyfully** *adv.*

joy·ous /ˈdʒɔɪəs/ *adj. literary* full of happiness, or likely to make people happy: *a joyous song* —**joyously** *adv.*

joy·ride /ˈdʒɔɪraɪd/ *n.* [C] a fast dangerous drive in a car, often after someone has stolen it for fun —**joyriding** *n.* [U] —**joyrider** *n.* [C]

joy·stick /ˈdʒɔɪˌstɪk/ *n.* [C] a handle that you use in order to control something such as an aircraft or a computer game

Jr. *adj.* the written abbreviation of **junior**

ju·bi·lant /ˈdʒubələnt/ *adj.* extremely happy and pleased because you have been successful —**jubilation** /ˌdʒubəˈleɪʃən/ *n.* [U]

Ju·da·ism /ˈdʒudiˌɪzəm, -deɪ-, -də-/ *n.* [U] the Jewish religion based on the Old Testament, the Talmud, and later TEACHINGS of the RABBIS

judge[1] /dʒʌdʒ/ *n.* [C] **1** the official in control of a court who decides how criminals should be punished

> **TOPIC**
>
> **defendant**, **defense**, **prosecution**, **jury**
> ➔ see Topic box at COURT[1]

2 someone who decides on the result of a competition: *a panel of judges at the Olympics* **3 a good/bad etc. judge of sth** someone who is usually right or wrong about something: *a **good judge of character***

judge[2] *v.* **1** [I,T] to form or give an opinion about someone or something after thinking about all the information: *Employees should be **judged on** the quality of their work.* | ***Judging by** her clothes, I'd say she's rich.*

> **THESAURUS**
>
> **evaluate** formal – to judge how good, useful, or successful someone or something is: *The survey was meant to evaluate customer satisfaction.*
> **assess** – to judge a person or situation after thinking carefully about it: *Psychologists will assess the child's behavior.*
> **appraise** – to judge how valuable, effective, or successful someone or something is: *The company regularly appraises the performance of its employees.*
> **gauge** – to judge what someone is likely to do or how s/he feels: *It can be difficult to gauge students' understanding.*

2 [T] to decide in court whether someone is guilty of a crime **3** [I,T] to decide the result in a competition: *Kim and I will be judging the writing competition.* **4** [I,T] to form an opinion about someone in an unfair or criticizing way: *I just want Mom to stop judging me.*

judg·ment /ˈdʒʌdʒmənt/ *n.* **1** [C,U] an opinion that you form after thinking about something: *It's still too early to **make a judgment about** the quality of her work.* | ***In my judgment*** (=in my opinion), *John is the best candidate.* **2** [U] the ability to make decisions about situations or people: *good/bad/poor judgment* | *I trust your judgment.* **3** [C,U] an official decision given by a judge or a court of law **4 judgment call** a decision you have to make yourself because there are no fixed rules in a situation

judg·ment·al /dʒʌdʒˈmɛntl/ *adj. disapproving* too quick to form opinions and criticize other people

ˈJudgment ˌDay *n.* [singular] a time after death when everyone is judged by God, according to some religions

ju·di·cial /dʒuˈdɪʃəl/ *adj.* relating to a court of law, judges, etc.: *the judicial system*

ju·di·ci·ar·y /dʒuˈdɪʃiˌɛri, -ʃəri/ *n.* **the judiciary** *formal* all the judges in a country who, as a group, form part of the system of government

ju·di·cious /dʒuˈdɪʃəs/ *adj. formal* sensible and careful: *a judicious use of money*

ju·do /ˈdʒudoʊ/ *n.* [U] a Japanese method of defending yourself, in which you try to throw your opponent onto the ground, usually done as a sport

jug /dʒʌg/ *n.* [C] a large deep container for liquids that has a narrow opening and a handle

jug·gle /ˈdʒʌgəl/ *v.* **1** [I,T] to keep three or more objects moving through the air by throwing and catching them very quickly **2** [T] to try to fit two or more jobs, activities, etc. into your life: *It's hard trying to juggle work and children.* —**juggler** *n.* [C]

jug·u·lar /ˈdʒʌgyələ˞/ *n.* [C] **1 go for the jugular** *informal* to criticize or attack someone very strongly **2** the large VEIN in your neck that takes blood from your head to your heart

juice /dʒus/ *n.* **1** [C,U] the liquid that comes from fruit and vegetables, or a drink made from this: *a glass of orange juice* **2** [U] the liquid that comes out of meat when it is cooked

juic·y /ˈdʒusi/ *adj.* comparative **juicier**, superlative **juiciest** **1** containing a lot of juice: *a juicy peach* **2 juicy gossip/details** *informal* interesting or shocking information —**juiciness** *n.* [U]

juke box /ˈdʒuk bɑks/ *n.* [C] a machine in BARS, restaurants, etc. that plays music when you put money in it

Ju·ly /dʒʊˈlaɪ, dʒə-/ *n.* [C,U] the seventh month of the year: *The package arrived **on July 3rd**.* | *Henry started working here **in July**.* | *We're getting married **next July**.* | *I haven't heard from him since **last July**.*

jum·ble /ˈdʒʌmbəl/ *n.* [singular] a messy mixture of things: *a **jumble of** papers* —**jumble** *v.* [T]

jum·bo /ˈdʒʌmboʊ/ *adj. informal* larger than other things of the same type: *a jumbo jet*

J

jump[1] /dʒʌmp/ *v.*
1 UP [I,T] to push yourself suddenly up in the air using your legs, or to go over something doing this: *A fan tried to* ***jump onto*** *the stage.* | *Lyle was* ***jumping up and down*** (=jumping many times) *and waving his arms.* ➔ see picture on page A9

THESAURUS

skip – to move forward with little jumps between your steps
hop – to move around by jumping on one leg
leap – to jump high into the air or over something
dive – to jump into water with your head and arms first
vault – to jump over something in one movement, using your hands or a pole to help you

2 DOWN [I] to let yourself drop from a place that is above the ground: *During the fire, two people* ***jumped out*** *of a window.*
3 MOVE FAST [I] to move quickly or suddenly in a particular direction: *Paul* ***jumped up*** *to answer the door.*
4 IN SURPRISE/FEAR [I] to make a sudden movement because you are surprised or frightened: *The sudden ring of the telephone* ***made us jump.***
5 INCREASE [I] if a number or amount jumps, it increases suddenly and by a large amount: *Profits jumped 20% last month.*
6 jump down sb's throat *informal* to suddenly speak angrily to someone: *All I did was ask a question, and he jumped down my throat!*
7 jump to conclusions to form an opinion about something before you have all the facts
8 jump the gun to start doing something too soon: *I know you wanted to tell Bill the news yourself but I'm afraid I jumped the gun.*
jump at sth *phr. v.* to eagerly accept the chance to do something: *Ruth* ***jumped at the chance*** *to study at Harvard.*
jump on sb *phr. v. informal* to criticize or punish someone, especially unfairly: *Dad* ***jumps on*** *Jeff* ***for*** *every little mistake.*

jump[2] *n.* [C] **1** an act of pushing yourself suddenly up into the air using your legs **2** an act of letting yourself drop from a place that is above the ground: *a parachute jump* **3** a sudden large increase in an amount or value: *a* ***jump in*** *prices* **4 get a jump on sth** *informal* to gain an advantage by doing something earlier than usual or earlier than someone else: *I want to get a jump on my Christmas shopping.*

jump·er /ˈdʒʌmpɚ/ *n.* [C] **1** a dress without SLEEVES, usually worn over a shirt **2** a person or animal that jumps

ˈjumper ˌcables *n.* [plural] thick wires used to connect the batteries (BATTERY) of two cars in order to start one car that has lost power

ˈjump rope *n.* [C] a long piece of rope that you pass over your head and under your feet as you jump, either as a game or for exercise ➔ see picture on page A9

ˈjump-start *v.* [T] **1** to help a process or activity start or become more successful: *the government's efforts to jump-start the economy* **2** to start a car whose BATTERY has lost power by connecting it to another BATTERY

jump·suit /ˈdʒʌmpsut/ *n.* [C] a single piece of clothing like a shirt attached to a pair of pants, worn especially by women

jump·y /ˈdʒʌmpi/ *adj.* worried or excited because you are expecting something bad to happen

junc·tion /ˈdʒʌŋkʃən/ *n.* [C] a place where one road, track, etc. meets another: *a railroad junction*

junc·ture /ˈdʒʌŋktʃɚ/ *n.* **at this juncture** *spoken formal* at this point in an activity or time

June /dʒun/ *n.* [C,U] the sixth month of the year: *Can you come to our party* ***on June 24th****?* | *Janet was born* ***in June.*** | *The movie will be released* ***next June.*** | *I graduated* ***last June.***

jun·gle /ˈdʒʌŋgəl/ *n.* [C,U] a thick tropical forest with many large plants that grow very close together

Jun·ior /ˈdʒunyɚ/ *adj.* **Jr.** used after the name of a man who has the same name as his father [➡ **Senior**]

junior[1] *n.* [C] **1** a student in the third year of HIGH SCHOOL or college [➡ **freshman**, **senior**, **sophomore**] **2 be two/five/ten etc. years sb's junior** to be two, five, etc. years younger than someone else

junior[2] *adj.* [only before noun] younger, less experienced, or of a lower rank [≠ **senior**]: *the junior senator from Georgia*

THESAURUS

senior, **chief**, **high-ranking**, **top**, **assistant**
➔ see Thesaurus box at POSITION[1]

junior ˈcollege *n.* [C,U] a college where students can study for two years [= **community college**]

ˌjunior 'high school **also ˌjunior 'high** *n.* [C,U] a school in the U.S. and Canada for students who are between 12 and 14 or 15 years old [➥ **middle school, high school**]

junk /dʒʌŋk/ *n.* [U] old or unwanted things that have no use or value: *an attic filled with junk*

jun·ket /ˈdʒʌŋkɪt/ *n.* [C] *disapproving* an unnecessary trip made by a public official that is paid for by government money

'junk food *n.* [U] *informal* food that is not healthy because it has a lot of fat or sugar ➔ see Thesaurus box at FOOD

> **THESAURUS**
> **fast food, health food, vegetarian food**
> ➔ see Thesaurus box at FOOD

junk·ie /ˈdʒʌŋki/ *n.* [C] **1** *informal* someone who takes dangerous drugs and is dependent on them **2** *humorous* someone who likes something so much that s/he seems to need it: *a political junkie*

'junk mail *n.* [U] mail that advertisers send to people who do not want it

> **THESAURUS**
> **advertisement, flier, spam**
> ➔ see Thesaurus box at ADVERTISEMENT

junk·yard /ˈdʒʌŋkˌyɑrd/ *n.* [C] a business that buys old cars, broken furniture, etc. and sells the parts of them that can be used again, or the place where this business keeps these things

jun·ta /ˈhʊntə, ˈdʒʌntə/ *n.* [C] a military government that has gained power by using force

Ju·pi·ter /ˈdʒupəṭɚ/ *n.* the largest PLANET, which is fifth from the sun

jur·is·dic·tion /ˌdʒʊrɪsˈdɪkʃən/ *n.* [U] the right to use an official power to make legal decisions, or the area where this right exists: *a matter* ***outside*** *the court's* ***jurisdiction***

ju·ror /ˈdʒʊrɚ/ *n.* [C] a member of a jury

ju·ry /ˈdʒʊri/ *n.* plural **juries** [C] **1** a group of 12 people who listen to details of a case in court and decide whether someone is guilty or not [➥ **grand jury**]

> **TOPIC**
> **defendant, defense, judge, prosecution**
> ➔ see Topic box at COURT[1]

2 a group of people chosen to judge a competition

'jury ˌduty *n.* [U] a period of time during which you must be ready to be part of a jury if necessary

just[1] /dʒʌst/ *adv.* **1** exactly: *My brother looks* ***just like*** *my dad.* | *The temperature was* ***just right.*** | *The $250 TV is* ***just as*** *good* ***as*** *the $300 one.* | ***Just then*** *Mr. Struthers walked in.* **2** only: *He was just a little boy when his mother died.* | *Don't be upset – I was just joking.* | *Can you wait five minutes? I just have to iron this.* **3** if something has just happened, it happened only a short time ago: *I just got back from Marilyn's house.*

> **THESAURUS**
> **recently, a little/short while ago, lately, freshly, newly**
> ➔ see Thesaurus box at RECENTLY

4 just about almost: *She calls her mother just about every day.* | *I'm just about finished.* **5 be just about to do sth** to be going to do something soon: *I was just about to call you.* **6 just before/after** only a short time before or after something else: *Theresa got home just before us.* **7 just (barely)** if something just happens, it does happen, but it almost did not: *Kurt just barely made it home before the storm.*

> **SPOKEN PHRASES**
> **8** used when politely asking or telling someone something: ***Could/Can I just*** *use your phone for a minute?* **9 just a minute/second/moment** used in order to ask someone to wait for a short time while you do something: *Just a second – I'm getting dressed.* **10** used in order to emphasize something that you are saying: *The young woman just kept getting angrier and angrier.* | *Just be quiet, will you?* **11 it's just that** used in order to explain the reason for something when someone thinks there is a different reason: *Boston is nice, it's just that I don't know anybody there.* **12 just now** a moment ago, or at this time: *He just now walked in the front door.* **13 I would just as soon do sth** if you would just as soon do something, you are saying in a polite way that you would prefer to do it: *I'd just as soon go with you, if that's okay.* **14 it's just as well** said when it is lucky that something has happened in the way it did because if not, there may have been problems: *It's just as well Scott didn't go to the party, because Lisa was there.* **15 just because ... (it) doesn't mean ...** used to say that although one thing is true, another thing is not necessarily true: *Just because you're older than me doesn't mean you can tell me what to do!*

just[2] *adj.* morally right and fair [≠ **unjust**]: *a just punishment*

> **THESAURUS**
> **fair, reasonable, equitable, balanced, even-handed**
> ➔ see Thesaurus box at FAIR[1]

jus·tice /ˈdʒʌstɪs/ *n.* **1** [U] fairness in the way people are treated [≠ **injustice**]: *If there were any justice in the world, teachers would earn more than athletes.* **2** [U] the system by which people are judged in courts of law and criminals are punished: *the criminal justice system* **3** [C] a judge in a court of law **4 do sb/sth justice also**

J

do justice to sb/sth to treat or represent someone or something in a way that is fair and shows his, her, or its best qualities: *This picture doesn't do you justice.*

ˌJustice of the ˈPeace *n.* [C] someone who judges less serious cases in small courts of law and can perform marriage ceremonies

jus·ti·fi·a·ble /ˌdʒʌstəˈfaɪəbəl/ *adj.* an action, decision, etc. that is justifiable is reasonable because it is done for good reasons: *justifiable pride* —**justifiably** *adv.*

jus·ti·fi·ca·tion /ˌdʒʌstəfəˈkeɪʃən/ *n.* [C,U] a good and acceptable reason for doing something: *There is no **justification for** terrorism.*

jus·ti·fied /ˈdʒʌstəˌfaɪd/ *adj.* having an acceptable explanation or reason: *Your complaints are certainly justified.*

jus·ti·fy /ˈdʒʌstəˌfaɪ/ *v.* past tense and past participle **justified**, third person singular **justifies** [T] to give an acceptable explanation for something that other people think is unreasonable: *How can you justify spending so much money on a coat?*

jut /dʒʌt/ *v.* past tense and past participle **jutted**, present participle **jutting** [I] **also jut out** to stick up or out farther than the other things in the same area: *a point of land that **juts out into** the ocean*

ju·ve·nile /ˈdʒuvənl, -ˌnaɪl/ *adj.* **1** *law* relating to young people who are not yet adults: *juvenile crime* **2** typical of a child, rather than an adult [= **childish**]: *a juvenile sense of humor* —**juvenile** *n.* [C]

ˌjuvenile deˈlinquent *n.* [C] a child or young person who behaves in a criminal way —**juvenile delinquency** *n.* [U]

jux·ta·pose /ˈdʒʌkstəˌpoʊz, ˌdʒʌkstəˈpoʊz/ *v.* [T] *formal* to put things that are different together, especially in order to compare them: *On his wall were photographs **juxtaposed with** drawings of the same scenes.* —**juxtaposition** /ˌdʒʌkstəpəˈzɪʃən/ *n.* [C,U]

K

K, k

K, k /keɪ/ the ELEVENTH letter of the English alphabet

K /keɪ/ *n.* the written abbreviation of **1,000**: *He earns $50K a year.*

ka·lei·do·scope /kəˈlaɪdəˌskoʊp/ *n.* [C] a tube with mirrors and pieces of colored glass at one end that shows colored patterns when you look into the tube and turn it

kangaroo

kan·ga·roo /ˌkæŋgəˈru/ *n.* [C] an Australian animal that has strong back legs for jumping and carries its babies in a pocket of skin on its stomach

ka·put /kəˈpʊt/ *adj. spoken* broken: *The TV **went kaput** right during the game.*

kar·at /ˈkærət/ *n.* [C] a unit for measuring how pure a piece of gold is: *Pure gold is 24 karats.*

karate

ka·ra·te /kəˈrɑt̬i/ *n.* [U] a Japanese fighting sport in which you use your hands and feet to hit and kick

kar·ma /ˈkɑrmə/ *n.* [U] **1** *informal* the feeling you get from a person, place, or action: *This house has a lot of **good/bad karma**.* **2** the force that is produced by the things you do in your life and that will influence you in the future, according to some religions

kay·ak /ˈkaɪæk/ *n.* [C] a type of boat, usually for one person, that has a hole for that person to sit in, and that is moved using a PADDLE → see picture on page A10

kebab /kəˈbɑb/ *n.* [C] SHISH KEBAB

keel¹ /kil/ *n.* **stay/remain on an even keel also keep an even keel** to continue doing the things you always do or feeling the way you always feel, without any sudden changes

keel² *v.*

keel over *phr. v.* to fall over sideways: *Rob looked as if he were ready to keel over.*

keen /kin/ *adj.* **1** very interested in something or eager to do it: *Most people are **keen to** do a job well.* | *I was never very **keen on** science.* **2** a keen sense of smell, sight, or hearing is an extremely good ability to smell, etc. **3** *formal* intelligent and quick to understand things: *a keen mind* —**keenly** *adj.*

keep¹ /kip/ *v.* past tense and past participle **kept** /kɛpt/

1 NOT GIVE BACK [T] to have something and not give it back to the person who had it before: *You can keep that sweater – it's too small for me.*
2 NOT LOSE [T] to continue to have something and not lose it or get rid of it: *They're keeping the house in Colorado and selling this one.* | *I've kept her photograph all these years.*
3 NOT CHANGE/MOVE [linking verb] to continue to be in a particular condition or place and not change or move [**= stay**]: *This blanket should help you **keep warm**.* | ***Keep still** so I can cut your hair.*
4 MAKE SB/STH NOT CHANGE OR MOVE [T] to make someone or something continue to be in a particular state, situation, or place: *They kept him in jail for two weeks.* | *It's hard to keep the house clean with three kids.* | *Her son **kept** her **waiting** for an hour.* | *I don't know **what's keeping** her. It's 8:00 already.* | ***Keep** those kids **out** of my yard!*
5 keep (on) doing sth to continue doing something, or repeat an action many times: *If he keeps on growing like this, he'll be taller than Dad.* | *Keep driving – I'll tell you when we're almost there.*
6 STORE STH [T] to leave something in one particular place so that you can find it easily: *I **keep** my keys **in** the top drawer of my dresser.*

THESAURUS

store – to put things away and keep them there until you need them: *Canned goods can be stored at room temperature.*
save – to keep something so that you can use or enjoy it in the future: *I'm saving this bottle of champagne for a special occasion.*
reserve – to keep something separate so that it can be used for a particular purpose: *These seats are reserved for people with tickets.*
file – to store papers or information in a particular order or a particular place: *All the contracts are filed alphabetically.*
collect – to get and keep objects of the same type because you think they are attractive or interesting: *Kate collects old postcards.*

7 keep a record/diary etc. to regularly write down information in a particular place: *She's kept a diary since she was 13.*
8 keep going *spoken* used to encourage something who is doing something and to tell them to continue: *Keep going, you're doing fine.*
9 keep your promise/word to do what you have promised to do: *The President kept his promise to appoint more women to his cabinet.*
10 keep sth quiet/keep quiet about sth to not say anything in order to avoid complaining, telling a secret, or causing problems: *I'll tell you what happened but you have to keep it quiet.*
11 keep sb posted to continue to tell someone the most recent news about someone or something: *Keep me posted – I'd like to know about any changes.*
12 FOOD [I] if food keeps, it stays fresh enough to still be eaten: *How long do you think this milk will keep?*

keep at sth *phr. v.* to continue working hard at something: *Just **keep at it** until you get it right.*

keep sb/sth ⇔ **away** *phr. v.* to avoid going somewhere or seeing someone, or to make someone or something do this: ***Keep away from** the fire.* | *Mom kept us away from school for a week.*

keep sth ⇔ **down** *phr. v.* **1** to control something in order to prevent it from increasing: *They promised to keep the rents down.* **2 keep it down** *spoken* said when you want someone to be quieter: *Keep it down! I'm on the phone.* **3** to succeed in keeping food in your stomach without VOMITING: *I haven't been able to keep anything down all day.*

keep from sb/sth *phr. v.* **1 keep sth from sb** to not tell someone something that you know: *He kept Angie's death from his family for 3 days.* **2 keep (sb/sth) from doing sth** to prevent someone from doing something or prevent something from happening: *She had to cover her mouth to keep from laughing.* | *Put foil over the pie to keep it from burning.*

keep sth **off** *phr. v.* to prevent something from affecting or damaging something else: *Wear a hat to keep the sun off your head.*

keep out *phr. v.* **1 Keep Out!** used on signs to tell people that they are not allowed into a place **2 keep sb/sth out** to prevent someone or something from getting into a place: *She closed the window to keep the dust out.*

keep out of sth *phr. v.* to try not to become involved with something: *My father warned us to keep out of trouble.*

keep to sb/sth *phr. v.* **1 keep to sth** to continue to do, use, or talk about one thing and not change: *You're better off keeping to the main roads.* | *Mullin kept to the same strategy throughout the game.* **2 keep sth to yourself** to not tell anyone else something that you know **3 keep to yourself** to not do things that involve other people because you want to be alone: *Nina kept to herself at the party.*

keep up *phr. v.* **1 keep** sth ⇔ **up** to prevent something from going to a lower level: *The shortage of supplies is keeping the price up.* **2 keep** sth ⇔ **up** to continue doing something, or to make something continue: *Keep up the good work!* **3** to move as fast as someone else: *Hey, slow down. I can't keep up!* **4** to learn as fast or do as much as other people: *Davey's having trouble **keeping up with** the other students.* **5** to continue to learn about a subject: *It's hard to **keep up on/with** changes in computer technology.* **6 keep** sb **up** to prevent someone from sleeping: *The dog has been keeping us up all night.*

keep² *n.* [C] **1 earn your keep** to do a job in order to pay for the basic things you need such as food, clothing, etc. **2 for keeps** *informal* forever

keep·ing /ˈkipɪŋ/ *n.* [U] **1 for safe keeping** so that something will not be damaged or lost: *I'll put the tickets here for safe keeping.* **2 in keeping with sth/out of keeping with sth** appropriate

K

or not appropriate for a particular occasion or purpose: *In keeping with tradition, we opened our presents on Christmas Eve.*

keep·sake /ˈkipseɪk/ *n.* [C] a small object that reminds you of someone or something

keg /kɛg/ *n.* [C] a large round container, used especially for storing beer

keg·ger /ˈkɛgɚ/ **also ˈkeg ˌparty** *n.* [C] *slang* a big party, usually outdoors, where beer is served from kegs

ken·nel /ˈkɛnl/ *n.* [C] a place where dogs are cared for while their owners are away, or the CAGE where they sleep

kept /kɛpt/ *v.* the past tense and past participle of KEEP

ker·nel /ˈkɚnl/ *n.* [C] **1** the center part of a nut or seed, usually the part you can eat **2** one of the small yellow parts of corn that you eat **3** a small but important part of a statement, idea, plan, etc.: *There may be a* ***kernel of truth*** *in what he says.*

ker·o·sene /ˈkɛrəˌsin, ˌkɛrəˈsin/ *n.* [U] a type of oil that is burned for heat and light

ketch·up /ˈkɛtʃəp, ˈkæ-/ *n.* [U] a red sauce made from tomatoes and used on food

ket·tle /ˈkɛtl̩/ *n.* [C] a special metal pot used for boiling and pouring water

key¹ /ki/ *n.* [C] **1** a specially shaped piece of metal that you put into a lock in order to lock or unlock a door, start a car, etc.: *I can't find my* ***car keys****.* **2 the key** the part of a plan, action, etc. that everything else depends on: *Exercise is* ***the key to*** *a healthy body.* **3** the part of a musical instrument, computer, or machine that you press with your fingers to make it work **4** a set of seven musical notes that have a particular base note, or the quality of sound these notes have: ***the key of*** *G*

key² *adj.* very important and necessary for success or to understand something: *a key player*

K

THESAURUS

important, **crucial**, **vital**, **essential**, **major**, **significant**

→ see Thesaurus box at IMPORTANT

key³ *v.*

key sth ⇔ **in** *phr. v.* to put information into a computer by using a keyboard: *Key in your password and press "Return."*

key·board /ˈkibɔrd/ *n.* [C] **1** a row or several rows of keys on a machine such as a computer, or a musical instrument such as a piano → see picture on page A11 **2** an electronic musical instrument with a keyboard similar to a piano

ˌkeyed ˈup *adj. informal* worried or excited: *I was so keyed up I couldn't sleep.*

key·hole /ˈkihoʊl/ *n.* [C] the hole in a lock that you put a key in

key·note /ˈkinoʊt/ *adj.* **1 keynote speech/address** the most important speech at an official event **2 keynote speaker** the person who gives the most important speech at an official event

ˈkey ring *n.* [C] a metal ring that you keep keys on

kg *n.* the written abbreviation of **kilogram**

kha·ki /ˈkæki/ *n.* **1** [U] a dull brown or green-brown color **2** [U] cloth of this color, especially when worn by soldiers **3 khakis** [plural] pants that are made from khaki —**khaki** *adj.*

kick¹ /kɪk/ *v.* **1** [T] to hit something with your foot: *Stop kicking me!* | *She* ***kicked*** *the pile of books* ***over****.* → see picture on page A9 **2** [I,T] to move one or both of your legs with short, quick movements as if you are hitting something with your foot: *a baby kicking its legs* | *Kyle collapsed on the floor* ***kicking and screaming****.* **3 kick the habit** *informal* to stop doing something, such as smoking, that is a harmful habit **4 kick yourself** *spoken* said when you are annoyed with yourself because you have made a mistake or missed an opportunity: *I wanted to kick myself for forgetting her name.* **5 kick the bucket** *humorous* to die

kick around *phr. v.* **1 kick** sth ⇔ **around** *informal* to think about something a lot or get people's opinions about it before making a decision: *We've been* ***kicking around*** *the* ***idea*** *of getting a dog.* **2 kick** sb ⇔ **around** to treat someone badly or unfairly: *He won't be kicking me around anymore!*

kick back *phr. v. informal* to relax: *I thought I'd kick back and watch some TV.*

kick in *phr. v.* **1** *informal* to begin to have an effect: *Those pills should kick in any time now.* **2 kick in** sth *informal* to join with others to give money or help with something: *Everyone kicked in $5 for gas.* **3 kick** sth ⇔ **in** to kick something so hard that it breaks open: *The police had to kick the door in.*

kick off *phr. v.* **kick** (sth ⇔) **off** *informal* to start, or to make an event start: *The festivities will* ***kick off with*** *a barbecue dinner.*

kick sb ⇔ **out** *phr. v. informal* to dismiss someone or make him/her leave a place: *Sean was* ***kicked out of*** *school for cheating.*

kick² *n.* [C] **1** an act of hitting something with your foot: *If the gate won't open, just* ***give it a good kick*** (=kick it hard). **2** *informal* a strong feeling of excitement or pleasure: *I* ***get a*** *real* ***kick out of*** *watching my two cats play.* | *She started stealing* ***for kicks****.* **3 be on a health/wine/swimming etc. kick** *informal* to have a strong new interest in something

kick·back /ˈkɪkbæk/ *n.* [C,U] *journalism* money that you pay someone for secretly or dishonestly helping you to make money [= **bribe**]

kick·off /ˈkɪk-ɔf/ *n.* [C,U] the time when a game of football or SOCCER starts, or the first kick that starts it: *Kickoff is at 3:00.*

kid¹ /kɪd/ *n.* **1** [C] *informal* a child: *Kim is really good with kids.* | *She's loved animals since she was a* ***little kid****.* **2** [C] *informal* a son or daughter: *How many kids do you have?* **3** [C] *informal* a young person: *college kids* **4 kid stuff** *informal disapproving* something that is very easy or boring **5** [C,U] a young goat, or the leather made from its skin

kid² *v.* past tense and past participle **kidded**, present participle **kidding** *informal* **1** [I,T] to say something that is not true, especially as a joke: *Don't get mad. I was* ***just kidding****.* **2 no kidding** *spoken* used when you are surprised by what someone says: *"You lived in Baltimore? I did, too." "No kidding."* **3 you're kidding** *spoken* said when it is difficult for you to believe that what someone is telling you is true: *They fired you? You're kidding!* **4 kid yourself** to make yourself believe something that is not true or not likely: *Don't kid yourself; she'll never change.*

kid³ *adj.* **kid brother/sister** *informal* your brother or sister who is younger than you

kid·nap /ˈkɪdnæp/ *v.* past tense and past participle **kidnapped**, present participle **kidnapping** **also** past tense and past participle **kidnaped** present participle **kidnaping** [T] to take someone away illegally and demand money for returning him/her: *She was kidnapped and held for ransom.* —**kidnapper** *n.* [C] —**kidnapping** *n.* [C,U]

kid·ney /ˈkɪdni/ *n.* plural **kidneys** [C] one of the two organs in your lower back that separate waste liquid from blood and make URINE ➔ see picture on page A3

ˈkidney bean *n.* [C] a dark red bean with a curved shape

kill¹ /kɪl/ *v.* **1** [I,T] to make a person or living thing die: *Kerr is accused of killing three men.* | *Too much water could kill the plants.* | *Who knows when he might kill again?* | *Smoking kills.*

THESAURUS

murder – to deliberately kill someone
commit manslaughter – to kill someone without intending to
commit suicide – to deliberately cause your own death
assassinate – to deliberately kill an important person, especially a politician
slaughter/massacre – to kill a large number of people in a violent way
execute sb/put sb to death – to kill someone as a punishment for a crime
➔ CRIME

2 [T] to make something stop or fail, or turn off the power to something: *Nothing that the doctor gives me kills the pain.* | *A group of bankers persuaded lawmakers to kill the proposal.* **3** [T] *informal* to be very angry at someone: *My wife will kill me if I don't get home soon.* **4 sth is killing me** *spoken* used to say that a part of your body is hurting a lot: *My head is killing me.* **5 kill time** *informal* to do something that is not very useful or interesting while you are waiting for something to happen: *We hung out at the mall to kill time.* **6 kill two birds with one stone** to achieve two things with one action

kill sb/sth ⇔ **off** *phr. v.* to cause the death of a lot of living things: *A new drug is being used to kill off the virus.*

kill² *n.* **1** [singular] an animal killed by another animal, especially for food: *The lion dragged its kill into the bushes.* **2** [C usually singular] the act of killing a hunted animal: *The hawk swooped in* ***for the kill****.*

kill·er¹ /ˈkɪlɚ/ *n.* [C] a person, animal, or thing that kills or has killed: *Police are still looking for the girl's killer.*

killer² *adj.* [only before noun] **1** *slang* very attractive or very good: *That looks like a killer movie.* **2** very harmful or likely to kill you: *a killer landslide*

kill·ing /ˈkɪlɪŋ/ *n.* [C] **1** a murder: *a series of brutal killings* **2 make a killing** *informal* to make a lot of money very quickly: *They planned to make a killing on the stock market.*

kiln /kɪln/ *n.* [C] a special OVEN for baking clay pots, bricks, etc.

ki·lo /ˈkiloʊ, ˈkɪ-/ *n.* plural **kilos** [C] a KILOGRAM

ki·lo·byte /ˈkɪləˌbaɪt/ *n.* [C] a unit for measuring computer information, equal to 1024 BYTES

kil·o·gram /ˈkɪləˌgræm/ **also kilo** *n.* [C] *written abbreviation* **kg** a unit for measuring weight, equal to 1,000 grams

ki·lo·me·ter /kɪˈlɑmət̬ɚ, ˈkɪləˌmit̬ɚ/ *n.* [C] *written abbreviation* **km** a unit for measuring length, equal to 1,000 meters

kil·o·watt /ˈkɪləˌwɑt/ *written abbreviation* **kW** *n.* [C] a unit for measuring electrical power, equal to 1,000 WATTS

kilt /kɪlt/ *n.* [C] a type of wool skirt with a pattern of lines and squares on it, traditionally worn by Scottish men

kil·ter /ˈkɪltɚ/ *n.* **out of kilter also off kilter** if something is out of kilter, it is not working the way it should be or not doing what it should

ki·mo·no /kəˈmoʊnoʊ/ *n.* plural **kimonos** [C] a traditional piece of Japanese clothing like a long coat, that is worn at special ceremonies

kin /kɪn/ *n.* [plural] **1 next of kin** *formal* your most closely related family **2** *old-fashioned* your family

kind¹ /kaɪnd/ *n.* **1** [C] a type or sort of person or thing: *What* ***kind of*** *dog is that?* | *We sell* ***all kinds of*** *hats.* | *She met people* ***of all kinds*** *while traveling.* | *This camera is* ***the best of its kind****.*

THESAURUS

type, sort, category, brand, make, model, genre
➔ see Thesaurus box at TYPE¹

2 kind of *spoken* **a)** slightly, or in some ways: *You must be kind of disappointed.* **b)** used when you are explaining something and want to avoid giving the details: *I kind of made it look like it was an accident.* **3 (a) kind of (a)** *spoken* used in

K

order to say that your description of something is not exact: *a kind of a reddish-brown color* **4 one of a kind** the only one of a particular type of something: *Each vase is handmade and is one of a kind.* **5 in kind** reacting by doing the same thing that someone else has just done: *The U.S. should **respond in kind** if other countries do not trade fairly.*

kind² *adj.* helpful, friendly, and caring toward other people: *Thank you for your kind invitation.* | *That was very **kind of** you.* | *Janine has been very **kind to** me lately.*

> **THESAURUS**
>
> **nice** – friendly and kind
> **considerate** – thinking about other people's feelings: *He used to be a good driver, and very considerate of others.*
> **thoughtful** – thinking of things you can do to make other people happy
> **caring** – kind to someone and willing to help him/her
> → NICE

kind·a /ˈkaɪndə/ a short form of "kind of," used in writing to show how people sound when they speak: *I'm kinda tired.*

kin·der·gar·ten /ˈkɪndɚˌgɑrt̚n, -ˌgɑrdn/ *n.* [C] a class for young children who are about five years old that prepares them for school [➡ **nursery school**]

ˌkind-ˈhearted *adj.* kind and generous: *a kind-hearted woman*

kin·dle /ˈkɪndl/ *v.* **1** [T] to make something start burning **2 kindle excitement/interest etc.** to make someone excited, interested, etc.

kin·dling /ˈkɪndlɪŋ/ *n.* [U] small pieces of dry wood, leaves, etc. that you use for starting a fire

kind·ly¹ /ˈkaɪndli/ *adv.* **1** in a kind way [=**generously**]: *Mr. Thomas has kindly offered to let us use his car.* **2 not take kindly to sth** to be annoyed or upset by something that someone says or does: *He didn't take kindly to having his picture taken.* **3** *spoken* a word meaning "please," often used when you are annoyed: ***Would you kindly** close that door?*

K

kindly² *adj. old-fashioned* kind and caring about other people: *a kindly woman*

kind·ness /ˈkaɪndnɪs/ *n.* [C,U] kind behavior, or a kind action: *We relied on the **kindness of** strangers.*

kin·dred /ˈkɪndrɪd/ *adj.* **a kindred spirit** someone who thinks and feels the way you do

ki·net·ic /kɪˈnɛt̬ɪk/ *adj. technical* relating to movement: *kinetic energy*

king /kɪŋ/ *n.* [C] **1** a man who is the ruler of a country because he is from a royal family [➡ **queen**]: *the **king of** Spain* | *King Edward*

> **THESAURUS**
>
> **queen** – the female ruler of a country, or the wife of a king
> **monarch** – a king or queen
> **ruler** – someone such as a king, who has official power over a country and its people
> **emperor** – the ruler of an empire (=group of countries)
> **sovereign** formal – a king or queen

2 someone who is considered to be the most important or best member of a group: *the **king of** comedy*

king·dom /ˈkɪŋdəm/ *n.* [C] **1** a country ruled by a king or queen **2 the animal/plant/mineral kingdom** one of the three parts into which the natural world is divided

king·pin /ˈkɪŋˌpɪn/ *n.* [C] the most important person in a group: *a drug kingpin*

ˈking-size also **ˈking-sized** *adj.* very large, and usually the largest of its type: *a king-size bed*

kink /kɪŋk/ *n.* [C] **1** a twist in something that is normally straight: *The hose has a **kink in** it.* **2 work out the kinks** to solve all the problems in a plan, situation, etc.

kink·y /ˈkɪŋki/ *adj. informal* **1** someone who is kinky, or who does kinky things, has strange ways of getting sexual excitement **2** kinky hair has a lot of tight curls

ki·osk /ˈkiɑsk/ *n.* [C] a small building where you can buy things such as newspapers or tickets

kiss¹ /kɪs/ *v.* **1** [I,T] to touch someone with your lips as a greeting, or to show love: *They stood on the beach and kissed.* | *She **kissed** me **on** the cheek.* | *He leaned forward and **kissed** her **goodnight**.* **2 kiss sth goodbye** *spoken* used in order to say that someone will lose his/her chance to get or do something: *If you don't start working harder, you can kiss medical school goodbye.*

kiss² *n.* [C] an act of kissing: *Come here and **give** me **a kiss**.*

kit /kɪt/ *n.* [C] **1** a set of tools, equipment, etc. that you use for a particular purpose or activity: *a first-aid kit* **2** something that you buy in parts and put together yourself: *a model airplane kit*

kitch·en /ˈkɪtʃən/ *n.* [C] the room where you prepare and cook food: *Jay's **in the kitchen** washing the dishes.* | *Put the groceries on the **kitchen table**.*

kite /kaɪt/ *n.* [C] a toy that you fly in the air on the end of a long string, made from a light frame covered in paper or plastic

kitsch /kɪtʃ/ *n.* [U] decorations, movies, etc. that seem to be cheap and without style, and often amuse people because of this —**kitsch**, **kitschy** *adj.*

kit·ten /ˈkɪt̚n/ *n.* [C] a young cat

kit·ty /ˈkɪt̬i/ *n.* plural **kitties** [C] **1** *spoken* also

kit·ty·cat /ˈkɪṭiˌkæt/ a word meaning a cat, used especially by children or when calling to a cat: *Here, kitty kitty!* **2** [usually singular] the money that people have collected for a particular purpose

ˈkitty-ˌcorner *adv.* **kitty-corner from sth** DIAGONALLY across from a particular place: *His store is kitty-corner from the bank.*

ki·wi /ˈkiwi/ **also ˈkiwi fruit** *n.* [C] a soft green fruit with small black seeds and a thin brown skin ➔ see picture at FRUIT

KKK *n.* **the KKK** the **Ku Klux Klan**

Kleen·ex /ˈklinɛks/ *n.* [C,U] *trademark* a piece of soft thin paper, used especially for blowing your nose

klutz /klʌts/ *n.* [C] *informal* someone who often drops things and falls easily —**klutzy** *adj.*

km *n.* [C] the written abbreviation of **kilometer**

knack /næk/ *n.* [singular] *informal* a natural ability to do something well: *Knight has always **had a knack for** teaching.*

THESAURUS

ability, skill, talent
➔ see Thesaurus box at ABILITY

knap·sack /ˈnæpsæk/ *n.* [C] a bag that you carry on your shoulders [= **backpack**]

knead /nid/ *v.* [T] to press DOUGH (=a mixture of flour, water, etc. for making bread) many times with your hands ➔ see picture on page A4

knee¹ /ni/ *n.* [C] **1** the joint where your leg bends: *a knee injury* | *He actually got **down on his knees** and asked me to forgive him.* ➔ see picture on page A3 **2** the part of your pants that covers your knee: *Billy's jeans had holes in both knees.* **3 bring sb/sth to their knees a)** to defeat a country or group of people in a war **b)** to have such a bad effect on an organization, activity, etc. that it cannot continue

knee² *v.* [T] to hit someone with your knee: *Victor **kneed** him **in** the stomach.*

knee·cap /ˈnikæp/ *n.* [C] the bone at the front of your knee ➔ see picture on page A3

ˌknee-ˈdeep *adj.* **1 a)** deep enough to reach your knees **b)** in something that is deep enough to reach your knees: ***knee-deep in** snow* **2 knee-deep in sth** *informal* very involved in something, or greatly affected by something that you cannot avoid: *Ralph lost his job, and we ended up knee-deep in debt.*

knee-deep

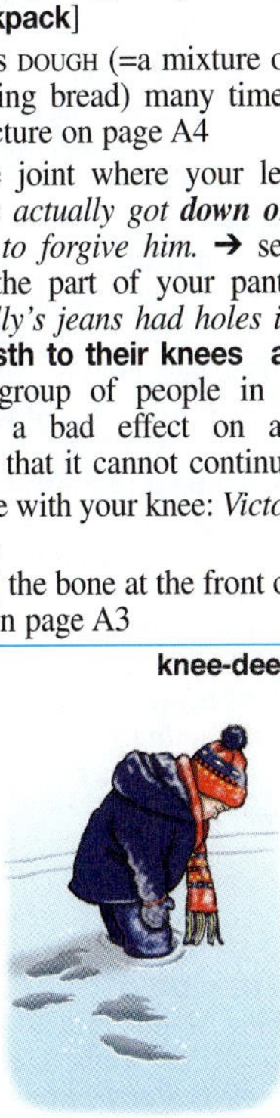

knee-deep in snow

ˌknee-ˈhigh *adj.* tall enough to reach your knees: *knee-high water*

ˈknee-jerk *adj.* *disapproving* a knee-jerk reaction, opinion, etc. is what you feel or say about a situation from habit, without thinking about it

kneel /nil/ **also kneel down** *v.* past tense and past participle **knelt** /nɛlt/ or **kneeled** [I] to be in or move into a position where your body is resting on your knees: *She **knelt down** on the floor to pray.* ➔ see picture on page A9

knew /nu/ *v.* the past tense of KNOW

knick·ers /ˈnɪkɚz/ *n.* [plural] short loose pants that fit tightly at your knees, worn especially in past times

knick-knack /ˈnɪk næk/ *n.* [C] *informal* a small object used as a decoration

knife¹ /naɪf/ *n.* plural **knives** /naɪvz/ [C] a tool used for cutting or as a weapon, consisting of a metal blade attached to a handle: *a knife and fork*

knife² *v.* [T] to put a knife into someone's body [= **stab**]: *The victim was **knifed in** the back.*

knight /naɪt/ *n.* [C] **1** a European man with a high rank in past times, who was trained to fight while riding a horse **2** the CHESS piece with a horse's head on it

knight·hood /ˈnaɪthʊd/ *n.* [C,U] a special title or rank that is given to someone by the British king or queen

knit

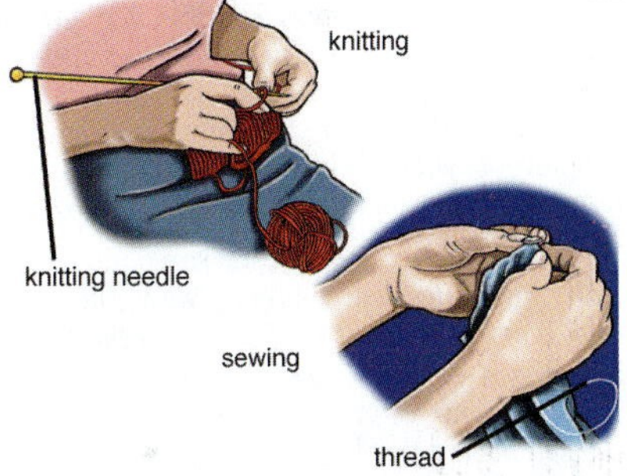

knit¹ /nɪt/ *v.* past tense and past participle **knit** or **knitted**, present participle **knitting** [I,T] **1** to make clothes out of YARN (=thick thread) using knitting needles or a special machine: *She's knitting me a sweater.* **2** to join people, things, or ideas more closely, or to be closely related: *The broken bone should **knit together** smoothly.* | *a **tightly/closely knit** community* **3 knit your brows** to show you are worried, thinking hard, etc. by moving your EYEBROWS together

knit² *adj.* [only before noun] made by knitting: *a gray knit sweater*

knit·ting /ˈnɪṭɪŋ/ *n.* [U] something that is being knitted

ˈknitting ˌneedle *n.* [C] one of the two long sticks that you use to knit something ➔ see picture at KNIT¹

knives /naɪvz/ *n.* the plural of KNIFE

knob /nɑb/ *n.* [C] a round handle that you turn or pull to open a door or drawer, turn on a radio, etc. [➥ **doorknob**]

K

knob·by /ˈnabi/ *adj.* with hard parts that stick out from under the surface of something: *knobby knees*

knock

knock[1] /nak/ *v.* **1** [I] to hit a door or window with your closed hand in order to attract the attention of the people inside: *I've been **knocking at/on** the door for five minutes.*

THESAURUS
bang, tap, pound, rap, hammer
→ see Thesaurus box at HIT[1]

2 [I,T] to hit someone or something with a quick hard hit, so that he, she, or it moves or falls down: *The ball was **knocked loose**.* | *A car **knocked into** a pole in the parking lot.* **3 knock sb unconscious** to hit someone so hard that s/he becomes unconscious

SPOKEN PHRASES
4 knock it off used in order to tell someone to stop doing something because it is annoying you **5 knock some sense into sb** to make someone learn to behave in a more sensible way: *Maybe getting arrested will knock some sense into him.* **6 knock on wood** an expression that is used after a statement about something good, in order to prevent your luck from becoming bad: *I haven't had a cold all winter, knock on wood.*

7 [T] to criticize someone or something, especially in an unfair or annoying way: *The mayor took every opportunity to knock his opponent.*

knock sth ⇔ **back** *phr. v. informal* to drink a large amount of alcohol very quickly: *We knocked back a few beers.*

knock sb/sth ⇔ **down** *phr. v.* **1** to hit or push someone so that s/he falls to the ground: *The horse knocked Laura down while she was cleaning the stable.* **2** to destroy a building or structure: *My elementary school was knocked down so a mall could be built.* **3** *informal* to reduce the price of something: *The new stove we bought was **knocked down from** $800 **to** $550.*

knock off *phr. v. informal* **1** to stop working: *We decided to knock off around 3.* **2 knock** sth ⇔ **off** to reduce the price of something by a particular amount: *I got him to knock $10 off the regular price.*

knock sb/sth ⇔ **out** *phr. v.* **1 knock** sb ⇔ **out** to make someone become unconscious: *He knocked out his opponent in the fifth round.* **2 knock** sb/sth ⇔ **out** to defeat a person or team in a competition so that he, she, or it cannot continue to take part in the competition: *Indiana **knocked** Kentucky **out of** the tournament.* **3 knock yourself out** *informal* to work very hard in order to do something well, especially so that you are very tired when you finish: *He's been knocking himself out trying to find a job.*

knock sb/sth ⇔ **over** *phr. v.* to hit or push someone or something so that he, she, or it falls down: *Scott knocked the lamp over.*

knock sb ⇔ **up** *phr. v. slang* to make a woman PREGNANT

knock[2] *n.* [C] **1** the sound of something hard hitting a hard surface: *a loud knock at the door* **2** the action of something hard hitting your body: *a **knock on** the head* **3 take a knock** *informal* to have some bad luck or trouble: *Lee's **taken** quite a few **hard knocks** lately.*

knock·er /ˈnakɚ/ *n.* [C] a piece of metal on an outside door that you use to knock loudly

knock·out /ˈnak-aʊt/ *n.* [C] **1** an act of hitting your opponent so hard in BOXING that s/he falls down and cannot get up again **2** *old-fashioned informal* a woman who is very attractive

knoll /noʊl/ *n.* [C] a small round hill

knot[1] /nat/ *n.* [C] **1** a place where two ends or pieces of rope, string, etc. have been tied together: *Her Brownie troop is learning how to **tie knots**.* **2** many hairs, threads, etc. that are twisted together **3** a hard round place in a piece of wood where a branch once joined the tree **4** a tight painful place in a muscle, or a tight uncomfortable feeling in your stomach: *a **knot in** my back* | *My stomach is **in knots**.* **5 tie the knot** *informal* to get married **6** a small group of people standing close together **7** a unit for measuring the speed of a ship that is about 1,853 meters per hour

knot[2] *v.* past tense and past participle **knotted**, present participle **knotting** **1** [T] to tie together two ends or pieces of rope, string, etc. **2** [I,T] if hairs, threads, etc. knot, or if something knots them, they become twisted together

know[1] /noʊ/ *v.* past tense **knew** /nu/, past participle **known** /noʊn/
1 HAVE INFORMATION [I,T] to have information about something: *Do you know the answer?* | *I don't **know** much **about** art.* | *We don't **know what** we're supposed to be doing.* | *Did you **know that** Andy was fired?* | *He **wants to know*** (=wants to be told) *what happened.*
2 BE SURE [I,T] to be sure about something: *"Is Bob coming?" "I don't know."* | *I **knew that** she didn't like him.* | *Barry didn't **know what** to say.*
3 BE FAMILIAR WITH SB/STH [T] to be familiar with a person, place, system, etc.: *She knows the city pretty well.* | *I've known Jack since we were in the army.* | *He said he'd like to **get to know** us better* (=would like to know more about us).
4 REALIZE [T] to realize or understand something: *I don't think he **knows how** stupid he sounds.* | *I **know** exactly **what** you mean.* | *You **know full/perfectly well** what I'm talking about.*
5 RECOGNIZE [T] to be able to recognize someone or something: *She **knew** it was Gail **by** her voice* (=she recognized Gail because of her voice).
6 know better to be wise or experienced enough

K

to avoid making mistakes: *He **should have known better than to** trust Rich.*

7 know your way around to be familiar with a place, organization, system, etc. so that you can use it effectively

SPOKEN PHRASES

8 you know a) said when you cannot quickly think of what to say next but you want to keep someone's attention: *And then I told him he could, you know, call me whenever he wants.* **b)** said when you are trying to explain something by giving more information: *I have some clothes for Matthew, you know, for the baby, if Carrie wants them.* **c)** said when you begin talking about a subject: *You know, I spoke to Eric last night.* **d)** said in order to check if someone understands what you are saying: *I can't stand it when people are late, you know?*

9 I know a) used to agree with someone or to say that you feel the same way: *"That meeting was so boring!" "I know, I couldn't wait to get out of there."* **b)** said when you suddenly have an idea or think of the answer to a problem: *I know, let's ask Luis for a ride.*

10 as far as I know said when you think something is true, but you are not sure: *As far as I know, Gail left at 6:00.*

11 you never know used to say that you are not sure what will happen: *You never know. You might win!*

know of sb/sth *phr. v.* **1** to have been told or to have read about someone or something, but not know much about them or it: *I only know of him – I've never met him.* **2** used to ask for or give advice: *Do you know of any good restaurants around here?* **3 not that I know of** used in order to say that the answer to a question is "no," but that there may be facts you do not know about: *"Does Chris smoke?" "Not that I know of."*

know² *n.* **in the know** having more information about something than most people: *Those in the know say that gas prices will be going up.*

'know-how *n.* [U] *informal* knowledge, practical ability, or skill

know·ing /'nouɪŋ/ *adj.* showing that you know all about something: *a knowing smile*

know·ing·ly /'nouɪŋli/ *adv.* **1** deliberately: *He'd never knowingly hurt you.* **2** in a way that shows you know all about something: *Tara nodded knowingly.*

'know-it-all *n.* [C] *informal disapproving* someone who behaves as if s/he knows everything

knowl·edge /'nɑlɪdʒ/ *n.* [U] **1** the information and understanding that you have gained through learning or experience: *His **knowledge of** American history is impressive.* **2** what someone knows or has information about: ***To the best of my knowledge**, each of the victims survived* (=I think this is true, although I may not have all the facts). | *The decision to attack was made **without my knowledge*** (=I did not know about it). | *"Has there been any improvement in the patient's condition?" **"Not to my knowledge** (=I do not think this is true, based on what I know)."*

knowl·edge·a·ble /'nɑlɪdʒəbəl/ *adj.* knowing a lot: *Steve's very **knowledgeable about** politics.*

known¹ /noun/ *v.* the past participle of KNOW

known² *adj.* known about, especially by many people: *a known criminal*

knuck·le¹ /'nʌkəl/ *n.* [C] one of the joints in your fingers ➔ see picture at HAND¹

knuckle² *v.*

knuckle under *phr. v. informal* to accept someone's authority or orders without wanting to: *She refused to **knuckle under to** company regulations.*

KO *n.* [C] the written abbreviation of **knockout**

ko·a·la /kou'ɑlə/ **also ko'ala bear** *n.* [C] an Australian animal like a small bear that climbs trees and eats leaves

Ko·ran /kə'ræn, -'rɑn/ *n.* **the Koran** the holy book of the Muslim religion

Ko·re·an¹ /kə'riən/ *adj.* **1** relating to or coming from Korea **2** relating to the Korean language

Korean² *n.* **1** [U] the language used in Korea **2** [C] someone from Korea

ko·sher /'kouʃɚ/ *adj.* **1** kosher food is prepared according to Jewish law **2** kosher restaurants or stores sell food prepared in this way **3** *informal* honest and legal, or socially acceptable: *I don't think the way she broke up with him was kosher.*

kow·tow /'kautau/ *v.* [I] *informal disapproving* to be too eager to please or obey someone who has more power than you: *I don't like the way this president **kowtows to** big business.*

Krem·lin /'krɛmlɪn/ *n.* **the Kremlin** the government of Russia and the former USSR, or the buildings that are this government's offices

KS the written abbreviation of **Kansas**

ku·dos /'kudous, -douz/ *n.* [U] admiration and respect that you get for being important or doing something important

Ku Klux Klan /ˌku klʌks 'klæn/ **KKK** *n.* **the Ku Klux Klan** a U.S. political organization whose members are Protestant white people, and who believe that people of other races or religions should not have any power or influence in American society

kung fu /ˌkʌŋ 'fu/ *n.* [U] an ancient Chinese fighting art in which you attack people with your feet and hands

kW *n.* [C] the written abbreviation of **kilowatt**

Kwanzaa /'kwɑnzə/ *n.* [C,U] a holiday celebrated by some African-Americans between December 26 and January 1

KY the written abbreviation of **Kentucky**

L, l

L, l /ɛl/ **1** the TWELFTH letter of the English alphabet **2** the ROMAN NUMERAL for 50

LA **1** the written abbreviation of **Louisiana** **2 L.A.** Los Angeles

lab /læb/ *n.* [C] *informal* **1** a LABORATORY: *a* ***research lab*** *at Columbia University* **2** a LABRADOR

la·bel[1] /ˈleɪbəl/ *n.* [C] **1** a piece of paper or other material that is attached to something and has information about that thing printed on it: *a beer label* | *Always read the instructions* ***on the label.*** **2** a famous name that represents a company that is selling a product: *Fischer recorded two albums for the Victor label.* **3** a word or phrase that is used in order to describe someone or something: *As a writer, he's proud of his "liberal" label.*

label[2] *v.* [T] **1** to attach a label to something or write information on something: *Make sure your charts are clearly labeled.* **2** to use a particular word or phrase in order to describe someone: *No one wants to be labeled a racist.*

THESAURUS

call, **describe**, **brand**, **characterize**, **portray**
→ see Thesaurus box at CALL[1]

la·bor[1] /ˈleɪbɚ/ *n.* [U] **1** work, especially work using a lot of physical effort: *farm labor* | ***manual labor*** (=physical work) **2** all the people who work for a company or in a country: *a shortage of* ***skilled labor*** (=trained workers) **3** the process in which a baby is born by being pushed from its mother's body, or the period when this happens: *Sandra was* ***in labor*** *for 17 hours.*

labor[2] *v.* [I] **1** *formal* to work very hard: *farmers laboring in the fields* **2** to try to do something that is difficult: *Writers can spend hours* ***laboring over*** *a single sentence.*

lab·ora·to·ry /ˈlæbrəˌtɔri/ *n.* plural **laboratories** [C] a special room or building in which scientists do tests and RESEARCH → —see also LANGUAGE LABORATORY

ˈlabor camp *n.* [C] a place where prisoners are forced to do hard physical work

ˈLabor Day *n.* [C] a public holiday in the U.S. and Canada on the first Monday in September

la·bor·er /ˈleɪbərɚ/ *n.* [C] someone whose job involves a lot of physical work

la·bo·ri·ous /ləˈbɔriəs/ *adj.* needing to be done slowly, and with a lot of effort: *Filmmaking can be a* ***laborious process.***

Lab·ra·dor /ˈlæbrəˌdɔr/ *n.* [C] a large dog with black or yellow fur

lab·y·rinth /ˈlæbəˌrɪnθ/ *n.* [C] a MAZE

lace[1] /leɪs/ *n.* **1** [U] a type of fine cloth made with patterns of very small holes: *lace curtains* **2** [C usually plural] a string that is pulled through special holes in shoes or clothing and tied, in order to pull the edges together and fasten them → see picture at SHOE[1]

lace[2] **also lace up** *v.* [T] to pull something together by tying a lace: *Paul laced up his boots.*

lac·er·ate /ˈlæsəˌreɪt/ *v.* [T] *technical* to badly cut or tear the skin —**laceration** /ˌlæsəˈreɪʃən/ *n.* [C,U]

lack[1] /læk/ *n.* [singular, U] the state of not having something, or of not having enough of it: *a* ***lack of*** *interest* | *The project was canceled* ***for lack of*** *money* (=because there was not enough).

lack[2] *v.* [T] to not have something, or to not have enough of it: *She's talented but lacks experience.*

lack·ing /ˈlækɪŋ/ *adj.* **1** not having enough of a particular thing or quality: *No one said she was* ***lacking in*** *determination.* **2** not existing or available: *Information about the cause of the crash was lacking.*

lack·lus·ter /ˈlækˌlʌstɚ/ *adj.* not very exciting or impressive: *a lackluster performance*

la·con·ic /ləˈkɑnɪk/ *adj.* using only a few words when you talk

lac·quer /ˈlækɚ/ *n.* [U] a clear substance painted on wood or metal to give it a hard shiny surface —**lacquered** *adj.*: *a lacquered box*

lac·tose /ˈlæktoʊs/ *n.* [U] a type of sugar found in milk

lac·y /ˈleɪsi/ *adj.* decorated with LACE, or looking like lace: *black lacy underwear*

lad /læd/ *n.* [C] *old-fashioned* a boy or young man

lad·der /ˈlædɚ/ *n.* [C] **1** a piece of equipment used for climbing up to high places, consisting of two long BARS connected with RUNGS (=steps): *The painter* ***climbed up/down*** *the ladder.* **2** the jobs you have to do in an organization in order to gradually become more powerful or important: *Stevens worked his way to* ***the top of the*** *corporate* ***ladder.***

lad·en /ˈleɪdn/ *adj.* carrying or containing a lot of something: *The table was* ***laden with*** *food.*

ˈladies' room *n.* [C] a room in a public building with toilets for women

la·dle /ˈleɪdl/ *n.* [C] a deep spoon with a long handle —**ladle** *v.* [T] *ladling soup into bowls*

la·dy /ˈleɪdi/ *n.* plural **ladies** [C] **1** a word meaning a woman, used in order to be polite: ***Ladies and gentlemen,*** *thank you for coming this evening.* | *a little old lady* **2** *spoken offensive* said when talking to a woman you do not know: *Hey, lady, get out of the way!*

la·dy·bug /ˈleɪdiˌbʌg/ *n.* [C] a small round insect that is red with black spots

lag[1] /læg/ *v.* past tense and past participle **lagged**, present participle **lagging** [I] to move or develop more slowly than other things or people: *Students' test scores are* ***lagging behind*** *last year's.*

lag[2] *n.* [C] a delay between two events → JET LAG

la·goon /ləˈgun/ *n.* [C] an area of ocean that is not very deep, and is nearly separated from the ocean by rocks, sand, or CORAL

laid /leɪd/ *v.* the past tense and past participle of LAY

ˌlaid-ˈback *adj.* relaxed and not seeming to worry about anything: *He's a pretty laid-back guy.*

THESAURUS
calm, relaxed, mellow, cool
➔ see Thesaurus box at CALM[2]

lain /leɪn/ *v.* the past participle of LIE

lair /lɛr/ *n.* [C] the place where a wild animal hides and sleeps: *a wolf's lair*

lais·sez-faire /ˌlɛseɪ ˈfɛr/ *n.* [U] the principle that the government should not control or INTERFERE with businesses or the economy

lake /leɪk/ *n.* [C] a large area of water surrounded by land: *We're going swimming in the lake.* | *Lake Michigan*

lamb /læm/ *n.* [C,U] a young sheep, or the meat of a young sheep

lam·bast /læmˈbeɪst, ˈlæmbeɪst/ *v.* [T] to severely criticize someone or something

lame[1] /leɪm/ *adj.* **1** *old-fashioned* unable to walk easily because your leg or foot is injured **2** *informal* too silly or stupid to believe: *a lame excuse* **3** *spoken* boring or not very good: *The party was lame.*

lame[2] *v.* [T] to make a person or animal lame

ˌlame ˈduck *n.* [C] someone in an official position, such as a president, who is powerless because his/her period in office will soon end

la·ment[1] /ləˈmɛnt/ *v.* [I,T] to express feelings of great sadness or disappointment about something

lament[2] *n.* [C] something such as a song that expresses great sadness

lam·en·ta·ble /ləˈmɛntəbəl/ *adj. formal* very disappointing

lam·i·nate /ˈlæməˌneɪt/ *v.* [T] to cover paper or wood with a thin layer of plastic in order to protect it —**laminated** *adj.*

lamp /læmp/ *n.* [C] an object that produces light by using electricity, oil, or gas: *a desk lamp* ➔ see picture at LIGHT[1]

lam·poon /læmˈpun/ *v.* [T] to write about someone such as a politician in a funny way that makes him/her seem stupid —**lampoon** *n.* [C]

lamp·shade /ˈlæmpʃeɪd/ *n.* [C] a decorative cover put over the top of a lamp in order to make the light less bright

lance /læns/ *n.* [C] a long thin pointed weapon used in past times by soldiers on horses

land[1] /lænd/ *n.* **1** [U] the ground, especially when owned by someone and used for buildings or farming [➥ **earth, soil**]: *A mall is being built on the land near the lake.* | *5,000 acres of agricultural land* ➔ see Thesaurus box at EARTH **2** [U] the solid dry part of the Earth's surface: *Frogs live **on land** and in the water.* **3** [C] *literary* a country or place: *a faraway land*

THESAURUS
country, nation, state, power
➔ see Thesaurus box at COUNTRY[1]

land

land[2] *v.* **1** [I,T] if an airplane lands, or if a pilot lands an airplane, the airplane moves down until it is safely on the ground [≠ **take off**]: *My flight landed in Chicago an hour late.*

THESAURUS
arrive, get to, reach, turn up, show up, get in, come in
➔ see Thesaurus box at ARRIVE

2 [I] to fall or come down onto something after moving through the air: *Chris slipped and **landed on** his back.* **3** [T] to finally succeed in getting a particular job, contract, or deal: *Kelly landed a job with a big law firm.* **4** [I] to arrive somewhere in a boat, airplane, etc.: *The immigrants landed in New York.* **5** [T] to put someone or something on land from an airplane or boat: *They landed 1,200 troops on the beach.*

land·fill /ˈlændfɪl/ *n.* [C] a place where waste is buried in large amounts

land·ing /ˈlændɪŋ/ *n.* [C] **1** the floor at the top of a set of stairs **2** the action of arriving on land, or of making something such as an airplane or boat come onto land [➥ **takeoff**]: *an **emergency landing*** (=a sudden landing made by an airplane because it is having trouble)

ˈlanding gear *n.* [U] an aircraft's wheels and wheel supports

ˈlanding pad *n.* [C] the area where a HELICOPTER comes down to earth

ˈlanding strip *n.* [C] a special road on which an airplane lands, especially one not at an airport [➥ **runway**]

land·la·dy /ˈlændˌleɪdi/ *n.* plural **landladies** [C] a woman who owns a building or other property and rents it to people [➥ **landlord**] ➔ see Topic box at RENT[1]

land·locked /ˈlændlɑkt/ *adj.* surrounded by land: *a landlocked country*

land·lord /ˈlændlɔrd/ *n.* [C] someone who owns a building or other property and rents it to other people [➥ **landlady**] ➔ see Topic box at RENT[1]

land·mark /ˈlændmɑrk/ *n.* [C] **1** something that helps you recognize where you are, such as a famous building **2** one of the most important events, changes, or discoveries that influences someone or something: *The treaty is an important landmark in U.S.-Mexico relations.*

'land mine, land·mine /'lændmaɪn/ *n.* [C] a type of bomb hidden in the ground that explodes when someone walks or drives over it

land·own·er /'lændˌoʊnɚ/ *n.* [C] someone who owns a large amount of land

land·scape¹ /'lændskeɪp/ *n.* [C] **1** a view across an area of land, including hills, forests, fields, etc. [➡ **scenery**]: *the beautiful landscape of Sonoma Valley* **2** a photograph or painting of a landscape ➔ see picture at PAINTING

landscape² *v.* [T] to arrange where the plants should grow in a park, yard, or garden —**landscaping** *n.* [U]

land·slide /'lændslaɪd/ *n.* [C] **1** the sudden falling of a lot of soil and rocks down the side of a hill, cliff, or mountain: *Part of Highway 101 is blocked by a landslide.* **2** a victory in which a person or political party wins a lot more votes than the others in an election: *The president was re-elected* ***in/by a landslide.***

lane /leɪn/ *n.* [C] **1** one of the parts of a main road that is divided by painted lines: *driving* ***in the fast/slow lane*** (=in the lane that is farthest left or farthest right) **2** a narrow country road

THESAURUS

road, **street**, **main street**, **avenue**, **main road**, **highway**, **freeway**, **expressway**, **toll road**, **turnpike**
➔ see Thesaurus box at ROAD

3 one of the narrow areas that a pool or race track is divided into

lan·guage /'læŋgwɪdʒ/ *n.* **1** [C] a system of words, phrases, and grammar, used by people who live in a country or area to communicate with each other: *the English language* | *Her* ***native language*** (=the first language she learned) *is Danish.* | *"Do you speak any* ***foreign languages****?" "Yes, I speak French."*

L

THESAURUS

dialect – a form of a language that is spoken in one area, which is different from the way it is spoken in other areas: *Cantonese is only one of many Chinese dialects.*
accent – a way of pronouncing words that someone has because of where s/he was born or lives: *She has a strong Southern accent.*
tongue – a particular language: *Winnie started school knowing only her native tongue.*
slang – very informal and sometimes offensive language, used especially by people who belong to a particular group: *Mudbugs is Louisiana slang for crawfish.*
jargon – technical words and phrases used by people in a particular profession: *a document full of legal jargon*
terminology formal – the technical words or expressions that are used in a particular subject: *the basic terminology used by geologists*

2 [U] the use of words, grammar, etc. to communicate with other people: *language skills* **3** [U] the kind of words that someone uses, or that are used when talking or writing about a particular subject: *the language of business* | ***bad language*** (=words that people consider offensive) **4** [C,U] *technical* a system of instructions used in computer programs **5** [C,U] any system of signs, movements, sounds, etc. that are used to express meanings or feelings: *the language of music*

'language ˌlaboratory also **'language lab** *n.* [C] a room in a school or college where students can listen to TAPES of a foreign language and practice speaking it

lan·guid /'læŋgwɪd/ *adj. literary* moving slowly and weakly, but in an attractive way

lan·guish /'læŋgwɪʃ/ *v.* [I] to be prevented from developing, improving, or being dealt with: *a case that has languished for years in the courts*

lank·y /'læŋki/ *adj.* someone who is lanky is very tall and thin

lan·tern /'læntɚn/ *n.* [C] a type of lamp you can carry that usually has a metal frame and glass sides ➔ see picture at LIGHT¹

lap¹ /læp/ *n.* [C] **1** the upper part of your legs when you are sitting down: *The little girl was sitting* ***on*** *her mother's* ***lap.*** **2** a single trip around a race track or between the two ends of a pool: *Patty swims 30 laps a day.*

lap² *v.* past tense and past participle **lapped**, present participle **lapping** **1** [I,T] if water laps something or laps against something, it touches something with small waves: *the sound of the lake* ***lapping against*** *the shore* **2** [T] **also lap up** to drink using quick movements of the tongue: *a cat lapping milk*

lap sth ⇔ **up** *phr. v. disapproving* to enjoy or believe something without criticizing or doubting it at all: *She's flattering him and he's just* ***lapping it up!***

la·pel /lə'pɛl/ *n.* [C] the front part of a coat or JACKET that is attached to the collar and folds back on both sides

lapse¹ /læps/ *n.* [C] **1** a short period of time when you forget something, do not pay attention, or fail to do something you should: *a memory lapse* **2** the period of time between two events: *There was a* ***lapse of*** *ten years before they met again.*

lapse² *v.* [I] to end, especially because an agreed time limit is finished: *The insurance policy has lapsed.*

lapse into sth *phr. v.* **1** to start behaving or speaking in a very different way, especially one that is more normal or usual for you: *Without* *thinking, he lapsed into French.* **2** to become very quiet, less active, or unconscious: *She **lapsed into silence**.*

lap·top /ˈlæptɑp/ **also** ˌ**laptop comˈputer** *n.* [C] a small computer that you can carry with you

lar·ce·ny /ˈlɑrsəni/ *n.* [U] *law* the crime of stealing something

lard /lɑrd/ *n.* [U] the thick white fat from pigs, used in cooking

large /lɑrdʒ/ *adj.* **1** big, or bigger than usual in size, number, or amount [≠ **small**]: *a large pepperoni pizza* | *What's the largest city in Canada?*

> **THESAURUS**
>
> **big**, **huge**, **enormous**, **vast**, **gigantic**, **massive**, **immense**, **colossal**, **substantial**
> ➔ see Thesaurus box at BIG

2 a large person is tall and often fat: *Aunt Betsy was a very large woman.*

> **THESAURUS**
>
> **fat**, **overweight**, **big**, **heavy**, **obese**, **chubby**, **plump**
> ➔ see Thesaurus box at FAT[1]

3 at large in general: *The risk is to American society at large.* **4 be at large** if a dangerous person or animal is at large, they have escaped from somewhere and may cause harm: *The suspect is still at large.* **5 larger than life** more attractive, exciting, or interesting than other people or things **6 by and large** used in order to say that something is generally true or usually happens, but not always: *By and large, the kids are well-behaved.* —**largeness** *n.* [U]

large·ly /ˈlɑrdʒli/ *adv.* mostly or mainly: *The delay was largely due to bad weather.*

> **THESAURUS**
>
> **mainly**, **chiefly**, **principally**, **primarily**
> ➔ see Thesaurus box at MAINLY

ˌ**large-ˈscale** *adj.* involving a lot of people, effort, money, supplies, etc.: *large-scale unemployment*

lark /lɑrk/ *n.* [C] a small wild brown bird that sings and has long pointed wings

lar·va /ˈlɑrvə/ *n.* plural **larvae** /ˈlɑrvi/ [C] a young insect with a soft tube-shaped body that will become an insect with wings ➔ see picture on page A2

lar·yn·gi·tis /ˌlærənˈdʒaɪtɪs/ *n.* [U] an illness in which your throat and LARYNX are swollen, making it difficult for you to talk

lar·ynx /ˈlærɪŋks/ *n.* [C] *technical* the part of your throat from which your voice is produced

la·sa·gna /ləˈzɑnyə/ *n.* [C,U] a type of Italian food made with flat pieces of PASTA, meat or vegetables, and cheese ➔ see picture on page A5

las·civ·i·ous /ləˈsɪviəs/ *adj.* *disapproving* showing a very strong sexual desire

la·ser /ˈleɪzɚ/ *n.* [C] a piece of equipment that produces a powerful narrow beam of light, or the beam of light itself: *laser surgery* | *a laser beam*

lash[1] /læʃ/ *v.* **1** [T] to hit someone very hard with a whip, stick, etc. **2** [T] to tie something tightly to something else using a rope: *The branches were lashed together.* **3** [I,T] to hit sharply against something: *waves lashing the rocks*

lash out *phr. v.* **1** to suddenly speak loudly and angrily: *He **lashed out at** critics.* **2** to suddenly try to hit someone with a lot of violent uncontrolled movements

lash[2] *n.* [C] **1** a hit with a whip, especially as a punishment **2** an EYELASH

las·so /ˈlæsoʊ/ *n.* [C] a rope with one end tied in a circle, used for catching cattle and horses —**lasso** *v.* [T]

last[1] /læst/ *determiner, adj.* **1** most recent [➡ **next**]: *Did you go to the last football game?* | *I saw Tim **last night/week/Sunday**.* | *The **last time** I saw Ken, we got into an argument.*

> **THESAURUS**
>
> **previous** – happening or existing before the particular event, time, or thing mentioned: *The increase in sales was smaller than in previous years.*
> **former** – happening or existing before, but not now: *the former owner of the property*

> **USAGE**
>
> Use **last** to mean "the one that happened most recently" or "the one before the present one": *our last vacation in Maine* | *my last job*
> Use **latest** to mean "new and most recent": *the latest news* | *the latest Paris fashions*

2 at the end, after everyone or everything else: *The last part of the song is sad.* | *He's **the last person** I'd ask for help* (=I do not want to ask him). **3** remaining after all others have gone: *The last guests were just putting on their coats.* | *Do you want the last piece of cake?* **4 on its last legs** likely to fail or break: *The truck was on its last legs.* **5 have the last word** to make the last statement in an argument, which gives you an advantage

last[2] *adv.* **1** most recently before now: *When did you see her last?* **2** after everything or everyone else: *Harris is going to speak last.* **3 last but not least** said when making a final statement, to show that it is just as important as your other statements: *Last but not least, I'd like to thank my mother.*

last³ *n., pron.* [C] **1 the last** the person or thing that comes after all the others: *Joe was the last of nine children* (=he was born last). | *Les was the last to go to bed that night.* **2 at (long) last** if something happens at last, it happens after you have waited a long time: *At last, we were able to afford a house.* **3 the day/week/year before last** the day, week, etc. before the one that has just finished **4 the last I/we...** *informal* used when telling someone the most recent news that you know: *The last we heard, Paul was in Cuba.* **5 the last of sth** the remaining part of something: *This is the last of the paint.*

last⁴ *v.* [I] **1** to continue to happen or exist: *Jeff's operation lasted 3 hours.* | *I wished this moment would last forever.* **2** to continue to be effective, useful, or in good condition: *Most batteries will **last for** up to 8 hours.*

ˌlast-ˈditch *adj.* **last-ditch effort/attempt etc.** a final attempt to achieve something before it becomes impossible to do

last·ing /ˈlæstɪŋ/ *adj.* continuing for a long time: *It has been difficult to achieve lasting peace in the Middle East.*

last·ly /ˈlæstli/ *adv. formal* used when telling someone the last thing in a series of statements: *Lastly, I'd like to suggest a few solutions.*

USAGE

Use **lastly** or **finally** to introduce the last point, action, or instruction in a list: *Lastly/Finally, I'd like to thank everyone for all their hard work.*
Use **finally** or **eventually** to say that something happens after a long time: *Finally/Eventually, we managed to get the car started.* | *She eventually/finally apologized.*
Use **at last** to emphasize that you are glad when something happens because you have been waiting a long time for it: *Spring's here at last!*
→ FIRST

ˌlast-ˈminute *adj.* [only before noun] happening or done as late as possible within a process, event, or activity: *a last-minute decision*

ˈlast name *n.* [C] your family's name, which in English comes after your other names [➡ **first name, middle name**] → —see Usage box at NAMES

latch¹ /lætʃ/ *n.* [C] a small metal BAR used for fastening a door, gate, window, etc.

latch² *v.*
latch onto sth *phr. v. informal* if you latch onto an idea, style, phrase, etc. you think it is so good, important, etc. that you start using it too

late¹ /leɪt/ *adj.* **1** arriving, happening, or done after the expected time: *Sorry I'm late. I got stuck in traffic.* | *Peggy was **late for** school.* | *a late breakfast* | *Is it **too late to** send in my forms?*

THESAURUS

overdue – not done or happening when expected: *He recently paid two overdue tax bills.*
be behind with sth – to be late or slow in doing something: *They were three months behind with the rent.*
be delayed – to make someone or something late: *The flight was delayed by bad weather.*
be held up – to be late because of something that has happened: *Sorry I'm late – I got held up.*

2 near the end of a period of time: *a house built in the late 19th century* **3** happening at night, especially when most people are asleep: *I watched the late show on TV.* **4** paid or given back after the arranged time: *I had to pay a fee because my payment was late.* **5** *formal* [only before noun] dead: *Marion and her late husband bought the house back in 1950.*

late² *adv.* **1** after the usual or expected time: *I probably won't be home until late.* | *Our flight arrived 2 hours late.* **2** near the end of a period of time: ***late in** the afternoon* | *taking a walk **late at night***

late·ly /ˈleɪtli/ *adv.* recently: *It hasn't rained much lately.* | *Lately, I've been really busy.*

USAGE

You must always use **lately** with the present perfect tense. It shows that the situation you are talking about is still continuing. You can use **recently** like this, too: *I've been very busy lately.* | *There hasn't been much rain recently.*
You can also use **recently** with the simple past tense to talk about something that happened not long ago: *They recently got married.*
→ see also Thesaurus box at RECENTLY

la·tent /ˈleɪtˀnt/ *adj.* present but not yet noticeable, active, or completely developed: *latent racism*

lat·er¹ /ˈleɪt̬ɚ/ *adv.* **1** after the present time or a time you are talking about: *I'll see you later.* | *They met in July, and two months later they got married.*

THESAURUS

after, afterward, next, subsequently
→ see Thesaurus box at AFTER¹, NEXT¹

2 later on at some time in the future, or after something else: *That's a decision we can make later on.*

later² *adj.* **1** coming in the future, or after something else: *This will be decided **at a later time/date**.* **2** [only before noun] more recent: *Later models of the car are much improved.*

lat·er·al /ˈlæt̬ərəl/ *adj. technical* relating to the side of something, or movement to the side

lat·est¹ /ˈleɪt̬ɪst/ *adj.* [only before noun] most

recent or newest: *What's **the latest** news?* | ***the latest** fashions*

THESAURUS

new, **recent**, **modern**
→ see Thesaurus box at NEW

USAGE

Use **latest** to mean "new and most recent": *the latest news* | *the latest Paris fashions*
Use **last** to mean "the one that happened most recently" or "the one before the present one": *our last vacation in Maine* | *my last job*

latest² *n.* **at the latest** no later than the time mentioned: *I want you home by 11 at the latest.*

la·tex /ˈleɪtɛks/ *n.* [U] a thick white liquid used for making products such as rubber, glue, and paint, and produced artificially or by some plants: *latex gloves*

lath·er¹ /ˈlæðɚ/ *n.* [singular, U] a lot of small white BUBBLES produced by rubbing soap with water

lather² *v.* [I,T] to produce a lather, or cover something with lather

Lat·in¹ /ˈlætˀn/ *adj.* **1** relating to or coming from Mexico, Central America, or South America **2** relating to the Latin language

Latin² *n.* [U] an old language that is now used mostly for legal, scientific, or medical words

La·ti·na /ləˈtinə/ *n.* [C] a woman in the U.S. whose family comes from a country in Latin America —**Latina** *adj.*

ˌLatin Aˈmerica *n.* [C] the land including Mexico, Central America, and South America —**Latin American** *adj.*

La·ti·no /ləˈtinoʊ/ *n.* [C] a man in the U.S. whose family comes from a country in Latin America ▶ In the plural, Latinos can mean a group of men and women, or just men. ◀ —**Latino** *adj.*

lat·i·tude /ˈlæt̬əˌtud/ *n.* **1** [C,U] *technical* the distance north or south of the EQUATOR, measured in degrees [➡ **longitude**] → see picture at GLOBE **2** [U] *formal* freedom to do or say what you like: *Students now have greater **latitude in** choosing their classes.*

la·trine /ləˈtrin/ *n.* [C] an outdoor toilet at a camp or military area

THESAURUS

toilet, **bathroom**, **restroom**, **women's/ladies' room**, **men's room**, **lavatory**
→ see Thesaurus box at TOILET

lat·ter¹ /ˈlæt̬ɚ/ *n.* **the latter** *formal* the second of two people or things that are mentioned [➡ **former**]: *Either glass or plastic would be effective, but the latter* (=plastic) *weighs less.*

latter² *adj.* **1 the latter sth** *formal* being the last person or thing that has just been mentioned: *Of the phrases "go crazy" and "go nuts," the latter term is used less frequently.* **2 the latter sth** closer to the end of a period of time: *the latter part of the 19th century*

laud·a·ble /ˈlɔdəbəl/ *adj. formal* deserving praise or admiration

laugh¹ /læf/ *v.* **1** [I] to make a sound with your voice, usually while smiling, because you think something is funny [➡ **laughter**, **smile**]: *How come no one ever **laughs at** my jokes?* | *The story **made** me **laugh** so hard I started crying.* | *Nancy and I **burst out laughing*** (=suddenly started laughing).

THESAURUS

giggle – to laugh quickly in a high voice, especially because you think something is very funny or because you are nervous or embarrassed
chuckle – to laugh quietly
cackle – to laugh in an unpleasant loud way
snicker – to laugh quietly in an unkind way
guffaw – to laugh loudly
(be) in stitches – to be laughing so much that you cannot stop

2 no laughing matter something serious that should not be joked about

laugh at sb/sth *phr. v.* to make unkind or funny remarks about someone: *If I told them my real feelings, they would just laugh at me.*

laugh sth ⇔ **off** *phr. v.* to joke about something in order to pretend that it is not very serious or important: *She laughed off their insults.*

laugh² *n.* **1** [C] the sound you make when you laugh [➡ **smile**]: *a loud laugh* **2 have the last laugh** to finally be successful after someone has criticized or defeated you

laugh·a·ble /ˈlæfəbəl/ *adj.* impossible to be treated seriously because of being so silly, bad, or difficult to believe [= **ridiculous**]

laugh·ing·stock /ˈlæfɪŋˌstɑk/ *n.* [C] someone who has done something silly or stupid, and whom people make jokes about and laugh at in a way that is not nice

laugh·ter /ˈlæftɚ/ *n.* [U] the action of laughing, or the sound of people laughing: *Everyone **burst into*** (=started laughing) *laughter.* | *The audience **roared with laughter**.*

launch¹ /lɔntʃ, lɑntʃ/ *v.* [T] **1** to start something new, such as an activity, plan, or profession: *the movie that launched his acting career* **2** to send a weapon or a space vehicle into the sky or into space **3** to put a boat or ship into the water

launch into sth *phr. v.* to suddenly start describing something or criticizing something: *He launched into the story of his life.*

launch² *n.* [C] an occasion at which a new product is shown or made available

ˈlaunch pad *n.* [C] the area from which a space vehicle, ROCKET, etc. is sent into space

laun·der /ˈlɔndɚ, ˈlɑn-/ *v.* [T] **1** to put stolen

L

money into legal businesses or bank accounts in order to hide it or use it **2** *formal* to wash clothes

Laun·dro·mat /ˈlɔndrəˌmæt, ˈlɑn-/ *n.* [C] *trademark* a place where you pay money to wash your clothes in machines

laun·dry /ˈlɔndri, ˈlɑn-/ *n.* [U] clothes, sheets, etc. that need to be washed, or that have already been washed: *I have to* ***do the laundry*** (=wash clothes, sheets, etc.). | *a* ***laundry basket***

lau·re·ate /ˈlɔriɪt, ˈlɑr-/ *n.* [C] someone who has been given an important prize: *a Nobel laureate*

lau·rel /ˈlɔrəl, ˈlɑr-/ *n.* [C] **1** a small tree with smooth shiny dark green leaves that do not fall off in winter **2 rest/sit on your laurels** to be satisfied with what you have achieved and therefore stop trying to achieve anything new

la·va /ˈlɑvə, ˈlævə/ *n.* [U] **1** hot melted rock that flows from a VOLCANO **2** this rock when it becomes cold and solid

lav·a·to·ry /ˈlævəˌtɔri/ *n.* plural **lavatories** [C] *formal* a room with a toilet in it

THESAURUS

toilet, bathroom, restroom, women's/ladies' room, men's room, latrine
→ see Thesaurus box at TOILET

lav·en·der /ˈlævəndɚ/ *n.* **1** [C,U] a plant with purple flowers that have a strong pleasant smell **2** [U] a pale purple color

lav·ish¹ /ˈlævɪʃ/ *adj.* very generous and often expensive or complicated: *lavish gifts* | *He is* ***lavish with*** *his praise.*

lavish² *v.*

lavish sth **on** sb *phr. v.* to give someone a lot of something good: *They lavish a lot of attention on their children.*

law /lɔ/ *n.* **1** [singular, U] the system of rules that people in a country, city, or state must obey [➡ **legal**]: *Drunk driving is* ***against the law*** (=illegal). | *He never intended to* ***break the law*** (=do something illegal). **2** [C] a rule that people in a particular country, city, or local area must obey: ***Under*** *a new* ***law***, *drivers may not use cell phones.*

L

THESAURUS

rule, regulation, restriction, guidelines, statute
→ see Thesaurus box at RULE¹

3 [U] the study of law, or the profession involving laws: *She* ***practices law*** (=works as a lawyer) *in New York.* **4 the law** the police: *Is he in trouble with the law?* **5 law and order** a situation in which people respect the law, and crime is controlled by the police, the prison system, etc.: *The national guard was sent in to restore law and order.* **6** [C] a statement that describes and explains how something works: *the* ***law of*** *gravity* | *the economic law of supply and demand*

ˈlaw-aˌbiding *adj.* respectful of the law and obeying it

law·ful /ˈlɔfəl/ *adj. formal* considered by the government or courts of law to be legal

law·less /ˈlɔlɪs/ *adj. formal* not obeying the law, or not controlled by law

lawn /lɔn/ *n.* [C] an area of ground around a house or in a park that is covered with grass: *I should* ***mow the lawn*** (=cut the grass) *today.*

ˈlawn ˌmower, lawn·mow·er /ˈlɔnˌmoʊɚ/ *n.* [C] a machine that you use to cut the grass

law·suit /ˈlɔsut/ *n.* [C] a problem or complaint that someone brings to a court of law to be settled, especially for money: *They have* ***filed a lawsuit*** *against the builders.*

law·yer /ˈlɔyɚ/ *n.* [C] someone whose job is to advise people about laws, write formal agreements, or represent people in court [= **attorney**]

lax /læks/ *adj.* not strict or careful about standards of behavior, work, safety, etc.: *The airport has been criticized for* ***lax security***. —**laxity** *n.* [U]

lax·a·tive /ˈlæksətɪv/ *n.* [C] a medicine or something that you eat that makes your BOWELS empty easily —**laxative** *adj.*

lay¹ /leɪ/ *v.* past tense and past participle **laid** **1** [T] to put someone or something carefully into a particular position: ***Lay*** *the peppers* ***on*** *the chicken.* | *Martha* ***laid*** *the baby* ***down***.

USAGE

Lay means to put something down in a flat position: *She laid the newspaper down and picked up the phone.*
Lie has two different meanings:
– to be or move into in a flat position on the floor, a bed, etc.: *She was lying on the sofa.* The past tense for this meaning of lie is **lay**: *He lay on the bed.*
– to say something that is not true: *Why did you lie to me?* The past tense for this meaning of lie is **lied**: *The police think that he lied.*

2 lay bricks/carpet/cable etc. to put or attach something in the correct place, especially onto something flat or under the ground: ***laying down*** *a new bedroom carpet* **3** [I,T] if a bird, insect, etc. lays eggs, it produces them from its body **4 lay a finger/hand on sb** to hurt someone, especially to hit him/her: *He never laid a finger on her.* **5 lay blame/criticism/emphasis etc.** *formal* to blame, criticize, emphasize, etc. **6 lay yourself open to blame/criticism etc.** to do something that makes you likely to be blamed, criticized, etc.

lay sth ⇔ **down** *phr. v.* to officially state rules, methods, etc. that someone must obey or use: *The rules have already been laid down.*

lay into sb *phr. v. informal* to attack someone physically or criticize him/her angrily: *You should have heard Dad laying into Tommy.*

lay off *phr. v.* **1 lay** sb ⇔ **off** to stop employing someone, especially when there is not much work to do: *500 auto workers were laid off.* **2 lay off** sth/sb *spoken* to stop doing, having, or using something that is bad or annoying: *Don't you think you should lay off alcohol for a while? | Just* ***lay off*** (=stop criticizing) *– I don't care what you think!*

lay sth ⇔ **out** *phr. v.* **1** to spread something out: *Pam laid her dress out on the bed.* **2** *informal* to explain or describe a plan, idea, etc.: *The mayor laid out her budget proposal at Tuesday's meeting.*

lay up *phr. v.* **be laid up (with sth)** to have to stay in bed because you are sick or injured: *He's laid up with a broken collarbone.*

lay² *v.* the past tense of LIE

lay³ *adj.* [only before noun] not trained in a particular profession or subject: *a lay preacher*

lay·a·way /ˈleɪəˌweɪ/ *n.* [U] a way of buying goods in which the goods are kept by the seller for a small amount of money until the full price is paid

lay·er¹ /ˈleɪɚ/ *n.* [C] **1** an amount of a substance that covers all of a surface: *a* ***layer of*** *dust on the desk* **2** something that is placed on or between other things: *several* ***layers of*** *clothing*

layer² *v.* [T] to put something down in layers: *a lemon cake* ***layered with*** *raspberries*

lay·man /ˈleɪmən/ *n.* [C] someone who is not trained in a particular subject or type of work: *a book on astronomy written for* ***the layman*** (=people in general)

lay·off /ˈleɪɔf/ *n.* [C] the act of stopping a worker's employment because there is not enough work: *layoffs in the steel industry*

lay·out /ˈleɪaʊt/ *n.* [C,U] **1** the way things are arranged in a particular area or place: *changes in the office layout* **2** the way in which writing and pictures are arranged on a page

lay·o·ver /ˈleɪˌoʊvɚ/ *n.* [C] a short stay somewhere between parts of a trip: *We'll have a two-hour layover in Dallas.*

lay·per·son /ˈleɪˌpɚsən/ *n.* [C] a word meaning a LAYMAN that is used when the person could be a man or a woman

laze /leɪz/ *v.* [I] to relax and enjoy yourself without doing very much: *Jeff spent the morning just lazing in the yard.*

la·zy /ˈleɪzi/ *adj.* comparative **lazier**, superlative **laziest** **1** not liking to do work or to make an effort: *the laziest boy in the class | I've gotten a little lazy about cooking.*

THESAURUS

idle old-fashioned – lazy and wasting time when there is work to do: *In the story, Jack is an idle boy who would rather play than work.*
indolent formal – lazy and living a comfortable life: *The news startled him out of his state of indolent contentment.*
shiftless – lazy and not at all interested in working: *Some politicians seem to think that anyone who doesn't have a job is shiftless.*
slack – lazy and not taking enough care to do things correctly: *Some of the students were slack, not bothering to even turn in their homework.*

2 a lazy time is spent relaxing: *lazy summer afternoons*

lb *n.* [C] the written abbreviation of **pound**

lead¹ /lid/ *v.* past tense and past participle **led** /lɛd/

1 GUIDE [T] to guide a person or animal to a place by going with or in front of the person or animal: *Isabel* ***led us up/down*** *some narrow stairs and into a small room. | We led the horses along the river.*

THESAURUS

guide – to take someone to a place and show him/her interesting things there: *She guides tourists around the White House.*
direct formal – to explain to someone how to get somewhere: *He directed them to the station.*
point – to show someone which direction to go: *a sign pointing the way*

2 GO IN FRONT [I,T] to go in front of a group of people or vehicles: *The high school band is leading the parade.*
3 DOOR/ROAD [I] if a door, road, etc. leads somewhere, you can get there by using it: *The second door* ***leads to*** *the principal's office.*
4 CONTROL [T] to be in charge of something, especially an activity or a group of people: *Who is leading the investigation?*
5 WIN [I,T] to be winning a game or competition: *At half time, Green Bay was leading 12–0.*
6 CAUSE STH [T] to be the thing that makes someone do something or think something: *What* ***led*** *you* ***to*** *study geology? | Rick* ***led me to believe*** (=made me believe) *he was going to return the money.*
7 lead a normal/dull etc. life to have a normal, boring, etc. type of life
8 SUCCESS [I,T] to be more successful than other people, companies, or countries in a particular activity or area of business: *Georgia* ***leads*** *the nation* ***in*** *peanut production.*
9 lead the way a) to guide someone in a particular direction **b)** to be the first to do something good or successful: *The Japanese led the way in using robots in industry.*
10 CONVERSATION [I,T] to direct a conversation or discussion so that it develops in the way you want: *She finally led the topic around to pay raises.*

lead off sth *phr. v.* to begin an event by doing something: *They* ***led off*** *the concert* ***with*** *a Beethoven overture.*

L

lead sb **on** *phr. v.* to make someone believe something that is not true: *I thought he was in love with me, but he was just leading me on.*

lead to sth *phr. v.* to make something happen or exist as a result of something else: *Opening the new lumber mill has led to the creation of 200 jobs.*

lead up to sth *phr. v.* **1** to come before something: *the days leading up to the election* **2** to gradually introduce a subject into a conversation: *remarks leading up to a request for money*

lead² *n.* **1** [singular] the position or situation of being in front of, or better than everyone else in a race or competition: *Lewis is still* ***in the lead.*** | *Joyner has* ***taken the lead*** (=moved into the front position in a race). **2** [singular] the distance, number of points, etc. by which one competitor is ahead of another: *The Bulls* ***have*** *a 5-point* ***lead over*** *the Celtics at halftime.* **3** [C] a piece of information that may help you to make a discovery or find the answer to a problem: *Police are pursuing all leads.* **4** [C] the main acting part in a play, movie, etc., or the main singer, dancer, etc. in a group: *Who has the lead in the school play?* | *the lead guitarist*

lead³ /lɛd/ *n.* **1** [U] a soft gray-blue metal that melts easily **2** [C,U] the substance in a pencil that makes the marks when you write

lead·er /ˈlidɚ/ *n.* [C] **1** the person who directs or controls a team, organization, country, etc.: *Most world leaders will attend the conference.* | *the* ***leader of*** *the Senate* **2** the person, organization, etc. that is better than all the others in a race or competition: ***leaders in*** *the field of medical science*

lead·er·ship /ˈlidɚˌʃɪp/ *n.* **1** [U] the quality of being good at leading a team, organization, country, etc.: *training to build leadership skills* **2** [U] the position of being the leader of a team, organization, etc.: ***Under*** *Brown's* ***leadership****, the magazine attracted new readers.* **3** [singular] the people who lead a country, organization, etc.

lead·ing /ˈlidɪŋ/ *adj.* **1** best, most important, or most successful: *a leading athlete* **2 a leading question** a question asked in a way that makes you give a particular answer

leaf¹ /lif/ *n.* plural **leaves** /livz/ **1** [C] one of the flat green parts of a plant that are joined to its stem or branches: *There are still some leaves on the trees.* → see picture at PLANT¹ **2** [C] a part of the top of a table that can be added to make the table larger **3** [U] gold or silver in a very thin sheet → **turn over a new leaf** at TURN¹

leaf² *v.*

leaf through sth *phr. v.* to turn the pages of a book quickly, without reading it carefully

leaf·let /ˈliflɪt/ *n.* [C] a small piece of printed paper that gives information or advertises something

leaf·y /ˈlifi/ *adj.* having a lot of leaves: *green leafy vegetables*

league /lig/ *n.* [C] **1** a group of sports teams or players who play games against each other to see who is best: *major league baseball* **2** a group of people or countries that have joined together because they have similar aims, political beliefs, etc.: *the League of Nations* **3 not in the same league/out of sb's league** not having the same abilities or qualities as someone or something else: *He knows a lot more than I do – he's way out of my league.*

leak¹ /lik/ *v.* **1** [I,T] to let a liquid or gas in or out of a hole or crack: *Somebody's car must be leaking oil.* | *The roof's leaking!* **2** [I] to pass through a hole or crack: *Gas was* ***leaking out*** *of the pipes.*

> **THESAURUS**
>
> **pour**, **flow**, **drip**, **ooze**, **gush**, **spurt**, **run**, **come out**
>
> → see Thesaurus box at POUR

3 [T] to deliberately give secret information to a newspaper, television company, etc.: *Details of the President's speech were* ***leaked to*** *reporters.* —**leakage** *n.* [C,U]

leak out *phr. v.* if secret information leaks out, a lot of people find out about it

leak² *n.* [C] **1** a small hole that lets liquid or gas flow into or out of something: *a leak in the water pipe*

> **THESAURUS**
>
> **hole**, **space**, **gap**, **crack**
>
> → see Thesaurus box at HOLE¹

2 a situation in which someone has secret information: *leaks about a secret deal* **3 take/have a leak** *slang* to URINATE

leak·y /ˈliki/ *adj.* having a hole or crack so that liquid or gas can pass through: *a leaky faucet*

lean¹ /lin/ *v.* **1** [I] to move or bend your body in a particular position: *He* ***leaned over*** *and kissed his wife.* **2** [I] to support yourself or be supported in a position that is not straight or upright: *Brad was* ***leaning on/against*** *a wall.* → see picture on page A9 **3** [T] to put something in a sloping position against something else: *Dad* ***leaned*** *the ladder* ***against*** *the wall.*

> **THESAURUS**
>
> **stand** – to put something in an almost upright position: *He stood the Christmas tree against the wall.*
>
> **rest** – to support an object by putting it on or against something: *I rested my head on the back of the chair.*
>
> **prop** – to support something or keep it in a particular position: *A small mirror was propped against the wall.*

lean on sb/sth *phr. v.* to get support and encour-

agement from someone: *I know I can always lean on my friends.*
lean toward sth *phr. v.* to tend to agree with or support a particular set of opinions, beliefs, etc.: *Most of the church's members lean toward the political right.*

lean² *adj.* **1** thin in a healthy and attractive way: *lean and athletic*

THESAURUS

thin, **slim**, **slender**, **skinny**, **underweight**, **emaciated**
→ see Thesaurus box at THIN¹

2 lean meat does not have much fat on it **3** difficult as a result of bad economic conditions or lack of money: *a lean year for the business*

lean·ing /ˈliniŋ/ *n.* [C] a tendency to prefer or agree with a particular set of beliefs, opinions, etc.: *liberal leanings*

leap¹ /lip/ *v.* past tense and past participle **leaped** or **leapt** /lɛpt/ [I] **1** to jump high into the air or over something: *One by one, the kids were leaping into the river.*

THESAURUS

jump, **skip**, **hop**, **dive**, **vault**
→ see Thesaurus box at JUMP¹

2 to move very quickly and with a lot of energy: *Jon **leaped up** to answer the phone.*
leap at sth *phr. v.* to accept an opportunity very eagerly: *The manager needed an assistant, and Paula **leaped at the chance**.*

leap² *n.* **1** [C] a big jump **2 by/in leaps and bounds** very quickly: *Your English is improving in leaps and bounds.*

leapfrog

leap·frog /ˈlipfrɑg/ *n.* [U] a children's game in which someone bends over and someone else jumps over him/her

ˈleap year *n.* [C] a year when February has 29 days instead of 28, which happens every four years

learn /lɚn/ *v.* **1** [I,T] to gain knowledge of a subject or of how to do something, through experience or study: *Lisa's learning Spanish.* | *I'd like to **learn (how) to** sew.* | *We've been **learning about** electricity in school.*

THESAURUS

study – to spend time going to classes, reading, etc. to learn about a subject: *Many students use computers to help them study.*
pick sth up – to learn something without much effort, by watching or listening to other people: *I picked up some Korean when I was in the army.*
get the hang of sth – to learn how to do something, especially by practicing it: *She's fallen off the bike a lot, but she's beginning to get the hang of it.*
master – to learn something so well that you understand it completely and have no difficulty with it: *Children are graduating from high school without mastering the basic skills needed to hold a job.*

USAGE

You **learn** a subject or skill when you study or practice it: *I'm thinking of learning Italian.* | *Jo's learning to drive.*
If you **teach** someone a subject or skill, you help him/her learn it: *Dad taught me to play the guitar.* You cannot say "Dad learned me to..."

2 [T] to get to know something so well that you can easily remember it: *Have you learned your lines for the play?* **3** [I,T] *formal* to find out information, news, etc. by hearing it from someone else: *We only **learned about** the accident later.* **4 learn sth the hard way** to understand something by learning from your mistakes and experiences: *I've learned the hard way that it's better to keep business and friendship separate.* **5 learn your lesson** to suffer so much after doing something wrong that you will not do it again: *I didn't punish him because I thought he had learned his lesson.* —**learner** *n.* [C] *a **fast/quick/slow learner***

learn·ed /ˈlɚnɪd/ *adj. formal* having a lot of knowledge because you have read and studied a lot

learn·ing /ˈlɚniŋ/ *n.* [U] knowledge gained through reading and study

ˈlearning curve *n.* [C] the rate at which you learn a new skill: *I like my new job, but it's been **a steep learning curve*** (=I had to learn a lot very quickly).

ˈlearning disaˌbility *n.* [C] a mental problem that affects a child's ability to learn

lease¹ /lis/ *n.* **1** [C] a legal agreement that allows you to use a building, property, etc. when you pay rent: *a two-year **lease on** the apartment* | *We **signed** the **lease** in December.* **2 a new/fresh lease on life** the feeling of being healthy, active, or happy again after being sick or unhappy

lease² *v.* [T] to use or let someone use buildings, property, etc. when s/he pays rent: *The lofts have been **leased to** artists.*

leash /liʃ/ *n.* [C] a piece of rope, leather, etc. fastened to a dog's collar in order to control the dog: *All dogs in the park must be kept **on a leash**.*

least¹ /list/ *determiner, pron.* [the superlative of "little"] **1 at least a)** not less than a particular number or amount: *The thunderstorm lasted at least two hours.* **b)** used when mentioning an advantage to show that a situation is not as bad as

it seems: *Well, at least you got your money back.* **c)** said when you want to correct or change something you have just said: *His name is Jerry. At least, I think it is.* **d)** even if nothing else is said or done: *Will you at least say you're sorry?*
2 the least sb could do said when you think someone should do something to help someone else: *The least he could do is help you clean up.*
3 to say the least used in order to show that something is more serious than you are actually saying: *Their living arrangements are unusual, to say the least.* **4** the smallest number or amount [➡ **less**]: *Compared to the other cakes, this one has the least amount of calories.*

least² *adv.* **1** less than anything or anyone else: *It always happens when you least expect it.* | *I'm the least experienced person on the team.* **2 least of all** especially not: *I don't like any of them, least of all Debbie.*

leath·er /ˈlɛðɚ/ *n.* [U] animal skin that has been treated to preserve it, and is used for making shoes, etc. [➡ **suede**]: *a leather belt* ➔ see picture at MATERIAL¹

leath·er·y /ˈlɛðəri/ *adj.* hard and stiff like leather: *leathery skin*

leave¹ /liv/ *v.* past tense and past participle **left** /lɛft/, present participle **leaving**
1 GO AWAY [I,T] to go away from a place or person: *Jones quickly left the room.* | *I'm* ***leaving for*** (=going to) *Paris in an hour!* | *I feel a little lonely now the kids have all left home* (=are no longer living at home).
2 leave sb alone *spoken* used in order to tell someone to stop annoying or upsetting someone else: *Just stop asking questions and leave me alone.*
3 leave sth alone *spoken* used in order to tell someone to stop touching something: *Timmy! Leave that alone – you'll break it!*
4 STAY IN POSITION/STATE [T] to make or let something stay in a particular state, place, or position when you are not there: *We're going to leave the car at the airport.*
5 PUT STH IN A PLACE [T] to put something in a place for someone: *Just leave the map on the table.* | *Please* ***leave a message*** *and I'll get back to you.*
6 FORGET [T] to forget to take something with you when you leave a place: *I think I left my keys in the car.*
7 be left to remain after everything else has been taken away: *Is there any coffee left?*
8 NOT DO STH [T] to not do something until later: *Let's* ***leave*** *the dishes* ***for*** *the morning.*
9 HUSBAND/WIFE [I,T] to stop living with your husband or wife: *Tammy's husband left her last year.*
10 LET SB DECIDE [T] to let someone decide something or be responsible for something: ***Leave*** *the details* ***to*** *me; I'll arrange everything.*
11 GIVE AFTER DEATH [T] to give something to someone after you die: *She* ***left*** *a lot of money* ***to*** *her son.* ➔ see Thesaurus box at GIVE¹
12 leave it at that *spoken* to not say or do anything more about a situation: *He's not going – let's just leave it at that.*
13 leave a mark/stain etc. to make a mark, STAIN, etc. that remains afterward: *Make sure that you don't leave any footprints.*
14 leave a lot to be desired to be very unsatisfactory: *Though the play leaves a lot to be desired, the costumes are beautiful.*
15 from where sb left off from the place where you stopped: *Tomorrow we'll start the reading from where we left off.*

leave sb/sth **behind** *phr. v.* to forget to take something with you when you leave a place, or to not take something on purpose: *Did you leave your umbrella behind in the restaurant?*

leave sb/sth **out** *phr. v.* **1** to not include someone or something in a group, list, activity, etc.: *The stew will still taste okay if we leave out the wine.* **2 be/feel left out** to feel as if you are not accepted or welcome in a social group: *I always felt left out when my sister's friends were here.*

leave² *n.* **1** [U] time that you are allowed to spend away from your work because you are sick, have had a baby, etc.: *How much* ***sick leave*** *have you taken?*

THESAURUS
vacation, holiday, break
➔ see Thesaurus box at VACATION

2 leave of absence a period of time that you are allowed to spend away from work for a particular purpose

leaves /livz/ *n.* the plural of LEAF

lech·er·ous /ˈlɛtʃərəs/ *adj. disapproving* a lecherous man is always thinking about sex

lec·tern /ˈlɛktɚn/ *n.* [C] a high desk that you stand behind when you give a speech

lec·ture¹ /ˈlɛktʃɚ/ *n.* [C] **1** a long talk to a group of people about a particular subject: *She's* ***giving a lecture on*** *modern art.* **2** a long serious talk that criticizes someone or warns him/her about something: *My parents* ***gave*** *me another* ***lecture about*** *my school work.*

lecture² *v.* **1** [T] to talk angrily or seriously to someone in order to criticize or warn him/her: *I wish you'd stop* ***lecturing*** *me* ***about*** *smoking.* **2** [I] to teach a group of people about a particular subject, especially at a college

led /lɛd/ *v.* the past tense and past participle of LEAD

ledge /lɛdʒ/ *n.* [C] **1** a narrow flat surface like a shelf that sticks out from the side of a building: *a window ledge* **2** a narrow flat surface of rock that is parallel to the ground

ledg·er /ˈlɛdʒɚ/ *n.* [C] a book in which a bank, business, etc. records the money received and spent ➔ see Thesaurus box at RECORD¹

leech /litʃ/ *n.* [C] a small soft creature that attaches itself to an animal in order to drink its blood

leek /lik/ *n.* [C] a vegetable with long straight green leaves, that tastes like an onion

leer /lɪr/ *v.* [I] to look at someone in an unpleasant way that shows that you think s/he is sexually attractive —**leer** *n.* [C]

leer·y /ˈlɪri/ *adj.* worried and unable to trust someone or something: *The girl was **leery of** strangers.*

lee·way /ˈliweɪ/ *n.* [U] freedom to do things in the way you want to: *Students **have** some **leeway** in what they can write about.*

left[1] /lɛft/ *adj.* **1** your left side is the side of your body that contains your heart [≠ **right**]: *He broke his left leg.* **2** on the same side of something as your left side [≠ **right**]: *the first house on the left side of the street*

left[2] *adv.* toward the left side [≠ **right**]: ***Turn left** at the next street.*

left[3] *n.* [C] **1** the left side or direction [≠ **right**]: *It's the second door **on your/the left**.* **2 the left** in politics, the left are people who believe that the government has a duty to pay for social services and to limit the power of businesses [≠ **right**]

left[4] *v.* the past tense and past participle of LEAVE

ˈleft field *n.* **1 in/from left field** *informal* unusual or strange compared to the way that people usually behave: *Some of his ideas are **way out in left field*** (=very strange). **2** [singular] the area in baseball in the left side of the OUTFIELD

ˌleft-ˈhand *adj.* on the left side of something: *the top left-hand drawer*

ˌleft-ˈhanded *adj.* **1** someone who is left-handed uses his/her left hand to do most things **2** done with the left hand: *a left-handed throw* **3** made to be used with the left hand: *left-handed scissors* —**left-handed** *adv.*

left·o·vers /ˈlɛftˌoʊvɚz/ *n.* [plural] food that remains at the end of a meal and is kept to be eaten later

ˌleft-ˈwing *adj.* supporting the political aims of the LEFT: *a left-wing newspaper* —**left-wing** *n.* [singular] —**left-winger** *n.* [C]

leg /lɛg/ *n.*

1 BODY PART [C] one of the two long parts of your body that you use to stand or walk, or a similar part on an animal or insect: *How did you hurt **your leg**? | Mia was sitting with her legs crossed. | She fell and broke her **left/right leg**.*

2 FURNITURE [C] one of the upright parts that supports a piece of furniture: *a table leg*

3 PANTS [C] the part of your pants that covers your leg

4 FOOD [C,U] the leg of an animal eaten as food: *roast leg of lamb*

5 TRIP/RACE ETC. [C] a part of a long trip, race, process, etc. that is done one part at a time: *She started the last leg of the tour last week.*

6 -legged having a particular number or type of legs: *a three-legged cat*

7 leg room space in which to put your legs comfortably when you are sitting in a car, theater, etc.: *There wasn't enough leg room.*

8 not have a leg to stand on *informal* to be in a situation where you cannot prove or legally support what you say → **on its last legs** at LAST[1]

leg·a·cy /ˈlɛgəsi/ *n.* plural **legacies** [C] **1** a situation that exists as a result of things that happened at an earlier time: *Racial tension in the country is a **legacy of** slavery.* **2** money or property that you receive from someone after s/he dies

le·gal /ˈligəl/ *adj.* **1** allowed, ordered, or approved by law [≠ **illegal**]: *Is it legal to park here overnight? | a legal agreement* **2** relating to the law: *the legal system | If you don't pay soon, we'll be forced to **take legal action*** (=go to court). —**legally** *adv.*: *You can't legally buy alcohol until you're 21.* —**legality** /lɪˈgæləṭi/ *n.* [U]

le·gal·ize /ˈligəˌlaɪz/ *v.* [T] to make something legal that was not legal before: *a campaign to legalize marijuana* —**legalization** /ˌligələˈzeɪʃən/ *n.* [C]

leg·end /ˈlɛdʒənd/ *n.* **1** [C,U] an old well-known story, often about brave people or adventures, or all stories of this kind: ***the legend of** King Arthur*

> **THESAURUS**
> **story, tale, myth, fable**
> → see Thesaurus box at STORY

2 [C] someone who is famous and admired for being extremely good at doing something: *Elvis Presley, the rock and roll legend*

leg·end·ar·y /ˈlɛdʒənˌdɛri/ *adj.* **1** famous and admired: *the legendary baseball player Ty Cobb*

> **THESAURUS**
> **famous, well-known, infamous, notorious**
> → see Thesaurus box at FAMOUS

2 talked or read about in legends

leg·gings /ˈlɛgɪŋz/ *n.* [plural] women's pants that stretch to fit the shape of the body

leg·i·ble /ˈlɛdʒəbəl/ *adj.* written or printed clearly enough for you to read [≠ **illegible**]: *His writing was barely legible.* —**legibly** *adv.*

le·gion /ˈlidʒən/ *n.* [C] a large group of soldiers or people

leg·is·late /ˈlɛdʒəˌsleɪt/ *v.* [I] to make a law about something: *plans to **legislate against** abortion*

leg·is·la·tion /ˌlɛdʒəˈsleɪʃən/ *n.* [U] **1** a law or set of laws: *human rights legislation* **2** the act of making laws

leg·is·la·tive /ˈlɛdʒəˌsleɪṭɪv/ *adj.* relating to laws or to making laws: *legislative leaders | the legislative branch of government*

leg·is·la·tor /ˈlɛdʒəˌsleɪṭɚ/ *n.* [C] an elected government official who is involved in making laws

L

leg·is·la·ture /ˈlɛdʒəˌsleɪtʃɚ/ *n.* [C] an institution that has the power to make or change laws: *the Ohio state legislature*

leg·it /lɪˈdʒɪt/ *adj. spoken* LEGITIMATE

le·git·i·mate /ləˈdʒɪt̬əmɪt/ *adj.* **1** fair or reasonable: *She has a legitimate reason for being late.* **2** operating legally or according to the law: *legitimate business activities* —**legitimacy** *n.* [U]

lei·sure /ˈliʒɚ/ *n.* [U] **1** time when you are not working and can do things you enjoy: *I spend most of my* ***leisure time*** *reading.* **2 at sb's leisure** as slowly as you want, and when you want: *Read it at your leisure.*

lei·sure·ly /ˈliʒɚli/ *adj.* moving or done in a relaxed way: *a leisurely walk around the park*

lem·on /ˈlɛmən/ *n.* [C,U] a yellow fruit that has a sour-tasting juice ➔ see picture at FRUIT

lem·on·ade /ˌlɛməˈneɪd/ *n.* [U] a drink made with lemon juice, sugar, and water

lend /lɛnd/ *v.* past tense and past participle **lent** /lɛnt/ [T] **1** to let someone borrow money or something that belongs to you for a short time: *Could you lend me your bike?*

USAGE

If you **lend** something to someone, you give it to him/her so that s/he can use it for a short time: *I lent that DVD to Rick.* | *Could you lend me some money?* You cannot say "Could you borrow me some money?"
If you **borrow** something from someone, you take something that belongs to him/her for a short time, with his/her permission, and then give it back: *Can I borrow your dictionary?* You cannot say "Can I lend your dictionary?"

2 if a bank lends money, it lets someone borrow it if s/he pays it back with an additional amount of money: *This bank* ***lends*** *a lot of money* ***to*** *local businesses.* **3 lend (sb) a hand** to help someone do something, especially something that needs physical effort: *Lend me a hand with this box.* **4 sth lends itself to sth** used to say that something is appropriate for being used in a particular way: *Nature lends itself to drawing and painting.* **5** to give something a particular quality: *The balloons lend a festive air to the park.* —**lender** *n.* [C]

length /lɛŋkθ, lɛnθ/ *n.* **1** [C,U] the measurement of something from one end to the other [➡ **height**, **width**]: *The* ***length of*** *the room is five feet.* | *a pole about 7 feet* ***in length*** **2** [C,U] the amount of time that you spend doing something or that something continues for: *the* ***length of*** *your stay in the hospital* **3** [C,U] the amount of writing in a book, article, etc., or the amount of time that a movie, play, etc. continues for: *His new film is nearly twice the length of his last one.* **4 go to great lengths to do sth** to be willing to use many different methods to achieve something you want: *She went to great lengths to help us.* **5 at length** for a long time: *She spoke* ***at length*** *on the dangers of smoking.* **6** [C] a piece of something that is long and thin: *two* ***lengths of*** *rope*

length·en /ˈlɛŋkθən/ *v.* [I,T] to make something longer, or to become longer [≠ **shorten**]: *I need this dress lengthened.*

THESAURUS

prolong, extend, drag out
➔ see Thesaurus box at PROLONG

length·wise /ˈlɛŋkθwaɪz/ **also length·ways** /ˈlɛŋkθweɪz/ *adv.* in the direction or position of the longest side: *Fold the cloth lengthwise.*

length·y /ˈlɛŋkθi/ *adj.* continuing for a long time: *a lengthy interview*

le·ni·ent /ˈliniənt, ˈlinyənt/ *adj.* not strict in the way you punish someone or control his/her behavior: *She was too* ***lenient with*** *the children.* —**leniency** *n.* [U]

lens /lɛnz/ *n.* [C] **1** a piece of curved glass or plastic that makes things look bigger, smaller, or clearer: *glasses with thick lenses* **2** the clear part inside your eye that FOCUSes so you can see things clearly

Lent /lɛnt/ *n.* [U] the 40 days before Easter, when some Christians stop eating particular things or stop particular habits

lent *v.* the past tense and past participle of LEND

len·til /ˈlɛnt̬əl/ *n.* [C] a small round seed which has been dried and can be cooked

Le·o /ˈlioʊ/ *n.* **1** [U] the fifth sign of the ZODIAC, represented by a lion **2** [C] someone born between July 23 and August 22

leopard

leop·ard /ˈlɛpɚd/ *n.* [C] a large wild cat with yellow fur and black spots, from Africa and southern Asia

le·o·tard /ˈliəˌtɑrd/ *n.* [C] a tight-fitting piece of woman's clothing that covers the body from the neck to the top of the legs, worn especially while exercising

lep·er /ˈlɛpɚ/ *n.* [C] someone who has leprosy

lep·ro·sy /ˈlɛprəsi/ *n.* [U] a serious infectious disease in which someone's flesh is gradually destroyed —**leprous** /ˈlɛprəs/ *adj.*

les·bi·an /ˈlɛzbiən/ *n.* [C] a woman who is sexually attracted to other women [➡ **homosexual**, **gay**]

L

less /lɛs/ *quantifier, pron., adv.* [the comparative of "little"] **1** a smaller amount, or to a smaller degree [≠ **more**]: *The job involves much less stress than my last one.* | *I'm trying to exercise more and eat less.* | *Women generally earn* ***less*** *money* ***than*** *men.* | *She spends* ***less of*** *her time playing tennis now.* **2 less and less** gradually becoming smaller in amount or degree: *We seem to be spending less and less time together.* **3 no less than sth** used to emphasize that an amount or number is large: *I watched him eat no less than three pizzas.* **4 nothing less than sth** used to emphasize how serious or important something is: *Her death was nothing less than a tragedy.*

GRAMMAR

less, fewer

Use **less** before U nouns: *We've had less sunshine this year than last year.*

Use **fewer** before plural noun forms: *In those days there were fewer cars on the roads.*

less·en /ˈlɛsən/ *v.* [I,T] to become smaller in size, amount, importance, or value, or to make something do this [➡ **reduce**]: *A low-fat diet can lessen the risk of heart disease.*

THESAURUS

reduce, **lower**, **decrease**, **cut**, **slash**, **roll back**, **relieve**, **ease**, **alleviate**

➔ see Thesaurus box at REDUCE

less·er /ˈlɛsɚ/ *adj.* **1** *formal* not as large, as important, or as much as something else: *These wounds would have killed* ***a lesser man*** (=someone not as strong or brave). **2 the lesser of two evils** the less bad or harmful of two bad choices —**lesser** *adv.*: *a lesser-known artist*

les·son /ˈlɛsən/ *n.* [C] **1** a period of time in which someone is taught a particular subject or skill: *I* ***have*** *a guitar* ***lesson*** *today.* | *Hannah is* ***taking*** *cooking* ***lessons from*** *a professional chef.* **2** an experience, especially a bad one, that makes you more careful in the future: *Our town's experience with the fire should serve as a lesson to the entire state.* ➔ **learn your lesson** at LEARN ➔ **teach sb a lesson** at TEACH

let /lɛt/ *v.* past tense and past participle **let**, present participle **letting** **1** [T] to allow someone to do something, or allow something to happen: *I wanted to go but my mother wouldn't let me.* | *Ed lets me borrow his car whenever I want.* | *Don't pick up the phone – let the answering machine get it.* | *Let me finish this, then we can go.* **2 let go** to stop holding someone or something: *You can* ***let go of*** *my hand when we've crossed the street.* **3 let sb go a)** to allow a person or animal to leave a place where they have been kept: *The police let her go after two hours.* **b)** to dismiss someone from his/her job: *I'm afraid we have to let you go.* **4 let sb know** to tell someone something: *Could you* ***let*** *me* ***know when*** *you're done?* **5 let alone** used to say that because one thing does not happen, is not true, etc. another thing cannot possibly happen or be true: *I don't have $10, let alone $10,000!* **6 let sth go/pass** to decide not to react to something bad or annoying that someone has said or done: *I'll let it go this time, but don't be late again.* **7 let sb/sth be also let sb/sth alone** to stop annoying someone, asking questions, or trying to change things: *Your mother's had a hard day, so just let her be.*

SPOKEN PHRASES

8 let's is the short form of "let us," used when you want to suggest that someone or a group of people do something with you: *I'm hungry; let's eat.* | ***Let's not*** *talk about this right now.* **9 let's see a)** said when you are going to try to do something: ***Let's see if/whether*** *Andy's home.* **b)** said when you pause because you cannot remember or find something: *Now let's see, where did I put it?* **c)** said to ask someone to show you something: *"I got a new dress." "Really? Let's see."* **10 let's hope (that)** said when you hope something is true or will happen: *Let's hope she didn't hear what we were saying.* **11 let me do sth** said when you are offering to help someone: *Let me carry that for you.* **12 let me tell you** said to emphasize that a feeling you had was very strong: *It was a really great party, let me tell you.*

let sb ⇔ **down** *phr. v.* to make someone feel disappointed because you have behaved badly or have not done what you said you would do ➔ LETDOWN

let sb/sth ⇔ **in** *phr. v.* **1** to open the door of a room, building, etc. so that someone can come in: *She unlocked the door to let him in.* **2** to allow light, water, etc. to enter a place: *The door opened, letting in a gust of wind.* **3 let sb in on sth** to tell someone a secret: *I'll let you in on a little secret.*

let sb ⇔ **into** sth *phr. v.* to allow someone to come into a room or building: *Security guards refused to let reporters into the building.*

let sb ⇔ **off** *phr. v.* to not punish someone, or to not make him/her do something: *The police officer* ***let*** *us* ***off with*** *a warning.*

let on *phr. v.* to behave in a way that shows you know a secret: *Don't* ***let on (that)*** *you know!*

let out *phr. v.* **1 let** sb ⇔ **out** to allow someone to leave a building, room, etc.: *Let the dog out, please.* **2** if a school, college, movie, etc. lets out, it ends, and people can leave: *School lets out at 3:30.* **3 let** sth ⇔ **out** to allow light, air, etc. to leave a place: *Close the door – you're letting all the heat out.* **4 let out a scream/cry etc.** to make a sound, especially a loud one

let up *phr. v.* if rain or snow lets up, it stops or there is less of it ➔ LETUP

let·down /ˈlɛtdaʊn/ *n.* [singular] *informal* something that makes you feel disappointed because it

L

is not as good as you expected [= **disappointment**]: *Our hotel was a big letdown.*

le·thal /'liθəl/ *adj.* able to kill someone: *a lethal dose of heroin*

le·thar·gic /lə'θɑrdʒɪk/ *adj.* having no energy, so that you feel lazy or tired —**lethargy** /'lɛθɚdʒi/ *n.* [U]

let's /lɛts/ ➔ LET

let·ter /'lɛt̬ɚ/ *n.* [C] **1** a written message that you put into an envelope and send to someone by mail: *Ken **wrote a letter to** the local newspaper.* | *Can you **mail** this **letter** on your way to work?* **2** one of the signs in writing that represents a sound in speech: *There are 26 letters in the English alphabet.* **3 to the letter** exactly: *He followed their instructions to the letter.*

let·ter·head /'lɛt̬ɚˌhɛd/ *n.* **1** [U] paper that has the name and address of a person or business printed at the top of it **2** [C] the name and address of a person or business printed at the top of a piece of paper

let·tuce /'lɛt̬ɪs/ *n.* [C,U] a round green vegetable with large thin leaves, eaten raw in SALADS ➔ see picture at VEGETABLE

let·up /'lɛt̬ʌp/ *n.* [singular, U] a pause or a reduction in a difficult, dangerous, or tiring activity: *We drove 24 hours straight without letup* (=without stopping).

leu·ke·mia /lu'kimiə/ *n.* [U] a serious disease that affects the blood and that can cause death

lev·ee /'lɛvi/ *n.* [C] a special wall built to stop a river from flooding

lev·el[1] /'lɛvəl/ *n.* [C] **1** the amount or degree of something, as compared to another amount or degree: ***a high/low level of** risk* | *The temperature will stay **at** these **levels** until Friday.* **2** the height or position of something in relation to the ground or another thing: *Check the water level in the radiator.* | *Hang the picture **at eye level*** (=at the same height as your eyes). ➔ SEA LEVEL **3** a standard of skill or ability in a particular subject, sport, etc.: *Students are given an exam to determine their level.* | *Few athletes can compete **at** this **level**.* **4** a particular position in a system that has different ranks: *high-level talks* (=discussions between important people) **5** a floor in a building that has several floors: *Housewares is on Level 3.* **6** a tool used for checking if a surface is flat

level[2] *adj.* **1** flat and not sloping, with no surface higher than the rest: *The floor isn't level.*

THESAURUS

flat, **smooth**, **even**, **horizontal**
➔ see Thesaurus box at FLAT[1]

2 at the same height or position as something else: *My head was **level with** his chin.*

level[3] *v.* [T] **1** to knock down or completely destroy a building or area: *An earthquake leveled several buildings in the city.* **2 level a charge/accusation/criticism etc.** to publicly criticize someone or say s/he is responsible for a crime, mistake, etc.: *Dunn **leveled** one criticism after another **at** the university.* **3** to make a surface flat and smooth: *Level the ground before laying the turf.*

level off/out *phr. v.* to stop going up or down, and continue at the same height or amount: *The plane climbed to 20,000 feet, then leveled off.* | *Oil prices have **leveled off at** $25 a barrel.*

level with sb *phr. v. informal* to speak honestly with someone and tell him/her what you really think

ˌlevel-'headed *adj.* calm and sensible in making judgments or decisions

lev·er /'lɛvɚ, 'li-/ *n.* [C] **1** a stick or handle attached to a machine that you move to make the machine work **2** a long thin piece of metal, wood, etc. that you put under a heavy object in order to lift it —**lever** *v.* [T]

lev·er·age /'lɛvərɪdʒ, 'li-/ *n.* [U] influence that you can use to make people do what you want: *Small businesses have less leverage in dealing with banks.*

lev·i·tate /'lɛvəˌteɪt/ *v.* [I] to rise and float in the air as if by magic —**levitation** /ˌlɛvə'teɪʃən/ *n.* [U]

lev·i·ty /'lɛvət̬i/ *n.* [U] *formal* the quality of telling jokes and having fun instead of being serious

lev·y[1] /'lɛvi/ *v.* past tense and past participle **levied**, third person singular **levies**, **levy a tax/charge etc.** to officially make someone pay a tax, etc.

levy[2] *n.* plural **levies** [C] an additional sum of money, usually paid as a tax

lewd /lud/ *adj.* using rude words or movements that make someone think of sex: *lewd jokes*

lex·i·cal /'lɛksɪkəl/ *adj.* relating to words

lex·i·con /'lɛksɪˌkɑn/ *n.* [C] **1** all the words used in a language or by people in a particular group, profession, etc. **2** a book containing lists of words and their meanings

li·a·bil·i·ty /ˌlaɪə'bɪlət̬i/ *n.* **1** [U] legal responsibility for something, especially for paying money that is owed, or for damage or injury: *The company has admitted **liability for** the accident.* **2** [singular] someone or something that is likely to cause problems for someone: *He became a **liability to** the team.*

li·a·ble /'laɪəbəl/ *adj.* **1 be liable to do sth** to be likely to do something, behave in a particular way, or be treated in a particular way: *Wayne and I are liable to start arguing if we discuss politics.* **2** legally responsible for the cost of something: *The university was not **held liable for** the damage done by its students.*

li·aise /li'eɪz/ *v.* [I] to work with other people and share information with them

li·ai·son /li'eɪˌzɑn/ *n.* **1** [C] someone who talks to different people, departments, groups, etc. and tells each of them about what the others are doing: *He's the **liaison between** the ruler and the local people.* **2** [C] a secret sexual relationship **3** [sin-

L

gular, U] a working relationship between two groups, companies, etc.

li·ar /ˈlaɪɚ/ *n.* [C] someone who tells lies

li·bel /ˈlaɪbəl/ *n.* [C,U] the act of writing or printing untrue statements about someone, so that other people are likely to have a bad opinion of him/her: *He is suing the magazine **for libel**.* —**libel** *v.* [T]

THESAURUS

lie, **slander**, **fib**, **white lie**
➔ see Thesaurus box at LIE[3]

lib·eral[1] /ˈlɪbrəl, -bərəl/ *adj.* **1** willing to understand or respect the different behavior, ideas, etc. of other people [≠ **conservative**]: *a liberal attitude toward sex* **2** supporting political ideas that include more involvement by the government in business and in people's lives, and willing to respect the different behaviors of other people in their private lives [≠ **conservative**]: *the liberal wing of the Democratic party* **3** supporting changes in political, social, or religious systems that allow people more freedom to do what they want: *a **liberal democracy*** **4** *formal* given in large amounts: *a liberal donation*

liberal[2] *n.* [C] someone with liberal opinions or principles [≠ **conservative**]

ˌliberal ˈarts *n.* [plural] subjects that develop someone's general knowledge and ability to think, rather than technical skills

lib·eral·is·m /ˈlɪbrəˌlɪzəm/ *n.* [U] liberal opinions and principles, especially on social and political subjects [➡ **conservatism**]

lib·eral·ize /ˈlɪbrəˌlaɪz/ *v.* [T] to make a system, laws, or moral attitudes less strict

lib·eral·ly /ˈlɪbrəli/ *adv.* in large amounts

lib·er·ate /ˈlɪbəˌreɪt/ *v.* [T] **1** to free someone from feelings or situations that make his/her life difficult: *These gadgets **liberated** housewives **from** many hard chores.* **2** to free prisoners, a city, a country, etc. from someone's control: *The city was liberated by the Allies in 1944.* —**liberator** *n.* [C] —**liberation** /ˌlɪbəˈreɪʃən/ *n.* [U] *the liberation of Eastern Europe*

lib·er·at·ed /ˈlɪbəˌreɪt̬ɪd/ *adj.* free to do the things you want, and not controlled by rules or other people

lib·er·ty /ˈlɪbɚt̬i/ *n.* plural **liberties** **1** [U] the freedom to do what you want without having to ask permission from people in authority: *principles of liberty and democracy* **2** [C usually plural] a particular legal right: *civil liberties* **3 be at liberty to do sth** to have the right or permission to do something: *I'm not at liberty to say where he is at the moment.* **4 take the liberty of doing sth** to do something without asking permission because you do not think it will upset or offend anyone: *I took the liberty of inviting Jeff along.*

li·bi·do /lɪˈbidoʊ/ *n.* [C,U] *technical* someone's desire to have sex

Li·bra /ˈlibrə/ *n.* **1** [U] the seventh sign of the ZODIAC, represented by a SCALE **2** [C] someone born between September 23 and October 23

li·brar·i·an /laɪˈbrɛriən/ *n.* [C] someone who works in a library

li·brar·y /ˈlaɪˌbrɛri/ *n.* plural **libraries** [C] a room or building containing books that you can borrow or read there

lice /laɪs/ *n.* the plural of LOUSE

li·cense[1] /ˈlaɪsəns/ *n.* **1** [C] an official document that gives you permission to own something or do something: *a driver's license* | *He was charged with possessing firearms **without a license**.* **2** [U] *formal* freedom to do or say whatever you want: *He thinks because he's famous he has **license to** be rude.*

license[2] *v.* [T] to give official permission for someone to own or do something: *Williams is not **licensed to** practice law in New York.*

ˈlicense plate *n.* [C] one of the signs with numbers and letters on it at the front and back of your car ➔ see picture on page A12

lick[1] /lɪk/ *v.* [T] **1** to move your tongue across the surface of something in order to taste it, clean it, etc.: *Judy's dog jumped up to lick her face.* **2** *informal* to defeat an opponent or solve a problem: *"It looks like we have the fire licked," said Chief Grafton.*

lick[2] *n.* [C usually singular] an act of licking something: *Can I have a lick of your ice cream cone?*

lick·ing /ˈlɪkɪŋ/ *n.* [singular] *informal* **1** a severe beating as a punishment **2** a heavy defeat in a sports competition

lic·o·rice /ˈlɪkərɪʃ/ *n.* [U] a type of strong-tasting black or red candy

lid /lɪd/ *n.* [C] **1** a cover for a pot, box, or other container: *He carefully lifted the **lid of** the box.*

THESAURUS

cover, **top**, **wrapper**, **wrapping**
➔ see Thesaurus box at COVER[2]

2 keep a lid on sth *informal* to control a situation so that it does not become worse: *Police try to keep a lid on crime in the area.* **3** ➔ EYELID

L

lie[1] /laɪ/ *v.* past tense **lay** /leɪ/ past participle **lain** /leɪn/ present participle **lying** [I] **1 a)** to be in a position in which your body is flat on the floor, a bed, etc.: *We **lay on** the beach all day.* | *I **lay awake** worrying.* **b) also lie down** to put yourself in this position: *I'm going upstairs to lie down.*

USAGE

Lay means to put something down in a flat position: *She laid the newspaper down and picked up the phone.*
Lie has two different meanings:
– to be or move into in a flat position on the floor, a bed, etc.: *She was lying on the sofa.* The

past tense for this meaning of lie is **lay**: *He lay on the bed.*
– to say something that is not true: *Why did you lie to me?* The past tense for this meaning of lie is **lied**: *The police think that he lied.*

2 to be in a particular place or position: *The town **lies to** the east of the lake.* | *The ship had **lain on** the ocean floor for decades.* **3** used to say where something such as a reason or answer can be found: *Mitchell's charm **lies in** his sense of humor.* **4** to be or remain in a particular condition or position: *The city **lay in ruins**.* | *The letters lay hidden in her attic for forty years.* **5 lie low** to remain hidden when someone is trying to find you: *Weaver decided to lie low at his sister's house.* **6 lie ahead** if something lies ahead, it is going to happen in the future: *There are difficulties that lie ahead.* → **not take sth lying down** at TAKE[1]

lie around *phr. v.* **1** to be left out of the correct place, so that things look messy: *Books and papers were lying around everywhere.* **2** to spend time being lazy, not doing anything useful: *We lay around the house all afternoon, watching TV.*

lie behind sth *phr. v.* to be the true reason for an action, decision, etc.: *I wonder what really lay behind her decision to quit her job.*

lie[2] *v.* past tense and past participle **lied** /laɪd/ present participle **lying** [I] to deliberately tell someone something that is not true: *She's **lying about** her age.* | *Don't **lie to** me!*

THESAURUS

make sth up – to invent a story, explanation, etc. in order to deceive someone: *"What'll you tell your mother?" "I'll make something up."*
invent – to think of an idea, story, etc. that is not true: *If I can't find a reason, I'll invent one.*
mislead – to make someone believe something that is not true by giving him/her false or incomplete information: *The ads were accused of misleading consumers.*
deceive – to make someone believe something that is not true: *Both sides sent false code messages to deceive the enemy.*
perjure – to tell a lie in a court of law: *Company executives may have perjured themselves in sworn testimony to Congress.*

L

lie[3] *n.* [C] something that you say or write that you know is not true: *I've never known him to **tell lies**.*

THESAURUS

fib informal – a small unimportant lie
white lie – a small lie that you tell someone, usually to avoid hurting his/her feelings
slander law – something untrue that is said about someone which could harm the opinion people have of him/her
libel law – something untrue that is written about someone which could harm the opinion people have of him/her

'lie de,tector *n.* [C] a machine used by the police to find out if someone is lying

lieu /lu/ *n. formal* **in lieu of sth** instead of something else

lieu·ten·ant /lu'tɛnənt/ *n.* [C] **a)** a fairly low rank in the Army, Navy, Air Force, or Marines, or an officer who has this rank **b)** a fairly high rank in the police force, or an officer who has this rank

life /laɪf/ *n.* plural **lives** /laɪvz/
1 PERIOD OF LIFE [C,U] the period of time between someone's birth and death: *Charles lived in New York City **all his life**.* | *It was the happiest day **of my life**.* | *She **spent her life** helping others.* | *I've never felt better **in my life**.*
2 BEING ALIVE [C,U] the state of being alive: *Surgery could **save** her **life**.* | *Firemen **risked their lives*** (=did something during which they could have been killed) *to save him.* | *Tragically, she **took her own life*** (=killed herself).
3 WAY OF LIVING [C,U] all the experiences and activities that are typical of a particular way of living: *How's life in Japan?* | *He's spent most of his **working life*** (=time spent working) *with one company.* | ***Married life** has been an adjustment.* | *Violence is a **way of life** for many teenagers.* | ***This is the life**, Joan* (=what we are doing is the most enjoyable way to live)*!*
4 EXPERIENCES [C] the type of experience that someone has during his/her life: *Tia had a full and happy life.* | *She wanted to save her son from **a life of** crime.* | *Then he started telling me his **life story*** (=all the things that happened in his life).
5 LIVING THINGS [U] living things such as people, animals, or plants: *Do you think there is life on other planets?*
6 private/sex/social etc. life activities in your life that are private, relate to sex, are done with friends, etc.: *I don't have much time for a social life.*
7 MOVEMENT [U] activity or movement: *We looked around for any **signs of life**.* | *Katie was young and **full of life*** (=very cheerful and active).
8 EXISTENCE [U] human existence, and all the things that can happen during someone's life: *Life can be hard sometimes.*
9 PRISON [U] **also life in prison** a LIFE SENTENCE: *The defendants were **sentenced to life**.*
10 real life what really happens rather than what only happens in stories or someone's imagination: *Things like that don't happen **in real life**.*
11 quality of life the level or quality of health, success, and comfort in someone's life: *Crime affects everyone's quality of life.*
12 WORKING/EXISTING [singular] the period of time during which something exists or continues to happen: *long-life batteries*
13 bring sb/sth to life **a)** to make someone or something live: *Doctors fought to bring the baby back to life.* **b)** to make something more exciting or interesting: *The movie really brings 19th century New York to life.*

SPOKEN PHRASES

14 that's life said when something bad has happened that you must accept
15 life is too short said when telling someone that something is not important enough to worry about: *Life is too short to hold grudges.*
16 Get a life! used to tell someone you think s/he is boring
17 Not on your life! used to say that you will definitely not do something
18 for the life of me said when you cannot do something, even when you try very hard: *I can't remember her name for the life of me!*

life·boat /ˈlaɪfboʊt/ *n.* [C] a small boat that is used for helping people who are in danger on the ocean

ˌlife exˈpectancy *n.* plural **life expectancies** [C] the length of time that a person or animal is expected to live

life·guard /ˈlaɪfgɑrd/ *n.* [C] someone whose job is to help swimmers who are in danger at the beach or a pool

ˈlife inˌsurance *n.* [U] a type of insurance that someone buys so that when s/he dies, his/her family will receive money

ˈlife ˌjacket *n.* [C] a piece of equipment that you wear around your chest to prevent you from sinking in the water

life·less /ˈlaɪflɪs/ *adj.* **1** lacking excitement, activity, or interest: *a lifeless party* **2** *literary* dead or seeming to be dead: *a lifeless body* ➔ see Thesaurus box at DEAD[1]

life·like /ˈlaɪflaɪk/ *adj.* very much like a real person or thing: *a lifelike statue*

life·line /ˈlaɪflaɪn/ *n.* [C] something that someone depends on completely: *The phone is my lifeline.*

life·long /ˈlaɪflɔŋ/ *adj.* continuing all through your life: ***lifelong friends***

life·sav·er /ˈlaɪfˌseɪvɚ/ *n.* [C] someone or something that helps you avoid a difficult or bad situation

ˌlife ˈsentence *n.* [C] the punishment of sending someone to prison for the rest of his/her life

ˈlife-size also **ˈlife-sized** *adj.* a life-size model, picture, etc. is the same size as the person or object it represents

life·style /ˈlaɪfstaɪl/ *n.* [C] the way someone lives, including his/her work and activities, and what things s/he owns: *an active, healthy lifestyle*

ˈlife supˌport *n.* [U] machines or methods that keep someone alive who is extremely sick

ˈlife-ˌthreatening *adj.* a life-threatening illness, injury, or situation could cause a person to die

life·time /ˈlaɪftaɪm/ *n.* [C] the period of time during which someone is alive: ***During** her **lifetime**, she had witnessed two world wars.*

ˈlife vest *n.* [C] a LIFE JACKET

lift[1] /lɪft/ *v.* **1** [T] to take something in your hands and raise it, move it, or carry it somewhere: *Can you help me lift this box?* ➔ see picture on page A9 **2** [I,T] **also lift up** to move something up into the air, or to move up into the air: *Lift up your feet so I can sweep the floor.* **3** [T] to remove a rule or a law that says that something is not allowed: *a promise to **lift the ban** on homosexuals in the military* **4** [I] if clouds or FOG lift, it begins to get sunny **5** [T] *informal* to steal something, or to copy the words, ideas, music, etc. that someone else has written: *Parts of her essay were lifted directly from an encyclopedia.*

lift[2] *n.* [C] **1** if you give someone a lift, you take him/her somewhere in your car [= **ride**]: *Can you **give** me **a lift** to the nearest gas station?* **2 give sb/sth a lift** to make someone feel happier, or to make something more successful: *The end of the war is expected to give the economy a lift.* **3** a movement in which something is lifted or raised

ˈlift-off *n.* [C,U] the moment when a vehicle that is about to travel in space leaves the ground [➥ **take-off**]

lig·a·ment /ˈlɪgəmənt/ *n.* [C] a band of strong material in your body that joins your bones together

light[1] /laɪt/ *n.*
1 LIGHT TO SEE [U] the energy from the sun, a lamp, etc. that allows you to see things: *Light was streaming in through the window.* | ***The light** is better over here.*
2 ELECTRIC LIGHT [C] something such as a lamp that uses electricity: *Can you **turn/switch the lights on/off** for me?*
3 TRAFFIC [C] one of a set of red, green, and yellow lights used for controlling traffic: *Turn left at the light.* | *He was fined for **running a** red **light*** (=driving past a red light).
4 ON A VEHICLE [C] one of the lights on a car, bicycle, etc., especially the HEADLIGHTS
5 a light a match or lighter that you use to light a cigarette: *Excuse me, do you **have a light**?*
6 come to light/be brought to light if new information comes to light, it becomes known: *New evidence has come to light since the trial.*
7 in light of sth because of something: *The highway has been closed in light of heavy snow.*
8 in a new/different/bad etc. light if someone or something is seen or shown in a new, different, etc. light, people begin to have a different opinion

of him/her or it: *A recent biography shows the actor in a new light.*
9 shed/throw/cast light on sth to provide new information about something so it is easier to understand: *This sheds some light on the cause of the disease.*
10 light at the end of the tunnel something that gives you hope that a bad situation will end soon
11 see the light to suddenly realize and understand something: *We're hoping that one of these days he'll see the light and quit drinking.*

light[2] *adj.*
1 COLOR a light color is pale and not dark [≠ **dark**]: *a light blue dress*

THESAURUS

pale – a pale color has more white in it than usual: *a dress made of pale yellow silk*
pastel – having a soft light color: *She was knitting a baby blanket in pastel blue yarn.*
faded – having lost color, for example by being washed many times or by being left out in the sun: *a pair of faded jeans*

2 WEIGHT not weighing very much [≠ **heavy**]: *My new cell phone is lighter than my old one.*
3 CLOTHES light clothes are thin and not very warm: *a light sweater*
4 ROOM if a room or building is light, a lot of light from the sun gets into it: *The house was light and airy.*
5 TOUCH very gentle and soft: *She gave him a light kiss on the cheek.*
6 FOOD a) having less fat or fewer CALORIES than usual: *light cream cheese* **b)** not having a strong taste: *a light wine*
7 NOT SERIOUS not serious in meaning or style: *light reading*
8 WIND blowing without much force [➡ **strong**]: *a light breeze*
9 it is/gets light used to say that there is enough natural light outside to see by: *It was still light when we got home.*
10 SMALL AMOUNT small in amount, or less than you expected: *Traffic was lighter than usual today.*
11 make light of sth to joke about something or to treat it as if it were not important

light[3] *v.* past tense and past participle **lit** /lɪt/ or **lighted 1** [I,T] to start burning, or to make something do this: *Derek stopped to light a cigarette.* **2** [T] to give light to something: *The room is lit by candles.* | *a **brightly/poorly/well lit** room*

light up *phr. v.* **1** to become bright or to make something bright: *Fireworks lit up the night sky.* **2** if your face or eyes light up, you show that you are pleased or excited: *Paula's eyes lit up when she saw all of her presents.* **3** *informal* to light a cigarette

light[4] *adv.* **travel light** to travel without carrying too many clothes, etc.

'light bulb *n.* [C] the glass object in a lamp that produces light

light·en /'laɪt˺n/ *v.* **1** [T] to reduce the amount of work, worry, debt, etc. that someone has: *Hiring extra men will **lighten the load**.* **2** [I,T] to become brighter, or make something become brighter [≠ **darken**]: *At 5 a.m. the sky started to lighten.* **3 lighten up!** *spoken* used in order to tell someone not to be so serious about something: *Hey, lighten up, it was just a joke!* **4** [I,T] to reduce the weight of something or become less heavy

light·er /'laɪt̬ɚ/ *n.* [C] a small object that produces a flame to light cigarettes, CIGARS, etc.

,light-'headed *adj.* not able to think clearly or move steadily because you are sick or have drunk too much alcohol [= **dizzy**]

,light-'hearted *adj.* **1** not intended to be serious: *a light-hearted comedy* **2** cheerful and happy

lighthouse

light·house /'laɪthaʊs/ *n.* [C] a tower with a bright light that guides ships away from danger near the shore

light·ing /'laɪt̬ɪŋ/ *n.* [U] the lights in a room, building, etc., or the quality of the light: *soft/bright/dim lighting*

light·ly /'laɪtli/ *adv.* **1** with only a small amount of weight or force: *I tapped her lightly on the shoulder.* **2** using or having only a small amount of something: *Sprinkle sugar lightly over the cake.* **3 take sth lightly** to do something without serious thought: *A bomb threat is not to be taken lightly.*

lightning

light·ning[1] /'laɪt˺nɪŋ/ *n.* [U] a bright flash of light in the sky that happens during a storm: *The tree was **struck** (=hit) **by lightning**.*

lightning[2] *adj.* extremely fast or sudden: *a lightning attack*

light·weight[1] /'laɪt˺weɪt/ *adj.* **1** weighing less than average: *a lightweight computer* **2** showing a lack of serious thought: *a lightweight novel*

lightweight[2] *n.* [C] *disapproving* **1** someone who you do not think has the ability to think about serious or difficult subjects **2** someone who has no importance or influence: *a political lightweight*

'light year *n.* [C] the distance that light travels in one year

L

lik·a·ble /ˈlaɪkəbəl/ *adj.* likable people are nice, and are easy to like

like¹ /laɪk/ *prep.* **1** similar in some way to something else: *You two are behaving **just like** children.* | *I'd love a car like yours.* | *Ken **looks like** his brother.* | *It **tastes like** chicken.* | *Was the movie **anything like** the book* (=was it similar in any way)? | ***There's nothing like*** (=there is nothing better than) *a day at the beach.* **2** typical of a particular person: *It's not **like** Dad **to** be late* (=it is unusual that Dad is late). **3** *nonstandard* used to give an example of something [**= such as**]: *Foods like spinach and broccoli are high in iron.* **4 what is sb/sth like?** used when asking someone to describe or give his/her opinion on a person or thing: *What's the new house like?*

SPOKEN PHRASES

5 like this/so said when showing someone how to do something or how something is done: *He was leaning against the wall, like this.* **6 more like** said when giving a number that you think is more correct than the one already mentioned: *"He's been in there for 15 minutes." "More like half an hour!"*

GRAMMAR

like, such as

Many teachers think that using **like** to give an example is wrong. It is better to use **such as**: *Games such as chess take a long time to learn.*

like² *v.* [T] **1** to enjoy something, or think that someone or something is nice or good [**≠ dislike**]: *Do you like Mexican food?* | *I like Billy a lot.* | *He **really likes** camping.* | *Pam doesn't **like to** walk home late at night.* | *Mom doesn't **like it** when we argue.*

THESAURUS

enjoy, love, have a good/great time, have fun
➔ see Thesaurus box at ENJOY

2 to prefer that something is done in one particular way or at one particular time rather than another: *Jim **likes to** get to the airport early.* | *How do you like your hamburger cooked?*

SPOKEN PHRASES

3 I/she etc. would like used to say politely what someone wants: *I'd like a large pizza with mushrooms.* | *He'd **like to** know how much it will cost.* | *We would like you to be there if you can.* **4 Would you like ...?** used to ask someone if s/he wants something: *Would you like some more coffee?* **5 How do you like sth?** used to ask someone for his/her opinion of something: *"How did you like the movie?" "It was okay."* **6 (whether you) like it or not** used to emphasize that something bad is true or will happen and cannot be changed: *They expect us to work together, whether we like it or not.*

GRAMMAR

Do not say "I am liking it" or "I am liking to do it." Say *"I like it"* or *"I like to do it."*
Do not say "I am liking very much Anna." Say *"I like Anna very much."*

like³ *adv. spoken nonstandard* **1 I'm like/he's like/Bob's like etc. a)** used in order to tell someone the exact words someone used: *He asked if he could use my car and I was like, no way.* **b)** said when describing an event, feeling, or person, when it is difficult to describe or when you use a noise instead of a word: *He was like, huh* (=he was really surprised)? | *We were like, oh no* (=we realized something was wrong)! **2** said when you pause because you do not know what to say, you are embarrassed, etc.: *Would it be OK if I, like, called you up sometime?* **3** said in order to give an example: *My neighbor's driving me crazy. Like last night I had to tell him to turn his radio down.* **4** said when what you are saying is not exact: *It was like 9 o'clock and she still wasn't home.* **5** said in order to emphasize something: *That's like so stupid.*

like⁴ *conjunction nonstandard* **1** as if: *He acts like he owns the place.* **2 like I said/told you/was saying** said when you are repeating something you have already said: *Like I said, we'll be there around ten.* **3** in the same way as: *I don't want you to turn out like your father.*

like⁵ *adj.* **1** *formal* similar in some way: *a chance to meet people **of like minds*** (=who think in a similar way)

THESAURUS

similar, alike, akin to, identical, matching
➔ see Thesaurus box at SIMILAR

2 -like typical of, or similar to something: *moving with cat-like grace*

like⁶ *n.* **sb's likes and dislikes** all the things you like and do not like

like·li·hood /ˈlaɪkliˌhʊd/ *n.* [singular, U] **1** how likely something is to happen: ***The likelihood of** an agreement being reached is high.* **2 in all likelihood** almost definitely

like·ly /ˈlaɪkli/ *adj.* something that is likely will probably happen or is probably true: *It's **likely to** rain tomorrow.* | *Young drivers are **more likely** to have accidents than older drivers.* —**likely** *adv.*: *I'd **very likely** have done the same thing.*

ˌlike-ˈminded *adj.* having similar interests and opinions

lik·en /ˈlaɪkən/ *v.*
liken sb/sth **to** sb/sth *phr. v. formal* to say that someone or something is similar to someone or something else: *She likened the new hospital to a five-star hotel.*

like·ness /ˈlaɪknɪs/ *n.* **1** [U] the quality of being similar in appearance to someone or something else: *a strong **likeness to** his father* **2** [C] the

L

image of someone in a painting or photograph: *It's a good **likeness of** Eva.*

like·wise /'laɪk-waɪz/ *adv.* **1** *formal* in the same way: *I brought a hat. You should **do likewise**.* **2** *spoken* said in order to return someone's greeting or polite remark: *"It's great to see you." "Likewise."*

lik·ing /'laɪkɪŋ/ *n.* [C] **1 liking for sb/sth** the feeling when you like someone or something: *He always **had a liking for** whiskey.* **2 take a liking to sb** *informal* to begin to like someone or something

li·lac /'laɪlək, -læk/ *n.* **1** [C] a small tree with pale purple or white flowers **2** [U] a pale purple color —**lilac** *adj.*

lilt /lɪlt/ *n.* [singular] the pleasant rise and fall in the sound of someone's voice or a piece of music

lil·y /'lɪli/ *n.* plural **lilies** [C] a plant with large, usually bell-shaped white flowers

li·ma bean /'laɪmə ˌbin/ *n.* [C] a pale green flat bean

limb /lɪm/ *n.* [C] **1** a large branch of a tree **2 be/go out on a limb** to do something risky without any help or support **3** an arm or leg

lim·bo /'lɪmboʊ/ *n.* **be in limbo** to be in an uncertain situation in which it is difficult to know what to do: *I'm in limbo until I know which college I'm going to.*

lime /laɪm/ *n.* **1** [C] a bright green fruit with a sour taste, or the tree this grows on ➔ see picture at FRUIT **2** [U] a white powdery substance used in making CEMENT

lime·light /'laɪmlaɪt/ *n.* **the limelight** the attention someone gets from newspapers and television

lim·er·ick /'lɪmərɪk/ *n.* [C] a humorous short poem with five lines

lim·it¹ /'lɪmɪt/ *n.* [C] **1** the greatest or least amount, number, etc. that is allowed or is possible: *a 65 mph **speed limit** | There is a **limit on/to** the time you have to complete the test. | **There's no limit to** her potential. | **Set a limit** before you go shopping. | Our finances are **stretched to the limit*** (=we do not have any more money to spend). **2** the furthest point or edge of a place, often one that must not be passed: *Los Angeles **city limits*** **3 off limits** beyond the area where someone is allowed to go: *The beach is off limits after dark.* **4 within limits** within the time, level, amount, etc. considered acceptable: *Employees can dress how they like – within limits.*

limit² *v.* [T] **1** to stop an amount or number from increasing beyond a particular point: *Class size is **limited to** 30.* **2** to allow someone to use only a particular amount of something: *Try to **limit** yourself **to** a glass of wine per night.* **3** to exist or happen only in a particular place or group: *The damage **was limited to** the roof.* —**limiting** *adj.*

lim·i·ta·tion /ˌlɪmə'teɪʃən/ *n.* **1** [C,U] the act or process of controlling or reducing something: *a nuclear limitation treaty | new **limitations on** parking* **2 limitations** [plural] things that limit how good something can be: *Computers **have** their **limitations**.*

lim·it·ed /'lɪmɪṭɪd/ *adj.* not very great in amount, number, degree, etc.: *The organization has very **limited resources**. | There are only a **limited number** of tickets available.*

lim·o /'lɪmoʊ/ *n. informal* [C] a LIMOUSINE

lim·ou·sine /'lɪməˌzin, ˌlɪmə'zin/ *n.* [C] a big expensive car, driven by someone who is paid to drive

limp¹ /lɪmp/ *adj.* not strong or firm: *The dog's body **went limp** as the drug took effect.*

limp² *v.* [I] to walk with difficulty because one leg is hurt ➔ see Thesaurus box at WALK¹

limp³ *n.* [C] the way someone walks when s/he is limping: *After my surgery, I **walked with a limp**.*

linch·pin /'lɪntʃˌpɪn/ *n.* **the linchpin of sth** the most important person or thing in a group, system, etc. on which everything depends: *My mother is the linchpin of the family.*

line¹ /laɪn/ *n.* [C]

1 LONG THIN MARK [C] a long, thin, usually continuous mark on a surface: *She **drew a line** on the map to show him how to get to the museum.* ➔ DOTTED LINE

THESAURUS

stripe – a long narrow line of color: *a tie with thin blue and white stripes*
streak – a colored line or thin mark, especially one that is not straight or has been made accidentally: *a streak of orange paint across the canvas*
band – a narrow area of color that is different from the areas around it: *The fish has a black band on its fin.*

2 LIMIT/END [C] a long thin mark used to show a limit or end of something: *You're supposed to park between the white lines. | crossing the **finish line*** ➔ FINISH LINE

3 PEOPLE/THINGS [C] a row of people or things: *a **line of** cars | We **stood/waited in line** for more than two hours.*

4 DIRECTION [C] the direction something travels, or the imaginary path between two points in space: *Light travels **in a straight line**.*

5 COMPUTER on line using a computer that is connected to the Internet or a computer system to get information or communicate with other people: *You can pay on line.* ➔ ONLINE

6 LAND [C] an imaginary line on the surface of the earth, for example one showing where one state or area of land stops and another begins: *I didn't stop driving until I crossed the **state line**.*

7 line of action/thought/reasoning etc. a way or method of doing something or thinking about something: *That line of thinking will get you into trouble.*

8 WAY OF DOING STH [C] a way of thinking about or doing something: *This meeting will be*

L

organized ***along the*** *same* ***lines*** (=in the same way) *as the last one.*
9 be out of line *informal* to say or do something that is not acceptable in a particular situation: *I thought what Kenny said was way out of line.*
10 be in line with sth if one thing is in line with another, they are similar to each other, or they operate in a similar way: *The company's actions are in line with state laws.*
11 ON SB'S FACE [C] a line on the skin of someone's face [= **wrinkle**]: *There were* ***fine lines*** *around her eyes.*
12 PLAY/POEM ETC. [C] **a)** a line of words in a poem, film, song, etc. **b)** the words of a play or performance that an actor learns: *He has trouble remembering his lines.*
13 PHONE [C] a telephone wire or connection [➡ **telephone, phone**]: *We were* ***on the line*** (=on the phone) *for almost two hours.* | *You'll have to try again later –* ***the line's busy*** (=someone is already using it). ➔ see Topic box at TELEPHONE[1]
14 RAILROAD [C] a track that a train travels along: *a* ***railroad line***
15 WAR [C] a row of military defenses in front of the area that an army controls during a war: *a raid inside* ***enemy lines***
16 be (first/second/next etc.) in line for sth to be very likely to be the first, next, etc. person to get something: *Carl is next in line for a raise.*
17 PRODUCTS [C] a type of goods for sale in a store: *a new* ***line of*** *computers*
18 COMPANY [C] a company that provides a system for moving goods by road, water, or air: *a large shipping line*
19 SHAPE [C usually plural] the outer shape of something long or tall: *the car's smooth, elegant lines*
20 the line a CLOTHESLINE
21 FAMILY [singular] the people that came or existed before you in your family: *She comes* ***from a long line of*** *politicians.*
22 SPORTS [C] a row of players with a particular purpose in a sport such as football: *the Bears' defensive line*
23 FISHING [C] a strong thin string, used to catch fish ➔ **draw the line (at sth)** at DRAW[1] ➔ **the poverty line/level** at POVERTY ➔ **read between the lines** at READ ➔ **somewhere along the line/way** at SOMEWHERE

line[2] *v.* [T] **1** to cover the inside of something with something else: *We* ***lined*** *the box* ***with*** *newspaper.* **2** to form rows along the edge of something: *Thousands of fans lined the streets.*
line up *phr. v.* **1 line** sb/sth ⇔ **up** to make a row, or arrange people or things in a row: *Customers lined up hours before the show.* | *Line the chairs up in rows of ten.* **2 line** sb/sth ⇔ **up** to make arrangements so that something will happen or someone will be available for an event: *They've lined up some dancers for the show.*

lin·e·age /ˈlɪniɪdʒ/ *n.* [C,U] *formal* the way in which members of a family are related to other members who lived in past times

lin·e·ar /ˈlɪniə/ *adj.* **1** consisting of lines, or in the form of a straight line: *a linear drawing* **2** related to length: *linear measurements* **3** involving a series of connected events, ideas, etc. that develop in stages

line·back·er /ˈlaɪnˌbækə/ *n.* [C,U] a football player whose job is trying to TACKLE the member of the other team who has the ball

lined /laɪnd/ *adj.* **1** a skirt, coat, etc. that is lined has a piece of material covering the inside: *a fur-lined coat* **2** lined paper has straight lines printed on it

line·man /ˈlaɪnmən/ *n.* plural **linemen** /-mən/ [C] a player who plays in the front line of a football team

lin·en /ˈlɪnən/ *n.* [U] **1** sheets, TABLECLOTHS, etc.: *bed/table linen* **2** cloth used to make high quality clothes, home decorations, etc.

lin·er /ˈlaɪnə/ *n.* [C] **1** a large ship for carrying people: *an ocean liner* ➔ see picture at TRANSPORTATION ➔ AIRLINER

THESAURUS

ship, **cruise ship**, **ferry**, **freighter**, **tanker**, **barge**, **aircraft carrier**, **battleship**, **cruiser**, **submarine**, **warship**
➔ see Thesaurus box at SHIP[1]

2 a piece of material used inside something in order to protect it

line·up /ˈlaɪnʌp/ *n.* [C] **1** a set of events, programs, performers, etc. arranged to follow each other: *The lineup of performers included Tony Curtis and Diana Ross.* **2** a group of people arranged in a row by the police so that a person who saw a crime can try to recognize the criminal ➔ STARTING LINEUP

lin·ger /ˈlɪŋgə/ *v.* [I] **1** to stay somewhere for a little longer, especially because you do not want to leave: *We found a small cafe where we could* ***linger over*** *our coffee.* **2 also linger on** if a smell, memory, etc. lingers, it does not disappear for a long time: *The smell of smoke lingered for days.*

lin·ge·rie /ˌlɑnʒəˈreɪ, ˌlɑndʒə-/ *n.* [U] women's underwear

lin·ger·ing /ˈlɪŋgərɪŋ/ *adj.* slow to finish or disappear: *lingering questions about the murder*

lin·go /ˈlɪŋgoʊ/ *n.* [C usually singular] *informal* **1** words used only by a group of people who do a particular job or activity: *computer lingo* **2** *informal* a language, especially a foreign one

lin·guist /ˈlɪŋgwɪst/ *n.* [C] **1** someone who studies or teaches linguistics **2** someone who speaks several languages well

lin·guis·tic /lɪŋˈgwɪstɪk/ *adj.* relating to language, words, or linguistics

lin·guis·tics /lɪŋˈgwɪstɪks/ *n.* [U] the study of

L

languages, including their structures, grammar, and history

lin·ing /ˈlaɪnɪŋ/ *n.* [C,U] a piece of material covering the inside of a box, a coat, etc.: *a jacket with a silk lining*

link[1] /lɪŋk/ *v.* [T] **1** if two things are linked, they are related, often because one strongly affects or causes the other: *Lung cancer has been **linked to/with** smoking cigarettes.* **2 also link up** to connect computers, communication systems, etc. so that electronic messages can be sent between them: *Each computer is **linked to/with** the Internet.* **3** to connect one place to another: *a highway linking two major cities*

link[2] *n.* [C] **1** a relationship or connection between two or more events, people, ideas, etc.: *Latin is the **link between** all of the Romance languages.* | *He is believed to have **links with** terrorist groups.* **2** one of the rings in a chain **3 a satellite/telephone/rail etc. link** something that makes communication or travel between two places possible **4** a word or picture on a WEBSITE or computer document that will take you to another page or document if you CLICK on it ➔ CUFF LINK

link·age /ˈlɪŋkɪdʒ/ *n.* [C,U] a link or connection between two things

ˈlinking ˌverb *n.* [C] *technical* in grammar, a verb that connects the subject of a sentence to a word or phrase that describes it. In the sentence "She seems friendly," "seems" is the linking verb.

li·no·le·um /lɪˈnoʊliəm/ *n.* [U] smooth shiny material that is used to cover a floor

lint /lɪnt/ *n.* [U] soft light pieces of thread or wool that come off cotton, wool, or other material

lion

li·on /ˈlaɪən/ *n.* [C] a large African and Asian wild cat, the male of which has long thick hair around his neck

li·on·ess /ˈlaɪənɪs/ *n.* [C] a female lion

lip /lɪp/ *n.* [C] **1** one of the two edges of your mouth where your skin is redder or darker: *a kiss **on the lips*** ➔ see picture on page A3 **2** the top edge of a container such as a bowl or cup **3 my lips are sealed** *spoken* said when promising someone that you will not tell a secret **4 thin-lipped/full-lipped etc.** with lips that are thin, round, etc. **5 pay/give lip service to sth** to say that you support or agree with something, without doing anything to prove this

ˈlip gloss *n.* [C,U] a substance used to make lips look very shiny

lip-read /ˈlɪp rid/ *v.* [I,T] to watch someone's lips move in order to understand what s/he is saying, especially because you cannot hear —**lip-reading** *n.* [U]

lip·stick /ˈlɪpˌstɪk/ *n.* [C,U] a substance used for adding color to your lips, or a small tube containing this

lip sync /ˈlɪp ˌsɪŋk/ *v.* [I] to pretend to sing by moving your lips at the same time as a recording is being played

liq·ue·fy /ˈlɪkwəˌfaɪ/ *v.* past tense and past participle **liquified**, third person singular **liquifies** [I,T] *formal* to become liquid, or make something become liquid

li·queur /lɪˈkɚ, lɪˈkyʊr/ *n.* [C,U] a strong sweet alcoholic drink usually drunk after a meal

liq·uid /ˈlɪkwɪd/ *n.* [C,U] a substance such as water that is not a solid or a gas: *Cook the rice until all the liquid is absorbed.* —**liquid** *adj.*: *liquid soap*

liq·ui·date /ˈlɪkwəˌdeɪt/ *v.* [I,T] to close a business or company and sell its goods in order to pay a debt —**liquidation** /ˌlɪkwəˈdeɪʃən/ *n.* [C,U]

ˌLiquid ˈPaper *n.* [U] *trademark* white liquid that is used to correct mistakes in writing and TYPING

liq·uor /ˈlɪkɚ/ *n.* [U] a strong alcoholic drink such as WHISKEY

ˈliquor store *n.* [C] a store where alcohol is sold ➔ see Thesaurus box at STORE[1]

lisp /lɪsp/ *n.* [C] someone who has a lisp pronounces "s" sounds like "th" —**lisp** *v.* [I,T]

list[1] /lɪst/ *n.* [C] a set of names, things, numbers, etc. written one below the other: *a **list of** questions* | ***Make a list** of the things you'll need.* | *a **shopping list*** | *Is my name **on the list**?* ▶ Don't say "in the list." ◀

THESAURUS

Types of lists

grocery list or **shopping list** – a list of food you need to buy
mailing list – a list of people who are all sent information or advertising material by mail or email
price list – a printed list of a company's goods or services, and their prices
checklist – a list of things you need to check
waiting list – a list of people who want something but will have to wait for it
guest list – a list of people invited somewhere

list[2] *v.* [T] to write a list, or mention things one after the other: *Each Monday the newspaper lists the ten most popular films.*

lis·ten /ˈlɪsən/ *v.* [I] **1** to pay attention to what someone is saying or to something that you hear: *This is very important so I need you to listen.* |

L

*Have you **listened to** this CD?* **2** *spoken* used to tell someone to pay attention to what you are saying: *Listen, can I call you back later?* **3** to consider what someone says to you and accept his/her advice: *I told him it was dangerous, but he wouldn't listen.*

listen for sth/sb *phr. v.* to pay attention so that you are sure you will hear a sound: *He put down the paper and listened for the telephone.*

listen in *phr. v.* to listen to what someone is saying without him/her knowing it: *I think someone's **listening in on** the other phone.*

listen up *phr. v. spoken* used in order to get people's attention so they will hear what you are going to say: *OK, people, listen up. I'm only going to say this once.*

lis·ten·er /'lɪsənɚ/ *n.* [C] **1** someone who listens, especially to the radio [➡ **viewer**] **2 a good listener** someone who listens in a patient and sympathetic way to other people

list·ing /'lɪstɪŋ/ *n.* **1** [C] something that is on a list **2 listings** [plural] lists of movies, plays, and other events with the times and places at which they will happen

list·less /'lɪstlɪs/ *adj.* feeling tired and not interested in things

lit[1] /lɪt/ *v.* the past tense and past participle of LIGHT

lit[2] *adj.* having light or burning: *a brightly-lit hallway*

lit·a·ny /'lɪt˺n-i/ *n.* **a litany of sth** a long list of problems, questions, complaints, etc.

lite /laɪt/ *adj. nonstandard* having fewer CALORIES than usual [➡ **light**]: *lite beer*

li·ter /'liṭɚ/ *n.* [C] *written abbreviation* **l** a unit for measuring liquids, equal to 2.12 PINTS or 0.26 gallons: *a **liter of** vodka*

lit·er·a·cy /'lɪṭərəsi/ *n.* [U] the ability to read and write

lit·er·al /'lɪṭərəl/ *adj.* the literal meaning of a word or expression is its basic or original meaning [➡ **figurative**]: *a literal interpretation of the Bible*

lit·er·al·ly /'lɪṭərəli/ *adv.* **1** according to the most basic meaning of a word or expression: *There are literally millions of students in these programs.* **2** *spoken* used in order to emphasize something you have just said: *The program has moved literally thousands of homeless people off the streets.* **3 take sb/sth literally** to think that a word or statement is literal when it is not: *Lou was joking, but Sara took it literally.*

lit·er·ar·y /'lɪṭəˌrɛri/ *adj.* **1** relating to literature: *a literary critic* **2** typical of writing used in literature rather than in ordinary writing and talking

lit·er·ate /'lɪṭərɪt/ *adj.* **1** able to read and write [≠ **illiterate**] **2** well educated

lit·er·a·ture /'lɪṭərətʃɚ, 'lɪtrə-/ *n.* [U] **1** books, plays, etc. that are considered very good and that people have liked for a long time: *the great classics of English literature* ➔ see Thesaurus box at BOOK[1] **2** printed information produced by organizations that want to sell something or tell people about something

lithe /laɪð/ *adj.* able to bend and move your body easily and gracefully

lit·i·ga·tion /ˌlɪṭə'geɪʃən/ *n.* [U] the process of taking a legal case to a court of law —**litigate** *v.* [I,T]

lit·mus test /'lɪt˺məs ˌtɛst/ *n.* [singular] a single action, situation, or quality that allows you to measure someone's attitude, beliefs, etc.: *The elections will be **a litmus test of** the political mood in the U.S.*

lit·ter[1] /'lɪṭɚ/ *n.* **1** [U] pieces of waste paper, etc. that people leave on the ground in public places

> **THESAURUS**
> **garbage, trash, refuse, waste**
> ➔ see Thesaurus box at GARBAGE

2 [C] a group of baby animals born at the same time to one mother: *a **litter of** puppies*

> **THESAURUS**
> **herd, flock, school, shoal, pack**
> ➔ see Thesaurus box at GROUP[1]

litter[2] *v.* **1** [I,T] to leave pieces of waste paper, etc. on the ground in a public place: *The sign says: Please Do Not Litter.* **2** [T] if a lot of things litter a place, they are spread all over it in a messy way: *The floor was **littered with** clothes.*

lit·tle[1] /'lɪṭl/ *adj.* **1** small in size: *a little house*

> **THESAURUS**
> **small, tiny, minute, cramped, petite**
> ➔ see Thesaurus box at SMALL

2 a little bit not very much: *It will only hurt a little bit.* | *Can I have **a little bit of*** (=a small amount of) *milk in my coffee, please?* **3** short in time or distance: *I'll wait **a little while** and then call again.* | *Anna walked **a little way** down the road with him.* **4** young and small: *a little boy* | *Amy's **little brother/sister*** (=younger brother or sister)

> **THESAURUS**
> **young, small, teenage, adolescent**
> ➔ see Thesaurus box at YOUNG[1]

5 not important: *He gets angry over little things.* | *There is one little problem.* **6** *spoken* used in order to emphasize an adjective: *She owns a nice little restaurant in the city.*

little[2] *quantifier* comparative **less**, superlative **least** **1** only a small amount of something: *Little is known about the disease.* | *We had **very little** money.* **2 a little** a small amount: *I only know a little Spanish.* | *She told him **a little** about it.* | *I need **a little more** time to finish the test.* | *Tony went out to see **a little of** the town.* **3** a short time or distance: *He must be **a little over** 60.* (=slightly

L

older than 60) | *Phoenix is **a little under** 50 miles from here* (=slightly fewer than 50 miles).

GRAMMAR

little, a little

Use **little** when you mean "not much": *I've got very little money left.*

Use **a little** when you mean "a small amount": *I accidentally spilled a little coffee on the carpet.*

Little and **a little** are always used with U nouns.

➔ FEW

little³ *adv.* **1** not much or only slightly [➡ **less, least**]: *He moved the table **a little** closer to the wall.* | *I was **a little** afraid of the dog.* | *She goes out very little.* **2 little by little** gradually: *Little by little, his playing improved.*

ˌlittle ˈfinger *n.* [C] the smallest finger on your hand

ˌLittle League ˈBaseball *n. trademark* [C] a group of baseball teams for children

lit·ur·gy /ˈlɪt̬ɚdʒi/ *n.* plural **liturgies** [C,U] prayers, songs, etc. that are said in a particular order in a religious ceremony —**liturgical** /lɪˈtɚdʒɪkəl/ *adj.*

liv·a·ble, **liveable** /ˈlɪvəbəl/ *adj.* good enough to live in, but not very good [= **habitable**]

live¹ /lɪv/ *v.* **1** [I] to be alive or to continue to stay alive: *My grandmother lived to be 88.* | *Thoreau lived in the mid-1800s.* **2** [I] to have your home in a particular place: *Where do you live?* | ***I live in** Boston.* | *They **live on** Bergen Street.* | *Kitty still **lives at home*** (=lives with her parents). **3** [I,T] to have a particular type of life, or to live in a particular way: *We earn enough to live comfortably.* | *children **living in poverty***

live for sb/sth *phr. v.* to consider someone or something to be the most important thing in your life: *She lives for her children.*

live off sth/sb *phr. v.* to get your food or money from someone or something other than a job: *He's living off money from his investments.*

live sth **down** *phr. v.* **not live sth down** to not be able to make people forget about something bad or embarrassing you have done: *You'll never live this evening down!*

live on *phr. v.* **1 live on** sth to have a particular amount of money to buy food and other necessary things: *I don't know how he can live on $600 a month.* **2 live on** sth to eat a lot of a particular kind of food: *These animals live on insects.* **3** to continue to exist: *She will live on in our memories.*

live together *phr. v.* to live with another person in a sexual relationship without being married: *Mark and I have been living together for two years.*

live through sth *phr. v.* to experience difficult or dangerous conditions and continue living: *Don didn't expect to live through the war.*

live up to sth *phr. v.* to do something as well, or be as good as someone expects: *Charles could never **live up to** his father's **expectations**.*

live with sb/sth *phr. v.* **1 live with** sth to accept a difficult situation even when it continues for a long time: *living with pain* **2 live with** sb to live with another person, especially in a sexual relationship without being married: *Tim's living with a girl he met in college.*

live² /laɪv/ *adj.* **1** not dead or artificial [≠ **dead**]: *He fed the snake live rats.* **2** broadcast as an event happens: *a live broadcast of the Rose Parade* **3** performed for people who are watching: *The club has live music six nights a week.* **4** having electricity flowing through it: *a live wire* **5** ready to explode: *a live bomb* ➔ **real live** at REAL¹

live³ /laɪv/ *adv.* **1** if something is broadcast live, it is broadcast on television or radio as it is actually happening: *Live, from New York, it's "Saturday Night!"* **2** performing in front of people: *The band is playing live in Houston this week.*

live·li·hood /ˈlaɪvliˌhʊd/ *n.* [C,U] the way you earn money in order to live: *Farming is their livelihood.*

live·ly /ˈlaɪvli/ *adj.* comparative **livelier**, superlative **liveliest** **1** very active and cheerful: *a lively group of children* **2** very exciting and interesting: *a lively debate* —**liveliness** *n.* [U]

liv·en /ˈlaɪvən/ *v.*

liven (sth ⇔) **up** *phr. v.* to become more exciting, or to make something more exciting: *Better music might liven the party up.*

liv·er /ˈlɪvɚ/ *n.* **1** [C] a large organ in your body that cleans your blood ➔ see picture on page A3 **2** [U] the liver of an animal used as food

lives /laɪvz/ *n.* the plural of LIFE

live·stock /ˈlaɪvstɑk/ *n.* [U] animals that are kept on a farm

liv·id /ˈlɪvɪd/ *adj.* extremely angry [= **furious**]

THESAURUS

angry, **annoyed**, **irritated**, **furious**, **mad**

➔ see Thesaurus box at ANGRY

liv·ing¹ /ˈlɪvɪŋ/ *adj.* **1** [only before noun] alive now [≠ **dead**]: *She is one of our greatest living writers.* | *The ocean is full of **living things*** (=animals and plants). **2** existing or being used now: *a living language*

living² *n.* **1** [C usually singular] the way that you earn money: *What does he **do for a living**?* | *It's hard to **make a living*** (=earn enough money) *as an actor.* **2** [U] the way that someone lives his/her life: *Sometimes I want to give up city living and move to the country.* **3 the living** all the people who are alive ➔ COST OF LIVING

ˈliving room *n.* [C] the main room in a house, where you relax, watch television, etc.

ˌliving ˈwill *n.* [C] a document that explains what

legal and medical decisions should be made for you if you are too sick to make them yourself

liz·ard /ˈlɪzɚd/ *n.* [C] a REPTILE that has rough skin, four short legs, and a long tail

lla·ma /ˈlɑmə/ *n.* [C] a large South American animal with thick hair like wool and a long neck

Ln. the written abbreviation of **lane**

load¹ /loʊd/ *n.* [C] **1** a large quantity of something that is carried by a person, a vehicle, etc.: *a ship carrying **a full load of** fuel and supplies* **2 carload/truckload etc.** the largest amount or number that a car, etc. can carry: *a busload of kids* **3** the amount of work that a machine or a person has to do: *a light/heavy **work load*** **4** a quantity of clothes that are washed at the same time: *Can you **do a load of** clothes later today?*

SPOKEN PHRASES

5 a load of sth/loads of sth a lot of something: *Don't worry, there's loads of time.* **6 get a load of sb/sth** said when you want someone to notice something funny or surprising

load² *v.* **1** [I,T] **also load up** to put a load of something on or into a vehicle or container: *They **loaded** all their luggage **into** the car.* | *He cleared the table and loaded the dishwasher.* **2** [T] to put bullets into a gun or film into a camera **3** [T] to put a program into a computer

load sb/sth ⇔ **down** *phr. v.* to make someone carry too many things or do too much work: *Mom was **loaded down with** groceries.*

load·ed /ˈloʊdɪd/ *adj.* **1** containing bullets or film: *a loaded gun* **2** carrying a load of something: *a loaded truck* **3** [not before noun] *informal* very rich: *His grandmother is loaded.* **4 loaded question** a question that is unfair because it makes you give a particular answer **5 loaded with sth** full of a particular quality, or containing a lot of something: *a cake loaded with nuts*

loaf¹ /loʊf/ *n.* plural **loaves** /loʊvz/ [C] bread that is shaped and baked in one large piece: *a **loaf of bread*** ➔ see picture at BREAD

loaf² *v.* [I] *informal* to waste time in a lazy way when you should be working: *He spends his days **loafing around** the house.*

Loaf·er /ˈloʊfɚ/ *n.* [C] *trademark* a flat leather shoe without LACES

loan¹ /loʊn/ *n.* **1** [C] an amount of money that you borrow from a bank: *We'll **take out a loan** to buy the car.* | *I'll be **paying off/back** the **loan** for at least five years.* | ***student loans*** (=money that students borrow to pay for college) **2 on loan** being borrowed: *The book is on loan from the library.* **3** [singular] the act of lending something

loan² *v.* [T] to lend someone something, especially money: *Can you loan me $20 until Friday?*

ˈloan shark *n.* [C] *disapproving* someone who lends money to people and charges a very high rate of INTEREST

loath /loʊθ, loʊð/ *adj.* **be loath to do sth** *formal* to be unwilling to do something

loathe /loʊð/ *v.* [T] *formal* to hate someone or something —**loathing** *n.* [U]

THESAURUS

hate, can't stand, detest, despise, abhor
➔ see Thesaurus box at HATE¹

loath·some /ˈloʊðsəm, ˈloʊθ-/ *adj. formal* very unpleasant [= **disgusting**]

loaves /loʊvz/ *n.* [C] the plural form of LOAF

lob /lɑb/ *v.* past tense and past participle **lobbed**, present participle **lobbing** [T] to throw or hit a ball so that it moves slowly in a high curve

lob·by¹ /ˈlɑbi/ *n.* plural **lobbies** [C] **1** a large hall inside the entrance of a building: *waiting in the hotel lobby* **2** a group of people who try to persuade the government to change or approve a particular law: *the environmental lobby*

lobby² *v.* past tense and past participle **lobbied**, third person singular **lobbies** [I,T] to try to persuade the government to change a particular law: *a group **lobbying for/against** the law* —**lobbyist** *n.* [C]

lobe /loʊb/ *n.* [C] ➔ EARLOBE

lob·ster /ˈlɑbstɚ/ *n.* [C,U] an ocean animal with eight legs, a shell, and two large CLAWS, or the meat of this animal

lobster

lo·cal¹ /ˈloʊkəl/ *adj.* **1** [usually before noun] relating to a particular place or area, especially the place you live in: *a good local hospital* | *The story appeared in the local newspaper.* | *It costs a quarter to make a **local call*** (=a telephone call to someone in the same area as you).

THESAURUS

near, close, not far (away), nearby, within walking distance, neighboring
➔ see Thesaurus box at NEAR¹

2 *technical* affecting a particular part of your body: *a local anesthetic*

local² *n.* **the locals** the people who live in a particular place

lo·cale /loʊˈkæl/ *n.* [C] *formal* the place where something happens

lo·cal·i·ty /loʊˈkæləṭi/ *n.* [C] plural **localities** *formal* a small area of a country, city, etc.

lo·cal·ized /ˈloʊkəˌlaɪzd/ *adj. formal* only within a small area: *localized pain*

lo·cal·ly /ˈloʊkəli/ *adv.* in or near the area where you are or the area you are talking about: *locally grown apples*

L

THESAURUS

nearby: *Do you live nearby?*
close by/close to here: *My folks live close by.*
around here: *Is there a bank around here?*
in the neighborhood: *Is there a good Chinese restaurant in the neighborhood?*
in/around these parts: *Most folk in these parts don't want the dam to be built.*
→ NEAR[1]

'local time *n.* [U] the time of day in a particular part of the world: *We'll arrive in Boston at 4:00 local time.*

lo·cate /ˈlooukeɪt/ *v.* **1** [T] to find the exact position of something: *Divers have located the shipwreck.*

THESAURUS

find, **discover**, **trace**, **track down**, **turn up**, **unearth**
→ see Thesaurus box at FIND[1]

2 be located to be in a particular place or position: *The bakery is located in the middle of town.* **3** [I,T] to come to a place and start a business there: *The company **located** its offices **in** New Jersey when rents went up in New York.*

lo·ca·tion /loʊˈkeɪʃən/ *n.* **1** [C] a particular place or position: *His apartment is in a really good location.* | *a map showing the **location of** the school*

THESAURUS

place, **position**, **spot**, **site**
→ see Thesaurus box at PLACE[1]

2 [C,U] a place where a movie is filmed, away from the STUDIO: *scenes shot **on location** in Montana*

lock[1] /lɑk/ *v.* **1** [I,T] to be fastened with a lock, or to fasten something with a lock [≠ **unlock**]: *Lock the door when you leave.* **2 lock sth up/away/in etc.** to put something in a safe place and fasten it with a lock: *He **locked** the money **in** a safe.* **3** [I] to become set in one position and be unable to move: *The brakes locked and we skidded.*

lock sb **in** *phr. v.* to prevent someone from leaving a place by locking the door

lock into sth *phr. v.* **be locked into** sth to be unable to change a situation: *families who are locked into a cycle of poverty*

lock sb **out** *phr. v.* to prevent someone from entering a place by locking the door

lock up *phr. v.* **1** *informal* **lock** sb **up** to put someone in prison **2 lock** (sth ⇔) **up** to make a building safe by locking all the doors

lock[2] *n.* [C] **1** a thing that keeps a door, drawer, etc. fastened or shut and is usually opened with a key: *There's no lock on the door.* **2 lock, stock, and barrel** including every part of something: *They sold everything, lock, stock, and barrel.* **3 under lock and key** kept safely in something that is locked **4** a small number of hairs on your head that hang together: *Carla twisted **a lock of hair** around her finger.* **5** a special area on a river where the water level can go up or down to raise or lower boats

lock·er /ˈlɑkɚ/ *n.* [C] a small cupboard with a lock where you leave books, clothes, etc., especially at school or when you are playing sports

'locker room *n.* [C] a room where you change your clothes and leave them in a LOCKER

lock·et /ˈlɑkɪt/ *n.* [C] a piece of jewelry like a small round box in which you put a picture of someone, worn on a chain around your neck

lock·smith /ˈlɑkˌsmɪθ/ *n.* [C] someone who makes and repairs locks

lo·co·mo·tive /ˌloʊkəˈmoʊt̬ɪv/ *n.* [C] a train engine

lo·cust /ˈloʊkəst/ *n.* [C] an insect similar to a GRASSHOPPER that flies in large groups and often destroys crops

lodge[1] /lɑdʒ/ *v.* **1** [I] to become stuck somewhere [≠ **dislodge**]: *He had a fish bone **lodged in** his throat.* **2 lodge a complaint/protest etc.** to officially complain, protest, etc. about something: *He has lodged a formal complaint with the club.* **3** [I] to pay someone rent in order to live in a room in his/her house

lodge[2] *n.* [C] **1** a building in the country where people can stay for a short time, especially in order to do a particular activity: *a ski lodge* **2** a local meeting place for some organizations: *the Masonic lodge*

lodg·ing /ˈlɑdʒɪŋ/ *n.* [U, plural] a place to stay: *The tourist office will give you information on lodging.*

loft /lɔft/ *n.* [C] **1** a space above a business, factory, etc. that was once used for storing goods, but has been changed into living space or work space for artists: *She's just bought a loft in Manhattan.* **2** a raised area above the main part of a room, usually used for sleeping **3** a raised level in a BARN where HAY is kept

loft·y /ˈlɔfti/ *adj.* comparative **loftier**, superlative **loftiest** **1** showing high standards or high moral qualities: *lofty ideals* **2** *literary* high

log[1] /lɔg, lɑg/ *n.* [C] **1** a thick piece of wood cut from a tree → see picture at PLANT[1] **2** an official record of events on a ship or airplane

log[2] *v.* past tense and past participle **logged**, present participle **logging** **1** [T] to make an official record of events, facts, etc., especially on a ship or airplane **2** [I,T] to cut down trees —**logger** *n.* [C]

log off/out *phr. v.* to stop using a computer or computer system by typing (TYPE) a special word

log on/in *phr. v.* to start using a computer or computer system by typing (TYPE) a special word

ˌlog 'cabin *n.* [C] a small house made of LOGS

log·ger·heads /ˈlɔgɚˌhɛdz, ˈlɑ-/ *n.* **be at loggerheads (with sb)** to disagree very strongly with someone

log·ging /ˈlɔgɪŋ, ˈlɑ-/ *n.* [U] the industry of cutting down trees for wood, paper, etc.

log·ic /ˈlɑdʒɪk/ *n.* [U] **1** a set of sensible and correct reasons: *There is no **logic in** releasing criminals just because the prisons are crowded.* **2** the science or study of thinking carefully about something, using formal methods

log·i·cal /ˈlɑdʒɪkəl/ *adj.* **1** seeming reasonable and sensible [≠ **illogical**]: *It's the logical place to build a new supermarket.* **2** based on the rules of logic: *a logical conclusion* —**logically** *adv.*

lo·gis·tics /loʊˈdʒɪstɪks, lə-/ *n.* **the logistics of sth** the practical organizing that is needed to make a complicated plan or activity successful —**logistical** *adj.* —**logistically** *adv.*

log·jam /ˈlɔgdʒæm, ˈlɑg-/ *n.* [C] a lot of problems or other things that are preventing something from being done: *a logjam of work*

lo·go /ˈloʊgoʊ/ *n.* plural **logos** [C] a small design that is the official sign of a company or organization

loin·cloth /ˈlɔɪnklɔθ/ *n.* [C] a piece of cloth that men in some hot countries wear around their waist

loins /lɔɪnz/ *n.* [plural] *literary* the part of the body below your waist where the sexual organs are

loi·ter /ˈlɔɪtə/ *v.* [I] to stand in a public place without having a reason to be there

loll /lɑl/ *v.* [I] **1** to sit or lie in a lazy or relaxed way: *We spent the afternoon **lolling around** on the beach.* **2** if someone's head or tongue lolls, it hangs down

lol·li·pop /ˈlɑliˌpɑp/ *n.* [C] a hard candy on the end of a stick

lone /loʊn/ *adj.* *literary* [only before noun] being the only person or thing in a place, or the only person or thing that does something: *a lone figure standing in the snow*

lone·ly /ˈloʊnli/ *adj.* **1** unhappy because you are alone: *She was very lonely after her husband died.* **2** *literary* far from where people live: *a lonely country road* —**loneliness** *n.* [U]

lon·er /ˈloʊnə/ *n.* [C] someone who wants to be alone or who has no friends

lone·some /ˈloʊnsəm/ *adj.* → LONELY

long[1] /lɔŋ/ *adj.*
1 MEASUREMENT measuring a great length, distance, or time [≠ **short**]: ***long hair*** | *There was a **long line** at the bank.* | *The book is good, but it's too long.* | *It **takes a long time** to drive to work.*
2 PARTICULAR LENGTH/TIME having a particular length or continuing for a particular amount of time: *The snake was at least 3 feet long.* | ***How long** is the movie?* | *O'Keeffe lived **long enough** to see her artwork become successful.*
3 SEEMING LONG *informal* seeming too long in time or distance because you are tired, bored, etc.: *It's been a **long day**.*
4 long hours a large amount of time: *She spent long hours working at the computer.*
5 BOOK/LIST/NAME ETC. a long book, list, etc. has a lot of pages, details, etc.
6 long weekend three days, including Saturday and Sunday, when you do not have to go to work or school
7 in the long run when something is finished, or at a later time: *All our hard work will be worth it in the long run.*
8 CLOTHES covering all of your arms or legs [≠ **short**]: *a long skirt* | *a **long-sleeved** shirt*

long[2] *adv.* **1** for a long time: *Have you been waiting long?* **2 long before/after** for a long time before or after a particular time or event: *The farm was sold long before you were born.* **3 for long** for a long time: *Have you known the Garretts for very long?* **4 as long as** if: *You can go as long as you're back by four o'clock.* **5 no longer also not any longer** used in order to show that something happened in the past, but does not happen now: *Mr. Allen no longer works for the company.* **6 so long** *spoken* goodbye **7 before long** soon: *It will be Christmas before long.*

long[3] *v.* [I] *formal* to want something very much: *The children **longed to** get outside.*

ˌlong-ˈdistance *adj.* [only before noun] **1** a long-distance telephone call is to a place that is far away [≠ **local**] **2** traveling, running, etc. between two places that are far away from each other: *long-distance flights* —**long-distance** *adv.*

ˌlong-drawn-ˈout *adj.* [only before noun] continuing for a longer time than is necessary: *a long-drawn-out discussion*

lon·gev·i·ty /lɑnˈdʒɛvət̬i, lɔn-/ *n.* [U] *formal* long life

long·hand /ˈlɔŋhænd/ *n.* [U] writing full words by hand rather than using a machine such as a computer

long·ing /ˈlɔŋɪŋ/ *n.* [singular, U] a strong feeling of wanting someone or something very much: *a **longing for** peace* —**longing** *adj.* —**longingly** *adv.*

lon·gi·tude /ˈlɑndʒəˌtud/ *n.* [C,U] a position on the Earth measured in degrees east or west of an imaginary line from the top of the Earth to the bottom [➡ **latitude**] —**longitudinal** /ˌlɑndʒəˈtudn-əl/ *adj.* → see picture at GLOBE

ˈlong johns *n.* [plural] *informal* warm underwear that covers your legs

ˈlong jump *n.* [U] a sport in which you jump as far as possible

ˌlong-ˈlasting *adj.* continuing for a long time: *the long-lasting effects of child abuse*

long-lived /ˌlɔŋ ˈlaɪvd◂/ *adj.* living or existing for a long time

ˌlong-ˈlost *adj.* [only before noun] lost or not seen for a long time: *a **long-lost friend***

ˌlong-ˈrange *adj.* [usually before noun] **1** relating to a time that continues far into the future: *long-range development plans* **2** covering a long distance: *a long-range missile*

ˌlong-ˈrunning *adj.* [usually before noun] having existed or happened for a long time: *a long-running show on Broadway*

L

long·shore·man /ˌlɔŋˈʃɔrmən, ˈlɔŋˌʃɔrmən/ *n.* [C] someone whose job is to load and unload ships

ˈlong shot *n.* [C usually singular] *informal* **1** someone or something with very little chance of success: *It's a long shot, but I may as well apply.* **2 not by a long shot** not at all or not nearly: *This isn't over, not by a long shot.*

ˌlong-ˈstanding *adj.* having continued or existed for a long time: *a long-standing agreement between the two countries*

ˌlong-ˈsuffering *adj.* [usually before noun] patient in spite of problems or unhappiness

ˌlong-ˈterm *adj.* continuing for a long period of time into the future [➡ **short-term**]: *The **long-term effects** of the drug are not known.* ➔ **in the long/short term** at TERM[1]

long·time /ˈlɔŋtaɪm/ *adj.* [only before noun] having existed for a long time, or having had a particular position for a long time: *her longtime boyfriend | a longtime goal*

ˌlong-ˈwinded *adj.* continuing to talk for too long in a way that is boring: *a long-winded speech*

look[1] /lʊk/ *v.* **1** [I] to turn your eyes toward something so that you can see it: *I didn't see it. I wasn't looking. | "I have to go," Mel said, **looking at** his watch.*

THESAURUS

glance – to look at someone or something for a short time and then look quickly away: *Kevin glanced at the clock.*
peek – to quickly look at something, especially something you are not supposed to see: *I peeked through the curtains, trying to see if they were home.*
peer – to look very carefully, especially because you cannot see something well: *Hansen peered through the windshield at the street signs.*
stare – to look at someone or something for a long time, especially without blinking your eyes: *He stood staring out into the street.*
gaze – to look at someone or something for a long time, often without realizing that you are doing it: *Helen gazed out the window at the shimmering water.*
gape – to look at something for a long time, usually with your mouth open, because you are very shocked or surprised: *She backed away as the children gaped at her.*

USAGE

You **look at** a picture, person, thing, etc. because you want to: *Hey, look at these jeans.*
You **see** something without planning to: *Two people saw him take the bag.*
You **watch** TV, a movie, or something that happens for a period of time: *Did you watch the football game last night? | The kids are watching TV.*
You can also say that you saw a movie, a program, etc., but you cannot say "see television": *I saw a great movie on TV last night.*

L

2 [I] to try to find someone or something using your eyes: *I've **looked** everywhere **for** the money. | Have you looked in here? | Brad was **looking for** you last night.*

THESAURUS

search – to look carefully for someone or something: *We searched the whole house for the keys.*
try to find sb/sth – to look for someone or something, especially when this is difficult: *He's been trying to find a job for several months.*
seek formal – to try to find someone or something: *The new graduates are seeking employment.*
go through sth – to examine something very thoroughly when looking for something: *Security officers went through our bags.*

3 [linking verb] to seem to be something, especially by having a particular appearance: *You **look nice/good** in that dress. | He **looks like** he hasn't slept for days. | Gina and Ron looked very happy.*

THESAURUS

seem, **appear**, **sound**, **come across as**
➔ see Thesaurus box at SEEM

4 -looking having a particular type of appearance: *That was a funny-looking dog! | weird-looking people* **5 look sb in the eye** to look directly at someone in order to show that you are not afraid of him/her

SPOKEN PHRASES

6 Look... said when you are annoyed and you want to emphasize what you are saying: *Look, I'm very serious about this.* **7** [T] said in order to make someone notice something: *Look how skinny she is. | Mom, look what I made!* **8 (I'm) just looking** used in a store in order to tell someone who works there that you do not need help: *"Can I help you?" "No thanks, I'm just looking."*

look after sb/sth *phr. v.* to take care of someone or something: *Paul helps look after his two younger brothers.*

look ahead *phr. v.* to think about what will happen in the future: *We need to look ahead and plan for next year.*

look around *phr. v.* **look around** sth to see, study, read, etc. many different things in order to find something or to learn about something: *We have about three hours to look around the downtown.*

look at sth *phr. v.* **1** to read something quickly: *Jane was looking at a magazine while she waited.* **2** to study and consider something in order to decide what to do: *The doctor looked at the cut on her head.* **3 look at** sb *spoken* used to give someone or something as an example of a situation: *Look at Eric. He didn't go to college and he's doing fine.*

look back also **look back on sth** *phr. v.* to think about something that happened in the past: *Looking back, I see my mistake.*

look down on sb/sth *phr. v.* to think that you are better than someone or something else: *He looks down on anyone who doesn't have a college education.*

look for sb/sth *phr. v.* **1** to try to find a particular type of thing or person that you need or want: *How long have you been looking for a job?* **2 be looking for trouble/a fight** *informal* to be behaving in a way that makes it likely that problems or a fight will happen

look forward to sth *phr. v.* to be excited and happy about something that is going to happen: *We're really looking forward to skiing in Tahoe.*

look into sth *phr. v.* to try to find out the truth about something: *The FBI will look into the cause of the fire.*

look on *phr. v.* **1** to watch something, without being involved in it: *Children ran through the playground as their mothers looked on.* **2 look on/upon** sth to think about something in a particular way: *My family **looks on** divorce **as** a sin.*

look out to pay attention to what is happening around you: *Look out! There's a car coming.*

look sth/sb ⇔ **over** *phr. v.* to examine something or someone quickly: *Can you look over my résumé before I send it?*

look through *phr. v.* **1 look through** sth to look for something in a pile of papers, a drawer, someone's pockets, etc.: *I found her looking through my old letters.* **2 look right through sb** to pretend that you have not seen someone

look up *phr. v.* **1** if a situation is looking up, it is becoming better: *Things are looking up for me.* **2 look sth ⇔ up** to try to find information in a book, on a computer, etc.: *If you don't know the word, look it up.* **3 look sb ⇔ up** to visit someone you know, especially when you go to the place where s/he lives for another reason: *Don't forget to look up my parents when you're in Boston.*

look up to sb *phr. v.* to admire and respect someone: *Everybody looks up to Hugh.*

look[2] *n.* **1** [C usually singular] an act of looking at something: *Let me **take/have a look at** that map again.* **2** [C] an expression that you make with your eyes or face to show how you feel: *She **gave** me an angry **look**.* **3** [C] the appearance of someone or something: ***I don't like the look of** that bruise – maybe you should see a doctor.* **4 looks** [plural] how attractive someone is: *He's got his father's **good looks**.*

look·a·like /ˈlʊkəˌlaɪk/ *n.* [C] *informal* someone who looks very similar to someone else, especially someone famous: *a Madonna lookalike*

look·out /ˈlʊk-aʊt/ *n.* **1 be on the lookout (for sb/sth)** to continuously watch a place or pay attention to a situation because you are looking for someone or something: *Be on the lookout for snakes.* **2** [C] someone whose duty is to watch carefully for danger, or the place where s/he does this

loom[1] /lum/ *v.* [I] **1** to appear as a large unclear threatening shape: *The mountain loomed in front of us.* **2** if a problem or difficult situation looms, it is likely to happen soon: *economic changes that loom ahead* **3 loom large** to seem important, worrying, and difficult to avoid: *Fear of failure loomed large in his mind.*

loom[2] *n.* [C] a frame or machine used for weaving cloth

loon·y /ˈluni/ *adj. informal* extremely silly or crazy

> **THESAURUS**
> **crazy, mentally ill, insane, disturbed, nuts**
> ➔ see Thesaurus box at CRAZY

loop[1] /lup/ *n.* **1** [C] a shape like a curve or a circle, or a line, piece of wire, string, etc. that has this shape: *belt loops* (=cloth loops used for holding a belt on pants) **2 be out of the loop** to not be part of a group of people that has information and makes decisions about something

loop[2] *v.* [I,T] to make a loop or to make something into a loop

loop·hole /ˈluphoʊl/ *n.* [C] a small mistake in a law or rule that makes it possible to legally avoid doing what the law says: *tax loopholes*

loose[1] /lus/ *adj.*

1 NOT FIRMLY ATTACHED not firmly attached to something: *a loose screw* | *The buttons on my shirt are **coming loose**.*

2 NOT TIED/FASTENED not tied or fastened very tightly: *My shoelaces are loose.*

3 CLOTHES loose clothes are big and do not fit tightly on your body [= **baggy**]

4 NOT CONTROLLED free from being controlled in a CAGE, prison, or institution: *Two of the prisoners **broke loose** from the guards.* | *Don't **let** your dog **loose** on the beach.*

5 not exact: *a **loose translation/interpretation***

6 loose ends parts of something such as work or an agreement that have not yet been completed: *I have to **tie up** a few **loose ends** before we go away.*

7 loose cannon someone who cannot be trusted because s/he says or does things you do not want him/her to

8 NOT MORAL *old-fashioned* behaving in a way that is considered to be sexually immoral: *a loose woman* —**loosely** *adv.*: *A towel was loosely wrapped around his neck.*

loose[2] *n.* **on the loose** if a criminal is on the loose, s/he has escaped from prison

ˌloose-ˈleaf *adj.* [only before noun] having pages that can be put in or taken out easily: *a loose-leaf notebook*

loos·en /ˈlusən/ *v.* [I,T] to become less tight or less firmly attached to something, or to make something do this: *He loosened his tie.* | *The screws in the shelf had loosened.*

loosen (sb/sth ⇔) **up** *phr. v.* **1** to become more relaxed and feel less worried, or to make someone feel this way: *Claire loosened up after a few drinks.* **2** if your muscles loosen up, or if you loosen them up, they stop feeling stiff

loot[1] /lut/ *v.* [I,T] to steal things, especially from stores that have been damaged in a war or RIOT: *Businesses were looted and burned in the riot.* —**looting** *n.* [U] —**looter** *n.* [C]

loot[2] *n.* [U] goods that are stolen by thieves or taken by soldiers who have won a battle

lop /lɑp/ *v.* past tense and past participle **lopped**, present participle **lopping** [T] **also lop off** to cut part of something off

lope /loʊp/ *v.* [I] *literary* to run easily using long steps

lop·sid·ed /ˈlɑpˌsaɪdɪd/ *adj.* having one side that is heavier, larger, or lower than the other side: *a lopsided smile*

Lord /lɔrd/ *n.* [C] **1 also the Lord** a title used for God or Jesus Christ **2 good/oh/my Lord!** *spoken* said when you are surprised, worried, or angry

lord *n.* [C] a man who has a particular position in the ARISTOCRACY

lore /lɔr/ *n.* [U] knowledge and TRADITIONS that people learn from other people rather than from books

lose /luz/ *v.* past tense and past participle **lost** /lɔst/

1 NOT HAVE [I] to stop having something important that you need: *Michelle lost her job.* | *Anna's family **lost everything** in the war.*

2 NOT FIND [T] to be unable to find someone or something: *Danny's always losing his keys.*

USAGE

If you **lose** something, you cannot find it: *I've lost my keys.*
If you **miss** a class, meeting, etc. that you regularly attend, you do not go to it: *Bill has missed several days of work.*
➔ LOST

3 NOT WIN [I,T] to not win a game, argument, war, etc.: *We **lost to** the Red Sox 5–0.* | *Sanders **lost** the election **by** 371 votes.*

4 HAVE LESS [T] to have less of something than before: *I need to **lose weight**.* | *She's lost a lot of blood.*

5 lose your sight/memory/voice etc. to stop being able to see, remember things, talk, etc.

6 STOP HAVING A QUALITY [T] to no longer have a particular quality, belief, attitude, etc.: *The kids were **losing interest** in the game.* | *Jake **lost** his **temper/cool*** (=became angry) *and started shouting.* | *Rich **lost control** of the car and drove into a ditch.*

7 lose an arm/eye etc. to have a serious injury in which your arm, etc. is cut off

8 lose your balance to become unsteady, especially so that you fall

9 lose your husband/mother etc. if you lose your husband, mother, etc., s/he dies: *Michael **lost** his wife **to** cancer.* | *Janet **lost the baby*** (=the baby died before being born).

10 lose your life to die: *5,000 soldiers lost their lives.*

11 WASTE [T] to waste time or opportunities: *Pam **lost no time** in finding a new boyfriend.* | *You lost your chance!*

12 lose sb *informal* to confuse someone when explaining something to him/her: *You've lost me. Can you repeat that?*

13 have nothing to lose if you have nothing to lose, it is worth taking a risk because you cannot make your situation any worse: *You might as well apply for the job – you've got nothing to lose.*

14 lose touch (with sb/sth) **a)** to not speak, see, or write to someone for so long that you do not know where s/he is: *I've lost touch with all my high school friends.* **b)** to not know the most recent information about a particular place, situation, event, etc.: *He's lost touch with his Mexican culture.*

15 lose it *spoken* **a)** to suddenly start shouting, laughing, or crying a lot because you think something is very bad, funny, or wrong: *When he started criticizing me again, I just completely lost it.* **b)** to become crazy

16 lose your mind *informal* to go crazy or to stop behaving sensibly: *What are you doing on the roof? Have you lost your mind?*

17 lose sight of sth to forget about the most important part of something you are doing: *We can't lose sight of our goals.*

18 lose your touch to stop having a special ability or skill

19 lose heart to become disappointed and unhappy

lose out *phr. v.* to not get something important such as a job because someone else gets it: *He **lost out on** a scholarship because his grades were low.*

los·er /ˈluzɚ/ *n.* [C] **1** someone who does not win: *a **bad/sore loser*** (=someone who becomes too upset when s/he loses) **2** *informal disapproving* someone who is never successful in life, work, or relationships: *Pam's boyfriend is such a loser!*

loss /lɔs/ *n.* **1** [C,U] the fact of not having something any longer, or the action of losing something: *weight loss* | *the **loss of** innocence* | *job losses*

COLLOCATIONS

loss of confidence – when you stop believing in your ability to do things well
loss of appetite – when you do not get hungry, for example because you are sick
loss of memory also **memory loss** – when you cannot remember things well
loss of blood also **blood loss** – when you bleed a lot, for example after an accident
weight loss – when you become thinner
hearing loss also **loss of hearing** – when you cannot hear as well as you could before

job losses – when a number of people lose their jobs in a company, industry, etc.

2 [C,U] money that has been lost by a company, government, person, etc.: *The auto industry **reported losses of** $10 million last year.* **3** [C] an occasion when you do not win a game: *3 wins and 4 losses so far this season* **4** [C,U] the death of someone: *Troops suffered **heavy losses*** (=many deaths) *in the first battle.* **5** [singular, U] the sadness you feel or disadvantage you have because someone or something leaves: *She felt a great **sense of loss** when her son left home.* **6 be at a loss** to not know what you should do or say: *I'm **at a loss to explain** what happened.* **7 it's sb's loss** *spoken* said when you think someone is stupid for not taking a good opportunity: *Well, if he doesn't want to come, it's his loss.*

lost[1] /lɔst/ *adj.* **1** not knowing where you are or how to find your way: *We **got lost** driving around the city.*

USAGE

Use **lost** in order to describe someone or something that you cannot find, or someone who does not know where s/he is: *We took a wrong turn and got lost.* | *Lost children should talk to a store employee.* | *a lost wallet*
Use **missing** in order to describe someone or something you have been looking for, especially when the situation is serious: *the missing jewels* | *the search for the two missing boys*

2 unable to be found: *a lost dog* **3** wasted: *lost opportunities* **4 be/feel lost** to not feel confident or able to take care of yourself: *I'd be lost without all your help.* **5 be lost on sb** if humor or intelligent thinking is lost on someone, s/he cannot understand it or does not want to accept it: *Your sarcasm was lost on him.* **6 Get lost!** *spoken* used in order to tell someone rudely to go away **7 lost cause** something that has no chance of succeeding: *Trying to interest my son in classical music is a lost cause.*

lost[2] *v.* the past tense and past participle of LOSE

ˌlost-and-ˈfound *n.* [singular] an office used for keeping things that people have lost until their owners can get them

lot /lɑt/ *n.* **1 a lot also lots** *informal* **a)** a large amount, quantity, or number of something: ***A lot of** people at work have the flu.* | *Mrs. Ruiz has **lots of** money.* | ***A lot of times*** (=usually or often) *we just sat and talked.* **b)** much: *You'll get there a lot quicker if you drive.* **2 have a lot on your mind** to have many problems you are thinking about **3** [C] an area of land used especially for building on ➔ PARKING LOT

GRAMMAR

a lot of, much, many

In negative sentences, you can use **much** or **many** instead of **a lot of**.
Much is used with uncountable nouns: *There isn't much wine left.*
Many is used with plural noun forms: *I didn't see many people there that I knew.*
A lot of can be used with both types of noun: *I don't have a lot of money.* | *She doesn't have a lot of friends.*

lo·tion /ˈloʊʃən/ *n.* [C,U] a liquid mixture that you put on your skin in order to make it soft or to protect it: *hand lotion*

lot·ter·y /ˈlɑt̬əri/ *n.* plural **lotteries** [C] a game of chance in which people buy tickets in order to try to win a lot of money: *Maybe I'll **win the lottery**.*

loud[1] /laʊd/ *adj.* **1** making a lot of noise [≠ **quiet**, **soft**]: *The TV's too loud!*

THESAURUS

noisy – making a lot of noise, or full of noise: *a classroom full of noisy kids* | *a noisy bar*
rowdy – behaving in a noisy and uncontrolled way: *rowdy football fans*
thunderous – extremely loud: *thunderous applause*
deafening – very loud, so that you cannot hear anything else: *a deafening roar*
ear-splitting – painfully loud: *The Saints scored and the crowd erupted in an ear-splitting din.*
shrill – a shrill sound is high and unpleasant: *a shrill voice*
➔ QUIET

2 *disapproving* loud clothes are too brightly colored —**loudly** *adv.*

loud[2] *adv.* loudly: *Can you talk a little louder, please?* ➔ **out loud** at OUT[1]

ˈloud-mouth *n.* [C] *disapproving* someone who talks too much, too loudly, and often in an offensive way —**loud-mouthed** *adj.*

loud·speak·er /ˈlaʊdˌspikɚ/ *n.* [C] a piece of equipment that makes messages loud enough to be heard in a public place

lounge[1] /laʊndʒ/ *n.* [C] a room in a public building where people can relax, sit down, or drink: *We were watching TV in the student lounge.*

lounge[2] *v.* [I] to stand or sit in a lazy way: *We were lounging by the pool.*

louse[1] /laʊs/ *n.* plural **lice** /laɪs/ [C] a very small insect that lives on the skin and hair of animals and people

louse[2] *v.*
louse sth ⇔ **up** *phr. v.* to make a mistake or do something badly, especially so that it affects other people: *I don't want to louse things up in our relationship.*

lous·y /ˈlaʊzi/ *adj. informal* very bad: *What lousy weather!* | *I'm still **feeling** pretty **lousy*** (=feeling ill).

L

THESAURUS

bad, **awful**, **terrible**, **horrible**, **appalling**, **horrific**, **horrendous**, **atrocious**, **abysmal**
➔ see Thesaurus box at BAD[1]

lov·a·ble /ˈlʌvəbəl/ *adj.* easy to love: *a lovable child*

love[1] /lʌv/ *v.* [T] **1** to care very much about someone, especially a member of your family or a close friend: *It's incredible how much she loves those two kids.*

THESAURUS

If you **are infatuated with** someone, you have unreasonably strong feelings of love for him/her.
If you **have a crush on** someone, you have a strong feeling of love for him/her, but it usually only continues for a short time: *Carrie has a crush on her brother's best friend.*
If you **are crazy about** someone, you love him/her very much, especially in a way that you cannot control.
If you **are devoted to** someone, you love him/her and are loyal to him/her: *He has always been devoted to his wife.*
If you **adore** someone, you love him/her very much and are proud of him/her: *She adores her grandchildren.*
➔ HATE

2 to have a strong feeling of caring for and liking someone, combined with sexual attraction: *I love you, Betty.* | *Tom was the only man she had ever really loved.* **3** to like something very much, or enjoy doing something very much: *Tom loves to read.* | *I love being out in the woods.* | *Mom really loved her new dress.*

THESAURUS

enjoy, **like**, **have a good/great time**, **have fun**
➔ see Thesaurus box at ENJOY

4 to have a strong feeling of loyalty to your country, an institution, etc.: *He loves his country.* **5 I would love to/I'd love to (do sth)** *spoken* said when you really want to do something: *I'd love to come with you but I have work to do.*

love[2] *n.* **1** [U] a strong romantic feeling for someone: *He* ***is in love with*** *Laura.* | *They* ***fell in love.*** | *It was* ***love at first sight.*** **2** [U] the strong feeling of caring very much about someone or something: *a mother's* ***love for*** *her child* **3** [C,U] something that you like very much, or that you enjoy doing very much: *his* ***love of*** *music* **4** [C] someone whom you have romantic feelings about: *Mike was my* ***first love.*** **5 make love (to/with sb)** to have sex with someone you love **6 love/lots of love/all my love** *informal* written at the end of a letter to a friend, parent, husband, etc.: *Take care. Lots of love, Dad.*

ˈlove afˌfair *n.* [C] a romantic sexual relationship: *a secret love affair*

love·ly /ˈlʌvli/ *adj.* very nice, beautiful, or enjoyable: *Thank you for a lovely evening.*

lov·er /ˈlʌvɚ/ *n.* [C] **1** a sexual partner, usually someone whom you are not married to: *Greg was once her lover.* | *a pair of* ***young lovers*** **2** someone who enjoys something very much: *music lovers*

ˈlove seat *n.* [C] a small SOFA for two people

love·sick /ˈlʌvˌsɪk/ *adj.* sad because the person you love is not with you or does not love you

lov·ing /ˈlʌvɪŋ/ *adj.* very caring: *a wonderful, loving husband*

low[1] /loʊ/ *adj.* **1** not high, or not far above the ground [≠ **high**]: *Move the toys onto a lower shelf.* | *a low ceiling* | *low clouds* **2** small in degree or amount [≠ **high**]: *low temperatures* | *Their profits were lower than expected.* **3** bad, or below an acceptable standard [≠ **high**]: *a low grade in math* | *a low opinion of his work* **4** if a supply is low, you have used almost all of it: *We're* ***running/getting low on*** *gas.* **5** unhappy: *I've been* ***feeling*** *pretty* ***low*** *since he left.*

THESAURUS

sad, **unhappy**, **miserable**, **upset**, **depressed**, **down**, **homesick**, **gloomy**, **glum**
➔ see Thesaurus box at SAD

6 a low voice, sound, etc. is quiet or deep [≠ **high**]

THESAURUS

quiet, **soft**, **muffled**, **hushed**, **subdued**
➔ see Thesaurus box at QUIET[1]

7 lights that are low are not bright

low[2] *adv.* in a low position or at a low level [≠ **high**]: *The helicopters seemed to be flying very low.*

low[3] *n.* [C] a low price, level, degree, etc.: *Prices dropped to an* ***all-time low*** (=the lowest they have ever been). | *Tomorrow's low will be 25°F.*

low·brow /ˈloʊbraʊ/ *adj. disapproving* a lowbrow book, movie, etc. is not about serious ideas or not of very good quality

low-cal /ˌloʊˈkæl◂ / *adj. informal* low-cal food or drinks do not have many CALORIES

low·down /ˈloʊdaʊn/ *n.* **get the lowdown on sb/sth** *informal* to be given the important facts about someone or something

ˈlow-end *adj.* [usually before noun] *informal* not the most expensive or not of the best quality: *low-end home computers*

low·er[1] /ˈloʊɚ/ *adj.* [only before noun] **1** below something else [≠ **upper**]: *He began to bite his lower lip.* **2** near or at the bottom of something [≠ **upper**]: *the lower floors of the building* **3** less important than other things [≠ **upper**]: *the lower levels of the organization*

lower[2] *v.* **1** [I,T] to become less, or to reduce something in amount, degree, strength, etc.: *We're*

L

lowering prices on all our products! | *Please* ***lower your voice*** (=speak more quietly)*!*

THESAURUS

reduce, **decrease**, **cut**, **slash**, **roll back**
➔ see Thesaurus box at REDUCE

2 [T] to move something down: *The flag was lowered at sunset.*

low·er·case /ˈloʊɚˌkeɪs/ *n.* [U] letters written in their small form, such as a, b, c, etc. [≠ **upper-case**]

ˌlower ˈclass *n.* **the lower class** the group of people in society who have less money, power, or education than anyone else [➡ **middle class**, **upper class**, **working class**] —**lower-class** *adj.*: *a lower-class family*

ˌlow-ˈfat *adj.* low-fat food has very little fat: *low-fat milk* | *a low-fat diet*

ˌlow-ˈkey *adj.* not intended to attract a lot of attention: *The reception was very low-key.*

ˈlow life *n.* [C] *informal* someone who is involved in crime or who is bad —**low-life** *adj.*

low·ly /ˈloʊli/ *adj.* low in rank or importance

ˌlow-ˈlying *adj.* **1** low-lying land is not much higher than the level of the ocean **2** not very high: *low-lying fog*

loy·al /ˈlɔɪəl/ *adj.* always supporting a particular person, set of beliefs, or country [≠ **disloyal**]: *a loyal friend* | *The army has remained* ***loyal to*** *the government.*

THESAURUS

faithful, **devoted**, **staunch**
➔ see Thesaurus box at FAITHFUL

loy·al·ty /ˈlɔɪəlti/ *n.* **1** [U] the quality of being loyal to a particular person, set of beliefs, or country: *The company demands loyalty from its workers.* **2** [C usually plural] a feeling of wanting to help and encourage someone or something: *political loyalties*

loz·enge /ˈlɑzəndʒ/ *n.* [C] a small candy that has medicine in it

LSAT /ˈɛlsæt/ *n.* [C] *trademark* **Law School Admission Test** an examination taken by students who have completed a first degree and want to go to LAW SCHOOL

LSD *n.* [U] an illegal drug that makes people HALLUCINATE

lube /lub/ *v.* [T] *informal* to LUBRICATE the parts of a car's engine

lu·bri·cant /ˈlubrəkənt/ *n.* [C,U] a substance such as oil that is used on things that rub together, making them move more smoothly and easily

lu·bri·cate /ˈlubrəˌkeɪt/ *v.* [T] to put a LUBRICANT on something —**lubrication** /ˌlubrəˈkeɪʃən/ *n.* [U]

lu·cid /ˈlusɪd/ *adj.* **1** clearly expressed and easy to understand: *a lucid and interesting article* **2** able to think clearly and understand what is happening around you: *He was rarely lucid during his long illness.*

luck[1] /lʌk/ *n.* [U] **1** success or something good that happens by chance: *Have you* ***had any luck*** *finding a new roommate?* | ***Wish me luck!*** | ***Good luck*** *with your interview!*

USAGE

You can use **have** with **luck** only when luck has something before it such as "bad," "good," "any," or "a little bit of": *I've been trying to reach Jane all morning, but I haven't had any luck.*
Or you can use **be** with **lucky**: *You're lucky to live by the sea.* You cannot say you "have luck to do something."

2 the way in which good or bad things happen to people by chance: *I've had nothing but* ***good/bad luck*** *since moving here.* **3 be in luck/be out of luck** to get or not get something that you want: *You're in luck – there's one ticket left!* **4 just my luck!** *spoken* said when you are disappointed but not surprised that something bad has happened: *Just my luck! The guys just left.* **5 better luck next time** *spoken* said when you hope that someone will be more successful the next time s/he tries to do something ➔ **tough!/tough luck!** at TOUGH[1]

luck[2] *v.*
luck out *phr. v. informal* to be lucky: *I lucked out and got an A.*

luck·y /ˈlʌki/ *adj.* comparative **luckier**, superlative **luckiest** **1** having good luck [= **fortunate**; ≠ **unlucky**]: *He's* ***lucky to*** *be alive.* | *"I just got the last bus." "That was lucky!"* ➔ see Usage box at LUCKY[1] **2** bringing good luck: *7 is my* ***lucky number***. —**luckily** *adv.*: *Luckily, no one was hurt.*

lu·cra·tive /ˈlukrət̬ɪv/ *adj. formal* making you earn a lot of money: *lucrative deals*

lu·di·crous /ˈludɪkrəs/ *adj.* silly, wrong, and unreasonable [= **ridiculous**]

lug /lʌg/ *v.* past tense and past participle **lugged**, present participle **lugging** [T] *informal* to pull or carry something that is very heavy: *We* ***lugged*** *our suitcases* ***up*** *to our room.*

THESAURUS

carry, **tote**, **cart**, **haul**, **schlep**, **bear**
➔ see Thesaurus box at CARRY

lug·gage /ˈlʌgɪdʒ/ *n.* [U] the bags, etc. carried by people who are traveling [= **baggage**]: *We had lost our luggage.*

GRAMMAR

Luggage does not have a plural form. You can say **some luggage**, **any luggage**, or **pieces of luggage**: *Do you have any more luggage?*

lu·gu·bri·ous /ləˈgubriəs/ *adj. literary* very sad and serious

L

luke·warm /ˌluk'wɔrm◂ / *adj.* **1** a liquid that is lukewarm is only slightly warm

THESAURUS

hot, **boiling**, **scalding**, **warm**
➔ see Thesaurus box at HOT

2 not showing very much interest or excitement: *His idea got only a* ***lukewarm response*** *from the committee.*

lull¹ /lʌl/ *v.* [T] **1** to make someone feel calm or sleepy: *Singing softly, she* ***lulled*** *us* ***to sleep***. **2** to make someone feel so safe and confident that you can easily deceive him/her: *She was* ***lulled into*** *believing that there was no danger.*

lull² *n.* [C] a short period when there is less activity or noise than usual: *a* ***lull in*** *the conversation*

lul·la·by /'lʌləˌbaɪ/ *n.* plural **lullabies** [C] a song that you sing to children in order to make them calm and sleepy

lum·ber¹ /'lʌmbɚ/ *n.* [U] trees that are cut down and used as wood for building

lumber² *v.* [I] to move in a slow awkward way, usually because you are heavy

lum·ber·jack /'lʌmbɚˌdʒæk/ *n.* [C] someone whose job is to cut down trees for wood

lumberjack

lu·mi·nar·y /'luməˌnɛri/ *n.* plural **luminaries** [C] someone who is famous and respected because of his/her knowledge or skills

lu·mi·nous /'lumənəs/ *adj.* able to shine in the dark without being lit: *luminous paint*

lump¹ /lʌmp/ *n.* **1** [C] a small piece of something solid that does not have a definite shape: *a* ***lump of*** *clay*

THESAURUS

piece, **scrap**, **chunk**, **fragment**, **crumb**
➔ see Thesaurus box at PIECE¹

2 [C] a hard swollen area on someone's skin or in his/her body **3 a lump in your throat** the tight feeling in your throat that happens when you want to cry

lump² *v.* [T] to put two or more different people or things together and consider them as a single group: *Do you think I can* ***lump*** *these ideas* ***into*** *one paragraph?*

ˌlump 'sum *n.* [C] an amount of money given in a single payment

lump·y /'lʌmpi/ *adj.* comparative **lumpier**, superlative **lumpiest** having lumps and therefore not smooth: *a lumpy mattress*

lu·na·cy /'lunəsi/ *n.* [U] actions or behavior that seem very stupid and unreasonable

lu·nar /'lunɚ/ *adj.* relating to the moon: *a lunar eclipse*

lu·na·tic /'lunətɪk/ *n.* [C] someone who behaves in a crazy, stupid, or very strange way —**lunatic** *adj.*

lunch /lʌntʃ/ *n.* [C,U] a meal eaten in the middle of the day, or that time of day: *What do you want* ***for lunch****? | When do you usually* ***eat lunch****? | We've already* ***had lunch****. | I'll see you* ***at lunch****. |* ***school lunches*** *for children*

COLLOCATIONS

have/eat lunch
have sth for lunch – to eat a particular food for lunch
go out for lunch – to go to eat lunch in a restaurant
take sb out to lunch – to take someone to a restaurant for lunch and pay the bill
be at lunch – to not be working because you are having lunch
break for lunch – to stop working in order to eat lunch
(brown) bag lunch also **sack lunch** – food, for example a sandwich, that you take to work or school for lunch
➔ MEAL

lunch·eon /'lʌntʃən/ *n.* [C,U] *formal* LUNCH

lunch·time /'lʌntʃtaɪm/ *n.* [C,U] the time in the middle of the day when people usually eat lunch: *Is it lunchtime yet? | I usually go for a walk* ***at lunchtime***.

lung /lʌŋ/ *n.* [C] one of two organs in your body that you use for breathing ➔ see picture on page A3

lunge /lʌndʒ/ *v.* [I] to make a sudden forceful movement toward someone or something: *She suddenly* ***lunged at*** *me.* —**lunge** *n.* [C]

lurch¹ /lɚtʃ/ *v.* [I] to walk or move in an unsteady uncontrolled way

lurch² *n.* **1** [C] a sudden movement **2 leave sb in the lurch** to leave someone at a time when you should stay and help him/her

lure¹ /lʊr/ *v.* [T] to persuade someone to do something by making it seem attractive, exciting, etc.: *Another company tried to lure him over by offering more money.*

lure² *n.* **1** [C usually singular, U] something that attracts people, or the quality of being able to do this: ***the lure of*** *power and money* **2** [C] an object used in order to attract animals or fish so that they can be caught

lu·rid /'lʊrɪd/ *adj. disapproving* a description, story, etc. that is lurid is deliberately shocking and involves sex or violence: *the lurid details of the murder*

lurk /lɚk/ *v.* [I] **1** to wait somewhere secretly, usually before doing something bad: *men lurking in the alley* **2** if you lurk in a CHAT ROOM on the

Internet, you read what other people are writing to each other, but you do not write any messages yourself

lus·cious /ˈlʌʃəs/ *adj.* extremely good to eat: *luscious ripe strawberries*

lush¹ /lʌʃ/ *adj.* having lots of very green and healthy plants or leaves: *New Zealand is a country of lush green hills.*

lush² *n.* [C] *informal* someone who drinks too much alcohol

lust¹ /lʌst/ *n.* [C,U] a very strong feeling of sexual desire, or a strong desire for something such as power or money: *his* ***lust for*** *power*

lust² *v.*

lust after/for sb/sth *phr. v.* **1** to have a strong feeling of sexual desire for someone **2** to want something very much that you do not have yet: *politicians lusting for power*

lus·ter /ˈlʌstɚ/ *n.* [singular, U] an attractive shiny appearance —**lustrous** /ˈlʌstrəs/ *adj.*

lust·y /ˈlʌsti/ *adj. literary* strong and healthy [= **powerful**]: *the lusty cry of a newborn baby* —**lustily** *adv.*

Lu·ther·an /ˈluθərən/ *adj.* relating to the Protestant church that follows the ideas of Martin Luther —**Lutheran** *n.* [C]

lux·u·ri·ant /lʌgˈʒʊriənt, lʌkˈʃʊ-/ *adj.* healthy and growing thickly and strongly

lux·u·ri·ate /lʌgˈʒʊrieɪt, lʌkˈʃʊ-/ *v.*

luxuriate in sth *phr. v.* to relax and enjoy the pleasure you feel: *She luxuriated in the hot bath.*

lux·u·ri·ous /lʌgˈʒʊriəs, lʌkˈʃʊ-/ *adj.* very comfortable, beautiful, and expensive: *a luxurious hotel*

lux·u·ry /ˈlʌkʃəri, ˈlʌgʒəri/ *n.* plural **luxuries** **1** [U] very great comfort and pleasure that you get from expensive food, beautiful houses, cars, etc.: *They lead* ***a life of luxury***. | *a* ***luxury car/hotel*** **2** [C] something expensive that you want but do not need: *Back in the 1950s, a washing machine was a luxury.*

Ly·cra /ˈlaɪkrə/ *n.* [U] *trademark* a cloth that stretches, used especially for making tight-fitting sports clothes

ly·ing /ˈlaɪ-ɪŋ/ *v.* the present participle of LIE

lynch /lɪntʃ/ *v.* [T] if a crowd of people lynches someone, they kill that person by HANGing him/her, without using the usual legal process —**lynching** *n.* [C]

lynch·pin /ˈlɪntʃˌpɪn/ *n.* [C] a LINCHPIN

lyr·ic /ˈlɪrɪk/ *n.* [C usually plural] the words of a song

lyr·i·cal /ˈlɪrɪkəl/ *adj.* expressing strong emotions in a beautiful way: *lyrical poetry*

lyr·i·cist /ˈlɪrəsɪst/ *n.* [C] someone who writes lyrics

M, m

M

M, m /em/ **1** the thirteenth letter of the English alphabet **2** the ROMAN NUMERAL for 1,000

m **1** the written abbreviation of **meter** **2** the written abbreviation of **million** **3** the written abbreviation of **male** **4** the written abbreviation of **mile** **5** the written abbreviation of **married** **6** the written abbreviation of **medium**, used especially in clothes

MA the written abbreviation of **Massachusetts**

ma /mɑ, mɔ/ *n.* [C] *old-fashioned* mother

M.A. *n.* [C] **Master of Arts** a university degree in a subject such as history or literature that you can get after you have your first degree [➡ **M.S.**]: *Eve* ***has*** *an* ***M.A. in*** *French.*

ma'am /mæm/ *n. spoken* [C] used in order to speak politely to a woman when you do not know her name [➡ **miss, sir**]: *May I help you, ma'am?*

ma·ca·bre /məˈkɑbrə, məˈkɑb/ *adj. literary* strange, frightening, and relating to death or injury: *a macabre tale*

mac·a·da·mi·a /ˌmækəˈdeɪmiə/ *n.* [C] a sweet white nut that grows on a tropical tree, or the tree that produces this nut

mac·a·ro·ni /ˌmækəˈroʊni/ *n.* [U] a type of PASTA in the shape of small curved tubes: ***macaroni and cheese*** (=macaroni cooked with a cheese sauce) ➔ see picture on page A5

Mace /meɪs/ *n.* [U] *trademark* a chemical that makes your eyes and skin sting painfully, which some people carry to defend themselves

ma·che·te /məˈʃɛt̬i, -ˈtʃɛ-/ *n.* [C] a large knife with a broad heavy blade, used as a tool for cutting or as a weapon

ma·chine¹ /məˈʃin/ *n.* [C] **1** a piece of equipment that uses power such as electricity to do a particular job: *a* ***washing/sewing machine*** | *Just hit that button to stop the machine.* | *I left a message on her machine* (=answering machine).

THESAURUS

appliance – a machine that is used in the home: *kitchen appliances such as refrigerators*
device – a piece of equipment that is usually small and usually electronic, that does a special job: *A seismograph is a device that measures earthquake activity.*
gadget – a small piece of equipment that makes a particular job easier to do: *a new gadget for opening wine bottles*

2 a computer: *My machine just crashed again.*

machine² *v.* [T] to make or shape something, especially metal parts, using a machine

maˈchine gun *n.* [C] a gun that fires a lot of bullets very quickly

ma,chine-'readable *adj.* able to be understood and used by a computer: *machine-readable text*

ma·chin·er·y /mə'ʃinəri/ *n.* [U] **1** machines, especially large ones: *farm machinery* | *You shouldn't drive or operate* ***heavy machinery*** *while taking this medication.* **2** the parts inside a machine that make it work **3** an official system or set of processes for organizing or achieving something: *The machinery of the law works slowly.*

M

ma·chin·ist /mə'ʃinɪst/ *n.* [C] someone who operates or makes machines

ma·cho /'mɑtʃoʊ/ *adj. informal* a man who is macho has qualities such as strength that are typical of men, but is not sensitive or sympathetic

mack·er·el /'mækərəl/ *n.* [C,U] a common sea fish that has a strong taste, or the meat from this fish

mac·ro·cos·m /'mækrə,kɑzəm/ *n.* [C] a large complicated system such as the whole universe or a society, considered as a single unit [➡ **microcosm**]

mad /mæd/ *adj.* comparative **madder**, superlative **maddest** **1** *informal* angry: *Are you still* ***mad at*** *me?* | *You* ***make*** *me so* ***mad!*** | *Lucy* ***got mad*** *and told us all to leave.*

THESAURUS

angry, **annoyed**, **irritated**, **livid**, **furious**
➔ see Thesaurus box at ANGRY

2 do sth like mad *informal* to do something as quickly as you can: *Carlos was writing like mad at the end of the exam.* **3** behaving in a wild, uncontrolled way, without thinking about what you are doing: *We made* ***a mad dash for*** (=ran wildly toward) *the door.* **4 power-mad/money-mad etc.** only thinking about power, money, etc.: *a power-mad dictator*

mad·am /'mædəm/ *n.* **1 Dear Madam** used at the beginning of a business letter to a woman whose name you do not know **2 Madam President/Ambassador etc.** used to address a woman who has an important official position **3** [C] a woman who is in charge of a BROTHEL

mad·den·ing /'mædn-ɪŋ, 'mædnɪŋ/ *adj.* very annoying: *maddening behavior*

made /meɪd/ *v.* **1** the past tense and past participle of MAKE **2 be made of sth** to be produced from a particular substance or material: *The frame is made of silver.*

USAGE

Use **made of** when you can clearly see what material has been used to make something: *a table made of wood* | *a handbag made of leather*
Use **made from** when the materials have been completely changed in the process of making something: *Paper is made from wood.* | *soap made from the finest ingredients*
Use **made by** to talk about the person or company that has made something: *furniture made by craftsmen*

3 be made for each other *informal* to be completely suitable for each other, especially as husband and wife: *I think Anna and Juan were made for each other.* **4 sb has (got) it made** *informal* to have everything that you need for a happy life or to be successful

mad·house /'mædhaʊs/ *n.* [C] a place that is very busy and noisy

mad·ly /'mædli/ *adv.* **1 madly in love (with sb)** very much in love **2** in a wild, uncontrolled way: *Shoppers were rushing madly through the store.*

mad·man /'mædmæn, -mən/ *n.* [C] plural **madmen** /-mɛn, -mən/ someone who behaves in a wild uncontrolled way: *He drives* ***like a madman.***

mad·ness /'mædnɪs/ *n.* [U] very stupid and often dangerous behavior: ***It's madness to*** *spend that kind of money on a car.*

Ma·don·na /mə'dɑnə/ *n.* **1 the Madonna** Mary, the mother of Jesus Christ in the Christian religion **2** [C] a picture or figure of the Madonna

mael·strom /'meɪlstrəm/ *n.* [C] *literary* a situation full of events that you cannot control or strong emotions that make people feel confused or frightened

mae·stro /'maɪstroʊ/ *n.* [C] someone who can do something very well, especially a musician

ma·fi·a /'mɑfiə/ *n.* **the Mafia** a large organization of criminals who control many illegal activities

mag·a·zine /,mægə'zin, 'mægə,zin/ *n.* [C] **1** a large thin book with a paper cover that contains news stories, articles, photographs, etc., and is sold weekly or monthly: *a* ***fashion/computer/news magazine*** | *He* ***subscribes to*** *several* ***magazines.*** | *a* ***magazine article*** **2** the part of a gun that holds the bullets

ma·gen·ta /mə'dʒɛntə/ *n.* [U] a dark purple-red color —**magenta** *adj.*

mag·got /'mægət/ *n.* [C] the LARVA (=young insect) of a fly that lives in decaying food or flesh

mag·ic[1] /'mædʒɪk/ *n.* [U] **1** a special power that makes strange or impossible things happen: *Do you believe in magic?*

THESAURUS

witchcraft – the use of magic, usually to do bad things: *Hundreds of women were accused of witchcraft in the 1600s.*
spell – a piece of magic that someone does, or the special words or ceremonies used in making it happen: *An evil witch cast a spell on him, turning him into a beast.*

curse – magic words that bring someone bad luck: *People believed the pharaoh would put a curse on anyone who broke into the tomb.*
the occult – the knowledge and study of magic and spirits: *stories that deal with the occult*

2 the skill of doing tricks that look like magic, or the tricks themselves **3** an attractive quality that makes someone or something interesting or exciting: *Christmas has lost some of its magic for me over the years.*

magic² *adj.* [only before noun] **1** a magic word or object has special powers that make strange or impossible things happen: *a magic sword | a book of **magic spells*** **2** relating to the skill of doing tricks that look like magic: *His best **magic trick** is sawing the lady in half.*

mag·i·cal /ˈmædʒɪkəl/ *adj.* **1** very enjoyable and exciting, in a strange or special way: *a magical evening beneath the stars* **2** containing magic, or done using magic: *magical powers* —**magically** *adv.*

ma·gi·cian /məˈdʒɪʃən/ *n.* [C] someone who entertains people by doing magic tricks

ˌMagic ˈMarker *n.* [C,U] *trademark* a large pen with a thick soft point

ma·gis·trate /ˈmædʒɪˌstreɪt, -strɪt/ *n.* [C] someone who judges less serious crimes in a court of law

mag·nan·i·mous /mægˈnænəməs/ *adj. formal* kind and generous toward other people —**magnanimity** /ˌmægnəˈnɪməṭi/ *n.* [U]

mag·nate /ˈmægneɪt, -nɪt/ *n.* **steel/oil/shipping etc. magnate** a wealthy and powerful person in the steel, etc. industry

mag·ne·si·um /mægˈniziəm, -ʒəm/ *n.* [U] a light silver-white metal that is often used in medicine and to make other metals

mag·net /ˈmægnɪt/ *n.* [C] **1** a piece of iron or steel that can make other metal objects move toward it **2** a person or place that attracts many other people or things: *The city has become **a magnet for** many new industries.* —**magnetize** /ˈmægnəˌtaɪz/ *v.* [T]

mag·net·ic /mægˈnɛṭɪk/ *adj.* **1** having the power of a magnet: *the Earth's magnetic field* **2 magnetic tape/disk etc.** a special TAPE, etc. that contains electronic information which can be read by a computer or other machine **3 magnetic personality** a quality that someone has that makes other people feel strongly attracted to him/her

mag·net·ism /ˈmægnəˌtɪzəm/ *n.* [U] **1** a quality that makes other people feel attracted to you: *He had a magnetism that drew women to him.* **2** the power that a magnet has to attract things

mag·nif·i·cent /mægˈnɪfəsənt/ *adj.* very impressive because of being big, beautiful, etc.: *The view was magnificent.* —**magnificence** *n.* [U]

mag·ni·fy /ˈmægnəˌfaɪ/ *v.* [T] past tense and past participle **magnified**, third person singular **magnifies** **1** to make something appear larger than it is: *A microscope magnifies the image so you can see the cells.* **2** to make something seem more important or worse than it really is: *The reports tend to magnify the risks involved.* —**magnification** /ˌmægnəfəˈkeɪʃən/ *n.* [C,U]

ˈmagnifying ˌglass *n.* [C] a round piece of glass with a handle, that magnifies things when you look through it ➔ see picture at MAGNIFY

mag·ni·tude /ˈmægnəˌtud/ *n.* [U] **1** how large or important something is: *I hadn't realized **the magnitude of** the problem.* **2** *technical* how strong an EARTHQUAKE is, or how bright a star is

mag·no·lia /mægˈnoʊlyə/ *n.* [C] a tree or bush with large white, yellow, pink, or purple sweet-smelling flowers

mag·pie /ˈmægpaɪ/ *n.* [C] a wild bird with black and white feathers and a loud cry

ma·hog·a·ny /məˈhɑgəni/ *n.* [U] a tropical American tree, or the hard dark wood of this tree

maid /meɪd/ *n.* [C] **1** a woman whose job is to clean rooms, serve meals, wash clothes, etc. in a large house **2** a woman whose job is to clean rooms in a hotel

maid·en¹ /ˈmeɪdn/ **also maid** *n.* [C] *literary* a young woman or girl who is not married

maiden² *adj.* **maiden flight/voyage** the first trip that an airplane or ship makes

ˈmaiden name *n.* [C] the family name that a woman had before she got married and began using her husband's name ➔ see Thesaurus box at NAME¹

ˌmaid of ˈhonor *n.* [C] the main BRIDESMAID in a wedding

TOPIC

bride, groom, best man, bridesmaids
➔ see Topic box at WEDDING

mail¹ /meɪl/ *n.* [U] **1** the system of collecting and delivering letters, packages, etc.: *What time does the mail come? | I just put the letter **in the mail**. | You can renew your passport **by mail**.* **2** the letters, packages, etc. that are delivered to a particular person or at a particular time: *They sent his mail to the wrong address.* **3** messages that are sent and received on a computer [= **email**] ➔ AIRMAIL

mail² *v.* [T] **1** to send a letter, package, etc. to someone: *I'll **mail** it **to** you tomorrow.* **2** to send a document to someone using a computer [= **email**]: *Can you mail it to me as an attachment?*

mail·box /ˈmeɪlbɑks/ *n.* [C] **1** a box, usually outside a house, where someone's letters are delivered or collected **2** a special box outdoors or at a POST OFFICE where you mail letters **3** the part of a computer's memory where email messages are stored

mail·ing /ˈmeɪlɪŋ/ *n.* [C,U] the act of sending a large number of letters, advertisements, etc. at the same time, or the total number of letters that you send

M

ˈmailing list *n.* [C] a list of people's names and addresses that a company keeps in order to send information or advertisements to them: *We have more than 1,000 names* ***on our mailing list.*** ➔ see Thesaurus box at LIST¹

mail·man /ˈmeɪlmæn, -mən/ *n.* [C] plural **mailmen** /-mɛn, -mən/ a man who delivers mail to people's houses

ˌmail ˈorder *n.* [U] a method of buying and selling in which you buy goods from a company that sends them by mail: *a* ***mail order catalog***

maim /meɪm/ *v.* [T] *formal* to injure someone very seriously and often permanently: *The accident* ***maimed*** *her* ***for life.***

main¹ /meɪn/ *adj.* [only before noun] **1** bigger or more important than all other things, ideas, etc. of the same kind: *Let's meet by the main entrance.* | *My main goal is to compete in the Olympics.* | *He left the job because of money – at least that was the* ***main reason.*** **2 the main thing** *spoken* used in order to say what the most important thing is in a situation: *As long as you're not hurt,* ***that's the main thing.***

main² *n.* [C] a large pipe carrying water or gas that is connected to people's houses by smaller pipes: *a frozen* ***water main***

main·frame /ˈmeɪnfreɪm/ *n.* [C] a large computer that can work very fast and that a lot of people can use at the same time

main·land /ˈmeɪnlænd, -lənd/ *n.* **the mainland** the main area of land that forms a country, as compared to islands near it that are also part of that country —**mainland** *adj.*: *mainland China*

main·ly /ˈmeɪnli/ *adv.* used in order to mention the main part or cause of something, the main reason for something, etc.: *Students in our program are mainly from Asia.* | *Their diet consists mainly of rice and beans.* | *I don't go out much,* ***mainly because*** *I have to look after the kids.*

THESAURUS

chiefly – mainly: *How quickly you recover depends chiefly on your state of health before the operation.*
principally – firstly and most importantly: *Foreign aid was sent principally to the south of the region.*
largely – mainly, and because of a particular reason: *The school is in a largely black neighborhood.*
primarily – mainly because of one reason or situation, which is more important than any other: *We are primarily concerned with the effect this will have on the students here.*

main·stay /ˈmeɪnsteɪ/ *n.* [C] the most important part of something that makes it possible for it to work correctly or to continue to exist: *Farming is still* ***the mainstay of*** *our country's economy.*

main·stream /ˈmeɪnstrim/ *n.* **the mainstream** the beliefs and opinions that represent the most usual way of thinking about or doing something, or the people who have these beliefs and opinions: *The Green Party is still outside the mainstream in American politics.* —**mainstream** *adj.*: *mainstream Hollywood movies*

main·tain /meɪnˈteɪn/ *v.* [T] **1** to make something continue in the same way or at the same standard as before: *The U.S. and Britain have maintained close ties.* | *It is important to maintain a healthy weight.* **2** to keep something in good condition by taking care of it: *It costs a lot of money to maintain a big house.* **3** to strongly express an opinion or attitude: *I've always* ***maintained that*** *any changes in the law will hurt the poor more than the rich.* | *From the beginning, James has* ***maintained*** *his* ***innocence.***

main·te·nance /ˈmeɪntˀn-əns/ *n.* [U] the work that is necessary to keep something in good condition: *car maintenance* | *the* ***maintenance of*** *school buildings*

ma·jes·tic /məˈdʒɛstɪk/ *adj.* looking very big and impressive: *a majestic view of the lake* —**majestically** *adv.*

THESAURUS

impressive, **imposing**, **dazzling**, **awe-inspiring**, **breathtaking**
➔ see Thesaurus box at IMPRESSIVE

maj·es·ty /ˈmædʒəsti/ *n.* **1** [U] the quality of being impressive and beautiful: *the majesty of the Great Pyramids* **2 Your/Her/His Majesty** used when talking to or about a king or queen

ma·jor¹ /ˈmeɪdʒɚ/ *adj.* [usually before noun] very large or important, especially when compared to other things or people of a similar kind [≠ **minor**]: *major surgery* | *There were no* ***major problems.*** | *Training new employees is a major part of her job.* ▶ Don't say "major than." Say "more important than" or "bigger than." ◀

THESAURUS

important, **crucial**, **vital**, **essential**, **significant**, **key**
➔ see Thesaurus box at IMPORTANT

major² *n.* [C] **1** the main subject that you study at a college or university [➡ **minor**]: *His major is history.* ➔ see Topic box at UNIVERSITY **2** someone who is studying a particular subject as his or her main subject at a college or university: *Darla was a biology major.* **3** a middle rank in the Army, Air Force, or Marines, or an officer who has this rank

major³ *v.*

major in sth *phr. v.* to study something as your

main subject at a college or university: *I'm majoring in biology.*

ma·jor·i·ty[1] /mə'dʒɔrət̬i, -'dʒɑr-/ *n.* plural **majorities** **1** [singular] most of the people or things in a particular group [≠ **minority**]: ***The majority of** people support the president.* | ***the vast majority*** (=nearly everyone) **2** [C usually singular] the difference between the number of votes gained by the winning party or person in an election and the number gained by other parties or people: *He won by **a majority of** 500 votes.*

majority[2] *adj.* [only before noun] happening as a result of the decision of most members of a group: *a **majority decision/ruling***

ˌmajor-'league *adj.* [usually before noun] **1** relating to the Major Leagues: *a major-league pitcher* **2** important or having a lot of power: *a major-league player in Michigan politics*

ˌMajor 'Leagues also **Majors** *n.* [plural] the group of teams that make up the highest level of American professional baseball [➡ **Minor Leagues**]

ma·jor·ly /'meɪdʒɚli/ *adv. spoken slang* very or extremely: *When they broke up, he was majorly depressed.*

make[1] /meɪk/ *v.* past tense and past participle **made** /meɪd/ present participle **making**

1 PRODUCE STH [T] to produce something by working or doing something: *Can I call you back? I'm making dinner.* | *She made the curtains herself.* | *My flute was made in Japan.*

2 DO STH [T] used before some nouns to show that someone does the action of the noun: *Maybe they **made** a **mistake**.* | *We've finally **made** a **decision**.* | *Do you want to **make** an **appointment** with the doctor?*

3 CAUSE [T] to cause a particular state or situation to happen: *Thanks for listening – you've really made me feel better.* | *That button makes the machine stop.* | *What made you decide to become a lawyer?* ▶ Don't say "What made you to decide to become a lawyer?" ◀

4 FORCE [T] to force someone to do something: *Mom, make Billy stop it!* | *I wasn't hungry, but I made myself eat something.*

5 EARN MONEY [T] to earn or get money: *He's working Saturdays to make some extra money.*

USAGE

Make is a less formal way of saying **earn**: *I make $20 an hour.*
Gain means to get something useful or necessary: *I've gained a lot of useful experience.* Do not use **gain** to talk about getting money for the work you do. Use **earn** or **make**: *He earns more than I do.*
Win means to get a prize in a game or competition: *The first person to get all the answers right will win $100.*

6 NUMBER [linking verb] to be a particular number or amount when added together: *2 and 2 make 4.* | *If you include us, that makes eight people for dinner.*

7 make time (for sb/sth) to leave enough time to do something: *She always makes time for exercise.*

8 BE SUITABLE [linking verb] to have the qualities that are necessary for a particular job, use, or purpose: *John will make a good father.* | *Sonia's life would make a good movie.*

9 make a difference to cause a change, especially one that improves a situation: *Having a car has **made a big difference** in our lives.*

10 make it a) to arrive somewhere: *We just **made it to** the hospital before the baby arrived.* **b)** to be able to go to an event, meeting, etc.: *I'm sorry I can't **make it to** your play.* **c)** to be successful in a particular business or activity: *He's **made it big*** (=has been very successful) *in Hollywood.* **d)** to live after a serious illness or injury, or to deal with a very difficult situation: *Mom **made it through** the operation all right.*

11 make the bed to pull the sheets and BLANKETS over a bed to make it look neat when you are not sleeping in it

12 that makes two of us *spoken* used in order to say that you feel the same way that someone else does: *"I'm so tired!" "Yeah, that makes two of us."*

13 make or break to cause either great success or failure: *The first year can make or break a new business.*

14 make do to manage to do something using the things you already have, even though they are not exactly what you want: *We'll have to **make do with** a quick sandwich.*

15 make believe to pretend that something is true, especially as a game ➔ **be made of** at MADE[2] ➔ **make a (big) difference/make all the difference** at DIFFERENCE ➔ **make love** at LOVE[2] ➔ **make sense** at SENSE[1] ➔ **make the best of sth** at BEST[3] ➔ **make friends (with sb)** at FRIEND ➔ **make up your mind** at MIND[1]

make for sth *phr. v.* **1** to go toward a place: *We made for the exit.* **2** to have a particular result or effect: *It should make for an interesting evening.* ➔ **be made for each other** at MADE[2]

make sth ⇔ **into** sth *phr. v.* to change something into something else: *We can make your room into a study.*

make sth **of** sb/sth *phr. v.* **1** to have a particular opinion about someone or something, or a particular way of understanding something: *I really don't know what to make of him.* **2 make the most of sth** to use an opportunity in a way that gives you as much advantage as possible: *I want to make the most of the time I have left in Europe.* **3 make too much of sth** to treat a situation as if it is more important than it really is: *He doesn't like to make too much of his birthday.* ➔ **make a fool of yourself** at FOOL[1]

make off with sth *phr. v.* to steal something: *They made off with our TV.*

make out *phr. v.* **1 make** (sth ⇔) **out** to be able to hear, see, or understand something: *I can't make out what the sign says.* **2 make a check out to sb** to write a check so that the money is paid to a particular person, company, store, etc. **3 make out (that)** *informal* to say that something is true when it is not: *The situation was never as bad as the media made out.* **4 how did sb make out ...?** *spoken* used in order to ask if someone did something well: *"How did you make out in the interview?" "I think it went well."* **5** *spoken* to kiss and touch someone in a sexual way

make up *phr. v.* **1 make** (sth ⇔) **up** to invent a story, explanation, etc. in order to deceive someone: *Ron made up an excuse so his mother wouldn't be mad.* **2 make** (sth ⇔) **up** to produce a new story, song, game, etc.: *"What are you singing?" "I don't know, I just made it up."* **3 make up** sth to combine together to form a substance, group, system, etc.: *the rocks and minerals that make up the earth's outer layer* | *Women make up 60% of our employees.* **4 make up** sth to add to an amount in order to bring it up to the level that is needed: *We're going to have to charge more to* ***make up the difference***. **5 make** (sth ⇔) **up** to work at times when you do not usually work because you have not done enough work at some other time: *I have to leave early, but I'll* ***make up the time/work*** *tomorrow.* **6 make** (sb ⇔) **up** to put MAKEUP on someone's face in order to make him/her look better or different: *They made him up to look like an old man.* **7 make it up to sb** to do something good for someone because you feel responsible for something bad that happened to him/her: *I'm sorry I forgot! I promise I'll make it up to you.* **8 make up** to become friends with someone again, after you have had an argument: *Have you two made up?*

make up for sth *phr. v.* **1** to make a bad situation or event seem better: *He bought everyone a drink to make up for being late.* **2** to have so much of one quality that it does not matter that you do not have others: *Jay lacks experience, but he makes up for it with hard work.* **3 make up for lost time** to do something very quickly because you started late or something made you work too slowly

make[2] *n.* **1** [C] a product made by a particular company: *"What make is your car?" "It's a Chevy."*

THESAURUS

type, **kind**, **sort**, **category**, **brand**, **model**, **genre**

→ see Thesaurus box at TYPE[1]

2 be on the make *disapproving* to be trying hard to get something such as money or sex

'make-be,lieve *adj., adv.* not real, but imagined or pretended: *Many small children have make-believe friends.*

mak·er /ˈmeɪkɚ/ *n.* [C] **1** a person, company, or machine that makes something or does something: *U.S. auto makers* | *a coffee maker* **2 decision maker/peacemaker etc.** someone who is good at or responsible for making decisions, stopping arguments, etc.

make·shift /ˈmeɪkˌʃɪft/ *adj.* [only before noun] made for temporary use when you need something and there is nothing better available: *a makeshift table made from boxes*

make·up /ˈmeɪk-ʌp/ *n.* **1** [U] substances such as powder, creams, and LIPSTICK that some people, usually women or actors, put on their faces: *I waited for Ginny to* ***put on her makeup***. **2** [singular] all the parts, members, or qualities that make up something: *We haven't yet been told what* ***the makeup of*** *the new government will be* (=who the members will be).

mak·ing /ˈmeɪkɪŋ/ *n.* **1** [U] the process or business of making something: *The making of the movie took four years.* | *the art of rug making* **2 in the making** in the process of being made or produced: *The deal was 11 months in the making.* **3 have the makings of sth** to have the qualities or skills needed to become a particular type of person or thing: *Sandy has the makings of a good doctor.*

mal·a·dy /ˈmælədi/ *n.* plural **maladies** [C] *formal* **1** an illness **2** something that is wrong with a system or organization

mal·aise /mæˈleɪz/ *n.* [U] *formal* a feeling of anxiety, and a lack of confidence and satisfaction

ma·lar·i·a /məˈlɛriə/ *n.* [U] a serious disease that is common in hot countries and is caused by the bite of an infected MOSQUITO

male /meɪl/ *adj.* **1** belonging to the sex that cannot have babies [≠ **female**]: *a male lion* | *Many women earn less than their male colleagues.* **2** typical of this sex [≠ **female**]: *a male voice* —**male** *n.* [C]

,male 'chauvinist also **,male ,chauvinist 'pig** *n.* [C] a man who believes that men are better than women —**male chauvinism** *n.* [U]

ma·lev·o·lent /məˈlɛvələnt/ *adj. formal* showing a desire to harm other people —**malevolence** *n.* [U]

mal·func·tion /mælˈfʌŋkʃən/ *n.* [C] a fault in the way a machine works: *a* ***malfunction in*** *the computer system* —**malfunction** *v.* [I]

mal·ice /ˈmælɪs/ *n.* [U] the desire to harm or upset someone: *The criticism was made* ***without malice***.

ma·li·cious /məˈlɪʃəs/ *adj.* showing a desire to harm or upset someone: *malicious gossip* —**maliciously** *adv.*

ma·lign /məˈlaɪn/ *v.* [T] *formal* to say or write unpleasant and untrue things about someone: *He's been* ***much maligned*** *by the press.*

ma·lig·nant /məˈlɪgnənt/ *adj. technical* a malignant TUMOR (=a group of growing cells) contains CANCER and may kill someone [≠ **benign**] —**malignancy** *n.* [U]

Picture Dictionary

Learner's Handbook

tail feathers
beak
throat
breast
claw
webbed foot
talon
antler
whiskers
fang
fur
horn
front leg
hind leg
paw
claw
tusk
trunk
pouch
hooves
antenna
wing
tail
scales
fin
chrysalis
eggs
gill
caterpillar/larva

face

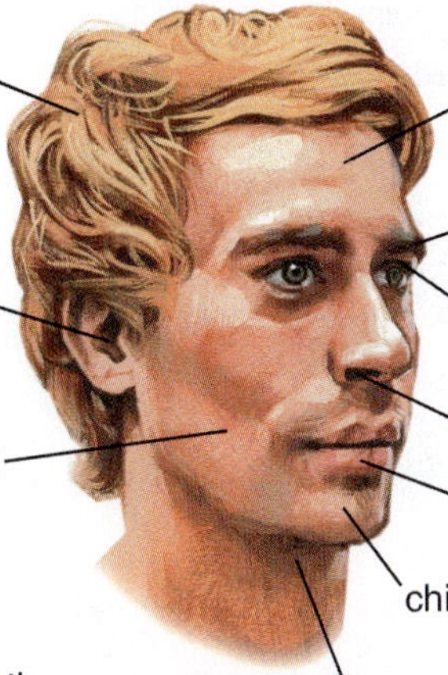

body

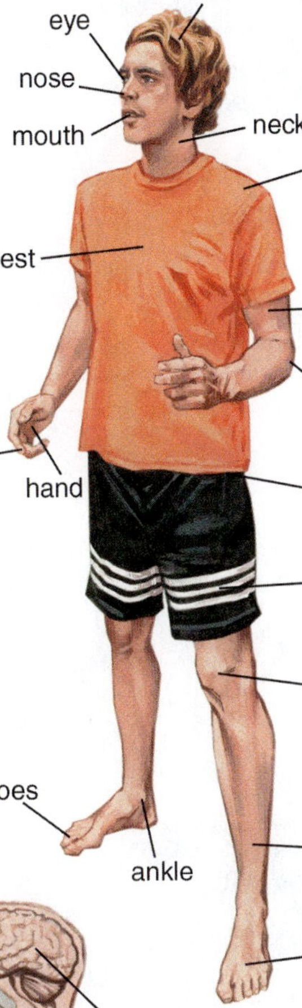

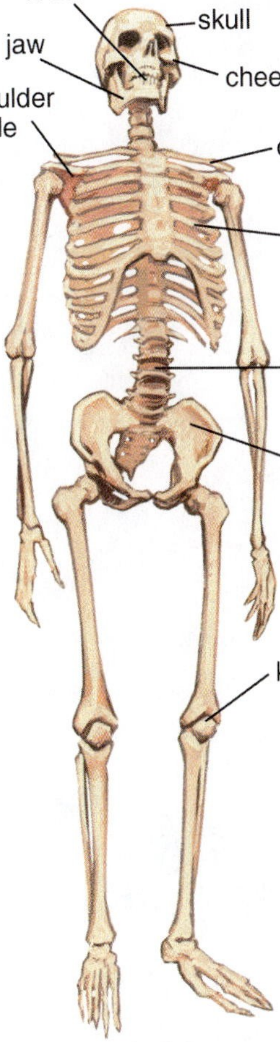

skeleton

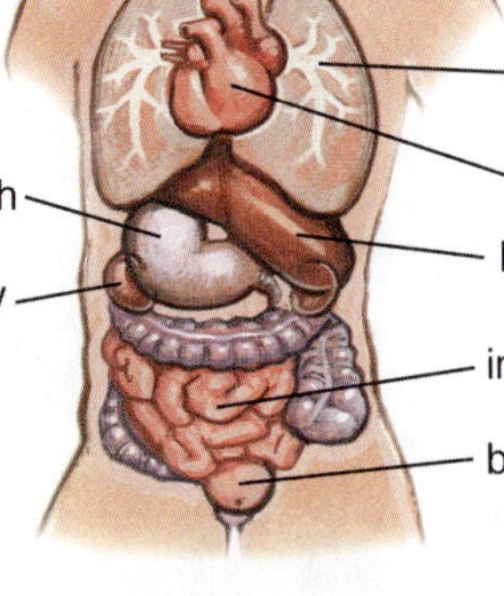

internal organs

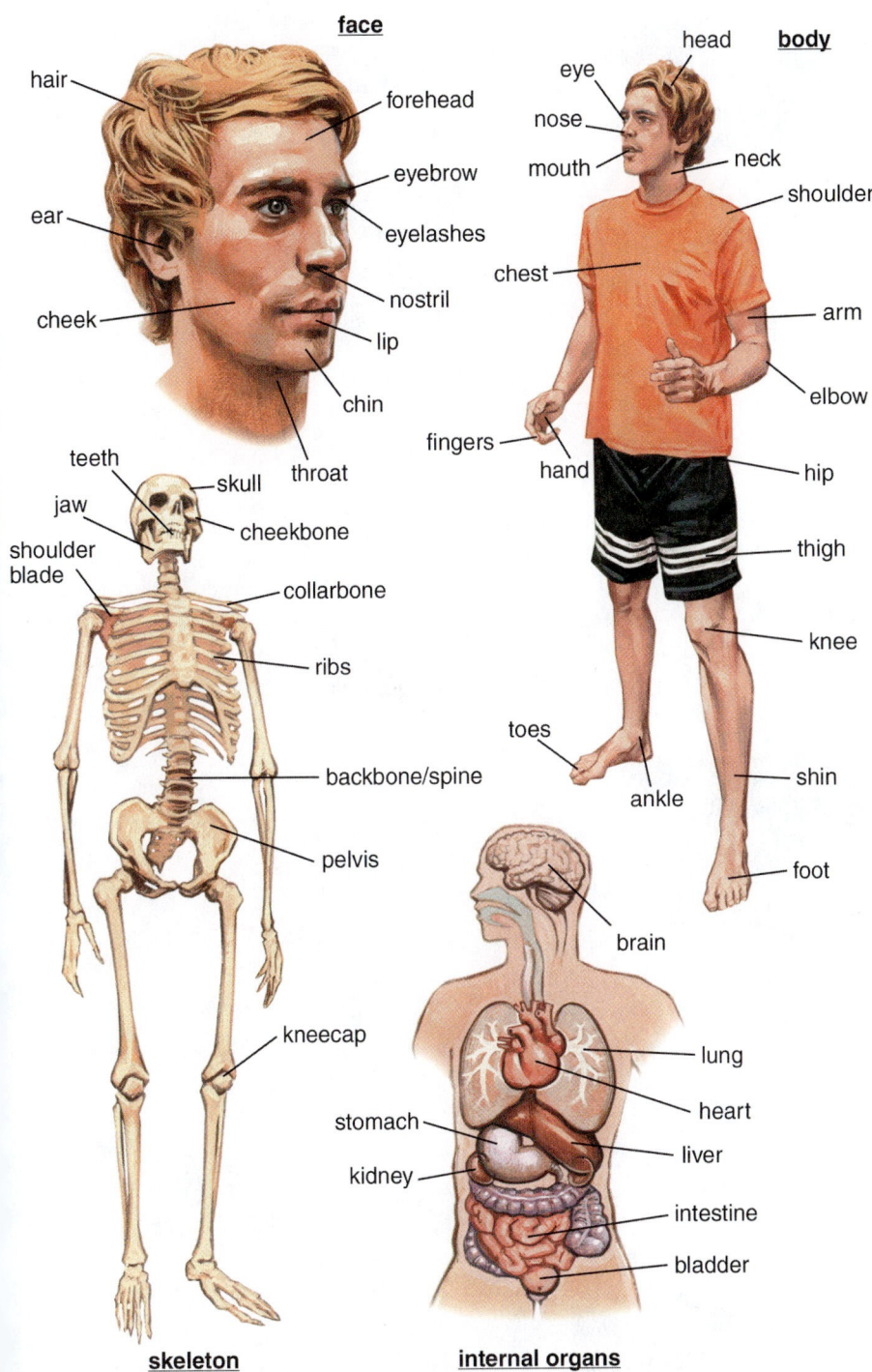

roll/roll out

beat

whisk

mix

strain

sprinkle

knead

spread

squeeze

crush

pour
stir

shish kebabs
salad
popcorn
chili
lasagna
soup
roast chicken
lemon pie
macaroni and cheese
muffins
spaghetti
soufflé
cookies
pancakes
stir-fry
quiche
waffles
grilled steak
pork chop

Musical Instruments

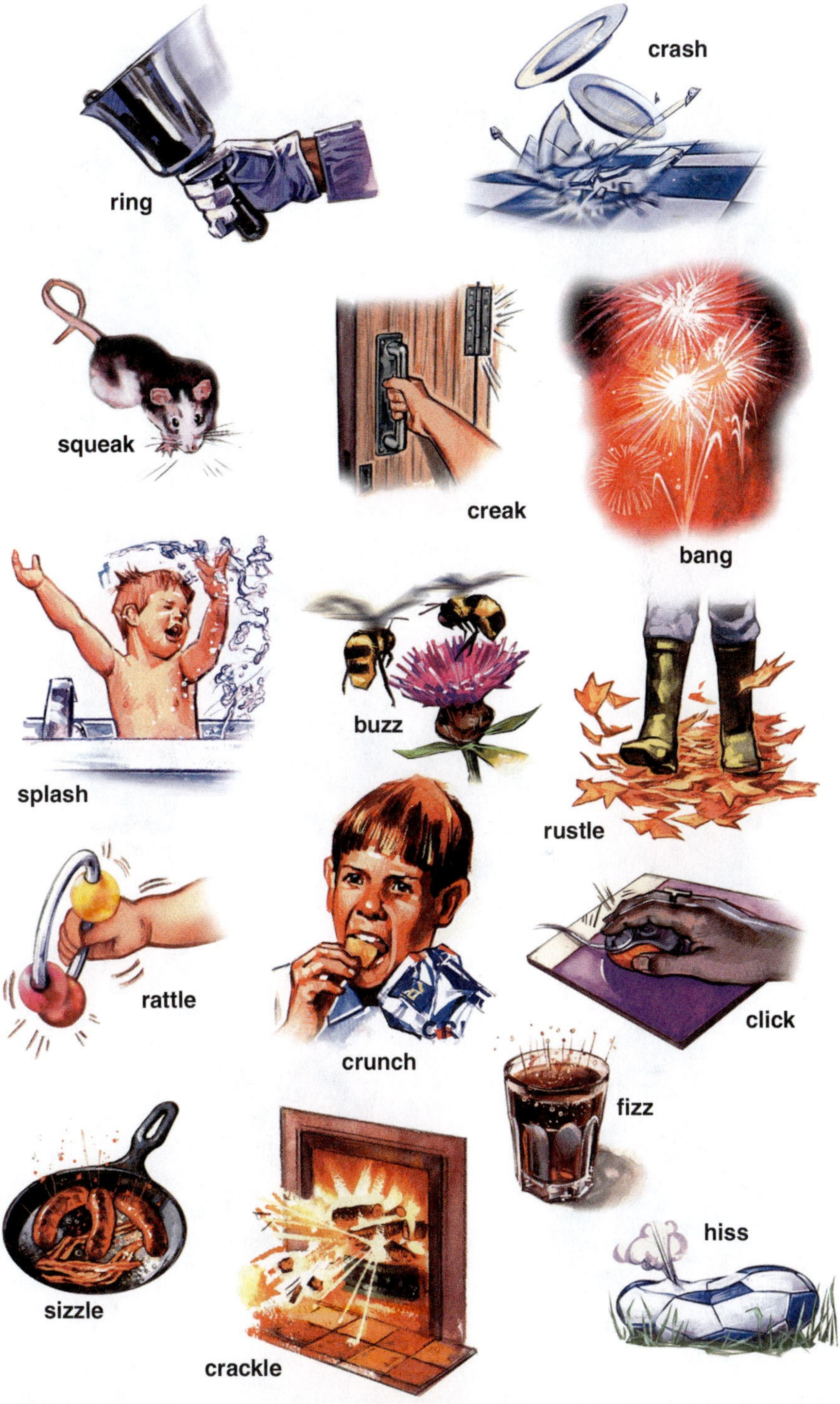
ring
crash
squeak
creak
bang
splash
buzz
rustle
rattle
crunch
click
fizz
sizzle
crackle
hiss

clap

flick

hold hands

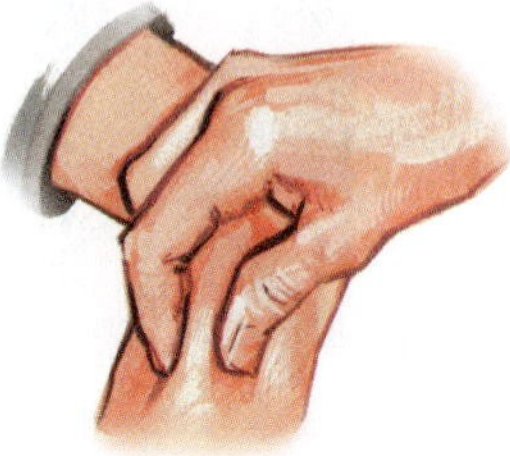

pinch

tap

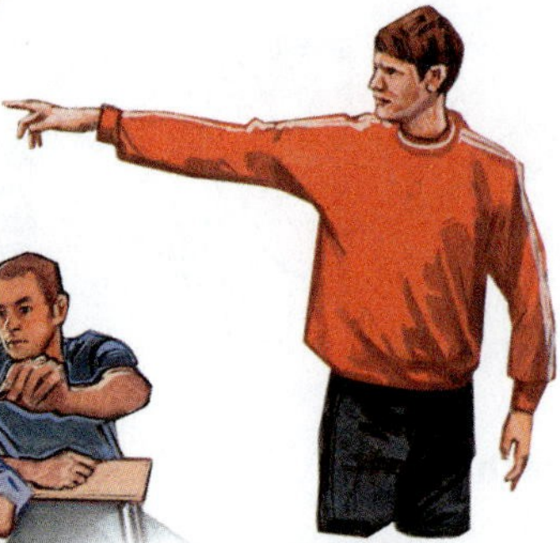

point

scratch

poke

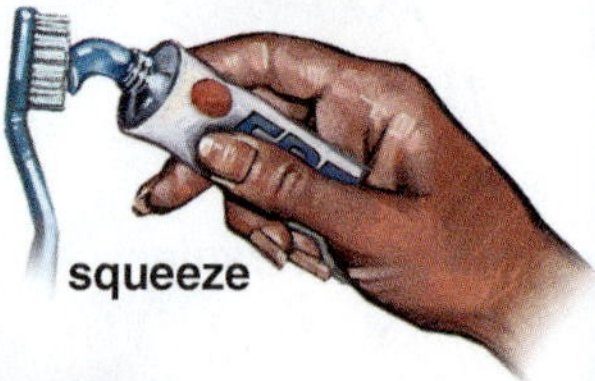

squeeze

pet/stroke

wave

pick up
put down
lift
carry
hold
stretch
bend
squat
kneel
hop
jump rope
jump
lean
crouch
drag
push
pull
drop
climb
fall
jog
walk
march
sit
crawl
tiptoe
run
hrow
kick
punch
catch

surfing
sailing
kayaking
windsurfing
rowing
hang gliding
parachuting
mountain biking
gliding
scuba diving
climbing
cycling
swimming
skiing
ice hockey
speed skating

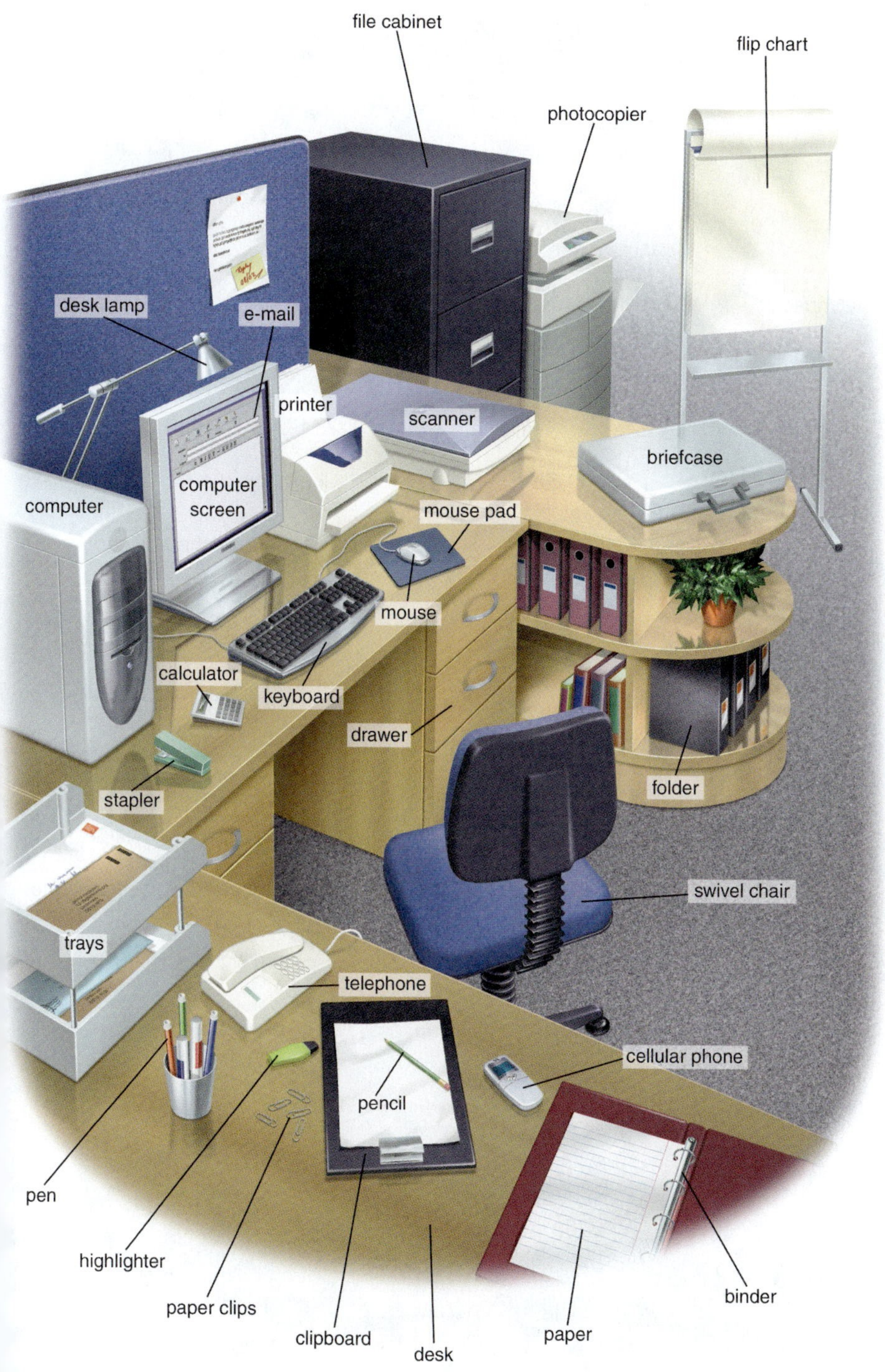
file cabinet
flip chart
photocopier
desk lamp
e-mail
printer
scanner
briefcase
computer
computer screen
mouse pad
mouse
calculator
keyboard
drawer
folder
stapler
swivel chair
trays
telephone
cellular phone
pencil
pen
highlighter
paper clips
clipboard
desk
paper
binder

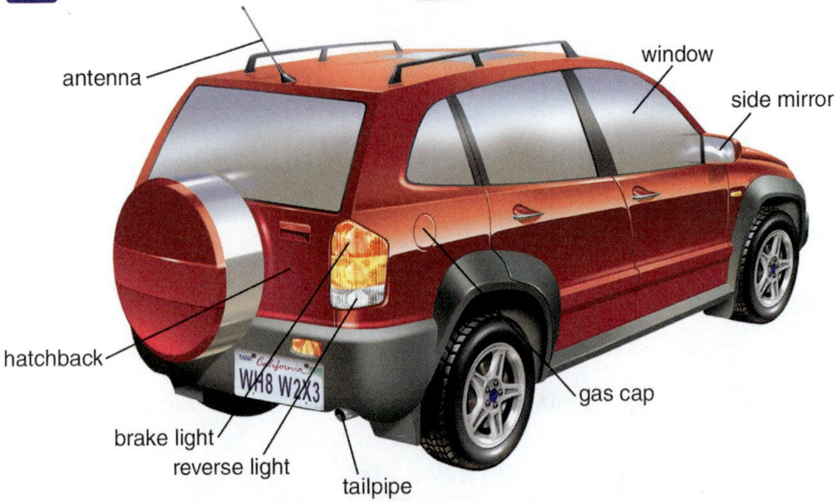
antenna
window
side mirror
hatchback
gas cap
brake light
reverse light
tailpipe

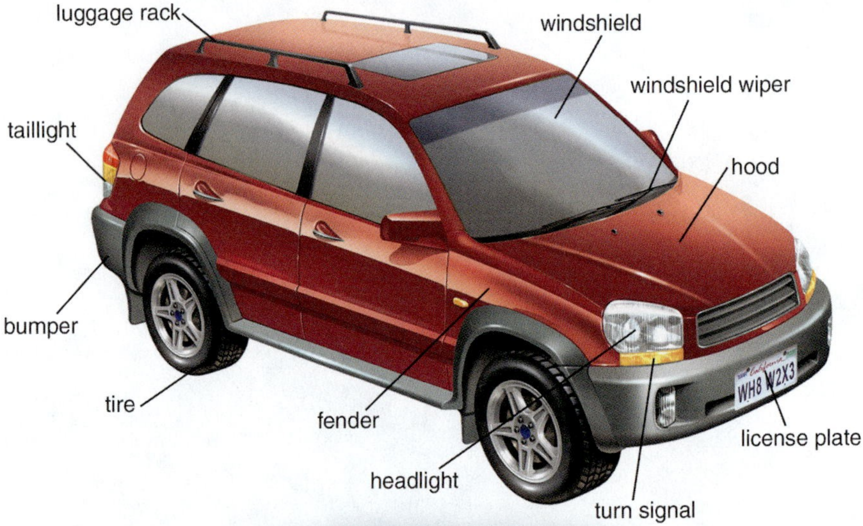
luggage rack
windshield
windshield wiper
taillight
hood
bumper
tire
fender
license plate
headlight
turn signal

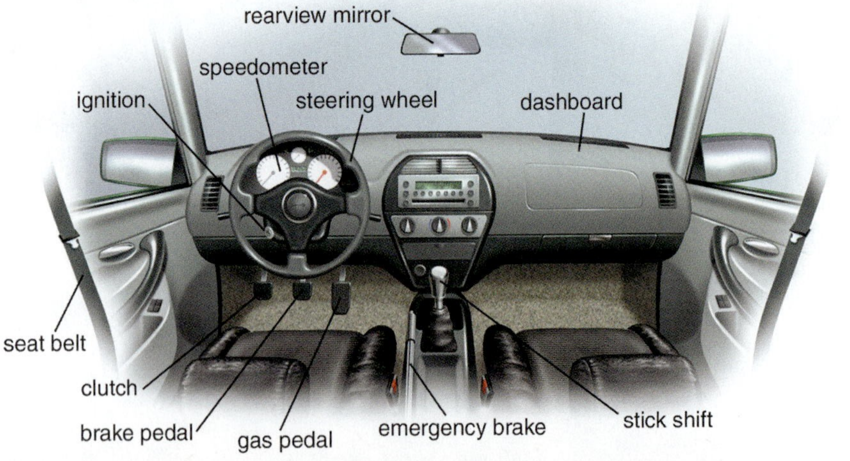
rearview mirror
speedometer
ignition
steering wheel
dashboard
seat belt
clutch
brake pedal
gas pedal
emergency brake
stick shift

Finding Words in the Dictionary

EXERCISE 1

To find a word in the dictionary, you will need to know the correct spelling, especially the first two or three letters. If you can't find a word, you may have the wrong spelling. Think what other spellings may be possible.

These words all contain spelling mistakes in the first two or three letters. What are the correct spellings?

1 fotograph **3** restle **5** brather **7** shure
2 sience **4** nife **6** tipical **8** accomodation

EXERCISE 2

The dictionary lists words in alphabetical order. Sometimes a word is made of two words that are written separately (**ice cream**) or joined with a hyphen (**role-play**). In this dictionary these words are listed alphabetically as if they were one word.

Write these groups of words in alphabetical order.

1	foggy	1	nose	4	unless	6	kind	3	guess	2	skinny	5
2	vote		scrap		day-to-day		tense		forget		slap	
3	trunk		thread		trinket		trade		turtle		trade secret	
4	fan club		flutter		flashy		fanatic		fluffy		floral	

EXERCISE 3

Some words are made from other words. For example, the adjective **overwhelmed** comes from the verb **overwhelm**, so it appears in the same entry.

The following words do not have separate entries in this dictionary. Which main entry would you go to to find them?

1 greatness ......great......
2 genuinely ....
3 impatience ....
4 encouragement ....
5 anthropologist ....
6 transparently ....
7 uncertainly ....
8 critically ....

Key Words

EXERCISE 4

Some entries begin with a word that is **red**. These are the most important words to learn and remember.

In the following groups of words, one word is *not* a "red" word and is less frequently used than the other words. Circle the word which is not a key word.

1 browse explore seek search
2 beautiful stunning pretty nice
3 part piece section segment
4 belief creed opinion view

Checking Spellings

EXERCISE 5

Use the dictionary to check words if you are unsure of their spelling.

Each of the following words has one letter missing. Correct the spelling. Look the words up in the dictionary if necessary.

1 bound^a^ry boundary
2 brige ....
3 matress ....
4 forsee ....
5 accomodation ....
6 relable ....
7 disatisfied ....
8 forteen ....

Pronunciation

Pronunciations in this dictionary are shown at the beginning of entries between slanting lines (/ /) using the International Phonetic Alphabet (IPA). Learning the IPA will help you pronounce English, since the normal spelling of English words does not always show you clearly how to pronounce them. The pronunciation table can be found on the inside front cover of this dictionary.

EXERCISE 6

Put the words below under the correct vowel symbol by looking in the dictionary to see which sound each word uses.

said need raw glue new bet field thought boot seed soft clean dead mood true do eat next taught malt

/i/	/ɛ/	/ɔ/	/u/
need	said	raw	glue

EXERCISE 7

Put the words below under the correct consonant symbol, by looking in the dictionary to see which sound each word starts with.

kite night city cool noon knead pneumatic key science psychiatrist cyberspace cream color seal

/s/	/k/	/n/
city	kite	night

EXERCISE 8

Circle the correct pronunciation of these six words.

1 chips tʃɪps / tʃɪpz
2 useful 'usfel / 'yusfəl
3 blue blou / blu
4 gorgeous 'gɔrdʒəs / 'gɔrdʒəz
5 houses 'haʊzɪz / 'haʊsɪz
6 sword swɔrd / sɔrd

EXERCISE 9

There are many irregularities in English spelling. Words can sound the same yet be spelled differently. Find the pairs of words in these lists that rhyme.

1 ball	straight
2 bread	drum
3 drain	high
4 laughter	sneeze
5 night	crawl
6 plate	wrote
7 tease	after
8 thumb	plane
9 try	fed
10 boat	white

Stress

EXERCISE 10

If a word has two or more syllables we put a stress on one of the syllables. In this dictionary, the symbol / ' / appears before the main stressed syllable. For example, the phonetic transcription of *discuss*, [dɪ'skʌs], shows that the second syllable is stressed.

Circle the stressed syllable in the following words.

1 decide
2 exciting
3 embarrass
4 explode
5 wonderful
6 responsible
7 spectacle
8 happiness

EXERCISE 11

Words may change their stress when they are used for different grammatical functions. Read these sentences and circle the correct stress pattern for the words in red type.

1 We keep a careful **record** of all expenses. reCORD / REcord
2 You should really **record** the amount of money you spend in a month. REcord / reCORD
3 The weather was **perfect**. perFECT / PERfect
4 Scientists still have to **perfect** the cloning process. perFECT / PERfect
5 There has been a sharp **increase** in car thefts. inCREASE / INcrease
6 Unless we **increase** our profits, the company will not survive. INcrease / inCREASE
7 You need a special **permit** to park here. PERmit / perMIT
8 They only **permit** employees to park here. perMIT / PERmit

Syllables and Hyphenation

EXERCISE 12

It helps to learn the pronunciation of a long word if you start by saying it one syllable at a time. This dictionary uses dots (=small round marks) between the syllables of a word to show where the syllable breaks are:

in•her•i•tance /ɪn'hɛrɪṭəns/ *n*

Say each syllable slowly:

in her i tance ɪn' hɛr ɪ ṭəns

Now say the word quickly. Remember to put the stress on /hɛr/: inheritance.

Look up the words below and mark the syllable breaks.

1 de/scent **2** capacity **3** latter **4** muffin **5** rather **6** tumble

Parts of Speech

EXERCISE 13

The dictionary tells you the grammatical function of each word. These functions are called "parts of speech."

What word classes do the following words belong to?

1 another	*noun*
2 soccer	*pronoun*
3 hot	*interjection*
4 slowly	*preposition*
5 us	*modal verb*
6 and	*adverb*
7 speak	*adjective*
8 into	*conjunction*
9 hurray	*verb*
10 should	*determiner*

EXERCISE 14

Sometimes the same word may have more than one part of speech. There is an entry for each different grammatical function of the same word. If you see a small raised number after the main word that begins an entry (**chip**[1]), it means there is more than one entry for this word.

Read the sentences and circle the correct word class for the word in **red** type.

1 The diamond he gave me was a **fake**.	*noun* / *verb*
2 The police found **fake** passports and identity papers.	*adjective* / *verb*
3 Crocodiles can run very **fast**.	*adjective* / *adverb*
4 She's a **fast** runner.	*noun* / *adjective*
5 Now **glue** the two pieces of paper together.	*noun* / *verb*
6 If we're out of tape, maybe we can use **glue**.	*noun* / *adjective*
7 Someone needs to **clear** a path through the forest.	*verb* / *adjective*
8 The lake is so **clear** that you can see the bottom.	*noun* / *adjective*

9 They used a **chemical** to kill the bacteria. *noun / adjective*
10 A **chemical** reaction occurs when the two substances are mixed. *verb / adjective*
11 We put out some **poison** to kill the rats. *noun / adjective*
12 He was sure someone was trying to **poison** his food. *verb / noun*
13 Buying that puppy was a big **mistake**. *adjective / noun*
14 People often **mistake** me for my brother. *verb / adjective*
15 The exchange rate has reached an all-time **low**. *noun / verb*
16 The plane was flying so **low** we could see people in it. *adjective / adverb*

Word Families

EXERCISE 15

Not every word has its own entry in the dictionary. Sometimes the entry for a very common word will have less common related words shown at the end of the entry.

Look up the words in the first column below in the dictionary. At the end of the entry for the main word, you will find words that are related to it. Write the related words in the columns on the right. Not every word will have related words in every column.

word	adj.	adv.	n.	n.	v.
angry		angrily			
respectable					
authentic					
takeout					
perplex					
babysit					
careless					
magnet					
permanent					

Countable and Uncountable Nouns

EXERCISE 16

Most English nouns (like *chair*, *house*, and *computer*) have plural forms (*chairs*, *houses*, *computers*). These are called *countable nouns* and are marked [C] in this dictionary. Nouns that don't have plurals (*laughter*, *money*, *information*) are *uncountable nouns* and are marked [U]. Some nouns can be countable and uncountable, depending on how they are used (*wine*, *cheese*, *coincidence*) and are marked [C, U].

Is the noun in **red** type in each sentence countable or uncountable? Write C or U next to it.

1 How many **cars** do they have? C
2 I need some **advice**. ☐
3 Have you heard the latest **news**? ☐

4 Al was in a bad car **accident**. ☐
5 I'm having **trouble** answering question #2. ☐
6 Would you like some more **soup**? ☐
7 Let's order **pizza** tonight. ☐
8 I just put a **pizza** in the oven. ☐

Irregular Plurals

EXERCISE 17

To form the plural of nouns in English, we usually add *-s* or *-es* to the singular form.

A few nouns have irregular plurals. These irregular forms are always shown in the dictionary at the beginning of the entry.

Here are eight irregular plural nouns. What are their singular forms?

1 men ......man......
2 feet ....
3 fish ....
4 teeth ....
5 mice ....
6 knives ....
7 children ....
8 sheep ....

Compound Nouns

EXERCISE 18

Look through the dictionary and you will notice two-word entries, for example *foul play*. This is because compounds are nouns in their own right.

How many of these compounds do you recognize and understand? Try to match them to the definitions listed below.

alarm clock **barbed wire** **game show** **global warming**
hit man **middle name** **open house** **theme park**

1 a television program in which people play games or answer questions in order to win money and prizes ......game show......
2 an increase in world temperatures, caused by an increase in carbon dioxide around the Earth ....
3 an occasion when a school or business allows the public to come in and see the work that is done there ....
4 a criminal whose job is to kill someone ....
5 a place where you can have fun riding on big machines that are all based on one subject such as water or space travel ....
6 the name that comes between your first name and your family name ....
7 a clock that will make a noise at a particular time to wake you up ....
8 wire with short sharp points on it, usually used for making fences ....

Transitive and Intransitive Verbs

EXERCISE 19

Many verbs normally have a direct object (noun or pronoun or clause). These are called *transitive* verbs and are marked [T] in this dictionary. Examples of these verbs include *hit*, *see*, *enjoy*, *contain*, and *need*.

We can't say *Did you see?* But we can say *Did you see the game yesterday?*

Many verbs do not normally have a direct object. These are called *intransitive* verbs and are marked [I] in this dictionary. Examples of these verbs include *happen*, *wait*, *snow*, *sleep*, *arrive*, and *rain*.

We can't say *Wait the others here*. We can only say *Wait here*. (or *Wait for the others here.*)

Some verbs can be used transitively and intransitively. They are marked [I,T] in this dictionary. Examples of these verbs include *begin*, *drop*, *open*, *win*, and *ring*.

We can say *Williams won the game* (transitive) or *Williams won* (intransitive).

Are the grammar codes for these verbs [I], [T], or [I,T]? Put a direct object (noun or pronoun) after these verbs wherever possible.

1 We need ......some money........ . T
2 The girl screamed .... ☐
3 I really enjoyed .... ☐
4 I started .... ☐
5 It's raining .... ☐
6 Did you see .... ? ☐
7 Will he win .... ? ☐
8 The bag contains .... ☐

Irregular Verbs

EXERCISE 20

For all irregular verbs, the dictionary gives the past tense, the past participle and the present participle (see the irregular verbs table on page 1142).

Complete this chart of irregular verbs. If necessary, check the verbs in the dictionary by looking up the infinitive form.

Infinitive	Past tense	Past participle	Present participle
bring	brought	brought	bringing
draw	drew	drawn	1 ....
feed	2	fed	feeding
forget	3	4	forgetting
read	read	5	reading
6	swept	swept	sweeping

Phrasal Verbs

EXERCISE 21

Phrasal verbs are special verbs that are made up of a verb + an adverb or preposition. Phrasal verbs can be found in this dictionary at the end of the entries for the verbs that they begin with. Try keeping your own lists of phrasal verbs. You will be surprised how soon you start to see verbs from your lists in different contexts.

Complete the sentences.

break feel fall run stand take throw touch

1 What does FBI ....stand.... for?
2 John's got two final exams on the same day. I really .... for him.
3 We're planning to go to Nepal. I hope the plans don't .... through.
4 These eggs are six weeks old. We'd better .... them away.
5 If we .... out of food, we'll just go to the store and buy more.
6 I .... after my father. We both get seasick.
7 Old cars .... down a lot more often than new cars.
8 The plane will .... down at 12:45 – if it's on time.

EXERCISE 22

Write each phrasal verb from the previous exercise in the blank next to its definition.

1 to feel sympathy for someone ....feel for....
2 to stop working ....
3 to get rid of something that you do not want or need ....
4 to be a short form of a word or phrase ....
5 to look or behave like an older member of your family ....
6 to use all of something, so that there is none left ....
7 to fail to happen or be completed ....
8 to land on the ground at an airport ....

Modal Verbs

EXERCISE 23

A modal verb is a special kind of verb that is usually used with another main verb to change its meaning somehow. Write the correct modal verb in these sentences.

can could may must should will would

1 She ....could.... read when she was 4.
2 Both teams are really good. It .... be a great game.
3 We .... not have time to finish by 5:00, but let's start anyway.
4 He .... be pretty rude sometimes, I've found.
5 You .... be tired after that long trip.
6 I'm sure she .... love your present.
7 I .... love to go to New York.

Interjections

EXERCISE 24

An interjection is a word that is used to express surprise, pleasure, pain, etc. or to attract people's attention. Do you recognize the interjections in this list? Which interjection would you use in each of the situations described below?

hey oops phew shh um wow yuck yum

1 You think something tastes good. ....yum....
2 You are not sure what to say next. ....
3 You feel tired, hot, or relieved. ....
4 You are telling somebody to be quiet. ....
5 You've made a small mistake or you've dropped something. ....
6 You see something very impressive or surprising. ....
7 You want to get your friend's attention. ....
8 You think something is unpleasant. ....

Finding and Understanding Meanings

EXERCISE 25

The definitions in this dictionary use a selected vocabulary of 2,000 words. This means that even definitions of difficult words are easy to understand.

The following verbs all describe ways of walking. Try and match them to the definitions below.

creep rush saunter skip stagger stride stroll

1 to walk with quick long steps ....stride....
2 to move very carefully and quietly so that no one will notice you ....
3 to walk in a slow relaxed way ....
4 to walk or move in an unsteady way, almost falling over ....
5 to move forward with quick jumps from one foot to the other ....
6 to move somewhere or do something very quickly ....
7 to walk in a slow and confident way ....

Words with More Than One Meaning

EXERCISE 26

Many words in English have more than one meaning. Different meanings are listed separately in the entry, each preceded by a number in bold type: **1**, **2**, **3** ...

When a word has more than one part of speech, you will find completely separate entries for each function.

Look up these words in the dictionary. How many meanings does each one have?

1 multiply 2
2 dizzy .....
3 setting .....
4 beaker .....
5 language .....
6 rotten .....
7 poach .....
8 gloom .....
9 yarn .....

EXERCISE 27

Read the following pairs of definitions. Each pair refers to the same word, but used in different meanings. What is the word?

diamond fair fine fly last park star sweet

1 *n.* a common small flying insect with two wings
v. to move through the air, or to make something do this ....fly........

2 *n.* a clear, very hard, valuable stone used in jewelry and in industry
n. a shape with four straight sides of equal length that stands on one of its points ....

3 *n.* a very large amount of burning gases in space that looks like a point of light in the sky at night
n. a famous performer in entertainment or sports ....

4 *adj.* kind, gentle, and friendly
adj. having a taste like sugar ....

5 *n.* a large open area with grass and trees in a town, where people can walk, play games, etc.
v. to put a car or other vehicle in a particular place for a period of time ....

6 *n.* money that you have to pay as a punishment for breaking a law or rule
adj. good enough or acceptable ....

7 *n.* an outdoor event at which there are large machines to ride on, games to play, and sometimes farm animals being judged and sold
adj. reasonable, right, and accepted by most people ....

8 *adj.* most recent
v. to continue to happen or exist ....

EXERCISE 28

To help you find the meaning of a word that you need, this dictionary lists the different meanings of words in order of frequency. The first definition is the most frequently used meaning of the word, but read all the meanings to make sure you have found the right one.

Read these pairs of sentences. Put a check mark next to the sentence that shows the more frequent use of the word in **red** type.

1 a Most schools do not place enough **emphasis** on art and music. ☑
b The **emphasis** should go on the word "would." ☐

2 a United flight 519 is now boarding at **Gate** 15. ☐
b Fred left the **gate** open and the dog ran off. ☐

3 a He was wearing a **light** blue shirt. ☐
b I'll only want a **light** meal. ☐

4 a I plan to study **medicine**. ☐
b Don't forget to take your **medicine**. ☐

5 a **Pick** a card but don't show it to me. ☐
b He **picked** all the cherries off the cake. ☐

6 a **Selling** the idea to the boss could be difficult. ☐
b I **sold** my bike to a girl in my class. ☐

Vocabulary Building (Thesaurus Boxes)

EXERCISE 29

The Thesaurus boxes in this dictionary help students to build their vocabulary by grouping together words with a similar meaning or which are used to talk about a particular topic. Go to the Thesaurus box at the word **group**, read the definitions for the various nouns, then look at the exercise below without referring to the Thesaurus box.

gang flock bunch crowd

Fill in the blanks with the best noun from the list above.

1 A ....flock.... of seagulls followed the fishing boat back to the shore.
2 A huge .... of people waited outside the hotel, hoping to see the movie star.
3 One of her teenage sons joined a .... and got involved in crime.
4 He gave us each cheese, crackers, and a .... of grapes.

EXERCISE 30

This time go to the Thesaurus box at the word **cold**, read the definitions for the various adjectives, then look at the exercise below without referring to the Thesaurus box.

cool chilly frosty freezing

Fill in the blanks with the best adjective from the list above.

1 It's nice and .... outside. Why don't we sit on the porch?
2 I'm not going outside. It's .... out there.
3 It's a little .... in here. I think I'll put on a sweater.
4 It was a beautiful .... morning, and the grass crunched under our feet.

EXERCISE 31

Now go to the Thesaurus box at the word **dirty**, read the definitions for the various adjectives, then look at the exercise below without referring to the Thesaurus box.

filthy dusty muddy greasy

Fill in the blanks with the best adjective from the list above.

1 It was so dry and windy that soon my hair and clothes were very ....
2 The bathroom is .... I don't think it's ever been cleaned.
3 These pans still feel .... Did you wash them carefully?
4 It rained during our hike and our boots got all ....

Using Words Together Correctly (Collocation Boxes)

Collocations are pairs or groups of words that are frequently used together. For example the verb **commit** is often used with the noun *crime*. You can find Collocation boxes throughout the dictionary that give important information that will help you to sound natural in English.

EXERCISE 32

Verbs and Nouns

The words in **red** below have their own collocation box in the dictionary.

Study the relevant Collocation boxes then choose a verb from the list below and use it in the correct form to complete these sentences.

nodded rent went study call sent out reply had

1 We're leaving soon. Can you ....call.... a **cab**?
2 I'm planning to .... to her **e-mail** as soon as I have time.
3 They .... to **jail** for armed robbery.
4 If we .... the **map** carefully we should find our way back to the campsite.
5 I'm going to .... a **video** and stay in tonight.
6 They .... over fifty **invitations** for their party.
7 She .... her **head** to show that she understood the question.
8 Have you already .... **lunch**?

EXERCISE 33

Adjectives and Nouns

The words in **red** below each have their own collocation box in the dictionary.

Fill in the blanks with the best adjectives from the Collocation boxes.

1 That job would have been great, but it's too late now. It was definitely a ....missed.... **opportunity**.
2 The country's .... **situation** is improving as inflation continues to fall.
3 Every newly married couple expects to have a .... **marriage**.
4 I take a .... **lunch** to school with me every day.
5 It won't take long. It's a fairly .... **task**.
6 There are only four of us in my .... **family**.
7 His car wasn't outside – a .... **sign** that he'd already left.
8 I felt a sudden .... **pain** and knew immediately that my leg was broken.

Prepositions

EXERCISE 34

The dictionary shows many examples of the correct prepositions to use with particular words.

Choose the correct preposition for these sentences. Compare your answers to the examples given in the dictionary.

after at behind by in in front of through under

1 Have you read any books ....by........ John Grisham?
2 She smiled .... me.
3 We crouched .... the bushes so they wouldn't see us.
4 She walked out halfway .... the film.
5 I couldn't see because a tall man was standing .... me.
6 He was driving .... the influence of alcohol.
7 She's been .... a bad mood all day.
8 I don't like walking home .... dark.

Idioms

EXERCISE 35

An idiom is an expression that has a special meaning that is different from the meanings of all the individual words put together.

Look at these idioms. The words in **red** type show you where you can find the idiom in the dictionary.

What do they mean?

a in small **doses**
b be up to your **ears** in something
c put your **foot** down
d out of the **blue**
e **stand** on your own two feet
f like a **shot**
g till you're **blue** in the face
h off the **top** of your head

Which idioms can be used in the sentences below? Write the correct letter from above in each blank below.

1 I'm ..b.. work right now.
2 It's about time you learned to ..... and stop depending on your parents.
3 She just called me up ..... and asked me out to dinner.
4 The kids ran out the door .....
5 You can talk ....., but I won't change my mind.
6 How much do you think it will cost, just .....?
7 As a parent, sometimes you have to ..... and make your kids do things they don't really want to do.
8 Robert's funny but I can only take him .....

Recording and Learning Vocabulary

EXERCISE 36

Make your own lists of words that you think will be useful or words that interest you. Organize your word lists under headings, such as:

- family
- sports
- describing people
- the street

Don't only list single words. Include:

- phrasal verbs, for example **take after**
- adjective + noun combinations, for example (**he's a**) **bad loser**
- verb + object combinations, for example **find fault** (**with**)

List these words under the following headings: *Ways of Talking*, *Personalities*, *Movies*

chat confident director extrovert interrupt laid-back multiplex mumble obnoxious praise shout shy special effects subtitles thriller touchy trailer whisper

Workbook Answer Key

EXERCISE 1

1 photograph **2** science **3** wrestle **4** knife **5** brother **6** typical **7** sure **8** accommodation

EXERCISE 2

1 foggy *1* nose *4* unless *6* kind *3* guess *2* skinny *5*
2 vote *6* scrap *3* day-to-day *1* tense *5* forget *2* slap *4*
3 trunk *5* trader *2* trinket *4* thread *1* turtle *6* trade secret *3*
4 fan club *2* flutter *6* flashy *3* fanatic *1* fluffy *5* floral *4*

EXERCISE 3

1 great **2** genuine **3** impatient **4** encourage **5** anthropology **6** transparent **7** uncertain **8** critical

EXERCISE 4

1 browse **2** stunning **3** segment **4** creed

EXERCISE 5

1 boundary **2** bridge **3** mattress **4** foresee **5** accommodation **6** reliable **7** dissatisfied **8** fourteen

EXERCISE 6

/i/	/ɛ/	/ɔ/	/u/
need	said	raw	glue
field	bet	thought	new
seed	dead	soft	boot
clean	next	taught	mood
eat		malt	true
			do

EXERCISE 7

/s/	/k/	/n/
city	kite	night
science	cool	noon
psychiatrist	key	knead
cyberspace	cream	pneumatic
seal	color	

EXERCISE 8

1 tʃɪps **2** 'yusfəl **3** blu **4** 'gɔrdʒəs **5** 'haʊzɪz **6** sɔrd

EXERCISE 9

1 ball – crawl **2** bread – fed **3** drain – plane **4** laughter – after **5** night – white **6** plate – straight **7** tease – sneeze **8** thumb – drum **9** try – high **10** boat – wrote

EXERCISE 10

1 deCIDE **2** exCITing **3** emBArrass **4** exPLODE **5** WONderful **6** resPONsible **7** SPECtacle **8** HAPpiness

EXERCISE 11

1 REcord **2** reCORD **3** PERfect **4** perFECT **5** INcrease **6** inCREASE **7** PERmit **8** perMIT

EXERCISE 12

1 de | scent
2 ca | pac | i | ty
3 lat | ter
4 muf | fin
5 rath | er
6 tum | ble

EXERCISE 13

1 another – determiner
2 soccer – noun
3 hot – adjective
4 slowly – adverb
5 us – pronoun
6 and – conjunction
7 speak – verb
8 into – preposition
9 hurray – interjection
10 should – modal verb

EXERCISE 14

1 noun **2** adjective **3** adverb **4** adjective **5** verb **6** noun **7** verb **8** adjective **9** noun **10** adjective **11** noun **12** verb **13** noun **14** verb **15** noun **16** adverb

EXERCISE 15

angry: angrily
respectable: respectably, respectability
authentic: authentically, authenticity
takeout: take-out
perplex: perplexed
babysit: babysitter, babysitting
careless: carelessly, carelessness
magnet: magnetize
permanent: permanence

EXERCISE 16

1 C **2** U **3** U **4** C **5** U **6** U **7** U **8** C

EXERCISE 17

1 man **2** foot **3** fish **4** tooth **5** mouse **6** knife **7** child **8** sheep

EXERCISE 18

1 game show **2** global warming **3** open house **4** hit man **5** theme park **6** middle name **7** alarm clock **8** barbed wire

EXERCISE 19

1 [T] **2** [I] **3** [T] **4** [I,T] **5** [I] **6** [T] **7** [I,T] **8** [T]

EXERCISE 20

1 drawing **2** fed **3** forgot **4** forgotten **5** read **6** sweep

EXERCISE 21

1 stand **2** feel **3** fall **4** throw **5** run **6** take **7** break **8** touch

EXERCISE 22

1 feel for **2** break down **3** throw away **4** stand for **5** take after **6** run out of **7** fall through **8** touch down

EXERCISE 23

1 could **2** should **3** may **4** can **5** must **6** will **7** would

EXERCISE 24

1 yum **2** um **3** phew **4** shh **5** oops **6** wow **7** hey **8** yuck

EXERCISE 25

1 stride **2** creep **3** stroll **4** stagger **5** skip **6** rush **7** saunter

EXERCISE 26

1 multiply – 2
2 dizzy – 2
3 setting – 3
4 beaker – 1
5 language – 5
6 rotten – 2
7 poach – 2
8 gloom – 2
9 yarn – 2

EXERCISE 27

1 fly **2** diamond **3** star **4** sweet **5** park **6** fine **7** fair **8** last

EXERCISE 28

1 a **2** b **3** a **4** b **5** a **6** b

EXERCISE 29

1 flock **2** crowd **3** gang **4** bunch

EXERCISE 30

1 cool **2** freezing **3** chilly **4** frosty

EXERCISE 31

1 dusty **2** filthy **3** greasy **4** muddy

EXERCISE 32

1 call **2** reply **3** went **4** study **5** rent **6** sent out **7** nodded **8** had

EXERCISE 33

1 wasted/lost/missed
2 economic
3 happy/good
4 (brown) bag/sack
5 easy/simple/routine
6 immediate
7 sure/clear
8 sharp

EXERCISE 34

1 by **2** at **3** behind **4** through **5** in front of **6** under **7** in **8** after

EXERCISE 35

1 b **2** e **3** d **4** f **5** g **6** h **7** c **8** a

EXERCISE 36

Ways of Talking: chat, interrupt, mumble, praise, shout, whisper
Personalities: confident, extrovert, laid-back, obnoxious, shy, touchy
Movies: director, multiplex, special effects, subtitles, thriller, trailer

Capitalization and Punctuation

WRITING TIP

- Learn the basic rules of capitalization and punctuation. They make your writing clearer and allow your readers to focus on what you are trying to say.

Capitalization

Use a capital letter at the start of:

- Every sentence:
  He lives downtown. | *Where are you going?* | *We won $100!*
- Names of places, people, organizations, languages, religions, and nationalities:
  Dallas, Texas | *Rachel Adams* | *the Red Cross* | *Spanish* | *Buddhism* | *American*
- Words like *college*, *high school*, and *place*, when they are a part of a name:
  I go to City College. (but *I go to college.*) | *We live at Columbus Place.*
- The first and last word in a title of a book, movie, etc., and all other words in the title except for articles, prepositions, coordinating conjunctions, and the *to* in infinitives:
  The Catcher in the Rye | *Lord of the Rings* | *Journey to the Center of the Earth*
- Names of days of the week and months of the year:
  Wednesday | *April*
- Titles and ranks used with people's names:
  Mrs. Davis | *Professor Jones* | *Colonel Bedell*
- Titles of family members, when they are used as names:
  Can I have some milk, Mom? (but *My mom works in a bank.*)
- The pronoun *I*, no matter where it is in the sentence:
  I heard that. | *Can I help you?*

Punctuation

Use a **period** (.):

- At the end of a sentence that makes a statement:
  I'll see you tomorrow. | *The tickets cost $30.*
- After some abbreviations:
  Mr. Lewis | *3 p.m.* | *etc.*

Use a **question mark** (?):

- At the end of a question:
  Why is it so cold in here? | *When did he tell you that?*

Use an **exclamation point** (!):

- At the end of a sentence that shows a strong emotion:
  I'm so excited to be here! | *Hurry up!*

Use a **comma** (,):

- Before a coordinating conjunction such as *and*, *or*, *so*, or *but* that joins two main clauses (each with a subject and verb) in one sentence:
  Rhonda finished the report, and then she left. | *You can come with us, or you can go with Ed.* | *I wanted to send Mike an invitation, but I didn't have his address.*

- After a word or phrase that introduces a sentence, such as *however*, *for example*, or *furthermore*:
  He has many ideas. However, not all of the ideas are practical. | *In the next six weeks, we will cover the first half of the book.*
- After a clause at the beginning of a sentence that begins with a subordinating conjunction, such as *if*, *while*, *when*, or *although*:
  If it smells funny, don't eat it. | *Although he promised to send the money, we never received it.*
- To separate spoken words from the rest of the sentence:
  "Hello," he said. | *She asked me, "What do you think you're doing?"*

Use a **colon** (:):

- After a sentence to introduce a list or example:
  You will need two of each of the following fruits: oranges, peaches, grapes, and bananas.

Use a **semi-colon** (;):

- Between two closely related sentences that are joined together in a single sentence:
  You've studied hard; I'm sure you'll do fine on the test.

Use an **apostrophe** ('):

- To represent missing letters:
  can't, *haven't*, *I'll*, *there's*
- To show a possessive:
  Andy's computer

Use **quotation marks** (" "):

- To show words which are spoken:
  "I'm sorry I'm late," she said.
- Around titles of short stories, essays, articles, chapters, etc.:
  His article "A New Approach to Gardening" appeared in last week's paper.
- Around words that are being treated in a special way or used with an ironic meaning:
  The word "rural" is difficult for many foreigners to pronounce. | *The "diamond" she kept talking about turned out to be fake.*

Commas and periods always go inside quotation marks. Question marks, exclamation points, and semi-colons go inside or outside depending on the meaning of the sentence.

Use **parentheses** (( )):

- Around extra information that you want to set off from the rest of the sentence.
  Johanna Kruse (born 1854) was among the first students in the school.

Use a **dash** (—):

- To set extra information off from the rest of the sentence. A dash draws more attention to the information than parentheses. If the extra information comes in the middle of a sentence, use a dash on both sides of the information.
  They built their home—a huge mansion on the top of a mountain—in the early 1980s.

Vocabulary Building:
Using the Thesaurus Boxes

WRITING TIPS

- Use synonyms in your writing to avoid repeating the same basic word again and again.
- Choose words with precise meanings.
- Choose words with the appropriate level of formality for what you are writing.

Throughout this dictionary you will find Thesaurus boxes at different entries. These boxes list words that are related in meaning to the word you are looking up. Using these Thesaurus boxes can help you build your vocabulary and improve your writing. Specifically, use the boxes to help you:

1. Vary Your Word Choice

English has more words than any other language, so there are always many words to choose from. If you choose one basic word and repeat it again and again, people will understand what you are writing. However, your writing will not be as interesting as it could be if you varied your vocabulary and used synonyms. For example, read the following paragraph:

> As I was talking to her, she suddenly started to **cry**. She **cried** very loudly for a while. Then she got quieter, but she continued to **cry** a lot. Finally, I asked her, "Why are you **crying**?"

cry[1] /kraɪ/ *v.* past tense and past participle **cried**, third person singular **cries** **1** [I] to produce tears from your eyes, usually because you are unhappy or hurt: *What are you **crying about**? | Sydney **cried for** her mother. | a woman **crying over** the death of her son | Sad movies always **make** me **cry**.*

THESAURUS

If someone **weeps**, s/he cries a lot because s/he feels very sad.
If someone **sobs**, s/he cries a lot in a noisy way.
If someone **is in tears**, s/he is crying.
If someone **bursts into tears**, s/he suddenly starts crying.

2 [I,T] to say something loudly: *"Stop!" she cried. | He **cried for help** | The crowd cried his*

The verb *cry*, which is a very basic word, is used four times. After looking at the Thesaurus box at *cry*, you could rewrite the paragraph like this:

> As I was talking to her, she suddenly **burst into tears**. She **sobbed** very loudly for a while. Then she got quieter, but she continued to **weep**. Finally, I asked her, "Why are you **crying**?"

2. Write More Precisely

Some words have very general meanings and others have more specific meanings. In general, it is best to use precise words with specific meanings so that your readers know exactly what you mean. The Thesaurus boxes can help you find precise words and understand small differences in meaning. Using more precise words makes your writing clearer and more interesting.

For example, *mark* is a very general word. If you write, "Todd has a mark on his left cheek," people will not know what kind of mark it is. You can of course describe the mark, but using a more precise word to start with will help your readers even more. The Thesaurus box at *mark* lists nine different words to refer to marks on people's skin and four words for marks on any surface. Using any of these words will give your readers much more precise information than using *mark* alone.

mark[2] *n.* [C]
1 DIRTY SPOT a spot or small dirty area on something that spoils its appearance: *What are these black marks on the couch?*

THESAURUS

Types of dirty marks

stain – a mark that is difficult to remove: *an ink stain on the shirt pocket*
spot – a small mark: *a grease spot on his shirt*
smudge – a dirty mark, made when something is rubbed against a surface: *a smudge of paint on her cheek*
smear – a mark that is left when a substance is spread on a surface: *There was a smear of blood on the chair.*

Types of marks on someone's skin

blemish – a mark on your skin that spoils its appearance
bruise – a purple or brown mark on your skin that you get because you have fallen or been hit
scar – a permanent mark on your skin, caused by a cut or by something that burns you
pimple – a small raised red mark or lump on your skin that teenagers often have
zit informal – a pimple
wart – a small hard raised mark on your skin caused by a virus (=a living thing that causes an infectious illness)
blister – a small area of skin that is swollen and full of liquid because it has been rubbed or burned
freckle – one of several small light brown marks on someone's skin
mole – a small usually brown mark on the skin that is often slightly higher than the skin around it

2 DAMAGE a small damaged area on someone or something: *Her injuries included scratch marks*

Sentences with Precise Vocabulary	What the Sentences Tell Us
Todd had a **bruise** on his left cheek.	Todd's cheek has been hit.
Todd has a **scar** on his left cheek.	Todd's cheek was cut or burnt a long time ago.
Todd has a **pimple** on his left cheek.	There is a small raised bump on Todd's cheek.
Todd has a **freckle** on his left cheek.	The mark on Todd's cheek is a natural part of his skin.
Todd has a **smudge** on his left cheek.	Something dirty has rubbed against Todd's cheek.

3. Choose the Appropriate Level of Formality

Some words are more formal or informal than others. When you are writing, it is important to choose words that match the level of formality of your writing. For example, if you look again at the Thesaurus box for *mark*, you will see that *pimple* and *zit* mean the same thing. However, *zit* is an informal word. If you were writing an essay or a story for a class, you could use the word *pimple* (*Pimples are caused by oil blocking pores.* | *The teenager had a pimple on his cheek.*). The word *zit* would not be appropriate, though, because it is too informal. On the other hand, *zit* would be a fine choice if you were writing an e-mail to a friend (*I have a big zit on my chin, and I wish it would go away.*).

Collocations

STUDY TIP

- When you learn a new noun, make a note of the verbs and the adjectives that are often used with it.

You can make your English sound more fluent and natural by using pairs or groups of words that are commonly used together by native speakers of English. These pairs or groups of words are called ***collocations***. When you write, practice using the collocations of English.

Adjectives That Go with Nouns

If you want to describe a noun, there are many adjectives to choose from. Some adjectives are always used with particular nouns. Somebody who eats a lot is *a **big** eater*, but somebody who smokes a lot is *a **heavy** smoker* (NOT *a **big** smoker*). When you look up a noun in the dictionary, the entry tells you if there are adjectives that often go with it. Look at the entry for **situation**. In the actual entry, you will see some collocations in bold. But there is also a Collocations box after the entry that lists a large number of adjective + noun collocations. These Collocation boxes can be found throughout the dictionary.

sit·u·a·tion /ˌsɪtʃuˈeɪʃən/ *n.* [C] a combination of all the things that are happening and all the conditions that exist at a particular time and place: *the present **economic/political situation** in the country* | ***In** this **situation**, it is unrealistic to expect a quick solution.*

COLLOCATIONS

difficult/bad/dangerous/tough situation – one that is bad and difficult to deal with
economic/political/financial situation
present/current situation – one that exists now
no-win situation – one that will end badly no matter what you decide to do
win-win situation – one that will end well for everyone involved in it
If a **situation improves**, it becomes better.
If a **situation worsens** or **deteriorates**, it becomes worse.

Nouns That Go with Nouns

Sometimes, when two or more nouns often appear together, they only sound correct in English if they are used in a particular order. For example, you always say **bread and butter**. If you say **butter and bread** it sounds very strange.

Here are examples of nouns matched with their correct partners (look them up in the dictionary if you are not sure what they mean):

knife and fork **bed and breakfast** **room and board** **dos and don'ts**
law and order **hustle and bustle** **ins and outs** **pros and cons** **salt and pepper**

Verbs That Go with Nouns

Some pairs of verbs and nouns sound right when they are used together and others do not. For example, you cannot say ***do** a mistake*. You have to say ***make** a mistake*. If you say ***do** a mistake*, people will understand what you mean, but your English will sound unnatural.

Common Mistakes with Verb + Noun Collocations

✗ People who ~~do~~ crimes often end up in jail.
✎ People who **commit** crimes often end up in jail.

✗ We have to ~~do~~ a speech for English class.
✎ We have to **make** a speech for English class.

✗ He ~~said~~ a remark about my haircut.
✎ He **made** a remark about my haircut.

This dictionary will tell you which verbs are used with which nouns. The entry for **mistake** shows that you "**make** mistakes," "**learn about** mistakes," and that you can "do something **by** mistake."

> **mis·take**[1] /mɪˈsteɪk/ *n.* [C] **1** something that has been done in the wrong way, or an opinion or statement that is incorrect: *spelling mistakes* | *I think you've **made a mistake** – I ordered fish, not beef.* | *The bill is $500? **There must be some mistake**.* → see Thesaurus box at ERROR **2** something you do that you later realize was not the right thing to do: *Marrying him was a **big mistake**.* | ***I made the mistake of** giving him my phone number.* | *We need to start **learning from** our **mistakes**.* **3 by mistake** if you do something by mistake, you do it without intending to: *I brought the wrong book home by mistake.*

make and *do*, *have* and *take*

Learning verb + noun combinations will improve your English and make it sound more correct and natural. Look at the following table. It shows collocations for *make*, *do*, *have*, and *take*.

	make	do	have	take		make	do	have	take
preparations					a picture				
damage					an exam				
a bath					a promise				
research					a complaint				
lessons					justice				
a test					breakfast				
an operation					progress				
a decision					fun				
a discovery					an effort				
a phone call					harm				
a look					a comment				
a baby					a break				
a party					a suggestion				
a noise					a list				

→ See also **Grammar Guide** on **Intensifying Adjectives and Adverbs**

Idioms

Using idioms in your writing can make your writing more natural and interesting. However, idioms are sometimes tricky to use, and not all idioms are appropriate for all types of writing. In fact, many idioms are best used only in spoken English or informal English. Most of the idioms below should not be used when writing essays or formal letters.

STUDY TIPS

- Always look idioms up in the dictionary and make sure you have understood their meaning.
- Check if the idiom is informal or slang. If it is, be careful when you use it, and do not use it in formal writing.
- Remember that you cannot usually translate idioms directly from one language into another.
- Learning and using idioms can be fun, but remember not to use too many idioms together, as this can sound strange or unnatural.

What Is an Idiom?

An idiom is a group of two or more words that have a special meaning. This meaning is different from the meanings of the individual words when they are used separately. For example, if you are told that somebody is in hot water, you cannot guess the meaning from the usual meanings of in + hot + water. This idiom actually means "in a lot of trouble."

In this dictionary, each idiom is shown in **bold** at the beginning of a new sense. For example, the entry for cold shows these four idioms after the main senses:

> **4 leave sb cold** *informal* to not interest someone at all: *Ballet just leaves me cold.* **5 get/have cold feet** *informal* to suddenly feel that you are not brave enough to do something: *She was getting cold feet about getting married.* **6 cold snap** a sudden short period of very cold weather **7 give sb the cold shoulder** to deliberately ignore someone or be unfriendly to him/her **8 in cold blood** in a cruel and deliberate way: *They shot him in cold blood.* —**coldness** *n.* [U]

Idiom Meanings

We saw above that in hot water means "in a lot of trouble." There are many idioms that people use to talk about problems and difficulties. The table below shows just a few of them. Look up the words in **bold** in the dictionary to find out exactly what they mean.

PROBLEMS AND DIFFICULTIES

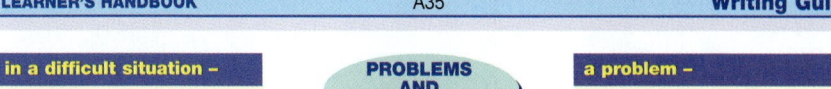

in a difficult situation –

- be in the **doghouse**
- be up the **creek** (without a paddle)
- in/into hot **water**
- be in a **fix**
- hit/reach **rock bottom**
- in **dire** straits
- not have a **leg** to stand on
- get/be **bog**ged down (in sth)

to cause problems for others or for yourself –

- **rock** the boat
- **deal** a blow (to sb/sth)
- put your **foot** in your mouth
- **stick** your neck out

a problem –

- a **stumbling block**
- a **thorny** question/problem/ issue etc.
- **growing pains**
- a **sticky** situation

When you learn a new idiom it is very important to make sure that you understand what it means. Do you know the difference between being **bogged down** and being **up the creek**? The dictionary will make it clear.

Metaphor in Idioms

If we say that someone is **in hot water**, we do not mean that they are literally in some water that is hot. **In hot water** has a metaphorical meaning – it is understood as a difficult situation to be in. A metaphor is a way of describing something by comparing it to something else that has similar qualities. Many idioms use metaphor in this way. For example, words related to explosions and being hot are often used as a metaphor for anger:

- hit the **roof**
- go **ballistic**
- lose your **cool**

Similarly, *cold* is associated with other types of emotion:

- give sb the **cold** shoulder
- have/get **cold** feet
- leave sb **cold**
- keep/lose your **cool** (see entry at *cool*)
- break the **ice** (see entry at *ice*)

Metaphorical Actions

Many idioms describe an action, but the meaning of the idiom is not the same as the meaning of the action. It can be very difficult to guess what these idioms mean. For example, *show somebody the **ropes*** means "to show someone how to do a job." Sometimes, two of these "action" idioms can look very similar but have very different meanings. For example:

- ***bite** the bullet* means "to start dealing with an unpleasant situation because you can no longer avoid it."
- ***bite** the dust* means "to die, fail, or be defeated."

Sometimes several different idioms can mean the same thing. For example, the following idioms all describe a situation in which someone reveals a secret:

- ***spill** the beans*
- *let the **cat** out of the bag*
- *let sth **slip***

→ If you want more information on idioms, the ***Longman American Idioms Dictionary*** shows clearly the meaning and use of thousands of spoken and written American idioms.

Writing Essays

WRITING TIPS

- Give your essay a clear structure with a beginning (introduction), middle (body), and end (conclusion).
- Use clear, short sentences. Use common words that you know well, but avoid very informal words.
- Do not use contracted forms such as *don't* and *can't*. These are used in spoken and informal English.
- After you write the first draft, reread your essay and make changes.
- Remember to proofread and check your punctuation, capitalization, and spelling.

There are many things you can do in an essay, but you should decide what type of essay you are writing before you start. Doing this will help you organize your ideas. In your essay, you can:

1. Compare two or more things and decide which is best.
2. Discuss the advantages and disadvantages of doing something.
3. Discuss a problem and suggest a solution.

Make sure that the topic you choose includes an opinion and is not just a collection of facts that everyone already knows. Remember your readers and make your essay as interesting or surprising as possible.

Organizing Your Essays

Your completed essay should have an introduction, a body, and a conclusion. Each part of the essay has a specific purpose:

Introduction (usually one paragraph)	**1.** Introduce the subject and say why the subject is important and interesting to your readers. **2.** Describe in a general way the areas that you will discuss in your essay. **3.** Give your thesis statement, usually at the end of the introduction. The thesis statement is a clear opinion that you will prove in your essay.
Body (one paragraph for each main idea)	**1.** Describe the main points of the situation or problem in a sensible order. Save your strongest points for the end of the essay. **2.** Organize your discussion into paragraphs and give each main point its own paragraph. **3.** Write a topic sentence for each paragraph that states the main point of the paragraph. Use the rest of the paragraph to give facts, details, and examples that support the topic sentence.
Conclusion (usually one paragraph)	**1.** Give a summary of the points you have made and present your conclusion. **2.** Make sure your conclusion matches your thesis statement in the introduction. If they express different opinions, you need to make changes until they do match. **3.** Do not introduce any major new ideas in the conclusion. If there is another idea you want to discuss, put it in the body of the essay.

Linking Your Ideas

You can use the following useful phrases to organize your essay and link your ideas together. If you understand and learn these useful phrases, it will make your arguments clearer. These phrases can all come at the beginning of sentences or paragraphs. Try to vary your use of these phrases and avoid using the same one over and over.

To Introduce the Subject	*It is a well-known fact that …* *Many people believe that …* *It is often claimed that …* *There are several ways of looking at the problem of …* *One of the most important issues in society today is …*
To Start the Discussion	*First of all,* / *Firstly,* / *To begin with,* / *In the first place, …* (NOT *Firstly of all*) *Let us begin by looking at …* *First of all, let us consider …* *The first thing that should be noted is …* *It is worth stating from the outset that …*
To Continue the Discussion	*Secondly, …* (NOT *Second* or *Secondly of all*) *Thirdly, …* (It is rare to use *Fourthly*, *Fifthly*, etc.) *Lastly,* / *Finally, …* (NOT *In the last* / *final place*) *As far as … is concerned* / *As regards …* / *As for …* *This brings us to the question of whether/how/who etc. …* *It should also be noted/stressed that …* *Furthermore,* / *Moreover,* / *In addition,* / *Besides this,* / *What is more, …*
To Show the Other Side of the Discussion	*However,* / *Nevertheless, …* *The opposite may also be true.* *There is more than one way of looking at this problem.* *(On the one hand, …) On the other hand, …* If you use *On the one hand …*, you should also use *On the other hand …* in the following sentence or paragraph.
To Show Similarities	*Likewise,* / *Similarly,* / *In the same way, …*
To Give Examples	*For example, …*
To State a Result or Effect	*Therefore,* / *As a result,* / *Thus, …*
To Present a Conclusion or a Solution to the Problem	*On balance, …* *To sum up,* / *In summary,* / *In conclusion, it would seem that …* *This brings us to the conclusion that …* *To conclude, it seems likely that …*
To Express Your Personal Opinion	*In my opinion, …* (do NOT write *I think* after this phrase) *My personal opinion is that …* *My own view of this is that …* *It is my opinion that …*

Writing Letters and E-mails

WRITING TIPS

- Choose the appropriate level of formality and make sure that you use the same level of formality from the beginning to the end. Use the boxes below to guide you.
- For a formal style, do not use contractions like *I'm*, *I've*, or *you'd*, and avoid abbreviations like *etc.* and *e.g.*
- Use paragraphs to organize the main points in your letter.

Writing Letters

You use different styles for different kinds of letter. The box below will help you to decide how to start and finish your letter.

	Formal Letters	Informal Letters
Ways of Opening a Letter (The Greeting or Salutation)	**In formal or business letters, use a colon (:) after the salutation:** ***Dear Mr./Mrs./Ms./Miss*** + family name: (In a business context, it is best to use **Ms.** rather than **Mrs.** or **Miss** as a title for a woman, and it should always be used when you do not know if the woman is married or not) ***Dear Dr./Professor*** + family name: (do NOT use the person's first name with **Dear Dr./Professor**) ***Dear Sir or Madam***: or ***Dear Sir/Madam***: (use this when you do not know whether you are writing to a man or a woman) ***Dear Sir***: (use this when you do not know the man's name) ***Dear Madam***: (use this when you do not know the woman's name) ***To Whom It May Concern***: (use this when you do not know the person's name and the letter is very formal)	**In informal or personal letters, use a comma (,) after the salutation:** ***Dear*** + first name, (use this when you know the person well enough to use their first name only) ***Hi/Hello*** (+ first name), (use this in letters to friends and people that you know well)

	Formal Letters	Informal Letters
Phrases Used in the Body of a Letter	*With regard to your letter of July 18* *I am writing to enquire about …* *I am writing to confirm that …* *I am writing to apologize for …* *I am writing to inform you that …* *I am writing in response to your advertisement in …* *I would appreciate it if you could …* *Please accept my apologies for …* *I am enclosing …* *Please do not hesitate to contact me if you have any questions/problems.* *I can be contacted at the address above or at (555) 555-1234.* *I look forward to hearing from you.* *Thank you in advance for ...*	*I was really pleased to get your letter./Thanks for your letter.* *It was great to see you/hear from you.* *Sorry it's been so long since I last wrote./Sorry I haven't written for so long.* *I hope you are well./How are you?/How're things?* *Just a quick note to let you know ...* *Give me a call and let me know whether you can make it.* *Let me know when you are free so we can get together.* *It would be great to hear from you.* *Hope to see you soon./Really looking forward to seeing you soon./Talk to you soon.* *Write soon./Keep in touch./Drop me a line when you get a chance.* *Give my love/regards to ...*
Ways of Ending a Letter (The Closing)	**Use one of these before signing your first and last name:** ***Sincerely,*** ***Sincerely yours,***	**Use one of these before signing your first name:** ***Love,/Lots of love (from),*** (use this in letters to your close friends and family) ***All the best,/Best wishes,*** ***Take care,*** ***Regards,/Best regards,*** (use this in letters to people you work with or do not know very well)

Writing E-mails

E-mails to companies and organizations are usually formal, and you can use the same beginnings and endings as in a formal letter. E-mails to friends and colleagues are usually written in a very brief and informal style:

Informal E-mails:

You can open the e-mail with:

Hi, *Hi* + first name, *Dear* + first name, (slightly more formal)
first name only, no name and no greeting

You can end the e-mail with:

All the best, + your first name
Best wishes, + your first name
Regards, (slightly more formal) + your first name
Love, (only to friends and family) + your first name
your first name only
the first letter of your first name only (informal)
Talk to you soon/later + your first name (informal)
the first letter of your first name only (informal)

2905 Forest Road, Boulder, CO 80302

March 7, 2005

Ms. Megan Gray
Director of Human Resources
Newstar Publishing
2816 Lincoln Avenue
Minneapolis, MN 55403

Dear Ms. Gray:

Thank you for taking the time to meet with me this morning and tell me more about the technical support position at Newstar. I really liked everyone I met and am excited about the possibility of working at your company. I feel sure that I could be an asset to your IT team.

As we discussed in the interview, I would be able to begin working as early as next month. If you have any further questions, please do not hesitate to contact me. My phone number, once again is (303) 555-4965. I look forward to speaking with you again soon.

Sincerely,

Luis Garcia

Luis Garcia

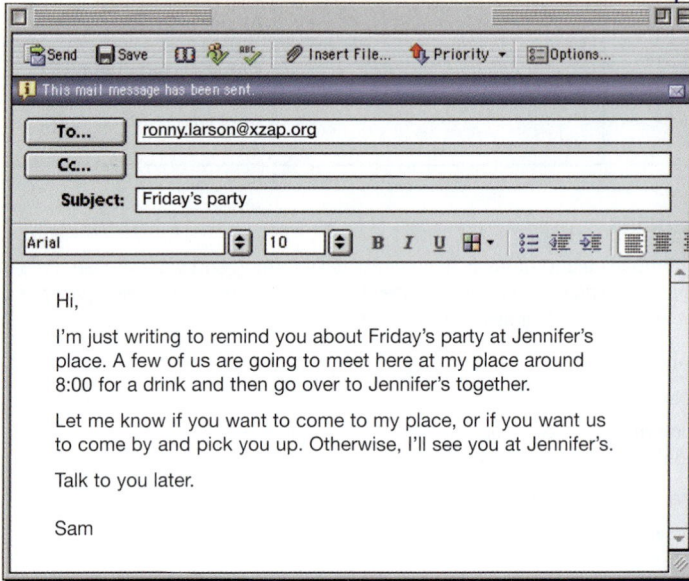

Send Save Insert File... Priority Options...

This mail message has been sent.

To... ronny.larson@xzap.org

Cc...

Subject: Friday's party

Arial 10 B I U

Hi,

I'm just writing to remind you about Friday's party at Jennifer's place. A few of us are going to meet here at my place around 8:00 for a drink and then go over to Jennifer's together.

Let me know if you want to come to my place, or if you want us to come by and pick you up. Otherwise, I'll see you at Jennifer's.

Talk to you later.

Sam

Writing Résumés and Cover Letters

WRITING TIPS

- Make your résumé and cover letter as concise as possible.
- Focus on your relevant work experience and your strongest points.
- Use short, clear sentences. Do not use contractions and informal language.

When you write to apply for a job, you should include a résumé and a cover letter that explains your interest in the job and your qualifications. Employers must look at many applications and often do not have time to read every word of what you write. Therefore, keep your explanations as brief and relevant as possible.

Writing a Résumé

A résumé is a document that lists your experience and qualifications. You can organize the information in whatever way or in whatever order you like. However, you should give each section a clear heading, keep explanations short, focus on what is relevant, and put the most important or relevant information first.

Résumés should usually be no more than one page (or in some cases the front and back of one sheet). Because there is not space, it is acceptable to drop the subject pronoun *I* and articles (for example, *worked in high-tech company* instead of *I worked in a high-tech company*), but be consistent.

It is a good idea to modify slightly your résumé depending on the job you are applying for in order to highlight your most relevant qualifications. Below are some of the most common types of information found in résumés:

Section Heading	Information to Include
Personal Information	Include your name, address, phone number, and e-mail address at the top of the first page. Do NOT include your age or birth date, height, weight, or marital status. It is not usual to attach a picture of yourself. If your résumé is more than a page, make sure your name is at the top of each page.
Work Experience	List your work experience in reverse order, starting with your most recent job. Give the title of your position, the name of your employer, and its location, and the dates you worked there. If you have had many previous jobs, you can list only your most relevant work experience. It is a good idea to explain gaps in your work history in your cover letter.
Education	List the degrees you have earned in reverse order and the names and locations of academic institutions you have attended. If you have attended a college or university, you do not usually mention your high school or earlier schools.
Awards and Achievements	List, in reverse order, any special awards or achievements that are relevant to the field of work you are applying for.
Skills	List skills that would be helpful in the job you are applying for. These can include foreign language skills or experience with different types of software.
Interests	List here any interests or hobbies you want the employer to know about.
References	You can list the names and phone numbers of two or three people who have worked with you or who know you and your work history well. You should also explain their relationship to you. Alternatively, you may simply write "Available upon request" under this heading.

Résumés should be typed or printed on good-quality paper. Résumés should NOT be handwritten. The paper does not have to be white. In fact, using a cream color or other color often helps to set your résumé apart from others. However, the paper should be a light enough color so that the text is still easy to read.

Writing a Cover Letter

A cover letter is a formal letter you write to accompany your résumé when you are applying for a job. It is your chance to highlight the most important points in your résumé and explain why you should be interviewed for the job. It should not be handwritten and should not be longer than one page.

Section	Information to Include	Sample Phrases
Your Address	Include your address (but not your name) at the top of the page.	*1839 Gallagher St.* *New Town, CA 97000*
Date	Include the date on a separate line below your address.	*October 13, 2004*
The Company's Address	Include the name and title of the person you are writing to (if you have it), the name of the company, and its address.	*Mr. Jenkins* *Director of Marketing* *Global Industries* *...*
Opening or Salutation	Write directly to the person who will look at your application. If the person's name does not appear in the job advertisement and you cannot find out the name by calling the company, use the appropriate title.	*Dear Mr. Jenkins:* *Dear Ms. Hu:* *Dear Human Resources Director:*
First Paragraph	State clearly the job you are applying for and how you learned about it. You can also state why you are particularly well qualified for the job. This paragraph can be just one or two sentences.	*I am writing to apply for the administrative assistant position advertised in the July 8 Register.* *My friend, Donna Garcia, told me about an open position in your sales department.*
Body Paragraph(s)	Talk about the highlights of your résumé here. List strongest qualities first. Explain in more detail experience or qualifications that are particularly relevant. Do not simply repeat the information in your résumé, and do not list details that are not relevant to the job you are applying for.	*As you can see from my enclosed/attached résumé I have worked for the past three years as the manager of a small restaurant.* *I also hold a B.A. in business from the University of Ohio.*
Last Paragraph(s)	Emphasize the qualities and skills that you will bring to the company you are applying to. State your availability for an interview and provide contact information.	*I am confident that I can bring many new ideas to your design team.* *I would like to meet with you to discuss my qualifications in person.* *You can reach me at 555-5893 or by e-mail at adam@...com* *I look forward to hearing from you.*
Closing	Close with "Sincerely," Type your first and last name below your signature.	*Sincerely,* Adam Lawson *Adam Lawson*

If you are writing an e-mail rather than a letter to apply for a job, you do not need to include the addresses or date at the top of the e-mail or the signature at the bottom. But the rest is the same. Be sure to attach your résumé.

2905 Forest Road, Boulder, CO 80302

February 4, 2005

Ms. Megan Gray
Director of Human Resources
Newstar Publishing
2816 Lincoln Avenue
Minneapolis, MN 55403

Dear Ms. Gray:

I am writing to apply for the technical support position that was advertised in today's *Star Tribune*. I believe that my technical background and work experience make me an ideal candidate for the job.

As you can see from my enclosed resumé, I hold a B.S. in computer science from Portland State College and have worked since my graduation in 2002 as an information technology associate at Ranger Books in Boulder, Colorado. During that time, I have worked closely with our editorial and design staff to make sure that our computer systems operate smoothly. I often took a leadership role on our tech support team.

Before that, I worked in the computer lab at my college. I also published a monthly newsletter and maintained the website for the Computer Science Department. So I am used to working with large groups of people, and I am good at solving the problems related to computers and publishing.

I have enjoyed my time at Ranger and have learned a great deal. But I am now ready for the challenges of working at a larger company with more opportunities for advancement. I am excited by the idea of being part of a leading publisher like Newstar. I am confident my technical expertise and interpersonal skills would make me an effective member of your team.

I would enjoy meeting with you in person to discuss my qualifications and learn more about the opening at your company. You can reach me by phone at (303) 555-4965 or by e-mail at luis@garcia.com to set up an appointment. I look forward to hearing from you.

Sincerely,

Luis Garcia

Luis Garcia

2905 Forest Road
Boulder, CO 80302
Tel: (303) 555-4965
Email: luis@garcia.com

Luis Garcia

Objective To find a technical support position in the field of publishing.

Experience

2002 – present Ranger Books Boulder, CO

Information Technology Associate

- Managed computer system of editorial and design staff.
- Worked on team of five IT associates to improve overall operations.

1999–2002 Portland State College Portland, OR

Computer Lab Assistant

- Helped students and faculty with a variety of computer problems.
- Set up and repaired computer equipment as needed.

2000–2002 Portland State College Portland, OR

Newsletter Publisher/Web Designer

- Published monthly departmental newsletter.
- Maintained department website.

Education

1999–2002 Portland State College Portland, OR

- B.S., Computer Science.
- Graduated with honors.

Skills Familiar with a variety of computer programs/languages including:

- Quark • PageMaker • Framemaker • HTML
- C++ • BASIC

Interests Hiking, yoga, computers.

References Available upon request.

LONGMAN WRITING GUIDE

Word Building

PREFIX	MEANING	EXAMPLE
a-, an-	opposite; without; not	amoral, atypical, antonym
anti-	opposed to; against	antifreeze, antidote
audi-, audio-	relating to sound; relating to hearing	audiovisual, auditorium
auto-	of or by yourself	autobiography, automobile
bi-	two; twice	bilingual, biannual
bio-	relating to living things	biology, biochemistry
cent-, centi-	100; 100th part of something	centipede, centimeter
circum-	all the way around something	circumstance, circumference
co-, col-, com-con-, cor-	with; together	coexist, collect, compassion, confederation, correlation
contra-	against	contraceptive
counter-	opposite; against	counterproductive
cyber-	relating to computers	cyberspace, cyberpunk
de-	to do or make the opposite of; remove from; reduce	decriminalize, decaffeinated, devalue
dis-	opposite	disapprove, dishonesty
down-	to a lower position; to or toward the bottom	downturn, downriver, downstairs
eco-	relating to the environment	ecological
electri-, electro-	relating to electricity	electrify, electrocute
em-, en-	to make something have a quality	empower, enlarge
ex-	no longer being or doing	ex-wife, ex-football player
ex-	out; from	exit, export
extra-	outside; beyond	extraterrestrial, extracurricular
geo-	relating to the earth	geology, geography
hydr-, hydro-	relating to or using water	hydroelectric, hydrant
il-, im-, in-, ir-	not	illogical, impossible, inconvenient, irrational
in-, im-	in; into	incoming, immerse
inter-, intro-, intra	between; together; within	international, introduce, intravenous
mis-	bad; badly	misfortune, misbehave
mono-	one	monogram, monologue
multi-	many	multicolored, multicultural
non-	not	nonsmoking, nonstandard
over-	too much; beyond; outer; additional	overpopulate, overhang, overcoat, overtime
poly-	many	polygon
post-	later than; after	postgraduate, postpone
pre-	before	prewar, preview
pro-	in favor of	pro-American
re-	again	rewrite, redo, rewind
semi-	half; partly	semicircle, semiprecious
sub-	under; below; less important or powerful	subway, substandard, subcommittee
super-	larger; greater; more powerful	supermarket, superhuman, supervisor
sym-, syn-	with; together	sympathy, synthesis
tele-	at or over a long distance	telescope, television
theo-	relating to God or gods	theology
therm-, thermo-	relating to heat	thermostat, thermometer
trans-	on or to the far side of something; between two things	transatlantic, transportation
tri-	three	tricycle, triangle
ultra-	beyond; extremely	ultrasonic, ultramodern
un-	not; opposite	unhappy, unfair, undress
under-	too little	underdeveloped, underage
uni-	one	unilateral
vice-	next in rank below the most important person	Vice-President, vice-captain

SUFFIX	MEANING	EXAMPLE
-ability, -ibility	used in order to make nouns from adjectives that end in -able and -ible	accountability, flexibility
-able, -ible	capable of; having a particular quality	manageable, comfortable, reversible, responsible
-al, -ial	relating to something; the act of doing something	electrical, financial, refusal, denial
-an, -ian, -ean	from or relating to a place; someone who has a particular job or knows about a particular subject; relating to or similar to a time, thing, or person; someone who has a particular belief	American, suburban, librarian, historian, subterranean, Victorian, Christian
-ant, -ent	someone or something that does something	servant, disinfectant, resident, repellent
-ar	relating to something	muscular, stellar
-ary	relating to something	customary, planetary
-ation, -tion, -ion	the act of doing something; the state or result of doing something	examination, combination, completion, election
-cy	used in order to make nouns	accuracy
-en	made of something; to make something have a particular quality	wooden, golden, darken, strengthen
-ence, -ance, -ency, -ancy	a state or quality; the act of doing something	intelligence, obedience, performance, tendency, presidency, pregnancy
-er, -or, -ar, -r	someone or something that does something	teacher, actor, beggar, writer, photocopier, accelerator
-ery, -ry	an act; a quality; a place where something is done or made	bribery, bravery, snobbery, distillery, bakery
-ful	full of	beautiful, harmful
-goer	someone who goes somewhere regularly	moviegoer, churchgoer
-graph, -graphy	something that is written or drawn	autograph, biography
-hood	the state or time of being something	childhood, manhood, womanhood
-ial, -al	relating to something	managerial, coastal
-ic, -ical	of; like; relating to a particular thing	photographic, historical
-ify	to affect in a particular way	purify, clarify, terrify
-ish	people or language; having a quality	Spanish, English, childish, selfish
-ism	a belief or set of ideas; the act of doing something	Buddhism, capitalism, criticism
-ist	relating to a political or religious belief	socialist, Methodist
-ity	having a particular quality	stupidity, regularity
-ive	having a particular quality	creative, descriptive
-ize	to make something have a quality; to change something into a different state	modernize, crystallize
-less	without something	childless, careless, endless
-logue, -log	relating to words	monologue, catalog
-ly	in a particular way; at regular times	slowly, quickly, hourly
-ment	the act or result of doing something	government, development
-ness	used in order to make nouns	happiness, softness
-ology	the study or science of something	geology, technology
-or	someone or something that does something	doctor, actor, inventor, radiator, incinerator, incubator
-ory	a place or thing used for doing something; having a particular quality	laboratory, satisfactory, obligatory
-ous, -ious	used in order to make adjectives from nouns	dangerous, furious
-proof	not allowing something to come in, come through, or destroy something	soundproof, waterproof, fireproof
-ship	having a particular position; an art or skill	membership, friendship, scholarship
-wear	clothes of a particular type	menswear, womenswear, sportswear
-y	full of or covered with something; tending to do something	hairy, fuzzy, sleepy, curly

Countable and Uncountable Nouns

Countable Nouns

Things that you can count are called **countable nouns**. These are often (but not always) objects such as *apple* and *house*:

an hour   two hours   a tree   six trees

In this dictionary, countable nouns appear with a label like this: [**C**]

REMEMBER

1. Countable nouns can be both singular (*chair*) and plural (*chairs*).
2. A singular countable noun is almost always used with an article or other determiner (for example, *a*, *another*, or *the*).
3. A plural countable noun is often used without a determiner. For example, when you are talking in general about something, *the* is not used: *Apples are sweeter than lemons.*
4. When a noun is singular, the following verb is also singular: *A chair has four legs.*
5. When a noun is plural, the following verb is also plural: *Chairs have four legs.*

Uncountable Nouns

Things that you cannot count are called **uncountable nouns**. Uncountable nouns are usually the names of substances (such as *water*, *grass*), qualities (such as *happiness*), collections (such as *furniture*, *money*) and other things that we do not see as individual objects (such as *electricity*).

In this dictionary, uncountable nouns appear with a label like this: [**U**]

Common Mistakes with Uncountable Nouns

Here are some common mistakes that students make with uncountable nouns:

✗ I want to give you ~~an~~ advice.
✎ I want to give you a piece of advice.

✗ I need to buy new ~~furnitures~~ for my home.
✎ I need to buy new furniture for my home.

✗ They have ~~many~~ furniture in their house.
✎ They have a lot of furniture in their house.

REMEMBER

1. Uncountable nouns NEVER have a plural form. You say *some furniture* (NOT *some furnitures*).
2. You do not use *a*, *an*, or *another*, or words such as *many*, *these*, or *three* with uncountable nouns. These determiners are only used with countable nouns.
3. You CAN use *the* with uncountable nouns when you are referring to a particular thing: *The weather was cold* (NOT *Weather was cold*) or *They gave me the information I needed* (NOT *They gave me information I needed*).
4. The verb that follows an uncountable noun is always singular. You say *The music was beautiful* (NOT *The music were beautiful*).

Quantity

As we have already seen, you use different words and expressions in English to describe the *number* of countable nouns and *amount* of uncountable nouns. The table below will help you to learn and remember the correct way to describe these two types of nouns:

Countable Nouns	Uncountable Nouns
How many apples? an apple some / several / a few / not many apples fewer apples not ... any / no apples none	How much luggage? luggage, a piece of luggage some / a little / not much luggage less luggage not ... any / no luggage none

Note that some nouns that are **countable** in your language may be **uncountable** in English. The nouns in the list below are all uncountable nouns in English:

advice, equipment, furniture, hardware/software, homework, housework, information, knowledge, machinery, money, scenery, stuff, traffic, weather

Counting Uncountable Nouns with *A Piece of ...*

If you want to talk about one or more individual examples of an uncountable noun, you cannot use *a* or *an*. For example, you cannot say *an advice*, you have to say *a piece of advice*. Here are some more uncountable nouns that can be used with a *piece of*:

information an interesting *piece of* information
furniture some new *pieces of* furniture
equipment a useful *piece of* equipment
bread Would you like *a piece of* bread?
research An interesting *piece of* research

Nouns That Are Countable AND Uncountable

Some nouns can have both a countable [C] and an uncountable [U] meaning. This often happens with the names of animals that are also a type of food:

> **chick·en**[1] /ˈtʃɪkən/ *n.* **1** [C] a farm bird that is kept for its meat and eggs ➔ see picture at FARM[1] **2** [U] the meat from this bird: *fried chicken* **3** [C] *informal* someone who lacks courage: *Don't be such a chicken!*

Some nouns are countable and uncountable in the same meaning. These are often things we eat and drink. You can talk about an amount of the food or drink (uncountable), or about different types of the food or drink (countable). In this dictionary, these nouns appear with a label like this: **[C,U]**:

> **wine**[1] /waɪn/ *n.* [C,U] an alcoholic drink made from GRAPES, or a type of this drink: *a glass of* ***red/white wine*** | *a fine selection of wines*

Verb Patterns

STUDY TIPS

- Whenever you learn a new verb, look it up in the dictionary and study the grammatical patterns that can follow it.
- Use the example sentences in the dictionary to help you to learn these patterns. There are many different patterns that can follow verbs but not all of them can be used with every verb.

Read the passage below:

Michael **wanted to buy** a present for his mother. He **finished doing** his homework and **asked his friend to come** with him to **help him decide** what to buy. He **thought about buying** a vase, but he **couldn't afford** it, so in the end his friend **advised him to buy** some flowers.

The patterns for the verbs in this passage are:
want **to do** sth, finish **doing** sth, ask sb **to do** sth, help (sb) **decide** sth, think **about doing** sth, (can't) afford **to do** sth, advise sb **to do** sth

Common Mistakes with Verb Patterns

✗ I want ~~that you come~~ to my party.
✎ I **want you to come** to my party.

✗ I am ~~waiting a call~~ from my sister.
✎ I am **waiting for a call** from my sister.

✗ You can ~~to~~ go there by bus.
✎ You **can go** there by bus.

The box below gives examples of different patterns that are used when one verb follows another in a sentence:

Types of Verb Patterns	Examples	In the dictionary, the verb patterns look like this:
verb + verb-*ing*	I **enjoy reading**. He **denies cheating** on the test. He **keeps forgetting**.	enjoy doing sth deny doing sth keep (on) doing sth
verb + infinitive with *to*	I **want to go** home. He **needs to study**. She always **forgets to close** the door.	want to do sth need to do sth forget to do sth
verb + direct object + infinitive with *to*	The doctor **advised me to rest**. I **asked him to go** with me.	advise sb to do sth ask sb to do sth
verb + direct object + infinitive without *to* (+ object)	She **let** me **drive** her car home. He **watched** her **dance**. I **saw** her leave the meeting early.	let sb do sth watch sb do sth see sb do sth
verb + preposition + verb-*ing*	He **thought about calling** the police. How long do you **plan on staying**?	think about doing sth plan on doing sth
verb + direct object + preposition + verb-*ing*	He **stopped me from leaving**. She **stopped the vase from falling**.	stop sb/sth from doing sth

Adjective Patterns

Choosing the Right Preposition or Pattern

When you use an adjective such as **interested**, you need to know which preposition or pattern to use with it. Do you say *interested about* something or *interested in* something? Do you say *interested to do* something or *interested in doing* something?

This dictionary shows you clearly which prepositions and patterns to use. Here is the entry for **interested**:

> **in·ter·est·ed** /ˈɪntrɪstɪd, ˈɪntəˌrɛstɪd/ *adj.* **1** giving a lot of attention to something because you want to find out more about it: *Tim's really* ***interested in*** *antique cars.* | *I'd be* ***interested to know*** *what you think about it.* **2** eager to do or have something: *Jill is* ***interested in*** *studying in Europe.*

As you can see, the usual preposition to use with **interested** is **in**. The verb pattern that you choose depends on the meaning of **interested**. If you want to talk about "wanting to know about something," you say **interested to hear/know/learn**. If you want to talk about "wanting to do something," you say **interested in doing something**.

Common Mistakes with Adjectives

✗ She is good ~~in~~ math.
✎ She is **good at** math.

✗ I'm tired ~~to wait~~ for the bus.
✎ I'm **tired of** wait**ing** for the bus.

✗ Are you interested ~~about~~ politics?
✎ Are you **interested in** politics?

✗ He's good ~~with~~ teaching.
✎ He's **good at** teach**ing**.

✗ She's bored ~~about~~ her job.
✎ She's **bored with** her job.

✗ I'm scared of ~~to walk~~ alone at night.
✎ I'm **scared of** walk**ing** alone at night.

Choosing the Right Pattern

Here is a list of some common adjectives and the patterns that can follow them:

+ Preposition + Verb-*ing*	+ Infinitive Verb Form	+ *that*
bored with do**ing** the same thing every day	**pleased to hear** the news	**surprised** (**that**) he didn't know
upset about/at be**ing** forgotten	**eager to get** married	**pleased** (**that**) she had remembered
excited about go**ing** on a trip	**unable to come** to class	**sure** (**that**) she would come soon
tired of wait**ing** for the bus	**reluctant to give** an answer	**determined** (**that**) he would go
proud of winn**ing** the competition	**determined to go** to college	**aware** (**that**) she was uncomfortable
fond of tell**ing** stories	**proud to be** chosen	
	surprised to learn the truth	

Prepositions

Prepositions are words that come before nouns and show the relationship between those nouns and the rest of the sentence. They can show location, direction, time, possession, etc. For example, in the sentence "The tree is behind the house," *behind* is a preposition. The pictures on these pages show some of the most common prepositions of location.

The glasses are **in** the cabinet **on** the top shelf. The plates are **on** the bottom shelf. The cabinet is **on** the wall **above/over** the counter. The toaster is **on** the counter. There is a drawer **under/below** the counter. The silverware is **in** the drawer.

There's a campground **below** the hill, **beside** the river. The campground is **near** the bridge that goes **over** the river. Cars are **on** the bridge, driving **over** it. The river flows **through** the valley **under** the bridge **past** the campground. There's a tent **under** a tree and a small campfire **next to** the tent. There's a rowboat **on** the river and someone is fishing **in** the river.

There is a large vase **on** the table. There are flowers **in** the vase. There is a candle **beside/next to** the vase. There are chairs **around** the table.

Shawn and Terry live **in** a city. They live **in** this apartment building. They live **on** East 135th Street. They live **on** the corner of East 135th Street and Ferndale Avenue. They live **at** 2963 East 135th Street **in** apartment 7B.

The truck is **in front of** the station wagon. The convertible is **between** the truck and the motorcycle. All the other vehicles are **behind** the motorcycle.

A woman is coming **out of** the bookstore. Two teenagers are going **into** the shoe store. A group of children are walking **toward** the toy store. A man is walking **away from** it.

The post office is **next to** the library. The library is **between** the post office and the clothes store. There are three buildings **across from** these buildings. The movie theater is directly **opposite** the library. The bank is **kitty-corner from** the park.

Phrasal Verbs

What Is a Phrasal Verb?

Read the passage below:

> My alarm **went off** at 7:00, but I didn't **get up** until 7:45. That's when my roommate yelled, "**Hurry up** if you want a ride—I'm about to leave." So I jumped out of bed, **threw on** some clothes, and ran out the door.

In this passage **go off**, **get up**, **hurry up**, and **throw on** are phrasal verbs, but *jump out of* and *run out* are not. Why?

A phrasal verb is a verb that is made up of two or three words. The first word is a verb, and the second word (and the third, if there is one) is a *particle*. A particle can be an adverb or a preposition.

But that is not all that is necessary to make a phrasal verb. In some verbs such as **fall over**, the particle does not change the meaning of the main verb. In phrasal verbs, however, the addition of the particle creates a completely new meaning. For example, the phrasal verb **get up to** (which means "to do something that might be slightly bad") is not connected with the usual meanings of the words **get** + **up** + **to**. It is often difficult to guess the meaning of a phrasal verb.

NOTE

- If a verb is followed by a preposition but keeps its ordinary meaning, it is NOT a phrasal verb. This is why *jump out of* and *run out* in the passage above are not phrasal verbs.

In this dictionary, phrasal verbs are labeled *phr. v.* and appear in blue at the end of the main verb entry. Some phrasal verbs must have an object, and the object can come either before or after the particle.

	Different Types of Phrasal Verbs
Phrasal Verbs with No Object	**get up** *phr. v.* **1** to wake up and get out of bed: *What time do you usually* ***get up****?* *He* ***got up*** *and went downstairs for breakfast.*
Phrasal Verbs with One Object	**1.** With some phrasal verbs, the object can come *either* before *or* after the particle. The **Longman Dictionary of American English** uses a special symbol ⇔ to show this is possible. **put sb/sth⇔up** *phr. v* **1** to build or make an upright structure: *The kids were* ***putting*** *a tent* ***up*** *in the back yard.* You can also say: *The kids were* ***putting up*** *a tent in the back yard.* **Note:** If the object is a pronoun (it/them/her/him etc.), the pronoun MUST always come before the particle: *They* ***put*** *it* ***up****.* NOT *They* ***put up*** *it.*

	2. With some phrasal verbs, the object must always come *between* the verb and the particle. **get sb/sth down** *phr. v.* **1** *informal* to make someone feel unhappy: *His problems at work are really **getting** him **down**.*
	3. With some phrasal verbs, the object must always come *after* the particle. **get over** *phr. v.* **1** *informal* **get over sth** to feel better after an illness or bad experience: *It will take a couple of weeks to **get over** the infection | Her son died in an accident and she never really **got over** it.*
Phrasal Verbs with Two Objects	With phrasal verbs that have two objects, one object comes after the verb and the other comes after the particle. **get out of** *phr. v.* **2 get sth out of sb** to persuade someone to tell or give you something: *She **got** about $200 **out** of him.* **3 get sth out of sth** to enjoy an activity and feel you have gained something from it: **get sth out of doing sth** *Do you **get** a lot **out** of playing the violin?*

Expand Your Vocabulary

Often there is a single word that has a similar meaning to a particular phrasal verb. For example, the single word **distribute** means the same as the phrasal verb **hand out** (they both mean "to give something to everyone in a group"). However, you should be careful when you use a single-word verb, because they are often more formal or more technical than the equivalent phrasal verb. Always check whether a verb is formal or informal, so that you use words that are appropriate for the situation. Here are some verbs that you can use when talking about telephoning someone, ending a telephone call, etc.

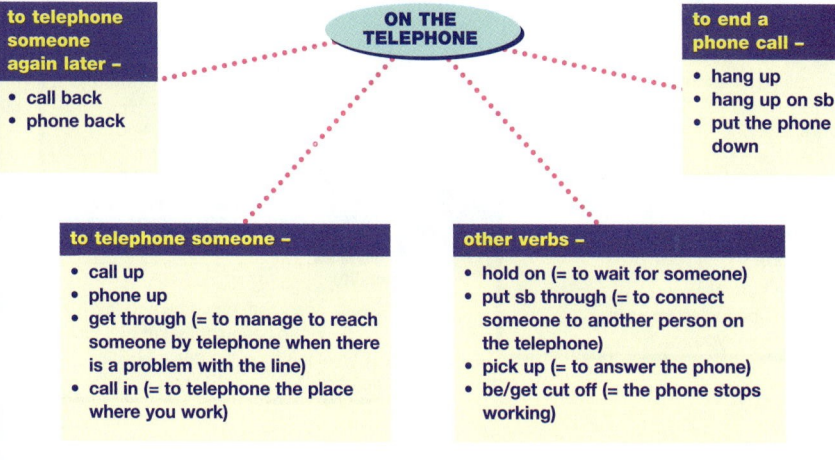

ON THE TELEPHONE

to telephone someone again later –
- call back
- phone back

to end a phone call –
- hang up
- hang up on sb
- put the phone down

to telephone someone –
- call up
- phone up
- get through (= to manage to reach someone by telephone when there is a problem with the line)
- call in (= to telephone the place where you work)

other verbs –
- hold on (= to wait for someone)
- put sb through (= to connect someone to another person on the telephone)
- pick up (= to answer the phone)
- be/get cut off (= the phone stops working)

→ If you want more information on phrasal verbs, the ***Longman Phrasal Verbs Dictionary*** explains the meaning of and shows how to use 5,000 phrasal verbs.

Modal Verbs

The modal verbs in English are **can**, **could**, **must**, **will**, **would**, **should**, **may**, **shall**, and **might**. These verbs are used before an infinitive verb without *to*. They are used to give extra information about the main verb. **Need (to)**, **ought to**, **have to** and **have got to** are also often used in similar ways.

Modal verbs are often contracted (=shortened), especially in speech and informal writing. So we say *I can't* rather than *I cannot*, *you shouldn't* rather than *you should not*, *they wouldn't* rather than *they would not*.

You can use modal verbs for offering help, advice, or suggestions, and for asking for and giving permission:

Making Requests: can, will, could, would

Can you help me, please?
Will you come here for a minute?
Could you tell me what time it is?
Would you pass me the salt, please?

Note: could and would are more formal and polite.

Offering to Help: can, may, shall, will

Can I give you a hand?
May I help you?
Shall I answer the phone?
I'll drive you home.

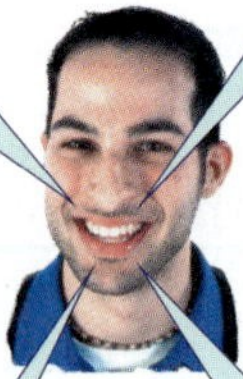

Asking for and Giving Permission: can, could, may

You can borrow my bike.
Can I have some of your French fries?
Could I speak to the manager, please?
May I use the car tonight?

Note: could is more polite than can, and may is used in more formal English.

Making Suggestions and Giving Advice: should, ought to, shall, have to

You should exercise more.
You ought to go to the doctor.
Shall we go?
You really have to try the fish – it's delicious.

Certainty: must, can't, will

He must be here already – there's his car.
She's late. She must have missed the bus.
You can't be finished already!

You use will/won't to say whether something is certain to happen in the future.

It will be summer soon.
We won't be fooled so easily.
I won't forget you.

Probability: should, ought to

They should be in New York by now.
The show ought to end around 10.00.
It's only a headache – I should feel better in the morning.

Possibility: may, could, might

I may have seen Tom downtown today.
It could be in the basement – I'm not sure.
I might have left it on the bus – I can't remember.

Or for talking about somebody's abilities or about necessity and obligations:

Ability: can, could

She **can** speak Chinese.
Can you see the mountains from here?
I **can't** afford a bigger apartment.
Could you understand what he was saying?
I **could** hear the neighbors arguing next door.

Necessity and Obligation: need to, have to, have got to, must

I **need to** go to the bathroom.
It **have to** call my parents today.
I**'ve got to** get up early in the morning.
Members **must** sign in before using the club.

You use will have to or will need to to say that it is necessary to do something in the future.

You**'ll have to** help me move this – it's too heavy.
You**'ll need to** learn some Japanese before you go to Tokyo.

Common Problems with Modal Verbs

Modal verbs are followed by a verb in the infinitive, without "to":

✗ I should ~~to~~ do my homework.
✎ I should **do** my homework.

They do not take "s" in the 3rd person singular:

✗ She ~~cans~~ answer your questions.
✎ She **can** answer your questions.

They cannot follow another verb. If you want to talk about the future, simply use the modal verb without *will*, or another verb or verb phrase such as *will be able to* or *will have to*:

✗ I ~~will can~~ meet you tomorrow.
✎ I **can** meet you tomorrow.
✎ I **will be able** to meet you tomorrow.

✗ He ~~will must~~ pay a large fine.
✎ He **will have to** pay a large fine.

STUDY TIP

- Avoid repetition by using different modal verbs to express the same meaning. For example, you can say: *Tonight **I have to** do my homework, then **I need to** write to Sally, and then **I've got to** go to bed early.*

Intensifiers

STUDY TIP

- When you look up a word in the dictionary, pay attention to the example sentences and to the examples in bold. This will help you learn which words belong together.

Intensifying Adjectives

You can make your English sound more natural and interesting by using a wider variety of adjectives and adverbs to emphasize what you are saying. Instead of saying that something is a **big problem** or a **big surprise**, you can say that it is a **serious problem** or a **complete surprise**.

Common Mistakes with Intensifying Adjectives

Sometimes it is hard to choose the correct adjective. For example, you can say that something is of **great importance**, but you can't say that it is of **big importance**.

✗ a ~~strong~~ lie
✎ a **big** lie

✗ a ~~big~~ interest in something
✎ a **great** interest in something

✗ a ~~strong~~ illness/infection/disease
✎ a **serious** illness/infection/disease

The box below shows you some of the different adjectives that are used to emphasize some common nouns:

	big	complete	total	serious	great	strong	distinct	huge
difficulty				✓	✓			✓
problem	✓			✓				✓
mistake	✓	✓	✓	✓	✓			✓
possibility						✓	✓	
disaster	✓	✓	✓					✓
difference	✓				✓			✓
surprise	✓	✓	✓		✓			✓
importance					✓			✓
lack (of)		✓	✓				✓	

Intensifying Adjectives

Instead of saying that something is **very difficult** or that somebody is **very intelligent**, you can say **extremely difficult**, or **highly intelligent**.

Common Mistakes with Intensifying Adverbs

Sometimes it is hard to choose the correct adverb. For example, you can say **highly intelligent**, but NOT **highly smart** (you have to say **very smart**).

✗ ~~strongly~~ sure
✎ **absolutely** sure

✗ ~~absolutely~~ different
✎ **completely** different

✗ ~~highly~~ certain
✎ **absolutely** certain

✗ ~~completely~~ hungry
✎ **very** hungry

✗ ~~strongly~~ disappointed
✎ **deeply** disappointed

The box below shows you some of the different adverbs that are used to emphasize some common adjectives:

	very	highly	completely	totally	seriously	extremely	absolutely	really
difficult								
interesting								
important								
funny								
exhausted								
sorry								
upset								
successful								
ill								
different								
impossible								

This dictionary gives a lot of useful information to help you learn which adverbs and adjectives to use to add emphasis. Look at the entry for **highly**:

> **high·ly** /ˈhaɪli/ *adv.* **1** very: *a* ***highly successful*** *meeting* | ***highly skilled*** *workers* **2** to a high level or degree: *a highly paid attorney*

NOTE

Often, different meanings of a word will collocate with different intensifying adjectives and adverbs. So you say:

- She was ***badly/seriously*** hurt (= injured) in the accident.

but

- I was ***deeply/very*** hurt (= upset) by her comments.

→ See also **Writing Guide** on **Collocations**.

Articles

Articles are special words that come before nouns that show which person, place, or thing you are talking about. The articles in English are **a** or **an**, and **the**. Adjectives come between articles and nouns, but do not use an article without a noun:

✘ ~~a~~ great.
✎ He's **a** great teacher.

Use *The*:

- When it is clear which person, place, or thing you are talking about:
  *I'm not going to **the** party* (= the person you are talking to knows which party you mean).
- When you refer to a particular thing, or when there is only one thing of this kind:
  *I live in **the** house with **the** blue door* (= there is only one house with a door like this).
  ***The** sun shone all day* (= there is only one sun).

Use *A* or *An*:

- When you refer to someone or something for the first time and it may not be clear which person, place, or thing you are talking about:
  *Would you like to go to **a** party* (= the person you are talking to does not know about the party yet)?
- When you are talking about one of several things in a general way:
  *I live in **a** house with **a** blue door* (= there is more than one house like this).
- When you talk about a type of person or thing:
  *My mother is **a** doctor.* | *Do you want **an** umbrella?*

A or *An*:

- Use **an** instead of **a** before a word that starts with a vowel sound:
  ✘ I bought ~~a~~ orange.
  ✎ I bought **an** orange.
  ✘ I bought ~~an~~ big orange.
  ✎ I bought **a** big orange.
- The choice between **a** or **an** depends on pronunciation, not spelling, so use **an** before any word that starts with a vowel sound, even if it is spelled with a consonant:
  ✘ I got there ~~a~~ hour early.
  ✎ I got there **an** hour early.
- The letter "u" is a vowel. But when a "u" at the beginning of a word is pronounced like "you" (as in *unit*) the word starts with a consonant sound. In this case, use **a** not **an**:
  ✘ ~~A~~ uncle
  ✎ **An** uncle
  BUT
  ✘ ~~An~~ university
  ✎ **A** university
- The letters *f*, *h*, *l*, *m*, *n*, *r*, *s*, and *x* are consonants, but the pronunciation of their names start with vowel sounds (e.g., "eff" and "aitch"). Use **an** before the NAMES of these letters:
  ✘ Do you spell "rise" with ~~a~~ *s* or a *z*?
  ✎ Do you spell "rise" with **an** *s* or a *z*?

→ You can Test Yourself on **a** or **an** by doing the exercises on **Articles** on the CD-ROM
See also **Grammar Guide** on **Countable and Uncountable Nouns**.

Saying Thank You

When Someone Does Something for You or Gives You Something

Thank you. / Thanks.

Let me help you with those bags.

Oh, thank you.

+ for

Thank you for getting the tickets. | Thanks for the suggestion.

Thank you very much. / Thanks a lot.

Thank you very much for all your help.

Here are those notes you wanted.

Thanks a lot.

To emphasize your thanks, especially in more formal situations, you can say:

That's very kind/nice of you.

I'll give you a ride home if you want.

Thanks. That's very kind of you.

I really appreciate it.

Thank you for helping me clean out the garage. I really appreciate it.

When You Are Writing a Letter

***Thank you for* (doing) sth.**

Thank you for the birthday card and the money. | Thank you for feeding my cat while I was away.

***Thank you very much for* (doing) sth.**

Thank you very much for sending me the information about the language courses at your school.

***Many thanks for* (doing) sth.** (FORMAL)

Many thanks for all your hard work on this year's campaign.

When Someone Says Something Nice to You

Thank you. / Thanks.

Your presentation was really good.

Thank you. I worked really hard on it.

Thank you very much. / Thanks a lot.

That dress looks really good on you.

Thanks a lot. I just got it last week.

Thanks is more informal than **thank you**. Don't say "very thanks" or "much thanks." "Thanks a lot" can sound like you are actually annoyed by what someone has done if it is said with the wrong intonation. So be careful how you say it.

Replying to Someone Who Thanks You

You're welcome.

Thanks for dinner.

Oh, you're welcome.

That's OK. / Don't mention it. / (It was) my pleasure.

Thank you for all your help.

Don't mention it.

Sure. / No problem. (FORMAL)

Thanks a lot for coming with me.

No problem.

Advice

Asking for Advice

Can I ask your advice/opinion about something?

Can I ask your opinion about something? What do you think the best way to ask my parents for a loan would be?

What do you think I should do?

I don't know whether to take the job or not. What do you think I should do?

Do you think I should* do sth*?

It only costs $15. Do you think I should buy it?

I'm thinking of* doing sth. *What do you think?

I'm thinking of dyeing my hair red. What do you think?

> ❗ Don't say, "Can you give me an advice?" Use one of the phrases above.

Giving Advice

***You should* do sth. / *You ought to* do sth.**

You should call Tom if you're so upset.

***You shouldn't* do sth.**

You shouldn't drive so fast.

***If I were you, I'd / I wouldn't* do sth.**

If I were you, I'd wait till Heather mentions it. | If I were you, I wouldn't lend him any more money.

***The best thing to do would be to* do sth.**

The best thing to do would be to sell the house.

***What you should do is* do sth.** (INFORMAL)

What you should do is write a letter and explain the situation.

***What you need is* sth.** (INFORMAL)

What you need is a nice long vacation.

***You'd better* do sth.** (INFORMAL)

You'd better hide that before Andy gets home.

***Make sure (that) you* do sth.** (INFORMAL)

Make sure you take enough warm clothing.

***I would advise you (not) to* do sth.** (FORMAL)

I would advise you not to tell anyone else about this.

Suggestions

Making a Suggestion

***Let's* do sth.**
Let's take a taxi.

***We/You could* do sth.**
We could meet at the bar next to the theater. | You could wear your brown jacket.

***Should I/we* do sth?**
Should I make the reservations?

***Why don't we/you* do sth?**
Why don't you try the other key?

***How/What about* (doing) sth?**
How about having a big Halloween party this year?

***Do you want to* do sth?**
Do you want to go fishing this weekend?

***Why not* do sth?**
Why not invite your sister to come along?

***I/You/We could always* do sth.**
You could always stay at my place if it gets too late.

Saying Yes or No to a Suggestion

YES

OK. / All right.

Let's take the bus.

All right. Are you going to pay?

Yes. / Yeah. (INFORMAL)

You could wear your brown jacket.

Yeah. That would go well with this shirt.

Good/Great idea!

How about having a big Halloween party this year?

Good idea! We could decorate the whole house.

That sounds good/great.

Do you want to go fishing this weekend?

That sounds great.

NO

***I'd rather* do sth. /**
***I'd prefer to* do sth.**

You could always stay at my place if it gets too late.

I'd rather go home, I think.

I'd rather not.

Why not invite your sister to come along?

I'd rather not.

How about* (doing) sth *instead?

We could meet at that bar next to the theater.

How about the new bar on the corner instead?

Making Requests
Asking Someone to Do Something for You

Use the polite phrases when you are talking to someone you do not know well, or when you are asking a friend to do something difficult or important.

When You Are Asking Someone You Know Well

***Can you* do sth?**

Can you help me move these boxes?

***Will you* do sth?**

Will you buy some cereal on the way home?

When You Are Asking Anyone

***Could you* do sth?**

Could you show me how to use the copy machine?

***Would you mind* doing sth?**

Would you mind mailing this letter for me?

When You Want To Be Especially Polite

Do you think you* could do sth, *please?

Do you think you could try the number again, please?

***I was wondering if you* could do sth.**

I was wondering if you could give me a ride to the airport on Saturday.

Saying Yes or No to a Request

YES

OK. / All right.

Will you buy some cereal on the way home?

OK. What kind?

Sure. / No problem. (INFORMAL)

Would you mind mailing this letter for me?

No problem.

Certainly. (FORMAL)

Do you think you could try the number again, please?

Certainly, sir. Just a moment.

NO

If you say no, it is polite to give a reason.

Sorry, but ...

Can you help me move these boxes?

Sorry, but I have a bad back.

I'm afraid ...

Could you show me how to use the copy machine?

I'm afraid I don't know how to use it either.

I really can't.

I was wondering if you could give me a ride to the airport Saturday morning?

I really can't. I've got soccer practice.

Asking For Permission
Asking Someone to Let You Do Something

Use the polite phrases when you are talking to someone you do not know well, or when you are asking a friend if you can do something important, such as borrow their car.

When You Are Asking Someone You Know Well

***Can I* do sth?**

Can I borrow your pen?

***Is it OK/all right if I* do sth?**

Is it OK if I use your phone?

When You Are Asking Anyone

***Could I* do sth?**

Could I look at the paper when you're finished?

***Do you mind if I* do sth?**

Do you mind if I smoke?

When You Want To Be Especially Polite

***May I* do sth?**

May I sit here?

***Would you mind if I* did sth?**

Would you mind if I closed the window?

***Would it be OK/all right if I* did sth?**

Would it be all right if I left early today?

Saying Yes or No to Someone's Request for Permission

YES

Yes, of course. / Please do. / Be my guest.

Is it OK if I use your phone?

Please do.

Sure. / No problem. (INFORMAL)

Can I borrow your pen?

No problem.

No, that's fine. / No, go right ahead.

Use this to respond to questions that start with *Do/Would you mind if …?*

Would you mind if I closed the window?

No, go right ahead.

NO

If you say no, it is polite to give a reason.

Sorry, but …

Could I look at the paper when you're finished?

Sorry, but I promised it to Paula.

No, sorry.

May I sit here?

No, sorry. That seat's taken.

I'm afraid …

Do you mind if I smoke?

I'm afraid smoking's not allowed in the building.

Agreeing

When You Agree

Yes. / Yeah.

We should give Becky a call.

Yeah, that's a good idea.

I know.

Class was so boring today.

I know.

I agree.

People should stop complaining and do something.

I agree.

Right. / That's right. / You're right.

We'll never finish this tonight.

You're right. Let's do it tomorrow.

When You Agree Strongly

Exactly! / Absolutely!

She shouldn't have accused him if she wasn't sure.

Exactly!

I couldn't agree more.

Parents need to take more responsibility for their children's behavior.

I couldn't agree more.

You're telling me! / You said it!
(INFORMAL)

Movie tickets have really gotten expensive.

You're telling me! I had to pay $11 last week.

When You Agree, but Not Strongly

I suppose/guess so.

It might be nice to try the new Japanese restaurant.

I guess so.

Disagreeing

When You Disagree, but Want to Be Polite

Yes, but ... / I know, but ...

It would be easier to meet at the restaurant.

I know, but I might get lost. Let's go together.

Not really.

You're lucky.

Not really.

I'm not so sure.

I think Greg would do a great job.

I'm not sure. He messed things up last time.

I see your point, but ...

Famous people can't really expect to keep their private lives private.

I see your point, but don't you think everyone has a right to privacy?

But don't you think ...?

We could go to Europe this summer.

But don't you think it'll be too expensive?

Giving When You Disagree Strongly

Use these phrases only with people you know well. You may sound rude if you say them to a stranger.

I don't think so.

The flowers would look really nice over by the window.

I don't think so. I think they look better here.

***No, it isn't. / No, they don't.* etc.**

The quickest way is to take the subway.

No, it isn't. It's a lot faster by car.

That's not true/right.

Everyone thought the show was great.

That's not true. A lot of people were disappointed.

You must be joking! / No way! / You can't be serious! (INFORMAL)

We'll have this finished in a half an hour.

You must be joking! There's at least two hours' work left to do.

Saying Yes to a Question

When the Answer is Yes

Yes.

Are these flowers real?

Yes, they are.

Yeah. (INFORMAL)

Are you going to Ben's party?

Yeah. Are you?

That's right.

You used to work with Liz, didn't you?

That's right.

I'm afraid so.

Use this when you think the person asking the question is hoping for a different answer.

The store's already closed, isn't it?

I'm afraid so.

When You Want to Emphasize That the Answer is Yes

Definitely!

Are you going to be there Sunday?

Definitely!

Of course!

Use this especially when you are surprised or annoyed that someone has asked you something.

Is it OK if I stay at your place?

Of course! You're always welcome.

When You Think That the Answer is Yes, but You Are Not Sure

I think/guess so.

Has Ted already left?

I guess so.

Probably.

Will there be food at the meeting?

Probably. They usually provide something to eat.

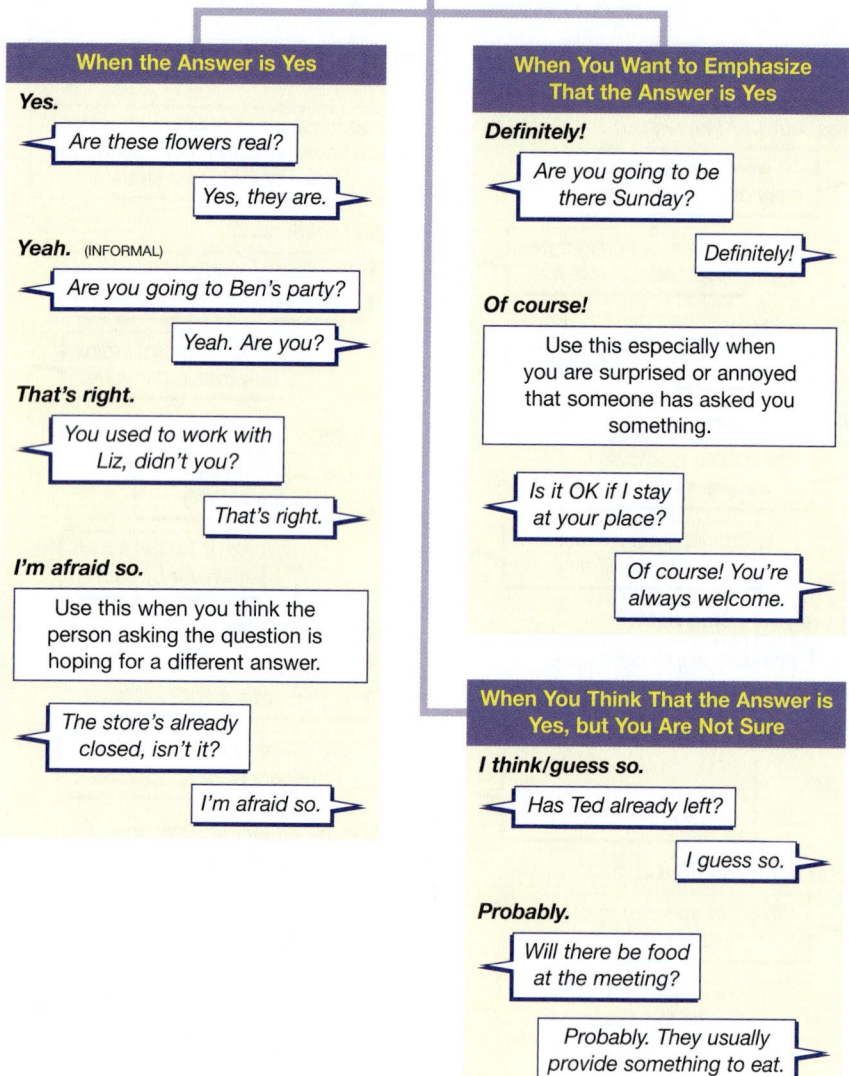

Saying No to a Question

When the Answer is No

No.

❗ It often sounds rude or angry if you use "no" on its own. People usually say something else after the word "no."

Were you looking for me?

No, but I think Carol was.

Not really.

Did you enjoy the movie?

Not really. It was kind of boring.

I'm afraid not.

Use this when you think the person asking the question is hoping for a different answer.

Did the package arrive yet?

I'm afraid not.

When You Think That the Answer is No, but You Are Not Sure

I don't think so.

Will it be ready tomorrow?

I don't think so. Maybe by Wednesday.

Probably not.

Do you think $50 will be enough?

Probably not. I'm taking $75.

I doubt it.

Do you think Anna will help us?

I doubt it. She's pretty busy these days.

When You Want to Emphasize That the Answer is No

Use these phrases only with people you know well. You may sound rude if you say them to a stranger.

Definitely not!

So would you travel with Jeff again?

Definitely not! He drove me crazy.

Of course not!

Use this especially when you are surprised or annoyed that someone has asked you something.

Did you tell her how bad she looked?

Of course not!

Of course I won't. / Of course she didn't. etc.

She won't tell anyone, will she?

Of course she won't. She can keep a secret.

No way! (INFORMAL)

Are you going to take the apartment?

No way! It was disgusting.

Saying Hello

Saying Hello to Someone That You Already Know

Hello. / Hi.

Hey. (INFORMAL)

Morning.

Use this when you see someone at the start of the day, for example when you arrive at work.

Saying Hello in a Formal or Business Situation

Hello.

Good morning. (= before 12 noon)

Good afternoon. (= 12 noon until about 6 p.m.)

Good evening. (= after about 6 p.m.)

! Use **Good night** only when you are saying goodbye in the evening, not when you are saying hello. Do not say **Good day**.

Saying Hello to Someone You Have Just Been Introduced to for the First Time

Nice/Pleased to meet you.

This is Erik, one of my co-workers.

Nice to meet you, Erik.

Saying Hello and Introducing Yourself

Hello/Hi, I'm ...

Hi, I'm Reggie, one of Lynn's friends.

Hello/Hi, my name's ...

Hello, my name's Sue. What's yours?

Introducing Other People

This is ... / Have you met ...? / Do You Know ...?

Sheryl, this is my fiancée, Lucinda.

I'd like you to meet ... (FORMAL)

I'd like you to meet Hugh Duncan. He's our new vice president of sales.

Saying Goodbye

Saying Godbye to Someone That You Know Well

Bye. / Goodbye. / See you.

***See you later/soon/Wednesday* etc.**

See you on Monday. Have a nice weekend.

Bye-bye.

> ❗ When you use this phrase with adults, be sure to stress the second syllable, not the first. Stress the first syllable, or stress them both equally, only when you are talking to small children.

Saying Goodbye in a Formal or Business Situation

Goodbye.

It was nice meeting you. / It was nice talking to you.

> Use this when you are saying goodbye to someone you have met for the first time.

Saying Goodbye at the End of the Evening or When You Are Going to Bed

Good night.

Night.

Saying Goodbye to a Friend That You May Not See for a While

See you around. / Take care.

Saying That You Have to Leave

> You usually give a reason when you tell someone that you have to leave.

I'd better be going. / I've got to go. / I have to go.

Well, I'd better be going, or I'll be late.

Having a Conversation

To Ask Someone to Repeat Something

Excuse me? / Sorry?

Sorry? Did you say Tuesday?

Could you repeat ...? / Could you say ... again?

Could you repeat the phone number, please?

I didn't quite catch ...

I didn't quite catch your name. Could you say it again?

To Interrupt Someone

When you want to interrupt, you usually show this by leaning forward, making a movement, or taking a breath. You can also use these words and phrases.

Uh ... / Um ... / Well ...

A: *So if we all meet here at 6:00 ...*
B: *Um ... I don't get off work till 6:30.*

Yes, but ... / I know, but ...

A: *Well, first we'll take out this wall. Then we'll replace all the carpeting, and ...*
B: *Yes, but how are we going to afford it all?*

Sorry to interrupt, but ...

Sorry to interrupt, but your 1:00 appointment is here.

Use this when you are interrupting a conversation which you were not involved in before.

To Check That Someone Understands or Agrees with You

(Do) you know what I mean?

It's not so easy when you're directly involved. You know what I mean?

..., you know?

I want to get one of those big leather bags, you know? One with a shoulder strap.

To Show That You Are Listening to What Someone is Saying

Uh-huh. / Mm-hmm. / Yeah. / Yes. / Right. / OK.

A: *You know my friend Alan.*
B: *Mm-hmm.*
A: *Well, he's trying to get a group together to go camping.*
B: *Uh-huh.*
A: *So would you like to come along?*
B: *OK.*

To Give Yourself More Time to Think

Um ... / Uh ... / Well ...

Um ... I don't really know.

I mean ...

It's so far away. And, I mean, if we have to be there by 2:00 ...

To Start a New Subject or Go Back to the Main Subject

So ...

So, I hear you're thinking of moving back to Ohio.

Anyway ...

Anyway, what I really want to know is how you two met.

To Start the Conversation Again After You Have Been Interrupted

Where were we?

Where were we? Oh yeah, I was going to tell you about Tom's new job.

Complaining

When You Are Complaining to Someone You Know Well

I'm sick/tired of you **doing sth.**

I'm sick of you criticizing me all the time.

I've had enough of you **doing sth.**

I've had enough of you two fighting. Stop right now!

You're always **doing sth.**

You're always making me wait while you talk on your cell phone.

You never **do sth.**

You never listen, do you?

When You Are Writing a Letter to Complain about Something

I am writing to complain about **sth.**

I am writing to complain about the way I was treated by a member of your staff.

When You Are Complaining in a Store, Restaurant, Hotel, etc.

The usual way to complain in one of these situations is simply to explain what is wrong. For example, *The shower in my room isn't working.* | *My steak isn't cooked enough.* You can then expect the person you are talking to to try to fix the problem.

Use the following phrases only when you have already done this and are complaining to someone else because you are still not satisfied.

I'd like to make a complaint about **sth.**

I'd like to make a complaint about these charges on my bill.

I'm not satisfied with **sth.**

I'm not satisfied with the repairs that you made.

Talking on the Phone

When You Are Making the Call

To Ask For the Person You Want To Speak To

Is ... there (, please)?

Hello, is Luis there?

> ❗ Don't say "Is there ..., please?"

Can/May/Could I speak to ..., please? (FORMAL)

Can I speak to Dr. Baldwin, please?

Is this ...?

> Use this when you think you are speaking to the right person, but you are not sure.

Hello. Is this Mary?

To Say Who You Are

This is ...

Hello, is Steve there? This is his brother.

> ❗ Don't say "Here is ..."

To Leave a Message

> Use these phrases only with people you know well. You may sound rude if you say them to a stranger.

Could you tell him/her ... called? / Could you ask him/her to call me back? etc.

Could you tell her that Roger Lind called?

When You Are Answering the Call

When You Pick Up the Phone

Hello.

> In business situations, you usually give your name, or the name of your company. At home, it is common just to say "hello."

Hello, Gail Doherty.

When Someone Asks Who You Are

It's ...

Is this Gary?

No, it's Ron. I'll go get Gary.

When the Call Is For You

Use these phrases only with people you know well. You may sound rude if you say them to a stranger.

Speaking.

May I speak to Vanessa Weiss, please?

Speaking. (= I am Vanessa Weiss.)

This is ....

Is Nick there?

This is Nick.

When the Call Is for Someone Else Who Is There

One moment, please. (FORMAL)

Hello, this is Heidi Williams. May I speak to Mr. Wallace?

One moment, please.

Use these phrases only with people you know well. You may sound rude if you say them to a stranger.

Hold on. / Hang on. / Just a second. (INFORMAL)

Hello. Is Jackie there?

Hang on. I'll see if she's here.

I'll (go) get him/her. (INFORMAL)

Is your mom there?

Yes, I'll go get her.

To Tell Someone Else the Call Is For Them?

You have a phone call. / ... is on the phone.

Jason, your dad's on the phone.

It's for you. / It's ...

Here, it's Jennifer. She wants to talk to you.

When the Call Is for Someone Else Who Is Not There

Use these phrases only with people you know well. You may sound rude if you say them to a stranger.

Sorry, he's/she's not here (right now).

Can I take a message? / Would you like to leave a message?

I'm afraid he's already left for the day. Would you like to leave a message?

Do you want to hold?

Use this to ask someone if they want to wait on the phone until the person they are calling is available.

I'm sorry, but her line's busy right now. Do you want to hold?

Apologizing

When You Have Done Something Wrong or When Someone May Be Upset

Sorry. (INFORMAL)

Sorry I'm late. Did I miss anything? | I forgot to tell you that Tom called. Sorry.

+ *about* *Sorry about losing my temper yesterday.*

I'm (really) sorry.

I'm sorry. I didn't know you wanted to go too.

+ *(that)* *I'm sorry I shouted at you. | I'm sorry that I forgot your birthday again.*

+ *about* *I'm really sorry about the damage. How much do you think it will cost to fix?*

+ *but* *I'm really sorry, but I lost the DVD you lent me.*

***I apologize for* (doing) sth.**
(SPOKEN FORMAL)

> Use this in formal spoken situations such as meetings or when you are speaking to a customer.

I apologize for the delay. | I apologize for bringing this up again, but we need to make a decision.

When You Have Made a Small Mistake, For Example, If You Accidentally Step on Someone's Foot

Sorry. (SPOKEN)

Sorry. I didn't see you standing there.

Excuse me. (SPOKEN)

Excuse me. I didn't mean to bump you!

Responding to an Apology

Don't worry about it. / That's OK. / Never mind. / It doesn't matter.

I'm really sorry, but I broke a glass.

Don't worry about it.

I'm sorry I forgot your birthday again.

Oh, that's OK.

M

mall /mɔl/ *n.* [C] a very large building with a lot of stores in it [= **shopping mall**; ➡ **strip mall**]: *Suzy's **at the mall**. | Do you want to **go to the mall**?*

mal·lard /ˈmælɚd/ *n.* [C] a type of common wild duck

mal·le·a·ble /ˈmæliəbəl/ *adj.* **1** something that is malleable is easy to press, pull, or bend into a new shape: *a malleable metal* **2** *formal* someone who is malleable is easily influenced or changed by people

mal·let /ˈmælɪt/ *n.* [C] a wooden hammer

mal·nour·ished /ˌmælˈnɚɪʃt, -ˈnʌrɪʃt/ *adj.* sick or weak because of not eating enough food, or because of not eating good food

mal·nu·tri·tion /ˌmælnuˈtrɪʃən/ *n.* [U] illness or weakness as a result of being malnourished

mal·prac·tice /ˌmælˈpræktɪs/ *n.* [C,U] the act of failing to do a professional duty, or of making a mistake while doing it

malt /mɔlt/ *n.* **1** [C] a drink made from milk, malt powder, ICE CREAM, and something such as chocolate **2** [U] grain, usually BARLEY, that is used for making beer, WHISKEY, etc.

malt·ed /ˈmɔltɪd/ **also** **ˌmalted ˈmilk** *n.* [C] a MALT

mal·treat /mælˈtrit/ *v.* [T] *formal* to treat an animal or person cruelly —**maltreatment** *n.* [U]

ma·ma /ˈmɑmə/ *n.* [C] *informal* a MOTHER

ˈmama's boy *n.* [C] *informal disapproving* a boy or man that people think is weak because his mother is too protective of him

mam·mal /ˈmæməl/ *n.* [C] the group of animals including humans that drink milk from their mother's breasts when they are young

mam·mo·gram /ˈmæməˌgræm/ *n.* [C] an X-RAY picture of a woman's breast

mam·moth /ˈmæməθ/ *adj.* very large: *a mammoth job*

man¹ /mæn/ *n.* plural **men** /mɛn/

1 MALE [C] an adult male human [➡ **woman**]: *Carl is a really nice man. | A group of middle-aged men came into the restaurant.*

THESAURUS

guy informal – a man: *He's such a great guy. | One of the guys at work is from Mexico.*
gentleman – a polite word for a man, often used in formal situations: *Good evening, ladies and gentlemen.*
boy – a young male person, usually a child or a teenager: *I took the boys swimming. | a teenage boy | The gang, including a boy of 10, had all been at the party.*
youth – a teenage boy or young man: *He teaches at a school for troubled youths in San Diego.*
➔ WOMAN

2 STRONG/BRAVE [C usually singular] a man who has the qualities that people think a man should have, such as being brave, strong, etc.: *If someone has something to say, **be a man** and speak up.*

3 ALL PEOPLE [U] all people, both male and female, considered as a group: *This is one of the worst diseases **known to man**.*

4 PERSON [C] *old-fashioned* a person, either male or female: *All men are equal in the eyes of the law.*

THESAURUS

Man can mean "people in general": *Man has always tried to understand the stars.*
Mankind means "all people, considered as a group": *the darkest time in the history of mankind*
Some people think that using **man** and **mankind** in this way seems to not include women. To avoid this problem, you can use **people** to mean "people in general" and **humankind** instead of **mankind**: *People have always tried to understand the stars. | the darkest time in the history of humankind*

5 WORKER [C] a man who does a job for you, usually repairing something: *The telephone man is supposed to come this morning.*

6 SOLDIER [C usually plural] a soldier, SAILOR, police officer, etc. who has a low rank: *General Lee ordered his men to retreat.*

7 WHAT SB LIKES [C] used in order to say that a man likes, or likes doing, a particular thing: *a gambling man | He's a meat and potatoes man* (=likes eating plain traditional food).

8 GAMES [C] one of the pieces you use in a game such as CHESS

9 man and wife *formal* to be or become married: *I now pronounce you man and wife* (=you are now officially married).

SPOKEN PHRASES

10 [C] used in order to speak to someone, especially an adult male: *Hey, man! How're you doing?*

11 my man said by some men when talking to a male friend

man² *v.* past tense and past participle **manned**, present participle **manning** [T] to use or operate a vehicle, piece of equipment, etc.: *the astronauts who manned the first spacecraft* ➔ MANNED

man³ *interjection* used in order to emphasize what you are saying: *Oh man! I'm going to be really late.*

man·a·cle /ˈmænəkəl/ *n.* [C] an iron ring on a chain that is put around the hand or foot of a prisoner

man·age /ˈmænɪdʒ/ *v.* [I,T] **1** to succeed in doing something difficult, such as dealing with a problem or living in a difficult situation: *Don't worry – we'll manage somehow. | Did you **manage to** get any sleep on the plane?* **2** to direct or control a business and the people who work in it: *Katie manages a restaurant in town.* **3** *spoken* to be able to do something or carry something without help: *"Can I help you with that?" "That's okay – I can manage."*

man·age·a·ble /ˈmænɪdʒəbəl/ *adj.* easy to control or deal with: *Break the task down into manageable chunks.*

man·age·ment /ˈmænɪdʒmənt/ *n.* **1** [U] the act or process of controlling and organizing the work of a company or organization and the people who work for it: *He studied Business Management.* **2** [singular, U] the people who are in charge of controlling and organizing a company or organization: *The management has agreed to talk with our union.* | *a member of the senior management team*

man·ag·er /ˈmænɪdʒɚ/ *n.* [C] someone who directs the work of something such as a business, organization, department, etc.: *That meal was terrible – I want to speak to the manager!* | *the* ***manager of*** *the Boston Red Sox*

man·a·ge·ri·al /ˌmænəˈdʒɪriəl/ *adj.* relating to the job of being a manager: *good managerial skills*

Man·da·rin /ˈmændərɪn/ *n.* [U] the official language of China

man·date /ˈmændeɪt/ *n.* [C] *formal* **1** the right or power that a government has to do something, given by the people in an election: *The governor was elected with a clear* ***mandate to*** *raise taxes.* **2** an official order given to a person or organization to do something —**mandate** *v.* [T]

man·da·to·ry /ˈmændəˌtɔri/ *adj.* something that is mandatory must be done: *mandatory safety inspections*

THESAURUS

compulsory, necessary, essential, vital
→ see Thesaurus box at NECESSARY

mane /meɪn/ *n.* [C] the long hair on the back of a horse's neck, or around the face and neck of a male lion

ma·neu·ver¹ /məˈnuvɚ/ *n.* **1** [C] a skillful movement or carefully planned action, especially to avoid something or go around it: *basic skiing maneuvers* **2 maneuvers** [plural] a military exercise like a battle used for training soldiers

maneuver² *v.* [I,T] to move or turn skillfully, or to move or turn something skillfully: *It was hard to* ***maneuver*** *the piano* ***through*** *the door.*

ma·neu·ver·a·ble /məˈnuvərəbəl/ *adj.* easy to move or turn

man·ger /ˈmeɪndʒɚ/ *n.* [C] a long open container that horses, cows, etc. eat from

man·gle /ˈmæŋgəl/ *v.* [T] to damage something badly by crushing or twisting it: *The car was badly mangled in the accident.*

man·go /ˈmæŋgoʊ/ *n.* [C] plural **mangos** or **mangoes** a sweet juicy tropical fruit with a large seed → see picture at FRUIT

man·grove /ˈmæŋgroʊv/ *n.* [C] a tropical tree that grows in or near water and grows new roots from its branches

mang·y /ˈmeɪndʒi/ *adj.* looking old, dirty, and in bad condition

man·han·dle /ˈmænˌhændl/ *v.* [T] to move someone or something roughly, using force

man·hole /ˈmænhoʊl/ *n.* [C] a hole on the surface of a road, covered by a lid, that people go down to examine pipes, wires, etc.

man·hood /ˈmænhʊd/ *n.* [U] **1** the qualities that people think a man should have: *He felt the need to prove* ***his manhood.*** **2** *formal* the state of being a man rather than a boy

man·hunt /ˈmænhʌnt/ *n.* [C] an organized search, usually for a criminal

ma·ni·a /ˈmeɪniə/ *n.* [C,U] **1** a very strong desire for something or interest in something, especially among a lot of people **2** *technical* a type of mental illness in which someone is extremely excited and active

ma·ni·ac /ˈmeɪniˌæk/ *n.* [C] *informal* **1** someone who is not responsible and behaves in a stupid or dangerous way: *He drives* ***like a maniac.*** **2** someone who is considered strange because s/he is too involved or interested in something: *a sex maniac*

ma·ni·a·cal /məˈnaɪəkəl/ *adj.* behaving as if you are crazy: *maniacal laughter*

man·ic /ˈmænɪk/ *adj.* behaving in a very excited and often anxious way: *She had a lot of manic energy.*

man·i·cure /ˈmænɪˌkyʊr/ *n.* [C,U] a treatment for the hands and FINGERNAILS that includes cleaning, cutting, etc. [➡ **pedicure**] —**manicure** *v.* [T] —**manicurist** *n.* [C]

man·i·fest¹ /ˈmænəˌfɛst/ *v. formal* **manifest itself** if something manifests itself, it appears or becomes easy to see: *The disease can manifest itself in many ways.*

manifest² *adj. formal* plain and easy to see [= **obvious**]: *a manifest error in his judgment* —**manifestly** *adv.*

man·i·fes·ta·tion /ˌmænəfəˈsteɪʃən/ *n.* [C,U] a very clear sign that a particular situation or feeling exists: *These latest riots are a clear* ***manifestation of*** *growing unhappiness.*

man·i·fes·to /ˌmænəˈfɛstoʊ/ *n.* plural **manifestos** [C] a written statement by a group, especially a political group, saying what it thinks and intends to do: *the Communist manifesto*

man·i·fold /ˈmænəˌfoʊld/ *adj. formal* many, and of different kinds: *The problems facing the government are manifold.*

ma·nil·a /məˈnɪlə/ *adj.* made of a strong brown paper: *a manila envelope*

ma·nip·u·late /məˈnɪpyəˌleɪt/ *v.* [T] **1** to make someone do exactly what you want by deceiving or influencing him/her: *I don't like the way he manipulates people.* **2** to skillfully handle, control, or move something —**manipulation** /mə,nɪpyə'leɪʃən/ *n.* [U]

ma·nip·u·la·tive /mə'nɪpyələt̬ɪv/ *adj. disapproving* good at controlling or deceiving people to get what you want: *a manipulative person* —**manipulator** /mə'nɪpyə,leɪt̬ɚ/ *n.* [C]

man·kind /,mæn'kaɪnd/ *n.* [U] all humans, considered as a group: *the worst war in **the history of mankind***

THESAURUS

mankind, man, people, humankind
➔ see Thesaurus box at MAN[1]

man·ly /'mænli/ *adj. approving* having qualities such as strength or courage that are considered to be typical of a man —**manliness** *n.* [U]

,man-'made *adj.* made of substances such as plastic that are not natural [➥ **artificial**]: *man-made fibers*

THESAURUS

artificial, processed, synthetic
➔ see Thesaurus box at NATURAL[1], ARTIFICIAL

manned /mænd/ *adj.* controlled or operated by people [≠ **unmanned**]: *a manned space flight*

man·ne·quin /'mænəkən/ *n.* [C] a model of a human body used for showing clothes

man·ner /'mænɚ/ *n.* **1** [singular] *formal* the way in which something is done or happens: *The issue should be resolved **in a manner** fair to both parties.* **2** [singular] the way in which someone talks or behaves with other people: *She has an easygoing manner.* | *Greet the customer **in a** friendly and courteous **manner**.*

THESAURUS

behavior, conduct, demeanor
➔ see Thesaurus box at BEHAVIOR

3 manners [plural] polite ways of behaving in social situations: *The girl had **good/bad manners**.* **4 all manner of sth** *formal* many different kinds of things or people: *The camp offers all manner of activities.*

man·nered /'mænɚd/ *adj.* **well-mannered/bad-mannered** *formal* polite or not polite to other people: *a bad-mannered old man*

man·ner·ism /'mænə,rɪzəm/ *n.* [C,U] a way of speaking, behaving, moving, etc. that is typical of a particular person or group of people: *Some of his mannerisms are exactly like his father's.*

man·nish /'mænɪʃ/ *adj.* a woman who is mannish looks or behaves like a man

man·or /'mænɚ/ *n.* [C] a large house with a large area of land around it

man·pow·er /'mæn,paʊɚ/ *n.* [U] all the workers available to do a particular type of work: *We don't have enough manpower right now to start the project.*

man·sion /'mænʃən/ *n.* [C] a very large house

THESAURUS

house, ranch house, ranch, cottage, row house, bungalow, duplex, apartment, condominium, condo, townhouse, mobile home, trailer
➔ see Thesaurus box at HOUSE[1]

man·slaugh·ter /'mæn,slɔt̬ɚ/ *n.* [U] *law* the crime of killing someone without intending to [➥ **murder**]

man·tel /'mæntl/ **also man·tel·piece** /'mæntl,pis/ *n.* [C] the shelf above a FIREPLACE

man·tle /'mæntl/ *n.* [C] **1 take on/assume/wear the mantle of sth** to accept or have a particular duty or responsibility: *He assumed the mantle of leadership when the Prime Minister died.* **2 a mantle of snow/darkness etc.** *literary* something that covers or surrounds a surface or area

man·tra /'mɑntrə/ *n.* [C] a repeated word or sound used as a prayer or to help people MEDITATE

man·u·al[1] /'mænyuəl/ *adj.* **1** manual work involves using your hands or your physical strength rather than your mind: *He makes a living doing **manual labor**.* **2** operated or done by hand or without the help of electricity, computer, etc.: *a manual pump* **3** relating to how well you use your hands to do or make things: *manual skills* —**manually** *adv.*

manual[2] *n.* [C] a book that gives instructions about how to do something such as use a machine: ***a computer manual***

man·u·fac·ture[1] /,mænyə'fæktʃɚ/ *v.* [T] to use machines to make goods, usually in large numbers: *I work for a company that manufactures aircraft engine parts.*

manufacture[2] *n.* [U] *formal* the process of making goods, usually in large numbers

man·u·fac·tur·er /,mænyə'fæktʃərɚ/ *n.* [C] a company that makes goods, usually in large numbers: *the world's largest shoe manufacturer*

man·u·fac·tur·ing /,mænyə'fæktʃərɪŋ/ *n.* [U] the process of making goods in factories

ma·nure /mə'nʊr/ *n.* [U] waste matter from animals that is put into the soil to produce better crops

man·u·script /'mænyə,skrɪpt/ *n.* [C] **1** a book or piece of writing before it is printed: *She sent a 350-page manuscript to the publisher.* **2** an old book written by hand before printing was invented: *an ancient Chinese manuscript*

man·y /'mɛni/ *quantifier, pron.* comparative **more**, superlative **most** **1** a large number of people or things [≠ **few**]: *I don't have many friends.* | ***How many** people are in your class?* | *There **aren't many** tickets left.* | ***Many of** the staff work part-time.* | *I've missed **too many** days off work* (=more than I should) *already.* | *Why did you bring **so many** pencils?* ➔ see Grammar box at LOT

M

THESAURUS

a large number: *They collected a large number of signatures on the petition.*
a lot/lots – a large amount, quantity, or number of something: *There are lots of other kids to play with in the neighborhood.* | *He has a lot of money.*
plenty – a large amount that is enough or more than enough: *Make sure you eat plenty of fruits and vegetables.*

USAGE

many, a lot of
In sentences that are not negative and not questions, it is more usual to say **a lot of** instead of **many**, especially in spoken English: *She has a lot of friends.*

2 as many the same number: *There weren't **as many** people at the meeting **as** we had hoped.* **3 a good/great many** *formal* a large number: *A great many men died in that battle.*

map[1] /mæp/ *n.* [C] a drawing of an area or country showing rivers, roads, cities, etc.: *a **map of** Texas* | *a **street/city map*** | *Do you see Smith Street **on the map**?*

COLLOCATIONS

You **look at a map** when you are trying to find your way to or around a place.
If you look very carefully at a map, you can say that you **study the map**.
If you can **read a map**, you can understand the information on a map.
If something is **on the map**, the map shows it: *I can't find Church Street on the map.*
A **detailed map** is one which includes a lot of information: *a detailed map showing the way to the campground*

map[2] *v.* past tense and past participle **mapped**, present participle **mapping** [T] to make a map of a particular area
map sth ⇔ **out** *phr. v.* to plan something carefully: *His future had been mapped out by his parents.*

ma·ple /ˈmeɪpəl/ *n.* [C,U] a tree in northern countries that has leaves with many points, or the wood from this tree

mar /mɑr/ *v.* past tense and past participle **marred**, present participle **marring** [T] *written* to make something less attractive or enjoyable [= **spoil**]: *His good looks were marred by a scar along his cheek.*

mar·a·thon[1] /ˈmærəˌθɑn/ *n.* [C] a race in which competitors run 26 miles and 385 yards: *She **ran the marathon** in just under three hours.*

marathon[2] *adj.* [only before noun] continuing for a very long time: *a marathon session of Congress*

ma·raud·ing /məˈrɔdɪŋ/ *adj.* searching for something to kill, steal, or destroy: *marauding soldiers*

mar·ble /ˈmɑrbəl/ *n.* **1** [U] a hard white rock that can be POLISHed and used for building, STATUES, etc.: *a marble floor* **2** [C] a small colored glass ball that children roll along the ground as part of a game **3 marbles** a game played by children using marbles

March /mɑrtʃ/ *n.* [C,U] the third month of the year: *We're going to meet **on March 15th**.* | *I might be going to California **in March**.* | *Julia had her baby **last March**.* | *The elections will take place **next March**.*

march[1] *v.* [I] **1** to walk quickly and with firm regular steps like a soldier: *The Union army **marched across** the field.* ➔ see picture on page A9

THESAURUS

walk, stride, stroll, amble, trudge, hike
➔ see Thesaurus box at WALK[1]

2 to walk quickly because you are angry or determined: *Mrs. Hawthorne stood up, turned around, and **marched out** the front door.* **3** to walk somewhere in a large group to protest about something: *The group plans to **march on** the White House next week.*

THESAURUS

protest, demonstrate, riot, hold/stage a sit-in, go on a hunger strike, boycott
➔ see Thesaurus box at PROTEST[2]

march[2] *n.* [C] **1** an organized event in which many people walk together to protest about something: *a civil rights march* **2** the act of walking with firm regular steps like a soldier **3** a piece of music with a regular beat for soldiers to march to

ˈmarching ˌband *n.* [C] a group of musicians who march while they play instruments

Mar·di Gras /ˈmɑrdi ˌgrɑ/ *n.* [singular] the day before Lent, or the music, dancing, etc. that celebrate this day

mare /mɛr/ *n.* [C] a female horse or DONKEY [➡ **stallion**]

mar·ga·rine /ˈmɑrdʒərɪn/ *n.* [U] a yellow food that is similar to butter

mar·gin /ˈmɑrdʒɪn/ *n.* [C] **1** the empty space at the side of a printed page: *I wrote some notes **in the margin**.*

THESAURUS

edge, border, rim
➔ see Thesaurus box at EDGE[1]

2 the difference in the number of votes, points, etc. that exists between the winners and the losers of an election or competition: *Polls show the senator leading by **a wide margin*** (=a lot of votes). **3 margin of error** the degree to which a calculation can be wrong without affecting the final results **4 ➔** PROFIT MARGIN

mar·gin·al /ˈmɑrdʒənl/ *adj.* small in importance or amount: *The film was a marginal success.* —**marginally** *adv.*

mar·i·jua·na /ˌmærəˈwɑnə/ *n.* [U] an illegal drug in the form of dried leaves that people smoke

ma·ri·na /məˈrinə/ *n.* [C] a small area of water where people keep boats used for pleasure

mar·i·nate /ˈmærəˌneɪt/ **also mar·i·nade** /ˌmærəˈneɪd, ˈmærəˌneɪd/ *v.* [T] to put meat or fish in a mixture of oil, wine, SPICES, etc. before you cook it: ***Marinate** the chicken **in** soy sauce for one hour.* —**marinade** *n.*

ma·rine¹ /məˈrin/ *adj.* relating to the ocean and the animals and plants that live there: ***marine life*** (=animals and fish that live in the ocean)

marine² *n.* [C] someone who is in the Marines

mar·i·ner /ˈmærənɚ/ *n.* [C] *literary* a sailor

Ma·rines /məˈrinz/ **also Maˈrine Corps** *n.* [U] the military organization of the U.S. consisting of soldiers who are on ships

mar·i·o·nette /ˌmæriəˈnɛt/ *n.* [C] a toy that looks like a person, animal, etc. that is moved by pulling strings attached to its body [➡ **puppet**] ➔ see picture at PUPPET

mar·i·tal /ˈmærət̬l/ *adj.* relating to marriage: *marital problems*

mar·i·time /ˈmærəˌtaɪm/ *adj.* **1** relating to the ocean or ships: *the maritime industry* **2** near the ocean: *the maritime provinces*

mark¹ /mɑrk/ *v.* **1** [T] to make a sign, shape, or word using a pen or pencil: *Check the envelopes that are marked "urgent" first.* | *a white banner **marked with** red lettering* **2** [T] to show where something is or was: *The grave is marked by a stone cross.* **3** [T] if a particular year, month, or week marks an important event, the event happened on that date during a previous year: *This year marks the company's 50th anniversary.* **4** [T] to GRADE a student's work **5** [I,T] to make a mark on something in a way that spoils or damages it: *The heels of his boots had marked the floor.*

mark sth ⇔ **down** *phr. v.* to reduce the price of things that are being sold: *Books have been marked down by 25%.* ➔ MARKDOWN

mark sth ⇔ **up** *phr. v.* to increase the price of an item in order to sell it for more than you paid for it ➔ MARKUP

mark² *n.* [C]

1 DIRTY SPOT a spot or small dirty area on something that spoils its appearance: *What are these black marks on the couch?*

THESAURUS

Types of dirty marks

stain – a mark that is difficult to remove: *an ink stain on the shirt pocket*
spot – a small mark: *a grease spot on his shirt*
smudge – a dirty mark, made when something is rubbed against a surface: *a smudge of paint on her cheek*
smear – a mark that is left when a substance is spread on a surface: *There was a smear of blood on the chair.*

Types of marks on someone's skin

blemish – a mark on your skin that spoils its appearance
bruise – a purple or brown mark on your skin that you get because you have fallen or been hit
scar – a permanent mark on your skin, caused by a cut or by something that burns you
pimple – a small raised red mark or lump on your skin that teenagers often have
zit informal – a pimple
wart – a small hard raised mark on your skin caused by a virus (=a living thing that causes an infectious illness)
blister – a small area of skin that is swollen and full of liquid because it has been rubbed or burned
freckle – one of several small light brown marks on someone's skin
mole – a small usually brown mark on the skin that is often slightly higher than the skin around it

2 DAMAGE a small damaged area on someone or something: *Her injuries included scratch marks on her face.*

3 WRITING a sign or shape that is written or printed: *She **made a mark** on the map to show where her house was.*

4 make/leave your mark to become successful or famous: *Portman first made her mark in "The Professional."*

5 a mark of sth a sign that something is true or exists: *We'd like to give you this gift as **a mark of** our **respect**.*

6 be off the mark/be wide of the mark to be incorrect: *My estimate was **way off the mark**.*

7 on your mark, get set, go! *spoken* said in order to start a race

mark·down /ˈmɑrkdaʊn/ *n.* [C] a reduction in the price of something

marked /mɑrkt/ *adj.* very easy to notice: *a marked improvement* —**markedly** /ˈmɑrkɪdli/ *adv.*

mark·er /ˈmɑrkɚ/ *n.* [C] **1** an object, sign, etc. that shows the position of something: *a marker at the edge of the football field* **2** a large pen with a thick point [➡ **Magic Marker**]

mar·ket¹ /ˈmɑrkɪt/ *n.*

1 PLACE TO BUY/SELL [C] **a)** an area outside where people buy and sell goods, food, etc.: *We buy all our vegetables from the **farmer's market**.* **b)** a GROCERY STORE [➡ **supermarket**]

2 the market the STOCK MARKET

3 on the market available for someone to buy: *Our house has been on the market for a year now.*

4 COUNTRY/AREA [C] a particular country or area where a company sells its goods: *our biggest* ***overseas/domestic market*** | *the Japanese market*
5 BUYERS [singular] the number or kind of people who want to buy something: *The* ***market for*** *used cars in the U.S. is getting smaller.* | *the youth market*
6 the housing/insurance etc. market the trade in buying houses, insurance, etc.
7 the job/labor market the number of people looking for work or the number of jobs available
8 be in the market for sth to be interested in buying something: *I'm in the market for a new car.*
9 a buyer's/seller's market a time that is better for buyers because prices are low, or better for sellers because prices are high ➔ BLACK MARKET ➔ **corner the market** at CORNER² ➔ FLEA MARKET, FREE MARKET

market² *v.* [T] to try to persuade someone to buy something by advertising it in a particular way: *The game is being* ***marketed as*** *a learning toy.* —**marketer** *n.* [C]

THESAURUS
advertise, **promote**, **hype**, **plug**
➔ see Thesaurus box at ADVERTISE

mar·ket·a·ble /ˈmɑrkɪṭəbəl/ *adj.* marketable goods, skills, etc. are easy to sell because people want them: *The program is designed to provide students with real,* ***marketable skills.*** —**marketability** /ˌmɑrkɪṭəˈbɪləṭi/ *n.* [U]

mar·ket·ing /ˈmɑrkɪṭɪŋ/ *n.* [U] the activity of deciding how to advertise a product, what price to charge for it, etc., or the type of job in which you do this: *a large* ***marketing campaign*** | *Reed works in marketing.*

mar·ket·place /ˈmɑrkɪt˺ˌpleɪs/ *n.* [C] **1 the marketplace** the business of buying and selling goods in competition with other companies **2** MARKET

mark·ing /ˈmɑrkɪŋ/ *n.* [C usually plural] **1** marks painted or written on something: *line markings on the highway* **2** the colored patterns and shapes on an animal's fur or skin: *a cat with black and gray markings*

marks·man /ˈmɑrksmən/ *n.* plural **marksmen** /-mən/ [C] someone who can shoot very well

mark·up /ˈmɑrk-ʌp/ *n.* [C] an increase in the price of something: *The usual markup is 20%.*

mar·ma·lade /ˈmɑrməˌleɪd/ *n.* [U] a JAM made with fruit such as oranges

ma·roon /məˈrun/ *n.* [U] a very dark red-brown color —**maroon** *adj.*

ma·rooned /məˈrund/ *adj.* if you are marooned somewhere, you are in a place from which you cannot leave and there are no people to help you: *The climbers were marooned on the mountain for three days.*

mar·quee /mɑrˈki/ *n.* [C] a large sign on a theater that gives the name of the movie or play

mar·riage /ˈmærɪdʒ/ *n.* **1** [C,U] the relationship between two people who are married, or the state of being married: *a long and happy marriage* | *She felt she wasn't ready for marriage.* | *She has two children from a* ***previous marriage.***

COLLOCATIONS
a happy/good marriage
an unhappy/broken/troubled/failed/loveless marriage
sb's marriage breaks up – someone's marriage ends because of problems and disagreement
the breakup of sb's marriage – the end of someone's marriage
sb's marriage ends in divorce
a proposal of marriage – an occasion when someone asks you to marry them
a mixed/interracial marriage – a marriage between people of different races
an arranged marriage – a marriage in which your parents choose the person you marry

2 [C] the ceremony in which two people get married [= **wedding**]

mar·ried /ˈmærid/ *adj.* having a husband or a wife: *How long have you been married?* | *Agnes and I have decided to* ***get married.*** | *Helen is* ***married to*** *a lawyer.* ➔ MARRY

THESAURUS
If someone is **single**, they are not married.
If someone is **engaged**, they have formally agreed to marry someone in the future.
If a husband and wife are **separated**, they are living apart because they are having problems in their marriage.
If a husband and wife get **divorced**, they officially end their marriage.
If two people are **living together**, they are in a romantic relationship and share a home together, but are not married.
If someone is **widowed**, his/her husband or wife has died.
➔ WEDDING

mar·row /ˈmæroʊ/ *n.* [U] the soft substance in the hollow center of bones [= **bone marrow**]

mar·ry /ˈmæri/ past tense and past participle **married**, third person singular **marries** *v.* **1** [I,T] to become someone's husband or wife: *I've asked Linda to marry me.* | *My uncle didn't marry until he was 50.* | *We* ***got married*** *last July.* | *She* ***married young*** (=at a young age). ▶ Don't say "married with." ◀ **2** [T] to perform the ceremony at which two people get married: *Rabbi Feingold will marry us.*
marry into sth *phr. v.* to join a family by marrying someone who belongs to it: *She married into a rich family.*

Mars /mɑrz/ *n.* the fourth PLANET from the sun

marsh /mɑrʃ/ *n.* [C,U] an area of low ground that is soft and wet [➡ **swamp**] —**marshy** *adj.*

mar·shal¹ /ˈmɑrʃəl/ *n.* [C] **1** a police officer in the U.S. whose job is to make sure that people obey an order that has been given by a court of law: *a U.S. marshal* **2** the officer in charge of a city's fire-fighting department: *the fire marshal*

marshal² *v.* **marshal your resources/forces etc.** to organize things or people so that they are used in the most effective way

marsh·mal·low /ˈmɑrʃˌmɛloʊ/ *n.* [C,U] a very soft white candy made of sugar

mar·su·pi·al /mɑrˈsupiəl/ *n.* [C] a type of animal that carries its baby in a pocket of skin on its body

mart /mɑrt/ *n.* **market**

mar·tial /ˈmɑrʃəl/ *adj.* related to war and fighting

ˌmartial ˈart *n.* [C usually plural] a sport such as KARATE, in which you fight with your hands and feet

ˌmartial ˈlaw *n.* [U] a situation in which the army controls a city, country, etc.

Mar·tian /ˈmɑrʃən/ *n.* [C] an imaginary creature from Mars

Mar·tin Lu·ther King Day /ˌmɑrt˺n ˌluθɚ ˈkɪŋ ˌdeɪ/ *n.* a public holiday in the U.S. on the third Monday in January when people remember Dr. Martin Luther King, Jr

mar·tyr /ˈmɑrt̬ɚ/ *n.* [C] someone who dies for his/her religious or political beliefs, and whose death makes people believe more strongly in those beliefs —**martyr** *v.* [T] —**martyrdom** *n.* [U]

mar·vel¹ /ˈmɑrvəl/ *v.* [I,T] to feel surprise or admiration for the quality of something: *We **marveled at** her courage.*

marvel² *n.* [C] something or someone that is extremely impressive: *Laser surgery is one of the **marvels of** modern medicine.*

mar·vel·ous /ˈmɑrvələs/ *adj.* extremely good, enjoyable, or impressive: *You are doing a marvelous job.* | *a marvelous opportunity*

Marx·is·m /ˈmɑrkˌsɪzəm/ *n.* [U] a political system based on Karl Marx's ideas that explains the changes in history as the result of the struggle between social classes —**Marxist** *n.* [C]

masc. the written abbreviation of **masculine**

mas·car·a /mæˈskærə/ *n.* [U] a dark substance that you use to color your EYELASHES

mas·cot /ˈmæskɑt/ *n.* [C] an animal, toy, etc. that represents a team or organization, and is thought to bring them good luck

mas·cu·line /ˈmæskyəlɪn/ *adj.* **1** having qualities that are considered to be typical of men [➡ **feminine**]: *a masculine voice* **2** *technical* in grammar, a masculine noun or PRONOUN has a form that means it relates to a male, such as "widower" or "him" [➡ **feminine**]

mas·cu·lin·i·ty /ˌmæskyəˈlɪnət̬i/ *n.* [U] qualities that are considered typical of a man [➡ **femininity**]

mash /mæʃ/ *v.* [T] to crush something, such as food that has been cooked, until it is soft: ***Mash** the **potatoes** until they're smooth.*

> **THESAURUS**
>
> **press, squash, crush, grind, squeeze**
> ➔ see Thesaurus box at PRESS¹

mask¹ /mæsk/ *n.* [C] something that covers all or part of your face, to protect or hide it: *a ski mask* | *The attackers wore masks.* ➔ GAS MASK

mask² *v.* [T] **1** to hide the truth about a situation, about how you feel, etc.: *Small children find it hard to mask their emotions.* **2** to prevent a smell, taste, sound, etc. from being noticed: *He used mints to mask the alcohol on his breath.*

masked /mæskt/ *adj.* wearing a mask: *a masked gunman*

ˈmasking tape *n.* [U] a special type of tape, made of paper

mas·och·ism /ˈmæsəˌkɪzəm/ *n.* [U] sexual behavior in which someone gets pleasure from being hurt —**masochist** *n.* [C] —**masochistic** /ˌmæsəˈkɪstɪk◂/ *adj.*

ma·son /ˈmeɪsən/ *n.* [C] **1** someone who builds walls, buildings, etc. with bricks, stones, etc. **2 Mason also Freemason** a man who belongs to a society in which each member helps the other members to become successful, and in which they also do work to help other people

ma·son·ry /ˈmeɪsənri/ *n.* [U] brick or stone from which a building, wall, etc. is made

mas·quer·ade¹ /ˌmæskəˈreɪd/ *n.* [C] a formal dance or party where people wear MASKS and unusual clothes

masquerade² *v.* [I] to pretend to be someone or something else: *Two men **masquerading as** police officers robbed a local bank.*

mass¹ /mæs/ *n.* **1** [C] a large amount or quantity of something: *The train wreck was **a mass of** twisted steel.* **2** [singular] a large crowd: *a **mass of** people*

> **THESAURUS**
>
> **group, crowd, gang, mob, bunch, flock**
> ➔ see Thesaurus box at GROUP¹

3 [C,U] **Mass** the main religious ceremony in some Christian churches, especially the Roman Catholic Church **4 the masses** [plural] all the ordinary people in a society **5** [U] *technical* the amount of material in something: *the **mass of** a star*

mass² *adj.* involving or intended for a large number of people: *weapons of mass destruction* | *a mass grave*

mass³ *v.* [I,T] to come together in a large group, or to make people or things do this: *Troops are massing at the border.*

mas·sa·cre¹ /ˈmæsəkɚ/ *n.* [C,U] the killing of a lot of people, especially people who cannot defend themselves: *the **massacre of** 17 unarmed peasants*

massacre² *v.* [T] to kill a lot of people, especially people who cannot defend themselves: *Government troops massacred hundreds of students.*

THESAURUS
kill, murder, slaughter
→ see Thesaurus box at KILL[1]

M

mas·sage /mə'sɑʒ, -'sɑdʒ/ *n.* [C,U] the action of pressing and rubbing someone's body with your hands to reduce pain or help him/her relax: *How much does it cost to **get a massage**? | Larry **gave** me **a massage** to help my back.* —**massage** *v.* [T]

mas·seur /mæ'sɚ, mə-/ *n.* [C] someone who gives people a massage

mas·seuse /mæ'suz, mə-/ *n.* [C] a woman who gives people a massage

mas·sive /'mæsɪv/ *adj.* **1** very large, solid, and heavy: *massive oil reserves beneath the ocean*

THESAURUS
big, large, huge, enormous, vast, gigantic, immense, colossal
→ see Thesaurus box at BIG

2 unusually large, powerful, or damaging: *Dad suffered a massive heart attack.*

ˌmass 'media *n.* **the mass media** all the people and organizations that provide information and news for the public, including television, radio, and newspapers

ˌmass 'murderer *n.* [C] someone who has murdered a lot of people

ˌmass-pro'duced *adj.* produced in large numbers using machinery, so that each object is the same and can be sold cheaply: *The computers will be mass-produced in Korea.* —**mass production** *n.* [U] —**mass-produce** *v.* [T]

mast /mæst/ *n.* [C] **1** a tall pole on which the sails on a ship are hung **2** a tall pole on which a flag is hung

mas·ter[1] /'mæstɚ/ *n.* [C] **1** someone who is very skilled at something: *a **master of** disguise* **2** a document, record, etc. from which other copies are made **3** *old-fashioned* a man who has authority over people or animals [➡ **mistress**]

master[2] *v.* [T] to learn something so well that you understand it completely and have no difficulty with it: *It only took him a few months to master French.*

THESAURUS
learn, pick up, get the hang of
→ see Thesaurus box at LEARN

master[3] *adj.* **1 master copy/list/tape etc.** the original thing from which copies are made **2 master plumber/chef etc.** someone who is very skillful at doing a particular job **3** most important or main: *the **master bedroom***

mas·ter·ful /'mæstɚfəl/ *adj.* skillfully done, made, or dealt with: *a masterful performance*

'master key *n.* [C] a key that will open all the door locks in a building

mas·ter·mind /'mæstɚˌmaɪnd/ *n.* [C usually singular] someone who organizes a complicated plan, especially a criminal plan: *the **mastermind behind** the bombings* —**mastermind** *v.* [T]

ˌMaster of 'Arts *n.* an M.A.

ˌmaster of 'ceremonies *n.* [C usually singular] someone who introduces speakers or performers at a social or public occasion [= **M.C.**] → EMCEE

ˌMaster of 'Science *n.* an M.S.

mas·ter·piece /'mæstɚˌpis/ *n.* [C] a work of art, piece of writing, music, etc. that is of the highest quality

'master's deˌgree also **master's** *n.* [C] a university degree that you get by studying for one or two years after your first degree

mas·ter·y /'mæstəri/ *n.* [U] complete control or power over someone or something: *Shakespeare's **mastery of** the English language*

mas·tur·bate /'mæstɚˌbeɪt/ *v.* [I,T] to touch or rub your sexual organs for pleasure —**masturbation** /ˌmæstɚ'beɪʃən/ *n.* [U]

mat /mæt/ *n.* [C] **1** a small piece of thick material that covers part of a floor **2** a piece of thick soft material used in some activities for people to sit on, fall onto, etc.

mat·a·dor /'mæṭəˌdɔr/ *n.* [C] someone who fights and tries to kill a BULL during a BULLFIGHT

match[1] /mætʃ/ *n.* **1** [C] a small wooden or paper stick with a special substance at the top, used to light a fire, cigarette, etc.: *a box of matches | He **lit/struck a match** so we could see.* **2** [C] a game or sports event: *a tennis/boxing/soccer match | a semifinal **match against** Korea | a classic **match between** McEnroe and Borg* **3 be no match for sb** to be much less strong, fast, etc. than an opponent: *Our defense was no match for theirs.* **4 a shouting match** a loud argument

match[2] *v.* **1** [I,T] if one thing matches another, or if two things match, they look good together because they have a similar color, pattern, etc.: *We found carpet to match the curtains in this room. | Do these socks match?* **2** [I,T] if two things match, or if one matches the other, they look or seem the same: *Police say the murder weapon matches a knife belonging to the suspect.* **3** [T] to be appropriate for a particular person, thing, or situation: *We'll try to help you find a job to match your skills.* **4** [T] to put two people or things together that are somehow related to each other: ***Match** the title of each book **with** its author.* **5** [T] to be equal to something in value, size, or quality: *His ambition was matched by a devotion to his family.*

match up *phr. v.* **1** to be of a similar level or of similar quality as something: *If the product doesn't **match up to** our standards, we don't sell it.* **2** to belong with or fit together with something: *The edges of the cloth don't match up.*

match·book /'mætʃbʊk/ *n.* [C] a small piece of thick folded paper containing paper matches

match·box /'mætʃbɑks/ *n.* [C] a small box containing matches

match·ing /ˈmætʃɪŋ/ *adj.* having the same color, style, or pattern as something else: *three girls in matching red, white, and blue outfits*

> **THESAURUS**
>
> **similar, like, alike, akin to, identical**
> ➔ see Thesaurus box at SIMILAR

match·less /ˈmætʃlɪs/ *adj. formal* better than all other things of the same kind

match·mak·er /ˈmætʃˌmeɪkɚ/ *n.* [C] someone who tries to find the right person for someone else to marry —**matchmaking** *n.* [U]

mate¹ /meɪt/ *n.* [C] **1 office/band/locker etc. mate** someone you work with, do an activity with, or share something with ➔ CLASSMATE, ROOMMATE **2** a husband, wife, or sexual partner, used especially in magazines: *He's still searching for the perfect mate.* **3** the sexual partner of an animal **4** one of a pair of objects: *I can't find the mate to this glove.*

mate² *v.* [I] if animals mate, they have sex to produce babies: *The male* ***mates with*** *several females.*

materials

ma·te·ri·al¹ /məˈtɪriəl/ *n.* **1** [C,U] cloth used for making clothes, curtains, etc.: *Mom bought some velvet material for the dress.* **2** [C,U] things such as wood, plastic, paper, etc. from which things can be made: *building materials* **3** [U] **also materials** the things that are used for making or doing something: ***reading/writing/teaching*** *material* **4** [U] information or ideas used in books, movies, etc.: *He's looking for new* ***material for*** *his next book.*

material² *adj.* **1** relating to your money, possessions, living conditions, etc. rather than the needs of your mind or soul: *We have very few* ***material possessions*** *but we have each other.* **2** relating to the real world or to physical objects, rather than religious matters: *the material world* **3** *law* important and needing to be considered when making a decision: *a* ***material witness*** *for the defense*

ma·te·ri·al·ism /məˈtɪriəˌlɪzəm/ *n.* [U] *disapproving* the belief that money and possessions are more important than art, religion, morality, etc. —**materialist** *adj., n.* [C] —**materialistic** /məˌtɪriəˈlɪstɪk/ *adj.*

ma·te·ri·al·ize /məˈtɪriəˌlaɪz/ *v.* [I] **1** to happen or appear in the way that you expected: *The student protest* ***failed to materialize/never materialized*** (=did not happen). **2** to appear in an unexpected and strange way: *A man materialized from the shadows.*

ma·ter·nal /məˈtɚnl/ *adj.* **1** typical of the way a good mother feels or acts [➥ **paternal**]: *maternal feelings* **2 maternal grandfather/aunt etc.** your mother's father, sister, etc.

ma·ter·ni·ty /məˈtɚnət̬i/ *adj.* relating to a woman who is PREGNANT, or who has had a baby, or to the time when she is pregnant: *maternity clothes*

maˈternity ˌleave *n.* [U] time that a woman is allowed away from her job when she has a baby: *Karen's still* ***on maternity leave****.*

maˈternity ˌward *n.* [C] a department in a hospital where a woman is cared for after having a baby

math /mæθ/ *n.* [U] *informal* the study or science of numbers and of the structure and measurement of shapes

math·e·mat·i·cal /mæθˈmæt̬ɪkəl, ˌmæθə-/ *adj.* related to or using mathematics: *a mathematical equation*

math·e·ma·ti·cian /ˌmæθməˈtɪʃən/ *n.* [C] someone who studies or teaches mathematics

math·e·mat·ics /ˌmæθˈmæt̬ɪks, ˌmæθə-/ *n.* [U] *formal* ➔ MATH

mat·i·née /ˌmætˀnˈeɪ/ *n.* [C] a performance of a play or movie in the afternoon

ma·tri·arch /ˈmeɪtriˌɑrk/ *n.* [C] a woman who has the most influence or power in a family or social group [➥ **patriarch**] —**matriarchal** /ˌmeɪtriˈɑrkəl/ *adj.*

ma·tri·ar·chy /ˈmeɪtriˌɑrki/ *n.* [U] a social system in which women hold all the power [➥ **patriarchy**]

ma·tric·u·late /məˈtrɪkyəˌleɪt/ *v.* [I] *formal* to officially begin studying at a school or college: *He* *majored in theater after* ***matriculating to*** *Northwestern.* —**matriculation** /məˌtrɪkyəˈleɪʃən/ *n.* [U]

mat·ri·mo·ny /ˈmætrəˌmoʊni/ *n.* [U] *formal* the state of being married —**matrimonial** /ˌmætrəˈmoʊniəl/ *adj.*

M

ma·tron /ˈmeɪtrən/ *n.* [C] *literary* an older married woman

ma·tron·ly /ˈmeɪtrənli/ *adj.* a polite word to describe a woman who is not thin, young, or attractive

matte /mæt/ *adj.* matte paint, color, or photographs are not shiny

mat·ted /ˈmæṭɪd/ *adj.* matted hair or fur is twisted and stuck together

mat·ter¹ /ˈmæṭɚ/ *n.*
1 SUBJECT/SITUATION [C] a subject or situation that you have to think about or deal with: *I need to speak with you about a* ***serious matter****.* | *The argument was strictly a* ***private/personal matter****.* | ***matters of*** *public concern* | *Whether he is guilty is* ***a matter for*** *the jury to decide.* | *financial matters*
2 matters [plural] a situation that you are in or have been describing: *She tried to apologize, but that only* ***made matters worse****.* | *It* ***didn't help matters*** (=made the situation worse) *when the money failed to arrive.*

SPOKEN PHRASES

3 the matter used to ask why something is not working normally, someone seems upset or sick, or something looks wrong: ***What's the matter?*** *Why are you crying?* | *Is there* ***something the matter with*** *the VCR?*
4 as a matter of fact said when giving a surprising or unexpected answer to a question or statement: *"Have you ever been to Paris?" "As a matter of fact I just came from there."*
5 the fact of the matter is (that) used when saying what you think is really true concerning a situation: *The fact of the matter is the company has had financial problems for years.*

6 no matter how/where/what etc. used to say that something is always the same whatever happens, or in spite of someone's efforts to change it: *No matter how hard she tried, she couldn't get the door open.*
7 it's only/just a matter of time used to say that something will definitely happen in the future: *It's only a matter of time before he loses his job.*
8 SUBSTANCE/THINGS [U] **a)** *technical* the material that everything in the universe is made of **b)** things of a particular kind or for a particular use: ***waste/vegetable matter*** | ***reading matter***
9 take matters into your own hands to deal with a problem yourself because other people have failed to deal with it: *Local people took matters into their own hands and hired their own security guards.*
10 sth is a matter of principle/money etc. used to say that what happens or what you decide depends on your judgment, how much something costs, how much time there is, etc.: *The planning is finished. Now it's just a matter of money and time.*
11 be a matter of doing sth used to say that you only have to do a particular thing, or do something in a particular way, in order to be successful: *I have a place to stay. Now it's just a matter of booking my flight.*
12 sth is a matter of opinion used to say that people have different opinions about something
13 a matter of life and death a very dangerous or serious situation
14 a matter of seconds/days/inches etc. only a few seconds, days, inches, etc.: *The bullet missed him by a matter of inches.*
15 for that matter used to say that what you have said about one thing is also true about another: *We don't have a TV yet, or even a bed for that matter.*

matter² *v.* [I] **1** to be important, or to have an effect on what happens: *Money is the only thing that* ***matters to*** *him.* | *Does it* ***matter which*** *road I take?* | *No* ***matter how*** *much suntan lotion I put on, I still burn.* **2 it doesn't matter** *spoken* **a)** used to say that you do not care which one of two things you have: *"Do you want tea or coffee?" "Oh, it doesn't matter."* **b)** used to tell someone you are not angry or upset: *"I lost the book you loaned me." "It doesn't matter – I have another copy."*

ˌmatter-of-ˈfact *adj.* showing no emotion when you are talking about something, especially something exciting, frightening, upsetting, etc.: *Jerry was very* ***matter-of-fact about*** *losing his job.*

THESAURUS

detached – not reacting to something in an emotional way: *She described what had happened in a detached way.*
impassive – not showing any emotions: *The witness remained impassive throughout questioning.*
cold – without friendly feelings: *a cold and distant man*

—**matter-of-factly** *adv.*

mat·tress /ˈmætrɪs/ *n.* [C] the soft part of a bed that you lie on

ma·ture¹ /məˈtʃʊr, məˈtʊr/ *adj.* **1** behaving in a reasonable way like an adult – used especially about a child or young person [≠ **immature**]: *She's young, but she's very* ***mature for*** *her* ***age****.* **2** fully grown and developed: *Eagles aren't sexually mature until age five.* | *mature wine* **3** a polite way of describing someone who is not young anymore

mature² *v.* [I] **1** to begin to behave in a reasonable way like an adult: *Pat's matured a lot since going to college.* **2** to become fully grown or developed: *The fly matures in only seven days.* | *It will mature into a small tree.* **3** if a financial arrangement such as a BOND or POLICY matures, it becomes ready to be paid

ma·tur·i·ty /mə'tʃʊrət̬i, -'tʊr-/ *n.* [U] **1** the quality of behaving in a sensible way like an adult: *He has a lot of maturity for a fifteen year old.* **2** the time when a person, animal, or plant is fully grown or developed: *Rabbits* ***reach maturity*** *in only five weeks.* **3** *technical* the time when a financial arrangement such as a BOND or POLICY is ready to be paid

maud·lin /'mɔdlɪn/ *adj. disapproving* talking or behaving in a sad and silly way: *moments of maudlin self-pity*

maul /mɔl/ *v.* [T] if an animal mauls someone, it injures him/her badly, tearing his/her flesh

mau·so·le·um /ˌmɔsə'liəm, -zə-/ *n.* [C] a large stone building containing many GRAVES or built over a grave

mauve /moʊv/ *n.* [U] a pale purple color —**mauve** *adj.*

mav·er·ick /'mævərɪk/ *n.* [C] someone who thinks or behaves in a way that is different from most people: *a political maverick* —**maverick** *adj.*

max[1] /mæks/ *n.* [U] **1** the written abbreviation of **maximum**: *Five people will fit, but that's the max.* **2 to the max** *slang* to the greatest degree possible —**max** *adj., adv.*: *It'll cost $50 max.*

max[2] *v.*

max out *phr. v. slang* **max** sth ⇔ **out** to use something such as money or supplies so that there is none left: *I maxed out my credit card.*

max·im /'mæksɪm/ *n.* [C] a well-known phrase that gives a rule for sensible behavior

max·i·mize /'mæksəˌmaɪz/ *v.* [T] **1** to increase something as much as possible [≠ **minimize**]: *We want to maximize the services available to our customers.* **2** to CLICK on a special part of a WINDOW on a computer screen so that it becomes as big as the screen [≠ **minimize**]

max·i·mum[1] /'mæksəməm/ *adj.* the maximum amount, quantity, speed, etc. is the largest that is possible or allowed [≠ **minimum**]: *The maximum penalty is five years in prison.*

maximum[2] *n.* [C usually singular] the largest number, amount, etc. that is possible or is allowed [≠ **minimum**]: *The road was designed for* ***a maximum of*** *35,000 vehicles a day.*

May /meɪ/ *n.* [C,U] the fifth month of the year: *Our anniversary is* ***on May 1st.*** | *We might be going to Texas* ***in May.*** | *Construction is scheduled to begin* ***next May.*** | *We haven't seen Tania since* ***last May.***

may *modal verb* **1** used to talk about what is or was possible [➡ **might**]: *You may have to come back next week.* | *This may not be enough money.* ▶ Don't say "mayn't." ◀ **2 may I...?** *spoken* used to ask politely if you can do something: *May I borrow your pen?* | *May I please speak to Carl?* **3** *formal* used to say that someone is allowed to do something: *You may start writing on your test forms now.* **4 may ... but ...** used to say that although one thing is true, something else which seems very different is also true: *This may taste bad but it's good for you.* **5 may as well ➔ might as well** at MIGHT[1]

GRAMMAR

May is not used in questions about possible events or situations. Use **might** instead: *Might there be problems?*

may·be /'meɪbi/ *adv.* **1** used to say that something may be true or may happen, but that you are not sure [= **perhaps**]: *Maybe Anna's stuck in traffic.* | *"Will you be there tomorrow night?" "Maybe."* | *Maybe this wasn't such a good idea.* | *Maybe you're right but* ***maybe not.***

USAGE

Use **maybe** to talk about something that is possible, especially as a way of suggesting or explaining something. Maybe usually goes at the beginning of a sentence: *Maybe we can get together this weekend.*
May be is a modal verb followed by "be," used to show that something is possible but not sure: *We may be getting together this weekend.*

2 used to make a suggestion: *Maybe Jeff could help you.*

'May Day *n.* [C,U] the first day of May, when people traditionally celebrate the arrival of spring

may·day /'meɪdeɪ/ *n.* [C usually singular] a radio signal used to ask for help when a ship or airplane is in danger

may·hem /'meɪhɛm/ *n.* [U] an extremely confused situation in which people are very frightened or excited: *There was complete mayhem after the explosion.*

may·o /'meɪoʊ/ *n.* [U] *spoken* mayonnaise

may·on·naise /'meɪəˌneɪz/ *n.* [U] a thick white sauce made of egg and oil

may·or /'meɪɚ, mɛr/ *n.* [C] someone who is elected to lead the government of a town or city

THESAURUS

politician, **president**, **congressman**, **congresswoman**, **senator**, **governor**
➔ see Thesaurus box at POLITICIAN

maze /meɪz/ *n.* [C] **1 a maze of streets/tunnels etc.** a complicated and confusing arrangements of streets, etc. **2** something that is complicated and difficult to understand: *a* ***maze of rules/laws/regulations*** **3** a specially designed system of paths that is difficult to find your way through, which people go to for fun

M.B.A. *n.* [C] **Master of Business Administration** a GRADUATE degree that teaches you the skills you need to be in charge of a business

MCAT /'ɛmkæt/ *n.* [C] *trademark* **Medical College Admission Test** an examination taken by

M

students who have completed a first degree and want to go to MEDICAL SCHOOL

Mc·Coy /mə'kɔɪ/ *n.* **the real McCoy** *informal* something that is real and not a copy

MD the written abbreviation of **Maryland**

M.D. *n.* [C] **Doctor of Medicine**

M

ME the written abbreviation of **Maine**

me /mi/ *pron.* **1** the object form of "I": *Cathy called me last night.* | *Give it to me.* **2 me too** *spoken* said when you agree with someone, or are going to do the same thing as they are: *"I'm hungry!" "Me too."* **3 me neither** *spoken* said when you agree with a negative statement someone has just made: *"I don't like fruitcake." "Me neither."*

mead·ow /'mɛdoʊ/ *n.* [C] a field with wild grass and flowers

mea·ger /'migɚ/ *adj.* very small in amount: *a meager salary*

meal /mil/ *n.* [C] a particular time when you eat food, or the food that is eaten then: *Would you like wine with your meal?* | *Don't **eat** a heavy **meal** before going to bed.* | *We **had** a nice **meal**.*

COLLOCATIONS

evening meal – dinner or supper
main meal – the most important and largest meal you eat during a day
three/four/five-course meal – a large meal that has three, etc. courses (=separate parts of a meal)
light/quick meal – a small meal
decent/good/full meal -a large meal with good food
have/eat a meal
cook/prepare/make a meal
go (out) for a meal – to go to a restaurant to eat
ask sb out for a meal also **take sb out for a meal** – to ask someone to come to a restaurant with you to eat, or to take someone there
→ LUNCH

THESAURUS

Types of meals
breakfast – a meal that you eat in the morning
lunch – a meal that you eat in the middle of the day
brunch – a meal that you eat in the late morning, instead of breakfast or lunch
dinner/supper – a meal that you eat in the evening
picnic – a meal that you eat outdoors, consisting of food that you cook or prepare earlier
barbecue – a meal that you cook and eat outdoors
→ CORNMEAL, OATMEAL

meal·time /'miltaɪm/ *n.* [C] a time during the day when you have a meal

mean¹ /min/ *v.* past tense and past participle **meant** /mɛnt/ [T] **1** to have or represent a particular meaning: ***What does** the word "Konbanwa" **mean**?* | *This light means you're running low on fuel.* ▶ Don't say "is meaning." ◀

THESAURUS

indicate, show, suggest, demonstrate, prove
→ see Thesaurus box at DEMONSTRATE

2 to intend a particular meaning when you say something: *I said Monday but I meant Tuesday.* | *When I said I didn't want the award, I just **meant that** I didn't want to take all the credit myself.* ▶ Don't say "I am meaning." ◀ **3** to intend to do something or intend that someone else should do something: *I've been **meaning to** ask you something.* | *He says he didn't **mean for** her **to** get hurt.* **4** to have a particular result: *An airline strike **meant that** he was stuck in Athens for another week.*

SPOKEN PHRASES

5 I mean a) said when you want to explain or give an example of something, or when you stop to think about what to say next: *She's always late for work. I mean, yesterday she showed up at 10:30.* **b)** said when you want to quickly correct what you have just said: *She plays the violin, I mean the viola.* **6 (do) you mean...?** said when you are checking that you understand something that someone has said: *You mean you want me to call you, or will you call me?* **7 (do) you know what I mean?** said when you are asking someone if s/he understands you: *He wore a hat like the one Sherlock Holmes had. You know what I mean?* **8 I know what you mean** used to tell someone that you understand or agree with what s/he is saying: *"I'm so tired of his complaining." "I know what you mean."* **9 I see what you mean** used to tell someone that you now understand what s/he has been saying **10 what do you mean (...)? a)** said when you do not understand someone **b)** said when you are very surprised or annoyed by something someone has said: *What do you mean, you sold the car?*

11 sb/sth means sth (to sb) used to say that someone or something is very important to someone: *It would **mean a lot to** your father if you offered to help.* **12 sb means business** to be determined to do something: *You have to be strict about the rules so they know you mean business.* **13 sth was meant to be** used to say that you think a situation was certain to happen and that no one could have prevented it: *Our marriage was never meant to be.*

mean² *adj.* **1** cruel or not kind: *Why do you say such mean things to me?* | *Don't be **mean to** your sister.* | ***It** was **mean of** you not to invite her.*

THESAURUS

cruel – deliberately making someone suffer or feel unhappy: *Kids can be very cruel to each other.*
unkind – treating people in a way that makes them unhappy or hurts their feelings: *She never says an unkind word.*
nasty – not kind and not pleasant, often deliberately: *Their neighbors were really nasty.*
thoughtless – not thinking about the needs and feelings of other people: *a thoughtless remark*

2 no mean feat/trick/achievement etc. something that is very difficult to do, so that someone who does it deserves to be admired: *It was no mean achievement for a woman to become a doctor in 1920.* **3 a mean sth** *informal* used to say that something is very good or someone is very good at doing something: *Ray plays a mean game of tennis.* **4** *technical* average: *The mean price for a single-family home was $170,000 last year.*

mean³ *n.* **1 means** [plural] a method, system, object, etc. that is used as a way of achieving a result: *We'll use any means we can to raise the money.* | *My bicycle is my main **means of** transportation.* | *The oil is transported **by means of*** (=using) *a pipeline.* **2 means** [plural] the money or income that you have: *They don't have **the means to** buy a car.* | *Try to live **within** your **means*** (=only spending what you can afford). | *a man **of means*** (=who is rich) **3 by all means** *spoken* used to mean "of course" when politely allowing someone to do something or agreeing with a suggestion: *"Can I invite Clarence?" "Oh, by all means."* **4 by no means** *formal* not at all: *The results are by no means certain.* **5 a means to an end** something that you do only to achieve a result, not because you want to do it: *This job is just a means to an end.* **6 the mean** *technical* the average amount, figure, or value: *The mean of 7, 9, and 14 is 10.*

me·an·der /mi'ændɚ/ *v.* [I] to move in a slow relaxed way, not in any particular direction: *I spent the afternoon **meandering through** the city.*

mean·ing /'minɪŋ/ *n.* **1** [C,U] the thing, idea, feeling, etc. that a word, phrase, or sign represents: *I don't understand the **meaning of** this word.* **2** [C,U] the thoughts or ideas that someone wants you to understand from what s/he says, does, writes, etc.: *The exact **meaning of** the king's statement was not clear.* **3** [U] the importance that something has in a particular situation: *Until today, I hadn't realized the full meaning of what had happened.* **4 (not) know the meaning of sth** to have, or not have, experience and understanding of a particular situation or feeling: *Those kids don't know the meaning of hard work.*

mean·ing·ful /'minɪŋfəl/ *adj.* **1** serious, useful, or important: *a meaningful relationship* | *meaningful work* **2** easy to understand: *The data isn't very meaningful to anyone but a scientist.* **3 a meaningful look/smile etc.** a look that clearly expresses the way someone feels

mean·ing·less /'minɪŋlɪs/ *adj.* having no purpose or importance and therefore not worth doing or having: *a meaningless job* | *a statistic that is **completely/totally/absolutely meaningless***

M

meant /mɛnt/ *v.* the past tense and past participle of MEAN

mean·time /'mintaɪm/ *n.* **in the meantime** in the period of time between now and a future event, or between two events in the past: *We want to buy a house, but in the meantime we're renting the apartment.*

mean·while /'minwaɪl/ *adv.* while something else is happening, or in the time between two events: *I was in the kitchen cleaning up. Meanwhile, Ray was in the living room watching TV.*

mea·sles /'mizəlz/ **also the measles** *n.* [U] an infectious illness in which you have a fever and small red spots on your face and body

mea·sly /'mizli/ *adj. informal* very small and disappointing in size, quantity, or value: *I only won a measly $5.*

meas·ur·a·ble /'mɛʒərəbəl/ *adj.* **1** able to be measured: *A manager should set measurable goals.* **2** important or large enough to have an effect: *The changes have not achieved any measurable results.* —**measurably** *adv.*

meas·ure¹ /'mɛʒɚ/ *v.* **1** [T] to find the size, length, or amount of something: *Measure the wall to see if the bookshelves will fit.* **2** [T] to judge the importance or value of something: *It's difficult to measure educational success.* **3** [linking verb] to be a particular size, length, or amount: *The table measures four feet by six feet.*

measure

measure sb/sth **against** sth *phr. v.* to judge someone or something by comparing him, her, or it to another person or thing

measure up *phr. v.* to be good enough to do a particular job or to reach a particular standard: *The test will allow us to see how our students measure up.*

measure² *n.* **1** [C] an official action that is intended to deal with a problem: *Congress passed a measure to control spending today.* | *We have **taken measures** to limit smoking to one area in the building.* | *Officials said they were satisfied with **security measures**.* **2 a measure of sth** an amount of something good or something that you want: *Over time, they developed a measure of trust.* **3 be a measure of sth** *formal* to be a sign of the importance, strength, etc. of something: *Profits are often used as a measure of a company's success.* **4** [C,U] a system or unit for measuring the weight, length, etc. of something: *A kilo is a measure of weight.*

meas·ure·ment /ˈmɛʒɚmənt/ *n.* [C,U] the length, height, value, etc. of something, or the act of measuring this: *We **took measurements** and realized that the table wouldn't fit through the doorway.*

M

meat /mit/ *n.* [U] the flesh of animals and birds eaten as food: *She never eats meat on Fridays.* | ***red meat*** (=dark meat such as beef) | ***white meat*** (=pale meat such as chicken)

THESAURUS

Types of meat
beef – the meat from a cow
veal – the meat from a young cow
pork – the meat from a pig
ham – meat from a pig, that has been preserved with salt or smoke
bacon – long thin pieces of meat from the back or sides of a pig, that have been preserved with salt or smoke
The meat from lamb, birds, or fish is called by the name of the animal: *We had chicken for dinner.* | *roast lamb* | *salmon steaks in tomato sauce*

meat·ball /ˈmitˀbɔl/ *n.* [C] a small round ball made from very small pieces of meat pressed together

meat·loaf /ˈmitloʊf/ *n.* [C,U] meat, egg, bread, etc. mixed and baked together in the shape of a LOAF

meat·y /ˈmit̬i/ *adj.* containing a lot of meat or having a strong meat taste: *a meaty stew*

mec·ca /ˈmɛkə/ *n.* [singular] **1 Mecca** a city in Saudi Arabia which is the holiest city of Islam **2** a place that many people want to visit for a particular reason: *Alaska is a **mecca for** nature lovers.*

me·chan·ic /mɪˈkænɪk/ *n.* **1** [C] someone whose job is to repair vehicles and machinery **2 mechanics** [U] the science that deals with the effects of forces on objects **3 the mechanics of (doing) sth** the way in which something works or is done: *The mechanics of bookkeeping can be complex.*

me·chan·i·cal /mɪˈkænɪkəl/ *adj.* **1** relating to machines, or using power from a machine: ***Mechanical failure** caused the jet to crash.* | *a mechanical device* **2** done or said without thinking, as if you were a machine: *a mechanical answer* —**mechanically** *adv.*

mech·a·nism /ˈmɛkəˌnɪzəm/ *n.* [C] **1** the part of a machine that does a particular job: *a car's steering mechanism* **2** a way in which something works or the process by which it is done: *the mechanisms of the brain* | *a **mechanism for** measuring employee performance*

mech·a·nized /ˈmɛkəˌnaɪzd/ *adj.* using machines instead of people or animals: *a highly mechanized factory* —**mechanize** *v.* [T]

med·al /ˈmɛdl/ *n.* [C] a round flat piece of metal given to someone who has won a competition or who has done something brave: *He **won** an Olympic gold **medal**.*

med·al·ist /ˈmɛdl-ɪst/ *n.* [C] someone who has won a medal in a competition: *a **gold/silver/bronze medalist***

me·dal·lion /məˈdælyən/ *n.* [C] a piece of metal shaped like a large coin, worn as jewelry on a chain around the neck

med·dle /ˈmɛdl/ *v.* [I] *disapproving* to try to influence a situation that does not concern you: *I don't want the government **meddling in** my affairs.* —**meddler** *n.* [C]

me·di·a /ˈmidiə/ *n.* [plural] all the organizations, such as television, radio, and newspapers, that provide news and information for the public, or the people who do this work: *the **news media*** | *The film attracted a lot of **media attention**.* → MASS MEDIA

me·di·an /ˈmidiən/ *n.* [C] **1** something that divides a road or HIGHWAY, such as a thin piece of land **2** *technical* the middle number in a set of numbers that are arranged in order

me·di·ate /ˈmidiˌeɪt/ *v.* [I,T] to try to help two groups, countries, etc. to stop arguing and make an agreement: *The court had to **mediate between** Hassel and his neighbors.* —**mediator** *n.* [C] —**mediation** /ˌmidiˈeɪʃən/ *n.* [U]

Med·i·caid /ˈmɛdɪˌkeɪd/ *n.* [U] a system by which the government helps to pay the cost of medical treatment for poor people

med·i·cal /ˈmɛdɪkəl/ *adj.* relating to medicine and the treatment of disease or injury: *medical school* | *The clinic provides free **medical care**.* | *new types of **medical treatment*** | *the **medical profession*** (=doctors, nurses, etc.) —**medically** *adv.*

Med·i·care /ˈmɛdɪˌkɛr/ *n.* [U] a system by which the government helps to pay for the medical treatment of old people

med·i·cat·ed /ˈmɛdɪˌkeɪt̬ɪd/ *adj.* containing medicine: *medicated shampoo*

med·i·ca·tion /ˌmɛdɪˈkeɪʃən/ *n.* [C,U] medicine given to people who are sick: *Are you **taking** any **medication**?* | *He's **on medication** for his heart.*

me·dic·i·nal /məˈdɪsənəl/ *adj.* helping to cure illness or disease: *The herbs are used **for medicinal purposes**.*

med·i·cine /ˈmɛdəsən/ *n.* **1** [C,U] a substance used for treating illness: *Remember to **take** your **medicine**.* | *Medicines should be kept away from children.*

THESAURUS

pill/tablet/capsule – a small hard piece of medicine that you swallow
eye/ear drops – liquid medicine that you put into your eye or ear
drug – a medicine or a substance for making medicines: *a new drug in the treatment of breast cancer*
dosage – the amount of medicine that you should take: *The usual dosage is 25 to 50 mg.*

2 [U] the treatment and study of illnesses and injuries: *She plans to study medicine at Harvard.*

me·di·e·val /mɪˈdivəl, mɛ-, mi-/ *adj.* relating to the MIDDLE AGES: *medieval poetry*

me·di·o·cre /ˌmidiˈoʊkɚ/ *adj.* not very good, but not extremely bad: *a mediocre student* —**mediocrity** /ˌmidiˈɑkrət̬i/ *n.* [U]

med·i·tate /ˈmɛdəˌteɪt/ *v.* [I] to make yourself very calm by relaxing completely, and thinking only about one thing such as a sound or a religious idea —**meditation** /ˌmɛdəˈteɪʃən/ *n.* [U]

med·i·ta·tive /ˈmɛdəˌteɪt̬ɪv/ *adj.* thinking deeply and seriously about something, or showing that you are doing this: *He was in a meditative mood.*

Med·i·ter·ra·ne·an /ˌmɛdɪtəˈreɪniən/ *n.* **the Mediterranean** the areas of land surrounding the Mediterranean Sea (=sea between northern Africa and southern Europe), and the islands in it —**Mediterranean** *adj.*

me·di·um[1] /ˈmidiəm/ *adj.* of middle size or amount: *"What size do you wear?" "Medium."* | *Cook the soup over medium heat for 30 minutes.* | *a man **of medium height***

medium[2] *n.* [C] **1** plural **media** /ˈmidiə/ a way of communicating or expressing something: *The Internet is a powerful advertising medium.* **2** plural **media** the material, paints, etc. that an artist uses: *This sculptor's favorite medium is wood.* **3** plural **mediums** someone who claims to speak to dead people and receive messages from them

ˈmedium-sized also **ˈmedium-size** *adj.* not small, but not large either: *medium-sized apples* | *a medium-size city*

med·ley /ˈmɛdli/ *n.* [C] tunes from different songs that are played one after the other as a single piece of music: *a **medley of** folk songs*

meek /mik/ *adj.* very quiet and gentle, and not willing to argue —**meekly** *adv.* —**meekness** *n.* [U]

meet[1] /mit/ *v.* past tense and past participle **met** /mɛt/

1 SEE SB FOR THE FIRST TIME [I,T] to see and talk to someone for the first time, or to be introduced to someone: *Mike and Sara met in college.* | *When did we first meet?* | *I saw Jim's wife once, but I never met her.*

2 BE IN THE SAME PLACE [I,T] to come to the same place as someone else because you have arranged to find him/her there: *Let's **meet for** lunch tomorrow.* | *I could meet you at the coffee shop at 11.*

THESAURUS

get together – to meet with someone or with a group of people: *Why don't we all get together and go out for a drink?*
gather – if people gather somewhere, or if someone gathers them, they come together in the same place: *Fans have started to gather outside the stadium.*
assemble – if you assemble people, or if people assemble, they are brought together in the same place: *The members of the tour group assembled at the airport before departure.*
come together – if people come together, they meet in order to discuss things, exchange ideas, etc.: *People came together from miles away to attend his funeral.*

3 nice/good/pleased to meet you *spoken* said when you meet someone for the first time: *"Paul, this is Jack." "Nice to meet you."*
4 (it was) nice meeting you *spoken* used when saying goodbye to someone you have just met for the first time
5 MEETING [I] to be together in the same place in order to discuss something: *The committee met to discuss goals for the coming year.*
6 meet a need/demand etc. to have or do enough of what is needed, or be good enough to reach a particular standard: *We're trying to find a way to **meet the needs** of all students.*
7 SB ARRIVING [T] to be at an airport, station, etc. when someone arrives: *I'm going to meet John's plane.* | *Alice will meet us at the station.*
8 JOIN [I,T] to join together at a particular place: *the place where two roads meet*
9 meet (sb) halfway to do some of the things that someone wants, if s/he does some of the things you want

meet up *phr. v.* to meet someone informally in order to do something together: *Let's meet up after the game.* | *We **met up with** Jan outside the museum.*

meet with sb/sth *phr. v.* **1** to have a meeting with someone: *The President met with European leaders today in Paris.* **2** to get a particular reaction or result: *His proposal **met with opposition/approval**.*

meet[2] *n.* [C] a sports competition: *a **swim/track meet***

meet·ing /ˈmit̬ɪŋ/ *n.* [C] **1** an organized gathering of people for the purpose of discussing something: *We **have a meeting** at two.* | *a **meeting of** world business leaders* | *a **meeting with** my boss* | *John has been **in a meeting** all morning.* **2 a meeting of the minds** a situation in which people agree about something

M

'meeting house *n.* [C] a building where Quakers go to WORSHIP

meg·a /'mɛgə/ *adj., adv. slang* very big, impressive, and enjoyable: *Their first record was a mega hit.*

meg·a·byte /'mɛgəˌbaɪt/ *n.* [C] a unit for measuring computer information equal to a million BYTES

M

meg·a·lo·ma·ni·a /ˌmɛgəloʊ'meɪniə/ *n.* [U] the belief that you are extremely important and powerful —**megalomaniac** /ˌmɛgəloʊ'meɪniˌæk/ *adj.*

meg·a·phone /'mɛgəˌfoʊn/ *n.* [C] a thing like a large CONE, that you talk through when speaking to a crowd in order to make your voice sound louder

meg·a·ton /'mɛgəˌtʌn/ *n.* [C] a measure of the power of an explosive that is equal to that of a million TONS of TNT (=a powerful explosive)

mel·an·chol·y¹ /'mɛlənˌkɑli/ *adj.* sad, or making you feel sad: *a melancholy look*

melancholy² *n.* [U] *literary* a feeling of sadness

mel·a·nin /'mɛlənɪn/ *n.* [U] a natural substance in human skin, hair, and eyes that gives them a dark color

meld /mɛld/ *v.* [I,T] to mix or combine two or more different things together

mel·low¹ /'mɛloʊ/ *adj.* **1** pleasant and smooth in sound or taste: *mellow jazz | a mellow wine* **2** friendly, relaxed, and calm: *Tim's more mellow now that he's older.*

THESAURUS

calm, relaxed, laid-back, cool
→ see Thesaurus box at CALM²

mellow² **also mellow out** *v.* [I,T] to become more relaxed and calm, or to make someone do this: *She's mellowed over the years.*

me·lod·ic /mə'lɑdɪk/ *adj.* **1** having a pleasant tune or a pleasant sound like music: *a sweet melodic voice* **2** relating to the main tune in a piece of music: *the melodic structure of Beethoven's symphonies*

me·lo·di·ous /mə'loʊdiəs/ *adj. literary* having a pleasant tune or a pleasant sound like music: *a melodious voice*

mel·o·dra·ma /'mɛləˌdrɑmə/ *n.* [C,U] a story or play with many exciting events in which people's emotions are shown very strongly

mel·o·dra·mat·ic /ˌmɛlədrə'mæṭɪk/ *adj. disapproving* having or showing emotions that are strong and unreasonable: *Stop being melodramatic!*

mel·o·dy /'mɛlədi/ *n.* [C,U] plural **melodies** a song or tune

THESAURUS

music, tune, song, arrangement, number, composition
→ see Thesaurus box at MUSIC

mel·on /'mɛlən/ *n.* [C,U] one of several types of large sweet juicy fruits with hard skins and flat seeds

melt /mɛlt/ *v.* **1** [I,T] to change something from solid to liquid by heating [➡ **freeze, thaw**]: *The snow's melting. | Melt the butter, and add the chopped onion.* **2** [I] to suddenly feel love or sympathy: *My **heart melted** when I saw her crying.* **3 melt in your mouth** if food melts in your mouth, it is smooth and tastes extremely good

melt away *phr. v.* to disappear quickly and easily: *He began to exercise regularly, and the weight melted away.*

melt·down /'mɛlt˺daʊn/ *n.* [C,U] a very dangerous situation in which the material in a NUCLEAR REACTOR melts and burns through its container

'melting pot *n.* [C] a place where people from different races, countries, or social classes come and live together: *The U.S. is often called a melting pot.*

mem·ber /'mɛmbɚ/ *n.* [C] **1** someone who has joined a particular club, group, or organization: *Are you a **member of** the French club? | Ben treats his dog like a **member of the family**. | Frank has been a **staff member** for 20 years.* **2** one of a group of similar people or things: *Cats and tigers are **members of** the same species.*

mem·ber·ship /'mɛmbɚˌʃɪp/ *n.* **1** [C,U] the state of being a member of a club, group, organization, or system: *Many countries have applied for **membership in** NATO. | I just **renewed** my gym **membership**. | The **membership fee*** (=money that you pay to become a member) *is $25.* **2** [singular] all the members of a club, group, or organization: *The membership will vote for a chairman tonight.*

mem·brane /'mɛmbreɪn/ *n.* [C,U] a very thin substance similar to skin that covers or connects parts of the body: *a membrane in the ear*

me·men·to /mə'mɛntoʊ/ *n.* plural **mementos** [C] a small object that you keep to remind you of someone or something: *a* ***memento of*** *my college days*

mem·o /'mɛmoʊ/ *n.* plural **memos** [C] a short official note to another person in the same company: *a* ***memo to*** *employees*

mem·oirs /'mɛmwɑrz/ *n.* [plural] a book written by a famous person about his/her life and experiences

mem·o·ra·bil·i·a /ˌmɛmərə'bɪliə, -'bil-/ *n.* [plural] things that you keep or collect because they relate to a famous person, event, or time: *sports memorabilia*

mem·ora·ble /'mɛmrəbəl/ *adj.* worth remembering: *a memorable evening* —**memorably** *adv.*

mem·o·ran·dum /ˌmɛmə'rændəm/ *n.* plural **memoranda** /-'rændə/ or **memorandums** [C] *formal* a MEMO

me·mo·ri·al¹ /mə'mɔriəl/ *adj.* [only before noun] made or done in order to remind people of someone who has died: *a* ***memorial service*** *for my grandfather*

memorial² *n.* [C] a public structure with writing on it that reminds people of someone who has died: *the Lincoln memorial* | *The wall was built as a* ***memorial to*** *soldiers who died in Vietnam.*

Me'morial ˌDay *n.* [U] a U.S. national holiday on the last Monday in May when people remember soldiers who were killed in wars

mem·o·rize /'mɛməˌraɪz/ *v.* [T] to learn and remember words, music, or other information: *You all should have your lines memorized by Friday.*

mem·o·ry /'mɛmri, -məri/ *n.* plural **memories** **1** [C,U] the ability to remember things, places, experiences, etc.: *My* ***memory*** *isn't as* ***good*** *as it used to be.* | *Could you draw the map* ***from memory*** (=by remembering it)*?* **2** [C usually plural] something that you remember from the past about a person, place, or experience [➡ **souvenir**]: *John talked about his* ***memories of*** *the war.* | *I have such* ***fond/happy memories*** *of my grandmother.* | *That song really* ***brings back memories*** (=makes me remember something). **3** [U] the amount of space that can be used for storing information on a computer: *256 megabytes of memory* **4** [C,U] the part of a computer in which information can be stored **5 in memory of sb** for the purpose of remembering someone who has died: *We observed a moment of silence in memory of the bombing victims.*

men /mɛn/ *n.* the plural of MAN

men·ace¹ /'mɛnɪs/ *n.* **1** [C] something or someone that is dangerous or extremely annoying: *That man is* ***a menace to society****!* **2** [U] a threatening quality or manner: *There was real menace in her voice.*

menace² *v.* [T] *formal* to threaten someone or something with danger or harm

men·ac·ing /'mɛnɪsɪŋ/ *adj.* making you expect something dangerous or bad [= **threatening**]: *a menacing laugh*

me·nag·er·ie /mə'nædʒəri, -ʒə-/ *n.* [C] *literary* a collection of animals kept privately or for people to see

mend¹ /mɛnd/ *v.* **1** [T] to repair a tear or hole in a piece of clothing: *You'd better mend that shirt.*

> **THESAURUS**
>
> **repair, fix, renovate, restore, service, rebuild**
> ➔ see Thesaurus box at REPAIR²

2 mend your ways to improve the way you behave after behaving badly for a long time

mend² *n.* **be on the mend** to be getting better after an illness

me·ni·al /'miniəl, -nyəl/ *adj.* *disapproving* menial work is boring and needs no skill

men·o·pause /'mɛnəˌpɔz/ *n.* [U] the time when a woman stops menstruating

me·no·rah /mə'nɔrə/ *n.* [C] a special CANDLESTICK, used in Jewish ceremonies

'men's room *n.* [C] a room in a public place with toilets for men

> **THESAURUS**
>
> **toilet, bathroom, restroom, women's/ladies' room, lavatory, latrine**
> ➔ see Thesaurus box at TOILET

men·stru·ate /'mɛnstruˌeɪt, -streɪt/ *v.* [I] *formal* when a woman menstruates every month, blood flows from her body [➡ **period**] —**menstrual** *adj.* —**menstruation** /ˌmɛnstru'eɪʃən, mɛn'streɪʃən/ *n.* [U]

men·tal /'mɛntəl/ *adj.* [only before noun] relating to the mind, or happening in the mind: *He has a history of severe* ***mental problems.*** | ***Mental illness*** *often runs in families.* | *The doctors were worried about her* ***mental health.*** | *I'm a little concerned about Jeremy's* ***mental state.*** | ***I made a mental note*** (=made an effort to remember) *to call Julie.* —**mentally** *adv.*: *She is obviously* ***mentally ill.***

'mental instiˌtution *n.* [C] a hospital for people who are mentally ill

men·tal·i·ty /mɛn'tæləṭi/ *n.* plural **mentalities** [C,U] a particular type of attitude or way of thinking: *It's hard to understand their mentality.*

men·thol /'mɛnθɔl, -θɑl/ *n.* [U] a substance that smells and tastes like MINT, used in medicine, candy, and cigarettes

men·tion¹ /'mɛnʃən/ *v.* [T] **1** to say or write about something in a few words: *I* ***mentioned*** *the idea* ***to*** *Joan, and she seemed to like it.* | *Helen* ***mentioned (that)*** *she had been feeling depressed.*

M

M

THESAURUS

refer to sth – to mention or speak about someone or something: *Palmer was referring to an article in the Times.*
raise – to begin to talk or write about something that you want someone to consider: *Becky raised the question of whether the students would learn better in smaller groups.*
allude to sth – to mention something in a way that is not direct: *Many stories and poems allude to this myth.*
bring sth up – to start to talk about a particular subject or person: *He waited until she was calmer to bring up the subject again.*
cite – to mention something as an example or proof of something else: *Collins cited the document as evidence that something had gone wrong.*
➔ see also Thesaurus box at SAY[1]

2 don't mention it *spoken* used in order to say in a friendly way that there is no need for someone to thank you [= **you're welcome**]: *"Thanks for helping me out." "Don't mention it."* **3 not to mention sth** said when you are adding a piece of information that emphasizes what you have been saying: *He already has two houses and two cars, not to mention the boat.*

mention² *n.* [C,U] the act of mentioning someone or something in a conversation or piece of writing: *Any* ***mention of*** *the accident upsets her.* | *The report* ***made no mention of*** *any profit figures.*

men·tor /ˈmɛntɔr, -tɚ/ *n.* [C] an experienced person who advises and helps a less experienced person

men·tor·ing /ˈmɛntərɪŋ/ *n.* [U] a system of using people who have a lot of experience and knowledge to advise other people

men·u /ˈmɛnyu/ *n.* [C] **1** a list of all the kinds of food that are available in a restaurant: *Can we see a menu, please?* | *the most popular dish* ***on the menu*** ➔ see Topic box at RESTAURANT **2** a list of things on a computer screen which you can ask the computer to do: *Go to the Edit menu and select Copy.* | *a* ***pull-down menu*** (=a list of choices which appears when you CLICK on a place on the screen)

me·ow /miˈaʊ/ *n.* [C] the crying sound that a cat makes —**meow** *v.* [I]

mer·ce·nar·y¹ /ˈmɚsəˌnɛri/ *n.* plural **mercenaries** [C] someone who fights for any country who pays him/her

mercenary² *adj. disapproving* only concerned with making money

mer·chan·dise /ˈmɚtʃənˌdaɪz, -ˌdaɪs/ *n.* [U] things that are for sale in stores: *Several thousand dollars' worth of merchandise was stolen.*

mer·chant /ˈmɚtʃənt/ *n.* [C] someone who buys and sells large quantities of goods: *a wine merchant*

ˌmerchant maˈrine *n.* **the merchant marine** all of a country's ships that are used for trade, not war, and the people who work on these ships

mer·ci·ful /ˈmɚsɪfəl/ *adj.* kind to people, rather than being cruel

mer·ci·ful·ly /ˈmɚsɪfli/ *adv.* fortunately, because a situation could have been much worse: *At least her death was mercifully quick.*

Mer·cu·ry /ˈmɚkyəri/ *n.* the smallest PLANET, which is nearest the sun

mercury *n.* [U] a liquid silver-white metal that is used in THERMOMETERS

mer·cy /ˈmɚsi/ *n.* **1** [U] kindness, pity, and a willingness to forgive: *The boy was* ***begging/pleading for mercy.*** | *The judge* ***showed*** *him* ***no mercy.*** **2 at the mercy of sb/sth** in a situation that is controlled by someone or something that has the power to hurt you: *We were at the mercy of the storm.*

ˈmercy ˌkilling *n.* [C,U] EUTHANASIA

mere /mɪr/ *adj.* [only before noun] **1** used in order to emphasize how small or unimportant someone or something is: *A mere 10% of the population voted in the last election.* **2** used in order to say that something small or unimportant has a big effect: ***The mere thought*** *of food made her feel sick.*

mere·ly /ˈmɪrli/ *adv. formal* used in order to emphasize that an action, person, or thing is very small, simple, or unimportant, especially when compared to what it could be [= **only, just**]: *For Ken, a job is merely a way to make money.* | *His behavior was* ***not merely*** *foolish but dangerous.*

merge /mɚdʒ/ *v.* **1** [I,T] to combine or join together to form one thing: *The two unions merged to form a larger one.* | *Her company* ***merged with*** *another.* **2** [I] if traffic merges, the cars from two roads come together onto the same road

merge into sth *phr. v.* to seem to disappear into something and become part of it: *a point where the mountains merged into the sky*

merg·er /ˈmɚdʒɚ/ *n.* [C] the act of joining together two more companies or organizations to form one larger one

me·rid·i·an /məˈrɪdiən/ *n.* [C] a line drawn from the North Pole to the South Pole to show the positions of places on a map

me·ringue /məˈræŋ/ *n.* [C,U] a light sweet food made by baking a mixture of sugar and the white parts of eggs: *lemon meringue pie*

mer·it¹ /ˈmɛrɪt/ *n.* **1** [C usually plural] one of the good qualities or features of something or someone: *Living downtown* ***has its merits.*** **2** [U] *formal* a good quality that makes something deserve praise or admiration: *a book* ***of*** *great* ***merit*** | *Each student will be judged* ***on merit.***

merit² *v.* [T] *formal* to deserve something: *The idea merits serious consideration.*

mer·maid /ˈmɚmeɪd/ *n.* [C] a woman in stories who has a fish's tail instead of legs

mer·ry /ˈmɛri/ *adj.* comparative **merrier**, superlative **merriest** **1 Merry Christmas!** used to say that you hope someone will have a happy time at Christmas **2** cheerful and happy

'merry-go-ˌround *n.* [C] a large round thing that children ride on for fun, which turns around and around

mesh¹ /mɛʃ/ *n.* [U] a piece of material made of threads or wires that have been woven together like a net: *a wire mesh screen*

mesh² *v.* [I] **1** if two or more ideas, qualities, people, etc. mesh, they go well together: *He wants a job that will **mesh with** his skills and interests.* **2** *technical* if two parts of an engine or machine mesh, they fit closely together

mes·mer·ize /'mɛzməˌraɪz/ *v.* [T] to make someone become completely interested in something: *The kids sat mesmerized in front of the TV.* —**mesmerizing** *adj.*

mess¹ /mɛs/ *n.* **1** [singular, U] a place or a group of things that is not organized or arranged neatly: *This house is a mess!* | *I'll help you **clean up** the **mess**.* | *The kids **made a mess** in their room again.* **2** [singular] *informal* a situation in which there are a lot of problems and difficulties, especially as a result of mistakes or people not being careful: *My life is such a mess.* | *How did we ever **get into** this **mess**?* **3** [singular] *informal* someone who has a lot of emotional problems: *Nell was a complete mess after the divorce.*

mess² *v.*

mess around *phr. v. informal* **1** to play or do silly things when you should be working or paying attention: *Stop messing around and do your homework.* **2** to have a sexual relationship with someone, especially when you should not: *Joe found his wife **messing around with** another man.*

mess with sb/sth *phr. v. informal* **1 mess with** sth to use something or make small changes to it: *Who's been messing with my computer?* **2 mess with** sb to make someone angry or argue with him/her: *I wouldn't mess with Nick if I were you.*

mess sth ⇔ **up** *phr. v. informal* **1** to spoil or ruin something: *I hope I haven't messed up your plans.* **2** to make something dirty or messy: *Stop it! You'll mess up my hair!* **3** to make a mistake or do something badly: *"How did you do on the test?" "Oh, I really messed up."* ➔ MESSED UP

mes·sage /'mɛsɪdʒ/ *n.* **1** [C] written or spoken information that you leave for someone, especially when you cannot speak to him/her directly: *Did you **get** my **message**?* | *Hugh **left a message** saying he would be late.* | *Sorry, Tony's not home yet. **Can I take a message**?* (=used during phone calls) | *I'll **send** you a **message*** (=an e-mail) *to let you know what time we're meeting.*

COLLOCATIONS

telephone/phone message
e-mail/mail message
fax message
text message – a written message on a cell phone
error message – a message on a computer screen, saying that the computer cannot do what you want it to do
message of thanks/congratulations/support/sympathy

2 [singular] the main idea or the most important idea in a movie, book, speech, etc.: *The message was clear: global warming will eventually affect us all.* | *an effective way of **getting** your **message across*** **3 get the message** *informal* to understand what someone means or what s/he wants you to do: *OK, I get the message – I'm going.*

ˌmessed 'up *adj. informal* if someone is messed up, s/he has a lot of emotional problems

mes·sen·ger /'mɛsəndʒɚ/ *n.* [C] someone who takes packages or messages to other people

'mess hall *n.* [C] a large room where soldiers eat

mes·si·ah /mə'saɪə/ *n.* **the Messiah** Jesus Christ in the Christian religion, or the leader sent by God to save the world in the Jewish religion

Messrs. /'mɛsɚz/ *n. formal* [C] the written plural of Mr.

mess·y /'mɛsi/ *adj.* comparative **messier**, superlative **messiest** **1** dirty, or not arranged in an organized way: *a messy desk* **2** a messy situation is complicated and difficult to deal with, especially because it involves people's emotions: *a **messy divorce***

met /mɛt/ *v.* the past tense and past participle of MEET

me·tab·o·lism /mə'tæbəˌlɪzəm/ *n.* [C,U] the chemical processes in your body that change food into the energy you need for working and growing —**metabolic** /ˌmɛt̬ə'bɑlɪk◂/ *adj.*

met·al /'mɛt̬l/ *n.* [C,U] a hard, usually shiny substance such as iron, gold, or steel: *a metal pipe* | *scrap metal*

'metal deˌtector *n.* [C] a machine used for finding metal, especially one used at airports for finding weapons

me·tal·lic /mə'tælɪk/ *adj.* made of metal, or similar to metal in color, appearance, or taste: *a car painted metallic blue*

met·al·lur·gy /'mɛt̬lˌɚdʒi/ *n.* [U] the scientific study of metals and their uses —**metallurgical** /ˌmɛt̬l'ɚdʒɪkəl/ *adj.*

met·a·mor·pho·sis /ˌmɛt̬ə'mɔrfəsɪs/ *n.* plural **metamorphoses** /-fəsiz/ [C,U] the process in which something changes into a completely different form: *a caterpillar's **metamorphosis into** a butterfly*

met·a·phor /'mɛt̬əˌfɔr/ *n.* [C,U] a way of describing something by comparing it to something else that has similar qualities, without using the words "like" or "as." "A river of tears" is a metaphor. [➡ **simile**] —**metaphorical** /ˌmɛt̬ə'fɔrɪkəl/ *adj.* —**metaphorically** *adv.*

M

met·a·phys·i·cal /ˌmɛt̬əˈfɪzɪkəl/ *adj.* relating to a study of PHILOSOPHY that is concerned with trying to understand and describe what REALITY is —**metaphysics** *n.* [U] —**metaphysically** *adv.*

mete /mit/ *v.*

mete sth ⇔ **out** *phr. v. formal* to give someone a punishment

M

me·te·or /ˈmit̬iɚ/ *n.* [C] a small piece of rock or metal that produces a bright burning line in the sky when it falls from space into the earth's ATMOSPHERE ➔ see Thesaurus box at SPACE[1]

me·te·or·ic /ˌmit̬iˈɔrɪk, -ˈɑr-/ *adj.* happening very suddenly and usually continuing for only a short time: *his **meteoric rise to** fame*

me·te·or·ite /ˈmit̬iəˌraɪt/ *n.* [C] a small meteor that has landed on the earth's surface

me·te·or·ol·o·gy /ˌmit̬iəˈrɑlədʒi/ *n.* [U] the scientific study of weather —**meteorologist** *n.* [C]

meter /ˈmit̬ɚ/ *n.* **1** [C] *written abbreviation* **m** a unit for measuring length, equal to 100 centimeters or 39.37 inches **2** [C] a piece of equipment that measures the amount of gas, electricity, time, etc. you have used: *Someone from the gas company came to look at the meter.* | *a taxi meter* ➔ PARKING METER **3** [C,U] the way that the words of a poem are arranged into a pattern of weak and strong beats

ˈmeter maid *n.* [C] *old-fashioned* a woman whose job is to check that cars are not parked illegally

meth·a·done /ˈmɛθəˌdoʊn/ *n.* [U] a drug that is often given to people who are trying to stop taking HEROIN

meth·ane /ˈmɛθeɪn/ *n.* [U] a gas with no color or smell, which can be burned to give heat

meth·od /ˈmɛθəd/ *n.* [C] a planned way of doing something: *I think we should try again using a different method.* | *an effective **method of** birth control* | *traditional teaching methods*

me·thod·i·cal /məˈθɑdɪkəl/ *adj.* done in a careful and well organized way, or always doing things this way: *They made a methodical search of the building.* —**methodically** *adv.*

THESAURUS

careful, **thorough**, **meticulous**, **systematic**, **painstaking**
➔ see Thesaurus box at CAREFUL

Meth·od·ist /ˈmɛθədɪst/ *adj.* relating to the Protestant church that follows the ideas of John Wesley —**Methodist** *n.* [C]

meth·od·ol·o·gy /ˌmɛθəˈdɑlədʒi/ *n.* plural **methodologies** [C,U] a set of methods and principles used when studying a particular subject or doing a particular type of work —**methodological** /ˌmɛθədəˈlɑdʒɪkəl/ *adj.*

me·tic·u·lous /məˈtɪkyələs/ *adj. approving* very careful about details, and always trying to do things correctly: *She kept meticulous records.* —**meticulously** *adv.*

THESAURUS

careful, **methodical**, **thorough**, **systematic**, **painstaking**
➔ see Thesaurus box at CAREFUL

met·ric /ˈmɛtrɪk/ *adj.* using the metric system, or relating to it: *All the tools are in metric sizes.*

ˈmetric ˌsystem *n.* **the metric system** the system of weights and measures based on the meter, the liter, and the gram

met·ro /ˈmɛtroʊ/ *adj.* [only before noun] relating to or belonging to a very large city: *the metro area* | *Metro Detroit*

me·trop·o·lis /məˈtrɑpəlɪs/ *n.* [C] a very large city, or the most important city of a country or area —**metropolitan** /ˌmɛtrəˈpɑlət̚n/ *adj.*: *the New York metropolitan area*

met·tle /ˈmɛt̬l/ *n.* [U] *literary* courage and determination: *Soldiers eager to **prove** their **mettle**.*

Mex·i·can[1] /ˈmɛksɪkən/ *adj.* relating to or coming from Mexico

Mexican[2] *n.* [C] someone from Mexico

mez·za·nine /ˈmɛzəˌnin, ˌmɛzəˈnin/ *n.* [C] the floor or BALCONY just above the main floor in a theater, hotel, store, etc.

mg the written abbreviation of **milligram**

MI the written abbreviation of **Michigan**

mice /maɪs/ *n.* the plural of MOUSE

mi·crobe /ˈmaɪkroʊb/ *n.* [C] an extremely small living creature that cannot be seen without a MICROSCOPE

mi·cro·bi·ol·o·gy /ˌmaɪkroʊbaɪˈɑlədʒi/ *n.* [U] the scientific study of very small living things —**microbiologist** *n.* [C]

mi·cro·brew·er·y /ˈmaɪkroʊˌbruəri/ *n.* plural **microbreweries** [C] a small company that makes beer to sell, and often has a restaurant where its beer is served

mi·cro·chip /ˈmaɪkroʊˌtʃɪp/ *n.* [C] a computer CHIP

mi·cro·cli·mate /ˈmaɪkroʊˌklaɪmɪt/ *n.* [C] the general weather patterns in a small area, which are different from the weather patterns in the surrounding area

mi·cro·cosm /ˈmaɪkrəˌkɑzəm/ *n.* [C,U] a small group, society, etc. that has the same qualities as a much larger one [➡ **macrocosm**]: *San Jose's mix of people is **a microcosm of** America.*

mi·cro·fiche /ˈmaɪkroʊˌfiʃ/ *n.* [C,U] a sheet of MICROFILM that can be read using a special machine, especially in a library

mi·cro·film /ˈmaɪkrəˌfɪlm/ *n.* [C,U] film used for making very small photographs of important documents, newspapers, maps, etc.

mi·cro·or·ga·nism /ˌmaɪkroʊˈɔrgəˌnɪzəm/ *n.* [C] an extremely small living creature that cannot be seen without a MICROSCOPE

mi·cro·phone /ˈmaɪkrəˌfoʊn/ *n.* [C] a piece of electrical equipment that makes your voice sound louder when you hold it in front of your mouth while you are singing, giving a speech, etc.: *Please speak clearly **into** the **microphone**.*

mi·cro·proc·es·sor /ˌmaɪkroʊˈprɑsɛsɚ/ *n.* [C] the main CHIP in a computer that controls most of its operations

mi·cro·scope /ˈmaɪkrəˌskoʊp/ *n.* [C] a scientific instrument that makes extremely small things appear large enough to be seen: *We looked at the insects **under** a **microscope**.*

microscope

mi·cro·scop·ic /ˌmaɪkrəˈskɑpɪk◂ / *adj.* extremely small: *microscopic organisms*

mi·cro·wave[1] /ˈmaɪkrəˌweɪv/ *n.* [C] **1 also microwave oven** a type of OVEN that cooks food very quickly by using electric waves instead of heat **2** a very short electric wave used especially for cooking food, sending radio messages, and in RADAR

microwave[2] *v.* [I] to cook something in a microwave

mid·air /ˌmɪdˈɛr◂ / *n.* **in midair** in the air or sky: *The plane exploded in midair.* —**midair** *adj.* [only before noun] *a midair collision*

mid·day /ˈmɪd-deɪ/ *n.* [U] the middle of the day, around 12:00 p.m. [= **noon**; ➡ **midnight**]

mid·dle[1] /ˈmɪdl/ *n.* **1 the middle** the part that is nearest the center of something, and furthest from the sides, edges, top, bottom, etc. [= **center**]: *Tom's the guy **in the middle**.* | *Hannah's toys were in the middle of the floor.* | *Why's your car parked **right in the middle of** the road?* **2 the middle** the part that is between the beginning and the end of a period of time or an event, story, etc.: *I fell asleep **in the middle of** class.* **3 be in the middle of (doing) something** to be busy doing something: *Can I call you back later? I'm **right in the middle of** cooking dinner.*

middle[2] *adj.* [only before noun] **1** nearest to the center of something: *The socks are in the middle drawer.* | *The middle lane was blocked off because of an accident.* **2** half way through an event, action, or period of time, or between the beginning and the end: *I missed the middle act of the play.* **3 middle child/daughter/brother etc.** the child, brother, daughter, etc. who is between the oldest and the youngest

ˌmiddle-ˈaged *adj.* belonging or relating to the period of your life when you are about 45 to 65 years old: *a middle-aged woman* —**middle age** *n.* [U]

ˌMiddle ˈAges *n.* **the Middle Ages** the period in European history between the 5th and 15th centuries A.D.

ˌMiddle Aˈmerica *n.* [U] **1** the MIDWEST **2** average Americans who have traditional ideas and beliefs

ˌmiddle ˈclass *n.* **the middle class** the group of people in society who are neither rich nor poor, especially people who are educated and work in professional jobs [➡ **lower class**, **upper class**, **working class**] —**middle-class** *adj.*: *middle-class families*

ˌMiddle ˈEast *n.* **the Middle East** the part of Asia that is between the Mediterranean Sea and the Arabian Sea, including countries such as Turkey and Iran [➡ **Far East**] —**Middle Eastern** *adj.*

ˌmiddle ˈfinger *n.* [C] the longest finger in the middle of the five fingers on your hand ➔ see picture at HAND[1]

mid·dle·man /ˈmɪdlˌmæn/ *n.* plural **middlemen** /-ˌmɛn/ [C] someone who buys things in order to sell them to someone else, or who helps to arrange business deals for other people

ˌmiddle ˈname *n.* [C] the name that, in English, comes between your first name and your family name

THESAURUS

first name, given name, last name, family name, surname, full name

➔ see Thesaurus box at NAME[1]

ˌmiddle-of-the-ˈroad *adj.* middle-of-the-road ideas, opinions, etc. are not extreme, so many people agree with them

ˈmiddle school *n.* [C] a school in the U.S. for students between the ages of 11 and 14

midg·et /ˈmɪdʒɪt/ *n.* [C] *offensive* a person who is very small because his/her body has not grown correctly

mid·life cri·sis /ˌmɪdlaɪf ˈkraɪsɪs/ *n.* [C usually singular] the worry and lack of confidence that some people feel when they are about 40 or 50 years old

mid·night /ˈmɪdnaɪt/ *n.* [U] 12 O'CLOCK at night [➡ **noon**, **midday**]: *We arrived **at midnight**.* | *I fell asleep a little **after/before midnight**.*

mid·riff /ˈmɪdrɪf/ *n.* [C] *formal* the front part of the body between your chest and your waist

midst /mɪdst/ *n.* **in the midst of sth** in the middle of something such as an event, situation, place, or group: *The city is **in the midst of a crisis**.*

mid·term /ˈmɪdtɚm/ *n.* **1** [C] an examination that students take in the middle of a SEMESTER: *I **have** a biology **midterm** on Friday.* ➔ see Topic box at UNIVERSITY **2** [U] the middle of the period when an elected government has power —**midterm** *adj.*

mid·way /ˌmɪdˈweɪ◂ / *adj.*, *adv.* at the middle point between two places, or in the middle of a period of time or an event: *There's a gas station **midway between** here and Fresno.* | *He went silent **midway through** his speech.*

mid·week /ˌmɪdˈwik◂ / *adj.*, *adv.* on one of the middle days of the week, such as Tuesday,

M

Wednesday, or Thursday: *midweek classes* | *I can see you midweek.*

Mid·west /ˌmɪdˈwest/ *n.* **the Midwest** the central area of the U.S. —**Midwestern** /mɪdˈwestərn/ *adj.*

mid·wife /ˈmɪdwaɪf/ *n.* plural **midwives** /-waɪvz/ [C] a specially trained nurse, usually a woman, whose job is to help women when they are having a baby

M

miffed /mɪft/ *adj. informal* annoyed

might¹ /maɪt/ *modal verb* **1** used in order to talk about what was or is possible: *I might be able to get free tickets.* | *They might not come until tomorrow morning.* | *She might have tried calling, but I've been out.* **2** used instead of "may" when reporting what someone said or thought: *I thought he might still be mad at me.* **3 might as well** *spoken* used in order to say that you will do something even though you are not very interested in it or excited about it: *I might as well go with you. I don't have anything else to do.* **4** used in order to give advice or make a suggestion: *You might try calling the store.* | *You* ***might want to*** *get your blood pressure checked.*

might² *n.* [U] *literary* strength and power: *She tried* ***with all*** *her* ***might*** *to push him away.*

might·y¹ /ˈmaɪt̬i/ *adj.* strong and powerful: *mighty warriors*

mighty² *adv. informal* very: *That was a mighty fine meal.*

mi·graine /ˈmaɪgreɪn/ *n.* [C] an extremely bad HEADACHE

mi·grant /ˈmaɪgrənt/ *n.* [C] **1** someone who goes to another area or country, especially in order to find work [➡ **immigrant**, **emigrant**]: ***migrant workers*** **2** a bird or animal that travels from one part of the world to another, especially in the fall and spring

mi·grate /ˈmaɪgreɪt/ *v.* [I] **1** if birds or animals migrate, they travel to a different part of the world, especially in the fall and spring: *More than 2 million ducks* ***migrate to*** *the lake each fall.*

THESAURUS

immigrate, emigrate
➔ see Thesaurus box at IMMIGRATE

2 to go to another area or country for a short time, usually in order to find a place to live or work

mi·gra·tion /maɪˈgreɪʃən/ *n.* [C] the action of a large group of birds, animals, or people moving from one area or country to another: *the yearly* ***migration of*** *geese* —**migratory** /ˈmaɪgrəˈtɔri/ *adj.*

mike /maɪk/ *n.* [C] *informal* a MICROPHONE

mild /maɪld/ *adj.* **1** not too severe or serious: ***a mild case of*** *the flu* | *mild criticism* **2** not strong-tasting or spicy: *mild cheddar cheese* **3** if the weather is mild, it is not too cold or wet and not too hot: *a mild winter* **4** if a soap or beauty product is mild, it is gentle to your skin, hair, etc.

mil·dew /ˈmɪldu/ *n.* [U] a white or gray substance that grows on walls and other surfaces in warm, slightly wet places —**mildewed** *adj.*

mild·ly /ˈmaɪldli/ *adv.* **1** slightly: *McKee was only mildly interested.* **2 to put it mildly** *spoken* said when you are saying something bad or severe in the most polite way that you can: *We were not welcome there, to put it mildly.* **3** in a gentle way without being angry: *"Perhaps," he answered mildly.*

mile /maɪl/ *n.* [C] **1** a unit for measuring distance, equal to 5,280 feet or about 1,609 meters: *Mark jogs at least five miles a day.* | *We're only a few hundred miles from Atlanta.* **2 miles** *informal* a very long distance: *We walked* ***for miles*** *without seeing anyone.* **3 talk a mile a minute** *spoken* to talk very quickly without stopping

mile·age /ˈmaɪlɪdʒ/ *n.* **1** [singular, U] the number of miles that a car has traveled since it was new: *a used car with low mileage* **2** [U] the number of miles a car can travel using each gallon of gasoline: *Our car gets really* ***good mileage*** (=a lot of miles per gallon). **3 get a lot of mileage out of sth** to make something be as useful for you as it can be: *I've gotten a lot of mileage out of that old joke.*

mile·stone /ˈmaɪlstoʊn/ *n.* [C] a very important event in the development of something: *a* ***milestone in*** *automotive history*

mi·lieu /milˈyu, mɪlˈyʊ/ *n.* plural **milieus** [C,U] *formal* all the things and people that surround you and influence you

mil·i·tant¹ /ˈmɪlət̬ənt/ *adj.* willing to use force or violence: *militant nationalists* —**militancy** *n.* [U]

militant² *n.* [C] someone who uses violence to achieve social or political change

mil·i·ta·ris·m /ˈmɪlət̬əˌrɪzəm/ *n.* [U] the belief that a country should increase its army, navy, etc. and use them to get what it wants —**militaristic** /ˌmɪlət̬əˈrɪstɪk/ *adj.*

mil·i·tar·y¹ /ˈmɪləˌtɛri/ *adj.* used by, involving, or relating to the army, navy, air force, or Marine Corps: *military aircraft* | *a military base in Greece* | *The U.S. was prepared to take* ***military action.*** —**militarily** /ˌmɪləˈtɛrəli/ *adv.*

military² *n.* **the military** the military organizations of a country, such as the army and navy: *My father is* ***in the military.***

mi·li·tia /məˈlɪʃə/ *n.* [C] a group of people trained as soldiers who are not members of the permanent army

milk¹ /mɪlk/ *n.* [U] **1** a white liquid that people drink, which is usually produced by cows or goats: *a glass of milk* | *Would you like milk in your coffee?*

THESAURUS

Types of milk
skim milk – milk that has had all the fat removed from it

low-fat/2% milk – milk that has had some of the fat removed from it
whole milk – milk that has not had any fat removed from it
buttermilk – the liquid that remains after butter has been made, used for drinking or cooking
half-and-half – a mixture of milk and cream, used in coffee

2 a white liquid produced by female animals and women for feeding their babies

milk² *v.* [T] **1** to take milk from a cow or goat **2 milk sb/sth for sth** *informal* to get all the money, advantages, etc. that you can from a person, thing, or situation: *I'm going to milk her for every penny she has.*

milk·man /ˈmɪlkmæn/ *n.* plural **milkmen** /-mɛn/ [C] someone who delivers milk to houses each morning

milk·shake /ˈmɪlkʃeɪk/ *n.* [C] a thick drink made from milk and ICE CREAM: *a chocolate milkshake*

milk·y /ˈmɪlki/ *adj.* **1** water or a liquid that is milky is not clear and looks like milk **2** milky skin is white and smooth

ˌMilky ˈWay *n.* **the Milky Way** the pale white band made up of large numbers of stars that you can see across the sky at night

mill¹ /mɪl/ *n.* [C] **1** a large machine used for crushing food such as corn, grain, or coffee into a powder **2** a building where materials such as paper, steel, or cotton cloth are made **3** a small machine used for crushing pepper or coffee

mill² *v.* [T] to crush grains in a mill
mill around *phr. v. informal* if a lot of people are milling around, they are moving around a place and do not seem to have a particular purpose: *Tourists were milling around the streets.*

mil·len·ni·um /məˈlɛniəm/ *n.* plural **millennia** /-niə/ [C] **1** a period of 1,000 years **2** the time when a new 1,000 year period begins: *the start of the new millennium*

mil·li·gram /ˈmɪləˌgræm/ *n.* [C] *written abbreviation* **mg** a unit for measuring weight, equal to 1/1000th of a gram

mil·li·li·ter /ˈmɪləˌlit̬ɚ/ *n.* [C] *written abbreviation* **ml** a unit for measuring liquids, equal to 1/1000th of a liter

mil·li·me·ter /ˈmɪləˌmit̬ɚ/ *n.* [C] *written abbreviation* **mm** a unit for measuring length, equal to 1/1000th of a meter

mil·lion /ˈmɪlyən/ *number* **1** 1,000,000: *$350 million* | *4 million people* ▶ Don't say "4 million of people." ◀ **2 also millions** an extremely large number of people or things: *I've heard that excuse a million times.* **3 not/never in a million years** *spoken* said in order to emphasize how impossible or unlikely something is: *I never would have guessed in a million years.* **4 one in a million** the best of all possible people or things: *People like Sue are one in a million.* —**millionth** /ˈmɪlyənθ/ *number*

mil·lion·aire /ˌmɪlyəˈnɛr/ *n.* [C] someone who is very rich and has at least one million dollars

mime¹ /maɪm/ *n.* [C] an actor who performs without using words, or a performance in which no words are used

mime² *v.* [I,T] to perform using actions and movements without any words: *She stretched out her arms, miming a swimmer.*

mim·ic¹ /ˈmɪmɪk/ *v.* past tense and past participle **mimicked**, present participle **mimicking** [T] **1** to copy the way someone speaks, moves, or behaves, usually to make people laugh: *Lily mimicked Sue's Southern accent.* **2** to behave or operate in exactly the same way as someone or something else: *The drug mimics the action of the body's own chemicals.* —**mimicry** *n.* [U]

mimic² *n.* [C] a person or animal that is good at mimicking someone's voice, appearance, etc. or something such as the sound of a machine

min. **1** the written abbreviation of **minimum** **2** the written abbreviation of MINUTE or MINUTES

mince /mɪns/ *v.* **1** [T] to cut food into extremely small pieces: *Mince the onion and garlic.* **2 not mince words** to say exactly what you think, even if this may offend people: *Stella has never been one to mince words.* **3** [I] to walk, using very small steps and moving your HIPS a lot

mince·meat /ˈmɪnsmit/ *n.* [U] a sweet mixture of apples, dried fruit, and SPICES, but no meat, used in PIES

mind¹ /maɪnd/ *n.*
1 BRAIN [C] your thoughts, or the part of your brain used for thinking and imagining things: *Grandma's mind is as sharp as ever.* | *What kind of plans did you **have in mind*** (=what have you thought of doing)*?* | *What's **on your mind*** (=what are you thinking about)*?*
2 change your mind to change your opinions or decision about something: *If you change your mind and want to come, give us a call.*
3 make up your mind to decide something, or become very determined to do something: *Have you made up your mind which college you want to go to?* | *Once she made up her mind to go, there was no stopping her.*
4 cross/enter your mind if something crosses your mind, you think about it for a short period: *It never **crossed** my **mind that** she might be unhappy.*
5 be out of your mind *informal* to behave in a crazy or stupid way: *Are you out of your mind?*
6 go out of your mind/lose your mind *informal* to start to become mentally ill or behave in a crazy way: *I'm going to lose my mind if I don't find a new apartment soon.*
7 on your mind if something is on your mind, you are thinking or worrying about it a lot: *Sorry I didn't call but I've **had a lot on my mind** lately.* | *Is there something on your mind?*

8 have sb/sth in mind to have an idea about who or what you want for a particular purpose: *Did you have anyone in mind for the job?*
9 with sb/sth in mind while thinking about something or someone or considering that person or thing: *Racing cars weren't built with safety in mind.*
10 come/spring to mind if something comes to mind, you suddenly think of it: *She was so nervous she just started saying whatever came to mind.*
11 state/frame of mind the way you are feeling, such as how happy or sad you are: *I have to be in the right frame of mind before a game.*
12 -minded having a particular attitude or believing that a particular thing is important: *He was a mean, **narrow/closed-minded** old man* (=he did not accept other ideas and opinions). | *politically-minded students*
13 keep/bear sth in mind to remember something: ***Keep in mind that** the bank will be closed tomorrow.*
14 no one in his/her right mind *informal* no one who is sensible: *No woman in her right mind would walk alone at night around here.*
15 have/keep an open mind to be willing to accept new ideas and opinions: *The mayor promises to keep an open mind on the issue of new schools.*
16 take/get/keep your mind off sth to make you stop thinking about something: *Dad needs a vacation to take his mind off work.*
17 keep your mind on sth to keep paying attention to something even if you want to think about something else: *He could hardly keep his mind on what she was saying.*
18 put your mind to sth to decide to do something and use a lot of effort in order to succeed: *You can win if you just put your mind to it.*
→ ONE-TRACK MIND → **sth blows your mind** at BLOW[1] → **slip your mind** at SLIP[1]

mind² *v.* **1** [I,T] to feel annoyed, worried, or angry about something: *Do you mind if I open the window?* | *This is a nice place to live if you don't mind the noise.* | *He doesn't mind sleeping on the couch.* | *She doesn't **mind that** her book has not been selling well.*

SPOKEN PHRASES

2 do/would you mind used to ask politely if you can do something or if someone will do something: ***Do you mind if** I use your phone?* | *Would you mind waiting here a minute?* **3 mind your own business** to not ask questions about a situation that does not involve you, often used to tell someone rudely not to do this: *Why doesn't she mind her own business?* **4 I wouldn't mind (doing) sth** said when you would like to do something: *I wouldn't mind living in Minneapolis.*

5 mind your manners to behave or speak in a polite way → **never mind** at NEVER

ˈmind-ˌboggling *adj. informal* very difficult to imagine because of being so big, strange, or complicated: *a mind-boggling amount of money*

mind·ful /ˈmaɪndfəl/ *adj.* behaving in a way that shows you remember a rule or fact: ***Mindful of** the guide's warning, they returned before dark.*

mind·less /ˈmaɪndlɪs/ *adj.* **1** so simple that you do not have to think about what you are doing: *mindless work* **2** stupid and without any purpose: *mindless violence/cruelty* —**mindlessness** *n.* [U]

mind·set /ˈmaɪndsɛt/ *n.* [C usually singular] someone's general attitude, and the way in which s/he thinks about things and makes decisions

mine¹ /maɪn/ *pron.* the thing or things belonging or relating to the person who is speaking: *Theresa's coat is black. Mine is blue.* | *He doesn't have a car so I let him borrow mine.* | *Tom's a good **friend of mine**.*

mine² *n.* [C] **1** a type of bomb that is hidden just below the ground or underwater, which explodes when someone or something touches it **2** a deep hole or holes in the ground from which gold, coal, etc. is dug: ***coal/gold etc. mines***

mine³ *v.* **1** [I,T] to dig into the ground in order to get gold, coal, etc.: *men **mining for** gold* **2** [T] to hide bombs under the ground or in the ocean

mine·field /ˈmaɪnfild/ *n.* [C] **1** an area of land that has mines hidden in it **2** a situation in which there are many hidden dangers: *The issue is a political minefield.*

min·er /ˈmaɪnɚ/ *n.* [C] someone who works in a mine: *a coal miner*

min·er·al /ˈmɪnərəl/ *n.* [C] a natural substance such as iron, coal, or salt that is present in some foods and in the earth: *Milk is full of valuable **vitamins and minerals**.*

ˈmineral ˌwater *n.* [C,U] water that comes from under the ground and contains minerals

min·gle /ˈmɪŋgəl/ *v.* **1** [I] to meet and talk with a lot of different people at a social event: *Reporters **mingled with** movie stars at the awards ceremony.* **2** [I,T] if smells, sounds, feelings, etc. mingle, they combine with each other: *anger **mingled with** disappointment and fear*

min·i- /ˈmɪni/ *adj. informal* small compared with others of the same type: *a minivan* | *a mini-market* (=a small food store)

min·i·a·ture¹ /ˈmɪniətʃɚ, ˈmɪnɪtʃɚ/ *adj.* very small: *a miniature camera*

miniature² *n.* [C] **1** something that has the same appearance as someone or something, but is much smaller: *This painting is **a miniature of** the one in the museum.* **2 in miniature** exactly like someone or something but much smaller: *She has her mother's face in miniature.*

ˌminiature ˈgolf *n.* [U] a golf game, played for fun, in which you hit a small ball through passages, over small bridges and hills, etc.

min·i·mal /ˈmɪnəməl/ *adj.* very small in degree or amount: *The fire caused minimal damage.* —**minimally** *adv.*

min·i·mize /ˈmɪnəˌmaɪz/ *v.* [T] **1** to make the degree or amount of something as small as possible [≠ **maximize**]: *To **minimize the risk** of* *getting heart disease, eat well and exercise daily.* **2** to make a document or program on your computer very small when you are not using it but still want to keep it open [≠ **maximize**]

min·i·mum¹ /ˈmɪnəməm/ *adj.* the minimum number, amount, or degree is the smallest that it is possible to have [≠ **maximum**]: *You will need to make a minimum payment of $50 a month.*

minimum² *n.* [C usually singular] the smallest number, amount, or degree that it is possible to have [≠ **maximum**]: *Jim works* ***a minimum of*** (=at least) *50 hours a week.* | *Costs were* ***kept to a minimum.***

ˌminimum ˈwage *n.* [singular, U] the lowest amount of money that can legally be paid per hour to a worker: *More than 4 million Americans earn* ***the minimum wage.***

min·ing /ˈmaɪnɪŋ/ *n.* [U] the action or industry of digging gold, coal, etc. out of the ground

min·i·se·ries /ˈmɪniˌsɪriz/ *n.* [plural] a television DRAMA that is divided into several parts and shown on different nights

min·i·skirt /ˈmɪniˌskɚt/ *n.* [C] a very short skirt

min·is·ter /ˈmɪnəstɚ/ *n.* [C] **1** a religious leader in some Christian churches [➡ **priest**] **2** a politician who is in charge of a government department in some countries: *the* ***Minister of*** *Defense*

min·is·te·ri·al /ˌmɪnəˈstɪriəl/ *adj.* relating to a minister, or done by a minister

min·is·try /ˈmɪnəstri/ *n.* plural **ministries** **1 the ministry** the profession of being a church leader: *Our son* ***entered/joined the ministry*** *two years ago* (=became a minister). **2** [C usually singular] the work done by a religious leader **3** [C] a government department in some countries: *the Foreign Ministry*

min·i·van /ˈmɪniˌvæn/ *n.* [C] a large vehicle with seats for six or more people ➔ see picture at TRANSPORTATION

mink /mɪŋk/ *n.* [C,U] a small animal with soft brown fur, or the valuable fur from this animal: *a mink coat*

min·now /ˈmɪnoʊ/ *n.* [C] a very small fish that lives in rivers, lakes, etc.

mi·nor¹ /ˈmaɪnɚ/ *adj.* small and not very important or serious, especially when compared with other things [≠ **major**]: *minor surgery* | *We made a few* ***minor changes*** *to the plan.* | *It's only a* ***minor injury.*** ▶ Don't say "minor than." ◀

minor² *n.* [C] **1** *law* someone who is not old enough to be considered legally responsible for his/her actions: *It's illegal to sell cigarettes to minors.* **2** the second main subject that you study at college for your degree [➡ **major**]: *She has* ***a minor in*** *history.* ➔ see Topic box at UNIVERSITY

minor³ *v.*

minor in sth *phr. v.* to study a second main subject as part of your college degree: *I'm minoring in history.*

mi·nor·i·ty¹ /məˈnɔrət̬i, maɪ-, -ˈnɑr-/ *n.* plural **minorities** **1** [C usually plural] a group of people of a different race or religion than most people in a country, or someone in one of these groups: ***ethnic/racial/religious minorities*** **2** [singular] a small part of a larger group of people or things [➡ **majority**]: *Only* ***a*** *small* ***minority of*** *senators were in favor of a tax increase.* **3 be in the minority** to be less in number than any other group: *Male teachers are very much in the minority at public schools.*

minority² *adj.* relating to a group of people who do not have the same opinion, religion, race, etc. as most of the larger group that they are in: *help for minority groups* | *minority students*

ˌminor ˈleague *n.* **the minor leagues also the Minor Leagues** the groups of teams that form the lower levels of American professional sports, especially baseball [➡ **Major Leagues**] —**minor-league** *adj.* [only before noun] *a minor-league team*

min·strel /ˈmɪnstrəl/ *n.* [C] **1** a white singer or dancer who tried to look like a black person and who performed in shows in the early part of the 20th century **2** a singer or musician in the Middle Ages

mint¹ /mɪnt/ *n.* **1** [C] a candy with a strong fresh taste **2** [U] a plant with strong fresh-tasting leaves, used in cooking and making medicine [➡ **peppermint**] **3** [C] a place where coins are officially made

mint² *adj.* **in mint condition** looking new and in perfect condition: *a 1957 Chevy in mint condition*

mint³ *v.* [T] to make a coin

mint·y /ˈmɪnti/ *adj.* tasting or smelling of mint

mi·nus¹ /ˈmaɪnəs/ *prep.* **1** used in mathematics when you SUBTRACT one number from another [➡ **plus**]: *17 minus 5 is 12 (17-5=12)* | *the value of your assets minus tax*

> **THESAURUS**
>
> **plus, add, subtract, take away, multiply, divide**
>
> ➔ see Thesaurus box at CALCULATE

2 *informal* without something that would normally be there: *He came back from the fight minus a couple of front teeth.*

minus² *n.* [C] **1** a MINUS SIGN **2** something bad about a situation [➡ **plus**]: *There are* ***pluses and minuses*** *to living in a big city.*

minus³ *adj.* **1 A minus/B minus etc.** a GRADE used in a system of judging a student's work. A minus is lower than A, but higher than B plus [➡ **plus**] **2 minus 5/20/30 etc.** less than zero, especially less than zero degrees in temperature [➡ **below**]: *At night the temperature can go as low as minus 30.*

min·us·cule /ˈmɪnəˌskyul/ *adj.* extremely small: *a minuscule amount of food*

ˈminus ˌsign *n.* [C] a sign (-) showing that a

M

number is less than zero, or that the second of two numbers is to be SUBTRACTed from the first

min·ute¹ /ˈmɪnɪt/ *n.* **1** [C] a period of time equal to 60 seconds: *Ethel's train arrives in fifteen minutes.* | *three **minutes to/before** 4:00* | *twelve **minutes after/past** one* **2** [C] a very short period of time: ***For a minute** I thought he was serious.* | *I'll be ready **in a minute**.* **3 wait a minute/just a minute/hold on a minute** *spoken* **a)** used to ask someone to wait a short period of time while you do something: *"Are you coming with us?" "Yes, just a minute."* **b)** used when you want to tell someone that you do not agree with something s/he has said or done: *Wait a minute – you said my car would be ready by 5:00!* **4 last minute** at the last possible time, just before something must be done or completed: *Frank changed his mind **at the last minute** and decided to come after all.* | *a few last-minute arrangements* **5 the minute (that)** as soon as: *I knew it was Jill the minute I heard her voice.* **6 any minute (now)** *spoken* very soon: *She should be here any minute now.* **7 minutes** [plural] an official written record of what is said and decided at a meeting

mi·nute² /maɪˈnut/ *adj.* **1** extremely small: *You only need a minute amount.*

THESAURUS

small, little, tiny, petite
➔ see Thesaurus box at SMALL

2 paying attention to the smallest things or parts: *Johnson explained the plan **in minute detail**.*

mir·a·cle /ˈmɪrəkəl/ *n.* [C] **1** something lucky that happens, that you did not think was possible: ***It's a miracle (that)** you weren't killed!* | *the country's **economic miracle*** **2** an action or event believed to be caused by God, which is impossible according to the ordinary laws of nature **3 miracle cure/drug** an effective treatment for a serious medical illness

mi·rac·u·lous /mɪˈrækyələs/ *adj.* completely unexpected and very lucky: *The patient made a miraculous recovery.* —**miraculously** *adv.*

mi·rage /mɪˈrɑʒ/ *n.* [C] something you think you see that is not actually there, caused by hot air in a desert

mire /maɪɚ/ *v.* **be mired in sth** **a)** to be in a very difficult situation: *an economy mired in recession* **b)** to be stuck in deep mud

mir·ror¹ /ˈmɪrɚ/ *n.* [C] **1** a piece of special flat glass that you can look at and see yourself in: *the bathroom mirror* | *a rearview mirror* (=a mirror in a car, for looking behind you) | *He looked at himself **in the mirror**.* **2 mirror image** a system or pattern that is almost exactly the same as another one: *This year's election is a mirror image of the one in 1984.*

mirror² *v.* [T] to represent or be very similar to something else: *The election results mirrored public opinion.*

mirth /mɚθ/ *n.* [U] *literary* happiness and laughter

mis·ad·ven·ture /ˌmɪsədˈvɛntʃɚ/ *n.* [C,U] bad luck or an accident

mis·ap·pro·pri·ate /ˌmɪsəˈproʊpriˌeɪt/ *v.* [T] *formal* to dishonestly take something, especially money, that a company, organization, etc. has trusted you to keep safe —**misappropriation** /ˌmɪsəˌproʊpriˈeɪʃən/ *n.* [U]

mis·be·have /ˌmɪsbɪˈheɪv/ *v.* [I] to behave badly: *Anne's being punished for misbehaving in class.* —**misbehavior** /ˌmɪsbɪˈheɪvyɚ/ *n.* [U]

misc. the written abbreviation of **miscellaneous**

mis·cal·cu·late /ˌmɪsˈkælkyəˌleɪt/ *v.* [I,T] **1** to make a mistake in deciding how long something will take to do, how much money you will need, etc.: *We miscalculated the time it would take to drive to Long Island.* **2** to make a mistake when you are judging a situation: *Republicans seem to have miscalculated the mayor's popularity.* —**miscalculation** /mɪsˌkælkyəˈleɪʃən/ *n.* [C]

mis·car·riage /ˈmɪsˌkærɪdʒ, ˌmɪsˈkærɪdʒ/ *n.* [C,U] **1** the act of accidentally giving birth too early for the baby to live [➡ **abortion**]: *She **had a miscarriage** and nearly died.* **2 miscarriage of justice** a situation in which someone is wrongly punished by a court of law for something s/he did not do

mis·car·ry /ˌmɪsˈkæri/ *v.* past tense and past participle **miscarried**, third person singular **miscarries** [I] to accidentally give birth to a baby too early for him/her to live

mis·cel·la·ne·ous /ˌmɪsəˈleɪniəs/ *adj.* made up of many different things or people that do not seem to be related to each other: *a stack of miscellaneous papers*

mis·chief /ˈmɪstʃɪf/ *n.* [U] bad behavior, especially by children, that causes trouble or damage but no serious harm: *A group of kids were running around and **making mischief*** (=behaving in a way that causes trouble). | *Sports **kept** me **out of mischief** when I was growing up.*

mis·chie·vous /ˈmɪstʃəvəs/ *adj.* a mischievous child likes to have fun by playing tricks on people or doing things to annoy or embarrass them —**mischievously** *adv.*: *He smiled mischievously.*

mis·con·cep·tion /ˌmɪskənˈsɛpʃən/ *n.* [C,U] an idea that is wrong or untrue, but that people still believe: *It's a **misconception that** red meat cannot be part of a healthy diet.*

mis·con·duct /ˌmɪsˈkɑndʌkt/ *n.* [U] *formal* bad or dishonest behavior by someone in a position of authority or trust: *an investigation into police misconduct*

mis·con·strue /ˌmɪskənˈstru/ *v.* [T] *formal* to not understand correctly what someone has said or done: *The research results have been misconstrued.*

mis·deed /ˌmɪsˈdid/ *n.* [C] *formal* a wrong or illegal action

mis·de·mean·or /ˌmɪsdɪˈminɚ/ *n.* [C] *law* a crime that is not very serious

mis·di·rect /ˌmɪsdəˈrɛkt/ *v.* [T] *formal* to use your efforts, emotions, or abilities in a way that is wrong or not appropriate: *misdirected anger*

mi·ser /ˈmaɪzɚ/ *n.* [C] *disapproving* someone who hates spending money and likes saving it —**miserly** *adj.*

mis·er·a·ble /ˈmɪzərəbəl/ *adj.* **1** very unhappy, especially because you are lonely or sick: *Dana was in the other day and she looked miserable.* | *She* ***made my life miserable****.*

THESAURUS

sad, **unhappy**, **upset**, **depressed**, **down**, **low**, **homesick**, **gloomy**, **glum**
➔ see Thesaurus box at SAD

2 very bad in quality: *miserable weather* —**miserably** *adv.*

mis·er·y /ˈmɪzəri/ *n.* plural **miseries** [C,U] great suffering or unhappiness: *the misery of the poor*

mis·fit /ˈmɪsˌfɪt/ *n.* [C] someone who does not seem to belong in a place because s/he is very different from the other people there: *a social misfit*

mis·for·tune /mɪsˈfɔrtʃən/ *n.* [C,U] bad luck, or something that happens to you as a result of bad luck: *We* ***had the misfortune of*** *being in an airport when the snow storm hit.*

mis·giv·ing /mɪsˈgɪvɪŋ/ *n.* [C usually plural,U] a feeling of doubt or fear about what might happen or about whether something is right: *He* ***had*** *some* ***misgivings about*** *letting me use his car.*

mis·guid·ed /mɪsˈgaɪdɪd/ *adj.* **1** intended to be helpful but actually making a situation worse: *a misguided attempt to impress her boss* **2** wrong because of being based on a wrong understanding of a situation: *He became a teacher on the misguided belief that the hours were short.*

mis·han·dle /ˌmɪsˈhændl/ *v.* [T] to deal with a situation badly, or not skillfully: *The University mishandled the situation.*

mis·hap /ˈmɪshæp/ *n.* [C,U] a small accident or mistake that does not have a very serious effect: *The pilot completed the rest of the flight* ***without mishap****.*

THESAURUS

accident, **crash**, **collision**, **disaster**, **catastrophe**, **wreck**
➔ see Thesaurus box at ACCIDENT

mis·in·form /ˌmɪsɪnˈfɔrm/ *v.* [T] to give someone information that is not correct: *Patients were misinformed about their treatment.*

mis·in·ter·pret /ˌmɪsɪnˈtɚprɪt/ *v.* [T] to not understand the correct meaning of something that someone says or does: *I think she misinterpreted my joke.* —**misinterpretation** /ˌmɪsɪnˌtɚprəˈteɪʃən/ *n.* [C,U]

mis·judge /ˌmɪsˈdʒʌdʒ/ *v.* [T] **1** to form a wrong or unfair opinion about a person or situation: *The White House has badly misjudged Congress's support for his bill.* **2** to guess an amount, distance, etc. wrongly: *Don misjudged the turn and wrecked his car.* —**misjudgment** *n.* [C,U]

mis·lead /mɪsˈlid/ *v.* past tense and past participle **misled** /-ˈlɛd/ [T] to make someone believe something that is not true by giving him/her false or incomplete information: *a deliberate attempt to mislead the public*

THESAURUS

deceive, **lie**, **perjure**
➔ see Thesaurus box at LIE[2]

mis·lead·ing /mɪsˈlidɪŋ/ *adj.* likely to make someone believe something that is not true: *Statistics can be very misleading.* —**misleadingly** *adv.*

THESAURUS

wrong, **incorrect**, **inaccurate**, **false**
➔ see Thesaurus box at WRONG[1]

mis·man·age /ˌmɪsˈmænɪdʒ/ *v.* [T] if someone mismanages something s/he is in charge of, s/he deals with it badly: *This project's been completely mismanaged from the beginning.* —**mismanagement** *n.* [U] *financial mismanagement*

mis·match /ˈmɪsmætʃ/ *n.* [C] a combination of things or people that do not work well together or are not appropriate for each other: *There seems to be a* ***mismatch between*** *skills and jobs.* —**mismatched** *adj.*

mis·no·mer /ˌmɪsˈnoʊmɚ/ *n.* [C] a wrong or inappropriate name: *The term "dry cleaning" is* ***something of a misnomer****, as fluids are actually used.*

mi·sog·y·nist /mɪˈsɑdʒənɪst/ *n.* [C] *formal* a man who hates women —**misogyny** *n.* [U] —**misogynistic** /mɪˌsɑdʒəˈnɪstɪk/ *adj.*

mis·place /ˌmɪsˈpleɪs/ *v.* [T] to put something somewhere and then forget where you put it: *I've misplaced my glasses again.*

mis·placed /ˌmɪsˈpleɪst/ *adj.* misplaced feelings of trust, love, etc. are inappropriate because the person that you have these feelings for does not deserve them: *a misplaced sense of loyalty*

mis·print /ˈmɪsˌprɪnt/ *n.* [C] a mistake in a book, magazine, etc.

mis·pro·nounce /ˌmɪsprəˈnaʊns/ *v.* [T] to pronounce a word or name wrongly —**mispronunciation** /ˌmɪsprəˌnʌnsiˈeɪʃən/ *n.* [C,U]

mis·quote /ˌmɪsˈkwoʊt/ *v.* [T] to make a mistake in reporting what someone else has said or written: *Morales claims the magazine misquoted him.*

mis·read /ˌmɪsˈrid/ *v.* past tense and past participle **misread** /-ˈrɛd/ [T] **1** to make a wrong judgment about a situation or person [➡ **misinterpret**]: *The U.N. badly misread the situation.* **2** to read something in the wrong way: *I misread the schedule and missed my bus.*

M

mis·rep·re·sent /ˌmɪsrɛprɪˈzɛnt/ *v.* [T] to deliberately give a wrong description of someone's opinions or of a situation: *Our aims have been misrepresented in the press.* —**misrepresentation** /mɪsˌrɛprɪzənˈteɪʃən/ *n.* [C,U]

M

THESAURUS

twist, **distort**
→ see Thesaurus box at CHANGE[1]

miss[1] /mɪs/ *v.* **1** [T] to not go somewhere or do something, especially when you want to but cannot: *Sorry I missed your call.* | *She didn't want to* ***miss a chance/opportunity to*** *work in Hollywood.*

USAGE

If you **miss** a class, meeting, etc. that you regularly attend, you do not go to it: *Bill has missed several days of work.*
If you **lose** something, you cannot find it: *I've lost my keys.*
→ MISSING

2 [T] to be too late for something: *By the time we got there, we'd missed the beginning of the movie.* | *You'll* ***miss*** *your* ***plane/train/bus*** *unless you leave now.* **3** [T] to feel sad because you are not with a particular person, or because you no longer have something or are no longer doing something: *Did you miss me while I was gone?* | *I miss living in London.* **4** [I,T] to not hit or catch something: *She fired at the target but missed.* | *Jackson missed an easy catch and the A's scored.* **5 miss the point** to not understand the main point of what someone is saying **6** [T] to not see, hear, or notice something: *Jody found an error that everyone else had missed.* | *It's a big red house with a small pond in front –* ***you can't miss it.*** **7** [T] to notice that something or someone is not in the place you expect him, her, or it to be: *I didn't miss my key until I got home.* **8 miss the boat** *informal* to fail to take an opportunity that will give you an advantage: *You'll be missing the boat if you don't buy these shares now.*

miss out *phr. v.* to not have the chance to do something that you enjoy: *You're the one who'll miss out if you don't come.* | *She got married very young, and now she feels she's* ***missing out on*** *life.*

miss[2] *n.* **1 Miss Smith/Jones etc.** used in front of the family name of a woman who is not married in order to speak to her politely, write to her, or talk about her [➡ **Mrs.**, **Ms.**] **2** [C] a failed attempt to hit, catch, or hold something **3** used to speak politely to a young woman when you do not know her name: *Excuse me, miss, you've dropped your umbrella.*

mis·shap·en /ˌmɪsˈʃeɪpən, ˌmɪˈʃeɪ-/ *adj.* not the normal or natural shape: *He was born with a misshapen spine.*

mis·sile /ˈmɪsəl/ *n.* [C] **1** a weapon that can fly over long distances and that explodes when it hits something: *a* ***nuclear missile*** **2** *formal* an object that is thrown at someone in order to hurt him/her

missing

one shirt button is missing

miss·ing /ˈmɪsɪŋ/ *adj.* **1** someone or something that is missing is not in the place where you would normally expect him, her, or it to be: *Police are still searching for the missing child.* | *A button on his shirt was missing.* | *$200 was* ***missing from*** *my desk drawer.*

USAGE

Use **lost** in order to describe someone or something that you cannot find, or someone who does not know where s/he is: *We took a wrong turn and got lost.* | *Lost children should talk to a store employee.* | *a lost wallet*
Use **missing** in order to describe someone or something you have been looking for, especially when the situation is serious: *the missing jewels* | *the search for the two missing boys*

2 not included, although it ought to have been: *Why is my name* ***missing from*** *the list?* **3 missing in action** a soldier who is missing in action has not been seen after a battle, and is probably dead

mis·sion /ˈmɪʃən/ *n.* [C] **1** an important job that someone has been given to do: *His mission was to help the president win re-election.* **2** a group of people who are sent by their government to another country for a particular purpose: *a Canadian trade mission to Japan* **3** the purpose or the most important aim of an organization: *Each school's central mission should be to teach reading, writing, and arithmetic.* **4** something that you feel you must do because it is your duty: *She feels her* ***mission in life*** *is to help poor people.* **5** a special trip made by a space vehicle or military airplane: *a mission to Mars* **6** the work of a missionary, or a building where s/he does this work

mis·sion·ar·y /ˈmɪʃəˌnɛri/ *n.* plural **missionaries** [C] someone who has gone to a foreign country in order to teach people about Christianity

mis·spell /ˌmɪsˈspɛl/ *v.* [T] to spell a word incorrectly —**misspelling** *n.* [C,U]

mis·step /ˈmɪs-stɛp/ *n.* [C] *written* a mistake, especially one that offends or upsets people: *political missteps*

M

mist¹ /mɪst/ *n.* [C,U] cloud that is close to the ground, making it difficult to see very far [➡ **fog**]: *The sun had burned through the early morning mist.*

mist² *v.* [I,T] to become covered with very small drops of water, or to make something do this: *The windows are all **misted up/over**.*

mis·take¹ /mɪˈsteɪk/ *n.* [C] **1** something that has been done in the wrong way, or an opinion or statement that is incorrect: *spelling mistakes* | *I think you've **made a mistake** – I ordered fish, not beef.* | *The bill is $500? **There must be some mistake**.* ➔ see Thesaurus box at ERROR **2** something you do that you later realize was not the right thing to do: *Marrying him was a **big mistake**.* | ***I made the mistake of** giving him my phone number.* | *We need to start **learning from** our **mistakes**.* **3 by mistake** if you do something by mistake, you do it without intending to: *I brought the wrong book home by mistake.*

THESAURUS

A **mistake** is something that you do by accident, or that is the result of a bad judgment: *I took Larry's coat by mistake.* | *We made a mistake in buying this car.*
An **error** is a mistake that you do not realize you are making, and that causes problems: *He made several errors when adding up the bill.*

mistake² *v.* past tense **mistook** /-ˈstʊk/ past participle **mistaken** /-ˈsteɪkən/
mistake sb/sth **for** sb/sth *phr. v.* to think that one person or thing is someone or something else: *I mistook him for his brother.*

mis·tak·en /mɪˈsteɪkən/ *adj.* wrong about something: *I think the party is next week but I might be mistaken.* | *We bought the rug in Turkey, **if I'm not mistaken**.* —**mistakenly** *adv.*

mis·ter /ˈmɪstɚ/ *n.* **1** MR. **2** *spoken old-fashioned* said in order to speak to a man when you do not know his name [➡ **sir**]: *Hey, mister, is this your wallet?*

mis·tle·toe /ˈmɪsəlˌtoʊ/ *n.* [U] a plant with small white berries that is often used as a decoration at Christmas

mis·took /mɪˈstʊk/ *v.* the past tense of MISTAKE

mis·treat /ˌmɪsˈtrit/ *v.* [T] to treat a person or animal cruelly: *The hostages said they had not been mistreated.* —**mistreatment** *n.* [U]

mis·tress /ˈmɪstrɪs/ *n.* [C] **1** a woman that a man has a sexual relationship with, even though he is married to someone else **2** *old-fashioned* a woman who has authority over servants or animals [➡ **master**]

mis·tri·al /ˈmɪstraɪl/ *n.* [C] a TRIAL during which a mistake in the law is made, so that a new trial has to be held

mis·trust /mɪsˈtrʌst/ *n.* [U] the feeling that you cannot trust someone: *Some Americans admit to a deep **mistrust of** the media.* —**mistrust** *v.* [T]

mist·y /ˈmɪsti/ *adj.* **1** misty weather is weather with a lot of mist **2** *literary* full of tears: *her eyes became misty*

mis·un·der·stand /ˌmɪsʌndɚˈstænd/ *v.* past tense and past participle **misunderstood** /-ˈstʊd/ [I,T] to fail to understand someone or something correctly: *I think you misunderstood what I was trying to say.*

mis·un·der·stand·ing /ˌmɪsʌndɚˈstændɪŋ/ *n.* **1** [C,U] a failure to understand a question, situation, or instruction: *There must be some misunderstanding. I didn't order all these books.* | *We've called a meeting to clear up any **misunderstandings about** the project.* **2** [C] an argument or disagreement that is not very serious: *We've had our misunderstandings in the past, but we're good friends now.*

mis·un·der·stood /ˌmɪsʌndɚˈstʊd/ *adj.* if someone is misunderstood, s/he has been treated unfairly because people have decided that they do not like him/her, without knowing what s/he is really like: *Albert's really a nice guy; he's just misunderstood.*

mis·use¹ /ˌmɪsˈyuz/ *v.* [T] to use something in the wrong way or for the wrong purpose: *Even harmless drugs can be misused.*

mis·use² /ˌmɪsˈyus/ *n.* [C,U] the use of something in the wrong way or for the wrong purpose: *a **misuse of** power*

mite /maɪt/ *n.* [C] **1** a very small insect that lives in plants, CARPETS, etc.: *dust mites* **2 a mite** *old-fashioned* a little: *The hotel was a mite expensive.*

mit·i·gate /ˈmɪt̬əˌgeɪt/ *v.* [T] *formal* to make a situation or the effects of something less bad, harmful, or serious: *Only foreign aid can mitigate the terrible effects of the war.* —**mitigation** /ˌmɪt̬əˈgeɪʃən/ *n.* [U]

mitt /mɪt/ *n.* [C] **1** a type of leather GLOVE used for catching a ball in baseball **2** a GLOVE made of thick material, worn to protect your hand: *an oven mitt*

mit·ten /ˈmɪt˺n/ *n.* [C] a type of GLOVE that does not have separate parts for each finger

mix¹ /mɪks/ *v.* **1** [I,T] if you mix two or more substances or if they mix, they combine to become a single substance: *Oil and water don't mix.* | ***Mix** the butter **and** sugar **together**, and then add the milk.* | ***Mix** the beans thoroughly **with** the sauce.* ➔ see picture on page A4

THESAURUS

combine – to join two or more things together, or to be joined together with another thing: *Combine the wet ingredients and beat until smooth.*
stir – to mix a liquid or food by moving a spoon around in it: *Reduce the heat and stir until thickened.*

blend – to mix together soft or liquid substances to form a single smooth substance: *Blend the yogurt with fresh fruit for a wonderful drink.*
beat – to mix food together quickly and thoroughly using a fork or kitchen tool: *Beat the eggs and add to the sugar mixture.*

M

2 [I,T] to combine two or more different activities, ideas, groups of things, etc.: *Their music **mixes** jazz **and** rock.* | *I don't **mix business with pleasure**.* **3** [I] to enjoy meeting, talking, and spending time with other people, especially people you do not know very well: *Strug **mixed** easily **with** the other members of the team.*

mix up *phr. v.* **1 mix** sb/sth ⇔ **up** to make the mistake of thinking that someone or something is another person or thing: *I keep **mixing** him **up with** his brother.* **2 mix** sth ⇔ **up** to change the way things have been arranged so that they are no longer in the same order: *Don't mix up those papers, or we'll never find the ones we need.* **3 mix** sb **up** *informal* to make someone feel confused: *Too many people were giving her advice and mixing her up.* → MIXED UP, MIX-UP

mix² *n.* **1** [C,U] a combination of substances that you mix together to make something: *cake mix* **2** [singular] the particular combination of things or people that form a group: *There was a strange **mix of** people at Larry's party.*

mixed /mɪkst/ *adj.* **1** consisting of many different types of things or people: *a mixed diet of fruit and vegetables* **2 have mixed emotions/feelings (about sth)** to be unsure about whether you like or agree with something or someone: *We had mixed feelings about moving to New York.* **3 a mixed blessing** something that is good in some ways but bad in others: *Having children is a mixed blessing.* **4 mixed response/reaction** if something gets a mixed response, some people say that they like it but others do not like it

ˌmixed ˈmarriage *n.* [C,U] a marriage between two people from different races or religions

ˌmixed ˈup *adj.* **1** confused: *I got mixed up and went to the wrong restaurant.* **2 be mixed up with sb** to be involved with someone who has a bad influence on you: *If you get mixed up with those people, you'll end up in jail.* **3 be mixed up in sth** to be involved in an illegal or dishonest activity: *I don't want my kids getting mixed up in drugs.* → **mix up** at MIX¹ → MIX-UP

mix·er /ˈmɪksɚ/ *n.* [C] a piece of equipment used for mixing different substances together: *Beat the eggs and sugar with an electric mixer.*

mix·ture /ˈmɪkstʃɚ/ *n.* **1** [C,U] a single substance made by mixing several substances together: *Pour the cake mixture into a pan and bake it for 45 minutes.*

THESAURUS

combination – two or more different things, substances, etc. that are used or put together: *Doctors use a combination of drugs to combat the disease.*
blend – a mixture of two or more things: *The salad dressing is an interesting blend of oil, vinegar, and spices.*
compound – a chemical compound is a substance that consists of two or more different substances: *Carbon dioxide is a common compound found in the air.*
solution – a liquid mixed with a solid or a gas: *a weak sugar solution*

2 [C usually singular] a combination of two or more people, things, feelings, or ideas that are different: *I listened to his excuse with **a mixture of** amusement and disbelief.*

ˈmix-up *n. informal* a mistake that causes confusion about details or arrangements: *There was a mix-up at the station and Eddie got on the wrong bus.* → **mix up** at MIX¹ → MIXED UP

ml the written abbreviation of **milliliter**

mm the written abbreviation of **millimeter**

MN the written abbreviation of **Minnesota**

MO the written abbreviation of **Missouri**

mo. the written abbreviation of **month**

moan¹ /moʊn/ *v.* [I] **1** to make the sound of a moan: *The victim was bleeding and moaning in pain.* **2** *informal* to complain in an annoying way, especially in an unhappy voice: *Stop **moaning about** your problems and get to work!* —**moaner** *n.* [C]

moan² *n.* [C] a long low sound expressing pain or sadness

moat /moʊt/ *n.* [C] a deep wide hole, usually filled with water, that was dug around a castle as a defense

mob¹ /mɑb/ *n.* [C] **1** a large noisy crowd, especially one that is angry and violent: ***mobs of** protesters*

THESAURUS

group, crowd, gang, bunch, mass, flock
→ see Thesaurus box at GROUP¹

2 the Mob *informal* MAFIA

mob² *v.* past tense and past participle **mobbed**, present participle **mobbing** [T] **1** to form a crowd around someone in order to express admiration or to attack him/her: *She's mobbed by her fans wherever she goes.* **2** if a place is mobbed, it has a lot of people in it: *The beach was **mobbed with** people.*

mo·bile¹ /ˈmoʊbəl/ *adj.* able to move or be moved easily [≠ **immobile**]: *I'm much more mobile now that I have a car.* —**mobility** /moʊˈbɪləṭi/ *n.* [U] *elderly people with limited mobility*

mo·bile² /ˈmoʊbil/ *n.* [C] a decoration made of small objects tied to string and hung up so that they move when air blows around them

ˌmobile ˈhome *n.* [C] a type of house made of

metal that can be pulled by a large vehicle and moved to another place

mobile 'phone *n.* [C] a CELL PHONE

mo·bi·lize /'moubə,laɪz/ *v.* [I,T] **1** to gather together or be brought together in order to work to achieve something difficult: *Forces have been mobilized to defend the capital.* **2 mobilize support/opposition** to encourage people to support or oppose something —**mobilization** /,moubələ'zeɪʃən/ *n.* [C,U]

mob·ster /'mɑbstɚ/ *n.* [C] *informal* a member of the Mafia

moc·ca·sin /'mɑkəsən/ *n.* [C] a flat comfortable shoe made of soft leather

mock[1] /mɑk/ *v.* [I,T] to laugh at someone or something and try to make him, her, or it seem stupid, especially by copying his or her actions or speech: *Wilson mocked Joe's southern accent.* | *Are you mocking me?* —**mockingly** *adv.*

mock[2] *adj.* not real: *a mock debate* | ***mock horror/surprise***

mock·er·y /'mɑkəri/ *n.* **1 make a mockery of sth** to make something such as a plan or system seem completely useless or ineffective: *The trial made a mockery of justice.* **2** [U] the act of laughing at someone or something and trying to make him, her, or it seem stupid or silly

mock·ing·bird /'mɑkɪŋ,bɚd/ *n.* [C] an American bird that copies the songs of other birds

modal 'verb also **modal** *n.* [C] *technical* in grammar, a verb that is used with other verbs to change their meaning by expressing ideas such as possibility, permission, or intention. In English, the modals are "can," "could," "may," "might," "shall," "should," "will," "would," "must," "ought to," "used to," "have to," and "had better." [➡ **auxiliary verb**]

mode /moud/ *n.* [C] *formal* a particular way or style of behaving, living, or doing something: *a very efficient **mode of** transportation*

mod·el[1] /'mɑdl/ *n.* [C] **1** someone whose job is to show clothes, hair styles, etc. by wearing them and being photographed: *a top **fashion model*** **2** a small copy of a vehicle, building, machine, etc., especially one that can be put together from separate parts: *They showed us a **model of** the building.* **3** someone who is employed by an artist or photographer in order to be painted or photographed **4** a person or thing that is a perfect example of something good and is therefore worth copying: *It served as a **model for** other cities.* | *Shelly's essay is a **model of** care and neatness.* ➔ ROLE MODEL **5** a particular type or design of a vehicle, machine, weapon, etc.: *Ford has two new models coming out in October.*

THESAURUS

type, **kind**, **sort**, **brand**, **make**
➔ see Thesaurus box at TYPE[1]

model[2] *adj.* **1 model airplane/train/car etc.** a small copy of an airplane, etc., especially one that can be put together from separate parts **2 model wife/employee/school etc.** a person or thing that is a perfect example of its type

model[3] *v.* **1** [I,T] to wear clothes in order to show them to possible buyers **2** [I,T] to be employed by an artist or photographer in order to be painted or photographed **3** [T] to copy a system or way of doing something: *Their education system is **modeled on** the French one.* **4 model yourself after sb** to try to be like someone else because you admire him/her: *The young singer modeled himself after Frank Sinatra.* **5** [T] to make small objects from materials such as wood or clay

mod·el·ing /'mɑdl-ɪŋ/ *n.* [U] **1** the work of a fashion model: *a career in modeling* **2** the activity of making models or objects: *clay modeling*

mo·dem /'moudəm/ *n.* [C] a piece of electronic equipment that allows information from one computer to be sent along telephone wires to another computer ➔ see Topic box at INTERNET

mod·er·ate[1] /'mɑdərɪt/ *adj.* **1** neither very big nor very small, very hot nor very cold, very fast nor very slow, etc.: *a moderate temperature* | *Moderate exercise can reduce the risk of heart disease.* **2** having opinions or beliefs, especially about politics, that are not extreme and that most people consider reasonable: *a **moderate Republican/Democrat*** | ***moderate voters***

mod·e·rate[2] /'mɑdə,reɪt/ *v.* [I,T] to make something less extreme or violent, or to become less extreme or violent: *To lose weight, moderate the amount of food you eat.*

mod·e·rate[3] /'mɑdərɪt/ *n.* [C] someone whose opinions or beliefs, especially about politics, are not extreme and are considered reasonable by most people

mod·er·ate·ly /'mɑdərɪtli/ *adv.* fairly but not very: *a moderately successful company*

mod·er·a·tion /,mɑdə'reɪʃən/ *n.* **1 in moderation** if you do something in moderation, you do not do it too much: *You've got to learn to drink in moderation.* **2** [U] *formal* control of your behavior, so that you keep your actions, feelings, habits, etc. within reasonable or sensible limits

mod·er·at·or /'mɑdə,reɪṭɚ/ *n.* [C] someone whose job is to control a discussion or argument and to help people reach an agreement

mod·ern /'mɑdɚn/ *adj.* **1** belonging to the present time or the most recent time [➡ **contemporary**]: *modern American history* | *Computers are an essential part of **modern life**.* | *The country is suffering one of its worst economic crises **in modern times**.* **2** using or willing to use very recent ideas, fashions, or ways of thinking: *The school is very modern in its approach to sex education.* **3** made or done using the most recent methods: *advances in **modern medicine*** | ***modern***

technology —**modernity** /mɑˈdɚnət̬i, -ˈdɛr-/ *n.* [U]

THESAURUS

new, **recent**, **latest**
→ see Thesaurus box at NEW

M

mod·ern·ize /ˈmɑdɚˌnaɪz/ *v.* [T] to change something so that it is more modern by using new equipment or methods: *We're modernizing the whole house, starting with a new bathroom.* —**modernization** /ˌmɑdɚnəˈzeɪʃən/ *n.* [C,U]

mod·est /ˈmɑdɪst/ *adj.* **1** *approving* unwilling to talk proudly about your abilities and achievements [≠ **immodest**]: *He was extremely* ***modest about*** *his contributions.* **2** not very big in size, quantity, value, etc.: *a modest salary* | *The film was only a* ***modest success****.* **3** shy about showing your body or attracting sexual interest —**modestly** *adv.*

mod·es·ty /ˈmɑdəsti/ *n.* [U] **1** *approving* the quality of being modest about your abilities or achievements **2** the quality of being modest about your body

mod·i·cum /ˈmɑdɪkəm/ *n. formal* **a modicum of sth** a small amount of something, especially a good quality: *Walker had a modicum of success as a football player.*

mod·i·fi·ca·tion /ˌmɑdəfəˈkeɪʃən/ *n.* **1** [C] a small change made in something such as a design, plan, or system: *We've made a few* ***modifications to*** *the original design.* **2** [U] the act of modifying something, or the process of being modified

mod·i·fi·er /ˈmɑdəˌfaɪɚ/ *n.* [C] *technical* in grammar, an adjective, adverb, or phrase that gives additional information about another word. In the sentence "The dog is barking loudly," "loudly" is a modifier.

mod·i·fy /ˈmɑdəˌfaɪ/ *v.* past tense and past participle **modified**, third person singular **modifies** [T] **1** to make small changes to something in order to improve it: *The car's been* ***modified to*** *use less fuel.*

THESAURUS

change, **alter**, **adapt**, **adjust**
→ see Thesaurus box at CHANGE[1]

2 *technical* to act as a modifier

mod·u·lar /ˈmɑdʒəlɚ/ *adj.* based on modules or made using modules: *modular furniture*

mod·u·late /ˈmɑdʒəˌleɪt/ *v.* [T] *technical* to change the sound of your voice or another sound —**modulation** /ˌmɑdʒəˈleɪʃən/ *n.* [U]

mod·ule /ˈmɑdʒul/ *n.* [C] **1** one of several separate parts that can be combined to form a larger object, such as a machine or building **2** a part of a SPACECRAFT that can be separated from the main part and used for a particular purpose

mo·gul /ˈmoʊgəl/ *n.* **media/business/movie etc. mogul** someone who has great power and influence in a particular industry or activity

mo·hair /ˈmoʊhɛr/ *n.* [U] expensive wool made from ANGORA

Mo·ham·med /moʊˈhæməd/ MUHAMMAD

moist /mɔɪst/ *adj.* slightly wet, in a pleasant way [➡ **damp**]: *Make sure the soil is moist before planting the seeds.* | *a moist chocolate cake*

THESAURUS

damp, **humid**
→ see Thesaurus box at DAMP

moist·en /ˈmɔɪsən/ *v.* [I,T] to become slightly wet, or to make something become slightly wet: *Moisten the clay with a little water.*

mois·ture /ˈmɔɪstʃɚ/ *n.* [U] small amounts of water that are present in the air, in a substance, or on a surface: *The nails were kept in a tin box to keep moisture out.*

mois·tur·iz·er /ˈmɔɪstʃəˌraɪzɚ/ *n.* [C] a creamy liquid you put on your skin to keep it soft

mo·lar /ˈmoʊlɚ/ *n.* [C] one of the large teeth at the back of the mouth, used for crushing food

mo·las·ses /məˈlæsɪz/ *n.* [U] a thick dark sweet liquid that is obtained from raw sugar plants when they are being made into sugar

mold[1] /moʊld/ *n.* **1** [U] a soft green or black substance that grows on old food and on objects that are in warm, slightly wet places **2** [C] a hollow container that you pour liquid into, so that when the liquid becomes solid, it takes the shape of the container: *a candle mold shaped like a star*

mold[2] *v.* [T] **1** to shape a solid substance by pressing or rolling it, or by putting it into a mold: *a figure of a man* ***molded out of*** *clay* **2** to influence the way someone's character or attitudes develop: *I try to take young athletes and* ***mold*** *them* ***into*** *team players.*

mold·ing /ˈmoʊldɪŋ/ *n.* [C,U] a thin line of stone, wood, plastic, etc. used as decoration around the edge of something such as a wall, car, or piece of furniture

mold·y /ˈmoʊldi/ *adj.* covered with mold: *moldy bread*

mole /moʊl/ *n.* [C] **1** a small brown mark on the skin that is sometimes slightly higher than the skin around it

THESAURUS

mark, **blemish**, **bruise**, **scar**, **pimple**, **zit**, **wart**, **blister**, **freckle**
→ see Thesaurus box at MARK[2]

2 a small animal with brown fur that lives in holes in the ground, and that cannot see well **3** someone who works for an organization, especially a government, in order to secretly give information about it to its enemy

mol·e·cule /ˈmɑləˌkyul/ *n.* [C] one or more atoms that form the smallest unit of a particular substance: *a single water molecule* —**molecular** /mə'lɛkyələ/ *adj.*

mo·lest /mə'lɛst/ *v.* [T] to attack or harm someone, especially a child, by touching him/her in a sexual way or trying to have sex with him/her: *She was sexually molested by her uncle.* —**molester** *n.* [C] *a child molester* —**molestation** /ˌmoʊlə'steɪʃən, ˌmɑ-/ *n.* [U]

mol·lusk /'mɑləsk/ *n.* [C] a type of sea or land animal with a soft body covered by a hard shell, for example a SNAIL or CLAM

molt /moʊlt/ *v.* [I] when a bird or animal molts, it loses hair, feathers, or skin so that new hair, feathers, or skin can grow

mol·ten /'moʊlt'n/ *adj.* molten metal or rock is liquid because it has been heated to a very high temperature

mom /mɑm/ *n.* [C] *informal* mother: *Can I go to David's house, Mom?* | *I called my mom.*

THESAURUS

relative, **parents**, **father**, **mother**, **daddy**, **dad**, **mommy**, **brother**, **sister**, **grandparents**, **grandfather**, **grandmother**, **grandpa**, **grandma**, **great-grandparents**, **uncle**, **aunt**, **nephew**, **niece**, **cousin**

→ see Thesaurus box at RELATIVE[1]

mo·ment /'moʊmənt/ *n.* [C] **1** a very short period of time [➡ **minute**]: *Robert paused* ***for a moment****.* | *I'll be back* ***in a moment****.* | *Could you wait* ***just a moment****?* | *He was here* ***a moment ago****.* | *Denise arrived moments later.* **2** a particular point in time: *Just* ***at that moment****, Shelly came in.* | *I knew it was you* ***the moment (that)*** *I heard your voice.* | *He said he loved her* ***from the moment (that)*** *he met her.* | ***At that very/exact/precise moment****, the phone rang.* **3 at the moment** now: *Japanese food is popular at the moment.* **4 any moment** soon: *The attack could come* ***at any moment****.* **5 for the moment** used in order to say that something is happening now but will probably change in the future: *For the moment, she decided not to argue.* **6** a particular period of time when you have a chance to do something: *It was her* ***big moment*** (=important chance)*; she took a deep breath and began to play.* | *Jo speaks out against sexism, but knows she has to* ***choose*** *her* ***moments*** (=choose the best time) *carefully.*

mo·men·tar·i·ly /ˌmoʊmən'tɛrəli/ *adv.* **1** for a very short time: *The car slowed down momentarily.* **2** very soon: *I'll be with you momentarily.*

mo·men·tar·y /'moʊmənˌtɛri/ *adj.* continuing for a very short time: *a momentary silence*

mo·men·tous /moʊ'mɛntəs, mə-/ *adj.* a momentous event, occasion, decision, etc. is very important, especially because of the effects it will have in the future: *the momentous events of the past year*

mo·men·tum /moʊ'mɛntəm, mə-/ *n.* [U] **1** the ability to keep increasing, developing, or being more successful: *Leconte won the first set, then seemed to* ***lose momentum****.* | *Cellular phone use has* ***gained/gathered momentum*** *in the past few years.* **2** the force that makes a moving object keep moving: *I'd* ***gained/gathered*** *so much* ***momentum*** (=moved faster and faster) *that I couldn't stop.*

mom·ma /'mɑmə/ *n.* [C] *spoken* mother

mom·my /'mɑmi/ *n.* plural **mommies** [C] *spoken* mother

THESAURUS

relative, **parents**, **father**, **mother**, **daddy**, **dad**, **mom**, **brother**, **sister**

→ see Thesaurus box at RELATIVE[1]

mon·arch /'mɑnək, 'mɑnɑrk/ *n.* [C] a king or queen

THESAURUS

king, **queen**, **ruler**, **emperor**, **sovereign**

→ see Thesaurus box at KING

mon·ar·chy /'mɑnəki/ *n.* plural **monarchies** **1** [U] the system in which a country is ruled by a king or queen [➡ **republic**]

THESAURUS

democracy, **republic**, **regime**, **dictatorship**, **police state**

→ see Thesaurus box at GOVERNMENT

2 [C] a country that is ruled by a king or queen

mon·as·ter·y /'mɑnəˌstɛri/ *n.* plural **monasteries** [C] a building or group of buildings in which MONKS live [➡ **convent**]

mo·nas·tic /mə'næstɪk/ *adj.* relating to MONKS or a monastery

Mon·day /'mʌndi, -deɪ/ *written abbreviation* **Mon.** *n.* [C] the second day of the week: *The results will be announced Monday.* | *It snowed* ***on Monday****.* | *We'll see you* ***next Monday****.* | *Kelly arrived* ***last Monday****.* | *I'll call you first thing* ***Monday morning****.*

mon·e·tar·y /'mɑnəˌtɛri/ *adj.* relating to money, especially all the money in a particular country: *France's monetary policy*

mon·ey /'mʌni/ *n.* [U] **1** what you earn by working and use in order to buy things, for example coins or special pieces of paper [➡ **cash**, **currency**]: *$250 is a lot of money.* | *the* ***amount of money*** *California spends on schools* | *Teachers don't* ***make/earn*** *a lot of* ***money****.* | *We're trying to* ***save*** *enough* ***money*** *for a trip to Europe.* | *Women tend to* ***spend*** *their* ***money*** *on their families.* | *I forgot my wallet – do you* ***have*** *enough* ***money*** *to pay for the meal?* | *Buying a used truck is a* ***waste of money****.* | *The raffle is to* ***raise money*** *for the*

M

school. | *Plumbers can make* ***good money*** (=good wages). | *a business that is* ***losing money*** (=earning less money than it spends)

THESAURUS

Types of money
bill – paper money: *a $20 bill*
coin – metal money: *old coins*
penny – a coin worth 1 cent
nickel – a coin worth 5 cents
dime – a coin worth 10 cents
quarter – a coin worth 25 cents
cash – money in the form of coins and bills: *I didn't have enough cash, so I paid by check.*
change – money in the form of coins: *Do you have any change for the phone?*
currency – the money used in a particular country: *He had $500 worth of Japanese currency.*

2 all the money that a person, country, or organization owns: *Is Ed just marrying her for her money?* | *I think he* ***made*** *his* ***money*** *on the stock market.* **3 get your money's worth** to think that something you have paid to do or see was worth the price that you paid: *Fans should get their money's worth.*

SPOKEN PHRASES

4 this/that kind of money a phrase meaning a lot of money, used when you think something costs too much, when someone earns a lot more than other people, etc.: *The rent was $5,250, and I just* ***don't have that kind of money***. **5 pay good money for sth** to spend a lot of money on something: *I paid good money for those shoes!* **6 for my money** used when giving your opinion about something, to emphasize that you believe it strongly: *For my money, Williams was a much better ballplayer.* **7 put your money where your mouth is** to show by your actions that you really believe what you say: *The legislature needs to put its money where its mouth is regarding the environment.* **8 money is no object** used in order to say that you can spend as much money as you want to on something

mon·ey·mak·er /ˈmʌniˌmeɪkɚ/ *n.* [C] a product or business that earns a lot of money

'money ˌmarket *n.* [C] the banks and other financial institutions that buy and sell BONDS, CURRENCY (=paper money), etc.

'money ˌorder *n.* [C] a special type of check that you buy and send to someone so that s/he can exchange it for money

mon·grel /ˈmɑŋɡrəl, ˈmʌŋ-/ *n.* [C] a dog that is a mix of several breeds of dog [➡ **mutt**]

mon·i·tor¹ /ˈmɑnət̬ɚ/ *n.* [C] **1** a piece of equipment that looks like a television and that shows information or pictures, especially on a computer: *a monitor showing the patient's heartbeat* **2** someone whose job is to make sure that something happens fairly or in the right way: *UN monitors will oversee the elections.* **3** a child who is chosen to help a teacher in some way

monitor² *v.* [T] to carefully watch, listen to, or examine something over a period of time, to check for any changes or developments: *Nurses are monitoring the patient's condition.* | *Army intelligence has been* ***closely monitoring*** *the enemy's radio broadcasts.*

monk /mʌŋk/ *n.* [C] a man who is a member of a group of religious men who live together in a MONASTERY (=special building) [➡ **nun**]

mon·key¹ /ˈmʌŋki/ *n.* plural **monkeys** [C] **1** a type of active animal that lives in hot countries and has a long tail that it uses with its hands to climb trees **2** *informal* a small child who is active and likes to play tricks **3 monkey business** behavior that may cause trouble or be dishonest

monkey² *v.* past tense and past participle **monkeyed**, third person singular **monkeys**

monkey (around) with sth *phr. v.* to touch or change something, usually when you do not know how to do it correctly: *They should stop monkeying around with the tax system.*

'monkey bars *n.* [plural] a structure of metal bars for children to climb on

'monkey wrench *n.* [C] a tool that is used for holding or turning things of different widths, especially NUTS

mon·o /ˈmɑnoʊ/ *n.* [U] *informal* an infectious illness that makes you feel weak and tired for a long time

mo·nog·a·my /məˈnɑɡəmi/ *n.* [U] the CUSTOM or practice of being married to only one person at one time [➡ **polygamy**] —**monogamous** /məˈnɑɡəməs/ *adj.*

mon·o·gram /ˈmɑnəˌɡræm/ *n.* [C] a design made from the first letters of someone's names that is put on things such as shirts or writing paper —**monogrammed** *adj.*

mon·o·lith·ic /ˌmɑnlˈɪθɪk◂ / *adj.* a monolithic organization, political system, etc. is very large and difficult to change —**monolith** /ˈmɑnəlɪθ/ *n.* [C]

mon·o·logue, **monolog** /ˈmɑnlˌɔɡ, -ˌɑɡ/ *n.* [C] a long speech by one character in a play, movie, or television show

mon·o·nu·cle·o·sis /ˌmɑnoʊˌnukliˈoʊsɪs/ *n.* [U] *technical* MONO

mo·nop·o·lize /məˈnɑpəˌlaɪz/ *v.* [T] *disapproving* to have complete control over something, especially a type of business, so that other people cannot get involved: *Big farming corporations are starting to monopolize the industry.* —**monopolization** /məˌnɑpələˈzeɪʃən/ *n.* [U]

Mo·nop·o·ly /məˈnɑpəli/ *n.* [U] *trademark* a game using artificial money in which you try to get more money and property than your opponents

monopoly *n.* plural **monopolies** [C usually singular] **1** the control of all or most of a business activity, or the company that has this control: *The* *train company has a* ***monopoly on/over*** *services to New Jersey.* **2 have a monopoly on sth** to have complete control or possession of something, so that other people cannot have it: *No country has a monopoly on bravery.* —**monopolistic** /məˌnɑpəˈlɪstɪk/ *adj.*

mon·o·rail /ˈmɑnəˌreɪl/ *n.* [C] a type of railroad that uses a single RAIL, or the train that travels on this type of railroad

mon·o·tone /ˈmɑnəˌtoʊn/ *n.* [singular] a way of talking that is boring because it does not get louder or softer: *She read aloud in a monotone.*

mo·not·o·nous /məˈnɑtˀn-əs/ *adj.* boring because nothing changes: *a monotonous job* —**monotony** *n.* [U] —**monotonously** *adv.*

THESAURUS

boring, **dull**, **tedious**, **not (very/that/all that) interesting**
➔ see Thesaurus box at BORING

mon·soon /mɑnˈsun/ *n.* [C] the season when it rains a lot in India and other southern Asian countries, or the rain or wind that happens during this season

mon·ster /ˈmɑnstɚ/ *n.* [C] **1** an imaginary large ugly frightening creature: *a sea monster* **2** someone who is cruel and evil: *Only a monster could kill an innocent child.* **3** an object, animal, etc. that is unusually large: *The storm was a monster.* —**monster** *adj.*

mon·stros·i·ty /mɑnˈstrɑsət̬i/ *n.* plural **monstrosities** [C] something large that is very ugly, especially a building

mon·strous /ˈmɑnstrəs/ *adj.* **1** very wrong, immoral, or unfair: *a monstrous crime* **2** unusually large: *a monstrous animal* —**monstrously** *adv.*

mon·tage /mɑnˈtɑʒ, moʊn-/ *n.* **1** [U] an art form in which a picture, movie, etc. is made by combining parts of different pictures, etc. **2** [C] a picture, movie, etc. made using this process

month /mʌnθ/ *n.* [C] **1** one of the 12 periods of time that a year is divided into: *the month of May* | *He's starting college at the end of* ***this month.*** | *the meeting* ***last/next month*** (=the month before or after this one) | *We see my parents* ***once/twice etc. a month.*** **2** any period of time equal to about four weeks: *a six-month-old baby* | *We'll be back* ***a month from today/tomorrow/Friday.*** **3 months** a long time: *He was in the hospital* ***for months.***

GRAMMAR

Talking about months

Use **in** to talk about a month but not about a particular date in that month: *He was born in February.*

Use **on** to talk about a particular date in a month: *He was born on February 20th.* | *She finishes school on the nineteenth of July.*

You can use **next** to talk about a month after the present one: *They're getting married next June.*

You can also use **this** or **this coming** to talk about a month in the very near future: *This coming October, my daughter turns 15.*

You can use **last** to talk about a month before the present one: *He died last October.*

You can also use **this** or **this past** to talk about a month in the very recent past: *He returned to Los Angeles this past July.*

M

month·ly /ˈmʌnθli/ *adj., adv.* **1** happening or done every month: *a monthly meeting* | *The windows are cleaned monthly.*

THESAURUS

regular, **hourly**, **daily**, **weekly**, **yearly**, **annual**, **annually**
➔ see Thesaurus box at REGULAR[1]

2 relating to a single month: *his monthly income*

mon·u·ment /ˈmɑnyəmənt/ *n.* [C] a building or other large structure that is built to remind people of an important event or famous person [➥ **statue**]: ***a monument to*** *soldiers killed in the war*

mon·u·men·tal /ˌmɑnyəˈmɛntl◂/ *adj.* **1** extremely large, bad, good, impressive, etc.: *a monumental task* **2** very important and having a lot of influence: *Darwin's monumental work on evolution*

moo /mu/ *n.* [C] the sound that a cow makes —**moo** *v.* [I]

mood /mud/ *n.* **1** [C,U] the way you feel at a particular time, or the way a group of people feel: *You're certainly* ***in a good/bad mood*** *today.* | *The mood of the country has changed.* **2 be in the mood** to want to do something or feel that you would enjoy something: *He wasn't* ***in the mood for*** *jokes.* **3 mood swings** occasions when someone's mood changes from being happy to being sad or angry, usually for no reason

mood·y /ˈmudi/ *adj.* comparative **moodier**, superlative **moodiest** **1** *disapproving* someone who is moody becomes angry or sad quickly: *a moody teenager* **2** making people feel sad, worried, or frightened: *moody music*

moon[1] /mun/ *n.* **1 the moon** the round object that shines in the sky at night: ***The moon rose*** *over the frozen lake.*

TOPIC

meteor, **asteroid**, **comet**, **constellation**, **galaxy**, **black hole**, **planet**, **star**, **sun**
➔ see Topic box at SPACE[1]

2 [singular] the shape of this object as it appears at a particular time: *There's no moon tonight* (=it cannot be seen). | *a* ***full moon*** | *the slender crescent that was the* ***new moon*** (=the moon when it first appears again in the sky) **3** [C] a large round object that moves around PLANETS other than the earth: *Saturn has several moons.* → **once in a blue moon** at ONCE[1]

moon² *v.* [I,T] *informal* to bend over and show your uncovered BUTTOCKS to someone as a rude joke

moon·less /ˈmunlɪs/ *adj.* without the moon showing in the sky: *a cloudy moonless night*

moon·light¹ /ˈmunlaɪt/ *n.* [U] the light of the moon: *The water looked silver **in the moonlight**.*

M

moonlight² *v.* [I] *informal* to have a second job in addition to your main job: *Clayton's been **moonlighting as** a security guard.* —**moonlighting** *n.* [U]

moon·lit /ˈmunˌlɪt/ *adj.* made brighter by the light of the moon: *a beautiful moonlit night*

moon·shine /ˈmunʃaɪn/ *n.* [U] *informal* strong alcohol that is produced illegally

moor /mʊr/ *v.* [I,T] to fasten a ship or boat to the land or the bottom of the sea, lake, etc. with a rope or chain

moor·ing /ˈmʊrɪŋ/ *n.* [C] the place where a ship or boat moors

moose /mus/ *n.* [C] a large wild North American, European, or Asian animal with large ANTLERS (=flat horns that look like branches) and a head like a horse

moose

moot /mut/ *adj.* a situation or possible action that is moot is no longer likely to happen or exist, or is no longer important: *The film's quality will be a **moot point** if it doesn't get finished.*

mop¹ /mɑp/ *n.* [C] **1** a thing for washing floors, made of a long stick with thick strings or a SPONGE fastened to one end **2** *informal* a large amount of thick messy hair: *a **mop of** curly **hair***

mop² *v.* past tense and past participle **mopped**, present participle **mopping** [T] **1** to wash a floor with a wet mop

THESAURUS

scrub, **scour**, **vacuum**, **sweep (up)**, **dust**, **polish**
→ see Thesaurus box at CLEAN²

2 to remove liquid from a surface by rubbing it with a cloth or something soft: *He mopped his face with a napkin.*

mop sth ⇔ **up** *phr. v.* to clean liquid off a surface using a mop, cloth, or something soft: *We mopped up the spill with a rag.*

mope /moʊp/ **also mope around** *v.* [I] to pity yourself and feel sad, without trying to be happier: *Jane moped and cried.*

mo·ped /ˈmoʊpɛd/ *n.* [C] a vehicle like a bicycle with a small engine

mor·al¹ /ˈmɔrəl, ˈmɑrəl/ *adj.* [usually before noun] **1** relating to the principles of what is right and wrong behavior, and the difference between good and evil [≠ **immoral**]: *a moral issue such as the death penalty* | *There are doubts about his ethical and **moral standards/values**.* | *a **moral responsibility/obligation/duty** to help the poor* **2 moral support** encouragement that you give by expressing approval or interest, rather than by giving practical help: *I went along to offer moral support.* **3 moral victory** a situation in which you show that your beliefs are right and fair, even if you do not win **4** always behaving in a way that is based on strong principles about what is right and wrong: *a moral man*

moral² *n.* **1 morals** [plural] principles or standards of good behavior, especially in matters of sex: *You're dealing with someone who has no morals or ethics.*

THESAURUS

ethics – moral rules or principles of behavior for deciding what is right and wrong: *Corporations should learn to care about ethics as much as profit.*
standards – moral principles about what kind of behavior and attitudes are acceptable: *Are the country's moral standards lower than in the past?*
values – your beliefs about what is right and wrong, or about what is important in life: *Children should learn values from their parents.*
principles – a set of rules or ideas about what is right and wrong that influences how you behave: *He tries to live according to his Christian principles.*
scruples – a belief about what is right and wrong that prevents you from doing something bad: *No one should set aside their moral scruples when they go to work.*

2 [C] a practical lesson about how to behave that you learn from a story or from something that happens to you: ***The moral of the story is** that crime doesn't pay.*

mo·rale /məˈræl/ *n.* [U] a person or group's morale is how good, bad, or confident they feel about their situation: *The employees' **morale** is **low/high*** (=bad/good).

mor·al·ist·ic /ˌmɔrəˈlɪstɪk, ˌmɑr-/ *adj. disapproving* having very strong beliefs about what is right and wrong, and about how people should behave —**moralist** /ˈmɔrəlɪst, ˈmɑ-/ *n.* [C]

mo·ral·i·ty /məˈræləṭi/ *n.* [U] **1** beliefs or ideas about what is right and wrong, and about how people should behave: *declining standards of morality* **2** the degree to which something is right or acceptable: *a discussion on the **morality of** the death penalty*

mor·al·ize /ˈmɔrəˌlaɪz, ˈmɑr-/ *v.* [I] *disapproving* to tell other people your ideas about right and wrong behavior, and about how people should behave

mor·al·ly /ˈmɔrəli, ˈmɑr-/ *adv.* **1** according to

moral principles about what is right and wrong: *It wasn't against the law, but it was **morally wrong**.* **2** in a way that is good and right: *the difficulty of behaving morally*

mo·rass /mə'ræs/ *n.* [singular] **1** a complicated and confusing situation that is very difficult to get out of: *California's economic morass* **2** a complicated amount of information: *a **morass of** details*

mor·a·to·ri·um /ˌmɔrə'tɔriəm, ˌmɑr-/ *n.* [C usually singular] an official announcement stopping an activity for a period of time: *a **moratorium on** nuclear weapons testing*

mor·bid /'mɔrbɪd/ *adj. disapproving* having a strong interest in unpleasant subjects, especially death: *a **morbid fascination** with instruments of torture* —**morbidly** *adv.*

more[1] /mɔr/ *adv.* **1** [used before an adjective or adverb to form the comparative] having a particular quality to a greater degree [≠ **less**]: *The second test was more difficult.* | *It was **more** expensive **than** I thought it would be.* | *People change careers **much/a lot/far more** frequently now.* | *Teenagers rely **more and more** on their friends.* | *Children are **no more** likely **than** adults to develop the disease.* **2** happening a greater number of times or for longer [≠ **less**]: *I promised I'd help more in the house.* | *We see our grandchildren **more than** we used to.* | *He's been working **a lot more** lately.* **3 not ... any more** used in order to show that something that used to happen or be true does not happen or is not true now [➡ **anymore**]: *Sarah doesn't live here any more.* ➔ **once more** at ONCE[1]

more[2] *quantifier* [the comparative of "many" and "much"] **1** a greater amount or number: ***More** new jobs were created **than** were lost in the industry.* | *The bus was **more than** two hours late.* | ***More and more** schools have their own website.* **2** an additional number or amount: *Would you like some more coffee?* | *I have to make **some/a few/many etc. more** phone calls.* | *Is there **any more** cake?* | *We had **no more** questions.* | *We had **5/12/20 more** people at the meeting **than** we expected.* | *Scott needed to see **more of** his father.*

THESAURUS

another – something in addition to a particular amount, distance, period of time, etc.: *Do you want another cup of coffee?*
extra – more than the usual or standard amount of something: *I always carry an extra key, in case I lose my other one.*
additional – more than you already have, or more than was agreed or expected: *Additional troops will be sent to the region.*
further – more, used especially when something happens again or is done again: *Further research is needed.*

3 more or less almost: *This report says more or less the same thing as the other one.*

more·o·ver /mɔr'oʊvɚ/ *adv. formal* a word meaning "in addition to this" that is used in order to add information to something that has just been said: *My father said I was old enough, and, moreover, he trusted me.*

mo·res /'mɔreɪz/ *n.* [plural] *formal* the CUSTOMS, social behavior, and moral values of a particular group: *American social mores*

morgue /mɔrg/ *n.* [C] a building or room where dead bodies are kept before they are buried or burned

M

Mor·mon /'mɔrmən/ *adj.* relating to a religious organization called The Church of Jesus Christ of Latter-Day Saints, that has strict moral rules such as not allowing its members to drink alcohol and coffee —**Mormon** *n.* [C] —**Mormonism** *n.* [U]

morn·ing /'mɔrnɪŋ/ *n.* **1** [C,U] the early part of the day, especially from when the sun rises until the middle of the day: *I got a letter from Wayne **this morning**.* | *The freeway is usually jammed **in the morning**.* | *Andy woke up at **two/three etc. in the morning*** (=during the night). | *the TV programs that are on **Saturday/Tuesday etc. morning*** | *a meeting **yesterday/tomorrow morning*** | *a **sunny/cloudy/foggy etc. morning*** | *I had my **morning coffee/walk/routine etc.*** (=coffee, etc. that you have in the morning) **2 (Good) Morning** *spoken* said in order to greet someone when you meet him/her in the morning: *Morning, Rick.*

'morning ˌsickness *n.* [U] a feeling of sickness that some women have when they are PREGNANT

mo·ron /'mɔrɑn/ *n.* [C] someone who is very stupid —**moronic** /mə'rɑnɪk/ *adj.*

mo·rose /mə'roʊs/ *adj. literary* unhappy, silent, and in a bad mood —**morosely** *adv.*

morph /mɔrf/ *v.* **1** [I,T] to make one image gradually change into a different image by using a computer, or to gradually change into a different image **2** [I] *informal* to gradually change into something different: *At that time I was **morphing into** being a single mom.*

mor·phine /'mɔrfin/ *n.* [U] a powerful drug used for stopping pain

Morse code /ˌmɔrs 'koʊd/ *n.* [U] a system of sending messages in which the alphabet is represented by short and long signals of sound or light

mor·sel /'mɔrsəl/ *n.* [C] a small piece of food: *a **morsel of** bread*

mor·tal[1] /'mɔrtl̩/ *adj.* **1** not living forever [≠ **immortal**]: *mortal creatures* **2 mortal injuries/blow/danger etc.** injuries, etc. that will cause death or are likely to cause death **3 mortal fear/terror/dread** extreme fear —**mortally** *adv.*: *He was mortally wounded.*

mortal[2] *n.* **1 lesser/ordinary/mere mortals** *humorous* an expression meaning ordinary people, as compared with people who are more important or more powerful **2** [C] *literary* a human

mor·tal·i·ty /mɔr'tæləṭi/ *n.* [U] **1 also mortality rate** the number of deaths during a particular period of time among a particular group of people or from a particular cause: *a decrease in the **infant mortality rate*** (=the rate at which babies die) **2** the condition of being human and having to die

mor·tar /ˈmɔrṭɚ/ *n.* **1** [C] a heavy gun that fires explosives in a high curve **2** [U] a mixture of LIME, sand, and water, used in building for sticking bricks or stones together

M

mor·tar·board /ˈmɔrṭɚˌbɔrd/ *n.* [C] a cap with a flat square top that you wear when you GRADUATE from a HIGH SCHOOL, college, or university

mort·gage¹ /ˈmɔrgɪdʒ/ *n.* [C] **1** an agreement in which you borrow money from a bank in order to buy a house, and pay back the money over a period of years: *We **took out a** bigger **mortgage*** (=borrowed money) *to pay for the work on the house.* | *a **mortgage on** the farm* **2** the amount of money lent on a mortgage: *a **mortgage of** $100,000*

mortgage² *v.* [T] to borrow money by giving someone, usually a bank, the right to own your house, land, or property if you do not pay back the money the person or bank lent you within a certain period of time

mor·ti·cian /mɔrˈtɪʃən/ *n.* [C] someone whose job is to arrange funerals and prepare bodies before they are buried

mor·ti·fy /ˈmɔrṭəˌfaɪ/ *v.* **be mortified** to feel extremely embarrassed or ashamed: *Harry was mortified by his mistake.* —**mortifying** *adj.* —**mortification** /ˌmɔrṭəfəˈkeɪʃən/ *n.* [U]

mor·tu·ar·y /ˈmɔrtʃuˌɛri/ *n.* plural **mortuaries** [C] the place where a body is kept before a funeral and where the funeral is sometimes held

mo·sa·ic /moʊˈzeɪ-ɪk/ *n.* [C,U] a pattern or picture made by fitting together small pieces of colored stone, glass, etc.

mosh /mɑʃ/ *v.* [I] *informal* to dance using a lot of energy at a concert with loud ROCK or PUNK music

Mos·lem /ˈmɑzləm, ˈmɑs-/ *n.* [C] a MUSLIM —**Moslem** *adj.*

mosque /mɑsk/ *n.* [C] a building where Muslims go to have religious services

mos·qui·to /məˈskiṭoʊ/ *n.* plural **mosquitoes** [C] a small flying insect that bites and sucks the blood of people and animals, making you ITCH and sometimes spreading diseases

moss /mɔs/ *n.* [U] a small flat green or yellow plant that looks like fur and often grows on trees and rocks —**mossy** *adj.*

most¹ /moʊst/ *adv.* **1** [used before an adjective or adverb to form the superlative] having the greatest amount of a particular quality: *Basketball is the most popular sport.* | *She has lived in France, Italy, and, most recently, Spain.* | *the most powerful man in the world* **2** to a greater degree or more times than anything else: *Which do you like most?* | *It's been challenging, but **most of all**, it's been fun.* **3** *spoken nonstandard* almost: *We eat at Joe's **most every** weekend.*

most² *quantifier* [the superlative of "many" and "much"] **1** almost all of the people or things in a group [➡ **majority**]: ***Most of the** books were old.* | *Polls show that most Americans don't eat enough fruit.* **2** a larger amount or number than anyone or anything else: *Which class has **the most** children?* | *The team that scores **the most** points wins.* **3** the largest number or amount possible: *How can we get **the most** power from the engine?* **4 at (the) most** used in order to say that a number or amount will not be larger than you say: *It'll take twenty minutes at the most.* **5 for the most part** used in order to say that something is generally true but not completely true: *For the most part, they did a pretty good job.* **6 make the most of sth/get the most out of sth** to get the greatest possible advantage from a situation: *It's your only chance, so make the most of it.*

> **GRAMMAR**
>
> **most, most of**
>
> Use **most** immediately before a plural noun form or an uncountable noun when you are talking about something in general: *I like most animals.* | *He thinks most poetry is boring.*
>
> Use **most of** before "the", "this," "my," etc. and a noun when you are talking about a particular group or thing: *I got most of the answers right.* | *He does most of his work at home.*

most·ly /ˈmoʊstli/ *adv.* in most cases, or most of the time: *The room was full of athletes, mostly football players.* | *Mostly, our friends have stayed close by.* ► Don't say "mostly all," "mostly everybody," etc. say "almost all," "almost everybody," etc. ◄

mo·tel /moʊˈtɛl/ *n.* [C] a hotel for people traveling by car, with a place for the car near each room

> **THESAURUS**
>
> **hotel, inn, bed and breakfast (B&B), campground**
>
> ➔ see Thesaurus box at HOTEL

moth /mɔθ/ *n.* [C] an insect similar to a BUTTERFLY that usually flies at night, especially toward lights

moth·ball¹ /ˈmɔθbɔl/ *v.* [T] *informal* to close a factory or operation, and keep all its equipment or plans for a long time without using them

mothball² *n.* [C] a small ball made of a strong-smelling chemical, used for keeping moths away from clothes

moth·er /ˈmʌðɚ/ *n.* [C] **1** a female parent: *My mother said I have to be home by 9:00.* | *a **mother of** three* (=with three children) | *a mother hen and her chicks*

> **THESAURUS**
>
> **relative, parents, father, daddy, dad, mommy, mom, brother, sister, grandparents, grandfather, grandmother, grandpa,**

grandma, **great-grandparents**, **uncle**, **aunt**, **nephew**, **niece**, **cousin**
➔ see Thesaurus box at RELATIVE[1]

2 *spoken* something that is a very good or very bad example of its type, or that is very impressive: *I woke up with **the mother of all** hangovers.* —**mother** *v.* [T]

moth·er·board /ˈmʌðɚˌbɔrd/ *n.* [C] *technical* the main CIRCUIT BOARD inside a computer

moth·er·hood /ˈmʌðɚˌhʊd/ *n.* [U] the state of being a mother

moth·er·ing /ˈmʌðərɪŋ/ *n.* [U] the activity of a mother taking care of her children

ˈmother-in-ˌlaw *n.* plural **mothers-in-law** [C] the mother of your husband or wife

moth·er·ly /ˈmʌðɚli/ *adj.* typical of a kind or concerned mother: *The teacher was a motherly woman.*

ˌMother ˈNature *n.* [U] an expression used in order to talk about the Earth, its weather, and the living creatures and plants on it

ˌmother-of-ˈpearl *n.* [U] a pale-colored smooth shiny substance on the inside of some shells, used for making buttons, jewelry, etc.

ˈMother's Day *n.* [C] a holiday in honor of mothers, celebrated in the U.S. and Canada on the second Sunday of May

ˌmother-to-ˈbe *n.* [C] a woman who is going to have a baby

mo·tif /moʊˈtif/ *n.* [C] an idea, subject, or pattern that is regularly repeated and developed in a book, movie, work of art, etc.

THESAURUS
pattern, **design**, **markings**
➔ see Thesaurus box at PATTERN

mo·tion[1] /ˈmoʊʃən/ *n.* **1** [U] the process of moving, or the way that someone or something moves: *the gentle rolling **motion of** the ship* **2** [C] a single movement of your head, hand, etc.: *One of the soldiers **made a** chopping **motion** with his hand.* **3** [C] a proposal that is made formally at a meeting and then decided on by voting: *The **motion to** increase the charges was **passed/carried** by 15 votes to 10.* | *Janke **made/proposed a motion** that the meeting be adjourned.* | *The **motion** was **seconded** by Levin.* **4 in slow motion** if something on television or in the movies is shown in slow motion, it is shown more slowly than usual so that all the actions can be clearly seen: *Let's look at that touchdown in slow motion.* **5 set sth in motion** to start a process or series of events that will continue: *The kidnapping set in motion a massive police investigation.* **6 go through the motions** to do something because you have to do it, without being very interested in it: *Too many students just go through the motions in school.*

motion[2] *v.* [I,T] to give someone directions or instructions by moving your head, hand, etc.: *The police officer **motioned for** me **to** stop the car.*

mo·tion·less /ˈmoʊʃənlɪs/ *adj.* not moving at all: *Kemp sat motionless as the verdict was read.*

ˌmotion ˈpicture *n.* [C] a MOVIE

mo·ti·vate /ˈmoʊt̬əˌveɪt/ *v.* [T] **1** to make someone feel determined or eager to do something: *Praise, rather than criticism, **motivates** children **to** do well.* **2 motivating factor/force** the reason why someone behaves in a particular way: *Freud thought that sex was **the motivating factor behind** much human behavior.*

mo·ti·vat·ed /ˈmoʊt̬əˌveɪt̬ɪd/ *adj.* **1** very eager to do or achieve something: *an intelligent and **highly motivated** student* **2** done for a particular reason: *The killings were thought to be **racially motivated*** (=done because someone hates other races).

mo·ti·va·tion /ˌmoʊt̬əˈveɪʃən/ *n.* **1** [U] the determination and desire to do something: *Jack is smart, but he lacks motivation.* **2** [C] the reason why you want to do something: *a student's **motivation for** learning* —**motivational** *adj.*: *a motivational speech*

mo·tive /ˈmoʊt̬ɪv/ *n.* [C] the reason that makes someone do something, especially when this reason is kept hidden: *Police are trying to find out the **motive for** the attack.* ➔ **ulterior motive** at ULTERIOR

THESAURUS
reason, **explanation**, **excuse**
➔ see Thesaurus box at REASON[1]

mot·ley /ˈmɑtli/ *adj.* *disapproving* **a motley crew/bunch/assortment etc.** a group of people or other things that do not seem to belong together

mo·tor[1] /ˈmoʊt̬ɚ/ *n.* [C] the part of a machine that makes it work or move [➡ **engine**]: *The drill is powered by a small electric motor.*

motor[2] *adj.* **1** using power provided by an engine: *a motor vehicle* **2** relating to the way muscles are controlled: *a child's motor skills*

mo·tor·bike /ˈmoʊt̬ɚˌbaɪk/ *n.* [C] a motorcycle, especially a small one ➔ see picture at TRANSPORTATION

mo·tor·cade /ˈmoʊt̬ɚˌkeɪd/ *n.* [C] a group of cars and other vehicles that travel together and surround a very important person's car

mo·tor·cy·cle /ˈmoʊt̬ɚˌsaɪkəl/ *n.* [C] a fast, usually large, two-wheeled vehicle with an engine

ˈmotor home *n.* [C] a large vehicle with beds, a kitchen, etc. in it, used for traveling [= **RV**; ➡ **mobile home**]

mo·tor·ist /ˈmoʊt̬ərɪst/ *n.* [C] *formal* someone who drives a car

mo·tor·ized /ˈmoʊt̬əˌraɪzd/ *adj.* having an engine, especially when something does not usually have an engine: *a motorized wheelchair*

ˈmotor ˌscooter *n.* [C] a SCOOTER

'motor ,vehicle *n.* [C] *formal* a car, bus, truck, etc.

mot·tled /'mɑtld/ *adj.* covered with spots of light and dark colors of different shapes: *mottled skin*

mot·to /'mɑtoʊ/ *n.* plural **mottoes** [C] a short statement that expresses the aims or beliefs of a person, school, or institution: *The motto of the Boy Scouts is "Be Prepared."*

M

mound /maʊnd/ *n.* [C] **1** a pile of dirt, stones, sand, etc.

THESAURUS

pile, heap
➔ see Thesaurus box at PILE[1]

2 a large pile of something: *a* ***mound of*** *papers*

mount[1] /maʊnt/ *v.* **1** [I] **also mount up** to increase gradually in size, degree, or amount [➡ **mounting**]: *His debts continued to mount up.* | ***Tensions mounted*** *as we waited for the result.* **2** [T] to plan, organize, and begin an event or a course of action: *The gallery mounted an exhibition of Weston's photographs.* | *Guerrillas* ***mounted*** *an* ***attack*** *on the village.* **3** [I,T] *formal* to get on a horse or bicycle [≠ **dismount**] **4** [T] *formal* to go up something such as a set of stairs: *He mounted the steps and shook hands with Bianchi.* **5 be mounted on sth** to be attached to something and supported by it: *paintings mounted on the wall*

mount[2] *n.* **1 Mount** part of the name of a mountain: *Mount Everest* **2** [C] *literary* an animal, especially a horse, that you ride on

mountain

moun·tain /'maʊnt̚n/ *n.* [C] **1** a very high hill: *the highest mountain in California* | *She was the first British woman to* ***climb*** *the* ***mountain***. | *the* ***mountain ranges*** (=lines of mountains) *in the west* | *snow-capped* ***mountain peaks*** (=tops of mountains) **2** a very large pile or amount of something: *a* ***mountain of*** *work to do*

'mountain ,bike *n.* [C] a strong bicycle with wide thick tires that you can ride on rough ground ➔ see picture on page A10

moun·tain·eer·ing /,maʊnt̚n'ɪrɪŋ/ *n.* [U] an outdoor activity in which you climb mountains —**mountaineer** *n.* [C]

'mountain goat *n.* [C] a type of goat that lives in the western mountains of North America

'mountain ,lion *n.* [C] a COUGAR

moun·tain·ous /'maʊnt̚n-əs/ *adj.* having a lot of mountains: *a mountainous region of Europe*

moun·tain·side /'maʊnt̚n,saɪd/ *n.* [C] the side of a mountain

moun·tain·top /'maʊnt̚n,tɑp/ *n.* [C] the top part of a mountain

Mount·ie /'maʊnti/ *n.* [C] a member of the national police force of Canada

mount·ing /'maʊntɪŋ/ *adj.* gradually increasing or becoming worse: *There was* ***mounting pressure*** *from the country's political leaders.*

mourn /mɔrn/ *v.* [I,T] to feel very sad because someone has died, and show this in the way you behave: *The whole country mourned Kennedy's death.* | *She was still* ***mourning for*** *her sister.*

mourn·er /'mɔrnɚ/ *n.* [C] *written* someone who attends a funeral, especially a relative of the dead person

mourn·ful /'mɔrnfəl/ *adj. literary* very sad: *slow mournful music*

mourn·ing /'mɔrnɪŋ/ *n.* [U] **1** great sadness because someone has died: *People wore black as a sign of mourning.* **2 be in mourning** to be very sad because someone has died: *She's still* ***in mourning for*** *her son.*

mouse /maʊs/ *n.* [C] **1** plural **mouses** or **mice** /maɪs/ a small object connected to a computer by a wire, that you move with your hand to give instructions to the computer ➔ see picture on page A11 **2** plural **mice** a small furry animal with a long tail and a pointed nose that lives in buildings or in fields

'mouse pad *n.* [C] a small piece of flat material on which you move a computer mouse ➔ see picture on page A11

mousse /mus/ *n.* [U] **1** a cold sweet food made from a mixture of cream, eggs, and fruit or chocolate: *chocolate mousse* **2** a slightly sticky substance that you put in your hair to make it look thicker or to hold it in place

mous·tache /'mʌstæʃ, mə'stæʃ/ *n.* [C] a MUSTACHE

mous·y /'maʊsi, -zi/ *adj. disapproving* **1** mousy hair is a dull brownish-gray color **2** a mousy girl or woman is small, quiet, not interesting, and not attractive

mouth[1] /maʊθ/ *n.* plural **mouths** /maʊðz/ [C] **1** the part of your face that you use for speaking and eating: *his round face and wide mouth* | *The beginnings of a smile touched the* ***corners of*** *her* ***mouth***. | *Don't talk with your* ***mouth full*** (=full of food). ➔ see picture on page A3 **2 open/shut your mouth** to start to speak, or to stop speaking: *Shut your mouth, Tonya!* | *He was afraid to open his mouth during the meeting.* **3 keep your mouth shut** *informal* to not say what you are thinking, or not tell someone a secret: *I was getting really mad, but I kept my mouth shut.*

4 an opening, entrance, or way out: *the mouth of a river* (=where it joins the sea) | *the mouth of a jar* **5 big mouth** *informal* someone who is a big mouth or has a big mouth often says things that s/he should not say **6 make your mouth water** if food makes your mouth water, it smells or looks so good you want to eat it immediately [➡ **mouth-watering**] **7 open-mouthed/wide-mouthed etc.** with an open, wide, etc. mouth → **shoot your mouth off** at SHOOT[1]

mouth² /maʊð/ *v.* [T] to move your lips as if you are saying words, but without making any sound: *Kim looked at me and mouthed, "It's O.K."* → BADMOUTH

mouth off *phr. v. informal* to talk angrily or rudely to someone: *Jack was* ***mouthing off to*** *the teacher.*

mouth·ful /ˈmaʊθfʊl/ *n.* [C] an amount of food or drink that you put into your mouth at one time: *He swallowed a* ***mouthful of*** *coffee.*

mouth·piece /ˈmaʊθpis/ *n.* [C] **1** the part of a musical instrument, telephone, etc. that you put in your mouth or next to your mouth **2** a person, newspaper, etc. that expresses the opinions of a government or a political organization, especially without ever criticizing these opinions: *Pravda used to be the* ***mouthpiece of*** *the Communist Party.*

mouth·wash /ˈmaʊθwɑʃ, -wɔʃ/ *n.* [U] a liquid you can use to make your mouth smell fresh or to get rid of an infection in your mouth

ˈmouth-ˌwatering *adj.* food that is mouth-watering looks or smells extremely good

mov·a·ble /ˈmuvəbəl/ *adj.* able to be moved [≠ **immovable**]: *dolls with movable arms and legs*

move¹ /muv/ *v.*

1 CHANGE POSITION [I,T] to change from one place or position to another, or to make something do this [➡ **motion**]: *Molly sat down and refused to move.* | *Could you move your car, please?* | *Pat* ***moved*** *closer* ***to/toward etc.*** *her.* | *She* ***moved slowly/quickly etc.*** *to the door.* | *The kids were* ***moving around*** *the classroom, choosing activities.*

2 NEW PLACE [I,T] to go to a new place to live, work, or study, or to make someone do this: *Her parents are* ***moving into*** *a retirement home.* | *The army paid to* ***move*** *our family* ***to*** *Germany.*

3 CHANGE JOB/CLASS ETC. [I,T] to change to a different job, class, etc., or to make someone change to a different job, class, etc.: *He* ***moved*** *easily* ***from*** *teaching* ***into*** *administration.* | *Some students were* ***moved into*** *the intermediate class.*

4 get moving also move it *spoken* used in order to say that someone needs to hurry: *If you don't get moving, you'll miss the bus.*

5 PROGRESS [I] to progress or change in a particular way: *The talks seem to be* ***moving*** *swiftly* ***toward*** *a deal.*

6 START DOING STH [I] to start doing something in order to achieve something: *U.S. leaders should* ***move*** *quickly* ***to*** *outlaw these weapons.* | *The Senate has not yet* ***moved on*** (=not done anything as a result of) *the suggestions from the committee.*

7 FEEL EMOTION [T] to make someone feel a strong emotion, especially sadness or sympathy [➡ **moving**]: *The song* ***moved*** *even the youngest of them* ***to tears*** (=made them cry). | *The audience,* ***deeply/genuinely moved****, was silent.*

8 CHANGE ARRANGEMENTS [T] to change the time or order of something: *The meeting's been* ***moved to*** *Tuesday.*

9 MEETING [I] *formal* to make an official suggestion at a meeting: *Dr. Reder* ***moved that*** *the proposal be accepted.*

10 GO FAST [I] *informal* to travel very fast: *That truck was really moving.*

move away *phr. v.* to go to live in a different area: *I lost touch with her when her family moved away.*

move in also move into *phr. v.* **1** to start living in a new house [≠ **move out**]: *When are you moving into your new house?* **2** to start living with someone in the same house: *After her father died, she* ***moved in with*** *her aunt.* | *Al and Bridget have* ***moved in together****.* **3** to start being involved in and controlling a situation that someone else controlled previously: *huge companies* ***moving in on*** *small businesses*

move on *phr. v.* **1** to leave your present job, class, or activity and start doing another one: *After 12 years as principal here, Garcia will* ***move on to*** *a new school this fall.* **2** to leave a place where you have been staying or doing something in order to continue to another place: *The play, a success in San Diego, has* ***moved on to*** *New York.* **3** to start talking or writing about a new subject in a speech, book, discussion, etc.: *Before we move on, does anyone have any questions?* **4** to develop in your life, and change your relationships, interests, activities, etc.: *Harry left a year ago; it's time for you to move on.* **5** to progress, improve, or become more modern as time passes: *By the time the software was ready, the market had moved on.*

move out *phr. v.* to leave the house where you are living in order to go to live somewhere else [≠ **move in**]: *When did Bob move out?*

move over *phr. v.* to change position so that there is space for someone or something else: *Move over a little, so I can sit down.*

move up *phr. v.* to get a better job, or change to a more advanced group, higher rank, or higher level: *Students have to pass oral and written exams before moving up.* | ***Moving up the*** *economic* ***ladder*** *is everyone's dream.*

move² *n.* [C] **1** something that you decide to do in order to achieve something or make progress: *The White House says the statement is a* ***move toward*** *peace.* | *I'm not sure that's a* ***good/bad/wise etc. move****.* | *Hogan has* ***made*** *no* ***move*** *to change his decision.* **2** an action in which someone moves in a particular direction: *dancers practicing their moves* | *Grover* ***made a move toward*** *the door.* | *They watched us but* ***made no move to***

M

stop us. **3 be on the move** to travel or move a lot: *These little fish are always on the move.* **4 get a move on** *spoken* said when you want someone to hurry: *Get a move on, or we'll be late!* **5** the process of leaving the place where you live or work and going to live or work somewhere else: *We visited Seattle several times before deciding to* ***make the move***. **6** the act of changing the position of one of the objects in a game: *It's your move, Jane.*

M

move·ment /ˈmuvmənt/ *n.* **1** [C,U] an action in which something or someone changes position or moves from one place to another: *the quick eye movements during sleep | troop movements in the desert | the* ***movement of*** *goods across the border* **2** [C] a group of people who share the same ideas or beliefs and work together to achieve a particular aim: *the* ***civil rights/antiwar/feminist etc. movement*** *| the* ***movement for*** *democracy* **3** [C] a change or development in a situation or in people's attitudes or behavior: *a* ***movement away from/toward*** *fairness in employment* **4** [C] one of the main parts into which a piece of music such as a SYMPHONY is divided **5** [C] the moving parts of a piece of machinery, especially a clock **6** [C] *formal* the action of getting rid of waste matter from your BOWELS

mov·er /ˈmuvə/ *n.* [C] **1** someone whose job is to help people move from one house to another **2 mover and shaker** an important person who has power and influence over what happens in a situation

mov·ie /ˈmuvi/ *n.* [C] **1** a story that is told using sound and moving pictures [= **film**]: *Shh! I want to* ***watch the movie****! | I've* ***seen*** *that* ***movie*** *twice. | a bad* ***TV movie***

THESAURUS

Types of movies
feature film – a movie made to be shown in movie theaters
comedy – a movie intended to make people laugh
romantic comedy – a movie about love that is intended to make the people who watch it feel happy
thriller – an exciting movie about murder or serious crimes
western – a movie with cowboys in it
action movie – a movie that has lots of fighting, explosions, etc.
horror movie – a frightening movie about ghosts, murders, etc.
science fiction movie – a movie about imaginary events in the future or in outer space
animated movie/cartoon – a movie with characters that are drawn or made using a computer
flick informal – a movie: *an action flick*
film – a movie, especially one that people think is very good or important: *a foreign film*

People who make movies
actor – a man or woman who acts in a movie
actress – a woman who acts in a movie
star – a famous actor or actress
director – the person who tells the actors and actresses in a movie what to do
producer – the person who makes the arrangements for a movie to be made and controls the movie's budget (=the money available to make the film)
film/movie crew – the people operating the camera, lights, etc. who help the director make a movie

2 the movies the theater where you go to watch a movie: *Do you want to* ***go to the movies*** *with us?*

ˈmovie star *n.* [C] a famous movie actor or actress

ˈmovie ˌtheater *n.* [C] a building where you go to watch movies

mov·ing /ˈmuvɪŋ/ *adj.* **1** making you feel strong emotions, especially sadness or sympathy: *a moving story | a* ***deeply/very moving*** *experience*

THESAURUS

emotional, touching, poignant, sentimental, schmalzy
→ see Thesaurus box at EMOTIONAL

2 [only before noun] changing from one position to another: *the* ***moving parts*** *of an engine |* ***fast/slow moving*** *traffic* —**movingly** *adv.*: *She spoke movingly about her father's last days.*

ˈmoving ˌvan *n.* [C] a large vehicle used for moving furniture from one house to another

mow /moʊ/ *v.* past tense **mowed**, past participle **mowed** or **mown** /moʊn/ [I,T] to cut grass with a machine: *When are you going to* ***mow the lawn****?*

THESAURUS

cut, saw, chop down, trim, snip
→ see Thesaurus box at CUT[1]

mow sb ⇔ **down** *phr. v.* to kill people or knock them down, especially in large numbers: *soldiers mowed down by machine-gun fire*

mow·er /ˈmoʊə/ *n.* [C] a LAWN MOWER

mpg miles per gallon – used when describing the amount of GAS used by a car: *a car that gets 35 mpg*

mph miles per hour – used when describing the speed of a vehicle: *a 65 mph speed limit*

Mr. /ˈmɪstə/ **1 Mr. Smith/Jones etc.** used before a man's family name to be polite when you are speaking to him, writing to him, or talking about him **2** a title used when speaking to a man in an official position: *Mr. Chairman | Mr. President* **3 Mr. Right** *informal* a man who would be the perfect husband for a particular woman: *Jill's still looking for Mr. Right.*

Mrs. /ˈmɪsɪz/ **Mrs. Smith/Jones etc.** used before a married woman's family name to be polite when you are speaking to her, writing to her, or talking about her [➡ **Miss, Ms.**]

MS the written abbreviation of **Mississippi**

Ms. /mɪz/ *n.* **Ms. Smith/Jones etc.** used before a woman's family name when she does not want to be called "Mrs." or "Miss," or when you do not know whether she is married or not

M.S., M.Sc. *n.* [C] **Master of Science** a university degree in science that you can earn after your first degree [➡ **M.A.**]

MSG *n.* [U] a chemical that is added to food to make it taste better

MT the written abbreviation of **Montana**

Mt. the written abbreviation of **mount**: *Mt. Everest*

much[1] /mʌtʃ/ *adv.* **1** [used before comparatives or superlatives] a lot: *I'm feeling much better.* | *This one is* ***much higher/bigger/longer etc.*** | *The job was* ***much more*** *difficult than I expected.* | *He was driving* ***much too*** *fast.*

USAGE

Use **much** with the comparative form of adjectives. Do not say "This school's very better." Use **much** instead: *This school's much better.*
➔ TOO

2 too much/so much/very much/how much etc. used in order to talk about the amount or degree to which someone does something or something happens: *Thank you very much!* | *How much further is it?* | *He's feeling so much better today.* **3 not ... much a)** only a little or hardly at all: *"Did you enjoy it?" "No, not much."* | *She isn't much younger than me.* | *Rob didn't like the movie very much.* **b)** used in order to say that something does not happen very often: *Kids* ***don't*** *play outside* ***as much as*** *they used to.* ➔ see Grammar box at LOT **4 much like sth/much as also much the same (as sth)** used in order to say that something is very similar to something else: *It tastes* ***very much like*** *butter.* **5 much less** used in order to say that something is even less true or less possible than another: *You'll never see him in a tie, much less a suit.*

much[2] *quantifier* **1** ["much" is used mainly in questions and negatives] a lot of something: *Was there much traffic?* | *We don't have much time.* | *The storm will bring rain to* ***much of*** *the state.* **2 how much** used in order to ask or talk about the amount or cost of something: *How much were the groceries* (=what did they cost)*?* | *It is not clear how much of the crime problem is gang-related.* **3 so much/too much** used in order to talk about an amount that is very large, especially one that is larger than it should be: *There was so much smoke we couldn't see anything.* | *Ray drinks too much.* **4 not ... much/nothing much** used in order to say that something is not important, interesting good, etc.: *"What's going on?" "Not much."* (=nothing that is interesting or important) | *I didn't think much of the book* (=I didn't like it). **5 as much (...) as** an amount that is equal and not less: *His bag weighed as much as he did.* **6 so much for sth** *spoken* said when a particular action, idea, statement, etc. was not useful or did not produce the result that was hoped for: *She wouldn't discuss it. So much for trying to compromise.* **7 be too much for sb** to be too difficult for someone: *The stairs were too much for her.*

GRAMMAR

much, a lot of
In sentences that are not negative and not questions, use **a lot of** rather than **much**: *There was a lot of traffic.* Do not say "There was much traffic."
➔ LOT

muck /mʌk/ *n.* [U] something such as dirt, mud, or another sticky substance: *the muck near the water's edge*

mu·cus /ˈmyukəs/ *n.* [U] a sticky liquid produced by parts of your body such as your nose —**mucous** *adj.*

mud /mʌd/ *n.* [U] **1** wet earth that is soft and sticky: *His boots were covered in mud.* **2 sb's name is mud** *spoken* said when people are annoyed at someone because s/he has caused trouble

mud·dle[1] /ˈmʌdl/ *v.*
muddle through (sth) *phr. v.* to continue doing something even though it is confusing or difficult

muddle[2] *n.* [C usually singular] a state in which things are confused, not organized correctly, or done badly: *a bureaucratic muddle*

mud·dled /ˈmʌdld/ *adj.* confused, messy, or not organized correctly: *a muddled line between reality and fantasy*

mud·dy[1] /ˈmʌdi/ *adj.* covered with mud, or containing mud: *muddy boots* | *muddy water*

THESAURUS

dirty, filthy, dusty, greasy
➔ see Thesaurus box at DIRTY[1]

muddy[2] *v.* past tense and past participle **muddied**, third person singular **muddies** [T] **1 muddy the issue/waters** to make a situation more complicated or more confusing than it was before **2** to make something dirty with mud

mud·slide /ˈmʌdslaɪd/ *n.* [C] a lot of very wet mud that has slid down the side of a hill

mud·sling·ing /ˈmʌdˌslɪŋɪŋ/ *n.* [U] the practice of saying bad things about someone so that other people will have a bad opinion of him/her: *political mudslinging* —**mudslinger** *n.* [C]

muf·fin /ˈmʌfən/ *n.* [C] a small, slightly sweet type of bread that often has fruit in it: *a blueberry muffin* → see picture on page A5

muffin

muf·fle /ˈmʌfəl/ *v.* [T] to make a sound less loud or clear: *Thick curtains muffled the traffic noise.* —**muffled** *adj.*: *the muffled sound of a TV in the next room*

muf·fler /ˈmʌflɚ/ *n.* [C] **1** a piece of equipment on a vehicle that makes the noise from the engine quieter **2** *old-fashioned* SCARF

mug¹ /mʌg/ *n.* [C] a large cup with straight sides and a handle: *a **mug of** coffee*

mug

mug² *v.* past tense and past participle **mugged**, present participle **mugging** [T] to attack and rob someone in a public place: *She was mugged in front of her apartment.* —**mugging** *n.* [U] —**mugger** *n.* [C]

> **THESAURUS**
> **steal, shoplift, burglarize, rob**
> → see Thesaurus box at STEAL¹

mug·gy /ˈmʌgi/ *adj.* comparative **muggier**, superlative **muggiest** *informal* muggy weather is unpleasant because it is too warm and wet [➡ **humid**] —**mugginess** *n.* [U]

mug·shot /ˈmʌgʃɑt/ *n.* [C] *informal* a photograph of a criminal's face taken by the police

Mu·ham·mad /moʊˈhæməd/ a PROPHET who taught ideas on which Islam is based

mulch /mʌltʃ/ *n.* [singular, U] decaying leaves that you put on the soil to improve its quality and to protect the roots of plants

mule /myul/ *n.* [C] an animal that has a DONKEY and a horse as parents

mull /mʌl/ *v.* [T] to heat wine or beer with sugar and SPICES

mull sth ⇔ **over** *phr. v.* to think about something carefully: *I decided to mull over his offer.*

mul·lah /ˈmʌlə/ *n.* [C] a religious leader or teacher in Islam

mul·ti·col·ored /ˈmʌltɪˌkʌlɚd/ *adj.* having many different colors: *a multicolored shirt*

mul·ti·cul·tur·al /ˌmʌltiˈkʌltʃərəl/ *adj.* involving people or ideas from many different countries, races, religions, etc.: *The U.S. is a multicultural society.* —**multiculturalism** *n.* [U]

mul·ti·lat·er·al /ˌmʌltɪˈlæt̬ərəl/ *adj.* involving several different countries, companies, etc. [➡ **bilateral, unilateral**]: *a **multilateral agreement** to stop the fighting*

mul·ti·me·di·a /ˌmʌltɪˈmidiə/ *adj.* [only before noun] using a mixture of sounds, words, pictures, etc. to give information, especially on a computer program —**multimedia** *n.* [U]

mul·ti·na·tion·al /ˌmʌltɪˈnæʃənl/ *adj.* **1** a multinational company has offices, businesses, etc. in several different countries

> **THESAURUS**
> **firm, business, corporation, subsidiary**
> → see Thesaurus box at COMPANY

2 involving people from several different countries: *a multinational peace-keeping force*

mul·ti·ple¹ /ˈmʌltəpəl/ *adj.* including or involving many parts, people, events, etc.: *He suffered multiple injuries to his legs. | She ordered multiple copies of the book.*

multiple² *n.* [C] a number that can be divided by a smaller number an exact number of times. For example, 20 is a multiple of 4 and 5

ˌmultiple ˈchoice *adj.* a multiple choice test or question shows several possible answers and you must choose the correct one

mul·ti·plex /ˈmʌltɪˌplɛks/ *n.* [C] a movie theater that has several rooms in which different movies are shown

mul·ti·pli·ca·tion /ˌmʌltəpləˈkeɪʃən/ *n.* [U] **1** a method of calculating in which you MULTIPLY numbers [➡ **division**] **2** *formal* a large increase in the size, amount, or number of something

mul·ti·plic·i·ty /ˌmʌltəˈplɪsət̬i/ *n.* [singular, U] *formal* a large number or great variety of things: *a **multiplicity of** views on the issue*

mul·ti·ply /ˈmʌltəˌplaɪ/ *v.* past tense and past participle **multiplied**, third person singular **multiplies** [I,T] **1** to increase greatly, or to make something do this: *The company's problems have multiplied over the past year.* **2** to do a calculation in which you add one number to itself a particular number of times [➡ **divide**]: *4 **multiplied by** 5 is 20* (4 x 5 = 20)

> **THESAURUS**
> **calculate, add, subtract, take away, divide, plus, minus**
> → see Thesaurus box at CALCULATE

mul·ti·pur·pose /ˌmʌltɪˈpɚpəs◂/ *adj.* having many different uses or purposes: *a multipurpose room*

mul·ti·ra·cial /ˌmʌltɪˈreɪʃəl◂/ *adj.* including or involving many different races of people [➡ **multicultural**]: *a multiracial society*

mul·ti·tude /ˈmʌltəˌtud/ *n. formal* **a multitude of sb/sth** a very large number of things or people: *a multitude of possible interpretations*

mum·ble /ˈmʌmbəl/ *v.* [I,T] to say something too quietly or not clearly enough, so that other people cannot understand you: *He mumbled something and left.*

THESAURUS

whisper, **mutter**, **murmur**
➔ see Thesaurus box at SAY[1]

mum·bo-jum·bo /ˌmʌmboʊ 'dʒʌmboʊ/ *n.* [U] *informal* something that is difficult to understand or that makes no sense: *legal mumbo-jumbo*

mum·mi·fy /'mʌməˌfaɪ/ *v.* [T] past tense and past participle **mummified**, third person singular **mummifies** to preserve a dead body as a MUMMY

mum·my /'mʌmi/ *n.* plural **mummies** [C] a dead body that has been preserved and often wrapped in cloth, especially in ancient Egypt

mumps /mʌmps/ *n.* **the mumps** an infectious illness in which your throat swells and becomes painful

munch /mʌntʃ/ *v.* [I,T] to eat something in a noisy way: *The kids were **munching on** popcorn.*

munch·ies /'mʌntʃiz/ *n.* [plural] *informal* **1 have the munchies** to feel hungry, especially for food such as cookies or POTATO CHIPS **2** foods such as cookies or POTATO CHIPS that are served at a party

mun·dane /mʌn'deɪn/ *adj.* ordinary and not interesting or exciting [= **boring**]: *Initially, the job was pretty mundane.* —**mundanely** *adv.*

mu·nic·i·pal /myu'nɪsəpəl/ *adj.* relating to the government of a town or city: *municipal elections*

mu·nic·i·pal·i·ty /myuˌnɪsə'pæləṭi/ *n.* plural **municipalities** [C] a town or city that has its own government

mu·ni·tions /myu'nɪʃənz/ *n.* [plural] military supplies such as bombs and large guns

mu·ral /'myʊrəl/ *n.* [C] a painting that is painted on a wall

mur·der[1] /'mɚdɚ/ *n.* **1** [C,U] the crime of deliberately killing someone: *Lowe has been **charged with murder**.* | *Police don't know who **committed** the **murders**.* | *the brutal **murder of** a young woman* | *Investigators have not yet found the **murder weapon**.*

THESAURUS

assault, **mugging**, **rape**
➔ see Thesaurus box at CRIME

2 get away with murder *informal* to not be punished for doing something wrong, or to be allowed to do anything you want: *The parents just let him get away with murder!*

murder[2] *v.* [T] to kill someone deliberately and illegally: *John Lennon was murdered in 1980.* —**murderer** *n.* [C] *a convicted murderer*

THESAURUS

kill, **commit manslaughter**, **commit suicide**, **assassinate**, **slaughter**, **massacre**, **execute sb**, **put sb to death**
➔ see Thesaurus box at KILL[1]

mur·der·ous /'mɚdərəs/ *adj.* very dangerous or violent and likely to kill someone: *He went into a murderous rage.*

murk·y /'mɚki/ *adj.* comparative **murkier**, superlative **murkiest** dark and difficult to see through: *murky water*

mur·mur[1] /'mɚmɚ/ *v.* [I,T] to say something in a soft quiet voice: *He softly murmured her name.* —**murmuring** *n.* [C,U]

THESAURUS

whisper, **mumble**, **mutter**
➔ see Thesaurus box at SAY[1]

murmur[2] *n.* [C] **1** a soft quiet sound made by someone's voice: *She answered in a low murmur.* **2 a murmur of approval/dissent/disbelief etc.** approval, etc. that is expressed in a soft or quiet way

mus·cle /'mʌsəl/ *n.* **1** [C,U] one of the pieces of flesh inside your body that join bones together and make your body move: *stomach/leg/thigh, etc. muscles* | *Weight lifting will strengthen your muscles.* | *I think I've **pulled** a **muscle*** (=injured a muscle). **2 military/political etc. muscle** military, etc. power or influence **3** [U] physical strength and power: *It **takes muscle** to move a piano.* **4 not move a muscle** to not move at all

mus·cu·lar /'mʌskyəlɚ/ *adj.* **1** having a lot of big muscles: *strong muscular arms* **2** related to or affecting the muscles: *a muscular disease*

muse /myuz/ *v.* [I] *formal* to imagine or think a lot about something

mu·se·um /myu'ziəm/ *n.* [C] a building where important objects are kept and shown to the public: *the Museum of Modern Art*

mush /mʌʃ/ *n.* [singular, U] a soft food that is part solid and part liquid

mush·room[1] /'mʌʃrum/ *n.* [C] one of several kinds of FUNGUS with stems and round tops, some of which can be eaten and some of which are poisonous ➔ see picture at VEGETABLE

mushroom[2] *v.* [I] to grow in size or numbers very quickly: *The city's population has mushroomed to over one million.*

'mushroom ˌcloud *n.* [C] a large cloud shaped like a MUSHROOM that is caused by a NUCLEAR explosion

mush·y /'mʌʃi/ *adj.* **1** soft and wet: *a mushy banana* **2** expressing love in a silly way: *mushy love stories*

mu·sic /'myuzɪk/ *n.* [U] **1** the arrangement of sounds made by instruments or voices in a way that is pleasant or exciting: *What kind of music does your band play?* | ***pop/country/classical etc. music*** | *I like to **listen to music**.* | *My favorite **piece of music** is Bach's "Magnificat."* | *Why don't you **put** some **music on*** (=turn on the radio or start playing a CD)?

THESAURUS

tune a series of musical notes that are nice to listen to: *Suzy was humming a tune.*
melody – a song or tune: *a lovely melody*

M

M

song – a short piece of music with words: *pop songs*
arrangement – a piece of music that has been written or changed for a particular instrument: *an arrangement for flute and guitar*
composition – a piece of music or art, or a poem: *one of Schubert's early compositions*
number – a piece of popular music, a song, a dance, etc. that forms part of a larger performance: *Spears sang several numbers from her most recent album.*

Types of music
pop (music), **rock (music)**, **rock'n'roll**, **heavy metal**, **reggae**, **house (music)**, **hip-hop**, **rap (music)**, **jazz**, **classical (music)**, **country (music)**, **folk (music)**

2 the art of writing or playing music: *music lessons* **3** a set of written marks representing music, or the paper that this is written on: *Jim plays the piano well, but he can't **read music**.* **4 face the music** to admit that you have done something wrong and accept punishment: *If he took the money, he'll have to face the music.*

mu·si·cal[1] /ˈmyuzɪkəl/ *adj.* **1** [only before noun] relating to music or consisting of music: *musical instruments* **2** good at playing or singing music: *I wasn't very musical as a child.* —**musically** *adv.*

musical[2] *n.* [C] a play or movie that uses songs and music to tell a story

TOPIC
play, **opera**, **ballet**
➔ see Topic box at THEATER

mu·si·cian /myuˈzɪʃən/ *n.* [C] someone who plays a musical instrument very well or as a job: *classical musicians*

musk /mʌsk/ *n.* [U] a strong smelling substance used to make PERFUME —**musky** *adj.*

mus·ket /ˈmʌskɪt/ *n.* [C] a type of gun used in past times

Mus·lim /ˈmʌzləm, ˈmʊz-, ˈmʊs-/ *adj.* relating to Islam —**Muslim** *n.* [C]

muss /mʌs/ *v.* [T] *informal* to make something messy, especially hair

mus·sel /ˈmʌsəl/ *n.* [C] a small sea animal with a black shell and a soft body that can be eaten

must[1] /məst; *strong* mʌst/ *modal verb* negative short form **mustn't** **1** past tense **had to** used in order to say that something is necessary because of a rule, or because it is the best thing to do: *The $60 passport fee must accompany your application.* | *It's getting late – I really must go.* ➔ see Grammar box at HAVE TO

USAGE
If an action is not necessary, you can say that you **don't need to** do it: *I don't need to leave until 10.*
If someone **must not** do something, s/he is not allowed to do it. **Must not** is quite formal and is used especially in written English: *You must not take any sharp objects on the plane.*
Do not say **don't need to** to mean **must not**.

2 past tense **must have** used in order to say that something is very likely to be true: *George must be almost eighty years old now.* | *We must have gone the wrong way.* **3** used in order to suggest that someone do something: ***You must** see his new film.*

must[2] /mʌst/ *n.* **a must** *informal* something that you must do or must have: *The Greens Cookbook is a must for any serious vegetarian.*

mus·tache /ˈmʌstæʃ, məˈstæʃ/ *n.* [C] hair that grows on a man's upper lip ➔ see picture at HAIR

mus·tang /ˈmʌstæŋ/ *n.* [C] a small wild horse

mus·tard /ˈmʌstɚd/ *n.* [U] a yellow SAUCE with a strong taste, usually eaten in small amounts with meat

mus·ter[1] /ˈmʌstɚ/ *v.* **muster (up) courage/support etc.** to find or gather as much courage, etc. as you can in order to do something difficult: *I'm still trying to muster up the courage to speak to her.*

muster[2] *n.* **pass muster** to be accepted as good enough for something

must·n't /ˈmʌsənt/ *modal verb* the short form of "must not": *You mustn't forget to tell her what I said.*

must·y /ˈmʌsti/ *adj.* having a wet unpleasant smell: *musty old books*

mu·ta·ble /ˈmyut̬əbəl/ *adj. formal* able or likely to change [≠ **immutable**] —**mutability** /ˌmyut̬əˈbɪlət̬i/ *n.* [U]

mu·tant /ˈmyutˀnt/ *n.* [C] an animal or plant that is different from others of the same kind because of a change in its GENES —**mutant** *adj.*

mu·tate /ˈmyuteɪt/ *v.* [I] if an animal or plant mutates, it becomes different from others of the same kind because of a change in its GENES —**mutation** /myuˈteɪʃən/ *n.* [C,U]

mute[1] /myut/ *v.* [T] to make a sound quieter, or to make it disappear completely: *He muted the TV during the commercials.*

mute[2] *adj.* unable to speak —**mutely** *adv.*

mut·ed /ˈmyut̬ɪd/ *adj.* **1 muted criticism/response etc.** criticism, etc. that is not expressed strongly **2** quieter than usual: *the muted sound of snoring from the next room* **3** a muted color is less bright than usual

mu·ti·late /ˈmyut̬lˌeɪt/ *v.* [T] to damage someone or something severely, especially by removing part of it: *bodies mutilated in the explosion* —**mutilation** /ˌmyut̬lˈeɪʃən/ *n.* [C,U]

mu·ti·nous /ˈmyutˀn-əs/ *adj.* involved in a mutiny: *mutinous soldiers*

mu·ti·ny /ˈmyutˀn-i/ *n.* plural **mutinies** [C,U] a situation in which soldiers or SAILORS refuse to obey someone in authority and try to take control for themselves —**mutiny** *v.* [I]

mutt /mʌt/ *n.* [C] *informal* a dog that does not belong to a particular breed

mut·ter /ˈmʌtə/ *v.* [I,T] to speak in a quiet voice, especially when you are complaining about something but do not want other people to hear you: *What are you muttering about?*

> **THESAURUS**
> **whisper**, **mumble**, **murmur**
> ➔ see Thesaurus box at SAY[1]

mut·ton /ˈmʌt̚n/ *n.* [U] the meat from a sheep

mu·tu·al /ˈmyutʃuəl/ *adj.* **1** a feeling that is mutual is felt by two or more people toward one another: *A good marriage is marked by* ***mutual respect***. | *European nations can live together in a spirit of* ***mutual trust***. **2 mutual agreement/consent** a situation in which two or more people both agree to something: *He has left the company* ***by mutual consent***. **3** shared by two or more people: *We were introduced by a mutual friend* (=someone we both know). **4 the feeling is mutual** *spoken* said when you have the same feeling about someone as s/he has toward you: *"You really drive me crazy sometimes!" "The feeling is mutual!"* —**mutuality** /ˌmyutʃuˈæləṭi/ *n.* [U]

ˈmutual fund *n.* [C] a company through which you can buy SHARES of other companies

mu·tu·al·ly /ˈmyutʃuəli, -tʃəli/ *adv.* **1** done, felt, or experienced by two or more people: *They have mutually agreed to go their separate ways.* **2 mutually exclusive** if two ideas, beliefs, etc. are mutually exclusive, they cannot both exist or be true at the same time

Mu·zak /ˈmyuzæk/ *n.* [U] *trademark* recorded music that is played continuously in airports, offices, etc.

muz·zle[1] /ˈmʌzəl/ *n.* [C] **1** the nose and mouth of an animal, especially a dog or horse **2** the end of the BARREL of a gun **3** something that you put over a dog's mouth so it cannot bite someone

muzzle[2] *v.* [T] **1** to prevent someone from speaking freely or from expressing his/her opinions: *an attempt to muzzle the press* **2** to put a muzzle over a dog's mouth so that it cannot bite someone

my /maɪ/ *determiner* belonging or relating to the person who is speaking: *That's my car over there.* | *I tried not to let my feelings show.* | *My son is in college.*

my·op·ic /maɪˈɑpɪk, -ˈoʊ-/ *adj. technical* NEARSIGHTED —**myopia** /maɪˈoʊpiə/ *n.* [U]

myr·i·ad /ˈmɪriəd/ *n.* [C] *literary* a very large number of something: ***a myriad of*** *stars in the sky* —**myriad** *adj.*

my·self /maɪˈsɛlf/ *pron.* **1** used by the person speaking or writing to show that s/he is affected by his/her own action: *I made myself a cup of coffee.* | *I blame myself for what has happened.* **2** used in order to emphasize "I" or "me": *They say it's a beautiful place, but I myself have never been there.* **3 (all) by myself a)** without help: *Look, Mommy – I tied my shoes all by myself!* **b)** alone: *I went to the movie by myself.* **4 (all) to myself** for my own use: *I* ***had*** *the whole swimming pool* ***to myself*** *today.* **5 not be myself** *spoken* said when you are not behaving or feeling as you usually do because you are sick or upset: *I'm sorry for what I said – I'm not myself these days.*

mys·te·ri·ous /mɪˈstɪriəs/ *adj.* **1** strange and difficult to explain or understand: *the mysterious disappearance of our neighbor*

> **THESAURUS**
> **strange**, **funny**, **peculiar**, **odd**, **weird**, **bizarre**
> ➔ see Thesaurus box at STRANGE[1]

2 not saying much about something because you want it to be a secret: *Oliver is being very* ***mysterious about*** *his plans.* —**mysteriously** *adv.*: *Modotti died mysteriously in 1945.*

mys·ter·y /ˈmɪstəri/ *n.* plural **mysteries** **1** [C] something that is difficult to explain or understand: *The location of the stolen money* ***remains a mystery***. | *It won't be easy to* ***solve*** *the* ***mystery***. **2** [C] a story, especially about a murder, in which events are not explained until the end: *the Sherlock Holmes mystery stories* **3** [U] a quality that makes someone or something seem strange, interesting, and difficult to explain or understand: *There's an* ***air of mystery*** *about him that intrigues people.*

mys·ti·cal /ˈmɪstɪkəl/ **also** **mys·tic** /ˈmɪstɪk/ *adj.* relating to religious or magical powers that people cannot understand —**mystically** *adv.*

mys·ti·cism /ˈmɪstəˌsɪzəm/ *n.* [U] a religious practice in which someone tries to gain knowledge about God and truth by praying and thinking very seriously —**mystic** /ˈmɪstɪk/ *n.* [C]

mys·ti·fy /ˈmɪstəˌfaɪ/ *v.* past tense and past participle **mystified**, third person singular **mystifies** [T] to make someone feel confused and unable to explain or understand something: *a case that mystified the police* —**mystifying** *adj.*

mys·tique /mɪˈstik/ *n.* [U] *formal* the quality that makes something seem mysterious, special, or interesting

myth /mɪθ/ *n.* [C,U] **1** an ancient story, especially one that explains a natural or historical event, or this type of story in general: *Greek myths*

> **THESAURUS**
> **story**, **tale**, **legend**, **fable**
> ➔ see Thesaurus box at STORY

2 an idea or story that many people believe, but that is not true: ***the myth that*** *older workers are not productive*

myth·i·cal /ˈmɪθɪkəl/ *adj.* **1** existing only in a myth: *mythical creatures such as the Minotaur* **2** imagined or invented

my·thol·o·gy /mɪˈθɑlədʒi/ *n.* [U] **1** ancient MYTHS in general, or the beliefs that they represent: *stories from Greek mythology* **2** ideas or stories that many people have, but that are not true —**mythological** /ˌmɪθəˈlɑdʒɪkəl/ *adj.*

M

N, n

N

N, n /ɛn/ the fourteenth letter of the English alphabet

N the written abbreviation of **north** or **northern**

n the written abbreviation of **noun**

N/A not applicable – used on a form to show that you do not need to answer a particular question

nab /næb/ *v.* past tense and past participle **nabbed**, present participle **nabbing** [T] *informal* to catch someone doing something illegal: *The police nabbed him for speeding.*

nag[1] /næg/ *v.* past tense and past participle **nagged**, present participle **nagging** [I,T] **1** to continuously ask someone to do something in an annoying way: *Shawna has been **nagging** me **to** fix the kitchen sink.* **2** to make someone feel continuously worried or uncomfortable over a period of time: *A problem had been **nagging at** me for days.*

nag[2] *n.* [C] *informal* someone who NAGS continuously

nag·ging /ˈnægɪŋ/ *adj.* [only before noun] making you worry or feel pain all the time: *I have this **nagging feeling** that he's lying.* | *a **nagging injury***

nail[1] /neɪl/ *n.* [C] **1** a thin pointed piece of metal with a flat end that you push into a piece of wood, etc. using a hammer **2** the hard flat part that covers the top end of your fingers and toes: *Stop **biting** your **nails**!* | *I need to **cut/file/paint** my **nails*** → **fight (sb/sth) tooth and nail** at TOOTH

COLLOCATIONS

You **cut/clip** your **nails** with **scissors** or **nail clippers**.
You **file** your **nails** (=rub them) with a **nail file** to make them the right shape.
Some women put **nail polish** on their nails.
If you **have a manicure**, someone shapes and polishes your nails for you.

nail[2] *v.* [T] **1** to fasten something to something else with a nail: *The windows were **nailed shut**.* | *She **nailed** the poster **to** the wall.* **2** *informal* to catch someone who has done something wrong and prove that s/he is guilty: *They finally **nailed** him **for** fraud.* **3** *informal* to do something exactly right, or to be exactly correct: *Jackson nailed his final shot, and the Bulls won the game.*

nail sth ⇔ **down** *phr. v.* to reach a final and definite decision about something: *The contract hasn't been nailed down yet.*

nail·brush /ˈneɪlbrʌʃ/ *n.* [C] a small stiff brush used for cleaning your nails

ˈnail file *n.* [C] a thin piece of metal with a rough surface, used for shaping your nails

ˈnail ˌpolish *n.* [U] colored or clear liquid that you paint on your nails to make them look attractive

na·ive /nɑˈiv/ *adj.* lacking any experience of life, so that you believe most people are honest and kind and that only good things will happen to you [➡ **innocent**]: *a naive young girl* —**naively** *adv.* —**naivety**, **naiveté** /nɑˈivəˌteɪ, nɑˌivˈteɪ/ *n.* [U] [C]

na·ked /ˈneɪkɪd/ *adj.* **1** not wearing any clothes [= **nude**]: *The child was running naked through the backyard.* | *He was **stark naked*** (=completely naked).

THESAURUS

nude – not wearing any clothes, used especially when talking about people in paintings, movies, etc.: *a nude photograph of a beautiful woman*
undressed – not wearing any clothes, especially because you have just taken them off in order to go to bed, take a bath, etc.: *Rachel got undressed and ready for bed.*
bare – not covered by clothes: *Their long bare legs dangled over the edge of the porch.*
have nothing on also **not have anything on**: *He didn't have anything on except a towel.*

2 the naked eye if you can see something with the naked eye, you can see it without using something such as a TELESCOPE to help you: *On a clear night, many other planets are **visible to the naked eye**.* —**nakedness** *n.* [U] —**nakedly** *adv.*

name[1] /neɪm/ *n.* **1** [C] the word that someone or something is called or known by: *My **first name** is Vera and my **last name** is Smith.* | *She **called** him **by** his first **name*** (=she used his first name when talking to him). | *Please write your **full name*** (=complete name) *and address.* | *I can't remember the **name of** the hotel.* | *They don't have a **name for** the baby yet.*

THESAURUS

Types of names
first name/given name – for example "Bret" in the name Bret Stern
last name/family name/surname – for example "Potter" in the name Harry Potter
middle name – the name between your first and last names
full name – your complete name
maiden name – a woman's family name before she got married and changed it
nickname – a name your friends and family use for you, not your real name
stage name – the name an actor uses that is not his/her real name
pen name/pseudonym – a name a writer uses that is not his/her real name
assumed name/alias – a false name, often one used by a criminal

2 a big/famous/household name *informal* someone who is famous: *the biggest names in Hollywood* **3** [singular] the opinion that people have about a person, company, etc. [= **reputa-**

tion]: *He has **given** baseball a **bad name*** (=made people have a bad opinion about it). | *He is determined to **clear his** family's good **name*** (=make people respect them again). **4 in sb's name** to officially belong to someone: *The house is in my wife's name.* **5 (do sth) in the name of science/religion etc.** to use science, religion, etc. as the reason for doing something, even if it is wrong **6 call sb names** to say something insulting to someone **7 the name of the game** the most important thing or quality in a particular activity

name² *v.* [T] **1** to give someone or something a particular name: *They named their son Jacob.* | *We **named** the baby Henry, **after** his grandfather* (=gave him the same name as his grandfather). | *RFK Stadium was **named for** Robert F. Kennedy* (=it was given his name to show respect for him). **2** to say what the name of someone or something is: *He refused to name his clients.* | *Wells was **named as** the leading suspect.* **3** to officially choose someone for a particular job: *Roy Johnson was **named as** the new manager.* **4 you name it** *spoken* said after a list of things to mean that there are many more that you could mention: *Beer, whiskey, wine – you name it and I've **got it**!* **5 name names** to give the names of people who are involved in something, especially something wrong or something they want to hide: *She did not name names, but I think she was referring to Richard.*

'name-ˌcalling *n.* [U] the act of using an unpleasant or insulting word to describe someone in order to hurt or embarrass him/her

name·drop·ping /'neɪmˌdrɑpɪŋ/ *n.* [U] *disapproving* the act of mentioning the name of a famous or important person to make it seem that you know them well —**namedrop** *v.* [I]

name·less /'neɪmlɪs/ *adj.* **1** not known by a name [= **anonymous**]: *a gift from a nameless businessman* **2 sb who shall remain nameless** *spoken* used when you want to say that someone has done something wrong, but without saying his/her name **3** having no name: *millions of nameless stars*

name·ly /'neɪmli/ *adv.* used when saying the name of the person or thing you are talking about: *The movie won two Oscars, namely "Best Actor" and "Best Director."*

name·sake /'neɪmseɪk/ *n.* **sb's namesake** someone or something that has the same name as someone or something else

'name tag *n.* [C] a small sign with your name on it that you attach to your clothes so that people know who you are

nan·ny /'næni/ *n.* plural **nannies** [C] a woman whose job is to take care of a family's children, usually in the children's own home

nap /næp/ *n.* [C] a short sleep during the day: *Dad usually **takes a nap** in the afternoon.* —**nap** *v.* [I]

na·palm /'neɪpɑm/ *n.* [U] a liquid used in bombs to burn people and things

nape /neɪp/ *n.* [singular] the back of your neck: *He kissed **the nape of** her **neck**.*

nap·kin /'næpkɪn/ *n.* a small piece of cloth or paper used for cleaning your mouth or hands when you are eating

narc¹ /nɑrk/ *n.* [C] *informal* a police officer who deals with catching people who use and sell illegal drugs

narc² *v.* [I] *slang* to tell the police about something illegal that someone is doing, especially when it involves drugs: *Tanya would never **narc on** us.*

nar·cis·sis·tic /ˌnɑrsə'sɪstɪk/ *adj. formal* having too much admiration for your own appearance or abilities —**narcissism** /'nɑrsəˌsɪzəm/ *n.* [U] —**narcissist** *n.* [C]

nar·cot·ic /nɑr'kɑt̬ɪk/ *n.* [C] a strong drug such as HEROIN that stops pain and makes people sleep —**narcotic** *adj.*

nar·rate /'næreɪt, næ'reɪt/ *v.* [T] if someone narrates a movie or television program, s/he describes or explains what is happening in the pictures: *a documentary narrated by Robert Redford* —**narration** /næ'reɪʃən/ *n.* [C,U]

nar·ra·tive /'nærət̬ɪv/ *n.* [C,U] *formal* a description of events that is told as a story —**narrative** *adj.*

nar·ra·tor /'næˌreɪt̬ɚ/ *n.* [C] someone who tells the story in a movie, book, etc.

nar·row¹ /'næroʊ/ *adj.* **1** only measuring a small distance from side to side [≠ **wide**]: *a long narrow street* | *The stairs were very narrow.* **2 narrow defeat/victory etc.** a defeat, victory, etc. that is achieved with difficulty or happens by only a small amount: *France finished in first place after a narrow victory over Brazil.* | *Kennedy **won** the election **by a narrow margin*** (=by a very small amount). **3** *disapproving* a narrow attitude or way of looking at a situation is too limited and does not consider enough possibilities: *She has a very **narrow view** of life.* **4 narrow escape** an occasion when you just avoid something bad or dangerous that almost happens to you —**narrowness** *n.* [U]

narrow² *v.* [I,T] **1** to become more narrow, or to make something do this: *The road narrows here.* | *She **narrowed** her **eyes** and frowned.* **2 also narrow down** to reduce the number of possibilities or choices: *The police have narrowed down their list of suspects.*

narrow³ *n.* → **the straight and narrow** at STRAIGHT³

nar·row·ly /'næroʊli/ *adv.* **1** only by a small amount: *Smith narrowly lost the election* | *They narrowly escaped death in the accident.* **2** in a limited way: *The law is being interpreted too narrowly.*

ˌnarrow-'minded *adj. disapproving* not willing to accept ideas or beliefs that are new and different [➡ **prejudiced**]

N

N

na·sal /ˈneɪzəl/ *adj.* **1** a nasal sound or voice comes mostly through your nose **2** [only before noun] relating to the nose: *the nasal cavity* —**nasally** *adv.*

nas·ty /ˈnæsti/ *adj.* comparative **nastier**, superlative **nastiest** **1** unkind or unpleasant: *Matt has been saying some nasty things about me.* | *a nasty old man* | *I don't understand why Stacy was so* ***nasty to*** *us.* | *nasty weather* | *a nasty habit*

> **THESAURUS**
> **mean**, **cruel**, **unkind**, **thoughtless**
> → see Thesaurus box at MEAN[2]

2 *spoken* having a bad appearance, smell, or taste: *That looks like a nasty bruise.* | *Those toilets are so nasty.* —**nastiness** *n.* [U] —**nastily** *adv.*

na·tion /ˈneɪʃən/ *n.* [C] **1** a country and its people, used especially when considering its political and economic structures: *The President is addressing the nation tomorrow.* | *People all across the nation were protesting against the war.* | *the major industrialized nations*

> **THESAURUS**
> **country**, **state**, **power**, **land**
> → see Thesaurus box at COUNTRY[1]

2 a large group of people of the same race who speak the same language: *the Cherokee nation*

> **THESAURUS**
> **race**, **people**, **tribe**, **ethnic group**
> → see Thesaurus box at RACE[1]

na·tion·al[1] /ˈnæʃənl/ *adj.* **1** relating to a whole nation rather than to part of it or to other nations [➡ **international**]: *the national news* | *an issue of national importance* **2** [only before noun] owned or controlled by the government: *Yosemite National Park*

national[2] *n.* [C] someone who is a citizen of one country but is living in another country [➡ **alien**, **citizen**]: *a Korean national living in the U.S.*

ˌnational ˈanthem *n.* [C] the official song of a nation that is sung or played at public occasions

na·tion·al·ism /ˈnæʃənlˌɪzəm/ *n.* [U] **1** the belief that your country is better than any other country **2** the desire of people who have the same race or who speak the same language, etc. to have their own country: *the rise of nationalism in Eastern Europe*

na·tion·al·ist /ˈnæʃənl-ɪst/ *adj.* wanting to become politically independent, or wanting to remain this way —**nationalist** *n.* [C] *Quebec nationalists*

na·tion·al·is·tic /ˌnæʃnəˈlɪstɪk/ *adj.* believing that your country is better than other countries [➡ **patriotic**]

na·tion·al·i·ty /ˌnæʃəˈnæləṭi/ *n.* plural **nationalities** [C,U] **1** the legal right of belonging to a particular country [= **citizenship**]: *He* ***has*** *British/Swiss, etc.* ***nationality***. ▶ Don't say "My nationality is Mexican/Swedish etc." Say "I come from Mexico/Sweden etc." ◀ **2** a large group of people who have the same race, language, or culture: *There are children of many different nationalities at our school.*

na·tion·al·ize /ˈnæʃənəˌlaɪz/ *v.* [T] if a government nationalizes a large company or an industry, it buys it or takes control of it [➡ **privatize**]

na·tion·al·ly /ˈnæʃənl-i/ *adv.* by or to everyone in a nation: *a series of nationally televised debates*

ˌnational ˈmonument *n.* [C] a building or a special place that is protected by the government for people to visit

ˌnational seˈcurity *n.* [U] the ways in which a country protects its citizens or keeps its secrets safe, for example by having a strong army

na·tion·wide /ˌneɪʃənˈwaɪd◂/ *adj.* happening or existing in every part of a nation: *nationwide price increases* | *The brewery employs about 3000 people nationwide.* —**nationwide** *adv.*

> **THESAURUS**
> **everywhere**, **all over**, **worldwide**, **everyplace**
> → see Thesaurus box at EVERYWHERE

na·tive[1] /ˈneɪṭɪv/ *adj.* **1 native country/land etc.** the place where you were born: *He returned to his native Poland.* **2 native Californian/New Yorker etc.** someone who was born in California, etc. **3** growing, living, or produced in a particular area: *a plant* ***native to*** *Ecuador* **4 native language/tongue** the language you first learned to speak

native[2] *n.* [C] **1** someone who was born in a particular country: *Andrea is a* ***native of*** *Brazil.* **2** [usually plural] a word used by white people in the past to refer to the people who lived in Africa, America, etc. before Europeans arrived. Many people now consider this word offensive.

ˌNative Aˈmerican *n.* [C] someone who belongs to one of the tribes who were living in North America before the Europeans arrived —**Native American** *adj.*

ˌnative ˈspeaker *n.* [C] someone who has learned a particular language as his/her first language, rather than as a foreign language [≠ **non-native speaker**]: *a* ***native speaker of*** *English*

NATO /ˈneɪṭoʊ/ *n.* **North Atlantic Treaty Organization** a group of countries in North America and Europe that give military help to each other

nat·u·ral[1] /ˈnætʃərəl/ *adj.* **1** normal or usual, and what you would expect in a particular situation [≠ **unnatural**]: ***It's only natural to*** (=it is completely normal) *have doubts before your wedding.* | *It's not* ***natural for*** *a four-year-old* ***to*** *be so quiet.* **2** existing in nature, not caused, made, or controlled by people: *earthquakes and other* ***natural disasters*** | *natural fibers like cotton* | *He died of* ***natural causes*** (=because of illness or old age).

THESAURUS

Describing things that are natural

wild – used about flowers, plants, and animals that are not controlled by people: *Wild dogs roamed the streets.*
pure – used about food or drink that has not had anything added to it: *pure orange juice*
organic – used about fruit, vegetables, meat, etc. that is produced without using chemicals: *organic tomatoes*

Describing things that are not natural

artificial – not made of natural materials or substances, but made to be like something natural: *The drink contains artificial coloring.*
processed – used about food that has been treated with chemicals to make it stay fresh or look good: *processed cheese*
man-made – made by people, but similar to something natural: *a man-made lake*
synthetic – used about cloth or substances made by a chemical process: *nylon, polyester, and other synthetic materials*

3 [only before noun] having a particular skill or ability without being taught: *a **natural athlete*** **4** behaving in a way that is normal and shows you are relaxed and not trying to pretend: *Just be natural – you'll do fine.* —**naturalness** *n.* [U]

natural[2] *n.* **be a natural** to be very good at doing something without being taught

ˌnatural ˈgas *n.* [U] gas used for cooking or heating that is taken from under the earth or ocean

ˌnatural ˈhistory *n.* [U] the study of plants, animals, and minerals

nat·u·ral·ist /ˈnætʃərəlɪst/ *n.* [C] someone who studies plants, animals, and other living things

nat·u·ral·ized /ˈnætʃərəˌlaɪzd/ *adj.* a naturalized citizen is someone who becomes a citizen of a country that s/he was not born in —**naturalization** /ˌnætʃərələˈzeɪʃən/ *n.* [U]

nat·u·ral·ly /ˈnætʃərəli/ *adv.* **1** in a way that you would expect: *Naturally, you'll want to discuss this with your wife.* | *Since her art is so unusual, it **naturally enough** attracts attention.* **2** *spoken* used in order to agree with what someone has said, or to answer "of course" to a question: *"Are you excited to be home?" "Naturally."* **3** as a natural feature or quality, not made or done by people: *Allison's hair is naturally curly.* | *Golf seemed to **come naturally** to him* (=he was good at it without being taught). **4** in a relaxed manner without trying to look or sound different from usual: *Just **speak naturally** and pretend the microphone isn't there.* | *Try to **act naturally**.*

ˌnatural ˈresources *n.* [plural] all the land, minerals, energy, etc. that exist in a country

ˌnatural seˈlection *n.* [U] *technical* the process by which only the plants and animals that are naturally appropriate for life in their environment will continue to live

na·ture /ˈneɪtʃɚ/ *n.* **1** [U] everything that exists in the world that is not made or controlled by humans, such as animals, plants, weather, etc.: *All of these minerals are found **in nature**.* | *the forces of nature* (=wind, rain, etc.) | *a nature walk/trail* **2** [C,U] the character or particular qualities of someone or something: *He was an optimist **by nature**.* | *The **nature of** my work requires a lot of traveling.* | *Of course she's jealous – it's **human nature*** (=the feelings and qualities that all people have). **3** [singular] a particular type of thing: *He provided support **of a** financial **nature**.* **4 let nature take its course** to allow events to happen without doing anything to change the results → SECOND NATURE

ˈnature reˌserve *n.* [C] an area of land in which animals and plants are protected

naught /nɔt/ *n.* [U] *old-fashioned* nothing: *All their plans **came to naught*** (=failed).

naugh·ty /ˈnɔṭi/ *adj.* comparative **naughtier**, superlative **naughtiest** a naughty child behaves badly and is rude or does not obey adults —**naughtiness** *n.* [U] —**naughtily** *adv.*

nau·se·a /ˈnɔziə, ˈnɔʒə, ˈnɔʃə/ *n.* [U] *formal* the feeling you have when you think you are going to VOMIT

nau·se·at·ed /ˈnɔziˌeɪṭɪd/ *adj.* feeling that you are going to VOMIT: *When I was pregnant I felt nauseated all the time.* —**nauseate** *v.* [T]

nau·se·at·ing /ˈnɔziˌeɪṭɪŋ/ *adj.* making you feel that you are going to VOMIT: *the nauseating smell of cigar smoke*

nau·seous /ˈnɔʃəs, -ʒəs/ *adj.* **1** feeling that you are going to VOMIT: *I suddenly **felt nauseous**.* **2** *formal* making you feel that you are going to VOMIT: *nauseous odors*

nau·ti·cal /ˈnɔṭɪkəl/ *adj.* relating to ships or sailing: *a distance of 300 **nautical miles*** —**nautically** *adv.*

na·val /ˈneɪvəl/ *adj.* relating to the navy: *a naval battle*

na·vel /ˈneɪvəl/ *n.* [C] *formal* BELLY BUTTON

nav·i·ga·ble /ˈnævɪgəbəl/ *adj.* a river, lake, etc. that is navigable is deep and wide enough for ships to travel on

nav·i·gate /ˈnævəˌgeɪt/ *v.* **1** [I,T] to plan the way a car, ship, or airplane travels to a place, using a map: *Rick usually drives and I navigate.* **2** [I,T] to find your way around a particular WEBSITE, or to move from one website to another: *The university's website is really easy to navigate.* **3** [I,T] to find your way through a complicated system, set of rules, etc.: *A social worker is helping Kelly navigate the legal system.* **4** [T] to sail along a river or other area of water —**navigation** /ˌnævəˈgeɪʃən/ *n.* [U]

nav·i·ga·tor /ˈnævəˌgeɪṭɚ/ *n.* [C] the officer on a ship or aircraft who plans the way along which it travels

na·vy /ˈneɪvi/ *n.* plural **navies** **1** [C usually singular] the part of a country's military forces that is organized for fighting a war at sea [➡ **air force**, **army**, **marines**]: *My dad was 20 when he* ***joined the navy***. | *Frank is* ***in the navy***. **2** [U] navy blue

ˌnavy ˈblue *adj.* very dark blue —**navy blue** *n.* [U]

NBC *n.* **National Broadcasting Company** one of the national television and radio companies in the U.S.

N

NC the written abbreviation of **North Carolina**

NCAA *n.* **National Collegiate Athletic Association** the organization that is in charge of sports at American colleges and universities

NCO *n.* **Noncommissioned Officer** a soldier such as a CORPORAL or SERGEANT

ND the written abbreviation of **North Dakota**

NE **1** the written abbreviation of **northeast** **2** the written abbreviation of **Nebraska**

near¹ /nɪr/ *adv., prep.* **1** only a short distance from someone or something: *Why don't we meet near the library?* | *I'd like to live* ***nearer to*** *the ocean.* | *Is there a bank near here?*

THESAURUS

close – not far from someone or something: *He sat close to his mom.*
not far (away) – not a long distance away: *The park's not far away.*
nearby – near here or near a particular place: *Do you live nearby?* | *a nearby farm*
within walking distance (of sth) – easy to walk to from somewhere: *The beach is within walking distance of the hotel.*
local – used about stores, schools, etc. that are in the area where you live: *your local library*
neighboring – used about towns, countries, etc. that are very near a particular place: *discussions between Egypt and neighboring states*
➔ LOCALLY

USAGE

Near and **close** are both used to talk about short distances between things.
Near can be followed directly by a noun: *Is the hotel near the beach?*
Close cannot be followed directly by a noun.
Close must be followed by the preposition "to" and then a noun: *They live close to the park.*

2 close in time to a particular event: *She got more and more nervous as the wedding* ***drew near*** (=became closer in time). | *The construction work is now near completion.* **3** **nowhere near** not at all close to a particular quality or state: *His latest movie is nowhere near as good as the last one.* | *We're nowhere near finished.* **4** **near perfect/impossible etc.** *informal* almost perfect, impossible, etc. [= **nearly**]: *a near perfect test score*

near

near² *adj.* **1** only a short distance from someone or something: *The nearest town* (=the town that is the closest) *is 20 miles away.* **2** very close to having a particular quality or being a particular thing: *His explanation is as* ***near to*** *the truth as we'll get.* **3** **in the near future** at a time that is not very far in the future: *We will have a new teacher joining us in the near future.* **4** **near miss** a situation in which something almost hits something else

near·by /ˌnɪrˈbaɪ◂/ *adj.* [only before noun] not far away: *Rita was taken to a nearby hospital.* —**nearby** *adv.*: *The teacher stood nearby.*

THESAURUS

close, close by, not far (away), within walking distance, local, in the neighborhood
➔ see Thesaurus box at NEAR¹, LOCALLY

near·ly /ˈnɪrli/ *adv.* almost, but not completely or exactly: *It took me nearly five hours to write the essay.* | ***Nearly all*** *of our students go on to college.* | *The team is* ***not nearly as*** *good as it could have been.*

near·sight·ed /ˈnɪrˌsaɪt̬ɪd/ *adj.* unable to see things clearly unless they are close to you [≠ **farsighted**] —**nearsightedness** *n.* [U]

neat /nit/ *adj.* **1** *spoken* very good, enjoyable, interesting, etc.: *What a neat idea!* | *He's a really neat guy.* **2** carefully arranged and not messy: *Chris looked neat and well shaven.* | *They keep their house* ***neat and clean***. **3** a neat person does not like his/her things or house to be messy **4** simple and effective: *a neat solution to the problem* —**neatly** *adv.* —**neatness** *n.* [U]

nec·es·sar·i·ly /ˌnɛsəˈsɛrəli/ *adv.* **not necessarily** used to say that something may not be true or may not always happen, even if it might be reasonable to expect it to: *Expensive restaurants do not necessarily have the best food.*

nec·es·sar·y /ˈnɛsəˌsɛri/ *adj.* **1** needed in order for you to do something or have something [➡ **essential**]: *Will you make all the necessary arrangements?* | *Don't call me unless it's* ***absolutely necessary***. | *He will do anything* ***necessary to*** *win.* | *It might be* ***necessary for*** *me to have an operation.* | *We're prepared to go to war,* ***if necessary***.

THESAURUS

essential – important and necessary: *Education is essential if you want a good job.*
vital – extremely important and necessary: *Vital information was not given to the decision makers.*
mandatory – if something is mandatory, it must be done because of a rule or law: *Parents do not want school uniform to become mandatory.*
compulsory – if something is compulsory, you must do it: *Service in the army was compulsory.*

2 a necessary evil something bad or unpleasant that you have to accept in order to achieve what you want: *He regarded work as a necessary evil.*

ne·ces·si·tate /nəˈsɛsəˌteɪt/ *v.* [T] *formal* to make something necessary

ne·ces·si·ty /nəˈsɛsət̬i/ *n.* plural **necessities** **1** [C] something that you need to have or that must happen: *A car is an **absolute necessity** in the suburbs.* | *A valid driver's license is a **necessity for** renting a car.* | ***basic necessities** like food and shelter* **2** [U] the fact of something being necessary: *Many parents are questioning **the necessity of** standardized tests.* | *She went back to work, but only **out of necessity**.*

neck¹ /nɛk/ *n.* [C] **1** the part of your body that joins your head to your shoulders: *She was wearing a gold chain **around** her **neck**.* | *Swans have long slender necks.* ➔ see picture on page A3 **2 V-necked/open-necked, etc.** also **v-neck/open-neck** if a piece of clothing is v-necked, open-necked, etc., it has that type of neck: *a V-neck sweater* | *an open-necked shirt* **3** the long, narrow part of something such as a bottle or a musical instrument **4 neck and neck** *informal* if two people, teams, etc. are neck and neck in a competition, they both have an equal chance of winning **5 in this neck of the woods** *informal* in this area or part of the country: *What are you doing in this neck of the woods?* **6 be up to your neck in sth** *informal* to be in a very difficult situation, or to be very busy doing something: *Mason is up to his neck in debt.*

neck² *v.* [I] *informal old-fashioned* if two people neck, they kiss for a long time in a sexual way

neck·lace /ˈnɛk-lɪs/ *n.* [C] a piece of jewelry that hangs around your neck: *a pearl necklace* ➔ see picture at JEWELRY

neck·line /ˈnɛk-laɪn/ *n.* [C] the shape made by the edge of a woman's dress, shirt, etc. around or below the neck: *a low neckline*

neck·tie /ˈnɛktaɪ/ *n.* [C] *formal* a TIE

nec·tar /ˈnɛktɚ/ *n.* [U] **1** thick juice made from some fruits: *peach nectar* **2** the sweet liquid that BEES collect from flowers

nec·ta·rine /ˌnɛktəˈrin/ *n.* [C] a round juicy yellow-red fruit that has a large rough seed and smooth skin

née /neɪ/ *adj.* used in order to show the family name that a woman had before she was married: *Lorna Brown, née Wilson*

need¹ /nid/ *v.* [T] **1** to feel that you must have or do something, or that something is necessary: *I need a vacation.* | *What do you **need** the money **for**?* | *He knows exactly what **needs to** be done.* | *David, I **need** you **to** pick up the dry cleaning.* | *Affordable housing is **badly/desperately needed** in the city.*

THESAURUS

could use sth spoken: *Let's stop. I could use a rest.*
be desperate for sth – to need something urgently: *a little boy who is desperate for attention*
can't do without sth – to be unable to manage without something: *I can't do without my morning coffee.*
be dependent on sth/sb – to be unable to live or continue normally without something or someone: *The refugees are dependent on outside food supplies.*
require: *This sport requires a lot of skill and strength.*

2 to have to do something: *There's something I **need to** tell you.* | *Do we **need to** bring anything?* | *You **don't need to** make a reservation.*

USAGE

Use **must not** or **mustn't** when saying that someone is not allowed to do something: *You mustn't tell anyone else about this.* **Must not** is quite formal and is used mainly in written English.
Use **don't have to** when saying that it is not necesssary for someone to do somethig: *You don't have to come with us if you don't want to.*
➔ MUST¹

3 sb does not need sth *spoken* used in order to say that something will make someone's life more difficult: *"He's always questioning everything I do." "Yeah, you don't need that."*

need² *n.* **1** [singular,U] a situation in which something must be done, especially to improve the situation: *I've never felt the **need to** diet.* | ***There is no need to** apologize.* | *a **need for** change* | *There's an **urgent need** for more nurses.* | *We will work all night **if need be*** (=if it is necessary). **2** [C usually plural] something that you need in order to be healthy, comfortable, successful, etc.: *We aim to **meet** the **needs** of our customers.* | *children with **special needs*** (=physical or learning problems) **3 in need of sth** needing attention, help, money, etc.: *a large population in need of doctors* **4 in need** not having enough food or money [➡ **needy**]: *We're collecting donations for families in need.*

nee·dle¹ /ˈnidl/ *n.* [C] **1** a small thin piece of steel used for sewing that has a point at one end and a hole at the other end: *a needle and thread* **2** the sharp hollow metal part on the end of a SYRINGE: *Drug users are at risk when they share needles.* **3** a small thin pointed leaf, especially from a PINE tree → see picture at PLANT[1] **4** the very small pointed part in a RECORD PLAYER that picks up sound from the records **5 sth is like looking for a needle in a haystack** used in order to say that something is almost impossible to find

needle² *v.* [T] to deliberately annoy someone by making a lot of unkind remarks or stupid jokes

N

need·less /ˈnid-lɪs/ *adj.* **1 needless to say** used when you are telling someone something that s/he probably already knows or expects: *Needless to say, with four children we're always busy.* **2** not necessary, and often easily avoided: *Why take needless risks?* —**needlessly** *adv.*

nee·dle·work /ˈnidlˌwɚk/ *n.* [U] the activity or art of sewing, or things made by sewing

need·y /ˈnidi/ *adj.* **1** having very little food or money: *a needy family*

THESAURUS

poor, destitute, impoverished, broke, disadvantaged, underprivileged, deprived
→ see Thesaurus box at POOR

2 the needy people who do not have enough food or money

ne·gate /nɪˈgeɪt/ *v.* [T] *formal* to prevent something from having any effect: *The decision would effectively negate last year's Supreme Court ruling.* —**negation** /nɪˈgeɪʃən/ *n.* [U]

neg·a·tive¹ /ˈnɛgət̬ɪv/ *adj.* **1** bad or harmful [≠ **positive**]: *The divorce had a **negative effect** on the children.* **2** considering only the bad qualities of a situation, person, etc. [≠ **positive**]: *a **negative attitude** | He has always been very **negative about** the U.S.* **3** saying or meaning no [≠ **affirmative**]: *a negative answer* **4** a medical or scientific test that is negative does not show any sign of what was being looked for [≠ **positive**]: *She **tested negative** for HIV. | The blood tests **came back/up/out negative**.* **5** *technical* having the type of electrical charge that is carried by ELECTRONS, shown by a (-) sign on a BATTERY [≠ **positive**] **6** *technical* a negative number or quantity is lower than zero. (-) is the negative sign. [≠ **positive**] —**negatively** *adv.*

negative² *n.* **1** [C] a piece of film that shows dark areas as light and light areas as dark, from which a photograph is printed **2** [U] a statement or expression that means no [≠ **affirmative**]: *He replied **in the negative**.* **3** [C] something bad or harmful [≠ **positive**]: *Another negative was the increase in unemployment.*

ne·glect¹ /nɪˈglɛkt/ *v.* [T] **1** to not pay enough attention to someone or something, or to not take care of him, her, or it very well: *Each year, 700,000 children are abused or neglected.* **2** to not do something or forget to do it, especially because you are lazy or careless: *Sarah **neglected to** tell us of the change in plans.* —**neglected** *adj.*

neglect² *n.* [U] **1** failure to take care of something or someone well: *cases of child abuse or neglect* **2** the condition something or someone is in when he, she, or it has not been taken care of: *inner cities in a state of neglect*

ne·glect·ful /nɪˈglɛktfəl/ *adj. formal* not taking care of something or someone very well: *neglectful parents*

neg·li·gee /ˌnɛglɪˈʒeɪ, ˈnɛglɪˌʒeɪ/ *n.* [C] a very thin pretty piece of clothing that a woman wears over a NIGHTGOWN

neg·li·gence /ˈnɛglɪdʒəns/ *n.* [U] the failure to do something that you are responsible for in a careful enough way, so that something bad happens or may happen: *They're suing the doctor for negligence.*

neg·li·gent /ˈnɛglɪdʒənt/ *adj.* not being careful enough about something that you are doing, so that serious mistakes are made: *The company had been **negligent in** its safety procedures.* —**negligently** *adv.*

neg·li·gi·ble /ˈnɛglɪdʒəbəl/ *adj.* too slight or unimportant to have any effect [= **insignificant**] —**negligibly** *adv.*

ne·go·tia·ble /nɪˈgoʊʃəbəl/ *adj.* prices, agreements, etc. that are negotiable can be discussed and changed: *Is the salary negotiable?*

ne·go·ti·ate /nɪˈgoʊʃiˌeɪt/ *v.* **1** [I,T] to discuss something in order to reach an agreement: *UN representatives are trying to negotiate a ceasefire. | The government refuses to **negotiate with** terrorists.* **2** [T] to succeed in getting past or over a difficult place on a road, path, etc.: *an old man carefully negotiating the steps* —**negotiator** *n.* [C]

ne·go·ti·a·tion /nɪˌgoʊʃiˈeɪʃən/ *n.* [C usually plural, U] official discussions between two groups who are trying to agree on something: *We can't discuss the details because they are still **under negotiation**. | Baseball owners have begun **negotiations with** the players' union. | budget **negotiations between** the White House and Congress*

Ne·gro /ˈnigroʊ/ *n.* plural **Negroes** [C] *old-fashioned* a Black person —**Negro** *adj.*

neigh /neɪ/ *v.* [I] to make a loud sound like a horse —**neigh** *n.* [C]

neigh·bor /ˈneɪbɚ/ *n.* [C] **1** someone who lives in a house or apartment very near you: *The Nelsons are our **next-door neighbors*** (=they live in the house next to ours). **2** someone who is sitting or standing next to you: *Discuss the questions with your neighbor.* **3** a country that has a border with another country: *Germany and its European neighbors*

neigh·bor·hood /ˈneɪbɚˌhʊd/ *n.* [C] **1** a small area of a town, or the people who live there: *a nice neighborhood in Boston | a neighborhood school | Are there any good restaurants **in the neighborhood*** (=in this area of town)*?*

THESAURUS

area, **region**, **zone**, **district**, **suburb**
➔ see Thesaurus box at AREA

2 in the neighborhood of sth either a little more or a little less than a particular number or amount: *The car cost* ***something/somewhere in the neighborhood of*** *$60,000.*

neigh·bor·ing /ˈneɪbərɪŋ/ *adj.* near the place where you are or the place you are talking about: *neighboring towns*

THESAURUS

near, **close**, **not far (away)**, **nearby**, **within walking distance**, **local**
➔ see Thesaurus box at NEAR[1]

neigh·bor·ly /ˈneɪbɚli/ *adj.* friendly and helpful toward your NEIGHBORS —**neighborliness** *n.* [U]

nei·ther[1] /ˈniðɚ, ˈnaɪ-/ *determiner, pron.* not one or the other of two people or things [➡ **either**, **none**]: ***Neither of*** *them was hungry, but they had a cup of coffee.* | *Neither leader would admit to being wrong.*

GRAMMAR

neither, neither of

Neither is used with a singular noun form and a singular verb: *Neither answer is right.*

Neither of is used with a plural noun form or pronoun, and the verb is usually singular: *Neither of us speaks Spanish.*

neither[2] *adv.* used in order to agree with a negative statement that someone has made, or to add a negative statement to one that has just been made: *"I don't like coffee." "Neither do I."* | *Bill can't sing at all, and neither can his brother.* | *"I haven't seen Greg in a long time." "Me neither."*

neither[3] *conjunction* **neither ... nor ...** used when mentioning two statements, facts, actions, etc. that are not true or possible: *Neither his mother nor his father spoke English.* | *The equipment is neither accurate nor safe.*

ne·on /ˈniɑn/ *n.* [U] a gas that shines brightly when electricity goes through it, used in lights and signs: *neon lights*

neph·ew /ˈnɛfyu/ *n.* [C] the son of your brother or sister, or the son of your husband's or wife's brother or sister [➡ **niece**]

THESAURUS

relative, **parents**, **father**, **mother**, **brother**, **sister**, **grandparents**, **grandfather**, **grandmother**, **great-grandparents**, **uncle**, **aunt**, **niece**, **cousin**
➔ see Thesaurus box at RELATIVE[1]

nep·o·tism /ˈnɛpəˌtɪzəm/ *n.* [U] *disapproving* the practice of giving the best jobs to members of your family when you are in a position of power

Nep·tune /ˈnɛptun/ *n.* the eighth PLANET from the sun

nerd /nɚd/ *n.* [C] *informal* someone who is not fashionable and does not know how to behave in social situations: *a computer nerd* (=someone who is interested only in computers) —**nerdy** *adj.*

nerve /nɚv/ *n.* **1** [U] the ability to stay calm in a dangerous, difficult, or frightening situation: *It* ***takes a lot of nerve*** *to give a speech in front of so many people.* | *He would've won if he hadn't* ***lost*** *his* ***nerve****.* **2 nerves** [plural] the feeling of being nervous because you are worried or a little frightened: *"What's wrong?" "It's just nerves. My exam is tomorrow."* **3** [C] one of the thin parts like threads inside your body that help control your movements, and along which your brain sends and receives feelings of heat, cold, pain, etc.: *He has some* ***nerve damage*** *in his left hand.* **4 get on sb's nerves** *informal* to annoy someone, especially by doing something again and again: *Joyce's complaining is getting on my nerves.* **5 have the nerve to do sth** *informal* to be rude without being ashamed or embarrassed about it: *He had the nerve to criticize my cooking.* **6 hit/touch/strike a (raw) nerve** *informal* to mention something that people feel strongly about or that upsets people: *I accidentally hit a raw nerve by asking him about his wife.*

ˈnerve-ˌracking, **nerve-wracking** *adj.* very worrying or frightening: *a nerve-racking wait for test results*

nerv·ous /ˈnɚvəs/ *adj.* **1** worried or frightened about something, and unable to relax: *Sam's* ***nervous about*** *taking his driving test again.* | *Would you stop staring? You're* ***making*** *me* ***nervous****.* | *nervous laughter* | *By the time I got to the interview, I was a* ***nervous wreck*** (=was extremely nervous).

THESAURUS

worried, **anxious**, **concerned**, **uneasy**, **stressed (out)**
➔ see Thesaurus box at WORRIED

2 often becoming worried or frightened and easily upset: *a thin nervous man* **3** relating to the nerves in your body: *a nervous disorder* —**nervously** *adv.* —**nervousness** *n.* [U]

ˌnervous ˈbreakdown *n.* [C] a mental illness in which someone becomes extremely anxious and tired and cannot live and work normally: *He almost* ***had/suffered a nervous breakdown*** *last year.*

ˈnervous ˌsystem *n.* [C usually singular] the system of nerves in your body, through which you feel pain, heat, etc. and control your movements

nest[1] /nɛst/ *n.* [C] **1** a hollow place made or chosen by a bird to lay its eggs in and to live in: *The robins were* ***building*** *a* ***nest*** *in our backyard.* **2** a place where insects or small animals live: *a*

N

hornets' nest **3 leave/fly the nest** *informal* to leave your parents' house when you are an adult

nest² *v.* [I] to build or use a nest: *owls nesting in a tree hole*

'nest egg *n.* [C] an amount of money that you have saved

nes·tle /'nɛsəl/ *v.* **1** [I,T] to move into a comfortable position by pressing against someone or something: *She nestled her head against his shoulder.* **2** [I] to be in a position that is protected from wind, rain, etc.: *a village **nestling among** the hills*

N

net¹ /nɛt/ *n.* **1** [C,U] a material made of strings, wires, or threads woven across each other with regular spaces between them: *a fishing net* **2** [C usually singular] a net used in particular games: *The ball went straight **into the net**.* **3 the Net** THE INTERNET: *I read about it **on the net**.*

net

casting a fishing net

net² *v.* past tense and past participle **netted**, present participle **netting** [T] **1** to earn a particular amount of money as a profit after paying taxes [➡ **gross**]: *Last year, they netted $52,000.* **2** to catch a fish in a net

net³ *adj.* [only before noun] **1** a net amount of money is the amount that remains after things such as taxes, etc. have been taken away [➡ **gross**]: *a **net profit/loss** of $500,000* **2 net weight** the weight of something without its container **3 net result** the final result, after all the effects are known: *The net result of the policy was higher prices in the stores.*

net·i·quette, **Netiquette** /'nɛt̬ɪkɪt/ *n.* [U] *informal* the commonly accepted rules for polite behavior when communicating with other people on the Internet

net·ting /'nɛt̬ɪŋ/ *n.* [U] material consisting of string, wire, etc. that has been woven into a net

net·tle /'nɛt̬l/ *n.* [C,U] a wild plant with rough leaves that sting you

net·work¹ /'nɛt˺wɚk/ *n.* [C] **1** a group of radio or television stations that broadcasts many of the same programs in different parts of the country: *the four biggest TV networks* **2** a set of computers that are connected to each other so that they can share information: *network administrators* | *I wasn't able to log onto the network.* **3** a system of lines, tubes, wires, roads, etc. that cross each other and are connected to each other: *the freeway network* | *the **network of** blood vessels in the body* **4** a group of people, organizations, etc. that are connected or that work together: *Trina had developed a good **network of** business contacts.*

network² *v.* **1** [I] to meet other people who do the same type of work in order to share information, help each other, etc. **2** [T] to connect several computers together so that they can share information

net·work·ing /'nɛt˺ˌwɚkɪŋ/ *n.* [U] the practice of meeting other people who do the same type of work, in order to share information, help each other, etc.

neu·rol·o·gy /nʊ'rɑlədʒi/ *n.* [U] the scientific study of the NERVOUS SYSTEM and the diseases that are related to it —**neurologist** *n.* [C] —**neurological** /ˌnʊrə'lɑdʒɪkəl/ *adj.*

neu·ro·sis /nʊ'roʊsɪs/ *n.* plural **neuroses** /-'roʊsiz/ [C,U] a mental illness that makes someone worried or frightened in an unreasonable way

neu·rot·ic /nʊ'rɑt̬ɪk/ *adj.* **1** unreasonably anxious or afraid: *My aunt is **neurotic about** cleanliness.* **2** *technical* relating to a neurosis: *neurotic disorders* —**neurotically** *adv.* —**neurotic** *n.* [C]

neu·ter¹ /'nut̬ɚ/ *adj.* *technical* in English grammar, a neuter PRONOUN such as "it" relates to something that has no sex, or does not show the sex of the person or animal that it relates to

neuter² *v.* [T] to remove part of the sex organs of a male animal so that it cannot produce babies [➡ **spay**]

neu·tral¹ /'nutrəl/ *adj.* **1** not supporting either side in an argument, competition, or war: *Switzerland was neutral during World War II.* **2** not showing any strong feelings or opinions: *"I see," she said in a **neutral tone**.* **3** a neutral color such as gray or brown is not strong or bright

neutral² *n.* [U] the position of the GEARS of a car or machine when it will not move forward or backward: *Start the car **in neutral**.*

neu·tral·i·ty /nu'træləṭi/ *n.* [U] the state of not supporting either side in an argument, competition, or war

neu·tral·ize /'nutrəˌlaɪz/ *v.* [T] to prevent something from having any effect: *Air freshener can help neutralize pet odors.* | *Higher taxes will neutralize increased wages.* —**neutralization** /ˌnutrələ'zeɪʃən/ *n.* [U]

neu·tron /'nutrɑn/ *n.* [C] a part of an atom that has no electrical CHARGE

nev·er /'nɛvɚ/ *adv.* **1** not at any time, or not once: *I've never been to Hawaii.* | *We waited until 11:00, but they never came.* | *I'll **never** make that mistake **again**.* | ***I never knew*** (=I did not know until now) *that you played the guitar!*

THESAURUS

never ever spoken – used to emphasize that you mean never: *I'll never ever forgive him.*
not in a million years spoken – used to say that something is completely impossible: *She wouldn't go without me – not in a million years!*
not once – used to show that you are surprised

or annoyed, or to emphasize something: *Craig didn't phone all week – not once!*
→ RARELY, OFTEN, SOMETIMES

2 never mind *spoken* used in order to tell someone that something was not important or that you do not want to say something again: *"What did you say?" "Never mind, it doesn't matter."* **3 you never know** *spoken* used in order to say that something that seems unlikely could happen: *You never know, maybe you'll win.*

GRAMMAR

Use **never** before a verb, unless the verb is "be": *He never listens to me.* | *Her father was never angry.*
If there are two or more verbs together, **never** comes after the first one: *I have never read any of her books.*

nev·er·the·less /ˌnɛvɚðəˈlɛs◂/ *adv.* in spite of what has just been mentioned: *I know he's telling the truth. Nevertheless, I don't trust him.*

new /nu/ *adj.* **1** recently made, built, invented, or developed [≠ **old**]: *The city is building a new football stadium.* | *Can the new drugs help her?* | *technology that is completely new*

THESAURUS

recent – used about something that was new or that happened a short time ago: *recent news reports*
modern – used about things that are different from earlier things of the same kind: *modern technology*
original – completely new and different from anything that has been done or thought of before: *original ideas*
fresh – used about food that was made, picked, etc. only a short time ago: *fresh bread*
latest – used about a film, book, fashion, etc. that is the newest one: *his latest movie*
→ OLD

2 recently bought: *Do you like my new dress?* **3** not used or owned by anyone before [≠ **used**]: *A used car costs a lot less than a new one.* | *a* ***brand new*** (=completely new) *CD player* **4** not experienced by someone before: *Do you like your new teacher?* | *Learning a new language is always a challenge.* | *The idea was* ***new to*** *me.* **5** having recently arrived in a place, or started a different job or activity: *Are you a new student here?* | *Charlie is* ***new to*** *the area and eager to meet people.* | *It's hard being* ***the new kid on the block*** (=the newest person in a job, school, etc.). **6** recently discovered: *new evidence* | *a new planet* **7 what's new?** *spoken* used as a friendly greeting to ask what is happening in someone's life —**newness** *n.* [U]

ˈNew Age *adj.* relating to a set of beliefs about religion, medicine, and ways of life that are not part of traditional Western religions

new·bie /ˈnubi/ *n.* [C] *informal humorous* someone who has just started doing something, especially using the Internet or computers [= **beginner**]

new·born /ˈnubɔrn/ *n.* [C] a baby that has recently been born —**newborn** /ˌnuˈbɔrn◂/ *adj.*

TOPIC

baby, infant, toddler
→ see Topic box at BABY

new·com·er /ˈnuˌkʌmɚ/ *n.* [C] someone who has recently arrived somewhere or recently started a particular activity: *a* ***newcomer to*** *the real estate business*

new·fan·gled /ˈnuˌfæŋgəld/ *adj.* [only before noun] *disapproving* newfangled ideas, machines, etc. have been recently invented but seem complicated or unnecessary: *newfangled ideas about raising children*

new·ly /ˈnuli/ *adv.* **newly elected/formed etc.** elected, etc. very recently: *the newly appointed chairman*

THESAURUS

recently, just, a little/short while ago, lately, freshly
→ see Thesaurus box at RECENTLY

new·ly·weds /ˈnuliˌwɛdz/ *n.* [plural] a man and a woman who have recently gotten married

news /nuz/ *n.* **1** [U] information about something that has happened recently: *Have you* ***heard*** (=received) *any* ***news about*** *your job application?* | *I have some* ***good/bad news*** *for you.* | *We were shocked by the* ***news that*** *Tom had left his wife.* | *I don't know how I'm going to* ***break the news*** *to her* (=tell her about something bad that has happened). | *an interesting* ***piece of news*** **2** [U] reports of recent events in the newspapers or on the radio or television: *There is more* ***news of*** *fighting in the area.* | *a* ***news story/report/item*** *on the plane crash* | ***local/national/international news*** | *20 years ago, environmental issues rarely* ***made the news*** (=were reported in newspapers, etc.). **3 the news** a regular television or radio program that gives you reports of recent events: *the eleven o'clock news* | *We usually* ***watch the*** *evening* ***news.*** | *The teachers' strike was* ***on the news.*** **4 that's news to me** *spoken* said when you are surprised or annoyed because you were not told something earlier: *The meeting's been canceled? That's news to me.*

GRAMMAR

News is always followed by a singular verb: *The news was very exciting.* You can say **some news, any news** etc., or **a piece of news**: *Is there any interesting news in the paper?*

ˈnews ˌagency *n.* [C] a company that supplies

reports on recent events to newspapers, television, and radio

'news ˌbulletin *n.* [C] a very short news program about something important that has just happened, that is broadcast suddenly in the middle of a television or radio program

news·cast /ˈnuzkæst/ *n.* [C] a news program on television or the radio

news·cast·er /ˈnuzˌkæstɚ/ *n.* [C] someone who reads the news on television or the radio

N

news·let·ter /ˈnuzˌlɛt̬ɚ/ *n.* [C] a short written report of news about a club, organization, or particular subject that is sent regularly to people: *our church newsletter*

news·pa·per /ˈnuzˌpeɪpɚ/ *n.* **1** [C] **also paper** a set of large folded sheets of paper containing news, pictures, advertisements, etc. that is printed and sold daily or weekly: *the local newspaper* | *I saw your picture* ***in the newspaper***. | *a* ***newspaper article***

> **THESAURUS**
>
> **Newspapers in general**
> **the papers**, **the press**, **the media** (=newspapers, TV, radio, etc.)
> **tabloid** – a newspaper that has small pages, a lot of photographs, short stories, and not much serious news
> **broadsheet** – a serious newspaper printed on large sheets of paper
>
> **Parts of a newspaper**
> **front page**, **sports/entertainment/food etc. section**, **the comics page**, **the funnies**, **editorial page**, **headlines**, **article**, **story**, **column**
>
> **People who write newspapers**
> **editor**, **reporter**, **journalist**, **correspondent**, **columnist**

2 [U] sheets of paper from old newspapers: *We packed the dishes in newspaper.*

news·print /ˈnuzˌprɪnt/ *n.* [U] cheap paper used mostly for printing newspapers

news·stand /ˈnuzˌstænd/ *n.* [C] a place on a street where newspapers are sold ➔ see Thesaurus box at STORE[1]

news·wor·thy /ˈnuzˌwɚði/ *adj.* important or interesting enough to be reported as news: *newsworthy events*

news·y /ˈnuzi/ *adj. informal* a newsy letter is from a friend or relative and contains a lot of information about him/her

newt /nut/ *n.* [C] a small animal with a long body, four legs, and a tail that lives in water

ˌNew 'Testament *n.* **the New Testament** the part of the Bible that is about Jesus Christ's life and what he taught [➡ **Old Testament**]

ˌnew 'wave *n.* [C usually singular] people who are trying to introduce new ideas in music, movies, art, politics, etc.: *a* ***new wave of*** *Hong Kong filmmakers* —**new-wave** *adj.*

ˌNew 'World *n.* **the New World** North, Central, and South America, used when talking about the time that Europeans first discovered these areas

ˌnew 'year *n.* [C] **1 New Year also New Year's** the time when you celebrate the beginning of the year: ***Happy New Year!*** | *Have you made any* ***New Year's resolutions*** (=promises to improve yourself)? **2 the new year** the year after the present year, especially the months at the beginning of it: *We're opening three new stores* ***in the new year***.

ˌNew Year's 'Day *n.* [singular, U] a holiday on January 1, the first day of the year in Western countries

ˌNew Year's 'Eve *n.* [singular, U] a holiday on December 31, the last day of the year in Western countries, when many people have parties to celebrate the start of the new year

next[1] /nɛkst/ *determiner, adj.* **1** the next day, time, event, etc. is the one that happens after the present one: ***The next*** *flight leaves in 45 minutes.* | *They returned to New York* ***the next day***. | ***Next time*** (=when this happens again) *be more careful.* | *See you* ***next week***. | *School starts* ***next Monday***. ▶ Don't say "the next Monday/month/year etc." ◀

> **THESAURUS**
>
> **following** – immediately after: *There will be a reception following the wedding.*
> **subsequent** formal – coming after or following something else: *In subsequent years, Dr. Kim devoted all of his time to research.*
> **succeeding** – coming after something else: *succeeding generations*
> **later** – coming in the future, or after something else: *We'll discuss this at a later time.*

2 the next place is the one closest to where you are now: *Turn left at the next corner.* | *the people at the next table* **3** the next person or thing on a list, in a series, etc. is the one that comes after the present one: *Who's the next person in line?* | *Read the next two chapters by Friday.* **4 the next best thing** the thing or situation that is almost as good as the one you really want: *If we can't be together, talking on the phone is the next best thing.*

next[2] *adv.* **1** immediately afterward: *What should we do next?* | *First, write your name at the top of the page. Next, read the instructions.*

> **THESAURUS**
>
> **after**, **afterward**, **later**, **subsequently**
> ➔ see Thesaurus box at AFTER[1]

2 next to sb/sth very close to someone or something, with nothing in between: *I sat next to a really nice lady on the plane.* | *The baby sleeps in the room next to ours.* **3 next to nothing** very little: *Phil earns next to nothing.* **4 next to**

impossible very difficult: *It's next to impossible to get tickets for the game.*

next[3] *pron.* **1** the person or thing in a list, series, etc. that comes after the person or thing you are dealing with now: *What's next on the shopping list?* | *We're next in line.* **2 the day/week etc. after next** the day, week, etc. that follows the next one: *The week after next is our spring break.*

next 'door *adv.* in the room, building, etc. that is next to yours or someone else's: *Deanna's office is right next door.* | *The Garcias just bought the house **next door to** my mother's.*

'next-door *adj.* [only before noun] relating to the room, building, etc. that is next to yours: *Our **next-door neighbor** will take care of the cats for us.*

ˌnext of 'kin *n.* [U] *law* your closest living relative or relatives, for example your mother, father, son, or daughter: *The victim will not be named until her next of kin are informed.*

NFC *n.* [C] **National Football Conference** a group of teams that is part of the NFL

NFL *n.* [C] **National Football League** the organization that is in charge of professional football in the U.S.

NH the written abbreviation of **New Hampshire**

NHL *n.* [C] **National Hockey League** the organization that is in charge of professional HOCKEY in the U.S. and Canada

nib·ble /'nɪbəl/ *v.* [I,T] to eat a small amount of food by taking very small bites: *Guests were **nibbling on** cheese and crackers.* —**nibble** *n.* [C]

nice /naɪs/ *adj.* **1** good, pleasant, attractive, or enjoyable: *Did you have a **nice time** last night?* | *That's a nice sweater.* | *Their apartment is much nicer than ours.* | *You **look nice** today.* | ***It's nice to** see you again.* | ***It would be nice if** Chris could come.* | ***It's** really **nice out*** (=the weather is good) *today.* | *Let's sit by the fire where it's **nice and warm**.*

THESAURUS

enjoyable – used for describing something that gives you pleasure because it is interesting, exciting, etc.: *an enjoyable day at the beach*
pleasant – used for describing something that you like, especially something that is peaceful or relaxing: *It had been a pleasant evening.*
great/fantastic/wonderful – used for describing something that you like very much: *"How was your vacation?" "Wonderful!"*
➔ HORRIBLE

2 friendly or kind: *Matt is a really nice guy.* | ***It was nice of you to** stop by.* | ***Be nice to** your little sister!* —**niceness** *n.* [U]

THESAURUS

kind, considerate, thoughtful, caring
➔ see Thesaurus box at KIND[2]

SPOKEN PHRASES

3 (it's) nice to meet you a polite phrase used when you meet someone for the first time **4 (it was) nice meeting you** a polite phrase used when you say goodbye after meeting someone for the first time **5 Have a nice day!** a phrase used when you say goodbye to someone, especially to a customer in a store, restaurant, etc. **6 Nice going/move/one!** said as a joke when someone makes a mistake or does something wrong: *"I just spilled my coffee!" "Nice going!"*

ˌnice-'looking *adj.* fairly attractive: *He's a really nice-looking guy.*

THESAURUS

attractive, good-looking, pretty, beautiful, handsome, gorgeous, stunning, cute, hot
➔ see Thesaurus box at ATTRACTIVE

nice·ly /'naɪsli/ *adv.* **1** in a satisfactory, pleasing, or skillful way [= **well**]: *Belinda is always so nicely dressed* (=wearing attractive clothes). | *His arm is healing nicely.* **2** in a polite or friendly way: *I'm sure he'll help if you ask him nicely.*

ni·ce·ty /'naɪsət̬i/ *n.* plural **niceties** [C] something small that is nice to have, but not necessary: *The rooms had little niceties like alarm clocks and ironing boards.*

niche /nɪtʃ/ *n.* [C] a job or activity that is perfect for the skills, abilities, and character that you have: *After many years, she **found her niche** as a fashion designer.*

nick[1] /nɪk/ *n.* [C] **1 in the nick of time** just before it is too late or before something bad happens: *The doctor arrived just in the nick of time.* **2** a very small cut on the surface or edge of something

nick[2] *v.* [T] to accidentally make a small cut on the surface or edge of something: *I nicked my chin when I was shaving.*

nick·el /'nɪkəl/ *n.* **1** [C] a coin used in the U.S. and Canada worth 5 cents (=1/20 of a dollar)

THESAURUS

coin, penny, dime, quarter
➔ see Thesaurus box at MONEY

2 [U] a hard silver-white metal that is an ELEMENT and is used for making other metals

nick·name /'nɪkneɪm/ *n.* [C] a silly name or a shorter form of someone's real name, usually given by friends or family: *His nickname was "Elephant" because of his ears.* —**nickname** *v.* [T] *The puppy was soon nicknamed "Trouble."*

THESAURUS

first name, given name, last name, family name, surname, middle name, full name, maiden name, stage name, pen name, pseudonym, assumed name, alias
→ see Thesaurus box at NAME[1]

nic·o·tine /ˈnɪkəˌtin/ *n.* [U] a dangerous substance in tobacco

niece /nis/ *n.* [C] the daughter of your brother or sister, or the daughter of your husband's or wife's brother or sister [➡ **nephew**]

N

THESAURUS

relative, parents, father, mother, brother, sister, grandparents, grandfather, grandmother, great-grandparents, uncle, aunt, nephew, cousin
→ see Thesaurus box at RELATIVE[1]

nif·ty /ˈnɪfti/ *adj. informal* very good, fast, or effective: *a nifty little machine*

nig·gling /ˈnɪglɪŋ/ *adj.* [only before noun] not very important, but continuing to annoy someone: *a* ***niggling doubt***

night /naɪt/ *n.* **1** [C,U] the dark part of each 24-hour period, when the sun cannot be seen [➡ **day**]: *a cold night* | *I stayed up* ***all night*** *to finish the paper.* | *You can see the stars really clearly here* ***at night.*** **2** [C,U] the evening [➡ **tonight**]: *Some friends are coming over* ***tomorrow night.*** | *What did you do* ***last night?*** | *I fly back to New Orleans* ***on Thursday night.*** | *I don't want to walk home alone* ***late at night.*** ▶ Don't say "this night," say "tonight." ◀ **3** [C,U] the time when most people are sleeping: *The baby cried* ***all night long.*** | *We'll* ***spend the night*** (=sleep) *at my parents' and come back Sunday.* | *I woke up* ***in the middle of the night.*** | *What you need is a* ***good night's sleep*** (=to sleep well all night). **4 nights** [plural] if you do something nights, you do it regularly or often at night: *Peter* ***works nights.*** **5 night and day also day and night** all the time: *We had to work night and day to get it finished.* **6 night after night** every night for a long period: *He goes out drinking night after night.*

night·club /ˈnaɪt˺klʌb/ *n.* [C] a place where people can drink and dance that is open late at night

night·fall /ˈnaɪtfɔl/ *n.* [U] *literary* the time in the evening when the sky becomes darker [= **dusk**]

night·gown /ˈnaɪt˺gaʊn/ *n.* [C] a piece of loose clothing, like a dress, that women wear in bed

night·ie /ˈnaɪţi/ *n.* [C] *informal* a NIGHTGOWN

night·in·gale /ˈnaɪt˺nˌgeɪl, ˈnaɪţɪŋ-/ *n.* [C] a small European wild bird that sings very beautifully, especially at night

night·life /ˈnaɪt˺laɪf/ *n.* [U] entertainment in places where you can dance, drink, etc. in the evening: *Las Vegas is famous for its nightlife.*

ˈnight light *n.* [C] a small, not very bright light, often used in a child's room at night, so that s/he will not be afraid of the dark

night·ly /ˈnaɪtli/ *adj., adv.* happening every night: *the nightly news* | *The restaurant is open nightly.*

night·mare /ˈnaɪt˺mɛr/ *n.* [C] **1** a very frightening dream: *I still* ***have*** *terrible* ***nightmares*** *about the accident.* **2** *informal* a person, thing, situation, etc. that is very bad or very difficult to deal with: *Living with my parents again would be a total nightmare!* —**nightmarish** *adj.*

ˈnight owl *n.* [C] *informal* someone who enjoys being awake or working late at night

ˈnight school *n.* [U] classes taught at night, for people who work during the day: *I learned how to make pottery in night school.*

night·stand /ˈnaɪtstænd/ **also ˈnight ˌtable** *n.* [C] a small table beside a bed

night·time /ˈnaɪt-taɪm/ *n.* [U] the time during the night when the sky is dark [≠ **daytime**]

nil /nɪl/ *n.* [U] *formal* nothing or zero: *His chances of winning the election are* ***almost/practically/virtually nil.***

nim·ble /ˈnɪmbəl/ *adj.* able to move quickly and skillfully [= **agile**]: *nimble fingers*

nin·com·poop /ˈnɪŋkəmˌpup/ *n.* [C] *old-fashioned informal* a stupid person [= **idiot**]

nine /naɪn/ *number* **1** 9 **2** 9 O'CLOCK: *I have to be in the office by nine.*

nine·teen /ˌnaɪnˈtin◂/ *number* 19 —**nineteenth** *number*

ˌnine-to-ˈfive *adj., adv.* from 9:00 a.m. until 5:00 p.m.; the hours that most people work in an office: *You* ***work nine-to-five,*** *right?* | *a nine-to-five job*

nine·ty /ˈnaɪnţi/ *number* **1** 90 **2 the nineties a)** the years between 1990 and 1999 **b)** the numbers between 90 and 99, especially when used for measuring temperatures **3 be in your nineties** to be between 90 and 99 years old —**ninetieth** /ˈnaɪnţiɪθ/ *number*

ninth /naɪnθ/ *number* **1** 9th **2** 1/9

nip[1] /nɪp/ past tense and past participle **nipped**, present participle **nipping** *v.* **1** [I,T] to bite someone or something with small sharp bites, or to try to do this: *This stupid dog keeps* ***nipping at*** *my ankles.* **2 nip sth in the bud** to prevent something from becoming a problem by stopping it as soon as it starts

nip[2] *n.* [C] a small sharp bite

nip·ple /ˈnɪpəl/ *n.* [C] **1** the dark raised circle in the middle of a woman's breast that a baby sucks in order to get milk **2** one of the two dark raised circles on a man's chest **3** the small piece of rubber on the end of a baby's bottle

nip·py /ˈnɪpi/ *adj. informal* weather that is nippy is cold enough that you need a coat [= **chilly**]

nit /nɪt/ *n.* [C] the egg of a LOUSE (=small insect)

nit·pick·ing /ˈnɪtˌpɪkɪŋ/ *n.* [U] *informal disapproving* the act of criticizing people about unimportant details —**nitpick** *v.* [I] —**nitpicking** *adj.*

ni·trate /ˈnaɪtreɪt/ *n.* [C,U] a chemical compound that is mainly used for improving the soil that crops are grown in

ni·tro·gen /ˈnaɪtrədʒən/ *n.* [U] **N** a gas that is an ELEMENT and is the main part of the Earth's air

nit·ty-grit·ty /ˈnɪṭi ˌgrɪṭi, ˌnɪṭi ˈgrɪṭi/ *n.* **the nitty-gritty** *informal* the basic and practical facts and details of an agreement or activity: *Let's* ***get down to the nitty-gritty*** *and work out the cost.*

nit·wit /ˈnɪtˀˌwɪt/ *n.* [C] *informal* a silly stupid person

nix /nɪks/ *v.* [T] *journalism* to answer no to something or refuse something: *They immediately nixed my idea.*

NJ the written abbreviation of **New Jersey**

NM the written abbreviation of **New Mexico**

no[1] /noʊ/ *adv.* **1** said in order to give a negative reply to a question, offer, or request [≠ **yes**]: *"Is she married?" "No, she's not."* | *"Do you want some more coffee?"* ***"No thanks."*** | *When I asked him, he* ***said no.*** **2** *spoken* said when you disagree with a statement [≠ **yes**]: *"Gary's weird." "No, he's just shy."* **3** *spoken* said when you do not want someone to do something [≠ **yes**]: *No, Jimmy, don't touch that.*

no[2] *determiner* **1** not any, or not at all: *No visitors are allowed.* | *There's no more milk.* | *He had no intention of returning the money.* | *There's no reason to be afraid.* **2** used on a sign in order to show that something is not allowed: *No smoking* | *No pets* ➔ **no good** at GOOD[1] ➔ **in no time** at TIME[1]

no[3] *n.* plural **noes** [C usually singular] a negative answer or decision: *Her answer was a definite no.*

no. plural **nos.** the written abbreviation of **number**

no·bil·i·ty /noʊˈbɪləṭi/ *n.* **1 the nobility** the group of people in particular countries who have the highest social class and have special titles **2** [U] the quality of being noble

no·ble[1] /ˈnoʊbəl/ *adj.* **1** morally good or generous in a way that should be admired: *a noble intention* **2** belonging to the group of people in particular countries who have the highest social class and special titles: *noble families* —**nobly** *adv.*

noble[2], **also no·ble·man** /ˈnoʊbəlmən/, **no·ble·wom·an** /ˈnoʊbəlˌwʊmən/ *n.* plural **noblemen** /-mən/, **noblewomen** /-ˌwɪmɪn/ [C] someone who belongs to the nobility

no·bod·y[1] /ˈnoʊˌbʌdi, -ˌbɑdi/ *pron.* no person [= **no one**]: *I knocked on the door, but nobody answered.*

nobody[2] *n.* plural **nobodies** [C] someone who is not important, successful, or famous

ˌno-ˈbrainer *n.* [C usually singular] *slang* something that you do not have to think about because it is easy to understand: *If you ask me, it's a no-brainer. Of course you should accept the job.*

noc·tur·nal /nɑkˈtɚnl/ *adj.* **1** *technical* nocturnal animals are active at night **2** *formal* happening at night

nod /nɑd/ *v.* past tense and past participle **nodded**, present participle **nodding** **1** [I,T] to move your head up and down, especially to show that you agree with or understand something: *Dora* ***nodded*** *her* ***head*** *in agreement.* | *He nodded and smiled.* **2** [I] to move your head up and down once toward someone or something, in order to greet someone or to give him/her a sign to do something: *I* ***nodded to*** *the waiter and asked for the bill.* | *"Sally's in there," Jim said,* ***nodding toward*** *the door.* —**nod** *n.* [C] *He gave a nod of agreement.*

nod off *phr. v.* to begin to sleep, often without intending to: *His speech was so boring I kept nodding off.*

node /noʊd/ *n.* [C] **1** *technical* a place where lines in a network, GRAPH, etc. meet or join **2** a LYMPH NODE

ˌno-ˈfault *adj.* [only before noun] **1** no-fault car insurance will pay for the damage done in an accident, even if you caused the accident **2** a no-fault DIVORCE does not blame either the husband or the wife

ˌno-ˈfrills *adj.* [only before noun] without any features that are not completely necessary: *a no-frills airline*

noise /nɔɪz/ *n.* [C,U] a sound or sounds that is or are too loud, annoying, or not intended: *the* ***noise of*** *the traffic* | *You're* ***making*** *too much* ***noise.*** | *Do you hear that squeaking noise?* | *There was* ***a lot of noise*** *outside.*

> **THESAURUS**
>
> A **sound** is anything that you can hear: *the sound of voices*
> A **noise** is usually a loud, unpleasant, or unexpected sound: *the deafening noise of overhead planes*

noise·less /ˈnɔɪzlɪs/ *adj. literary* not making any sound —**noiselessly** *adv.*

ˈnoise polˌlution *n.* [U] very loud continuous noise in the environment that is harmful to people

nois·y /ˈnɔɪzi/ *adj.* comparative **noisier**, superlative **noisiest** making a lot of noise, or full of noise: *a noisy crowd* | *a noisy restaurant* | *Their lawn mower is really noisy.* —**noisily** *adv.*

> **THESAURUS**
>
> **loud**, **rowdy**, **thunderous**, **deafening**, **ear-splitting**, **shrill**
> ➔ see Thesaurus box at LOUD[1]

no·mad /ˈnoʊmæd/ *n.* [C] a member of a tribe that travels from place to place, usually to find fields for his/her animals —**nomadic** /noʊˈmædɪk/ *adj.*

ˈno-man's ˌland *n.* [singular, U] land that no one owns or controls, especially between two opposing armies

no·men·cla·ture /ˈnoʊmənˌkleɪtʃɚ/ *n.* [C,U] *formal* a system of naming things

N

N

nom·i·nal /ˈnɑmənl/ *adj.* **1 a nominal price/fee/sum etc.** a small amount of money: *You can get the new telephone service for a nominal fee.* **2 nominal leader/head etc.** someone who has the title of leader, etc. but does not actually do that job

nom·i·nal·ly /ˈnɑmənl-i/ *adv. formal* officially described as something or as doing something, although the truth may be different: *The country is nominally Catholic.*

nom·i·nate /ˈnɑməˌneɪt/ *v.* [T] **1** to officially choose someone so that s/he can be one of the competitors in an election, competition, etc.: *Ferraro was the first woman to be* ***nominated for*** *the job of vice president.* **2** to choose someone for a particular job or position: *Margaret was* ***nominated (as)*** *club representative.*

nom·i·na·tion /ˌnɑməˈneɪʃən/ *n.* [C,U] **1** the act of officially choosing someone to be a competitor in an election, competition, etc., or the official choice: *Who will get the Republican* ***nomination for*** *president?* **2** the act of choosing someone for a particular job, or the person chosen: *the* ***nomination of*** *O'Connor* ***to*** *the United States Supreme Court*

nom·i·nee /ˌnɑməˈni/ *n.* [C] someone who has been nominated for a prize, duty, etc.: *the Democratic Party's presidential nominee*

non·ag·gres·sion /ˌnɑnəˈgrɛʃən/ *n.* [U] the state of not fighting or attacking: *a* ***nonaggression pact/treaty*** (=a country's promise not to attack)

non·al·co·hol·ic /ˌnɑnælkəˈhɔlɪk/ *adj.* a nonalcoholic drink does not have any alcohol in it

non·cha·lant /ˌnɑnʃəˈlɑnt/ *adj.* calm and not seeming interested in or worried about anything: *She tried to look nonchalant.* —**nonchalance** *n.* [U] —**nonchalantly** *adv.*

non·com·bat·ant /ˌnɑnkəmˈbætˀnt/ *n.* [C] someone who is in the military during a war but does not actually fight, for example a doctor

non·com·mit·tal /ˌnɑnkəˈmɪtl̩/ *adj. formal* not giving a definite answer, or not willing to express your opinions: *The lawyer was* ***noncommittal about*** *Jones' chances of going to prison.* —**noncommittally** *adv.*

non·con·form·ist /ˌnɑnkənˈfɔrmɪst/ *n.* [C] someone who deliberately does not accept the beliefs and ways of behaving that most people in a society accept

non·count /nɑnˈkaʊnt/ *adj. technical* **noncount noun** an UNCOUNTABLE noun

ˌnon-ˈdairy *adj.* containing no milk, and used instead of a product that contains milk: *non-dairy creamer*

ˌnon-denomiˈnational *adj.* not related to a particular religion or religious group: *a non-denominational chapel*

non·de·script /ˌnɑndɪˈskrɪpt◂/ *adj.* not having any noticeable or interesting qualities: *a nondescript man in a plain gray suit*

none¹ /nʌn/ *quantifier, pron.* **1** not any of something: *"Can I have some more pie?" "Sorry, there's none left."* **2** not one person or thing: ***None of*** *my friends has a bike.* | *An old car is better than* ***none at all.*** **3 none other than sb** used in order to emphasize a fact when you are surprised that it is true: *Pam's writing was praised by none other than Toni Morrison.*

> **GRAMMAR**
>
> When you use **none** with an uncountable noun, the verb is singular: *None of the food was left.*
> When you use **none** with a plural noun form, the verb can be singular or plural: *None of the packages was for me.* | *None of my friends were there.*

none² *adv.* **1 none the worse/wiser etc.** not any worse than before, not knowing any more than before, etc.: *She seems* ***none the worse for*** *her experience.* **2 none too soon/likely etc.** not at all soon, not at all likely, etc.: *Consumers are none too happy about the price increase.*

non·en·ti·ty /nɑnˈɛntət̬i/ *n.* plural **nonentities** [C] someone who has no importance, power, or ability

none·the·less /ˌnʌnðəˈlɛs◂/ *adv. formal* in spite of what has just been mentioned [**= nevertheless**]: *The paintings are complex, but have plenty of appeal nonetheless.*

non·ex·ist·ent /ˌnɑnɪgˈzɪstənt◂/ *adj.* not existing at all in a particular place or situation: *Airplanes were practically nonexistent in those days.*

non·fat /ˌnɑnˈfæt◂/ *adj.* nonfat milk, YOGURT, etc. has no fat in it

non·fic·tion /ˌnɑnˈfɪkʃən/ *n.* [U] articles, books, etc. about real facts or events, not imagined ones [**≠ fiction**] —**nonfiction** *adj.*

> **THESAURUS**
>
> **fiction, literature, science fiction**
> → see Thesaurus box at BOOK¹

non·flam·ma·ble /ˌnɑnˈflæməbəl/ *adj.* difficult or impossible to burn [**≠ flammable**]

non·im·mi·grant /nɑnˈɪməgrənt/ *n.* [C] someone who is living in or visiting a foreign country, but is not planning to live there permanently —**nonimmigrant** *adj.*: *a nonimmigrant student visa*

non·in·ter·ven·tion /ˌnɑnɪntəˈvɛnʃən/ *n.* [U] the refusal of a government to become involved in the affairs of other countries

ˌnon-ˌnative ˈspeaker *n.* [C] someone who has learned a particular language as a foreign language

ˈno-no *n.* [singular] *informal* something that is not allowed, or not socially acceptable: *Chewing gum during a job interview is a definite no-no.*

ˌno-ˈnonsense *adj.* very practical, direct, and unwilling to waste time: *a no-nonsense attitude toward work*

non·pay·ment /ˌnɑnˈpeɪmənt/ *n.* [U] failure to pay bills, taxes, or debts: ***nonpayment of*** *rent*

non·plussed /ˌnɑnˈplʌst/ *adj.* so surprised that you do not know what to say or do

THESAURUS

surprised, amazed, shocked, astonished, astounded, flabbergasted, stunned, dumbfounded

➔ see Thesaurus box at SURPRISED

non·prof·it /ˌnɑnˈprɑfɪt/ *adj.* a nonprofit organization, school, hospital, etc. uses the money it earns to help people instead of making a profit, and therefore does not have to pay taxes —**nonprofit** *n.* [C] *Danson works for a Seattle nonprofit.*

non·pro·lif·er·a·tion /ˌnɑnprəˌlɪfəˈreɪʃən/ *n.* [U] the act of limiting the number of NUCLEAR or chemical weapons that are being made across the world

non·re·fund·a·ble /ˌnɑnrɪˈfʌndəbəl/ *adj.* if something you buy is nonrefundable, you cannot get your money back after you have paid for it: *nonrefundable airline tickets*

non·re·new·a·ble /ˌnɑnrɪˈnuəbəl/ *adj.* nonrenewable types of energy, such as coal or gas, cannot be replaced after they have been used

non·res·i·dent /ˌnɑnˈrɛzɪdənt/ *n.* [C] someone who does not live permanently in a particular place or country

non·sense /ˈnɑnsɛns, -səns/ *n.* [U] **1** ideas, statements, or opinions that are not true or that seem very stupid: *That's* ***complete/total/utter nonsense!*** **2** behavior that is stupid and annoying: *She won't* ***take any nonsense*** *from the kids in her class.* **3** speech or writing that has no meaning or cannot be understood: *nonsense words* —**nonsensical** /nɑnˈsɛnsɪkəl/ *adj.*

non se·qui·tur /ˌnɑn ˈsɛkwɪt̬ɚ/ *n.* [C] *formal* a statement that does not seem related to the statements that were made before it

non·smok·er /ˌnɑnˈsmoʊkɚ/ *n.* [C] someone who does not smoke

non·smok·ing /ˌnɑnˈsmoʊkɪŋ◂/ *adj.* a nonsmoking area, building, etc. is one where people are not allowed to smoke

non·stand·ard /ˌnɑnˈstændɚd◂/ *adj. technical* nonstandard words, expressions, or pronunciations are usually considered incorrect by educated speakers of a language [➡ **standard**]

non·stick /ˌnɑnˈstɪk◂/ *adj.* nonstick pans have a special surface inside that food will not stick to

non·stop /ˌnɑnˈstɑp◂/ *adj., adv.* without stopping or without a stop: *Dan worked nonstop for 12 hours.* | *a nonstop flight to New York*

non·vi·o·lence /ˌnɑnˈvaɪələns/ *n.* [U] the practice of opposing a government without fighting, for example by not obeying laws

non·vi·o·lent /ˌnɑnˈvaɪələnt/ *adj.* not using or not involving violence: *nonviolent protests*

noo·dle /ˈnudl/ *n.* [C usually plural] a long thin piece of soft food made from flour, water, and usually eggs that is cooked by being boiled: *egg noodles*

nook /nʊk/ *n.* [C] **1** a small quiet place or corner: *a shady nook* **2 every nook and cranny** every part of a place: *We've searched every nook and cranny for that key.*

noon /nun/ *n.* [U] 12 O'CLOCK in the middle of the day [➡ **midnight**]: *Lunch will be right* ***at noon.*** | *The gallery is open from noon to 5:00 pm.*

'no one *pron.* not anyone: *I tried calling last night, but no one was home.* | *No one could remember her name.*

noose /nus/ *n.* [C] a circle of a rope that becomes tighter as it is pulled, used for killing someone by hanging

nope /noʊp/ *adv. spoken informal* no: *"Aren't you hungry?" "Nope."*

no·place, 'no place /ˈnoʊpleɪs/ *adv. informal* NOWHERE

nor /nɚ; *strong* nɔr/ *conjunction* **1 neither ... nor** used in order to show that not one of a set of facts, people, qualities, actions, etc. is true: *My mother's family was neither rich nor poor.* | *Neither Julie nor Mark said anything.* **2** *formal* used after a negative statement when adding another negative statement: *She didn't reply, nor did she look at him.*

norm /nɔrm/ *n.* [C] the usual or generally accepted way of doing something: *Working at home is becoming* ***the norm*** *for many employees.* | *the* ***social/cultural norms*** *of American society*

nor·mal¹ /ˈnɔrməl/ *adj.* **1** usual, typical, or expected: *The store is open during normal business hours.* | ***It's normal to*** *feel nervous when you start a new job.*

THESAURUS

ordinary – not special or unusual: *an ordinary day*

average – typical of a normal person or thing: *the average family*

standard – used about products or methods that are the most usual type: *shoes in standard sizes*

routine – used about something that is done regularly and is part of a normal system: *a routine check of the plane*

conventional – used when comparing a piece of equipment, method, etc. that has been used for a long time with something that is new and different: *microwaves and conventional ovens*

➔ NATURAL

2 a normal person is mentally and physically healthy and does not behave strangely [≠ **abnormal**]: *He seems like a* ***perfectly normal*** *child to me.*

normal² *n.* [U] the usual state, level, or amount: *The temperatures have been slightly* ***above/below***

normal. | *Things are finally getting* ***back to normal.***

nor·mal·i·ty /nɔr'mæləṭi/ **also** **nor·mal·cy** /'nɔrməlsi/ *n.* [U] a situation in which everything happens in the usual or expected way

nor·mal·ize /'nɔrmə,laɪz/ *v.* [I,T] to become normal again, or to make a situation become normal again: *The two countries have* ***normalized relations*** (=become friendly again after a period of disagreement). —**normalization** /,nɔrmələ'zeɪʃən/ *n.* [U]

N

nor·mal·ly /'nɔrməli/ *adv.* **1** usually: *I normally go to bed around eleven.* | *Normally, it takes me about twenty minutes to get to work.* **2** in the usual or expected way: *Try to relax and breathe normally.*

north

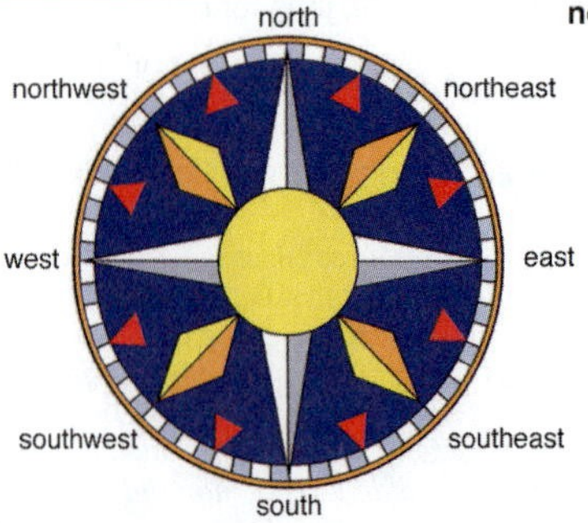

north¹, **North** /nɔrθ/ *n.* [singular, U] **1** the direction toward the top of the world, or to the left of someone facing the rising sun: *Which way is north?* **2 the north** the northern part of a country, state, etc.: *My relatives live* ***in the north*** *of the state.* **3 the North** the part of the U.S. east of the Mississippi River and north of Washington, D.C.

USAGE

Use **north/south/east/west of sth** in order to describe where a place is in relation to another place: *Chicago is south of Milwaukee.*
Use **in the north/south/east/west of sth** in order to say which part of a place you are talking about: *The mountains are in the west of the province.*
Use **northern**, **southern**, **eastern**, **western** with the name of a place: *They have a cabin in northern Ontario.*
Don't say "in the north of Ontario."

north² *adj.* **1** in, to, or facing north: *a town 20 miles* ***north of*** *Salem* | *the north side of the street* **2 north wind** a wind coming from the north

north³ *adv.* toward the north: *Go north on I-5 to Portland.* | *The window faces north.*

,North A'merica *n.* [C] one of the seven CONTINENTS that includes land between the Arctic Ocean and the Caribbean Sea —**North American** *adj.*

north·bound /'nɔrθbaʊnd/ *adj.* traveling or leading toward the north: *northbound traffic*

north·east¹ /,nɔrθ'ist◂/ *n.* [U] **1** the direction that is exactly between north and east ➔ see picture at NORTH¹ **2 the Northeast** the northeast part of a country, state, etc. —**northeastern** *adj.*

northeast² *adj., adv.* in, from, or toward the northeast: *traveling northeast* | *a northeast wind*

north·er·ly /'nɔrðəli/ *adj.* **1** in or toward the north: *sailing in a northerly direction* **2** a northerly wind comes from the north

north·ern /'nɔrðən/ *adj.* in or from the north part of an area, country, state, etc.: *northern California* ➔ see Usage box at NORTH¹

north·ern·er, **Northerner** /'nɔrðənə/ *n.* [C] someone who comes from the northern part of a country

,Northern 'Lights *n.* **the Northern Lights** bands of colored lights that are seen in the night sky in the most northern parts of the world

north·ern·most /'nɔrðən,moʊst/ *adj.* farthest north: *the northernmost tip of Maine*

,North 'Pole *n.* **the North Pole** the most northern point on the surface of the earth, or the area around it ➔ see picture at GLOBE

north·ward /'nɔrθwəd/ *adj., adv.* toward the north

north·west¹ /,nɔrθ'wɛst◂/ *n.* [U] **1** the direction that is exactly between north and west ➔ see picture at NORTH¹ **2 the Northwest** the northwest part of a country, state, etc. —**northwestern** *adj.*

northwest² *adj., adv.* in, from, or toward the northwest: *driving northwest* | *a northwest wind*

nose¹ /noʊz/ *n.* [C]
1 FACE the part of your face that you use for smelling and breathing: *a broken nose* | *He took out a tissue and* ***blew*** *his* ***nose*** (=cleared it by blowing). | *Don't* ***pick your nose*** (=clean it with your finger). ➔ see picture on page A3
2 sb's nose is running/sb has a runny nose if someone's nose is running, or if s/he has a runny nose, liquid is slowly coming out of it because s/he has a cold
3 red-nosed/long-nosed etc. having a nose that is red, long, etc.
4 (right) under sb's nose so close to someone that s/he should notice, but does not: *Lynn's husband had been having an affair right under her nose.*
5 stick/poke your nose into sth *informal* to show too much interest in private matters that do not concern you: *Jana's always sticking her nose into other people's business.*
6 keep your nose out (of sth) *informal* to avoid becoming involved in a situation that should not involve you
7 look down your nose at sb *informal* to think that you are much better than someone else
8 turn your nose up (at sth) *informal* to refuse to accept something because you do not think it is good enough for you
9 on the nose *informal* exactly: *Tanya guessed the price right on the nose.*

10 AIRPLANE the pointed front end of an airplane, ROCKET, etc.
11 keep your nose to the grindstone to continue working very hard, without stopping to rest
➔ **pay through the nose** at PAY

nose² *v.* [I,T] to move forward, or move something forward, slowly and carefully: *The ship nosed forward.*

nose around (sth) *phr. v.* to try to find out private information about someone or something: *Why were you nosing around my office?*

nose·bleed /ˈnoʊzblid/ *n.* [C] blood that is coming out of your nose: *Bill **has a nosebleed**.*

nose·dive /ˈnoʊzdaɪv/ *n.* [C] **1** a sudden drop in amount, price, rate, etc.: *The company's profits **took a nosedive** last year.* **2** a sudden steep drop by an airplane, with its front end pointing toward the ground —**nosedive** *v.* [I]

ˈnose job *n.* [C] *informal* a medical operation on someone's nose in order to improve its appearance

ˌno-ˈshow *n.* [C] *informal* someone who does not go to an event that s/he has promised to go to: *The room was crowded even though there were a dozen no-shows.*

nos·tal·gia /nɑˈstældʒə, nə-/ *n.* [U] the slightly sad feeling you have when you remember happy events from the past: ***nostalgia for** the good old days* —**nostalgic** *adj.* —**nostalgically** *adv.*

nos·tril /ˈnɑstrəl/ *n.* [C] one of the two holes at the end of your nose, through which you breathe ➔ see picture on page A3

nos·y /ˈnoʊzi/ *adj. disapproving* always trying to find out private information about someone or something: *Our neighbors are really nosy.* —**nosiness** *n.* [U]

not /nɑt/ *adv.* **1** used in order to make a word, statement, or question negative [➡ **no**]: *The museum is not open on Mondays.* | *She's not a very nice person.* | *I don't* (=do not) *smoke.* **2** used instead of a whole phrase to mean the opposite of what has been mentioned before it: *No one knows if the story is true **or not*** (=or if it is not true). | *"Is Mark still sick?" **"I hope not."*** (=I hope he is not still sick.) **3** used in order to make a word or phrase have the opposite meaning: *The food is **not very good** there.* | ***Not a lot/not much*** (=little) *is known about the disease.* | *Most of the hotels were **not that** cheap* (=they were fairly expensive). **4 not only** in addition to being or doing something: *She's **not only** funny, she's **also** smart.* **5 not a sth/not one sth** not any person or thing [= **no**]: *Not one of the students knew the answer.* | *Look! Not a cloud in the sky!* **6 not bad!** *spoken* said when you want to praise something, or when something is better than you expected: *"See, I got a B+ on my test!" "Not bad!"* **7 not that...** used before a negative sentence: *Sarah has a new boyfriend – **not that I care*** (=I do not care). **8 ...not!** *slang* said at the end of a sentence when you mean the opposite of what you have just been saying: *Yeah, she's pretty – not* (=she is ugly)*!*

no·ta·ble /ˈnoʊt̬əbəl/ *adj.* [usually before noun] important, interesting, or unusual enough to be noticed: *Freeman is the most notable player on the Texas team.* | *Most teachers agreed with the principal, with a few **notable exceptions*** (=a few teachers did not).

no·ta·bly /ˈnoʊt̬əbli/ *adv.* especially or particularly: *Some politicians, most notably the President, refused to comment.*

no·ta·rized /ˈnoʊt̬əˌraɪzd/ *adj. law* signed by a notary

no·tar·y /ˈnoʊt̬əri/ **also ˌnotary ˈpublic** *n.* plural **notaries** [C] someone who has the legal power to make a signed document official

no·ta·tion /noʊˈteɪʃən/ *n.* [C,U] a system of written marks or signs used for representing musical sounds, mathematical problems, or scientific ideas

notch¹ /nɑtʃ/ *n.* [C] **1** a V-shaped cut in a surface or edge: *Cut a notch near one end of the stick.* **2** a level of achievement or a social position: *Losing the game **brought** the team **down a few notches**.*

notch² *v.* [T] **1** to cut a V-shaped mark into something **2 also notch up** to win or achieve something: *Craven just notched the third goal of the season.*

note¹ /noʊt/ *n.* **1** [C] a short informal letter: *I **wrote/sent** Tina **a note** to thank her for helping.* | *Renee wasn't there, so we **left a note** on her door.* **2** [C] something that you write down in order to remind you of something: *She **made a note of** my new address.* **3 notes** [plural] information that a student writes down during a class, from a book, etc. so s/he will remember it: *Did you **take** any **notes*** (=write them) *in history class?* **4** [C] a particular musical sound or PITCH, or the sign in written music that represents this **5 take note (of sth)** to pay careful attention to something: *Take note of the instructions at the top of the page.* **6** [singular] a particular quality or feeling that you notice in a particular person or situation: *You could hear **a note of** weariness in her voice.* | *The story ended **on a** happy **note**.* **7 sb/sth of note** *formal* important or famous: *a writer of note*

note² *v.* [T] **1** *formal* to notice or pay careful attention to something: *Please **note that** these prices may change.* **2** *formal* to mention something because it is important or interesting: *A lawyer **noted that** Miller had no previous criminal record.* **3 also note down** to write something down so you will remember it: *He noted my telephone number.*

note·book /ˈnoʊt˺bʊk/ *n.* [C] **1** a book of plain paper in which you can write notes **2** a small computer that is about the size of a book [➡ **laptop**]

not·ed /ˈnoʊt̬ɪd/ *adj.* well-known or famous: *a noted author*

N

note·pa·per /ˈnoʊt˺ˌpeɪpɚ/ *n.* [U] paper used for writing letters or notes

note·wor·thy /ˈnoʊt˺ˌwɚði/ *adj. formal* important or interesting enough to deserve your attention: *a noteworthy event*

noth·ing¹ /ˈnʌθɪŋ/ *pron.* **1** not anything or no thing: *There's nothing in the bag.* | *I know nothing about her family.* | *Nothing you can say will change my mind.* | *There was* ***nothing else*** *the doctors could do.* | *I* ***have nothing against*** *New York* (=I have no reason for not liking it) – *I just don't want to live there.*

N

THESAURUS

zero, O, zip
➔ see Thesaurus box at ZERO¹

2 something that you do not consider to be important or interesting: *There's nothing on TV tonight.* | *I have nothing to wear to the wedding.* **3** zero: *The Red Sox won the game three nothing* (=the Red Sox had 3; the other team had no points). **4 for nothing a)** without getting the results you expected or wanted: *We drove all the way down there for nothing* **b)** without paying or being paid: *My dad said he'd fix it for nothing.* **5 have nothing to do with sb/sth a)** if something has nothing to do with a fact or situation, it is not related to that fact or situation: *"He's mad because of what I said, isn't he?" "No, that has nothing to do with it."* **b)** if someone has nothing to do with a situation or person, he or she is not involved in that situation or with that person: *"What happened?" "I don't know. I had nothing to do with it."* **6 nothing special** having no very good or very bad qualities: *The play was good, but nothing special.* **7 nothing but sth** only: *We've had nothing but rain for two weeks now.* | *He's nothing but trouble*

SPOKEN PHRASES

8 nothing much *spoken* very little: *"What did you do last weekend?" "Oh, nothing much."* **9 it was nothing** used when someone thanks you, in order to say that you did not mind helping: *"Thanks a lot!" "It was nothing."* **10 (there's) nothing to it/sth** used in order to say that something is easy to do: *Anyone can use a computer. There's nothing to it.* **11** *nonstandard* anything: *Nobody said nothing.*

nothing² *adv.* **1 be nothing like sb/sth** to have no qualities that are similar to someone or something else: *Tommy is nothing like his father.* **2 be nothing less than sth also be nothing short of sth** if something is nothing less than or nothing short of a particular quality, then it has that quality: *She thought his ideas were nothing less than ridiculous.*

noth·ing·ness /ˈnʌθɪŋnɪs/ *n.* [U] the state of complete emptiness where nothing exists

no·tice¹ /ˈnoʊt̬ɪs/ *v.* [I,T] to see, feel, or hear someone or something: *I don't think I've ever noticed that painting before.* | *I* ***noticed that*** *his hands were trembling.* | *Did you* ***notice how*** *tired Frances looked?*

THESAURUS

see, spot, catch a glimpse of, make out, catch sight of, witness
➔ see Thesaurus box at SEE

notice² *n.* **1** [C] a written or printed statement that gives information or a warning to people: *Put the notice up here so everyone can see it.* **2** [U] information or a warning about something that will happen: *You must* ***give*** *the bank* ***three days'/two weeks'/a month's notice*** *before closing the account.* **3 take notice (of sb/sth)** to pay attention to someone or something: *Critics are really starting to* ***take notice*** *of Gwen's poetry.* | *Mother kept talking, but nobody* ***took*** *any* ***notice****.* **4 give notice/hand in your notice** to tell your employer that you will be leaving your job soon [= **resign**]: *Ross gave notice yesterday.* ➔ see Topic box at JOB **5 on short notice** without much warning, so that you have only a short time to do something: *It will be hard to find a substitute teacher on such short notice.* **6 until further notice** from now until another change is announced: *The store will be closed until further notice.*

no·tice·a·ble /ˈnoʊt̬ɪsəbəl/ *adj.* easy to notice: *There's been a noticeable improvement in your work.* —**noticeably** *adv.*

THESAURUS

clear – impossible to doubt or make a mistake about: *clear evidence of his guilt*
obvious – easy to notice: *an obvious mistake*
conspicuous – very noticeable, especially because something is different from other things: *I felt conspicuous in my red coat.*
striking – unusual or interesting enough to be noticed: *He bears a striking resemblance to his father.*
eye-catching – noticeable and attractive: *an attractive eye-catching design*

no·ti·fi·ca·tion /ˌnoʊt̬əfəˈkeɪʃən/ *n.* [C,U] *formal* an act of officially telling someone about something

no·ti·fy /ˈnoʊt̬əˌfaɪ/ *v.* [T] past tense and past participle **notified**, third person singular **notifies** *formal* to tell someone something formally or officially [= **inform**]: *Have you notified the police?*

no·tion /ˈnoʊʃən/ *n.* [C] an idea, belief, or opinion about something, especially one that you think is wrong: *She rejects* ***the notion that*** *women are weaker than men.*

no·to·ri·e·ty /ˌnoʊt̬əˈraɪət̬i/ *n.* [U] the state of being famous for doing something bad

no·to·ri·ous /noʊˈtɔriəs/ *adj.* famous for something bad: *The city is **notorious for** rainy weather.* | *a notorious criminal* —**notoriously** *adv.*: *Their statistics are notoriously unreliable.*

THESAURUS
famous, **well-known**, **legendary**, **infamous**
→ see Thesaurus box at FAMOUS

not·with·stand·ing /ˌnɑtˈwɪθˈstændɪŋ/ *prep., adv. formal* if something is true notwithstanding something else, it is true even though the other thing has happened: *Their friendship notwithstanding, the two Senators have very different ideas.*

noun /naʊn/ *n.* [C] in grammar, a word or group of words that represents a person, place, thing, quality, action, or idea. In the sentence "Pollution is a problem in some cities," "pollution," "problem," and "cities" are nouns.

nour·ish /ˈnɚɪʃ, ˈnʌrɪʃ/ *v.* [T] to give a person or plant the food that is needed in order to live, grow, and be healthy: *healthy **well-nourished** children*

nour·ish·ing /ˈnɚɪʃɪŋ, ˈnʌr-/ *adj.* food that is nourishing makes you strong and healthy: *a nourishing meal*

nour·ish·ment /ˈnɚɪʃmənt, ˈnʌr-/ *n.* [U] *formal* food that is needed so you can live, grow, and be healthy

nov·el¹ /ˈnɑvəl/ *n.* [C] a long book in which the characters and events are usually imaginary: *a novel by Hemingway* | *She's written several novels.* | *a **romance/historical/mystery novel***

THESAURUS
book, **nonfiction**, **fiction**, **literature**, **reference book**, **text book**, **hardcover**, **hardback**, **paperback**, **science fiction**, **biography**, **autobiography**
→ see Thesaurus box at BOOK¹

novel² *adj.* new, different, and unusual: *a novel idea*

nov·el·ist /ˈnɑvəlɪst/ *n.* [C] someone who writes NOVELS

nov·el·ty /ˈnɑvəlti/ *n.* plural **novelties** **1** [U] the quality of being new, different, and unusual: *It was fun for a while, but the **novelty wore off*** (=it became boring). **2** [C] something new and unusual that attracts people's attention and interest: *I remember when the Internet was still a novelty.*

No·vem·ber /noʊˈvɛmbɚ, nə-/ *written abbreviation* **Nov.** *n.* [C] the 11th month of the year: *The festival starts **on November 6th**.* | *Valerie's turning 30 **in November**.* | *Ben will be three years old **next November**.* | *The project began **last November**.*

nov·ice /ˈnɑvɪs/ *n.* [C] someone who has just begun learning a skill or activity: *I'm still a novice at chess.*

No·vo·cain /ˈnoʊvəˌkeɪn/ *n.* [U] *trademark* a drug used in order to stop pain during a small operation or treatment, especially on your teeth

now¹ /naʊ/ *adv.* **1** at the present time: *Where is Heather working now?* | *Judy should have been home **by now*** (=before now). | *Mom says we have to be home by 9:00 **from now on*** (=starting now and continuing into the future). | *Let's leave the boxes in the closet **for now*** (=for a short time).

THESAURUS
at the moment – now: *Both men are in jail at the moment.*
for the moment – happening now but likely to change in the future: *The club is not for sale, at least for the moment.*
at present/at the present time – happening or existing now: *At present, my kids are all at college.*
currently – happening or existing now: *I'm currently writing a new novel.*
presently formal – at this time: *The company presently employs over 1,000 people.*

2 immediately: *You'd better go now – you're late.* | *Call her **right now** before she leaves.* **3** used when you know or understand something because of something you have just seen, just been told, etc.: *"I've just been talking to the landlord." "So, now do you see why I'm worried?"* **4 3 weeks/2 years etc. now** used in order to say how long ago something started: *I've been here for four years now.* **5 (every) now and then** used in order to say that something happens sometimes but not very often: *We go out to dinner every now and then.*

SPOKEN PHRASES
6 said when you pause because you cannot think what to say or when you want to get someone's attention: *Now, what did you say your name was?* | *OK, now. Watch me.* **7 any day/minute etc. now** very soon: *She's going to have the baby any day now.* **8 now you tell me!** said when you are annoyed because someone has just told you something s/he should have told you before

now² also **'now that** *conjunction* because or after something has happened: *I don't see as much of Mona now that she's married.*

now·a·days /ˈnaʊəˌdeɪz/ *adv.* in the present, compared to what happened in past times: *There's a lot more violence on television nowadays.*

no·where /ˈnoʊwɛr/ *adv.* **1** not any place: *There was nowhere to sit.* | *There are plants on the island that grow **nowhere else*** (=in no other place). **2 get/go nowhere** to have no success, or make no progress: *His career is going nowhere.* **3 be nowhere to be seen/found also be nowhere in sight** to be impossible to find: *We looked everywhere, but the money was nowhere to be found.* **4 nowhere near a)** far from a particular place: *Buffalo is in New York State, but it's nowhere near New York City.* **b)** not at all: *They've sold a lot of bikes, but nowhere near as many as they needed to.* **5 out of/from nowhere** happening or appearing suddenly and without warning: *The car came out of nowhere and just missed hitting her.*

nox·ious /ˈnɑkʃəs/ *adj. formal* harmful or poisonous: *a noxious gas*

noz·zle /ˈnɑzəl/ *n.* [C] a short tube attached to the end of a pipe or HOSE that controls the flow of liquid coming out

N

NPR **National Public Radio** a company in the U.S. that broadcasts radio programs without advertisements

-n't /ənt/ *adv.* the short form of "not": *He isn't* (=is not) *here.* | *She can't* (=cannot) *see him.* | *I didn't* (=did not) *do it.*

nu·ance /ˈnuɑns/ *n.* [C,U] a very slight difference in meaning, color, or feeling —**nuanced** *adj.*

nu·cle·ar /ˈnukliə/ *adj.* **1** relating to or involving the use of nuclear weapons: *nuclear war* **2** using nuclear power, or relating to nuclear energy: *a nuclear submarine* | *a nuclear reactor* **3** relating to the NUCLEUS (=central part) of an atom: *nuclear physics*

ˌnuclear disˈarmament *n.* [U] the activity of getting rid of NUCLEAR WEAPONS

ˌnuclear ˈenergy *n.* [U] the powerful force that is produced when the NUCLEUS of an atom is either split or joined to another atom

ˌnuclear ˈfamily *n.* [C] a family that has a father, mother, and children [➡ **extended family**]

ˌnuclear ˈpower *n.* [U] power, usually in the form of electricity, produced from nuclear energy

ˌnuclear reˈactor *n.* [C] a large machine that produces NUCLEAR ENERGY, especially as a means of producing electricity

ˌnuclear ˈwaste *n.* [U] waste from NUCLEAR REACTORS, which is RADIOACTIVE

ˌnuclear ˈweapon *n.* [C] a very powerful weapon that uses NUCLEAR ENERGY to destroy large areas

nu·cle·us /ˈnukliəs/ *n.* plural **nuclei** /-kliaɪ/ [C] **1** the central part of an atom or cell **2 the nucleus of sth** the central or most important part of something: *Moore and Lane form the nucleus of the team.*

nude¹ /nud/ *adj.* not wearing any clothes [**= naked**] —**nudity** *n.* [U]

THESAURUS

naked, undressed, bare, have nothing on, not have anything on

➔ see Thesaurus box at NAKED

nude² *n.* **1 in the nude** without wearing any clothes: *sleeping in the nude* **2** [C] a painting or STATUE of someone who is not wearing clothes

nudge /nʌdʒ/ *v.* [T] to push someone or something gently, especially with your elbow: *Ken nudged me and said, "Look, there's Cindy."* —**nudge** *n.* [C]

THESAURUS

push, roll, poke, shove, elbow

➔ see Thesaurus box at PUSH¹

nu·dist /ˈnudɪst/ *n.* [C] someone who enjoys not wearing any clothes because s/he believes it is natural and healthy —**nudist** *adj.*

nug·get /ˈnʌgɪt/ *n.* [C] a small rough piece of a valuable metal found in the earth: *a gold nugget*

nui·sance /ˈnusəns/ *n.* [C usually singular] someone or something that annoys you or causes problems: *Jon is **making a nuisance of** himself, always phoning Rachel late at night.*

nuke¹ /nuk/ *v.* [T] *informal* **1** to attack a place using NUCLEAR WEAPONS **2** *spoken* to cook food in a MICROWAVE

nuke² *n.* [C usually plural] *informal* a NUCLEAR WEAPON

null and void /ˌnʌl ən ˈvɔɪd/ *adj. law* an agreement, contract, etc. that is null and void has no legal force

nul·li·fy /ˈnʌləˌfaɪ/ *v.* past tense and past participle **nullified**, third person singular **nullifies** [T] *law* to state officially that something will have no legal force: *The election results were nullified because of voter fraud.*

numb¹ /nʌm/ *adj.* **1** unable to feel anything: *My feet are **getting numb** from the cold.* **2** unable to think, feel, or react in a normal way: *She was **numb with** grief after her mother's death.* —**numbness** *n.* [U] —**numbly** *adv.*

numb² *v.* [T] to make someone unable to feel anything: *The cold wind numbed my face.*

num·ber¹ /ˈnʌmbə/ *n.*

1 SIGN [C] a word or sign that represents an amount or quantity: *Pick any number between one and ten.* | *Add the numbers 7, 4, and 3.* | *an **even number*** (=2, 4, 6, 8, etc.) | *an **odd number*** (=1, 3, 5, 7, etc.)

USAGE

Number is used with countable nouns: *a large number of cities*

Amount is used with uncountable nouns: *a large amount of money*

2 ON A PHONE [C] a set of numbers that you press on a telephone when you are calling someone: *Ann's phone number is 555–3234.* | *I think I dialed the **wrong number**.* | *He gave me his **work/home number**.*

3 IN A SERIES [C] a number used in order to show the position of something in an ordered set, list, series, etc.: *Look at question number five.* | *What's his room number?*

4 FOR RECOGNIZING PEOPLE/THINGS [C] a set of numbers used in order to name or recognize someone or something: *a social security number* | *What's your account number?*

5 AMOUNT [C,U] an amount of something that can be counted: ***The number of** smokers is decreasing.* | *We have been friends for **a number of*** (=several) *years.* | *People are moving to the southwest **in increasing/growing numbers**.* | *Doctors believe that **a large/great/small number of** people are at risk.*
6 number one *informal* the best or most important person or thing in a group: *California continues to be the number one travel destination in the U.S.*
7 MUSIC [C] a piece of popular music, a song, a dance, etc. that forms part of a larger performance

number² *v.* [T] **1** to give a number to something that is part of a set or list: ***Number** the items **from** one **to** ten.* **2** if people or things number a particular amount, that is how many there are: *The crowd numbered around 20,000.* **3 sb's/sth's days are numbered** used in order to say that someone or something cannot live or continue much longer: *These injuries mean his days as a player are numbered.*

nu·mer·al /ˈnumərəl, ˈnumrəl/ *n.* [C] a written sign that represents a number, such as 5, 22, etc.

nu·mer·i·cal /nuˈmɛrɪkəl/ *adj.* expressed in numbers, or relating to numbers: *Are the pages **in numerical order*** (=numbered 1, 2, 3, etc.)? —**numerically** *adv.*

num·er·ous /ˈnumərəs/ *adj. formal* many: *We discussed the plans **on numerous occasions**.*

nun /nʌn/ *n.* [C] a woman who is a member of a group of religious women who live together in a CONVENT [➡ **monk**]

nup·tials /ˈnʌpʃəlz/ *n.* [plural] *formal* a wedding

nurse¹ /nɚs/ *n.* [C] someone whose job is to take care of people who are sick or injured, usually in a hospital: *The nurse is coming to give you an injection.*

nurse² *v.* **1** [T] to take care of people who are sick or injured: *Michael **nursed** his wife **back to health**.* **2** [T] to rest when you have an illness or injury so you will get better: *He's nursing a sprained ankle.* **3** [I,T] to BREASTFEED

nurs·er·y /ˈnɚsəri/ *n.* plural **nurseries** [C] **1** a place where plants and trees are grown and sold ➔ see Thesaurus box at STORE¹ **2** *old-fashioned* a bedroom for a baby

ˈnursery rhyme *n.* [C] a short well-known song or poem for children

ˈnursery ˌschool *n.* [C] a school for children from three to five years old [➡ **preschool, kindergarten**]

nurs·ing /ˈnɚsɪŋ/ *n.* [U] the job of taking care of people who are sick, injured, or very old: *Joanne plans to go into nursing.*

nursing home *n.* [C] a place where people who are too old or sick to take care of themselves can live [➡ **retirement home**]

nur·ture¹ /ˈnɚtʃɚ/ *v.* [T] *formal* **1** to feed and take care of a child or a plant while it is growing: *children nurtured by loving parents* **2** to help a plan, idea, feeling, etc. develop: *new democracies that need to be nurtured*

nurture² *n.* [U] *formal* the education and care that are given to a child who is growing and developing

nut /nʌt/ *n.* [C] **1** a large seed that you can eat that usually grows in a hard brown shell: *a cashew nut* **2** a small piece of metal with a hole in the middle that is screwed onto a BOLT to fasten things together: *Use a wrench to loosen the nut.* **3 golf/opera etc. nut** *informal* someone who is very interested in golf, etc.: *a golf nut* **4** *informal* someone who is crazy or behaves strangely **5** [usually plural] *slang* TESTICLE **6 the nuts and bolts of sth** the practical details of a subject, plan, job, etc.

nut·crack·er /ˈnʌt˺ˌkrækɚ/ *n.* [C] a tool for cracking the shells of nuts

nutcracker

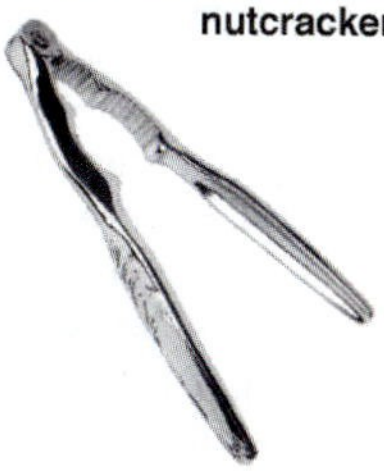

nut·meg /ˈnʌt˺mɛg/ *n.* [U] a brown powder used as a spice to give a particular taste to food

nu·tri·ent /ˈnutriənt/ *n.* [C] a chemical or food that helps plants, animals, or people to live and grow: *Plants take nutrients from the soil.*

nu·tri·tion /nuˈtrɪʃən/ *n.* [U] the process of getting the right types of food for good health and growth: ***good/poor nutrition*** —**nutritional** *adj.*: *food that has little nutritional value* —**nutritionally** *adv.*

nu·tri·tious /nuˈtrɪʃəs/ *adj.* food that is nutritious has a lot of substances that your body needs to stay healthy and grow

nuts /nʌts/ *adj. informal* crazy, silly, or angry: *His stupid comments **drive me nuts*** (=annoy me very much).

THESAURUS

crazy, mentally ill, insane, disturbed, loony
➔ see Thesaurus box at CRAZY

nut·shell /ˈnʌt˺ʃɛl/ *n.* [C] **1 (to put it) in a nutshell** *informal* used in order to show that you are going to give the main facts about something in a way that is short and clear **2** the hard outer part of a nut

nut·ty /ˈnʌţi/ *adj.* **1** tasting like nuts: *a nutty flavor* **2** *informal* crazy: *a nutty idea*

nuz·zle /ˈnʌzəl/ *v.* [I,T] to gently rub your face or head against someone in a loving way: *a new mother gently nuzzling her baby's head*

NV the written abbreviation of **Nevada**

NW the written abbreviation of **northwest**

NY the written abbreviation of **New York**

ny·lon /ˈnaɪlɑn/ *n.* [U] **1** a strong artificial material that is used for making plastic, cloth, rope, etc.: *nylon running shorts* **2 nylons** [plural] a

N

piece of clothing that women wear on their legs, that is very thin and made of nylon

nymph /nɪmf/ *n.* [C] one of the spirits of nature who appears in the form of a young girl, in ancient Greek and Roman stories

nym·pho·ma·ni·ac /ˌnɪmfəˈmeɪniˌæk/ *n.* [C] a woman who wants to have sex often, usually with a lot of different men —**nymphomania** /ˌnɪmfəˈmeɪniə/ *n.* [U]

O, o

O, o /oʊ/ **1** the fifteenth letter of the English alphabet **2** *spoken* zero: *room 203* (=two o three)

o' /ə/ *prep. nonstandard* a way of writing "of" as it is often said in speech: *a cup o' coffee*

oaf /oʊf/ *n.* [C] *old-fashioned* a large, stupid, awkward man or boy —**oafish** *adj.*

oak /oʊk/ *n.* [C,U] a large tree that is common in northern countries, or the hard wood of this tree

oar /ɔr/ *n.* [C] a long pole with a wide blade at one end, used for rowing a boat

oasis

o·a·sis /oʊˈeɪsɪs/ *n.* plural **oases** /oʊˈeɪsiz/ [C] a place with trees and water in a desert

oat /oʊt/ *n.* **oats** [plural] a grain that is eaten by people and animals —**oat** *adj.* [only before noun] *hot oat cereal*

oath /oʊθ/ *n.* plural **oaths** /oʊðz, oʊθs/ [C] **1 be under oath** to have made an official promise to tell the truth in a court of law: *The witness **testified under oath**.* **2** a formal and serious promise: *New U.S. citizens **take/swear an oath** of allegiance* (=promise to be loyal to the U.S.).

oat·meal /ˈoʊt˺mil/ *n.* [U] crushed oats that are boiled and eaten for breakfast, or used in cooking

o·be·di·ence /əˈbidiəns, oʊ-/ *n.* [U] doing what you are supposed to do, according to a law or to someone in authority [≠ **disobedience**; ➡ **obey**]: *Kay acted **in obedience to** her parents.*

o·be·di·ent /əˈbidiənt, oʊ-/ *adj.* always obeying laws, rules, or people in authority [≠ **disobedient**; ➡ **obey**]: *an obedient child* —**obediently** *adv.*

o·bese /oʊˈbis/ *adj.* very fat in a way that is unhealthy —**obesity** *n.* [U]

> **THESAURUS**
>
> **fat**, **overweight**, **big**, **heavy**, **large**, **chubby**, **plump**
> → see Thesaurus box at FAT[1]

o·bey /əˈbeɪ, oʊ-/ *v.* past tense and past participle **obeyed**, third person singular **obeys** [I,T] to do what you are supposed to do, according to the law or to what someone in authority says [≠ **disobey**; ➡ **obedient**]: *Children should be taught to **obey the law**. | "Sit!" he said, and the dog obeyed him immediately.*

> **THESAURUS**
>
> **do what sb says**: *I don't ask questions – I just do what the coach says.*
> **do what you are told/do as you are told**: *Maybe next time you'll do what you are told.*
> **follow sb's orders/instructions**: *Follow the manufacturer's instructions. | You must follow your doctor's orders.*

o·bit·u·ar·y /əˈbɪtʃuˌɛri, oʊ-/ *n.* plural **obituaries** [C] a report of someone's death in a newspaper

ob·ject¹ /ˈɑbdʒɪkt, ˈɑbdʒɛkt/ *n.* **1** [C] a thing that you can see, hold, or touch: *a small metal object*

> **THESAURUS**
>
> **thing**, **item**, **article**
> → see Thesaurus box at THING

2 [singular] the purpose of a plan, action, or activity: ***The object of** the game is to improve children's math skills.* **3 an object of desire/pity etc.** someone or something that you desire, pity, etc. **4** [C] *technical* **a)** in grammar, the person or thing that is affected by the action of the verb, for example "door" in the sentence "Sheila closed the door." [= **direct object**] **b)** in grammar, the person who is involved in the result of an action, for example "her" in the sentence "I gave her a book." [= **indirect object**] **c)** in grammar, the person or thing that is connected by a PREPOSITION to another word, for example "table" in the sentence "We sat at the table."

ob·ject² /əbˈdʒɛkt/ *v.* [I] to say that you do not like or approve of something: *Reynolds **objected to** the plan.*

ob·jec·tion /əbˈdʒɛkʃən/ *n.* [C] a reason you give for not approving of an idea or plan: *The group **has** strong **objections to** the death penalty. | Several Senators **raised objections*** (=they objected) *to the bill.* → see Thesaurus box at OPPOSITION

COLLOCATIONS

have an objection: *I have no objection to comedians making fun of politicians.*
raise an objection: *Opponents of the plan have raised other objections.*
state an objection: *The President stated three main objections to the legislation.*
voice an objection: *The church has voiced strong objections to the movie.*
make an objection: *She was granted bail after the prosecution made no objection.*
lodge/register an objection formal (=make one): *Players have registered their strong objection to the new contracts.*

ob·jec·tion·a·ble /əbˈdʒɛkʃənəbəl/ *adj.* likely to offend people [= **offensive**]: *The program contains material that some people may **find objectionable**.*

ob·jec·tive¹ /əbˈdʒɛktɪv/ *n.* [C] something that you are working hard to achieve: *The company's **main objective** is to increase sales overseas.*

THESAURUS

purpose, aim, goal
➔ see Thesaurus box at PURPOSE

objective² *adj.* not influenced by your own feelings, beliefs, or ideas [≠ **subjective**]: *objective news reporting* —**objectively** *adv.*: *We need to look at the situation objectively.* —**objectivity** /ˌɑbdʒɛkˈtɪvət̮i/ *n.* [U]

ob·li·gat·ed /ˈɑbləˌgeɪt̮ɪd/ *adj.* **be/feel obligated (to do sth)** to feel that it is your duty to do something: *I don't want them to feel obligated to pay for dinner.*

ob·li·ga·tion /ˌɑbləˈgeɪʃən/ *n.* [C,U] a moral or legal duty to do something: *Every father **has an obligation to** take care of his child.* | *You are **under no obligation to*** (=do not have to) *answer these questions.*

o·blig·a·to·ry /əˈblɪgəˌtɔri/ *adj. formal* having to be done because of a law, rule, etc. [= **mandatory**]

o·blige /əˈblaɪdʒ/ *v.* **1 be/feel obliged (to do sth)** to feel that it is your duty to do something: *You shouldn't feel obliged to work overtime.* **2** [I,T] *formal* to do something that someone has asked you to do: *He asked to borrow my car, and I was **happy/glad to oblige**.* **3 (I'm/we're) much obliged** *spoken old-fashioned* said in order to thank someone very politely

o·blig·ing /əˈblaɪdʒɪŋ/ *adj.* willing and eager to help: *a cheerful and obliging woman* —**obligingly** *adv.*

o·blique /əˈblik, oʊ-/ *adj. formal* not expressed in a direct way [= **indirect**]: *oblique references to his drinking problem*

ob·lit·er·ate /əˈblɪt̮əˌreɪt/ *v.* [T] to destroy something completely: *Large areas of the city were obliterated during World War II.* —**obliteration** /əˌblɪt̮əˈreɪʃən/ *n.* [U]

ob·liv·i·on /əˈblɪviən/ *n.* [U] *formal* **1** the state of being completely forgotten: *Old movie stars who have **faded into oblivion**.* **2** the state of being unconscious or of not knowing what is happening: *He spent the night drinking himself **into oblivion**.*

ob·liv·i·ous /əˈblɪviəs/ *adj.* not knowing about or not noticing something happening around you [= **unaware**]: *She seemed completely **oblivious to/of** the danger.*

ob·long /ˈɑblɔŋ/ *adj.* having a shape that is longer than it is wide: *an oblong mirror* —**oblong** *n.* [C]

ob·nox·ious /əbˈnɑkʃəs/ *adj.* very offensive or rude: *Her friends were loud and obnoxious.* —**obnoxiously** *adv.*

o·boe /ˈoʊboʊ/ *n.* [C] a wooden musical instrument, shaped like a narrow tube, that you play by blowing into it ➔ see picture on page A6

ob·scene /əbˈsin, ɑb-/ *adj.* **1** offensive and shocking in a sexual way: *obscene photographs* | *He made an **obscene gesture**.* **2** extremely immoral or unfair: *Some players earn obscene amounts of money.*

ob·scen·i·ty /əbˈsɛnət̮i/ *n.* plural **obscenities** **1** [C usually plural] a sexually offensive word or action: *kids shouting obscenities* **2** [U] offensive language or behavior involving sex, especially in a book, play, etc.: *laws against obscenity*

ob·scure¹ /əbˈskyʊr/ *adj.* **1** unclear or difficult to understand: *Jarrett didn't like the plan for some obscure reason.* **2** known about only by a few people: *an obscure poet*

obscure² *v.* [T] **1** to prevent something from being seen or heard clearly: *Parts of the coast were obscured by fog.* **2** to make something difficult to know or understand: *Recent successes have **obscured the fact that** the company is still in trouble.*

ob·scur·i·ty /əbˈskyʊrət̮i/ *n.* plural **obscurities** **1** [U] the state of not being known or remembered: *O'Brien retired from politics and died **in obscurity**.* **2** [C,U] something that is difficult to understand, or the quality of being difficult to understand

ob·serv·a·ble /əbˈzɚvəbəl/ *adj.* able to be seen or noticed

ob·serv·ance /əbˈzɚvəns/ *n.* [U] the practice of obeying laws, religious rules, etc.: *the **observance of** Yom Kippur*

ob·serv·ant /əbˈzɚvənt/ *adj.* **1** good or quick at noticing things: *I can see you're very observant.* **2** obeying laws, religious rules, etc.: *observant Hindus*

ob·ser·va·tion /ˌɑbzɚˈveɪʃən, -sɚ-/ *n.* **1** [C,U] the act or process of carefully watching someone or something, or one of the facts you learn from doing this: *The psychologist's theories are based on his **observation of** children's behavior.* | *The patient is **under** close **observation*** (=being continuously watched). **2** [C] a remark about something that you have noticed: *I'd like to* ***make*** *an* ***observation***.

ob·serv·a·to·ry /əbˈzɚvəˌtɔri/ *n.* plural **observatories** [C] a special building from which scientists watch the moon, stars, weather, etc.

ob·serve /əbˈzɚv/ *v.* [T] **1** to watch someone or something carefully: *The police have been observing his movements.* **2** *formal* to see or notice something in particular: *Doctors* ***observed that*** *the disease only occurs in women over 50.* **3** to obey a law, agreement, or religious rule: *Both sides are observing the ceasefire.*

O

ob·serv·er /əbˈzɚvɚ/ *n.* [C] **1** someone who goes to a meeting, class, event, etc. to officially watch or check what is happening: *International observers monitored the elections.* **2** someone who sees or notices something

ob·sess /əbˈsɛs/ *v.* **1** [T] to think about someone or something all the time, so that you cannot think of anything else: *William* ***is obsessed with*** *making money.* **2** [I] *informal* to think about something or someone much more than is necessary and sensible: *Stop* ***obsessing about/over*** *your weight. You look great!*

ob·ses·sion /əbˈsɛʃən/ *n.* [C,U] an extreme unhealthy interest in something or worry about something, which prevents you from thinking about other things: *an unhealthy* ***obsession with*** *sex*

ob·ses·sive /əbˈsɛsɪv/ *adj.* thinking or worrying too much about someone or something so that you do not think about other things enough: *She's* ***obsessive about*** *exercise.* —**obsessively** *adv.*

ob·so·lete /ˌɑbsəˈlit◂ / *adj.* no longer useful or needed because something newer and better has been made: *The old computers have* ***become obsolete***. —**obsolescence** /ˌɑbsəˈlɛsəns/ *n.* [U]

ob·sta·cle /ˈɑbstɪkəl/ *n.* [C] **1** something that makes it difficult for you to succeed: *Lack of confidence can be a big* ***obstacle to*** *success.* | *The team has had to* ***overcome obstacles*** *this season.* **2** something that blocks your way, so that you must go around it: *an obstacle in the road*

ˈobstacle course *n.* [C] a line of objects that a runner must jump over, go under, etc.

ob·stet·rics /əbˈstɛktrɪks, ɑb-/ *n.* [U] the part of medical science that deals with the birth of children —**obstetrician** /ˌɑbstəˈtrɪʃən/ *n.* [C]

ob·sti·nate /ˈɑbstənɪt/ *adj.* refusing to change your opinions, ideas, behavior, etc. [= **stubborn**] —**obstinacy** *n.* [U]

ob·struct /əbˈstrʌkt/ *v.* [T] **1** to block a road, path, passage, or someone's view of something: *The truck was on its side, obstructing two lanes of traffic.* **2** to try to prevent someone from doing something by making it difficult: *Federal officers accused Robbins of obstructing their investigation.* —**obstructive** *adj.*

obstruction

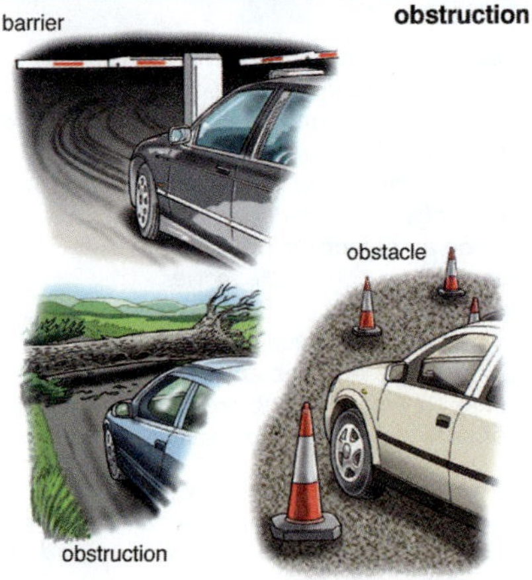

ob·struc·tion /əbˈstrʌkʃən/ *n.* **1** [C,U] something that blocks a road, passage, tube, etc., or the fact of blocking a road, etc.: *The accident* ***caused an obstruction*** *on the freeway.* **2** [U] the act of preventing something from happening: *The judge is charged with* ***obstruction of justice*** *in the Martel case.*

ob·tain /əbˈteɪn/ *v.* [T] *formal* to get something that you want: *Information about passports can be* ***obtained from*** *the embassy.*

ob·tru·sive /əbˈtrusɪv/ *adj. formal* noticeable in a bad or annoying way [≠ **unobtrusive**]: *The waitresses were friendly but never obtrusive.*

ob·tuse /əbˈtus, ɑb-/ *adj.* **1** *formal* stupid or slow to understand something **2 obtuse angle** *technical* an angle between 90 and 180 degrees [➡ **acute angle**]

ob·vi·ous /ˈɑbviəs/ *adj.* easy to notice or understand: *the obvious choice* | ***It was obvious (that)*** *he hadn't actually read the book.* | *The need for change seemed* ***obvious to*** *everyone.*

THESAURUS

noticeable, clear, conspicuous, striking, eye-catching
➔ see Thesaurus box at NOTICEABLE

ob·vi·ous·ly /ˈɑbviəsli/ *adv.* used when something is easily noticed or understood: *Obviously, I was scared.* | *Patrick is obviously a good father.*

oc·ca·sion /əˈkeɪʒən/ *n.* **1** [C] a time when something happens: *I met with him* ***on*** *several* ***occasions***. **2** [C] an important event or ceremony: *We're saving the champagne for* ***a special occasion***. | *a* ***joyous/happy/solemn etc. occasion*** **3 on occasion** sometimes, but not often: *Craig helps out on occasion.* **4** [U] a cause or reason to do something: *I'm sure we will* ***have occasion to*** *discuss this further.*

oc·ca·sion·al /əˈkeɪʒənl/ *adj.* happening sometimes but not often: *He has **the/an occasional** drink.*

oc·ca·sion·al·ly /ə'keɪʒənl-i/ *adv.* sometimes, but not regularly or often: *We occasionally see each other.* | *Heat the soup, stirring occasionally.*

THESAURUS

sometimes, (every) once in a while, every so often, from time to time
➔ see Thesaurus box at SOMETIMES

oc·cult /ə'kʌlt/ *n.* **the occult** the knowledge and study of magic and spirits —**occult** *adj.*

oc·cu·pan·cy /'ɑkyəpənsi/ *n.* [U] *formal* someone's use of a building or other space for living or working

oc·cu·pant /'ɑkyəpənt/ *n.* [C] *formal* someone who lives in a building, room, etc., or who is in it at a particular time: *a letter addressed to the occupant*

oc·cu·pa·tion /ˌɑkyə'peɪʃən/ *n.* **1** [C] *formal* a job or profession [➡ **employment**, **work**]: *the occupations available to women* **2** [U] the act of entering a place and getting control of it, especially by military force [➡ **occupy**]: *the German **occupation of** France in the war* **3** [U] *formal* a way of spending your time

oc·cu·pa·tion·al /ˌɑkyə'peɪʃənəl/ *adj.* relating to your job

oc·cu·pied /'ɑkyəˌpaɪd/ *adj.* **1** busy doing or thinking about something: *toys to **keep** the kids **occupied*** | *His father was **occupied with** work.* **2** being used: *All the rooms on the first floor are occupied.* **3** an occupied place is controlled by an army: *the occupied territories*

oc·cu·py /'ɑkyəˌpaɪ/ *v.* past tense and past participle **occupied**, third person singular **occupies** [T] **1** to live, work, stay, etc. in a particular place: *Salem Press occupies the seventh floor of the building.* **2** if something occupies you or your time, you are busy doing it: *Reading instruction occupies two hours of each day.* **3** to fill a particular amount of space: *Family photos occupied almost the entire wall.* **4** to enter a place and get control of it, especially by military force [➡ **invade**]

oc·cur /ə'kɚ/ *v.* past tense and past participle **occurred**, present participle **occurring** [I] *formal* **1** to happen, especially without being planned first: *Earthquakes occur without any warning signs.* **2** to exist or be present in a particular place: *The disease mainly **occurs in** young children.* —**occurrence** *n.* [C, singular] *Stress-related illness is now a fairly common occurrence.*

occur to sb *phr. v.* to suddenly come into your mind: ***It** never **occurred to** me **to** ask.*

o·cean /'oʊʃən/ *n.* **1** [C] a particular area of salt water somewhere on Earth: *the Indian Ocean* **2 the ocean** the great quantity of salt water that covers most of the Earth's surface —**oceanic** /ˌoʊʃi'ænɪk/ *adj.*

o·cean·og·ra·phy /ˌoʊʃə'nɑgrəfi/ *n.* [U] the scientific study of the ocean —**oceanographer** *n.* [C]

o'clock /ə'klɑk/ *adv.* **one/two/three etc. o'clock** one of the times when the clock shows the exact hour as a number from 1 to 12

oc·ta·gon /'ɑktəˌgɑn/ *n.* [C] a flat shape with eight sides and eight angles —**octagonal** /ɑk'tægənəl/ *adj.*

Oc·to·ber /ɑk'toʊbɚ/ *n. written abbreviation* **Oct.** [C] the tenth month of the year: *The group will be performing **on October 22nd**.* | *Clare's going to be two **in October**.* | *We have been in this apartment since **last October**.* | *Our membership expires **next October**.*

oc·to·pus /'ɑktəpəs/ *n.* plural **octopuses** or **octopi** /'ɑktəpaɪ/ [C] a sea creature with a soft body and eight TENTACLES (=arms)

OD *v.* past tense and past participle **OD'd**, present participle **OD'ing** [I] *slang* **overdose** to take too much of a dangerous drug

odd /ɑd/ *adj.* **1** different from what is expected or normal [= **strange**]: *an odd guy* | ***It's odd** that she hasn't phoned by now.*

THESAURUS

strange, funny, peculiar, mysterious, weird, bizarre, eccentric
➔ see Thesaurus box at STRANGE[1]

2 odd jobs small jobs of different types, for example fixing or cleaning things **3** an odd number cannot be divided by 2. For example, 1, 3, 5, etc. are odd numbers [➡ **even**] **4** [only before noun] separated from its pair or set: *an odd sock* **5 20-odd/30-odd etc.** *informal* a little more than 20, 30, etc. ➔ ODDS

odd·ball /'ɑdbɔl/ *adj. informal* strange or unusual —**oddball** *n.* [C]

odd·i·ty /'ɑdət̬i/ *n.* plural **oddities** [C] a strange or unusual person or thing

odd·ly /'ɑdli/ *adv.* in a strange or unusual way ➔ **strangely/oddly/funnily enough** at ENOUGH

odds /ɑdz/ *n.* [plural] **1 the odds** how likely it is that something will or will not happen [= **chance**]: ***The odds are** about 1 in 12 **that** a boy will be colorblind.* | *Doctors have improved **the odds of** survival for these babies.* **2** difficulties that make a good result seem very unlikely: *Our team won the title **against all the odds*** (=in spite of difficulties). **3 at odds (with sb)** disagreeing with someone: *Mark's account of what happened is at odds with Dan's.*

ˌodds and 'ends *n.* [plural] *informal* various small things that have little value

ode /oʊd/ *n.* [C] a long poem that is written in order to praise a person or thing

o·di·ous /ˈoʊdiəs/ *adj. formal* very bad or disgusting

o·dor /ˈoʊdɚ/ *n.* [C] a smell, especially a bad one

> **THESAURUS**
> **smell, stink, stench**
> ➔ see Thesaurus box at SMELL²

o·dor·less /ˈoʊdɚlɪs/ *adj.* not having a smell: *an odorless gas*

od·ys·sey /ˈɑdəsi/ *n.* [C] *literary* a long trip

O

of /əv, ə; *strong* ʌv/ *prep.* **1** used in order to show a quality or feature that someone or something has: *the color of his shirt* | *the size of the building* | *It was stupid of me to say that.* **2** used in order to show that something is a part of something else: *the first part of the story* | *the tips of your fingers* **3** used in order to show that something belongs to or relates to someone or something: *an old shirt of his* | *a friend of Bobby's* **4** used with words that show a particular type of group: *a bunch of grapes* | *a herd of elephants* **5** used in order to show an amount or measurement: *a cup of coffee* | *lots of room* | *a drop of water* **6** used in order to show that someone or something is from a larger group: *That's one of her best poems.* | *members of a rock group* **7** used in dates: *the 23rd of January, 2004* **8** *spoken* used in giving the time, to mean "before": *It's ten of five* (=ten minutes before 5:00). **9** used when giving the name of something: *the city of New Orleans* | *the game of chess* **10** used when giving the reason for or the cause of something: *She died of cancer.* **11** used in order to say what something shows: *a picture of his family* | *a map of the world* **12** used in order to say what something is about or what type of thing it is: *Do you know the story of Tom Thumb?* | *the problem of crime in schools* **13** used in order to show direction or distance: *I live just north of here.* | *The school is within a mile of the park* (=it is less than a mile from the park). **14** used after nouns describing actions to show to whom the action is done or who did the action: *the testing of river water for chemicals* | *the crying of a child* **15** *literary* made from: *a dress of pure silk* **16** written, made, produced, etc. by someone or something: *the early plays of Shakespeare* **17** used in order to say where someone lives: *the people of Malaysia* ➔ **of course** at COURSE

off /ɔf/ *adv., prep., adj.* **1** away from or out of a place or position: *She waved and drove off.* | *Get your feet off the couch!* | *He took his shoes off.* | *The bus stopped, and she got off.* **2** a machine, light, etc. that is off is not working or operating [≠ **on**]: *Why are all the lights off?* | ***Turn** the lights **off** when you leave.* | *Does the machine **shut** itself **off**?* **3** lower in price: *You **get** **10%/15% off** if you buy $100 worth of groceries.* **4** how far away something is, or how much time there is between now and a future event: *Spring is still **a long way off**.* | *mountains **way off** in the distance* **5** away from a particular place: *Oak Hills – isn't that off Route 290?* | *a hotel **just off** the main street* **6** not at work or school because you are sick or on vacation: *Dave's off tomorrow.* | *Monday is my **day off**.* | *I'm **taking the day/week off**.* **7** if an event is off, it will not now take place: *The wedding's off.* **8** not as good as usual: *Sales are a little off compared with last year.* **9** not correct or not of good quality: *His calculations are off by 20%.* **10 have an off day/week etc.** *spoken* to have a day, week, etc. when you are not doing something as well as you usually do **11 off and on/on and off** for short periods of time, but not regularly: *We've been going out together for two years, off and on.* ➔ WELL-OFF

ˌoff-ˈbalance *adj.* [not before noun] **1** in an unsteady position and likely to fall: *He staggered back, off-balance.* **2 catch/throw sb off-balance** to surprise or shock someone because s/he is not prepared: *American forces were caught off-balance by the tactics.*

off·beat /ˌɔfˈbit◂/ *adj. informal* unusual and not what people expect, in an interesting way: *an offbeat style of comedy*

of·fend /əˈfɛnd/ *v.* **1** [T] to make someone angry or upset [➡ **offensive**]: *The senator's remarks offended many women.* **2** [I] *formal* to do something that is a crime

of·fend·er /əˈfɛndɚ/ *n.* [C] someone who is guilty of a crime: *As a **first-time offender**, Joe received a fine.*

> **THESAURUS**
> **criminal, thief, robber, burglar, shoplifter, pickpocket, attacker, mugger, murderer, rapist**
> ➔ see Thesaurus box at CRIMINAL²

of·fense¹ /əˈfɛns/ *n.* **1** [C] a crime: *Drinking and driving is a **serious offense**.* | *Anyone charged with a **criminal offense** is entitled to a trial.* | *programs to prevent teenagers from **committing** more serious **offenses*** **2 no offense** *spoken* said in order to show that you hope what you are saying will not offend someone: *No offense, but that's not a smart thing to do.* **3 take offense/cause offense** to feel offended or to offend someone: *Many women **took offense at** the tone of his speech.*

of·fense² /ˈɔfɛns/ *n.* [U] the action of trying to get points and win in a sports game, or the group of players responsible for doing this [≠ **defense**]: *The team needs to work on their offense.*

of·fen·sive¹ /əˈfɛnsɪv/ *adj.* **1** used or intended for attacking [≠ **defensive**]: *offensive weapons* **2** very insulting and likely to upset people [≠ **inoffensive**]: *offensive jokes* **3** relating to trying to get points and win in sports games, or relating to the players who do this [≠ **defensive**]: *the Bears' offensive lineup* —**offensively** *adj.*

offensive² *n.* [C] **1** an attack made on a place by an army: *a **military offensive***

THESAURUS

rude, impolite, insulting, tactless
→ see Thesaurus box at RUDE

2 be/go on the offensive also take the offensive to attack or criticize people

of·fer¹ /ˈɔfɚ, ˈɑfɚ/ *v.* **1** [T] to say that you are willing to give something to someone, or to hold something out to someone so that s/he can take it: *I offered them a drink.* | *Did they offer you the job?* | *They **offered** us $175,000 **for** the house.* | *The company **offers** scholarships **to** inner-city students.* | *Stewart **offers advice/help/support** to women in this difficult position.*

COMMUNICATION

Ways of offering something
Have sth informal: *Here, have a bite.*
Would you like sth?: *Would you like some wine?*
Can I get you sth?: *Can I get you something to drink?*
Do you want sth? informal: *Do you want some more spaghetti?*
Can I offer you sth? formal: *Can I offer you a beverage?*
Help yourself to sth (=take something, especially food, whenever you want it): *Help yourself to some fruit.*

2 [I,T] to say that you are willing to do something: *She didn't even **offer to** help.*

offer² *n.* [C] **1** a statement that you are willing to give something to someone or do something for someone: *an **offer of** help* | *a **job offer***

COLLOCATIONS

make someone an **offer**
have/receive an **offer** from someone
consider an **offer** – to think about an offer carefully before making a decision
accept/take an **offer** – to say yes
refuse/reject an **offer** or **turn** it **down** – to say no
→ ACCEPT, REFUSE

2 something that is offered, especially an amount of money: *The company **made an offer of** $5 million for the site.*

of·fer·ing /ˈɔfrɪŋ, ˈɑ-/ *n.* [C] something you give someone, especially God

off ˈguard *adj.* **catch/take sb off guard** to surprise someone by doing something or happening when s/he is not expecting anything: *The storm caught everyone off guard.*

off·hand¹ /ɔfˈhænd/ *adv.* immediately, without time to think: *I can't give you an answer offhand.*

off·hand² /ˌɔfˈhænd◂/ *adj.* said or done without thinking, or said in a way that makes something seem unimportant: *an offhand remark*

of·fice /ˈɔfɪs, ˈɑ-/ *n.* **1** [C] a room with a desk, telephone, etc. in it where you do your work: *the manager's office* | *Is Shaw **in** his **office**?* | *a small **home office*** **2** [C] the building of a company or organization where people work: *Are you going to **the office** today?* | *the **main/central office** of the company* | *the **branch/local office** of the FBI*

TOPIC

Many modern offices are not divided into separate rooms. Instead, people sit at **desks** in small **cubicles** or **cubes**. The part of an office where you work, including your **desk**, **computer/PC**, etc. is your **workstation**. Somewhere in the office there is a **printer**, a **photocopier**, a **fax (machine)**, and **file/filing cabinets**. The office building may have several **floors**. There is often a **cafeteria** where you can eat.

3 [C,U] an important job or position, especially in government: *Richardson's achievements **in office*** | *Muller **took/left office** in 1997.* | *It takes a lot of money to **run for office*** (=try to be elected). **4** [C] the place where a doctor or DENTIST sees patients → BOX OFFICE → POST OFFICE

of·fi·cer /ˈɔfəsɚ, ˈɑ-/ *n.* [C] **1** someone who has a position of authority in the army, navy, etc. **2** a member of the police: *the officers at the scene* | *Officer Johnson* **3** someone who has an important position in an organization [➡ **CEO**, **official**]

of·fi·cial¹ /əˈfɪʃəl/ *adj.* approved of or done by someone in authority, especially the government: *an official investigation* | *The governor was on an official visit to Mexico.*

official² *n.* [C] someone who has a responsible position in an organization: *senior bank officials*

of·fi·cial·ly /əˈfɪʃəli/ *adv.* **1** publicly and formally: *The new bridge was officially opened this morning.* **2** according to what you say publicly, even though this may not be true: *Officially, they are not counted as unemployed.*

of·fi·ci·ate /əˈfɪʃiˌeɪt/ *v.* [I] *formal* to perform special duties, especially at a religious ceremony

of·fi·cious /əˈfɪʃəs/ *adj.* *disapproving* someone who is officious is always telling other people what to do

off·ing /ˈɔfɪŋ/ *n.* **be in the offing** to be about to happen: *Big changes are in the offing.*

off·line /ˌɔfˈlaɪn◂/ *adv.* **1** with your computer not connected to the Internet [➡ **online**]: *writing emails offline* **2** not connected to or controlled by a computer: *Problems with the server kept the system offline until noon.* —**offline** *adj.*

'off-ramp *n.* [C] a road for driving off a HIGHWAY or FREEWAY [≠ **on-ramp**]

,off 'season *n.* [singular] the time in the year when a sport is not usually played —**off-season** *adj.* [only before noun]

off·set /ˌɔf'sɛt, 'ɔfsɛt/ *v.* past tense and past participle **offset**, present participle **offsetting** [T] if something offsets another thing, it has an opposite effect so that the situation remains the same: *The new contracts should help to offset the recent losses.*

off·shoot /'ɔfʃut/ *n.* [C] an organization, system of beliefs, etc. that has developed from a larger or earlier one: *The business was an **offshoot of** IBM.*

O

off·shore /ˌɔf'ʃɔr◂ / *adj., adv.* in the water, at a distance from the shore: *America's offshore oil reserves*

off·spring /'ɔfˌsprɪŋ/ *n.* plural **offspring** [C] *formal* **1** someone's child or children **2** an animal's baby or babies

off·stage /ˌɔf'steɪdʒ/ *adv.* **1** just behind or to the side of a stage in a theater: *There was a loud crash offstage.* **2** when an actor is not acting: *Olivier's life offstage*

,off-the-'record *adj.* an off-the-record remark is not supposed to be made public → **off the record** at RECORD

,off-the-'wall *adj. informal* strange or unusual: *an off-the-wall TV comedy*

of·ten /'ɔfən, 'ɔftən/ *adv.* **1** if something happens often, it happens regularly, many times, or in many situations [= **frequently**]: *She often works weekends.* | ***How often** do you come to New Orleans?* | *This happens **more often** than you might think.*

THESAURUS

a lot informal: *I've been to Boston a lot of times.*
frequently – very often: *He's frequently late for work.*
regularly – often and at regular times, for example every day, every week, or every month: *You should exercise regularly.*
repeatedly – use this to emphasize that someone did something many times: *I asked him repeatedly to tell me what was wrong.*
constantly – very often over a long period of time: *He talked constantly about his old girlfriend.*
continuously – without stopping: *He's been ill almost continuously for the last year.*
again and again/over and over (again) – many times, and more often than you would expect: *Fans of the show go to see it again and again.* | *I get bored doing the same thing over and over again.*
→ NEVER, RARELY, SOMETIMES

2 all too often used in order to say that something sad or wrong happens too much: *All too often, fathers don't see their children much after a divorce.* **3 every so often** sometimes, but not regularly: *We go out for coffee every so often.*

GRAMMAR

often, very often
Use **often** before a verb, unless the verb is "be": *Dad often gets home late.* | *This is often not possible.*
If there are two or more verbs together, **often** comes after the first one: *I don't often go to the cinema.*
Very often is used at the end of a negative sentence: *He doesn't telephone very often.*

of·ten·times /'ɔfənˌtaɪmz/ *adv. informal* often: *Oftentimes the situation can get out of control.*

o·gle /'oʊgəl/ *v.* [I,T] to look at someone in an offensive way that shows you think s/he is sexually attractive

o·gre /'oʊgɚ/ *n.* [C] **1** someone who seems cruel and frightening **2** a large ugly person in children's stories who eats people

OH the written abbreviation of **Ohio**

oh /oʊ/ *interjection* **1** used in order to express strong emotions or to emphasize what you think about something: *Oh, thank goodness you're safe!* | ***Oh, no!** My wallet is gone!* **2** said in order to make a slight pause, especially before replying to a question or giving your opinion on something: *"Why?" "Oh, I don't know."* | *"I'm finished." "**Oh, yeah**, how does it look?"* | *"We lost." "**Oh, well**, better luck next time."*

ohm /oʊm/ *n.* [C] a unit for measuring electrical RESISTANCE

oil[1] /ɔɪl/ *n.* **1** [U] a thick dark liquid from under the ground, from which GASOLINE and other products are made [= **petroleum**]: *the price of oil* | *the oil industry* **2** [U] a smooth thick liquid that is burned to produce heat or used for making machines run easily: *motor oil* **3** [C,U] a smooth thick liquid made from plants or animals, used in cooking or for making beauty products: *Fry in a little oil.* | *a tablespoon of **olive/sunflower/vegetable oil*** **4 oils** [plural] paints that contain oil

oil[2] *v.* [T] to put oil into or onto something

oiled /ɔɪld/ *adj.* covered with oil: *Place the fish in a lightly oiled pan.*

'oil ,painting *n.* [C,U] a picture painted with paint that contains oil, or the art of painting with oil paint

'oil slick *n.* [C] a layer of oil floating on water

'oil well *n.* [C] a special hole dug in the ground so that oil can be taken out

oil·y /'ɔɪli/ *adj.* **1** covered with oil, or containing a lot of oil: *shampoo for oily hair* | *an oily fish* **2** looking or feeling like oil: *an oily liquid*

oink /ɔɪŋk/ *n.* [C] the sound that a pig makes —**oink** *v.* [I]

oint·ment /'ɔɪntˀmənt/ *n.* [C,U] a soft oily substance that you rub into your skin, especially as a medical treatment

OJ *n.* [U] *spoken* orange juice

OK the written abbreviation of **Oklahoma**

okay[1], **OK** /oʊˈkeɪ/ *adj. spoken* **1** not sick, injured, unhappy, etc.: *Do you **feel okay** now?* | *The kids are **doing OK**.* **2** satisfactory or acceptable: *Does my hair look okay?* | *I did okay on the test.* **3** used in order to ask if you can do something, or to tell someone that s/he can do something: *"**Is it okay** if I leave early?"* | ***It's okay** for you to go.* —**okay** /ˌoʊˈkeɪ/, **OK** *adv.*: *Is your computer working OK?*

okay[2], **OK** *interjection* **1** said when you start talking, or continue to talk after a pause: *OK, can we go now?* **2** said when you agree with someone or when you give permission: *"We'd better be there by four." "Okay."* **3** said to ask if someone agrees or will give permission: *I'll go first, okay?*

okay[3], **OK** *v.* past tense and past participle **okayed**, third person singular **okays** [T] *informal* to say officially that you will agree to something or allow it to happen: *Are you sure the bank will okay the loan?*

okay[4], **OK** *n. informal* **give the okay/get the okay** to give or get permission to do something: *I got the okay to leave early.*

old /oʊld/ *adj.* **1** having existed or been used for a long time [≠ **new**]: *We sell old and new books.* | *an old building*

THESAURUS

ancient – used about buildings, cities, languages, etc. that existed long ago: *ancient history* | *ancient cultures*
antique – used about furniture, jewelry, etc. that is old and valuable: *an antique rug*
vintage – used about things that are old but of high quality: *vintage cars*
classic – used about movies, books, television programs, and cars that are old but of very good quality: *Lumet's classic film "12 Angry Men"*
secondhand – used about cars, books, clothes, etc. that were owned by someone else and then sold
used – used about cars or other products which are being sold that are not new: *a used car dealer*
stale – used about bread, cakes, etc. that are no longer fresh
rotten – used about food, especially fruit or eggs, that is no longer good to eat
→ NEW, YOUNG

2 a) having lived for a long time [≠ **young**; ➡ **elderly**]: *an old man* | *My parents are **getting old**.* **b) the old** old people **3** having a particular age: *Our dog is three years old.* | *my ten-year-old daughter* | ***How old** is Kenny?* **4 old house/job/teacher etc.** *informal* a house, etc. that you had before but do not have now [= **former**]: *I saw your old girlfriend last night.* **5 good/poor/silly old etc. sb** *spoken* used in order to talk to or about someone you know and like: *Good old Larry hadn't changed a bit.* **6** experienced, heard, or seen many times before [= **familiar**]: *all the old familiar faces* | *I'm tired of listening to **the same old** music all the time.* **7 an old friend/enemy etc.** a friend, etc. that you have known for a long time **8 the old days** times in the past: ***In the old days**, only a few people were well educated.* | *She sat listening to her mother talk about **the good old days**.*

old·en /ˈoʊldən/ *adj. literary* **in olden days/times** a long time ago

ˌold-ˈfashioned *adj.* not considered to be modern or fashionable anymore: *old-fashioned values* | *a good old-fashioned ghost story*

THESAURUS

outdated/out-of-date – no longer useful or modern: *The equipment at the school is hopelessly outdated.* | *outdated laws* | *If the rules are out-of-date or unrealistic, they should be changed.*
dated – looking old-fashioned: *The film looks a bit dated now, but the story is still very contemporary.*

old·ie /ˈoʊldi/ *n.* [C] *informal* someone or something that is old, especially a song or movie

ˌOld ˈTestament *n.* **the Old Testament** the part of the Bible that tells about the time before the birth of Jesus Christ [➡ **New Testament**]

ˌold-ˈtimer *n.* [C] *informal* someone who has been in a particular job, place, etc. for a long time

ˌOld ˈWorld *n.* **the Old World** Europe, and parts of Asia and Africa [➡ **New World**] —**Old World** *adj.*

ol·ive /ˈɑlɪv/ *n.* **1** [C] a small black or green fruit, eaten as a vegetable or used for making oil **2** [U] **also olive green** a dull pale green color —**olive** *adj.*

O·lym·pic Games /əˌlɪmpɪk ˈgeɪmz/ *n.* **the Olympic Games** [plural] **also the Olympics** an international sports event held every four years —**Olympic** *adj.*

ome·let, **omelette** /ˈɑmlɪt/ *n.* [C] eggs that have been beaten together and cooked, often with other foods added: *a cheese omelet*

o·men /ˈoʊmən/ *n.* [C] a sign of what will happen in the future: *a **good/bad omen***

om·i·nous /ˈɑmənəs/ *adj.* making you feel that something bad is going to happen: *ominous black clouds* —**ominously** *adv.*

o·mis·sion /oʊˈmɪʃən, ə-/ *n.* **1** [U] the act of not including or doing something **2** [C] something that has been omitted: *The report is full of mistakes and omissions.*

o·mit /oʊˈmɪt, ə-/ *v.* past tense and past participle **omitted**, present participle **omitting** [T] *formal* to not include something, either deliberately or because you forgot to do it [= **leave out**]: *Important details had been omitted.*

om·nip·o·tent /ɑmˈnɪpət̬ənt/ *adj. literary* able to do everything —**omnipotence** *n.* [U]

om·ni·scient /ɑmˈnɪʃənt/ *adj. literary* knowing everything —**omniscience** *n.* [U]

on /ɔn, ɑn/ *prep., adj., adv.* **1** touching, being supported by, or hanging from something: *I got mud on my pants.* | *pictures hanging on the wall* | *a child sitting on her dad's shoulders* **2** if you have a piece of clothing on, you are wearing it: *He came to the door with his coat on.* **3** in a particular place or area of land: *The answer is on page 44.* | *They built a fence on our land.* **4** at the side of something such as a street, road, or river: *a restaurant on the river* | *the stores on Rodeo Drive* **5** at some time during a particular day: *Is there a meeting on Monday?* | *a party on her birthday* | *On May 10, Jo had a baby girl.* **6** continuing without stopping: *Go on, Cheryl. What happened next?* | *The peace talks dragged on* (=continued slowly) *for months.* **7** forward or ahead, toward a particular place: *We drove on to Dillon.* | *You guys go on without me.* **8** later or after a particular time: ***From that day/point/time on** he started eating healthy foods and exercising.* **9** being broadcast by a television or radio station, or recorded on something: *Keillor's program on the radio* | *a movie available on video* | *The news will be on at six.* **10** about a particular subject: *a book on China*

> **THESAURUS**
>
> **about, concerning, regarding, re**
> → see Thesaurus box at ABOUT[1]

11 used in order to show who or what is affected by an action: *a new tax on imported wine* | *The divorce was hard on Jill.* | *medical testing done on rats* **12** using something: *Sam's on the phone.* | *a piece featuring Hawkins on saxophone* | *a report done on the computer* | *I cut myself on a piece of glass.* **13** in a particular direction: *The Mayor was sitting on my right.* **14** in or into a vehicle such as a bus, airplane, train, etc.: *Did you sleep on the plane?* | *I **got on** at Vine Street.* **15** taking part in an activity or traveling somewhere: *They met on a trip to Spain.* **16** included in a team or group, or in a list: *She's on the volleyball team.* | *an item on the agenda* **17** operating or working [≠ **off**]: *The TV was on.* | ***Turn on** the light.* **18** taking a medicine or drugs: *She's on antibiotics.* **19 have/carry sth on you** *informal* to have something with you now: *Do you have a pen on you?* **20** *spoken* used in order to say that someone is paying for something: *Dinner's on me tonight.* **21** if an event is on, it will happen: *There's a jazz festival on this weekend.* **22** *informal* if something bad happens on someone, it happens when s/he is not expecting it: *You can't just quit on me!* → HEAD-ON → **later on** at LATER[1] → **on and off** at OFF

once[1] /wʌns/ *adv.* **1** on one occasion, or at a time in the past: *I've only met her once.* | *I once ran 21 miles.* | *He tried skiing **once before**, but he didn't like it.* **2 once a week/year etc.** one time every week, year, etc. as a regular activity: *She goes to the gym once a week.* **3 (every) once in a while** sometimes, but not often: *We see each other every once in a while.* **4 once more** one more time [= **again**]: *I'll call him once more, but then we have to leave.* **5 at once a)** at the same time: *I can't do two things at once!* **b)** *formal* immediately or without waiting: *I recognized him at once.* **6 all at once a)** suddenly: *All at once, the room went quiet.* **b)** at the same time: *A lot of things needed to be dealt with all at once.* **7** in the past, but not now: *They were once good friends.* **8 for once** *spoken* used in order to say that something should happen more often: *"Where's Mark?" "He's washing the dishes, for once."* **9 once and for all** definitely and finally: *Let's settle this once and for all.* **10 once upon a time** a long time ago – used at the beginning of children's stories **11 once in a blue moon** very rarely: *He comes to see us once in a blue moon.*

once[2] *conjunction* from the time something happens: *Once you try this, you'll never want to stop.*

on·com·ing /ˈɔnˌkʌmɪŋ, ˈɑn-/ *adj.* **oncoming car/traffic etc.** a car, etc. that is coming toward you

one[1] /wʌn/ *number* **1** 1 **2** one O'CLOCK: *I have a meeting at one.* **3** one year old: *Katie's almost one.*

one[2] *pron.* **1** someone or something that has been mentioned or is known about: *"Do you have a bike?" "No, but I'm getting one for my birthday."* | *"Where are those books?" "Which ones?"* | *"Which candy bar do you want?" **"This/that one."*** | *Jane's **the one** with the red hair.* **2 one by one** if people do something one by one, first one person does it, then the next, etc.: *One by one, the passengers got off the bus.* **3 one after the other/one after another** if events or actions happen one after the other, they happen without much time between them: *He's had one problem after another this year.* **4 (all) in one** if someone or something is many different things all in one, s/he or it is all those things: *This is a TV, radio, and VCR all in one.* **5** *formal* **a)** people in general: *One must be careful to keep exact records.* **b)** *old-fashioned* used in order to mean "I": *One is tempted to ignore the whole problem.*

> **GRAMMAR**
>
> **One of** is followed by a plural noun form but a singular verb: *One of the computers isn't working.*

one[3] *determiner* **1** used to emphasize a particular person or thing: *One reason I like the house is because of the big kitchen.* | ***One of*** *the children is sick.* ▶ Don't say "One of the children are sick." ◀ **2 one day/afternoon etc. a)** a particular day, etc. in the past: *There was one week in April when we had two feet of snow.* **b)** any day, etc. in the future: *We should go for a meal one evening.* **3 for one thing** used in order to introduce a reason for what you have just said **4** *spoken* used in order to emphasize your description of someone or something: *That is one cute kid!*

one[4] *n.* [C] a piece of paper money worth $1: *Do you have five ones?*

ˌone anˈother *pron. formal* EACH OTHER

ˌone-ˈliner *n.* [C] a very short joke

THESAURUS

joke, gag, wisecrack, pun
➔ see Thesaurus box at JOKE[1]

ˌone-night ˈstand *n.* [C] an occasion when two people have sex, but do not intend to meet each other again

ˌone-of-a-ˈkind *adj.* special because no one or nothing else is like him, her, or it: *one-of-a-kind handmade carpets*

ˌone-on-ˈone *adj.* between only you and one other person: *one-on-one English lessons* —**one-on-one** *adv.*

on·er·ous /ˈɑnərəs, ˈoʊ-/ *adj. formal* difficult and tiring: *onerous duties*

ˌone-ˈsided *adj.* **1** considering or showing only one side of a question, subject, etc. in a way that is unfair: *a one-sided account of the war* **2** an activity or competition that is one-sided is one in which one person or team is much stronger or does more than the other: *a one-sided football game*

one·time /ˈwʌntaɪm/ *adj.* former: *a onetime TV star*

ˌone-to-ˈone *adj.* **1** between only two people: *one-to-one talks* **2** matching one other person, thing, etc. exactly: *a one-to-one correspondence between sound and symbol*

ˌone-track ˈmind *n.* **have a one-track mind** *disapproving* to think about only one thing all the time

ˌone-ˈway *adj.* **1** moving or allowing movement in only one direction: *one-way traffic* | *a one-way street* **2** a one-way ticket is for taking a trip from one place to another, but not back again [➡ **round-trip**]

on·go·ing /ˈɔnˌgoʊɪŋ, ˈɑn-/ *adj.* continuing: *ongoing discussions*

on·ion /ˈʌnyən/ *n.* [C,U] a round white vegetable with brown, red, or white skin and many layers that has a strong taste and smell ➔ see picture at VEGETABLE

on·line /ˌɔnˈlaɪn◂, ˌɑn-/ *adj., adv.* **1** connected to other computers through the Internet, or available through the Internet [≠ **offline**]: *All the city's schools will* ***be/go online*** *by the end of the year.* **2** directly connected to or controlled by a computer [≠ **offline**]: *an online printer*

on·look·er /ˈɔnˌlʊkɚ, ˈɑn-/ *n.* [C] someone who watches something happening without being involved in it: *A crowd of onlookers had gathered at the scene of the accident.*

on·ly[1] /ˈoʊnli/ *adv.* **1** not more than a particular amount, number, age, etc., especially when this is unusual: *Tammy was only 9 months old when she started walking.* | *It's only eight o'clock.* **2** nothing or no one except the person or thing mentioned: *You're only wearing a T-shirt. No wonder you're cold.* | *parking for restaurant customers only* **3** in one place, situation, or way and no other, or for one reason and no other: *You can only exit through this door.* | *The contract will be renewed* ***only if*** *the work has been done to the correct standard.* | *The aquarium light should be on* ***only when*** *the fish are being displayed.* **4** not very important, serious, good, etc. compared to something else: *The job's interesting, but it's only temporary.* | *I was only kidding.* **5 not only... (but also)** used in order to say that something is even better, worse, or more surprising than what you have just said: *Math is not only easy for her, it's fun.* **6** *formal* no earlier than a particular time: *Congress passed the law only last year.* | *She finally tapped his shoulder, and* ***only then*** *did he look up.* **7 if only a)** used in order to give a reason for something, and say that it is not the best one: *He was thinking about joining the Navy, if only to get away from his parents.* **b)** used in order to express a strong wish: *If only they'd let us know in time!* **8 only too** very or completely: *He was only too ready to leave.*

only[2] *adj.* **1** used in order to say that there is one person, thing, or group in a particular situation and no others: *Walking is the only exercise I get.* | *He's* ***the only one*** *who did a good job.* **2 an only child** a child who does not have any brothers or sisters **3 the only thing is...** *spoken* used before you begin to talk about something that might be a problem: *The only thing is, I have to be back by eight.*

only[3] *conjunction* except that [= **but**]: *I'd help, only I'm really busy that day.*

ˈon-ramp *n.* [C] a road for driving onto a HIGHWAY or FREEWAY [≠ **off-ramp**]

on·set /ˈɔnsɛt, ˈɑn-/ *n.* **the onset of sth** the beginning of something: *the onset of a bad cold*

on·slaught /ˈɑnslɔt, ˈɔn-/ *n.* [C usually singular] a very strong attack or criticism

ˈon-the-job *adj.* [only before noun] while working, or at work: *on-the-job training*

on·to / *before consonants* ˈɔntə, ˈɑn-; *before vowels and strong* ˈɔntu, ˈɑn-/ *prep.* **1** used in order to show movement to a position on a surface, area, or object: *The cat leaped onto the* *table.* | *Turn onto River Road.* | *Claire jumped **out/back/over onto** the sidewalk.* **2 be onto sb** *informal* to know who did something wrong or illegal: *Briggs knew the cops were onto him.*

o·nus /ˈoʊnəs/ *n.* **the onus** the RESPONSIBILITY for something: ***The onus is on** the company **to** provide safety equipment.*

on·ward[1] /ˈɔnwərd, ˈɑn-/ **also onwards** *adv.* **1 from ... onward** beginning at a particular time and continuing after that: *European history from 1900 onward* **2** *formal* forward: *The ship moved onward through the fog.*

onward[2] *adj. formal* moving forward, continuing, or developing: *the onward march of scientific progress*

O

oo·dles /ˈudlz/ *n. informal* **oodles of sth** a large amount of something: *oodles of fun*

oops /ʊps, ups/ *interjection* said when someone has fallen, dropped something, or made a small mistake: *Oops! I spilled the milk.*

ooze /uz/ *v.* [I,T] **1** if a liquid oozes from something or if something oozes a liquid, liquid flows from it very slowly: *Blood was **oozing from** the cut.*

> **THESAURUS**
>
> **pour**, **flow**, **drip**, **leak**, **gush**, **spurt**, **run**, **come out**
>
> → see Thesaurus box at POUR

2 *informal* to show a lot of a particular quality: *Leo positively oozes charm.*

o·pal /ˈoʊpəl/ *n.* [C,U] a white stone with changing colors in it, used in jewelry

o·paque /oʊˈpeɪk/ *adj.* **1** difficult to see through [≠ **transparent**] **2** hard to understand

o·pen[1] /ˈoʊpən/ *adj.*

1 OPEN not closed or covered [≠ **closed, shut**]: *an open door* | *A book lay open on the table.* | *I can barely **keep** my **eyes open**, I'm so tired.* | *All the windows were **wide open**.*

2 STORES/BANKS ETC. ready or available for people to use, visit, etc.: *a museum that is open daily* | *When is the new library going to be open?* | *The restaurant's **open for** lunch and dinner.* | *Stores were **open for business** as usual.* | *The pool is only **open to the public** in the summer.*

3 NOT RESTRICTED available to anyone, so that anyone can take part: *The competition is **open to** children aged 7 to 14.* | *an open meeting*

4 NOT ENCLOSED not enclosed or covered by buildings, walls, etc.: *Lang grew up in the **open spaces** of the prairie.* | *classes held out in the **open air*** (=outdoors) | *an open fire*

5 NOT SECRET not hiding anything: *Ralph looked at her with open admiration.* | *testimony given in open court* (=in a court where everything is done in public) | *My husband and I try to be **open with** each other.*

6 WILLING TO LISTEN willing to listen to other people: ***Keep an open mind*** (=listen without judging) *until you've heard everyone's ideas.* | *We're **open to suggestions** on how to improve our service.*

7 be open to criticism/discussion etc. able to be criticized, discussed, etc.: *Her comments were open to misunderstanding.*

8 NOT DECIDED not finally decided: *The location of the peace talks is still **an open question**.* | *The rules are not **open to** negotiation.* | *It's a possibility. I'm **keeping** my **options open*** (=not deciding between the things I might do).

9 an open mind if you have an open mind, you deliberately do not make a decision or form a definite opinion about something: *Jurors must try to **keep an open mind** during the trial.*

10 keep your eyes/ears open *spoken* to keep looking or listening so that you will notice anything that is important

11 welcome/greet sb with open arms to greet someone with happiness and excitement

open[2] **also open up** *v.* **1** [I,T] to move something so that something is not closed or covered, or to be moved in this way: *Dan's opening his birthday presents.* | *a door that opens automatically* | *Meg opened her eyes wide.* | *She opened the curtains.* | ***Open up** the window, will you?*

> **THESAURUS**
>
> **unlock** – to open a door, drawer, etc. with a key
>
> **unscrew** – to open a lid on a bottle, container, etc. by turning it
>
> **unwrap** – to open a package by removing the paper that covers it
>
> **unfold** – to open a piece of paper, a cloth, etc. that was folded
>
> **unfasten/undo** – to open something that is fastened or tied, for example a seat belt or a piece of clothing
>
> → CLOSE

> **USAGE**
>
> Do not use **open** and **close** to talk about things that use electricity or things that provide water or gas. Use **turn on/off** instead: *Can you turn off the stove?* | *I turned on the TV.*
>
> For things that use electricity, you can also use **switch on/off**: *Don't forget to switch off the lights.*

2 [I] if a store, bank, or public building opens at a particular time, it begins to allow people inside at that time: *What time does the bookstore open on Sundays?* **3** [I,T] to start, or to make something start: *The restaurant opens next month.* | *a new play opening on Broadway* | *He **opened up** a checking account.* **4** [I,T] to spread something out, or become spread out: *I can't open my umbrella.* | *The roses are starting to **open up**.* | *Open your books to page 153.* **5** [T] to make something available to be used or visited: *Snow-*

plows were out ***opening up*** *the streets.* | *Parts of the White House will be opened to the public.* **6 open fire (on sth/sb)** to start shooting at someone or something

open up *phr. v.* **1 open** sth ⇔ **up** to become available or possible, or to make something available or possible: *Education opens up all kinds of opportunities.* **2** to stop being shy and say what you really think

open³ *n.* **(out) in the open a)** outdoors **b)** not hidden or secret: *The truth is finally out in the open.*

open-air

an open-air concert

ˌopen-ˈair *adj.* outdoor: *open-air concerts*

ˌopen-ˈended *adj.* without a definite ending time, rules, or an answer: *an open-ended investigation*

o·pen·er /ˈoʊpənɚ/ *n.* [C] **1** a tool or machine used in order to open letters, bottles, or cans: *a* ***can opener*** **2** the first of a series of things such as sports games: *the season opener against the Celtics*

ˌopen-heart ˈsurgery *n.* [U] a medical operation in which doctors operate on someone's heart

ˌopen ˈhouse *n.* [C] **1** an occasion when a school or business allows the public to come in and see the work that is done there **2** a party that you can come to or leave at any time during a particular period: *an open house from 2–6 p.m.*

o·pen·ing¹ /ˈoʊpənɪŋ/ *n.* [C] **1** an occasion when a new business, building, etc. is ready for use: *the* ***opening of*** *the exhibition* **2** the beginning of something: *the* ***opening of*** *the concert season* **3** a job or position that is available: ***job openings*** *for high school graduates* **4** a hole or space in something: *an* ***opening in*** *the fence* **5** a chance to do or say something: *This provides an opening for you to praise the student's effort.*

opening² *adj.* first or beginning: *the opening paragraph* | *Are you going to* ***opening night*** (=the first night of a new play, movie, etc.)*?*

o·pen·ly /ˈoʊpənli/ *adv.* honestly and not secretly: *They talk openly about their problems.*

ˌopen-ˈminded *adj.* willing to consider and accept new ideas, opinions, etc. —**open-mindedness** *n.* [U]

o·pen·ness /ˈoʊpənnɪs/ *n.* [U] **1** the quality of being honest and not keeping things secret: *the openness of a small child* **2** the quality of being willing to accept new ideas or people: *an organization with an* ***openness to*** *different kinds of people*

op·er·a /ˈɑprə, ˈɑpərə/ *n.* [C,U] a musical play in which all of the words are sung, or these plays considered as a form of art [➡ **musical**] —**operatic** /ˌɑpəˈrætɪk◂ / *adj.*

TOPIC

play, musical, ballet
➔ see Topic box at THEATER

op·era·ble /ˈɑprəbəl/ *adj.* **1** able to be treated by a medical operation [≠ **inoperable**]: *The cancer is operable.* **2** working and ready to use [≠ **inoperable**]: *an operable machine*

op·er·ate /ˈɑpəˌreɪt/ *v.* **1** [I,T] if a machine operates or you operate it, it works or you make it work: *technicians who are trained to operate the scanning equipment* | *The engine seems to be operating smoothly.* **2** [I] to cut open someone's body in order to repair or remove a part that is damaged: *the surgeon that* ***operated on*** *his knee* **3** [I,T] if a business or organization operates, or if you operate it, it is organized to do its work: *an agreement to build and operate a cellular phone network* | *factories* ***operating in*** *Mexico* **4** [I,T] if a system, process, or service operates, or if you operate it, it works or has a particular purpose: *How does the new security system operate?* | *The cloth* ***operates as*** *a filter.*

ˈoperating ˌsystem *n.* [C] a system in a computer that helps all the programs to work

op·er·a·tion /ˌɑpəˈreɪʃən/ *n.* **1** [C] the process of cutting into someone's body to repair or remove a part that is damaged: *a knee operation* | *He needed an* ***operation on*** *his brain.* | *Taylor has* ***had/undergone*** *a heart bypass* ***operation.*** **2** [C] a set of planned actions or activities for a particular purpose: *a rescue operation* **3** [U] the way the parts of a machine or system work together: *Wear protective glasses when the machine is* ***in operation.*** **4** [C,U] a business or company, or the work of a business: *The company is expanding its overseas operations.* | *A literacy program has been* ***in operation*** (=been working) *for ten years.* **5** [C] *technical* an action done by a computer: *a machine performing millions of operations per second* **6** [U] the way something such as a law has an effect or achieves a result: *the operation of the tax laws*

op·er·a·tion·al /ˌɑpəˈreɪʃənl/ *adj.* **1** working and ready to be used: *The system is now* ***fully operational.*** **2** relating to the operation of a business, government, etc.: *operational costs* —**operationally** *adv.*

op·er·a·tive /ˈɑpərətɪv/ *n.* [C] someone who does work that is secret in some way: *a CIA operative*

op·er·a·tor /ˈɑpəˌreɪt̬ɚ/ *n.* [C] **1** someone who works for a telephone company giving information to people and helping to connect calls **2** someone who operates a machine or piece of equipment: *a radio operator*

oph·thal·mol·o·gy /ˌɑfθəlˈmɑlədʒi, -θəˈmɑ-, ˌɑp-/ *n.* [U] *technical* the medical study of the eyes and diseases that affect them —**ophthalmologist** *n.* [C]

o·pin·ion /əˈpɪnyən/ *n.* **1** [C,U] your ideas or beliefs about a particular subject: *What's your **opinion on/of** the death penalty? | Teachers were not asked their **opinions about** the curriculum. | **In my opinion**, getting a divorce is too easy. | people who aren't afraid to **express/give their opinions** | Polls are taken to discover **public opinion*** (=what ordinary people think about something).

COLLOCATIONS

general/popular/public opinion – what most people think: *Television has a big influence on popular opinion.*
give/state/express/voice an opinion: *He knows baseball and he's not afraid to give his opinion.*
ask for sb's opinion: *Asked for his opinion on the law, he confessed that he wasn't sure.*
in sb's opinion – used in order to say what your opinion is: *In my opinion, it's a total waste of time.*
keep your opinion to yourself – to not say what you think about something

COMMUNICATION

Ways of giving your opinion
I think (that)...: *I think you should apologize.*
If you ask me...: *If you ask me, he should apologize.*
It seems to me...: *It seems to me there isn't enough time.*
In my opinion/view...: *In my opinion, you should accept the offer.*
Personally: *Personally, I really like the idea.*
I guess spoken: *I guess it could have been worse.*

THESAURUS

view – your opinion about something: *What are your views about global warming?*
point of view – a particular way of thinking about or judging something: *The story is told from the man's point-of-view.*
position – used especially about the opinion of a government or organization: *The president has made his position perfectly clear.*
attitude – your opinions and feelings about something: *If you go into the game with a positive attitude, you have more chance of winning. | his permissive attitude towards drugs*

2 [C] judgment or advice from a professional person about something: *We got **a second opinion** (=we asked two people) before replacing the furnace.* **3 have a high/low/good etc. opinion of sb/sth** to think that someone or something is very good or very bad: *On the whole, people have a low opinion of politicians.*

o·pin·ion·at·ed /əˈpɪnyəˌneɪt̬ɪd/ *adj. disapproving* expressing very strong opinions about things

o'pinion poll *n.* [C] a POLL

o·pi·um /ˈoʊpiəm/ *n.* [U] an illegal drug made from POPPY seeds

o·pos·sum /əˈpɑsəm, ˈpɑsəm/ *n.* [C] an American animal that looks like a large rat and can hang from trees by its tail

op·po·nent /əˈpoʊnənt/ *n.* [C] **1** someone who tries to defeat another person or team in a competition, game, argument, etc.: *This week Oregon faces its toughest opponent.* **2** someone who disagrees with a plan, idea, etc.: ***opponents of** abortion*

op·por·tune /ˌɑpɚˈtun/ *adj. formal* **an opportune moment/time/place etc.** a time, etc. that is appropriate for doing something

op·por·tun·ist /ˌɑpɚˈtunɪst/ *n. disapproving* [C] someone who uses every chance to gain power or advantages over others —**opportunism** *n.* [U] —**opportunistic** /ˌɑpɚtuˈnɪstɪk/ *adj.*

op·por·tu·ni·ty /ˌɑpɚˈtunət̬i/ *n.* plural **opportunities** [C] **1** an occasion when it is possible for you to do something [➡ **chance**]: *Children will **get/have** an **opportunity to** try several different sports. | The program **gives** students **the/an opportunity to** see live drama. | I'd like to **take this opportunity to** thank everyone who helped me. | Under the law, women were guaranteed **equal opportunities*** (=chances to do things that are equal to men's chances). | *This is a **great/good opportunity** for investors.*

COLLOCATIONS

An **opportunity comes along/up** or **arises**.
You **have/are given** the **opportunity** to do something.
You **take/seize/use** an **opportunity** by doing something when you have the chance to do it.
A **wasted/lost/missed opportunity** is a good opportunity that you did not take.
An **ideal/perfect/unique/golden opportunity** is one that is very good or special, and may not happen again.
A **rare opportunity** is one that does not happen very often.

2 a chance to get a job: *There are good opportunities for graduates in your field.*

op·pose /əˈpoʊz/ *v.* [T] to disagree strongly with an idea or action: *A local group opposes the plan for environmental reasons.*

op·posed /əˈpoʊzd/ *adj.* **1** disagreeing strongly with someone or something, or feeling strongly that someone or something is wrong: *militants who are **opposed to** the peace process | groups that are **strongly opposed to** abortion* **2 as opposed to sth** used in order to show that two things are different from each other: *The teaching is geared to practical problems, as opposed to theory.*

op·pos·ing /əˈpoʊzɪŋ/ *adj.* **1** opposing teams, groups, etc. are competing, arguing, etc. with each other **2** opposing ideas, opinions, etc. are completely different from each other

op·po·site[1] /ˈɑpəzɪt, -sɪt/ *n.* [C] a person or thing that is completely different from someone or something else: *Hot and cold are opposites.* | *Most people think work and play are* ***the opposite of*** *each other.* | *the* ***exact opposite*** *of the truth* | *He said he'd do one thing, and then did* ***the opposite****.*

opposite[2] *adj.* **1** completely different: *Ray walked off in the opposite direction.* | *the two men are at* ***opposite ends*** *of the political spectrum* **2** facing something or directly across from something: *a building on the opposite side of the river* **3 the opposite sex** the other sex. If you are a man, women are the opposite sex.

opposite[3] *prep., adv.* if one thing or person is opposite another, they are facing each other: *the wall opposite the door* | *He's moved into the house opposite.*

op·po·si·tion /ˌɑpəˈzɪʃən/ *n.* [U] strong disagreement with, or protest against something: *the residents'* ***opposition to*** *plans for a new highway* | *There was* ***stiff/strong/intense opposition*** *from the teachers' union.*

THESAURUS

objection – a reason you give for not approving of an idea or plan: *Lawyers raised no objections to the plan.*
antagonism – strong opposition to or hatred of someone else: *antagonism between the two political parties*
antipathy formal – a feeling of strong dislike or opposition: *a growing antipathy towards the government*

op·press /əˈprɛs/ *v.* [T] to treat people in an unfair and cruel way —**oppressor** /əˈprɛsɚ/ *n.* [C]

op·pressed /əˈprɛst/ *adj.* treated unfairly or cruelly: *oppressed minority groups* | *the poor and* ***the oppressed*** (=people who are oppressed)

op·pres·sion /əˈprɛʃən/ *n.* [U] the act of oppressing people, or the state of being oppressed

op·pres·sive /əˈprɛsɪv/ *adj.* **1** cruel and unfair: *an oppressive military government* **2** making you feel uncomfortable: *oppressive heat*

opt /ɑpt/ *v.* [T] to choose one thing or do one thing instead of another: *If you prefer quiet,* ***opt for*** *a smaller resort.* | *More high school students are* ***opting to*** *go to college.*
opt out *phr. v.* to choose not to join in a group or system: *Parents can* ***opt out of*** *the public school system by home schooling.*

op·tic /ˈɑptɪk/ *adj.* relating to the eyes

op·ti·cal /ˈɑptɪkəl/ *adj.* relating to the way light is seen, or relating to the eyes: *an optical instrument* —**optically** *adv.*

ˌoptical ilˈlusion *n.* [C] a picture or image that tricks your eyes and makes you see something that is not actually there

op·ti·cian /ɑpˈtɪʃən/ *n.* [C] someone who makes glasses

op·ti·mism /ˈɑptəˌmɪzəm/ *n.* [U] a tendency to believe that good things will happen [≠ **pessimism**]: ***optimism about*** *the country's economic future* | *The results give* ***reason/cause/grounds for optimism****.*

op·ti·mist /ˈɑptəmɪst/ *n.* [C] someone who believes that good things will happen [≠ **pessimist**]

op·ti·mist·ic /ˌɑptəˈmɪstɪk/ *adj.* believing that good things will happen in the future [≠ **pessimistic**]: *Students were* ***optimistic about*** *their future.* | *We're* ***optimistic that*** *the changes will be beneficial.* —**optimistically** *adv.*

op·ti·mum /ˈɑptəməm/ *adj.* best or most appropriate for a particular purpose: *the optimum diet for good health*

op·tion /ˈɑpʃən/ *n.* [C] **1** a choice you can make in a particular situation: *career options* | *The jury* ***had the option of*** *finding him guilty but mentally ill.* | *Dropping out of school* ***is not an option*** (=you cannot do it). | *Press 4 to select the printer control option* (=on a computer). **2 keep/leave your options open** to wait before making a decision: *Leave your options open until you have the results of the test.* **3** the right to buy or sell something in the future: *stock options*

op·tion·al /ˈɑpʃənl/ *adj.* something that is optional is something you do not need to do or have, but can choose if you want it [≠ **required**]: *Attendance at the meeting is optional.*

op·tom·e·trist /ɑpˈtɑmətrɪst/ *n.* [C] someone who examines people's eyes and orders glasses for them —**optometry** /ɑpˈtɑmətri/ *n.* [U]

op·u·lent /ˈɑpyələnt/ *adj.* decorated in an expensive way: *an opulent hotel* —**opulence** *n.* [U]

OR the written abbreviation of **Oregon**

or /ɚ; *strong* ɔr/ *conjunction* **1** used between two possibilities or before the last in a series of possibilities [➡ **either**]: *Would you like pie, cake, or some ice cream?* | *a project receiving state or federal funds* | *You can use* ***either*** *milk* ***or*** *cream in the sauce.* | *They speak only a little Spanish,* ***or else*** *none at all.* **2 or anything/something** *spoken* something that is similar to what you have just mentioned: *Do you want to go out for a drink or anything?* **3** used after a negative verb when you mean not one thing and not another thing: *Elena never learned to read or write English.* **4** used in order to warn or advise someone: *Hurry or you'll miss your plane.* | *Businesses will have to raise prices,* ***or else*** *their profits will drop.* | *Don't be late,* ***or***

else... (=used as a threat) **5** used when you are guessing at a number, time, distance, etc. because you cannot be exact: *a little girl four or five years old* | *There's a gas station a mile* ***or so*** *down the road.* **6** used in order to give more specific information or to correct what has been said before: *biology, or the study of living things* **7** used in order to explain why something happened or why something must be true: *She must be tired, or she wouldn't be so crabby.*

o·ral¹ /'ɔrəl/ *adj.* **1** spoken, not written: *an oral report* **2** relating to the mouth: *oral hygiene*

oral² *n.* [C] a test in a university in which questions and answers are spoken rather than written

O

or·ange /'ɔrɪndʒ, 'ɑr-/ *n.* [U] **1** a round fruit that has sweet juice and thick skin, which you do not eat: *orange juice* → see picture at FRUIT **2** the color of an orange —**orange** *adj.*

o·rang·u·tan /ə'ræŋəˌtæn/ **also o·rang·u·tang** /ə'ræŋəˌtæŋ/ *n.* [C] a large APE that has long arms and long orange-brown hair

or·a·tor /'ɔrət̬ɚ, 'ɑr-/ *n.* [C] *formal* someone who makes speeches and is good at persuading people —**oration** /ɔ'reɪʃən, ə-/ *n.* [C,U]

or·a·tory /'ɔrəˌtɔri, 'ɑr-/ *n.* [U] *formal* the skill of making public speeches

or·bit¹ /'ɔrbɪt/ *n.* [C] the path traveled by an object that is moving around a larger object: *the Moon's orbit around the Earth* —**orbital** *adj.*

orbit² *v.* [I,T] to travel in a circle around a larger object: *a satellite that orbits the Earth*

or·chard /'ɔrtʃɚd/ *n.* [C] a place where fruit trees are grown: *a cherry orchard*

or·ches·tra /'ɔrkɪstrə/ *n.* [C] a large group of musicians who play CLASSICAL MUSIC on different instruments —**orchestral** /ɔr'kɛstrəl/ *adj.*

TOPIC

Sections of an orchestra
the woodwind/wind section also **the winds** – the instruments made mostly of wood that you blow through
the strings/the string section – the instruments that have strings
the brass (section) – the instruments made of metal that you blow through
the percussion (section) – the instruments such as drums

People in an orchestra:
conductor – the person who directs the music and musicians
cellist – a person who plays the cello
flutist – a person who plays the flute
violinist – a person who plays the violin
percussionist – a person who plays percussion

'orchestra pit *n.* [C] the space below the stage in a theater where the musicians sit

or·ches·trate /'ɔrkɪˌstreɪt/ *v.* [T] to organize an important event or a complicated plan, especially secretly: *a rebellion orchestrated by the army*

or·chid /'ɔrkɪd/ *n.* [C] a tropical, often brightly colored flower with three PETALS

or·dain /ɔr'deɪn/ *v.* [T] to officially make someone a religious leader [➡ **ordination**]: *John was ordained a priest.*

or·deal /ɔr'dil/ *n.* [C] a very bad experience that continues for a long time: *She had to* ***go through*** *a terrible* ***ordeal.***

or·der¹ /'ɔrdɚ/ *n.*

1 in order (for sb/sth) to do sth so that something can happen or so that someone can do something: *In order for you to graduate next year, you'll have to go to summer school.* | *Plants need light in order to live.*

2 ARRANGEMENT [C,U] the way that several things are arranged, organized, or put on a list: *Are all the slides* ***in order****?* | *The names were written* ***in alphabetical order.*** | *I think these pages are* ***out of order*** (=not correctly arranged). | *State the main points* ***in order of*** *importance.* | *We've got to* ***get*** *our finances* ***in order*** (=organize them).

3 REQUEST FOR GOODS [C] a request for goods from a company or for food in a restaurant, or the goods or food that you ask for: *We've received more* ***orders for*** *car alarms this year than ever before.* | *The school's just* ***placed an order*** *for more books.* | *May I* ***take*** *your* ***order*** (=used to ask what a customer in a restaurant wants)*?* | *Your order will be ready soon.*

4 NO CRIME/TROUBLE [U] a situation in which people obey rules and respect authority: *Police are working hard to maintain* ***law and order*** *in the area.*

5 COMMAND [C] a command given by someone in authority: *Captain Marshall* ***gave*** *the* ***order*** *to advance.* | *The soldiers had been trained to* ***obey/follow orders.***

6 out of order a phrase meaning "not working," used especially on signs: *The pay phone was out of order.*

7 in order legal and correct: *Your passport seems to be in order.*

8 POLITICS ETC. [singular] the political, social, or economic situation at a particular time: *the present economic order* → **in short order** at SHORT

order² *v.* **1** [I,T] ask for food or drink in a restaurant, bar, etc.: *Are you ready to order?* | *We ordered coffee and dessert.*

THESAURUS

ask, **demand**, **request**, **beg**, **question**, **interrogate**, **inquire**, **enquire**
→ see Thesaurus box at ASK

2 [T] to ask a company to make or send you something: *They've ordered a new carpet for the bedroom.* **3** [T] to tell someone that s/he must do something: *The judge* ***ordered*** *him* ***to*** *pay $1 million.* **4** [T] to arrange something in a particular way: *a list of names ordered alphabetically*

order sb **around** *phr. v.* to continuously tell someone what to do in an annoying way: *I wish she'd stop ordering me around.*

or·der·ly[1] /'ɔrdɚli/ *adj.* **1** peaceful or behaving well: *Please leave the building* ***in an orderly fashion***. **2** arranged or organized in a neat way: *an orderly desk*

orderly[2] *n.* plural **orderlies** [C] someone who does unskilled jobs in a hospital

'ordinal ˌnumber *n.* [C] one of the numbers such as first, second, third, etc. that show the order of things [➡ **cardinal number**]

or·di·nance /'ɔrdn-əns/ *n.* [C] a law of a city or town: *parking ordinances*

or·di·nar·i·ly /ˌɔrdn'ɛrəli/ *adv.* usually: *I don't ordinarily go to sleep so early.*

or·di·nar·y /'ɔrdnˌɛri/ *adj.* **1** average or usual, and not different or special in any way: *All the candidates are trying to reach out to* ***ordinary people***. | *Art should be part of* ***ordinary life***. | *It was just an ordinary day.*

THESAURUS

normal, average, standard, routine, conventional
➔ see Thesaurus box at NORMAL[1]

2 out of the ordinary very different from what is usual: *Did you notice anything out of the ordinary?*

or·di·na·tion /ˌɔrdn'eɪʃən/ *n.* [C,U] the act or ceremony of making someone a religious leader [➡ **ordain**]

ore /ɔr/ *n.* [C,U] rock or earth from which metal can be obtained

o·reg·a·no /ə'rɛgəˌnoʊ/ *n.* [U] a plant used in cooking, especially Italian cooking

or·gan /'ɔrgən/ *n.* [C] **1** a part of the body of an animal or plant that has a particular purpose: *an organ transplant* ➔ see picture on page A3 **2** a large musical instrument like a piano, with large pipes to make the sound, or an electric instrument that makes similar sounds

or·gan·ic /ɔr'gænɪk/ *adj.* **1** living, or relating to living things [≠ **inorganic**]: *organic matter* | *organic chemistry* **2** using farming methods that do not use chemicals, or produced by these methods: *organic vegetables* ➔ see Thesaurus box at ENVIRONMENT, NATURAL[1] —**organically** *adv.*: *organically grown vegetables*

or·ga·nism /'ɔrgəˌnɪzəm/ *n.* [C] a living thing: *a microscopic organism*

or·gan·ist /'ɔrgənɪst/ *n.* [C] someone who plays the organ

or·ga·ni·za·tion /ˌɔrgənə'zeɪʃən/ *n.* **1** [C] a group such as a club or business that has been formed for a particular purpose: *student organizations* | *a non-profit organization*

THESAURUS

institution – a large important organization such as a bank or university
association – an organization for people who do the same kind of work or have the same interests
(political) party – an organization of people with the same political aims
club/society – an organization for people who share an interest
union – an organization formed by workers in order to protect their rights

2 [U] the act of planning and arranging things effectively: *Anne is responsible for the* ***organization of*** *the reception.* **3** [U] the way in which the different parts of a system are arranged and work together: *I still need to work on the* ***organization of*** *my essay.* —**organizational** *adj.*

or·ga·nize /'ɔrgəˌnaɪz/ *v.* **1** [T] to plan or arrange something: *I agreed to help organize the company picnic.* | *Organize your ideas on paper before you write your essay.* **2** [I,T] to form a UNION (=an organization that protects workers' rights) or persuade people to join one

or·ga·nized /'ɔrgəˌnaɪzd/ *adj.* **1** planned or arranged in an effective way [≠ **disorganized**]: *Her presentation was* ***well organized***.

THESAURUS

efficient – working well, without wasting time or energy: *an energy efficient refrigerator* | *efficient workers*
well-run – organized efficiently: *a well-run hotel*
businesslike – sensible and practical in the way you do things: *a businesslike attitude*

2 an organized person is able to plan and arrange things in an effective way [≠ **disorganized**]: *Barbara's a very organized person.* | *I need to* ***get*** *more* ***organized***. **3** an organized activity is arranged for and done by many people: *organized religion*

ˌorganized 'crime *n.* [U] illegal activities involving powerful well-organized groups of criminals [➡ **mafia**]

or·ga·niz·er /'ɔrgəˌnaɪzɚ/ *n.* [C] someone who organizes an event or group of people: *The organizers had expected about 50,000 people to attend the event.*

or·gasm /'ɔrˌgæzəm/ *n.* [C,U] the moment when you have the greatest sexual pleasure during sex

or·gy /'ɔrdʒi/ *n.* plural **orgies** [C] a wild party with a lot of sexual activity

O·ri·ent /'ɔriənt/ *n.* **the Orient** *old-fashioned* the eastern part of the world, especially China and Japan

o·ri·ent /'ɔriˌɛnt/ *v.* [T] **1** to make someone familiar with a place or situation: *It takes a while to* ***orient yourself*** *in a new city.* **2** to find your position using a map or a COMPASS

O·ri·en·tal /ˌɔri'ɛntl/ *adj.* **1** relating to the eastern part of the world, especially China or Japan **2** *old-fashioned* a word for someone from Asia, now considered offensive [➡ **Asian**]

o·ri·en·ta·tion /ˌɔriən'teɪʃən/ *n.* **1** [C,U] the beliefs, aims, or interests that a person or group chooses to have: *the group's right-wing political orientation* **2** [U] training and preparation for a new job or activity: *orientation week for new students* **3 sexual orientation** the fact of being HETEROSEXUAL or HOMOSEXUAL **4** [C] the direction in which something faces

o·ri·ent·ed /'ɔriˌɛntɪd/ *adj.* giving attention to a particular type of person or thing: *She's very career-oriented.* | *a service **oriented towards** the needs of business people*

O

or·i·gin /'ɔrədʒɪn, 'ɑr-/ *n.* [C,U] **1** when, where, or how something began: *a word **of** Latin **origin*** | *a theory that explains **the origins of** the universe* **2** the country, race, or social class from which someone comes: *Nine percent of the city's population is **of** Hispanic **origin**.*

o·rig·i·nal[1] /ə'rɪdʒənl/ *adj.* **1** [only before noun] first or earliest: *Our original plan was to go to Florida.* | *The original version of the song is much better.*

THESAURUS

new, **recent**, **modern**, **fresh**, **latest**
➔ see Thesaurus box at NEW

2 completely new and different: *Steve comes up with a lot of **original ideas**.* | *Her writing is truly original.* **3** [only before noun] not copied, or not based on something else: *an original screenplay*

original[2] *n.* [C] a painting, document, etc. that is not a copy: *I'll keep a copy of the lease and you can have **the original**.*

o·rig·i·nal·i·ty /əˌrɪdʒə'nælət̮i/ *n.* [U] the quality of being completely new and different: *Marie's work **shows** a lot of **originality**.*

o·rig·i·nal·ly /ə'rɪdʒənl-i/ *adv.* in the beginning: *I'm originally from Texas.* | *Originally, we hoped to be finished by June.*

o·rig·i·nate /ə'rɪdʃəˌneɪt/ *v.* [I] *formal* to start to develop in a particular place or from a particular situation: *The custom of having a Christmas tree **originated in** Germany.*

o·ri·ole /'ɔriˌoʊl, 'ɔriəl/ *n.* [C] a wild bird that is black with a red and a yellow STRIPE on its wings

or·na·ment /'ɔrnəmənt/ *n.* [C] an object that you use for decoration because it is beautiful rather than useful: *Christmas ornaments*

or·na·men·tal /ˌɔrnə'mɛntl◂/ *adj.* designed to decorate something: *ornamental vases*

or·nate /ɔr'neɪt/ *adj.* having a lot of decoration: *ornate furniture* —**ornately** *adv.*

or·ne·ry /'ɔrnəri/ *adj. informal* behaving in an unreasonable and angry way

or·ni·thol·o·gy /ˌɔrnə'θɑlədʒi/ *n.* [U] the scientific study of birds —**ornithologist** *n.* [C]

or·phan[1] /'ɔrfən/ *n.* [C] a child whose parents are dead

orphan[2] *v.* **be orphaned** to become an orphan

or·phan·age /'ɔrfənɪdʒ/ *n.* [C] a place where orphans live

or·tho·don·tist /ˌɔrθə'dɑntɪst/ *n.* [C] a DENTIST who makes teeth straight when they have not been growing correctly —**orthodontics** *n.* [U] —**orthodontic** *adj.*

or·tho·dox /'ɔrθəˌdɑks/ *adj.* **1** officially accepted, or considered to be normal by most people: *orthodox methods of treating disease* **2** following the traditional beliefs of a religion: *an orthodox Jew* —**orthodoxy** *n.* [C,U]

ˌOrthodox 'Church *n.* **the Orthodox Church** one of the Christian churches in eastern Europe and parts of Asia

or·tho·pe·dics /ˌɔrθə'pidɪks/ *n.* [U] the area of medicine that treats problems that affect people's bones —**orthopedic** *adj.*

Os·car /'ɑskɚ/ *n.* [C] one of the prizes given each year to the best movies, actors, etc. in the movie industry: *Who **won** the **Oscar for** best actor?*

os·ten·si·ble /ɑ'stɛnsəbəl/ *adj.* [only before noun] *written* the ostensible purpose or reason for something is the one which is openly stated, but which is probably not the true reason or purpose —**ostensibly** *adv.*

os·ten·ta·tious /ˌɑstən'teɪʃəs/ *adj. disapproving* designed or done in order to be impressive to other people: *a big ostentatious engagement ring* —**ostentation** /ˌɑstən'teɪʃən/ *n.* [U]

ostracize /'ɑstrəˌsaɪz/ *v.* [T] to behave in a very unfriendly way toward someone and not allow him/her to be part of a group: *He was ostracized by the other students.* —**ostracism** /'ɑstrəˌsɪzəm/ *n.* [U]

os·trich /'ɑstrɪtʃ, 'ɔ-/ *n.* [C] a very large African bird with long legs that runs very quickly but cannot fly

oth·er[1] /'ʌðɚ/ *determiner, adj.* **1** used in order to mean one or more of the rest of a group of people or things, when you have already mentioned one person or thing: *I could do it, but none of **the other** boys in the class could.* | *Here's one sock, but where's **the other one**?* **2** used in order to mean someone or something that is different from, or exists in addition to, the person or thing you have already mentioned: *He shares an apartment with three other guys.* | *Sue went to the mall with some of her other friends.* | *Does anyone have **any other** questions?* | *Let's discuss this **some other** time.* | *A taxi stopped on **the other side** of the road.* **3 the other day/morning etc.** *spoken* recently: *I talked to Ted the other day.* **4 other than** except: *I know she has brown hair, but other than that I don't remember much about her.* **5 every other day/week etc.** on one of every two days, weeks, etc.: *The class meets every other Thursday.* **6 in other words** used in order to express an idea or opinion in a way that is easier to understand: *There are TV sets in 68.5 million homes; in other words, 97 percent of the population watches TV.* ➔ EACH OTHER ➔ **on the one hand ... on the other hand** at HAND[1]

GRAMMAR

Do not use **other** after "an." Use **another**: *There must be another way of doing it.*

other[2] *pron.* **1** one or more people or things that form the rest that you are talking about: *We ate one pizza and froze the other.* | *It looks like* ***all the others*** *have left.* | *Some stereos are better than others.* **2 someone/something etc. or other** used when you cannot be certain or definite about what you are saying: *We'll get the money somehow or other.*

oth·er·wise /ˈʌðɚˌwaɪz/ *adv.* **1** a word meaning "if not," used when there will be a bad result if something does not happen: *You'd better go now, otherwise you'll be late.* **2** except for what has just been mentioned: *The sleeves are too long, but otherwise the dress fits.* **3** in a different way: *Adam was ready to buy the house, but his wife decided otherwise.*

ot·ter /ˈɑt̬ɚ/ *n.* [C] a small animal that can swim, has brown fur, and eats fish

ouch /aʊtʃ/ *interjection* said when you feel sudden pain: *Ouch! That hurt!*

ought to /ˈɔt̬ə; *strong* ˈɔtu/ *modal verb* **1** used to say that someone should do something: *We ought to give Jane a call.* | *You ought to be ashamed of yourself.* **2** used in order to say that you expect something to happen or be true: *The weather ought to be nice there in October.*

ounce /aʊns/ *n.* [C] **1** *written abbreviation* **oz** a unit for measuring weight, equal to 1/16 of a pound or 28.35 grams ➔ FLUID OUNCE **2 an ounce of truth/sense etc.** a small amount or a particular quality: *Don't you have even an ounce of sense?*

our /ɑr; *strong* aʊɚ/ *determiner* belonging or relating to the person who is speaking and one or more other people: *We don't have curtains on our windows.* | *Our daughter is at college.*

ours /aʊɚz, ɑrz/ *pron.* the thing or things belonging or relating to the person who is speaking and one or more other people: *"Whose car is that?" "It's ours."* | *They have their tickets, but ours haven't come yet.*

our·selves /aʊɚˈsɛlvz, ɑr-/ *pron.* **1** the REFLEXIVE form of "we": *It was strange seeing ourselves on television.* **2** the strong form of "we," used in order to emphasize the subject or object of a sentence: *We started this business ourselves.* **3 (all) by ourselves a)** without help: *Amy and I made supper all by ourselves.* **b)** alone: *Dad left us by ourselves for an hour.* **4 to ourselves** not having to share with other people: *We'll have the house to ourselves next week.*

oust /aʊst/ *v.* [T] *journalism* to force someone out of a position of power: *an attempt to* ***oust*** *the communists* ***from*** *political power*

out[1] /aʊt/ *adv., adj.* **1** away from the inside of a place or container [≠ **in**]: *Close the door on your way out.* | *The keys must have fallen* ***out of*** *my pocket.* **2** away from the place where you usually are, such as home or work [≠ **in**]: *Did anyone call while I was out?* | *He* ***asked*** *me* ***out*** *for dinner tonight* (=invited me to dinner). | *We* ***eat out*** (=eat in a restaurant) *all the time.*

USAGE

out – away from the building where you live or work: *Tom's out. He should be back soon.*
outside – not inside a room or building but near it: *I'll wait for you outside.*
outdoors – not inside a building: *We spent most of the summer outdoors.*
outdoor (without an -s) – used to describe things that are outside, or that happen outside: *an outdoor swimming pool* | *outdoor sports*

3 outside: *Why don't you go out and play?* **4** in or to a place that is far away or difficult to get to: *a little hotel out in the country* | *He's moved out to Arizona.* **5** completely or carefully: *Clean out the cupboard before you put the dishes in.* | *I'm worn out* (=very tired). **6** if power, electricity, etc. is out, it is not working correctly, or not on: *The electricity was out for an hour last night.* | *The lights are out – I don't think anyone's home.* **7** not having power any more: *The only way to lower taxes is to vote the Democrats out!* | *He may face prosecution when he is* ***out of office.*** **8** used in order to say that something has appeared: *It looks like the sun is finally going to come out.* **9 out loud** done in a way so that people can hear your voice: *parents reading out loud to their kids* **10** available to be bought: *Morrison has a new book out this month.* **11** *spoken* not possible: *"Where should we go?" "Well, skiing's out because it costs too much."* **12 be out for sth/be out to do sth** *informal* to intend to do or get something: *Don't listen to Danny – he's just out to get attention.* **13** *informal* **a)** asleep: *Billy was* ***out like a light*** *by 6:00.* **b)** not conscious: *You must have hit him pretty hard. He's* ***out cold.*** **14** a player in a game who is out is no longer allowed to play, or has lost one of his/her chances to get a point **15** clothes or styles that are out are no longer fashionable **16** someone who is out has told people that s/he is HOMOSEXUAL **17** if the tide is out, the ocean is at its lowest level

out[2] *prep.* **1** from inside something, or through something: *He was looking out the window at the beach.* **2 out of a)** from a particular place or time: *I got a coke out of the refrigerator.* | *a nail sticking out of the wall* | *The tango is a dance that comes out of Buenos Aires.* **b)** from a larger group of the same kind: *Three out of four dentists recommend the toothpaste.* | *Kathy was chosen out*

O

of all the kids in her class. **c)** having none of something that you had before: *We're almost out of gas.* | *The car was completely out of control.* **d)** used in order to show what something is made from: *a box made out of wood* **3 out of it** *informal* not able to think clearly because you are very tired, drunk, etc.: *I'm really out of it today.* **4 out of the way** finished: *Good. Now that's out of the way, we can start working.*

out³ *n.* **1** [C] an act of making a player in baseball lose the chance to get a RUN **2 an out** *informal* an excuse for not doing something: *I'm busy Sunday, so that gives me an out.*

out⁴ *v.* [T] to publicly say that someone is HOMOSEXUAL when that person wants it to be a secret

O

out·age /'aʊtɪdʒ/ *n.* [C] a period of time when a service, especially the electricity supply, is not provided: ***a power outage***

,out-and-'out *adj.* [only before noun] having all the qualities of a particular type of person or thing [= **complete**]: *an out-and-out lie*

out·back /'aʊt˺bæk/ *n.* **the outback** the Australian COUNTRYSIDE far away from cities, where few people live

out·bid /aʊt˺'bɪd/ *v.* past tense and past participle **outbid**, present participle **outbidding** [T] to offer more money than someone else for something that you want to buy

out·bound /'aʊt˺baʊnd/ *adj.* moving away from you or away from a city, country, etc.: *outbound flights*

out·break /'aʊt˺breɪk/ *n.* [C] the start or sudden appearance of something bad such as a war or disease: *an **outbreak of** malaria*

out·burst /'aʊt˺bəst/ *n.* [C] a sudden powerful expression of strong emotion: *an angry outburst*

out·cast /'aʊt˺kæst/ *n.* [C] someone who is not accepted by other people: *a social outcast*

out·class /aʊt˺'klæs/ *v.* [T] to be much better than someone or something else

out·come /'aʊt˺kʌm/ *n.* [singular] the final result of a meeting, process, etc.: *We were eager to know what the **outcome of** the experiment would be.*

THESAURUS

result, consequences, effect, upshot
→ see Thesaurus box at RESULT¹

out·cry /'aʊt˺kraɪ/ *n.* [singular, U] an angry protest by a lot of people: ***public outcry against** the war*

out·dat·ed /,aʊt'deɪtɪd◂/ *adj.* no longer useful or modern: *The textbooks are outdated.*

THESAURUS

old-fashioned, out-of-date, dated
→ see Thesaurus box at OLD-FASHIONED

out·dis·tance /aʊt'dɪstəns/ *v.* [T] to go faster or farther than someone else in a race

out·do /aʊt'du/ *v.* past tense **outdid** /-'dɪd/ past participle **outdone** /-'dʌn/ third person singular **outdoes** /-'dʌz/ [T] to be better or more successful than someone else: *The skaters were trying to outdo each other.* | *You've really **outdone yourself*** (=done something extremely well) *this time!*

out·door /'aʊtdɔr/ *adj.* [only before noun] happening, existing, or used outside and not in a building [≠ **indoor**]: *outdoor activities* | *an outdoor swimming pool*

USAGE

outdoor (without an -s) – used to describe things that are outside, or that happen outside: *an outdoor swimming pool* | *outdoor sports*
outdoors – not inside a building: *We spent most of the summer outdoors.*
outside – not inside a room or building but near it: *I'll wait for you outside.*
out – away from the building where you live or work: *Tom's out. He should be back soon.*

out·doors /aʊt'dɔrz/ *adv.* outside, not inside a building [≠ **indoors**]: *I prefer working outdoors.*

out·door·sy /aʊt'dɔrzi/ *adj. informal* someone who is outdoorsy enjoys outdoor activities, such as HIKING and camping

out·er /'aʊtə/ *adj.* [only before noun] **1** on the outside of something [≠ **inner**]: *Peel off the outer leaves of lettuce.* **2** far from the middle of something [≠ **inner**]: *the outer suburbs*

out·er·most /'aʊtə,moʊst/ *adj.* [only before noun] farthest from the middle [≠ **innermost**]: *the outermost planets*

,outer 'space *n.* [U] the space outside the Earth's air where the stars and PLANETS are

out·field /'aʊtfild/ *n.* [singular] the part of a baseball field that is farthest from the player who is BATting —**outfielder** *n.* [C]

out·fit¹ /'aʊt,fɪt/ *n.* [C] **1** a set of clothes worn together: *She bought a new outfit for the party.* **2** *informal* a group of people who work together as an organization: *a small advertising outfit in San Diego*

outfit² *v.* past tense and past participle **outfitted**, present participle **outfitting** [T] to provide someone or something with the clothes or equipment s/he needs for a special purpose

out·fit·ter /'aʊt,fɪtə/ *n.* [C] a store that sells equipment for outdoor activities such as camping

out·go·ing /'aʊt˺,goʊɪŋ/ *adj.* **1** wanting to meet and talk to new people, or showing this quality [= **friendly**]: *Sally is really outgoing and easy to talk to.* | *an outgoing personality*

THESAURUS

sociable, extroverted, gregarious
→ see Thesaurus box at SOCIABLE

2 the outgoing president/CEO etc. someone who is finishing a job as president, etc. **3** [only before noun] going out from or leaving a place [≠ **incoming**]: *outgoing phone calls*

out·grow /aʊt˺ˈgroʊ/ *v.* past tense **outgrew** /-ˈgru/ past participle **outgrown** /-ˈgroʊn/ [T] **1** to grow too big for something: *Kara's already outgrown her shoes.* **2** to no longer enjoy something that you used to enjoy

out·growth /ˈaʊt˺groʊθ/ *n.* [C] a natural result of something: *Crime is often an* ***outgrowth of*** *poverty.*

out·house /ˈaʊthaʊs/ *n.* [C] a small building over a hole in the ground that is used as a toilet

out·ing /ˈaʊt̬ɪŋ/ *n.* [C] a short enjoyable trip for a group of people: *a Sunday* ***outing to*** *the park*

out·land·ish /aʊtˈlændɪʃ/ *adj.* strange and unusual: *outlandish clothes*

out·last /aʊtˈlæst/ *v.* [T] to continue to exist or do something longer than someone else: *The whole point of the game is to outlast your opponent.*

out·law[1] /ˈaʊt˺lɔ/ *v.* [T] to say officially that something is illegal: *an agreement outlawing chemical weapons*

outlaw[2] *n.* [C] *old-fashioned* a criminal who is hiding from the police

out·lay /ˈaʊt˺leɪ/ *n.* plural **outlays** [C,U] an amount of money that is spent for a particular purpose: *There will be an initial outlay of $2,500 for tools and equipment.*

out·let /ˈaʊt˺lɛt, -lɪt/ *n.* [C] **1** a place on a wall where you can connect electrical equipment to the electricity supply **2** a store that sells things for less than the usual price: *an outlet mall* **3** a way of expressing or getting rid of strong feelings: *I use judo as* ***an outlet for*** *stress.* **4** a way out through which something such as a liquid or gas can flow

out·line[1] /ˈaʊt˺laɪn/ *n.* **1** [C,U] the main ideas or facts about something without all the details: *Here is an* ***outline of*** *the company's plan.* **2** [C] a plan for a piece of writing in which each new idea is separately written down: *The teacher wants an* ***outline of*** *our essays by Friday.* **3** [C,U] a line around the edge of something that shows its shape

outline[2] *v.* [T] **1** to describe the main ideas or facts about something, but not all the details: *The president outlined his peace plan for the Middle East.* **2** to draw or put a line around the edge of something to show its shape: *We could see the huge Ferris wheel* ***outlined in*** *colored lights.*

out·live /aʊt˺ˈlɪv/ *v.* [T] to live longer than someone else: *She outlived her husband by 10 years.*

out·look /ˈaʊt˺lʊk/ *n.* **1** [C] your general attitude to life and the world: *Nels has a very* ***positive outlook on*** *life.* **2** [singular] what is expected to happen in the future: *The* ***outlook for*** *the health care professions is good.*

out·ly·ing /ˈaʊt˺ˌlaɪ-ɪŋ/ *adj.* [only before noun] far from cities, people, etc.: *Housing prices are lower in some* ***outlying areas****.*

out·ma·neu·ver /ˌaʊt˺məˈnuvɚ/ *v.* [T] to gain an advantage over someone by using skillful movements or plans

out·mod·ed /aʊt˺ˈmoʊdɪd/ *adj.* OUTDATED

out·num·ber /aʊt˺ˈnʌmbɚ/ *v.* [T] to be more in number than another group: *Men outnumber women in Congress.*

ˌout of ˈbounds *adj.* **1** not inside the official playing area in a sports game: *The referee said the ball was out of bounds.* **2** not allowed or acceptable: *Some topics, such as sex, are out of bounds for discussion.* —**out of bounds** *adv.*: *The ball was knocked out of bounds.*

ˌout-of-ˈdate *adj.* OUTDATED

> **THESAURUS**
>
> **old-fashioned, outdated, dated**
>
> ➔ see Thesaurus box at OLD-FASHIONED

ˌout-of-ˈstate *adj., adv.* from, to, or in another state: *out-of-state license plates*

ˌout-of-the-ˈway *adj.* far from cities and people, and often difficult to find: *They met in an out-of-the-way hotel.*

out·pa·tient /ˈaʊt˺ˌpeɪʃənt/ *n.* [C] someone who goes to the hospital for treatment, but does not stay there [➡ **inpatient**]

out·per·form /ˌaʊt˺pɚˈfɔrm/ *v.* [T] to do something better than other things or people

out·place·ment /ˈaʊt˺ˌpleɪsmənt/ *n.* [U] a service that a company provides to help its workers find other jobs when it cannot continue to employ them

out·post /ˈaʊt˺poʊst/ *n.* [C] a small town or group of buildings in a place that is far away from big cities

out·pour·ing /ˈaʊt˺ˌpɔrɪŋ/ *n.* [C] a large amount of something that is produced suddenly, such as strong emotions, ideas, or help: *an* ***outpouring of*** *grief*

out·put /ˈaʊt˺pʊt/ *n.* [C,U] **1** the amount of work, goods, etc. produced by someone or something [= **production**]: *Economic output is down 10% this year.* **2** the results produced by a computer or other process

out·rage[1] /ˈaʊt˺reɪdʒ/ *n.* [C,U] a feeling of great anger or shock, or something that causes this: *a deep sense of* ***moral outrage*** | *The prices they charge are an outrage!*

outrage[2] *v.* [T] to make someone feel very angry or shocked: *I was outraged by his sexist comments.* —**outraged** *adj.*

out·ra·geous /aʊt˺ˈreɪdʒəs/ *adj.* very shocking or unreasonable: *outrageous lies* —**outrageously** *adv.*: *outrageously expensive clothes*

out·reach /ˈaʊt˺ritʃ/ *n.* [U] the practice of trying to help people with particular problems, especially through an organization: *the church's community outreach program*

out·right[1] /ˈaʊt̚raɪt/ *adj.* [only before noun] **1** complete and total: *an outright refusal* **2** clear and direct: *an outright lie*

out·right[2] /aʊt̚ˈraɪt, ˈaʊt̚raɪt/ *adv.* **1** clearly and directly: *Nadine laughed outright at the suggestion.* **2 buy/own sth outright** to own something such as a house completely because you have paid the full price with your own money

out·run /aʊt̚ˈrʌn/ *v.* past tense **outran** /-ˈræn/ past participle **outrun**, present participle **outrunning** [T] **1** to run faster or farther than someone **2** to develop more quickly than something else: *The company's spending was outrunning its income.*

O

out·set /ˈaʊtsɛt/ *n.* **at/from the outset** at or from the beginning of an event or process: *The rules were agreed **at the outset of** the game.*

out·shine /aʊtˈʃaɪn/ *v.* past tense and past participle **outshined** or **outshone** /-ˈʃoʊn/ present participle **outshining** [T] to be much better at something than someone else

out·side[1] /ˌaʊtˈsaɪd, ˈaʊtsaɪd/ **also outside of** *adv., prep.* **1** not inside a building or room, but near it [≠ **inside**]: *Mom, can I **go outside** and play?* | *He left an envelope outside my door.*

USAGE

out – away from the building where you live or work: *Tom's out. He should be back soon.*
outside – not inside a room or building but near it: *I'll wait for you outside.*
outdoors – not inside a building: *We spent most of the summer outdoors.*
outdoor (without an -s) – used to describe things that are outside, or that happen outside: *an outdoor swimming pool* | *outdoor sports*

2 beyond the limits of a city, country, etc.: *We live **just outside** Pittsburgh.* **3** beyond the limits of a situation, activity, etc.: *Teachers can't control what students do outside school.* | *I'm afraid that subject is outside the scope of this discussion.*

outside[2] *adj.* [only before noun] **1** not inside a building: *We turned off the outside lights.* **2** involving people who do not belong to the same group or organization as you: *We may need some **outside help**.* **3 the outside world** the rest of the world: *Since the attack, the city has been cut off from the outside world.* **4 outside interests** things you do or that you are interested in, that are not related to your work

outside[3] *n.* [C] **1 the outside** the outer part or surface of something [≠ **inside**]: *They painted **the outside of** the building pink.* | ***From the outside** the house looked very nice.* **2 on the outside** used in order to describe the way someone or something appears to be: *Their marriage seemed so perfect on the outside.*

out·sid·er /aʊtˈsaɪdɚ/ *n.* [C] someone who does not belong to a particular group, organization, etc.: *Corran is a Washington outsider who has never been in office before.*

out·skirts /ˈaʊtskɚts/ *n.* [plural] the parts of a city or town that are farthest from the center: *He lived **on the outskirts of** town.*

out·smart /aʊtˈsmɑrt/ *v.* [T] to gain an advantage over someone using tricks or your intelligence

out·sourc·ing /ˈaʊtˌsɔrsɪŋ/ *n.* [U] the practice of using workers from outside a company, or of buying supplies, parts, etc. from another company instead of producing them yourself —**outsource** *v.* [T]

out·spo·ken /aʊtˈspoʊkən/ *adj.* expressing your opinions honestly and directly, even if they shock or offend other people: *an outspoken critic of the program* —**outspokenness** *n.* [U]

out·stand·ing /aʊtˈstændɪŋ/ *adj.* **1** better than anyone or anything else [= **excellent**]: *an outstanding performance*

THESAURUS

good, **great**, **excellent**, **wonderful**, **fantastic**, **exceptional**, **first-class**
→ see Thesaurus box at GOOD[1]

2 not yet done, paid, or solved: *an outstanding debt*

out·stretched /ˌaʊtˈstrɛtʃt◂/ *adj.* reaching out to full length: *I took hold of his **outstretched arm/hand**.*

out·strip /aʊtˈstrɪp/ *v.* past tense and past participle **outstripped**, present participle **outstripping** [T] to be larger, greater, or better than someone or something else: *The gains will outstrip the losses.*

out·ward[1] /ˈaʊt̚wɚd/ *adj.* **1** relating to how people, things, etc. seem to be rather than how they are [≠ **inward**]: *Amy answered with a look of outward calm.* **2** going away from a place or toward the outside: *The outward flight was bumpy.*

outward[2] **also outwards** *adv.* toward the outside [≠ **inward**]: *The door opens outward.*

out·ward·ly /ˈaʊt̚wɚdli/ *adv.* according to how people, things, etc. seem to be rather than how they are inside [≠ **inwardly**]: *Outwardly, he seems to be very happy.*

out·weigh /aʊt̚ˈweɪ/ *v.* [T] to be more important or valuable than something else: *The advantages **far outweigh** the disadvantages.*

out·wit /aʊt̚ˈwɪt/ *v.* past tense and past participle **outwitted**, present participle **outwitting** [T] OUTSMART

o·val /ˈoʊvəl/ *n.* [C] a shape that is like a circle, but longer than it is wide —**oval** *adj.* → see picture at SHAPE[1]

THESAURUS

square, circle, semicircle, triangle, rectangle, cylinder
➔ see Thesaurus box at SHAPE[1]

ˌOval ˈOffice *n.* **the Oval Office** the office of the U.S. President, in the White House in Washington, D.C.

o·va·ry /ˈoʊvəri/ *n.* plural **ovaries** [C] the part of a female that produces eggs —**ovarian** /oʊˈvɛriən/ *adj.*

o·va·tion /oʊˈveɪʃən/ *n. formal* [C] if people give someone an ovation, they CLAP their hands to show approval: *The performance received a* ***standing ovation*** (=people stood up and clapped their hands).

ov·en /ˈʌvən/ *n.* [C] a piece of equipment that food is cooked inside, shaped like a metal box with a door on it: *Preheat the oven to 350 degrees.*

o·ver[1] /ˈoʊvɚ/ *prep.* **1** above or higher than something, without touching it [≠ **under**]: *I leaned over the desk.* | *The sign over the door said "No Exit."* | *The ball went* ***way over*** (=a long way above) *my head.* **2** moving across the top of something, or from one side of it to the other: *We walked over the hill.* | *One of the men jumped over the counter and grabbed the money.* **3** on something or someone so that he, she, or it is covered [≠ **under**]: *I put the blanket over the baby.* **4** more than a particular amount, number, or age: *Mike makes over $100,000 a year.* | *The game is designed for children over seven years old.* **5** during: *Where did you go over summer vacation?* **6** down from the edge of something: *Hang the towel over the back of the chair.* **7 be/get over sth** to feel better after being sick or upset: *He's mad, but he'll get over it.* **8** about or concerning something: *They had an argument over who would take the car.* **9** using the telephone or a radio: *The salesman explained it to me over the phone.* ➔ **all over** at ALL[2]

over[2] *adv.* **1** down from an upright position: *Kate fell over and hurt her ankle.* | *The wind blew the table over.* **2** used in order to show where someone or something is: *I'm over here!* | *There's a mailbox* ***over on*** *the corner.* **3** to or in a particular place: *Pat came over to our place last night.* | *The weather's awful. Why don't you* ***stay over*** (=spend the night at my house)*?* **4** above: *You can't hear anything when the planes fly over.* **5** again: *I got mixed up and had to* ***start over****.* | *If you make a mistake in the recording, we can always* ***do it over****.* | *They just keep playing the same songs* ***over and over again*** (=repeatedly). **6 think/read/talk sth over** to think, read, or talk about something carefully or thoroughly before deciding what to do: *I'll need to read the contract over before I sign it.* **7** so that another side is showing: ***Turn*** *your papers* ***over*** *and begin.* | *He rolled over and went to sleep.* **8** from one person or group to another: *The land was* ***handed over*** (=given) *to the government.* **9** more or higher than a particular amount, number, or age: *"Did you guess the right number?" "No, I was* ***over by*** *two."* (=the number I guessed was two higher) | *a game for children ages six* ***and over***

over[3] *adj.* **1** finished: *The game's over – Dallas won.*

THESAURUS

done, finished, complete, through
➔ see Thesaurus box at DONE[2]

2 get sth over with *informal* to do something that you do not want to do, but that is necessary, so that you do not have to worry about it anymore: *Well, call her and get it over with.*

o·ver·all[1] /ˈoʊvɚˌɔl/ *adj.* including everything: *The overall cost of the trip is $500.*

o·ver·all[2] /ˌoʊvɚˈɔl/ *adv.* **1** generally: *Overall, the situation looks good.* **2** including everything: *Inflation is growing at 3% a year overall.*

o·ver·alls /ˈoʊvɚˌɔlz/ *n.* [plural] heavy cotton pants with a piece that covers your chest, held up by two bands that go over your shoulders ➔ see picture at CLOTHES

o·ver·bear·ing /ˌoʊvɚˈbɛrɪŋ/ *adj. disapproving* always trying to control other people without considering their feelings or needs [= **domineering**]

o·ver·board /ˈoʊvɚˌbɔrd/ *adv.* **1** over the side of a ship into the water: *He* ***fell overboard*** *in the storm.* **2 go overboard** to do or say something that is too extreme for a particular situation, for example by being too emotional or expensive: *She managed to find a nice present, without going overboard.*

o·ver·bur·dened /ˌoʊvɚˈbɚdnd/ *adj.* carrying or doing too much: *a manager overburdened with work* | *the overburdened court system*

o·ver·cast /ˈoʊvɚˌkæst/ *adj.* dark because of clouds: *a gray overcast sky*

o·ver·charge /ˌoʊvɚˈtʃɑrdʒ/ *v.* [I,T] to charge someone too much money for something [≠ **undercharge**]

o·ver·coat /ˈoʊvɚˌkoʊt/ *n.* [C] a long thick warm coat

o·ver·come /ˌoʊvɚˈkʌm/ *v.* past tense **overcame** /-ˈkeɪm/ past participle **overcome** **1** [T] to succeed in controlling a feeling or problem: *I'm trying to overcome my fear of flying.* **2** [T] to make someone very emotional, sick, or weak: *She was* ***overcome by*** *smoke.* | *Charles was* ***overcome with*** *grief.* **3** [I,T] to fight and win against someone or something: *Union troops finally overcame rebel forces in the south.*

o·ver·com·pen·sate /ˌoʊvɚˈkɑmpənˌseɪt/ *v.* [I] to try to correct a weakness or mistake by doing too much of the opposite thing —**overcompensation** /ˌoʊvɚˌkɑmpənˈseɪʃən/ *n.* [U]

o·ver·crowd·ed /ˌoʊvɚˈkraʊdɪd◂ / *adj.* filled with too many people or things: *an overcrowded bus*

o·ver·do /ˌoʊvɚˈdu/ *v.* past tense **overdid** /-ˈdɪd/ past participle **overdone** /-ˈdʌn/ third person singular **overdoes** /-ˈdʌz/ [T] to do or use too much of something: *When exercising, you have to be careful not to **overdo it**.*

o·ver·done /ˌoʊvɚˈdʌn/ *adj.* cooked too much: *an overdone steak*

o·ver·dose /ˈoʊvɚˌdoʊs/ *n.* [C] too much of a drug taken at one time: *He died from a heroin overdose.* —**overdose** *v.* [I]

O

o·ver·drawn /ˌoʊvɚˈdrɔn/ *adj.* having spent more money than you have in the bank, so you owe the bank money: *If you are overdrawn, there's a $50 fee to pay.* ➔ see Topic box at ACCOUNT[1]

o·ver·due /ˌoʊvɚˈdu◂ / *adj.* **1** not done or happening when expected [= **late**]: *an overdue library book*

THESAURUS

late, behind, delayed, held up
➔ see Thesaurus box at LATE[1]

2 something that is overdue should have happened or been done a long time ago: *Salary increases are **long overdue**.*

o·ver·eat /ˌoʊvɚˈit/ *v.* past tense **overate** /-ˈeɪt/ past participle **overeaten** /-ˈitˀn/ [I] to eat too much, or more than is healthy

o·ver·es·ti·mate /ˌoʊvɚˈɛstəˌmeɪt/ *v.* [I,T] to think that someone or something is larger, more expensive, or more important than it really is: *Rosa had overestimated the strength of her opponent.* | *The importance of education **cannot be overestimated*** (=it is very important).

o·ver·ex·tend /ˌoʊvɚɪkˈstɛnd/ *v.* [T] to try to do too much or use too much of something, causing problems: *Even with extra people working, they're **overextending themselves**.* —**overextended** *adj.*

o·ver·flow[1] /ˌoʊvɚˈfloʊ/ *v.* [I,T] **1** if a liquid or river overflows, it goes over the edges of the container or place where it is: *a sink **overflowing with** water* **2** if people overflow a place, or if a place overflows with people, there are too many people to fit into it

o·ver·flow[2] /ˈoʊvɚˌfloʊ/ *n.* [C,U] the people, water, etc. that cannot be contained in a place because it is already full: *the **overflow of** people from the concert*

o·ver·grown /ˌoʊvɚˈgroʊn◂ / *adj.* covered with plants that have grown without being controlled: *a yard **overgrown with** weeds*

o·ver·hand /ˈoʊvɚˌhænd/ *adj., adv.* thrown with your arm above the level of your shoulder [≠ **underhand**]: *an overhand pitch*

o·ver·hang /ˌoʊvɚˈhæŋ/ *v.* past tense and past participle **overhung** /-ˈhʌŋ/ [I,T] to hang over something or stick out above it: *tree branches overhanging the path*

o·ver·haul /ˌoʊvɚˈhɔl, ˈoʊvɚˌhɔl/ *v.* [T] to repair or change all the parts of a machine, system, etc. that need it —**overhaul** /ˈoʊvɚˌhɔl/ *n.* [C] *The truck needs a complete overhaul.*

o·ver·head[1] /ˌoʊvɚˈhɛd◂ / *adj., adv.* above your head: *A plane flew overhead.* | *We put our bags in the overhead compartment.*

o·ver·head[2] /ˈoʊvɚˌhɛd/ *n.* [C] money that you spend for rent, etc. to keep a business operating

o·ver·hear /ˌoʊvɚˈhɪr/ *v.* past tense and past participle **overheard** /-ˈhɚd/ [T] to hear by accident what other people are saying when they do not know that you are listening [➡ **eavesdrop**]: *I overheard some people saying that the food was bad.*

o·ver·joyed /ˌoʊvɚˈdʒɔɪd/ *adj.* extremely happy because something good has happened: *We were **overjoyed to hear** that they are getting married.*

o·ver·kill /ˈoʊvɚˌkɪl/ *n.* [U] *informal* more of something than is necessary or desirable: *If your speech were any longer, it would be overkill.*

o·ver·land /ˈoʊvɚˌlænd/ *adj., adv.* across land, not by sea or air: *overland travel*

o·ver·lap /ˌoʊvɚˈlæp/ *v.* past tense and past participle **overlapped**, present participle **overlapping** [I,T] **1** if two or more things overlap, part of one thing covers part of another thing: *a pattern of overlapping circles* **2** if two subjects, activities, ideas, etc. overlap, they share some but not all of the same parts or qualities: *Our jobs overlap in certain areas.* —**overlap** /ˈoʊvɚˌlæp/ *n.* [C,U]

o·ver·load /ˌoʊvɚˈloʊd/ *v.* [T] **1** to load something with too many things or people: *Don't **overload** the washing machine **with** clothes.* **2** to give someone too much work to do **3** to damage an electrical system by causing too much electricity to flow through it —**overload** /ˈoʊvɚˌloʊd/ *n.* [C,U]

o·ver·look /ˌoʊvɚˈlʊk/ *v.* [T] **1** to not notice something, or to not realize how important it is: *It's easy to overlook mistakes when reading your own writing.* **2** to forgive someone's mistake, bad behavior, etc.: *I can't overlook his drinking any longer.* **3** to have a view of something from above: *a room overlooking the beach*

o·ver·ly /ˈoʊvɚli/ *adv.* too much, or very: *It is a problem, but we are **not overly** concerned about it.*

o·ver·night[1] /ˌoʊvɚˈnaɪt/ *adv.* **1** for or during the night: *She's **staying overnight** at a friend's house.* **2** *informal* suddenly: *You can't expect to lose the weight overnight.*

o·ver·night[2] /ˈoʊvɚˌnaɪt/ *adj.* [only before noun] continuing all night: *an overnight flight to Japan*

o·ver·pass /ˈoʊvɚˌpæs/ *n.* [C] a structure like a bridge that allows one road to go over another road

o·ver·pop·u·lat·ed /ˌoʊvɚˈpɑpyəˌleɪt̬ɪd/ *adj.*

having too many people: *an overpopulated city* —**overpopulation** /ˌoʊvɚˌpɑpyəˈleɪʃən/ *n.* [U]

o·ver·pow·er /ˌoʊvɚˈpaʊɚ/ *v.* [T] to defeat someone because you are stronger

o·ver·pow·er·ing /ˌoʊvɚˈpaʊərɪŋ/ *adj.* very strong [= **intense**]: *an overpowering smell*

o·ver·priced /ˌoʊvɚˈpraɪst◂/ *adj.* too expensive: *overpriced restaurants*

> **THESAURUS**
>
> **expensive, high, pricey, extortionate, astronomical, exorbitant**
> ➔ see Thesaurus box at EXPENSIVE

o·ver·qual·i·fied /ˌoʊvɚˈkwɑləˌfaɪd/ *adj.* having more experience or education than is needed for a particular job: *Sara's* ***overqualified for*** *most sales jobs.*

o·ver·rat·ed /ˌoʊvɚˈreɪt̬ɪd◂/ *adj.* not as good or important as some people think or say [≠ **underrated**]: *I think her books are overrated.* —**overrate** *v.* [T]

o·ver·re·act /ˌoʊvəriˈækt/ *v.* [I] to react to something with too much anger or surprise, or by doing more than is necessary: *You always* ***overreact to*** *criticism.* —**overreaction** /ˌoʊvəriˈækʃən/ *n.* [C,U]

o·ver·ride /ˌoʊvɚˈraɪd/ *v.* past tense **overrode** /-ˈroʊd/ past participle **overridden** /-ˈrɪdn/ present participle **overriding** [T] **1** to change someone's decision because you have the authority to do so: *Congress has overridden the President's veto.* **2** to be more important than something else: *The state of the economy seems to override other political and social questions.*

o·ver·rid·ing /ˌoʊvɚˈraɪdɪŋ/ *adj.* [only before noun] more important than anything else: *Security is of overriding importance.*

o·ver·rule /ˌoʊvɚˈrul/ *v.* [T] to officially change someone's order or decision because you think that it is wrong: *The Supreme Court overruled the lower court's decision.*

o·ver·run /ˌoʊvɚˈrʌn/ past tense **overran** /-ˈræn/ past participle **overrun** *v.* [T] to spread over a place quickly and in great numbers, harming that place: *a town* ***overrun with*** *tourists*

o·ver·seas /ˌoʊvɚˈsiz/ *adj., adv.* to or in a foreign country that is across the ocean [➡ **abroad**]: *overseas travel*

o·ver·see /ˌoʊvɚˈsi/ *v.* past tense **oversaw** /-ˈsɔ/ past participle **overseen** /-ˈsin/ [T] to watch a group of workers to be sure that a piece of work is done correctly [= **supervise**]: *Bentley is overseeing the project.* —**overseer** /ˈoʊvɚˌsiɚ/ *n.* [C]

o·ver·shad·ow /ˌoʊvɚˈʃædoʊ/ *v.* [T] to make someone seem less important: *His work has been overshadowed by that of newer writers.*

o·ver·shoot /ˌoʊvɚˈʃut/ *v.* past tense and past participle **overshot** /-ˈʃɑt/ [I,T] to accidentally go a little further or spend more than you intended: *The plane overshot the runway.*

o·ver·sight /ˈoʊvɚˌsaɪt/ *n.* **1** [C,U] a mistake in which you forget something or do not notice something: *If Butler didn't receive the report, it was an oversight.* **2** [U] if someone has oversight of something, s/he must make sure it is done in the correct way

o·ver·sim·pli·fy /ˌoʊvɚˈsɪmpləˌfaɪ/ *v.* past tense and past participle **oversimplified**, third person singular **oversimplifies** [I,T] *disapproving* to make a problem or situation seem more simple than it really is, by ignoring important facts —**oversimplification** /ˌoʊvɚˌsɪmpləfəˈkeɪʃən/ *n.* [C,U]

o·ver·sleep /ˌoʊvɚˈslip/ *v.* past tense and past participle **overslept** /-ˈslɛpt/ [I] to sleep for longer than you intended

> **THESAURUS**
>
> **sleep, doze, doze off, take a nap, toss and turn, not sleep a wink**
> ➔ see Thesaurus box at SLEEP[1]

o·ver·spend /ˌoʊvɚˈspɛnd/ *v.* past tense and past participle **overspent** /-ˈspɛnt/ [I,T] to spend more money than you can afford

o·ver·state /ˌoʊvɚˈsteɪt/ *v.* [T] to talk about something in a way that makes it seem more important, serious, etc. than it really is [= **exaggerate**; ≠ **understate**]: *A child's need for a routine* ***cannot be overstated*** (=it is very important).

o·ver·step /ˌoʊvɚˈstɛp/ *v.* [T] to go beyond an acceptable limit: *Wilson has clearly* ***overstepped his authority***.

o·vert /oʊˈvɚt, ˈoʊvɚt/ *adj. formal* done or shown in public or in an open way [≠ **covert**]: *overt discrimination* —**overtly** *adv.*

o·ver·take /ˌoʊvɚˈteɪk/ *v.* past tense **overtook** /-ˈtʊk/ past participle **overtaken** /-ˈteɪkən/ [T] **1** to have a sudden strong effect on someone: *He was overtaken by exhaustion.* **2** to develop or increase more quickly than someone or something else: *DVDs seem to be rapidly overtaking video.*

ˌover-the-ˈcounter *adj.* over-the-counter medicines can be bought without a PRESCRIPTION (=written order) from a doctor

o·ver·throw /ˌoʊvɚˈθroʊ/ *v.* past tense **overthrew** /-ˈθru/ past participle **overthrown** /-ˈθroʊn/ [T] to remove a leader or government from power by force: *Rebel forces have made an attempt to overthrow the government.* —**overthrow** /ˈoʊvɚˌθroʊ/ *n.* [U]

o·ver·time /ˈoʊvɚˌtaɪm/ *n.* [U] time that you work on your job in addition to your usual working hours: *Tom's been* ***working/doing*** *a lot of* ***overtime*** *lately.*

o·ver·ture /ˈoʊvɚtʃɚ, -ˌtʃʊr/ *n.* [C] **1** a piece of music written as an introduction to a longer musical piece, especially an OPERA **2 also overtures** an attempt to be friendly with a person,

O

group, or country: *They began* ***making overtures to*** *the Japanese government.*

o·ver·turn /ˌoʊvɚˈtɚn/ *v.* **1** [I,T] if something overturns or you overturn it, it turns upside down or falls over on its side: *an overturned car* **2 overturn a ruling/verdict/law etc.** to change a decision made by a court so that it becomes the opposite of what it was before

o·ver·view /ˈoʊvɚˌvyu/ *n.* [C] a short description of a subject or situation that gives the main ideas without explaining all the details: ***an overview of*** *developments in the Middle East*

o·ver·weight /ˌoʊvɚˈweɪt◂/ *adj.* too heavy or too fat: *He was* ***10/20 etc. pounds overweight.***

THESAURUS

fat, **big**, **heavy**, **large**, **obese**, **chubby**, **plump**
→ see Thesaurus box at FAT[1]

o·ver·whelm /ˌoʊvɚˈwɛlm/ *v.* [T] **1** if work, a problem, etc. overwhelms someone, it is too much or too difficult to deal with: *a sensitive child who is* ***overwhelmed by*** *the demands of school* **2** if a feeling overwhelms someone, s/he feels it very strongly: *I was* ***overwhelmed by/with*** *grief.* —**overwhelmed** *adj.*

o·ver·whelm·ing /ˌoʊvɚˈwɛlmɪŋ/ *adj.* **1** affecting someone very strongly: *an overwhelming sense of guilt* **2** extremely large or great: *an* ***overwhelming number/majority*** *of voters* —**overwhelmingly** *adv.*

o·ver·worked /ˌoʊvɚˈwɚkt◂/ *adj.* working too much and for too long: *an overworked teacher* —**overwork** *n.* [U]

ow /aʊ/ *interjection* said in order to show that something hurts you: *Ow! That hurt!*

owe /oʊ/ *v.* [T] **1** to need to pay someone because s/he has allowed you to borrow money: *Bob owes me $20.* | *How much do you still owe on your college loans?*

THESAURUS

be in debt – to owe an amount of money
be overdrawn – to owe money to your bank, as a result of spending more money than you have in your bank account
be in the red – to have spent more money than you have

2 to feel that you should do something for someone or give something to someone, especially because s/he has done something for you: *Jane will watch the kids – she* ***owes me a favor*** *anyway.* | *You* ***owe it to*** *your kids to teach them about healthy eating.* | *I think I* ***owe*** *you* ***an apology.***

ˈowing to *prep. formal* because of: *Greely was unable to accept the job, owing to a serious illness.*

owl /aʊl/ *n.* [C] a bird that hunts at night and has large eyes and a loud call → NIGHT OWL

owl

own[1] /oʊn/ *determiner, pron.* **1** belonging to or done by a particular person and no one else: *his own car* | *She makes a lot of her own clothes.* | *I'd love a place* ***of*** *my* ***own.*** **2 (all) on your own a)** alone: *Many older people still live on their own.* **b)** without help: *It's a decision you have to make on your own.*

own[2] *v.* [T] to legally have something because you bought it or have been given it [= **possess**]: *The city owns the buildings.*

THESAURUS

possess *formal* – to own or have something: *Philips was charged with possessing cocaine.*
have – to own something: *How many students have a cell phone?*
belong to sb – if something belongs to you, you own it: *The ring belonged to my grandmother.*

own up *phr. v.* to admit that you have done something wrong: *He'll never* ***own up to*** *his mistakes.*

own·er /ˈoʊnɚ/ *n.* [C] someone who owns something: *pet owners* | *the* ***owner of*** *the business* —**ownership** *n.* [U]

ox /ɑks/ *n.* plural **oxen** /ˈɑksən/ [C] a male cow that has had part of its sex organs removed

ox·ide /ˈɑksaɪd/ *n.* [C,U] *technical* a substance that is produced when a substance is combined with oxygen

ox·i·dize /ˈɑksəˌdaɪz/ *v.* [I,T] *technical* to combine with oxygen, or to make something combine with oxygen, especially in a way that causes RUST

ox·y·gen /ˈɑksɪdʒən/ *n.* [U] **O** a gas in the air that has no color, smell, or taste, and that all plants and animals need in order to live

ox·y·mo·ron /ˌɑksiˈmɔrɑn/ *n.* [C] a combination of words that seem to mean the opposite of each other, such as "new classics"

oys·ter /ˈɔɪstɚ/ *n.* [C,U] a small sea animal that has a shell and can produce a jewel called a PEARL, or the meat of this animal

oz the written abbreviation of **ounce**

o·zone /ˈoʊzoʊn/ *n.* [U] a poisonous blue gas that is a type of oxygen

ˈozone ˌlayer *n.* [singular] a layer of ozone above the Earth that prevents harmful RADIATION from the sun from reaching the Earth's surface

P, p

P, p /pi/ the sixteenth letter of the English alphabet

p. plural **pp.** the written abbreviation of **page** and pages

PA¹ the written abbreviation of **Pennsylvania**

PA² *n.* [C usually singular] **public address system** electronic equipment that makes someone's voice loud enough to be heard by a large group of people

pa /pɑ/ *n.* [C] *old-fashioned* father

PAC /pæk/ *n.* [C] **political action committee** an organization that tries to influence politicians so that they will support the organization's aims

pace¹ /peɪs/ *n.* **1** [singular] the speed or rate at which something happens or is done: *We started walking uphill **at a steady/slow/rapid/fast etc. pace**. | Students are encouraged to work **at** their **own pace**.*

COLLOCATIONS

pace of life – the amount of activity in people's lives and how busy they are
pace of change/reform/growth – how quickly change, reform, or growth happens
at your own pace – at a pace that is comfortable for you
at a rapid/slow/steady etc. pace
at a snail's pace – very slowly
keep up the pace – continue to do something or happen as quickly as before
keep pace with sth – do something at the same speed or rate as something else

2 keep pace (with sb/sth) to move or change as fast as something or someone else

pace² *v.* [I,T] **1** to walk first in one direction and then in another, again and again, when you are waiting or worried about something: *Darren **paced back and forth** in the waiting room.* **2 pace yourself** to do something at a steady speed so you do not get tired too quickly

pace·mak·er /ˈpeɪsˌmeɪkɚ/ *n.* [C] a very small machine that is attached to someone's heart to help it beat regularly

Pa·cif·ic O·cean /pəˌsɪfɪk ˈoʊʃən/ *n.* **the Pacific Ocean, the Pacific** the large ocean between Asia and Australia in the west, and North and South America in the east

Paˌcific ˈRim *n.* **the Pacific Rim** the land and islands that are around the edges of the Pacific Ocean, especially in Asia

pac·i·fi·er /ˈpæsəˌfaɪɚ/ *n.* [C] a plastic or rubber object that a baby sucks on so that s/he does not cry

pac·i·fism /ˈpæsəˌfɪzəm/ *n.* [U] the belief that all wars and forms of violence are wrong —**pacifist** *n.* [C]

pac·i·fy /ˈpæsəˌfaɪ/ *v.* past tense and past participle **pacified**, third person singular **pacifies** [T] to make someone calm and quiet after s/he has been angry or upset, or to make a group or area peaceful: *"You're right," Rita said, in order to pacify him.*

pack¹ /pæk/ *v.* **1** [I,T] **also pack up** to put things into boxes, SUITCASES, bags, etc. in order to take or store them somewhere: *The Olsons **packed** their **bags/suitcases**. | I still need to pack tonight. | They packed up and moved back to Tucson. | eggs packed in cartons* **2** [I,T] if a crowd of people packs a place, there are so many of them that the place is too full: *50,000 fans packed the stadium.* **3** [T] to cover, fill, or surround something closely with material to protect it: ***Pack** some newspaper **around** the bottles.* **4** [T] to press soil, snow, etc. down firmly: ***Pack** the soil firmly **around** the roots.*

pack sb/sth ⇔ **in** *phr. v.* **1** *informal* to fit a lot of people, information, ideas, etc. into a limited space: *The Lollapalooza concerts really packed in the fans.* **2 pack it in** *informal* to stop doing something: *Mike was ready to pack it in for the night.*

pack sth **into** sth *phr. v.* to fit a lot of something into a space, place, or period of time: *We packed a lot of sightseeing into two weeks.*

pack sb/sth **off** *phr. v. informal* to send someone or something away quickly, especially in order to get rid of him/her: *Our folks **packed** us **off to** camp every summer.*

pack up *phr. v. informal* to finish work and put things away: *The band packed up at midnight.*

pack² *n.* [C] **1** a small container that holds a set of things: *a **pack of** cigarettes/cards/gum* **2** a group of wild animals that live and hunt together: *a wolf pack*

THESAURUS

herd, flock, school, shoal, litter
→ see Thesaurus box at GROUP¹

3 a group of people: *a **pack of** reporters yelling questions* **4** several things wrapped or tied together to make them easy to sell, carry, or send: *a **pack of** three t-shirts | a six-pack of beer*

pack·age¹ /ˈpækɪdʒ/ *n.* [C] **1** something packed into a box and wrapped in paper, especially for mailing **2** the box, bag, etc. that food is put into and in order to be sold: *Nutrition information is listed on the side of the package.* **3** a set of related things or services that are sold or offered together: *a new software package | a financial aid package for students*

package² *v.* [T] **1** to put something in a special package, ready to be sold or sent: *Meat is packaged and dated in this area here.* **2** to try to make an idea, person, etc. seem interesting or attractive so that people will like it or buy it: *a new band that's been packaged to appeal to teenage girls*

pack·ag·ing /ˈpækɪdʒɪŋ/ *n.* [U] the container or material that a product is sold in: *cardboard packaging*

packed /pækt/ *adj.* **1** extremely full of people or things: *The theater was packed.* | *a forest **tightly/densely/closely packed** with pine trees*

THESAURUS

full, filled with, crammed, stuffed (full of), bursting (with), overflowing
➔ see Thesaurus box at FULL[1]

2 if you are packed, you have put everything you need into boxes or SUITCASES before going on a trip

P

pack·er /ˈpækɚ/ *n.* [C] someone whose job is to pack things that are to be moved or sold

pack·et /ˈpækɪt/ *n.* [C] **1** a small envelope containing something: *a **packet of** sugar* **2** *technical* a quantity of information that is sent as a single unit from one computer to another on a network or on the Internet

pack·ing /ˈpækɪŋ/ *n.* [U] **1** the act of putting things into boxes, cans, SUITCASES, etc. so that you can send or take them somewhere: *I've still got to **do** my **packing**.* **2** paper, plastic, cloth, etc. used for packing things

ˈpack rat *n.* [C] *informal* someone who collects and stores things that s/he does not really need

pact /pækt/ *n.* [C] a formal or serious agreement between two groups, nations, or people: *The U.S. signed a trade **pact with** Canada.* | *We **made a pact to** help each other out.*

pad[1] /pæd/ *n.* [C] **1** a thick piece of soft material, used for protecting or cleaning something, or for making something more comfortable: *the helmets and pads of a football player* | *a heating pad* **2** many sheets of paper fastened together, used for writing or drawing: *a **sketch pad*** ➔ LAUNCH PAD

pad[2] *v.* past tense and past participle **padded**, present participle **padding** **1** [I] to walk softly and quietly: *a cat padding across the floor* **2** [T] to fill or cover something with a soft material in order to protect it or make it more comfortable **3** [T] *informal* to add something unnecessary to a document or speech to make it longer, or to a price to make it higher: *He was padding his expense accounts.*

pad·ded /ˈpædɪd/ *adj.* filled or covered with a soft material: *a padded jacket*

pad·ding /ˈpædɪŋ/ *n.* [U] material that fills or covers something to make it softer or more comfortable

pad·dle[1] /ˈpædl/ *n.* [C] **1** a short pole with a wide flat end, used for moving a small boat along [➡ **oar**] **2** an object used for hitting the ball in PING-PONG, consisting of a round flat top on a short handle

paddle[2] *v.* **1** [I,T] to move a small boat through water, using a paddle **2** [T] to hit a child with a piece of wood as a punishment ➔ DOG PADDLE

pad·dy /ˈpædi/ **also rice paddy** *n.* plural **paddies** [C] a field in which rice is grown in water

pad·lock /ˈpædlɑk/ *n.* [C] a lock with a curved bar at the top that you can put on a door, bicycle, etc. —**padlock** *v.* [T]

pa·gan /ˈpeɪgən/ *n.* [C] someone who does not believe in any of the main modern religions of the world —**pagan** *adj.*

page[1] /peɪdʒ/ *n.* [C] **1** one side of a sheet of paper in a book, newspaper, etc., or the sheet of paper itself: *Do the exercises **on page** 10 for homework.* | *The story was on the **front page** of every newspaper.* | *Callie **turned** the **page** and continued reading.* **2** all the writing and pictures that you can see at one time on a computer screen: *a **web page*** **3** a young person who works in a government office for a short time in order to gain experience

page[2] *v.* [T] **1** to call someone's name in a public place, especially using a LOUDSPEAKER: *We couldn't find Jan at the airport, so we had her paged.* **2** to call someone using a BEEPER (=small machine that receives messages)

page down/up *phr. v.* to press a special key on a computer that makes the screen show the page after or before the one you are reading

pag·eant /ˈpædʒənt/ *n.* [C] **1** a competition for young women in which their beauty and other qualities are judged: *a **beauty pageant*** **2** a public show or ceremony that usually shows an event in history

pag·eant·ry /ˈpædʒəntri/ *n.* [U] *formal* impressive ceremonies or events, involving many people wearing special clothes: *the pageantry of a royal wedding*

pag·er /ˈpeɪdʒɚ/ *n.* [C] a BEEPER

pa·go·da /pəˈgoʊdə/ *n.* [C] an Asian TEMPLE that has several levels, with a decorated roof at each level

paid /peɪd/ *v.* the past tense and past participle of PAY

pail /peɪl/ *n.* [C] **1** a container with a handle, used for carrying liquids or by children when playing on the beach [= **bucket**]: *a pail of water* **2** a container used for carrying or holding something: *a garbage pail* | *a lunch pail*

pain[1] /peɪn/ *n.* **1** [C,U] the feeling you have when part of your body hurts: *Soldiers lay groaning **in pain*** (=feeling pain) *on the ground.* | *drugs that **ease/relieve pain*** (=make it hurt less) | *patients suffering from **shoulder/chest/back pain*** | *As soon as I stood up, I **felt the pain**.*

COLLOCATIONS

A **terrible**, **severe**, **intense**, or **unbearable pain** is very bad.
A **sharp pain** is short but severe.
A **dull pain** is not severe, but it continues for a long time.
If you have pain over a long period of time, you can call it **chronic pain**.

Another word for a pain that continues but is not very strong is an **ache**.
If you are **in pain**, you take **medicine** or **painkillers** to **lessen/ease/relieve/kill the pain**.

2 be a pain (in the neck/butt) *spoken* to be very annoying: *This pan is a pain to wash.* **3** [C,U] the feeling of unhappiness you have when you are sad, upset, etc.: *the pain children feel when their parents divorce* **4 take pains to do sth** to make a special effort to do something well: *I **took great pains** not **to** upset them.* **5 be at pains to do sth** *formal* to be very careful to do something

pain² *v.* [T] *formal* to make someone feel unhappy: ***It pains me to** see my mother growing old.*

pained /peɪnd/ *adj.* worried, upset, or slightly annoyed: *a **pained look/expression***

pain·ful /ˈpeɪnfəl/ *adj.* **1** making you feel physical pain: *a painful injury* | *He was finding it **painful to** walk.*

THESAURUS

tender – a tender part of your body is painful if someone touches it: *Her feet still felt tender.*
stiff – if a part of your body is stiff, your muscles hurt and it is difficult to move, usually because you have exercised too much or you are sick: *My legs are so stiff!*
sore – painful as a result of a wound, infection, or too much exercise: *a sore throat and fever*
➔ HURT¹

2 making you feel very upset or unhappy: ***painful memories** of the war* | *The divorce was **painful for** both of us.* | *a **painful decision** to leave* **3** very bad and embarrassing for other people to watch, hear, etc.: *The acting in the movie was so bad that it was painful to watch.*

pain·ful·ly /ˈpeɪnfəli/ *adv.* **1** with pain, or causing pain: *Mike walked slowly and painfully to the door.* | *People can be painfully cruel to each other.* **2** very – used to emphasize a bad or harmful quality or that something makes you upset: *It was **painfully obvious** that she wasn't well.* **3** needing a lot of effort, or causing a lot of trouble: *Real change is a painfully slow process.*

pain·kill·er /ˈpeɪnˌkɪlɚ/ *n.* [C] a medicine that reduces or removes pain

pain·less /ˈpeɪnlɪs/ *adj.* **1** without pain, or causing no pain: *a painless death* **2** *informal* needing no effort or hard work: *a painless way to learn Spanish*

pains·tak·ing /ˈpeɪnzˌteɪkɪŋ, ˈpeɪnˌsteɪ-/ *adj.* very careful and thorough: *painstaking research* —**painstakingly** *adj.*

THESAURUS

careful, **methodical**, **thorough**, **meticulous**, **systematic**
➔ see Thesaurus box at CAREFUL

paint¹ /peɪnt/ *n.* **1** [U] a colored liquid that you put on a surface to make it a particular color: *a can of yellow paint* | *The kitchen needs a fresh **coat of paint*** (=layer of paint). **2** [C,U] a colored substance in a small tube or block, used for painting pictures: *a set of oil paints*

paint² *v.* [I,T] **1** to put paint on a surface: *How much will it cost to paint the house?* | *The door had been painted blue.* | *the **freshly painted** (=recently painted) walls* **2** to make a picture of someone or something using paint: *He painted a portrait of Allen's wife.* **3 paint a picture/portrait of sth** to describe something in a particular way: *The report paints a grim picture of family life.*

paint·brush /ˈpeɪntˌbrʌʃ/ *n.* [C] a special brush used for painting pictures or for painting rooms, houses, etc. ➔ see picture at BRUSH¹

P

paint·er /ˈpeɪntɚ/ *n.* [C] **1** someone who paints pictures [= **artist**]: *a landscape painter*

THESAURUS

artist, **photographer**, **sculptor**, **potter**
➔ see Thesaurus box at ARTIST

2 someone whose job is painting houses, rooms, etc.

painting

paint·ing /ˈpeɪntɪŋ/ *n.* **1** [C] a painted picture: *a **painting of** Thomas Jefferson* (=that shows Thomas Jefferson) | *a **painting by** Mondrian* (=painted by him)

THESAURUS

drawing, **photography**, **sculpture**, **pottery**, **ceramics**
➔ see Thesaurus box at ART

2 [U] the act or skill of making a picture using paint: *Monet's style of painting* **3** [U] the act of covering a wall, house, etc. with paint

ˈpaint ˌthinner *n.* [U] a liquid that you add to paint to make it less thick

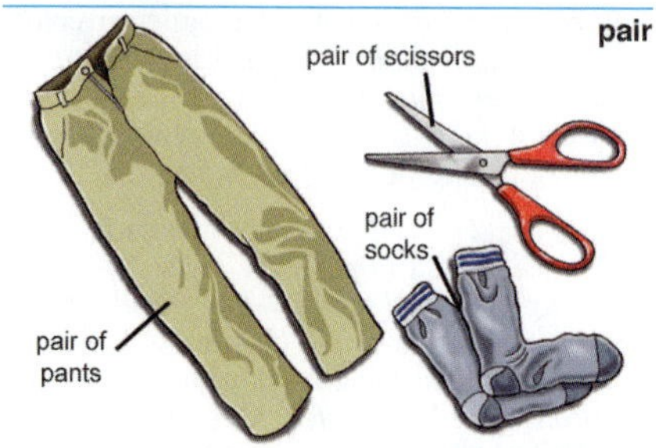

pair[1] /pɛr/ *n.* plural **pairs** or **pair** [C] **1** something made of two similar parts that are joined together: *a **pair of** scissors | two pairs of jeans | a pair of glasses* **2** two things of the same kind that are used together: *a **pair of** earrings | She has 12 pairs of shoes!* **3** two people who are standing or doing something together: *a **pair of** dancers | Work **in pairs*** (=in groups of two) *on the next exercise.*

pair[2] **also pair up** *v.* [I,T] to form or be put into groups of two: *We were each **paired with** a newcomer to help with training.*

pair (sb ⇔) **off** *phr. v.* to come together or bring two people together: *The guests paired off for the first dance.*

pa·ja·mas /pəˈdʒɑməz, -ˈdʒæ-/ *n.* [plural] a pair of loose pants and a loose shirt that you wear in bed

pal /pæl/ *n.* [C] *old-fashioned* a close friend: *a college pal* ➔ PEN PAL

pal·ace /ˈpælɪs/ *n.* [C] a large house where a king or queen officially lives: *Buckingham Palace*

pal·at·a·ble /ˈpælət̬əbəl/ *adj. formal* **1** palatable food or drinks have an acceptable taste: *a palatable wine* **2** an idea, suggestion, etc. that is palatable is acceptable: *a plan that is more palatable to local residents*

pal·ate /ˈpælɪt/ *n.* [C] **1** the top inside part of the mouth **2** [usually singular] *formal* someone's ability to taste things: *flavors to please the palate*

pa·la·tial /pəˈleɪʃəl/ *adj.* very large and beautifully decorated: *a palatial hotel*

pale[1] /peɪl/ *adj.* **1** having a much lighter skin color than usual because you are sick, frightened, etc.: *Her father looked pale and nervous.* **2** a pale color has more white in it than usual: *pale green walls*

THESAURUS

light, pastel, faded
➔ see Thesaurus box at LIGHT[2]

pale[2] *v.* [I] **1 pale in/by comparison** to seem less important, good, etc. when compared to something else: *Today's economic problems **pale in comparison with** those of the 1930s.* **2 pale into insignificance** to seem much less important when compared to something else: *All our troubles paled into insignificance when we heard about the war.* **3** *literary* if you pale, your face becomes much whiter than usual because you are sick, frightened, etc.

pa·le·on·tol·o·gy /ˌpeɪliənˈtɑlədʒi, -liɑn-/ *n.* [U] the study of FOSSILS (=ancient animals and plants that have been preserved in rock) —**paleontologist** *n.* [C]

pal·ette /ˈpælɪt/ *n.* [C] **1** a board with a curved edge and a hole for the thumb, on which a painter mixes colors **2** the particular set of colors a painter uses: *a bright palette*

pall[1] /pɔl/ *n.* **1** [C] a low dark cloud of smoke, dust, etc.: *a **pall of** black **smoke*** **2** [singular] something that spoils an event or occasion that should have been happy: *The drug scandal **cast a pall over*** (=spoiled the happy feelings at) *the Olympics.*

pall[2] *v.* [I] *literary* to become less interesting or enjoyable: *Gradually, the novelty of city life began to pall.*

pall·bear·er /ˈpɔlˌbɛrɚ/ *n.* [C] someone who helps to carry a CASKET (=a box with a dead body inside) at a funeral

pal·let /ˈpælɪt/ *n.* [C] a large flat wooden frame on which heavy goods can be lifted, stored, or moved

pal·lid /ˈpælɪd/ *adj. literary* looking pale and unhealthy: *pallid skin*

pal·lor /ˈpælɚ/ *n.* [singular] *literary* a pale unhealthy color of your skin or face

palm[1] /pɑm/ *n.* [C] **1** the inside surface of your hand between the base of your fingers and your wrist: *The boy held a penny **in the palm of** his **hand**.* ➔ see picture at HAND[1] **2** a PALM TREE

palm[2] *v.* [T]

palm sth ⇔ **off** *phr. v.* to persuade someone to accept or buy something, especially by deceiving him/her

ˌPalm ˈSunday *n.* [C] the Sunday before Easter in Christian religions

palm·top /ˈpɑmtɑp/ *n.* [C] a very small computer that you can hold in your hand

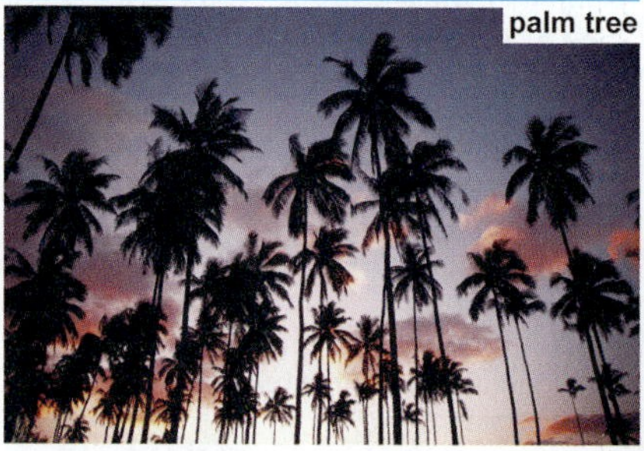
palm tree

ˈpalm tree *n.* [C] a tall tropical tree with large pointed leaves at its top that grows near beaches or in deserts

pal·pa·ble /ˈpælpəbəl/ *adj. formal* easily and clearly noticed: *Rosanne's disappointment was palpable.* —**palpably** *adv.*

pal·pi·ta·tions /ˌpælpəˈteɪʃənz/ *n.* [plural] irregular or extremely fast beating of your heart

pal·try /ˈpɔltri/ *adj. disapproving* too small to be useful or important: *a paltry pay raise*

pam·per /ˈpæmpɚ/ *v.* [T] to give someone a lot of care and attention, sometimes in a way that is bad for him/her: *a pampered dog*

pam·phlet /ˈpæmflɪt/ *n.* [C] a very thin book with paper covers, giving information about something

pan¹ /pæn/ *n.* [C] **1** a round metal container used for cooking, usually with a handle: *a large* ***pan of*** *boiling water* | ***pots and pans*** | *a* ***frying pan*** **2** a metal container used for baking food, or the food that this contains: *Spoon half the batter into a greased pan.* | *a* ***pan of*** *sweet rolls* **3** a container with low sides, used for holding liquids: *an oil pan*

pan² *v.* past tense and past participle **panned**, present participle **panning** **1** [T] *journalism* to strongly criticize a movie, play, etc. in a newspaper or on television or radio: *The critics panned his first play.* **2** [I,T] to move a camera while taking a picture, or follow a moving object with a camera: *The camera panned across the crowd.* **3** [I] to wash soil in a pan in order to separate gold from it: ***panning for*** *gold*

pan out *phr. v. informal* to happen or develop in the expected way: *I got a few job interviews, but nothing panned out.*

pan·a·ce·a /ˌpænəˈsiə/ *n.* [C usually singular] something that people think will make everything better or cure any illness: *Money is not a* ***panacea for*** *the problems in our schools, but it can help.*

pa·nache /pəˈnæʃ, -ˈnɑʃ/ *n.* [U] a way of doing things that is exciting and makes them seem easy: *Mr. Seaton danced* ***with*** *real* ***panache***.

pan·cake /ˈpænkeɪk/ *n.* [C] a flat round type of bread made from flour, milk, and eggs that is cooked in a pan and eaten for breakfast → see picture on page A5

pan·cre·as /ˈpæŋkriəs/ *n.* [C] a GLAND in your body that helps your body to use the food you eat —**pancreatic** /ˌpæŋkriˈæṭɪk/ *adj.*

pan·da /ˈpændə/ *n.* [C] a large black and white animal, similar to a bear, that lives in China

pan·de·mo·ni·um /ˌpændəˈmoʊniəm/ *n.* [U] a situation in which there is a lot of noise and movement because people are angry, frightened, excited, etc.: *For the next hour, there was pandemonium in the classroom.*

pan·der /ˈpændɚ/ *v.*

pander to sth/sb *phr. v. disapproving* to give someone what s/he wants in order to please him/her, even if it seems unreasonable or unnecessary: *a president who panders to big business*

pane /peɪn/ *n.* [C] a piece of glass in a window or door: *a* ***window pane*** | *a* ***pane of glass***

pan·el¹ /ˈpænl/ *n.* [C] **1** a group of people who are chosen to discuss something, decide something, or answer questions: *Six Congressmen are* ***on the panel*** *looking into the issue.* | *a* ***panel of*** *experts* **2** a flat sheet of wood, glass, etc. that fits into a frame to form part of a door, wall, or ceiling: *an oak door with three panels* **3 instrument/control panel** the place in an airplane, boat, etc. where the instruments or controls are

panel² *v.* [T] to cover or decorate something such as a wall with flat pieces of wood, glass, etc.: *an oak-paneled room*

pan·el·ing /ˈpænl-ɪŋ/ *n.* [U] wood in long pieces that is used for covering walls, etc.: *pine paneling*

pan·el·ist /ˈpænl-ɪst/ *n.* [C] a member of a panel, especially on a radio or television program

pang /pæŋ/ *n.* [C] a sudden strong and unpleasant feeling: *strong* ***hunger pangs*** | *a* ***pang of*** *regret*

pan·han·dle¹ /ˈpænˌhændl/ *v.* [I] to ask people for money in the streets [= **beg**] —**panhandler** *n.* [C]

panhandle² *n.* [C] a thin piece of land that is joined to a larger area: *the Texas panhandle*

pan·ic¹ /ˈpænɪk/ *n.* [C,U] a sudden feeling of fear or anxiety that makes you do things without thinking carefully about them: *People fled the area* ***in (a) panic***. | *The announcement caused widespread panic.*

panic² *v.* past tense and past participle **panicked**, present participle **panicking** [I,T] to suddenly feel so frightened that you do things without thinking clearly, or to make someone feel this way: *Johnson panicked and ran.* | ***Don't panic*** (=stay calm) – *we're getting you out of there right now.* —**panicky** *adj.*

ˈpanic-ˌstricken *adj.* so frightened that you cannot think clearly: *Panic-stricken parents swarmed around the school.*

pan·o·ram·a /ˌpænəˈræmə, -ˈrɑ-/ *n.* [C] an impressive view over a wide area of land: *a* ***panorama of*** *the Rocky Mountains* —**panoramic** /ˌpænəˈræmɪk◂/ *adj.*: *a panoramic view of the valley*

pan·sy /ˈpænzi/ *n.* plural **pansies** [C] a small flat brightly colored garden flower

pant¹ /pænt/ *v.* [I] to breathe quickly with short noisy breaths, especially after exercising or because it is hot: *Eddie was panting with the effort of the climb.*

THESAURUS

wheeze, be short of breath, be out of breath, gasp for breath/air
→ see Thesaurus box at BREATHE

pant² *adj.* [only before noun] relating to, or part of, a pair of pants: *We rolled up our* ***pant legs*** *and waded in the creek.*

pan·the·ism /ˈpænθiˌɪzəm/ *n.* [U] the religious idea that God is present in all natural things in the universe

pan·ther /ˈpænθɚ/ *n.* [C] a large wild black cat that is good at hunting

pant·ies /ˈpæntiz/ *n.* [plural] a piece of women's

underwear that covers the area between the waist and the top of the legs ➔ see picture at CLOTHES

pan·to·mime /ˈpæntəˌmaɪm/ *n.* [C,U] a method of performing using only actions and not words, or a play performed using this method

pan·try /ˈpæntri/ *n.* plural **pantries** [C] a small room near a kitchen where food, dishes, etc. are kept

pants /pænts/ *n.* [plural] a piece of clothing that covers you from your waist to your feet and has a separate part for each leg: *a black **pair of pants** | He put it in his **pants pocket**.* ➔ see picture at CLOTHES

pant·suit /ˈpæntsut/ *n.* [C] a women's suit consisting of a JACKET and matching pants

pan·ty·hose /ˈpæntiˌhoʊz/ *n.* [plural] a very thin piece of women's clothing that covers the legs from the feet to the waist, usually worn with dresses or skirts

P

pan·ty·lin·er /ˈpæntiˌlaɪnɚ/ *n.* [C] a very thin SANITARY NAPKIN

pa·pa /ˈpɑpə/ *n. old-fashioned* [C] FATHER

pa·pa·cy /ˈpeɪpəsi/ *n.* **the papacy** the position and authority of the POPE

pa·pal /ˈpeɪpəl/ *adj.* relating to the POPE

pa·pa·raz·zi /ˌpɑpəˈrɑtsi/ *n.* [plural] people who take photographs of famous people by following them around

pa·pa·ya /pəˈpaɪə/ *n.* [C,U] a sweet juicy tropical fruit with many small seeds inside it

pa·per¹ /ˈpeɪpɚ/ *n.* **1** [U] thin sheets used for writing or drawing, wrapping things, etc.: *a letter written on blue paper | Kellen looked at the **piece/sheet of paper** on his desk. | She jotted her phone number on a **slip/scrap of paper*** (=small piece of paper). | *a piece of **wax/tissue/wrapping etc. paper** | a brown paper bag* ➔ see picture on page A11 **2** [C] a newspaper: *Have you seen today's paper? | an article **in the paper** | an ad in the **local paper*** (=the newspaper for the area you live in) **3** [C] a piece of writing that is done as part of a class: *My history paper is due tomorrow.* **4 papers** important or official documents or letters, such as documents you use in your work, your WILL, your PASSPORT, etc.: *legal papers | a set of identity papers* **5 on paper a)** if an idea seems good on paper, it seems good or true but has not been tested or does not work in a real situation: *On paper, the company's policy of flexible working hours sounded great.* **b)** if you put ideas or information on paper, you write them down **6** [C] a piece of writing or a speech by someone who has studied a particular subject: *Einstein's first **paper on** relativity* **7** [C,U] WALLPAPER

paper² *v.* [T] to decorate the walls of a room by covering them with WALLPAPER

pa·per·back /ˈpeɪpɚˌbæk/ *n.* [C] a book with a stiff paper cover: *Her novel's available **in paperback**.*

THESAURUS

hardcover, hardback
➔ see Thesaurus box at BOOK¹

ˈpaper boy *n.* [C] a boy who delivers newspapers to people's houses

ˈpaper clip *n.* [C] a small piece of curved wire used for holding sheets of paper together ➔ see picture on page A11

ˈpaper girl *n.* [C] a girl who delivers newspapers to people's houses

pa·per·weight /ˈpeɪpɚˌweɪt/ *n.* [C] a small heavy object that you put on top of papers so that they stay on a desk

pa·per·work /ˈpeɪpɚˌwɚk/ *n.* [U] **1** work such as writing letters or reports, which must be done but is not very interesting: *Social workers have far too much paperwork to do.* **2** the documents that you need for a business deal, a trip, etc.: *I went to the insurance office to fill out the paperwork.*

pa·pier-mâ·ché /ˌpeɪpɚ məˈʃeɪ/ *n.* [U] a soft substance made from a mixture of paper, water, and glue, which becomes hard when it dries

Pap smear /ˈpæp smɪr/ *n.* [C] a medical test that takes cells from a woman's CERVIX and examines them for signs of CANCER

par /pɑr/ *n.* [U] **1 be on a par (with sth)** to be of the same standard as something else: *Their military forces are on a par with ours.* **2 not be up to par also be below par** to be less good or well than usual: *Several students are not performing up to par.* **3 be par for the course** to be what you would normally expect to happen: *"Lisa was late again." "That's par for the course."* **4** the number of STROKES a good player should take to hit the ball into a hole in golf

par·a·ble /ˈpærəbəl/ *n.* [C] a short simple story that teaches a moral or religious lesson

par·a·chute¹ /ˈpærəˌʃut/ *n.* [C] a large piece of cloth that is attached to the back of someone who jumps out of an AIRPLANE, which makes him/her fall slowly and safely to the ground

parachute

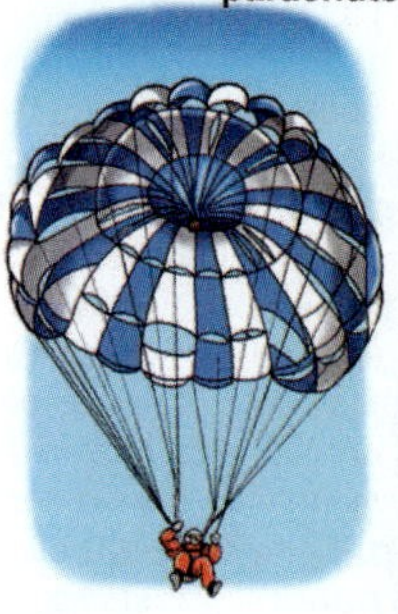

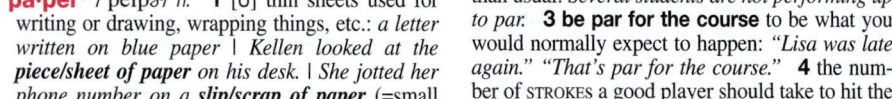

parachute² *v.* **1** [I] to jump from an AIRPLANE using a parachute: *Soldiers **parachuted into** the field during the night.* **2** [T] to drop something from an AIRPLANE with a parachute: *Supplies were **parachuted into** the area.*

pa·rade¹ /pəˈreɪd/ *n.* [C] **1** a public celebration when musical bands, decorated vehicles, etc. move down the street: *the Rose Parade on New Year's Day | a band marching in the parade* **2** a military ceremony in which soldiers stand on march together so that they can be examined: *cadets **on parade***

parade² *v.* **1** [I] to march together to celebrate or protest something: *Peace demonstrators **paraded through/along/in** the streets.* **2** [I] *disapproving* to walk around an area in order to attract attention: *A couple of teenage girls were **parading around** the pool in their bikinis.* **3** [T] to show someone to the public, especially in order to prove that you have control or power over him/her: *The prisoners were paraded in front of the TV cameras.* **4** [T] to show a particular quality or possession in order to make people notice you: *Young athletes will get a chance to parade their skills.*

par·a·digm /ˈpærəˌdaɪm/ *n.* [C] *formal* a model or typical example of something that explains an idea or process very clearly: *The Holocaust is a **paradigm of** evil.* —**paradigmatic** /ˌpærədɪgˈmæt̬ɪk/ *adj.*

par·a·dise /ˈpærəˌdaɪs, -ˌdaɪz/ *n.* **1** [U] a place or situation that is extremely pleasant, beautiful, or enjoyable: *an island paradise* **2** [singular] a place that has everything you need to do a particular activity: *This mall is a shopper's paradise.* **3** [U] HEAVEN

par·a·dox /ˈpærəˌdɑks/ *n.* [C] a statement or situation that seems strange or impossible because it contains two ideas or qualities that are very different but are both true: *It's a paradox that such a rich country has so many poor people.* —**paradoxical** /ˌpærəˈdɑksɪkəl/ *adj.* —**paradoxically** *adv.*

par·af·fin /ˈpærəfɪn/ *n.* [U] a soft white substance used for making CANDLES

par·a·gon /ˈpærəˌgɑn/ *n.* [C] someone who is a perfect example of something: *Alice was a **paragon of** wifely **virtue**.*

par·a·graph /ˈpærəˌgræf/ *n.* [C] a group of several sentences that start on a new line and deal with one idea in a piece of writing: *I've only read the first paragraph of the article.* | *Your closing paragraph should sum up your argument.*

par·a·keet /ˈpærəˌkit/ *n.* [C] a small brightly colored bird with a long tail that is often kept as a pet

par·a·le·gal /ˌpærəˈligəl/ *n.* [C] someone whose job is to help a lawyer do his/her work

par·al·lel¹ /ˈpærəˌlɛl/ *n.* [C] **1** a relationship or similarity between two things, especially things that happen or exist in different places or at different times: *The article **draws a parallel between** the political situation now and the situation in the 1930s* (=it shows how they are similar). | *The administration would like us to see **parallels with** World War II in today's conflict.* **2** an imaginary line drawn on a map of the Earth that is parallel to the EQUATOR

parallel² *adj.* **1** two lines that are parallel to each other are the same distance apart along their whole length: *a street **parallel to/with** the railroad* **2** similar and happening at the same time: *two parallel murder investigations*

parallel³ *v.* [T] *formal* to be very similar to something else: *The movie's plot closely parallels a play by Shakespeare.*

pa·ral·y·sis /pəˈræləsɪs/ *n.* [U] **1** the loss of the ability to move or feel part of your body: *Such injuries can cause permanent paralysis.* **2** a lack of ability to operate correctly or to do anything: *the political paralysis caused by Congress's lack of cooperation with the White House*

par·a·lyze /ˈpærəˌlaɪz/ *v.* [T] **1** to make someone lose the ability to move part of his/her body, or to feel anything in it **2** to make something or someone unable to operate normally: *Heavy snow has paralyzed several cities in the eastern States.* | *He was paralyzed by fear.* —**paralyzed** *adj.*: *The stroke left him paralyzed and unable to feed himself.*

P

par·a·med·ic /ˌpærəˈmɛdɪk/ *n.* [C] someone who usually works in an AMBULANCE and is trained to help sick or injured people, but is not a doctor or nurse

pa·ram·et·er /pəˈræmət̬ɚ/ *n.* [C usually plural] a limit that controls the way that something should be done: *Congress will decide on **parameters for** the investigation.*

par·a·mil·i·tar·y /ˌpærəˈmɪləˌtɛri/ *adj.* organized like an army, but not part of the legal military forces of a country: *extremist paramilitary groups* —**paramilitary** *n.* [C]

par·a·mount /ˈpærəˌmaʊnt/ *adj.* more important than anything else: *The needs of the customer should be paramount.*

par·a·noid /ˈpærəˌnɔɪd/ *adj.* **1** believing unreasonably that you cannot trust other people, or that they are trying to harm you: *All the stress about job losses is making me a little paranoid.* **2** suffering from a mental illness that makes you believe that other people are trying to harm you —**paranoia** /ˌpærəˈnɔɪə/ *n.* [U]

par·a·pher·na·lia /ˌpærəfɚˈneɪlyə, -fəˈneɪl-/ *n.* [U] a lot of small things that belong to someone or that are used for a particular activity: *photographic paraphernalia*

par·a·phrase /ˈpærəˌfreɪz/ *v.* [T] to express what someone has written or said in a way that is shorter or easier to understand: *Write a paragraph that paraphrases the story.* —**paraphrase** *n.* [C]

par·a·ple·gic /ˌpærəˈplidʒɪk/ *n.* [C] someone who is unable to move the lower part of his/her body

par·a·site /ˈpærəˌsaɪt/ *n.* [C] **1** a plant or animal that lives on or in another plant or animal and gets food from it **2** a lazy person who does not work but depends on other people —**parasitic** /ˌpærəˈsɪt̬ɪk/ *adj.*

par·a·sol /ˈpærəˌsɔl, -ˌsɑl/ *n.* [C] a type of UMBRELLA used for protection from the sun

par·a·troop·er /ˈpærəˌtrupɚ/ *n.* [C] a soldier

who is trained to jump out of an AIRPLANE using a PARACHUTE

par·cel¹ /ˈpɑrsəl/ *n.* [C] **1** PACKAGE **2** an area of land that is part of a larger area that has been divided: *a 50-acre parcel in the foothills*

parcel² *v.*

parcel sth ⇔ **out** *phr. v.* to divide or share something among several people or groups: *The foundation receives the money, then parcels it out to various projects.*

ˈparcel post *n.* [U] the cheapest way of sending packages by mail because it uses trains and trucks rather than AIRPLANES

parched /pɑrtʃt/ *adj.* **1** *literary* extremely dry: *parched fields* **2 be parched** *informal* to be very THIRSTY: *I'm parched!*

par·don¹ /ˈpɑrdn/ *v.* [T] **1 pardon me** *spoken* **a)** used in order to politely say sorry after you have made an impolite sound such as a BURP or a YAWN **b)** used in order to politely say sorry when you have accidentally pushed someone, interrupted him/her etc.: *Oh, pardon me, I didn't realize you were on the phone.* **c) also Pardon?** used in order to politely ask someone to repeat what s/he has just said because you did not hear it correctly **d)** used in order to politely get someone's attention in order to ask a question: *Pardon me, do you know what time it is?* **e)** used before you politely correct someone or disagree with him/her: *Pardon me, but I don't think that's true.* **2** to officially allow someone to be free without being punished, although a court has decided s/he is guilty of a crime: *Before he could serve his term, he was pardoned by the President.*

pardon² *n.* [C] an official order allowing someone to be free without being punished, although a court has decided s/he is guilty of a crime: *The governor was persuaded to **grant/give** Davis **a pardon**.* ➔ **I beg your pardon** at BEG

par·don·a·ble /ˈpɑrdn-əbəl/ *adj. formal* possible to forgive or excuse: *a pardonable error*

pare /pɛr/ *v.* [T] to cut off the thin outer part of a fruit or vegetable: *Pare the apples and slice them into chunks.*

pare sth **down** *phr. v.* to gradually reduce an amount or number: *Production costs have to be pared down.*

par·ent /ˈpɛrənt, ˈpær-/ *n.* [C] the father or mother of a person or animal: *My parents are coming to visit next week.* | ***single parents*** (=who do not live with their child's other parent) *who cannot afford childcare* —**parental** /pəˈrɛntl/ *adj.*: *parental rights*

par·ent·age /ˈpɛrəntɪdʒ, ˈpær-/ *n.* [U] *formal* someone's parents and the country they are from: *children of French-Canadian parentage*

pa·ren·the·sis /pəˈrɛnθəsɪs/ *n.* plural **parentheses** /-siz/ [C usually plural] one of the marks ( ), used in writing to separate additional information from the main information: *The numbers **in parentheses** refer to page numbers.*

par·ent·hood /ˈpɛrəntˌhʊd, ˈpær-/ *n.* [U] the state of being a parent: *They felt that they were not yet ready for parenthood.*

par·ish /ˈpærɪʃ/ *n.* **1** [C] the area that a priest in some Christian churches is responsible for **2 the parish** the members of a particular church —**parishioner** /pəˈrɪʃənə/ *n.* [C]

par·i·ty /ˈpærəti/ *n.* [U] the state of being equal, especially having equal pay, rights, or power: *Our employees are demanding **parity with** other workers in the industry.*

park¹ /pɑrk/ *n.* [C] **1** a large open area with grass and trees in a town, where people can walk, play games, etc.: *We went for a walk **in the park**.* | *a park bench* | *Central Park* **2** a large area of land in the country that has been kept in its natural state to protect the plants and animals there: *a **state/national park*** **3** a field where baseball is played: *Fenway Park* ➔ AMUSEMENT PARK, BALL PARK, THEME PARK, TRAILER PARK

park² *v.* [I,T] to put a car or other vehicle in a particular place for a period of time: *Is it okay if I park here?* | *Park your car in the back lot.* ➔ see Topic box at DRIVE¹

par·ka /ˈpɑrkə/ *n.* [C] a thick warm coat with a HOOD

ˌpark and ˈride *n.* [U] a system in which you leave your car in a special place in one part of a city, and then take a bus or train from there to the center of town

park·ing /ˈpɑrkɪŋ/ *n.* [U] **1** the act of parking a car: *The sign said "No Parking."* **2** spaces in which you can leave a car: *Parking is available on Lemay Street.* | *We found a **parking space/place** near the door.*

ˈparking gaˌrage *n.* [C] a building with several floors or an area underground where cars can be parked: *an underground parking garage*

ˈparking lot *n.* [C] an open area where cars can be parked

ˈparking ˌmeter *n.* [C] a machine which you put money into when you park your car next to it

park·way /ˈpɑrkweɪ/ *n.* [C] a wide road, usually with grass and trees in the middle or along the sides

par·lay /ˈpɑrleɪ, -li/ *v.* past tense and past participle **parlayed**, third person singular **parlays**

parlay sth **into** sth *phr. v. journalism* to use something that you already have, such as your skills, experience, or money, to become successful or get something that you want: *She parlayed a $600 investment into the state's largest home decorating company.*

par·lia·ment /ˈpɑrləmənt/ *n.* [C] the group of people in some countries who are elected to make laws and discuss important national affairs —**parliamentary** /ˌpɑrləˈmɛntri, -ˈmɛntəri/ *adj.*

par·lor /ˈpɑrlə/ *n.* [C] **1** a store or type of business that provides a particular service: *a beauty parlor* | *a funeral parlor* **2** *old-fashioned* a room in a house which has comfortable chairs and is used for meeting guests

Par·me·san /ˈpɑrmə,zɑn/ **also** ˈ**Parmesan** ,**cheese** *n.* [U] a hard strong-tasting Italian cheese

pa·ro·chi·al /pəˈroʊkiəl/ *adj.* **1** relating to a particular church: *a **parochial school*** (=a private school that is run by a particular church) **2** *disapproving* only interested in the things that affect you and your local area: *Brian has a very parochial world view.*

par·o·dy[1] /ˈpærədi/ *n.* plural **parodies** [C,U] a performance or a piece of writing or music that copies a particular well-known style in a funny way: *a **parody of** a romance novel*

parody[2] *v.* past tense and past participle **parodied**, third person singular **parodies** [T] to copy someone's style or attitude in a funny way

pa·role /pəˈroʊl/ *n.* [U] permission for someone to leave prison, on the condition that s/he promises to behave well: *He was released **on parole** after serving 5 years.* —**parole** *v.* [T]

par·quet /pɑrˈkeɪ, ˈpɑrkeɪ/ *n.* [U] small flat blocks of wood laid in a pattern that cover the floor of a room

par·rot[1] /ˈpærət/ *n.* [C] a brightly colored tropical bird with a curved beak that can be taught to copy human speech

parrot[2] *v.* [T] *disapproving* to repeat someone else's words or ideas without really understanding them

pars·ley /ˈpɑrsli/ *n.* [U] a plant with groups of curled leaves, used in cooking or as a decoration on food

part[1] /pɑrt/ *n.*

1 OF A WHOLE [C,U] one of the pieces or features of something, such as an object, place, event, or period of time: *Which **part of** town do you live in?* | ***The best/worst part** of the movie was the ending.* | *Getting Dad to agree will be **the hard/easy part**.* | ***A large/good part of*** (=a lot of) *my time is spent reading.* | *We waited for **the better part of*** (=most of) *an hour.*

THESAURUS

piece – one of several different parts that you join together to make something: *One of the pieces of the jigsaw puzzle was missing.*
section – one of several parts that something is divided into: *the sports section of the newspaper*
chapter – one of the parts that a book is divided into: *I've read the first two chapters.*
scene – one of the parts that a play or movie is divided into: *the opening scene* | *a love scene*
department – one part of a large organization, which is responsible for a particular kind of work: *the marketing department*
→ STAGE[1]

2 SEPARATE PIECE [C usually plural] one of the separate pieces that a machine or piece of equipment is made of: *Do you sell parts for Ford cars?*

3 play/have a part (in sth) to be one of several things that make something happen or be successful: *The school's excellent reputation **played a big/important/major part in** her decision to go there.*

4 take part to be involved in an activity, event, etc. together with other people [= **participate**]: *Ten runners **took part in** the race.*

5 WHAT SB DID [C,U] what someone did in an activity, especially one that was shared by several people: *We'd like to thank Walter for his **part in** organizing the concert.* | *It was a huge mistake **on her part*** (=that she made).

6 IN A PLAY/MOVIE [C] the words and actions of a particular character in a play, movie, etc., performed by an actor: *Kessler **played/had the part of** Hamlet.*

7 QUANTITY [C] a particular quantity used when measuring different substances together into a mixture: *Mix two parts sand to one part cement.*

8 HAIR [C] the line on your head made by dividing your hair with a comb

9 for the most part also in large part mostly, in most places, or most of the time: *She is, for the most part, a fair person.*

10 in part *formal* to some degree, but not completely: *The accident was due in part to the bad weather.*

part[2] *v.* **1** [I,T] to pull the two sides of something apart, or to move apart in this way, making a space in the middle: *He parted the curtains and looked out into the street.* **2** [I] *formal* to separate from someone, or end a relationship with him/her: *Sharon and I parted on friendly terms.* **3** [T] if you part your hair, you comb some of your hair in one direction and the rest in the other direction **4 part company a)** to separate from someone, or end a relationship with someone: *Dick **parted company with** Rogers after a property deal that lost money.* **b)** to no longer agree with someone

part with sth *phr. v.* to get rid of something although you do not want to: *She couldn't bear to part with the dress.*

part[3] *adv.* **part sth, part sth** if something is part one thing, part another, it consists of both those things: *The English test is part written, part spoken.*

par·tial /ˈpɑrʃəl/ *adj.* **1** not complete: *The airline released a partial list of the flight's passengers.* **2 be partial to sth** *formal* to like something very much: *The Beals are partial to country music.* **3** unfairly supporting one person or one side against another [≠ **impartial**]

par·ti·al·i·ty /,pɑrʃiˈæləṭi/ *n.* [U] unfair support of one person or group more than another

par·tial·ly /ˈpɑrʃəli/ *adv.* not completely: *He's only partially to blame.*

par·tic·i·pant /pɑrˈtɪsəpənt, pə-/ *n.* [C] someone who is taking part in an activity or event:

participants in *the negotiations* | *Jesse is an* ***active participant*** *in class.*

par·tic·i·pate /pɑrˈtɪsəˌpeɪt, pɚ-/ *v.* [I] to take part in an activity or event: *If you'd like to participate, send us your name and address.* | *Thanks to everyone who* ***participated in*** *the festival.*

par·ti·ci·pa·tion /pɑrˌtɪsəˈpeɪʃən, pɚ-/ *n.* [U] the act of taking part in something: *The suspect was charged with* ***participation in*** *an illegal organization.*

par·ti·ci·ple /ˈpɑrt̬əˌsɪpəl/ *n.* [C] *technical* in grammar, the form of a verb, usually ending in "-ing" or "-ed," that is used in compounds to make verb tenses, or as an adjective or GERUND ➔ PAST PARTICIPLE, PRESENT PARTICIPLE

par·ti·cle /ˈpɑrt̬ɪkəl/ *n.* [C] a very small piece of something: *dust particles*

P

par·tic·u·lar¹ /pɚˈtɪkyəlɚ/ *adj.* **1** [only before noun] a particular thing or person is the one that you are talking about, and not any other: *There's one particular song I've been trying to find.* | *Consumers can easily find out how much caffeine a particular product contains.* **2** [only before noun] special or important enough to mention separately: *Police say there was* ***no particular reason*** *why the victim was attacked.* | *There was nothing in the letter* ***of particular importance***. **3** very careful about choosing exactly what you like, and not easily satisfied [**= fussy**]: *He's very* ***particular about*** *what he eats.*

particular² *n.* **in particular** special or specific: *Is there* ***anything/something in particular*** *I can help you with?*

par·tic·u·lar·ly /pɚˈtɪkyələ·li, -ˈtɪkyəli/ *adv.* **1** especially: *We are hoping to expand our business, particularly in Europe.* **2 not particularly a)** not very: *She's not particularly pretty.* **b)** *spoken* not very much or not really: *"Do you like cats?" "No, not particularly."*

part·ing¹ /ˈpɑrt̬ɪŋ/ *n.* [C,U] *literary* an occasion when two people leave each other: *an emotional parting at the airport*

parting² *adj.* **1 parting kiss/gift/glance etc.** something that you give someone as you leave **2 parting shot** a cruel or severe remark that you make just as you are leaving: *As a parting shot, Ashley told him never to call her again.*

par·ti·san /ˈpɑrt̬əzən, -sən/ *adj.* showing support for a particular political party, plan, or leader, and criticizing all others: *a partisan speech* —**partisan** *n.* [C]

par·ti·tion¹ /pɑrˈtɪʃən, pɚ-/ *n.* **1** [C] a thin wall that separates one part of a room from another **2** [U] the separation of a country into two or more independent countries: *the* ***partition of*** *India*

partition² *v.* [T] to divide a country, room, or building into two or more parts

partition sth ⇔ **off** *phr. v.* to divide part of a room from the rest using a partition

part·ly /ˈpɑrtli/ *adv.* to some degree, but not completely: *The accident was partly my fault.* | *The company's success is* ***partly due to*** *a strong economy.* | *The forecast is for* ***partly cloudy*** *skies.*

part·ner /ˈpɑrtˀnɚ/ *n.* [C] **1** someone with whom you do a particular activity, for example dancing, or playing a game against two other people: *my tennis partner* **2** one of the owners of a business: *She's a partner in a law firm.* **3** one of two people who are married, or who live together and have a sexual relationship: *Discuss your worries with your partner.*

part·ner·ship /ˈpɑrtˀnɚˌʃɪp/ *n.* **1** [U] the state of being a partner, especially in business: *We've been* ***in partnership with*** *them for five years.* **2** [C] a relationship in which two or more people, organizations, etc. work together to achieve something: *a* ***partnership between*** *the college and the local business community* **3** [C] a business owned by two or more partners

ˌpart of ˈspeech *n.* plural **parts of speech** [C] *technical* in grammar, any of the types into which words are divided according to their use, such as noun, verb, or adjective

par·tridge /ˈpɑrtrɪdʒ/ *n.* [C,U] a fat brown bird with a short tail which some people shoot as a sport or for food

ˌpart-ˈtime *adj., adv.* someone who has a part-time job works for only part of each day or week [➡ **full-time**]: *I* ***worked part-time*** *at a bookstore when I was in college.* | *a part-time job*

part·way /ˌpɑrtˀˈweɪ◂/ *adv.* after part of a distance has been traveled, or after part of a period of time has passed: *Dave arrived* ***partway through*** *the lecture.*

par·ty¹ /ˈpɑrt̬i/ *n.* plural **parties** [C] **1** an occasion when people meet together to enjoy themselves by eating, drinking, dancing, etc.: *We're* ***having/giving/throwing a party*** *on Saturday.* | *a birthday party* | *a surprise party*

THESAURUS

get-together – a small informal party
bash informal – a party
dinner party – a party where people are invited to someone's house for an evening meal
birthday party – a party to celebrate someone's birthday, especially a child's
house-warming party – a party that you have when you move into a new house
cocktail party – a party that people go to in order to talk and drink together for a few hours
bachelor party – a social event that is just for men, which happens before a wedding
baby/wedding/bridal shower – an event at which people give presents to a woman who is going to have a baby or get married
reception – a large formal party, for example after a wedding
celebration – a party that is organized in order to celebrate something

2 an organization of people with the same political aims that you can vote for in elections: *the Democratic Party* **3** a group of people that has been organized in order to do something: *A* ***search party*** *was formed to find the missing girl.* | *Foster,* ***party of*** *six, your table is ready.*

THESAURUS

group, **crowd**, **team**, **crew**, **gang**, **mob**, **bunch**, **flock**, **mass**
➔ see Thesaurus box at GROUP[1]

4 *formal* one of the people or groups involved in an argument, agreement, etc., especially a legal one: *The two parties will meet to discuss a settlement.* **5 party animal** *informal* someone who enjoys parties a lot

party² *v.* past tense and past participle **partied**, third person singular **parties** [I] *informal* to enjoy yourself, especially by drinking alcohol, eating, dancing, etc.: *We were out partying until 4 a.m.*

pass

pass¹ /pæs/ *v.*
1 GO PAST [I,T] **also pass by** to move to a particular point, object, person, etc. and go past him, her, or it: *Angie waved at me as she passed.* | *A car passed us doing at least 90 miles an hour.* | *I pass by her house every day.*

USAGE

Passed is the past tense and past participle of the verb **pass**: *We've just passed Tim's house.*
Past is an adjective or noun which is used to talk about a period of time before now: *The past year has been very difficult.* | *things that happened in the past*
Past is also an adverb and a preposition used in order to describe something's movement or position in relation to other things: *She drove past us on her way to work.* | *The hotel is just past the church.*

2 MOVE IN A DIRECTION [I] to move from one place to another, following a particular direction: *We* ***passed through*** *Texas on our way to Mexico.* | *A plane* ***passed over*** *the fields.*
3 GO THROUGH/ACROSS ETC. [I,T] to go across, through, around, etc. something else, or to make something do this: *The road* ***passes through*** *some pretty little towns.* | *She was* ***just passing through*** (=traveling through a place) *on her way to Miami.* | *Pass the rope around the tree.*
4 GIVE [T] to take something and put it in someone's hand: *Please pass the salt.* | *Can you pass me a napkin?*
5 SPORTS [I,T] to kick, throw, or hit a ball or other object to another member of your team: *My dad taught me how to pass a football.*

THESAURUS

throw, **toss**, **chuck**, **hurl**, **fling**, **pitch**
➔ see Thesaurus box at THROW[1]

6 TIME a) [I] if time passes, it goes by: *A year passed before I learned the truth.* **b)** [T] to spend time in a particular way: *I cleaned my apartment to* ***pass the time***.
7 TEST/CLASS a) [I,T] to succeed in a test or class [≠ **fail**]: *You'll never pass if you don't start studying.* | *He's worried he won't pass history.* **b)** [T] to officially decide that someone has passed a test [≠ **fail**]: *Do you think Mrs. Cox will pass us?*
8 LAW/DECISION [T] to officially accept a law or proposal, especially by voting: *The motion was passed, 15 votes to 3.*

THESAURUS

approve, **ratify**
➔ see Thesaurus box at APPROVE

9 let sth pass to deliberately not say something when someone says or does something that you do not like: *Carla made some comment about my work, but I decided to* ***let it pass***.
10 END [I] to stop existing or happening [= **end**]: *The storm soon passed.* | *Ann will be upset for a while, but it'll pass.*
11 pass judgment (on sb) to say whether you think someone or something is right or wrong: *I'm only here to listen, not to pass judgment.*
12 DON'T KNOW THE ANSWER [I] *spoken* to say that you do not know the answer to a question: *I had to* ***pass on*** *the last question.*

pass sth ⇔ **around** *phr. v.* to give something to one person in a group, who then gives it to another person etc.: *Pass these papers around, will you?*

pass away *phr. v.* to die – used in order to avoid saying this directly

pass sb **by** *phr. v.* if something passes you by, it happens, but you are not involved in it: *Robin felt that* ***life was passing*** *her* ***by***.

pass sth ⇔ **down** *phr. v.* to give or teach something to people who are younger than you or who live after you: *These traditions have been* ***passed down from*** *one generation* ***to*** *the next.*

pass for sb/sth *phr. v.* to seem very similar to someone or something else, so that people might

P

not realize what or who they are looking at: *With her hair cut like that, she could pass for a boy.*

pass sb/sth **off as** sth *phr. v.* to try to make people think that someone or something is something that he, she, or it is not: *He tried to pass himself off as a police officer.*

pass on *phr. v.* **1 pass** sth ⇔ **on** to tell someone a piece of information that someone else has told you: *She said she'd* ***pass*** *the message* ***on to*** *Ms. Chen.* **2 pass** sth ⇔ **on** to give something to someone else: *Take one and* ***pass*** *the rest* ***on to*** *the next person.*

pass out *phr. v.* **1** to become unconscious **2 pass** sth ⇔ **out** to give something to each one of a group of people: *Please* ***pass out*** *the dictionaries* ***to*** *the class.*

P

THESAURUS

give out, hand, hand out, share, distribute
→ see Thesaurus box at GIVE OUT

pass sb ⇔ **over** *phr. v.* if you pass over someone for a job, you give the job to someone else who is younger or lower in the organization than s/he is

pass sth ⇔ **up** *phr. v.* **pass up a chance/opportunity/offer etc.** to not use a chance to do something: *I couldn't pass up an opportunity to meet the president.*

pass[2] *n.* [C] **1** the act of kicking, throwing, or hitting a ball or other object to another member of your team during a game: *a 30-yard pass* **2** an official document that proves you are allowed to enter a building or travel on something without paying: *a bus pass* | *a museum pass* **3** a road or path that goes between mountains to the other side: *a narrow mountain pass* **4 make a pass at sb** *informal* to try to kiss or touch another person with the intention of having sex with him/her

pass·a·ble /'pæsəbəl/ *adj.* **1** *formal* good enough to be acceptable, but not very good: *Al speaks passable Spanish.* **2** a road or river that is passable is not blocked, so you can travel along or across it [≠ **impassable**]

pas·sage /'pæsɪdʒ/ *n.* **1** [C] **also pas·sage·way** /'pæsɪdʒˌweɪ/ a narrow area with walls on each side that connects one room or place to another: *a dark passage at the back of the building* **2** [C] a short part of a book, poem, speech, piece of music, etc.: *a* ***passage from*** *the Bible* **3** [U] the process of having a new law accepted by Congress or a similar organization: *Supporters say that passage of the bill will reduce crime.* **4** *formal* [U] the action of going across, over, or along something: *The bridge isn't strong enough to allow the* ***passage of*** *heavy vehicles.* **5** [C] a tube in your body that air or liquid can pass through: *nasal passages* **6 the passage of time** the passing of time: *Her condition improved with the passage of time.*

pass·book /'pæsbʊk/ *n.* [C] a book for keeping a record of the money you put into and take out of your bank account

pas·sé /pæ'seɪ/ *adj.* no longer modern or fashionable: *a writing style that has become passé*

pas·sen·ger /'pæsəndʒɚ/ *n.* [C] someone who is traveling in a car, AIRPLANE, boat, etc., but is not driving it: *There were only a few other passengers.* | *Police found a gun under the car's* ***passenger seat*** (=the seat next to the driver).

THESAURUS

traveler, tourist, explorer, commuter
→ see Thesaurus box at TRAVEL[1]

pass·er·by /ˌpæsɚ'baɪ/ *n.* plural **passersby** [C] someone who is walking past a place by chance: *Several passersby saw the accident.*

pass·ing[1] /'pæsɪŋ/ *adj.* **1** going past: *A passing motorist gave her a ride.* **2** continuing or lasting for only a short time: *He gave the report only a passing glance.* | *It's just a passing fad.*

passing[2] *n.* **1 in passing** if you say something in passing, you mention it while you are mainly talking about something else: *The actress* ***mentioned in passing*** *that she had once worked in a factory.* **2** [U] someone's death – used in order to avoid saying this directly

pas·sion /'pæʃən/ *n.* **1** [C,U] a very strongly felt emotion, especially of love, hatred, or anger: *He spoke* ***with passion*** *about the situation in his country.* | *her* ***passion for*** *two men* **2** [C] a strong liking for something: *a* ***passion for*** *golf*

pas·sion·ate /'pæʃənɪt/ *adj.* showing passion, or full of passion: *a passionate kiss* | *a passionate speech* —**passionately** *adv.*

pas·sive[1] /'pæsɪv/ *adj.* **1** tending to accept situations or things that other people do, without attempting to change or fight against them: *"I'm a very passive person," she admitted.* **2** not actively involved in something that is happening: *Traditional classroom learning is usually very passive.* —**passively** *adv.* —**passivity** /pæ'sɪvəṭi/ *n.* [U]

passive[2] *n.* **the passive (voice)** *technical* in grammar, in the passive voice, the action of the verb has an effect on the subject of the sentence. It is shown in English by the verb "be" followed by a past participle. In the sentence, "Oranges are grown in California," the verb is in the passive voice [➡ **active**]

ˌpassive 'smoking *n.* [U] the act of breathing in smoke from someone else's cigarette, pipe, etc., although you do not want to

Pass·o·ver /'pæsˌoʊvɚ/ *n.* [singular,U] a Jewish holiday in the spring to remember when the Jews in ancient Egypt became free

pass·port /'pæspɔrt/ *n.* [C] a small official document given by a government to a citizen, which proves who that person is and allows them to leave the country and enter other countries

COLLOCATIONS

A **passport holder** is the person who a passport belongs to.
If you travel to a foreign country, you must **show** your **passport** at immigration (=the place in an airport, at a border, etc. where officials check your documents) when you enter the country and may **have/get** your **passport stamped**.
A **valid passport** is officially acceptable.
A **passport** that has **expired** is too old to be acceptable.
→ AIRPORT, TRAVEL

pass·word /ˈpæswɚd/ *n.* [C] **1** a secret group of letters or numbers that you must type into a computer before you can use a system or program: *Enter your username and password.* | *I've* ***forgotten*** *my* ***password.*** **2** a secret word or phrase that you must use before being allowed to enter a place that is guarded

past[1] /pæst/ *adj.* **1** [only before noun] having happened, existed, or been experienced before now: *He knew from past experience not to argue.* | *Our current problems are the result of past mistakes.* **2** [only before noun] a little earlier than the present, or up until now: *Tim's been out of town for the past week.* | *the past six months* **3** finished or having come to an end: *The time for discussion is past.* **4** [only before noun] achieving something in the past, or holding an important position in the past [= **former**]: *She's a past president of the club.*

past[2] *prep.* **1** farther than: *My house is* ***just past*** *the bridge.* **2** up to and beyond: *She walked* ***right past*** *me without saying hello.* | *We drove past Al's old house.* **3** after a particular time: *It's ten past nine* (=ten minutes after nine o'clock). | *It was* ***way past*** *midnight when the party ended.* **4 I wouldn't put it past sb (to do sth)** *spoken* used in order to say that you would not be surprised if someone did something bad or unusual because it is typical of him/her: *I wouldn't put it past Colin to lie to his wife.*

past[3] *n.* **1 the past** the time that existed before now, and the things that happened during that time: *People travel more now than they did* ***in the past.*** | *We should ignore the past and concentrate on the future.* **2** [singular] all the things that have happened to you in the time before now: *I'd like to forget my past and start all over.*

past[4] *adv.* **1** up to and beyond a particular place: *Hal and his friends drove past at top speed.* **2 go past** if a period of time goes past, it passes: *Several weeks went past without any news from home.*

USAGE

Past is an adjective or noun which is used to talk about a period of time before now: *The past year has been very difficult.* | *things that happened in the past*
Past is also an adverb and a preposition used in order to describe something's movement or position in relation to other things: *She drove past us on her way to work.* | *The hotel is just past the church.*
Passed is the past tense and past participle of the verb **pass**: *We've just passed Tim's house.*

pas·ta /ˈpɑstə/ *n.* [U] an Italian food made from flour, water, and sometimes eggs, and cut into various shapes, usually eaten with a sauce

paste[1] /peɪst/ *n.* **1** [U] a type of thick glue that is used for sticking paper onto things **2** [C,U] a soft thick mixture that can be easily shaped or spread: *Mix the water and the powder into a smooth paste.* | *tomato paste*

paste[2] *v.* **1** [I,T] to make words that you have removed or copied appear in a new place on a computer screen [➡ **copy**, **cut**] **2** [T] to stick something to something else using paste

pas·tel /pæˈstɛl/ *n.* **1** [C] a soft pale color, such as pale blue or pink

THESAURUS

light, pale, faded
→ see Thesaurus box at LIGHT[2]

2 [C,U] a small colored stick used for drawing pictures, made of a substance like CHALK —**pastel** *adj.*: *soft* ***pastel colors***

pas·teur·ize /ˈpæstʃəˌraɪz, -stəˌraɪz/ *v.* [T] to heat a liquid, especially milk, in a special way that kills any BACTERIA in it —**pasteurization** /ˌpæstʃərəˈzeɪʃən/ *n.* [U]

pas·time /ˈpæs-taɪm/ *n.* [C] something enjoyable that you do when you are not working: *His pastimes include watching TV and reading.*

pas·tor /ˈpæstɚ/ *n.* [C] a minister in some Protestant churches

pas·tor·al /ˈpæstərəl/ *adj.* **1** *formal* relating to the duties of a priest, minister, etc. toward the members of his/her religious group: *pastoral visits* **2** *literary* typical of the simple peaceful life in the country: *a pastoral scene*

ˌpast ˈparticiple *n.* [C] *technical* in grammar, a PARTICIPLE that is usually formed by adding "-ed" to a verb, but that can be IRREGULAR. It can be used in compounds to make PERFECT tenses, or as an adjective. In the sentence "Look what you have done," "done" is a past participle.

ˌpast ˈperfect *n.* **the past perfect** *technical* in grammar, the tense of a verb that shows that an action was completed before another event or time in the past. In the sentence "I had finished my breakfast before Rick called," "had finished" is in the past perfect.

pas·tra·mi /pæˈstrɑmi/ *n.* [U] smoked BEEF that contains a lot of spices and is usually eaten in sandwiches

pas·try /ˈpeɪstri/ *n.* plural **pastries** **1** [U] a mixture of flour, butter, and milk or water, used for making the outer part of baked foods such as PIES [➡ **dough**, **crust**] **2** [C] a small sweet cake

ˌpast ˈtense *n.* **the past tense** *technical* in grammar, the tense of a verb that shows that an action or state began and ended in the past. In the sentence "We walked to school yesterday," "walked" is in the past tense.

pas·ture /ˈpæstʃɚ/ *n.* [C,U] land that is covered with grass and is used for cattle, sheep, etc. to eat

past·y /ˈpeɪsti/ *adj.* looking very pale and unhealthy: *a pasty face*

pat¹ /pæt/ *v.* past tense and past participle **patted**, present participle **patting** **1** [T] to touch someone or something lightly again and again, with your hand flat: *He knelt down to pat the dog.*

THESAURUS

touch, **feel**, **stroke**, **rub**, **scratch**, **brush**, **caress**, **fondle**, **tickle**, **grope**

➔ see Thesaurus box at TOUCH¹

2 pat sb/yourself on the back *informal* to praise someone or yourself for doing something well

pat² *n.* [C] **1** an act of touching someone or something with your hand flat, especially in a friendly way: *She **gave** the little boy **a pat** on the head.* **2 a pat on the back** *informal* praise for something that you have done well: *Alex deserves a pat on the back for all his hard work.* **3 a pat of butter** a small flat piece of butter

pat³ *adv.* **have sth down pat** to know something thoroughly so that you can say it, perform it, etc. without thinking about it

patch¹ /pætʃ/ *n.* [C] **1** a small piece of material used for covering a hole in something, especially clothes: *There were **patches on** the elbows of his jacket.* **2** a part of an area that is different or looks different from the parts that surround it: *We finally found a **patch of** grass to sit down on.* **3** a small area of ground for growing fruit or vegetables: *a cabbage patch*

patch² **also patch up** *v.* [T] to put a small piece of material over a hole, especially in a piece of clothing

patch sth ⇔ **up** *phr. v.* **1** to end an argument and become friendly with someone: *I've **patched things up with** my girlfriend.* **2** to fix something quickly but not carefully: *We patched up his wound until we could get him to a hospital.*

patch·work /ˈpætʃwɚk/ *n.* [U] a type of sewing in which many different colored pieces of cloth are sewn together to make one large piece: *a patchwork quilt*

patch·y /ˈpætʃi/ *adj.* **1** happening or existing in some areas but not in others: *patchy fog* **2** not complete enough to be useful: *My knowledge of biology is pretty patchy.*

pâ·té /pɑˈteɪ, pæ-/ *n.* [U] a thick smooth food made from meat or fish, that you spread on bread

pa·tent¹ /ˈpætˀnt/ *n.* [C] a special document that says that you have the right to make or sell a new invention or product and that no one else is allowed to do so

patent² *v.* [T] to obtain a patent for a new invention or product: *a patented system that turns old cans into aluminum sheets*

patent³ *adj.* *formal* clear and easy to notice [= **obvious**]: *a patent lie*

ˌpatent ˈleather *n.* [U] thin shiny leather that is usually black

pa·tent·ly /ˈpætˀntli/ *adv.* *formal* **patently obvious/false/unfair etc.** completely clear, untrue, unfair, etc., in a way that anyone can notice: *patently offensive language*

pa·ter·nal /pəˈtɚnl/ *adj.* **1** typical of the way a father feels or acts [➡ **maternal**] **2 paternal grandmother/uncle etc.** your father's mother, brother, etc. [➡ **maternal**] —**paternally** *adv.*

pa·ter·nal·ism /pəˈtɚnlˌɪzəm/ *n.* [U] *disapproving* the practice of making decisions for people or organizations, so that they are never able to be responsible themselves —**paternalistic** /pəˌtɚnlˈɪstɪk/ *adj.*

pa·ter·ni·ty /pəˈtɚnəṭi/ *n.* [U] *law* the state of being a father [➡ **maternity**]

path /pæθ/ *n.* plural **paths** /pæðz, pæθs/ [C] **1** a track that people walk along over an area of ground: *a path through the woods* | *I **followed** the **path** until I came to the river.* **2** a way through something, made by opening a space to allow you to move forward: *The police cleared a **path through** the crowd.* | *There was a truck blocking our path.* **3** the direction or line along which someone or something moves: *The storm destroyed everything **in** its **path**.*

pa·thet·ic /pəˈθeṭɪk/ *adj.* very bad, useless, or weak: *Vicky made a pathetic attempt to apologize.* —**pathetically** *adv.*

path·o·log·i·cal /ˌpæθəˈlɑdʒɪkəl/ *adj.* **1** pathological behavior or feelings are unreasonable and impossible to control: *a **pathological liar*** **2** a mental or physical condition that is pathological is caused by disease: *a pathological condition*

pa·thol·o·gy /pəˈθɑlədʒi, pæ-/ *n.* [U] the study of the causes and effects of diseases —**pathologist** *n.* [C]

pa·thos /ˈpeɪθoʊs, -θɑs, ˈpæ-/ *n.* [U] *literary* the quality that a person or a situation has that makes you feel pity and sadness

path·way /ˈpæθweɪ/ *n.* [U] a PATH

pa·tience /ˈpeɪʃəns/ *n.* [U] the ability to wait calmly for a long time or deal with difficulties without becoming annoyed or anxious [≠ **impatience**]: *Finally I **lost my patience with** him and started shouting.* | *The kids are beginning to **try my patience** (=make me stop being patient).* | *She **has** no **patience for** people who make excuses.*

pa·tient¹ /ˈpeɪʃənt/ *n.* [C] someone who is getting medical treatment: *cancer patients* | *Dr. Ross is very popular with his patients.*

patient² *adj.* able to wait calmly for a long time

or to deal with difficulties without becoming annoyed or anxious [≠ **impatient**]: ***Be patient*** *– I'll be off the phone in a minute.* | *Wendy is very* ***patient with*** *her students.* —**patiently** *adv.*: *Simpson* ***waited patiently*** *for his chance.*

pat·i·o /ˈpæt̬iˌoʊ/ *n.* plural **patios** [C] a flat hard area next to a house, where people can sit outside: *Sylvia was sitting* ***out on the patio****.*

pa·tri·arch /ˈpeɪtriˌɑrk/ *n.* [C] *formal* a man who is respected as the head of a family or tribe [➡ **matriarch**]

pa·tri·arch·al /ˌpeɪtriˈɑrkəl/ *adj. formal* **1** ruled or controlled only by men: *a patriarchal society* **2** relating to being a patriarch, or typical of a patriarch

pa·tri·arch·y /ˈpeɪtriˌɑrki/ *n.* [U] a social system in which men hold all the power [➡ **matriarchy**]

pa·tri·ot /ˈpeɪtriət/ *n.* [C] *approving* someone who loves his/her country and is willing to defend it

pa·tri·ot·ic /ˌpeɪtriˈɑt̬ɪk/ *adj. approving* having or expressing a great love of your country: *a patriotic citizen* | *patriotic songs* —**patriotism** /ˈpeɪtriəˌtɪzəm/ *n.* [U]

pat·rol¹ /pəˈtroʊl/ *v.* past tense and past participle **patrolled**, present participle **patrolling** [I,T] to regularly check an area in order to prevent problems or crime: *Two tanks patrolled the city center.*

patrol² *n.* **1** [C,U] the action of regularly checking different parts of an area to prevent problems or crime: *Guards were* ***on patrol*** *throughout the night.* **2** [C] a group of police, soldiers, AIRPLANES, etc. that patrol a particular area: *the California Highway Patrol*

paˈtrol car *n.* [C] a police car that drives around the streets of a city

pa·trol·man /pəˈtroʊlmən/ *n.* plural **patrolmen** /-mən/ [C] a police officer who patrols a particular area

pa·tron /ˈpeɪtrən/ *n.* [C] **1** someone who supports an organization, artist, musical performer, etc., especially by giving money: *a* ***patron of*** *the arts* **2** *formal* someone who uses a particular store, restaurant, company, etc. [= **customer**]

pa·tron·age /ˈpeɪtrənɪdʒ, ˈpæ-/ *n.* [U] **1** *formal* the support that you give a particular store, restaurant, company, etc. by buying their goods or using their services: *Thank you for your patronage.* **2** the support that a patron gives to an organization, etc. **3** a system in which a powerful person gives money or important jobs to people who support him/her

pa·tron·ize /ˈpeɪtrəˌnaɪz, ˈpæ-/ *v.* [T] **1** *disapproving* to talk to someone in a way which seems friendly but shows that you think s/he is less important or intelligent than you: *Don't patronize me.* | *Some of his employees believed that he patronized women.* **2** *formal* to regularly use a particular store, restaurant, company, etc.

pa·tron·iz·ing /ˈpeɪtrəˌnaɪzɪŋ, ˈpæ-/ *adj. disapproving* talking to someone or treating someone as if you think s/he is less important or intelligent than you: *a patronizing attitude*

pat·ter /ˈpæt̬ɚ/ *n.* **1** [singular] the sound of something lightly hitting a hard surface again and again: *the* ***patter of*** *footsteps* **2** [singular, U] very fast and continuous talk: *a car salesman's patter* —**patter** *v.* [I]

pat·tern /ˈpæt̬ɚn/ *n.* [C] **1** the regular way in which something happens, develops, or is done: ***patterns of*** *behavior* | *Romantic novels tend to* ***follow*** *a similar* ***pattern****.* **2** a regularly repeated arrangement of shapes, colors, lines, etc.: *a* ***pattern of*** *red and white squares* | *a dress with a rose pattern*

THESAURUS

design – a pattern used for decorating something: *curtains with a floral design*
markings – the colored patterns and shapes on an animal's fur, feathers, or skin: *the tiger's black and orange markings*
motif – a pattern that is regularly repeated: *a light blue wallpaper with a rose motif*

3 a shape that you copy onto cloth, paper, etc. when making something, especially clothing: *a skirt pattern*

pat·terned /ˈpæt̬ɚnd/ *adj.* decorated with a pattern: *a gold and black patterned tie*

pat·ty /ˈpæt̬i/ *n.* plural **patties** [C] a round flat piece of cooked meat or other food: *beef patties*

pau·ci·ty /ˈpɔsət̬i/ *n.* **a/the paucity of sth** *formal* less than is needed of something: *a paucity of evidence*

paunch /pɔntʃ, pɑntʃ/ *n.* [C] a man's fat stomach —**paunchy** *adj.*

pau·per /ˈpɔpɚ/ *n.* [C] *old-fashioned* someone who is very poor

pause¹ /pɔz/ *v.* **1** [I] to stop speaking or doing something for a short time before starting again: *Tom* ***paused for*** *a moment, and then asked, "So what should I do?"* | *Amanda* ***paused to*** *admire the view.*

THESAURUS

stop, **have/take a break**, **break**
➔ see Thesaurus box at STOP¹

2 [I,T] to push a button on a CD PLAYER, TAPE RECORDER, computer, etc. in order to make a CD, tape, etc. stop playing for a short time

pause² *n.* [C] a short time when you stop speaking or doing something: *a* ***pause in*** *the conversation* | *After a* ***long pause*** *Rick said, "You're right."*

pave /peɪv/ *v.* [T] **1** to cover a path, road, etc. with a hard level surface such as CONCRETE **2 pave the way** to do something that will make an event, development, etc. possible in the future:

Galileo's achievements ***paved the way for*** *Newton's scientific laws.*

pave·ment /ˈpeɪvmənt/ *n.* [U] the hard surface of a road: *As she fell off the bike, her arm hit the pavement.*

pa·vil·ion /pəˈvɪlyən/ *n.* [C] a structure built in a park or at a FAIR, and used as a place for public entertainment, EXHIBITIONS, etc.

ˈpaving stone *n.* [C] one of the flat pieces of stone used to make a hard surface to walk on

paw¹ /pɔ/ *n.* [C] an animal's foot that has nails or CLAWS: *a lion's paw* ➔ see picture on page A2

paw² *v.* [I,T] **1** if an animal paws something, it touches the thing with its paw: *The dog's* ***pawing at*** *the door again.* **2** *informal* to touch someone in a way that is too rough or too sexual: *He kept trying to paw me in the car.*

P

pawn¹ /pɔn/ *n.* [C] **1** one of the eight smallest and least valuable pieces in the game of CHESS **2** someone who is used by a more powerful person or group: *We're just* ***pawns in*** *a big political game.*

pawn² *v.* [T] to leave a valuable object with a pawnbroker in order to borrow money

pawn·bro·ker /ˈpɔnˌbroʊkɚ/ *n.* [C] someone whose business is to lend people money in exchange for valuable objects

pay¹ /peɪ/ *v.* past tense and past participle **paid**, third person singular **pays**

1 GIVE MONEY [I,T] to give someone money for something in order to buy it, or for something s/he has done for you: *They ran off without paying.* | *Have you paid the babysitter yet?* | *The company's* ***paying for*** *my plane tickets.* | *She claims the publisher refused to* ***pay*** *her* ***for*** *the book she wrote.* | *How much did you* ***pay for*** *those shoes?* | *You can* ***pay by check****.*

2 BILL/DEBT [T] to give a person, company, etc. the money that you owe for a bill or debt: *We need to* ***pay*** *the electricity* ***bill*** *soon.*

3 JOB [I,T] to give someone money for the job s/he does: *How much do they pay you?* | *Plumbers* ***get paid*** *$40 an hour.* | *workers who are* ***well/highly/poorly paid***

4 pay attention (to sb/sth) to carefully listen to or watch someone or something, or to be careful about what you are doing: *Sorry, I wasn't paying attention. What did you say?*

5 pay a visit to sb also pay sb a visit to go to see a particular person: *It's about time you paid a visit to the dentist.*

6 pay sb a compliment to say nice things about someone's appearance, behavior, etc.

7 pay your way to pay for your bills, food, etc. without needing to use anyone else's money: *She paid her own way through law school.*

8 GOOD RESULT [I] to be worth doing, and result in an advantage for you: *Crime doesn't pay.* | ***It pays to*** *be on time.*

9 PROFIT [I] if a shop or business pays, it makes a profit: *We worked hard but couldn't* ***make*** *the business* ***pay****.*

10 pay tribute to sb/sth to show how much you admire or respect someone or something

11 pay your respects (to sb) *formal* to greet someone politely or visit a place, especially in order to say or show that you are sorry that someone has died: *Sam came over to pay his respects to the family.*

12 pay your dues to work at the lowest levels of a profession or organization in order to earn the right to move up to a better position

13 pay through the nose (for sth) *informal* to pay far too much money for something ➔ **pay/give lip service** at LIP

pay sb/sth ⇔ **back** *phr. v.* to give someone the money that you owe him/her [= **repay**]: *Can I borrow $10? I'll pay you back tomorrow.*

pay for sth *phr. v.* to suffer or be punished for doing something: *If you drink any more, you'll be paying for it in the morning.*

pay sth ⇔ **in/into** (sth) *phr. v.* to put money into a bank account: *The check was paid into your account on Friday.* | *How much do you pay in each month?*

pay off *phr. v.* **1 pay** sth ⇔ **off** to pay all the money that you owe for something: *We've finally paid off the mortgage.* **2** if something that you try to do pays off, it is successful after a long time: *My efforts finally paid off when they called me in for an interview.* **3 pay** sb ⇔ **off** to give someone money so that s/he will not tell people about something illegal or dishonest

pay out *phr. v.* **pay sth** ⇔ **out** to pay a lot of money for something: *Last year, $123 million was paid out in health benefits.*

pay up *phr. v.* *informal* to pay all the money that you owe

pay² *n.* [U] money that you are given for working [= **salary**]: *The pay will be better at my new job.* | *Workers say they haven't had a* ***pay raise/increase*** *in two years.* | *Teachers have refused to accept a* ***pay cut****.*

COLLOCATIONS

base pay – the pay that you always receive, without payment for any extra hours
overtime pay – payment for extra hours that you work
take-home pay – the money you receive after tax, etc. has been taken away
vacation pay – payment for the time when you are on vacation
sick pay – payment for the times when you are sick and not at work
➔ MONEY, PENSION

THESAURUS

income – money that you receive from working, investments, etc.: *families on a low income*
salary – the pay that professional people such

as teachers or lawyers earn every year: *a salary of $34,000 a year*
wages – the pay that someone earns every hour or every week: *Her wages barely cover the rent.*
earnings – all the money that you earn by working: *Record your earnings on the income tax form.*

pay·a·ble /ˈpeɪəbəl/ *adj.* **1** a bill, debt, etc. that is payable must be paid: *A standard fee of $35 is payable every three months.* **2 payable to sb** able to be paid to a particular person or organization: *Please **make the check payable to** Al's Service Station* (=write this name on the check).

pay·check /ˈpeɪtʃɛk/ *n.* [C] a check that pays a worker his/her salary: *a weekly paycheck*

pay·day /ˈpeɪdeɪ/ *n.* [C usually singular] the day when you get your paycheck

ˈpay dirt *n.* **hit/strike pay dirt** *informal* to make a valuable or useful discovery: *a group of scientists who struck pay dirt*

pay·ee /peɪˈi/ *n.* [C] *technical* the person who should be paid money, especially by check

pay·load /ˈpeɪloʊd/ *n.* [C,U] the amount of goods or passengers carried by a vehicle or aircraft

pay·ment /ˈpeɪmənt/ *n.* **1** [C] an amount of money that must be paid or has been paid: *How much are your **car/house/loan payments**? | He couldn't afford to **make** the **payments on** his house. | She agreed to repay the loan in **monthly payments** of $200.* **2** [U] the act of paying: *Late payment will result in a $10 fine.*

pay·off /ˈpeɪɔf/ *n.* [C] **1** the good result or the advantage that you get because of doing something: *With electric cars, the development costs are high but there is a big environmental payoff.* **2** a payment that is made to someone, often illegally, in order to stop him/her from causing you trouble

ˈpay phone *n.* [C] a public telephone that you can use when you put in coins or a CREDIT CARD number

pay·roll /ˈpeɪroʊl/ *n.* [C usually singular] **1** the list of people who are employed by a company and the amount of money they are paid: *We have 127 staff **on the payroll**.* **2** the total amount of money that a company pays the people who work there

PBS *n.* [U] **Public Broadcasting System** a company in the U.S. that broadcasts television programs without advertisements

PC¹ *n.* [C] **personal computer** a small computer that is used by one person at a time, at work or at home

PC² *adj.* POLITICALLY CORRECT

pdf, PDF *n.* [C] **portable document format** a type of computer FILE that can be opened on most personal computers, even those that do not have the same software program that was used to produce the file

PE *n.* [U] **physical education** sports and exercises that are taught as a school subject

pea /pi/ *n.* [C] a small round green seed that is cooked and eaten as a vegetable

peace /pis/ *n.* **1** [singular,U] a situation or period of time in which there is no war or fighting: *working for **world peace** | Germany has been **at peace with** France since 1945. | My hope is that one day our countries can **live in peace**. | The prime minister promised to **bring peace to** the region.* **2** [U] a situation that is very calm, quiet, and pleasant: *All I want is some **peace and quiet**. | Mary, let your sister read **in peace*** (=without being interrupted). **3** [U] a feeling of being calm, happy, and not worried: *I decided to see a doctor, just for **peace of mind**.* **4 disturbing the peace** *law* the crime of being too noisy or too violent in a public place **5 make (your) peace** to agree to stop fighting with a person or group: *He was anxious to **make peace with** Jill before she left.*

peace·a·ble /ˈpisəbəl/ *adj.* not liking to argue, or not causing any arguments or fights: *peaceable citizens* —**peaceably** *adv.*

ˈPeace Corps *n.* **the Peace Corps** a U.S. government organization that helps poorer countries by sending VOLUNTEERS to teach skills in education, health, farming, etc.

peace·ful /ˈpisfəl/ *adj.* **1** calm, quiet, and without problems or excitement: *It's peaceful out here in the woods.*

THESAURUS
quiet, calm, tranquil, sleepy
➔ see Thesaurus box at QUIET¹

2 not fighting a war, or deliberately not being violent: *a peaceful relationship between countries | a peaceful protest* —**peacefully** *adv.*

peace·keep·ing /ˈpisˌkipɪŋ/ *adj.* trying to prevent fighting or violence: *peacekeeping troops* —**peacekeeper** *n.* [C]

peace·mak·er /ˈpisˌmeɪkɚ/ *n.* [C] someone who tries to persuade people or countries to stop fighting

peace·time /ˈpis-taɪm/ *n.* [U] a period of time when a country is not fighting a war [≠ **wartime**]

peach /pitʃ/ *n.* **1** [C] a round juicy yellow-red fruit that has a large rough seed and skin that feels FUZZY, or the tree that it grows on ➔ see picture at FRUIT **2** [U] a pale pink-orange color

pea·cock /ˈpikɑk/ *n.* [C] a large bird, the male of which has long blue and green tail feathers that it can spread out

peak¹ /pik/ *n.* [C] **1** the time when someone or something is biggest, most successful, or best: *Trenton is now **at the peak of** his career. | The company's profits **reached a peak** in 1992.* **2** the pointed top of a mountain, or a mountain with a pointed top: *the Alps' snow-covered peaks*

peak² *v.* [I] to become the biggest, most successful, or best that someone or something can be: *In the 1950s, Chicago's population **peaked at** around 3.6 million.*

peal /pil/ *n.* [C] *literary* a sudden loud repeated sound, such as laughter, THUNDER, or bells RINGING: *I could hear* ***peals of laughter*** *coming from upstairs.* —**peal** *v.* [I]

pea·nut /ˈpinʌt/ *n.* **1** [C] a small nut you can eat that has a soft light brown shell **2 peanuts** [plural] *informal* a very small amount of money: *I'm tired of* ***working for peanuts.***

peanut

ˈpeanut ˌbutter *n.* [U] a soft food made from crushed peanuts, usually eaten on bread: *a peanut butter and jelly sandwich*

pear /pɛr/ *n.* [C] a sweet juicy fruit with a round wide bottom that becomes thinner on top near the stem, or the tree on which it grows ➔ see picture at FRUIT

pearl /pɚl/ *n.* [C] a valuable small white round object, that forms inside an OYSTER and is used in jewelry: *a pearl necklace*

peas·ant /ˈpɛzənt/ *n.* [C] a poor farmer who owns or rents a small amount of land, either in past times or in poor countries

peat /pit/ *n.* [U] a substance formed under the surface of the ground from decaying plants, used as soil or as FUEL

peb·ble /ˈpɛbəl/ *n.* [C] a small smooth stone that is usually in a river or on a beach

pe·can /pɪˈkɑn, -ˈkæn/ *n.* [C] a long thin sweet nut with a dark smooth shell, or the tree on which these nuts grow: *pecan pie*

peck¹ /pɛk/ *v.* [I,T] if a bird pecks something or pecks at something, it quickly moves its beak to hit, bite, or pick up that thing

peck² *n.* [C] **1** a quick kiss: *He gave Jill a* ***peck on the cheek.*** **2** the action of a bird pecking something with its beak

pe·cu·liar /pɪˈkyulyɚ/ *adj.* **1** strange and a little surprising: *This cheese has a peculiar smell.* | *The new guy in the office is a little peculiar.*

> **THESAURUS**
>
> **strange**, **funny**, **mysterious**, **odd**, **weird**, **bizarre**, **eccentric**
> ➔ see Thesaurus box at STRANGE¹

2 be peculiar to sth to be a quality that only one particular person, place, or thing has: *The problem of racism is not peculiar to this country.* —**peculiarly** *adv.*

pe·cu·li·ar·i·ty /pɪˌkyuliˈærəti/ *n.* plural **peculiarities** [C,U] an unusual or slightly strange habit or quality, especially one that only a particular person, place, etc. has: *the* ***peculiarities of*** *the newspaper business* | *Over time, she grew to love his peculiarities.*

ped·a·gog·i·cal /ˌpɛdəˈgɑdʒɪkəl/ *adj. formal* relating to methods of teaching —**pedagogy** /ˈpɛdəˌgɑdʒi/ *n.* [U]

ped·al¹ /ˈpɛdl/ *n.* [C] the part of a bicycle, car, or MOTORCYCLE that you push with your foot in order to make it move: *the gas pedal* ➔ see picture at BICYCLE

pedal² *v.* [I,T] to ride a bicycle by pushing the pedals with your feet

pe·dan·tic /pəˈdæntɪk/ *adj. disapproving* paying too much attention to small details and rules: *The book is fascinating, although some readers will find it pedantic.*

ped·dle /ˈpɛdl/ *v.* [T] to go from place to place trying to sell something, especially something illegal or cheap: *Eric was caught* ***peddling drugs.*** —**peddler** *n.* [C]

> **THESAURUS**
>
> **sell**, **auction**, **export**
> ➔ see Thesaurus box at SELL

ped·es·tal /ˈpɛdəstl/ *n.* [C] **1** the base on which a STATUE or a PILLAR stands **2 put/place sb on a pedestal** *disapproving* to admire someone so much that you treat him/her or talk about him/her as though s/he is perfect

pe·des·tri·an¹ /pəˈdɛstriən/ *n.* [C] someone who is walking instead of driving a car, riding a bicycle, etc.

pedestrian² *adj. formal* ordinary, and not very interesting or exciting: *It is a piece of real journalism, rather than the usual pedestrian stuff.*

pe·di·a·tri·cian /ˌpidiəˈtrɪʃən/ *n.* [C] a doctor who treats children

> **THESAURUS**
>
> **physician**, **surgeon**, **specialist**, **psychiatrist**
> ➔ see Thesaurus box at DOCTOR¹

pe·di·at·rics /ˌpidiˈætrɪks/ *n.* [U] the area of medicine that deals with children and their illnesses

ped·i·cure /ˈpɛdɪˌkyʊr/ *n.* [C,U] a treatment for the feet that includes cleaning them and cutting the TOENAILS [➡ **manicure**]

ped·i·gree /ˈpɛdəˌgri/ *n.* [C,U] the parents and other past family members of an animal or person, or the written record of them —**pedigree** *adj.*: *a pedigree Great Dane*

pee /pi/ *v.* [I] *informal* to pass liquid waste from your body [= **urinate**] —**pee** *n.* [U]

peek¹ /pik/ *v.* [I] to quickly look at something, especially something you are not supposed to see: *Paula opened the box and peeked inside.*

> **THESAURUS**
>
> **look**, **glance**, **peer**, **stare**, **gaze**, **gape**
> ➔ see Thesaurus box at LOOK¹

peek² *n.* [C] a quick look at something: ***Take a peek*** *down the hall and see if anyone's coming.*

P

peek·a·boo /ˈpikəˌbu/ *interjection, n.* [U] a game played with babies and young children, in which you hide your face and then show it again and again, saying "peekaboo!"

peel

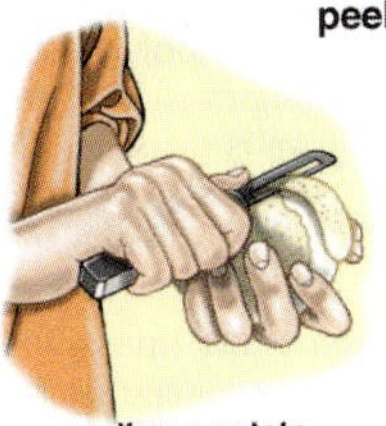

peeling a potato

peel[1] /pil/ *v.* **1** [T] to remove the skin of a fruit or vegetable: *Peel the potatoes and cut them in half.*

THESAURUS

cut, **chop (up)**, **slice**, **dice**, **carve**, **shred**, **grate**
➔ see Thesaurus box at CUT[1]

2 [T] to remove a thin outside layer from the surface of an object: ***Peel*** *the labels* ***off/from*** *the jars before recycling.* **3** [I] if skin, paper, or paint is peeling, it is loose and coming off in small thin pieces: *I got sunburned and now my face is peeling.*

peel sth ⇔ **off** *phr. v.* to take off your clothes, especially if they are wet or tight: *He peeled off his uniform and stepped into the shower.*

peel[2] *n.* [U] the thick skin of a fruit or vegetable, such as an orange, a potato, or a BANANA: *orange peel* ➔ see picture at FRUIT

peel·ings /ˈpilɪŋz/ *n.* [plural] pieces of skin that have been removed from a fruit or vegetable: *carrot peelings*

peep[1] /pip/ *v.* [I] **1** to look at something quickly and secretly: *I saw Joe* ***peeping through*** *the curtains.* **2** to appear from behind or under something: *The sun finally* ***peeped out*** *from behind the clouds.*

peep[2] *n.* [C] **1** [usually singular] a sound: ***I didn't hear a peep out of*** *the kids all afternoon.* **2** [usually singular] a quick or secret look at something: *Did you* ***get/take a peep at*** *the audience?* **3** a short weak high sound that some young birds make

peep·hole /ˈpiphoʊl/ *n.* [C] a small hole in a door that you can look through

peeping Tom /ˌpipɪŋ ˈtɑm/ *n.* [C] someone who secretly watches people, especially people who are taking off their clothes

peer[1] /pɪr/ *n.* **sb's peer** someone who is the same age as another person, or who has the same type of job, rank, etc.: *Barton has gained the respect of his peers.*

peer[2] *v.* [I] to look very carefully, especially because you cannot see something well: *Harris* ***peered into*** *the dark closet.*

THESAURUS

look, **glance**, **peek**, **stare**, **gaze**, **gape**
➔ see Thesaurus box at LOOK[1]

peer·less /ˈpɪrlɪs/ *adj. formal* better than anyone or anything else: *B.B King's peerless guitar playing*

ˈpeer ˌpressure *n.* [U] the strong feeling that young people have that they should do the same things that their peers are doing: *It can be difficult not to* ***give in to peer pressure*** (=do something just because other people are doing it).

peeve /piv/ *n.* **pet peeve** *informal* something that always annoys you, but that may not annoy other people: *One of my pet peeves is people being late for meetings.*

peg[1] /pɛg/ *n.* [C] **1** a short piece of wood or metal that fits into a hole or is fastened to a wall, and can be used for fastening furniture together, for hanging things, etc.: *a coat peg* **2 also tent peg** a pointed piece of wood or metal used for keeping a tent attached to the ground

peg[2] past tense and past participle **pegged**, present participle **pegging** *v.* [T] **1** to believe or say that someone has a particular type of character: *Teachers* ***had*** *him* ***pegged as*** *a troublemaker.* **2** to set prices, salaries, etc. in relation to a particular value: *loan payment rates that are* ***pegged to*** *the national rates*

pe·jor·a·tive /pɪˈdʒɔrət̬ɪv, -ˈdʒɑr-/ *adj. formal* a pejorative word or phrase is used in order to insult someone or to show disapproval

pel·i·can /ˈpɛlɪkən/ *n.* [C] a large bird that catches fish for food and holds them in the part of its large beak that is shaped like a bag

pel·let /ˈpɛlɪt/ *n.* [C] a small hard ball made from metal, ice, paper, food, etc.

pelt[1] /pɛlt/ *v.* [T] to attack someone by throwing a lot of things at him/her: *Two kids were* ***pelting*** *each other* ***with*** *snowballs.*

pelt[2] *n.* [C] the skin of a dead animal with the fur or hair still on it

pel·vis /ˈpɛlvɪs/ *n.* [C] the set of large wide curved bones at the base of your SPINE, to which your legs are joined —**pelvic** *adj.* ➔ see picture on page A3

pen[1] /pɛn/ *n.* **1** [C,U] an instrument used for writing and drawing in ink: *a ballpoint pen* | *Write your essays* ***in pen*** (=using a pen), *not pencil.* ➔ see picture on page A11 **2** [C] a small area surrounded by a fence that farm animals are kept in ➔ PIGPEN

pen[2] *v.* past tense and past participle **penned**, present participle **penning** [T] *literary* to write a letter, note, etc. with a pen

pen sb/sth **in/up** *phr. v.* to prevent a person or animal from leaving an enclosed area: *The protesters were kept penned up behind the fence.*

pe·nal /ˈpinl/ *adj.* **1** relating to the legal punishment of criminals: *the penal system* **2 penal offense** *law* a crime

ˈpenal ˌcode *n.* [C] a set of laws and the punishments for not obeying these laws

pe·nal·ize /ˈpinlˌaɪz, ˈpɛn-/ *v.* [T] **1** to punish someone or treat him/her unfairly: *If Glenda's been trying her best, she shouldn't be* ***penalized for*** *her low grades.* **2** to punish a player or sports

P

team by giving an advantage to the other team: *The Bears were **penalized for** taking too much time.*

pen·al·ty /ˈpɛnlti/ *n.* plural **penalties** [C] **1** a punishment for not obeying a law, rule, or legal agreement: *The maximum **penalty for** the crime is five years in prison.* | *He was given **the death penalty*** (=killed as a punishment).

THESAURUS

punishment, sentence, fine, community service, corporal punishment, capital punishment
➔ see Thesaurus box at PUNISHMENT

2 a disadvantage given to a player or sports team for not obeying the rules

P

pen·ance /ˈpɛnəns/ *n.* [C,U] *literary* a punishment that you accept, especially for religious reasons, to show that you are sorry for doing a bad thing

pen·chant /ˈpɛntʃənt/ *n.* [C] a liking for something that you do as a habit: *Bill **has a penchant for** fast cars.*

pen·cil[1] /ˈpɛnsəl/ *n.* [C,U] an instrument used for writing and drawing, made of wood with a gray or colored center: *Do the math problems **in pencil*** (=using a pencil), *not pen.* | *a sharp pencil* ➔ see picture on page A11

pencil[2] *v.* [T] to write something with a pencil or make a mark with a pencil

pencil sb/sth ⇔ **in** *phr. v.* to make an arrangement for a meeting or other event, knowing that it might have to be changed later: *I'll **pencil in** a meeting **for** next Tuesday.*

ˈpencil ˌsharpener *n.* [C] an object with a small blade inside it, used for making the pointed end of a pencil sharp

pend·ant /ˈpɛndənt/ *n.* [C] a jewel or small decoration that hangs from a NECKLACE: *a diamond pendant*

pend·ing[1] /ˈpɛndɪŋ/ *prep. formal* until something happens, or while something happens: *The decision has been delayed pending further research.*

pending[2] *adj. formal* not yet decided, agreed on, or finished: *Their divorce is still pending.*

pen·du·lum /ˈpɛndʒələm/ *n.* [C] a long stick with a weight on the end of it that hangs down and swings from side to side, especially in a large clock

pen·e·trate /ˈpɛnəˌtreɪt/ *v.* **1** [I,T] to enter something or pass through it, especially when this is difficult: *bullets that can penetrate metal* | *Explorers **penetrated** deep **into** unknown regions.* **2** [T] to join and be accepted by an organization, business, etc. in order to find out secret information: *Spies had penetrated the highest ranks of both governments.* **3** [T] to understand something difficult: *scientists trying to penetrate the mysteries of nature* —**penetration** /ˌpɛnəˈtreɪʃən/ *n.* [U]

pen·e·trat·ing /ˈpɛnəˌtreɪtɪŋ/ *adj.* **1 penetrating eyes/look/gaze etc.** someone who has penetrating eyes, etc. seems able to see what another person is thinking **2** a penetrating noise or voice is so loud that you hear it very clearly **3** showing an ability to understand things quickly and completely: *a penetrating mind*

pen·guin /ˈpɛŋgwɪn/ *n.* [C] a large black and white Antarctic sea bird that cannot fly but uses its wings for swimming

pen·i·cil·lin /ˌpɛnəˈsɪlən/ *n.* [U] a substance used as a medicine to destroy BACTERIA

pe·nin·su·la /pəˈnɪnsələ/ *n.* [C] a piece of land that is almost completely surrounded by water —**peninsular** *adj.*

pe·nis /ˈpinɪs/ *n.* [C] the outer sex organ of males

pen·i·tent /ˈpɛnətənt/ *adj. literary* feeling sorry about doing something bad, and showing you do not intend to do it again —**penitence** *n.* [U]

pen·i·ten·tia·ry /ˌpɛnəˈtɛnʃəri/ *n.* plural **penitentiaries** [C] a prison: *the state penitentiary*

pen·knife /ˈpɛn-naɪf/ *n.* plural **penknives** /-naɪvz/ [C] a POCKET KNIFE

ˈpen name *n.* [C] a name used by a writer instead of his/her real name [**= pseudonym**]

pen·nant /ˈpɛnənt/ *n.* [C] a long pointed flag used by schools, sports teams, etc., or on ships as a sign

pen·ni·less /ˈpɛnɪlɪs/ *adj.* having no money

pen·ny /ˈpɛni/ *n.* plural **pennies** [C] **1** a coin used in the U.S. and Canada worth 1 cent (=1/100 of a dollar)

THESAURUS

coin, nickel, dime, quarter
➔ see Thesaurus box at MONEY

2 not a penny no money at all: *I don't owe her a penny!* **3 every (last) penny** all of your money: *He spent every penny on his car.* | *The new carpet wasn't cheap, but it was **worth every penny*** (=I am happy I bought it).

ˈpen pal *n.* [C] someone to whom you write letters in order to become his/her friend

pen·sion /ˈpɛnʃən/ *n.* [C] the money that a company pays regularly to someone after s/he RETIRES (=stops working because s/he is old): *Howe **draws** a yearly **pension** of $15,000.* ➔ see Topic box at RETIRE

ˈpension fund *n.* [C] a large amount of money that a company, organization, etc. INVESTS and uses for paying pensions

ˈpension plan *n.* [C] a system for organizing the type of pension that a company will give you

pen·sive /ˈpɛnsɪv/ *adj. literary* thinking about something a lot and seeming slightly sad

Pen·ta·gon /ˈpɛntəˌgɑn/ *n.* **the Pentagon** the U.S. government building in Washington, D.C. from which the army, navy, etc. are controlled, or the military officers who work in this building

pentagon *n.* [C] a flat shape with five sides and five angles —**pentagonal** /pɛnˈtægənl/ *adj.*

Pen·te·cos·tal /ˌpɛntɪˈkɑstl/ *adj.* relating to the Christian church whose members believe that the spirit of God can help them to cure diseases and pray in special languages —**Pentecostal** *n.* [C]

pent·house /ˈpɛnthaʊs/ *n.* [C] a very expensive and comfortable apartment on the top floor of a tall building

ˌpent-ˈup *adj.* pent-up emotions are not expressed for a long time: *All the pent-up anger she was feeling came out as she cried.*

pe·on /ˈpiɑn/ *n.* [C] *informal* someone who works at a boring or physically hard job for low pay: *the office peons*

peo·ple¹ /ˈpipəl/ *n.* **1** [plural] the usual plural form of PERSON: *I like the people I work with.* | *How many people were at the wedding?*

USAGE

people – many men, women, and children. In this meaning, **people** is the plural of **person**: *There were about 100 people at the wedding.*
people – a particular race or group that lives in a particular country. In this meaning, the plural is **peoples**: *the peoples of the Caribbean*
person – a man, woman, or child: *She's a really generous person.*
persons formal – more than one man, woman, or child – used only in official language: *Police are looking for the person or persons responsible for her death.*

2 the people [plural] all the ordinary people in a country or a state: *The mayor should remember that he was elected to serve the people.*

THESAURUS

the public – ordinary people, not people who work for the government or other special organizations: *It's the job of the media to inform the public.*
society – all the people who live in a country: *responsible members of society*
the human race/mankind/humankind – all the people in the world, considered as a group: *the origins of the human race*
population – the number of people or animals living in a particular area, country, etc.: *What's the population of Los Angeles?* | *the planet's rapid population growth*
➔ GROUP

3 [plural] people in general, or people other than yourself: *People sometimes make fun of my name.* | *Computer people seem to speak a language of their own.* **4 of all people** *spoken* used in order to say that someone is the only person who you would not have expected to do something: *You of all people should have realized the risks.* **5** [C] *formal* a race or nation: *all the peoples of the world*

people² *v.* **be peopled with/by sb** *literary* to be filled with people of a particular type

pep¹ /pɛp/ *v.* past tense and past participle **pepped**, present participle **pepping**

pep sb/sth ⇔ **up** *phr. v. informal* to make something or someone more active, interesting, or full of energy: *I had some coffee to pep myself up.*

pep² *n.* [U] *informal* physical energy —**peppy** *adj.*

pep·per¹ /ˈpɛpɚ/ *n.* **1** [U] a spicy black, pale yellow, or red powder, used in cooking: *salt and pepper* **2** [C] a hollow red, green, or yellow fruit with a sweet or spicy taste that is eaten as a vegetable or added to other foods ➔ see picture at VEGETABLE

pepper² *v.* [T] **1** to scatter things all over or all through something: *The article is* ***peppered with*** *quotations.* **2** to put pepper in food

pep·per·mint /ˈpɛpɚˌmɪnt/ *n.* **1** [U] a MINT plant with sweet-smelling strong-tasting leaves used in making candy, tea, and medicine **2** [C] a candy that has a taste like peppermint

pep·pe·ro·ni /ˌpɛpəˈroʊni/ *n.* [U] a spicy dry Italian SAUSAGE

ˈpep ˌrally *n.* [C] an event at a school before a sports event, when people give speeches or shout to encourage and support a team

ˈpep talk *n.* [C] *informal* a speech that is intended to encourage people to work harder, win a game, etc.: *The coach was* ***giving*** *the team a* ***pep talk****.*

per /pɚ/ *prep.* for each: *Bananas are 60 cents per pound.* | *You need at least half a bottle of wine per person for the party.*

per ca·pi·ta /pɚ ˈkæpət̬ə/ *adj., adv. formal* calculated by dividing the total amount of something by the number of people in a particular place: *The average per capita income in the area is $40,000 a year.*

per·ceive /pɚˈsiv/ *v.* [T] *formal* **1** to understand or think about something in a particular way: *It is a difficult situation, but we don't* ***perceive*** *it* ***as*** *anything we can't deal with.* | *Everyone could* ***perceive that*** *their marriage was in trouble.* **2** to notice something that is difficult to notice: *The sound is too high to be perceived by humans.*

per·cent¹ /pɚˈsɛnt/ *n.* **five/ten etc. percent also 5%/10% etc.** five, ten, etc. in every hundred: *The interest rate at the bank is six percent* (=6%, or six cents on every dollar).

percent² *adj., adv.* **1 %** equal to a particular amount in every hundred: *Leave the waitress a 15% tip* (=a tip of 15 cents for every dollar you have spent on the meal). **2 a/one hundred percent** completely: *I agree with you a hundred percent.*

per·cent·age /pɚˈsɛntɪdʒ/ *n.* **1** [C,U] a particular amount out of every hundred: *What* ***percentage of*** *the population is elderly?* | *A* ***small/large percentage*** *of students receive financial aid.* **2** [C usually singular] a share of profits equal to a particular amount in every dollar: *He gets a percentage for every book that is sold.*

P

per·cep·ti·ble /pɚˈsɛptəbəl/ *adj. formal* noticeable [≠ **imperceptible**]: *The sound was **barely perceptible**.*

per·cep·tion /pɚˈsɛpʃən/ *n.* **1** [C,U] the way you understand something and your beliefs about what it is like: *Our eating habits and our **perception of** nutrition have changed in the last 50 years.* | *There's a **perception that** Margaret is not an effective leader.* **2** [U] the way you use your senses to notice things: *drugs that alter perception* **3** [U] the natural ability to understand or notice something quickly: *I was impressed by her perception and her grasp of the facts.*

per·cep·tive /pɚˈsɛptɪv/ *adj.* good at noticing and understanding what is happening or what someone is thinking or feeling: *a perceptive young man* | *perceptive comments*

P

perch[1] /pɚtʃ/ *n.* **1** [C] a branch, stick, etc. where a bird sits **2** [C] *informal* a high place where someone can sit or where a building is placed: *He watches from his perch halfway up the mountain.* **3** [C,U] plural **perch** a fish with sharp pointed FINS that lives in rivers, lakes, etc., or the meat from this fish

perch[2] *v.* **1 be perched on/over etc. sth** to be in a position on top of or on the edge of something: *a house perched on a hill* **2 perch (yourself) on sth** to sit on top of or on the edge of something: *Wally perched on the gate and stared at us.* **3** [I] if a bird perches on something, it sits on it

per·co·late /ˈpɚkəˌleɪt/ *v.* [I] if a liquid percolates through something, it passes slowly through a material that has small holes in it

per·co·la·tor /ˈpɚkəˌleɪt̬ɚ/ *n.* [C] a pot in which coffee is made by passing hot water again and again through crushed coffee beans

per·cus·sion /pɚˈkʌʃən/ *n.* [U] drums and other musical instruments which you play by hitting or shaking them

pe·ren·ni·al[1] /pəˈrɛniəl/ *adj.* **1** [only before noun] happening again and again, or existing for a long time: *the perennial problem of poverty* **2** a plant that is perennial lives for more than two years

perennial[2] *n.* [C] a plant that lives for more than two years

per·fect[1] /ˈpɚfɪkt/ *adj.* **1** complete and without any mistakes or problems [≠ **imperfect**; ➡ **perfectly**]: *a car in perfect condition* | *Your English is perfect.* **2** as good as possible, or the best of its kind [➡ **perfectly**]: *John was in perfect health.* | *a perfect solution to the problem* **3** exactly right for a particular purpose: *This rug's **perfect for** the living room.* | *a perfect day for a picnic*

THESAURUS

ideal – being the best that something could possibly be: *It's an ideal vacation spot for families.*
just right – being the best or most appropriate for something: *The dress was just right for the occasion.*

4 used in order to emphasize what you are saying: *She has a date with **a perfect stranger**.* **5 nobody's perfect** *spoken* used when you are answering someone who has criticized you: *Yes, I made a mistake – nobody's perfect.*

per·fect[2] /pɚˈfɛkt/ *v.* [T] to make something perfect or as good as you are able to: *She's spending a year in France to perfect her French.*

per·fect[3] /ˈpɚfɪkt/ *n.* [U] *technical* ➔ FUTURE PERFECT, PAST PERFECT, PRESENT PERFECT

per·fec·tion /pɚˈfɛkʃən/ *n.* [U] **1** the state of being perfect: *Claire's parents demanded perfection from her.* | *The steak was cooked **to perfection**.* **2** the process of making something perfect: *the **perfection of** his golf swing*

per·fec·tion·ist /pɚˈfɛkʃənɪst/ *n.* [C] someone who is not satisfied with anything unless it is completely perfect: *You look fine. Don't be such a perfectionist.*

per·fect·ly /ˈpɚfɪktli/ *adv.* **1** used in order to emphasize what you are saying: *It's perfectly normal to feel nervous before a performance.* | *They had thrown away a **perfectly good** stereo.* **2** in a perfect way: *She speaks English perfectly.*

per·fo·rat·ed /ˈpɚfəˌreɪt̬ɪd/ *adj.* a piece of paper that is perforated has a line of small holes in it so that part of it can be torn off easily

per·form /pɚˈfɔrm/ *v.* **1** [I,T] to do something to entertain people: *The drama group performed "Hamlet" last week.* | *Karen will be performing with her band on Friday.* **2** [T] to do something such as a job or piece of work, especially something difficult or complicated: *Surgeons performed an emergency operation.* | *software that performs a specific function* **3 perform well/badly** to work or do something well, badly, etc.: *The bike performs well on mountain trails.* | *The team has been performing poorly.*

per·form·ance /pɚˈfɔrməns/ *n.* **1** [C] an act of performing a play, piece of music, etc., or the occasion when something is performed: *a beautiful **performance of** Swan Lake* | *The next performance is at 8 o'clock.* **2** [U] how well or badly someone or something does something: *Linda's performance at school has greatly improved.* | *The car's performance on wet roads was good.* **3** [U] the act of doing something, especially your work: *the **performance of** his official duties*

per·form·er /pɚˈfɔrmɚ/ *n.* [C] an actor, musician, etc. who performs in order to entertain people: *a circus performer*

perˌforming ˈarts *n.* [plural] arts such as dance, music, or DRAMA, that are performed to entertain people

per·fume /ˈpɚfyum, pɚˈfyum/ *n.* [C,U] **1** a liquid with a strong pleasant smell that women put on their skin: *She never **wears perfume**.* **2** a pleasant smell: *the rose's sweet perfume* —**perfumed** *adj.*: *perfumed soap*

THESAURUS

smell, aroma, scent, fragrance
→ see Thesaurus box at SMELL²

per·haps /pəˈhæps/ *adv.* **1** possibly [= **maybe**]: *Perhaps it'll be warmer tomorrow.* | *This is perhaps Irving's finest novel.* **2** *spoken* used in order to ask or suggest something politely [= **maybe**]: *Perhaps you'd like to join us?*

per·il /ˈpɛrəl/ *n. literary* **1** [U] danger of being harmed or killed: *Everyone feared that the sailors were* ***in*** *great* ***peril****.* **2 the perils of sth** the dangers involved in a particular activity: ***the perils of*** *drug use*

per·il·ous /ˈpɛrələs/ *adj. literary* very dangerous: *a perilous journey*

pe·rim·e·ter /pəˈrɪmət̬ɚ/ *n.* [C] **1** the border around an area of land: *the* ***perimeter of*** *the airfield* **2** the whole length of the border around an area or shape [➡ **circumference**]: *the* ***perimeter of*** *a triangle*

pe·ri·od /ˈpɪriəd/ *n.* [C] **1** a length of time: *We worked together over a 15-month period.* | *James finished the research within a short* ***period of time****.* **2** a particular length of time in history or in a person's life: *We're studying the Civil War period.* | *the blue period in Picasso's painting* **3** the monthly flow of blood from a woman's body **4** the mark (.) used in writing that shows the end of a sentence or an abbreviation **5** one of the equal parts that the school day is divided into: *I have a history test during* ***first/second/third etc. period*** *on Tuesday.* **6** one of the equal parts that a game is divided into in a sport such as HOCKEY **7 period!** *spoken* said at the end of a sentence when you have made a decision and you do not want to discuss the subject any more: *I just won't do it, period!*

pe·ri·od·ic /ˌpɪriˈɑdɪk◂/ **also periodical** *adj.* happening again and again, usually at regular times: *Dale gets periodic headaches.*

pe·ri·od·i·cal /ˌpɪriˈɑdɪkəl/ *n.* [C] a magazine, especially one about a serious or technical subject

pe·ri·od·i·cally /ˌpɪriˈɑdɪkli/ *adv.* happening again and again, usually at regular times: *The river periodically floods the valley.* | *Athletes are periodically tested for drugs.*

ˌperiodic ˈtable *n.* **the periodic table** a specially arranged list of the ELEMENTS (=simple chemical substances)

pe·riph·e·ral¹ /pəˈrɪfərəl/ *adj.* **1** *formal* relating to the main idea, question, activity, etc., but less important than it: *He had only a peripheral role in the negotiations.* **2 peripheral vision** what you can see to the side of you when you look straight ahead **3** *technical* peripheral equipment can be connected to a computer and used with it

peripheral² *n.* [C] *technical* a piece of equipment that is connected to a computer and used with it

pe·riph·er·y /pəˈrɪfəri/ *n.* [singular] the outside area or edge of something: *a new neighborhood* ***on the periphery of*** *the city*

per·i·scope /ˈpɛrəˌskoʊp/ *n.* [C] a long tube with mirrors fitted in it that is used for looking over the top of something, especially in a SUBMARINE

per·ish /ˈpɛrɪʃ/ *v.* [I] *literary* to die: *Hundreds perished when the Titanic sank.*

per·ish·a·ble /ˈpɛrɪʃəbəl/ *adj.* food that is perishable can become bad quickly: *milk and other perishable items* —**perishables** *n.* [plural]

per·jure /ˈpɚdʒɚ/ *v.* **perjure yourself** to tell a lie in a court of law

THESAURUS

lie, make up, invent, mislead, deceive
→ see Thesaurus box at LIE²

per·ju·ry /ˈpɚdʒəri/ *n.* [U] the crime of telling a lie in a court of law

perk¹ /pɚk/ *n.* [C] money, goods, or other advantages that you get from your work in addition to your pay: *a few extra perks like a company car and travel expenses*

perk² *v. informal*

perk (sb ⇔) **up** *phr. v.* to become more cheerful and interested in what is happening around you, or to make someone feel this way: *A cup of coffee will perk you up.* | *Meg perked up when the music started.*

perk (sth ⇔) **up** *phr. v.* to become better, more interesting, etc., or to make something do this: *A little more pepper will perk up the sauce.*

perk·y /ˈpɚki/ *adj. informal* confident, happy, and full of interest: *a perky little girl*

perm¹ /pɚm/ *n.* [C] a way of putting curls into straight hair by treating it with chemicals

perm² *v.* [T] to put curls into straight hair using chemicals: *Did you* ***have*** *your* ***hair permed****?*

per·ma·frost /ˈpɚməˌfrɔst/ *n.* [U] a layer of soil that is always frozen, in places such as Alaska and northern Canada

per·ma·nent /ˈpɚmənənt/ *adj.* continuing to exist for a long time or for all time [≠ **temporary**]: *There was not any* ***permanent damage*** *to the muscle.* | *The UN Security Council has five permanent members.* —**permanence** *n.* [U]

per·ma·nent·ly /ˈpɚmənəntli/ *adv.* always, or for a very long time: *Do you plan to live here permanently?* | *The accident left him permanently disabled.*

THESAURUS

always, forever, for life, for good
→ see Thesaurus box at ALWAYS

ˌpermanent ˈpress *n.* [U] a way of treating cloth so that it stays smooth, or cloth that has been treated in this way

per·me·ate /ˈpɚmiˌeɪt/ *v.* [I,T] *formal* to spread

through every part of something: *The smell of smoke permeated the house.* | *A feeling of sadness permeates his music.*

per·mis·si·ble /pɚˈmɪsəbəl/ *adj. formal* allowed by law or by the rules: *In some religions, divorce is not permissible.*

per·mis·sion /pɚˈmɪʃən/ *n.* [U] the act of allowing someone to do something: *You have to* ***ask permission*** *if you want to leave class early.* | *You must* ***have permission*** *to enter these areas.* | *Did your dad* ***give*** *you* ***permission*** *to use the car?* ▶ Don't say "the permission." ◀

COMMUNICATION

Ways of asking for permission to do something
Can I...?: *"Can I borrow your book?" "Sure."*
Could/May I...? more formal: *"May I use your phone?" "Of course – go ahead."*
Do you mind if I...?: *"Do you mind if I open the window?" "No, that's fine."*
Is it all right if I...? also **Would it be all right if I...?**: *"Is it all right if I leave a little bit early?" "Of course you can."*
Would it be possible to...?: *"Would it be possible to borrow more?" "I think so, but let me check."*

P

per·mis·sive /pɚˈmɪsɪv/ *adj.* allowing actions or behavior that many people disapprove of: *permissive parents*

per·mit[1] /pɚˈmɪt/ *v.* past tense and past participle **permitted**, present participle **permitting** *formal* **1** [T] to allow something to happen, especially by a rule or law: *Smoking is not permitted inside the building.* | *Each employee is* ***permitted to*** *bring a guest to the party.* **2** [I] to make it possible for something to happen: *We'll probably go to the beach,* ***weather permitting***.

per·mit[2] /ˈpɚmɪt/ *n.* [C] an official written statement giving you the right to do something: *You can't park here without a permit.* | *a* ***travel/work permit***

per·mu·ta·tion /ˌpɚmyʊˈteɪʃən/ *n.* [C] one of the different ways in which a set of things can be arranged, or put together to make something else

per·ni·cious /pɚˈnɪʃəs/ *adj. formal* very harmful, especially in a way that is not easily noticeable: *the pernicious effects of advertising*

per·ox·ide /pəˈrɑkˌsaɪd/ *n.* [U] a chemical liquid used in order to make dark hair lighter, or to kill BACTERIA

per·pen·dic·u·lar /ˌpɚpənˈdɪkyəlɚ/ *adj.* **1 be perpendicular to sth** if one line is perpendicular to another line, they form an angle of 90° [➡ **horizontal, vertical**] **2** exactly upright and not leaning to one side or the other [= **vertical**]: *a perpendicular pole*

per·pe·trate /ˈpɚpəˌtreɪt/ *v.* [T] *formal* to do something that is wrong or illegal: *crimes perpetrated by young people*

per·pe·tra·tor /ˈpɚpəˌtreɪt̬ɚ/ *n.* [C] *formal* someone who does something that is a crime

per·pet·u·al /pɚˈpɛtʃuəl/ *adj.* continuing forever or for a long time: *the perpetual noise of the machinery* | *her perpetual complaining* —**perpetually** *adv.*

per·pet·u·ate /pɚˈpɛtʃuˌeɪt/ *v.* [T] to make a situation, attitude, etc., especially a bad one, continue to exist for a long time: *The movie perpetuates stereotypes about women.*

per·plex /pɚˈplɛks/ *v.* [T] if a problem perplexes you, it confuses you and worries you, because it is difficult to understand: *Shea's symptoms perplexed the doctors.* —**perplexed** *adj.*

per·qui·site /ˈpɚkwəzɪt/ *n.* [C] *formal* a PERK

per se /ˌpɚ ˈseɪ/ *adv. formal* used in order to show that something is being considered alone, apart from anything else: *Money, per se, is not usually why people change jobs.*

per·se·cute /ˈpɚsɪˌkyut/ *v.* [T] to treat someone cruelly and unfairly, especially because of his/her religious or political beliefs: *a writer* ***persecuted for*** *criticizing the government* —**persecutor** *n.* [C]

per·se·cu·tion /ˌpɚsɪˈkyuʃən/ *n.* [U] the act of persecuting someone: *the* ***persecution of*** *religious groups*

per·se·ver·ance /ˌpɚsəˈvɪrəns/ *n.* [U] *approving* determination to keep trying to do something difficult: *It took perseverance to overcome his reading problems.*

per·se·vere /ˌpɚsəˈvɪr/ *v.* [I] *approving* to continue trying to do something difficult in a determined way: *The team has persevered through a lot of tough times.*

per·sist /pɚˈsɪst/ *v.* [I] *formal* **1** to continue to do something, even though it is difficult or other people do not like it: *Students must* ***persist in*** *their efforts if they wish to do well.* **2** to continue to exist or happen: *Call a doctor if the pain persists for more than a few days.*

per·sist·ence /pɚˈsɪstəns/ *n.* [U] determination to do something even though it is difficult or other people oppose it: *Claudia's persistence paid off and she got the job.*

per·sist·ent /pɚˈsɪstənt/ *adj.* **1** continuing to exist or happen, especially for longer than is usual or desirable: *persistent problems* | *There have been* ***persistent rumors*** *that the chairman is going to quit.* **2** continuing to do something even though it is difficult or other people oppose it: *You have to be persistent if you want to get a job.* —**persistently** *adv.*: *He persistently denies doing anything wrong.*

per·son /ˈpɚsən/ *n.* plural **people** /ˈpipəl/ [C] **1** a man, woman, or child: *Diane is a really nice person.* | *I was the last person to be called.* | *Abby's a* ***computer/cat/night etc. person*** (=someone who likes computers, cats, etc.).

USAGE

person – a man, woman, or child: *She's a really generous person.*
persons formal – more than one man, woman, or child – used only in official language: *Police are looking for the person or persons responsible for her death.*
people – many men, women, and children. In this meaning, **people** is the plural of **person**: *There were about 100 people at the wedding.*
people – a particular race or group that lives in a particular country. In this meaning the plural is **peoples**: *the peoples of the Caribbean*

2 in person if you do something in person, you do it when you are in a place, not by sending a letter or using the telephone: *You'll have to apply for your passport in person.* → FIRST PERSON, SECOND PERSON, THIRD PERSON

per·so·na /pɚˈsoʊnə/ *n.* plural **personas** or **personae** /-ni/ [C] the way you behave when you are with other people: *You always wonder how different movie stars are from their* ***public personas.***

per·son·a·ble /ˈpɚsənəbəl/ *adj.* having a pleasant way of talking and behaving

per·son·al /ˈpɚsənəl/ *adj.*
1 RELATING TO YOU [only before noun] belonging or relating to one particular person, rather than to other people or to people in general: *Please keep all bags and other* ***personal belongings*** *with you.* | *I know* ***from personal experience*** *how difficult this kind of work can be.* | *My* ***personal opinion*** *is that we began the project too late.*
2 PRIVATE private and concerning only you: *Can I ask you a* ***personal question****?* | *He won't talk about his* ***personal life****.* | *Beth had a lot of* ***personal problems*** *at that time.*

THESAURUS

private, **secret**, **innermost**
→ see Thesaurus box at PRIVATE[1]

3 ONLY YOU used in order to emphasize that someone does something directly, instead of asking someone else to do it: *The president made a personal visit to the scene of the accident.* | *I will give this my* ***personal attention****.*
4 CRITICISM involving rude or upsetting criticism of someone: *Making* ***personal remarks*** *like that isn't professional.* | ***It's nothing personal*** (=I am not criticizing you) – *I just don't agree with you.*
5 personal friend someone you know well, especially someone famous or important: *The editor is* ***a personal friend of*** *his.*
6 NOT WORK not relating to your work or business: *We're not allowed to make personal phone calls at work.*
7 YOUR BODY [only before noun] relating to your body or the way you look: *personal hygiene*

ˌpersonal comˈputer *n.* [C] PC

per·son·al·i·ty /ˌpɚsəˈnæləti/ *n.* plural **personalities** **1** [C,U] someone's character, especially the way s/he behaves toward other people: *an ambitious woman with a strong personality* | *Childhood experiences can affect personality.* **2** [C] someone who is well known to the public: *a TV personality* **3** [U] *informal* the qualities that make someone or something interesting: *We liked the name because we thought it had personality.*

per·son·al·ize /ˈpɚsənəˌlaɪz/ *v.* [T] **1** to put your name or INITIALS on something: *cars with personalized license plates* **2** to decorate something in a way you like: *Becky has personalized her office with photos and drawings.* **3** to make something appropriate for what a particular person needs: *All products can be personalized to the client's requirements.*

per·son·al·ly /ˈpɚsənəli/ *adv.* **1** *spoken* used in order to emphasize that you are giving your own opinion: *Personally, I think it's a bad idea.* **2** doing or having done something yourself: *I delivered the letter personally.* | *She's* ***personally responsible*** *for all the arrangements.* **3 take sth personally** to get upset by the things other people say or do because you think their remarks or behavior are directed at you: *Don't take it personally – he's rude to everyone.* **4** as a friend, or as someone you have met: *I don't* ***know*** *her* ***personally****, but I like her books.*

ˌpersonal ˈpronoun *n.* [C] *technical* in grammar, a PRONOUN used for the person who is speaking, being spoken to, or being spoken about, such as "I," "you," and "they"

per·so·nals /ˈpɚsənəlz/ *n.* **the personals** [plural] a part of a newspaper in which people can have private messages printed

per·son·i·fi·ca·tion /pɚˌsɑnəfəˈkeɪʃən/ *n.* **1 the personification of sth** someone who has a lot of a particular quality, so that s/he is used as an example of that quality: *Mrs. Grant is the personification of kindness.* **2** [C,U] the REPRESENTATION of a thing or a quality as a person: *the personification of Justice as a woman holding scales*

per·son·i·fy /pɚˈsɑnəˌfaɪ/ *v.* past tense and past participle **personified**, third person singular **personifies** [T] **1** to have a lot of a particular quality or be a typical example of something: *In front of a classroom, she personifies control.* **2 sb is sth personified** used in order to say that someone perfectly represents a quality or idea: *Theresa was kindness personified.* **3** to think of or represent a quality or thing as a person: *Time is usually personified as an old man with a beard.*

per·son·nel /ˌpɚsəˈnɛl/ *n.* **1** [plural] the people who work in a company or for a particular kind of employer: *All personnel need to have identification cards.* | *military personnel* **2** [U] HUMAN RESOURCES: *the personnel department*

per·spec·tive /pɚˈspɛktɪv/ *n.* **1** [C] a way of thinking about something that is influenced by the type of person you are or by your experiences:

P

Becoming a mother gave Helen a whole new ***perspective on*** *life.* | *The novel is written* ***from*** *a child's* ***perspective****.* **2** [U] the ability to think about something sensibly, so that it does not seem worse than it is: *I think Tony's* ***lost*** *all* ***sense of perspective****.* | *You've got to* ***keep*** *things* ***in perspective****.* **3** [U] a method of drawing a picture that makes objects look solid and shows distance and depth: *the artist's use of perspective*

per·spi·ra·tion /ˌpɚspəˈreɪʃən/ *n.* [U] *formal* SWEAT

per·spire /pɚˈspaɪɚ/ *v.* [I] *formal* to SWEAT

per·suade /pɚˈsweɪd/ *v.* [T] **1** to make someone agree to do something by giving good reasons why s/he should: *We eventually* ***persuaded*** *Mark* ***to*** *come with us.*

THESAURUS

talk sb into sth – to persuade someone to do something: *I should never have let my mother talk me into buying this dress.*
get sb to do sth – to persuade or force someone to do something: *I tried to get Jill to come, but she said she was too tired.*
encourage – to persuade someone to do something, especially by telling him/her that it is good for him/her: *More high schools are encouraging their students to do community service.*
influence – to have an effect on what someone does or thinks: *Sports figures influence kids' ideas about what's cool.*
convince – to persuade someone to do something, especially something s/he does not want to do: *I convinced him to stay another night.*
coax – to persuade someone to do something by talking gently and kindly: *"Come for Christmas," Jody coaxed over the phone.*
cajole – to persuade someone to do something by praising him/her or making promises to him/her: *I managed to cajole a colleague into taking her case.*

2 to make someone believe something or feel sure about something [= **convince**]: *Members of the jury were not persuaded by the lawyer's arguments.* | *She'll only take me back if I can* ***persuade*** *her* ***(that)*** *I've changed.*

per·sua·sion /pɚˈsweɪʒən/ *n.* **1** [U] the act or skill of persuading someone to do something: *With a little persuasion, Debbie agreed to come with us.* | *It took all of my* ***powers of persuasion*** *to convince him.* **2** [C] a particular belief, especially a political or religious one: *Jake and his brother are of different political persuasions.*

per·sua·sive /pɚˈsweɪsɪv/ *adj.* able to influence other people to believe or do something: *Erin can be very persuasive.* | *It was not a very* ***persuasive argument****.*

pert /pɚt/ *adj.* **1** small and attractive: *a pert nose* **2** *literary* amusing in a way that shows a slight lack of respect: *a pert answer*

per·tain /pɚˈteɪn/ *v.*
pertain to sth *phr. v. formal* to relate directly to something: *laws pertaining to welfare benefits*

per·ti·nent /ˈpɚt˺n-ənt/ *adj. formal* directly relating to something that is being considered [= **relevant**]: *Reporters asked a few pertinent questions.*

per·turbed /pɚˈtɚbd/ *adj. formal* worried and annoyed: *We weren't too perturbed by the delay.* —**perturb** *v.* [T]

pe·ruse /pəˈruz/ *v.* [T] *formal* to read something in a careful way —**perusal** *n.* [U]

per·vade /pɚˈveɪd/ *v.* [T] *formal* to spread through all parts of something: *A feeling of hopelessness pervaded the country.*

per·va·sive /pɚˈveɪsɪv/ *adj.* existing or spreading everywhere: *the pervasive influence of violence on TV*

per·verse /pɚˈvɚs/ *adj.* behaving in an unreasonable way by doing the opposite of what people want you to do: *He takes perverse pleasure in arguing with everyone.*

per·ver·sion /pɚˈvɚʒən/ *n.* [C,U] **1** a type of sexual behavior that is considered unnatural and unacceptable **2** the act of changing something so that it is no longer right, reasonable, or true: *a* ***perversion of*** *the truth*

per·vert¹ /pɚˈvɚt/ *v.* [T] to change someone or something in a harmful way: *TV violence perverts the minds of young children.*

per·vert² /ˈpɚvɚt/ *n.* [C] someone whose sexual behavior is considered unnatural and unacceptable

per·vert·ed /pɚˈvɚţɪd/ *adj.* **1** relating to unacceptable and unnatural sexual thoughts or behavior **2** morally wrong or unnatural: *perverted logic*

pes·ky /ˈpɛski/ *adj. informal* annoying and causing trouble: *Those pesky kids!*

pes·si·mis·m /ˈpɛsəˌmɪzəm/ *n.* [U] a tendency to believe that bad things will happen [≠ **optimism**]: *a feeling of* ***pessimism about*** *the future*

pes·si·mist /ˈpɛsəmɪst/ *n.* [C] someone who always expects that bad things will happen [≠ **optimist**]

pes·si·mis·tic /ˌpɛsəˈmɪstɪk/ *adj.* expecting that bad things will happen or that a situation will have a bad result [≠ **optimistic**]: *Jonathan is* ***pessimistic about*** *his chances.*

pest /pɛst/ *n.* [C] **1** a small animal or insect that destroys crops or food **2** *informal* an annoying person: *The kids next door can be real pests.*

pes·ter /ˈpɛstɚ/ *v.* [T] to annoy someone by asking for something again and again: *She kept pestering her parents to let her go out.*

pes·ti·cide /ˈpɛstəˌsaɪd/ *n.* [C] a chemical substance that kills insects that destroy crops

pets

pet¹ /pɛt/ *n.* [C] an animal that you keep at home: *Do you have any pets?* ➔ TEACHER'S PET

pet² *v.* past tense and past participle **petted**, present participle **petting** [T] to touch and move your hand gently over an animal's fur: *Our cat loves being petted.* ➔ see picture on page A8

pet³ *adj.* [only before noun] **1 pet project/subject etc.** a plan, subject, etc. that you particularly like or are interested in: *Congressmen are always looking for funding for their pet projects.* **2** a pet animal is one that someone keeps at home: *a pet hamster* **3 pet peeve** something that always annoys you, that may not annoy other people: *One of my pet peeves is people being late for meetings.*

pet·al /ˈpɛṭl/ *n.* [C] the colored part of a flower that is shaped like a leaf: *rose petals* ➔ see picture at PLANT¹

pe·ter /ˈpiṭɚ/ *v.*
peter out *phr. v.* to gradually become smaller, fewer, quieter, etc. and then no longer exist or happen: *After a few minutes, the conversation began to peter out.*

pe·tite /pəˈtit/ *adj. approving* a woman who is petite is short and thin in an attractive way

> **THESAURUS**
> **small**, **little**, **tiny**
> ➔ see Thesaurus box at SMALL

pe·ti·tion¹ /pəˈtɪʃən/ *v.* [I,T] to formally ask someone in authority to do something, especially by sending him/her a petition: *Residents are **petitioning against** a new prison in the area.*

petition² *n.* [C] a piece of paper that asks someone in authority to do or change something, and is signed by a lot of people: *Will you **sign** our **petition**?* | *a **petition against** nuclear testing*

pet·ri·fied /ˈpɛtrəˌfaɪd/ *adj.* **1** extremely frightened: *I'm absolutely **petrified of** dogs.*

> **THESAURUS**
> **frightened**, **afraid**, **scared**, **terrified**
> ➔ see Thesaurus box at FRIGHTENED

2 petrified wood wood that has changed into stone over millions of years —**petrify** *v.* [T]

pet·ro·chem·i·cal /ˌpɛtroʊˈkɛmɪkəl/ *n.* [C] a chemical substance obtained from PETROLEUM or natural gas: *the petrochemical industry*

pe·tro·le·um /pəˈtroʊliəm/ *n.* [U] oil that is obtained from below the surface of the Earth and is used in order to make GASOLINE and other chemical substances: *petroleum-based products*

pet·ty /ˈpɛṭi/ *adj.* **1** something that is petty is not serious or important: *Don't bother me with petty details.* **2** someone who is petty cares too much about things that are not very important or serious: *Sometimes he's so petty about money* (=he thinks too much about exactly how much people owe him). **3 petty crime** a crime that is not serious, for example, stealing things that are not expensive —**pettiness** *n.* [U]

ˌpetty ˈcash *n.* [U] money that is kept in an office for making small payments

ˌpetty ˈofficer, **Petty Officer** *n.* [C] an officer who has the lowest rank in the Navy

pet·u·lant /ˈpɛtʃələnt/ *adj. formal* behaving in an impatient and angry way, like a child

pew¹ /pyu/ *n.* [C] a long wooden seat in a church

pew² *interjection* said when something smells very bad: *Pew! There must be a farm near here.*

pew·ter /ˈpyuṭɚ/ *n.* [U] a gray metal made by mixing LEAD and TIN

PG *adj.* **parental guidance** – used in order to show that a movie may include parts that are not appropriate for young children

PG-13 /ˌpi dʒi θɚˈtin/ *adj.* **parental guidance-13** – used in order to show that a movie may include parts that are not appropriate for children under the age of 13

phal·lic /ˈfælɪk/ *adj.* like a PENIS, or relating to the PENIS

phal·lus /ˈfæləs/ *n.* [C] the male sex organ, or a model of it

phan·tom /ˈfæntəm/ *n.* [C] *literary* **1** a GHOST

> **THESAURUS**
> **ghost**, **spirit**, **specter**, **apparition**
> ➔ see Thesaurus box at GHOST

2 something that exists only in your imagination

Phar·aoh /ˈfɛroʊ, ˈfær-/ *n.* [C] a ruler of ancient Egypt

phar·ma·ceu·ti·cal /ˌfɑrməˈsuṭɪkəl/ *n.* [C usually plural] a medicine or drug —**pharmaceutical** *adj.* [only before noun] *large pharmaceutical companies*

phar·ma·cist /ˈfɑrməsɪst/ *n.* [C] someone whose job is to prepare drugs and medicine in a store or hospital

phar·ma·col·o·gy /ˌfɑrməˈkɑlədʒi/ *n.* [U] the

scientific study of drugs and medicines —**pharmacologist** *n.* [C]

phar·ma·cy /ˈfɑrməsi/ *n.* plural **pharmacies** [C] a store or a part of a store where medicines are prepared and sold

phase¹ /feɪz/ *n.* [C] **1** one of the stages of a process of development or change: *The first* ***phase of*** *renovation should be finished by January.* | *The work will be carried out* ***in phases****.* | *Your child is just* ***going through a phase****.*

THESAURUS

stage, part
→ see Thesaurus box at STAGE¹

2 *technical* one of the changes in the appearance of the moon or a PLANET when it is seen from the Earth

P

phase² *v.*
phase sth ⇔ **in** *phr. v.* to introduce something gradually: *New rules are being phased in over the next two months.*
phase sth ⇔ **out** *phr. v.* to gradually stop using or providing something: *Leaded gas was phased out in the 1970s.*

Ph.D. /ˌpi eɪtʃ ˈdi/ *n.* [C] **Doctor of Philosophy** the highest university degree that can be earned, or someone who has this degree

pheas·ant /ˈfɛzənt/ *n.* [C,U] a large colorful bird with a long tail that is hunted for food and sport, or the meat from this bird

phe·nom·e·nal /fɪˈnɑmənl/ *adj.* very great or impressive: *New York's* ***phenomenal success*** *in reducing crime* —**phenomenally** *adv.*: *phenomenally popular*

phe·nom·e·non /fɪˈnɑmənən, -ˌnɑn/ *n.* plural **phenomena** /-mənə/ [C] **1** something that happens or exists in society, science, or nature that is unusual or difficult to understand: *Homelessness is not a* ***new phenomenon****.* | ***natural phenomena*** *such as earthquakes*

THESAURUS

event, occurrence, incident, happening
→ see Thesaurus box at EVENT

2 a person or thing that has a rare ability or quality

phew /fyu, hyu/ *interjection* said when you feel tired, hot, or RELIEVED: *Phew! I'm glad that's over.*

phi·lan·der·er /fɪˈlændərə/ *n.* [C] *disapproving* a man who has sex with many women but does not want a serious relationship —**philandering** *n.* [U]

phi·lan·thro·pist /fɪˈlænθrəpɪst/ *n.* [C] a rich person who gives a lot of money to help poor people

phi·lan·thro·py /fɪˈlænθrəpi/ *n.* [U] the practice of giving money and help to people who need it —**philanthropic** /ˌfɪlənˈθrɑpɪk/ *adj.*

phil·is·tine /ˈfɪləˌstin/ *n.* [C] *disapproving* someone who does not like or understand art, music, literature, etc.

phi·los·o·pher /fɪˈlɑsəfə/ *n.* [C] someone who studies or teaches philosophy: *ancient Greek philosophers*

phil·o·soph·i·cal /ˌfɪləˈsɑfɪkəl/ *adj.* **1** relating to philosophy: *a philosophical discussion* **2** accepting difficult or bad situations calmly: *Anderson remains* ***philosophical about*** *his defeat.* —**philosophically** *adv.*

phi·los·o·phize /fɪˈlɑsəˌfaɪz/ *v.* [I] to talk or think about important subjects and ideas in a serious way

phi·los·o·phy /fɪˈlɑsəfi/ *n.* plural **philosophies** **1** [U] the study of what it means to exist, what good and evil are, what knowledge is, or how people should live: *She graduated from Yale with a degree in philosophy.* **2** [C] a set of ideas about these subjects: *the* ***philosophy of*** *Plato* **3** [C] a set of beliefs about how you should live your life, do your job, etc.: *a new business philosophy* | *We share a similar* ***philosophy of life****.*

phlegm /flɛm/ *n.* [U] a thick sticky substance produced in your nose and throat, especially when you have a cold [= **mucus**]

phleg·mat·ic /flɛgˈmæṭɪk/ *adj. formal* calm and not easily excited or worried

pho·bi·a /ˈfoʊbiə/ *n.* [C] a strong unreasonable fear of something: *Holly* ***has a phobia*** *about snakes.* —**phobic** *adj.*

phoe·nix /ˈfinɪks/ *n.* [C] a bird in ancient stories that burns itself at the end of its life and is born again from the ASHES

phone¹ /foʊn/ *n.* [C] **1** a piece of equipment that you use in order to talk with someone in another place: *I got up to* ***answer the phone****.* | *I was* ***on the phone*** (=talking to someone else using a telephone) *for an hour, talking to Lynn.* | *Will you get* ***off the phone****? I'm expecting a call.* | *What's your* ***phone number****?* | *Just as we sat down to dinner the* ***phone rang****.* | *Tickets can be ordered* ***by phone****.* **2** the part of a telephone that you hold close to your ear and mouth: *She* ***picked up the phone*** *and dialed.*

TOPIC

When you want to **make a phone call/call sb/phone sb**, you **lift/pick up** the **receiver** (=part you speak into) and **dial** the **number** you want. If the telephone **rings**, someone may **answer** it, or there may be **no answer**. If the number is **busy**, someone is already speaking on that **line**, and you cannot **get through**. If the person you are **calling** has an **answering machine** or **voice mail**, you can **leave a message** for the person to listen to later. If you **get the wrong number** by mistake, try **dialing** again. When you finish speaking on the phone, **hang up** (=put the receiver down).
→ CELL PHONE

phone² *v.* [I,T] to talk to someone using a phone

[= **call**]: *Several people phoned the radio station to complain.*

'phone book *n.* [C] a book containing an alphabetical list of the names, addresses, and telephone numbers of all the people and businesses that have a telephone in the area

'phone booth *n.* [C] a partly enclosed structure containing a telephone that the public can use

phone booth

'phone card *n.* [C] a special card that you buy and use to make phone calls on a public phone

pho·net·ic /fə'nɛṭɪk/ *adj.* relating to the sounds of human speech: *a phonetic alphabet* (=one that uses signs to represent the sounds) —**phonetically** *adv.*

pho·net·ics /fə'nɛṭɪks/ *n.* [U] *technical* the science and study of speech sounds

phon·ics /'fɑnɪks/ *n.* [U] a method of teaching people to read in which they are taught to recognize the sounds that letters represent

pho·no·graph /'foʊnə,græf/ *n.* [C] *old-fashioned* a RECORD PLAYER

pho·ny /'foʊni/ *adj. informal* false or not real, and intended to deceive someone [= **fake**]: *Dirk gave the cops a phony address.* | *a phony passport* —**phony** *n.* [C] *She's such a phony!*

THESAURUS

fake, false, imitation, counterfeit, forged
➔ see Thesaurus box at FAKE[2]

phoo·ey /'fui/ *interjection old-fashioned* used in order to express strong disbelief or disappointment

phos·phate /'fɑsfeɪt/ *n.* [C,U] one of the various forms of a salt of phosphorus, used in industry

phos·pho·res·cent /,fɑsfə'rɛsənt/ *adj.* shining slightly in the dark but producing little or no heat —**phosphorescence** *n.* [U]

phos·pho·rus /'fɑsfərəs/ *n.* [U] a poisonous chemical that starts to burn when it is brought out into the air —**phosphoric** /fɑs'fɔrɪk, -'fɑr-/ *adj.*

pho·to /'foʊṭoʊ/ *n.* plural **photos** [C] *informal* a PHOTOGRAPH: *Who's the girl in this photo?* | *a* ***photo of*** *Babe Ruth* | *This camera* ***takes*** *quite good* ***photos****.*

pho·to·cop·i·er /'foʊṭə,kɑpiɚ/ *n.* [C] a machine that quickly copies documents onto paper by photographing them ➔ see picture on page A11

pho·to·cop·y /'foʊṭə,kɑpi/ *n.* plural **photocopies** [C] a copy of a document made by a photocopier: ***Make a photocopy of*** *this article for me.* —**photocopy** *v.* [T]

,photo 'finish *n.* [C] the end of a race in which the leaders finish so close together that a photograph has to be taken to show who won

pho·to·gen·ic /,foʊṭə'dʒɛnɪk/ *adj.* a photogenic person always looks attractive in photographs: *Julie is very photogenic.*

pho·to·graph[1] /'foʊṭə,græf/ *n.* [C] a picture that is made using a camera: *The book includes more than 100 color photographs.* | *an old* ***photograph of*** *my grandfather* | *Visitors are not allowed to* ***take photographs****.* ➔ PICTURE[1]

photograph[2] *v.* [T] to take a photograph of someone or something: *She was photographed by Vogue.*

pho·tog·ra·pher /fə'tɑgrəfɚ/ *n.* [C] someone who takes photographs, especially as a job: *a news photographer*

THESAURUS

artist, painter, sculptor, potter
➔ see Thesaurus box at ARTIST

pho·to·graph·ic /,foʊṭə'græfɪk◂/ *adj.* **1** relating to photographs: *a photographic image* **2 photographic memory** an ability that some people have to remember exactly every detail of something s/he has seen

pho·tog·ra·phy /fə'tɑgrəfi/ *n.* [U] the art, profession, or process of producing photographs or the scenes in movies: *fashion photography*

THESAURUS

painting, drawing, sculpture, pottery, ceramics
➔ see Thesaurus box at ART

'photo oppor,tunity *n.* [C] an occasion when someone such as a politician is photographed by the newspapers or filmed for television doing something that will make him/her look good

pho·to·syn·the·sis /,foʊṭoʊ'sɪnθəsɪs/ *n.* [U] *technical* the way that green plants make their food using the light from the sun

,phrasal 'verb *n.* [C] *technical* in grammar, a verb that changes its meaning when it is used with an adverb or PREPOSITION. In the sentence "The rocket blew up," "blew up" is a phrasal verb.

phrase[1] /freɪz/ *n.* [C] **1** a group of words that together have a particular meaning: *Darwin's famous phrase, "the survival of the fittest"*

THESAURUS

expression – a word or phrase that has a particular meaning
idiom – a group of words that have a special meaning that is different from the usual meaning of each word
cliché – a phrase that has been repeated so often that it is not interesting
saying/proverb – a phrase that many people know, that expresses a sensible idea and is used to give advice

P

2 *technical* in grammar, a group of words without a main verb that together make a subject, an object, or a verb tense. In the sentence "We have a brand new car," "a brand new car" is a noun phrase. [➡ **clause**, **sentence**]

phrase² *v.* [T] to express something in a particular way: *He phrased his question politely.* —**phrasing** *n.* [U] *I don't remember her exact phrasing.*

phys·i·cal¹ /ˈfɪzɪkəl/ *adj.* **1** relating to someone's body rather than his/her mind or soul [➡ **mental**]: ***physical fitness*** | *a woman of great physical strength* | *She was in constant physical pain.* | *your* ***physical appearance*** (=the way you look) **2** relating to real things that can be seen, tasted, felt, etc.: *our physical environment* | *There is no* ***physical evidence*** *to connect him to the crime scene.* **3** someone who is physical touches people a lot **4** involving touching someone in a rough or violent way: *Hockey is a very physical game.* **5** relating to or following the laws of nature: *the physical force of gravity* **6** a physical science such as PHYSICS studies things that are not living [➡ **organic**]: *physical chemistry*

physical² also **ˌphysical examiˈnation** *n.* [C] a medical examination by a doctor to check that you are healthy, especially when you start a new job

ˌphysical eduˈcation *n.* [U] PE

phys·i·cally /ˈfɪzɪkli/ *adv.* **1** in relation to the body rather than the mind or soul [➡ **mentally**]: *He was physically exhausted.* | *I try to keep myself* ***physically fit*** (=having strong muscles and not much fat). **2 physically impossible** not possible according to the laws of nature: *It's physically impossible for penguins to fly.*

ˌphysical ˈtherapy *n.* [U] a treatment for injuries and muscle problems that uses special exercises, rubbing, heat, etc. —**physical therapist** *n.* [C]

phy·si·cian /fɪˈzɪʃən/ *n.* [C] *formal* a DOCTOR

> **THESAURUS**
>
> **doctor**, **surgeon**, **specialist**, **dentist**
> ➔ see Thesaurus box at DOCTOR¹

phys·ics /ˈfɪzɪks/ *n.* [U] the science that deals with the study of physical objects and substances, and natural forces such as light, heat, and movement —**physicist** /ˈfɪzəsɪst/ *n.* [C]

phys·i·ol·o·gy /ˌfɪziˈɑlədʒi/ *n.* [U] a science that deals with the study of how the bodies of living things work —**physiological** /ˌfɪziəˈlɑdʒɪkəl/ *adj.*

phys·i·o·ther·a·py /ˌfɪzioʊˈθɛrəpi/ *n.* [U] PHYSICAL THERAPY

phy·sique /fɪˈzik/ *n.* [C] the shape, size, and appearance of someone's body: *a man with a powerful physique*

pi·an·ist /piˈænɪst, ˈpiənɪst/ *n.* [C] someone who plays the piano

pi·an·o /piˈænoʊ/ *n.* plural **pianos** [C] a large musical instrument that you play by pressing the KEYS (=narrow black and white bars) ➔ see picture on page A6

pick¹ /pɪk/ *v.* [T]

1 CHOOSE to choose something or someone from a group of people or things: *In the end, Katie picked the blue dress.* | *Have you* ***picked*** *a date* ***for*** *the wedding yet?* | *He* ***picked*** *the Giants* ***to*** *win the division.* | *The board* ***picked*** *Kertzman* ***as*** *the man to run the company.* | *She can* ***pick and choose*** *her jobs* (=she can choose only the ones she likes).

> **THESAURUS**
>
> **choose**, **select**, **opt for**, **decide on**
> ➔ see Thesaurus box at CHOOSE

2 FLOWER/FRUIT to pull off or break off a flower, fruit, etc. from a plant or tree: *We're going out to the farm on Saturday to pick apples.* | *Amy picked a bunch of flowers from her garden.*

3 REMOVE/PULL OFF to remove small things from something, or to pull off small pieces from something: ***picking*** *meat* ***off*** *the bone* | *Michael, stop* ***picking*** *your* ***nose*** (=cleaning the inside of it with your finger).

4 pick your way through/across/among etc. sth to move carefully through an area, choosing exactly where to walk or drive: *Rescue workers picked their way through the rubble.*

5 pick a fight (with sb) to deliberately begin an argument or fight with someone: *Adam's always picking fights with the younger kids.*

6 pick sb's pocket to quietly steal something from someone's pocket, bag, etc.

7 pick sb's brain(s) to ask someone who knows a lot about a subject for information or advice about it: *Can I pick your brains about a legal issue?*

8 pick a lock to use something that is not a key to unlock a door, window, etc. ➔ PICKPOCKET

pick at sth *phr. v.* to eat only a small amount of your food because you do not feel hungry or do not like the food: *I was so nervous I could only pick at my lunch.*

pick sb/sth ⇔ **off** *phr. v.* to shoot people or animals one at a time from a long distance away: *Snipers were picking off anyone who came outdoors.*

pick on sb *phr. v.* to treat someone in a way that is not kind: *Greg, stop picking on your sister!*

pick sb/sth ⇔ **out** *phr. v.* **1** to choose someone or something carefully from a group: *We had a lot of fun picking out a present for Leslie's baby.* **2** to recognize someone or something in a group of people or things: *The victim was able to pick out her attacker from a police lineup.*

pick sth ⇔ **over** *phr. v.* to examine a group of things carefully in order to choose the ones you want: *Wash and pick over the beans.*

pick up *phr. v.*

1 LIFT UP pick sb/sth ⇔ **up** to lift something or someone up: *Pick me up, Daddy!* | *He knelt down to pick up his keys.* | *I* ***picked up the phone*** (=answered the phone) *just as it stopped ringing.*

2 GO GET SB/STH pick sb/sth ⇔ **up** to go somewhere, usually in a vehicle, in order to get someone or something: *I'll pick up my stuff around six, okay?* | *What time should we pick you up at the airport?*
3 BUY pick sth ⇔ **up** to buy something: *Will you pick up something for dinner on your way home?* | *The company is **picking up the bill/tab*** (=paying) *for my computer.*
4 CLEAN A PLACE pick sth ⇔ **up** to put things away neatly, or to clean a place by doing this: *Straighten your room and pick all those papers up.* | *Pick up the living room, please.* | *He never **picks up after** himself* (=puts away the things he has used).
5 GET BETTER to improve: *Sales should pick up before Christmas.*
6 INCREASE pick up sth to increase or get faster: *The car was gradually picking up speed* (=going faster). | *The wind had picked up considerably.*
7 LEARN pick sth ⇔ **up** to learn something without much effort by watching or listening to other people: *I picked up some Korean when I was in the army.*
8 ILLNESS pick sth ⇔ **up** to get an illness from someone, or to become sick: *She's picked up a cold from a child at school.*
9 NOTICE pick sth ⇔ **up** to notice, smell, or hear something, especially when this is difficult: *The dogs were able to pick up the scent.*
10 RADIO/SIGNALS if a machine picks up a sound, movement, or signal, it is able to notice it or receive it: *We didn't pick anything up on radar.* | *Our TV doesn't pick up channel 26 very well.*
11 START AGAIN pick sth ⇔ **up** to begin a conversation, meeting, etc. again, starting from the point where it stopped earlier: *We'll **pick up where we left off** after lunch.*
12 POLICE pick sb ⇔ **up** if the police pick someone up, they find him/her and take him/her to the police station: *Carr was picked up and taken in for questioning.*
13 SEX pick sb ⇔ **up** to talk to someone you do not know because you want to have sex with him/her: *Some guy at the bar was trying to pick up Audrey.*
14 pick up the pieces (of sth) to get a situation back to normal after something bad has happened: *Republicans will try to pick up the pieces after major losses in the last election.*

pick up on sth *phr. v.* to notice something about the way someone is behaving, especially when it is not easy to notice: *Children quickly pick up on tensions between their parents.*

pick² *n.* **1** [U] choice: *There are four kinds of cake, so you can **take your pick**.* | *She'll be able to **have** her **pick of** colleges* (=choose any one she wants). **2 the pick of sth** *informal* the best thing or things in a group: *The Doles will get the pick of the puppies.* **3** [C] a PICKAX **4** [C] a small flat object that you use for playing an instrument such as a GUITAR

pick·ax /ˈpɪk-æks/ *n.* [C] a large tool that you use for breaking up the ground. It consists of a curved iron bar with a sharp point on each end, and a long handle

pick·er /ˈpɪkɚ/ *n.* [C] a person or machine that picks things such as fruit, cotton, etc.

pick·et¹ /ˈpɪkɪt/ **also ˈpicket line** *n.* [C] a group or line of people who picket a factory, store, etc.: *Two workers were hurt today trying to **cross the picket line*** (=trying to work during a STRIKE).

picket² *v.* [I,T] to stand or march in front of a factory, store, etc. to protest something, or to stop people from going in to work during a STRIKE (=time when a group of workers refuse to work): *Protesters are still picketing outside the White House gates.*

ˈpicket ˌfence *n.* [C] a fence made of a line of strong pointed sticks fastened in the ground

pick·le¹ /ˈpɪkəl/ *n.* **1** [C,U] a CUCUMBER preserved in VINEGAR or salt water, or a piece of this: *a dill pickle* **2 be in a pickle** *old-fashioned* to be in a difficult situation

pickle² *v.* [T] to preserve food in VINEGAR or salt water —**pickled** *adj.*: *pickled onions*

ˈpick-me-up *n.* [C] *informal* something that makes you feel cheerful or gives you more energy, especially a drink or medicine

pick·pock·et /ˈpɪkˌpɑkɪt/ *n.* [C] someone who steals things from people's pockets, especially in a crowd

THESAURUS

offender, thief, robber, burglar, shoplifter, attacker, mugger, murderer, rapist
→ see Thesaurus box at CRIMINAL²

pick·up /ˈpɪkʌp/ *n.* **1** [C] **also pickup truck** a small truck with low sides that is used for carrying goods **2** [C] an occasion when someone or something is taken away from a place: *There is a regular garbage pickup on Tuesdays.* **3** [U] the ability of a car to reach a high speed in a short time: *My old car didn't have much pickup.* **4** [C] an increase or improvement in something: *a **pickup in** sales*

pick·y /ˈpɪki/ *adj.* comparative **pickier**, superlative **pickiest** *informal disapproving* someone who is picky is difficult to make happy because s/he only likes certain things [= **fussy**]: *He's not a very **picky eater**.*

pic·nic¹ /ˈpɪknɪk/ *n.* [C] **1** an occasion when people take food and eat it outdoors, for example in a park: *We used to **have picnics** down by the creek.* | *Do you want to **go for a picnic** this Saturday?*

THESAURUS

meal, breakfast, lunch, brunch, dinner, supper, barbecue
→ see Thesaurus box at MEAL

P

2 be no picnic *informal* to be difficult or unpleasant: *Riding the bus to work every day is no picnic!*

picnic² *v.* past tense and past participle **picnicked**, present participle **picnicking** [I] to have a picnic

pic·to·ri·al /pɪk'tɔriəl/ *adj.* relating to or using pictures: *a pictorial history of Montana*

pic·ture¹ /'pɪktʃɚ/ *n.*

1 IMAGE [C] a painting, drawing, or photograph: *a* ***picture of*** *Nelson Mandela* | ***Draw/paint a picture of*** *your house.* | *a group of tourists* ***taking pictures*** (=taking photographs) | *Leo's picture* (=photograph of him) *is in the newspaper.*

THESAURUS

sketch – a picture that is drawn quickly
snapshot – a photograph that is taken quickly
portrait – a painting, drawing, or photograph of a person
cartoon – a funny drawing in a newspaper or magazine that tells a story or a joke
caricature – a funny drawing of someone that makes a particular feature of his/her face or body look bigger, worse, etc. than it really is
illustration – a picture in a book
poster – a large picture printed on paper, used in order to advertise something or as a decoration on a wall
→ CAMERA, DRAWING

2 SITUATION [singular] the general situation in a place, organization, etc.: *The* ***political picture*** *has greatly changed since March.* | *You're missing the* ***big/bigger/wider picture*** (=the situation considered as a whole).

3 DESCRIPTION [C usually singular] a description that gives you an idea of what something is like: *To get a better* ***picture of*** *how the company is doing, look at sales.* | *The book* ***paints a*** *clear* ***picture*** *of life in Ancient Rome.*

4 be in/out of the picture *informal* to be involved or not be involved in a situation: *With his main rival out of the picture, the mayor has a chance of winning the election.*

5 ON A SCREEN [C] the image that you see on a television or in a movie: *Something's wrong with the picture.*

6 get the picture *spoken* to understand something: *I don't want you around here any more, get the picture?*

7 MOVIE [C] *old-fashioned* a MOVIE: *Grandma loved going to the pictures.*

picture² *v.* [T] **1** to imagine something, especially by making an image in your mind: *I can still picture him standing there with his uniform on.* | *I can't* ***picture*** *myself* ***as*** *a mother.*

THESAURUS

imagine, **visualize**, **conceive of**
→ see Thesaurus box at IMAGINE

2 to show something or someone in a photograph, painting, or drawing: *The governor is pictured here with his wife and children.*

'picture book *n.* [C] a children's story book that has a lot of pictures in it

pic·tur·esque /ˌpɪktʃə'rɛsk◂/ *adj.* attractive and interesting: *a picturesque seaside town*

pid·dling /'pɪdlɪŋ/ *adj. informal* small and unimportant: *a piddling amount of money*

pidg·in /'pɪdʒən/ *n.* [C,U] a language that is a mixture of two other languages, which people who do not speak each other's languages will use to talk to each other

pie /paɪ/ *n.* [C,U] **1** a food usually made with fruit baked inside a covering of PASTRY: *a* ***piece/slice*** *of apple pie* **2 as easy as pie** *informal* very easy **3 a piece/share/slice of the pie** *informal* a share of something such as money or profit: *Landers wants a bigger slice of the pie.* **4 pie in the sky** *informal* a good plan or promise that you do not think will happen: *Hope of a cure is just pie in the sky.*

piece¹ /pis/ *n.* [C]

1 PART OF A WHOLE a part of something that has been separated, broken, or cut off from the rest of it: *Do you want a* ***piece of*** *pizza?* | *There were pieces of broken glass everywhere.* | *The vase lay* ***in pieces*** (=in small parts) *on the floor.* | ***Cut*** *the chicken* ***into pieces****, and put it in a roasting pan.*

THESAURUS

scrap – a small piece of paper, cloth, etc.: *He took out the scrap of paper on which he'd written the address.*
chunk – a thick piece of something solid that does not have an even shape: *a stew filled with large chunks of chicken*
lump – a small piece of something solid that does not have a definite shape: *a lump of metal*
fragment – a small piece that has broken off something, especially glass or metal: *Fragments of glass from the crash were still on the street.*
crumb – a very small piece of bread, cake, etc.: *She scattered crumbs for the birds.*
slice – a thin, flat piece of bread, meat, etc. cut from a larger piece: *a slice of blueberry pie*

2 PART OF A SET a single thing of a particular type, often part of a set of things or part of a larger thing: *a* ***piece of*** *paper* | *a chess piece* | *We found this perfect piece of land on the river.* | *a* ***five-piece band*** (=one with five members) → see Thesaurus box at PART¹

3 CONNECTED PART one of several different parts that can be connected together to make something: *the* ***pieces of*** *a jigsaw puzzle* | *The cars were shipped* ***in pieces*** (=separated into pieces) *and then reassembled.*

4 a piece of advice/information/gossip etc. some advice, information, etc.: *Let me give you a piece of advice: don't ask her about her mother.*

5 go to pieces to become so upset or nervous

that you cannot think or behave normally: *When he died, Liz just went to pieces.*
6 smash/tear/rip etc. sth to pieces to damage something severely by breaking it into many parts: *A dog had torn the bird to pieces.*
7 (all) in one piece not damaged or injured: *I'm glad the china arrived all in one piece.*
8 give sb a piece of your mind *informal* to tell someone that you are very angry with him/her: *I went back to the store and gave the manager a piece of my mind.*
9 be a piece of cake *informal* to be very easy to do: *Raising four children hasn't been a piece of cake.*
10 ART/MUSIC ETC. something that has been written or made by an artist, musician, or writer: *an impressive* ***piece of*** *art | They performed a piece by Mozart.*

piece² *v.*
piece sth ⇔ **together** *phr. v.* **1** to use all the facts or information that you have in order to understand a situation: *Police are still trying to piece together a motive for the shooting.* **2** to put all the parts of something back into the correct position or order

piece·meal /ˈpismil/ *adj., adv.* happening or done slowly in separate stages that are not planned or related: *Changes were introduced in piecemeal fashion. | The house was filled with old furniture they'd bought piecemeal.*

piece·work /ˈpiswɚk/ *n.* [U] work for which you are paid according to the number of things you produce rather than the number of hours you work

ˈpie ˌchart *n.* [C] a circle divided into several parts that shows how big the different parts of a total amount are

pier /pɪr/ *n.* [C] **1** a structure that is built out into the water so that boats can stop next to it or people can walk along it: *We were standing at the end of the pier, watching the boats.* **2** a thick stone, wooden, or metal post used for supporting something such as a bridge

pierce /pɪrs/ *v.* [T] **1** to make a hole in or through something using an object with a sharp point: *Tiffany's* ***getting*** *her* ***ears pierced*** (=having a hole put in her ears for wearing jewelry). | *A bullet pierced his body.*

THESAURUS

make a hole in sth – to cause a hole to appear in something: *Make a hole in the bottom of the can using a hammer and nail.*
prick – to make a small hole in the surface of something, using a sharp point: *She pricked her finger with the needle.*
punch – to make a hole in something using a metal tool or other sharp object: *I had to punch an extra hole in the belt to get it to fit.*
drill – to make a hole using a special tool: *They drilled a 180-foot-deep well.*
bore – to make a deep round hole in a hard surface: *Workers bored a hole in the wall.*

2 *literary* if light or sound pierces something, you suddenly see or hear it: *The car's headlights pierced the darkness.*

pierc·ing /ˈpɪrsɪŋ/ *adj.* **1** a piercing sound is high, loud, and not nice to listen to: *a piercing cry/scream*

THESAURUS

high, high-pitched, shrill
→ see Thesaurus box at HIGH¹

2 a piercing wind is very cold **3** someone with piercing eyes seems to know what you are thinking when s/he looks at you: *her piercing gaze*

pi·e·ty /ˈpaɪəṭi/ *n.* [U] respect for God and religion, shown in the way you behave

pig¹ /pɪg/ *n.* [C] **1** a farm animal with short legs, a fat body, and a curled tail. Pigs are kept for their meat. **2** *spoken* an impolite word meaning someone who eats too much, is very dirty, or is offensive in some way: *You ate all the pizza, you pig.*

pig² *v.* past tense and past participle **pigged**, present participle **pigging**
pig out *phr. v. informal* to eat a lot of food all at once: *We* ***pigged out on*** *ice cream last night.*

pi·geon /ˈpɪdʒən/ *n.* [C] a gray bird with short legs that is common in cities

pi·geon·hole¹ /ˈpɪdʒənˌhoʊl/ *n.* [C] one of a set of small boxes built into a desk, or into a frame on a wall, into which letters or papers can be put

pigeonhole² *v.* [T] to decide unfairly that someone or something belongs to a particular group or type: *Hijuelos resists being* ***pigeonholed as*** *strictly a "Latino writer."*

ˈpigeon-ˌtoed *adj.* having feet that point in rather than straight forward when you walk

pig·gy /ˈpɪgi/ *n.* plural **piggies** [C] *spoken* a pig – used especially by children or when talking to children

pig·gy·back ride /ˈpɪgiˌbæk ˌraɪd/ *n.* [C] a way of carrying a child by putting him/her on your back —**piggyback** *adv.*

ˈpiggy bank *n.* [C] a small container, sometimes in the shape of a pig, used especially by children for saving coins

pig·head·ed /ˈpɪgˌhɛdɪd/ *adj. disapproving* determined to do things the way you want even if there are good reasons not to [= **stubborn**]

pig·let /ˈpɪglɪt/ *n.* [C] a young pig

pig·ment /ˈpɪgmənt/ *n.* [C,U] a natural substance that makes skin, hair, plants, etc. a particular color

pig·men·ta·tion /ˌpɪgmənˈteɪʃən/ *n.* [U] the natural color of living things

pig·pen /ˈpɪgpɛn/ **also pig·sty** /ˈpɪgstaɪ/ *n.* [C] **1** a place on a farm where pigs are kept **2** *informal* a place that is very dirty or messy: *Your bedroom is a pigpen!*

pig·tail /ˈpɪgteɪl/ *n.* [C] one of two long lengths of hair that has been pulled together and tied at either side of the head, worn especially by young girls: *a girl with her hair **in pigtails*** ➔ BRAID[1], PONYTAIL, HAIRSTYLE

pike /paɪk/ *n.* [C] **1** plural **pike** a large fish that eats other fish and lives in rivers and lakes **2** *informal* a TURNPIKE

pile[1] /paɪl/ *n.* **1** [C] a large mass of things collected or thrown together in the shape of a small hill: *huge **piles of** garbage | a pile of snow | He raked the leaves **into** small **piles**.*

THESAURUS

heap – a large messy pile of things: *A heap of books and papers lay on the floor.*
mound – a pile of something with a round shape: *a small mound of rice on the plate*

2 [C] a neat collection of similar things put one on top of the other [= **stack**]: *a **pile of** folded clothes* **3 piles of sth/a pile of sth** *informal* a lot of something: *I have piles of work to do tonight. | She's making **piles of money** at her new job.*

pile[2] *v.* **1** [I,T] **also pile up** to make a pile by collecting things together: *A lot of dishes had piled up in the sink.* **2** [T] to fill something or cover a surface with a lot of something: *a plate **piled high with** spaghetti*

pile in/into sth *phr. v. informal* if a group of people pile into a place or vehicle, they all try to get into it quickly and at the same time: *We all piled into the car and left.*

pile out *phr. v. informal* if a group of people pile out of a place or vehicle, they all try to get out of it quickly and at the same time: *As soon as we stopped, the kids piled out and ran to the beach.*

pile up *phr. v.* to become larger in quantity or amount, in a way that is difficult to manage: *Debts from the business were piling up quickly.*

pile·up /ˈpaɪlʌp/ *n.* [C] a traffic accident involving many vehicles: *a 16-car pileup*

pil·fer /ˈpɪlfɚ/ *v.* [I,T] to steal things that are not worth much: *He was caught **pilfering from** the office.*

pil·grim /ˈpɪlgrəm/ *n.* [C] a religious person who travels a long way to a holy place

pil·grim·age /ˈpɪlgrəmɪdʒ/ *n.* [C,U] a trip to a holy place for a religious reason: *Every year, about two million Muslims **make** the **pilgrimage to** Mecca.*

pil·ing /ˈpaɪlɪŋ/ *n.* [C] a heavy post made of wood, cement, or metal, used for supporting a building or bridge

pill /pɪl/ *n.* [C] **1** a small solid piece of medicine that you swallow: *She's **taking pills** to control her blood pressure. | sleeping pills*

THESAURUS

medicine, **tablet**, **capsule**, **eye/ear drops**, **drug**
➔ see Thesaurus box at MEDICINE

2 the Pill a pill taken regularly by some women in order to avoid having babies: *Mary has been **on the pill** for years now.*

pil·lage /ˈpɪlɪdʒ/ *v.* [I,T] if soldiers pillage a place in a war, they steal a lot of things and do a lot of damage

pil·lar /ˈpɪlɚ/ *n.* [C] **1** a tall solid post used as a support for part of a building: *Eight massive stone pillars supported the roof.* **2 a pillar of the community/church etc.** an active and important member of a group, organization, etc.

pil·low /ˈpɪloʊ/ *n.* [C] a cloth bag filled with soft material that you put your head on when you sleep ➔ see picture at BED[1]

pil·low·case /ˈpɪloʊˌkeɪs/ *n.* [C] a cloth cover for a pillow

pi·lot /ˈpaɪlət/ *n.* [C] **1** someone who operates the controls of an aircraft or spacecraft: *an airline pilot* **2** a television program that is made in order to test whether people like it and would watch it again in the future **3 pilot program/project/study etc.** a test that is done to see if an idea or product will be successful —**pilot** *v.* [T]

ˈpilot light *n.* [C] a small gas flame that burns all the time and is used for lighting larger gas burners

pimp /pɪmp/ *n.* [C] a man who makes money by controlling PROSTITUTES (=women who have sex with men for money)

pim·ple /ˈpɪmpəl/ *n.* [C] a small raised red spot on your skin, especially on your face —**pimply** *adj.*

THESAURUS

mark, **blemish**, **zit**
➔ see Thesaurus box at MARK[2]

PIN /pɪn/ *n.* **Personal Identification Number** a number that you use when you get money from a machine using a plastic card

pin[1] /pɪn/ *n.* [C] **1** a short thin piece of metal with a sharp point at one end, used especially for fastening pieces of cloth together **2** a piece of metal, sometimes containing jewels, that you fasten to your clothes to wear as a decoration **3** one of the bottle-shaped objects that you try to knock down in a game of BOWLING **4** a thin piece of metal used to fasten things together, especially broken bones: *He has to have pins put in his ankle.* ➔ CLOTHESPIN, PINS AND NEEDLES, ROLLING PIN, SAFETY PIN

pin[2] *v.* past tense and past participle **pinned**, present participle **pinning** **1** [T] to fasten something somewhere, or join things together with a pin or pins: *Can you **pin** this announcement **on** the bulletin board for me? | He wore campaign buttons **pinned to** his lapels.* **2 pin your hopes on sth/sb** to hope that something will happen or someone will help you because all your plans depend on this: *I hope she's not pinning all her hopes on winning.* **3** [T] to make someone unable to move by putting a lot of pressure or weight on him/her: *He **pinned** her arms **to** her sides.* | *He was **pinned under** the car.*

pin sb/sth **down** *phr. v.* **1** to make someone decide something or tell you what the decision is: *I couldn't pin him down to a definite date for the meeting.* **2** to understand something clearly or be able to describe exactly what it is: *I can't pin down his accent.*

pin·ball /ˈpɪnbɔl/ *n.* [U] a game played on a machine with a sloping board. You push buttons to try to keep a ball from rolling off the board: *a pinball machine*

pin·cer /ˈpɪnsɚ, ˈpɪntʃɚ/ *n.* [C] one of the pair of CLAWS (=sharp curved nails) that some insects and SHELLFISH have

pinch[1] /pɪntʃ/ *v.* **1** [T] to press a part of someone's skin very tightly between your finger and thumb: *She leaned over and pinched his cheeks.* ➔ see picture on page A8 **2** [I,T] if your clothes, shoes, etc. pinch you, they are too tight and hurt you **3 pinch pennies** to be careful to spend as little money as possible

pinch[2] *n.* [C] **1 pinch of salt/pepper etc.** a small amount of salt, pepper, etc. that you can hold between your finger and thumb **2** an act of pinching someone: *She **gave him a pinch** on the cheek.* **3 in a pinch** if necessary in a difficult or urgent situation: *I have room for four more people, five in a pinch.*

pinched /pɪntʃt/ *adj.* **1** not having enough money to do what you want: *financially pinched schools* **2** a pinched face looks thin and unhealthy, for example because the person is sick, cold, or tired

ˈpinch-hit *v.* [I] **1** to BAT[2] instead of another player in a game of baseball **2** to do something for someone else because s/he is suddenly not able to do it: *Could you pinch-hit for Larry in the meeting today?* —**pinch-hitter** *n.* [C]

pin·cush·ion /ˈpɪnˌkʊʃən/ *n.* [C] a small soft object into which you stick pins until you need to use them

pine[1] /paɪn/ **also ˈpine tree** *n.* [C,U] a tree with long leaves shaped like needles, or the wood of this tree

pine[2] **also pine away** *v.* [I] to gradually become weaker, less active, and less healthy because you are very unhappy

pine for sb/sth *phr. v.* to be unhappy because you cannot be with a person, be in a place, or experience something that happened in the past again: *Ten years after Amanda left he was still pining for her.* | *After two months in France I was pining for home.*

pine·ap·ple /ˈpaɪnˌæpəl/ *n.* [C,U] a large yellow-brown tropical fruit, or its sweet yellow flesh ➔ see picture at FRUIT

pine cone *n.* [C] the brown seed container of the pine

ping /pɪŋ/ *n.* [C] a short high RINGING sound —**ping** *v.* [I]

ping-pong, **Ping Pong** /ˈpɪŋpɑŋ, -pɔŋ/ *n.* [U] *trademark* an indoor game played on a large table, in which two people use PADDLES to hit a small ball to each other across a low net [**= table tennis**]

pink /pɪŋk/ *adj.* pale red: *a pink dress* —**pink** *n.* [C,U]

pink·ie, **pinky** /ˈpɪŋki/ *n.* [C] the smallest finger on your hand ➔ see picture at HAND[1]

ˌpink ˈslip *n.* [C] *informal* a written warning telling you that your job is going to end because there is not enough work

pin·na·cle /ˈpɪnəkəl/ *n.* **1** [singular] the most successful, powerful, or exciting part of something: *It took Carlson only eight years to **reach the pinnacle of** his profession.* **2** [C] the top of a high mountain **3** [C] a pointed stone decoration like a small tower on top of a church or castle

pin·point[1] /ˈpɪnpɔɪnt/ *v.* [T] to say exactly what something is, or exactly where someone or something is: *It was impossible to pinpoint the cause of the crash.* | *Can you **pinpoint where** you last saw him?*

pinpoint[2] *adj.* **with pinpoint accuracy** very exactly: *the plane's ability to drop bombs with pinpoint accuracy*

pinpoint[3] *n.* [C] a very small area or amount of something: *a tiny **pinpoint of** light*

pin·prick /ˈpɪnˌprɪk/ *n.* [C] a very small hole or mark in something, like one made by a pin

ˌpins and ˈneedles *n.* **1** [U] an uncomfortable feeling which you get especially when you have not moved part of your body for a long time, and the supply of blood has stopped flowing correctly **2 be on pins and needles** to be very nervous: *Mom's been on pins and needles waiting to hear from you.*

pin·stripe /ˈpɪnstraɪp/ *n.* [C] one of the thin light-colored lines that form a pattern on dark cloth: *a blue pinstripe suit* —**pinstriped** *adj.*

pint /paɪnt/ *n.* [C] a unit for measuring liquid, equal to 2 cups or 0.4732 liters: *a **pint of** milk*

pin·up /ˈpɪnʌp/ *n.* [C] **1** a picture of an attractive or famous person, often a woman wearing little clothing **2** someone who appears in one of these pictures

pi·o·neer[1] /ˌpaɪəˈnɪr/ *n.* [C] **1** one of the first people to do something that other people will later develop or continue to do: *one of the **pioneers of** the personal computer industry* **2** one of the first people to travel to a new or unknown place and begin living there, farming, etc.

pioneer[2] *v.* [T] to be the first person to do, invent, or use something: *a hospital pioneering a new type of surgery*

pi·ous /ˈpaɪəs/ *adj.* having strong religious beliefs, and showing this in the way you behave

pipe[1] /paɪp/ *n.* [C] **1** a tube through which a liquid or gas flows: *a **water pipe*** | *The **pipes** had **frozen** and we had no water.* **2** a thing used for smoking tobacco, consisting of a small tube with a container shaped like a bowl at one end: *Harry* *stood on the porch, **smoking** his **pipe**.* **3** one of the metal tubes that air is forced through in an ORGAN **4** a simple musical instrument like a tube that you blow through

pipe[2] *v.* [T] to send a liquid or gas through a pipe to another place: *oil piped from Alaska*

pipe down *phr. v. spoken* to stop talking or making a noise, and become calmer and less excited: *Pipe down! I'm trying to listen to this!*

pipe up *phr. v. informal* to suddenly say something, especially when you have been quiet until then: *Dennis piped up, saying he didn't agree.*

'pipe dream *n.* [C] a hope, idea, plan, etc. that will probably never work or happen: *Money and fame – isn't that all a pipe dream?*

pipe·line /'paɪp-laɪn/ *n.* [C] **1** a long line of connecting pipes, used for carrying gas, oil, etc. over long distances **2 be in the pipeline** if a plan, idea, or event is in the pipeline, it is still being prepared, but it will happen or be completed soon

P

pip·ing[1] /'paɪpɪŋ/ *n.* [U] **1** several pipes, or a system of pipes, used for carrying a liquid or gas: *Something's wrong with the piping in the building.* **2** thin cloth CORDS used as decorations on clothes and furniture

piping[2] *adj.* **piping hot** very hot: *a pot of piping hot tea*

pip·squeak /'pɪpskwik/ *n.* [C] *spoken old-fashioned* someone whom you think is not worth attention or respect, especially because s/he is small or young: *Shut up, you little pipsqueak!*

pi·quant /pi'kɑnt, 'pikənt/ *adj. formal* **1** having a pleasantly spicy taste: *a piquant chili sauce* **2** interesting and exciting: *piquant photos of life in Paris* —**piquancy** /'pikənsi/ *n.* [U]

pique[1] /pik/ *v.* [T] **1 pique sb's interest/curiosity** to make someone very interested in something: *Emker's life story piqued the public's interest.* **2** *formal* to make someone feel annoyed or upset

pique[2] *n.* [U] *formal* a feeling of being annoyed or upset: *Greta left **in a fit of pique**.*

pi·ra·cy /'paɪrəsi/ *n.* [U] **1** the act of illegally copying and selling books, tapes, videos, computer programs, etc.: *software piracy* **2** the crime of attacking and stealing from ships at sea

pi·ra·nha /pə'rɑnə, -'ræn-/ *n.* [C] a South American fish with sharp teeth that lives in rivers and eats flesh

pi·rate[1] /'paɪrɪt/ *n.* [C] **1** someone who sails on the oceans, attacking other boats and stealing things from them **2** someone who illegally copies and sells another person's work: *We're losing thousands of dollars to video pirates.*

pirate[2] *v.* [T] to illegally copy and sell another person's work: *pirated CDs*

> **THESAURUS**
>
> **copy, photocopy, forge**
> → see Thesaurus box at COPY[2]

pir·ou·ette /ˌpɪru'ɛt/ *n.* [C] a dance movement in which the dancer turns very quickly, standing on one toe or the front part of one foot —**pirouette** *v.* [I]

Pis·ces /'paɪsiz/ *n.* **1** [U] the twelfth sign of the ZODIAC, represented by two fish **2** [C] someone born between February 19 and March 20

pis·ta·chi·o /pɪ'stæʃiˌoʊ/ *n.* plural **pistachios** [C] a small green nut

pis·tol /'pɪstl/ *n.* [C] a small gun that you can use with one hand

pis·ton /'pɪstən/ *n.* [C] a part of an engine consisting of a short solid piece of metal inside a tube that moves up and down to make the other parts of the engine move

pit[1] /pɪt/ *n.* [C]

1 HOLE a hole in the ground, especially one made by digging: *a barbecue pit | Many of the victims were buried in large pits.*

2 MARK a small hollow mark in the surface of something: *There are tiny scratches and pits on the windshield.*

3 MESSY PLACE *spoken* a house or room that is dirty, messy, or in bad condition: *Erica's house is a total pit!*

4 be the pits *spoken* to be very bad: *My job is the pits.*

5 in the pit of your stomach if you have a feeling in the pit of your stomach, you have a sick or tight feeling in your stomach, usually because you are nervous or afraid: *The strange noises gave her a funny feeling in the pit of her stomach.*

6 IN FRUIT the single large hard seed in some fruits: *a peach pit* → see picture at FRUIT

7 FOR CARS a place beside a race track where a race car can quickly get more gas or be repaired

8 → ORCHESTRA PIT

9 → MINE[2]

pit[2] *v.* past tense and past participle **pitted**, present participle **pitting** [T] **1** to take out the single large hard seed inside some fruits **2** to put small marks or holes in the surface of something: *The disease had pitted and scarred his skin.*

pit sb/sth **against** sb/sth *phr. v.* to test your strength, ability, power, etc. against someone else: *This week's big game pits Houston against Miami.*

pi·ta /'pitə/ **also 'pita bread** *n.* [C,U] a type of flat bread that can be opened so you can put food into it

'pit bull also ˌpit bull 'terrier *n.* [C] a short, extremely strong, and often violent dog

pitch[1] /pɪtʃ/ *v.*

1 BASEBALL [I,T] to aim and throw the ball to the BATTER in baseball: *Who's pitching for the Red Sox today? | He **pitched** three **innings** in Monday night's game.*

> **THESAURUS**
>
> **throw, toss, chuck, hurl, fling, pass**
> → see Thesaurus box at THROW[1]

2 THROW [T] to throw something, especially with a lot of force: *Carl tore up Amy's letter and **pitched** it **into** the fire.*
3 FALL [I,T] to fall suddenly and heavily in a particular direction, or to make someone or something fall in this way: *A sudden stop **pitched** her **into** the windshield.* | *Daley **pitched forward** and fell from the stage.*
4 VOICE/MUSIC [T] to make a sound be produced at a particular level: *The song is pitched too high for me.*
5 pitch a tent to set up a tent
6 SELL/PERSUADE [I,T] *informal* to try to persuade someone to buy or do something: *The meeting is your chance to **pitch** your ideas **to** the boss.*
7 SAY/WRITE [T] to aim a product, film, etc. at a particular group of people, or to describe something in a particular way in order to sell it: *a TV show **pitched at** children*
8 SHIP/PLANE [I] if a ship or an aircraft pitches, it moves up and down in an uncontrolled way with the movement of the water or air
pitch in *phr. v. informal* to join others and help with an activity: *If we all pitch in, it won't take very long to finish.*

pitch² *n.* **1** [C] a throw of the ball to the BATTER in baseball: *The first pitch was a strike.* **2** [C] how high or low a musical note or someone's voice is **3** [C] *informal* the things someone says in order to persuade people to buy or do something: *a sales pitch* **4** [singular, U] the strength of your feelings or opinions about something: *Their excitement rose to **fever pitch*** (=a very excited level). **5** [U] a dark sticky substance that is used on roofs, the bottoms of ships, etc. to stop water coming through

ˌpitch 'black *adj.* completely black or dark: *She turned off the lights, and suddenly it was pitch black.*

pitch·er /ˈpɪtʃɚ/ *n.* [C] **1** a container used for holding and pouring liquids, with a handle and a SPOUT (=shaped part for pouring): *a **pitcher of** beer* **2** the baseball player who throws the balls to the BATTER

pitch·fork /ˈpɪtʃfɔrk/ *n.* [C] a farm tool with a long handle and two or three long curved metal points, used especially for lifting HAY (=dried cut grass)

pit·e·ous /ˈpɪt̬iəs/ *adj. literary* making you feel pity: *a piteous cry*

pit·fall /ˈpɪtfɔl/ *n.* [C] a problem or difficulty that is likely to happen: *the **pitfalls of** fame*

pith·y /ˈpɪθi/ *adj.* spoken or written in strong clear language without wasting any words: *pithy comments*

pit·i·ful /ˈpɪt̬ɪfəl/ *adj.* **1** making you feel pity or sympathy: *a pitiful sight* **2** very bad in quality: *His grades this semester are pitiful.* —**pitifully** *adv.*

pit·i·less /ˈpɪt̬ɪlɪs/ *adj.* showing no pity: *a pitiless dictator*

'pit stop *n.* **1 make a pit stop** *spoken* to stop when driving on a long trip in order to get food, gas, etc., or to use the toilet **2** [C] a time when a race car stops beside the track in order to get more gas or be quickly repaired

pit·tance /ˈpɪtˀns/ *n.* [singular] a very small amount of money: *She works for a pittance.*

pit·y¹ /ˈpɪt̬i/ *n.* **1** [U] sympathy you feel for someone who is suffering or unhappy: *I don't need your pity!* | *He doesn't appear to have any **pity for** the victims of the war.* **2** [singular] used to show that you are disappointed about something and you wish things could happen differently: ***It's a pity (that)** so much time was wasted.* | *"We're leaving tomorrow." **"What a pity!"*** **3 take/have pity on sb** to feel sympathy for someone and do something to help him/her

pity² *v.* past tense and past participle **pitied**, third person singular **pities** [T] to feel sympathy for someone because s/he is in a bad situation: *I pity anyone who has to live with Sherry.*

piv·ot¹ /ˈpɪvət/ *n.* [C] **1** a central point or pin on which something balances or turns **2 also pivot point** the most important idea or event on which all the other parts of a plan, situation, process, etc. are based

pivot² *v.* [I,T] to turn or balance on a central point, or to make something do this: *The table-top **pivots on** two metal pins.*
pivot on sth *phr. v.* to depend on or be planned around one important thing, event, idea, etc.: *Her future pivoted on their answer.*

piv·ot·al /ˈpɪvət̬əl/ *adj.* a pivotal time, event, or person has a very important effect on the way something develops: *Parker played **a pivotal role** in getting the deal.*

pix·el /ˈpɪksəl/ *n.* [C] *technical* the smallest unit of an image on a computer screen

pix·ie /ˈpɪksi/ *n.* [C] a very small imaginary creature with magic powers that looks like a person

piz·za /ˈpitsə/ *n.* [C,U] a thin flat round bread, baked with TOMATO, cheese, and usually vegetables or meat on top: *a slice of pizza*

piz·zazz /pəˈzæz/ *n.* [U] an exciting quality or style: *a theater show that needs more pizzazz*

piz·ze·ri·a /ˌpitsəˈriə/ *n.* [C] a restaurant that serves pizza

pj's, PJ's /ˈpi dʒeɪz/ *n.* [plural] *spoken* PAJAMAS

plac·ard /ˈplækɚd, -kɑrd/ *n.* [C] a large sign or advertisement that you carry or put on a wall

pla·cate /ˈpleɪkeɪt, ˈplæ-/ *v.* [T] *formal* to make someone stop feeling angry: *The airline gave out free drinks in an effort to placate angry customers.*

place¹ /pleɪs/ *n.* [C]
1 AREA/SPACE/BUILDING ETC. any space or area, for example a particular point on a surface or a room, building, town, city, etc.: *Keep your money **in** a safe **place**.* | *a beautiful place sur-*

P

rounded by mountains | *She was born in a place called Black River Falls.* | *The water is 30 feet deep* ***in places*** (=in some areas). | *a sore place on my knee*

THESAURUS

position – the exact place where someone or something is, in relation to other things: *We need to know the enemy's position.*
spot informal – a place, especially a pleasant one where you spend time: *It's a favorite spot for picnics.*
location – the place where a hotel, store, office, etc. is, or where a movie is made: *The apartment's in an ideal location.*
site – a place where something is going to be built, or where something important happened: *the site for the new airport* | *an archeological site*
point – an exact place, for example on a map: *At this point the path gets narrower.*

P

2 WHERE YOU DO STH a building or area that is used for, or is suitable for, a particular purpose or activity: *I spent 20 minutes trying to find a* ***place to*** *park.* | *a* ***place of worship*** (=a church, mosque, etc.) | *There's a nice Korean place* (=restaurant) *on the corner.* | *Mexico's a great* ***place for*** *a vacation.* | *A library* ***is no place*** *for a party.*
3 take place to happen: *The earthquake took place at about 5:00 this morning.*
4 WHERE SB LIVES *informal* the house, apartment, or room where someone lives: *I'm going over to Jeff's place* (=his house) *for dinner.* | *For months I've been looking for a new* ***place to live****.*
5 SEAT/POSITION IN LINE a space where you can sit, or a position in a line: *Is this place taken* (=being used)*?* | *Can you* ***save my place*** (=not let anyone else use it)*?*
6 RIGHT POSITION/ORDER the right or usual position or order: *Put the CDs back in their place.* | *By six o'clock, everything was* ***in place*** *for the party.*
7 in place of sb/sth instead of someone or something: *Try using mixed herbs in place of salt on vegetables.*
8 in sb's place used when talking about what you would do if you were in someone else's situation: *What would you do in my place?*
9 IMPORTANCE the importance or position that someone or something has, compared to other people or things: *No one could ever* ***take*** *her* ***place*** (=be as important or loved as she is). | *Carla has friends* ***in high places*** (=with important ranks in society). | *By the1950s, cars had* ***taken the place of*** (=were used instead of) *trains.* | *There will always be* ***a place for*** *you here* (=a position for you to have).
10 RIGHT OCCASION the right occasion or situation: *This* ***isn't the place to*** *talk business.*
11 first/second/third etc. place first, second, etc. position in a race or competition: *Jerry finished* ***in*** *third* ***place****.*
12 in the first/second/third place *spoken* used in order to introduce a series of points in an argument or discussion: *Well, in the first place, I can't afford it, and in the second place I'm not really interested.*
13 all over the place *informal* everywhere: *There were children all over the place!*
14 it is not sb's place (to do sth) if it is not your place to do something, you do not have the duty or right to do it: *It's not her place to tell me how to raise my kids.*
15 out of place not appropriate for or comfortable in a particular situation: *I felt really out of place at Cindy's wedding.*
16 put sb in his/her place to show someone that s/he is not as important, intelligent, etc. as s/he thinks s/he is
17 go places *informal* to become successful: *Work hard and you could really go places.*
18 also Place used in the names of short streets: *I live at 114 Seaview Place.*

place² *v.* [T] **1** to put something somewhere, especially with care [**= put**]: *Seth* ***placed*** *his trophy* ***on*** *the top shelf.* | *She* ***placed*** *the money* ***in*** *a large brown envelope.* **2** to put someone or something in a particular situation: *You'll be placed with the advanced students.* | *This places me in a very difficult position.* **3** to decide that someone or something is important or valuable: *Your father has placed great trust in you.* **4 can't place sb** to recognize someone, but be unable to remember where you have met him/her before: *I know the name, but I can't quite place her.* **5** to arrange for something to be done: *The police department* ***placed an order*** *for six new cars.* | *He* ***placed an ad/advertisement*** *in the local paper.* **6** to find a job or place to live for someone: *The agency had* ***placed*** *her* ***in*** *a local firm.* | *He was later* ***placed with*** *a foster family.*

pla·ce·bo /plə'sibou/ *n.* plural **placebos** [C] a harmless substance such as water that is given to a patient instead of medicine, without telling him/her it is not a medicine, often as part of a test

place·ment /'pleɪsmənt/ *n.* [C,U] **1** the act of finding a place for someone to live, work, or go to college: *a job placement* | *the college* ***placement office*** (=where they help you find work) **2** the act of putting something or someone in a position: *He wasn't satisfied with the furniture placement.* | *You'll need to take a* ***placement test*** (=test that decides which level of class you can take).

place·name /'pleɪsneɪm/ *n.* [C] the name of a particular city, mountain, etc.

pla·cen·ta /plə'sɛntə/ *n.* [C] an ORGAN that forms inside a woman's UTERUS to feed a baby that has not been born yet

plac·id /'plæsɪd/ *adj.* calm and peaceful: *a placid expression* | *The hotel sits on the seashore of a placid bay.* —**placidly** *adv.*

pla·gia·rism /'pleɪdʒəˌrɪzəm/ *n.* [C,U] the act of using someone else's words, ideas, or work and pretending they are your own, or the words, etc. themselves: *She was accused of plagiarism in writing her thesis.* | *an article full of plagiarisms* —**plagiarist** *n.* [C]

pla·gia·rize /'pleɪdʒəˌraɪz/ *v.* [I,T] to take someone else's words, ideas, etc. and copy them, pretending that they are your own: *The teacher accused me of having plagiarized.*

plague[1] /pleɪg/ *n.* **1** [C,U] any disease that causes death and spreads quickly to a large number of people **2 a plague of rats/locusts etc.** a very large and dangerous number of rats, etc.

plague[2] *v.* [T] to make someone suffer over a long period of time, or to cause trouble again and again: *Gloria had always been plagued by ill health.*

plaid /plæd/ *n.* [C,U] a pattern of crossed lines and squares, used especially on cloth —**plaid** *adj.*: *a plaid work shirt*

plain[1] /pleɪn/ *adj.* **1** very clear, and easy to understand or recognize: ***It's** quite **plain that** you don't agree.* | *Why don't you tell me **in plain English*** (=without using technical or difficult words)*?* **2** without anything added or without decoration [= **simple**]: *plain yogurt* | *a plain blue suit* | *a sheet of **plain paper*** (=paper with no lines on it) **3** showing clearly and honestly what you think about something: *Albright was known for her plain speaking.* **4** a woman or girl who is plain is unattractive – used in order to avoid saying this directly

plain[2] *n.* [C] **also plains** a large area of flat land: *a grassy plain* | *countless miles of plains*

plain[3] *adv.* **plain stupid/wrong/rude etc.** *spoken* clearly and simply stupid, wrong, etc.: *They're just plain lazy.*

plain·clothes /'pleɪnklouz, -klouðz/ *adj.* plainclothes police wear ordinary clothes so that they can work without being recognized

plain·ly /'pleɪnli/ *adv.* **1** in a way that is easy to see, hear, or understand: *Tony was plainly nervous as he began his speech.* **2** simply or without decoration: *a plainly dressed young girl*

plain·tiff /'pleɪntɪf/ *n.* [C] *law* the person in a court of law who ACCUSES someone else of doing something illegal [➡ **defendant**]

plain·tive /'pleɪntɪv/ *adj.* *literary* a plaintive sound is high, like someone crying, and sounds sad: *the **plaintive cry** of the wolf*

plan[1] /plæn/ *n.* [C] **1** something that you have decided to do or achieve: *She has no **plans to** retire.* | *Brown's **plans for** the future* | *We **made plans** to go out and see him in the fall.* | *Do you **have** any **plans** for Friday night?*

THESAURUS

plot/conspiracy – a secret plan to do something bad or illegal, especially a plan that involves a lot of people: *a plot to assassinate the President*
scheme – a plan, especially to do something bad or illegal: *He created an elaborate scheme to steal from his employer.*
strategy – a careful plan aimed at achieving something difficult: *the government's economic strategy*
schedule – a plan of what someone is going to do and when s/he is going to do it: *My schedule looks pretty busy.*
timetable – a plan that shows the exact times when something should happen: *We had to adjust the timetable for construction.*

2 a set of actions for achieving something in the future: ***plans for** dealing with a major earthquake* | ***Under the plan**, 700 acres will become a park.* | *a **business plan*** (=what your business will do) *for the 21st century* | *the zoo's **master plan*** (=main plan for the future) **3 health/pension/retirement etc. plan** an arrangement in which you pay money to a company, and they give you money back if you need medical care, stop working, etc. **4** a drawing of something such as a building, room, or machine, as it would be seen from above, showing the shape, size, parts, etc.: *the **plans for** the new library*

plan[2] *v.* past tense and past participle **planned**, present participle **planning** **1** [I,T] **also plan out** to think about something you want to do, and how you will do it: *Mary's planning a 21st birthday party for her son.* | *Most problems can be avoided by **careful/good planning**.* **2** [T] to intend to do something: *How long do you **plan on** staying?* | *David **plans to** work part-time.* **3** [T] to think about something you are going to make or build, and decide what it will look like: *Planning a small garden is often difficult.*

plane /pleɪn/ *n.* [C] **1** a vehicle that flies in the air and has wings and at least one engine [= **airplane**]: *What time does your **plane take off**?* | *The **plane landed** at O'Hare Airport.* | *My son held my hand as we **boarded the plane**.* **2** a level or standard of thought, conversation, etc.: *a **higher plane** of intellectual curiosity* **3** a tool that has a flat bottom with a sharp blade in it, used for making wooden surfaces smooth **4** *technical* a completely flat surface in GEOMETRY

plan·et /'plænɪt/ *n.* [C] **1** a very large round object in space that moves around a star, such as the sun: *Mercury is the smallest planet.*

TOPIC

meteor, **asteroid**, **comet**, **moon**, **star**, **sun**, **constellation**, **galaxy**, **black hole**
➔ see Topic box at SPACE[1]

2 the planet the Earth: *weapons capable of destroying the planet* | *the richest gold mine **on the planet*** —**planetary** /'plænəˌtɛri/ *adj.*

plan·e·tar·i·um /ˌplænə'tɛriəm/ *n.* [C] a build-

P

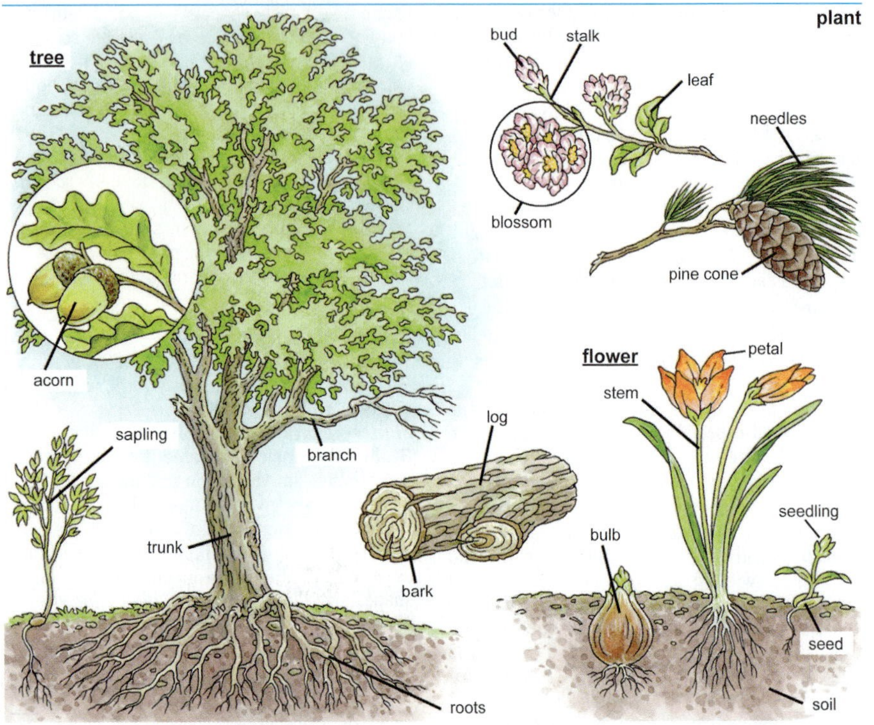

ing where lights on a curved ceiling show the movements of PLANETS and stars

plank /plæŋk/ *n.* [C] **1** a long narrow flat piece of wood used for building **2** a feature or principle that a political party says is one of its aims [➡ **platform**]: *a* ***central plank*** *in the candidate's platform*

plank·ton /'plæŋktən/ *n.* [U] very small plants and animals that live in the ocean and are eaten by fish

plan·ner /'plænə/ *n.* [C] someone who plans something, especially someone who plans the way cities grow and develop: ***city planners*** | *He works as a* ***financial planner****.*

plant¹ /plænt/ *n.* [C] **1** a living thing that has leaves and roots and grows in the ground, especially one that is smaller than a tree [➡ **houseplant**]: *a plant that grows well in the shade* | *a bean plant* **2** a factory and all its equipment: *a manufacturing plant*

plant² *v.* [T] **1** to put plants or seeds in the ground to grow: *Plant tomatoes in a sunny place.* | *a hillside* ***planted with*** *pine trees* **2** *informal* to hide stolen or illegal goods in someone's clothes, bags, room, etc. in order to make him/her seem guilty of a crime: *The police were accused of planting evidence against him.* **3** to put something firmly somewhere: *He stood, his feet planted slightly apart.* **4 plant an idea/doubt/suspicion (in sb's mind)** to mention something that makes someone begin to have an idea, doubt, etc.: *Don't plant ideas in the boy's head!* —**planting** *n.* [C,U]

plan·ta·tion /plæn'teɪʃən/ *n.* [C] a large farm, especially in a hot country, where a single crop such as tea, cotton, or sugar is grown: *a rubber plantation*

plant·er /'plæntə/ *n.* [C] **1** a container in which plants are grown **2** someone who owns or is in charge of a PLANTATION

plaque /plæk/ *n.* **1** [C] a piece of flat metal or stone with writing on it: *A bronze plaque on the house read: Walt Whitman was born here.* **2** [U] a harmful substance that forms on your teeth, that BACTERIA can live and grow in

plas·ma /'plæzmə/ *n.* [U] the yellowish liquid part of the blood that carries the blood cells

plas·ter¹ /'plæstə/ *n.* [U] a substance used for covering walls and ceilings to give them a smooth surface

plaster² *v.* [T] **1** to spread or stick something all over a surface so that it is thickly covered: *a wall* ***plastered with*** *posters* **2** to cover a surface with plaster

plas·tered /'plæstəd/ *adj. informal* very drunk

plaster of Par·is /ˌplæstə əv 'pærɪs/ *n.* [U] a mixture of a white powder and water that dries quickly, used especially for making STATUES or MOLDS

plas·tic¹ /'plæstɪk/ *n.* **1** [C,U] a light strong material that is produced by a chemical process that can be made into different shapes when it is soft: *toys made of plastic* **2** [U] *informal* a CREDIT CARD: *Some customers are worried about paying with plastic on the Internet.*

plastic² *adj.* **1** made of plastic: *a plastic bag | plastic cups* ➔ see picture at MATERIAL¹ **2** *disapproving* seeming artificial or not natural: *a plastic smile | plastic-tasting food* **3** *technical* a plastic substance such as clay can be formed into many different shapes and then keeps the shape until someone changes it

plas·tic·i·ty /plæˈstɪsət̬i/ *n.* [U] *technical* the quality of being easily made into any shape

plastic 'surgery *n.* [U] the medical practice of changing the appearance of people's faces or bodies, either to improve their appearance or to repair injuries

plate /pleɪt/ *n.* **1** [C] a flat, usually round, dish that you eat from or serve food on: *a china plate | Even Jon* ***cleaned*** *his* ***plate*** (=ate all the food that was on his plate). **2** [C] **also plateful** /ˈpleɪtfʊl/ the amount of food on a plate [➡ **dish**]: *a* ***plate of*** *scrambled eggs and toast* **3** [C] a flat piece of metal, glass, bone, etc.: *a metal plate on the heel of the shoe* **4 gold/silver etc. plate** [U] ordinary metal with a thin covering of gold, silver, etc. **5** [C] *informal* a LICENSE PLATE: *New Jersey plates* **6** [singular] the place where the person hitting the ball stands in the sport of baseball: *Reid* ***stepped up to the plate****, swung, and hit the ball.* **7** [C] a thin piece of plastic with FALSE TEETH in it

pla·teau /plæˈtoʊ/ *n.* [C] **1** a large area of flat land that is higher than the land around it **2** a period during which the level or amount of something does not change: *I had* ***reached a plateau*** *in my career.* —**plateau** *v.* [I]

plat·ed /ˈpleɪt̬ɪd/ *adj.* covered with a thin layer of metal, especially gold or silver: *a silver-plated spoon*

,plate 'glass *n.* [U] clear glass made in large thick sheets, used especially in store windows —**plate-glass** *adj.*: *a* ***plate-glass window***

plat·form /ˈplætfɔrm/ *n.* [C] **1** a raised structure for people to stand or work on: *He climbed on to the wooden platform and began to speak. | an oil platform* **2** the main ideas and aims of a political party, especially the ones that they state just before an election: *Tax cuts may be included in the* ***party platform*** *for the next election.* **3** the type of computer system or software that someone uses: *a multimedia platform* **4** a chance for someone to express his/her opinions: *He used the TV interview as a* ***platform for*** *his views on education.* **5** the place in a railroad station or SUBWAY where you get on and off a train: *We were waiting* ***on*** *the* ***platform****.* ➔ see Topic box at TRAIN¹

plat·ing /ˈpleɪt̬ɪŋ/ *n.* [U] a thin layer of metal that covers another metal surface: *silver plating*

plat·i·num /ˈplætˀnəm, ˈplætˀn-əm/ *n.* [U] **Pt** an expensive heavy silver-white metal that is an ELEMENT and is used in making jewelry

plat·i·tude /ˈplæt̬əˌtud/ *n.* [C] *disapproving* a boring statement that has been made many times before: *a speech full of platitudes*

pla·ton·ic /pləˈtɑnɪk/ *adj.* a relationship that is platonic is friendly, but not sexual

pla·toon /pləˈtun/ *n.* [C] a small group of soldiers that is part of a COMPANY

plat·ter /ˈplæt̬ɚ/ *n.* [C] **1** a large plate, used for serving food **2 chicken/seafood etc. platter** chicken, etc. arranged on a plate with other foods and served in a restaurant

plat·y·pus /ˈplæt̬əpəs/ *n.* [C] a small Australian animal that lays eggs and has a beak, but also has fur and feeds milk to its babies

plau·dit /ˈplɔdɪt/ *n.* [C usually plural] *formal* praise and admiration: *The magazine has* ***won plaudits*** *from media critics.*

plau·si·ble /ˈplɔzəbəl/ *adj.* easy to believe and likely to be true [≠ **implausible**]: *a plausible story*

play¹ /pleɪ/ *v.*

1 SPORT/GAME a) [I,T] to take part or compete in a game or sport: *men playing poker | Kara played basketball in college. | Garcia* ***plays for*** *the Hornets. | The 49ers are playing the Vikings on Saturday* (=they are competing against the Vikings). **b)** [T] to use a particular piece, card, person, etc. in a game or sport: *Coach Nelson will play Williams at quarterback.*

2 CHILDREN/TOYS [I,T] to do things that you enjoy, especially to pretend things or to use toys: *a little girl who likes* ***playing with*** *dolls | Outside, the kids were* ***playing tag/catch/house etc.*** *| Parents need to spend time just* ***playing with*** *their children.*

3 MUSIC a) [I,T] to perform a piece of music on an instrument: *The band played for 10,000 people at the Newport Festival. | Matt plays drums.* **b)** [I,T] to make a radio, STEREO, etc. produce sounds, especially music: *a story tape to play for the kids in the car*

4 play a part/role to have an effect or influence on something: *Police believe he may have* ***played a role in*** *the boy's death.*

5 THEATER/MOVIE a) [T] to act as one of the characters in a movie, television, or theater performance: *Kidman* ***plays the role/part of*** *Virginia Woolf in the movie. | He plays a shy, nervous man.* **b)** [I] to be performed or shown at a theater, etc.: *Where's the movie playing?*

6 BEHAVE [linking verb, T] *informal* to behave in a particular way, or pretend to have a particular quality, in order to achieve something: *If he asks, just* ***play dumb*** (=pretend you do not know the answer). *| the accusation that scientists are* ***playing God*** *| Doctors warned parents to* ***play it safe*** (=do the safest thing) *by immunizing their children. | Tracy forced herself to* ***play it cool*** (=stay calm and not be too eager) *with Brad.*

7 play ball a) to throw, hit, kick, or catch a ball

P

as a game or activity: *Just don't play ball in the house.* **b)** *informal* to agree to do something that someone wants you to do: *They threatened to stop advertising if the magazine didn't play ball.*
8 play a trick/joke/prank on sb to do something to surprise or deceive someone, and make other people laugh
9 play tricks (on you) if your mind, memory, sight, etc. plays tricks on you, you feel confused and not sure about what is happening
10 play it by ear *informal* to decide what to do as things happen, instead of planning anything: *We'll see what the weather's like and play it by ear.*
11 play sth by ear to be able to play music after you have heard it instead of by reading the notes
12 play games *disapproving* to not be serious about what you are doing or not say what you really think, especially in a way that tricks or deceives other people: *Stop playing games and just tell me what you want.*
13 play with fire to do something that could have a very bad result: *If you invest in high-risk stocks, you're playing with fire.*
14 play your cards right to behave in an effective way in a situation, in order to get what you want: *If you play your cards right, eventually you'll get promoted.*
15 play second fiddle to sb/sth to be involved in an activity, but not be as important as the main person or group that is involved in it

GRAMMAR

Do not use a preposition or "the" after **play** when you are talking about playing a game or sport. Say: *They're playing football.*
Do not say "They're playing at football" or "They're playing the football."
Always use "the" after the verb **play** and before the names of musical instruments: *Anna plays the piano.*

play around *phr. v.* **1** to spend time having fun, but without having a particular purpose: *I didn't get good grades because I played around a lot.* **2** *informal* to have a sexual relationship with someone who is not your husband or wife

play sth ⇔ **back** *phr. v.* to let someone hear or see again something that has been recorded on a TAPE, VIDEO, etc.: *Jody rewound the tape and played it back.*

play sth ⇔ **down** *phr. v.* to make something seem less important or bad than it really is: *The White House tried to play down the latest economic figures.*

play on sth *phr. v.* to use a feeling or idea in order to get what you want, often in an unfair way: *His campaign plays on people's fear of crime.*

play sth ⇔ **up** *phr. v.* to make something seem better or more important than it really is: *The town has played up its location to attract tourists.*

play with sth *phr. v.* **1** to keep touching or moving something: *Stop playing with the remote control!* **2 also play around with sth** to organize or think about something in different ways, to see what works: *I've been playing with the design of the newsletter.*

play² *n.* **1** [C] a story that is written to be performed by actors, especially in a theater: *a play by Shakespeare* | *a* ***play about*** *two men on trial for murder* | *Each year the drama department* ***puts on/performs a play*** *in the spring.*

TOPIC

musical, opera, ballet
→ see Topic box at THEATER

2 [C,U] the actions of the people who are playing a game or sport: *Jackson scores with a three-point play* (=he makes three points by doing one action)*!* **3** [U] the things that people, especially children, do for fun, such as using toys: *the shouts of children* ***at play*** | *Children learn* ***through play.*** | *a play area with slides and swings* **4** [U] the effect or influence of something: *All of these factors are* ***at play*** (=having an effect) *in any human relationship.* | *Cultural differences* ***come into play*** (=begin to have an effect) *when trying to sell a product in a foreign country.* | *A complex system of muscles is* ***brought into play*** (=begun to be used) *for each body movement.* **5 play on words** a use of a word or phrase that is interesting or funny because it has more than one meaning [➡ **pun**]

play·act·ing /ˈpleɪˌæktɪŋ/ *n.* [U] *disapproving* behavior in which someone pretends to be serious or sincere, but is not

play·boy /ˈpleɪbɔɪ/ *n.* [C] *old-fashioned* a rich man who does not work and who spends time enjoying himself with beautiful women, fast cars, etc.

ˌplay-by-ˈplay *adj.* **play-by-play commentary/description** a description of the action in a sports game as it happens, given on television or the radio

ˈPlay-Doh *n.* [U] *trademark* a soft substance like colored clay, used by children for making shapes

play·er /ˈpleɪɚ/ *n.* [C] **1** someone who plays a game, sport, or musical instrument: *a piano player* | *a basketball player* **2** one of the people, companies, organizations, etc. that is involved in a situation: *a* ***major/dominant/key player*** *in the stock market* **3 a CD/record/cassette etc. player** a machine that is used to play CDs, etc.

play·ful /ˈpleɪfəl/ *adj.* **1** intended to be fun rather than serious, or showing that you are having fun: *playful tunes* | *She gave him a playful poke.* **2** very active and happy: *playful children tumbling in the snow* —**playfully** *adv.* —**playfulness** *n.* [U]

play·ground /ˈpleɪgraʊnd/ *n.* [C] an area where children can play, especially at a school or in a park, that often has special equipment that children can climb on, ride on, etc.

play·house /ˈpleɪhaʊs/ *n.* [C] **1** a theater, often

used as part of a theater's name: *the Pasadena Playhouse* **2** a small structure like a house that children can play in

playing card

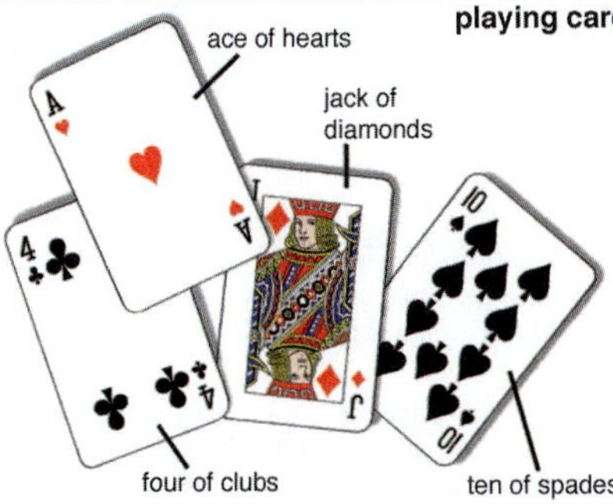

'playing card *n.* [C] a CARD

'playing field *n.* [C] **1** a large piece of ground with particular areas marked on it for playing football, baseball, etc. **2 a level playing field** a situation in which different people, companies, countries, etc. can all compete fairly with each other because no one has special advantages: *Canada limits election spending in an attempt to create a level playing field.*

play·mate /ˈpleɪmeɪt/ *n.* [C] *old-fashioned* a friend you play with when you are a child

play·off /ˈpleɪɔf/ *n.* [C usually plural] a game or series of games played by the best teams or players in a sports competition, in order to decide the final winner: *The Chicago Cubs are* ***in the playoffs***.

> **THESAURUS**
> **competition**, **championship**, **tournament**, **contest**
> ➔ see Thesaurus box at COMPETITION

play·pen /ˈpleɪpɛn/ *n.* [C] an enclosed area like an open box with a net or wooden BARS around it, in which very young children can play safely

play·room /ˈpleɪrum, -rʊm/ *n.* [C] a room for children to play in

play·thing /ˈpleɪˌθɪŋ/ *n.* [C] a toy

play·time /ˈpleɪtaɪm/ *n.* [U] a period of time during which a child can play: *Don't let TV take up too much playtime.*

play·wright /ˈpleɪraɪt/ *n.* [C] someone who writes plays

pla·za /ˈplɑzə, ˈplæzə/ *n.* [C] an outdoor public place, usually with a lot of stores and small businesses

plea /pli/ *n.* [C] **1** a request that is urgent and full of emotion: *a* ***plea for*** *help* | *They* ***made a plea*** *for more resources.* **2** *law* a statement by someone in a court of law saying whether s/he is guilty or not: *The defendant* ***entered a plea of*** *"not guilty."*

'plea-ˌbargain *v.* [I] to avoid punishment for a serious crime by agreeing to say you are guilty of a less serious one

plead /plid/ *v.* **1** [I] past tense and past participle **pleaded** to ask for something you want very much, in an urgent and emotional way [= **beg**]: *Mother* ***pleaded with*** *Dad* ***to*** *be gentler with us.* | *He* ***pleaded for*** *forgiveness.* **2** [I,T] past tense and past participle **pleaded** or **pled** /plɛd/ *law* to officially say in a court of law whether or not you are guilty of a crime: *"How do you plead?" "Not guilty."* | *Parker* ***pled guilty to*** *four charges of theft.*

pleas·ant /ˈplɛzənt/ *adj.* **1** enjoyable, nice, or good: *It had been a pleasant evening.* | *a pleasant surprise*

> **THESAURUS**
> **enjoyable**, **great**, **fantastic**, **wonderful**
> ➔ see Thesaurus box at NICE

2 polite, friendly, or kind: *a really nice, pleasant man* —**pleasantly** *adv.*: *We were pleasantly surprised by how welcoming everyone was.*

> **THESAURUS**
> **nice**, **friendly**, **kind**, **likeable**, **sweet**, **great**
> ➔ see Thesaurus box at KIND2

pleas·ant·ry /ˈplɛzəntri/ *n.* plural **pleasantries** [C] *formal* something that you say in order to be polite

please1 /pliz/ *interjection* **1** used in order to be polite when asking someone to do something: *Patty, sit down, please.* | *Could you please hold the line?* **2** used in order to be polite when asking for something: *Can I have a cookie, please?* | *Can I please go to Becky's party?* **3** *spoken* said in order to politely accept something that someone offers you: *"Coffee?" "Yes, please."*

please2 *v.* **1** [I,T] to make someone feel happy or satisfied: *a business that wants to please its customers* | *a boss who is* ***hard to please*** | *Children are often* ***eager to please***. **2** [I] used in some phrases to show that someone can do or have what s/he wants: *Students can study* ***whatever*** *they* ***please***. | *You can come and go* ***as you please***.

pleased /plizd/ *adj.* **1** happy or satisfied: *Your mom will be really pleased.* | *We're very* ***pleased with*** *the results.* | *Ellen was* ***pleased that*** *Toby had remembered.* | *I was* ***pleased to hear/see/learn etc.*** *that things had improved.*

> **THESAURUS**
> **happy**, **glad**, **content**, **delighted**, **ecstatic**
> ➔ see Thesaurus box at HAPPY

2 (I'm) pleased to meet you *spoken* said in order to be polite when you meet someone for the first time

pleas·ing /ˈplizɪŋ/ *adj. formal* giving pleasure, enjoyment, or satisfaction: *a pleasing flavor* | *The sculpture's smooth edges are very* ***pleasing to the eye*** (=nice to look at).

P

pleas·ur·a·ble /ˈplɛʒərəbəl/ *adj. formal* enjoyable: *pleasurable activities*

pleas·ure /ˈplɛʒɚ/ *n.* **1** [U] a feeling of happiness, satisfaction, or enjoyment [➡ **pleasant**]: *Marie laughed **with pleasure**. | a book to read **for pleasure** | He **took pleasure in** his work. | The park has **given pleasure to** many people. | The kids yelled for the **sheer/pure pleasure** of it.* **2** [C] an activity or experience that you enjoy very much: *Chocolate is one of my chief pleasures. | **It's a pleasure to** finally meet you.* **3 (it is) my pleasure** *spoken* a polite phrase used in order to say that you are glad you can do something nice for someone: *"Thanks for walking me home." "It was my pleasure."*

pleat /plit/ *n.* [C usually plural] a flat fold in a piece of clothing —**pleat** *v.* [T]

P

pleat·ed /ˈplit̬ɪd/ *adj.* a pleated skirt, pair of pants, dress, etc. has a lot of flat narrow folds

pled /plɛd/ *v.* a past tense and past participle of PLEAD

pledge¹ /plɛdʒ/ *n.* [C] **1** a serious promise or agreement to do something or give money to something: *a pledge of support | Parents **make a pledge** to take their children to rehearsals. | a pledge of $100 to the public television station* **2** someone who promises to become a member of a college FRATERNITY or SORORITY

pledge² *v.* [T] **1** to make a formal, usually public, promise: *Canada **pledged to** provide medical aid.* **2** to make someone formally promise something: *Employees were **pledged to** secrecy.* **3** to promise to become a member of a college FRATERNITY or SORORITY

ˌPledge of Alˈlegiance *n.* **the Pledge of Allegiance** an official statement said by Americans in which they promise to be loyal to the United States. It is usually said by children every morning at school.

plen·ti·ful /ˈplɛntɪfəl/ *adj.* more than enough in amount or number: *a plentiful supply* —**plentifully** *adv.*

plen·ty¹ /ˈplɛnti/ *pron.* a large amount that is enough or more than enough: *Eat **plenty of** fruits and vegetables. | We have **plenty to** worry about.*

THESAURUS
many, **a large number**, **a lot**, **lots**
→ see Thesaurus box at MANY

plenty² *adv. spoken* more than enough [= **a lot**]: *There's **plenty more** room in the car.*

THESAURUS
enough, **sufficient**, **adequate**
→ see Thesaurus box at ENOUGH

pleth·o·ra /ˈplɛθərə/ *n.* **a plethora of sth** *formal* a very large number of something

Plex·i·glas /ˈplɛksiˌglæs/ *n.* [U] *trademark* a strong clear type of plastic that can be used instead of glass

pli·a·ble /ˈplaɪəbəl/ *adj. formal* **1** able to bend without breaking or cracking [= **flexible**]: *Roll the clay until it is soft and pliable.* **2 also pli·ant** /ˈplaɪənt/ easily influenced by others, or willing to accept new ideas: *a pliant legislature*

pli·ers /ˈplaɪɚz/ *n.* [plural] a small metal tool used for bending wire or cutting it: *a pair of pliers*

plight /plaɪt/ *n.* [C usually singular] a bad, serious, or sad situation that someone is in: *the **plight of** women in that society | the university's financial plight*

plod /plɑd/ *v.* past tense and past participle **plodded**, present participle **plodding** [I] to move or do something very slowly, especially in a way that is boring or that shows you are tired: *We plodded uphill. | The movie **plods along** without very much ever happening.* —**plodding** *adj.*

plop¹ /plɑp/ *v.* past tense and past participle **plopped**, present participle **plopping** [T] to sit down, fall down, or drop something somewhere in a careless way: *Jaime **plopped down** on the bed. | I plopped a couple of ice cubes into a glass.*

plop² *n.* [C] the sound made by something when it falls or is dropped into liquid

plot¹ /plɑt/ *n.* [C] **1** the events that form the main story of a book, movie, or play: *The movie has a very complicated plot.* **2** a secret plan you make with other people to do something illegal or harmful: *a plot to kill the President*

THESAURUS
plan, **conspiracy**, **scheme**, **strategy**
→ see Thesaurus box at PLAN¹

3 a small piece of land for building or growing things on: *a two-acre **plot of land***

plot² past tense and past participle **plotted**, present participle **plotting** *v.* **1** [I,T] to make a secret plan, especially one intended to harm a particular person or organization: *The group had **plotted to** smuggle explosives into the country. | rebels **plotted against** the dictator* **2** [T] **also plot out** to make lines and marks on a CHART or map that represent facts, numbers, etc.: *graphs that plot the company's progress*

plow¹ /plaʊ/ *n.* [C] **1** a large piece of equipment used on farms that cuts up the surface of the ground so that seeds can be planted **2** *informal* a SNOWPLOW

plow² *v.* **1** [I,T] to use a plough in order to cut earth, push snow off streets, etc.: *newly plowed fields* **2** [I] to move with a lot of effort or force: *a ship **plowing through** the waves*

plow ahead *phr. v.* to continue to do something in spite of difficulties or opposition: *She was silent, but I **plowed ahead with** my questions.*

plow sth ⇔ **back** *phr. v.* to use money that you have earned from a business to make the business

bigger and more successful: *Profits are* ***plowed back into*** *equipment and training.*
plow into sth *phr. v.* to hit something hard with a car, truck, etc.: *We plowed into a parked car.*
plow through sth *phr. v.* to read or look at all of something even though it is difficult, long, or boring: *Investigators plowed through the phone records.*

ploy /plɔɪ/ *n.* plural **ploys** [C] a way of tricking someone in order to gain an advantage: ***a ploy to*** *advance his political career*

pluck¹ /plʌk/ *v.* [T] **1** to pull something quickly in order to remove it: *flowers plucked from the garden* | *She* ***plucks her eyebrows*** (=pulls out hairs from the edges of them). **2** to take someone away from a place or situation: *Rescue teams* ***plucked*** *people* ***from*** *the rooftops as the water rose.* **3 pluck up the courage** to make yourself be brave or confident enough to do something: *I finally* ***plucked up the courage to*** *ask for a raise.* **4** to pull the feathers off a chicken or other bird before cooking it **5** to quickly pull the strings of a musical instrument

pluck² *n.* [U] *old-fashioned* courage and determination to do something that is difficult: *It* ***takes*** *a lot of* ***pluck*** *to do what he's done.* —**plucky** *adj.*

plug¹ /plʌg/ *n.* [C] **1** the small object at the end of a wire that is used for connecting a piece of electrical equipment to a SOCKET (=supply of electricity) **2** a round flat piece of rubber used for blocking the hole in a bathtub or SINK **3** *informal* a way of advertising a book, movie, etc. by talking about it on a radio or television program

plug² *v.* past tense and past participle **plugged**, present participle **plugging** [T] **1 also plug up** to fill a hole or block it: *The drain was plugged up with paper.* **2** to advertise a book, movie, etc. by talking about it on a radio or television program: *Susan was on the show to plug her new novel.*

THESAURUS

advertise, promote, market, hype
➔ see Thesaurus box at ADVERTISE

plug away *phr. v.* to continue working hard at something: *Scientists have been* ***plugging away at*** *the problem.*
plug sth ⇔ **in** *phr. v.* to connect a piece of electrical equipment to a SOCKET (=supply of electricity) [≠ **unplug**]: *Is the TV plugged in?*
plug sth **into** sth *phr. v.* to connect one piece of electrical equipment to another: *Can you plug the speakers into the stereo for me?*

plum /plʌm/ *n.* [C] **1** a soft round usually purple fruit with a single large seed, or the tree on which it grows ➔ see picture at FRUIT **2** something very good that other people wish they had, such as a good job, part in a play, etc.: *The governorship of California is a bigger political plum than a seat in Congress.* —**plum** *adj.* [only before noun] *a* ***plum job/role/assignment***

plum·age /ˈplumɪdʒ/ *n.* [U] *formal* the feathers covering a bird's body

plumb /plʌm/ *adv. spoken informal* exactly or completely: *He's plumb crazy.* | *Sorry, I just plumb forgot.*

plumb·er /ˈplʌmɚ/ *n.* [C] someone whose job is to repair water pipes, SINKS, toilets, etc.

plumb·ing /ˈplʌmɪŋ/ *n.* [U] the system of water pipes in a house or building

plume /plum/ *n.* [C] **1** a small cloud of smoke, dust, gas, etc.: ***plumes of*** *black smoke coming from the garage* **2** a large feather

plum·met /ˈplʌmɪt/ *v.* [I] **1** to suddenly and quickly decrease in value: *House prices have plummeted.*

THESAURUS

decrease, go down, drop, fall, diminish, decline
➔ see Thesaurus box at DECREASE¹

2 to fall suddenly and very quickly from a very high place: *The plane plummeted to the ground.*

plump¹ /plʌmp/ *adj.* **1** attractively round and slightly fat: *plump juicy strawberries* **2** fat – used in order to be polite: *He was 67, short, and a little plump.*

THESAURUS

fat, overweight, big, heavy, large, obese, chubby
➔ see Thesaurus box at FAT¹

plump² **also plump up** *v.* [T] to make a PILLOW rounder and softer by shaking or hitting it

plun·der¹ /ˈplʌndɚ/ *v.* [I,T] to steal money or property from a place while fighting in a war: *The Vikings invaded and plundered the town.*

plunder² *n.* [U] things that are stolen by the fighters during an attack or war

plunge¹ /plʌndʒ/ *v.* **1** [I,T] to move, fall, or be thrown or pushed suddenly forward or downward: *The plane* ***plunged into*** *the Atlantic shortly after takeoff.* ➔ see Thesaurus box at DIVE¹ **2** [I] to suddenly decrease in amount or value: *The stock market plunged more than 1,200 points.*
plunge (sb/sth) **into** sth *phr. v.* to suddenly experience a bad or difficult situation, or to make someone or something do this: *The company was plunged into bankruptcy.*

plunge² *n.* **1 take the plunge** to decide to do something risky, usually after delaying or worrying about it: *Deming took the plunge and started his own business.* **2** [C] a sudden decrease in amount, or a sudden fall

plung·er /ˈplʌndʒɚ/ *n.* [C] a tool used for clearing waste that is blocking a kitchen or bathroom

P

pipe. It consists of a straight handle with a large rubber cup on the end

plunk /plʌŋk/ *v.* [I,T] *informal* to put something somewhere in a noisy, sudden, or careless way, or to suddenly sit down: *Grover* ***plunked down*** *in front of the TV.*

plunk sth ⇔ **down** *phr. v.* to spend a lot of money for something: *He plunked down $30 for a box of chocolates.*

plu·per·fect /ˌpluˈpɚfɪkt/ *n.* **the pluperfect** *technical* PAST PERFECT

plu·ral /ˈplʊrəl/ *n.* **the plural** *technical* in grammar, the form of a word that represents more than one person or thing. For example, "dogs" is the plural of "dog" [➡ **singular**] —**plural** *adj.*: *a* ***plural noun/verb***

plu·ral·i·ty /plʊˈræləṭi/ *n.* plural **pluralities** [C,U] the largest number of votes in an election, especially when this is less than the total number of votes that all the other people or parties have received

P

plus¹ /plʌs/ *prep.* used when one number or amount is added to another: *Three plus six equals nine. (3+6=9)* | *The jacket costs $49.95 plus tax.*

THESAURUS

add, **subtract**, **take away**, **multiply**, **divide**, **minus**

➔ see Thesaurus box at CALCULATE

plus² *conjunction* and also: *He's going to college, plus he's working 20 hours a week.*

plus³ *adj., adv.* **1 A plus/B plus/C plus etc.** a GRADE used in a system of marking students' work. For example, a C plus is higher than a C, but lower than a B MINUS. [➡ **minus**] **2** greater than zero or than a particular amount [➡ **minus**]: *a temperature of plus 12°* | *She makes $50,000 a year plus.* **3 plus or minus** used in order to say that a number may be more or less by a certain amount: *The poll's margin of error was plus or minus 3 percentage points.* **4 plus sizes** sizes for women's clothes that are larger than regular sizes

plus⁴ *n.* [C] **1** a PLUS SIGN **2** something that is an advantage or a quality that you think is good: *The restaurant's location is* ***a big/major plus***.

plush¹ /plʌʃ/ *adj.* comfortable, expensive, and of good quality: *a plush resort*

plush² *n.* [U] a type of cloth with a thick soft surface: *a plush rabbit*

ˈplus sign *n.* [C] the sign (+)

Plu·to /ˈpluṭoʊ/ *n.* the ninth PLANET from the sun

plu·to·ni·um /pluˈtoʊniəm/ *n.* [U] **Pu** a metal that is an ELEMENT and is used for producing NUCLEAR power

ply¹ /plaɪ/ *n.* [U] a unit for measuring the thickness of thread, rope, PLYWOOD, etc. based on the number of threads or layers that it has: ***two-/three-ply etc.*** *toilet paper*

ply² *v.* past tense and past participle **plied**, third person singular **plies** **1 ply your trade/craft** *written* to work at your business or special skill: *an elderly musician still plying his trade* **2** [I,T] *literary* a boat or vehicle that plies between two places travels to those two places regularly

ply sb **with** sth *phr. v.* to continue giving someone large amounts of something, especially food and drinks

ply·wood /ˈplaɪwʊd/ *n.* [U] a material made of thin sheets of wood stuck together to form a hard board

p.m. used when talking about times that are between NOON and MIDNIGHT: *I get off work at 5:30 p.m.*

PMS *n.* [U] **premenstrual syndrome** the uncomfortable physical and emotional feelings that many women have before their PERIOD starts

pneu·mat·ic /nʊˈmæṭɪk/ *adj.* **1** filled with air: *a pneumatic tire* **2** able to work using air pressure: *a pneumatic drill* —**pneumatically** *adv.*

pneu·mo·nia /nʊˈmoʊnyə/ *n.* [U] a serious illness that affects your lungs and makes it difficult to breathe

P.O. *n.* the written abbreviation of **post office**

P.O. Box /ˌpi ˈoʊ ˌbɑks/ *n.* [C] **post office box** a box in a post office that has a special number, to which you can have mail sent instead of to your home

P.O.W. *n.* [C] **prisoner of war**: *a P.O.W. camp*

poach /poʊtʃ/ *v.* **1** [T] to cook food such as eggs or fish in a small amount of boiling liquid **2** [I,T] to illegally catch or shoot animals, birds, or fish, especially from private land

poach·er /ˈpoʊtʃɚ/ *n.* [C] someone who illegally catches or shoots animals, birds, or fish, especially on private land

pock·et¹ /ˈpɑkɪt/ *n.* [C] **1** a small bag sewn into or onto shirts, coats, pants, or skirts that you can put keys, money, etc. in: *a key in his pants pocket* **2** the amount of money you have that you can spend: *Over $20 million was taken* ***out of the pockets*** *of American taxpayers.* | *a corporation with* ***deep pockets*** (=a lot of money) **3** a small bag or piece of material that is attached to something such as a car seat, used for holding maps, magazines, etc. **4** a small area or amount that is different from what surrounds it: ***pockets of*** *poverty in the city*

pocket² *v.* [T] **1** to put something in your pocket **2** to get money in a way that is very easy or dishonest: *a judge who pocketed $500,000 in bribes*

pocket³ **also ˈpocket-sized** *adj.* small enough to fit into a pocket: *a pocket calendar*

pock·et·book /ˈpɑkɪtˌbʊk/ *n.* [C] **1** the amount of money you have, or your ability to pay for things: *Some voters are worried that the changes could hurt their pocketbooks* (=cause them to have less money). **2** *old-fashioned* a WALLET or PURSE

pock·et·ful /ˈpɑkɪtfʊl/ *n.* [C] the amount that

will fill a pocket, or a large amount: *a **pocketful of** small change*

'pocket knife *n.* [C] a small knife with a blade that you can fold into its handle

pod /pɑd/ *n.* [C] the long green part of plants such as beans and PEAS that the seeds grow in

po·di·a·trist /pəˈdaɪətrɪst/ *n.* [C] a doctor who takes care of people's feet and treats foot diseases —**podiatry** *n.* [U]

po·di·um /ˈpoʊdiəm/ *n.* [C] **1** a tall narrow desk that you stand behind when giving a speech to a lot of people: *Several speakers **took the podium*** (=spoke from it) *that night.* **2** a small raised area for a performer, speaker, or musical CONDUCTOR to stand on

po·em /ˈpoʊəm/ *n.* [C] a piece of writing that expresses emotions, experiences, and ideas, especially in short lines using words that RHYME (=have a particular pattern of sounds)

po·et /ˈpoʊɪt/ *n.* [C] someone who writes poems

po·et·ic /poʊˈɛt̬ɪk/ *adj.* **1** relating to poetry, or typical of poetry: *poetic language* **2** graceful and expressing deep emotions: *a poetic and powerful ballet* —**poetically** *adv.*

po,etic 'justice *n.* [U] a situation in which someone who has done something bad suffers in a way that you think s/he deserves

po,etic 'license *n.* [U] the freedom to change facts, not obey grammar rules, etc. because you are writing poetry or making art

po·et·ry /ˈpoʊətri/ *n.* [U] poems, or the art of writing them [➡ **prose**]: *a book of Emily Dickenson's poetry*

pog·rom /ˈpoʊgrəm/ *n.* [C] a planned killing of large numbers of people, especially Jews, done for reasons of race or religion [➡ **genocide**]

poign·ant /ˈpɔɪnyənt/ *adj.* making you feel sad or full of pity: *a simple melody and poignant lyrics* —**poignancy** *n.* [U] —**poignantly** *adv.*

> **THESAURUS**
> **emotional, moving, touching, sentimental, schmalzy**
> ➔ see Thesaurus box at EMOTIONAL

poin·set·ti·a /pɔɪnˈsɛt̬iə/ *n.* [C] a plant with groups of large bright red or white leaves that look like flowers

point[1] /pɔɪnt/ *n.*

1 ONE IDEA [C] a single fact, idea, or opinion in an argument or discussion: *There were a lot of **good points** in his speech.* | *I **made** that **point** at a staff meeting last week.* | *I didn't like his attitude, but I could **see his point*** (=understand his idea). | *I had to admit that he **had a point*** (=his opinion is correct).

2 MAIN IDEA the point the main meaning or idea in something that is said or done: *Come on, Charlie, **get to the point*** (=say your idea directly)*!* | ***The point is (that)** he had been proven wrong.* | ***What's your point**, Rob?* | *I think you're **missing the point*** (=do not understand the most important thing). | *He's a nice guy, but **that's beside/not the point**.* | ***The important/main/crucial point** is that no one is wholly good or wholly evil.*

3 PURPOSE [U] the purpose or aim of doing something: ***The whole point of** traveling is to experience new things.* | ***There's no point in** continuing.* ▶ Don't say "There's no point to continue." ◀

4 IN TIME/DEVELOPMENT [C] a specific moment, time, or stage in something's development: ***At this/that/one/some point**, Moore decided to tell him.* | *She had **reached the point** where she knew something had to change.* | *It's a good **starting point** for any future negotiations.* | *the **turning point** in the investigation* (=the time when it changed)

> **THESAURUS**
> **stage, part, phase**
> ➔ see Thesaurus box at STAGE[1]

5 PLACE [C] a particular position or place: *the point where two lines cross each other*

> **THESAURUS**
> **place, spot, position, location, site**
> ➔ see Thesaurus box at PLACE[1]

6 QUALITY [C] a particular quality or feature that someone or something has: *Teachers should try to focus on a learner's **strong points*** (=best qualities or abilities)*, and then work on his or her **weak points**.*

7 GAME/SPORT [C] a unit used for showing the SCORE in a game or sport: *The Rams beat the Giants by six points.*

8 IN NUMBERS [C] the sign (.) used for separating a whole number from the DECIMALS that follow it: *four point five percent* (=4.5%)

9 MEASURE [C] a measure on a scale: *Stocks were down 12 points today at 8,098.*

10 the high/low point of sth the best or worst part of something, or the best or worst moment: *It was the high point of their trip.*

11 SHARP END [C] the sharp end of something: *the point of a needle*

> **THESAURUS**
> **end, tip**
> ➔ see Thesaurus box at END[1]

12 up to a point partly, but not completely: *He believed her story, up to a point.*

13 make a point of doing sth to deliberately do something: *Don makes a point of spending Saturdays with his kids.*

14 SMALL SPOT [C] a very small spot: *a tiny point of light*

15 LAND [C] a long thin piece of land that stretches out into the ocean

16 to the point only talking about the most

P

important facts or ideas: *Your business letters should be short and to the point.*

17 the point of no return a stage in a process or activity when it becomes impossible to stop it or do something different: *We've* ***reached the point of no return****, so we might as well finish the project.* → GUNPOINT, POINT OF VIEW

point² *v.* **1** [I] to show someone something by holding your finger out toward it: *John* ***pointed to/toward*** *two of the players.* | *"That's my car," she said,* ***pointing at*** *a white Ford.* → see picture on page A8 **2** [I,T] to aim something or to be aimed in a particular direction: *He* ***pointed*** *a gun* ***at*** *the old man's head.* | *Dozens of cameras were* ***pointed toward*** *them.* | *What time is it when the little hand* ***points to*** *the eight, and the big hand points to the twelve?* **3** [T] to show someone which direction to go: *There should be signs* ***pointing the way*** *to the beach.*

THESAURUS

lead, guide, direct
→ see Thesaurus box at LEAD¹

4 point the finger at sb *informal* to blame someone [= **accuse**]

point out *phr. v.* **1 point** sth ⇔ **out** to tell someone something that s/he does not already know or has not yet noticed: *The manager* ***pointed out that*** *he would have to raise rents to pay for the improvements.* **2 point** sb/sth ⇔ **out** to show a person or thing to someone by pointing at him, her, or it: *The little girl* ***pointed out*** *her mother* ***to*** *us.*

point to/toward sb/sth *phr. v.* to show that something is probably true: *The report points to stress as a cause of heart disease.*

ˌpoint-ˈblank *adv., adj.* **1** if you say something point-blank, you say it in a very direct way: *I* ***asked/told*** *him* ***point-blank*** *what was going on.* **2** if you shoot a gun point-blank, the person or thing you are shooting is directly in front of you: *Ralston was* ***shot point-blank*** *in the chest.* | *He was* ***shot at point-blank range****.*

point·ed /ˈpɔɪntɪd/ *adj.* **1** having a point at the end: *cowboy boots with pointed toes* **2 a pointed question/look/remark etc.** a direct question, look, etc. that deliberately shows that you are bored, annoyed, or do not approve of something

point·ed·ly /ˈpɔɪntɪdli/ *adv.* deliberately, so that people notice that you are bored, annoyed, or do not approve of something: *Wilton looked pointedly at the clock.*

point·er /ˈpɔɪntə/ *n.* [C] **1** a helpful piece of advice [= **tip**]: *I gave him some* ***pointers on*** *his golf technique.* **2** the thin ARROW that points to a particular place, number, or direction on a piece of equipment such as a computer or scale **3** a long stick used for pointing at things on a map, board, etc.

point·less /ˈpɔɪntlɪs/ *adj.* without any purpose or meaning, or not likely to have an effect: *pointless violence on TV* | ***It's pointless*** *trying to call him; he isn't home.*

THESAURUS

futile – having no chance of being effective or successful: *a futile attempt to prevent the war*
useless – not useful or effective in any way: *The information he provided was useless.*
be a waste of time/money/effort – to use time, money, or effort in a way that is not effective, useful, or sensible: *I thought the class was a waste of time.*

ˈpoint man *n.* [C usually singular] **1** a soldier who goes ahead of a group to see if there is any danger **2** someone who is in charge of a particular subject in a company or organization: *the administration's* ***point man on*** *health care*

ˌpoint of ˈview *n.* [C] **1** a particular way of thinking about or judging a situation: *I began writing about families* ***from*** *a father's* ***point of view****.*

THESAURUS

opinion, view, position, attitude
→ see Thesaurus box at OPINION

2 someone's own personal opinion or attitude about something: *My parents never seem to be able to see my point of view.*

poin·ty /ˈpɔɪnti/ *adj. informal* POINTED: *a pointy beard*

poise¹ /pɔɪz/ *n.* [U] **1** a calm confident way of behaving, and the ability to control how you feel: *She spoke to the police* ***with*** *perfect* ***poise****.* **2** a graceful way of moving or standing: *the poise of a dancer*

poise² *v.* [T] to put something in a carefully balanced position, or to hold it there: *He* ***poised*** *the bottle* ***over*** *her glass, ready to pour.*

poised /pɔɪzd/ *adj.* **1** completely prepared to do something or for something to happen, when it is likely to happen soon: *a team* ***poised to*** *win the championships.* **2** not moving, but completely ready to move: *I could sense that she was* ***poised to*** *run at any second.* | *a rocket* ***poised for*** *launch* **3** behaving in a calm confident way, and able to control your feelings and reactions: *a poised and talented girl*

poi·son¹ /ˈpɔɪzən/ *n.* [C,U] **1** a substance that can kill you or make you sick if you eat it, breathe it, etc.: *rat poison* **2** a person, feeling, idea, etc. that makes you behave badly or makes you feel very unhappy: *Hatred is a poison for the soul.*

poison² *v.* [T] **1** to kill or harm someone by giving him/her poison: *She poisoned the neighbor's dog.* **2** to make land, lakes, rivers, air, etc. dirty and dangerous, especially by using harmful chemicals: *Pesticides are poisoning our rivers.*

3 to have harmful effects on someone's mind or emotions, or on a situation: *Money has poisoned American politics.*

poi·son·ing /ˈpɔɪzənɪŋ/ *n.* [C,U] an illness that is caused by swallowing, touching, or breathing a poisonous substance: *children suffering from* ***food/lead poisoning***

ˌpoison ˈivy *n.* [U] a plant with an oily substance on its leaves that makes your skin hurt and ITCH

ˌpoison ˈoak *n.* [U] a plant that has leaves that make your skin hurt and ITCH

poi·son·ous /ˈpɔɪzənəs/ *adj.* containing poison or producing poison: *a poisonous chemical | poisonous snakes* —**poisonously** *adv.*

THESAURUS

harmful, **toxic**, **detrimental**, **damaging**
➔ see Thesaurus box at HARMFUL

poke /poʊk/ *v.* **1** [I,T] to quickly push your finger or some other pointed object into something or someone: *Polly* ***poked*** *me* ***in*** *the ribs. | David* ***poked at*** *the campfire with a stick.* ➔ see picture on page A8

THESAURUS

push, **roll**, **shove**, **nudge**, **elbow**
➔ see Thesaurus box at PUSH[1]

2 [I,T] to push something through a space or out of an opening, so that you can see part of it, or to be partly through a space or opening: *Eve* ***poked*** *her head* ***around*** *the door and told us to be quiet. | Weeds were* ***poking through*** *the cracks.* **3 poke a hole** to make a hole in something by pushing a pointed object through it **4 poke fun at sb** to joke about someone in an unkind way: *an article poking fun at Hollywood celebrities* —**poke** *n.* [C]

poke along *phr. v. informal* to move or travel slowly

poke around *phr. v.* to look for something, especially by moving things: *I began poking around in the cupboard.*

pok·er /ˈpoʊkɚ/ *n.* **1** [U] a card game that people usually play for money **2** [C] a metal stick used for moving coal or wood in a fire to make it burn better

pok·ey, **poky** /ˈpoʊki/ *adj. informal* doing things very slowly, especially in a way that you find annoying: *a pokey driver*

po·lar /ˈpoʊlɚ/ *adj.* **1** relating to the North Pole or the South Pole: *polar ice* **2 polar opposite** someone or something that is completely opposite to another person or thing in character or style: *Presidents Kennedy and Johnson were polar opposites in terms of style and background.*

polar bear

ˈpolar ˌbear *n.* [C] a large white bear that lives near the North Pole

po·lar·ize /ˈpoʊləˌraɪz/ *v.* [I,T] *formal* to divide into two opposing groups, or to make people do this: *The trial polarized the city.* —**polarization** /ˌpoʊlərəˈzeɪʃən/ *n.* [U]

Po·lar·oid /ˈpoʊləˌrɔɪd/ *n.* [C] *trademark* a camera that uses a special film to produce a photograph very quickly, or a photograph taken with this kind of camera

Pole /poʊl/ *n.* [C] someone from Poland

pole *n.* [C] **1** a long stick or post: *a telephone pole* (=holding up telephone wires outside) | *a fishing pole* **2** the most northern and southern point on a PLANET: *an expedition to the North Pole* **3 be poles apart** to be very different from someone or something else: *The two classes were poles apart in atmosphere.* **4** one of two points at the end of a MAGNET where its power is strongest **5** one of the two points at which wires can be attached to a BATTERY in order to use its electricity

po·lem·ic /pəˈlɛmɪk/ *n.* [C,U] strong arguments that criticize or defend a particular idea, opinion, or person —**polemical** *adj.*

ˈpole vault *n.* **the pole vault** a sport in which you jump over a high BAR using a special long pole —**pole vaulter** *n.* [C]

po·lice[1] /pəˈlis/ *n.* **1 the police** an official organization whose job is to catch criminals, make sure that people obey the law, and protect people and property: *Her neighbors called the police.*

THESAURUS

People in the police
police officer/policeman/policewoman
detective – a police officer whose job is to discover who is responsible for crimes
plain-clothes police officer – a police officer who is wearing ordinary clothes instead of a uniform
cop informal – a police officer

Things the police do
investigate crimes
find/collect evidence
arrest sb
question/interrogate/interview sb
hold/keep sb in custody – to keep someone in

P

prison while collecting more information about a crime, or before s/he goes to court
charge sb with a crime – to state officially that someone might be guilty of a crime

2 [plural] the people who work for this organization: *Police broke down the door.* | *police records/reports*

police² *v.* [T] **1** to keep control over a place using police **2** to control a particular activity or industry by making sure people obey the rules: *an agency that polices the nuclear power industry* —**policing** *n.* [U]

po'lice de,partment *n.* [C] the official police organization in a particular area or city

po'lice force *n.* [C] the official police organization in a country or area

po·lice·man /pə'lismən/ *n.* plural **policemen** /-mən/ [C] a male police officer

po'lice ,officer *n.* [C] a member of the police

po'lice state *n.* [C] *disapproving* a country where the government strictly controls most of the activities of its citizens

THESAURUS

democracy, republic, monarchy, regime, dictatorship, totalitarian country/state
➔ see Thesaurus box at GOVERNMENT

po'lice ,station *n.* [C] the local office of the police in a town or city

po·lice·wom·an /pə'lis,wʊmən/ *n.* plural **policewomen** /-,wɪmɪn/ [C] a female police officer

pol·i·cy /'pɑləsi/ *n.* plural **policies** **1** [C,U] a way of doing things that has been officially agreed and chosen by a political party, business, or organization: *our **foreign/economic/immigration etc. policy*** | *the company's **policy on** maternity leave* | *government officials who **make policy*** **2** [C] a written agreement with an insurance company: *a health **insurance policy*** **3** [C,U] a particular principle that you believe in: ***It's** my **policy** not **to** gossip.*

po·li·o /'poʊli,oʊ/ *n.* [U] a serious infectious disease of the nerves in the SPINE that often results in someone being permanently unable to move particular muscles

po·li sci /,pɑli 'saɪ/ *n.* [U] *informal* POLITICAL SCIENCE

Po·lish¹ /'poʊlɪʃ/ *adj.* relating to or coming from Poland

Polish² *n.* **1** [U] the language used in Poland **2 the Polish** [plural] the people of Poland

pol·ish¹ /'pɑlɪʃ/ *v.* [T] to make something smooth, bright, and shiny by rubbing it: *He polished his shoes each night.*

THESAURUS

clean, scour, scrub, dust, sweep (up), mop
➔ see Thesaurus box at CLEAN²

polish sth ⇔ **off** *phr. v. informal* to finish food, work, etc. quickly or easily: *The kids polished off the rest of the cake.*

polish² *n.* **1** [C,U] a liquid, powder, or other substance that you rub into a surface to make it shiny: *furniture polish* | *shoe polish* **2** [U] a high level of skill and style in the way someone performs, writes, or behaves: *experiences that will give you social polish* **3** [singular] the smooth shiny appearance of something that is produced by polishing ➔ NAIL POLISH

pol·ished /'pɑlɪʃt/ *adj.* **1** shiny because of being rubbed with polish: ***highly polished** wood* **2** done with great skill and style, or doing something with skill and style: *a polished performance* | *a polished ballerina* **3** polite and confident: *a polished and sophisticated woman*

po·lite /pə'laɪt/ *adj.* behaving or speaking in a way that is correct for the social situation you are in, or showing good manners: *polite young people* | ***It's** not **polite to** talk with your mouth full.* | *a polite smile* | *Len sipped at his drink to be polite.* | *They weren't just making **polite conversation**; they really wanted to know.* —**politely** *adv.* —**politeness** *n.* [U]

THESAURUS

have good manners – to behave in a polite way in social situations: *Parents want to teach their children to have good manners.*
well-behaved – behaving in a polite or socially acceptable way: *My kids are generally well-behaved.*
courteous – polite and respectful: *You should be courteous to other drivers.*
civil – polite but not very friendly: *I know you don't like him, but try to be civil.*

po·lit·i·cal /pə'lɪt̬ɪkəl/ *adj.* **1** relating to the government, politics, and the public affairs of a country: *The U.S. has two main political parties.* | *the political issues that are important to senior citizens* **2** relating to the way that different people or groups have power within a system, organization, etc.: *He was promoted for political reasons.* **3** [not before noun] interested in or active in politics: *Mike's never been political.* —**politically** *adv.*: *She's becoming more politically active.*

po,litically cor'rect, P.C. *adj.* politically correct language, behavior, and attitudes are carefully chosen so that they do not offend or insult anyone: *politically correct literature textbooks that include African and women writers* —**political correctness** *n.* [U]

po,litical 'prisoner *n.* [C] someone who is put in prison because s/he criticizes the government

po,litical 'science also **poli sci** *informal n.* [U] the study of politics and government

pol·i·ti·cian /,pɑlə'tɪʃən/ *n.* [C] someone who

works in politics, especially an elected member of the government

THESAURUS

president – someone who is elected to be the official leader of a country that does not have a king or queen
congressman/congresswoman – someone who is elected to be in Congress
senator – someone who is elected to be a member of the Senate
governor – someone who is elected to lead the government of a state
mayor – someone who is elected to lead the government of a town or city
→ GOVERNMENT

po·lit·i·cize /pə'lɪt̬ə,saɪz/ v. [T] to make a situation, position, or organization more political or more involved in politics: *The Olympic Games should not be politicized.* —**politicized** adj.

pol·i·tics /'pɑlətɪks/ n. **1** [U] ideas and activities relating to gaining and using power in a country, city, etc.: *an important figure in European politics* | *a debate about* ***local/national/international politics*** | *They like to* ***talk/discuss politics.*** **2** [U] the profession of being a politician: *Smith* ***went into politics*** *as a young man.* **3** [plural] the activities of people who are concerned with gaining personal advantage within a group: *Working at home frees you from* ***office politics.*** **4** [plural] someone's political beliefs and opinions: *I don't agree with her politics.*

pol·ka /'poʊlkə, 'poʊkə/ n. [C] a very quick simple dance for people dancing in pairs, or the music for this dance —**polka** v. [I]

'polka dot n. [C] one of a number of round spots that form a pattern, especially on cloth used for clothing: *a white dress with red polka dots* —**polka-dot** adj.: *a polka-dot scarf*

poll[1] /poʊl/ n. **1** [C] the process of finding out what people think about something by asking many people the same question, or the record of the result [➡ **survey**]: *a recent* ***opinion poll*** | *a* ***poll conducted/taken/done*** *by the New York Times*

THESAURUS

survey – a set of questions that you ask a large number of people in order to find out about their opinions and behavior: *According to a recent survey, most Americans think there is too much violence on television.*
questionnaire – a written set of questions about a particular subject that is given to a large number of people, in order to collect information: *Would you have a moment to fill out this questionnaire?*

2 the polls [plural] the voting in an election: *Voters will* ***go to the polls*** (=vote) *on Tuesday.*

poll[2] v. [T] to ask a lot of people the same questions in order to find out what they think about a subject: *35% of those polled had been on a diet recently.*

pol·len /'pɑlən/ n. [U] a powder produced by flowers, which is carried by the wind or insects to make other flowers of the same type produce seeds

pol·li·nate /'pɑlə,neɪt/ v. [T] to make a flower or plant produce seeds by giving it pollen: *flowers pollinated by bees* —**pollination** /,pɑlə'neɪʃən/ n. [U]

'polling place also **'polling ,station** n. [C] the place where you can go to vote in an election

poll·ster /'poʊlstɚ/ n. [C] someone who carries out a POLL (=asks questions to find out what people think about a particular subject)

pol·lut·ant /pə'lut⁊nt/ n. [C] a substance that makes air, water, soil, etc. dangerously dirty

pol·lute /pə'lut/ v. [I,T] to make air, water, soil, etc. dangerously dirty: *toxic waste that is* ***polluting*** *the* ***air/ocean/environment*** —**polluter** n. [C]

pollution

the result of pollution

pol·lut·ed /pə'lut̬ɪd/ adj. full of pollution: ***heavily/highly/badly polluted*** *air*

pol·lu·tion /pə'luʃən/ n. [U] **1** the process of polluting a place: *Toxic waste is a major cause of pollution.*

TOPIC

the greenhouse effect, **global warming**, **acid rain**, **deforestation**, **environmentally friendly**, **eco-friendly**, **recycle**, **biodegradable**, **organic**
→ see Topic box at ENVIRONMENT

2 substances that pollute a place: *a plan to reduce pollution*

po·lo /'poʊloʊ/ n. [U] an outdoor game played between two teams riding horses, who use long wooden hammers to hit a small ball → WATER POLO

'polo shirt n. [C] a shirt with short SLEEVES and a collar, usually made of cotton

pol·y·es·ter /'pɑli,ɛstɚ, ,pɑli'ɛstɚ/ n. [U] an artificial material used especially to make cloth: *a polyester suit*

pol·y·eth·yl·ene /,pɑli'ɛθə,lin/ n. [U] strong light plastic used for making bags, small containers, etc.

po·lyg·a·my /pə'lɪgəmi/ n. [U] *technical* the practice of having more than one husband or wife at the same time —**polygamous** adj. —**polygamist** n. [C]

pol·y·gon /'pɑli,gɑn/ n. [C] *technical* a flat shape with three or more sides

pol·y·graph /'pɑli,græf/ n. [C] *technical* a LIE DETECTOR: *The suspect later passed a* ***polygraph test.***

pol·y·mer /ˈpɑləmɚ/ *n.* [C] a chemical compound that has a simple structure of large MOLECULES

pol·yp /ˈpɑləp/ *n.* [C] a small LUMP that grows inside someone's body and is caused by an illness

pol·y·tech·nic /ˌpɑliˈtɛknɪk/ *n.* [C] a college where you can study technical or scientific subjects

pol·y·un·sat·u·rat·ed /ˌpɑliʌnˈsætʃəˌreɪt̬ɪd/ *adj.* polyunsaturated fats or oils come from vegetables and plants, and are considered to be better for your health than animal fats [➡ **saturated fat**]

pom·e·gran·ate /ˈpɑməˌgrænɪt/ *n.* [C] a round fruit with thick red skin and many juicy red seeds that you can eat

pomp /pɑmp/ *n.* [U] *formal* all the impressive clothes, decorations, music, etc. that are traditional for an important public ceremony

P

pom·pom /ˈpɑmpɑm/ **also** **pom·pon** /ˈpɑmpɑn/ *n.* [C] **1** a large round ball of loose plastic strings connected to a handle, used by CHEERLEADERS **2** a small wool ball used as a decoration on clothing, especially hats

pomp·ous /ˈpɑmpəs/ *adj. disapproving* trying to make people think you are important, especially by using a lot of formal words: *pompous politicians* —**pomposity** /pɑmˈpɑsət̬i/ *n.* [U]

pon·cho /ˈpɑntʃoʊ/ *n.* plural **ponchos** [C] a type of coat that is made from a single piece of thick cloth, with a hole in the middle for your head, and sometimes a HOOD (=cover for your head)

pond /pɑnd/ *n.* [C] a small area of fresh water that is smaller than a lake

pon·der /ˈpɑndɚ/ *v.* [I,T] *formal* to spend time thinking carefully and seriously about something: *Travers took a deep breath as he **pondered** the **question**.*

pon·der·ous /ˈpɑndərəs/ *adj.* **1** moving slowly or awkwardly because of being very big and heavy: *an elephant's ponderous walk* **2** boring and too serious: *His films are ponderous.*

pon·tiff /ˈpɑntɪf/ *n.* [C] *formal* the POPE

pon·tif·i·cate /pɑnˈtɪfəˌkeɪt/ *v.* [I] to give your opinion about something in a way that shows you think you are always right: *Anthony likes to **pontificate about** how wonderful capitalism is.*

pon·toon /pɑnˈtun/ *n.* [C] one of the floating metal containers that are attached to bridges, airplanes, etc. in order to make them float

po·ny¹ /ˈpoʊni/ *n.* plural **ponies** [C] a small horse

pony² *v.* past tense and past participle **ponied**, third person singular **ponies**

pony up (sth) *phr. v. informal* to pay for something: *Fans who pony up $34.95 will see a four-hour opera special.*

ˌPony Exˈpress *n.* [singular] a mail service in the 1860s that used horses and riders to carry the mail

po·ny·tail /ˈpoʊniˌteɪl/ *n.* [C] long hair that you tie together at the back of your head: *Chrissy pulled her hair back **in a ponytail**.* ➔ see picture at HAIR

pooch /putʃ/ *n.* [C] *informal* a dog

poo·dle /ˈpudl/ *n.* [C] a dog with thick curly hair

pooh-pooh /ˌpu ˈpu/ *v.* [T] *informal* to say that you think that an idea, suggestion, etc. is not very good: *At first they pooh-poohed the idea.*

pool¹ /pul/ *n.* **1 also swimming pool** [C] a structure that has been specially built and filled with water so that people can swim or play in it: *They have a nice pool in their backyard.* **2** [U] a game in which you use a stick to hit numbered balls into holes in the sides and corners of a table: *Let's **play/shoot** some **pool**.* **3 pool of blood/water/oil etc.** a small area of liquid on a surface: *Creighton lay there in a pool of blood.* **4 pool of light** a small area of light shining on something **5** [C] a small area of still water in the ground: *Mosquitoes breed in stagnant pools of water.* **6** [C] a group of people who are available to work or to do an activity when they are needed: *a **pool of** volunteers | a jury pool* **7** [C] a group of things or an amount of money that is owned or shared by a group of people: *the huge **pool of** money investors have put into the stockmarket*

pool² *v.* [T] to combine your money, ideas, skills, etc. with those of other people so that you can all use them: *If we **pool** our **resources**, we can start our own business.*

ˈpool hall *n.* [C] a building where people go to play pool

ˈpool ˌtable *n.* [C] a cloth-covered table with pockets at the corners and sides, used for playing pool

poop¹ /pup/ *n.* [singular, U] *spoken* solid waste from your BOWELS, or the act of passing waste: *dog poop*

poop² *v.* [I,T] *informal* to pass solid waste from your BOWELS

pooped /pupt/ **also** **ˌpooped ˈout** *adj. spoken* very tired: *I'm pooped!*

poop·er scoop·er /ˈpupɚ ˌskupɚ/ *n.* [C] *informal* a small SHOVEL and a container, used by dog owners for removing their dogs' solid waste from the streets

poor /pʊr, pɔr/ *adj.* **1** having very little money and not many possessions: *She comes from a poor family. | a poor country*

THESAURUS

needy – having very little food or money: *The program provides health care to needy families.*
destitute formal – having no money, no place to live, no food, etc.: *The Depression left many farmers completely destitute.*
impoverished formal – very poor: *an impoverished neighborhood in Chicago*
broke – not having any money for a period of time: *I'm broke and I need a job.*
disadvantaged – having social problems, such as a lack of money, that make it difficult to

succeed: *students from disadvantaged backgrounds*
underprivileged – poor and not having the advantages of most other people in society: *The center helps underprivileged children.*
deprived – not having the things that are considered necessary for a comfortable or happy life: *a deprived area in the inner city*

2 the poor people who are poor: *a charity that distributes food to the poor* **3** not as good as it could be or should be: *The soil in this part of the country is poor.* | *poor health* **4** [only before noun] *spoken* said in order to show pity for someone because s/he is unlucky, unhappy, etc.: *Poor Stacy – her mother's very sick.* | *The* ***poor thing*** *looks like she hasn't eaten in days.* **5** not good at doing something: *a poor student*

poor·ly /ˈpʊrli, ˈpɔr-/ *adv.* badly: *a poorly lit room*

pop[1] /pɑp/ *v.* past tense and past participle **popped**, present participle **popping** **1** [I,T] to suddenly make a short sound like a small explosion, or to make something do this: *Jody squeezed the* ***balloon*** *until it* ***popped***.

THESAURUS
break, **smash**, **shatter**, **crack**, **tear**, **snap**, **burst**
➔ see Thesaurus box at BREAK[1]

2 [I] *spoken* to go somewhere quickly, suddenly, or without planning: *I need to* ***pop into*** *the drug store for a second.* | *Maybe I'll just* ***pop in on*** *Terry* (=visit him for a short time). **3** [I] to come suddenly or without warning out of or away from something: *A button* ***popped off*** *my jacket.* | *The ball* ***popped out*** *of her hands and rolled under the sofa.* **4** [T] to cook POPCORN until it bursts open **5** [I] if your ears pop, you feel the pressure in them suddenly change, for example, when you go up in an airplane **6 pop the question** *informal* to ask someone to marry you: *Has Dan popped the question yet?* **7** [T] *informal* to hit someone: *If you say that again, I'll pop you.*

pop up *phr. v. informal* to happen or appear suddenly or without warning: *Her name keeps popping up in the newspapers.*

pop out *phr. v. informal* to say something suddenly without thinking about it first: *I didn't mean to say that – it just popped out.*

pop[2] *n.* **1 also ˈpop ˌmusic** [U] modern music that is popular with young people: *a pop concert*

THESAURUS
rock (music), **rock'n'roll**, **heavy metal**, **reggae**, **house (music)**, **hip-hop**, **rap (music)**, **jazz**, **classical (music)**, **country (music)**, **folk (music)**
➔ see Thesaurus box at MUSIC

2 [C usually singular] *old-fashioned* FATHER **3** [U] *informal* SOFT DRINK

THESAURUS
soft drink, **soda**, **soda pop**
➔ see Thesaurus box at SOFT DRINK

4 [C] a sudden short sound like a small explosion: *the pop of an air rifle* **5 pops** [U] CLASSICAL MUSIC that is known and liked even by people who do not usually like classical music: *the Boston Pops Orchestra*

pop·corn /ˈpɑpkɔrn/ *n.* [U] a type of corn that swells and bursts open when heated, usually eaten warm with butter and salt ➔ see picture on page A5

Pope /poʊp/ *n.* [C] the leader of the Roman Catholic Church: *the Pope's recent visit* | *Pope Paul VI*

pop·lar /ˈpɑplɚ/ *n.* [C] a very tall thin tree that grows very fast

ˌpop psyˈchology *n.* [U] the ways in which people's personal problems are dealt with on television or in books, but which are not considered scientific

pop·py /ˈpɑpi/ *n.* plural **poppies** [C] a brightly colored flower, usually red, with small black seeds

ˈpop quiz *n.* [C] a short test that is given without any warning in order to check that students have been studying

Pop·si·cle /ˈpɑpsɪkəl/ *n.* [C] *trademark* frozen fruit juice on a stick

pop·u·lace /ˈpɑpyələs/ *n.* [singular] *formal* the ordinary people living in a country

pop·u·lar /ˈpɑpyəlɚ/ *adj.* **1** liked by a lot of people: *His movies have become very popular.* | *the most popular kid in school* | *Tom is very* ***popular with*** *women.*

THESAURUS
bestseller – a book that a lot of people buy
blockbuster – a movie that a lot of people watch, especially an exciting movie
hit – a movie, song, play, etc. that a lot of people pay to see or listen to
craze/fad – a fashion, game, etc. that is very popular for a short time
cult – a movie or a performer that is very popular among a certain group of people: *cult movies*
be all the rage – to be very popular and fashionable: *Disco was all the rage in the 80s.*

2 shared, accepted, or done by a lot of people: *The party had managed to gain massive popular support.* | *Despite* ***popular opinion/belief*** (=what most people think), *not everybody in Fayette County is rich.* **3** relating to ordinary people, or intended for ordinary people: *Ramsay believes there's too much violence in American* ***popular culture*** (=TV, pop music, action films, etc.).

pop·u·lar·i·ty /ˌpɑpyəˈlærət̬i/ *n.* [U] the quality of being liked or supported by a large number of people: *the growing* ***popularity of*** *electronic music*

pop·u·lar·ize /ˈpɑpyələˌraɪz/ *v.* [T] to make

something well known and liked: *Hawking's books have helped popularize science.*

pop·u·lar·ly /ˈpɑpyələ̆li/ *adv.* by most people: *It's popularly believed that people need eight hours of sleep every night.*

pop·u·late /ˈpɑpyəˌleɪt/ *v.* [T] if an area is populated by a particular group of people, they live there: *a neighborhood that is* ***densely/heavily populated*** *by students* (=has a lot of students living there) | *a* ***sparsely populated*** *area* (=with few people)

pop·u·la·tion /ˌpɑpyəˈleɪʃən/ *n.* [C,U] **1** the number of people or animals living in a particular area, country, etc.: *What's the* ***population of*** *New York?* | *There was a* ***population explosion*** (=a sudden large increase in population) *between 1944 and 1964 in the U.S.* **2** all of the people who live in a particular area or share a particular condition: *Most of the population of Canada lives near the U.S. border.* | *Florida's large Hispanic population*

P

THESAURUS

people, the public, society, the human race, mankind, humankind
➔ see Thesaurus box at PEOPLE[1]

pop·u·lous /ˈpɑpyələs/ *adj. formal* having a large population: *the most populous country in Africa*

por·ce·lain /ˈpɔrsəlɪn/ *n.* [U] a hard shiny white substance that is used for making expensive plates, cups, etc., or objects made of this

porch /pɔrtʃ/ *n.* [C] a structure built onto a house at its front or back entrance, with a floor and roof but no walls

por·cu·pine /ˈpɔrkyəˌpaɪn/ *n.* [C] an animal with long, sharp, needle-like parts growing all over its back and sides

pore[1] /pɔr/ *n.* [C] one of the small holes in your skin or in a leaf that liquid can pass through

pore[2] *v.*

pore over sth *phr. v.* to read or look at something very carefully for a long time: *We spent all day poring over wedding magazines.*

pork /pɔrk/ *n.* [U] **1** the meat from pigs: *pork chops*

THESAURUS

meat, beef, veal, ham, bacon
➔ see Thesaurus box at MEAT

2 *slang disapproving* government money spent in a particular area in order to get political advantages

por·nog·ra·phy /pɔrˈnɑgrəfi/ **also porn** /pɔrn/ *n.* [U] magazines, movies, etc. that show sexual acts and images in a way that is intended to make people feel sexually excited —**pornographer** *n.* [C] —**pornographic** /ˌpɔrnəˈgræfɪk◂/ *adj.*

po·rous /ˈpɔrəs/ *adj.* allowing liquid, air, etc. to pass through slowly: *porous soil*

por·poise /ˈpɔrpəs/ *n.* [C] a large sea animal, similar to a DOLPHIN, that breathes air

por·ridge /ˈpɔrɪdʒ, ˈpɑ-/ *n.* [U] cooked OATMEAL

port /pɔrt/ *n.* **1** [C,U] a place where ships can be loaded and unloaded: *The ship was back* ***in port*** *after a week at sea.* **2** [C] a town or city with a HARBOR: *the port of Veracruz* **3** [C] a place on the outside of a computer where you can connect another piece of equipment, such as a PRINTER **4** [U] a strong sweet Portuguese wine **5** [U] the left side of a ship or aircraft when you are looking toward the front [➡ **starboard**]

portable

a portable TV

port·a·ble /ˈpɔrt̬əbəl/ *adj.* light and easily carried or moved: *a portable phone/computer* —**portable** *n.* [C]

por·tal /ˈpɔrt̬l/ *n.* [C] **1** a website that helps you find other websites **2** *literary* a large gate or entrance to a building

por·tend /pɔrˈtɛnd/ *v.* [T] *literary* to be a sign that something is going to happen, especially something bad: *strange events that portend some great disaster* —**portent** /ˈpɔrtɛnt/ *n.* [C]

por·ter /ˈpɔrt̬ə̆/ *n.* [C] **1** someone whose job is to carry travelers' bags at airports, hotels, etc. **2** someone whose job is to take care of the part of a train where people sleep

port·fo·li·o /pɔrtˈfoʊliˌoʊ/ *n.* plural **portfolios** [C] **1** a large flat case used especially for carrying pictures, documents, etc. **2** a collection of pictures or other pieces of work by an artist, photographer, etc.: *You'll need to submit a* ***portfolio of*** *your work along with your application.* **3** a collection of STOCKS owned by a particular person or company: *an investment portfolio*

port·hole /ˈpɔrthoʊl/ *n.* [C] a small window on the side of a ship or airplane

por·ti·co /ˈpɔrt̬ɪˌkoʊ/ *n.* plural **porticoes** or **porticos** [C] a covered entrance to a building, consisting of a roof supported by PILLARS

por·tion[1] /ˈpɔrʃən/ *n.* [C] **1** a part of something larger: *The news showed only a* ***portion of*** *the interview.* | *He sends a* ***large portion*** *of his salary home to Slovakia.* **2** an amount of food for one person, especially when served in a restaurant: *Do you have children's portions?* | *Everyone was given a small* ***portion of*** *rice and beans.* **3** a share of something such as blame or a duty: *Both drivers must bear a* ***portion of*** *the blame.*

portion[2] *v.*

portion sth ⇔ **out** *phr. v.* to divide something into parts and give them to several people

port·ly /ˈpɔrtli/ *adj. written* someone who is portly, especially an old man, is fat and round: *a portly gentleman*

por·trait /ˈpɔrtrɪt/ *n.* [C] **1** a painting, drawing, or photograph of a person: *a family portrait* ➔ see picture at PAINTING

THESAURUS
picture, **sketch**, **snapshot**, **cartoon**, **caricature**, **illustration**, **poster**
➔ see Thesaurus box at PICTURE[1]

2 a description of someone or something in a book, movie, etc.: *The movie is a* ***portrait of*** *life in Harlem in the 1940s.*

por·trai·ture /ˈpɔrtrɪtʃɚ/ *n.* [U] *formal* the art of painting or drawing pictures of people

por·tray /pɔrˈtreɪ, pɚ-/ *v.* past tense and past participle **portrayed**, third person singular **portrays** [T] **1 portray sb/sth as sth** to describe or show someone or something in a particular way, according to your opinion of him/her: *Each candidate portrayed himself as an enemy of big business.*

THESAURUS
call, **describe**, **label**, **brand**, **characterize**
➔ see Thesaurus box at CALL[1]

2 to describe or represent something or someone: *a movie that portrays the life of Charlie Chaplin* **3** to act the part of a character in a play: *Robin Williams portrayed Peter Pan in the movie.*

por·tray·al /pɔrˈtreɪəl, pɚ-/ *n.* [C,U] the way someone or something is described or shown in a book, film, play, etc.: *an* ***accurate portrayal*** *of pioneer life*

Por·tu·guese[1] /ˌpɔrtʃəˈgiz◂/ *adj.* relating to or coming from Portugal

Portuguese[2] *n.* **1** [U] the language of Portugal, Brazil, and some other countries **2 the Portuguese** [plural] the people of Portugal

pose[1] /poʊz/ *v.* **1 pose a problem/threat/challenge etc.** to exist in a way that may cause a problem, danger, difficulty, etc.: *Nuclear waste* ***poses*** *a threat* ***to*** *the environment.* **2** [I,T] to sit or stand in a particular position in order to be photographed or painted, or to make someone do this: *The astronauts* ***posed for*** *pictures near the shuttle.* **3 pose a question** to ask a question that needs to be thought about carefully: *Nielsen's essay poses some tough questions.* **4 pose as sb** to pretend to be someone else in order to deceive people: *The thief got in by posing as a repairman.*

pose[2] *n.* [C] the position in which someone deliberately stands or sits, especially in a painting or photograph: *She* ***struck a pose*** (=stood or sat in a particular position) *with her head to one side.*

pos·er /ˈpoʊzɚ/ *n.* [C] someone who pretends to have a quality or social position s/he does not have, in order to seem impressive to other people

posh /pɑʃ/ *adj.* expensive and used by rich people: *a posh hotel*

THESAURUS
expensive, **high**, **pricey**, **overpriced**, **extortionate**, **astronomical**, **exorbitant**
➔ see Thesaurus box at EXPENSIVE

po·si·tion[1] /pəˈzɪʃən/ *n.*
1 STANDING/SITTING [C] the way someone stands, sits, or lies, or the direction in which an object is pointing: *You should be* ***in*** *a comfortable* ***position*** *when driving.* | *This exercise is done in* ***a sitting/standing/kneeling position.***
2 SITUATION [C usually singular] the situation that someone or something is in: *The company is in a dangerous financial position right now.* | *I'm not sure what I would do if I were* ***in*** *your* ***position.*** | *I'm afraid I'm* ***not in a position to*** *help you* (=do not have the power or money to help you).
3 OPINION [C] an opinion about a particular subject: *The governor has changed his* ***position on*** *abortion.*

THESAURUS
opinion, **view**, **point of view**, **attitude**
➔ see Thesaurus box at OPINION

4 PLACE [C,U] the place where someone or something is, in relation to other things: *Help me put the furniture back* ***in position.*** | *The army took up* ***strategic positions*** *around the capital.*

THESAURUS
place, **spot**, **location**
➔ see Thesaurus box at PLACE[1]

5 JOB [C] a job: *He decided to give up his* ***position as*** *coach of the football team.*

THESAURUS

Describing types of positions
senior – used about someone who has an important position in a company or organization: *a senior executive*
chief – used about someone who has the most important or one of the most important positions in a company or organization, used especially in job titles: *the company's chief financial officer*
high-ranking – used about someone who has a high position in an organization such as the police, the army, or the government: *high-ranking military officers*
top – used about someone who is in a very high position in a large company or organization, or someone in an important profession, for example a lawyer or a doctor, who is very successful in his/her job: *the top executives of some of the country's biggest corporations* | *one of the agency's top lawyers*
junior – used about someone who does not have an important position or who has less experience than someone doing the same job: *the junior senator from Mississippi*

P

> **assistant** – an assistant manager, director, editor, etc. has a position just below a manager, etc.: *the store's assistant manager*

6 RANK [C] the level or rank someone has in a society or organization: *Ask someone in a **position of authority**. | a study on the **position of** minorities **in** our society*
7 SPORTS [C] the area where someone plays in a sport, or the type of actions s/he is responsible for doing in a game: *"What **position** do you **play**?" "Second base."*
8 RACE/COMPETITION [C,U] the place of someone or something in a race or competition in relation to the other people or things [= **place**]: *Paldi has moved into **first/second/third etc. position**.*

position² *v.* [T] to put something or someone in a particular place: *Police positioned themselves around the bank.*

P

pos·i·tive¹ /ˈpɑzət̬ɪv/ *adj.* **1** [not before noun] very sure that something is right or true: *"Are you sure you don't want a drink?" "Positive." | I'm **positive that** I told her to meet us here at 2.* **2** hopeful and confident, and thinking about what is good in a situation rather than what is bad [≠ **negative**]: *The president sounded very **positive about** the state of the economy. | I always try to have a **positive attitude**.* **3** good or useful [≠ **negative**]: *At least **something positive** has come out of the situation. | Living abroad has been **a positive experience** for Jim.* **4** expressing support, agreement, or approval [≠ **negative**]: *So far, we've had mostly positive reactions to the new show.* **5** a medical or scientific test that is positive shows signs of what is being looked for [≠ **negative**]: *He **tested positive** for drugs. | Her pregnancy test **came back/up/out positive**.* **6** *technical* a positive number or quantity is higher than zero. (+) is the positive sign [≠ **negative**] **7** *technical* having the type of electrical charge that is carried by PROTONS, shown by a (+) sign on a BATTERY [≠ **negative**]

positive² *n.* [C] a quality or feature that is good or useful [≠ **negative**]: *You can find positives in any situation.*

pos·i·tive·ly /ˈpɑzət̬ɪvli, ˌpɑzəˈtɪvli◂/ *adv.* **1** *informal* used in order to emphasize what you are saying: *Some patients positively enjoy being in the hospital. | This is positively the last time I'm going to say this.* **2** in a way that shows you agree with something and want it to succeed: *News of the changes was received positively.* **3** in a way that leaves no doubt: *Don't tell anyone unless you're positively certain you can trust them.* → **think positively** at THINK

pos·se /ˈpɑsi/ *n.* [C] **1** a group of men gathered together in past times by a SHERIFF (=local law officer) to help catch criminals **2** *informal* someone's group of friends – used especially by young people

pos·sess /pəˈzɛs/ *v.* [T] **1** *formal* to own or have something: *Neither of them possessed a credit card. | Bauer was charged with possessing illegal weapons.*

> **THESAURUS**
>
> **own, have, belong to**
> → see Thesaurus box at OWN²

2 what possessed sb (to do sth)? *spoken* said when you cannot understand why someone did something stupid: *What possessed you to buy such an expensive gift?* —**possessor** *n.* [C]

pos·sessed /pəˈzɛst/ *adj.* controlled by an evil spirit

pos·ses·sion /pəˈzɛʃən/ *n.* **1** [C usually plural] something that you own [= **belongings**]: *When they left, they had to sell most of their possessions.* **2** [U] *formal* the state of having or owning something: *He was found **in possession of** illegal drugs. | China **took possession of** Hong Kong in 1997.*

pos·ses·sive¹ /pəˈzɛsɪv/ *adj.* **1** *disapproving* wanting someone to have feelings of love or friendship only for you: *I love Dave, but he's very possessive.* **2** unwilling to let other people use something you own: *As a child, she was very **possessive of** her toys.*

possessive² *n.* **the possessive** *technical* in grammar, a word such as "my," "its," "their," etc., used in order to show that one thing or person belongs to another thing or person, or is related to that thing or person —**possessive** *adj.*: *a possessive adjective/pronoun*

pos·si·bil·i·ty /ˌpɑsəˈbɪlət̬i/ *n.* plural **possibilities** **1** [C,U] if there is a possibility that something is true or that something will happen, it might be true or it might happen: *There's always the **possibility (that)** we may all lose our jobs. | There's a **strong possibility** he won't be able to play on Sunday. | a **possibility of** getting a scholarship* **2** [C] an opportunity to do something, or something that can be done or tried: *We want to **explore** all the **possibilities**. | the almost endless **possibilities for** growth*

pos·si·ble /ˈpɑsəbəl/ *adj.* **1 as long/much/soon etc. as possible** as long, soon, etc. as you can: *They need the tapes as quickly as possible. | Keep him busy for as long as possible.* **2** able to be done or likely to happen, exist, or be true [➡ **impossible**]: *Icy conditions are possible along the coast. | **Is it possible to** use the program on a Macintosh? | Computer technology now **makes it possible** for people to work at home. | This is the **best/worst possible** result* (=it can be no better or worse). **3 would it be possible (for sb) to do sth?** *spoken* said when asking politely if you can do or have something: *Would it be possible to exchange these gloves?* **4 whenever/wherever possible** every time you have an opportunity to do something: *She visits her grandmother whenever possible.*

pos·si·bly /ˈpɑsəbli/ *adv.* **1** used when saying

that something may be true or likely [= **perhaps**]: *The trial will take place soon, possibly next week.* | *This new drug could* ***quite possibly*** (=very likely) *save thousands of lives.* **2** used with MODAL VERBS, especially "can" and "could," to emphasize that something is or is not possible: *I couldn't possibly eat all that!* | *We did everything we possibly could to help them.* **3 could/can you possibly...?** *spoken* said when politely asking someone to do something: *Could you possibly turn the radio down?*

pos·sum /ˈpɑsəm/ *n.* [C] *informal* an OPOSSUM

post¹ /poʊst/ *n.* [C] **1** a strong upright piece of wood, metal, etc. that is set into the ground, especially to support something: *a fence post* | *the goal posts* **2** *formal* an important job, especially in the government or military: *She decided to leave her post at the Justice Department.* **3** the place where a soldier, guard, etc. is expected to be in order to do his or her job: *The guards cannot* ***leave*** *their* ***posts***. **4** a military BASE

post² *v.* [T] **1 a)** to put a public notice about something on a wall or BULLETIN BOARD: *They've posted warning signs on the gate.* **b)** to put a message or computer document on the Internet so that other people can see it: *FBI agents have posted a message on the Internet describing the suspect.* **2** if someone who works for the government or military is posted somewhere, he or she is sent to work there, usually for several years: *His regiment have been* ***posted to*** *Germany.* **3** if a company posts its profits, sales, losses, etc., it records the money gained or lost in its accounts: *In the final quarter, the company posted $12.4 million in earnings.*

post·age /ˈpoʊstɪdʒ/ *n.* [U] the money charged for sending a letter, package, etc. by mail: *Please add $3.95 for* ***postage and handling*** (=the charge for packing and sending something you have bought).

ˈpostage stamp *n.* [C] *formal* a STAMP

post·al /ˈpoʊstl/ *adj.* relating to the official mail system that takes letters from one place to another: *postal workers*

ˈpostal ˌservice *n.* **the postal service** the public service for carrying letters, packages, etc. from one part of the country to another

post·card /ˈpoʊstkɑrd/ *n.* [C] a card, often with a picture on the front, that can be sent in the mail without an envelope: ***Send*** *me* ***a postcard*** *while you're away.*

post·date /ˌpoʊstˈdeɪt/ *v.* [T] to write a check with a date that is later than the actual date, so that it cannot be used until that time

post·er /ˈpoʊstɚ/ *n.* [C] a large printed notice, picture, etc. used in order to advertise something or as a decoration: *a poster of Bob Marley*

THESAURUS

picture, illustration, advertisement, billboard
→ see Thesaurus box at PICTURE¹, ADVERTISEMENT

pos·te·ri·or /pɑˈstɪriɚ, poʊ-/ *n.* [C] *humorous* the part of the body you sit on

pos·ter·i·ty /pɑˈstɛrəṭi/ *n.* [U] all the people in the future who will be alive after you are dead: *I'm saving these pictures* ***for posterity***.

post·grad·u·ate /ˌpoʊstˈgrædʒuɪt/ *n.* [C] someone who is studying to obtain a higher degree after college —**postgraduate** *adj.*: *a postgraduate scholarship*

post·hu·mous /ˈpɑstʃəməs/ *adj.* happening after someone's death: *a posthumous award* —**posthumously** *adv.*

ˈPost-it *n.* [C] *trademark* a small piece of paper that sticks to things, used for leaving notes for people

post·man /ˈpoʊstmən/ *n.* plural **postmen** /-mən/ [C] a MAILMAN

post·mark /ˈpoʊstmɑrk/ *n.* [C] an official mark made on a letter, package, etc. that shows the place and time it was sent —**postmark** *v.* [T] *The card is postmarked Dec. 2.*

post·mas·ter /ˈpoʊstˌmæstɚ/ *n.* [C] the person in charge of a post office

post·mor·tem /ˌpoʊstˈmɔrṭəm/ *n.* [C] an examination of a dead body to discover why the person died

ˈpost ˌoffice *n.* [C] a place where you can buy stamps, and send letters, packages, etc.

ˈpost office ˌbox *n.* [C] a P.O. BOX

post·par·tum /ˌpoʊstˈpɑrṭəm◂/ *adj. technical* relating to the time just after a woman has a baby: *postpartum depression*

post·pone /poʊstˈpoʊn/ *v.* [T] to change an event to a later time or date [➡ **cancel**]: *The game was postponed because of rain.* —**postponement** *n.* [C,U]

THESAURUS

delay, put off, procrastinate
→ see Thesaurus box at DELAY¹

post·script /ˈpoʊstˌskrɪpt/ *n.* [C] P.S.

pos·tu·late /ˈpɑstʃəˌleɪt/ *v.* [T] *formal* to suggest that something might have happened or might be true

pos·ture /ˈpɑstʃɚ/ *n.* [C,U] the position you hold your body in when you sit or stand: *Poor posture can lead to back trouble.*

post·war /ˈpoʊstwɔr/ *adj.* [only before noun] happening or existing after a war: *the postwar years* | *postwar prosperity*

po·sy /ˈpoʊzi/ *n.* plural **posies** [C] *literary* a small BUNCH of flowers

pot¹ /pɑt/ *n.* **1** [C] a container used for cooking, that is round, deep, and usually made of metal, or the amount this container holds [➡ **pan, saucepan, jar**]: *pots and pans* | *a* ***pot of*** *soup* **2** [C] a container with a handle and a small tube for pouring, used for making coffee or tea [➡ **jug**]: *a coffee pot* **3** [C] a container for a plant [= **flowerpot**]: *The plant needs a new pot.* **4 go to pot** *informal* if an organization or a place goes to pot, its condition becomes worse because no one takes care of it: *The university has gone to pot since we were there.* **5 the pot** *informal* all the money that people have risked in a game of cards **6** *informal* [U] MARIJUANA

pot² *v.* [T] to put a plant in a pot filled with soil

po·tas·si·um /pəˈtæsiəm/ *n.* [U] a silver-white soft metal that is used in making soaps and FERTILIZERS

po·ta·to /pəˈteɪt̬oʊ, -t̬ə/ *n.* plural **potatoes** [C,U] a hard round white root with a brown, red, or pale yellow skin, cooked and eaten as a vegetable [➡ **sweet potato**]: ***mashed/baked/fried/boiled potatoes*** ➔ see picture at VEGETABLE

po'tato chip *n.* [C] one of many thin hard pieces of potato that have been cooked in oil, and that are sold in packages: *a **bag of potato chips***

P

pot·bel·ly /ˈpɑt˺ˌbɛli/ *n.* plural **potbellies** [C] a large round stomach that sticks out —**potbellied** *adj.*

po·ten·cy /ˈpoʊt˺nsi/ *n.* [U] **1** the strength of the effect of a drug, medicine, alcohol, etc. on your mind or body: *high-potency vitamins* **2** a man's ability to have sex

po·tent /ˈpoʊt˺nt/ *adj.* powerful and effective: *a potent weapons system* | *potent drugs*

po·ten·tial¹ /pəˈtɛnʃəl/ *adj.* likely to develop into a particular type of person or thing in the future: *Brush regularly and avoid potential problems with your teeth.* | ***potential customers/buyers***

potential² *n.* **1** [singular,U] the possibility that something will develop or happen in a particular way: *There's **a potential for** conflict in the area.* | *It hasn't lived up to its potential.* **2** [U] a natural ability that could develop to make you very good at something: *She **has/shows potential** as a singer.*

po·ten·tial·ly /pəˈtɛnʃəli/ *adv.* something that is potentially dangerous, useful, etc. is not dangerous, etc. now, but may become so in the future: *a potentially embarrassing situation* | *a potentially fatal disease* (=one that could kill you)

pot·hold·er /ˈpɑtˌhoʊldɚ/ *n.* [C] a piece of thick material used for holding hot cooking pans

pot·hole /ˈpɑthoʊl/ *n.* [C] a hole in the surface of a road that makes driving difficult

po·tion /ˈpoʊʃən/ *n.* [C] *literary* a drink intended to have a special or magic effect on the person who drinks it: *a love potion*

pot·luck¹ /ˌpɑtˈlʌk◂/ *n.* **take potluck** *informal* to choose something without knowing very much about it: *Nobody knew about any good restaurants, so we took potluck.*

potluck² *adj.* **a potluck meal/dinner etc.** a meal in which everyone who is invited brings something to eat

ˌpot ˈpie *n.* [C] meat and vegetables covered with PASTRY and baked in a deep dish: *chicken pot pie*

pot·pour·ri /ˌpoʊpʊˈri/ *n.* [U] a mixture of dried flowers and leaves kept in a bowl to make a room smell nice

pot·ter·y /ˈpɑt̬əri/ *n.* [U] **1** the activity of making objects out of baked clay: *a pottery class*

> **THESAURUS**
>
> **painting**, **drawing**, **photography**, **sculpture**, **ceramics**
> ➔ see Thesaurus box at ART

2 objects made out of baked clay: *Native American pottery* —**potter** *n.* [C]

pot·ty /ˈpɑt̬i/ *n.* plural **potties** [C] *spoken* a word meaning a toilet, used when speaking to children

pouch /paʊtʃ/ *n.* [C] **1** a small leather or cloth bag that you can keep things in **2** a pocket of skin on the stomach that MARSUPIALS keep their babies in ➔ see picture on page A2

poul·try /ˈpoʊltri/ *n.* [U] birds such as chickens that are kept on farms for supplying eggs and meat, or the meat from these birds

pounce /paʊns/ *v.* [I] to suddenly jump on a person or animal after waiting to catch him, her, or it: *He **pounced on** my back, forcing me to the ground.*

pounce on sb/sth *phr. v.* to criticize someone's mistakes or ideas very quickly and eagerly: *Republicans quickly pounced on the president's proposal.*

pounce

pound¹ /paʊnd/ *n.* [C] **1** *written abbreviation* **lb** a unit for measuring weight, equal to 16 OUNCES or 453.6 grams: *a **pound of** apples* | *Jim **weighs** 175 **pounds**.* | *She's **lost/gained** 10 **pounds** this year* (=her weight has gone down or up by 10 pounds). **2 the pound** a place where lost dogs and cats are kept until the owner claims them **3** the standard unit of money in the U.K. and some other countries: *a ten-pound note*

pound² *v.* **1** [I,T] to hit something several times to make a lot of noise, damage it, make it lie flat, etc.: *Thomas **pounded on** the desk with his fist.* | *The man suddenly began **pounding** his head **against** the wall.* | *The boys pounded the bottles with their sticks until they had all broken.*

> **THESAURUS**
>
> **hit**, **punch**, **slap**, **beat**, **smack**, **whack**, **strike**, **bang**, **knock**, **tap**, **rap**, **hammer**
> ➔ see Thesaurus box at HIT¹

2 [T] to attack a place continuously for a long time with bombs: *Enemy guns pounded the city until morning.* **3** [I] if your heart pounds, it beats very quickly **4** [I] to walk or run quickly with heavy loud steps: *I heard the sound of heavy boots pounding on the floor.*

pound cake *n.* [C] a heavy cake made from flour, sugar, eggs, and butter

pour /pɔr/ *v.* **1** [T] to make a liquid or a substance such as salt or sand flow out of or into something: *She poured coffee for everyone.* | *Could you pour me a glass of lemonade, please?* **2** [I] to rain heavily without stopping: *It's been pouring all afternoon.* **3** [I] to flow quickly and in large amounts: *Fuel **poured out of** the plane.*

THESAURUS

flow – to move in a steady continuous stream: *This is the place where the river flows into the sea.*
drip – to produce small drops of liquid, or to fall in drops: *Water dripped onto the floor.*
leak – if a liquid leaks, it passes through a hole or crack: *Oil leaked from the damaged tanker.*
ooze – to flow from something very slowly: *Blood oozed through the bandages.*
gush – to flow or pour out quickly in large quantities: *Water gushed from the fountain.*
spurt – to flow out suddenly with a lot of force: *Blood spurted from the wound.*
run – to flow: *Tears ran down her cheeks.*
come out – to pour out of a container, place, etc.: *I turned on the faucet, but no water came out.*

4 [I] if people or things pour into or out of a place, a lot of them arrive or leave at the same time: *Letters are **pouring in** from people all over the state.* | *People **poured out of** their houses into the streets.* **5 pour money/aid etc. into sth** to invest a lot of money in something over a period of time in order to make it successful: *Thomas has poured thousands of dollars into his shop.*

pour sth ⇔ **out** *phr. v.* to tell someone everything about your thoughts, feelings, etc.: *Sonia **poured out** all her frustrations **to** Val.*

pout /paʊt/ *v.* [I,T] to push out your lower lip because you are annoyed, or in order to look sexually attractive: *Stop pouting and eat your dinner.* —**pout** *n.* [C]

pov·er·ty /ˈpɑvəṭi/ *n.* **1** [U] the situation or experience of being poor: *families **living in poverty*** | *I was shocked by the **abject/extreme poverty** that I saw.* **2 the poverty line/level** the income below which someone is officially considered to be very poor and in need of help: *Fifteen percent of the city's residents live **below the poverty level**.*

ˈpoverty-ˌstricken *adj.* extremely poor: *a poverty-stricken neighborhood*

pow·der¹ /ˈpaʊdə/ *n.* [C,U] a dry substance in the form of very small grains: *talcum powder* | *baking powder*

powder² *v.* [T] **1** to put powder on your skin **2 powder your nose** a phrase meaning to go to the toilet, used by women in order to be polite

pow·dered /ˈpaʊdəd/ *adj.* produced or sold in the form of powder: *powdered milk*

ˈpowder room *n.* [C] *old-fashioned* a polite phrase meaning a women's public toilet

pow·der·y /ˈpaʊdəri/ *adj.* like powder or easily broken into powder: *powdery snow*

pow·er¹ /ˈpaʊə/ *n.*

1 CONTROL SB/STH [U] the ability or right to control people or events [➡ **powerful**, **powerless**]: *We all felt that the chairman had too much power.* | *The new law gives the chancellor complete **power over** the city's schools.* | ***the power of** the media*

2 POLITICAL [U] political control of a country or government: *The current leader has been **in power** for ten years.* | *He **came to power*** (=began to control the country) *after the revolution.*

3 ENERGY [U] energy such as electricity that can be used to make a machine, car, etc. work: *The plane **lost power** and had to make an emergency landing.* | *The storm caused a **power failure/cut*** (=a time when there is no electricity) *in our area.* | *electricity produced by **nuclear/solar/wind power***

4 AUTHORITY [C,U] the legal right or authority to do something: *Congress has the **power to** declare war.* | *Only the police have the **power of** arrest.*

5 COUNTRY [C] a country that is very strong and important: *Germany is a major **industrial power** in Europe.* | *a meeting of **world powers*** (=the strongest countries in the world)

THESAURUS

country, **nation**, **state**, **land**
➔ see Thesaurus box at COUNTRY¹

6 PHYSICAL [U] the physical strength of something such as an explosion, natural force, or animal: *The **power of** the eruption blew away the whole mountainside.*

THESAURUS

force, **strength**
➔ see Thesaurus box at FORCE¹

7 NATURAL ABILITY [C,U] a natural or special ability to do something: *the **power of** sight/speech* | *She has the **power to** make an audience laugh or cry.*

8 do everything in your power to do everything that you are able or allowed to do: *I did everything in my power to save her.*

9 a power struggle a situation in which groups or leaders try to defeat each other and get complete control

10 earning/purchasing etc. power the ability to earn money, buy things, etc.: *the purchasing power of middle-class teenagers*

11 be in sb's power to be in a situation in which someone has control over you

12 the powers that be *informal* the people who have positions of authority, and whose decisions affect your life: *The hardest part will be persuading the powers that be at City Hall to agree.*

13 to the power of 3/4/5 etc. *technical* if a

number is increased to the power of three, four, five, etc., it is multiplied by itself three, four, five, etc. times

power² *v.* **1 solar-powered/nuclear-powered etc.** working or moving by means of , the sun, etc.: *a battery-powered flashlight* **2** [T] to supply power to a vehicle or machine: *a car* ***powered by*** *solar energy* **3** [I,T] to do something quickly and with a lot of strength: *North Carolina* ***powered*** *its way* ***through*** *the tournament.*

power sth ⇔ **up** *phr. v.* to make a machine start working: *Never move a computer while it is powered up.*

'power base *n.* [C] the group of people in a particular area that supports a politician or leader

pow·er·boat /'paʊɚˌboʊt/ *n.* [C] a boat with a powerful engine that is used for racing

P

pow·er·ful /'paʊɚfəl/ *adj.* **1** able to control and influence events and other people's actions: *a meeting of the world's most powerful leaders* | *the most powerful political party in the country*

THESAURUS

influential – having a lot of power to influence what happens: *a meeting of influential business leaders*
strong – having a lot of power, influence, or ability: *He is a strong voice in the state assembly.*
dominant – more powerful than other people or groups, and able to control what happens: *England was once the dominant power in the world.*

2 having a lot of power, strength, or force: *a powerful engine* | *a powerful man* | *a powerful explosion* **3** having a strong effect on someone's feelings or ideas: *a powerful speech* | *a* ***powerful argument*** *against eating meat* **4** having a strong effect on your body: *a powerful drug/medicine* —**powerfully** *adv.*

pow·er·house /'paʊɚˌhaʊs/ *n.* [C] *informal* **1** a country, company, organization, etc. that has a lot of power or influence **2** someone who has a lot of energy

pow·er·less /'paʊɚlɪs/ *adj.* unable to stop or control something because you do not have the power, strength, or right to do so: *The small group of soldiers was* ***powerless to*** *stop the attack.* —**powerlessness** *n.* [U]

'power line *n.* [C] a large wire carrying electricity above or under the ground

ˌpower of at'torney *n.* [C,U] *law* the legal right to do things for someone else in his/her business or personal life, or the document that gives this right

'power plant also **'power ˌstation** *n.* [C] a building where electricity is produced to supply a large area

'power ˌsteering *n.* [U] a special system that makes it easier for the driver of a vehicle to STEER (=change the direction of the vehicle)

'power tool *n.* [C] a tool that works by using electricity

pow·wow /'paʊwaʊ/ *n.* [C] **1** *humorous* a meeting or discussion **2** a meeting or council of Native American tribes

pp. the written abbreviation of **pages**: *Read pp. 20–35.*

PR *n.* **1** [U] PUBLIC RELATIONS **2** the written abbreviation of Puerto Rico

prac·ti·ca·ble /'præktɪkəbəl/ *adj. formal* possible in a particular situation: *The only practicable course of action is to sell the company.*

prac·ti·cal /'præktɪkəl/ *adj.* **1** relating to real situations and events rather than ideas: *Do you have a lot of* ***practical experience*** *as a mechanic?* | *I deal with* ***practical matters,*** *like finding people places to stay.* **2** practical plans, methods, etc. are likely to succeed or be effective: *Is that a practical solution to the problem?* | *Treganowan's book gives* ***practical advice*** *for keeping your car on the road.* **3** a practical person is good at dealing with problems and making decisions based on what is possible and what will really work: *Be practical – at least wait for the storm to pass.* **4** useful, or appropriate for a particular purpose: *practical gifts, such as clothes* | *a practical car for a family* **5 for all practical purposes** used in order to describe what the real effect of a situation is: *For all practical purposes, the election is over* (=we already know who the winner is).

prac·ti·cal·i·ty /ˌpræktɪ'kæləṭi/ *n.* **1 practicalities** [plural] the real facts of a situation, rather than ideas about how it might be: *the* ***practicalities of*** *rearing children* **2** [U] how appropriate something is, and whether it will work: *You need to think about comfort and practicality when choosing walking shoes.*

ˌpractical 'joke *n.* [C] a trick that is intended to surprise someone and make other people laugh —**practical joker** *n.* [C]

prac·ti·cally /'præktɪkli/ *adv.* **1** *spoken* almost: *Practically everyone was there.* | *She practically jumped out of her chair.* | *I've read* ***practically all*** *of his books.* **2** in a sensible way: *Vasko just doesn't think practically.*

prac·tice¹ /'præktɪs/ *n.*

1 SKILL [U] **a)** regular activity that you do in order to improve a skill or ability: *It* ***takes a lot of practice*** *to be a good piano player.* | *Your English will improve* ***with practice.*** **b)** [C,U] the period of time in which you do this: ***football/choir etc. practice***

2 STH THAT IS USUALLY DONE [C,U] **a)** something that people do often and in a particular way: *unsafe sexual practices* | *It's* ***common/standard/normal practice*** *to do the payroll in this way.* **b)** something that you do often because of your religion or your society's tradition [**= custom**]: ***the practice of*** *kissing someone as a greeting*

3 in practice used in order to describe what the

real situation is rather than what seems to be true: *Annette is the head of the company, but in practice Sue runs everything.*
4 DOCTOR/LAWYER [C] the work of a doctor or lawyer, or the place where s/he works: *She has a successful* ***medical/legal practice****.*
5 be out of practice to be unable to do something well because you have not done it for a long time: *I'd like to sing with you, but I'm really out of practice.*
6 put sth into practice if you put an idea, plan, etc. into practice, you start to use it and see if it is effective: *Now's your chance to put the skills you've learned into practice.*

practice² *v.* **1** [I,T] to do an activity regularly to improve your skill or ability: *Gail practices the piano more than an hour every day.* | *The Giants spent the afternoon* ***practicing for*** *their game on Sunday.*

THESAURUS

rehearse – to practice something such as a play or concert before giving a public performance: *The band was rehearsing for the show that night.*
work on sth – to practice a skill, musical instrument, etc. in order to improve: *Jessie has been working on her tennis serve.*
train – to prepare for a sports event by exercising and practicing: *Olympic swimmers train for hours every day.*
drill – to teach people something by making them repeat the same exercise, lesson, etc. many times: *The program allows you to drill yourself on grammar, vocabulary, and dictation.*

2 [I,T] to work as a doctor or lawyer: *Bill is* ***practicing law/medicine*** *in Ohio now.* **3** [T] to do an activity as a habit, or to live according to the rules of a religion: *The posters encourage young people to practice safe sex.*

prac·ticed /ˈpræktɪst/ *adj.* good at doing something because you have done it many times before: *a practiced pilot*

prac·tic·ing /ˈpræktɪsɪŋ/ *adj.* **1 a practicing Catholic/Jew/Muslim etc.** someone who obeys the rules of a particular religion

THESAURUS

religious, devout
➔ see Thesaurus box at RELIGIOUS

2 a practicing doctor/lawyer/architect etc. someone who is working as a doctor, lawyer, etc.

prac·ti·tion·er /prækˈtɪʃənɚ/ *n.* [C] *formal* someone who is trained to do a particular type of work that involves a lot of skill: *a tax practitioner* | *a medical practitioner*

prag·mat·ic /prægˈmæṭɪk/ *adj.* dealing with problems in a sensible practical way, instead of strictly following a set of ideas: *The diet gives you pragmatic suggestions for eating healthily.*

prag·ma·tism /ˈprægməˌtɪzəm/ *n.* [U] a tendency to deal with problems in a pragmatic way —**pragmatist** *n.* [C]

prai·rie /ˈprɛri/ *n.* [C] a large area of flat land in North America that is covered in grass

ˈprairie dog *n.* [C] a North American animal with a short tail that lives in holes on a prairie

praise¹ /preɪz/ *v.* [T] **1** to say publicly that someone has done something well or that you admire him/her: *Mr. Bonner* ***praised*** *Jill* ***for*** *the quality of her work.* | *a* ***highly praised*** *speech*

THESAURUS

congratulate – to tell someone that you are happy that they have achieved something
flatter – to say nice things about someone, sometimes when you do not really mean it, often in order to get something you want
compliment sb/pay sb a compliment – to say something nice to someone in order to praise them

2 to give thanks or honor to God

praise² *n.* [U] **1** words that you say or write to praise someone or something: *The papers* ***were full of praise for*** *the quick actions of the fire department.* | *Teachers need to* ***give*** *plenty of* ***praise*** *and encouragement to students.* **2** an expression of respect or thanks to God: *Let us give praise unto the Lord.*

praise·wor·thy /ˈpreɪzˌwɚði/ *adj. formal* deserving praise

prance /præns/ *v.* [I] *disapproving* to walk or dance with high steps or large movements in a way that makes people notice you: *He started* ***prancing around*** *in front of the video camera.*

prank /præŋk/ *n.* [C] a trick that is intended to make someone look silly: *Chris and Keith love to* ***play/pull pranks*** *on each other.*

prank·ster /ˈpræŋkstɚ/ *n.* [C] someone who plays pranks on people

prawn /prɔn/ *n.* [C] a sea animal like a large SHRIMP that is used for food

pray /preɪ/ *v.* [I,T] **1** to speak to a god or gods in order to ask for help or give thanks: *You don't have to go to church to pray.* | *people* ***praying for*** *peace at the Wailing Wall* | *She got down on her knees and* ***prayed to*** *God.* **2** to wish or hope for something very strongly: *We're* ***praying for*** *good weather tomorrow.* | *I'm just* ***praying that*** *I graduate in time.*

prayer /prɛr/ *n.* **1** [C] words that you say when praying to a god or gods: *I closed my eyes and* ***said*** *a* ***prayer****.* | *Our thoughts and prayers go out to the victims.* | *a* ***prayer for*** *the dead* **2** [U] the act or regular habit of praying: *a time of prayer* | *They bowed their heads* ***in prayer****.* **3 not have a prayer** *informal* to have no chance of succeeding: *The Seahawks* ***don't have a prayer of*** *winning.*

preach /pritʃ/ *v.* **1** [I,T] to give a speech, usually in a church, about a religious subject: *The minister*

***preaches to** large crowds every Sunday.* **2** [T] to talk about how good or important something is and to try to persuade other people to do or accept it: *He's always preaching **the value/virtue/gospel etc. of** hard work.* **3** [I] to give advice in a way that annoys people: *I wish you would stop **preaching at** me like this.*

preach·er /ˈpritʃɚ/ *n.* [C] someone who talks about religious subjects, usually in a church

preach·y /ˈpritʃi/ *adj. informal* trying very hard to persuade people to accept a particular opinion, in a way that annoys them: *I don't like the preachy tone in her writing.*

pre·am·ble /ˈpriˌæmbəl/ *n.* [C] *formal* a statement at the beginning of a book, speech, etc.: *the **preamble to** the Constitution*

P

pre·ar·ranged /ˌpriəˈreɪndʒd◂/ *adj.* planned before: *We can have a driver pick you up at a prearranged time.*

pre·car·i·ous /prɪˈkɛriəs, -ˈkær-/ *adj.* **1** a precarious situation may easily or quickly become worse: *The newspaper is in a **precarious** financial **position**.* **2** likely to fall, or likely to cause something to fall: *We had to cross a precarious rope bridge.* —**precariously** *adv.*

pre·cau·tion /prɪˈkɔʃən/ *n.* [C] something that you do to prevent something bad or dangerous from happening: *safety precautions* | *People were warned to stay inside **as a precaution**.* | *You have to **take precautions** when working with chemicals.*

pre·cau·tion·a·ry /prɪˈkɔʃəˌnɛri/ *adj.* done as a PRECAUTION: *The doctors have put him in the hospital as a **precautionary measure**.*

pre·cede /prɪˈsid/ *v.* [T] *formal* to happen or exist before something else: *The fire was preceded by a loud explosion.*

prec·e·dence /ˈprɛsədəns/ *n.* **take/have precedence (over sth)** to be more important or urgent than someone or something else: *This project takes precedence over everything else.*

prec·e·dent /ˈprɛsədənt/ *n.* [C] an action or official decision that is used as an example for a similar action or decision at a later time: *The trial **set a precedent** for civil rights legislation.*

pre·ced·ing /prɪˈsidɪŋ, ˈprisidɪŋ/ *adj.* [only before noun] *formal* happening or coming before something else: *The events of the preceding week worried him.*

pre·cept /ˈprisɛpt/ *n.* [C] *formal* a rule that helps you decide how to think or behave in a situation: *basic moral precepts*

pre·cinct /ˈprisɪŋkt/ *n.* [C] a part of a city that has its own police force, government officials, etc.: *the 12th precinct*

pre·cious[1] /ˈprɛʃəs/ *adj.* **1** something that is precious is valuable or important and should not be wasted: *We cannot afford to waste **precious time/days/minutes etc.*** **2** precious memories or possessions are very important to you because they remind you of people or events in your life: *The doll is **precious to** me because it was my grandmother's.* **3** valuable because of being rare or expensive: *a **precious jewel/stone/metal***

THESAURUS

valuable, priceless, worth a lot/a fortune
→ see Thesaurus box at VALUABLE

4 *spoken* used in order to describe someone or something that is small and pretty: *What a precious little girl!*

precious[2] *adv.* **precious little/few** *informal* very little or very few: *We had precious little time to prepare for the trip.*

prec·i·pice /ˈprɛsəpɪs/ *n.* [C] a very steep side of a mountain or cliff

pre·cip·i·tate[1] /prɪˈsɪpəˌteɪt/ *v.* [T] *formal* to make something happen suddenly: *The President's death precipitated a political crisis.*

pre·cip·i·tate[2] /prɪˈsɪpətɪt/ *adj. formal* done too quickly, especially without thinking carefully enough

pre·cip·i·ta·tion /prɪˌsɪpəˈteɪʃən/ *n.* [C,U] *formal* rain or snow

pre·cip·i·tous /prɪˈsɪpət̬əs/ *adj. formal* **1** very sudden: *a **precipitous drop/decline** in property values* **2** dangerously high or steep: *precipitous cliffs*

pre·cise /prɪˈsaɪs/ *adj.* **1** exact or correct in every detail: *The precise cause of the accident is unknown.* | *The **precise location** of the ship is still unknown.* | *At that **precise moment**, the telephone rang.* | *a **precise figure/number/amount*** **2 to be precise** used when you add exact details about something: *He was born in April, on the 4th to be precise.*

pre·cise·ly /prɪˈsaɪsli/ *adv.* **1** exactly or completely correct in every detail: *I do not remember **precisely** what happened.* | *at precisely 4 o'clock* **2** *spoken* used in order to agree with what someone has just said: *"So Clark is responsible for the mistake." "Precisely."*

pre·ci·sion /prɪˈsɪʒən/ *n.* [U] the quality of being very exact: *The weight of an atom can be measured **with** great **precision**.* —**precision** *adj.*: *precision bombing*

pre·clude /prɪˈklud/ *v.* [T] *formal* to prevent something or make it impossible to happen: *Poor eyesight may **preclude** you **from** driving.*

pre·co·cious /prɪˈkoʊʃəs/ *adj.* a precocious child shows skill or intelligence at a young age, or behaves in an adult way

pre·con·ceived /ˌprikənˈsivd◂/ *adj.* [only before noun] preconceived ideas are formed about something before you know what it is really like: *He has a lot of **preconceived ideas/notions** about what living in America is like.*

pre·con·cep·tion /ˌprikənˈsɛpʃən/ *n.* [C] an idea that is formed about something before you know what it is really like

pre·con·di·tion /ˌprikənˈdɪʃən/ *n.* [C] something that must happen before something else can happen: *An end to the fighting is a* ***precondition for*** *peace negotiations.*

pre·cur·sor /'pri,kɚsɚ, prɪ'kɚsɚ/ *n.* [C] *formal* something that happened or existed before something else and influenced its development: *This machine is* ***a precursor of*** *the computer.*

pre·date /pri'deɪt/ *v.* [T] to happen or exist earlier than something else: *His troubles actually predated the arrest.*

pred·a·tor /'prɛdət̬ɚ/ *n.* [C] an animal that kills and eats other animals

pred·a·to·ry /'prɛdə,tɔri/ *adj.* **1** predatory animals kill and eat other animals **2** *disapproving* trying to use someone's weakness to get an advantage for yourself

pred·e·ces·sor /'prɛdə,sɛsɚ/ *n.* [C] **1** the person who had a job before someone else began to do it: *My predecessor worked here for ten years.* **2** something such as a machine or system that existed before another one: *a computer that is much faster than its predecessors*

pre·des·ti·na·tion /,pridɛstə'neɪʃən/ *n.* [U] the belief that God or FATE has decided everything that will happen and that no one can change this

pre·des·tined /pri'dɛstɪnd/ *adj.* something that is predestined is certain to happen and cannot be changed

pre·de·ter·mined /,pridɪ'tɚmɪnd/ *adj. formal* decided or arranged before: *The doors unlock at a predetermined time.*

pre·dic·a·ment /prɪ'dɪkəmənt/ *n.* [C] a difficult situation in which you do not know what is the best thing to do: *It was Raoul who got us* ***in this predicament*** *in the first place.*

pred·i·cate /'prɛdɪkɪt/ *n.* [C] *technical* in grammar, the part of a sentence that has the main verb, and that tells what the subject is doing or describes the subject. In the sentence "He ran out of the house," "ran out of the house" is the predicate. [➡ **subject**]

pred·i·ca·tive /'prɛdɪkət̬ɪv, -,keɪt̬ɪv/ *adj. technical* in grammar, a predicative adjective or phrase comes after a verb and describes the subject, such as "sad" in "She is sad."

pre·dict /prɪ'dɪkt/ *v.* [T] to say that something will happen before it happens: *The newspapers are predicting a close election.* | *Analysts* ***predict (that)*** *college costs will continue to rise.* | *It's difficult to* ***predict*** *exactly* ***what*** *the effects will be.*

THESAURUS

prophesy – to use religious or magical knowledge to say what will happen in the future: *The priestess at Delphi prophesied that Laius would be killed by his own son.*
forecast – to say what is likely to happen in the future, based on information you have: *The number of passengers using the airport is forecast to rise.*
foresee – to know that something will happen before it happens: *No one could have foreseen what happened next.*
have a premonition – to have a feeling that something bad is about to happen: *He had a premonition of impending danger.*

pre·dict·a·ble /prɪ'dɪktəbəl/ *adj.* behaving or happening in a way that you expect: *You're so predictable!* | *The ending of the movie was too predictable.* —**predictably** *adv.* —**predictability** /prɪ,dɪktə'bɪlət̬i/ *n.* [U]

pre·dic·tion /prɪ'dɪkʃən/ *n.* [C,U] a statement saying that something is going to happen, or the act of making statements of this kind: *It's hard to* ***make*** *a* ***prediction*** *about who will win.* | ***predictions of*** *climate change* —**predictive** *adj.*

pred·i·lec·tion /,prɛdl'ɛkʃən, ,prid-/ *n.* [C] *formal* the tendency to like a particular kind of person or thing: *a* ***predilection for*** *apple pie*

pre·dis·posed /,pridɪ'spoʊzd/ *adj.* **predisposed to/toward sth** likely to behave or think in a particular way, or to have a particular health problem: *Some people are predisposed to depression.*

pre·dis·po·si·tion /,pridɪspə'zɪʃən/ *n.* [C] a tendency to behave in a particular way or suffer from a particular health problem: *a* ***predisposition to/toward*** *skin cancer*

pre·dom·i·nance /prɪ'dɑmənəns/ *n. formal* **1** [singular] if there is a predominance of one type of thing or person in a group, there are more of them than any other type of person or thing: *the* ***predominance of*** *male students in the class* **2** [U] the most power or importance in a particular group or area: *American* ***predominance in*** *world economics*

pre·dom·i·nant /prɪ'dɑmənənt/ *adj.* more powerful, common, or noticeable than others: *Racism in American society is a predominant theme in Wright's novels.*

pre·dom·i·nant·ly /prɪ'dɑmənəntli/ *adv.* mostly or mainly: *a predominantly middle class neighborhood*

pre·dom·i·nate /prɪ'dɑmə,neɪt/ *v.* [I] to have the most importance, or to be the most in number: *a district where Democrats predominate*

pree·mie /'primi/ *n.* [C] *informal* a PREMATURE baby

pre·em·i·nent /pri'ɛmənənt/ *adj.* much more important or powerful than all others in a particular group: *a preeminent political figure* —**preeminence** *n.* [U]

pre·empt /pri'ɛmpt/ *v.* [T] to make what someone is about to do unnecessary or not effective, by doing something else first: *Approval of the plan would preempt the strike.* —**preemptive** *adj.*: *a preemptive attack*

preen /prin/ *v.* **1** [I,T] if a bird preens or preens itself, it cleans itself and makes its feathers smooth **2 preen yourself** *disapproving* to spend a lot of time making yourself look good: *He's always preening himself in the mirror.*

pre·ex·ist·ing /ˌpriɪgˈzɪstɪŋ◂/ *adj.* [only before noun] existing already, or before something else: *a pre-existing medical condition*

pre·fab·ri·cat·ed /priˈfæbrəˌkeɪt̬ɪd/ **also pre·fab** /priˈfæb, ˈprifæb/ *adj.* built from parts made in a factory and put together somewhere else: *prefabricated homes*

pref·ace¹ /ˈprɛfɪs/ *n.* [C] an introduction at the beginning of a book or speech: *the* ***preface to*** *the novel*

preface² *v.* [T] *formal* to say or do something first before saying or doing something else: *He* ***prefaced*** *his remarks* ***with*** *an expression of thanks to the audience.*

pre·fer /prɪˈfɚ/ *v.* past tense and past participle **preferred**, present participle **preferring** [T] **1** to like someone or something more than someone or something else: *Which color do you prefer?* | *Many companies* ***prefer to*** *hire young workers.* | *I* ***would prefer*** *not to talk about it at the moment.* | *She* ***prefers*** *walking* ***to*** *driving.* **2 I would prefer it if** *spoken* used in order to tell someone politely not to do something: *I'd prefer it if you didn't smoke in the house.*

pref·er·a·ble /ˈprɛfərəbəl/ *adj.* better or more appropriate: *Anything is* ***preferable to*** *war.*

pref·er·a·bly /ˈprɛfərəbli/ *adv.* used in order to show which person, thing, place, or idea you think would be the best choice: *You should see a doctor, preferably a specialist.*

pref·er·ence /ˈprɛfrəns, -fərəns/ *n.* [C,U] **1** if someone has a preference for something, s/he likes it more than another thing: *We have always* ***had a preference for*** *small cars.* | *It's a matter of* ***personal preference.*** **2 give/show preference (to sb)** to treat someone better than you treat other people: *Doctors should give preference to patients who are seriously ill.*

pref·er·en·tial /ˌprɛfəˈrɛnʃəl◂/ *adj.* treating one person or group better than others: *Why should she get* ***preferential treatment****?*

pre·fix /ˈprifɪks/ *n.* [C] *technical* in grammar, a group of letters that is added to the beginning of a word in order to make a new word, such as "mis-" in "misunderstand" [➡ **suffix**]

preg·nan·cy /ˈprɛgnənsi/ *n.* plural **pregnancies** [C,U] the condition of being PREGNANT, or the period of time when a woman is pregnant: *You should not drink alcohol during your pregnancy.* | *a pregnancy test*

preg·nant /ˈprɛgnənt/ *adj.* **1** having a baby that has not been born yet growing in your body: *a pregnant woman* | *She's three months pregnant.* | *Marie* ***got pregnant*** *when she was 16.* | *She's* ***pregnant with*** *her first child.* **2 a pregnant silence/pause** *literary* a silence or pause which is full of meaning or emotion

pre·heat /priˈhit/ *v.* [T] to heat an OVEN to a particular temperature before cooking food in it

pre·his·tor·ic /ˌprihɪˈstɔrɪk◂/ *adj.* relating to the time in history before anything was written down: *prehistoric cave drawings* —**prehistory** /priˈhɪstəri/ *n.* [U]

pre·judge /ˌpriˈdʒʌdʒ/ *v.* [T] *disapproving* to form an opinion about someone or something before knowing all the facts

prej·u·dice¹ /ˈprɛdʒədɪs/ *n.* [C,U] an unfair feeling of dislike against someone who is of a different race, sex, religion, etc.: ***racial prejudice*** | ***prejudice against*** *single mothers*

THESAURUS

Types of prejudice

racism – unfair treatment of people because they belong to a different race: *accusations of police brutality and racism*

discrimination – the practice of treating one group of people differently from another in an unfair way: *She accused the company of sexual discrimination.*

intolerance – the fact of not being willing to accept ways of thinking or behaving that are different from your own: *religious intolerance*

anti-Semitism – a strong feeling of hatred toward Jewish people: *Is anti-Semitism on the rise in America and Europe?*

People who are prejudiced

racist: *When he expressed his opinion, he was branded a racist.*

bigot – someone who has strong unreasonable opinions, especially about race or religion: *He was known to be a bigot.*

prejudice² *v.* [T] to influence someone so that s/he has an unfair opinion about someone or something before s/he knows all the facts: *Watson's wild appearance may* ***prejudice*** *the jury* ***against*** *him.*

prej·u·diced /ˈprɛdʒədɪst/ *adj.* having an unfair feeling of dislike for someone who is of a different race, sex, religion, etc.: *Kurt is so* ***prejudiced against*** *gay people!*

prej·u·di·cial /ˌprɛdʒəˈdɪʃəl/ *adj. formal* influencing people so that they have a bad opinion of someone or something: *prejudicial remarks*

pre·lim·i·nar·y¹ /prɪˈlɪməˌnɛri/ *adj.* happening before something that is more important, often in order to prepare for it: *a preliminary investigation* | *preliminary talks/discussions*

preliminary² *n.* plural **preliminaries** [C usually plural] something that is done at the beginning of an activity, event, etc., often in order to prepare for it: *the preliminaries of the competition*

prel·ude /ˈpreɪlud, ˈprɛlyud/ *n.* **1 be a prelude to sth** to happen just before something else, often as an introduction to it: *The attack may be a prelude to full-scale war.* **2** [C] a short piece of music that comes before a large musical piece: *Chopin's preludes*

pre·mar·i·tal /ˌpri'mærətl/ *adj.* happening or existing before marriage: *premarital sex*

pre·ma·ture /ˌpriməˈtʃʊr◂, -'tʊr◂/ *adj.* **1** happening too early or before the right time: *a premature death* **2** a premature baby is born before the usual time: *The baby was six weeks premature.* —**prematurely** *adv.*: *The sun causes your skin to age prematurely.* | *The baby was born prematurely.*

pre·med, **pre-med** /'primɛd/ *adj. informal* relating to classes that prepare a student for medical school, or to students who are taking these classes: *a premed student*

pre·med·i·tat·ed /pri'mɛdəˌteɪt̬ɪd/ *adj.* a premeditated action has been planned and done deliberately: *a premeditated murder* —**premeditation** /priˌmɛdə'teɪʃən/ *n.* [U]

pre·men·strual /pri'mɛnstrəl/ *adj. technical* happening just before a woman's PERIOD (=monthly flow of blood)

preˌmenstrual 'syndrome *n.* [U] PMS

pre·mier¹, **Premier** /prɪ'mɪr, -'myɪr, 'primɪr/ *n.* [C] the leader of a government

premier² *adj. formal* best or most important: *a premier wine from Bordeaux*

pre·miere, **première** /prɪ'mɪr, -'myɪr, -'myɛr/ *n.* [C] the first public performance of a movie or play: *the 1955* ***premiere of*** *"Cat on a Hot Tin Roof"* —**premiere** *v.* [I,T]

prem·ise /'prɛmɪs/ *n.* **1 premises** [plural] the buildings and land that a store, company, etc. uses: *He was ordered* ***off the premises*** (=out of the building). | *Do not smoke* ***on the premises*** (=in the building). **2** [C] *formal* a statement or idea that you think is true and use as a base for developing other ideas: *His theory is based on the* ***premise that*** *there may be life on other planets.*

pre·mi·um /'primiəm/ *n.* [C] **1** an amount of money that you pay for something such as insurance: *annual premiums* **2 be at a premium** difficult to get because a lot of people want it: *Hotel rooms are at a premium around major holidays.* **3 put/place a premium on sth** to think that one quality or activity is much more important than others: *The club puts a premium on loyalty.*

pre·mo·ni·tion /ˌpriməˈnɪʃən, ˌprɛ-/ *n.* [C] a feeling that something bad is about to happen: *She* ***had*** *a horrible* ***premonition that*** *something would happen to the children.*

pre·na·tal /ˌpri'neɪt̬l◂/ *adj. technical* relating to unborn babies and the care of women who are PREGNANT [➡ **postpartum**]: *prenatal care*

pre·oc·cu·pa·tion /priˌɑkyə'peɪʃən/ *n.* **1** [singular, U] the state of being preoccupied: *His growing* ***preoccupation with*** *his health began to affect his work.* **2** [C] something that you give all your attention to: *Brad's main preoccupations were eating and sleeping.*

pre·oc·cu·pied /pri'ɑkyəˌpaɪd/ *adj.* thinking or worrying about something a lot, so that you do not pay attention to other things: *What's wrong? You seem* ***preoccupied with*** *something today.*

pre·oc·cu·py /pri'ɑkyəˌpaɪ/ *v.* past tense and past participle **preoccupied**, third person singular **preoccupies** [T] if something preoccupies you, you think or worry about it a lot

pre·or·dained /ˌpriɔr'deɪnd/ *adj. formal* certain to happen because God or FATE has already decided it

prep /prɛp/ *v.* past tense and past participle **prepped**, present participle **prepping** [T] *informal* to prepare for something

pre·paid /ˌpri'peɪd◂/ *adj.* if something is prepaid, it is paid for before it is needed or used: *a prepaid phone card*

prep·a·ra·tion /ˌprɛpə'reɪʃən/ *n.* **1** [U] the act or process of preparing something: *Flowers have been ordered* ***in preparation for*** *the wedding.* | *the* ***preparation of*** *the report* | *income tax preparation* **2 also preparations** [plural] arrangements for something that is going to happen: *They are* ***making preparations for*** *the President's visit.*

pre·par·a·to·ry /prɪ'pærəˌtɔri, -'pɛr-, 'prɛprə-/ *adj.* [only before noun] done in order to get ready for something: *preparatory work*

pre·pare /prɪ'pɛr/ *v.* **1** [T] to make something ready to be used: *The rooms still need to be* ***prepared for*** *the guests.* | *You need to prepare the soil before planting the seeds.*

THESAURUS

get sth ready: *I've been getting everything ready for the party.*
set sth up – to make a piece of equipment ready to be used: *Kim's setting up the computer in the meeting room.*
make preparations – to prepare for an important event: *They spent six months making preparations for the trip.*

2 [I,T] to make plans or arrangements for something that will happen soon: *I hope you've begun to* ***prepare for*** *the test.* | *The Bears are* ***preparing to*** *play the Redskins next week.* | *We need to prepare a plan for raising the money.* **3** [T] to make yourself or someone else ready to deal with something that will happen soon: *You should probably* ***prepare yourself for*** *some bad news.* **4** [T] to give someone the training, skill, etc. that s/he needs to do something: *The program* ***prepares*** *students* ***for*** *a career in business.* **5** [T] to make food or a meal ready to eat: *This dish can be prepared the day before.*

pre·pared /prɪ'pɛrd/ *adj.* **1** [not before noun] ready to do something or to deal with a particular situation: *He wasn't really* ***prepared for*** *all their questions.* **2 be prepared to do sth** to be willing to do something if it is necessary: *Is he prepared to accept the offer?* | *I am not prepared to discuss this any further.* **3** [only before noun] arranged and ready to be used, before it is needed: *The police read out a **prepared statement** to the press.*

pre·par·ed·ness /prɪˈpɛrɪdnɪs/ *n.* [U] the state of being ready for something: *military preparedness*

pre·pon·der·ance /prɪˈpɑndərəns/ *n.* [singular] *formal* a larger number or amount of one type of thing or person in a group than of any other type: *There's **a preponderance of** women in the orchestra.*

prep·o·si·tion /ˌprɛpəˈzɪʃən/ *n.* [C] *technical* in grammar, a word or phrase that is used before a noun, PRONOUN, or GERUND to show place, time, direction, etc. In the phrase "at the bank," "at" is a preposition. —**prepositional** *adj.*: *a prepositional phrase*

pre·pos·ter·ous /prɪˈpɑstərəs/ *adj.* completely unreasonable or silly [= **absurd**]: *That's a preposterous story!*

P

prep·py /ˈprɛpi/ *adj. informal* preppy styles or clothes are very neat and CONSERVATIVE in a way that is typical of people who go to expensive private schools

'prep school *n.* [C] *informal* a private school that prepares students for college

pre·quel /ˈprikwəl/ *n.* [C] a book or film that tells the story of what happened before the story told in a previous popular book or film

pre·reg·is·ter /priˈrɛdʒɪstɚ/ *v.* [I] to put your name on a list for a particular course of study, school, etc. before the official time to do so —**preregistration** /ˌprirɛdʒɪˈstreɪʃən/ *n.* [U]

pre·req·ui·site /priˈrɛkwəzɪt/ *n.* [C] *formal* something that is necessary before something else can happen or be done: *A degree in French is a **prerequisite for** the job.*

pre·rog·a·tive /prɪˈrɑgət̬ɪv/ *n.* [C] a special right that someone has: *If you want to leave early, that's your prerogative.*

pres·age /ˈprɛsɪdʒ, prɪˈseɪdʒ/ *v.* [T] *literary* to be a sign that something is going to happen, especially something bad

Pres·by·te·ri·an /ˌprɛzbəˈtɪriən, ˌprɛs-/ *adj.* relating to the Protestant church that is one of the largest churches in the U.S. and the national church of Scotland —**Presbyterian** *n.* [C]

pre·school /ˈpriskul/ *n.* [C] a school for young children between two and five years of age: *Emma is **in preschool** now.* —**preschool** *adj.*: *preschool children* —**preschooler** *n.* [C]

pre·scribe /prɪˈskraɪb/ *v.* [T] **1** to say what medicine or treatment a sick person should have: *Doctors commonly **prescribe** steroids **for** children with asthma.* **2** *formal* to state officially what should be done in a particular situation: *a punishment prescribed by the law*

pre·scrip·tion /prɪˈskrɪpʃən/ *n.* **1** [C] a piece of paper on which a doctor writes what medicine a sick person should have, or the medicine itself: *a **prescription for** painkillers* **2 by prescription** a drug that you get by prescription can only be obtained with a written order from the doctor [≠ **over the counter**]

pre·scrip·tive /prɪˈskrɪptɪv/ *adj. formal* saying how something should be done or what someone should do

pres·ence /ˈprɛzəns/ *n.* **1** [U] the state of being present in a particular place [≠ **absence**]: *The ambassador's presence at the reception was a surprise.* | *Tests revealed **the presence of** poison in the blood.* **2 in sb's presence/in the presence of sb** with someone or in the same place as him/her: *Everyone was afraid to voice an opinion in his presence.* | *He blushed whenever he was in the presence of women.* **3** [singular] a group of people, especially the army or the police, who are in a place to watch or control what is happening: *the American **military presence** in Vietnam* | *There's a heavy **police presence** at the embassy.* **4 have the presence of mind to do sth** to have the ability to deal with a dangerous situation calmly and quickly: *Bill had **the presence of mind to** call 911 after the fire started.* **5 make your presence felt** to have a strong effect on other people or situations: *Hanley has made his presence felt since joining the company.* **6** [U] the ability to appear impressive to people with your appearance or manner: *an actor who has a powerful stage presence.*

pres·ent¹ /ˈprɛzənt/ *adj.* **1 be present** *formal* to be in a particular place [≠ **absent**]: *How many people were **present at** the board meeting?* **2** [only before noun] happening or existing now: *We are unable to answer your questions **at the present time**.* | *Many people are unhappy with the **present situation**.*

> **THESAURUS**
>
> **current** – happening, existing, or being used now: *What is your current address?*
> **existing** – present now and available to be used: *The existing system is not working.*

3 the present day *formal* in modern times: *Traditional Indian pottery designs are still used in the present day.*

pre·sent² /prɪˈzɛnt/ *v.* [T] **1** to give something to someone, especially at an official or public occasion: *Mr. Davis **presented** the winning team **with** a gold cup.* **2** to give or show information in a particular way: *The evidence was **presented to** the court by Conor's lawyer.* **3 present yourself** the way you present yourself is the way you talk and behave when you meet new people: *She presents herself as confident and experienced.* **4** to cause something such as a problem or difficulty to happen or exist: *The heavy rains **presented** a new **difficulty** for the rescue workers.* **5** to give a performance in a theater, etc., or broadcast it on television or radio: *The Roxy is presenting a production of "Waiting for Godot" this week.* **6** *formal* to introduce someone formally to someone else: *May I present my parents, Mr. and Mrs. Benning.*

pre·sent[3] /ˈprɛzənt/ *n.* [C] **1** something that you give to someone on a special occasion [= **gift**]: *a **birthday/Christmas/anniversary present** | He didn't even **give** me a **present**.* **2 the present** the time that is happening now: *Live in the present – don't worry about the past!* **3 at present** at this time: *We have no plans at present for closing the factory.*

pre·sent·a·ble /prɪˈzɛntəbəl/ *adj.* attractive and neat enough to be seen or shown in public: *Do I **look presentable**? | Let me try to **make** the house a little bit more **presentable**.*

pres·en·ta·tion /ˌprizənˈteɪʃən, ˌprɛ-/ *n.* **1** [C] the act of giving someone a prize or present at a formal ceremony: *the **presentation of** the awards* **2** [C] a formal talk about a particular subject: *She **gave** a short **presentation on/about** the new product.* **3** [U] the way in which something is shown, said, etc. to others: *As a chef I care about the **presentation of** food as well as its taste.*

ˈpresent-day *adj.* modern or existing now: *The colonists settled near present-day Charleston.*

pres·ent·ly /ˈprɛzəntli/ *adv. formal* **1** at this time: *I presently live in Berlin.*

> **THESAURUS**
>
> **now, at the moment, for the moment, at present, at the present time, currently**
> → see Thesaurus box at NOW[1]

2 *old-fashioned* in a short time: *The doctor will see you presently.*

ˌpresent ˈparticiple *n.* [C] *technical* in grammar, a PARTICIPLE that is formed by adding "-ing" to a verb. It can be used in compounds to make CONTINUOUS tenses, as in "she's sleeping," as an adjective, as in "the sleeping child," or as a GERUND, as in "I like cooking."

ˌpresent ˈperfect *n.* **the present perfect** *technical* in grammar, the tense of a verb that shows a time up to and including the present, and is formed with "have" and the past participle. In the sentence "Ken has traveled all over the world," "has traveled" is in the present perfect.

ˌpresent ˈtense *n.* **the present tense** *technical* in grammar, the form of a verb that shows what is true, what exists, or what is happening now. In the sentence "I always leave for work at 8:00," "leave" is in the present tense.

pres·er·va·tion /ˌprɛzɚˈveɪʃən/ *n.* [U] the act of keeping something unharmed or unchanged, or the degree to which it is unharmed or unchanged: *the **preservation of** the rainforest | The painting was **in a good/bad state of preservation**.*

pre·serv·a·tive /prɪˈzɚvət̬ɪv/ *n.* [C,U] a chemical substance that prevents food or wood from decaying: *food that contains no **artificial preservatives***

pre·serve[1] /prɪˈzɚv/ *v.* [T] **1** to keep something or someone from being harmed, destroyed, or changed too much: *The group is dedicated to preserving historic buildings. | We want to preserve as much open land as possible.*

> **THESAURUS**
>
> **protect, guard, shield, give/offer/provide protection, shelter**
> → see Thesaurus box at PROTECT

2 to add something so that it will stay in good condition for a long time: *cucumbers **preserved in** vinegar*

preserve[2] *n.* **1** [C] an area of land or water in which animals, fish, or trees are protected: *the nation's first wilderness preserve* **2** [singular] an activity that only one particular group of people can do, or a place that only those people can use: *Politics is no longer the **preserve of** wealthy white males.* **3 preserves** [plural] a sweet food such as JAM made from large pieces of fruit boiled with sugar: *strawberry preserves*

pre·side /prɪˈzaɪd/ *v.* [I] to be in charge of a formal meeting, ceremony, important situation, etc.: *Judge Baxter **presided over** the trial.*

pres·i·den·cy /ˈprɛzədənsi/ *n.* plural **presidencies** [C] the job of being a president or the period of time when someone is a president: *his first attempt to win the presidency*

pres·i·dent, **President** /ˈprɛzədənt/ *n.* [C] **1** the official leader of a country that does not have a king or queen: *the **President of** Mexico | President Lincoln*

> **THESAURUS**
>
> **politician, congressman, congresswoman, senator, governor, mayor**
> → see Thesaurus box at POLITICIAN

2 someone who is in charge of a business, bank, club, college, etc.: *the **President of** Brown University*

pres·i·den·tial /ˌprɛzəˈdɛnʃəl◂ / *adj.* relating to the job or office of president: *the presidential campaign/election | the presidential nominee/candidate/contender*

ˈPresidents' Day *n.* a U.S. holiday on the third Monday in February to remember the BIRTHDAYS of George Washington and Abraham Lincoln

press[1] /prɛs/ *v.*
1 WITH FINGER [T] to push something with your finger in order to make a machine start, a bell ring, etc.: *What happens if I **press** this **button**? | Mrs. Mott pressed the doorbell again. | Press F3 to save the document.*
2 PUSH AGAINST [T] to push something firmly against a surface: *He **pressed** some money **into** her hand. | Their faces were **pressed against** the window.*

3 IRON [T] to make clothes smooth using heat [= **iron**]: *I need to have this suit cleaned and pressed.*
4 press charges to say officially that someone has done something illegal so that a court must decide if s/he is guilty
5 PERSUADE [T] to try very hard to persuade someone to do something or tell you something: *He **pressed** me **to** accept the job.* | *Detectives had been **pressing** him **for** details.*
6 MOVE [I] to move in a particular direction by pushing: *The crowd **pressed forward** to see what was happening.*
7 HEAVY WEIGHT [T] to put pressure or weight on something to make it flat, crush it, etc.: *a machine for pressing grapes*

P

THESAURUS

squash – to press something and damage it by making it flat: *Put the tomatoes where they won't get squashed.*
crush – to press something very hard so that it is broken or destroyed: *His leg was crushed in the accident.*
mash – to press fruit or cooked vegetables until they are soft and smooth: *Mash the potatoes well.*
grind – to press something into powder using a special machine: *Can you grind the coffee beans?*
squeeze – to press something from both sides, usually with your fingers: *Squeeze the toothpaste tube from the bottom.* | *fresh-squeezed orange juice*

press on/ahead *phr. v.* to continue doing something without stopping: *The army crossed the river and pressed on to the border.*

press² *n.* **1 the press** newspapers, magazines, etc. or the people who work for them: *Taylor refuses to speak to the press.* | *the **freedom of the press*** | *Mary's new play is getting the attention of **the national/local press**.* **2 good/bad press** the praise or criticism that someone is given by newspapers, radio, or television: *I don't think Kurt deserves all the **bad press** that he's **getting**.* **3** [C] a business that prints and sometimes sells books: *the University Press* **4** [C] PRINTING PRESS **5 go to press** if a newspaper, magazine, or book goes to press, it begins to be printed: *All information was correct at the time we went to press.* **6** [C] a piece of equipment that makes something flat or forces liquid out of something: *a flower press* | *a wine press*

'press ˌagent *n.* [C] someone whose job is to give photographs or information about a famous person to newspapers, radio, or television

'press ˌconference *n.* [C] a meeting at which someone makes official statements to people who write news reports: *The Governor **held a press conference** last night.*

'press corps *n.* [C] a group of people who usually write the news reports that come from a particular place: *the White House press corps*

pressed /prɛst/ *adj.* **be pressed for time/money etc.** to not have enough time, money, etc.: *I can't stop now – I'm pressed for time.*

press·ing /'prɛsɪŋ/ *adj.* a pressing problem, matter, question, etc. needs to be dealt with very soon [= **urgent**]: *Poverty is the country's most **pressing problem**.*

'press reˌlease *n.* [C] an official statement that gives information to the newspapers, radio, or television

pres·sure¹ /'prɛʃɚ/ *n.* **1** [U] an attempt to make someone do something by using influence, arguments, threats, etc.: *Kay's family is **putting pressure on** her to get married.* | *The company is **under pressure** to reduce costs.* | *The president faces **pressure from** militants in his own party.* **2** [C,U] the conditions of your work, family, or way of living that make you anxious and cause problems: *I've been **under** a lot of **pressure** at work lately.* | *There is a lot of **pressure on** children these days.* | *the **pressures of** modern life* **3** [C,U] the force that a gas or liquid has when it is pushed and held inside a container: *The air pressure in the tires might be low.* **4** [U] the force produced by pressing on someone or something: *the **pressure of** his hand on her shoulder*

pressure² *v.* [T] to try to make someone do something by using influence, arguments, threats, etc.: *She was **pressured into** signing the statement.*

THESAURUS

force, make, coerce, compel
➔ see Thesaurus box at FORCE²

'pressure ˌcooker *n.* [C] a tightly covered cooking pot that cooks food very quickly using hot steam

pres·sured /'prɛʃɚd/ *adj.* feeling a lot of worry because of the number of things that you have to do: *Her job makes her **feel pressured** all the time.*

'pressure group *n.* [C] a group of people or an organization that tries to influence what the public thinks about things, and what the government does about things

pres·sur·ized /'prɛʃəˌraɪzd/ *adj.* if an aircraft is pressurized, the air pressure inside it is similar to the pressure on the ground

pres·tige /prɛ'stiʒ, -'stidʒ/ *n.* [U] if you have prestige, you are respected and admired because of your job or something that you have achieved: *My present job has a certain amount of prestige attached to it.*

pres·tig·ious /prɛ'stɪdʒəs, -'sti-/ *adj.* admired or respected as one of the best and most important: *a prestigious award for writers*

pre·sum·a·bly /prɪ'zuməbli/ *adv.* used in order to say that something is likely to be true, although you are not certain: *Presumably, he's going to come back and get this stuff.*

pre·sume /prɪ'zum/ *v.* **1** [T] to think that something is likely to be true, although you are not certain [= **assume**]: ***I presume (that)** this price includes all transportation and hotels.* **2** [T] to accept that something is true until it is proved untrue, especially in law: *She is missing and **is presumed dead**.* **3** [I] *formal* to behave rudely by doing something that you do not have the right to do: *Don't **presume to** tell me how to raise my children!*

pre·sump·tion /prɪ'zʌmpʃən/ *n.* **1** [C] something that you think must be true or is very likely to be true: *There should always be **a presumption of** innocence until someone is proven guilty.* **2** [U] *formal* behavior that seems rude and too confident

pre·sump·tu·ous /prɪ'zʌmptʃuəs/ *adj.* doing something that you have no right to do and that seems rude: ***It would be presumptuous** of me to try to tell you what to do.*

pre·sup·pose /ˌprisə'poʊz/ *v.* [T] *formal* to depend on something that is thought to be true [= **assume**]: *All your plans **presuppose that** the bank will be willing to lend us the money.* —**presupposition** /ˌprisʌpə'zɪʃən/ *n.* [C,U]

pre·teen /'pritin/ *n.* [C] someone who is 12 or 13 years old —**preteen** *adj.*: *my preteen daughter*

pre·tend[1] /prɪ'tɛnd/ *v.* [I,T] **1** to behave as if something is true when you know it is not: *Terry **pretended to** be asleep.* | *We can't go on **pretending (that)** everything is OK.* **2** to imagine that something is true or real, as a game: *Let's **pretend (that)** we're on the moon!*

pretend[2] *adj.* a word meaning IMAGINARY, used especially by or when talking to children: *We sang songs around a pretend campfire.*

pre·tense /'pritɛns, prɪ'tɛns/ *n.* **1** [singular, U] an attempt to pretend that something is true: *Kevin **made no pretense of** being surprised.* | *We had to **keep up the pretense** that we were married.* **2 under false pretenses** if you do something under false pretenses, you do it by pretending that something is true when it is not: *He would get women to come into his home under false pretenses, and then attack them.*

pre·ten·sion /prɪ'tɛnʃən/ *n.* [C usually plural, U] an attempt to seem more important, rich, or intelligent than you really are: *his honesty and lack of pretension*

pre·ten·tious /prɪ'tɛnʃəs/ *adj.* trying to seem more important, rich, or intelligent than you really are: *There were a bunch of pretentious people at the gallery opening.*

pre·text /'pritɛkst/ *n.* [C] a false reason that is given for doing something, in order to hide the real reason: *He got into the building **on the pretext** of checking the heating.*

pret·ty[1] /'prɪṭi/ *adv. informal* **1** fairly, but not completely: *I thought the test was pretty easy.* | *"How are you feeling?" "Oh, pretty good."* | *That car was going pretty quickly.*

> **THESAURUS**
>
> **rather, fairly, quite**
> → see Thesaurus box at RATHER

2 very: *Dad was pretty angry about it.* **3 pretty much** almost completely: *I'm pretty much done with my homework.*

pretty[2] *adj.* comparative **prettier**, superlative **prettiest** **1** a woman or child who is pretty is attractive: *a very pretty little girl* | *Laura is much prettier than her sister.*

> **THESAURUS**
>
> **attractive, good-looking, beautiful, handsome, gorgeous, stunning, nice-looking, cute, hot**
> → see Thesaurus box at ATTRACTIVE

2 attractive or pleasant to look at or listen to: *a pretty pink dress* | *a song with a pretty tune* **3 not a pretty picture/sight** very ugly, upsetting, or worrying: *The plane was completely destroyed – it's not a pretty picture.*

pret·zel /'prɛtsəl/ *n.* [C] a salty type of bread, baked in the shape of a loose knot

pretzel

pre·vail /prɪ'veɪl/ *v.* [I] *formal* **1** if a person, idea, or principle prevails, they achieve success after a struggle: *Justice prevailed in the end.* **2** if a belief or opinion prevails, it is common among a group of people: *After the riots, a mood of uncertainty still **prevails in** the neighborhood.*

prevail on/upon sb *phr. v. formal* to persuade someone: *I might be willing to prevail upon the committee to reconsider its decision.*

pre·vail·ing /prɪ'veɪlɪŋ/ *adj.* **1** very common in a particular place at a particular time [= **current**]: *Williams' books challenged prevailing views of U.S. history.* **2 prevailing wind** the direction in which the wind usually blows over a particular area at a particular time of the year

prev·a·lent /'prɛvələnt/ *adj.* common at a particular time or in a particular place: *The disease is more **prevalent among** young people.* —**prevalence** *n.* [U] *the prevalence of crime in the inner city*

pre·vent /prɪ'vɛnt/ *v.* [T] to stop something from happening, or stop someone from doing something: *an accident that could have been prevented* | *A knee injury **prevented** him **from** playing.* —**preventable** *adj.*: *preventable diseases*

pre·ven·ta·tive /prɪ'vɛnṭəṭɪv/ *adj.* PREVENTIVE

pre·ven·tion /prɪ'vɛnʃən/ *n.* [U] the act of preventing something, or the actions that you take in order to prevent something: *crime prevention* | *the **prevention of** accidents*

pre·ven·tive /prɪ'vɛntɪv/ *adj.* intended to prevent something you do not want to happen: *pre-*

P

ventive medicine (=treatment to prevent people from becoming sick)

pre·view /ˈprivyu/ *n.* [C] **1** an occasion when you see a movie, play, etc. before it is shown to the public **2** an advertisement for a movie or television program that often consists of short parts of it —**preview** *v.* [T]

pre·vi·ous /ˈpriviəs/ *adj.* [only before noun] happening or existing before a particular event, time, or thing: *She has two children from a previous marriage.* | *Have you had any previous experience in accounting?*

THESAURUS

last, former
→ see Thesaurus box at LAST[1]

P

pre·vi·ous·ly /ˈpriviəsli/ *adv.* before now, or before a particular time: *She previously worked at Bank of Boston.*

THESAURUS

before, prior to, earlier
→ see Thesaurus box at BEFORE[1]

pre·war /ˌpriˈwɔr◂ / *adj., adv.* happening or existing before a war, especially World War I or World War II: *the country's prewar population*

prey[1] /preɪ/ *n.* **1** [U] an animal that is hunted and eaten by another animal: *a tiger stalking its prey* **2 fall prey to sth** to be affected by something unpleasant: *More teenagers are falling prey to gang violence.*

prey[2] *v.*
prey on sb/sth *phr. v.* **1** if an animal or bird preys on another animal or bird, it hunts and eats it **2** to try to influence or deceive weaker people: *dishonest salesmen who prey on old people*

price[1] /praɪs/ *n.* **1** [C,U] the amount of money that must be paid in order to buy something: *What's the* ***price of*** *this book?* | *Gas* ***prices*** *have* ***gone up*** *again.* | *I can't believe how* ***high/low*** *their* ***prices*** *are.* | *Stock* ***prices fell*** *yesterday.* | *We could rent a car or take the train – there's almost no difference* ***in price***. | *price cuts*

COLLOCATIONS

go up/rise/increase – to become higher
increase/raise prices – to make them higher
go down/fall/drop – to become lower
cut/lower/slash prices – to make them lower
rocket/soar – to suddenly become much higher
tumble/plummet – to suddenly become much lower
fluctuate – to keep becoming higher and then lower
level out/off – to stop going up or down, and continue at the same amount

THESAURUS

cost, expense, charge, fee, fare, rent
→ see Thesaurus box at COST[1]

2 [C,U] something bad that you must deal with in order to have or do something else: *He's very busy, but I guess that's the* ***price of*** *success.* | *She's gotten the job she wanted, but* ***at what price?*** **3 at/for a price** used in order to say that you can buy something, but only if you pay a lot of money: *You can buy excellent wine here – at a price.* **4 at any price** even if something is extremely difficult: *They were determined to have a child at any price.* **5 asking price** the price that someone who is selling something says s/he wants for it: *The asking price was $500, but we paid $350 for it.*

price[2] *v.* [T] **1** to give a price to something that is for sale: *a reasonably priced pair of shoes* **2** to put a sign on goods that shows how much they cost

price·less /ˈpraɪslɪs/ *adj.* **1** so valuable that you cannot calculate a financial value: *priceless antiques*

THESAURUS

valuable, precious, worth a lot/a fortune
→ see Thesaurus box at VALUABLE

2 extremely important or useful: *priceless information* **3** *informal* very funny or silly: *The look on his face when I walked in the room was priceless.*

pric·ey, **pricy** /ˈpraɪsi/ *adj. informal* expensive: *a pricey restaurant*

THESAURUS

expensive, high, overpriced, extortionate, astronomical, exorbitant
→ see Thesaurus box at EXPENSIVE

prick[1] /prɪk/ *v.* **1** [T] to make a small hole in the surface of something, using a sharp point: *Prick the pie dough all over with a fork.* | *She* ***pricked*** *her* ***finger*** *with the needle.*

THESAURUS

pierce, make a hole in, punch, drill, bore
→ see Thesaurus box at PIERCE

2 prick up its ears if an animal pricks up its ears, it raises them and points them toward a sound **3 prick up your ears** to start listening to what someone is saying because it is interesting

prick[2] *n.* [C] **1** a slight pain you get when something sharp goes into your skin: *She felt a sharp prick when the needle went into her finger.* **2** a small hole in the surface of something, made by a sharp point

prick·le[1] /ˈprɪkəl/ *n.* [C] **1** a long thin sharp point on the skin of some plants and animals **2** a stinging feeling on your skin

prickle[2] *v.* [I,T] if your skin prickles, or if something prickles your skin, you feel a slight stinging pain on your skin: *That sweater always prickles me.*

prick·ly /ˈprɪkli/ *adj.* **1** covered with PRICKLES: *prickly bushes* **2** causing a stinging feeling on your skin: *a prickly wool jacket*

pride¹ /praɪd/ *n.* [U] **1** a feeling of satisfaction and pleasure in what you have done, or in what someone connected with you has done [➡ **proud**]: *Everyone on our team* ***takes*** *great* ***pride in*** (=is very proud of) *the quality of their work.* | *They always talk about their son* ***with pride***. **2** a feeling that you like and respect yourself and that you deserve to be respected by other people: *Losing his job really* ***hurt*** *his* ***pride***. **3** a feeling that you are better than other people: *I had too much pride to ask for money.* **4 sb's pride and joy** someone or something that is very important to someone: *Ken's new car is his pride and joy.* **5 swallow your pride** to ignore your feelings of pride and do something that seems necessary, even though you do not want to do it: *You're just going to have to swallow your pride and apologize.*

pride² *v.* **pride yourself on sth** to be very proud of something that you do well, or of a quality that you have: *Sandy prides herself on her ability to speak four languages.*

priest /prist/ *n.* [C] someone who performs religious duties and ceremonies in some religions [➡ **minister**]

priest·ess /ˈpristɪs/ *n.* [C] a woman with religious authority and duties in some non-Christian religions

priest·hood /ˈpristhʊd/ *n.* **the priesthood** the position of being a priest: *Angelo has decided to* ***enter the priesthood*** (=become a priest).

prim /prɪm/ *adj.* very formal in the way you behave, and easily shocked by anything rude: *Janet's much too* ***prim and proper*** *to laugh at a joke like that.* —**primly** *adv.*

pri·ma·cy /ˈpraɪməsi/ *n.* [U] the state of being the thing or person with the most importance or authority: *No one ever questioned* ***the primacy of*** *the church in their lives.*

pri·ma don·na /ˌprimə ˈdɑnə, ˌprɪmə-/ *n.* [C] *disapproving* someone who thinks that s/he is very good at what s/he does, and demands a lot of attention and admiration from other people

pri·mal /ˈpraɪməl/ *adj.* [only before noun] primal feelings are basic and seem to come from ancient times when humans were more like animals: *primal instincts*

pri·mar·i·ly /praɪˈmɛrəli/ *adv.* mainly: *We do sell paintings, but this is primarily a furniture store.*

THESAURUS

mainly, **chiefly**, **principally**, **largely**
➔ see Thesaurus box at MAINLY

pri·mar·y¹ /ˈpraɪˌmɛri, -məri/ *adj.* [only before noun] **1** most important [= **main**]: *Our primary concern is the safety of the children.* **2** relating to the education of children who are between 5 and 11 years old: *primary education*

primary² *n.* plural **primaries** [C] an election in the U.S. in which people vote to decide who will be their political party's CANDIDATE for a political position

ˌprimary ˈcare *n.* [U] the main medical help that you get, unless your doctor decides that you need to see a SPECIALIST (=doctor with special skills)

ˌprimary ˈcolor *n.* [C] one of the three colors – red, yellow, and blue – that you can mix together to make any other color

ˈprimary ˌschool *n.* [C] ELEMENTARY SCHOOL

pri·mate /ˈpraɪmeɪt/ *n.* [C] a member of the group of MAMMALS that includes humans and monkeys

prime¹ /praɪm/ *adj.* [only before noun] **1** most important: *Smoking is the prime cause of lung disease.* **2** very good: *The house is in a* ***prime location***. | *The church is a* ***prime example*** *of Gothic architecture.*

prime² *n.* **be in your prime/be in the prime of life** to be at the time in your life when you are strongest and most active

prime³ *v.* [T] **1** to prepare someone for a situation so that s/he knows what to do: *The senators were primed to ask some tough questions.* **2** to put a special layer of paint on a surface, to prepare it for the main layer **3** to prepare a PUMP to work by filling it with a liquid

ˌprime ˈminister *n.* [C] the leader of the government in countries that have a PARLIAMENT

ˌprime ˈnumber *n.* [C] a number that can only be divided by itself and the number one

prim·er /ˈpraɪmɚ/ *n.* [C,U] a special paint that you put on wood, metal, etc. before you put on the main layer of paint

ˈprime ˌtime *n.* [U] the time in the evening when the largest number of people are watching television

pri·me·val /praɪˈmivəl/ *adj.* belonging to the earliest time in the existence of the Earth or the UNIVERSE: *primeval forests*

prim·i·tive /ˈprɪmət̬ɪv/ *adj.* **1** belonging to a simple way of life that existed in the past, or to an early stage in the development of humans or animals [≠ **modern**]: *primitive societies* **2** very simple, uncomfortable, or without modern features: *primitive living conditions*

pri·mor·di·al /praɪˈmɔrdiəl/ *adj.* existing at the beginning of time or the beginning of the Earth: *the primordial seas*

prince /prɪns/ *n.* [C] **1** the son of a king or queen, or one of his or her close male relatives **2** a male ruler of some small countries: *Prince Rainier of Monaco*

prince·ly /ˈprɪnsli/ *adj.* impressive or large: *a* ***princely sum*** *of money*

prin·cess /ˈprɪnsɪs, -sɛs/ *n.* [C] **1** the daughter

of a king or queen, or one of his or her close female relatives **2** the wife of a prince

prin·ci·pal[1] /ˈprɪnsəpəl/ *n.* **1** [C] someone who is in charge of a school: *a high school principal* | *Helen Davies is the* ***principal of*** *Ferry Elementary School.* **2** [U] *technical* the original amount of money that is lent to someone or saved by someone, not including any of the INTEREST **3** [C] the main person in a business or organization, who can make business decisions

principal[2] *adj.* most important [= **main**]: *Magic is a principal ingredient in fairy tales.*

prin·ci·pal·i·ty /ˌprɪnsəˈpæləti/ *n.* plural **principalities** [C] a country ruled by a prince

prin·ci·pally /ˈprɪnsəpli/ *adv.* mainly: *an audience made up principally of women*

P

THESAURUS

mainly, **chiefly**, **largely**, **primarily**
➔ see Thesaurus box at MAINLY

prin·ci·ple /ˈprɪnsəpəl/ *n.* **1** [C,U] a moral rule or set of ideas about what is right and wrong, that influences how you behave: *the* ***principle that*** *everyone is equal* | *I refused to accept the contract as a* ***matter of principle*** (=because the contract included things I believed were wrong). | *our society's values and* ***moral principles*** **2** [C] the basic idea that a plan or system is based on: *the* ***principles of*** *business management* | *The law is a violation of the* ***basic principles*** *of a free society.* **3** [C] a rule that explains the way something works: *the* ***basic/fundamental principles*** *of physics* **4 in principle a)** if something is possible in principle, there is no good reason why it should not happen: *In principle, you can leave work early on Friday, but it's not always possible.* **b)** if you agree to something in principle, you agree about a general plan or idea without the details: *The arrangement has been agreed to in principle.*

prin·ci·pled /ˈprɪnsəpəld/ *adj. written* having strong beliefs about what is morally right and wrong: *a* ***strongly/highly principled*** *woman*

print[1] /prɪnt/ *v.* **1** [I,T] to produce words, numbers, or pictures on paper, using a machine that puts ink onto the surface: *The books are printed in China.* | *Why isn't my document printing?* **2** [T] to produce many copies of a book, newspaper, etc.: *About 100 copies of the report have been printed.* **3** [T] to print an article, letter, speech, etc. in a newspaper, book, or magazine: *The Times printed a story about it this week.* **4** [I,T] to write words by hand without joining the letters: *Please print your name in capital letters.* **5** [T] to produce a photograph on special paper

print sth ⇔ **off/out** *phr. v.* to produce a printed copy of a computer document

print[2] *n.* **1** [U] writing that has been printed in books, newspapers, etc.: *The print is awfully small.* | *People learn many words by seeing them* ***in print****, rather than hearing them said.* **2 be in print/be out of print** if a book is in print, it is available to buy, and if it is out of print, it is not available to buy anymore **3 the fine/small print** the details of a legal document, which are often in very small writing: *the fine print in the contract* **4** [C] a picture that has been printed from a small sheet of metal or block of wood, or a copy of a painting **5** [C] a photograph printed on paper: *Why don't you order an extra* ***set of prints****?* **6** [C] a mark made on a surface or in a soft substance by something that has been pressed onto it [➡ **footprint**]: *muddy paw prints all over the floor* **7 prints** [plural] someone's FINGERPRINTS **8** [C,U] cloth that has a colored pattern on it: *a print dress*

print·er /ˈprɪntɚ/ *n.* [C] **1** a machine connected to a computer that can copy documents from a computer onto paper: *a laser printer* ➔ see Topic box at OFFICE ➔ see picture on page A11 **2** someone who owns or works in a printing business

print·ing /ˈprɪntɪŋ/ *n.* **1** [U] the act or process of making a book, magazine, etc. using a machine: *a printing error* **2** [C] an act of printing a number of copies of a book: *a novel in its third printing* **3** [U] a method of writing, in which you write each letter of a word separately rather than joining them together

ˈprinting press *n.* [C] a machine that prints newspapers, books, etc.

print·out /ˈprɪntaʊt/ *n.* [C,U] paper with printed information on it, produced by a computer PRINTER

pri·or /ˈpraɪɚ/ *adj. formal* **1 prior to sth** before: *the week prior to the election* **2** [only before noun] done, planned, or existing earlier than something else [= **previous**]: *No change can be made without prior approval.*

pri·or·i·tize /praɪˈɔrəˌtaɪz/ *v.* [T] to deal with something important first, or to list several things, problems, etc. in order of importance: *Ask your boss to prioritize your projects.* —**prioritization** /praɪˌɔrətəˈzeɪʃən/ *n.* [U]

pri·or·i·ty /praɪˈɔrəti/ *n.* **1** [C,U] the thing that you think is most important and that needs attention before anything else: *Education is his* ***top priority****.* | *The company considers training to be a* ***high/low priority****.* **2** [U] the right to be given attention first and before other people or things: *Children who live near the school are* ***given priority over*** *those who live farther away.*

prism /ˈprɪzəm/ *n.* [C] a transparent block of glass that breaks up white light into different colors

pris·on /ˈprɪzən/ *n.* [C,U] a large building where people are kept as a punishment for a crime, or while waiting to go to court for their TRIAL: *He spent ten months* ***in prison****.* | *Williams was* ***sent to***

prison** for rape.* | *a **prison sentence/term (=time that must be spent in prison)

COLLOCATIONS

go to prison: *He could go to prison for 25 years.*
put sb in prison: *If he's caught, they'll put him in prison.*
send sb to prison: *Her husband was sent back to prison after violating his parole* (=disobeying the rules which allowed him to leave prison early).
spend time in prison – to be in prison for committing a crime: *He will spend the rest of his life in prison.*
release sb from prison – to let someone leave prison: *He was released from prison after serving a two-year sentence.*
get out of prison – to be released from prison: *The day he got out of prison, he stole a car.*
escape from prison: *He died trying to escape from prison.*
➔ PUNISHMENT, CRIME, CRIMINAL

pris·on·er /ˈprɪzənɚ/ *n.* [C] **1** someone who is kept in a prison as a punishment for a crime [= **convict**] **2** someone who is taken by force and kept somewhere, for example during a war: *Six soldiers were **taken prisoner**.* | *They **kept/held** her **prisoner** for three months.*

THESAURUS

captive – someone who is kept as a prisoner, especially in a war: *The rebels are holding 54 captives.*
hostage – someone who is kept as a prisoner by an enemy, so that the other side will do what the enemy demands: *The group demanded that 400 prisoners be released in exchange for the hostages.*

ˌprisoner of ˈwar, P.O.W. *n.* [C] a member of the military who is caught by the enemy during a war and kept as a prisoner

pris·sy /ˈprɪsi/ *adj. informal disapproving* behaving very correctly, and easily shocked by anything rude

pris·tine /ˈprɪˌstin, prɪˈstin/ *adj.* extremely clean, and not spoiled at all by use: *a 1973 Volkswagen Beetle **in pristine condition*** | *the pristine white sand*

pri·va·cy /ˈpraɪvəsi/ *n.* [U] **1** the state of being able to be alone, and not seen or heard by other people: *the things people do **in the privacy of** their own homes* **2** the state of being able to keep your own affairs secret: *reporters who **invade** the **privacy** of celebrities*

pri·vate[1] /ˈpraɪvɪt/ *adj.* **1** for use by one person or group, not for everyone [≠ **public**]: *a private jet* | *Rooms are available for private parties.* | *They were arrested for trespassing on **private property**.* **2** secret or personal and not for sharing with others: *her private thoughts* | *You had no right to look at my private papers.*

THESAURUS

secret – known or felt only by you, and not talked about or shown to anyone else: *Dreams may reveal our secret desires.*
personal – concerning only you: *He asked a lot of personal questions.*
innermost – your innermost feelings, desires, etc. are the ones you feel most strongly and keep private: *Collins expressed her innermost feelings in her poetry.*
be none of sb's business – if something is none of your business, it is private and you should not ask about it: *It's none of your business what I do in my free time.*

3 not relating to, owned by, or paid for by the government [≠ **public**]: *a private college* **4** separate from your work or your official position, and not related to it: *Should reporters be prying into the **private lives** of politicians?* **5** quiet and without lots of people: *Is there a private corner where we can talk?* —**privately** *adv.*: *Is there someplace we can talk privately?*

private[2] *n.* **1 in private** without other people listening or watching: *Miss Schultz, I need to speak to you in private.* **2** [C] a soldier of the lowest rank in the Army or Marines

ˌprivate ˈenterprise *n.* [U] the economic system in which private businesses can compete, and the government does not control industry

THESAURUS

business, commerce, industry, trade
➔ see Thesaurus box at BUSINESS

ˌprivate inˈvestigator also **ˌprivate deˈtective, ˈprivate eye** *informal n.* [C] someone whom you pay to do things such as look for information or missing people, or follow someone and report on what s/he does

ˌprivate ˈparts also **pri·vates** /ˈpraɪvɪts/ *n.* [plural] *informal* the sex organs – used in order to avoid naming them directly

ˈprivate school *n.* [C] a school that is not supported by government money, where education must be paid for by the children's parents [➥ **public school**]

pri·va·tion /praɪˈveɪʃən/ *n.* [C,U] *formal* a lack of the things that everyone needs, such as food, warmth, and shelter

pri·vat·ize /ˈpraɪvəˌtaɪz/ *v.* [T] if a government privatizes an industry, service, etc. that it controls or owns, it sells it or gives contracts to private companies [➥ **nationalize**] —**privatization** /ˌpraɪvət̬əˈzeɪʃən/ *n.* [U]

priv·i·lege /ˈprɪvlɪdʒ, -vəlɪdʒ/ *n.* **1** [C] a special advantage that is given only to one person or group of people: *These soldiers were given **spe-***

P

cial privileges. | *Good health care should not be just a* ***privilege of*** *the wealthy.* **2** [singular] something that you are lucky to have the chance to do, and that you enjoy very much: ***It's*** *been* ***a privilege to*** *meet you, sir.* | *I* ***had the privilege of*** *working with some very interesting people.* **3** [U] a situation in which people who are rich or of a high social class have many more advantages than other people: *a life of wealth and privilege* —**privileged** *adj.*

priv·y¹ /ˈprɪvi/ *adj. formal* **be privy to sth** to share secret knowledge of something: *I was not privy to the discussion.*

privy² *n.* plural **privies** [C] *old-fashioned* an OUTHOUSE

prize¹ /praɪz/ *n.* [C] something that is given to someone who is successful in a competition, race, game of chance, etc.: *Her roses won* ***first/second/third prize*** *at the flower show.* | *Bohr* ***won*** *the Nobel* ***Prize*** *in 1922.* | *the Pulitzer* ***Prize for*** *fiction*

prize² *adj.* **1** good enough to win a prize or to have won a prize: *prize cattle* **2 prize money** money that is given to the person who wins a competition, race, etc.

prize³ *v.* [T] to think that someone or something is very important or valuable: *a necklace that his mother had prized*

prized /praɪzd/ *adj.* very important or valuable to someone: *Education is* ***highly prized***. | *all her most* ***prized possessions***

prize·fight /ˈpraɪzfaɪt/ *n.* [C] a BOXING match in which the competitors are paid —**prizefighter** *n.* [C]

pro /proʊ/ *n.* plural **pros** [C] **1** *informal* a PROFESSIONAL: *a golf pro* **2** something that is an advantage: *We discussed* ***the pros and cons*** (=the advantages and disadvantages) *of starting our own business.* —**pro** *adj.*: *pro basketball*

prob·a·bil·i·ty /ˌprɑbəˈbɪləṭi/ *n.* **1** [singular, U] how likely it is that something will happen, exist, or be true: *the* ***probability of*** *delay* | *a* ***high/low probability*** *of success* **2 in all probability** very probably: *There will, in all probability, be parts that you do not understand.* **3** [singular] something that is likely to happen or exist: *War is a real probability unless the talks succeed.*

prob·a·ble /ˈprɑbəbəl/ *adj.* likely to happen, exist, or be true: ***It is probable that*** *both genes and the environment play a role in the disease.* | *the probable cause of the accident*

prob·a·bly /ˈprɑbəbli/ *adv.* likely to happen, exist, or be true: *It will probably take about a week.* | *"Is Julie going?"* ***"Probably not."***

pro·ba·tion /proʊˈbeɪʃən/ *n.* [U] **1** a system that allows some criminals to leave prison early or not to go to prison at all, if they promise to behave well for a specific period of time: *Preston's been* ***on probation*** *for three years.* **2** a period of time during which an employer can see if a new worker is good enough —**probationary** /proʊˈbeɪʃəˌnɛri/ *adj.*

pro'bation ˌofficer *n.* [C] someone whose job is to watch, advise, and help people who have broken the law and are on probation

probe¹ /proʊb/ *v.* [I,T] **1** to ask questions in order to find things out: *reporters* ***probing into*** *the personal lives of politicians* **2** to look for something or examine something, using a long thin instrument —**probing** *adj.*: *probing questions*

probe² *n.* [C] **1** a long thin instrument that doctors and scientists use to examine parts of the body **2** a SPACECRAFT without people in it that is sent into space to collect information

TOPIC

spacecraft, **spaceship**, **rocket**, **(space) shuttle**, **satellite**

➔ see Topic box at SPACE¹

3 *journalism* a process of asking many questions in order to find the truth about something

prob·lem /ˈprɑbləm/ *n.* [C] **1** a difficult situation or person that has to be dealt with or thought about: *I've been* ***having*** *a few* ***problems*** *with my car.* | *There are* ***problems with*** *the equipment.* | *The governor has done nothing to* ***solve*** *these* ***problems***. | *a* ***drug problem*** *in the school* | *the* ***problem of*** *teen pregnancy* | *Unemployment remains a* ***serious problem***. ▶ Don't say "an important problem." ◀

THESAURUS

setback – a problem that stops you from making progress: *The space program suffered a major setback when the space shuttle, Discovery, exploded.*
snag informal – a problem, especially one that you had not expected: *The project has hit a major snag.*
hitch – a small problem that delays or prevents something: *There have been a few last-minute hitches.*
trouble – when something does not work in the way it should: *The plane developed engine trouble.*
hassle spoken – a situation that is annoying because it causes problems: *I wish clothes shopping was less of a hassle.* | *With a digital camera you get pictures without the hassle of getting them developed.*
➔ DEFECT¹

2 something wrong with your health or with part of your body: *a woman with serious* ***health problems*** | *He has a* ***back/heart/knee etc. problem***. **3** a question that must be answered, especially one relating to numbers or facts: *The test will have 20 algebra problems.*

SPOKEN PHRASES

4 no problem a) used in order to say that you are very willing to do something: *"Can you help?" "Sure, no problem."* **b)** used after someone has thanked you or said s/he is sorry: *"Thanks a lot." "Oh, no problem."* **5 that's your/his/their etc. problem** used in order to say that someone else is responsible for dealing with a situation, not you: *If you can't get yourself there on time, that's your problem.* **6 what's your problem?** used in order to ask someone what is wrong, in a way that shows you think s/he is not being reasonable: *Look, what's your problem? It's my decision!*

prob·lem·at·ic /ˌprɑbləˈmæt̬ɪk/ *adj.* full of problems and difficult to deal with: *Painkillers can be problematic when combined with other medicines.* —**problematically** *adv.*

pro·ce·dure /prəˈsidʒɚ/ *n.* [C,U] a way of doing something, especially the correct or normal way [➡ **process**]: *the **procedure for** dealing with a fire* | *Officials must **follow** the correct **procedure**.* | *a common **medical procedure*** —**procedural** *adj.*

pro·ceed /prəˈsid, proʊ-/ *v.* [I] **1** to continue to do something that has already been planned or started: *We will **proceed with** the negotiations.* **2 proceed to do sth** to do something next: *He took out his wallet, and proceeded to count out enough money to pay for the meal.* **3** *formal* to move in a particular direction: *Please **proceed to** the nearest exit.*

pro·ceed·ings /prəˈsidɪŋz, proʊ-/ *n.* [plural] **1** an event or series of actions: *A crowd gathered to watch the proceedings.* **2** actions taken in a court of law or in a legal case: *legal proceedings*

pro·ceeds /ˈproʊsidz/ *n.* [plural] the money that has been gained from doing something or selling something: *The **proceeds from** the carnival will **go to** local children's charities.*

pro·cess[1] /ˈprɑsɛs, ˈproʊ-/ *n.* [C] **1** a series of actions, developments, or changes that happen naturally: *the aging process* | *the **natural process** of evolution* **2** a series of actions that someone does to achieve a particular result: *the peace process* | *Medical research is a **slow process**.* **3 be in the process of doing sth** to have started doing something and not yet be finished: *Grady is in the process of collecting data for the study.* **4 in the process** while you are doing something or something is happening: *I spilled my coffee, burning myself in the process.* **5** a system or a treatment of materials that is used for producing goods: *an industrial process*

process[2] *v.* [T] **1** to deal with information in an official way: *This department processes mail order requests.* **2** to make food, materials, or goods ready to be used or sold, for example by preserving or improving them in some way: *methods for processing beef* **3** to put information into a computer to be examined —**processed** *adj.*: *processed cheese* —**processing** *n.* [U]

pro·ces·sion /prəˈsɛʃən/ *n.* [C] **1** a line of people or vehicles moving slowly as part of a ceremony [➡ **parade**]: *a funeral procession* **2** several people or things of the same kind, appearing or happening one after the other: *an endless **procession of** legal experts*

pro·ces·sor /ˈprɑsɛsɚ/ *n.* [C] a CPU → FOOD PROCESSOR

ˌpro-ˈchoice *adj.* believing that women have a right to have an ABORTION [➡ **pro-life**]

pro·claim /proʊˈkleɪm, prə-/ *v.* [T] *formal* to say officially or publicly that something is true or exists: *In 1948, Israel proclaimed its independence.*

proc·la·ma·tion /ˌprɑkləˈmeɪʃən/ *n.* [C] an official public statement about something important: *the Emancipation Proclamation* (=the speech about freeing the SLAVES in the U.S. in 1863)

pro·cras·ti·nate /prəˈkræstəˌneɪt/ *v.* [I] to delay doing something that you ought to do: *People tend to **procrastinate about** paperwork.* —**procrastinator** *n.* [C] —**procrastination** /prəˌkræstəˈneɪʃən/ *n.* [U]

THESAURUS

delay, **postpone**, **put off**
→ see Thesaurus box at DELAY[1]

pro·cre·ate /ˈproʊkriˌeɪt/ *v.* [I,T] *formal* to produce children or baby animals —**procreation** /ˌproʊkriˈeɪʃən/ *n.* [U]

pro·cure /proʊˈkyʊr, prə-/ *v.* [T] *formal* to obtain something, especially something that is difficult to get: *Clark was accused of **procuring** guns **for** the rebels.* —**procurement** *n.* [U]

prod /prɑd/ *v.* past tense and past participle **prodded**, present participle **prodding** [I,T] **1** POKE **2** to strongly encourage someone to do something, especially when s/he is lazy or not willing: *Teachers are having to **prod** students **into** completing their work.*

pro·di·gious /prəˈdɪdʒəs/ *adj. formal* very large or skillful in a surprising or impressive way: *The Internet contains **prodigious amounts** of information.* —**prodigiously** *adv.*

prod·i·gy /ˈprɑdədʒi/ *n.* plural **prodigies** [C] a young person who has a great natural ability in a subject or skill [➡ **genius**]: *Mozart was a **child prodigy**.*

pro·duce[1] /prəˈdus/ *v.* [T] **1** to grow something or make it naturally [➡ **product**, **production**]: *the areas where cotton is produced* | *Trees produce carbon dioxide.* **2** to make something happen or develop, or have a particular result or effect: *The drug can produce side effects in some people.* **3** to show something so it can be seen or considered: *Officer Ryan asked the suspect to produce his driver's license.* **4** to make something, especially using an industrial process [➡ **product**]: *the costs of producing goods and services* **5** if someone produces a movie, play, or television program, s/he finds the money for it and controls the way it is made [➡ **producer**] **6** to make something using skill and imagination: *Diane produced a fantastic meal.* **7** to give birth to a baby or young animals

prod·uce² /ˈprɑdus, ˈproʊ-/ *n.* [U] food that has been grown or farmed, especially fresh fruits and vegetables [➡ **product**]: *The restaurant uses **fresh** local **produce**.*

pro·duc·er /prəˈdusɚ/ *n.* [C] **1** a person, company, or country that makes or grows goods, foods, or materials: *Scotland is a **producer of** high quality wool.* | *oil producers in Venezuela* **2** someone whose job is to control the preparation of a play, movie, etc., but who does not direct the actors: *a TV producer*

P

TOPIC

actor, **actress**, **director**, **film/movie crew**
→ see Topic box at MOVIE

prod·uct /ˈprɑdʌkt/ *n.* **1** [C,U] something that is grown, made in a factory, or taken from nature, usually in order to be sold [➡ **produce**, **production**]: *None of our products are tested on animals.* | *milk and other **dairy products*** **2 be the product of sth** to be the result of particular experiences, situations, or processes: *Abusive husbands tend to be the product of violent homes.* | *The report was the product of four years' hard work.* **3** [C] *technical* the number you get by multiplying two or more numbers

pro·duc·tion /prəˈdʌkʃən/ *n.* **1** [U] the process of making or growing things, or the amount that is produced: *Steel production has decreased by 35%.* **2** [C,U] a play, movie, etc. that is produced for the public, or the process of producing it: *a new Broadway production of "My Fair Lady"*

pro·duc·tive /prəˈdʌktɪv/ *adj.* producing or achieving a lot [≠ **unproductive**]: *productive land* | *Some workers become **more/less productive** under this system.* —**productively** *adv.*

pro·duc·tiv·i·ty /ˌproʊdəkˈtɪvət̬i, ˌprɑ-/ *n.* [U] the rate at which goods are produced, and the amount produced: *ways of **increasing/raising/improving productivity***

prof /prɑf/ *n.* [C] **1** *spoken* a PROFESSOR **2 Prof.** the written abbreviation of **professor**

pro·fane /proʊˈfeɪn, prə-/ *adj.* showing a lack of respect for God or for holy things, by using rude words or religious words wrongly [➡ **obscene**]: *profane language*

pro·fan·i·ty /proʊˈfænət̬i, prə-/ *n.* plural **profanities** [C,U] a swear word, or a religious word used wrongly, that shows a lack of respect for God or for holy things [➡ **obscenity**]

pro·fess /prəˈfɛs, proʊ-/ *v.* [T] *formal* **1** to say that you do something or are something, often when it is not really true [= **claim**]: *He **professed to** be surprised by the verdict.* **2** to express a personal feeling or belief openly: *Soon, Frank was **professing** his **love** and asking her to marry him.* —**professed** *adj.*

pro·fes·sion /prəˈfɛʃən/ *n.* **1** [C] a job that needs special education and training: *professions such as nursing or teaching* | *He's a lawyer **by profession*** (=as his job).

THESAURUS

job, **work**, **position**, **occupation**, **career**, **vocation**
→ see Thesaurus box at JOB

2 [singular] all the people in a particular profession: *the medical/legal/teaching etc. profession* **3** [C] *formal* a statement of your belief, opinion, or feeling

pro·fes·sion·al¹ /prəˈfɛʃənl/ *adj.* **1** doing a job, sport, or activity for money [≠ **amateur**]: *professional athletes* | *a professional army* **2** professional sports are played by people who are paid [≠ **amateur**]: *professional hockey* **3** relating to a job that needs special education and training: *You should speak to a lawyer for professional advice.* **4** showing that someone has been well trained and is good at his/her work: *This report looks very professional.* —**professionally** *adv.*

professional² *n.* [C] **1** someone who works in a job that needs special education and training: *a health care professional* **2** someone who earns money by doing a job, sport, or activity that other people do just for enjoyment [≠ **amateur**]: *In this competition, the amateurs play alongside the professionals.*

pro·fes·sion·al·ism /prəˈfɛʃənlˌɪzəm/ *n.* [U] the skill and high standards of behavior expected of a professional person

pro·fes·sor /prəˈfɛsɚ/ *n.* [C] a teacher at a university or college, especially one who has a high rank: *Thank you, Professor Drexler.* | *my history professor* | *a **professor of** economics*

THESAURUS

teacher, **lecturer**, **instructor**, **coach**
→ see Thesaurus box at TEACHER

prof·fer /ˈprɑfɚ/ *v.* [T] *formal* to offer something to someone

pro·fi·cien·cy /prəˈfɪʃənsi/ *n.* [U] the ability to do something with a high level of skill: *a student's **proficiency in** math* | *The classes were geared to our **level of proficiency**.*

pro·fi·cient /prəˈfɪʃənt/ *adj.* able to do something with a high level of skill: *a proficient typist* —**proficiently** *adv.*

pro·file¹ /ˈprouфaɪl/ *n.* **1** [C,U] a side view of someone's head: *Callan photographed her* ***in profile.*** **2** [C] a short description that gives important details about someone or something: *a* ***profile of*** *her career* **3 keep a low profile** to behave quietly and avoid doing things that would make people notice you **4 high profile** something that is high profile is noticed by many people and gets a lot of attention: *Luria has a high profile in the arts community.*

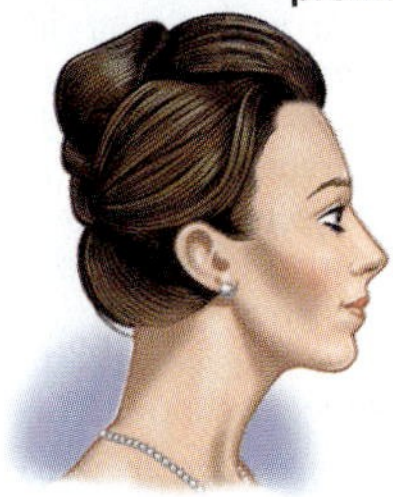
profile

profile² *v.* [T] to write or give a short description of someone or something: *the artists who are profiled in his book*

pro·fil·ing /ˈprouˌfaɪlɪŋ/ *n.* [U] the process of examining information about a particular group, in order to know what they might want or do, or in order to know who might belong to that group: *Profiling has helped U.S. Customs officers spot drug smugglers.*

prof·it¹ /ˈprɑfɪt/ *n.* **1** [C,U] money that you gain by selling things or doing business: *NovaCorp* ***made a*** *pretax* ***profit*** *of $39 million.* | *They sold the company* ***at a*** *huge* ***profit.*** **2** [U] an advantage that you gain from doing something: *reading for profit and pleasure*

profit² *v. formal* **1** [I,T] to be useful or helpful to someone: *Everyone* ***profits from*** *an education.* **2** [I] to get money from doing something: *The states have* ***profited from*** *cigarette taxes.*

prof·it·a·bil·i·ty /ˌprɑfɪṭəˈbɪləṭi/ *n.* [U] the state of producing a profit, or the degree to which a business or activity is profitable

prof·it·a·ble /ˈprɑfɪṭəbəl/ *adj.* producing a profit or a useful result: *The company has had a profitable year.* —**profitably** *adv.*

ˈprofit ˌmargin *n.* [C] the difference between the cost of producing something and the price you sell it at to make a profit

ˈprofit ˌsharing *n.* [U] a system in which workers are allowed to share some of their company's profits

prof·li·gate /ˈprɑfləgɪt/ *adj. formal* wasting money in a careless way

pro·found /prəˈfaʊnd/ *adj.* **1** very great, important, or strong: *Davis had a* ***profound impact/effect/influence*** *on jazz music.* **2** showing strong serious feelings [= **deep**]: *a profound sense of guilt* **3** showing great knowledge and understanding [= **deep**]: *a profound book* —**profoundly** *adv.*: *Their lives had been profoundly affected by the war.* —**profundity** /prəˈfʌndəṭi/ *n.* [C,U]

pro·fuse·ly /prəˈfyusli/ *adv.* many times, or in large numbers or amounts: *Keiko thanked them profusely.* —**profuse** *adj.*

pro·fu·sion /prəˈfyuʒən/ *n.* [singular, U] *formal* a very large amount: *a* ***profusion of*** *wildflowers*

prog·e·ny /ˈprɑdʒəni/ *n.* [U] *literary* the babies of a person or animal

prog·no·sis /prɑgˈnoʊsɪs/ *n.* plural **prognoses** /-siz/ [C] *technical* **1** a doctor's opinion of how an illness or disease will develop [➡ **diagnosis**] **2** a judgment about what will happen in the future, based on information or experience

pro·gram¹ /ˈproʊgræm, -grəm/ *n.* [C] **1** a show on television or radio: *a popular TV program* | *a* ***program about*** *whales* ➔ see Topic box at TELEVISION **2** a set of instructions given to a computer to make it do a particular job: *an educational software program* **3** a series of actions, services, courses, etc. which are designed to achieve something: *Stanford's MBA program* | *government programs that benefit poor people* | *an exercise program* **4** a small book or piece of paper that gives information about a play, concert, etc. and who the performers are ➔ see Topic box at THEATER **5 get with the program** *spoken* used in order to tell someone to pay attention to what needs to be done, and do it

program² *v.* past tense and past participle **programmed**, present participle **programming** [T] **1** to set a machine to operate in a particular way: *I programmed the VCR to record that movie you wanted.* **2 be programmed** if a person or animal is programmed socially or BIOLOGICALLY to do something, he, she, or it does it without thinking: *Our bodies seem* ***programmed to*** *want the type and amounts of foods we need.* **3** to give a set of instructions to a computer to make it do a particular job: *a computer* ***programmed to*** *play chess*

pro·gram·mer /ˈproʊˌgræmɚ, -grəmɚ/ *n.* [C] someone whose job is to write programs for computers

pro·gram·ming /ˈproʊˌgræmɪŋ/ *n.* [U] **1** television or radio programs, or the planning of these broadcasts: *quality children's programming* **2** the activity of writing programs for computers, or something written by a programmer

prog·ress¹ /ˈprɑgrəs, -grɛs/ *n.* [U] **1** the process of developing or improving, or getting closer to achieving something: *a country which has* ***made*** *great economic* ***progress*** | *tests to measure the* ***progress of*** *individual students* | *The patients had made* ***progress in*** *changing their eating habits.* | ***Progress on*** *the report has been slow.* **2 in progress** happening now, and not yet finished: *Please do not enter while there is a class in progress.* **3** movement toward a place: *The ship* ***made*** *slow* ***progress through*** *the rough sea.*

pro·gress² /prəˈgrɛs/ *v.* [I] **1** to develop, improve, or become more complete over a period of time: *Work on the new building progressed quickly.* **2** if an activity, event, time, etc.

P

progresses, it continues and time passes: *As the talks progressed, a deal became certain.*

pro·gres·sion /prəˈgrɛʃən/ *n.* [singular, U] a process of change or development: *the rapid progression of her illness*

pro·gres·sive¹ /prəˈgrɛsɪv/ *adj.* **1** supporting new or modern ideas and methods: *the ideas behind progressive education* **2** becoming better, worse, or more complete over a period of time: *a progressive disease* —**progressively** *adv.*

progressive² *n. technical* **the progressive** the CONTINUOUS

pro·hib·it /proʊˈhɪbɪt, prə-/ *v.* [T] **1** to say that an action is illegal or not allowed, especially officially: *Smoking is strictly prohibited.* | *Stores are* ***prohibited from*** *selling alcohol to people under 21.*

P

THESAURUS

forbid, not allow/permit/let, ban, bar
➔ see Thesaurus box at FORBID

2 to make something impossible or prevent it from happening

pro·hi·bi·tion /ˌproʊəˈbɪʃən/ *n.* **1** [C,U] *formal* the act of saying that something is illegal or not allowed, or an order that does this: *a* ***prohibition on*** *cigarette advertising* **2 Prohibition** the period from 1919 to 1933 in the U.S., when it was illegal to produce or sell alcoholic drinks

pro·hib·i·tive /proʊˈhɪbət̬ɪv, prə-/ *adj.* preventing people from doing or buying something: *The* ***cost*** *of the trip was* ***prohibitive*** (=too high). —**prohibitively** *adv.*

proj·ect¹ /ˈprɑdʒɛkt, -dʒɪkt/ *n.* **1** [C] a carefully planned piece of work: *the new highway project* | *a research project involving people with cancer* **2 the projects** *informal* [plural] HOUSING PROJECTS

project

overhead projector

pro·ject² /prəˈdʒɛkt/ *v.* **1** [T] to calculate or plan what will happen in the future, using the information you have now: *The new freeway is projected to cost $230 million.* | *A national tour is projected for 2005.* **2** [T] to make other people have a particular idea about you: *Jim always* ***projects an image*** *of self-confidence.* **3** [I,T] to speak or sing loudly enough to be heard by everyone in a big room or theater **4** [T] to make the picture of a movie, photograph, etc. appear in a larger form on a screen or flat surface **5** [I,T] to stick out beyond an edge or surface: *The roof projects over the driveway.* **6** [T] *formal* to make something move up or forward with great force

pro·jec·tile /prəˈdʒɛktl, -ˌtaɪl/ *n.* [C] *formal* an object that is thrown or fired from a weapon

pro·jec·tion /prəˈdʒɛkʃən/ *n.* **1** [C] a statement about something you think will happen, based on information you have now: *this year's sales projections* **2** [C] something that sticks out beyond an edge or surface **3** [C,U] the act of making a movie, photograph, etc. appear on a screen, or the image itself: *film projection*

pro·jec·tion·ist /prəˈdʒɛkʃənɪst/ *n.* [C] someone whose job is to operate a projector

pro·jec·tor /prəˈdʒɛktɚ/ *n.* [C] a piece of equipment that uses light to make a movie, photograph, etc. appear on a screen

pro·le·tar·i·at /ˌproʊləˈtɛriət/ *n.* **the proletariat** the people in a society who are poor, own no property, etc. —**proletarian** *adj.*

ˌpro-ˈlife *adj.* opposing ABORTION [➡ **pro-choice**]

pro·lif·er·ate /prəˈlɪfəˌreɪt/ *v.* [I] *formal* to increase very quickly in number and spread to many different places: *In the Triassic period, dinosaurs proliferated.* —**proliferation** /prəˌlɪfəˈreɪʃən/ *n.* [singular, U]

pro·lif·ic /prəˈlɪfɪk/ *adj.* producing a lot of something: *Agatha Christie was a prolific writer.* —**prolifically** *adv.*

pro·logue /ˈproʊlɑg, -lɔg/ *n.* [C] the introduction to a book, movie, or play

pro·long /prəˈlɔŋ/ *v.* [T] to make something such as a feeling, activity, or state continue longer [**= lengthen**]: *high-tech machinery that prolongs people's lives* —**prolonged** *adj.*: *a prolonged illness*

THESAURUS

lengthen – to make something continue longer: *The bill would lengthen prison sentences.*
extend – to continue for a longer period of time, or to make something continue longer: *The board is considering extending the school day by half an hour.*
drag out – to make a situation or event last longer than necessary: *Each side accused the other of dragging out the negotiations.*

prom /prɑm/ *n.* [C] a formal dance party for HIGH SCHOOL students, usually held at the end of a school year: *the* ***senior prom*** (=dance for students in their last year of school)

> **THESAURUS**
>
> **dance**, **ball**
>
> → see Thesaurus box at DANCE[2]

prom·e·nade /ˌprɑməˈneɪd, -ˈnɑd/ *n.* [C] *old-fashioned* a walk for pleasure in a public place, or a wide path where you can do this —**promenade** *v.* [I]

prom·i·nence /ˈprɑmənəns/ *n.* [U] the fact of being important and famous: *Chavez* ***rose to prominence*** (=became famous) *in the 1960s.*

prom·i·nent /ˈprɑmənənt/ *adj.* **1** famous or important: *a prominent biotech company* **2** large and sticking out: *prominent cheekbones* **3** **a prominent place/position** somewhere that is easily seen: *The sculpture has a prominent position in the park.* —**prominently** *adv.*

pro·mis·cu·ous /prəˈmɪskyuəs/ *adj.* *formal* having sex with a lot of people —**promiscuity** /ˌprɑmɪˈskyuət̬i/ *n.* [U]

prom·ise[1] /ˈprɑmɪs/ *v.* **1** [I,T] to tell someone that you will definitely do something or that something will definitely happen: *Police have promised a full investigation.* | *I* ***promised*** *Barbara* ***(that)*** *I'd meet her after work.* | *I* ***promise (that)*** *I'll never do that again.* | *Both candidates* ***promised to*** *get tougher on crime.* | *I've already promised them a ride to the dance.*

> **THESAURUS**
>
> **swear** – to make a very serious promise: *He had sworn not to reveal her secret.*
>
> **take/swear an oath** – to make a very serious promise in public: *You must take an oath of loyalty to your country.*
>
> **vow** – to make a serious promise, often to yourself: *She vowed that she would never drink alcohol again.*
>
> **guarantee** – to promise something that you feel very sure about: *I can guarantee you a ten percent increase on your current salary.*
>
> **give sb your word** – to promise someone very sincerely that you will do something: *He gave us his word and I believe him.*

2 [T] to make people expect that something will happen: *The game* ***promises to be*** *exciting.* **3** **I can't promise anything** *spoken* used in order to tell someone that you will try to do what s/he wants, but you may not be able to do it

promise[2] *n.* **1** [C] a statement that you will definitely do something or that something will definitely happen: *She* ***made a promise*** *to take care of her neighbor's dog.* | *I didn't want to* ***break*** *my* ***promise*** (=not do what I said I would do). | *Has the president* ***kept*** *his* ***promise*** *to increase funding for education?* | *a* ***promise of*** *help* **2** [U] signs that something or someone will be good or successful: *He* ***shows*** *a lot of* ***promise*** *as a writer.*

prom·is·ing /ˈprɑmɪsɪŋ/ *adj.* showing that someone or something is likely to be successful in the future: *a promising young singer* —**promisingly** *adv.*

pro·mo /ˈproʊmoʊ/ *n.* plural **promos** [C] *informal* PROMOTION

prom·on·to·ry /ˈprɑmənˌtɔri/ *n.* plural **promontories** [C] *technical* a high piece of land that goes out into the ocean

pro·mote /prəˈmoʊt/ *v.* [T] **1** to help something develop and be successful: *The bureau's job is to promote tourism to the area.* **2** to give someone a better, more responsible position at work [≠ **demote**]: *Ted was* ***promoted to*** *senior sales manager.* **3** to advertise a product or event: *The author went on a national tour to promote the book.*

> **THESAURUS**
>
> **advertise**, **market**, **hype**, **plug**
>
> → see Thesaurus box at ADVERTISE

4 to be responsible for arranging a large public event such as a concert or a sports game

pro·mot·er /prəˈmoʊt̬ɚ/ *n.* [C] someone whose job is to arrange large public events such as concerts or sports games

pro·mo·tion /prəˈmoʊʃən/ *n.* [C,U] **1** a move to a better, more responsible position at work: *She received a* ***promotion to*** *lieutenant.* → see Topic box at JOB **2** an activity intended to advertise a product or event, or the thing that is being advertised: *a sales promotion*

pro·mo·tion·al /prəˈmoʊʃənl/ *adj.* promotional products and activities are made or organized in order to advertise something

prompt[1] /prɑmpt/ *v.* **1** [T] to make someone do something, or to help him/her remember to do it: *The changes prompted several people to resign from the committee in protest.* **2** [I,T] to remind someone, especially an actor, of the next words in a speech

prompt[2] *adj.* **1** done quickly, immediately, or at the right time: *Prompt payment is requested.* **2** someone who is prompt arrives at the right time or does something on time —**promptly** *adv.*: *Callan dealt with the problem promptly.*

prompt[3] *n.* [C] a sign on a computer screen that shows that the computer has finished one operation and is ready to begin the next

prone /proʊn/ *adj.* **1** likely to do something or suffer from something: *a narrow river that is* ***prone to*** *flooding* | *a boy who seems* ***accident prone*** (=he often has accidents) **2** *formal* lying down flat, with the front of your body facing down —**prone** *adv.*

prong /prɔŋ, prɑŋ/ *n.* [C] **1** one of the thick sharp pointed parts on the end of something, such as a PLUG or a PITCHFORK [➡ **tine**] **2** one of two or three ways of achieving something, which are used at the same time: *the second* ***prong of*** *the attack* —**pronged** *adj.*: *a two-pronged fork*

pro·noun /'proʊnaʊn/ *n.* [C] *technical* in grammar, a word that is used instead of a noun or noun phrase, such as "he" instead of the name "Peter" or the noun phrase "the man"

pro·nounce /prə'naʊns/ *v.* [T] **1** to make the sound of a letter, word, etc. in the correct way [➡ **pronunciation**]: *Her name is Tea, pronounced "Tay-uh."* **2** to state something officially and formally: *He was **pronounced dead** at 11:00 p.m.*

pro·nounced /prə'naʊnst/ *adj.* very strong or noticeable: *Nicole still has a pronounced French accent.*

pro·nounce·ment /prə'naʊnsmənt/ *n.* [C] *formal* an official public statement

pron·to /'prɑntoʊ/ *adv. spoken* quickly or immediately – used especially when you are annoyed: *Get in the house, pronto!*

P

pro·nun·ci·a·tion /prə,nʌnsi'eɪʃən/ *n.* **1** [C,U] the way in which a language or a particular word is pronounced: *the correct pronunciation of English words* **2** [singular, U] a particular person's way of pronouncing a word or words

proof /pruf/ *n.* **1** [U] facts, information, documents, etc. that prove something is true: *There is no **proof that** the suspect was home when he said he was.* | *Drivers should carry **proof of** insurance.* | *The tests are used **as proof** that the students are making progress.* **2** [C] *technical* a printed copy of a piece of writing that is checked carefully before the final printing is done **3** [U] a measurement of how much alcohol is in a drink. For example, 40 proof is 20% alcohol. **4** [C] a test in mathematics of whether a calculation is correct, or a list of reasons that shows a THEOREM (=statement) in GEOMETRY to be true

proof·read /'pruf-rid/ *v.* past tense and past participle **proofread** /-rɛd/ [I,T] to read something in order to correct any mistakes in it —**proofreader** *n.* [C]

prop[1] /prɑp/ *v.* past tense and past participle **propped**, present participle **propping** [T] to support something or keep it in a particular position: *He **propped** his bike **against** the fence.* | *The gate had been **propped open** with a brick.*

THESAURUS

lean, **stand**, **rest**
➔ see Thesaurus box at LEAN[1]

prop sth ⇔ **up** *phr. v.* **1** to prevent something from falling by putting something against it or under it: *Steel poles prop up the crumbling walls.* | *Frank propped himself up on his elbows.* **2** to help something to continue to exist: *Military spending props up the economies of several states.*

prop[2] *n.* [C] **1** an object placed under or against something to hold it in a position **2** an object such as a book, weapon, etc. used by actors in a play or movie

prop·a·gan·da /,prɑpə'gændə/ *n.* [U] information which is false or which emphasizes just one part of a situation, used by a government or other group to make people agree with them: *Soviet propaganda about the evils of capitalism* —**propagandist** *n.* [C] —**propagandize** *v.* [I,T]

prop·a·gate /'prɑpə,geɪt/ *v. formal* **1** [T] to share ideas, information, or beliefs with many people **2** [I,T] to grow or produce new plants, or to make a plant do this —**propagation** /,prɑpə'geɪʃən/ *n.* [U]

pro·pane /'proʊpeɪn/ *n.* [U] a colorless gas used for cooking and heating

pro·pel /prə'pɛl/ *v.* past tense and past participle **propelled**, present participle **propelling** [T] **1** to make someone achieve something, or to make something happen or develop: *Pearl Harbor was the attack that **propelled** America **into** World War II.* **2** to move, drive, or push something forward: *old ships propelled by steam*

pro·pel·ler /prə'pɛlɚ/ *n.* [C] a piece of equipment that consists of two or more blades that spin around to make an airplane or ship move

pro·pen·si·ty /prə'pɛnsət̬i/ *n.* plural **propensities** [C] *formal* a natural tendency to behave or develop in a particular way: *Doug **has a propensity to** gain weight.*

prop·er /'prɑpɚ/ *adj.* **1** correct, or right for a particular situation: *You need the proper tools for the job.* **2** socially correct and acceptable: *her views on proper behavior for young girls* **3** [only after noun] inside the limits of an area or subject: *We don't live in Boston proper; it's a suburb of Boston.*

prop·er·ly /'prɑpɚli/ *adv.* correctly, in a way that is right or appropriate: *When used properly, car air bags save lives.*

,proper 'noun also **,proper 'name** *n.* [C] *technical* in grammar, a noun that is the name of a particular person, place, or thing and is spelled with a capital letter, such as "Mike," "Paris," or "Easter"

prop·er·ty /'prɑpɚt̬i/ *n.* **1** [U] something that someone owns: *Police recovered some of the **stolen property**.* | *his **personal property***

THESAURUS

possessions – the things that you own: *The fire destroyed most of their possessions.*
things – the things that you own or are carrying: *Just put your things over there.*
stuff informal – the things that you own or are carrying with you: *All our stuff is still in cardboard boxes.*
belongings – things you own, especially things you are carrying with you: *The bell rang, and the students began gathering up their belongings.*
effects formal – the things that someone owns: *After Harding's death, the army sent his personal effects to his parents.*

2 [C,U] land, a building, or both together: *The property is worth about $5 million.* | *The building* *is* ***private/public property*** (=it is owned by a person or business/it is owned by the government). **3** [C usually plural] a natural quality of something: *an herb with* ***healing properties***

THESAURUS

characteristic, feature, quality, attribute
➔ see Thesaurus box at CHARACTERISTIC[1]

proph·e·cy /'prɑfəsi/ *n.* plural **prophecies** [C] a statement that tells what will happen in the future, often made by someone with religious or magical power

proph·e·sy /'prɑfə,saɪ/ *v.* past tense and past participle **prophesied**, third person singular **prophesies** [I,T] to use religious or magical knowledge to say what will happen in the future

THESAURUS

predict, forecast, foresee, have a premonition
➔ see Thesaurus box at PREDICT

proph·et /'prɑfɪt/ *n.* **1** [C] someone who says what will happen in the future and teaches people more about a religion **2 the Prophet** Mohammed, who began the religion of Islam

pro·phet·ic /prə'fɛṭɪk/ *adj.* correctly saying what will happen in the future: *His words turned out to be prophetic.* —**prophetically** *adv.*

pro·po·nent /prə'poʊnənt/ *n.* [C] someone who supports something or persuades people to do something [≠ **opponent**]: *a* ***proponent of*** *the new airport*

pro·por·tion /prə'pɔrʃən/ *n.* **1** [C,U] a part or share of a larger amount or number of something: *The* ***proportion of*** *adults who smoke is lower than before.* | *He won a* ***large/high proportion*** *of the vote.* **2** [C,U] the relationship between the amounts, numbers, or sizes of related things: *Girls outnumber boys at the school by a* ***proportion of*** *three* ***to*** *one.* | *Taxes rise* ***in proportion to*** *the amount you earn.* **3 proportions** [plural] the size or importance of something: *The flu outbreak has* ***reached*** *epidemic* ***proportions****.* **4** [U] the correct relationship between the size or shape of the different parts of something: *Her head seems large* ***in proportion to*** *her thin figure.* **5 get/ blow things out of proportion** to react to a situation as if it is worse or more serious than it really is **6 sense of proportion** the ability to judge what is most important in a situation

pro·por·tion·al /prə'pɔrʃənl/ **also pro·por·tion·ate** /prə'pɔrʃənɪt/ *adj.* staying in a particular relationship with another thing in size, amount, or importance: *The number of Representatives each state has* ***is proportional to*** *its population.* —**proportionally** *adv.*

pro·pos·al /prə'poʊzəl/ *n.* **1** [C,U] a plan or idea that is officially suggested for someone to consider, or the act of suggesting this: *a* ***proposal to*** *raise bus fares* **2** [C] the act of asking someone to marry you

pro·pose /prə'poʊz/ *v.* **1** [T] to officially suggest that something be done: *Smith* ***proposes that*** *the rules be changed.* **2** [I] to ask someone to marry you: *Has he proposed yet?* **3** [T] *formal* to intend to do something: *What does the candidate* ***propose to*** *do about unemployment?*

prop·o·si·tion[1] /,prɑpə'zɪʃən/ *n.* [C] **1** a statement in which you express a judgment or opinion: *the* ***proposition that*** *all people are created equal under the law* **2** an offer, plan, or idea, especially in business or politics: *Jack went to Robards with a proposition.* | *Proposition 13 on the ballot*

proposition[2] *v.* [T] to suggest to someone that s/he have sex with you, especially in exchange for money

pro·pri·e·tar·y /prə'praɪə,tɛri/ *adj. formal* information or products that are proprietary can only be known about or sold by a particular company

pro·pri·e·tor /prə'praɪəṭɚ/ *n.* [C] *formal* an owner of a business

pro·pri·e·ty /prə'praɪəṭi/ *n.* [singular, U] *formal* correct social or moral behavior [≠ **impropriety**]: *the* ***propriety of*** *physically punishing children*

pro·pul·sion /prə'pʌlʃən/ *n.* [U] *technical* the force that moves a vehicle forward, or the system used in order to make this happen: *jet propulsion*

pro·rate /'proʊreɪt, proʊ'reɪt/ *v.* [T] to calculate a price, salary, etc. according to exactly how much of something is used or how much work is done

pro·sa·ic /proʊ'zeɪ-ɪk/ *adj. formal* boring, ordinary, or lacking in imagination: *a prosaic style of writing* —**prosaically** *adv.*

pro·scribe /proʊ'skraɪb/ *v.* [T] *formal* to officially stop the existence or use of something: *laws to proscribe child labor* —**proscription** /proʊ'skrɪpʃən/ *n.* [C,U]

prose /proʊz/ *n.* [U] written language in its usual form, not as poetry

pros·e·cute /'prɑsə,kyut/ *v.* [I,T] to say officially that you think someone is guilty of a crime and must be judged by a court of law: *He was* ***prosecuted for*** *theft.*

pros·e·cu·tion /,prɑsə'kyuʃən/ *n.* **1 the prosecution** the people in a court of law who are trying to prove that someone is guilty of a crime [➡ **defense**]: *a witness for the prosecution* ➔ see Topic box at COURT[1] **2** [C,U] the process or act of prosecuting someone

pros·e·cu·tor /'prɑsə,kyuṭɚ/ *n.* [C] a lawyer who is trying to prove in a court of law that someone is guilty of a crime [➡ **district attorney**]

pros·pect[1] /'prɑspɛkt/ *n.* **1** [C,U] something that is possible or likely to happen in the future: *I was excited at* ***the prospect of*** *going to Europe.* | *a company with good* ***prospects for*** *growth* **2 prospects** [plural] chances of success in the future: *Going to college will improve your* ***job prospects****.*

prospect[2] *v.* [I,T] to look for things such as gold,

silver, or oil in the ground or under the ocean: *men* ***prospecting for*** *gold* —**prospector** *n.* [C]

pro·spec·tive /prəˈspɛktɪv/ *adj.* **1** likely to do a particular thing: *a prospective buyer for the house* **2** likely to happen: *the prospective annual costs*

pro·spec·tus /prəˈspɛktəs/ *n.* [C] a document that describes a business opportunity or advertises something

pros·per /ˈprɑspɚ/ *v.* [I] to grow and develop in a successful way, especially by making money: *an environment in which small businesses can prosper*

pros·per·i·ty /prɑˈspɛrət̬i/ *n.* [U] the condition of having money and being successful: *a time of peace and prosperity*

pros·per·ous /ˈprɑspərəs/ *adj.* successful and rich: *a prosperous community*

P

THESAURUS

rich, **well-off**, **wealthy**, **well-to-do**, **rolling in it**, **loaded**
→ see Thesaurus box at RICH

pros·tate /ˈprɑsteɪt/ *n.* [C] a part in the body of a man or a male animal that produces a liquid in which SPERM are carried

pros·ti·tute /ˈprɑstəˌtut/ *n.* [C] someone who has sex with people to earn money

pros·ti·tu·tion /ˌprɑstəˈtuʃən/ *n.* [U] the work of prostitutes

pros·trate[1] /ˈprɑstreɪt/ *adj., adv. formal* **1** lying flat on the ground with your face down **2** so shocked or upset that you cannot do anything: *Mrs. Klinkman was* ***prostrate with*** *grief.*

prostrate[2] *v.* **prostrate yourself** *literary* to lie flat on the ground with your face down, in order to show praise or respect

pro·tag·o·nist /proʊˈtægənɪst/ *n.* [C] *formal* the main character in a play, movie, or story

pro·tect /prəˈtɛkt/ *v.* [T] to keep someone or something safe from harm, damage, or illness: *We must protect the environment.* | *vaccines that* ***protect*** *you* ***against*** *disease* | *The laws are meant to* ***protect*** *minorities* ***from*** *discrimination.* —**protected** *adj.*: *a protected species* —**protector** *n.* [C] *a chest protector*

THESAURUS

guard – to protect someone or something from being attacked or stolen: *The building is guarded by security officers.*
shield – to protect someone or something from being hurt, damaged, or upset: *She brought up her arms to shield her face.*
give/offer/provide protection – to protect someone from something harmful: *lotions that provide protection from the sun*
shelter – to provide a place where someone is protected from the weather or from danger: *At great risk to themselves, they sheltered Jews from the Nazis.*
preserve – to keep someone or something from being harmed, destroyed, or changed too much: *Efforts are being made to preserve the reef.*

pro·tec·tion /prəˈtɛkʃən/ *n.* [C,U] something that protects someone or something, or the act of protecting something: *environmental protections* | *the* ***protection of*** *civil rights* | *a hat offers/provides/gives* ***protection against*** *the sun*

pro·tec·tive /prəˈtɛktɪv/ *adj.* **1** used or intended for protection: *a crab's protective shell* **2** wanting to protect someone from danger or harm: *She's fiercely* ***protective of*** *her children.*

pro·té·gé /ˈproʊt̬əˌʒeɪ, ˌproʊt̬əˈʒeɪ/ *n.* [C] a young person who is taught or helped by an older more experienced person

pro·tein /ˈproʊtin/ *n.* [C,U] one of the many substances in foods such as meat and eggs that helps your body to grow and be healthy

pro·test[1] /ˈproʊtɛst/ *n.* **1** [C] a strong complaint that shows you disagree with something that you think is wrong or unfair: *Almirez led a* ***protest against*** *the new road.* | *Six teachers quit* ***in protest*** *of the board's decision.* | *He cleaned his room* ***without protest.*** **2 do sth under protest** to do something in a way that shows you do not want to do it because you think it is wrong or unfair

pro·test[2] /ˈproʊtɛst, prəˈtɛst/ *v.* **1** [I,T] to say or do something publicly to show that you disagree with something or think that it is wrong or unfair: *a group* ***protesting against*** *human rights abuses* | *Students carried signs protesting the war.*

THESAURUS

march – to protest while walking with a group of people from one place to another: *Over a million people marched to protest against the war.*
demonstrate – to protest while walking or standing somewhere with a group of people: *A crowd of people were demonstrating outside the embassy.*
riot – to protest by behaving in a violent and uncontrolled way: *People were rioting in the streets in reaction to the elections.*
hold/stage a sit-in – to protest by refusing to leave a place: *Hundreds of students staged a sit-in.*
go on a hunger strike – to protest by refusing to eat: *The prisoners went on a hunger strike.*
boycott – to protest about the actions of a company or country by refusing to buy something, go somewhere, etc.: *Some countries have threatened to boycott the Olympic Games.*

2 [T] to state very strongly that something is true, especially when other people do not believe you: *Throughout the trial, he kept* ***protesting*** *his* ***innocence.*** —**protestation** /ˌprɑt̬əˈsteɪʃən, ˌproʊ-/ *n.* [C]

Prot·es·tant /ˈprɑt̬əstənt/ *adj.* relating to a part of the Christian church that separated from the Roman Catholic church in the 16th century —**Protestant** *n.* [C] —**Protestantism** *n.* [U]

pro·test·er, **protestor** /ˈproʊˌtɛstɚ, proʊˈtɛstɚ/ *n.* [C] someone who takes part in a public event to show his/her opposition to something: *anti-war protesters*

pro·to·col /ˈproʊt̬əˌkɔl, -ˌkɑl/ *n.* **1** [singular, U] the system of rules for the correct way to behave on official occasions: *Even touching the Queen is a* ***breach of protocol*** (=it is not allowed). **2** [C] an official statement of the rules that a group of countries have agreed to follow in dealing with a particular problem: *the Montreal Protocol on greenhouse gases*

pro·ton /ˈproʊtɑn/ *n.* [C] *technical* a part of an atom that has a positive electrical CHARGE

pro·to·type /ˈproʊt̬əˌtaɪp/ *n.* [C] a model of a new car, machine, etc., used in order to test the design before it is produced in large numbers

pro·tract·ed /proʊˈtræktɪd, prə-/ *adj.* continuing for a long time, usually longer than necessary: *a protracted strike*

pro·trac·tor /proʊˈtræktɚ, prə-/ *n.* [C] a flat tool shaped like a half circle, used for measuring and drawing angles

pro·trude /proʊˈtrud/ *v.* [I] *formal* to stick out from somewhere: *a rock* ***protruding from*** *the water* —**protrusion** /proʊˈtruʒən/ *n.* [C,U]

proud /praʊd/ *adj.* **1** feeling pleased because you think that something you have achieved or are connected with is very good [➡ **pride**]: *My husband and I are very* ***proud of*** *her.* | *We're* ***proud to*** *announce the birth of our son.* | *I'm* ***proud (that)*** *the team's done so well.* **2** *disapproving* thinking that you are better, more important, more skillful, etc. than other people

> **THESAURUS**
>
> **conceited/big-headed** – very proud of yourself, especially of what you can do, in a way that other people dislike
> **vain** – very proud of yourself, especially of your appearance, in a way that other people dislike
> **arrogant** – showing that you think you are better than other people

3 too embarrassed or ashamed to allow other people to help you when you need it: *Terry was too proud to ask his family for money.* **4 do sb proud** to make someone feel proud of you by doing something well: *Vicki hopes to do her school proud.* —**proudly** *adv.* ➔ PRIDE[1]

prove /pruv/ *v.* past tense **proved**, past participle **proved** or **proven** /ˈpruvən/ [T] **1** to show that something is definitely true [➡ **proof**]: *They have enough evidence to* ***prove that*** *she is guilty.* | *I know he's innocent, and I'm going to* ***prove*** *it* ***to*** *you.*

> **THESAURUS**
>
> **demonstrate**, **show**, **mean**, **indicate**, **suggest**
> ➔ see Thesaurus box at DEMONSTRATE

2 to show over time that someone or something has a particular quality: *Any delay will prove costly.* | *The weather* ***proved to be*** *beautiful.* **3 prove yourself also prove sth to sb** to show that you are able to do something well: *At seventeen years old, she had yet to prove herself on the pro golf tour.* —**provable** *adj.*

prov·en[1] /ˈpruvən/ *adj.* shown to be real or true: *a proven method of learning*

proven[2] *v.* a past participle of PROVE

prov·erb /ˈprɑvɚb/ *n.* [C] a short statement that most people know, that contains advice about life. For example, "A journey of a thousand miles begins with a single step" is a proverb.

> **THESAURUS**
>
> **phrase**, **expression**, **idiom**, **cliché**, **saying**
> ➔ see Thesaurus box at PHRASE[1]

P

pro·ver·bi·al /prəˈvɚbiəl/ *adj.* **the proverbial sth** used when you describe something using a well-known expression: *Ice cream was selling like the proverbial hotcakes.* —**proverbially** *adv.*

pro·vide /prəˈvaɪd/ *v.* [T] **1** to give or supply something to someone: *a charity that* ***provides*** *shelter* ***for*** *the homeless* | *Rescuers* ***provided*** *the lost hikers* ***with*** *blankets and food.* **2 provide that** *formal* if a law or rule provides that something must happen, it states that it must happen

provide for sb/sth *phr. v.* **1** to give someone the things s/he needs, such as money, food, or clothing: *Dad always thought a man should provide for his family.* **2** to make plans in order to deal with something that might happen in the future: *The hotel is examining ways to provide for the disabled.*

pro·vid·ed /prəˈvaɪdɪd/ **also pro'vided that** *conjunction* used in order to say that something will only happen if another thing happens first: *Talks will take place in July, provided that enough progress has been made.*

prov·i·dence /ˈprɑvədəns/ *n.* [singular, U] a force that some people believe controls our lives in the way God wants: *an act of* ***divine providence***

pro·vid·er /prəˈvaɪdɚ/ *n.* [C] **1** a person or company that provides a service: *a health-care provider* **2** someone who supports a family

pro·vid·ing /prəˈvaɪdɪŋ/ **also pro'viding that** *conjunction* used in order to say that something will only happen if another thing happens first: *You can borrow the car, providing that I have it back by six o'clock.*

prov·ince /ˈprɑvɪns/ *n.* **1** [C] one of the large areas into which some countries are divided: *the provinces of Canada* **2 the provinces** [plural] the parts of a country that are not near a large city, especially the capital city: *In Boston, he received a more sophisticated schooling than he had* ***in the provinces.***

pro·vin·cial /prəˈvɪnʃəl/ *adj.* **1** *disapproving* not interested in anything new or different: *provincial attitudes* **2** relating to a province, or the parts of a country that are not near the capital: *the provincial government of Quebec*

pro·vi·sion /prə'vɪʒən/ *n.* **1** [C,U] the act of providing something that someone needs now or will need in the future: *the **provision of** services for the elderly | He has **made provisions for** his wife in his will* (=he arranged for her to have money when he dies). **2** [C] a condition in an agreement or law: *the **provisions of** the treaty* **3 provisions** [plural] food supplies, especially for a trip: *We had enough provisions for two weeks.*

pro·vi·sion·al /prə'vɪʒənl/ *adj.* intended to exist for only a short time and likely to be changed in the future: *a provisional government*

pro·vi·so /prə'vaɪzoʊ/ *n.* plural **provisos** [C] *formal* something that you say must happen before another thing is allowed to happen: *Tom's grandson inherited his money **with the proviso that** he go to college.*

P

prov·o·ca·tion /ˌprɑvə'keɪʃən/ *n.* [C,U] an action or event that makes someone angry, or that is intended to do this: *My client was attacked **without provocation**!*

pro·voc·a·tive /prə'vɑkət̬ɪv/ *adj.* **1** intending to make someone angry or cause a lot of discussion: *provocative comments* **2** intending to make someone sexually excited: *a provocative dress* —**provocatively** *adv.*

pro·voke /prə'voʊk/ *v.* [T] **1** to make someone very angry, especially by deliberately annoying him/her: *She did hit him, but he **provoked** her **into** doing it.* **2** to cause a sudden reaction or feeling: *The president's speech provoked criticism from Democrats.*

pro·vost /'proʊvoʊst/ *n.* [C] an important official at a university

prow /praʊ/ *n.* [C] the front part of a ship or boat

prow·ess /'praʊɪs/ *n.* [U] *formal* great skill at doing something: *a man of great athletic prowess*

prowl¹ /praʊl/ *v.* [I,T] to move around an area quietly, trying not to be seen or heard: *a tiger prowling through the jungle*

prowl² *n.* **1 be on the prowl** if an animal is on the prowl, it is hunting **2 be on the prowl for sth/sb** if someone is on the prowl for something, s/he is moving around looking for something or someone in different places: *She's always on the prowl for bargains.*

prowl·er /'praʊlɚ/ *n.* [C] someone who moves around quietly at night, especially near your house, in order to steal something or harm you

prox·im·i·ty /prɑk'sɪmət̬i/ *n.* [U] *formal* nearness in distance or time: *We chose this house because of its **proximity to** the school.*

prox·y /'prɑksi/ *n.* plural **proxies** **1** [C] someone whom you choose to represent you, especially to vote for you **2 by proxy** if you do something by proxy, you arrange for someone else to do it for you

prude /prud/ *n.* [C] *disapproving* someone who is very easily shocked by anything relating to sex —**prudish** *adj.*

pru·dent /'prudnt/ *adj.* sensible and careful, especially by avoiding risks that are not necessary: *It would not **be prudent to** invest all of your money in the same place.* —**prudence** *n.* [U]

prune¹ /prun/ **also prune back** *v.* [T] to cut some of the branches of a tree or bush to make it grow better

prune² *n.* [C] a dried PLUM (=type of fruit)

pru·ri·ent /'prʊriənt/ *adj.* *formal* showing too much interest in sex

pry /praɪ/ *v.* past tense and past participle **pried**, third person singular **pries** **1** [T] to force something open, or to force it away from something else: *They finally **pried** the window **open**. | I had to use a screwdriver to **pry** the lid **off** the paint can.* **2** [I] to try to find out details about someone's private life in an impolite way: *I don't want to pry, but I need to ask you one or two questions.*

P.S. *n.* [C] **postscript** a note that you add to the end of a letter, that gives more information

psalm /sɑm/ *n.* [C] a song or poem praising God

pseu·do·nym /'sudnˌɪm, 'sudəˌnɪm/ *n.* [C] a false name used by someone, especially a writer, instead of his/her real name

psych /saɪk/ *v.*

psych sb ⇔ **out** *phr. v. informal* to do or say things that will make your opponent feel nervous or confused: *He would psych out opponents by screaming and jumping up and down before each game.*

psych sb/yourself **up** *phr. v. informal* to build up your confidence before doing something difficult by telling someone or telling yourself that you can do it: *soldiers trying to psych themselves up for combat*

psy·che /'saɪki/ *n.* [C usually singular] *technical* someone's mind or basic nature that controls how s/he thinks or behaves

psyched /saɪkt/ **also ˌpsyched 'up** *adj.* *spoken* **be psyched (up)** to be mentally prepared for an event and excited about it: *Bryony's totally **psyched about/for** her date.*

psy·che·del·ic /ˌsaɪkə'dɛlɪk◂ / *adj.* **1** psychedelic drugs such as LSD make you see things that do not really exist **2** psychedelic art, clothing, etc. has a lot of bright colors and patterns

psy·chi·a·trist /saɪ'kaɪətrɪst, sə-/ *n.* [C] a doctor who studies and treats mental illness [➡ **psychologist**]

THESAURUS

doctor, **physician**, **surgeon**, **specialist**, **pediatrician**
→ see Thesaurus box at DOCTOR¹

psy·chi·a·try /saɪ'kaɪətri, sə-/ *n.* [U] the study and treatment of mental illness —**psychiatric** /ˌsaɪki'ætrɪk◂ / *adj.*: *a psychiatric hospital*

psy·chic[1] /ˈsaɪkɪk/ *adj.* **1** relating to strange events involving the power of the human mind: *a mysterious **psychic phenomenon** | She claims to have **psychic powers**.* **2** someone who is psychic has the ability to know what other people are thinking or what will happen in the future **3** affecting the mind rather than the body: *psychic pain/scar/wound | people who are in **psychic pain***

psychic[2] *n.* [C] someone who has strange powers such as the ability to know what will happen in the future

psy·cho /ˈsaɪkoʊ/ *n.* plural **psychos** [C] *informal* someone who is likely to behave in a violent or crazy way

psy·cho·a·nal·y·sis /ˌsaɪkoʊəˈnæləsɪs/ *n.* [U] a way of treating someone who is mentally ill by talking to him/her about his/her life, feelings, etc. to find out the cause of the illness —**psychoanalyze** /ˌsaɪkoʊˈænlˌaɪz/ *v.* [T]

psy·cho·an·a·lyst /ˌsaɪkoʊˈænl-ɪst/ *n.* [C] someone who treats people using psychoanalysis

psy·cho·log·i·cal /ˌsaɪkəˈlɑdʒɪkəl/ *adj.* **1** relating to the way people's minds work and the way this affects their behavior: *The patient has a history of **psychological problems**.* **2** relating to psychology: *a psychological test* —**psychologically** *adv.*: *psychologically disturbed patients*

psy·chol·o·gist /saɪˈkɑlədʒɪst/ *n.* [C] someone who is trained in psychology [➡ **psychiatrist**]

psy·chol·o·gy /saɪˈkɑlədʒi/ *n.* plural **psychologies** **1** [U] the study of the mind and how it works: *a professor of psychology* **2** [C usually singular,U] what someone thinks or believes, and how this affects what s/he does: *the **psychology of** a serial killer*

psy·cho·path /ˈsaɪkəˌpæθ/ *n.* [C] someone who has a mental illness that makes him/her behave in a violent or criminal way —**psychopathic** /ˌsaɪkəˈpæθɪk/ *adj.*

psy·cho·sis /saɪˈkoʊsɪs/ *n.* plural **psychoses** /-siz/ [C,U] *technical* a serious mental illness that may cause changes in someone's behavior

psy·cho·so·mat·ic /ˌsaɪkoʊsəˈmæt̬ɪk/ *adj.* *technical* a psychosomatic illness is caused by fear or anxiety, not by any physical problem

psy·cho·ther·a·py /ˌsaɪkoʊˈθɛrəpi/ *n.* [U] the treatment of mental illness by talking to someone and discussing problems, rather than by using drugs or medicine —**psychotherapist** *n.* [C]

psy·chot·ic /saɪˈkɑt̬ɪk/ *adj. technical* relating to mental illness, or resulting from it: *psychotic behavior* —**psychotic** *n.* [C]

PTA *n.* [C] **Parent-Teacher Association** an organization of teachers and parents that works to improve a particular school

pub /pʌb/ *n.* [C] a comfortable BAR that often serves food

pu·ber·ty /ˈpyubɚt̬i/ *n.* [U] the time when your body develops from being a child to being an adult: *Our daughter is just **reaching puberty*** (=starting to develop physically).

pu·bes·cent /pyuˈbɛsənt/ *adj.* a pubescent boy or girl is going through puberty

pu·bic /ˈpyubɪk/ *adj.* relating to or near the sex organs: *pubic hair*

pub·lic[1] /ˈpʌblɪk/ *adj.* **1** relating to all the ordinary people in a country or city: *We acted out of concern for public welfare. | The judge ruled that allowing the broadcast of the trial would be **in the public interest**. | The mayor seems to have **public opinion** on his side.* **2** available for anyone to use [≠ **private**]: *a public restroom | public transportation* **3** relating to the government and the services that it provides [≠ **private**]: *It has been eight years since she was elected to **public office*** (=a job in the government). | *Republicans want to cut **public spending*** (=money the government spends on roads, hospitals, etc.). **4** known about by most people: *Last night the name of the killer was **made public**. | a **public figure*** (=well-known person) **5** intended for anyone to know, see, or hear [≠ **private**]: ***public display of affection/emotion/anger etc.*** (=showing your emotions so that everyone can see) **6 go public** to tell everyone about something that was secret: *They finally went public with news of their engagement.* ➔ PUBLICLY

public[2] *n.* **1 the public** all the ordinary people in a country or city: *The museum is **open to the public** five days a week. | This product is not for sale to **the general public**.* **2 in public** in a place where anyone can know, see, or hear [≠ **in private**]: *She was careful not to criticize him in public.* **3** [singular, U] the people who like a particular singer, writer, etc.: *A star has to try to please her public.*

ˌpublic ˈaccess *n.* [U] a situation in which anyone can enter a place or use a service: *Public access to the beach is blocked by private property.*

ˌpublic adˈdress ˌsystem *n.* a PA

ˌpublic afˈfairs *n.* [plural] events or questions, especially political ones, that affect everyone

ˌpublic asˈsistance *n.* [U] the government programs that help poor people get food, homes, and medical care [➡ **welfare**]

pub·li·ca·tion /ˌpʌbləˈkeɪʃən/ *n.* **1** [U] the process of printing a book, magazine, etc. and offering it for sale [➡ **publish**]: *She was in England for the **publication of** her new book. | There may be a delay of up to eight weeks before publication.* **2** [C] a book, magazine, etc.: *a monthly publication for stamp collectors* **3** [U] the act of making something known to the public: *The authorities tried to stop the publication of the test results.*

ˌpublic deˈfender *n.* [C] a lawyer who is paid

by the government to defend people who cannot pay for a lawyer themselves

ˌpublic ˈfigure *n.* [C] someone who is well-known because s/he is on television or in the newspapers a lot

ˌpublic ˈhousing *n.* [U] houses or apartments built by the government for poor people

pub·li·cist /ˈpʌbləsɪst/ *n.* [C] someone whose job is to make sure that famous people or new products, movies, books, etc. get a lot of publicity

pub·lic·i·ty /pəˈblɪsət̬i/ *n.* [U] **1** the attention that someone or something gets from newspapers, television, etc.: *His new novel has **received** a lot of **publicity**.* | ***good/bad/negative publicity*** **2** the business of making sure that people know about what a famous person is doing, or about a new product, movie, book, etc.: *a publicity campaign*

pub·li·cize /ˈpʌbləˌsaɪz/ *v.* [T] to tell people about a new film, book, event, etc.: *a **well/highly publicized** crime*

pub·lic·ly /ˈpʌblɪkli/ *adv.* **1** in a way that is intended for anyone to know, see, or hear: *None of the players were willing to comment publicly.* | *Lozansky was jailed for publicly criticizing the government.* **2** by the government, as part of its services: *The hospitals are publicly operated in cities, suburbs, and rural areas.* **3** a company that is publicly owned has sold STOCK in it to the public **4** among the ordinary people in a country or city: *publicly elected bodies*

ˌpublic reˈlations, PR *n.* **1** [plural] the relationship between an organization and the public: *Organizing events for charity is always good for public relations.* **2** [U] the work of explaining what a company does so the public will approve of it: *the public relations department*

ˌpublic ˈschool *n.* [C] a free local school that is controlled and paid for by the government [➡ **private school**]

ˌpublic ˈtelevision *n.* [U] a television program or service that is paid for by the government, large companies, and the public

ˌpublic transporˈtation *n.* [U] buses, trains, etc. that are available for everyone to use

pub·lish /ˈpʌblɪʃ/ *v.* **1** [I,T] to arrange for a book, magazine, etc. to be written, printed, and sold: *a book that was first published in 1851* | *We publish mainly educational materials.* **2** [T] if a newspaper, magazine, etc. publishes something such as a letter, it prints it for people to read: *The article was published in the Los Angeles Times.* **3** [T] to make official information available for everyone to use: *New guidelines for social studies education were published this year.* —**publishing** *n.* [U] *I work in publishing.*

pub·lish·er /ˈpʌblɪʃɚ/ *n.* [C] a person or company that arranges the writing, printing, and sale of books, newspapers, etc.

puck /pʌk/ *n.* [C] a hard flat circular piece of rubber that you hit with a stick in the game of HOCKEY

puck·er /ˈpʌkɚ/ **also pucker up** *v.* **1** [I,T] *informal* if your mouth puckers, or if you pucker it, your lips are pulled together tightly, for example because you are going to kiss someone **2** [I] if cloth puckers, it gets folds in it so that it is no longer flat —**puckered** *adj.*

pud·ding /ˈpʊdɪŋ/ *n.* [C,U] a thick sweet creamy food made with milk, eggs, sugar, and flour that is eaten cold: *chocolate pudding*

puddle

pud·dle /ˈpʌdl/ *n.* [C] a small pool of rain on a road, path, etc.: *children splashing in the puddles*

pudg·y /ˈpʌdʒi/ *adj.* fatter than usual: *short pudgy fingers* —**pudginess** *n.* [U]

pu·er·ile /ˈpyʊrəl, -raɪl/ *adj. formal* silly and stupid [= **childish**]: *puerile humor*

puff¹ /pʌf/ *v.* **1** [I,T] to breathe in and out while smoking a cigarette, pipe, etc.: *William sat there **puffing on** his pipe.* **2** [I] to breathe quickly and with difficulty after running, carrying something heavy, etc.: *Max was puffing heavily after climbing the stairs.* **3** [I,T] to blow steam or smoke out of something: *The boiler was puffing thick black smoke.*

puff sth ⇔ **out** *phr. v.* to make something bigger by filling it with air: *a frog with its throat puffed out*

puff up *phr. v.* **1 also puff** sth ⇔ **up** to become bigger by filling with air, or to make something do this: *Birds puff up their feathers to stay warm.* **2** if your eye, face, etc. puffs up, it swells: *My eye puffed up where he hit me.*

puff² *n.* [C] **1** the action of breathing smoke into your mouth and blowing it out again: *He **took a puff on** his cigar.* **2** a sudden short movement of air, smoke, or wind: *puffs of smoke coming from the chimney*

puffin

puf·fin /ˈpʌfɪn/ *n.* [C] a North Atlantic bird with a black and white body and a large brightly colored beak

puff·y /ˈpʌfi/ *adj.* puffy eyes, cheeks, or faces are swollen: *Her eyes were red and puffy from crying.* —**puffiness** *n.* [U]

pug·na·cious /pʌg'neɪʃəs/ *adj. formal* very eager to argue or fight with people

puke /pyuk/ *v.* [I,T] *slang* VOMIT —**puke** *n.* [U]

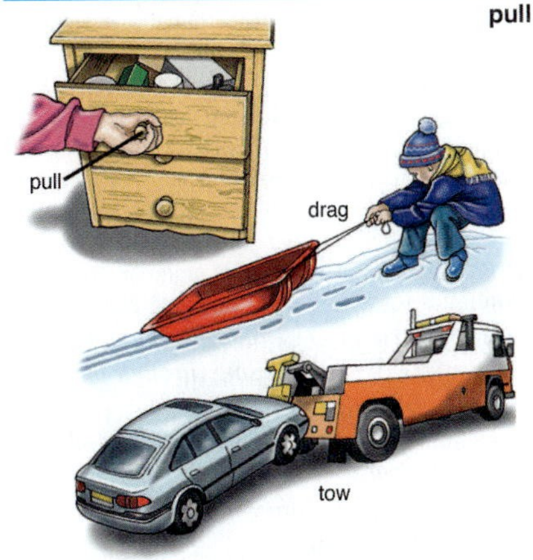

pull¹ /pʊl/ *v.*

1 MOVE TOWARD YOU [I,T] to use your hands to move something toward you [≠ **push**]: *Mom, Sara's pulling my hair!* | *When I count to three, start pulling.* | *Wilson quickly* ***pulled*** *the door* ***open/shut****.* | *Help me* ***pull*** *the trunk* ***into*** *the corner.*

THESAURUS

tug – to pull something suddenly, especially several times with small movements: *The little boy was tugging at her sleeve.*
drag – to pull something somewhere, usually along the ground: *I dragged the chair upstairs.*
haul – to pull something heavy, often using a rope: *fishermen hauling in their nets*
tow – to pull another vehicle or boat: *pickup trucks towing trailers*
heave – to pull or lift something very heavy, especially with one movement: *We managed to heave the piano into position.*
→ PUSH

2 REMOVE [T] to remove something from its place, especially by using force: *She has to have her wisdom teeth pulled.* | *The baby's* ***pulled*** *everything* ***out*** *of the cupboards.*
3 MAKE STH FOLLOW YOU [I,T] to use a rope, chain, your hands, etc. to make something move behind you in the direction you are moving [≠ **push**]: *a car pulling a camper behind it*
4 MUSCLE [T] to injure a muscle by stretching it too much during physical activity: *Martinez* ***pulled*** *a groin* ***muscle*** *and had to leave the game.*
5 pull sb's leg *informal* to tell someone something that is not true, as a joke: *I think he was just pulling your leg.*
6 pull strings to secretly use your influence with important people in order to get something or to help someone: *Barry pulled some strings and got us tickets for the football game.*
7 MOVE YOUR BODY a) [I,T] to move your body or part of your body away from someone or something: *She* ***pulled away from*** *him in horror.* **b)** [T] to use force to move your body somewhere: *The kids* ***pulled*** *themselves* ***up*** *onto the platform.*
8 CLOTHING [I,T] to put on or take off clothing, usually quickly: *He* ***pulled off*** *his gloves and placed them on the dresser.*
9 pull your weight to do your share of the work: *If you don't start pulling your weight around here, you'll be fired!*
10 pull a stunt/trick/joke/prank *informal* to do something that annoys or harms other people: *Don't you ever pull a stunt like that again!*
11 TRICK [T] *spoken* to deceive or trick someone: *What are you trying to pull?* | *Are you trying to* ***pull a fast one*** *on me?*
12 pull the strings to control something, especially when you are not the person who is supposed to be controlling it: *Who is really pulling the strings in the White House?*
13 SWITCH [T] to move a control such as a SWITCH or TRIGGER toward you to make a piece of equipment work: *She raised the gun and pulled the trigger.*
14 GUN/KNIFE [T] to take out a gun or knife ready to use it: *Suddenly the man* ***pulled*** *a* ***gun*** *and began shooting.*
15 pull the rug out from under sb to suddenly take away something that someone was depending on to achieve what s/he wanted

pull sth ⇔ **apart** *phr. v.* to separate something into two or more pieces or groups: *Loosen the roots and gently pull the plants apart.* | *the ethnic problems that pulled Yugoslavia apart*

pull away *phr. v.* **1** to move ahead of a competitor by going faster or being more successful: *Chicago pulled away in the third quarter to win 107–76.* **2** to start to drive away from the place where your car was stopped: *Grant* ***pulled away from*** *the curb.*

pull sth ⇔ **down** *phr. v.* to destroy a building, wall, etc.: *Many of the houses were pulled down to make way for a new highway.*

pull for sb *phr. v. informal* to encourage a person or team to succeed: *Which team are you pulling for?*

pull in *phr. v.* **1 pull** sth ⇔ **in** to move a car into a particular space and stop it: *Kevin pulled in behind me and parked.* **2 pull** sth ⇔ **in** *informal* if you pull in a lot of money, you earn it

pull off *phr. v.* **1 pull** sth ⇔ **off** *informal* to succeed in doing something difficult: *Cruz expects to win the fight but no one else thinks he can* ***pull it off****.* **2 pull off** sth to leave a road in order to stop or to turn into another road

pull out *phr. v.* **1** to drive a car onto a road from where you have stopped **2** to get out of a bad situation or dangerous place: *Investors pulled out,* *selling all their shares.* | *We plan to pull our troops out of the area.* **3 pull** sb/sth ⇔ **out** to get someone out of a bad situation or dangerous place: *We plan to pull our troops out of the area.*

pull sb/sth ⇔ **over** *phr. v.* to drive to the side of a road and stop your car, or to make someone do this: *We didn't realize we were speeding until the highway patrol pulled us over.*

pull (sb) **through** *phr. v. informal* **1** to stay alive after a serious injury or illness, or to help someone do this: *We all prayed that he would pull through.* **2** to continue to live or exist after being in a difficult or upsetting situation: *The city managed to pull through its financial crisis.*

pull together *phr. v.* **1** to work hard with other people to achieve something: *After the hurricane, neighbors pulled together to help each other.* **2 pull yourself together** *informal* to force yourself to stop being nervous, afraid, or disorganized: *A year after the accident, she's finally starting to pull herself together.*

pull up *phr. v.* **1** to stop the vehicle you are driving: *A red Buick pulled up at the stop lights.* **2 pull up a chair/stool etc.** to get a chair and sit down near someone who is already sitting

pull² *n.* **1** [C] an act of using force to move something toward you or in the same direction as you are going: ***Give** the **rope a** good **pull.*** **2** [C usually singular] a strong force such as GRAVITY that makes things move in a particular direction: *the pull of the ocean's tide* **3** [singular, U] *informal* power that gives you an unfair advantage: *a family with a lot of political pull*

pul·ley /ˈpʊli/ *n.* plural **pulleys** [C] a piece of equipment used for lifting heavy things, consisting of a wheel over which you pull a chain or rope

pull·out /ˈpʊlaʊt/ *n.* [C] **1** the act of an army, business, etc. leaving a particular place: *the pull-out of NATO troops from the region* **2** part of a book or magazine that can be removed

pull·o·ver /ˈpʊlˌoʊvɚ/ *n.* [C] a SWEATER without buttons

ˈpull-up *n.* [C] an exercise in which you use your arms to pull yourself up toward a BAR that is above your head

pul·mo·nar·y /ˈpʊlməˌnɛri, ˈpʌl-/ *adj. technical* relating to or affecting the lungs: *pulmonary disease*

pulp¹ /pʌlp/ *n.* [U] **1** the soft inside part of a fruit or vegetable: *Cut the melon in half and scoop out the pulp.* **2** a very soft substance that is almost liquid: ***Mash** the bananas **to a pulp.*** | *timber grown for **wood pulp**, used for making paper* **3 beat sb to a pulp** *informal* to hit someone until s/he is seriously injured

pulp² *adj.* pulp magazines, stories, etc. are usually of poor quality and tell stories about sex and violence: *pulp fiction*

pul·pit /ˈpʊlpɪt, ˈpʌl-/ *n.* [C] a structure like a tall box at the front of a church that a priest or minister stands behind when s/he speaks: *Reverend Dawson addressed the congregation **from the pulpit**.*

pul·sate /ˈpʌlseɪt/ *v.* [I] to make sounds or movements that are strong and regular like a heart beating: *loud pulsating music* —**pulsation** /pʌlˈseɪʃən/ *n.* [C,U]

pulse¹ /pʌls/ *n.* **1** [C usually singular] the regular beat that can be felt as your heart pumps blood around your body: *He doesn't **have a pulse**.* | *Her **pulse rate*** (=the number of beats per minute) *is high.* | *A nurse came in and **took** my **pulse*** (=counted the number of beats in a minute). **2** [C] an amount of light, sound, or energy that continues for a very short time: *an electric pulse*

pulse² *v.* [I] to move or flow quickly with a steady beat or sound: *blood **pulsing through** the veins*

pul·ver·ize /ˈpʌlvəˌraɪz/ *v.* [T] **1** to crush something into powder: *a machine that pulverizes rocks* **2** *informal* to defeat someone completely

pu·ma /ˈpumə, ˈpyumə/ *n.* [C] a COUGAR

pum·mel /ˈpʌməl/ *v.* [T] to hit someone or something many times with your FISTS

pump¹ /pʌmp/ *n.* [C] **1** a machine that forces liquid or gas into or out of something: *a **water/fuel/gas etc. pump*** | *an air/a bicycle pump* ➔ see picture at BICYCLE **2** a woman's plain shoe that does not fasten: *a pair of black pumps* **3 also gas pump** a machine at a GAS STATION, used to put gasoline into a car

pump² *v.* **1** [T] to make liquid or gas move in a particular direction, using a pump: *a machine that **pumps** water **into** the fields* **2** [I] to move liquid very quickly in and out or up and down: *His heart was pumping fast.* **3 pump sb (about sth)** *informal* to ask someone a lot of questions in order to find out information **4 pump iron** *informal* to do exercise by lifting heavy weights

pump sth **into** sth *phr. v.* **pump money into sth** *informal* to spend a lot of money on something such as a project: *He had to pump $10,000 of his own money into the company.*

pump out *phr. v.* **1 pump** sth ⇔ **out** to remove liquid from something using a pump: *We had to pump the basement out after the pipes burst.* **2 pump** sth ⇔ **out** to produce or supply something in large amounts: *I pump out a new novel every year.*

pump up *phr. v.* **1 pump** sth ⇔ **up** to fill something such as a tire or ball with air until it is full [= **inflate**] **2 pump** sb ⇔ **up** to increase someone's interest or excitement about something: *Hutchison traveled around the state the day before the election to pump up voters.*

pum·per·nick·el /ˈpʌmpɚˌnɪkəl/ *n.* [U] a heavy dark brown bread

pump·kin /ˈpʌmpkɪn, ˈpʌŋkɪn/ *n.* [C,U] a very large orange fruit that grows on the ground, or the inside of this eaten as food: *pumpkin pie* ➔ see picture at VEGETABLE

pun /pʌn/ *n.* [C] an amusing use of a word or phrase that has two meanings, or of words with the same sound but different meanings —**pun** *v.* [I]

THESAURUS

joke, **gag**, **wisecrack**, **one-liner**, **funny story**
➔ see Thesaurus box at JOKE[1]

punch[1] /pʌntʃ/ *v.* [T] **1** to hit someone or something hard with your FIST (=closed hand): *Bill was suspended from school for punching another student.* ➔ see picture on page A9

THESAURUS

hit, **slap**, **beat**, **smack**, **whack**, **strike**, **bang**, **knock**, **tap**, **pound**, **rap**, **hammer**
➔ see Thesaurus box at HIT[1]

2 to make a hole in something using a metal tool or other sharp object: *The conductor came along and punched our tickets.*

THESAURUS

pierce, **make a hole in**, **prick**, **drill**, **bore**
➔ see Thesaurus box at PIERCE

3 punch a clock to record the time that you start or finish work by putting a card into a special machine

punch in *phr. v.* to record the time that you arrive at work by putting a card into a special machine

punch out *phr. v.* to record the time that you leave work by putting a card into a special machine

punch[2] *n.* **1** [C] a quick strong hit made with your FIST (=closed hand): *a punch in the stomach* **2** [U] a drink made from fruit juice, sugar, water, and sometimes alcohol: *fruit punch* **3** [C] a metal tool for cutting holes or for pushing something into a small hole **4** [U] a strong effective quality that makes people interested: *We need something to give the ad campaign some punch.*

'punching bag *n.* **1** [C] a heavy leather bag that hangs from a rope, that is punched for exercise **2 use sb as a punching bag** *informal* to hit someone hard, or to criticize someone a lot, even though s/he has done nothing wrong

'punch line, **punch·line** /'pʌntʃlaɪn/ *n.* [C] the last few words of a joke or story that make it funny or surprising

punc·tu·al /'pʌŋktʃuəl/ *adj.* arriving, happening, etc. at exactly the time that has been arranged: *My boss demands that we be punctual for work.* —**punctuality** /ˌpʌŋktʃu'ælət̬i/ *n.* [U]

punc·tu·ate /'pʌŋktʃuˌeɪt/ *v.* [T] **1** to divide written work into sentences, phrases, etc. using COMMAS, PERIODS, etc. **2 be punctuated by/with sth** to be interrupted many times by something: *The president's speech was punctuated by occasional cheers.*

punc·tu·a·tion /ˌpʌŋktʃu'eɪʃən/ *n.* [U] the way that punctuation marks are used in a piece of writing

ˌpunctu'ation mark *n.* [C] a sign, such as a COMMA or QUESTION MARK, that is used in dividing a piece of writing into sentences, phrases, etc.

punc·ture[1] /'pʌŋktʃɚ/ *n.* [C] a small hole made when something is punctured

puncture[2] *v.* [I,T] to make a small hole in something, so that air or liquid can get out: *One bullet punctured his lung.*

pun·dit /'pʌndɪt/ *n.* [C] someone who knows a lot about a particular subject, and is often asked for his/her opinion: *political pundits*

pun·gent /'pʌndʒənt/ *adj.* having a strong smell or taste: *the pungent smell of onions*

pun·ish /'pʌnɪʃ/ *v.* [T] to make someone suffer because s/he has done something wrong or broken the law: *We will catch the people responsible for this crime, and we will punish them.* | *Don't* ***punish*** *him* ***for*** *one small mistake.* | *Any student caught destroying school property will be* ***severely punished****.*

P

pun·ish·a·ble /'pʌnɪʃəbəl/ *adj.* deserving legal punishment: *Murder is* ***punishable by*** *life imprisonment.*

pun·ish·ing /'pʌnɪʃɪŋ/ *adj.* difficult, tiring, or extreme: *a punishing walk*

pun·ish·ment /'pʌnɪʃmənt/ *n.* **1** [C] something that is done to punish someone: *Mason wants tougher* ***punishments for*** *youths involved with gangs.* | *A year in prison seems like a* ***harsh/severe punishment*** *for a minor offense.* ▶ Don't say "strict/strong punishments." ◀

THESAURUS

sentence – a punishment given by a judge in a court: *a prison sentence* | *He faces a death sentence* (=death as punishment for a crime).
penalty – a punishment given to someone who has broken a law, rule, or agreement: *Drug dealers face severe penalties.* | *The prosecution will seek the death penalty* (=death as punishment for a crime) *for the murder.*
fine – an amount of money that you must pay as a punishment for breaking a rule or law: *I got a fine for speeding.*
community service – unpaid work helping other people that someone does as punishment for a crime: *He was ordered to do 60 hours of community service.*
corporal punishment – the act of punishing a child by hitting him/her: *Corporal punishment is illegal in schools.*
capital punishment – the practice of killing someone as punishment for a crime

2 [U] the act of punishing someone, or the process of being punished: *The terrorists will not escape punishment.* | *As* ***punishment****, Marshall had to stay after school.*

pu·ni·tive /ˈpyunəṭɪv/ *adj.* intended as punishment: *The company will seek* ***punitive damages*** (=money that a court orders someone to pay as a punishment) *related to the fraud conviction.*

punk /pʌŋk/ *n.* **1** [U] **also punk rock** a type of loud music popular in the late 1970s and 1980s **2** [C] *informal* a boy or young man who likes to start fights, do things that are illegal, etc. **3** [C] **also punk rocker** someone who likes punk music and wears things that are typical of it, such as torn clothes, metal chains, and colored hair

punt /pʌnt/ *n.* [C] in football, a long kick that you make after dropping the ball from your hands —**punt** *v.* [I,T]

pu·ny /ˈpyuni/ *adj.* small, thin, and weak: *a puny little kid*

P

pup /pʌp/ *n.* [C] **1** a PUPPY **2** a young SEAL or OTTER

pu·pil /ˈpyupəl/ *n.* [C] **1** *formal* a child or young person in school [➡ **student**] **2** the small black round area in the middle of your eye ➔ see picture at EYE[1]

puppet

pup·pet /ˈpʌpɪt/ *n.* [C] **1** a model of a person or animal that you can move by pulling strings that are attached to parts of its body, or by putting your hand inside it: *a puppet show* **2** *disapproving* a person or organization that is controlled by someone else and does not make any independent decisions: *a puppet government*

pup·pet·eer /ˌpʌpɪˈtɪr/ *n.* [C] someone who performs with puppets

pup·py /ˈpʌpi/ *n.* plural **puppies** [C] a young dog

ˈpuppy love *n.* [U] a young boy's or girl's romantic love for someone that people do not think of as serious

pur·chase[1] /ˈpɚtʃəs/ *v.* [T] *formal* to buy something: *The couple recently purchased a $4 million mansion in Beverly Hills.* | *Tickets may be* ***purchased from*** *the box office.*

THESAURUS

buy, acquire, get, snap up
➔ see Thesaurus box at BUY[1]

purchase[2] *n. formal* **1** [C,U] the act of buying something: *Please have your credit card ready when* ***making*** *your* ***purchase***. | *The law requires a five-day waiting period for the* ***purchase of*** *handguns.* **2** [C] something that has been bought: *The store will deliver your purchases.*

pure /pyʊr/ *adj.* **1** not mixed with anything else [≠ **impure**]: *rings made of* ***pure gold*** | *pure wool blankets*

THESAURUS

natural, wild, organic
➔ see Thesaurus box at NATURAL[1]

2 [only before noun] complete: *a smile of* ***pure joy*** | *It was* ***pure chance*** *that we were there at the same time.* **3** clean, without anything harmful or unhealthy [≠ **impure**]: *pure drinking water* | *In the mountains, the air is purer.* **4 pure and simple** used to emphasize that there is only one thing involved or worth considering: *This was murder, pure and simple.* **5** *literary* without any sexual experience or evil thoughts [≠ **impure**] **6 pure science/math etc.** work done in order to increase our knowledge of something rather than to make practical use of it [➡ **applied**]

pu·rée /pyʊˈreɪ/ *n.* [C,U] food that is boiled or crushed until it is almost a liquid: *tomato purée* —**purée** *v.* [T]

pure·ly /ˈpyʊrli/ *adv.* completely and only: *He did it for purely selfish reasons.* | *We met purely by chance.*

pur·ga·to·ry /ˈpɚgəˌtɔri/ *n.* [U] **1 Purgatory** a place where, according to Roman Catholic beliefs, the souls of dead people must suffer for the bad things they have done, until they are good enough to enter heaven **2** a place, situation, or time when you suffer a lot

purge /pɚdʒ/ *v.* [T] **1** to force people to leave a place or organization because the people in power do not like them: *The army was* ***purged of*** *anyone the government considered dangerous.* **2** *technical* to get rid of something bad that is in your body **3** *literary* to remove bad feelings: *We must purge ourselves of hatred.* —**purge** *n.* [C]

pu·ri·fy /ˈpyʊrəˌfaɪ/ *v.* past tense and past participle **purified**, third person singular **purifies** [T] to remove the dirty or unwanted parts from something: *The water should be purified before drinking.* —**purification** /ˌpyʊrəfəˈkeɪʃən/ *n.* [U]

pur·ist /ˈpyʊrɪst/ *n.* [C] someone who has very strict ideas about what is right or correct in a particular subject

pur·it·an /ˈpyʊrətən, -rətˀn/ *n.* [C] **1** someone with strict moral views who thinks that pleasures such as sex or drinking alcohol are wrong **2 Puritan** a member of a Protestant religious group in the 16th and 17th centuries, who wanted to make religion simpler

pu·ri·tan·i·cal /ˌpyʊrəˈtænɪkəl/ *adj. disapproving* having strict attitudes about religion and moral behavior: *a puritanical and deeply religious woman*

pu·ri·ty /ˈpyʊrət̬i/ *n.* [U] the quality or state of being pure: *the purity of the water* | *religious purity*

pur·ple /ˈpɚpəl/ *n.* [U] a dark color made from red mixed with blue —**purple** *adj.*

ˌPurple ˈHeart *n.* [C] a MEDAL given to U.S. soldiers who have been wounded in battle

pur·port /pɚˈpɔrt/ *v.* [I,T] *formal* to claim to be or do something, even if this is not true: *He* ***purports to be*** *the son of the wealthy Italian banker.* | *The painting* ***is purported to be*** *the work of Monet.* —**purportedly** *adv.*

pur·pose /ˈpɚpəs/ *n.* **1** [C] the thing that an event, process, or activity is supposed to achieve: *The* ***purpose of*** *this exercise is to increase your strength.* | *The Red Cross sent supplies* ***for*** *medical* ***purposes***. | ***For the purposes*** *of the report, low income was defined as $30,000 a year for a family of four.* | *He came here* ***with the purpose of*** *carrying out the attack.*

THESAURUS

aim – something that you want to achieve: *Our main aim is to find the child before dark.*
goal – something that you hope to achieve in the future: *Athletes set personal goals for themselves.*
objective – something that you are working hard to achieve: *The major objectives have been achieved.*

2 on purpose deliberately: *Firefighters believe the fire was started on purpose.* **3** [U] determination to succeed in what you want to do: *She came back from vacation with a new sense of purpose.*

pur·pose·ful /ˈpɚpəsfəl/ *adj.* having a clear aim or purpose [= **determined**]: *She kept walking, with long, purposeful strides.*

pur·pose·ly /ˈpɚpəsli/ *adv.* deliberately: *They purposely left him out of the discussion.*

purr /pɚ/ *v.* [I] if a cat purrs, it makes a soft low sound in its throat to show that it is pleased —**purr** *n.* [C]

purse¹ /pɚs/ *n.* **1** [C] a bag used by women to carry money and personal things: *I think my glasses are still in my purse.* ➔ see picture at BAG¹ **2 control/hold the purse strings** to control the money in a family, company, etc.

purse² *v.* **purse your lips** to bring your lips together tightly in a circle, especially to show disapproval

purs·er /ˈpɚsɚ/ *n.* [C] an officer who is responsible for the money on a ship and is in charge of the passengers' rooms, comfort, etc.

pur·sue /pɚˈsu/ *v.* [T] **1** to continue doing an activity or trying to achieve something over a long time: *He left home to* ***pursue a career*** *in acting.*

THESAURUS

follow, **chase**, **run after**, **tail**, **stalk**
➔ see Thesaurus box at FOLLOW

2 to chase or follow someone or something in order to catch him, her, or it: *A police car pursued the suspect along Nordhoff Blvd.* **3 pursue the matter/question/argument** to continue trying to ask about, find out about, or persuade someone about a particular subject: *The company plans to pursue the matter in court.*

pur·suit /pɚˈsut/ *n.* **1** [U] the act of chasing or following someone: *With the officers* ***in (hot) pursuit*** (=following close behind), *Parker pulled off the freeway and ran into the woods.* **2** [U] *formal* the act of trying to achieve something in a determined way: *the right to life, liberty, and the* ***pursuit of*** *happiness* **3** [C usually plural] *formal* an activity that you spend a lot of time doing: *Nancy enjoys outdoor pursuits.*

pur·vey·or /pɚˈveɪɚ/ *n.* [C] *formal* a business that supplies information, goods, or services: *purveyors of fine cheeses* —**purvey** *v.* [T]

pus /pʌs/ *n.* [U] a thick yellowish liquid produced in an infected part of your body

push¹ /pʊʃ/ *v.*
1 MOVE [I,T] to move a person or thing away from you by pressing him, her, or it with your hands [≠ **pull**]: *A couple of guys were pushing an old Volkswagen down the street.* | *Lisa* ***pushed*** *Amy* ***into*** *the pool.* | *She tried to* ***push*** *him* ***away***. | *Can you push harder? It's not moving.* ➔ see picture on page A9

THESAURUS

roll – to push a round object so that it moves forward: *He rolled the wheel over to the car.*
poke – to push someone or something with your finger or something sharp: *Jill poked the fish to see if it was alive.*
shove – to push someone or something roughly: *He shoved her against a wall.*
nudge – to push someone gently with your elbow to get their attention: *"Move over," she said, nudging my arm.*
elbow – to push someone with your elbows, especially in order to move past him/her: *As he left the field, he elbowed jeering spectators out of his way.*
➔ PULL

2 MAKE STH START/STOP [I,T] to press a button, SWITCH, etc. to make a machine start or stop working: *Push the green button to start the engine.*
3 TRY TO GET PAST SB [I,T] to move somewhere

P

by pushing people away from you: *Heather **pushed past** us without speaking.* | *people trying to **push** their **way** to the front*

4 PERSUADE [I,T] to try to persuade someone to accept or do something: *The agency is **pushing to** increase U.S. exports.* | *citizens **pushing for** stricter gun controls* | *My parents **pushed** me **into** going to college.*

5 WORK HARD [T] to make someone work very hard: *Royce has been **pushing himself** too much lately.* | *Coach Koepple **pushes** his players pretty **hard**.*

6 INCREASE/DECREASE [I,T] to increase or decrease an amount, number, or value: *New medical technology has **pushed** the cost of health care **up/higher**.* | *The recession has **pushed** stock market prices **down/lower**.*

7 DRUGS [T] *informal* to sell illegal drugs

8 push your luck/push it *informal* to do something or ask for something again, when this is likely to annoy someone or be risky: *I want to ask my boss for another day off but I don't want to push my luck.*

push ahead *phr. v.* to continue with a plan or activity in a determined way: *The airport is **pushing ahead with** its program to expand.*

push sb ⇔ **around** *phr. v. informal* to tell someone what to do in a rude or threatening way: *Don't let your boss push you around.*

push on *phr. v.* to continue traveling somewhere or doing an activity: *The others stopped for a rest, but I pushed on to the top.* | *Even with disagreement growing, they decided to **push on with** the negotiations.*

push sth ⇔ **through** *phr. v.* to get a plan, law, etc. officially accepted, especially quickly: *Wilson pushed through a measure to increase the state sales tax.*

push² *n.* [C usually singular] **1** the act of pushing someone or something: *Just **give** the door **a push** if it's stuck.* **2** an attempt to get or achieve something: *Eastern Europe's **push to** modernize their economies* | *a **push for** longer prison terms* **3 if/when push comes to shove** when or if a situation becomes extremely difficult: *If push comes to shove, I can always rent out the house.*

push·er /ˈpʊʃɚ/ *n.* [C] *informal* someone who sells illegal drugs

push·o·ver /ˈpʌʃˌoʊvɚ/ *n. informal* **be a pushover** to be easy to persuade, influence, or defeat

ˈpush-up *n.* [C] an exercise in which you lie on the floor facing the ground, and push yourself up with your arms: *I can only do about twenty push-ups*

push·y /ˈpʊʃi/ *adj. disapproving* so determined to succeed and get what you want that you behave in a rude way: *pushy salespeople*

puss·y·cat /ˈpʊsiˌkæt/ *n.* [C] **1** a cat, a word used by children or when speaking to children **2** *informal* someone who is kind and gentle: *Jake's a real pussycat once you get to know him.*

puss·y·foot /ˈpʊsiˌfʊt/ *v.* [I] *informal* to be too careful and afraid to do something: *Stop **pussyfooting around** and decide!*

put

put on — take off

put /pʊt/ *v.* past tense and past participle **put**, present participle **putting** [T]

1 MOVE TO PLACE/POSITION to move someone or something into a particular place or position: *Where did you put the newspaper?* | *Put the scissors in the drawer when you're finished.* | *I put some money into our account.* | *It's time to **put** the kids **to bed*** (=make them go into their beds).

2 CHANGE to change someone's situation or the way s/he feels: *Ohio State's win put them in the playoffs.* | *The recent layoffs put 250 people out of work.* | *Higher insurance costs may **put** many companies **out of business*** (=make the companies close down). | *Politics **puts** me **to sleep**.* | *He **put** himself **in danger** to save the lives of others.* | *music to **put** you **in a** relaxed **mood*** (=make you feel relaxed)

3 WRITE to write or print something: *Put your name at the top of your answer sheet.* | *We put an ad in the paper.*

4 put emphasis/pressure/blame etc. on sb/sth to emphasize something, make someone feel pressure, blame someone, etc.: *People are starting to put pressure on Congress to pass gun control laws.*

5 put an end/a stop to sth to stop an activity that is harmful or not acceptable: *We want the president to put an end to this war.*

6 EXPRESS to say or express something in a particular way: ***How can I put this?*** (=said to someone when you want to tell them something that they may not like) | ***To put it bluntly**, a lot of people just don't like her.* | *Well, let me **put it this way**: he's lied to us before.*

7 HAVE IMPORTANCE/QUALITY to consider something to have a particular level of importance or quality: *Responsible parents always put their*

children first. | *The new study puts UCLA among the top five research universities in the U.S.*
8 put sth behind you to try to forget about a bad experience or a mistake so that it does not affect you now: *Vietnam veterans talked of the need to put the war behind them.*
9 put faith/confidence/trust etc. in sb/sth to trust or believe in someone or something: *These people put little trust in doctors.* → **put your mind to sth** at MIND[1]

put sth ⇔ **across** *phr. v.* to explain your ideas, beliefs, etc. in a way that people can understand: *I had a hard time putting my message across to the students.*

put sth ⇔ **aside** *phr. v.* **1** to ignore a problem or disagreement because you want to achieve something: *Try to put your feelings aside and look at the facts.* **2** to save money regularly, usually for a particular purpose: *I have money put aside for emergencies.*

put sth ⇔ **away** *phr. v.* to put something in the place where it is usually kept: *Could you put the dishes away before you go to bed?*

put sth ⇔ **back** *phr. v.* to put things or people in the place or situation they were before: *Put the milk back in the fridge, please.* | *a program to put people back to work*

put down *phr. v.* **1 put** sb **down** *informal* to criticize someone and make him/her feel silly or stupid: *Her father is always putting her down.* **2 put** sth ⇔ **down** *informal* to write something on a piece of paper: *I put down that I'd be available to work on Saturdays.* **3 put** sb/sth ⇔ **down** to use force to stop people who are fighting against a government: *Soldiers were sent to put down the rebellion.*

put sth ⇔ **forward** *phr. v.* to suggest a plan, idea, etc.: *a treaty put forward by the Dutch*

put sth ⇔ **in** *phr. v.* **1** to put a piece of equipment somewhere and connect it so that it is ready to be used: *We had to have a new furnace put in.* **2** to spend time or effort doing something: *Doug is putting in a lot of hours at work* (=he is working a lot). **3** to ask for something in an official way: *Sawyer put in his expenses claim last week.* | *Jones* ***put in for*** *a transfer to our Dallas office.*

put sth **into** sth *phr. v.* **1** to make money available to be used for a particular purpose: *The company plans to put more money into computer technology.* **2 put energy/effort/enthusiasm etc. into sth** to use energy, etc. when you are doing something: *Koskoff put a lot of time and effort into this project.* **3 put sth into action/effect/practice** to start using something such as an idea or plan: *The college hopes to put the changes into effect by August 1.*

put off *phr. v.* **1 put** sth ⇔ **off** to delay something, or to delay doing something: *Many Americans put off filling out their tax forms as long as possible.* | *We've decided to put off our trip to Europe until next year.* **2 put** sb ⇔ **off** to make you dislike something or not want to do something: *Don't be put off by the restaurant's decor; the food is excellent.*

put on *phr. v.*
1 CLOTHES put sth ⇔ **on** to put a piece of clothing on your body [➡ **take off**]: *Put your coat on – it's cold.*
2 AFFECT/INFLUENCE put sth ⇔ **on** sth to do something that affects or influences something else: *The government put a freeze on the construction of new nuclear power plants* (=they stopped it).
3 put on weight/5 pounds etc. to become fatter and heavier
4 START EQUIPMENT put sth ⇔ **on** to make a piece of equipment begin working: *It's cold in here. Why don't you put on the heat?*
5 MUSIC put sth ⇔ **on** to begin to play a record, tape, video, etc.: *Let's put on some music.*
6 ON SKIN put sth ⇔ **on** to use MAKEUP, etc. on your skin: *I hardly ever put on lipstick.*
7 EVENT/PLAY put sth ⇔ **on** to arrange an event, concert, play, etc., or to perform in one: *The orchestra is putting on a concert for charity.*
8 FOOD put sth ⇔ **on** to start cooking something: *Let me just put the potatoes on.*

put out *phr. v.* **1 put** sth ⇔ **out** to make a fire, cigarette, etc. stop burning: *It took nearly three hours to put out the fire.* **2 put** sth ⇔ **out** to produce something, such as a book, record, movie, etc.: *They've put out three books now on vegetarian cooking.* **3 put** sth ⇔ **out** to place things where people can find and use them: *I'm just going to put out cold cuts, bread, and stuff for lunch.* **4 put** sth ⇔ **out** to put something outside the house: *Has anybody put the trash out yet?* **5 put** sth ⇔ **out** to broadcast or produce something for people to read or listen to: *The company has put out a statement saying that they will replace all the defective products.* **6 put** sb ⇔ **out** to make more work or cause problems for someone: *Will it put you out if I bring another guest?* **7 put your hand/foot/arm out** to move your hand, etc. away from your body: *Jack put out his foot and tripped her.*

put through *phr. v.* **1 put** sb **through** sth to make someone do something that is very bad or difficult: *My father's drinking problem put my mother through hell.* **2 put sb through school/college/university** to pay for someone to go to school, etc.: *He worked part-time to put himself through school.* **3 put** sb **through** to connect someone to someone else on the telephone

put sth **to** sb *phr. v.* to suggest something such as a plan to a person or group: *The proposal was put to the committee on January 9.*

put sth ⇔ **together** *phr. v.* **1** to build or fix something by joining its different parts together: *The store will put the bicycle together for you.* **2** to prepare or produce something by collecting pieces of information, ideas, etc.: *Franklin has put together a program to help families in need.*

P

3 put together combined: *He earns **more than** the rest of us **put together**.*

put up *phr. v.* **1 put** sth ⇔ **up** to build something such as a wall or building, or to raise something so that it is upright: *The developers plan to put up a 15-story office building.* **2 put** sth ⇔ **up** to attach a picture, etc. to a wall or decorate things, so people can see them: *Stores are already putting up Christmas decorations.* **3 put sth up for sale/discussion/review etc.** to make something available to be sold, discussed, etc.: *We put our house up for sale.* **4 put** sb **up** *informal* to let someone stay in your house: *I can put Jared up for the night.* **5 put up money/$500/$3 million etc.** to give money to be used for a particular purpose: *Furth put up $42,000 in prize money for the contest.* **6 put up resistance/a fight/a struggle** to argue against or oppose something in a determined way, or to fight against someone who is attacking you: *Opponents of the bill are putting up a good fight in the Assembly.*

put sb **up to** sth *phr. v.* to encourage someone to do something wrong, silly, or dangerous: *Jim wouldn't usually play such a stupid trick; someone must have put him up to it.*

put up with sb/sth *phr. v.* to accept a bad situation or person without complaining: *I'm not going to put up with being treated like that.*

'put-down *n.* [C] *informal* something you say that is intended to make someone feel stupid and unimportant

pu·tre·fy /ˈpyutrəˌfaɪ/ *v.* past tense and past participle **putrefied**, third person singular **putrefies** [I,T] *formal* to decay and smell very bad

pu·trid /ˈpyutrɪd/ *adj.* decaying and smelling very bad

putt /pʌt/ *v.* [I,T] to hit a GOLF ball gently a short distance along the ground toward the hole —**putt** *n.* [C]

put·ter /ˈpʌt̬ɚ/ *v.* [I] to spend time doing things that are not very important, in a relaxed way: *He's been **puttering around** the yard all morning.*

put·ty /ˈpʌt̬i/ *n.* [U] a soft substance that becomes hard when it dries, used for example for fixing glass into window frames

'put up,on *adj.* **be/feel put upon** to think that other people are treating you unfairly by expecting you to do too much

puz·zle¹ /ˈpʌzəl/ *n.* [C] **1** a game or toy that has a lot of pieces that you have to fit together: *a 500-piece **jigsaw puzzle*** **2** a game in which you have to think hard to solve a difficult question or problem: *a book of crossword puzzles* **3** something that is difficult to understand or explain: *The way the stock market works has always been a puzzle to me.*

puzzle² *v.* **1** [T] to confuse someone because s/he does not understand something: *The results of the study puzzled scientists.* **2** [I,T] to think for a long time about something because you cannot understand it: *Jill **puzzled over** the first question on the exam for ten minutes.*

puz·zled /ˈpʌzəld/ *adj.* confused and unable to understand something: *a puzzled look*

puz·zling /ˈpʌzlɪŋ/ *adj.* difficult to understand: *a puzzling question* | *I find his work puzzling.*

pyg·my /ˈpɪgmi/ *n.* plural **pygmies** [C] **1 also Pygmy** someone who belongs to a race of very small people from parts of Asia and Africa **2** a very small type of animal: *a pygmy rabbit*

py·lon /ˈpaɪlɑn/ *n.* [C] a tall metal structure that supports wires carrying electricity

pyr·a·mid /ˈpɪrəmɪd/ *n.* [C] **1** a large stone building with a flat base and sides shaped like TRIANGLES that form a point at the top ➔ see picture at SHAPE¹ **2** something that has this shape

pyre /paɪɚ/ *n.* [C] a high pile of wood on which a dead body is placed to be burned in a funeral ceremony: *a funeral pyre*

Py·rex /ˈpaɪrɛks/ *n.* [U] *trademark* a special type of strong glass that does not break at high temperatures and is used for making cooking dishes

py·thon /ˈpaɪθɑn, -θən/ *n.* [C] a large tropical snake that kills animals for food by crushing them

Q, q

Q, q /kyu/ *n.* the seventeenth letter of the English alphabet

Q *written* **question**

Q-tip /ˈkyu tɪp/ *n.* [C] *trademark* a small thin stick with cotton at each end, used for cleaning places that are difficult to reach, such as your ears

quack¹ /kwæk/ *v.* [I] to make the sound that ducks make

quack² *n.* [C] **1** *informal* someone who pretends to be a doctor **2** the sound a duck makes

quad /kwɑd/ *n.* [C] *informal* **1** a square open area with buildings all around it, especially in a school or college **2 quads** [plural] *informal* QUADRICEPS

quad·ran·gle /ˈkwɑdræŋgəl/ *n.* [C] **1** *technical* a flat shape that has four straight sides **2** a QUAD

quad·rant /ˈkwɑdrənt/ *n.* [C] **1** a quarter of a circle **2** a quarter of an area, especially of land: *the town's southwest quadrant* **3** a tool for measuring angles

quad·ri·ceps /ˈkwɑdrəˌsɛps/ *n.* [plural] *technical* the large muscle at the front of your THIGH

quad·ri·lat·er·al /ˌkwɑdrəˈlæt̬ərəl/ *n.* [C] a flat shape with four straight sides —**quadrilateral** *adj.*

quad·ri·ple·gic /ˌkwɑdrəˈplidʒɪk/ *n.* [C] someone who is permanently unable to move any part of his/her body below his/her neck [➡ **paraplegic**] —**quadriplegic** *adj.*

quad·ru·ped /ˈkwɑdrəˌpɛd/ *n.* [C] *technical* an animal that has four feet

quad·ru·ple¹ /kwɑˈdrupəl/ *v.* [I,T] to increase and become four times as big or as high, or to make something do this: *The city's population has quadrupled since the 1930s.*

quadruple² *adj., quantifier* four times as big, as many, or as much: *quadruple the normal dose*

quad·ru·plet /kwɑˈdruplɪt/ *n.* [C] one of four babies born at the same time to the same mother

quag·mire /ˈkwægmaɪɚ, ˈkwɑg-/ *n.* [C] **1** a difficult or complicated situation: *Vietnam became a political and military quagmire.* **2** an area of soft wet muddy ground

quail /kweɪl/ *n.* [C,U] a small fat bird with a short tail that is hunted and shot for food and sport, or the meat from this bird

quaint /kweɪnt/ *adj.* unusual and attractive, especially in an old-fashioned way: *a quaint little restaurant*

quake¹ /kweɪk/ *v.* [I] **1** to shake, usually because you are afraid: *He quaked in terror.* **2** if the earth, a building, etc. quakes, it shakes violently

quake² *n.* [C] *informal* an EARTHQUAKE

Quak·er /ˈkweɪkɚ/ *adj.* relating to the Society of Friends, a Christian religious group that opposes violence, has no religious leaders or ceremonies, and holds its religious meetings in silence —**Quaker** *n.* [C]

qual·i·fi·ca·tion /ˌkwɑləfəˈkeɪʃən/ *n.* **1** [C usually plural] a skill, personal quality, or type of experience that makes you right for a particular job or position: *What are the key* ***qualifications for*** *the presidency? | Does he have the right* ***qualifications to*** *become a Supreme Court Justice?* **2** [C,U] the official standard that must be achieved in order to do a job, enter a sports competition, etc., or the achievement of this standard: *her* ***qualification for*** *the Olympic swimming team | educational qualifications* **3** [C,U] something that you add to a statement to limit its effect or meaning: *You have the right to refuse without qualification.*

qual·i·fied /ˈkwɑləˌfaɪd/ *adj.* **1** having the right knowledge, experience, skills, etc. for a particular job: *a qualified teacher | The employees here are* ***highly qualified.*** **2** [usually before noun] qualified agreement, approval, etc. is limited in some way because you do not completely agree: *Is it worth the money? The answer is* ***a qualified yes.***

qual·i·fi·er /ˈkwɑləˌfaɪɚ/ *n.* [C] **1** someone who has reached the necessary standard for entering a competition **2** a word or phrase that limits or adds to the meaning of another word or phrase. In the phrase "her new red bike," "new" and "red" are qualifiers.

qual·i·fy /ˈkwɑləˌfaɪ/ *v.* past tense and past participle **qualified**, third person singular **qualifies** **1** [I] to pass an examination or reach the standard of knowledge or skill that you need in order to do something: *I* ***qualified as*** *a pilot. | She has* ***qualified for*** *the 100-meter race.* **2** [I,T] to have the right to have or do something, or to give someone this right: *They* ***qualify for*** *food stamps.* **3** [I] to have all the necessary qualities to be considered a particular thing: *The organization* ***qualifies as*** *a charity.* **4** [T] to add something to what has already been said, in order to limit its effect or meaning: *Let me qualify that statement.*

qual·i·ta·tive /ˈkwɑləˌteɪt̬ɪv/ *adj.* relating to the quality or standard of something, rather than amount or number [➡ **quantitative**]: *a qualitative study of the health care program*

qual·i·ty¹ /ˈkwɑləṭi/ *n.* plural **qualities** **1** [C,U] the degree to which something is good or bad: *today's air quality | concern about the* ***quality of*** *education |* ***high/low quality*** *recording equipment | drugs that improve* ***the quality of life*** *for cancer sufferers* **2** [C usually plural] something that someone has as part of his/her character, especially good things [➡ **characteristic**]: *She has many of the qualities he lacks. | leadership qualities | the* ***qualities of*** *honesty and independence*

> **THESAURUS**
> **characteristic, feature, property, attribute**
> ➔ see Thesaurus box at CHARACTERISTIC¹

3 [C] something that is typical of something and makes it different from other things: *the qualities of the rock* **4** [U] a high standard: *a guarantee of quality*

quality² *adj.* of a high standard: *quality products*

ˈquality conˌtrol *n.* [U] the practice of checking goods as they are produced, to make sure their quality is good enough

ˈquality ˌtime *n.* [U] the time that you spend giving someone your full attention, especially time you spend with your children

qualm /kwɑm, kwɔm/ *n.* [C usually plural] a feeling of slight worry or doubt because you are not sure that what you are doing is right: *He* ***has no qualms about*** *proceeding.*

quan·da·ry /ˈkwɑndəri/ *n.* [C] **be in a quandary about/over sth** to be unable to decide what to do about a difficult problem or situation: *We were* ***in a quandary*** *over whether to go or not.*

quan·ti·fi·er /ˈkwɑntəˌfaɪɚ/ *n.* [C] *technical* in grammar, a word or phrase that is used with a noun to show quantity. In the sentence "There were only a few people at the party," "few" is a quantifier.

quan·ti·fy /ˈkwɑntəˌfaɪ/ *v.* past tense and past participle **quantified**, third person singular **quan-**

tifies [T] to measure something and express it as a number: *The damage to the company is difficult to quantify.* —**quantifiable** /ˌkwɑntəˈfaɪəbəl/ *adj.*

quan·ti·ta·tive /ˈkwɑntəˌteɪt̬ɪv/ *adj.* relating to amounts rather than to the quality or standard of something [➡ **qualitative**]: *a quantitative improvement in production*

quan·ti·ty /ˈkwɑntət̬i/ *n.* plural **quantities** [C,U] an amount of something that can be counted or measured: *the **quantity of** evidence proving his guilt* | ***large/great quantities** of natural gas*

quan·tum leap /ˌkwɑntəm ˈlip/ *n.* [C] a very large and important improvement

quar·an·tine /ˈkwɔrənˌtin, ˈkwɑr-/ *n.* [C,U] a time when a person or animal is kept apart from others in case she, he, or it has a disease: *The dogs were kept **in quarantine** for three months.* —**quarantine** *v.* [T]

quark /kwɑrk/ *n.* [C] *technical* a very small piece of matter that forms part of an atom

Q

quar·rel¹ /ˈkwɔrəl, ˈkwɑrəl/ *n.* [C] **1** an angry argument: *He'd **had a quarrel** with his wife.* | *a **quarrel over** money* **2** *formal* a reason to dislike someone or disagree with an idea, decision, etc.: *We **have no quarrel with** the court's decision.*

quarrel² *v.* [I] to have an angry argument: *I had **quarreled with** my parents.* | *Downstairs, the children were **quarreling over** a game.*

> **THESAURUS**
>
> **argue, have an argument, fight, have a fight, have a quarrel, squabble, bicker**
> ➔ see Thesaurus box at ARGUE

quar·rel·some /ˈkwɔrəlsəm, ˈkwɑr-/ *adj.* too ready to argue about things

quar·ry /ˈkwɔri, ˈkwɑri/ *n.* plural **quarries** [C] **1** a place where large amounts of stone, sand, etc. are dug out of the ground **2** an animal or person that you are hunting or chasing —**quarry** *v.* [T]

quart /kwɔrt/ *n.* [C] a unit for measuring liquid, equal to 2 PINTS or 0.9463 liters: *a **quart of** milk*

quar·ter /ˈkwɔrt̬ɚ/ *n.* [C] **1** one of four equal parts into which something can be divided [➡ **half, third**]: *Cut the sandwiches into quarters.* | *A **quarter of** Canada's population is French speaking.* | ***three-quarters of** (=75%) the country's voters* **2** a period of fifteen minutes: *Can you be ready in **a quarter (of an) hour**?* | *It's **a quarter to/after five*** (=15 minutes before or after 5 o'clock). | *The unloading took **three-quarters of an hour*** (=45 minutes). **3** a coin used in the U.S. and Canada worth 25 cents (=1/4 of a dollar)

> **THESAURUS**
>
> **coin, penny, nickel, dime**
> ➔ see Thesaurus box at MONEY

4 a period of three months – used when discussing business and financial matters: *Profits were down in the fourth quarter.* **5** one of the four periods into which a year at school or college is divided [➡ **semester**] ➔ see Topic box at UNIVERSITY **6** one of the four equal periods of time into which games of some sports are divided: *The score was 66–58 in the third quarter.* **7 quarters** [plural] the house or rooms where you live, especially if you are a servant or in the army: *Upstairs were spacious **living quarters**.*

quar·ter·back /ˈkwɔrt̬ɚˌbæk/ *n.* [C] the player in football who directs the OFFENSE and throws the ball

quar·ter·fi·nal /ˌkwɔrt̬ɚˈfaɪnl/ *n.* [C] one of the set of four games near the end of a competition, whose winners play in the two SEMIFINALS

quar·ter·ly /ˈkwɔrt̬ɚli/ *adj., adv.* produced or happening four times a year: *a quarterly report*

quar·tet /kwɔrˈtɛt/ *n.* [C] **1** a piece of music written for four performers: *a **string quartet*** (=four people playing musical instruments with strings, such as violins) **2** a group of four things or people

quartz /kwɔrts/ *n.* [U] a hard mineral substance that is used in making electronic watches and clocks

qua·sar /ˈkweɪzɑr/ *n.* [C] *technical* a very bright, very distant object similar to a star

quash /kwɑʃ/ *v.* [T] *formal* **1** to officially state that a judgment or decision is no longer legal or correct: *The judge quashed the decision of a lower court.* **2** to say or do something to stop something from continuing: *an attempt to quash rumors*

qua·ver /ˈkweɪvɚ/ *v.* [I,T] if your voice quavers, it shakes as you speak, especially because you are nervous

quay /keɪ, ki/ *n.* [C] a place where boats can be tied up or loaded

quea·sy /ˈkwizi/ *adj.* feeling that you are going to VOMIT [= **nauseous**] —**queasiness** *n.* [U]

queen /kwin/ *n.* [C] **1 also Queen** the female ruler of a country who is from a royal family, or the wife of a king: *Queen Elizabeth*

> **THESAURUS**
>
> **king, monarch, ruler, emperor, sovereign**
> ➔ see Thesaurus box at KING

2 a large female BEE, ANT, etc. that lays the eggs for a whole group **3** the woman who wins a beauty competition

ˈqueen-size *adj.* larger than the standard size: *a queen-size bed*

queer¹ /kwɪr/ *adj.* **1** *old-fashioned* strange: *a queer expression* **2** *informal offensive* HOMOSEXUAL

queer² *n.* [C] *informal offensive* a HOMOSEXUAL

quell /kwɛl/ *v.* [T] **1** to make a violent situation end: *The military were sent in to **quell the rioting**.* **2** to stop feelings of doubt, worry, and anxiety from getting stronger: *I struggled to quell my sense of panic.*

quench /kwɛntʃ/ *v.* **quench your thirst** if a

drink quenches your thirst, it makes you stop feeling thirsty

que·ry /ˈkwɪri/ *n.* plural **queries** [C] *formal* a question: *Staff are available to **answer** your **queries**.* —**query** *v.* [T]

quest /kwɛst/ *n.* [C] *literary* a long search for something —**quest** *v.* [I]

ques·tion[1] /ˈkwɛstʃən, ˈkwɛʃtʃən/ *n.* **1** [C] a sentence or phrase used in order to ask for information [≠ **answer**]: *Can I **ask** you a **question**? | Does anyone **have** any **questions**? | **questions about/on** health habits | I'm not sure I can **answer** that **question**.*

COLLOCATIONS

ask a question
answer a question
have a question – to want to ask one
put a question to sb – to ask someone a question in a formal situation
pose a question – to ask a difficult question
bombard sb with questions – to ask someone a lot of questions
rephrase a question – to ask it in a different way
avoid/evade/sidestep a question – to avoid giving a direct answer

2 [C] a subject or problem that needs to be discussed or dealt with [= **issue**]: ***the question of** what should be done with nuclear waste | Their actions **raise the question** of whether they should be treated as war criminals.* **3** [U] a feeling of doubt about something: *The accuracy of the data has been **called into question*** (=people have doubts about it). | ***There is no question** that teachers prefer smaller classes.* **4 without question a)** definitely: *The most beautiful fish here is without question the angelfish.* **b)** without complaining or asking why: *He followed Dennison's advice without question.* **5 in question** the person or thing that is in question is the one that is being discussed: *The document in question is a report dated June 18, 1948.* **6 be a question of sth** used in order to say what the most important fact, part, or feature of something is: *It's a question of all working together to solve these problems.* **7 be out of the question** if something is out of the question, it is definitely not possible or not allowed: *Ticket prices are so high that going to the game is out of the question.* **8 (that's a) good question!** *spoken* said when you are admitting you do not know the answer to a question: *"How did she and Luke meet?" "Good question."*

question[2] *v.* [T] **1** to ask someone questions, especially about a crime: *Police are **questioning** three men **about** the murder.*

THESAURUS

ask, **order**, **demand**, **request**, **beg**, **interrogate**, **inquire**, **enquire**
→ see Thesaurus box at ASK

2 to have or express doubts about whether something is true, good, or necessary: *Are you questioning my honesty? | Fans are **questioning whether** the team can win.*

ques·tion·a·ble /ˈkwɛstʃənəbəl/ *adj.* **1** not likely to be good, honest, or morally correct: *questionable business activities* **2** not certain or possibly not correct: ***It is questionable whether** the tests are worthwhile.*

ques·tion·ing[1] /ˈkwɛstʃənɪŋ/ *n.* [U] the process of asking questions: *a witness undergoing questioning*

questioning[2] *adj.* a questioning look or expression shows that you need more information or that you doubt something

ˈquestion mark *n.* [C] the mark (?), used in writing at the end of a question

ques·tion·naire /ˌkwɛstʃəˈnɛr/ *n.* [C] a written set of questions about a particular subject that is given to a large number of people, in order to collect information

THESAURUS

poll, **survey**
→ see Thesaurus box at POLL[1]

quib·ble /ˈkwɪbəl/ *v.* [I] to argue about something that is not very important —**quibble** *n.* [C]

quiche /kiʃ/ *n.* [C] a type of food that consists of PASTRY filled with a mixture of eggs, cheese, vegetables, etc. → see picture on page A5

quick[1] /kwɪk/ *adj.* **1** quick actions or events continue for, or are done, in a short time: *I'll just take a quick shower first. | a quick response | It'd be quicker to drive.* **2** people who are quick are fast or do something fast: *I promise I'll be quick. | People are **quick to** complain but slow to help.* **3** able to learn and understand things in a short time [= **intelligent**]: *Carolyn's a **quick learner/study**.*

quick[2] *adv. spoken nonstandard* quickly: *Come quick! Larry's on TV! | It was all over pretty quick.*

quick·en /ˈkwɪkən/ *v.* [I,T] *written* to become quicker, or to make something do this: *Elaine **quickened** her **pace*** (=walked faster).

quick·ie /ˈkwɪki/ *adj.* happening or done quickly: *a quickie divorce* (=one that is done cheaply and quickly) —**quickie** *n.* [C]

quick·ly /ˈkwɪkli/ *adv.* **1** fast, or done in a short amount of time: *Don't eat too quickly. | Firefighters quickly put out the blaze.*

THESAURUS

fast, **swiftly**, **rapidly**, **speedily**
→ see Thesaurus box at FAST[2]

2 after a very short time: *I quickly realized it wasn't going to be easy.* **3** for a short amount of time: *I'll just run into the store quickly, and then we can go.*

Q

quicksand

quick·sand /ˈkwɪksænd/ *n.* [C,U] wet sand that is dangerous because it pulls you down into it if you walk on it

ˌquick-ˈwitted *adj.* able to understand things quickly and say things that are funny and smart

quid pro quo /ˌkwɪd proʊ ˈkwoʊ/ *n.* [C] *formal* something that you give or do in exchange for something else, especially when this arrangement is not official

Q

qui·et¹ /ˈkwaɪət/ *adj.* **1** not making much noise: ***Be quiet!*** *I'm on the phone.* | *a quiet car* | *The classroom suddenly became quiet.*

THESAURUS

Words used to describe a quiet voice or sound

low – a low voice or sound is quiet and deep: *A low humming noise was coming from the refrigerator.*

soft – quiet in a way that is pleasant: *He spoke with a soft southern accent.*

muffled – a muffled sound is very difficult to hear: *the muffled sound of voices in the next room*

hushed – if people speak in **hushed tones**, they speak with quiet voices, especially so that other people cannot hear them: *They huddled together in a corner, speaking in hushed tones.*

subdued – if a person is subdued, s/he is quiet and looks sad: *She looked subdued after her interview.*

➔ LOUD

COMMUNICATION

Ways of telling someone to be quiet

Be quiet!

Sh/Ssh

Shut up! informal

Keep it down informal

Hush – used especially when talking to a child who is crying

2 not busy, or not full of people or activity: *a quiet neighborhood* | *Finally, the house was quiet.* | *Business has been really quiet recently.*

THESAURUS

Words to describe a quiet place

calm – quiet and without activity or trouble: *The streets remained calm again after last week's riots.*

tranquil/peaceful – quiet in a way that is pleasant and relaxing: *a tranquil spot for a picnic*

sleepy – quiet with very little happening: *a sleepy little town*

3 not speaking or not likely to say much: *a quiet, hardworking boy* | *Why are you so quiet tonight?*
➔ **keep (sth) quiet** at KEEP

quiet² **also quiet down** *v.* [I,T] to become calmer and less active or noisy, or to make someone do this: *Quiet down and get ready for bed!*

quiet³ *n.* [U] the state of being quiet and not active: *I was looking for some* ***peace and quiet****.*

qui·et·ly /ˈkwaɪətli/ *adv.* **1** without making much or any noise: *Ron shut the door quietly.* | *"I'm sorry," he said quietly.* **2** in a way that does not attract attention: *The council has been quietly preparing for the changes.*

quill /kwɪl/ *n.* [C] **1** a large feather, or a pen made from a large feather, used in past times **2** one of the sharp needles on the backs of some animals, such as the PORCUPINE

quilt /kwɪlt/ *n.* [C] a warm thick cover for a bed, made by sewing two layers of cloth together with a filling of cloth or feathers: *a patchwork quilt*

quilt·ed /ˈkwɪltɪd/ *adj.* quilted cloth consists of layers held together by lines of stitches that cross each other

quint·es·sen·tial /ˌkwɪntəˈsɛnʃəl/ *adj.* being a perfect example of a particular type of person or thing: *New York is the quintessential big city.* —**quintessentially** *adv.* —**quintessence** /kwɪnˈtɛsəns/ *n.* [U]

quin·tet /kwɪnˈtɛt/ *n.* [C] five singers or musicians who perform together

quin·tu·plet /kwɪnˈtʌplɪt, -ˈtu-/ *n.* [C] one of five babies who are born at the same time to the same mother

quip /kwɪp/ *v.* past tense and past participle **quipped**, present participle **quipping** [I] to make an amusing remark —**quip** *n.* [C]

quirk /kwɚk/ *n.* [C] **1** a strange habit or feature that someone or something has: *a* ***quirk in*** *the law* **2** something strange that happens by chance: *Years later, by a strange* ***quirk of fate****, she met him again on a plane.*

quirk·y /ˈkwɚki/ *adj.* slightly strange or unusual: *a quirky comedy*

quit /kwɪt/ *v.* past tense and past participle **quit**, present participle **quitting** **1** [I,T] *informal* to leave a job, school, etc., usually without finishing it, especially because you are annoyed or unhappy: *He quit school when he was 16.* | *Betty quit her job to stay home with the children.*

THESAURUS

give up – to stop doing something, or stop trying to do something: *She gave up her job to care for her ailing parents.*

resign – to officially leave your job or position: *Three board members have resigned.*
give notice – to officially tell your employer that you will be leaving your job soon: *She left without giving notice.*
drop out – to stop going to school or stop an activity before you have finished it: *Tucker dropped out of high school when he was 16.*

2 [T] *informal* to stop doing something that is bad: *I quit smoking three years ago.*

quite /kwaɪt/ *adv., quantifier* **1** very, but not extremely [= **pretty**]: *He's quite fat.* | *It became quite clear that we needed help.*

THESAURUS

rather, **fairly**, **pretty**
➔ see Thesaurus box at RATHER

2 not quite not completely or not exactly: *I'm not quite ready.* | *It wasn't quite the way he had imagined it.* | *Lewis* ***isn't quite as*** *fast as he used to be.* **3** used when an amount or number is large, but not extremely large: *They've had* ***quite a bit*** *of snow this year* (=a lot of snow). | *There were* ***quite a few*** *people at the party* (=a lot of people). | *We saved* ***quite a lot*** *of money.* | *We haven't seen each other in* ***quite a while*** (=a long time). **4** used in order to emphasize the fact that something is unusually good, bad, etc.: *That's* ***quite a*** *coat; where did you buy it?* | *Ruby made* ***quite an*** *impression on the kids.*

quits /kwɪts/ *adj. informal* **call it quits** to stop doing something: *Baird will call it quits after two terms as mayor.*

quit·ter /ˈkwɪt̬ɚ/ *n.* [C] *informal disapproving* someone who stops doing a job, activity, or duty because it becomes difficult

quiv·er[1] /ˈkwɪvɚ/ *v.* [I] to shake slightly because you are angry, upset, or anxious: *Diana's voice* ***quivered with*** *emotion.*

quiver[2] *n.* [C] **1** a slight shaking movement **2** a long case used for carrying ARROWS

quix·ot·ic /kwɪkˈsɑt̬ɪk/ *adj.* having ideas and plans that are based on hopes and are not practical

quiz[1] /kwɪz/ *n.* plural **quizzes** [C] **1** a short test: *a math quiz* | *Mr. Wilson gave us a* ***pop quiz*** (=an unexpected test). **2** a competition or game in which you have to answer questions: *a love quiz in a magazine*

quiz[2] *v.* past tense and past participle **quizzed**, present participle **quizzing** [T] to ask someone a lot of questions: *Webster quizzed 20 possible jurors.*

quiz·zi·cal /ˈkwɪzɪkəl/ *adj.* **a quizzical look/smile/expression** a look, etc. that shows you have a question

quo·rum /ˈkwɔrəm/ *n.* [C] the smallest number of people that must be at a meeting in order for official decisions to be made

quo·ta /ˈkwoʊt̬ə/ *n.* [C] **1** an official limit on the number or amount of something that is allowed in a particular period: *a* ***quota on*** *the amount of fish you may catch* **2** an amount of something that someone is expected to do or achieve: *The department is* ***meeting*** *its sales* ***quota.***

quo·ta·tion /kwoʊˈteɪʃən/ *n.* **1** [C] words from a book, poem, etc. that you repeat in your own speech or piece of writing: *a* ***quotation from*** *Shakespeare* **2** [C] a written statement of the exact amount of money that a service will cost [➡ **estimate**]: *Get quotations from two or more insurance companies.* **3** [U] the act of quoting something

quoˈtation ˌmark *n.* [C usually plural] a mark (" or ") used in writing before and after any words that are being quoted

quote[1] /kwoʊt/ *v.* **1** [I,T] to repeat exactly what someone else has said or written: *A doctor was* ***quoted as saying*** *he would not give the vaccine to his children.* | *a verse* ***quoted from*** *the Bible* **2** [T] to give something as an example to support what you are saying: *Dr. Morse quoted three successful cases in which patients used the new drug.* **3** [T] to tell a customer the price you will charge him/her for a service or product: *The airline has been quoting a standard fare of $358.* **4 quote ... unquote** *spoken* used when you are repeating the exact words someone else used: *He said it was the fault of "those people," quote unquote.*

R

quote[2] *n.* [C] *informal* a QUOTATION

quo·tient /ˈkwoʊʃənt/ *n.* [C] *technical* a number that is the result of one number being divided by another

R, r

R[1], **r** /ɑr/ the eighteenth letter of the English alphabet

R[2] *adj.* **restricted** – used in order to show that no one under the age of 17 can go to a particular movie unless an adult goes with him/her

R & B *n.* [U] **rhythm and blues** a type of popular music that is a mixture of BLUES and JAZZ

R & D *n.* [U] **research and development** the part of a business concerned with studying new ideas and planning new products

R & R *n.* [U] **rest and relaxation** a vacation given to people in the army, navy, etc. after a long time of hard work or during a war

rab·bi /ˈræbaɪ/ *n.* [C] plural **rabbis** a Jewish religious leader

rab·bit /ˈræbɪt/ *n.* [C] a small animal with long ears and soft fur that lives in a hole in the ground ➔ see picture at PET[1]

rab·ble /ˈræbəl/ *n.* [singular] a noisy crowd of people who are likely to cause trouble

rab·id /ˈræbɪd/ *adj.* **1** very extreme and often

unreasonable: *rabid anti-Americanism* **2** suffering from RABIES: *a rabid dog*

ra·bies /'reɪbiz/ *n.* [U] a disease that affects animals, that people can catch if they are bitten by an infected animal

raccoon

rac·coon /ræ'kun/ *n.* [C] an animal with black fur around its eyes and black and white bands on its tail

race

race[1] /reɪs/ *n.* **1** [C] a competition to find out who can run, drive, swim, etc. the fastest: *The colt has **won** nine **races** already.* | *She finished second **in the race**.* **2** [C,U] one of the groups that humans can be divided into, based on their skin color and other physical features: *The census has questions about race and ethnicity.*

THESAURUS

nation – a country and its social and political structure, or a group of people with the same history and language: *The leaders of several Western nations are meeting in Paris this week.* | *the Mandan tribe of the Sioux nation*
race – one of the groups that people are divided into, based on skin color and other physical features: *The survey was given to people of different races and ages.*
people – a race or group of people that live in a particular country. The plural of this meaning of "people" is "peoples": *the native peoples of the United States*
tribe – a group of people within a country who are the same race, and who have the same traditions and the same leader: *The Navajo tribe is the second largest in the U.S.*
ethnic group – a group of people of the same race, nation, or tribe: *the many different ethnic groups that call the city home*

3 [C] a competition for power, a prize, or a political position: *the presidential race* **4** [C] a situation in which one group tries to obtain or achieve something before another group does: *the **race to** put a man on the moon* **5 a race against time** a situation in which something difficult must be done before a particular time **6 the races** an event at which horses are raced against each other
→ ARMS RACE, HUMAN RACE

race[2] *v.* **1** [I,T] to compete in a race: *I'll race you to the corner!* | *She'll be **racing against** some of the world's top athletes.* **2** [I,T] to go very quickly, or to make someone or something do this: *I raced home after school.* | *Victims were **raced to** the hospital.*

THESAURUS

rush, dash, charge, speed, sprint
→ see Thesaurus box at RUSH[1], RUN[1]

3 [I] to try to do something very quickly, especially because there is little time or you want to be the first: *Doctors **raced to** solve this medical mystery.* **4** [I] if your heart or mind races, it is working harder and faster than usual: *Her mind was racing – would David be there?* **5** [I,T] if an engine races or you race it, its parts are moving too fast

'race re,lations *n.* [plural] the relationship between two groups of people who are from different races but who live in the same city, country, or area

race·track /'reɪs-træk/ *n.* [C] a track around which runners, cars, horses, etc. race

ra·cial /'reɪʃəl/ *adj.* **1** relating to the relationships between different races of people: *a fight against **racial discrimination*** (=unfair treatment of people because of their race) **2** relating to people's race: *racial groups* —**racially** *adv.*: *a racially motivated attack*

rac·ing /'reɪsɪŋ/ *n.* **horse/car/bicycle etc. racing** the sport of racing horses, cars, etc.

rac·ism /'reɪsɪzəm/ *n.* [U] **1** unfair treatment of people, or violence against them, because they belong to a different race from yours: *the struggle against racism and poverty*

THESAURUS

prejudice, discrimination, intolerance, anti-Semitism
→ see Thesaurua box at PREJUDICE

2 the belief that some races of people are better than others —**racist** *adj., n.* [C] *racist remarks*

rack[1] /ræk/ *n.* [C] a frame or shelf for holding things, usually with BARS or hooks: *a coat rack*

rack[2] *v.* [T] **1 rack your brain(s)** to think very hard or for a long time **2** to make someone feel great physical or mental pain: *Afterwards, he was **racked with** guilt and shame.*

rack sth ⇔ **up** *phr. v. informal* to make the value,

amount, or level of something increase: *They racked up a nine-game winning streak.*

rack·et /ˈrækɪt/ *n.* **1** [singular] *informal* a loud noise: *Laura was* ***making*** *a terrible* ***racket*** *in the kitchen.* **2** [C] a thing used for hitting the ball in games such as tennis, consisting of a light stick with a circle filled with tight strings at the top **3** [C] *informal* a dishonest way of obtaining money – sometimes used about an ordinary business to show that you think it is somehow unfair: *the insurance racket*

rack·et·ball /ˈrækɪtˀˌbɔl/ *n.* [U] an indoor game in which two players use rackets to hit a small rubber ball against the four walls of a square court

rack·et·eer·ing /ˌrækəˈtɪrɪŋ/ *n.* [U] a crime that consists of getting money dishonestly, using a carefully planned system —**racketeer** *n.* [C]

rac·y /ˈreɪsi/ *adj.* exciting in a sexual way

ra·dar /ˈreɪdɑr/ *n.* [C,U] a piece of equipment that uses radio waves to find the position of things and watch their movement, or the process of doing this: *The missile didn't show up* ***on radar****.*

ra·di·al tire /ˌreɪdiəl ˈtaɪɚ/ **also radial** *n.* [C] a car tire with wires inside the rubber to make it stronger and safer

ra·di·ance /ˈreɪdiəns/ *n.* [U] **1** soft shining light: *the moon's radiance* **2** great happiness or love that shows in the way someone looks: *the radiance of youth*

ra·di·ant /ˈreɪdiənt/ *adj.* **1** full of happiness and love, in a way that shows in your face: *a radiant smile* **2** *technical* sending out light or heat —**radiantly** *adv.*

ra·di·ate /ˈreɪdiˌeɪt/ *v.* **1** [I,T] if someone radiates a feeling or quality, or if it radiates from him/her, s/he shows it in a way that is easy to see: *Janine radiates confidence.* **2** [I,T] if something radiates light or heat, or if light or heat radiates, it is sent out in all directions: *The fireplace radiated a comforting warmth.* **3** [I] to spread out from a central point: *pain* ***radiating down*** *his leg*

ra·di·a·tion /ˌreɪdiˈeɪʃən/ *n.* [U] **1** energy in the form of heat or light sent out as waves that you cannot see [➡ **radioactive**]: *cancer treated with radiation* **2** a form of energy that comes from NUCLEAR reactions, which in large amounts is harmful to living things [➡ **radioactive**]: *radiation exposure*

ra·di·a·tor /ˈreɪdiˌeɪt̬ɚ/ *n.* [C] **1** the part of a car or airplane that stops the engine from getting too hot **2** a piece of equipment used for heating a room, consisting of a hollow metal container fastened to a wall, through which hot water passes

rad·i·cal[1] /ˈrædɪkəl/ *adj.* **1** thorough and complete, so that something is very different: ***radical changes*** *in family life* **2** relating to a political or social idea that is very different from what exists now, or supporting these ideas: *Radical demonstrators clashed with riot police.* —**radically** *adv.*: *a radically different idea*

radical[2] *n.* [C] someone who wants thorough and complete social and political change —**radicalism** *n.* [U]

ra·di·o[1] /ˈreɪdiˌoʊ/ *n.* **1** [C,U] a piece of electronic equipment that you use to listen to music or programs that are broadcast, or the programs themselves: *the latest hits* ***on the radio*** | *Kelly was* ***listening to the radio****.* | *J.D.* ***turned on the radio****.* **2** [U] the activity of making and broadcasting programs that can be heard on a radio: *He'd like a job* ***in radio****.* | *a San Diego* ***radio station*** **3** [C,U] a piece of electronic equipment that can send and receive spoken messages, or the sending or receiving of these messages: *We've lost radio contact.*

radio[2] *v.* past tense and past participle **radioed** [I,T] to send a message using a radio: *The ship* ***radioed for*** *help.*

ra·di·o·ac·tive /ˌreɪdioʊˈæktɪv/ *adj.* containing RADIATION: *radioactive waste*

ra·di·o·ac·tiv·i·ty /ˌreɪdioʊækˈtɪvət̬i/ *n.* [U] the sending out of RADIATION, when the NUCLEUS (=central part) of an atom has broken apart

ra·di·ol·o·gist /ˌreɪdiˈɑlədʒɪst/ *n.* [C] a hospital doctor who is trained in the use of RADIATION to find out what is causing an illness and to treat people

ra·di·ol·o·gy /ˌreɪdiˈɑlədʒi/ *n.* [U] the study of the use of RADIATION and X-RAYS in medical treatment

ra·di·o·ther·a·py /ˌreɪdioʊˈθɛrəpi/ *n.* [U] the treatment of illnesses using RADIATION

rad·ish /ˈrædɪʃ/ *n.* [C] a small red or white root that has a slightly hot taste and is eaten raw as a vegetable

ra·di·um /ˈreɪdiəm/ *n.* [U] a very RADIOACTIVE metal that is an ELEMENT

ra·di·us /ˈreɪdiəs/ *n.* plural **radii** /ˈreɪdiaɪ/ [C] **1** the distance from the center to the edge of a circle, or a line drawn from the center to the edge **2 within a 10-mile/100-meter etc. radius** within a distance of 10 miles, etc. in all directions from a particular place: *The bomb caused damage within a half-mile radius.*

ra·don /ˈreɪdɑn/ *n.* [U] a RADIOACTIVE gas that is an ELEMENT

raf·fle[1] /ˈræfəl/ *n.* [C] a type of competition or game in which people buy tickets with numbers on them in order to try to win prizes

raffle[2] **also raffle off** *v.* [T] to offer something as a prize in a RAFFLE

raft /ræft/ *n.* [C] **1** a small flat rubber boat filled with air, used for example if a boat sinks: *He helped her onto the* ***life raft*** (=used when a boat sinks). **2** a flat floating structure, usually made of pieces of wood tied together, used as a boat **3 a raft of sth** a large number of things or a large amount of something: ***A whole raft of*** *popular players will attend.*

raf·ter /ˈræftɚ/ *n.* [C] one of the large sloping pieces of wood that form the structure of a roof

raft·ing /ˈræftɪŋ/ *n.* [U] the sport of traveling down a fast-flowing river in a rubber raft

rafting

rag¹ /ræg/ *n.* [C] **1** a small piece of old cloth: *a dirty rag* **2 in rags** wearing old torn clothes **3 from rags to riches** becoming very rich after starting your life very poor

rag² *v.* past tense and past participle **ragged**, present participle **ragging**

rag on sb *phr. v. spoken* **1** to make jokes and laugh at someone in order to embarrass him/her [= **tease**] **2** to criticize someone in an angry way: *The coach was ragging on me for missing my free throws.*

ˌrag ˈdoll *n.* [C] a soft DOLL made of cloth

rage¹ /reɪdʒ/ *n.* [C,U] a strong feeling of anger that you cannot control: *She was shaking* ***with rage.***

R

rage² *v.* [I] **1** to continue happening with great force or violence: *The rioting raged for four days.* | *a raging blizzard* **2** to feel extremely angry about something and to show this in the way you behave or speak: *Tom raged at himself for having been so stupid.*

rag·ged /ˈrægɪd/ **also rag·ged·y** /ˈrægɪdi/ *adj.* **1** torn and in bad condition: *a ragged shirt* **2** not straight or neat, but with rough uneven edges: *a ragged beard* **3** wearing clothes that are old, torn, and dirty: *ragged children* **4** not regular or smooth, or not done together: *ragged breathing*

rag·tag /ˈrægtæg/ *adj.* looking messy and wearing dirty torn clothes: *a ragtag army*

rag·time /ˈrægtaɪm/ *n.* [U] a type of JAZZ music with a quick strong beat, popular in the U.S. in the early 1900s

raid¹ /reɪd/ *n.* [C] **1** a short attack on a place by soldiers, airplanes, or ships, intended to cause damage but not to take control: *an air raid*

THESAURUS

attack, invasion, assault, ambush, counterattack, assault
→ see Thesaurus box at ATTACK¹

2 a surprise visit by the police when they are searching for something: *an FBI* ***raid on*** *the apartment*

raid² *v.* [T] **1** if the police raid a place, they enter it suddenly to search for something illegal: *Police raided his home and seized his computer.* **2** *informal* to take or use something that does not belong to you: *Governors have raided education budgets to pay for more prisons.* | *The kids* ***raided the refrigerator*** *after school* (=ate a lot of food). **3** to make a sudden attack on a place **4** *informal* to go into a place and steal things —**raider** *n.* [C]

rail¹ /reɪl/ *n.* **1** [C] a bar that is fastened along or around something, especially to keep you from falling, hang something on, etc.: *Tourists stood at the rail taking pictures of the falls.* | *a towel rail* **2** [U] a railroad system: *The city is promoting* ***light rail*** (=a railroad that only carries passengers) *as an alternative to cars.* **3** [C] one of the two long metal tracks attached to the ground that trains move along

rail² *v.* [I] *formal* to complain angrily about something that you think is unfair: *Business leaders have been* ***railing against*** *the proposed tax increases.*

rail·ing /ˈreɪlɪŋ/ **also railings** *n.* [C] a short fence consisting of upright bars or lengths of wood or metal supported by upright posts, which keeps people from falling over an edge, supports them going up stairs, etc.: *the porch railing*

rail·road¹ /ˈreɪlroʊd/ *n.* **1** [U] a method of traveling or moving things around using trains, and things relating to this: *livestock shipped* ***by railroad*** | *a* ***railroad station*** **2** [C] the tracks and ground that a train travels on **3** [C] a company that owns trains and tracks: *the Southern Pacific railroad* **4 the railroad** the system of trains, and all the companies, work, equipment, etc. relating to it: *My grandfather* ***worked on/for the railroad*** *all his life.*

railroad² *v.* [T] to force or persuade someone to do something without giving him/her enough time to think about it: *The workers were* ***railroaded into*** *signing the agreement.*

rain¹ /reɪn/ *n.* **1** [U] water that falls in small drops from clouds in the sky: *I hate going out* ***in the rain.*** | *He walked through* ***the pouring/driving/heavy rain*** (=a lot of rain). | *A* ***light rain*** (=a small amount of rain) *fell on the crowd.*

THESAURUS

drizzle – light rain with very small drops of water: *a steady drizzle*
shower – a short period of rain: *a light shower*
downpour – a lot of rain that falls in a short period of time: *a heavy downpour*
storm – very bad weather with a lot of wind and rain: *violent storms* | *a tropical storm*
hail – frozen rain that falls in the form of **hailstones** (=small balls of ice): *A hail storm flattened crops.*
sleet – a mixture of snow and rain: *sleet and snow showers*
→ SNOW, WEATHER, WIND

2 the rains a time in the year when there is a lot of rain in tropical countries [= **monsoon**]

rain² *v.* **it rains** if it rains, drops of water fall from clouds in the sky: *Is it still raining?* | *It suddenly started* ***raining hard*** (=raining a lot).

THESAURUS

It's pouring (rain) – it's raining very heavily
It's drizzling – a small amount of rain is falling
It's sleeting – it's raining and snowing at the same time
It's hailing – small balls of ice are falling
→ WEATHER

rain down (sth) *phr. v.* if something rains down or is rained down, it falls in large quantities: *Bombs rained down on the city.*

rain sth ⇔ **out** *phr. v.* if an event is rained out, it has to stop because there is too much rain

rainbow

rain·bow /ˈreɪnboʊ/ *n.* [C] a large curve of different colors that can appear in the sky when there is both sun and rain

ˈrain check *n.* [C] **1 take a rain check** *spoken* used in order to say that you would like to accept an invitation or offer later, but you cannot right now: *I'm sorry, but I'm busy on Saturday – can I take a rain check?* **2** a piece of paper that allows you to buy something at a special price, given to people when the thing they want to buy is not available **3** a ticket for an outdoor event, game, etc. that you can use again if the event has to stop because of rain

rain·coat /ˈreɪnkoʊt/ *n.* [C] a coat that you wear to protect yourself from the rain

rain·drop /ˈreɪndrɑp/ *n.* [C] a single drop of rain

rain·fall /ˈreɪnfɔl/ *n.* [C,U] the amount of rain that falls on an area in a particular time: *six inches of annual rainfall*

rain ˌforest *n.* [C] an area of thick forest with tall trees that are very close together, growing in a place where it rains a lot

THESAURUS

woods, **woodland**, **forest**, **jungle**
→ see Thesaurus box at TREE

rain·storm /ˈreɪnstɔrm/ *n.* [C] a storm with a lot of rain and strong winds

rain·water /ˈreɪnˌwɔt̬ɚ, -ˌwɑ-/ *n.* [U] water that has fallen as rain

rain·y /ˈreɪni/ *adj.* **1** having a lot of rain: *a rainy weekend* **2 rainy day** a difficult time when you will need money that you do not need now: *We have a little extra money* ***saved for a rainy day****.*

raise[1] /reɪz/ *v.* [T]
1 MOVE to move or lift something to a higher position or to an upright position [≠ **lower**]: *The flag is raised at school every morning.* | ***Raise*** *your* ***hand*** *if you know the answer.*

USAGE

People **raise** things to a higher position: *She raised her glass to make a toast.*
When things move upward on their own, they **rise**: *The balloon rose high into the air.*

2 INCREASE to increase an amount, number, or level [≠ **lower**]: *a plan to raise taxes* | *She hopes the story will raise awareness of mental illness* (=increase people's understanding of it). | *In my family, no one ever* ***raised*** *their* ***voices*** (=spoke loudly and angrily).
3 IMPROVE to improve the quality or standard of something [≠ **lower**]: *Public schools have been trying hard to raise standards.*
4 CHILDREN to take care of your children until they are adults: *a single parent raising her children alone*
5 GET MONEY/SUPPORT to collect money, support, etc. so that you can use it to help people: ***raising*** *money* ***for*** *cancer research*
6 FARMING to grow plants or keep animals, especially to sell: *chickens raised in cages*
7 CAUSE A REACTION to cause a particular emotion or reaction: *The accident has raised concerns about safety.*
8 START A SUBJECT to begin to talk or write about something that you want someone to consider [= **bring up**]: *The article raises questions about the fairness of the trial.*
9 raise your eyebrows to show surprise, a question, doubt, disapproval, etc. by moving your EYEBROWS upward
10 raise eyebrows if something raises eyebrows, it surprises and shocks people: *The police chief's actions have raised eyebrows.*
11 raise your glass (to sth) to celebrate something by holding up your glass and drinking from it: *Members of the club raised their glasses to salute the President.*

raise[2] *n.* [C] an increase in the money you earn: *a raise of $100 a month*

rai·sin /ˈreɪzən/ *n.* [C] a dried GRAPE

rake[1] /reɪk/ *n.* [C] a tool used for removing dead leaves from areas of grass or making soil level

rake[2] *v.* **1** [I,T] **also rake up** to move a rake across a surface in order to remove dead leaves from an area of grass or make the soil level **2** [T] to move something such as a gun or a light across an area: *Soldiers raked the building with gunfire.* **3 rake your fingers/nails** to pull your fingers or nails through something or across a surface: *She raked his face with her nails.* **4 rake sb over the coals** to speak angrily to someone who has done something wrong

rake sth ⇔ **in** *phr. v. informal* to earn a lot of

R

money without trying very hard: *One lawyer raked in $3.5 million on a case.*

ral·ly¹ /ˈræli/ *n.* plural **rallies** [C] **1** a large public meeting to support a political idea, sports event, etc.: *a campaign rally* **2** an occasion when something becomes stronger or better again, after a period of weakness or defeat: *The Cubs scored three runs in a late rally.*

rally² *v.* past tense and past participle **rallied**, third person singular **rallies** **1** [I,T] to come together or bring people together to support an idea, a political party, etc.: *Women's groups **rallied to** her defense.* **2** [I] to become stronger or better again after a time of weakness or defeat: *The Kings rallied to beat the Knicks.*

rally around (sb/sth) *phr. v.* if a group of people rally around, they all try to help you in a difficult situation: *Her friends all rallied around when her father died.*

RAM /ræm/ *n.* [U] *technical* **random access memory** the part of a computer that keeps information for a short time so that it can be used immediately [➡ **ROM**]

ram¹ /ræm/ past tense and past participle **rammed**, present participle **ramming** *v.* [T] **1** to run or drive into something, or to push something using a lot of force: *A truck rammed into a line of cars.* **2 ram sth down sb's throat** to try to make someone accept an idea or opinion by repeating it again and again

ram sth ⇔ **through** *phr. v.* to try to make someone accept something, without giving him/her time to consider it carefully: *Democrats were trying to ram the bill through Congress.*

ram² *n.* [C] a fully grown male sheep

Ram·a·dan /ˈrɑməˌdɑn/ *n.* [singular] the ninth month of the Muslim year, during which no food may be eaten during the hours of the day when it is light

ram·ble¹ /ˈræmbəl/ *v.* [I] **1** to talk in a way that is not clearly organized, and move from one subject to another in a confusing way: *His speeches tend to ramble.* **2** to go on a walk for pleasure

ramble on *phr. v.* to talk or write for a long time in a way that other people think is boring: *Sara rambled on about her trip.*

ramble² *n.* [C] a long walk for pleasure

ram·bling /ˈræmblɪŋ/ *adj.* **1** speech or writing that is rambling is very long and does not seem to have any clear organization or purpose: *a long rambling letter* **2** a building that is rambling has an irregular shape and covers a large area: *a rambling old house*

ram·bunc·tious /ræmˈbʌŋkʃəs/ *adj.* noisy, full of energy, and behaving in a way that cannot be controlled: *a rambunctious kid*

ram·i·fi·ca·tion /ˌræməfəˈkeɪʃən/ *n.* [C usually plural] *formal* a result of something you do, that affects things in a way that you may not have expected: *the ramifications of rising oil prices*

ramp /ræmp/ *n.* [C] **1** a road for driving onto or off a large main road [➡ **on-ramp**, **off-ramp**] **2** a slope that has been built to connect two places that are at different levels: *ramps for wheelchair users*

ram·page /ˈræmpeɪdʒ, ræmˈpeɪdʒ/ *v.* [I] to behave wildly or violently, especially in groups: *Rioters **rampaged through** the city, destroying property.* —**rampage** *n.* [C] *a gunman **on** a bloody **rampage***

ramp·ant /ˈræmpənt/ *adj.* spread across or affecting a large area, and difficult to control: *rampant inflation* —**rampantly** *adv.*

ram·rod /ˈræmrɑd/ *n.* **ramrod stiff/straight** sitting or standing with your back straight and your body stiff

ram·shack·le /ˈræmˌʃækəl/ *adj.* badly built and needing to be repaired: *a ramshackle farm house*

ran /ræn/ *v.* the past tense of RUN

ranch /ræntʃ/ *n.* [C] a very large farm where cattle, horses, or sheep are raised

ranch·er /ˈræntʃɚ/ *n.* [C] someone who owns or works on a RANCH: *a cattle rancher* —**ranch** *v.* [I] —**ranching** *n.* [U]

ˈranch house *n.* [C] a type of house built on one level, with a roof that does not slope much

ran·cid /ˈrænsɪd/ *adj.* food such as milk, butter, or meat that is rancid smells or tastes unpleasant because it is no longer fresh: *rancid butter*

ran·cor /ˈræŋkɚ/ *n.* [U] *formal* a feeling of hatred, especially when you cannot forgive someone [= **resentment**]: *the political rancor that has marked this election campaign* —**rancorous** /ˈræŋkərəs/ *adj.*

ran·dom /ˈrændəm/ *adj.* **1** happening or chosen without any definite plan, aim, or pattern: *a **random sample** of 635 patients* **2 at random** in a completely unplanned way: *The winning numbers will be chosen at random.* —**randomly** *adv.*: *The lottery numbers are randomly chosen.*

ˌrandom ˈaccess ˌmemory *n.* [U] *technical* RAM

rang /ræŋ/ *v.* the past tense of RING

range¹ /reɪndʒ/ *n.*

1 GROUP [C] a number of people or things that are different, but belong to the same general type: *students with a **range of** interests | books on a **wide/broad range** of subjects*

2 NUMBER LIMITS [C] the limits within which amounts, levels, ages, etc. can be different from each other: *games for the 8–12 age range | The house is **beyond/out of** our **price range*** (=more than our limit).

3 PRODUCTS [C] a set of similar products made by a particular company or available in a particular store: *a new range of mountain bikes*

4 DISTANCE a) [U] the distance within which something can be seen or heard or at which a particular weapon can hit things: *Luckily, we were not **within range** when they began firing. | I was **out of** her **range** of vision.* **b)** [C] the distance at which a vehicle such as an aircraft can travel

before it needs more FUEL: *missiles with **a range of** more than 300 miles*
5 LIMITS TO POWER/ACTIVITY [C] the limits to the amount of power or RESPONSIBILITY that a person or organization has, or the types of activity they are allowed to do: *The issue falls outside the range of the investigation.*
6 MOUNTAINS [C] a line of mountains or hills: *the Cascade Range*
7 FOR PRACTICE [C] an area of land where you can practice using weapons: *a rifle range*
8 LAND [C,U] a large area of land covered with grass, used by cattle
9 COOKING [C] a STOVE

range² *v.* [I] **1** to include the two things mentioned and other things in between them: *toys **ranging in** price from $5 to $25* **2** to deal with a large number of subjects: *Republicans challenged him on issues **ranging from** abortion **to** taxes.* **3** if animals range somewhere, they move over a wide area of land

rang·er /'reɪndʒɚ/ *n.* [C] someone whose job is to watch and take care of a forest or area of public land and the people and animals that use it: *a park ranger*

rank¹ /ræŋk/ *n.* [C,U] the position or level that someone has in an organization: *an officer of **high/low rank** | He **held** the **rank** of sergeant.*

rank² *v.* **1** [I] to have a particular position in a list of people or things that are put in order of quality or importance: *The team is ranked fourth in the city.* **2** [T] to decide the position someone or something should have on a list, based on quality or importance: *a list of wines ranked by quality and price*

rank³ *adj.* having a very strong and unpleasant smell or taste: *rank meat*

ˌrank and 'file *n.* **the rank and file** the ordinary members of an organization rather than the leaders

rank·ing¹ /'ræŋkɪŋ/ *n.* [C] the position or level that someone has on a list of people who have a particular skill: *the skater's national ranking*

ranking² *adj.* a ranking person has a high position in an organization or is one of the best at an activity: *the ranking officer*

ran·kle /'ræŋkəl/ *v.* [I,T] if something rankles or rankles you, it still annoys you a long time after it happened

ran·sack /'rænsæk/ *v.* [T] **1** to go through a place stealing things and causing damage: *The victim's house had been ransacked.* **2** to search a place very thoroughly: *She ransacked her closet for something to wear.*

ran·som /'rænsəm/ *n.* [C,U] an amount of money paid to free someone who is held as a prisoner: *a ransom note | The kidnappers demanded $200,000 **in ransom**.* —**ransom** *v.* [T]

rant /rænt/ *v.* [I] to talk or complain in a loud, excited, and confused way: *She **ranted about** the misleading claims of diet books.* —**rant** *n.* [C]

rap¹ /ræp/ *n.* **1 also 'rap music** [C,U] a type of popular music in which the words are not sung, but spoken in time to music with a steady beat

THESAURUS

pop (music), rock (music), rock'n'roll, heavy metal, reggae, house (music), hip-hop, jazz, classical (music), country (music), folk (music)
→ see Thesaurus box at MUSIC

2 [C] a quick light hit or knock: *a rap on the door* **3** [singular] blame or punishment for a mistake or crime: *a murder rap | He got himself a good lawyer to **beat the rap*** (=avoid punishment). | *I'd rather drive, so I don't have to **take the rap*** (=be blamed) *for getting lost.* **4 get a bad/bum rap** to be unfairly criticized, or to be treated badly: *Diet food has gotten a bad rap for the way it tastes.*

rap² *v.* past tense and past participle **rapped**, present participle **rapping** **1** [I,T] to hit or knock something quickly and lightly: *Henry **rapped on** the door.*

THESAURUS

hit, punch, slap, beat, smack, whack, strike, bang, knock, tap, pound, hammer
→ see Thesaurus box at HIT¹

2 [T] to criticize or blame someone: *a movie rapped by critics for its violence* **3** [I] to say the words of a rap song

rape¹ /reɪp/ *v.* [T] to force someone to have sex by using violence

rape² *n.* **1** [C,U] the crime of forcing someone to have sex by using violence: *a rape victim*

THESAURUS

assault, mugging, murder
→ see Thesaurus box at CRIME, ATTACK¹

2 [singular] unnecessary destruction, especially of the environment: *the rape of our rain forests*

rap·id /'ræpɪd/ *adj.* done very quickly, or happening in a short time [= **fast**, **quick**]: *rapid population growth* —**rapidly** *adv.*: *Technology is rapidly changing.* —**rapidity** /rə'pɪdəṭi/ *n.* [U]

rap·ids /'ræpɪdz/ *n.* [plural] part of a river where the water looks white because it is moving very fast over rocks

ˌrapid 'transit also **ˌrapid 'transit ˌsystem** *n.* [C] a system of trains, buses, etc. for moving people around a city

rap·ist /'reɪpɪst/ *n.* [C] someone who has forced someone else to have sex by using violence

THESAURUS

criminal, offender, attacker, mugger, murderer
→ see Thesaurus box at CRIMINAL²

rap·per /'ræpɚ/ *n.* [C] someone who speaks the words of a RAP song

rap·port /ræ'pɔr, rə-/ *n.* [C,U] friendly agree-

R

ment and understanding between people: *a teacher who has a **rapport with** her students*

rap·proche·ment /ˌræproʊʃˈmɑn/ *n.* [singular, U] *formal* the establishment of good relations between two countries or groups of people, after a time of unfriendly relations: *the U.S. **rapprochement with** China in the 1970s*

rapt /ræpt/ *adj.* so interested in something that you do not notice anything else: *The children listened with **rapt attention**.*

rap·ture /ˈræptʃɚ/ *n.* [U] great excitement, pleasure, and happiness: *He looked **with/in rapture** at her face.* —**rapturous** *adj.*

rare /rɛr/ *adj.* **1** not seen or found very often, or not happening very often [≠ **common**]: *a rare form of cancer* | ***It is rare for** her **to** miss school.*

USAGE

Use **rare** when something is valuable and there is not much of it: *a rare coin worth a lot of money*
Use **scarce** when there is not enough of something available at a particular time: *During the war, food was scarce.*

R

2 meat that is rare has only been cooked for a short time and is still red

rare·ly /ˈrɛrli/ *adv.* not often [≠ **frequently**]: *She's rarely home.*

THESAURUS

not very often: *I go to the movies, but not very often.*
hardly ever – almost never: *The kids hardly ever call* (=telephone) *me.*
seldom more formal – very rarely: *We seldom see her nowadays.*
➔ OFTEN, NEVER, SOMETIMES

rar·ing /ˈrɛrɪŋ/ *adj.* **raring to go** *informal* very eager to start an activity: *We got up early, raring to go.*

rar·i·ty /ˈrɛrət̬i/ *n.* **be a rarity** to not happen or exist very often: *In 1975, women lawyers were a rarity.*

ras·cal /ˈræskəl/ *n.* [C] *humorous* a child who behaves badly but whom you still like

rash¹ /ræʃ/ *adj.* done too quickly without thinking carefully first, or behaving in this way: *rash promises* | *a rash young man*

THESAURUS

impulsive, **hotheaded**, **hasty**
➔ see Thesaurus box at IMPULSIVE

rash² *n.* **1** [C] a lot of red spots on someone's skin, caused by an illness or a reaction to food, plants, medicine, etc. **2 a rash of sth** *informal* a large number of unpleasant events, changes, etc. within a short time: *a rash of injuries on the team*

rasp·ber·ry /ˈræzˌbɛri/ *n.* plural **raspberries** [C] a soft sweet red BERRY ➔ see picture at FRUIT

rasp·y /ˈræspi/ *adj.* making a rough unpleasant sound: *his raspy voice* —**rasp** *v.* [I] —**rasp** *n.* [singular]

rat¹ /ræt/ *n.* [C] **1** an animal that looks like a large mouse with a long tail **2** *informal* someone who has been disloyal to you or has deceived you: *That rat Bruce just did it for the money.* ➔ RAT RACE

rat² *v.* past tense and past participle **ratted**, present participle **ratting** [I] *old-fashioned* to tell someone in authority about something wrong that someone has done, in a way that is considered disloyal: *I never **ratted on** Huey.*

rate¹ /reɪt/ *n.* [C] **1** the number of times something happens over a period of time: *a country with a low **birth/unemployment/crime etc. rate*** | *an area with a **low/high rate** of crime* **2** a charge or payment set according to a standard scale: *The Federal Reserve lowered **interest rates** today.* | *the hourly **rate of** pay* **3** the speed at which something happens over a period of time: *Children learn **at different rates**.* | *Car thefts have increased **at an alarming rate**.* **4 at any rate** *spoken* used when you are giving one definite fact in a situation that is not sure or not satisfactory: *He's what, seventeen? At any rate, he's old enough to go on his own.* **5 at this rate** *spoken* used in order to say what will happen if things continue to happen in the same way: *At this rate, we'll never afford a vacation.* **6 first-rate/second-rate/third-rate** of good, bad, or very bad quality: *a third-rate movie*

rate² *v.* **1** [T] to have a particular opinion about the value or worth of someone or something: *38% rated him a weak leader.* **2 X-rated/rated R etc.** used in order to show that a movie has been officially approved for people of a particular age to see **3** [T] *informal* to deserve something: *You all rate a big thank-you for your work.*

rath·er /ˈræðɚ/ *adv.*, *quantifier* **1 rather than** a phrase meaning instead of, used when you are comparing two things or situations: *We usually travel by train, rather than by plane.* **2 would rather** used when you would prefer to do or have one thing more than another: *I hate sitting doing nothing; I'd rather be busy.* | *Dave **would rather** have a dog **than** a cat, but I like cats.* | *"Why don't you ask her?" **"I'd rather not."*** **3** *formal* used in order to give more correct or specific information about what you have said: *Lucy, or Susie rather, asked me to come tonight.* **4** fairly or to some degree: *Some of the photographs are rather blurred.*

THESAURUS

fairly: *The test was fairly easy.* | *It's a fairly long way.*
pretty spoken: *Her French is pretty good.* | *It's pretty tough work.*
quite formal: *It's quite late.* | *That's quite an interesting problem.*

rat·i·fy /ˈræt̬əˌfaɪ/ *v.* [T] to make a written agreement official by signing it: *Both nations ratified the treaty.* —**ratification** /ˌræt̬əfəˈkeɪʃən/ *n.* [U]

THESAURUS

approve, pass
➔ see Thesaurus box at APPROVE

rat·ing /ˈreɪṱɪŋ/ *n.* **1** [C] a level on a scale that shows how popular, good, important, etc. someone or something is: *The governor's **approval rating** is high.* **2** [singular] a letter that shows what age someone should be before s/he can see a particular movie, television show, etc.: *a rating system used for video games* | *an R rating* **3 the ratings** [plural] a list that shows which movies, television programs, etc. are the most popular: *The show finished 20th **in the ratings**.*

ra·ti·o /ˈreɪʃiˌoʊ, ˈreɪʃoʊ/ *n.* plural **ratios** [C] a relationship between two amounts, represented by two numbers that show how much bigger one amount is than the other [➡ **proportion**]: *The **ratio of** boys **to** girls in the class is 2:1* (=two boys for each girl).

ra·tion¹ /ˈræʃən, ˈreɪ-/ *n.* **1** [C] a limited amount of something such as food or gas that you are allowed to have when there is not much available: *a ration of sugar* **2 rations** [plural] a particular amount of food given to a soldier or a member of a group

ration² *v.* [T] to control the supply of something by allowing people to have only a limited amount of it: *Coffee was rationed during the war.* —**rationing** *n.* [U]

ra·tion·al /ˈræʃənəl/ *adj.* **1** rational thoughts, decisions, etc. are based on reason rather than on emotion [≠ **irrational**]: *a rational decision* **2** a rational person is able to think clearly and make good decisions [= **sensible**; ≠ **irrational**]: *Let's try to discuss this like rational human beings.* —**rationally** *adv.*: *We were too shocked to think rationally.* —**rationality** /ˌræʃəˈnæləṱi/ *n.* [U]

ra·tion·ale /ˌræʃəˈnæl/ *n.* [C,U] *formal* the reasons and principles on which a decision, plan, etc. is based: *the Pope's **rationale for** not allowing women to be priests*

ra·tion·al·ize /ˈræʃnəˌlaɪz/ *v.* [I,T] if you rationalize behavior that is wrong, you think of reasons for it so that it does not seem as bad: *We rationalize that junk food is part of childhood, but we're setting our kids up for health problems.* —**rationalization** /ˌræʃnələˈzeɪʃən/ *n.* [C,U]

ˈrat race *n.* **the rat race** *informal* the unpleasant situation in business, politics, etc. in which people are always competing against each other

rat·tle¹ /ˈræṱl/ *v.* **1** [I,T] if you rattle something, or it rattles, it shakes and makes a short repeated knocking sound: *There was something **rattling around** in the trunk.* ➔ see picture on page A7

THESAURUS

shake, tremble, shiver, wobble, vibrate
➔ see Thesaurus box at SHAKE¹

2 [T] *informal* to make someone lose his/her confidence and become nervous: *She's a good player, but **gets rattled** easily.*

rattle sth ⇔ **off** *phr. v.* to say something very quickly and easily, especially from memory: *He rattled off his phone number.*

rattle² *n.* [C] **1** a baby's toy that makes a noise when it is shaken **2** [usually singular] the noise that you hear when the parts of something knock against each other

rat·tler /ˈrætlɚ, ˈræṱl-ɚ/ *n.* [C] *informal* a RATTLESNAKE

rat·tle·snake /ˈræṱlˌsneɪk/ *n.* [C] a poisonous American snake that makes a noise with its tail

rau·cous /ˈrɔkəs/ *adj.* a raucous voice or noise is very loud and unpleasant: *a raucous laugh* —**raucously** *adv.*

raun·chy /ˈrɔntʃi, ˈrɑn-/ *adj. informal* intended to make you think about sex, in a way that seems shocking: *a raunchy movie*

rav·age /ˈrævɪdʒ/ *v.* [T] to destroy, ruin, or damage something badly [= **devastate**]: *a forest **ravaged by** fire*

rav·ag·es /ˈrævɪdʒɪz/ *n.* **the ravages of sth** *literary* damage or destruction caused by something such as war, disease, time, etc.: *a building that has survived **the ravages of time***

rave¹ /reɪv/ *v.* [I] **1** to talk in an excited way about something because you think it is very good: *Customers **rave about** their chili.* **2** to talk in an angry or crazy way: *He was **ranting and raving** about something she'd done.* —**raving** *adj., adv.*: *raving drunk*

rave² *adj.* **rave reviews** strong praise for something such as a new movie, book, etc.: *The book has **won rave reviews**.*

rave³ *n.* [C] **1** an event at which young people dance all night to loud music with a strong beat **2** strong praise for something such as a new movie, book, etc.

ra·ven /ˈreɪvən/ *n.* [C] a large black bird

rav·en·ous /ˈrævənəs/ *adj.* extremely hungry

ra·vine /rəˈvin/ *n.* [C] a deep narrow valley with steep sides

rav·ish·ing /ˈrævɪʃɪŋ/ *adj. literary* very beautiful – used especially to describe people

raw /rɔ/ *adj.* **1** not cooked: *raw onions* **2** raw substances are in a natural state and have not been treated or prepared for people to use: *The paper company imports its **raw materials** from North America.* **3** skin that is raw is red and sore **4** not experienced or not fully trained: ***raw recruits** in the army* (=people who have just joined the army) **5** not organized, examined, or developed: *raw data* | *This idea was the **raw material*** (=an idea that is not developed) *for his new play.* **6** a raw emotion or quality is strong, natural, and easy to notice: *raw courage* **7 a raw deal** unfair treatment: *She deserved a raise – I think she's **getting a raw deal**.*

ray /reɪ/ *n.* [C] **1** a narrow beam of light from the sun, a lamp, etc.: *the **rays** of the sun* **2 ray of**

R

hope/comfort etc. something that provides a small amount of hope, comfort, etc.

ray·on /ˈreɪɑn/ *n.* [U] a smooth artificial material like silk used for making clothes

raze /reɪz/ *v.* [T] to destroy a city, building, etc. completely: *The old theater had been razed.*

ra·zor /ˈreɪzɚ/ *n.* [C] a sharp instrument for removing hair from the body: *an electric razor*

ˈrazor blade *n.* [C] a small flat blade with a very sharp cutting edge, used in some razors

ˌrazor-ˈsharp *adj.* **1** very sharp **2** showing intelligence and the ability to think quickly: *a razor-sharp sense of humor*

Rd. *n.* the written abbreviation of **road**

RDA *n.* [singular] **recommended daily allowance** the amount of substances such as VITAMINS that you should have every day

re /ri/ *prep.* used in business letters to introduce the main subject: *Re your letter of June 10...*

THESAURUS

about, **on**, **concerning**, **regarding**
➔ see Thesaurus box at ABOUT[1]

R

reach[1] /ritʃ/ *v.* **1** [I,T] to move your hand or arm in order to touch, hold, or pick up something: *David **reached for** the wine.* | *He **reached out** and took her hand.* | *Jean can't reach the cans on the top shelf.* **2** [T] to increase, decrease, or develop to a particular level, standard, or situation over time: *The temperature will reach 95° today.* | *John had **reached the point*** (=reached a situation) *in his life at which he knew he had to make some changes.* **3 reach a decision/agreement/verdict etc.** to succeed in deciding something, agreeing on something, etc. **4** [T] to speak to someone, especially by telephone: *Hughes could not be reached for comment.* **5** [T] to arrive at a particular place: *Peary's first attempt to reach the North Pole, in 1898*

THESAURUS

arrive, **get to**, **turn up**, **show up**
➔ see Thesaurus box at ARRIVE

6 [I,T] to be big enough, long enough, etc. to get to a particular level or point: *Will the ladder reach the roof?*

THESAURUS

go: *The road only goes as far as the farmhouse.*
go up/down to sth: *The water went up almost to the top of the dam.*
come up/down to sth: *Alex is taller; he comes up to Pat's shoulder now.*

7 [T] if a message, television program, etc. reaches a lot of people, they hear or see it: *a TV program that reaches millions of homes*

reach[2] *n.* **1** [singular, U] the distance that you can stretch out your arm to touch something: *The boat floated away, **out of reach**.* | *He breaks everything **within reach**.* **2 within reach (of sth) a)** within a distance that you can easily travel: *We live **within easy reach of** the city.* **b) also in reach** able to be achieved or gotten with the skills, power, money, etc. that you have: *An agreement is **within reach**.* **3 beyond the reach/out of reach** difficult to achieve or get because you do not have enough skill, power, or money: *A permanent solution is still **out of reach**.*

re·act /riˈækt/ *v.* [I] **1** to behave in a particular way because of what someone has done or said to you [➡ **overreact**]: *How did she **react to** the news?* | *The audience **reacted by** shouting and booing.* **2** to become ill when a chemical or drug goes into your body, or when you eat a particular food: *Health workers sometimes react to the latex in gloves.* **3** *technical* if a chemical substance reacts, it changes when mixed with another substance

react against sth *phr. v.* to show that you do not like or agree with something by deliberately doing the opposite: *He reacted against his religious upbringing.*

re·ac·tion /riˈækʃən/ *n.* **1** [C,U] something that you feel or do because of something that has happened or been said: *The public **reaction to** the decision was furious.* | *My **first/initial/immediate reaction** to the book was quite negative.* **2** [C] if you have a reaction to a drug or to something you have eaten, it makes you sick: *an **allergic reaction** to seafood* **3 reactions** [plural] your ability to move quickly when something dangerous happens: *an athlete with quick reactions* **4** [singular] a change in someone's attitudes, behavior, etc. that happens because s/he disapproves of the way things were done in the past: *The attitudes of my generation are a **reaction against** the selfish values of the 1980s.* **5** [C,U] a change that happens when two or more chemical substances are mixed together ➔ **gut reaction/feeling etc.** at GUT[1]

re·ac·tion·ar·y /riˈækʃəˌnɛri/ *adj.* *disapproving* strongly opposed to social or political change —**reactionary** *n.* [C]

re·ac·tor /riˈæktɚ/ *n.* [C] a NUCLEAR REACTOR

read /rid/ *v.* past tense and past participle **read** /rɛd/ **1** [I,T] to look at written words, numbers, or signs and understand what they mean: *children learning to read* | *She sat reading a magazine.* | *I can't read music.*

THESAURUS

flip/thumb through sth – to look at parts of a book, magazine, etc. quickly
browse through sth – to look at parts of a book, magazine, etc. slowly
skim/scan (through) sth – to read something quickly to get the main ideas or to find what you want
pore over sth – to read something very carefully for a long time

devour sth – to read something quickly and eagerly
plow/wade through sth – to read something long and boring
→ WRITE

2 [I,T] to find out information from books, newspapers, etc.: *The class has been* ***reading about*** *the Mayans.* | *He had* ***read that*** *walking was good for your health.* **3** [I,T] to say written or printed words to other people: *Will you read me a story?* | ***Read to*** *your kids every day.* | *a good book to* ***read aloud*** **4 read between the lines** to guess what someone really feels or means, even when his/her words do not show it **5 read sb's mind/thoughts** to guess what someone is thinking: *"Coffee?" "You must have read my mind."* **6** [T] if a measuring instrument reads a particular number, it shows that number: *The thermometer read 46 degrees.* **7** [T] to understand a remark, situation, etc. in a particular way: *The movie could be read as a protest against the Church.* **8 well-read** having read a lot of books

read sth **into** sth *phr. v.* to think that a situation, action, etc. means more than it really does: *People shouldn't read too much into the court's decision.*

read sth ⇔ **out** *phr. v.* to read and say words that are written down, so that people can hear: *He read out the name of the winner.*

read up on sth *phr. v.* to read a lot about something so that you know a lot about it: *Patients should try to read up on their illness.*

read·a·ble /ˈridəbəl/ *adj.* **1** interesting, enjoyable, or easy to read: *a very readable book* **2** clear and able to be read → MACHINE-READABLE

read·er /ˈridɚ/ *n.* [C] **1** someone who reads a lot, or reads in a particular way: *an* ***avid/voracious reader*** (=someone who likes to read a lot) | *a book for young readers* | *a fast/slow reader* **2** someone who reads a particular book, newspaper, etc.: *a newspaper with 30,000 readers*

read·er·ship /ˈridɚˌʃɪp/ *n.* [C,U] the people who read a particular newspaper, magazine, etc.

read·i·ly /ˈrɛdl-i/ *adv.* **1** quickly and easily: *The information is* ***readily available*** *on the Internet.* **2** quickly, willingly, and without complaining: *Chip readily agreed to help.*

read·i·ness /ˈrɛdinɪs/ *n.* **1** [singular,U] willingness to do something: *I admire his* ***readiness to*** *help people.* **2** [U] the state of being prepared and ready for something that might happen: *The army was standing by* ***in readiness for*** *an attack.*

read·ing /ˈridɪŋ/ *n.* **1** [U] the activity of looking at and understanding written words: *Paula loves reading.* **2** [U] the books, articles, etc. that you read: *I have a lot of reading to do for class.* | *It's* ***light reading*** (=easy to read and not very serious). **3** [singular] the act of reading something: *a* ***close reading*** *of the text* **4** [C] your way of understanding what a particular statement, situation, event, etc. means [= **interpretation**]: *What's your* ***reading of*** *the situation, Herb?* **5** [C] a number or amount shown on a measuring instrument: *The man came to* ***take*** *a* ***reading*** *from the electric meter.* **6** [C] an occasion when something is read to people: *a poetry reading*

re·ad·just /ˌriəˈdʒʌst/ *v.* **1** [I] to change the way you do things because of a new job, situation, or way of life: *After the war, I needed time to* ***readjust to*** *life at home.* **2** [T] to make a small change to something, or move something to a new position: *We lifted him up and readjusted the back of the chair.* —**readjustment** *n.* [C,U]

ˌread-only ˈmemory *n.* [U] ROM

read·out /ˈrid-aʊt/ *n.* [C] a record of information produced by a computer that is shown on a screen or in print

read·y /ˈrɛdi/ *adj.* [not before noun] **1** someone who is ready is prepared or able to do something: *Aren't you ready yet?* | *We're just about* ***ready to*** *eat.* | *Go* ***get ready*** *for bed.* | *I don't think he's* ***ready for*** *marriage yet.* **2** something that is ready has been prepared and can be used, eaten, etc. immediately: *Is supper ready?* | *The computer is now set up and* ***ready to*** *use.* | *Is everything* ***ready for*** *the party?* | *I've got to* ***get*** *a room* ***ready*** *for our guests.* | ***Have*** *your passport* ***ready*** *when you go through immigration.* **3** willing or likely to do something: *She's always* ***ready to*** *help.*

ˌready-ˈmade *adj.* already prepared and ready to be used immediately: *ready-made curtains*

real¹ /ril/ *adj.* **1** not imaginary but actually existing: *The new system has real advantages.* | *There is a* ***very real danger/possibility/risk*** *of an explosion.* **2** [only before noun] true and not pretended: *What's the real reason you were late?* | *That's not her real name.* **3** not false or artificial [≠ **fake**]: *real leather* | *I don't want a plastic Christmas tree – I want* ***the real thing*** (=a real Christmas tree). **4** *informal* used in order to emphasize what you are saying: *Matt's a real jerk.* | *It's a real pleasure to meet you.* **5 the real world also real life** the world that people actually live in, as opposed to an imaginary one: *Things don't happen like that in the real world.*

SPOKEN PHRASES

6 said when something is the way you think it should be: *Now that's real coffee!* **7 real live** used in order to emphasize how rare or unusual something is: *Wow! A real live movie star!* **8 are you for real?** used when you are very surprised or shocked by what someone has done or said **9 for real** seriously, not just pretending: *He quit smoking? For real?* **10 get real!** used in order to tell someone that that s/he is being silly or unreasonable: *Get real! He'll never make the team.* **11 keep it real** *slang* something young people say when they mean to behave in an honest way and not pretend to be different from how they really are

real² *adv. spoken nonstandard* very: *I'm real sorry!*

ˈreal esˌtate *n.* [U] **1** property such as houses or

R

land: *Real estate prices fell again last year.* **2** the business of selling houses or land

'real estate ˌagent *n.* [C] someone whose job is to sell houses or land

re·al·ism /ˈriəˌlɪzəm/ *n.* [U] **1** the ability to deal with situations in a practical or sensible way **2** the quality of seeming real: *the gritty realism of the novel*

re·al·ist /ˈriəlɪst/ *n.* [C] someone who thinks in a realistic way

re·al·is·tic /ˌriəˈlɪstɪk/ *adj.* **1** practical and sensible, or dealing with situations in this way: *You have to be* ***realistic about*** *your chances of winning* (=realize that you may not win). | *realistic goals* (=sensible ones, that can be achieved) **2** showing things as they are in real life: *His paintings are so realistic, they look like photographs.*

re·al·is·tic·al·ly /ˌriəˈlɪstɪkli/ *adv.* **1** in a realistic way: *We can't realistically hope for any improvement so soon.* **2** in a way that is very similar to real life: *a realistically drawn picture*

R

re·al·i·ty /riˈælət̬i/ *n.* plural **realities** **1** [C,U] what is true or what actually happens, not what is imagined or not real: *Crime is one of the* ***realities of*** *living in the city.* | *She refuses to* ***face reality****.* | ***The reality is that*** *we can't depend on him.* **2 in reality** used in order to say that something is different from what seems to be true: *He said he'd retired, but in reality, he was fired.* **3 become a reality/make sth a reality** to begin to exist or happen, or to make something do this: *Frank's dream of opening a restaurant became a reality last May.* **4 reality check** *informal* an occasion when you consider the facts of a situation, as opposed to what you would like or what you have imagined

re·al·i·za·tion /ˌriələˈzeɪʃən/ *n.* [singular, U] **1** the act of understanding or realizing something that you did not know before: *We finally* ***came to the realization that*** *the business wasn't going to work.* **2** *formal* the act of achieving what you had planned or hoped to do: ***the realization of*** *a lifelong ambition*

re·al·ize /ˈriəˌlaɪz/ *v.* [T] **1** to know or understand the importance of something that you did not know before: *Do you* ***realize (that)*** *you're an hour late?* | *It was only later that I realized my mistake.*

THESAURUS

become aware – to gradually realize that something is happening or is true: *I became aware that two girls were watching me.*
dawn on sb – to realize something for the first time: *It dawned on me that he was making fun of me.*
sink in – to begin to understand something or realize its full meaning: *It took a few minutes for the doctor's words to sink in.*

2 realize a hope/goal/dream etc. to achieve something you have been hoping to achieve **3 sb's (worst) fears were realized** used in order to say that the thing that you were afraid of has actually happened: *Morris's worst fears were realized when the police came to his door.*

real·ly /ˈrili/ *adv.* **1** very or very much: *Tom's a really nice guy.* | *His letter really irritated me.* | *I'm* ***really, really*** *sorry.*

USAGE

Do not use **very** with adjectives and adverbs that already have a strong meaning, for example "huge" or "terrible." Say "a terrible war," not "a very terrible war." You can use **really** instead: *That was a really awful movie.*
Do not use **very** with the comparative form of adjectives. Do not say "This school's very better." Use **much** instead: *This school's much better.*
→ TOO

2 used when you are talking about what actually happened or is true, rather than what people might wrongly think: *Kevin's not really his brother.* | *What do you really think?*

SPOKEN PHRASES

3 used in order to emphasize something you are saying: *I really don't mind.* | *No, really, I'm fine. Don't worry.* **4 really?** used when you are surprised about or interested in what someone has said: *"Meg's getting married." "Really? When?"* **5 not really** used in order to say "no," especially when something is not completely true: *"Are you hungry yet?" "Not really."* **6 (yeah) really** used in order to agree with someone: *"Greg can be such a jerk sometimes." "Yeah, really."*

realm /rɛlm/ *n.* [C] **1** *formal* an area of knowledge, interest, or thought: *new discoveries in the* ***realm of*** *science* **2** *literary* a country ruled over by a king or queen

'real-time *adj.* [only before noun] *technical* a real-time computer system deals with information as fast as it receives it —**real time** *n.* [U]

real·tor /ˈriltɚ/ *n.* [C] REAL ESTATE AGENT

real·ty /ˈrilti/ *n.* [U] REAL ESTATE

ream /rim/ *n.* **1 reams of sth** *informal* a lot of something: *He took reams of notes.* **2** [C] *technical* 500 sheets of paper

reap /rip/ *v.* **1** [T] to get something good because of the hard work that you have done: *Paula is starting to* ***reap the benefits*** *of all her hard work.* **2** [I,T] to cut and gather a crop of grain

rear[1] /rɪr/ *n.* [C] **1 the rear** the back part of an object, vehicle, building, etc.: *There are more seats* ***at the rear of*** *the theater.* **2** REAR END **3 bring up the rear** to be at the back of a line or group of people that is moving forward: *The kids came around the corner with Donny bringing up the rear.*

rear[2] *v.* **1** [T] to care for a person, animal, or plant until s/he or it is fully grown [= **raise**]: *She reared seven children by herself.* **2** [I] **also rear up** if an animal rears, it rises up on its back legs: *The horse reared and threw me off.*

rear[3] *adj.* [only before noun] relating to the back of something [≠ **front**]: *the rear wheels of the car* | *the rear entrance of the hospital*

'rear end *n.* [C] *spoken* the part of your body that you sit on [= **buttocks**]

'rear-end *v.* [T] *informal* to hit the back of someone's car with another car: *Someone rear-ended us on the freeway.*

re·ar·range /ˌriə'reɪndʒ/ *v.* [T] to change the position or order of things: *We rearranged the furniture in the living room.* —**rearrangement** *n.* [C,U]

rear·view mir·ror /ˌrɪrvyu 'mɪrɚ/ *n.* [C] the mirror in a car that you use to see what is behind you → see picture on page A12

rear·ward /'rɪrwɚd/ *adv.* in, toward, or at the back of something

rea·son[1] /'rizən/ *n.* **1** [C] the cause or fact that explains why something happens or exists: *Did he* ***give*** *any* ***reason for*** *quitting?* | *There are many* ***reasons why*** *people develop heart disease.* | *One of the* ***reasons (that)*** *she came to Boston is her family.*

THESAURUS

explanation – a reason that you give for why something happened or why you did something: *Is there any explanation for his behavior?*
excuse – a reason that you give for why you did something bad: *I hope she has a good excuse for being late again.*
motive – a reason that makes someone do something, especially something bad: *The police have found no motive for the attack.*

2 [C,U] a fact that makes it right or fair to do something: *There is* ***no reason to*** *panic.* | *You* ***had every reason*** *to be suspicious.* **3** [U] sensible judgment or advice: *He won't* ***listen to reason*** (=be persuaded by sensible advice). | *You can go anywhere you want,* ***within reason*** (=within sensible limits). **4** [U] the ability to think, understand, and make good judgments [➡ **logic**]: *a conflict between reason and emotion* **5 all the more reason to do sth** used in order to say that what has just been mentioned is another reason for doing what you have suggested: *"We can't agree about anything." "Well, that's all the more reason for us to sit down and talk."*

reason[2] *v.* **1** [T] to form a particular judgment about something after thinking about the facts: *The jury* ***reasoned that*** *he could not have committed the crimes.* **2** [I] to think about facts clearly and make judgments: *the ability to reason*

reason with sb *phr. v.* to talk to someone in order to persuade him/her to be more sensible: *I tried to reason with her, but she wouldn't listen.*

rea·son·a·ble /'riznəbəl/ *adj.* **1** fair and sensible [≠ **unreasonable**]: *a reasonable request* | ***Be reasonable*** *– you can't expect her to do all the work on her own!* | *He seemed like a reasonable guy.*

THESAURUS

fair, **just**, **equitable**, **balanced**, **even-handed**
→ see Thesaurus box at FAIR[1]

2 a reasonable amount, number, or price is not too much or too big: *good food at a reasonable price* —**reasonableness** *n.* [U]

THESAURUS

cheap, **inexpensive**, **good/great/excellent value**
→ see Thesaurus box at CHEAP[1]

rea·son·a·bly /'riznəbli/ *adv.* **1** fairly but not completely: *I did reasonably well on the test.* **2** in a way that is fair or sensible: *"I'm sure we can find an answer," Steve said reasonably.*

rea·soned /'rizənd/ *adj.* based on careful thought [= **logical**]: *a reasoned argument*

rea·son·ing /'rizənɪŋ/ *n.* [U] the process of thinking carefully about something in order to make a judgment: *What's the* ***reasoning behind*** *this proposal?*

re·as·sur·ance /ˌriə'ʃʊrəns/ *n.* [C,U] something that you say or do to make someone feel less worried about a problem: *people seeking* ***reassurance that*** *pensions would be paid*

re·as·sure /ˌriə'ʃʊr/ *v.* [T] to make someone feel calm and less worried about a problem: *Kids need to be* ***reassured that*** *their parents love them no matter what.* | *She* ***reassured*** *me* ***that*** *everything would be okay.*

re·as·sur·ing /ˌriə'ʃʊrɪŋ/ *adj.* making someone feel less worried: *a reassuring smile* —**reassuringly** *adv.*

re·bate /'ribeɪt/ *n.* [C] an amount of money that is paid back to you when you have paid too much rent, taxes, etc.: *a tax rebate*

reb·el[1] /'rɛbəl/ *n.* [C] **1** someone who opposes or fights against people in authority: *Rebels have overthrown the government.* **2** someone who does not do things in the way that other people want him/her to do them: *She was a rebel at school.*

re·bel[2] /rɪ'bɛl/ *v.* past tense and past participle **rebelled**, present participle **rebelling** [I] to oppose or fight against someone who is in authority: *teenagers who* ***rebel against*** *their parents*

THESAURUS

disobey, **break a rule/law**, **defy**, **violate**
→ see Thesaurus box at DISOBEY

re·bel·lion /rɪ'bɛlyən/ *n.* [C,U] **1** an organized

R

attempt to change the government using violence [➡ **revolution**]: *He led an armed* ***rebellion against*** *the government.*

THESAURUS

revolution, revolt, uprising, coup
➔ see Thesaurus box at REVOLUTION

2 opposition to someone in authority: *teenage rebellion*

re·bel·lious /rɪ'bɛlyəs/ *adj.* **1** deliberately disobeying someone in authority: *a rebellious child* **2** fighting against the government by using violence: *rebellious troops*

re·birth /ri'bɚθ, 'ribɚθ/ *n.* [singular] *formal* a change that results in an old idea, method, etc. becoming popular again

re·boot /ri'but/ *v.* [I,T] if you reboot a computer, you start it again after it has stopped working

TOPIC

start up/boot up a computer, log in/on, shut down, crash, restart
➔ see Topic box at COMPUTER

R

re·bound¹ /'ribaʊnd, rɪ'baʊnd/ *v.* [I] **1** if a ball rebounds, it moves quickly back after hitting something solid: *The ball* ***rebounded off*** *the hoop.* **2** to increase again after decreasing [= **recover**]: *Oil prices rebounded this week.*

re·bound² /'ribaʊnd/ *n.* **on the rebound** if someone is on the rebound, s/he has recently stopped being in a romantic relationship, and is likely to start another romantic relationship soon

re·buff /rɪ'bʌf/ *v.* [T] *formal* to be unkind to someone who is trying to be friendly or helpful —**rebuff** *n.* [C]

re·build /ri'bɪld/ *v.* past tense and past participle **rebuilt** /-'bɪlt/ [T] **1** to build something again, after it has been damaged or destroyed: *The freeway system was quickly rebuilt after the earthquake.*

THESAURUS

repair, fix, mend, renovate, restore, service
➔ see Thesaurus box at REPAIR²

2 to make something strong and successful again: *We try to help drug addicts* ***rebuild*** *their* ***lives****.*

re·buke /rɪ'byuk/ *v.* [T] *formal* to criticize someone because s/he has done something wrong —**rebuke** *n.* [C,U]

re·but /rɪ'bʌt/ *v.* past tense and past participle **rebutted**, present participle **rebutting** [T] *formal* to give reasons to show that a statement or a legal charge that has been made against you is false —**rebuttal** /rɪ'bʌtl/ *n.* [C]

re·cal·ci·trant /rɪ'kælsətrənt/ *adj. formal* refusing to obey or be controlled, even after being punished —**recalcitrance** *n.* [U]

re·call¹ /rɪ'kɔl/ *v.* [T] **1** to remember something: *I don't recall meeting him.* | *I seem to* ***recall (that)*** *we had problems finding the place.* **2** if a company recalls a product, it asks people to return the product because something is wrong with it

re·call² /rɪ'kɔl, 'rikɔl/ *n.* **1** [U] the ability to remember something you have learned or experienced: *She has* ***total recall*** (=ability to remember everything) *of what she has read.* **2** [C] a situation in which a company recalls a product

re·cant /rɪ'kænt/ *v.* [I,T] *formal* to say publicly that you no longer have a particular religious or political belief

re·cap /'rikæp/ *n.* [C usually singular] *informal* the act of repeating the main points of something that has just been said: *And now for a recap of tonight's news.* —**recap** /'rikæp, ri'kæp/ *v.* [I,T]

re·cap·ture /ri'kæptʃɚ/ *v.* [T] **1** to make someone experience or feel something again: *a movie that recaptures the innocence of childhood* **2** to catch a prisoner or animal that has escaped

re·cede /rɪ'sid/ *v.* [I] **1** if something you see, feel, or hear recedes, it gets further and further away until it disappears: *The sound of her footsteps* ***receded into the distance****.* **2** if your hair recedes, you gradually lose the hair at the front of your head: *He has a* ***receding hairline****.* **3** if water recedes, it moves back from an area that it was covering

re·ceipt /rɪ'sit/ *n.* **1** [C] a piece of paper that shows that you have received money or goods: *Keep your receipts for tax purposes.* | *credit card receipts* **2** [U] *formal* the act of receiving something: *The contract becomes valid* ***on/upon receipt of*** (=when we receive) *your letter.*

re·ceive /rɪ'siv/ *v.* [T] **1** to be given something officially: *He* ***received*** *an award* ***from*** *the college.* **2** *formal* to get a letter, telephone call, etc.: *Have you received my letter?* **3** to react to something in a particular way: *Her first novel was* ***well received*** (=people said it was good). **4** *formal* if you receive medical treatment, an injury, etc., it happens or is done to you: *He is still in the hospital* ***receiving treatment*** *for the cuts on his hands.* **5** *formal* to accept or welcome someone officially as a guest or member of a group: *Perez was received at the White House and given the award.*

re·ceiv·er /rɪ'sivɚ/ *n.* [C] **1** the part of a telephone that you hold next to your mouth and ear ➔ see Topic box at TELEPHONE¹ **2** a piece of electronic equipment in a STEREO that changes electrical signals into sound, then makes them loud enough to hear **3** in football, the player who catches the ball

re·cent /'risənt/ *adj.* having happened or begun to exist only a short time ago: *a recent photo* | *the* ***most recent*** *edition of the magazine* | *The situation has improved* ***in recent years/months****.*

THESAURUS

new, modern, latest
➔ see Thesaurus box at NEW

re·cent·ly /ˈrisəntli/ *adv.* not long ago: *We recently moved from Ohio.* | *Have you seen Anna recently?* | *He worked as a teacher* ***until recently***.

THESAURUS

just – only a few minutes, hours, or days ago: *The show just started.* | *They just got back from France.*
a little/short while ago – only a few minutes, hours, or days ago: *Ned called a little while ago.*
lately – in the recent past: *I haven't been to the movies lately.*
freshly – used to say that something was recently made, picked, etc.: *freshly baked bread* | *freshly cut flowers*
newly – used to say that something happened recently, or that something was made, done, etc. recently: *the newly elected governor of New York* | *a newly married couple* | *newly built homes*

USAGE

You can use **recently** and **lately** with the present perfect tense to talk about a situation that is still continuing: *I've been very busy lately.* | *There hasn't been much rain recently.* You can also use **recently** with the simple past tense to talk about something that happened not long ago: *They recently got married.*

re·cep·ta·cle /rɪˈsɛptəkəl/ *n.* [C] *formal* a container

re·cep·tion /rɪˈsɛpʃən/ *n.* **1** [C] a large formal party to celebrate something or to welcome someone: *a wedding reception* | *a reception for the visiting professors*

THESAURUS

party, **get-together**, **bash**, **baby/wedding/bridal shower**, **celebration**
➔ see Thesaurus box at PARTY[1], WEDDING

2 [C usually singular] a way of reacting to a person or idea that shows what you think of him, her, or it: *He got a* ***warm reception*** (=a friendly greeting) *from the crowd.* **3** [U] the quality of the sound of your radio or the picture of your television: *My TV* ***gets good/poor reception***. **4 reception desk/area** the desk or area where visitors who are arriving in a hotel or large organization go first

re·cep·tion·ist /rɪˈsɛpʃənɪst/ *n.* [C] someone whose job is to answer the telephone and help people when they arrive at an office

re·cep·tive /rɪˈsɛptɪv/ *adj.* willing to listen to new ideas or new opinions: *Ron isn't very* ***receptive to*** *other people's suggestions.*

re·cess /ˈrisɛs, rɪˈsɛs/ *n.* **1** [U] a time when children are allowed to go outside to play during the school day: *Charlie got into a fight* ***during/at recess***. **2** [C,U] the time between when work stops and starts again in a court of law or other institution where people have been elected to make laws: *Congress is* ***in recess*** *until January.* **3** [C] a space in the wall of a room for shelves, cupboards, etc.

re·ces·sion /rɪˈsɛʃən/ *n.* [C] a period of time when there is less business activity, trade, etc. than usual: *an* ***economic recession*** | *The economy is* ***going into recession***. | *a country struggling* ***out of recession***

THESAURUS

depression – a long period when businesses do not buy, sell, or produce very much and many people do not have jobs: *During the depression, many young people were unable to find any work at all.*
slump – a period when there is a reduction in business and many people lose their jobs: *a slump in the airline industry*
crash – an occasion when the value of stocks on a stock market falls suddenly and by a large amount, causing economic problems: *the effects of the 1987 stock market crash*

re·charge /riˈtʃɑrdʒ/ *v.* [T] to put a new supply of electricity into a BATTERY —**rechargeable** *adj.*

rec·i·pe /ˈrɛsəpi/ *n.* **1** [C] a set of instructions that tells you how to cook something: *recipes from a French cookbook* | *a* ***recipe for*** *chocolate cake* **2 be a recipe for sth** *informal* to be likely to cause a particular result: *Inviting Paul and his ex-wife to the party was a* ***recipe for disaster***.

re·cip·i·ent /rɪˈsɪpiənt/ *n.* [C] *formal* someone who receives something: *Bauer has been the* ***recipient of*** *many honors.*

re·cip·ro·cal /rɪˈsɪprəkəl/ *adj. formal* a reciprocal agreement, relationship, etc. is one where two groups of people do or give the same things to each other

re·cip·ro·cate /rɪˈsɪprəˌkeɪt/ *v.* [I,T] *formal* to do or give something because something similar has been done for or given to you

re·cit·al /rɪˈsaɪtl̩/ *n.* [C] a public performance of a piece of music or poetry, usually by one person: *a piano recital*

re·cite /rɪˈsaɪt/ *v.* [I,T] to say something such as a poem, story, etc. that you know by memory —**recitation** /ˌrɛsəˈteɪʃən/ *n.* [C,U]

reck·less /ˈrɛklɪs/ *adj.* not caring about danger or the bad results of your behavior, or showing this quality: ***reckless driving*** —**recklessly** *adv.* —**recklessness** *n.* [U]

reck·on /ˈrɛkən/ *v.* [T] **1** to guess a number, amount, etc. without calculating it exactly: *The software company reckons it will sell 2.5 million units this year.* **2** *spoken* to think or suppose: *I reckon they'll be late.*

reckon with sb/sth *phr. v.* to consider a possible problem when you think about the future: *The new team is a* ***force to be reckoned with*** (=something to consider seriously).

reck·on·ing /ˈrɛkənɪŋ/ *n.* [U] calculation that is

not exact: ***By** my **reckoning**, we should be there by now.*

re·claim /rɪˈkleɪm/ *v.* [T] **1** to ask for something to be given back to you: *reclaiming lost luggage* **2** to make land able to be used for farming, building, etc., when it has never been used or has not been used for a while: *Large areas of land will be reclaimed for a new airport.* —**reclamation** /ˌrɛkləˈmeɪʃən/ *n.* [U]

recline

re·cline /rɪˈklaɪn/ *v.* **1** [I,T] to push the back of a seat or chair so that it slopes backward, so that you can lean back in it: *The front seats of the car recline.* **2** [I] to lie or sit back in a relaxed way: *people **reclining on** the grass in the sunshine*

rec·luse /ˈrɛklus/ *n.* [C] someone who likes to live alone and avoids other people —**reclusive** /rɪˈklusɪv/ *adj.*: *the reclusive novelist Thomas Pynchon*

rec·og·ni·tion /ˌrɛkəgˈnɪʃən/ *n.* **1** [singular, U] public admiration and thanks for someone's work or achievements: *She was given an award **in recognition of** 25 years of service.* | *He **gained** international **recognition** after winning the competition.* **2** [singular,U] the act of realizing and accepting that something is important or true: *There is a growing **recognition of** the importance of early childhood education.* **3** [U] the act of recognizing someone or something: *He looked past me with no sign of recognition.* | *The city had changed **beyond recognition*** (=so much that I could not recognize it).

rec·og·nize /ˈrɛkəgˌnaɪz/ *v.* [T] **1** to realize when you see someone that you know him/her because you have seen him/her before: *He'd lost so much weight I hardly recognized him!* | *Social workers have been trained to recognize the signs of child abuse.* **2** to accept officially that an organization, government, etc. is legal: *The UN has refused to recognize the new government.* **3** to accept and admit that something is true or real: *It's important to **recognize that** stress can affect your health.* **4** to thank someone officially for something s/he has done: *His contribution to classical music should be recognized.* —**recognizable** /ˌrɛkəgˈnaɪzəbəl, ˈrɛkəgˌnaɪ-/ *adj.* —**recognizably** *adv.*

re·coil /ˈrikɔɪl, rɪˈkɔɪl/ *v.* [I] **1** to feel a strong dislike for something and want to avoid it: *Most people **recoil from** such racist views.* **2** to move back suddenly from something that you do not like or are afraid of: *Emily **recoiled at** the sight of the snake.*

rec·ol·lect /ˌrɛkəˈlɛkt/ *v.* [T] to remember something: *I don't recollect her name.*

rec·ol·lec·tion /ˌrɛkəˈlɛkʃən/ *n.* [C,U] *formal* something from the past that you remember, or the act of remembering it: *He **has no recollection** of the crash.*

rec·om·mend /ˌrɛkəˈmɛnd/ *v.* [T] **1** to advise someone to do something: *Dentists **recommend that** you change your toothbrush every few months.* | *We **strongly recommend** buying a bicycle helmet.*

THESAURUS

advise, **urge**
→ see Thesaurus box at ADVISE

2 to say that someone or something is good: *Can you recommend a local restaurant?* | *I **recommend** this book **to** anyone who likes adventure stories.* **3 sth has little/nothing etc. to recommend it** used in order to say that something has few or no good qualities: *The hotel has little to recommend it except that it's cheap.*

rec·om·men·da·tion /ˌrɛkəmənˈdeɪʃən/ *n.* **1** [C] advice given to someone, especially about what to do: *The committee was able to **make** detailed **recommendations** to the school.* | *the **recommendation that** babies should sleep on their backs*

THESAURUS

advice, **tip**, **guidance**
→ see Thesaurus box at ADVICE

2 [U] a suggestion that someone or something is appropriate or useful for a particular situation: *We took the tour **on** a friend's **recommendation**.* **3** [C] **also letter of recommendation** a letter which states that someone would be a good person to do a job, study at a college, etc.: *Can you **write a recommendation** for me?*

rec·om·pense /ˈrɛkəmˌpɛns/ *v.* [T] *formal* to give someone a payment for trouble or losses that you have caused —**recompense** *n.* [singular, U]

rec·on·cile /ˈrɛkənˌsaɪl/ *v.* **1 be reconciled (with sb)** to have a good relationship with someone again after arguing with him/her: *His parents are now reconciled with each other.* **2** [T] to show that two different ideas, situations, etc. can exist together and are not opposed to each other: *How can he **reconcile** his religious beliefs **with** all this gambling?*

reconcile sb/yourself **to** sth *phr. v.* to make someone able to accept a bad situation: *I've reconciled myself to the fact that our marriage is over.*

rec·on·cil·i·a·tion /ˌrɛkənˌsɪliˈeɪʃən/ *n.* [singular,U] a situation in which two people, countries, etc. become friendly again after arguing or fighting with each other: *There are signs of a **reconciliation between** the two countries.*

re·con·di·tion /ˌrikən'dɪʃən/ *v.* [T] to repair a machine so that it can be sold again

re·con·nais·sance /rɪ'kɑnəsəns, -zəns/ *n.* [C,U] the activity of sending out aircraft or soldiers in order to get information about the enemy —**reconnoiter** /ˌrikə'nɔɪtɚ/ *v.* [I,T]

re·con·sid·er /ˌrikən'sɪdɚ/ *v.* [I,T] to think again about something in order to decide if you should change your opinion: *Won't you reconsider our offer?* —**reconsideration** /ˌrikənˌsɪdə'reɪʃən/ *n.* [U]

re·con·sti·tute /ri'kɑnstəˌtut/ *v.* [T] **1** to make a group, organization, etc. exist in a different form: *The four political groups will be reconstituted as a new party.* **2** to change dried food to its original form by adding water to it

re·con·struct /ˌrikən'strʌkt/ *v.* [T] **1** to produce a complete description of something that happened by collecting pieces of information: *Police have reconstructed the events leading up to the crime.* **2** to build something again after it has been destroyed or damaged

re·con·struc·tion /ˌrikən'strʌkʃən/ *n.* **1** [U] work that is done to repair damage to a city, industry, etc. especially after a war: *the reconstruction of Europe after the war* **2** [C usually singular] a description or copy of something that you produce by collecting information about it: *a **reconstruction of** the crime*

re·con·struc·tive /ˌrikən'strʌktɪv/ *n.* [only before noun] a reconstructive operation is one done to make a part of someone's body the right shape, for example after a bad injury: ***reconstructive surgery***

re·cord¹ /'rɛkɚd/ *n.* **1** [C,U] information about something or someone, which is either written on paper or stored on a computer: ***Keep a record of** how much you spend on this trip.* | ***medical records*** | *This summer has been the dryest **on record*** (=that has been written in records).

THESAURUS

diary/journal – a book in which you write down the things that have happened to you each day
file – a set of written records, or information stored on a computer under a particular name
accounts – an exact record of the money that a company has received and spent
books – written records of a company's financial accounts
ledger – a book in which a company's financial records are kept
roll – an official list of names, for example of the people attending a school
log (book) – an official record of events, especially on a ship or airplane

2 [C] the fastest speed, longest distance, highest or lowest level, etc. ever: *a **record high/low** temperature* | *She **holds** the world **record** for the 1500 meter run.* | *The movie **broke** all box office **records**.* **3** [singular] the known facts about someone's past behavior and how good or bad it has been: *an airline with a **good/bad** safety **record*** | *Does he have a **criminal record*** (=has he committed any crimes)*?* **4** [C] a round flat piece of plastic on which music is stored: *a huge **record collection*** **5 off/on the record** not official and not meant to be repeated, or official and able to be repeated **6 for the record** used in order to tell someone that what you are saying should be remembered

re·cord² /rɪ'kɔrd/ *v.* **1** [T] to write information down so that it can be looked at in the future: *All the events were recorded.* **2** [I,T] to store music, sound, television programs, etc. on tape or DISKS, etc. so that people can listen to them or watch them again: *The group has just recorded a new album.* | *Are we recording yet?* **3** [T] to measure the size, speed, temperature, etc. of something so that it can be seen

'record-ˌbreaking *adj.* better, higher, faster, etc. than anything done before: *record-breaking temperatures*

re·cord·er /rɪ'kɔrdɚ/ *n.* [C] **1** TAPE RECORDER **2** a small wooden musical instrument shaped like a tube that you play by blowing into it

re·cord·ing /rɪ'kɔrdɪŋ/ *n.* [C] a piece of music, speech, etc. that has been recorded: *a **recording of** Vivaldi's "Gloria"*

'record ˌlabel *n.* [C] a company that records and produces a singer's, group of musicians', etc. music

'record ˌplayer *n.* [C] a piece of equipment for playing records

re·count¹ /rɪ'kaʊnt/ *v.* [T] *formal* to tell a story or describe a series of events

re·count² /'rikaʊnt/ *n.* [C] a process of counting votes again

re·coup /rɪ'kup/ *v.* [T] to get back money you have lost or spent

re·course /'rikɔrs, rɪ'kɔrs/ *n.* [U] *formal* something you can do to help yourself in a difficult situation, or the act of doing this: *The police **had no recourse but to** shoot* (=shooting was their only choice).

re·cov·er /rɪ'kʌvɚ/ *v.* **1** [I] to get better after an illness, injury, shock, etc.: *My uncle is **recovering from** a heart attack.* **2** [I] to return to a normal condition after a period of trouble or difficulty: *The economy will take years to recover.* **3** [T] to get back something that was taken from you, lost, or almost destroyed: *The stolen paintings have been recovered.* **4** [T] to get back your ability to control your feelings or your body: *He never recovered the use of his arm.*

re·cov·er·y /rɪ'kʌvəri/ *n.* **1** [singular,U] the process of getting better after an illness, injury, etc.:

R

his slow ***recovery from*** *a knee injury | Doctors expect Kelly to* ***make*** *a* ***full recovery***. **2** [singular,U] the process of returning to a normal condition after a period of trouble or difficulty: *economic recovery* **3** [U] the act of getting back something that is lost, stolen, or owed: *the* ***recovery of*** *the stolen jewels*

re·cre·ate /ˌrikri'eɪt/ *v.* [T] to make something exist again or be experienced again: *The zoo tries to recreate the animals' natural habitats.*

rec·re·a·tion /ˌrɛkri'eɪʃən/ *n.* [C,U] an activity that you do for pleasure or fun: *outdoor recreation*—**recreational** *adj.*

> **THESAURUS**
>
> **game**, **sport**, **hobby**
> ➔ see Thesaurus box at GAME[1]

re·crim·i·na·tion /rɪˌkrɪmə'neɪʃən/ *n.* [C usually plural,U] a situation in which people blame each other, or the things they say when they are blaming each other

re·cruit[1] /rɪ'krut/ *v.* [I,T] to find new people to work in a company, join an organization, do a job, etc.: *The coaches are visiting colleges in order to recruit new players.* —**recruitment** *n.* [U] —**recruiter** *n.*

recruit[2] *n.* [C] someone who has recently joined a company or an organization: *You could tell he was a* ***new recruit***.

rec·tan·gle /'rɛkˌtæŋgəl/ *n.* [C] a shape with four straight sides, two of which are usually longer than the other two, and four RIGHT ANGLES —**rectangular** /rɛk'tæŋgyələ/ *adj.* ➔ see picture at SHAPE[1]

> **THESAURUS**
>
> **square**, **circle**, **semicircle**, **triangle**, **oval**, **cylinder**
> ➔ see Thesaurus box at SHAPE[1]

rec·ti·fy /'rɛktəˌfaɪ/ *v.* past tense and past participle **rectified**, third person singular **rectifies** [T] *formal* to correct something that is wrong: *All efforts to rectify the problem have failed.*

rec·tor /'rɛktə/ *n.* [C] **1** a priest who is in charge of a local Episcopal church **2** the person in charge of some colleges or schools

rec·tum /'rɛktəm/ *n.* [C] *technical* the lowest part of your BOWELS —**rectal** /'rɛktl/ *adj.*

re·cu·per·ate /rɪ'kupəˌreɪt/ *v.* [I] to get better after an illness, injury, etc.: *Jan is still* ***recuperating from*** *her operation.* —**recuperation** /rɪˌkupə'reɪʃən/ *n.* [U]

re·cur /rɪ'kə/ *v.* past tense and past participle **recurred**, present participle **recurring** [I] to happen again, or to happen several times: *a recurring dream* —**recurrence** *n.* [C,U] —**recurrent** *adj.*

re·cy·cla·ble /ri'saɪkləbəl/ *adj.* able to be recycled: *recyclable bottles* —**recyclable** *n.* [C usually plural]

re·cy·cle /ri'saɪkəl/ *v.* [I,T] to put used objects or materials through a special process, so that they can be used again: *bottles that can be recycled* —**recycled** *adj.*: *recycled paper* —**recycling** *n.* [U]

> **TOPIC**
>
> **pollution**, **the greenhouse effect**, **global warming**, **acid rain**, **deforestation**, **environmentally friendly**, **eco-friendly**, **biodegradable**, **organic**
> ➔ see Topic box at ENVIRONMENT

red[1] /rɛd/ comparative **redder**, superlative **reddest** *adj.* **1** having the color of blood: *a red dress |* ***bright red*** *lipstick* **2** hair that is red is an orange-brown color **3** skin that is red is a bright pink color —**redness** *n.* [U]

red[2] *n.* **1** [C,U] a red color **2 be in the red** to owe more money than you have [≠ **be in the black**] **3 see red** to become very angry

ˌred-'blooded *adj.* **red-blooded male/American etc.** *humorous* used in order to emphasize that someone has all of the qualities that a typical man, American, etc. is supposed to have

ˌred 'carpet *n.* **the red carpet** special treatment that you give someone important who is visiting you

ˌRed 'Cross *n.* [singular] an international organization that helps people who are suffering as a result of war, floods, disease, etc.

red·den /'rɛdn/ *v.* [I,T] to become red, or to make something do this

re·dec·o·rate /ri'dɛkəˌreɪt/ *v.* [I,T] to change the way a room looks by painting, changing the furniture, etc.

re·deem /rɪ'dim/ *v.* [T] *formal* **1 redeem yourself** to do something to improve other people's opinion of you, after you have behaved badly or failed **2** to exchange a piece of paper representing an amount of money for the money that it is worth: *You can redeem the coupon at any store.* **3 redeeming quality/value etc.** a good quality, etc. that keeps someone or something from being completely bad or wrong: *Maybe she has redeeming qualities, but I can't see them.* **4** to make something less bad: *Nothing could redeem this awful movie.* —**redeemable** *adj.*

re·demp·tion /rɪ'dɛmpʃən/ *n.* [U] **1 past/beyond redemption** too bad to be saved or improved **2** the state of being freed from the power of evil, believed by Christians to be made possible by Jesus Christ

re·de·vel·op /ˌridə'vɛləp/ *v.* [T] to make an area more modern by putting in new buildings or changing old ones —**redevelopment** *n.* [C,U]

'red-eye *n.* [U] *informal* an airplane with PASSENGERS on it that makes a trip that starts late at night and arrives early in the morning: *the red-eye from Chicago to Seattle*

ˌred 'flag *n.* [C] something that shows or warns you that something might be wrong, illegal, etc.

ˌred-ˈhanded *adj.* **catch sb red-handed** *informal* to catch someone at the moment when s/he is doing something wrong: *She was caught red-handed taking money from the register.*

red·head /ˈrɛdhɛd/ *n.* [C] someone who has red hair

ˌred ˈherring *n.* [C] a fact or idea that is not important but is introduced in order to take your attention away from something that is important

ˌred-ˈhot *adj.* extremely hot: *red-hot metal*

re·di·rect /ˌridɪˈrɛkt, -daɪ-/ *v.* [T] to send something in a different direction, or use something for a different purpose: *She needs to redirect her energy into something more useful.*

re·dis·tri·bu·tion /ˌridɪstrəˈbyuʃən/ *n.* [U] the act of sharing something between people in a way that is different from in the past: *the **redistribution of wealth/income/land etc.*** —**redistribute** /ˌridɪˈstrɪbyut/ *v.* [T]

ˌred-ˈlight ˌdistrict *n.* [C] the area of a city where there are many PROSTITUTES

ˌred ˈmeat *n.* [U] dark colored meat such as BEEF

red·neck /ˈrɛdnɛk/ *n.* [C] *informal disapproving* someone who lives in a country area, is not educated, and has strong unreasonable opinions

re·do /riˈdu/ *v.* past tense **redid** /-ˈdɪd/ past participle **redone** /-ˈdʌn/ third person singular **redoes** /-ˈdʌz/ [T] to do something again: *You'll have to redo this essay.*

re·dou·ble /riˈdʌbəl/ *v.* **redouble your efforts** to greatly increase your efforts to do something

re·dress /rɪˈdrɛs/ *v.* [T] *formal* to correct something that is wrong, not equal, or unfair —**redress** /ˈridrɛs, rɪˈdrɛs/ *n.* [U]

ˌred ˈtape *n.* [U] official rules that seem unnecessary and that delay action: *The new policies are intended to **cut red tape**.*

re·duce /rɪˈdus/ *v.* [T] to make something become less in amount, size, price, etc.: *Reduce the heat and simmer the rice for another 10 minutes.* | *a jacket **reduced from** $75 **to** $35*

THESAURUS

To reduce prices, numbers, or amounts
lower: *The candidate promised to lower tax rates.*
decrease: *Salaries of middle managers have decreased in the last few years.*
cut: *Stores cut prices after Christmas to get rid of excess merchandise.*
slash – to reduce an amount or price by a large amount: *attempts to slash government spending*
roll back informal – to reduce prices, costs, etc. to a previous level: *a proposal to roll back the gas tax*

To reduce pain
relieve: *Aspirin is effective at relieving headaches.*
ease – to reduce pain and make someone feel more comfortable: *Massage can ease the pain from tight muscles.*
lessen: *drugs to lessen pain*
alleviate formal: *Sitting in a warm bath may alleviate the discomfort.*

reduce sb/sth **to** sth *phr. v.* **1 reduce sb to tears/silence etc.** to make someone cry, be silent, etc.: *Many of us were reduced to tears by the tragedy.* **2 reduce sb to doing sth** to make someone do something which s/he would prefer not to, especially behaving or living in a way that is not as good as before: *They were reduced to begging on the streets.* **3 reduce sth to rubble/ashes/ruins** to destroy something completely, especially a building or city

re·duc·tion /rɪˈdʌkʃən/ *n.* [C,U] a decrease in size, amount, price, etc.: *a **reduction in** the price of gasoline* | *a **reduction of** 30% on all sale items* | *an **arms reduction** treaty*

re·dun·dant /rɪˈdʌndənt/ *adj.* not necessary because something else means or does the same thing. —**redundancy** *n.* [U]

red·wood /ˈrɛdwʊd/ *n.* [C,U] a very tall tree that grows near the coast in Oregon and California

reed /rid/ *n.* [C] **1** a tall plant like grass that grows near water **2** a thin piece of wood in some musical instruments that produces a sound when you blow over it

reef /rif/ *n.* [C] a line of sharp rocks or a raised area of sand near the surface of the sea

reek /rik/ *v.* [I] to have a strong bad smell: *His breath **reeked of** garlic.* —**reek** *n.* [singular]

reel¹ /ril/ *n.* [C] **1** a round object onto which things such as film or string for fishing can be wound **2** the amount that one of these objects will hold: *a **reel of** film*

reel² *v.* **1** [I] to walk in an unsteady way and almost fall over, as if you are drunk: *A guy **came reeling** down the hallway.* **2** [I] to be confused or shocked: *People **are** still **reeling from** the hurricane that hit the town on Sunday.* **3** [T] to wind or unwind string for FISHING on a reel: *It took almost an hour to **reel** the fish **in**.*

reel sth ⇔ **off** *phr. v. informal* to repeat a lot of information quickly and easily: *Andy can reel off the names of all the state capitals.*

re·e·lect /ˌriəˈlɛkt/ *v.* [T] to elect someone again —**reelection** /ˌriəˈlɛkʃən/ *n.* [C,U]

re-en·act /ˌriɪˈnækt/ *v.* [T] to perform the actions of a story, crime, etc. that happened in the past: *children re-enacting the Christmas story* —**re-enactment** *n.*

re·en·try /riˈɛntri/ *n.* plural **reentries** [C,U] an act of entering a place or situation again: *a spacecraft's **reentry into** the Earth's atmosphere*

ref /rɛf/ *n.* [C] *spoken* REFEREE

re·fer /rɪˈfɚ/ *v.* past tense and past participle **referred**, present participle **referring**

refer to *phr. v.* **1 refer to** sb/sth to mention or speak about someone or something: *Rachel didn't*

R

mention names, but everyone knew who she was referring to. | *He likes to be* ***referred to as*** *"Doctor Mills."* **2 refer to** sth to look at a book, map, piece of paper, etc. for information: *Refer to page 14 for instructions.* **3 refer to** sb/sth if a statement, number, report, etc. refers to someone or something, it is about that person or thing: *The blue line on the graph refers to sales.* **4 refer** sb/sth **to** sb/sth to send someone or something to another place or person for information, advice, or a decision: *My doctor referred me to a specialist.*

ref·er·ee[1] /ˌrɛfəˈri/ *n.* [C] someone who makes sure that the rules are followed during a game in sports such as football, basketball, or BOXING

THESAURUS

Referee and **umpire** mean the same but are used for different sports.
Use **referee** when you are talking about football, soccer, ice hockey, basketball, boxing, wrestling, or volleyball.
Use **umpire** when you are talking about baseball or tennis.

R

referee[2] *v.* [I,T] to be the referee for a game

ref·erence /ˈrɛfrəns/ *n.* **1** [C,U] something you say or write that mentions another person or thing: *Her writing is full of* ***references to*** *Chicago.* | *The article* ***made*** *no* ***reference to*** *previous research.* **2** [C,U] the act of looking at something for information, or the book, magazine, etc. you get the information from: *I'll keep a copy of the document* ***for future reference.*** | *the reference section of the library* **3** [C] **a)** a letter containing information about you, written by a former employer or someone who knows you well to a new employer **b)** the person who writes this letter **4** [C] a note that tells you where the information that is used in a book, article, etc. comes from: *a list of references at the end of the article*

ˈreference book *n.* [C] a book such as a dictionary that you look at to find information

THESAURUS

nonfiction, fiction, literature, text book, novel, science fiction, biography, autobiography
→ see Thesaurus box at BOOK[1]

ˈreference ˌlibrary also **ˈreference ˌroom** *n.* [C] a public library or a room in a library that contains reference books that you can use but not take away

ref·er·en·dum /ˌrɛfəˈrɛndəm/ *n.* plural **referenda** /-də/ or **referendums** [C,U] an occasion when you vote in order to make a decision about a particular subject, rather than voting for a person: *a* ***referendum on*** *independence*

re·fer·ral /rɪˈfʌrəl, -ˈfɚ-/ *n.* [C,U] *formal* an act of sending someone or something to another place for help, information, etc.: *The doctor will* ***give*** *you a* ***referral to*** *a specialist.*

re·fill /riˈfɪl/ *v.* [T] to fill something again: *A waiter refilled our glasses.* —**refill** /ˈrifɪl/ *n.* [C] *Would you like a refill?*

re·fi·nance /riˈfaɪnæns, ˌrifəˈnæns/ *v.* [T] to replace a LOAN that you have with another loan: *We plan to refinance our mortgage.*

re·fine /rɪˈfaɪn/ *v.* [T] **1** to make a substance more pure using an industrial process: *The sugar is refined and then shipped abroad.* **2** to improve a method, plan, system, etc. by making small changes to it

re·fined /rɪˈfaɪnd/ *adj.* **1** made more pure using an industrial process: *refined flour* **2** improved and made more effective: *a more refined technique* **3** polite and well-educated

re·fine·ment /rɪˈfaɪnmənt/ *n.* **1** [U] the process of improving something or making a substance more pure: *the* ***refinement of*** *sugar* | *the* ***refinement of*** *their economic theories* **2** [C] a change to an existing product, plan, system, etc. that improves it: *We've added a number of refinements to the design.* **3** [U] the quality of being polite and well-educated

re·fin·er·y /rɪˈfaɪnəri/ *n.* plural **refineries** [C] a factory where something such as oil, sugar, or metal is REFINED

re·fin·ish /riˈfɪnɪʃ/ *v.* [T] to give the surface of something, especially wood, a new appearance by painting or POLISHING it: *The hardwood floors were sanded and refinished.*

re·flect /rɪˈflɛkt/ *v.* **1 be reflected in sth** if an object, person, view, etc. is reflected in a mirror or in the water, you can see the person or thing in it: *We could see the mountains* ***reflected in*** *the lake.* **2** [T] if a surface reflects light, heat, or sound, it sends back the light, etc. that hits it: *Wear something white – it reflects the heat.* **3** [T] to show or be a sign of a particular situation, idea, or feeling: *The fact that people are living longer is reflected in the latest census statistics.* **4** [I] to think carefully: *Please take some time to* ***reflect on*** *our offer.*

reflect on sb/sth *phr. v.* to influence people's opinion of someone or something, especially in a bad way: *behavior that* ***reflects badly on*** *the school*

reflection

re·flec·tion /rɪˈflɛkʃən/ *n.* **1** [C] an image that is reflected in a mirror, glass, or water: *We looked* *at our reflections in the pool.* **2** [C,U] careful thought, or an idea or opinion based on this: *a writer's* ***reflections on*** *America in the 1920s* | *At first I disagreed, but* ***on/upon reflection*** (=after thinking carefully about it), *I realized she was right.* **3** [singular] something that shows, or is a sign of, a particular situation, fact, or feeling: *The rise in crime is a* ***reflection of*** *a violent society.* | *If your kids are bad, it's a* ***reflection on*** *you* (=a sign that you are a bad parent). **4** [U] the light or heat that is reflected from something

re·flec·tive /rɪ'flɛktɪv/ *adj.* **1** a reflective surface REFLECTS light: *reflective tape* **2** thinking quietly, or showing that you are doing this: *He was in a reflective mood.*

re·flec·tor /rɪ'flɛktɚ/ *n.* [C] a small piece of plastic that REFLECTS light ➔ see picture at BICYCLE

re·flex /'riflɛks/ *n.* [C usually plural] a sudden physical reaction that you have without thinking about it: *basketball players with* ***good reflexes*** (=the ability to react quickly)

re·flex·ive /rɪ'flɛksɪv/ *adj. technical* in grammar, a reflexive verb or PRONOUN refers back to the person or thing that does the action. In the sentence "I enjoyed myself," "myself" is reflexive.

re·form¹ /rɪ'fɔrm/ *v.* **1** [T] to improve an organization or system by making a lot of changes to it: *plans to reform the tax laws*

THESAURUS

change, **alter**, **adapt**, **adjust**, **modify**, **reorganize**, **restructure**, **transform**, **revolutionize**

➔ see Thesaurus box at CHANGE¹

2 [I,T] to improve your behavior by making a lot of changes to it, or to make someone do this: *a* ***reformed alcoholic/smoker etc.*** (=someone who is no longer an alcoholic, etc.)

reform² *n.* [C,U] a change made to an organization or system in order to improve it: *the* ***reform of*** *the legal system* | ***economic/political/educational reform***

re·form·er /rɪ'fɔrmɚ/ *n.* [C] someone who works hard to make a lot of changes in order to improve a government or society

re'form school *n.* [C] a special school where young people who have broken the law are sent

re·frain¹ /rɪ'freɪn/ *v.* [I] *formal* to stop yourself from doing something: *Please* ***refrain from*** *smoking.*

refrain² *n.* [C] part of a song that is repeated, especially at the end of each VERSE

re·fresh /rɪ'frɛʃ/ *v.* **1** [T] to make someone feel less tired or hot: *A shower will refresh you.* **2 refresh sb's memory** to say something that makes someone remember something: *Please refresh my memory – what was your last job?* —**refreshed** *adj.*

re'fresher ˌcourse *n.* [C] a training class that teaches you about new developments in a subject or skill you have already studied or learned

re·fresh·ing /rɪ'frɛʃɪŋ/ *adj.* **1** making you feel less tired or less hot: *a refreshing drink* **2** pleasantly different from what is familiar and boring: *The movie is a* ***refreshing change*** *from the usual Hollywood blockbusters.* —**refreshingly** *adv.*

re·fresh·ment /rɪ'frɛʃmənt/ *n.* **1** [C usually plural] food and drinks that are provided at a meeting, party, sports event, etc.: *Refreshments will be served after the concert.* **2** [U] food and drinks in general

re·fried beans /ˌrifraɪd 'binz/ *n.* [plural] a Mexican dish in which beans that have already been cooked are crushed and FRIED with spices

re·frig·er·ate /rɪ'frɪdʒəˌreɪt/ *v.* [T] to make something such as food and drinks cold in order to preserve them: *Refrigerate the sauce overnight.* —**refrigeration** /rɪˌfrɪdʒə'reɪʃən/ *n.* [U]

re·frig·er·a·tor /rɪ'frɪdʒəˌreɪtɚ/ *n.* [C] a large piece of kitchen equipment used for keeping food and drinks cold, shaped like a metal cupboard and kept cold by electricity [= **fridge**]

re·fuel /ri'fyul/ *v.* [I,T] to fill a vehicle or airplane with FUEL again before continuing on a trip

ref·uge /'rɛfyudʒ/ *n.* [C,U] a place that provides protection or shelter from bad weather or danger: *About 50 families have* ***taken refuge*** (=found protection) *in a Red Cross shelter.* | *We* ***sought refuge*** (=looked for protection) *from the 37-degree heat.*

ref·u·gee /ˌrɛfyʊ'dʒi/ *n.* [C] someone who has been forced to leave his/her country, especially during a war: *Refugees were streaming across the border.* | ***refugee camps***

re·fund /'rifʌnd/ *n.* [C] an amount of money that is given back to you if you are not satisfied with the goods or services you have paid for: *If you're not completely satisfied, we'll* ***give*** *you* ***a refund.*** —**refund** /rɪ'fʌnd, 'rifʌnd/ *v.* [T]

re·fur·bish /rɪ'fɚbɪʃ/ *v.* [T] to repair and improve a building: *The hotel was recently refurbished.* —**refurbishment** *n.* [C,U]

re·fus·al /rɪ'fyuzəl/ *n.* [C,U] an act of saying or showing that you will not do, accept, or allow something: *His* ***refusal to*** *pay the fine means he may go to prison.*

re·fuse¹ /rɪ'fyuz/ *v.* **1** [I,T] to say firmly that you will not do or accept something: *I asked her to marry me, but she refused.* | *Steen* ***refused to*** *answer any questions.* | *an offer that's* ***too good to refuse*** (=so good that you cannot say no)

THESAURUS

reject, **turn down**, **say no**, **decline**

➔ see Thesaurus box at REJECT¹

COMMUNICATION

Ways of refusing

No, thanks: *"Do you want some coffee?" "No, thanks."*

R

Thanks, but...: *"Anything I can do to help?" "Thanks, but everything's pretty well taken care of."*
I'd love to, but...: *"Why don't you stay another day?" "I'd love to, but I have to get back."*
I can't...: *"Are you coming to the party?" "I can't. I have exams tomorrow."*
I'd better not: *"Another drink?" "I'd better not, I'm driving."*
→ ACCEPT, AGREE, REJECT

2 [T] to not give or allow someone to have something that s/he wants, especially when s/he has asked for it officially: *We were refused permission to enter the country.*

ref·use² /ˈrɛfjus/ *n.* [U] *formal* waste material

THESAURUS
garbage, **trash**, **litter**, **waste**
→ see Thesaurus box at GARBAGE

re·fute /rɪˈfyut/ *v.* [T] *formal* to prove that a statement or idea is not correct or fair: *Several scientists have attempted to refute Moore's theories.*

R

re·gain /rɪˈgeɪn/ *v.* [T] to get something back, especially an ability or quality that you have lost: *The doctors don't know if Maria will ever regain the use of her legs.*

re·gal /ˈrigəl/ *adj.* typical of a king or queen and therefore very impressive

re·ga·lia /rɪˈgeɪlyə/ *n.* [U] traditional clothes and decorations, used at official ceremonies: *a Native American chief* ***in full regalia*** (=wearing traditional clothes, decorations, etc.)

re·gard¹ /rɪˈgɑrd/ *n. formal* **1** [U] respect for someone or something, or when you show respect to someone or something: *Doctors are* ***held in high regard*** (=respected very much) *by society.* | *You have no* ***regard for*** *my feelings!* **2 with/in regard to sth** *formal* used in order to say what you are talking or writing about: *Several changes have been made with regard to security.* **3 regards** [plural] used in order to send good wishes to someone in a polite and slightly formal way: ***Give*** *my* ***regards*** *to your parents.*

regard² *v.* [T] **1** [not in progressive] to think about someone or something in a particular way: *I've always* ***regarded*** *you* ***as*** *my friend.* | *Carl's work is* ***highly regarded*** *by critics.* **2** *formal* to look at someone or something, especially in a particular way: *She regarded him thoughtfully.*

re·gard·ing /rɪˈgɑrdɪŋ/ *prep. formal* a word used especially in business letters to introduce the particular subject you are writing about: *Regarding your recent inquiry, I've enclosed a copy of our new brochure.*

THESAURUS
about, **on**, **concerning**, **re**
→ see Thesaurus box at ABOUT¹

re·gard·less /rɪˈgɑrdlɪs/ *adv.* **1 regardless of sth** without being affected by different situations, problems, etc.: *The law requires equal treatment for all, regardless of race, religion, or sex.* **2** if you continue doing something regardless, you do it in spite of difficulties or people telling you not to do it: *He does what he wants* ***regardless of*** *what I say.*

re·gat·ta /rɪˈgɑṭə, -ˈgæ-/ *n.* [C] a race for rowing or sailing boats

re·gen·er·ate /rɪˈdʒɛnəˌreɪt/ *v.* [I,T] *formal* to develop and grow strong again, or to make something do this: *Given time, the forest will regenerate.* —**regeneration** /rɪˌdʒɛnəˈreɪʃən/ *n.* [U]

re·gent /ˈridʒənt/ *n.* [C] a member of a small group of people that makes decisions about education in a U.S. state, or that governs a university

reg·gae /ˈrɛgeɪ/ *n.* [U] a type of popular music from Jamaica

THESAURUS
pop (music), **rock (music)**, **rock'n'roll**, **heavy metal**, **house (music)**, **hip-hop**, **rap (music)**, **jazz**, **classical (music)**, **country (music)**, **folk (music)**
→ see Thesaurus box at MUSIC

re·gime /reɪˈʒim, rɪ-/ *n.* [C] a government, especially one that was not elected fairly or that you disapprove of: *a brutal* ***military regime***

THESAURUS
democracy, **republic**, **monarchy**, **dictatorship**, **totalitarian country/state**, **police state**
→ see Thesaurus box at GOVERNMENT

re·gi·men /ˈrɛdʒəmən/ **also regime** *n.* [C] a special plan for eating, exercising, etc. that is intended to improve your health

reg·i·ment /ˈrɛdʒəmənt/ *n.* [C] a large group of soldiers consisting of several BATTALIONS —**regimental** /ˌrɛdʒəˈmɛntl◂/ *adj.*

reg·i·ment·ed /ˈrɛdʒəˌmɛnṭɪd/ *adj.* controlled very strictly: *Prisoners follow a highly regimented schedule.* —**regimentation** /ˌrɛdʒəmənˈteɪʃən/ *n.* [U]

re·gion /ˈridʒən/ *n.* [C] **1** a fairly large area of a state, country, etc., usually without exact limits: *Snow is expected in mountain regions.* | *the Burgundy* ***region of*** *France*

THESAURUS
area, **zone**, **district**, **neighborhood**, **suburb**
→ see Thesaurus box at AREA

2 the area around a particular part of your body: *pain in the lower back region* **3 (somewhere) in the region of sth** about [= **approximately**]: *It will cost in the region of $750.*

re·gion·al /ˈridʒənl/ *adj.* relating to a particular region: *a regional accent* —**regionally** *adv.*

reg·is·ter¹ /ˈrɛdʒəstɚ/ *n.* **1** [C] a book containing an official list or record of something: *the National Register of Historic Places* **2** [C] the place where the warm or cool air of a heating system comes into a room, with a metal cover you can open or close [= **vent**] **3** [C,U] a way of speaking or writing that is formal, informal, humorous, etc. that you use when you are in a particular situation **4** [C] CASH REGISTER

register² *v.* **1** [I,T] to record a name, details about something, etc. on an official list: *The car is registered in my sister's name.* **2** [I,T] to officially arrange to attend a particular school, university, or course [= **enroll**]: *How many students have **registered for** the European History class?* **3** [T] *formal* to express a feeling or opinion about something: *Her face registered surprise and shock.* **4** [I,T] if an instrument registers an amount, or if an amount registers on it, the instrument shows or records that amount: *The thermometer registered 74°F.*

ˌregistered ˈmail *n.* [U] a service in which the post office records the time when your mail is sent and delivered

ˌregistered ˈnurse, RN *n.* [C] someone who has been trained and is officially allowed to work as a nurse

reg·is·trar /ˈrɛdʒəˌstrɑr/ *n.* [C] someone who is in charge of official records, especially in a college

reg·is·tra·tion /ˌrɛdʒəˈstreɪʃən/ *n.* **1** [U] the process of officially arranging to attend a particular school, university, or class [= **enrollment**] **2** [U] the act of recording names and details on an official list **3** [C] an official piece of paper containing details about a vehicle and the name of its owner: *May I see your **license and registration**, Ma'am?*

reg·is·try /ˈrɛdʒəstri/ *n.* plural **registries** [C] a place where official records are kept

re·gress /rɪˈgrɛs/ *v.* [I] to go back to an earlier, less developed state [≠ **progress**] —**regression** /rɪˈgrɛʃən/ *n.* [U]

re·gret¹ /rɪˈgrɛt/ *v.* past tense and past participle **regretted**, present participle **regretting** [T] **1** to feel sorry about something you have done and wish you had not done it: *We've always regretted selling that car.* | *He **regrets that** he never went to college.* | *You'll **regret it** if you leave your job now.* **2** *formal* [not in progressive] to be sorry and sad about a situation: *I **regret that** I will be unable to attend.*

regret² *n.* [C,U] sadness that you feel about something because you wish it had not happened or that you had not done it: *The company **expressed** deep **regret at** the accident.* | *Carl said he **had** no **regrets about** his decision.* —**regretfully** *adv.* —**regretful** *adj.*

re·gret·ta·ble /rɪˈgrɛt̬əbəl/ *adj.* something that is regrettable is something that you wish had not happened: *a regrettable mistake* —**regrettably** *adv.*

re·group /ˌriˈgrup/ *v.* [I,T] to form a group again in order to be more effective, or to make people do this: *The party needs time to regroup politically.*

reg·u·lar¹ /ˈrɛgyələ/ *adj.*

1 REPEATED happening every hour, every week, every month, etc., usually with the same amount of time in between: *His heartbeat is strong and regular.* | *We hear from him **on a regular basis**.* | *Planes were taking off **at regular intervals**.*

THESAURUS

hourly – happening or done every hour: *Legal advisors usually charge an hourly fee.* | *The tour of the studio departs hourly.*
daily – happening or done every day: *a daily newspaper* | *The park is open daily from 10:00 am.*
weekly – happening or done every week: *She writes a weekly column for the Boston Globe.* | *Our Website is updated weekly.*
monthly – happening or done every month: *regular monthly meetings* | *The magazine is published monthly.*
yearly – happening or done every year: *yearly visits to his mother* | *The hospital keeps a record of the number of the operations performed yearly.*
annual – happening every year: *We hold our annual convention in May.*
annually – every year: *The Museum of Science attracts 1.7 million visitors annually.*

2 SAME TIME happening or doing something very often: *He's one of our regular customers.* | *Regular exercise will help you lose weight.*
3 USUAL normal or usual: *She's not our regular babysitter.*
4 ORDINARY ordinary, without any special features or qualities: *He's just **a regular guy**.*
5 NORMAL SIZE of standard size: *fries and a regular coke*
6 EVENLY SHAPED evenly shaped with parts or sides of equal size: *regular features* (=an evenly shaped face)
7 GRAMMAR *technical* a regular verb or noun changes its forms in the same way as most verbs or nouns. The verb "walk" is regular, but "be" is not. —**regularity** /ˌrɛgyəˈlærət̬i/ *n.* [U]

regular² *n.* **1** [C] *informal* a customer who goes to the same store, restaurant, etc. very often: *The bartender knows all the regulars by name.* **2** [U] gas that contains LEAD

reg·u·lar·ly /ˈrɛgyələli, ˈrɛgyəli/ *adv.* **1** at regular times, for example every day, week, or month: *Brush your teeth and see your dentist regularly.* **2** often: *Janet comes to visit regularly.*

THESAURUS

often, a lot, frequently, repeatedly, constantly, continuously, again and again, over and over (again)
→ see Thesaurus box at OFTEN

R

reg·u·late /ˈrɛgyəˌleɪt/ *v.* [T] **1** to control an activity or process, usually by having rules: *The use of these drugs is strictly regulated.* **2** *formal* to make a machine or your body work at a particular speed, temperature, etc.: *People sweat to regulate their body heat.*

reg·u·la·tion /ˌrɛgyəˈleɪʃən/ *n.* **1** [C] an official rule or order: *safety regulations* | *There seem to be so many* ***rules and regulations****.*

> **THESAURUS**
>
> **rule, law, restriction, guidelines, statute**
> ➔ see Thesaurus box at RULE[1]

2 [U] control over something, especially by rules: *government* ***regulation of*** *arms sales*

reg·u·la·to·ry /ˈrɛgyələˌtɔri/ *adj. formal* having the purpose of controlling an activity or process, especially by rules: *the Nuclear Regulatory Commission*

re·gur·gi·tate /rɪˈgɚdʒəˌteɪt/ *v. formal* **1** [I,T] VOMIT **2** [T] *disapproving* to repeat facts, ideas, etc. that you have heard or read without understanding them clearly yourself —**regurgitation** /rɪˌgɚdʒəˈteɪʃən/ *n.* [U]

re·hab /ˈrihæb/ *n.* [U] *informal* treatment to help someone who takes drugs or drinks too much alcohol: *Frank's been* ***in rehab*** *for six weeks.*

re·ha·bil·i·tate /ˌriəˈbɪləˌteɪt, ˌrihə-/ *v.* [T] **1** to help someone to live a healthy or useful life again after s/he has been sick or in prison: *rehabilitating young criminals* **2** to improve a building or area so that it is in a good condition again —**rehabilitation** /ˌriəˌbɪləˈteɪʃən, ˌrihə-/ *n.* [U]

re·hash /riˈhæʃ/ *v.* [T] *informal disapproving* to use the same ideas again in a new form that is not really different or better: *He keeps rehashing the same old speech.* —**rehash** /ˈrihæʃ/ *n.* [C]

re·hears·al /rɪˈhɚsəl/ *n.* [C,U] a period of time or a particular occasion when all the people in a play, concert, etc. practice it before giving a public performance: *a* ***rehearsal for*** *"Romeo and Juliet"*

re·hearse /rɪˈhɚs/ *v.* [I,T] to practice something such as a play or concert before giving a public performance: *They* ***rehearsed*** *the* ***scene*** *in her dressing room.*

> **THESAURUS**
>
> **practice, work on, train, drill**
> ➔ see Thesaurus box at PRACTICE[2]

reign[1] /reɪn/ *n.* **1** [C] the period of time during which someone rules a country: *the* ***reign of*** *Queen Anne* **2** [singular] a period of time during which someone is in control of an organization, business, etc.: *his 4-year reign as team coach* **3 reign of terror** a period during which a government, army, etc. uses violence to control people

reign[2] *v.* [I] **1** to be the ruler of a country **2 the reigning champion** the most recent winner of a competition **3** *literary* if a feeling or quality reigns, it is the main feature of the situation: *For a few moments* ***confusion reigned****.*

re·im·burse /ˌriɪmˈbɚs/ *v.* [T] *formal* to pay money back to someone: *The company will* ***reimburse*** *you* ***for*** *your travel expenses.* —**reimbursement** *n.* [U]

rein /reɪn/ *n.* **1** [C usually plural] a long narrow band of leather that is fastened around a horse's head in order to control it **2 give sb (a) free rein** to give someone complete freedom to say or do things the way s/he wants to **3 keep a tight rein on sb/sth** to control someone or something strictly: *The government is trying to keep a tight rein on public spending.*

re·in·car·nate /ˌriɪnˈkɑrˌneɪt/ *v.* **be reincarnated** to be born again in another body after you have died

re·in·car·na·tion /ˌriɪnkɑrˈneɪʃən/ *n.* **1** [U] the belief that people return to life in another body after they have died **2** [C] the person or animal that a person becomes when they are reincarnated

rein·deer /ˈreɪndɪr/ *n.* [C] a type of DEER with long horns that lives in very cold places

reindeer

re·in·force /ˌriɪnˈfɔrs/ *v.* [T] **1** to support an opinion, feeling, system, etc. and make it stronger: *The fire safety rules will be reinforced by regular drills.* **2** to make something such as a part of a building, a piece of clothing, etc. stronger: *a wall reinforced with concrete*

re·in·force·ment /ˌriɪnˈfɔrsmənt/ *n.* **1** [U] the act of doing something to make an opinion, statement, feeling, etc. stronger: *We need to* ***give*** *students* ***positive reinforcement*** (=say that his/her work is good). **2 reinforcements** [plural] more soldiers or police who are sent to help make a group stronger: *The police* ***called for reinforcements****.* **3** [U] the act of making something stronger: *The bridge needs some structural reinforcement.*

re·in·state /ˌriɪnˈsteɪt/ *v.* [T] **1** to put someone back into a job that s/he had before: *Two employees who were wrongfully fired will be reinstated.* **2** if a law, system, or practice is reinstated, it begins to be used after not being used —**reinstatement** *n.* [C,U]

re·in·vent /ˌriɪnˈvɛnt/ *v.* [T] **1 reinvent yourself** to completely change your appearance and image: *Madonna has constantly reinvented herself.* **2** to make changes to an existing idea, method, system, etc. in order to improve it or make it more modern: *his plan to reinvent the*

American educational system **3 reinvent the wheel** *informal* to waste time trying to find a way of doing something, when someone else has already discovered the best way to do it

re·is·sue /ri'ɪʃu/ *v.* [T] to produce a record, book, etc. again, after it has not been available for some time —**reissue** *n.* [C]

re·it·e·rate /ri'ɪt̬əˌreɪt/ *v.* [T] *formal* to say something more than once: *Lawyers* ***reiterated that*** *there was no direct evidence against Mr. Evans.* —**reiteration** /riˌɪt̬ə'reɪʃən/ *n.* [C,U]

re·ject[1] /rɪ'dʒɛkt/ *v.* [T] **1** to not accept someone or something: *She rejected our offers of help.* | *Tom was rejected by several law schools.*

THESAURUS

reject – to say firmly that you will not accept an offer or suggestion: *Morse's book was rejected by many publishers.*
refuse – to say firmly that you do not want something that you have been offered: *They refused all offers of help.*
turn down informal – to say that you do not want something that you have been offered – use this especially when this is surprising: *An advertising company offered her a job, but she turned it down.*
say no spoken – to say you do not want something or will not accept a suggestion: *I asked him if he wanted a drink, but he said no.*
decline formal – to say politely that you cannot or will not accept an offer: *Mr. and Mrs. Forester declined the invitation.*
→ ACCEPT, AGREE, REFUSE

2 to not give someone love or attention: *She feels rejected by her parents.*

re·ject[2] /'ridʒɛkt/ *n.* [C] **1** a product that is thrown away because it is damaged or imperfect **2** *spoken* someone who is not accepted or liked by other people

re·jec·tion /rɪ'dʒɛkʃən/ *n.* **1** [C,U] the act of not accepting something: *The council's* ***rejection of*** *the proposal was unexpected.* | *She received many rejections before the novel was published.* **2** [U] a situation in which someone stops giving you love or attention: *fear of rejection*

re·joice /rɪ'dʒɔɪs/ *v.* [I] *literary* to feel or show that you are very happy —**rejoicing** *n.* [U]

re·join /rɪ'dʒɔɪn/ *v.* [T] to return to a group or person: *She rejoined her friends in the lounge.*

re·join·der /rɪ'dʒɔɪndə/ *n.* [C] *formal* a reply, especially one that is rude

re·ju·ve·nate /rɪ'dʒuvəˌneɪt/ *v.* [T] **1** to make someone feel or look young and strong again: *After a workout, I feel rejuvenated.* **2** to make a system or place better again: *the rejuvenated downtown area* —**rejuvenation** /rɪˌdʒuvə'neɪʃən/ *n.* [singular, U]

re·kin·dle /ri'kɪndl/ *v.* [T] to make someone have a particular feeling, thought, etc. again: *a chance to rekindle an old romance*

re·lapse /rɪ'læps/ *n.* [C,U] a situation in which someone feels sick again after seeming to improve: *He's* ***had/suffered a relapse.*** —**relapse** *v.* [I]

re·late /rɪ'leɪt/ *v.* **1** [T] to show or prove a connection between two or more things: *I don't understand how the two ideas relate.* **2** [T] to be concerned with or directly connected to a particular subject: *How does this job* ***relate to*** *your career goals?* **3** [T] *formal* to tell someone about something that has happened: *He later* ***related*** *the whole story* ***to*** *us.*

relate to sb/sth *phr. v.* to understand how someone feels: *I find it hard to relate to kids.*

re·lat·ed /rɪ'leɪt̬ɪd/ *adj.* **1** connected by similar ideas or dealing with similar subjects: *Police believe the murders are related.* | *diseases* ***related to*** *smoking* | *Politics and economics are* ***closely related.*** **2 stress-related/drug-related etc.** caused by or relating to stress, drugs, etc.: *alcohol-related violence* **3** connected by a family relationship: *Are you* ***related to*** *Paula?*

re·la·tion /rɪ'leɪʃən/ *n.* **1 in relation to sb/sth** used when comparing two things or showing the relationship between them: *The area of land is tiny in relation to the population.* **2 relations** [plural] official connections and attitudes between countries, organizations, groups, etc.: *Are the* ***relations between*** *the staff and students good?* | *Israel's* ***relations with*** *its Arab neighbors* | *The U.S. has maintained* ***diplomatic relations*** *with Laos.* **3** [C,U] a connection between two things: *Is there any* ***relation between*** *the drugs he was taking and his death?* | *This case* ***bears no relation to*** (=is not connected with or similar to) *the Goldman trial.* **4** [C] a member of your family [= **relative**]

THESAURUS

family, relative, folks
→ see Thesaurus box at FAMILY, RELATIVE[1]

re·la·tion·ship /rɪ'leɪʃənˌʃɪp/ *n.* **1** [C] the way in which two people or groups behave toward each other: *They seem to* ***have*** *a* ***good relationship.*** | *a mother's* ***relationship with*** *her children* | *the special* ***relationship between*** *the U.S. and Britain* **2** [C] a situation in which two people have sexual or romantic feelings for each other: *a* ***sexual relationship*** | *He's much happier now that he's* ***in a relationship.*** **3** [C,U] the way in which two or more things are related to each other: *the* ***relationship between*** *pay and performance at work*

rel·a·tive[1] /'rɛlət̬ɪv/ *n.* [C] a member of your family: *a* ***close relative*** (=mother, brother, cousin, etc.) | ***distant relatives*** (=second or third cousins, etc. that you rarely see)

R

THESAURUS

parents
father/mother
dad/daddy informal, **mom/mommy** informal
brother/sister
grandparents
grandfather/grandmother
grandpa/grandma informal
great-grandparents
uncle/aunt
nephew/niece
cousin
→ FAMILY

relative[2] *adj.* **1** having a particular quality when compared with something else: *The 1950s were a time of **relative peace/calm/prosperity** for the country.* **2 relative to sth** relating to or compared with a particular subject: *Demand for corn is low relative to the supply.*

ˌrelative ˈclause *n.* [C] *technical* in grammar, a part of a sentence that has a verb in it and is joined to the rest of the sentence by a RELATIVE PRONOUN. In the sentence "The dress that I bought is too small," "that I bought" is the relative clause.

R

rel·a·tive·ly /ˈrɛlət̬ɪvli/ *adv.* to a particular degree, especially when compared to something similar: *It's a relatively inexpensive restaurant.*

ˌrelative ˈpronoun *n.* [C] *technical* in grammar, a PRONOUN such as "who," "which," or "that," which connects a RELATIVE CLAUSE to the rest of the sentence. In the sentence "The dress that I bought is too small," "that" is the relative pronoun.

rel·a·tiv·i·ty /ˌrɛləˈtɪvət̬i/ *n.* [U] *technical* in PHYSICS, the relationship between time, space, and movement: *Einstein's theory of relativity*

re·lax /rɪˈlæks/ *v.* **1** [I,T] to become more calm and less worried, or to make someone do this: *What do you do to relax? | A hot bath should help to relax you.* **2** [I,T] if a part of your body relaxes, or if you relax it, it becomes less stiff and tight: *Try to relax your neck. | Let your muscles relax.* **3** [T] to make rules, controls, etc. less strict: *plans to relax the law*

re·lax·a·tion /ˌrilækˈseɪʃən/ *n.* **1** [C,U] the state of being relaxed in your mind and body, or the process of becoming this way: *I like to cook **for relaxation**.* **2** [U] the process of making rules, controls, etc. less strict: *the **relaxation of** travel restrictions*

re·laxed /rɪˈlækst/ *adj.* **1** calm and not worried or angry: *Gail was lying in the sun, looking happy and relaxed.*

THESAURUS

calm, **laid-back**, **mellow**, **cool**
→ see Thesaurus box at CALM[2]

2 a situation or attitude that is relaxed is informal and not strict: *There's a **relaxed atmosphere** in class.*

re·lax·ing /rɪˈlæksɪŋ/ *adj.* making you feel calm: *relaxing music*

re·lay[1] /ˈrileɪ, rɪˈleɪ/ *v.* past tense and past participle **relayed**, third person singular **relays** [T] to send a message or information from one person, thing, or place to another person, thing, or place: *Could you **relay** the message **to** Mary for me?*

re·lay[2] /ˈrileɪ/ **also ˈrelay race** *n.* [C] a race in which each member of a team runs or swims part of the distance

re·lease[1] /rɪˈlis/ *v.* [T] **1** to allow someone to be free after you have kept him/her somewhere: *Three hostages were released this morning. | He was **released from** the hospital this morning.* **2** to stop holding something: *He released her arm when she screamed.* **3** to let news or information be known publicly: *Details of the crime have not been released.* **4** to make a movie, record, etc. available for people to buy or see: *The band has just released a new album.*

release[2] *n.* **1** [singular] the act of allowing someone to be free after s/he has been kept somewhere: *After his **release from** prison, he worked as a carpenter.* **2** [C] a new movie, record, etc. that is available for people to see or buy: *the singer's latest release* **3** [U] a feeling that you are free from worry or pain: *a sense of emotional release*

rel·e·gate /ˈrɛləˌgeɪt/ *v.* [T] *formal* to make someone or something less important than before: *He's been **relegated to** the role of assistant.*

re·lent /rɪˈlɛnt/ *v.* [I] to let someone do something that you refused to let him/her do before: *At last, her father relented and she moved into her own apartment.*

re·lent·less /rɪˈlɛntlɪs/ *adj.* **1** if something bad is relentless, it continues without stopping or getting less severe: *There's relentless pressure on top athletes. | the relentless heat of the desert* **2** someone who is relentless continues to do something in a determined way: *We will be **relentless in** our pursuit of criminals.* —**relentlessly** *adv.*

rel·e·vant /ˈrɛləvənt/ *adj.* directly relating to the subject or problem being discussed [≠ **irrelevant**]: *The question is not **relevant to** my point. | We told the police all the relevant facts.* —**relevance** *n.* [U]

re·li·a·ble /rɪˈlaɪəbəl/ *adj.* someone or something that is reliable can be trusted or depended on [= **dependable**; ≠ **unreliable**]: *a reliable car | We need a more reliable babysitter.* —**reliably** *adv.* —**reliability** /rɪˌlaɪəˈbɪlət̬i/ *n.* [U]

re·li·ance /rɪˈlaɪəns/ *n.* [singular, U] the state of being dependent on something: *the country's **reliance on** imported oil*

re·li·ant /rɪˈlaɪənt/ *adj.* **be reliant on/upon sb/sth** to depend on something or someone [➡ **rely**]: *She's still reliant on her parents for money.*

rel·ic /ˈrɛlɪk/ *n.* [C] something from the past that still exists: ***relics of** ancient Egypt*

re·lief /rɪˈlif/ *n.* **1** [singular, U] the happy feeling you have when something frightening, worrying, or painful has ended or has not happened: *Exams* *are finally over.* ***What a relief!*** | ***It was a relief*** *to finally be alone.* | *No one was hurt, and we all* ***breathed a sigh of relief.*** | *She listened to the news* ***with relief.*** **2** [U] the reduction of pain: *a medicine for* ***pain relief*** | ***relief from*** *the intense heat* **3** [U] money, food, clothing, etc. given to people who need them by a government or other organization: ***disaster/earthquake/flood relief*** *operations* | ***Relief workers*** *distributed bottles of water.* **4** [C] a person or group of people that replaces another one and does their work after they have finished: *a relief pitcher*

re·lieve /rɪ'liv/ *v.* [T] **1** to make a pain, problem, bad feeling, etc. less severe: *The county is building a new school to relieve overcrowding.* | *We tried to* ***relieve the boredom/tension*** *by singing.*

> **THESAURUS**
>
> **reduce, lower, decrease, ease, lessen, alleviate**
>
> → see Thesaurus box at REDUCE

2 to replace someone else at a job or duty: *The guards are relieved at six o'clock.*

relieve sb **of** sth *phr. v. formal* to help someone by carrying something heavy or by doing something difficult for him/her: *He rose and relieved her of her bags.*

re·lieved /rɪ'livd/ *adj.* feeling happy because something bad did not happen or is finished [➡ **relief**]: *I was* ***relieved to be*** *out of the hospital.* | *We were* ***relieved that*** *Brian was home safe.*

re·li·gion /rɪ'lɪdʒən/ *n.* [C,U] belief in one or more gods, or a particular system of beliefs in one or more gods: *the study of religion* | *people* ***of different religions***

> **THESAURUS**
>
> **faith, belief, creed**
>
> → see Thesaurus box at FAITH

re·li·gious /rɪ'lɪdʒəs/ *adj.* **1** relating to religion: *We don't share the same* ***religious beliefs.***

> **THESAURUS**
>
> **devout** – having very strong religious beliefs: *a devout Catholic*
>
> **practicing** – obeying the rules of a particular religion: *a practicing Muslim*

2 believing strongly in your religion and obeying its rules: *a very religious woman*

re·li·gious·ly /rɪ'lɪdʒəsli/ *adv.* **1** regularly and thoroughly or completely: *He exercises religiously.* **2** in a way that is related to religion: *a religiously diverse country* (=one with many different religions)

re·lin·quish /rɪ'lɪŋkwɪʃ/ *v.* [T] *formal* to give up your position, power, rights, etc.

rel·ish[1] /'rɛlɪʃ/ *v.* [T] to enjoy something or like it: *Jamie* ***didn't relish the idea of*** *getting up early.*

relish[2] *n.* **1** [C,U] a cold SAUCE eaten especially with meat to add taste: *pickle relish* **2** [U] great enjoyment of something: *Barry ate* ***with*** *great* ***relish.***

re·live /ˌri'lɪv/ *v.* [T] to experience something again that happened in past times, or to remember it clearly: *I'm focusing on the future, not reliving the past.*

re·load /ˌri'loʊd/ *v.* [I,T] **1** to put something into a container again, especially bullets into a gun **2** if you reload a page on the Internet, you ask for the information shown on that page to be sent to your computer again

re·lo·cate /ri'loʊˌkeɪt/ *v.* [I,T] to move to a new place: *Our company* ***relocated to*** *the West Coast.* —**relocation** /ˌriloʊ'keɪʃən/ *n.* [U]

re·luc·tant /rɪ'lʌktənt/ *adj.* unwilling and slow to do something: *a reluctant smile* | *She was* ***reluctant to*** *ask for help.* —**reluctance** *n.* [singular, U] —**reluctantly** *adv.*

re·ly /rɪ'laɪ/ *v.* past tense and past participle **relied**, third person singular **relies**

rely on/upon sb/sth *phr. v.* to trust or depend on someone or something: *We're relying on him to help.*

re·main /rɪ'meɪn/ *v.* **1** [I, linking verb] to stay in the same place or condition: *The others left while I remained at home.* | *Veltman* ***remained silent.*** **2** [I] to continue to exist after other things or parts have gone or been destroyed: *Only half the statue remains.* **3** [I] if something remains to be done, said, etc., it still needs to be done, said, etc.: *Many questions remain to be answered.* | *It* ***remains to be seen*** *whether the operation was successful* (=we do not know yet whether it was successful).

re·main·der /rɪ'meɪndɚ/ *n.* **the remainder (of sth)** the rest of something after everything else has gone or been dealt with: *the remainder of the semester*

re·main·ing /rɪ'meɪnɪŋ/ *adj.* still left when other similar things or people have gone or been dealt with: *The remaining puppies were given away.*

re·mains /rɪ'meɪnz/ *n.* [plural] **1** the parts of something that are left after the rest has been destroyed: *We visited* ***the remains of*** *the temple.* **2** *formal* a person's body after s/he has died

re·make /'rimeɪk/ *n.* [C] a movie or song that has the same story as one that was made before: *a* ***remake of*** *"The Wizard of Oz"* —**remake** /ri'meɪk/ *v.* [T]

re·mark[1] /rɪ'mɑrk/ *n.* [C] something that you say: *Carl* ***made*** *a sarcastic* ***remark.***

remark[2] *v.* [T] to say something, especially your opinion about something: *One woman* ***remarked that*** *he was handsome.* | *Several people* ***remarked on/upon*** *the poor service.*

re·mark·a·ble /rɪ'mɑrkəbəl/ *adj.* very unusual or noticeable in a way that deserves attention or praise: *Josephine was a truly remarkable woman.*

re·mark·a·bly /rɪ'mɑrkəbli/ *adv.* in a way that is surprising: *Charlotte and her cousin look remarkably similar.*

re·mar·ry /ri'mæri/ *v.* past tense and past parti-

R

ciple **remarried**, third person singular **remarries** [I,T] to marry again: *After her husband's death, Carol never remarried.* —**remarriage** *n.* [C,U]

re·mas·ter /ri'mæstɚ/ *v.* [T] to improve the quality of a MOVIE or musical recording, using a computer

re·me·di·al /rɪ'midiəl/ *adj.* **1 remedial class/education etc.** a special class, etc. for students who are having difficulty learning something **2** *formal* intended to provide a cure or improvement in something

rem·e·dy¹ /'rɛmədi/ *n.* plural **remedies** [C] **1** a successful way of dealing with a problem: *a* ***remedy for*** *unemployment* **2** a medicine that cures pain or illness: *a cold remedy*

remedy² *v.* past tense and past participle **remedied**, present participle **remedying**, third person singular **remedies** [T] to deal successfully with a problem or improve a bad situation: *The hospital is trying to remedy the problem.*

re·mem·ber /rɪ'mɛmbɚ/ *v.* **1** [I,T] to have a picture or idea in your mind of people, events, etc. from the past: *Do you remember that guy Anthony from school?* | *I don't remember meeting her before.* | *I* ***remember (that)*** *he had a broken leg that summer.* | *Mr. Daniels has lived there* ***for as long as I can remember.*** **2** [I,T] to bring information or facts that you know back into your mind: *She suddenly* ***remembered (that)*** *she had to go to the dentist.* | *I can't remember her phone number.* **3** [I,T] to not forget to do something: ***Remember to*** *get some milk at the store today!* **4** [T] to think about someone who has died, with special respect and honor: *On Memorial Day, we remember those who have died in wars.* **5 be remembered for/as sth** to be famous for something important that you did

USAGE

remember – to think of something that you must do, and not forget about it: *I hope he remembers to bring the wine.*
remind – to make someone remember something s/he must do or something s/he needs to know: *Remind me to take a bottle of wine to the party.*

re·mem·brance /rɪ'mɛmbrəns/ *n.* [U] the act of remembering and giving honor to someone who has died: *She planted a tree* ***in remembrance of*** *her husband.*

re·mind /rɪ'maɪnd/ *v.* [T] to make someone remember something that s/he must do: ***Remind*** *me* ***to*** *tell you the story sometime.* | *Let me call Frank to* ***remind*** *him* ***that*** *we're picking him up at 8:00.* ➔ see Usage box at REMEMBER

remind sb **of** sb/sth *phr. v.* to seem similar to someone or something else: *Carl reminds me of his father.*

re·mind·er /rɪ'maɪndɚ/ *n.* [C] something that makes you notice or remember something else: *a painful* ***reminder of*** *the war*

rem·i·nisce /ˌrɛmə'nɪs/ *v.* [I] to talk or think about pleasant events in your past: *We sat* ***reminiscing about*** *our college days.* —**reminiscence** *n.* [C,U]

rem·i·nis·cent /ˌrɛmə'nɪsənt/ *adj.* **reminiscent of sth** reminding you of something: *His voice is reminiscent of Frank Sinatra's.*

re·miss /rɪ'mɪs/ *adj. formal* careless about doing something that you ought to do: *Investigators would* ***be remiss*** *if they didn't pursue every possible lead.*

re·mis·sion /rɪ'mɪʃən/ *n.* [C,U] a period of time when an illness improves: *Her cancer* ***is in remission.***

re·mit /rɪ'mɪt/ *v.* past tense and past participle **remitted**, present participle **remitting** [I,T] *formal* to send a payment by mail

re·mit·tance /rɪ'mɪt⁻ns/ *n.* [C,U] *formal* the act of sending money by mail, or the amount of money that is sent

rem·nant /'rɛmnənt/ *n.* [C] a small part of something that remains after the rest has been used or destroyed: ***remnants of*** *a lost civilization*

re·mod·el /ˌri'mɑdl/ *v.* [T] to change the shape or appearance of something: *We've had the kitchen remodeled.*

rem·on·strate /'rɛmənˌstreɪt, rɪ'mɑnˌstreɪt/ *v.* [I] *formal* to tell someone that you strongly disapprove of what s/he has done

re·morse /rɪ'mɔrs/ *n.* [U] a strong feeling of being sorry for doing something very bad: *Keating* ***showed/expressed no remorse*** *for his crime.* —**remorseless** *adj.*: *a remorseless killer* —**remorseful** *adj.*

THESAURUS

guilt, **shame**, **conscience**
➔ see Thesaurus box at GUILT

re·mote /rɪ'moʊt/ *adj.* **1** far away in distance or time: *a remote forest area* | *the remote past* **2** very slight or small: *There's* ***a remote possibility/chance that*** *the operation will not work.* | *The prospects for peace seem very remote.* **3** very different from something else, or not closely related to it: *subjects that are* ***remote from*** *everyday life* **4** unfriendly, and not interested in people: *Her father was a remote, stern man.* —**remoteness** *n.*

reˌmote con'trol also **remote** *n.* [C] a piece of equipment that you use to control a television, video, etc. from a distance ➔ see Topic box at TELEVISION —**remote-controlled** *adj.*: *a remote-controlled car*

re·mote·ly /rɪ'moʊtli/ *adv.* used in order to emphasize a negative statement: *This is* ***not even remotely*** *funny.*

re·mov·a·ble /rɪ'muvəbəl/ *adj.* able to be removed: *chairs with removable covers*

re·mov·al /rɪ'muvəl/ *n.* [C,U] the act of removing something: *the* ***removal of*** *foreign troops from the country* | *his* ***removal from*** *power*

re·move /rɪ'muv/ *v.* [T] **1** to take something away from, out of, or off the place where it is: *The old paint will have to be removed first.* | ***Remove*** *the pan* ***from*** *the oven to cool.*

THESAURUS

take off – to remove clothing: *She began to take off her clothes.*
tear off – to remove part of a piece of paper or cloth by tearing it: *Tear off the coupon below.*
break off – to remove a part of something by breaking it: *Ted broke off a piece of chocolate.*
scrape off – to remove something using a knife or sharp tool: *We began by scraping off the wallpaper.*
wipe off/up – to remove dirt, liquid, etc. with a cloth: *He wiped the sweat off his forehead.* | *Julie wiped up the spilled milk.*
rub off – to remove dirt, marks, etc. with a cloth or brush: *He rubbed off some of the rust.*

2 to get rid of something so it does not exist anymore: *What's the best way to remove red wine stains?* **3 be (far) removed from sth** to be very different from something else: *This job is far removed from anything that I've done before.* **4** *formal* to make someone leave a job: *The Mayor has been* ***removed from*** *office.*

re·mov·er /rɪ'muvɚ/ *n.* **paint/stain etc. remover** a substance that removes paint, etc. from something else

re·mu·ner·ate /rɪ'myunə,reɪt/ *v.* [T] *formal* to pay someone for something s/he has done —**remuneration** /rɪ,myunə'reɪʃən/ *n.* [C,U]

ren·ais·sance /'rɛnə,zɑns, -,sɑns, ,rɛnə'sɑns/ *n.* **1** [singular] a new interest or development in something that has not been popular: *the* ***renaissance in*** *women's sports* **2 the Renaissance** the time in Europe between the 14th and 17th centuries when a lot of new art and literature was produced

re·name /ri'neɪm/ *v.* [T] to change the name of something

ren·der /'rɛndɚ/ *v.* [T] *formal* **1** to cause someone or something to be in a particular state: *The accident rendered her left leg useless.* **2** to give someone something: *It is the jury's responsibility to render a fair verdict.* | *payment* ***for services rendered*** (=for work someone has done)

ren·der·ing /'rɛndərɪŋ/ *n.* [C] the particular way a painting, story, etc. is expressed

ren·dez·vous /'rɑndeɪ,vu, -dɪ-/ *n.* plural **rendezvous** /-,vuz/ [C] an arrangement to meet someone at a particular time and place, or the place where you meet: *a midnight* ***rendezvous with*** *her lover* —**rendezvous** *v.* [I]

ren·di·tion /rɛn'dɪʃən/ *n.* [U] the way that a play, piece of music, art, etc. is performed or made: *a powerful* ***rendition of*** *"America the Beautiful"*

ren·e·gade /'rɛnə,geɪd/ *n.* [C] someone who joins the opposing side in a war, argument, etc. —**renegade** *adj.*: *renegade soldiers*

re·nege /ri'nɛg, -'nɪg/ *v.* [I] to not do something that you promised to do: *He* ***reneged on*** *his* ***promise*** *to send the money.*

re·new /rɪ'nu/ *v.* [T] **1** to arrange for something such as a contract to continue: *It's time to renew our insurance.* | *Library books can be renewed by phone.* **2** *formal* to begin to do something again [= **resume**]: *The search will be renewed in the morning.* —**renewal** *n.* [C,U]

re·new·a·ble /rɪ'nuəbəl/ *adj.* **1** a renewable contract, ticket, etc. can be made to continue after the date that it is supposed to end [≠ **nonrenewable**] **2** able to be replaced by natural processes so that it is never used up: ***renewable energy*** *such as solar power*

re·newed /rɪ'nud/ *adj.* increasing again after not being very strong: *his* ***renewed interest*** *in religion*

re·nounce /rɪ'naʊns/ *v.* [T] **1** to say publicly that you will no longer try to keep something, or will not stay in an important position: *Grayson* ***renounced his claim to*** *the family fortune.* **2** to say publicly that you no longer believe in or support something: *We absolutely renounce all forms of terrorism.*

ren·o·vate /'rɛnə,veɪt/ *v.* [T] to repair something such as a building so that it is in good condition again —**renovation** /,rɛnə'veɪʃən/ *n.* [C,U]

THESAURUS

repair, **fix**, **mend**, **restore**, **service**, **rebuild**
➔ see Thesaurus box at REPAIR²

re·nowned /rɪ'naʊnd/ *adj.* known and admired by a lot of people [= **famous**]: *a renowned architect* | *She was* ***renowned for*** *her beauty.* —**renown** *n.* [U]

rent¹ /rɛnt/ *v.* **1** [I,T] to pay money regularly to live in a place that belongs to someone else: *They're renting an apartment near the beach.* | *I rented for years before buying a place.*

TOPIC

When you rent a house or apartment, you are called the **tenant**. You usually have to **pay a deposit** before moving in. The **deposit/security deposit** is usually an amount of money equal to a month's rent, or equal to the first and last month's rent. After that you **pay the rent** every month to the **landlord/landlady** (=owner). If you do not pay the rent or behave well, the landlord can **evict** you (=force you to leave). If you want to stop renting the house or apartment, you have to **give notice** (=tell the landlord you want to leave), usually a month before you want to leave.

2 [T] to pay money for the use of something for a short period of time: *We're probably going to rent a car while we're there.* | *Do you want to rent a movie?* **3** [I,T] **also rent** sth ⇔ **out** to let some-

R

one live in a place that you own in return for money: *They've rented out their house for the summer.* | *He refused to* ***rent to*** *gay people.* —**renter** *n.*

rent[2] *n.* [C,U] **1** the amount of money you pay for the use of a house, room, car, etc. that belongs to someone else: *I don't know how we're going to* ***pay*** *the* ***rent*** *next month.*

THESAURUS

cost, expense, price, charge, fee, fare
➔ see Thesaurus box at COST[1]

2 for rent available to be rented: *She put the house up for rent a month ago.*

rent·al[1] /ˈrɛntl/ *n.* **1** [C,U] an arrangement by which you rent something: *car rental companies* **2** [U] the money that you pay to rent something: *Ski rental is $14.*

rental[2] *adj.* available to be rented or being rented: *a rental car* | *rental properties*

ˈrent conˌtrol *n.* [U] official action taken by a city or state to limit the price of renting apartments

re·nun·ci·a·tion /rɪˌnʌnsiˈeɪʃən/ *n.* [C,U] *formal* the act of renouncing (RENOUNCE) something

re·or·ga·nize /riˈɔrgəˌnaɪz/ *v.* [I,T] to arrange or organize something in a new and better way: *The filing system needs to be reorganized.* —**reorganization** /riˌɔrgənəˈzeɪʃən/ *n.* [U]

THESAURUS

change, alter, adapt, adjust, modify, reform, restructure, transform, revolutionize
➔ see Thesaurus box at CHANGE[1]

rep /rɛp/ *n.* [C] **1** *informal* someone who represents an organization or a company and its products [= **representative**]: *a sales rep* **2** *slang* REPUTATION

re·pair[1] /rɪˈpɛr/ *n.* **1** [C usually plural, U] something that you do to fix something that is broken or damaged: *They're* ***doing repairs*** *on/to the bridge.* | *The roof is badly* ***in need of repair.*** | *It's damaged* ***beyond repair*** (=so damaged that it cannot be repaired). **2 in good/bad repair** *formal* in good or bad condition

repair

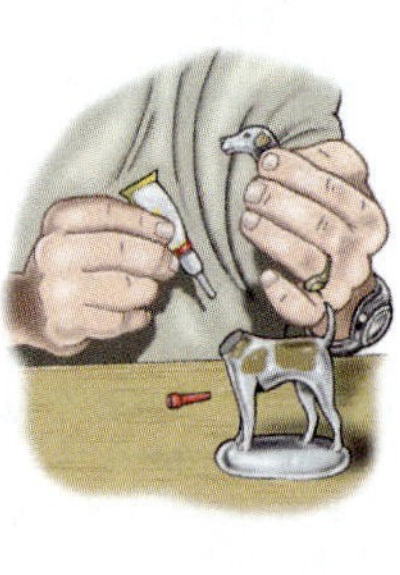

repair[2] *v.* [T] to fix something that is broken or damaged: *I have to* ***get*** *the TV* ***repaired.*** | *Jones had surgery to* ***repair*** *the* ***damage*** *to his knees.*

THESAURUS

fix – to repair something that is broken or not working correctly: *Someone's coming to fix the washing machine.*

mend – to repair a hole in something, especially a piece of clothing: *She was mending a pair of jeans.*

renovate – to repair a building or furniture so that it is in good condition again: *a renovated 19th century hotel*

restore – to repair something so that it looks new: *The church was carefully restored after the war.*

service – to examine a machine or vehicle and repair it if necessary: *I need to take the car in to get it serviced.*

rebuild – to build something again, after it has been damaged or destroyed: *This government aid will help rebuild homes damaged by the storm.*

re·pair·man /rɪˈpɛrmæn/ *n.* [C] someone whose job it is to fix a particular type of thing: *a TV repairman*

rep·a·ra·tion /ˌrɛpəˈreɪʃən/ *n.* [C,U] *formal* payment made to someone for damage, injury, etc. that you have caused: *The government agreed to* ***pay reparations*** *to victims.*

re·pa·tri·ate /riˈpeɪtriˌeɪt/ *v.* [T] to send someone back to his/her own country —**repatriation** /riˌpeɪtriˈeɪʃən/ *n.* [U]

re·pay /riˈpeɪ/ *v.* past tense and past participle **repaid**, third person singular **repays** [T] **1** to pay back money that you have borrowed: *How long will it take to repay the loan?* **2** to show someone that you are grateful for his/her help: *How can I ever repay you?* —**repayment** *n.* [C,U]

re·peal /rɪˈpil/ *v.* [T] to officially end a law: *In 1933, Prohibition was finally repealed.* —**repeal** *n.* [U]

re·peat[1] /rɪˈpit/ *v.* [T] **1** to say or do something again: *Sally kept repeating, "It wasn't me, it wasn't me."* | *You'll have to repeat the class.* | *He's always* ***repeating himself*** (=saying the same thing again).

COMMUNICATION

Ways of asking someone to repeat something
Excuse me?/Pardon (me)?/Sorry?
What? informal
I didn't quite catch that
Could you repeat that?/Would you mind repeating that? formal

2 to say something that you have heard someone else say: *Please don't* ***repeat*** *any of this* ***to*** *Bill.*

repeat[2] *n.* [C] an event that is just like something that happened before: *I don't want to see* ***a repeat performance*** *of last year* (=have the same thing happen).

re·peat·ed /rɪˈpit̬ɪd/ *adj.* done or happening again and again: *her repeated attempts to lose weight* —**repeatedly** *adv.*: *He has repeatedly denied the rumor.*

re·pel /rɪ'pɛl/ *v.* past tense and past participle **repelled**, present participle **repelling** **1** [T] to use force to make someone who is attacking you go away: *Tear gas was used to repel the rioters.* **2** [T] if something repels you, you dislike it a lot and want to avoid it **3** [I,T] *technical* if two things repel each other, they push each other away with a MAGNETIC force

re·pel·lent[1] /rɪ'pɛlənt/ *n.* [C,U] a substance that keeps insects away from you: *mosquito repellent*

repellent[2] *adj.* disgusting: *The sight of blood is repellent to some people.*

re·pent /rɪ'pɛnt/ *v.* [I,T] *formal* to be sorry for something that you have done, especially something that breaks a religious law —**repentance** *n.* [U] —**repentant** *adj.*

re·per·cus·sions /ˌripɚ'kʌʃən/ *n.* [plural] the effects of an action or event, especially bad effects that happen much later: *The collapse of the company will **have repercussions** for the whole industry.*

rep·er·toire /'rɛpɚˌtwɑr/ *n.* [C usually singular] all the plays, pieces of music, etc. that a performer or group can perform

rep·e·ti·tion /ˌrɛpə'tɪʃən/ *n.* [C,U] the act of saying or doing the same thing again, or many times [➡ **repeat**]: *We don't want a **repetition of** last year's disaster.* | *kids learning the times tables **by repetition***

rep·e·ti·tious /ˌrɛpə'tɪʃəs/ *adj.* saying or doing the same thing many times, so that people become bored: *a repetitious speech*

re·pet·i·tive /rɪ'pɛţəţɪv/ *adj.* done many times in the same way: *repetitive exercises*

re·phrase /ri'freɪz/ *v.* [T] to express something in different words so that its meaning is clearer or more acceptable: *Let me **rephrase** the **question**.*

re·place /rɪ'pleɪs/ *v.* [T] **1** to start doing something, or being used instead of another person or thing: *Typewriters have been replaced by computers.* **2** to remove someone from his/her job or something from its place, and put a different person or thing there: *They have **replaced** thousands of full-time workers **with** part-timers.* **3** to buy something that is newer or better in order to use it instead of something that is old or broken: *The tires need to be replaced.* **4** to put something back in its correct place: *Please replace the books when you are finished.*

re·place·ment /rɪ'pleɪsmənt/ *n.* **1** [C] someone or something that replaces another person or thing: *We're waiting for Mr. Dunley's replacement.* **2** [U] the act of replacing something

re·play /'ripleɪ/ *n.* [C] a sports game or particular part of the game that has been recorded and is shown again: *an **instant replay*** (=immediate replay) *of the touchdown*

re·plen·ish /rɪ'plɛnɪʃ/ *v.* [T] *formal* to put new supplies into something, or to fill something again —**replenishment** *n.* [U]

re·plete /rɪ'plit/ *adj. formal* full of something: *a new car **replete with** leather seats*

rep·li·ca /'rɛplɪkə/ *n.* [C] a very good copy of a piece of art, a building, etc.

rep·li·cate /'rɛpləˌkeɪt/ *v.* [T] *formal* to do or make something again, so that you get the same result or make an exact copy: *Scientists are trying to replicate Hudson's experiment.* —**replication** /ˌrɛplə'keɪʃən/ *n.* [C,U]

re·ply[1] /rɪ'plaɪ/ *v.* past tense and past participle **replied**, third person singular **replies** [I,T] to answer someone by saying or writing something: *"Of course," she replied.* | *He never **replied to** our letters.* | *Deagal **replied that** he had not known what would happen.*

THESAURUS
answer, respond
➔ see Thesaurus box at ANSWER[1]

reply[2] *n.* plural **replies** [C,U] something that is said, written, or done in order to reply to someone: *There haven't been any **replies to** the ad.* | *Billy **made** no **reply**.*

re·port[1] /rɪ'pɔrt/ *n.* [C] **1** a written or spoken description of a situation or event, giving people information: *a police **report on** the accident* | *a weather report* **2** a piece of writing in which someone carefully examines a particular subject: *a book report* | *an environmental impact report* **3** *formal* the noise of an explosion or shot

report[2] *v.* **1** [I,T] to tell someone about something, especially in newspapers and on television: *The Daily Gazette reported the story.* | *a journalist **reporting on** the election* **2** [T] to tell someone in authority that a crime or accident has happened: *Three boys were reported missing.* | *Only 4% of burglaries are **reported to** police.* **3 be reported to be/do sth** used in order to say that a statement has been made about someone or something, but you do not know if it is true: *Cummings was reported to be furious.* **4** [I,T] to tell someone, especially your manager, about what has been happening or what you are doing as part of your job: *Each naval station **reports to** an admiral.* **5** [I] to state officially to someone in authority that you have arrived in a place: *Visitors should **report to** reception.* | *One of the soldiers had not **reported for duty**.* **6** [T] to complain officially about someone to people in authority: *A customer reported her to her supervisor.*

report back *phr. v.* to bring someone information that s/he asked you to find: *The committee **reported back to** Congress.*

re'port card *n.* [C] a written statement by teachers about a child's work at school

re·port·ed·ly /rɪ'pɔrţɪdli/ *adv.* according to what

some people say, but when it is not known for certain: *Two soldiers reportedly were injured.*

re,ported 'speech *n.* [U] *technical* in grammar, the style of speech or writing that is used for reporting what someone says, without repeating the actual words. The sentence "She said she didn't feel well" is an example of reported speech.

re·port·er /rɪ'pɔrtə/ *n.* [C] someone whose job is to write or tell about events in a newspaper or on radio or television [➡ **journalist**]: *a newspaper reporter*

TOPIC

editor, **journalist**, **correspondent**, **columnist**
➔ see Topic box at NEWSPAPER

re·pos·i·to·ry /rɪ'pɑzə,tɔri/ *n.* plural **repositories** [C] *formal* a place where things are kept safely: *a repository for nuclear waste*

re·pos·sess /,ripə'zɛs/ *v.* [T] to take back something such as a car or furniture that someone has paid part of the money for because s/he cannot pay the rest of the money

R

rep·re·hen·si·ble /,rɛprɪ'hɛnsəbəl/ *adj. formal* reprehensible behavior is very bad and deserves criticism

THESAURUS

bad, **evil**, **wicked**, **immoral**, **wrong**
➔ see Thesaurus box at BAD[1]

rep·re·sent /,rɛprɪ'zɛnt/ *v.* **1** [T] to do things or speak officially for someone else, or to express his/her views or opinions: *She represents the 5th congressional district of Texas.* | *They want a school board that represents their educational values.* **2** [linking verb] to form or be something: *The talks represent a significant step toward peace.* **3** [T] to be a sign or mark for something else [= **stand for**]: *The green triangles on the map represent campgrounds.* **4** [T] if art represents something, it shows or means a thing or idea: *a painting representing heaven and hell* **5** [T] to describe someone or something in a particular way, especially in a way that is not true: *The author was criticized for the way he represents women.*

rep·re·sen·ta·tion /,rɛprɪzɛn'teɪʃən, -zən-/ *n.* **1** [U] the state of having someone to speak, vote, or make decisions for you: *There is no representation on the council for the Hispanic community.* **2** [U] the state of being present in a place, or of taking part in something: *the representation of minorities among the faculty* **3** [C] something, for example a painting or sign, that shows or describes something else: *The model is a* ***representation of*** *a water molecule.*

rep·re·sent·a·tive[1] /,rɛprɪ'zɛntətɪv/ *n.* [C] **1** someone who is chosen to act, speak, vote, etc. for someone else **2 also Representative** a member of the House of Representatives in the U.S. Congress

representative[2] *adj.* **1** like other members of the same group [= **typical**]: *The sample is* ***representative of*** *the total population.* **2** relating to a system of government in which people elect other people to represent them: *representative democracy*

re·press /rɪ'prɛs/ *v.* [T] **1** to stop yourself from expressing a feeling, remembering something, or doing something you want to do: *Boys learn to repress their need to cry.* **2** to control people by using force

re·pressed /rɪ'prɛst/ *adj. disapproving* having feelings or desires that you do not express: *a sexually repressed man*

re·pres·sion /rɪ'prɛʃən/ *n.* [U] **1** the use of force to control people: *Stalin's repression of religious groups* **2** the action of stopping yourself from feeling an emotion, or the state of having done this

re·pres·sive /rɪ'prɛsɪv/ *adj.* controlling people in a cruel and severe way: *a repressive society*

re·prieve /rɪ'priv/ *n.* [C] **1** a delay before something bad happens or continues: *a* ***reprieve from*** *the pain* **2** an official order that prevents a prisoner from being killed as a punishment [➡ **pardon**] —**reprieve** *v.* [T]

rep·ri·mand /'rɛprə,mænd/ *v.* [T] to tell someone officially that s/he has done something wrong: *He was* ***reprimanded for*** *failing to do his duty.* —**reprimand** *n.* [C,U]

re·pris·al /rɪ'praɪzəl/ *n.* [C,U] a violent action that punishes your enemy for something bad that s/he has done

re·prise /rɪ'priz/ *v.* [I,T] to act the same part again, play the same tune again, etc.

re·proach[1] /rɪ'proʊtʃ/ *n.* **1** [C,U] criticism or disapproval, or a remark that expresses this: *The reproach in her voice made me pause.* **2 above/beyond reproach** impossible to criticize [= **perfect**]: *The actions of the police should be above reproach.*

reproach[2] *v.* [T] to criticize someone and try to make him/her sorry for doing something: *His daughter* ***reproached*** *him* ***for*** *not telling her the truth.* —**reproachful** *adj.*

re·pro·duce /,riprə'dus/ *v.* **1** [I,T] to produce young plants or animals: *Most fish reproduce by laying eggs.* **2** [T] to make a copy of something: *The colors were difficult to reproduce.*

re·pro·duc·tion /,riprə'dʌkʃən/ *n.* **1** [U] the act or process of producing babies, young animals, or plants: *sex and reproduction* **2** [C,U] the act of copying something such as a book or painting, or the copy itself: *a reproduction of Homer's painting*

re·pro·duc·tive /,riprə'dʌktɪv/ *adj.* relating to the process of producing babies, young animals, or plants: *the reproductive system of mammals*

re·prove /rɪ'pruv/ *v.* [T] *formal* to criticize someone for doing something bad

rep·tile /'rɛptaɪl, 'rɛptl/ *n.* [C] a type of animal, such as a snake or LIZARD, that lays eggs, and whose body temperature changes according to the temperature around it —**reptilian** /rɛp'tɪliən/ *adj.*

re·pub·lic /rɪ'pʌblɪk/ *n.* [C] a country governed by elected representatives and led by a president [➡ **monarchy**]

THESAURUS

democracy, **monarchy**, **regime**, **dictatorship**, **totalitarian country/state**, **police state**
➔ see Thesaurus box at GOVERNMENT

re·pub·li·can[1] /rɪ'pʌblɪkən/ *adj.* **1 Republican** relating to or supporting the Republican Party of the U.S. [➡ **Democratic**]: *a Republican candidate for the Senate* **2** relating to or supporting a system of government that is not led by a king or queen and is elected by the people: *a republican system of government* —**Republicanism** *n.* [U]

republican[2] *n.* [C] **1 Republican** a member or supporter of the Republican Party of the U.S. [➡ **Democrat**] **2** someone who believes in government by elected representatives only, with no king or queen

Re'publican ˌParty *n.* **the Republican Party** one of the two main political parties of the U.S. [➡ **Democratic Party**]

re·pu·di·ate /rɪ'pyudiˌeɪt/ *v.* [T] *formal* to refuse to accept or continue with something, especially because you disagree strongly with it [= **reject**]: *The senator repudiated attacks on the candidate's patriotism.* —**repudiation** /rɪˌpyudi'eɪʃən/ *n.* [U]

re·pug·nance /rɪ'pʌgnəns/ *n.* [U] *formal* a feeling of strong dislike [= **disgust**]

re·pug·nant /rɪ'pʌgnənt/ *adj.* *formal* very unpleasant and offensive: *Slavery is* ***morally repugnant****.*

re·pulse /rɪ'pʌls/ *v.* [T] **1** if something or someone repulses you, you think that he, she, or it is so unpleasant that it makes you feel sick: *The terrorist attacks repulsed the nation.* **2** to defeat a military attack

re·pul·sion /rɪ'pʌlʃən/ *n.* **1** [singular, U] a sick feeling that you get from seeing or thinking about something extremely unpleasant [= **revulsion**] **2** [U] *technical* the electric or MAGNETIC force by which one object pushes another one away from it

re·pul·sive /rɪ'pʌlsɪv/ *adj.* extremely unpleasant, so that you almost feel sick: *a repulsive, oily man*

rep·u·ta·ble /'rɛpyət̬əbəl/ *adj.* respected for being honest and doing good work: *a reputable construction company*

rep·u·ta·tion /ˌrɛpyə'teɪʃən/ *n.* [C] the opinion that people have of someone or something because of what has happened in the past: *Denver has a* ***reputation as*** *a livable city.* | *a* ***reputation for*** *honesty*

re·pute /rɪ'pyut/ *n.* [U] *formal* reputation: *a pianist* ***of*** *great* ***repute***

re·put·ed /rɪ'pyut̬ɪd/ *adj.* *formal* according to what most people think or say: *He* ***is reputed to be*** *a millionaire.* —**reputedly** *adv.*

re·quest[1] /rɪ'kwɛst/ *n.* [C] the act of asking for something politely or formally: *a* ***request for*** *more funding* | *Aladdin* ***made a request*** *of the genie.* | *a* ***formal/polite/written request*** | *Drinks are available* ***on request*** (=if you ask for them).

request[2] *v.* [T] to ask for something politely or formally: *She* ***requested that*** *everyone attend a meeting at 2 p.m.* | *Harris* ***requested permission/information/aid****.*

THESAURUS

ask, **order**, **demand**, **beg**
➔ see Thesaurus box at ASK

R

req·ui·em /'rɛkwiəm/ *n.* [C,U] a Christian ceremony of prayers for someone who has died, or a piece of music written for this ceremony

re·quire /rɪ'kwaɪɚ/ *v.* [T] **1** to need something: *The program requires 16 megabytes of memory.* ➔ see Thesaurus box at NEED[1] **2** *formal* to demand officially that someone do something because of a law or rule: *Doctors are* ***required to*** *report certain serious diseases.*

re·quire·ment /rɪ'kwaɪɚmənt/ *n.* [C] **1** something that someone needs or asks for: *The refugees' main requirements are for food and shelter.* | *a vitamin pill that* ***meets*** *all your daily* ***requirements*** **2** something that must be done because of a rule or law: *English 4 is a* ***requirement for*** *English majors* (=they must take this class). | *the* ***legal requirements*** *regarding marriage*

req·ui·site /'rɛkwəzɪt/ *adj.* *formal* needed for a particular purpose

req·ui·si·tion /ˌrɛkwə'zɪʃən/ *n.* [C,U] *formal* an official demand to have something, usually made by the army —**requisition** *v.* [T]

re·route /ri'raʊt, ri'rut/ *v.* [T] to make vehicles, aircraft, etc. go a different way from the way they usually go: *Traffic has been rerouted across the bridge.*

re·run /'rirʌn/ *n.* [C] a television program or a movie that is being shown again: *a rerun of "Cheers"* —**rerun** /ri'rʌn/ *v.* [T]

re·sale /'riseɪl/ *n.* [U] the state of being sold again: *the* ***resale value*** *of the house*

re·scind /rɪ'sɪnd/ *v.* [T] to officially end a law, agreement, or decision

rescue

a mountain rescue

res·cue[1] /ˈreskyu/ *v.* [T] to save someone or something from harm or danger: *Survivors of the crash were rescued by helicopter.* | *He rescued two people **from** the fire.* —**rescuer** *n.* [C]

rescue[2] *n.* [C,U] an act of saving someone or something from harm or danger: *a **rescue mission/operation*** | *A nearby boat **came to the rescue*** (=saved or helped someone).

re·search[1] /ˈrisɚtʃ, rɪˈsɚtʃ/ *n.* [U] serious study of a subject that is intended to discover new facts about it: *scientific **research on/into** heart disease* | *Holmes is **doing research*** (=finding information) *for a book on the Middle Ages.*

re·search[2] /rɪˈsɚtʃ, ˈrisɚtʃ/ *v.* [I,T] to study a subject in detail, in order to discover new facts about it: *a psychologist researching the causes of teen suicide* —**researcher** *n.* [C]

re·sem·blance /rɪˈzɛmbləns/ *n.* [C,U] if there is a resemblance between two things or people, they are similar to each other: *There's a slight **resemblance between** Mike and his cousin* (=they look like each other).

re·sem·ble /rɪˈzɛmbəl/ *v.* [T] to look like, or be similar to, someone or something: *She resembles her mother in many ways.*

re·sent /rɪˈzɛnt/ *v.* [T] to feel angry and upset about something that you think is unfair: *The new rules were **bitterly/deeply resented** by the students.*

re·sent·ful /rɪˈzɛntfʊl/ *adj.* feeling angry and upset about something that you think is unfair: *a resentful look*

re·sent·ment /rɪˈzɛntˀmənt/ *n.* [U] a feeling of anger about something that you think is unfair

res·er·va·tion /ˌrɛzɚˈveɪʃən/ *n.* **1** [C] an arrangement that you make so that a place in a hotel, on an airplane, etc. is kept for you to use: *a plane reservation* | *Have you **made reservations** at the restaurant yet?* **2** [C,U] a feeling of doubt because you do not agree completely with a plan, idea, etc.: *They **have** serious **reservations about** the proposal.* **3** [C] an area of land in the U.S. that is kept separate, especially an area for Native Americans to live on

re·serve[1] /rɪˈzɚv/ *v.* [T] **1** to arrange for a place in a hotel, on an airplane, etc. to be kept for you to use: *I'd like to reserve a table for 8:00.* **2** to keep something separate so that it can be used for a particular purpose: *a parking space **reserved for** the disabled*

> **THESAURUS**
> **keep, store, save, file, collect**
> ➔ see Thesaurus box at KEEP[1]

reserve[2] *n.* **1** [C usually plural] an amount of something that is kept to be used if it is needed: *oil reserves* | *A month's supply of food is **kept in reserve** for emergencies.* **2** [U] the quality of not liking to express your emotions or talk about your problems [➡ **shyness**]: *John's natural reserve* **3** [C] an area of land where wild animals, plants, etc. are protected: *a wetlands reserve* **4** [U] **also reserves** a military force that a country has in addition to its usual army

re·served /rɪˈzɚvd/ *adj.* not liking to express your emotions or talk about your problems: *a quiet, reserved man*

> **THESAURUS**
> **shy, timid, bashful, introverted, withdrawn, antisocial, retiring**
> ➔ see Thesaurus box at SHY[1]

res·er·voir /ˈrɛzəˌvwɑr, -zɚ-, -ˌvwɔr/ *n.* [C] **1** a special lake where water is stored to be used by people in a city **2** a large amount of something that has not been used yet: *a reservoir of oil beneath the desert*

re·shuf·fle /riˈʃʌfəl/ *v.* [T] to REORGANIZE something

re·side /rɪˈzaɪd/ *v.* [I] *formal* to live in a particular place

res·i·dence /ˈrɛzədəns/ *n. formal* **1** [C] the place where you live: *a private residence*

> **THESAURUS**
> **home, place, house**
> ➔ see Thesaurus box at HOME[4]

2 [U] the state of living in a place **3 in residence** living or working in a place: *the job of poet in residence at UCLA*

res·i·den·cy /ˈrɛzədənsi/ *n.* [U] **1** a period of time during which a doctor receives special training in a particular type of medicine **2** the state of living in a place, or legal permission to live in a country: *After five years of residency, you may apply for citizenship.*

res·i·dent /ˈrɛzədənt/ *n.* [C] **1** someone who lives in a particular place: *a park for local residents* **2** a doctor working at a hospital where s/he is being trained —**resident** *adj.*

res·i·den·tial /ˌrɛzəˈdɛnʃəl◂/ *adj.* a residential area consists of private houses, with no offices or businesses: *a quiet, residential neighborhood*

re·sid·u·al /rɪˈzɪdʒuəl/ *adj. formal* remaining after a process, event, etc. is finished: *the residual effects of radiation exposure*

res·i·due /ˈrɛzəˌdu/ *n.* [C,U] a substance that remains after something else has disappeared or been removed: *an oily residue*

re·sign /rɪˈzaɪn/ *v.* [I,T] **1** to officially leave your job or position [➡ **quit**]: *Burton* ***resigned from*** *the company yesterday.*

THESAURUS

quit, **give notice**
➔ see Thesaurus box at QUIT

2 resign yourself to (doing) sth to accept something that is unpleasant but cannot be changed: *I resigned myself to paying the fees.*

res·ig·na·tion /ˌrɛzɪgˈneɪʃən/ *n.* **1** [C,U] the act of resigning, or a written statement to say you are doing this: *Morris* ***handed in/submitted*** *his* ***resignation*** (=give his resignation to the manager). **2** [U] the feeling of accepting an unpleasant situation that you cannot change: *I could hear the resignation in his voice.*

re·signed /rɪˈzaɪnd/ *adj.* accepting an unpleasant situation that you cannot change, or showing that you feel this: *patients who seem* ***resigned to*** *the pain* | *a resigned voice/look*

re·sil·ient /rɪˈzɪliənt/ *adj.* **1** able to become strong, happy, or successful again after a difficult situation or event: *a resilient economy* **2** strong and not easily damaged by being pulled, pressed, etc.: *resilient materials* —**resilience** *n.* [U]

res·in /ˈrɛzən/ *n.* **1** [U] a thick sticky liquid that comes from some trees **2** [C,U] a chemical substance used for making plastics

re·sist /rɪˈzɪst/ *v.* **1** [I,T] to stop yourself from having something that you like or doing something that you want to do: *I* ***couldn't resist*** *the temptation to peek.* | *Carter found their offer* ***hard/difficult to resist.*** **2** [I,T] to not accept changes, or to try to prevent changes from happening: *People generally resist change.* **3** [I,T] to use force to stop something from happening: *The suspect resisted arrest.* | *I pulled her to me and she did not resist.* **4** [T] to not be changed or harmed by something: *Vitamin C is supposed to help you resist colds.*

re·sist·ance /rɪˈzɪstəns/ *n.* **1** [singular, U] a refusal to accept new ideas or changes: *people's* ***resistance to*** *change* | *The plan met with* ***resistance from*** *the U.S. ambassador.* **2** [singular, U] fighting against someone or something: *a resistance fighter* | *The rebels* ***put up*** *fierce* ***resistance.*** **3** [singular, U] the natural ability to avoid the effects of a disease or drug: *Some types of infections have developed a* ***resistance to*** *antibiotics.* **4** [U] *technical* the degree to which a substance can stop electricity from going through it

re·sis·tant /rɪˈzɪstənt/ *adj.* **1** not easily harmed or damaged by something: *flame-resistant pajamas* **2** unwilling to accept something: *companies that are* ***resistant to*** *change*

res·o·lute /ˈrɛzəˌlut/ *adj.* doing something because you feel very strongly that you are right —**resolutely** *adv.*

res·o·lu·tion /ˌrɛzəˈluʃən/ *n.* **1** [C] a formal or official decision agreed on by a group, especially after a vote: *A Congressional resolution allowed the U.S. to enter the war.* **2** [singular, U] the final solution to a problem or difficulty: *a peaceful* ***resolution to*** *the conflict* **3** [C] a promise that you make to yourself to do something: *Have you made any* ***New Year's resolutions?*** **4** [U] the quality of having strong beliefs and determination: *his resolution to continue*

re·solve[1] /rɪˈzɑlv/ *v.* **1** [T] to find an answer to a problem or a way of dealing with it: *The training helps children resolve conflicts without fighting.* | *We're hoping they'll* ***resolve*** *their* ***differences*** (=stop arguing and become friendly again) *soon.* **2** [I] to make a definite decision to do something: *I* ***resolved to*** *lose weight.*

THESAURUS

decide, **make up your mind**, **choose**
➔ see Thesaurus box at DECIDE

3 [I,T] to make a formal decision to do something, especially by voting

resolve[2] *n.* [U] *formal* strong determination to succeed in doing something

res·o·nant /ˈrɛzənənt/ *adj.* having a deep clear loud sound that continues for a long time: *a resonant voice* —**resonance** *n.* [U]

res·o·nate /ˈrɛzəˌneɪt/ *v.* [I] **1** to make a deep clear loud sound that continues for a long time **2** if an event or idea resonates with people, it seems important to them or means a lot to them

re·sort[1] /rɪˈzɔrt/ *n.* **1** [C] a place where many people can go for a vacation, with hotels, swimming pools, etc.: *a beach resort* **2 last resort** what you will do if everything else fails: ***As a last resort,*** *doctors will try an experimental drug.*

resort[2] *v.*

resort to sth *phr. v.* to do something or use something in order to succeed, even if it is bad: *Police fear the demonstrators will resort to violence.*

re·sound /rɪˈzaʊnd/ *v.* [I] **1** to be full of sound: *The room* ***resounded with*** *laughter.* **2** if a sound resounds, it continues loudly and clearly for a long time

re·sound·ing /rɪˈzaʊndɪŋ/ *adj.* **1** a resounding noise is loud and clear: *a resounding crash* **2 a resounding success/victory etc.** a very great and complete success, victory, etc. —**resoundingly** *adv.*

re·source /ˈrisɔrs, rɪˈsɔrs/ *n.* **1** [C usually plural] something such as land, minerals, or natural energy that exists in a country and can be used in order to increase its wealth: *a country rich in* ***natural resources*** **2** [C] something that can be used in order to make a job or activity easier: *an electronic resource for lesson plans* **3 resources**

R

[plural] all the money, property, skills, etc. that you have available to use: *the organization's financial resources* ➔ HUMAN RESOURCES

re·source·ful /rɪ'sɔrsfəl/ *adj.* good at finding ways to deal with problems effectively —**resourcefulness** *n.* [U]

re·spect[1] /rɪ'spɛkt/ *n.* **1** [U] the attitude of believing that something or someone is important, and so being careful not to be rude or not to harm him, her, or it [≠ **disrespect**]: *In Japan, people* ***show*** *more* ***respect to*** *the elderly.* | *These kids* ***have*** *no* ***respect for*** *other people's property.* | ***Out of respect for*** *the flag, you should stand.* **2** [U] admiration for someone because of his/her knowledge, skill, personal qualities, etc.: *I* ***have*** *a lot of* ***respect for*** *this team.* | *Earhart had* ***earned the respect of*** *the other pilots.* **3 in one respect/in some respects/in every respect** used in order to say that something is true in one way, some ways, or in every way: *In some respects, very little has changed.* **4 respects** [plural] *formal* polite greetings: ***Give my respects to*** *your parents.* **5 pay your (last/final) respects** to go to a funeral to show that you liked and respected someone **6 with (all due) respect** *formal* used before disagreeing with someone when you want to be polite: *With all due respect, I don't think that will work.* **7 with respect to sth** *formal* relating to a particular thing, or relating to something that has just been mentioned [= **regarding**]: *The article examines what the Bible says with respect to marriage.*

respect[2] *v.* [T] **1** to admire someone because of his/her knowledge, skill, personal qualities, etc.: *The students like and respect him.*

> **THESAURUS**
> **admire, look up to, idolize**
> ➔ see Thesaurus box at ADMIRE

2 to be careful not to do anything against someone's wishes, rights, etc.: *Parents should respect a teenager's need for privacy.* | *When traveling abroad, I always try to respect local customs.* **3 respect the law/Constitution etc.** to be careful not to disobey the law, Constitution, etc.

re·spect·a·ble /rɪ'spɛktəbəl/ *adj.* **1** showing standards of behavior or appearance that people approve of and admire: *a respectable family* **2** good or satisfactory: *She jumped a respectable five and a half feet.* —**respectably** *adv.* —**respectability** /rɪˌspɛktə'bɪləṭi/ *n.* [U]

re·spect·ed /rɪ'spɛktɪd/ *adj.* admired by many people because of your work, skills, etc.: *a* ***highly/widely respected*** *musician*

re·spect·ful /rɪ'spɛktfəl/ *adj.* feeling or showing respect [≠ **disrespectful**] —**respectfully** *adv.*

re·spec·tive /rɪ'spɛktɪv/ *adj.* people's respective jobs, houses, etc. are the separate ones that each of them has: *the two sisters and their respective husbands*

re·spec·tive·ly /rɪ'spɛktɪvli/ *adv.* each separately in the order mentioned: *The dollar and yen rose 2% and 3% respectively.*

res·pi·ra·tion /ˌrɛspə'reɪʃən/ *n.* [U] *technical* the process of breathing ➔ ARTIFICIAL RESPIRATION

res·pi·ra·tor /'rɛspəˌreɪṭɚ/ *n.* [C] a piece of equipment that covers the nose and mouth and helps someone to breathe

res·pira·to·ry /'rɛsprəˌtɔri/ *adj. technical* relating to breathing: *the respiratory system*

res·pite /'rɛspɪt/ *n.* [singular, U] a short time when something bad stops happening: *a brief* ***respite from*** *the rain*

re·splend·ent /rɪ'splɛndənt/ *adj. formal* very beautiful in appearance, in a way that looks expensive

re·spond /rɪ'spɑnd/ *v.* **1** [I] to react to something that has been said or done: *Engine Company 29* ***responded to*** *the fire.* | *The Federal Reserve* ***responded by*** *raising interest rates.* **2** [I,T] to say or write something as a reply: *He* ***responded that*** *he didn't want to see her.* | *The mayor's office has not* ***responded to*** *requests for comments.*

> **THESAURUS**
> **answer, reply**
> ➔ see Thesaurus box at ANSWER[1]

3 [I] to improve as a result of a particular medical treatment: *Her cancer is* ***responding*** *well* ***to*** *the drugs.*

re·sponse /rɪ'spɑns/ *n.* [C,U] something that is said, written, or done as a reaction or reply to something else: *"No," Thompson said* ***in response to*** *the question.* | *We've had a good* ***response to*** *our appeal for help.*

re·spon·si·bil·i·ty /rɪˌspɑnsə'bɪləṭi/ *n.* plural **responsibilities** **1** [U] a duty to be in charge of or take care of something: *Do you think he's ready for more responsibility?* | *It's your* ***responsibility to*** *inform us of any changes.* | *The students* ***take responsibility for*** *planning their projects.* | *The federal government* ***has responsibility for*** *enforcing immigration laws.* **2** [C] something that you have a duty to do, be in charge of, or take care of: *a single parent trying to balance work and family responsibilities* **3** [U] blame for something bad: *No one has* ***accepted/taken responsibility for*** *the bombing.*

re·spon·si·ble /rɪ'spɑnsəbəl/ *adj.* **1** if you are responsible for something bad, it is your fault: *the people* ***responsible for*** *the mail bombs* | *Can parents be* ***held responsible*** *when their children commit a crime?* **2** in charge of or taking care of something: *The Forest Service is* ***responsible for*** *fighting fires in national forests.* | *Mills is responsible for a budget of over $5 million.* **3** sensible and able to be trusted: *a responsible young man* **4 responsible job/position/post** a job in which the ability to make good judgments and decisions is needed **5 be responsible to sb** if you are responsible to someone, that person is in charge of your work and you must explain your actions to him/her

re·spon·si·bly /rɪ'spɑnsəbli/ *adv.* in a sensible way that makes people trust you: *Are reporters acting responsibly?*

re·spon·sive /rɪ'spɑnsɪv/ *adj.* **1** reacting quickly, in a useful or helpful way: *a company that is* ***responsive to*** *your business needs* **2** able or eager to communicate with people, and to react to them in a positive way: *a happy and responsive baby* —**responsiveness** *n.* [U]

rest¹ /rɛst/ *n.* **1 the rest** the part of a group, thing, etc. that is left after everything else has been used, dealt with, etc.: *I'll read you the rest tomorrow night.* | *Each child does a dance while the rest watch.* | *He will have to take the medication for* ***the rest of*** *his life.* **2** [C,U] a period of time when you can relax or sleep: *You'd better* ***get some rest.*** **3 put/set sb's mind at rest** to make someone feel less anxious or worried **4 come to rest** to stop moving: *The ball came to rest near the hole.* **5 lay/put sth to rest** to stop people from believing, talking, or worrying about something: *He has put to rest speculation that he would run for president.* **6 at rest** *technical* not moving **7** [C] a period of silence of a particular length in a piece of music, or the written sign that shows this

rest² *v.* **1** [I] to stop doing something and relax or sleep for a period of time: *I usually rest for a while after lunch.* **2 rest your feet/legs/eyes etc.** to stop using a part of your body for a period of time because it is feeling sore or tired: *The snow is so bright you have to close your eyes to rest them.* **3** [T] to support an object or part of your body by putting it on or against something: *The baby* ***rested*** *his head* ***on*** *my shoulder.* | *His briefcase* ***rested against*** *his chair.*

> **THESAURUS**
>
> **lean**, **stand**, **prop**
> ➔ see Thesaurus box at LEAN¹

4 rest assured (that) *formal* used in order to tell someone not to worry because what you say is true: *You can rest assured that we'll do all we can.* **5 sb will not rest until...** *literary* if someone will not rest until something happens, s/he will not be satisfied until it happens **6** [I] if a dead person rests somewhere, s/he is buried there: *My mother, may she* ***rest in peace****, is buried there.*

rest on/upon sth *phr. v. formal* to depend on or be based on something: *Their chance at going to the playoffs rests on this game.*

rest with sb *phr. v.* if a decision rests with someone, s/he is responsible for it: *The final decision rests with the Public Health Service.*

re·state /ri'steɪt/ *v.* [T] to say something again in a different way, so that it is clearer or more strongly expressed: *Jackson restated his intention to retire.* —**restatement** *n.* [C,U]

res·tau·rant /'rɛsˌtrɑnt, 'rɛstəˌrɑnt, 'rɛstərənt/ *n.* [C] a place where you can buy and eat a meal: *a small Italian restaurant*

> **THESAURUS**
>
> **cafe/coffee shop** – a place where you can get drinks, cakes, and small meals
> **fast food restaurant** – one where you can get meals such as hamburgers, french fries, etc.
> **diner** – a restaurant where you can eat cheap and simple food
> **cafeteria** – a place at work or school where you can get a meal which you take to a table yourself

> **TOPIC**
>
> In a restaurant, the **waiter** or **waitress** brings you the **menu** and you choose what you want to eat. The menu may be divided into **appetizers** (=first courses), **main courses/entrées**, and **desserts** (=sweet food eaten at the end). When you have finished your meal, you ask for the **check/bill**. People usually **leave a tip** unless waiter **service** is **included** in the cost.

rest·ful /'rɛstfəl/ *adj.* peaceful and quiet: *a restful weekend*

'rest home *n.* [C] a NURSING HOME

res·ti·tu·tion /ˌrɛstə'tuʃən/ *n.* [U] *formal* the act of giving back to the owner something that was lost or stolen, or of paying for damage

res·tive /'rɛstɪv/ *adj. formal* bored or not satisfied with your situation, and wanting it to change

rest·less /'rɛstlɪs/ *adj.* **1** unable to keep still, especially because you are nervous or bored: *The kids have been inside all day, and they're* ***getting restless.*** **2** not satisfied and wanting new experiences: *a restless man, always changing jobs* —**restlessness** *n.* [U] —**restlessly** *adv.*

re·store /rɪ'stɔr/ *v.* [T] **1** to make something exist again or return to its former state: *The army was called in to* ***restore order.*** | *ways to* ***restore*** *her* ***confidence*** **2** to repair something so that it is in its original condition: *They're restoring a Victorian house.*

> **THESAURUS**
>
> **repair**, **fix**, **mend**, **renovate**, **service**, **rebuild**
> ➔ see Thesaurus box at REPAIR²

3 *formal* to give something back to someone: *The change in the law will* ***restore*** *benefits* ***to*** *legal immigrants.* —**restoration** /ˌrɛstə'reɪʃən/ *n.* [C,U] *a building in need of restoration*

re·strain /rɪ'streɪn/ *v.* [T] **1** to prevent someone from doing something, often by using physical force: *They attacked a policeman who tried to* ***restrain*** *them* ***from*** *driving drunk.* **2** to control something: *Raising prices should restrain consumer spending.*

re·strained /rɪ'streɪnd/ *adj.* behavior that is restrained is calm and controlled

re·straint /rɪ'streɪnt/ *n.* **1** [U] calm and controlled behavior: *He urged the protestors to* ***show***

R

restraint. **2** [C,U] something that controls what you can say or do: *Budget cuts have put **restraints on** public spending.* **3** [C] something that prevents someone from moving freely: *a prisoner in restraints*

re·strict /rɪ'strɪkt/ *v.* [T] to control something or keep it within limits: *The army **restricted** helicopter pilots **to** four hours of flight time per day.*

re·strict·ed /rɪ'strɪktɪd/ *adj.* **1** controlled or limited: *The sale of alcohol is restricted.* **2** only allowed to be seen or used by a particular group of people: *a restricted area*

re·stric·tion /rɪ'strɪkʃən/ *n.* [C,U] a rule or set of laws that limits what you can do or what is allowed to happen: ***restrictions on** cigarette advertising | freedom to travel without restriction*

THESAURUS

rule, **law**, **regulation**, **guidelines**, **statute**
→ see Thesaurus box at RULE[1]

re·stric·tive /rɪ'strɪktɪv/ *adj.* stopping people doing what they want to do: *restrictive trade policies*

R

rest·room /'rɛstrum, -rʊm/ *n.* [C] a room with a toilet, in a public place such as a restaurant or theater: *Employees must wash their hands after **using the restroom**.*

THESAURUS

toilet, **bathroom**, **women's/ladies' room**, **men's room**
→ see Thesaurus box at TOILET

re·struc·ture /ˌri'strʌktʃɚ/ *v.* [T] to change the way in which something such as a business or system is organized —**restructuring** *n.* [U]

THESAURUS

change, **alter**, **modify**, **reform**, **reorganize**, **transform**, **revolutionize**
→ see Thesaurus box at CHANGE[1]

re·sult[1] /rɪ'zʌlt/ *n.* **1** [C,U] something that happens or exists because of something that happened before: *The **end/final result** will be a delicious loaf of bread. | Will more students attend college **as a result of** the tax breaks? | Some teachers already use the system, **with** excellent **results**.*

THESAURUS

consequences – the things that happen as a result of an action, event, etc.: *the tragic consequences of the accident*
effect – a change that is the result of something: *the harmful effects of pollution*
outcome – the final result of a meeting, election, war, etc.: *the final outcome of the talks*
upshot – the final result of a situation: *The upshot of higher interest rates is that products cost more to manufacture.*

2 [C] information or answers that are produced by examining something carefully, especially in a scientific way: *a blood test result | the **results of** the police investigation*

result[2] *v.* [I] to happen or exist because of something: *injuries **resulting from** car accidents*
result in sth *phr. v.* to make something happen: *The fire resulted in the death of two children.*

re·sult·ant /rɪ'zʌltənt, -tˀnt/ *adj. formal* happening or existing because of something else

re·sume /rɪ'zum/ *v.* [I,T] *formal* to start doing something again after a pause: *Thielen hopes to resume his duties soon.* —**resumption** /rɪ'zʌmpʃən/ *n.* [singular, U]

ré·su·mé /'rɛzəˌmeɪ, ˌrɛzə'meɪ/ *n.* [C] a written list and description of your education and your previous jobs that you use when you are looking for a job: *I'll put this job **on** my **résumé**.*

re·sur·face /ˌri'sɚfɪs/ *v.* **1** [I] to appear again: *I… was successful until old back injuries resurfaced.* **2** [I] to come back up to the surface of the water **3** [T] to put a new surface on a road

re·sur·gence /rɪ'sɚdʒəns/ *n.* [singular, U] if there is a resurgence of a belief or activity, it appears again and becomes stronger, after a time when it was not common: *a **resurgence of** racism* —**resurgent** *adj.*

res·ur·rect /ˌrɛzə'rɛkt/ *v.* [T] to bring an old practice, belief, etc. back into use or fashion: *Designers have resurrected the styles of the 1960s.*

res·ur·rec·tion /ˌrɛzə'rɛkʃən/ *n.* **1 the Resurrection** the return of Jesus Christ to life after his death on the cross, which is one of the main beliefs of the Christian religion **2** [U] the act of bringing an old practice, belief, etc. back into use or fashion

re·sus·ci·tate /rɪ'sʌsəˌteɪt/ *v.* [T] to make someone breathe again after s/he has almost died —**resuscitation** /rɪˌsʌsə'teɪʃən/ *n.* [U]

re·tail[1] /'riteɪl/ *n.* [U] the sale of goods in stores to people for their own use [➡ **wholesale**]: *retail stores | a retail price of $16.95* —**retailing** *n.* [U]

retail[2] *v.* **retail for/at sth** to be sold at a particular price in stores: *The wine retails for $8.95 a bottle.*

retail[3] *adv.* if you buy or sell something retail, you buy or sell it in a shop

re·tail·er /'riˌteɪlɚ/ *n.* [C] someone who sells goods to the public, using a store [➡ **wholesaler**]

re·tain /rɪ'teɪn/ *v.* [T] **1** to keep something or to continue to have something: *Steamed vegetables retain more of their flavor. | The Republicans retained control of Congress.* **2** to keep facts in your memory: *She retains most of what she reads.* —**retention** /rɪ'tɛnʃən/ *n.* [U]

re·tain·er /rɪ'teɪnɚ/ *n.* [C] **1** an amount of money that you pay regularly to someone such as a lawyer, so that s/he will continue to work for you **2** a small plastic and wire object that you wear in your mouth to make your teeth stay straight

re·take /ˌri'teɪk/ *v.* past tense **retook** /-'tʊk/ past participle **retaken** /-'teɪkən/ [T] **1** to get control of something again: *Rebels have retaken the city.* **2** to take a test or class again because you failed it before → see Topic box at SCHOOL[1]

re·tal·i·ate /rɪ'tælieɪt/ *v.* [I] to do something bad to someone because s/he has done something bad to you: *Police **retaliated by** using tear gas.*

re·tal·i·a·tion /rɪˌtæli'eɪʃən/ *n.* [U] the act of retaliating: *The shooting appeared to be **in retaliation for** an attack last week.*

re·tard /rɪ'tɑrd/ *v.* [T] *formal* to delay the development of something, or to make something happen more slowly —**retardation** /ˌritɑr'deɪʃən/ *n.* [U]

re·tard·ed /rɪ'tɑrdɪd/ *adj.* less mentally developed than other people. This word is considered by many people to be offensive.

retch /rɛtʃ/ *v.* [I] if you retch, you feel like you are VOMITing but nothing comes out of your stomach

re·think /ˌri'θɪŋk/ *v.* past tense and past participle **rethought** /-'θɔt/ [I,T] to think about a plan or idea again in order to decide if any changes should be made

ret·i·cent /'rɛṭəsənt/ *adj.* not willing to talk about what you know or how you feel —**reticence** *n.* [U]

ret·i·na /'rɛt˺nə/ *n.* [C] the area at the back of your eye that sends an image of what you see to your brain

ret·i·nue /'rɛt˺nˌu/ *n.* [C] a group of helpers or supporters who are traveling with an important person: *a retinue of aides*

re·tire /rɪ'taɪɚ/ *v.* **1** [I,T] to stop working, usually because of old age, or to make someone do this: *Quigley retired from the army in September.*

> **TOPIC**
>
> In the United States, most people retire when they are 65. This is the usual **retirement age**, but some people **take early retirement**. When you retire, you must live on your **pension**, **Social Security**, or your **savings**.
> → PENSION, WORK[1]

2 [I] *formal* to go away to a quiet place: *He **retired to** his room.* **3** [I] *formal* to go to bed

re·tired /rɪ'taɪɚd/ *adj.* retired people have stopped working, usually because they are old: *a retired teacher*

re·tire·ment /rɪ'taɪɚmənt/ *n.* **1** [C,U] the act of retiring from your job: *his **retirement from** the Senate* **2** [singular, U] the period of time after you have retired: *a long and happy retirement*

re'tirement ˌhome *n.* [C] a place where old people can live, where various services are provided such as food, social activities, and medical care [➡ **nursery home**]

re·tir·ing /rɪ'taɪərɪŋ/ *adj.* **1** not wanting to be with other people: *a shy and retiring woman*

> **THESAURUS**
>
> **shy, timid, bashful, reserved, introverted, withdrawn, antisocial**
> → see Thesaurus box at SHY[1]

2 the retiring president/manager etc. a president, etc. who is soon going to RETIRE

re·tort /rɪ'tɔrt/ *v.* [T] to reply quickly, in an angry or humorous way: *"None of your business!" he retorted.* —**retort** *n.* [C]

re·trace /ri'treɪs/ *v.* [T] **1** to go back the way you have come: *I tried to **retrace** my **steps**, but I can't find the campsite.* **2** to repeat exactly the same trip that someone else has made: *The ships retraced Columbus's route.*

re·tract /rɪ'trækt/ *v.* **1** [T] to make an official statement saying that something you said earlier is not true: *He confessed to the crime but later retracted his statement.* **2** [I,T] if a part of something retracts or is retracted, it moves back into the main part —**retraction** /rɪ'trækʃən/ *n.* [C,U]

re·tract·a·ble /rɪ'træktəbəl/ *adj.* a retractable part of something can be pulled back into the main part: *a knife with a retractable blade*

re·treat[1] /rɪ'trit/ *v.* [I] **1** to decide not to do what you have planned because it seems too difficult or not popular: *The president seems to be **retreating from** his pledge to cut taxes.* **2** to move away from a place or person: *He shouted, and the dogs retreated.* **3** to stop being involved with society or other people: *His way of coping is to **retreat into** his own world.* **4** if an army retreats, it stops fighting and moves away from the enemy

retreat[2] *n.* **1** [singular, U] the act of deciding to not do what you had planned because it is too difficult or not popular: *The United States must not **retreat from** its international responsibilities.* **2** [C,U] an army's movement away from the enemy: *Napoleon's **retreat from** Moscow* **3** [C] a place you can go to that is quiet or safe: *a mountain retreat* **4** [C,U] an occasion when you go away from people, especially to pray or study, or the action of doing this: *a weekend retreat for people who do yoga* **5** [singular, U] a movement away from a place or person

re·tri·al /ˌri'traɪl, 'ritraɪl/ *n.* [C] the process of judging a law case in court again: *My lawyer demanded a retrial.*

ret·ri·bu·tion /ˌrɛtrə'byuʃən/ *n.* [singular, U] punishment that is deserved: *Victims are demanding **retribution for** the attacks.*

re·trieve /rɪ'triv/ *v.* [T] **1** to find something and bring it back: *I ran to retrieve the ball.* | *It took four days to **retrieve** all the bodies **from** the crash.* **2** to get back information that has been stored in the memory of a computer —**retrieval** *n.* [U]

re·triev·er /rɪ'trivɚ/ *n.* [C] a type of dog that can

R

be trained to find and bring back birds that its owner has shot

ret·ro·ac·tive /ˌrɛtroʊ'æktɪv/ *adj.* a law or decision that is retroactive is effective from a particular date in the past: *a retroactive pay increase* —**retroactively** *adv.*

ret·ro·spect /'rɛtrəˌspɛkt/ *n.* **in retrospect** thinking back to a time in the past, and knowing more now than you did then: *In retrospect, I should have left him much earlier.*

re·tro·spec·tive /ˌrɛtrə'spɛktɪv/ *adj.* relating to or thinking about the past: *a retrospective look at Capra's movies*

re·turn[1] /rɪ'tɚn/ *v.*
1 GO BACK [I] to go or come back to a place where you were before: *Kevin has just* ***returned from*** *Texas.* | *Are you planning to* ***return to*** *Spain?* | *She didn't return until after 8 o'clock.* ▶ Don't say "return back." ◀
2 PREVIOUS STATE [I] to be in a previous state or condition again: *Her heartbeat* ***returned to*** *normal.* | *Will the Democrats* ***return to*** *power in the next election?*
3 GIVE BACK [T] to give something back, or put something back in its place: *I have to* ***return*** *these books* ***to*** *the library.* | *It didn't fit, so I returned it* (=took it back to the store).
4 HAPPEN AGAIN [I] to start to happen or exist again: *Take two of these pills if the pain returns.*
5 START AGAIN [I] to go back to an activity, discussion, etc. that was stopped or interrupted: *He smiled and* ***returned to*** *his book.* | *Hannah* ***returned to*** *work part-time.*
6 DO STH SIMILAR [T] to react to something someone has done by doing something similar: *Why didn't you return my call?* | *Lisa returned his smile.*
7 return a verdict if a JURY returns a VERDICT, they say whether someone is guilty or not
8 MONEY [T] if an INVESTMENT returns a particular amount of money, that is how much profit it produces

return[2] *n.*
1 GOING BACK [singular, U] the act of going or coming back to a place where you were before: *Jefferson's* ***return from*** *France* | *I want you to have dinner ready* ***on/upon*** *my* ***return*** (=when I come back).
2 GIVING STH BACK [U] the act of giving, putting, or sending something back: *the safe* ***return of*** *the prisoners of war*
3 CHANGING BACK [singular] a change back to a previous state or situation: *We must prevent a* ***return to*** *Communist rule.*
4 STH HAPPENING AGAIN [C] the fact of something starting to happen or to exist again: *the* ***return of*** *spring*
5 STH STARTING AGAIN [singular] the act of starting an activity, discussion, etc. again after stopping for a time: *her* ***return to*** *full-time work*
6 MONEY [C,U] the amount of profit that you get from something: *a big* ***return on*** *his investment*
7 COMPUTER [U] the key that you press on a computer at the end of an instruction or to move to a new line [**= enter**]
8 in return (for sth) in exchange for, or as payment for something: *One student does child care in return for room and board.*
9 STATEMENT [C] a statement or set of figures given as a reply to an official demand: *a tax return*

re·turn·a·ble /rɪ'tɚnəbəl/ *adj.* returnable bottles, containers, etc. can be given back to the store

re·un·ion /ri'yunyən/ *n.* **1** [C] a meeting of people who have not met for a long time: *a high-school reunion* | *a family reunion* **2** [U] the state of being brought together again after a period of being separated: *a day of* ***reunion with*** *friends*

re·u·nite /ˌriyu'naɪt/ *v.* [I,T] to come together again, or to be brought together again after a period of being separated: *The children were* ***reunited with*** *their families.*

Rev. the written abbreviation of **Reverend**

rev[1] /rɛv/ *n.* [C usually plural] *informal* one REVOLUTION of an engine

rev[2] **also rev up** *v.* past tense and past participle **revved**, present participle **revving** [I,T] if you rev an engine, or if it revs, it works faster

re·vamp /ri'væmp/ *v.* [T] *informal* to change something in order to improve it: *a promise to revamp the welfare system*

re·veal /rɪ'vil/ *v.* [T] **1** to show something that was previously hidden: *The curtains opened to reveal a darkened stage.* **2** to make something known that was previously secret: *The giant's wife reveals the secret of the castle.* | *The report* ***revealed that*** *many children were not reading at grade level.*

re·veal·ing /rɪ'vilɪŋ/ *adj.* **1** showing something about someone's character, thoughts, or feelings: *a revealing comment* **2** revealing clothes show parts of your body that are usually kept covered

rev·el /'rɛvəl/ *v.*
revel in sth *phr. v.* to enjoy something very much: *Bobby reveled in my undivided attention.*

rev·e·la·tion /ˌrɛvə'leɪʃən/ *n.* [C,U] a surprising and previously secret fact that suddenly becomes known, or the act of making this fact known: *strange* ***revelations about*** *her past* | ***revelations that*** *two senior officers had lied in court*

rev·el·er /'rɛvələ/ *n.* [C] someone who is enjoying singing, dancing, etc. in a noisy way

rev·el·ry /'rɛvəlri/ *n.* [U] wild noisy dancing, eating, drinking, etc., usually to celebrate something

re·venge[1] /rɪ'vɛndʒ/ *n.* [U] something you do in order to punish someone who has harmed or offended you: *The voters* ***took revenge*** *on election day.* | *He vowed that someday he would* ***get revenge****.*

revenge[2] *v.* [T] to punish someone who has harmed or offended you [➡ **avenge**]

rev·e·nue /ˈrɛvəˌnu/ *n.* [U] **1** money that is earned by a company **2** money that the government receives from tax

re·ver·ber·ate /rɪˈvɚbəˌreɪt/ *v.* [I] **1** if a loud sound reverberates, it is heard many times as it is sent back from different surfaces: *Their voices **reverberated around** the empty church.* **2** to have a strong effect that continues for a long time: *News of the verdict reverberated through the city.* —**reverberation** /rɪˌvɚbəˈreɪʃən/ *n.* [C,U]

re·vere /rɪˈvɪr/ *v.* [T] *formal* to greatly respect and admire someone

rev·er·ence /ˈrɛvrəns/ *adj. formal* respect and admiration [≠ **irreverence**]: *a reverence for tradition* —**reverent** *adj.* —**reverently** *adv.*

Rev·er·end /ˈrɛvrənd, -ərənd/ used in the title of a minister in a Christian church: *Reverend Larson*

rev·er·ie /ˈrɛvəri/ *n.* [C,U] a state of imagining or thinking about pleasant things [= **daydream**]

re·ver·sal /rɪˈvɚsəl/ *n.* [C,U] the act of changing an arrangement, process, or action in order to do the opposite: *a **reversal of** the court's decision* | *Their **role reversal**, in which Mike is the stay-at-home parent, benefits everyone.*

re·verse[1] /rɪˈvɚs/ *v.* **1** [T] to change something, such as a decision, judgment, or process, so that it is the opposite of what it was before: *The court reversed the original ruling.* | *Unions want to reverse the decline in membership.* **2 reverse yourself** to change your opinion or position in an argument **3** [T] to change around the usual order of the parts of something, or the usual things two people do: *As your parents age, you may find yourself reversing roles.* **4** [I,T] to move backward, especially in a vehicle [= **back up**] —**reversible** *adj.*: *a reversible coat*

reverse[2] *n.* **1 the reverse** the opposite: *Some people get sleepy after one drink; for others it's the reverse.* **2 in reverse** done in the opposite way or with the opposite effect: *Welfare is taxation in reverse.* **3** [U] the control in a vehicle that makes it go backward: *I started the car and put it **in reverse**.*

reverse[3] *adj.* opposite of what is usual or to what has just been stated: *She answered their questions in reverse order.*

reˌverse discrimiˈnation *n.* [U] a situation in which a woman or someone from a MINORITY group is chosen for a job, even though s/he is not the best person, because they were unfairly treated in the past [➡ **affirmative action**]

re·vert /rɪˈvɚt/ *v.* **revert to sth** to go back to a previous situation, condition, use, or habit: *Leningrad reverted to its former name of St. Petersburg.* —**reversion** /rɪˈvɚʒən/ *n.* [singular, U]

re·view[1] /rɪˈvyu/ *n.* **1** [C,U] a careful examination of a situation or process: *an urgent **review of** safety procedures* | *the main issue **under review*** (=being considered) | *a review committee* **2** [C] an article that gives an opinion about a new book, play, movie, etc.: *His book got very good reviews.*

review[2] *v.* **1** [T] to examine, consider, and judge a situation or process carefully: *The policy is being reviewed by federal wildlife officials.* **2** [I,T] to write an article describing and judging a new book, play, movie, etc.: *He writes a column reviewing computer software.* **3** [I,T] to prepare for a test by studying books, notes, reports, etc.

re·view·er /rɪˈvyuɚ/ *n.* [C] someone who writes articles that give his/her opinion about new books, plays, movies, etc.

re·vile /rɪˈvaɪl/ *v.* [T] *formal* to express hatred of someone or something

re·vise /rɪˈvaɪz/ *v.* [T] **1** to change your opinions, plans, etc. because of new information or ideas: *Plans for the building are being revised.* **2** to improve a piece of writing

re·vi·sion /rɪˈvɪʒən/ *n.* **1** [C,U] the process of changing something to improve it, especially a piece of writing: *a **revision of** the labor laws* **2** [C] a piece of writing that has been improved

re·vi·tal·ize /riˈvaɪtl̩ˌaɪz/ *v.* [T] to make something become strong, active, or powerful again: *The city has begun to revitalize the downtown area* (=make businesses stronger, rebuild buildings, etc.). —**revitalization** /riˌvaɪtl̩-əˈzeɪʃən/ *n.* [U]

re·viv·al /rɪˈvaɪvəl/ *n.* **1** [C,U] a process in which something becomes active, strong, or popular again: *a **revival of** interest in traditional crafts* **2** [C] a new performance of a play that has not been performed for a long time: *a revival of "Oklahoma!"* **3** [C] **revival meeting** a public religious meeting that is intended to make people interested in Christianity

re·vive /rɪˈvaɪv/ *v.* **1** [I,T] to become conscious, healthy, or strong, or to make someone or something do this: *measures to revive a sagging economy* **2** [T] to bring something back into use or existence: *The workshop will help revive the ancient craft of storytelling.*

re·voke /rɪˈvoʊk/ *v.* [T] to officially state that a law, decision, etc. is no longer effective [= **cancel**]: *Her driver's license has been revoked.*

re·volt[1] /rɪˈvoʊlt/ *v.* **1** [I] to refuse to obey a government, law, etc., often using violence against it [= **rebel**; ➡ **revolution**]: *Rebels in the south **revolted against** the government.* **2** [T] to make you feel sick and shocked [➡ **revulsion**]: *The idea revolted me.*

revolt[2] *n.* [C,U] a refusal to obey a government, law, etc., sometimes expressed by violent action against it: *Henry VIII led England **in revolt** against the Pope.* | *a slave revolt in 1791*

THESAURUS

revolution, **rebellion**, **uprising**, **coup**
→ see Thesaurus box at REVOLUTION

R

re·volt·ing /rɪˈvoʊltɪŋ/ *adj.* extremely unpleasant: *a revolting stench*

THESAURUS

horrible, **disgusting**, **awful**, **foul**, **terrible**, **dreadful**
➔ see Thesaurus box at HORRIBLE

rev·o·lu·tion /ˌrɛvəˈluʃən/ *n.* **1** [C,U] a time when people change a ruler or political system by using force or violence: *the Russian Revolution*

THESAURUS

rebellion – an organized attempt to change the government of a country using violence: *an armed rebellion*
revolt – a refusal to obey a government, law, etc., or an occasion when people try to change the government of a country, often by using violence: *Troops loyal to the President crushed the revolt.*
uprising – an occasion when a large group of people use violence to try to change the rules, laws, etc. in an institution or country: *a popular uprising* (=involving ordinary people, not the army)
coup – an action in which a group of people, especially soldiers, suddenly take control of their country: *The President was deposed in a violent military coup.*

2 [C] a complete change in ways of thinking, methods of working, etc.: *Computer technology has caused a revolution in business practices.* | *the sexual revolution* **3** [C,U] one complete circular movement or spin around a central point [➡ **revolve**]: *The earth makes one* ***revolution around*** *the sun each year.*

rev·o·lu·tion·ar·y[1] /ˌrɛvəˈluʃəˌnɛri/ *adj.* **1** completely new and different: *a revolutionary new treatment for cancer* **2** relating to a political or social revolution: *a revolutionary army*

revolutionary[2] *n.* plural **revolutionaries** [C] someone who joins in or supports a political or social revolution

rev·o·lu·tion·ize /ˌrɛvəˈluʃəˌnaɪz/ *v.* [T] to completely change the way people think or do things: *His work revolutionized the treatment of this disease.*

THESAURUS

change, **alter**, **modify**, **reform**, **reorganize**, **restructure**, **transform**
➔ see Thesaurus box at CHANGE[1]

re·volve /rɪˈvɑlv/ *v.* [I,T] to spin around a central point, or to make something do this: *The wheels began to revolve slowly.* —**revolving** *adj.*: *a revolving door*

THESAURUS

turn, **twist**, **spin**, **go around**, **rotate**
➔ see Thesaurus box at TURN[1]

revolve around sb/sth *phr. v.* **1** to have something as a main subject or purpose: *Jess's life has revolved around basketball.* **2** to move in circles around something: *The moon revolves around the earth.*

re·volv·er /rɪˈvɑlvɚ/ *n.* [C] a type of small gun that you hold in one hand

re·vue /rɪˈvyu/ *n.* [C] a show in a theater that includes singing, dancing, and telling jokes

re·vul·sion /rɪˈvʌlʃən/ *n.* [U] a strong feeling of being sick and shocked

re·ward[1] /rɪˈwɔrd/ *n.* [C,U] something that you get because you have done something good or helpful or have worked hard [➡ **prize**, **award**]: *The police are offering a* ***reward for*** *information.*

reward[2] *v.* [T] to give something to someone because s/he has done something good or helpful or has worked for it: *The students are* ***rewarded for*** *hard work.* | *They* ***rewarded*** *him* ***with*** *a free ticket.*

re·ward·ing /rɪˈwɔrdɪŋ/ *adj.* making you feel happy and satisfied: *a rewarding job*

re·wind /riˈwaɪnd/ *v.* past tense and past participle **rewound** /-ˈwaʊnd/ [I,T] to make a TAPE go back to the beginning

re·work /riˈwɚk/ *v.* [T] to change or improve a plan, piece of music, story, etc.: *He spent some time reworking the last paragraph.*

re·write /riˈraɪt/ *v.* past tense **rewrote** /-ˈroʊt/ past participle **rewritten** /-ˈrɪtˀn/ [T] to write something again using different words in order to make it clearer or more effective —**rewrite** /ˈriraɪt/ *n.* [C]

rhap·so·dy /ˈræpsədi/ *n.* plural **rhapsodies** [C] a piece of music that is written to express emotion, and does not have a regular form

rhet·o·ric /ˈrɛt̬ərɪk/ *n.* [U] **1** speech or writing that sounds impressive, but is not actually sincere or very useful: *slick speeches and political rhetoric* **2** the art of speaking or writing in order to persuade or influence people —**rhetorical** /rɪˈtɔrɪkəl/ *adj.* —**rhetorically** *adv.*

rhe,torical 'question *n.* [C] a question that you ask as a way of making a statement, without expecting an answer

rheu·ma·tism /ˈruməˌtɪzəm/ *n.* [U] a disease that makes your joints or muscles painful and stiff

rhine·stone /ˈraɪnstoʊn/ *n.* [C,U] a jewel made from glass or a rock that is intended to look like a DIAMOND

rhi·noc·er·os /raɪˈnɑsərəs/ **also rhi·no** /ˈraɪnoʊ/ *n.* [C] a large heavy animal with thick rough skin and one or two horns on its nose

rho·do·den·dron /ˌroʊdəˈdɛndrən/ *n.* [C] a large bush with groups of red, purple, pink, or white flowers

rhu·barb /ˈrubɑrb/ *n.* [U] a plant with long thick red stems that are cooked and eaten as a fruit

rhyme[1] /raɪm/ *v.* **1** [I] if two words or lines of poetry rhyme, they end with the same sound:

*"House" **rhymes with** "mouse."* **2** [T] to put two or more words together to make them rhyme: *You can't **rhyme** "box" **with** "backs."*

rhyme² *n.* **1** [U] the use of words that rhyme in poetry, especially at the ends of lines: *Parts of Shakespeare's plays are written **in rhyme**.* **2** [C] a short poem or song, especially for children, using words that rhyme [➡ **nursery rhyme**] **3** [C] a word that ends with the same sound as another word: *I can't find a **rhyme for** "donkey."* **4 no rhyme or reason also without rhyme or reason** in a way that cannot be reasonably explained: *The movie goes from fantasy to romance to horror without rhyme or reason.*

rhythm /ˈrɪðəm/ *n.* [C,U] a regular repeated pattern of sounds in music, speech, etc.: *the **rhythm of** the music*

rhythm and ˈblues *n.* [U] the long form of R & B

rhyth·mic /ˈrɪðmɪk/ *adj.* having rhythm: *a rhythmic swinging motion*

RI the written abbreviation of **Rhode Island**

rib¹ /rɪb/ *n.* [C] **1** one of the 12 pairs of curved bones that surround your lungs, or one of the similar bones in an animal ➔ see picture on page A3 **2** a piece of meat that includes an animal's rib: *beef ribs*

rib² *v.* past tense and past participle **ribbed**, present participle **ribbing** [T] *informal* to make jokes about someone and laugh at him/her, but in a friendly way [= **tease**] —**ribbing** *n.* [U]

ri·bald /ˈraɪbɔld, ˈrɪbəld/ *adj.* ribald jokes, remarks, songs, etc. are humorous and usually about sex

ribbed /rɪbd/ *adj.* having a pattern of raised lines: *a ribbed sweater*

rib·bon /ˈrɪbən/ *n.* **1** [C,U] a long narrow piece of cloth, used for tying things or as a decoration: *a red ribbon in her hair* **2** [C] a colored ribbon that is given as a prize in a competition [➡ **blue ribbon**]

ˈrib cage *n.* [C] the structure of RIBS around your lungs and heart

rice /raɪs/ *n.* [U] a white or brown grain grown in wet fields that is eaten after it has been boiled

ˈrice ˌpaddy *n.* [C] a PADDY

rich /rɪtʃ/ *adj.* **1** having a lot of money or valuable possessions [≠ **poor**]: *one of the richest women in America | a rich and powerful nation | a bright young lawyer who wants to **get rich***

THESAURUS

well-off – fairly rich, so that you can live very comfortably
wealthy – used especially about people whose families have been rich for a long time
prosperous formal – rich and successful
well-to-do – rich and having a high position in society
rolling in it/loaded informal – extremely rich
➔ POOR

2 rich foods contain a lot of butter, cream, or eggs, and make you feel full very quickly [≠ **light**]: *rich desserts* **3** containing a lot of something good: *Oranges are **rich in** vitamin C. | a rich cultural heritage* **4 the rich** people who have a lot of money or valuable possessions **5** very deep, strong, and pleasant: *the rich colors of Brett's illustrations | the rich tone of a cello | the wine's rich flavor* **6** good for growing plants in: *rich soil* **7** expensive and beautiful: *rich silk* —**richness** *n.* [U]

rich·es /ˈrɪtʃɪz/ *n.* [plural] *literary* a lot of money or valuable possessions

rich·ly /ˈrɪtʃli/ *adv.* **1** in a beautiful or expensive way: *a richly colored window | The woman was richly dressed.* **2** in large amounts: *Their efforts were richly rewarded. | a richly forested area* **3 richly deserve** to completely deserve something: *They got the punishment they so richly deserved.*

rick·et·y /ˈrɪkət̬i/ *adj.* a rickety piece of furniture, set of stairs, etc. is in bad condition and is likely to break if you use it

rick·shaw /ˈrɪkʃɔ/ *n.* [C] a small vehicle used in Asia for carrying one or two passengers that is pulled by someone walking or riding a bicycle

ric·o·chet /ˈrɪkəˌʃeɪ/ *v.* [I] if something such as a bullet or a thrown rock ricochets, it changes direction when it hits a surface —**ricochet** *n.* [C]

rid¹ /rɪd/ *adj.* **1 get rid of sb/sth a)** to throw away something you do not want or use: *Get rid of all your old clothes that don't fit.* **b)** to make something that is unpleasant go away, stop happening, or stop existing: *I can't get rid of this cold.* **c)** to make someone leave because s/he annoys you or causes problems: *It can be difficult to get rid of under-performing employees.* **2 be rid of sb/sth** to have gotten rid of someone who annoys you or something that is unpleasant: *He's gone, and I'm glad to be rid of him.*

rid² *v.* past tense and past participle **rid**, present participle **ridding**

rid sb/sth **of** sth *phr. v.* **1** to remove something or someone that is bad or harmful from a place, organization, etc.: *The diet is supposed to rid the body of toxins.* **2 rid yourself of sth** to stop having a feeling, thought, or problem that was causing you trouble: *She's taking classes to rid herself of her Southern accent.*

rid·dance /ˈrɪdns/ *n.* **good riddance** *spoken* said when you are glad that someone or something has gone away

rid·dle /ˈrɪdl/ *n.* [C] **1** a difficult and amusing question that you must guess the answer to **2** a mysterious action, event, or situation that you do not understand and cannot explain: *His disappearance is a riddle.*

rid·dled /ˈrɪdld/ *adj.* **riddled with sth** very full of something, especially something bad or unpleasant: *a street riddled with potholes*

ride¹ /raɪd/ *v.* past tense **rode** /roʊd/ past participle **ridden** /ˈrɪdn/ present participle **riding**

R

1 [I,T] to sit on an animal, especially a horse, or on a bicycle, and make it move along: *He rode his bike to school.* | *In the movies, the bad guys* ***ride on*** *black horses.* **2** [I,T] to travel in a car, train, or other vehicle [➡ **drive**]: *We rode the bus into New York City.* | *Mrs. Turnbull rode in silence.* | *My three-year-old loves to ride the escalators in Bloomingdales.* **3 let sth ride** *spoken* to take no action about something that is wrong or unpleasant: *I didn't like what he was saying, but I let it ride.* **4** [T] *spoken* to annoy someone by continuously criticizing him/her or asking him/her to do a lot of things: *Why are you riding her so hard?*

ride on sth *phr. v.* if something is riding on something else, it depends on it: *The actor's hopes are riding on a small part in Spielberg's new movie.*

ride sth ⇔ **out** *phr. v.* if you ride out a difficult situation or experience, you are not badly harmed by it: *The company managed to ride out the recession.*

ride² *n.* [C] **1** a trip in a car, train, or other vehicle, when you are not driving: *Have you* ***gone for a ride*** *in Peggy's new car yet?* | *a 30-minute* ***train/bus/car etc. ride*** | *Mick* ***gave*** *me* ***a ride*** *to work.* **2** a large machine that people ride on for pleasure at a FAIR or AMUSEMENT PARK: *a new ride at Disneyland* **3** a trip on an animal, especially a horse, or on a bicycle: *a fifteen-mile* ***bike ride*** | *Want to* ***go for a ride****?*

rid·er /'raɪdɚ/ *n.* [C] someone who rides a horse, bicycle, etc.

ridge /rɪdʒ/ *n.* [C] **1** a long area of high land, especially at the top of a mountain: *a ridge overlooking the valley* **2** something long and thin that is raised above the things around it: *There are still ridges and ruts left in the ground by wagon wheels.*

rid·i·cule¹ /'rɪdəˌkyul/ *n.* [U] unkind laughter, or remarks intended to make someone or something seem stupid: *The other children made her an* ***object/target of ridicule****.*

ridicule² *v.* [T] to laugh at a person, idea, etc., or to make unkind remarks about him, her, or it: *At the time, his ideas were ridiculed.*

ri·dic·u·lous /rɪ'dɪkyələs/ *adj.* silly or unreasonable: *That's ridiculous. I never even met him.* | *He looked ridiculous.* —**ridiculously** *adv.*

rid·ing /'raɪdɪŋ/ *n.* [U] the sport of riding horses: *Let's* ***go riding****.*

rife /raɪf/ *adj.* **1 rife with sth** full of something bad: *The office is rife with rumors.* **2** if something bad is rife, it is very common

riff /rɪf/ *n.* [C] a repeated series of notes in popular music

ri·fle¹ /'raɪfəl/ *n.* [C] a long gun that you hold up to your shoulder to shoot

rifle² *v.* [T] to search through a place and steal things from it: *Someone had been* ***rifling through*** *my desk.*

rift /rɪft/ *n.* [C] **1** a serious disagreement: *a growing* ***rift between*** *the two countries* **2** a crack or narrow opening in a large piece of rock, group of clouds, etc.

rig¹ /rɪg/ *v.* past tense and past participle **rigged**, present participle **rigging** [T] **1** to dishonestly arrange or influence the result of an election, competition, etc., or the price that will be charged for something: *The opposition charged that the election had been rigged.* **2 also rig sth ⇔ up** to arrange something so that it will do something in a particular way: *She rigged a mosquito net over the bed.* **3** to provide a ship with ropes, sails, etc.

rig sth ⇔ **up** *phr. v.* to make a piece of equipment, furniture, etc. from objects that you find around you: *He'd rigged up a buzzer by his bed so he could call his wife.*

rig² *n.* [C] **1** a large structure used for digging to find oil **2** *informal* a large TRUCK

rig·a·ma·role /'rɪgəməˌroʊl/ *n.* [singular, U] another spelling of RIGMAROLE

rig·ging /'rɪgɪŋ/ *n.* [U] all the ropes, sails, etc. on a ship

right¹ /raɪt/ *adj.* **1** correct or true [≠ **wrong**]: *Did you get the right answer?* | *You were right – it's really busy tonight.*

THESAURUS

correct – used about answers, facts, etc. that are right: *Is this information correct?*
accurate – used about measurements, descriptions, etc. that are completely right: *Can you give us an accurate description of the man?*
➔ WRONG

2 on the right, which is the side of the body that has the hand most people write with [≠ **left**]: *Make a right turn after the gas station.* | *Raise your right hand.* **3** best or most appropriate for a particular situation or purpose [≠ **wrong**]: *the right choice* | *the right person for the job* **4** morally correct, or done according to the law [≠ **wrong**]: *I'm only trying to do what's right.* | *Was I* ***right to*** *report him to the police?* **5 be in the right place at the right time** to be in a place or position where something useful becomes available or is being offered —**rightness** *n.* [U] ➔ ALL RIGHT

SPOKEN PHRASES

6 that's right said in order to agree with what someone says, to answer "yes" to a question, or when you remember something or are reminded of it: *"You're Steve?" "That's right."* | *"No, it's on Friday." "Oh, that's right."* **7** said in order to check if what you have said is correct: *There's a meeting at two, right?* **8 yeah, right** said when you do not believe what has just been said: *He says, "I'll call you," and I'm like, "yeah, right."* **9** used in order to check that someone understands and agrees with what you have said: *If people are comfortable, they're more likely to talk, right?*

right² *adv.* **1** exactly in a particular position or place: *Shut up, he's* ***right behind*** *you!* | *I left the* *keys* ***right there/here****.* **2** immediately: *Call me back* ***right away****.* | *I need it* ***right now****!* | *It's on* ***right after*** *the six o'clock news.* | *I'll* ***be right there*** (=I am coming now). | *She'll* ***be right back*** (=come back soon). **3** correctly [≠ **wrong**]: *They didn't spell my name right.* **4** toward the right side [≠ **left**]: ***Turn right*** *at the lights.* **5** all the way to something, through something, etc.: *The school is right on the other side of town.* | *You can see right through her bathing suit!* **6 sb will be right with you** used in order to say that someone will come soon to help or talk to you: *Your waitress will be right with you.*

right[3] *n.* **1** [C] something that you are allowed to do or have according to the law or according to moral ideas: *Women didn't* ***have the right to*** *vote until 1920.* | *a defendant's* ***right to*** *a trial* | *the fight for* ***equal rights*** (=rights that are the same for everyone) ➔ CIVIL RIGHTS ➔ HUMAN RIGHTS **2** [singular] the side of your body that has the hand that most people write with, or the direction toward this side [≠ **left**]: *Traffic in England drives* ***on the right****.* | *the door* ***to your right*** **3** [U] behavior that is morally correct: *Teach your kids to* ***know right from wrong*** (=know what is morally correct and what is not). **4 in his/her/its own right** considered alone, without depending on anyone or anything else: *San Jose is a city in its own right, not just a suburb of San Francisco.* **5 have a right to be/do sth** to have a good reason to do something, feel something, expect something, etc.: *Weil* ***has every right to be*** *angry.* | *You* ***have no right to*** *tell me what to do!* **6 the right** in politics, the right are people who believe that the government should not try to change or control social problems or businesses by making too many rules or limits [= **conservative**; ≠ **left**] **7 rights** [plural] legal permission to print or use a story, movie, etc. in another form: ***the*** *movie* ***rights to*** *his new book*

right[4] *v.* [T] **1** to put something back in an upright position: *We righted the canoe.* **2** to correct something: *an attempt to* ***right the wrong*** (=correct something bad that was done) *of discrimination*

'right ˌangle *n.* [C] an angle of 90°, like the angles at the corners of a square —**right-angled** *adj.*

ˌright-'click *v.* [I,T] to press the right button on a computer MOUSE to make the computer do something

right·eous /ˈraɪtʃəs/ *adj.* **1 righteous indignation/anger etc.** strong feelings of anger when you think a situation is not morally right or fair **2** *literary* morally good and fair: *a righteous man* **3** *slang* extremely good —**righteousness** *n.* [U] —**righteously** *adv.*

'right field *n.* [singular] the area in baseball in the right side of the OUTFIELD

right·ful /ˈraɪtfəl/ *adj.* according to what is legally and morally correct: *Racism denied them their rightful place in society.* —**rightfully** *adv.*

ˌright-'hand *adj.* **1** on your right side: *Make a right-hand turn.* **2 sb's right-hand man** the person who supports and helps someone the most, especially in his/her job

ˌright-'handed *adj.* **1** someone who is right-handed uses his/her right hand for most things **2** done with the right hand: *a right-handed punch* —**right-handed** *adv.*

right·ly /ˈraɪtli/ *adv.* correctly, or for a good reason: *The book has rightly been called "an American Classic."* | *The organization decided,* ***rightly or wrongly****, that the problem was limited.*

ˌright of 'way *n.* [U] the right to drive into or across a road before other vehicles

ˌright-'wing *adj.* supporting the political aims of the RIGHT: *a right-wing newspaper* —**right-winger** *n.* [C] —**right wing** *n.* [singular]

rig·id /ˈrɪdʒɪd/ *adj.* **1** rigid methods, systems, etc. are very strict and difficult to change [≠ **flexible**]: *parents who set rigid rules* **2** someone who is rigid is very unwilling to change his/her ideas [≠ **flexible**] **3** stiff and not moving or bending [≠ **flexible**]: *a tent supported on a rigid frame* —**rigidly** *adv.* —**rigidity** /rɪˈdʒɪdəṭi/ *n.* [U]

rig·ma·role /ˈrɪgməˌroʊl/ *n.* [singular, U] a set of actions that seems silly: *the rigmarole of filling out all these forms*

rig·or /ˈrɪgɚ/ *n.* **1** [U] the action of taking great care and being thorough in making sure that something is correct: *students who lack intellectual rigor* **2 the rigors of sth** the problems and difficulties of a situation: *the rigors of a Canadian winter*

rig·or mor·tis /ˌrɪgɚ ˈmɔrṭɪs/ *n.* [U] the condition in which someone's body becomes stiff after s/he dies

rig·or·ous /ˈrɪgərəs/ *adj.* **1** careful and thorough: *rigorous safety checks* **2** very strict or severe: *rigorous education standards* —**rigorously** *adv.*

rile /raɪl/ **also rile up** *v.* [T] *informal* to make someone very angry

rim /rɪm/ *n.* [C] **1** the outside edge of something, especially something circular such as a glass: *the rim of the Grand Canyon*

> **THESAURUS**
>
> **edge, border, margin**
> ➔ see Thesaurus box at EDGE[1]

2 -rimmed with a particular type of rim: *gold-rimmed glasses*

rind /raɪnd/ *n.* [C,U] the thick outer skin of some foods or fruits, such as cheese or LEMONS

ring[1] /rɪŋ/ *n.* [C] **1** a piece of jewelry that you wear on your finger: *a* ***wedding ring*** | *a* ***diamond ring*** ➔ see picture at JEWELRY **2** a circular line or mark: *a dirty ring around the tub* **3** an object in the shape of a circle: *a key ring* **4** a group of people or things arranged in a circle: *a ring of young birch trees* **5** a group of people who

R

illegally control a business or criminal activity: *a drug ring* **6** the sound made by a bell, or the act of making this sound: *a ring at the door* ➔ see picture on page A7 **7** a small square area where people BOX or WRESTLE, or the large circular area surrounded by seats at a CIRCUS

ring² *v.* past tense **rang** /ræŋ/ past participle **rung** /rʌŋ/ **1** [I,T] to make a bell make a sound, especially to call someone's attention to you: *Benjy rang the doorbell.* **2** [I] if a bell rings, it makes a noise: *The telephone's ringing.* **3** [I] if your ears ring, they are filled with a continuous sound that only you can hear **4 ring a bell** *informal* if something rings a bell, you think you have heard it before: *Frank Gordon – it rings a bell, but I can't be sure.* **5 not ring true** if something does not ring true, you do not believe it: *None of these explanations rang true.*

ring out *phr. v.* if a voice, bell, etc. rings out, it makes a loud and clear sound: *Shouts rang out from the schoolyard.*

ring sth ⇔ **up** *phr. v.* to press buttons on a CASH REGISTER to record how much money needs to be put inside it: *She rang up our purchases.*

R

ring³ *v.* past tense and past participle **ringed** [T] to surround something: *a house ringed by trees*

ring·lead·er /ˈrɪŋˌlidɚ/ *n.* [C] someone who leads a group that is doing something illegal or wrong

ring·let /ˈrɪŋlɪt/ *n.* [C] a long curl of hair that hangs down

ring·side /ˈrɪŋsaɪd/ *n.* [singular] the area nearest to the performance in a CIRCUS or BOXING match: *a ringside seat*

ring·worm /ˈrɪŋwɚm/ *n.* [U] a common disease that gives you red rough circles on your skin

rink /rɪŋk/ *n.* [C] a building with a specially prepared area with a smooth surface where you can SKATE: *an ice rink*

rinse¹ /rɪns/ *v.* [T] to use running water and no soap in order to remove dirt, soap, etc.: *He used a hose to* ***rinse off*** *the car.* | ***Rinse*** *the lettuce* ***in*** *cold water.*

rinse sth ⇔ **out** *phr. v.* to wash something with clean water but not soap: *Chuck rinsed out his cup.*

rinse² *n.* **1** [C,U] a product used for slightly changing the color of hair: *a brown rinse* **2** [C] an act of rinsing something: *a hot rinse*

ri·ot¹ /ˈraɪət/ *n.* **1** [C] a situation in which a crowd of people behaves in a violent and uncontrolled way: *the* ***race riots*** (=caused by problems between different races of people) *of the late 1960s* **2** [singular] someone or something that is very funny or enjoyable **3 read sb the riot act** *informal* to warn someone angrily that s/he must stop doing something wrong

riot² *v.* [I] if a crowd of people riots, they all behave violently in a public place —**rioter** *n.* [C]

THESAURUS

protest, march, demonstrate, hold/stage a sit-in, go on a hunger strike, boycott
➔ see Thesaurus box at PROTEST²

ri·ot·ing /ˈraɪətɪŋ/ *n.* [U] violent and uncontrolled behavior from a crowd that is out of control: ***Rioting broke out*** *in the city late last night.*

ri·ot·ous /ˈraɪətəs/ *adj.* **1** noisy, exciting, and fun in an uncontrolled way: *the kids cheered with riotous pleasure* **2** noisy, possibly dangerous, and not controlled: *riotous crowds*

RIP Rest in Peace – written on a GRAVESTONE

rip¹ /rɪp/ *v.* past tense and past participle **ripped**, present participle **ripping** [I,T] to tear something or be torn quickly and violently: *Dave ripped his jacket on the fence.* | *Don't pull on it; it'll rip.* | *I ripped a sheet of paper from my notebook.* | *Impatiently, Sue* ***ripped*** *the letter* ***open***.

rip sth ⇔ **apart** *phr. v.* to destroy something by separating it into pieces: *Their family has been ripped apart by the murder.* | *The bomb ripped apart a bus.*

rip into sb *phr. v.* to criticize someone angrily

rip sb/sth **off** *phr. v. spoken* **1** to charge someone too much money for something: *The cab driver tried to rip me off!* **2** to steal something: *Someone ripped off the liquor store.*

rip through sth *phr. v.* to move through a place quickly and violently: *typhoons that rip through the islands*

rip sth ⇔ **up** *phr. v.* to tear something into several pieces: *In frustration, she ripped up her story.*

rip² *n.* [C] a long tear or cut

ripe /raɪp/ *adj.* **1** ripe food or crops are ready to eat: *ripe peaches* **2 be ripe for sth** to be in the right condition for something: *The company is weak and ripe for a takeover.* **3 the time is ripe (for sth)** used in order to say it is the right time for something to happen: *She'll grab for power when the time is ripe.* **4 ripe old age** if you live to a ripe old age, you are very old when you die —**ripeness** *n.* [U]

rip·en /ˈraɪpən/ *v.* [I,T] to become ripe, or to make something do this

rip·off, rip-off /ˈrɪpɔf/ *n.* [C] *spoken* **1** something that is unreasonably expensive, and makes you feel cheated: *Most diet products are a complete ripoff.* **2** a piece of music or art or a movie that copies something else without admitting it

rip·ple¹ /ˈrɪpəl/ *v.* **1** [I,T] to move in small waves, or to make something do this: *a soft breeze rippled the wheat* **2** [I] to make a noise like water that is flowing gently: *water rippling over rocks* **3** [I] to pass from one person to the next like a wave: *Laughter* ***rippled through/around*** *the crowd.*

ripple² *n.* [C] **1** a small low wave on the surface of a liquid: *ripples on the pond* **2** a feeling or sound that spreads through a person or group because of something that happens: *A* ***ripple of*** *laughter ran through the audience.* **3 ripple effect** a situation in which one action causes another, which then causes a third, etc.

rise¹ /raɪz/ *v.* past tense **rose** /roʊz/ past participle **risen** /ˈrɪzən/ present participle **rising** [I]
1 INCREASE to increase in number, amount, quality, or value [≠ **fall**]: *Ocean temperatures are rising.* | *Tourism* ***rose by*** *4% last year.* | *The population has* ***risen steadily/sharply*** *since the 1950s.* | *rising crime/unemployment*

THESAURUS
increase, **go up**, **grow**, **double**, **shoot up**
→ see Thesaurus box at INCREASE¹

2 GO UP to go up [≠ **fall**]: *Smoke rose from the chimney.* | *The tide had risen.*

USAGE
Rise is not followed by an object: *The balloon rose high into the air.*
Raise is always followed by an object: *Raise your hand if you know the answer.*

3 STAND to stand up: *Thornton* ***rose to his feet*** *and turned to speak to them.*
4 BECOME SUCCESSFUL to become important, powerful, successful, or rich: *Presley* ***rose to*** *fame in the 1950s.*
5 VOICE/SOUND to be heard, especially by getting louder or stronger: *The sound of traffic rose from the street below.*
6 SUN/MOON/STAR to appear in the sky [≠ **set**]: *The moon rose over the lake.*
7 EMOTION to get stronger: *You could feel the excitement rising as we waited.*
8 MOUNTAIN/BUILDING to be or seem taller than anything else around: *the skyscrapers that* ***rise above*** *the Manhattan skyline*
9 BREAD/CAKES if bread, cakes, etc. rise, they become bigger as they bake because there is air inside them
10 rise to the occasion/challenge to deal with a difficult situation or problem successfully by doing things better than you have done them before
11 all rise *spoken formal* used in order to tell people to stand up when a judge enters a court of law
12 BED *literary* to get out of bed in the morning
13 AGAINST A GOVERNMENT *literary* **also rise up** to try to defeat the government or army that is in control of your country [= **rebel**]

rise above sth *phr. v.* to be good or wise enough to not let a bad situation or influence affect you: *He rose above his poverty-stricken childhood to become a top lawyer.*

rise² *n.* **1** [C] an increase in number, amount, or value [≠ **fall**]: *a* ***rise in*** *college costs* | *price rises* **2** [singular] the achievement of importance, success, or power [≠ **fall**]: *a book about his* ***rise to fame/power/prominence*** **3 give rise to sth** to be the reason something happens or begins to exist: *The book's popularity gave rise to a number of imitations.* **4** [C] a movement upward: *the rise and fall of her chest as she breathed* **5** [C] an upward slope: *a slight rise in the road* **6 get a rise out of sb** *informal* to make someone annoyed or embarrassed by making a joke about him/her

ris·er /ˈraɪzɚ/ *n.* **1 early/late riser** someone who usually wakes up very early or very late **2 risers** [plural] a set of steps for a group of people to stand on

risk¹ /rɪsk/ *n.* **1** [C,U] the chance that something bad may happen: *the* ***risk of*** *injury to workers* | *There was a* ***risk (that)*** *the herd would stampede.* | *There is no* ***risk to*** *public health.* | *Healthy eating* ***reduces the risk of*** *cancer.*

THESAURUS
danger, **threat**, **hazard**
→ see Thesaurus box at DANGER

2 take a risk/run the risk to do something even though there is a chance that something bad will happen: *The nurses run the risk of infection.* **3 at risk** likely to be harmed or put in a bad situation: *The firm's reputation is at risk.* | *Small children* ***at risk from*** *car airbags.* | *men* ***at risk of/for*** *diabetes* | *people whose lifestyles* ***put*** *them* ***at risk*** *for AIDS* **4 at your own risk** if you do something at your own risk, no one else is responsible if something bad happens: *Parking is at your own risk.* **5** [C] something that is likely to hurt you or be dangerous: *Oily rags are a fire risk.* | *the* ***risk factors*** *for heart disease* (=things that make you likely to get sick) **6** [C] a person or business to whom it is a good or bad idea to give insurance or lend money: *Drivers under 21 are considered poor* ***insurance risks.***

risk² *v.* [T] **1** to put something in a situation in which it could be lost, destroyed, or harmed: *I'm not going to* ***risk*** *my life* ***to*** *save a cat!* | *If she told the police, she risked losing her job.* **2** to do something that you know may have bad results: *She risked a glance back over her shoulder.*

risk·y /ˈrɪski/ *adj.* involving a risk that something bad will happen: *Doctors said that operating*

R

would be too risky. | *Investing in the stock market is* ***risky business*** (=a risky thing to do). —**riskiness** *n.* [U]

ris·qué /rɪsˈkeɪ/ *adj.* a joke, remark, etc. that is risqué is slightly shocking because it is about sex

rite /raɪt/ *n.* [C] **1** a ceremony that is always performed in the same way, often for a religious purpose: *funeral rites* **2 rite of passage** a special ceremony or action that is a sign of a new time in someone's life

rit·u·al¹ /ˈrɪtʃuəl/ *n.* [C,U] a ceremony or set of actions that is always done in the same way: *religious rituals* | *the Christmas ritual of decorating the tree*

ritual² *adj.* **1** done as part of a rite or ritual: *ritual sacrifice* **2** done in a particular, expected way, but without real meaning: *ritual campaign promises*

ritz·y /ˈrɪtsi/ *adj. informal* fashionable and expensive: *a ritzy neighborhood*

ri·val¹ /ˈraɪvəl/ *n.* [C] a person, group, or organization that you compete with: *a business rival*

R

rival² *adj.* **rival company/team/player etc.** a person, group, or organization that competes against you: *rival airlines*

rival³ *v.* [T] to be as good or important as someone or something else: *The band rivaled The Doors as L.A.'s finest rock band.*

ri·val·ry /ˈraɪvəlri/ *n.* plural **rivalries** [C,U] competition over a long period of time: *sibling rivalry* | *the* ***rivalry between*** *the two teams*

river

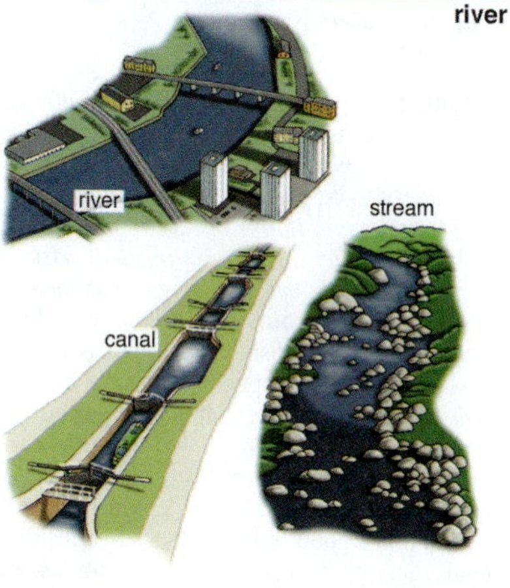

riv·er /ˈrɪvɚ/ *n.* [C] **1** a natural and continuous flow of water in a long line that goes into an ocean, lake, etc.: *the Colorado River* | *trees on the* ***river bank*** (=land on the edge of a river) | *a boat sailing* ***up/down river*** (=in the opposite direction that a river is flowing, or in the same direction) **2** a large amount of moving liquid: *a* ***river of*** *tears*

riv·er·bed /ˈrɪvɚˌbɛd/ *n.* [C] the ground over which a river flows

riv·er·side /ˈrɪvɚˌsaɪd/ *n.* [singular] the land on the sides of a river: *a cottage on the riverside*

riv·et¹ /ˈrɪvɪt/ *n.* [C] a metal pin for fastening flat pieces of metal together

rivet² *v.* [T] **1** to attract and hold someone's attention: *People sat* ***riveted to*** *their TVs during the trial.* **2** to fasten something with RIVETS

riv·et·ing /ˈrɪvət̬ɪŋ/ *adj.* extremely interesting: *a riveting tale of suspense*

R.N. *n.* [C] **registered nurse**

RNA *n.* [U] **ribonucleic acid** an important chemical that exists in all living cells and controls chemical activity in cells [➡ **DNA**]

roach /routʃ/ *n.* [C] a COCKROACH

road /roud/ *n.* **1** [C,U] a specially prepared hard surface for vehicles to travel on [➡ **street, highway**]: *Tom's dad lives just* ***up/down the road*** (=farther along the road). | *the* ***main road*** *out of town* | *a* ***side/back road*** (=a small one that is not used very much) | *the traffic on Mission Road* | *ice* ***on the roads*** (=on all the streets and roads in an area)

THESAURUS

Types of roads

street – a road in a town, with houses or stores on each side
main street – a road in the middle of a town where many stores, offices, etc. are
avenue – a road in a town, often with trees on each side
lane – a narrow road in the country, or one of the two or three parallel areas on a road which are divided by painted lines to keep traffic apart
main road – a large and important road
the main drag informal – the main road through a town
highway – a very wide road for traveling fast over long distances
freeway/expressway – a very wide road in a city or between cities, on which cars can travel very fast without stopping
toll road – a road that you pay to use
turnpike – a large road for fast traffic that you pay to use

2 on the road a) traveling for a long distance, especially in a car: *We've been on the road since 7:00 a.m.* **b)** if a sports team, group of actors, etc. are on the road, they are traveling to different places playing games or giving performances: *Oregon had two losses on the road.* **3 on the road to success/recovery etc.** developing in a way that will result in success, health, etc. **4 down the road** in the future: *That may cause problems further down the road.*

road·block /ˈroudblɑk/ *n.* [C] **1** something that stops the progress of a plan: *Lack of education is a* ***roadblock to*** *success.* **2** a place where the police are blocking the road to stop traffic:

Police ***put/set up roadblocks*** *to catch drunk drivers.*

road·house /ˈroʊdhaʊs/ *n.* [C] a restaurant or BAR on a road outside a city

road·kill /ˈroʊdkɪl/ *n.* [U] *informal* animals that are killed by cars on a road or HIGHWAY

road·run·ner /ˈroʊdˌrʌnɚ/ *n.* [C] a small bird that runs very fast and lives in the southwest U.S.

road·side /ˈroʊdsaɪd/ *n.* [singular] the edge of a road: *a roadside restaurant*

ˈroad trip *n.* [C] **1** a long trip in a car, taken for pleasure **2** an occasion when a sports team travels to other places to play: *a four-game road trip*

road·way /ˈroʊdweɪ/ *n.* [singular] the part of the road that is used by vehicles

roam /roʊm/ *v.* [I,T] to walk or travel for a long time with no clear purpose: *Buffalo roamed the prairie.* | *I spent the summer* ***roaming around/through*** *Europe.*

roar[1] /rɔr/ *v.* **1** [I] to make a deep, very loud noise: *lions roaring* | *Jets roared overhead.* **2** [I] if a vehicle roars somewhere, it moves very quickly and in a noisy way: *Two motorcycles* ***roared down*** *the street.* **3** [I,T] to say something or laugh with a loud voice: *"What are you doing?" he roared.* | *The audience* ***roared with laughter.***

roar[2] *n.* [C] a deep loud continuous sound: *a roar of laughter* | *the roar of the engine*

roar·ing /ˈrɔrɪŋ/ *adj.* **roaring fire** a fire that burns with a lot of flames and heat

roast[1] /roʊst/ *v.* [I,T] to cook meat or vegetables in an OVEN or over a fire

THESAURUS

cook, bake, fry, broil, grill, sauté, boil, steam, deep fry
→ see Thesaurus box at COOK[1]

roast[2] *n.* [C] **1** a large piece of roasted meat **2** an outdoor party at which food is cooked on an open fire: *a hot dog roast* **3** an occasion at which people celebrate someone by telling funny stories and giving speeches about him/her

roast[3] *adj.* having been roasted: *roast beef*

rob /rɑb/ *v.* past tense and past participle **robbed**, present participle **robbing** [T] to steal money or things from a person, bank, etc.: *The boys robbed a convenience store.*

USAGE

Use **rob** to talk about the place or the person that money is taken from: *Someone robbed the bank last night.*
Use **steal** to talk about the things that were taken: *Matt's bike was stolen yesterday.*

THESAURUS

steal, burglarize, rob, mug, shoplift, rip off sth
→ see Thesaurus box at STEAL[1]

rob sb/sth ⇔ **of** sth *phr. v.* to take away an important quality, ability, etc. from someone or something: *A hamstring injury robbed him of his speed.*

rob·ber /ˈrɑbɚ/ *n.* [C] someone who steals things, especially from stores or banks: *a bank robber*

THESAURUS

thief, burglar, shoplifter, pickpocket attacker, mugger, murderer, rapist, offender
→ see Thesaurus box at CRIMINAL[2]

rob·ber·y /ˈrɑbəri/ *n.* plural **robberies** [C,U] the crime of stealing money or things from a person or place: *Most home robberies are drug related.* | *the* ***armed robbery*** (=robbery using a gun) *of a bank*

THESAURUS

theft, burglary, shoplifting, mugging
→ see Thesaurus box at CRIME

robe /roʊb/ *n.* [C] a long loose piece of clothing: *pajamas and a robe* | *a judge's black robe*

rob·in /ˈrɑbɪn/ *n.* [C] a common wild bird with a red chest and brown back

ro·bot /ˈroʊbɑt, -bʌt/ *n.* [C] a machine that can move and do some of the work of a person, and is controlled by a computer: *industrial robots* —**robotic** /roʊˈbɑṭɪk/ *adj.*

ro·bot·ics /roʊˈbɑṭɪks/ *n.* [U] the study of how robots are made and used

ro·bust /roʊˈbʌst, ˈroʊbʌst/ *adj.* strong and healthy, or not likely to have problems: *a robust 70-year-old man* | *robust economic growth*

rock[1] /rɑk/ *n.* **1** [U] a type of stone that forms part of the Earth's surface: *a tunnel cut through solid rock* **2** [C] a large piece of stone: *A ship hit the rocks in the storm.* | *He sat on a rock by the river, fishing.* **3 also rock music** [U] a type of popular modern music with a strong loud beat, played on GUITARS and drums: *a rock band* | *a rock concert*

THESAURUS

pop (music), rock'n'roll, heavy metal, reggae, house (music), hip-hop, rap (music), jazz, classical (music), country (music), folk (music)
→ see Thesaurus box at MUSIC

4 be between a rock and a hard place to have a choice between two things, both of which are unpleasant **5 on the rocks a)** alcoholic drinks that are served on the rocks have ice in them **b)** a relationship or marriage that is on the rocks is failing

rock[2] *v.* **1** [I,T] to move gently, leaning from one side to the other, or to make something do this: *She rocked the cradle until the baby slept.* | *Hilda rocked back and forth, crying.* | *The boat rocked*

R

gently. **2** [T] to make the people in a place feel very shocked or surprised: *a city rocked by violence* **3 rock the boat** *informal* to cause problems for other members of a group by criticizing something or trying to change the way something is done **4 sb/sth rocks** *spoken* said in order to show that you strongly approve of someone or something

ˌrock and ˈroll *n.* [U] another spelling of ROCK'N'ROLL

ˌrock ˈbottom *n.* **hit/reach rock bottom** *informal* to become as bad as something can possibly be: *By June, their marriage had hit rock bottom.*

ˈrock-bottom *adj.* rock-bottom prices are as low as they can possibly be

rock·er /ˈrɑkɚ/ *n.* [C] **1** a ROCKING CHAIR **2 be off your rocker** *spoken* to be crazy

rock·et¹ /ˈrɑkɪt/ *n.* [C] **1** a vehicle used for traveling or carrying things into space, which is shaped like a big tube

> **TOPIC**
>
> **spacecraft**, **spaceship**, **(space) shuttle**, **satellite**, **probe**
> → see Topic box at SPACE¹

R

2 a weapon shaped like a big tube [➡ **missile**]: *They began* ***firing rockets*** *at the ship.* **3** a type of FIREWORK

rocket² *v.* [I] **1** to move somewhere very fast: *Her serve rocketed over the net.* **2** to achieve a successful position very quickly: *The song rocketed to number one in the charts.* **3 also rocket up** if a price or amount rockets, it increases quickly and suddenly: *The company's shares rocketed up 46%.*

ˈrocking chair *n.* [C] a chair that has two curved pieces of wood fixed under it, so that it ROCKS → see picture at SEAT¹

ˈrocking horse *n.* [C] a toy horse for children that ROCKS when you sit on it

rock'n'roll /ˌrɑkənˈroʊl/ *n.* [U] a type of music with a strong loud beat that is played on GUITARS and drums, that first became popular in the 1950s

> **THESAURUS**
>
> **pop (music)**, **rock (music)**, **heavy metal**, **reggae**, **house (music)**, **hip-hop**, **rap (music)**, **jazz**, **classical (music)**, **country (music)**, **folk (music)**
> → see Thesaurus box at MUSIC

rock·y /ˈrɑki/ *adj.* **1** covered with rocks or made of rock: *the rocky coast of Maine* **2** *informal* a relationship or situation that is rocky is difficult and may not continue or be successful: *The team has* ***gotten off to a rocky start*** *this season.*

rod /rɑd/ *n.* [C] a long thin pole or stick: *a fishing rod*

rode /roʊd/ *v.* the past tense of RIDE

ro·dent /ˈroʊdnt/ *n.* [C] one of a group of small animals with long sharp front teeth, such as rats or rabbits

ro·de·o /ˈroʊdiˌoʊ, roʊˈdeɪoʊ/ *n.* plural **rodeos** [C] a competition in which COWBOYS ride wild horses, and catch cattle with ropes

roe /roʊ/ *n.* [C,U] fish eggs eaten as a food

rogue¹ /roʊg/ *adj.* [only before noun] a rogue person or organization does not follow the usual rules or methods and often causes trouble: *The government is concerned about* ***rogue states*** *that may have nuclear weapons.*

rogue² *n.* [C] *old-fashioned* a man who often behaves in a slightly bad or dishonest way, but whom people still like

rogu·ish /ˈroʊgɪʃ/ *adj.* typical of a ROGUE, or behaving like a rogue: *the actor's roguish image*

role /roʊl/ *n.* [C] **1** the position, job, or FUNCTION someone or something has in a particular situation or activity: *The company has* ***played a major/key role in*** *medical research over the years.* | *He has traditional views about the* ***role of*** *women in society.* | *Parents should* ***take an active role*** *in their child's education.* **2** the character played by an actor: *Brendan will* ***play the role of*** *Romeo.* | *Kate has a* ***leading/starring role*** *in the movie.*

ˈrole ˌmodel *n.* [C] someone whose behavior or attitude people try to copy because they admire him/her: *She's a* ***good/bad/positive role model*** *for teenagers.*

ˈrole-play *n.* [C,U] an exercise in which you behave in the way that someone else would behave in a particular situation: *ideas for classroom role-plays* —**role-play** *v.* [I,T]

roll¹ /roʊl/ *v.*

1 ROUND OBJECT [I,T] to move by turning over and over, or from side to side, or to make something do this: *The ball* ***rolled down*** *the street.* | *One of the eggs* ***rolled off*** *the counter.* | ***Roll*** *the chicken breasts* ***in*** *flour.*

> **THESAURUS**
>
> **push**, **poke**, **shove**, **nudge**
> → see Thesaurus box at PUSH¹

2 PERSON/ANIMAL also roll over [I,T] to turn your body over when you are lying down, or to turn someone else's body over: *We tried to* ***roll*** *him* ***onto*** *his side.* | *Beth's dog has been* ***rolling in*** *the mud.*

3 SHAPE OF TUBE/BALL [T] to make something into the shape of a tube or ball: ***Roll*** *the dough* ***into*** *small balls.*

4 STH WITH WHEELS [I,T] to move on wheels, or make something that has wheels move: *The van was starting to* ***roll backwards***. | *The waitress* ***rolled*** *the dessert cart* ***over*** *to our table.*

5 MAKE STH FLAT also roll out [T] to make something flat by moving something round and heavy over it: *Roll the pie crust thin.* → see picture on page A4

6 DROP OF LIQUID [I] to move over a surface

smoothly without stopping: *A tear **rolled down** her cheek.*
7 roll your eyes to move your eyes around and up to show that you think someone or something is stupid
8 WAVES/CLOUDS [I] to move continuously in a particular direction: *We watched the waves **rolling** onto the beach.* | *We could see the fog starting to **roll in**.*
9 GAME [I,T] if you roll DICE, you throw them as part of a game
10 SOUND [I] if a drum or THUNDER rolls, it makes a long deep sound
11 MACHINE/CAMERA [I] if a machine such as a movie camera or a PRINTING PRESS rolls, it operates: *Quiet! The cameras are rolling!*
12 (all) rolled into one including several things in one thing: *The class was a history, art, and language course all rolled into one.*

SPOKEN PHRASES

13 be ready to roll used in order to say that you are ready to do something or go somewhere: *After months of planning, we were finally ready to roll.*
14 let's roll used in order to suggest to a group of people that you all begin doing something or go somewhere
15 be rolling in money/dough/cash/it to have or earn a lot of money

roll around *phr. v. informal* if a regular time or event rolls around, it arrives or happens again: *By the time Friday night rolled around, we were too tired to go out.*
roll sth ⇔ **back** *phr. v.* to reduce the price of something: *a promise to roll back taxes*
roll sth ⇔ **down** *phr. v.* **roll a window down** to open a car window
roll in *phr. v.* **1** *informal* to arrive in large numbers or quantities: *Investors will expect profits to start rolling in soon.* **2** *informal* to arrive later than expected: *They finally rolled in at 4:00.*
roll up *phr. v.* **1 roll sth up** to curl something so that it is in the shape of a ball or a tube: *Painters arrived and rolled up the carpet.* **2 roll your sleeves up** to start doing a job even though it is difficult or you do not want to do it **3 roll a window up** to close a car window

roll² *n.* [C] **1** a piece of paper, film, money, etc. that has been curled into the shape of a tube: *I need to buy a **roll of** film.* | *rolls of toilet paper* **2** a small round LOAF of bread for one person: *The soup comes with a roll.* **3** an official list of the names of people at a meeting, in a class, etc. [➡ **roll call, honor roll**] ➔ see Thesaurus box at RECORD¹ **4 be on a roll** *informal* to be having a lot of success with what you are trying to do: *I don't want to stop playing – I'm on a roll!* **5** a thick layer of skin or fat, usually just below your waist: *the **rolls of fat** on his stomach* **6** a long deep sound: *There was a **roll of thunder** and then the rain started coming down.* **7** an action of throwing DICE as part of a game

'roll call *n.* [C,U] the act of reading out an official list of names to check who is present at a meeting or in a class

roll·er /ˈroʊlɚ/ *n.* [C] **1** a tube-shaped piece of wood, metal, etc. that can be rolled over and over: *paint rollers* **2** a CURLER

Roll·er·blade /ˈroʊlɚˌbleɪd/ *n.* [C] *trademark* a special boot with a single row of wheels fixed under it that you wear for skating (SKATE) [➡ **roller skate**] —**rollerblade** *v.* [I] —**rollerblading** *n.* [U]

'roller ˌcoaster *n.* [C] **1** a track with sudden steep slopes and curves that people ride on in special cars at FAIRS and AMUSEMENT PARKS **2** a situation that is impossible to control because it keeps changing very quickly: *I feel like I'm on an **emotional roller coaster**.*

'roller skate *n.* [C] a special boot with four wheels fixed under it that you wear for skating (SKATE) —**rollerskate** *v.* [I] —**rollerskating** *n.* [U]

rol·lick·ing /ˈrɑlɪkɪŋ/ *adj.* [only before noun] noisy and cheerful: *a rollicking good time*

roll·ing /ˈroʊlɪŋ/ *adj.* rolling hills have many long gentle slopes

'rolling pin *n.* [C] a long tube-shaped piece of wood used for making PASTRY flat and thin before you cook it

ro·ly-po·ly /ˌroʊli ˈpoʊli/ *adj.* a roly-poly person is short and fat

ROM /rɑm/ *n.* [U] *technical* **read-only memory** the part of a computer where permanent instructions and information are stored [➡ **RAM**]

Ro·man Cath·olic /ˌroʊmən ˈkæθlɪk/ *adj.* relating to the part of the Christian religion whose leader is the Pope: *the Roman Catholic Church* —**Roman Catholic** *n.* [C]

ro·mance /ˈroʊmæns, roʊˈmæns/ *n.* **1** [C] an exciting relationship between two people who love each other: *a summer romance* **2** [C] a story about love between two people **3** [U] the feeling of excitement and adventure that is related to a particular place, activity, etc.: *the **romance of** traveling to distant places.*

ˌRoman 'numeral *n.* [C] a number in a system that was used in ancient Rome, that uses letters instead of numbers: *XXVII is the Roman numeral for 27.*

ro·man·tic¹ /roʊˈmæntɪk/ *adj.* **1** showing strong feelings of love: *"Paul gave me roses for our anniversary." "How romantic!"* **2** involving feelings of love: *I'm not ready for a romantic relationship.* **3** a romantic story or movie is about love: *a new romantic comedy* **4** *disapproving* romantic ideas are not practical because they are based on how you would like things to be rather than how they really are [≠ **realistic**]: *the **romantic notion** that Christmas shopping is a magical event* —**romantically** *adv.*: *They were never romantically involved.*

romantic² *n.* [C] **1** someone who shows strong feelings of love and likes doing things that are

R

related to love, such as buying flowers, presents, etc. **2** someone who is not practical and bases his/her actions too much on an imagined idea of the world [≠ **realist**]

ro·man·ti·cize /roʊˈmæntəˌsaɪz/ *v.* [T] to talk or think about things in a way that makes them seem more attractive than they really are: *a romanticized idea of country life*

romp /rɑmp/ *v.* [I] **1** to play in a noisy way by running, jumping, etc.: *They could hear the children romping around upstairs.* **2** to win a race/competition/election etc. very easily: *the Yankees romped over the Red Sox*

roof¹ /ruf, rʊf/ *n.* [C] **1** the part of a building or vehicle that covers the top of it: *They finally found the cat up on the roof.* | *The roof is leaking.* | *We can probably strap the bikes to the* ***roof of*** *the car.* **2** the top of a passage under the ground: *The roof of the tunnel suddenly collapsed.* **3 the roof of your mouth** the top part of the inside of your mouth **4 a roof over your head** a place to live: *I may not have a job, but at least I've got a roof over my head.* **5 under one roof/under the same roof** in the same building or house: *If we're going to live under the same roof, we need to get along.*

roof² *v.* [T] to put a roof on a building: *a house* ***roofed with*** *tiles*

roof·ing /ˈrufɪŋ/ *n.* [U] material for making or covering roofs

roof·top /ˈruftɑp/ *n.* [C] the top surface of a building: *People were standing on rooftops to watch the parade.*

rook·ie /ˈrʊki/ *n.* [C] someone who has just started doing a job or playing a professional sport, and has little experience: *a rookie policeman*

room¹ /rum, rʊm/ *n.* **1** [C] a part of the inside of a building that has its own walls, floor, and ceiling: *The room is quite big.* | *the* ***living room/dining room/bathroom*** | *a* ***hotel/motel room*** | *Amanda, can you clean up* ***your room*** (=your bedroom), *please?* **2** [U] enough space for a particular purpose: *There isn't any more* ***room in*** *the closet.* | *Save* ***room for*** *dessert!* | *The kids don't have much* ***room to*** *play in the yard.* **3** [U] the possibility that something may exist or will happen: *I always try to* ***make room*** *for exercise.* | *There was little* ***room for doubt*** *that he was guilty.* | *Good work is being done, but there's still* ***room for improvement*** (=the possibility of doing better). **4** [singular] all the people in a room: ***The whole room*** *started singing "Happy Birthday."*

room² *v.* **room with sb** to share the room that you live in with someone, for example at college

ˌroom and ˈboard *n.* [U] a room to sleep in, and meals: *Room and board at school costs $600 a month.*

room·mate /ˈrum-meɪt, ˈrʊm-/ *n.* [C] someone with whom you share a room, apartment, or house: *college roommates*

ˈroom ˌservice *n.* [U] a service provided by a hotel, by which food, drinks, etc. can be brought to a guest's room: *We decided to* ***order room service.***

room·y /ˈrumi, ˈrʊmi/ *adj.* with plenty of space inside: *a roomy car*

roost /rust/ *n.* [C] a place where birds rest and sleep —**roost** *v.* [I]

roost·er /ˈrustɚ/ *n.* [C] a male chicken

root¹ /rut, rʊt/ *n.* [C]
1 PLANT the part of a plant or tree that grows under the ground: *Cover the roots with plenty of soil.* ➔ see picture at PLANT¹
2 PROBLEM the basic or main part of a problem or idea: *The love of money is* ***the root of*** (=is the cause of) *all evil.* | *the* ***root causes*** *of crime.* | *A good mechanic will* ***get to the root of*** *the problem.*
3 roots [plural] the origin or main part of something such as a CUSTOM, law, activity, etc. from which other things have developed: *Jazz* ***has its roots in*** *African music.*
4 sb's roots someone's connection with a place because s/he was born there or his/her family lived there: *She's proud of her Polish roots.*
5 put down roots to start to feel that a place is your home
6 TOOTH/HAIR the part of a tooth, hair, etc. that is fixed to the rest of the body
7 take root a) if an idea takes root, people begin to accept or believe it: *helping democracy take root* **b)** if a plant takes root, it grows into the ground
8 LANGUAGE *technical* in grammar, the basic part of a word that shows its main meaning. For example, the root of "disagree" is "agree". ➔ GRASS ROOTS, SQUARE ROOT

root² *v.* **1 be rooted in sth** to have developed from something and be strongly influenced by it: *moral values rooted in conservative religious beliefs* **2** [I] to search for something by moving things around: *I* ***rooted through*** *my purse for a pen and paper.* **3** [I,T] to grow roots or to fix a plant firmly by its roots: *The bulbs will root in spring.*

root for sb *phr. v. informal* to support and encourage someone to succeed in a competition, test, or difficult situation: *We're all rooting for you, Bill.*

root sth ⇔ **out** *phr. v.* to find out where a particular problem exists and get rid of it: *efforts to root out corruption in the police force*

ˈroot beer *n.* [C,U] a sweet non-alcoholic drink made from the roots of some plants

root·less /ˈrutlɪs/ *adj.* having nowhere that you feel is really your home

rope¹ /roʊp/ *n.* **1** [C,U] very strong thick string, made by twisting together many threads: *They tied a piece of rope around my waist and pulled me up.* **2 the ropes** [plural] the things someone needs to know in order to do a job: *I spent the first month **learning the ropes**. | New employees are assigned a buddy to **show** them **the ropes**.* **3 be at/near the end of your rope** to have no more strength or ability to deal with a difficult situation

rope² *v.* [T] to tie things together using rope: *Harvey **roped** his horse **to** a nearby tree. | The climbers were **roped together** for safety.*

rope sb ⇔ **in/into** sth *phr. v. informal* to persuade someone to help you in a job or activity: *My wife and I have been roped into going to this fund-raising dinner.*

rope sth ⇔ **off** *phr. v.* to surround an area with ropes in order to separate it from another area: *Police roped off the area of the robbery.*

ro·sa·ry /ˈroʊzəri/ *n.* plural **rosaries** [C] a string of BEADS used by Roman Catholics for counting prayers

rose¹ /roʊz/ *n.* [C] a common sweet-smelling flower that grows on a bush that has THORNS (=sharp points on a stem): *a dozen **red roses***

rose² *v.* the past tense of RISE

ro·sé /roʊˈzeɪ/ *n.* [U] pink wine

Rosh Ha·sha·nah /ˌrɑʃ həˈʃɑnə/ *n.* Jewish New Year, in late September or early October

ros·ter /ˈrɑstɚ/ *n.* [C] **1** a list of the names of people on a sports team, in an organization, etc.: *the company's **roster of** top executives | Williams took Carney's place **on the** Miami Dolphin **roster**.* **2** a list of people's names showing the jobs they must do and when they must do them

ros·trum /ˈrɑstrəm/ *n.* [C] a small PLATFORM (=raised area) that you stand on in front of an AUDIENCE

ros·y /ˈroʊzi/ comparative **rosier**, superlative **rosiest** *adj.* **1** seeming to offer hope of success or happiness: *The company has a **rosy future**.* **2** pink: *rosy cheeks*

rot¹ /rɑt/ *v.* past tense and past participle **rotted**, present participle **rotting** [I,T] to decay by a gradual natural process, or to make something do this: *Sugar rots your teeth. | old buildings that were left to rot*

> **THESAURUS**
> **decay, decompose**
> ➔ see Thesaurus box at DECAY¹

rot² *n.* [U] the natural process of decaying, or the part of something that has decayed: *a tree full of rot*

ro·ta·ry /ˈroʊt̬əri/ *adj.* turning in a circle around a fixed point, like a wheel

ro·tate /ˈroʊteɪt/ *v.* **1** [I,T] to turn around a fixed point, or to make something do this: *The Earth rotates every 24 hours. | **Rotate** the handle **to** the right.*

> **THESAURUS**
> **turn, twist, spin, go around, revolve**
> ➔ see Thesaurus box at TURN¹

2 [I,T] if a job rotates or people rotate jobs, they each do the job for a fixed period of time: *We try to rotate the boring jobs.* **3** [T] to regularly change the crops grown on a piece of land —**rotation** /roʊˈteɪʃən/ *n.* [C,U] *crop rotation*

ROTC /ˈrɑtsi, ˌɑr oʊ ti ˈsi/ *n.* **Reserve Officers Training Corps** an organization that trains students to be U.S. army officers

rote /roʊt/ *n.* **learn sth by rote** to learn something by repeating it until you remember it, without really understanding it

ro·tis·ser·ie /roʊˈtɪsəri/ *n.* [C] a piece of equipment for cooking meat by turning it around and around on a metal ROD

ro·tor /ˈroʊt̬ɚ/ *n.* [C] the part of a machine that turns around on a fixed point

rot·ten /ˈrɑtˀn/ *adj.* **1** badly decayed: *rotten apples*

> **THESAURUS**
> **old, used, stale**
> ➔ see Thesaurus box at OLD

2 *informal* very bad: *I'm a rotten cook. | She felt rotten about having to fire him.*

ro·tund /roʊˈtʌnd/ *adj.* having a fat round body

ro·tun·da /roʊˈtʌndə/ *n.* [C] a round building or hall, especially one with a DOME

rouge /ruʒ/ *n.* [U] BLUSH

rough¹ /rʌf/ *adj.* **1** having an uneven surface [➡ **flat, smooth**]: *Our jeep's good for traveling over rough ground.* **2** not exact or not containing many details: *Can you give us a **rough idea** of the cost? | a **rough draft** of an essay* **3** using force or violence: *Ice hockey is a rough sport.* **4** a rough area has a lot of violence and crime: *a rough part of the city* **5** a rough period of time is one when you have a lot of problems and difficulties: *It sounds like you had a **rough day** at work. | I had a **rough night*** (=I did not sleep well). *| We've been through some **rough times** together.* **6** with strong winds or storms: *Their boat sank in **rough seas**.* **7** not fair or kind: *Don't be so **rough on** her* (=be kinder). —**roughness** *n.* [U]

rough² *v.*, **rough it** *informal* to live in conditions that are not very comfortable: *We're going to rough it in the mountains for a few days.*

rough sb ⇔ **up** *phr. v. informal* to attack someone by hitting him/her

rough³ *adv.* **play rough** to play in a fairly violent way

rough·age /ˈrʌfɪdʒ/ *n.* [U] a substance in some foods that helps your BOWELS to work [**= fiber**]

ˌrough-and-ˈtumble *adj.* full of people compet-

R

ing, often in a cruel way: *the rough-and-tumble world of politics*

rough·house /ˈrʌfhaʊs/ *v.* [I] to play in a noisy physical way

rough·ly /ˈrʌfli/ *adv.* **1** not exactly [= **approximately**, **about**]: *Roughly 100 people came.*

THESAURUS

about, **approximately**, **around**, **or so**
→ see Thesaurus box at ABOUT[2]

2 not gently or carefully: *Don't pet the cat so roughly!*

rough·shod /ˈrʌfʃɑd/ *adv.* **ride roughshod over sb/sth** to behave in a way that ignores other people's feelings or opinions

rou·lette /ruˈlɛt/ *n.* [U] a game in which people try to win money by guessing which hole a small ball on a spinning wheel will fall into

round[1] /raʊnd/ *adj.* **1** shaped like a circle or a ball: *a round table* | *a tree with round berries* | *the baby's round cheeks* **2** a round number is a whole number, often ending in 0, that is usually not exact: *Let's make it a round number – $50.* | ***In round numbers*** (=to the nearest 10, 100, 1000, etc.) *we supply 50 percent of the trucks in the area.* —**roundness** *n.* [U]

R

THESAURUS

circular, **square**, **semicircular**, **triangular**, **rectangular**, **oval**, **cylindrical**
→ see Thesaurus box at SHAPE[1]

round[2] *n.* [C]
1 CONNECTED EVENTS a number of events that are related: *the latest* ***round of*** *peace talks*

THESAURUS

stage, **part**, **phase**
→ see Thesaurus box at STAGE[1]

2 DRINKS if you buy a round of drinks, you buy an alcoholic drink for all the people in your group: *I'll buy the next round.*
3 COMPETITION one of the parts of a competition that you have to finish or win before you can go to the next part: *She made it to the second round.* | *the final* ***round of*** *the championship*
4 round of applause a time when people CLAP to show that they enjoyed a performance: *Let's* ***give*** *them* ***a round of applause****.*
5 rounds [plural] the usual visits or checks that someone makes as a part of his/her job, especially a doctor: *The theft was discovered by a security guard who was* ***making*** *his* ***rounds****.*
6 SHOT a single shot from a gun: *The soldier fired several rounds before escaping.*
7 GOLF a complete game of golf
8 BOXING one of the periods in a BOXING match: *a 15-round heavyweight bout*
9 SONG a song for three or four singers who each start the same tune at different times, until all of them are singing

round[3] *v.* [T] **1** to go around something such as a bend or the corner of a building: *The Porsche* ***rounded the bend*** *at 120 mph.* **2** to make something round: *The edges of the counter have been rounded to make them safer.*
round sth ⇔ **off** *phr. v.* to change an exact figure to the nearest whole number
round sth ⇔ **out/off** *phr. v.* to do something pleasant at the end of an activity or event that makes the experience more satisfying: *Chocolate cake served with vanilla ice cream rounded out the meal.*
round sth ⇔ **up** *phr. v.* **1** to find and gather together a group of people or things: *Police rounded up 20 people for questioning.* **2** to increase an exact figure to the next highest whole number

round[4] *adv.* → **all year round** at YEAR → AROUND

round·a·bout /ˈraʊndəˌbaʊt/ *adj.* [only before noun] not done in the shortest most direct way: *a roundabout route to avoid heavy traffic*

ˌround-the-ˈclock *adj.* all the time, both day and night: *round-the-clock hospital care*

ˈround-trip *adj.* a round-trip ticket is for taking a trip from one place to another and back again [≠ **one-way**] —**round trip** *n.* [C]

round·up /ˈraʊndʌp/ *n.* [C] **1** an occasion when a lot of people or animals are brought together, often by force: *a* ***roundup of*** *criminal suspects* **2** a short description of the main parts of the news, on the radio or on television

rouse /raʊz/ *v.* [T] **1** to make someone want to do something: *The speech* ***roused*** *King's supporters* ***to*** *action.* **2** *formal* to wake up, or wake someone up

rous·ing /ˈraʊzɪŋ/ *adj.* making people feel excited and eager to do something: *a rousing speech*

rout /raʊt/ *v.* [T] to defeat someone completely —**rout** *n.* [C]

route[1] /rut, raʊt/ *n.* [C] the way from one place to another: *What is the shortest* ***route from*** *Memphis* ***to*** *Atlanta?* | *the most* ***direct route*** *home* | *We had to* ***take a*** *longer* ***route*** *because of the snow.*

route[2] *v.* [T] to send something or someone by a particular route [➡ **en route**]: *All the military supplies were* ***routed through*** *Turkey.*

rou·tine[1] /ruˈtin/ *n.* **1** [C,U] the usual or normal way in which you do things: *Harry doesn't like any change in his* ***daily routine****.* | *It took us a little while to* ***get into*** *our old* ***routine****.* **2** [C] a series of movements performed one after the other: *an* ***exercise routine***

routine[2] *adj.* **1** regular and usual: *a routine medical test* | *a few routine questions*

THESAURUS

normal, **ordinary**, **average**, **standard**, **conventional**
→ see Thesaurus box at NORMAL[1]

2 ordinary and boring: *a routine job* —**routinely** *adv.*

rov·ing /ˈroʊvɪŋ/ *adj.* traveling or moving from one place to another: *a roving reporter*

row[1] /roʊ/ *n.* [C] **1** a line of things or people next to each other: *a* ***row of*** *houses | children standing* ***in a row*** **2** a line of seats in a theater, large room, etc.: *I sat* ***in the front row***. **3 three/four etc. in a row** happening three times, four times, etc. in exactly the same way or with the same result: *We've lost four games in a row.*

row[2] *v.* [I,T] to make a boat move by using OARS: *Slowly, she* ***rowed across*** *the lake.* —**rowing** *n.* [U] ➔ see picture on page A10

row·boat /ˈroʊboʊt/ *n.* [C] a small boat that you move by using OARS ➔ see picture at TRANSPORTATION

row·dy /ˈraʊdi/ *adj.* behaving in a noisy way that is not controlled: *a group of rowdy children* —**rowdiness** *n.* [U]

> **THESAURUS**
>
> **loud**, **noisy**
> ➔ see Thesaurus box at LOUD[1]

ˈrow house *n.* [C] a house that is part of a line of houses that are joined to each other

> **THESAURUS**
>
> **ranch house**, **ranch**, **cottage**, **mansion**, **bungalow**, **duplex**, **apartment**, **condominium**, **condo**, **townhouse**, **mobile home**, **trailer**
> ➔ see Thesaurus box at HOUSE[1]

roy·al /ˈrɔɪəl/ *adj.* relating to or belonging to a king or queen: *the royal family*

roy·al·ty /ˈrɔɪəlti/ *n.* **1** [U] members of a royal family **2 royalties** [plural] payments made to the writer of a book or piece of music

rpm *n.* **revolutions per minute** a unit for measuring the speed of an engine

RSI *n.* [U] **repetitive strain injury** pain in your hands or arms caused by doing the same movement many times, especially typing (TYPE)

RSVP an abbreviation that is written on invitations in order to ask someone to reply

rub[1] /rʌb/ *v.* [I,T] past tense and past participle **rubbed**, present participle **rubbing** **1** to move your hand, a cloth, etc. over a surface while pressing against it: *Laura took off her glasses and rubbed her eyes. | The stain will come out if you* ***rub harder***. *| Can you* ***rub*** *some lotion* ***on*** *my back, please?*

> **THESAURUS**
>
> **touch**, **feel**, **stroke**, **scratch**, **pat**, **brush**, **caress**, **fondle**, **tickle**, **grope**
> ➔ see Thesaurus box at TOUCH[1]

2 to move around while pressing against another surface: *The cat was* ***rubbing against*** *my legs. | They were* ***rubbing*** *their hands* ***together***, *trying to stay warm.* **3 rub it in** *informal* to remind someone of something embarrassing that you know s/he wants to forget: *Okay, there's no need to rub it in!* **4 rub sb the wrong way** *informal* if someone rubs you the wrong way, s/he annoys you, usually without intending to **5 rub shoulders with sb also rub elbows with sb** *informal* to meet and spend time with important or famous people

rub off on sb *phr. v.* if a feeling, quality, or habit rubs off on someone, s/he starts to have it because someone else has it: *Her positive attitude seemed to rub off on everyone.*

rub[2] *n.* [C] an act of rubbing something or someone: *Could you* ***give*** *me a back* ***rub***?

rub·ber /ˈrʌbɚ/ *n.* **1** [U] a substance used for making tires, boots, etc. that is made from chemicals or the liquid that comes out of tropical trees: *rubber gloves* ➔ see picture at MATERIAL[1] **2** [C] *informal* a CONDOM

ˌrubber ˈband *n.* [C] a thin circular piece of rubber used to hold things together

rub·ber·neck /ˈrʌbɚˌnɛk/ *v.* [I] *informal* to look around at something such as an accident while you are driving or walking past

ˌrubber-ˈstamp *v.* [T] *disapproving* to give official approval to something without really thinking about it

rub·ber·y /ˈrʌbəri/ *adj.* looking or feeling like rubber

rub·bish /ˈrʌbɪʃ/ *n.* [U] GARBAGE

rub·ble /ˈrʌbəl/ *n.* [U] broken stones or bricks from a building, wall, etc. that has been destroyed: *a pile of rubble*

rub·down /ˈrʌbdaʊn/ *n.* **give sb a rubdown** to give someone a MASSAGE in order to make him/her relax, especially after exercise

ru·bel·la /ruˈbɛlə/ *n.* [U] *technical* GERMAN MEASLES

ru·by /ˈrubi/ *n.* plural **rubies** [C,U] a dark red jewel, or the color of this jewel —**ruby** *adj.*

ruck·us /ˈrʌkəs/ *n.* [singular] *informal* a noisy argument or confused situation: *What's all the ruckus about?*

rud·der /ˈrʌdɚ/ *n.* [C] a flat part at the back of a boat or aircraft that is turned in order to change the direction in which the vehicle moves

rud·dy /ˈrʌdi/ *adj.* a ruddy face looks pink and healthy

rude /rud/ *adj.* **1** speaking or behaving in a way that is not polite: *a rude remark | Don't be* ***rude to*** *your grandmother!* ▶ Don't say "rude with." ◀ ***It's rude to*** *stare.*

> **THESAURUS**
>
> **impolite** formal: *You might touch the person next to you and that would be impolite.*
> **insulting** – saying or doing something that insults someone: *comments that are insulting to women*
> **tactless** – carelessly saying or doing things that are likely to upset someone: *a tactless remark*
> **offensive** – likely to upset or offend people: *His remarks are offensive to African Americans.*

2 a rude awakening a situation in which someone suddenly realizes something upsetting or bad —**rudely** *adv.* —**rudeness** *n.* [U]

ru·di·men·ta·ry /ˌrudəˈmɛntri, -ˈmɛntəri/ *adj. formal* very simple and basic: *a **rudimentary knowledge of** geometry*

ru·di·ments /ˈrudəmənts/ *n.* [plural] *formal* the most basic parts of a subject: *They know **the rudiments of** grammar.*

rue /ru/ *v.* [T] *literary* to wish that you had not done something [= **regret**]: *She'll **rue the day that** she met him.*

rue·ful /ˈrufəl/ *adj.* showing that you wish something had not happened but you accept it: *a rueful smile* —**ruefully** *adv.*

ruf·fle[1] /ˈrʌfəl/ *v.* [T] **1** to make a smooth surface uneven or messy: *He reached over and **ruffled** my **hair**.* **2** to offend, annoy, or upset someone: *I don't want to **ruffle** his **feathers*** (=upset him).

ruffle[2] *n.* [C] a band of cloth sewn in folds as a decoration around the edges of a shirt, skirt, etc. —**ruffled** *adj.*

R

rug

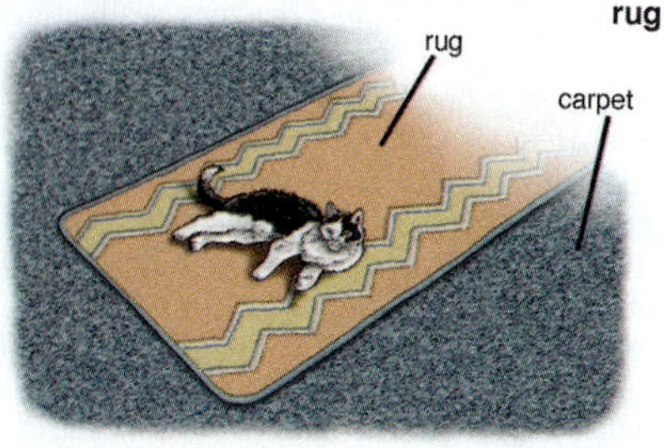

rug /rʌg/ *n.* [C] a piece of thick cloth or wool that covers part of a floor, used for warmth or as a decoration [➡ **carpet**]

rug·by /ˈrʌgbi/ *n.* [U] an outdoor game played by two teams with an OVAL ball that you kick or carry

rug·ged /ˈrʌgɪd/ *adj.* **1** land that is rugged is rough, rocky, and uneven **2** a man who is rugged is attractive and has strong features which may not be perfect: *his rugged good looks*

ru·in[1] /ˈruɪn/ *v.* [T] **1** to spoil or destroy something completely: *The new road will ruin the countryside.* | *One stupid comment had ruined everything.* **2** to make someone lose all his/her money: *A long strike would ruin the company.*

ruin[2] *n.* **1** [U] a situation in which someone loses his/her social position or money, especially because of a business failure: *small businesses facing **financial ruin*** **2 also ruins** [plural] the part of a building that is left after the rest has been destroyed: *the **ruins of** the temple* **3 be/lie in ruins** to be badly damaged or destroyed: *The country's economy is in ruins.* **4 fall into ruin** if something falls into ruin, it becomes damaged or destroyed because no one is taking care of it: *The 18th century mansion has fallen into ruin.*

ru·in·ous /ˈruɪnəs/ *adj.* causing great destruction or loss of money: *a ruinous decision*

rule[1] /rul/ *n.* **1** [C] an official instruction that says how something is to be done or what is allowed, especially in a game, organization, or job: *Erin knows the **rules of** the game.* | ***strict rules** about what you can wear* | *If you **follow** the **rules**, you won't get into trouble.* | *Well, that's what happens if you **break** the **rules*** (=disobey them). | *It's **against the rules** to pick up the ball* (=it is not allowed). | *Can't we **bend the rules*** (=allow something that is usually not allowed) *just this once?*

THESAURUS

law – a rule that people in a particular country, city, or state must obey: *The law requires motorcyclists to wear helmets.*
regulation – an official rule or order: *environmental regulations on air pollution*
restriction – a rule or set of laws that limits what you can do or what is allowed to happen: *new restrictions on immigration*
guidelines – rules or instructions about the best way to do something: *the Department of Health's guidelines for a healthy diet*
statute formal – a law or rule: *a federal statute prohibiting sex discrimination*

2 [U] the government of a country by a particular group of people or by using a particular system: *At that time, Vietnam was **under** French **rule.*** | ***majority rule*** (=government by the political party that most people voted for) **3** [singular] something that is the case or is usually true: ***As a general rule**, vegetable oils are much better for you than animal fats.* | *I worked last weekend but that's **the exception rather than the rule**.* **4** [C] a statement about what is usually allowed in the grammar of a language, or according to a particular system: *the **rules of** grammar* **5 rule of thumb** a principle that is based on practical experience, and that works most of the time: *As a rule of thumb, chicken should be cooked 15 minutes for each pound.*

rule[2] *v.* **1** [I,T] to have the official power to control a country and its people: *The King ruled for 30 years.* | *Alexander the Great **ruled over** a huge empire.* **2** [I,T] to make an official decision about something such as a legal problem: *The judge **ruled that** the mother should have custody of the children.* | *The Supreme Court has not **ruled on** the case yet.* **3** [T] if a feeling or desire rules someone, it controls his/her life, so that s/he does not have time for other things: *Don't let your job **rule** your **life**.* **4 sb/sth rules** *spoken* used in order to say that the team, school, place, etc. mentioned is better than any other: *Jefferson High rules!*

rule sth/sb **out** *phr. v.* to decide that something is not possible or appropriate: *We can't **rule out the possibility** that he has left the country.*

ruled /ruld/ *adj.* ruled paper has parallel lines printed across it

rul·er /'rulɚ/ *n.* [C] **1** someone such as a king who has official power over a country and its people

THESAURUS

king, **queen**, **monarch**, **emperor**, **sovereign**
➔ see Thesaurus box at KING

2 a flat narrow piece of plastic, wood, or metal that you use for measuring things and drawing straight lines

rul·ing¹ /'rulɪŋ/ *n.* [C] an official decision, especially one made by a court of law: *the Supreme Court's **ruling on** the case*

ruling² *adj.* **the ruling class/party** the group that controls a country or organization

rum /rʌm/ *n.* [C,U] a strong alcoholic drink made from sugar

rum·ble /'rʌmbəl/ *v.* [I] to make a lot of long low sounds: *Thunder rumbled in the distance.* —**rumble** *n.* [singular]

ru·mi·nate /'rumə,neɪt/ *v.* [I] *formal* to think carefully about something

rum·mage /'rʌmɪdʒ/ *v.* [I] to search for something by moving things around: *Kerry was **rummaging through** a drawer looking for a pen.*

'rummage sale *n.* [C] an event at which old clothes, furniture, toys, etc. are sold

ru·mor /'rumɚ/ *n.* [C,U] information that is passed from one person to another and which may not be true: *Have you heard the **rumor about** Sam and Kelly?* | *Knox denied **rumors that** he might be running for office.* | ***Rumor has it (that)*** (=people are saying that) *Jean's getting married again.*

ru·mored /'rumɚd/ *adj.* if something is rumored to be true, people are saying that it may be true but no one knows for certain: ***It was rumored that** a magazine had offered a lot of money for her story.* | *He's **rumored to** be running for president.*

rump /rʌmp/ *n.* [C,U] the part of an animal's back that is just above its legs

rum·pled /'rʌmpəld/ *adj.* rumpled hair, clothes, etc. are messy

run¹ /rʌn/ *v.* past tense **ran** /ræn/ past participle **run**, present participle **running**
1 MOVE [I] to move very quickly, moving your legs faster than when you walk: *If we run, we can still catch the bus.* | *I **ran down** the stairs as fast as I could.* | *Billy **ran over** to the playground.* | *Stephen **came running** into the house.* ➔ see picture on page A9

THESAURUS

sprint – to run as fast as you can for a short distance: *I sprinted toward the end zone.*
dash/tear – to run very fast in a hurried way: *He's always dashing off somewhere.*
jog/go jogging – to run quite slowly for exercise over a long distance
race – to go somewhere very quickly: *I raced home from school.*
➔ WALK

2 BE IN CHARGE OF STH [T] to control, organize, or operate a business, organization, etc.: *Ann runs a restaurant in Atlanta.* | *The hotel is **well-run/badly-run**.*
3 IN A RACE [I,T] to run in a race: *I'm **running in** a marathon at the end of this month.*
4 GO SOMEWHERE QUICKLY *spoken* to go somewhere quickly, either walking or in a car: *I need to run out to my car; I left my books in it.* | *I need to **run to** the store for some milk.*
5 MACHINES [I,T] if a machine runs, or if you run it, it is operating: *The radio **runs on/off** batteries* (=uses batteries to work). | *I forgot to run the dishwasher.* | *Nate left the engine running.* | *We should have the telescope **up and running*** (=working) *by the weekend.*
6 COMPUTER [T] to start or use a computer program: *You can run this software on any PC.*
7 be running late to be doing things late: *Sorry you had to wait – I've been running late all day.*
8 ELECTION [I] to try to be elected: *It looks like he is going to **run for** president.* | *Johnstone is **running against** Pershing.*
9 NEWS/STORIES/ADVERTISEMENTS [I,T] to print or broadcast a story, etc.: *What does it cost to run an ad in the local paper?* | *They ran the item on the 6 o'clock news.*
10 run a check/test/experiment etc. to arrange for someone or something to be checked or tested: *The doctors say they need to run a few tests first.*
11 MONEY/NUMBERS [I,T] to be at a particular level, length, amount, price, etc.: *Unemployment is **running at** 5%.* | *The cost of repairs could **run to** $500.*
12 WATER/LIQUIDS [I] to flow: *Tears ran down her face.* | *Who left the water running* (=still flowing from a pipe)? | *My **nose is running*** (=liquid is coming out).

THESAURUS

pour, **flow**, **drip**, **leak**, **ooze**, **gush**, **spurt**, **come out**
➔ see Thesaurus box at POUR

13 HAPPEN [I] to happen in a particular way or for a particular time: *The play **ran for*** (=was performed for) *two years* | *The teacher kept things **running smoothly**.*
14 STH LONG [I,T] if something long such as a road or wire runs in a particular direction, that is its position, or that is where you put it: *Develop-*

R

ers want to run a road right through his farm. | *Run the cables under the carpet.*

15 BUSES/TRAINS [I] to take people from one place to another: *The bus doesn't run on Sunday.* | *The trains should* ***run on time*** (=arrive and leave at the correct time).

16 be running short of sth also be running low on sth to have very little of something left: *I'm* ***running low on*** *money.*

17 TOUCH [T] to touch something by moving your hand along its surface: *She ran her fingers through her hair.*

18 sth runs in the family if something such as a quality, disease, or skill runs in the family, many people in that family have it

19 run drugs/guns to bring drugs or guns illegally into a country in order to sell them

20 COLOR [I] if color or MAKEUP runs, it spreads from one area of cloth or skin to another when it gets wet

21 HOLE IN CLOTHES [I] if a hole in PANTY HOSE runs, it gets longer in a straight line

22 be running a temperature/fever to have a body temperature that is higher than normal because you are sick

R

23 FEELING [I] if thoughts or feelings run through you, you feel them in a very strong way: *I felt a sharp pain run down my leg.*

run across sb/sth *phr. v.* to meet or find someone or something by chance: *I ran across some old love letters the other day.*

run after sb/sth *phr. v.* to chase someone or something: *She started to leave, but Smith ran after her.*

run around *phr. v.* to be very busy doing many small jobs: *She's been running around all day getting things ready for the wedding.*

run away *phr. v.* **1** to leave a place in order to escape from someone or something: *Kathy* ***ran away from home*** *at the age of 16.* **2** to try to avoid an unpleasant situation: *You can't* ***run away from*** *your problems.*

run sth **by** sb *phr. v.* to tell someone about something so that s/he can give you his/her opinion: *Can you run that by me again* (=repeat what you said because I did not understand)*?*

run sb/sth ⇔ **down** *phr. v.* **1** to hit a person or animal with a car while you are driving, and kill or injure him, her, or it: *A drunk driver ran down a 14-year-old girl.* **2** to gradually lose power, or to make something do this: *Don't leave it switched on – you'll run down the batteries.* **3** *informal* to criticize someone or something: *Her boyfriend's always running her down.*

run into sb/sth *phr. v.* **1** *informal* to meet someone by chance: *I ran into him in town.* **2** to hit someone or something with a car: *He lost control and ran into another car.* **3 run into trouble/problems/debt etc.** to begin to have trouble, problems, etc.: *She ran into trouble when she couldn't pay the hospital bills.*

run off *phr. v.* **1** to leave your husband or wife and live with or marry someone else: *Her husband had run off, leaving her and the children.* **2 run** (sth ⇔) **off** to quickly print copies of something: *I'll need to run off 100 copies of this.*

run off with sb/sth *phr. v.* **1** to go away with someone because you are having a sexual relationship with him/her and other people do not approve: *Her husband ran off with an old girlfriend.* **2** to steal something and leave on foot: *A thief ran off with her cell phone.*

run out *phr. v.* **1** to use all of something, so that there is none left: *We've* ***run out of*** *sugar.* | *I'm running out of ideas.* **2** if something is running out, there will soon be none left: *They need to make a deal, but* ***time is running out.*** **3** to come to the end of a period of time when something is allowed to be done or used: *My membership runs out in September.*

run sb/sth ⇔ **over** *phr. v.* to hit someone or something with a car or other vehicle, and drive over him, her, or it: *I think you just ran over some broken glass.*

run through sth *phr. v.* **1** to read, check, or practice something quickly: *I'd like to run through the agenda with you before the meeting.* **2** if a quality or feature runs through something, it exists in all parts of it: *a theme which runs through the book*

run up sth *phr. v.* to make a debt, cost, price, etc. greater: *We ran up a huge phone bill.*

run up against sth *phr. v.* to suddenly have to deal with a problem when you are trying to do something: *The school board has run up against opposition to its proposals.*

run² *n.*

1 RUNNING [C] a period of time spent running, or a distance that you run: *He usually* ***goes for a run*** *before breakfast.* | *a 5-mile run*

2 in the short/long run in the near future, or later in the future: *I think in the long run you'll be happier without him.*

3 BASEBALL [C] a point in a baseball game: *The Cubs* ***scored*** *three* ***runs*** *in the sixth inning.*

4 be on the run a) to be trying to escape from someone, especially the police: *He's been* ***on the run from*** *the police for years.* **b)** to be very busy doing a lot of different things and going to different places: *It's hard to eat well when you're on the run all day.*

5 PLAY/MOVIE ETC. [C] a period of time during which a play, movie, or television show is shown or performed regularly: *The play starts an 8-week run on Friday.*

6 a run of good/bad luck several lucky or unlucky things happening quickly one right after another: *Losing my job was the start of a run of bad luck that year.*

7 a run on sth a situation in which a lot of people take their money out of a bank or buy a lot of one particular thing at the same time: *There's always a run on sleds at this time of year.*

8 ELECTION [C usually singular] an attempt to be

elected: *Turner is **making** his first **run for** public office.*

9 HOLE IN CLOTHES [C] a long hole in a pair of PANTYHOSE

10 make a run for sth also make a run for it to suddenly start running because you want to get to another place very quickly: *It was still raining, but we decided to make a run for the car.*

11 have the run of sth to be allowed to go anywhere or do anything in a place: *We had the run of the house for the weekend.*

12 REGULAR TRIP [C usually singular] a regular trip made by a person or a vehicle that carries a lot of people: *the daily ferry run*

13 give sb a run for his/her money to make an opponent or competitor work very hard to beat you: *The White Sox gave the A's a run for their money, but lost in the ninth inning.*

run·a·round /ˈrʌnəˌraʊnd/ *n.* **give sb the runaround** *informal* to deliberately avoid giving someone the information or help s/he has asked for: *I keep calling to find out about my insurance, but they just keep giving me the runaround.*

run·a·way[1] /ˈrʌnəˌweɪ/ *n.* [C] someone, especially a child, who has left home or the place where s/he is supposed to be

runaway[2] *adj.* [only before noun] **1** a runaway vehicle is out of control **2** happening quickly and suddenly: *The movie was a **runaway success**.*

ˌrun-ˈdown *adj.* **1** a building or area that is run-down is in very bad condition: *a run-down motel* **2** [not before noun] someone who is run-down is very tired and not very healthy: *He's been feeling run-down lately.*

THESAURUS

tired, **exhausted**, **worn out**, **weary**, **beat**
→ see Thesaurus box at TIRED

run·down /ˈrʌndaʊn/ *n.* [singular] a quick report or explanation of a situation, event, etc.: *Can you **give me a rundown on** what happened while I was gone?*

rung[1] /rʌŋ/ *v.* the past participle of RING

rung[2] *n.* [C] **1** one of the steps of a LADDER **2** *informal* a particular level or position in an organization: *I started on the bottom rung of the company.*

ˈrun-in *n.* [C] an argument or disagreement with someone in authority: *Barry **had a run-in with** the police.*

run·ner /ˈrʌnɚ/ *n.* [C] **1** someone who runs as a sport: *a long-distance runner* **2** one of the long thin blades of metal on the bottom of a SLED **3 drug/gun runner** someone who brings drugs or guns illegally into a country in order to sell them

ˌrunner-ˈup *n.* plural **runners-up** [C] the person or team that finishes in second place in a race or competition

run·ning[1] /ˈrʌnɪŋ/ *n.* [U] **1** the activity of running: *running shoes* | *Do you want to **go running**?* **2 be in the running/be out of the running** to have some chance of winning or being successful, or to have no chance: *Is Sam still **in the running for** the swim team?* **3 the running of sth** the way that a business, organization, etc. is managed or organized: *He is not involved in **the day-to-day running of** the business.*

running[2] *adj.* **1 running water** water that comes from a FAUCET: *a house with no running water* **2 running battle/argument** an argument that continues over a long period of time **3 running commentary** a spoken description of an event while it is happening, especially a sports event **4 running total** a total that is always being increased as new costs, amounts, etc. are added to it

running[3] *adv.* **three years/five times etc. running** for three years, five times, etc. without a change: *This is the fourth day running that it has rained.*

ˌrunning ˈback *n.* [C] in football, a player whose main job is to run with the ball

ˈrunning mate *n.* [C] the person who is chosen by someone who is trying to become president, who will then be the VICE PRESIDENT if s/he wins the election

run·ny /ˈrʌni/ *adj. informal* **1** a runny nose has liquid coming out of it because you are sick **2** food that is runny is not as thick as normal or as you want: *runny eggs*

ˌrun-of-the-ˈmill *adj.* not special or interesting [= **ordinary**]: *a run-of-the-mill job*

ˈrun-on ˌsentence *n.* [C] a sentence that has two main CLAUSES without connecting words or correct PUNCTUATION

runt /rʌnt/ *n.* [C] the smallest and least developed baby animal of a group born at the same time

ˈrun-through *n.* [C] a short practice before a performance, test, etc.

ˈrun-up *n.* **the run-up to sth** the period of time just before an important event: *Most stores are hiring more staff in the run-up to Christmas.*

run·way /ˈrʌnweɪ/ *n.* [C] a very long surface like a wide road that aircraft leave from and come down on → see Topic box at AIRPORT

rup·ture[1] /ˈrʌptʃɚ/ *n.* [C,U] an occasion when something suddenly breaks apart or bursts: *the **rupture of** a blood vessel*

rupture[2] *v.* [I,T] to break or burst, or to make something do this: *An oil pipeline ruptured early this morning.*

ru·ral /ˈrʊrəl/ *adj.* relating to country areas rather than the city [≠ **urban**]: *a peaceful rural setting*

ruse /ruz/ *n.* [C] *formal* something you do in order to deceive someone [= **trick**]

rush[1] /rʌʃ/ *v.* **1** [I,T] to move somewhere or do something very quickly: *David **rushed into** the room.* | *There's no need to rush – we have plenty of time.* | *Everyone was **rushing to** catch the last bus.*

R

THESAURUS

race – to go somewhere as fast as you can: *Carter raced downstairs.*
dash – to run somewhere very fast, especially only a short distance: *I dashed into my bedroom and grabbed my notebook.*
charge – to move quickly forward: *The boys charged up the trail, laughing and yelling.*
speed – to move very fast, used about cars, trains, etc., or the people traveling in them: *The train sped toward San Francisco.*
→ RUN[1]

2 [T] to take or send something somewhere very quickly: *We had to **rush** Helen **to** the hospital.* **3** [I,T] to do or decide something too quickly, without taking the time to think carefully, or to make someone do this: *Don't rush me – let me think.* | *My mother's worried that I'm **rushing into** getting married.*
rush around *phr. v.* to try to do a lot of things quickly in a short period of time
rush sth ⇔ **through** *phr. v.* to get something such as a new law approved more quickly than usual
rush² *n.* **1** [singular] a sudden fast movement of things or people: *There was **a rush for** the door.* **2** [singular, U] a situation in which you need to hurry, especially because a lot of people want to do or get something: *We have plenty of time. There's no rush.* | *I can't stop. I'm **in a rush**.* | *There's a big **rush to** get tickets.* **3 the rush** the time when a place or group of people are very busy: *the Christmas rush* **4** [singular] a sudden strong feeling: *Mark felt **a rush of** anger.*

rush hour

'rush hour *n.* [C,U] the time of day when there are a lot of vehicles on the road because people are going to and from work: *rush hour traffic*
Rus·sian¹ /ˈrʌʃən/ *adj.* **1** relating to or coming from Russia **2** relating to the Russian language
Russian² *n.* **1** [U] the language used in Russia **2** [C] someone from Russia
rust¹ /rʌst/ *n.* [U] the reddish-brown substance that forms on iron, steel, etc. when it gets wet
rust² *v.* [I,T] to become covered with rust, or to make something do this: *a lock that has rusted shut*
rus·tic /ˈrʌstɪk/ *adj.* simple and old-fashioned in a way that is attractive and typical of the COUNTRYSIDE: *a rustic mountain cabin*
rus·tle¹ /ˈrʌsəl/ *v.* [I,T] if leaves, papers, etc. rustle, or if you rustle them, they make a soft noise as they rub against each other
rustle sth ⇔ **up** *phr. v.* to find or make something quickly, especially food for a meal
rustle² *n.* [singular] the noise made when something rustles: *the **rustle of** dry leaves* → see picture on page A7
rust·proof /ˈrʌstpruf/ *adj.* metal that is rustproof will not RUST
rust·y /ˈrʌsti/ *adj.* **1** covered with RUST: *rusty nails* **2** if a skill that you have is rusty, you are not as good at doing something as you used to be because you have not practiced it for a long time: *My tennis is a little rusty.*
rut /rʌt/ *n.* **1 in a rut** *informal* living or working in a situation that does not change, and so is boring: *I was **stuck in a rut** and decided to look for a new job.* **2** [C] a deep narrow track left in the ground by a wheel
ru·ta·ba·ga /ˈrut̬əˌbeɪgə/ *n.* [C] a large round yellow vegetable that grows under the ground
ruth·less /ˈruθlɪs/ *adj.* not caring if you have to harm other people to get what you want: *a ruthless dictator* | *ruthless determination* —**ruthlessly** *adv.* —**ruthlessness** *n.* [U]
RV *n.* [C] **recreational vehicle** a large vehicle with cooking equipment, beds, etc. that a family uses for traveling or camping
rye /raɪ/ *n.* [U] a type of grain that is used for making bread and WHISKEY (=alcohol)

S, s

S, s /ɛs/ *n.* [C] the nineteenth letter of the English alphabet
S the abbreviation of **south** or **southern**
S & L *n.* [C] *informal* **savings and loan**
Sab·bath /ˈsæbəθ/ *n.* **the Sabbath** the day of the week that Jews or Christians consider to be a day for resting and praying, either Saturday or Sunday
sab·bat·i·cal /səˈbæt̬ɪkəl/ *n.* [C,U] a period when someone who teaches stops doing his/her usual work in order to study or travel: *Prof. Morris **is on sabbatical** this semester.*
sa·ber /ˈseɪbɚ/ *n.* [C] a military sword
sa·ble /ˈseɪbəl/ *n.* [C,U] an expensive fur used for making coats, or the small animal this fur comes from
sab·o·tage¹ /ˈsæbəˌtɑʒ/ *v.* [T] **1** to secretly damage or destroy something so that an enemy cannot use it: *Soldiers sabotaged road and rail*

lines. **2** to deliberately spoil someone's plans because you do not want him/her to succeed: *Senior managers sabotaged plans to change working practices.* —**saboteur** /ˌsæbəˈtɚ/ *n.* [C]

sabotage² *n.* [U] **1** deliberate damage done to equipment, vehicles, etc., in order to prevent an enemy or opponent from using them: *an **act of sabotage** at the factory* **2** a situation in which someone deliberately spoils someone else's plans, because s/he does not want him/her to succeed: *campaign sabotage*

sac /sæk/ *n.* [C] *technical* a part shaped like a small bag inside a plant or animal, that contains air or liquid

sac·cha·rin /ˈsækərɪn/ *n.* [U] a chemical substance that tastes very sweet and is used instead of sugar

sac·cha·rine /ˈsækəˌrin/ *adj.* very romantic or involving a lot of emotion, in a way that seems silly and not sincere: *a saccharine view of motherhood*

sack¹ /sæk/ *n.* [C] **1** a large bag made of strong cloth, plastic, or paper in which you carry or keep things: *a **sack of** potatoes* **2 also sackful** the amount that a sack can contain ➔ **hit the sack** at HIT

sack² *v.* [T] **1** to steal and destroy things in a city that has been defeated by an army: *The Vandals sacked Rome in 455 A.D.* **2** to knock down the QUARTERBACK in football

sack out *phr. v. informal* to go to sleep: *Karl was **sacked out on** the sofa.*

sac·ra·ment /ˈsækrəmənt/ *n.* [C] an important Christian ceremony such as marriage or COMMUNION

sa·cred /ˈseɪkrɪd/ *adj.* **1** relating to a god or religion, and believed to be holy: *the sacred places of Japan* **2** extremely important or greatly respected: *Life is sacred.*

ˌsacred ˈcow *n.* [C] *disapproving* a belief, object, etc. that is so important to someone that s/he will not let anyone criticize or change it

sac·ri·fice¹ /ˈsækrəˌfaɪs/ *n.* [C,U] **1** something that you decide not to have or not to do in order to get something that is more important: *Her parents **made** a lot of **sacrifices** to put her through college.* | *Rugiero was willing to **sacrifice** his life **for** his country.* **2** the act of offering something to a god, or an object or animal that is killed in order to be offered to a god —**sacrificial** /ˌsækrəˈfɪʃəl◂/ *adj.*

sacrifice² *v.* **1** [T] to willingly stop having or doing something in order to get something that is more important: *Ellis **sacrificed** a high-paying legal career **to** work in the inner city.* **2** [I,T] to offer something to a god as part of a ceremony, often by killing it

sac·ri·lege /ˈsækrəlɪdʒ/ *n.* [C,U] an occasion when someone treats something holy or important in a way that does not show respect —**sacrilegious** /ˌsækrəˈlɪdʒəs/ *adj.*

sac·ro·sanct /ˈsækroʊˌsæŋkt/ *adj.* very important, so that it should never be changed or criticized in any way: *Marriage no longer seems to be sacrosanct.*

sad /sæd/ *adj.* comparative **sadder**, superlative **saddest** **1** unhappy, especially because something unpleasant has happened [≠ **happy**]: *Ted **looked** tired and **sad**.* | *We **were sad to** see him go.* | *a sad face*

THESAURUS

unhappy: *an unhappy marriage* | *We're unhappy with your performance.*
miserable – very sad, especially because you are lonely or sick: *I couldn't help feeling miserable.* | *I had a miserable time at college.*
upset – sad because something bad or disappointing has happened: *She's still very upset about her father's death.*
depressed – sad for a long time because things are wrong in your life: *Patients will get depressed over their symptoms.*
down/low informal – a little sad about things in your life: *Whenever I felt down, I'd read his letter.*
homesick – sad because you are away from your home, family, and friends: *Many students get homesick in their first year.*
gloomy – sad because you think a situation will not improve: *a gloomy mood*
glum – used especially to say that someone looks sad: *You look glum.*

2 a sad event, story, etc. makes you feel unhappy: *sad news* | *It was a sad day for us all.* | *a story with a sad ending* | ***It's sad that** James couldn't come.* **3** very bad or unacceptable: *The house was in a **a sad state of** neglect.* | ***It's sad that** these students don't get the help they need.* —**sadness** *n.* [singular, U]

sad·den /ˈsædn/ *v.* [T] *formal* to make someone feel sad or disappointed: *We were deeply **saddened by** her death.*

sad·dle¹ /ˈsædl/ *n.* [C] **1** a seat made of leather that is put on a horse's back so that you can ride it **2** a seat on a bicycle or a MOTORCYCLE

saddle² *v.* [T] **also saddle up** to put a SADDLE on a horse

saddle sb **with** sth *phr. v.* to give someone a job, problem, etc. that is difficult or boring: *small businesses saddled with debts*

sad·dle·bag /ˈsædlˌbæg/ *n.* [C] a bag that you carry things in, that is attached to a saddle on a horse or a bicycle

sa·dism /ˈseɪdɪzəm/ *n.* [U] behavior in which someone gets pleasure, especially sexual pleasure, from being cruel to someone [➡ **masochism**] —**sadist** *n.* [C] —**sadistic** /səˈdɪstɪk/ *adj.*: *a sadistic ruler*

sad·ly /ˈsædli/ *adv.* **1** in a way that shows you are sad: *Jimmy nodded sadly.* **2** in a way that you wish were not true [= **unfortunately**]: *Sadly, most small businesses fail in the first year.*

sa·fa·ri /sə'fɑri/ *n.* [C] a trip through the country areas of Africa in order to watch wild animals: *tourists **on safari** in Zaire*

safe[1] /seɪf/ *adj.* **1** not in danger of being harmed or stolen: *People don't **feel safe** in their own homes.* | *Nothing can **keep** a city **safe from** terrorist attacks.* | *Both children were found, **safe and sound*** (=unharmed). **2** not likely to cause or allow any physical injury or harm: *safe drinking water* | ***It's** not **safe to** walk there at night.* | *Have a **safe trip**.* | *He stopped the car **a safe distance** away.* **3** a safe place is one where something is not likely to be stolen or lost: *Keep your passport in a safe place.* **4** not involving any risk and very likely to succeed: *a safe investment* | *U.S. Treasury bonds are a **safe bet**.* **5** not likely to cause disagreement: *I think **it's safe to say** that few people read the entire document.* **6 to be on the safe side** *spoken* used when you are being very careful in order to avoid an unpleasant situation: *We'll each keep a copy of the lease to be on the safe side.* **7 better (to be) safe than sorry** *spoken* used in order to say that it is better to be careful, even if this takes time or effort, than to take a risk —**safely** *adv.*: *Drive safely!*

S

safe[2] *n.* [C] a strong metal box or cupboard with a lock on it, where you keep money and valuable things

'safe-deposit ˌbox *n.* [C] a small box used for keeping valuable objects, usually in a special room in a bank

safe·guard /'seɪfgɑrd/ *n.* [C] a law, agreement, etc. that is intended to protect someone or something from possible dangers or problems: ***safeguards against** the exploitation of children* —**safeguard** *v.* [T]

ˌsafe 'haven *n.* [C] a place where someone can go in order to escape from possible danger or attack

safe·keep·ing /ˌseɪf'kipɪŋ/ *n.* **for safekeeping** if you put something somewhere for safekeeping, you put it in a place where it will not get damaged, lost, or stolen

ˌsafe 'sex *n.* [U] ways of having sex that reduce the risk of getting a sexual disease, especially by using a CONDOM

safe·ty /'seɪfti/ *n.* [U] **1** the state of being safe from danger or harm: *Some students are concerned about safety on campus.* **2** how safe someone or something is: *Police have expressed **fears for** the girl's **safety**.* | *People have questioned the **safety of** the fireworks show.*

'safety belt *n.* [C] a SEAT BELT

'safety net *n.* [C] **1** a system or arrangement that helps people if they get into a difficult situation or have serious problems: *a safety net for the country's poorest people* **2** a large net that is placed below someone who is performing high above the ground, to catch him/her if s/he falls

'safety pin *n.* [C] a wire pin with a cover that its point fits into so that it cannot hurt you

'safety valve *n.* [C] **1** something you do that allows you to express strong feelings such as anger without doing any harm: *Exercise is a good safety valve for stress.* **2** a part of a machine that allows gas, steam, etc. to be let out when the pressure is too high

sag /sæg/ *v.* past tense and past participle **sagged**, present participle **sagging** [I] **1** to hang down or bend in the middle, especially because of the weight of something: *The bookcases sagged under hundreds of books.* **2** to become weaker or less valuable: *a sagging economy*

sa·ga /'sɑgə/ *n.* [C] a long story or description of events

sage /seɪdʒ/ *n. literary* **1** [C] someone, especially someone old, who is very wise **2** [U] an HERB with gray-green leaves **3** [U] sagebrush —**sage** *adj.*: *sage advice*

sage·brush /'seɪdʒbrʌʃ/ *n.* [U] a small bush with a strong smell, that grows on dry land in western North America

Sag·it·tar·i·us /ˌsædʒə'tɛriəs/ *n.* **1** [U] the ninth sign of the ZODIAC, represented by a man with a BOW and ARROWS **2** [C] someone born between November 22 and December 21

said[1] /sɛd/ *v.* the past tense and past participle of SAY

said[2] *adj. law* used when giving more information about someone or something that has just been mentioned: *The said robbery happened about 5:00.*

sail[1] /seɪl/ *v.* **1** [I] to travel across an area of water in a boat or ship: *Melville **sailed to** Hawaii.* | *the first Europeans to **sail across** the Atlantic*

THESAURUS

drive, **fly**, **go by train/bus**, **walk**, **bike**
➔ see Thesaurus box at TRAVEL[1]

2 [I,T] to direct or control the movement of a boat or ship: *We sailed the boat along the coast.* | *I'd like to learn how to sail.* **3** [I] to start a trip by boat or ship: *The Dawn Princess will sail from San Juan.*

sail through sth *phr. v.* to succeed in doing something very easily

sail[2] *n.* [C] **1** a large piece of strong cloth attached to a boat, so that the wind will push the boat along **2 set sail** to begin a trip by boat or ship: *The ship will set sail at dawn.*

sail·boat /'seɪlboʊt/ *n.* [C] a small boat with one or more sails

sail·ing /'seɪlɪŋ/ *n.* [U] the sport of traveling through water in a sailboat ➔ see picture on page A10

sail·or /'seɪlɚ/ *n.* [C] **1** someone who works on a ship **2** someone who is in the Navy ➔ see picture at ARMED FORCES

saint /seɪnt/ *n.* [C] **1 also Saint** someone who

is honored by the Catholic Church after death because s/he has suffered for his/her religious beliefs: *St. Jude* **2** *spoken* someone who is very good, kind, or patient: *I'm certainly no saint!* —**sainthood** /ˈseɪnthʊd/ *n.* [U]

Saint Ber·nard /ˌseɪnt bɚˈnɑrd/ *n.* [C] a very large strong dog with long hair

sake /seɪk/ *n.* [U] **1 for the sake of sb also for sb's sake** in order to help, improve, or please someone or something: *She stayed in the marriage for the sake of the children.* | *Be nice to her, for Kathy's sake.* **2 for goodness'/Pete's/heaven's etc. sake** *spoken* said when you are annoyed, surprised, etc., or when you want to emphasize what you are saying: *Why didn't you tell me, for heaven's sake?*

sal·a·ble, saleable /ˈseɪləbəl/ *adj.* something that is salable can be sold, or is easy to sell

sal·ad /ˈsæləd/ *n.* [C,U] **1** a mixture of raw vegetables, for example LETTUCE, CUCUMBER, and TOMATO ➔ see picture on page A5 **2** raw or cooked food cut into small pieces and served cold: *potato salad*

ˈsalad bar *n.* [C] a place in a restaurant where you can make your own salad

ˈsalad ˌdressing *n.* [C,U] a liquid mixture for putting on salads to give them a special taste

sal·a·man·der /ˈsæləˌmændɚ/ *n.* [C] a small animal similar to a LIZARD, that can live in water and on land

sa·la·mi /səˈlɑmi/ *n.* [C,U] a large SAUSAGE with a strong taste, that is eaten cold

sal·a·ried /ˈsælərid/ *adj.* receiving a salary: *salaried workers*

sal·a·ry /ˈsæləri/ *n.* plural **salaries** [C,U] money that you receive every month as payment from the organization you work for [➡ **wages**]: *the average **yearly/annual salary*** | *The university may need to **pay** higher **salaries** to attract top faculty.*

THESAURUS

pay, income, wages, earnings
➔ see Thesaurus box at PAY², WORK¹

sale /seɪl/ *n.* **1** [C,U] the act of selling something, or an occasion when you sell something: *The **sale of** alcohol is strictly controlled.* | *a **yard/garage sale*** (=occasion when you sell things you no longer need) **2 sales a)** [plural] the total number of products that are sold during a particular period of time: *a company with **sales of** $60 million per year* | *Sales of the album have been strong.* **b)** [U] the part of a company that deals with selling products: *Sally got a job as sales manager.* **3 for sale** available to be bought: *They had to **put** their home **up for sale**.* | *postcards for sale in the gift shop* **4 on sale a)** available to be bought: *Tickets **go on sale** Monday.* **b)** available to be bought for a lower price than usual: *The sweaters were on sale.* **5** [C] a time when stores sell their goods at lower prices than usual: *Nordstrom's summer sale*

ˈsales clerk *n.* [C] someone who sells things in a store

sales·man /ˈseɪlzmən/ *n.* [C] a man whose job is to sell things: *a used car salesman*

sales·person /ˈseɪlzˌpɚsən/ *n.* [C] someone whose job is to sell things

ˈsales repreˌsentative also ˈsales rep *n.* [C] someone who travels around selling his/her company's products

ˈsales slip *n.* [C] a small piece of paper that you are given in a store when you buy something [**= receipt**]

ˈsales tax *n.* [C,U] a tax that you pay in addition to the cost of something you are buying

sales·wom·an /ˈseɪlzˌwʊmən/ *n.* [C] a woman whose job is selling things

sa·li·ent /ˈseɪliənt/ *adj. formal* most noticeable or important: *the **salient points** of the plan* —**salience** *n.* [U]

sa·line /ˈseɪlin, -laɪn/ *adj.* containing or consisting of salt: *a **saline solution*** (=liquid with salt in it) —**saline** *n.* [U]

sa·li·va /səˈlaɪvə/ *n.* [U] the liquid that is produced naturally in your mouth

sal·i·vate /ˈsæləˌveɪt/ *v.* [I] *technical* **1** to produce more saliva in your mouth than usual, because you see or smell food **2** to show interest in something in a way that shows you like or want it: *Newspapers are **salivating over** the story.*

sal·low /ˈsæloʊ/ *adj.* sallow skin looks slightly yellow and unhealthy

salm·on /ˈsæmən/ *n.* [C,U] a large ocean fish with silver skin and pink flesh, or the meat from this fish

sal·mo·nel·la /ˌsælməˈnɛlə/ *n.* [U] a type of BACTERIA in food that makes you sick

sa·lon /səˈlɑn/ *n.* [C] a place where you can get your hair cut, have a MANICURE, etc.: *a beauty salon*

sa·loon /səˈlun/ *n.* [C] a place where alcoholic drinks were sold and drunk in the western U.S. in the 19th century

sal·sa /ˈsælsə, ˈsɔl-/ *n.* [U] **1** a SAUCE made from onions, TOMATOes, and hot-tasting PEPPERS that you put on Mexican food **2** a type of Latin American dance music

salt¹ /sɔlt/ *n.* **1** [U] a natural white mineral that is added to food to make it taste better: *Add some salt and pepper.* **2** [C] *technical* a type of chemical, formed by combining an acid with another substance **3 salts** [plural] a mineral substance like salt that is used as a medicine or to make your bath smell good

salt² *v.* [T] to add salt to food to make it taste better

salt sth ⇔ **away** *phr. v.* to save money for future use, especially dishonestly

S

salt[3] *adj.* **1** preserved by salt: *salt pork* **2** containing salt or salt water: *a salt lake*

'salt ˌshaker *n.* [C] a small container for salt

salt·wa·ter /'sɔlt˺ˌwɔtɚ, -ˌwɑ-/ *adj.* living in salty water: *saltwater fish*

salt·y /'sɔlti/ *adj.* tasting like or containing salt —**saltiness** *n.* [U]

> **TOPIC**
>
> **sweet**, **sour**, **hot**, **spicy**, **bland**
> ➔ see Topic box at TASTE[1]

sal·u·ta·tion /ˌsælyə'teɪʃən/ *n.* [C,U] *formal* a word or phrase used to greet someone at the beginning of a letter or speech, such as "Dear Mr. Roberts"

sa·lute[1] /sə'lut/ *v.* [I,T] to move your right hand to your head in order to show respect to an officer in the Army, Navy, etc.: *He turned around and saluted the captain.*

salute[2] *n.* [C] **1** an act of saluting **2** an occasion when guns are fired into the air in order to show respect for someone: *a 21-gun salute*

sal·vage[1] /'sælvɪdʒ/ *v.* [T] to save something from a situation in which other things have already been damaged, destroyed, or lost: *He's trying to salvage his political reputation.* | *a sofa **salvaged from** the dump*

S

salvage[2] *n.* [U] the act of salvaging something, or the things that are salvaged

sal·va·tion /sæl'veɪʃən/ *n.* [U] **1** the state of being saved from evil by God, according to the Christian religion **2** something that prevents danger, loss, or failure: *Education seemed their best chance of salvation.*

Salˌvation 'Army *n.* **the Salvation Army** a Christian organization that tries to help poor people

salve /sæv/ *n.* [C,U] a substance that you put on sore skin to make it less painful —**salve** *v.* [T]

sal·vo /'sælvoʊ/ *n.* plural **salvos** [C] *formal* **1** one of a series of actions or statements, especially in a situation in which people are arguing: *the **opening salvo** of the election campaign* **2** the act of shooting several guns in a battle or as part of a ceremony

Sa·mar·i·tan /sə'mærət˺n/ **also good Samaritan** *n.* [C] someone who helps you when you have problems

same[1] /seɪm/ *adj.* [only before noun] **1 a)** one particular person, place, etc. and not a different one: *We work at **the same** place.* | *Their birthdays are on **the same** day.* **b)** used in order to say that two or more people, things, etc. are exactly like each other [= **identical**]: *I told him **the same** thing.* | *The two of them looked **exactly the same**.* | *She does **the same** job **as** I do, but in a bigger company.* ▶ Don't say "She does the same job like I do." ◀ **2** used in order to say that a particular person or thing does not change: *He's still **the same old** Peter!* **3 at the same time** if two things happen at the same time, they happen together: *I wanted to laugh and cry at the same time.* **4 the same old story/excuse etc.** *informal disapproving* something that you have heard many times before: *politicians repeating the same old promises* **5 same difference** *spoken* used in order to say that different actions, behavior, etc. have the same result: *"Should I e-mail them or fax a letter?" "Same difference."* **6 by the same token** in the same way or for the same reasons: *Some mothers are committed to their careers. By the same token, some fathers want to spend more time with their families.* **7 be in the same boat** to be in the same difficult situation that someone else is in

> **GRAMMAR**
>
> Do not say "a same." Say *the same sort of*: *I'd like the same sort of car as that.*

same[2] *pron.* **1 the same a)** used in order to say that two or more people, actions, or things are exactly like each other: *Thanks – I'll do the same for you sometime.* | *The houses look the same, but one's slightly larger.* **b)** used in order to say that a particular person or thing does not change: *It won't be the same without you.* | *"How's Danny?" "Oh, he's the same as ever."* ▶ Don't say "He's same as ever." ◀ **2 (and the) same to you!** *spoken* used as a reply to a greeting, or as an angry reply to a rude remark: *"Happy New Year!" "Same to you!"* **3 same here** *spoken* said in order to tell someone that you feel the same way as him/her: *"I'd love to see you again." "Same here."*

same·ness /'seɪmnɪs/ *n.* [U] a boring lack of variety, or the quality of being very similar to something else: *the sameness of the landscape*

ˌsame-'sex *adj.* **same-sex marriage/relationship etc.** a marriage, etc. between two men or two women

sam·ple[1] /'sæmpəl/ *n.* **1** a small part or amount of something that is examined or used in order to find out what the rest is like: *Do you have a **sample of** your work?* | *a **blood/urine/tissue sample*** (=that a doctor examines for a disease) | *a **free sample** of shampoo* **2** a group of people who have been chosen to give information by answering questions: *a **random sample of** 500 college students* **3** a small part of a song from a CD or record that is used in a new song

sample[2] *v.* [T] **1** to taste a food or drink in order to see what it is like: *We sampled several kinds of cheese.* **2** to choose some people from a larger group in order to ask them questions: *25% of the people sampled were college-educated.* **3** to use a small part of a song from a CD or record in a new song —**sampling** *n.* [C]

sanc·ti·fy /'sæŋktəˌfaɪ/ *v.* past tense and past participle **sanctified**, third person singular **sanctifies** [T] to make something holy

sanc·ti·mo·ni·ous /ˌsæŋktə'moʊniəs/ *adj. dis-*

approving behaving as if you are morally better than other people

sanc·tion¹ /ˈsæŋkʃən/ *n.* **1 sanctions** [plural] official orders or laws stopping trade, communication, etc. with another country, as a way of forcing its leaders to make political changes: *Trade **sanctions** were **imposed on** South Africa before apartheid ended.* | *U.S. **sanctions against** Cuba* **2** [U] official permission, approval, or acceptance: *The protest march was held without government sanction.* **3** [C] something, such as a punishment, that makes people obey a rule or law: *Sex outside of marriage was punished by powerful social sanctions.*

sanction² *v.* [T] *formal* to officially accept or allow something: *The UN refused to sanction the use of force.*

sanc·ti·ty /ˈsæŋktət̬i/ *n.* **the sanctity of sth** the quality that makes something so important that it must be respected and preserved: *the sanctity of marriage*

sanc·tu·ar·y /ˈsæŋktʃuˌɛri/ *n.* plural **sanctuaries** **1** [C,U] a peaceful place that is safe and provides protection, especially for people who are in danger: *The rebel leader **took sanctuary** in an embassy.* **2** [C] an area for birds or animals where they are protected and cannot be hunted **3** [C] the room where Christian religious services take place

sanc·tum /ˈsæŋktəm/ *n.* [C] **1 the inner sanctum** *humorous* a place that only a few important people are allowed to enter **2** a holy place inside a TEMPLE

sand¹ /sænd/ *n.* [U] the substance that forms deserts and BEACHES, and consists of many small grains of rock

sand² *v.* [T] **1** to make a surface smooth by rubbing it with SANDPAPER or a special piece of equipment **2** to put sand on a frozen road to make it safer

san·dal /ˈsændl/ *n.* [C] a light open shoe that you wear in warm weather ➔ see picture at SHOE¹

sand·bag /ˈsændbæg/ *n.* [C] a bag filled with sand, used for protection from floods, explosions, etc.

sand·bank /ˈsændbæŋk/ *n.* [C] a raised area of sand in a river, ocean, etc.

sand·blast /ˈsændblæst/ *v.* [T] to clean or POLISH metal, stone, glass, etc. with a machine that sends out a powerful stream of sand

sand·box /ˈsændbɑks/ *n.* [C] a special area of sand for children to play in

sand·cas·tle /ˈsændˌkæsəl/ *n.* [C] a small model of a castle made out of sand, usually by children on a BEACH

ˈsand dune *n.* [C] a DUNE

sand·man /ˈsændmæn/ *n.* [singular] a man in children's stories who makes children sleep by putting sand in their eyes

sand·pa·per /ˈsændˌpeɪpɚ/ *n.* [U] strong paper covered on one side with sand or another rough substance, used for rubbing wood in order to make it smooth —**sandpaper** *v.* [T]

sand·pip·er /ˈsændˌpaɪpɚ/ *n.* [C] a small bird with long legs and a long beak, that lives by the ocean

sand·stone /ˈsændstoʊn/ *n.* [U] a type of soft yellow or red rock

sand·storm /ˈsændstɔrm/ *n.* [C] a storm in the desert in which sand is blown around by strong winds

sand·wich¹ /ˈsændwɪtʃ/ *n.* [C] two pieces of bread with cheese, meat, egg, etc. between them, usually eaten for LUNCH: *tuna fish sandwiches*

sandwich² *v.* **be sandwiched between sth** to be in a very small space between two other things: *a motorcycle sandwiched between two vans*

sand·y /ˈsændi/ *adj.* **1** covered with sand: *a sandy beach* **2** sandy hair is dark BLONDE

sane /seɪn/ *adj.* **1** able to think in a normal and reasonable way [≠ **insane**] **2** reasonable and based on sensible thinking: *a sane solution to a difficult problem*

sang /sæŋ/ *v.* the past tense of SING

san·guine /ˈsæŋgwɪn/ *adj. formal* happy and hopeful about the future: *Smith's lawyers aren't very sanguine about the outcome of the trial.*

san·i·tar·i·um /ˌsænəˈtɛriəm/ *n.* [C] a hospital for sick people who are getting better but still need rest and care

san·i·tar·y /ˈsænəˌtɛri/ *adj.* **1** relating to the ways that dirt, infection, and waste are removed, so that places are clean and healthy for people to use: *the lack of **sanitary facilities*** (=toilets and sinks) **2** clean and not involving any danger to your health: *All food is stored under sanitary conditions.*

ˈsanitary ˌnapkin *n.* [C] a piece of soft material that a woman wears in her underwear when she has her PERIOD

san·i·ta·tion /ˌsænəˈteɪʃən/ *n.* [U] the protection of public health by removing and treating waste, dirty water, etc.

san·i·tize /ˈsænəˌtaɪz/ *v.* [T] **1** to make news, literature, etc. less offensive by taking out anything unpleasant: *a sanitized version of the story* **2** to clean something thoroughly, removing dirt and BACTERIA

san·i·ty /ˈsænət̬i/ *n.* [U] **1** the ability to think in a normal and reasonable way: *I went away for the weekend to try and **keep** my **sanity**.* **2** the condition of being mentally healthy: *I feared for my mother's fragile sanity.* | *She wondered if she was **losing** her **sanity**.*

sank /sæŋk/ *v.* the past tense of SINK

San·ta Claus /ˈsæntə ˌklɔz/ **also Santa** *n.* an old man with red clothes and a long white BEARD, who children believe brings them presents at Christmas

sap¹ /sæp/ *n.* **1** [U] the substance like water that

S

carries food through a plant **2** [C] *informal* a stupid person who is easy to deceive or treat badly

sap² *v.* past tense and past participle **sapped**, present participle **sapping** [T] to gradually make something weak or destroy it: *The heat and humidity* ***sapped*** *my* ***strength***.

sap·ling /'sæplɪŋ/ *n.* [C] a young tree → see picture at PLANT¹

sap·phire /'sæfaɪɚ/ *n.* [C,U] a transparent bright blue jewel

sap·py /'sæpi/ *adj. disapproving* expressing love and emotions in a way that seems silly: *a sappy love song*

Sa·ran Wrap /sə'ræn ˌræp/ *n.* [U] *trademark* thin transparent plastic used for wrapping food

sar·casm /'sɑrˌkæzəm/ *n.* [U] a way of speaking or writing in which you say the opposite of what you really mean in order to make an unkind joke or to show that you are annoyed: *"I'm glad you came early," said Jim, with* ***heavy sarcasm***. | *His voice* ***dripped with sarcasm*** (=showed a lot of sarcasm).

sar·cas·tic /sɑr'kæstɪk/ *adj.* using sarcasm: *He can be very sarcastic.* —**sarcastically** *adv.*

sar·dine /sɑr'din/ *n.* [C,U] **1** a young HERRING (=a type of fish), or the meat from this fish, usually sold in cans **2 be packed like sardines** to be packed tightly together in a small space

S

sar·don·ic /sɑr'dɑnɪk/ *adj.* speaking or smiling in an unpleasant way that shows you do not have a good opinion of someone or something

sa·ri /'sɑri/ *n.* [C] a type of loose clothing worn by many Indian and Bangladeshi women, and some Pakistani women

SASE *n.* [C] **self-addressed stamped envelope** an envelope that you put your name, address, and a stamp on, so that someone else can send you something

sash /sæʃ/ *n.* [C] **1** a long piece of cloth that you wear around your waist like a belt: *a white dress with a blue sash* **2** a long piece of cloth that you wear over one shoulder and across your chest as a sign of a special honor

sass /sæs/ *v.* [T] *spoken* to talk in a rude way to someone you should respect: *Don't sass me, young lady!* —**sass** *n.* [U]

sass·y /'sæsi/ *adj. informal* **1** a sassy child is rude to someone s/he should respect **2** a sassy woman is confident and does not really care what other people think about her

SAT *n.* [C] *trademark* **Scholastic Aptitude Test** an examination that high school students take before they go to college

sat /sæt/ *v.* the past tense and past participle of SIT

Sa·tan /'seɪtˀn/ *n.* [singular] the Devil, considered to be the main evil power and God's opponent

sa·tan·ic /sə'tænɪk, seɪ-/ *adj.* **1** relating to practices that treat the Devil like a god: *satanic rites* **2** extremely cruel or evil: *satanic laughter*

sa·tan·is·m /'seɪtˀnˌɪzəm/ *n.* [U] the practice of treating the Devil like a god —**satanist** *n.* [C]

satellite

a satellite photo

sat·el·lite /'sæt̬lˌaɪt/ *n.* [C] **1** a machine that has been sent into space and goes around the Earth in order to send and receive electronic information: *a live broadcast coming in* ***by/via satellite*** | *a satellite communications network*

> **TOPIC**
>
> **spacecraft**, **spaceship**, **rocket**, **(space) shuttle**, **probe**
>
> → see Topic box at SPACE¹

2 a natural object such as the moon that moves around a PLANET **3** a country, town, or organization that is controlled by or is dependent on another larger one

'satellite ˌdish *n.* [C] a large circular piece of metal that receives the signals for satellite television

ˌsatellite 'television also **ˌsatellite T'V** *n.* [U] television programs that are broadcast using SATELLITES in space

sat·in /'sætˀn/ *n.* [U] a type of cloth that is very smooth and shiny

sat·in·y /'sætˀn-i/ *adj.* smooth, shiny, and soft like SATIN: *satiny material*

sat·ire /'sætaɪɚ/ *n.* **1** [U] a way of criticizing someone or something, in which you show his, her, or its faults in a funny way: *a comedian who does* ***political satire*** | *a* ***satire of*** *the movie industry* **2** [C] a play, story, etc. written in this way —**satirical** /sə'tɪrɪkəl/ *adj.* —**satirically** *adv.*

sat·i·rist /'sæt̬ərɪst/ *n.* [C] someone who writes satire

sat·i·rize /'sæt̬əˌraɪz/ *v.* [T] to use satire to make people see someone or something's faults: *a movie satirizing the fashion industry*

sat·is·fac·tion /ˌsæt̬ɪs'fækʃən/ *n.* **1** [C,U] a feeling of happiness or pleasure because you have achieved something or gotten what you wanted [≠ **dissatisfaction**]: *He looked around the room* ***with satisfaction***. | *Liz found* ***satisfaction in*** *her job.* | *the* ***satisfaction of*** *knowing that I was right* **2** [U] the act of getting something you want, need, or have demanded: *the satisfaction of biological needs* **3 to sb's satisfaction** as well or completely as someone wants: *I'm not sure I can answer that question to your satisfaction.*

sat·is·fac·to·ry /ˌsæt̬ɪsˈfæktəri, -tri/ *adj.* good enough for a particular situation or purpose, or good enough to please you [≠ **unsatisfactory**; ➡ **satisfying**]: *a satisfactory explanation | Progress has been satisfactory. | a satisfactory result | an agreement that is **satisfactory to** both sides*

THESAURUS

good enough – having a standard that is satisfactory for a particular purpose or situation: *Is he good enough to play in the major leagues?*
acceptable – good enough for a particular purpose: *Some students said it was easy to get acceptable grades without doing much work.*
adequate – enough in quantitiy or of a good enough quality for a particular purpose: *Are they given adequate training before starting work?*
all right/okay – acceptable, but not excellent: *The school's all right; most kids graduate.*

sat·is·fied /ˈsæt̬ɪsˌfaɪd/ *adj.* **1** pleased because something has happened in the way that you want, or because you have achieved something [≠ **dissatisfied**]: *satisfied customers | Are you **satisfied with** your job?* **2** feeling sure that something is right or true: *I'm **satisfied (that)** he's telling the truth.* **3 satisfied?** *spoken* said in an annoyed way when you say or do something that you do not really want to say or do: *Okay, okay, I was wrong – satisfied?*

sat·is·fy /ˈsæt̬ɪsˌfaɪ/ *v.* past tense and past participle **satisfied**, third person singular **satisfies** [T] **1** to make someone happy by providing what s/he wants or needs: *One bite satisfied my craving for chocolate. | Can the school **satisfy the needs** of special learners?* **2** to make someone feel sure that something is true or has been done correctly: *The evidence did not **satisfy** the jury **that** he was guilty.* **3** *formal* to be good enough for a particular purpose, standard, etc.: *students who have not satisfied the requirements for graduation*

sat·is·fy·ing /ˈsæt̬ɪsˌfaɪ-ɪŋ/ *adj.* **1** making you feel pleased and happy, especially because you have got what you wanted [≠ **unsatisfying**; ➡ **satisfactory**]: *a satisfying victory* **2** food that is satisfying makes you feel that you have eaten enough: *a satisfying meal*

sat·u·rate /ˈsætʃəˌreɪt/ *v.* [T] **1** to make something completely wet: *The ground is completely **saturated with** rain.* **2** to make something very full of a particular type of thing: *an area **saturated with** radio stations* —**saturation** /ˌsætʃəˈreɪʃən/ *n.* [U]

saturated 'fat *n.* [C,U] a type of fat from meat and milk products

Sat·ur·day /ˈsæt̬ɚdi, -deɪ/ *written abbreviation* **Sat.** *n.* [C] the seventh day of the week: *The documents were released Saturday. | Jim's going to Phoenix **on Saturday**. | Would **next Saturday** be a good time for me to visit? | I went out and played golf **last Saturday**. | What are you doing **Saturday night**?*

Sat·urn /ˈsæt̬ɚn/ *n.* the second largest PLANET, which is sixth from the sun

sauce /sɔs/ *n.* [C,U] a thick cooked liquid that is served with food to give it a particular taste: *spaghetti with tomato sauce*

sauce·pan /ˈsɔs-pæn/ *n.* [C] a deep round metal container with a handle, used for cooking

sau·cer /ˈsɔsɚ/ *n.* [C] a small round plate that you put a cup on

sau·cy /ˈsɔsi/ *adj.* about sex or relating to sex, in a way that is amusing but not shocking: *a saucy comedy*

sau·er·kraut /ˈsaʊɚˌkraʊt/ *n.* [U] a salty German food made of CABBAGE

sau·na /ˈsɔnə/ *n.* [C] **1** a room that is filled with steam to make it very hot, in which people sit because it is considered healthy **2** a time when you sit or lie in a room like this

saun·ter /ˈsɔnt̬ɚ, ˈsɑn-/ *v.* [I] to walk in a slow and confident way: *Myers sauntered up to her desk.*

sau·sage /ˈsɔsɪdʒ/ *n.* [C,U] a mixture of meat and SPICES, usually in a small tube shape, that is cooked and often eaten for breakfast

sau·té /sɔˈteɪ/ *v.* [T] to cook something quickly in a little hot oil or fat: *sautéed mushrooms*

sav·age¹ /ˈsævɪdʒ/ *adj.* **1** very cruel and violent: *a savage murder* **2** criticizing someone or something very severely: *a savage attack on the newspaper industry* **3** very severe and harmful: *savage budget cuts* **4** *old-fashioned* PRIMITIVE —**savagely** *adv.*

savage² *n.* [C] *old-fashioned offensive* someone from a country where the way of living seems simple and undeveloped

savage³ *v.* [T] **1** to criticize someone or something very severely: *a movie savaged by the critics* **2** if an animal savages someone, it attacks him/her, and causes serious injuries

sav·age·ry /ˈsævɪdʒri/ *n.* [U] extremely cruel and violent behavior

save¹ /seɪv/ *v.*
1 FROM HARM/DANGER [T] to make someone or something safe from danger, harm, or destruction: *We are working to **save** the rain forest **from** destruction. | The new treatment could **save** his **life**.*
2 MONEY [I,T] **also save up** to keep money so that you can use it later: *We're trying to **save** money **to** buy a house. | I'm **saving up for** a trip to Europe.*
3 NOT WASTE [T] to use less time, money, energy, etc. so that you do not waste any: *We'll save time if we take a cab. | Buying new equipment will actually save the company money.*
4 TO USE LATER [T] to keep something so that you can use or enjoy it in the future: *I'm **saving** this bottle of champagne **for** a special occasion.*

THESAURUS

keep, store, reserve, file, collect
➔ see Thesaurus box at KEEP¹

S

5 HELP TO AVOID [T] to help someone by making it unnecessary for him/her to do something that is inconvenient or difficult: *Could you get the medicine on your way home? It would save me a trip to the pharmacy.*
6 COLLECT [T] **also save** (sth ⇔) **up** to keep all the objects of a particular kind that you can find so that they can be used for a special purpose: *I'm **saving** all the bottles and cans **for** recycling.*
7 KEEP FOR SB [T] to stop people from using something so that it is available for someone else: *We'll **save** some dinner **for** you. | Will you save me a seat?*
8 COMPUTER [I,T] to make a computer keep the work that you have done on it: *Don't forget to save before you close the file.*
9 SPORT [T] to stop the other team from scoring a GOAL in games such as SOCCER or HOCKEY
10 saving grace the one good thing that makes someone or something acceptable: *His sense of humor was his only saving grace.* ➔ **lose/save face** at FACE[1]
save on sth *phr. v.* to avoid wasting something by using as little as possible of it: *We turn the heat down during the day to save on electricity.*

save² *n.* [C] an action by the GOALKEEPER in SOCCER, HOCKEY, etc. that prevents the other team from getting a point

S

sav·er /'seɪvɚ/ *n.* **1 time-saver/money-saver/energy-saver etc.** something that prevents loss or waste: *Shopping by mail is a great time-saver.* **2** [C] someone who saves money in a bank

sav·ing /'seɪvɪŋz/ *n.* **1 savings** [plural] all the money that you have saved, especially in a bank: *She lost their **life savings** in a Vegas casino.* **2** [C] an amount of something that you have not used or do not have to spend: *Enjoy 25% **savings on** our regular prices. | a **saving of** $15*

'savings ac,count *n.* [C] a bank account that pays INTEREST on the money you have in it

THESAURUS

checking account, **joint account**, **online account**
➔ see Thesaurus box at ACCOUNT[1]

,savings and 'loan *n.* [C] a business similar to a bank where you can save money, and that also lends money for things such as houses

'savings bank *n.* [C] a bank whose business is mostly from SAVINGS ACCOUNTS and from LOANS on houses

sav·ior /'seɪvyɚ/ *n.* **1** [C] someone or something that saves you from a difficult or dangerous situation: *Many believed he would be the **savior of** the organization.* **2 the/our Savior** another name for Jesus Christ, used in the Christian religion

sa·vor /'seɪvɚ/ *v.* [T] to make an activity or experience last as long as you can, because you are enjoying every moment of it: *Drink it slowly and savor every drop.*

sa·vor·y /'seɪvəri/ *adj.* savory food has a pleasant spicy or salty smell or taste: *savory snacks*

sav·vy /'sævi/ *n.* [U] practical knowledge and ability: *marketing savvy* —**savvy** *adj.*: *a savvy businesswoman*

saw¹ /sɔ/ *v.* the past tense of SEE

saw² *n.* [C] a tool that has a flat blade with a row of sharp points, used for cutting wood

saw³ *v.* past tense **sawed**, past participle **sawed** or **sawn** /sɔn/ [I,T] to cut something using a saw: *We decided to **saw off** the lower branches of the apple tree.*

THESAURUS

cut, **chop down**, **mow**, **trim**, **snip**
➔ see Thesaurus box at CUT[1]

saw·dust /'sɔdʌst/ *n.* [U] very small pieces of wood that are left when you cut wood with a SAW

saw·mill /'sɔmɪl/ *n.* [U] a factory where trees are cut into boards

sawn /sɔn/ *v.* the past particple of SAW

sax /sæks/ *n.* [C] *informal* a saxophone

sax·o·phone /'sæksə,foʊn/ *n.* [C] a metal musical instrument that you play by blowing into it and pressing special KEYS ➔ see picture on page A6

say¹ /seɪ/ *v.* past tense and past participle **said** /sɛd/ third person singular **says** /sɛz/
1 EXPRESS STH [T] to express a thought or feeling in words: *"I'm so tired," she said. | They left without **saying goodbye**. | Dave **said (that)** he'd call back. | Did she **say what** happened? | Tom didn't **say why** he was angry. | That was **a nice/mean/strange** thing **to say**. | What did you **say to** them?*

THESAURUS

mention – to say something but without giving many details: *He mentioned something about a party.*
add – to say something more about something: *Is there anything you'd like to add?*
express – to say how you feel about something: *It's hard to express how I felt.*
point out – to say something that other people had not noticed or thought of: *"It's upside down," Liz pointed out.*
suggest/imply – to say something in a way that is not direct, especially something bad: *He seemed to be suggesting that I'd stolen it!*
whisper – to say something very quietly: *"Is the baby asleep?" she whispered.*
mumble/mutter/murmur – to say something quietly so that your words are not clear: *He mumbled something about working late. | "It's not fair," she muttered.*

USAGE

Say cannot have a person as its object. Do not use "say me." Use "**tell** me" instead. Compare these sentences: *He said that he was tired. | He told me that he was tired.*

2 PRONOUNCE [T] to pronounce a word or sound: ***How do** you **say** your last name?*

3 WITHOUT WORDS [I,T] to express something without using words: *What is Hopper trying to say in this painting?* | *Her smile **says it all*** (=her smile expresses her happiness).

4 GIVE INFORMATION [T] to give information in writing, pictures, or numbers: *The clock said quarter after six.* | *The instructions **say (that)** you cook it for ten minutes.*

5 sth goes without saying used when what you have said or written is so clear that it really did not need to be stated: ***It goes without saying** that a well-rested person is a better worker.*

6 say to yourself to think something: *I was worried about it, but I said to myself, "You can do this."*

7 to say the least used when what you have said could have been stated much more strongly: *The house needs work, to say the least.*

8 having said that used before saying something that makes the opinion you have given seem less strong: *The movie is poorly made, but having said that, it's still a cute picture to take the kids to.*

9 that is to say used before describing what you mean in more detail or more clearly: *Things still aren't equal. That is to say, women still are not paid as much as men.*

SPOKEN PHRASES

10 be saying used in phrases to emphasize that you are trying to explain what you mean in a way that someone will understand better, especially in a situation in which you are arguing with someone and do not want him/her to be angry: ***All I'm saying is** that he should have been more careful.* | ***I'm not saying** it's a bad idea, just that we need to think about it.* | ***I'm just saying** it would be easier if we made a copy.* | *Teachers have to try to understand their students more, **(do you) know what I'm saying*** (=do you understand me)*?*

11 [T] to suggest or suppose that something might happen or might be true: *Say you were going to an interview. What would you wear?* | ***Let's say** they don't approve our plan. What do we do then?*

12 what do you say? used in order to ask someone if s/he agrees with a suggestion: ***What do you say we** all go to a movie?*

13 you can say that again used in order to say that you completely agree with someone: *"It's cold in here." "You can say that again."*

14 say when used when you want someone to tell you when you have given him/her the correct amount of something, especially a drink

15 Say what? *slang* said when you have not heard something that someone said, or when you cannot believe that something is true

say² *n.* [singular, U] **1** the right to help decide something: *Citizens should **have a say in** how their tax money is spent.* | *Members felt that they **had no say in** the proposed changes.* | *The chairman **has the final say*** (=has the right to make the final decision about something). **2 have your say** to have the opportunity to give your opinion about something: *You'll all have the chance to have your say.*

say·ing /ˈseɪ-ɪŋ/ *n.* [C] a well-known statement that expresses an idea most people believe is true and wise

THESAURUS

phrase, expression, idiom, cliché, proverb
→ see Thesaurus box at PHRASE[1]

SC the written abbreviation of **South Carolina**

scab /skæb/ *n.* [C] **1** a hard layer of dried blood that forms over a cut or wound **2** *informal* an insulting word for someone who works in a place where other people are on STRIKE (=refusing to work because of a disagreement with an employer)

scads /skædz/ *n.* [plural] *informal* large numbers or quantities of something: ***scads of** money*

scaf·fold /ˈskæfəld, -foʊld/ *n.* [C] **1** a structure built next to a building or high wall, for people to stand on while they work on the building or wall **2** a structure used in past times for killing criminals by hanging them from it

scaf·fold·ing /ˈskæfəldɪŋ/ *n.* [U] poles and boards that are built into a structure for people to stand on when they are working on a high wall or the outside of a building

scaffolding

scald /skɔld/ *v.* [T] to burn yourself with hot liquid or steam

scald·ing /ˈskɔldɪŋ/ *adj., adv.* extremely hot: ***scalding hot** coffee*

THESAURUS

hot, boiling, boiling hot, sweltering
→ see Thesaurus box at HOT

scale¹ /skeɪl/ *n.*

1 SIZE [singular, U] the size or level of something, when compared to what is normal: *The **scale of** the problem soon became clear.* | *There has been housing development **on a** massive **scale** since 1980.* | *a **large/small scale** research project*

2 MEASURING SYSTEM [C usually singular] a system for measuring the force, speed, amount, etc. of something, or for comparing it with something else: *The earthquake measured 7 **on** the Richter **scale**.* | *Your performance will be judged **on a scale of** 1 **to** 10.*

3 RANGE [C usually singular] the whole range of different types of people, things, ideas, etc. from the lowest level to the highest: *Some rural schools*

have 50 students while ***at the other end of the scale*** *are city schools with 5,000 students.*
4 FOR WEIGHING [C] a machine or piece of equipment for weighing people or objects: *The nurse asked me to get* ***on the scale.*** → see picture at WEIGH
5 MEASURING MARKS [C] a set of marks with regular spaces between them on an instrument that is used for measuring: *a ruler with a metric scale*
6 MAP/DRAWING [C,U] the relationship between the size of a map, drawing, or model and the actual size of the place or thing that it represents: *a* ***scale of*** *1 inch to the mile*
7 MUSIC [C] a series of musical notes that have a fixed order and become gradually higher or lower in PITCH
8 ON FISH [C usually plural] one of the small flat pieces of hard skin that cover the bodies of fish, snakes, etc. → see picture on page A2

scale² *v.* [T] to climb to the top of something that is high: *They scaled a 40-foot wall and escaped.*
scale sth ⇔ **back/down** *phr. v.* to reduce the size of something such as an organization or plan: *Military operations in the area have been scaled down.*

scal·lop /ˈskæləp, ˈskɑləp/ *n.* [C] a small sea animal that has a hard flat shell, or the meat from this animal

scal·loped /ˈskæləpt, ˈskɑ-/ *adj.* cloth or objects that have scalloped edges are cut in a series of small curves as a decoration

scalp¹ /skælp/ *n.* [C] the skin on the top of your head, where your hair grows

scalp² *v.* [T] **1** *informal* to buy tickets for an event and sell them again at a much higher price **2** to cut the scalp off a dead enemy as a sign of victory

scal·pel /ˈskælpəl/ *n.* [C] a small and very sharp knife used by doctors during operations

scalp·er /ˈskælpɚ/ *n.* [C] someone who makes money by buying tickets for an event and selling them again at a very high price

scal·y /ˈskeɪli/ *adj.* **1** an animal that is scaly is covered with small flat pieces of hard skin **2** scaly skin is dry and rough

scam /skæm/ *n.* [C] *informal* a smart but dishonest plan to get money: *an insurance scam*

scam·per /ˈskæmpɚ/ *v.* [I] to run with short quick steps, like a small animal: *A mouse* ***scampered into*** *its hole.*

scan¹ /skæn/ *v.* past tense and past participle **scanned**, present participle **scanning** **1** [I,T] **also scan through** to read something quickly in order to understand its main meaning or to find a particular piece of information [➡ **skim**]: *I had a chance to scan through the report on the plane.* **2** [T] to examine an area carefully, because you are looking for a particular person or thing: *They anxiously* ***scanned*** *the streets* ***for*** *Billy.* **3** [T] if a machine scans an object or a part of your body, it produces a picture of what is inside [➡ **scanner**]: *All luggage has to be scanned at the airport.* **4** [T] to copy a picture or piece of writing onto a computer by putting it into a machine attached to the computer [➡ **scanner**]

scan² *n.* [C] a medical test in which a special machine produces a picture of something inside your body: *a bone/brain scan*

scan·dal /ˈskændl/ *n.* [C,U] something that has happened that people think is immoral or shocking: *He was involved in a major* ***sex/financial scandal.***

scan·dal·ize /ˈskændlˌaɪz/ *v.* [T] to do something that shocks people very much

scan·dal·ous /ˈskændl-əs/ *adj.* completely immoral and shocking: *scandalous behavior*

scan·ner /ˈskænɚ/ *n.* [C] **1** a machine that passes a BEAM of ELECTRONS over an object or a part of your body in order to produce a picture of what is inside **2** a piece of computer equipment that copies an image from paper onto the computer → see picture on page A11

scant /skænt/ *adj.* not enough: *The story has received* ***scant attention*** *in the press.*

scant·y /ˈskænti/ *adj.* very little in size or amount: *a scanty bikini* —**scantily** *adv.*: *scantily dressed*

scape·goat /ˈskeɪpgoʊt/ *n.* [C] someone who is blamed for something bad that happens, even if it is not his/her fault: *He's been made a* ***scapegoat for*** *their lack of success.* —**scapegoat** *v.* [T]

scar¹ /skɑr/ *n.* [C] **1** a permanent mark on your skin from a cut or wound: *The cut will* ***leave a*** *permanent* ***scar.***

THESAURUS

mark, **blemish**, **bruise**, **pimple**, **zit**, **wart**, **blister**, **freckle**, **mole**
→ see Thesaurus box at MARK²

2 a feeling of fear and sadness that stays with a person after a bad experience: *The war has* ***left*** *a deep* ***scar*** *on this community.*

scar² *v.* past tense and past participle **scarred**, present participle **scarring** [T] **1** to have or be given a permanent mark on your skin from a cut or wound: *The fire had left him* ***scarred for life.*** **2** if a bad experience scars you, it leaves you with a feeling of sadness and fear that continues for a long time: *She was* ***deeply scarred*** *by her father's suicide.*

scarce /skɛrs/ *adj.* if food, clothing, water, etc. is scarce, there is not enough of it available

USAGE

Use **scarce** when there is not enough of something available at a particular time: *During the war, food was scarce.*
Use **rare** when something is valuable and there is not much of it: *a rare coin worth a lot of money*

scarce·ly /ˈskɛrsli/ *adv.* **1** almost not at all, or

almost none at all [= **hardly**]: *Their teaching methods have scarcely changed in the last 10 years.* | *The country has* ***scarcely any*** *industry.* **2** definitely not, or almost certainly not: *Owen is really angry, and you can scarcely blame him.*

scar·ci·ty /ˈskɛrsət̬i/ *n.* [singular, U] a situation in which there is not enough of something: *a* ***scarcity of*** *medical supplies*

scare¹ /skɛr/ *v.* **1** [T] to make someone feel frightened: *I didn't mean to scare you.* | *We were* ***scared to death*** (=very scared). | *The alarm* ***scared the life out of*** *me* (=scared me very much)! **2** [I] to become frightened: *I don't* ***scare easily****, you know.*

scare sb/sth ⇔ **off/away** *phr. v.* **1** to make someone or something go away by frightening him, her, or it: *A barking dog had scared the attackers away.* **2** to make someone uncertain or nervous so that s/he does not do something s/he was going to do: *I'd like to call him, but I don't want to scare him off.*

scare sth ⇔ **up** *phr. v. spoken* to make something although you have very few things to make it from: *I'll try to scare up some breakfast.*

scare² *n.* **1** [singular] a sudden feeling of fear: *You really* ***gave us a scare****.* **2** [C] a situation in which a group of people become frightened about something: *a* ***bomb scare***

scare·crow /ˈskɛrkroʊ/ *n.* [C] an object made to look like a person, that is put in a field to frighten birds away

scarecrow

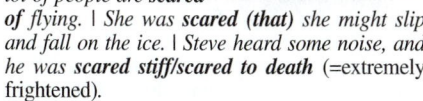

scared /skɛrd/ *adj.* frightened by something or nervous about something [= **afraid**]: *A lot of people are* ***scared of*** *flying.* | *She was* ***scared (that)*** *she might slip and fall on the ice.* | *Steve heard some noise, and he was* ***scared stiff/scared to death*** (=extremely frightened).

THESAURUS

frightened, afraid, terrified, petrified
➔ see Thesaurus box at FRIGHTENED

scarf¹ /skɑrf/ *n.* plural **scarves** /skɑrvz/ or **scarfs** [C] a piece of material that you wear around your neck, head, or shoulders to keep you warm or make you look attractive ➔ see picture at CLOTHES

scarf² *v.* [I,T] *slang*

scarf sth ⇔ **down/up** *phr. v.* to eat something very quickly: *I scarfed down a candy bar between classes.*

scar·let /ˈskɑrlɪt/ *n.* [U] a very bright red color —**scarlet** *adj.*

scarves /skɑrvz/ *n.* a plural of SCARF

scar·y /ˈskɛri/ *adj.* comparative **scarier**, superlative **scariest** frightening: *a scary movie*

scath·ing /ˈskeɪðɪŋ/ *adj.* scathing remarks, COMMENTS, etc. criticize someone or something very severely: *a* ***scathing attack*** *on the president*

scat·ter /ˈskæt̬ɚ/ *v.* **1** [T] to throw or drop a lot of things over a wide area: ***Scatter*** *the seeds* ***over*** *the soil.* **2** [I,T] if people or animals scatter, or if something scatters them, they move quickly in different directions: *The sound of gunfire made the crowd scatter.*

scat·ter·brained /ˈskæt̬ɚˌbreɪnd/ *adj. informal* tending to forget or lose things because you do not think in a practical way

scat·tered /ˈskæt̬ɚd/ *adj.* spread over a wide area or over a long period of time: *The weather forecast is for* ***scattered showers*** (=short periods of rain).

scav·enge /ˈskævɪndʒ/ *v.* [I,T] to search for food or useful objects among things that have been thrown away —**scavenger** *n.* [C]

sce·nar·i·o /sɪˈnɛriˌoʊ, -ˈnær-/ *n.* plural **scenarios** [C] a situation that could possibly happen but has not happened yet: *Even in the* ***worst-case scenario*** (=if the worst possible thing happens), *we'll still get the money back.*

scene /sin/ *n.*

1 PLAY/MOVIE [C] a part of a play or movie during which the action all happens in one place over a short period of time: *She comes on in Act 2, Scene 3.* | *a love scene*

THESAURUS

part, section, chapter
➔ see Thesaurus box at PART¹

2 ACCIDENT/CRIME [singular] the place where an accident or crime happened: *Firefighters arrived* ***on/at the scene*** *within minutes.* | *the* ***scene of the crime***

3 VIEW/PICTURE [C] a view or picture of a place: *a peaceful country scene* ▶ Don't say "There's a nice scene from my window." Say "There's a nice view from my window." ◀

4 the music/fashion/political etc. scene a particular set of activities and the people who are involved in them: *a newcomer to the political scene*

5 ARGUMENT [C] a loud angry argument, especially in a public place: *Sit down and stop* ***making a scene****!*

6 not sb's scene *informal* not the type of thing someone likes: *Loud parties aren't really my scene.*

7 behind the scenes secretly, while other things are happening publicly: *People are working hard behind the scenes.*

8 set the scene a) to provide the conditions in which an event can happen: *This agreement* ***sets the scene for*** *democratic elections.* **b)** to describe the situation before you begin to tell a story

S

sce·ner·y /ˈsinəri/ *n.* [U] **1** the natural features of a place, such as mountains, forests, etc.: *What beautiful scenery!*

USAGE

View is used to talk about all the things you can see from a place: *We had a spectacular view of the ocean from the hotel.*
Scenery is used to talk about the natural features of a place, such as mountains, forests, etc.: *the breathtaking scenery in Arizona*
You cannot say "sceneries."

2 the painted background, furniture, etc. used on a theater stage

sce·nic /ˈsinɪk/ *adj.* with beautiful views of nature: *Let's take the **scenic route** home.*

scent /sɛnt/ *n.* [C] **1** a particular smell, especially a pleasant one: *the **scent of** roses*

THESAURUS

smell, aroma, fragrance, perfume
→ see Thesaurus box at SMELL[2]

2 the smell left behind by an animal or person

scent·ed /ˈsɛntɪd/ *adj.* having a pleasant smell: *scented soap*

S

sched·ule[1] /ˈskɛdʒəl, -dʒul/ *n.* **1** [C,U] a plan of what someone is going to do and when s/he is going to do it: *What's your schedule like on Wednesday?* | *I have a very **busy/full/tight schedule** this week* (=I am very busy). | *The project is six months **behind schedule*** (=progressing more slowly than planned). | *The building was finished **ahead of schedule*** (=earlier than the planned time). | *We are right **on schedule*** (=doing things at the planned times).

THESAURUS

plan, timetable
→ see Thesaurus box at PLAN[1]

2 [C] a list showing the times that buses, trains, etc. leave or arrive at a particular place

schedule[2] *v.* [T] to plan that something will happen at a particular time: *The meeting has been **scheduled for** Friday.* | *Another new store is **scheduled to** open in three weeks.*

scheme[1] /skim/ *n.* [C] **1** a plan, especially to do something bad or illegal: *a **scheme to** avoid paying taxes*

THESAURUS

plan, plot, conspiracy
→ see Thesaurus box at PLAN[1]

2 color scheme the different colors in which a room or house is painted

scheme[2] *v.* [I] to secretly make dishonest plans to get or achieve something: *politicians **scheming to** win votes* —**schemer** *n.* [C]

schism /ˈsɪzəm, ˈskɪzəm/ *n.* [C,U] *formal* the SEPARATION of a group of people into two groups as the result of a disagreement

schiz·o·phre·ni·a /ˌskɪtsəˈfriniə/ *n.* [U] a serious mental illness in which someone's thoughts and feelings become separated from what is really happening around him/her —**schizophrenic** /ˌskɪtsəˈfrɛnɪk/ *adj., n.* [C]

schlep /ʃlɛp/ *v.* past tense and past participle **schlepped**, present participle **schlepping** [T] *informal* to carry or pull something heavy: *I don't want to **schlep** this all the way **across** town.*

THESAURUS

carry, tote, lug, cart, haul, bear
→ see Thesaurus box at CARRY

schlock /ʃlɑk/ *n.* [U] *informal* things that are cheap, bad, or useless

schmaltz·y /ˈʃmɔltsi, ˈʃmɑl-/ *adj. informal disapproving* dealing with strong emotions such as love and sadness in a way that seems silly: *a schmaltzy love song* —**schmaltz** *n.* [U]

schmooze /ʃmuz/ *v.* [I] *informal disapproving* to talk about unimportant things at a social event in a friendly way that is not always sincere

schmuck /ʃmʌk/ *n.* [C] *informal* a stupid person

schnapps /ʃnæps/ *n.* [U] a strong alcoholic drink

schol·ar /ˈskɑlɚ/ *n.* [C] someone who studies a subject and knows a lot about it

schol·ar·ly /ˈskɑlɚli/ *adj.* **1** relating to the serious study of a particular subject: *a scholarly journal* **2** someone who is scholarly spends a lot of time studying, and knows a lot about a particular subject

schol·ar·ship /ˈskɑlɚˌʃɪp/ *n.* **1** [C] an amount of money that is given to someone by an organization to help pay for his/her education: *a football/music/academic etc. scholarship* | *Michael **got a scholarship** to college.* **2** [U] the knowledge, work, or methods used in serious studying: *Burns's book is a work of great scholarship.*

scho·las·tic /skəˈlæstɪk/ *adj. formal* relating to schools or teaching [➡ **academic**]: *an excellent scholastic record*

school[1] /skul/ *n.*

1 BUILDING [C, U] a place where children are taught: *Which **school** did you **go to*** (=attend)? | *I can get some work done while the kids are **at school*** (=studying in the school building).

COLLOCATIONS

(school) curriculum – the subjects that are taught at school
school playground/library/bus
school lunch/school meal
school uniform

TOPIC

At school, **schoolchildren/students** have classes with a **teacher** and **study/learn** a range of **subjects**. In class, students **do classwork**. After school, they **do homework**. Students **take tests/exams**. If they **pass a test/an exam**, they succeed in the test. If they **fail a test/an exam**, they do not succeed in the test, and may have to **retake** it.

2 TIME AT SCHOOL [U] **a)** the time spent at school: *What are you doing* ***after school****?* **b)** the time during your life when you go to a school: *Joanne's one of my old friends from school.*
3 in school attending a school, as opposed to having a job: *Are your boys still in school?*
4 UNIVERSITY **a)** [C,U] *informal* a college or university, or the time when you study there: *"Where did you go to school?" "UC San Diego."* **b)** [C] a department that teaches a particular subject at a university: *the Harvard* ***School of*** *Law* | *I worked my way through* ***law/medical/graduate school****.*
5 FOR ONE SUBJECT [C,U] a place where a particular subject or skill is taught: *an art school*
6 TEACHERS/STUDENTS [singular,U] the students and teachers at a school: *The whole school was sorry when she left.*
7 ART/IDEAS [C] a number of artists, writers, etc. who are considered as a group because their style of work or their ideas are very similar: *the Dutch school of painting*
8 school of thought an opinion or way of thinking about something that is shared by a group of people: *There are many schools of thought on how yoga should be taught.*
9 FISH [C] a large group of fish or other sea creatures that are swimming together: *a* ***school of*** *dolphins*

THESAURUS

herd, **flock**, **shoal**, **pack**, **litter**
➔ see Thesaurus box at GROUP[1]

GRAMMAR

Do not use "the" before **school** when you are talking about someone studying or teaching there: *What time do you leave for school in the morning?*
Use "the" before **school** if someone goes there for some other reason, not to study or teach: *We all went to see the play at the school.*
You must also use "the" if you describe exactly which school you are talking about: *the school on Court Street*

school² *v.* [T] *formal* to train or teach someone: *The children are* ***schooled in*** *music and art from a very early age.*
school·ing /ˈskulɪŋ/ *n.* [U] education at school
schoo·ner /ˈskunɚ/ *n.* [C] a fast sailing ship with two sails
sci·ence /ˈsaɪəns/ *n.* **1** [U] knowledge about the physical world that is based on testing and proving facts, or work that results in this knowledge: *the teaching of science in schools* | *developments in* ***science and technology*** **2** [C,U] the study of a particular type of human behavior: *political science*
ˌscience ˈfiction *n.* [U] books and stories about the future, for example about traveling in time and space

THESAURUS

nonfiction, **fiction**, **literature**, **biography**, **autobiography**
➔ see Thesaurus box at BOOK[1]

sci·en·tif·ic /ˌsaɪənˈtɪfɪk◂/ *adj.* **1** relating to science: *scientific discoveries* | *a* ***scientific experiment*** **2** using an organized system: *We do keep records, but we're not very scientific about it.*
sci·en·tist /ˈsaɪəntɪst/ *n.* [C] someone who works in science
sci-fi /ˌsaɪˈfaɪ/ *n.* [U] *informal* SCIENCE FICTION
scin·til·lat·ing /ˈsɪntlˌeɪt̬ɪŋ/ *adj. formal* very interesting, exciting, and impressive: *a scintillating speech*
scis·sors /ˈsɪzɚz/ *n.* [plural] a tool for cutting paper, cloth, etc., made of two sharp blades fastened together in the middle, and handles with holes for your finger and thumb: *Hand me that* ***pair of scissors****, please.*
scoff /skɔf, skɑf/ *v.* [I,T] to laugh at a person or idea, or to say something in a way that shows you think he, she, or it is stupid: *David* ***scoffed at*** *my fears.*
scold /skoʊld/ *v.* [T] to tell someone in an angry way that s/he has done something wrong: *Mom* ***scolded*** *the boys* ***for*** *taking the candy without asking first.* —**scolding** *n.* [C,U]
scoop¹ /skup/ *n.* [C] **1** a deep spoon for serving food, or the amount that a scoop contains: *two* ***scoops of*** *ice cream* **2** an important or exciting news story that is reported by one newspaper, television station, etc. before any of the others know about it
scoop² *v.* [T] to pick something up with a scoop, a spoon, or with your curved hand: *Cut the melon and* ***scoop out*** *the seeds.*
scoot /skut/ *v.* [I] *informal* **1** to move to one side, especially to make room for someone or something else: *Can you* ***scoot over****?* **2** to move quickly: *Go to bed, Andrew – scoot!*
scoot·er /ˈskut̬ɚ/ *n.* [C] **1** a small two-wheeled vehicle like a bicycle with an engine ➔ see picture at TRANSPORTATION **2** a child's vehicle with two small wheels, an upright handle, and a narrow board that you stand on with one foot, while the other foot pushes the vehicle along the ground
scope¹ /skoʊp/ *n.* [U] **1** the range of things that a subject, activity, book, etc. deals with: *A thorough discussion of this subject is* ***beyond the***

S

***scope of** this paper.* **2** the opportunity to do or develop something: *I want a job with **scope for** promotion.*

scope² *v.*

scope sb/sth ⇔ **out** *phr. v. informal* to look at someone or something to see what he, she, or it is like: *A couple of guys were scoping out the girls.*

scorch /skɔrtʃ/ *v.* [I,T] if you scorch something, or if it scorches, its surface burns slightly and changes color: *Turn down the iron or you'll scorch your shirt.* —**scorch** *n.* [C] *scorch marks from the fire*

scorch·er /ˈskɔrtʃɚ/ *n.* [C usually singular] *informal* an extremely hot day

scorch·ing /ˈskɔrtʃɪŋ/ *adj. informal* extremely hot: *the **scorching heat** of summer in New Orleans*

score¹ /skɔr/ *n.* [C] **1** the number of points that each team or player has won in a game or competition: *What's the score?* | *The **final score** was 35 to 17.* | *Who's going to **keep score*** (=keep a record of the points won)*?* **2** the number of points that a student has earned for correct answers on a test: *Average **test scores** have fallen in recent years.* | *I got a **higher/lower score** than Tracy on the geometry test.* **3 sb knows the score** *informal* if someone knows the score, they know the real facts of a situation, including any unpleasant ones: *He knew the score when he decided to get involved.* **4** a printed copy of a piece of music: *a jazz score* **5 on that score** *spoken* concerning the subject you have just mentioned: *We've got plenty of money, so don't worry on that score.* **6 scores of sth** a large number of people or things: *Scores of reporters gathered outside the courthouse.* **7 settle a score** to do something to harm someone who has harmed you in the past

score² *v.* **1** [I,T] to win or earn points in a game, competition, or test: *How many **goals** has he **scored** this year?* | *Dallas scored in the final minute of the game.* | *Anyone who scored under 70% has to take the exam again.* **2** [T] to give a particular number of points in a game, competition, or test: *The exams will be scored by computer.* **3 score points (with sb)** *informal* to do or say something to please someone or to make him/her feel respect for you: *You'll score points with your girlfriend if you send her flowers.* **4** [I,T] *slang* to manage to get something you want, especially sex or illegal drugs

score·board /ˈskɔrbɔrd/ *n.* [C] a sign on which the SCORE of a game is shown as it is played

score·card /ˈskɔrkɑrd/ *n.* [C] a printed card used for writing the score of a game as it is played

scor·er /ˈskɔrɚ/ *n.* [C] **1** someone who scores a GOAL, point, etc. in a game **2 also scorekeeper** someone who records the number of points won in a game or competition as it is played

scorn¹ /skɔrn/ *n.* [U] strong criticism of someone or something that you think is stupid or not as good as other people or things: *He could barely disguise his **scorn for** her.* —**scornful** *adj.*

scorn² *v.* [T] *formal* to show in an unkind way that you think that a person, idea, or suggestion is stupid or not worth considering: *Skinner's ideas were scorned by many American psychologists.*

Scor·pi·o /ˈskɔrpiˌoʊ/ *n.* **1** [U] the eighth sign of the ZODIAC, represented by a scorpion **2** [C] someone born between October 24 and November 21

scor·pi·on /ˈskɔrpiən/ *n.* [C] a tropical creature like an insect with a curving tail and a poisonous sting

Scotch /skɑtʃ/ *n.* [C,U] a type of WHISKEY (=a strong alcoholic drink) made in Scotland, or a glass of this drink

ˌScotch ˈtape *n.* [U] *trademark* sticky thin clear plastic in a long narrow band, used for sticking paper and other light things together

scot-free /ˌskɑt ˈfri/ *adv.* **get off scot-free** *informal* to avoid being punished although you deserve to be

Scot·tish /ˈskɑt̬ɪʃ/ *adj.* relating to or coming from Scotland

scoun·drel /ˈskaʊndrəl/ *n.* [C] *old-fashioned* a bad or dishonest man

scour /skaʊɚ/ *v.* [T] **1** to search very carefully and thoroughly through an area or a document: *Police have **scoured** the area **for** evidence.* **2** to clean something very thoroughly by rubbing it with a rough material [= **scrub**]

THESAURUS

clean, do/wash the dishes, scrub, dust, polish, vacuum, sweep (up), mop
→ see Thesaurus box at CLEAN²

scourge /skɚdʒ/ *n.* [C] *formal* something that causes a lot of harm or suffering: *the **scourge of** war* —**scourge** *v.* [T]

scout¹ /skaʊt/ *n.* [C] **1** a soldier who is sent to search an area in front of an army and get information **2** someone whose job is to look for good sports players, musicians, etc. in order to employ them: *a talent scout* **3** a member of the GIRL SCOUTS or BOY SCOUTS

scout² *v.* **1** [I] **also scout around** to look for something in a particular area: *I'll **scout around for** a place to eat.* **2** [T] **also scout for** to look for good sports players, musicians, etc. in order to employ them

scowl /skaʊl/ *v.* [I] to look at someone or something in an angry or disapproving way: *Tom **scowled at** me from across the room.* —**scowl** *n.* [C]

Scrab·ble /ˈskræbəl/ *n.* [U] *trademark* a game using a special board and small objects with letters on them, in which you try to make words out of the letters

scrabble *v.* [I] to quickly feel around with your fingers in order to find something

scrag·gly /ˈskrægli/ *adj.* growing in a way that looks uneven and messy: *a scraggly beard*

scram /skræm/ *v.* past tense and past participle **scrammed**, present participle **scramming** [I] *informal* to leave a place very quickly, used especially to tell someone to leave: *Get out of here! Scram!*

scram·ble¹ /ˈskræmbəl/ *v.* **1** [I] to climb up or over something quickly and with difficulty, using your hands to help you: *The kids were* ***scrambling over*** *the rocks.* | *They tried to* ***scramble up*** *the cliff.* **2** [I] to compete and struggle with other people in order to get or reach something: *people* ***scrambling for*** *safety* **3** [I] to try to do something difficult very quickly: *Builders are* ***scrambling to*** *keep up with demand for their services.* **4** [T] to mix electronic signals so that they cannot be understood without a special piece of equipment: *All messages are scrambled for security reasons.* **5** [T] to mix up the order of letters, words, etc., so that the meaning is not clear

scramble² *n.* [singular] **1** a quick and difficult climb in which you have to use your hands to help you: *a rough scramble over loose rocks* **2** a situation in which people rush and struggle with each other in order to get or reach something: *a* ***scramble for*** *the best seats*

ˌscrambled ˈeggs *n.* [plural] eggs that have been cooked after mixing the white and yellow parts together

scrap¹ /skræp/ *n.* **1** [C] a small piece of paper, cloth, etc.: *He wrote his address on a* ***scrap of*** *paper.*

> **THESAURUS**
> **piece, chunk, lump, fragment**
> ➔ see Thesaurus box at PIECE¹

2 [C] a small amount of information, truth, etc.: *There isn't a* ***scrap of*** *evidence to support her story.* **3** [U] materials or objects that are damaged or not used anymore, but can be used again in another way: *He collects and sells* ***scrap metal*** (=metal from old cars, machines, etc. that is melted and used again). **4 scraps** [plural] pieces of food that are left after you have finished eating: *scraps for the dog* **5** [C] *informal* a short fight or argument that is not very serious: *Katie got into a little scrap at school.*

> **THESAURUS**
> **fight, brawl, free-for-all, scuffle**
> ➔ see Thesaurus box at FIGHT²

scrap² *v.* past tense and past participle **scrapped**, present participle **scrapping** **1** [T] *informal* to decide not to do or use something because it is not practical: *We've decided to* ***scrap*** *the whole* ***idea*** *of renting a car.* **2** [T] to get rid of an old machine, vehicle, etc., and use its parts in some other way: *equipment to be sold or scrapped*

scrap·book /ˈskræpbʊk/ *n.* [C] a book with empty pages in which you can stick pictures, newspaper articles, or other things you want to keep

scrape¹ /skreɪp/ *v.* **1** [T] to remove something from a surface, using the edge of a knife, stick, etc.: *Jerry bent to* ***scrape*** *the mud* ***off*** *his boots.* **2** [I,T] to rub against a rough surface in a way that causes slight damage or injury, or to make something do this: *I* ***scraped*** *my knee* ***on*** *the sidewalk.* **3** [I,T] to make an unpleasant noise by rubbing roughly against a surface: *Metal scraped when he turned the key.*

scrape by *phr. v.* to have just enough money to live: *They just manage to scrape by on her salary.*

scrape sth ⇔ **together/up** *phr. v.* to get enough money for a particular purpose, when this is difficult: *We're trying to scrape together enough money for a vacation.*

scrape² *n.* [C] **1** a mark or slight injury caused by rubbing against a rough surface: *Steve only got a few* ***cuts and scrapes****.*

> **THESAURUS**
> **injury, wound, bruise, cut, sprain, bump**
> ➔ see Thesaurus box at INJURY

2 *informal* a situation in which you get into trouble or have difficulties: *Harper has had previous* ***scrapes with*** *the law.* **3** the noise made when one surface rubs roughly against another: *the scrape of chalk on the blackboard*

ˈscrap ˌpaper *n.* [U] used paper on which you can write notes, lists, etc.

scrap·py /ˈskræpi/ *adj. informal approving* always wanting to compete, argue, or fight

scratch¹ /skrætʃ/ *v.* **1** [I,T] to rub your skin with your nails [➥ **itch**]: *Will you scratch my back?* | *Try not to scratch those mosquito bites.* ➔ see picture on page A8

> **THESAURUS**
> **touch, feel, stroke, rub, pat, brush, caress, fondle, tickle, grope**
> ➔ see Thesaurus box at TOUCH¹

2 [T] to cut someone's skin slightly with your nails or with something sharp: *Did the cat scratch you?* | *The tree's branches had scratched her hands.* **3** [T] to damage a surface by pulling something sharp against it: *Don't drag the chair – you'll scratch the floor.* **4** [I] if an animal scratches, it rubs its foot against something, making a noise: *The dog kept* ***scratching at*** *the door to be let in.* **5 scratch the surface** to deal with only a very small part of a subject: *We've been studying the stars for years, but we've only scratched the surface.* **6** [T] *informal* to stop planning to do something because it is no longer possible or practical: *I guess we can scratch that idea.* **7** [T] to remove a person or thing from a list: *Her name had been* ***scratched from/off*** *the list of competitors.*

S

scratch² *n.* **1** [C] a long thin cut or mark on the surface of something or on someone's skin: *Where did this scratch on the car come from?* **2 from scratch** without using anything that was prepared before: *I made the cake from scratch.* **3 without a scratch** *informal* without being injured at all: *Stuart was hurt in the accident, but Max escaped without a scratch.*

'scratch ˌpaper *n.* [U] cheap paper, or paper that has already been used on one side, that you can write notes or lists on

scratch·y /'skrætʃi/ *adj.* **1** scratchy clothes or materials have a rough surface and are uncomfortable to wear or touch: *a scratchy pair of wool socks* **2** a voice that is scratchy sounds deep and rough **3** a scratchy throat is sore

scrawl /skrɔl/ *v.* [T] to write something in a fast, careless, or messy way: *a telephone number scrawled on a piece of paper* —**scrawl** *n.* [C,U]

scraw·ny /'skrɔni/ *adj.* thin and weak: *a scrawny little kid*

scream¹ /skrim/ *v.* **1** [I] to make a loud high noise with your voice because you are hurt, frightened, excited, etc.: *There was a loud bang and people started screaming.* | *She lay there **screaming in pain**.*

> **THESAURUS**
>
> **shout**, **call (out)**, **yell**, **cry out**, **raise your voice**, **cheer**, **bellow**, **holler**
>
> → see Thesaurus box at SHOUT¹

2 [I,T] to shout something in a very loud high voice because you are angry or afraid [= **yell**]: *I **screamed for** help.* | *The girls were **screaming at** each other.*

scream² *n.* [C] **1** a loud high noise that you make when you are hurt, frightened, excited, etc.: *He **let out a scream**.*

> **COLLOCATIONS**
>
> **shrill/piercing** – very loud, high, and annoying
> **high-pitched** – very high
> **ear-splitting** – very loud
> **bloodcurdling** – very frightening
>
> → SHOUT

2 a very loud high sound: *the scream of the jet engines* **3 be a scream** *informal* to be very funny: *"How was the show?" "It was a scream."*

screech /skritʃ/ *v.* **1** [I,T] to shout loudly in a high voice, especially because you are upset: *"Get out of my way!" she screeched.* **2** [I] if a vehicle screeches, its wheels make a loud high noise: *The car **screeched to a halt**.* —**screech** *n.* [C]

screen¹ /skrin/ *n.* **1** [C] the flat glass part of a television or a computer, on which you see words, pictures, etc.: *a computer with an 18-inch screen* | *It's easier to correct your work **on screen** than on paper.* → see picture on page A11 **2** [C] a large flat white surface that movies are shown on in a movie theater **3** [singular, U] movies in general: *his first appearance **on screen*** | *Her play was adapted for **the big screen**.* **4** [C] a wire net that covers an open door or window so that air can get inside a house but insects cannot: *screens on the windows* | *a screen door* **5** [C] a piece of furniture like a thin wall that can be moved around and is used for dividing one part of a room from another **6** [C] something that hides a place or thing: *The house was hidden behind a **screen of** bushes.*

screen² *v.* [T] **1** to do medical tests on people in order to discover whether they have a particular illness: *Women over the age of 50 are **screened for** breast cancer.* **2** to find out information about people in order to decide whether they can be trusted in a particular job: *People wanting to work with children are thoroughly screened.* **3 also screen off** to hide or protect something by putting something in front of it: *The hedge screens the back yard from the street.* **4 screen (your) calls** to let your telephone calls be answered by an ANSWERING MACHINE, so that you can decide whether or not to talk to the person who calls you **5** to show a movie or television program

screen·ing /'skrinɪŋ/ *n.* **1** [C,U] the showing of a film or television program: *a screening of Spielberg's new movie* **2** [U] medical tests that are done on a lot of people to make sure that they do not have a particular disease: ***screening for** breast cancer* **3** [U] tests or checks that are done to make sure that people or things are acceptable or useful for a particular purpose: *security screening of airline passengers*

screen·play /'skrinpleɪ/ *n.* [C] a story written for a movie or a television show

'screen ˌsaver *n.* [C] a moving picture that appears on a computer screen while you are not using the computer

screen·writ·er /'skrinˌraɪt̬ɚ/ *n.* [C] someone who writes SCREENPLAYS

screw¹ /skru/ *n.* **1** [C] a thin pointed piece of metal that you push and turn in order to fasten pieces of wood or metal together [➡ **nail**, **screwdriver**] **2 have a screw loose** *informal* to be slightly crazy

screw² *v.* **1** [T] to fasten one thing to another, using a screw: ***Screw** the shelf **to** the wall.* **2** [T] to fasten or close something by turning it until it cannot be turned any more: *Don't forget to **screw** the top back **on**.*

screw around *phr. v. spoken* to waste time or behave in a silly way: *Stop screwing around and get back to work!*

screw sb/sth ⇔ **up** *phr. v. informal* **1** to make a bad mistake that ruins what you intended to do: *You'd better not screw up again!* | *He's always screwing everything up.* **2** *informal* to make someone feel extremely unhappy, confused, or anxious, especially for a long time: *Carole's family really screwed her up.*

screw·ball /'skrubɔl/ *n.* [C] *informal* **1** someone

who seems very strange, silly, or crazy **2 screwball comedy** a film or television program that is funny because silly or crazy things happen

screw·driv·er /ˈskruˌdraɪvɚ/ *n.* [C] a tool that you use to turn screws

screwed ˈup *adj. informal* **1** very unhappy, confused, or anxious because you have had bad experiences in the past: *These poor kids, they're so screwed up from their parents' divorce.* **2** not working, or in a bad condition: *My left leg **got screwed up** playing football.*

screw·y /ˈskrui/ *adj. informal* slightly strange or crazy: *a screwy plan*

scrib·ble /ˈskrɪbəl/ *v.* **1 also scribble down** [T] to write something quickly in a messy way: *He scribbled down his phone number on a business card.* **2** [I] to draw marks that do not mean anything —**scribble** *n.* [C,U]

THESAURUS

draw, **sketch**, **doodle**, **trace**
➔ see Thesaurus box at DRAW[1]

scribe /skraɪb/ *n.* [C] someone in past times whose job was to copy or record things by writing them

scrimp /skrɪmp/ *v.* **scrimp and save** to try to save as much money as you can, even though you have very little

script /skrɪpt/ *n.* **1** [C] the written form of a speech, play, movie, etc. **2** [C,U] the set of letters used in writing a language [= **alphabet**]: *Arabic script*

script·ed /ˈskrɪptɪd/ *adj.* a scripted speech or broadcast has been planned and written down so that it can be read

scrip·ture /ˈskrɪptʃɚ/ *n.* **1** [U] **also the (Holy) Scripture** the Bible **2** [C,U] the holy books of a particular religion —**scriptural** *adj.*

script·writ·er /ˈskrɪptˌraɪt̬ɚ/ *n.* [C] someone who writes SCRIPTS for movies, television programs, etc.

scroll[1] /skroʊl/ *n.* [C] a document that is rolled up, especially an official document from the past

scroll[2] *v.* [I,T] to move information up or down a computer screen so that you can read it

scrooge /skrudʒ/ *n.* [C] *informal* someone who hates to spend money

scro·tum /ˈskroʊt̬əm/ *n.* [C] the bag of flesh on a man or male animal that contains the TESTICLES

scrounge /skraʊndʒ/ *v. informal* **1** [T] to get money or something you want by asking other people to give it to you instead of earning it or paying for it yourself: *We managed to **scrounge up** enough money to pay the bills.* **2** [I] to search for something such as food or supplies: *We saw children **scrounging around for** food in garbage cans.*

scrub[1] /skrʌb/ *v.* past tense and past participle **scrubbed**, present participle **scrubbing** [I,T] to clean something by rubbing it very hard with a stiff brush or rough cloth: *Tom was on his knees, scrubbing the floor.*

THESAURUS

clean, **do/wash the dishes**, **scour**, **dust**, **polish**, **vacuum**, **sweep (up)**, **scrub**, **mop**
➔ see Thesaurus box at CLEAN[2]

scrub[2] *n.* [U] low bushes and trees that grow in very dry soil

scruff /skrʌf/ *n.* **by the scruff of the neck** by the back of a person's or animal's neck: *The cat had a kitten by the scruff of its neck.*

scruff·y /ˈskrʌfi/ *adj.* dirty and messy: *a scruffy kid*

scrump·tious /ˈskrʌmpʃəs/ *adj. informal* food that is scrumptious tastes very good

scrunch /skrʌntʃ/ *v.*

scrunch sth ⇔ **up** *phr. v.* to twist and press a piece of paper into a ball

scru·ple /ˈskrupəl/ *n.* [C usually plural] a belief about what is right and wrong that prevents you from doing something bad: *He **has no scruples** about lying.*

scru·pu·lous /ˈskrupyələs/ *adj.* **1** done very carefully so that every detail is correct: *This job requires scrupulous attention to detail.* **2** careful to be honest and fair —**scrupulously** *adv.*

scru·ti·nize /ˈskrutˀnˌaɪz/ *v.* [T] to examine someone or something very carefully and completely

scru·ti·ny /ˈskrutˀn-i/ *n.* [U] the process of examining something carefully and completely: ***Closer scrutiny** shows that the numbers don't add up.* | *The senator's office later **came under scrutiny** from the Justice Department.*

scu·ba div·ing /ˈskubə ˌdaɪvɪŋ/ *n.* [U] the sport of swimming under water while breathing from a container of air on your back ➔ see picture on page A10

scuff /skʌf/ *v.* [T] to make a mark on a smooth surface by rubbing something rough against it: *I've already scuffed my new shoes.*

scuf·fle /ˈskʌfəl/ *n.* [C] a short fight: *A policeman was injured in a scuffle with demonstrators yesterday.* —**scuffle** *v.* [I,T]

THESAURUS

fight, **brawl**, **free-for-all**, **scrap**
➔ see Thesaurus box at FIGHT[2]

sculp·tor /ˈskʌlptɚ/ *n.* [C] an artist who makes sculptures

THESAURUS

artist, **painter**, **photographer**, **potter**
➔ see Thesaurus box at ARTIST

sculp·ture /ˈskʌlptʃɚ/ *n.* **1** [C,U] a work of art made from stone, wood, clay, etc.: *a bronze sculpture by Peter Helzer*

THESAURUS

painting, **drawing**, **photography**, **pottery**, **ceramics**
→ see Thesaurus box at ART

2 [U] the art of making objects out of stone, wood, clay, etc.: *a sculpture class*

sculp·tured /ˈskʌlptʃɚd/ *adj.* **1** cut or formed from wood, clay, stone, etc., or decorated with SCULPTURES **2 sculptured muscles/features etc.** muscles, etc. that have a smooth attractive shape

scum /skʌm/ *n.* **1** [singular, U] the thick dirty substance that forms on the surface of a liquid: *a pond covered with green scum* **2** [C] *spoken* a SCUMBAG

scum·bag /ˈskʌmbæg/ *n.* [C] *spoken* an unpleasant person that you do not like, trust, or respect

scur·ry /ˈskɚi, ˈskʌri/ *v.* past tense and past participle **scurried**, third person singular **scurries** [I] to move very quickly with small steps: *workers* ***scurrying around*** *the factory floor*

scut·tle /ˈskʌtl/ *v.* **1** [T] *informal* to ruin someone's plans or chance of being successful: *The issue threatens to scuttle the peace talks.* **2** [I] to run quickly with small steps, especially because you are afraid: *Eddie scuttled down the hall.* **3** [T] to sink a ship, especially in order to prevent it from being used by an enemy

S

scythe /saɪð/ *n.* [C] a farming tool with a long curved blade, used for cutting grain or long grass

SD the written abbreviation of **South Dakota**

SE the written abbreviation of **southeast**

sea /si/ *n.* **1** [C] a large area of salty water that is smaller than an ocean, or that is enclosed by land: *the Mediterranean Sea* **2** [singular, U] a word meaning the ocean that is used when talking about traveling in a ship or boat: *The boat was heading* ***out to sea*** (=away from land). | *four days* ***at sea*** (=on a boat in the ocean) **3 a sea of sth** a large number or amount of something: *a sea of people* **4 the seas** *literary* the ocean

sea·bed /ˈsibɛd/ *n.* [singular] the SEA FLOOR

sea·board /ˈsibɔrd/ *n.* [C] the east side of the U.S., next to the Atlantic Ocean: *the* ***eastern/Atlantic seaboard***

ˌsea ˈfloor *n.* **the sea floor** the land at the bottom of the sea

sea·food /ˈsifud/ *n.* [U] ocean animals such as fish and SHELLFISH that can be eaten

sea·gull /ˈsigʌl/ *n.* [C] a common gray and white bird that lives near the sea and has a loud cry

sea·horse /ˈsihɔrs/ *n.* [C] a small sea fish that has a head and neck that look like those of a horse

seal¹ /sil/ *n.* [C] **1** a large sea animal that has smooth fur, eats fish, and lives around coasts **2** an official mark that is put on documents, objects, etc. in order to prove that they are legal or real: *the seal of the Department of Justice* **3** a piece of rubber or plastic used on something such as a pipe, machine, or container in order to prevent something such as water or air from going into or out of it: *a rubber seal in the booster rocket* **4** a piece of paper, plastic, WAX, etc., that you break in order to open a letter or container: *Do not use this product if the* ***seal*** *on the bottle is* ***broken.*** **5 seal of approval** if you give something your seal of approval, you say that you accept or approve of it, especially officially: *a diet that has the Medical Association's seal of approval*

seal² *v.* [T] **1 also seal up** to close an entrance, container, or hole with something that stops air, water, etc. from coming in or out of it: *Many of the tombs have remained sealed since the 16th century.* **2** to close an envelope, package, etc. using something sticky, such as TAPE or glue **3 seal a deal/agreement etc.** to do something that makes a promise, agreement, etc. seem more definite or official: *We shook hands, sealing the bargain.*

seal sth ⇔ **in** *phr. v.* to stop something from going out of the thing it is contained in: *Fry the steak quickly to seal in the flavor.*

seal sth ⇔ **off** *phr. v.* to stop people entering a particular area or building, especially because it is dangerous: *Police sealed off the street to traffic.*

sealed /sild/ *adj.* something that is sealed is completely closed and cannot be opened unless it is broken, cut, or torn: *a sealed envelope*

ˈsea ˌlevel *n.* [U] the average level of the sea, used as a standard for measuring the height of an area of land, such as a mountain: *200 feet above sea level*

ˈsea ˌlion *n.* [C] a large type of SEAL that lives on the coasts of the Pacific Ocean

seam /sim/ *n.* [C] **1** the line where two pieces of cloth have been sewn together **2** a layer of a mineral, such as coal, that is under the ground **3** the line where two pieces of metal, wood, etc. have been joined together

sea·man, **Seaman** /ˈsimən/ *n.* [C] someone who has the lowest rank in the Navy

seam·less /ˈsimlɪs/ *adj.* done or made so well, that you do not notice where one part ends and another part begins: *The show is a seamless blend of song, dance, and storytelling.*

seam·stress /ˈsimstrɪs/ *n.* [C] a woman whose job is to make and sew clothes

seam·y /ˈsimi/ *adj.* involving unpleasant things such as crime, violence, or immoral behavior: *the seamy side of politics*

sé·ance /ˈseɪɑns/ *n.* [C] a meeting where people try to talk to the spirits of dead people, or to receive messages from them

ˈsea plane *n.* [C] an airplane that can land on water

sear /sɪr/ *v.* **1** [I,T] to burn something with a sudden very strong heat: *The firestorm seared the ground.* **2** [T] to cook the outside of a piece of meat quickly at a very high temperature **3** [I,T] to have a very strong unpleasant effect on you: *The images sear themselves into the viewer's mind.*

search[1] /sɚtʃ/ *n.* **1** [C] an attempt to find someone or something that is difficult to find: *The company has begun a* ***search for*** *a new president.* | *The tiger goes* ***in search of*** *food.* | *Police have* ***called off the search*** *for* (=officially stopped looking for) *the missing children.* **2** [C] a series of actions done by a computer to find information: *I* ***ran a search*** *for information on diabetes.* **3** [singular] an attempt to find the answer to or explanation of a difficult problem: *the* ***search for*** *genetic causes of disease*

search[2] *v.* **1** [I,T] to try to find someone or something by looking very carefully: *Denise* ***searched*** *her purse* ***for*** *a photo of Ben.* | *Jackie's* ***searching for*** *a job.* | *I* ***searched through*** *the papers on my desk, looking for the receipt.*

> **THESAURUS**
> **look, try to find, seek, go through**
> ➔ see Thesaurus box at LOOK[1]

2 [T] if the police or someone in authority searches you or your house, bags, etc., they look for things you might be hiding: *Police* ***searched*** *the house* ***for*** *weapons.* **3** [T] to use a computer to find information, especially on the Internet: ***searching*** *the Web* ***for*** *cheap flights* **4** [I] to try to find an answer or explanation for a difficult problem: *The Center is* ***searching for*** *solutions to campus overcrowding.*

'search ˌengine *n.* [C] a computer program that helps you find information on the Internet ➔ see Topic box at INTERNET

search·ing /ˈsɚtʃɪŋ/ *adj.* trying hard to find out details, facts, or someone's feelings and thoughts: *searching questions*

search·light /ˈsɚtʃlaɪt/ *n.* [C] a large bright light used for finding people, vehicles, etc. at night

'search ˌparty *n.* [C] a group of people who are organized to look for someone who is lost or missing

'search ˌwarrant *n.* [C] a legal document that officially allows the police to search a building

sear·ing /ˈsɪrɪŋ/ *adj.* **1** searing pain is very severe **2** extremely hot: *the searing heat of the desert*

sea·shell /ˈsiʃɛl/ *n.* [C] an empty shell that once covered some types of ocean animals

sea·shore /ˈsiʃɔr/ *n.* **the seashore** the land along the edge of the ocean [➡ **beach**]

> **THESAURUS**
> **shore, coast, beach, bank**
> ➔ see Thesaurus box at SHORE[1]

sea·sick /ˈsiˌsɪk/ *adj.* feeling sick because of the movement of a boat or ship —**seasickness** *n.* [U]

sea·side /ˈsisaɪd/ *adj.* relating to the land next to the sea or the ocean: *a seaside restaurant*

sea·son[1] /ˈsizən/ *n.* **1** [C] one of the four main periods in the year, which are winter, spring, summer, and fall: *the change of the seasons* **2** [C usually singular] a period of time in a year when something happens most often or when something is usually done: *The* ***rainy/wet season*** *usually starts in May.* | *the first game of the season* (=the time when a particular sport is played) | *the* ***hunting/football, etc. season*** | *the* ***holiday season*** (=the period from Thanksgiving to New Year) **3 be in season** if particular vegetables or fruit are in season, it is the time of year when they are ready to be eaten **4 out of season** if someone hunts or catches fish out of season, s/he is doing it when it is not legal

season[2] *v.* [T] to add salt, pepper, etc. to food in order to make it taste better

sea·son·a·ble /ˈsizənəbəl/ *adj.* **seasonable weather/temperatures** weather that seems typical for a particular season [≠ **unseasonable**]

sea·son·al /ˈsizənəl/ *adj.* only happening, available, or needed during a particular season: *seasonal farm workers*

sea·soned /ˈsizənd/ *adj.* [only before noun] having a lot of experience of something: *a seasoned diplomat*

sea·son·ing /ˈsizənɪŋ/ *n.* [C,U] salt, pepper, SPICES, etc. that you add to food to make it taste better

'season ˌticket *n.* [C] a ticket that allows you to go on a trip, go to a theater, watch a sports team, etc. as often as you want during a period of time

> **THESAURUS**
> **one-way ticket, round-trip ticket, off-peak ticket, e-ticket**
> ➔ see Thesaurus box at TICKET[1]

seats

seat[1] /sit/ *n.* **1** [C] a place where you can sit, especially one in a vehicle, restaurant, theater, etc.: *Lucy sat* ***in the front/back seat.*** | *We had great seats at the Giants game.*

S

COLLOCATIONS

back/rear/front seat – the back or front seat in a car
driver's seat – where the driver sits
passenger seat – the seat next to the driver's
window/aisle seat – a seat next to the window or aisle on an airplane
front row seat – a seat in a theater, stadium, etc. that is closest to the stage, field, etc.
good seat – one in a theater, stadium, etc. from which you can see well
empty/vacant seat – one that is not being used
book/reserve a seat – to arrange to have a seat in a theater, on an airplane, etc. at a particular time in the future

2 take/have a seat to sit down **3** [C] the part of a chair, bicycle, etc. that you sit on: *the toilet seat* **4** [C] a position as a member of the government or a group that makes official decisions: *a **seat in** the Senate | a **seat on** the school board* **5** [singular] the part of your pants that you sit on **6 baby/child/car/safety seat** a special seat that you put in a car for a baby or small child **7 seat of learning/government etc.** *formal* a place, usually a city, where a university or government is based ➔ **take a back seat** at BACK SEAT

S

seat² *v.* [T] **1 seated** sitting down: *We **were seated** at the table. | Please **be seated**. | **Remain seated** and fasten your seat belts. | The boy seated next to me had red hair.* **2 seat yourself** to sit down somewhere **3** to make someone sit in a particular place: *The hostess will seat you soon.* **4** if a room, vehicle, theater, etc. seats a number of people, it has enough seats for that number: *The new Olympic stadium seats over 70,000.*

'seat belt *n.* [C] a strong belt attached to the seat of a car or airplane, that you fasten around yourself for protection in an accident: *Please **fasten** your **seat belts**.* ➔ see picture on page A12

seat·ing /'siṭɪŋ/ *n.* [U] **1** all the seats in a theater, restaurant, etc. **2** the places where people will sit, according to an arrangement: *a **seating plan** for the reception*

'sea ˌurchin *n.* [C] a small round sea animal that is covered with sharp points

sea·weed /'siwid/ *n.* [U] a common plant that grows in the ocean

sec /sɛk/ *n.* [C] *spoken* a short form of "second": *Wait a sec, will you?*

se·cede /sɪ'sid/ *v.* [I] *formal* to formally stop being part of a country, especially because of a disagreement: *The southern states wanted to **secede from** the U.S. in the 1850s.* —**secession** /sɪ'sɛʃən/ *n.* [singular, U]

se·clud·ed /sɪ'kludɪd/ *adj.* very private and quiet: *a secluded beach*

se·clu·sion /sɪ'kluʒən/ *n.* [U] the state of being private and away from other people: *The family lives **in seclusion**.*

sec·ond¹ /'sɛkənd/ *number, pron.* **1** 2nd; someone or something that is after the first one: *September 2nd | Jane's second husband | She **came in second** in the women's marathon.* **2** another example of the same thing, or another in addition to the one you have: *A second woman came into the room.* **3 have second thoughts** to start having doubts about a decision you have made: *I had second thoughts about going to graduate school.* **4 a second chance** an opportunity to try to do something again, after you failed the first time **5 be second to none** to be better than anyone or anything else: *His generosity is second to none.*

second² *n.* **1** [C] a unit for measuring time. There are 60 seconds in a minute: *Players have five seconds to take a shot.* **2** [C usually singular] *spoken* a very short period of time: ***For a second**, I thought he was joking. | I'll be off the phone **in a second**! | **Just a second**, I'm almost ready.* **3 seconds** [plural] **a)** another serving of the same food, after you have eaten your first serving **b)** goods sold cheaply because they are not perfect: *factory seconds*

sec·ond·ar·y /'sɛkənˌdɛri/ *adj.* **1** not as important or valuable as something else: *Some of the students behave as though studying is **secondary to** their social life.* **2** developing from something of the same type, or coming from it: *a secondary infection* **3** relating to secondary schools: *secondary education*

'secondary ˌschool *n.* [C] a school that children go to after ELEMENTARY SCHOOL and before college [➡ **high school**]

ˌsecond 'base *n.* [singular] in baseball, the second place that a player must touch before s/he can gain a point

ˌsecond 'class *n.* [U] a way of traveling, especially on trains, that is cheaper but not as comfortable as FIRST CLASS

ˌsecond-'class *adj.* **1** considered to be less important than other people or things: *They treated us like **second-class citizens*** (=people who are not as important as other people in society). **2** relating to cheaper and less comfortable seats on a train, bus, etc.: *second-class tickets*

ˌsecond-'guess *v.* [T] **1** to criticize something after it has already happened, by saying what should have been done: *A lot of people have been second-guessing the police investigation.* **2** to try to say what will happen or what someone will do before s/he does it

sec·ond·hand /ˌsɛkənd'hænd◂ / *adj.* **1** secondhand clothes, furniture, books, etc. have already been owned or used by someone else: *a cheap secondhand car*

THESAURUS

old, **vintage**, **used**
➔ see Thesaurus box at OLD

2 a secondhand report, information, etc. is told to

you by someone who is not the person who originally said it —**secondhand** *adv.*

sec·ond·ly /ˈsɛkəndli/ *adv.* used in order to give a second fact or reason, etc.: *Secondly, the script is really poor.*

ˌsecond ˈnature *n.* [U] something you have done so often that you now do it without thinking a lot about it: *After you get used to driving a car, it becomes second nature.*

ˌsecond ˈperson *n.* [singular] *technical* in grammar, a form of a verb or PRONOUN that you use to show the person you are speaking to. "You" is a second person pronoun, "you are" is the second person singular of the verb "to be".

ˌsecond-ˈrate *adj.* not very good: *second-rate artists*

second wind /ˌsɛkənd ˈwɪnd/ *n.* [singular] a new feeling of energy after you have been working or exercising very hard, and had thought you were too tired to continue

se·cre·cy /ˈsikrəsi/ *n.* [U] the act of keeping something such as information secret, or the state of being secret: *She **swore** him **to secrecy*** (=made him promise to keep a secret). | *talks conducted **in secrecy***

se·cret[1] /ˈsikrɪt/ *adj.* known about by only a few people: *The deal was **kept secret** until the contracts were signed.* | *He **kept** his marriage **secret from** his parents* (=he did not tell his parents about it). | *secret government files*

> **THESAURUS**
>
> **Confidential** information is secret and not intended to be shown or told to other people: *confidential FBI files*
> **Classified** information, documents, etc. are kept secret by the government or an organization: *a spy who passed classified documents to the enemy*
> **Covert** activities are done secretly, especially by a government or official organization: *covert operations run by the CIA*
> **Undercover** work is done secretly by the police in order to catch criminals or find out information: *The police mounted an undercover operation to break the drug-smuggling ring.*
> → PRIVATE[1]

—**secretly** *adv.*: *I secretly recorded our conversation.*

secret[2] *n.* [C] **1** something that is kept hidden or that is known about by only a few people: *Can you **keep a secret*** (=not tell a secret)? **2 in secret** in a private way or place that other people do not know about: *The meetings took place **in secret**.* **3** a particular way of achieving a good result: ***The secret to** good French bread is steam in the oven.*

ˌsecret ˈagent *n.* [C] someone who secretly collects information or watches people for a government

sec·re·tar·y /ˈsɛkrəˌtɛri/ *n.* plural **secretaries** [C] **1** someone whose job is to TYPE letters, keep records, arrange meetings, answer telephones, etc. in an office **2** an official who is in charge of a large government department in the U.S.: *the Secretary of Defense* **3** an official in an organization whose job is to write down notes from meetings, write letters, etc.: *the secretary of the PTA* —**secretarial** /ˌsɛkrəˈtɛriəl/ *adj.*

se·crete /sɪˈkrit/ *v.* [T] **1** if part of a plant or animal secretes a substance, it produces that substance: *The animal secretes a scent to keep attackers away.* **2** *formal* to hide something —**secretion** /sɪˈkriʃən/ *n.* [C,U]

se·cre·tive /ˈsikrəṭɪv/ *adj.* behaving in a way that shows you do not want to tell people your thoughts, plans, etc.

ˌsecret ˈservice *n.* **the Secret Service** a U.S. government department whose main purpose is to protect the President

sect /sɛkt/ *n.* [C] a group of people who have their own set of beliefs or religious habits, especially a group that has separated from a larger group

> **THESAURUS**
>
> **church, denomination, cult**
> → see Thesaurus box at CHURCH

sec·tar·i·an /sɛkˈtɛriən/ *adj.* supporting a particular religious group and its beliefs, or relating to the differences between religious groups: *sectarian violence*

sec·tion[1] /ˈsɛkʃən/ *n.* [C] **1** one of the parts that an object, group, place, etc. is divided into: *the eastern **section of** the city* | *a seat in the **smoking section*** | *The rocket is built **in sections*** (=in parts that are then fitted together).

> **THESAURUS**
>
> **part, piece, department**
> → see Thesaurus box at PART[1]

2 one of the parts of a book or newspaper: *the **sports/travel/business, etc. section*** | *the topic discussed in section 3* —**sectional** *adj.*

section[2] *v.* [T] *technical* to separate something into parts

section sth ⇔ **off** *phr. v.* to divide an area into parts: *The old part of the graveyard had been sectioned off by trees.*

sec·tor /ˈsɛktɚ/ *n.* [C] **1** a part of an area of activity, especially of business, industry, or trade: *jobs in the **public/private sector*** (=the part controlled by the government or by private companies) **2** one of the parts that an area is divided into for military purposes: *the former eastern sector of Berlin*

sec·u·lar /ˈsɛkyəlɚ/ *adj.* not religious or not controlled by a religious authority: *a secular government*

se·cure[1] /sɪˈkyʊr/ *adj.* **1** not likely to change or be at risk: *a secure job* **2** safe and protected from danger: *The bank's deposits remain secure.*

3 fastened, locked, or guarded: *Keep your passport in a secure place.* **4** confident about yourself and your abilities [≠ **insecure**]: *children who feel* ***secure in*** *their parents' love* **5** feeling certain about a situation and not worried that it might change: *He was successful and* ***financially secure*** (=did not need to worry about having enough money).

secure² *v.* [T] **1** to get or achieve something important, especially after a lot of effort: *a treaty designed to secure peace* **2** to make something safe from being attacked or harmed: *Troops secured the border.* **3** to fasten or tie something tightly in a particular position: *Her ponytail was secured with an elastic band.* —**securely** *adv.*

se·cu·ri·ty /sɪˈkyʊrət̬i/ *n.* [U] **1** the state of being safe, or the things you do to keep someone or something safe: *national security* | *airport security checks* | *security cameras* | ***tight security*** *at the conference* **2** protection from change, risks, or bad situations: *employees with* ***job security*** | *Rules and order can give a child a* ***sense of security***. **3** the guards who protect a business's buildings, equipment, and workers: *The receptionist called security.*

se·dan /sɪˈdæn/ *n.* [C] a large car that has seats for at least four people and has a TRUNK

S

se·date /sɪˈdeɪt/ *adj.* slow, formal, or not very exciting: *a sedate private club*

se·dat·ed /sɪˈdeɪt̬ɪd/ *adj.* made sleepy or calm by being given a special drug

sed·a·tive /ˈsɛdət̬ɪv/ *n.* [C] a drug used in order to make someone sleepy or calm

sed·en·tar·y /ˈsɛdnˌtɛri/ *adj.* a sedentary job involves sitting down or not moving very much

sed·i·ment /ˈsɛdəmənt/ *n.* [singular, U] the solid material, such as dirt, that settles at the bottom of a liquid

sed·i·ment·a·ry /ˌsɛdəˈmɛntri, -ˈmɛntəri/ *adj.* made of the SEDIMENT at the bottom of lakes, oceans, etc.: *sedimentary rock*

se·di·tion /sɪˈdɪʃən/ *n.* [U] *formal* speech, writing, or actions that try to encourage people to disobey a government —**seditious** *adj.*

se·duce /sɪˈdus/ *v.* [T] **1** to persuade someone to do something, especially to have sex, by making it seem extremely attractive: *He's talking to her, trying to seduce her.* **2** to make someone want to do something by making it seem very attractive or interesting: *young people who are seduced by Hollywood* —**seduction** /sɪˈdʌkʃən/ *n.* [C,U]

se·duc·tive /sɪˈdʌktɪv/ *adj.* **1** sexually attractive: *a seductive look* **2** very attractive to you: *a seductive job offer*

see /si/ *v.* past tense **saw** /sɔ/ past participle **seen** /sin/

1 NOTICE [T] to notice someone or something, using your eyes: *He saw her go into the house.* | *Can I see your ticket, please?* | *Did you* ***see where*** *the car went off the road?*

THESAURUS

notice – to see something interesting or unusual: *I noticed a police car outside their house.*

spot – to notice or recognize someone or something that is difficult to see: *Nick spotted the advertisement in the paper.*

catch a glimpse of sth/sb – to see something or someone, but only for a short time: *I caught a glimpse of his face as he ran past the window.*

make sth out – to see something, but only with difficulty: *Ahead, I could just make out the figure of a woman.*

catch sight of sb/sth – to suddenly see someone or something: *She caught sight of Alec, waiting in a doorway.*

witness – to see something bad happen, especially an accident or a crime: *Several people witnessed the attack.*

→ HEAR

USAGE

You **look at** a picture, person, thing, etc. because you want to: *Hey, look at these jeans.*
You **see** something without planning to: *Two people saw him take the bag.*
You **watch** TV, a movie, or something that happens for a period of time: *Did you watch the football game last night?* | *The kids are watching TV.*
You can also say that you **saw** a movie, a program, etc., but you cannot say "see television": *I saw a great movie on TV last night.*

2 UNDERSTAND [I,T] to understand or realize something: *Do you* ***see how*** *it works?* | *I could* ***see (that)*** *something was terribly wrong.* | ***(You) see,*** *you have to put in this part first* (=used when you are explaining something). | *"It goes in the red box." "Oh,* ***I see*** (=I understand)." | *At 14, he couldn't* ***see the point of*** (=understand the reason for) *staying in school.* | *It's all coming apart here,* ***see what I mean/see what I'm saying?*** (=used to check that someone understands)

3 ABILITY TO SEE [I,T] to be able to use your eyes to look at things and know what they are: *I* ***can't see*** *a thing without my glasses.*

4 VISIT/MEET [T] to visit, meet, or have a meeting with someone: *I'm seeing Margo and Rod on Saturday.* | *You ought to see a doctor.*

5 FIND OUT [T] to find out information or a fact: *Plug it in and* ***see if*** *it's working.* | *Marion looked out to* ***see what*** *was happening.* | *We could see that it was dangerous.*

6 WATCH [T] to watch a television program, play, movie, etc.: *Karl's seen "Star Wars" about eight times.*

7 CONSIDER [T] to consider someone or something in a particular way: *I thought I'd done the right thing, but Bill saw it differently.* | *Fights on TV can make children* ***see*** *violence* ***as*** *normal.* |

*Well, **the way I see it**, that school is no worse than any other.*
8 EXPERIENCE [T] to have experience of something: *The attorney said he had never seen a case like this before.*
9 HAPPEN [T] to be the time when something happens, or the place where something happens: *This year has seen a 5% increase in burglaries.*
10 FUTURE [I,T] to find out something about the future, or to imagine what might happen in the future: *Just **wait and see** if anything improves.* | *Call them and **see if** we can schedule a meeting.* | *I don't know – I'll **see how it goes/things go**.* | *I **can't see** her **as** a teacher.*
11 MAKE SURE [T] to make sure or check that something is done correctly: *Their duty is to **see that** the rules are kept.* ➔ —see also SEE TO
12 be seeing sb to be having a romantic relationship with someone
13 see eye to eye to agree with someone: *My mother and I have never really seen eye to eye.*
14 see fit to do sth *formal* to decide that it is right to do something, even though many people disagree: *The government has seen fit to start testing more nuclear weapons.*

SPOKEN PHRASES

15 see you used in order to say goodbye to someone you will meet again: *Okay, I'll **see you** later.* | *See you, Ben.*
16 let's see/let me see said when you are trying to remember something or think about something: *Let me see, that's two per person, so 24.*
17 I don't see why not said when you mean yes: *"Would that be possible?" "I don't see why not."*
18 I'll/we'll see said when you do not want to make a decision immediately, especially when you are talking to a child: *"Can Denise come too?" "We'll see."*
19 you should have seen sb/sth said when you think someone or something you have seen was very funny, surprising, etc.: *You should've seen the look on her face!*
20 we'll see about that said when you intend to stop someone doing something: *"She says she's leaving early today." "Really? We'll see about that."*

see about sth *phr. v.* to make arrangements for someone to do something: *I made some phone calls to see about getting him a job.*
see sb ⇔ **off** *phr. v.* to go to an airport, station, etc. to say goodbye to someone who is leaving: *My friends came to see me off at the airport.*
see sb ⇔ **out** *phr. v.* to go with someone to the door when s/he leaves: *No, that's okay, I'll **see myself out*** (=leave without anyone coming with me).
see through *phr. v.* **1 see through** sb/sth to be able to recognize the truth when someone is trying to deceive you: *I can't lie to her; she sees right through me.* **2 see** sb/sth **through** (sth) to continue doing something difficult until it is finished, or to give help and support to someone during a difficult time: *I managed to earn enough to see me through the rest of the year.* | *He'd promised to stay long enough to see it through.* **3 see sth through sb's eyes** to see something or think about it in the way that someone else does
see to sth *phr. v.* to deal with something or make sure that it happens: *Klein **saw to it** that she got free tickets.*

seed¹ /sid/ *n.* **1 a)** [C] a small hard object produced by plants, from which a new plant will grow: *an apple seed* ➔ see picture at PLANT¹ **b)** [U] a quantity of seeds: *grass seed* **2 (the) seeds of sth** the beginning of something that will grow and develop: *The World War I peace agreement **sowed the seeds of** World War II.*

seed² *v.* [T] to plant seeds in the ground

seed·ling /ˈsidlɪŋ/ *n.* [C] a young plant grown from seed ➔ see picture at PLANT¹

seed·y /ˈsidi/ *adj. informal* looking dirty or poor, and often being related to illegal or immoral activity: *a seedy bar*

see·ing /ˈsiɪŋ/ *conjunction* because a particular fact or situation is true: *You can stay out later tonight, **seeing that/as** it's Friday.*

ˌSeeing ˈEye ˌdog *n.* [C] *trademark* a dog that is trained to guide blind people

Seeing Eye dog

seek /sik/ *v.* past tense and past participle **sought** /sɔt/ [T] **1** to try to find or get something: *graduates seeking employment* | *Local schools are **seeking to** reduce the dropout rate.* | *Ted **sought advice/approval/help** from his parents.* | *Refugees **sought refuge** from the civil war.*

THESAURUS

look, **search**, **try to find**, **go through**
➔ see Thesaurus box at LOOK¹

2 *formal* to try to achieve or do something: *The governor will seek re-election.*

seem /sim/ *v.* [linking verb] **1** to appear to exist or be true, or to have a particular quality or feeling: ***It seemed** very strange.* | *The nausea **seems to be** a side effect from the medication.* | *It **seems to** me you don't have much choice.* | *He **seems to** like his job.* | *The town **seemed like** a nice place.* | *It just didn't **seem** right **to** me.*

THESAURUS

appear formal – to seem to have particular

S

qualities: *Light colors make a room appear bigger than it is.*
look – to seem to be something, especially by having a particular appearance: *William looked very tired.*
sound – to seem to have a particular quality when you hear or read about someone or something: *It sounds like a wonderful trip.*
come across as sth – to seem to have certain qualities: *She comes across as a really happy person.*

2 can't/couldn't seem to do sth used to say that you have tried to do something but cannot do it: *I can't seem to relax.* **3** used to make what you are saying less strong or certain, and more polite: *We **seem to** have turned onto the wrong road.*

seem·ing /'simɪŋ/ *adj. formal* appearing to be true even though it may not be: *her seeming calm*

seem·ing·ly /'simɪŋli/ *adv.* in a way that appears to be true but may not be [= **apparently**]: *a seemingly endless road | a seemingly simple task*

seen /sin/ *v.* the past participle of SEE

seep /sip/ *v.* [I] to flow slowly through small holes or cracks: *Blood **seeped through/into** the bandages.* —**seepage** *n.* [singular, U]

see·saw¹ /'sisɔ/ *n.* [C] a long board on which children play, that is balanced in the middle so that when one end goes up the other end goes down

seesaw² *v.* [I] to move suddenly up and down or from one condition to another and back again: *Stock prices seesawed throughout the morning.*

seethe /sið/ *v.* [I] to be so angry that you are almost shaking: *Holly was **seething with** rage.* —**seething** *adj.*

seg·ment /'sɛgmənt/ *n.* [C] a part of something that is different from or divided from the whole: *a **segment of** the entertainment market | an orange segment* —**segmentation** /ˌsɛgmən'teɪʃən/ *n.* [U] —**segmented** /'sɛgmɛntɪd/ *adj.*

seg·re·gate /'sɛgrəˌgeɪt/ *v.* [T] to separate one group of people from others because of race, sex, religion, etc. [≠ **integrate**]: *The classes are segregated by ability.* —**segregation** /ˌsɛgrə'geɪʃən/ *n.* [U] *racial segregation*

THESAURUS
separate, divide, split, break up
➔ see Thesaurus box at SEPARATE²

seg·re·gat·ed /'sɛgrəˌgeɪt̬ɪd/ *adj.* segregated buildings or areas can only be used by members of a particular race, sex, religion, etc.: *racially segregated schools*

seis·mic /'saɪzmɪk/ *adj. technical* relating to or caused by EARTHQUAKES: *a period of seismic activity*

seis·mol·o·gy /saɪz'mɑlədʒi/ *n.* [U] the scientific study of EARTHQUAKES —**seismologist** *n.* [C]

seize /siz/ *v.* [T] **1** to take hold of something quickly and in a forceful way [= **grab**]: *Thomas seized her hand.* **2** to take control of a place suddenly, using military force: *Rebels **seized control** of the embassy.* **3** to take away something such as illegal guns, drugs, etc.: *Police seized 10 kilos of cocaine.*

sei·zure /'siʒɚ/ *n.* **1** [U] the act of taking control or possession of something suddenly: *the seizure of illegal firearms* **2** [C] a short time when someone is unconscious and cannot control the movements of his/her body: *an epileptic seizure*

sel·dom /'sɛldəm/ *adv.* very rarely: *Glenn seldom eats breakfast.*

THESAURUS
rarely, not very often, hardly ever
➔ see Thesaurus box at RARELY

se·lect¹ /sɪ'lɛkt/ *v.* [T] to choose something or someone [= **pick**]: *The entertainers were **selected to** appeal to both adults and children. | the five students **selected for** the program | The university **selected** Garrett **as** athletics director.*

THESAURUS
choose, pick, opt for, decide on
➔ see Thesaurus box at CHOOSE

select² *adj. formal* consisting of or used by a small group of specially chosen people: *a select club*

se·lec·tion /sɪ'lɛkʃən/ *n.* **1** [C,U] the act of choosing something or someone, or the thing or person that is chosen [= **choice**]: *his **selection as** the Democratic candidate | the **selection of** a new leader | **Make** a **selection** from the list.* **2** [C] a collection of things of one type, especially things for sale: *a wide **selection of** jewelry*

se·lec·tive /sɪ'lɛktɪv/ *adj.* careful about what you choose to do, buy, etc.: *a **highly selective** college*

self /sɛlf/ *n.* plural **selves** /sɛlvz/ [C,U] the type of person you are, including your character, abilities, etc.: *He's starting to feel like his **old self** again* (=feel normal again, after feeling bad or sick). *| the need for a child to develop a **sense of self*** (=idea of who s/he is as a person who is different from other people)

ˌself-ab'sorbed *adj.* interested only in yourself and the things that affect you

ˌself-ap'pointed *adj. disapproving* giving yourself a duty or job without the agreement of other people: *a self-appointed guardian of morality*

ˌself-as'sured *adj.* confident about what you are doing —**self-assurance** *n.* [U]

ˌself-'centered *adj.* interested only in yourself and never thinking about other people [= **selfish**]: *a vain, self-centered man*

ˌself-'confident *adj.* sure that you can do things well, that people like you, etc. [= **confident**] —**self-confidence** *n.* [U]

ˌself-'conscious *adj.* worried and embarrassed about what you look like or what other people think of you: *"Hi," I said, suddenly* ***self-conscious about*** *my accent.*

ˌself-conˈtained *adj.* complete in itself and not needing other things to make it work: *a self-contained army base*

ˌself-conˈtrol *n.* [U] the ability to control your feelings and behavior even when you are angry, excited, or upset: *children learning to* ***exercise self-control***

ˌself-deˈfeating *adj.* making a situation have a bad result for you: *the self-defeating attempt to stay young*

ˌself-deˈfense *n.* [U] the use of force to protect yourself from attack: *She shot him* ***in self-defense****.*

ˌself-deˈnial *n.* [U] the practice of not having or doing the things that you enjoy, either because you cannot afford it or for moral or religious reasons

ˌself-deˈstructive *adj.* self-destructive actions are likely to harm or kill the person who is doing them

ˌself-ˈdiscipline *n.* [U] the ability to make yourself do the things that you ought to do, without someone else making you do them: *Working at home takes self-discipline.* —**self-disciplined** *adj.*

ˌself-emˈployed *adj.* working for yourself rather than for a company

ˌself-esˈteem *n.* [U] the feeling of being satisfied with your own abilities, and that you deserve to be liked or respected: *Lack of success at school often leads to* ***low/poor self-esteem****.*

ˌself-ˈevident *adj.* clearly true and needing no proof [= **obvious**]

ˌself-exˈplanatory *adj.* clear and easy to understand, with no need for explanation: *The VCR controls are pretty self-explanatory.*

ˌself-fulˌfilling ˈprophecy *n.* [C] a statement about what will happen in the future, that becomes true because you changed your behavior to make it happen

ˌself-ˈhelp *n.* [U] the use of your own efforts to deal with your problems instead of depending on other people: *self-help books*

ˌself-ˈimage *n.* [C] the idea that you have of your own abilities, appearance, and character: *a* ***poor/good/positive, etc. self-image***

ˌself-imˈportant *adj. disapproving* thinking you are more important than other people

ˌself-imˈprovement *n.* [U] the activity of trying to learn more skills or deal with your problems better

ˌself-inˈdulgent *adj. disapproving* allowing yourself to have or enjoy something that you do not need: *He's irresponsible and self-indulgent.* —**self-indulgence** *n.* [singular, U]

ˌself-inˈflicted *adj.* a self-inflicted injury, problem, etc. is one that you have caused yourself: *a self-inflicted gunshot wound*

ˌself-ˈinterest *n.* [U] the state of caring most about what is best for you, and less about what is best for other people: *an action that is* ***in*** *the national* ***self-interest***

self·ish /ˈsɛlfɪʃ/ *adj. disapproving* caring only about yourself and not about other people [≠ **unselfish**]: *Don't be selfish.* —**selfishness** *n.* [U] —**selfishly** *adv.*

self·less /ˈsɛlflɪs/ *adj.* caring about other people more than about yourself

ˌself-ˈmade *adj.* successful and rich because of your own efforts: *a self-made millionaire*

ˌself-ˈpity *n.* [U] the feeling of being too sorry for yourself

ˌself-ˈportrait *n.* [C] a picture that you make of yourself

ˌself-posˈsessed *adj.* calm and confident because you are in control of your feelings

ˌself-preserˈvation *n.* [U] keeping yourself from being harmed or killed: *the instinct for self-preservation*

ˌself-reˈliance *n.* [U] the ability to act and make decisions by yourself without depending on other people —**self-reliant** *adj.*

ˌself-reˈspect *n.* [U] a feeling of confidence and happiness about your abilities, ideas, and character: *She needs to regain her confidence and self-respect.* —**self-respecting** *adj.*

ˌself-reˈstraint *n.* [U] the ability to control what you do or say in situations that upset you

ˌself-ˈrighteous *adj. disapproving* very proud and sure that your beliefs, attitudes, etc. are right, in a way that annoys other people

ˌself-ˈsacrifice *n.* [U] *approving* the act of giving up what you need or want in order to help someone else —**self-sacrificing** *adj.*

ˌself-ˈsatisfied *adj.* SMUG

self-ˈservice **also** **ˌself ˈserve** *adj.* relating to stores, restaurants, etc. where you get things for yourself, rather than being served: *a self-service gas station*

ˌself-ˈserving *adj. disapproving* showing that you will only do something if it gains you an advantage: *self-serving politicians*

ˈself-styled *adj. disapproving* having given yourself a title, position, etc. without having a right to it: *a self-styled expert*

ˌself-sufˈficient *adj.* able to provide all the things you need without help from other people: *a country that is* ***self-sufficient in*** *food production* —**self-sufficiency** *n.* [U]

ˌself-supˈporting *adj.* able to earn enough money to support yourself: *a self-supporting museum*

sell /sɛl/ *v.* past tense and past participle **sold** /soʊld/ **1** [I,T] to give something to someone in exchange for money [≠ **buy**]: *I sold him my baseball card collection.* | *We* ***sold*** *the car* ***for*** *$5,000.* | *It is illegal to* ***sell*** *alcohol* ***to*** *minors.*

S

THESAURUS

put sth up – to give money to be used for a particular purpose: *Her brother put up $70,000 to start the business.*
auction – to sell things at a special event to the person who offers the most money: *The artist's drawings and posters were auctioned off.*
peddle – to go from place to place trying to sell something, especially something illegal or cheap: *He was peddling souvenirs outside the Sears Tower.*
export – to sell goods to another country: *countries that export oil to the United States.*

2 [I,T] to offer something for people to buy: *a store selling hand-crafted jewelry* | *Avocados* **sell for** *only a few cents each in Mexico.* **3** [I,T] to make someone want to buy something: *Advertisers know that sex sells.* **4** [I,T] to be bought by people in large numbers or amounts: *Her novels have sold millions of copies.* | *Lower-priced homes continue to* **sell well/badly**. **5** [I,T] to try to make someone accept a new plan, idea, etc., or to become accepted: *the candidate's attempts to* **sell** *his policies* **to** *the voters*

sell sth ⇔ **off** *phr. v.* to sell something, especially cheaply, because you need the money or want to get rid of it: *The company is selling off everything but its core business.*

S

sell out *phr. v.* **1** to sell all of something, so that there is none left: *The concert is almost sold out.* **2** *informal* to do something that is against your beliefs or principles, in order to get power or money: *a politician who has sold out to the gun lobby*

sell·er /'sɛlɚ/ *n.* [C] **1** a person or company that sells something [≠ **buyer**] **2 good/best/biggest etc. seller** a product that a company sells a lot of [➡ **best-seller**]

'selling point *n.* [C] a special feature of a product that will make people want to buy it

sell·out /'sɛlaʊt/ *n.* [singular] **1** a performance, sports event, etc. for which all the tickets have been sold: *a sellout crowd* **2** *informal* a situation in which someone does not do something s/he promised, or in which s/he does something that is against his/her beliefs or principles: *Environmental groups labeled the deal a sellout.*

selves /sɛlvz/ *n.* the plural of SELF

se·man·tics /sə'mæntɪks/ *n.* [U] **1** the meaning of a word **2** the study of the meanings of words —**semantic** *adj.*

sem·blance /'sɛmbləns/ *n.* **a/some semblance of sth** a condition or quality that is similar to another one: *Life was returning to some semblance of normality.*

se·men /'simən/ *n.* [U] the liquid that is produced by the male sex organs and contains SPERM

se·mes·ter /sə'mɛstɚ/ *n.* [C] one of two periods into which a year at school or college is divided [➡ **quarter**]: *the* ***spring/fall semester*** ➔ see Topic box at UNIVERSITY

sem·i /'sɛmi/ *n.* [C] *informal* **1** a very large heavy truck consisting of two connected parts **2** a SEMIFINAL

sem·i·cir·cle /'sɛmi,sɚkəl/ *n.* [C] **1** half a circle

THESAURUS

square, **circle**, **triangle**, **rectangle**, **oval**, **cylinder**
➔ see Thesaurus box at SHAPE[1]

2 a group arranged in a curved line: *chairs arranged* ***in a semicircle*** —**semicircular** /,sɛmi'sɚkyəlɚ/ *adj.*

sem·i·co·lon /'sɛmi,koʊlən/ *n.* [C] the mark (;) used in writing to separate independent parts of a sentence or list

sem·i·con·duct·or /'sɛmikən,dʌktɚ/ *n.* [C] a substance such as SILICON that is used in electronic equipment to allow electricity to pass through it

sem·i·fi·nal /'sɛmi,faɪnl, 'sɛmaɪ-, ,sɛmi'faɪnl/ *n.* [C] one of two sports games whose winners then compete against each other to decide who wins the whole competition [➡ **quarterfinal**]

sem·i·nal /'sɛmənəl/ *adj.* new and important, and influencing the way something develops in the future: *Darwin's seminal work on evolution*

sem·i·nar /'sɛmə,nɑr/ *n.* [C] a short course or a special meeting that people attend in order to study a particular subject: *a* ***seminar on*** *effective management*

sem·i·nary /'sɛmə,nɛri/ *n.* plural **seminaries** [C] a college at which people study religion and can train to be priests or ministers

Se·mit·ic /sə'mɪtɪk/ *adj.* relating to the race of people that includes Jews, Arabs, and, in ancient times, Babylonians and Assyrians [➡ **anti-Semitic**]

sen·ate /'sɛnɪt/ *n.* **the Senate** the smaller of the two groups of people who make the laws in countries such as the U.S. and Australia [➡ **House of Representatives**]

sen·a·tor, **Senator** /'sɛnətɚ/ *n.* [C] a member of the Senate: *Senator Feinstein* —**senatorial** /,sɛnə'tɔriəl/ *adj.*

THESAURUS

politician, **president**, **congressman**, **congresswoman**, **governor**, **mayor**
➔ see Thesaurus box at POLITICIAN

send /sɛnd/ *v.* past tense and past participle **sent** /sɛnt/ [T] **1** to arrange for something to go or be taken to another place, especially by mail: *Taryn sent some pictures of the baby.* | *I sent you an e-mail yesterday.* | *Do you want me to* **send** *a copy* **to** *you?* | *a letter* **sent by** *fax* **2** to ask or tell someone to go somewhere: *The UN is* **sending** *troops* **to** *the region.* | *Doris and I were* **sent back** *to bed.* | *Frank came, but I* **sent** *him* **away**. **3** to arrange for someone to go somewhere and stay there: *Morrison was **sent to** jail for five years.* **4 send your love/best wishes etc.** to ask someone to give your greetings, good wishes, etc. to someone else: *Mark sends his love.* **5** to make someone or something do something: *The blast sent people running for safety.* | *The film sent me to sleep.*

send away for sth *phr. v.* to order something through the mail

send sth ⇔ **down** *phr. v.* to make something lose value: *The news sent shares down.*

send for sb/sth *phr. v.* to ask or order someone to come to you, or that something be brought or mailed to you: *An ambulance was sent for.* | *Send now for your free catalog.*

send sb/sth ⇔ **in** *phr. v.* **1** to send something, usually by mail, to a place where it can be dealt with: *Did you send in your application?* **2** to send soldiers, police, etc. somewhere to deal with a dangerous situation: *The FBI sent in agents to investigate.*

send sb/sth ⇔ **off** *phr. v.* **1** to mail something somewhere: *She sent off the completed book to her publisher.* **2** to make someone go somewhere: *We got sent off to camp every summer.*

send sb/sth ⇔ **out** *phr. v.* to make something or someone go from one place to various other places: *The wedding invitations were sent out weeks ago.*

'send-off *n.* [C] *informal* an occasion when people gather together to say goodbye to someone who is leaving: *We wanted to **give** you a big **send-off**.*

se·nile /'sinaɪl/ *adj.* mentally confused or behaving strangely, because of old age —**senility** /sɪ'nɪləṭi/ *n.* [U]

Se·nior /'sinyɚ/ *adj.* **Sr.** used after the name of a man who has the same name as his son [➡ **Junior**]: *Robert Burrelli, Sr.*

senior[1] *n.* [C] **1** a student in the last year of HIGH SCHOOL or college [➡ **junior**, **sophomore**, **freshman**]

THESAURUS

chief, **high-ranking**, **top**
→ see Thesaurus box at POSITION[1]

2 be two/five/ten etc. years sb's senior to be two, five, ten, etc. years older than someone

senior[2] *adj.* older, or of higher rank [➡ **junior**]: *a senior officer*

,senior 'citizen *n.* [C] an old person, especially someone over the age of 65

,senior 'high school *n.* [C] HIGH SCHOOL

se·nior·i·ty /ˌsin'yɔrəṭi, -'yɑr-/ *n.* [U] **1** if you have seniority in a company or organization, you have worked there a long time and have some official advantages: *a worker with ten years' seniority at the plant* **2** the state of being older or higher in rank than someone else: *an important position of seniority*

sen·sa·tion /sɛn'seɪʃən/ *n.* **1** [C,U] the ability to feel, or a feeling that you get from one of your five senses: *Matt **had a** burning **sensation** in his arm.* | *Jerry realized that he had no sensation in his legs.* **2** [C] a feeling that is difficult to describe, caused by a particular event, experience, or memory: *I **had the** strangest **sensation that** I was being watched.* **3** [C usually singular] extreme excitement or interest, or someone or something that causes this: *The band's first album **caused a sensation** among rap fans.*

sen·sa·tion·al /sɛn'seɪʃənl/ *adj.* **1** very interesting or exciting: *a sensational finish to the race* **2** *disapproving* intended to excite or shock people: *sensational news stories* **3** *informal* very good: *She looked sensational.*

sen·sa·tion·al·ism /sɛn'seɪʃənlˌɪzəm/ *n.* [U] *disapproving* a way of reporting events or stories that is intended to shock or excite people

sense[1] /sɛns/ *n.*

1 JUDGMENT [U] good understanding and judgment, especially about practical things, that allows you to make sensible decisions [➡ **common sense**]: *Earl **had the sense** not **to** move the injured man much.* | ***There's no sense in** waiting any longer* (=it is not sensible to continue waiting).

2 FEELING [singular] a feeling about something: *She **felt a** strong **sense of** accomplishment.* | *A sense of panic has spread over the country.*

3 make sense a) to have a clear meaning and be easy to understand: *Do these instructions make any sense to you?* | *I can't **make sense of*** (=understand) *the report.* **b)** if something makes sense, there seems to be a good reason for it: *Why would she wander off alone? It doesn't make sense.* **c)** to be a sensible thing to do: *It **makes sense to** take care of your health while you're young.*

4 SEE/SMELL ETC. [C] one of the five natural powers of sight, hearing, touch, taste, and smell: *a dog with a strong **sense of smell***

5 sense of humor the ability to understand and enjoy things that are funny, or to make people laugh: *Larry **has a** great **sense of humor**.*

6 in a sense/in one sense/in some senses used to say that something is true or correct in a particular way but there may be other ways in which it is not true or correct: *We're all competitors in a sense but we also want each other to succeed.*

7 sb's senses someone's ability to know and do what is sensible in a situation: *I'm glad that Lisa finally **came to** her **senses*** (=realized what was sensible) *and sold that car.* | *Have you **lost your senses*** (=are you crazy)*?* | *It's too bad it took a lawsuit to **bring** them **to** their **senses*** (=make them think clearly and behave sensibly).

8 ABILITY [singular] a natural ability to judge something: *When we were in the woods, I lost all **sense of direction*** (=ability to know where I was).

9 in the sense that used in order to say that

S

something you have just said is true in a particular way: *The experiment was a success in the sense that we got the results we were looking for.*
10 MEANING [C] the meaning of a word, phrase, sentence, etc.: *The word "record" has many senses.* | *In what sense is the term used?*

sense² *v.* [T] to feel that something exists or is true without being told or having proof: *I could sense something was wrong.* | *Sonya **sensed that** David wanted to be alone.* | *I could **sense how** disappointed she was.*

sense·less /ˈsɛnslɪs/ *adj.* **1** happening or done for no good reason or with no purpose: *the senseless killing of innocent people* **2** *informal* if someone is knocked, beaten, etc. senseless, s/he is hit until s/he is unconscious

sen·si·bil·i·ty /ˌsɛnsəˈbɪləṭi/ *n.* plural **sensibilities** [C,U] the way that someone reacts to particular subjects or types of behavior: *We apologize if we have **offended the sensibilities of** our viewers.* | *our moral sensibility*

sen·si·ble /ˈsɛnsəbəl/ *adj.* **1** showing good judgment: *Come on, be sensible.* | *a sensible approach to the problem*

USAGE

Use **sensible** in order to talk about someone who makes good reasonable decisions and who does not behave in a stupid or dangerous way: *She's sensible enough not to drive when she's had a drink.*
Use **sensitive** in order to talk about someone who is easily upset or offended: *He's a little sensitive about his height.*

2 suitable for a particular purpose, and practical rather than fashionable: *Wear sensible shoes.* —**sensibly** *adv.*

sen·si·tive /ˈsɛnsəṭɪv/ *adj.* **1** a sensitive person is able to understand the feelings, problems, etc. of other people [≠ **insensitive**]: *a husband who is **sensitive to** his wife's needs* **2** easily offended or hurt by the things that other people do or say: *a very sensitive child* | *Chrissy is very **sensitive about** her weight.* | *Alan is very **sensitive to** criticism.* ➔ see Usage box at SENSIBLE **3** easily affected, hurt, or damaged by a substance or temperature: *My teeth are really **sensitive to** cold.* | ***sensitive skin*** **4** a sensitive situation or subject needs to be dealt with very carefully because it is secret or because it may offend people: *a sensitive issue/subject/topic* | ***highly sensitive** information* **5** reacting to very small changes in light, temperature, sound, etc.: *a **highly sensitive** listening device* —**sensitively** *adv.* —**sensitivity** /ˌsɛnsəˈtɪvəṭi/ *n.* [U]

sens·or /ˈsɛnsɚ, -sɔr/ *n.* [C] *technical* a piece of equipment that is used to find light, heat, movement, etc., even in very small amounts

sen·so·ry /ˈsɛnsəri/ *adj.* relating to your senses of sight, hearing, smell, taste, or touch: ***sensory overload*** (=too many sights, sounds, tastes, etc.)

sen·su·al /ˈsɛnʃuəl/ *adj.* relating to or enjoying physical pleasure, especially sexual pleasure: *a sensual massage* | *She believes that food can be a **sensual pleasure**.* —**sensuality** /ˌsɛnʃuˈæləṭi/ *n.* [U]

sen·su·ous /ˈsɛnʃuəs/ *adj.* pleasing to your senses: *the sensuous feel of silk*

sent /sɛnt/ *v.* the past tense and past participle of SEND

sen·tence¹ /ˈsɛntˀns, -təns/ *n.* [C] **1** a group of written or spoken words that has a subject and a verb, and expresses a complete thought or asks a question. Sentences written in English begin with a capital letter and end with a PERIOD, a QUESTION MARK, or an EXCLAMATION POINT. **2** a punishment that a judge gives to someone who is guilty of a crime: *a 10-year **prison sentence*** | *Harris is **serving a** 28-year **sentence*** (=spending 28 years in prison). | *He has just begun a **life sentence** for murder.* | *The defendant faces a possible **death sentence*** (=punishment by death).

THESAURUS

penalty, **fine**, **community service**, **corporal punishment**, **capital punishment**
➔ see Thesaurus box at PUNISHMENT

sentence² *v.* [T] if a judge sentences someone who is guilty of a crime, s/he gives him/her a punishment: *He was **sentenced to** life in prison for the murder.*

sen·ti·ment /ˈsɛnṭəmənt/ *n.* **1** [C,U] *formal* an opinion or feeling that you have about something: ***Public/Popular sentiment*** (=what many people believe) *against the war was growing.* | *"Anderson ought to be fired." **"My sentiments exactly** (=I completely agree)."* **2** [U] feelings such as pity, love, or sadness that are considered to be too strong or not appropriate for a particular situation: *There's no room for sentiment in business!*

sen·ti·men·tal /ˌsɛnṭəˈmɛnṭl◂/ *adj.* **1** showing emotions such as love, pity, and sadness too strongly: *a sentimental movie* | *Laurie still gets **sentimental about** our old house.*

THESAURUS

emotional, **moving**, **touching**, **poignant**, **schmalzy**
➔ see Thesaurus box at EMOTIONAL

2 based on or relating to feelings rather than being practical: *a sentimental view of the past* | *The watch wasn't worth much, but it had great **sentimental value**.* —**sentimentality** /ˌsɛnṭəmɛnˈtæləṭi/ *n.* [U]

sen·try /ˈsɛntri/ *n.* plural **sentries** [C] *old-fashioned* a soldier standing outside a building as a guard

sep·a·ra·ble /ˈsɛpərəbəl/ *adj.* able to be separated from something else [≠ **inseparable**]

sep·a·rate¹ /ˈsɛprɪt/ *adj.* **1** not related to or not affected by something else: *He keeps his profes-*

sional life ***separate from*** *his private life.* | *It's a completely separate issue.* **2** different: *a word with four separate meanings* | *In 1995, AT&T announced it would split into three separate companies.* **3** not joined to each other or touching something else: *There is a small smoking area* ***separate from*** *the main dining room.* —**separately** *adv.*

sep·a·rate² /ˈsɛpəˌreɪt/ *v.* **1** [I,T] to divide or split something into two or more parts, or to make something do this: *Ms. Barker* ***separated*** *the class* ***into*** *four groups.* | *At this point the satellite* ***separates from*** *the rocket.*

THESAURUS

divide – to separate something into a number of smaller parts: *The teacher divided the class into groups.*
split – to separate something into two or more groups, parts, etc.: *We split the money between us.*
break up – to separate something into smaller parts: *The phone company was broken up to encourage competition.*
segregate – to separate one group of people from others because of race, sex, religion, etc.: *Schools were racially segregated.*

2 [T] to be between two things so that they cannot touch each other or connect to each other: *A curtain* ***separated*** *one patient's area* ***from*** *another.* **3** [I] to start to live apart from your husband, wife, or sexual partner: *When did Lyle and Jan separate?*

THESAURUS

divorce, split up, break up, leave
→ see Thesaurus box at DIVORCE²

4 [I,T] to move apart, or to make people do this: *Police moved in to separate the crowd.* | *In the fog, they got* ***separated from*** *the rest of their group.*

sep·a·rat·ed /ˈsɛpəˌreɪt̬ɪd/ *adj.* no longer living with your husband, wife, or sexual partner: *Her parents are separated.*

THESAURUS

married, single, engaged, divorced, widowed
→ see Thesaurus box at MARRIED

sep·a·ra·tion /ˌsɛpəˈreɪʃən/ *n.* **1** [U] *formal* the act of separating or the state of being separate: *the* ***separation of*** *powers between Congress and the President* **2** [C,U] a period of time when two or more people live apart from each other: *Separation from the family is hard on children.* **3** [C] a situation in which a husband and wife agree to live apart even though they are still married

Sep·tem·ber /sɛpˈtɛmbɚ/ **Sept.** *n.* the ninth month of the year: *School starts* ***in September.*** | *We have to turn in the papers* ***on September 2nd.*** | *Laura moved here* ***last September.*** | *They're getting married* ***next September.***

se·quel /ˈsikwəl/ *n.* [C] **1** a movie, book, etc. that continues the story of an earlier one: *another* ***sequel to*** *"Jurassic Park"* **2** an event that is related to an earlier event

se·quence /ˈsikwəns/ *n.* [C,U] **1** the order that things are supposed to have, or in which actions are supposed to be done: *Two of the pages were* ***out of sequence*** (=not in the correct order). | *Try to place the following pictures* ***in sequence*** (=in the correct order). **2** a series of related events, actions, etc. that happen or are done in a particular order: *the* ***sequence of events*** *that led to World War I* —**sequential** /sɪˈkwɛnʃəl/ *adj.*

se·quin /ˈsikwɪn/ *n.* [C] a small shiny flat round piece of metal that is sewn on clothes for decoration

se·quoi·a /sɪˈkwɔɪə/ *n.* [C] a REDWOOD

ser·e·nade /ˌsɛrəˈneɪd/ *n.* [C] a love song —**serenade** *v.* [T]

se·rene /səˈrin/ *adj.* very calm or peaceful —**serenity** /sɪˈrɛnət̬i/ *n.* [U]

ser·geant /ˈsɑrdʒənt/ *n.* [C] a low rank in the Army, Air Force, police, etc., or an officer who has this rank

se·ri·al¹ /ˈsɪriəl/ *adj.* **1** arranged or happening one after the other in the correct order: *serial processing on a computer* **2 serial killer/rapist etc.** someone who commits the same crime several times

serial² *n.* [C] a story that is broadcast or printed in several separate parts on television, in a newspaper, etc.

ˈserial ˌnumber *n.* [C] a number put on things that are produced in large quantities, so that each one has its own different number

se·ries /ˈsɪriz/ *n.* plural **series** [C] **1** a group of events, actions, or things of the same kind that happen one after the other: *There has been a* ***series of*** *accidents along this road.* | *the first novel in a series* **2** a set of television or radio programs with the same characters or on the same subject: *a new comedy series* **3** a set of sports games played between the same two teams: *the World Series* (=in baseball)

se·ri·ous /ˈsɪriəs/ *adj.* **1** a serious problem, situation, etc. is extremely bad or dangerous: *Luckily, the damage was not serious.* | *Drugs are a* ***serious problem*** *in many communities.* | *Her mother's been in a* ***serious accident.*** **2 be serious** to say what you really mean, and not joke or pretend: *John is* ***serious about*** *finding a new career.* | *You can't be serious* (=I do not believe you)*!* **3** important and deserving a lot of attention: *Raising children is a* ***serious business.*** **4** a serious romantic relationship is intended to continue for a long time —**seriousness** *n.* [U]

se·ri·ous·ly /ˈsɪriəsli/ *adv.* **1** in a way that is bad or dangerous: *Two of the victims were* ***seriously injured.*** | *Something was* ***seriously wrong.***

2 in a way that shows that you think something is important: *He's thinking seriously about running for governor.* | *Don't* ***take*** *everything he says so* ***seriously*** (=think that it is important). **3** [sentence adverb] *spoken* used to show that what you say next is not a joke: *Seriously, I really need you to be there on time.*

ser·mon /ˈsɚmən/ *n.* [C] **1** a talk about a religious subject, usually given at a church and based on the Bible **2** *informal disapproving* a long talk in which someone tries to give you unwanted moral advice: *a* ***sermon on*** *the virtues of hard work* → PREACH

ser·pent /ˈsɚpənt/ *n.* [C] *literary* a snake

ser·rat·ed /səˈreɪt̬ɪd, ˈsɛˌreɪt̬ɪd/ *adj.* having a sharp edge made of a row of connected V-shaped points: *a serrated knife*

se·rum /ˈsɪrəm/ *n.* [C,U] *technical* a liquid containing substances that fight infection or poison, that is put into a sick person's blood

serv·ant /ˈsɚvənt/ *n.* [C] someone who is paid to clean someone's house, cook food for him/her etc.

serve¹ /sɚv/ *v.*

1 FOOD/DRINKS [I,T] to give someone food or drinks as part of a meal: *Dinner will be served at 8:00.* | *The crab was* ***served with*** *melted butter and a slice of lemon.* | *Why aren't you out there serving the guests?*

2 BE USED [I,T] to be appropriate for a particular purpose: *The couch can also* ***serve as*** *a bed.* | *Critics claim that the weapon* ***serves*** *no useful military* ***purpose****.*

3 DO A JOB [I,T] to spend time doing a particular job, especially one that is helpful: *Kelly* ***served*** *a three-year term* ***in*** *the Army.* | *In 1993, Campbell became the first woman to* ***serve as*** *Canada's prime minister.*

4 PROVIDE STH [T] to provide an area or a group of people with something that they need or use: *We're your local Ford dealers, serving Sioux Falls for over 25 years.*

5 IN PRISON [T] to spend time in prison: *Baxter* ***served a*** *five-year* ***sentence for*** *theft.*

6 LEGALLY [T] to officially give or send someone a legal document to appear in court: *Jones was* ***served*** *a* ***summons*** *to appear in court.*

7 SPORTS [I,T] to start playing a game such as tennis by throwing the ball into the air and hitting it to your opponent

8 it serves sb right *spoken* used in order to say that someone deserves something bad, because s/he has done something stupid or unkind: *"I failed my test." "Serves you right for not studying."*

serve² *n.* [C] the action in a game such as tennis in which you throw the ball into the air and hit it to your opponent

serv·er /ˈsɚvɚ/ *n.* [C] **1** the main computer on a NETWORK that controls all the others **2** someone who brings you food in a restaurant

serv·ice¹ /ˈsɚvɪs/ *n.*

1 IN A STORE ETC. [U] the help that people who work in a restaurant, hotel, store etc. give you: *The food is terrific but the service is lousy.* | *the* ***customer service*** *department*

2 WORK DONE [C,U] the work that you do for someone or an organization: *He retired after 20* ***years of service****.* | *You may need the* ***services of*** *a lawyer.* | *She was given an award in honor of her years of* ***service to*** *the Democratic Party.*

3 BUSINESS [C] a business that provides help or does jobs for people rather than producing things: *a cleaning service*

4 public services things such as hospitals, schools, etc. that are provided by the government for the public to use

5 CEREMONY [C] a formal religious ceremony, especially in a church: *a funeral service*

6 HELP [singular, U] *formal* help that you give to someone: *"Thank you so much." "I'm glad to* ***be of service*** *(=to help)."* | *We're* ***at your service*** (=available to help), *Ma'am.*

7 the service a country's military forces, especially considered as a job

8 GOVERNMENT [C] an organization that works for the government: *the foreign service*

9 SPORTS [C] an act of hitting the ball to your opponent to start a game such as tennis

10 CAR/MACHINE [C] a regular examination of a car or machine to make sure that it works correctly

11 in service/out of service to be available or not available for people to use: *an elevator/bus/telephone, etc. that is out of service*

service² *v.* [T] **1** to examine a machine or vehicle and fix it if necessary: *When's the last time you had the car serviced?*

THESAURUS

repair, **fix**, **mend**, **renovate**, **restore**, **rebuild**
→ see Thesaurus box at REPAIR²

2 to provide people with something that they need: *buses that service the local community*

serv·ice·a·ble /ˈsɚvɪsəbəl/ *adj.* ready or able to be used

ˈservice ˌcharge *n.* [C] an amount of money that is added to the price of something in order to pay for extra services that you use when buying it: *For phone orders, there's a $1 service charge.*

serv·ice·man /ˈsɚvɪsˌmæn, -mən/ *n.* plural **servicemen** /-ˌmɛn, -mən/ [C] a man who is a member of the military

ˈservice ˌstation *n.* [C] a GAS STATION

serv·ice·wom·an /ˈsɚvɪsˌwʊmən/ *n.* plural

servicewomen /-ˌwɪmɪn/ [C] a woman who is a member of the military

ser·vile /ˈsɚvəl, -vaɪl/ *adj. disapproving* very eager to obey and please someone

serv·ing /ˈsɚvɪŋ/ *n.* [C] an amount of food that is enough for one person

ser·vi·tude /ˈsɚvəˌtud/ *n.* [U] the condition of being a SLAVE or being forced to obey someone

ses·sion /ˈsɛʃən/ *n.* [C] **1** a period of time used for a particular purpose, especially by a group of people: *a question-and-answer session | teacher-training sessions* **2** a formal meeting or group of meetings, especially of a court of law or government organization: *The State Court is now **in session**.* **3** a part of the year when classes are given at a university

set[1] /sɛt/ *v.* past tense and past participle **set**, present participle **setting**

1 PUT STH SOMEWHERE [T] to carefully put something down somewhere: *Just **set** that bag **down** on the floor. | He took off his watch and **set** it **on** the dresser.*

2 STANDARD [T] to decide something that other things are compared to or measured against: *The agency has **set standards** for water cleanliness. | Parents should **set an example** for their children* (=behave in the way they want their children to behave).

3 PRICE/TIME ETC. [T] to decide that something will happen at a particular time, cost a particular amount, etc.: *The judge plans to **set** a **date** for the trial. | Officials have not yet **set** a **price** on how much the study will cost.*

4 CLOCK/MACHINE [T] to move part of a clock or a piece of equipment so that it will do what you want it to do: *I **set** my **alarm** for 6:30. | Do you know how to set the VCR?*

5 START STH HAPPENING [I,T] to make something start happening or to make someone start doing something: *Angry mobs **set** the building **on fire**. | Careless campers **set fire to** the dry brush. | A study by military experts was immediately **set in motion**. | Volunteers set to work clearing trash from the field.*

6 MOVIE/STORY ETC. [I, T] if a play, movie, story, etc. is set in a place or at a particular time, the action takes place there or then: *Clavell's epic novel is **set in** 17th century Japan.*

7 set a record to run faster, jump higher, etc. than anyone else: *Bailey set a world record in the 100 meters.*

8 set the table to put knives, forks, etc. on a table so that you can eat a meal

9 set sb/sth straight to correct something or someone: *The company wants to **set the record straight*** (=explain the true situation) *about its safety procedures.*

10 set the stage/scene to make it possible for something to happen: *Recent pay cuts set the stage for a strike.*

11 SUN/MOON [I] when the sun or moon sets, it moves lower in the sky and disappears [≠ **rise**]

12 set your mind/sights/heart on (doing) sth to be determined to achieve something or decide that you definitely want to have it: *Heath had set her sights on the U.S. Senate seat for Colorado.*

13 set foot in/on sth to go into or onto a place: *The event is attracting people who have never before set foot in a museum.*

14 set sb/sth free/loose to allow a person or animal to be free: *All the other hostages were finally set free.*

15 set sail to start sailing somewhere

16 BECOME SOLID [I] if a substance sets, it becomes hard: *The concrete will set within two hours.*

17 set sth to music a) to write music for a story or poem: *poems set to music by Lloyd Webber* **b)** to arrange something so that it can be done while music plays: *exercise routines set to music*

18 set a trap a) to make a trap ready to catch an animal **b)** to invent a plan that will catch someone doing something wrong: *Police set a trap for the thieves.*

19 BONE a) [T] to move the ends of a broken bone into position so that they are in the right place to grow together again **b)** [I] if a broken bone sets, it joins together again

20 HAIR [T] to arrange someone's hair while it is wet, so that it will have a particular style when it is dry

set about sth *phr. v.* **set about (doing)** sth to begin doing something: *Johnny set about improving his Spanish before his trip.*

set sb **against** sb *phr. v.* to make someone start to argue or fight with someone else: *The civil war set brother against brother.*

set sb/sth ⇔ **apart** *phr. v.* to make someone or something different from or better than other similar people or things: *The movie's realistic characters **set** it **apart from** other gangster pictures.*

set sth ⇔ **aside** *phr. v.* **1** to save something for a special purpose: *Hotels must **set aside** 50% of their rooms **for** non-smokers.* **2** to decide not to be affected by a particular belief, idea, etc. because something else is more important: *They should set politics aside and do what is best for the country.*

set back *phr. v.* **1 set** sb/sth ⇔ **back** to delay the progress or development of someone or something: *Officials fear that the incident will set back race relations.* **2 set** sb **back** *informal* to cost someone a lot of money: *My new stereo set me back $2000.*

set sth ⇔ **down** *phr. v.* to write about something so that you have a record of it, such as a set of rules: *The rules of the game were clearly set down.*

set in *phr. v.* if something unpleasant sets in, it begins and is likely to continue: *Winter seems to be setting in early this year.*

S

set off *phr. v.* **1** to start to go somewhere: *Thousands of people* ***set off for*** *the West during the 1800s.* **2 set** sth ⇔ **off** to make something start happening: *The attack set off another round of fighting.* | *The rains set off a mudslide that killed 15 people.* **3 set** sth ⇔ **off** to make something explode: *The bomb was set off by a remote control device.* **4 set** sth ⇔ **off** to make an ALARM start working: *A fire in the kitchen set off the smoke alarms.*

set forth *phr. v.* **1 set** sth ⇔ **forth** *formal* to write or talk about an idea, rule, etc. in a clear and organized way, especially in an official document or speech [= **set out**]: *the principles set forth in the treaty* **2** *literary* to start a trip [= **set out**]

set out *phr. v.* **1** to start a trip, especially a long trip: *The couple* ***set out for*** *Fresno at 9:30.* **2 set out to do** sth to deliberately start doing something in order to achieve a particular result: *He set out to make a movie about his experiences in Vietnam.* **3 set out** sth to write or talk about ideas, rules, etc. in a clear and organized way: *He is the first candidate to set out his foreign policy proposals.*

set up *phr. v.* **1 set** sth ⇔ **up** to start a company, organization, business, etc.: *The county has set up a special education program for teenage mothers.* **2 set** sth ⇔ **up** to prepare equipment so that it is ready for an event, activity, or situation: *Chris, could you help me set up the computer?* **3 set** sth ⇔ **up** to arrange for something to happen: *Call the doctor's office and set up an appointment.* **4 set** sth ⇔ **up** to build or place something somewhere: *The police have set up a roadblock.* **5 set** sb ⇔ **up** to deliberately make people think that someone has done something wrong: *Hudson accused his partners of setting him up.* **6 set up shop** to start a business: *They set up shop in 1993 in Mason's basement.*

S

set² *n.* [C] **1** a group of things that belong together or are related in some way: *a* ***set of*** *dishes* | *a set of rules* | *a chess set* ➔ see picture at COLLECTION **2** a television: *a TV set* **3 a)** a place where a movie or television program is filmed: *OK, everybody, quiet* ***on the set!*** **b)** the SCENERY, furniture, etc. used in a play, movie, or television show **4** one part of a game such as tennis or VOLLEYBALL: *Hewitt leads two sets to one.* **5** a performance by a band, singer, or DJ: *They played a 90-minute set.*

set³ *adj.* **1** [only before noun] a set time, amount, price, etc. is fixed and is never changed: *We meet at a set time each week.* | *I invest a set amount of money each month.* **2** [not before noun] *informal* ready to do something: *If everyone is* ***all set****, we'll start the meeting.* | *I was just* ***set to*** *leave when the phone rang.* **3 be set on/upon/against (doing) sth** *informal* to be very determined about something: *Jerry's* ***dead set against*** *paying the extra money for the trip.* **4** in a particular place or position: *a castle* ***set on*** *a hill*

set·back /ˈsɛtˌbæk/ *n.* [C] something that delays your progress or makes things worse than they were: *a* ***major setback*** | *The peace talks* ***suffered a setback*** *when fighting resumed this week.*

> **THESAURUS**
> **problem, hitch, trouble, snag, hassle**
> ➔ see Thesaurus box at PROBLEM

set·ting /ˈsɛtɪŋ/ *n.* [C] **1** the place where something is or where something happens, and all the things that surround it: *a cabin in a mountain setting* | *the* ***perfect setting*** *for a wedding* **2** the position in which you put the controls on a machine or instrument: *Turn the microwave to its* ***highest setting****.* **3** the place or time in which the events in a book, movie, etc. happen: *London is the setting for his most recent novel.*

set·tle /ˈsɛtl/ *v.*

1 END ARGUMENT [I,T] to end an argument or solve a disagreement: *an attempt to* ***settle*** *the* ***case/claim/lawsuit*** | *The union finally* ***settled with*** *management after a two-day strike.* | *They might be willing to* ***settle out of court*** (=come to an agreement without going to a court of law). | *They met recently to try and* ***settle their differences*** (=agree to stop arguing).

2 COMFORTABLE POSITION [I,T] to move into a comfortable position: *Dave* ***settled back*** *and turned on the TV.* | *Roger settled himself on a park bench for a photograph.*

3 DECIDE STH [T] to decide on something, or organize the details of something that will happen in the future: *So it's settled — I'll meet you in front of the theater at 7:00.*

4 IN A NEW PLACE a) [I,T] to go to a place where no people have lived permanently before and start to live there: *the men and women who settled Alaska* **b)** [I] to begin to live in a place where you intend to live for a long time: *My family moved around a lot before* ***settling in*** *Los Angeles.*

5 SNOW/DUST [I] if snow, dust, etc. settles, it falls to the ground and stays there

6 BILL/DEBT [T] if you settle a bill, account, debt, etc., you pay all the money that you owe

7 settle a score to do something bad to someone because s/he has done something bad to you

8 STOMACH [I,T] if your stomach settles, or if something settles it, it stops feeling uncomfortable or making you sick

9 settle your nerves to do something to make yourself stop being nervous or upset: *He took a deep breath to settle his nerves.*

settle down *phr. v.* **1 settle** sb ⇔ **down** to become quiet and calm, or to make someone quiet and calm: *Kids, settle down and eat your dinner.* | *Sometimes we take the baby for a ride in the car to settle him down.* **2** to start living a quiet and calm life in one place, especially when you get married: *My parents want me to marry Jim and* *settle down.* **3** to begin to do something and to give it all your attention: *When he finally* ***settled down to*** *work, it was 10:30.*

settle for sth *phr. v.* to accept something that is less than what you wanted: *We looked at some nice apartments, but we had to settle for the cheapest one.*

settle in **also** **settle into** sth *phr. v.* to become happier and more comfortable in a new situation or place: *Adam seems to have settled in at his new school.*

settle on/upon sth *phr. v.* to decide or agree on something: *They haven't settled on a name for the baby yet.*

settle up *phr. v. informal* to pay money that you owe for something: *I'll* ***settle up with*** *the bartender, then let's go.*

set·tled /'sɛtld/ *adj.* **1 feel/be settled** to feel comfortable about living or working in a particular place: *We don't feel settled in our new house yet.* **2** unlikely to change: *the settled life of a farmer*

set·tle·ment /'sɛtlmənt/ *n.* **1** [C,U] an official agreement or decision that ends an argument: *The two sides have* ***reached a settlement*** (=made an agreement) *in the land dispute.* **2** [C,U] a payment of money that you owe someone or that someone owes to you: *He accepted a financial settlement of $500.* **3** [U] the movement of a large number of people into a new place in order to live there: *the* ***settlement of*** *the Oklahoma territory* **4** [C] a group of houses and buildings where people live, in a place where no group lived before: *a Stone Age settlement*

set·tler /'sɛtlɚ, 'sɛtl-ɚ/ *n.* [C] someone who goes to live in a new place, usually where there were few people before: *early* ***settlers of*** *the American West*

set·up /'sɛtʌp/ *n.* [C usually singular] **1** a way of organizing or arranging something: *Do you like the new setup at work?* **2** *informal* a dishonest plan that is intended to trick someone: *I knew immediately that the whole thing was a setup.*

sev·en /'sɛvən/ *number* **1** 7 **2** seven O'CLOCK: *The movie starts at seven.*

sev·en·teen /ˌsɛvən'tin◂/ *number* 17 —**seventeenth** *number*

sev·enth /'sɛvənθ/ *number* **1** 7th **2** 1/7 **3 be in seventh heaven** *informal* to be extremely happy

sev·en·ty /'sɛvənti/ *number* **1** 70 **2 the seventies a)** the years between 1970 and 1979 **b)** the numbers between 70 and 79, especially when used for measuring temperature **3 be in your seventies** to be aged between 70 and 79: *She's* ***in*** *her* ***early/mid/late seventies.*** —**seventieth** /'sɛvəntiɪθ/ *number: her seventieth birthday*

sev·er /'sɛvɚ/ *v.* [T] *formal* **1** to cut through something completely: *His finger was severed in the accident.* **2** to end a relationship or agreement with someone: *The deal* ***severs*** *all* ***ties*** *between the two organizations.* —**severance** *n.* [U]

sev·eral /'sɛvrəl/ *quantifier* a number of people or things that is more than a few, but not a lot [➡ **few**]: *I called her several times on the phone.* | *I've talked to* ***several of*** *my students about this.*

sev·erance pay /'sɛvrəns ˌpeɪ/ *n.* [U] money you get from a company that you worked for when they no longer have a job for you

se·vere /sə'vɪr/ *adj.* **1** very bad or serious: *severe head injuries* | *severe problems* **2** very strict or extreme: *severe criticism* | *The president's plan calls for severe penalties for underage criminals.* **3** not kind or friendly: *a severe look on her face* —**severity** /sɪ'vɛrəti/ *n.* [C,U]

se·vere·ly /sə'vɪrli/ *adv.* very badly or to a great degree: *The building was severely damaged in the fire.* | *She was punished severely for her actions.*

sew /soʊ/ *v.* past tense **sewed**, past participle **sewn** /soʊn/ or **sewed** [I,T] to use a needle and thread to make or repair clothes, or to attach something such as a button to them: *My mother taught me to sew.* | *Can you* ***sew*** *a button* ***on*** *this shirt for me?* —**sewing** *n.* [U] ➔ see picture at KNIT[1]

sew sth ⇔ **up** *phr. v. informal* to gain control over a situation so that you are sure to win or get an advantage: *The Republicans think they* ***have*** *the election* ***sewn up.***

sew·age /'suɪdʒ/ *n.* [U] the waste material and used water that is carried away from houses by sewers: *a sewage treatment plant*

sew·er /'suɚ/ *n.* [C] a pipe or passage under the ground that carries away waste material and used water from houses, factories, etc.

sewn /soʊn/ *v.* a past participle of SEW

sex /sɛks/ *n.* **1** [U] the physical activity that people do together in order to produce babies or for pleasure: *They believe it's wrong to* ***have sex*** *before they're married.* | *She said she wouldn't* ***have sex with*** *him until she knew him better.* | *the need to practice* ***safe sex*** (=wear something that will protect you from sexual diseases) **2** [U] the condition of being male or female: *I don't care what sex the baby is, as long as it's healthy.* **3** [C] one of the two groups of people or animals, male and female: *He isn't comfortable with members of* ***the opposite sex*** (=people that are not his own sex). | *people of* ***both sexes*** (=men and women)

'sex drive *n.* [C usually singular] someone's ability or need to have sex regularly

'sex eduˌcation *n.* [U] education in schools about sexual activity and sexual relationships

sex·ism /'sɛkˌsɪzəm/ *n.* [U] the belief that one sex, especially the female sex, is weaker, less intelligent, or less important than the other, especially when this results in someone being treated unfairly

sex·ist /'sɛksɪst/ *adj.* relating to or showing sexism: *sexist remarks* —**sexist** *n.* [C]

'sex life *n.* [C] someone's sexual activities: *an active and fulfilling sex life*

'sex ˌsymbol *n.* [C] someone famous who many people think is very sexually attractive

sex·u·al /ˈsɛkʃuəl/ *adj.* **1** relating to sex: *sexual contact | a sexual relationship* **2** relating to the social relationships between men and women: *children learning their sexual roles* —**sexually** *adv.*: *the age when teenagers become sexually active* (=start having sex)

ˌsexual 'harassment *n.* [U] sexual remarks, looks, or touching done to someone who does not want it, especially from someone that s/he works with

ˌsexual 'intercourse *n.* [U] *formal* the physical act of sex between two people

sex·u·al·i·ty /ˌsɛkʃuˈæləṭi/ *n.* [U] the things people do and feel that are related to their desire or ability to have sex

sex·y /ˈsɛksi/ *adj.* comparative **sexier**, superlative **sexiest** sexually exciting or attractive: *sexy clothes*

Sgt. *n.* the written abbreviation of **sergeant**

sh, shh /ʃʃ/ *interjection* used in order to tell someone to be quiet: *Shh! I can't hear what he's saying.*

S

shab·by /ˈʃæbi/ *adj.* **1** shabby clothes, places, or objects are old and in bad condition: *shabby hotel rooms* **2** unfair or wrong: *I don't deserve this kind of **shabby treatment**.* —**shabbily** *adv.*

shack¹ /ʃæk/ *n.* [C] a small building that has not been built very well

shack² *v.*

shack up *phr. v. informal disapproving* to start living with someone who you have sex with but are not married to: *I found out that she was **shacked up with** some guy from Florida.*

shack·le¹ /ˈʃækəl/ *n.* [C usually plural] **1** one of a pair of metal rings joined by a chain, that is used for keeping a prisoner's hands or feet together **2 the shackles of sth** *written* limits that something puts on your freedom: *We need to free ourselves from the shackles of the past.*

shackle² *v.* [T] **1** to restrict what someone can do: *a company shackled by debts* **2** to put shackles on someone

shade¹ /ʃeɪd/ *n.* **1** [singular, U] an area that is cooler and darker because the light of the sun cannot reach it [➡ **shadow**]: *Let's find a table **in the shade**. | boys sitting **in the shade of** a tree*

USAGE

Shade is a cool dark area where the sun does not reach: *We ate our lunch in the shade.*
A **shadow** is a dark shape made by something that blocks the sun or a light: *She saw his shadow on the wall.*

2 [C] something that reduces or blocks light, especially a cover that you pull across a window **3** [C] a particular degree of a color: *a darker shade of red* **4 shades** [plural] *informal* SUNGLASSES **5 shade of meaning/opinion etc.** a meaning, etc. that is slightly different from other ones: *a word with many shades of meaning* **6 a shade** very slightly, a little bit: *The room is a shade too hot for me.*

shade² *v.* [T] to protect something from direct light or heat: *She used her hand to **shade** her eyes **from** the sun.*

shad·ow¹ /ˈʃædoʊ/ *n.* **1** [C] a dark shape that an object or a person makes on a surface when s/he or it is between that surface and the light: *The sun began to **cast** long **shadows*** (=make long shadows) *across a grassy field.* ➔ see Usage box at SHADE¹ **2** [C,U] darkness caused when light is prevented from coming into a place: *Margaret's face was half hidden **in shadow**. | He waited **in the shadows**.* **3 without/beyond a shadow of a doubt** without any doubt at all: *I think he's guilty beyond a shadow of a doubt.* **4 cast a shadow over/on sth** to make something seem less attractive or impressive: *The scandal cast a shadow over his reputation for the rest of his career.*

shadow² *v.* [T] to follow someone closely in order to watch what s/he is doing

shad·ow·y /ˈʃædoʊi/ *adj.* **1** mysterious and secret: *a **shadowy figure** from his past* **2** full of shadows and difficult to see: *a shadowy corner*

shad·y /ˈʃeɪdi/ *adj.* **1** protected from the sun or producing shade: *a shady spot for a picnic* **2** *informal* not honest or legal: *a **shady** business **deal***

shaft /ʃæft/ *n.* [C] **1** a passage that goes up through a building or down into the ground, so that someone or something can get in or out: *an elevator shaft* **2** a long handle on a tool, SPEAR, etc. **3 shaft of light/sunlight** a narrow beam of light

shag·gy /ˈʃægi/ *adj.* **1** shaggy hair or fur is long and messy: *a shaggy beard* **2** having shaggy hair

shake

shaking hands

shake¹ /ʃeɪk/ *v.* past tense **shook** /ʃʊk/ past participle **shaken** /ˈʃeɪkən/ present participle **shaking** **1** [I,T] to move up and down or from side to side with quick movements, or to make someone or something do this: *His hands were shaking. | Shake the bottle before you open it. | She shook him by the shoulders and told him to pay attention.*

THESAURUS

tremble – to shake because you are frightened or upset: *The dog was trembling with fear.*
shiver – to shake because you are very cold: *I jumped up and down to stop myself shivering.*
wobble – to shake from side to side: *The pile of books wobbled and fell.*
vibrate – to shake continuously with small fast movements: *The music was so loud that the whole room vibrated.*
rattle – to shake and make a noise: *The windows rattled in the wind.*

2 shake your head to move your head from side to side as a way of saying no [➡ **nod**] **3 shake sb's hand/shake hands (with sb)** to hold someone's hand in your hand and move it up and down, as a greeting or a sign that you have agreed on something **4** [I] if your voice shakes, it sounds unsteady, usually because you are nervous or angry **5** [T] to make someone feel less confident or certain about something: *This experience has **shaken** my **confidence/faith/belief** in the legal system.* **6 be/look/feel shaken** to be frightened, shocked, or upset: *Mark looked shaken as he put down the phone.*

shake sb ⇔ **down** *phr. v. informal* to get money from someone by using threats

shake off *phr. v.* **1 shake** sth ⇔ **off** to get rid of an illness, problem, etc.: *I can't seem to shake off this cold.* **2 shake** sb ⇔ **off** to escape from someone who is chasing you

shake sth ⇔ **out** *phr. v.* to shake something such as a cloth so that small pieces of dirt, dust, etc. come off

shake sb/sth ⇔ **up** *phr. v.* **1** if an unpleasant experience shakes someone up, s/he is shocked or upset by it: *The accident really shook her up.* **2** to make changes to an organization, country, etc. to make it more effective ➔ SHAKEUP

shake² *n.* [C] **1** an act of shaking: ***Give** the ketchup bottle **a** good **shake**.* **2** a MILKSHAKE: *a vanilla shake*

shake·down /ˈʃeɪkdaʊn/ *n.* [C] **1** *informal* the act of getting money from someone by using threats **2** a final test of a vehicle or system for problems before it is put into general use

shak·en /ˈʃeɪkən/ *v.* the past participle of SHAKE

shake·up /ˈʃeɪk-ʌp/ *n.* [C] a process in which an organization, company, etc. makes a lot of changes in a short time in order to be more effective

shak·y /ˈʃeɪki/ *adj.* **1** weak and unsteady because of illness, old age, or shock: *a shaky voice* | *She stood up, still feeling a little bit shaky.* **2** likely to fail or be unsuccessful: *a shaky marriage* | *The team got off to a **shaky start*** (=they started badly). **3** not solid or firm: *a shaky ladder*

shall /ʃəl; *strong* ʃæl/ *modal verb* **1** *formal* used in official documents to state an order, law, promise, etc.: *The right to a trial by jury shall be preserved.* **2 shall I/we?** used in order to ask a question, especially as a way of suggesting something: *Shall I turn on the air conditioner?* **3** *formal* used in order to say what will happen in the future: *I shall keep her picture always.*

shallow

shal·low /ˈʃæloʊ/ *adj.* **1** measuring only a short distance from the top to the bottom [≠ **deep**]: *a shallow baking dish* | *a shallow pool* **2** *disapproving* not interested in or not showing any understanding of important or serious matters [≠ **deep**]: *a shallow argument* | *If he's only interested in your looks, that shows how shallow he is.*

sham¹ /ʃæm/ *n.* [singular] *disapproving* someone or something that is not what s/he is claimed to be: *Our marriage is a sham.*

sham² *adj.* made to appear real in order to deceive people: *sham jewelry*

sham·bles /ˈʃæmbəlz/ *n. informal* **be (in) a shambles a)** to be very badly organized, and fail completely: *The whole evening was a shambles – the food never even arrived.* **b)** to be very messy or damaged: *The apartment was a shambles.*

shame¹ /ʃeɪm/ *n.* [U] **1 it's/what a shame** *spoken* used in order to say that a situation is disappointing, and you wish things had happened differently: ***It's such a shame (that)** Margaret couldn't come.* | *"Our game was cancelled because of the rain." "Oh, **that's a shame**."* | ***What a shame** we missed the wedding.* **2** the feeling of being guilty or embarrassed that you have after doing something that is wrong [➡ **ashamed**]: *a deep sense of shame*

THESAURUS

guilt, **remorse**, **conscience**
➔ see Thesaurus box at GUILT

3 Shame on you! *spoken* used in order to tell someone that s/he should feel ashamed of something that s/he has done: *Shame on you, Patrick. I trusted you.* **4 put sb/sth to shame** to be so much better than someone or something else that it makes the other thing seem very bad or ordinary: *This party puts my little dinner to shame.* **5** loss of honor: *His behavior **brought shame on** the whole family.* | ***There's no shame in** finishing second* (=it should not make you feel ashamed).

S

shame² *v.* [T] to make someone feel ashamed: *It shames me to say it, but I lied.*

shame·ful /ˈʃeɪmfəl/ *adj.* so bad that someone should be ashamed: *a shameful secret* —**shamefully** *adv.*

shame·less /ˈʃeɪmlɪs/ *adj.* not seeming to be ashamed of your bad behavior, although other people think you should be ashamed: *a shameless liar* —**shamelessly** *adv.*

sham·poo¹ /ʃæmˈpu/ *n.* [C,U] a liquid soap used for washing your hair

shampoo² *v.* [T] to wash something with shampoo: *She showered and* ***shampooed*** *her* ***hair***.

shan·ty /ˈʃænti/ *n.* plural **shanties** [C] a small building that has not been built very well

shape

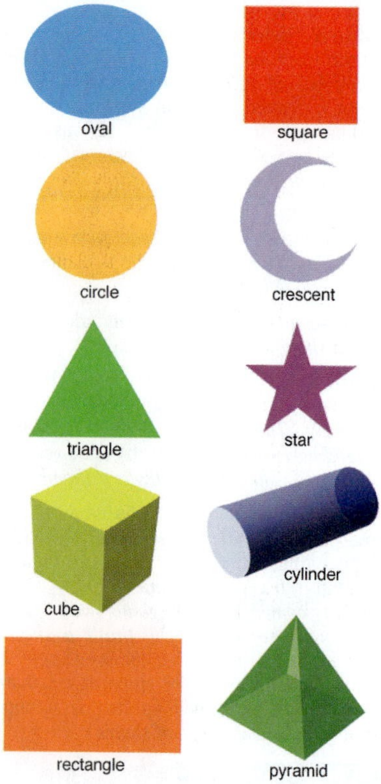

shape¹ /ʃeɪp/ *n.* **1** [C,U] the form that something has, for example round, square, TRIANGULAR, etc. [➡ **shaped**]: *a cake* ***in the shape of*** *a heart* | *What shape is your kitchen table?*

THESAURUS

Types of shapes
square – a shape with four straight sides that are equal in length and four angles of 90 degrees
circle – a round shape that is like an O
semicircle – half a circle
triangle – a shape with three straight sides and three angles
rectangle – a shape with four straight sides and four angles of 90 degrees
oval – a shape like a circle, but which is longer than it is wide
cylinder – an object in the shape of a tube

Describing types of shapes
square – shaped like a square: *a square box*
circular/round – shaped like a circle: *a circular table*
semicircular – shaped like a semi-circle: *a semi-circular arch above the door*
triangular – shaped like a triangle: *sails divided into triangular sections*
rectangular – shaped like a rectangle: *a simple rectangular building*
oval – shaped like an oval: *an oval swimming pool*
cylindrical – shaped like a cylinder: *The statue is on top of a tall cylindrical column.*

2 in good/bad/poor shape in good, bad, etc. condition or health: *The old car's still in good shape.* **3 in shape/out of shape** in a good or bad state of health or physical FITNESS: *I need to* ***get in shape***. **4 take shape** to develop into a clear and definite form **5** [C] something or someone that you cannot see clearly enough to recognize: *He was just a shape in the mist.*

shape² *v.* [T] **1** to influence something such as a belief or opinion and make it develop in a particular way: *an event that shaped public opinion* **2** to make something have a particular shape: ***Shape*** *the clay* ***into*** *small balls.*

shape up *phr. v. informal* **1** to improve your behavior or work: *You better shape up John, or you're off the team.* **2** to make progress in a particular way: *The team is starting to shape up nicely.*

shaped /ʃeɪpt/ *adj.* having a particular shape: ***heart-shaped/star-shaped, etc.*** *flowers* | *a trophy* ***shaped like*** *a football*

shape·ly /ˈʃeɪpli/ *adj.* having an attractive shape: *her long shapely legs*

share¹ /ʃɛr/ *v.* **1** [I,T] to have or use something with other people: *She* ***shares*** *an office* ***with*** *her boss.* | *There's only one book – we'll have to share.* **2** [T] to let someone have or use something that belongs to you: *Will you* ***share*** *your toys* ***with*** *Ronnie?* **3** [I,T] to divide something between two or more people: *I took the cookies to work to* ***share with*** *everybody.* | *We share the expenses for the house.*

THESAURUS

give out, pass, hand, hand out, pass out, distribute
➔ see Thesaurus box at GIVE OUT

4 [T] to have the same interest, opinion, etc. as someone else: *We* ***share*** *an* ***interest in*** *cooking.*

5 [T] to tell someone else about an idea, secret, problem, etc.: *Thank you for **sharing** your feelings **with** me.*

share[2] *n.* **1** [singular] the part of something that you own or are responsible for: *I paid my **share of** the bill and left.* | *Becky deserves a large share of the credit.* **2 have/get your (fair) share** to get as much of something as you could reasonably expect to have: *Rob's certainly **getting** his **share of** attention from the women.* | *Don't worry – you'll get your fair share.* **3** [C] one of the equal parts into which the OWNERSHIP of a company is divided, that people can buy and sell [➡ **stock**]: *He wants to **buy/sell** 500 **shares** in CNN.* | ***shares in** General Electric*

share·hold·er /ˈʃɛrˌhoʊldɚ/ *n.* [C] someone who owns STOCK

shark /ʃɑrk/ *n.* [C] a large sea fish with very sharp teeth

sharp[1] /ʃɑrp/ *adj.*
1 ABLE TO CUT something that is sharp has a very thin edge or point that can cut things easily [≠ **blunt**; ➡ **dull**]: *a sharp knife* | *It's **razor sharp*** (=very sharp).
2 DIRECTION a sharp turn or bend changes direction suddenly: *a **sharp turn** in the road* | *Make a **sharp left/right** onto Grant Avenue.*

sharp

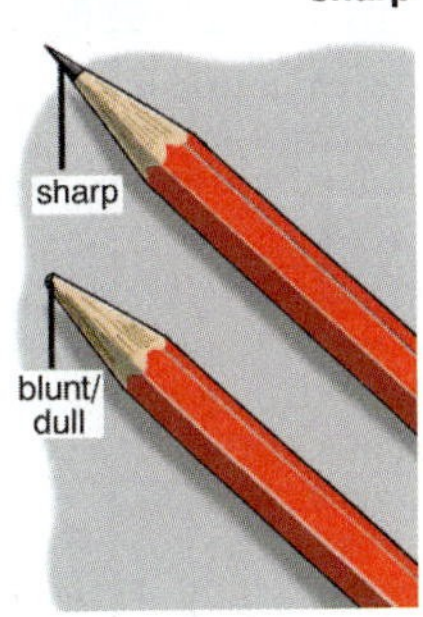

3 CHANGE a sharp increase, fall, etc. is very sudden and very big: *a **sharp rise/increase** in prices* | *a **sharp decline/drop** in the number of smokers*
4 DIFFERENCE clear and definite, so that there is no doubt: *The crowd's support was in **sharp contrast*** (=very different) *to the criticism he has received lately.* | *a **sharp difference** of opinion*
5 INTELLIGENT able to think and understand things very quickly: *She's a very sharp lawyer.* | *her **sharp wit***
6 PAIN sudden and very bad: *a **sharp pain** in my chest*
7 REMARK criticizing in a severe and angry way: *The proposal has drawn **sharp criticism** from the president.* | *He's known for his **sharp tongue**.*
8 EYES able to see or notice things very easily: *Lenny has **a sharp eye for detail**.*
9 CLOTHES attractive and STYLISH: *My grandfather was a sharp dresser* (=wore stylish clothes).
10 SOUNDS loud, short, and sudden: *a sharp cry*
11 PICTURE if an image or picture is sharp, you can see all the details very clearly: *a sharp picture on the TV*
12 MUSIC a) F/C etc. sharp a musical note that is a half TONE higher than the note F, C, etc., and is shown by the sign (#) **b)** a musical note that is sharp is played or sung slightly higher than it should be [➡ **flat**]
13 TASTE having a strong taste: *sharp Cheddar cheese* —**sharply** *adv.* —**sharpness** *n.* [U]

sharp[2] *adv.* **at 8 o'clock/two-thirty etc. sharp** at exactly 8:00, 2:30, etc.: *I expect you to be here at 10:30 sharp.*

sharp·en /ˈʃɑrpən/ *v.* [I,T] to make something sharper, or become sharper: *sharpening a pencil*

sharp·en·er /ˈʃɑrpənɚ/ *n.* [C] a tool or machine that sharpens pencils, knives, etc.

shat·ter /ˈʃæt̬ɚ/ *v.* **1** [I,T] to break suddenly into very small pieces, or to make something do this: *My cup fell to the floor and shattered.*

THESAURUS
break, **smash**, **crack**, **tear**, **snap**, **burst**, **pop**
➔ see Thesaurus box at BREAK[1]

2 [T] to completely destroy someone's hopes, beliefs, or confidence: *A knee injury shattered his hopes of becoming a baseball player.*

shave[1] /ʃeɪv/ *v.* [I,T] to cut off hair very close to the skin, especially from your face or legs, using a RAZOR: *Brian had **cut** himself **shaving**.* | *She **shaves** her **legs**.*

shave[2] *n.* [C usually singular] **1** an act of shaving: *I need a shave.* **2 a close shave** a situation in which you only just avoid an accident or something bad

shav·er /ˈʃeɪvɚ/ *n.* [C] a tool used for shaving

shav·ings /ˈʃeɪvɪŋz/ *n.* [plural] very thin pieces of something such as wood that are cut from a surface

shawl /ʃɔl/ *n.* [C] a piece of cloth that is worn around the shoulders or head for warmth, especially by women

s/he /ˌʃi ɚ ˈhi/ *pron.* used in writing when the subject of the sentence can be either male or female

she[1] /ʃi/ *pron.* a female person or animal who has been mentioned or is known about: *"Where's Kate?" "She went out to the car."* | *"I saw Suzy today." "Oh really, how is she?"* | *She's* (=she is) *a nurse.*

she[2] *n.* [singular] a female: *What a cute dog! Is it a she or a he?*

sheaf /ʃif/ *n.* plural **sheaves** /ʃivz/ [C] several pieces of paper held or tied together

shear /ʃɪr/ *v.* past tense **sheared**, past participle **sheared** or **shorn** /ʃɔrn/ [T] to cut the wool off a sheep

shears /ʃɪrz/ *n.* [plural] a tool like a large pair of scissors

sheath /ʃiθ/ *n.* plural **sheaths** /ʃiðz, ʃiθs/ [C] a cover for the blade of a knife or sword

sheaves /ʃivz/ *n.* the plural of SHEAF

she'd /ʃid/ **1** the short form of "she had": *She'd forgotten to close the door.* **2** the short form of "she would": *She said she'd love to come.*

shed[1] /ʃɛd/ *n.* [C] a small building used especially for storing things: *a tool shed*

shed[2] *v.* past tense and past participle **shed** [T] **1** to get rid of something that you do not want: *I'd like to* ***shed*** *a few* ***pounds*** (=lose some weight) *before summer.* **2** to allow something to fall off, especially as part of a natural process: *Snakes regularly shed their skin.* **3 shed tears** to cry: *She had not shed a single tear during the funeral.* **4 shed blood** to kill someone **5 shed light on sth** to make something easier to understand: *Recent research has shed light on the causes of the disease.*

sheen /ʃin/ *n.* [singular, U] a smooth shiny appearance

sheep /ʃip/ *n.* plural **sheep** [C] a farm animal that is kept for its wool and its meat ➔ see picture at FARM[1]

sheep·ish /ˈʃipɪʃ/ *adj.* uncomfortable or embarrassed because you have done something silly or wrong: *Renny apologized, looking sheepish.* —**sheepishly** *adv.*

sheer /ʃɪr/ *adj.* **1 sheer joy/luck/bliss etc.** joy, luck, etc. with no other feeling or quality mixed with it: *people dancing and singing with sheer joy* **2 the sheer size/weight/numbers etc.** used in order to emphasize that something is very big, heavy, etc.: *The most impressive thing about Alaska is its sheer size.* **3** a sheer drop, cliff, etc. is extremely steep **4** material that is sheer is fine or thin, so that you can almost see through it

sheet /ʃit/ *n.* [C] **1** a large piece of thin cloth that you put on a bed to lie on or under: *Have you* ***changed the sheets*** (=put clean sheets on the bed)? ➔ see picture at BED[1] **2** a thin flat piece of something such as paper, metal, or glass: *a* ***sheet of*** *paper* **3** a large flat area of something such as ice or water that is spread over a surface: *The road was covered with a* ***sheet of ice****.*

sheik, **sheikh** /ʃik, ʃeɪk/ *n.* [C] **1** an Arab chief or prince **2** a Muslim religious teacher or leader

shelf /ʃɛlf/ *n.* plural **shelves** /ʃɛlvz/ [C] a long flat board attached to a wall, in a frame, etc., that you can put things on: *shelves of books* | *Could you get me that bowl off the* ***top shelf****?*

she'll /ʃil/ the short form of "she will"

shell[1] /ʃɛl/ *n.* [C] **1** the hard outer part that covers and protects nuts, eggs, seeds, and some types of animals: *sea shells* | *peanut shells* **2** a metal tube containing a bullet and an explosive substance, which is fired from a large gun

shell

shell[2] *v.* [T] to fire shells at something, using a large gun

shell out *phr. v. informal* to pay money for something, often when you do not want to: *We had to shell out over $400 to get the car fixed.*

shell·fish /ˈʃɛlˌfɪʃ/ *n.* plural **shellfish** [C,U] a small sea or water animal that has a shell, or this animal eaten as a food

shel·ter[1] /ˈʃɛltɚ/ *n.* **1** [C,U] a place with a roof over it that protects you from danger or the weather, or the protection that it gives: *a bomb shelter* | *a bus shelter* | *The family* ***took shelter*** *in the cellar when the tornado hit.* **2** [C] a place where people or animals can go if they have no home or are in danger from someone who treats them badly: *a shelter for battered women* **3** [U] a place to live, considered as one of the basic needs of life: *providing food and shelter for the homeless*

shelter[2] *v.* **1** [T] to provide a place where someone is protected from the weather or from danger: *families who* ***sheltered*** *Jews* ***from*** *the Nazis*

> **THESAURUS**
>
> **protect**, **guard**, **shield**, **give/offer/provide protection**
>
> ➔ see Thesaurus box at PROTECT

2 [I] to stay somewhere in order to be protected from bad weather or danger: *People were sheltering in doorways, under bridges, anywhere.*

shel·tered /ˈʃɛltɚd/ *adj.* **1** protected from anything that might hurt, upset, or shock you: *Gina had a sheltered childhood.* **2** protected from the weather: *a sheltered valley*

shelve /ʃɛlv/ *v.* [T] to decide not to continue with a plan, although you might continue with it later: *The project has been shelved due to lack of funding.*

shelves /ʃɛlvz/ *n.* the plural of SHELF

shelv·ing /ˈʃɛlvɪŋ/ *n.* [U] a set of shelves, or the material used for them

she·nan·i·gans /ʃəˈnænɪgənz/ *n.* [plural] *informal* tricks or slightly dishonest behavior

shep·herd /ˈʃɛpɚd/ *n.* [C] someone whose job is to take care of sheep

sher·bet /ˈʃɚbət/ *n.* [U] a frozen sweet food made from water, fruit, sugar, and milk

sher·iff /ˈʃɛrɪf/ *n.* [C] a chief police officer in a COUNTY who is elected

sher·ry /ˈʃɛri/ *n.* plural **sherries** [C,U] a strong Spanish wine, or a glass of this drink

she's /ʃiz/ **1** the short form of "she is": *She's my little sister.* **2** the short form of "she has": *She's invited us to a party.*

shield[1] /ʃild/ *n.* [C] **1** something that protects someone or something from being hurt or damaged: *police carrying riot shields* | *the heat shield on a rocket* **2** a broad piece of metal or leather used in past times by soldiers to protect themselves in battle

shield[2] *v.* [T] to protect someone or something from being hurt, damaged, or upset: *Of course,* *you try to **shield** your children **from** bad influences.* | *a hat to **shield** your face **from** the sun*

> **THESAURUS**
> **protect**, **guard**, **give/offer/provide protection**, **shelter**
> → see Thesaurus box at PROTECT

shift[1] *v.* [I,T] **1** to change your opinion or attitude: *Washington's policy toward Taiwan appears to have shifted.* **2** to move from one place or position to another, or make something do this: *Jan shifted uncomfortably in her seat.* | *Amos shifted his chair around to get a better look.* **3** to change the GEARS when you are driving: ***Shift into** second gear.*

shift[2] /ʃɪft/ *n.* [C] **1** a change in the way most people think about something, or in the way something is done: *Polls show a **shift in** public opinion.* | *the **shift from** communism to capitalism* **2** one of the periods during each day and night when workers in a factory, hospital, etc. are at work: *Lou's on the **night/day shift** this week.* → GEAR SHIFT

shift·less /ˈʃɪftlɪs/ *adj.* lazy and not at all interested in working

> **THESAURUS**
> **lazy**, **idle**, **indolent**, **slack**
> → see Thesaurus box at LAZY

shift·y /ˈʃɪfti/ *adj.* someone who is shifty looks dishonest

shim·mer /ˈʃɪmɚ/ *v.* [I] to shine with a soft light that seems to shake slightly: *a lake shimmering in the moonlight* —**shimmer** *n.* [singular]

> **THESAURUS**
> **shine**, **flash**, **flicker**, **twinkle**, **glow**, **sparkle**
> → see Thesaurus box at SHINE[1]

shin /ʃɪn/ *n.* [C] the front part of your leg between your knee and your foot → see picture on page A3

shine[1] /ʃaɪn/ *v.* past tense and past participle **shone** /ʃoʊn/ present participle **shining** **1** [I] to produce light: *The **sun** was **shining**.* | *The bright TV lights were **shining in** her eyes.*

> **THESAURUS**
> **flash** – to shine brightly for a very short time: *Lightning flashed across the sky.*
> **flicker** – to shine with an unsteady light: *The candle flickered and went out.*
> **twinkle** – to shine in the dark but not very brightly or continuously: *stars twinkling in the sky*
> **glow** – to shine with a warm soft light: *I could see a lamp glowing in the window.*
> **sparkle** – to shine with many small bright points of light: *diamonds sparkling in the light*
> **shimmer** – to shine with a soft light that seems to shake slightly: *The lake shimmered in the moonlight.*

2 [I] to look bright and smooth: *Dan polished the car until it shone.* **3** past tense and past participle **shined** [T] to make something bright by rubbing it: *When's the last time you **shined** your **shoes**?* **4** [T] to point a light toward a particular place or in a particular direction: *Shine the flashlight over here.* **5** [I] if your eyes or face shine, they show you are happy **6** [I] to be very good at something: *The concert will give young musicians a chance to shine.*

shine[2] *n.* [singular, U] the brightness that something has when light shines on it: *Lucy's dark hair seemed to have lost its shine.*

shin·gle /ˈʃɪŋgəl/ *n.* [C,U] one of many thin pieces of wood or other material used for covering a roof or a wall

shin·ny /ˈʃɪni/ *v.* past tense and past participle **shinnied**, third person sigular **shinnies** **shinny up/down** *informal* to climb quickly up or down a tree or a pole

shin·y /ˈʃaɪni/ *adj.* comparative **shinier**, superlative **shiniest** bright and smooth looking: *shiny hair* | *shiny leather boots*

ship[1] /ʃɪp/ *n.* [C] **1** a large boat used for carrying people and things on the ocean: *a cruise ship* | *Supplies came **by ship**.*

> **THESAURUS**
> **Ships that carry people**
> **cruise ship**, **liner**, **ferry**
> **Ships that carry goods**
> **freighter**, **tanker**, **barge**
> **Fighting ships**
> **aircraft carrier**, **battleship**, **cruiser**, **submarine**, **warship**

2 a space vehicle: *a rocket ship*

ship[2] *v.* past tense and past participle **shipped**, present participle **shipping** [T] **1** to deliver goods: *The books will be shipped out to you within 24 hours.* **2** to send or carry something by sea

ship·load /ˈʃɪploʊd/ *n.* [C] the number of people or things a ship can carry

ship·ment /ˈʃɪpmənt/ *n.* [C,U] a load of goods being delivered, or the act of sending them: *a **shipment of** grain* | *The goods are ready for shipment.*

ship·ping /ˈʃɪpɪŋ/ *n.* **1 shipping and handling** the price charged for delivering goods: *Please add $2.95 to cover **shipping and handling**.* **2** [U] ships considered as a group, or anything that is related to business done by ships: *The canal has been closed to shipping.*

ship·wreck[1] /ˈʃɪp-rɛk/ *n.* [C,U] the destruction of a ship by a storm or an accident, or a ship that has been destroyed in this way: *survivors of a shipwreck*

S

shipwreck² *v.* **be shipwrecked** to have been in a ship that has been destroyed by a storm or an accident

ship·yard /ˈʃɪp-yɑrd/ *n.* [C] a place where ships are built or repaired

shirk /ʃɚk/ *v.* [I,T] *formal* to avoid doing something you should do: *parents who* ***shirk*** *their* ***duties/responsibilities*** *towards their children*

shirt /ʃɚt/ *n.* [C] a piece of clothing that covers the upper part of your body and your arms, and has a collar and usually buttons down the front [➡ **blouse**, **T-shirt**]: *She was wearing a white silk shirt.* | *I have to wear a* ***shirt and tie*** *to work.* ➔ see picture at CLOTHES

shirt·sleeves /ˈʃɚtslivz/ *n.* **in (your) shirtsleeves** wearing a shirt but no JACKET

shish ke·bab /ˈʃɪʃ kəˌbɑb/ *n* [C] small pieces of meat and sometimes vegetables, cooked on a stick ➔ see picture on page A5

shiv·er¹ /ˈʃɪvɚ/ *v.* [I] to shake slightly because you are cold or frightened: *Come inside – you're shivering.*

THESAURUS

shake, **tremble**, **wobble**, **vibrate**, **rattle**
➔ see Thesaurus box at SHAKE¹

shiver² *n.* [C] a shaking movement of your body that happens when you are cold or afraid: *A* ***shiver ran down*** *my* ***spine*** (=I felt afraid). —**shivery** *adj.*

shoal /ʃoʊl/ *n.* [C] a large group of fish that swim together

THESAURUS

herd, **flock**, **school**, **pack**, **litter**
➔ see Thesaurus box at GROUP¹

shock¹ /ʃɑk/ *n.* **1** [C usually singular] an unexpected and unpleasant event or piece of news that makes you extremely upset: *Rob's death* ***came as a*** *complete* ***shock*** *to us.* **2** [singular,U] the feeling of surprise and DISBELIEF you have when something unexpected and unpleasant happens: *She looked like she was* ***in shock.*** | *the* ***shock of*** *seeing someone in such pain* **3** [C] a sudden painful feeling caused by a flow of electricity passing through your body: *Ow! The toaster* ***gave*** *me* ***a shock.*** **4** [U] *technical* a medical condition in which someone is very weak, often after an unpleasant experience: *The crash victims are* ***suffering from shock.*** | *He is clearly* ***in a state of shock.*** **5** [C] SHOCK WAVE **6** [C] SHOCK ABSORBER

shock² *v.* **1** [I,T] to make someone feel very surprised, and usually upset or offended: *We were* ***shocked to hear*** *of his arrest.* **2** [T] to give someone an electric shock —**shocked** *adj.*

ˈshock abˌsorber *n.* [C] a piece of equipment connected to each wheel of a vehicle to make it travel smoothly over uneven ground

shock·ing /ˈʃɑkɪŋ/ *adj.* very offensive or upsetting: *a shocking crime*

THESAURUS

surprising, **extraordinary**, **amazing**, **astonishing**, **astounding**, **staggering**, **stunning**
➔ see Thesaurus box at SURPRISING

ˈshock wave *n.* [C] **1** a strong feeling of shock that people have when something bad happens without warning: *The news* ***sent shock waves through*** *the world's stock markets.* **2** a strong movement of air, heat, or the earth from an explosion, EARTHQUAKE, etc.

shod¹ /ʃɑd/ *adj. literary* wearing shoes

shod² *v.* the past tense and past participle of SHOE

shod·dy /ˈʃɑdi/ *adj.* **1** badly or cheaply made, or not done well: *shoddy goods* **2** unfair and dishonest: *He treated me in a pretty shoddy way.*

shoes

shoe¹ /ʃu/ *n.* [C] **1** something that you wear to cover your feet, that is made of leather or some other strong material: *a* ***pair of shoes*** | *high-heeled shoes* **2 be in sb's shoes** to be in the situation that someone else is in: ***I wouldn't like to be in*** *his* ***shoes*** *when his wife finds out what happened.*

shoe² *v.* past tense and past participle **shod** /ʃɑd/ [T] to put a HORSESHOE (=curved piece of metal) on a horse's foot

shoe·horn /ˈʃuhɔrn/ *n.* [C] a curved piece of plastic or metal that you use to help you put a shoe on easily

shoe·lace /ˈʃuleɪs/ *n.* [C] a thin piece of string or leather that you use to tie your shoes [= **lace**]

shoe·string /ˈʃuˌstrɪŋ/ *n.* **on a shoestring** done or made without spending very much money: *a movie made on a shoestring*

shone /ʃoʊn/ *v.* the past tense and past participle of SHINE

shoo /ʃu/ *interjection* said in order to tell an annoying child or animal to go away —**shoo** *v.* [T]: *Aunt Betty shooed us out of the kitchen.*

ˈshoo-in *n.* [C usually singular] *informal* someone

who is expected to win an election or race easily: *He looked like a shoo-in to win the election.*

shook /ʃʊk/ *v.* the past tense of SHAKE

shook-'up *adj. spoken* [not before noun] very frightened, shocked, or upset because of something that has happened

shoot[1] /ʃut/ *v.* past tense and past participle **shot** /ʃɑt/
1 GUN [I,T] to fire a gun at someone, or kill or injure someone with a gun: *Stop or I'll shoot!* | *She pulled out a gun and shot him.* | *Someone on the roof was **shooting at** her.* | *He had been shot in the leg while trying to escape.* | *One police officer was **shot dead** in the incident.*
2 MOVE QUICKLY [I,T] to move quickly in a particular direction, or to make something move in this way: *The fountain shoots water 20 feet into the air.* | *A sharp pain suddenly **shot through** his right arm.*
3 PHOTO/MOVIE [I,T] to take photographs or make a movie: *The movie was shot in Rome.*
4 SPORTS [I,T] to throw, kick, or hit a ball toward the place where you can make points: *We were waiting for him to shoot.*
5 shoot *spoken* used in order to tell someone to start speaking: *"I've got a question." "Okay, shoot."*
6 shoot the breeze *informal* to have a friendly conversation about unimportant things: *Cal and I were sitting on the porch, shooting the breeze.*
7 shoot your mouth off *informal* to talk too much, especially about your opinions or a secret: *Don't go shooting your mouth off about this.*
shoot sb/sth ⇔ **down** *phr. v.* **1** to destroy an enemy airplane while it is flying: *The plane was shot down over the ocean.* **2** to say that what someone suggests is wrong or stupid: *Terry's boss shot down all her ideas.*
shoot for sth *phr. v. informal* to try to achieve something: *Okay, we'll shoot for 1:30* (=try to do something by then).
shoot up *phr. v.* to quickly increase in number, size, or amount: *Prices shot up by 60%.*

shoot[2] *n.* [C] **1** an occasion when someone takes photographs or makes a movie: *a **photo shoot*** **2** a new part of a plant

shoot[3] *interjection* said when you are annoyed, disappointed, or surprised: *Oh shoot, I forgot to go to the bank.*

shoot·ing /'ʃuṭɪŋ/ *n.* [C] a situation in which someone is killed or injured by a gun

shooting 'star *n.* [C] a piece of rock or metal from space that burns brightly as it falls toward the earth

shop[1] /ʃɑp/ *n.* **1** [C] a small store that sells only a particular type of goods: *a card shop* **2** [C] a place where things are made or repaired: *a bicycle repair shop* **3** [U] a subject taught in school, in which students use tools and machinery to make or repair things → **set up shop** at SET[1]

shop[2] *v.* past tense and past participle **shopped**, present participle **shopping** [I] to go to one or more stores to buy things: *I was out **shopping for** food.* —**shopper** *n.* [C] *Christmas shoppers*
shop around *phr. v.* to compare the price and quality of different things before you decide which to buy

shop·lift /'ʃɑpˌlɪft/ *v.* [I,T] to take something from a store without paying for it —**shoplifting** *n.* [U] —**shoplifter** *n.* [C]

> **THESAURUS**
> **steal, burglarize, rob, mug**
> → see Thesaurus box at STEAL[1]

shop·ping /'ʃɑpɪŋ/ *n.* **1** [U] the activity of going to stores to buy things: *I've got to **do** some **shopping*** (=buy the food, etc. that you use regularly). | *Christmas shopping* **2 go shopping** to go to stores to buy things, often for enjoyment **3** [singular] the things you have bought, usually food: *The boys helped me bring the shopping in from the car.*

'shopping ˌcenter *n.* [C] a group of stores built together in one area

'shopping mall *n.* [C] a MALL

shore[1] /ʃɔr/ *n.* [C,U] the land along the edge of a large area of water: *We could see a boat about a mile from shore.* | *The cabin stood **on the shores** of Lake Erie.*

> **THESAURUS**
> **coast** – the land next to the ocean: *The island is 15 miles off the coast of Newfoundland.*
> **beach** – an area of sand or small stones at the edge of an ocean or lake: *We spent the day at the beach.* | *Let's take a walk on the beach at sunset.* | *Palm Beach, Florida*
> **seashore** – the area of land next to the ocean: *hotels directly on the seashore*
> **bank** – the edge of a river: *the banks of the Mississippi river*

shore[2] *v.*
shore sth ⇔ **up** *phr. v.* **1** to support a wall with large pieces of wood, metal, etc. to stop it from falling down **2** to help or support something that is likely to fail or is not working well: *The money is needed to shore up the failing bank.*

shorn /ʃɔrn/ *v.* a past participle of SHEAR

short[1] /ʃɔrt/ *adj.*
1 LENGTH/DISTANCE not very long in length or far in distance [≠ **long**]: *His hair is very short.* | *a short skirt* | *It's only a **short distance** from here to the river.*
2 TIME happening for only a little time or for less time than usual [≠ **long**]: *a short meeting* | *I've just been living here **a short time**.* | ***Life's** too **short** to stay angry.*
3 PERSON not as tall as average height [≠ **tall**]: *a short fat man*
4 NOT ENOUGH not having enough of something

S

you need: *I'm **short of cash** right now.* | *I'm five dollars short.*

5 on short notice with very little warning that something is going to happen: *Sorry – we can't come on such short notice.*

6 in the short run/term during a short period of time after the present: *The crisis will affect the peace process, at least in the short term.*

7 be short for sth to be a shorter way of saying a name: *Her name is Becky, short for Rebecca.*

8 short of breath unable to breathe easily, especially because of being unhealthy

9 be in short supply to not be available in large quantities: *Fruit and sugar were in short supply then.*

10 be short with sb to speak to someone in a rude or unfriendly way: *Sorry I was so short with you on the phone.*

11 in short order very quickly: *His demands were met in short order.*

12 get the short end of the stick *informal* to be given something difficult or bad to do, especially when other people have been given something better —**shortness** *n.* [U]

short² *adv.* **short of (doing) sth** without actually doing something: *They've cut the budget and the workforce – everything short of canceling the project altogether.* ➔ **cut sth short** at CUT¹ ➔ **fall short (of sth)** at FALL¹ ➔ **be running short of sth** at RUN¹ ➔ **stop short of sth** at STOP¹

S

short³ *n.* **1 shorts** [plural] **a)** short pants that end at or above the knees: *a **pair of shorts*** **b)** loose underwear for men [= **boxer shorts**] **2 in short** used when you want to say the most important point in a few words: *In short, I don't think we can do it.* **3 for short** as a shorter way of saying a name: *It's called the Message Handling System – MHS for short.* **4** [C] *informal* a short movie that is shown before the main movie in a theater **5** [C] *informal* SHORT CIRCUIT

short⁴ *v.* [I,T] *informal* to have a bad electrical connection that makes a machine stop working correctly, or to make something do this

short·age /ˈʃɔrt̬ɪdʒ/ *n.* [C,U] a situation in which there is not enough of something that people need: *food shortages* | *a **shortage of** medicine*

short·bread /ˈʃɔrt˺brɛd/ *n.* [U] a hard sweet cookie made with a lot of butter

short·cake /ˈʃɔrt˺ˌkeɪk/ *n.* [U] cake over which a sweet fruit mixture is poured: *strawberry shortcake*

ˌshort-ˈchange *v.* [T] **1** to treat someone unfairly by not giving him/her what s/he deserves: *The miners felt short-changed by the new contract.* **2** to give back too little money to someone who has paid you for something

ˌshort ˈcircuit *n.* [C] a bad electrical connection that makes a machine stop working correctly —**short circuit** *v.* [I,T]

short·com·ing /ˈʃɔrt˺ˌkʌmɪŋ/ *n.* [C usually plural] a fault in something or someone, that makes it, him, or her less effective: *the **shortcomings of** the new law* | ***shortcomings in** his research*

ˌshort ˈcut *n.* [C] **1** a quicker more direct way of going somewhere: *Let's **take a short cut** across the park.* **2** a quicker way of doing something: *There are no **short cuts to** finding a job.*

short·en /ˈʃɔrt˺n/ *v.* [I,T] to become shorter, or to make something shorter [≠ **lengthen**]: *Her name is often shortened to Pat.* | *in fall, when the days shorten*

short·en·ing /ˈʃɔrt˺n-ɪŋ, -nɪŋ/ *n.* [U] fat made from vegetable oil that you mix with flour when making PASTRY

short·fall /ˈʃɔrtfɔl/ *n.* [C] the difference between the amount you have and the amount you need or expect: ***shortfalls in** the city's budget*

short·hand /ˈʃɔrthænd/ *n.* [U] a fast method of writing using special signs and short forms of words: *taking notes **in shorthand***

ˈshort list *n.* [C] a list of the most appropriate people for a job, chosen from all the people who were first considered for it

short-lived /ˌʃɔrtˈlɪvd◂/ *adj.* existing only a short time: *a short-lived fashion*

short·ly /ˈʃɔrtli/ *adv.* **1** very soon: *I expect him home shortly.* | *The President left for Washington shortly before noon.*

THESAURUS

soon, in a minute, any minute now, before long, in the near future

➔ see Thesaurus box at SOON

2 speaking in a way that is not patient: *"Yes, yes, I understand," he said shortly.*

ˌshort-order ˈcook *n.* [C] someone in a restaurant kitchen who makes the food that can be prepared easily or quickly

ˌshort-ˈrange *adj.* [only before noun] short-range weapons are designed to travel or be used over a short distance

short·sight·ed, **short-sighted** /ˌʃɔrtˈsaɪt̬ɪd◂/ *adj.* **1** not considering the future effects of something: *short-sighted planning* **2** NEARSIGHTED

short·stop /ˈʃɔrtstɑp/ *n.* [C,U] the position in baseball between SECOND BASE and THIRD BASE, or the person who plays this position

ˌshort ˈstory *n.* [C] a short written story, usually about imaginary events

ˌshort-ˈterm *adj.* continuing for only a short time into the future [≠ **long-term**]: *a short-term solution* ➔ **in the long/short term** at TERM¹

ˈshort wave *n.* [U] a range of radio waves used for broadcasting around the world

shot¹ /ʃɑt/ *n.* [C]

1 GUN an act of FIRING a gun, or the sound that this makes: *We heard a shot.* | *He quickly **fired** three **shots**.*

2 SPORTS an attempt to throw, kick, or hit the ball toward the place where you can get a point:

Nice shot! | *Shaw* ***made the shot*** *and turned to run down the court.*

3 MOVIES/PHOTOGRAPHS **a)** a photograph: *a beautiful* ***shot of*** *the countryside around Prague* **b)** the view of something in a movie, television program, or photograph: *a* ***close-up shot*** | *In the* ***opening shot****, we see a man walking down a street.*

4 ATTEMPT *informal* an attempt to do something or achieve something: *Marty always wanted to* ***take a shot at*** *acting.* | *I'll* ***give it*** *my* ***best shot*** (=try as hard as possible).

5 DRINK a small amount of a strong alcoholic drink: *a* ***shot of*** *whiskey*

6 DRUG the act of putting medicine into your body using a needle: *Have you* ***had*** *your tetanus* ***shot****?*

7 a shot in the dark an attempt to guess something without having any facts or definite ideas: *My answer to the last question was a complete shot in the dark.*

8 like a shot very quickly: *He jumped up like a shot and ran to the door.* ➔ BIG SHOT, LONG SHOT

shot² *adj.* **be shot** *informal* to be in bad condition or useless: *This battery is shot – do we have another one?*

shot³ *v.* the past tense and past participle of SHOOT

shot·gun /ˈʃɑt˺gʌn/ *n.* [C] a long gun, used for shooting animals and birds

ˌshotgun ˈwedding *n.* [C] a wedding that has to take place immediately because the woman is going to have a baby

ˈshot put *n.* [singular] a sport in which you throw a heavy metal ball as far as you can —**shot putter** *n.*

should /ʃəd; *strong* ʃʊd/ *modal verb* **1** used when giving or asking for advice or an opinion: *You* ***should have*** *called me right away.* | *Should I wear my gray dress?* | *Children shouldn't* (=should not) *take candy from strangers.* **2** used in order to say that you expect something to happen or be true: *Yvonne* ***should be*** *back by 8:00.* | *It should be a nice day tomorrow.* **3** *formal* used like "if" in formal CONDITIONAL sentences that use the present tense: *Should you decide to accept the offer, please return the enclosed form.*

shoul·der¹ /ˈʃoʊldɚ/ *n.* [C] **1** one of the two parts of the body at each side of the neck where the arm is connected: *Andy put his arm around his wife's shoulders.* | *When we asked him what was wrong, he just* ***shrugged his shoulders*** (=raised them to show that he did not know or care). ➔ see picture on page A3 **2 watch/look over sb's shoulder** to watch carefully what someone is doing, sometimes so that you can criticize him/her: *I can't work at the computer when someone is watching over my shoulder.* **3** the part of a shirt, coat, etc. that covers your shoulders **4 a shoulder to cry on** someone who gives you sympathy: *Diane's always there when I* ***need a shoulder to cry on****.* **5** an area of ground beside a road where drivers can stop their cars if they are having trouble

shoulder² *v.* **1 shoulder the responsibility/blame/cost etc.** to accept a difficult or unpleasant RESPONSIBILITY, duty, etc.: *Carrie shouldered the burden of taking care of three young kids alone.* **2 shoulder your way through/into etc.** to move through a large crowd of people by pushing with your shoulders: *He shouldered his way through the crowd.*

ˈshoulder bag *n.* [C] a woman's PURSE that hangs from the shoulder by a long piece of material

ˈshoulder blade *n.* [C] one of the two flat bones on each side of your back ➔ see picture on page A3

should·n't /ˈʃʊdnt/ *modal verb* the short form of "should not"

should've /ˈʃʊdəv/ *modal verb* the short form of "should have"

shout¹ /ʃaʊt/ *v.* [I,T] to say something very loudly: *"Get out of the way!" she shouted.* | *I wish he'd stop* ***shouting at*** *the children.* | *They* ***shouted for*** *help.*

THESAURUS

call (out) – to shout in order to get someone's attention
scream – to shout in a very loud high voice because you are so angry, excited, etc. that you cannot control your voice
yell – to shout, for example because you are angry or excited, or because you want to get someone's attention
cry out – to make a sudden loud noise, for example when you are suddenly hurt or afraid
raise your voice – to say something more loudly than usual, often because you are angry about something
cheer – to shout to show that you like a team, performance, etc.
bellow – to shout loudly in a deep voice
holler informal – to shout loudly
➔ SCREAM

shout sb ⇔ **down** *phr. v.* to shout so that someone who is speaking cannot be heard: *She tried to argue, but was quickly shouted down.*

shout sth ⇔ **out** *phr. v.* to say something suddenly in a loud voice: *Don't shout out the answer.*

shout² *n.* **1** [C] a loud call that expresses anger, excitement, etc.: *She heard a shout from upstairs.* **2 give sb a shout** *spoken* to go and find someone and tell him/her something: *Give me a shout if you need any help.*

shove /ʃʌv/ *v.* **1** [I,T] to push someone or something in a rough or careless way, using your hands or shoulders: *People were* ***pushing and shoving*** *to get a better view.*

THESAURUS

push, **poke**, **nudge**, **roll**, **elbow**
→ see Thesaurus box at PUSH[1]

2 [T] *informal* to put something somewhere quickly and carelessly: *Just shove those papers into the drawer for now.*

THESAURUS

stick – to put something somewhere in a careless way: *Just stick the books on the table for now.*
thrust – to push something somewhere suddenly or forcefully: *David thrust his hands into his pockets.*
dump – to drop or put something somewhere in a careless way: *Don't just dump your coat on the floor!*

3 shove it *spoken* an impolite phrase said when you are very annoyed or angry and you do not want to talk to someone any longer: *They can take their job and shove it.* —**shove** *n.* [C]
shove off *phr. v.* to push a boat away from the land, usually with a pole

shov·el[1] /ˈʃʌvəl/ *n.* [C] a tool with a long handle, used for digging or moving earth, stones, etc.

S

shovel[2] *v.* **1** [I,T] to dig or move earth, stones, etc. with a shovel: *I'm going out to* ***shovel the driveway/sidewalk*** (=shovel snow from the driveway or sidewalk). **2 shovel sth into/onto sth** to put something into a place quickly: *He sat at the table shoveling his dinner into his mouth.*

show[1] /ʃoʊ/ *v.* past tense **showed**, past participle **shown** /ʃoʊn/
1 LET SB SEE [T] to let someone see something: *Karen showed us her wedding pictures.* | *I* ***showed*** *the letter* ***to*** *Ruth.*
2 MAKE STH CLEAR [T] to make it clear that something is true or exists by providing facts or information: *The report shows a rise in employment.* | *Studies have* ***shown (that)*** *consumers are buying more organic produce.* | *Applicants must* ***show how*** *their qualifications make them suitable for the job.*

THESAURUS

demonstrate, **indicate**, **suggest**, **explain**, **prove**
→ see Thesaurus box at DEMONSTRATE, EXPLAIN

3 HOW YOU FEEL [T] to show how you feel by the way that you behave: *Alan tried not to show his disappointment.*
4 EXPLAIN STH [T] to tell someone how to do something or where something is: *I'll show you what to do.* | *My grandma* ***showed*** *me* ***how to*** *make cornbread.*
5 GUIDE SB [T] to go with someone and guide him/her to a place: *Did Rachel show you where to leave your coat?* | *I'll* ***show*** *you* ***the way.***
6 CAN BE SEEN [I,T] if something shows, people can see or notice it easily: *His anger showed on his face.* | *Ellen was tired, and* ***it showed.***
7 MOVIE [I,T] if a movie or television program is shown, people are able to see it at a theater or on television: *The movie was shown on HBO.*
8 show signs of sth used in order to say that something is starting to become noticeable: *At 65, Nelson* ***shows no signs of*** *slowing down.* | *Data from the second quarter* ***showed some signs of*** *improvement.*
9 INFORMATION [T] if a picture, map, etc. shows something, you can see it on the picture, map, etc.: *a map showing all the stations*
10 have something/nothing to show for sth to have achieved something or nothing as a result of your efforts: *I've been practicing so hard, and I still have nothing to show for it.*
show sb **around** *phr. v.* to go with someone around a place and show him/her what is important, interesting, etc.: *His wife showed us around the house.*
show off *phr. v.* **1** *disapproving* to try to make people admire your abilities, achievements, or possessions: *Ignore him. He's just showing off.* **2 show** sth ⇔ **off** to show something to many people because you are very proud of it: *Jen proudly showed off her engagement ring.*
show up *phr. v.* **1** *informal* to arrive at the place where someone is waiting for you: *It was 9:20 when he finally showed up.* **2** to be easy to see or notice: *The bacteria showed up under the microscope.* **3 show** sb ⇔ **up** to do something that embarrasses someone or make him/her seem stupid when other people are there

show[2] *n.* [C] **1** a performance in a theater or on radio or television: *a new show opening on Broadway* | *a popular TV show* → see Topic box at TELEVISION **2** a collection of things for the public to look at: *the spring flower show* | *a Paris* ***fashion show*** **3 a show of sth** something that someone does in order to make a particular feeling or quality clear to someone else: *The army marched through the town in* ***a show of force.***
4 make a show of sth *disapproving* to do something in a very clear way so that other people notice that you are doing it: *She made a show of interest.* **5 on show** if something is on show, it is in a place where it can be seen by the public: *The photographs will be on show until the end of the month.* **6 let's get this show on the road** *spoken* said when you want to tell people it is time to start working or start a trip

ˌshow and ˈtell *n.* [U] an activity for children in which they bring an object to school and tell the other children about it

show biz /ˈʃoʊ bɪz/ *n.* [U] *informal* SHOW BUSINESS

ˈshow ˌbusiness *n.* [U] the entertainment industry

show·case /ˈʃoʊkeɪs/ *n.* [C] an event or situation that is designed to show the good qualities of a person, organization, etc.: *a **showcase for** new musical talent* —**showcase** *v.* [T]

show·down /ˈʃoʊdaʊn/ *n.* [C] a meeting, argument, fight, etc. that will settle a disagreement or competition that has continued for a long time: *a **showdown between** the top two teams in the league*

show·er[1] /ˈʃaʊɚ/ *n.* [C] **1** a thing that you stand under to wash your whole body: *The phone always rings when I'm **in the shower**.* **2** an act of washing your body while standing under the shower: *Hurry up! I want to **take a shower** too.* **3** a short period of rain: *Showers are expected later today.*

THESAURUS

rain, **drizzle**, **downpour**, **storm**, **hail**, **hailstones**, **sleet**
➔ see Thesaurus box at RAIN[1]

4 a party at which presents are given to a woman who is going to get married or have a baby: *We're having a **baby shower** for Paula on Friday.*

shower[2] *v.* **1** [I] to wash your whole body while standing under a SHOWER **2** [I,T] to cover a person or place with a lot of small things: *People standing near the window were showered with broken glass.* **3** [T] to give someone a lot of something: *Mother **showered** us **with** gifts.*

show·ing /ˈʃoʊɪŋ/ *n.* **1** [C] an occasion when a movie, art show, etc. can be seen or looked at: *a special **showing of** Georgia O'Keeffe's paintings* **2** [C usually singular] something that shows how well or badly you are doing: *The senator **made** a strong **showing** at the polls.*

show·man /ˈʃoʊmən/ *n.* plural **showmen** /-mən/ [C] someone who is good at entertaining people and getting a lot of public attention —**showmanship** *n.* [U]

shown /ʃoʊn/ *v.* the past participle of SHOW

ˈshow-off *n.* [C] *informal disapproving* someone who always tries to show how smart s/he is or how much skill s/he has so that other people will admire him/her: *Don't be such a show-off!*

show·piece /ˈʃoʊpis/ *n.* [C] something that an organization, government, etc. wants people to see because it is a successful example of what they are doing

show·room /ˈʃoʊrum, -rʊm/ *n.* [C] a large room where you can look at things that are for sale: *a car showroom*

show·y /ˈʃoʊi/ *adj.* very colorful, big, expensive, etc. in a way that attracts people's attention: *a showy ring*

shrank /ʃræŋk/ *v.* the past tense of SHRINK

shrap·nel /ˈʃrapnəl/ *n.* [U] small pieces of metal from a bomb or bullet that has exploded

shred[1] /ʃrɛd/ *n.* [C] **1** a small thin piece that is torn or cut roughly from something: *The kitten had **torn/ripped** the toy **to shreds**.* **2** a very small amount: *There's **not a shred of evidence** against him* (=there is none at all).

shred[2] *v.* past tense and past participle **shredded**, present participle **shredding** [T] **1** to cut or tear something into shreds ➔ see picture at CUT[1] **2** to put a document into a shredder

THESAURUS

chop (up), **slice**, **dice**, **peel**, **carve**, **grate**
➔ see Thesaurus box at CUT[1]

shred·der /ˈʃrɛdɚ/ *n.* [C] a machine that cuts documents into small pieces so that no one can read them

shrewd /ʃrud/ *adj.* good at judging what people or situations are really like, especially in a way that makes you successful: *a shrewd businesswoman*

shriek /ʃrik/ *v.* [I,T] to shout loudly, or to say something in a very loud voice, especially because you are frightened, excited, angry, etc. [= **scream**]: *They were dragged from their homes, shrieking and weeping.* | *"I'll kill you," Anne **shrieked at** him.* —**shriek** *n.* [C]

shrill /ʃrɪl/ *adj.* a shrill sound is high and unpleasant: *shrill voices*

THESAURUS

high, **high-pitched**, **piercing**, **squeaky**
➔ see Thesaurus box at HIGH[1], LOUD[1]

shrimp /ʃrɪmp/ *n.* [C,U] a small curved sea animal that has ten legs and a soft shell, or the meat from this animal

shrine /ʃraɪn/ *n.* [C] **1** a place that is related to a holy event or holy person, and that people visit for religious reasons **2** a place that people visit and respect because it is related to a famous person: *Elvis Presley's home has become a shrine.*

shrink[1] /ʃrɪŋk/ *v.* past tense **shrank** /ʃræŋk/ past participle **shrunk** /ʃrʌŋk/ **1** [I,T] to become smaller or to make something smaller: *My sweater shrank in the dryer.* **2** [I,T] to become smaller in amount, size, or value: *Profits have been shrinking over the last year.* **3** [I] to move away because you are afraid: *She **shrank back** in fright.*

shrink from sth *phr. v.* to avoid doing something difficult or unpleasant: *Many people shrink from discussing such personal issues.*

shrink[2] *n.* [C] *informal humorous* a PSYCHIATRIST

shrink·age /ˈʃrɪŋkɪdʒ/ *n.* [U] the act of shrinking, or the amount that something shrinks

ˌshrink-ˈwrapped *adj.* goods that are shrink-wrapped are wrapped tightly in plastic —**shrink-wrap** *n.* [U]

shriv·el /ˈʃrɪvəl/ **also shrivel up** *v.* [I,T] if something shrivels or if it is shriveled, it becomes smaller and its surface is covered in lines because it is dry or old: *The flowers had shriveled up.* —**shriveled** *adj.*: *her shriveled hands*

S

shroud[1] /ʃraʊd/ *n.* [C] **1** a cloth that is wrapped around a dead person's body before it is buried **2** something that hides or covers something: *a* ***shroud of*** *fog*

shroud[2] *v.* **1 be shrouded in darkness/mist/cloud etc.** to be so dark that you cannot see anything, or be completely covered and hidden by mist, cloud, etc.: *mountains shrouded in clouds* **2 be shrouded in mystery/secrecy etc.** to be mysterious, secret, etc.

shrub /ʃrʌb/ *n.* [C] a small bush

shrub·ber·y /ˈʃrʌbəri/ *n.* [U] shrubs planted close together in a group

shrug /ʃrʌg/ *v.* past tense and past participle **shrugged**, present participle **shrugging** [I,T] to raise and then lower your shoulders in order to show that you do not know something or do not care about something: *Dan shrugged and went back to what he was doing.* | *Melanie* ***shrugged*** *her* ***shoulders****.* —**shrug** *n.* [C] *"I don't know," he said with a shrug.*

shrug sth ⇔ **off** *phr. v.* to treat something as unimportant and not worry about it: *Marge tried to shrug off her failure.*

shrunk /ʃrʌŋk/ *v.* the past participle of SHRINK

shrunk·en /ˈʃrʌŋkən/ *adj.* having become smaller or been made smaller: *a shrunken sweater*

shuck /ʃʌk/ *v.* [T] to remove the outer cover of a vegetable such as corn or PEAS, or the shell of OYSTERS or CLAMS

shucks /ʃʌks/ *interjection old-fashioned* said in order to show you are a little disappointed about something

shud·der /ˈʃʌdɚ/ *v.* [I] to shake because you are frightened or cold, or because you think something is very unpleasant: *She* ***shuddered at*** *the thought.* —**shudder** *n.* [C]

shuf·fle[1] /ˈʃʌfəl/ *v.* **1** [I] to walk slowly and in a noisy way, without lifting your feet off the ground: *an old man* ***shuffling across*** *the room* **2 shuffle your feet** to keep moving your feet slightly because you are bored or embarrassed: *Ernie looked nervous and shuffled his feet.* **3** [T] to move something such as papers into a different order or into different positions: *Ginny shuffled the papers on her desk.* **4** [I,T] to mix playing cards into a different order before playing a game with them

shuffle[2] *n.* **be/get lost in the shuffle** to not be noticed or considered because there are so many other things to deal with

shuf·fle·board /ˈʃʌfəlˌbɔrd/ *n.* [U] a game in which you use a long stick to push a flat round object along a smooth surface toward an area with numbers on it

shun /ʃʌn/ *v.* past tense and past participle **shunned**, present participle **shunning** [T] to avoid someone or something deliberately: *She shuns publicity.*

shunt /ʃʌnt/ *v.* [T] to move someone or something to another place or position, especially in a way that seems unfair: *Some of the children had been* ***shunted aside*** *into slower classes.*

shush /ʃʌʃ, ʃʊʃ/ *v.* **1 shush!** *spoken* said in order to tell someone, especially a child, to be quiet **2** [T] to tell someone to be quiet: *She started to complain, but Betty shushed her.*

shut[1] /ʃʌt/ *v.* past tense and past participle **shut**, present participle **shutting** [I,T] to close something, or to become closed: *Do you want me to shut the window?* | *I heard the back door shut.* | *She leaned back and* ***shut*** *her* ***eyes****.*

shut sb/sth **away** *phr. v.* to put someone or something in a place away from other people: *He* ***shut himself away*** *in his office.*

shut down *phr. v.* **shut** sth ⇔ **down** if a company, factory, machine, etc. shuts down, or if you shut it down, it stops operating: *Three nuclear generators were shut down for safety reasons.* | *How do I shut down this machine?*

shut off *phr. v.* **1 shut** sth ⇔ **off** if a machine, tool, etc. shuts off, or if you shut it off, it stops operating: *We shut the engine off before it overheated.* | *The heat shuts off automatically.* **2 shut** sth ⇔ **off** to prevent goods or supplies from being available or being delivered: *Food, oil, and gas supplies were shut off during the fighting.* **3 shut yourself off** to avoid meeting and talking to other people: *After his wife's death, Pete* ***shut himself off from*** *the rest of the family.*

shut sb/sth **out** *phr. v.* **1 shut** sb ⇔ **out** to deliberately not let someone join in an activity, process, etc.: *Many of the working poor are being shut out of the health care system.* **2 shut** sth ⇔ **out** to stop yourself from seeing, hearing, or thinking about something: *He can shut out the rest of the world when he's working.* **3 shut out** sb to defeat an opposing team and prevent them from getting any points: *The Blue Jays shut out the Phillies 3–0.*

shut sb/sth ⇔ **up** *phr. v.* **1 shut up!** *spoken* said in order to tell someone rudely to stop talking **2 shut** sb ⇔ **up** to make someone stop talking or be quiet: *The chairman tried to shut us up.*

shut[2] *adj.* [not before noun] not open [= **closed**]: *We heard the door* ***slam shut*** *behind us.* | *Squeeze your* ***eyes shut****.*

shut·down /ˈʃʌtdaʊn/ *n.* [C] the closing of a factory, business, or piece of machinery: *the* ***shutdown of*** *a paper mill*

ˈshut-eye *n.* [U] *informal* sleep: *I really need to* ***get/catch some shut-eye*** (=go to sleep).

shutter

shut·ter /ˈʃʌt̬ɚ/ *n.* [C] **1** a wooden or metal cover that can be closed over the outside of a window **2** a part of a camera that opens to let light onto the film

shut·tle[1] /ˈʃʌt̬l/ *n.* [C] **1** an airplane, bus, or train that makes regular short trips between two places: *the Washington-New York shuttle* | *The hotel provides a free* ***shuttle service*** *to restaurants downtown.* **2** a SPACE SHUTTLE

shuttle² *v.* [T] to travel or move people regularly between two places: *The visitors were* ***shuttled between*** *the hotel and the conference center twice a day.*

shut·tle·cock /ˈʃʌtl̩ˌkɑk/ *n.* [C] a small light object that you hit over the net in the game of BADMINTON [= **birdie**]

shy¹ /ʃaɪ/ *adj.* **1** nervous and embarrassed about meeting and speaking to other people, especially people you do not know: *As a teenager, I was* ***painfully shy*** (=extremely shy). | *She's* ***too shy*** *to speak up for herself.*

THESAURUS

timid – not brave or confident: *She's a good player, but timid on the court.*
bashful – shy and not willing to say very much: *Rachel blushed and gave me a bashful smile.*
reserved – not liking to express your emotions or talk about your problems: *a quiet, reserved man*
introverted – thinking a lot about your own interests, problems, etc., and not liking to be with other people: *She was an introverted person who did not become involved in campus activities.*
withdrawn – quiet, and not wanting to talk to other people: *After the accident, he became anxious and withdrawn.*
antisocial – not liking to meet people and talk to them: *My family was fairly antisocial and we seldom had visitors.*
retiring formal – not wanting to be with other people: *a shy and retiring woman*
→ see also Thesaurus box at INSECURE, SOCIABLE

2 sb is not shy about sth used in order to say that someone is very willing to do something or get involved in something: *John has strong opinions, and he's* ***not shy about*** *voicing them.* —**shyly** *adv.*: *She smiled shyly.* —**shyness** *n.* [U]

shy² *v.* past tense and past participle **shied** third person singular **shies** [I] if a horse shies, it makes a sudden movement away from something because it is frightened

shy away from sth *phr. v.* to avoid doing something because you are not confident enough about it: *Erik had always shied away from speaking in public.*

shy·ster /ˈʃaɪstɚ/ *n.* [C] *informal* a dishonest person, especially a lawyer or politician

sib·ling /ˈsɪblɪŋ/ *n.* [C] **1** *formal* your brother or sister: *All of her siblings are still in Korea.* **2 sibling rivalry** competition between brothers and sisters for the attention of their parents

sic /sɪk/ *adv.* used after a word that you have copied into a piece of writing in order to show that you know it was not spelled or used correctly

sick /sɪk/ *adj.* **1** suffering from a disease or illness: *His mother's very sick.* | *Everyone ate the same thing, but I was the only one who* ***got sick.*** | *Leslie* ***called in sick*** (=telephoned to say she would not come to work because she was sick) *today.*

THESAURUS

feel sick – to feel sick in your stomach and as if you might vomit
not feel good/well – to feel sick: *Mommy, I don't feel good.*
ill – sick: *More than 50 school children became ill.*
not very well: *You don't look very well* (=you look sick).
under the weather spoken – slightly sick: *I've been a little under the weather lately.*

2 be sick to bring food up from your stomach through your mouth [= **vomit**]: *I think I'm going to be sick.* **3 the sick** people who are sick: *nurses taking care of the sick and wounded* **4 feel sick (to your stomach)** to feel as if you are going to VOMIT: *I felt so sick after eating all that popcorn.* **5 be sick (and tired) of/be sick to death of** to be angry and bored with something that has been happening for a long time: *I'm sick and tired of her excuses.* **6 make me sick** *spoken* **a)** to make you feel strong anger and disapproval: *People who treat animals like that make me sick.* **b)** to make someone feel very JEALOUS – used humorously: *You got an A? You make me sick!* **7 be worried sick** to be extremely worried: *Why didn't you call? We were worried sick about you.* **8** someone who is sick does things that are strange and cruel: *The murders are obviously the work of a* ***sick mind.*** **9** sick stories, jokes, etc. deal with death and suffering in a cruel or unpleasant way

sick·en /ˈsɪkən/ *v.* **1** [T] to make you feel strong anger and disapproval: *We were sickened by newspaper reports of child abuse.* **2** [I] to become sick

sick·en·ing /ˈsɪkənɪŋ/ *adj.* **1** very shocking, annoying, or upsetting: *It's sickening to see so many poor people in such a wealthy country.* **2** disgusting and making you feel as if you want to VOMIT: *the sickening smell of rotting meat*

sick·le /ˈsɪkəl/ *n.* [C] a tool with a blade in the shape of a hook, used for cutting wheat or long grass

ˈsick leave *n.* [U] the time you are allowed to be away from work because of sickness

sick·ly /ˈsɪkli/ *adj.* **1** weak, unhealthy, and often sick: *a sickly child* **2** a sickly smell, taste, etc. is disgusting and makes you feel sick: *the sickly sweet smell of cheap perfume*

sick·ness /ˈsɪknɪs/ *n.* **1** [U] the state or feeling of being sick: *soldiers suffering from hunger and sickness* | ***motion/car/sea, etc. sickness*** (=sickness caused by traveling in a car, boat, etc.) **2** [C] a

S

particular illness: *common sicknesses such as colds and ear infections* → MORNING SICKNESS

sick·o /ˈsɪkoʊ/ *n.* plural **sickos** [C] *informal* someone who gets pleasure from things that most people find disgusting or upsetting: *What kind of sicko would write something like that?*

ˈsick pay *n.* [U] money paid by an employer to a worker who cannot work because of illness

side[1] /saɪd/ *n.* [C]
1 PART OF AN AREA one of the two areas that something is divided into: *Jim grew up on Detroit's east side.* | *They own a house* ***on the other side of*** *the lake.* | *She tilted her head* ***to one side****, considering the question.*
2 NEXT TO STH [usually singular] the place or area directly next to someone or something: *Stand on this side of me so Dad can get a photo.* | *Her mother was always* ***at/by*** *her* ***side*** *in the hospital.*
3 side by side a) next to each other: *They walked side by side.* **b)** if people live, work, etc. side by side, they do it together, have a good relationship, and help each other: *Doctors and scientists are working side by side to find a cure for AIDS.*
4 EDGE the part of an object or area that is farthest from the middle, at or near the edge: *We pulled over to* ***the side of the road****.*
5 OF A BUILDING/VEHICLE, ETC. a part of something that is not the front, back, top, or bottom: *A truck ran into the left* ***side of*** *the bus.*
6 OF A THIN OBJECT one of the two surfaces of a thin flat object: *You can write on both* ***sides of*** *the paper.*
7 FLAT SURFACE one of the flat surfaces of something: *A cube has six sides.* | *a five-sided shape*
8 from side to side moving continuously from right to left: *The boat swayed from side to side as waves hit it.*
9 from all sides from every direction: *enemy gunfire coming from all sides*
10 SUBJECT/SITUATION one part of a subject, problem, or situation: *I'd like to hear her side of the story.* | *You should* ***look on the bright side*** (=think about the positive parts of the situation). | *Who's in charge of the creative side of the project?*
11 ARGUMENT/WAR, ETC. one of the people, groups, teams, or countries opposing each other in an argument, war, etc.: *Nancy's* ***on our side*** (=agrees with us). | *We were on* ***the winning/losing side****.* | *Teachers should never* ***take sides*** (=support just one person or opinion).
12 FOOD a dish that you eat in addition to the main dish of a meal in a restaurant [= **side dish**, **side order**]: *I'll have the roast beef sandwich with* ***a side of*** *fries.*
13 on the side a) in addition to your regular job: *He runs a little business on the side.* **b)** in addition to the main dish that you order in a restaurant: *Could I have a salad on the side?*
14 PART OF YOUR BODY the left or right part of your body from your shoulder to the top of your leg: *Turn over and* ***lie on*** *your right* ***side****.*
15 OF A FAMILY the parents, grandparents, etc. of your mother or father: *There's a history of heart disease* ***on*** *my mother's* ***side****.*
16 MOUNTAIN/VALLEY one of the sloping areas of a hill, valley, etc.

side[2] *adj.* [only before noun] **1** in or on the side of something: *You can leave by the side door.* **2 side street/road etc.** a street, road, etc. that is smaller than a main street: *We parked the car on a side street.* **3** from the side of something: *a side view of the statue*

side[3] *v.*
side against sb *phr. v.* to argue against a person or group in an argument, fight, etc.
side with sb *phr. v.* to support a person or group in an argument, fight, etc.: *It seems like Frank always sides with Dad.*

side·board /ˈsaɪdbɔrd/ *n.* [C] a long low piece of furniture in a DINING ROOM that you store dishes and glasses in

side·burns /ˈsaɪdbɚnz/ *n.* [plural] hair that grows down the sides of a man's face in front of his ears

side·car /ˈsaɪdkɑr/ *n.* [C] an enclosed seat that is joined to the side of a MOTORCYCLE and has a separate wheel

ˈside dish *n.* [C] a dish that is served along with the main food at a meal

ˈside efˌfect *n.* [C] **1** an effect that a drug has on your body in addition to the intended effect: *The drug has no* ***harmful side effects****.* **2** an unexpected result of an activity, situation, or event

side·kick /ˈsaɪdˌkɪk/ *n.* [C] *informal* someone who is a close friend or helper of a more important person, especially in movies, etc.

side·line[1] /ˈsaɪdlaɪn/ *n.* [C] **1** one of the two lines that form the edges of a field where sports are played, and the area just outside these lines **2** something that you do to earn money in addition to your regular job: *Mark does translation work* ***as a sideline****.* **3 on the sidelines** not taking part in an activity even though you want to: *There are still buyers on the sidelines waiting to get stocks.*

sideline[2] *v.* **be sidelined** to not be included in a game or event because you are injured or because you are not as good as someone else: *Their quarterback was sidelined with a knee injury.*

side·long /ˈsaɪdlɔŋ/ *adj.* **a sidelong look/glance** a way of looking at someone by moving your eyes to the side, done secretly or when you are nervous

ˈside ˌorder *n.* [C] a small amount of a food ordered in a restaurant to be eaten with a meal, but served on a separate dish: *a* ***side order of*** *onion rings*

side·show /ˈsaɪdʃoʊ/ *n.* [C] a separate small part of a CIRCUS or a fair, that often has very unusual performers

S

side·step /ˈsaɪdstɛp/ *v.* past tense and past participle **sidestepped**, present participle **sidestepping** [T] to avoid a difficult question or decision: *Congressman Howell sidestepped the reporters' questions.*

side·swipe /ˈsaɪdswaɪp/ *v.* [T] to hit the side of a car or other vehicle with the side of your car

side·track /ˈsaɪdtræk/ *v.* [T] to make someone stop doing or saying something by making him/her interested in something else: *I think we're **getting sidetracked** from the main issue here.*

ˌside-view ˈmirror *n.* [C] a mirror attached to the side of a car

side·walk /ˈsaɪdwɔk/ *n.* [C] a hard surface or path for people to walk on along the side of a street

side·ways /ˈsaɪdweɪz/ *adv.* toward one side, or with the side facing forward: *Mel's car slid sideways as it hit the ice.*

sid·ing /ˈsaɪdɪŋ/ *n.* [U] wood, metal, or plastic in long narrow pieces, used for covering the sides of houses: *They've put new **aluminum siding** on their home.*

si·dle /ˈsaɪdl/ *v.* [I] to walk toward someone or something slowly, as if you do not want to be noticed: *Theo **sidled up to** me with an embarrassed look.*

siege /sidʒ/ *n.* [C,U] a situation in which an army surrounds a place and stops supplies of food, weapons, etc. from getting to it: *a city **under siege*** (=surrounded by an army)

si·es·ta /siˈɛstə/ *n.* [C] a short sleep in the afternoon, often taken by people in warm countries [➡ **nap**]

sieve /sɪv/ *n.* [C] a kitchen tool that looks like a wire net, used for separating solids from liquids —**sieve** *v.* [T]

sift /sɪft/ *v.* [T] **1** to put flour, sugar, etc. through a SIFTER in order to remove large pieces **2 also sift through** to examine something very carefully in order to find something: *It will take a while to sift through all these files.*

sifter /ˈsɪftɚ/ *n.* [C] **1** a kitchen tool made of a tube with a wire net inside, through which you put flour, sugar, etc. in order to remove or break up large pieces

sigh¹ /saɪ/ *v.* [I] to breathe out loudly and slowly, especially when you are tired or in order to express a strong emotion: *She **sighed deeply** and shook her head.*

sigh² *n.* [C] an act or sound of sighing: *Judy sat down with a **sigh of** relief.*

sight¹ /saɪt/ *n.*

1 ABILITY TO SEE [U] the physical ability to see [➡ **eyesight**]: *My grandmother is **losing** her **sight*** (=going blind).

2 ACT OF SEEING [singular,U] the act of seeing something: *He can't stand **the sight of** blood.* | *We **caught sight of*** (=suddenly saw) *Henry as we turned the corner.*

3 STH YOU SEE [C] something you can see, especially if it is something beautiful, unusual, etc.: *The Wrigley Building is one of the most famous sights in Chicago.* | *It was a **common sight** to see children begging on the streets.*

4 in/within sight (of sth) **a)** inside the area that you can see: *There was nobody in sight.* | *We camped within sight of the lake.* **b)** likely to happen soon: *Peace is in sight.*

5 out of sight (of sth) outside the area that you can see: *Keep your car windows rolled up and your valuables out of sight.*

6 not let sb out of your sight to make sure that someone stays near you: *Stay here, and don't let the baby out of your sight.*

7 lose sight of sth to forget an important part of something because you are too concerned about the details: *We have **lost sight of the fact that** the computer is only a tool.*

8 out of sight, out of mind used to say that you will soon forget someone or something if you do not see him, her, or it for a short period of time

9 ON A WEAPON [C usually plural] the part of a gun or weapon that helps you aim at something

sight² *v.* [T] to see something from a long distance away, especially something you have been looking for: *Two bears have been sighted in the area.*

sight·ed /ˈsaɪṭɪd/ *adj.* able to see [≠ **blind**]

sight·ing /ˈsaɪṭɪŋ/ *n.* [C] an occasion when something is seen, especially when it is something unusual or rare

sight-read /ˈsaɪtˀrid/ *v.* past tense and past participle **sight-read** /-rɛd/ [I,T] to play or sing written music that you are looking at for the first time, without practicing it first

sight·see·ing /ˈsaɪtˌsiɪŋ/ *n.* [U] the activity of visiting famous or interesting places, especially as a tourist: *We **went sightseeing** and saw a play.* —**sightseer** *n.* [C]

sign¹ /saɪn/ *n.* [C] **1** a piece of paper, metal, etc. with words or a picture that gives people information, warnings, or instructions: *Follow the **signs** that **say** "Montlake Bridge."* | *a no smoking sign* **2** an event, fact, etc. that shows that something exists or is happening, or that it will happen in the future: *The house **showed** no **signs of** a forced entry.* | *That's a **good/bad sign**!* | *Extreme tiredness is an early **sign of** the disease.* | ***There are** worrying **signs** that the agreement will fail.*

COLLOCATIONS

clear/obvious/visible sign – one that you can clearly see or understand
good/positive/encouraging sign – one that tells you that something good might happen
bad/warning sign – one that tells you that something bad might happen
early sign – one that shows what is happening at the beginning of a process, situation, etc.
sure sign – one that proves that something is true

3 a picture or shape that has a particular meaning

S

[= **symbol**]: *A dollar sign looks like "$."* **4** a movement or sound that you make without speaking, in order to tell someone something: *a thumbs-up sign* **5** one of the SYMBOLS of the ZODIAC

sign² *v.* **1** [I,T] to write your name on a letter or document to show that you wrote it or agree with it, or to make it official: *Rundon signed the agreement last week.* | *Underneath, she had **signed** her **name**.* | *The players **signed autographs** after the game.* ➔ see picture at CHECK² **2** [T] to officially agree to employ someone: *Columbia Records **signed** her **to** a three-year contract.* **3** [I] to tell someone something by using movements: *She **signed to** us **to** get out of the way.*

sign sth ⇔ **away** *phr. v.* to sign a document that gives your property or legal rights to someone else: *The Puyallup Tribe signed away much of their land rights.*

sign for sth *phr. v.* to sign a document to prove that you have received something: *He signed for a letter from a New York law firm.*

sign (sb) ⇔ **in** *phr. v.* to write your name or someone's name in a book when you enter a hotel, an office building, etc.

sign off *phr. v.* **1** to officially say or show that you approve of a document, plan, or idea: *Both sides **signed off on** the agreement.* **2** to say goodbye at the end of a radio or television broadcast, or at the end of a letter

sign on *phr. v.* to agree to work for someone or to do something, and usually to sign a document showing this: *Several boys **signed on as** volunteers.*

sign out *phr. v.* **1 sign** (sb) **out** to write your name in a book when you leave a hotel, an office building, etc. **2 sign** sth ⇔ **out** to write your name on a form or in a book to show that you have taken or borrowed something

sign sth ⇔ **over** *phr. v.* to sign an official document that gives your property or legal rights to someone else: *Daley **signed over** his shares **to** his partner.*

sign up *phr. v.* **1 sign** sb ⇔ **up** if someone is signed up by an organization, s/he signs a contract and agrees to work for that organization: *Navy recruiters want to sign up people with technical abilities.* **2** to put your name on a list because you want to take a class, belong to a group, etc.: *500 children have **signed up for** the music classes.*

sig·nal¹ /ˈsɪgnəl/ *n.* [C] **1** a sound, action, or event that gives information or tells someone to do something: *He **gave the signal** to start.* | *I phoned, but only got a **busy signal*** (=a sound telling you the phone is being used). | *The governor is sending **signals that** he will run for president.* **2** a series of light waves, sound waves, etc. that carry an image, sound, or message to something such as a radio or television: *broadcasting signals*

signal² *v.* **1** [I,T] to make a movement or sound, without speaking, that gives information or tells someone to do something: *Marshall **signaled for** coffee.* **2** [T] to make something clear by what you say or do: *Carter has signaled his intention to run for mayor.* **3** [T] to be a sign or proof of something: *Bad behavior may signal a learning problem.* **4** [I] to show the direction you intend to turn in a car, but using lights: *Don't forget to signal before you change lanes.*

sig·na·to·ry /ˈsɪgnəˌtɔri/ *n.* plural **signatories** [C] *formal* one of the people or countries that sign an agreement

sig·na·ture /ˈsɪgnətʃɚ/ *n.* [C] your name written the way you usually write it, for example at the end of a letter, on a check, etc.: *We need your signature on these documents.*

sig·nif·i·cance /sɪgˈnɪfəkəns/ *n.* [U] the importance or meaning of something, especially something that might affect you in the future: *the historical **significance of** the battle*

sig·nif·i·cant /sɪgˈnɪfəkənt/ *adj.* **1** noticeable or important [≠ **insignificant**]: *a significant 20th century artist* | *significant differences between the two groups*

> **THESAURUS**
>
> **important**, **crucial**, **vital**, **essential**, **major**, **key**
> ➔ see Thesaurus box at IMPORTANT

2 having a special meaning that is not known to everyone: *Tom gave her a significant look.* —**significantly** *adv.*

sigˌnificant ˈother *n.* [C] *humorous* your husband, wife, girlfriend, or boyfriend

sig·ni·fy /ˈsɪgnəˌfaɪ/ *v.* past tense and past participle **signified**, third person singular **signifies** [T] **1** to represent, mean, or be a sign of something: *The move **signified that** our old lives were over.* **2** to express a wish, feeling, or opinion by doing something: *Everyone nodded to signify their agreement.*

sign·ing /ˈsaɪnɪŋ/ *n.* [U] the act of signing something such as an agreement or a contract: *the **signing of** the peace agreement*

ˈsign ˌlanguage *n.* [C,U] a language that uses hand movements instead of spoken words, used by people who cannot hear

sign·post /ˈsaɪnpoʊst/ *n.* [C] **1** something that is used for holding a street sign up **2** something that shows you what is happening or what you should do: *The employment figures are a key signpost of the economy's performance.*

si·lence¹ /ˈsaɪləns/ *n.* **1** [C,U] complete quiet because no one is talking, or a period of complete quiet: *There was a **stunned/awkward/embarrassed, etc. silence**.* | *a **brief/short/long silence*** | *The family sat eating **in silence**.* **2** [U] complete absence of sound or noise: ***the silence of** space* | *A blackbird's call **broke the silence**.*

silence² *v.* [T] **1** *written* to make someone stop criticizing or giving his/her opinions: *Critics of the government were silenced.* **2** to make someone stop talking, or to stop something making noise: *A shout from the soldier silenced everybody.*

si·lenc·er /ˈsaɪlənsɚ/ *n.* [C] a thing that is put on the end of a gun so that it makes less noise when it is fired

si·lent /ˈsaɪlənt/ *adj.* **1** not saying anything or making any noise [= **quiet**]: *silent prayer* | *The crowd* ***fell silent*** (=became quiet) *when the President appeared.* **2** failing or refusing to talk about something: *"Well?" Maria* ***remained silent.*** **3** [only before noun] a silent movie has pictures but no sound **4** a silent letter in a word is not pronounced —**silently** *adv.*

ˌsilent ˈpartner *n.* [C] someone who owns part of a business but does not make decisions about how it operates

sil·hou·ette¹ /ˌsɪluˈɛt, ˈsɪluˌɛt/ *n.* [C] a dark shape or shadow, seen against a light background

silhouette² *v.* [T] to appear as a silhouette: *skyscrapers* ***silhouetted against*** *the sky*

sil·i·con /ˈsɪlɪˈkɑn, -kən/ *n.* [U] an ELEMENT that is often used for making glass, bricks, parts for computers, etc.

silk /sɪlk/ *n.* [C,U] a thin thread produced by a SILKWORM, or the soft, usually shiny cloth made from this thread: *a silk shirt*

silk·en /ˈsɪlkən/ *adj. literary* soft and smooth like silk, or made of silk: *her silken hair*

silk·worm /ˈsɪlk-wɚm/ *n.* [C] a type of CATERPILLAR (=insect) that produces silk

silk·y /ˈsɪlki/ *adj.* soft and smooth like silk: *silky fur*

sill /sɪl/ *n.* [C] the narrow flat piece of wood at the base of a window frame

sil·ly /ˈsɪli/ *adj.* comparative **sillier**, superlative **silliest** not sensible or serious: *a silly thing to do* | *You're being silly.* —**silliness** *n.* [U]

si·lo /ˈsaɪloʊ/ *n.* plural **silos** [C] **1** a tall round building used for storing grain, animal food, etc. **2** a large structure under the ground from which a MISSILE can be fired

silt /sɪlt/ *n.* [U] sand or mud that is carried by the water in a river, and settles in a bend of the river or in the entrance to a port

sil·ver¹ /ˈsɪlvɚ/ *n.* [U] **1** a valuable shiny white metal that is an ELEMENT and is used for making jewelry, spoons, etc. **2** the color of this metal

silver² *adj.* **1** made of silver: *a silver spoon* ➔ see picture at MATERIAL¹ **2** colored silver: *a silver dress*

ˌsilver anniˈversary *n.* [C] the date that is exactly 25 years after an important event, especially a wedding

ˌsilver ˈmedal *n.* [C] a prize made of silver that is given to someone who finishes second in a race or competition

sil·ver·ware /ˈsɪlvɚˌwɛr/ *n.* [U] objects such as knives, spoons, and forks that are made of silver or a similar metal

sim·i·lar /ˈsɪmələ/ *adj.* almost the same but not exactly the same [≠ **dissimilar**; ➡ **alike**]: *kids with similar backgrounds* | *The system is* ***similar to*** *one used in other schools.* | *The two cheeses are* ***similar in*** *flavor.*

THESAURUS

like – similar in some way to something else: *It tastes a little like chicken.*
alike – very similar: *She and her sister look alike.*
akin to sth – similar to something: *He looked at me with something akin to awe.*
identical – exactly the same: *The two pictures were identical.*
matching – having the same color, style, or pattern as something else: *The twins were dressed in matching outfits.*

sim·i·lar·i·ty /ˌsɪməˈlærət̬i/ *n.* plural **similarities** [C,U] the quality of being similar, or a particular way in which things or people are similar: ***There are similarities*** *with German, but Yiddish is a distinct language.* | *his* ***similarity to*** *my brother* | *Discuss the* ***similarities and differences*** *between the two writers.*

sim·i·lar·ly /ˈsɪmələli/ *adv.* in a similar way: *The two cities are laid out similarly.*

sim·i·le /ˈsɪməli/ *n.* [C] an expression in which you compare two things using the words "like" or "as," for example "as red as blood" [➡ **metaphor**]

sim·mer /ˈsɪmɚ/ *v.* **1** [I,T] to cook food in liquid and not allow it to boil **2 simmer down** *spoken* to become less excited or angry and more calm —**simmer** *n.* [singular]

sim·per /ˈsɪmpɚ/ *v.* [I] to smile in a way that is silly and annoying

sim·ple /ˈsɪmpəl/ *adj.* **1** not difficult or complicated [= **easy**]: *a simple math problem* | *The solution is* ***fairly/pretty/relatively simple.*** | *It's* ***simple to*** *make.*

THESAURUS

easy – not difficult: *It was an easy class.*
straightforward – simple and easy to understand: *a straightforward task*

2 made in a plain style, without a lot of decoration or things that are not necessary: *a simple white dress* **3** not involving anything else: *He plays for the love of music,* ***pure/plain and simple.*** | ***The simple fact/truth is*** *we don't have the money.* ▶ Don't say "The fact is simple." ◀ **4** consisting of only one or a few necessary parts: *simple tools like a hammer and saw* **5** ordinary and not special in any way: *I live a very simple life.* **6 simple past/present/future** *technical* a tense of a verb that is not formed with an AUXILIARY such as "have" or "be"

ˌsimple ˈinterest *n.* [U] INTEREST that is calculated on the sum of money that you first INVESTED,

S

and does not include the interest it has already earned [➡ **compound interest**]

ˌsimple-ˈminded *adj.* not able to understand complicated things

sim·plic·i·ty /sɪmˈplɪsət̬i/ *n.* [U] the quality of being simple and not complicated, especially when this is attractive or useful: *the simplicity of their clothes* | ***For simplicity*** (=to make something easy), *divide the class into three groups.*

sim·pli·fy /ˈsɪmpləˌfaɪ/ *v.* past tense and past participle **simplified**, third person singular **simplifies** [T] to make something clearer and easier to do or understand [➡ **oversimplify**]: *a promise to simplify the tax forms* —**simplification** /ˌsɪmpləfəˈkeɪʃən/ *n.* [U]

sim·plis·tic /sɪmˈplɪstɪk/ *adj. disapproving* treating difficult subjects in a way that is too simple: *a simplistic view of the problem*

sim·ply /ˈsɪmpli/ *adv.* **1** only [= **just**]: *You shouldn't buy something **simply because** it's on sale.* **2** used in order to emphasize what you are saying: *The movie simply isn't any good.* **3** in a way that is easy to understand: *To **put it simply*** (=explain it in a simple way), *the students are not prepared for college work.* **4** in a plain and ordinary way: *Alanna was dressed quite simply.*

S

sim·u·late /ˈsɪmyəˈleɪt/ *v.* [T] to make or do something that is not real but looks, sounds, or feels as though it is real: *Computer models have simulated conditions on Mars.* —**simulator** *n.* [C] *a flight simulator* —**simulated** *adj.*

sim·u·la·tion /ˌsɪmyəˈleɪʃən/ *n.* [C,U] something you do or make in order to practice what you would do in a real situation: *a computer simulation used to train airline pilots*

si·mul·ta·ne·ous /ˌsaɪməlˈteɪniəs/ *adj.* happening or done at exactly the same time: *a simultaneous broadcast on TV and radio* —**simultaneously** *adv.*

sin¹ /sɪn/ *n.* **1** [C] something you do that is against religious laws: *He **confessed** his **sins** to one of the priests.* **2** [singular] *informal* something that you do not approve of: ***It's a sin** to waste food.*

sin² *v.* past tense and past participle **sinned**, present participle **sinning** [I] to do something wrong that is against religious laws

since /sɪns/ *conjunction, prep., adv.* **1** at or from a particular time in the past until now: *I haven't seen him since we graduated from high school.* | *Paul had been waiting since 2 o'clock.* | *His ex-wife has since remarried, but he's still single.* | *We've lived here **ever since** we got married.* | *He had a car accident in 2002. **Since then**, he has been unemployed.* **2** because: *You'll have to get up early, since the bus leaves at 7 a.m.* **3 since when?** *spoken* used in questions to show anger or surprise: *Since when did you start smoking?*

sin·cere /sɪnˈsɪr/ *adj.* honest and true, or based on what you really feel or believe [≠ **insincere**]: *a sincere apology*

sin·cere·ly /sɪnˈsɪrli/ *adv.* **1** in a sincere way: *Both men sincerely admired each other's work.* **2 Sincerely/Sincerely yours/Yours sincerely** an expression you write at the end of a formal letter before you sign your name

sin·cer·i·ty /sɪnˈsɛrət̬i/ *n.* [U] the quality of being honest, and really meaning or believing what you say: *I don't doubt her sincerity, but I think she's got her facts wrong.*

sin·ew /ˈsɪnju/ *n.* [C,U] *technical* a strong CORD in the body that connects a muscle to a bone

sin·ew·y /ˈsɪnyui/ *adj.* showing strong muscles

sin·ful /ˈsɪnfəl/ *adj.* **1** morally wrong [= **wicked**]: *a sinful man* **2** *informal* very bad or wrong: *a sinful waste of money*

sing /sɪŋ/ *v.* past tense **sang** /sæŋ/ past participle **sung** /sʌŋ/ **1** [I,T] to make musical sounds, songs, etc. with your voice: *The kids **sang songs** about peace.* | *Jana sings in the church choir.* | *She started **singing** Georgie **to sleep**.* **2** [I] if birds sing, they produce high musical sounds —**singing** *n.* [U]

sing along *phr. v.* to sing with someone else who is already singing or playing music: ***Sing along to/with** all your favorite tunes.*

sing out *phr. v.* to sing or shout loudly and clearly

sing. the written abbreviation of **singular**

singe /sɪndʒ/ *v.* [I,T] to burn something slightly on the surface or edge, or to be burned in this way

sing·er /ˈsɪŋɚ/ *n.* [C] someone who sings, especially as a job: *an opera singer*

sin·gle¹ /ˈsɪŋgəl/ *adj.* **1** only one: *We lost the game by a single point.* | *a single sheet of paper* **2** not married: *Is he single?* | *a club for single men/women*

THESAURUS

married, engaged, separated, divorced, widowed

➔ see Thesaurus box at MARRIED

3 single parent/mother/father a mother or father who takes care of her/his children by herself or himself, because s/he is not married **4** used in order to emphasize a separate thing: *Smoking is the **single most** important cause of lung cancer.* | *This is the **single biggest/greatest** problem we face.* | *She visits her mother **every single** day.* **5** intended to be used by only one person [➡ **double**]: *a single bed* ➔ see picture at BED¹

single² *n.* [C] **1** a musical recording of only one song: *her hit single* **2** a one-dollar bill: *Do you have any singles?* **3 singles** [plural] people who are not married: *a singles bar* (=where single people can go to drink and meet people)

ˌsingle ˈfile *n.* [U] a line with one person behind the other: *The children walked **in single file** to the field.*

ˌsingle-ˈhandedly **also** **ˌsingle-ˈhanded** *adv.* done by one person with no help from anyone else

THESAURUS
alone, on your own, (all) by yourself, solo
➔ see Thesaurus box at ALONE

ˌsingle-ˈminded *adj.* having one clear purpose and working hard to achieve it: *a **single-minded determination** to succeed*

sin·gly /ˈsɪŋgli/ *adv.* alone, or one at a time: *people walking singly or in groups*

sing·song /ˈsɪŋsɔŋ/ *n.* [singular] a way of speaking in which your voice keeps rising and falling —**singsong** *adj.*

sin·gu·lar¹ /ˈsɪŋgyələ˞/ *adj.* **1** relating to the singular **2** [usually before noun] very great or noticeable: *a singular achievement*

singular² *n.* **the singular** *technical* in grammar, the form of a word that represents only one person or thing. For example, "child" is in the singular. [➡ **plural**]

sin·gu·lar·ly /ˈsɪŋgyələ˞li/ *adv. formal* in a way that is very noticeable or unusual: *She wore a singularly inappropriate dress.*

sin·is·ter /ˈsɪnɪstə˞/ *adj.* seeming to be bad or evil: ***There was something/nothing sinister** about his financial dealings.*

sink¹ /sɪŋk/ *v.* past tense **sank** /sæŋk/ or **sunk** /sʌŋk/, past participle **sunk**

1 IN WATER [I,T] to go down below the surface of water, mud, etc., or to make something do this [➡ **drown**]: *The Titanic **sank to** the bottom of the sea.* | *Submarines were ordered to sink enemy ships.* ➔ see picture at FLOAT¹

THESAURUS
dive, plunge, submerge
➔ see Thesaurus box at DIVE¹

2 FALL/SIT DOWN [I] to fall down heavily, especially because you are weak or tired: *I **sank down into** one of the soft chairs.*

3 MOVE LOWER [I] to move down slowly to a lower level: *The sun **sank beneath** the horizon.*

4 GET WORSE [I] to gradually get into a worse state: *In the 1930s, America **sank** deeper **into** the Depression.*

5 DECREASE [I] to decrease in amount, number, value, etc.: *House prices in the area are sinking fast.*

6 be sunk *informal* to be in a situation in which you are certain to fail or have a lot of problems: *If he doesn't lend us the money, we're sunk!*

7 your heart sinks/your spirits sink if your heart or spirits sink, you lose your hope or confidence

8 a sinking feeling a feeling that you get when you realize that something very bad is beginning to happen

9 sink or swim to succeed or fail without help from anyone else

10 MONEY [T] to spend a lot of money on something; [= **invest**]: *They had **sunk** thousands **into** that house.*

11 SPORTS [T] to get a basketball or GOLF ball into a basket or hole

sink in *phr. v.* if information, facts, etc. sink in, you begin to understand them or realize their full meaning: *At first, what she said didn't really sink in.*

sink² *n.* [C] an open container in a kitchen or BATHROOM that you fill with water to wash dishes, your hands, etc.: *There was a pile of dirty dishes in the sink.*

sin·ner /ˈsɪnə˞/ *n.* [C] someone who SINS

si·nus /ˈsaɪnəs/ *n.* [C] *technical* one of the pair of hollow spaces in the bones of your face behind your nose

sip¹ /sɪp/ *v.* past tense and past participle **sipped**, present participle **sipping** [I,T] to drink something slowly, swallowing only small amounts: *Mrs. Hong sipped her tea.*

THESAURUS
drink, gulp down, slurp, knock back, swig
➔ see Thesaurus box at DRINK²

sip² *n.* [C] a very small amount of a drink: *He **took a sip of** coffee.*

si·phon¹ /ˈsaɪfən/ *v.* [T] **1** to take something away from the person, organization, etc. for which it was intended, especially to dishonestly take money: *Aid was **siphoned off** by government officials for their own use.* **2** to remove liquid from a container using a siphon

siphon² *n.* [C] a bent tube that you use to get liquid out of a container, by holding one end of the tube at a lower level than the container

sir /sə˞/ *n.* **1** *spoken* used in order to speak politely to a man when you do not know his name or when you want to show respect: *Can I help you, sir?* | *"Do you understand, Louise?" "Yes, sir."* | *Dear Sir* (=used at the beginning of a business letter to a man when you do not know his name) **2 Sir** a title used before the name of a KNIGHT: *Sir Lancelot*

sire /saɪə˞/ *v.* [T] *written* **1** to be the father of a child **2** to be the father of an animal —**sire** *n.* [C]

si·ren /ˈsaɪrən/ *n.* [C] a piece of equipment that makes very loud warning sounds, used on police cars, fire engines, etc.: *I heard police sirens in the distance.*

sir·loin /ˈsə˞lɔɪn/ **also** **ˌsirloin ˈsteak** *n.* [C,U] a good piece of meat cut from the back of a cow

sis·sy /ˈsɪsi/ *n.* plural **sissies** [C] *informal* a boy that other boys do not approve of because he likes doing things that girls do —**sissy** *adj.*

sis·ter /ˈsɪstə˞/ *n.* [C] **1** a girl or woman who has the same parents as you [➡ **brother**]: *Mary is my **big/older** sister, and Kim is my **little/younger** sister.*

S

THESAURUS

relative, parents, father, mother, brother, grandparents, grandfather, grandmother, great-grandparents, uncle, aunt, nephew, niece, cousin
→ see Thesaurus box at RELATIVE[1]

2 used by women to talk about other women and to show that they have feelings of friendship and support toward them: *Susan B. Anthony and other sisters fought for our right to vote.* **3 also Sister** a NUN: *Sister Frances* —**sisterly** *adj.*

sis·ter·hood /ˈsɪstɚˌhʊd/ *n.* [U] a strong loyalty among women who share the same ideas and aims [➡ **brotherhood**]

ˈsister-in-ˌlaw *n.* plural **sisters-in-law** [C] **1** the sister of your husband or wife **2** the wife of your brother, or the wife of your husband or wife's brother

sit /sɪt/ *v.* past tense and past participle **sat** /sæt/ present participle **sitting**
1 ON A SEAT [I] **a)** to be on a chair, a seat, or the ground with the top half of your body upright and your weight resting on your BUTTOCKS: *The children **sat** around her **on** the floor.* | *I was **sitting at** my desk writing a letter.* | ***Sit still*** (=sit without moving) *and let me fix your hair.* **b) also sit down** to move to a sitting position after you have been standing: *He came and **sat beside/next to** her.*
2 OBJECTS/BUILDINGS [I] to lie or be in a particular position or condition: *Several books **sat on** the desk.* | *The house sat empty for two years.*
3 NOT DO ANYTHING [I] to stay in one place for a long time, especially doing nothing useful: *I can't **sit here** all day, I have work to do.* | *He was just **sitting there**, staring into space.*
4 MAKE SB SIT [T] **also sit** sb **down** to make someone sit somewhere: *She **sat** the boy **in** a corner.*
5 TAKE CARE OF [I] to take care of a baby or child while his/her parents are not home [= **babysit**]
6 sit tight to stay where you are and not move, or to stay in the same situation and not do anything, while you are waiting for something: *Investors should sit tight and not panic.*
7 not sit well with sb if a situation, plan, etc. does not sit well with someone, s/he does not like it: *A tax raise won't sit well with the voters.*
8 sit on the fence to avoid saying which side of an argument you support or what your opinion is about something
9 MEET [I] to have an official meeting: *The court sits once a month.*

sit around *phr. v.* to spend time resting or not doing anything useful or to spend a lot of time sitting and doing nothing useful: *We were just sitting around talking.*

sit back *phr. v.* **1** to get into a comfortable position and relax: *Just sit back and relax – I'll make dinner.* **2** to make no effort to get involved in something: *You can't just sit back and then complain about what happens.*

sit in *phr. v.* to be present somewhere but not get involved in the activity: *I **sat in on** one of his classes.*

sit in for sb *phr. v.* to do a job, go to a meeting, etc. instead of the person who usually does it: *He's sitting in for Sally while she's gone.*

sit on sth *phr. v.* to be a member of an organization or other official group: *Hawkins sits on several committees.*

sit sth ⇔ **out** *phr. v.* to stay where you are and not take part in something until it finishes: *Due to injuries, Herrera sat out the last two games.*

sit through sth *phr. v.* to go to a meeting, performance, etc. and stay until it finishes, even if it is very long or boring: *We had to sit through a three-hour meeting this morning.*

sit up *phr. v.* **1** to be in a sitting position or move to a sitting position after you have been lying down: *He finally was able to sit up in bed and eat something.* | *Maria **sat up straight*** (=with her back very upright) *and looked upset.* **2** to stay awake and not go to bed: *He sat up all night reading it.* **3 sit up and take notice** to suddenly start paying attention to someone or something: *The success of writers like Paretsky has **made** publishers **sit up and take notice**.*

sit·com /ˈsɪtˀkɑm/ *n.* [C,U] a funny television program in which the same characters appear in different situations each week

THESAURUS

movie, film, soap opera, game show, talk show, cartoon, drama series, documentary, the news
→ see Thesaurus box at TELEVISION

ˈsit-down *adj.* **1** a sit-down meal or restaurant is one in which you sit at a table and eat a formal meal **2 sit-down protest/strike etc.** an occasion when a large group of people protest something by not moving from a particular area until their demands are listened to

site[1] /saɪt/ *n.* [C] **1** a place where something important or interesting happened: *the site where the Pilgrims landed*

THESAURUS

place, spot, location
→ see Thesaurus box at PLACE[1]

2 an area where something is being built or will be built: *a construction site* **3** a WEBSITE

site[2] *v.* **be sited** to be put or built in a particular place: *The zoo is sited in the middle of the city.*

ˈsit-in *n.* [C] a protest in which people sit down and refuse to leave a place until their demands are listened to

sit·ter /ˈsɪt̬ɚ/ *n.* [C] *spoken* a babysitter, especially one who is taking care of older children

sit·ting /ˈsɪt̬ɪŋ/ *n.* **at/in one sitting** during one continuous period of time when you are sitting in a chair: *Morris read the whole book in one sitting.*

sit·u·at·ed /ˈsɪtʃuˌeɪt̬ɪd/ *adj.* **be situated** to be in a particular place or position: *The hotel is* ***situated in/near*** *the old market district.*

sit·u·a·tion /ˌsɪtʃuˈeɪʃən/ *n.* [C] a combination of all the things that are happening and all the conditions that exist at a particular time and place: *the present* ***economic/political situation*** *in the country* | ***In this situation****, it is unrealistic to expect a quick solution.*

COLLOCATIONS

difficult/bad/dangerous/tough situation – one that is bad and difficult to deal with
economic/political/financial situation
present/current situation – one that exists now
no-win situation – one that will end badly no matter what you decide to do
win-win situation – one that will end well for everyone involved in it
If a **situation improves**, it becomes better.
If a **situation worsens** or **deteriorates**, it becomes worse.

ˌsituation ˈcomedy *n.* [C] a SITCOM

ˈsit-up *n.* [C usually plural] an exercise for your stomach, in which you sit up from a lying position while keeping your feet on the floor [➡ **crunch**]

six /sɪks/ *number* **1** 6 [➡ **sixth**] **2** six O'CLOCK: *I get out of class at six.*

ˈsix-pack *n.* [C] six bottles or CANS of a drink sold together as a set: *a six-pack of beer*

six·teen /ˌsɪkˈstin◂/ *number* 16 —**sixteenth** *number*

sixth /sɪksθ/ *number* **1** 6th **2** 1/6

ˌsixth ˈsense *n.* [singular] a special ability to feel or know something without using any of your five usual senses such as hearing or sight [➡ **intuition**]

six·ty /ˈsɪksti/ *number* **1** 60 **2 the sixties a)** the years between 1960 and 1969 **b)** the numbers between 60 and 69, especially when used for measuring temperature **3 be in your sixties** to be aged between 60 and 69: *He's* ***in his early/mid/late*** *sixties.* —**sixtieth** /ˈsɪkstiɪθ/ *number*

siz·a·ble, **sizeable** /ˈsaɪzəbəl/ *adj.* fairly large: *a sizable crowd*

size¹ /saɪz/ *n.* **1** [C,U] how big or small something is: *Class sizes are smaller at private schools.* | *an orange that is* ***the size of*** (=the same size as) *a softball* | *Abby and Kate are about* ***the same size****.* | *Shrimp vary* ***in size****.* **2** [U] the fact of being very big: *You should see the size of their house!* | *The company's* ***sheer size*** *gives it an advantage.* **3** [C] one of the standard measures in which clothes, goods, etc. are made and sold: *This shirt is the wrong size.* ▶ Don't say "have a size." ◀ *They didn't have anything* ***in my size****.* | *a size 10 shoe* **4 large-sized/medium-sized etc.** large, average, etc. in size: *a pocket-sized calculator*

size² *v.*
size sb/sth ⇔ **up** *phr. v. informal* to look at or consider a person or situation and make a judgment about them: *He sized up the situation in a glance.*

siz·zle /ˈsɪzəl/ *v.* [I] to make a sound like water falling on hot metal: *bacon sizzling in the pan* ➔ see picture on page A7

skate¹ /skeɪt/ *n.* [C] **1** an ICE SKATE **2** a ROLLER SKATE

skate² *v.* [I] to move on skates —**skating** *n.* [U] *Let's* ***go skating****.* —**skater** *n.* [C]

skate·board /ˈskeɪt˺bɔrd/ *n.* [C] a short board with two wheels at each end, on which you stand and ride, pushing your foot along the ground in order to move —**skateboarding** *n.* [U] ➔ see picture at BOARD¹

ˈskate park *n.* [C] a special place where children can ride skateboards

skel·e·ton /ˈskɛlət˺n/ *n.* [C] **1** the structure consisting of all the bones in a human or animal body: *the human skeleton* ➔ see picture on page A3 **2 have a skeleton in the closet** to have a secret about something embarrassing or unpleasant that happened to you in the past **3 skeleton staff/crew/service** only enough people to keep an operation or organization working —**skeletal** *adj.*

skep·tic /ˈskɛptɪk/ *n.* [C] someone who does not believe something unless s/he has definite proof

skep·ti·cal /ˈskɛptɪkəl/ *adj.* doubting or not believing something: *Voters are highly* ***skeptical about/of*** *the proposal.* —**skepticism** /ˈskɛptəˌsɪzəm/ *n.* [U]

sketch¹ /skɛtʃ/ *n.* [C] **1** a drawing that you do quickly and without a lot of details: *a pencil* ***sketch of*** *a bird*

THESAURUS

picture, **snapshot**, **portrait**, **cartoon**, **caricature**, **illustration**, **poster**
➔ see Thesaurus box at PICTURE¹

2 a short humorous scene that is part of a longer performance: *a comedy sketch* **3** a short written or spoken description without a lot of details: *a brief sketch of each candidate*

sketch² *v.* [I,T] **1** to draw a sketch of something

THESAURUS

draw, **doodle**, **scribble**, **trace**
➔ see Thesaurus box at DRAW¹

2 also sketch out to describe something in a general way, giving the basic ideas: *Deming sketched out his plans for the new business.*

sketch·y /ˈskɛtʃi/ *adj.* not thorough or complete, and not having enough details to be useful: *sketchy information*

skew /skyu/ *v.* [T] if something skews the result of a test, election, RESEARCH, etc. it affects the results, making them incorrect: *Money is skewing* *our political system.* —**skewed** *adj.*: *Sometimes the data can be badly skewed.*

skew·er /ˈskyuɚ/ *n.* [C] a long metal or wooden stick that you put through a piece of raw food that you want to cook —**skewer** *v.* [T]

ski¹ /ski/ *n.* plural **skis** [C] one of a pair of long narrow pieces of wood or plastic that you fasten to boots so you can move easily on snow

ski² *v.* past tense and past participle **skied** [I] to move over snow on SKIS —**skiing** /ˈskiɪŋ/ *n.* [U] *We're* ***going skiing*** *this weekend.* —**skier** *n.* [C] ➔ see picture on page A10

skid¹ /skɪd/ *v.* past tense and past participle **skidded**, present participle **skidding** [I] if a vehicle skids, it suddenly slides sideways and it is difficult to control: *A car* ***skidded on*** *the ice.* ➔ see picture at SLIDE¹

skid² *n.* [C] **1** a sudden sliding movement of a vehicle, that you cannot control: *skid marks* | *He* ***went into a skid*** *on an icy road.* **2 be on the skids/hit the skids** *informal* to begin to fail: *That was when his career hit the skids.*

skill /skɪl/ *n.* [C,U] an ability to do something very well, especially because you have learned and practiced it [➡ **talent**]: *a test of basic* ***skills in*** *reading and math* | *an employee's* ***writing/technical/social, etc. skills*** | *The boys are playing* ***with*** *increasing* ***skill.***

THESAURUS

ability, talent, knack
➔ see Thesaurus box at ABILITY

skilled /skɪld/ *adj.* having the training and experience needed to do something well [≠ **unskilled**]: *a* ***highly skilled*** *mechanic*

skil·let /ˈskɪlɪt/ *n.* [C] a FRYING PAN

skill·ful /ˈskɪlfəl/ *adj.* good at doing something that you have learned and practiced: *a skillful doctor* —**skillfully** *adv.*

skim /skɪm/ *v.* past tense and past participle **skimmed**, present participle **skimming** **1** [T] to remove something that is floating on the surface of a liquid: ***Skim*** *the fat* ***off*** *the soup.* **2** [I,T] **also skim through** to read something quickly to find the main facts or ideas in it: *Helen skimmed the headlines.* **3** [T] to move along quickly, nearly touching the surface of something: *birds skimming the trees*

skim sth ⇔ **off** *phr. v.* to take the best people, best part of something, or money for yourself: *Corrupt leaders have skimmed off much of the country's wealth.*

ˈskim milk *n.* [U] milk that has had most of its fat removed from it

THESAURUS

milk, low-fat/2% milk, whole milk, buttermilk, half-and-half
➔ see Thesaurus box at MILK¹

skimp /skɪmp/ *v.* [I,T] to not use enough money, time, effort, etc. on something, so it is unsuccessful or of bad quality: *Don't* ***skimp on*** *buying good shoes for your children.*

skimp·y /ˈskɪmpi/ *adj.* too small in size or quantity: *a skimpy little dress*

skin¹ /skɪn/ *n.*

1 ON A BODY [C,U] the natural outer covering of a human's or animal's body: *her beautiful dark skin* | *The snake was shedding its skin.*

COLLOCATIONS

fair/pale skin
dark/olive skin
dry/oily/sensitive skin
smooth/soft skin
rough/leathery skin
good/bad skin – healthy or unhealthy skin
➔ HAIR

2 FOOD [C,U] the natural outer layer of some fruits and vegetables: *banana skins*
3 ANIMAL SKIN [C,U] the skin of an animal used as leather, clothes, etc.: *a tiger skin rug*
4 dark-skinned/smooth-skinned etc. having a particular type or color of skin: *a fair-skinned woman*
5 LAYER [C,U] a thin solid layer that forms on the top of a liquid such as paint or milk when it gets cool or is left uncovered
6 COMPUTER [C,U] the way particular information appears on a computer screen, especially when this can be changed quickly and easily
7 get under sb's skin *informal* to annoy someone, especially by the way you behave: *I could tell my comment had gotten under his skin.*
8 have thin/thick skin to be easily upset or not easily upset by criticism
9 (do sth) by the skin of your teeth *informal* to succeed in doing something, when you have almost failed to do it: *We made it there by the skin of our teeth.*
10 make sb's skin crawl to make someone feel uncomfortable, nervous, or slightly afraid
11 sth is only skin deep used in order to say that something may seem important or effective, but it really is not because it only affects the way things appear: ***Beauty is only skin deep.***

skin² *v.* past tense and past participle **skinned**, present participle **skinning** [T] to remove the skin from an animal, fruit, or vegetable

skin·flint /ˈskɪnˌflɪnt/ *n.* [C] *informal disapproving* someone who hates spending or giving away money [= **miser**]

skin·head /ˈskɪnhɛd/ *n.* [C] a young person who SHAVES off his/her hair and often behaves violently toward people who are not white

skin·ny /ˈskɪni/ *adj.* comparative **skinnier**, superlative **skinniest** very thin, especially in a way that is not attractive: *a tall, skinny kid*

THESAURUS

thin, **slim**, **slender**, **lean**, **underweight**, **emaciated**
→ see Thesaurus box at THIN[1]

ˈskinny ˌdipping *n.* [U] *informal* swimming without any clothes on

ˌskin-ˈtight *adj.* clothes that are skin-tight fit tightly against your body: *skin-tight jeans*

skip /skɪp/ *v.* past tense and past participle **skipped**, present participle **skipping** **1** [T] to not do something that you would usually do or that you should do: *I'd skipped breakfast.* | *Brad got in trouble for* ***skipping school***. **2** [I] to move forward with quick jumps from one foot to the other: *children* ***skipping down/across*** *the street*

THESAURUS

jump, **hop**, **leap**, **dive**, **vault**
→ see Thesaurus box at JUMP[1]

3 [I,T] to not read, mention, or deal with something that would normally come or happen next: *I skipped question four.* | *Readers occasionally* ***skip over*** *a word they don't know.* **4** [I] to go from one subject, place, etc. to another in no particular order: *She* ***skips from*** *one topic* ***to*** *another.*

skip·per /ˈskɪpɚ/ *n.* [C] *informal* someone who is in charge of a ship [= **captain**]

skir·mish /ˈskɚmɪʃ/ *n.* [C] a military fight between small groups of people or soldiers: *a border skirmish*

skirt[1] /skɚt/ *n.* [C] a piece of women's clothing that fits around the waist and hangs down like the bottom part of a dress: *She was wearing a white blouse and a plain black skirt.* | *a* ***short/long skirt***
→ see picture at CLOTHES

skirt[2] **also skirt around** *v.* [T] **1** to go around the outside edge of a place: *The soldiers skirted around the town and crossed the river.* **2** to avoid talking about an important problem, subject, etc.: *The company spokesman skirted the question.* **3** if you skirt the rules or the law, you do something that is not illegal, but that does not exactly follow the rules

skit /skɪt/ *n.* [C] a short funny play

skit·tish /ˈskɪt̮ɪʃ/ *adj.* nervous, frightened, or not sure about something: *a skittish horse*

skulk /skʌlk/ *v.* [I] to hide or move around quietly because you do not want to be seen: *Two men were* ***skulking in*** *the shadows.*

skull /skʌl/ *n.* [C] the bones of a person's or animal's head → see picture on page A3

skull·cap /ˈskʌlkæp/ *n.* [C] a YARMULKE

skunk /skʌŋk/ *n.* [C] a small black and white animal that produces a very bad smell if it feels threatened

sky /skaɪ/ *n.* plural **skies** **1** [C,U] the space above the earth where the sun, clouds, and stars are: *a* ***clear/cloudless/overcast, etc.*** *sky* | *a few clouds* ***in the sky*** **2 skies** [plural] the sky – used especially when talking about the weather: *clear skies* **3 the sky's the limit** *spoken* used in order to say that there is no limit to what someone can achieve, spend, win, etc.

sky·div·ing /ˈskaɪˌdaɪvɪŋ/ *n.* [U] the sport of jumping from an aircraft and falling through the sky before opening a PARACHUTE —**skydiver** *n.* [C]

ˌsky-ˈhigh *adj. informal* extremely high or expensive: *Prices at the auction were sky-high.* —**sky-high** *adv.*

sky·light /ˈskaɪlaɪt/ *n.* [C] a window in the roof of a building

skyline

sky·line /ˈskaɪlaɪn/ *n.* [C] the shape made by tall buildings or hills against the sky: *the New York City skyline*

sky·rock·et /ˈskaɪˌrɑkɪt/ *v.* [I] to increase suddenly and by large amounts: *Property values have skyrocketed.*

sky·scrap·er /ˈskaɪˌskreɪpɚ/ *n.* [C] a very tall building in a city

skyscrapers

slab /slæb/ *n.* [C] a thick flat piece of a hard material such as stone: *a concrete slab*

slack[1] /slæk/ *adj.* **1** hanging loosely, or not pulled tight: *a slack rope* **2** with less business activity than usual: *People get laid off when things are slack.* **3** *disapproving* not taking enough care to do things correctly: *The waiters were slack.*

THESAURUS

lazy, **idle**, **indolent**, **shiftless**
→ see Thesaurus box at LAZY

slack[2] *n.* **1 slacks** [plural] a pair of pants **2 take/pick up the slack** **a)** to do something that needs to be done because the person or organization that usually does it is no longer doing it: *As the government cuts programs, charities try to pick up the slack.* **b)** to make a rope tighter **3 cut/give sb some slack** *informal* to allow someone to do something without criticizing him/her or making it more difficult: *They have no reason to cut the opposing team any slack.* **4** [U] looseness in the way something such as a rope hangs or is fastened: *He **gave** the line some **slack**, then slowly began reeling it in.*

slack³ also slack off *v.* [I] **1** to not work as quickly as you should on your job: *Everything was going well, and I thought I could slack off a little.* **2** SLACKEN —**slacker** *n.* [C]

slack·en /ˈslækən/ *v.* [I,T] to gradually become slower, weaker, or less active, or to make something do this: *The rain slackened briefly.*

slag /slæg/ *n.* [U] waste material that is left when metal is obtained from rock

slain /sleɪn/ *v.* the past participle of SLAY

slake /sleɪk/ *v. literary* **slake your thirst** to drink so that you are not THIRSTY

slam¹ /slæm/ *v.* past tense and past participle **slammed**, present participle **slamming** **1** [I,T] if a door, gate, etc. slams, or someone slams it, it shuts loudly with a lot of force: *Baxter left the room, slamming the door.* | *The door **slammed shut**.* **2** [I,T] to hit something or someone against a surface with a lot of force, or to hit something with a lot of force: *Manya **slammed** the phone **down**.* | *He was going 80 mph when he **slammed into** the back of a stopped car.* **3** [T] *informal written* to criticize someone strongly: *Watson was slammed for not acting sooner.*

S

slam² *n.* [C usually singular] the noise or action of hitting or closing something hard

ˈslam dunk *n.* [C] an action in basketball when a player jumps up high and throws the ball down through the basket —**slam dunk** *v.* [I]

slan·der /ˈslændɚ/ *n.* [C,U] a spoken statement about someone that is not true and is intended to damage the good opinion that people have of him/her —**slander** *v.* [T] —**slanderous** *adj.*

THESAURUS

lie, fib, libel
➔ see Thesaurus box at LIE³

slang /slæŋ/ *n.* [U] very informal, sometimes offensive, language that is used especially by people who belong to a particular group

THESAURUS

language, jargon, terminology
➔ see Thesaurus box at LANGUAGE

—**slangy** *adj.*

slant¹ /slænt/ *v.* **1** [I,T] to slope, or to make something slope in a particular direction: *a hat slanted over his forehead* **2** [T] to provide information in a way that unfairly supports one opinion, gives an advantage to one group, etc.

slant² *n.* [singular] **1** a sloping position or angle: *She cut it **on a slant**.* **2** a way of writing or thinking about a subject that shows support for a particular set of ideas or beliefs: ***a** feminist **slant on** Dickens's novels*

slan·ted /ˈslæntɪd/ *adj.* **1** *disapproving* providing facts or information in a way that unfairly supports only one side of an argument or one opinion: *The article was slanted.* **2** sloping: *a slanted roof*

slap¹ /slæp/ *v.* past tense and past participle **slapped**, present participle **slapping** [T] **1** to hit someone quickly with the flat part of your hand: *She **slapped** his **face**.*

THESAURUS

hit, punch, beat, smack, whack, strike
➔ see Thesaurus box at HIT¹

2 *informal* to suddenly make someone do something more, pay more money, etc.: *In 1990, the U.S. **slapped** sanctions **on** Iraq.* **3 slap sb on the back** to hit someone on the back in a friendly way, often as a way of praising him/her

slap sth ⇔ **on** *phr. v.* to put or spread something quickly on a surface in a careless way: *Just slap on a coat of paint.*

slap² *n.* [C] **1** a quick hit with the flat part of your hand **2 a slap in the face** an action that seems to be deliberately intended to offend or upset someone: *The offer was so low as to be a slap in the face.* **3 a slap on the wrist** *informal* a punishment that is not very severe

slap·dash /ˈslæpdæʃ/ *adj.* careless and done too quickly: *a slapdash job*

slap·stick /ˈslæpˌstɪk/ *n.* [U] humorous acting in which the actors fall over, throw things at each other, etc.

slash¹ /slæʃ/ *v.* **1** [I,T] to cut or try to cut something in a violent way with a sharp weapon, making a long deep cut: *Her throat had been slashed.* **2** [T] *informal written* to greatly reduce an amount or price: *a campaign promise to slash taxes*

THESAURUS

reduce, lower, decrease, cut, roll back
➔ see Thesaurus box at REDUCE

slash² *n.* [C] **1 also slash mark** a line (/) used in writing to separate words, numbers, or letters **2** a long narrow cut in something

slat /slæt/ *n.* [C] a thin flat piece of wood, plastic, or metal, used especially in furniture

slate¹ /sleɪt/ *n.* **1** [U] a dark gray rock that can be easily split into thin flat pieces **2** [C] a list of people that voters can choose in an election

slate² *v.* **be slated to do sth/be slated for sth** if something is slated to happen, it is planned to happen in the future: *The committee is slated to vote on the bill next week.* | *The corner office buildings are slated for demolition.*

slath·er /ˈslæðɚ/ *v.* [T] *informal* to cover something with a thick layer of a soft substance: *fresh bread slathered with butter*

slaugh·ter /ˈslɔt̬ɚ/ *v.* [T] **1** to kill a lot of people in a cruel or violent way: *Hundreds of innocent* *civilians had been slaughtered by government troops.*

THESAURUS

kill, **murder**, **massacre**
➔ see Thesaurus box at KILL[1]

2 to kill an animal for food **3** *informal* to defeat an opponent by a large number of points: *New York slaughtered Boston, 11–2.* —**slaughter** *n.* [U] *the slaughter of innocent people*

slaugh·ter·house /ˈslɔt̬ɚˌhaʊs/ *n.* [C] a building where animals are killed for their meat

slave[1] /sleɪv/ *n.* [C] **1** someone who is owned by another person and is forced to work without pay for him/her **2 be a slave to/of sth** *disapproving* to be so strongly influenced by something that you cannot make your own decisions: *a* ***slave to fashion***

slave[2] *v.* [I] to work very hard with little time to rest: *Hector grew up watching his father* ***slaving away*** *at a factory job.*

ˈslave ˌdriver *n.* [C] *informal disapproving* someone who makes people work extremely hard

ˌslave ˈlabor *n.* [U] **1** *informal* work for which you are paid a very small amount of money **2** work done by slaves, or the slaves that do this work

slav·er·y /ˈsleɪvəri/ *n.* [U] the system of having slaves, or the condition of being a slave: ***Slavery*** *was* ***abolished*** (=officially ended) *after the Civil War.*

slav·ish /ˈsleɪvɪʃ/ *adj. disapproving* too willing to do what you are told to do or to behave like someone else, without thinking for yourself: *slavish devotion to duty*

slay /sleɪ/ *v.* past tense **slew** /slu/ past participle **slain** /sleɪn/ [T] *journalism* to kill someone violently: *The victim was slain in his driveway by a masked gunman.* —**slaying** *n.* [C]

sleaze /sliz/ *n.* [U] immoral behavior, usually involving sex or lies: *allegations of political sleaze*

slea·zy /ˈslizi/ *adj.* comparative **sleazier**, superlative **sleaziest** *disapproving* **1** a sleazy place is dirty, cheap, or in bad condition: *sleazy bars* **2** relating to sex or dishonest behavior: *a sleazy lawyer*

sled /slɛd/ *n.* [C] a vehicle that slides over snow, often used by children —**sled** *v.* [I]

sledge ham·mer /ˈslɛdʒ ˌhæmɚ/ *n.* [C] a large heavy hammer

sleek /slik/ *adj.* **1** sleek hair or fur is smooth, shiny, and healthy-looking: *a cat's sleek fur* **2** having a smooth attractive shape: *a sleek car*

sleep[1] /slip/ *v.* past tense and past participle **slept** /slɛpt/ **1** [I] to rest your mind and body by lying down with your eyes closed [➡ **asleep**]: *"Did you* ***sleep well****?"* | *He was* ***sleeping soundly*** *when the phone rang.* | *I* ***couldn't sleep*** *last night.* | *If you're tired, why don't you* ***sleep late*** (=sleep until late in the morning) *tomorrow?* | *Goodnight,* ***sleep tight*** (=sleep well). ▶ Don't say "I slept early." Say "I went to sleep/bed early." ◀

COLLOCATIONS

sleep well/badly
sleep soundly – to sleep deeply and peacefully
sleep like a baby/sleep like a log – to sleep very well, without waking up at all
sleep late/sleep in – to deliberately sleep later than usual in the morning
sleep lightly – to wake up very easily if there is any noise

THESAURUS

doze – to sleep lightly for a short time, especially when you did not intend to: *He was dozing in front of the TV.*
doze off – to fall asleep, especially when you did not intend to: *Several times I dozed off, lulled by the gentle sound of the waves against the shore.*
take a nap – to sleep for a short time during the day: *He said he was going upstairs to take a nap.*
oversleep – to sleep for longer than you intended: *I overslept and missed my plane.*
toss and turn – to keep changing your position in bed because you cannot sleep: *I lay awake, tossing and turning.*
not sleep a wink – to not be able to sleep at all: *Peter didn't sleep a wink that night.*

USAGE

Use **sleep** when you are giving more information, for example how long someone sleeps, or where s/he sleeps: *Most people sleep for about eight hours.* | *He slept downstairs.*
Do not use **sleep** to talk about starting to sleep. Use **fall asleep** or **go to sleep**: *She fell asleep in front of the TV.*

2 sleep on it *spoken* to not make a decision about something important until the next day **3** [T] to have enough beds for a particular number of people: *The tent sleeps six.*

sleep around *phr. v. disapproving* to have sex with many people without having a serious relationship with any of them

sleep in *phr. v.* to sleep later than usual in the morning: *I slept in till 10:00 on Saturday.*

sleep sth ⇔ **off** *phr. v.* to sleep until you are no longer drunk: *Why don't you take him home so he can* ***sleep it off****.*

sleep over *phr. v.* to sleep at someone's house for a night: *Mom, can I* ***sleep over at*** *Ann's tonight?*

sleep through sth *phr. v.* to continue sleeping while something noisy is happening: *How could you have slept through the earthquake?*

S

sleep together *phr. v. informal* if people sleep together, they have sex with each other

sleep with sb *phr. v. informal* to have sex with someone, especially someone you are not married to: *Everyone knows he's sleeping with Diana.*

sleep² *n.* **1** [U] the natural state of being asleep [➥ **asleep**]: *I rarely get more than 6 hours of sleep a night.* | *What time did you* ***get to sleep*** (=start sleeping)? | *I didn't* ***get*** *much* ***sleep*** *last night.* | *Ed sometimes talks* ***in*** *his* ***sleep*** (=while he is sleeping). **2** [singular] a period when you are sleeping: *You'll feel better after a* ***good night's sleep*** (=a night when you sleep well). | *A sudden noise woke me from a* ***deep sleep.*** **3 go to sleep a)** to start sleeping: *Katherine went to sleep about 7:00 last night.* **b)** *informal* if a part of your body goes to sleep, you cannot feel it for a short time because it has not been getting enough blood **4 not lose (any) sleep over sth** *spoken* to not worry about something: *I won't* ***lose any sleep over it.*** **5 put a dog/cat etc. to sleep** to give an animal drugs so that it dies without pain

sleep·er /'slipɚ/ *n.* [C] **1** someone who is asleep or who sleeps in a particular way: *Sam's a* ***heavy/light sleeper*** (=he sleeps well or wakes up easily). **2** a movie, book, etc. that is successful, even though people did not expect it to be

S

'sleeping bag *n.* [C] a large warm bag for sleeping in, especially when camping

'sleeping pill *n.* [C] a PILL that helps you to sleep

sleep·less /'sliplɪs/ *adj.* **a sleepless night** a night when you are unable to sleep —**sleeplessness** *n.* [U]

sleep·walk·er /'slip͵wɔkɚ/ *n.* [C] someone who walks while s/he is sleeping —**sleepwalk** *v.* [I] —**sleepwalking** *n.* [U]

sleep·y /'slipi/ *adj.* comparative **sleepier**, superlative **sleepiest** **1** tired and ready for sleep: *I don't know why I'm so sleepy.* **2** a sleepy place is quiet and without much activity: *a sleepy little town* —**sleepily** *adv.* —**sleepiness** *n.* [U]

THESAURUS

quiet, peaceful, calm, tranquil
➔ see Thesaurus box at QUIET¹

sleep·y·head /'slipi͵hɛd/ *n.* [C] *spoken* someone, especially a child, who looks as if s/he wants to go to sleep: *It's time for bed, sleepyhead.*

sleet /slit/ *n.* [U] freezing rain—**sleet** *v.* [I]

THESAURUS

snow, slush, frost, hail
➔ see also Thesaurus box at SNOW¹, RAIN¹

sleeve /sliv/ *n.* [C] **1** the part of a piece of clothing that covers your arm or part of your arm: *a blouse with short/long sleeves* **2 long-sleeved/short-sleeved** with long or short sleeves: *a long-sleeved shirt* **3 have sth up your sleeve** *informal* to have a secret plan that you are going to use later: *Janssen usually has a few surprises up his sleeve.*

sleeve·less /'slivlɪs/ *adj.* without sleeves: *a sleeveless dress*

sleigh /sleɪ/ *n.* [C] a large vehicle pulled by animals, used for traveling on snow

sleight of hand /͵slaɪt̬ əv 'hænd/ *n.* [U] quick skillful movements with your hands when performing magic tricks

slen·der /'slɛndɚ/ *adj.* thin, graceful, and attractive: *long slender fingers*

THESAURUS

thin, slim, skinny, lean, underweight, emaciated
➔ see Thesaurus box at THIN¹

slept /slɛpt/ *v.* the past tense and past participle of SLEEP

sleuth /sluθ/ *n.* [C] *old-fashioned* someone who tries to find out information about a crime

slew¹ /slu/ *n.* **a slew of sth** *informal* a large number: *Her work as a reporter has won her a slew of awards.*

slew² *v.* the past tense of SLAY

slice¹ /slaɪs/ *n.* [C] **1** a thin flat piece of bread, meat, etc. cut from a larger piece: *a* ***slice of*** *pizza* | ***Cut*** *the tomato* ***into*** *thin/thick* ***slices.*** ➔ see Thesaurus box at PIECE¹ **2** a part or a piece of something: *The German company wants a* ***slice of*** *the U.S. market.* **3 a slice of life** a film, play, or book which shows life as it really is

slice² *v.* **1 also slice up** [T] to cut meat, bread, etc. into thin flat pieces: *Could you slice the bread?* ➔ see picture at CUT¹

THESAURUS

cut, chop (up), dice, peel, carve, shred, grate
➔ see Thesaurus box at CUT¹

2 [I,T] to cut something easily with one movement of a sharp knife or edge: *Careful – that blade could* ***slice through*** *your finger.*

slick¹ /slɪk/ *adj.* **1** *disapproving* good at persuading people, often in a way that does not seem honest: *a slick salesman* **2** *disapproving* attractive or skillful, but not containing any important or interesting ideas: *slick commercials* **3** smooth and slippery: *The roads are* ***slick with*** *ice.*

slick² *n.* [C] an OIL SLICK

slick³ *v.*

slick sth ⇔ **down/back** *phr. v.* to make hair smooth and shiny by putting oil, water, etc. on it

slide

slide[1] /slaɪd/ *v.* past tense and past participle **slid** /slɪd/ **1** [I,T] to move smoothly over a surface while continuing to touch it, or to make something move in this way: *children **sliding on** the ice* | *She **slid** the box **across** the floor.* | *The door **slides open** automatically.* **2** [I,T] to move somewhere quietly without being noticed, or to move something in this way: *She **slid out** of the room without waking anyone.* | *He **slid** the gun **into** his pocket.* **3** [I] to become lower in value, number, or amount: *Car sales slid 0.5% in July.* **4** [I] to gradually become worse, or to begin to have a problem: *Morrison gradually slid into alcohol and drug abuse.* **5 let sth slide** *informal* to ignore something: *I didn't agree, but I **let it slide**.*

slide[2] *n.* [C] **1** a large structure for children to slide down while playing **2** a photograph in a frame that you shine a light through to show a picture on a SCREEN or wall: *slides of our vacation* **3** a decrease in the amount, value, standard, or quality of something: *a **slide in** interest rates* | *The school is worried about the **slide in** student performance.* **4** a sudden fall of earth, stones, snow, etc. down a slope: *a rock slide* **5** a small piece of thin glass used for holding something when you look at it under a MICROSCOPE

'slide pro,jector *n.* [C] a piece of equipment that makes slides appear on a screen

,sliding 'scale *n.* [C] a system for calculating how much you pay for taxes, medical treatment, etc., in which the amount that you pay changes according to different conditions: *Fees are calculated **on a sliding scale**.*

slight[1] /slaɪt/ *adj.* **1** small in degree, and not serious or important: *a slight delay* | *a slight increase* | *a slight headache* **2 not the slightest chance/doubt/difference etc.** no doubt, chance, etc. at all: *I didn't have the slightest idea who that man was.* **3** someone who is slight is thin and delicate: *a slight old lady*

slight[2] *v.* [T] to offend someone by treating him/her rudely: *Meg **felt slighted** at not being invited to the party.*

slight[3] *n.* [C] *formal* a remark or action that offends someone: *I consider the comment a **slight on** the quality of our work!*

slight·ly /ˈslaɪtli/ *adv.* **1** a little: *She raised her eyebrow slightly.* | *The official gave a **slightly different** version of events.* | *The trip took **slightly more** than an hour.* **2 slightly built** having a thin and delicate body

slim[1] /slɪm/ *adj.* **1** attractively thin: *tall and slim*

THESAURUS

thin, **slender**, **skinny**, **lean**, **underweight**, **emaciated**
➔ see Thesaurus box at THIN[1]

2 very small in amount or number: *a slim lead in the polls* | *We have only **a slim chance** of winning.*

slim[2] *v.* past tense and past participle **slimmed**, present participle **slimming**

slim down *phr. v.* **1** to reduce the size or number of something: *Apex Co. is slimming down its workforce to cut costs.* **2** to become thinner by eating less or exercising more: *I've been trying to slim down since Christmas.*

slime /slaɪm/ *n.* [U] a thick slippery substance that looks or smells bad

slim·y /ˈslaɪmi/ *adj.* **1** covered with slime: *slimy rocks* **2** *informal disapproving* friendly in a way that does not seem sincere: *a slimy politician*

sling[1] /slɪŋ/ *v.* past tense and past participle **slung** /slʌŋ/ [T] to throw or put something somewhere in a way that is careless and forceful: *She **slung** her purse **over** her shoulder.*

sling[2] *n.* [C] **1** a piece of cloth tied around your neck to support your injured arm or hand: *Emily's arm has been **in a sling** for six weeks.* **2** a set of ropes or strong pieces of cloth that are used to lift and carry heavy objects

sling·shot /ˈslɪŋʃɑt/ *n.* [C] a stick in the shape of a Y with a thin band of rubber across the top, used especially by children to throw stones

slink /slɪŋk/ *v.* past tense and past participle **slunk** /slʌŋk/ [I] to move somewhere quietly and secretly, especially because you are afraid or ashamed: *He lowered his eyes and slunk back into his office.*

slip[1] /slɪp/ *v.* past tense and past participle **slipped**, present participle **slipping** **1** [I] to accidentally slide a short distance quickly, or to fall by sliding in this way: *Joan slipped and fell.* | *Be careful not to **slip on** the ice.* | *The knife slipped and cut her finger.* ➔ see picture at SLIDE[1]

THESAURUS

fall, **trip**, **stumble**, **lose your balance**
➔ see Thesaurus box at FALL[1]

2 [I] to go somewhere, without attracting other people's attention: *I managed to **slip out** of the office before 5:00.* **3** [T] to put something some-

S

where or give someone something quietly or secretly: *Dad slipped me $50 when Mom wasn't looking.* | *Someone slipped a note under my door.* **4** [I,T] to put on or take off a piece of clothing quickly and smoothly: *I'll just **slip into** something more comfortable.* | *He **slipped off** his coat and went upstairs.* **5** [I] to become worse or lower than before [= **fall**]: *Standards have slipped in the restaurant since the head chef left.* **6 let sth slip** to say something without meaning to, when you had wanted it to be a secret: *Lance **let it slip that** Julie was planning to quit.* **7 slip your mind** if something slips your mind, you forget to do it: *I meant to call you but it completely slipped my mind.*

slip out *phr. v.* if something slips out, you say it without intending to: *I'm sorry I spoiled the surprise; it just slipped out.*

slip up *phr. v.* to make a mistake: *They slipped up and sent me the wrong form.*

slip² *n.* [C] **1** a small or narrow piece of paper: *a **slip of paper** with her phone number on it* **2 a slip of the tongue** something that you say when you meant to say something else **3** a piece of underwear, similar to a thin dress or skirt, that a woman wears under a dress or skirt **4 give sb the slip** *informal* to escape from someone who is chasing you: *He gave the police the slip.*

S

slip·knot /ˈslɪpnɑt/ *n.* [C] a knot that you can make tighter by pulling one of its ends

ˌslipped ˈdisc, **slipped disk** *n.* [C] a painful injury caused when a connecting part between the bones in your back moves out of place

slip·per /ˈslɪpɚ/ *n.* [C] a light soft shoe that you wear in your house ➔ see picture at SHOE¹

slip·per·y /ˈslɪpəri/ *adj.* **1** something that is slippery is difficult to hold, walk on, etc. because it is wet or GREASY: *Careful, the sidewalk's slippery.* **2 a/the slippery slope** the beginning of something that will be hard to stop and will develop into something very bad

slip·shod /ˈslɪpʃɑd/ *adj. disapproving* done too quickly and carelessly: *slipshod work*

ˈslip-up *n.* [C] a careless mistake: *We cannot afford another slip-up.*

slit /slɪt/ *v.* past tense and past participle **slit**, present participle **slitting** [T] to make a straight narrow cut in cloth, paper, etc.: *Slit the pie crust before baking.* —**slit** *n.* [C]

slith·er /ˈslɪðɚ/ *v.* [I] to slide or move across a surface, twisting and moving like a snake

sliv·er /ˈslɪvɚ/ *n.* [C] a very small narrow piece of something: *a **sliver of** glass* | *You can just see a sliver of the ocean from our hotel.*

slob /slɑb/ *n.* [C] *informal* someone who is lazy, dirty, and messy

slob·ber /ˈslɑbɚ/ *v.* [I] to let SALIVA (=liquid produced in your mouth) come out of your mouth and run down: *The dog's slobbered all over the rug!*

slog /slɑg/ *v.* past tense and past participle **slogged**, present participle **slogging** [I] **1** to work very hard at something without stopping: *I've been **slogging through** a boring 400 page novel.* **2** to walk somewhere with difficulty: *soldiers **slogging through** the mud*

slo·gan /ˈsloʊgən/ *n.* [C] a short phrase that is easy to remember, used by politicians, companies that are advertising, etc.: *The crowd shouted anti-racist slogans.*

slop¹ /slɑp/ *v.* past tense and past participle **slopped**, present participle **slopping** [I,T] to make liquid move around or over the edge of something, or to move in this way: *The coffee slopped out of the cup and all over me.*

slop² *n.* [U] **1** food waste that is used for feeding animals **2** food that is too soft and tastes bad: *I'm not eating that slop!*

slope¹ /sloʊp/ *n.* **1** [C] a piece of ground or a surface that is higher at one end than the other: *a ski slope* **2** [singular] the angle at which something slopes: *a **slope of** 30°*

slope² *v.* [I] if the ground or a surface slopes, it is higher at one end than the other: *They looked out over a broad meadow that sloped toward the water.*

slop·py /ˈslɑpi/ *adj.* **1** not done carefully or thoroughly: *sloppy work* | *sloppy handwriting* **2** sloppy clothes are loose-fitting and not neat: *a sloppy old sweater* **3** wet and disgusting: *a sloppy kiss* —**sloppily** *adv.* —**sloppiness** *n.* [U]

slosh /slɑʃ/ *v.* [I] **1** to walk through water or mud in a noisy way: *kids sloshing through puddles* **2** if a liquid in a container sloshes, it moves against the sides of the container: *water **sloshing around** in the bottom of the boat*

sloshed /slɑʃt/ *adj. informal* drunk: *Gus was sloshed even before the party started.*

slot¹ /slɑt/ *n.* [C] **1** a long narrow hole made in a surface: *Which slot do the coins go in?* **2** a short period of time allowed for one particular event on a program: *the most popular TV show in its **time slot***

slot² *v.* past tense and past participle **slotted**, present participle **slotting** [I,T] to put something into a slot, or to go in a slot: *The cassette **slots in** here.*

sloth /slɔθ, sloʊθ/ *n.* **1** [C] a slow-moving animal from Central and South America **2** [U] *literary* laziness —**slothful** *adj.*

ˈslot maˌchine *n.* [C] a machine in which you put coins so that you can play games or try to win money

slouch¹ /slaʊtʃ/ *v.* [I] to stand, sit, or walk with your shoulders bent forward in a way that makes you look tired or lazy: *Stanley was slouched against the wall, fast asleep.*

slouch² *n.* **1** [singular] the position of your body when you slouch **2 be no slouch (at sth)** *informal* to be very good or skillful at something: *He's no slouch with a camera.*

slov·en·ly /ˈslʌvənli, ˈslɑ-/ *adj.* dirty, messy, and careless: *a slovenly old woman*

slow¹ /sloʊ/ *adj.* **1** not moving, being done, or happening quickly [≠ **fast**]: *The slowest runners started at the back.* | *They've been **slow in** answering our letter* (=took a long time to answer it). | *The police were **slow to** respond* (=took too long to do something). | *Progress has been **painfully slow*** (=far too slow). **2** [not before noun] showing time that is earlier than the true time [≠ **fast**]: *My watch is a few minutes slow.* **3** if business is slow, there are not many customers: *It's been a slow day.* **4** someone who is slow does not understand things quickly or easily: *The school gives extra help for slower students.*

slow² also **slow up** *v.* [I,T] to become slower or make something slower: *Her breathing slowed and she fell asleep.* | *Road work slowed up traffic this morning.*

slow down *phr. v.* **slow** sth ⇔ **down** to become slower or make something slower: *Slow down or you'll get a speeding ticket.* | *Dave's back trouble is slowing him down.*

slow³ *adv.* SLOWLY: *Can you run a little slower? I can't keep up.*

slow·down /ˈsloʊdaʊn/ *n.* [C usually singular] **1** a reduction in activity or speed: *a slowdown in the tourist trade* **2** a period when people deliberately work slowly in order to protest about something

slow·ly /ˈsloʊli/ *adv.* at a slow speed or rate: *Doctors slowly removed the bandages from her arm.* | *Things have begun to change slowly.*

ˌslow ˈmotion *n.* [U] movement in a movie or television program shown at a much slower speed than the speed at which it happened: *a replay of the goal shown **in slow motion***

slow·poke /ˈsloʊpoʊk/ *n.* [C] *spoken* someone who moves or does things too slowly

ˌslow-ˈwitted *adj.* not quick to understand things

sludge /slʌdʒ/ *n.* [U] a soft thick substance made of mud, waste, oil, etc.

slug¹ /slʌg/ *n.* [C] **1** a small creature with a soft body, that moves very slowly and eats garden plants **2** *informal* a bullet **3** *informal* a piece of metal used illegally instead of a coin in machines that sell things

slug² *v.* past tense and past participle **slugged**, present participle **slugging** [T] **1** *informal* to hit someone hard with your closed hand [= **punch**]: *I stood up and he slugged me again.* **2 slug it out** to argue or fight until someone wins or something has been decided: *The two sides are slugging it out in court.* **3** to hit a baseball hard

slug·gish /ˈslʌgɪʃ/ *adj.* moving, working, or reacting more slowly than normal: *The traffic was sluggish downtown.*

sluice¹ /slus/ *n.* [C] a passage for water to flow through, with a gate that can stop the water if necessary

sluice² *v.* [T] to wash something with a lot of water

slum¹ /slʌm/ *n.* [C] an area of a city with old buildings in very bad condition, where many poor people live: *She grew up in **the slums** of L.A.* ➔ see Thesaurus box at AREA

slum² *v.* past tense and past participle **slummed**, present participle **slumming** [I,T] to spend time in conditions that are much worse than those you are used to: *We traveled around the country, **slumming it**.*

slum·ber /ˈslʌmbɚ/ *n.* [singular] *literary* to sleep —**slumber** *v.* [I]

ˈslumber ˌparty *n.* [C] a party in which a group of children sleep at one child's house

slump¹ /slʌmp/ *v.* [I] **1** to suddenly go down in price, value, or number: *Car sales have slumped recently.* **2** to fall or lean against something because you are not strong enough to stand: *He was found **slumped over** the steering wheel of his car.*

slump² *n.* [C] **1** a sudden decrease in prices, sales, profits, etc.: *a **slump in** the housing market*

> **THESAURUS**
>
> **recession**, **depression**, **crash**
> ➔ see Thesaurus box at RECESSION

2 a period when there is a reduction in business and many people lose their jobs: *an economic slump* **3** a time when a player or team does not play well: *The Yankees needed this win to pull them out of a slump.*

slung /slʌŋ/ *v.* the past tense and past participle of SLING

slunk /slʌŋk/ *v.* the past tense and past participle of SLINK

slur¹ /slɚ/ *v.* past tense and past participle **slurred**, present participle **slurring** **1** [I,T] to speak unclearly without separating words or sounds: *After a few drinks, he started to **slur** his **words**.* **2** [T] to criticize someone or something unfairly

slur² *n.* [C] an unfair criticism, or an offensive remark: ***racial slurs***

slurp /slɚp/ *v.* [I,T] to drink a liquid while making a noisy sucking sound —**slurp** *n.* [C]

> **THESAURUS**
>
> **sip**, **gulp down**, **knock back**, **take/have a swig**
> ➔ see Thesaurus box at DRINK²

slush /slʌʃ/ *n.* **1** [U] partly melted snow

> **THESAURUS**
>
> **snow**, **sleet**, **frost**, **hail**
> ➔ see Thesaurus box at SNOW¹

2 [C] a drink made with crushed ice and a sweet liquid: *orange slush* —**slushy** *adj.*

ˈslush fund *n.* [C] a sum of money kept for dishonest purposes, especially by a politician

S

sly /slaɪ/ *adj.* comparative **slier** or **slyer** superlative **sliest** or **slyest** **1** using tricks and dishonesty to get what you want: *He's sly and greedy.* **2** showing that you know something that others do not know: *a sly smile* **3 on the sly** *informal* secretly doing something you are not supposed to be doing: *He's been seeing someone else on the sly.* —**slyly** *adv.*

smack[1] /smæk/ *v.* [T] **1** to hit someone or something, especially with your open hand [➡ **punch**]: *She smacked him hard across the face.*

THESAURUS

hit, **punch**, **slap**, **beat**, **whack**, **strike**
➔ see Thesaurus box at HIT[1]

2 smack your lips to make a short loud noise with your lips because you are hungry
smack of sth *phr. v.* to seem to have a particular bad quality: *a policy that smacks of age discrimination.*

smack[2] *n.* [C] a hit with your open hand, or a noise like the sound of this: *a smack on the head*

smack[3] *adv. informal* **1** exactly or directly in the middle of something, in front of something, etc.: *an old building* ***smack (dab) in the middle of*** *campus* **2** if something goes smack into something, it hits it with a lot of force: *The van ran smack into the wall.*

small /smɔl/ *adj.* **1** not large in size or amount [≠ **big**]: *a small dark woman* | *Rhode Island is the smallest state.* | *a store selling small appliances* | *This jacket is too small.*

THESAURUS

little – small in size: *a little house*
tiny – very small: *a tiny baby*
minute – extremely small: *Even in minute amounts, the chemical is very harmful.*
cramped – used about a space that is too small: *cramped working conditions*
petite – used about a woman who is short and thin in an attractive way
➔ BIG

2 unimportant or easy to deal with: *a small problem* | *We may have to make a few small changes.* **3 small business/farm** a business that does not involve large amounts of money or does not employ a large number of people **4** a small child is young

THESAURUS

young, **little**
➔ see Thesaurus box at YOUNG[1]

5 a small fortune a lot of money: *That house must have* ***cost*** *him* ***a small fortune***. —**small** *adv.*: *He writes so small I can't read it.*

ˌsmall ˈarms *n.* [plural] guns that are held in one or both hands for firing

ˌsmall ˈchange *n.* [U] money in coins of low value

ˌsmall ˈclaims court *n.* [C] a court that deals with cases that involve small amounts of money

ˈsmall fry *n.* [U] *informal* **1** children **2** people or things that are not important when compared to other people or things

ˌsmall-ˈminded *adj. disapproving* only interested in things that affect you, and too willing to judge people according to your own opinions: *greedy small-minded people*

ˌsmall poˈtatoes *adj. informal* not very big or important: *Compared to his salary, mine is small potatoes.*

small·pox /ˈsmɔlpɑks/ *n.* [U] a serious disease that causes spots that leave permanent marks on your skin

ˌsmall-ˈscale *adj.* not involving a lot of people, money, etc.: *a small-scale project*

ˈsmall talk *n.* [U] polite friendly conversation about unimportant subjects: *He's not very good at* ***making small talk***.

ˈsmall-time *adj.* unimportant or not successful: *a small-time drug dealer*

smart[1] /smɑrt/ *adj.* **1** intelligent or showing good judgment [≠ **stupid**]: *Jill's a smart kid.* | *I was smart enough to take advantage of a good opportunity.* | *I don't think that would be a very* ***smart move*** (=sensible thing to do).

THESAURUS

intelligent, **bright**, **brilliant**, **wise**, **clever**
➔ see Thesaurus box at INTELLIGENT

2 smart machines, weapons, etc. use computers or advanced technology to work: *smart bombs* **3** saying funny things in a way that is not respectful: *Don't* ***get smart with*** *me, young lady!* **4** *old-fashioned* neat and fashionable: *a smart suit* —**smartly** *adv.*: *smartly dressed men*

smart[2] *v.* [I] **1** to be upset because someone has offended you: *He's still* ***smarting from*** *the insult.* **2** if a part of your body smarts, it hurts with a stinging pain

smart al·eck /ˈsmɑrt̬ ˌælɪk/ *n.* [C] *informal* someone who says funny or intelligent things in a rude or annoying way

ˈsmart card *n.* [C] a small plastic card with an electronic part that records and remembers information

smarts /smɑrts/ *n.* [U] *spoken informal* intelligence: *Julie impressed her boss with her smarts and hard work.*

smarty pants /ˈsmɑrt̬i ˌpænts/ *n.* [C] *humorous* a SMART ALECK

smash[1] /smæʃ/ *v.* **1** [I,T] to break into many small pieces in a forceful way, or to make something do this by dropping, throwing, or hitting it: *The plates smashed on the floor.* | *Rioters smashed store windows and set fire to cars.*

THESAURUS

break, **shatter**, **crack**, **tear**, **snap**, **burst**, **pop**
→ see Thesaurus box at BREAK[1]

2 [I,T] to hit an object or surface in a forceful way, or to make something do this: *Murray **smashed** his fist **against** the wall.* | *Thompson died when his motorcycle **smashed into** a parked car.* **3** [T] to destroy something such as a political system or criminal organization: *Police have smashed a drug smuggling ring.*

smash sth ⇔ **in** *phr. v.* to hit something with so much force that you damage it: *The door had been smashed in.*

smash sth ⇔ **up** *phr. v.* to damage or destroy something: *She smashed up the truck in an accident.*

smash[2] **also smash hit** *n.* [C] a very successful new play, movie, song, etc.: *the latest Broadway smash*

smashed /smæʃt/ *adj. informal* drunk

smat·ter·ing /ˈsmæṭərɪŋ/ *n.* **a smattering of sth** a small number or amount of something: *a smattering of applause* | *He **has a smattering of** French* (=he knows a little French).

smear[1] /smɪr/ *v.* **1** [I,T] to spread a liquid or soft substance on a surface, or to become spread on a surface: *Jill **smeared** lotion **on** Rick's back.* | *The note was damp and the ink had smeared.* **2** [T] to spread an untrue story about someone important in order to harm him/her: *an attempt to smear the party leadership*

smear[2] *n.* [C] **1** a mark that is left when a substance is spread on a surface: *a blood smear*

THESAURUS

mark, **stain**, **spot**, **smudge**
→ see Thesaurus box at MARK[2]

2 an untrue story about someone important that is meant to harm him/her

smell[1] /smɛl/ *v.* **1** [I] to have a particular smell: *The room **smelled of** fresh bread.* | *This wine **smells like** berries.* **2** [I] to have an unpleasant smell [= **stink**]: *Something in the refrigerator smells.* **3** [I,T] to notice or recognize a particular smell, or to be able to do this: *I could smell alcohol on his breath.* **4** [T] to put your nose near something in order to discover what type of smell it has: *Come and smell these roses.*

smell[2] *n.* **1** [C] the quality that you recognize by using your nose: *the **smell of** flowers* | *the **strong smell** of gasoline* | *the fresh smell of the ocean*

THESAURUS

aroma – a strong pleasant smell, used especially about food: *the aroma of fresh coffee*
scent/fragrance/perfume – a pleasant smell: *the sweet fragrance of roses*

2 [C] a bad smell: *What's that smell in the basement?*

THESAURUS

stink: *the stink of rotting fish*
stench: *the stench of burning rubber*
odor: *the odor of alcohol on his breath*

3 [U] the ability to notice or recognize smells: *an excellent **sense of smell***

smell·y /ˈsmɛli/ *adj.* having a strong bad smell: *smelly socks*

smelt /smɛlt/ *v.* [T] to melt a rock that contains metal in order to remove the metal

smidg·en /ˈsmɪdʒən/ **also smidge** /smɪdʒ/ *n.* [singular] *informal* a small amount of something: *Add just **a smidgen of** salt.*

smile /smaɪl/ *v.* **1** [I] to have a happy expression on your face in which your mouth curves up: *Keith **smiled at** me.* | *a smiling baby*

THESAURUS

grin – to smile continuously with a very big smile: *He walked out of the bathroom grinning from ear to ear.*
beam – to smile because you are very pleased about something: *Jenny ran across the room, beaming with pleasure.*
smirk – to smile in an unpleasant way, for example because you are pleased about someone else's bad luck: *Some of the snowboarders were smirking at my efforts.*

2 [T] to say or express something with a smile: *"You're welcome," she smiled.* —**smile** *n.* [C] *a big smile*

smirk /smɚk/ *v.* [I] to smile in a way that is not nice, and that shows that you are pleased by someone else's bad luck: *Both officers smirked and laughed at him.* → see Thesaurus box at SMILE —**smirk** *n.* [C]

smith /smɪθ/ *n.* [C] **1 goldsmith/silversmith etc.** someone who makes things from gold, silver, etc. **2** a BLACKSMITH

smith·er·eens /ˌsmɪðəˈrinz/ *n.* **blow/smash etc. sth to smithereens** *informal* to destroy something completely by breaking it violently into very small pieces

smit·ten /ˈsmɪt˺n/ *adj.* **be smitten** to suddenly feel that you love someone very much: *He's absolutely **smitten with** that new girl.*

smock /smɑk/ *n.* [C] a loose piece of clothing like a long shirt, worn especially by artists to protect their clothes

smog /smɑg, smɔg/ *n.* [U] dirty air caused by smoke from cars and factories in cities —**smoggy** *adj.*

smoke[1] /smoʊk/ *n.* **1** [U] the white, gray, or black gas that is produced by something burning: *cigarette smoke* | *The fire sent up a huge **cloud of smoke**.* **2** [C] an act of smoking a cigarette, etc.: *He went outside for a smoke.* **3** [C] *informal* a cigarette: *Do you have a smoke?* **4 go up in**

S

smoke *informal* if your plans go up in smoke, you cannot do what you intended to do

smoke² *v.* **1** [I,T] to suck or breathe in smoke from your cigarette, PIPE, etc., or to do this regularly as a habit: *Do you mind if I smoke?* | *We sat on the porch smoking cigarettes.* | *I only smoke when I'm drinking.* **2** [I] to produce or send out smoke: *a smoking chimney* **3** [T] to give fish or meat a special taste by hanging it in smoke: *smoked salmon* —**smoking** *n.* [U]

smok·er /ˈsmoʊkɚ/ *n.* [C] someone who smokes [≠ **nonsmoker**]: *She used to be a* ***heavy smoker*** (=someone who smokes a lot).

ˈsmoke screen *n.* [C] something that you say or do to hide your real plans or actions

smoke·stack /ˈsmoʊkstæk/ *n.* [C] a tall CHIMNEY at a factory or on a ship

ˌsmoking ˈgun *n.* [C usually singular] *informal* definite proof of who is responsible for something bad or how something really happened

smok·y /ˈsmoʊki/ *adj.* **1** filled with smoke: *a smoky room* **2** producing a lot of smoke: *a smoky fire* **3** having the taste, smell, or appearance of smoke: *smoky cheese*

smol·der /ˈsmoʊldɚ/ *v.* [I] **1** to burn slowly without a flame: *The factory is still smoldering after last night's blaze.* **2** to have strong feelings that are not expressed: *Nick left Judy* ***smoldering with*** *anger.*

S

smooch /smutʃ/ *v.* [I] *informal* if two people smooch, they kiss each other in a romantic way —**smooch** *n.* [C]

smooth¹ /smuð/ *adj.* **1** having an even surface, without any BUMPS or holes [≠ **rough**]: *a smooth road* | *smooth skin* ➔ see picture at BUMPY

THESAURUS

flat, level, even, horizontal
➔ see Thesaurus box at FLAT¹

2 a liquid mixture that is smooth is thick but has no big pieces in it: *smooth peanut butter* **3** with no sudden movements or changes of direction, especially in a way that is graceful or comfortable: *Swing the tennis racket in one smooth motion.* | *a smooth flight* **4** operating or happening without problems: *a* ***smooth transition*** *from dictatorship to democracy* **5** *disapproving* polite and confident in a way that people do not trust: *a* ***smooth talker*** —**smoothly** *adv.*: *My talk went smoothly.* —**smoothness** *n.* [U]

smooth² *v.* [T] **1 also smooth out/down** to make something flat by moving your hands across it: *Tanya sat down, smoothing her skirt.* **2** to make a rough surface flat and even: *Make sure you* ***smooth down*** *all the surfaces before you start painting.*

smooth sth ⇔ **over** *phr. v.* to make problems or difficulties seem less important: *He depended on Nancy to smooth over any troubles.*

smooth·ie /ˈsmuði/ *n.* [C] a thick drink made of fruit and fruit juices that have been mixed together until they are smooth

smor·gas·bord /ˈsmɔrgəsˌbɔrd/ *n.* [C,U] a meal in which people serve themselves from a large number of different foods

smoth·er /ˈsmʌðɚ/ *v.* [T] **1** to kill someone by putting something over his/her face so that s/he cannot breathe **2** to cover the whole surface of something with something else: *a cake* ***smothered with/in*** *chocolate* **3** to give someone so much love and attention that s/he feels like s/he is not free and becomes unhappy **4** to make a fire stop burning by preventing air from reaching it: *We used a wet towel to smother the fire.*

smudge¹ /smʌdʒ/ *n.* [C] a dirty mark: *There was a* ***smudge of*** *lipstick on the cup.*

THESAURUS

mark, stain, spot, smear
➔ see Thesaurus box at MARK²

—**smudgy** *adj.*

smudge² *v.* [I,T] if a substance such as ink or paint smudges or is smudged, it becomes messy or unclear because someone has touched or rubbed it: *Now look, you've smudged my drawing!* | *Your lipstick is smudged.*

smug /smʌg/ *adj. disapproving* showing that you are very satisfied with how smart, lucky, or good you are: *a smug smile* —**smugly** *adv.*

smug·gle /ˈsmʌgəl/ *v.* [T] to take someone or something illegally from one place to another: *cocaine* ***smuggled from*** *South America* ***into*** *the United States* —**smuggler** *n.* [C] *drug smugglers* —**smuggling** *n.* [U]

smut /smʌt/ *n.* [U] *disapproving* books, stories, pictures, etc. that offend some people because they are about sex —**smutty** *adj.*: *a smutty T.V. show*

snack¹ /snæk/ *n.* [C] a small amount of food that you eat between meals or instead of a meal: *I only had time to grab a quick snack.* | *a* ***bedtime*** *snack* ➔ see picture at DINE

snack² *v.* [I] to eat a small amount of food between main meals or instead of a meal

ˈsnack bar *n.* [C] a place where you can buy snacks

sna·fu /ˈsnæfu, snæˈfu/ *n.* [C] *informal* a situation in which something does not happen the way it should

snag¹ /snæg/ *n.* [C] **1** *informal* a disadvantage or problem, especially one that is not very serious: *The project* ***hit a snag*** *when costs got out of hand.*

THESAURUS

problem, setback, hitch, trouble
➔ see Thesaurus box at PROBLEM

2 a thread that has been accidentally pulled out of a piece of cloth because it has gotten stuck on something sharp or pointed

snag² *v.* past tense and past participle **snagged,**

present participle **snagging** **1** [I,T] to damage something by getting it stuck on something, or to become damaged in this way: *Marty's fishing line snagged on a tree branch.* **2** [T] *informal* to get someone to notice you, or to succeed in getting something that is difficult to get: *Can you snag that waiter for me?* | *I snagged two tickets for tonight's show.*

snail /sneɪl/ *n.* [C] **1** a small soft creature that moves very slowly and has a hard shell on its back **2 at a snail's pace** extremely slowly

'snail mail *n.* [U] the system of sending letters through the mail, rather than by email

snake

snake[1] /sneɪk/ *n.* [C] an animal with a long thin body and no legs: *Paul was bitten by a* ***poisonous snake****.*

snake[2] *v.* [I] *literary* to move in long twisting curves: *The train* ***snaked its way through*** *the hills.*

snap[1] /snæp/ *v.* past tense and past participle **snapped**, present participle **snapping** **1** [I,T] if something snaps, or if you snap it, it breaks with a short loud noise: *Dry branches snapped under their feet.* | *I* ***snapped*** *the ends* ***off*** *the beans and dropped them into a bowl.* | *He* ***snapped*** *the chalk* ***in two/half*** (=into two pieces).

THESAURUS

break, smash, shatter, crack, tear, burst, pop
➔ see Thesaurus box at BREAK[1]

2 [I,T] to move into a particular position with a short loud noise, or to make something do this: *The pieces just* ***snap together*** *like this.* | *She* ***snapped*** *her briefcase* ***open/shut****.* **3** [I,T] to speak quickly in an angry way: *I'm sorry I* ***snapped at*** *you.* | *"Don't be ridiculous," she snapped.* **4** [I] if a dog snaps at you, it tries to bite you **5 snap your fingers** to make a short loud noise by moving a finger quickly across the thumb on the same hand **6** [I] to suddenly become unable to control a strong feeling such as anger or worry: *I don't know what happened – I guess I just snapped.* **7** [T] *journalism* to stop a series of events: *Tampa snapped an eight-game losing streak on Saturday.* **8** [T] *informal* to take a photograph: *We asked a policeman to snap our picture.*

snap out of sth *phr. v. informal* to suddenly stop being sad, tired, upset, etc.: *Come on, Gary,* ***snap out of it****.*

snap up *phr. v.* **1 snap** sth ⇔ **up** to buy something immediately, especially because it is very cheap: *People initially snapped up shares in dot-com companies.* **2 snap** sb ⇔ **up** to eagerly take an opportunity to have someone as part of your company, team, etc.: *It would shock the hockey world if the Bruins didn't snap him up.*

snap[2] *n.* **1** [singular] a sudden short loud noise, especially of something breaking or closing: *I heard a snap, and then the tree just fell over.* **2** [C] a small metal object that fastens clothes when you press its two parts together **3 be a snap** *informal* to be very easy to do: *Making pie crust is a snap.* ➔ **cold snap** at COLD[1]

snap[3] *adj.* **snap judgment/decision** a judgment or decision made quickly, without careful thought or discussion

snap·py /ˈsnæpi/ *adj.* **1** spoken or written in a short, clear, and often funny way: *Keep your answer* ***short and snappy****.* **2 make it snappy** *spoken* said in order to tell someone to hurry, in a way that is not polite: *Get me a drink, and make it snappy.* **3** *informal* snappy clothes are attractive and fashionable: *a snappy blue blazer*

snap·shot /ˈsnæpʃɑt/ *n.* [C] a photograph taken quickly and often not very skillfully

THESAURUS

picture, sketch, portrait, cartoon, caricature, illustration, poster
➔ see Thesaurus box at PICTURE[1]

snare[1] /snɛr/ *n.* [C] a trap for catching an animal

snare[2] *v.* [T] **1** to catch an animal using a snare **2** to catch someone, especially by tricking him/her: *Ships patrol the coast to snare drug smugglers.*

snarl /snɑrl/ *v.* **1** [I,T] to speak or say something in an angry way: *"Shut up!" he snarled.* **2** [I] if an animal snarls, it makes a low angry sound and shows its teeth **3 also snarl up** [I,T] if traffic snarls or is snarled, it cannot move **4** [I] if hair, thread, wires, etc. snarl, they become twisted and messy and are difficult to separate —**snarl** *n.* [C]

snatch[1] /snætʃ/ *v.* [T] **1** to take something away from someone with a quick violent movement: *I saw two kids snatch her purse.* **2** to take someone or something away from a place by force: *Vargas was snatched from his home by two armed men.* **3** to quickly take the opportunity to do something: *I managed to* ***snatch*** *an hour's* ***sleep*** *on the bus.*

snatch[2] *n.* **a snatch of conversation/song etc.** a short and incomplete part of something that you hear

snaz·zy /ˈsnæzi/ *adj. informal* very bright, attractive, and fashionable: *a snazzy new car*

sneak[1] /snik/ *v.* past tense and past participle **sneaked** or **snuck** /snʌk/ **1** [I] to go somewhere quietly and secretly: *She* ***snuck out*** *of the house once her parents were asleep.* ➔ see Thesaurus

S

box at WALK[1] **2** [T] to take something somewhere secretly: *He had tried to **sneak** drugs **across** the border.* **3 sneak a look/glance at sth** to look at something quickly and secretly: *I sneaked a look at her diary.*

sneak up *phr. v.* to come near someone very quietly, so s/he does not see or hear you: *Don't **sneak up on** me like that!*

sneak² *n.* [C] *informal* someone who does things secretly and cannot be trusted

sneak·er /ˈsnikɚ/ *n.* [C] TENNIS SHOE

sneak·ing /ˈsnikɪŋ/ *adj.* **have a sneaking suspicion/feeling (that)** to think you know something without being sure: *I had a sneaking suspicion that he was lying.*

sneak·y /ˈsniki/ *adj.* doing things in a secret and often dishonest way

sneer /snɪr/ *v.* [I] to smile or speak in a way that is not nice and shows you have no respect for someone or something: *He **sneered at** her taste in music.* —**sneer** *n.* [C]

sneeze /sniz/ *v.* [I] **1** when you sneeze, air suddenly comes out of your nose and mouth in an uncontrolled way, for example when you are sick: *The dust is **making** me **sneeze**.* | *I've been coughing and sneezing all day.* **2 sth is nothing to sneeze at** *informal* used in order to say that something is impressive enough to be considered important: *With 35 nations involved, the competition is nothing to be sneezed at.* —**sneeze** *n.* [C]

snick·er /ˈsnɪkɚ/ *v.* [I] to laugh quietly in a way that is not nice at something that is not supposed to be funny —**snicker** *n.* [C]

> **THESAURUS**
> **laugh, giggle, chuckle, cackle, guffaw, (be) in stitches**
> ➔ see Thesaurus box at LAUGH[1]

snide /snaɪd/ *adj.* funny but unkind: *She started making **snide remarks/comments** about him.*

sniff /snɪf/ *v.* **1** [I,T] to breathe in through your nose in order to smell something: *cats **sniffing at** their food* **2** [I] to breathe air into your nose with a loud sound, especially in short breaths: *She sniffed a few times and then stopped crying.* —**sniff** *n.* [C]

sniff at sth *phr. v.* to refuse something in a proud way: *A job with them is **nothing to sniff at*** (=something you should not refuse).

sniff sth ⇔ **out** *phr. v.* to discover or find something by its smell: *dogs that sniff out drugs*

snif·fle /ˈsnɪfəl/ *v.* [I] to sniff continuously in order to stop liquid from running out of your nose, especially when you are crying or when you are sick

snif·fles /ˈsnɪfəlz/ *n.* **the sniffles** a slight cold: *Max has **had the sniffles** all week.*

snip /snɪp/ *v.* past tense and past participle **snipped**, present participle **snipping** [I,T] to cut something with scissors, making quick small cuts —**snip** *n.* [C]

> **THESAURUS**
> **cut, saw, chop down, mow, trim**
> ➔ see Thesaurus box at CUT[1]

snipe /snaɪp/ *v.* [I] **1** to shoot at people from a hidden position **2** to criticize someone in an unkind way

snip·er /ˈsnaɪpɚ/ *n.* [C] someone who shoots at people from a hidden position

snip·pet /ˈsnɪpɪt/ *n.* [C] a small piece of information, music, etc.: *a few **snippets of** conversation*

snit /snɪt/ *n.* **be in a snit** *informal* to be annoyed about something in a way that seems unreasonable

snitch¹ /snɪtʃ/ *v. informal* **1** [I] *disapproving* to tell someone in authority that someone else has done something wrong because you want him/her to be punished **2** [T] to steal something, especially something that is small and not valuable

snitch² *n.* [C] someone who is not liked because s/he tells people in authority when other people do things that are wrong or against the rules

snivel /ˈsnɪvəl/ *v.* [I] to behave or speak in a weak complaining way, especially while crying

snob /snɑb/ *n.* [C] **1** someone who thinks s/he is better than other people: *Ellen is such a snob.* **2 music/wine etc. snob** someone who knows a lot about music, etc. and thinks his/her opinions are better than other people's

snob·ber·y /ˈsnɑbəri/ *n.* [U] the attitudes and behavior of snobs

snob·bish /ˈsnɑbɪʃ/ **also snob·by** /ˈsnɑbi/ *adj.* having attitudes and behavior that are typical of a snob

snoop /snup/ *v.* [I] to try to find out about someone's life or activities by secretly looking at his/her things: *I caught her **snooping in/around** my office.* —**snoop** *n.* [C]

snoot·y /ˈsnut̬i/ *adj.* rude and unfriendly because you think you are better than other people

snooze /snuz/ *v.* [I] *informal* to sleep for a short time —**snooze** *n.* [C]

snore /snɔr/ *v.* [I] to make a loud noise each time you breathe while you are asleep —**snore** *n.* [C]

snor·kel¹ /ˈsnɔrkəl/ *n.* [C] a tube that allows a swimmer to breathe air when his/her face is under water

snorkel² *v.* [I] to swim using a snorkel —**snorkeling** *n.* [U]

snort /snɔrt/ *v.* [I,T] to make a noise by forcing air out through your nose, especially in order to express anger or when laughing: *Olsen **snorted at** the suggestion.* —**snort** *n.* [C]

snot /snɑt/ *n. informal* **1** [U] an impolite word for the thick MUCUS (=liquid) produced in your nose **2** [C] someone who is snotty

'snot-nosed *adj.* **snot-nosed kid/brat/etc.** *informal* an annoying child

snot·ty /'snɑṭi/ *adj. informal* **1** showing that you think you are better than other people [= **snobbish**] **2** wet and dirty with MUCUS from your nose: *a snotty handkerchief*

snout /snaʊt/ *n.* [C] the long nose of some kinds of animals, such as pigs

snow¹ /snoʊ/ *n.* **1** [U] water frozen into soft white pieces that fall like rain in cold weather: ***Snow** was **falling** on the quiet street.* | *We are expecting six **inches of snow**.* | *The **snow** is already **melting**.* | *High winds and **heavy snow*** (=a lot of snow that is falling) *caused chaos on the roads.* | *The rain was turning to **light snow**.*

THESAURUS

snowflakes – pieces of falling snow
sleet – a mixture of snow and rain
slush – snow on the road that has partly melted and is very wet
blizzard – a storm with a lot of snow and a strong wind
frost – white powder that covers the ground when it is cold
hail – drops of **rain** that fall as ice, which are called **hailstones**
➔ RAIN, WEATHER, WIND

2 [C] a period of time during which snow falls: *the first snow of the winter*

snow² *v.* **1 it snows** if it snows, snow falls from the sky: *Look, it's snowing!* | *We got back home before it started snowing.* **2 be snowed in** to be unable to leave a place because so much snow has fallen: *We were snowed in for a week.* **3 be snowed under (with sth)** *informal* to have more work than you can deal with: *I'd love to go, but I'm totally snowed under right now.* **4** [T] *informal* to make someone believe or support something that is not true: *Even the banks were snowed by this charming conman.*

snow·ball¹ /'snoʊbɔl/ *n.* [C] a ball made out of snow that someone has pressed together: *The kids were **having** a **snowball fight** outside.*

snowball² *v.* [I] if a problem or situation snowballs, it quickly gets bigger or harder to control

snow·board /'snoʊbɔrd/ *n.* [C] a long wide board made of plastic, which people stand on to go down snow-covered hills as a sport

snow·board·ing /'snoʊˌbɔrdɪŋ/ *n.* [U] the sport of going down snow-covered hills on a snowboard —**snowboarder** *n.* [C]

snow·bound /'snoʊbaʊnd/ *adj.* unable to leave a place because there is too much snow

snow·drift /'snoʊˌdrɪft/ *n.* [C] a large amount of snow piled up by the wind

snow·fall /'snoʊfɔl/ *n.* [C,U] an occasion when snow falls from the sky, or the amount that falls in a particular period of time: *a **light/heavy snowfall***

snow·flake /'snoʊfleɪk/ *n.* [C] a small soft white piece of frozen water that falls as snow

'snow job *n.* [C] *informal* an act of making someone believe something that is not true

snow·man /'snoʊmæn/ *n.* plural **snowmen** /-mɛn/ [C] a figure of a person made out of snow

snow·plow /'snoʊplaʊ/ *n.* [C] a vehicle or piece of equipment attached to the front of a vehicle, used for pushing snow off roads

snow·shoe /'snoʊʃu/ *n.* [C] one of a pair of wide flat frames used for walking on snow without sinking

snow·storm /'snoʊstɔrm/ *n.* [C] a storm with strong winds and a lot of snow

snow·y /'snoʊi/ *adj.* if it is snowy, the ground is covered with snow or snow is falling: *a snowy January day*

snub /snʌb/ *v.* past tense and past participle **snubbed**, present participle **snubbing** [T] to be rude to someone, especially by ignoring him/her when you meet —**snub** *n.* [C]

snuck /snʌk/ *v.* a past tense and past participle of SNEAK

snuff¹ /snʌf/ *v.*
snuff sth ⇔ **out** *phr. v.* **1** to put out a CANDLE by covering it or pressing the flame with your fingers **2** *informal* to end something in a sudden way: *laws intended to snuff out smoking in public places*

snuff² *n.* [U] **1** tobacco made into a powder, which some people breathe in through their noses **2 not be up to snuff** *informal* to not be good enough: *Her performance just wasn't up to snuff.*

snug /snʌg/ *adj.* **1** warm and comfortable: *The children were safe and snug in their beds.* **2** clothes that are snug fit fairly tightly —**snugly** *adv.*

snug·gle /'snʌgəl/ **also snuggle up** *v.* [I] to get into a warm comfortable position: *couples **snuggling up** on cold winter nights*

so¹ /soʊ/ *adv.* **1** used in order to emphasize what you are saying: *He was so weak that he could hardly stand up.* | ***So many** kids come from broken homes these days.* | *I feel so embarrassed.* | *That party was so boring!* **2** used in order to refer back to something that has already been mentioned: *If you have not sent in your payment yet, please **do so** immediately.* | *"Will I need my coat?" "**I don't think so.**"* **3 so do I/so is he/so would John etc.** used in order to say that something is also true about someone else: *"I have a lot to do today." "So do I."* | *If you're going to have dessert then so will I.* **4 be so** to be true or correct: *"It belongs to my father." "**Is that so?**"* | *Please say **it isn't so!*** **5 or so** used when you cannot be exact about a number, amount, or period of time: *He left a week or so ago.* | *Dena had five drinks or so.* **6 and so on/forth** used after a list to show that there are other similar things that could also be mentioned: *a room full of old furniture, paintings, rugs, and so forth* **7 be just/exactly so** to be arranged neatly, with every-

S

thing in the right place: *Everything has to be just so at Maxine's dinner parties.* **8 so as (not) to do sth** *formal* in order to do or not do something: *Try to remain calm so as not to alarm anyone.*

SPOKEN PHRASES

9 said in order to get someone's attention, especially in order to ask him/her a question: *So, Lisa, how's the new job going?* **10** said when you are making sure that you have understood something: *So you aren't actually leaving until Friday?* **11** used with a movement of your hand when you are describing how big, tall, etc. something or someone is, or how to do something: *It was about so big.* | *Then you fold the paper* ***like so.*** **12 also so what?** used in order to say impolitely that you do not think that something is important: *"I'm going to tell Mom what you said." "So?"* | *Yes, I'm late. So what?* **13** *slang* definitely: *He is* ***so not*** *the right person for her.* **14 so long!** used in order to say goodbye **15 so be it** used in order to show that you do not like or agree with something, but you will accept it: *If this means delaying the trip, then so be it.* **16 so much for sb/sth** used in order to say that something you tried to do did not work, or something that was promised did not happen: *Well, so much for getting out of here at five o'clock.* **17 so help me also so help me God** said in order to emphasize how determined you are: *So help me God, I will not let you down.*

so² *conjunction* **1** used in order to show why something happens: *I got hungry, so I made a sandwich.* ► Don't say "Since I got hungry, so I made a sandwich." ◄ **2 so (that)** in order to make something happen, or make something possible: *I put your keys in the drawer so they wouldn't get lost.*

soak /soʊk/ *v.* [I,T] **1** if you soak something, or if you let it soak, you cover it with liquid for a period of time: *Just put that dish in the sink to soak.* | *Soak the beans overnight.* **2** to make something completely wet, or to become completely wet: *If you don't take your umbrella, you're going to* ***get soaked.*** | *The blood had* ***soaked through*** *the bandage.*

soak sth ⇔ **up** *phr. v.* **1** if something soaks up a liquid, it takes the liquid into itself [**= absorb**]: *The bread will soak up the milk.* **2** to enjoy everything about an experience: *I just wanted to* ***soak up*** *the* ***sun.***

soak·ing /ˈsoʊkɪŋ/ **also** **ˌsoaking ˈwet** *adj.* completely wet

ˈso-and-so *n.* [U] *spoken* used in order to talk about someone, without saying his/her name: *All they care about is whether so-and-so is going to be at the party.*

soap¹ /soʊp/ *n.* **1** [U] the substance that you use with water to wash things, especially your body: *a* ***bar of soap*** | *Wash your hands with* ***soap and water.*** **2** [C] *informal* a SOAP OPERA

soap² *v.* [T] to rub soap on someone or something

soap·box /ˈsoʊpbɑks/ *n.* **be/get on your soapbox** *informal disapproving* to tell people your opinions about something in a loud and forceful way

ˈsoap ˌopera *n.* [C] a television or radio story about the daily lives of the same group of people, which is broadcast regularly

THESAURUS

movie, film, sitcom, game show, talk show, cartoon, drama series, documentary, the news
→ see Thesaurus box at TELEVISION

soap·y /ˈsoʊpi/ *adj.* containing soap: *soapy water*

soar /sɔr/ *v.* [I] **1** to increase quickly to a high level: *The temperature soared to 97°.* **2** to fly, especially very fast or very high up in the air: *birds soaring overhead* **3** buildings, mountains, or cliffs, etc. that soar look very tall and impressive: *The cliffs soar 500 feet above the sea.* —**soaring** *adj.*

sob /sɑb/ *v.* past tense and past participle **sobbed**, present participle **sobbing** [I] to cry while breathing in short sudden bursts: *He began* ***sobbing uncontrollably.*** —**sob** *n.* [C]

so·ber¹ /ˈsoʊbɚ/ *adj.* **1** not drunk **2** extremely serious: *Much sober thought is required to make the right choice.* —**soberly** *adv.* —**sobriety** /soʊˈbraɪət̬i, sə-/ *n.* [U]

sober² *v.*

sober sb ⇔ **up** *phr. v.* to gradually become less drunk, or to make someone do this: *Some black coffee might sober you up.*

so·ber·ing /ˈsoʊbərɪŋ/ *adj.* making you feel very serious: *a* ***sobering thought***

ˈsob ˌstory *n.* [C] *informal disapproving* a story that someone tells you in order to make you feel sorry for him/her

ˈso-called *adj.* [only before noun] **1** used in order to show that you think the name that someone or something is called is wrong: *these so-called freedom fighters* **2** used in order to show that something or someone is usually called a particular name: *Only so-called "safe and sane" fireworks are allowed.*

soc·cer /ˈsɑkɚ/ *n.* [U] a sport played by two teams of 11 players who try to kick a ball into their opponents' GOAL

so·cia·ble /ˈsoʊʃəbəl/ *adj.* someone who is sociable is friendly and likes to be with other people: *I wish my son was a bit more sociable.*

THESAURUS

outgoing – liking to meet and talk to new people: *an outgoing, popular girl*
extroverted – confident, and enjoying being with other people: *an extroverted salesman*
gregarious – friendly and enjoying being and talking with other people: *a gregarious man who loves telling stories*
→ SHY

so·cial /ˈsoʊʃəl/ *adj.* **1** relating to human society and the way it is organized: ***social issues*** *such as unemployment and education* | *The students come from a variety of* ***social classes*** (=groups of people who have the same social position). **2** relating to meeting people, forming relationships with them, and spending time with them: *Ellis always had an active* ***social life****.* | *a range of* ***social events*** *for employees* | *Children need to develop their* ***social skills****.* **3** social animals live together in groups, rather than alone —**socially** *adv.*: *socially acceptable behavior*

ˌsocial ˈclimber *n.* [C] *disapproving* someone who tries very hard to move into a higher social class

so·cial·is·m /ˈsoʊʃəˌlɪzəm/ *n.* [U] an economic and political system that tries to give equal opportunities to all people, and in which most businesses belong to the government [➡ **capitalism, communism**] —**socialist** *adj., n.* [C]

so·cia·lite /ˈsoʊʃəˌlaɪt/ *n.* [C] a rich person who is well known for going to many fashionable parties

so·cial·ize /ˈsoʊʃəˌlaɪz/ *v.* [I] to spend time with other people in a friendly way: *I hate having to* ***socialize with*** *strangers.*

ˌsocial ˈscience *n.* [C,U] subjects such as history, politics, and ECONOMICS, or one of these subjects

ˌSocial Seˈcurity *n.* [U] a U.S. government program into which workers must pay money, that gives money to old people and others who cannot work

TOPIC

pension, savings
➔ see Topic box at RETIRE

ˈsocial ˌstudies *n.* [plural] SOCIAL SCIENCE

ˈsocial ˌworker *n.* [C] someone who is trained to help people with particular social problems —**social work** *n.* [U]

so·ci·e·ty /səˈsaɪəṭi/ *n.* plural **societies** **1** [C,U] all the people who live in the same country and share the same laws and CUSTOMS: *a modern industrial society* | *Children are the least powerful* ***members of society****.*

THESAURUS

people, the public, the human race, mankind, humankind, population
➔ see Thesaurus box at PEOPLE[1]

2 [C] an organization with members who share similar interests, aims, etc.: *the American Cancer Society*

THESAURUS

organization, institution, association, (political) party, club
➔ see Thesaurus box at ORGANIZATION

3 [U] the rich and fashionable people in a country: *a society wedding*

so·ci·o·ec·o·nom·ic /ˌsoʊsioʊˌɛkəˈnɑmɪk, -ˌikə-/ *adj.* relating to both social and economic conditions

so·ci·ol·o·gy /ˌsoʊsiˈɑlədʒi/ *n.* [U] the scientific study of societies and the behavior of people in groups —**sociologist** *n.* [C]

so·cio·path /ˈsoʊsiəˌpæθ, -ʃiə-/ *n.* [C] someone whose behavior toward other people is strange and possibly dangerous

sock[1] /sɑk/ *n.* [C] **1** a piece of clothing that you wear on your foot inside your shoe: *a* ***pair of socks*** ➔ see picture at CLOTHES **2 knock/blow sb's socks off** *informal* to surprise and excite someone a lot

sock[2] *v.* [T] *informal* to hit someone very hard

sock·et /ˈsɑkɪt/ *n.* [C] **1** the place in a wall where you can connect electrical equipment to the supply of electricity [= **outlet**] **2** the hollow part of something that another part fits into: *eye sockets*

sod /sɑd/ *n.* [U] a piece of dirt with grass growing on top of it

so·da /ˈsoʊdə/ *n.* [C,U] **1** a SOFT DRINK

THESAURUS

soft drink, pop, soda pop
➔ see Thesaurus box at SOFT DRINK

2 also soda water water that contains BUBBLES, often added to alcoholic drinks

sod·den /ˈsɑdn/ *adj.* very wet and heavy: *sodden clothing*

so·di·um /ˈsoʊdiəm/ *n.* [U] a silver-white metal that produces salt when mixed with CHLORINE

so·fa /ˈsoʊfə/ *n.* [C] a comfortable seat that is wide enough for two or three people to sit on [= **couch**]: *She sat down on the sofa.*

soft /sɔft/ *adj.* **1** not hard, firm, or stiff, but easy to press [≠ **hard**]: *a soft pillow* **2** smooth and pleasant to touch [≠ **rough**]: *soft skin* | *a cat with soft fur* **3** a soft sound, voice, or music is quiet and often pleasant to listen to: *There was some soft music playing in the background.* | *Her* ***voice*** *was* ***soft*** *and calming.*

THESAURUS

quiet, low, muffled, hushed, subdued
➔ see Thesaurus box at QUIET[1]

4 soft colors or lights are not too bright [≠ **harsh**]: *Soft lighting is much more romantic.* **5** soft drugs are illegal drugs and are considered to be less harmful than some other drugs **6** *informal* a soft job, life, etc. is too easy and does not involve hard work or difficulties **7** *informal* not strict enough or not treating people severely enough when they have done something wrong: *The Governor does not want to seem* ***soft on*** *crime.* | *Some of his rivals think he's* ***gone soft****.* **8 have a soft spot for sb** to like someone **9 a**

S

soft touch *informal* someone who is easy to deceive or persuade to do something such as give you money **10** soft water does not contain a lot of minerals and forms bubbles from soap easily —**softly** *adv.* —**softness** *n.* [U]

soft·ball /'sɔftbɔl/ *n.* **a)** [U] an outdoor game similar to baseball but played with a slightly larger and softer ball **b)** [C] the ball used in this game

ˌsoft-'boiled *adj.* an egg that is soft-boiled has been boiled until the white part is solid, but the yellow part is still liquid

'soft drink *n.* [C] a sweet drink that contains BUBBLES and has no alcohol in it: *cola and other soft drinks*

THESAURUS

Soft drink, **soda**, **pop**, and **soda pop** all mean the same thing. **Soft drink** is a general word that is used everywhere in the U.S. **Soda** is mainly used in the Northeast and Southwest. **Pop** is used mainly in the Midwest and West. **Soda pop** is fairly old-fashioned, but it is still used in some parts of the U.S., especially in the Midwest.

soft·en /'sɔfən/ *v.* [I,T] **1** to become softer, or to make something do this [≠ **harden**]: *a lotion that helps to soften your skin* **2** to become less severe and more gentle, or to make something do this: *His voice softened as he spoke to her.* | *Goldberg tried to **soften the blow*** (=make bad news less upsetting) *with a joke.*

soften sb ⇔ **up** *phr. v.* to be nice to someone so that s/he will do something for you

soft·en·er /'sɔfənɚ/ *n.* [C] a substance that you add to water to make clothes feel soft after washing

soft·heart·ed /ˌsɔft'hɑrt̬ɪd◂/ *adj.* kind and sympathetic

soft·ie, **softy** /'sɔfti/ *n.* [C] *informal* someone who is very kind and sympathetic, or is easily persuaded: *He's just a big softy really.*

ˌsoft-'spoken *adj.* having a quiet gentle voice

soft·ware /'sɔft-wɛr/ *n.* [U] the sets of programs that tell a computer how to do a particular job [➥ **hardware**]: *She **loaded** the new **software**.* | *a software company*

sog·gy /'sɑgi/ *adj.* very wet and soft: *The pie crust was kind of soggy.*

soil[1] /sɔɪl/ *n.* [C,U] the top layer of the earth in which plants grow: *The soil here is very poor.* | *rich, fertile soil* ➔ see picture at PLANT[1]

THESAURUS

ground, **land**, **earth**
➔ see Thesaurus box at GROUND[1]

soil[2] *v.* [T] *formal* to make something dirty —**soiled** *adj.*

so·journ /'soʊdʒɚn/ *n.* [C] *formal* a period of time that you stay in a place that is not your home —**sojourn** *v.* [I]

sol·ace /'sɑlɪs/ *n.* [U] a feeling of happiness after having been very sad or upset: *After the death of her son, Val **found solace in** the church.*

solar

so·lar /'soʊlɚ/ *adj.* relating to the sun or the sun's power [➥ **lunar**]: *a solar eclipse* | *solar energy*

'solar ˌsystem *n.* **the solar system** the earth and all the PLANETS, moons, etc. that move around the sun

sold /soʊld/ *v.* the past tense and past participle of SELL

sol·der /'sɑdɚ, 'sɔ-/ *v.* [T] to join metal surfaces together or to repair them using melted metal

sol·dier[1] /'soʊldʒɚ/ *n.* [C] a member of the army, especially someone who is not an officer ➔ see picture at ARMED FORCES

soldier[2] *v.*

soldier on *phr. v.* to continue doing something in spite of difficulties: *It won't be easy without him, but we'll have to soldier on.*

ˌsold-'out *adj.* if a concert, movie, etc. is sold-out, all the tickets for it have been sold

sole[1] /soʊl/ *adj.* [only before noun] **1** only: *He was the **sole survivor** of the crash.* | *His **sole purpose** in going there was to see Rachel.* **2** not shared with anyone else: *The women had to take **sole responsibility** for their children.*

sole[2] *n.* **1** [C] the bottom of your foot or shoe: *The **soles of** his **feet** were perfectly clean.* ➔ see picture at SHOE[1] **2** [C,U] a flat ocean fish, or the meat from this fish

sole·ly /'soʊli/ *adv.* only, or not involving anyone or anything else: *Scholarships are awarded solely on the basis of financial need.*

sol·emn /'sɑləm/ *adj.* **1** very serious: *His face grew solemn.* | *a solemn ceremony* **2** [only before noun] a solemn promise is a promise that you will definitely keep —**solemnly** *adv.* —**solemnity** /sə'lɛmnət̬i/ *n.* [U]

so·lic·it /sə'lɪsɪt/ *v.* [T] *formal* to ask someone for money, help, or information —**solicitation** /səˌlɪsə'teɪʃən/ *n.* [C,U]

so·lic·i·tor /sə'lɪsət̬ɚ/ *n.* [C] *formal* **1** someone who goes from place to place trying to sell goods **2** the main lawyer of a city, town, or government department

so·lic·it·ous /sə'lɪsəţəs/ *adj. formal* caring very much about someone's safety, health, or comfort

sol·id[1] /'sɑlɪd/ *adj.* **1** firm and usually hard, without spaces or holes: *solid rock* | *The lake in the park is* ***frozen solid***.

> **THESAURUS**
>
> **hard**, **firm**, **stiff**
> → see Thesaurus box at HARD[1]

2 strong and well made: *a good solid chair* **3** a solid achievement or solid work is of real, practical, and continuing value: *Kids need a good solid education in high school.* | *Julia has a* ***solid foundation*** *for a career in design.* **4** someone or something that is solid can be depended on or trusted: *a bank with a* ***solid reputation*** | *The prosecution has no* ***solid evidence***. **5 solid gold/silver/oak etc.** completely made of gold, etc.: *a solid gold necklace* **6** *informal* continuous, without any pauses: *She didn't talk to me for three solid weeks.* —**solidly** *adv.* —**solidity** /sə'lɪdəţi/ *n.* [U]

solid[2] *n.* [C] **1** an object or substance that has a firm shape: *Water is a liquid and wood is a solid.* **2 solids** [plural] food that is not liquid: *Is the baby eating solids yet?* **3** *technical* a shape that has length, width, and height

sol·i·dar·i·ty /ˌsɑlə'dærəţi/ *n.* [U] the loyalty and support of a group of people that share the same aim or opinions: *We are going on strike to* ***show solidarity with*** *the nurses.*

so·lid·i·fy /sə'lɪdəˌfaɪ/ *v.* past tense and past participle **solidified**, third person singular **solidifies** [I,T] to become solid, or to make a substance become solid

so·lil·o·quy /sə'lɪləkwi/ *n.* plural **soliloquies** [C] a long speech made by an actor who is alone on the stage

sol·i·taire /'sɑləˌtɛr/ *n.* **1** [U] a card game for one player **2** [C] a piece of jewelry that has only one jewel in it: *a diamond solitaire ring*

sol·i·tar·y /'sɑləˌtɛri/ *adj.* **1** [only before noun] a solitary person or thing is the only one in a place: *A solitary figure waited by the door.* **2** [only before noun] done or experienced without anyone else around: *Helena took long solitary walks to the lake.* **3** spending a lot of time alone, usually because you like being alone [≠ **sociable**]: *Hamilton was described as a solitary man.*

ˌsolitary con'finement *n.* [U] a punishment in which a prisoner is kept alone

sol·i·tude /'sɑləˌtud/ *n.* [U] the state of being alone, especially when this is what you enjoy: *She spent most of her life living* ***in solitude***.

so·lo[1] /'soʊloʊ/ *adj.* **1** performed by one musician, rather than by a group: *I don't really like his solo album.* **2** done alone, without anyone else helping you: *his first solo flight* —**solo** *adv.*

> **THESAURUS**
>
> **alone**, **on your own**, **(all) by yourself**, **single-handedly**
> → see Thesaurus box at ALONE

solo[2] *n.* plural **solos** [C] a piece of music written for one performer

so·lo·ist /'soʊloʊɪst/ *n.* [C] a musician who performs a solo

sols·tice /'sɑlstɪs, 'sɔl-/ *n.* [C] the longest or shortest day of the year: *the* ***summer/winter solstice***

sol·u·ble /'sɑlyəbəl/ *adj.* a soluble substance can be DISSOLVED in a liquid [≠ **insoluble**]

so·lu·tion /sə'luʃən/ *n.* [C] **1** a way of solving a problem or dealing with a difficult situation: *the perfect* ***solution to*** *all our problems* | *Both sides are trying to* ***find*** *a peaceful* ***solution***. | *The* ***only solution*** *was to move into a quieter apartment.* **2** the correct answer to a question or problem: *The* ***solution to*** *the puzzle is on page 14.* **3** a liquid mixed with a solid or a gas: *a weak sugar solution* | *saline solution*

> **THESAURUS**
>
> **mixture**, **combination**, **blend**, **compound**
> → see Thesaurus box at MIXTURE

solve /sɑlv/ *v.* [T] **1** to find a way of dealing with a problem or difficult situation: *Mike thinks money will* ***solve*** *all his* ***problems***. **2** to find the correct answer to a question or problem, or the explanation for something that is difficult to understand: *I couldn't solve the equation.* | *Police are still trying to* ***solve*** *the* ***crime/case/mystery***. —**solvable** *adj.*

sol·vent[1] /'sɑlvənt/ *adj.* having enough money to pay your debts —**solvency** *n.* [U]

solvent[2] *n.* [C] a chemical substance that can change a solid substance into a liquid, or that can remove a substance from a surface

som·ber /'sɑmbɚ/ *adj.* **1** sad and serious: *a somber mood* **2** dark, or not having any bright colors: *a somber room*

some[1] /səm; *strong* sʌm/ *quantifier* **1** a number of people or things, or an amount of something, when the exact number or amount is not said or shown: *Do you want some coffee?* | *Of course you'll make some new friends in college.*

> **USAGE**
>
> Use **some** in questions when you think the answer will be "yes": *Would you like some coffee?*
> Use **any** when you do not know what the answer will be: *Were there any letters for me?*

2 a number of people or things, or an amount of something, but not all: *The team has* ***some of*** *the best young players in the country.* | *Some people believe in life after death.* | *In some cases, the damage can be repaired.* **3** *formal* a fairly large

S

amount of something: *It was some time before the police finally arrived.*

some² *pron.* **1** a number of people or things, or an amount of something, but not all: *Many local businesses are having difficulties, and some have even gone bankrupt.* | *Some will live and some will not.* **2** a number of people or things, or an amount of something, when the exact number or amount is not stated: *We're out of milk. Could you buy some on your way home?* **3 and then some** *informal* and more: *He has enough money to buy the house and then some!*

some³ *determiner* **1** *informal* used when you are talking about a person or thing that you do not know, remember, or understand: *Can you give me some idea of the cost?* | ***For some reason or other** they decided to move to Detroit.* | *He's receiving **some kind/type/sort of** award.* **2 some friend/help! etc.** *spoken* said when you are annoyed because someone or something has disappointed you: *I can't believe you told Mom. Some brother you are!*

some⁴ *adv.* **1** a little more or a little less than a particular number or amount: *Some 700 homes were damaged by the storm.* **2 some more** an additional number or amount of something: *Would you like some more cake?* **3** *spoken* a little: *We could work some and then rest a while.*

S

some·bod·y /ˈsʌmˌbɑdi, -ˌbʌdi/ *pron.* SOMEONE

some·day /ˈsʌmdeɪ/ *adv.* at an unknown time in the future: *Someday I'm going to go to Spain.*

some·how /ˈsʌmhaʊ/ *adv.* **1** in some way, although you do not know how: *We'll get there somehow.* | *I knew he was connected **somehow or other** with the CIA.* **2** for some reason, but you are not sure why: *Somehow it seemed like the right thing to do.*

some·one /ˈsʌmwʌn/ *pron.* a word meaning a particular person, used when you do not know or do not say who that person is [**= somebody**]: *Be careful! Someone could get hurt.* | *"Does Mike still live here?" "No, **someone else** (=a different person) is renting it now."*

GRAMMAR

someone, anyone

In questions and negative sentences, we usually use **anyone** and not **someone**: *Have you told anyone about this?* | *I didn't see anyone there.*

some·place /ˈsʌmpleɪs/ *adv. spoken* SOMEWHERE

som·er·sault /ˈsʌmɚˌsɔlt/ *n.* [C] a movement in which you roll forward until your feet go over your head and touch the ground again —**somersault** *v.* [I]

some·thing /ˈsʌmθɪŋ/ *pron.* **1** used to mention a particular thing when you do not know its name, do not know exactly what it is, etc. [➡ **anything, everything, nothing**]: *There's something in my eye.* | *He said **something about** a party.* | *There's **something wrong** (=a problem) with the phone.* | *Can you **do something about** that noise?* | *I don't eat eggs. Could I have **something else**?*

THESAURUS

thing, object, item, article

➔ see Thesaurus box at THING

2 something to eat/drink some food or a drink: *We went out for something to eat after the movie.* **3 have/be something to do with sb/sth** to be connected with or related to a particular person or thing, but in a way that you are not sure about: *I know Steve's job has something to do with investments.* **4 make something of yourself** to become successful through your own efforts **5 something like 100/2,000 etc.** APPROXIMATELY: *There are something like 3,000 homeless people in this city.* **6 twenty-something/thirty-something** *informal* used when someone is between the ages of 20 to 29, 30 to 39, etc., when you do not know exactly

SPOKEN PHRASES

7 or something... said when you cannot remember or cannot be exact: *Maybe I cooked it too long or something.* **8 be (really) something** used when something is impressive or unusual: *It's really something to see all the hot air balloons taking off together.* **9 a little something** a small gift that is not very expensive: *Here's a little something for you.*

GRAMMAR

something, anything

In questions and negative sentences, we usually use **anything** and not **something**, but if you are offering someone some food, a drink, etc., it sounds more polite to use **something**: *Would you like something to eat?*

some·time /ˈsʌmtaɪm/ *adv.* at an unknown time in the past or future: *I'll call you sometime next week.*

some·times /ˈsʌmtaɪmz/ *adv.* on some occasions, but not always: *Sometimes I don't get home until 9:00 at night.* | *"Do you miss your old school?" "Sometimes."*

THESAURUS

occasionally – sometimes but not often: *We see each other occasionally.*

(every) once in a while/every so often – sometimes but not regularly: *It would be nice if he would call every once in a while.*

from time to time – sometimes but not often or regularly: *A situation like this arises from time to time.*

➔ OFTEN, NEVER, RARELY

some·way /ˈsʌmweɪ/ *adv. informal* SOMEHOW

some·what /ˈsʌmwʌt/ *adv.* slightly, but not very much: *I feel somewhat responsible for the accident.*

some·where /ˈsʌmwɛr/ *adv.* **1** in a place or to

a place that is not specific: *My wallet must be around here somewhere.* | *Let's find* ***somewhere to eat.*** | *I want to live* ***somewhere else*** (=somewhere different). | *They're made somewhere in Europe.* **2 somewhere around/between etc.** a little more or a little less than a particular number or amount [= **approximately**]: *A good CD player costs somewhere around $500.* **3 be getting somewhere** to be making progress: *At last we're getting somewhere!* **4 somewhere along the line/way** used in order to say that you are not sure when something happened: *Somewhere along the line I made a mistake.*

GRAMMAR

somewhere, anywhere

In questions and negative sentences, we usually use **anywhere** and not **somewhere**: *I haven't seen it anywhere.*

son /sʌn/ *n.* **1** [C] your male child: *My son is 12 years old.* | *She has two daughters and one son.* | *Bill was the* ***son of*** *German immigrants.* **2** [singular] used by an older person as a friendly way to talk to a boy or young man: *What's your name, son?*

so·na·ta /sə'nɑṭə/ *n.* [C] a piece of CLASSICAL MUSIC usually for two instruments, one of which is a piano

song /sɔŋ/ *n.* **1** [C] a short piece of music with words: *She* ***sang a song.*** | *a* ***pop/folk/love song*** | *He suddenly* ***burst/broke into song*** (=started singing).

THESAURUS

music, **tune**, **melody**, **arrangement**, **composition**, **number**
➔ see Thesaurus box at MUSIC

2 [U] songs in general: *a celebration of music, song and dance* **3** [C,U] the musical sounds made by birds

son·ic /'sɑnɪk/ *adj. technical* relating to sound

'son-in-,law *n.* [C] the husband of your daughter

son·net /'sɑnɪt/ *n.* [C] a poem that has 14 lines that RHYME with each other in a particular pattern

so·no·rous /'sɑnərəs/ *adj.* having a deep pleasantly loud sound: *a sonorous voice*

soon /sun/ *adv.* **1** in a short time from now, or a short time after something has happened: *It will be dark soon.* | *Paula became pregnant* ***soon after*** *they were married.*

THESAURUS

in a minute spoken – used when talking about something that will happen within a few minutes: *I'll be ready in a minute.*
any minute now spoken – used when something will happen in a very short time from now, but you do not know exactly when: *The train should be here any minute now.*
before long – soon or in a short time: *Those two will be getting married before long.*
shortly formal: *Davis made a confession shortly after his arrest.*
in the near future – in the next few weeks or months: *They promised to contact us again in the near future.*

2 quickly: *I'll get it fixed* ***as soon as possible.*** | ***How soon*** *can you get here?* **3 as soon as** immediately after something has happened: *I tried to call you as soon as I heard the news.* **4 sooner or later** used to say that something will definitely happen, but you are not sure when: *She's bound to find out sooner or later.* **5 the sooner...the better** used to say that something should happen as quickly as possible: *The sooner you finish this report, the better.* **6 no sooner had ... than** used when something has happened almost immediately after something else: *No sooner had I stepped in the shower than the phone rang.* **7 I would sooner/I would just as soon** used when you are saying what you would prefer to happen: *I would just as soon stay in and watch TV.* ➔ **would (just) as soon** at WOULD

soot /sʊt/ *n.* [U] black powder that is produced when something burns

soothe /suð/ *v.* [T] **1** to make someone feel calmer and less worried, angry, or upset: *Lucy soothed the baby by rocking him in her arms.* **2** to make a pain stop hurting as much: *A massage would soothe your aching muscles.* —**soothing** *adj.*: *gentle, soothing music*

sop /sɑp/ *v.* past tense and past participle **sopped**, present participle **sopping**

sop sth ⇔ **up** *phr. v.* to remove a liquid from a surface using something that will ABSORB the liquid: *Jesse sopped up the spilled drink with a towel.*

so·phis·ti·cat·ed /sə'fɪstə,keɪṭɪd/ *adj.* **1** confident and having a lot of experience of life and good judgment about socially important things such as art, fashion, etc.: *She's beautiful, sophisticated, and wealthy.* **2** having a lot of knowledge and experience of difficult or complicated subjects and therefore able to understand them well: *today's more sophisticated investors* **3** made or designed well, and often complicated: *a* ***highly sophisticated*** *alarm system*

THESAURUS

advanced, **high-tech**, **state-of-the-art**, **cutting-edge**
➔ see Thesaurus box at ADVANCED

—**sophistication** /sə,fɪstə'keɪʃən/ *n.* [U]

soph·o·more /'sɑfmɔr/ *n.* [C] a student in the second year of HIGH SCHOOL or college

soph·o·mor·ic /sɑf'mɔrɪk/ *adj.* very silly and unreasonable: *sophomoric humor*

sop·o·rif·ic /,sɑpə'rɪfɪk/ *adj. formal* making you feel ready to sleep

sop·ping /ˈsɑpɪŋ/ **also** **ˌsopping ˈwet** *adj.* very wet

so·pra·no /səˈprænoʊ/ *n.* plural **sopranos** [C,U] a woman, girl, or young boy singer with a very high voice

sor·bet /sɔrˈbeɪ, ˈsɔrbət/ *n.* [C,U] a sweet frozen food made from fruit juice, sugar, and water

sor·cer·er /ˈsɔrsərə-/ *n.* [C] a man in stories who uses magic [= **wizard**]

sor·cer·ess /ˈsɔrsərɪs/ *n.* [C] a woman in stories who uses magic [= **witch**]

sor·cer·y /ˈsɔrsəri/ *n.* [U] magic, especially evil magic

sor·did /ˈsɔrdɪd/ *adj.* involving immoral or dishonest behavior: *all the **sordid details** of the scandal*

sore¹ /sɔr/ *adj.* **1** painful as a result of a wound, infection, or too much exercise: *My knee's a little sore from running yesterday.* | *a **sore throat***

THESAURUS

painful, **tender**, **stiff**
→ see Thesaurus box at PAINFUL

2 sore point/spot (with sb) something that is likely to make someone upset or angry if you talk about it: *Don't mention marriage – it's a sore point with him.* **3** *old-fashioned* upset, angry, or annoyed —**soreness** *n.* [U]

sore² *n.* [C] a painful place on your body where your skin is cut or infected: *They were starving and covered with sores.*

sore·ly /ˈsɔrli/ *adv.* very much: *He will be **sorely missed** by everyone.*

so·ror·i·ty /səˈrɔrəṯi, -ˈrɑr-/ *n.* plural **sororities** [C] a club for women at a college or university [➡ **fraternity**]

sor·row /ˈsɑroʊ, ˈsɔ-/ *n.* [C,U] a feeling of great sadness, or an event that makes you feel great sadness: *a time of **great/deep sorrow*** | *Our prayers are with you in your time of sorrow.* —**sorrowful** *adj.*

sor·ry /ˈsɑri, ˈsɔri/ *adj.* **1 sorry/I'm sorry** *spoken* **a)** used to tell someone that you feel bad about doing something that has upset or annoyed him/her: *I'm really sorry. I didn't mean to hurt your feelings.* | *"Kevin! Don't do that!" "Sorry."* | ***Sorry about** the mess.* | *I'm **sorry (that)** I was late.* **b)** used when politely saying something that disappoints or disagrees with someone: *I'm sorry – we're not going to be able to come.* | *I'm **sorry to** call you so late, but this is important.* **2** [not before noun] feeling bad about a situation and wishing it were different: *Casey was **sorry (that)** he had gotten so angry.* | *I was **sorry to** hear of your father's death.* **3 be/feel sorry for sb** to feel pity or sympathy for someone because s/he is in a bad situation: *He was lonely and I felt sorry for him.* | *Stop **feeling sorry for yourself** and do something!* **4 sorry?** *spoken* used to ask someone to repeat something that you have not heard correctly [= **pardon**] **5** [only before noun] *informal* very bad: *That's the sorriest excuse I've ever heard.*

sort¹ /sɔrt/ *n.* **1** [C] a type or kind of something: *What **sort of** work does he do?* | *They had **all sorts of** (=many different kinds of) seafood on the menu.*

THESAURUS

type, **kind**, **category**, **make**, **model**, **brand**, **genre**
→ see Thesaurus box at TYPE¹

2 sort of *spoken* used when what you are saying or describing is not very definite or exact: *I still feel sort of tired.* | *"Do you like him then?" "Sort of."* **3** [singular] if a computer does a sort, it arranges a list of things in order

sort² *v.* [T] to put things in a particular order, or to arrange them in groups according to size, type, etc.: *Eggs are **sorted according to** size.* | *Applications will be **sorted into** three piles.*

sort sth ⇔ **out** *phr. v.* **1** to organize something that is messy, complicated, or in the wrong order: *I need to sort out all the paperwork.* **2** to deal with a problem: *Mike's still trying to sort out his personal life.*

sort through sth *phr. v.* to look at a lot of things in order to find something or arrange things in order: *We sorted through all his papers after he died.*

sort·a /ˈsɔrṯə/ a short form of "sort of", used in writing to show how people sound when they speak: *He's sorta cute.*

SOS *n.* [singular] a signal or message that a ship or airplane is in danger and needs help

ˈso-so *adj., adv. spoken* neither very good nor very bad: *"How was the movie?" "So-so."*

souf·flé /suˈfleɪ/ *n.* [C,U] a baked food that is light and made from eggs, flour, milk, and sometimes cheese

sought /sɔt/ *v.* the past tense and past participle of SEEK

ˈsought-ˌafter *adj.* wanted by a lot of people, but difficult to get: *a sought-after chef*

soul /soʊl/ *n.* **1** [C] the part of a person that is not physical and contains his/her thoughts, feelings, character, etc. Many people believe the soul continues to exist after death: *the immortality of the **human soul*** | *He knew **in his soul** that Linda was never going to change.* **2** [C] a person: *There wasn't a soul in sight.* **3** [U] a type of popular modern music that often expresses deep emotions, usually performed by black singers and musicians **4** [U] a special quality that gives something its true character: *the soul of the Old Town area* **5** [U] a special quality that makes you feel strong emotions: *His poetry lacks soul.*

soul·ful /ˈsoʊlfəl/ *adj.* expressing deep, usually sad, emotions: *a soulful performance*

soul·less /ˈsoʊl-lɪs/ *adj.* lacking the qualities that

make people feel interest, emotions, or excitement: *a soulless suburb*

ˈsoul-ˌsearching *n.* [U] the act of carefully examining your thoughts and feelings in order to make a decision: *soul-searching questions*

sound[1] /saʊnd/ *n.* **1** [C,U] something that you hear, or something that can be heard: *the **sound of** breaking glass* | ***Turn the sound down/up*** (=make it quieter or louder) *on the TV, will you?*

THESAURUS

A **sound** is anything that you can hear: *the sound of voices*
A **noise** is usually a loud, unpleasant, or unexpected sound: *the deafening noise of overhead planes*

2 like the sound of sth to be interested in a plan, idea, what someone says, etc.: *"Things will be changing." "I **don't like the sound of** that."* **3 from the sound of it/things** *spoken* according to what you have heard or read about something: *From the sound of it, they're having marriage problems.* **4** [C] a long wide area of water that connects two larger areas of water

sound[2] *v.* **1** [linking verb] if someone or something sounds good, strange, etc., he, she, or it seems that way when you hear or read about him, her, or it: *Mike **sounds like** a nice guy.* | ***It sounded** wonderful – a dream trip.* **2** [linking verb] to seem to show a particular quality or emotion with your voice: *You sound upset.* | *He **sounded as though/if** he were having second thoughts.* | *You **sound like** you have a cold.*

THESAURUS

seem, **appear**, **look**, **come across as**
→ see Thesaurus box at SEEM

3 [linking verb] if a noise sounds like a particular thing, that is how it seems to you when you hear it: *That **sounded like** thunder.* **4 sound a warning/the alarm** to give a public warning or tell people to be careful **5 sounds good** *spoken* said in order to accept something that someone has suggested: *"Do you want Thai food?" "Sounds good."* **6** [I,T] to produce a noise, or to make something do this: *The church bells sounded.*

sound sb/sth ⇔ **out** *phr. v.* **1** to talk to someone in order to find out what s/he thinks about a plan or idea: *He used polls to sound out public opinion.* **2** to make the sounds of the letters as you try to read a word: *The children were **sounding out** words in class.*

sound[3] *adj.* **1** practical, based on good judgment, and likely to produce good results: *His advice was sound.* | *a sound investment* **2** in good condition and not damaged in any way **3 of sound mind** *law* not mentally ill

sound[4] *adv.* **sound asleep** completely asleep

ˈsound ˌbarrier *n.* **the sound barrier** the point when an aircraft reaches the speed of sound

ˈsound bite *n.* [C] a short phrase from a speech or statement that presents an important idea and that is meant to be used on a radio or television news program

ˈsound card *n.* [C] a CIRCUIT BOARD in a computer that makes the computer able to produce sounds

ˈsound efˌfects *n.* [plural] special sounds used in order to make a movie, television show, etc. seem more real

ˈsounding board *n.* [C] someone you discuss your ideas with before using them

sound·ly /ˈsaʊndli/ *adv.* **1 sleep soundly** to sleep well and peacefully **2** completely or severely: *Washington was soundly defeated.* **3** in a way that is strong and unlikely to break: *The building is soundly designed.*

sound·proof /ˈsaʊndpruf/ *adj.* a soundproof wall, room, etc. is one that sound cannot pass through, into, or out of —**soundproof** *v.* [T]

sound·track /ˈsaʊndtræk/ *n.* [C] the recorded music from a movie: *the **soundtrack to** "The Mission"*

soup /sup/ *n.* [C,U] a hot liquid food that often has pieces of meat or vegetables in it: *chicken noodle soup* | *a **bowl of soup*** → see picture on page A5

ˈsoup ˌkitchen *n.* [C] a place where free food is given to people who have no home

S

sour[1] /saʊɚ/ *adj.* **1** having an acid taste, like the taste of a LEMON: *sour apples*

THESAURUS

sweet, salty, hot, spicy, bland
→ see Thesaurus box at TASTE[1]

2 milk or other food that is sour is not fresh and has a bad taste and smell: *The milk had **gone sour**.* **3** unfriendly or unhappy: *a sour expression* **4 turn/go sour** *informal* to stop being enjoyable or satisfactory: *Their marriage had turned sour.*

sour[2] *v.* **1** [I] to stop being enjoyable, friendly, or satisfactory: *Relations between the two countries had soured.* **2** [I,T] to become sour, or to make a food do this

source /sɔrs/ *n.* [C] **1** the thing, place, person, etc. that you get something from: *gasoline and other **sources of** energy* | *Tourism is the city's **main/major/primary source** of income.* **2** the cause of a problem, or the place where it starts: *Technicians located the **source of** the problem.* **3** a person, book, or document that you get information from: ***Reliable sources** say the company is going bankrupt.* **4** the place where a stream or river starts

ˌsour ˈcream *n.* [U] a thick white cream with a sour taste, used in cooking

sour·dough /ˈsaʊɚdoʊ/ **also ˌsourdough ˈbread** *n.* [U] a type of bread with a slightly sour taste

south[1], **South** /saʊθ/ *n.* [singular, U] **1** the direction that is at the bottom of a map of the world, or to the right of someone facing the rising sun: *Which way is south?* ➔ see picture at NORTH[1] **2 the south** the southern part of a country, state, etc.: *Rain will spread* ***to the south*** *later today.* | *the* ***south of*** *France* **3 the South** the southeastern states of the U.S. **4 down South** in or to the south of an area, especially the southeastern part of the U.S.: *We moved down South in 1996.*

USAGE

Use **north/south/east/west etc. of sth** in order to describe where a place is in relation to another place: *Memphis is south of St. Louis.*
Use **in the north/south/east/west etc. of sth** in order to say which part of a place you are talking about: *The mountains are in the west of the province.*
Use **northern/southern/eastern/western etc.** with the name of a place: *They have a cabin in northern Ontario.* Don't say "in the north of Ontario."

south[2] *adj.* **1** in, to, or facing south: *The hotel's about two miles* ***south of*** *Monterey.* | *the south wall* **2 south wind** a wind coming from the south

S

south[3] *adv.* toward the south: *Go south on I-35.* | *The window faces south.*

South A·mer·i·ca /ˌsaʊθ əˈmɛrəkə/ *n.* one of the seven CONTINENTS, that includes land south of the Caribbean Sea and north of Antarctica —**South American** *adj.*

south·bound /ˈsaʊθbaʊnd/ *adj.* traveling or leading toward the south: *the southbound lanes of the freeway*

south·east[1] /ˌsaʊθˈist◂/ *n.* [U] **1** the direction that is exactly between south and east ➔ see picture at NORTH[1] **2 the Southeast** the southeast part of a country, state, etc. —**southeastern** *adj.*

southeast[2] *adj., adv.* in, from, or toward the southeast: *We drove southeast.* | *a southeast wind*

south·er·ly /ˈsʌðəli/ *adj.* **1** in or toward the south: *a southerly direction* **2** a southerly wind comes from the south

south·ern /ˈsʌðən/ *adj.* in or from the south part of an area, state, country, etc.: *southern New Mexico* ➔ see Usage box at SOUTH

south·ern·er /ˈsʌðənə/ *n.* [C] someone who comes from the southern part of a country or the southern HEMISPHERE

south·ern·most /ˈsʌðənˌmoʊst/ *adj.* farthest south

South Pa·cif·ic /ˌsaʊθ pəˈsɪfɪk/ *n.* **the South Pacific** the southern part of the Pacific Ocean where there are groups of islands, such as New Zealand and Polynesia

ˌSouth ˈPole *n.* **the South Pole** the most southern point on the surface of the earth, or the area around it ➔ see picture at GLOBE

south·ward /ˈsaʊθwəd/ *adj., adv.* toward the south

south·west[1] /ˌsaʊθˈwɛst◂/ *n.* [U] **1** the direction that is exactly between south and west ➔ see picture at NORTH[1] **2 the Southwest** the southwest part of a country, state, etc. —**southwestern** *adj.*

southwest[2] *adj., adv.* in, from, or toward the southwest: *We drove southwest.* | *a southwest wind*

sou·ve·nir /ˌsuvəˈnɪr, ˈsuvəˌnɪr/ *n.* [C] an object that you keep to remind yourself of a special occasion or a place that you have visited: *I bought a model of the Eiffel Tower* ***as a souvenir of*** *Paris.* | *a* ***souvenir shop***

sov·er·eign[1] /ˈsɑvərɪn/ *adj.* **1** having the highest power or authority in a country **2** a sovereign country is independent and governs itself —**sovereignty** *n.* [U]

sovereign[2] *n.* [C] *formal* a king or queen

THESAURUS

king, queen, monarch, ruler, emperor
➔ see Thesaurus box at KING

So·vi·et /ˈsoʊviɪt, -viˌɛt/ *adj.* relating to or coming from the former Soviet Union

sow[1] /soʊ/ *v.* past tense **sowed**, past participle **sown** /soʊn/ or **sowed** [I,T] to plant or scatter seeds on a piece of ground: *Sow herbs indoors in February.*

sow[2] /saʊ/ *n.* [C] a female pig

soy·bean /ˈsɔɪbin/ *n.* [C] a bean from which oil and food containing a lot of PROTEIN is produced

spa /spɑ/ *n.* [C] **1 also health spa** a place that people go to in order to improve their health, especially a place where the water has special minerals in it **2** a special bathtub that sends currents of hot water around you

space[1] /speɪs/ *n.* **1** [U] the amount of an area, room, container, etc. that is empty or available to be used: *The class has* ***space for*** *five more students.* | *There's not enough space in the computer's memory.* **2** [C,U] an empty area that is used for a particular purpose: *parking spaces* | *storage space* **3** [U] the area beyond the Earth where the stars and PLANETS are: *the first man* ***in space*** | *space exploration* | *an alien from* ***outer space*** (=far away in space)

TOPIC

Things in space
meteor, asteroid, comet, moon, planet, star, sun, constellation, galaxy, black hole
Vehicles used in space
spacecraft, spaceship, rocket, (space) shuttle, satellite, probe
Someone who travels in space
astronaut

4 [C] the empty area between two things: *the* ***spaces between*** *the words* | *an* ***empty space*** *at the* *back of the stage* **5 in the space of sth** within a particular period of time: *They went from first place to last in the space of a season.* **6** [C,U] empty land that does not have anything built on it: *a fight to save the city's* ***open spaces*** **7** [U] freedom to do what you want or to be alone: *I want to* ***give*** *my students* ***space*** *to think for themselves.*

space² *v.* **1** [T] to arrange objects, events, etc. so that they have an equal amount of space or time between them: ***Space*** *the plants four inches* ***apart.*** **2** [I] **also space out** *slang* to stop paying attention and begin to look in front of you without thinking —**spacing** *n.* [U]

'space-age *adj. informal* very modern: *space-age design*

'space ca,det also 'space case *n.* [C] *slang* someone who is SPACEY

space·craft /'speɪs-kræft/ *n.* [C] a vehicle that can travel in space ➔ see Topic box at SPACE¹

spaced /speɪst/ **also ,spaced 'out** *adj. slang* SPACEY

space·ship /'speɪs,ʃɪp/ *n.* [C] a spacecraft – used especially in stories ➔ see Topic box at SPACE¹

'space ,shuttle *n.* [C] a spacecraft for carrying people into space, that can be used more than once

space·y /'speɪsi/ *adj. spoken* someone who is spacey does not pay attention, forgets things, and often behaves slightly strangely

spa·cious /'speɪʃəs/ *adj.* having a lot of space in which you can move around: *a spacious house*

spade /speɪd/ *n.* [C] **1** a SHOVEL **2** a playing card with one or more black shapes like pointed leaves on it ➔ see picture at PLAYING CARD

spa·ghet·ti /spə'geṭi/ *n.* [U] long thin pieces of PASTA that look like strings ➔ see picture on page A5

spam¹ /spæm/ *n.* [U] email messages that a computer user has not asked for and does not want to read, for example from someone who is advertising something ➔ see Thesaurus box at ADVERTISEMENT

spam² *v.* [I,T] *disapproving* to send spam to many different people —**spamming** *n.* [U]

span¹ /spæn/ *n.* [C] **1** the amount of time during which something continues to exist or happen: *Most children have a short* ***attention span.*** | *The mayfly has a two-day* ***life span.*** **2** a period of time between two dates or events: ***Over a span of*** *five years, they planted 10,000 new trees.* | *a short* ***time span*** **3** the distance from one side of something to the other: *the bird's* ***wing span***

span² *v.* past tense and past participle **spanned**, present participle **spanning** [T] **1** to include all of a period of time: *a career spanning four decades* **2** to include all of a particular area: *The Internet spans the globe.* **3** to go from one side of something to the other: *a bridge spanning the river*

span·iel /'spænyəl/ *n.* [C] a dog with long hair and long ears

Span·ish¹ /'spænɪʃ/ *adj.* **1** relating to or coming from Spain **2** relating to the Spanish language

Spanish² *n.* **1** [U] the language used in places such as Mexico, Spain, and South America **2 the Spanish** [plural] the people of Spain, considered as a single group

spank /spæŋk/ *v.* [T] to hit a child on the BUTTOCKS with your open hand —**spanking** *n.* [C,U]

spar /spɑr/ *v.* past tense and past participle **sparred**, present participle **sparring** [I] **1** to practice BOXING with someone **2** to argue with someone: *The parties have been* ***sparring over*** *the health bill.*

spare¹ /spɛr/ *adj.* **1 spare key/battery etc.** a key, etc. that you have in addition to the one you usually use, so that it is available if it is needed **2** not being used by anyone and therefore available for use: *a spare bedroom* **3 spare time** time when you are not working: *I play tennis in my spare time.* **4 spare change** coins that you can afford to give to someone

spare² *v.* [T] **1** to prevent someone from having to do something difficult or unpleasant: *I wanted to spare the kids the pain of our divorce.* **2 money/time etc. to spare** money or time that is left in addition to what you have used or need: *We made it to the airport with 10 minutes to spare.* **3** to make something such as time, money, or workers available for someone, especially when this is difficult: *I guess I* ***can spare*** *a few dollars.* | ***Could*** *you* ***spare*** *me twenty minutes?* **4 spare no expense/effort etc.** to use as much money, effort, etc. as necessary to do something **5** to not damage or harm someone or something, when other people or things are being killed or damaged: *If they surrendered, their lives would be spared.*

spare³ *n.* [C] an additional key, BATTERY, etc. that you keep so that it is available if it is needed: *There's a spare* (=additional tire) *in the trunk.*

spar·ing·ly /'spɛrɪŋli/ *adv.* using or giving only a little of something: ***Use*** *water* ***sparingly*** *this summer.* —**sparing** *adj.*

spark¹ /spɑrk/ *n.* [C] **1** a very small piece of fire coming from a larger fire or from hitting two hard objects together: *sparks from the fire* **2** a flash of light caused by electricity passing across a small space **3 spark of interest/intelligence etc.** a small amount of a feeling or quality: *As she spoke, she saw a spark of hope in Tony's eyes.*

spark² *v.* **1** [T] to make something start happening: *The verdict* ***sparked off*** *riots.* **2** [I] to produce sparks

spar·kle /'spɑrkəl/ *v.* [I] **1** to shine in small bright flashes: *diamonds sparkling in the light*

THESAURUS

shine, flash, flicker, twinkle, glow, shimmer
➔ see Thesaurus box at SHINE¹

2 if someone's eyes sparkle, they shine because s/he is happy or excited —**sparkle** *n.* [C,U]

S

spark·ler /ˈspɑrklɚ/ *n.* [C] a type of FIREWORK that you can hold in your hand, consisting of a thin stick that burns with colored SPARKS

spark·ling /ˈspɑrklɪŋ/ *adj.* **1** shining brightly with points of flashing light: *a sparkling brook* **2** very clean: *the sparkling kitchen*

ˈspark plug *n.* [C] a part in a car engine that produces the SPARK to make the gas burn

spar·row /ˈspæroʊ/ *n.* [C] a common small brown or gray bird

sparse /spɑrs/ *adj.* small in number or amount, and usually scattered over a large area: *sparse vegetation* —**sparsely** *adv.*: *sparsely populated*

spar·tan /ˈspɑrt̚n/ *adj.* very simple and without comfort: *a spartan room*

spasm /ˈspæzəm/ *n.* [C] **1** an occasion when your muscles suddenly become tight, causing you pain: *back spasms* **2** a short period during which you have a sudden strong feeling or reaction to something: *spasms of laughter*

spas·mod·ic /spæzˈmɑdɪk/ *adj.* **1** happening for short periods of time but not regularly or continuously: *my spasmodic efforts to stop smoking* **2** relating to a muscle SPASM —**spasmodically** *adv.*

spas·tic /ˈspæstɪk/ *adj. old-fashioned* having uncontrolled SPASMS as a result of a disease

S

spat¹ /spæt/ *n.* [C] *informal* an argument or disagreement that is not important [**= quarrel**]

spat² *v.* a past tense and the past participle of SPIT

spate /speɪt/ *n.* **a spate of sth** a large number of similar events that happen in a short period of time: *a spate of burglaries*

spa·tial /ˈspeɪʃəl/ *adj. technical* relating to the position, size, or shape of things

spat·ter /ˈspæt̬ɚ/ *v.* [I,T] if a liquid spatters, or if you spatter it, drops of it fall onto a surface: *a t-shirt **spattered with** paint*

spat·u·la /ˈspætʃələ/ *n.* [C] a kitchen tool with a wide flat part, used for lifting or spreading food

spawn¹ /spɔn/ *v.* **1** [T] to make something happen or start to exist: *The book "Dracula" has spawned a number of movies.* **2** [I,T] if a fish or FROG spawns, it lays a lot of eggs

spawn² *n.* [U] the eggs of a fish or FROG laid together in a soft group

spay /speɪ/ *v.* [T] to remove part of a female animal's sex organs so that she cannot produce babies [**= neuter**]

speak /spik/ *v.* past tense **spoke** /spoʊk/ past participle **spoken** /ˈspoʊkən/

1 TALK TO SB [I] to talk to someone about something or have a conversation: *Hello, can I **speak to** Mr. Sherwood, please?* | *Solomon **spoke with** a reporter.* | *He **spoke of/about** his love of the theater.*

2 SAY WORDS [I] to use your voice to say words: *He spoke very softly.*

3 LANGUAGE [T] to be able to talk in a particular language: *My brother speaks French.* ► Don't say "My brother speaks in French." ◄ ***Can** you **speak** English?*

4 OPINIONS [I] to say something that expresses your ideas or opinions: ***Generally speaking**, money issues matter most to voters.* | *He **spoke highly/well of** (=said good things about) her.*

5 so to speak *spoken* used in order to say that the words you have used do not have their usual meaning: *He found the problem in his own back yard, so to speak* (=affecting him or his family, or the area he lives in).

6 speaking of sb/sth *spoken* used when you want to say more about someone or something that has just been mentioned: *Speaking of Jody, how is she?*

7 speak your mind to say exactly what you think

8 no sth to speak of also without any sth to speak of nothing large or important enough to mention: *There is no industry in the town to speak of.*

9 GIVE A SPEECH [I] to make a formal speech: *Burnett **spoke at** the graduation ceremony.*

speak for sb/sth *phr. v.* **1 also speak on behalf of sb** to express the feelings, thoughts, etc. of another person or group of people: *Mr. Miles spoke for all the parents at the school.* **2 sth speaks for itself** to show something so clearly that no explanation is necessary: *Our profits speak for themselves* (=our profits show how good or bad our business is). **3 be spoken for** to be promised to someone else: *This puppy is already spoken for.*

speak out *phr. v.* to say publicly what you think about something, especially as a protest: *people **speaking out against** human rights abuses*

speak up *phr. v.* **1** *spoken* used in order to ask someone to speak more loudly: *Could you speak up please, I can't hear you.* **2** to say publicly what you think about something: *If you don't like what's happening, speak up!*

speak·er /ˈspikɚ/ *n.* [C] **1** someone who makes a speech: *the guest speaker for the evening* **2** the part of a radio, CD PLAYER, etc. where the sound comes out **3 English/French etc. speaker** someone who speaks English, French, etc. **4 also Speaker of the House** the politician who controls discussions in the U.S. House of Representatives

spear¹ /spɪr/ *n.* [C] a pole with a sharp pointed blade at one end, used as a weapon

spear² *v.* [T] to push a pointed object such as a fork into something

spear·head /ˈspɪrhɛd/ *v.* [T] to lead an attack or an organized action: *the troops who spearheaded the rescue mission*

spe·cial¹ /ˈspɛʃəl/ *adj.* **1** different in some way from what is ordinary or usual, and often better or more important: *a special place in the classroom for reading* | *Give her **something special** this Christmas.* | *a dish served on **special occasions***
2 particularly important to someone and deserv-

ing love, attention, etc.: *He made me **feel special.*** | *her special friends* **3 special care/attention etc.** more care, attention, etc. than is usual: *We try to **give special care** to the youngest patients.*

special² *n.* [C] **1** something that is not ordinary or usual, but is made or done for a particular purpose: *a TV special on the election* **2** a lower price than usual for a particular product for a short period of time: *today's lunch special* | *Chickens are **on special**.*

ˌspecial eduˈcation *n.* [U] education for children who have physical or mental problems

ˌspecial efˈfects *n.* [plural] images or sounds that have been produced artificially to be used in a movie or television program

spe·cial·ist /ˈspɛʃəlɪst/ *n.* [C] someone who knows a lot about a particular subject or has a lot of skill in it: *a heart specialist*

THESAURUS

expert, **authority**, **connoisseur**
→ see Thesaurus box at EXPERT, DOCTOR[1]

spe·cial·ize /ˈspɛʃəˌlaɪz/ *v.* [I] to limit most of your study, business, etc. to a particular subject or activity: *a lawyer who **specializes in** divorce cases* —**specialization** /ˌspɛʃələˈzeɪʃən/ *n.* [C,U]

spe·cial·ized /ˈspɛʃəˌlaɪzd/ *adj.* developed for a particular purpose: *soldiers going through specialized training*

spe·cial·ly /ˈspɛʃəli/ *adv.* **1** for one particular purpose: *specially trained dogs used by blind people* **2** *spoken* especially: *I had it made specially for you.*

spe·cial·ty /ˈspɛʃəlti/ *n.* plural **specialties** [C] **1** a subject that you know a lot about, or a skill that you have: *his academic specialty* **2** a food or product that is very good, produced in a particular restaurant, area, etc.: *The **house specialty** is chicken enchiladas.* **3** a particular product or business that has one purpose or sells one type of thing: *specialty magazines*

spe·cies /ˈspiʃiz, -siz/ *n.* plural **species** [C] a group of animals or plants of the same kind that can breed with each other: *Three different **species of** deer live in the forest.* → ENDANGERED SPECIES

spe·cif·ic /spɪˈsɪfɪk/ *adj.* **1** detailed and exact: *specific questions* | *Can you **be more specific**?* **2** used when talking about a particular thing, person, time, etc.: *Set a specific time aside to do homework.*

spe·cif·i·cally /spɪˈsɪfɪkli/ *adv.* **1** for a particular type of person or thing: *a book written specifically for teenagers* **2** in a detailed or exact way: *You were specifically requested to leave by 4 p.m.*

spec·i·fi·ca·tion /ˌspɛsəfəˈkeɪʃən/ *n.* [C usually plural] a detailed instruction about how something should be done, made, etc.: *The airport tower was built **to** FAA **specifications**.*

spe·cif·ics /spɪˈsɪfɪks/ *n.* [plural] particular and exact details: ***the specifics of** the deal*

spe·ci·fy /ˈspɛsəˌfaɪ/ *v.* past tense and past participle **specified**, third person singular **specifies** [T] to state something in an exact and detailed way: *The governor did not **specify what** changes would be made.*

spec·i·men /ˈspɛsəmən/ *n.* [C] **1** a small amount or piece of something that is taken so that it can be tested or examined: *a blood specimen* **2** a single example of something, from a group of similar things: *a specimen of tropical fish*

spe·cious /ˈspiʃəs/ *adj. formal* seeming to be true or correct, but really false: *a specious argument*

speck /spɛk/ *n.* [C] a very small mark, spot, or piece of something: *a **speck of** dust*

speck·led /ˈspɛkəld/ *adj.* covered with a lot of small spots or marks: *speckled eggs*

spec·ta·cle /ˈspɛktəkəl/ *n.* [C] **1** *disapproving* an unusual or strange thing or situation that you see: *He got drunk and **made a spectacle of** himself.* **2** a public scene or show that is very impressive: *the spectacle of the Thanksgiving parade* **3 spectacles** [plural] *old-fashioned* GLASSES

spec·tac·u·lar¹ /spɛkˈtækyələ˞/ *adj.* very impressive or exciting: *a spectacular view of the Grand Canyon* —**spectacularly** *adv.*

spectacular² *n.* [C] an event or performance that is very big and impressive

spec·ta·tor /ˈspɛkˌteɪt̬ə˞/ *n.* [C] someone who watches an event, game, etc.

spec·ter /ˈspɛktə˞/ *n.* **1 the specter of sth** something that frightens you because it may affect you badly: *The failure of the talks **raised the specter of** war.* **2** [C] *literary* a GHOST

THESAURUS

ghost, **spirit**, **phantom**, **apparition**
→ see Thesaurus box at GHOST

spec·trum /ˈspɛktrəm/ *n.* plural **spectra** /-trə/ **1** [singular] a complete or very wide range of opinions, ideas, people, etc.: *The policy appeals to a **wide/broad spectrum** of voters.* | *women from **across the** social **spectrum*** **2** [C] the set of different colors that is produced when light passes through a PRISM

spec·u·late /ˈspɛkyəˌleɪt/ *v.* **1** [I,T] to guess why something happened or what will happen next, without knowing all the facts: *Officials would not **speculate on/about** the cause of the crash.* **2** [I] to buy goods, property, etc., hoping to make a large profit when you sell them —**speculator** *n.* [C] —**speculation** /ˌspɛkyəˈleɪʃən/ *n.* [C,U] ***speculation that** he will resign*

spec·u·la·tive /ˈspɛkyələt̬ɪv, -ˌleɪt̬ɪv/ *adj.* **1** based on guessing, not facts: *a speculative article* **2** bought or done in order to make a profit later: *a speculative investment*

S

sped /spɛd/ *v.* the past tense and past participle of SPEED

speech /spitʃ/ *n.* **1** [C] a talk, especially a formal one about a particular subject, given to a group of people: *a campaign speech* | *Walters **gave/made a speech** at graduation.* | *a **speech on/about** immigration* **2** [U] the ability to speak, or the way someone speaks: *Her speech was slow.* **3** [U] spoken language rather than written language: *In speech we use a smaller vocabulary than in writing.*

speech·less /ˈspitʃlɪs/ *adj.* unable to speak because you are angry, shocked, upset, etc.: *Boyd's answer **left** her **speechless**.*

speed¹ /spid/ *n.* **1** [C,U] how fast something moves or travels: *a car traveling **at high/low speed*** ▶ Don't say "in high speed." ◀ *an air **speed of** 400 miles an hour*

COLLOCATIONS

at high/low speed
at great speed
at top/full speed
at lightning speed – extremely fast
at breakneck speed – dangerously fast
at the speed of light

2 [U] the rate at which something happens or is done: *a high-speed computer* | *the **speed of** change* **3** [U] the quality of being fast: *a player with speed and power* **4 five-speed/ten-speed etc.** having a particular number of GEARS **5** [U] *slang* an illegal drug that makes you very active

speed² *v.* past tense and past participle **sped** /spɛd/ or **speeded** **1** [I] to move or happen quickly: *The train **sped along/by/past**.*

THESAURUS

rush, race, dash, charge
→ see Thesaurus box at RUSH¹

2 be speeding to be driving faster than the legal limit

speed up *phr. v.* to move or happen faster, or to make something do this: *an attempt to speed up production* | *We sped up to pass the car in front of us.*

speed·boat /ˈspidboʊt/ *n.* [C] a small boat with a powerful engine that can go very fast

speed·ing /ˈspidɪŋ/ *n.* [U] the action of traveling too fast in a vehicle: *Police stopped him **for speeding**.*

ˈspeed ˌlimit *n.* [C] the fastest speed that you are allowed to drive on a particular road: *a 40 mph speed limit*

speed·om·e·ter /spɪˈdɑmət̬ɚ/ *n.* [C] an instrument in a vehicle that shows how fast it is going → see picture on page A12

ˈspeed trap *n.* [C] a place on a road where police wait to catch drivers who are going too fast

speed·y /ˈspidi/ *adj.* comparative **speedier**, superlative **speediest** happening or done quickly, or working quickly: *a speedy recovery* —**speedily** *adv.*

spell¹ /spɛl/ *v.* **1** [I,T] to form a word by writing or saying the letters in the correct order: *My last name is Haines, spelled H-A-I-N-E-S.* | *a list of words that are often **spelled wrong*** **2 spell trouble/defeat/danger etc.** if a situation spells trouble, etc., it makes you expect trouble: *Too many tourists could spell danger for the wilderness.* **3** [T] if letters spell a word, they form it

spell sth ⇔ **out** *phr. v.* to explain something clearly and in detail: *an advert spelling out the dangers of smoking*

spell² *n.* [C] **1** a piece of magic that someone does, or the special words or ceremonies used in making it happen: *The witches **cast a spell on/over** the young prince.*

THESAURUS

magic, witchcraft, curse, the occult
→ see Thesaurus box at MAGIC¹

2 a period of a particular type of weather, activity, etc.: *a dizzy spell* | *We've had **a cold/warm/wet/dry spell** for most of January.*

spell·bound /ˈspɛlbaʊnd/ *adj.* extremely interested in something you are listening to: *His stories **kept/held** us **spellbound**.*

ˈspell-ˌchecker *n.* [C] a computer program that tells you when you have not spelled a word correctly —**spell-check** *v.* [I,T]

spell·ing /ˈspɛlɪŋ/ *n.* **1** [U] the ability to spell words in the correct way: *His spelling has improved.* **2** [C] the way that a word is spelled: *the correct spelling*

ˈspelling bee *n.* [C] a spelling competition done by students

spend /spɛnd/ *v.* past tense and past participle **spent** /spɛnt/ **1** [I,T] to use your money to buy or pay for something: *We **spend** $150 a week **on** groceries.* | ***Spending** their own **money** teaches kids about budgets.* **2** [T] to use time doing a particular activity: *I want to **spend** more **time with** my family.* | *We **spent the day/morning etc.** by the pool.*

spend·ing /ˈspɛndɪŋ/ *n.* [U] the amount of money spent on something, especially by the government: *a cut in **defense/public spending***

spend·thrift /ˈspɛndˌθrɪft/ *n.* [C] someone who spends a lot of money in a careless way

spent¹ /spɛnt/ *v.* the past tense and past participle of SPEND

spent² *adj.* **1** already used and now empty or useless: *spent cartridges* **2** *literary* extremely tired

sperm /spɚm/ *n.* plural **sperm** **1** [C] a cell produced by the male sex organ that joins with an egg to produce new life **2** [U] SEMEN

spew /spyu/ **also spew out** *v.* [I,T] to flow out of something in large quantities, or to make something do this: *factories **spewing out** pollution*

S

sphere /sfɪr/ *n.* [C] **1** the shape of a ball: *The earth is a sphere.* **2** a particular area of work, interest, knowledge, etc.: *women's **sphere of** activity* **3 sphere of influence** an area of the world or a situation in which a particular country, group, or person can influence what happens

spher·i·cal /ˈsfɪrɪkəl, ˈsfɛr-/ *adj.* having a round shape like a ball

sphinx /sfɪŋks/ *n.* [C] an ancient Egyptian image of a lion with a human head

spice[1] /spaɪs/ *n.* **1** [C,U] a powder or seed taken from plants that is put into food to give it a special taste: *herbs and spices* **2** [singular, U] interest or excitement that is added to something: *Travel **adds spice** to your life.* —**spiced** *adj.*

spice[2] **also spice up** *v.* [T] **1** to add interest or excitement to something: *Graphics **spice up** your marketing materials.* **2** to add SPICE to food

spick-and-span /ˌspɪk ən ˈspæn/ *adj.* very clean and neat

spic·y /ˈspaɪsi/ *adj.* food that is spicy contains a lot of spices: *a **hot and spicy** chili*

> **THESAURUS**
> **sweet, tasty, sour, salty, hot, bland**
> ➔ see Thesaurus box at TASTE[1]

spi·der /ˈspaɪdɚ/ *n.* [C] a small creature with eight legs that makes WEBS (=sticky nets) to catch insects

spi·der·web /ˈspaɪdɚˌwɛb/ *n.* [C] a WEB [➡ **cobweb**]

spi·der·y /ˈspaɪdəri/ *adj.* covered with or made of lots of long thin uneven lines: *spidery handwriting*

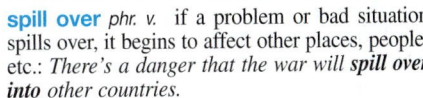

spiel /ʃpil, spil/ *n.* [C,U] *informal* a speech that the speaker has used many times before, usually intended to persuade someone to buy something

spike[1] /spaɪk/ *n.* [C] **1** something that is long and thin with a sharp point, especially a piece of metal **2** a sudden large increase in the number, price, rate, etc. of something: *a spike in share prices* —**spiky** *adj.*

spike[2] *v.* **1** [T] to add something, especially alcohol or a drug, to a drink: *The orange juice had been **spiked with** gin.* **2** [I] if a number, price, rate, etc. spikes, it increases quickly: *His temperature had spiked.*

spill[1] /spɪl/ *v.* **1** [I,T] if a liquid spills or you spill it, it flows over the edge of a container by accident: *I **spilled** coffee **on** my shirt.* **2** [I] if people spill out of a place, they move out in large groups **3 spill your guts** *informal* to tell someone a lot of personal things, especially because you are upset

spill over *phr. v.* if a problem or bad situation spills over, it begins to affect other places, people, etc.: *There's a danger that the war will **spill over into** other countries.*

spill[2] *n.* [C,U] an act of spilling something, or the amount that is spilled: *an oil spill*

spin[1] /spɪn/ *v.* past tense and past participle **spun** /spʌn/ present participle **spinning** **1** [I,T] to turn around and around very quickly, or to make something do this: *The ceiling fans were spinning.* | *He grabbed Lisa by the arm and **spun** her **around*** (=turned her around).

> **THESAURUS**
> **turn, twist, go around, revolve, rotate**
> ➔ see Thesaurus box at TURN[1]

2 [T] to describe a situation or information in a way that is intended to influence the way people think about it – used especially about what politicians do: *In the book, he admits his affair but spins it as best he can.* **3** [I,T] to make cotton, wool, etc. into thread by twisting it together **4 sb's head is spinning** if your head is spinning, you feel confused or as though you might FAINT (=become unconscious) **5 be spinning your wheels** *informal* to continue trying to do something without having any success **6** [T] if an insect spins a WEB or a COCOON, it produces thread and makes it **7 spin a tale/yarn/story** to tell a story that you have invented

spin (sth ⇔) **off** *phr. v.* to make part of a company into a separate company, or to become a separate company: *The company may spin off its engineering division.*

spin[2] *n.* **1** [C,U] an act of turning around quickly: *the spin of the wheel* **2** [singular, U] the way someone, especially a politician, talks about information or a situation, in order to influence the way people think about it [➡ **spin doctor**]: *A spokesman tried to **put** a positive **spin** on the report.* | *political **spin control*** (=the attempt to control the way people think about an event) **3** [singular] *informal* a short trip in a car for pleasure

spin·ach /ˈspɪnɪtʃ/ *n.* [U] a vegetable with large dark green leaves

spi·nal /ˈspaɪnl/ *adj.* relating to or affecting the SPINE: *a spinal injury*

ˈspinal cord *n.* [C] the long string of nerves that go from your brain down your back, through your SPINE

spin·dly /ˈspɪndli/ *adj.* long and thin and not strong: *spindly legs*

ˈspin ˌdoctor *n.* *informal* [C] someone who describes a situation in a way that is intended to influence people's opinions of it: *a White House spin doctor*

spine /spaɪn/ *n.* [C] **1 also ˈspinal ˌcolumn** the long row of bones down the center of your back ➔ see picture on page A3 **2** a stiff sharp point on

S

an animal or plant: *cactus spines* **3** the part of a book that the pages are attached to

spine·less /ˈspaɪnlɪs/ *adj.* lacking courage and determination

ˈspinning wheel *n.* a simple machine used in past times to make thread

ˈspin-off *n.* [C] a television program using characters that were originally on a different program

spin·ster /ˈspɪnstɚ/ *n. old-fashioned* [C] a woman who is not married, especially one who is no longer young and seems unlikely to marry

spi·ral¹ /ˈspaɪrəl/ *n.* [C] **1** a curve in the form of a continuous line that winds around a central point **2** a process in which something gradually but continuously gets worse or better: *the peso's* ***downward spiral*** (=in which it continues to lose value) —**spiral** *adj.*: *a spiral staircase*

spiral² *v.* [I] **1** to move up or down in the shape of a spiral: *a leaf* ***spiraling to*** *the ground* **2** to gradually but continuously get worse in a way that cannot be controlled: *The economy has spiraled downward.* | *He felt his life was* ***spiraling out of control.***

spire /spaɪɚ/ *n.* [C] a tower that rises steeply to a point, especially on a church

spir·it /ˈspɪrɪt/ *n.* **1** [C,U] the qualities that make someone live the way s/he does, and make him/her different from other people, and which many people believe continues to exist after death [➡ **soul**]: *He has a* ***generous/free/independent spirit.*** | *I can still feel her spirit in this house.* | *The Olympic flame symbolizes the best of the* ***human spirit*** (=the qualities that make us human). **2 spirits** [plural] how happy or sad someone feels at a particular time: *The children were* ***in high/good spirits*** (=happy and excited). | *Her* ***spirits rose/sank*** (=she became happy or unhappy) *when she heard the news.* | *The music helped* ***lift*** *her* ***spirits*** (=made her happier). **3** [C] a creature without a physical body, such as an ANGEL or GHOST: *the spirits of our ancestors*

THESAURUS

ghost, **phantom**, **specter**, **apparition**
➔ see Thesaurus box at GHOST

4 [U] courage, energy, and determination: *the team's* ***fighting spirit*** **5** [singular] the attitude that you have toward something: *a* ***spirit of*** *cooperation* **6 team/community/public etc. spirit** the strong feeling of belonging to a particular group and wanting to help it

spir·it·ed /ˈspɪrɪt̬ɪd/ *adj.* having a lot of courage, determination, and energy: *a spirited discussion*

spir·i·tu·al¹ /ˈspɪrɪtʃuəl, -tʃəl/ *adj.* **1** relating to the spirit rather than the body or mind: *spiritual health* **2** relating to religion: *a spiritual leader* —**spiritually** *adv.*

spiritual² *n.* [C] a religious song first sung by the black people of the U.S. when they were SLAVES

spit¹ /spɪt/ *v.* past tense and past participle **spit** or **spat** /spæt/ present participle **spitting** [I,T] to force a small amount of liquid, blood, food, etc. from your mouth: *He* ***spat on*** *the ground.* | *She tasted the drink and immediately* ***spat it out.***

spit up *phr. v.* if a baby spits up, it brings back milk from its stomach out of its mouth

spit² *n.* **1** [U] *informal* SALIVA **2** [C] a long thin stick that you put through meat to cook it over a fire

spite¹ /spaɪt/ *n.* [U] **1 in spite of sth** without being affected or prevented by something [= **despite**]: *Mrs. Hetland, in spite of her age, is still beautiful.* **2** a feeling of wanting to hurt, annoy, or upset someone: *Lois refused to let her ex-husband see the children* ***out of spite*** (=because of spite).

spite² *v.* [T] to annoy or upset someone deliberately: *He's doing this just to spite me!*

spite·ful /ˈspaɪt˺fəl/ *adj.* being unkind deliberately in order to annoy or upset someone

splash¹ /splæʃ/ *v.* **1** [I,T] if a liquid splashes, or if you splash it, it falls on something or hits against it: *He* ***splashed*** *some cold water* ***on*** *his face.* | *water splashed down onto the rocks* **2** [I] to move around in water in a noisy way: *The children were* ***splashing around*** *in the pool.*

splash² *n.* [C] **1** the sound water makes when something hits it: *Jerry jumped into the water* ***with a loud splash.*** ➔ see picture on page A7 **2** a mark made by a liquid splashing onto something else: ***splashes of*** *paint on my pants* **3 a splash of color** a small area of bright color **4 make a splash** *informal* to do something that gets a lot of public attention: *The story made a splash in the newspapers.*

splash·y /ˈsplæʃi/ *adj.* big, bright, and very easy to notice: *a splashy tie*

splat /splæt/ *n.* [singular] the sound made when something wet hits a hard surface

splat·ter /ˈsplæt̬ɚ/ *v.* [I,T] if a liquid splatters, or if someone splatters it, it hits against a surface: *rain* ***splattering against*** *the window*

splay /spleɪ/ **also splay out** *v.* [I,T] to spread your fingers, arms, or legs wide apart: *He sat with his legs splayed out in front of him.*

splen·did /ˈsplɛndɪd/ *adj.* **1** excellent: *a splendid performance* **2** beautiful or impressive: *a splendid view from the balcony* —**splendidly** *adv.*

splen·dor /ˈsplɛndɚ/ *n.* [U] impressive beauty: *the* ***splendor of*** *Yosemite Valley*

splice /splaɪs/ *v.* [T] to join the ends of two pieces of film, wire, etc. so they form one piece

splint /splɪnt/ *n.* [C] a flat piece of wood, metal, etc. used for keeping a broken bone in position while it HEALS

splin·ter¹ /ˈsplɪntɚ/ *n.* [C] **1** a small sharp piece of wood, glass, or metal that has broken off of a larger piece: *I have a splinter in my finger.* **2 splinter group/organization** a group of people that separate from a larger organization because they have different ideas

splinter² *v.* [I,T] **1** to break into thin sharp pieces, or to cause something to do this **2** if a group or organization splinters, or if it is splintered by something such as a disagreement, it separates into smaller groups or organizations

split¹ /splɪt/ *v.* past tense and past participle **split**, present participle **splitting** **1** [I,T] **also split up** to divide or make something divide into two or more groups, parts, etc.: *We'll **split (up) into** three work groups.* | *Try **splitting** this section **into two.***

THESAURUS

separate, **divide**, **break up**
→ see Thesaurus box at SEPARATE²

2 [I,T] to tear or break something along a straight line, or to be torn or broken in this way: *The board had **split in two**.* | *One of the boxes had **split open**.* **3** [I,T] if a group of people splits, or if something splits them, they divide into smaller groups after disagreeing strongly about something: *It was feared that the issue would split the church.* **4** [T] to divide something among two or more people in equal parts: *Do you want to split a pizza?* | *We decided to **split** the money **between** us.* **5** [I] *informal* to leave a place quickly

split up *phr. v.* to end a marriage or a relationship: *Eve's parents split up when she was three.*

split² *n.* [C] **1** a long straight hole caused when something breaks or tears: *a **split in** the seam of my skirt* **2** a serious disagreement that divides an organization or group of people into smaller groups: *a **split in** the Republican Party*

ˌsplit-ˈlevel *adj.* a split-level house, room, or building has floors at different heights in different parts

ˌsplit ˈsecond *n.* **a split second** an extremely short period of time: *For a split second, I thought I was going to die.* —**split-second** *adj.*: *a split-second decision* (=one taken very quickly)

split·ting /ˈsplɪt̬ɪŋ/ *adj.* **splitting headache** a very painful HEADACHE

splurge /splɚdʒ/ *v.* [I] *informal* to spend more money than you can usually afford: *We went shopping and **splurged on** clothes.*

spoil /spɔɪl/ *v.* **1** [T] to ruin something by making it less attractive, enjoyable, useful, etc.: *Don't let his bad mood spoil your evening.* **2** [T] to let a child do or have whatever they want, with the result that they behave badly: *We've been careful not to spoil our kids.* **3** [T] to treat someone in a way that is very kind or too generous: *a hotel that spoils its guests* **4** [I] if food spoils, it starts to decay

spoiled /spɔɪld/ *adj.* someone, especially a child, who is spoiled is rude and behaves badly because s/he is always allowed to do or have whatever s/he wants: *a **spoiled brat***

spoils /spɔɪlz/ *n.* [plural] things taken by an army from a defeated enemy, or things taken by thieves

spoil·sport /ˈspɔɪlspɔrt/ *n.* [C] *informal* someone who spoils other people's fun: *Come on and play, **don't be a spoilsport**.*

spoke¹ /spoʊk/ *v.* the past tense of SPEAK

spoke² *n.* [C] one of the thin metal bars that connect the outer edge of a wheel to the center, especially on a bicycle → see picture at BICYCLE

spok·en¹ /ˈspoʊkən/ *v.* the past participle of SPEAK

spoken² *adj.* **1 spoken English/language** the form of language that you speak rather than write **2 softly-spoken/soft-spoken/well-spoken** speaking quietly or in an educated way: *a soft-spoken man* (=he speaks quietly)

spokes·man /ˈspoʊksmən/ *n.* plural **spokesmen** /-mən/ [C] a male spokesperson: *a **spokesman for** the victims' families*

spokes·per·son /ˈspoʊksˌpɚsən/ *n.* [C] someone who has been chosen to speak officially for a group, organization, government, etc.: *a White House spokesperson*

spokes·wom·an /ˈspoʊksˌwʊmən/ *n.* plural **spokeswomen** /-ˌwɪmɪn/ [C] a female spokesperson

sponge¹ /spʌndʒ/ *n.* **1** [C,U] a piece of a very light substance that is full of small holes and is used for washing or cleaning something **2** [C] a sea animal with a soft body, from which some sponges are made

sponge² *v.* **1** [T] **also sponge down** to wash something with a wet sponge **2** [T] to remove liquid from a surface using a sponge **3** [I] *informal disapproving* to get money, food, etc. from someone without working for it: *He's been **sponging off** his friends for years.*

ˈsponge cake *n.* [C,U] a light cake made with eggs, sugar, and flour but usually no fat

spong·y /ˈspʌndʒi/ *adj.* soft and full of holes like a sponge: *spongy wet earth*

spon·sor¹ /ˈspɑnsɚ/ *n.* [C] **1** a person or company that sponsors a television show, sports event, etc.: *the **sponsor of** the French Open* **2** someone who sponsors a person for CHARITY

sponsor² *v.* [T] **1** to give money to a television show, sports event, etc. in exchange for the right to advertise your products at the event: *a competition sponsored by Campbell's Soup* **2** to officially support a proposal for a new law **3** to agree to give someone money for a CHARITY if s/he walks, runs, swims, etc. a particular distance

spon·ta·ne·ous /spɑnˈteɪniəs/ *adj.* happening or done without being planned or organized, because you suddenly want to do it: *a spontaneous decision* —**spontaneously** *adv.* —**spontaneity** /ˌspɑntəˈneɪət̬i, ˌspɑntˀnˈeɪ-/ [U]

spoof /spuf/ *n.* [C] a funny book, movie, or play, etc. that copies a serious or important book, etc. and makes it seem silly: *a **spoof on/of** Shakespeare's "Richard III"* —**spoof** *v.* [T]

spook¹ /spuk/ *n.* [C] *informal* a GHOST

spook² *v.* [T] *informal* to frighten someone: *Being alone all night really spooked me.* | *The drop in share prices spooked investors.*

spook·y /'spuki/ *adj. informal* strange or frightening [= **eerie**]: *a spooky old house*

spool /spul/ *n.* [C] an object shaped like a small wheel that you wind wire, thread, camera film, etc. around

spoon¹ /spun/ *n.* [C] a tool used for eating, cooking, and serving food, shaped like a small bowl with a long handle

spoon² *v.* [T] to pick up or move food with a spoon: ***Spoon** the sauce **over** the fish.*

'spoon-feed *v.* past tense and past participle **spoon-fed** [T] *disapproving* to give too much help to someone: *Spoon-feeding students does not help them remember things.*

spoon·ful /'spunfʊl/ *n.* [C] the amount that a spoon can hold: *a **spoonful of** sugar*

spo·rad·ic /spə'rædɪk/ *adj.* happening often but not regularly or continuously: *sporadic bombing* —**sporadically** *adv.*

sport¹ /spɔrt/ *n.* [C] **1** a physical activity in which people compete against each other: *What's your favorite sport?* | *Do you **play** any **sports**?* | *Soccer and basketball are **team sports**.* | *Baseball is America's most popular **spectator sport*** (=one watched by a lot of people).

THESAURUS

Places where people play sports
field – a large area of ground, usually covered with grass, where team sports are played: *a football/baseball/soccer field* | *The athletic fields are next to the school.*
stadium – a large sports field with seats all around it for people to watch team sports or track and field competitions: *a football stadium*
court – an area with lines painted on the ground, for tennis, basketball, etc.: *a tennis court*
diamond – the area in a baseball field that is within the shape formed by the four bases, also used to refer to the whole field
track – a special area for running on
gym – a large room with machines which you can use to do exercises
(swimming) pool – a place where you can swim
health club – a building where you can do various different sports

2 an activity such as hunting or fishing

THESAURUS

game, **recreation**, **hobby**
→ see Thesaurus box at GAME¹

3 a good sport someone who does not get angry when they lose at a game or sport **4 a bad/poor sport** someone who gets angry very easily when they lose at a game or sport

sport² *v.* **be sporting sth** to be wearing or showing something in a proud way: *Martin walked in sporting a tall white cowboy hat.*

sport·ing /'spɔrt̬ɪŋ/ *adj.* [only before noun] relating to sports: *a store selling **sporting goods*** (=sports equipment) | *one of the biggest **sporting events** of the year*

sports /spɔrts/ *adj.* **1** relating to sports or used for sports: *a sports club* | *sports equipment* **2** on the subject of sports: *I like reading the **sports pages/section*** (=in a newspaper).

'sports car *n.* [C] a low fast car, often with a roof that can be folded back

sports·cast /'spɔrts-kæst/ *n.* [C] a television program of a sports game

'sports ˌjacket also **'sports coat** *n.* [C] a man's comfortable jacket, worn on informal occasions

sports·man·ship /'spɔrtsmənˌʃɪp/ *n.* [U] behavior that is fair, honest, and polite in a game or sports competition: *We try to teach the kids **good sportsmanship**.*

sports·wear /'spɔrtswɛr/ *n.* [U] clothes that are appropriate for informal occasions

ˌsport-u'tility ˌvehicle *n.* [C] an SUV

sport·y /'spɔrt̬i/ *adj. informal* designed to look attractive in a bright informal way: *a sporty red car*

spot¹ /spɑt/ *n.* [C]
1 PLACE a particular place: *Oh, sorry, I'm sitting in your spot.* | *a popular vacation spot* | *a parking spot*

THESAURUS

place, **position**, **location**, **site**
→ see Thesaurus box at PLACE¹

2 COLORED AREA a small round area on a surface, that is a different color from the rest: *a white dog with black spots*
3 MARK a small mark on something: *grease spots* | *There are **spots of** blood on his jacket.*

THESAURUS

mark, **stain**, **smudge**, **smear**
→ see Thesaurus box at MARK²

4 on the spot *informal* **a)** immediately: *Cathy was offered the job on the spot.* **b)** at the place where something is happening: *He lit up a cigar on the spot.*
5 APPEARANCE a short appearance or advertisement on TV, radio, etc.: *an advertising spot* | *a guest spot on the Tonight Show*
6 POSITION a position in a competition: *The top finisher will earn a spot in the U.S. Olympic team.*
7 put sb on the spot to deliberately ask someone a question that is difficult or embarrassing to answer

8 bright spot something that is good in a bad situation: *Foreign trade is the one bright spot in the economy.* ➔ **hit the spot** at HIT[1]

spot² *v.* past tense and past participle **spotted**, present participle **spotting** [T] **1** to notice or recognize someone or something that is difficult to see: *A helicopter pilot spotted the wreckage of the plane.* | *She has a good eye for spotting talent.* | *I spotted something moving in the trees.*

THESAURUS

see, notice, catch a glimpse of, make out, catch sight of

➔ see Thesaurus box at SEE

2 to give the other player in a game an advantage: *Come on, I'll spot you 10 points if you play.*

ˌspot 'check *n.* [C] an examination of a few things or people in a group, to see whether everything is correct or satisfactory: *Health inspectors will make spot checks throughout the state.*

spot·less /ˈspɑtlɪs/ *adj.* **1** completely clean: *Donna keeps her car spotless.* **2** completely honest and good: *a spotless reputation*

spot·light¹ /ˈspɑtlaɪt/ *n.* **1** [C] a very powerful light that can be directed at someone or something, or the light made by this. Spotlights are often used to light a stage when actors or singers are performing. **2 the spotlight** a lot of attention in newspapers, on television, etc.: *Russia is back **in the** media **spotlight** again.*

spotlight² *v.* [T] to make people pay attention to someone or something: *a music festival that spotlights modern composers*

spot·ty /ˈspɑt̬i/ *adj.* good in some parts but not in others: *The stock market showed spotty gains.*

spouse /spaʊs/ *n.* [C] *formal* a husband or wife

spout¹ /spaʊt/ *n.* [C] a small pipe on the side of a container that you pour liquid out through

spout² *v.* **1** [I,T] if a liquid spouts or fire spouts from somewhere, it comes out very quickly in a powerful stream: *A leak **spouted from** the garden hose.* **2** [I] *informal* **also spout off** to talk a lot in a boring or annoying way: *He's always **spouting off about** politics.*

sprain /spreɪn/ *v.* [T] to injure a joint in your body by suddenly twisting it: *Amy **sprained** her **ankle** when she fell.* —**sprain** *n.* [C]

sprang /spræŋ/ *v.* the past tense of SPRING

sprawl /sprɔl/ *v.* [I] **1 also sprawl out** to lie or sit with your arms or legs stretched out: *When we got home, Carey was **sprawled on** the sofa.* **2** if a building or town sprawls, it spreads out over a wide area in an unattractive way —**sprawl** *n.* [singular, U] *urban sprawl* (=growth in the size of a town or city)

spray¹ /spreɪ/ *v.* **1** [T] to make a liquid come out of a container, HOSE, etc. in a stream of very small drops: ***Spray** a little perfume **on** the backs of your knees too.* | *She **sprayed** herself **with** perfume.* ➔ see picture at SQUIRT[1] **2** [I] to be scattered in small drops or pieces through the air: *Water **sprayed from** the garden hose.*

spray² *n.* **1** [C,U] liquid that is forced out of a container in a stream of very small drops: *hair spray* **2** [C] a special container from which liquid comes out in small drops: *a non-aerosol spray* **3** [U] water that is thrown up into the air in very small drops: *The boat scattered sea spray over us as it rocked up and down.*

spread¹ /sprɛd/ *v.* past tense and past participle **spread**

1 OPEN/ARRANGE [T] **also spread out** to open something so that it covers a big area, or to arrange a number of things so that they cover a flat surface: *Tracy had a map spread out over the floor.* | *The population is evenly **spread across** the state.* | *He sat with books and papers **spread over** the table.*

2 AFFECT MORE PEOPLE/PLACES/THINGS [I,T] to move and affect more people, places, or a larger area, or to make something do this: *Rain will **spread throughout** the area by tonight.* | *Cancer has **spread to** her lungs.* | *Only a small number of insects **spread disease**.*

3 INFORMATION/IDEAS [I,T] to tell a lot of people about something or to become known by a lot of people: *His neighbors began **spreading rumors** that he was a spy.* | *News of her arrest quickly spread.*

4 SOFT SUBSTANCE [T] to put a soft substance onto a surface in order to cover it: ***Spread** some honey **on** the bread.* ➔ see picture on page A4

5 PUSH APART [I,T] **also spread apart** to push your arms, legs, or fingers wide apart

6 DO STH GRADUALLY [T] **also spread out** to do something gradually over time: *You can **spread** the payments **over** a year.*

7 spread yourself too thin to try to do too many things at the same time so that you do not do any of them effectively

8 WINGS [T] **also spread open** if a bird or insect spreads its wings, it stretches them wide

spread out *phr. v.* if a group of people spread out, they move apart from each other in order to cover a wide area: *If we spread out, it should be easier to find her.*

spread² *n.* **1** [singular] the increase in the area or number of people that something has an effect on: ***the spread of** TB* **2** [C,U] a soft food that you put on bread: ***cheese/chocolate, etc. spread*** **3** [C] *informal* a large meal for several people on a special occasion: *There was a nice spread at the reception after the wedding.* **4** [C] a special article or advertisement in a newspaper or magazine: *a two-page spread* **5** [C] a large farm or RANCH: *a 300-acre spread*

spread·sheet /ˈsprɛdʃit/ *n.* [C] *technical* **1** a computer program that can show and calculate financial information **2** a document that contains rows and COLUMNS of numbers that can be used to calculate something

spree /spri/ *n.* [C] a short period in which you do something that you enjoy, especially spending money or drinking: *I see you* ***went on a shopping spree****!*

sprig /sprɪg/ *n.* [C] a small stem or part of a branch with leaves or flowers on it: *a* ***sprig of*** *parsley*

spring[1] /sprɪŋ/ *n.* **1** [C,U] the season between winter and summer, when leaves and flowers appear: *The park opens* ***in the spring****.* | *I'm going to Cancun* ***this spring****.* | ***last/next spring*** (=the spring before or after this one) **2** [C] a twisted piece of metal that has been made so that it will return to its original shape after it has been pressed down **3** [C] a place where water comes up naturally from the ground: *a hot spring* **4** [U] the ability of a chair, bed, etc. to return to its normal shape after being pressed down **5** [C] a sudden quick movement or jump in a particular direction

spring[2] *v.* past tense **sprang** /spræŋ/ also **sprung** /sprʌŋ/ past participle **sprung** [I] **1** to jump or move suddenly and quickly in a particular direction: *He turned off the alarm and* ***sprang out of*** *bed.* | *He* ***sprang to*** *his* ***feet*** (=stood up suddenly) *and rushed after her.* | *The lid of the box* ***sprang open/shut*** (=suddenly opened or shut). | *The branch* ***sprang back/up*** (=moved quickly back to its original position or shape) *and hit him in the face.* **2 spring to mind** if someone or something springs to mind, you immediately think of him, her, or it: *Pam's name springs to mind as someone who could do the job.* **3 spring into action/spring to life** to suddenly become active or start doing things: *The whole school springs into action at Homecoming.* **4 spring to sb's defense** to immediately help someone who is being attacked or criticized: *Molly sprang to her daughter's defense.* **5 spring a leak** if a boat or a container springs a leak, it begins to let liquid in or out through a crack or hole

spring for sth *phr. v. informal* to pay for something: *Carol said she'd spring for lunch.*

spring from sth *phr. v.* to be caused by something: *health problems that spring from living in a cold, wet country*

spring sth **on** sb *phr. v. informal* to tell someone something or ask him/her to do something when s/he does not expect it and is not ready for it.: *I'm sorry to have to spring this on you.*

spring up *phr. v.* to suddenly appear or start to exist: *All along the railroad, new towns sprang up.*

spring·board /ˈsprɪŋbɔrd/ *n.* [C] **1** something that helps you to start doing something: *His computer knowledge provided a* ***springboard for*** *his career.* **2** a strong board that bends, used in order to jump high, especially into water

ˌspring ˈbreak *n.* [C] a vacation from school in the spring that is usually one week long

ˌspring ˈchicken *n.* **be no spring chicken** *humorous* to no longer be young

ˌspring ˈfever *n.* [U] a sudden feeling of energy and wanting to do something new and exciting, that you get in the spring

spring·time /ˈsprɪŋtaɪm/ *n.* [U] the time of year when it is spring

spring·y /ˈsprɪŋi/ *adj.* returning quickly to its original shape after being pressed: *springy grass*

sprin·kle[1] /ˈsprɪŋkəl/ *v.* **1** [T] to scatter small drops of liquid or small pieces of something onto something else: *spaghetti* ***sprinkled with*** *parmesan* | *She* ***sprinkled*** *some cookie crumbs* ***on*** *the ice cream.* ➔ see picture on page A4 **2 it is sprinkling** if it is sprinkling, it is raining lightly

sprinkle[2] *n.* [C] **1** small pieces of food, or a light layer of these: *chocolate sprinkles* | *a* ***sprinkle of*** *grated cheese* **2** a light rain

sprin·kler /ˈsprɪŋklɚ/ *n.* [C] a piece of equipment used for scattering drops of water on grass

sprint /sprɪnt/ *v.* [I] to run very fast for a short distance —**sprint** *n.* [C] —**sprinter** *n.* [C]

> **THESAURUS**
> **run, dash, tear, race**
> ➔ see Thesaurus box at RUN[1]

sprout[1] /spraʊt/ *v.* **1** [I,T] to start to grow, or produce new leaves, BUDS, or SHOOTS: *a plant sprouting new flowers* | *seeds beginning to sprout* **2** [I] **also sprout up** to appear suddenly in large numbers: *new homes sprouting up in the suburbs*

sprout[2] *n.* [C] **1** a new growth on a plant **2** a bean or other plant that is not fully grown and is eaten in SALADS: *alfalfa sprouts* **3** BRUSSELS SPROUT

spruce[1] /sprus/ *n.* [C,U] a tree with short leaves shaped like needles, or the wood of this tree

spruce[2] *v.*

spruce (sth/sb) **up** *phr. v. informal* to make yourself or a place look better or neater: *I want to spruce up a little before dinner.*

sprung /sprʌŋ/ *v.* the past tense and past participle of SPRING

spry /spraɪ/ *adj.* a spry old person is active and cheerful

spud /spʌd/ *n.* [C] *informal* a POTATO

spun /spʌn/ *v.* the past tense and past participle of SPIN

spunk·y /ˈspʌŋki/ *adj. informal* brave and full of energy and determination: *the film's spunky heroine* —**spunk** *n.* [U]

spur[1] /spɚ/ *n.* [C] **1 on the spur of the moment** without planning ahead of time: *We got married on the spur of the moment.* **2** a sharp pointed object attached to the heel of a rider's boot that s/he presses against the side of a horse to encourage it to go faster

spur[2] *v.* past tense and past participle **spurred**, present participle **spurring** [T] **1** to make an improvement or change happen faster: *Growth in the city was spurred by cheap housing.* **2 also spur sb on** to encourage someone to do or continue doing something: *Her sister's success **spurred** her **on** to practice harder.*

spu·ri·ous /ˈspyʊriəs/ *adj. formal* not based on correct facts or good reasoning, and so likely to be wrong: *spurious arguments*

spurn /spɚn/ *v.* [T] *literary* to refuse to accept something or to have a relationship with someone, in an unkind way: *a spurned lover*

spurt¹ /spɚt/ *v.* [I] **1** to flow out suddenly with a lot of force: *Blood **spurted from** his arm.*

THESAURUS

flow, **drip**, **leak**, **ooze**, **gush**, **run**, **come out**
→ see Thesaurus box at POUR

2 to suddenly move forward very quickly: *Liz **spurted past** the other runners.*

spurt² *n.* [C] **1** a stream of liquid, flames, etc. that comes out of something suddenly: *Water was coming out of the faucet **in spurts*** (=quickly for short periods). **2** a short sudden increase in activity, effort, or speed: *a growth spurt*

sput·ter /ˈspʌt̬ɚ/ *v.* **1** [I] to work badly or not effectively, used especially in news reports: *Pittsburgh's offense sputtered through the whole game.* **2** [I] if an engine sputters, it makes sounds like very small explosions, because it is not working correctly: *The engine sputtered and died.* **3** [I,T] to talk quickly in short confused phrases, especially because you are angry or shocked: *"They think I'm a fool," she sputtered.*

spy /spaɪ/ *v.* past tense and past participle **spied**, third person singular **spies** [I] to secretly collect information or watch people, usually for a government or company: *She hired a private detective to **spy on** her husband.* | *He confessed to **spying for** North Korea.* —**spy** *n.* [C] *a government spy*

squab·ble /ˈskwɑbəl/ *v.* [I] to argue about something unimportant: *What are those kids **squabbling about** now?* —**squabble** *n.* [C]

THESAURUS

argue, **have an argument**, **fight**, **have a fight**, **quarrel**, **have a quarrel**, **bicker**
→ see Thesaurus box at ARGUE

squad /skwɑd/ *n.* [C] a group of people who work together and do a job that needs special skills: *soldiers in the bomb squad*

ˈsquad car *n.* [C] a car used by police

squad·ron /ˈskwɑdrən/ *n.* [C] a military force consisting of a group of aircraft or ships

squal·id /ˈskwɑlɪd/ *adj.* extremely dirty, unhealthy, and unsafe: *squalid living conditions*

squall /skwɔl/ *n.* [C] a sudden strong wind that brings rain or snow

squal·or /ˈskwɑlɚ/ *n.* [U] extremely dirty, unhealthy, and unsafe conditions: *people living **in squalor***

squan·der /ˈskwɑndɚ/ *v.* [T] to carelessly waste money, time, opportunities, etc.: *They've **squandered** thousands **on** that old house.*

square¹ /skwɛr/ *adj.* **1** having four equal straight sides and four right angles: *a square window* **2 square inch/mile etc.** the measurement of an area that is a square shape with sides an inch, mile, etc. long: *two square acres of land* **3** like a square in shape: *a square corner* | *a square jaw* **4 be (all) square** if two people are square, they do not owe each other any money: *Here's your $20, so now we're square.* **5 a square meal** a complete satisfying meal **6 a square deal** honest and fair treatment from someone: *a car dealer that gives customers a square deal* **7** *old-fashioned* honest: *I'm **being square with** you.*

THESAURUS

circular, **round**, **semicircular**, **triangular**, **rectangular**, **oval**, **cylindrical**
→ see Thesaurus box at SHAPE¹

square² *n.* [C] **1** a shape with four straight equal sides forming four RIGHT ANGLES → see picture at SHAPE¹

THESAURUS

circle, **semicircle**, **triangle**, **rectangle**, **oval**, **cylinder**
→ see Thesaurus box at SHAPE¹

2 a broad open area with buildings around it in the middle of a town: *Times Square* **3 be back to square one** to be back in exactly the same situation that you started from: *The development deal fell through and now we're back to square one.* **4** the result of multiplying a number by itself. For example, the square of 5 is 25. [= **square root**]

square³ *v.* [T] to multiply a number by itself

square sth ⇔ **away** *phr. v.* to finish dealing with something: *Peter needs another day to **get** things **squared away** at home.*

square off *phr. v.* to get ready to fight someone

square up *phr. v.* to pay money that you owe: *I'll get the drinks, and we can square up later.*

square⁴ *adv. spoken* SQUARELY

ˈsquare dance *n.* [C] a type of dance in which four pairs of dancers face each other in a square

square·ly /ˈskwɛrli/ *adv.* **1** exactly or directly: *The ball landed squarely in the palm of his hand.* **2** completely and with no doubt: *The report puts the blame **squarely on** the senior managers.*

ˌsquare ˈroot *n.* [C] the number that, when multiplied by itself, equals a particular number. For example, the square root of 9 is 3.

squash¹ /skwɑʃ, skwɔʃ/ *v.* **1** [T] to press

S

something into a flat shape, often damaging it: *My hat got squashed on the flight.*

THESAURUS

press, **crush**, **mash**, **grind**
➔ see Thesaurus box at PRESS[1]

2 [I,T] to push yourself or someone else into a space that is too small [= **squeeze**]: *Seven of us **squashed into** the car.*

squash² *n.* **1** [C,U] one of a group of large vegetables with solid flesh and hard skins, such as PUMPKINS ➔ see picture at VEGETABLE **2** [U] an indoor game similar to RACKETBALL

squat¹ /skwɑt/ *v.* [I] **1 also squat down** to balance on your feet with your legs bent under you and your bottom near the ground ➔ see picture on page A9 **2** to live in a building or on a piece of land without permission and without paying rent

squat² *adj.* short and thick, or low and wide: *small squat houses | He is short and squat.*

squawk /skwɔk/ *v.* [I] if a bird squawks, it makes a loud angry cry —**squawk** *n.* [C]

squeak /skwik/ *v.* [I] **1** to make a very short high noise or cry: *Is that your chair squeaking?* ➔ see picture on page A7 **2 squeak by/through** *informal* to manage to succeed, but not by very much: *The Bulls have **squeaked through** into the playoffs.* —**squeak** *n.* [C] *the squeak of new leather*

squeak·y /'skwiki/ *adj.* **1** making very high noises that are not loud: *a squeaky voice | squeaky bed springs*

THESAURUS

high, **high-pitched**, **piercing**, **shrill**
➔ see Thesaurus box at HIGH[1]

2 squeaky clean *informal* **a)** never having done anything morally wrong: *The incident has ruined McIntyre's squeaky clean image.* **b)** completely clean: *squeaky clean hair*

squeal¹ /skwil/ *v.* [I] **1** to make a long loud high sound or cry: *squealing tires | children **squealing with** excitement* **2 squeal (on sb)** *informal* to tell the police or someone in authority about someone you know who has done something wrong

squeal² *n.* [C] a long loud high sound or cry: ***squeals of** delight*

squeam·ish /'skwimɪʃ/ *adj.* easily shocked or upset, or easily made to feel sick by disgusting sights: *I couldn't be a doctor – I'm too squeamish.*

squeeze¹ /skwiz/ *v.* **1** [T] to press something firmly together with your fingers or hands: *She squeezed Jim's shoulder gently.* ➔ see picture on page A8 **2** [T] to twist or press something in order to get liquid out of it: ***Squeeze** some lemon juice **onto** the salad.* ➔ see picture on page A4

THESAURUS

press, **squash**, **crush**, **mash**, **grind**
➔ see Thesaurus box at PRESS[1]

3 [I,T] to try to make a person or thing fit into a small space [= **squash**]: *Can you **squeeze in** next to Rick? | She had to **squeeze past** boxes of books to get to the front door.* **4 squeeze sb/sth in** *informal* to manage to do something although you are very busy: *Professor Lang can **squeeze you in** at 2:00.* **5 squeeze sb out (of sth)** to not let someone take part in something: *Some small businesses are being squeezed out of the market.* **6** [T] to strictly limit the amount of money that is available to an organization: *a school squeezed by budget cuts*

squeeze² *n.* **1 a (tight) squeeze** a situation in which there is only just enough room for things or people to fit somewhere: *It'll be a tight squeeze with six of us in the car.* **2** [C] an act of pressing something firmly with your fingers or hand: *Laurie **gave** his hand **a** little **squeeze**.* **3** [C] a small amount of something you get by squeezing: *a **squeeze of** lime juice* **4** [singular] a situation in which salaries, prices, borrowing money, etc. are strictly controlled: *a **squeeze on** farm programs*

squelch /skwɛltʃ/ *v.* **1** [T] *informal* to stop something from spreading or continuing: *Store owners said the law would squelch competition.* **2** [I] SQUISH

squid /skwɪd/ *n.* [C] a sea creature with a long soft body and ten arms

squig·gle /'skwɪgəl/ *n.* [C] a short line in writing or drawing that curls and twists —**squiggly** *adj.*

squint /skwɪnt/ *v.* [I] to look at something with your eyes partly closed in order to see better: *He looked at me, squinting in the sun.* —**squint** *n.* [C]

squire /skwaɪə/ *n.* [C] a young man in the Middle Ages who learned how to be a KNIGHT by serving one

squirm /skwəm/ *v.* [I] to twist your body from side to side because you are uncomfortable or nervous: *Stop squirming so I can comb your hair!*

squirrel

squir·rel /'skwəəl/ *n.* [C] a small animal with a long furry tail that lives in trees and eats nuts

squirt

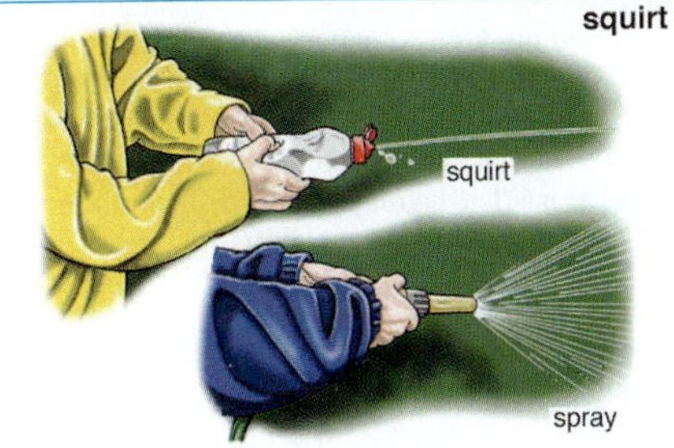

squirt[1] /skwɚt/ *v.* **1** [I,T] if you squirt liquid or it squirts, it is forced out of a narrow hole in a thin fast stream: *Orange juice **squirted onto** her dress.* | *You need to **squirt** some oil **in** the lock.* **2** [T] to hit or cover someone or something with a stream of liquid: *The children **squirted** each other **with** the hose.*

squirt[2] *n.* [C] **1** a fast thin stream of liquid: *a **squirt of** ketchup* **2** *spoken* a word used when speaking to a small child: *Hey squirt — it's time to wake up.*

squish /skwɪʃ/ *v.* **1** [I,T] *informal* to SQUASH something soft or wet, or to become squashed **2** [I] to make a sucking sound by moving through something soft and wet, such as mud

squish·y /ˈskwɪʃi/ *adj.* soft, wet, and easy to SQUEEZE: *squishy mud*

Sr. *n.* the written abbreviation of **Senior**

St. *n.* **1** the written abbreviation of **street** **2** the written abbreviation of **Saint**

stab[1] /stæb/ *v.* past tense and past participle **stabbed**, present participle **stabbing** **1** [T] to push a sharp object into someone or something: *He was **stabbed to death** in a fight.* | *I was **stabbed** several times **in** the arm/chest/etc.* | *She says he **stabbed** her **with** the bread knife.* **2 stab sb in the back** *informal* to do something bad to someone who likes and trusts you [= **betray**]

stab[2] *n.* **1** [C] an act of stabbing or trying to stab someone: *The victim had four **stab wounds**.* **2 take a stab at (doing) sth** *informal* to try to do something that is difficult or that you have never done: *Carla decided to take a stab at learning to sail.*

stab·bing /ˈstæbɪŋ/ *n.* [C] a crime in which someone is stabbed

sta·bil·i·ty /stəˈbɪləti/ *n.* [U] the condition of being strong, steady, and not changing [≠ **instability**]: *a long period of political stability*

sta·bi·lize /ˈsteɪbəˌlaɪz/ *v.* [I,T] to become firm, steady, or unchanging, or to make something firm or steady [➡ **stable**]: *The financial markets are finally stabilizing.* | *A rod is put in to stabilize the broken bone.* —**stabilization** /ˌsteɪbələˈzeɪʃən/ *n.* [U]

sta·ble[1] /ˈsteɪbəl/ *adj.* **1** steady and not likely to move or change: *Be careful – the ladder doesn't look stable.* | *a stable marriage* **2** calm, reasonable, and not easy to upset: *He was clearly not a very stable person.*

stable[2] *n.* [C] a building where horses are kept

stack[1] /stæk/ *n.* [C] a neat pile of things: *a **stack of** magazines on the table*

> **THESAURUS**
> **pile, heap, mound**
> ➔ see Thesaurus box at PILE[1]

stack[2] *v.* **1** [I,T] **also stack up** to form a neat pile, or put things into a neat pile: *Just stack the dishes in the sink for now.* | *chairs that are designed to stack easily* **2** [T] to put piles of things on something: *Al has a job stacking shelves in the supermarket.*

stack up *phr. v. informal* used to talk about how good something is compared with something else: *a new PC that stacks up well against the others on the market*

sta·di·um /ˈsteɪdiəm/ *n.* plural **stadiums** or **stadia** /-diə/ [C] a building for sports, large rock concerts, etc., consisting of a field surrounded by rows of seats: *a football stadium*

> **THESAURUS**
> **field, court, track, diamond, gym, (swimming) pool, health club**
> ➔ see Thesaurus box at SPORT[1]

staff[1] /stæf/ *n.* [C] the people who work for an organization: *a meeting of library **staff members*** | *Joan is the only lawyer we have **on staff**.* | *Reiter manages a **staff of** forty.* | *a **staff meeting*** ➔ see Thesaurus box at WORK[1]

> **TOPIC**
> **employee, employer, colleagues, co-workers**
> ➔ see Topic box at WORK[1]

staff[2] *v.* [T] to be or provide the workers for an organization: *a hospital staffed by experienced nurses* —**staffing** *n.* [U] *staffing costs*

staff·er /ˈstæfɚ/ *n.* [C] one of the people who works for an organization

stag /stæg/ *n.* [C] a fully grown male DEER

stage[1] /steɪdʒ/ *n.* **1** [C] a particular point or time in a process that something or someone reaches before going to the next one: *The disease is still **in its early stages**.* | ***At this stage*** (=right now) *no one is sure what to do next.* | *The government has promised elections **at some stage** in the next 12 months.* | *Children go through various **stages of** development.* | *the planning stage of the project*

> **THESAURUS**
> **part** – one of the pieces or features of something, such as an event or period of time: *The early part of his life was spent in New York.*
> **phase** – a separate part in a process of

S

> development or change: *Schools will receive extra funding in both phases of the plan.*
> **point** – a specific moment, time, or stage in something's development: *The team is playing better than I thought they would at this point.*
> **round** – one of a number of events that are related: *the first round of the negotiations*

2 [C] the raised floor in a theater where actors, singers, musicians, etc. perform **3** [singular, U] the profession of acting: *Lina's always wanted to be* ***on stage*** (=be an actor). ➔ see Topic box at THEATER **4** [C] a place where something important happens: *the world political stage* **5 s/he's going through a stage** *informal* used in order to say that someone young will soon stop behaving badly or strangely ➔ **set the stage/scene** at SET[1]

stage[2] *v.* [T] **1** to organize a public event: *They're staging five plays this summer.* | *Workers are* ***staging*** *a* ***strike****.* **2** to start doing something again after you have stopped for a while: *After five years, Johnson* ***is staging a comeback*** *in basketball.*

stage·coach /ˈsteɪdʒkoʊtʃ/ *n.* [C] a closed vehicle pulled by horses, that carried passengers and mail in past times

ˈstage fright *n.* [U] nervousness that some people feel before they perform in front of a lot of people

ˈstage ˌmanager *n.* [C] someone who is responsible for a theater stage during a performance

stag·ger[1] /ˈstægɚ/ *v.* **1** [I] to walk or move in an unsteady way, almost falling over: *A man came staggering down the stairs.* | *Somehow he managed to stagger to a hospital.* **2** [T] to arrange for things to be done at different times, so that they do not all happen at the same time: *Student registration will be staggered to avoid delays.*

stagger[2] *n.* [C] an unsteady movement of someone who has difficulty walking

stag·ger·ing /ˈstægərɪŋ/ *adj.* extremely great or surprising: *She spends a staggering amount of money on clothes.*

> **THESAURUS**
>
> **surprising**, **extraordinary**, **amazing**, **shocking**, **astonishing**, **astounding**, **stunning**
> ➔ see Thesaurus box at SURPRISING

stag·ing /ˈsteɪdʒɪŋ/ *n.* [C,U] the activity or art of performing a play, or the way this is done: *a modern* ***staging of*** *"Romeo and Juliet"*

stag·nant /ˈstægnənt/ *adj.* **1** stagnant water or air does not move or flow and often smells bad **2** not changing or improving: *Steel production has stayed stagnant.*

stag·nate /ˈstægneɪt/ *v.* [I] to stop developing or improving: *a stagnating economy* —**stagnation** /stægˈneɪʃən/ *n.* [U] *political stagnation*

staid /steɪd/ *adj.* serious, old-fashioned, and boring: *a staid old bachelor*

stain[1] /steɪn/ *v.* **1** [I,T] to accidentally make a colored mark on something, especially one that is difficult to remove, or to be marked in this way: *This carpet stains easily.* | *a tablecloth* ***stained with*** *wine* **2** [T] to paint wood with a stain

stain[2] *n.* **1** [C] a mark that is difficult to remove: *I got coffee* ***stains on*** *my shirt.*

> **THESAURUS**
>
> **mark**, **spot**, **smudge**, **smear**
> ➔ see Thesaurus box at MARK[2]

2 [C,U] a special liquid that you use to change the color of wood

ˌstainless ˈsteel *n.* [U] a type of steel that does not RUST

stair /stɛr/ *n.* **1 stairs** [plural] a set of steps built for going from one level of a building to another: *Bev ran* ***up/down the stairs****.* | *Please leave your shoes at* ***the bottom/foot of the stairs****.* | *I left my briefcase at the* ***top of the stairs****.* | *The office is up one* ***flight of stairs*** (=set of stairs). **2** [C] one of the steps in a set of stairs: *Jane sat on the bottom stair.* ➔ DOWNSTAIRS, UPSTAIRS

stair·case /ˈstɛrkeɪs/ *n.* [C] a set of stairs inside a building, and the structure that supports it

stair·way /ˈstɛrweɪ/ *n.* [C] a set of stairs and the structure that supports it, either inside or outside a building

stake[1] /steɪk/ *n.* **1 be at stake** if something that you value very much is at stake, you will lose it if a plan or action is not successful: *The team goes into the game knowing their coach's job is at stake.* **2 have a stake in sth a)** to have an important part or share in a business, plan, etc.: *a 5% stake in the company* **b)** if you have a stake in something, you will get advantages if it is successful, and you feel that you have an important connection with it: *Young people don't feel they have a stake in the country's future.* **3** [C] a pointed piece of wood, metal, etc. that is pushed into the ground to hold a rope, mark a particular place, etc.: *tent stakes* **4** [C usually plural] money risked on the result of a game, race, etc.

stake[2] *v.* [T] **1** to risk losing something valuable on the result of a game, race, etc., or on the result of a plan or action [= **bet**]: *The President is* ***staking*** *his reputation* ***on*** *the peace plan.* **2 stake (out) a claim** to say publicly that you think you have a right to have or own something: *The two tribes have both* ***staked a claim to*** *the territory.*

stake sth ⇔ **out** *phr. v. informal* to watch a place secretly and continuously: *The police have been staking out the club for weeks.*

stake·out /ˈsteɪkaʊt/ *n.* [C] an activity in which the police watch a place secretly and continuously in order to catch someone doing something illegal

stale /steɪl/ *adj.* **1** no longer fresh [≠ **fresh**]: *stale bread* **2** no longer interesting: *a stale old joke*

stale·mate /'steɪlmeɪt/ *n.* [C,U] a situation in which neither side in an argument, battle, etc. can gain an advantage: *an attempt to* ***break the stalemate***

stalk¹ /stɔk/ *n.* [C] a long narrow part of a plant that supports leaves, fruits, or flowers: *celery stalks* ➔ see picture at PLANT¹

stalk² *v.* **1** [T] to follow a person or animal quietly in order to catch, attack, or kill him, her, or it: *We know the rapist stalks his victims at night.*

THESAURUS

follow, chase, pursue, run after, tail
➔ see Thesaurus box at FOLLOW

2 [I] to walk in a proud or angry way: *Sheryl turned and* ***stalked out*** *of the room.*

stalk·er /'stɔkɚ/ *n.* [C] someone who often follows someone else in a way that is annoying or threatening —**stalking** *n.* [U]

stall¹ /stɔl/ *n.* [C] **1** a table or a small store with an open front, especially outdoors, where goods are sold: *a market stall* **2** a small enclosed private area for washing or using the toilet: *a shower/bathroom stall* **3** an enclosed area in a building for an animal, especially a horse

stall² *v.* [I,T] **1** if an engine stalls or you stall it, it suddenly stops working: *My car always stalls when it's cold.* **2** *informal* to deliberately delay doing something, or to make someone else do this: *Quit stalling and answer my question!* | *I'll try to stall him for a few minutes.*

stal·lion /'stælyən/ *n.* [C] a fully grown male horse

stal·wart /'stɔlwɚt/ *n.* [C] someone who strongly supports a particular organization or set of ideas —**stalwart** *adj.*: *a stalwart supporter*

stam·i·na /'stæmənə/ *n.* [U] physical or mental strength that lets you continue doing something for a long time without getting tired

stam·mer /'stæmɚ/ *v.* [I,T] to speak with a lot of pauses or to repeat the first letter of some words, either because you have a speech problem or because you are nervous [➡ **stutter**] —**stammer** *n.* [singular]

stamp¹ /stæmp/ *n.* [C] **1 also postage stamp** *formal* a small piece of paper that you stick onto an envelope or package that shows you have paid to mail it: *a 37-cent stamp* | *a* ***sheet/book of stamps*** (=set of stamps that you buy) **2** a tool for printing a mark onto a surface, or the mark made by this tool: *a stamp in your passport* **3 sb's stamp of approval** someone's statement that s/he accepts something or gives permission for something: *The Board of Education has* ***given its stamp of approval to*** *new standardized tests.* ➔ FOOD STAMP

stamp² *v.* **1** [I,T] to lift up your foot and put it down hard, or to walk in this way: *She* ***stamped out*** *of the room.* | *The audience applauded and* ***stamped*** *their* ***feet***. **2** [T] to put a pattern, sign, or letters on something using a special tool: *Please* ***stamp*** *the date* ***on*** *all incoming mail.*

stamp sth ⇔ **out** *phr. v.* to prevent something bad from continuing: *efforts to stamp out drug abuse*

stam·pede /stæm'pid/ *n.* [C] **1** an occasion when a large number of animals suddenly start running together **2** a sudden rush by a lot of people who all want to do the same thing or go to the same place —**stampede** *v.* [I,T]

stance /stæns/ *n.* [C usually singular] **1** an opinion that is stated publicly: *the Senator's tough* ***stance on*** *crime* **2** the way in which you stand during a particular activity

stanch /stæntʃ/ *v.* [T] ➔ STAUNCH²

stand¹ /stænd/ *v.* past tense and past participle **stood** /stʊd/

1 STAND [I] to be on your feet in an upright position: *Anna was standing in front of me.* | *Hundreds of people stood watching.* | *Could you* ***stand still*** (=stand without moving) *and listen to me?* | *Don't just* ***stand there*** (=stand doing nothing) – *help me!* | *A policeman told everyone to* ***stand back/aside*** (=move and stand farther away from something).

2 START STANDING [I] **also stand up** to rise onto your feet after you have been sitting, bending, or lying down: *She stood up and put her coat on.*

3 BE IN A PLACE/POSITION [I,T] to be in a place or position, or to put something in a place or position: *There's now a parking lot where the theater once stood.* | *A lamp stood on the table.* | *Few houses were* ***left standing*** *after the tornado hit.* ➔ see Thesaurus box at LEAN¹

4 can't stand *spoken* to dislike something or someone very much: *Dave can't stand dogs.* | *Allison* ***can't stand the sight of*** *blood.* | *I* ***can't stand to*** *be around cigarette smoke.*

5 IN A STATE/CONDITION [linking verb] to be in a particular state or condition: *The kitchen door* ***stood open***. | *The house has* ***stood empty*** *for 20 years.* | ***Where/how*** *do negotiations* ***stand*** *right now?* | *The offer,* ***as it stands*** (=the present offer), *is not acceptable.*

6 BE GOOD ENOUGH [T] to be good enough or strong enough to remain unharmed or unchanged by something: *jeans that can stand the rough wear kids give them* | *Their marriage has certainly* ***stood the test of time***.

7 ACCEPT A SITUATION [T] to be able to accept or deal well with a difficult situation [= **tolerate**]: *He* ***could*** *hardly* ***stand*** *the pain.*

8 HEIGHT [I] to have a particular height: *The Eiffel Tower* ***stands*** *300 meters* ***high***.

9 LEVEL/AMOUNT [I] to be at a particular level or amount: *The unemployment rate* ***stood at*** *8% in January.*

S

10 DECISION/OFFER [I not in progressive] if a decision, offer, etc. stands, it continues to exist or be correct: *The court has ruled that the conviction should stand.* | *My offer of help still stands.*
11 OPINION **where sb stands** if you know where someone stands, or how someone stands on a particular matter, you know what his/her opinion is: *Where do you stand on the issue of gun control?* | *You just never **know where you stand with** Walter.*
12 SUGGEST STH TO SB **could stand** *spoken* used in order to say that someone should do something or that something should be different: *He could stand to lose a little weight.*
13 stand a chance (of doing sth) to be likely to succeed in doing something: *You **don't stand a chance** of going out with her.*
14 stand to do sth to be likely to do or have something: *The company stands to make more than $12 million on the deal.*
15 stand in the way/in sb's way to prevent someone from doing something, or prevent something from happening or developing: *I always encouraged Brian. I didn't want to stand in his way.* | *You can't stand in the way of progress!*
16 stand on your own two feet *informal* to be independent and not need help from other people
17 it stands to reason (that) used in order to say that something is clearly true: *It stands to reason that children will copy their parents.*
18 stand trial to be brought to a court of law to have your case examined and judged
19 stand pat to refuse to change a decision or plan
20 stand on your head/hands to support yourself on your head or hands in an upright position, with your feet in the air

stand around *phr. v.* to stand somewhere and not do anything: *Everybody was just standing around talking.*

stand back *phr. v.* to move backward away from something, or stand some distance away from something: *Stand back from the edge of the platform*

stand by *phr. v.* **1 stand by sth** to continue to believe that something you said, did, or believed is still correct or true: *I stand by what I said earlier.* **2 stand by sb** to stay loyal to someone and support him/her in a difficult situation: *Matt's parents have stood by him through his drug problem.* **3** to be ready to do something: *Fire crews are now standing by.* **4** to not do anything to help someone, or to not prevent something from happening: *People just stood by and watched him being attacked.*

stand for sth *phr. v.* **1** to be a short form of a word or phrase: *VA stands for Veterans Administration.* **2** to support an idea, principle, etc.: *Martin Luther King stood for fairness and racial equality.* **3 not stand for sth** if someone will not stand for something, s/he will not allow it to happen: *Ms. Smith won't stand for any nonsense.*

stand in for sb *phr. v.* to do someone else's job while he or she is away: *Karen stood in for me when I was sick.*

stand out *phr. v.* **1** to be clearly better than other things or people: *Morrison **stands out as** the most experienced candidate.* **2** to be very easy to see or notice: *In her red dress, she really **stood out in the crowd**.*

stand up *phr. v.* **1** to be on your feet, or to rise to your feet: *We stood up when the judge came in.* | ***Stand up straight** and don't slouch!* **2** to be proven to be true, useful, or strong when tested: *The accusations will never **stand up in court**.* **3 stand sb up** to not meet someone when you have promised to meet him/her: *My date stood me up last night.*

stand up for sb/sth *phr. v.* to support or defend someone or something when s/he or it is being attacked or criticized: *Don't be afraid to stand up for what you believe in.*

stand up to sb *phr. v.* to be brave and refuse to do or say what someone is trying to make you do or say: *He became a kind of hero for standing up to local gangs.*

stand[2] *n.* [C] **1** a piece of furniture or equipment for supporting something: *a music stand* **2** a table or small structure, usually outside or in a large building, used for selling or showing things to people: *a hotdog stand* **3** an opinion that you state publicly: *Bradley was unwilling to **take a stand** (=say what his opinion was) on the issue.* **4 the stand** the place in a court of law where someone sits when the lawyers ask him/her questions: *Shaw had lied **on the stand** (=when he was answering questions).* | *Epstein will **take the stand** (=begin answering questions) Friday.* **5** an effort to defend yourself or to oppose something: *We have to **make/take a stand against** racism.* **6 stands** [plural] the place where people sit to watch a sports game

stan·dard[1] /ˈstændɚd/ *n.* **1** [C,U] a level of quality, skill, or ability that is considered to be acceptable: *teachers who have **high/low standards*** | *Tricia's parents **set** very high **standards**.* | *Students have to **meet/reach a** certain **standard** or they won't pass.* | *national **academic/health/environmental** standards* **2 by ... standards** compared to the normal or expected level of something else: ***By** American **standards**, Rafael's salary is pretty low.* **3 standards** [plural] moral principles about what kind of behavior or attitudes are acceptable: *She has very high **moral standards**.*

standard[2] *adj.* normal or usual: *The shoes are available in all standard sizes.* | *Security checks are now **standard practice/procedure**.*

THESAURUS

normal, **ordinary**, **average**, **routine**, **conventional**
➔ see Thesaurus box at NORMAL¹

stan·dard·ize /ˈstændɚˌdaɪz/ *v.* [T] to make all the things of one particular type the same as each other: *national standardized tests* —**standardization** /ˌstændɚdəˈzeɪʃən/ *n.* [U]

ˌstandard of ˈliving *n.* plural **standards of living** [C] the amount of wealth and comfort that a person, group, or country has: *a nation with a **high/low standard of living***

stand·by /ˈstændbaɪ/ *n.* plural **standbies** [C] **1** someone or something that is ready to be used when needed: *a standby power generator* **2 on standby a)** ready to be used when needed: *The police have been kept on standby in case of trouble.* **b)** if you are on standby for an airplane ticket, you will be allowed to travel if there are any seats that are not being used

ˈstand-in *n.* [C] someone who does the job or takes the place of someone else for a short time

stand·ing¹ /ˈstændɪŋ/ *adj.* [only before noun] **1** permanently agreed or arranged: *We have a **standing invitation** to use their beach cabin.* **2** done from a standing position: *a **standing ovation*** (=when people stand to CLAP after a performance)

standing² *n.* [U] someone's rank or position in a system, organization, etc., based on what other people think of him/her: *The scandal damaged the governor's **standing in** the polls.*

stand·off /ˈstændɔf/ *n.* [C] a situation in which neither side in a fight or battle can gain an advantage

stand·off·ish /stænˈdɔfɪʃ/ *adj. informal disapproving* unfriendly and formal

stand·out /ˈstændaʊt/ *n.* [C] someone who is better at doing something than other people in a group —**standout** *adj.*

stand·point /ˈstændpɔɪnt/ *n.* [C] one way of thinking about a situation [= **point of view**]: *Let's look at this **from a** practical **standpoint**.*

stand·still /ˈstændˌstɪl/ *n.* [singular] a situation in which there is no movement or activity at all: *The funeral **brought** the city **to a standstill**.* | *The traffic **came to a standstill**.*

stand·up /ˈstændʌp/ *adj.* [only before noun] *informal* standup COMEDY involves one person telling jokes as a performance —**standup** *n.* [U]

stank /stæŋk/ *v.* the past tense of STINK

stan·za /ˈstænzə/ *n.* [C] a group of lines that forms part of a poem

sta·ple¹ /ˈsteɪpəl/ *n.* [C] **1** a small piece of thin wire that is used in order to hold pieces of paper together **2** a food that is needed and used all the time: *staples like flour and rice*

staple² *v.* [T] to fasten things together with a STAPLE

THESAURUS

fasten, **attach**, **join**, **glue**, **tape**, **clip**, **tie**, **button (up)**, **zip (up)**
➔ see Thesaurus box at FASTEN

sta·pler /ˈsteɪplɚ/ *n.* [C] a tool used for putting STAPLES into paper ➔ see picture on page A11

star¹ /stɑr/ *n.* [C] **1** a very large amount of burning gases in space, that looks like a point of light in the sky at night: *I lay on my back and looked up at the stars.* | *The **stars** were **out*** (=shining).

TOPIC

moon, **planet**, **sun**
➔ see Topic box at SPACE¹

2 a famous performer in entertainment or sports: *a movie star* | *By the age of twenty, she was already a **big star**.* **3 a)** a shape with five or six points, that is supposed to look like a star in the sky: *The U.S. flag's fifty stars represent fifty states.* ➔ see picture at SHAPE¹ **b)** a mark in the shape of a star that is used in order to mark something as important: *I put stars next to the items we still need to buy.* **4** *informal* someone who is particularly good at something: *Jim is definitely our **star player**.* **5 the star of the show** the person who gives the best performance in a play, movie, etc. **6** a mark used in a system for showing how good a hotel or restaurant is: *a **three-star/four-star/five-star** restaurant*

star² *v.* past tense and past participle **starred**, present participle **starring** [I,T] if a movie, play, etc. stars someone, or if someone stars in a movie, play, etc., that person has one of the main parts in it: *a movie starring Bruce Willis* | *He has also **starred in** comedies.* | *Nicole Kidman **stars as** Emma.*

star·board /ˈstɑrbɚd/ *n.* [U] the right side of a ship or aircraft when you are looking toward the front [➡ **port**]

starch¹ /stɑrtʃ/ *n.* **1** [C,U] a substance in such foods as bread, rice, and potatoes **2** [U] a substance used for making cloth stiff

starch² *v.* [T] to make cloth stiff using STARCH

starch·y /ˈstɑrtʃi/ *adj.* starchy foods contain a lot of starch

star·dom /ˈstɑrdəm/ *n.* [U] the situation of being a famous performer

stare /stɛr/ *v.* [I] to look at someone or something for a long time: *Sue **stared at** him in disbelief.* | *He sat **staring into space*** (=looking at nothing for a long time). —**stare** *n.* [C] *She gave him a hard stare.*

THESAURUS

look, **glance**, **peek**, **glare**, **peer**, **gaze**, **gape**
➔ see Thesaurus box at LOOK¹, EYE¹

star·fish /ˈstɑrˌfɪʃ/ *n.* [C] a flat sea animal that is shaped like a star

stark[1] /stɑrk/ *adj.* **1** very simple and severe in appearance: *the stark beauty of the desert* **2** unpleasantly clear and impossible to avoid: *the* ***stark realities*** *of drug addiction* —**starkly** *adv.*

stark[2] *adv.* **stark naked** *informal* not wearing any clothes

star·let /ˈstɑrlɪt/ *n.* [C] a young actress who plays small parts in movies and is hoping to become famous

star·light /ˈstɑrlaɪt/ *n.* [U] the light that comes from the stars

star·ling /ˈstɑrlɪŋ/ *n.* [C] a greenish-black bird that is very common in Europe and North America

star·lit /ˈstɑrˌlɪt/ *adj. literary* made brighter by the light of the stars: *a starlit night*

star·ry /ˈstɑri/ *adj.* having many stars: *a starry sky*

ˌstarry-ˈeyed *adj. informal* hopeful about things in a way that is silly or unreasonable: *a starry-eyed teenager*

ˌStars and ˈStripes *n.* **the Stars and Stripes** the flag of the U.S.

ˌStar-Spangled ˈBanner *n.* **the Star-Spangled Banner** the national ANTHEM (=song) of the U.S.

S

ˈstar-ˌstudded *adj.* including many famous performers: *a star-studded cast*

start[1] /stɑrt/ *v.*

1 BEGIN DOING STH [I,T] to begin doing something: *Have you started making dinner?* | *It's* ***starting to*** *rain.* | *Mark's* ***starting school/college*** *in the fall.* | *It's late, so we should* ***get started.***

2 BEGIN HAPPENING [I,T] to begin happening, or to make something do this: *The race starts in ten minutes.* | *The fire was started by a loose wire.*

3 BUSINESS/ORGANIZATION, ETC. [T] **also start up** to create a new business or business activity: *Brad left his father's company to start a business of his own.*

4 TRIP [I] **also start off/out** to begin a trip: *You'll have to start early if you want to get there by noon.*

5 CAR/ENGINE/MACHINE [I,T] **also start up** if you start a car or engine, or if it starts, it begins to work: *Can't you* ***get*** *that* ***engine started****?*

6 to start with *spoken* **a)** used in order to emphasize the first of a list of things you want to mention: *There's a lot wrong with those kids – to start with, they're rude.* **b)** at the beginning of a situation: *I was nervous to start with, but then I was fine.*

7 PRICES start at/from sth if prices start at or from a particular figure, that is the lowest figure at which you can buy something: *Tickets start from $12.*

8 ROAD/RIVER [I] if a road, river, etc. starts somewhere, it begins in that place: *The Red River* ***starts in*** *New Mexico.*

9 MOVE SUDDENLY [I] to move suddenly because you are surprised or afraid

USAGE

Start and **begin** usually mean the same thing, but **start** has several meanings for which you cannot use **begin**.
Use **start** in order to talk about making a machine work: *I couldn't start the car this morning.*
Use **start** in order to talk about making something begin to exist: *Starting a new business is hard work.*

start off *phr. v.* to begin an activity: *Let's start off by reviewing what we did last week.*

start on sth *phr. v.* **start on sth** to begin working on something: *You'd better get started on your homework.*

start out *phr. v.* **1** to begin happening or existing in a particular way, especially when this changes later: *The book* ***started out as*** *a short article.* **2** to begin your life, profession, or an important period of time: *Laura* ***started out as*** *a teacher, and later got into writing.*

start over *phr. v.* to start doing something again from the beginning: *If you make a mistake, just erase it and start over.*

start[2] *n.* **1** [C usually singular] the beginning of an activity, event, or situation: *Hurry, or we'll miss the* ***start of*** *the show.* | *They've had problems* ***(right) from the start.*** | *It was a close race* ***from start to finish.*** | *The day* ***got off to a good/bad start.*** **2 it's a start** *informal* used in order to say that something you have achieved may not be impressive, but it will help with a bigger achievement: *We only have $2 million of the $60 million needed, but it's a start.* **3 for a start** *informal* said in order to emphasize the first of a list of facts or opinions: *I don't think she'll get the job. She's too young, for a start.* **4** [singular] a sudden movement caused by fear or surprise: *Ed woke up* ***with a start.***

start·er /ˈstɑrt̬ɚ/ *n.* [C] **1** a person, horse, etc. that is in a race when it starts: *Of the eight starters, only three finished the race.* **2 for starters** *informal* used in order to emphasize the first thing in a list: *You've spelled the name wrong, for starters.* **3** someone who gives the signal for a race to begin **4 also starter motor** a piece of equipment for starting an engine

ˈstarting ˌlineup *n.* [C usually singular] the best players on a sports team, who play when the game begins

start·le /ˈstɑrt̬l/ *v.* [T] to make someone suddenly feel surprised or slightly shocked: *Sorry, I didn't mean to startle you.* —**startling** *adj.*: *startling news*

ˈstart-up[1] *adj.* [only before noun] start-up costs are related to beginning and developing a new business

ˈstart-up² *n.* [C] a new small company: *an Internet start-up*

star·va·tion /stɑrˈveɪʃən/ *n.* [U] suffering or death caused by not having enough to eat: *people dying of starvation*

starve /stɑrv/ *v.* **1** [I,T] to suffer or die because you do not have enough to eat, or to make someone do this: *Thousands of people could **starve to death**.* | *starving refugees* **2 be starving/starved** *spoken* to be very hungry: *When do we eat? I'm starving!* **3 be starved for/of sth** to not be given something very important: *That poor kid's just **starved for** attention.*

stash¹ /stæʃ/ *v.* [T] *informal* to keep something in a safe, often secret, place: *He has money **stashed away** in a Swiss bank.*

stash² *n.* [C] *informal* an amount of something, especially drugs or money, that is kept in a secret place: *a **stash of** drugs*

state¹ /steɪt/ *n.* **1** [C] the condition that someone or something is in: *We are concerned about the **state of** the economy.* | *Exercise can improve your **state of mind*** (=the way you think and feel). | *They found him **in a state of shock**.* | *The house was in a **sorry state*** (=in a bad condition). **2** [C] **also State** one of the areas with limited lawmaking powers that some countries, such as the U.S., are divided into: *the state of Oklahoma* **3** [C,U] **also State** a country or its government: *a meeting between **heads of state*** | ***state-owned** industries*

> **THESAURUS**
>
> **country**, **nation**, **power**, **land**
> → see Thesaurus box at COUNTRY¹

4 the States *spoken* the U.S., used especially by someone when s/he is outside of the U.S. **5 a state of affairs** a situation: *It is **a sad/sorry state of affairs** when you can kill someone and only spend a year in jail.* **6 state visit/ceremony/opening etc.** an important official visit, ceremony, etc. involving governments or rulers: *the President's state visit to Moscow*

state² *v.* [T] *formal* **1** to give a piece of information or your opinion, especially by saying it clearly: *Please state your name.* | *The witness **stated that** he had never seen the woman before.* **2** if a document, ticket, etc. states information, it contains the information written clearly

state·ly /ˈsteɪtli/ *adj.* impressive in style or size: *a stately mansion*

state·ment /ˈsteɪt˺mənt/ *n.* [C] **1** something that you say or write officially and publicly: *The president is expected to **make a statement** later today.* | *the candidate's **statement about/on** the economy* | *He **gave a statement** to the police.* **2** a list showing amounts of money paid, received, etc. and their total: *a bank statement* **3 make a statement** to do something that shows your beliefs or political opinions: *Why get your nose pierced? Are you trying to make a statement?*

ˌstate-of-the-ˈart *adj.* using the newest methods, materials, or knowledge: *state-of-the-art technology*

> **THESAURUS**
>
> **advanced**, **sophisticated**, **high-tech**, **cutting-edge**
> → see Thesaurus box at ADVANCED

states·man /ˈsteɪtsmən/ *n.* plural **statesmen** /-mən/ [C] a political or government leader, especially one who is known as being wise and fair —**statesmanship** *n.* [U]

stat·ic¹ /ˈstæt̬ɪk/ *adj.* not moving, changing, or developing: *static prices*

static² *n.* [U] **1** noise caused by electricity in the air that spoils the sound on a radio or TV **2** static electricity

ˌstatic elecˈtricity *n.* [U] electricity that is not flowing in a current, but collects on the surface of an object and gives you a small electric shock

sta·tion¹ /ˈsteɪʃən/ *n.* [C] **1** a place where public vehicles stop so that passengers can get on and off, goods can be loaded, etc.: *a **bus/train station*** **2** a building or place that is a center for a particular type of service or activity: *a **police station*** | *a **gas station*** **3** a company that broadcasts on radio or television, or its programs that you receive: *a **radio/TV station*** | *I can only **get** a few **stations** on this radio.*

station² *v.* [T] to put someone in a particular place in order to do a particular job or military duty: *My uncle's stationed in Germany right now.*

sta·tion·a·ry /ˈsteɪʃəˌnɛri/ *adj.* not moving: *a stationary vehicle*

sta·tion·er·y /ˈsteɪʃəˌnɛri/ *n.* [U] special paper for writing letters on, usually with matching envelopes

ˈstation ˌwagon *n.* [C] a car with a door at the back, and a lot of space for boxes, cases, etc.

sta·tis·tic /stəˈtɪstɪk/ *n.* [singular] **1 statistics a)** [plural] a collection of numbers which represents facts or measurements: ***Statistics show** that the crime rate is falling.* **b)** [U] the science of using numbers to represent facts or measurements: *Statistics is a branch of mathematics.* **2** a single number that represents a fact or measurement: *Is he aware of the statistic that two out of three marriages fail?* —**statistical** *adj.*: *statistical analysis* —**statistically** *adv.*

stat·is·ti·cian /ˌstæt̬əˈstɪʃən/ *n.* [C] someone who works with STATISTICS

stats /stæts/ *n.* [plural] *informal* statistics

stat·ue /ˈstætʃu/ *n.* [C] an object that looks like a person or animal, and is made of stone, metal, etc.: *a **statue of** Abraham Lincoln*

statue

stat·u·ette /ˌstætʃuˈɛt/ *n.* [C] a very small STATUE

stat·ure /ˈstætʃɚ/ *n.* [U] *formal* **1** the degree to which someone is admired or regarded as important: *a musician of great stature* **2** someone's height

sta·tus /ˈsteɪt̬əs, ˈstæ-/ *n.* **1** [C,U] the legal and social position of a person, group, country, etc.: *Please state your name, age and **marital status*** (=whether you are married or not). | *the social **status of** women* **2** [U] your social or professional rank or position, considered in relation to other people: ***high-status/low-status** jobs* | *Doctors have traditionally enjoyed **high social status**.* **3 the status of sth** what is happening at a particular time in a situation: *No one would comment on the status of her application.*

status quo /ˌsteɪt̬əs ˈkwoʊ, ˌstæ-/ *n.* **the status quo** the state of a situation at a particular time

ˈstatus ˌsymbol *n.* [C] something that you own that suggests you are rich or important

stat·ute /ˈstætʃut/ *n.* [C] *formal* a law or rule

> **THESAURUS**
>
> **rule, law, regulation, restriction, guidelines**
> → see Thesaurus box at RULE[1]

stat·u·to·ry /ˈstætʃəˌtɔri/ *adj. formal* fixed or controlled by law: *statutory rights*

ˌstatutory ˈrape *n.* [C] the crime of having sex with someone who is below a particular age

staunch[1] /stɔntʃ, stɑntʃ/ *adj.* very loyal: *a staunch supporter* —**staunchly** *adv.*

> **THESAURUS**
>
> **faithful, loyal, devoted**
> → see Thesaurus box at FAITHFUL

staunch[2] **also stanch** /stæntʃ/ *v.* [T] to stop the flow of a liquid, especially of blood from a wound

stave /steɪv/ *v.*

stave sth ⇔ **off** *phr. v.* to stop someone or something from reaching you or affecting you for a period of time: *She ate an apple to stave off hunger.*

stay[1] /steɪ/ *v.* **1** [I] to remain in the same place, job, school, etc., and not leave: *I had to **stay late** at work.* | *She decided to **stay home**.* | ***Stay right there!** I'll be back in a minute.* **2** [I, linking verb] to continue to be in a particular state and not change: *It was hard to **stay awake**.* | *The town has **stayed the same** for centuries.* | *Let's just **stay calm** and try to figure out what to do.* **3** [I] to live in a place for a short time as a visitor or guest: *She's **staying with** us for a week.* | *Where are you staying while you're here?* ▶ Don't say "Where do you stay?" ◀ **4 stay put** *informal* to remain in one place and not move

stay away *phr. v.* to not go near someone or something: ***Stay away from** my sister!*

stay behind *phr. v.* to stay in a place after the other people have left

stay in *phr. v.* to stay in your home and not go out: *Let's stay in and watch TV.*

stay on *phr. v.* to continue to do a job or to study after the usual or expected time for leaving: *Rachelle is staying on for a fifth year in college.*

stay out *phr. v.* to remain away from home during the evening or night: *She stayed out until midnight.*

stay up *phr. v.* to not go to bed: *We **stayed up late** last night.*

stay[2] *n.* [C] a short period of time that you spend somewhere: *We hope you enjoy your stay.*

stead /stɛd/ *n.* **1 stand sb in good stead** to be very useful for someone in the future: *a skill that has stood me in good stead as an actor* **2** *formal* **do sth in sb's stead** to do something instead of someone else

stead·fast /ˈstɛdfæst/ *adj. literary* faithful and very loyal

stead·y[1] /ˈstɛdi/ *adj.* **1** not moving or shaking: *Keep the ladder steady.* **2** continuing or developing at the same rate, without stopping or changing: *He has made steady progress.* | *a steady speed of 50 mph* **3 steady job/work/income** a job, etc. that will continue over a long period of time **4 steady boyfriend/girlfriend** someone that you have had a romantic relationship with for a long time —**steadily** *adv.* —**steadiness** *n.* [U]

steady[2] *v.* past tense and past participle **steadied**, third person singular **steadies** [I,T] to hold someone or something so s/he or it becomes more balanced or controlled, or to become more balanced or controlled: *He put out his hand to steady himself.*

steady[3] *adv.* **go steady (with sb)** to have a long romantic relationship with someone

steak /steɪk/ *n.* [C,U] a thick flat piece of meat or fish → see picture on page A5

steal[1] /stil/ *v.* past tense **stole** /stoʊl/ past participle **stolen** /ˈstoʊlən/ **1** [I,T] to take something that belongs to someone else without his/her permission: *Two local men were arrested for stealing a car.* | *When did you find out your partner was **stealing from** you?*

> **THESAURUS**
>
> **burglarize** – to go into a building, car, etc. and steal things from it: *The office had been burglarized.*

rob – to steal money or other things from a bank, store, or person: *He robbed several gas stations in the area.*
mug – to attack someone in the street and steal something from him/her: *He had been mugged at gunpoint.*
shoplift – to steal something from a store by leaving without paying for it
rip off sth informal – to steal something: *Someone had ripped off $3000 worth of stereo equipment.*
➔ CRIME, CRIMINAL

USAGE

Use **steal** to talk about the things that were taken: *Matt's bike was stolen yesterday.*
Use **rob** to talk about the person that money is taken from, or the place, especially a bank: *Someone robbed the bank last night.*

2 [I] *literary* to move quietly without anyone noticing you

steal² *n.* **a steal** something that costs much less than it is worth: *At $15 a bottle, their Merlot* ***is a*** *real* ***steal.***

stealth /stɛlθ/ *n.* [U] the action of doing something quietly and secretly —**stealthy** *adj.*

steam¹ /stim/ *n.* **1** [U] the mist that hot water produces: *The kitchen was full of steam.* | *a* ***steam engine*** (=one that uses the power produced by steam to operate) **2 let/blow off steam** to get rid of your anger or energy by doing something active **3 run out of steam** to no longer have the energy or the support you need to continue doing something

steam² *v.* **1** [I] to produce steam: *a cup of steaming coffee* **2** [T] to cook something using steam: *Steam the vegetables for five minutes.*

THESAURUS

cook, **bake**, **fry**, **roast**, **broil**, **grill**, **sauté**, **boil**, **deep fry**
➔ see Thesaurus box at COOK¹

steam sth ⇔ **up** *phr. v.* to cover or be covered with steam: *My glasses are steamed up.*

steam·roll /ˈstimroʊl/ *v.* [T] *informal* to defeat an opponent or force someone to do something by using all your power or influence

steam·roll·er /ˈstimˌroʊlɚ/ *n.* [C] a heavy vehicle with very wide wheels for making road surfaces flat

steam·y /ˈstimi/ *adj.* **1** full of steam, or covered with steam: *steamy windows* **2** sexually exciting: *a steamy love scene*

steel¹ /stil/ *n.* [U] **1** a strong metal that can be shaped easily, consisting of iron and CARBON **2 nerves of steel** the ability to be brave and calm in a dangerous or difficult situation

steel² *v.* **steel yourself** to prepare yourself to do something unpleasant

ˌsteel ˈwool *n.* [U] a rough material made of steel wires, used in order to make surfaces smooth, remove paint, etc.

steel·y /ˈstili/ *adj.* extremely strong and determined: *a steely expression*

steep¹ /stip/ *adj.* **1** a road, hill, etc. that is steep goes down or up at a sharp angle **2** a steep increase or rise in something is large and happens quickly **3** *informal* very expensive —**steeply** *adv.* —**steepness** *n.* [U]

steep² *v.* [I,T] **1 be steeped in history/tradition etc.** to contain a lot of a particular quality: *Yale is an old university steeped in tradition.* **2** to put something such as food in a liquid and leave it there for some time: *Leave the tea bag to steep for two minutes.*

stee·ple /ˈstipəl/ *n.* [C] a tall pointed tower on a church

steer¹ /stɪr/ *v.* **1** [I,T] to control the direction that a vehicle goes in: *Maria steered while I gave directions.* **2** [T] to influence someone's behavior or the way a situation develops: *Helen tried to* ***steer the conversation*** *away from school.* | *My parents* ***steered*** *me* ***towards*** *a medical career.* **3** [T] to guide someone to a place: *Bobby took my arm and* ***steered*** *me* ***into*** *the next room.* **4 steer clear (of sb/sth)** *informal* to try to avoid someone or something

steer² *n.* [C] a young male cow that has had part of its sex organs removed

steer·ing /ˈstɪrɪŋ/ *n.* [U] the parts of a vehicle that allow you to control the direction it goes in: *power steering*

ˈsteering wheel *n.* [C] a wheel that you turn to control the direction a vehicle goes in ➔ see picture on page A12

stel·lar /ˈstɛlɚ/ *adj.* done extremely well: *a stellar performance*

stem¹ /stɛm/ *n.* [C] a long thin part of a plant, from which leaves or flowers grow ➔ see picture at FRUIT ➔ see picture at PLANT¹

stem² *v.* past tense and past participle **stemmed**, present participle **stemming** [T] **stem the tide/flow of sth** to stop something from spreading or growing: *an effort to stem the rising tide of crime*
stem from sth *phr. v.* to develop as a result of something else: *A lot of her emotional problems stem from her childhood.*

stench /stɛntʃ/ *n.* [C] a strong unpleasant smell: *the* ***stench of*** *rotting food*

THESAURUS

smell, **stink**, **odor**
➔ see Thesaurus box at SMELL²

sten·cil /ˈstɛnsəl/ *n.* [C] a piece of paper or plastic with patterns or letters cut out of it, which you use for painting patterns or letters onto a surface —**stencil** *v.* [T]

S

ste·nog·ra·pher /stəˈnɑgrəfɚ/ *n.* [C] someone whose job is to write down what someone else is saying by using SHORTHAND —**stenography** *n.* [U]

step¹ /stɛp/ *n.* [C]
1 MOVEMENT the movement you make when you put one foot in front of the other when walking: *He **took** a few **steps** and then stopped.* | *Jamie took a **step forward/back**.*
2 ACTION one of a series of things that you do in order to deal with a problem or achieve something: *We must **take steps*** (=take action) *to make sure it never happens again.* | *an important **first step** toward peace* | *Environmentalists called the change **a step in the right direction*** (=a good thing to do).
3 STAIR a flat narrow surface, especially one in a series, that you put your foot on when you are going up or down, especially outside a building [➡ **stairs**]: *Ellen ran up the steps and knocked on the door.*
4 STAGE IN A PROCESS a stage in a process or a position on a scale: *That promotion was quite a **step up** for her.* ➔ STEP-BY-STEP
5 DANCING a movement of your feet in dancing
6 in step/out of step a) having ideas that are the same as, or different from, other people's: *The president needs to **keep in step with** public opinion.* **b)** moving your feet in the same way as, or a different way from, people you are walking or marching with
7 SOUND the sound you make when you take a step ➔ FOOTSTEP

step² *v.* past tense and past participle **stepped**, present participle **stepping** [I] **1** to move somewhere by putting one foot down in front of the other: ***Step aside/back** and let the doctor through.* **2** to bring your foot down on something: *Sorry – I didn't mean to **step on** your foot.* **3 step on it/step on the gas** *spoken* to drive faster: *If you don't step on it we'll miss the plane.* **4 step on sb's toes** to offend or upset someone, especially by trying to do his/her work **5 step out of line** to behave badly by breaking a rule or disobeying an order
step down/aside *phr. v.* to leave your job or official position because you want to or think you should: *He's decided to step down at the end of the year.*
step forward *phr. v.* to come and offer help: *Several volunteers have kindly stepped forward.*
step in *phr. v.* to become involved in a situation, especially to stop trouble: *The police stepped in and stopped the fight.*
step out *phr. v.* to go out for a short time: *Molly just stepped out – may I take a message?*
step sth ⇔ **up** *phr. v.* to increase the amount of an activity or the speed of a process: *The airlines are stepping up security checks.*

step·broth·er /ˈstɛpˌbrʌðɚ/ *n.* [C] the son of someone who has married one of your parents

ˌstep-by-ˈstep *adj.* a step-by-step plan, method, etc. deals with things carefully and in a particular order: *a **step-by-step guide** to buying a house*

step·child /ˈstɛpˌtʃaɪld/ *n.* plural **stepchildren** /-ˌtʃɪldrən/ [C] a stepdaughter or stepson

step·daugh·ter /ˈstɛpˌdɔt̬ɚ/ *n.* [C] a daughter that your husband or wife has from a relationship before your marriage

step·fa·ther /ˈstɛpˌfɑðɚ/ *n.* [C] a man who is married to your mother but who is not your father

step·lad·der /ˈstɛpˌlædɚ/ *n.* [C] a LADDER with two sloping parts that are attached at the top so that it can stand without support

step·moth·er /ˈstɛpˌmʌðɚ/ *n.* [C] a woman who is married to your father but who is not your mother

ˈstepped-up *adj.* [only before noun] done more quickly or with more effort than before [➡ **step up**]: *the **stepped-up security** at the airport*

ˈstepping-ˌstone *n.* [C] **1** something that helps you to improve or become more successful: *a stepping-stone to a better job* **2** one of a row of stones that you walk on to get across a stream

step·sis·ter /ˈstɛpˌsɪstɚ/ *n.* [C] the daughter of someone who has married one of your parents

step·son /ˈstɛpsʌn/ *n.* [C] a son that your husband or wife has from a relationship before your marriage

ster·e·o /ˈstɛriˌoʊ, ˈstɪr-/ *n.* plural **stereos** [C] **1** a machine for playing records, CDS, etc. that produces sound from two SPEAKERS **2 in stereo** if music or a broadcast is in stereo, the sound it makes is directed through two SPEAKERS

ster·e·o·type¹ /ˈstɛriəˌtaɪp, ˈstɪr-/ *n.* [C] *disapproving* an idea of what a particular type of person is like, especially one which is wrong or unfair: *racial stereotypes* | ***stereotypes about** women* —**stereotypical** /ˌstɛrioʊˈtɪpɪkəl/ *adj.*

stereotype² *v.* [T] *disapproving* to decide, usually unfairly, that some people have particular qualities or abilities because they belong to a particular race, sex, etc.: *Too many children's books **stereotype** girls **as** helpless and weak.*

ster·ile /ˈstɛrəl/ *adj.* **1** unable to have children [**= infertile**; **≠ fertile**] **2** completely clean and not containing any BACTERIA: *a sterile bandage* **3** lacking new ideas or imagination —**sterility** /stəˈrɪlət̬i/ *n.* [U]

ster·il·ize /ˈstɛrəˌlaɪz/ *v.* [T] **1** to make something completely clean and kill any BACTERIA in it: *sterilized surgery equipment* **2** to perform an operation that makes a person or animal unable to have babies —**sterilization** /ˌstɛrələˈzeɪʃən/ *n.* [C,U]

ster·ling /ˈstɚlɪŋ/ *adj.* **sterling qualities/character/record etc.** excellent qualities, character, etc.

ˌsterling ˈsilver also **sterling** *n.* [U] a metal that is over 92% pure silver

stern¹ /stɚn/ *adj.* very strict and severe: *stern warnings* | *a **stern voice/face*** —**sternly** *adv.*

stern[2] *n.* [C] the back part of a ship

ste·roid /ˈstɛrɔɪd, ˈstɪrɔɪd/ *n.* [C] a drug used especially for treating injuries, that people sometimes use illegally to improve their sports performance

steth·o·scope /ˈstɛθəˌskoʊp/ *n.* [C] an instrument used by doctors to listen to someone's heart or breathing

stew[1] /stu/ *n.* [C,U] a meal made by cooking meat or fish and vegetables together slowly for a long time: *beef stew*

stew[2] *v.* [T] to cook something slowly in liquid: *stewed tomatoes*

stew·ard /ˈstuɚd/ *n.* [C] **1** *old-fashioned* a man who is a FLIGHT ATTENDANT **2 also shop steward** a worker who represents the members of a UNION

stew·ard·ess /ˈstuɚdɪs/ *n. old-fashioned* [C] a woman who is a FLIGHT ATTENDANT

stick[1] /stɪk/ *v.* past tense and past participle **stuck** /stʌk/ **1** [I,T] to attach something to something else using a sticky substance, or to become attached to a surface: *Did you remember to **stick** a stamp **on** the envelope?* | *leaves **sticking to** the windshield* | *The papers were all **stuck together**.* **2** [I] to push a pointed object into something, or to be pushing into something in this way: *The nurse stuck a needle in my arm.* | *There's a nail **sticking through** the board here.* **3** [T] *informal* to put something somewhere: *Just **stick** your coat **on** that chair.* **4** [I,T] if something sticks or is stuck, it is fixed and difficult to move: *Hey, this door is stuck.* **5 stick in sb's mind** if something sticks in your mind, you remember it well because it was surprising, interesting, etc. **6 stick your neck out** *informal* to take the risk of saying or doing something that may be wrong, or that other people may disagree with

stick around *phr. v. informal* to stay in a place or wait somewhere for someone

stick by sb *phr. v.* to help and support someone who is in a difficult situation: *My wife has always stuck by me.*

stick out *phr. v.* **1** if part of something sticks out, it comes out further than the rest of a surface or comes out through a hole: *Paul's legs were sticking out from under the car.* **2 stick** sth ⇔ **out** to deliberately move part of your body forward or push it out: *Don't stick your tongue out at me!* **3 stick out (like a sore thumb)** *informal* to be easily noticed because of looking very different from everyone or everything else **4 stick it out** *informal* to continue doing something that is difficult, boring, etc.

stick to sth *phr. v.* **1** to decide what to do, say, or believe, and not change this: *That's my story and I'm sticking to it.* **2 stick to your guns** to continue to say or do something, although people disagree with you

stick together *phr. v. informal* if people stick together, they continue to support each other

stick up *phr. v.* if a part of something sticks up, it is raised up or points upward above a surface

stick up for sb *phr. v. informal* to defend someone who is being criticized: *You'll have to learn to **stick up for yourself**.*

stick with *phr. v. informal* **1 stick with** sb to stay close to someone when there is a risk you could be separated **2 stick with** sb/sth to continue doing something or supporting someone: *Let's just stick with the original plan.* **3 stick** sb **with** sth to give someone a difficult or unpleasant responsibility: *I'll go as long as I don't get stuck with paying the bill again!* **4 stick with it** to continue doing something that is difficult, boring, etc. **5 stick with** sb to remain in your memory: *One thing he said has stuck with me ever since.*

stick[2] *n.* [C] **1** a long thin piece of wood that has fallen or been cut from a tree **2** a long thin piece of something: *a **stick of** chewing gum* **3** a long thin piece of wood or metal that you use for a particular purpose: *a walking stick* **4 the sticks** [plural] an area that is very far away from a town or city: *a kid **from the sticks*** → **get the short end of the stick** at SHORT[1]

stick·er /ˈstɪkɚ/ *n.* [C] a small piece of paper or plastic with a picture or writing on it, that you can stick onto something

ˈstick-in-the-ˌmud *n.* [C] someone who is not willing to try anything new, or does not want to go out and have fun

stick·ler /ˈstɪklɚ/ *n.* **be a stickler for rules/punctuality etc.** to think that rules, etc. are extremely important, and expect people to follow them

ˈstick shift *n.* [C] a piece of equipment in a car that you move with your hand to control its GEARS [➡ **automatic**]

ˈstick-up *n.* [C] *informal* a situation in which someone steals money from people in a bank, store, etc. by threatening them with a gun

stick·y /ˈstɪki/ *adj.* **1** made of or covered with a substance that sticks to surfaces: *sticky candy* | *Your hands are sticky.* **2** *informal* a sticky situation, question, or problem is difficult to deal with **3** weather that is sticky is very hot and the air feels wet [= **humid**] —**stickiness** *n.* [U]

stiff[1] /stɪf/ *adj.* **1** if a part of your body is stiff, your muscles hurt and it is difficult to move: *I've got a **stiff neck**.* | *My back was stiff and sore.*

THESAURUS

painful, tender, sore
→ see Thesaurus box at PAINFUL

2 difficult to bend or move: *stiff cardboard*

THESAURUS

hard, firm, solid
→ see Thesaurus box at HARD[1]

S

3 more difficult, strict, or severe than usual: *a **stiff penalty/fine/sentence*** 4 thick and almost solid: *Beat the egg whites until stiff.* 5 unfriendly or very formal: *a stiff smile* 6 **a stiff drink** a very strong alcoholic drink 7 **a stiff wind/breeze** a fairly strong wind —**stiffly** *adv.* —**stiffness** *n.* [U]

stiff[2] *adv.* **bored/scared/worried stiff** *informal* extremely bored, etc.

stiff[3] *n.* [C] 1 *slang* the body of a dead person 2 **working stiff** *informal* an ordinary person who works to earn enough money to live

stiff[4] *v.* [T] *slang* to not pay someone money that you owe him/her or that s/he expects to be given

stiff·en /ˈstɪfən/ *v.* [I] to suddenly stop moving, especially because you are frightened or worried

sti·fle /ˈstaɪfəl/ *v.* [T] to stop something from happening, developing, or being expressed: *laws that stifle competition* —**stifling** *adj.*: *stifling heat*

stig·ma /ˈstɪgmə/ *n.* [singular, U] a strong feeling in society that a type of behavior or a particular illness or condition is something to be ashamed of: *the **stigma attached to** mental illness* —**stigmatize** /ˈstɪgməˌtaɪz/ *v.* [T]

still[1] /stɪl/ *adv.* 1 up to a particular point in time and continuing at that moment: *Andy's still asleep.*

S

USAGE

Still is used to say that a situation that began in the past has not changed and is continuing: *He still lives with his parents.*

Always means "all the time" or "every time": *Her house is always clean.* | *I always see him on Tuesdays.*

Yet is used in negative sentences and questions to talk about something that you expect to happen, but which has not happened: *I haven't finished the book yet.* | *Is Mark back from lunch yet?*

2 in spite of what has just been said or done: *Clare didn't study much, but she still passed the exam.* 3 used in order to say that something continues to be possible: *We can still catch the bus if we hurry.* 4 **still colder/harder/better etc. also colder/harder/better etc. still** even colder, harder, etc. than something else: *Dan found biology difficult, and physics harder still.* 5 **be still going strong** to continue to be active or successful, even after a long time: *We've been married for 25 years, and we're still going strong.*

GRAMMAR

Use **still** before a verb unless the verb is "be": *She still calls me regularly.* | *It was still dark outside.*

If there are two or more verbs together, **still** comes after the first one: *I can still remember them.*

Still usually comes before any negative word: *She still isn't ready.*

still[2] *adj.* 1 not moving: *Just **keep/stand/stay still** while I tie your shoes.* 2 quiet and calm: *The forest was completely still.* —**stillness** *n.* [U]

still[3] *n.* [C] a photograph of a scene from a movie

still·born /ˌstɪlˈbɔrn◂/ *adj.* born dead

ˌstill ˈlife *n.* plural **still lifes** [C,U] a picture of an arrangement of objects, especially flowers and fruit ➔ see picture at PAINTING

stilt·ed /ˈstɪltɪd/ *adj.* stilted writing or speaking is formal and unnatural

stilts /stɪlts/ *n.* [plural] a pair of poles you can stand on, used for walking high above the ground

stim·u·lant /ˈstɪmyələnt/ *n.* [C] a drug or substance that makes you feel more awake and active: *Caffeine is a stimulant.*

stim·u·late /ˈstɪmyəˌleɪt/ *v.* [T] 1 to encourage more of an activity, or to help a process develop faster: *efforts to **stimulate** the **economy*** 2 to make someone excited about and interested in something: *We hope the project will **stimulate** students' **interest** in science.* —**stimulating** *adj.*: *a stimulating conversation* —**stimulation** /ˌstɪmyəˈleɪʃən/ *n.* [U]

stim·u·lus /ˈstɪmyələs/ *n.* plural **stimuli** /-laɪ/ [C,U] something that causes a development or reaction: *a **stimulus to** industrial development*

sting[1] /stɪŋ/ *v.* past tense and past participle **stung** /stʌŋ/ [I,T] 1 if an insect or plant stings you, it causes a sharp pain and that part of your body swells: *Jamie was stung by a bee.* 2 to feel a sudden sharp pain in your eyes, throat, or skin, or to make someone feel this: *The antiseptic might sting a little.*

THESAURUS

hurt, ache, throb

➔ see Thesaurus box at HURT[1]

3 if you are stung by something, you are upset or badly affected by it: *Pearson was **stung** by her **criticism**.*

sting[2] *n.* 1 [C] a wound made when an insect or plant stings you: *a bee sting* 2 [singular] a sharp pain that you feel in your eyes, throat, or skin 3 [C] a trick used for catching someone while s/he is doing something illegal: *an undercover sting operation*

sting·er /ˈstɪŋɚ/ *n.* [C] the point on a creature's body that contains poison, for example on a BEE

sting·ray /ˈstɪŋreɪ/ *n.* [C] a large flat fish that has a long tail like a whip with stingers on it

stin·gy /ˈstɪndʒi/ *adj.* not willing to spend money or share something even though you have enough: *She's so stingy.* —**stinginess** *n.* [U]

stink[1] /stɪŋk/ *v.* past tense **stank** /stæŋk/ past participle **stunk** /stʌŋk/ [I] 1 to have a very strong bad smell: *The dog's breath stinks!* | *The room **stank of** cigar smoke.* 2 **sth stinks** *spoken* said when you think something is bad or unfair: *I think the whole thing stinks.* —**stinky** *adj.*

stink sth ⇔ **up** *phr. v. informal* to fill a place with a very strong bad smell

stink² *n.* [singular] **1 make/cause/raise a stink** to complain very strongly about something **2** a very strong bad smell

> **THESAURUS**
> **smell, stench, odor**
> ➔ see Thesaurus box at SMELL²

stink·er /ˈstɪŋkɚ/ *n. informal* [C] someone who behaves badly

stink·ing /ˈstɪŋkɪŋ/ *adj.* having a very strong bad smell: *a dump full of stinking garbage*

stint¹ /stɪnt/ *n.* [C] a period of time that you spend doing something: *a five-year* ***stint in*** *the army*

stint² *v.* [I] ➔ SKIMP

sti·pend /ˈstaɪpɛnd, -pənd/ *n.* [C] an amount of money paid regularly to someone such as a priest or student as a salary: *a monthly stipend*

stip·u·late /ˈstɪpyəˌleɪt/ *v.* [T] *formal* if an agreement, law, or rule stipulates something, it must be done: *The contract* ***stipulates that*** *we receive 25% of the profits.* —**stipulation** /ˌstɪpyəˈleɪʃən/ *n.* [C]

stir¹ /stɚ/ *v.* past tense and past participle **stirred**, present participle **stirring** **1** [T] to mix a liquid or food by moving a spoon around in it: *Could you stir the sauce for me?* | ***Stir*** *the flour* ***into*** *the mixture.* ➔ see picture on page A4

> **THESAURUS**
> **mix, combine, blend, beat**
> ➔ see Thesaurus box at MIX¹

2 [I,T] to move slightly, or to make someone or something do this: *Rachel stirred in her sleep.* **3** [T] to make someone feel a strong emotion: *The killings* ***stirred*** *citizens* ***to*** *protest.*

stir sth ⇔ **up** *phr. v.* to deliberately cause problems or arguments: *John was always* ***stirring up trouble****.*

stir² *n.* [C usually singular] **1** a strong feeling such as excitement or anger, felt by many people: *The nude drawings at the library have* ***caused/created*** *quite* ***a stir****.* | *The movie* ***caused such a stir*** *that it was finally banned.* **2** an act of stirring something: ***Give*** *the soup* ***a stir****.*

ˈstir-fry *v.* past tense and past participle **stir-fried**, third person singular **stir-fries** [T] to quickly cook meat, vegetables, etc. in a little oil over very high heat —**stir-fry** *n.* ➔ see picture on page A5

stir·rup /ˈstɚəp, ˈstɪrəp/ *n.* [C] one of the two metal parts on a horse's SADDLE that you put your foot in

stitch¹ /stɪtʃ/ *n.* [C] **1** one of the small lines of thread where a piece of cloth has been sewn: *tiny stitches in the sleeves* **2** a piece of special thread that a doctor uses to sew together a cut or wound: *Nancy had 14 stitches in her leg.* **3** one of the small circles that you KNIT when you are making a SWEATER **4 in stitches** *informal* laughing so much that you cannot stop: *Her jokes* ***had*** *us all* ***in stitches****.* **5 not a stitch (of clothing)** *informal* no clothes at all: *He stood there without a stitch on.*

stitch² *v.* [T] to sew two pieces of cloth together, or to sew something onto a piece of cloth —**stitching** *n.* [U]

stitch sth ⇔ **up** *phr. v.* to sew together the edges of a wound or two pieces of cloth: *The nurse stitched up the cut and left it to heal.*

stock¹ /stɑk/ *n.* **1** [C,U] a supply of something that is kept to be sold or used later: ***stocks of*** *canned food in the cupboard* | *Their new album is now* ***in stock/out of stock*** (=available or unavailable to be sold). **2** [C,U] a SHARE or shares in a company **3** [U] a liquid made from boiling meat, bones, or vegetables, used especially for making soups: *chicken stock* **4 take stock (of sth)** to think carefully about everything that has happened so that you can decide what to do next: *We need to take stock of the situation.*

stock² *v.* [T] to have a supply of something available to be sold or used: *Do you stock camping equipment?*

stock up *phr. v.* to buy a lot of something that you intend to use later: *I need to stock up on groceries.*

stock·brok·er /ˈstɑkˌbroʊkɚ/ *n.* [C] a person or company whose job is to buy and sell STOCKS, BONDS, etc. for other people —**stockbroking** *n.* [U]

ˈstock cerˌtificate *n.* [C] an official document that proves you own STOCK in a company

ˈstock exˌchange *n.* [C] the business of buying and selling STOCKS, BONDS, etc., or the place where this happens

stock·hold·er /ˈstɑkˌhoʊldɚ/ *n.* [C] someone who owns STOCK

stock·ing /ˈstɑkɪŋ/ *n.* [C] **1** a very thin close-fitting piece of clothing that covers a woman's foot and most of her leg: *silk stockings* **2** a large sock that is hung by the FIREPLACE before Christmas to be filled with presents

ˈstock ˌmarket *n.* [C usually singular] **1** ➔ STOCK EXCHANGE **2** the average value of STOCKS sold in the STOCK EXCHANGE

stock·pile /ˈstɑkpaɪl/ *n.* [C] a large supply of something that you collect in order to use it in the future: *a stockpile of weapons* —**stockpile** *v.* [T]

ˌstock-ˈstill *adv.* not moving at all

stock·y /ˈstɑki/ *adj.* having a short, heavy, strong-looking body: *a stocky policeman*

stock·yard /ˈstɑkyɑrd/ *n.* [C] a place where cattle are kept before being sold or killed for their meat

stodg·y /ˈstɑdʒi/ *adj.* boring, formal, and old-fashioned

sto·ic /ˈstoʊɪk/ **also sto·i·cal** /ˈstoʊɪkəl/ *adj.* not showing your emotions or not complaining when something bad happens to you —**stoicism** /ˈstoʊɪˌsɪzəm/ *n.* [U]

S

stoke /stoʊk/ *v.* [I,T] **1** to add more wood or FUEL to a fire **2** to cause something to increase: *High economic growth could stoke inflation.*

stoked /stoʊkt/ *adj. slang* very happy and excited about something

stole¹ /stoʊl/ *v.* the past tense of STEAL

stole² *n.* [C] a long straight piece of cloth or fur that a woman wears over her shoulders

sto·len /'stoʊlən/ *v.* the past participle of STEAL

stol·id /'stɑlɪd/ *adj.* not showing a lot of emotion —**stolidly** *adv.*

stom·ach¹ /'stʌmək/ *n.* [C] **1** the organ in your body that DIGESTS the food you eat: *Sam's* ***stomach growled*** (=made a noise). | *Don't drink on an* ***empty stomach.*** ➔ see picture on page A3 **2** the front part of your body, below your chest: *I always sleep on my stomach.* **3** the ability and willingness to do something unpleasant: *I didn't* ***have the stomach to*** *watch him fight.* ➔ **feel sick to your stomach** at SICK

stomach² *v.* [T] to be able to deal with something that is unpleasant: *I just* ***can't stomach*** *moving again.*

stom·ach·ache /'stʌmək,eɪk/ *n.* [C] a pain in your stomach

stomp /stɑmp, stɔmp/ *v.* [I] to walk with very heavy steps or put your foot down hard, usually because you are angry

S

stone¹ /stoʊn/ *n.* **1** [U] rock, or a hard mineral substance: *a stone fireplace* **2** [C] a small rock or a piece of rock: *A few of the protesters began throwing stones at the police.* **3** [C] a jewel: *a ring set with* ***precious stones*** **4** [C] a ball of hard material that can form in an organ such as the KIDNEY or BLADDER

stone² *adv.* **stone cold/deaf/dead** completely cold, DEAF, or dead

stone³ *v.* [T] to kill or hurt someone by throwing stones at him/her

stoned /stoʊnd/ *adj. slang* feeling very excited or very relaxed, because you have taken an illegal drug

stone·wall /'stoʊnwɔl/ *v.* [I,T] to deliberately delay doing something or refuse to give information about it: *The union is stonewalling on the contract.*

ston·y /'stoʊni/ *adj.* **1** covered with stones or containing stones **2** showing no emotion or pity: *a stony silence*

stood /stʊd/ *v.* the past tense and past participle of STAND

stool /stul/ *n.* [C] **1** a seat that has three or four legs, but no back or arms: *a piano stool* ➔ see picture at SEAT¹ **2** *technical* a piece of solid waste from the body

stoop¹ /stup/ *v.* [I] **1** to bend your body forward and down: *Troy stooped to pick up his pencil.* **2** to do something that other people consider to be bad or morally wrong: *I never thought you'd* ***stoop so low.***

stoop² *n.* [C] **1** the position you hold your body in when you STOOP **2** a set of stairs leading up to a city house, or the flat area at the top of them

stop¹ /stɑp/ *v.* past tense and past participle **stopped**, present participle **stopping** **1** [I,T] to end an action, activity, movement, or event, or to make something end: *He finally stopped smoking.* | *The rain's stopping.* | *Doctors stopped the bleeding.* | *He's been stopped twice by the police for speeding.* **2** [I] to pause during an activity, trip, etc. in order to do something: *We* ***stopped for*** *gas in Louisville.* | *Let's find a place to* ***stop and*** *eat.* | *She* ***stopped to*** *tie her shoe.*

THESAURUS

have/take a break – to stop doing something for a short time in order to rest: *Are you feeling tired? Let's take a break.*
break – to stop for a short time in order to rest or eat something: *Should we break for lunch?*
pause – to stop speaking or doing something for a short time before starting again: *He paused for a moment to consider the question.*

3 [T] to prevent someone from doing something: *I'm leaving, and you can't stop me.* | *We must do everything we can to* ***stop*** *this* ***from*** *happening again.* **4 stop it/that!** *spoken* said when you want someone to stop annoying or upsetting you: *Stop it! That hurts!* **5 stop short of sth** to stop before you do one more thing that would be too dangerous, risky, etc.: *Tom stopped short of calling her a liar.* **6 stop at nothing** to be ready to do anything to achieve something you want: *They've said they'll stop at nothing to save the redwood trees.*

stop by *phr. v.* to make a short visit to a person or place, especially before going somewhere else: *It was nice of Judy to stop by.*

stop in *phr. v. informal* to make a short visit to a place or person, especially when you are going somewhere else: *Let's* ***stop in at*** *Gary's on the way home.*

stop off *phr. v.* to quickly visit a place that is on the way to where you are going: *I need to* ***stop off at*** *the post office.*

stop² *n.* [C] **1** the action of stopping or of being stopped: *The taxi* ***came to a stop*** *outside his hotel.* | *Mrs. Drayton* ***put a stop to*** *the gossip.* **2** a place where you stop during a trip, or the short period you spend at that place: *Paris will be the first stop of the tour.* **3** a place where a bus or train regularly stops for its passengers: *This is my stop.* | *the* ***bus/subway/train stop*** *at 45th Street* ➔ **pull out all the stops** at PULL¹ ➔ TRUCK STOP

stop·gap /'stɑpgæp/ *n.* [C] a solution, plan, person, etc. that you use until you have a better one: *a* ***stopgap measure*** *to deal with the parking problem*

stop·light /'stɑplaɪt/ *n.* [C] a set of red, yellow, and green lights used for controlling traffic

stop·o·ver /'stɑp,oʊvɚ/ *n.* [C] a short time

between parts of a trip, especially a long airplane trip: *a three-hour stopover in Atlanta*

stop·page /'stɑpɪdʒ/ *n.* [C] an occasion when workers stop working for a short time as a protest

stop·per /'stɑpɚ/ *n.* [C] a piece of plastic, CORK etc. that you put in the top of a bottle to close it

stop·watch /'stɑpwɑtʃ/ *n.* [C] a watch used for measuring the exact time it takes to do something, such as run a race ➔ see picture at WATCH[2]

stor·age /'stɔrɪdʒ/ *n.* [U] the act or state of keeping something in a special place when it is not being used: *the safe* ***storage of*** *chemical weapons* | *The furniture is* ***in storage***.

store[1] /stɔr/ *n.* [C] **1** a place where goods are sold to the public: *a street lined with small stores* | *a* ***grocery/book/shoe, etc. store*** | *I'm* ***going to the store*** (=to a food store) *to get some milk.*

THESAURUS

Stores that sell particular types of goods
bookstore/clothes store/record store etc. – a store that sells one type of goods
grocery store – a store that sells food and other things used in the home
supermarket – a large store that sells many different kinds of food and things people need for the house
bakery – a place or area within a grocery store where bread, cakes, cookies, etc. are made or sold
delicatessen/deli – a small store or an area within a grocery store that sells cheese, cooked meat, bread, etc.
liquor store – a small store where alcohol is sold
drugstore – a store where you can buy medicines, beauty products, etc.
hardware store – a store that sells equipment and tools that you use in your home and yard
nursery/garden center – a place where plants and trees are grown and sold
newsstand – a place on a street where newspapers and magazines are sold
boutique – a small store that sells fashionable clothes or decorations
Stores that sell different types of goods
convenience store – a store where you can buy food, newspapers, etc., that is often open 24 hours each day
department store – a large store that sells many different products, such as clothes, kitchen equipment, etc.
chain store – one of a group of stores owned by the same company
superstore – a very big store, especially one that has many different types of products, or one that has a lot of one type of product
Stores that sell goods more cheaply
outlet store – a store that sells things for less than the usual price
warehouse store – a store that sells things in large amounts at lower prices
People who use or work in stores
customer – someone who buys the things sold in a store
sales assistant/clerk – someone whose job it is to help customers to buy things
cashier – someone whose job is to receive and pay out money in a store

2 a supply of something that you keep to use later: *secret stores of weapons* **3 be in store** to be about to happen to someone: *There's a surprise in store for you!*

store[2] *v.* [T] **1 also store away** to put things away and keep them there until you need them: *photos* ***stored in*** *shoe boxes*

THESAURUS

keep, save, reserve, file, collect
➔ see Thesaurus box at KEEP[1]

2 to keep facts or information in a computer: *data* ***stored on*** *the hard drive*

store·front /'stɔrfrʌnt/ *n.* [C] **1** the part of a store that faces the street **2 storefront church/office/school etc.** a small church, etc. in a shopping area

store·house /'stɔrhaʊs/ *n.* **a storehouse of information/memory etc.** something that contains a lot of information, memories, etc.

store·keep·er /'stɔrˌkipɚ/ *n.* [C] someone who owns or is in charge of a store

store·room /'stɔr-rum, -rʊm/ *n.* [C] a room where goods are stored

sto·rey /'stɔri/ *n.* [C] ➔ STORY

stork /stɔrk/ *n.* [C] a tall white water bird with long legs and a long beak

storm[1] /stɔrm/ *n.* [C] **1** a period of bad weather when there is a lot of wind, rain, snow, etc.: *a snow storm* | *a* ***winter/summer storm***

THESAURUS

hurricane, tornado, typhoon
➔ see Thesaurus box at WIND[1]

2 a situation in which people suddenly become angry and excited: *The changes raised* ***a storm of opposition/criticism/protest***. **3 dance/talk/work etc. up a storm** *informal* to do something with a lot of excitement and effort: *Jenny and I cooked up a storm.* **4 take sb/sth by storm** to suddenly become very successful in a particular place: *a new show that's taking Broadway by storm*

storm[2] *v.* **1** [T] to attack a place and enter it using a lot of force: *Police officers stormed the building.* **2** [I] to go somewhere in a fast, noisy way because you are very angry: *Jack* ***stormed in***, *demanding an explanation.*

storm·y /'stɔrmi/ *adj.* **1** with rain, strong winds, snow, etc.: *stormy weather* | *a stormy day* **2** a

S

stormy relationship or situation is one in which people often feel angry

sto·ry /ˈstɔri/ *n.* plural **stories** [C] **1** a description of an event that is intended to entertain people: *a **story about/of** her father's rodeo days* | *The movie is based on a **true story**.* | *a **ghost/detective/love story*** | *Grandma used to **read/tell** us **stories** every night.*

THESAURUS

tale – a story about things that happened long ago, or things that may not have really happened: *tales of adventure*
myth – a very old story about gods, magical creatures, etc.: *the Greek myths about Zeus*
legend – an old story about brave people or magical events: *the legend of King Arthur*
fable – a traditional story that teaches a moral lesson: *the legendary fable of the race between the tortoise and the hare*
yarn – a long story that is not completely true: *He spins (=tells) wonderful yarns about his boyhood and his early career as a sailor.*

2 a report in a newspaper or news broadcast about a recent event: *The Post published a **story on** his White House visit.*

TOPIC

article, **column**
➔ see Topic box at NEWSPAPER

3 a floor or level of a building: *a **three-story** building* (=with three levels) **4 it's a long story** *spoken* said when you think something will take too long to explain: *It's a long story – I'll tell you later.* **5 to make a long story short** *spoken* said when you want to finish explaining something quickly: *To make a long story short, she got mad and left.* **6** an excuse, explanation, or lie: *Do you believe his story?*

sto·ry·tell·er /ˈstɔriˌtɛlɚ/ *n.* [C] someone who tells stories

stout /staʊt/ *adj.* **1** fairly fat and heavy **2** brave and determined: *a stout defender of human rights*

stove /stoʊv/ *n.* [C] **1** a piece of kitchen equipment on which you cook food in pots and pans, and that contains an OVEN: *There's a pan of rice **on the stove**.* **2** a thing inside which you burn wood, coal, etc. in order to heat a room: *an old wood stove*

stow /stoʊ/ **also stow away** *v.* [T] to put something away neatly in a place until you need it again: *Please stow all carry-on baggage under your seat.*

stow·a·way /ˈstoʊəˌweɪ/ *n.* [C] someone who hides on an aircraft, ship, etc. in order to travel without paying

strad·dle /ˈstrædl/ *v.* [T] **1** to sit or stand with your legs on either side of something: *Nick straddled a chair.* **2** if something straddles a line, road, river, etc., part of it is on one side and part on the other side: *a town that straddles the U.S. – Canadian border* **3** to include different areas of activity, groups, time, etc.: *immigrants who straddle two cultures*

strag·gle /ˈstrægəl/ *v.* [I] if people in a large group straggle, they move away from the group one at a time: *Travelers were beginning to straggle out of Customs.*

strag·gly /ˈstrægli/ *adj.* *informal* growing or spreading out in a messy uneven way: *straggly hair*

straight¹ /streɪt/ *adv.* **1** in a line or direction that is not bent, curved, or leaning: *Stand up straight!* | *The bathroom's **straight down** the hall.* | *She sat there, staring **straight ahead**.* **2** immediately and without any delay: *Why didn't you go straight to the police?* **3** happening one after the other in a series: *He worked 18 hours straight.* **4 not see/think straight** to be unable to see or think clearly: *It was so noisy, I could hardly think straight.*

straight² *adj.* **1** not bent or curved: *a straight line* | *long straight hair* ➔ see picture at HAIR **2** level or upright, and not bent or leaning: *Is this sign straight?* | *straight teeth* **3** honest and direct: *I wish you'd give me a **straight answer**.* **4** one after the other: *three straight victories* **5 get/keep sth straight** *spoken* to correctly understand the facts about a situation without being confused: *I can't keep all their names straight.* **6 get straight A's/B's etc.** to earn the GRADE "A", etc. in all of your school subjects **7 a straight face** a serious expression on your face even though you want to laugh or smile: *How did you **keep a straight face**?* **8** *informal* HETEROSEXUAL **9** alcoholic drinks that are straight do not have any ice, water, etc. added to them **10** *informal* not liking to take risks or do things that are not ordinary, and often following strict moral rules: *"What's his girlfriend like?" "She's pretty straight."*

straight³ *n.* **1** [C] *informal* someone who is HETEROSEXUAL [≠ **gay**] **2 the straight and narrow** a sensible and moral way of living

straight·en /ˈstreɪtˀn/ *v.* **1** [I,T] **also straighten out** to become straight, or make something straight: *She straightened a picture on the wall.* **2** [I] **also straighten up** to make your back straight, or to stand up straight after bending down **3** [T] **also straighten up** to clean a room that is messy

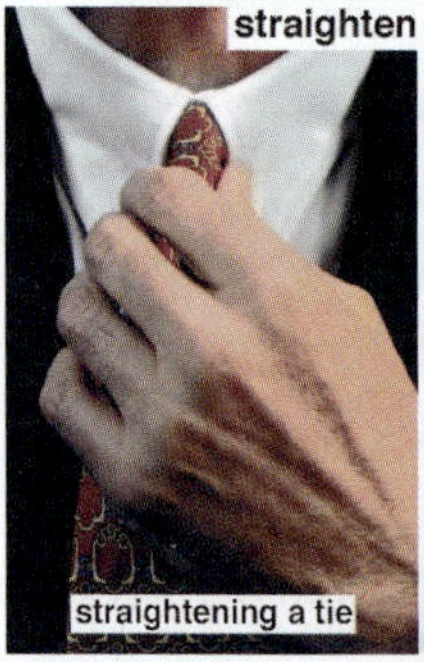
straighten
straightening a tie

straighten sb/sth ⇔ **out** *phr. v.* **1** to deal with a difficult situation or solve a problem: *I'll talk to him and see if I can straighten things out.* **2** to improve your bad behavior or deal with personal problems, or to help someone do this: *He's back in school and getting himself straightened out.*

straighten up *phr. v.* to start behaving well: *You straighten up right now, young man!*

straight·for·ward /ˌstreɪtˈfɔrwɚd◂/ *adj.* **1** simple or easy to understand: *The task was **relatively/fairly straightforward**.* ➔ see Thesaurus box at SIMPLE **2** honest and not hiding what you think: *a straightforward response*

THESAURUS

frank, **candid**, **direct**, **blunt**, **forthright**
➔ see Thesaurus box at HONEST

straight·jack·et /ˈstreɪtˌdʒækɪt/ *n.* ➔ STRAITJACKET

strain¹ /streɪn/ *n.* **1** [C,U] worry that is caused by always being busy or always dealing with problems: *She's been **under** a lot of **strain** lately.* **2** [C] a problem or difficulty caused when someone or something has too much to do or too many problems to deal with: *The flu epidemic has **put a strain on** health organizations.* | ***strains in** their marriage* **3** [U] a situation in which something is being pulled, stretched, or pushed: *The rope snapped **under the strain**.* **4** [C,U] an injury caused by stretching a muscle or using part of your body more than you should [➡ **sprain**]: *eye strain* **5** [C] one of the particular varieties of a plant, animal, or living thing: *a new **strain of** the virus* **6 strains** [plural] the sound of music being played: *the familiar **strains of** "Happy Birthday"*

strain² *v.* **1** [T] to injure part of your body by stretching it or using it more than you should: *Kevin strained a muscle in his neck.* **2** [I,T] to try very hard to do something: *She was **straining to** hear what they said.* **3** [T] to cause problems or difficulties for someone or something: *Tuition costs have strained the family's finances.* **4** [T] to separate solid things from a liquid by pouring the mixture through a STRAINER or cloth ➔ see picture on page A4 **5** [I] to pull hard at something or push hard against something: *a boat **straining against** the wind*

strained /streɪnd/ *adj.* **1** unfriendly, not relaxed, and showing a lack of trust: *a strained conversation* **2** worried and tired: *Alex's pale, strained face*

strain·er /ˈstreɪnɚ/ *n.* [C] a kitchen tool used for separating solid food from a liquid

strait /streɪt/ *n.* [C] a narrow passage of water that joins two larger areas of water: *the Strait of Gibraltar*

strait·jack·et, **straightjacket** /ˈstreɪtˌdʒækɪt/ *n.* [C] a special coat for violent or mentally ill people that prevents them from moving their arms

strand /strænd/ *n.* [C] a single thin piece of thread, hair, wire, etc.: *He reached out and brushed a **strand of hair** away from her face.*

strand·ed /ˈstrændɪd/ *adj.* needing help because you are unable to move from a particular place: *I was stranded at the airport without any money.*

strange¹ /streɪndʒ/ *adj.* **1** unusual or surprising, in a way that is difficult to understand [≠ **normal**]: *strange noises* | *It looked kind of strange.* | ***It's strange that** Brad isn't here yet.* | *There was **something strange about** him.*

THESAURUS

funny – a little strange or unusual: *I heard a funny noise downstairs.*
peculiar – strange, unfamiliar, or a little surprising: *a peculiar taste*
mysterious – strange in a way that is hard to explain or understand: *his mysterious disappearance*
odd – strange, especially in a way that you disapprove of or cannot understand: *It seemed like an odd thing to say.*
weird – strange and different from what you are used to: *a weird experience* | *weird clothes*
bizarre – very unusual and strange in a way that is hard to explain or understand: *In a bizarre twist, the judge was later arrested for impersonating a police officer.*
eccentric – an eccentric person is strange and different in a way that people think is slightly amusing: *an eccentric old man*

2 not familiar: *I was all alone in a strange country.* —**strangeness** *n.* [U]

strange² *adv. spoken nonstandard* strangely

strange·ly /ˈstreɪndʒli/ *adv.* in an unusual or surprising way: *Their son was **acting/behaving strangely**.* | *It was strangely quiet.*

strang·er /ˈstreɪndʒɚ/ *n.* [C] **1** someone you do not know: *Never talk to strangers.* | *a phone call from a **total/perfect/complete stranger*** **2** someone in a new and unfamiliar place or situation: *a **stranger to** New York* **3 be no stranger to sth** to have had a lot of experience of something: *an artist who is no stranger to controversy*

stran·gle /ˈstræŋgəl/ *v.* [T] to kill someone by tightly pressing his/her throat with your hands, a rope, etc.: *The victim was found **strangled to death** in her home.* —**strangulation** /ˌstræŋgyəˈleɪʃən/ *n.* [U]

stran·gle·hold /ˈstræŋgəlˌhoʊld/ *n.* [C] the power to completely control something: *Just a few companies have a **stranglehold on** the market.*

strap¹ /stræp/ *n.* [C] a strong band of cloth, leather, or plastic that is used to fasten, hand, or hold onto something: *a watch strap* ➔ see picture at WATCH²

strap² *v.* past tense and past participle **strapped**, present participle **strapping** [T] to fasten someone or something to a place using one or more straps: *Keller strapped on his helmet.*

strap·less /ˈstræplɪs/ *adj.* a strapless dress, BRA, etc. does not have any STRAPS over the shoulders

S

strapped /stræpt/ *adj. informal* having little or no money to spend: *I'm a little **strapped for cash**.*

stra·ta /'stræṭə, 'streɪṭə/ *n.* [C] the plural of STRATUM

strat·a·gem /'stræṭədʒəm/ *n.* [C] a trick or plan used for deceiving an enemy or gaining an advantage

stra·te·gic /strə'tidʒɪk/ *adj.* **1** done as part of a military, business, or political plan: *the strategic position of U.S. armed forces in Europe* **2** useful for a particular purpose, especially fighting a war: *strategic missiles*

strat·e·gy /'stræṭədʒi/ *n.* plural **strategies** **1** [C] a planned series of actions for achieving something: *a **strategy for** raising funds | the company's **marketing/business/development strategy***

THESAURUS

plan, plot, conspiracy, scheme, schedule, timetable
➔ see Thesaurus box at PLAN¹

2 [C,U] the skill of planning the movements of armies in a war, or an example of this: *military strategy*

S

strat·i·fied /'stræṭəˌfaɪd/ *adj.* **1** separated into different social classes: *a stratified society* **2** containing layers of earth, rock, etc. —**stratify** *v.* [T]

strat·o·sphere /'stræṭəˌsfɪr/ *n.* **the stratosphere** the outer layer of air surrounding the earth, starting about six miles above the earth

strat·um /'stræṭəm, 'streɪ-/ *n.* plural **strata** /-ṭə/ [C] **1** a layer of a particular type of rock or dirt **2** a social class in society

straw /strɔ/ *n.* **1** **a)** [U] dried stems of wheat or similar plants, used for animals to eat or sleep on or for making things such as baskets: *a straw hat* **b)** [C] a single stem of this **2** [C] a thin tube of plastic used for sucking a drink from a bottle or cup **3 the last/final straw** the last problem in a series of problems that finally makes you get angry, give up, or refuse to accept the situation any more **4 be grasping/clutching at straws** to be trying everything you can to succeed, even though the things you are doing are not likely to help or work

straw·ber·ry /'strɔˌbɛri/ *n.* plural **strawberries** [C] a soft sweet red berry with small pale seeds on its surface ➔ see picture at FRUIT

stray¹ /streɪ/ *v.* [I] **1** to move away from the place where you should be, especially without intending to: *The plane had **strayed from** its flight plan.* **2** to begin to deal with or think about a different subject from the main one, especially without intending to: *an article that **strays from** the facts*

stray² *adj.* **1** a stray animal is lost or has no home: *We took in a stray dog.* **2** accidentally separated from a larger group: *a few stray hairs*

stray³ *n.* [C] an animal that is lost or has no home

streak¹ /strik/ *n.* [C] **1** a colored line or thin mark: *gray streaks in her hair*

THESAURUS

line, stripe, band
➔ see Thesaurus box at LINE¹

2 a quality you have that seems different from the rest of your character: *a streak of independence* **3** a period of time when you are always successful or always failing: *The Ducks **were on a** four-game **winning/losing streak**.* —**streaky** *adj.*

streak² *v.* **1** [T] to cover something with STREAKS: *Marcia's face was **streaked with** sweat.* **2** [I] to move or run very quickly: *A fighter jet **streaked across** the sky.*

stream¹ /strim/ *n.* [C] **1** a natural flow of water that is smaller than a river: *a clear mountain stream* ➔ see picture at RIVER **2** a long continuous series of people, vehicles, events, etc.: *a **stream of** cars | a **steady/endless/constant stream** of complaints* **3** a flow of water, gas, smoke, etc.: *a **stream of** warm air*

stream² *v.* **1** [I] to move quickly and continuously in one direction, especially in large amounts: *Tears were **streaming down** his cheeks. | People **streamed out of** the theater.* **2** [I] if light streams somewhere, it shines through an opening: *Sunlight **streamed in** through the window.* **3** [T] if you stream sound or video, you play it on your computer while it is being DOWNLOADed from the Internet, rather than saving it as a FILE and then playing it

stream·er /'strimɚ/ *n.* [C] a long narrow flag or piece of colored paper used as a decoration for special events

stream·line /'strimlaɪn/ *v.* [T] **1** to make something such as a business or process become simpler and more effective: *The city has streamlined the permit process.* **2** to make something have a smooth shape so that it moves easily through the air or water —**streamlined** *adj.*

street /strit/ *n.* [C] **1** a road in a town or city with houses, stores, etc. on one or both sides: *Be careful crossing the street. | the building **down/across/up the street***

THESAURUS

road, main street, avenue, lane, main road, highway, freeway, expressway, toll road, turnpike
➔ see Thesaurus box at ROAD

2 the streets the busy public parts of a city, where there is a lot of activity, excitement, and crime: *homeless people living **on the streets***

streetcar

street·car /ˈstritˈkɑr/ *n.* [C] an electric bus that moves along metal tracks in the road

street light, **streetlight** /ˈstrit-laɪt/ *n.* [C] a light on a long pole that stands next to a street

strength /strɛŋkθ, strɛnθ/ *n.*
1 PHYSICAL [U] the physical power and energy that makes someone strong [≠ **weakness**]: *She hardly* ***had the strength to*** *move.*

THESAURUS
force, **power**
→ see Thesaurus box at FORCE[1]

2 DETERMINATION [U] the quality of being brave or determined in dealing with difficult situations: *I wasn't sure I* ***had the strength to*** *go ahead if my parents disapproved.*
3 COUNTRY/SYSTEM ETC. [U] the power of an organization, country, or system: *the* ***military/economic/political strength*** *of the U.S.*
4 FEELING/BELIEF ETC. [U] how strong a feeling, belief, or relationship is: *the* ***strength of*** *her religious beliefs*
5 QUALITY/ABILITY [C] a particular quality or ability that makes someone or something successful and effective: *the* ***strengths of*** *the argument* | *her father's* ***strengths and weaknesses***
6 ALCOHOL/MEDICINE [C,U] how strong a liquid such as an alcoholic drink, medicine, or cleaning liquid is: *a* ***full-strength*** *fabric cleaner*
7 MONEY [U] the value of a particular type of money when compared to other types: *The yen gained in strength against the dollar today.*
8 NUMBER OF PEOPLE [U] the number of people on a team, in an army, etc.: *At* ***full strength****, the squad has 12 men.*
9 on the strength of sth because of something that persuaded or influenced you: *She was hired mainly on the strength of her ability to translate Russian.*

strength·en /ˈstrɛŋkθən, ˈstrɛnθən/ *v.* **1** [I,T] to become stronger, or to make something such as a feeling, belief, or relationship stronger [≠ **weaken**]: *Her determination to succeed has strengthened.* | *Family dinners* ***strengthen*** *your* ***ties/bonds/connections*** *with your children.* **2** [T] to make something such as your body or a building stronger [≠ **weaken**]: *an exercise to strengthen your arms* **3** [I,T] to increase in value or improve, or to make something do this [≠ **weaken**]: *new trade agreements to strengthen the economy*

stren·u·ous /ˈstrɛnyuəs/ *adj.* using a lot of effort, strength, or determination: *strenuous exercise* | *strenuous objections to the plan* —**strenuously** *adv.*

strep throat /ˌstrɛp ˈθroʊt/ *n.* [U] *informal* a fairly common medical condition in which your throat is very sore

stress¹ /strɛs/ *n.* **1** [C,U] continuous feelings of worry about your work or personal life, that prevent you from relaxing: *Baxter's* ***under*** *a lot of* ***stress*** *at work.* **2** [U] special attention or importance given to an idea or activity [= **emphasis**]: *He* ***put/laid stress on*** *the need for more teachers.* **3** [C,U] the physical force or pressure on an object: *rocks subjected to stress* **4** [C,U] the degree of force or loudness with which you say a word or part of a word, or play a note of music

stress² *v.* **1** [T] to emphasize a statement, fact, or idea: *Herman* ***stressed that*** *participation is voluntary.* | *She* ***stressed the need for*** *more health education.*

THESAURUS
emphasize, **highlight**, **underline**, **accentuate**, **underscore**
→ see Thesaurus box at EMPHASIZE

2 [I] *spoken* **also stress out** to feel stressed: *Terry's stressing out about his midterms.* **3** [T] to say a word or part of a word loudly or with more force, or play a note of music more loudly

stressed /strɛst/ **also** **ˌstressed ˈout** *adj. spoken* so worried and tired that you cannot relax: *I was stressed out and exhausted.*

stress·ful /ˈstrɛsfəl/ *adj.* making you worry a lot: *a stressful job*

stretch¹ /strɛtʃ/ *v.* **1** [I,T] **also stretch out** to become bigger or looser as a result of being pulled, or to make something become bigger or looser by pulling it: *My sweater has stretched all out of shape.* **2** [I,T] to reach out your arms, legs, or body to full length: *Maxie got up and stretched.* | *Klein* ***stretched out*** *his hand to Devlin.* → see picture on page A9 **3** [I] to spread out over a large area, or continue for a long period: *The line of people* ***stretched around*** *the corner.* | *The project will probably* ***stretch into*** *next year.* **4** [I] if cloth stretches, it changes shape when you pull or wear it, and becomes its original shape when you stop: *The shorts stretch to fit.* **5** [T] to pull something so it is tight: *Stretch a rope between two trees.* **6 be stretched (to the limit)** to have hardly enough money, supplies, energy, time, etc. to do something: *Our resources are already stretched to the limit.* **7 stretch your legs** *informal* to go for a walk

stretch out *phr. v. informal* to lie down so you can rest or sleep: *He* ***stretched out on*** *the bed.*

S

stretch[2] *n.* **1** [C] an area of water or land: *a dangerous **stretch of** road* **2** [C] a continuous period of time: *Nurses are working up to 12 hours **at a stretch*** (=without stopping). **3** [C] the action of stretching part of your body **4** [U] the ability of a material to become bigger or longer without tearing **5 not by any stretch (of the imagination)** *spoken* used in order to say that something is definitely not true: *She's not fat, by any stretch of the imagination.*

stretch·er /ˈstrɛtʃɚ/ *n.* [C] a covered frame on which you carry someone who is injured or too sick to walk

strew /stru/ *v.* past participle **strewn** /strun/ or **strewed** [T] to throw or drop a number of things over an area in a messy way: *Papers were **strewn all over** the floor.*

strick·en /ˈstrɪkən/ *adj.* *formal* very badly affected by trouble, illness, sadness, etc.: *a woman **stricken by** grief* ➔ POVERTY-STRICKEN

strict /strɪkt/ *adj.* **1** expecting people to obey rules or do what you say: *Her parents are very strict.* **2** a strict rule, order, etc. must be obeyed: *Gun regulations aren't strict enough.* | *a school with **strict rules/limits/controls*** **3** very exact and correct: *He practices Chinese medicine, so is not a doctor **in the strict sense**.*

S

strict·ly /ˈstrɪktli/ *adv.* **1** in a way that must be obeyed: *Smoking is **strictly forbidden**.* **2** exactly and correctly: *That is not strictly true.* | ***Strictly speaking**, spiders are not insects.* **3** used in order to emphasize what you are saying: *The drug treatment program is strictly voluntary.* **4** only for a particular purpose, thing, or person: *These bowls are **strictly for** decoration.*

stride[1] /straɪd/ *v.* past tense **strode** /stroʊd/ past participle **stridden** /ˈstrɪdn/ present participle **striding** [I] to walk with quick long steps: *He **strode across** the room.*

> **THESAURUS**
>
> **walk**, **march**, **stroll**, **amble**, **wander**, **creep**, **sneak**, **trudge**, **limp**, **wade**, **hike**
> ➔ see Thesaurus box at WALK[1]

stride[2] *n.* [C] **1** a long step that you make when you walk **2 make (great) strides** to develop or make progress quickly: *Doctors have **made great strides in** treating this type of injury.* **3 take sth in stride** to deal with a problem calmly without becoming annoyed or upset: *Most children take this type of teasing in stride.*

stri·dent /ˈstraɪdnt/ *adj.* **1** showing determination and a strong opinion in a way that other people may think is unpleasant: *strident attacks on his opponent* **2** a sound that is strident is loud and unpleasant: *her strident voice*

strife /straɪf/ *n.* [U] *formal* trouble or disagreement between two people or groups [= **conflict**]: *a period of **ethnic/political/marital strife***

strike[1] /straɪk/ *v.* past tense and past participle **struck** /strʌk/

1 HIT [T] *formal* to hit someone or something: *Paul fell, striking his head.* | *three soldiers struck by shrapnel* | *She struck him across the face.*

> **THESAURUS**
>
> **hit**, **punch**, **slap**, **beat**, **smack**, **whack**, **bang**, **knock**, **tap**, **pound**, **rap**, **hammer**
> ➔ see Thesaurus box at HIT[1]

2 THOUGHT/IDEA [T] if a thought or idea strikes you, you suddenly realize it, notice it, or think of it: *It **struck** me **that** he was probably nervous as well.*

3 strike sb as sth to seem to someone to have a particular quality: *She strikes me as a very intelligent woman.*

4 WORK [I] to deliberately stop working for a time because of a disagreement about pay, working conditions, etc.: *The dock workers are **striking for** shorter work days.*

5 ATTACK/CRITICIZE [I] to attack or criticize someone quickly and suddenly: *Police fear the killer will strike again.*

6 strike a balance to give the correct amount of attention or importance to two opposing ideas or situations: *It's never easy to **strike a balance between** work and family.*

7 STH UNPLEASANT [I] if something bad strikes, it happens suddenly: *A magnitude 7 earthquake struck near San Francisco.*

8 strike a deal to agree to do something if someone else does something for you: *The company finally struck a deal with the union.*

9 strike a chord to make someone feel that s/he agrees with, likes, or is similar to someone or something: *This idea has struck a chord with voters.*

10 strike a match to make a match burn

11 strike oil/gold etc. to discover oil, gold, etc. in the ground

12 CLOCK [I,T] if a clock strikes or strikes one, three, six, etc., its bell makes a sound one, three, six, etc. times to show what time it is: *The clock **struck four*** (=4 o'clock).

strike sth ⇔ **down** *phr. v.* to say that a law or formal decision is no longer legal or officially accepted: *The Supreme Court struck down a law against flag burning.*

strike out *phr. v.* **1 strike** (sb ⇔) **out** to get three STRIKES in baseball so that you are not allowed to continue to try to hit, or to make someone do this: *The first batter was struck out.* **2** to start a difficult trip or experience: *They struck out for a better life in America.* **3 strike out on your own** to start doing something or living independently **4** *informal* to be unsuccessful at something: *"Did she say she'd go out with you?" "No, I struck out."*

strike up *phr. v.* **1 strike up a conversation/friendship etc.** to start a conversation, friendship, etc. with someone **2 strike up (sth)** to begin to play or sing something: *The band struck up an Irish tune.*

strike² *n.* [C] **1** a time when a group of workers STRIKE: *The union decided to **go on strike**.* **2** a military attack: *threats of an **air strike*** **3 two/three etc. strikes against** a condition, situation, or quality that makes it extremely difficult for someone or something to be successful: *Children from poor backgrounds have several strikes against them before even starting school.* **4** in baseball, an attempt to hit the ball that fails, or a ball that is thrown toward the hitter within the correct area, but is not hit

strik·er /ˈstraɪkɚ/ *n.* [C] someone who is not working because s/he is on STRIKE

strik·ing /ˈstraɪkɪŋ/ *adj.* **1** unusual or interesting enough to be noticed: *a **striking similarity/difference** between the two girls*

THESAURUS

noticeable, clear, obvious, conspicuous, eye-catching
➔ see Thesaurus box at NOTICEABLE

2 very attractive, often in an unusual way: *a man with a striking face*

string¹ /strɪŋ/ *n.* **1** [C,U] a strong thread made of several threads twisted together, used for tying things: *We tied a string around the box.* | *a short **piece of string*** **2** [C] a number of similar things or events that happen one after the other: ***a string of** arrests for drug offenses* **3 (no) strings attached** having no special conditions or limits on an agreement, relationship, etc., or having conditions or limits: *the strings attached to the grant* **4 first/second/third string** relating to or being a member of a team or group with the highest, second highest, etc. level of skill: *the second string quarterback* **5 a string of pearls/beads etc.** a lot of PEARLS, BEADS etc. on a string **6** [C] one of the long thin pieces of wire that is stretched across a musical instrument to produce sound **7 the strings** the people in an ORCHESTRA who play instruments such as the VIOLIN, CELLO, etc. ➔ **control/hold the purse strings** at PURSE¹ ➔ **pull strings** at PULL¹ ➔ **pull the strings** at PULL¹

string² *v.* past tense and past participle **strung** /strʌŋ/ [T] **1** to put things together onto a string, chain, etc.: *Girls were stringing beads to make necklaces.* **2** to hang a wire or string in the air, or hang things on a wire or string, especially for decoration: *a clothesline strung between two posts*

string sb **along** *phr. v. informal* to continue to promise to do something that you do not intend to do, especially in relationships: *Jerry's been stringing her along for years.*

string sth ⇔ **together** *phr. v.* to combine things in order to make something: *words strung together into sentences*

ˌstring ˈbean *n.* [C] ➔ GREEN BEAN

strin·gent /ˈstrɪndʒənt/ *adj.* stringent rules, laws, etc. strictly control something

string·y /ˈstrɪŋi/ *adj.* **1** food that is stringy has long thin pieces in it that are difficult to eat **2** stringy hair looks like string because it is dirty

strip¹ /strɪp/ *v.* past tense and past participle **stripped**, present participle **stripping** **1** [I,T] **also strip off** to take off your clothes, or take off someone else's clothes: *He stripped and got into the shower.* | *I **stripped off** her snowsuit.* **2** [T] to remove something that is covering the surface of something else: ***Strip off** the old wallpaper.*

strip sb **of** sth *phr. v.* to take away something important from someone such as his/her possessions, rank, or property: *The doctor was found guilty and stripped of his medical license.*

strip² *n.* [C] **1** a long narrow piece of cloth, paper, etc.: *Tear the paper into one-inch strips.* **2** a long narrow area of land: *a strip of sand*

stripe /straɪp/ *n.* [C] a long narrow line of color: *a shirt with blue and red stripes*

THESAURUS

line, streak, band
➔ see Thesaurus box at LINE¹

striped /straɪpt, ˈstraɪpɪd/ *adj.* having a pattern of stripes: *a blue and white striped shirt*

ˈstrip mall *n.* [C] a row of small stores built together, with an area for parking cars in front of it

strip·per /ˈstrɪpɚ/ *n.* [C] someone whose job is to perform by taking off his/her clothes in a sexually exciting way

strip·tease /ˈstrɪptiz/ *n.* [C,U] the dance that a stripper does

strive /straɪv/ *v.* past tense **strove** /stroʊv/ or **strived**, past participle **striven** /ˈstrɪvən/ or **strived**, present participle **striving** [I] *formal* to try very hard to get or do something: *teachers who are **striving to** meet the needs of their students*

strode /stroʊd/ *v.* the past tense of STRIDE

stroke¹ /stroʊk/ *n.* [C] **1** a sudden illness in which an ARTERY (=tube carrying blood) in your brain bursts or becomes blocked: *Since Tom **had a stroke** he's had trouble talking.* **2** a repeated movement of your arms in a sport such as swimming, or a particular style of swimming or rowing: *the back stroke* **3** an action done to achieve something: *The change is a **bold stroke** on the mayor's part.* | *Getting those two to work together was a **stroke of genius**.* | *He managed to improve his election chances **at a stroke*** (=with one sudden action). **4 stroke of luck** something lucky that happens to you **5** a single movement of a pen or brush, or a line made by doing this: *With **a stroke of the pen**, the deal was finalized.*

stroke² *v.* [T] to move your hand gently over something: *She stroked the baby's face.* ➔ see picture on page A8

S

THESAURUS

touch, **feel**, **rub**, **scratch**, **pat**, **brush**, **caress**, **fondle**, **tickle**, **grope**
→ see Thesaurus box at TOUCH[1]

stroll /stroʊl/ *v.* [I] to walk in a slow relaxed way: *We **strolled along** the beach.* —**stroll** *n.* [C] *We went for a stroll after dinner.*

THESAURUS

march, **stride**, **amble**, **wander**, **creep**, **sneak**, **trudge**, **limp**, **wade**, **hike**
→ see Thesaurus box at WALK[1]

stroll·er /ˈstroʊlɚ/ *n.* [C] a chair on wheels in which a small child sits and is pushed along: *a **baby stroller*** → see Topic box at BABY

strong /strɔŋ/ *adj.*
1 PHYSICAL having a lot of physical power: *He was small but strong.* | *the strongest muscles in your body*
2 NOT EASILY BROKEN not easily broken or damaged: *a strong rope* | *The door was solid and strong.*
3 POWER having a lot of power, influence, or ability: *a strong leader* | *a strong army*

THESAURUS

powerful, **influential**, **dominant**
→ see Thesaurus box at POWERFUL

4 FEELINGS strong feelings, ideas, etc. are ones that are very important to you: *a strong interest in art* | *a strong sense of duty*
5 ARGUMENT a strong reason, opinion, etc. is one that is likely to persuade other people: *There's strong evidence to suggest that he's innocent.*
6 ABLE TO DEAL WITH DIFFICULTY determined and able to deal with problems without becoming upset or worried by them: *Do you think she's strong enough to handle this?* | *a strong character*
7 GOOD AT STH good at something: *a strong team* | *Jarvis's performance was very strong.*
8 LIKELY likely to succeed or happen: *He has a strong chance of winning in Florida.*
9 AFFECT having a large affect or influence: *a strong desire* | *He made a strong impression on me.*
10 TASTE/SMELL having a taste, smell, color, etc. that is easy to notice: *strong coffee*
11 RELATIONSHIP a strong relationship or friendship is likely to last a long time: *a strong bond between the two brothers*
12 50/1000/75,000 etc. strong used in order to give the number of people in a group: *Our staff is over a thousand strong.*

strong·hold /ˈstrɔŋhoʊld/ *n.* [C] **1** an area where there is a lot of support for a particular attitude, way of life, political party, etc.: *a Republican stronghold* **2** an area that is strongly defended: *a rebel stronghold*

strong·ly /ˈstrɔŋli/ *adv.* **1** if you feel or believe something strongly, you are very sure and serious about it: *I **feel strongly** that medical records should be private.* | *She is **strongly opposed** to abortion.* **2** in a way that persuades someone to do something: *I **strongly urge/advise/encourage** you **to** get more facts before deciding.* **3** in a way that is easy to notice: *The house smelled strongly of gas.*

ˌstrong-ˈwilled *adj.* having a lot of determination to do what you want [= **stubborn**]: *a strong-willed child*

strove /stroʊv/ *v.* the past tense of STRIVE

struck /strʌk/ *v.* the past tense and past participle of STRIKE

struc·tur·al /ˈstrʌktʃərəl/ *adj.* relating to the structure of something: *structural damage to the aircraft*

struc·ture[1] /ˈstrʌktʃɚ/ *n.* **1** [C,U] the way in which the parts of something connect with each other to form a whole, or the thing that these parts make up: *Children need a stable family structure to feel secure.* | *chemical structure* | *the city's **political/social structure*** **2** [C] something that has been built: *a huge steel structure*

structure[2] *v.* [T] to arrange something carefully in an organized way: *a **loosely/carefully/highly structured** novel*

strug·gle[1] /ˈstrʌgəl/ *v.* [I] **1** to try very hard to do or achieve something, even though it is difficult: *We're **struggling to** pay the bills.* **2** to fight someone who is attacking you or holding you: *She **struggled with** him, pushing him away.* **3** to move somewhere with a lot of difficulty: *He struggled up the stairs with the luggage.*

struggle[2] *n.* [C] **1** a long hard fight for freedom, political rights, etc.: *a **struggle for** equality* | *a **power struggle***

THESAURUS

fight, **battle**, **campaign**
→ see Thesaurus box at FIGHT[2]

2 a fight or argument between two people for something: *a long **struggle with** Congress over the budget*

strum /strʌm/ *v.* past tense and past participle **strummed**, present participle **strumming** [I,T] to play an instrument such as a GUITAR by moving your fingers across the strings

strung /strʌŋ/ *v.* the past tense and past participle of STRING

strut[1] /strʌt/ *v.* past tense and past participle **strutted**, present participle **strutting** [I] **1** to walk in a proud way with your head up and your chest pushed forward: *boys strutting down the street* **2 strut your stuff** *informal* to show proudly what you can do, especially in a performance

strut[2] *n.* [C] a long thin piece of metal or wood used for supporting a part of a bridge, the wing of an aircraft, etc.

stub[1] /stʌb/ *n.* [C] **1** the short part of something that is left after the rest has been used: *a pencil stub* **2** the part of a ticket that is returned to you as proof that you have paid: *a **ticket stub***

stub[2] *v.* past tense and past participle **stubbed**, present participle **stubbing** [T] **stub your toe** to hurt your toe by hitting it against something
stub sth ⇔ **out** *phr. v.* to stop a cigarette from burning by pressing the end of it against something

stub·ble /ˈstʌbəl/ *n.* [U] the very short stiff hairs on a man's face when he has not SHAVED —**stubbly** *adj.* → see picture at CLEAN-SHAVEN

stub·born /ˈstʌbərn/ *adj.* determined not to change your opinions, beliefs, etc., because you believe you are right: *a stubborn woman* | *his stubborn refusal to cooperate*

stub·by /ˈstʌbi/ *adj.* short and thick or fat: *his stubby fingers*

stuc·co /ˈstʌkoʊ/ *n.* [U] a CEMENT mixture used especially for covering the outside walls of houses

stuck[1] /stʌk/ *v.* the past tense and past participle of STICK

stuck[2] *adj.* **1** not able to move: *I tried to open the window, but it was stuck.* | *We **got stuck** in traffic.* **2** not able to continue working on something because it is too difficult: *Can you help me with this? I'm stuck.* **3** not able to get away from a boring or unpleasant situation: *I'm stuck at home all day with the kids.*

ˌstuck-ˈup *adj. informal* proud and unfriendly because you think you are better than other people

stud /stʌd/ *n.* **1** [C,U] an animal such as a horse that is kept for breeding: *a stud farm* **2** [C] a small round EARRING **3** [C] *slang* a man who is very active sexually **4** [C] a small round piece of metal that is put on a surface for decoration: *a leather jacket with silver studs*

stud·ded /ˈstʌdɪd/ *adj.* decorated with a lot of STUDS or jewels: *a bracelet **studded with** diamonds* → STAR-STUDDED

stu·dent /ˈstudnt/ *n.* [C] **1** someone who is studying at a school, university, etc.: *She has 30 students in her class.* | *Sally's an **A/B/C student*** (=she earns A's, etc.). | *a first-year **law/medical student*** **2 a student of sth** someone who is very interested in a particular subject: *He's obviously an excellent student of human nature.*

ˌstudent ˈbody *n.* [C] all the students in a school, university, etc.

stud·ied /ˈstʌdid/ *adj.* studied behavior is deliberate and intended to have a particular effect on other people: *She spoke with a studied politeness.*

stu·di·o /ˈstudiˌoʊ/ *n.* [C] **1** a room where television and radio programs are made and broadcast, or where music is recorded: *a **recording studio** in Nashville* | *a studio audience* **2** a movie company or the place where movies are made: *the big Hollywood studios* **3** a room where a painter or photographer works: *an art studio* **4 also studio apartment** a small apartment with one main room

stu·di·ous /ˈstudiəs/ *adj.* spending a lot of time reading and studying

stud·y[1] /ˈstʌdi/ *n.* plural **studies** **1** [C] a piece of work that is done to find out more about a particular subject or problem, and that is usually written in a report: *Several **studies showed** the drug can cause birth defects.* | *a **study on/of** 100 patients* **2** [U] the process of learning about a subject: *the **study of** ancient history* | *ways to improve your **study skills/habits*** **3** [C] a room in a house that is used for work or study **4 studies** [plural] the work you do in order to learn about something: *She began graduate studies at Berkeley.*

TOPIC

education, **university**, **college**, **lecture**, **class**, **seminar**
→ see Topic box at UNIVERSITY

study[2] *v.* past tense and past participle **studied**, third person singular **studies** **1** [I,T] to spend time going to classes, reading, etc. to learn about a subject: *I need to **study for** a midterm.* | *She **studied at** Harvard.* | *I'm **studying English/psychology/medicine etc.*** → see Topic box at SCHOOL[1] **2** [T] to examine something carefully to find out more about it: *An accounting firm is studying the problem.* | *Dr. Brock is **studying how** the disease affects children.*

stuff[1] /stʌf/ *n.* [U] *informal* **1** a substance or material of any sort: *What's this stuff on the floor?* **2** a number of different things: *I've got to pack my stuff.* | *She brought me some books **and stuff*** (=other things). **3 sb's stuff** things that belong to someone: *You can put your stuff over here for now.*

THESAURUS

property, **possessions**, **things**, **belongings**
→ see Thesaurus box at PROPERTY

4 all the activities that someone does: *I have a lot of stuff to do.* | *He likes biking and skateboarding and **stuff like that**.* **5** different subjects, information, or ideas: *a magazine with a lot of interesting stuff in it*

stuff[2] *v.* [T] **1** to push things into a small space quickly: *He **stuffed** some clothes **into** a bag and left.* **2** to fill something until it is full: *a pillow **stuffed with** feathers* | *Campaign workers stuffed envelopes.* **3** to fill a chicken, vegetable, etc. with a mixture of bread, rice, etc. before cooking it **4** to fill the skin of a dead animal in order to make the animal look alive

stuffed /stʌft/ *adj.* **1** [not before noun] *informal* completely full, so that you cannot eat any more: *The cake looks great, but I'm stuffed.* **2 stuffed animal/toy/bear etc.** a toy animal covered and filled with soft material

ˌstuffed-ˈup *adj. informal* unable to breathe because you have a cold

stuff·ing /ˈstʌfɪŋ/ *n.* [U] **1** a mixture of bread, rice, etc. that you put inside a chicken, vegetable, etc. before cooking it **2** material that is used for filling something such as a PILLOW

stuff·y /ˈstʌfi/ *adj.* **1** not having enough fresh air: *The room was hot and stuffy.* **2** boring, formal, and old-fashioned: *stuffy lawyers*

stum·ble /ˈstʌmbəl/ *v.* [I] **1** to almost fall down while you are walking: *Scott* ***stumbled over/on*** *the step.*

> **THESAURUS**
> **fall**, **trip**, **slip**, **lose your balance**
> ➔ see Thesaurus box at FALL[1]

2 to stop or make a mistake when you are reading or speaking to people: *He* ***stumbled over*** *the words as he read his speech.*

stumble on/across/upon sth *phr. v.* to discover something or meet someone by chance: *Hubbard stumbled across the notebooks in a yard sale.*

ˈstumbling ˌblock *n.* [C] a problem that prevents you from achieving something: *the main* ***stumbling block to*** *passage of the new law*

stump¹ /stʌmp/ *n.* **1** [C] the part of a tree that remains in the ground after the rest has been cut down **2** [C] the part of an arm, leg, etc. that remains when the rest has been cut off **3** [singular] a place or occasion when a politician makes a speech to try to gain political support: ***On the stump****, he talked a lot about health care.*

stump² *v.* [T] if you are stumped by a question or problem, you are unable to find an answer to it: *It's a question that has stumped everyone.* | *I* ***was*** *completely* ***stumped****.*

stun /stʌn/ *v.* past tense and past participle **stunned**, present participle **stunning** [T] **1** to surprise or shock someone so much that s/he does not react: *There was a stunned silence.* **2** to make someone unconscious for a short time by hitting him/her on the head

stung /stʌŋ/ *v.* the past tense and past participle of STING

stunk /stʌŋk/ *v.* the past tense and past participle of STINK

stun·ning /ˈstʌnɪŋ/ *adj.* **1** extremely attractive or beautiful: *You look stunning in that dress.*

> **THESAURUS**
> **attractive**, **good-looking**, **pretty**, **beautiful**, **handsome**, **gorgeous**, **nice-looking**, **cute**, **hot**
> ➔ see Thesaurus box at ATTRACTIVE

2 very surprising or shocking: *stunning news*

> **THESAURUS**
> **surprising**, **extraordinary**, **amazing**, **shocking**, **astonishing**, **astounding**, **staggering**
> ➔ see Thesaurus box at SURPRISING

stunt¹ /stʌnt/ *n.* [C] **1** something that is done to attract people's attention: *a* ***publicity stunt*** **2** a dangerous action that is done to entertain people, usually in a movie **3 pull a stunt** to do something that is silly or that is slightly dangerous: *Don't ever pull a stunt like that again!*

stunt² *v.* [T] to stop someone or something from growing or developing correctly: *Lack of food has* ***stunted*** *their* ***growth****.*

stuntman

ˈstunt man *n.* [C] a man or woman whose job is to take the place of an actor when something dangerous has to be done in a movie

stu·pe·fied /ˈstupəˌfaɪd/ *adj.* so surprised or bored that you cannot think clearly —**stupefy** *v.* [T]

stu·pe·fy·ing /ˈstupəˌfaɪ-ɪŋ/ *adj.* making you feel extremely surprised or bored

stu·pen·dous /stuˈpɛndəs/ *adj.* extremely large or impressive: *a stupendous achievement*

stu·pid /ˈstupɪd/ *adj.* **1** showing bad judgment or a lack of intelligence: *How could you be so stupid?* | *a stupid question* | *It was* ***stupid of*** *me* ***to*** *listen to him.* **2** *spoken* used when talking about something or someone that annoys you: *I can't get this stupid door open!* —**stupidity** /stuˈpɪdət̬i/ *n.* [C,U]

stu·por /ˈstupɚ/ *n.* [C,U] a state in which you cannot think, see, etc. clearly: *We found him in a* ***drunken stupor****.*

stur·dy /ˈstɚdi/ *adj.* comparative **sturdier**, superlative **sturdiest** strong and not likely to break or be hurt: *sturdy walking shoes*

stut·ter /ˈstʌt̬ɚ/ *v.* [I,T] to speak with difficulty because you repeat the first sound of a word [➡ **stammer**] —**stutter** *n.* [singular]

style¹ /staɪl/ *n.* **1** [C,U] a way of doing, making, painting, etc. something that is typical of a particular period of time, place, or group of people: *He's trying to copy Van Gogh's* ***style of*** *painting.* | *architecture in the Gothic style* **2** [C] the particular way that someone behaves, works, or deals with other people: *Carolyn has an informal* ***style of*** *teaching.* | *Yelling at her students is* ***not*** *her* ***style*** (=is not the way she usually behaves). | *I don't like loud parties – a quiet night at home is* ***more*** *my* ***style*** (=I prefer quiet nights at home).

3 [C,U] a particular design or fashion for something such as clothes, hair, furniture, etc.: *They have over two hundred* ***styles of*** *wallpaper to choose from.* | *Long hair is* ***in style/out of style*** (=fashionable or not fashionable). **4** [U] the particular way you do things that makes people admire you: *You may not like him, but you have to admit that he* ***has style.*** | *an actor* ***with style***

style² *v.* [T] to cut someone's hair in a particular way

styl·ish /ˈstaɪlɪʃ/ *adj.* attractive in a fashionable way: *a very stylish woman* | *stylish clothes*

THESAURUS

fashionable, trendy, designer
➔ see Thesaurus box at FASHIONABLE

sty·lis·tic /staɪˈlɪstɪk/ *adj.* relating to the style of a piece of writing or art: *I've made a few stylistic changes to your report.*

styl·ized /ˈstaɪəˌlaɪzd/ *adj.* done in an artificial style that is not natural or like real life

sty·mie /ˈstaɪmi/ *v.* [T] *informal* to prevent someone from doing what s/he has planned or wants to do: *The police investigation has been stymied by a lack of witnesses.*

suave /swɑv/ *adj.* attractive, confident, and relaxed, but often in a way that is not sincere

sub /sʌb/ *n.* [C] **1** *informal* a SUBMARINE **2** *informal* a SUBSTITUTE **3** a large long SANDWICH

sub·com·mit·tee /ˈsʌbkəˌmɪt̬i/ *n.* [C] a small group formed from a committee to deal with a particular subject in more detail

sub·con·scious /ˌsʌbˈkɑnʃəs/ *adj.* subconscious thoughts and feelings are in your mind and affect your behavior, but you do not realize that they exist —**subconscious** *adj.* —**subconsciously** *adv.*

sub·con·ti·nent /sʌbˈkɑntˀn-ənt, -tənənt/ *n.* [C] a large area of land that forms part of a CONTINENT

sub·cul·ture /ˈsʌbˌkʌltʃɚ/ *n.* [C] a particular group of people in a society whose behavior, beliefs, activities, etc. make them different from the rest of the society: *the drug subculture*

sub·di·vide /ˌsʌbdəˈvaɪd, ˈsʌbdəˌvaɪd/ *v.* [T] to divide into smaller parts something that is already divided

sub·di·vi·sion /ˈsʌbdəˌvɪʒən/ *n.* [C] an area of land for building a number of houses on, or these houses once they are built

sub·due /səbˈdu/ *v.* [T] to control someone, especially by using force: *The nurses were trying to subdue a violent patient.*

sub·dued /səbˈdud/ *adj.* **1** a person or sound that is subdued is unusually quiet: *Jason looked subdued after talking to the principal.*

THESAURUS

quiet, low, soft, muffled, hushed
➔ see Thesaurus box at QUIET¹

2 subdued colors, lights, etc. are less bright than usual

sub·ject¹ /ˈsʌbdʒɪkt/ *n.* [C] **1** the thing you are talking about or considering in a conversation, discussion, book, movie, etc.: *Bashkiroff is the* ***subject of*** *the book, "For Sasha, With Love."* | *While we're* ***on the subject of*** *money, do you have the $10 you owe me?* | *Stop trying to* ***change the subject*** (=talk about something else)*!* | *A member of the audience* ***raised the subject*** (=started talking about it) *of the president's age.* **2** something that you study at a school or university: *"What's your favorite subject?" "Science."* ➔ see Topic box at UNIVERSITY **3** *technical* in grammar, a noun, noun phrase, or PRONOUN that usually comes before the verb in a sentence, and represents the person or thing that does the action of the verb. In the sentence "Jean loves her cats," "Jean" is the subject. [➡ **object**] **4 subject matter** the subject that is being discussed in a book, shown in a movie or play, etc. **5** a person or animal that is used in a test or EXPERIMENT: *All the subjects were men between the ages of 18 and 25.* **6** the thing or person that is shown in a painting or photograph: *Degas frequently used dancers as his subjects.* **7** *formal* someone who is from a country that has a king or queen

subject² *adj.* **be subject to sth** **a)** to be likely to be affected by something: *All prices are* ***subject to change.*** **b)** to be dependent on something: *The deal is subject to approval by the bank.* **c)** if you are subject to a law, you must obey it: *Congress is subject to the same laws as everyone else.*

sub·ject³ /səbˈdʒɛkt/ *v.*

subject sb/sth **to** sth *phr. v. formal* to force someone or something to experience something very bad, upsetting, or difficult: *He subjected his victims to extreme torture.*

sub·jec·tive /səbˈdʒɛktɪv/ *adj.* a statement, attitude, etc. that is subjective is influenced by personal opinion or feelings rather than facts [≠ **objective**]

sub·ju·gate /ˈsʌbdʒəˌgeɪt/ *v.* [T] *formal* to force a person or group to obey you —**subjugation** /ˌsʌbdʒəˈgeɪʃən/ *n.* [U]

sub·junc·tive /səbˈdʒʌŋktɪv/ *n.* [C] *technical* in grammar, a verb form used in order to express doubt, wishes, or possibility. For example, in "If I were you," the verb "to be" is in the subjunctive.

sub·let /sʌbˈlɛt, ˈsʌblɛt/ *v.* past tense and past participle **sublet**, present participle **subletting** [I,T] to rent to someone else a property that you rent from its owner: *I'm subletting the room for the summer.* —**sublet** /ˈsʌblɛt/ *n.* [C]

sub·lime /səˈblaɪm/ *adj.* excellent in a way that makes you feel very happy

sub·lim·i·nal /sʌbˈlɪmənl/ *adj.* subliminal messages, suggestions, etc. affect the way you think without you noticing it

sub·ma·rine /ˈsʌbməˌrin, ˌsʌbməˈrin/ *n.* [C] a ship that can stay under water

THESAURUS

ship, **cruise ship**, **liner**, **ferry**, **freighter**, **tanker**, **barge**, **aircraft carrier**, **battleship**, **cruiser**, **warship**
→ see Thesaurus box at SHIP[1]

sub·merge /səbˈmɚdʒ/ *v.* [I,T] to go or put something under the surface of water: *Many cars were submerged by the flood.* —**submerged** *adj.*: *partially submerged houses* —**submersion** /səbˈmɚʒən/ *n.* [U]

sub·mis·sion /səbˈmɪʃən/ *n.* **1** [U] the state of being controlled by a powerful person or organization and accepting that you must obey him, her, or it: *The prisoners were starved* ***into submission***. **2** [C,U] the act of giving a piece of writing to someone so s/he can consider or approve it, or the piece of writing itself: *All submissions must be received by the 15th of March.*

sub·mis·sive /səbˈmɪsɪv/ *adj.* always willing to obey someone and never disagreeing with him/her: *a submissive wife*

sub·mit /səbˈmɪt/ *v.* past tense and past participle **submitted**, present participle **submitting** **1** [T] to give a plan, piece of writing, etc. to someone in authority so that s/he can consider or approve it: *I* ***submitted*** *my plan* ***to*** *the committee yesterday.* **2** [I,T] *formal* to obey someone who has power over you, especially because you have no choice: *We refused to* ***submit to*** *the kidnapper's demands.*

sub·or·di·nate[1] /səˈbɔrdənɪt/ *n.* [C] *formal* someone who has a lower position or less authority than someone else

subordinate[2] *adj.* *formal* less important than something else, or lower in rank or authority: *a subordinate position*

sub·or·di·nate[3] /səˈbɔrdnˌeɪt/ *v.* [T] to put someone or something in a less important job or position —**subordination** /səˌbɔrdnˈeɪʃən/ *n.* [U]

sub·poe·na /səˈpinə/ *n.* [C] *law* a legal document ordering someone to come to a court of law and be a witness —**subpoena** *v.* [T]

sub·scribe /səbˈskraɪb/ *v.* [I] to pay money regularly to have a newspaper or magazine sent to you, or for a particular service: *What magazines do you* ***subscribe to****? | households that subscribe to cable TV* —**subscriber** *n.*

subscribe to sth *phr. v.* to agree with or support an idea, opinion, etc.: *They obviously don't subscribe to his theory.*

sub·scrip·tion /səbˈskrɪpʃən/ *n.* [C] an amount of money that you pay regularly to have copies of a newspaper or magazine sent to you, or to receive a particular service

sub·se·quent /ˈsʌbsəkwənt/ *adj.* [only before noun] *formal* coming after or following something else: *Subsequent investigations did not uncover any new evidence.* —**subsequently** *adv.*: *The charges against him were subsequently dropped.*

THESAURUS

next, **following**, **succeeding**, **later**
→ see Thesaurus box at NEXT[1]

sub·ser·vi·ent /səbˈsɚviənt/ *adj.* *disapproving* too willing to do what other people want you to do —**subservience** *n.* [U]

sub·side /səbˈsaɪd/ *v.* [I] to become less strong or loud: *The storm subsided around dawn.*

sub·sid·i·ar·y[1] /səbˈsɪdiˌɛri/ *n.* plural **subsidiaries** [C] a company that is owned or controlled by another larger company

THESAURUS

company, **firm**, **business**, **corporation**, **multinational**
→ see Thesaurus box at COMPANY

subsidiary[2] *adj.* related to, but less important than something else: *He played a subsidiary role in the negotiations.*

sub·si·dize /ˈsʌbsəˌdaɪz/ *v.* [T] to pay part of the cost of something: *housing that is subsidized by the government* —**subsidized** *adj.*: *subsidized health care*

sub·si·dy /ˈsʌbsədi/ *n.* plural **subsidies** [C] money that is paid by a government or organization in order to reduce the cost of something: ***government subsidies*** *for small farmers*

sub·sist /səbˈsɪst/ *v.* [I] to stay alive when you only have small amounts of food or money: *The prisoners* ***subsisted on*** *rice and water.* —**subsistence** *n.* [U] *subsistence farming*

sub·stance /ˈsʌbstəns/ *n.* **1** [C] a particular type of solid, liquid, or gas: *The bag was covered with a sticky substance. | a poisonous/hazardous/toxic substance |* ***illegal substances*** (=drugs) **2** [singular, U] the most important ideas in a document, speech, report, etc.: *The news report said little about the* ***substance of*** *the peace talks.* **3** [U] *formal* if something has substance, it is true: *There's* ***no substance to*** *his arguments.*

ˈsubstance aˌbuse *n.* [U] *technical* the habit of taking too many illegal drugs so that you are harmed by them

sub·stand·ard /ˌsʌbˈstændɚd◂/ *adj.* not as good as the average, and not acceptable: *substandard health care*

sub·stan·tial /səbˈstænʃəl/ *adj.* **1** large in amount or number: *She earns a substantial income. | substantial evidence*

THESAURUS

big, **large**, **huge**, **enormous**, **vast**, **gigantic**, **massive**, **immense**, **colossal**
→ see Thesaurus box at BIG

2 large and strongly made: *a substantial piece of furniture*

sub·stan·tial·ly /səbˈstænʃəli/ *adv.* very much: *Prices have increased substantially.*

S

sub·stan·ti·ate /səbˈstænʃiˌeɪt/ *v.* [T] *formal* to prove the truth of something that someone has said: *The evidence failed to substantiate his claims.*

sub·sti·tute¹ /ˈsʌbstəˌtut/ *n.* [C] **1** someone who does someone else's job for a limited period of time: *a **substitute teacher*** **2** something new or different that you use or do instead of what you used or did before: *a sugar substitute* | *There is **no substitute for*** (=nothing better than) *a good diet.*

substitute² *v.* **1** [T] to use something new or different instead of something else: *You can **substitute** margarine **for** butter in this recipe.* **2** [I,T] to do someone's job for a short time until s/he is able to do it again —**substitution** /ˌsʌbstəˈtuʃən/ *n.* [C,U]

sub·ter·fuge /ˈsʌbtɚˌfyudʒ/ *n.* [C,U] *formal* a trick or dishonest way of doing something, or the use of this

sub·ter·ra·ne·an /ˌsʌbtəˈreɪniən/ *adj. technical* under the surface of the earth: *a subterranean lake*

sub·ti·tles /ˈsʌbˌtaɪṭlz/ *n.* [plural] words that translate what the actors in a foreign movie are saying, that appear on the bottom of the screen —**subtitled** *adj.*

sub·tle /ˈsʌṭl/ *adj.* **1** not easily noticed unless you pay careful attention: *She noticed some subtle changes in his personality.* **2** subtle smells, colors, etc. are pleasant because they are not too strong: *the subtle scent of mint in the air* **3** behaving in a skillful and intelligent way, especially in order to hide what you are trying to do: *I think we need a more subtle approach.* —**subtly** /ˈsʌṭl-i, ˈsʌtli/ *adv.*

sub·tle·ty /ˈsʌṭlti/ *n.* plural **subtleties** **1** [U] the quality that something has when it has been done in an intelligent or skillful way: *the **subtlety of** the wine's flavor* **2** [C usually plural] something that is important but difficult to notice: *The subtleties of the story do not translate well into other languages.*

sub·tract /səbˈtrækt/ *v.* [T] to take a number or amount from something larger [➡ **add**]: *If you **subtract** 15 **from** 25 you get 10.* —**subtraction** /səbˈtrækʃən/ *n.*

sub·urb /ˈsʌbɚb/ *n.* [C] an area away from the center of a city, where a lot of people live: *We moved to **the suburbs** last year.* | *a **suburb of** Chicago*

> **THESAURUS**
>
> **area, region, zone, district, neighborhood**
> ➔ see Thesaurus box at AREA

sub·ur·ban /səˈbɚbən/ *adj.* relating to a suburb, or in a suburb: *suburban life* | *suburban Miami* (=the suburbs around Miami)

sub·ur·bi·a /səˈbɚbiə/ *n.* [U] all suburbs in general: *life in suburbia*

sub·ver·sive /səbˈvɚsɪv/ *adj.* intending to destroy or damage a government, society, religion, etc.: *subversive activities*

sub·vert /səbˈvɚt/ *v.* [T] to try to destroy the power or influence of a government, belief, etc.

sub·way /ˈsʌbweɪ/ *n.* plural **subways** [C] a railroad that runs under the ground in cities: *a **subway station*** | *We **took the subway** home.* ➔ see picture at TRANSPORTATION

suc·ceed /səkˈsid/ *v.* **1** [I] to do what you have tried to do, or to do well in something such as your job [≠ **fail**]: *She gave herself five years to **succeed as** a writer.* | *Finally, I **succeeded in** convincing Anna that I was right.* | *skills that help students succeed in the classroom* **2** [I] to have the result or effect that something is intended to have [≠ **fail**]: *Our advertising campaign **succeeded in** attracting more customers.* **3** [I,T] to be the next person to take a position or do a job after someone else: *Mr. Harvey will **succeed** Mrs. Lincoln **as** chairman.*

suc·ceed·ing /səkˈsidɪŋ/ *adj.* coming after something else: *Sales improved in succeeding years.*

> **THESAURUS**
>
> **next, following, subsequent, later**
> ➔ see Thesaurus box at NEXT¹

suc·cess /səkˈsɛs/ *n.* **1** [C,U] something that has the result or effect that you intended, or the act of achieving this [≠ **failure**]: *We **had no/some success in** developing a better engine.* | *Jackie's wedding **was a big/huge/great success**.* | *Eventually she was able to **make a success of** the business.* | *Business leaders demanded, **without success**, that the government build new roads.* **2** [C] someone who does very well in his/her job, classes, in society, etc. [≠ **failure**]: *He was not much of a **success as** a comedian.*

suc·cess·ful /səkˈsɛsfəl/ *adj.* **1** having the result or effect you intended [≠ **unsuccessful**]: *The surgery was completely successful.* **2** making or earning a lot of money: *a successful businessman* | *a successful movie* —**successfully** *adv.*

suc·ces·sion /səkˈsɛʃən/ *n.* **1 in succession** happening one after the other: *The team has won four championships in succession.* **2 a succession of sth** a number of people or things that happen or follow one after another: *She's had a succession of rich husbands.* **3** [U] the act of taking over an important job, position, etc., or the right to do this

suc·ces·sive /səkˈsɛsɪv/ *adj.* coming or following one after the other: *Babe Ruth hit three successive home runs in one game.* —**successively** *adv.*

suc·ces·sor /səkˈsɛsɚ/ *n.* [C] someone who takes a job or position that was held before by someone else: *No one was certain who Mao's successor would be.*

S

suc·cinct /sək'sɪŋkt, sə'sɪŋkt/ *adj.* clearly expressed in a few words —**succinctly** *adv.*

suc·cu·lent /'sʌkyələnt/ *adj.* juicy and tasting very good: *a succulent steak* —**succulence** *n.* [U]

suc·cumb /sə'kʌm/ *v.* [I] *formal* **1** to stop opposing someone or something, and allow him, her, or it to take control: *Eventually, she **succumbed to** his charms.* **2** to become very sick or die from an illness

such /sʌtʃ/ *determiner, pron.* **1** used in order to talk about a person or thing that is like the one that you have just mentioned: *Such behavior is not acceptable here.* | *"Did you get the job?" **"No such luck** (=I wasn't lucky)."* **2 such as** used when giving an example of something: *big cities such as New York, Tokyo, and London* **3** used in order to emphasize an amount or degree: *We had such fun at your party!* | *Mandy's such a nice person.* | *I was in such a hurry that I forgot my purse.* **4 there's no such person/thing as sb/sth** used in order to say that a particular person or thing does not exist: *There's no such thing as a perfect job.* **5 not (...) as such** used to say that the word you are using to describe something is not exactly correct: *She's not retired as such, she's just taking a long break.*

GRAMMAR

such, so

Use **such** and **so** to emphasize a quality that someone or something has.

Use **so** before an adjective or an adverb: *Your dress is so pretty.* | *Some people are so rude.* | *He talks so loudly.*

Use **such** before a noun, or before an adjective and noun: *It was such a shock.* | *Mark is such a good swimmer.* | *She has such beautiful eyes.*

'such-and-such *determiner spoken* used instead of the name of something: *They will ask you to come on such-and-such a day, at such-and-such a time.*

suck /sʌk/ *v.* **1** [I,T] to hold something in your mouth and pull on it with your tongue and lips: *Don't suck your thumb, Katie.* | *Ben was **sucking on** a piece of candy.* **2** [I,T] to take air, liquid, etc. into your mouth by making your lips form a small hole and using the muscles of your mouth to pull it in: *Michael put the cigarette to his lips and **sucked in** the smoke.* **3** [T] to pull someone or something with a lot of force to a particular place: *A man almost got **sucked under** by the current.* **4 get/be sucked into (doing) sth** to become involved in something you do not want to be involved in: *I'm not going to get sucked into an argument with you guys.* **5 sth sucks** *slang* used to say that something is bad, unfair, dishonest, etc.: *That movie sucked.*

suck up to sb *phr. v. spoken disapproving* to say or do a lot of nice things in order to make someone like you or to get what you want: *She's always sucking up to her boss.*

suck·er /'sʌkɚ/ *n.* [C] **1** *informal* someone who is easily tricked: *Ellen always was a sucker.* **2 be a sucker for sth** to like something so much that you cannot refuse it: *I'm a sucker for old movies.* **3** *slang* a thing: *Do you know how much this sucker cost me?*

suc·tion /'sʌkʃən/ *n.* [U] the process of removing air or liquid from a container or space so that another substance can be pulled in, or so that two surfaces stick together

sud·den /'sʌdn/ *adj.* **1** done or happening quickly or in a way you did not expect: *We've had a **sudden change** of plans.* | *Don't make any sudden moves around the animals.* **2 all of a sudden** suddenly: *All of a sudden, the lights went out.* —**suddenness** *n.* [U]

sud·den·ly /'sʌdnli/ *adv.* quickly and in a way you did not expect: *She suddenly realized what she'd done.* | *Smith died suddenly of a heart attack.*

suds /sʌdz/ *n.* [plural] the BUBBLES that form on top of water with soap in it —**sudsy** *adj.*

sue /su/ *v.* [I,T] to make a legal claim against someone, especially for money, because s/he has harmed you in some way: *She plans to **sue** the company **for** $1 million.* | *Aaron is being sued for fraud.*

suede /sweɪd/ *n.* [U] soft leather with a slightly rough surface: *a suede jacket*

suf·fer /'sʌfɚ/ *v.* **1** [I,T] to feel pain or the effects of a sickness: *Neil suffered a heart attack last year.* | *Marnie **suffers from** headaches.* **2** [I,T] to experience a situation and be badly affected by it: *Small businesses are suffering financially right now.* | *The team **suffered** its worst **defeat** in ten years.* **3** [I] to become worse in quality: *Andy's work began to suffer after his divorce.* —**sufferer** *n.* [C] —**suffering** *n.* [C,U] *The war has caused so much pain and suffering.*

suf·fice /sə'faɪs/ *v.* [I] *formal* to be enough: *A light lunch **will suffice**.*

suf·fi·cient /sə'fɪʃənt/ *adj. formal* as much as you need for a particular purpose [= **enough**; ≠ **insufficient**]: *Will $100 be sufficient?* | *They had **sufficient** evidence **to** send him to prison.* —**sufficiency** *n.* [singular, U]

THESAURUS

enough, **plenty**, **adequate**
→ see Thesaurus box at ENOUGH

suf·fix /'sʌfɪks/ *n.* [C] *technical* in grammar, a letter or letters added to the end of a word in order to make a new word, such as "ness" at the end of "kindness" [➡ **prefix**, **affix**]

suf·fo·cate /'sʌfəˌkeɪt/ *v.* **1** [I,T] to die because there is not enough air to breathe, or to be killed in this way: *One firefighter was suffocated by the smoke.* **2 be suffocating** *informal* to feel uncomfortable because there is not enough fresh air —**suffocation** /ˌsʌfə'keɪʃən/ *n.* [U]

suf·frage /ˈʃʌfrɪdʒ/ *n.* [U] *formal* the right to vote

sug·ar /ˈʃʊgɚ/ *n.* [U] a sweet white or brown substance that is obtained from plants and used for making food and drinks sweet: *Do you take sugar in your coffee?* —**sugary** *adj.*: *sugary snacks*

sug·ared /ˈʃʊgɚd/ *adj.* covered in sugar: *sugared almonds*

sug·gest /səgˈdʒɛst, səˈdʒɛst/ *v.* [T] **1** to tell someone your ideas about what should be done: *They suggested meeting for drinks first.* | *Don* ***suggested (that)*** *we go swimming.* | *Wilson* ***suggested ways*** *students can improve their study habits.*

COMMUNICATION

Ways of suggesting something
let's...: *Let's get together this weekend.*
do you want to...?: *Do you want to go out to dinner?*
what do you say...?: *What do you say we all go to a movie?*
how/what about...?: *What about asking Tim over?*
why don't we...?: *Why don't we go to the park?*
→ ACCEPT, AGREE

2 to say or show that something may be true: *The article* ***suggested that*** *Nachez might run for mayor.* | *Are you suggesting that I cheated?*

THESAURUS

say, imply, indicate
→ see also Thesaurus box at DEMONSTRATE, SAY[1]

3 to say that someone or something is suitable for a particular job or purpose [= **recommend**]: *Gina Reed's name has been* ***suggested for*** *the job.*

sug·ges·tion /səgˈdʒɛstʃən, səˈdʒɛs-/ *n.* **1** [C] an idea or plan that someone suggests, or the act of suggesting it: *We've* ***had*** *some* ***suggestions*** *on good plays to see in New York.* | *Can I* ***make a suggestion****?* | *They accepted the* ***suggestion that*** *Todd go first.* | *My boss is always* ***open to suggestions*** (=willing to listen to ideas). | *I took the class* ***at*** *my adviser's* ***suggestion****.* **2** [singular,U] a possibility of something: *The police said that there was no* ***suggestion of*** *murder.*

sug·ges·tive /səgˈdʒɛstɪv, səˈdʒɛs-/ *adj.* **1** making you think of sex: *a suggestive remark* **2** similar to something: *a spotted rug,* ***suggestive of*** *leopard skin*

su·i·ci·dal /ˌsuəˈsaɪdl/ *adj.* **1** wanting to kill yourself: *suicidal thoughts* **2** likely to result in death: *a suicidal attack*

su·i·cide /ˈsuəˌsaɪd/ *n.* **1** [C,U] the act of killing yourself: *Her brother* ***committed suicide*** *last year.* | *Did she leave a* ***suicide note*** (=a note or letter saying why she killed herself)? **2 political/social etc. suicide** something you do that ruins your job or position in society

suit¹ /sut/ *n.* **1** [C] a set of clothes made of the same material, including a jacket with pants or a skirt: *a dark gray business suit* **2** [C] a piece of clothing or set of clothes used for a special purpose: *a* ***bathing suit*** **3** [C,U] a LAWSUIT: *A homeowner* ***filed suit against*** *the county and lost.* **4** [C] one of the four types of cards in a set of playing cards

suit² *v.* [T] **1** to be acceptable or right for a person or situation: *It takes time to find a college that will suit your child's needs.* **2** clothes, colors, etc. that suit you make you look attractive: *Short hair suits you.* **3** to have the right qualities to do something: *Lucy's well/ideally* ***suited for*** *the job.* **4 suit yourself** *spoken* used to tell someone that s/he can do whatever s/he wants to do, even though you are annoyed or upset: *"I'm not sure I want to go tonight." "Suit yourself."*

suit·able /ˈsuṭəbəl/ *adj.* right or acceptable for a particular person, purpose, or situation: *This book isn't* ***suitable for*** *young children.* —**suitably** *adv.* —**suitability** /ˌsuṭəˈbɪləṭi/ *n.* [U]

THESAURUS

appropriate, suited
→ see Thesaurus box at APPROPRIATE[1]

suit·case /ˈsut˺keɪs/ *n.* [C] a bag or box with a handle, for carrying your clothes and possessions when you travel: *She folded up the clothes and packed* (=put) *them in the suitcase.* → see picture at CASE

suite /swit/ *n.* [C] **1** a set of expensive rooms in a hotel or large building: *the honeymoon suite* | *a* ***suite of offices*** *in West Palm Beach* **2** a piece of music made up of several short parts: *the Nutcracker Suite* **3** *technical* a group of related computer programs

suit·or /ˈsuṭɚ/ *n.* [C] *old-fashioned* a man who wants to marry a particular woman

sul·fur /ˈsʌlfɚ/ *n.* [U] a yellow strong-smelling chemical substance

sulk /sʌlk/ *v.* [I] to show that you are annoyed about something by being silent and looking unhappy

sul·len /ˈsʌlən/ *adj.* showing that you are angry or in a bad mood by being silent and looking unhappy

sul·phur /ˈsʌlfɚ/ *n.* [U] SULFUR

sul·tan /ˈsʌlt˺n/ *n.* [C] a ruler in some Muslim countries

sul·try /ˈsʌltri/ *adj.* **1** weather that is sultry is hot with air that feels wet **2** a woman who is sultry is very sexually attractive

sum¹ /sʌm/ *n.* [C] **1** an amount of money: *The city has spent* ***a*** *large* ***sum of money*** *on parks.* **2** the total when you add two or more numbers together: ***The sum of*** *4 and 5 is 9.*

sum² *v.* past tense and past participle **summed**, present participle **summing**

sum up *phr. v.* to end a discussion or speech by giving the main information about it in a short statement: *So, to sum up, we need to organize our time better.*

sum·ma·rize /ˈsʌməˌraɪz/ *v.* [I,T] to give only the main information about an event, plan, report, etc., not all the details: *The authors summarize their views in the introduction.*

sum·ma·ry[1] /ˈsʌməri/ *n.* plural **summaries** [C] a short statement that gives the main information about an event, plan, report, etc.: *Read the article and write a **summary of** it.* | ***In summary**, more research is needed.*

summary[2] *adj.* [only before noun] done immediately without following the usual processes or rules: ***summary executions***

sum·mer /ˈsʌmɚ/ *n.* [C,U] the season between spring and fall, when the weather is hottest: *The pool is open **in the summer**.* | *We're going to Mt. Whitney **this summer**.* | ***last/next summer*** (=the summer before or after this one)

ˈsummer school *n.* [C,U] classes that you can take in the summer at a school or college

sum·mer·time /ˈsʌmɚˌtaɪm/ *n.* [U] the time of year when it is summer

ˌsummer vaˈcation *n.* [C,U] the time during the summer when schools are closed, or a trip you take during this time

S

sum·mit /ˈsʌmɪt/ *n.* [C] **1** a set of important meetings among the leaders of several governments: *an economic summit* **2** the top of a mountain: *Many people have now reached **the summit of** Mount Everest.*

sum·mon /ˈsʌmən/ *v.* [T] *formal* **1** to order someone to come to a particular place: *I was **summoned to** the principal's office.* **2 also summon up** to make a great effort to use your strength, courage, etc.: *It took her 11 years to summon the courage to leave her husband.*

sum·mons /ˈsʌmənz/ *n.* [C] plural **summonses** an official order to appear in a court of law

sump·tu·ous /ˈsʌmptʃuəs/ *adj.* very impressive and expensive: *a sumptuous meal*

sun[1] /sʌn/ *n.* **1 the sun/the Sun** the large bright star in the sky that gives us light and heat, and around which the Earth moves **2** [singular, U] the heat and light that come from the sun: *Val lay **in the sun**, listening to the radio.* **3** [C] any star around which PLANETS move

TOPIC

meteor, asteroid, comet, moon, planet, star, constellation, galaxy, black hole
→ see Topic box at SPACE[1]

sun[2] *v.* past tense and past participle **sunned**, present participle **sunning** [T] to sit or lie outside when the sun is shining

sun·bathe /ˈsʌnbeɪð/ *v.* [I] to sit or lie outside in the sun in order to get a TAN (=darker skin) —**sunbathing** *n.* [U]

sun·block /ˈsʌnblɑk/ *n.* [U] a cream that you put on your skin in order to completely prevent the sun from burning you [➡ **sunscreen**]

sun·burn /ˈsʌnbɚn/ *n.* [U] the condition of having skin that is red and painful from spending too much time in the sun —**sunburned** *adj.*

sun·dae /ˈsʌndi, -deɪ/ *n.* [C] a dish of ICE CREAM, fruit, nuts, and sweet sauce: *a hot fudge sundae*

Sun·day /ˈsʌndi, -deɪ/ *written abbreviation* **Sun.** *n.* [C] the first day of the week: *Anna is coming back Sunday.* | *I have to work **on Sunday**.* | *We're going to a baseball game **next Sunday**.* | *We had friends over **last Sunday**.* | *She usually wakes up early on **Sunday morning**.*

ˈSunday School *n.* [C,U] a place where children are taught about Christianity on Sundays

sun·dial /ˈsʌndaɪl/ *n.* [C] an object used in the past for telling the time. The shadow of a pointed piece of metal shows the time and moves round as the sun moves.

sun·down /ˈsʌndaʊn/ *n.* [U] SUNSET

sun·dry /ˈsʌndri/ *adj. formal* MISCELLANEOUS

sunflower

sun·flow·er /ˈsʌnˌflaʊɚ/ *n.* [C] a tall plant with a large yellow flower and seeds that can be eaten

sung /sʌŋ/ *v.* the past participle of SING

sun·glass·es /ˈsʌnˌglæsɪz/ *n.* [plural] dark glasses that you wear in order to protect your eyes when the sun is bright

sunk /sʌŋk/ *v.* the past tense and past participle of SINK

sunk·en /ˈsʌŋkən/ *adj.* **1** having fallen to the bottom of the sea: *a sunken ship* **2** built or placed at a lower level than the surrounding area: *a sunken garden* **3** sunken cheeks or eyes have fallen inward, making someone look sick

sun·light /ˈsʌnlaɪt/ *n.* [U] natural light that comes from the sun: *Plants need sunlight.*

sun·lit /ˈsʌnˌlɪt/ *adj.* made brighter by light from the sun: *a sunlit kitchen*

sun·ny /ˈsʌni/ *adj.* **1** full of light from the sun: *a sunny day* **2** cheerful and happy: *a sunny personality*

sun·rise /ˈsʌnraɪz/ *n.* [U] the time when the sun first appears in the morning

sun·roof /ˈsʌnruf/ *n.* [C] a part of the roof of a car that you can open

sun·screen /ˈsʌnskrin/ *n.* [C,U] a cream that

you put on your skin to stop the sun from burning you [➡ **sunblock**]

sun·set /'sʌnsɛt/ *n.* **1** [U] the time of day when the sun disappears and night begins **2** [C,U] the colored part of the sky when the sun disappears and night begins

sun·shine /'sʌnʃaɪn/ *n.* [U] the light and heat that comes from the sun: *Let's go out and enjoy the sunshine.*

sun·tan /'sʌntæn/ *n.* [C] a TAN

sun·up /'sʌnʌp/ *n.* [U] SUNRISE

su·per[1] /'supɚ/ *adj. informal* extremely good: *You guys really did a super job.*

super[2] *n.* [C] *spoken* a building SUPERINTENDENT

super[3] *adv. spoken* extremely: *a super expensive restaurant*

su·perb /sʊ'pɚb/ *adj.* extremely good [= **excellent**]: *The hotel was superb.* —**superbly** *adv.*

'Super Bowl *n.* [C] a football game played once a year in order to decide which professional team is the best in the U.S.

su·per·fi·cial /ˌsupɚ'fɪʃəl/ *adj.* **1** based only on the first things you notice, not on complete knowledge: *a superficial understanding of physics* **2** affecting only the surface of your skin or the outside part of something, and therefore not serious: *She had some superficial cuts on her arm.* **3** *disapproving* someone who is superficial does not think about things that are serious or important [= **shallow**] —**superficially** *adv.*

su·per·flu·ous /sʊ'pɚfluəs/ *adj. formal* more than is needed or wanted [= **unnecessary**]: *superfluous details*

su·per·he·ro /'supɚˌhɪroʊ/ *n.* plural **superheroes** [C] a character in COMIC BOOKS, movies, etc. who uses special powers, such as great strength or the ability to fly, to help people

su·per·high·way /ˌsupɚ'haɪweɪ/ *n.* [C] a very large road on which you can drive fast for long distances

su·per·hu·man /ˌsupɚ'hyumən◂/ *adj.* using powers that are much greater than those of ordinary people: *a* ***superhuman effort*** *to finish the job*

su·per·im·pose /ˌsupɚɪm'poʊz/ *v.* [T] to put one picture, image, or photograph on top of another so that both can be partly seen: *The picture had Mary's head superimposed on Greg's body.* —**superimposition** /ˌsupɚɪmpə'zɪʃən/ *n.* [U]

su·per·in·tend·ent /ˌsupɚɪn'tɛndənt/ *n.* [C] **1** someone who is responsible for all the schools in a particular area of the U.S. **2** someone who takes care of an apartment building **3** someone who is responsible for a place, job, activity, etc.

su·pe·ri·or[1] /sə'pɪriɚ, sʊ-/ *adj.* **1** better than other similar people or things [≠ **inferior**]: *I believe Matisse's work is* ***superior to*** *Picasso's.* ▶ Don't say "superior than." ◀ **2** extremely good in quality: *superior wines* **3** *disapproving* showing that you think you are better than other people: *She had that superior tone of voice.*

superior[2] *n.* [C] someone who has a higher rank or position than you in a job: *I'll have to discuss it with my superiors.*

su·pe·ri·o·ri·ty /səˌpɪri'ɔrət̬i, -'ɑr-/ *n.* [U] **1** the quality of being better than other people or things: *the country's military* ***superiority over*** *its neighbors* **2** *disapproving* an attitude that shows you think you are better than other people: *Janet always spoke with an air of superiority.*

su·per·la·tive[1] /sə'pɚlət̬ɪv, sʊ-/ *adj.* excellent: *superlative views of the city*

superlative[2] *n.* **the superlative** *technical* in grammar, the form of an adjective or adverb that shows the highest degree of a particular quality. For example, "fastest" is the superlative of "fast".

su·per·mar·ket /'supɚˌmɑrkɪt/ *n.* [C] a very large store that sells many different kinds of food and things people need for the house [➡ **grocery store**]

> **THESAURUS**
>
> **drugstore, hardware store, department store, liquor store, convenience store, superstore, warehouse store**
> ➔ see Thesaurus box at STORE[1]

su·per·mod·el /'supɚˌmɑdl/ *n.* [C] a very famous fashion model

su·per·nat·u·ral /ˌsupɚ'nætʃərəl◂, -tʃrəl◂/ *n.* **the supernatural** events, powers, abilities, or creatures that are impossible to explain by science or natural causes —**supernatural** *adj.*: *supernatural powers*

sup·er·pow·er /'supɚˌpaʊɚ/ *n.* [C] a country that has very great military and political power

su·per·sede /ˌsupɚ'sid/ *v.* [T] to replace something that is older or less effective with something new or better: *TV had superseded radio by the 1960s.*

su·per·son·ic /ˌsupɚ'sɑnɪk◂/ *adj.* faster than the speed of sound: *supersonic jets*

su·per·star /'supɚˌstɑr/ *n.* [C] an extremely famous performer, especially a musician or movie actor

su·per·sti·tion /ˌsupɚ'stɪʃən/ *n.* [C,U] *disapproving* a belief that some objects or actions are lucky and some are unlucky or cause particular results

su·per·sti·tious /ˌsupɚ'stɪʃəs/ *adj. disapproving* influenced by superstitions

su·per·struc·ture /'supɚˌstrʌktʃɚ/ *n.* [singular, U] a structure that is built on top of the main part of something such as a ship or building

su·per·vise /'supɚˌvaɪz/ *v.* [I,T] to be in charge of an activity or person, and make sure that things are done in the correct way: *Griffin closely supervised the research.* —**supervision** /ˌsupɚ'vɪʒən/ *n.* [U] *working* ***under supervision***

su·per·vis·or /'supɚˌvaɪzɚ/ *n.* [C] someone who supervises a person or activity

S

—**supervisory** /ˌsupɚˈvaɪzəri/ *adj.*: *a supervisory role*

sup·per /ˈsʌpɚ/ *n.* [C] the meal that is eaten in the early evening [= **dinner**]: *What's **for supper*** (=what will we eat)?

THESAURUS
breakfast, **lunch**, **brunch**, **dinner**
➔ see Thesaurus box at MEAL

sup·plant /səˈplænt/ *v.* [T] *formal* to take the place of another person or thing: *The old factories have all been supplanted by new high-tech industries.*

sup·ple /ˈsʌpəl/ *adj.* able to bend and move easily

sup·ple·ment¹ /ˈsʌpləmənt/ *n.* [C] **1** something that is added to something else to improve it: *dietary supplements*

THESAURUS
additive, **addition**
➔ see Thesaurus box at ADDITION

2 an additional part of something such as a newspaper, magazine, etc.: *the Sunday supplement*

S

sup·ple·ment² /ˈsʌpləˌmɛnt/ *v.* [T] to add something, especially to what you earn or eat, in order to improve it: *He took a night job to supplement their income.*

sup·ple·men·tal /ˌsʌpləˈmɛntl/ **also sup·ple·men·ta·ry** /-ˈmɛntri, -ˈmɛntəri/ *adj.* additional: *supplementary vitamins*

sup·pli·er /səˈplaɪɚ/ *n.* [C] a company that provides a particular product: *medical suppliers*

sup·ply¹ /səˈplaɪ/ *n.* plural **supplies** **1** [C,U] an amount of something that is available to be used, or the process of providing this: *the nation's fuel supplies* | *the **supply of** oxygen **to** the brain* | *an **ample/plentiful/endless, etc. supply of cash*** **2 supplies** [plural] food, clothes, and things that are necessary for daily life, especially for a particular period: *Emergency supplies are being sent to the flooded region.* **3 gas/electricity/water etc. supply** a system that is used to supply gas, electricity, water, etc. ➔ **be in short supply** at SHORT¹

supply² *v.* past tense and past participle **supplied**, third person singular **supplies** [T] to provide people with something that they need or want, especially regularly over a long time: *Workers are **supplied with** masks and special clothing.* | *He refused to **supply** any information **to** the police.*

sup·port¹ /səˈpɔrt/ *v.* [T] **1** to say that you agree with an idea, group, person, etc. and want him, her, or it to succeed: *I don't support any one political party.* | *We need to **support** teachers **in** their aims.* **2** to help and encourage someone: *I appreciate your supporting me during my divorce.* **3** to provide enough money for someone to have all the things s/he needs: *I **have** a wife and two children **to support**.* | *You've got to learn to **support yourself**.* **4** to hold the weight of something in order to prevent it from falling: *The bridge is supported by two columns.* **5** to show or prove that something is true: *There is now enough data to support the theory.*

support² *n.* **1** [U] approval and encouragement for a person, idea, plan, etc.: *There is a lot of **support for** the war.* | *Many people have **given us support** in our campaign.* **2** [U] money given to a person or organization in order to help pay for the cost of something: *He provides **financial support** to his ex-wife.* **3** [U] sympathy and help that you give to someone: *Thanks for all your support.* **4** [C,U] an object that holds up something else

sup·port·er /səˈpɔrt̬ɚ/ *n.* [C] someone who supports a particular person, group, or plan: ***supporters of** the governor*

supˈport group *n.* [C] a group of people who meet to help each other with a particular problem, for example ALCOHOLISM

sup·port·ing /səˈpɔrt̬ɪŋ/ *adj.* **supporting actor/part/role etc.** an actor who has a small part in a movie or play, or the part that they act

sup·port·ive /səˈpɔrt̬ɪv/ *adj.* giving help or encouragement: *All the team members are very **supportive of** each other.*

sup·pose /səˈpoʊz/ *v.* [T] **1 be supposed to do/be sth a)** used in order to say what someone should or should not do, especially because of official rules: *You're not supposed to smoke in here.* **b)** used in order to say what is expected or intended to happen, especially when it did not happen: *The checks were supposed to arrive two weeks ago.* **c)** used in order to say that something is believed to be true by many people: *This is supposed to be the best Chinese restaurant in town.*

SPOKEN PHRASES
2 I suppose a) used in order to say that you think something is probably true, although you are not sure: ***I suppose (that)** you're right.* **b)** used when you are agreeing to let someone do something, especially when you do not really want him/her to do it: *"Can we come with you?" "**I suppose so.**"* **c)** used when saying in an angry way that you think something is true: ***I suppose (that)** you thought that was funny!* **3 suppose/supposing** used in order to ask someone to imagine what might happen: *Suppose you do get the job. Who'd take care of the kids?* **4 what's that supposed to mean?** said when you are annoyed by what someone has just said: *"I'll keep your idea in mind." "Keep it in mind! What's that supposed to mean?"* **5 do you suppose (that)...?** used in order to ask someone's opinion about something: *Do you suppose people will ever live on Mars?*

sup·posed /səˈpoʊzd/ *adj.* used in order to say that what you are talking about is believed to be true, but you do not believe or agree with it yourself: *the supposed link between violent movies and crime*

sup·pos·ed·ly /səˈpoʊzɪdli/ *adv.* used when saying what other people say or believe is true, especially when you do not think they are right: *He comes from a very wealthy family, supposedly.* | *How could a supposedly intelligent person make so many mistakes?*

sup·po·si·tion /ˌsʌpəˈzɪʃən/ *n.* [C,U] *formal* something that you think is true even though you are not certain and cannot prove it

sup·press /səˈprɛs/ *v.* [T] **1** to stop people from opposing the government, especially by using force: *The army has suppressed the revolt.* **2** to control a feeling, so that you do not show it: *Andy could barely* ***suppress*** *his* ***anger***. **3** to prevent important information or opinions from becoming known: *His lawyer suppressed some of the evidence.* —**suppression** /səˈprɛʃən/ *n.* [U]

su·prem·a·cy /səˈprɛməsi, sʊ-/ *n.* [U] a situation in which a group or idea is more powerful or advanced than anything else

su·preme /səˈprim, sʊ-/ *adj.* **1** having the highest position of power, importance, or influence: *the supreme commander of the fleet* **2** [only before noun] the greatest possible: *He made a* ***supreme effort***.

Suˌpreme ˈCourt *n.* **the Supreme Court** the court of law with the most authority in the U.S.

su·preme·ly /səˈprimli, sʊ-/ *adv.* extremely: *a* ***supremely confident*** *athlete*

sur·charge /ˈsɚtʃɑrdʒ/ *n.* [C] money that you have to pay in addition to the basic price of something

sure[1] /ʃʊr, ʃɚ/ *adj.* **1** [not before noun] certain about something: *"That's Sarah's cousin." "Are you sure?"* | *I'm* ***sure (that)*** *I had the keys when we left the house.* | *I'm* ***not sure what*** *happened.* | *Are you always so* ***sure about*** *everything?* **2 make sure (that) a)** to check that something is true or that something has been done: *He called to make sure that we got home okay.* **b)** to do something so that you can be certain of the result: *Make sure you get there early.* **3** certain to happen or be true: *He's* ***sure to*** *say something stupid.* | *Investing in the stock market is not* ***a sure thing*** (=it is risky). **4 be sure of sth** to be certain to get something or certain that something will happen: *The Giants are now sure of a place in the playoffs.* **5 sure of yourself** confident about your own abilities and opinions **6 for sure** *informal* **a)** certainly: *I think he's married, but I don't know for sure.* **b)** used in order to emphasize that something is certain: *We'll always need teachers –* ***that's for sure***. **7 sure thing** *spoken* said in order to agree to something: *"See you Friday." "Yeah, sure thing."*

sure[2] *adv.* **1 sure enough** *informal* used in order to say that something happened that you expected to happen: *Sure enough, we got lost.*

SPOKEN PHRASES

2 said in order to say yes to someone: *"Can I read your paper?" "Sure."* **3** used as a way of replying when someone thanks you: *"Hey, thanks for your help." "Sure."* **4** said in order to emphasize a statement [= **certainly**] : *It sure is hot out here.* **5** used in order to admit that something is true, before you say something very different: *Sure, he's cute, but I'm still not interested.*

sure·ly /ˈʃʊrli, ˈʃɚli/ *adv.* **1** used in order to show that you are surprised at something: *Surely you're not leaving so soon?* **2** used in order to show that you think something must be true: *This will surely result in more problems.*

surf[1] /sɚf/ *v.* [I,T] **1** to ride on ocean waves standing on a special board → see picture on page A10 **2 surf the Internet/Net/Web** to look quickly at different places on the INTERNET for information that interests you —**surfer** *n.* [C] —**surfing** *n.* [U] *Didn't you* ***go surfing*** *at Ventura?* → **channel hop/surf** at CHANNEL

surf[2] *n.* [U] the white part that forms on the top of waves as they move toward the shore

sur·face[1] /ˈsɚfəs/ *n.* [C] **1** the outside or top layer of something: *the Earth's surface* | *leaves floating* ***on the surface of*** *the lake* **2 the surface** the qualities that someone or something seems to have until you learn more about him, her, or it: ***On the surface*** *she seems happy enough.* | *I sensed a lot of tension* ***below/beneath the surface***. **3** a flat area, for example on top of a cupboard, on which you can work: *a cleaner for all your kitchen surfaces*

surface[2] *v.* **1** [I] to become known: *Rumors have* ***begun to surface*** *in the press.* **2** [I] to appear again after being hidden or absent: *Three years later he surfaced again.* **3** [I] to rise to the surface of water: *Whales were surfacing near our boat.* **4** [T] to put a surface on a road

surf·board /ˈsɚfbɔrd/ *n.* [C] a long special board that you stand on to ride on ocean waves

surge[1] /sɚdʒ/ *v.* [I] **1** to suddenly move very quickly in a particular direction: *The crowd* ***surged forward***. **2 also surge up** to begin to feel an emotion very strongly: *Rage surged up inside her.*

surge[2] *n.* [C] **1** a sudden large increase in something: *a* ***surge of*** *excitement* | *a* ***surge in*** *oil prices* **2** a sudden movement of a lot of people

sur·geon /ˈsɚdʒən/ *n.* [C] a doctor who does operations in a hospital

THESAURUS

doctor, **physician**, **specialist**, **psychiatrist**, **pediatrician**
→ see Thesaurus box at DOCTOR[1]

S

sur·ger·y /ˈsɚdʒəri/ *n.* [U] medical treatment in which a doctor cuts open your body to fix or remove something inside: *heart surgery* | *Jenny is* ***having surgery*** *tomorrow.*

sur·gi·cal /ˈsɚdʒɪkəl/ *adj.* relating to or used for medical operations: *surgical gloves*

sur·ly /ˈsɚli/ *adj.* unfriendly and rude

sur·mise /sɚˈmaɪz/ *v.* [T] *formal* to guess that something is true, using the information you have

sur·mount /sɚˈmaʊnt/ *v.* [T] *formal* to succeed in dealing with a problem or difficulty [= **overcome**]

sur·name /ˈsɚneɪm/ *n.* [C] a LAST NAME

sur·pass /sɚˈpæs/ *v.* [T] to be better or greater than someone or something else: *He surpassed the previous record by 11 seconds.* | *The trip* ***surpassed*** *all our* ***expectations*** (=it was better than we hoped it would be).

sur·plus¹ /ˈsɚplʌs/ *n.* [C,U] **1** more of something than is needed or used: *a* ***surplus of*** *goods* **2** money that a country or company has after it has paid for the things it needs [≠ **deficit**]: *a budget surplus*

surplus² *adj.* more than what is needed or used: *surplus corn*

S

sur·prise¹ /sɚˈpraɪz, səˈpraɪz/ *n.* **1** [U] the feeling you have when something unexpected or unusual happens: *Bill looked at us* ***in surprise.*** | ***To*** *my* ***surprise,*** *she agreed.* | ***It came as no surprise*** *when he left.* **2** [C,U] something that is unexpected or unusual: *What a surprise to see you here!* | *Dad, I* ***have a surprise*** *for you!* | *a* ***surprise party*** **3 catch/take sb by surprise** to happen in an unexpected way: *The heavy snowfall caught everyone by surprise.*

surprise² *v.* [T] **1** to make someone feel surprised: *Her reaction surprised me.* | *"Pam got fired." "****It doesn't surprise me.****"* **2** to find, catch, or attack someone when s/he does not expect it: *A security guard surprised the robber.*

sur·prised /sɚˈpraɪzd, sə-/ *adj.* having a feeling of surprise: *Robert* ***looked surprised*** *to see me there.* | *I'm* ***surprised at*** *how much it costs.* | *We were* ***surprised (that)*** *David got the job.*

THESAURUS

amazed – very surprised: *I was amazed at how hard the exam was.*
shocked – feeling surprised, and often upset or offended: *We were all shocked by the news.*
astonished – very surprised: *Her lawyer was astonished at the verdict.*
astounded – very surprised: *I was astounded at how bad the play was.*
flabbergasted – very surprised and shocked: *People were flabbergasted; something like this couldn't happen.*
stunned – too surprised and shocked to speak: *We watched in stunned disbelief.*
dumbfounded – too surprised and confused to speak: *Coach Jones is dumbfounded by the team's performance.*
nonplussed – so surprised that you do not know what to say or do: *The stock market seems nonplussed by the figures.*

sur·pris·ing /sɚˈpraɪzɪŋ, sə-/ *adj.* unusual or unexpected: ***It's surprising how*** *quickly she finished the job.* | *A surprising number of people came.* | *It's* ***hardly/scarcely surprising that*** *they lost the game.*

THESAURUS

extraordinary – unusual and surprising: *He spends an extraordinary amount of money on clothes.*
amazing – very surprising or unexpected, and sometimes difficult to believe: *It's amazing how fast some animals can run.*
shocking – surprising and upsetting: *It is shocking that a policeman could lie to the public.*
astonishing – very surprising, and often difficult to believe: *The population of the world is growing at an astonishing rate.*
astounding – very surprising, and almost impossible to believe: *the astounding success of her second novel, published when she was 58*
staggering – very surprising and shocking, especially because something is so large: *a staggering sum of money*
stunning – very surprising and shocking: *In a stunning announcement, the senator said he was retiring.*

—**surprisingly** *adv.*: *The test was surprisingly easy.*

sur·real /səˈril/ **also sur·re·a·lis·tic** /səˌriəˈlɪstɪk/ *adj.* very strange, like something from a dream

sur·ren·der /səˈrɛndɚ/ *v.* **1** [I] to stop fighting because you know that you cannot win, or to stop trying to escape from the police: *The rebel forces have surrendered.* | *The man finally* ***surrendered to*** *the police.*

THESAURUS

give in – to accept that you have lost a fight, game, etc.: *Neither side was willing to give in.*
concede – to admit that you are not going to win a game, argument, battle, etc.: *Davis conceded defeat in the election.*
admit/accept defeat – to accept that you have not won something: *In July 1905, Russia admitted defeat in its war with Japan.*

2 [T] *formal* to give something to someone in authority, for example weapons or official documents: *They had to* ***surrender*** *their* ***passports.*** —**surrender** *n.* [U]

sur·rep·ti·tious·ly /ˌsɚəpˈtɪʃəsli, ˌsʌrəp-/ *adv.* done secretly or quietly so that other people do not notice —**surreptitious** *adj.*

sur·ro·gate /ˈsɚəgɪt, ˈsʌrə-/ *adj.* [only before noun] taking the place of someone or something else: *a surrogate family* —**surrogate** *n.* [C]

ˌsurrogate ˈmother *n.* [C] a woman who has a baby for another woman who cannot have children

sur·round /səˈraʊnd/ *v.* [T] **1** to be all around someone or something: *a lake **surrounded by** trees* | *The police surrounded the house.* **2 be surrounded by sb/sth** to have a lot of a particular type of people or things near you: *She is surrounded by friends.* **3** to be closely related to a situation or event: *Some of the issues surrounding alcohol abuse are very complex.* —**surrounding** *adj.*: *the surrounding countryside*

sur·round·ings /səˈraʊndɪŋz/ *n.* [plural] the place that you are in and all the things in it: *It took me a few weeks to get used to my **new surroundings**.*

sur·veil·lance /sɚˈveɪləns/ *n.* [U] the act of watching a particular person or place carefully, usually in order to catch a criminal or prevent a crime: *Police have the suspect **under surveillance**.* | *surveillance cameras*

sur·vey¹ /ˈsɚveɪ/ *n.* [C] **1** a set of questions that you ask a large number of people in order to find out about their opinions and behavior: *ABC News **conducted** a **survey** of working women.* | ***Surveys show** that most Americans support the president.*

> **THESAURUS**
> **poll, questionnaire**
> ➔ see Thesaurus box at POLL¹

2 a careful examination of an area of land, done in order to make a map of it

sur·vey² /sɚˈveɪ, ˈsɚveɪ/ *v.* [T] **1** to ask a large number of people a set of questions in order to find out about their opinions or behavior: *More than 50% of the students surveyed said they exercise regularly.* **2** to look at someone or something carefully so that you can make a decision, or find out more information: *I **surveyed** the **damage** to the car.* **3** to examine and measure an area of land in order to make a map

sur·vey·or /sɚˈveɪɚ/ *n.* [C] someone whose job is to measure and record the details of an area of land

sur·viv·al /sɚˈvaɪvəl/ *n.* [U] the state of continuing to live or exist, especially after a difficult or dangerous situation: *The operation will increase his **chances of survival**.* | *It's **survival of the fittest*** (=a situation in which only the strongest people, animals, or organizations can continue to exist).

sur·vive /sɚˈvaɪv/ *v.* [I,T] **1** to continue to live after an accident, illness, etc.: *Only one person survived the crash.* **2** to continue to live normally or exist in spite of difficulties: *Few small businesses survived the recession.* | *How do you manage to **survive on** such a low salary?* | *It's been a tough few months, but **I'll survive**.*

sur·vi·vor /sɚˈvaɪvɚ/ *n.* [C] **1** someone who continues to live after an accident, illness, etc.: *There were no survivors.* **2** *approving* someone who continues to live a normal life even when s/he has many difficulties or problems: *He's a survivor.*

sus·cep·ti·ble /səˈsɛptəbəl/ *adj.* likely to be affected by a particular illness or problem: *I've always been very **susceptible to** colds.*

su·shi /ˈsuʃi/ *n.* [U] Japanese food consisting of raw fish eaten with cooked rice

sus·pect¹ /ˈsʌspɛkt/ *n.* [C] someone who may be guilty of a crime: *the police's **prime suspect*** (=main one)

sus·pect² /səˈspɛkt/ *v.* [T] **1** to think that someone may be guilty of a crime: *She is **suspected of** murder.* **2** to think that something is probably true, especially something bad: *She **suspected (that)** Sandra had been lying.*

> **THESAURUS**
> **think, believe, consider, figure, guess**
> ➔ see Thesaurus box at THINK

3 to think that someone or something is not completely honest, sincere, or real: *Do you have reason to suspect his motives?*

sus·pect³ /ˈsʌspɛkt/ *adj.* difficult to believe or trust: *Her story is **highly suspect**.*

sus·pend /səˈspɛnd/ *v.* [T] **1** to officially stop someone from working, driving, or going to school for a fixed period, because s/he has broken the rules: *Joey was **suspended from** school.* | *Her driver's **license** was **suspended**.* **2** to officially stop something from continuing, usually for a short time: *The bus service has been suspended until further notice.* **3** *formal* if something is suspended somewhere, it is hanging down from there: *a chandelier **suspended from** the ceiling*

sus·pend·ers /səˈspɛndɚz/ *n.* [plural] two bands of cloth that go over your shoulders and are attached to your pants to hold them up

sus·pense /səˈspɛns/ *n.* [U] a feeling of not knowing what is going to happen next: *Don't **keep** us **in suspense**. What happened?*

sus·pen·sion /səˈspɛnʃən/ *n.* **1** [U] the act of officially stopping something from continuing for a period of time: *a **suspension of** military activity* **2** [C,U] an act of removing someone from a school or job for a short time, in order to punish him/her: *a three-day suspension for cheating* **3** [U] equipment attached to the wheels of a vehicle to make it comfortable to ride in

sus·pi·cion /səˈspɪʃən/ *n.* **1** [C,U] a feeling that someone is probably guilty of doing something wrong or dishonest: *Potter was arrested **on suspicion of** robbery.* | *I'm not sure who erased the file, but **I have my suspicions**.* **2** [U] a feeling that

S

you do not trust someone: *She always **treated** us **with suspicion**.*

sus·pi·cious /sə'spɪʃəs/ *adj.* **1** feeling that you do not like or trust someone or something: *I'm **suspicious of** her intentions.* | *Her behavior **made** me **suspicious**.* **2** making you think that something bad or illegal is happening: *He died under **suspicious circumstances**.* —**suspiciously** *adv.*: *They were acting suspiciously.*

sus·tain /sə'steɪn/ *v.* [T] **1** to make something continue to exist or happen over a period of time: *The nation's economy was largely sustained by foreign aid.* **2** *formal* to be injured or damaged, or to lose a lot of money or soldiers: *Two people **sustained** minor **injuries**.*

sus·tained /sə'steɪnd/ *adj.* continuing for a long time: *A sustained effort is needed.*

SUV *n.* [C] **sport utility vehicle** a type of vehicle that is bigger than a car and is made for traveling over rough ground

svelte /svɛlt/ *adj.* a svelte woman is thin and graceful

SW the written abbreviation of **southwest**

swab /swɑb/ *n.* [C] a small stick with a piece of material on the end, used for cleaning wounds or doing medical tests: *a cotton swab* —**swab** *v.* [T]

S

swag·ger /'swægɚ/ *v.* [I] to walk proudly, swinging your shoulders in a way that seems too confident —**swagger** *n.* [singular, U]

swal·low¹ /'swɑloʊ/ *v.* **1** [T] to make food or drink go down your throat: *She swallowed her coffee and got up to leave.* **2** [I] to make liquid in your mouth go down your throat, especially because you are nervous or afraid: *He swallowed anxiously before answering.* **3** [T] *informal* to believe a story or explanation that is not actually true: *I found his story a little **hard to swallow**.*

THESAURUS

believe, accept, take sb's word, fall for, buy
→ see Thesaurus box at BELIEVE

4 swallow your pride to do something that seems necessary even though you feel embarrassed or ashamed

swallow sth ⇔ **up** *phr. v.* to make something disappear or become part of something else: *As the city grew, local farms were swallowed up.*

swallow² *n.* [C] **1** an act of making food or drink go down your throat: *Mike drank his beer in one swallow.* **2** a common small bird with pointed wings and a tail with two points

swam /swæm/ *v.* the past tense of SWIM

swamp¹ /swɑmp, swɔmp/ *n.* [C,U] land that is always very wet or covered with water —**swampy** *adj.*

swamp² *v.* [T] **1** *informal* to suddenly give someone more work, problems, etc. than s/he can deal with: *We've been swamped with job applications.* **2** to suddenly cover something with a lot of water so that it causes damage: *Huge waves swamped the town.*

swan /swɑn/ *n.* [C] a large white bird with a long neck, that lives near lakes and rivers

swank /swæŋk/ **also swank·y** /'swæŋki/ *adj.* *informal* very fashionable or expensive: *a swank New York hotel*

swap /swɑp/ *v.* past tense and past participle **swapped**, present participle **swapping** [I,T] to exchange something you have for something that someone else has: *Can I **swap** seats **with** you?*

THESAURUS

exchange, trade
→ see Thesaurus box at EXCHANGE²

—**swap** *n.* [C]

'swap ˌmeet *n.* [C] an occasion when people meet to buy and sell used goods, or to exchange them

swarm¹ /swɔrm/ *v.* [I] if people swarm somewhere, they quickly move there together

swarm with sth *phr. v.* to be full of people, birds, or insects: *The beaches are swarming with people in the summer.*

swarm² *n.* [C] a large group of insects that move together: *a **swarm of** bees*

swarth·y /'swɔrði, -θi/ *adj.* someone who is swarthy has dark skin

swat /swɑt/ *v.* past tense and past participle **swatted**, present participle **swatting** [I,T] to hit an insect to try to kill it: *He **swatted at** a fly that was buzzing near his ear.* —**swat** *n.* [C]

swatch /swɑtʃ/ *n.* [C] a small piece of cloth that is used as an example of a type of material or its quality

swath /swɑθ, swɔθ/ *n.* [C] *formal* a long thin area of something, especially land

sway¹ /sweɪ/ *v.* **1** [I,T] to move slowly from one side to another: *palm trees swaying in the breeze* **2** [T] to try to influence someone to make a particular decision: *Nothing you say will sway her.*

sway² *n.* [U] **1** a swinging movement from one side to another: *the sway of the ship* **2** *literary* the power to rule or influence people: *Superstitious beliefs still **hold sway** in the country.*

swear /swɛr/ *v.* past tense **swore** /swɔr/ past participle **sworn** /swɔrn/ **1** [I] to use offensive language: *Don't swear in front of the children.* | *I'm sorry I **swore at** you.* **2** [I,T] to promise that you will do something: *Do you **swear to** tell the truth?*

THESAURUS

promise, take/swear an oath, vow, guarantee, give sb your word
→ see Thesaurus box at PROMISE¹

3 [T] *informal* used in order to emphasize that something is true: *She swore that she had never seen him before.* | ***I swear (to God)** I didn't take anything out of your room.* **4 I could have**

sworn (that)... *spoken* used in order to say that you were sure about something, but now you are not sure: *I could have sworn I left my keys here.*

swear by sth *phr. v.* to strongly believe that something is effective: *Heidi swears by vitamin C for preventing colds.*

swear sb ⇔ **in** *phr. v.* **1** to make someone publicly promise to be loyal to a country or an important job: *The new governor was sworn in today.* **2** to make someone give an official promise in a court of law: *The jury had to be sworn in.*

swear off sth *phr. v.* to decide to stop doing something that is bad for you: *I'm swearing off alcohol after last night!*

'swear word *n.* [C] a word that is considered rude or shocking

sweat¹ /swɛt/ *v.* **1** [I] to have liquid coming out through your skin, especially when you are hot or nervous: *The heat was making us sweat.* | *He was* ***sweating heavily/profusely*** (=a lot). **2** [I] *informal* to work hard: *I spent all night* ***sweating over*** *my term paper.* **3 don't sweat it** *spoken* used in order to tell someone not to worry about something: *Don't sweat it – I'll lend you the money.*

sweat sth ⇔ **out** *phr. v.* to continue doing something until it is finished, even though it is difficult: *We had to* ***sweat it out*** *until they arrived.*

sweat² *n.* **1** [U] liquid that comes out through your skin, especially when you are hot or nervous [= **perspiration**]: *His shirt was soaked with sweat.* | *We had both* ***worked up a sweat*** (=started sweating because of working hard). | *Sweat poured from his exhausted body.* **2 a cold sweat** nervousness or fear that makes you sweat even though you are not hot: *I woke up from the nightmare* ***in a cold sweat.*** **3 sweats** [plural] *informal* a SWEAT SUIT or the pants of a sweat suit **4 no sweat** *spoken* used in order to say that you can do something easily: *"Can I have a ride home?" "Yeah, no sweat!"*

sweat·er /ˈswɛt̬ɚ/ *n.* [C] a piece of warm wool or cotton clothing with long SLEEVES, which covers the top half of your body: *She put her sweater on.* | *a* ***wool/cotton/cashmere sweater*** → see picture at CLOTHES

'sweat pants *n.* [plural] soft thick pants, worn especially for sports

sweat·shirt /ˈswɛt-ʃɚt/ *n.* [C] a thick soft cotton shirt with long sleeves, no collar, and no buttons, worn especially for sports

sweat·shop /ˈswɛt-ʃɑp/ *n.* [C] a factory where people work hard in bad conditions for very little money

'sweat suit, sweat·suit /ˈswɛtsut/ *n.* a set of clothes made of thick soft material, worn especially for sports → see picture at CLOTHES

sweat·y /ˈswɛti/ *adj.* covered with SWEAT, or smelling like sweat: *I felt hot and sweaty.* | *sweaty hands*

sweep¹ /swip/ *v.* past tense and past participle **swept** /swɛpt/ **1** [T] **also sweep up** to clean the dirt from the floor or ground using a BROOM: *I've just swept the kitchen floor.* **2** [I,T] to move somewhere quickly or to move something quickly: *The crowd* ***swept through*** *the gates.* | *I* ***swept*** *the papers quickly* ***into*** *the drawer.* **3 sweep the country/nation** to quickly affect or become popular with most of the people in a country: *a fashion trend that is sweeping the nation* **4 sweep sb off his/her feet** to make someone feel suddenly and strongly attracted to you in a romantic way **5 sweep sth under the rug** to try to hide something bad that has happened

sweep sth ⇔ **away** *phr. v.* to completely destroy something or make something disappear: *Entire houses were swept away by the floods.*

sweep² *n.* **1** [C] a long swinging movement of your arm, a weapon, etc. **2** [C] a long curved line or area of land: ***the sweep of*** *the hills in the distance* **3** [C usually singular] a search or attack that moves through a particular area: *Soldiers made a sweep of the village.*

sweep·ing /ˈswipɪŋ/ *adj.* **1** affecting many things, or affecting one thing very much: *sweeping changes* **2 sweeping statement/generalization** *disapproving* a statement that is too general and does not consider all the facts

sweep·stakes /ˈswipsteɪks/ *n.* plural **sweepstakes** [C] **1** a type of competition in which you have a chance to win a prize if your name is chosen **2** a type of BETting in which the winner gets all the money risked by everyone else

sweet /swit/ *adj.* **1** having a taste like sugar: *sweet, juicy peaches*

> **THESAURUS**
> **sour, salty, hot, spicy, bland**
> → see Thesaurus box at TASTE¹

2 having a pleasant smell or sound: *a* ***sweet-smelling*** *rose* **3** kind, gentle, and friendly: *Fran is such a sweet person.* | *It was* ***sweet of*** *you to help.*

> **THESAURUS**
> **nice, kind, considerate, thoughtful, caring**
> → see Thesaurus box at KIND²

4 pretty and pleasant – used when you are talking about children and small things [= **cute**]: *Her baby is so sweet.* **5** making you feel happy and satisfied: *Revenge is sweet!* **6 have a sweet tooth** to like to eat sweet foods **7 Sweet!** *spoken* used in order to show that you think something is very good: *"I got four tickets to the concert." "Sweet!"* —**sweetly** *adv.*: *She smiled sweetly.* —**sweetness** *n.* [U]

sweet·en /ˈswitˀn/ *v.* **1** [I,T] to become or make something sweeter: *Sweeten the mixture with honey.* **2 sweeten the deal/pot/offer etc.** *informal* to make a deal seem more acceptable, usually by offering more money

S

sweet·en·er /ˈswitˀn-ɚ, -nɚ/ *n.* [C,U] a substance used instead of sugar to make food or drinks taste sweeter: *Many diet foods are full of* ***artificial sweeteners****.*

sweet·heart /ˈswithɑrt/ *n.* [C] **1** a way of talking to someone you love: *Good night, sweetheart.* **2** *old-fashioned* the person that you love: *He married his* ***childhood sweetheart****.*

sweet·ie /ˈswiţi/ *n.* [C] *spoken* **1** a way of talking to someone you love **2** someone who is kind and easy to love: *Pat's such a sweetie!*

ˌsweet poˈtato *n.* [C] a root that looks like an orange potato, is yellow inside, and tastes sweet

sweets /swits/ *n.* [plural] *informal* sweet food or candy

swell¹ /swɛl/ *v.* past tense **swelled**, past participle **swollen** /ˈswoʊlən/ **1** [I] **also swell up** to gradually increase in size, especially because of an injury: *My ankle swelled up like a balloon.* **2** [I,T] to increase to a much bigger amount or number: *The city's population has* ***swollen to*** *2 million.* **3 swell with pride/anger etc.** to feel very proud, angry, etc.

swell² *n.* [singular] the movement of the ocean as waves go up and down

swell³ *adj. old-fashioned* very good: *I had a really swell time.*

swell·ing /ˈswɛlɪŋ/ *n.* [C,U] an area on your body that becomes larger than usual because of injury or sickness: *This medicine should help* ***reduce the swelling****.*

swel·ter·ing /ˈswɛltərɪŋ/ *adj.* unpleasantly hot: *a sweltering summer day*

> **THESAURUS**
>
> **hot**, **warm**, **humid**, **boiling hot**
> → see Thesaurus box at HOT

swept /swɛpt/ *v.* the past tense and past participle of SWEEP

swerve /swɚv/ *v.* [I] to make a sudden movement to the left or right while moving forward, usually in order to avoid hitting something: *Mark swerved to avoid hitting the dog.*

swift /swɪft/ *adj.* happening or moving very quickly: *a swift response* —**swiftly** *adv.*

swig /swɪg/ *v.* past tense and past participle **swigged**, present participle **swigging** [T] *informal* to drink something by taking large amounts into your mouth —**swig** *n.* [C]

> **THESAURUS**
>
> **drink**, **sip**, **slurp**, **gulp down**, **knock back**
> → see Thesaurus box at DRINK²

swill¹ /swɪl/ *n.* [U] food for pigs

swill² *v.* [T] to drink a lot of something, especially beer

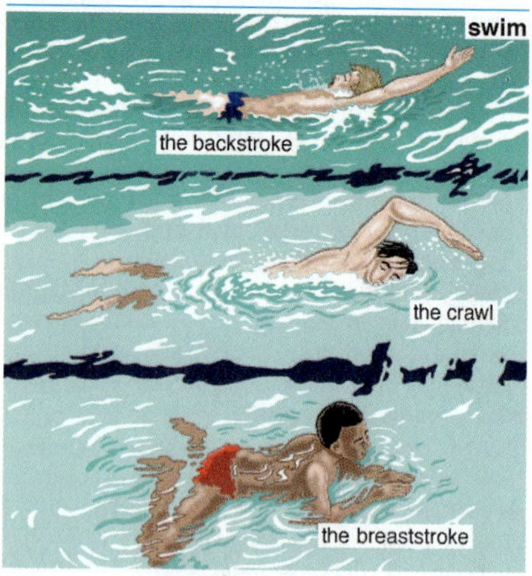

swim¹ /swɪm/ *v.* past tense **swam** /swæm/ past participle **swum** /swʌm/ present participle **swimming** **1** [I,T] to move through the water, using your arms and legs: *Can Lucy swim?* | *He swims 20 laps a day.* | *We used to* ***swim in*** *the lake.* **2** [I] if your head swims, you feel confused or as if everything is spinning around **3** [I] if something you are looking at swims, it seems to move around, usually because you are sick: *The room swam around her.* **4 be swimming in/with sth** to be covered by a lot of liquid: *meatballs swimming in sauce* —**swimming** *n.* [U] *Do you want to* ***go swimming****?*

swim² *n.* [C] a time when you swim: *Would you like to* ***go for a swim*** *after work?*

ˈswimming pool *n.* [C] a structure that has been built and filled with water for people to swim in [= **pool**]

ˈswimming suit *n.* [C] a SWIMSUIT

ˈswimming trunks *n.* [plural] a piece of clothing like SHORTS, worn by men for swimming

swim·suit /ˈswɪmsut/ *n.* [C] a piece of clothing worn for swimming

swin·dle¹ /ˈswɪndl/ *v.* [T] to get money from someone by tricking him/her —**swindler** *n.* [C]

swindle² *n.* [C] a situation in which someone gets money from someone else by tricking him/her

swine /swaɪn/ *n.* plural **swine** [C] *old-fashioned* a pig

swing¹ /swɪŋ/ *v.* past tense and past participle **swung** /swʌŋ/ **1** [I,T] to move backward and forward while hanging from a particular point, or to make something move in this way: *They walked hand in hand, swinging their arms.* | *a sign swinging in the wind* **2** [I,T] to move smoothly in a curved direction, or to make something move this way: *The screen door kept* ***swinging open/shut****.* **3** [I] if opinions or feelings swing, they change a lot: *Her mood* ***swung from*** *happiness* ***to*** *despair.*

swing around *phr. v.* to turn around quickly, or to make something do this: *Mitch swung around to face her.*

swing at sb/sth *phr. v.* to try to hit someone or

something with your hand or with an object that you are holding: *He swung at the ball and missed.*
swing by (sth) *phr. v. informal* to quickly visit a person or place before going somewhere else: *Can we swing by the store on the way home?*

swing² *n.* [C] **1** a seat hanging from ropes or chains, on which children swing: *a bunch of kids* ***playing on the swings*** **2** an attempt to hit someone or something by swinging your arm, an object, etc.: *Then he tried to* ***take a swing at*** *me.* **3** a change from one feeling, opinion, etc. to another: *mood swings* | *a big* ***swing in*** *public opinion* **4 be in full swing** if a party, event, etc. is in full swing, it is at its highest level of activity

swipe /swaɪp/ *v.* **1** [I,T] **also swipe at** to hit or try to hit someone or something by swinging your arm very quickly **2** [T] *informal* to steal something: *Somebody swiped my wallet.* **3** [T] to pull a plastic card through a machine that can read the electronic information on it —**swipe** *n.* [C]

swirl /swɚl/ *v.* [I,T] to turn around and around, or to make something do this: *mist* ***swirling around*** *the mountain peaks* —**swirl** *n.* [C]

swish /swɪʃ/ *v.* [I,T] to move or make something move quickly through the air with a soft sound like a whistle: *a cow swishing its tail* —**swish** *n.* [singular]

Swiss¹ /swɪs/ *adj.* relating to or coming from Switzerland

Swiss² *n.* **the Swiss** [plural] the people of Switzerland, considered as a single group

switch¹ /swɪtʃ/ *v.* **1** [I,T] to change from doing or using one thing to doing or using something else: *If you* ***switch to*** *a low-fat diet, your health will improve.* | *He kept* ***switching from*** *one subject* ***to*** *another.* | *He* ***switched sides*** *just days before the election.* **2** [T] to replace an object with a similar object, especially secretly or accidentally: *We must have accidentally switched umbrellas.*
switch sth ⇔ **off** *phr. v.* to turn off a machine, radio, light, etc. by using a switch: *Be sure to* ***switch off the lights*** *when you leave.*
switch sth ⇔ **on** *phr. v.* to turn on a machine, radio, light, etc. by using a SWITCH: *Could you switch the radio on?*
switch over *phr. v.* to start using a different product, system, etc.: *More and more people are switching over to Internet banking.*

switch² *n.* [C] **1** the part that you press or push on a machine, radio, light, etc. so that it starts or stops operating: *Where's the* ***on/off switch****?* | *a light switch* **2** a change from one thing to another: *More shoppers are* ***making the switch*** *to organic food.*

switch·board /ˈswɪtʃbɔrd/ *n.* [C] a piece of equipment that connects all the telephone calls made to or from a particular business, hotel, etc.

swiv·el /ˈswɪvəl/ **also swivel around** *v.* [I,T] to turn around while remaining in the same place, or to make something do this: *She wants a chair that swivels.* ➔ see picture on page A11

swol·len¹ /ˈswoʊlən/ *v.* the past participle of SWELL

swollen² *adj.* **1** a part of your body that is swollen is bigger than usual because of injury or sickness: *My knee is still really swollen from the accident.* **2** a swollen river has more water in it than usual

swoon /swun/ *v.* [I] *old-fashioned* to feel so much emotion that you almost FAINT (=lose consciousness)

swoop /swup/ *v.* [I] **1** to suddenly and quickly move down through the air, especially to attack something: *An owl* ***swooped down*** *and grabbed a mouse.* **2** if soldiers or the police swoop, they go somewhere very quickly and without warning in order to attack or ARREST someone —**swoop** *n.* [C]

sword /sɔrd/ *n.* [C] a weapon with a long sharp blade and a handle

sword·fish /ˈsɔrdˌfɪʃ/ *n.* [C] a large fish with a long pointed upper jaw

swore /swɔr/ *v.* the past tense of SWEAR

sworn¹ /swɔrn/ *v.* the past participle of SWEAR

sworn² *adj.* **1 sworn statement/testimony** something you say or write that you have officially promised is the truth **2 sworn enemies** two people or groups who will always hate each other

swum /swʌm/ *v.* the past participle of SWIM

swung /swʌŋ/ *v.* the past tense and past participle of SWING

syc·a·more /ˈsɪkəˌmɔr/ *n.* [C,U] an eastern North American tree with broad leaves, or the wood from this tree

syc·o·phant /ˈsɪkəfənt/ *n.* [C] *formal disapproving* someone who always praises an important person in order to gain an advantage, not in an honest way —**sycophantic** /ˌsɪkəˈfæntɪk◂/ *adj.*

syl·la·ble /ˈsɪləbəl/ *n.* [C] *technical* each part of a word that contains a single vowel sound. For example, "cat" has one syllable and "butter" has two.

syl·la·bus /ˈsɪləbəs/ *n.* plural **syllabi** /-baɪ/ or **syllabuses** [C] a plan that shows a student what s/he will be studying in a particular subject

sym·bol /ˈsɪmbəl/ *n.* [C] **1** a picture, person, object, etc. that represents a particular quality, idea, organization, etc.: *The cross is the most important symbol in Christianity.* | *The dove is a* ***symbol of*** *peace.* **2** a letter, number, or sign that represents a sound, amount, chemical substance, etc.: *Fe is the chemical* ***symbol for*** *iron.*

sym·bol·ic /sɪmˈbɑlɪk/ *adj.* **1** representing a particular idea or quality: *A red rose is* ***symbolic of*** *love.* **2** important but not having any real effect: *The president's trip to Russia was mostly symbolic.* —**symbolically** *adv.*

sym·bol·ism /ˈsɪmbəˌlɪzəm/ *n.* [U] the use of symbols to represent things: *There's a lot of religious symbolism in his paintings.*

sym·bol·ize /ˈsɪmbəˌlaɪz/ *v.* [T] if something symbolizes a quality, feeling, etc., it represents it: *A wedding ring symbolizes a couple's vows to each other.*

S

sym·met·ri·cal /sə'mɛtrɪkəl/ **also sym·met·ric** /sə'mɛtrɪk/ *adj.* having two sides that are exactly the same size and shape [≠ **asymmetrical**]

sym·me·try /'sɪmətri/ *n.* [U] the quality of being symmetrical

sym·pa·thet·ic /ˌsɪmpə'θɛt̬ɪk◂ / *adj.* **1** showing that you understand how sad, hurt, lonely, etc. someone feels [≠ **unsympathetic**]: *a sympathetic nurse | Parents aren't always very* ***sympathetic towards*** *their children.* **2** [not before noun] willing to support someone's plans, actions, ideas, etc. [≠ **unsympathetic**]: *He's fairly* ***sympathetic to*** *the staff's concerns.* —**sympathetically** *adv.*

sym·pa·thize /'sɪmpəˌθaɪz/ *v.* [I] **1** to understand how sad, hurt, lonely, etc. someone feels: *I can* ***sympathize with*** *the way you're feeling.* **2** to support someone's ideas or actions: *Very few people* ***sympathize with*** *his views.*

sym·pa·thiz·er /'sɪmpəˌθaɪzɚ/ *n.* [C] someone who supports the aims and ideas of a political organization

sym·pa·thy /'sɪmpəθi/ *n.* plural **sympathies** [C,U] **1** a feeling of support for someone who is sad, hurt, lonely, etc.: *I* ***have*** *absolutely* ***no sympathy for*** *students who get caught cheating on tests. | I'm sorry to hear Bill died; you have my* ***deep sympathy.*** **2** support for someone's plan, actions, ideas, etc.: *I do have some* ***sympathy with*** *their aims.*

sym·pho·ny /'sɪmfəni/ *n.* plural **symphonies** [C] a long piece of music written for an ORCHESTRA

symp·tom /'sɪmptəm/ *n.* [C] **1** a physical condition that shows you may have a particular disease: *Common* ***symptoms of*** *diabetes are weight loss and fatigue.* **2** a sign that a serious problem exists: *Rising crime rates are another* ***symptom of*** *a society in trouble.* —**symptomatic** /ˌsɪmptə'mæt̬ɪk/ *adj.*

syn·a·gogue /'sɪnəˌgɑg/ *n.* [C] a building where Jewish people go to have religious services

sync /sɪŋk/ *n. informal* **1 in sync** working together at the same time or speed or in the same way **2 out of sync** working at a different time or speed or in a different way

syn·chro·nize /'sɪŋkrəˌnaɪz/ *v.* [T] to make two or more things happen or move at the same time —**synchronization** /ˌsɪŋkrənə'zeɪʃən/ *n.* [U]

syn·di·cate /'sɪndəkɪt/ *n.* [C,U] a group of people or companies that join together to achieve a particular aim: *the city's largest crime syndicate*

syn·di·cat·ed /'sɪndəˌkeɪt̬ɪd/ *adj.* a syndicated newspaper COLUMN, television program, etc. is bought and used by several different newspapers or broadcasting companies —**syndication** /ˌsɪndə'keɪʃən/ *n.* [U]

syn·drome /'sɪndroʊm/ *n.* [C] a set of physical or mental conditions that show you have a particular disease

syn·o·nym /'sɪnəˌnɪm/ *n.* [C] *technical* a word with the same meaning as another word in the same language. For example, "mad" and "angry" are synonyms. [≠ **antonym**]

syn·on·y·mous /sɪ'nɑnəməs/ *adj.* **1** having a strong association with another quality, idea, situation, etc.: *He thinks that being poor is* ***synonymous with*** *being a criminal.* **2** two words that are synonymous have the same or nearly the same meaning

syn·op·sis /sɪ'nɑpsɪs/ *n.* plural **synopses** /-siz/ [C] a short description of the main parts of a story

syn·tax /'sɪntæks/ *n.* [U] *technical* the way words are arranged in order to form sentences or phrases

syn·the·sis /'sɪnθəsɪs/ *n.* [C,U] the act of combining several things into a single complete unit, or the combination that is produced

syn·the·size /'sɪnθəˌsaɪz/ *v.* [T] to combine different things in order to produce something: *Scientists can now synthesize the drug.*

syn·the·siz·er /'sɪnθəˌsaɪzɚ/ *n.* [C] an electronic musical instrument that can produce the sounds of various different musical instruments

syn·thet·ic /sɪn'θɛt̬ɪk/ *adj.* made from artificial substances, not natural ones: *synthetic fabrics like acrylic and polyester* —**synthetically** *adv.*

THESAURUS

artificial, fake, imitation, false, man-made
→ see Thesaurus box at ARTIFICIAL, NATURAL[1]

syph·i·lis /'sɪfəlɪs/ *n.* [U] a very serious disease that is passed from one person to another during sex

sy·ringe /sə'rɪndʒ/ *n.* [C] a hollow tube and needle used for removing blood or other liquids from your body, or putting drugs, etc. into it

syr·up /'sɚəp, 'sɪrəp/ *n.* [U] thick sticky liquid made from sugar: *pancakes with* ***maple syrup*** —**syrupy** *adj.*

sys·tem /'sɪstəm/ *n.* [C] **1** a group of things or parts that work together as a whole for a particular purpose: *the public school system | a new computer system | the digestive system* **2** a way of organizing or doing something: *a filing system | a* ***system of*** *government* **3 sb's system** someone's body – used when you are talking about its medical or physical condition **4 get sth out of your system** *informal* to do something that helps you stop feeling angry, annoyed, or upset **5 the system** *informal* the official rules and powerful organizations that restrict what you can do: *You can't* ***beat the system*** (=avoid or break the rules).

sys·tem·at·ic /ˌsɪstə'mæt̬ɪk/ *adj.* organized carefully and done thoroughly: *a* ***systematic approach*** *to training* —**systematically** *adv.*

T, t

T, t /ti/ **1** the twentieth letter of the English alphabet **2 to a T/to a tee** *informal* exactly or perfectly: *a dress that fits her to a T*

tab /tæb/ *n.* [C] **1** an amount of money that you owe for a meal or drinks you have had, or for a service: *Our lunch tab came to $53.* | *I'll* ***put it on*** *your* ***tab***. | *The city is* ***picking up the tab for*** *street repairs* (=is paying for them).

THESAURUS

bill, **check**, **invoice**
→ see Thesaurus box at BILL[1]

2 keep tabs on sb/sth *informal* to carefully watch what someone or something is doing: *The police are* ***keeping close tabs on*** *her.* **3** a small piece of metal, plastic, or paper that you pull to open a container **4** a small piece of paper, cloth, plastic, etc. that sticks out from the edge of something, so that you can find it more easily

tab·by /ˈtæbi/ *n.* plural **tabbies** [C] a cat with light and dark lines on its fur

ta·ble[1] /ˈteɪbəl/ *n.* [C] **1** a piece of furniture with a flat top supported by legs: *a picnic table* | *He sat* ***at the*** *kitchen* ***table***, *reading.* | *I'll* ***set the table*** (=put knives, forks, dishes, etc. on a table before a meal). | *Can you* ***clear the table*** (=take the plates, etc. off the table after a meal), *please.* **2** a table at a restaurant: ***Reserve a table*** *for four and invite your sisters.* | *The whole table* (=all the people sitting at a table in a restaurant) *got up and left.* **3** a list of numbers, facts, or information arranged in rows across and down a page: *the book's* ***table of contents*** **4 under the table** *informal* money that is paid under the table is paid secretly and illegally **5 turn the tables (on sb)** to change a situation completely so that someone loses an advantage and you gain one

table[2] *v.* **table a bill/proposal/offer etc.** to decide to deal with an offer, idea, etc. later

ta·ble·cloth /ˈteɪbəlˌklɔθ/ *n.* [C] a cloth used for covering a table

ta·ble·spoon /ˈteɪbəlˌspun/ *n.* [C] **1** *written abbreviation* **tbsp a)** a special large spoon used for measuring food **b) also ta·ble·spoon·ful** /-spunˌfʊl/ the amount this spoon holds **2** a large spoon used for eating or serving food

tab·let /ˈtæblɪt/ *n.* [C] **1** a small round piece of medicine that you swallow [= **pill**]: *vitamin C tablets*

THESAURUS

pill, **capsule**, **eye/ear drops**
→ see Thesaurus box at MEDICINE

2 a set of pieces of paper for writing on that are glued together at the top **3** a flat piece of hard clay or stone that has words cut into it

ˈtable ˌtennis *n.* [U] PING-PONG

tab·loid /ˈtæblɔɪd/ *n.* [C] a newspaper that has small pages, a lot of photographs, short stories, and not much serious news [➡ **broadsheet**] → see Thesaurus box at NEWSPAPER

ta·boo /təˈbu, tæ-/ *n.* plural **taboos** [C,U] a religious or social CUSTOM which means a particular activity or subject must be avoided —**taboo** *adj.*: *a taboo subject*

tab·u·late /ˈtæbyəˌleɪt/ *v.* [T] to arrange facts, numbers, or information together in lists, rows, etc. —**tabulation** /ˌtæbyəˈleɪʃən/ *n.* [U]

tac·it /ˈtæsɪt/ *adj.* tacit agreement, approval, or support is given without anything actually being said: *a* ***tacit agreement*** *between the three big companies* —**tacitly** *adv.*

tac·i·turn /ˈtæsəˌtɚn/ *adj.* a taciturn person does not talk a lot, and seems unfriendly

tack[1] /tæk/ **also tack up** *v.* [T] to attach something to a wall, board, etc. using a THUMBTACK

tack sth ⇔ **on** *phr. v. informal* to add something new to something that is already complete: *Joan tacked a few words on the end of my letter.*

tack[2] *n.* **1** [C,U] the way you deal with a particular situation or a method that you use to achieve something: *If polite requests don't work, you'll have to* ***try a different tack***. **2** [C] a THUMBTACK **3** [C] a small nail with a sharp point and a flat top: *carpet tacks*

tack·le[1] /ˈtækəl/ *v.* [T] **1** to try to deal with a difficult problem: *a new attempt to tackle homelessness*

THESAURUS

deal with, **handle**, **attend to**, **take care of**
→ see Thesaurus box at DEAL WITH

2 to force someone to the ground to stop him/her from running, especially in football: *Edwards was tackled on the play.*

tackle[2] *n.* **1** [C] the act of tackling (TACKLE) someone **2** [C] in football, one of the players who play on the outside of the GUARDS **3** [U] the equipment used in some sports such as fishing

tack·y /ˈtæki/ *adj.* **1** showing that you do not have good judgment about what is fashionable, socially acceptable, etc.: *It's kind of tacky to give her a present that someone else gave you.* **2** cheaply made and of bad quality: *tacky furniture* **3** slightly sticky —**tackiness** *n.* [U]

ta·co /ˈtɑkoʊ/ *n.* plural **tacos** [C] a type of Mexican food made from a TORTILLA, that is folded and filled with meat, beans, etc.

tact /tækt/ *n.* [U] the ability to say or do things carefully and politely so that you do not embarrass or upset someone

tact·ful /ˈtæktfəl/ *adj.* careful not to say or do something that will upset or embarrass someone else [≠ **tactless**]: *There was no tactful way of saying what he wanted to say.* —**tactfully** *adv.*

tac·tic /ˈtæktɪk/ *n.* [C usually plural] **1** a skillfully planned action used for achieving something: *aggressive sales tactics* **2 tactics** [plural] the way in which soldiers, weapons, etc. are arranged in a battle

tac·ti·cal /ˈtæktɪkəl/ *adj.* **1** done in order to help you achieve what you want: *a tactical move to avoid criticism* **2 tactical aircraft/missile etc.** an aircraft, MISSILE, etc. that is used over a short distance during a battle —**tactically** *adv.*

tact·less /ˈtæktfəl/ *adj.* carelessly saying or doing things that are likely to upset someone [≠ **tactful**] —**tactlessly** *adv.*

THESAURUS

rude, **impolite**, **insulting**, **offensive**
➔ see Thesaurus box at RUDE

tad /tæd/ *n. spoken* **a tad** a small amount: *Could you turn up the sound just a tad?*

tad·pole /ˈtædpoʊl/ *n.* [C] a small creature with a long tail that lives in water and grows into a FROG or TOAD

taf·fy /ˈtæfi/ *n.* [U] a type of soft CHEWY candy

tag¹ /tæg/ *n.* **1** [C] a small piece of paper, plastic, etc., attached to something to show what it is, who owns it, what it costs, etc.: *I can't find the* ***price tag*** *on these jeans.* **2** [U] a children's game in which one player chases and tries to touch the others

T

tag² *v.* past tense and past participle **tagged**, present participle **tagging** [T] to attach a tag to something: *Scientists have now tagged most of the bay's seals.*

tag along *phr. v. informal* to go somewhere with someone, especially when s/he has not invited you: *Do you mind if I tag along?*

tail¹ /teɪl/ *n.* **1** [C] the movable part that sticks out at the back of an animal's body: *The dog* ***wagged*** *its* ***tail.*** ➔ see picture on page A2 **2** [C] the back part of an aircraft ➔ see picture at AIRPLANE **3** [C] the end or back part of something, especially something long and thin: *the* ***tail of*** *a comet* **4 tails a)** [plural] a man's jacket with two long parts that hang down the back, worn to formal events **b)** [U] the side of a coin that does not have a picture of someone's head on it [≠ **heads**] **5 the tail end of sth** the last part of an event, situation, or period of time: *the tail end of the century*

tail² *v.* [T] *informal* to secretly watch and follow someone such as a criminal

THESAURUS

follow, **chase**, **pursue**, **run after**, **stalk**
➔ see Thesaurus box at FOLLOW

tail off *phr. v.* to gradually become quieter, smaller, weaker, etc.: *His voice tailed off as he saw his father approaching.*

tail·gate¹ /ˈteɪlgeɪt/ *v.* [I,T] to drive too closely to the vehicle in front of you

tailgate² *n.* [C] **1** a door at the back of a car or truck that opens out and down **2** a TAILGATE PARTY

ˈtailgate ˌparty *n.* [C] a party before a sports event or concert where people eat and drink in the PARKING LOT of the place where the event is taking place

tail·light /ˈteɪl-laɪt/ *n.* [C] one of the two red lights at the back of a vehicle ➔ see picture on page A12

tai·lor¹ /ˈteɪlɚ/ *n.* [C] someone whose job is to make clothes, especially men's clothes, that are measured to fit each customer perfectly

tailor² *v.* **tailor sth to/for sb** to make something so that it is exactly what someone wants or needs: *a music class tailored to children*

tai·lor·ing /ˈteɪlərɪŋ/ *n.* [U] the way that clothes are made, or the job of making them

ˌtailor-ˈmade *adj.* **1** exactly right for someone or something: *The job seems* ***tailor-made for*** *him.* **2** made by a tailor: *a tailor-made suit*

tail·pipe /ˈteɪlpaɪp/ *n.* [C] EXHAUST ➔ see picture on page A12

tail·spin /ˈteɪlspɪn/ *n.* **1 in/into a tailspin** in or into a bad situation that keeps getting worse in a way that you cannot control: *Raising interest rates could* ***send*** *the economy* ***into a tailspin.*** **2** [C] an occasion when an airplane falls through the air, with the front pointing down and the back spinning in a circle

taint /teɪnt/ *v.* [T] **1** to make someone or something seem less honest, respectable, or good: *Her reputation was tainted by the scandal.* **2** to damage something by adding an unwanted substance to it: *The blood supplies were* ***tainted with*** *bacteria.* —**taint** *n.* [C]

taint·ed /ˈteɪntɪd/ *adj.* **1** a tainted substance is not safe because it is spoiled or contains poison: *a tainted blood supply* **2** affected or influenced by something illegal, dishonest, or morally wrong: *tainted witnesses*

Tai·wan·ese /ˌtaɪwɑˈniz◂/ *adj.* relating to or coming from Taiwan

take¹ /teɪk/ *v.* past tense **took** /tʊk/ past participle **taken** /ˈteɪkən/ [T]

1 MOVE to move someone or something from one place to another: *Merritt was* ***taken*** *by ambulance* ***to*** *the nearest hospital.* | *Remember to* ***take*** *a jacket* ***with*** *you.* | *I was going to* ***take*** *some work* ***home***.

USAGE

bring – to take something or someone to a place: *We should bring a bottle of wine.* | *I bought the truck in Texas and brought it back to Mexico.*
take – to move something from one place to another, or help someone go from one place to another: *Don't forget to take your umbrella.* | *I can take you home after the concert.*
get – to go to another place and come back with something or someone: *Just a minute while I get my jacket.*

2 DO STH used with a noun to show that an action is being done: *Here, take a look.* | *I'm going to take a shower first.* | *Would you mind **taking a picture/photo** of us?* | *The new rules **take effect** May 1.* | *He **took the lead*** (=went into first place) *on the final lap.*
3 REMOVE to remove something from a particular place: *Can you **take** the turkey **out** of the oven for me?*
4 STEAL/BORROW to steal something or borrow something without asking someone's permission: *They took all her jewelry.*
5 HOLD/PUT to get hold of something in your hands: *Let me take your coat.*
6 TIME/MONEY/EFFORT if something takes a particular amount of time, money, etc., that amount of time, money, etc. is needed in order for it to happen or succeed: *It takes about three days to drive there.* | *It'll take a lot of planning, but I think it can be done.*
7 ACCEPT/RECEIVE to accept or receive something: *Are you going to take the job?* | *Do you take Visa?* | ***Take** my **advice** and go see a doctor.* | *Why should I **take the blame**?*
8 STUDY to study a particular subject: *We had to take two years of English.*
9 take a test/exam to write or do a test: *I'm taking my driving test next week.*
10 GET CONTROL to get possession or control of something: *Rebel forces have **taken control** of the airport.* | *The communists **took power** in 1948.*
11 ACCEPT STH BAD to accept a bad situation without becoming upset: *Jeff can't take the stress.* | *She's taken a lot of abuse from him.* | *His constant drinking was **hard to take*** (=difficult to accept).
12 MACHINE/VEHICLE if a vehicle, machine, etc. takes a particular type of gasoline or BATTERY, etc., you have to use that type of gasoline, etc. in order for it to work: *What kind of gas does your car take?*
13 MEDICINE/DRUG to swallow or INJECT a medicine or drug: *He doesn't smoke, drink, or take drugs* (=use illegal drugs). | *Why don't you take an aspirin or something?*
14 TRAVEL to use a car, bus, train, etc. to go somewhere, or to travel using a particular road: *I'll take the subway home.* | *Take Route 78 to Exit 18.*
15 REACT/CONSIDER to react to someone or something or consider him, her, or it in a particular way: *He takes his job very seriously.* | *I didn't mean for you to take what I said literally.*
16 WRITE also take down to write down information: *He's not here; can I **take a message**?* | *Let me take down your phone number.*
17 FEELINGS/REACTIONS to have a particular feeling or reaction when something happens: *His family **took** the news pretty **hard*** (=were very upset). | *She doesn't seem to take a lot of interest in her kids.*
18 MEASURE to measure the amount, level, or rate of something: *Sit here and we'll take your blood pressure.*
19 HAVE SPACE FOR SB/STH to have enough space to contain a particular number of people or things: *The station wagon takes six people.*
20 BUY to decide to buy something: *He gave me a discount so I said I'd take it.*
21 SIZE to wear a particular size of clothing or shoes: *Jim takes an extra large shirt.*
22 not take sth lying down to refuse to accept being treated badly
23 take it upon yourself to decide to do something even though no one has asked you to do it: *Parents have taken it upon themselves to raise extra cash for the school.*
24 do you take sugar/milk/cream etc.? *spoken* used to ask someone whether s/he likes to have sugar or milk in a drink such as tea or coffee → **take care** at CARE[2] → **take care of sb/sth** at CARE[2] → **take part** at PART[1] → **take place** at PLACE[1]

take after sb *phr. v.* to look or behave like another member of your family: *Jenny takes after her dad.*

take sth ⇔ **apart** *phr. v.* to separate something into all its different parts [≠ **put together**]: *Vic took apart the faucet and put in a new washer.*

take sb/sth ⇔ **away** *phr. v.* to remove someone or something: *One more speeding ticket and your license will be taken away.* | *He was taken away to begin a four-year prison sentence.*

take sth ⇔ **back** *phr. v.* **1** to admit that you were wrong to say something: *All right, I'm sorry, I **take it back**.* **2** to return something to the store where you bought it because it does not fit, is not what you wanted, etc.

take sth ⇔ **down** *phr. v.* to remove something from its place, especially by separating it into pieces [≠ **put up**]: *We take down the Christmas tree on January 6.*

take in *phr. v.* **1 take** sth ⇔ **in** to collect or earn an amount of money: *We've taken in $100,000 so far for charity.* **2 take** sb/sth ⇔ **in** to let someone or something stay in your house or a shelter, because she, he, or it has nowhere else to stay: *The Humane Society took in almost 38,000 cats and dogs last year.* **3 take** sth ⇔ **in** to notice, understand, and remember things: *Babies take in an amazing amount of information.* **4 take** sth ⇔ **in** to bring something to a place in order to be repaired: *I need to take the car in for a tune-up.* **5 take in** sth to go to see something, such as a movie, play, etc.: *tourists taking in the sights* **6 be taken in (by sth)** to be deceived by someone who lies to you: *Don't be taken in by his promises.* **7 take** sth ⇔ **in** to make a piece of clothing fit you by making it narrower: *If we take in the waist, the dress will fit you.*

take off **1 take** sth ⇔ **off** to remove something [≠ **put on**]: *Your name has been taken off the list.* | *Take your shoes off in the house.* **2** if an aircraft takes off, it rises into the air from the ground **3** *informal* to leave a place: *We packed everything*

T

in the car and took off. **4 take time/a day/a week etc. off also take time, etc. off work** to not go to work for a period of time: *I'm taking some time off work to go to the wedding.* **5** to suddenly become successful: *He died just as his film career was taking off.*

take on *phr. v.* **1 take** sb ⇔ **on** to compete or fight against someone: *The winner of this game will take on Houston in the championship.* **2 take on** sth to begin to have a particular quality or appearance: *Once we had children, Christmas took on a different sort of importance.* **3 take** sth ⇔ **on** to start doing some work or to start being responsible for something: *Ethel agreed to take on the treasurer's position.* **4 take** sb ⇔ **on** to start to employ someone: *The team has taken on a new coach.*

take out *phr. v.* **1 take** sb **out** to go with someone to a restaurant, movie, party, etc., and pay for his/her meal and entertainment: *We're **taking** Sabina **out for** dinner.* **2 take** sth ⇔ **out** to arrange to get something from a bank, court, insurance company, etc.: *The couple took out a $220,000 mortgage.*

take sth ⇔ **out on** sb *phr. v.* to treat someone badly when you are angry or upset, even though it is not his/her fault: *Don't **take it out on** me just because you've had a bad day.*

take sth ⇔ **over** *phr. v.* to take control of something: *His son will take over the business.*

take to *phr. v.* **1 take to** sb/sth to start to like someone or something: *The two women took to each other right away.* **2 take to doing sth** to begin doing something regularly: *Sandra has taken to getting up early to go jogging.*

take up *phr. v.* **1 take** sth ⇔ **up** to begin doing a job or activity: *I've just taken up tennis.* **2 take up** sth to fill a particular amount of time or space: *The program takes up a lot of memory on the hard drive.* | *Our new car takes up the whole garage.* **3 take** sth ⇔ **up** to begin discussing or considering something: *The Senate will take up the bill in the next few weeks.*

take sb **up on** sth *phr. v.* to accept an offer, invitation, etc.: *A number of students have taken him up on his offer of extra help.*

take sth ⇔ **up with** sb *phr. v.* to discuss something with someone, especially a complaint or problem: *You should take it up with the police.*

take² *n.* [C] **1** an occasion when a scene for a movie or television program is filmed **2** [usually singular] *informal* the amount of money earned by a store or business in a particular period of time

tak·en /ˈteɪkən/ *v.* the past participle of TAKE

take·off /ˈteɪk-ɔf/ *n.* **1** [C,U] the time when an airplane leaves the ground and begins to fly: *The plane crashed shortly after takeoff.* → see picture at LAND² **2** [C] a funny performance that copies the style of a particular show, movie, or performer

take·out /ˈteɪk-aʊt/ *n.* [C] **1** a meal you buy at a restaurant to eat at home **2** a restaurant that sells this food —**take-out** *adj.*

take·o·ver /ˈteɪkˌoʊvɚ/ *n.* [C] **1** the act of getting control of a company by buying over half of its STOCK **2** the act of getting control of a country or political group, often using force: *a military takeover*

tal·cum pow·der /ˈtælkəm ˌpaʊdɚ/ *n.* [U] a powder which you put on your skin after washing to make it smell nice

tale /teɪl/ *n.* [C] a story about imaginary events: *a **fairy tale** by Hans Christian Andersen* | ***tales of** adventure*

THESAURUS

story, myth, legend, fable
→ see Thesaurus box at STORY

tal·ent /ˈtælənt/ *n.* **1** [C,U] a natural ability to do something well: *great musical talent* | *his **talent for** painting* | *Vinny **has** a real **talent** for basketball.*

THESAURUS

ability, skill, knack
→ see Thesaurus box at ABILITY

2 [U] a person or people who have talent: *The Marlins have some of the best young talent in baseball.*

tal·ent·ed /ˈtæləntɪd/ *adj.* having a natural ability to do something well: *a talented actor*

tal·is·man /ˈtælɪsmən, -lɪz-/ *n.* plural **talismans** [C] an object that some people believe has the power to protect them

talk¹ /tɔk/ *v.* **1** [I] to say things to someone as part of a conversation [➡ **speak**]: *How old was your baby when she started to talk?* | *Who's he **talking to** on the phone?* | *English people love to **talk about** the weather.* | *I was just **talking with** Louis the other day.* ▶ Don't say "talk English/Chinese etc." say "speak English/Chinese etc." ◀

THESAURUS

have a conversation – to talk informally to another person or people in order to ask questions, exchange ideas, etc.: *I had a brief conversation with him last week.*
chat (with/to sb)/have a chat – to talk to someone in a friendly way about things that are not very important: *She's chatting with Chris.* | *We ended up having a chat about sailing.*
converse formal – to have a conversation with someone: *Students like her because she can converse with them in their own language.*
visit with sb informal – to have a conversation with someone, especially about your personal lives
discuss – to talk seriously about ideas or plans: *We'll discuss the matter at the meeting.*
gossip – to talk about other people's private

lives when they are not there: *People have started to gossip about his wife.*
whisper – to talk quietly, usually because you do not want other people to hear what you are saying: *He turned to his mother and whispered something in her ear.* | *"I love you," she whispered.*

2 [I,T] to discuss something with someone, especially something important: *I'd like to* ***talk with*** *you in private.* | *Grandpa never* ***talks about*** *the war.* | *Those guys are always* ***talking sports/business/politics, etc.*** (=discussing them). **3 talk your way out of sth** *informal* to use excuses or explanations to escape from a bad situation: *My brother always manages to talk his way out of trouble.* **4** [I] to give a speech: *Professor Wilson will* ***talk on/about*** *the recent election in Canada.* **5** [I] to tell someone secret information because you are forced to: *Prisoners who refused to talk were shot.*

SPOKEN PHRASES

6 talk tough (on sth) to tell people your opinions very strongly: *The President is talking tough on crime.* **7 what are you talking about?** used when you think what someone has said is stupid or wrong: *What are you talking about? I paid you yesterday.* **8 we're/you're talking $500/three days etc.** used to tell someone how much something will cost, how long something will take to do, etc.: *We're talking at least ten days to fix the car.* **9 talk about funny/stupid/rich etc.** said in order to emphasize that something is very funny, stupid, etc.: *Talk about lucky. That's the second time he's won this week.*

talk back *phr. v.* to rudely answer someone who is older or has more authority than you: *Don't* ***talk back to*** *your father!*

talk down to sb *phr. v.* to speak to someone as if s/he is stupid, although s/he is not: *He always explained things but never talked down to me.*

talk sb ⇔ **into** sth *phr. v.* to persuade someone to do something: *Maybe I can talk Vicky into driving us to the mall.*

talk sb ⇔ **out of** sth *phr. v.* to persuade someone not to do something: *Brenda talked me out of quitting my job.*

talk sth ⇔ **over** *phr. v.* to discuss a problem with someone before deciding what to do

talk² *n.* **1** [C] a conversation: *Steve and I* ***had a long talk*** *last night.* | *I need to* ***have a talk with*** *Suzanne.* **2 talks** [plural] formal discussions between governments, organizations, etc.: *the latest trade talks* **3** [C] a speech: *Ms. Mason will be* ***giving a talk on/about*** *the Civil War.* **4** [U] news that is not official or not completely true: *There was* ***talk of*** *the factory closing down.* **5** [U] a particular type of conversation or way of talking: *I'm tired of all this football talk.* → SMALL TALK, TRASH TALK

talk·a·tive /ˈtɔkət̬ɪv/ *adj.* liking to talk a lot

talk·er /ˈtɔkɚ/ *n.* [C] *informal* someone who talks a lot or talks in a particular way: *a fast talker*

ˌtalk ˈradio *n.* [U] radio programs on which people talk about various subjects, for example sports or politics

ˈtalk show *n.* [C] a television show in which famous people answer questions about themselves

THESAURUS

movie, soap opera, sitcom, game show, cartoon, drama series, documentary, the news
→ see Thesaurus box at TELEVISION

tall /tɔl/ *adj.* **1** having a greater than average height [≠ **small**]: *the tallest boy in the class* | *tall buildings* **2** having a particular height: *My brother's almost 6 feet tall.*

USAGE

Use **tall** to talk about the height of people and trees: *She's only five feet tall.* | *a road with tall trees on either side*
Use **tall** to talk about other narrow objects: *an old house with tall chimneys* | *the tall mast of a ship*
Use **high** to talk about mountains, walls, fences, etc.: *the highest mountain in the world* | *How high will the wall be?*
Use **high** to talk about how far something is from the ground: *The shelf's too high for the kids to reach.*
You can use both **tall** and **high** to talk about buildings: *one of the highest buildings in the world* | *a city with crowded streets and tall buildings*

3 a tall tale something someone tells you that is so unlikely that it is difficult to believe **4 a tall order** *informal* a piece of work or a request that will be extremely difficult to do: *Finding a witness to this crime is going to be a tall order.*

tal·low /ˈtæloʊ/ *n.* [U] hard animal fat used for making CANDLES

tal·ly¹ /ˈtæli/ *n.* plural **tallies** [C] a record of how much you have won, spent, used, etc. by a particular point in time: *Somebody should be* ***keeping a tally of*** (=writing down) *how much we owe.*

tally² *v.* past tense and past participle **tallied**, third person singular **tallies** **1** [T] **also tally up** to calculate the total number of points won, things done, etc.: *Can you tally up the scores?* **2** [I] if two numbers, statements, dates, etc. tally, they match exactly: *The signatures should* ***tally with*** *the names on the list.*

tal·on /ˈtælən/ *n.* [C] one of the sharp curved nails on the feet of some birds that hunt → see picture on page A2

T

tam·bou·rine /ˌtæmbəˈrin/ *n.* [C] a small drum with small pieces of metal around the edge, that you hold in your hand and play by hitting or shaking it ➔ see picture on page A6

tame[1] /teɪm/ *adj.* **1** a tame animal is not wild any longer, because it has been trained to live with people [➡ **wild**]: *tame elephants* **2** *informal* boring and disappointing: *"How was the movie?" "Pretty tame."*

tame[2] *v.* [T] to train a wild animal so that it will not hurt people

tam·per /ˈtæmpɚ/ *v.*

tamper with sth *phr. v.* to change something without permission, usually in order to damage it: *Several bottles of aspirin had been tampered with.*

tam·pon /ˈtæmpɑn/ *n.* [C] a tube-shaped piece of cotton that a woman puts in her VAGINA during her PERIOD (=monthly flow of blood)

tan[1] /tæn/ *adj.* **1** having a pale yellow-brown color **2** having darker skin after spending a lot of time in the sun: *Your face is really tan.*

tan[2] *n.* **1** [C] the attractive brown color that someone with pale skin gets after s/he has been in the sun [= **suntan**]: *Monica **got a** nice **tan** during her trip.* **2** [U] a pale yellow-brown color

tan[3] *v.* past tense and past participle **tanned**, present participle **tanning** **1** [I,T] if you tan, or if the sun tans you, your skin becomes darker because you spend time in the sun: *I don't tan easily.* **2** [T] to change animal skin into leather by putting a special acid on it

tan·dem /ˈtændəm/ *n.* **1 in tandem** *formal* together or at the same time: *Police are working **in tandem with** local schools to reduce car thefts.* **2** [C] a bicycle built for two riders sitting one behind the other

tan·gent /ˈtændʒənt/ *n.* **go off on a tangent** to suddenly start talking or thinking about a completely different subject

tan·ger·ine /ˌtændʒəˈrin/ *n.* [C] a sweet fruit that looks like a small orange

tan·gi·ble /ˈtændʒəbəl/ *adj.* **1** clear enough or definite enough to be easily seen or noticed [≠ **intangible**]: *tangible proof* **2** *technical* if something is tangible, you can touch or feel it

tangle[1] *v.* [I,T] to become twisted together, or make something become twisted together, in a messy way: *My hair tangles easily.*

tangle with sb *phr. v. informal* to argue or fight with someone

tan·gle[2] /ˈtæŋgəl/ *n.* [C] hair, threads, knots, etc. that have become twisted together: *a **tangle of** branches*

tan·gled /ˈtæŋgəld/ **also tangled up** *adj.* **1** twisted together in a messy way: *The phone cord is all tangled up.* **2** complicated and confusing: *tangled emotions*

tangled

tangled cord

tan·go /ˈtæŋgoʊ/ *n.* plural **tangos** [C] a lively dance from South America, or the music for this dance

tang·y /ˈtæŋi/ *adj.* having a pleasantly strong sharp taste or smell: *chunks of tangy rhubarb* —**tang** *n.* [singular]

tank /tæŋk/ *n.* [C] **1** a large container for holding liquid or gas: *a fish tank* | *a car's **gas tank*** **2** a heavy military vehicle with a large gun and metal belts over its wheels

tan·kard /ˈtæŋkɚd/ *n.* [C] a large metal cup used for drinking beer

tank·er /ˈtæŋkɚ/ *n.* [C] a vehicle or ship used for carrying a large amount of liquid or gas: *an oil tanker*

THESAURUS

ship, cruise ship, liner, ferry, freighter, barge, aircraft carrier, battleship, cruiser, submarine, warship
➔ see Thesaurus box at SHIP[1]

tan·ta·lize /ˈtæntlˌaɪz/ *v.* [T] to show or promise something that someone really wants, but then not allow him/her to have it

tan·ta·liz·ing /ˈtæntlˌaɪzɪŋ/ *adj.* making you want something very much: *tantalizing smells coming from the kitchen*

tan·ta·mount /ˈtæntəˌmaʊnt/ *adj.* **be tantamount to sth** to be almost the same thing as something else that is bad: *His refusal to speak was tantamount to admitting he was guilty.*

tan·trum /ˈtæntrəm/ *n.* [C] if someone, especially a child, throws or has a tantrum, s/he suddenly becomes very angry, noisy, and unreasonable: ***temper tantrums***

tap[1] /tæp/ *v.* past tense and past participle **tapped**, present participle **tapping** **1** [I,T] to gently hit your fingers or foot against something: *Someone was **tapping on** the window outside.* | *Caroline tapped her feet in time to the music.* | *He turned as someone tapped him on the shoulder.* ➔ see picture on page A8

THESAURUS

hit, punch, slap, beat, smack, whack, strike, bang, knock, pound, rap, hammer
➔ see Thesaurus box at HIT[1]

2 [I,T] to use or take what you need from a supply of something: *With the Internet you can **tap into***

information from around the world. | *tapping the country's natural resources* **3** [T] to put a tap on someone's telephone: *Murray began to suspect that his **phone** had been **tapped**.*

tap² *n.* **1** [C] an act of hitting something gently, especially to get someone's attention: *Suddenly I felt a **tap on** my shoulder.* **2** [C] an object used for letting liquid, especially beer, out of a BARREL **3** [C] a small electronic object that allows you to secretly listen to someone's telephone conversations **4 on tap** beer that is on tap comes from a BARREL **5** [C] FAUCET

'tap ˌdancing *n.* [U] a type of dancing in which you wear shoes with pieces of metal on the bottom, which make a sound as you move —**tap dance** *v.* [I]

tape¹ /teɪp/ *n.* **1 a)** [U] a thin narrow band of plastic material used for recording sounds, video pictures, or computer information [➡ **videotape**]: *Did you get the interview **on tape*** (=recorded on tape)*?* **b)** [C] a flat plastic case that contains this type of tape: *I'll listen to the tape tomorrow.* | *a **blank tape*** (=one with nothing recorded on it) **2** [C,U] a narrow band of sticky material used for sticking things together [= **Scotch tape**]: *a photo stuck to the wall with tape*

tape² *v.* **1** [I,T] to record sounds or pictures onto a tape [➡ **videotape**]: *Did you tape the movie?* **2** [T] to stick something onto something else using tape: *He has lots of postcards **taped to** his wall.*

THESAURUS

fasten, attach, join, glue, staple, clip, tie, button (up), zip (up)
→ see Thesaurus box at FASTEN

3 [T] **also tape up** to firmly tie a BANDAGE around an injury

'tape deck *n.* [C] the part of a STEREO used for recording and playing sounds on a tape

'tape ˌmeasure *n.* [C] a long band of cloth or metal with inches, CENTIMETERS etc. marked on it, used for measuring things

ta·per /'teɪpɚ/ *v.* [I,T] to become gradually narrower toward one end, or to make something become narrower at one end —**tapered** *adj.*: *pants with tapered legs*

taper off *phr. v.* to decrease gradually: *The rain finally tapered off in the afternoon.*

'tape reˌcorder *n.* [C] a piece of electronic equipment used for recording and playing sounds on a tape —**tape record** *v.* [T]

tap·es·try /'tæpɪstri/ *n.* plural **tapestries** [C,U] heavy cloth with colored threads woven into it to make a picture, or a large piece of this cloth

tape·worm /'teɪpwɚm/ *n.* [C] a long flat PARASITE that lives inside the INTESTINES of people and animals and can make them sick

'tap ˌwater *n.* [U] water that comes out of a FAUCET

tar¹ /tɑr/ *n.* [U] **1** a black substance that is thick and sticky, used on road surfaces, or on roofs in order to protect them from water **2** a sticky dark brown substance that is produced when tobacco burns

tar² *v.* past tense and past participle **tarred**, present participle **tarring** [T] to cover something with tar

ta·ran·tu·la /tə'ræntʃələ/ *n.* [C] a large hairy poisonous SPIDER

tar·dy /'tɑrdi/ *adj.* late, or done too slowly: *If you are tardy once more you'll have to stay after school.* —**tardiness** *n.* [U]

tar·get¹ /'tɑrgɪt/ *n.* [C] **1** an aim or result that you try to achieve: *We're trying to reach a **target of** $2 million in sales.* | *It will take a lot of hard work to **meet*** (=achieve) *our **target** this year.* **2** an object, person, or place that is deliberately chosen to be attacked: *a military target* | *Cars without security devices are an **easy target** for thieves.* **3** the person or place that is most directly affected by an action, especially a bad one: *The country is a **target of** criticism for its human rights record.* **4** something that you practice shooting at: *Pete missed the target by two inches.*

target² *v.* [T] **1** to aim something at someone or something: *missiles **targeted on/at** European cities* **2** to make something have an effect on a limited group or area: *welfare programs **targeted at** the unemployed* **3** to choose a particular person or place to attack: *Thieves have targeted smaller banks with less security.*

tar·iff /'tærɪf/ *n.* [C] a tax on goods that are brought into a country or taken out of it: *The government may impose **tariffs on** imports.*

tar·mac /'tɑrmæk/ *n.* [U] **1** ASPHALT **2 the tarmac** the large area at an airport where airplanes land and take off

tar·nish /'tɑrnɪʃ/ *v.* **1** [T] to make someone or something less impressive or respectable: *More violence will **tarnish** the school's **reputation**.* **2** [I] if a metal tarnishes, it becomes less shiny and loses its color

tar·ot /'tæroʊ/ **also 'tarot cards** *n.* [singular, U] a set of cards used for telling what might happen to someone in the future

tarp /tɑrp/ **also tar·pau·lin** /tɑr'pɔlən/ *n.* [C,U] a heavy cloth or piece of thick plastic that water cannot go through, used to protect things from the rain

tar·ry /'tæri/ *v.* past tense and past participle **tarried**, third person singular **tarries** [I] *literary* to stay in a place too long, or delay going somewhere

tart¹ /tɑrt/ *adj.* tart food has a sour taste: *tart green apples*

tart² *n.* [C] a small PIE without a top, usually containing fruit

tar·tan /'tɑrtˀn/ *n.* [C,U] a traditional Scottish pattern with colored squares and lines, or cloth with this pattern

T

tar·tar /ˈtɑrt̬ɚ/ *n.* [U] a hard substance that forms on teeth, damaging them

ˈtartar ˌsauce *n.* [U] a cold white thick sauce often eaten with fish

task /tæsk/ *n.* **1** [C] a job or particular thing that you have to do, especially a difficult or annoying one: *We were given **the task of** rescuing crash victims.* | *A computer can **perform** (=do) several **tasks** at the same time.*

> **COLLOCATIONS**
>
> **easy/simple/routine task** – one that is easy to do
> **difficult/impossible task** – one that is difficult to do
> **arduous task** – one that needs a lot of hard work and continuous effort
> **daunting task** – one that causes you to worry or be frightened
> **odious task** – one that is unpleasant to do
> **thankless task** – one that is difficult and you do not get much praise for
> **menial task** – one that is boring and does not need skill to do
> **mundane task** – one that is ordinary and not interesting or exciting

2 take sb to task to angrily criticize someone for doing something wrong

ˈtask force *n.* [C] a group formed for a short time to deal with a particular problem, especially a military or political one

tas·sel /ˈtæsəl/ *n.* [C] a group of threads tied together at one end and hung as a decoration on curtains, clothes, etc. —**tasseled** *adj.*

taste[1] /teɪst/ *n.* **1** [singular, U] the feeling that is produced when your tongue touches a particular food or drink, for example how sweet it is: *I don't like the **taste of** garlic.* | *a bitter/sour/sweet etc. taste* | *He no longer has any **sense of taste** or smell.*

> **THESAURUS**
>
> **delicious** – very good
> **disgusting/horrible/awful** – very bad
> **sweet** – like sugar
> **tasty** – having a pleasant taste, but not sweet
> **sour** – like a lemon (=yellow fruit)
> **salty** – containing a lot of salt
> **hot/spicy** – containing spices that give you the feeling that your mouth is burning
> **bland** – not having an interesting taste

2 [C,U] the kind of things that someone likes: *We have similar **tastes in** clothes.* | *She never lost her **taste for** travel.* **3** [U] someone's judgment when they choose clothes, decorations, etc.: *She has really good **taste in** music.* **4** [C usually singular] a small amount of a food or drink, eaten to find out what it is like: *Here, **have a taste** and tell me what you think.* **5 be in good/bad/poor taste** to be appropriate or inappropriate for a particular occasion: *a joke in very bad taste* **6 a taste of sth** a short experience of something: *The trip gave us a taste of life on board a ship.*

taste[2] *v.* **1** [I] to have a particular type of taste: *The chicken tastes really good.* | *This milk tastes a little sour.* ▶ Don't say "is tasting." ◀ *What does the soup **taste like** (=how would you describe its taste)?* **2** [T] to put a small amount of food or drink in your mouth in order to find out what it is like: *Taste this and see if it needs more salt.* **3** [T] to recognize the taste of a food or drink: *My cold's so bad I can't taste a thing.* ▶ Don't say "I am not tasting." ◀

taste·ful /ˈteɪstfəl/ *adj.* chosen, decorated, or made with good taste: *Frank was dressed in casual but tasteful clothes.* —**tastefully** *adv.*: *a tastefully furnished apartment*

taste·less /ˈteɪstlɪs/ *adj.* **1** chosen, decorated, or made with bad taste: *tasteless jokes* **2** tasteless food is unpleasant because it does not have a strong taste

tast·er /ˈteɪstɚ/ *n.* [C] someone whose job is to test the quality of a food or drink by tasting it: *wine tasters*

tast·ing /ˈteɪstɪŋ/ *n.* [C] an event where you can try different kinds of food and drinks: *a cheese tasting*

tast·y /ˈteɪsti/ *adj.* having a very good taste: *a tasty meal* ➔ see Thesaurus box at TASTE[1]

tat·tered /ˈtæt̬ɚd/ *adj.* old and torn: *tattered curtains*

tat·ters /ˈtæt̬ɚz/ *n.* **in tatters a)** clothes that are in tatters are old and torn **b)** completely ruined: *All his great plans **lay in tatters**.*

tat·tle /ˈtæt̬l/ *v.* [I] if a child tattles, s/he tells a parent or teacher that another child has done something bad

tat·tle·tale /ˈtæt̬lˌteɪl/ *n.* [C] *spoken* someone who tattles

tattoo

tat·too /tæˈtu/ *n.* plural **tattoos** [C] a picture, word, etc. that is put permanently onto your skin using a needle and ink: *He has a tattoo of a snake on his left arm.* —**tattooed** *adj.* —**tattoo** *v.* [T]

taught /tɔt/ *v.* the past tense and past participle of TEACH

taunt /tɔnt, tɑnt/ *v.* [T] to try to make someone upset or angry by saying something unkind: *The other kids **taunted** him **about** his weight.* —**taunt** *n.* [C]

Tau·rus /ˈtɔrəs/ *n.* **1** [U] the second sign of the ZODIAC, represented by a BULL **2** [C] someone born between April 20 and May 20

taut /tɔt/ *adj.* **1** stretched tight: *a taut rope*

2 seeming worried: *a taut look on his face* —**tautly** *adv.*

tav·ern /ˈtævərn/ *n.* [C] a BAR

taw·dry /ˈtɔdri/ *adj.* cheap and of bad quality: *tawdry jewelry* —**tawdriness** *n.* [U]

taw·ny /ˈtɔni/ *adj.* having a light gold-brown color: *tawny fur*

tax[1] /tæks/ *n.* [C,U] the money you must pay the government, based on how much you earn, what you buy, where you live, etc.: *a 13% **tax on** cigarettes* | *Everyone who works **pays tax**.* | *The city will have to **raise taxes** to pay for the roads.* | *If elected, she promised to **cut taxes**.* | *I only earn $25,000 a year **after taxes*** (=after paying tax). | ***a tax increase/cut***

tax[2] *v.* [T] **1** to charge a tax on something: *Incomes of under $30,000 are **taxed at** 15%.* **2 tax sb's patience/strength etc.** to use almost all of someone's PATIENCE, strength, etc.: *His constant questions had begun to tax her patience.*

tax·a·tion /tækˈseɪʃən/ *n.* [U] the system of charging taxes, or the money collected from taxes

ˌtax-exˈempt *adj.* not taxed, or not having to pay tax: *tax-exempt savings* | *a tax-exempt charity*

tax·i[1] /ˈtæksi/ **also tax·i·cab** /ˈtæksiˈkæb/ *n.* [C] a CAB ➔ see picture at TRANSPORTATION

taxi[2] *v.* past tense and past participle **taxied**, third person singular **taxis** or **taxies** [I] if an airplane taxis, it moves slowly on the ground before taking off or after landing

tax·i·der·my /ˈtæksəˌdəmi/ *n.* [U] the process or skill of filling the body of a dead animal, bird, or fish with a special material so that it looks alive

tax·ing /ˈtæksɪŋ/ *adj.* needing a lot of effort: *a taxing job*

ˈtaxi stand *n.* [C] a place where taxis wait in order to get passengers

tax·pay·er /ˈtæksˌpeɪə/ *n.* [C] someone who pays taxes

ˈtax ˌshelter *n.* [C] a plan or method that allows you to legally avoid paying taxes

TB *n.* the written abbreviation of TUBERCULOSIS

tbsp. *n.* the written abbreviation of TABLESPOON

tea /ti/ *n.* **1 a)** [C,U] a drink made by pouring boiling water onto dried leaves, or a cup of this drink: *a **cup of tea*** | *We'll have two teas and a coffee, please.* **b)** [U] dried leaves used for making tea **2 mint/herbal etc. tea** a hot drink made by pouring boiling water onto the leaves or flowers of a particular plant

ˈtea bag *n.* [C] a small paper bag with dried leaves in it, used for making tea

teach /titʃ/ *v.* past tense and past participle **taught** /tɔt/ **1** [I,T] to give someone lessons, especially in a school or college: *Mr. Rochet has been teaching for 17 years.* | *She **teaches** math **at** Jackson High School.* | *Firstly, we **teach** the children **to** read.* | *All students are taught basic computer skills.* | *We **teach** students **about** the dangers of drugs.*

USAGE

You **learn** a subject or skill when you study or practice it: *I'm thinking of learning Italian.* | *Jo's learning to drive.*
If you **teach** someone a subject or skill, you help him/her learn it: *Dad taught me to play the guitar.* You cannot say "Dad learned me to..."

2 [T] to tell or show someone how to do something: *Can you teach me one of your card tricks?* | *My dad **taught me (how) to** swim.* **3 teach sb a lesson** *informal* to punish someone for something s/he has done, so that s/he will not want to do it again

teach·er /ˈtitʃə/ *n.* [C] someone whose job is to teach: *my history teacher*

THESAURUS

A **teacher** is usually someone who works in a school: *Marie is a high school teacher.*
A **teacher** can also be someone who helps a person learn something: *a guitar teacher*
A **professor**, **lecturer**, or an **instructor** teaches in a university or college. A **professor** has a higher rank than a **lecturer** or an **instructor**.
An **instructor** is also someone who teaches a sport or practical skill such as swimming or driving: *a driving instructor* | *an aerobics instructor*
A **coach** trains a person or team in a sport: *a football coach*
➔ SCHOOL, UNIVERSITY

ˌteacher's ˈpet *n.* [C] a child who everyone thinks is the teacher's favorite student and is therefore disliked by the other students

teach·ing /ˈtitʃɪŋ/ *n.* [U] **1** the work that a teacher does, or the profession of being a teacher: *I'd like to **go into teaching*** (=become a teacher) *when I finish college.* **2 also teachings** [plural] the moral, religious, or political ideas spread by a particular person or group: *the **teachings of** the Buddha*

tea·cup /ˈtikʌp/ *n.* [C] a cup that you serve tea in

teak /tik/ *n.* [C,U] a very hard yellowish-brown wood that is used for making ships and good quality furniture, or the tree that this wood comes from

team[1] /tim/ *n.* [C] **1** a group of people who compete against another group in a sport, game, etc.: *Which team is winning?* | ***a baseball/football, etc. team***

THESAURUS

group, crowd, crew, gang, mob, bunch, flock, mass, party
➔ see Thesaurus box at GROUP[1]

2 a group of people who are chosen to work together to do a particular job: *a* ***team of*** *doctors*

team² *v.*

team up *phr. v.* to form a team with another person, company, etc. in order to work together: *We're* ***teaming up with*** *another publisher to do the book.*

team·mate /ˈtim-meɪt/ *n.* [C] someone who plays or works on the same team as you

ˈteam ˌplayer *n.* [C] someone who works well as a member of a team

team·ster /ˈtimstɚ/ *n.* [C] someone whose job is to drive a truck

team·work /ˈtimwɚk/ *n.* [U] the ability of a group to work well together, or the effort the group makes

tea·pot /ˈtipɑt/ *n.* [C] a container used for serving tea, that has a handle and a SPOUT

tear¹ /tɛr/ *v.* past tense **tore** /tɔr/ past participle **torn** /tɔrn/ **1** [I,T] if you tear paper, cloth, etc., or if it tears, you make a hole in it or it breaks into small pieces [**= rip**]: *You've torn your sleeve.* | *He* ***tore*** *the envelope* ***open****.* | *Oh no, I* ***tore a hole in*** *my jeans!* | *Someone had* ***torn*** *some pages* ***out of*** *the book.* | *Be careful, you don't want your dress to tear!*

> **THESAURUS**
> **break**, **smash**, **shatter**, **crack**, **snap**, **burst**, **pop**
> → see Thesaurus box at BREAK¹

2 [T] to pull something violently from a person or place: *The storm actually* ***tore*** *the door* ***off*** *its hinges.* **3** [I] to move very quickly, often in a careless or dangerous way: *Two kids came* ***tearing around*** *the corner.*

> **THESAURUS**
> **run**, **sprint**, **dash**, **race**
> → see Thesaurus box at RUN¹

tear apart *phr. v.* **1 tear** sth ⇔ **apart** to make a group, organization, etc. start having problems: *Scandal is tearing the government apart.* **2 tear** sb **apart** to make someone feel extremely unhappy or upset: *It tore me apart to see her leave.*

tear sth ⇔ **down** *phr. v.* to deliberately destroy a building: *The old train station was torn down in the early '90s.*

tear into sb/sth *phr. v. informal* to strongly criticize someone or something: *Then he started tearing into her for spending money.*

tear sth ⇔ **up** *phr. v.* to tear a piece of paper or cloth into small pieces: *He tore up all of Linda's old letters.*

tear² /tɪr/ *n.* [C] a drop of liquid that comes out of your eyes when you cry: *She ran away with tears in her eyes.* | *Garner left the courtroom* ***in tears*** (=crying). | *Suddenly Brian* ***burst into tears*** (=started crying).

tear³ /tɛr/ *n.* [C] a hole in a piece of paper, cloth, etc. where it has been torn: *There was a* ***tear in*** *his shirt.*

tear·drop /ˈtɪrdrɑp/ *n.* [C] a single tear

tear·ful /ˈtɪrfəl/ *adj.* crying or almost crying

tease¹ /tiz/ *v.* **1** [I,T] to make jokes about someone in order to embarrass or annoy him/her because you think it is funny: *Don't cry. I was just teasing.* | *His friends* ***teased*** *him* ***about*** *his accent.* **2** [T] to comb your hair in the wrong direction so that it looks thicker

tease² *n.* [C] someone who enjoys teasing people

tea·spoon /ˈtispun/ *n.* [C] **1** *written abbreviation* **tsp** a small spoon used for STIRring a cup of tea or coffee **2 a)** a special spoon used for measuring food **b) also tea·spoon·ful** /ˈti- spunfʊl/ the amount this spoon holds

teat /tit/ *n.* [C] a NIPPLE on a female animal

tech·ni·cal /ˈtɛknɪkəl/ *adj.* **1** relating to the practical skills, knowledge, and methods used in science or industry: *technical experts* | *technical training* **2** relating to a particular subject or profession: *a legal document full of technical terms*

tech·ni·cal·i·ty /ˌtɛknɪˈkæləṭi/ *n.* plural **technicalities** [C] **1** a small detail in a law or rule: *The case against him had to be dropped because of a technicality.* | *He* ***got off on a technicality*** (=because of a technicality). **2 technicalities** [plural] the details of a system or process that you need special knowledge to understand

tech·ni·cally /ˈtɛknɪkli/ *adv.* **1** according to the exact details of a rule or law: *Technically, he's responsible for fixing all the damage.* **2** relating to the way machines are used in science and industry: *a* ***technically advanced*** *engine*

tech·ni·cian /tɛkˈnɪʃən/ *n.* [C] a skilled scientific or industrial worker: *a lab technician*

tech·nique /tɛkˈnik/ *n.* [C,U] a special way of doing something: *new* ***techniques for*** *teaching English*

tech·nol·o·gy /tɛkˈnɑlədʒi/ *n.* plural **technologies** [C,U] knowledge about scientific or industrial methods, or the use of these methods: *medical technology* | *developing new technologies* —**technological** /ˌtɛknəˈlɑdʒɪkəl/ *adj.*

ted·dy bear /ˈtɛdi ˌbɛr/ *n.* [C] a soft toy shaped like a bear

te·di·ous /ˈtidiəs/ *adj.* boring, and continuing for a long time: *a tedious discussion*

> **THESAURUS**
> **boring**, **dull**, **not (very/that/all that) interesting**, **monotonous**
> → see Thesaurus box at BORING

te·di·um /ˈtidiəm/ *n.* [U] the quality of being tedious

tee /ti/ *n.* [C] a small object used for holding a GOLF ball, or the raised area from which you hit the ball

teem /tim/ *v.*
teem with sth *phr. v.* to be full of people or animals that are all moving around: *lakes teeming with fish* —**teeming** *adj.*: *the teeming streets of Cairo*

teen /tin/ *n.* [C] *informal* **1** TEENAGER **2 teens** [plural] the period of your life when you are between 13 and 19 years old: *She got married when she was still **in** her **teens**.* —**teen** *adj.*

teen·age /ˈtineɪdʒ/ *adj.* between 13 and 19 years old, or relating to someone who is: *teenage pregnancy* | *our teenage son* ▶ Don't say "our son is teenage." ◀

THESAURUS
young, adolescent
➔ see Thesaurus box at YOUNG[1]

teen·ag·er /ˈtiˌneɪdʒɚ/ *n.* [C] someone who is between 13 and 19 years old

THESAURUS
baby, child, kid
➔ see Thesaurus box at CHILD

tee·ny /ˈtini/ **also tee·ny-wee·ny** /ˌtini ˈwini◂ / *adj. spoken* very small [= **tiny**]

ˈtee ˌshirt *n.* [C] T-SHIRT

tee·ter /ˈtiṭɚ/ *v.* [I] **1** to move or stand in an unsteady way: *teetering in high-heeled shoes* **2 be teetering on (the brink/edge of) sth** to be very likely to become involved in a dangerous situation: *a country teetering on the brink of revolution*

teeth /tiθ/ *n.* the plural of TOOTH

teethe /tið/ *v.* [I] if a baby is teething, his/her first teeth are growing

tee·to·tal·er /ˈtiˌtoʊṭlɚ/ *n.* [C] someone who never drinks alcohol —**teetotal** *adj.*

Tef·lon /ˈtɛflɑn/ *n.* [U] *trademark* a special material that stops things from sticking to it, often used in making pans

tel·e·com·mu·ni·ca·tions /ˌtɛləkəˌmyunəˈkeɪʃənz/ *n.* [U] the process of sending and receiving messages by telephone, radio, SATELLITE etc.

tel·e·com·mut·er /ˈtɛləkəˌmyuṭɚ/ *n.* [C] someone who works for a company at home using a computer connected to the main office

tel·e·con·ference /ˈtɛləˌkɑnfrəns/ *n.* [C] a discussion between people in different places who talk to each other using telephones and video equipment —**teleconference** *v.* [I]

tel·e·gram /ˈtɛləˌgræm/ *n.* [C] a message sent by telegraph

tel·e·graph /ˈtɛləˌgræf/ *n.* [C,U] an old-fashioned method of sending messages using electrical signals, or the equipment used for sending these messages

te·lep·a·thy /təˈlɛpəθi/ *n.* [U] a way of communicating in which thoughts are sent from one person's mind to another person's mind —**telepathic** /ˌtɛləˈpæθɪk◂ / *adj.*

tel·e·phone[1] /ˈtɛləˌfoʊn/ *n.* [C] a PHONE ➔ see picture on page A11

telephone[2] *v.* [I,T] to PHONE

tel·e·pho·to lens /ˌtɛləˌfoʊṭoʊ ˈlɛnz/ *n.* [C] a special camera LENS used for taking clear photographs of things that are far away

tel·e·scope /ˈtɛləˌskoʊp/ *n.* [C] a piece of scientific equipment shaped like a tube, used for making distant objects such as stars and PLANETS look larger and closer

tel·e·scop·ic /ˌtɛləˈskɑpɪk◂ / *adj.* relating to a telescope, or using a telescope: *a telescopic lens*

tel·e·thon /ˈtɛləˌθɑn/ *n.* [C] a television show in which famous people provide entertainment and ask the people who are watching to give money to help people who need it

tel·e·vise /ˈtɛləˌvaɪz/ *v.* [T] to broadcast something on television: *Is the game going to be televised?*

tel·e·vi·sion /ˈtɛləˌvɪʒən/ **also TV** *n.* **1 also ˈtelevision ˌset** [C] a piece of electronic equipment shaped like a box with a screen, on which you can watch programs: ***turn on/off** the television* **2** [U] the programs that you can watch and listen to on a television: *He's been **watching television** all day.* | *What's **on television** tonight?*

THESAURUS
Types of television programs
movie/film: *There's a good movie on Channel 7 at 9 o'clock.*
soap opera – a program that is on TV regularly, often every day, about the same group of people
sitcom – a funny TV program which has the same people in it every week in a different story
game show – a program in which people play games in order to try and win prizes
talk show – a program in which people answer questions about themselves
cartoon – a movie or program that uses characters that are drawn and not real
drama series – a set of TV programs about the same group of people or about a particular subject, shown regularly: *a new drama series about cops and lawyers*
documentary – a program that gives information about a subject
the news: *the 6 o'clock news*

T

TOPIC

When you want to **watch TV**, you look in the **TV guide** (=a list of TV programs) to see **what's on**. When you decide which **program/show** you want to watch, you **turn on the TV**, usually by using a **remote control**. Many people just turn on the TV and **change channels** (=television stations) until they find a program they want to watch. If you change channels a lot, you can call it **channel hopping/surfing**. A lot of people have **cable TV** or **satellite TV**, which gives them a lot of channels to choose from. People who watch a lot of TV are sometimes called **couch potatoes**.

3 [U] the activity of making and broadcasting programs on television: *a job **in television***

tell /tɛl/ *v.* past tense and past participle **told** /toʊld/

1 INFORMATION [T] to give someone facts or information in speech or writing: ***Tell** Mark **(that)** I said hi.* | *Did you **tell** Jennifer **about** the party?* | *Could you **tell** me **how** to make that cheesecake?* | *She wouldn't **tell** me **why** she was angry.* | *I don't think he's **telling the truth**.* | *Dad used to tell us bedtime stories.*

THESAURUS

explain, **show**, **demonstrate**, **go through**
→ see Thesaurus box at EXPLAIN

USAGE

Tell must be followed by a direct object. This is usually the person who is being told something. If there is no direct object, use **say**. Compare these sentences: *What did they say?* | *What did they tell you?*

2 RECOGNIZE [I,T] to be able to recognize or judge something correctly: *I **could tell (that)** it was a serious discussion.* | *Use plain yogurt instead of sour cream – you **can't tell the difference**.* | *"How long will it take?" "**It's hard to tell**."*

3 WHAT SB SHOULD DO [T] to say that someone must do something: ***Tell** her **to** put on her coat – it's cold.* | *Stop **telling** me **what to do**!*

4 tell yourself to persuade yourself to do something or that something is true: *I kept telling myself to relax.*

5 SIGN [T] to give information in a way other than speech or writing: *This red light tells you it's recording.*

6 tell time to be able to know what time it is by looking at a clock

7 there's no telling what/how/whether etc. used in order to say that it is impossible to know what has happened or what will happen next: *There's no telling how long it will take.*

8 all told in total: *All told, 40,000 airline workers have lost their jobs this year.*

9 STH WRONG [I,T] *spoken* to tell someone in authority about something wrong that someone else has done: *I was afraid my little sister would **tell on** us.*

SPOKEN PHRASES

10 (I'll) tell you what said in order to suggest something: *Tell you what, call me on Friday, and we'll make plans then.*

11 I tell you/I'm telling you/let me tell you said in order to emphasize something: *I'm telling you, the gossip in this place is unbelievable!*

12 tell me about it said in order to say that you already know how bad something is: *"She's so arrogant!" "Yeah, tell me about it."*

13 (I) told you (so) said when someone does something you have warned him/her about, and it has a bad result: *I told you. You can't trust her.*

14 to tell (you) the truth said in order to emphasize that you are being honest: *I don't know how you cope, to tell you the truth.*

15 you never can tell/you can never tell used in order to say that you can never be certain about what will happen in the future: *They're not likely to win, but you never can tell.*

tell sb ⇔ **apart** *phr. v.* to be able to see the difference between two people or things, even though they are similar: *Carol puts the twins in different color booties so you **can tell** them **apart**.*

tell sb ⇔ **off** *phr. v.* to talk angrily to someone when s/he has done something wrong: *She told him off in front of the whole office.*

tell·er /ˈtɛlɚ/ *n.* [C] someone whose job is to receive and pay out money in a bank

tell·ing /ˈtɛlɪŋ/ *adj.* a remark that is telling shows what you really think, although you may not intend it to

tell·tale /ˈtɛlteɪl/ *adj.* clearly showing something has happened or exists, often something that is a secret: *the **telltale signs** of drug addiction*

temp¹ /tɛmp/ *n.* [C] an office worker who is only employed for a limited period of time

temp² *v.* [I] to work as a temp: *Anne's temping until she can find another job.*

tem·per¹ /ˈtɛmpɚ/ *n.* **1** [C,U] a tendency to become suddenly angry: *John needs to learn to control his temper.* **2 lose/keep your temper** to suddenly become very angry, or to stay calm **3 have a quick/hot/slow etc. temper** to get angry very easily, or not very easily: *Her father has a violent temper.* **4 -tempered** having a particular type of temper: *a **bad-tempered** old man* | *an **even-tempered** child* (=one who is calm and does not get angry easily)

temper² *v.* [T] **1** *formal* to make something less difficult or severe: *criticism **tempered with** humor* **2** to make metal harder by heating it and then making it cold: *tempered steel*

tem·pera·ment /ˈtɛmprəmənt/ *n.* [C,U] the part of your character that makes you likely to be happy, angry, sad, etc.: *a baby with a calm temperament*

tem·pera·men·tal /ˌtɛmprəˈmɛntl/ *adj.* **1** tending to get upset, excited, or angry very easily **2** a temperamental machine does not always work correctly

tem·perance /ˈtɛmprəns/ *n.* [U] the practice of never drinking alcohol

tem·perate /ˈtɛmprɪt/ *adj.* weather or a part of the world that is temperate is never very hot or very cold: *a temperate climate*

tem·pera·ture /ˈtɛmprətʃɚ/ *n.* **1** [C,U] how hot or cold something is: *Water freezes* ***at a temperature of*** *32°F.* | *The* ***temperature rose*** *to 102 degrees.* | ***Temperatures*** *could* ***drop*** *to below zero tonight.* | *Store this product at* ***room temperature*** (=the normal temperature in a room). **2 sb's temperature** the temperature of your body, used as a measure of whether you are sick or not: *The nurse* ***took*** *my* ***temperature****.* **3 have a temperature** to be hot because you are sick

tem·pest /ˈtɛmpɪst/ *n.* [C] *literary* a violent storm

tem·pes·tu·ous /tɛmˈpɛstʃuəs/ *adj.* always full of strong emotions: *a tempestuous relationship*

tem·plate /ˈtɛmpleɪt/ *n.* [C] **1** a sheet of paper, plastic, or metal in a particular shape, used in order to help you cut other materials in the same shape **2** *technical* a computer document that you use as a model for producing many similar documents

tem·ple /ˈtɛmpəl/ *n.* [C] **1** a building where people go to worship in some religions: *a Buddhist temple* **2** [usually plural] one of the two fairly flat areas on each side of your FOREHEAD

tem·po /ˈtɛmpoʊ/ *n.* plural **tempos** [C] **1** the speed at which something happens [= **pace**]: *the tempo of city life* **2** the speed at which music is played

tem·po·rar·y /ˈtɛmpəˌrɛri/ *adj.* existing or happening for only a limited period of time [≠ **permanent**]: *a temporary visa* | *Linda was employed* ***on a temporary basis****.* —**temporarily** /ˌtɛmpəˈrɛrəli/ *adv.*: *The library is temporarily closed.*

tempt /tɛmpt/ *v.* **1** [T] to persuade someone to do something by making it seem attractive: *They're offering free gifts to* ***tempt*** *people* ***to*** *join.* **2 be tempted to do sth** to consider doing something that may not be a good idea: *I was tempted to correct him, but I didn't want to hurt his feelings.* **3 tempt fate** to say or do something that may cause problems —**tempting** *adj.*: *a tempting offer*

temp·ta·tion /tɛmpˈteɪʃən/ *n.* [C,U] **1** a strong desire to have or do something even though you know you should not: *I had to* ***resist the temptation to*** *slap her.* | *I finally* ***gave in to temptation*** *and had a cigarette.* **2** something that you want to have or do, even though you know you should not: *Selling alcohol at rest stops is an unnecessary temptation for drivers.*

ten[1] /tɛn/ *number* **1** 10 **2** ten O'CLOCK: *I have a meeting* ***at ten****.*

ten[2] *n.* [C] a piece of paper money worth $10

te·na·cious /təˈneɪʃəs/ *adj.* very determined to do something, and unwilling to stop trying —**tenaciously** *adv.* —**tenacity** /təˈnæsət̬i/ *n.* [U]

ten·an·cy /ˈtɛnənsi/ *n.* plural **tenancies** [C,U] the period of time that someone rents a house, room, etc., or the right to use a house, room, etc. that has been rented

ten·ant /ˈtɛnənt/ *n.* [C] someone who lives in a house, room, etc. and pays rent to the person who owns it [➡ **landlord**]: *The desk was left by the previous tenant.* ➔ see Topic box at RENT[1]

tend /tɛnd/ *v.* **1 tend to do sth** to be likely to do a particular thing: *People tend to need less sleep as they get older.* **2** [T] **also tend to sb/sth** to take care of someone or something: *Rescue teams were tending to the survivors.*

tend·en·cy /ˈtɛndənsi/ *n.* plural **tendencies** [C] **1** if someone or something has a tendency to do something, s/he is likely to do it: *He* ***has a tendency to*** *talk too much.* **2** the way in which a situation is beginning to develop or a change that is happening to it: ***There is a tendency for*** *men to marry younger women.*

ten·der[1] /ˈtɛndɚ/ *adj.* **1** gentle in a way that shows love: *a tender look* **2** a tender part of your body is painful if someone touches it: *My arm is still tender where I bruised it.*

THESAURUS

stiff, **sore**
➔ see Thesaurus box at PAINFUL

3 tender food is easy to cut and eat [≠ **tough**] **4 tender age** *literary* young and inexperienced: *He lost his father* ***at the tender age of*** *seven.* —**tenderly** *adv.* —**tenderness** *n.* [U]

tender[2] *v.* [T] *formal* to formally offer something to someone: *Maria has* ***tendered*** *her* ***resignation*** (=officially said that she is going to leave her job).

ten·der·heart·ed /ˌtɛndɚˈhɑrt̬ɪd◂/ *adj.* very kind and gentle

ten·don /ˈtɛndən/ *n.* [C] a thick strong part inside your body that connects a muscle to a bone

ten·dril /ˈtɛndrəl/ *n.* [C] a thin curling piece on the stem of a climbing plant, by which the plant fastens to a wall

ten·e·ment /ˈtɛnəmənt/ *n.* [C] a large building divided into apartments, especially in a poor area of a city

ten·et /ˈtɛnɪt/ *n.* [C] a principle or belief: *the tenets of Buddhism*

ten·nis /ˈtɛnɪs/ *n.* [U] a game in which two or four people use RACKETS to hit a ball to each other across a net

ˈtennis shoe *n.* [C] a light shoe used for sports

ten·or /ˈtɛnɚ/ *n.* **1** [C] a male singer with a high voice **2 the tenor of sth** *formal* the general

T

meaning or quality of something: *the tenor of the president's speech*

tense[1] /tɛns/ *adj.* **1** nervous and anxious: *You seem really tense – what's wrong? | a **tense atmosphere/situation/moment*** **2** tense muscles feel tight and stiff

tense[2] **also tense up** *v.* [I,T] to become tight and stiff, or to make your muscles do this

tense[3] *n.* [C,U] *technical* in grammar, one of the forms of a verb that shows actions or states in the past, the present, or in the future. For example, "he studied" is in the past tense, "he studies" is in the present tense, and "he will study" is in the future tense.

ten·sion /ˈtɛnʃən/ *n.* **1** [C,U] the feeling that exists when people do not trust each other and may suddenly attack each other or start arguing: *the **racial tension** in American society | **tension between** the union workers and management* **2** [U] a nervous and anxious feeling: *The room was filled with tension as students waited for their exams.* **3** [U] tightness or stiffness in a wire, rope, muscle, etc.: ***Muscle tension** can be a sign of stress.*

tent /tɛnt/ *n.* [C] a shelter that you can easily move, made of cloth or plastic and supported by poles and ropes: *Where should we **pitch the tent*** (=put up the tent)*?*

ten·ta·cle /ˈtɛntəkəl/ *n.* [C] one of the long thin parts like arms of a sea creature such as an OCTOPUS

ten·ta·tive /ˈtɛntət̬ɪv/ *adj.* **1** not definite or certain: *tentative plans* **2** done without confidence: *a tentative smile* —**tentatively** *adv.*

tenth /tɛnθ/ *number* 10th

ten·u·ous /ˈtɛnyuəs/ *adj.* a situation or relationship that is tenuous is uncertain, weak, or likely to change: *There is only a **tenuous connection** between the two events.* —**tenuously** *adv.*

ten·ure /ˈtɛnyɚ/ *n.* [U] **1** the right to stay permanently in a teaching job at a university **2** *formal* the period of time when someone has an important job: *the Mayor's tenure in office*

te·pee, **teepee** /ˈtipi/ *n.* [C] a round tent used by some Native Americans

tep·id /ˈtɛpɪd/ *adj.* tepid liquid is slightly warm

te·qui·la /təˈkilə/ *n.* [U] a strong alcoholic drink made in Mexico

term[1] /tɚm/ *n.* [C]

1 in terms of sth if you explain something in terms of a particular fact or event, you talk about it only in relation to that fact or event and no others: *In terms of sales the book hasn't been very successful.*

2 in financial/artistic etc. terms if you describe or consider something in financial, etc. terms, you are thinking of it in a financial, etc. way: *A million years isn't a very long time in geological terms.*

3 WORD/EXPRESSION a word or expression that has a particular meaning, especially in a technical or scientific subject: *I don't understand these **legal/medical/technical terms**.*

4 CONDITIONS terms [plural] the conditions of an agreement, contract, legal document, etc.: ***Under the terms of the agreement**, the debt will be repaid over twenty years.*

5 be on good/bad/friendly etc. terms (with sb) to have a particular type of relationship with someone: *He hasn't been on good terms with his father for years.*

6 SCHOOL/COLLEGE one of the periods that a school or college year is divided into [➡ **semester**, **quarter**]: *When does the spring term start?*

7 PERIOD OF TIME a fixed period of time during which someone does something or something happens: *The president hopes to be elected for a second term. | Reynolds could get a **prison term** of up to 85 years.*

8 be on speaking terms to be able to talk to someone and have a friendly relationship with him/her: *We're barely on speaking terms now.*

9 come to terms with sth to understand and deal with a difficult situation: *It was hard to come to terms with Marie's death.*

10 in the long/short term during a long or short period from now: *The company's prospects look better in the long term.*

term[2] *v.* [T] *formal* to use a particular word or phrase to describe something: *The meeting could hardly be termed a success.*

ter·mi·nal[1] /ˈtɚmənəl/ *adj.* a terminal disease cannot be cured, and causes death: *terminal cancer* —**terminally** *adv.*: *terminally ill*

terminal[2] *n.* [C] **1** a big building where you go to get onto airplanes, buses, or ships: *Our flight leaves from Terminal B.*

> **TOPIC**
>
> **check-in counter/desk**, **security**, **departure gate**, **baggage claim**, **immigration**, **customs**
> → see Topic box at AIRPORT

2 a computer KEYBOARD and screen connected to a computer that is somewhere else

ter·mi·nate /ˈtɚməˌneɪt/ *v.* [I,T] *formal* if something terminates, or if you terminate it, it ends —**termination** /ˌtɚməˈneɪʃən/ *n.* [C,U]

ter·mi·nol·o·gy /ˌtɚməˈnɑlədʒi/ *n.* [U] the technical words or expressions that are used in a particular subject: *scientific terminology*

> **THESAURUS**
>
> **language**, **slang**, **jargon**
> → see Thesaurus box at LANGUAGE

ter·mi·nus /ˈtɚmənəs/ *n.* [C] the place at the end of a railroad or bus line

ter·mite /ˈtɚmaɪt/ *n.* [C] an insect that eats wood from trees and buildings

ter·race /ˈtɛrɪs/ *n.* [C] **1** a flat outdoor area next to a building or on a roof, where you can sit outside to eat, relax, etc. **2** a flat area cut out of the side of a hill, often used for growing crops on

ter·ra·cot·ta /ˌtɛrəˈkɑṭə◂/ *n.* [U] hard red-brown baked clay: *a terracotta pot*

ter·rain /təˈreɪn/ *n.* [C,U] land of a particular type: *rocky terrain*

ter·res·tri·al /təˈrɛstriəl/ *adj. technical* **1** relating to the earth rather than to the moon, stars, or other PLANETS **2** living on or relating to land rather than water

ter·ri·ble /ˈtɛrəbəl/ *adj.* very bad [= **awful**]: *The food at the hotel was terrible.* | *a terrible accident* | *You're making a terrible mistake.*

THESAURUS

bad, awful, horrible, appalling, horrific, lousy, horrendous, atrocious, abysmal
→ see Thesaurus box at BAD[1], HORRIBLE

ter·ri·bly /ˈtɛrəbli/ *adv.* **1** very badly: *The team played terribly.* **2** extremely: *I'm terribly sorry, but the answer is no.*

ter·ri·er /ˈtɛriə/ *n.* [C] a type of small dog

ter·rif·ic /təˈrɪfɪk/ *adj.* **1** *informal* very good or enjoyable: *That's a terrific idea.* | *She looked terrific.* **2** *formal* very large in size or degree: *a terrific shock* —**terrifically** *adv.*

ter·ri·fied /ˈtɛrəˌfaɪd/ *adj.* very frightened: *The children were **terrified of** the dog.* | *We were **terrified that** the bridge would collapse.*

THESAURUS

frightened, afraid, scared, petrified
→ see Thesaurus box at FRIGHTENED

ter·ri·fy /ˈtɛrəˌfaɪ/ *v.* past tense and past participle **terrified**, third person singular **terrifies** [T] to make someone extremely afraid: *The thought of giving a speech terrified her.* —**terrifying** *adj.*: *a terrifying experience*

ter·ri·to·ri·al /ˌtɛrəˈtɔriəl/ *adj.* **1** [only before noun] relating to land that is owned or controlled by a particular country: *U.S. territorial waters* **2** territorial animals or people closely guard the place they consider to be their own

ter·ri·to·ry /ˈtɛrəˌtɔri/ *n.* plural **territories** **1** [C,U] land that is owned or controlled by a particular country: *Canadian territory* | *The plane was flying over **enemy territory**.* **2** [U] land of a particular type: ***unexplored territory*** **3** [C] land that belongs to a country, but is not a state, PROVINCE, etc.: *the U.S. territory of Guam* **4** [C,U] the area that an animal considers to be its own **5** [U] a particular area of experience or knowledge: *We are in **unfamiliar/uncharted territory*** (=an area that we do not yet know about) *with the new drug.* **6 come/go with the territory** to be a natural and accepted part of a particular job, situation, place, etc.: *You'd better get used to criticism from the press – it comes with the territory.*

ter·ror /ˈtɛrə/ *n.* **1** [C,U] a feeling of extreme fear, or something that causes this: *She ran away **in terror**.* | *the **terrors of** war* **2** [U] violent action for political purposes [= **terrorism**]: *a campaign of terror against the West*

ter·ror·ism /ˈtɛrəˌrɪzəm/ *n.* [U] the use of bombs and violence, especially against ordinary people, to achieve political aims: *an **act of terrorism*** | *efforts to **combat terrorism***

ter·ror·ist /ˈtɛrərɪst/ *n.* [C] someone who uses bombs and violence, usually against ordinary people, in order to achieve political aims: *a suspected terrorist* —**terrorist** *adj.*: *a terrorist attack*

ter·ror·ize /ˈtɛrəˌraɪz/ *v.* [T] to deliberately frighten people by threatening to harm them, especially so they will do what you want

ter·ry·cloth /ˈtɛriˌklɔθ/ *n.* [U] thick cotton cloth used for making TOWELS

terse /tɜs/ *adj.* a terse reply, message, etc. uses very few words and shows that you are annoyed —**tersely** *adv.*

test[1] /tɛst/ *n.* [C] **1** a set of questions or exercises to measure someone's skill or knowledge: *I have a history test tomorrow.* | *Paul **passed/failed** his driver's **test**.* | *All students must **take a** placement **test**.* ▶ Don't say "make a test." Say "take a test." ◀ **2** a medical examination on a part of your body: *a blood test* | *a **test for** HIV* | *They don't know what's wrong with her yet – they're **running/doing** some **tests**.* **3** a process used to find out whether something works, whether it is safe, etc.: *a **test for** chemicals in the water* **4** a situation in which the qualities of something are clearly shown: *Today's race is a real **test of** skill.* | *Living together will really **put** their relationship **to the test*** (=find out how good it is).

test[2] *v.* [T] **1** to measure someone's skill or knowledge, using a test: *We're being **tested on** grammar tomorrow.* **2** to use or check something to find out whether it works or is successful: *None of our products are tested on animals.* **3** to do a medical check on part of someone's body: *You need to get your eyes tested.* | *They **tested** her **for** diabetes.* **4** to show how good or strong something is: *The next six months will test your powers of leadership.*

tes·ta·ment /ˈtɛstəmənt/ *n. formal* **a testament to sth** something that shows or proves something else very clearly: *His latest record is a testament to his growing musical abilities.*

ˈtest ban *n.* [C] an agreement between countries to stop testing NUCLEAR WEAPONS

ˈtest case *n.* [C] a legal case that makes a particular principle of law clear and is used as a model for similar cases in the future

ˈtest drive *n.* [C] an occasion when you drive a car and decide if you want to buy it —**test-drive** *v.* [T]

tes·ti·cle /ˈtɛstɪkəl/ *n.* plural **testicles** or **testes** /ˈtɛstiz/ [C] one of the two round organs below a man's PENIS that produce SPERM

T

tes·ti·fy /ˈtɛstəˌfaɪ/ *v.* past tense and past participle **testified**, third person singular **testifies** [I,T] to make a formal statement of what is true, especially in a court of law: *Two men **testified that** they saw you there.* | *She refused to **testify against** my husband.*

tes·ti·mo·ni·al /ˌtɛstəˈmoʊniəl/ *n.* [C] a formal statement about someone's qualities and character

tes·ti·mo·ny /ˈtɛstəˌmoʊni/ *n.* plural **testimonies** [C,U] **1** a formal statement of what is true, especially one made in a court of law: ***In her testimony**, Susan denied the allegations.* → see Topic box at COURT[1] **2 (a) testimony to sth** something that clearly shows or proves that something is true: *This achievement is a testimony to your hard work.*

tes·tos·ter·one /tɛˈstɑstəˌroʊn/ *n.* [U] the HORMONE in men that gives them their male qualities

ˈtest tube *n.* [C] a small glass container shaped like a tube that is used in scientific tests

tes·ty /ˈtɛsti/ *adj.* impatient and easily annoyed: *It had been a long day, and we were all getting a little testy.* —**testily** *adv.*

tet·a·nus /ˈtɛtˀn-əs, -nəs/ *n.* [U] a serious disease caused by infection in a cut or wound

teth·er /ˈtɛðɚ/ *n.* [C] a rope or chain that is used to tie something to something else —**tether** *v.* [T]

Tex-Mex /ˌtɛks ˈmɛks◂/ *adj.* [only before noun] *informal* relating to the music, cooking, etc. of Mexican-American people: *a Tex-Mex restaurant*

T

text /tɛkst/ *n.* **1** [U] any written material: *a book with pictures but no text* | *a disk that can store huge quantities of text* **2** [C] a book or other piece of writing that is related to learning or intended for study: *religious texts* **3 the text of sth** the exact words of something: *The entire text of the speech was printed in the newspaper.*

text·book¹ /ˈtɛkstbʊk/ **also text** *n.* [C] a book about a subject which students use: *a history textbook*

textbook² *adj.* **a textbook example/case (of sth)** a very clear and typical example of how something should happen or be done

tex·tile /ˈtɛkstaɪl/ *n.* [C] any material that is made by weaving

ˈtext ˌmessage *n.* [C] a written message that you send to someone using a CELL PHONE —**text messaging** *n.* [U]

tex·ture /ˈtɛkstʃɚ/ *n.* [C,U] the way that a surface, material, etc. feels when you touch it, and how smooth or rough it looks: *fabric with a coarse texture*

tex·tured /ˈtɛkstʃɚd/ *adj.* having a surface that is not smooth

than /ðən; *strong* ðæn/ *conjunction, prep.* used when comparing two things or people that are different: *Jean's taller than Stella.* | *a car that costs less than $2000* | *I can swim better than you.*

thank /θæŋk/ *v.* [T] **1** to tell someone that you are pleased and grateful for a gift or for something that s/he has done: *We would like to **thank** everyone **for** helping.* **2 thank God/goodness/heavens** *spoken* said when you are very glad about something: *Thank God no one was hurt!* **3 have sb to thank (for sth)** *spoken* used in order to say who you are grateful to: *I have Phil to thank for getting me my first job.*

thank·ful /ˈθæŋkfəl/ *adj.* glad and grateful that something good has happened: *Our family has a lot to **be thankful for**.* | *I'm **thankful that** no one was hurt.* —**thankfully** *adv.*: *Thankfully, everything turned out all right.*

thank·less /ˈθæŋklɪs/ *adj.* a thankless job is difficult and you do not get much praise for doing it

thanks¹ /θæŋks/ *interjection informal* **1** used to tell someone that you are grateful for something s/he has done for you or given you [= **thank you**]: *Can I borrow your pen? **Thanks**.* | ***Thanks for** the drink.* | ***Thanks a lot for** helping out.* **2** *spoken* used when politely answering someone's question about you: *"How are you?" **"Fine, thanks."*** **3 thanks/no thanks** *spoken* said in order to accept or refuse something that someone is offering you: *"Do you want another cup of coffee?" "Oh, thanks."*

thanks² *n.* [plural] **1** something that you say or do to show that you are grateful to someone: *He left without **a word of thanks**.* **2 thanks to sb/sth** because of someone or something: *We're late, thanks to you.*

Thanks·giv·ing /ˌθæŋksˈgɪvɪŋ/ *n.* [C,U] a holiday in the U.S. and Canada in the fall when families have a large meal together to celebrate and be thankful for food, health, families, etc.: *Where are you going **for Thanksgiving**?*

ˈthank you¹ *interjection* **1** said in order to tell someone that you are grateful for something that s/he has done: *I really liked the book. Thank you.* | ***Thank you very much**.* | ***Thank you for** the perfume.* **2 thank you/no thank you** said in order to accept or refuse something that someone is offering you: *"Would you like another cookie?" "No thank you."*

ˈthank you² *adj.* **thank you letter/gift/note etc.** a letter, gift, etc. that is given to someone to thank him/her for something

ˈthank you³ *n.* [C usually singular] something that you say or do to thank someone for something: *Please accept this gift as **a thank you** for your support.*

COMMUNICATION

Ways of saying thank you

thanks: *Pass the salt, please ... thanks.*

thanks a lot: *"Would you like a drink?" "Yes, thanks a lot."*

thank you very much/thanks very much: *Thanks very much for all your help.*

many thanks especially written: *Many thanks for your letter of the 19th.*

thank you so much formal: *Thank you so much for coming.*

that¹ /ðæt/ *determiner, pron.* plural **those** /ðoʊz/ **1** used to talk about someone or something that is a distance away from you [➡ **this**]: *My office is in that building.* | *Who are those boys over there?* **2** used when talking about someone or something that has already been mentioned or is already known about [➡ **this**]: *I've never seen that movie.* | *Who told you that?* | *Those were her exact words.* **3** used after a noun as RELATIVE PRONOUN instead of "which" or "who": *a ticket that I bought last week* | *Have you met the couple that moved in next door?*

USAGE

The relative pronoun **that** is often left out when it is the object of a verb: *She's the woman (that) I love.*

You can use **that** instead of **which** or **who** when you are saying which thing or person you mean: *This is the man that/who called the police.*

You cannot use **that** instead of **which** or **who** if you are simply adding information: *This is my father, who lives in Dublin.* | *She owns an old Rolls Royce, which she bought in 1954.*

4 that's it a) used when what you have mentioned is all of something or the end of something: *It rains in February and that's it for the year.* **b)** *spoken* used in order to tell someone that s/he has done something correctly: *Turn the wheel to the left, yes, that's it.* **5 that is** used in order to correct a statement or give more exact information about something: *It's a seven-day trip. That is, it's five days there plus two days driving.*

SPOKEN PHRASES

6 that's life/men/politics etc. used to say that something is typical of a particular situation, group of people, etc.: *I guess I made a mistake, but hey, that's life.* **7 that's that** said when something is completely finished or when a decision will not be changed: *You're not going and that's that!* **8 that's all there is to it** said in order to emphasize that something is simple to do, explain, etc.: *We lost because we didn't play well. That's all there is to it.*

that² /ðət; *strong* ðæt/ *conjunction* used in order to introduce a CLAUSE that is the object of a sentence, shows a result, or gives information about a person, thing, time, etc. that has already been mentioned: *The rules state that if the ball hits the line, it's in.* | *Is it true that the Nelsons are moving?* | *They're showing the movie that you wanted to see.* | *Have you gotten the letter that I sent you?* ➔ **so (that)** at SO²

that³ /ðæt/ *adv.* **1 that long/much/big etc.** *spoken* used when talking about the size of something and showing it with your hands: *It's about that long.* **2 that good/bad/difficult etc.** as good, bad, etc. as someone has already mentioned: *I didn't realize things were that bad.* **3 not that much/long/big etc.** *spoken* not very much, long, etc.: *It won't cost all that much.*

thatch /θætʃ/ *n.* [C,U] dried STRAW used for making roofs —**thatched** *adj.*

thaw¹ /θɔ/ *v.* **1** [I,T] **also thaw out** if ice or snow thaws or is thawed, it becomes warmer and turns into water [≠ **freeze**]: *The snow was beginning to thaw.* **2** [I,T] **also thaw out** if frozen food thaws or is thawed, it becomes soft so it is ready to be cooked [≠ **freeze**] **3** [I] to become more friendly and less formal: *Relations between the two countries are beginning to thaw.*

thaw² *n.* [singular] **1** a period of warm weather during which snow and ice melt: *the spring thaw* **2** a time when a relationship becomes more friendly

the¹ /ðə, *before a vowel* ði; *strong* ði/ *definite article* **1** used before nouns to show that you are talking about a particular person or thing, especially when it has already been mentioned or when there is only one [➡ **a**]: *the tallest building in the world* | *the woman I saw yesterday* | *That's the dress I want.* **2** used as part of the names of some countries, rivers, oceans, etc.: *the United States* | *the Pacific Ocean* **3** used before an adjective to make it into a noun that refers to a particular group of people: *the economic gap between* ***the rich*** *and* ***the poor*** **4** used before a singular noun to show that you are talking about that thing in general: *The computer has changed our lives.* **5** each or every: *He's paid by the hour.* **6** used before the names of musical instruments: *Kira's learning to play the piano.* **7** used in order to talk about a part of the body: *The ball hit him right in the eye!* **8** used before a particular date or period of time: *the 1960s* | *the third of May* **9** used in order to emphasize that someone or something is important or famous: *It's definitely the movie to see.*

GRAMMAR

Do not use **the** when you are talking about something in general using an uncountable noun or a plural noun form: *I like ice cream.* | *Cats often hunt at night.*

Use **the** when you are talking about a particular thing: *I like the ice cream you bought.* | *The cats on our street make a lot of noise.*

Do not use **the** before the names of airports, train stations, or streets: *We arrived at O'Hare.* | *The train leaves from Grand Central.* | *She lives on Carr Avenue.*

Use **the** when you are talking about a particular airport, train station, or street without naming it: *We arrived at the airport.* | *The train was just leaving the station.* | *They live on the same street.*

the² *adv.* **1 the ... the ...** used in comparisons to show that two things happen together: *The more you practice, the better you'll play.* | *"When do you want this?" "The sooner the better."* **2** used in front of the SUPERLATIVE form of adjectives and adverbs to emphasize that something is as big, good, etc. as it is possible to be: *He likes you the best.*

the·a·ter /ˈθiət̬ɚ/ *n.* **1** [C] a building with a stage where plays are performed: *the Apollo Theater*

TOPIC

You **go to the theater** to **see** a **play**, **musical**, **opera**, or **ballet**. Before you go to the theater, you can **reserve tickets** at the **box office**. The place that you pay to sit in is called a **seat**. You have seats on **the floor** (=lowest level) or in the **balcony** (=highest level). You can buy a **program** (=small book telling you about the play, the actors, etc.). In front of the **audience** (=people watching), there may be an **orchestra** (=group of musicians) below the **stage**. During the play there is usually an **intermission** (=when the performance stops for a short time and people can have a drink).

2 [U] the work of acting in, writing, or organizing plays: *She's been working **in theater** for many years.* **3** [C] a building where movies are shown

the·at·ri·cal /θiˈætrɪkəl/ *adj.* **1** relating to the theater: *an expensive theatrical production* **2** behaving in a way that is intended to make people notice you —**theatrics** *n.* [plural]

theft /θɛft/ *n.* [C,U] the act or crime of stealing something: *car theft* | *the **theft of** $200 from the office*

T

THESAURUS

robbery, **burglary**, **shoplifting**, **mugging**
→ see Thesaurus box at CRIME

their /ðɚ; *strong* ðɛr/ *determiner* **1** belonging or relating to the people, animals, or things that have been mentioned, or are known about: *The guests left their coats on the bed.* | *Their daughter is a teacher.* **2** *spoken* used instead of "his" or "her" after words such as someone, anyone, everyone, etc.: *Everybody has their own ideas about it.*

theirs /ðɛrz/ *pron.* **1** the thing or things belonging to or relating to the people or things that have been mentioned, or are known about: *When our washing machine broke the neighbors let us use theirs.* **2** *spoken* used instead of "his" or "hers" after words such as someone, anyone, everyone, etc.: *Okay, get your coats. Does everyone have theirs?*

them /ðəm, əm; *strong* ðɛm/ *pron.* **1** the object form of "they": *Has anybody seen my keys? I can't find them.* | *My friends want me to go out with them tonight.* **2** *spoken* used instead of "him" or "her" after words such as someone, anyone, everyone, etc.: *If anyone calls, can you tell them to call back later?*

theme /θim/ *n.* [C] **1** the main subject or idea in a book, movie, speech, etc.: *Love is the main **theme of** the book.* **2 theme music/song/tune** music or a song that is always played during a particular television or radio program —**thematic** /θiˈmæt̬ɪk/ *adj.*

ˈtheme park *n.* [C] an AMUSEMENT PARK that is based on one subject such as water or space travel

them·selves /ðəmˈsɛlvz, ðɛm-/ *pron.* **1** the REFLEXIVE form of "they": *People usually like to talk about themselves.* **2** used in order to emphasize the subject or object of a sentence: *Doctors themselves admit that the treatment does not always work.* **3 (all) by themselves a)** alone: *Many old people live by themselves.* **b)** without help: *The kids made cookies all by themselves.* **4 (all) to themselves** for their own use: *The kids had the pool to themselves today.*

then[1] /ðɛn/ *adv.* **1** after something has happened: *We could have lunch and then go shopping.* **2** at a particular time in the past or future: ***Just then**, the phone rang.* | ***By then**, he was married.* | *My family lived in New York **back then**.* **3** *spoken* said in order to show that what you are saying is related in some way to what has been said before: *"He can't come on Friday." "Then how about Saturday?"* | *So you're going into nursing then?* **4** used in order to say that if one thing is true, the other thing is also true or should be the correct result: *"I have to pick Bobby up at school." "Then you should leave by 2:30."* **5** used in order to add something to what you have just said: *He's really busy at work, and then there's the new baby, too!* **6 then and there** immediately: *I would have given up then and there if my parents hadn't encouraged me.* → **but then (again)...** at BUT[1] → **(every) now and then** at NOW[1]

then[2] *adj.* [only before noun] used when talking about someone who did a job at a particular time in the past: *the then-President of the U.S.*

the·o·lo·gian /ˌθiəˈloʊdʒən/ *n.* [C] someone who studies or writes about THEOLOGY

the·ol·o·gy /θiˈɑlədʒi/ *n.* [U] the study of religion —**theological** /ˌθiəˈlɑdʒɪkəl/ *adj.*

the·o·rem /ˈθiərəm, ˈθɪrəm/ *n.* [C] *technical* a statement that can be shown to be true, especially in mathematics

the·o·ret·i·cal /ˌθiəˈrɛt̬ɪkəl/ *adj.* **1** relating to scientific ideas rather than practical situations: *theoretical physics* **2** a theoretical situation could exist but does not yet exist —**theoretically** *adv.*

the·o·rist /ˈθiərɪst/ **also the·o·re·ti·cian** /ˌθiərəˈtɪʃən/ *n.* [C] someone who develops ideas that explain why particular things happen or are true

the·o·rize /ˈθiəˌraɪz/ *v.* [I,T] to think of a possible explanation or reason for a particular event, fact, etc.: *Police **theorize that** the two men were working together.*

the·o·ry /ˈθiəri, ˈθɪri/ *n.* plural **theories** **1** [C] an idea that explains how something works, why something happens, etc., especially one that has not yet been proven to be true: *Darwin's **theory of** evolution | different **theories about** how the brain works | a **theory that** light is made up of waves* **2 in theory** something that is true in theory should be true, but may not actually be true: *In theory, the crime rate should decrease as employment increases.* **3** [U] the general principles or ideas of a subject: *music theory*

ther·a·peu·tic /ˌθɛrəˈpyut̬ɪk/ *adj.* **1** relating to the treatment or cure of a disease: *therapeutic drugs* **2** making you feel calm and relaxed

ther·a·py /ˈθɛrəpi/ *n.* plural **therapies** **1** [C,U] the treatment of an illness or injury over a fairly long period of time: *Ted's having physical therapy for his back.* **2** [U] the treatment or examination of someone's mental problems by talking to him/her for a long time about his/her feelings: *He's been **in therapy** for years.* —**therapist** *n.* [C] *a speech therapist*

there¹ /ðɛr/ *pron.* **there is/are/was/were etc.** used in order to say that something exists or happens: *There were several people hurt in the accident. | Suddenly, there was a loud crash. | Are there any questions?*

there² *adv.* **1** in or to a particular place that is not where you are or near you [➡ **here**]: *Would you hand me that glass **over there**? | I know Boston well because I used to live there. | The party was almost over by the time I **got there*** (=arrived). **2** at a particular point in time, in a situation, story, etc.: *I'll read this chapter and stop there.* **3** if something is there, it exists: *The money's there if you need it.* **4 be there (for sb)** to be ready to help someone if s/he needs help: *My folks are great – they're always there for me.*➔ **then and there** at THEN¹

SPOKEN PHRASES

5 there is sth also there it is a) said to make someone look or pay attention to something: *There's the statue I was telling you about.* **b)** said when you have found something you were looking for: *"Where's my purse?" "There it is, on the couch."* **6 there (you go)** *informal* **a) also there you are** used when giving something to someone or when you have done something for someone: *I'll just get you the key – there you are.* **b)** used in order to tell someone that s/he has done something correctly or understood something: *Can you turn just a little to the left? There you go.* **7 there** used when you have finished something: *There, that's the last piece of the puzzle.* **8 hello/hi there** used when greeting someone, especially when you have just noticed him/her **9 there, there** used in order to comfort a child: *There, there, it's all right.*

there·a·bouts /ˌðɛrəˈbaʊts, ˈðɛrəˌbaʊts/ *adv.* near a particular number, amount, or time, but not exactly: *The chair costs $50 **or thereabouts**.*

there·af·ter /ðɛrˈæftɚ/ *adv. formal* after a particular event or time [= **afterwards**]: *The store caught fire and closed **shortly thereafter**.*

there·by /ðɛrˈbaɪ, ˈðɛrbaɪ/ *adv. formal* with the result that: *Expenses were cut 12%, thereby increasing efficiency.*

there·fore /ˈðɛrfɔr/ *adv. formal* for the reason that has just been mentioned: *The gang were armed, and therefore more dangerous. | It was clear that Lucy was unhappy. Therefore, it wasn't surprising when she quit.*

there·in /ðɛrˈɪn/ *adv. formal* **1** in that place, or in that piece of writing: *We have studied the report and the information contained therein.* **2 therein lies sth** used in order to state the cause of something: *The two sides will not talk to each other, and therein lies the problem.*

there·of /ðɛrˈʌv/ *adv. formal* relating to something that has just been mentioned: *Money, or the **lack thereof*** (=lack of money), *played a major role in their marital problems.*

there·up·on /ˈðɛrəˌpɑn, ˌðɛrəˈpɑn/ *adv. formal* immediately after something happens and as a result of it

ther·mal /ˈθɚməl/ *adj.* **1** relating to or caused by heat: *thermal energy* **2** thermal clothing is made from special material to keep you warm in very cold weather: *thermal underwear*

ther·mom·e·ter /θɚˈmɑmət̬ɚ/ *n.* [C] a piece of equipment that measures the temperature of the air, your body, etc.

Ther·mos /ˈθɚməs/ *n.* [C] *trademark* a special container like a bottle that keeps hot drinks hot or cold drinks cold

ther·mo·stat /ˈθɚməˌstæt/ *n.* [C] an instrument that keeps a room, machine, etc. at a specific temperature

the·sau·rus /θɪˈsɔrəs/ *n.* plural **thesauruses** or **thesauri** /-ˈsɔraɪ/ [C] a book in which words are put into groups with other words that have a similar meaning

these /ðiz/ *determiner, pron.* the plural form of THIS

the·sis /ˈθisɪs/ *n.* plural **theses** /ˈθisiz/ [C] **1** a long piece of writing about a particular subject that you do for a university degree: *He wrote his **thesis on** 18th century literature.* **2 also thesis statement** the statement in a piece of writing that gives the main idea or the writer's opinion

they /ðeɪ/ *pron.* **1** the people or things that have already been mentioned or that are already known about: *Ken gave me these flowers – aren't they beautiful? | I stopped at Doris and Ed's place, but they weren't home.* **2** a particular group or organization, or the people involved in it: *Where are they going to build the new highway? | "Naranjas" is what they call oranges in Spain.* **3 they say/think** *spoken* used in order to say what people in general say or think: *They say it's bad luck to spill salt.* **4** *spoken* used instead of "he" or "she" after words such as someone, anyone, everyone,

T

etc.: *Somebody at work said they saw you at the party.*

they'd /ðeɪd/ **1** the short form of "they had": *They'd been missing for three days.* **2** the short form of "they would": *They'd like to visit us soon.*

they'll /ðeɪl, ðɛl/ the short form of "they will": *They'll have to wait.*

they're /ðɚ; *strong* ðɛr/ the short form of "they are": *They're very nice people.*

they've /ðeɪv/ the short form of "they have": *They've been here before.*

thick

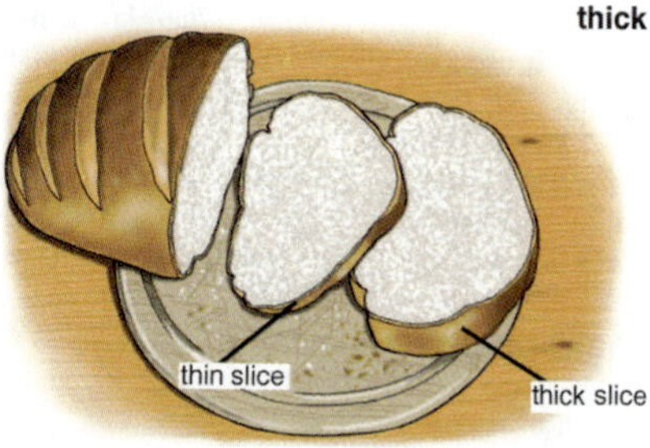

thick¹ /θɪk/ *adj.* **1** something that is thick is wide and not thin [≠ **thin**]: *a thick piece of bread | a thick layer of paint* **2 2 feet thick/12 inches thick etc.** used in order to describe how thick something is: *The wall is about 16 inches thick.* **3** a substance that is thick has very little water in it: *thick soup* **4** difficult to see through or breathe in: *The air was **thick with** smoke. | driving in **thick fog*** **5** growing very close together with not much space in between: *a thick forest | He has thick black hair.* —**thickly** *adv.*

thick² *n.* **1 be in the thick of sth** to be involved in the most active, dangerous, etc. part of a situation: *U.S. troops are right in the thick of the action.* **2 through thick and thin** in spite of any difficulties or problems: *They stayed married through thick and thin.*

thick·en /ˈθɪkən/ *v.* [I,T] to become thick, or make something thick: *Thicken the soup with flour.*

thick·et /ˈθɪkɪt/ *n.* [C] a group of bushes and small trees

thick·ness /ˈθɪknɪs/ *n.* [C,U] how thick something is: *Roll out the dough to a thickness of 1 inch.*

ˌthick-ˈskinned *adj.* not easily offended or upset by criticism

thief /θif/ *n.* plural **thieves** /θivz/ [C] someone who steals things: *a car thief | Thieves broke in and stole some valuable jewelry.*

> **THESAURUS**
>
> **robber**, **burglar**, **shoplifter**, **mugger**, **pickpocket**, **offender**, **attacker**, **murderer**, **rapist**
>
> → see Thesaurus box at CRIMINAL²

thigh /θaɪ/ *n.* [C] the top part of your leg above your knee → see picture on page A3

thim·ble /ˈθɪmbəl/ *n.* [C] a small hard cap that you put over the end of your finger to protect it when you are sewing

thin¹ /θɪn/ *adj.* comparative **thinner**, superlative **thinnest** **1** something that is thin is not very wide or thick [≠ **thick**]: *a thin slice of cheese | The walls here are **paper-thin*** (=very thin). **2** having little fat on your body [≠ **fat**]: *He's tall, very thin, and has dark hair.*

> **THESAURUS**
>
> **slim** and **slender** – used about someone who is thin in an attractive way
>
> **skinny** – used about someone who is very thin in a way that is not attractive
>
> **lean** – used about someone who is thin in a healthy way: *He has a runner's physique: long legs and a lean body.*
>
> **underweight** – used, especially by doctors, about someone who is too thin, in a way that is not healthy
>
> **emaciated** – used about someone who is extremely thin and weak because of illness or not eating
>
> → FAT

3 if someone has thin hair, they do not have very much hair [≠ **thick**] **4** air that is thin is difficult to breathe because there is not much OXYGEN in it **5** a substance that is thin has a lot of water in it [≠ **thick**]: *thin broth* —**thinness** *n.* [U]

thin² *v.* past tense and past participle **thinned**, present participle **thinning** [T] to make something thinner or to become thinner: *his thinning hair | paint thinned with water*

thin out *phr. v.* if a crowd thins out, people gradually leave so there are fewer of them

thing /θɪŋ/ *n.* [C] **1** a fact, idea, statement, action, or event: *A funny thing happened last week. | That's a terrible **thing to say**. | I have better things to do with my time. | I kept wondering if I was **doing the right thing**.* **2** used to talk about an object without saying its name, or when you do not know its name: *Do you know how to turn this thing off?*

> **THESAURUS**
>
> **object** especially written – a thing, especially a hard solid thing: *a sharp metal object*
>
> **something** – a thing, used especially when you do not know its name or what it is: *There's something in my eye.*
>
> **item** – one of the things in a set, group, or list: *He saved a few items and threw away the rest.*
>
> **article** – a thing, especially one of a group of things: *an article of clothing*

3 things [plural] life in general and the way it is affecting people: ***How are things going** at work? | We can't change **the way things are**.* **4 sb's**

things [plural] the things you own or the things you are carrying: *Just put your things over there.* **5 not know/feel/see etc. a thing** to know, feel, see, etc. nothing: *It was so dark I couldn't see a thing.* **6 there's no such thing (as sth)** used in order to emphasize that someone or something does not exist or does not happen: *There's no such thing as Santa Claus!* **7 the last thing sb wants/expects etc.** something that someone does not want, expect, etc. at all: *The last thing we wanted was to start a fight.* **8 do your own thing** *informal* to do what you want, and not what someone else wants you to do

SPOKEN PHRASES

9 the thing is said when explaining a problem or the reason for something: *We want to come, but the thing is we can't find a babysitter.* **10 for one thing** said when giving a reason for something: *I don't think she'll get the part – for one thing she can't sing!* **11 it's a good thing (that)** used in order to say that it is lucky or good that something happened: *It's a good thing the drug store's open late.* **12 first thing** at the beginning of the day or morning: *Let's talk about the report **first thing in the morning**.* **13 (it's) just one of those things** used in order to say that something that has happened is not someone's fault or could not have been avoided **14 it's (just) one thing after another** said when a lot of bad or unlucky things keep happening to you

thing·a·ma·jig /ˈθɪŋəmə,dʒɪg/ *n.* [C] *spoken* said when you cannot remember the real name of the thing you want to mention

think /θɪŋk/ past tense and past participle **thought** /θɔt/ *v.* **1** [T] to have an opinion about something: *I **think that** New York is a great place to live.* | *I **don't think (that)** he likes me* (=I think that he does not like me). | *What do you **think of** my new car?*

THESAURUS

believe – to think that it is true: *We believe that the risk is small.*
suspect – to think that something, especially something bad, is true but not be sure: *She suspected that he was seeing another woman.*
consider – to think about something carefully before deciding what to do: *He did not even consider the possibility of leaving.*
figure – used to say what your opinion is: *I figure he's at least 19.*
guess – to try to answer a question or make a judgment without knowing all the facts: *We guessed right this time.*

2 [T] to believe that something is true, although you are not sure: *I **think (that)** you're right.* | *I thought it was going to be sunny.* **3** [I] to use your mind to decide something, solve problems, have ideas, etc.: *What are you **thinking about**?* | *I couldn't **think of** anything to say.* | *Just a second, I'm thinking.* **4** [I] use your mind to remember something: *I can't **think of** her name.* **5 think about/of doing sth** to consider the possibility of doing something: *I'm thinking about moving to Boston.* **6 think of sb** to consider the feelings and wishes of another person, rather than just doing what you want: *Bill's always thinking of others.* **7 think better of sth** to decide not to do something that you had intended to do: *He reached for his cigarettes and then thought better of it.* **8 think nothing of (doing sth)** to do something easily that other people consider to be difficult or unusual: *Purdey thinks nothing of driving two hours to work every day.* **9 think twice** to consider a decision very carefully before you decide if you will do it or not: *You should **think twice before** signing the contract.* **10 who would have thought?** used in order to say that something is very surprising: *Who'd have thought being a mother would make you so happy?* **11 think well/highly of sb/sth** to admire or approve of someone or his/her work: *His teachers seem to think highly of him.* **12 think positively** to believe that you are going to be successful or that a situation is going to have a good result → UNTHINKABLE

SPOKEN PHRASES

13 I think so/I don't think so used when answering a question to say that you do or do not believe something is true: *"Will she be back on Friday?" "I think so."* **14 I think I'll...** said when telling someone what you will probably do: *I think I'll go to bed early tonight.* **15 I thought (that)** used when you are politely suggesting something to do: *I thought we could go to the lake this weekend.* **16 do you think (that)...?** used when you are asking someone politely to do something for you: *Do you think that you could give me a ride?* **17 you would think (that) also you would have thought (that)** used in order to say that you expect something to be true although it is not: *You would think someone who can sing that well would take better care of their voice.* **18 just think!** said when asking someone to imagine or consider something: *Just think – tomorrow we'll be in Hawaii!* **19 come to think of it** said when you have just remembered something that is related to your conversation: *Come to think of it, I did see Rita yesterday.*

think back *phr. v.* to think about things that happened in the past: *Thinking back, it amazes me we survived on so little money.*

think sth ⇔ **out** *phr. v.* to think about something carefully, considering all the possible problems, results, etc.: *The arguments had not been thought out very carefully.*

think sth ⇔ **over** *phr. v.* to consider something carefully before making a decision: *Take a few days to think over the offer.*

T

think sth ⇔ **through** *phr. v.* to think carefully about the possible results of doing something: *Give us time to think it through.*

think sth ⇔ **up** *phr. v.* to produce an idea, plan, etc. that is completely new: *Who thinks up the stories for these stupid TV shows?*

think·ing /ˈθɪŋkɪŋ/ *n.* [U] **1** an opinion about something, or an attitude toward something: *They have a different **way of thinking** about the issue.* **2** the activity of using your mind to solve a problem, produce thoughts, etc.: *Lance's **quick thinking** had saved her life.*

ˈthink tank *n.* [C] a committee of people with experience in a particular subject that an organization or government establishes to produce ideas and give advice: *a right-wing think tank*

thin·ly /ˈθɪnli/ *adv.* **1** if something is cut thinly, it is cut into thin pieces: *a **thinly sliced** onion* **2** with only a small number of people or things spread over a large area: *a **thinly populated** area*

thin·ning /ˈθɪnɪŋ/ *adj.* if your hair is thinning, some of it has fallen out

ˌthin-ˈskinned *adj.* too easily offended or upset by criticism

third /θɚd/ *number* **1** 3rd **2** 1/3

ˌthird ˈbase *n.* [singular] in baseball, the third place that a player must touch before s/he can gain a point

ˌthird deˈgree *n.* **give sb the third degree** *informal* to ask someone a lot of questions in order to get information from him/her

ˌthird-degree ˈburn *n.* [C] a very severe burn that goes through someone's skin

ˌthird ˈparty *n.* [singular] someone who is not one of the two main people involved in something, but who is involved in it or affected by it

ˌthird ˈperson *n.* [singular] *technical* in grammar, a form of a verb or PRONOUN that you use to show the person or thing that is being mentioned. "He," "she," "it," and "they" are all third person pronouns. [➡ **first person**, **second person**]

ˌthird-ˈrate *adj.* of very bad quality

ˌThird ˈWorld *n.* **the Third World** a phrase meaning the poorer countries of the world that do not have developed industries, which some people consider to be offensive —**Third World** *adj.*

thirst /θɚst/ *n.* **1** [singular] the feeling of wanting or needing a drink [➡ **hunger**]: *a drink to **quench** your **thirst*** (=stop you being thirsty) ▶ Don't say "I have thirst." Say "I am thirsty." ◀ **2** [U] the state of not having enough to drink: *Many of the animals had **died of thirst**.* **3 a thirst for sth** a strong need or desire for something: *a thirst for knowledge*

thirst·y /ˈθɚsti/ *adj.* feeling that you want to drink something [➡ **hungry**]: *I'm thirsty – can I have a glass of water?* —**thirstily** *adv.*

thir·teen /ˌθɚˈtin◂/ *number* 13 —**thirteenth** /ˌθɚˈtinθ◂/ *number*

thir·ty /ˈθɚṭi/ *number* **1** 30 **2 the thirties a)** the years between 1930 and 1939 **b)** the numbers between 30 and 39, especially when used for measuring temperature **3 be in your thirties** to be aged between 30 and 39: *She's **in** her **early/mid/late thirties**.* —**thirtieth** /ˈθɚṭiɪθ/ *number*

this[1] /ðɪs/ *determiner, pron.* plural **these** /ðiz/ **1** used when talking about someone or something that is close to you [➡ **that**]: *My mother gave me this necklace.* | *What should I do with this* (=something I am holding and showing you)*?* **2** used in order to talk about something that has just been mentioned or that is already known about: *I'm going to make sure this doesn't happen again.* **3** used in order to talk about the present time or a time that is close to the present [➡ **last**, **next**]: *What are you doing this week?* | *We'll be seeing Malcolm this Friday* (=on Friday of the present week). **4** *spoken* used in conversation to mention a particular person or thing: *This friend of mine said he could get us tickets.* | *We saw this really cool movie last night.* **5 this is...** *spoken* used in order to introduce someone to someone else: *Nancy, this is my wife, Elaine.*

this[2] *adv.* used when talking about the size, number, degree, or amount of something: *I've never stayed up this late before.* | *Katie's about this tall now* (=said when using your hands to show a size).

this·tle /ˈθɪsəl/ *n.* [C] a wild plant with purple flowers and leaves that have sharp points

thong /θɔŋ, θɑŋ/ *n.* **1 thongs** [plural] a pair of open summer shoes, held on your feet by a v-shaped band that fits between your toes **2** [C] a piece of underwear or the bottom part of a BIKINI that has a single string instead of the back part

thorn /θɔrn/ *n.* [C] **1** a sharp point that grows on a plant such as a rose **2 a thorn in your side** someone or something that annoys you or causes you problems over a long time

thorn·y /ˈθɔrni/ *adj.* **1 thorny question/problem/issue etc.** a question, problem, etc. that is very difficult to deal with **2** having a lot of THORNS

thor·ough /ˈθɚoʊ, ˈθʌroʊ/ *adj.* **1** including every possible detail: *The police conducted a thorough search of the property.*

> **THESAURUS**
>
> **careful**, **methodical**, **meticulous**, **systematic**, **painstaking**
>
> ➔ see Thesaurus box at CAREFUL

2 careful to do everything that you should and avoid mistakes: *As a scientist, Madison is methodical and thorough.* —**thoroughness** *n.* [U]

thor·ough·bred /ˈθɚəˌbrɛd, ˈθɚoʊ-, ˈθʌr-/ *n.* [C] a horse that has parents of the same very good breed

thor·ough·fare /ˈθɚəˌfɛr, ˈθɚoʊ-, ˈθʌr-/ *n.* [C] the main road through a city

thor·ough·ly /ˈθɚoʊli, ˈθʌr-/ *adv.* **1** completely or very much: *Thanks for dinner; I thoroughly enjoyed it.* **2** carefully and completely: *Rinse the vegetables thoroughly.*

those /ðoʊz/ *determiner, pron.* the plural of THAT

though¹ /ðoʊ/ *conjunction* **1** used in order to introduce a statement that is surprising, unexpected, or different from your other statements [➡ **although**]: *Though Beattie is almost 40, she still plans to compete.* | *I seem to keep gaining weight* ***even though*** *I'm exercising regularly.* **2** used like "but" in order to add a fact or opinion to what you have said: *I thought he'd been drinking though I wasn't completely sure.* **3 as though** used like "as if" in order to say how something seems or appears: *She was staring at me as though she knew me.*

though² *adv. spoken* in spite of that: *Raleigh's a nice city. Mark doesn't want to leave Georgia, though.*

thought¹ /θɔt/ *v.* the past tense and past participle of THINK

thought² *n.* **1** [C] something that you think of, think about, or remember [➡ **idea**]: *I've just* ***had a thought****. I'll ask Terry to come.* | *Even* ***the thought of*** *flying scares me.* | ***The thought that*** *I might not have a job next year made me nervous.* | *What are your* ***thoughts on*** *the subject* (=what is your opinion)*?* **2** [U] the act of thinking: *She sat at her desk,* ***lost/deep in thought*** (=thinking so much she did not notice anything else). **3** [U] the act of considering something carefully and seriously: *You need to* ***give*** *the decision* ***plenty of thought****.* **4 (it's) just a thought** *spoken* said when you have made a suggestion and you have not thought about it very much **5** [C,U] a feeling of caring about someone: *Michael never* ***gave*** *any* ***thought to*** *others.* | *You are always* ***in my thoughts*** (=used in order to tell someone that you think and care about him/her a lot). **6** [U] a way of thinking that is typical of a particular group, period of history, etc.: *ancient Greek thought* **7** [C,U] an intention or wish: *He has no thoughts of running for President.*

thought·ful /ˈθɔtfəl/ *adj.* **1** serious and quiet because you are thinking about something: *a* ***thoughtful look*** *on his face* | *a* ***thoughtful silence*** **2** kind and always thinking of things you can do to make other people happy: *You have a very thoughtful husband.* | ***It was*** *really* ***thoughtful of*** *you to remember my birthday.* —**thoughtfully** *adv.* —**thoughtfulness** *n.* [U]

> **THESAURUS**
> **kind, nice, considerate, caring**
> ➔ see Thesaurus box at KIND²

thought·less /ˈθɔtlɪs/ *adj.* not thinking about the needs and feelings of other people: *a thoughtless remark*

> **THESAURUS**
> **mean, cruel, unkind, nasty**
> ➔ see Thesaurus box at MEAN²

thou·sand /ˈθaʊzənd/ *number* **1** 1000 **2 thousands** *informal* a lot of: *We've received* ***thousands of*** *letters from fans.* —**thousandth** *adj.*

thrash /θræʃ/ *v.* **1** [T] to hit someone violently, often as a punishment **2** [I] to move from side to side in an uncontrolled way: *a fish* ***thrashing around*** *on dry land* —**thrashing** *n.* [C,U]

thrash sth ⇔ **out** *phr. v.* to discuss a problem thoroughly until you find an answer: *Officials are still trying to thrash out an agreement.*

thread¹ /θrɛd/ *n.* **1** [C,U] a long thin line of cotton, silk, etc. that you use to sew cloth: *a needle and thread* ➔ see picture at KNIT¹ **2** [singular] the relation between different parts of a story, explanation, etc.: *He* ***lost the thread*** (=forgot the main part) *of his argument.*

thread² *v.* [T] **1** to put thread, string, rope, etc. through a hole: *Will you* ***thread*** *the* ***needle*** *for me?* **2 thread your way through/down etc.** to move through a place by carefully going around things that are in the way: *a biker threading his way through traffic*

thread·bare /ˈθrɛdbɛr/ *adj.* clothes, CARPETS etc. that are threadbare are very thin because they have been used a lot

threat /θrɛt/ *n.* **1** [C,U] a statement in which you tell someone that you will cause harm or damage if s/he does not do what you want: *He* ***made a threat*** *against my family.* | ***threats of*** *violence* | *a* ***bomb threat*** **2** [C usually singular] someone or something that may cause damage or harm to another person or thing: *a* ***threat to*** *national security*

> **THESAURUS**
> **danger, risk, hazard**
> ➔ see Thesaurus box at DANGER

3 [C usually singular] the possibility that something bad will happen: *the* ***threat of*** *famine*

threat·en /ˈθrɛtˀn/ *v.* **1** [T] to say that you will cause someone trouble, pain, etc. if s/he does not do what you want: *Sandra* ***threatened to*** *run away from home.* | *Don't you threaten me!* **2** [T] to be likely to harm or destroy something: *Pollution is threatening the historical buildings of Athens.* **3** [I,T] if something unpleasant threatens to happen, it seems likely to happen: *The fighting* ***threatens to*** *become a major war.*

threat·en·ing /ˈθrɛtˀn-ɪŋ/ *adj.* making threats or intended to threaten someone: *a threatening letter*

three /θri/ *number* **1** 3 **2** three O'CLOCK: *I'll meet you* ***at three****.*

ˌthree-diˈmensional, 3-D *adj.* having or seeming to have length, depth, and height: *a 3-D movie*

thresh·old /ˈθrɛʃhoʊld, -ʃoʊld/ *n.* [C] **1 on**

the threshold of sth at the beginning of a new and important event or development: *We're on the threshold of a new period in telecommunications.* **2** the level at which something begins to happen or have an effect on something: *She has a **high/low pain threshold**.* **3** the entrance to a room, or the area of floor at the entrance

threw /θru/ *v.* the past tense of THROW

thrift /θrɪft/ *n.* [U] *old-fashioned* wise and careful use of money —**thrifty** *adj.*

'thrift store *n.* [C] a store that sells used goods, especially clothes, often in order to get money for a CHARITY

thrill[1] /θrɪl/ *n.* [C] a strong feeling of excitement and pleasure, or the thing that makes you feel this: ***the thrill of** driving a fast car*

thrill[2] *v.* [I,T] to feel strong excitement and pleasure, or make someone else feel this: *His music continues to thrill audiences.* —**thrilled** *adj.*: *We're thrilled with the results.* —**thrilling** *adj.*: *a thrilling game*

thrill·er /ˈθrɪlɚ/ *n.* [C] a movie or book that tells an exciting story about murder, crime, etc.

> **THESAURUS**
>
> **comedy, romantic comedy, western, action movie, horror movie, science fiction movie, animated movie/cartoon**
> ➔ see Thesaurus box at MOVIE

T

thrive /θraɪv/ *v.* past tense **thrived** or **throve** /θroʊv/ past participle **thrived**, present participle **thriving** [I] *formal* to become very successful or very strong and healthy: *a plant that is able to **thrive in** dry conditions* —**thriving** *adj.*: *a thriving business*

throat /θroʊt/ *n.* [C] **1** the passage from the back of your mouth down the inside of your neck: *I have **a sore throat**.* ➔ see picture on page A3 **2** the front of your neck: *The attacker grabbed Mark by the throat.* **3 force/ram sth down sb's throat** *informal* to force someone to accept your ideas or listen to your opinions when s/he does not want to **4 be at each other's throats** if two people are at each other's throats, they are fighting or arguing with each other ➔ **clear your throat** at CLEAR[2] ➔ **jump down sb's throat** at JUMP[1]

throat·y /ˈθroʊt̬i/ *adj.* a throaty sound is low and rough

throb[1] /θrɑb/ *v.* past tense and past participle **throbbed**, present participle **throbbing** [I] **1** if a part of your body throbs, you get a regular feeling of pain in it: *I woke up with a **throbbing headache**.*

> **THESAURUS**
>
> **hurt, ache, sting**
> ➔ see Thesaurus box at HURT[1]

2 to beat strongly and regularly

throb[2] *n.* [C] a strong regular beat: *the low throb of the music*

throes /θroʊz/ *n.* **in the throes of sth** in the middle of a very difficult situation: *Nigeria was in the throes of a bloody civil war.*

throne /θroʊn/ *n.* [C] **1** the chair on which a king or queen sits **2 the throne** the position and power of being king or queen: *In 2002, Queen Elizabeth celebrated her 50th year **on the throne**.*

throng[1] /θrɔŋ, θrɑŋ/ *n.* [C] *literary* ➔ CROWD[1]

throng[2] *v.* [I,T] *literary* if people throng a place, they go there in large numbers: *crowds thronging St. Peter's Square*

throt·tle[1] /ˈθrɑt̬l/ *v.* [T] ➔ STRANGLE

throttle[2] *n.* [C] *technical* a piece of equipment that controls the amount of gas going into an engine

through[1] /θru/ *prep., adv.* **1** from one side or end of something to the other: *He climbed in through the window.* | *a train going through a tunnel* | *We found a gap in the fence and climbed through.* **2** from the beginning to the end, including all parts of something: *She slept through the movie.* | *I've searched through my files but I can't find the receipt.* | *Make sure you **read** the contract **through** before signing it.* **3** if you see or hear something through a window, wall, etc., the window, wall, etc. is between you and it: *I could see him through the window.* | *music coming through the walls* **4** because of someone or with the help of something or someone: *She succeeded through sheer hard work.* | *I got the job through an employment agency.* **5** going into an area, group, etc. and moving across it or within it: *a plane flying through the air* | *a trip through Europe* **6 Friday through Sunday/March through May etc.** from Friday until the end of Sunday, from March until the end of May, etc.: *The exhibit will be here through July 31st.* **7 through and through** completely: *He came in from the rain soaked through and through.* ➔ **come through** at COME ➔ **get through** at GET ➔ **go through** at GO[1] ➔ **pull through** at PULL[1]

through[2] *adj. informal* **1 be through (with sth)** *informal* to have finished using something, doing something, etc.: *I'm through with the phone now if you still need it.*

> **THESAURUS**
>
> **done, finished, complete, over**
> ➔ see Thesaurus box at DONE[2]

2 be through (with sb) to no longer have a romantic relationship with someone: *Steve and I are through!*

through·out /θruˈaʊt/ *adv., prep.* **1** in every part of a place: *Thanksgiving is celebrated throughout the U.S.* **2** during all of a particular time: *She was calm throughout the interview.*

throve /θroʊv/ *v.* a past tense of THRIVE

throw[1] /θroʊ/ *v.* past tense **threw** /θru/ past participle **thrown** /θroʊn/

1 THROW A BALL/STONE ETC. [I,T] to make an object move quickly from your hand through the air by moving your arm: *Kids were **throwing** snowballs **at** each other.* | ***Throw** the ball **to** Daddy.* ➔ see picture on page A9

THESAURUS

toss – to throw something, especially in a careless way: *She tossed her coat onto the bed.*
chuck informal: *Kids were chucking snowballs at passing cars.*
hurl – to throw something with a lot of force: *They hurled a brick through his window.*
fling – to throw something somewhere with a lot of force, often in a careless way: *He flung her keys into the river.*

to throw a ball in a sport
pass – to throw, kick, or hit a ball to another member of your team
pitch – to throw the ball to the person who is trying to hit the ball in a game of baseball

2 PUT STH CARELESSLY [T] to put something somewhere quickly and carelessly: *Just **throw** your coat **on** the bed.*
3 PUSH ROUGHLY [T] to push someone roughly toward a particular direction or position: *Police **threw** the man **to the ground**.* | *She **threw open** the windows.*
4 throw yourself on/down etc. to move somewhere suddenly and with force: *Elise threw herself on the bed and started to cry.*
5 throw yourself into sth to start doing something with a lot of effort and energy: *I threw myself into my work.*
6 throw sb/sth into confusion/crisis/chaos etc. to do something that causes people to be confused, worried, etc.: *The changes to welfare will throw millions of children deeper into poverty.*
7 MOVE HANDS/HEAD ETC. [T] to suddenly move your hands, arms, head, etc. in a particular direction: *Vic **threw** his head **back** and laughed.*
8 throw sb in jail/prison *informal* to put someone in prison
9 throw sb *spoken* to confuse or shock someone, especially by suddenly saying something: *His reaction **threw** me **for a loop*** (=completely confused me).
10 throw a party to organize a party and invite people
11 throw a glance/look/smile etc. (at sb) to quickly look at someone, smile at someone, etc., especially in a way that shows what you are feeling: *He threw her a worried look.*
12 throw a game/fight to deliberately lose a game or fight that you could have won
13 throw the book at sb to punish someone as severely as possible
14 MAKE SB FALL [T] if a horse throws its rider, it makes him/her fall off

throw sth ⇔ **away** *phr. v.* **1** to get rid of something that you do not want or need: *junk mail that we throw away* **2** to lose or waste a chance, advantage, etc.: *The Democrats are just throwing away their shot at the presidency.*

throw in *phr. v.* **1 throw** sth ⇔ **in** to add something, especially to what you are selling: *a computer with some software thrown in* **2 throw in the towel** *informal* to admit that you have been defeated

throw sb/sth ⇔ **off** *phr. v.* **1** to take off a piece of clothing quickly and carelessly **2** to escape from someone or become free from something or someone: *The Serbs threw off 500 years of Ottoman rule.* **3** to confuse a situation or make it not work correctly: *The changes will throw off the schedule.*

throw sth ⇔ **on** *phr. v.* to put on a piece of clothing quickly and carelessly

throw sb/sth ⇔ **out** *phr. v.* **1** to get rid of something that you do not want or need: *I threw a lot of stuff out.* **2** to make someone leave a place quickly because s/he has behaved badly: *Cooper got **thrown out of** the Navy for taking drugs.* **3** if people throw out a plan or suggestion, they refuse to accept it

throw sth ⇔ **together** *phr. v.* to make something quickly and not very carefully: *How about throwing some sandwiches together?*

throw up *phr. v. informal* to VOMIT

throw[2] *n.* [C] an action in which someone throws something: *a good throw to first base*

throw·a·way /ˈθroʊəˌweɪ/ *adj.* **1 throwaway remark/line etc.** a short remark that is said quickly and without thinking carefully **2 throwaway society** a society that wastes things instead of caring about the environment

throw·back /ˈθroʊbæk/ *n.* [C usually singular] something that is similar to something that existed in the past: *The machine looks like **a throwback to** an earlier era.*

thrown /θroʊn/ *v.* the past participle of THROW

thru /θru/ *prep., adj., adv. nonstandard* THROUGH

thrust[1] /θrʌst/ *v.* past tense and past participle **thrust** [T] **1** to push something somewhere with a sudden or violent movement: *Dean **thrust** some money **into** the driver's hand.*

THESAURUS

shove, stick, dump
➔ see Thesaurus box at SHOVE

2 to be put in a difficult situation or forced to accept it: *The incident **thrust** the nation **into** an economic crisis.*

thrust[2] *n.* **1 the thrust** the main meaning or most important part of what someone says or does: *The **main/major/whole thrust** of his argument is that all of life is political.* **2** [U] the force of an engine that makes a car, train, or airplane move forward

thru·way /ˈθruweɪ/ *n.* [C] a wide road for fast traffic

thud /θʌd/ *n.* [C] the low sound that is made by a

heavy object hitting something else: *He landed **with a thud**.* —**thud** *v.* [I]

thug /θʌg/ *n.* [C] a violent man

thumb¹ /θʌm/ *n.* [C] **1** the short thick finger on the side of your hand that helps you to hold things ➔ see picture at HAND¹ **2 the thumbs up/down** to show that you approve or disapprove of something, or that you are ready to do something: *His new movie **got the thumbs up** from the public.* | *Ralph gave Captain Baker **the thumbs-up sign**.* **3 be under sb's thumb** if you are under someone's thumb, they control what you do ➔ **rule of thumb** at RULE¹ ➔ **stick out (like a sore thumb)** at STICK¹

thumb² *v.* **thumb your nose at sb/sth** to show that you do not respect rules, laws, someone's opinion, etc.: *Protesters feel the government is thumbing its nose at citizens' basic rights.*

thumb through sth *phr. v.* to look through a book, magazine, etc. quickly

thumb·nail¹ /ˈθʌmneɪl/ *n.* [C] the nail on your thumb

thumbnail² *adj.* **thumbnail sketch/description** a short description that gives only the main facts

thumb·tack /ˈθʌmtæk/ *n.* [C] a short pin with a wide flat top, used for attaching papers to walls

thump /θʌmp/ *v.* **1** [I,T] to make a dull sound by hitting against something: *a dog thumping his tail on the floor* **2** [I] if your heart thumps, it beats very quickly because you are frightened or excited **3** [T] *informal* to hit someone: *Brasco thumped him on the back.* —**thump** *n.* [C]

T

thun·der¹ /ˈθʌndɚ/ *n.* [U] the loud noise that you hear during a storm, usually after a flash of LIGHTNING: *a storm with **thunder and lightning*** | *Suddenly, there was a great **clap/crack of thunder**.*

thunder² *v.* **1 it thunders** if it thunders, a loud noise comes from the sky, usually after LIGHTNING **2** [I] to make a very loud noise: *The kids came thundering downstairs.*

thun·der·bolt /ˈθʌndɚˌboʊlt/ *n.* [C] a flash of LIGHTNING that hits something

thun·der·clap /ˈθʌndɚˌklæp/ *n.* [C] a loud noise of THUNDER

thun·der·cloud /ˈθʌndɚˌklaʊd/ *n.* [C] a large dark cloud in a storm

thun·der·ous /ˈθʌndərəs/ *adj.* extremely loud: *thunderous applause*

> **THESAURUS**
>
> **loud**, **noisy**, **rowdy**, **deafening**, **ear-splitting**
> ➔ see Thesaurus box at LOUD¹

thun·der·storm /ˈθʌndɚˌstɔrm/ *n.* [C] a storm with THUNDER and LIGHTNING

thun·der·struck /ˈθʌndɚˌstrʌk/ *adj.* extremely surprised or shocked

Thurs·day /ˈθɚzdi, -deɪ/ *written abbreviation* **Thurs.** *n.* the fifth day of the week: *I tried to call you Thursday.* | *Kim is leaving for Chicago **on Thursday**.* | *He was arrested **last Thursday**.* | *I made the appointment for **next Thursday**.* | *Jason arrived late **Thursday night**.*

thus /ðʌs/ *adv. formal* **1** as a result of something that you have just mentioned [= **so**]: *Traffic will become heavier, thus increasing pollution.* **2** in this way: *The oil spill could thus contaminate the water supply.* **3 thus far** until now: *Reviewers have said it's the best movie thus far this year.*

thwart /θwɔrt/ *v.* [T] to prevent someone from doing what s/he is trying to do

thy·roid /ˈθaɪrɔɪd/ **also** **ˈthyroid ˌgland** *n.* [C] an organ in your neck that produces HORMONES (=substances that affect the way your body grows and the way you behave)

ti·a·ra /tiˈɑrə, tiˈɛrə/ *n.* [C] a piece of jewelry like a small CROWN

tic /tɪk/ *n.* [C] a sudden movement of a muscle in your face, that you cannot control

tick¹ /tɪk/ *n.* [C] **1** the short repeated sound that a clock or watch makes every second **2** a small creature with eight legs that attaches itself to animals and sucks their blood

tick² *v.* **1** [I] if a clock or watch ticks, it makes a short sound every second **2 what makes sb tick** *informal* the reasons that someone behaves in a particular way

tick sb/sth ⇔ **off** *phr. v.* **1** *informal* to annoy someone: *Her attitude really ticks me off.* **2** to tell someone a list of things: *McCoy ticked off a list of the speakers.*

ˌticked-ˈoff *adj. informal* very annoyed

tick·et¹ /ˈtɪkɪt/ *n.* [C] **1** a printed piece of paper that shows that you have paid to do something, for example see a movie or travel on an airplane: *two **tickets to/for** the Lakers game* | *a **concert/bus/airplane ticket***

> **THESAURUS**
>
> **Types of tickets**
>
> **one-way ticket** – a ticket that lets you go to a place but not back again
>
> **round-trip ticket** – a ticket that lets you go to a place and back again
>
> **off-peak ticket** – a ticket that is cheaper than the usual price because you cannot use it at the busiest times
>
> **season ticket** – a ticket that lets you make the same trip every day for a particular period of time
>
> **e-ticket** – a ticket that you buy over the Internet, which you print from your computer or which you pick up when you arrive at the airport to go on your trip

2 a printed note saying that you must pay money because you have done something illegal while driving or parking your car: *a **speeding/parking ticket*** **3** a list of the people supported by a particular political party in an election: *the Democratic ticket*

ticket² *v.* [T] to give someone a ticket for parking

his/her car in the wrong place or for driving too fast

tick·le¹ /'tɪkəl/ *v.* **1** [T] to move your fingers lightly over someone's body in order to make him/her laugh: *Stop tickling me!*

THESAURUS

touch, feel, stroke, rub, scratch, pat, brush, caress, fondle, grope
→ see Thesaurus box at TOUCH¹

2 [I,T] if something touching your body tickles you, it makes you want to rub your body because it is uncomfortable: *Mommy, this blanket tickles.* **3** [T] if a situation, remark, etc. tickles you, it amuses or pleases you: *Mom will be **tickled pink/tickled to death*** (=very pleased) *when she hears you're coming.*

tickle² *n.* [C] a feeling in your throat that makes you want to cough

tick·lish /'tɪklɪʃ/ *adj.* **1** someone who is ticklish is very easy to tickle **2** *informal* a ticklish situation or problem must be dealt with very carefully

tic-tac-toe /ˌtɪk tæk 'toʊ/ *n.* [U] a children's game in which two players draw the marks X and O in a pattern of nine squares, trying to get three in a row

tid·al /'taɪdl/ *adj.* relating to the regular rising and falling of the sea: *tidal pools*

'tidal wave *n.* [C] a very large ocean wave that flows over the land and destroys things

tid·bit /'tɪdˌbɪt/ *n.* [C] **1** a small piece of food that tastes good **2** a small piece of interesting information, news, etc.

tide

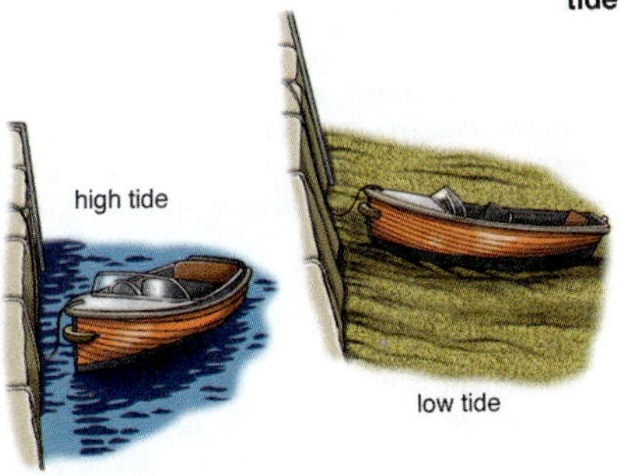

tide¹ /taɪd/ *n.* [C] **1** the regular rising and falling of the level of the ocean: *It's **high/low tide**.* **2** the way in which events or people's opinions are developing: *The **tide** has **turned**, and more jobs are being created than lost.* **3** a large amount of something that is increasing: *a **rising tide** of hate crimes*

tide² *v.*
tide sb **over** *phr. v.* to help someone deal with a difficult time: *Could you lend me $50 to tide me over until payday?*

ti·dy /'taɪdi/ *adj.* NEAT

tie¹ /taɪ/ *v.* past tense and past participle **tied**, present participle **tying**, third person singular **ties** **1** [I,T] to fasten something or hold it in a particular position using a rope, string, etc.: *The dress ties in the back.* | *She **tied** the scarf **around** her neck.* | *a dog **tied to** the fence*

THESAURUS

fasten, attach, join, glue, tape, staple, clip, button (up), zip (up)
→ see Thesaurus box at FASTEN

2 [T] to make a knot in a rope, string, etc.: *Can you tie your shoelaces yet?* **3** [I] **also be tied** to have the same number of points in a competition: *two teams that are **tied for** first place* | *The score is tied.* **4 be tied to sth** to be related to something and dependent on it: *Pay is tied to performance.*

tie sb **down** *phr. v.* to stop someone from being free to do what s/he wants to do: *I didn't want to be tied down with a child.*

tie in *phr. v.* if one idea or statement ties in with another one, they are similar or related: *The displays **tie in with** the advertising campaign.*

tie sb/sth ⇔ **up** *phr. v.* **1** to tie someone's arms, legs, etc. so that s/he cannot move: *They had tied her up so she couldn't escape.* **2** to fasten something together by using string or rope: *a package **tied up with** string* **3** to use something so much that it is prevented from working effectively: *Sorry I'm late – I got tied up in traffic.* | *The case could tie up the courts for months.* **4 be tied up a)** to be very busy **b)** if your money is tied up in something, it is all being used for that thing: *Our money's **tied up in** real estate.*

tie² *n.* [C] **1** a long narrow piece of cloth that men wear around their neck, tied in a knot outside their shirts → see picture at CLOTHES **2** a relationship between two people, groups, or countries: ***close** family **ties*** | ***diplomatic/economic/political, etc. ties** with Japan* **3** a piece of string, wire, etc. used in order to fasten or close something such as a bag **4** the result of a game, competition, or election in which two or more people get the same number of points, votes, etc.: *The game ended **in a tie**.*

tie·break·er /'taɪˌbreɪkɚ/ *n.* [C] an additional question or point that decides the winner when two people or teams are tied

'tie-dye *v.* [T] to make a pattern on clothing or other material by tying string around it and coloring it with DYE

tier /tɪr/ *n.* [C] **1** one of several layers or levels that rise up one above another: *the top tier of seats* **2** one of several levels in an organization or system: *four tiers of management*

tiff /tɪf/ *n.* [C] a slight argument between friends

T

ti·ger /ˈtaɪgɚ/ *n.* [C] a large strong wild cat with orange and black lines on its fur

tight¹ /taɪt/ *adj.*

1 CLOTHES fitting part of your body very closely: *These shoes feel too tight.* | *tight jeans*

2 FIRMLY PULLED pulled or stretched firmly: *a tight bandage*

3 FIRMLY FIXED firmly fixed and difficult to move: *Make sure the screws are tight.*

4 FIRMLY CONTROLLED controlled very strictly and firmly: *Security is tight for the President's visit.*

5 MONEY a) *informal* if money is tight, you do not have enough of it **b)** *disapproving* someone who is tight tries hard to avoid spending money

6 TIME if time is tight, it is difficult for you to do the things you need to do in the time you have: *a* ***tight schedule***

7 COMPETITION a tight election, game, competition, etc. is one in which the competitors have an almost equal chance of winning: *a tight race for the Senate seat* —**tightly** *adv.*

tight² *adv.* very firmly or closely [= **tightly**]: ***Hold tight*** *and don't let go.* | *Put the lid on tight.* | ***tight-fitting*** *jeans*

tight·en /ˈtaɪtˀn/ *v.* **1** [T] to close or fasten something firmly by turning it: *Tighten the clamps in place.* **2** [I,T] if you tighten a rope, wire, STRAP, etc., or if it tightens, it is stretched or pulled until it is tight: *I tightened the bindings of the snowshoes.* **3** [T] **also tighten up** to make a rule, law, or system more strict: *The government has tightened border controls.* **4** [I,T] if your muscles or a part of your body tightens, or you tighten it, it becomes stiff: *Miguel's lips tightened in anger.* **5** [I,T] to close firmly around something: *Richard* ***tightened*** *his* ***grip*** *on her arm.* **6 tighten your belt** *informal* to try to spend less money than you usually spend

ˌtight-ˈfisted *adj. informal disapproving* not generous with money [= **stingy**]

ˌtight-ˈlipped *adj.* not willing to talk about something

tight·rope /ˈtaɪtˀroʊp/ *n.* [C] a rope or wire high above the ground that someone walks along in a CIRCUS

tights /taɪts/ *n.* [plural] a piece of women's clothing made of thick colored material that fits tightly over the feet and legs and goes up to the waist

tile /taɪl/ *n.* [C] a thin square piece of baked clay or other material that is used for covering roofs, walls, or floors —**tile** *v.* [T]

till¹ /tɪl, tl/ *prep., conjunction spoken* until: *I was up till 1:00 a.m.*

USAGE

Until and **till** are used to talk about the time when something stops: *They stayed until/till after midnight.*

As far as is used to talk about the place where something stops: *Does the bus go as far as the station?*

Up to is used mainly to talk about the final number or the biggest possible number: *The children had to count up to fifty.*

till² *v.* [T] to prepare land for growing crops

tilt /tɪlt/ *v.* [I,T] **1** to move into a position where one side is higher than the other, or to make something do this: *She listened, her head tilted to one side.* **2** if an opinion or situation tilts, or something tilts it, it changes to that people start to prefer one person, belief, or action to others: *Public opinion has been* ***tilting toward*** *the Right.* —**tilt** *n.* [C,U]

tim·ber /ˈtɪmbɚ/ *n.* [U] trees that are cut down and used for building or making things

time¹ /taɪm/ *n.*

1 MINUTES/HOURS ETC. [U] the thing that is measured in minutes, hours, years, etc. using clocks: ***Time*** *seemed to* ***pass/go by*** *very quickly.* | *a three-month* ***period of time***

2 ON THE CLOCK [singular] a particular point in time that is shown on a clock in hours and minutes: *What time is it?* | *Evan is just learning to* ***tell time*** (=look at a clock to see what time it is).

3 OCCASION [C] an occasion when something happens or someone does something: *We visit him two or three times a month.* | *When was the* ***first/last time*** *you saw Kelly?* | *It makes me laugh* ***every/each time*** *I see it.* | *The* ***next time*** *you come, we'll go to a show.* | *Smoking is not allowed* ***at any time.***

4 HOW OFTEN/HOW LONG [singular, U] a period of time during which something happens or someone does something, used especially to emphasize how often or how long it happens: *I used to play tennis* ***all the time*** (=often). | *They seem to spend* ***most of the time*** *arguing* (=they argue a lot). | *Mandy's been gone for* ***a long/short time.*** | *Patty whined* ***the whole time*** (=during all of a period of time). | *These pictures were taken* ***some time ago*** (=a fairly long time ago).

5 WHEN STH HAPPENS [C,U] the particular minute, hour, day, etc. when something happens or someone does something: ***At that/the time*** (=at that particular time in the past), *few people had cars.* | *I was really hungry* ***by the time*** *I got home.* | *We left the building* ***at the same time.*** ▶ Don't say "in the same time." ◀ *The program's on at* ***breakfast/supper time.*** | *You've caught me* ***at***

T

a bad time (=a time that is not convenient) – *can I call you back later? | This isn't* ***the right time*** *to ask for a raise.*

6 it's time... used in order to say when something should be done, should happen, or is expected to happen: ***It's time for*** *dinner. |* ***It's time to*** *go.*

7 TIME NEEDED [U] the amount of time that is available or needed to do something: *Learning a language* ***takes time*** (=takes a long time). *| I won't* ***have time to*** *cook dinner. | I want to* ***spend*** *more* ***time*** *with my family. | Come on – stop* ***wasting time****. |* ***There is time*** *for questions afterward.*

8 be on time to arrive or happen at the correct time or the time that was arranged: *The buses are never on time.* ▶ Don't say "be in time." ◀

9 in time early or soon enough to do something: *They arrived* ***in time for*** *dinner.* ▶ Don't say "on time to" or "on time for." ◀

10 from time to time sometimes, but not regularly or very often: *He comes up to visit from time to time.*

11 ahead of time before an event or before you need to do something, in order to be prepared: *We need to get there ahead of time to get a good seat.*

12 at all times always: *Keep your hands inside the car at all times.*

13 in no time soon or quickly: *We'll be there in no time.*

14 it's about time *spoken* said when you feel strongly that something should happen soon or should already have happened: *It's about time you got a job!*

15 half the time if something happens half the time, it happens quite often: *Half the time, Alan doesn't even return her phone calls.*

16 when the time comes when something that you expect to happen actually happens, or when something becomes necessary: *She'll make the right choice when the time comes.*

17 one/two etc. at a time allowing only a specific number of things to happen or exist at the same time: *You can borrow three books at a time.*

18 take your time to do something slowly or carefully without hurrying: *Take your time and look over your essay before turning it in.*

19 for the time being for a short period of time from now, but not permanently: *For the time being, she's living with her father.*

20 good/bad/difficult etc. time a period of time or occasion when you have experiences that are good, bad, etc.: *That was the happiest time of my life. | Did you* ***have a good time*** *at Laura's?*

21 IN HISTORY [C] a particular period in history: *It happened in the time of the Romans.*

22 times [plural] the present time or a particular period in history, and the ways that people do or did things during that period: *modern times | Their technology is 30 years* ***behind the times****.*

23 time's up *spoken* said in order to tell people to stop doing something because there is no more time left: *Okay, time's up. Put down your pencils.*

24 in time to sth if you do something in time to a piece of music, you do it using the same RHYTHM and speed as the music

25 do time *informal* to spend time in prison

time² *v.* [T] **1** to do something or arrange for something to happen at a particular time: *The bomb was* ***timed to*** *go off at 5:00. | an* ***ill-timed/well-timed*** *announcement* (=one that happens at a bad or good time) **2** to measure how fast someone or something is going, how long it takes to do something, etc.: *Christie was* ***timed at*** *10.02 seconds.*

ˌtime and a ˈhalf *n.* [U] one and a half times the normal rate of pay

ˈtime bomb *n.* [C] **1** a situation that is likely to become a very serious problem: *It's an environmental time bomb.* **2** a bomb that is set to explode at a particular time

ˈtime card *n.* [C] a card on which the hours you have worked are recorded by a machine

ˈtime-conˌsuming *adj.* needing a long time to do: *a time-consuming process*

ˈtime frame *n.* [C] the period of time during which you expect or agree that something will happen or be done

ˈtime-ˌhonored *adj.* a time-honored method, CUSTOM etc. is one that has existed or worked well for a long time

time·keep·er /ˈtaɪmˌkipɚ/ *n.* [C] someone who officially records how long it takes to do something, especially at a sports event

time·less /ˈtaɪmlɪs/ *adj.* always remaining beautiful, attractive, etc.: *timeless melodies*

ˈtime ˌlimit *n.* [C] the longest time that you are allowed to do something in: *a* ***time limit for*** *using the library computer*

time·ly /ˈtaɪmli/ *adj.* done or happening at exactly the right time: *a timely decision*

ˌtime ˈoff *n.* [U] time when you are officially allowed not to be at work or studying

ˌtime ˈout *n.* [C] **1 take time out** to rest or do something different from your usual job or activities **2** a short time during a sports game when the teams can rest and get instructions from the COACH

tim·er /ˈtaɪmɚ/ *n.* [C] an instrument for measuring time, when you are doing something such as cooking

times /taɪmz/ *prep.* multiplied by: *Two times two equals four.*

time·ta·ble /ˈtaɪmˌteɪbəl/ *n.* [C] a plan of events and activities, with their dates and times: *a* ***timetable for*** *withdrawing the troops*

> **THESAURUS**
>
> **plan, schedule, scheme, strategy**
>
> → see Thesaurus box at PLAN¹

ˈtime warp *n.* [singular] *informal* the feeling that you are in a different time in history or in the future, instead of in the present: *Some of the professors seemed caught* ***in a time warp****.*

T

'time zone *n.* [C] one of the 24 areas the world is divided into, each of which has its own time

tim·id /'tɪmɪd/ *adj.* not brave or confident: *a timid child* —**timidly** *adv.* —**timidity** /tə'mɪdəṭi/ *n.* [U]

THESAURUS

shy, **bashful**, **reserved**, **introverted**, **withdrawn**
➔ see also Thesaurus box at SHY[1]

tim·ing /'taɪmɪŋ/ *n.* **1** [U] the skill of doing something at exactly the right time: *a comedian with **good/bad/wonderful timing*** **2** [C,U] the time when someone does something or when something happens: *the **timing of** his resignation*

tin /tɪn/ *n.* [U] a soft white metal used for making cans, building materials, etc.: *a tin can*

tin·der /'tɪndɚ/ *n.* [U] material that burns easily, used for lighting fires

tine /taɪn/ *n.* [C] a pointed part of something that has several points, for example on a fork

tin·foil /'tɪnfɔɪl/ *n.* [U] *old-fashioned* FOIL

tinge /tɪndʒ/ *n.* [C] a very small amount of a color, emotion, or quality: *a **tinge of** sadness in her voice* | *white paint with a yellow tinge* —**tinged** *adj.*

tin·gle /'tɪŋgəl/ *v.* [I] to feel a slight sting on your skin: *My fingers **tingled with** the cold.* —**tingle** *n.* [C]

tin·ker /'tɪŋkɚ/ *v.* [I] *informal* to make small changes to something in order to repair it or improve it: *Dad was **tinkering with** the engine.*

T

tin·kle /'tɪŋkəl/ *v.* [I] to make high soft RINGING sounds: *a tinkling bell* —**tinkle** *n.* [C]

tin·ny /'tɪni/ *adj.* a tinny sound is unpleasant to listen to, and sounds like it is coming from something made of metal: *tinny music*

tin·sel /'tɪnsəl/ *n.* [U] thin pieces of shiny silver paper, used especially as Christmas decorations

tint[1] /tɪnt/ *n.* [C] a small amount of a light color [**= shade**]: *The sky had a pink tint.*

tint[2] *v.* [T] to change the color of something, especially hair

ti·ny /'taɪni/ *adj.* extremely small: *thousands of **tiny little** fish* | *a tiny fraction of the budget*

THESAURUS

small, **little**, **minute**, **cramped**
➔ see Thesaurus box at SMALL

tip[1] /tɪp/ *n.* [C] **1** the end of something, especially something pointed: *the tip of your nose* | *the northern tip of the island*

THESAURUS

end, **point**
➔ see Thesaurus box at END[1]

2 a small amount of additional money that you give to someone such as a WAITER or taxi driver for his/her service: *Did you **leave a tip**?* | *a $5 tip* **3** a helpful piece of advice: *tips **on/for** losing weight* | *He **gave** me some **tips** on taking good pictures.*

THESAURUS

advice, **recommendation**, **guidance**
➔ see Thesaurus box at ADVICE

4 on the tip of your tongue if a word, name, etc. is on the tip of your tongue, you know it but cannot remember it immediately **5 the tip of the iceberg** a small sign of a problem that is much larger: *These figures are just the tip of the iceberg.*

tip[2] *v.* past tense and past participle **tipped**, present participle **tipping** **1** [I,T] to lean at an angle, or to make something do this: *The boat tipped a little to that side.* | *Jesse **tipped** his chair **back**.* **2** [I,T] to give a tip to a WAITER, taxi driver, etc. for his/her service: *I tipped him $5.* **3 tipped** having something at the tip: *red-tipped feathers* | *an arrow **tipped in/with** poison*

tip sb ⇔ **off** *phr. v. informal* to give someone such as the police secret information about something illegal: *The police must have been tipped off about the robbery.*

tip (sth ⇔) **over** *phr. v.* to fall or turn over, or to make something do this: *The canoe suddenly tipped over.* | *The baby tipped the plant over.*

ti·pi /'tipi/ *n.* [C] a TEPEE

'tip-off *n.* [C] *informal* **1** a warning or message about something illegal that is given secretly to the police, a government, etc. **2** the beginning of a basketball game, when the ball is thrown in the air and two players jump for it

tip·ster /'tɪpstɚ/ *n.* [C] *written* someone who gives the police, a REPORTER, etc. secret information about something that is going to happen

tip·sy /'tɪpsi/ *adj. informal* slightly drunk

tip·toe[1] /'tɪptoʊ/ *n.* **on tiptoe** standing on your toes, with the rest of your feet off the ground: *Matt **stood on tiptoe** to see.*

tiptoe[2] *v.* [I] to walk on TIPTOE: *Rita tiptoed downstairs.* ➔ see picture on page A9

ti·rade /'taɪreɪd/ *n.* [C] a long angry speech criticizing someone or something: *a **tirade against/at** polluters*

tire[1] /taɪɚ/ *n.* [C] a thick round piece of rubber that fits around the wheel of a car, bicycle, etc.: *I **had a flat tire*** (=all the air went out of it) *on the way home.* ➔ see picture on page A12

tire[2] *v.* **1** [I,T] to become tired, or to make someone feel tired: *Even short walks tire her.* **2 tire of sth** to become bored with something: *We never tired of her stories.*

tire sb ⇔ **out** *phr. v.* to make someone very tired: *All that walking tired me out.*

tired /taɪɚd/ *adj.* **1** feeling that you want to sleep or rest: *I was too tired to move.* | *Ben looks **tired out**.*

THESAURUS

exhausted – extremely tired: *I was completely exhausted after the long trip.*
worn out – very tired because you have been working or playing hard: *By the end of the season, many players are worn out.*
weary – very tired, especially because you have been doing something for a long time: *She grew weary* (=became weary) of spending every day in the car. | *weary travelers*
run-down – tired and unhealthy: *If you're feeling run-down, you probably need a holiday.*
beat informal: *I'm beat.*

2 tired of (doing) sth bored or annoyed with something: *I'm **tired of** waiting.*

tire·less /ˈtaɪɚlɪs/ *adj.* working very hard in a determined way: *a tireless worker* —**tirelessly** *adv.*

THESAURUS

energetic, **vigorous**, **full of energy**, **dynamic**
➔ see Thesaurus box at ENERGETIC

tire·some /ˈtaɪɚsəm/ *adj.* annoying and boring [➡ **tiring**]: *a tiresome conversation*

tir·ing /ˈtaɪərɪŋ/ *adj.* making you feel tired: *The trip had been tiring.*

tis·sue /ˈtɪʃu/ *n.* [U] **1** [C] a piece of soft thin paper, used for blowing your nose **2** [U] the material forming animal or plant cells: *damaged lung tissue*

tit-for-tat /ˌtɪt fɚ ˈtæt/ *n. informal* something bad that you do to someone because s/he has done something bad to you

tit·il·late /ˈtɪṭlˌeɪt/ *v.* [T] to make someone feel excited or interested, especially sexually: *a story to titillate the readers*

ti·tle[1] /ˈtaɪṭl/ *n.* **1** [C] the name given to a book, painting, play, etc.: *the title of this remarkable book* **2** [C] *written* a book: *this year's best-selling titles* **3** [C] a word or name that describes someone's rank or position: *Her official title is editorial manager.* **4** [C] a word such as "Mrs.," "Dr.," "Senator," etc. that is used before someone's name to show whether s/he is married or what his/her rank or position is **5** [C] the position of being the winner of an important sports competition: *the National League batting title* **6** [singular, U] *technical* the legal right to own something: *Who has the **title to** this land?*

title[2] *v.* [T] to give a name to a book, play, etc.: *a concert titled "Home for the Holidays"*

ˈtitle role also **ˈtitle ˌcharacter** *n.* [C] the main character in a play, movie, etc., which is the same as the name of the play, etc.

tit·ter /ˈtɪṭɚ/ *v.* [I] to laugh quietly, especially in a nervous way —**titter** *n.* [C]

tiz·zy /ˈtɪzi/ *n. informal* **in a tizzy** feeling nervous, upset, and sometimes confused

TLC *n.* [U] *informal* **tender loving care** kindness and love that you give to someone when s/he is sick or upset

TN the written abbreviation of **Tennessee**

TNT *n.* [U] a powerful explosive

to[1] /tə; *before vowels* tʊ; *strong* tu/ [used with the basic form of a verb to make the infinitive.] ▶ Do not use "to" with modal verbs. ◀ **1** used after a verb, noun, or adjective when the INFINITIVE completes its meaning: *I'd love to go!* | *It's starting to rain.* | *The men were told to leave the bar.* | *If you get a chance to see the play, you should.* | *Dad says he's not ready to retire yet.* | *It's great to see you!* **2** used by itself instead of an INFINITIVE in order to avoid repeating the same verb: *You can go if you want to.* **3** used after "how," "where," "who," "whom," "whose," "which," "when," "what," or "whether": *Can you show me how to do this?* | *Maria didn't know whether to call Tim or not.* **4** used in order to show the purpose of an action: *He covered the child to keep her from getting cold.* | *To begin with, let's look at chapter three.* **5** used after "too" and an adjective: *It's too cold to go outside.* **6** used after an adjective and "enough": *Are you feeling well enough to go back to work?* **7** used after "there is" and a noun: *There's nothing to do here.*

to[2] *prep.* **1** in order to be in a particular place, event, state, etc.: *The drive to the city takes five hours.* | *I couldn't go to sleep.* | *Are you going to the wedding?* **2** toward or in the direction of a place: *She went to the door.* | *Throw the ball to me.* **3** used in order to show the position of something, especially in relation to something else: *The water came up to our knees.* | *a town 50 miles to the south* | *My back was to the door* (=facing the door). **4** used in order to show who receives or owns something, or to whom speech is directed: *Angie said "hi" to me this morning.* | *The ring belongs to her mother.* **5** used in order to show where something is touching, fastened, or connected: *We tied the rope to a tree.* | *The computers are linked to a server.* **6** used to show a relationship with someone or something: *She's married to Gary's cousin.* **7** starting with one thing or in one place and ending with or in another: *A to Z* | *Count to 10.* | *It's 30 miles **from** here **to** Toronto.* **8** used when showing who or what is affected by an action or situation: *Mr. Reger is nice to everyone.* | *The chemicals are a danger to ocean life.* **9** fitting or being part of a machine or piece of equipment: *I have a key to the office.* **10** used when comparing two numbers, things, etc.: *The Bears won, 27 to 10.* **11** used in order to mean "before" when you are giving the time: *It's ten to four.* | *two weeks to Christmas*

toad /toʊd/ *n.* [C] an animal like a large FROG but brown in color

toad·stool /ˈtoʊdstul/ *n.* [C] a plant that looks like a MUSHROOM, but is usually poisonous

to and fro /ˌtu ən ˈfroʊ/ *adv.* moving in one

T

direction and then back again: *They swung to and fro.*

toast[1] /toʊst/ *n.* **1** [U] bread that has been heated until it is brown and CRISP: *a* ***slice/piece of toast*** ➔ see picture at BREAD[1] **2** [C] an occasion when you TOAST someone: *They* ***raised*** *their* ***glasses in a toast*** *to the happy couple.*

toast[2] *v.* [T] **1** to drink a glass of wine, etc. with other people in order to thank someone, wish someone luck, or celebrate something: *We toasted our victory with champagne.* **2** to make bread or other food turn brown by heating it

toast·er /ˈtoʊstɚ/ *n.* [C] a machine used for making toast

toast·y /ˈtoʊsti/ *adj. spoken* warm in a way that makes you feel comfortable

to·bac·co /təˈbækoʊ/ *n.* [U] dried brown leaves that are smoked in cigarettes, CIGARS etc., or the plant that these come from

to·bog·gan·ing /təˈbɑgənɪŋ/ *n.* [U] the sport of sliding down snow-covered hills on a special wooden or plastic board that curves up at the front —**toboggan** *n.* [C] —**toboggan** *v.* [I]

to·day[1] /təˈdeɪ/ *n.* [U] **1** the day that is happening now: *Today is Wednesday.* | *today's paper* **2** the present time: *young people of today*

today[2] *adv.* **1** during the day that is happening now: *Mom, can we go to the park today?* **2** in the present time: *Today, cancer is the leading cause of death in women.*

T

tod·dle /ˈtɑdl/ *v.* [I] to walk with short unsteady steps, like a very young child does

tod·dler /ˈtɑdlɚ/ *n.* [C] a child between the ages of about 1 and 3

TOPIC

newborn, infant, baby, child, teenager
➔ see Topic box at BABY, CHILD

to-ˈdo *n.* [singular] *informal* unnecessary excitement or angry feelings about something [= **fuss**]

toe[1] /toʊ/ *n.* [C] **1** one of the five separate parts at the end of your foot: *I hurt my* ***big toe*** (=largest toe). ➔ see picture on page A3 **2 on your toes** ready for anything that might happen: *The managers come to the factory floor, just to* ***keep*** *us* ***on*** *our* ***toes***. ➔ **step on sb's toes** at STEP[2]

toe[2] *v.* **toe the line** to do what you are told to do by people in authority

TOEFL /ˈtoʊfəl/ *n.* **Test of English as a Foreign Language** a test that students can take if their first language is not English, that proves that they can understand English

toe·hold /ˈtoʊhoʊld/ *n.* [singular] your first involvement in a particular activity, from which you can develop and become stronger: *It took us five years to* ***gain a toehold*** *in the market.*

toe·nail /ˈtoʊneɪl/ *n.* [C] the hard flat part that covers the top end of your toe

ˌtoe-to-ˈtoe *adj.* ➔ HEAD-TO-HEAD

tof·fee /ˈtɔfi, ˈtɑfi/ *n.* [C,U] a sticky brown candy made from sugar and butter, or a piece of this

to·fu /ˈtoʊfu/ *n.* [U] a soft white food that is made from SOYBEANS

to·ga /ˈtoʊgə/ *n.* [C] a long loose piece of clothing worn by people in ancient Greece and Rome

to·geth·er[1] /təˈgɛðɚ/ *adv.* **1** if two or more things are put together, they form a single subject, group, mixture, or object: *Add the numbers together.* | *We put the puzzle together last night.* **2** with or next to each other: *Kevin and I went to school together.* | *Keep everything together in a folder.* | *We were* ***crowded/packed, etc. together*** *in one little room.* **3** if two people are together, they are married or have a romantic relationship: *Mark and Sarah decided to* ***live together***. **4** at the same time: *Why do all the bills seem to come together?* ➔ **get your act together** at ACT[2]

together[2] *adj. spoken* thinking clearly, being very organized, etc.: *Carla seems really together.*

to·geth·er·ness /təˈgɛðɚnɪs/ *n.* [U] a feeling of having a close relationship with other people

tog·gle /ˈtɑgəl/ *n.* [C] something such as a key on a computer that lets you change from one operation to another —**toggle** *v.* [I,T]

togs /tɑgz, tɔgz/ *n.* [plural] *informal* clothes

toil /tɔɪl/ *v.* [I] *literary* to work very hard for a long period of time —**toil** *n.* [U]

toi·let /ˈtɔɪlɪt/ *n.* [C] a large bowl that you sit on to get rid of waste matter from your body

THESAURUS

Do not use **toilet** to talk about a room with a toilet in it.

bathroom – a room in a house with the toilet in it

restroom, women's/ladies' room, men's room – a room in a public place that has one or more toilets in it

lavatory – a room with a toilet in it, especially a room in a public building such as a school or on an airplane

latrine – an outdoor toilet at a camp or military area

ˈtoilet ˌpaper *n.* [U] soft thin paper used for cleaning yourself after you have used the toilet

toi·let·ries /ˈtɔɪlətriz/ *n.* [plural] things such as soap and TOOTHPASTE that are used for washing and cleaning yourself

to·ken[1] /ˈtoʊkən/ *n.* [C] **1** a round piece of metal that you use instead of money in some machines **2** something that represents a feeling, fact, event, etc.: *This is a* ***token of*** *our appreciation.*

token[2] *adj.* **1** a token action, change, etc. is small and not very important, but is done to show that you are dealing with a problem or will keep a promise: *He receives a token salary for his help.* **2 token woman/minority/black etc.** someone who is included in a group to make everyone think that it has all types of people in it, when this is often not really true

to·ken·ism /ˈtoʊkəˌnɪzəm/ *n.* [U] actions that are intended to make people think that an organization deals fairly with people or problems when in fact it does not

told /toʊld/ *v.* the past tense and past participle of TELL

tol·er·a·ble /ˈtɑlərəbəl/ *adj.* something that is tolerable is not very good, but you are able to accept it [≠ **intolerable**]: *The heat was barely tolerable.* —**tolerably** *adv.*

tol·er·ance /ˈtɑlərəns/ *n.* **1** [U] willingness to allow people to do, say, or believe what they want: *society's need for* ***religious/racial tolerance*** | *He had little* ***tolerance for/of*** *mistakes.* **2** [C,U] the degree to which someone or something can suffer pain, difficulty, etc. without being harmed: *plants with limited* ***tolerance for/to*** *the cold*

tol·er·ate /ˈtɑləˌreɪt/ *v.* [T] to accept something, even though you do not like it: *The school will not tolerate sexual harassment.* | *My stepmother* ***barely tolerated*** *me.* —**tolerant** *adj.* —**toleration** /ˌtɑləˈreɪʃən/ *n.* [U]

THESAURUS

accept – to agree or deal with a situation you do not like but cannot change: *She found it hard to accept his death.*
put up with sth – to accept an annoying situation or someone's annoying behavior, without trying to stop it or change it: *I don't see how you can put up with the constant noise.*
live with sth – to accept a bad situation as a permanent part of your life that you cannot change: *Stress is just something you have to learn to live with.*

toll¹ /toʊl/ *n.* [C] **1** [usually singular] the number of people killed or injured at a particular time: *The* ***death toll*** *has risen to 83.* **2** [usually singular] a bad effect that something has on someone or something over a long period of time: *Years of smoking have* ***taken*** *their* ***toll*** *on his health.* **3** the money you have to pay to use a particular road, bridge, etc.

toll² *v.* [I,T] if a bell tolls, or you toll it, it keeps ringing slowly

ˈtoll booth *n.* [C] a place where you pay to use a particular road, bridge, etc.

ˌtoll-ˈfree *adj.* a toll-free telephone call does not cost any money: *Call our* ***toll-free number*** *now.*

tom·a·hawk /ˈtɑməˌhɔk/ *n.* [C] a light AX used by some Native Americans in past times

to·ma·to /təˈmeɪt̬oʊ/ *n.* plural **tomatoes** [C] a soft round red fruit, eaten as a vegetable raw or cooked: *a tomato sauce* ➔ see picture at VEGETABLE

tomb /tum/ *n.* [C] a grave, especially a large one above the ground: *the* ***tomb of*** *China's first emperor*

tom·boy /ˈtɑmbɔɪ/ *n.* [C] a girl who likes to play the same games as boys

tomb·stone /ˈtumstoʊn/ *n.* [C] a GRAVESTONE

tom·cat /ˈtɑmkæt/ *n.* [C] a male cat

tome /toʊm/ *n.* [C] *literary* a large heavy book

to·mor·row¹ /təˈmɑroʊ, -ˈmɔr-/ *adv.* on or during the day after today: *Hanson is leaving tomorrow.* | *I'll see you* ***tomorrow morning/afternoon/night.***

tomorrow² *n.* [U] **1** the day after today [➡ **today, yesterday**]: *Tomorrow is Thursday.* **2** the future, especially the near future: *the schools of tomorrow* **3 do sth like there's no tomorrow** to do something without worrying about the future: *We're spending money like there's no tomorrow.*

ton /tʌn/ *n.* [C] **1** a unit for measuring weight, equal to 2000 pounds **2** *informal* a very large quantity or weight: *Your suitcase* ***weighs a ton!*** | *She spent* ***tons of*** *money.*

tone¹ /toʊn/ *n.* **1** [C,U] the way your voice sounds, which shows how you are feeling or what you mean: *Ben's calm, relaxed* ***tone of voice*** | *"Yes," she replied,* ***in an*** *amused* ***tone.*** **2** [singular, U] the general feeling or attitude expressed in a piece of writing, activity, etc.: *The argument* ***set the tone*** (=began a feeling that continued) *for the evening.* | *the formal* ***tone of*** *her poems* **3** [C] a sound made by a piece of electronic equipment: *Please leave a message after the tone.* **4** [U] the quality of a sound, especially the sound of a musical instrument or someone's voice **5** [U] how strong and firm your muscles, skin, etc. are: *exercises to improve* ***muscle tone*** **6** [C] a SHADE of a particular color

tone² **also tone up** *v.* [T] to improve the strength and firmness of your muscles, skin, etc.: *exercises to tone your stomach muscles*

tone sth ⇔ **down** *phr. v.* to make something such as a speech or piece of writing less offensive, exciting, etc.: *Advisers told him to tone down his statement.*

ˌtone-ˈdeaf *adj.* unable to hear the difference between different musical notes

ton·er /ˈtoʊnɚ/ *n.* [U] a type of ink that is used in machines that print or copy documents

tongs /tɑŋz, tɔŋz/ *n.* [plural] a tool for picking up objects, made of two movable BARS that are attached at one end

tongue /tʌŋ/ *n.* [C] **1** the soft part in your mouth that you can move and that you use for tasting and speaking **2 bite/hold your tongue** to stop yourself from saying something: *Jim struggled to hold his tongue.* **3** a language: *your* ***mother/native tongue*** (=the language you learned as a child)

THESAURUS

language, dialect
➔ see Thesaurus box at LANGUAGE

4 the part of a shoe under the LACES (=strings that

T

you tie them with) ➔ **on the tip of your tongue** at TIP[1] ➔ **a slip of the tongue** at SLIP[2]

ˌtongue-in-ˈcheek *adv.* said or done seriously, but meant as a joke

ˈtongue-tied *adj.* unable to speak easily because you are nervous

ˈtongue ˌtwister *n.* [C] a word or phrase with many similar sounds that is difficult to say quickly

ton·ic /ˈtɑnɪk/ *n.* **1** [C,U] **also tonic water** a bitter-tasting drink with BUBBLES, that you mix with some alcoholic drinks **2** [C] something, especially a medicine, that gives you more energy or strength

to·night[1] /təˈnaɪt/ *adv.* on or during the night of today: *I think I'll go to bed early tonight.*

tonight[2] *n.* [U] the night of today: *Tonight is a very special occasion.* | *tonight's news*

ton·nage /ˈtʌnɪdʒ/ *n.* [U] **1** the number of TONS that something weighs **2** the size of a ship or the amount of goods it can carry, shown in TONS

ton·sil /ˈtɑnsəl/ *n.* [C] one of two small organs at the sides of your throat near the back of your tongue

ton·sil·li·tis /ˌtɑnsəˈlaɪt̬ɪs/ *n.* [U] an infection of the tonsils

To·ny /ˈtoʊni/ *n.* plural **Tonies** [C] a prize given each year to the best plays, actors, etc. in New York's theaters

T

too /tu/ *adv.* **1** more than is needed, wanted, or possible: *You're going too fast!* | *He was **too** sick **to** travel.*

USAGE

Too is usually used to show that you do not like or approve of something: *This happens too often.* | *You're too old to go clubbing.* | *Help came too late to save the struggling animal.*
Very is used to emphasize something which can be either good or bad: *It's very hot today.* | *She's always very busy.*

2 also: *Sheila wants to come too.* | *"I'm really hungry." "I am too!"*

USAGE

Also is more formal than **too**, and is used more often in writing than in speech: *Tom was also hungry.*
Too and **as well** are less formal and more often used in spoken English: *Tom's hungry, and I am too.*
In negative sentences, use **either** rather than **also** or **too**. Do not say "Tom was also not hungry." or "Tom was not hungry too." Say "Tom was not hungry either."

3 very: *It shouldn't be too long until dinner's ready.* **4 be too much for sb** used in order to say that something is so difficult, tiring, or upsetting that someone cannot do it **5 I am too!/I did too! etc.** *spoken* used when you disagree with what someone has said about you: *"You're not old enough." "I am too!"*

took /tʊk/ *v.* the past tense of TAKE

tool[1] /tul/ *n.* [C] **1** something such as a hammer, SCREWDRIVER, etc. that you use to make or repair things: *He has all the tools needed for the job.* | *a **tool box/kit*** (=set of tools that you keep together) **2** something such as a piece of equipment or skill that is useful for a particular purpose: *Music can be a **useful/valuable/powerful tool** for learning.*

tool[2] *v.*

tool around/along *phr. v. informal* to drive, especially for fun

toot /tut/ *v.* [I,T] if a horn toots, or if you toot it, it makes a short sound —**toot** *n.* [C]

tooth /tuθ/ *n.* plural **teeth** /tiθ/ [C] **1** one of the hard objects in your mouth that you use for biting and chewing your food: *The wolf had fierce eyes and **sharp teeth**.* | *Did you **brush** your **teeth*** (=clean them)*?* ➔ see picture on page A3 **2** one of the pointed parts that sticks out from a comb, saw, etc. **3 fight (sb/sth) tooth and nail** to try with a lot of effort and determination to do something: *Neighborhood groups fought tooth and nail against the closing of the school.* ➔ **have a sweet tooth** at SWEET

tooth·ache /ˈtuθeɪk/ *n.* [C] a pain in a tooth

tooth·brush /ˈtuθbrʌʃ/ *n.* [C] a small brush for cleaning your teeth ➔ see picture at BRUSH[1]

tooth·paste /ˈtuθpeɪst/ *n.* [U] a substance used for cleaning your teeth

tooth·pick /ˈtuθˌpɪk/ *n.* [C] a small pointed piece of wood used for removing pieces of food from between your teeth

top[1] /tɑp/ *n.* [C]
1 HIGHEST PART the highest part of something [≠ **bottom**]: *the **tops of** the mountains* | *Write your name **at the top** of the page.* | *an ice cream sundae with nuts **on top** of it*
2 UPPER SURFACE the flat upper surface of an object: *The table has a glass top.* | *pictures **on top of** the piano*
3 on top of sth a) in addition to something: *On top of everything else, I need $700 to fix my car!* **b)** in control of a situation: *He felt alert and **on top of** things.*
4 the top the best, most successful, or most important position in an organization, company, competition, etc.: *The people **at the top** make the decisions.* | *men who have **reached the top** of their professions*

THESAURUS

senior, **chief**, **high-ranking**
➔ see Thesaurus box at POSITION[1]

5 CLOTHING clothing that you wear on the upper part of your body: *a pink top*
6 COVER a cover for a pen, container, etc., especially something that you push or turn: *I can't get the top off this jar.*

THESAURUS

cover, **lid**, **wrapper**, **wrapping**
➔ see Thesaurus box at COVER²

7 off the top of your head *informal* said without checking the facts: *Off the top of my head I'd say there were about 50.*
8 at the top of your voice/lungs shouted or sung as loudly as you can
9 TOY a toy that spins and balances on its point when you twist it
10 on top of the world *informal* extremely happy

top² *adj.* **1** at the top [≠ **bottom**]: *the top button of my shirt* **2** best or most successful: *a top salesman* | *the top score*

top³ *v.* past tense and past participle **topped**, present participle **topping** [T] **1** to be higher, better, or more than something: *Their profits have topped $5 million this year.* **2 be topped by/with sth** to have something on top: *ice cream* ***topped with*** *maple syrup*
top sth ⇔ **off** *phr. v. informal* to do one final thing before finishing something: *She topped it off by being named the most valuable player.*
top out *phr. v.* if something that is increasing tops out, it reaches its highest point and stops rising: *The Dow Jones average* ***topped out at*** *5999.75 today.*

top 40 /ˌtɑp ˈfɔrt̬i/ *n.* **the top 40** the list of the 40 most popular records in a particular week

ˌtop ˈhat *n.* [C] a man's tall hat with a flat top, worn in past times ➔ see picture at HAT

ˌtop-ˈheavy *adj.* **1** too heavy at the top and therefore likely to fall over **2** a top-heavy organization has too many managers

top·ic /ˈtɑpɪk/ *n.* [C] a subject that people talk or write about: *a discussion* ***on the topic*** *of human rights* | *the main* ***topic of conversation*** | *a* ***hot topic*** (=important topic) *during this election year*

top·i·cal /ˈtɑpɪkəl/ *adj.* relating to something that is important at the present time: *a show dealing with topical issues*

top·less /ˈtɑplɪs/ *adj.* a woman who is topless is not wearing any clothes on the upper part of her body

top·most /ˈtɑpmoʊst/ *adj.* highest: *the topmost branches*

ˌtop-ˈnotch *adj. informal* having the highest quality or standard: *top-notch schools*

to·pog·ra·phy /təˈpɑgrəfi/ *n.* [U] **1** the science of describing or making a map of an area of land **2** the shape of an area of land, including its hills, valleys, etc. —**topographer** *n.* [C] —**topographical** /ˌtɑpəˈgræfɪkəl/ *adj.*

top·ping /ˈtɑpɪŋ/ *n.* [C,U] food that you put on top of other food to make it taste or look better: *pizza toppings*

top·ple /ˈtɑpəl/ *v.* **1** [I,T] to fall over, or to make something do this: *Several trees* ***toppled over*** *in the storm.* **2** [T] to take power away from a leader or government: *The scandal could topple the government.*

ˌtop-ˈsecret *adj.* top-secret documents or information must be kept completely secret

top·sy-tur·vy /ˌtɑpsi ˈtɚvi◂/ *adj. informal* in a state of complete disorder or CONFUSION

torch¹ /tɔrtʃ/ *n.* [C] a long stick that you burn at one end for light or as a symbol: *the Olympic torch*

torch² *v.* [T] *written* to start a fire deliberately in order to destroy something: *Someone torched the old warehouse.*

tore /tɔr/ *v.* the past tense of TEAR

tor·ment¹ /ˈtɔrmɛnt/ *n.* [C,U] severe pain and suffering, or something that causes this

tor·ment² /tɔrˈmɛnt/ *v.* [T] to make someone suffer a lot of mental or physical pain: *He was* ***tormented by*** *guilt.* —**tormentor** *n.* [C]

torn /tɔrn/ *v.* the past participle of TEAR

tor·na·do /tɔrˈneɪdoʊ/ *n.* plural **tornadoes** [C] an extremely violent storm consisting of air that spins very quickly

THESAURUS

storm, **hurricane**, **typhoon**
➔ see Thesaurus box at WIND¹

tor·pe·do /tɔrˈpidoʊ/ *n.* plural **torpedoes** [C] a weapon that is fired under the surface of the ocean and explodes when it hits something —**torpedo** *v.* [T]

torrent

tor·rent /ˈtɔrənt, ˈtɑr-/ *n.* **1 a torrent of sth** a lot of something: *a torrent of criticism* **2** [C] a large amount of water moving very quickly in a particular direction —**torrential** /təˈrɛnʃəl, tɔ-/ *adj.*: *torrential rain*

tor·rid /ˈtɔrɪd, ˈtɑr-/ *adj.* **1** involving strong emotions, especially sexual excitement: *a torrid love affair* **2** extremely hot

tor·so /ˈtɔrsoʊ/ *n.* plural **torsos** [C] your body, not including your arms, legs, or head

tort /tɔrt/ *n.* [C] *law* an action that is wrong but not criminal and can be dealt with in a CIVIL court of law

tor·ti·lla /tɔrˈtiyə/ *n.* [C] a thin flat Mexican bread made from CORNMEAL or flour

tor·toise /ˈtɔrt̬əs/ *n.* [C] a slow-moving animal

that can put its legs and head inside the shell that covers its body

tor·tu·ous /ˈtɔrtʃuəs/ *adj.* **1** complicated, long, and therefore confusing: *a tortuous process* **2** a tortuous road has a lot of turns and is difficult to travel on

tor·ture[1] /ˈtɔrtʃɚ/ *n.* [C,U] **1** the act of torturing someone **2** mental or physical suffering: *The waiting must be torture for you.*

torture[2] *v.* [T] to deliberately hurt someone in order to force him/her to tell you something, to punish him/her, or to be cruel: *He was **tortured to death** in prison.*

toss /tɔs/ *v.* **1** [T] to throw something without much force: *Could you toss me my keys?* | *He **tossed** the apples **into** a barrel.*

> **THESAURUS**
>
> **throw**, **chuck**, **hurl**, **fling**, **pass**, **pitch**
> → see Thesaurus box at THROW[1]

2 [I,T] to move around continuously in a violent or uncontrolled way, or to make something do this: *The kite was being tossed by the wind.* | *I was **tossing and turning*** (=changing my position in bed because I could not sleep) *all night.* **3 also toss** sth ⇔ **out** [T] *informal* to get rid of something: *"Where's the newspaper?" "I tossed it."* **4** [T] to cover food in a liquid by moving it around in the liquid: *Toss the carrots in butter.* —**toss** *n.* [C] → **toss/flip a coin** at COIN[1]

T

ˈtoss-up *n.* **it's a toss-up** *spoken* said when you do not know which of two things will happen, or which of two things to choose: *So far the election is a toss-up.*

tot /tɑt/ *n.* [C] *informal* a small child

to·tal[1] /ˈtoʊtl/ *adj.* **1** complete, or as great as is possible: *Their marriage was a **total disaster**.* | *She has been slowed down by the almost total loss of her sight.* **2 total number/amount/cost etc.** the number, amount, etc. that is the total: *The total cost of the building will be $6 million.*

total[2] *n.* [C] the number that you get when you have added everything together: *The city spent **a total of** two million dollars on the library.* | *I was out of work for 34 days **in total**.*

total[3] *v.* **1** [linking verb] to add up to a particular amount: *Prize money totaling $5000 will be awarded.* **2** [T] *informal* to damage a car so badly that it cannot be repaired: *Chuck totaled his dad's new Toyota.*

to·tal·i·tar·i·an /toʊˌtæləˈtɛriən/ *adj.* based on a political system in which people are completely controlled by the government —**totalitarianism** *n.* [U]

to·tal·i·ty /toʊˈtæləti/ *n.* [U] *formal* the whole of something

to·tal·ly /ˈtoʊtl-i/ *adv.* completely: *I totally agree.* | *He's become a **totally different** person.* | *These mistakes are **totally unacceptable**.*

> **THESAURUS**
>
> **completely**, **absolutely**, **entirely**, **utterly**
> → see Thesaurus box at COMPLETELY

tote /toʊt/ *v.* [T] *informal* to carry something

> **THESAURUS**
>
> **carry**, **lug**, **cart**, **haul**, **schlep**, **bear**
> → see Thesaurus box at CARRY

ˈtote bag *n.* [C] a large bag in which you carry things

to·tem pole /ˈtoʊtəm poʊl/ *n.* [C] a tall wooden pole with images of animals or faces cut into it, made by some Native American tribes

tot·ter /ˈtɑtɚ/ *v.* [I] to walk or move in an unsteady way

touch[1] /tʌtʃ/ *v.* **1** [T] to put your finger, hand, etc. on something or someone: *Don't touch the paint – it's still wet!* | *She reached out to touch his arm.*

> **THESAURUS**
>
> **feel** – to touch something with your fingers to find out about it: *Feel this teddy bear – it's so soft!*
> **stroke** – to move your hand gently over something: *She stroked the baby's face.*
> **rub** – to move your hand or fingers over a surface while pressing it: *Bill yawned and rubbed his eyes.*
> **scratch** – to rub your finger nails on part of your skin: *Try not to scratch those mosquito bites.*
> **pat** – to touch someone or something lightly again and again, with your hand flat: *He knelt down to pat the dog.*
> **brush** – to touch someone or something lightly as you pass by: *Her hand brushed mine.*
> **caress** – to gently move your hand over a part of someone's body in a loving or sexual way: *Miguel gently caressed her hair.*
> **fondle** – to gently touch and move your fingers over part of someone's body in a way that shows love or sexual desire: *Tom fondled the dog's soft ears.*
> **tickle** – to move your fingers lightly over someone's body in order to make him/her laugh: *Minna tickled the baby's feet and he gurgled.*
> **grope** – to touch someone's body in a sexual way when s/he does not want to be touched: *One victim said he groped her.*

2 [I,T] if two things are touching, there is no space in between them: *Make sure the wires aren't touching.* **3 not touch sth a)** to not use or handle something: *My brother won't let me touch his bike.* **b)** to not eat or drink something: *She didn't touch her breakfast.* **c)** to refuse to deal with or become involved in a particular situation or problem: *Our lawyer said he wouldn't touch the case.* **4 not touch sb/sth** to not hurt someone or not damage something: *I swear Mom, I* *didn't touch him!* **5** [T] to affect someone's emotions, especially by making him/her feel pity or sympathy: *His speech touched everyone present.* **6 touch base** to talk to someone in order to find out how s/he is or what is happening: *I wanted to* ***touch base with*** *you before the meeting.* ➔ TOUCHED

touch down *phr. v.* if an aircraft touches down, it lands on the ground

touch sth ⇔ **off** *phr. v.* to cause a bad situation or violent event to begin: *The report touched off a fierce debate.*

touch on/upon sth *phr. v.* to mention something when you are talking or writing: *Her songs touch on social issues.*

touch sth ⇔ **up** *phr. v.* to improve something by making small changes to it: *Norma touched up her makeup for the picture.*

touch² *n.* **1** [C] the action of putting your finger, hand, etc. on someone or something: *Rita felt the* ***touch of*** *his hand on her shoulder.* **2 in touch (with sb)** talking or writing to someone: *I've been trying to* ***get in touch with*** (=phone or talk to) *you all morning.* | *Bye. I'll* ***be in touch.*** | *We've* ***stayed/kept in touch*** (=continued to write or call each other, even though we do not see each other often) *since college.* | *I've* ***lost touch with*** (=stopped writing or talking to) *my high school friends.* **3 in touch/out of touch** having or not having the latest information or knowledge about a subject, situation, or the way people feel: *I think he's* ***out of touch with*** *the American people.* **4** [U] the ability to know what something is like when you feel it with your fingers: *Her skin was cool* ***to the touch.*** **5 a touch of sth** a small amount of something: *a touch of sadness in her voice* | *salad dressing with a touch of lemon juice* **6** [C] a small detail or change that improves something: *Becky put the* ***finishing touches*** *on the cake.* **7** [U] a particular way of doing something skillful: *I must be* ***losing my touch*** *– I can't hit anything today.*

ˌtouch-and-ˈgo *adj. informal* if a situation is touch-and-go, there is a risk that something bad could happen: *After Dad's operation, it was touch-and-go for a while.*

touch·down /ˈtʌtʃdaʊn/ *n.* [C] **1** the action in football of moving the ball into the opponents' END ZONE in order to gain points **2** the moment that a space vehicle lands on the ground

touched /tʌtʃt/ *adj.* feeling happy and grateful because of what someone has done for you: *We* ***were touched by*** *their concern.*

touch·ing /ˈtʌtʃɪŋ/ *adj.* making you feel sympathy or sadness: *Fox gave a touching tribute to his late father.*

> **THESAURUS**
>
> **emotional**, **moving**, **poignant**, **sentimental**, **schmalzy**
> ➔ see Thesaurus box at EMOTIONAL

touch·stone /ˈtʌtʃstoʊn/ *n.* [C] a standard used for measuring the quality of something

touch·y /ˈtʌtʃi/ *adj.* **1** easily offended or annoyed [➡ **sensitive**]: *She is very* ***touchy about*** *her past.*

> **THESAURUS**
>
> **grumpy**, **cranky**, **crabby**, **grouchy**, **cantankerous**, **irritable**
> ➔ see Thesaurus box at GRUMPY

2 touchy subject/question etc. a subject, etc. that needs to be dealt with very carefully because it may offend or upset people

tough¹ /tʌf/ *adj.* **1** difficult and needing a lot of effort: *Working as a fireman is tough.* | *a tough question* | *a tough choice/decision* **2** a tough person is very strong or determined: *a tough businesswoman* **3** very strict: *tough anti-smoking laws* **4** tough material is not easily broken or damaged: *tough, durable plastic* **5** tough meat is difficult to cut or eat [≠ **tender**]: *a tough steak* **6 tough!/tough luck!** *spoken* said when you do not have any sympathy for someone else's problems: *"I'm freezing!" "Tough! You should have worn your coat."* **7** a tough place, area, etc. is likely to have a lot of violence and crime: *He grew up in a tough neighborhood.* —**toughness** *n.* [U]

tough² *v.*

tough sth ⇔ **out** *phr. v.* to deal with a very difficult situation by being determined to continue: *He could've gone home, but he stayed and* ***toughed it out.***

tough·en /ˈtʌfən/ **also toughen up** *v.* [I,T] to become tougher, or to make someone or something do this: *Hard work has toughened her up.*

tou·pee /tuˈpeɪ/ *n.* [C] a piece of artificial hair that a man can wear when he has no hair on part of his head

tour¹ /tʊr/ *n.* [C] **1** a trip to several different places in a country, area, etc.: *a 7-day* ***tour of*** *Egypt* **2** a short trip through a place to see it: *We* ***went on a tour through/of*** *the Smithsonian.* | *Sue once worked as a* ***tour guide*** *in Boston.* **3** a planned trip by a group of musicians, a sports team, etc. in order to play in several places: *The band goes* ***on tour*** *later this year.*

tour² *v.* [I,T] to visit a place on a tour: *We're going to tour New England this summer.*

tour·ism /ˈtʊrɪzəm/ *n.* [U] the business of providing tourists with places to stay and things to do: *The island depends on tourism for most of its income.*

tour·ist /ˈtʊrɪst/ *n.* [C] someone who visits a place for pleasure: *San Francisco is always full of tourists in the summer.* | *The Statue of Liberty is a major* ***tourist attraction.***

> **THESAURUS**
>
> **traveler**, **explorer**
> ➔ see Thesaurus box at TRAVEL¹

T

tour·na·ment /ˈtʊrnəmənt, ˈtɚ-/ *n.* [C] a competition in which many players or teams compete against each other until there is one winner

THESAURUS
competition, championship, contest, playoff
➔ see Thesaurus box at COMPETITION

tour·ni·quet /ˈtʊrnɪkɪt, ˈtɚ-/ *n.* [C] a band of cloth that is twisted tightly around an injured arm or leg to make blood stop coming out

tou·sle /ˈtaʊzəl, -səl/ *v.* [T] to make someone's hair look messy —**tousled** *adj.*

tout /taʊt/ *v.* [T] to praise someone or something in order to persuade people that he, she, or it is important or worth a lot: *Paul's band is being* ***touted as*** *the next big thing.*

tow[1] /toʊ/ *v.* [T] if one vehicle tows another one, it pulls the other vehicle along behind it: *Our car had to* ***be towed away****.*

THESAURUS
pull, tug, drag, haul, heave
➔ see Thesaurus box at PULL[1]

➔ see picture at PULL[1]

tow[2] *n.* [C] **1** an act of towing a vehicle or ship **2 in tow** following closely behind someone or something: *Mattie arrived with all her children in tow.*

to·ward /tɔrd, təˈwɔrd/ **also towards** *prep.* **1** in a particular direction: *All the windows face toward the river.* | *I saw a man coming toward me.* ▶ Don't say "I saw a man coming to me." ◀ **2** concerning someone or something: *How do you feel toward her?* | *different attitudes towards divorce* **3** in a process that will produce a particular result: *working towards world peace* **4** money put, saved, or given toward something is used to pay for it: *So far I've saved $4000 toward a new car.* **5** just before a particular time: *I felt tired toward the end of the day.* **6** near a particular place: *We're building a pipeline down toward Abilene.*

tow·el[1] /ˈtaʊəl/ *n.* [C] a piece of cloth used for drying something: *a bath towel* (=for drying yourself) | *a dish towel*

towel[2] **also towel off/down** *v.* [I,T] to dry your body using a towel

tow·er[1] /ˈtaʊɚ/ *n.* [C] **1** a tall narrow building or part of a building: *the Eiffel Tower* | *a church tower* **2** a tall structure used for signaling or broadcasting: *a radio/television tower*

tower[2] *v.* [I] to be much taller than the people or things around you: *Lewis* ***towered over*** *his opponent.* —**towering** *adj.*

town /taʊn/ *n.* **1** [C] a place with houses, stores, offices, etc. where people live and work, that is smaller than a city: *a little town on the coast* **2** [U] the town or city where you live: *How long have you been* ***in town****?* | *She's* ***from out of town*** (=lives in a different town). | *I'll be* ***out of town*** *this weekend.* **3** [U] the business or shopping center of a town: *"Where's Dad?" "He's gone* ***into town****."* **4** [singular] all the people who live in a particular town: *The whole town got involved in the celebrations.* **5 (out) on the town** *informal* going to restaurants, theaters, etc. for entertainment in the evening: *Everyone went out for* ***a night on the town****.* **6 go to town (on sth)** *informal* to do something eagerly and with a lot of energy: *Larry really went to town on those pancakes* (=ate them quickly).

ˌtown ˈhall *n.* [C] a public building used for a town's local government

town·house /ˈtaʊnhaʊs/ *n.* [C] a house in a group of houses that share one or more walls

THESAURUS
house, ranch house, ranch, cottage, row house, mansion, bungalow, duplex, apartment, condominium, condo, mobile home, trailer
➔ see Thesaurus box at HOUSE[1]

town·ship /ˈtaʊnʃɪp/ *n.* [C] an area where people live and work that is organized under a local government

towns·peo·ple /ˈtaʊnzˌpipəl/ **also towns·folk** /ˈtaʊnzfoʊk/ *n.* [plural] all the people who live in a particular town

ˈtow truck *n.* [C] a strong vehicle that can pull cars behind it

tox·ic /ˈtɑksɪk/ *adj.* poisonous: *toxic chemicals* —**toxicity** /tɑkˈsɪsət̬i/ *n.* [U]

THESAURUS
harmful, poisonous, detrimental, damaging
➔ see Thesaurus box at HARMFUL

tox·i·col·o·gy /ˌtɑksɪˈkɑlədʒi/ *n.* [U] the medical study of poisons and their effects

ˌtoxic ˈwaste *n.* [C,U] waste products from industry that are harmful to people, animals, or the environment

tox·in /ˈtɑksɪn/ *n.* [C] a poisonous substance, especially one made by BACTERIA

toy[1] /tɔɪ/ *n.* [C] an object for children to play with: *Her husband brought home some new toys for the baby.* | *a toy car* | *The children were* ***playing with*** *their new* ***toys****.*

toy[2] *v.*
toy with sb/sth *phr. v.* **1 toy with** sth to think about an idea, plan, etc. for a short time and not very seriously: *She* ***toyed with the idea of*** *becoming an actress.* **2 toy with** sb/sth to lie to someone or trick him/her, for example saying that you love him/her when you do not

trace[1] /treɪs/ *v.* [T] **1** to study or describe the history, development, or origin of something: *He* ***traced*** *his family history* ***(back) to*** *the 17th century.* **2** to copy a picture by putting a thin piece of paper over it and drawing the lines that you can see through the paper

THESAURUS

draw, sketch, doodle, scribble
→ see Thesaurus box at DRAW[1]

3 to find someone or something that has disappeared: *Police are still trying to trace the missing child.*

THESAURUS

find, discover, locate, track down, turn up, unearth
→ see Thesaurus box at FIND[1]

4 to find out where a telephone call is coming from, using electronic equipment: *Keep him on the line so we can* ***trace the call.*** —**traceable** *adj.*

trace[2] *n.* **1** [C,U] a sign that someone or something has been in a place: *We found* ***no trace of*** *them on the island.* | *He disappeared* ***without a trace*** (=completely). **2** [C] a very small amount of a substance, quality, emotion, etc. that is difficult to notice: *There was a* ***trace of*** *poison in the glass.* | *a trace of sorrow in his voice*

track[1] /træk/ *n.*
1 keep/lose track of sb/sth to pay attention to someone or something so that you know what is happening, or to fail to do this: *She lost track of all the money she spent.*
2 be on the right/wrong track to think in a way that is likely to lead to a correct or incorrect result: *Keep going, you're on the right track.*
3 FOR RACING [C] a course with a special surface on which people, cars, horses, etc. race

THESAURUS

field, stadium, court, diamond
→ see Thesaurus box at SPORT[1]

4 SPORT [U] the sport of running on a track: *He* ***ran track*** *in high school.*
5 be on/off track to be in a state or situation that will lead to success or failure: *I feel that my career is back on track now.*
6 RAILROAD [C] the two metal lines that a train travels on: *railroad tracks* → see Topic box at TRAIN[1]
7 tracks [plural] marks on the ground made by a moving animal, person, or vehicle: *We saw bear tracks in the mud.*
8 SONG [C] one of the songs or pieces of music on a record: *the best track on the album*
9 make tracks *informal* to leave somewhere quickly, or hurry when going somewhere → **off the beaten track/path** at BEATEN → **fast track** at FAST → ONE-TRACK MIND

track[2] *v.* [T] **1** to search for a person or animal by following a smell or tracks on the ground: *We tracked the moose for hours.* **2** to follow the movements of an aircraft or ship by using RADAR **3** to leave mud or dirt behind you when you walk: *Who tracked mud all over the floor?*
track sb/sth ⇔ **down** *phr. v.* to find someone or something after searching in different places: *We finally were able to track down her parents.*

ˌtrack and ˈfield *n.* [U] the sports that involve running races, jumping, and throwing things

ˈtrack meet *n.* [C] a sports competition with a variety of running, jumping, and throwing events

ˈtrack ˌrecord *n.* [singular] all the things that a person or organization has done in the past that show how well she, he, or it is likely to do similar things in the future: *The company has* ***a track record of*** *promoting women to high positions.*

tract /trækt/ *n.* [C] **1 the digestive/respiratory/urinary etc. tract** a system of connected organs in your body that have one purpose **2** a large area of land: *a tract of forest*

trac·tion /ˈtrækʃən/ *n.* [U] **1** the force that prevents something such as a wheel from sliding on a surface: *The car lost traction and ran off the road.* **2** the process of treating a broken bone with special medical equipment that pulls it

trac·tor /ˈtræktɚ/ *n.* [C] a strong vehicle with large wheels, used for pulling farm equipment

trade[1] /treɪd/ *n.* **1** [U] the business of buying and selling things, especially between countries: *foreign trade* | ***the trade in*** *oil*

THESAURUS

business, commerce, industry, private enterprise
→ see Thesaurus box at BUSINESS

2 the banking/retail/tourist etc. trade the business that comes from or is done by banks, etc. **3** [C] an exchange: *Let's* ***make a trade*** *– my frisbee for your baseball.* **4** [C,U] a particular job, especially one in which you work with your hands: *Jerry's a plumber* ***by trade.***

trade[2] *v.* **1** [I,T] to buy and sell goods and services: *Penalties were imposed on U.S. companies that* ***traded with*** *Cuba.*

THESAURUS

exchange, swap
→ see Thesaurus box at EXCHANGE[2]

2 [I,T] to exchange one thing for another: *I'll* ***trade*** *my apple* ***for*** *your candy bar.* **3 trade insults/blows etc.** to insult or hit each other during an argument or fight
trade sth ⇔ **in** *phr. v.* to give something old that you own, such as a car, as part of the payment for something new: *I* ***traded*** *my Chevy* ***in for*** *a Honda.*
trade on sth *phr. v.* to use a situation or someone's kindness in order to gain an advantage for yourself: *She's trading on her father's fame to try to make it in the music business.*

T

trade up *phr. v.* to sell something such as a car or house so you can buy a better car or house

'trade-in *n.* [C] a car, piece of equipment, etc. that you give as part of the payment for the newer one that you are buying

trade·mark /'treɪdmɑrk/ *n.* [C] a special word or picture on a product that shows it is made by a particular company, that cannot be used by any other company

'trade-off *n.* [C] an acceptable balance between two opposing things: *The boats are difficult to build, but the trade-off is that I get a good price for them.*

trad·er /'treɪdɚ/ *n.* [C] someone who buys and sells goods or STOCKS

'trade ˌschool *n.* [C] a school where people go in order to learn a particular TRADE[1]

ˌtrade 'secret *n.* [C] a piece of secret information about a particular business, that is only known by the people who work there

tra·di·tion /trə'dɪʃən/ *n.* **1** [C,U] something that people have done for a long time, and continue to do: *an old family/Jewish/American etc. tradition* | *This country has a* ***long tradition*** *of welcoming immigrants.* | *It's* ***a tradition that*** *the groom should not see the bride before the wedding.*

THESAURUS

habit, **custom**
→ see Thesaurus box at HABIT

2 (be) in the tradition of sth to have many of the same features as something made or done in the past: *an entertainer in the great tradition of vaudeville*

tra·di·tion·al /trə'dɪʃənl/ *adj.* **1** relating to the traditions of a country or group of people: *a traditional Irish folk song* | *traditional Mexican food* | ***It is traditional to*** *exchange gifts at Christmas.* **2** following ideas, methods, etc. that have existed for a long time rather than doing something new or different: *a woman's* ***traditional role*** *as mother* —**traditionally** *adv.*

tra·di·tion·al·ist /trə'dɪʃənl-ɪst/ *n.* [C] someone who likes traditional ideas and does not like change

traf·fic /'træfɪk/ *n.* [U] **1** the vehicles moving along a particular road: *We left early to avoid the traffic.* | ***heavy/light traffic*** (=a small or large amount of traffic) **2** the movement of aircraft, ships, or trains from one place to another: *air traffic control*

'traffic ˌjam *n.* [C] a long line of vehicles on the road that cannot move, or that move very slowly: *We were* ***stuck in a traffic jam*** *for two hours!*

traf·fick·ing /'træfɪkɪŋ/ *n.* **drug/arms trafficking** the activity of buying and selling illegal drugs or weapons —**trafficker** *n.* [C] —**traffic** *v.* [T]

'traffic light **also** **'traffic ˌsignal** *n.* [C] → LIGHT

traffic light

trag·e·dy /'trædʒədi/ *n.* plural **tragedies** [C,U] **1** a very sad and shocking event: *the* ***tragedy of*** *a child's death* **2** a serious play that ends sadly, or this style of writing: *Shakespeare's tragedies*

tra·gic /'trædʒɪk/ *adj.* very sad and shocking: *Holly's* ***tragic death*** *in a plane crash* —**tragically** *adv.*

trail[1] /treɪl/ *v.* **1** [I,T] **also trail behind** to be losing a game, competition, or election: *The Cowboys are trailing 21–14.* **2** [I,T] to pull something behind you, especially along the ground, or to be pulled in this way: *The wedding dress trailed on the ground behind her.* **3** [I] to follow someone: *The two mothers walked along with their kids* ***trailing behind*** *them.* **4** [T] to follow someone by looking for signs that s/he has gone in a particular direction

trail off *phr. v.* if your voice trails off, it becomes quieter and quieter until it cannot be heard: *Her words trailed off as Mrs. Hellman walked into the room.*

trail[2] *n.* **1** [C] a path across open country or through the forest: *a hiking trail in the mountains* **2 trail of blood/clues/destruction etc.** a series of marks or signs left behind by someone or something that is moving **3 be on the trail of sb/sth** to be looking for a person or information that is difficult to find: *a reporter on the trail of a big story*

trail·blaz·er /'treɪlˌbleɪzɚ/ *n.* [C] *informal* someone who is the first to discover or develop new methods of doing something: *a trailblazer in the field of medical research*

trail·er /'treɪlɚ/ *n.* [C] **1** a vehicle that can be pulled behind a car, used for living in during a vacation **2** a vehicle that can be pulled behind another vehicle, used for carrying something heavy **3** a short advertisement for a movie or television program

'trailer park *n.* [C] an area where trailers are parked and used as people's homes

train[1] /treɪn/ *n.* [C] **1** a long vehicle which travels along a railroad carrying people or goods. It consists of a line of carriages pulled by an engine: *the* ***train to*** *Detroit* | *It'll take about 4 hours* ***by train.*** | *I* ***take the train*** *to work.* | *Hurry up or we'll* ***miss*** *our* ***train.*** → see picture at TRANSPORTATION

TOPIC

You decide which train you are going to **get/catch**. You buy your ticket at the **ticket office**. You look at the **departure board** to check which **platform/track** your train **leaves from**. Sometimes the train is **on time** but sometimes it is **running late** or **delayed**. When your train **arrives**, you **get on** and find a **seat** in one of the **cars** (=one of the connected parts of a train). You can usually get a drink or small meal in the **dining car**.

2 train of thought a related series of thoughts that are developing in your mind: *Sorry, I've **lost** my **train of thought**.* **3** a long line of moving animals, vehicles, or people: *a camel train* **4** a part of a dress that spreads out over the ground behind the person wearing it

train² *v.* **1** [I,T] to teach someone or be taught the skills of a particular job or activity: *Sally spent two years **training as** a nurse.* | *He's **training to** be a pilot.*

THESAURUS

practice, **rehearse**, **work on**, **drill**
→ see Thesaurus box at PRACTICE²

2 [T] to teach an animal to do something or to behave correctly: *I've **trained** the dog **to** sit.* **3** [I,T] to prepare for a sports event by exercising and practicing, or to make someone do this: *He is **training for** the Olympics.* —**trained** *adj.*

train·ee /treɪ'ni/ *n.* [C] someone who is being trained for a job: *a sales trainee*

train·er /'treɪnɚ/ *n.* [C] someone whose job is to train people or animals to do something

train·ing /'treɪnɪŋ/ *n.* **1** [singular, U] the process of teaching or being taught skills for a particular job: *Myers has no formal **training in** music.* **2** [U] special physical exercises that you do to stay healthy or prepare for a competition: *weight training* | *She's **in training** for the Boston Marathon.*

trait /treɪt/ *n.* [C] a particular quality in someone's character [= **characteristic**]: *His jealousy is one of his worst traits.*

trai·tor /'treɪṭɚ/ *n.* [C] someone who is not loyal to his/her country, friends, etc.: *He had been a **traitor to** his country.*

tra·jec·to·ry /trə'dʒɛktəri/ *n.* plural **trajectories** [C] *technical* the curved path of an object that is fired or thrown through the air

tram /træm/ *n.* [C] a STREETCAR

tramp¹ /træmp/ *n.* [C] *old-fashioned* someone who has no home or job and moves from place to place, often asking for food or money

tramp² *v.* [I,T] to walk somewhere with heavy steps: *kids **tramping through** the snow*

tram·ple /'træmpəl/ *v.* [I,T] **1** to step on something heavily so that you crush it with your feet: *One woman was **trampled to death** by the crowd.* **2** to ignore or not care about someone's rights or feelings: *a rule that **tramples on** people's right to free speech*

tram·po·line /ˌtræmpə'lin, 'træmpəˌlin/ *n.* [C] a piece of sports equipment that you jump up and down on, made of a sheet of material tightly stretched across a large frame

trance /træns/ *n.* [C] a state in which you seem to be asleep but you are still able to hear and understand what is said to you: *He seemed to be **in a trance**.*

tran·quil /'træŋkwəl/ *adj.* pleasantly calm, quiet, and peaceful: *a tranquil spot for a picnic* —**tranquility** /træŋ'kwɪləṭi/ *n.* [U]

THESAURUS

quiet, **peaceful**, **calm**, **sleepy**
→ see Thesaurus box at QUIET¹

tran·qui·liz·er /'træŋkwəˌlaɪzɚ/ *n.* [C] a drug used in order to make a person or animal calm or unconscious —**tranquilize** *v.* [T]

trans·act /træn'zækt/ *v.* [I,T] *formal* to do business

trans·ac·tion /træn'zækʃən/ *n.* [C] *formal* a business deal: *the company's **financial transactions***

trans·at·lan·tic /ˌtrænzət'læntɪk/ *adj.* crossing the Atlantic Ocean, or involving people on both sides of the Atlantic: *a transatlantic flight* | *a transatlantic business deal*

tran·scend /træn'sɛnd/ *v.* [T] *formal* to go above or beyond the usual limits of something: *The appeal of baseball transcends age and class.* —**transcendence** *n.* [U]

tran·scen·den·tal /ˌtrænsɛn'dɛntl/ *adj.* existing above or beyond human knowledge or understanding

trans·con·ti·nen·tal /ˌtrænskɑntən'ɛntl, ˌtrænz-/ *adj.* crossing a CONTINENT: *the first transcontinental railroad*

tran·scribe /træn'skraɪb/ *v.* [T] to write down the words that someone has said, or the notes of a piece of music —**transcription** /træn'skrɪpʃən/ *n.* [C,U]

tran·script /'trænˌskrɪpt/ *n.* [C] **1** an exact written or printed copy of something that was said: *a **transcript of** the witness's testimony* **2** an official college document that has a list of the classes you took as a student and the GRADES you received

trans·fer¹ /'trænsfɚ, træns'fɚ/ *v.* past tense and past participle **transferred**, present participle **transferring** **1** [I,T] to move from one place, job, etc. to another, or to make someone or something do this: *After his first year he **transferred to** UCLA.* | *They're **transferring** him **from** accounts **to** the shipping department.* **2** [T] to move money from one account or institution to another: *I'd like*

T

to ***transfer*** *$500* ***to*** *my checking account.* **3** [T] *law* to officially give property or money to someone else —**transferable** /træns'fɚəbəl/ *adj.*

trans·fer² /'trænsfɚ/ *n.* **1** [C,U] the process of transferring someone or something: *the* ***transfer of*** *funds between banks | a job transfer* **2** [C] a ticket that allows a passenger to change from one bus, train, etc. to another without paying more money: *You should ask the bus driver for a transfer.*

trans·fixed /træns'fɪkst/ *adj.* unable to move because you are shocked, frightened, etc.: *We were transfixed by the pictures of the storm on TV.*

trans·form /træns'fɔrm/ *v.* [T] to change the appearance, character, etc. of someone or something completely, especially in a good way: *attempts to* ***transform*** *the country* ***into*** *a democracy* —**transformation** /ˌtrænsfɚ'meɪʃən/ *n.* [C,U] *the complete transformation of the city*

THESAURUS

change, **alter**, **adapt**, **adjust**, **modify**, **reform**, **reorganize**, **restructure**

➔ see Thesaurus box at CHANGE¹

trans·form·er /træns'fɔrmɚ/ *n.* [C] a piece of equipment for changing electricity from one VOLTAGE to another

trans·fu·sion /træns'fyuʒən/ *n.* [C,U] the process of putting one person's blood into the body of someone else as a medical treatment

trans·gress /trænz'grɛs/ *v.* [I,T] *formal* to do something that is against the rules of a religion or society —**transgression** /trænz'grɛʃən/ *n.* [C,U]

tran·sient¹ /'trænʒənt/ *adj. formal* **1** continuing only for a short time **2** working or staying somewhere for only a short time: *transient workers*

transient² *n.* [C] someone who has no home and moves from place to place

tran·sis·tor /træn'zɪstɚ/ *n.* [C] a piece of electronic equipment that controls the flow of electricity in radios, televisions, etc.

tran·sit /'trænzɪt/ *n.* [U] the process of moving people, products, etc. from one place to another: *The shipment must have been lost* ***in transit.***

tran·si·tion /træn'zɪʃən/ *n.* [C,U] *formal* the process of changing from one form or condition to another: *the* ***transition from*** *full-time work* ***to*** *retirement*

tran·si·tion·al /træn'zɪʃənl/ *adj.* relating to a period of change from one form or condition to another: *transitional housing | a transitional period between jobs*

tran·si·tive verb /ˌtrænzət̬ɪv 'vɚb/ *n.* [C] *technical* in grammar, a transitive verb has an object. In the sentence "She makes her own clothes," "makes" is a transitive verb [➡ **intransitive verb**]

tran·si·to·ry /'trænzəˌtɔri/ *adj.* TRANSIENT

trans·late /'trænzleɪt, ˌtrænz'leɪt/ *v.* **1** [I,T] to change speech or writing from one language to another [➡ **interpret**]: *He* ***translated*** *the book* ***into*** *German.* **2 translate into sth** if one thing translates into another, the second thing happens as a result of the first: *Will more investment translate into more jobs?* —**translation** /trænz'leɪʃən/ *n.* [C,U]

trans·la·tor /'trænzˌleɪt̬ɚ/ *n.* [C] someone who changes writing or speech into a different language [➡ **interpreter**]

trans·lu·cent /trænz'lusənt/ *adj.* not transparent, but clear enough for some light to pass through —**translucence** *n.* [U]

trans·mis·sion /trænz'mɪʃən/ *n.* **1** [C,U] the process of sending out radio or television signals, or the program itself **2** [C] the part of a vehicle that uses the power from the engine to turn the wheels: *The car has* ***automatic transmission.*** **3** [U] *formal* the process of sending or passing something from one place, person, etc. to another: *the* ***transmission of*** *disease*

trans·mit /trænz'mɪt/ *v.* past tense and past participle **transmitted**, present participle **transmitting** **1** [I,T] to send out electric signals for radio or television [= **broadcast**] **2** [T] to send or pass something from one place, person, etc. to another: *The virus is transmitted through the blood.*

trans·mit·ter /trænz'mɪt̬ɚ, 'trænzˌmɪt̬ɚ/ *n.* [C] equipment that sends out radio or television signals

trans·par·ent /træns'pærənt, -'pɛr-/ *adj.* **1** if something is transparent, you can see through it: *transparent glass* **2** easy to notice and not deceiving anyone [= **obvious**]: *a transparent attempt to fool the voters* —**transparency** *n.* [U] —**transparently** *adv.*

tran·spire /træn'spaɪɚ/ *v.* [T] *formal* to happen: *Nobody knows what transpired that day.*

trans·plant¹ /træns'plænt/ *v.* [T] **1** to move an organ, piece of skin, etc. from one person's body to another **2** to move a plant from one place and put it in another

trans·plant² /'trænsplænt/ *n.* [C,U] a medical operation in which an organ from someone's body is put into another person, or the organ itself: *a heart transplant*

trans·port /træns'pɔrt/ *v.* [T] to move or carry goods, people, etc. from one place to another in a vehicle: *Helicopters will transport the equipment.*

trans·por·ta·tion /ˌtrænspɚ'teɪʃən/ *n.* [U] **1** a system or method for carrying passengers or goods from one place to another: *Buses are the main form of* ***public transportation.*** **2** the process or business of taking goods from one place to another: *the* ***transportation of*** *goods*

trans·pose /træns'poʊz/ *v.* [T] *formal* to change

transportation

the order or position of two or more words, letters, etc.

trans·sex·u·al /trænz'sɛkʃuəl/ *n.* [C] someone who has had a medical operation to become a person of the opposite sex

trans·ves·tite /trænz'vɛstaɪt/ *n.* [C] someone, especially a man, who enjoys dressing like a person of the opposite sex

trap¹ /træp/ *n.* [C] **1** a piece of equipment for catching animals: *a mouse trap* **2** a bad situation from which it is difficult to escape: *the deadly trap of drug addiction* **3** a trick that is intended to catch someone or make him/her say or do something that s/he did not intend to

trap² *v.* past tense and past participle **trapped**, present participle **trapping** [T] **1** to prevent someone from escaping from somewhere, especially a dangerous place: *Up to 25 people may be trapped in the burning building.*

THESAURUS

catch, **capture**, **arrest**, **corner**
→ see Thesaurus box at CATCH¹

2 to trick someone so that s/he says or does something that s/he did not intend to: *The police **trapped** him **into** confessing.* **3 be/feel trapped** to be in a bad situation from which it is difficult to escape: *She was trapped in an unhappy marriage.* **4** to catch an animal in a trap **5** to prevent something such as water, dirt, heat, etc. from escaping or spreading: *a filter that traps dust*

'trap door *n.* [C] a small door that covers an opening in a floor or roof

tra·peze /træ'piz/ *n.* [C] a short BAR hanging from two ropes high above the ground, used by ACROBATS

trap·e·zoid /'træpəzɔɪd/ *n.* [C] *technical* a shape with four sides, only two of which are parallel

trap·per /'træpɚ/ *n.* [C] someone who traps wild animals for their fur

trap·pings /'træpɪŋz/ *n.* [plural] all the clothes, possessions, etc. that show how rich, famous, or powerful someone is: *He has all the **trappings of** stardom.*

trash¹ /træʃ/ *n.* [U] **1** things that you throw away, such as old food, dirty paper, etc. [= **garbage**]: *Just put it **in the trash**.* | *Will someone please **take out the trash*** (=take it outside the house)*?*

THESAURUS

garbage, **refuse**, **litter**, **waste**
→ see Thesaurus box at GARBAGE

2 *informal* something that is of very poor quality: *There's so much trash on TV these days.*

trash² *v.* [T] *informal* **1** to destroy something completely: *You can't have parties if your friends are going to trash the place.* **2** to criticize someone or something severely: *Critics have trashed the movie.*

'trash can *n.* [C] GARBAGE CAN

'trash com,pactor *n.* [C] a machine used for pressing trash into a small mass

'trash talk also **'trash ,talking** *n.* [U] the act of saying rude or insulting things to or about a sports player during a game or competition

trash·y /'træʃi/ *adj.* of extremely bad quality: *trashy novels*

trau·ma /'trɔmə, 'traʊmə/ *n.* [C,U] a state of extreme shock that is caused by a very bad or frightening experience, or the experience itself: *the **trauma of** divorce | soldiers suffering from trauma*

trau·mat·ic /trə'mæṭɪk, trɔ-/ *adj.* very shocking and upsetting: *a traumatic experience*

trau·ma·tize /'trɔmə,taɪz, 'traʊ-/ *v.* [T] to shock someone so badly that s/he is affected by it for a very long time: *He was traumatized by his war experiences.*

T

trav·el¹ /'trævəl/ *v.* **1** [I,T] to make a trip from one place to another, especially to distant places: *Rick's **traveling across/through** the U.S. with a backpack. | We always **travel light** (=without taking many bags). | We **traveled by bus/train etc.** through France. | He spent years **traveling the country/world**.*

THESAURUS

Ways of traveling
drive or **go by car**
fly or **go by plane**
sail or **go by boat/ship**
take a train/bus/taxi/cab or **go by train/bus etc.**
walk/hike or **go on foot**
bike or **go by bike**

Someone who travels
traveler – any person who is traveling
passenger – someone who is traveling in a car, bus, train, airplane, etc.
tourist – someone who is traveling somewhere for a vacation
explorer – someone who travels to places that people have not visited before
commuter – someone who travels a long distance to work every day
→ AIRPORT, JOURNEY, PASSPORT

2 [I] to move from one place or person to another: *News travels fast in a small town.* **3** [I,T] to go a particular distance or at a particular speed: *We traveled over 400 miles the first day of our trip. | The bus was **traveling at** a high speed.*

travel² *n.* [U] **1** the act or activity of traveling: *Heavy rain is making road travel difficult.*

THESAURUS

travel/traveling – the general activity of going from one place to another, especially for long distances and long periods of time: *a special ticket for train travel around Europe | I haven't really done much traveling.*
trip – the time spent and the distance traveled in going from one place to another: *a trip to the grocery store | They're planning a trip to Hawaii.*
journey formal – a trip that is long or difficult: *the journey across the plains in a covered wagon*
travels – trips to places that are far away, or the act of moving from place to place over a period of time: *her travels in South America*
voyage – a trip in which you travel by ship or in a spacecraft, used mainly in stories: *Columbus's voyage across the ocean*

USAGE

You can **take**, **make**, or **go on** a **trip**, **journey**, or **voyage**, but you cannot use these verbs with **travel**.

2 travels [plural] trips, especially to places that are far away: *She made a lot of friends **on her travels**.*

'travel ,agency *n.* [C] a business that arranges travel and vacations

'travel ,agent *n.* [C] someone who works in a travel agency

trav·el·er /'trævələ/ *n.* [C] someone who is on a trip or who travels often → see Thesaurus box at TRAVEL¹

'traveler's ,check *n.* [C] a special check that can be exchanged for the money of a foreign country

tra·verse /trə'vəs/ *v.* [T] *formal* to move across, over, or through something, especially land or water

trav·es·ty /'trævɪsti/ *n.* plural **travesties** [C] something that is very bad because it is not what it should be: *The trial was described as **a travesty of justice**.*

trawl /trɔl/ *n.* [C] a wide net that is pulled along the bottom of the ocean to catch fish —**trawl** *v.* [I,T]

trawl·er /'trɔlə/ *n.* [C] a fishing boat that uses a trawl

tray /treɪ/ *n.* [C] a flat piece of plastic, metal, or wood with raised edges, that is used for carrying things such as plates, food, etc. → see picture on page A11

treach·er·ous /'trɛtʃərəs/ *adj.* **1** someone who is treacherous cannot be trusted because s/he secretly intends to harm you **2** extremely dangerous because you cannot see the dangers: *Black ice on the roads made driving treacherous.*

treach·er·y /ˈtrɛtʃəri/ *n.* [U] actions that are not loyal to someone who trusts you

tread¹ /trɛd/ *v.* past tense **trod** /trɑd/ past participle **trodden** /ˈtrɑdn/ **1 tread carefully/lightly etc.** to be very careful about what you say or do in a difficult situation: *It's best to tread lightly when the boss is in a bad mood.* **2 tread water** to stay floating upright in deep water by moving your legs as if you were riding a bicycle **3** [I,T] *old-fashioned* to walk or step on something

tread² *n.* **1** [C,U] the pattern of lines on the part of a tire that touches the road **2** [C] the part of a stair that you put your foot on

tread·mill /ˈtrɛdmɪl/ *n.* **1** [C] a piece of exercise equipment that has a large belt around a set of wheels, that you can walk or run on while staying in the same place **2** [singular] work or a way of life that seems very boring because you always have to do the same things

trea·son /ˈtrizən/ *n.* [U] the crime of being disloyal to your country or government, especially by helping its enemies

treas·ure¹ /ˈtrɛʒɚ/ *n.* **1** [U] a group of valuable things, such as gold, silver, jewels, etc.: *a story about **buried treasure*** **2** [C] a very valuable and important object such as a painting or ancient document: *the treasures of the Art Institute of Chicago*

treasure² *v.* [T] to treat something or someone as very special, important, or valuable: *I'll always treasure the memories of this day.*

ˈtreasure ˌhunt *n.* [C] a game in which you have to find something that has been hidden by answering questions that are left in different places

treas·ur·er /ˈtrɛʒərɚ/ *n.* [C] someone who takes care of the money for an organization

treas·ur·y /ˈtrɛʒəri/ *n.* plural **treasuries** [C] **1** the money in an organization's accounts **2** a government office that controls a country's money: *the Treasury Department*

treat¹ /trit/ *v.* [T] **1** to behave toward someone in a particular way: *Why do you **treat** me **like** an idiot?* | *My parents always **treated** me **as** an equal.* | *Mr. Parker **treats** everyone **equally/fairly**.* **2** to consider something in a particular way: *You can **treat** these costs **as** business expenses.* **3** to give someone medical attention for a sickness or injury: *Eleven people were **treated for** minor injuries.* **4** to buy or arrange something special for someone: *We're **treating** Mom **to** dinner for her birthday.* **5** to put a special substance on something or use a chemical process in order to protect or clean it: *The wood has been treated to make it waterproof.*

treat² *n.* **1** [C] something special that you give someone or do for him/her: *If you're good, I'll buy you a treat.* **2** [singular] an unexpected event that gives you a lot of pleasure: *Getting your letter was **a real treat**.* **3 my treat** *spoken* used in order to tell someone that you will pay for something: *Put away your money – dinner's my treat.*

treat·a·ble /ˈtriṭəbəl/ *adj.* able to be medically treated: *The disease is treatable with antibiotics.*

trea·tise /ˈtriṭəs/ *n.* [C] a serious book or article about a particular subject: *a **treatise on** political philosophy*

treat·ment /ˈtritˀmənt/ *n.* **1** [C,U] a method that is intended to cure an injury or sickness: *a new **treatment for** cancer* | *She was **given** emergency **treatment** by paramedics.* **2** [U] a particular way of behaving toward someone or of dealing with him/her: *society's **treatment of** women* | *The coach denied giving his son **preferential/special treatment**.* **3** [C,U] a particular way of dealing with or talking about a subject: *I didn't think the film gave the issue serious treatment.* **4** [U] a process by which something is cleaned, protected, etc.: *a waste treatment plant*

trea·ty /ˈtriṭi/ *n.* plural **treaties** [C] a formal written agreement between two or more countries: *a **peace treaty***

tre·ble¹ /ˈtrɛbəl/ *n.* [C] the upper half of the whole range of musical notes

treble² *v.* [I,T] to TRIPLE

tree /tri/ *n.* [C] a very tall plant that has a TRUNK (=thick wooden stem), branches, and leaves: *an apple tree* | *As a kid, I loved to climb trees.*

THESAURUS

the woods – a large area with many trees
woodland – an area of land that is covered with trees
forest – a very large area with a lot of trees growing closely together
rain forest – a tropical forest with tall trees, in an area where it rains a lot
jungle – a tropical forest with trees and large plants

→ see picture at PLANT¹

tree·top /ˈtritɑp/ *n.* [C usually plural] the top branches of a tree

trek /trɛk/ *v.* past tense and past participle **trekked**, present participle **trekking** [I] to make a long and difficult trip on foot: ***trekking across** the Rockies* —**trek** *n.* [C] *a **trek across** the country* —**trekking** *n.* [U]

trel·lis /ˈtrɛlɪs/ *n.* [C] a wooden frame for supporting climbing plants

trem·ble /ˈtrɛmbəl/ *v.* [I] to shake because you are upset, afraid, or excited: *Her lip trembled as she spoke.* | *Ray's voice was **trembling with fear/anger**.*

THESAURUS

shake, shiver, wobble, vibrate, rattle
→ see Thesaurus box at SHAKE¹

tre·men·dous /trɪˈmɛndəs/ *adj.* **1** very great in amount, size, power, etc.: *I have tremendous respect for her.* | *a runner with tremendous speed*

T

2 excellent: *The play was a tremendous success.* —**tremendously** *adv.*

trem·or /ˈtrɛmɚ/ *n.* [C] **1** a small EARTHQUAKE **2** a slight shaking movement in your body that you cannot control: *There was a* ***tremor in*** *her hands.*

trench /trɛntʃ/ *n.* [C] a long narrow hole that is dug along the ground

tren·chant /ˈtrɛntʃənt/ *adj. written* expressed very strongly, effectively, and directly: *a trenchant critic of big business*

ˈtrench coat *n.* [C] a long RAINCOAT with a belt

trend /trɛnd/ *n.* [C] **1** the way a situation is generally developing or changing [= **tendency**]: *There's a* ***trend toward*** *more part-time employment.* | *recent* ***trends in*** *education* **2 set the trend** to start doing something that other people copy

trend·y /ˈtrɛndi/ *adj.* comparative **trendier**, superlative **trendiest** *informal* modern and fashionable: *the trendiest club in town*

> **THESAURUS**
> **fashionable, stylish, designer**
> → see Thesaurus box at FASHIONABLE

trep·i·da·tion /ˌtrɛpəˈdeɪʃən/ *n.* [U] *formal* a feeling of anxiety or fear about something that is going to happen

T

tres·pass /ˈtrɛspæs/ *v.* [I] to go onto someone's land without permission —**trespasser** *n.* [C]

> **THESAURUS**
> **enter, go in, come in, barge in, sneak in, get in**
> → see Thesaurus box at ENTER[1]

tres·tle /ˈtrɛsəl/ *n.* [C] a wooden support made of beams in an "A" shape under a table or bridge

tri·al /ˈtraɪəl/ *n.* **1** [C,U] a legal process in which a court of law examines a case to decide whether someone is guilty of a crime [➡ **try**]: *a murder trial* | *Holt is* ***on trial for*** (=being judged in a court for) *bank robbery.* | *He* ***stands trial*** (=will be judged in a court) *in June.* | *The defendant has a right to a* ***fair trial.*** **2** [C,U] a test to know if something works well and is safe: ***clinical trials*** *of a new drug* **3** [C,U] a short period during which you use something or employ someone to find out whether s/he or it is satisfactory for a particular purpose or job: *Bonnie's been hired* ***on a trial basis.*** **4 trial and error** testing different ways of doing something in order to find the best one: *I learned to cook* ***by/through trial and error.*** **5 trials** [plural] a sports competition in which people who want to be on a team are tested to find out who is best [= **tryout**]: *the Olympic swimming trials* **6 trials and tribulations** difficult experiences and troubles: *all the trials and tribulations of being a teenager*

ˌtrial ˈrun *n.* [C] an occasion when you test something new in order to see if it works

tri·an·gle /ˈtraɪˌæŋgəl/ *n.* [C] **1** a flat shape with three straight sides and three angles ➔ see picture at SHAPE[1]

> **THESAURUS**
> **square, circle, semicircle, rectangle, oval, cylinder**
> → see Thesaurus box at SHAPE[1]

2 a small musical instrument shaped like a triangle, that you play by hitting it with a small metal BAR —**triangular** /traɪˈæŋgyəlɚ/ *adj.*

tri·ath·lon /traɪˈæθlɑn, -lən/ *n.* [C] a sports competition in which you run, swim, and ride a bicycle

tribe /traɪb/ *n.* [C] a social group that consists of people of the same RACE who have the same beliefs, CUSTOMS, language, etc. and live in one area ruled by a chief: *the tribes of the Amazon jungle* —**tribal** *adj.*: *tribal art* | *tribal leaders*

> **THESAURUS**
> **race, nation, people, ethnic group**
> → see Thesaurus box at RACE[1]

trib·u·la·tion /ˌtrɪbyəˈleɪʃən/ *n.* [C,U] *formal* serious trouble or a serious problem ➔ **trials and tribulations** at TRIAL

tri·bu·nal /traɪˈbyunl, trɪ-/ *n.* [C] a type of court that has official authority to deal with a particular situation or problem: *a war crimes tribunal*

trib·u·tar·y /ˈtrɪbyəˌtɛri/ *n.* plural **tributaries** [C] a river or stream that flows into a larger river

trib·ute /ˈtrɪbyut/ *n.* [C,U] something that you say, do, or give in order to express your respect or admiration for someone: *The concert will be a* ***tribute to*** *Bob Dylan.* ➔ **pay tribute to sb/sth** at PAY[1]

tri·ceps /ˈtraɪsɛps/ *n.* [C] the large muscle at the back of your upper arm

trick[1] /trɪk/ *n.* [C] **1** something you do in order to deceive someone: *It was just a trick to get me to agree.* **2** something you do to surprise someone and make other people laugh: *The kids like* ***playing tricks on*** *the grownups.* **3** a skillful set of actions that seem like magic, done in order to entertain people: *a* ***magic trick*** **4 do the trick** *spoken* if something does the trick, it solves a problem or achieves what you want: *A little salt should do the trick.* **5** an effective way of doing something: *There's* ***a trick to*** *getting the audience's attention.*

trick[2] *v.* [T] to deceive someone in order to get something from him/her or make him/her do something: *Believe me, we're not trying to trick you.* | *Clients were* ***tricked into*** *believing he'd invest the money.*

trick·er·y /ˈtrɪkəri/ *n.* [U] the use of tricks to deceive or cheat people

trick·le /ˈtrɪkəl/ *v.* [I] **1** if liquid trickles somewhere, it flows slowly in drops or in a thin stream: *Sweat **trickled down** his face.* **2** if people, vehicles, goods, etc. trickle somewhere, they move there slowly in small groups or amounts: *Refugees have begun to **trickle across** the border.* —**trickle** *n.* [C] *a trickle of blood*

ˌtrick or ˈtreat *v.* **go trick or treating** if children go trick or treating, they put on COSTUMES and go from house to house on Halloween and say "trick or treat" in order to get candy

trick·ster /ˈtrɪkstɚ/ *n.* [C] someone who deceives or cheats people

trick·y /ˈtrɪki/ *adj.* comparative **trickier**, superlative **trickiest** something that is difficult to deal with or do because it is complicated and full of problems: *Finding out how the trouble started will be tricky.*

tri·cy·cle /ˈtraɪsɪkəl/ *n.* [C] a small vehicle, used especially by young children, with one wheel at the front and two wheels at the back

tri·dent /ˈtraɪdnt/ *n.* [C] a weapon with three points that looks like a large fork

tried[1] /traɪd/ *v.* the past tense and past participle of TRY

tried[2] *adj.* **tried and tested/true** used successfully many times: *tried and tested methods*

tri·fle /ˈtraɪfəl/ *n.* [C] **1 a trifle...** a little [= **slightly**]: *The soup is a trifle salty.* **2** something that has little value or importance

trig·ger[1] /ˈtrɪgɚ/ *n.* [C] **1** the part of a gun that you press with your finger to fire it: *Carter aimed and **pulled the trigger**.* **2 be the trigger (point)** to be the thing that causes a serious problem

trigger[2] **also trigger off** *v.* [T] to make something happen: *Heavy rain may trigger mudslides.*

THESAURUS

cause, make, be responsible for, bring about, result in, lead to
➔ see Thesaurus box at CAUSE[2]

trig·o·nom·e·try /ˌtrɪgəˈnɑmətri/ *n.* [U] the part of mathematics that is concerned with the relationship between the angles and sides of TRIANGLES

trike /traɪk/ *n. informal* ➔ TRICYCLE

tri·lat·er·al /ˌtraɪˈlætərəl◂/ *adj.* including three groups or countries: *a trilateral agreement*

trill /trɪl/ *n.* [C] a musical sound made by quickly repeating two notes that are very similar: *a bird's trill* —**trill** *v.* [I,T]

tril·lion /ˈtrɪlyən/ *number* 1,000,000,000,000

tril·o·gy /ˈtrɪlədʒi/ *n.* plural **trilogies** [C] a group of three books, plays, movies, etc. that have the same subject or characters

trim[1] /trɪm/ *v.* past tense and past participle **trimmed**, present participle **trimming** [T] **1** to cut a small amount off something, especially to make it look neater: ***Trim off** the excess fat.*

THESAURUS

saw, chop down, mow, snip
➔ see Thesaurus box at CUT[1]

2 to reduce the size or amount of something, especially to save money: *plans to trim the city's budget* **3** to decorate something around its edges: *a coat **trimmed with** velvet*

trim[2] *adj.* thin and healthy looking: *a trim figure*

trim[3] *n.* **1** [singular] an act of cutting something in order to make it look neater: *Your beard needs a trim.* **2** [singular, U] a decoration around the edges of a car, piece of clothing, etc.: *a blue car with white trim*

tri·mes·ter /ˈtraɪmɛstɚ, traɪˈmɛstɚ/ *n.* [C] **1** one of three periods into which a year at school or college is divided **2** one of the three-month periods of a woman's PREGNANCY: *Many women feel sick during the first trimester of pregnancy.*

trim·mings /ˈtrɪmɪŋz/ *n.* **all the trimmings** all the other types of food that are traditionally served with the main dish of a meal: *a turkey dinner with all the trimmings*

trin·i·ty /ˈtrɪnəti/ *n.* **the (Holy) Trinity** in the Christian religion, the union of Father, Son, and Holy Spirit in one God

trin·ket /ˈtrɪŋkɪt/ *n.* [C] a piece of jewelry or a small pretty object that is not worth much money

tri·o /ˈtrioʊ/ *n.* [C] **1** a group of three people or things: *a jazz trio* **2** a piece of music for three performers

trip[1] /trɪp/ *n.* [C] **1** an occasion when you go from one place to another, often to visit a place or person: *a **trip to** the grocery store* | *I'd met him **on** my last **trip** to Japan.* | *They recently **took a trip** to Florida.* | *a **camping/fishing/ski trip*** | *a week-long **business trip***

THESAURUS

travel, journey, voyage
➔ see Thesaurus box at TRAVEL[2]

2 *slang* the strange mental experiences someone has when s/he takes an illegal drug such as LSD

trip[2] *v.* past tense and past participle **tripped**, present participle **tripping** **1** [I] to hit something with your foot by accident so that you fall or almost fall: *Jack **tripped on/over** the bottom step.*

THESAURUS

fall, slip, stumble, lose your balance
➔ see Thesaurus box at FALL[1]

2 [T] **also trip up** to make someone fall by putting your foot in front of him/her when s/he is moving **3** [T] to accidentally make an electrical system operate by moving part of it: *An intruder had tripped the alarm.* **4** [I] **also trip out** *slang* to experience the effects of illegal drugs

trip (sb ⇔) **up** *phr. v.* to make a mistake, or to cause someone to make a mistake: *The question was intended to trip him up.*

T

tripe /traɪp/ *n.* [U] the stomach of a cow or pig, used as food

tri·ple[1] /ˈtrɪpəl/ *adj.* having three parts, or involving three people or groups: *a triple gold medal winner*

triple[2] *v.* [I,T] to increase by three times as much, or to make something do this: *The landlord tripled the rent.*

tri·plet /ˈtrɪplɪt/ *n.* [C] one of three children born at the same time to the same mother

trip·li·cate /ˈtrɪpləkɪt/ *n.* **in triplicate** if a document is written in triplicate, there are three copies of it

tri·pod /ˈtraɪpɑd/ *n.* [C] a support with three legs, used for a camera, TELESCOPE, etc.

trite /traɪt/ *adj.* a trite remark, idea, etc. has been used so often that it seems boring and not sincere

tri·umph[1] /ˈtraɪəmf/ *n.* **1** [C] an important success or victory, especially after a difficult struggle: *a foreign policy triumph* | *San Francisco's* ***triumph over*** *Cincinnati in the Super Bowl* **2** [U] a feeling of pleasure and satisfaction that you get from victory or success: *shouts of triumph* —**triumphant** /traɪˈʌmfənt/ *adj.*: *a triumphant army*

triumph[2] *v.* [I] to gain a victory or success, especially after a difficult struggle: *Good will* ***triumph over*** *evil.*

tri·um·phal /traɪˈʌmfəl/ *adj.* done or made in order to celebrate a victory or success: *a triumphal parade*

T

triv·i·a /ˈtrɪviə/ *n.* [plural] **1** detailed facts about history, famous people, sports, etc.: *movie trivia* | *a* ***trivia quiz/game/contest*** **2** unimportant or useless details: *meaningless trivia*

triv·i·al /ˈtrɪviəl/ *adj.* not important, valuable, or serious: *This issue is not a* ***trivial matter***.

triv·i·al·ize /ˈtrɪviəˌlaɪz/ *v.* [T] to make something important seem less important than it really is: *The media seemed to trivialize the court's decision.*

trod /trɑd/ *v.* the past tense of TREAD

trod·den /ˈtrɑdn/ *v.* the past participle of TREAD

troll /troʊl/ *n.* [C] an imaginary creature in ancient Scandinavian stories, like a very large or very small ugly person

trol·ley /ˈtrɑli/ *n.* [C] an electric vehicle for carrying passengers, that moves along the street on metal tracks

trom·bone /trɑmˈboʊn/ *n.* [C] a metal musical instrument, that you play by blowing into it and moving a long sliding tube → see picture on page A6

tromp /trɑmp, trɔmp/ *v.* [I,T] *informal* → TRAMP[2]

troop[1] /trup/ *n.* **1 troops** [plural] soldiers in an organized group: *Troops were sent in to stop the riots.* **2 troop movement/withdrawal/morale/readiness etc.** the movements, etc. of soldiers **3** [C] a group of soldiers, especially on horses or in TANKS **4** [C] an organized group of people or animals: *a Girl Scout troop*

troop[2] *v.* [I] *informal* to move together in a group: *People* ***trooped across/along/down etc.*** *the street.*

troop·er /ˈtrupɚ/ *n.* [C] a member of a state police force in the U.S.

tro·phy /ˈtroʊfi/ *n.* plural **trophies** [C] a prize for winning a competition, especially a silver cup or a PLAQUE: *He was presented with the* ***championship trophy***.

trop·i·cal /ˈtrɑpɪkəl/ *adj.* **1** coming from or existing in the hottest and wettest parts of the world: *tropical flowers* **2** weather that is tropical is hot and the air seems wet

trop·ics /ˈtrɑpɪks/ *n.* **the tropics** the hottest and wettest parts of the world, near the Equator

trot /trɑt/ *v.* past tense and past participle **trotted**, present participle **trotting** [I] **1** if a horse trots, it moves fairly quickly with short steps **2** to run fairly slowly with short steps: *Jimmy* ***trotted along*** *behind his parents.* —**trot** *n.*

trot sb/sth ⇔ **out** *phr. v. informal* to use an explanation, idea, opinion, etc. that has been used many times before: *He trotted out the same old excuses.*

trou·ba·dour /ˈtrubəˌdɔr/ *n.* [C] a singer and poet who traveled around in past times

trou·ble[1] /ˈtrʌbəl/ *n.*

1 PROBLEMS [C,U] problems that make something difficult, make you worry, spoil your plans, etc.: *They're* ***having*** *some* ***trouble with*** *their car.* | *We* ***had trouble*** *getting reservations.* | *a plane with engine trouble* | *the company's financial troubles* | *It took her mind off her troubles.*

THESAURUS

problem, setback, snag, hitch, hassle
→ see Thesaurus box at PROBLEM

2 BAD POINT [singular] *spoken* used when saying what is not satisfactory about something or someone or what causes problems: ***The trouble with*** *you is you don't listen.* | *There isn't enough time.* ***That's the trouble.***

3 in/into/out of trouble a) if someone or something is in trouble, she, he, or it is in a situation that has a lot of problems or that is difficult or dangerous: *Their marriage was in trouble.* | *The agency was* ***in serious/big/deep trouble***. **b)** if someone is in trouble, s/he has done something which someone will punish him/her for or be angry about: *My daughter's* ***gotten into trouble*** *at school.* | *Joe's* ***in trouble with*** *the police.* | *After-school activities help kids* ***stay/keep out of trouble.***

4 HEALTH [U] *informal* a problem that you have with your health: *He has* ***heart/back trouble***.

5 EFFORT [U] an amount of effort and time that is needed to do something: *She* ***took the trouble to*** *explain it to us again.* | *"Could you help me carry* *this?" "Sure, **it's no trouble*** (=I am happy to help)."

6 be asking for trouble *informal* to take risks or do something stupid that is likely to cause problems: *You're asking for trouble if you don't get those brakes fixed.*

7 ARGUMENT/VIOLENCE [C,U] a situation in which people argue or fight with each other: *recent troubles on college campuses*

trouble² *v.* [T] *formal* **1** if a problem troubles you, it makes you feel worried or upset: *His behavior toward her troubled me.* **2** to say something or ask someone to do something which may use his/her time or upset him/her: *I won't trouble you again.*

trou·bled /ˈtrʌbəld/ *adj.* **1** worried or anxious: *Clayton looked troubled.* **2** having many problems: *our troubled public schools* | *We are living in **troubled times**.* **3** having many mental or emotional problems: *a **deeply troubled** man*

trou·ble·mak·er /ˈtrʌbəlˌmeɪkɚ/ *n.* [C] someone who deliberately causes problems

trou·ble·shoot·er /ˈtrʌbəlˌʃuṭɚ/ *n.* [C] someone whose job is to deal with serious problems in a company, organization, etc. —**troubleshooting** *n.* [U]

trou·ble·some /ˈtrʌbəlsəm/ *adj.* causing problems: *troublesome questions*

ˈtrouble ˌspot *n.* [C] a place where trouble often happens, especially war or violence: *troops being sent to trouble spots abroad*

trou·bling /ˈtrʌblɪŋ/ *adj.* worrying: *The results raise some troubling questions.*

trough /trɔf/ *n.* [C] a long narrow open container that holds water or food for animals

trounce /traʊns/ *v.* [T] to defeat someone completely: *Colorado trounced Minnesota, 58–7.*

> **THESAURUS**
>
> **beat, defeat, clobber, cream**
>
> → see Thesaurus box at BEAT³

troupe /trup/ *n.* [C] a group of singers, actors, dancers, etc. who work together

trou·sers /ˈtraʊzɚz/ *n.* [plural] → PANTS

trout /traʊt/ *n.* [C,U] a common river fish, or the meat from this fish

trove /troʊv/ *n.* [C usually singular] a large number of special or valuable things: *a **treasure trove of** antique furniture*

trow·el /ˈtraʊəl/ *n.* [C] a small garden tool used for digging

tru·ant /ˈtruənt/ *adj.* staying away from school without permission —**truancy** *n.* [U] —**truant** *n.* [C]

truce /trus/ *n.* [C] an agreement between two enemies to stop fighting or arguing for a short time: *The warring sides have **called/declared a truce**.*

truck¹ /trʌk/ *n.* [C] a large road vehicle that is used for carrying heavy loads: *a truck driver* | *a **garbage/dump/delivery, etc. truck*** → PICKUP → see picture at TRANSPORTATION

truck² *v.* [T] to take something somewhere by truck: *Food and medicine were **trucked in**.*

truck·er /ˈtrʌkɚ/ *n.* [C] someone whose job is driving a truck

ˈtruck farm *n.* [C] a farm that grows vegetables and fruit for sale directly to customers

truck·ing /ˈtrʌkɪŋ/ *n.* [U] the business of taking goods from place to place by truck

truck·load /ˈtrʌkloʊd/ *n.* [C] the amount of something that a truck can carry

ˈtruck stop *n.* [C] a cheap place to eat and buy gas on a HIGHWAY, used especially by truck drivers

truc·u·lent /ˈtrʌkyələnt/ *adj.* *formal* easily annoyed and always willing to argue with people

trudge /trʌdʒ/ *v.* [I] to walk with slow heavy steps because you are tired, or it is difficult to walk: *A group of soldiers **trudged up/down** the hill.*

> **THESAURUS**
>
> **walk, march, stride, stroll, amble, wander, creep, sneak, limp, wade, hike**
>
> → see Thesaurus box at WALK¹

true /tru/ *adj.* **1** based on facts and not imagined or invented [≠ **false**]: ***It is true that** people are living longer.* | *a movie based on a **true story*** **2** [only before noun] real and correct: *the true meaning of Christmas* | *The house was sold for only a fraction of its true value.* **3** *spoken* used when admitting that something is a fact: *True, he has a college degree, but he doesn't have enough job experience.* **4 true love/courage/friend etc.** love, a friend, etc. that has all the qualities that he, she, or it should have: *He's a true friend.* **5 come true** if dreams, wishes, etc. come true, they happen: *Their wish for a child finally came true.* **6** faithful and loyal, or doing what you have promised to do: *She stayed **true to** her husband during the trial.* | *He was **true to** his **word** and didn't say anything to anyone.*

ˌtrue-ˈlife *adj.* based on what really happened, and not invented: *a true-life adventure*

truf·fle /ˈtrʌfəl/ *n.* [C] **1** a soft chocolate candy **2** a FUNGUS you can eat that grows under the ground

tru·ism /ˈtruɪzəm/ *n.* [C] a statement that is clearly true, so that there is no need to say it

tru·ly /ˈtruli/ *adv.* **1** used in order to emphasize that the way you are describing something is true [= **really**]: *What is truly important?* | *I truly believe Alex saved my life.* **2** in an exact or correct way: *A spider can't truly be called an insect.* → **yours (truly)** at YOURS

trump¹ /trʌmp/ *n.* [C] **1** a SUIT or a playing card that is chosen to be of a higher value than the others in a particular card game **2 trump card** something that you can do or use in a situation, which gives you an advantage

T

trump² *v.* [T] to play a trump that beats someone else's card in a game

trump sth ⇔ **up** *phr. v.* to use false information to make someone seem guilty of a crime —**trumped-up** *adj.*: *trumped-up charges*

trum·pet¹ /ˈtrʌmpɪt/ *n.* [C] **1** a musical instrument that you blow into, that consists of a long bent metal tube that is wide at one end ➔ see picture on page A6 **2** the loud noise made by some animals, such as ELEPHANTS

trumpet² *v.* [T] to tell everyone about something you think is important or are proud of: *The headlines trumpeted their victory.*

trun·cat·ed /ˈtrʌŋˌkeɪt̬ɪd/ *adj.* made short, or shorter than before: *a truncated speech*

trun·dle /ˈtrʌndl/ *v.* [I,T] to move slowly on wheels, or to make something do this by pushing it or pulling it

trunk /trʌŋk/ *n.* [C] **1** the thick central wooden stem of a tree that branches grow from: *a sign tacked to a* ***tree trunk*** ➔ see picture at PLANT¹ **2** an enclosed space at the back of a car where you can put bags, tools, etc.: *Put the suitcases in the trunk.* **3** the very long nose of an ELEPHANT ➔ see picture on page A2 **4** a large box made of wood or metal, in which clothes, books, etc. are stored or packed for traveling **5 trunks** [plural] short pants that men wear when swimming **6** *technical* the main part of your body, not including your head, arms, or legs [➥ **torso**]

T

trust¹ /trʌst/ *v.* **1** [T] to believe that someone is honest and will not do anything bad or wrong: *I've never trusted her.* | *Can you* ***trust*** *him* ***with*** *your car* (=believe he will not damage it)*?* | *Managers must* ***trust*** *employees* ***to*** *get the job done.*

THESAURUS

depend, **rely on/upon**, **count on**
➔ see Thesaurus box at DEPEND

2 [T] to depend on something and believe it is correct or will work: *I trust his judgment.* | *Not trusting her voice, she nodded.* **3 I trust** *spoken formal* used in order to say that you hope something is true: *The reasons, I trust, are clear.*

trust in sb/sth *phr. v. formal* to believe that you can depend on someone or something

trust² *n.* **1** [U] the belief that you can trust someone [≠ **distrust**]: *It took three years to earn his trust.* | *At first, there was a* ***lack of trust*** *between them.* | *I had* ***put*** *my* ***trust in*** *the doctor.* **2** [U] an arrangement in which someone legally controls your money or property, usually until you are old enough to use it: *$100,000 is being* ***held in trust*** *for his daughter.* **3** [C usually singular] an organization or group that has control over money that will be used to help someone else: *the J. Paul Getty trust* **4** [C] a group of companies that work together to reduce competition: *a railroad trust*

trust·ee /trʌˈsti/ *n.* [C] a person or company that has control of money or property that is in a trust for someone else

ˈtrust fund *n.* [C] money belonging to someone that is controlled for him/her by a trustee

trust·ing /ˈtrʌstɪŋ/ *adj.* willing to believe that other people are good and honest: *a trusting little child*

trust·wor·thy /ˈtrʌstˌwɚði/ *adj.* able to be trusted or depended on

trust·y /ˈtrʌsti/ *adj. humorous* a trusty weapon, horse, friend, etc. is one you can depend on

truth /truθ/ *n.* **1 the truth** the true facts about something: *Do you think he's* ***telling the truth****?* | ***the truth about*** *what he had done in the war* | *It was months before* ***the whole truth*** *was discovered.* **2** [U] the state or quality of being true: *There was no* ***truth in*** *the rumor.* **3** [C] *formal* an important fact or idea that is accepted as being true: *scientific truths* **4 to tell (you) the truth** *spoken* used when you admit something or tell someone your true opinion: *To tell you the truth, I just don't care.*

truth·ful /ˈtruθfəl/ *adj.* giving the true facts about something: *truthful answers* —**truthfully** *adv.*

try¹ /traɪ/ *v.* past tense and past participle **tried**, third person singular **tries** **1** [I,T] to attempt to do something: *Try again when you're not so tired.* | *Please* ***try to*** *come early.* | *Greg* ***tried hard*** *not to laugh.*

THESAURUS

attempt – to try to do something, especially something difficult: *He was attempting to climb Mt. Everest without oxygen.*
see if you can do sth spoken – to try to do something: *I'll see if I can get you a ticket.*
do your best – to try very hard, even if something is difficult and you are not sure you will succeed: *They'll do their best to get it finished by Friday.*
make an effort to do sth – to try to do something, especially something difficult: *The teachers make an effort to identify a student's strengths and weaknesses.*
endeavor formal – to try very hard to do something: *The company endeavors to satisfy its customers.*

2 [T] to do or use something, go somewhere, taste something, etc. in order to find out if it is useful, successful, or enjoyable: *Try logging off and logging on again.* | *Doctors are trying some new drugs in the cancer battle.* | *Have you tried Thai food?* **3** [T] to examine and judge a person or a legal case in a court of law: *Three men were* ***tried for*** *the murder.* **4 try sb's patience/nerves/temper etc.** to make someone start to feel impatient, nervous, angry, etc.

try sth ⇔ **on** *phr. v.* to put on a piece of clothing to find out if it fits or makes you look attractive: *I tried on one of her silk dresses.*

try sth ⇔ **out** *phr. v.* **1** to use something such as a method or piece of equipment in order to find out if it works or is good: *Are you going to try out your new bike?* **2** to show your skills in an attempt to be chosen as a member of a team, an actor in a play, etc.: *Sandra's **trying out for** the girls' basketball team.*

try² *n.* plural **tries** [C usually singular] an attempt to do something: *It looks hard, but I'll **give it a try**.* | *Good try, kid.*

try·ing /'traɪ-ɪŋ/ *adj.* difficult and unpleasant to deal with: *a trying time*

try·out /'traɪ-aʊt/ *n.* [C] an occasion when someone shows his/her skills in an attempt to be chosen for a sports team, play, etc. [➡ **audition**]

tsar /zɑr, tsɑr/ *n.* ➔ CZAR

T-shirt /'ti ʃɚt/ *n.* [C] a soft cotton shirt, with short SLEEVES and no collar ➔ see picture at CLOTHES

tsp. *n.* the written abbreviation of **teaspoon**

tub /tʌb/ *n.* [C] **1** ➔ BATHTUB **2** a plastic or paper container with a lid, that food is sold in: *a **tub of** ice cream* **3** a large round container used for washing things, storing things, etc.

tu·ba /'tubə/ *n.* [C] a large metal musical instrument with a wide opening that points straight up, that you play by blowing and that produces very low sounds ➔ see picture on page A6

tub·by /'tʌbi/ *adj. informal* short and fat

tube /tub/ *n.* [C] **1** a pipe made of metal, plastic, glass, etc., especially one that liquids or gases go through: *The patients are fed through tubes.* **2** a container for a soft substance, that you SQUEEZE to push the substance out: *a **tube of** toothpaste* **3** a tube-shaped part inside your body: *a fallopian tube* (=part of a woman's organs for having babies) **4 the tube** *spoken* the television: *What's on the tube?* **5 go down the tubes** if a situation goes down the tubes, it suddenly becomes bad: *Small businesses are going down the tubes.*

tu·ber·cu·lo·sis /tʊˌbɚkyə'loʊsɪs/ *n.* [U] a serious infectious disease that affects the lungs and other parts of the body

tub·ing /'tubɪŋ/ *n.* [U] tubes, usually connected together in a system: *copper tubing*

tu·bu·lar /'tubyələ˞/ *adj.* made of tubes or shaped like a tube

tuck¹ /tʌk/ *v.* [T] **1** to push the edge of a cloth or piece of clothing into something so that it stays in place: *He **tucked in** his shirt.* **2** to put something in a small space or a safe place: *She **tucked** the money **into** her pocket.* **3** to move the arms, legs, or head close to the body and keep it there: *The duck had its head tucked under its wing.*

tuck sth ⇔ **away** *phr. v.* **1** to put something in a safe or hidden place: *She tucked it away in a drawer.* **2 be tucked away** to be in a safe or hidden place: *a cabin tucked away in the mountains*

tuck sb ⇔ **in** *phr. v.* to make a child feel comfortable in bed by arranging the BLANKETS around him or her

tuck² *n.* [C] **1** a fold of cloth sewn flat in a piece of clothing **2** a medical operation to make someone look thinner or younger: *a tummy tuck*

Tues·day /'tuzdi, -deɪ/ *written abbreviation* **Tues.** *n.* the third day of the week: *He'll be back Tuesday.* | *Martha is going to St. Louis **on Tuesday**.* | *I'll see you **next Tuesday**.* | *We had the exam **last Tuesday**.* | *The meeting is scheduled for **Tuesday afternoon**.*

tuft /tʌft/ *n.* [C] a short thick group of hairs, feathers, grass, etc.: *a tuft of hair* —**tufted** *adj.*

tug¹ /tʌg/ *v.* past tense and past participle **tugged**, present participle **tugging** [I,T] to pull something suddenly and hard: *Alice **tugged at** my hand.*

THESAURUS

pull, drag, haul, tow, heave
➔ see Thesaurus box at PULL¹

tug² *n.* [C] **1 also tug boat** a small strong boat used for pulling ships **2** a sudden strong pull

ˌtug-of-'war *n.* [singular] **1** a competition in which two teams pull on the opposite ends of a rope **2** a situation in which two people or groups compete to get or keep the same thing

tu·i·tion /tu'ɪʃən/ *n.* [U] **1** the money you pay for being taught: *the cost of tuition at a private college* **2** the act of teaching

tu·lip /'tulɪp/ *n.* [C] a tall brightly colored garden flower, shaped like a cup

tum·ble /'tʌmbəl/ *v.* [I] **1** to fall or roll in a sudden uncontrolled way: *Rocks **tumbled down** the hillside.* **2** to decrease suddenly: *Oil prices have tumbled.* —**tumble** *n.* [C]

tum·bler /'tʌmblɚ/ *n.* [C] a glass with a flat bottom and no handle

tum·my /'tʌmi/ *n.* plural **tummies** [C] *informal* stomach – used especially by or to children

tu·mor /'tumɚ/ *n.* [C] a group of cells in the body that grow too quickly and cause sickness or health problems: *a brain tumor*

tu·mult /'tumʌlt/ *n.* [C,U] *formal* a state of CONFUSION, excitement, or other strong emotions: *the tumult of civil war* —**tumultuous** /tʊ'mʌltʃuəs/ *adj.*

tu·na /'tunə/ *n.* [C,U] a large common ocean fish, or the meat from this fish, usually sold in cans

tun·dra /'tʌndrə/ *n.* [U] the large flat areas of land in northern areas where it is very cold and there are no trees

tune¹ /tun/ *n.* **1** [C] a series of musical notes that are nice to listen to: *a pretty tune* | *It's sung **to the tune of** "Happy Birthday."*

THESAURUS

music, melody, song, arrangement, composition, number
➔ see Thesaurus box at MUSIC

T

2 in tune/out of tune playing or singing the correct musical notes, or playing or singing notes that are slightly too high or low: *My guitar's completely out of tune.* **3 in tune with sb/sth, out of tune with sb/sth** able or unable to realize, understand, or agree with what someone else thinks or wants: *a president who is in tune with ordinary Americans* **4 to the tune of $100/$15 million etc.** *informal* used in order to emphasize how large an amount or number is **5 change your tune** to suddenly have a different opinion about something

tune² *v.* [T] **1** to make a musical instrument play the correct PITCH: *The piano needs to be tuned.* **2** to make a television or radio receive broadcasts from a particular CHANNEL or STATION: ***Stay tuned** for more great music on KHPI.* **3 also tune up** to make small changes to an engine so that it works better

tune in *phr. v.* **1** to watch or listen to a particular television or radio program, or to make your television or radio receive that program: *I **tuned in to** the Giants' game.* **2** *informal* to realize or understand what is happening or what other people are thinking: *Try to **tune in to** your spouse's needs.*

tune (sb/sth ⇔) **out** *phr. v. informal* to ignore or stop listening to someone or something: *It's hard to tune out the noise in the office sometimes.*

tune up *phr. v.* when musicians tune up, they prepare their instruments so that they play at the same PITCH

'tune-up *n.* [C] an occasion when someone fixes and cleans your car's engine, or the process of doing this

T

tu·nic /'tunɪk/ *n.* [C] **1** a long loose piece of clothing, usually without SLEEVES, worn in the past **2** a woman's long loose shirt

tun·nel¹ /'tʌnl/ *n.* [C] a passage that has been dug under the ground or through a mountain, usually for cars or trains

tunnel

railroad tunnel

tunnel² *v.* [I] to dig a TUNNEL

,tunnel 'vision *n.* [U] **1** the tendency to think about only one subject, so that you forget other things that may be important too **2** a condition in which someone's eyes are damaged so that they can only see straight ahead

Tup·per·ware /'tʌpɚ,wɛr/ *n.* [U] *trademark* a type of plastic container with a tight lid, used for storing food

tur·ban /'tɚbən/ *n.* [C] a long piece of cloth that is worn twisted around the top of your head

tur·bine /'tɚbaɪn, -bɪn/ *n.* [C] an engine that works when the pressure from a liquid or gas moves a special wheel around

tur·bu·lence /'tɚbyələns/ *n.* [U] **1** irregular and strong movements of air or water that are caused by the wind: *There was a lot of turbulence during the flight.* **2** a situation in which people's thoughts, actions, and emotions are always changing: *political turbulence*

tur·bu·lent /'tɚbyələnt/ *adj.* **1** experiencing a lot of sudden changes and often wars or violence: *the turbulent years before the Revolution* **2** turbulent winds, oceans, etc. move around a lot with strong movements

turd /tɚd/ *n.* [C] *informal* a piece of solid brown waste passed from the body

tu·reen /tʊ'rin/ *n.* [C] a large dish with a lid, used especially for serving soup

turf /tɚf/ *n.* [U] **1** grass and soil on the ground's surface, or an artificial substance made to look like this: *thick green turf* **2** *informal* an area that someone knows well and feels that s/he controls or owns: *Davis's political turf*

tur·gid /'tɚdʒɪd/ *adj.* **1** boring and difficult to understand: *turgid poetry* **2** swollen, especially with liquid

tur·key /'tɚki/ *n.* [C,U] a bird similar to a chicken but larger, or the meat from this bird → COLD TURKEY

tur·moil /'tɚmɔɪl/ *n.* [singular, U] a state of CONFUSION, excitement, and trouble: *In 1967 the country was **in** racial **turmoil**.*

turn¹ /tɚn/ *v.*

1 YOUR BODY [I] to move your body so that you are looking in a different direction: *Alison turned and walked away.* | ***Turn around** so I can zip you up.* | *He **turned to** look behind him.*

2 OBJECT [T] to move an object so that it is facing in a different direction: *She **turned** the box **around/over** to look at the label.* | *A boat was **turned upside down** on the beach.*

3 DIRECTION [I] **a)** to go in a new direction when you are walking, driving, etc.: *Turn right at the next light.* **b)** if a road, river, etc. turns, it curves and starts to go in a new direction: *Further on the river turns east.*

4 MOVE AROUND A CENTRAL POINT [I,T] to move around a central point that does not move: *The wheels turned slowly.*

THESAURUS

twist – to turn something using a circular movement: *She twisted her hair up into a bun.*
spin – to turn around and around very quickly: *skaters spinning on the ice*
go around – to move in a continuous circular movement: *The fans go around to move the air and cool the room.*
revolve – to turn around a central point: *People in the past believed that the Sun revolved around the Earth.*
rotate – to turn around a particular point: *The Earth rotates every 24 hours.*

5 AGE [linking verb] to become a particular age: *Megan's just turned four.*
6 CHANGE [linking verb] to start to have a different quality than before: *The weather will turn colder.* | *The protests turned violent.* | *His hair is turning gray.* | *Helen turned bright red* (=because she was embarrassed).
7 PAGE [T] to move a page in a book or magazine so that you can see the next one
8 ATTENTION/THOUGHTS [I,T] to start to think about, deal with, look at, etc. a particular person, thing, or subject, instead of what you were thinking about, etc. before: *The reporters **turned** their **attention** to Dugan.* | *The conversation **turned to** events in Eastern Europe.*
9 turn your back (on sb/sth) to refuse to help or be involved with someone or something: *She wouldn't turn her back on her friends.*
10 turn over a new leaf to decide that you will change your behavior to make it better
11 turn a deaf ear/turn a blind eye to ignore what someone is saying or doing: *The administration turned a blind eye to the arms shipments.*
12 turn sb/sth loose to allow a person or animal to be free to do what she, he, or it wants
13 turn a profit to make a profit ➔ **turn your nose up (at sth)** at NOSE[1] ➔ **turn the tables (on sb)** at TABLE[2] ➔ **turn sth upside down** at UPSIDE DOWN

turn (sb) **against** sb/sth *phr. v.* to make someone stop liking or agreeing with someone or something: *His experiences in Vietnam turned him against the war.*

turn around *phr. v.* **1 turn** (sth ⇔) **around** if a situation, business, game, etc. turns around, or if someone turns it around, it changes and starts to become successful or to develop in the way you want: *The economy appears to be turning around.* | *They've turned the business around.* **2 turn around and say/do sth** to say or do something that is unexpected or that seems unreasonable: *I don't want him to turn around and sue us.*

turn away *phr. v.* **1 turn** sb ⇔ **away** to refuse to let people into a theater, restaurant, etc. because it is too full: *By 6:00, we were turning people away.* **2 turn** (sb ⇔) **away** to refuse to give sympathy, help, or support: *The hospital will never turn a sick child away.* | *The U.S. cannot just **turn away from** the world's problems.*

turn back *phr. v.* **1 turn** (sb ⇔) **back** to go in the opposite direction, or to tell someone to do this: *Snow covered the trail, and we had to turn back.* | *The journalists were turned back at the border.* **2** to return to doing something in the way it was done before: *Once you've left her, there will be **no turning back**.* ➔ **turn/set the clock back** at CLOCK[1]

turn sb/sth ⇔ **down** *phr. v.* **1** to make a machine such as a television, OVEN, etc. produce less sound, heat, etc.: *Turn the TV down!* **2** to refuse an offer, request, or invitation: *She was offered promotion, but turned it down.*

turn in *phr. v.* **1 turn** sth ⇔ **in** to give something to someone in authority: *They turned in a petition with more than 160,000 signatures.* **2 turn** sth ⇔ **in** to give work that you have done to your teacher: *Have you turned in your homework?* **3 turn** sb ⇔ **in** to tell the police where a criminal is **4** *informal* to go to bed: *I think I'll turn in.*

turn (sth) **into** sth *phr. v.* to become something different, or to make someone or something do this: *The argument turned into a fight.* | *The witch turned the frog into a prince.*

turn off *phr. v.* **1 turn** sth ⇔ **off** to stop a supply of water, electricity, etc., especially so that a machine stops working: *Turn off the TV – it's dinner time.* **2 turn off** sth to drive off one road and onto another, often a smaller one: *We turned off the highway looking for a place to eat.* **3 turn** sb **off** to make someone decide that s/he does not like someone or something: *voters who are turned off by politics* | *She says skinny men turn her off* (=she is not attracted to them sexually). ➔ TURN-OFF

turn on *phr. v.* **1 turn** sth ⇔ **on** to make the supply of water, electricity, etc. begin to flow through a pipe, machine, etc., so that it starts working: *Alice turned on a light.* **2 turn on** sb to suddenly attack someone physically or using unpleasant words: *"That's right, cry!" he said, turning on me.* **3 turn** sb **on** to make someone sexually excited

turn out *phr. v.* **1** to happen in a particular way, or to have a particular result: *Luckily, everything **turned out okay/all right/fine/well**.* | ***It turned out that** we were right.* | *The trail **turned out to be** much rougher than they expected.* **2 turn** sth ⇔ **out** if you turn out a light, you push a button to stop the flow of electricity **3** if people turn out for an event, they go to it or take part in it: *Only about 30 people **turned out for** the show.* ➔ TURNOUT **4 turn** sth ⇔ **out** to produce or make something: *The factory turns out 100,000 trucks a year.* **5 turn** sb **out** to make someone leave his/her home

turn over *phr. v.* **1 turn** sth ⇔ **over to** sb to give someone the right to own something such as a plan, business, piece of property, or to make him/her responsible for it: *Some of the work is being turned over to private firms.* **2 turn** sb/sth ⇔ **over** to bring a criminal or information to the police or another official organization: *Benson was **turned over to** the FBI yesterday.* | *The documents will be **turned over to** the IRS.* **3 turn over** sth if a business turns over a particular amount of money, it makes that amount during a period of time ➔ TURNOVER

turn to *phr. v.* **1 turn to** sb/sth to try to get help, advice, or sympathy from someone: *Biotechnology firms turned to Wall Street for financing.* **2 turn to** sth to go to a particular page in a book, magazine, etc.: *Turn to page 45.* **3 turn to** sth to

T

begin thinking about or doing something new: *Bateman turned to politics after law school.* **4 turn** (sth) **to** sth to become different in some way, or to make something do this: *The land is turning to desert.*

turn up *phr. v.* **1 turn** sth ⇔ **up** to make a machine such as a radio, OVEN, etc. produce more sound, heat, etc.: *Turn up the radio a little.* **2** to be found, especially by chance, after being searched for: *The keys turned up in the silverware drawer.* **3 turn** sth ⇔ **up** to find something by searching for it thoroughly: *An inspection of the brakes turned up no defects.* **4** to arrive: *Danny turned up late as usual.* **5** if an opportunity or situation turns up, it happens, especially when you are not expecting it: *Don't worry, a job will turn up soon.*

turn² *n.*

1 CHANCE TO DO STH [C] the time when it is your chance, duty, or right to do something that a group of people are doing, one after another: *Whose* ***turn*** *is it* ***to*** *set the table?* | ***It's*** *your* ***turn****, Bob.*

2 take turns if a group of people take turns doing something, one person does it, then another person does it, etc.: *We took turns driving.* | *Take turns on the swing!*

3 in turn a) one after another: *He spoke to each of the students in turn.* **b)** as a result of something: *Interest rates were cut, and in turn, share prices rose.*

4 CHANGE DIRECTION [C] a change in the direction you are moving in: ***Make a left/right turn*** *at the stop sign.*

5 TWO ROADS JOIN [C] a place where a road joins another road: *I think we missed our turn.* | ***Take*** *the second* ***turn*** *on the left.*

6 CHANGE IN EVENTS [C] a sudden or unexpected change that makes a situation develop in a different way: *Her health* ***took a turn for the worse/better****.* | *Monday's* ***turn of events*** *was an embarrassment for the administration.*

7 MOVE STH [C] the act of turning something: *Give the wheel another turn.*

8 the turn of the century the beginning of a century

9 do sb a good turn to help someone

turn·a·round /ˈtɚnəˌraʊnd/ *n.* [singular] **1** an important and complete change from a bad situation to a good one: *Brock has been key to the team's turnaround.* **2** the time it takes to receive something, deal with it, and send it back: *the* ***turnaround time*** *on maintenance requests*

turn·coat /ˈtɚnkoʊt/ *n.* [C] someone who stops supporting a political party or group and joins the opposite group

ˈturning point *n.* [C] the time when an important change starts to happen: *The win was a* ***turning point in*** *his athletic career.*

tur·nip /ˈtɚnɪp/ *n.* [C,U] a large round pale yellow or white root, cooked and eaten as a vegetable

turn·off, **turn-off** /ˈtɚnɔf/ *n.* [C] **1** a smaller road that leads off a main road: *Take the Ramsey Canyon turnoff.* **2** something that makes you dislike or lose interest in something, usually sex

turn·out /ˈtɚnaʊt/ *n.* [singular] the number of people who go to an event such as a party, meeting, or election: *Voter turnout was 93%.*

turn·o·ver /ˈtɚnˌoʊvɚ/ *n.* **1** [singular] the amount of money a business earns in a particular period: *an annual turnover of $35 million* **2** [U] the rate at which people leave an organization and are replaced by others: *The company has a high rate of turnover.* **3** [C] a small fruit PIE: *apple turnovers*

turn·pike /ˈtɚnpaɪk/ *n.* [C] a main road that you have to pay a TOLL to use

> **THESAURUS**
>
> **highway**, **freeway**, **expressway**, **toll road**
> ➔ see Thesaurus box at ROAD

ˈturn ˌsignal *n.* [C] one of the lights on a vehicle that flash to show which way the vehicle is turning ➔ see picture on page A12

turn·stile /ˈtɚnstaɪl/ *n.* [C] a gate that spins around and only lets one person through at a time

turn·ta·ble /ˈtɚnˌteɪbəl/ *n.* [C] a piece of equipment used for playing RECORDS

tur·pen·tine /ˈtɚpənˌtaɪn/ *n.* [U] a strong-smelling oil used for removing paint

tur·quoise /ˈtɚkwɔɪz, -kɔɪz/ *n.* [U] a bright blue-green color —**turquoise** *adj.*

tur·ret /ˈtɚɪt, ˈtʌrɪt/ *n.* [C] a small tower on a large building, especially a CASTLE

tur·tle /ˈtɚt̬l/ *n.* [C] a REPTILE (=type of animal) that has four legs and a soft body covered with a hard shell

tur·tle·neck /ˈtɚt̬lˌnɛk/ *n.* [C] a type of shirt or SWEATER with a high, close-fitting collar that covers most of your neck

tush /tʊʃ/ *n.* [C] *informal* the part of your body that you sit on

tusk /tʌsk/ *n.* [C] one of the two very long teeth that stick out of an animal's mouth, for example an ELEPHANT's ➔ see picture on page A2

tus·sle /ˈtʌsəl/ *n.* [C] a struggle or fight —**tussle** *v.* [I]

tu·tor /ˈtut̬ɚ/ *n.* [C] someone who is paid to teach only one or a few students, especially students who are having difficulty with a subject: *my French tutor* —**tutor** *v.* [T] *He's tutoring me in math.*

tu·to·ri·al /tuˈtɔriəl/ *adj.* relating to a TUTOR or the teaching that s/he does

tux·e·do /tʌkˈsidoʊ/ **also tux** /tʌks/ *n.* [C] a man's suit that is usually black, worn on formal occasions

TV *n.* [C,U] television: *What's* ***on TV****?* | *The kids*

were **watching TV**. | Sue just bought a new TV. | a good **TV show/program/series**

ˌTV ˈdinner *n.* [C] a frozen prepared meal you can buy from the store, that you heat up and eat at home

ˈTV set *n.* [C] a television

twang /twæŋ/ *n.* [C usually singular] **1** a quality in the way someone speaks, when the sound comes through the nose as well as the mouth **2** a short RINGing sound like the one made by pulling a tight string and quickly letting it go —**twang** *v.* [I,T]

twas /twʌz/ *literary* it was – used in past times

tweak /twik/ *v.* [T] **1** to make small changes to something in order to improve it: *Congress has tweaked the tax system again.* **2** to quickly pull or twist something: *Grandpa tweaked my nose.*

tweed /twid/ *n.* [U] a rough wool cloth used especially for making JACKETS

tweet /twit/ *v.* [I] to make a quick high sound like a small bird —**tweet** *n.* [C]

tweez·ers /ˈtwizɚz/ *n.* [plural] a small tool made from two thin pieces of metal joined at one end, used in order to pull or move very small objects: *a **pair of tweezers***

twelfth /twɛlfθ/ *number* **1** 12th **2** one of twelve equal parts of something

twelve /twɛlv/ *number* **1** 12 **2** twelve O'CLOCK: *I'm going to lunch at twelve.* **3** twelve years old: *He's twelve.*

twen·ty¹ /ˈtwɛnti/ *number* **1** 20 **2** twenty years old: *She's almost twenty.* **3 the twenties a)** the years between 1920 and 1929 **b)** the numbers between 20 and 29, especially when used for measuring temperature **4 sb's twenties** the time when someone is 20 to 29 years old: *a woman in her **early/late twenties*** —**twentieth** /ˈtwɛntiɪθ/ *number*

twenty² *n.* [C] a piece of paper money worth $20

ˌtwenty-four/ˈseven usually written as **24/7** *adv. informal* if something happens twenty-four/seven, it happens all day, every day

ˌtwenty-ˈone *n.* [U] ➔ BLACKJACK

twerp /twɚp/ *n.* [C] *spoken* a stupid or annoying person

twice /twaɪs/ *adv.* two times: *I've seen that movie twice.* | *an island twice the size of Massachusetts* | *He makes **twice as** much money as I do.* ➔ see Thesaurus box at TWO

twid·dle /ˈtwɪdl/ *v.* [T] to move your fingers around, or to turn something with them many times, usually because you are bored

twig /twɪg/ *n.* [C] a very thin branch that grows on a larger branch of a tree

twi·light /ˈtwaɪlaɪt/ *n.* [U] the time between day and night when the sky starts to become dark, or the pale light at this time

twins

identical twins

twin¹ /twɪn/ *n.* [C] one of two children who are born at the same time to the same mother: *Jenny and Julie are **identical twins*** (=twins who look exactly the same). | *I have a twin brother.*

twin² *adj.* **1** like something else and considered with it as a pair: *the jet's twin engines* **2** used in order to describe two things that happen at the same time and are related to each other: *the twin problems of poverty and unemployment*

ˌtwin ˈbed *n.* [C] a bed for one person

twine¹ /twaɪn/ *n.* [U] thick strong string

twine² *v.* [I,T] to twist something, or to twist around something: *Morning glories had **twined around** the fence.*

twinge /twɪndʒ/ *n.* [C] **1** a sudden pain **2** a sudden slight feeling of guilt, etc.: *He felt **a twinge of guilt** for not calling.*

twin·kle /ˈtwɪŋkəl/ *v.* [I] **1** if a star or light twinkles, it shines in the dark with an unsteady light

THESAURUS

shine, flash, flicker, glow, sparkle, shimmer
➔ see Thesaurus box at SHINE¹

2 if someone's eyes twinkle, s/he has a happy expression: *Her eyes **twinkled with** amusement.* —**twinkle** *n.* [C usually singular]

twirl /twɚl/ *v.* [I,T] to continue turning around quickly, or to make something do this: *dancers twirling on stage* —**twirl** *n.* [C]

twist¹ /twɪst/ *v.* **1** [I,T] to bend, turn, or wind something, such as wire, hair, or cloth, especially several times: *Twist the ends together.* | *The sheets were **twisted** tightly **around** him.* | ***Twist off** the bottle cap* (=remove it by twisting).

THESAURUS

turn, spin, go around, revolve, rotate
➔ see Thesaurus box at TURN¹

2 [I,T] to turn a part of your body around or change your position by turning: *He **twisted around** to look at me.* | *I **twisted my ankle*** (=hurt it by turning it in the wrong direction) *playing soccer.* **3** [T] to change the true or intended meaning of someone's statement: *He accused her of twisting his words for political reasons.*

THESAURUS

change, **alter**, **distort**, **misrepresent**
→ see Thesaurus box at CHANGE[1]

4 [I] if a road, river, etc. twists, it has a lot of curves in it **5 twist sb's arm** *informal* to persuade someone to do something that s/he does not want to do

twist² *n.* [C] **1** an unexpected change in a story or situation: *The lemon grass gives a new **twist on/to** a classic dish.* **2** something that is twisted into a shape: *pasta twists* **3** a bend in a road, river, etc.

twist·ed /ˈtwɪstɪd/ *adj.* **1** bent in many directions or turned many times: *twisted metal* → see picture at BENT²

THESAURUS

bent, **curved**, **warped**, **crooked**, **wavy**
→ see Thesaurus box at BENT²

2 strange and slightly cruel: *a twisted joke*

twist·er /ˈtwɪstɚ/ *n.* [C] *informal* → TORNADO

twit /twɪt/ *n.* [C] *spoken* a stupid or silly person

twitch /twɪtʃ/ *v.* [I] if a part of your body twitches, it makes a sudden small uncontrolled movement: *A muscle near his mouth twitched.* —**twitch** *n.* [C]

twit·ter /ˈtwɪt̬ɚ/ *v.* [I] if a bird twitters, it makes a lot of short high sounds —**twitter** *n.* [singular]

T

two /tu/ *number* **1** 2 [➥ **second**]

THESAURUS

a pair (of sth) – two things of the same type that you use together: *a pair of shoes*
a couple (of sth) – two things of the same type: *a couple of stamps*
a couple – two people who are married or have a romantic relationship: *a married couple*
twins – two children who were born on the same day to the same mother
double room/bed etc. – a room, bed, etc. for two people
twice – two times: *I phoned her twice yesterday.*
for two – for two people: *A table for two, please.*

2 two o'clock: *The game begins **at two**.* **3** two years old: *My daughter is two.*

ˈtwo-bit *adj. slang* not very good or important: *a two-bit actor*

ˌtwo-by-ˈfour *n.* [C] a long piece of wood that is two inches thick and four inches wide

ˌtwo-diˈmensional *adj.* flat: *a two-dimensional drawing*

ˌtwo-ˈfaced *adj. informal disapproving* changing what you say according to who you are talking to, in a way that is not honest or sincere

two·fold /ˈtufoʊld/ *adj.* two times as much or as many of something: *a twofold increase in cases of TB* —**twofold** *adv.*

ˈtwo-piece *adj.* a two-piece suit has a coat and pants that match

two·some /ˈtusəm/ *n.* [C] a group of two people

ˈtwo-time *v.* [T] *informal* to have a secret relationship with someone who is not your regular girlfriend, husband, etc.

ˈtwo-tone *adj.* having two different colors

ˌtwo-ˈway *adj.* **1** moving or allowing movement in both directions: *two-way traffic* **2** a two-way radio sends and receives messages **3** involving two people, groups, countries, etc., in a way so that each person, etc. is doing something with the other: *two-way trade*

TX the written abbreviation of **Texas**

ty·coon /taɪˈkun/ *n.* [C] someone who is very successful in business and has a lot of money: *an oil tycoon*

ty·ing /ˈtaɪ-ɪŋ/ *v.* the present participle of TIE

tyke /taɪk/ *n.* [C] *informal* a small child

type¹ /taɪp/ *n.* **1** [C] a group of people or things that have similar features or qualities, and that are different from other people or things: *different **types of** people* | *What's your blood type?* | *Romantic novels **of this type** sell well.*

THESAURUS

kind: *What kind of fish is this?*
sort: *They carry all sorts of toys for indoor and outdoor play.*
category – a group of people or things that are all of the same type: *The novels are divided into three categories: romances, mysteries, and science fiction.*
brand – a type of produce made by a particular company: *several different brands of soap*
make – a type of product made by a particular company: *"What make of car do you drive?" "A Ford."*
model – one particular type or design of a vehicle, machine, weapon, etc.: *The new models come out in September.*
genre – a type of art, music, literature, etc. that has a particular style or feature: *He has written novels in several genres, most notably science fiction.*

2 [C] someone with particular qualities, interests, appearance, etc.: *the athletic type* **3 not be sb's type** *informal* to not be the kind of person that someone is attracted to: *Alex is OK – but he's not really my type.* **4** [U] printed letters: *italic type*

type² *v.* [I,T] to write something using a computer or TYPEWRITER

type·cast /ˈtaɪpkæst/ *v.* past tense and past participle **typecast** [T] to always give an actor the same type of character to play: *He does not want to **be typecast as** a bad guy.*

type·face /ˈtaɪpfeɪs/ *n.* [C] a group of letters, numbers, etc. of the same style and size, used in printing

type·writ·er /ˈtaɪpˌraɪt̬ɚ/ *n.* [C] a machine that

prints letters, numbers, etc. onto paper [➡ **printer**]

type·writ·ten /ˈtaɪpˌrɪtˀn/ *adj.* written using a TYPEWRITER: *a typewritten manuscript*

ty·phoid /ˈtaɪfɔɪd/ **also ˌtyphoid ˈfever** *n.* [U] a serious infectious disease that is caused by BACTERIA in food or water

ty·phoon /taɪˈfun/ *n.* [C] a very strong tropical storm

> **THESAURUS**
> **storm, hurricane, tornado**
> ➔ see Thesaurus box at WIND[1]

ty·phus /ˈtaɪfəs/ *n.* [U] a serious infectious disease that is caused by the bite of an insect

typ·i·cal /ˈtɪpɪkəl/ *adj.* **1** having the usual features or qualities of a particular thing, person, or group: *the typical American diet* | *At age 2, the typical child talks in two-word sentences.* | *Cool weather is* ***typical of*** *early April.* **2 (that's) typical!** *spoken* said when you are annoyed that something bad has happened again: *The car won't start – typical!*

typ·i·cally /ˈtɪpɪkli/ *adv.* **1** in the way that something usually happens: *Summer classes typically last six weeks.* **2** in the way that a person or group usually behaves, or that shows the usual features of something: *The female is typically smaller than the male.*

typ·i·fy /ˈtɪpəˌfaɪ/ *v.* past tense and past participle **typified**, third person singular **typifies** [T] to be a typical example or feature of something: *a dark painting that typifies her work*

typ·ing /ˈtaɪpɪŋ/ *n.* [U] the activity of writing using a TYPEWRITER or KEYBOARD

typ·ist /ˈtaɪpɪst/ *n.* [C] someone who uses a TYPEWRITER or KEYBOARD

ty·po /ˈtaɪpoʊ/ *n.* [C] *informal* a small mistake in the way something has been TYPEd or printed

ty·ran·ni·cal /tɪˈrænɪkəl/ *adj.* behaving in an unfair or cruel way toward someone you have power over: *a brutal and tyrannical government* —**tyrannize** /ˈtɪrəˌnaɪz/ *v.* [T]

tyr·an·ny /ˈtɪrəni/ *n.* **1** [U] strict, unfair, and often cruel control over someone: *her husband's abusive tyranny* **2** [C,U] government by a cruel ruler who has complete power: *the country's decades of tyranny*

ty·rant /ˈtaɪrənt/ *n.* [C] someone, especially a ruler, who uses his/her power in an unfair or cruel way

tzar /zɑr, tsɑr/ *n.* [C] ➔ CZAR

U, u

U, u /yu/ the twenty-first letter of the English alphabet

u·biq·ui·tous /yuˈbɪkwət̬əs/ *adj. formal* seeming to be everywhere: *New York's ubiquitous yellow cabs* —**ubiquity** *n.* [U]

ud·der /ˈʌdɚ/ *n.* [C] the part of a cow, female goat, etc. that produces milk

UFO *n.* [C] **Unidentified Flying Object** a strange moving object in the sky that some people believe is a SPACESHIP from another world

ugh /ʌg, ʌk, ʌh/ *interjection* used in order to show strong dislike: *Ugh! That tastes terrible!*

ug·ly /ˈʌgli/ *adj.* comparative **uglier**, superlative **ugliest** **1** very unattractive, and not nice to look at: *an ugly building* | *She's not pretty, but she's not ugly either.* **2** very unpleasant or violent in a way that makes you feel frightened: *The game* ***turned ugly*** *as fans threw coins at the players.* | *an* ***ugly scene*** *at the bus stop* —**ugliness** *n.* [U]

uh /ʌ/ *interjection* said when you are deciding what to say next: *I, uh, I'm sorry I'm late.*

UHF *n.* [U] **ultra-high frequency** a range of radio WAVES that produces very good sound quality

uh huh /nˈhn, mˈhm, əˈhʌ/ *interjection informal* used in order to say yes or to show that you understand something: *"Is this the one you want?" "Uh huh."*

uh oh /ˈˀʌ ˀoʊ/ *interjection informal* said when you have made a mistake or have realized that something bad has happened: *Uh oh, I forgot my keys.*

uh uh /ˈˀʌn ˀʌn, ˈˀmˀm/ *interjection informal* used in order to say no: *"Did Ann call?" "Uh uh."*

ul·cer /ˈʌlsɚ/ *n.* [C] a sore area on your skin or inside your body: *a stomach ulcer*

ul·te·ri·or /ʌlˈtɪriɚ/ *adj.* **ulterior motive** a reason for doing something that you hide in order to get an advantage for yourself: *He's just being nice. I don't think he* ***has any ulterior motives***.

ul·ti·mate[1] /ˈʌltəmɪt/ *adj.* [only before noun] **1** an ultimate purpose, aim, reason, etc. is the final and most important one: *Her* ***ultimate goal*** *is a career in politics.* **2** better, bigger, worse, etc. than all other people or things of the same kind: *A Rolls Royce is the ultimate symbol of wealth.* **3** the ultimate result of a long process is what happens at the end of it: *the ultimate failure of the project*

ultimate[2] *n.* **the ultimate in sth** the best or most modern example of something: *The Orient Express is the ultimate in rail travel.*

ul·ti·mate·ly /ˈʌltəmɪtli/ *adv.* [sentence adverb] after everything else has been done or considered: *Ultimately it's your decision.* | *Their efforts ultimately resulted in his release from prison.*

U

ul·ti·ma·tum /ˌʌltəˈmeɪṭəm/ *n.* [C] a statement saying that if someone does not do what you want, s/he will be punished: *She finally* ***gave him an ultimatum****: either stop drinking or move out.*

ul·tra·son·ic /ˌʌltrəˈsɑnɪk◂/ *adj. technical* ultrasonic sounds are too high for humans to hear

ul·tra·sound /ˈʌltrəˌsaʊnd/ *n.* [C,U] a medical process that uses sound waves to produce images of something inside of your body

ul·tra·vi·o·let /ˌʌltrəˈvaɪəlɪt◂/ *adj.* ultraviolet light cannot be seen but makes your skin darker when you are in the sun

um /m, əm/ *interjection* said when you are deciding what to say next: *Um, yeah, I guess so.*

um·bil·i·cal cord /ʌmˈbɪlɪkəl ˌkɔrd/ *n.* [C] a tube that joins a baby that has not been born yet to its mother

um·brage /ˈʌmbrɪdʒ/ *n.* **take umbrage (at sth)** *formal* to be offended by something that someone has done or said

um·brel·la /ʌmˈbrɛlə/ *n.* [C] an object that you hold above your head to protect yourself from the rain: *He stood there under his umbrella, watching the rain.*

umbrella

ump /ʌmp/ *n. informal* [C] UMPIRE

um·pire /ˈʌmpaɪə/ *n.* [C] the person who makes sure that the players obey the rules in sports such as baseball and tennis —**umpire** *v.* [I,T]

U

THESAURUS

Umpire and **referee** mean the same but are used for different sports.
Use **umpire** when you are talking about baseball or tennis.
Use **referee** when you are talking about football, soccer, ice hockey, basketball, boxing, wrestling, or volleyball.

ump·teenth /ˈʌmptinθ, ˌʌmˈtinθ/ *quantifier informal disapproving* if something happens for the umpteenth time, it happens too many times: *They're showing "The Wizard of Oz"* ***for the umpteenth time****.* —**umpteen** *quantifier*

UN *n.* [U] **the United Nations** an international organization that tries to find peaceful solutions to world problems

un·a·bashed /ˌʌnəˈbæʃt◂/ *adj.* not shy or embarrassed about something: *the child's unabashed curiosity*

un·a·bat·ed /ˌʌnəˈbeɪṭɪd/ *adj.* continuing without becoming weaker or less violent: *The storm* ***continued unabated****.*

un·a·ble /ʌnˈeɪbəl/ *adj.* not able to do something [➡ **inability**]: *She was* ***unable to*** *sleep.* | *I'm sorry; I'm unable to help you.*

un·a·bridged /ˌʌnəˈbrɪdʒd◂/ *adj.* a piece of writing, speech, etc. that is unabridged has not been made shorter

un·ac·cept·a·ble /ˌʌnəkˈsɛptəbəl/ *adj.* something that is unacceptable is wrong or bad and should not be allowed to continue: *Nancy's behavior is unacceptable.* —**unacceptably** *adv.*

un·ac·count·a·ble /ˌʌnəˈkaʊnṭəbəl/ *adj.* **1** not having to explain your actions or decisions to anyone else **2** very surprising and difficult to explain: *a product that flopped for unaccountable reasons* —**unaccountably** *adv.*

un·ac·cus·tomed /ˌʌnəˈkʌstəmd◂/ *adj. formal* **1 unaccustomed to (doing) sth** not used to something: *He was unaccustomed to dealing with children.* **2** [only before noun] not usual, typical, or familiar: *this winter's unaccustomed warmth*

un·a·dul·ter·at·ed /ˌʌnəˈdʌltəˌreɪṭɪd/ *adj.* complete or pure: *pure unadulterated pleasure*

un·af·fect·ed /ˌʌnəˈfɛktɪd/ *adj.* not changed or influenced by something: *Parts of the city remained* ***unaffected by*** *the fire.*

un·aid·ed /ʌnˈeɪdɪd/ *adj.* without help

un-A'merican *adj.* not supporting or loyal to American CUSTOMS, ideas, etc.

u·nan·i·mous /yuˈnænəməs/ *adj.* a unanimous decision, vote, etc. is one on which everyone agrees —**unanimously** *adv.* —**unanimity** /ˌyunæˈnɪməṭi/ *n.* [U]

un·an·nounced /ˌʌnəˈnaʊnst◂/ *adj.* happening without anyone knowing about it or expecting it: *Several people arrived unannounced.*

un·an·swered /ˌʌnˈænsəd/ *adj.* an unanswered telephone call, letter, question, etc. has not been replied to

un·ap·peal·ing /ˌʌnəˈpilɪŋ◂/ *adj.* not pleasant or attractive: *an unappealing brown color*

un·armed /ˌʌnˈɑrmd◂/ *adj.* not carrying any weapons: *An officer shot an unarmed man.*

un·as·sum·ing /ˌʌnəˈsumɪŋ◂/ *adj.* quiet and showing no desire for attention [= **modest**]

un·at·tached /ˌʌnəˈtætʃt◂/ *adj.* not involved in a romantic relationship

un·at·tend·ed /ˌʌnəˈtɛndɪd◂/ *adj.* left alone without anyone in charge: *Do not* ***leave*** *your children* ***unattended****.*

un·at·trac·tive /ˌʌnəˈtræktɪv◂/ *adj.* **1** not physically attractive or beautiful **2** not good or desirable: *two unattractive options*

un·au·thor·ized /ʌnˈɔθəˌraɪzd/ *adj.* done without official approval or permission: *an unauthorized biography*

un·a·vail·a·ble /ˌʌnəˈveɪləbəl/ *adj.* **1** not able to be obtained: *an album previously unavailable on CD* **2** not able or willing to meet with someone: *Mr. Foster is* ***unavailable for comment*** (=not able or willing to speak to reporters).

un·a·void·a·ble /ˌʌnəˈvɔɪdəbəl/ *adj.* impossible to prevent: *an unavoidable delay*

un·a·ware /ˌʌnəˈwɛr/ *adj.* not noticing or realizing what is happening: *He was **unaware of** his legal rights.*

un·a·wares /ˌʌnəˈwɛrz/ *adv.* **catch/take sb unawares** if something catches you unawares, it happens when you are not prepared for it: *Events in the Middle East caught the CIA unawares.*

un·bal·anced /ʌnˈbælənst/ *adj.* **1** slightly crazy: *mentally unbalanced* **2** an unbalanced report, argument, etc. is unfair because it emphasizes one opinion too much

un·bear·a·ble /ʌnˈbɛrəbəl/ *adj.* too bad, painful, or annoying for you to deal with: *Her pain had become unbearable.* —**unbearably** *adv.*

un·beat·a·ble /ʌnˈbit̬əbəl/ *adj.* something that is unbeatable is the best of its kind: *unbeatable prices*

un·beat·en /ʌnˈbitˀn/ *adj.* a team, player, etc. that is unbeaten has not been defeated

un·be·liev·a·ble /ˌʌnbɪˈlivəbəl/ *adj.* **1** used to emphasize how good, bad, surprising, etc. something is: *The sound quality of this stereo is unbelievable.* | *an unbelievable amount of money* **2** very difficult to believe and probably not true: *Yvonne's excuse was totally unbelievable.* —**unbelievably** *adv.*

un·bi·ased /ʌnˈbaɪəst/ *adj.* unbiased information, opinions, advice, etc. is fair because the person giving it is not influenced by their own or other people's opinions [= **impartial**]: *We aim to provide a service that is balanced and unbiased.* | *an unbiased observer*

un·born /ˌʌnˈbɔrn◂/ *adj.* [only before noun] not yet born: *an unborn child*

un·bound·ed /ˌʌnˈbaʊndɪd/ *adj. formal* very great and seeming to have no limit: *unbounded optimism*

un·bri·dled /ˌʌnˈbraɪdld/ *adj.* not controlled and too extreme: *unbridled anger*

un·but·ton /ʌnˈbʌtˀn/ *v.* [T] to undo the buttons on a piece of clothing

un·called-for /ʌnˈkɔld ˌfɔr/ *adj.* behavior or remarks that are uncalled-for are insulting, unfair, or inappropriate

un·can·ny /ʌnˈkæni/ *adj.* very strange and difficult to explain: *The team has an **uncanny ability** to win close games.* —**uncannily** *adv.*

un·cer·tain /ʌnˈsɚtˀn/ *adj.* **1** feeling doubt about something: *I'm **uncertain about** what to say to her.* | *She was **uncertain of** whether to confront him.* **2** not clear, definite, or decided: *His **future** with the company **is uncertain**.* **3 in no uncertain terms** if you say something in no uncertain terms, you say it in a clear way, without trying to be polite: *We were told in no uncertain terms not to come back.* —**uncertainty** *n.* [C,U] *uncertainty about the future* —**uncertainly** *adv.*

un·chang·ing /ʌnˈtʃeɪndʒɪŋ/ **also un·changed** /ʌnˈtʃeɪndʒd/ *adj.* always staying the same

un·chart·ed /ʌnˈtʃɑrt̬ɪd/ *adj.* **uncharted territory/waters** a situation or activity that you have never experienced or tried before

un·checked /ˌʌnˈtʃɛkt◂/ *adj.* if something bad goes unchecked, it is not controlled or stopped and continues or gets worse: ***Left unchecked**, the disease will spread.*

un·civ·i·lized /ʌnˈsɪvəˌlaɪzd/ *adj.* **1** behavior that is uncivilized is rude or socially unacceptable **2** *old-fashioned* societies that are uncivilized have a very simple way of life [= **primitive**]

un·cle /ˈʌŋkəl/ *n.* [C] the brother of your mother or father, or the husband of your AUNT: *I went to stay with my aunt and uncle for a few days.* | *Uncle Bill*

THESAURUS

relative, **parents**, **father**, **mother**, **brother**, **sister**, **grandparents**, **grandfather**, **grandmother**, **great-grandparents**, **aunt**, **nephew**, **niece**, **cousin**
→ see Thesaurus box at RELATIVE[1]

un·clean /ˌʌnˈklin◂/ *adj.* dirty

un·clear /ˌʌnˈklɪr◂/ *adj.* difficult to understand or know about: *The terms of the contract are very unclear.*

Uncle Sam /ˌʌŋkəl ˈsæm/ *n.* [singular] *informal* the U.S., or U.S. government, represented by the figure of a man with a white BEARD and tall hat

Uncle Tom /ˌʌŋkəl ˈtɑm/ *n.* [C] *disapproving* a black person who is too respectful to white people

un·com·fort·a·ble /ʌnˈkʌmftəbəl, ʌnˈkʌmfɚt̬əbəl/ *adj.* **1** not feeling physically comfortable, or not making you feel comfortable: *These shoes are uncomfortable.* **2** unable to relax because you are embarrassed: *I feel uncomfortable talking about sex.* | *an uncomfortable silence* —**uncomfortably** *adv.*

un·com·mon /ʌnˈkɑmən/ *adj.* rare or unusual: ***It is not uncommon for*** (=it is fairly common for) *employees **to** work sixty hours a week.* —**uncommonly** *adv.*

un·com·pro·mis·ing /ʌnˈkɑmprəˌmaɪzɪŋ/ *adj.* determined not to change your opinions or intentions: *an uncompromising supporter of gun control*

un·con·cerned /ˌʌnkənˈsɚnd◂/ *adj.* not worried about something, or not interested in it: *Americans cannot be **unconcerned about** the problem of the world's poor.*

un·con·di·tion·al /ˌʌnkənˈdɪʃənəl◂/ *adj.* not limited by or depending on any conditions: *We are demanding the unconditional release of the hostages.* —**unconditionally** *adv.*

un·con·firmed /ˌʌnkənˈfɚmd◂/ *adj.* not proved or supported by official information: *an **unconfirmed report/rumor etc.** of a nuclear accident*

un·con·scion·a·ble /ʌnˈkɑnʃənəbəl/ *adj. formal* morally wrong or unacceptable

un·con·scious[1] /ˌʌnˈkɑnʃəs◂/ *adj.* **1** unable to see, move, feel, etc. because you are not conscious: *The car's driver was **knocked unconscious**.* **2** an

U

unconscious feeling is one that you have without realizing it [= **subconscious**]: *unconscious feelings of guilt* **3 be unconscious of sth** to not realize the effect of something you have said or done: *Barb seemed unconscious of the attention her dress was attracting.* —**unconsciously** *adv.* —**unconsciousness** *n.* [U]

unconscious² *n.* **the/sb's unconscious** the part of your mind in which there are thoughts and feelings that you do not realize that you have [➡ **subconscious**]

un·con·sti·tu·tion·al /ˌʌnkɑnstəˈtuʃənəl/ *adj.* not allowed by the rules that govern a country or organization

un·con·trol·la·ble /ˌʌnkənˈtroʊləbəl/ *adj.* impossible to control or stop: *uncontrollable rage*

un·con·trolled /ˌʌnkənˈtroʊld/ *adj.* **1** uncontrolled emotions or behavior continue because no one stops or controls them **2** without rules or laws: *an uncontrolled free market*

un·con·ven·tion·al /ˌʌnkənˈvɛnʃənəl/ *adj.* very different from the normal way people behave, think, dress, or do things

un·cool /ˌʌnˈkul◂ / *adj. informal* not fashionable or acceptable – used especially by young people: *a hopelessly uncool 13-year-old*

un·co·op·era·tive /ˌʌnkoʊˈɑprət̬ɪv◂ / *adj.* not willing to work with or help someone

un·count·a·ble /ʌnˈkaʊntəbəl/ *adj.* **uncountable noun** *technical* in grammar, a noun that has no plural form, such as "water," "gold," or "furniture" [≠ **countable**]

un·couth /ʌnˈkuθ/ *adj.* behaving or speaking in a way that is rude and unacceptable

U

un·cov·er /ʌnˈkʌvɚ/ *v.* [T] **1** to discover something that has been kept secret or hidden: *Customs officials uncovered a plot to smuggle drugs into the country.* **2** to remove the cover from something

un·cut /ˌʌnˈkʌt◂ / *adj.* **1** a movie, book, etc. that is uncut has not been made shorter, for example by having violent or sexual scenes removed **2** an uncut jewel has not yet been cut into a particular shape

un·daunt·ed /ˌʌnˈdɔntɪd◂ , -ˈdɑn-/ *adj.* not afraid to continue doing something in spite of difficulties or danger: *Nelson was **undaunted by** the opposition to his plan.*

un·de·cid·ed /ˌʌndɪˈsaɪdɪd◂ / *adj.* not having made a decision about something: *A majority of voters were **undecided about** which candidate to choose.*

un·de·ni·a·ble /ˌʌndɪˈnaɪəbəl◂ / *adj.* definitely true or certain: *an undeniable fact* —**undeniably** *adv.*

un·der /ˈʌndɚ/ *prep., adv.* **1** below or at a lower level than something, or covered by it [≠ **over**]: *She's hiding under the blanket.* | *a dog sleeping under the bed* | *Lee wore a sweater under his jacket.* | *He pushed Lonnie's head under the water.* **2** less than a particular age, number, amount, or price [≠ **over**]: *a ticket for under $10* | *Children six and under can ride the bus for free.* | *I can't buy beer – I'm **under age*** (=not old enough). **3** controlled or governed by a particular leader, government, system, etc.: *a country under Marxist rule* **4 be under discussion/construction/attack etc.** to be in the process of being discussed, built, etc.: *The new library is still under construction.* **5 under way** happening or in the process of being done: *Construction is already under way on the new airport.* **6** affected by a particular influence, condition, or situation: *She performs well **under pressure**.* | *He was accused of driving while **under the influence of alcohol/drugs**.* **7** if you work under someone, that person is in charge of what you do at work: *She had a total staff of ten working under her.* **8** according to a particular law, agreement, etc.: *Under state law, we are entitled to inspect your accounts.* **9** used to say in which part of a book, list, or system you can find particular information: *The baby's records are filed under the mother's name.* ➔ **be under the impression (that)** at IMPRESSION

un·der·a·chiev·er /ˌʌndərəˈtʃivɚ/ *n.* [C] someone who does not do as well at school or at work as s/he could do if s/he worked harder —**underachieve** *v.* [I] —**underachievement** *n.* [U]

un·der·age /ˌʌndɚˈeɪdʒ◂ / *adj.* too young to legally buy alcohol, drive a car, etc.: *underage drinking*

un·der·charge /ˌʌndɚˈtʃɑrdʒ/ *v.* [I,T] to charge someone too little money for something [≠ **overcharge**]

un·der·class /ˈʌndɚˌklæs/ *n.* [singular] the lowest social class, consisting of people who are very poor

un·der·class·man /ˌʌndɚˌklæsmən/ *n.* plural **underclassmen** /-mən/ [C] a student in the first two years of HIGH SCHOOL or college [➡ **upperclassman**]

un·der·cov·er /ˌʌndɚˈkʌvɚ◂ / *adj.* undercover work is done secretly by the police in order to catch criminals or find out information: *an undercover agent/cop*

un·der·cur·rent /ˈʌndɚˌkɚənt, -ˌkʌr-/ *n.* [C] a feeling that someone does not express openly: *There was an **undercurrent of** suspicion about the newcomers.*

un·der·cut /ˌʌndɚˈkʌt, ˈʌndɚˌkʌt/ *v.* past tense and past participle **undercut**, present participle **undercutting** [T] **1** to make something weaker or less effective: *Such activity could undercut public confidence in Congress.* **2** to sell something more cheaply than someone else

un·der·dog /ˈʌndɚˌdɔg/ *n.* **the underdog** the person or team in a competition that is not expected to win

un·der·es·ti·mate /ˌʌndɚˈɛstəˌmeɪt/ *v.* **1** [I,T] to think that something is smaller, cheaper, easier, etc. than it really is [≠ **overestimate**]: *They underestimated the cost of the construction.*

2 [T] to think that someone is less skillful, intelligent, etc. than s/he really is

un·der·go /ˌʌndɚˈgoʊ/ *v.* past tense **underwent** /-ˈwɛnt/ past participle **undergone** /-ˈgɔn/ [T] if you undergo a change, a bad experience, etc., it happens to you or is done to you: *He'll have to undergo major heart surgery.*

un·der·grad·u·ate /ˌʌndɚˈgrædʒuɪt/ *n.* [C] a student in college, who is working for his/her BACHELOR'S DEGREE [➡ **graduate**, **postgraduate**] —**undergraduate** *adj.*

un·der·ground /ˌʌndɚˈgraʊnd◂/ *adj., adv.* **1** under the earth's surface: *an underground tunnel | creatures that live underground* **2** an underground political organization is secret and illegal **3 go underground** to start doing something secretly, or hide in a secret place: *The Ukrainian church went underground during the Communist era.*

un·der·growth /ˈʌndɚˌgroʊθ/ *n.* [U] bushes, small trees, etc. that grow around and under bigger trees

un·der·hand /ˈʌndɚˌhænd/ *adj., adv.* thrown with your arm under the level of your shoulder [≠ **overhand**]

un·der·hand·ed /ˈʌndɚˌhændɪd/ *adj.* dishonest and done secretly: *an underhanded deal*

un·der·line /ˈʌndɚˌlaɪn, ˌʌndɚˈlaɪn/ *v.* [T] **1** to draw a line under a word **2** to show that something is important: *The rise in crime underlines the need for more jobs.*

THESAURUS

emphasize, **stress**, **highlight**, **accentuate**, **underscore**
→ see Thesaurus box at EMPHASIZE

un·der·ly·ing /ˈʌndɚˌlaɪ-ɪŋ/ *adj.* **underlying reason/cause/problem etc.** the reason, cause, etc. that is most important but that is not easy to discover: *the underlying causes of her depression*

un·der·mine /ˈʌndɚˌmaɪn, ˌʌndɚˈmaɪn/ *v.* [T] to gradually make someone or something less strong or effective: *This could seriously undermine the peace process.*

un·der·neath /ˌʌndɚˈniθ/ *prep., adv.* directly below or under something [➡ **beneath**]: *We turned some rocks over to see what was underneath. | There's nice wood underneath all that paint.*

un·der·nour·ished /ˌʌndɚˈnɚɪʃt, -ˈnʌrɪʃt/ *adj.* not healthy because you have not eaten enough food or the right type of food

un·der·paid /ˌʌndɚˈpeɪd◂/ *adj.* earning less money than you deserve —**underpay** /ˌʌndɚˈpeɪ/ *v.* [I,T]

un·der·pants /ˈʌndɚˌpænts/ *n.* [plural] a short piece of underwear worn on the lower part of the body → see picture at CLOTHES

un·der·pass /ˈʌndɚˌpæs/ *n.* [C] a road or path that goes under another road or path

un·der·priv·i·leged /ˌʌndɚˈprɪvlɪdʒd◂/ *adj.* very poor and not having the advantages of most other people in society: *underprivileged children*

THESAURUS

poor, **needy**, **destitute**, **impoverished**, **broke**, **disadvantaged**, **deprived**
→ see Thesaurus box at POOR

un·der·rat·ed /ˌʌndɚˈreɪt̬ɪd◂/ *adj.* better than people think or say [≠ **overrated**]: *an underrated actor* —**underrate** *v.* [T]

un·der·score /ˈʌndɚˌskɔr/ *v.* [T] to emphasize that something is important: *The survey underscores the division between rich and poor in America.*

THESAURUS

emphasize, **stress**, **highlight**, **underline**, **accentuate**
→ see Thesaurus box at EMPHASIZE

un·der·shirt /ˈʌndɚˌʃɚt/ *n.* [C] a piece of underwear worn under a shirt

un·der·side /ˈʌndɚˌsaɪd/ *n.* **the underside of sth** the bottom side or surface of something

un·der·sized /ˌʌndɚˈsaɪzd◂/ *adj.* too small

un·der·staffed /ˌʌndɚˈstæft◂/ *adj.* not having enough workers, or having fewer workers than usual: *The lines are so long because we're understaffed right now.*

un·der·stand /ˌʌndɚˈstænd/ *v.* past tense and past participle **understood** /-ˈstʊd/ **1** [I,T] to know the meaning of what someone is saying to you, or the language that s/he speaks: *Do you understand Spanish? | I could barely understand what he was saying. | I'm not very good at German but I can* ***make*** *myself* ***understood*** (=make what I say clear to other people). ▶ Don't say "I am understanding." ◀ **2** [I,T] to know how someone feels and why s/he behaves the way s/he does, and to be sympathetic: *Believe me, John – I* ***understand how*** *you feel. | Just tell him what happened – I'm sure he'll understand.* **3** [I,T] to know how or why a situation, event, etc. happens, especially through learning or experience: *My father never understood baseball. | Do you* ***understand how*** *this works?* **4** [I,T] to believe that something you have heard or read is true: *I* ***understand (that)*** *you want to buy a car.*

un·der·stand·a·ble /ˌʌndɚˈstændəbəl/ *adj.* understandable behavior, reactions, etc. seem reasonable because of the situation you are in: *It's* ***understandable that*** *he's a little afraid. | Your anger toward him is* ***perfectly understandable****.*

un·der·stand·ing[1] /ˌʌndɚˈstændɪŋ/ *n.* **1** [singular, U] knowledge about something, based on learning and experience: *She* ***has a*** *basic* ***understanding of*** *computers.* **2** [singular, U] sympathy toward someone's character and behavior: *Harry thanked us for our understanding.* **3** [C] an informal private agreement about something: *I*

U

thought we had ***come to an understanding*** *about the price.* **4** [U] the ability to think and learn

understanding² *adj.* showing sympathy and pity for other people's problems: *an understanding boss*

un·der·state /ˌʌndɚˈsteɪt/ *v.* [T] to describe something in a way that makes it seem less important or serious than it really is [≠ **overstate**]: *The report understates the severity of the problem.*

un·der·stat·ed /ˌʌndɚˈsteɪt̬ɪd◂/ *adj. approving* simple in a way that is attractive: *the understated decoration of his office*

un·der·state·ment /ˈʌndɚˌsteɪtˀmənt/ *n.* [C] a statement that is not strong enough to express how good, impressive, bad, etc. something really is: *To say the movie was bad* ***is an understatement.***

un·der·stood /ˌʌndɚˈstʊd/ *v.* the past tense and past participle of UNDERSTAND

un·der·stud·y /ˈʌndɚˌstʌdi/ *n.* plural **understudies** [C] an actor who learns a part in a play so that s/he can act if the usual actor cannot perform

un·der·take /ˌʌndɚˈteɪk/ *v.* past tense **undertook** /-ˈtʊk/ past participle **undertaken** /-ˈteɪkən/ [T] *formal* **1** to start to do a piece of work, especially one that is long and difficult: *The country undertook a massive reform of its legal system.* **2 undertake to do sth** to promise or agree to do something

un·der·tak·er /ˈʌndɚˌteɪkɚ/ *n.* [C] *old-fashioned* someone whose job is to arrange funerals [= **funeral director**]

U

un·der·tak·ing /ˈʌndɚˌteɪkɪŋ/ *n.* [C usually singular] an important job, piece of work, etc. for which you are responsible: *Holding the Olympic Games is a massive undertaking.*

un·der·tone /ˈʌndɚˌtoʊn/ *n.* [C] a feeling or quality that exists but which is not easy to notice: *an* ***undertone of*** *sadness in her voice*

un·der·tow /ˈʌndɚˌtoʊ/ *n.* [C] a strong current under the ocean's surface that pulls water away from the shore

underwater

swimming underwater

un·der·wa·ter /ˌʌndɚˈwɔt̬ɚ◂, -ˈwɑ-/ *adj.* [only before noun] below the surface of the water, or able to be used there: *an underwater camera* —**underwater** *adv.*

un·der·wear /ˈʌndɚˌwɛr/ *n.* [U] clothes that you wear next to your body under your other clothes

un·der·weight /ˌʌndɚˈweɪt◂/ *adj.* weighing less than is expected or usual [≠ **overweight**]: *an underweight baby*

> **THESAURUS**
>
> **thin**, **slim**, **slender**, **skinny**, **lean**, **emaciated**
> → see Thesaurus box at THIN¹

un·der·world /ˈʌndɚˌwɚld/ *n.* [singular] the criminals in a particular place and the activities they are involved in

un·der·write /ˈʌndɚˌraɪt, ˌʌndɚˈraɪt/ *v.* past tense **underwrote** /-roʊt/ past participle **underwritten** /-rɪtˀn/ [T] *formal* to support an activity, business, etc. with money: *The project is underwritten by a National Science Foundation grant.*

un·de·sir·a·ble /ˌʌndɪˈzaɪrəbəl◂/ *adj. formal* bad, or not wanted because it may have a bad effect: *The drug can produce undesirable side effects.*

un·de·ter·mined /ˌʌndɪˈtɚmɪnd◂/ *adj.* not known, decided, or calculated: *The cause of death is undetermined.*

un·de·vel·oped /ˌʌndɪˈvɛləpt◂/ *adj.* undeveloped land has not been built on or used for a particular purpose

un·dis·closed /ˌʌndɪsˈkloʊzd◂/ *adj.* not known publicly: *an* ***undisclosed amount/sum*** *of money*

un·dis·guised /ˌʌndɪsˈgaɪzd◂/ *adj.* an undisguised feeling is clearly shown and not hidden: *undisguised hatred*

un·dis·put·ed /ˌʌndɪˈspyut̬ɪd◂/ *adj.* **undisputed leader/master/champion etc.** someone whom everyone agrees is the leader, etc.

un·dis·turbed /ˌʌndɪˈstɚbd◂/ *adj., adv.* not interrupted or moved: *They let her rest undisturbed.*

un·di·vid·ed /ˌʌndɪˈvaɪdɪd◂/ *adj.* complete: *Please give me your* ***undivided attention.***

un·do /ʌnˈdu/ *v.* past tense **undid** /-ˈdɪd/ past participle **undone** /-ˈdʌn/ third person singular **undoes** /-ˈdʌz/ [T] **1** to untie or open something that is tied or closed: *I can't get the clasp on my necklace undone.*

> **THESAURUS**
>
> **open**, **unlock**, **unscrew**, **unwrap**, **unfold**, **unfasten**
> → see Thesaurus box at OPEN²

2 to try to remove the bad effects of something: *The courts have tried to undo the legal abuses of the past.* **3** to change something back to the state or condition it was before improvements were made: *Changing the law will undo decades of progress.*

un·do·ing /ʌnˈduɪŋ/ *n.* **be sb's undoing** to

cause someone's failure, defeat, shame, etc.: *Borrowing too much money proved to be his undoing.*

un·done /ˌʌn'dʌn◂ / *adj.* **1** not tied or closed: *Your shirt button has **come undone**.* **2** not finished or completed: *Much of the work on the bridge has been **left undone**.*

un·doubt·ed·ly /ʌn'daʊt̬ɪdli/ *adv.* used in order to emphasize that something is definitely true: *He's undoubtedly one of the best guitar players of all time.*

un·dress /ʌn'drɛs/ *v.* [I,T] to take your clothes off, or take someone else's clothes off: *Yvonne undressed and got into bed.*

un·dressed /ʌn'drɛst/ *adj.* not wearing any clothes: *He started to **get undressed*** (=take his clothes off).

> **THESAURUS**
> **naked, nude, bare**
> → see Thesaurus box at NAKED

un·due /ˌʌn'du◂ / *adj. formal* more than is reasonable, appropriate, or necessary: *The tax creates an undue burden on farmers.*

un·du·ly /ʌn'duli/ *adv. formal* more than is normal or reasonable: *unduly harsh punishment*

un·dy·ing /ˌʌn'daɪ-ɪŋ◂ / *adj. literary* continuing for ever: *undying love*

un·earth /ʌn'ɚθ/ *v.* [T] **1** to find something that was buried in the ground: *Scientists have unearthed eight more skeletons at Pompeii.*

> **THESAURUS**
> **find, discover, trace, locate, track down, turn up**
> → see Thesaurus box at FIND[1]

2 to find out information or the truth about something

un·earth·ly /ʌn'ɚθli/ *adj.* very strange and unnatural: *an unearthly greenish light*

un·eas·y /ˌʌn'izi◂ / *adj.* worried and anxious because you think something bad might happen: *We **felt uneasy about** his decision.* —**unease** *n.* [U] —**uneasiness** *n.* [U] —**uneasily** *adv.*

> **THESAURUS**
> **worried, anxious, concerned, nervous, stressed (out)**
> → see Thesaurus box at WORRIED

un·ed·u·cat·ed /ʌn'ɛdʒəˌkeɪt̬ɪd/ *adj.* not having much education, or showing that someone is not well educated

un·em·ployed /ˌʌnɪm'plɔɪd◂ / *adj.* without a job: *an unemployed actor* | *I've been unemployed for six months.*

un·em·ploy·ment /ˌʌnɪm'plɔɪmənt/ *n.* [U] **1** the condition of not having a job, or the number of people who do not have a job: ***Unemployment** remains relatively **low/high**.* | *The **unemployment rate** is rising.* **2** money paid regularly by the government to people who have no job: *He's been **on unemployment** for three months.*

un·end·ing /ʌn'ɛndɪŋ/ *adj.* something, especially something bad, that is unending seems as if it will continue for ever: *an unending stream of people*

un·e·qual /ʌn'ikwəl/ *adj.* **1** unfairly treating different people or groups in different ways: *the unequal treatment of minorities* **2** not the same in size, amount, value, rank, etc.: *two rooms of unequal size*

un·e·quiv·o·cal /ˌʌnɪ'kwɪvəkəl/ *adj. formal* completely clear and definite with no doubts

un·er·ring /ʌn'ɛrɪŋ, ʌn'ɚɪŋ/ *adj.* always right: *Madsen's unerring judgment*

un·eth·i·cal /ʌn'ɛθɪkəl/ *adj.* considered to be morally wrong

un·e·ven /ʌn'ivən/ *adj.* **1** not flat, smooth, or level: *uneven ground* **2** not equal or balanced: *The racial mix of the school is uneven.* **3** good in some parts and bad in others: *a music album of uneven quality* —**unevenly** *adv.*

un·ex·cused /ˌʌnɪk'skuzd◂ / *adj.* **unexcused absence** an occasion when you are away from school or work without permission

un·ex·pect·ed /ˌʌnɪk'spɛktɪd◂ / *adj.* surprising because of not being expected: *the unexpected death of his father* —**unexpectedly** *adv.*

un·fail·ing /ʌn'feɪlɪŋ/ *adj.* always there, even in times of difficulty or trouble: *his unfailing kindness*

un·fair /ˌʌn'fɛr◂ / *adj.* not right or fair: *an unfair decision* | *The system is **unfair to** the poor.* —**unfairly** *adv.* —**unfairness** *n.* [U]

un·faith·ful /ʌn'feɪθfəl/ *adj.* someone who is unfaithful has sex with someone who is not his/her wife, husband, or usual partner: *Kurt had been **unfaithful to** his wife on several occasions.*

un·fa·mil·iar /ˌʌnfə'mɪlyɚ/ *adj.* not known to you: *an unfamiliar face* | *I am **unfamiliar with** his books.* —**unfamiliarity** /ˌʌnfəˌmɪl'yærət̬i/ *n.* [U]

un·fas·ten /ˌʌn'fæsən/ *v.* [T] UNDO: *Lewis unfastened his seat belt.*

> **THESAURUS**
> **open, unlock, unscrew, unwrap, unfold, undo**
> → see Thesaurus box at OPEN[2]

un·fa·vor·a·ble /ʌn'feɪvərəbəl/ *adj.* **1** showing that you do not like something: *an unfavorable review of the movie* **2** unfavorable conditions, events, etc. are not good: *an unfavorable weather report*

un·feel·ing /ʌn'filɪŋ/ *adj.* not showing sympathy for others: *How can she be so **cold and unfeeling**?*

un·fet·tered /ʌn'fɛt̬ɚd/ *adj.* not restricted in any way

un·fit /ʌn'fɪt/ *adj.* not good enough to do something or to be used for something: *That woman is **unfit to** raise a child!* | *land **unfit for** cultivation*

U

un·fold /ʌn'foʊld/ *v.* [I,T] **1** if a story, plan, etc. unfolds, it becomes clearer as you hear or learn more about it: *The case began to slowly unfold in court.* **2** to open something that was folded: *She unfolded the map.*

THESAURUS

open, unlock, unscrew, unwrap, unfasten, undo

➔ see Thesaurus box at OPEN[2]

un·fore·seen /ˌʌnfɔr'sin◂ , -fɚ-/ *adj.* an unforeseen situation is one that you did not expect to happen: *an unforeseen delay* | ***Due to unforeseen circumstances****, the play has been canceled.*

un·for·get·ta·ble /ˌʌnfɚ'gɛṭəbəl/ *adj.* something that is unforgettable is so beautiful, good, exciting, etc. that you remember it for a long time: *an unforgettable sight*

un·for·tu·nate /ʌn'fɔrtʃənɪt/ *adj.* **1** happening because of bad luck: *an* ***unfortunate accident*** **2** someone who is unfortunate has something bad happen to him/her: *When we entered the room, the teacher was yelling at some unfortunate student.* **3** an unfortunate situation, condition, quality, etc. is one that you wish was different: ***It's unfortunate (that)*** *so few people seem willing to help.*

un·for·tu·nate·ly /ʌn'fɔrtʃənɪtli/ *adv.* [sentence adverb] used when you are mentioning a fact that you wish were not true: *Unfortunately, it's too late for me to do anything about it.*

un·found·ed /ʌn'faʊndɪd/ *adj.* not based on facts or EVIDENCE [= **wrong**]: *The company insisted that our complaints were unfounded.*

U

un·friend·ly /ʌn'frɛndli/ *adj.* **1** not kind or friendly: *The neighbors seemed unfriendly.* **2** not helping or wanting a type of person or thing: *We have created cities that are* ***unfriendly to*** *pedestrians.* **3** an unfriendly government or nation is one that opposes yours

un·furl /ʌn'fɚl/ *v.* [T] to unroll and open a flag, sail, etc.

un·gain·ly /ʌn'geɪnli/ *adj.* awkward and not graceful: *an ungainly teenager*

un·grate·ful /ʌn'greɪtfəl/ *adj.* not thanking someone for something s/he has given to you or done for you

un·hap·py /ʌn'hæpi/ *adj.* **1** not happy: *an unhappy childhood* | *She had been unhappy for a long time.*

THESAURUS

sad, miserable, upset, depressed, down, low, homesick, gloomy, glum

➔ see Thesaurus box at SAD

2 feeling worried or annoyed because you do not like what is happening: *Americans are deeply* ***unhappy with*** *the state of the nation.* | *Dennis is* ***unhappy about*** *having to work on a Saturday.* —**unhappiness** *n.* [U] —**unhappily** *adv.*

un·health·y /ʌn'hɛlθi/ *adj.* **1** likely to make you sick: *unhealthy city air* **2** not physically healthy: *an unhealthy baby* **3** not normal or natural and likely to cause harm: *Any obsession is unhealthy.*

un·heard-of /ʌn'hɚd ʌv/ *adj.* so unusual that it has never happened or been known before: *The opera raised the price of its seats to an unheard-of $100 each!*

un·ho·ly /ʌn'hoʊli/ *adj.* **1 an unholy alliance** an agreement between two people or organizations who would not normally work together, usually for a bad purpose **2** very great and very bad: *We're in an* ***unholy mess****.*

un·hook /ʌn'hʊk/ *v.* [T] to unfasten or remove something from a hook

UNICEF /'yunəˌsɛf/ *n.* [U] **the United Nations Children's Fund** an organization that helps children who suffer from disease, HUNGER etc.

u·ni·corn /'yunəˌkɔrn/ *n.* [C] an imaginary animal like a white horse with a long straight horn on its head

un·i·den·ti·fied /ˌʌnaɪ'dɛntə'faɪd◂ , ˌʌnə-/ *adj.* an unidentified person or thing is one that you do not know the name of: *an unidentified body*

u·ni·fi·ca·tion /ˌyunəfə'keɪʃən/ *n.* [U] the act of combining two or more groups, countries, etc. to make a single group or country: *the* ***unification of*** *Germany*

u·ni·form[1] /'yunəˌfɔrm/ *n.* [C] **1** a particular type of clothing that the members of an organization wear to work: *a picture of me* ***wearing*** *my football* ***uniform*** **2 in uniform a)** wearing a uniform **b)** in the army, navy, etc. —**uniformed** *adj.*: *uniformed police officers*

uniform[2] *adj.* things that are uniform are all the same shape, size, etc.: *Grade A eggs must be of uniform size.* —**uniformly** *adv.* —**uniformity** /ˌyunə'fɔrməṭi/ *n.* [U]

u·ni·fy /'yunəˌfaɪ/ *v.* past tense and past participle **unified**, third person singular **unifies** [T] to combine the parts of a country, organization, etc. to make a single unit [➡ **unification**]: *Spain was unified in the 16th century.* —**unified** *adj.*

u·ni·lat·er·al /ˌyunə'læṭərəl◂ / *adj.* a unilateral action or decision is made by only one of the groups involved in a situation without the agreement of the others [➡ **bilateral**, **multilateral**]: *a unilateral ceasefire*

un·i·ma·gin·a·ble /ˌʌnɪ'mædʒənəbəl◂ / *adj.* not possible to imagine: *unimaginable wealth* —**unimaginably** *adv.*

un·i·ma·gin·a·tive /ˌʌnɪ'mædʒənəṭɪv◂ / *adj.* **1** lacking the ability to think of new or unusual ideas **2** ordinary and boring, and not using any new ideas: *unimaginative architecture*

un·im·por·tant /ˌʌnɪm'pɔrt̚nt◂ / *adj.* not important

un·im·pressed /ˌʌnɪm'prɛst/ *adj.* not thinking that someone or something is good, interesting, etc.: *Board members were **unimpressed with/by** the plan.*

un·im·pres·sive /ˌʌnɪmˈprɛsɪv◂/ *adj.* not as good, large, etc. as expected or necessary: *The school's test results were unimpressive.*

un·in·formed /ˌʌnɪnˈfɔrmd◂/ *adj.* not having enough knowledge or information: *He seemed **uninformed about** foreign policy.*

un·in·hab·it·ed /ˌʌnɪnˈhæbɪtɪd◂/ *adj.* an uninhabited place does not have anyone living there [= **deserted**]: *an **uninhabited island***

THESAURUS

empty, bare, deserted
→ see Thesaurus box at EMPTY[1]

un·in·hib·it·ed /ˌʌnɪnˈhɪbɪt̬ɪd◂/ *adj.* confident or relaxed enough to do or say what you want to

un·in·spired /ˌʌnɪnˈspaɪɚd◂/ *adj.* not showing any imagination, and so not interesting or exciting: *an uninspired performance*

un·in·sured /ˌʌnɪnˈʃʊrd◂/ *adj.* having no insurance: *uninsured drivers*

un·in·tel·li·gi·ble /ˌʌnɪnˈtɛlədʒəbəl/ *adj.* impossible to understand: *Most of what he said was unintelligible.*

un·in·ten·tion·al /ˌʌnɪnˈtɛnʃənəl◂/ *adj.* not done deliberately: *unintentional errors on his tax form* —**unintentionally** *adv.*

un·in·ter·est·ed /ʌnˈɪntrɪstɪd, -ˈɪntəˌrɛs-/ *adj.* not interested

USAGE

In spoken English, many people use **disinterested** to mean "not interested." However, many teachers think that this is not correct. If you want to say that someone is "not interested," use **uninterested**: *She seemed uninterested in how it works.*

un·in·ter·rupt·ed /ˌʌnɪntəˈrʌptɪd◂/ *adj.* continuous without stopping or being interrupted: *eight hours of uninterrupted sleep*

un·ion /ˈyunyən/ *n.* **1** [C] LABOR UNION: *the teachers' union | Are you going to **join** the **union**?*

THESAURUS

organization, institution, association, (political) party
→ see Thesaurus box at ORGANIZATION

2 [singular] a group of countries or states with the same central government: *the Soviet Union* **3** [singular, U] *formal* the act of joining two or more things together, or the state of being joined together: *the **union** of East Germany **with** West Germany* **4** [C,U] *formal* marriage

un·ion·ized /ˈyunyəˌnaɪzd/ *adj.* having formed a union, or belonging to one —**unionize** *v.* [I,T]

u·nique /yuˈnik/ *adj.* **1** *informal* unusually good and special: *a unique opportunity to study with an artist* **2** being the only one of its kind: *Every person is unique.* **3 unique to sb/sth** existing only in a particular place, person, or group, etc.: *The issues being discussed here are not unique to the U.S.* —**uniquely** *adv.*

u·ni·sex /ˈyunəˌsɛks/ *adj.* appropriate for both men and women: *a unisex jacket*

u·ni·son /ˈyunəsən/ *n.* **in unison** if a group of people do something in unison, they all do it together at the same time

u·nit /ˈyunɪt/ *n.* [C] **1** a person or thing that is one whole part of something larger: *The family is the smallest social unit. | an eight-unit apartment building* (=it has 8 apartments) **2** a group of people who work together as part of a larger group: *the emergency unit of the hospital* **3** an amount of something used as a standard of measurement: *The dollar is the basic **unit of** money in the U.S.* **4** one of the numbered parts into which a TEXTBOOK (=a book used in schools) is divided [➡ **chapter**] **5** a piece of furniture that can be attached to others of the same type: *a kitchen unit* **6** a piece of equipment that is part of a larger machine: *The cooling unit is broken.*

U·ni·tar·i·an /ˌyunəˈtɛriən/ *n.* [C] a member of a Christian group that does not believe in the Trinity —**Unitarian** *adj.*

u·nite /yuˈnaɪt/ *v.* [I,T] to join together as one group, or to make people join together in this way, especially in order to achieve something: *Congress **united behind** the President. | The deal would unite two of the country's oldest electronics firms.*

u·nit·ed /yuˈnaɪt̬ɪd/ *adj.* **1** involving or done by everyone: *a united effort to clean up the environment* **2** closely joined by sharing feelings, aims, etc.: *a united community*

Uˌnited ˈNations *n.* the UN

u·ni·ty /ˈyunət̬i/ *n.* [U] a state or situation in which people work together to achieve something that they all agree on: *The team suffers from a lack of unity.*

u·ni·ver·sal /ˌyunəˈvɚsəl◂/ *adj.* **1** involving everyone in the world or in a particular group: *universal voting rights | a universal health care program* **2** true or appropriate in every situation: *a universal truth* —**universally** *adv.*

u·ni·verse /ˈyunəˌvɚs/ *n.* **the universe** all of space, including all the stars and PLANETS

u·ni·ver·si·ty /ˌyunəˈvɚsət̬i/ *n.* plural **universities** [C] a school at the highest level, where you study for a DEGREE [➡ **college**]: *a graduate of Harvard University | He later **attended** the **University** of California.*

TOPIC

People who **go to university/college** to **study** a **subject** are called **students**. Students choose a **major** (=main subject to study) and sometimes a **minor** (=second subject to study). Students must also study subjects that are not related to their main subjects, in order to get a good

U

general education. During the four or five years that they go to university, students **go to/attend**, **lectures**, **classes**, and **seminars**. They are taught by **professors** or sometimes by **teaching assistants (TA's)**, who are **graduate students** in the subject they are teaching. Students must write **papers** and, in science subjects, do **laboratory** work, and they take **midterm** and **final exams**. Final exams take place at the end of each **semester** or **quarter** (=periods of time that the college year is divided into). Students earn **credits** for each class. Once a student has earned enough credits, s/he **graduates** and **gets a degree** (=a document that shows s/he has graduated).

un·just /ˌʌn'dʒʌst◂/ *adj.* not fair or reasonable: *unjust laws*

un·jus·ti·fied /ˌʌn'dʒʌstəˌfaɪd/ *adj.* done without a good reason: *an unjustified attack* —**unjustifiable** *adj.*

un·kempt /ˌʌn'kɛmpt◂/ *adj.* not neat: *Her hair was dirty and unkempt.*

un·kind /ˌʌn'kaɪnd◂/ *adj.* cruel or not nice: *an unkind remark*

THESAURUS

mean, **cruel**, **nasty**, **thoughtless**
➔ see Thesaurus box at MEAN[2]

un·know·ing·ly /ʌn'noʊɪŋli/ *adv.* without realizing what you are doing or what is happening: *Millions of people may have been unknowingly infected.*

U

un·known¹ /ˌʌn'noʊn◂/ *adj.* **1** not known about: *An unknown number of rebels are in hiding.* **2** not famous: *an unknown musician*

unknown² *n.* [C] someone who is not famous: *Early in her career, she was still an unknown.*

un·law·ful /ʌn'lɔfəl/ *adj.* not legal

un·lead·ed /ˌʌn'lɛdɪd◂/ *n.* [U] gas that does not contain any LEAD [➡ **regular**]

un·leash /ʌn'liʃ/ *v.* [T] to cause or make something start happening suddenly and with a strong effect: *The ceremony unleashed memories of the war.*

un·less /ən'lɛs, ʌn-/ *conjunction* used in order to say that something will happen or be true if another thing does not happen or is not true: *We can go in my car unless you want to walk.* | *He won't go to sleep unless you tell him a story.* ▶ Don't say "unless if." ◀

un·li·censed /ʌn'laɪsənst/ *adj.* without a LICENSE (=official document that gives you permission to do or have something): *unlicensed guns*

un·like /ˌʌn'laɪk◂/ *prep.* **1** completely different from another person or thing: *Unlike me, she's intelligent.* **2** not typical of someone: *It's unlike Judy to leave without telling us.*

un·like·ly /ʌn'laɪkli/ *adj.* not likely to happen: ***It's unlikely (that)*** *I'll be able to get an earlier flight.* | *The weather is* ***unlikely to*** *improve over the next few days.* —**unlikelihood** *n.* [U]

un·lim·it·ed /ʌn'lɪmɪt̬ɪd/ *adj.* without any limit: *a rental car with unlimited mileage*

un·list·ed /ˌʌn'lɪstɪd◂/ *adj.* not in the list of numbers in the telephone book: *an unlisted phone number*

un·load /ʌn'loʊd/ *v.* **1** [I,T] to remove goods from a vehicle or large container, or to have them removed: *I unloaded the dishwasher* | *The ship took a long time to unload.* **2** [T] *informal* to get rid of something by selling it quickly: *The warehouse is trying to unload a huge quantity of goods at discount prices.* **3** [I,T] to take film out of a camera or bullets out of a gun

un·lock /ʌn'lɑk/ *v.* [T] to undo the lock on a door, box, etc.

THESAURUS

open, **unscrew**, **unwrap**, **unfold**, **unfasten**, **undo**
➔ see Thesaurus box at OPEN[2]

un·luck·y /ˌʌn'lʌki◂/ *adj.* **1** having bad luck: *Chicago was* ***unlucky to*** *lose in the final minute of the game.* | *She's been* ***unlucky in love*** (=not able to find someone to love romantically). **2** happening as a result of bad luck: *It was* ***unlucky*** *for us* ***that*** *the bank closed just as we got there.* **3** believed to cause bad luck: *Some people think black cats are unlucky.*

un·manned /ˌʌn'mænd◂/ *adj.* an unmanned vehicle or building does not have anyone in it: *an unmanned spacecraft*

un·marked /ˌʌn'mɑrkt◂/ *adj.* something that is unmarked has no words or signs on it: *an unmarked police car*

un·mar·ried /ˌʌn'mærid◂/ *adj.* not married [**= single**]

un·mask /ʌn'mæsk/ *v.* [T] to make a truth that has been hidden become known: *He was unmasked as an enemy spy.*

un·mis·tak·a·ble /ˌʌnmɪ'steɪkəbəl◂/ *adj.* easy to recognize: *the unmistakable taste of garlic*

un·mit·i·gat·ed /ʌn'mɪt̬əˌgeɪt̬ɪd/ *adj.* [only before noun] used to emphasize how bad something is: *The night turned into an* ***unmitigated disaster***. | *He had the* ***unmitigated gall*** *to complain.*

un·moved /ˌʌn'muvd/ *adj.* feeling no pity, sympathy, or sadness: *The judge was unmoved by his excuses.*

un·named /ˌʌn'neɪmd◂/ *adj.* an unnamed person, place, or thing is one who is mentioned, especially by a newspaper, but whose name is not given: *The newspaper quoted an unnamed diplomatic source.*

un·nat·u·ral /ˌʌn'nætʃərəl/ *adj.* **1** different from normal, especially in a way that is strange or wrong: *It's unnatural for a child to spend so much time alone.* **2** seeming false, or not real or natural: *Julia's laugh seemed forced and unnatural.* **3** different from what is produced in nature: *an unnatural shade of red* **4** different from normal human behavior in a way that seems morally wrong: *unnatural sexual practices* —**unnaturally** *adv.*

un·nec·es·sar·y /ʌn'nɛsəˌsɛri/ *adj.* not needed, or more than is needed: *unnecessary risks* —**unnecessarily** *adv.*

un·nerve /ʌn'nɚv/ *v.* [T] to upset or frighten someone so that s/he loses his/her confidence or ability to think clearly: *Dave was completely unnerved by the argument with Terry.* —**unnerving** *adj.*

un·no·ticed /ʌn'noʊt̬ɪst/ *adj.* without being noticed: *She sat unnoticed at the back.*

un·ob·served /ˌʌnəb'zɚvd/ *adj., adv.* not seen, or without being seen: *Bret left the meeting unobserved.*

un·ob·tru·sive /ˌʌnəb'trusɪv◂/ *adj.* not easily noticed or not trying to be noticed: *an efficient unobtrusive waiter*

un·oc·cu·pied /ʌn'ɑkyəˌpaɪd/ *adj.* a seat, house, room, etc. that is unoccupied has no one in it

un·of·fi·cial /ˌʌnə'fɪʃəl◂/ *adj.* **1** done or produced without the approval of or permission from someone in authority: *According to unofficial results, Carey received 52 percent of the vote.* **2** not done as part of official duties: *The President made an unofficial visit to a children's hospital.* —**unofficially** *adv.*

un·or·tho·dox /ʌn'ɔrθəˌdɑks/ *adj.* different from what is usual or accepted by most people: *unorthodox behavior*

un·pack /ʌn'pæk/ *v.* [I,T] to take everything out of a box or SUITCASE: *I haven't had a chance to unpack yet.*

un·paid /ˌʌn'peɪd◂/ *adj.* **1** an unpaid bill or debt has not been paid: *unpaid taxes* **2** done without getting any money: *unpaid work* | ***unpaid leave/time off*** (=unpaid time away from work)

un·par·al·leled /ʌn'pærəˌlɛld/ *adj. formal* much bigger, better, or worse than anything else: *Those years were a time of unparalleled happiness in our lives.*

un·planned /ˌʌn'plænd◂/ *adj.* not planned or expected: *an unplanned pregnancy*

un·pleas·ant /ʌn'plɛzənt/ *adj.* **1** not pleasant or enjoyable [≠ **nice**]: *an unpleasant surprise* **2** not kind or friendly [≠ **nice**]: *He said some very unpleasant things.*

un·plug /ʌn'plʌg/ *v.* past tense and past participle **unplugged**, present participle **unplugging** [T] to disconnect a piece of electrical equipment by taking its PLUG out of a SOCKET

un·plugged /ʌn'plʌgd/ *adj.* if a group of musicians performs unplugged, they perform without electric instruments

un·pop·u·lar /ʌn'pɑpyəlɚ/ *adj.* not liked by most people: *an unpopular decision* | *The plans were* ***unpopular with*** *voters,*

un·prec·e·dent·ed /ʌn'prɛsəˌdɛntɪd/ *adj.* never having happened before, or never having happened so much: *The Steelers won an unprecedented four Super Bowls in six years.*

un·pre·dict·a·ble /ˌʌnprɪ'dɪktəbəl◂/ *adj.* changing so much that you do not know what to expect: *unpredictable weather*

un·pre·pared /ˌʌnprɪ'pɛrd◂/ *adj.* not ready to deal with something: *I was totally* ***unprepared for*** *that question.*

un·pre·pos·sess·ing /ˌʌnpripə'zɛsɪŋ/ *adj.* not special, attractive, or interesting, and not likely to be noticed: *an unprepossessing girl of 14*

un·prin·ci·pled /ʌn'prɪnsəpəld/ *adj. formal* not caring whether what you do is morally right

un·print·a·ble /ʌn'prɪntəbəl/ *adj.* unprintable words, jokes, songs, etc. are so rude or shocking that they cannot be printed in a newspaper or magazine

un·pro·duc·tive /ˌʌnprə'dʌktɪv◂/ *adj.* not achieving very much: *an unproductive meeting*

un·pro·fes·sion·al /ˌʌnprə'fɛʃənəl/ *adj.* behaving in a way that is not acceptable in a particular profession: *Osborn was fired for unprofessional conduct.*

un·prof·it·a·ble /ʌn'prɑfɪt̬əbəl/ *adj.* **1** making no profit: *an unprofitable business* **2** *formal* producing no advantage

un·pro·tect·ed /ˌʌnprə'tɛktɪd◂/ *adj.* **1** not protected against damage or harm: *Without a roof it was unprotected from the weather.* **2 unprotected sex/intercourse** sex without a CONDOM

un·pro·voked /ˌʌnprə'voʊkt◂/ *adj.* unprovoked anger, attacks, etc. are directed at someone who has not done anything to deserve them

un·qual·i·fied /ʌn'kwɑləˌfaɪd/ *adj.* **1** not having the right knowledge, experience, or education to do something: *The hospital was accused of hiring unqualified health workers.* **2** complete: *The movie is an* ***unqualified success.***

un·ques·tion·a·bly /ʌn'kwɛstʃənəbli/ *adv.* in a way that leaves no doubt: *This is unquestionably the coldest winter in years.*

un·ques·tioned /ʌn'kwɛstʃənd/ *adj.* accepted by everyone: *his unquestioned right to rule*

un·quote /'ʌnkwoʊt/ *v. spoken* → **quote... unquote** at QUOTE[1]

un·rav·el /ʌn'rævəl/ *v.* **1** [T] to understand or explain something that is very complicated: *Detectives are still trying to unravel the mystery surrounding her death.* **2** [I,T] if you unravel threads or if they unravel, they become separated

un·real /ˌʌn'ril◂/ *adj.* **1** an experience, situation, etc. that is unreal seems so strange that you think you must be imagining it: *It seemed unreal to be sitting and talking to someone so famous.* **2** not relating to real things that happen: *Test questions often deal with unreal situations.*

un·re·al·is·tic /ˌʌnriə'lɪstɪk/ *adj.* unrealistic ideas or hopes are not reasonable or sensible: *unrealistic job expectations* | ***It's unrealistic to*** *expect her to be happy all the time.*

un·rea·son·a·ble /ʌn'rizənəbəl/ *adj.* **1** not

U

fair or sensible: ***It's unreasonable to*** *give a 10-year-old so much responsibility.* | *He has a talent for dealing with the kids when they're being unreasonable.* **2** behaving in a way that is not pleasant, not sensible, and often silly **3** unreasonable prices, costs, etc. are too high

un·rec·og·niz·a·ble /ˌʌnrɛkəgˈnaɪzəbəl/ *adj.* changed or damaged so much that you cannot recognize someone or something: *The downtown area is almost unrecognizable.*

un·rec·og·nized /ʌnˈrɛkəgˌnaɪzd/ *adj.* **1** not receiving the respect someone deserves: *an unrecognized jazz musician of the 1930s* **2** not noticed or not thought to be important: *Violence in the home had* ***gone unrecognized*** *in the courts for years.*

un·re·cord·ed /ˌʌnrɪˈkɔrdɪd◂ / *adj.* not written down or recorded: *Their courage went largely unrecorded.*

un·re·fined /ˌʌnrɪˈfaɪnd◂ / *adj.* **1** an unrefined substance is in its natural form: *unrefined sugar* **2** *formal* not polite or educated

un·re·lat·ed /ˌʌnrɪˈleɪt̬ɪd◂ / *adj.* events, actions, situations, etc. that are unrelated are not connected with each other: *He will now stand trial on unrelated charges.*

un·re·lent·ing /ˌʌnrɪˈlɛntɪŋ◂ / *adj. formal* an unpleasant situation that is unrelenting continues for a long time without stopping or improving: *two days of unrelenting rain*

un·re·li·a·ble /ˌʌnrɪˈlaɪəbəl◂ / *adj.* unable to be trusted or depended on: *unreliable information* | *My old car is unreliable in the winter.*

un·re·lieved /ˌʌnrɪˈlivd◂ / *adj.* a bad situation that is unrelieved continues for a long time because nothing happens to change it: *unrelieved pain*

U

un·re·mit·ting /ˌʌnrɪˈmɪt̬ɪŋ◂ / *adj. formal* continuing for a long time and not likely to stop: *unremitting criticism*

un·re·quit·ed /ˌʌnrɪˈkwaɪt̬ɪd◂ / *adj.* **unrequited love** romantic love that you feel for someone who does not feel the same love for you

un·re·solved /ˌʌnrɪˈzɑlvd◂ / *adj.* an unresolved problem or question has not been answered or solved

un·re·spon·sive /ˌʌnrɪˈspɑnsɪv/ *adj.* not reacting to something or not affected by it: *a disease that is* ***unresponsive to*** *drugs*

un·rest /ʌnˈrɛst/ *n.* [U] a political situation in which people protest or behave violently: ***civil/political etc. unrest*** *in the country*

un·re·strained /ˌʌnrɪˈstreɪnd◂ / *adj.* not controlled or limited: *unrestrained laughter*

un·ri·valed /ʌnˈraɪvəld/ *adj. formal* better than any other: *an unrivaled collection of 19th century art*

un·roll /ʌnˈroʊl/ *v.* [I,T] to open something that was in the shape of a ball or tube, and make it flat, or to become open in this way: *He unrolled the sleeping bag.*

un·ru·ly /ʌnˈruli/ *adj.* **1** violent or difficult to control: *unruly children* **2** unruly hair is messy

un·safe /ʌnˈseɪf/ *adj.* **1** dangerous and likely to cause harm: *It's unsafe to swim in the river.* **2** in danger and likely to be harmed: *Many people feel unsafe walking alone at night.*

un·said /ʌnˈsɛd/ *adj.* **be left unsaid** if something is left unsaid, you do not say it although you think it: *Some things are better left unsaid* (=it is better not to mention them).

un·san·i·tar·y /ʌnˈsænəˌtɛri/ *adj.* dirty and likely to cause disease: *unsanitary conditions*

un·sat·is·fac·to·ry /ˌʌnsæt̬ɪsˈfæktəri/ *adj.* not good enough: *Your work is unsatisfactory.*

un·sa·vor·y /ʌnˈseɪvəri/ *adj.* bad, dishonest, or morally unacceptable: *unsavory business deals*

un·scathed /ʌnˈskeɪðd/ *adj.* not hurt by a bad or dangerous situation: *The driver came out of the crash unscathed.*

un·screw /ʌnˈskru/ *v.* [T] **1** to open something by twisting it: *Turn off the light before unscrewing the bulb.*

> **THESAURUS**
>
> **open, unlock, unwrap, unfold, unfasten, undo**
> → see Thesaurus box at OPEN[2]

2 to take the screws out of something

un·scru·pu·lous /ʌnˈskrupyələs/ *adj.* behaving in an unfair or dishonest way: *an unscrupulous lawyer*

un·sea·son·a·bly /ʌnˈsizənəbli/ *adv.* **unseasonably warm/cold/mild etc.** used for saying that the weather is warmer, colder, etc. than usual at a particular time of year —**unseasonable** *adj.*

un·seat /ʌnˈsit/ *v.* [T] to remove someone from a position of power: *Two candidates are trying to unseat the mayor.*

un·seem·ly /ʌnˈsimli/ *adj. formal* unseemly behavior is not polite or appropriate: *It was considered unseemly for women to smoke.*

un·seen /ˌʌnˈsin◂ / *adj., adv. formal* not noticed or seen: *She left the office unseen.*

un·self·ish /ʌnˈsɛlfɪʃ/ *adj.* caring about other people and thinking about their needs and wishes rather than your own —**unselfishly** *adv.* —**unselfishness** *n.* [U]

un·set·tled /ˌʌnˈsɛt̬ld◂ / *adj.* **1** making people feel unsure about what will happen: *The country faces an unsettled future.* **2** slightly worried, upset, or nervous: *The children are feeling unsettled by the divorce.* **3** an unsettled argument continues without reaching any agreement: *The issue remains unsettled.* **4** if the weather is unsettled, it keeps changing and there is a lot of rain **5** feeling slightly sick: *My stomach's a little unsettled after all that rich food.*

un·set·tling /ʌnˈsɛt̬l-ɪŋ/ *adj.* causing worry: *unsettling changes in the software industry*

un·shav·en /ʌnˈʃeɪvən/ *adj.* a man who is unshaven has short hairs growing on his face because he has not SHAVED → see picture at CLEAN-SHAVEN

un·sight·ly /ʌn'saɪtli/ *adj.* not nice to look at: *unsightly office buildings*

un·skilled /ˌʌn'skɪld◂ / *adj.* **1** not trained for a particular type of job: *unskilled workers* **2** unskilled work does not need people with special skills

un·so·lic·it·ed /ˌʌnsə'lɪsɪt̬ɪd◂ / *adj.* not asked for and often not wanted: *unsolicited advice*

un·so·phis·ti·cat·ed /ˌʌnsə'fɪstəˌkeɪt̬ɪd/ *adj.* **1** not having much knowledge or experience of modern and fashionable things: *unsophisticated audiences* **2** unsophisticated tools, methods, or processes are simple or not very modern

un·sound /ˌʌn'saʊnd◂ / *adj.* **1** unsound arguments, methods, etc. are not based on fact or reason **2** an unsound building or structure is in bad condition

un·speak·a·ble /ʌn'spikəbəl/ *adj.* extremely bad: *unspeakable crimes*

un·spe·ci·fied /ʌn'spɛsəˌfaɪd/ *adj.* not known or not stated: *The ticket is valid for an unspecified period of time.*

un·spoiled /ˌʌn'spɔɪld◂ / *adj.* an unspoiled place is beautiful because it has not changed and there are no buildings there: *unspoiled beaches*

un·spo·ken /ʌn'spoʊkən/ *adj.* understood but not discussed: *There was an* ***unspoken agreement*** *between us that we would tell Dee.*

un·sports·man·like /ʌn'spɔrtsmənˌlaɪk/ *adj.* not behaving in a fair honest way when playing sports

un·sta·ble /ʌn'steɪbəl/ *adj.* **1** likely to change suddenly and become worse: *an unstable economy* **2** dangerous and likely to fall over: *an unstable wall* **3** someone who is unstable changes very suddenly so that you do not know how s/he will react or behave

un·stead·y /ʌn'stɛdi/ *adj.* shaking or moving in an uncontrolled way, or likely to move or shake: *I felt unsteady on my feet.* | *The old bridge had become unsteady.*

un·stop·pa·ble /ʌn'stɑpəbəl/ *adj.* unable to be stopped: *The team seems unstoppable this year.*

un·sub·stan·ti·at·ed /ˌʌnsəb'stænʃiˌeɪt̬ɪd/ *adj.* not proved to be true: *unsubstantiated allegations of child abuse*

un·suc·cess·ful /ˌʌnsək'sɛsfəl◂ / *adj.* not achieving what you wanted to achieve: *an unsuccessful attempt to win the election* —**unsuccessfully** *adv.*: *We tried, unsuccessfully, to convince Hererra of the truth.*

un·suit·a·ble /ʌn'sut̬əbəl/ *adj.* not having the right qualities for a particular person, purpose, or situation: *This movie is* ***unsuitable for*** *young children.*

un·sung /ˌʌn'sʌŋ◂ / *adj.* not praised or famous for something you have done, although you deserve to be: *the* ***unsung heroes*** *of the war against crime*

un·sure /ˌʌn'ʃʊr◂ / *adj.* **1** not certain about something or about what you have to do: *If you're* ***unsure of*** *the rules, ask the teacher.* **2 unsure of yourself** not having enough confidence: *Clara seemed shy and unsure of herself.*

un·sus·pect·ing /ˌʌnsə'spɛktɪŋ◂ / *adj.* not knowing that something bad is about to happen: *Criminals can make easy money from mugging unsuspecting tourists.*

un·swerv·ing /ʌn'swɚvɪŋ/ *adj.* never changing in spite of difficulties: *unswerving loyalty*

un·tan·gle /ʌn'tæŋgəl/ *v.* [T] **1** to make things straight that are twisted together: *conditioner that helps untangle your hair* **2** to understand something that is very complicated

un·tapped /ˌʌn'tæpt◂ / *adj.* an untapped RESOURCE, market, etc. has not yet been used

un·ten·a·ble /ʌn'tɛnəbəl/ *adj.* an untenable situation has become so difficult that it is impossible to continue: *The scandal put the President in an* ***untenable position***.

un·think·a·ble /ʌn'θɪŋkəbəl/ *adj.* impossible to accept or imagine: *It was* ***unthinkable*** *a few years ago* ***for*** *a woman to run for President.*

un·ti·dy /ʌn'taɪdi/ *adj. formal* messy: *an untidy room*

un·tie /ʌn'taɪ/ *v.* [T] to undo the knots in something, or undo something that has been tied: *Mommy, can you untie my shoelaces?*

un·til /ən'tɪl, ʌn-/ *prep., conjunction* **1** if something happens until a particular time, it continues and then stops at that time: *I have classes until 7 p.m. today.* | *Debbie's on vacation until Monday.*

USAGE

Until and **till** are used to talk about the time when something stops: *They stayed until/till after midnight.*
As far as is used to talk about the place where something stops: *Does the bus go as far as the station?*
Up to is used mainly to talk about the final number or the biggest possible number: *The children had to count up to fifty.*

2 not until used in order to say that something will not happen before a particular time: *The movie doesn't start until 8 p.m.* | *The doctor's not available until tomorrow.*

un·time·ly /ʌn'taɪmli/ *adj.* happening earlier than it should or than you expected: *an* ***untimely death***

un·tir·ing /ʌn'taɪərɪŋ/ *adj. approving* never stopping while working or trying to do something: *untiring efforts to help the homeless*

un·told /ˌʌn'toʊld◂ / *adj.* too much or too many to be counted: *Floods did* ***untold damage*** *to farmland.*

un·touch·a·ble /ʌn'tʌtʃəbəl/ *adj.* someone who is untouchable is in such a strong position that s/he cannot be affected by, or punished for, anything: *These drug dealers think they're untouchable.*

U

un·touched /ʌn'tʌtʃt/ *adj.* not changed, affected, or damaged in any way: *a town almost* ***untouched by*** *the war*

un·toward /ˌʌn'tɔrd/ *adj. formal* unexpected, unusual, or not wanted: *Neighbors say that* ***nothing untoward*** *had happened on the night of the shooting.*

un·tried /ˌʌn'traɪd◂ / *adj.* not yet tested to see whether it is successful: *an untried theory*

un·true /ʌn'tru/ *adj.* not based on facts that are correct [= **false**]

un·truth·ful /ʌn'truθfəl/ *adj.* dishonest or not true

un·used[1] /ˌʌn'yuzd◂ / *adj.* not being used, or never used: *unused plane tickets*

un·used[2] /ʌn'yust/ *adj.* **unused to (doing) sth** not experienced in dealing with something: *She's unused to driving at night.*

un·u·su·al /ʌn'yuʒuəl, -ʒəl/ *adj.* different from what is usual or normal: *Our team has an unusual number of talented players.* | *unusual clothes* | ***It's unusual for*** *Dave to be late.*

un·u·su·al·ly /ʌn'yuʒuəli, -ʒəli/ *adv.* **unusually hot/difficult etc.** more hot, difficult, etc. than is usual

un·veil /ʌn'veɪl/ *v.* [T] **1** to show or tell people something that was a secret: *The mayor will unveil plans for a new park.* **2** to remove the cover from something as part of a formal ceremony

un·want·ed /ˌʌn'wʌntɪd◂ , -'wɑn-, -'wɔn-/ *adj.* not wanted or needed: *an unwanted pregnancy*

un·war·rant·ed /ʌn'wɔrəntɪd, -'wɑr-/ *adj.* not done for any good reason: *Shafer said the criticism was unwarranted.*

un·wel·come /ʌn'wɛlkəm/ *adj.* not wanted: *This is unwelcome news for farmers.* | *Many minority students* ***felt unwelcome*** *at the southern university.*

un·wield·y /ʌn'wildi/ *adj.* an unwieldy object is heavy and difficult to carry

un·will·ing /ʌn'wɪlɪŋ/ *adj.* not wanting to do something: *He's still* ***unwilling to*** *admit he was wrong.* | *unwilling participants*

un·wind /ʌn'waɪnd/ *v.* past tense and past participle **unwound** /-'waʊnd/ **1** [I] to relax and stop feeling anxious: *Swimming helps me unwind.* **2** [I,T] to undo something that is wrapped or twisted around something else

un·wise /ˌʌn'waɪz◂ / *adj.* not based on good judgment: *It would be* ***unwise to*** *make him mad.*

un·wit·ting·ly /ʌn'wɪṭɪŋli/ *adv.* without knowing or realizing something: *Several employees unwittingly became involved in illegal activities.* —**unwitting** *adj.*

un·wor·thy /ʌn'wɚði/ *adj.* not deserving respect, attention, etc.: *an idea that's* ***unworthy of*** *serious consideration*

unwrap

unwrapping a present

un·wrap /ʌn'ræp/ *v.* past tense and past participle **unwrapped**, present participle **unwrapping** [T] to remove the paper, plastic, etc. that is around something: *Brianna was unwrapping her birthday presents.*

THESAURUS

open, unlock, unscrew, unfold, unfasten, undo
→ see Thesaurus box at OPEN[2]

un·writ·ten /ˌʌn'rɪtˀn◂ / *adj.* known about and understood by everyone but not written down: *an* ***unwritten rule***

un·yield·ing /ʌn'yildɪŋ/ *adj. formal* not willing to change your ideas or beliefs: *The senator expressed her unyielding support for the president.*

un·zip /ʌn'zɪp/ *v.* past tense and past participle **unzipped**, present participle **unzipping** [T] to unfasten the ZIPPER on a piece of clothing, bag, etc.

up[1] /ʌp/ *adv., prep.* **1** toward a higher place or position [≠ **down**]: *Duncan climbed up into the tree.* | *Walk up the hill and turn right.* | *Could you come up here and help us?* | *Put your hand up if you know the answer.* **2** in a higher place or position [≠ **down**]: *"Where's Dave?" "He's up in his room."* | *The cat's up a tree.* | *a balloon floating up above us* **3** in or to a place that is further along something such as a road or path [= **down**]: *I'm going up the road to see Jill.* **4** into an upright or raised position: *The choir stood up to sing.* | *The hair on the dog's back was sticking up.* **5** toward or in the north [≠ **down**]: *I'm driving up to see my parents.* | *His relatives all live up north.* **6** very close to someone or something: *The cop came* ***up to*** *the car and asked Chad for his license.* **7** increasing in loudness, strength, heat, activity, etc. [≠ **down**]: *Turn up the TV.* | *Violent crime was up 3% this month.* **8** completely done, used, etc., so that there is nothing left: *All the space in the basement is filled up.* | *Eat up your dinner!* **9** broken or divided completely: *She tore the letter up into tiny pieces.* | *We'll split the money up evenly.* **10** firmly fastened, covered, or joined: *a box tied up with string* | *Her dad covered her up and said goodnight.* **11** brought or gathered together: *Add up the following numbers.* | *He gathered up all the pens he could find.* **12** toward the place where a river starts: *sailing up the river* **13** above and including a particular number or amount: *This movie is suitable for children aged 12 and up.* **14 up to sth a)** used in order to show the highest amount or level of something, or the latest time something can happen: *Up to 10 people are allowed in the elevator at one time.* | *This offer is valid up to December 15.* **b)** used in order to say or ask what someone is doing: *What have you been up to lately?* | *I'm sure Bob's* ***up to something*** (=doing something secret or bad). **c)** good enough or well enough to do something: *The local police just aren't* ***up to the job*** (=not good enough to do it). | *Do you feel up to a walk today?* **15 up and down a)** higher and lower: *kids* ***jumping up and down*** **b)** to one end of something and then back again: *We walked up and down the street trying to find the house.* **16 it's up to you** *spoken* said to tell someone that you want him/her to make a decision: *"Do you think I should get the dress?" "It's up to you."* **17 up close** very near someone or something: *If you look up close, you can see the cracks.* **18 meet/see/know etc. up close** to meet someone or experience something that you had previously only read or heard about: *I was surprised by how short he was when I met him up close.*

up² *adj.* **1** awake: *"Sorry, were you in bed?" "No, I'm still up."* **2** a computer system that is up is working [≠ **down**] **3** a level, number, or amount that is up is higher than before [≠ **down**]: *Profits were up by 4% this year.* **4** beating your opponent by a certain number of points [≠ **down**]: *With 5 minutes left, Boston is up by 8 points.* **5** *informal* if a period of time is up, it is finished: *I'll give you a signal when the ten minutes are up.* **6 be up against sb/sth** to have to deal with a difficult situation or fight an opponent: *We're up against some of the biggest companies in the world.* **7 be up for sth a)** to be intended for a particular purpose: *The house is up for sale.* | *the topic up for discussion at the meeting* **b)** *spoken* to be interested in doing something, or willing to do something: *Is anybody up for a game of tennis?* **8 be up and running** if a machine or process is up and running, it is working correctly: *The equipment should be up and running in about three weeks.* **9 be up before sb/sth** to be judged in a court of law: *He was up before the grand jury on charges of fraud.*

SPOKEN PHRASES

10 What's up? used in order to greet someone, or to ask if there is a problem: *Hey, Mark! What's up?* **11 be up on (sth)** to know a lot about something: *I'm not really up on the way things work here.*

up³ *n.* **1 ups and downs** the good things and bad things that happen in a particular situation: *We've had our ups and downs like all couples.* **2 be on the up and up** *spoken* if a person or business is on the up and up, s/he or it is honest and does things legally

up⁴ *v. informal* **1** past tense and past participle **upped**, present participle **upping** [T] to increase the amount or level of something: *They've upped Don's salary by $2,500.* **2 up and do sth** to suddenly do something different or surprising: *Without saying another word, he* ***up and left.***

ˌup-and-ˈcoming *adj.* likely to be successful and popular: *an up-and-coming actor*

up·beat /ˌʌpˈbit◂/ *adj.* cheerful and making you feel that good things will happen: *We remained calm and upbeat about the situation.*

up·bring·ing /ˈʌpˌbrɪŋɪŋ/ *n.* [singular, U] the way that your parents care for you and teach you to behave when you are growing up: *He had a very* ***strict upbringing.***

up·chuck /ˈʌp-tʃʌk/ *v.* [I] *spoken informal* VOMIT

up·com·ing /ˈʌpˌkʌmɪŋ/ *adj.* happening soon: *the upcoming elections*

up·date¹ /ˈʌpdeɪt, ˌʌpˈdeɪt/ *v.* [T] **1** to add the most recent information to something: *The system needs to be updated.* **2** to make something more modern in the way it looks or operates: *We need to update our image.*

up·date² /ˈʌpdeɪt/ *n.* [C] the most recent news about something: *an* ***update on*** *the earthquake*

up·end /ʌpˈɛnd/ *v.* [T] to turn something over so that it is upside down

up·front /ʌpˈfrʌnt/ *adj.* **1** talking or behaving in a direct and honest way: *Jill's always been upfront with him.* **2** paid before any work has been done or before goods are supplied —**upfront** *adv.*: *We'll need $300 upfront.*

up·grade /ˈʌpgreɪd, ˌʌpˈgreɪd/ *v.* [T] to improve something, or to exchange something for something better: *I was upgraded to first class on the flight back.* | *We need to upgrade our computer.* —**upgrade** /ˈʌpgreɪd/ *n.* [C]

up·heav·al /ʌpˈhivəl, ˈʌpˌhivəl/ *n.* [C,U] a very big change that often causes problems: *political upheaval*

up·hill /ˌʌpˈhɪl◂/ *adj., adv.* **1** toward the top of a hill [≠ **downhill**]: *an uphill climb* **2** an uphill battle, job, etc. is very difficult and needs a lot of effort: *Kent faces an* ***uphill battle*** *if he wants to win.*

up·hold /ʌpˈhoʊld/ *v.* past tense and past participle **upheld** /-ˈhɛld/ [T] **1** to defend or support a law, system, or principle so that it is not made weaker: *They want to uphold family values.* **2** if a court upholds a decision that is made by another court, it states that the decision was correct

up·hol·ster /əˈpoʊlstɚ, ʌpˈhoʊl-/ *v.* [T] to cover a chair with material —**upholstered** *adj.*

up·hol·ster·y /əˈpoʊlstəri/ *n.* [U] material that is used for covering chairs, or the process of doing this

up·keep /ˈʌpkip/ *n.* [U] the care that is needed to keep something in good condition: ***the upkeep of*** *a big house*

up·lift·ing /ˌʌpˈlɪftɪŋ◂/ *adj.* making you feel more cheerful: *uplifting music*

up·on /əˈpɑn, əˈpɔn/ *prep. formal* on: *We are*

U

completely dependent upon your help. | *sitting upon the throne*

up·per /ˈʌpɚ/ *adj.* [only before noun] **1** in a higher position than something else [≠ **lower**]: *the upper jaw* **2** near or at the top of something [≠ **lower**]: *the upper floors of the building* **3** more important or higher in rank than other parts in an organization [≠ **lower**]: *upper management* **4 have/gain the upper hand** to have more power than someone else, so that you are able to control a situation: *Rebels have gained the upper hand in some areas.*

up·per·case /ˌʌpɚˈkeɪs◂/ *n.* [U] letters written in their large form, such as A, B, C, etc. [➡ **capital**; ≠ **lowercase**]

ˌupper ˈclass *n.* **the upper class** the group of people who belong to the highest social class [➡ **lower class**, **middle class**, **working class**] —**upper-class** *adj.*: *upper-class communities*

up·per·class·man /ˌʌpɚˈklæsmən/ *n.* plural **upperclassmen** /-mən/ [C] a student in the last two years of HIGH SCHOOL or college [➡ **underclassman**]

up·per·most /ˈʌpɚˌmoʊst/ *adj.* **1** most important: *Your safety is **uppermost in** my **mind*** (=I think it is most important). **2** highest: *the uppermost branches of the tree*

up·pi·ty /ˈʌpət̬i/ *adj. spoken informal* behaving as if you are more important than you really are, or not showing someone enough respect

up·right /ˈʌp-raɪt/ *adj., adv.* **1** standing, sitting, or pointing straight up: *Andy **stood upright** when he heard the noise.* | *Please put your seat in an **upright position**.* **2** always behaving in an honest way: *upright citizens*

U

up·ris·ing /ˈʌpˌraɪzɪŋ/ *n.* [C] an occasion when a large group of people use violence to try to change the rules, laws, etc. in an institution or country: *a **popular uprising*** (=by the ordinary people in a country)

THESAURUS

revolution, **rebellion**, **revolt**, **coup**
➔ see Thesaurus box at REVOLUTION

up·riv·er /ʌpˈrɪvɚ/ *adv.* toward the place where a river begins, in the opposite direction from the way the water is flowing

up·roar /ˈʌp-rɔr/ *n.* [singular, U] a lot of noise or angry protest about something: *The announcement **caused** an **uproar**.*

up·root /ˌʌpˈrut/ *v.* [T] **1** to pull a plant and its roots out of the ground **2** to make someone leave his/her home and move to a new place, especially when this is difficult: *Steven's new job will mean uprooting the family.*

up·scale /ˌʌpˈskeɪl◂/ *adj.* made for or relating to people from a high social class who have a lot of money: *an upscale department store*

up·set¹ /ˌʌpˈsɛt◂/ *adj.* **1** [not before noun] unhappy and worried because something bad or disappointing has happened: *What are you so **upset about**?* | *He was **upset that** Helen had lied to him.* | *When I told him he'd failed, he **got** very **upset**.*

THESAURUS

sad, **unhappy**, **miserable**, **depressed**, **down**, **low**, **homesick**, **gloomy**, **glum**
➔ see Thesaurus box at SAD

2 an upset stomach/tummy an illness that has an effect on the stomach and makes you sick

up·set² /ʌpˈsɛt/ *v.* past tense and past participle **upset**, present participle **upsetting** [T] **1** to make someone feel unhappy or worried: *Kopp's comments upset many of his listeners.* **2** to change something in a way that causes problems: *I hope I haven't upset all your plans.* **3 upset sb's stomach** to make someone feel sick

up·set³ /ˈʌpsɛt/ *n.* [C] an occasion when a person or team that is not expected to win defeats a stronger opponent in a competition, election, etc.

up·set·ting /ʌpˈsɛt̬ɪŋ/ *adj.* making you feel upset: *an upsetting experience*

up·shot /ˈʌpʃɑt/ *n.* **the upshot (of sth)** the final result of a situation: *The upshot is that she's decided to take the job.*

THESAURUS

result, **consequences**, **effect**, **outcome**
➔ see Thesaurus box at RESULT¹

up·side /ˈʌpsaɪd/ *n.* **the upside** the positive part of a situation [≠ **downside**]

ˌupside ˈdown *adj., adv.* **1** with the top at the bottom and the bottom at the top: *Isn't that picture upside down?* **2 turn sth upside down a)** to move a lot of things and make a place messy because you are looking for something: *We turned the house upside down looking for my keys.* **b)** to change something completely: *Her life had been turned upside down by the accident.*

up·stage /ˌʌpˈsteɪdʒ/ *v.* [T] to do something that takes people's attention away from a more important person or event

upstairs

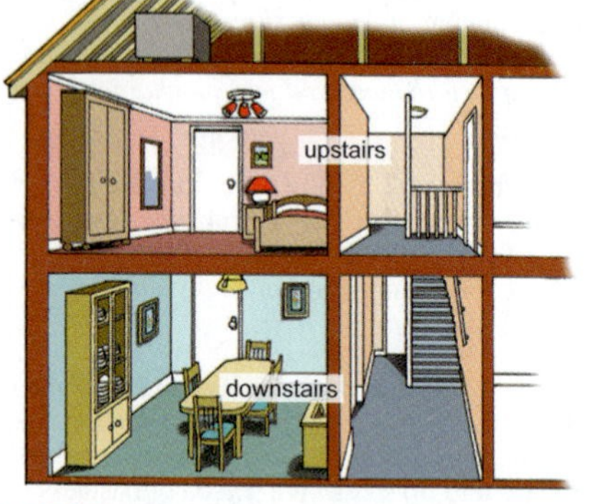

up·stairs /ˌʌpˈstɛrz◂/ *adj., adv.* **1** on or toward a higher floor of a building [≠ **downstairs**]: *Her* *office is upstairs on your right.* | *the upstairs bathroom* **2 the upstairs** one or all of the upper floors of a building: *Would you like to see the upstairs?*

up·stand·ing /ʌp'stændɪŋ/ *adj. formal* honest and responsible: *an upstanding citizen*

up·start /'ʌpstɑrt/ *n.* [C] someone who is new in his/her job and behaves as if s/he is more important than s/he is

up·state /ˌʌp'steɪt◂ / *adj.* in or toward the northern part of a state [≠ **downstate**]: *upstate New York* —**upstate** *adv.*

up·stream /ˌʌp'strim◂ / *adv.* along a river, in the opposite direction from the way the water is flowing [≠ **downstream**] —**upstream** *adj.*

up·surge /'ʌpsɚdʒ/ *n.* [C] a sudden increase: *a recent* ***upsurge in*** *car sales*

up·swing /'ʌpswɪŋ/ *n.* [C] an improvement or increase in the level of something [➡ **upturn**]: *an* ***upswing in*** *the economy* | *Incomes are* ***on the upswing***.

up·take /'ʌpteɪk/ *n.* **be slow/quick on the uptake** *informal* to be slow or fast at learning or understanding things

up·tight /ˌʌp'taɪt◂ / *adj. informal* behaving in an annoyed way because you are feeling nervous and worried: *You shouldn't* ***get*** *so* ***uptight about*** *it.*

ˌup-to-'date *adj.* **1** including all the newest information: *up-to-date travel information* | *Doctors must* ***keep up-to-date with*** *medical research.* **2** modern or fashionable: *the most up-to-date technology* | *The old system should be* ***brought up-to-date*** (=made modern).

ˌup-to-the-'minute *adj.* including the most recent information, details, etc.: *up-to-the-minute news on the negotiations*

up·town /ˌʌp'taʊn◂ / *adj., adv.* to or in the northern area of a city or town, or the area where the richer people live [➡ **downtown**]: *The Parkers live uptown.*

up·turn /'ʌptɚn/ *n.* [C] a time when business activity is increased and conditions improve [≠ **downturn**; ➡ **upswing**]: *an* ***upturn in*** *oil production*

up·turned /'ʌptɚnd, ˌʌp'tɚnd/ *adj.* **1** pointing upward at the end: *an upturned nose* **2** turned upside down: *upturned boxes*

up·ward[1] /'ʌpwɚd/ *adj.* [only before noun] **1** moving or pointing toward a higher position [≠ **downward**]: *an upward movement of the hand* **2** increasing to a higher level [≠ **downward**]: *the upward trend in house prices*

upward[2] **also upwards** *adv.* **1** from a lower place or position to a higher one [≠ **downward**]: *Billy pointed upward at the clouds.* **2** increasing to a higher level [≠ **downward**]: *Salaries have been moving upwards.*

u·ra·ni·um /yʊ'reɪniəm/ *n.* [U] a heavy RADIOACTIVE white metal that is used in producing NUCLEAR energy and weapons

U·ra·nus /yʊ'reɪnəs, 'yʊrənəs/ *n.* the seventh PLANET from the sun

ur·ban /'ɚbən/ *adj.* in or relating to a town or city [➡ **rural**, **suburban**]: *the growth of* ***urban areas*** | *the urban poor*

ur·bane /ɚ'beɪn/ *adj.* behaving in a relaxed and confident way in social situations

ˌurban re'newal *n.* [U] the process of improving poor city areas by building new houses, stores, etc.

ˌurban 'sprawl *n.* [U] the spread of city buildings and houses into an area that was COUNTRYSIDE

ur·chin /'ɚtʃɪn/ *n.* [C] *old-fashioned* a small dirty child

urge[1] /ɚdʒ/ *v.* [T] to strongly advise someone to do something: *Cal's family* ***urged*** *him* ***to*** *find another job.* | *Environmental groups have* ***urged that*** *the land remain undeveloped.*

> **THESAURUS**
>
> **advise, recommend**
> → see Thesaurus box at ADVISE

urge sb ⇔ **on** *phr. v.* to encourage someone to try harder, go faster, etc.: *Urged on by the crowd, they scored two more goals.*

urge[2] *n.* [C] a strong wish or need: *sexual urges* | *I felt a sudden* ***urge to*** *hit him.*

ur·gent /'ɚdʒənt/ *adj.* very important and needing to be dealt with immediately: *an urgent message* | *She's* ***in urgent need of*** *medical attention.* —**urgency** /'ɚdʒənsi/ *n.* [U] *a matter of great urgency* —**urgently** *adv.*: *Help is urgently needed.*

u·ri·nate /'yʊrəˌneɪt/ *v.* [I] *technical* to make URINE flow out of your body

u·rine /'yʊrɪn/ *n.* [U] the liquid waste that comes out of your body when you go to the toilet

urn /ɚn/ *n.* [C] **1** a container that holds and pours a large amount of coffee or tea **2** a decorated container, especially one that is used for holding the ASHes of a dead body

us /əs; *strong* ʌs/ *pron.* the object form of "we": *He walked by, but he didn't see us.*

U.S., **U.S.** *n.* **the U.S.** the United States of America

U.S.A., **USA** *n.* **the U.S.A.** the United States of America

us·a·ble /'yuzəbəl/ *adj.* something that is usable can be used: *The software converts raw data into usable information.*

us·age /'yusɪdʒ/ *n.* **1** [C,U] the way that words are used in a language: *a book on modern English usage* **2** [U] the way in which something is used, or the amount of it that is used: *plans to cut water usage*

use[1] /yuz/ *v.* **1** [T] if you use something, you do something with it for a particular purpose: *Can I use your phone?* | *I need to* ***use the bathroom*** (=go to the toilet). | ***Use*** *a food processor* ***to*** *grate the vegetables.* | *The system is* ***easy to use***. | *We*

U

only ***use*** *the car* ***for*** *driving in the city.* **2** [T] to need or take an amount of food, gas, money, etc.: *These light bulbs use less electricity.* | *Our car's using too much oil.* **3** [T] to treat someone in an unkind and unfair way in order to get something that you want: *Can't you see that Andy is just using you?* **4** [T] to say or write a particular word or phrase: *I try not to use bad language around the kids.* **5** [I,T] to take illegal drugs

use sth ⇔ **up** *phr. v.* to use all of something: *Who used up all the toothpaste?*

use² /yus/ *n.*

1 ACT OF USING STH [singular, U] the act of using something: *the* ***use of*** *computers in education*

2 WAY STH IS USED [C] a purpose for which something can be used: *The drug* ***has*** *many* ***uses.***

3 the use of sth the right or ability to use something: *Joe's given me the use of his office.* | *She lost the use of both legs.*

4 make use of sth to use something that is available in order to achieve something or to get an advantage for yourself: *It's a shame that teachers don't make use of the new computer lab.* | *Try to* ***make good use of*** *your time.*

5 put sth to (good) use to use knowledge, skills, etc. for a particular purpose: *a chance to put your medical training to good use*

6 be (of) no use (to sb) to be completely useless: *The books are of no use to me now.*

7 it's no use doing sth *spoken* used in order to tell someone not to do something because it will have no effect: *It's no use arguing with Kathy. She won't listen.*

8 it's no use! *spoken* used in order to say that you are going to stop doing something because you do not think it will be successful: *It's no use! I can't fix this.*

9 have no/little use for sb/sth to not like or respect someone or something: *She has no use for people who are always complaining.*

10 be in use being used: *The computer room's in use all morning.*

11 for the use of sb for a particular person or group to use: *The gym is for the use of employees only.*

12 WORDS [C] one of the meanings of a word, or the way that a particular word is used [➡ **usage**]: *an interesting use of the word "brave"*

used¹ /yust/ *adj.* **be used to (doing) sth** if you are used to something, you have experienced it many times before and it no longer seems surprising, difficult, etc.: *Kathy is used to getting up early.* | *He still hasn't* ***gotten used to*** *the weather here.*

used² /yuzd/ *adj.* **used cars/clothes/books etc.** cars, clothes, etc. that have already had an owner [= **secondhand**]

used to /ˈyustə; *final or before a vowel* ˈyustu/ *modal verb* if something used to happen, it happened often or regularly in the past but does not happen now: *We used to go to the movies every week.* | *"Do you play golf?" "No, but I used to."*

USAGE

Used to is used in order to talk about something that someone did regularly in the past but does not do anymore: *I used to play tennis twice a week, but I don't have time now.*
Be used to and **get used to** are used in order to talk about being or becoming more comfortable with a situation or activity, so that it does not seem surprising, difficult, etc. anymore: *Are you used to the cold winters yet?* | *I can't get used to living in a big city.*

use·ful /ˈyusfəl/ *adj.* helping you to do or to get what you want: *useful information* | ***It's useful to*** *make a list before you start.* —**usefully** *adv.* —**usefulness** *n.* [U]

use·less /ˈyuslɪs/ *adj.* not useful or effective in any way: *These scissors are* ***completely/totally*** *useless.* | ***It's useless to*** *complain.*

THESAURUS

pointless, futile, be a waste of time/money/effort
➔ see Thesaurus box at POINTLESS

us·er /ˈyuzɚ/ *n.* [C] someone who uses a product, service, etc.: *The CD-ROM allows the user to hear how all of the words are pronounced.* | *ramps designed for wheelchair users* | ***users of*** *cell phones*

ˌuser-ˈfriendly *adj.* easy to use or operate

us·er·name, **user name** /ˈyuzɚˌneɪm/ *n.* [C] a name or special word that proves who you are and allows you to enter a computer system or use the Internet

ush·er¹ /ˈʌʃɚ/ *n.* [C] someone who shows people to their seats at a theater, wedding, etc.

usher² *v.* [T] to take someone into or out of a room or building: *His secretary* ***ushered*** *us* ***into*** *the office.*

usher in sth *phr. v.* to make something new start happening: *Gorbachev ushered in a new era of reform.*

u·su·al /ˈyuʒuəl, -ʒəl/ *adj.* **1** the same as what happens most of the time or in most situations: *Let's meet at the usual place.* | *I woke up a little earlier/later* ***than usual.*** **2 as usual** in the way that happens or exists most of the time: *They were late, as usual.*

u·su·al·ly /ˈyuʒuəli, -ʒəli/ *adv.* used when describing what happens on most occasions or in most situations: *We usually go out for dinner on Saturday.* | *Usually, I just get a sandwich for lunch.*

u·surp /yuˈsɚp/ *v.* [T] *formal* to take someone else's power, position, job, etc.

UT the written abbreviation of **Utah**

u·ten·sil /yuˈtɛnsəl/ *n.* [C] a tool or object that you use to prepare, cook, or eat food: *cooking utensils*

U

u·ter·us /ˈyut̬ərəs/ *n. technical* [C] the organ in a woman or female MAMMAL where babies develop

u·til·i·ty /yuˈtɪləti̬/ *n.* plural **utilities** [C usually plural] a service such as gas or electricity that is provided for people to use: *Does the rent include utilities?*

u·til·ize /ˈyutl̬ˌaɪz/ *v.* [T] *formal* to use something —**utilization** /ˌyutl̬-əˈzeɪʃən/ *n.* [U]

ut·most[1] /ˈʌtˀmoʊst/ *adj.* **the utmost importance/care/etc.** the greatest possible importance, care, etc.: *This is a matter of the utmost importance.*

utmost[2] *n.* [singular] **1 to the utmost** to the highest limit, EXTENT, degree, etc. possible: *The piece challenges singers to the utmost.* **2 do your utmost** to try as hard as you can in order to achieve something: *We've done our utmost to make them feel welcome.*

u·to·pi·a /yuˈtoʊpiə/ *n.* [C,U] an imaginary perfect world where everyone is happy —**utopian** *adj.*

ut·ter[1] /ˈʌt̬ɚ/ *adj.* complete or extreme: *We watched in utter amazement.* —**utterly** *adv.*: *He felt utterly exhausted.*

utter[2] *v.* [T] *literary* to say something: *No one uttered a word.* —**utterance** *n.* [C]

U-turn /ˈyu tɚn/ *n.* [C] a turn that you make in a vehicle, so that you go back in the direction you came from: *Shea **made a U-turn** and drove away.*

V, v

V, v /vi/ **1** the twenty-second letter of the English alphabet **2** the number 5 in the system of ROMAN NUMERALS

VA the written abbreviation of **Virginia**

va·can·cy /ˈveɪkənsi/ *n.* plural **vacancies** [C] **1** a room in a hotel that is available for someone to stay in: *a motel sign saying "no vacancies"* **2** *formal* a job that is available for someone to start doing: *The principal is interviewing candidates to **fill** several **vacancies** at the school.*

va·cant /ˈveɪkənt/ *adj.* **1** empty and available for someone to use: *vacant apartments* **2** *formal* if a position in an organization is vacant, the job is available because no one is doing it **3** if someone has a vacant expression, s/he does not seem to be thinking about anything —**vacantly** *adv.*: *Cindy was staring vacantly out into empty space.*

va·cate /ˈveɪkeɪt/ *v.* [T] *formal* to leave a seat, room, etc. so that someone else can use it: *Guests must vacate their rooms by noon.*

va·ca·tion /veɪˈkeɪʃən, və-/ *n.* **1** [C,U] a time that is spent not working or not at school, especially time spent in another place for enjoyment: *They're **on vacation** for the next two weeks.* | *How did you spend your **summer vacation**?* | *We'd like to **take a vacation** in the Virgin Islands.*

> **THESAURUS**
>
> **vacation** – time you spend away from school or work: *a two-week vacation in Mexico* | *a real family vacation*
> **holiday** – a day when no one officially has to go to work or school: *the Thanksgiving holiday*
> **break** – a time when you stop working or studying in order to rest, or a short vacation from school: *a ten-minute coffee break* | *We spent spring break in Florida.*
> **leave** – a time when you are allowed not to work for a special reason: *Angela is on maternity leave.*

2 [U] the number of days, weeks, etc. that you are allowed as paid holiday by your employer: *All employees get three weeks' **paid vacation** each year.* —**vacation** *v.* [I]

vac·ci·nate /ˈvæksəˌneɪt/ *v.* [T] to protect someone from a disease by giving him/her a vaccine [= **immunize**]: *Have you been **vaccinated against** measles?* —**vaccination** /ˌvæksəˈneɪʃən/ *n.* [C,U]

vac·cine /vækˈsin/ *n.* [C,U] a substance that is used to protect people from a disease, that contains a weak form of the VIRUS that causes the disease: *a polio vaccine*

vac·il·late /ˈvæsəˌleɪt/ *v.* [I] *formal* to continue to change your opinions, ideas, etc. because you cannot decide between two choices

vac·uum[1] /ˈvækyum/ *n.* **1** [C] → VACUUM CLEANER **2** [C] a space that is completely empty of all air or gas **3** [singular] a situation in which someone or something is missing or lacking: *Her husband's death left a vacuum in her life.*

vacuum[2] *v.* [I,T] to clean a place using a VACUUM CLEANER: *She vacuumed the living room.*

> **THESAURUS**
>
> **clean, do the housework, dust, polish, sweep up, scrub, mop**
> → see Thesaurus box at CLEAN[2]

ˈvacuum ˌcleaner *n.* [C] a machine that cleans floors by sucking up the dirt from them

ˈvacuum-ˌpacked *adj.* vacuum-packed food is packed in a container from which the air is removed, in order to keep the food fresh

va·ga·ries /ˈveɪgəriz/ *n.* [plural] *formal* unexpected changes in a situation that you cannot control: ***the vagaries of** the weather*

va·gi·na /vəˈdʒaɪnə/ *n.* [C] the passage from a woman's outer sexual organs to her UTERUS —**vaginal** /ˈvædʒənl/ *adj.*

va·grant /ˈveɪgrənt/ *n. formal* [C] someone who has no home or work

vague /veɪg/ *adj.* **1** unclear because someone does not give enough details or say exactly what s/he means: *John was a little **vague about** where* *he was going.* | ***vague promises*** *to end the war* **2 have a vague idea/feeling etc.** to think that something might be true or that you remember something, although you are not sure

vague·ly /ˈveɪgli/ *adv.* **1** slightly: *She looked vaguely familiar.* **2** not clearly: *His statement was very vaguely worded.* **3** in a way that shows you are not thinking about what you are doing: *He smiled vaguely.*

vain /veɪn/ *adj.* **1** *disapproving* too proud of your appearance or your abilities [➡ **vanity**]: *Men can be just as vain as women.*

THESAURUS

proud, conceited, big-headed, arrogant
➔ see Thesaurus box at PROUD

2 in vain without success: *I tried in vain to convince Paul to come.* **3 vain attempt/hope etc.** an attempt, hope, etc. that is not successful —**vainly** *adv.*

val·en·tine /ˈvælən,taɪn/ *n.* [C] **1** a card given on Valentine's Day **2** a name for someone you love on VALENTINE'S DAY: *Will you be my valentine?*

ˈValentine's ˌDay *n.* [C] a holiday in some countries when people give special cards, candy, or flowers to people they love

val·et /væˈleɪ, ˈvæleɪ/ *n.* [C] **1** someone who parks your car for you at a hotel or restaurant **2** a male servant who takes care of a man's clothes, serves his meals, etc.

val·iant /ˈvælyənt/ *adj. formal* very brave: *a valiant rescue attempt*

val·id /ˈvælɪd/ *adj.* **1** a valid ticket, document, or agreement can be used legally or is officially acceptable [≠ **invalid**]: *a valid passport* **2** based on strong reasons or facts: *They had some valid concerns about the safety of the airplane.* —**validity** /vəˈlɪdəṭi/ *n.* [U] *Scientists are questioning the validity of his research.*

val·i·date /ˈvælə,deɪt/ *v.* [T] *formal* to show or prove that something is true or correct [≠ **invalidate**]

val·ley /ˈvæli/ *n.* [C] an area of lower land between two lines of hills or mountains: *the San Fernando Valley*

val·or /ˈvælə·/ *n.* [U] *literary* great courage, especially in war

val·u·a·ble /ˈvælyəbəl, -yuəbəl/ *adj.* **1** worth a lot of money: *a valuable ring*

THESAURUS

precious – valuable because of being rare or expensive: *precious gems*
priceless – so valuable that you cannot calculate a financial value: *a priceless painting by Rembrandt*
worth a lot/a fortune – to be worth a very large amount of money: *Their house is now worth a fortune.*

2 valuable help, advice, etc. is very useful [➡ **invaluable**]: *I think we've all learned a valuable lesson today.*

val·u·a·bles /ˈvælyəbəlz/ *n.* [plural] things that you own that are worth a lot of money, such as jewelry, cameras, etc.: *Guests should leave their valuables in the hotel safe.*

THESAURUS

property, possessions, things, stuff, belongings
➔ see Thesaurus box at OWN[2]

val·ue¹ /ˈvælyu/ *n.* **1** [C,U] the amount of money that something is worth: *the **value of** the house* | *The dollar has been steadily **increasing in value**.* | *Did the thieves take anything **of value*** (=worth a lot of money)? **2** [U] the importance or usefulness of something: *His research was **of great value** to doctors working with this disease.* | *These earrings **have sentimental value*** (=are important to you because they were a gift, remind you of someone, etc.). **3 values** [plural] your beliefs about what is right and wrong, or about what is important in life: *traditional family values* **4 good/great etc. value** something that is worth the amount you pay for it

value² *v.* [T] **1** to think that something is important and worth having: *I value your friendship.* **2** to say how much something is worth: *a painting **valued at** $5 million*

valve /vælv/ *n.* [C] a part of a tube or pipe that opens and closes like a door in order to control the flow of liquid, gas, air, etc. passing through ➔ see picture at BICYCLE

vam·pire /ˈvæmpaɪə·/ *n.* [C] in stories, a dead person who sucks people's blood by biting their necks

van /væn/ *n.* [C] **1** a TRUCK with an enclosed back, used for carrying goods: *a moving van* **2** a large box-like car

van·dal /ˈvændl/ *n.* [C] someone who deliberately damages things, especially public property

van·dal·ism /ˈvændl,ɪzəm/ *n.* [U] the crime of deliberately damaging things, especially public property

van·dal·ize /ˈvændl,aɪz/ *v.* [T] to damage or destroy things deliberately, especially public property: *The church property had been vandalized.*

van·guard /ˈvængɑrd/ *n.* **in the vanguard (of sth)** involved in an important activity, and trying to achieve something or develop new ideas: *a group in the vanguard of political reform*

va·nil·la /vəˈnɪlə/ *n.* [U] a substance with a slightly sweet taste, used in ICE CREAM and other foods

van·ish /ˈvænɪʃ/ *v.* [I] to disappear suddenly, especially in a way that cannot be easily explained: *When I looked again, he'd vanished.* | *The ship **vanished without a trace*** (=disappeared, leaving no sign of what had happened to it).

V

van·i·ty /ˈvænət̬i/ *n.* [U] *disapproving* the quality of being too proud of yourself [➡ **vain**]

van·quish /ˈvæŋkwɪʃ/ *v.* [T] *literary* to defeat someone or something completely

van·tage point /ˈvæntɪdʒ ˌpɔɪnt/ *n.* [C] **1** a good position from which you can see something **2** a way of thinking about things that is influenced by your own situation [= **point of view**]

va·por /ˈveɪpɚ/ *n.* [C,U] many small drops of liquid that float in the air: *water vapor*

var·i·a·ble¹ /ˈvɛriəbəl, ˈvær-/ *adj.* likely to change often or be different: *a variable rate of interest* | *Hospital food is* ***highly variable*** *in quality.*

variable² *n.* [C] something that may be different in different situations: *A number of variables can affect a student's performance.* —**variability** /ˌvɛriəˈbɪlət̬i, ˌvær-/ *n.* [U]

var·i·ance /ˈvɛriəns, ˈvær-/ *n.* **be at variance (with sth/sb)** *formal* if two people or things are at variance with each other, they do not agree or are very different

var·i·ant /ˈvɛriənt, ˈvær-/ *n.* [C] something that is slightly different from the usual form of something: *a spelling variant* —**variant** *adj.*

var·i·a·tion /ˌvɛriˈeɪʃən, ˌvær-/ *n.* **1** [C,U] a difference between similar things, or a change from the usual amount or form of something: ***variations in*** *prices from store to store* **2** [C] something that is done in a slightly different way from normal: *This is the traditional recipe, but of course there are many variations.*

var·i·cose veins /ˌværəkoʊs ˈveɪnz/ *n.* [plural] a medical condition in which the VEINS in your leg become swollen and painful

var·ied /ˈvɛrid, ˈvær-/ *adj.* including many different types of things or people: *a varied diet*

va·ri·e·ty /vəˈraɪət̬i/ *n.* plural **varieties** **1 a variety of sth** a lot of different things or people: *The girls come from* ***a variety of*** *different backgrounds.* | *The T-shirts are available in* ***a wide variety of*** *colors.* **2** [U] the differences within a group, set of actions, etc. that make it interesting: *She wants more variety in her work.* **3** [C] a particular type of something that is different from other things of a similar kind: *different* ***varieties of*** *apples*

vaˈriety ˌshow *n.* [C] a television or radio program or a play that consists of many different performances, especially funny ones

var·i·ous /ˈvɛriəs, ˈvær-/ *adj.* several different: *This coat comes in various colors.* | *He decided to leave school* ***for various reasons.***

var·i·ous·ly /ˈvɛriəsli, ˈvær-/ *adv.* in many different ways: *He's been variously called a genius and a madman.*

var·nish¹ /ˈvɑrnɪʃ/ *n.* [C,U] a clear liquid that is painted onto things that are made of wood, to protect them and give them a shiny surface

varnish² *v.* [T] to paint something with VARNISH

var·si·ty /ˈvɑrsət̬i/ *n.* plural **varsities** [C,U] the main team that represents a university, college, or school in sports: *the varsity basketball team*

var·y /ˈvɛri, ˈværi/ *v.* past tense and past participle **varied**, third person singular **varies** **1** [I] if several things of the same type vary, they are all different from each other: *Prices* ***vary from*** *$10* ***to*** *$50.* | *The flowers* ***vary in*** *color and size.* **2** [I] to change often: *The price of seafood* ***varies according to*** *the season.* | *"How often do you play tennis?" "Oh,* ***it varies.***" **3** [T] to regularly change what you do or the way that you do it: *You need to vary your diet.* —**varying** *adj.*: *varying degrees of success*

vase /veɪs, veɪz, vɑz/ *n.* [C] a container used to put flowers in

va·sec·to·my /vəˈsɛktəmi/ *n.* plural **vasectomies** [C,U] a medical operation that makes a man unable to produce children

Vas·e·line /ˈvæsəˌlin, ˌvæsəˈlin/ *n.* [U] *trademark* a thick clear substance used on the skin to make it less dry

vast /væst/ *adj.* **1** extremely large: ***vast areas*** *of rainforest*

> **THESAURUS**
>
> **big, large, huge, enormous, gigantic, massive, immense, colossal, substantial**
> ➔ see Thesaurus box at BIG

2 the vast majority (of sth) almost all of a group of people or things

vast·ly /ˈvæstli/ *adv.* very greatly: *vastly different opinions*

vat /væt/ *n.* [C] a very large container for keeping liquids in

vault¹ /vɔlt/ *n.* [C] **1** a room with thick walls and a strong door, where money, jewels, etc. are kept safely **2** a room where people from the same family are buried **3** a jump over something

vault² also **vault over** *v.* [T] to jump over something in one movement, using your hands or a pole to help you: *He vaulted over the fence and ran off.*

> **THESAURUS**
>
> **jump, skip, hop, leap, dive**
> ➔ see Thesaurus box at JUMP¹

V chip /ˈvi tʃɪp/ *n.* [C] a CHIP in a television that allows parents to prevent their children from watching programs that are violent or have sex in them

VCR *n.* [C] **video cassette recorder** a machine that is used for recording television shows or watching VIDEOTAPES

VD *n.* [U] *old-fashioned* **venereal disease** a disease that is passed from one person to another during sex [= **STD**]

VDU *n.* [C] **visual display unit** a computer screen [= **monitor**]

V

vegetables

veal /vil/ *n.* [U] the meat from a CALF (=young cow)

> **THESAURUS**
>
> **meat, beef, pork, ham, bacon**
> ➔ see Thesaurus box at MEAT

V

veer /vɪr/ *v.* [I] to change direction suddenly: *The car **veered** sharply **to** the left.*

veg /vɛdʒ/ **also veg out** *v.* [I] *informal* to relax and not do anything important

ve·gan /ˈvigən, ˈveɪ-, ˈvɛdʒən/ *n.* [C] someone who does not eat meat, fish, eggs, or milk products

vege·ta·ble /ˈvɛdʒtəbəl/ *n.* [C] a plant such as corn or potatoes, which you can eat: *fresh **fruits and vegetables** | We have a small **vegetable garden**.*

veg·e·tar·i·an /ˌvɛdʒəˈtɛriən/ *n.* [C] someone who does not eat meat or fish: *I'm thinking about **becoming a vegetarian**.* —**vegetarian** *adj.*

veg·e·ta·tion /ˌvɛdʒəˈteɪʃən/ *n.* [U] plants in general, especially all the plants in one particular area: *a meadow with thick vegetation*

veg·gie[1] /ˈvɛdʒi/ *n.* [C usually plural] *informal* a vegetable

veggie[2] *adj.* **a veggie burger/sandwich etc.** *informal* a HAMBURGER, SANDWICH, etc. that is made using vegetables or grain, rather than meat

ve·he·ment /ˈviəmənt/ *adj.* showing very strong feelings or opinions: *his vehement opposition to the plan* —**vehemently** *adv.*

ve·hi·cle /ˈviɪkəl/ *n. formal* [C] **1** a thing such as a car, bus, etc. that is used for carrying people or things from one place to another: *a description of the stolen vehicle* **2 a vehicle for (doing) sth** something that you use as a way of spreading your ideas, opinions, etc.: *The newspaper is a vehicle for government propaganda.*

veil /veɪl/ *n.* [C] **1** a thin piece of material that women wear to cover their faces: *a bridal veil* **2 a veil of secrecy/silence etc.** something that stops you knowing the full truth about a situation: *A veil of mystery surrounded Gomez's death.*

veiled /veɪld/ *adj.* **1 veiled criticism/threats etc.** criticisms, threats, etc. that are not said directly **2 be veiled in mystery/secrecy** if something is veiled in mystery, secrecy, etc., very little is known about it

vein /veɪn/ *n.* [C] **1** one of the tubes through which blood flows to your heart from other parts of your body [➡ **artery**] **2** one of the thin lines on a leaf or on the wing of an insect **3** a thin layer of coal, gold, etc. in rock **4 in a ... vein** in a particular style of speaking or writing: *Her speech continued **in the same vein**.*

Vel·cro /ˈvɛlkroʊ/ *n.* [U] *trademark* a material used for fastening shoes, clothes, etc., made from two special pieces of cloth that stick to each other

ve·loc·i·ty /vəˈlɑsət̬i/ *n.* plural **velocities** [C,U] *technical* the speed at which something moves in a particular direction: *the velocity of light*

vel·vet /ˈvɛlvɪt/ *n.* [U] cloth with a soft surface on one side

vel·vet·y /ˈvɛlvɪṭi/ *adj.* looking, feeling, tasting, or sounding smooth and soft: *a velvety voice*

ven·det·ta /vɛnˈdɛṭə/ *n.* [C] a situation in which one person tries for a long time to harm another person

vend·ing ma·chine /ˈvɛndɪŋ məˌʃin/ *n.* [C] a machine that you can get cigarettes, candy, drinks, etc. from by putting in money

ven·dor /ˈvɛndɚ/ *n.* [C] someone who sells things, especially in the street: *street vendors*

ve·neer /vəˈnɪr/ *n.* **1** [C,U] a thin layer of good quality wood that covers the outside of a piece of furniture that is made of a cheaper material: *oak veneer* **2 a veneer of sth** *formal* behavior that hides someone's real character or feelings: *a veneer of politeness*

ven·er·a·ble /ˈvɛnərəbəl/ *adj. formal* a venerable person or organization is very old and respected: *venerable institutions*

ven·er·ate /ˈvɛnəˌreɪt/ *v.* [T] *formal* to treat someone or something with great respect, especially because she, he, or it is old, holy, or connected with the past

ve·ne·re·al dis·ease /vəˈnɪriəl dɪˌziz/ *n.* [C,U] ➔ VD

Ve·ne·tian blind /vəˌniʃən ˈblaɪnd/ *n.* [C] a covering for a window, made of long flat bars that can be raised or lowered to let in light

venge·ance /ˈvɛndʒəns/ *n.* [singular, U] **1** something violent or harmful that you do to someone in order to punish him/her for hurting you: *a desire for vengeance* **2 with a vengeance** with much more force or effort than is expected or normal: *The music started up again with a vengeance.*

venge·ful /ˈvɛndʒfəl/ *adj. literary* very eager to punish someone who has hurt you

ven·i·son /ˈvɛnəsən/ *n.* [U] the meat of a DEER

ven·om /ˈvɛnəm/ *n.* [U] **1** a liquid poison that some snakes, insects, etc. produce **2** extreme anger or hatred: *a speech full of venom* —**venomous** *adj.*

vent[1] /vɛnt/ *n.* [C] **1** a hole or pipe through which gases, smoke, or liquid can enter or go out: *an air vent* **2 give vent to sth** *formal* to do something to express a strong feeling

vent[2] *v.* [T] to do something to express your feelings, often in a way that is unfair: *Jay* ***vented*** *his anger* ***on/at*** *his family.*

ven·ti·late /ˈvɛntlˌeɪt/ *v.* [T] to let fresh air into a room, building, etc. —**ventilated** *adj.*: *Mechanics should work in a well-ventilated space.* —**ventilation** /ˌvɛntlˈeɪʃən/ *n.* [U]

ven·ti·la·tor /ˈvɛntlˌeɪṭɚ/ *n.* [C] ➔ RESPIRATOR

ven·tril·o·quist /vɛnˈtrɪləkwɪst/ *n.* [C] someone who speaks without using his/her lips, in a way that makes the sound seem to come from somewhere else, especially from a PUPPET —**ventriloquism** *n.* [U]

ven·ture[1] /ˈvɛntʃɚ/ *n.* [C] a new business activity that involves taking risks: *a new* ***joint venture*** (=an agreement between two companies to do something together)

venture[2] *v. formal* **1** [I] to risk going somewhere when it could be dangerous: *Several boats* ***ventured out*** *to sea, despite the weather.* **2** [T] to say or do something although you are not sure of it, or are afraid of how someone may react to it: *No one else ventured an opinion.*

ven·ue /ˈvɛnyu/ *n.* [C] a place where an organized meeting, concert, etc. takes place: *a popular jazz venue*

Ve·nus /ˈvinəs/ *n.* the second PLANET from the sun

ve·ran·da /vəˈrændə/ *n.* [C] ➔ PORCH

verb /vɚb/ *n.* [C] *technical* in grammar, a word or group of words that is used in order to describe an action, experience, or state. In the sentence "They arrived late," "arrived" is a verb.

ver·bal /ˈvɚbəl/ *adj.* **1** spoken, not written: *a verbal agreement* **2** relating to words or using words: *verbal skills* —**verbally** *adv.*

ver·ba·tim /vɚˈbeɪṭɪm/ *adj., adv.* repeating the actual words that were spoken or written

ver·bose /vɚˈboʊs/ *adj. formal* using or containing too many words

ver·dict /ˈvɚdɪkt/ *n.* [C] **1** an official decision that is made by a JURY in a court of law about whether someone is guilty or not guilty of a crime: *Has the jury* ***reached a verdict*** (=made a decision)*?*

> **TOPIC**
>
> **testimony**, **evidence**, **defendant**, **defense**, **prosecution**, **judge**, **jury**
>
> ➔ see Topic box at COURT[1]

2 an official decision or opinion made by a person or group that has authority: *The panel will* ***give*** *their* ***verdict*** *tomorrow.*

verge[1] /vɚdʒ/ *n.* **be on the verge of sth** to be about to do something: *Andy was on the verge of tears.*

verge[2] *v.*

verge on/upon sth *phr. v.* to be very close to a harmful or extreme state: *Their behavior sometimes verges on insanity.*

ver·i·fy /ˈvɛrəˌfaɪ/ *v.* [T] past tense and past participle **verified**, third person singular **verifies** to find out if a fact, statement, etc. is correct or true: *There was no way to verify his story.* —**verification** /ˌvɛrəfəˈkeɪʃən/ *n.* [U]

ver·i·ta·ble /ˈvɛrəṭəbəl/ *adj. formal* used in order to emphasize your description of someone or something: *a veritable army of tourists* (=a very large number of them)

ver·min /ˈvɚmɪn/ *n.* [plural] small animals or insects that are harmful or difficult to control

ver·nac·u·lar /vəˈnækyələ/ *n.* [C] the language or DIALECT that ordinary people in a country or area speak, especially when this is not the official language

ver·sa·tile /ˈvəsəṭl/ *adj.* **1** good at doing a lot of different things and able to learn new skills quickly and easily: *a versatile singer* **2** having many different uses: *Cotton is a versatile material.* —**versatility** /ˌvəsəˈtɪləṭi/ *n.* [U]

verse /vəs/ *n.* **1** [C] a set of lines that forms one part of a poem or song, and that usually has a pattern that is repeated in other parts **2** [U] words arranged in the form of poetry: *a book of verse*

versed /vəst/ *adj.* **be (well) versed in sth** to know a lot about a subject or to have a lot of skill in doing something: *lawyers who are well-versed in these matters*

ver·sion /ˈvəʒən/ *n.* [C] **1** a copy of something that is slightly different from other forms of it: *the* ***original version*** *of the movie* | *a* ***new version*** *of an old song* **2** a description of an event that is given by one person: *I'm not sure I believe Bobby's* ***version of*** *the story.*

ver·sus /ˈvəsəs/ *prep.* **1 vs. or v.** used in order to show that two people or teams are against each other in a game or a court case: *the Knicks versus the Lakers* **2** used when comparing the advantages of two different things or ideas: *It's a question of quantity versus quality.*

ver·te·bra /ˈvəṭəbrə/ *n.* plural **vertebrae** /-breɪ, -bri/ [C] one of the small hollow bones down the center of your back

ver·ti·cal /ˈvəṭɪkəl/ *adj.* pointing straight upward [➡ **horizontal**, **diagonal**]: *a vertical line* —**vertically** *adv.*

ver·ti·go /ˈvəṭɪˌgoʊ/ *n.* [U] a sick DIZZY feeling that is caused by looking down from a very high place

V

verve /vəv/ *n.* [U] *literary* if someone does something with verve, s/he does it with energy and excitement

ve·ry[1] /ˈvɛri/ *adv.* **1** used in order to emphasize an adjective, adverb, or expression [➡ **really**]: *It's a very good book.* | *My family is very important to me.* | *Sid gets embarrassed very easily.* | *Carter went to the very best schools.* | *The two brothers died on* ***the very same*** (=exactly the same) *day.*

USAGE

Do not use **very** with adjectives and adverbs that already have a strong meaning, for example "huge" or "terrible." Say "a terrible war," not "a very terrible war." You can use **really** instead: *That was a really awful movie.*
Do not use **very** with the comparative form of adjectives. Do not say "This school's very better." Use **much** instead: *This school's much better.*
➔ TOO

2 not very a) used before a quality to mean exactly the opposite of that quality: *She wasn't very happy about working overtime* (=she was angry). **b)** only slightly: *"Was the game very exciting?" "Not very."* **3 your very own** used in order to emphasize that something belongs to one particular person: *I finally have my very own bedroom.* **4 very much** a lot: *It didn't cost very much.* ▶ Don't say "It cost very much." Say "It cost a lot." ◀ *I enjoyed my visit very much.* ▶ Don't say "I very much enjoyed my visit." ◀

very[2] *adj.* [only before noun] used in order to emphasize that you are talking about one particular thing or person: *Start again from the very beginning.* | *You come here* ***this very minute*** (=now)*!* | *The* ***very thought*** (=just thinking about it) *of food makes me feel sick.*

ˌvery high ˌfrequency *n.* [U] ➔ VHF

ves·sel /ˈvɛsəl/ *n.* [C] *formal* a ship or large boat ➔ BLOOD VESSEL

vest /vɛst/ *n.* [C] **1** a piece of clothing without SLEEVES that has buttons down the front, worn over a shirt as part of a suit **2** a piece of special clothing without SLEEVES that is worn to protect your body: *a* ***bulletproof vest***

vest·ed in·terest /ˌvɛstɪd ˈɪntrɪst/ *n.* [C] if you have a vested interest in something happening, you have a strong reason for wanting it to happen because you will get money or advantages from it

ves·ti·bule /ˈvɛstəˌbyul/ *n. formal* [C] a wide passage or small room inside the front door of a public building

ves·tige /ˈvɛstɪdʒ/ *n. formal* [C] a small part or amount of something that remains when most of it no longer exists: *a policy that is one of* ***the last vestiges of*** *the Cold War*

vet /vɛt/ *n.* [C] **1 veterinarian** someone who is trained to give medical care and treatment to sick animals **2** *informal* a **veteran**: *Vietnam vets*

vet·er·an /ˈvɛṭərən/ *n.* [C] **1** someone who has been a soldier, sailor, etc. in a war: ***veterans of*** *the Korean War* **2** someone who has had a lot of experience in a particular activity: *a veteran journalist*

vet·er·i·nar·i·an /ˌvɛṭərəˈnɛriən, ˌvɛtrə-, ˌvɛtˀn-/ *n.* [C] ➔ VET

vet·er·i·nar·y /ˈvɛṭərəˌnɛri, ˈvɛtrə-, ˈvɛtˀn-/ *adj. technical* relating to the medical care and treatment of sick animals

ve·to[1] /ˈviṭoʊ/ *v.* [T] past tense and past participle **vetoed**, third person singular **vetoes** to officially refuse to allow something to happen, especially something that other people or organizations have agreed: *The President* ***vetoed*** *the* ***bill.***

veto[2] *n.* plural **vetoes** [C,U] a refusal to give official permission for something, or the right to refuse to give such permission: *the governor's* ***veto of*** *a bill*

vex /vɛks/ *v.* [T] *old-fashioned* to make someone feel annoyed or worried

VHF *n.* [U] *technical* **very high frequency** radio

waves that move very quickly and produce good sound quality

VHS *n.* [U] *trademark* a type of VIDEOTAPE

vi·a /ˈvaɪə, ˈviə/ *prep.* **1** traveling through a place on the way to another place: *We're flying to Denver via Chicago.* **2** using a particular machine, system, person, etc. to send, receive, or broadcast something: *The concert was broadcast around the world via satellite.*

vi·a·ble /ˈvaɪəbəl/ *adj.* something that is viable is able to exist or succeed: *Solar energy is a* ***viable alternative*** *to coal or gas.* | *The plan isn't* ***economically/commercially viable****.*

vi·a·duct /ˈvaɪəˌdʌkt/ *n.* [C] a long high bridge across a valley

vi·al /ˈvaɪəl/ *n.* [C] a very small bottle, used especially for liquid medicines

vibe /vaɪb/ *n.* [C usually plural] *informal* the feelings that a particular person, group, or situation seems to produce and that you react to: *I'm getting* ***good/bad vibes*** *from this guy.*

vi·brant /ˈvaɪbrənt/ *adj.* **1** exciting, full of energy, and interesting: *a vibrant personality* **2** a vibrant color is bright and strong

vi·brate /ˈvaɪbreɪt/ *v.* [I,T] to shake continuously with small fast movements, or to make something do this: *The music got louder and the walls began to vibrate.*

THESAURUS

shake, tremble, shiver, wobble, rattle
➔ see Thesaurus box at SHAKE[1]

vi·bra·tion /vaɪˈbreɪʃən/ *n.* [C,U] a continuous slight shaking movement: *the vibrations of the plane's engine*

vic·ar /ˈvɪkɚ/ *n.* [C] a priest in the Church of England or in the Episcopal church

vi·car·i·ous /vaɪˈkɛriəs/ *adj.* experienced by watching or reading about someone else doing something, rather than by doing it yourself: *Parents get* ***vicarious pleasure/satisfaction*** *from their children's success.*

vice /vaɪs/ *n.* **1** [U] criminal activities that involve sex or drugs **2** [C] a bad habit: *Smoking is my only vice.* **3** [C] a bad or immoral quality in someone's character [≠ **virtue**]: *the vice of greed*

ˌvice ˈpresident *n.* [C] **1** the person who is next in rank to the president of a country **2** someone who is responsible for a particular part of a company: *the vice president of marketing*

ˈvice squad *n.* [C] the part of the police force that deals with crimes involving sex or drugs

vi·ce ver·sa /ˌvaɪs ˈvɚsə, ˌvaɪsə-/ *adv.* used when the opposite of a situation you have just described is also true: *Whatever Susie wants, James doesn't, and vice versa.*

vi·cin·i·ty /vəˈsɪnət̬i/ *n.* **in the vicinity (of sth)** in the area around a particular place: *The car was found in the vicinity of the bus station.*

vi·cious /ˈvɪʃəs/ *adj.* **1** violent and dangerous, and likely to hurt someone: *a vicious dog* **2** cruel and deliberately trying to upset someone: *a* ***vicious rumor*** —**viciously** *adv.* —**viciousness** *n.* [U]

ˌvicious ˈcircle *n.* [singular] a situation in which one problem causes another problem that then causes the first problem again

vic·tim /ˈvɪktɪm/ *n.* [C] **1** someone who has been hurt or killed by someone or something, or who has been affected by a bad situation: ***victims of*** *gang violence* | *a* ***murder/rape victim*** | *an aid program for* ***flood/earthquake/famine victims*** **2** something that is badly affected or destroyed by a situation or action: *Some small businesses have* ***fallen victim to*** *budget cuts.*

vic·tim·ize /ˈvɪktəˌmaɪz/ *v.* [T] to deliberately treat someone unfairly

vic·tor /ˈvɪktɚ/ *n. formal* [C] the winner of a battle or competition

vic·to·ri·ous /vɪkˈtɔriəs/ *adj.* successful in a battle or competition

vic·to·ry /ˈvɪktəri/ *n.* plural **victories** [C,U] the success you achieve by winning a battle, game, election, etc. [≠ **defeat**]: *Napoleon's military victories* | *the Lakers'* ***victory over/against*** *the Celtics* | *The government has* ***won*** *an important* ***victory****.* | *This ruling represents a* ***victory for*** *all women.*

vid·e·o[1] /ˈvɪdioʊ/ *n.* plural **videos** **1** [C] a copy of a movie or television program that is recorded on VIDEOTAPE [➡ **DVD**, **tape**]: *Let's* ***rent*** *a* ***video*** *tonight.* | *Has the movie come out* ***on video*** *yet?*

COLLOCATIONS

go to a video store
get/rent a video
watch a video
rewind a video – to press a button to go back to an earlier part
fast forward a video – to press a button to go to a later part
pause a video – to stop the video or DVD for a short time
make a video – to use a video camera to film someone or something

2 [C,U] a VIDEOTAPE: *Do we have a* ***blank video*** (=one with nothing recorded on it) *anywhere?* **3** [U] the process of recording and showing television programs, movies, real events, etc. using video equipment: *the use of video in the classroom*

video[2] *adj.* [only before noun] relating to recording and broadcasting sound and pictures on a VIDEOTAPE [➡ **audio**]: *video equipment*

ˌvideo casˈsette reˌcorder *n.* [C] ➔ VCR

vid·e·o·disk /ˈvɪdioʊˌdɪsk/ *n.* [C] a round flat piece of plastic from which movies can be played in the same way as from a VIDEOTAPE [➡ **DVD**]

ˈvideo ˌgame *n.* [C] a game in which you move images on a screen by pressing electronic controls

vid·e·o·tape¹ /ˈvɪdioʊˌteɪp/ *n.* [C] a long narrow band of MAGNETIC material in a plastic container, on which movies, television programs, etc. can be recorded

videotape² *v.* [T] to record a movie, television program, etc. on a videotape

vie /vaɪ/ *v.* past tense and past participle **vied**, present participle **vying**, third person singular **vies** [I] to compete very hard with someone in order to get something: *The two brothers* ***vied for*** *her attention.*

view¹ /vyu/ *n.* **1** [C] your belief, opinion, or attitude about something [➡ **point of view**]: *We have different* ***views on*** *this issue.* | *Not all her friends* ***shared*** *her* ***views***. | *What are your* ***views about*** *global warming?* | ***In my view***, *our civil liberties are just as important as national security.*

THESAURUS

opinion, **point of view**, **position**, **attitude**
➔ see Thesaurus box at OPINION

2 [C,U] what you are able to see or the possibility of seeing it: *We* ***had*** *a really good* ***view of*** *the stage.* | *I sat behind a tall guy who* ***blocked*** *my* ***view*** (=stopped me from seeing something). | *Suddenly the pyramids* ***came into view*** (=began to be seen). **3** [C] the whole area that you can see from somewhere, especially when it is very beautiful or impressive: *a spectacular* ***view of*** *the mountains* | *A new factory now* ***spoils the view*** (=makes it look less beautiful) *of the park.*

USAGE

View is used to talk about all the things you can see from a place: *We had a spectacular view of the ocean from the hotel.*
Scenery is used to talk about the natural features of a place, such as mountains, forests, etc.: *the breathtaking scenery in Arizona*
You cannot say "sceneries."

4 [C] a photograph or picture that shows a beautiful or interesting place: *The postcards show* ***scenic views of*** *New York.* **5 on view** paintings, photographs, etc. that are on view are in a public place where people can go to look at them **6 in view of sth** *formal* used in order to introduce the reason for a decision, action, or situation: *In view of all that has happened, Smith is expected to resign.*

view² *v.* **1** [T] to think of something or someone in a particular way: *My grandparents* ***viewed*** *the United States* ***as*** *a land of opportunity.* | *Some of the local people* ***view*** *tourists* ***with*** *suspicion.* **2** [T] *formal* to look at or watch something: *The mountain is best viewed from the north side.*

view·er /ˈvyuɚ/ *n.* [C] someone who watches television: *The series is watched by millions of viewers.*

view·point /ˈvyupɔɪnt/ *n.* [C] a particular way of thinking about a problem or subject [= **point of view**]: *From his* ***viewpoint***, *he had done nothing wrong.*

vig·il /ˈvɪdʒəl/ *n.* [C,U] **1** a silent political protest in which people gather outside, especially during the night: *Demonstrators* ***held a*** *candlelight* ***vigil*** *at the site of the bombing.* **2** a time, especially during the night, when you stay awake in order to pray or stay with someone who is sick: *John's been* ***keeping a vigil*** *beside his son in the hospital.*

vig·i·lant /ˈvɪdʒələnt/ *adj. formal* giving careful attention to what is happening, so that you will notice if something bad happens: *Doctors should* ***remain vigilant*** *for signs of infection.* —**vigilance** *n.* [U]

vig·i·lan·te /ˌvɪdʒəˈlænti/ *n.* [C] someone who tries to catch and punish criminals without having any legal authority to do so

vig·or /ˈvɪgɚ/ *n.* [U] physical and mental energy and determination

vig·or·ous /ˈvɪgərəs/ *adj.* **1** using a lot of energy and strength or determination: ***vigorous exercise*** | *a vigorous opponent of gun control*

THESAURUS

energetic, **full of energy**, **dynamic**, **tireless**
➔ see Thesaurus box at ENERGETIC

2 strong and very healthy: *a vigorous athlete*

vile /vaɪl/ *adj. informal* very bad or disgusting: *The act was unspeakably vile.*

vil·i·fy /ˈvɪləˌfaɪ/ *v.* [T] past tense and past participle **vilified**, third person singular **vilifies** *formal* to say bad things about someone in order to make other people have a bad opinion of him/her: *He was vilified by the press.*

vil·la /ˈvɪlə/ *n.* [C] a big country house

vil·lage /ˈvɪlɪdʒ/ *n.* [C] **1** a very small town: *My parents live in a small village in Mexico.* **2 the village** the people who live in the village: *The whole village came to the wedding.*

vil·lag·er /ˈvɪlɪdʒɚ/ *n.* [C] someone who lives in a village

vil·lain /ˈvɪlən/ *n.* [C] the main bad character in a movie, play, or story

vil·lain·y /ˈvɪləni/ *n.* [U] *literary* evil or criminal behavior

vin·di·cate /ˈvɪndəˌkeɪt/ *v.* [T] *formal* to prove that what someone said or did was right, especially when many people believe s/he was wrong —**vindication** /ˌvɪndəˈkeɪʃən/ *n.* [U]

vin·dic·tive /vɪnˈdɪktɪv/ *adj.* deliberately cruel and unfair

vine /vaɪn/ *n.* [C] a climbing plant that grows long stems that attach themselves to other plants, trees, buildings, etc.: *grape vines*

vin·e·gar /ˈvɪnɪgɚ/ *n.* [U] a sour-tasting liquid that is made from wine, used for improving the taste of food or preserving it

vine·yard /ˈvɪnyɚd/ *n.* [C] a piece of land where GRAPES are grown in order to make wine

vin·tage¹ /ˈvɪntɪdʒ/ *adj.* [only before noun]

1 vintage wine is good quality wine that is made in a particular year 2 old and showing high quality: *a vintage car*

THESAURUS

antique, classic
➔ see Thesaurus box at OLD

vintage² *n.* [C] a particular year or place in which a wine is made, or the wine itself

vi·nyl /ˈvaɪnl/ *n.* [U] a type of strong plastic

vi·o·la /viˈoʊlə/ *n.* [C] a wooden musical instrument shaped like a VIOLIN but larger and with a lower sound

vi·o·late /ˈvaɪəˌleɪt/ *v.* [T] to disobey or do something against a law, rule, agreement, etc.: *The military action violated international law.*

THESAURUS

disobey, break a rule/law, rebel, defy
➔ see Thesaurus box at DISOBEY

vi·o·la·tion /ˌvaɪəˈleɪʃən/ *n.* [C] an action that breaks a law, rule, agreement, etc.: *human rights violations | traffic violations*

vi·o·lence /ˈvaɪələns/ *n.* [U] 1 behavior that is intended to hurt other people physically: *There's too much violence on TV. | **violence against** women | We condemn any **act of violence**.* 2 extreme force: *the violence of a tornado*

vi·o·lent /ˈvaɪələnt/ *adj.* 1 violent actions are intended to hurt people: *an increase in **violent crime** | The riots ended in the **violent deaths** of three teenagers.* 2 someone who is violent is likely to attack, hurt, or kill other people: *a violent and dangerous criminal | The demonstrators suddenly **turned violent*** (=became violent). 3 **violent movie/play etc.** a movie, play, etc. that shows a lot of violence 4 violent feelings or reactions are strong and very difficult to control: *Joe has a **violent temper**. | a violent coughing fit* 5 **violent storm/earthquake etc.** a storm, EARTHQUAKE etc. that happens with a lot of force

vi·o·let /ˈvaɪəlɪt/ *n.* [C] a small sweet-smelling dark purple flower

vi·o·lin /ˌvaɪəˈlɪn/ *n.* [C] a wooden musical instrument that you hold under your chin and play by pulling a BOW (=special stick) across the strings ➔ see picture on page A6

VIP *n.* [C] **very important person** someone who is famous or powerful and is treated with respect

vi·per /ˈvaɪpɚ/ *n.* [C] a small poisonous snake

vi·ral /ˈvaɪrəl/ *adj.* relating to or caused by a VIRUS: *viral pneumonia*

vir·gin¹ /ˈvɚdʒɪn/ *n.* [C] someone who has never had sex

virgin² *adj.* **virgin land/forest etc.** land, forest, etc. that is still in its natural state and has not been used or changed by people

vir·gin·i·ty /vɚˈdʒɪnəṭi/ *n.* [U] the condition of never having had sex: *He was 20 when he **lost his virginity*** (=had sex for the first time).

Vir·go /ˈvɚgoʊ/ *n.* 1 [U] the sixth sign of the ZODIAC, represented by a VIRGIN 2 [C] someone born between August 23 and September 22

vir·ile /ˈvɪrəl/ *adj. approving* a man who is virile is strong in a sexually attractive way —**virility** /vəˈrɪləṭi/ *n.* [U]

vir·tu·al /ˈvɚtʃuəl/ *adj.* [only before noun] 1 very nearly a particular thing: *The two countries are locked in a virtual state of war.* 2 made, done, seen, etc. on the Internet, rather than in the real world: *The website allows you to take a virtual tour of the art gallery.* ➔ see Thesaurus box at ARTIFICIAL

vir·tu·al·ly /ˈvɚtʃuəli, -tʃəli/ *adv.* almost completely: *He was virtually unknown until the elections.*

ˌvirtual reˈality *n.* [U] an environment produced by a computer that looks and seems real to the person experiencing it

vir·tue /ˈvɚtʃu/ *n.* [C,U] 1 *formal* behavior that is morally good, or a good quality in someone's character [≠ **vice**]: *a life of virtue | Stella has many virtues.* 2 an advantage that makes something better or more useful than something else: *the virtues of organic farming* 3 **by virtue of sth** *formal* by means of or as a result of something: *He became chairman by virtue of hard work.*

vir·tu·o·so /ˌvɚtʃuˈoʊsoʊ/ *n.* plural **virtuosos** [C] someone who is a very skillful performer, especially in music: *a piano virtuoso* —**virtuoso** *adj.*: *a virtuoso performance*

vir·tu·ous /ˈvɚtʃuəs/ *adj. formal* behaving in a very honest and moral way

vir·u·lent /ˈvɪrələnt, ˈvɪryə-/ *adj.* 1 *formal* full of hatred: *virulent racism* 2 a poison, disease, etc. that is virulent is very dangerous and affects people very quickly

vi·rus /ˈvaɪrəs/ *n.* [C] 1 a very small living thing that causes infectious illnesses, or the illness caused by this: *the common cold virus* 2 a set of instructions secretly put into a computer that can destroy information stored in the computer

vi·sa /ˈvizə/ *n.* [C] an official mark that is put on your PASSPORT, that allows you to enter or leave another country: *a three-month **tourist/visitor's visa** | He has been **granted** a **visa** by the State Department.*

vis·age /ˈvɪzɪdʒ/ *n. literary* [C] a face

vis-à-vis /ˌvizəˈvi/ *prep. formal* in relation to or in comparison with something or someone

vis·cous /ˈvɪskəs/ *adj. technical* a viscous liquid is thick and does not flow easily —**viscosity** /vɪˈskɑsəṭi/ *n.* [U]

vise /vaɪs/ *n.* [C] a tool that holds an object firmly so that you can work on it using both of your hands

vis·i·bil·i·ty /ˌvɪzəˈbɪləṭi/ *n.* [U] the distance that it is possible to see at a particular time: *There is **poor visibility** on the roads due to heavy fog.*

vis·i·ble /ˈvɪzəbəl/ *adj.* something that is visible can be seen or noticed [≠ **invisible**]: *The mountains weren't visible because of the clouds.* | *a **visible change** in her attitude* —**visibly** *adv.*: *She was visibly upset by the news.*

vi·sion /ˈvɪʒən/ *n.* **1** [U] the ability to see [= **sight**]: *Will the operation improve my vision?* | *She has **good/poor vision**.* **2** [U] the area that you can see: *For a moment, the passing car was outside my **field of vision**.* **3** [C] an idea of what you think something should be like: *He had a clear **vision of** how he hoped the company would develop.* | *The President outlined his **vision for** the future.* **4** [C] something you seem to see, especially in a dream as part of a religious experience, especially in a dream: *She said that an angel appeared to her **in a vision**.* **5** [U] the knowledge and imagination that are needed in planning for the future with a clear purpose: *We need a leader with vision.*

vi·sion·ar·y /ˈvɪʒəˌnɛri/ *adj.* having clear ideas of how the world can be better in the future —**visionary** *n.* [C]

vis·it¹ /ˈvɪzɪt/ *v.* **1** [I,T] to go and spend time with someone: *Eric went to Seattle to visit his cousins.* | *My aunt is **coming to visit** next week.*

THESAURUS

You **go to** a movie, museum, theater, etc.: *Everyone likes to go to the movies.*
You **go to see** or **go and see** a person or place: *We went to see my aunt last week.*
If you **go sightseeing**, you visit places of interest in a country.
If someone **comes by/over**, s/he visits you informally in your home.
If someone **drops in/by**, or **stops by/in**, s/he visits you in your home, especially on the way to another place.

2 [I,T] to go and spend time in a place, especially as a tourist: *We want to visit the Grand Canyon on our trip.* **3** [T] to look at a website on the Internet: *Over 1,000 people visit our site every week.* **4** [I] *informal* to talk socially with someone: *We watched TV while Mom **visited with** Mrs. Levinson.*

visit² *n.* [C] **1** an occasion when someone visits a place or person: *a **visit to** London* | *We're just here **on a** short **visit**.* | *When are you going to **pay** us **a visit**?* | *We've just **had a visit from** the police.* **2** *informal* an occasion when you talk socially with someone, or the time you spend doing this: *Barbara and I had a nice long visit.*

vis·it·a·tion /ˌvɪzəˈteɪʃən/ **also** **ˌvisiˈtation ˌrights** *n.* [U] *law* the right that a parent who is DIVORCED has to see his/her children

vis·i·tor /ˈvɪzət̬ɚ/ *n.* [C] someone who comes to visit a place or a person: *a guidebook for **visitors** to Mexico City* | *Let's not bother them now – they **have visitors*** (=people are visiting them).

vi·sor /ˈvaɪzɚ/ *n.* [C] **1** the curved part of a hat or HELMET that sticks out above your eyes, or a special hat that consists only of this **2** the part of a HELMET that can be lowered to protect your face **3** a flat object above the front window of a car that you pull down to keep the sun out of your eyes

vis·ta /ˈvɪstə/ *n. literary* [C] a view, especially over a large area of land

vis·u·al¹ /ˈvɪʒuəl/ *adj.* relating to seeing or to your sight: *The movie has a strong visual impact.* —**visually** *adv.*

visual² *n.* [C usually plural] something such as a picture or part of a movie, video, etc. that you can see, not the parts that you hear: *the movie's stunning visuals*

ˌvisual ˈaid *n.* [C] something such as a map, picture, or movie that is used for helping people to learn

ˌvisual ˈarts *n.* [plural] art such as painting, SCULPTURE, etc. that you look at, rather than literature or music

vis·u·al·ize /ˈvɪʒuəˌlaɪz/ *v.* [T] to form a picture of someone or something in your mind [= **imagine**]: *I tried to visualize the house as he described it.*

THESAURUS

imagine, **picture**, **conceive of**, **fantasize**, **daydream**
→ see Thesaurus box at IMAGINE

vi·tal /ˈvaɪt̬l/ *adj.* **1** extremely important or necessary: *These computer systems are **vital to** our business.* | *Regular exercise is **vital for** your health.* | *Tourism plays a **vital role** in the country's economy.*

THESAURUS

important, **crucial**, **essential**, **major**, **significant**, **key**
→ see Thesaurus box at IMPORTANT, NECESSARY

2 full of life and energy: *Their music still sounds as fresh and vital as the day it was written*

vi·tal·i·ty /vaɪˈtæləṭi/ *n.* [U] life and energy: *He has the vitality of a man half his age.*

vi·tal·ly /ˈvaɪt̬l-i/ *adv.* in an extremely important or necessary way: *It's **vitally important** that you attend the meeting.*

ˌvital staˈtistics *n.* [plural] facts about people such as their age, race, and whether they are married, especially in official records

vi·ta·min /ˈvaɪt̬əmɪn/ *n.* [C] a chemical substance found in food that is necessary for good health: *Oranges are full of vitamin C.*

vit·ri·ol·ic /ˌvɪtriˈɑlɪk/ *adj.* something you say that is vitriolic is very cruel and angry toward someone: *a vitriolic attack*

vi·va·cious /vɪˈveɪʃəs, vaɪ-/ *adj.* someone, especially a woman, who is vivacious has a lot of energy and is fun to be with —**vivaciously** *adv.*

viv·id /ˈvɪvɪd/ *adj.* **1** vivid memories, dreams,

descriptions, etc. are so clear that they seem real: *He had a vivid picture of her in his mind.* **2 vivid imagination** an ability to imagine unlikely situations very clearly **3** vivid colors or patterns are very bright —**vividly** *adv.*

viv·i·sec·tion /ˌvɪvəˈsɛkʃən/ *n.* [U] the practice of operating on animals in order to do scientific tests on them

V-neck /ˈvi nɛk/ *n.* [C] a type of shirt or SWEATER with a collar that is shaped like the letter V

vo·cab·u·lar·y /voʊˈkæbyəˌlɛri, və-/ *n.* [C,U] plural **vocabularies** **1** all the words that someone knows, learns, or uses: *Reading is one of the best ways to improve your vocabulary.* **2** the words that are used when talking about a particular subject: *Most technical jobs use a specialized vocabulary.* **3** all the words in a particular language: *English has the largest vocabulary of any language.*

vo·cal[1] /ˈvoʊkəl/ *adj.* **1** expressing your opinion strongly or loudly: *a **vocal critic/opponent** of the president* **2** relating to the voice: *vocal music* —**vocally** *adv.*

vocal[2] *n.* [C usually plural] the part of a piece of music that is sung rather than played on an instrument: *The song has Maria McKee **on vocals**.*

ˈvocal cords, vocal chords *n.* [plural] thin pieces of muscle in your throat that produce sound when you speak or sing

vo·cal·ist /ˈvoʊkəlɪst/ *n.* [C] someone who sings, especially with a band

vo·ca·tion /voʊˈkeɪʃən/ *n.* [C,U] the feeling that the purpose of your life is to do a particular job, or the job itself: *Teaching isn't just a job to her – it's her vocation.*

THESAURUS

job, work, occupation, profession, career
→ see Thesaurus box at JOB

vo·ca·tion·al /voʊˈkeɪʃənəl/ *adj.* **vocational school/training/education etc.** a school or method of training that teaches you the skills you need to do a particular job

vo·cif·er·ous /voʊˈsɪfərəs/ *adj. formal* loud and determined in expressing your opinions: *a vociferous opponent of the plan* —**vociferously** *adv.*

vod·ka /ˈvɑdkə/ *n.* [U] a strong clear alcoholic drink, first made in Russia

vogue /voʊg/ *n.* **be in vogue/be the vogue** to be fashionable and popular: *Long skirts are back in vogue.*

voice[1] /vɔɪs/ *n.* **1** [C,U] the sound you make when you speak or sing, or the ability to make this sound: *I thought I heard voices downstairs.* | *Andrea has a really **deep voice** for a woman.* | *He called out **in a loud voice**.* | *He's caught a bad cold and **lost his voice*** (=cannot speak). | *I can hear you – you don't have to **raise your voice*** (=speak louder, especially in an angry way). | ***Keep your voice down*** (=speak more quietly) *– we don't want to wake everyone up.* **2** [C,U] an opinion or wish that is expressed: *Shouldn't parents **have a voice in** deciding how their children are educated?* **3** [singular] a person, organization, newspaper, etc. that expresses the wishes or opinions of a group of people: *Dr. King became the voice of the civil rights movement.* **4 the voice of reason/experience etc.** opinions or ideas that are reasonable, based on experience, etc., or someone who has these ideas: *Ben has been the voice of reason throughout the crisis.*

voice[2] *v.* [T] to tell people your opinions or feelings about a particular subject: *We all **voiced our concerns** about the plan.*

ˈvoice mail *n.* [U] a system that records telephone calls so you can listen to them later [➡ **answering machine**] → see Topic box at TELEPHONE[1]

void[1] /vɔɪd/ *adj.* **1** a contract or agreement that is void is officially no longer legal: *They were demanding that the elections be **declared void**.* **2 be void of sth** *literary* to completely lack something: *Her eyes were void of all expression.*

void[2] *n.* [C] **1** a feeling of great sadness that you have when someone you love dies or when something important is missing from your life: *Work helped to **fill the void** after his wife died.* **2** an empty space where nothing exists

void[3] *v.* [T] to make a contract or agreement VOID so that it has no legal effect: *The cashier will void the sale.*

vol·a·tile /ˈvɑlət̬l/ *adj.* **1** a volatile situation is likely to change suddenly and without much warning **2** someone who is volatile can suddenly become angry or violent —**volatility** /ˌvɑləˈtɪlət̬i/ *n.* [U]

vol·ca·no /vɑlˈkeɪnoʊ/ *n.* plural **volcanoes** or **volcanos** [C] a mountain with a large hole at the top out of which rocks, LAVA, and ASH sometimes explode: *This island has several **active volcanoes*** (=volcanoes that may explode at any time). —**volcanic** /vɑlˈkænɪk/ *adj.*: *volcanic rocks*

volcano

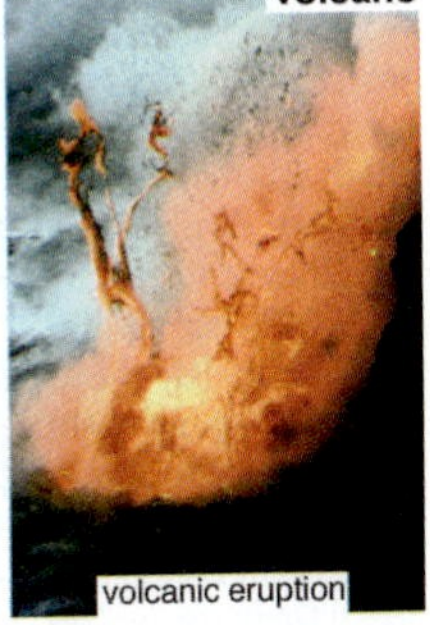

volcanic eruption

vo·li·tion /vəˈlɪʃən, voʊ-/ *n.* **of your own volition** *formal* because you want to do something and not because you are forced to do it: *Robin left the company of her own volition.*

vol·ley /ˈvɑli/ *n.* [C] **1** a large number of bullets, ARROWS, rocks, etc. fired or thrown at the same time: *a **volley of** shots* **2** a lot of questions, insults, attacks, etc. that are all said or made at the same time: *a **volley of** abuse*

vol·ley·ball /ˈvɑliˌbɔl/ *n.* **1** [U] a game in which two teams hit a ball to each other across a net with

V

their hands and try not to let it touch the ground **2** [C] the ball used in this game

volt /voʊlt/ *n.* [C] a unit for measuring the force of an electric current

volt·age /ˈvoʊltɪdʒ/ *n.* [C,U] the force of an electric current measured in VOLTS

vol·ume /ˈvɑlyəm, -yum/ *n.* **1** [U] the amount of sound produced by a television, radio, etc.: *Can you* ***turn the volume up/down****?* **2** [U] the amount of space that a substance fills or an object contains: *Let the dough double in volume before you bake it.* **3** [C,U] the total amount of something: *an increase in the* ***volume of*** *traffic* **4** [C] a book, especially one of the books into which a very long book is divided: *a 12-volume set of poetry*

vo·lu·mi·nous /vəˈlumənəs/ *adj. formal* **1** very large: *a voluminous skirt* **2** voluminous books, documents, etc. are very long and contain a lot of information

vol·un·tar·y /ˈvɑlənˌtɛri/ *adj.* done willingly and without being forced or paid: *voluntary work* | *We're asking for people to help* ***on a voluntary basis*** (=without being paid). —**voluntarily** /ˌvɑlənˈtɛrəli/ *adv.*

vol·un·teer¹ /ˌvɑlənˈtɪr/ *v.* **1** [I,T] to offer to do something without expecting any reward: *Ernie* ***volunteered to*** *wash the dishes.* | *I* ***volunteered for*** *the job.* **2** [T] to tell someone something without being asked: *Michael volunteered the information before I had a chance to say anything.* **3** [I] to offer to join the army, navy, etc.: *When the war began, my brother immediately volunteered.*

volunteer² *n.* [C] **1** someone who does something without being paid, or who is willing to offer to help someone: *We need volunteers to help look for the children.* **2** someone who offers to join the army, navy, or air force

vo·lup·tu·ous /vəˈlʌptʃuəs/ *adj.* a woman who is voluptuous has large breasts and a soft curved body

vom·it¹ /ˈvɑmɪt/ *v.* [I,T] *formal* if you vomit, food or drink comes up from your stomach and out through your mouth

vomit² *n.* [U] the food or drink that comes out when someone VOMITS

voo·doo /ˈvudu/ *n.* [U] magical beliefs and practices used as a form of religion, especially in parts of Africa, Latin America, and the Caribbean

vo·ra·cious /vəˈreɪʃəs, vɔ-/ *adj. formal* wanting to do something a lot, especially eating: *He had a* ***voracious appetite****.* —**voracity** /vəˈræsət̬i/ *n.* [U]

vor·tex /ˈvɔrtɛks/ *n.* plural **vortices** /ˈvɔrtəsiz/ or plural **vortexes** [C] a large area of wind or water that spins quickly and pulls things into its center

vote¹ /voʊt/ *v.* **1** [I,T] to show which person you want to elect, which plan you support, etc by doing something such as raising your hand, marking a paper using a pen or machine, CLICKing on a web page on the Internet, etc.: *Who did you* ***vote for****?* | *Only Stevens* ***voted against*** *the measure.* | *If we can't agree, we'll have to* ***vote on*** *it.* | *Congress* ***voted to*** *reduce taxes by 2%.* **2** [T] to choose someone or something for a particular prize by voting for him/her: *Berry was voted Best Actress.*

vote² *n.* [C] **1** a choice or decision that you make by voting: *He's certainly not going to get my vote!* | *There were 1,079* ***votes for*** *Mr. Swanson, and 766 for Mr. Reynolds.* | *You have until 8:00 to* ***cast your vote*** (=vote). **2** an act of making a choice or decision by voting: *We couldn't decide, so we* ***took a vote on*** *it.* | *Congress will* ***put*** *the bill* ***to a vote*** *tomorrow.* **3 the vote a)** the total number of votes made in an election or the total number of people who vote: *Davis won the election with 57% of the vote.* | *efforts to win* ***the African American/Irish/Jewish vote*** (=all the votes of African Americans, Irish people, etc.) **b)** the right to vote: *In France, women didn't get the vote until 1945.* **4 vote of confidence** the action of showing publicly that you support someone

vot·er /ˈvoʊt̬ɚ/ *n.* [C] someone who votes or has the right to vote: *The state decided to let the voters decide the issue.*

ˈvoting booth *n.* [C] an enclosed place where you can vote without being seen

vouch /vaʊtʃ/ *v.*

vouch for sb/sth *phr. v.* **1** to say that you have a firm belief that something is true or good because of your experience or knowledge of it: *I'll vouch for the accuracy of that report.* **2** to say that you believe that someone will behave well and that you will be responsible for his/her behavior, actions, etc.: *Don't worry about Andy – I can vouch for him.*

vouch·er /ˈvaʊtʃɚ/ *n.* [C] a type of ticket that can be used for a particular purpose instead of money

vow¹ /vaʊ/ *n.* [C] a serious promise: *marriage vows* | *She* ***made a vow*** *to herself that she would never go back.*

vow² *v.* [T] to make a serious promise to yourself or someone else: *Supporters have* ***vowed to*** *continue the protest until Adams is released.* | ***I vowed (that)*** *I would never drink again.*

THESAURUS

promise, **swear**, **take/swear an oath**, **guarantee**, **give sb your word**
→ see Thesaurus box at PROMISE¹

vow·el /ˈvaʊəl/ *n.* [C] *technical* the sounds represented in English by the letters a, e, i, o, or u, and sometimes y [➡ **consonant**]

voy·age /ˈvɔɪ-ɪdʒ/ *n.* [C] a long trip, especially in a ship or a space vehicle: *the voyage from England to America* —**voyage** *v.* [I] *literary*

THESAURUS

travel, **trip**, **journey**
→ see Thesaurus box at TRAVEL²

voy·eur /vɔɪˈɚ/ *n.* [U] someone who gets sexual pleasure from secretly watching other people's

V

sexual activities —**voyeurism** /ˈvɔɪəˌrɪzəm/ *n.* [U] —**voyeuristic** /ˌvɔɪəˈrɪstɪk/ *adj.*

vs. /ˈvɚsəs/ the written abbreviation of **versus**

VT the written abbreviation of **Vermont**

vul·gar /ˈvʌlgɚ/ *adj.* **1** vulgar language, humor, etc. is not polite because it talks about things such as sex or going to the toilet in a rude way: *vulgar jokes* **2** not showing good judgment about what is attractive or appropriate: *a vulgar display of wealth* —**vulgarity** /vəlˈgærət̬i/ *n.* [U]

vul·ner·a·ble /ˈvʌlnərəbəl/ *adj.* easy to harm, hurt, or attack [≠ **invulnerable**]: *The army was in a vulnerable position.* | *She looked so young and vulnerable.* —**vulnerability** /ˌvʌlnərəˈbɪlət̬i/ *n.* [U]

vul·ture /ˈvʌltʃɚ/ *n.* [C] a large wild bird that eats dead animals

vy·ing /ˈvaɪ-ɪŋ/ *v.* the present participle of VIE

W, w

W **1** the written abbreviation of **west** or **western** **2** the written abbreviation of **watt**

W, w /ˈdʌbəlˌyu, ˈdʌbəyu/ the twenty-third letter of the English alphabet

WA the written abbreviation of **Washington**

wack·y /ˈwæki/ *adj. informal* silly in an amusing way

wad¹ /wɑd/ *n.* [C] **1** a thick pile of thin sheets of something, especially money: *a **wad of** dollar bills* **2** a thick soft mass of material that has been pressed together: *a **wad of** bubble gum*

wad² **also wad up** *v.* past tense and past participle **wadded**, present participle **wadding** [T] to press something such as a piece of paper or cloth into a small tight ball: *Aaron wadded up his napkin.*

wad·dle /ˈwɑdl/ *v.* [I] to walk with short steps, swinging from one side to another like a duck —**waddle** *n.* [C]

wade /weɪd/ *v.* [I,T] to walk through water that is not deep

THESAURUS

walk, march, stride, stroll, amble, wander, creep, sneak, trudge, limp, hike
→ see Thesaurus box at WALK¹

wade in/into sth *phr. v.* to start taking part in a discussion, argument, attack, etc., in a forceful or annoying way: *Celebrities waded in to complain about the tabloids.*

wade through sth *phr. v.* to read or deal with a lot of long and boring written work: *Preston was wading through a 500-page report.*

wa·fer /ˈweɪfɚ/ *n.* [C] a very thin cookie

waf·fle¹ /ˈwɑfəl/ *n.* [C] a flat bread with a pattern of deep squares, often eaten for breakfast

waffle

waffle² *v.* [I] *informal* to be unable to decide what action to take: *He cannot continue to waffle on this issue.*

waft /wɑft, wæft/ *v.* [I,T] to move gently through the air: *The smell of bacon **wafted up** from the kitchen.*

wag /wæg/ *v.* past tense and past participle **wagged**, present participle **wagging** [I,T] **1** if a dog wags its tail, or the tail wags, it shakes from one side to another **2** to move your head, finger, etc. from side to side, especially in order to show disapproval: *"Not now," said Ralph, wagging his finger at the girls.* —**wag** *n.* [C]

wage¹ /weɪdʒ/ *n.* **1** [singular] the amount of money you earn, usually for each hour that you work: *He **earns a good wage**.* | *an hourly wage* | *the minimum wage* ▶ Don't say "an annual wage." say "an annual salary." ◀ **2 wages** [plural] the money you are paid each day, week, or month [➡ **salary**]: *Unskilled workers are paid lower wages.*

THESAURUS

pay, income, salary, earnings
→ see Thesaurus box at PAY², WORK

wage² *v.* [T] to be involved in a war, struggle, or fight against someone or something: *The police are **waging a campaign/war** against drug pushers.*

wa·ger¹ /ˈweɪdʒɚ/ *n.* [C] **1** an agreement to risk money on the result of a race, game, etc. [= **bet**] **2** the money that you risk: *a $10 wager*

wager² *v.* [T] to risk money on the result of a race, game, etc.: *Brad **wagered** $20 **on** the game.*

wag·on /ˈwægən/ *n.* [C] **1** a strong vehicle with four wheels, pulled by horses **2** a small CART with four wheels and a long handle in the front, used as a toy for children **3** *informal* ➔ STATION WAGON **4 be on the wagon** *informal* to no longer drink alcohol

ˈwagon train *n.* [C] a large group of WAGONS traveling together in past times

waif /weɪf/ *n.* [C] someone, especially a child or a young woman, who is pale and thin and looks as if s/he does not have a home

wail /weɪl/ *v.* **1** [I] to make a long high sound with your voice because you are in pain or very sad, or to make a sound like this: *sirens wailing in the distance* **2** [T] to say something in a loud, sad, and complaining way: *"My money's gone!" she wailed.* —**wail** *n.* [C]

waist /weɪst/ *n.* [C] **1** the part in the middle of your body just above your HIPS: *a slim waist* **2** the part of a piece of clothing that goes around your waist: *These pants are too big **in the waist**.*

waist·band /ˈweɪstbænd/ *n.* [C] the part of a skirt, pants, etc. that fastens around your waist

waist·line /ˈweɪstlaɪn/ *n.* **1** [singular] the measurement around your waist **2** [C] the position of the waist of a piece of clothing

wait¹ /weɪt/ *v.* **1** [I] to not do something until something else happens, someone arrives, etc.: *Hurry up! Everyone's waiting.* | ***Wait*** *right here* ***until*** *I come back.* | *people* ***waiting for*** *the bus* | *Henson has been* ***waiting to*** *hear from Miller.*

USAGE

Wait is never followed directly by a noun. You must say "wait for": *I'm waiting for a phone call.* Or you can say "wait to do something": *We're waiting to hear the news.*
Expect can be followed directly by a noun. Use it to say that you strongly believe that something will come, happen, etc.: *I'm expecting a phone call.* | *The police are expecting trouble.*
Look forward to means to be excited and pleased about something that you know is going to happen: *I'm looking forward to seeing you all.*

2 wait tables to serve food to people at their table in a restaurant **3 wait a minute/second** said in order to ask someone to wait for a short time: *Wait a second, I'll get my coat.*

COMMUNICATION

Ways of asking someone to wait

hold on/hang on informal
just a minute/second
I won't be a minute
wait up (=used in order to tell someone to stop walking or moving away, so that you can talk to him/her or go with him/her)
one moment, please formal
bear with me (=used in order to politely ask someone to wait while you do something)
please hold (the line) (=used on the telephone by someone who is trying to connect you)

W

4 sb can't wait/can hardly wait said to emphasize that someone is very excited about something and eager for it to happen: *I* ***can't wait to*** *see the look on his face.* **5 sth can/can't wait** if something can wait, it does not have to be done immediately. If something can't wait, it must be done now: *Which bills have to be paid and which can wait?* **6 wait and see** used in order to say that someone should be patient because they will find out about something later **7 wait until/till** used when you are excited about telling or showing someone something: *Wait till I tell Janice!* **8 wait your turn** to wait until it is your turn to do something

wait around *phr. v.* to do nothing while you are waiting for something to happen, someone to arrive, etc.: *I waited around for 10 minutes.*

wait on sb/sth *phr. v.* **1** to serve food to someone at his/her table, especially in a restaurant **2 wait on sb hand and foot** *humorous* to do everything for someone

wait up *phr. v.* **1** to wait for someone to return before you go to bed: *Please don't* ***wait up for*** *me.* **2 Wait up!** *spoken* used to tell someone to stop and wait for you: *Hey, wait up, you guys.*

wait² *n.* [singular] a period of time in which you wait for something to happen, someone to arrive, etc.: *a three-hour* ***wait for*** *our flight* | *They'll* ***have*** *a long* ***wait****.*

wait·er /ˈweɪt̬ɚ/ *n.* [C] a man who serves food in a restaurant

TOPIC

waitress
➔ see Topic box at RESTAURANT

ˈwaiting list also ˈwait list *n.* [C] a list of people who want to do or buy something, but who must wait before they can have or do it: *Over 500 students are* ***on the waiting list****.* ➔ see Thesaurus box at LIST¹

ˈwaiting room *n.* [C] a room for people to wait in, for example to see a doctor

wait·ress /ˈweɪtrɪs/ *n.* [C] a woman who serves food at the tables in a restaurant ➔ see Topic box at RESTAURANT

waive /weɪv/ *v.* [T] to state officially that a right, rule, etc. can be ignored: *She* ***waived her right*** *to a lawyer.*

waiv·er /ˈweɪvɚ/ *n.* [C] an official statement saying that a right, rule, etc. can be ignored

wake¹ /weɪk/ *v.* past tense **woke** /woʊk/ past participle **woken** /ˈwoʊkən/ present participle **waking** [I,T] **also wake up** to stop sleeping, or to make someone stop sleeping: *Try not to wake the baby.* | *I woke up early.*

wake up to sth *phr. v.* to start to realize and understand a danger, an idea, etc.: *The public is just beginning to wake up to the impact of these changes.*

wake² *n.* [C] **1 in the wake of/in sth's wake** as a result of something: *Five councilors resigned in the wake of the scandal.* **2** the track or path made behind a car, boat, etc. as it moves along: *The car left clouds of dust* ***in*** *its* ***wake****.* **3** the time before a funeral when people meet to remember the dead person

wak·en /ˈweɪkən/ *v.* [I,T] *formal* to wake, or to wake someone: *The sound had wakened him.*

wak·ing /ˈweɪkɪŋ/ *adj.* **waking hours/moments etc.** all the time when you are awake: *He spends* ***every waking moment*** *with that girl!*

walk¹ /wɔk/ *v.* **1** [I,T] to move forward by putting one foot in front of the other: *We must have walked ten miles.* | *Do you* ***walk to*** *work?* | *Lori* ***walked into*** *his office.* | *tourists* ***walking around*** *the downtown area* ➔ see picture on page A9

THESAURUS

march – to walk like soldiers, with regular steps
stride – to walk with long steps in a determined way
stroll – to walk in a relaxed way, especially for pleasure
amble – to walk slowly in a relaxed way
wander – to walk slowly, often when you are not going to any particular place
creep/sneak – to walk quietly when you do not want to be seen or heard
trudge – to walk in a tired way or when it is difficult to continue walking
limp – to walk with difficulty because one leg is hurt
wade – to walk through water
hike – to take a long walk in the country, mountains, etc.
➔ RUN, TRAVEL

2 [T] to walk through or across a particular area: *It's not safe to* ***walk the streets*** *at night.* | *He spent two years walking the Baja coastline.* **3** [T] to walk somewhere with someone: *It's late – I'll walk you home.* **4 walk the dog** to take a dog outside to walk **5 walk all over sb** *informal* to treat someone very badly: *She lets those kids walk all over her.* **6** [I] **also walk free** *informal* to leave a court of law without being punished or sent to prison **7 walk the walk** *informal* to do the things that a particular type of person is expected to do: *She doesn't call herself a feminist, but she walks the walk.*

walk away *phr. v.* to leave a bad or difficult situation: *You can't just walk away from eight years of marriage!*

walk away with sth *phr. v.* to win something easily: *Bradley won, walking away with $50,000.*

walk in on sb *phr. v.* to go into a place and accidentally interrupt someone whom you did not expect to be there

walk into sth *phr. v.* **1** to hit an object accidentally as you are walking: *She walked* ***straight/right into*** *a tree.* **2** to become involved in an unpleasant situation without intending to: *The soldiers walked into an ambush.* **3** to do something that makes you seem stupid: *You* ***walked straight into*** *that one!*

walk off *phr. v.* to leave someone by walking away from him or her

walk off with sth *phr. v.* to steal something, or to take something by mistake: *Someone walked off with my new jacket!*

walk out *phr. v.* **1** to stop working or leave a situation as a protest: *Most miners have walked out.* **2** to leave your husband, wife, etc. suddenly: *Mary just* ***walked out on*** *him one day.*

walk² *n.* **1** [C] a trip that you make by walking: *Let's* ***go for a walk.*** | *I like to* ***take a walk*** *after lunch.* | *It's only a* ***ten minute/two mile walk*** *from here.* **2** [C] a particular path or ROUTE for walking: *popular walks in Yellowstone National Park* **3** [U] the way someone walks ➔ WALK OF LIFE

walk·er /ˈwɔkɚ/ *n.* [C] **1** a metal frame that old or sick people use to help them walk **2** someone who is walking, especially at a particular speed, in a particular place, etc.: *a nice area for walkers* | *He's a* ***fast/slow walker.***

walk·ie-talk·ie /ˌwɔki ˈtɔki/ *n.* [C] one of a pair of radios that you can carry with you, and use to speak to the person who has the other radio

ˈwalk-in *adj.* big enough for a person to walk inside: *a walk-in closet*

ˈwalking stick *n.* [C] a long thin stick, used to help support you when you walk

Walk·man /ˈwɔkmən/ *n.* [C] *trademark* a small machine that plays TAPES and has HEADPHONES, that you carry with you to listen to music

ˌwalk of ˈlife *n.* [C] the position in society that someone has: *The club has members from* ***all walks of life.***

ˈwalk-on *n.* [C] a small acting part in a play or movie in which the actor has no words, or an actor who has this part —**walk-on** *adj.*

walk·out /ˈwɔk-aʊt/ *n.* [C] an occasion when people stop working or leave somewhere as a protest: *City employees* ***staged a walkout.***

ˈwalk-up *n.* [C] *informal* an apartment that you have to walk up the stairs to, because there is no ELEVATOR in the building

walk·way /ˈwɔk-weɪ/ *n.* [C] a path, often above the ground, built to connect two parts of a building or two buildings

wall /wɔl/ *n.* [C] **1** one of the sides of a room or building: *The walls were covered with posters.* **2** an upright structure made of stone or brick, that divides one area from another **3** the side of something hollow, such as a pipe or tube: *the walls of the blood vessels* **4** something that prevents you from doing something or going somewhere: *A wall of people was blocking my way.* —**walled** *adj.* ➔ **have your back to/against the wall** at BACK² ➔ **drive sb up the wall** at DRIVE¹

wal·let /ˈwɑlɪt, ˈwɔ-/ *n.* [C] a small object that you keep money in, that is usually made of leather and that you carry in your pocket or PURSE

wal·lop /ˈwɑləp/ *v.* [T] *informal* to hit someone or something very hard —**wallop** *n.* [C]

wal·low /ˈwɑloʊ/ *v.* [I] **1** *disapproving* to spend too long feeling an emotion, especially a negative emotion: *You don't have time to* ***wallow in*** *self-pity.* **2** to roll around in mud or water

wall·pa·per /ˈwɔlˌpeɪpɚ/ *n.* [U] **1** paper that you stick onto the walls of a room in order to decorate it **2** the picture that you have as the background on the screen of a computer —**wallpaper** *v.* [T]

ˈWall Street *n.* **1** a street in New York City where the American STOCK EXCHANGE is **2** the American STOCK EXCHANGE

W

ˌwall-to-ˈwall *adj.* covering the whole floor: *wall-to-wall carpeting*

wal·nut /ˈwɔlnʌt/ *n.* **1** [C] a slightly bitter nut with a large light brown shell, or the tree on which this grows **2** [U] the dark brown wood of this tree

wal·rus /ˈwɔlrəs, ˈwɑl-/ *n.* [C] a large sea animal with two long thick teeth coming down from the sides of its mouth

waltz¹ /wɔlts/ *n.* [C] a fairly slow dance with a RHYTHM consisting of patterns of three beats, or the music for this dance

waltz² *v.* [I] **1** to dance a WALTZ **2** *informal disapproving* to walk somewhere calmly and confidently: *Eric* ***waltzed in*** *late again.*

wan /wɑn/ *adj.* looking pale, weak, or tired: *a wan smile*

wand /wɑnd/ *n.* [C] a thin stick you hold in your hand to do magic tricks

wan·der /ˈwɑndɚ/ *v.* **1** [I,T] to walk slowly across or around an area, usually without having a clear direction or purpose: *We* ***wandered around*** *the city.* | *Homeless people wandered the streets.*

THESAURUS

walk, march, stride, stroll, amble, creep, sneak, trudge, limp, wade, hike
→ see Thesaurus box at WALK¹

2 [I] **also wander off** to move away from where you are supposed to stay: *The kids got bored and started to wander off.* **3** [I] to start to talk or write about something not related to the main subject that you were talking or writing about before **4** [I] if your mind, thoughts, etc. wander, you no longer pay attention to something: *He began to read, but his* ***mind wandered.*** —**wanderer** *n.* [C]

wane¹ /weɪn/ *v.* [I] **1** if something such as power, influence, or a feeling wanes, it becomes gradually less strong or less important: *My enthusiasm for the project was waning.* **2** when the moon wanes, you gradually see less of it

W

wane² *n.* **on the wane** becoming smaller, weaker, or less important: *The show's popularity is on the wane.*

wan·gle /ˈwæŋgəl/ *v.* [T] *informal* to get something by persuading or tricking someone: *I managed to wangle an invitation.*

wan·na /ˈwʌnə, ˈwɑnə/ a short form of "want to" or "want a," used in writing to show how people sound when they speak: *I don't wanna go.*

wan·na·be /ˈwɑnəˌbi/ *n.* [C] *informal* someone who tries to look, behave, or do something like a famous or popular person: *an Elvis wannabe*

want¹ /wʌnt, wɑnt, wɔnt/ *v.* [T] to have a desire or need for something: *What do you want for your birthday?* | *This is a team that really* ***wants to*** *win.* | *Do you* ***want*** *me* ***to*** *read you a story?* | *Want* (=do you want) *a drink?* | *I can pick it up on my way to work* ***if you want*** (=if you would like that).

want for sth *phr. v.* to not have something that you need: *Those kids have never wanted for anything.*

want² *n.* [C,U] something that you desire or need but do not have: *They are dying* ***for want of*** *food and medicine.*

ˈwant ad *n.* [C] a small advertisement that you put in a newspaper if you want to employ someone to do a job

want·ed /ˈwʌntɪd/ *adj.* someone who is wanted is being looked for by the police: *He is* ***wanted for*** *murder.*

want·ing /ˈwʌntɪŋ/ *adj.* lacking or missing something that is needed: *Security procedures were* ***found wanting.***

wan·ton /ˈwɑntˀn, ˈwɔn-/ *adj.* **1** deliberately causing damage or harm for no reason: *wanton destruction* **2** *old-fashioned* sexually uncontrolled: *She felt wanton and wild.*

war /wɔr/ *n.* [C,U] **1** a time when two or more countries or opposing groups within a country fight each other with soldiers and weapons [≠ **peace**]: *World War II* | *In 1793 England* ***was at war*** *with France.* | *the* ***war with/against*** *Germany* | *the soldiers killed* ***in the war*** | *Was it right to* ***go to war*** (=take part in a war)? | *the* ***war between*** *the states*

THESAURUS

warfare – the activity of fighting in a war – used especially when talking about particular methods of fighting: *guerrilla warfare*
fighting – an occasion when people or groups fight each other in a war, in the street etc: *One thousand people have died since the fighting began.*
conflict – fighting or a war: *the conflict in the Middle East*
combat – fighting during a war: *The soldiers were wounded in combat.*
action – fighting in a war: *He had been killed in action.*
hostilities – fighting in a war: *the formal cessation of hostilities*

2 a struggle to control or stop a bad or illegal activity: *the* ***war on/against*** *drugs* **3** a situation in which a person or group is fighting for power, influence, or control: *a trade war* —**war** *v.* [I]

war·ble /ˈwɔrbəl/ *v.* [I,T] to sing with a high, continuous, but quickly changing sound, the way a bird does

ˈwar crime *n.* [C] an illegal and cruel act done during a war —**ˈwar ˌcriminal** *n.* [C]

ward¹ /wɔrd/ *n.* [C] **1** a part of a hospital where people who need medical treatment stay: *the maternity ward* (=for women who are having babies) | *the children's ward* **2** *law* someone, especially a child, who is under the legal protection of another person or of a court of law **3** one of the small areas that a city has been divided into for the purpose of local elections

ward² *v.*
ward sth ⇔ **off** *phr. v.* to do something to protect yourself from an illness, danger, attack, etc.: *a spray to ward off insects*
war·den /ˈwɔrdn/ *n.* [C] the person in charge of a prison
war·drobe /ˈwɔrdroʊb/ *n.* [C] the clothes that someone has: *her large wardrobe*
ware·house /ˈwɛrhaʊs/ *n.* [C] a large building for storing large quantities of goods
ˈwarehouse ˌstore *n.* [C] a type of store that sells things in large amounts at lower prices ➔ see Thesaurus box at STORE¹
wares /wɛrz/ *n.* [plural] *written* things that are for sale, usually not in a store: *craftspeople* ***selling/peddling*** *their* ***wares***
war·fare /ˈwɔrfɛr/ *n.* [U] the activity of fighting in a war – used especially when talking about particular methods of fighting: *chemical warfare*

> **THESAURUS**
> **war**, **fighting**, **conflict**, **combat**, **action**, **hostilities**
> ➔ see Thesaurus box at WAR

ˈwar ˌgame *n.* [C] an activity in which soldiers fight an imaginary battle in order to test military plans
war·head /ˈwɔrhɛd/ *n.* [C] the explosive part at the front of a MISSILE
war·like /ˈwɔrlaɪk/ *adj.* threatening war or attack, or seeming to like war: *a warlike gesture*
war·lock /ˈwɔrlɑk/ *n.* [C] a man who has magic powers, especially to do bad things
war·lord /ˈwɔrlɔrd/ *n.* [C] a leader of an unofficial military or fighting group
warm¹ /wɔrm/ *adj.* **1** slightly hot, especially in a pleasant way [≠ **cool**]: *Are you warm enough? | warmer weather | a warm bath | They huddled together to* ***keep warm***.

> **THESAURUS**
> **hot**, **humid**, **boiling hot**, **sweltering**
> ➔ see Thesaurus box at HOT

2 able to keep in heat or keep out cold: *warm clothes* **3** friendly: *a warm smile* —**warmly** *adv.*

> **THESAURUS**
> **friendly**, **cordial**, **welcoming**, **hospitable**
> ➔ see Thesaurus box at FRIENDLY

warm² **also warm up** *v.* [I,T] to become warm or warmer, or to make someone or something do this: *There's some soup warming up on the stove.* ➔ GLOBAL WARMING
warm to sb/sth **also warm up to** sb/sth *phr. v.* to begin to like someone or something: *Bruce didn't warm to him as he had to Casey.*
warm up *phr. v.* **1** to do gentle physical exercises to prepare your body for exercise, singing, etc.: *The girls are warming up before the game.* **2 warm** (sth ⇔) **up** if a machine or engine warms up, or if you warm it up, it becomes ready to work after being turned on
ˌwarm-ˈblooded *adj.* having a body temperature that remains fairly high whether the temperature around it is hot or cold [➡ **cold-blooded**]: *Mammals are warm-blooded animals.*
ˌwarmed ˈover *adj.* **1** food that is warmed over has been cooked before and then is heated again for eating **2** an idea or argument that is warmed over has been used before and is no longer interesting or useful
ˌwarm-ˈhearted *adj.* friendly and kind: *a warm-hearted old lady*
war·mon·ger /ˈwɔrˌmʌŋgɚ, -ˌmɑŋ-/ *n.* [C] someone who is eager to start a war —**warmongering** *n.* [U]
warmth /wɔrmθ/ *n.* [U] **1** a feeling of being warm: *the warmth of the sun* **2** friendliness: *the warmth of her smile*
ˈwarm-up *n.* [C] a set of gentle exercises that you do to prepare your body for exercise, dancing, singing, etc.
warn /wɔrn/ *v.* [I,T] to tell someone that something bad or dangerous may happen, so that s/he can avoid it or prevent it: *A sign* ***warned of/about*** *the presence of snakes. |* ***I warned*** *you* ***not to*** *walk home alone. | The label* ***warns that*** *pregnant women should not drink alcohol.*

> **COMMUNICATION**
> **Ways of warning someone**
> **be careful**: *Be careful on the ice.*
> **look out** or **watch out**: *Look out! There's a car coming.*
> **beware of sth** written: *Beware of the dog.*
> **mind**: *Mind the step.*

warn·ing /ˈwɔrnɪŋ/ *n.* [C,U] something that tells you that something bad or dangerous might happen, so that you avoid it or prevent it: *a* ***warning of/about*** *the risks involved | The planes attacked* ***without warning***. *| a* ***warning to*** *women over 50 | You've been* ***given*** *several* ***warnings*** *already. | Be aware of* ***warning signs*** (=pain, etc. that shows that an illness is coming) *such as tiredness and headaches.*
warp /wɔrp/ *v.* [I,T] **1** to become bent or twisted, or to make something do this: *The wood had warped in the heat.* **2** to influence someone in a way that has a harmful effect on how s/he thinks or behaves ➔ TIME WARP
war·path /ˈwɔrpæθ/ *n.* **be on the warpath** *humorous* to be angry about something and want to punish someone for it
warped /wɔrpt/ *adj.* **1** someone who is warped has ideas or thoughts that most people think are unpleasant or not normal: *a warped sense of humor* **2** bent or twisted into the wrong shape: *a warped door*

THESAURUS

bent, **twisted**, **curved**, **crooked**, **wavy**
➔ see Thesaurus box at BENT[2]

'warp speed *n.* [U] *informal* a speed that is very fast

war·rant¹ /'wɔrənt, 'wɑ-/ *v.* [T] to be a good enough reason for something to happen or be done [➡ **unwarranted**]: *The story doesn't warrant the attention it's been given.*

warrant² *n.* [C] an official paper that allows the police to do something: *a **warrant for** Bryson's arrest* | *The local judge **issued** the **warrant**.*

war·ran·ty /'wɔrənti, 'wɑ-/ *n.* plural **warranties** [C,U] a written promise that a company will fix or replace something if it breaks after you have bought it: *The TV comes with a 3-year warranty.*

war·ren /'wɔrən, 'wɑ-/ *n.* [C] **1** a set of holes and passages under the ground that rabbits live in **2** a lot of narrow passages in a building or between buildings: *a warren of corridors*

war·ring /'wɔrɪŋ/ *adj.* fighting in a war: *warring factions*

war·ri·or /'wɔriɚ, 'wɑ-/ *n.* [C] *literary* a soldier, especially an experienced and skillful one

war·ship /'wɔrʃɪp/ *n.* [C] a navy ship with guns

THESAURUS

ship, **cruise ship**, **liner**, **ferry**, **freighter**, **tanker**, **barge**, **aircraft carrier**, **battleship**, **cruiser**, **submarine**
➔ see Thesaurus box at SHIP[1]

wart /wɔrt/ *n.* [C] a small hard raised spot on your skin caused by a VIRUS

THESAURUS

mark, **blemish**, **bruise**, **scar**, **pimple**, **zit**, **blister**, **freckle**, **mole**
➔ see Thesaurus box at MARK[2]

W

war·time /'wɔrtaɪm/ *n.* [U] the time during which a war is happening: *his wartime experiences*

'war-torn *adj.* being damaged or destroyed by war: *his war-torn homeland*

war·y /'wɛri/ *adj.* careful and worried about danger or problems: *Teach children to be **wary of** strangers.* —**warily** *adv.*

was /wəz; *strong* wʌz, wɑz/ *v.* the past tense of BE in the first and third person singular

wash¹ /wɑʃ, wɔʃ/ *v.* **1** [T] to clean something with water and usually soap: *She helped Penny wash the dishes.* | ***Wash** the mud **off** the truck.* **2** [I,T] to clean your body with water and usually soap: *Wash your hands thoroughly.* | *I'm going upstairs to wash.* **3** [I,T] if water, a river, the ocean, etc. washes, it flows somewhere or makes something move somewhere: *waves **washing against** the shore* | *Floods **washed** much of the topsoil **away**.* | *Their boat **washed up/ashore** about five miles south.* **4 sth doesn't/won't wash** *spoken* said when you do not believe or accept someone's explanation, reasons, etc.: *His explanation just didn't wash.* **5 wash your hands of sth** to refuse to be responsible for something: *Congress can't wash its hands of this.*

wash sth ⇔ **down** *phr. v.* **1** to drink something in order to help you swallow food or medicine: *He **washed down** a mouthful of toast **with** coffee.* **2** to clean something using a lot of water: *Ted was washing down the driveway.*

wash off *phr. v.* if a substance washes off, you can remove it from the surface of something by washing: *Will this paint wash off?*

wash out *phr. v.* **1** if a substance washes out, you can remove it from a material by washing it: *I don't know if that ink will wash out.* **2 wash** sth ⇔ **out** to wash the inside of something: *Will you wash out the cups?*

wash up *phr. v.* to wash your hands: *Go wash up for supper.*

wash² *n.* **1** [C,U] clothing, sheets, etc. that have been washed or that need washing: *I **did** three loads of **wash**.* | *Your blue shirt is **in the wash*** (=being washed or waiting to be washed). **2** [C] a river in a desert area that has no water in it most of the time **3 it will all come out in the wash** *spoken* said when you think that a problem will be solved without you having to do anything about it ➔ CAR WASH

wash·a·ble /'wɑʃəbəl/ *adj.* able to be washed without being damaged: *a **machine washable** sweater*

wash·basin /'wɑʃˌbeɪsən/ **also wash·bowl** /'wɑʃboʊl/ *n.* [C] a SINK

wash·cloth /'wɑʃklɔθ/ *n.* [C] a small square piece of cloth that you use to wash yourself

ˌwashed-'out *adj.* very tired and pale: *his washed-out blue eyes*

ˌwashed-'up *adj.* *informal* someone who is washed-up is no longer successful: *a washed-up rock star*

wash·er /'wɑʃɚ/ *n.* [C] **1** a washing machine **2** a small ring of plastic or metal that you put between a NUT and a BOLT, or between two pipes, to make them fit together tightly

wash·ing /'wɑʃɪŋ/ *n.* [U] clothes, etc. that need to be washed or have just been washed

'washing maˌchine *n.* [C] a machine that washes clothes

wash·room /'wɑʃrum, -rʊm/ *n.* [C] *old-fashioned* ➔ RESTROOM

was·n't /'wʌzənt, 'wɑzənt/ *v.* the short form of "was not": *He wasn't there.*

WASP, **Wasp** /wɑsp/ *n.* [C] **white Anglo-Saxon Protestant** a white American whose family was originally from northern Europe and who is therefore considered to be part of the most powerful group in society

wasp /wɑsp, wɔsp/ *n.* [C] a black and yellow flying insect similar to a BEE, that can sting you

waste[1] /weɪst/ *n.* **1** [singular, U] the use of something such as money or skills in a way that is not effective, useful, or sensible: *a **waste of** resources* | *My father thought college would be a **waste of time/money**.* **2 go to waste** if something goes to waste, it is not used: *A lot of the food ended up going to waste.* **3** [C,U] unwanted things or substances that are left after you have used something: *recycle **household waste*** | *the safe disposal of **nuclear/toxic/hazardous wastes***

THESAURUS

garbage, **trash**, **refuse**, **litter**
➔ see Thesaurus box at GARBAGE

waste[2] *v.* [T] **1** to use something in a way that is not effective, or to use more of it than you should: *Don't waste electricity!* | *They **wasted** a lot of **time** trying to fix it themselves.* **2 be wasted on sb** if something is wasted on someone, s/he does not understand it or does not think it is worth anything: *The joke was wasted on him.* **3** *slang* to kill someone

waste away *phr. v.* to gradually become thinner and weaker because you are sick

waste[3] *adj.* not being used effectively or no longer useful: *waste paper*

waste·bas·ket /ˈweɪst̬ˌbæskɪt/ *n.* [C] a container into which you put paper, etc. that you want to get rid of

wast·ed /ˈweɪstɪd/ *adj.* **1** useless: *It had been a wasted trip.* **2** *spoken* having drunk too much or taken drugs: *Chuck **got wasted** at Bryan's party.*

waste·ful /ˈweɪstfəl/ *adj.* using more than is needed of something or using it badly, so that it is wasted: *wasteful packaging on groceries*

waste·land /ˈweɪstlænd/ *n.* [C,U] **1** an area of land that is not or cannot be used for anything: *a desert wasteland* **2** a place, situation, or time that has no excitement or interest: *Television is a vast wasteland.*

waste·pa·per bas·ket /ˈweɪst̬ˌpeɪpɚ ˌbæskɪt/ *n.* [C] ➔ WASTEBASKET

watch[1] /wɑtʃ, wɔtʃ/ *v.* **1** [I,T] to look at and pay attention to something or someone: *Harry was watching the game on TV.* | *I watched him go.* | ***Watch closely** – can you see it moving?*

USAGE

You **look at** a picture, person, thing, etc. because you want to: *Hey, look at these jeans.*
You **see** something without planning to: *Two people saw him take the bag.*
You **watch** TV, a movie, or something that happens for a period of time: *Did you watch the football game last night?* | *The kids are watching TV.*
You can also say that you **saw** a movie, a program, etc., but you cannot say "see television": *I saw a great movie on TV last night.*

2 [T] to be careful about something, in order to avoid an accident or unwanted situation: *Watch your head; the door's low.* | ***Watch your weight*** (=be careful not to become fat) *and exercise.* | *Why don't you **watch where** you're **going**?* | *Hey, **watch it** – you stepped on my toes.* **3 watch your language/mouth/tongue** to not say things that might hurt or offend other people: *Watch your language, Bill, there's ladies present.* **4** [T] to take care of someone or guard something: *Could you watch the kids for me Saturday night?* **5 watch the clock** to keep looking to see what time it is because you are bored or do not want to work

watch (out) for sth *phr. v.* to look for something, so that you are ready to deal with it: *I watched for the White Oak exit.* | *You can ride your bike, but watch out for cars.*

watch out *phr. v.* used in order to tell someone to be careful: *Watch out! It's hot.*

watch over sth *phr. v.* to take care of something or guard it: *The eldest child watches over the younger ones.*

watch

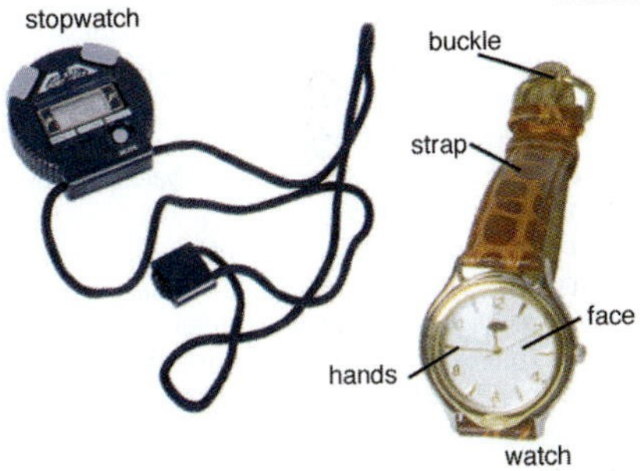

watch[2] *n.* **1** [C] a small clock that you wear on your wrist or carry in your pocket: *Scott looked at his watch.* **2** [singular,U] the process of checking a situation or a place carefully so that you always know what is happening and are ready to deal with it: *Police **kept** a 24-hour **watch on** the house.* | *Several soldiers **stood watch**.* | *Douglas **kept watch** while the others slept.* **3 be on the watch for sb/sth** to be looking and waiting for something that might happen or someone you might see: *Be on the watch for pickpockets.* **4** [C,U] people employed to guard or protect someone or something, or the fixed period of the day or night when they do this: *the night watch* | *Who has first watch?*

watch·dog /ˈwɑtʃdɔg/ *n.* [C] **1** a person or group that makes sure other people follow rules: *a consumer watchdog group* **2** a dog that protects someone's property

watch·ful /ˈwɑtʃfəl/ *adj.* careful to notice what is happening, in order to prevent something bad happening: *She learned to bake **under the watchful eye** of her mother.*

watch·mak·er /ˈwɑtʃˌmeɪkɚ/ *n.* [C] someone who makes and repairs watches and clocks

watch·man /ˈwɑtʃmən/ *n.* [C] someone whose job is to guard a building or area: *the night watchman*

watch·word /ˈwɑtʃwɚd/ *n.* [singular] the main principle or rule that you think about in a particular situation: *The school's watchword is "a community of learners."*

wa·ter¹ /ˈwɔt̬ɚ, ˈwɑ-/ *n.* [U] **1** the clear colorless liquid that falls from the sky as rain, forms lakes, rivers, and oceans, and is used for drinking, washing, etc.: *a drink of water* | *Mike waded out into the water.* | *floods left the area* ***under water*** | *a cabin with no* ***running water*** (=water from pipes) | ***fresh water*** (=from a lake, river, etc. not an ocean) *fish* **2 waters** [plural] **a)** the part of the ocean near or belonging to a particular country: *boats fishing in Icelandic waters* **b)** the water in a particular lake, river, etc.: *The waters of the Amazon flow into the sea.* **3 in/into hot water** in a situation in which you have a lot of trouble: *My brother got into hot water at school.*

water² *v.* **1** [T] to pour water on a plant or seeds in the ground to help them grow **2** [I] if your eyes water, they fill with water because they hurt: *Her eyes watered and her throat hurt.* **3** [I] if your mouth waters, it fills with water because you see something that looks good to eat

water sth ⇔ **down** *phr. v.* **1** to make something weaker by adding water: *The whiskey had been watered down.* **2** to make an idea, statement, etc. less strong so that it does not offend or upset anyone: *The bill got watered down in the Senate.*

wa·ter·bed /ˈwɔt̬ɚˌbɛd/ *n.* [C] a bed made of rubber or soft plastic and filled with water

wa·ter·borne /ˈwɔt̬ɚˌbɔrn/ *adj.* carried by water: *waterborne bacteria*

wa·ter·col·or /ˈwɔt̬ɚˌkʌlɚ/ *n.* [C,U] a special paint mixed with water, or a painting made with these

W

ˈwater ˌcooler *n.* [C] a WATER FOUNTAIN

ˌwatered-ˈdown *adj.* a watered-down statement, plan, etc. is not as strong or offensive as a previous one: *a watered-down version of the proposal*

wa·ter·fall /ˈwɔt̬ɚˌfɔl/ *n.* [C] water that falls straight down over a rock or from the top of a mountain

waterfall

ˈwater ˌfountain *n.* [C] a piece of equipment in a public place that produces a stream of water that you can drink from

wa·ter·front /ˈwɔt̬ɚˌfrʌnt/ *n.* [C] land at the edge of a lake, river, etc.: *a restaurant* ***on the waterfront***

wa·ter·hole /ˈwɔt̬ɚˌhoʊl/ *n.* [C] a WATERING HOLE

ˈwatering can *n.* [C] a container with a long hollow part on the front for pouring water on plants

ˈwatering hole *n.* [C] *informal* **1** a place such as a club or BAR where people can buy drinks: *the students' favorite watering hole* **2** a small area of water in a dry place where wild animals go to drink

wa·ter·logged /ˈwɔt̬ɚˌlɔgd, -ˌlɑgd/ *adj.* land or an object that is waterlogged is so wet it cannot hold any more water

wa·ter·mark /ˈwɔt̬ɚˌmɑrk/ *n.* [C] **1** a special design on a piece of paper that you can only see when it is held up to the light **2** the mark showing the highest level of a lake, river, etc.

wa·ter·mel·on /ˈwɔt̬ɚˌmɛlən/ *n.* [C,U] a large round green fruit with juicy dark pink flesh and black seeds ➔ see picture at FRUIT

ˈwater ˌpolo *n.* [U] a game played in a swimming pool, in which two teams of players try to throw a ball into their opponents' GOAL

wa·ter·proof /ˈwɔt̬ɚˌpruf/ *adj.* not allowing water to go through: *waterproof boots*

ˈwater reˌsistant *adj.* not letting water in easily, but not keeping all water out: *a water resistant watch*

wa·ter·shed /ˈwɔt̬ɚˌʃɛd/ *n.* **1** [singular] the point at which an important change happens: *The beginning of television was* ***a watershed in*** *20th century culture.* **2** [C] the high land separating two river systems

wa·ter·side /ˈwɔt̬ɚˌsaɪd/ *adj.* at the edge of a lake, river, etc.: *a waterside restaurant* —**waterside** *n.* [singular]

ˈwater ˌskiing *n.* [U] a sport in which someone is pulled along on SKIS over water by a boat: *Do you want to* ***go water skiing****?* —**water ski** *v.* [I] —**water skier** *n.* [C]

wa·ter·tight /ˈwɔt̬ɚˌtaɪt/ *adj.* not allowing water to get in: *a watertight container*

wa·ter·way /ˈwɔt̬ɚˌweɪ/ *n.* [C] an area of water, often part of a river, that ships can go through

wa·ter·works /ˈwɔt̬ɚˌwɚks/ *n.* [plural] buildings, pipes, and supplies of water that form a public water system

wa·ter·y /ˈwɔt̬əri/ *adj.* containing too much water: *watery soup* | *watery eyes*

watt /wɑt/ *n.* [C] a unit for measuring electrical power: *a 100 watt light bulb*

wave[1] /weɪv/ *n.* [C] **1** a area of raised water that moves across the surface of the ocean or another large area of water: ***waves breaking*** *on the beach* **2** a sudden increase in a particular emotion, activity, number, etc.: *a recent* ***crime wave*** | *a* ***wave of*** *nostalgia for his childhood* | *a sudden wave of nausea* | *a* ***great wave*** *of immigrants from Eastern Europe* **3** the movement you make when you wave your hand: *She left with* ***a wave of*** *her* ***hand****.* **4** a part of your hair that curls slightly: *a wave in her hair* **5** the form in which some types of energy move: *light/sound/radio waves* **6 make waves** *informal* to cause problems: *We have a job to finish, so don't make waves, OK?* ➔ HEAT WAVE

wave[2] *v.* **1** [I,T] to move your hand, or something you hold in your hand, from side to side as a signal or greeting, or to express something: *demonstrators waving their signs* | *The boys* ***waved at*** *her.* | *John* ***waved to*** *the waiter, asking for the check.* | ***I waved goodbye.*** | *One of the cops* ***waved*** *me* ***through/away*** (=moved his hand to show me which way to go). ➔ see picture on page A8 **2** [I] if a flag waves, it moves with the wind

wave sth ⇔ **aside** *phr. v.* to refuse to pay attention to a person or to his or her opinions, questions, ideas, etc.: *"Not true!" she said, waving aside any further questions.*

wave·length /ˈweɪvleŋkθ/ *n.* [C] **1** the size of a radio wave or the distance between two waves of energy such as sound or light **2 be on the same wavelength** *informal* to think in the same way about something as someone else does

wa·ver /ˈweɪvɚ/ *v.* [I] **1** to be unsteady: *Her voice wavered slightly.* **2** to become weaker or less certain: *Their faith in me never wavered.* **3** to not make a decision because you have doubts: *Harland is* ***wavering between*** *two options.*

wav·y /ˈweɪvi/ *adj.* having waves (=even curved shapes): *wavy hair*

THESAURUS

bent, twisted, curved, warped, crooked
➔ see Thesaurus box at BENT[2]

➔ see picture at HAIR

wax[1] /wæks/ *n.* [U] **1** a thick substance made of fats or oils, used for making things such as CANDLES **2** a natural sticky substance in your ears

wax[2] *v.* **1** [T] to put wax on something to protect it or make it shine **2 wax romantic/eloquent etc.** *often humorous* to talk eagerly about someone or something you admire, especially for a long time: *He waxed nostalgic about the one-room schools of his youth.* **3** [I] when the moon waxes, it seems to get bigger every night **4** [T] to use wax to remove the hair from your legs

ˌwaxed ˈpaper also **ˈwax ˌpaper** *n.* [U] paper with a thin layer of WAX on it, used for wrapping food

wax·y /ˈwæksi/ *adj.* made of wax, covered in wax, or feeling like wax: *apples with a waxy skin* —**waxiness** *n.* [U]

way[1] /weɪ/ *n.*

1 ROAD/PATH [C] the road, path, etc. that you have to follow in order to get to a particular place: *Which way should we go?* | *Can you mail this on your* ***way downtown/home****?* | *Could you tell me the* ***way to*** *the police station* ***from*** *here?* | *Ben* ***knows the way****.* | *I can give you a ride; it's* ***on my/the way****.* | *Can you move your bag; it's* ***in the way****.*

USAGE

Use **on the way** when you will do something or pass something as you go to a place: *I'll get some gas on the way home.*
Use **in the way** when something is preventing you from getting to the place you are going: *I couldn't get out of the driveway because Mark's car was in the way.*

2 DIRECTION [C] a particular direction: *Which way is north?* | *Face this way, please.*

3 METHOD [C] a manner or method of doing something or thinking about something: *Is there any* ***way to*** *tell how old it is?* | *I'd like to tell her* ***in my own way****.* | *Drugs do not affect everyone* ***in the same way****.* | *Look at the way that guy's dressed!* | *Ryan has a funny* ***way of*** *talking.*

4 in a way/in some ways/in one way used in order to say that something is partly true: *In a way, I like working alone better.*

5 DISTANCE/TIME [singular] **also ways** the distance or time between two places or events, especially if it is long: *a* ***long way*** *from home* | *We have a way to go yet before we're done.* | *Did he actually come* ***all the way*** (=the whole distance) *from Bali?*

6 have/get your way to do what you want even if someone else wants something different: *They always let that kid* ***get his own way****.*

7 the way/sb's way where someone wants to go: *There was a big truck* ***in the way*** (=preventing people from going past). | *Get* ***out of my way*** (=move aside)*!*

8 get in the way of sth to prevent something from happening: *Don't let your social life get in the way of your studying.*

9 come a long way to have developed a lot: *Psychiatry has come a long way since the 1920s.*

W

10 a long way to go to need a lot of time to develop or reach a particular standard: *There is a long way to go before democracy is accepted there.*
11 under way happening or moving: *Building work is scheduled to* ***get under way*** (=start happening) *today.*
12 be on the way/its way/sb's way to be arriving soon or traveling to a place: *The check is on its way.* | *Carla's already on her way here.*
13 way around/up a particular order or position that something should be in: *Which way around does this skirt go?* | *Make sure all the pictures are the* ***right way up****.*
14 give way to sth if one thing gives way to another thing, this other thing replaces it or controls it: *fear gave way to anger*
15 go out of your way to do sth to do something that involves making a special effort, especially for someone else: *Ben went out of his way to help us.*
16 you can't have it both ways used in order to say that you cannot have the advantages of two different possible decisions
17 make way a) to move to one side so that someone or something can pass **b)** if one thing makes way for something else, this other thing replaces it: *Several houses were torn down to* ***make way for*** *a new fire station.*

SPOKEN PHRASES

18 by the way said when you want to begin talking about a new subject that you have just remembered: *Oh, by the way, I saw Marie yesterday.*
19 no way! a) used in order to say that you will definitely not do or allow something: *No way am I letting him know about this.* **b)** used in order to say that you do not believe something or are surprised by it: *She's 45? No way!*
20 that's the way used in order to tell someone that they are doing something correctly: *Keep your arms straight out – that's the way.*
21 way to go! used in order to tell someone that s/he has done something good, or done something very well ➔ **out of the way** at OUT²

way² *adv.* **1** long in distance or time: *a boat* ***way out*** *on the lake* | *a movie made* ***way back*** *before they used sound* **2 way more/bigger/longer etc.** *spoken nonstandard* a lot more, bigger, longer, etc.: *This test was way harder than the last one.*

way·lay /ˈweɪleɪ/ *v.* past tense and past participle **waylaid** [T] to stop someone when s/he is trying to go some place, so that you can talk to him/her, or in order to rob or attack him/her

ˌway of ˈlife *n.* plural **ways of life** [C] the way someone lives, or the way people in a society usually live: *the* ***American way of life***

ˌway-ˈout *adj. spoken* very modern and strange: *I like jazz, but not the way-out stuff.*

way·side /ˈweɪsaɪd/ *n.* **fall/go by the wayside** to stop being successful, important, popular, etc.: *My dream of college fell by the wayside.*

way·ward /ˈweɪwɚd/ *adj.* not following rules, and causing problems: *a wayward teenager*

we /wi/ *pron.* **1** the person who is speaking and one or more other people: *We went to a movie.* | *We live in Dallas.* **2** people in general: *We know almost nothing about what causes the disease.* | ***We all*** *dream of being rich one day.*

weak /wik/ *adj.* **1** not physically strong: *He felt weak and dizzy.* | *a weak heart* | *Nina was* ***weak from/with*** *hunger.* **2** not strong in character, and easily influenced: *He's weak and indecisive.* **3** not having much ability or skill in a particular activity or subject: *I'm good at math, but* ***weak at/in*** *science.* | *the team's weak shooting* **4** not having much power or influence: *a weak leader* **5** not being good enough to persuade, influence, or interest people: *a weak excuse* | *a weak joke* **6** not financially successful: *the country's weak economy* **7** containing a lot of water or having little taste: *weak tea* —**weakly** *adv.*

weak·en /ˈwikən/ *v.* [I,T] **1** to become less powerful or physically strong, or to make someone or something do this: *The disease has weakened her heart.* | *a country weakened by war* **2** to become less determined, or to make someone do this: *Nothing could* ***weaken*** *her* ***resolve.*** **3** if money, the economy, etc. weakens, or if they are weakened, their value is reduced: *the country's weakened economy*

weak·ling /ˈwik-lɪŋ/ *n.* [C] *disapproving* someone who is not physically strong

weak·ness /ˈwiknɪs/ *n.* **1** [C] a fault in someone's character or in a system, organization, design, etc.: *What are your* ***strengths and weaknesses****?* | *a* ***major weakness*** *in the program* **2** [U] the state of lacking strength in your body or character: ***weakness in*** *the muscles* **3** [U] lack of power, strength, or influence: *moral* ***weakness in*** *our society* | *the* ***weakness of*** *our currency* **4 a weakness for sth** if you have a weakness for something, you like it very much even though it may not be good for you: *She's always had a weakness for chocolate.*

wealth /wɛlθ/ *n.* **1** [U] a large amount of money and possessions: *their family's personal wealth* | *the nation's mineral wealth* **2 a wealth of sth** a lot of something useful or good: *the wealth of information on the Internet*

wealth·y /ˈwɛlθi/ *adj.* comparative **wealthier**, superlative **wealthiest** **1** having a lot of money or valuable possessions: *a very wealthy man*

THESAURUS

rich, **well-off**, **prosperous**, **well-to-do**, **rolling in it**, **loaded**
➔ see Thesaurus box at RICH

2 the wealthy people who have a lot of money or valuable possessions

wean /win/ *v.* [I,T] to gradually stop feeding a baby his/her mother's milk and start giving him/her ordinary food

wean sb **off/from** sth *phr. v.* to make someone gradually stop doing something you disapprove of: *He'll need to be weaned off the drug slowly.*

be weaned on sth *phr. v.* to be influenced by something from a very early age: *young movie directors who were weaned on MTV videos*

weap·on /ˈwɛpən/ *n.* [C] **1** something that you use to fight with, especially a knife or gun: *soldiers carrying their weapons | the danger posed by **nuclear/chemical/biological weapons*** **2** an action, piece of information, piece of equipment, etc. that you can use to win or be successful in doing something: *a new weapon in the fight against cancer* —**weaponry** *n.* [U]

wear¹ /wɛr/ *v.* past tense **wore** /wɔr/ past participle **worn** /wɔrn/ **1** [T] to have something on your body, especially clothes or jewelry: *Why aren't you wearing your glasses? | a girl wearing a pink sun dress | His wife was **wearing black/white/blue*** (=wearing black, etc. clothes). **2** [T] to have your hair in a particular style: *Fay wore her hair in braids.* **3** [I,T] to become thinner, weaker, etc. by continued use, or to make something do this: *He's **worn a hole in** his pants already.* **4** [T] to have a particular expression on your face: *She was wearing a smile.* **5 wear well** to remain in good condition after a period of time: *Expensive fabrics don't always wear well.* **6 sth is wearing thin** *informal* if an excuse, explanation, opinion, etc. is wearing thin, it has been used so often that you no longer believe or accept it **7 wear the pants** *informal* to be the person in a family who makes the decisions

wear (sth ⇔) **away** *phr. v.* to gradually become thinner, weaker, etc., or to make something do this by using it, rubbing it, etc.: *The paint is almost all worn away. | The water is gradually wearing away the rock.*

wear down *phr. v.* **1 wear** (sth ⇔) **down** to gradually become smaller, or to make something do this by using it, rubbing it, etc.: *My shoes have worn down at the heel.* **2 wear** sb ⇔ **down** to gradually make someone physically weaker or less determined: *The constant stress is wearing her down.*

wear off *phr. v.* if pain or the effect of something wears off, it gradually stops: *The anesthesia was starting to wear off.*

wear on *phr. v.* if time wears on, it passes very slowly: *It became hotter as the day wore on.*

wear sb/sth ⇔ **out** *phr. v.* **1** to become weak, broken, or useless, or to make something do this by using it a lot or for a long time: *I think these batteries have worn out.* **2** to feel extremely tired, or to make someone feel this way: *You look really worn out.* **3 wear out your welcome** to stay at someone's house longer than s/he wants you to

wear² *n.* [U] **1** clothes of a particular type, or worn for a particular activity: *evening wear* **2** normal damage caused by continuous use over a long period: *Check the tires for **wear and tear**.* **3** the amount of use you can expect to get from something: *You'll **get** a lot of **wear out of** a sweater like that.*

wea·ri·some /ˈwɪrisəm/ **also wear·ing** /ˈwɛrɪŋ/ *adj. formal* making you feel bored, tired, or annoyed: *a wearisome task*

wea·ry¹ /ˈwɪri/ *adj.* comparative **wearier**, superlative **weariest** very tired: *She was **weary of** arguing. | The nation is **weary of** war.* —**wearily** *adv.* —**weariness** *n.* [U]

> **THESAURUS**
>
> **tired, exhausted, worn out, run-down, beat**
> ➔ see Thesaurus box at TIRED

weary² *v.* past tense and past participle **wearied**, third person singular **wearies** [I,T] *formal* to become very tired or no longer enjoy something, or to make someone feel this way: *Jacobs **wearied of** his job at the bank.*

wea·sel¹ /ˈwizəl/ *n.* [C] **1** an animal like a long thin rat that kills other small animals **2** *informal* someone who has not been loyal to you or has deceived you

weasel² *v.*

weasel out of sth *phr. v. informal* to avoid doing something you should do by using dishonest excuses or lies: *He's in court trying to weasel out of his debts.*

weath·er¹ /ˈwɛðɚ/ *n.* **1** [singular, U] the temperature and other conditions such as sun, rain, and wind: ***What's the weather like** today? | Our flight was delayed because of **bad weather**. | very **cold/warm/hot/dry weather***

> **COMMUNICATION**
>
> **Ways of talking about the weather**
> **It's sunny/nice/beautiful.**
> **It's rainy/wet/cloudy/windy/foggy.**
> **It's cool/chilly.**
> **It's warm.**
> **It's (boiling) hot.**
> **It's (freezing) cold.**
> **It's snowing.**
> **It's raining.**
> **It's pouring (rain)** (=raining a lot).
> **It's drizzling** (=raining a little).

2 under the weather *informal* slightly sick: *I'm feeling a little under the weather.*

weather² *v.* **1** [T] to come through a very difficult situation without failing: *Business was bad, but we knew we would **weather the storm**.* **2** [I,T] if a surface is weathered, or if it weathers, the wind, rain, and sun gradually change its appearance: *a weathered stone monument | Her face was weathered by the sun.*

ˈweather ˌforecast *n.* [C] a report on the television or radio that says what the weather will be like —**weather forecaster** *n.* [C]

W

'weather vane *n.* [C] a metal object attached to the top of a building, that moves to show the direction the wind is blowing

weave¹ /wiv/ *v.* **1** past tense **wove** /woʊv/ past participle **woven** /ˈwoʊvən/ [I,T] to make cloth, a CARPET, a basket, etc. by crossing threads or thin pieces under and over each other by hand or on a LOOM: *traditional basket weaving* **2** past tense **wove**, past participle **woven** [T] to put many different ideas, subjects, stories, etc. together and connect them smoothly: *Her novels weave together suspense and romance.* **3** past tense and past participle **weaved** [I,T] to move somewhere by turning and changing direction a lot: *The car was **weaving in and out of** traffic.*

weave² *n.* [C] the way in which a material is woven, and the pattern formed by this: *a fine weave*

web /wɛb/ *n.* [C] **1 the Web** the system that connects computers around the world together so that people can use and find information on the Internet [= **World Wide Web**]: *popular sites **on the Web*** **2** a net of sticky thin threads made by a SPIDER to catch insects: *a spider **spinning** its **web*** ➔ see picture at SPIDER **3 a web of sth** a closely related set of things that can be very complicated: *a web of lies*

webbed /wɛbd/ *adj.* webbed feet or toes have skin between the toes ➔ see picture on page A2

web·cam /ˈwɛbkæm/ *n.* [C] a video camera that is connected to a computer and broadcasts images onto a website

web·cast /ˈwɛbkæst/ *v.* [I,T] to broadcast an event on the Internet, at the time the event happens

'web page *n.* [C] all the information that you can see in one part of a website

web·site /ˈwɛbsaɪt/ *n.* [C] a place on the Internet where you can find information about something, especially a particular organization: *For more information, **visit** our **website**.* ➔ see Topic box at INTERNET

W

we'd /wid/ **1** the short form of "we had": *We'd better go now.* **2** the short form of "we would": *We'd rather stay.*

wed /wɛd/ *v.* past tense and past participle **wedded** or **wed** **1** [I,T] *literary* to marry someone **2 be wedded to sth** to believe strongly in a particular idea or way of doing things

wed·ding /ˈwɛdɪŋ/ *n.* [C] a marriage ceremony, especially one with a religious service: *Have you been invited to their wedding?* | *a simple **wedding reception*** (=a special meal or party after a wedding) | *a **wedding dress/cake/present***

TOPIC

At a **wedding ceremony/service** the most important people are the **bride** (=woman getting married) and the **groom** (=man getting married). The **best man** helps the groom and the **maid of honor** and the **bridesmaids** help the bride. After the ceremony, there is usually a **reception**. Then the bride and groom **go on a honeymoon** (=special vacation).
➔ ENGAGED, MARRIED

'wedding ring *n.* [C] a ring that you wear to show that you are married

wedge¹ /wɛdʒ/ *n.* [C] **1** a piece of wood, metal, etc. that has one thick edge and one pointed edge, used for keeping a door open, splitting wood, etc. **2** something shaped like a wedge: *a **wedge of** chocolate cake*

wedge² *v.* [T] **1** to force something firmly into a narrow space: *We **wedged** a towel **under** the door to keep the cold air out.* **2 wedge sth open/shut** to put something under a door, window, etc. to make it stay open or shut

wed·lock /ˈwɛdlɑk/ *n. old-fashioned* **born out of wedlock** if a child is born out of wedlock, his/her parents are not married when s/he is born

Wednes·day /ˈwɛnzdi, -deɪ/ *n.* [C] **Wed.** the fourth day of the week: *Classes start Wednesday.* | *What time are you coming **on Wednesday**?* | *I have to work **next Wednesday**.* | *Eva had surgery **last Wednesday**.* | *We're all going out to dinner on **Wednesday night**.*

wee /wi/ *adj.* **1** *literary* very small: *a wee child* **2 the wee hours** the early hours of the morning, just after MIDNIGHT

weed¹ /wid/ *n.* [C] a wild plant that grows where you do not want it to grow: *She was **pulling weeds** in the back yard.* | *The lilacs were growing **like weeds*** (=very quickly and easily).

weed² *v.* [I,T] to remove WEEDs from a place

weed sb/sth ⇔ **out** *phr. v.* to get rid of people or things that are not very good: *Weaker students were weeded out of the program.*

week /wik/ *n.* [C] **1** a period of time equal to seven days, beginning on Sunday and ending on Saturday: *I can't see you **this week**.* | ***last/next week*** (=the week before or after this one) **2** any period of time equal to seven days and nights: *I've been living here for six weeks.* | *This is the second time the Yankees have lost **in a week**.* | *I'll be back **a week from today/tomorrow/Friday*** (=a week after today, etc.). | *Are you busy **the week after next*** (=the week that follows next week)? **3 also work week** the part of the week when you go to work, usually from Monday to Friday: *a 40-hour week* | *I don't see the kids much **during the week**.*

week·day /ˈwikdeɪ/ *n.* [C] any day of the week except Saturday and Sunday

week·end /ˈwikɛnd/ *n.* [C] Saturday and Sunday: *What are you doing **this weekend**?* | *Jerry sees the children mainly **on weekends**.* | ***last/next weekend*** (=the weekend before or after this one) | *We went to the beach **over the weekend*** (=during the weekend).

week·ly /ˈwikli/ *adj.* happening or done every week: *a weekly radio show* | *weekly meetings*

THESAURUS

regular, **hourly**, **daily**, **monthly**, **yearly**, **annual**
→ see Thesaurus box at REGULAR[1]

—**weekly** *adv.*

week·night /ˈwiknaɪt/ *n.* [C] any night except Saturday or Sunday

wee·nie /ˈwini/ *n.* [C] *spoken* a HOT DOG

weep /wip/ *v.* past tense and past participle **wept** /wɛpt/ [I,T] *literary* to cry: *She wept quietly for a few moments.*

weigh /weɪ/ *v.* **1** [conjunction] to have a particular weight: *The baby weighs 12 pounds.* | ***How much** do you **weigh**?* **2** [T] to measure how heavy someone or something is: *Have you weighed yourself lately?* **3** [T] **also weigh up** to consider something carefully before making a decision: *I had to weigh the options pretty carefully.*

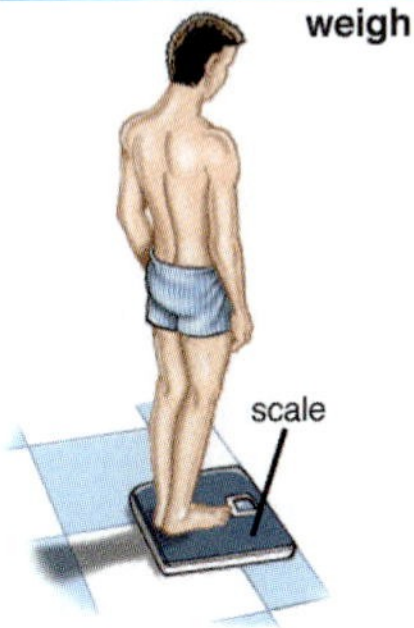

weigh sb ⇔ **down** *phr. v.* **1** if something weighs you down, it is heavy and difficult to carry **2** if you are weighed down by your problems and difficulties, you worry a lot about them: *He felt weighed down by his responsibilities.*

weigh in *phr. v.* **1** to have your weight measured before taking part in a competition **2** to add a remark to a discussion or an argument: *The chairman then **weighed in with** his own opinion.*

weigh on sb *phr. v.* to make someone feel worried: *The problem's been **weighing on** my **mind** for a long time.*

weight[1] /weɪt/ *n.*
1 WHAT SB/STH WEIGHS [U] how heavy someone or something is: *She's always worried about her weight.* | *Have you **lost weight** (=become thinner)?* | *I think he's **put on** some **weight*** (=become fatter). | *I'm **watching** my **weight*** (=being careful not to gain weight).
2 HEAVINESS [U] the fact of being heavy: *The weight of her boots made it hard for her to run.*
3 HEAVY THING [C] something that is heavy: *I can't lift heavy weights because of my bad back.*
4 RESPONSIBILITY/WORRY [singular] something that makes you worry: *the **weight of** responsibility* | *Selling the house was **a** great **weight off** my **mind**.*
5 IMPORTANCE [U] if something has weight, it is important and influences people: *Tina's opinion doesn't **carry** much **weight** around here.*
6 FOR MEASURING QUANTITIES [C] a piece of metal weighing a particular amount that is balanced against something else to measure what it weighs
7 weights [plural] heavy pieces of metal, usually fixed to a metal bar, that people lift to make their muscles bigger [➡ **weightlifting**]: *I've been **lifting weights** for years.* → **pull your weight** at PULL

weight[2] **also weight down** *v.* [T] to add something heavy to something or put a weight on it, especially in order to keep it in place: *fishing nets weighted with lead*

weight·ed /ˈweɪt̮ɪd/ *adj.* giving an advantage or disadvantage to one particular group or activity: *The voting system is **weighted against** the smaller parties.*

weight·less /ˈweɪtlɪs/ *adj.* having no weight, especially when you are floating in space —**weightlessness** *n.* [U]

weight·lift·ing /ˈweɪtˌlɪftɪŋ/ *n.* [U] the sport of lifting weights attached to the ends of a bar —**weight-lifter** *n.* [C]

weight·y /ˈweɪt̮i/ *adj.* important and serious: *a weighty problem*

weird /wɪrd/ *adj. informal* unusual and strange: *I had a really weird dream.* | *There's something weird about him.* | *The **weird thing** is that no one else seemed to notice.*

THESAURUS

strange, **funny**, **peculiar**, **mysterious**, **odd**, **bizarre**, **eccentric**
→ see Thesaurus box at STRANGE[1]

weird·o /ˈwɪrdoʊ/ *n.* plural **weirdos** [C] *spoken* someone who seems strange

wel·come[1] /ˈwɛlkəm/ *interjection* said in order to greet someone who has just arrived: ***Welcome to** Chicago!* | ***Welcome back** – it's good to see you again.*

welcome[2] *adj.* **1** if you are welcome in a place, the other people want you to be there: *I had the feeling I wasn't really welcome.* | *They did their best to **make** me **feel welcome**.* **2** if something is welcome, people are pleased that it has happened because it is useful, pleasant, etc.: *a welcome suggestion* | *a welcome breeze on a hot day*

SPOKEN PHRASES

3 you're welcome! said in order to reply politely to someone who has just thanked you for something: *"Thanks for the coffee." "You're welcome."* **4 be welcome to sb/sth** used in order to say that someone can be with someone or have something if s/he wants to, because you do not want to: *If Rob wants that job he's welcome to it!* **5 be welcome to do sth** used in order to say that someone can do something if s/he wants to: *You're welcome to stay for lunch.*

welcome[3] *v.* [T] **1** to say hello in a friendly way to someone who has just arrived: *Jill was welcoming guests at the door.* | *They **welcomed** us **warmly**.* **2** to be glad when something happens or is done, or to say that you are glad: *We would welcome a change in the law.*

welcome[4] *n.* [C] the way in which you greet someone when s/he arrives at a place: *They **gave***

W

him a very ***warm welcome*** *when he returned to work.* → **wear out your welcome** at WEAR[1]

wel·com·ing /ˈwɛlkəmɪŋ/ *adj.* making you feel happy and relaxed: *a welcoming smile*

THESAURUS

friendly, **warm**, **cordial**, **hospitable**
→ see Thesaurus box at FRIENDLY

weld /wɛld/ *v.* [T] to join metal objects to each other by heating them and pressing them together when they are hot —**welder** *n.* [C]

wel·fare /ˈwɛlfɛr/ *n.* [U] **1 also Welfare** money paid by the government to people who are very poor, not working, sick, etc.: *Most of the people in this neighborhood are* ***on welfare***. **2** someone's welfare is his/her health, comfort, and happiness: *We're only concerned with your welfare.*

we'll /wil/ the short form of "we will": *We'll have to leave soon.*

well[1] /wɛl/ *adv.* comparative **better**, superlative **best** **1** in a good, successful, or satisfactory way: *Did you sleep well?* | *She doesn't hear very well.* | *Is the business* ***doing well***? | *I hope your party* ***goes well***.

USAGE

Use **well** to talk about the way someone does something: *He plays tennis very well.*
Use **good** to describe the quality of something or someone: *a good teacher* | *Was the movie good?*

2 thoroughly or completely: *I don't know her very well.* | *Mix the flour and eggs well.* **3 as well (as sb/sth)** in addition to something or someone else: *I'm learning French as well as Italian.* **4 may/might/could well** used in order to say that something is likely to happen or is likely to be true: *What you say may well be true.* **5 sb may/might as well do sth** *informal* **a)** used in order to say that you will do something even though you do not particularly want to do it: *We may as well get started.* **b)** used in order to say that doing something else would have an equally good result: *You might as well buy the chair here since it costs the same as in the other place.* **6** very much, or very long in time: *I'm* ***well aware*** *of the problem.* | *It was* ***well after*** *2:00 by the time we finished.*

W

well[2] *adj.* comparative **better**, superlative **best** **1** healthy: *My mother's not very well.* | *I'm a lot better, thanks.* | *I hope you* ***get well soon***. **2 all is well/all is not well** *formal* used in order to say that a situation is satisfactory or not satisfactory: *All is not well with their marriage.* **3 it's just as well (that)** *spoken* used in order to say that things have happened in a way that is lucky or good: *It's just as well I took the train today – I heard the traffic was really bad.* **4 it's/that's all very well** *spoken* used in order to say that you are not happy or satisfied with something: *It's all very well for you to say you're sorry, but I've been waiting here for two hours!*

well[3] *interjection* **1** used in order to pause before saying something, or to emphasize what you are saying: *Well, let's see now, I could meet you on Thursday.* | ***Well, I mean****, you shouldn't just take things without asking.* | *"Jim doesn't want to come."* *"****Well then****, let's go on our own."* **2 also oh well** said in order to show that you accept a situation even though it is not a good one: *Oh well, at least you did your best.* **3 also well, well** used in order to express surprise or amusement: *Well, so Steve got the job?* **4** said in order to connect two parts of a story that you are telling: *You know that guy I was telling you about? Well, he's been arrested!* **5 Well?** used in order to ask someone to reply to you or tell you what has happened: *Well? What did he say?*

well[4] *n.* [C] **1** a deep hole in the ground from which water is taken **2** a very deep hole in the ground from which oil is taken

well[5] **also well up** *v.* [I] *literary* if a liquid wells up, it rises and may start to flow: ***Tears began to well up*** *in her eyes.*

ˌwell-adˈjusted *adj.* emotionally healthy and able to deal well with the problems of life: *a happy, well-adjusted child*

ˌwell-ˈbalanced *adj.* **1** a well-balanced person is sensible and does not suddenly become angry, upset, etc. **2** a well-balanced meal or DIET contains all the things you need to stay healthy

ˌwell-beˈhaved *adj.* behaving in a polite or socially acceptable way: *a well-behaved child*

THESAURUS

polite, **courteous**, **civil**
→ see Thesaurus box at POLITE

ˌwell-ˈbeing *n.* [U] a feeling of being comfortable, healthy, and happy

ˌwell-brought-ˈup *adj.* a child who is well-brought-up has been taught to be polite and to behave well

ˌwell-ˈdone *adj.* meat that is well-done has been cooked thoroughly [➡ **medium**, **rare**]: *He likes his steak well-done.*

ˌwell-ˈdressed *adj.* wearing attractive fashionable clothes: *an attractive, well-dressed young woman*

ˌwell-ˈearned *adj.* deserved because you have worked hard: *a well-earned vacation*

ˌwell-ˈfed *adj.* having plenty of good food to eat: *well-fed children*

ˌwell-ˈgroomed *adj.* someone who is well-groomed has a very neat and clean appearance: *a well-groomed young man*

ˌwell-ˈheeled *adj. informal* rich

ˌwell-inˈtentioned *adj.* → WELL-MEANING

ˌwell-ˈknown *adj.* known by a lot of people: *a well-known artist*

THESAURUS

famous, **legendary**, **infamous**, **notorious**
→ see Thesaurus box at FAMOUS

ˌwell-ˈmeaning *adj.* intending or intended to be helpful, but often failing or making things worse: *well-meaning advice*

well·ness /ˈwɛlnɪs/ *n.* [U] the state of being healthy: *The gym offers a variety of* ***wellness programs*** (=programs to help people stay healthy).

ˌwell-ˈoff *adj.* having enough money to have a very good standard of living: *Stella's family is well-off.*

THESAURUS

rich, **wealthy**, **prosperous**, **well-to-do**, **rolling in it**, **loaded**
→ see Thesaurus box at RICH

ˌwell-ˈpaid *adj.* providing or receiving good wages: *a well-paid job | well-paid executives*

well-read /ˌwɛl ˈrɛd◂/ *adj.* someone who is well-read has read many books and knows a lot about different subjects

ˌwell-ˈrounded *adj.* someone who is well-rounded has had a wide variety of experiences in life

ˌwell-ˈspoken *adj.* able to speak in a clear and polite way

ˌwell-ˈthought-of *adj.* liked and admired by other people

ˌwell-ˈtimed *adj.* said or done at the most appropriate time: *My arrival wasn't very well-timed.*

ˌwell-to-ˈdo *adj.* rich: *a well-to-do family*

THESAURUS

rich, **well-off**, **wealthy**, **prosperous**, **rolling in it**, **loaded**
→ see Thesaurus box at RICH

ˈwell-ˌwisher *n.* [C] someone who does something to show that s/he wants someone to succeed, be healthy, etc.: *She received hundreds of cards from well-wishers.*

Welsh /wɛlʃ/ *adj.* relating to or coming from Wales

welt /wɛlt/ *n.* [C] a raised mark on someone's skin where s/he has been hit

wel·ter /ˈwɛltɚ/ *n. formal* **a welter of sth** a large and confusing number of different details, emotions, etc.: *a welter of information*

went /wɛnt/ *v.* the past tense of GO

wept /wɛpt/ *v.* the past tense and and past participle of WEEP

we're /wɪr/ the short form of "we are": *We're going to the library.*

were /wɚ/ *v.* the past tense of BE

weren't /wɚnt, ˈwɚənt/ *v.* the short form of "were not": *Why didn't you tell me that you weren't happy?*

were·wolf /ˈwɛrwʊlf/ *n.* [C] a person in stories who changes into a WOLF

west¹, **West** /wɛst/ *n.* [singular, U] **1** the direction toward which the sun goes down: *Which way is west?* → see picture at NORTH¹ **2 the west** the western part of a country, state, etc.: *Rain will spread* ***to the west*** *later today. | the* ***west of*** *Ireland* **3 the West a)** the countries in North America and the western part of Europe **b)** the part of the U.S. west of the Mississippi River **4 out West** in or to the west of a particular area, especially the U.S.: *I've always wanted to travel out west.*

USAGE

Use **north/south/east/west of sth** in order to describe where a place is in relation to another place: *Chicago is south of Milwaukee.*
Use **in the north/south/east/west of sth** in order to say which part of a place you are talking about: *The mountains are in the west of the province.*
Use **northern**, **southern**, **eastern**, **western** with the name of a place: *They have a cabin in northern Ontario.*
Don't say "in the north of Ontario."

west² *adj.* **1** in, to, or facing the west: *four miles* ***west of*** *Toronto | the west coast of Florida* **2 west wind** a wind coming from the west

west³ *adv.* toward the west: *Go west on I-90 to Spokane. | The window faces west.*

west·bound /ˈwɛstbaʊnd/ *adj.* traveling or leading toward the west: *westbound traffic | the westbound lanes of the freeway*

west·er·ly /ˈwɛstɚli/ *adj.* **1** in or toward the west: *sailing in a westerly direction* **2** a westerly wind comes from the west

west·ern¹ /ˈwɛstɚn/ *adj.* **1** in or from the west part of an area, country, state, etc.: *western Iowa* **2 Western** in or from the countries in North America and the western part of Europe: *Western technology* → see Usage box at WEST¹

western² *n.* [C] a movie about life in the 19th century in the American West

THESAURUS

comedy, **romantic comedy**, **thriller**, **action movie**, **horror movie**, **science fiction movie**, **animated movie/cartoon**
→ see Thesaurus box at MOVIE

W

west·ern·er, **Westerner** /ˈwɛstɚnɚ/ *n.* [C] someone who comes from the WESTERN part of a country or the western HEMISPHERE

ˌWestern ˈEurope *n.* the western part of Europe, including places such as Great Britain and Italy —**ˌWestern Euroˈpean** *adj.*

west·ern·ized /ˈwɛstɚˌnaɪzd/ *adj.* [only before noun] influenced by and behaving like the people in North America and western Europe —**westernize** *v.* [T]

west·ern·most /ˈwɛstɚnˌmoʊst/ *adj.* farthest west: *the westernmost part of the island*

west·ward /ˈwɛstwɚd/ *adj., adv.* toward the west

wet¹ /wɛt/ *adj.* comparative **wetter**, superlative **wettest** **1** covered in or full of liquid [≠ **dry**]: *Try not to* ***get*** *your feet* ***wet****. | a wet sponge | We were* ***soaking wet*** (=extremely wet). **2** rainy: ***It's*** *very* ***wet*** *outside.* **3** not yet dry: *wet paint* **4 wet**

behind the ears *informal* very young and without much experience —**wetness** *n.* [U]

wet² *v.* past tense and past participle **wet** or **wetted**, present participle **wetting** [T] **1** to make something wet: *Wet this cloth and put it on her forehead.* **2 wet the bed/wet your pants** to make your bed or pants wet because you URINATE by accident

'wet suit *n.* [C] a thick piece of clothing, usually made of rubber, that swimmers wear to keep warm when they are in the water

we've /wiv/ the short form of "we have": *We've got to leave by 6:00.*

whack¹ /wæk/ *v.* [T] *informal* to hit someone or something hard

THESAURUS

hit, punch, slap, beat, smack, strike, bang, knock, tap, pound, rap, hammer
➔ see Thesaurus box at HIT¹

whack² *n. informal* **1 out of whack** if a machine or system is out of whack, it is not working correctly **2 take a whack at sth** to try to do something: *I can't open this jar; do you want to take a whack at it?* **3** [C] the act of hitting something hard, or the noise this makes

whacked /wækt/ **also ˌwhacked 'out** *adj. spoken* **1** very tired **2** behaving in a very strange way

whale¹ /weɪl/ *n.* [C] a very large animal that swims in the ocean and breathes through a hole on the top of its head

whale² *v.*

whale on sb/sth ⇔ *phr. v.* to start hitting someone or something

whal·er /'weɪlɚ/ *n.* [C] **1** someone who hunts whales **2** a boat used for hunting whales

whal·ing /'weɪlɪŋ/ *n.* [U] the activity of hunting whales

wham¹ /wæm/ *interjection* **1** said when describing the sound of one thing hitting another thing very hard: *The car went wham into the wall.* **2** said in order to show that something very unexpected suddenly happens: *Everything is going OK and then, wham, you lose your job.*

W

wham² *n.* [C] the sound made when something is hit very hard

wharf /wɔrf/ *n.* plural **wharves** /wɔrvz/ [C] a structure that is built out into the water so that boats can stop next to it [= **pier**]

what /wət; *strong* wʌt, wɑt/ *determiner, pron.* **1** used in order to ask for information about something: *What are you doing?* | *What did Ellen say?* | *What kind of dog is that?* | *"I didn't think it would be like this." "What do you mean?"*

USAGE

Which and **what** are both used when you are asking about one thing out of a number of possible things.
Use **which** when there is a small number of possibilities: *Which house does Tom live in?*
Use **what** when there is a very large number of possibilities: *What have they named the baby?* | *What is the answer to question 12?*
Which can be followed by "of" but **what** cannot: *Which of these dresses do you like best?*

2 used in order to talk about something that is not known or certain: *No one knows what happened.* | *I'm not sure* ***what to*** *do.* **3** the thing which: *Show me what you bought.* | *I believe what he told me.* **4** used at the beginning of a sentence to emphasize what you are saying: *What an idiot!* | *What I need is a nice hot bath.* **5 have what it takes** to have the ability or courage to do something: *Whitman didn't have what it takes to do the job.* ➔ **guess what/you'll never guess** at GUESS¹ ➔ **so what?** at SO¹

SPOKEN PHRASES

6 what? a) used in order to ask someone to repeat something that s/he has just said because you did not hear it very well: *"Do you want a fried egg?" "What?"* **b)** used when you have heard someone calling your name and you are asking him/her what s/he wants: *"Anita?" "What?" "Can you come here for a minute?"* **c)** used in order to show that you are surprised by what someone has said **7 what about...? a)** used in order to make a suggestion: *What about sending him an e-mail?* **b)** used in order to introduce a new person or thing into the conversation: *What about Patrick? What's he doing nowadays?* **8 What's up?** used when saying hello to someone you know well: *"Hey Chris! What's up?" "Not much"* **9 what's up with sb/sth?** used in order to ask what is wrong or what is happening: *What's up with this printer – does it work?* **10 what (...) for? a)** used in order to ask the reason for something or purpose of something: *What's this thing for?* **b)** why: *"She's decided to work part-time." "What for?"* **11 what if...? a)** used in order to ask what will happen, especially when it could be something bad or frightening: *What if we get stuck out there in the snow?* **b)** used when making a suggestion: *What if you just take that part out of the speech?* **12 what's his/her/its name** used when talking about a person or thing whose name you cannot immediately remember: *Is what's his name still working here?* **13 ...or what? a)** used in order to ask if there is another possibility: *Are they doing that to save money, or what?* **b)** used in order to show you are impatient when asking a question: *Are you coming now, or what?* **14 what's what** the real facts about a situation that are important to know: *She's been working here long enough to know what's what.* **15 what's with sb?** used in order to ask why someone is behaving strangely or why something strange is happening: *What's with Nicky? He seems really mad.* **16 what's with sth?** used in order to ask the reason for something: *What's with all the sad faces?*

what·cha·ma·call·it /ˈwʌtʃəmə,kɔlɪt/ *n.* [C] *spoken* a word you use when you cannot remember the name of something

what·ev·er[1] /wətˈɛvɚ/ *determiner, pron.* **1** any or all of the things that are wanted, needed, or possible: *Just take whatever you need.* | *He needs whatever help he can get.* **2** used in order to say it is not important what happens, what you do, etc. because it does not change the situation: *Whatever I say, she always disagrees.* **3 ...or whatever** *spoken* used in order to refer to other things of the same kind: *You can go swimming, scuba diving, or whatever.* **4** *spoken* used in order to say that you do not know the exact meaning of something or the exact name of someone or something: *Why don't you invite Steve, or whatever he's called, to supper?* **5 whatever you say/think/want** *spoken* used in order to tell someone that you agree with him/her or will do what s/he wants, especially when you do not really agree or want to do it: *"How about camping, just for a change?" "OK, whatever you want."* **6** used as a reply to say that you do not care what is done or chosen, or that the exact details of something do not matter: *"What flavor do you want? Strawberry, vanilla...?" "Whatever."*

whatever[2] **also what·so·ev·er** /,wʌtsoʊˈɛvɚ/ *adv.* used in order to emphasize a negative statement: *She had no money whatsoever.*

what·not /ˈwʌt˺nɑt/ *n.* **and whatnot** *spoken* an expression used at the end of a list of things when you do not want to give the names of everything: *Put all your paper, pencils, and whatnot in this drawer.*

wheat /wit/ *n.* [U] a plant that produces a grain used for making flour, or this grain

whee·dle /ˈwidl/ *v.* [I,T] to persuade someone to do something by saying pleasant things that you do not really mean: *She managed to* ***wheedle*** *$15* ***out of*** *him.*

wheel[1] /wil/ *n.* [C] **1** one of the round things under a car, bicycle, etc. that turns and allows it to move: *the car's* ***front/rear wheels*** ➔ see picture at BICYCLE **2** a STEERING WHEEL: *He had fallen asleep* ***at the wheel*** (=while driving). **3** a flat round part in a machine that turns when the machine operates: *a gear wheel*

wheel[2] *v.* **1** [T] to move something that has wheels: *She* ***wheeled*** *her bike* ***into*** *the garage.* **2** [I] to turn around suddenly: *Anita* ***wheeled around*** *and started yelling at us.* ➔ WHEELING AND DEALING

wheel·bar·row /ˈwil,bæroʊ/ *n.* [C] a small CART with one wheel in the front and two long handles for pushing it, that you use outdoors to carry things

wheel·chair /ˈwil-tʃɛr/ *n.* [C] a chair with wheels, used by people who cannot walk

wheel·ie /ˈwili/ *n.* **do/pop a wheelie** *informal* to balance on the back wheel of a bicycle or MOTORCYCLE that you are riding

,wheeling and ˈdealing *n.* [U] activities that involve a lot of complicated and sometimes dishonest deals, especially in politics or business —**wheeler-dealer** *n.*

wheeze /wiz/ *v.* [I] to breathe with difficulty, making a whistling sound in your chest —**wheezy** *adj.*

> **THESAURUS**
>
> **breathe, pant, be short of breath, be out of breath, gasp for breath, gasp for air**
> ➔ see Thesaurus box at BREATHE

when /wɛn/ *adv., conjunction* **1** used when asking what time something will happen: *When are we leaving?* | *I'll tell you* ***when to*** *stop.* **2** at or during the time that something happens: *He was nine when his father died.* | *I was in the shower when the doorbell rang.* | *The best moment was when Barnes scored the winning goal.*

> **THESAURUS**
>
> **at the time** – used in order to talk about a particular time in the past when two things happened at the same time: *I couldn't go to the wedding as I was in New York at the time.*
> **by the time** – used in order to say that one thing has or will have already happened when something else happens: *By the time a child is five, he will have watched hundreds of hours of television.*
> **by that time** – used in order to mention a particular time when something has already happened: *She called at six, but at that time we had already left.*

3 after or as soon as something happens: *I'll phone you when I get home.* **4** even though something is true: *Why do you want a new bike when this one is perfectly good?* ➔ **since when** at SINCE[2]

when·ev·er /wɛˈnɛvɚ, wə-/ *adv., conjunction* **1** every time: *Whenever we come here, we see someone we know.* **2** at any time: *Come over whenever you want.* **3** *spoken* used in order to say that it does not matter when something happens: *"Should I come over around six?" "Whenever."*

W

where /wɛr/ *adv., conjunction* **1** at, to, or from a particular place or position: *Where do you live?* | *I asked Lucy where she was going.* | *Do you know where my glasses are?* **2** used in order to ask or talk about the situation or state of something: *Where do you see yourself in ten years?* | *Where do we go from here* (=what do we do now)*?*

where·a·bouts[1] /ˈwɛrə,baʊts, ,wɛrəˈbaʊts/ *adv. spoken* used to ask in a general way where a place is: *Whereabouts do you live?*

where·a·bouts[2] /ˈwɛrə,baʊts/ *n.* [U] the place where someone or something is: *His whereabouts are still a mystery.*

where·as /wɛrˈæz; *weak* wɛrəz/ *conjunction formal* used in order to say that although something is true of one thing, it is not true of another: *Nowa-*

days the journey takes six hours, whereas then it took several weeks.

where·by /wɛr'baɪ/ *adv. formal* by means of which, or according to which: *a law whereby all children receive free education*

where·in /wɛr'ɪn/ *adv., conjunction formal* in which place or part: *the San Francisco house, wherein he and his family live*

where·u·pon /ˌwɛrə'pɑn, 'wɛrəˌpɑn/ *conjunction formal* after which: *One of them called the other a liar, whereupon a fight broke out.*

wher·ev·er /wɛr'ɛvɚ/ *adv., conjunction* **1** to or at any place: *If you could go wherever you wanted to in the world, where would you go? | Sit wherever you like.* **2 wherever possible** when it is possible to do something: *We try to use locally produced food wherever possible.* **3** *spoken* used at the beginning of a question to show surprise: *Wherever did you find that old thing?*

where·with·al /'wɛrwɪˌðɔl, -ˌθɔl/ *n.* **the wherewithal to do sth** the money or ability you need in order to do something: *He just didn't have the wherewithal to do more with his life.*

whet /wɛt/ *v.* past tense and past participle **whetted**, present participle **whetting whet sb's appetite (for sth)** to make someone want more of something by letting him/her try it or see what it is like

wheth·er /'wɛðɚ/ *conjunction* **1** used when talking about a choice between different possibilities: *He asked her whether she was coming. | I couldn't decide* ***whether or not*** *I wanted to go.* **2** used in order to say that something definitely will or will not happen in spite of what the situation is: ***Whether*** *you like it* ***or not****, you have to take that test.*

whew /hwyu, hwu/ *interjection* ➔ PHEW

W

which /wɪtʃ/ *determiner, pron.* **1** used in order to ask or state what things you mean when a choice has to be made: ***Which of*** *these books is yours? | Ask him which one he wants.*

USAGE

Which and **what** are both used when you are asking about one thing out of a number of possible things.
Use **which** when there is a small number of possibilities: *Which house does Tom live in?*
Use **what** when there is a very large number of possibilities: *What have they named the baby? | What is the answer to question 12?*
Which can be followed by "of" but **what** cannot: *Which of these dresses do you like best?*

2 used in order to show what specific thing or things you mean: *This is the book which I told you about.* **3** used in order to add more information about something, especially in written language after a COMMA: *The house, which was completed in 1856, was famous for its huge marble staircase. | The train only takes two hours, which is quicker than the bus.*

which·ev·er /wɪ'tʃɛvɚ/ *determiner, pron.* **1** used in order to say that it does not matter which person or thing is chosen because the result will be the same: *You get the same result whichever way you do it.* **2** any of a group of things or people: *You can have whichever you like best.*

whiff /wɪf/ *n.* [C] a smell of something that is not strong: *As she walked past, I* ***caught a whiff of*** (=smelled) *her perfume.*

while[1] /waɪl/ *n.* **a while** a period of time, especially a short one: *Can you wait a while? |* ***For a while*** *I worked in the Sales Department. | I'll be back* ***in a little while****.* ➔ AWHILE ➔ **worth your while** at WORTH[1]

while[2] *conjunction* **1** during the time that something is happening: *They arrived while we were having dinner. | I like to listen to music while I'm taking a bath.* **2** in spite of the fact that [= **although**]: *While it was a good school, I was not happy there.* **3** used in order to say that although something is true of one thing, it is not true of another [= **whereas**]: *That region has plenty of water, while this one has little.*

while[3] *v.* **while away the hours/evening/days etc.** to spend time in a pleasant and lazy way: *We whiled away the summer evenings talking and drinking wine.*

whim /wɪm/ *n.* [C] a sudden desire to do or have something, especially when there is no good reason for it: *I went to visit her* ***on a whim****.*

whim·per /'wɪmpɚ/ *v.* [I] to make low crying sounds because you are sad, frightened, or in pain: *The dog ran off whimpering.* —**whimper** *n.* [C]

whim·si·cal /'wɪmzɪkəl/ *adj.* unusual or strange and often amusing: *whimsical drawings*

whine /waɪn/ *v.* [I] **1** to complain in a sad annoying voice about something: *Stop whining! | She was* ***whining about*** *how hard her life is.* **2** to make a long high sound because you are in pain or unhappy: *The dog was whining at the door.* —**whine** *n.* [C]

whin·ny /'wɪni/ *v.* past tense and past participle **whinnied**, third person singular **whinnies** [I] if a horse whinnies, it makes a high sound

whip[1] /wɪp/ *n.* [C] a long thin piece of rope or leather with a handle, used for making animals move faster or for hitting people as a punishment

whip[2] past tense and past participle **whipped**, present participle **whipping** *v.* **1** [T] to hit a person or animal with a whip **2** [I] to move suddenly or violently: *Bill* ***whipped around*** *to see what was happening.* **3** [T] *informal* to move something with a quick sudden movement: *He* ***whipped out*** *a gun.* **4 whip sb/sth into shape** *informal* to make a system, group of people, etc. start to work in an organized way **5** [T] to mix cream or the clear part of an egg very hard until it becomes stiff [= **beat**]: *Whip the cream until thick.*

whip up *phr. v.* **1 whip** sb ⇔ **up** to try to make people feel strongly about something: *an attempt to whip up opposition to the plan* **2 whip** sth ⇔ **up** *informal* to quickly make something to eat: *I could whip up a salad.*

whip·lash /ˈwɪplæʃ/ *n.* [U] a neck injury caused when your head moves forward and back again suddenly and violently, especially in a car accident

whip·ping /ˈwɪpɪŋ/ *n.* [C] a punishment given to someone by hitting him/her, especially with a whip

whir /wɚ/ *v.* past tense and past participle **whirred**, present participle **whirring** [I] if a machine whirrs , it makes a continuous low sound —**whir** *n.* [singular] *the whir of a lawnmower*

whirl¹ /wɚl/ *v.* [I,T] to turn or spin around very quickly, or to make someone or something do this: *He* ***whirled*** *her* ***around*** *the dance floor.*

whirl² *n.* **1 give sth a whirl** *informal* to try something that you are not sure you are going to like or be able to do **2** [singular] a lot of activity of a particular kind: *a* ***whirl of*** *social activity* **3 be in a whirl** to feel very excited or confused about something **4** [C usually singular] a spinning movement, or the shape of a substance that is spinning: *a* ***whirl of*** *dust*

whirl·pool /ˈwɚlpul/ *n.* [C] a powerful current of water that spins quickly and pulls things down into it

whirl·wind /ˈwɚlˌwɪnd/ *n.* [C] **1 a whirlwind romance/tour etc.** something that happens much more quickly than usual **2** an extremely strong wind that moves quickly with a circular movement, causing a lot of damage **3 a whirlwind of activity/emotions etc.** a situation in which you quickly experience a lot of different activities or emotions one after another

whisk¹ /wɪsk/ *v.* [T] **1** to mix liquids, eggs, etc. very quickly, using a fork or a whisk [➡ **beat**, **whip**]: *Whisk the yolks and sugar in a bowl.* ➔ see picture on page A4 **2** to quickly take something or someone somewhere: *They* ***whisked*** *her* ***off*** *to the hospital.*

whisk² *n.* [C] a small kitchen tool made of curved pieces of wire, used for whisking eggs, cream, etc.

whisk·er /ˈwɪskɚ/ *n.* [C] **1** one of the long stiff hairs that grow near the mouth of a cat, mouse, etc. ➔ see picture on page A2 **2 whiskers** [plural] the hair that grows on a man's face

whis·key /ˈwɪski/ *n.* plural **whiskeys** or **whiskies** [C,U] a strong alcoholic drink made from grain, or a glass of this drink

whis·per /ˈwɪspɚ/ *v.* **1** [I,T] to speak or say something very quietly, using your breath rather than your voice: *He leaned over to* ***whisper*** *something* ***to*** *her.* | *"I love you," she* ***whispered in*** *his* ***ear****.*

THESAURUS

mumble, mutter, murmur
➔ see Thesaurus box at SAY¹, TALK¹

2 [I] *literary* to make a soft sound: *The wind whispered in the trees.* —**whisper** *n.* [C] *She spoke in a whisper.*

whis·tle¹ /ˈwɪsəl/ *v.* **1** [I,T] to make a high or musical sound by blowing air out through your lips: *Adam* ***whistled to/at*** *me from across the street.* **2** [I] to make a high sound by blowing into a whistle: *The referee whistled and the game began.* **3** [I] to move quickly with a high sound: *Bullets were* ***whistling through*** *the air.* **4** [I] to make a high sound when air or steam is forced through a small hole: *a whistling kettle*

whistle² *n.* [C] **1** a small object that produces a high sound when you blow into it: *The referee* ***blew*** *his* ***whistle****.* **2** a high sound made by blowing air through a whistle, your lips, etc. ➔ **blow the whistle (on sb)** at BLOW¹

white¹ /waɪt/ *adj.* **1** having the color of milk, salt, or snow: *white paint* **2** belonging to the race of people with pale skin who were originally from Europe: *The suspect is a young white man.* **3** looking pale because of illness, strong emotion, etc.: *Are you OK? You're* ***as white as a sheet*** (=extremely pale). —**whiteness** *n.* [U]

white² *n.* **1** [U] the color of milk, salt, or snow: *She was dressed completely in white.* **2** [C] **also White** someone who belongs to the race of people with pale skin who were originally from Europe **3** [C,U] the part of an egg which surrounds the YOLK and becomes white when cooked

ˈwhite-bread *adj. informal* relating to people who are white and who have traditional American values, and who are often considered boring: *a white-bread suburban family*

ˌwhite-ˈcollar *adj.* [only before noun] white-collar workers have jobs in offices, banks, etc. rather than jobs working in factories, building things, etc. [➡ **blue-collar**]

ˈWhite House *n.* **1 the White House** the official home in Washington D.C. of the President of the U.S. **2** [singular] the President of the U.S. and the people who advise him/her: *an election that resulted in a Democratic White House* —**White House** *adj.*: *a White House spokesperson*

ˌwhite ˈlie *n.* [C] *informal* a lie that is not very important, especially one that you tell in order to avoid hurting someone's feelings

THESAURUS

lie, fib
➔ see Thesaurus box at LIE³

whit·en /ˈwaɪtˀn/ *v.* [I,T] to become white, or to make something do this

ˌWhite ˈPages *n.* **the White Pages** the white part of a telephone DIRECTORY containing the

W

names, addresses, and telephone numbers of people with telephones [➡ **Yellow Pages**]

ˌwhite ˈtrash *n.* [U] *informal* an insulting expression meaning white people who are poor and uneducated

white·wash /ˈwaɪtˀwɑʃ, -wɔʃ/ *n.* **1** [C usually singular] an attempt to hide the true facts about a serious accident or illegal action: *One magazine called the report a whitewash.* **2** [U] a white liquid mixture used for painting walls, fences, etc. —**whitewash** *v.* [T]

white·wa·ter /ˈwaɪtˀˌwɔt̬ɚ, -ˌwɑ-/ *n.* [U] a part of a river that looks white because the water is flowing very quickly over rocks

whit·tle /ˈwɪt̬l/ *v.* **1** [I,T] to cut a piece of wood into a particular shape by cutting off small pieces **2** [T] **also whittle down** to gradually make something smaller by taking parts away: *I've whittled down the list of guests from 30 to 16.*

whittle (sth) away *phr. v.* to gradually make something smaller or less effective: *Congress has been* ***whittling away at*** *our freedom of speech.*

whiz¹ /wɪz/ *v.* past tense and past participle **whizzed**, present participle **whizzing**, third person singular **whizzes** [I] *informal* to move very quickly: *Marty* ***whizzed past*** *us on his motorbike.*

whiz² *n.* [C] *informal* someone who is very skilled at something

ˈwhiz kid *n.* [C] *informal* a young person who is very skilled or successful at something

who /hu/ *pron.* **1** used in order to ask or talk about which person is involved, or what the name of a person is: *"Who is that?" "That's Amy's brother." | Who locked the door? | I know who sent you that card.* ➔ —see also THAT¹ **2** used in order to add more information about someone: *That's the woman who owns the house. | She asked her English teacher, who had also studied Latin.*

whoa /woʊ, hwoʊ, hoʊ/ *interjection* **1** used in order to tell someone to become calmer or do something more slowly **2** used in order to show that you are surprised or that you think something is impressive

who'd /hud/ **1** the short form of "who had": *a young girl who'd been attacked* **2** the short form of "who would": *Who'd know where I can get tickets?*

who·dun·it /huˈdʌnɪt/ *n.* [C] *informal* a book, movie, etc. about a murder, in which you do not find out who the murderer is until the end

who·ev·er /huˈɛvɚ/ *pron.* **1** used in order to talk about someone when you do not know who s/he is: *Whoever did this is in big trouble.* **2** used in order to show that it does not matter which person does something: *Whoever gets there first can find a table.*

whole¹ /hoʊl/ *n.* **1 the whole of sth** all of something: *The whole of the morning was wasted.* **2 on the whole** generally or usually: *On the whole, life was much quieter after John left.* **3 as a whole** used in order to say that all the parts of something are being considered: *We must look at our educational system as a whole.* **4** [C usually singular] something that consists of a number of parts, but is considered as a single unit: *Two halves make a whole.*

whole² *adj.* **1** all of something [= **entire**]: *She drank a whole bottle of wine. |* ***The whole thing*** (=everything about a situation) *just makes me sick.* **2** complete and not divided or broken into parts: *Place a whole onion inside the chicken.*

whole·heart·ed /ˌhoʊlˈhɑrt̬ɪd◂/ *adj.* involving all your feelings, interest, etc.: *You have our* ***wholehearted support****.* —**wholeheartedly** *adv.*

whole·sale /ˈhoʊlseɪl/ *adj.* **1** relating to the sale of goods in large quantities, usually at low prices, to people or stores that then sell to other people [➡ **retail**]: *a wholesale price* **2** *disapproving* affecting almost everything or everyone, and often done without any concern for the results: *the wholesale destruction of the rainforest* —**wholesale** *adv.* —**wholesaler** *n.* [C]

whole·some /ˈhoʊlsəm/ *adj.* **1** likely to make you healthy: *a good wholesome breakfast* **2** considered to be morally good or acceptable: *a nice clean wholesome kid*

ˈwhole wheat *adj.* whole wheat flour or bread is made using every part of the WHEAT grain, including the outer layer

who'll /hul/ the short form of "who will": *This is Denise, who'll be your guide today.*

whol·ly /ˈhoʊli/ *adv. formal* completely: *The club is wholly responsible for the damage.*

whom /hum/ *pron.* **1** *formal* the object form of "who": *To whom am I speaking? | He spoke to a man with whom he used to work.* **2 many/all/some etc. of whom** many, all, etc. of the people just mentioned: *They had four sons, one of whom died young.*

whoop /hup, wup/ *v.* [I] to shout loudly and in a happy way —**whoop** *n.* [C]

whoops /wʊps/ *interjection* said when you make a small mistake, drop something, or fall

whoosh /wʊʃ, wuʃ/ *v.* [I] *informal* to move very fast with a soft rushing sound: *cars whooshing past* —**whoosh** *n.* [C]

whop·per /ˈwɑpɚ/ *n.* [C] *informal* something that is unusually large

whop·ping /ˈwɑpɪŋ/ *adj.* [only before noun] *informal* very large: *a whopping 28% increase*

who're /ˈhuɚ, hʊr/ the short form of "who are": *Who're those two guys?*

who's /huz/ **1** the short form of "who is": *Who's sitting next to Reggie?* **2** the short form of "who has": *That's Karl, the guy who's studied in Brazil.*

whose /huz/ *determiner, pron.* **1** used in order to ask which person or people a particular thing belongs to: *Whose jacket is this?* **2** used in order to show the relationship between a person and something that belongs to that person: *That's the man whose house burned down.*

who've /huv/ the short form of "who have"

why /waɪ/ *adv., conjunction* **1** for what reason: *Why are these books so cheap?* | *Why haven't you finished it yet?* | *I don't know why she won't talk to me.* **2 why don't you/why doesn't he ... etc.** *spoken* used in order to make a suggestion: *Why don't you try this one?* **3 why not?** *spoken* **a)** used in order to ask someone why s/he has not done something: *"I haven't done my homework." "Why not?"* **b)** used in order to agree to do something: *"Do you want to come along?" "Yeah, why not?"*

WI the written abbreviation of **Wisconsin**

wick /wɪk/ *n.* [C] the string on a CANDLE or in an oil lamp that is burned

wick·ed /ˈwɪkɪd/ *adj.* **1** morally bad or evil: *the wicked stepmother in "Cinderella"*

> **THESAURUS**
> **bad, evil, immoral, wrong, reprehensible**
> → see Thesaurus box at BAD[1]

2 bad in a way that is amusing: *a wicked grin* | *his* ***wicked sense of humor*** **3** *slang* very good: *a wicked concert*

wick·er /ˈwɪkɚ/ *adj.* made from thin dry branches woven together: *a wicker chair*

wide[1] /waɪd/ *adj.* **1** measuring a large distance from one side to the other [≠ **narrow**]: *a wide street* | *The quake was felt over a wide area.* | *Roberto's face broke into a* ***wide grin****.* **2** measuring a particular distance from one side to the other: *The bathtub's three feet wide and five feet long.* | *How wide is the door?* **3** including a lot of different people, things, or situations: *We offer* ***a wide range of*** *vegetarian dishes.* | *We want to reach a* ***wider audience****.* **4** happening among many people or in many places: *The trial was given wide coverage in the media.* | *We fear that the fighting will develop into a* ***wider conflict****.* **5 statewide/citywide/company-wide etc.** affecting all the people in a place: *Teen drug use is a citywide problem.* **6 wide difference/gap etc.** a large and noticeable difference: *wide differences of opinion*

wide[2] *adv.* **1** completely, or as much as possible: *Somebody left the door* ***wide open****.* | *It was 3 a.m., but I was* ***wide awake****.* | *The guards stood with their legs wide apart.* | *He stretched his arms wide, waiting for her hug.* **2 wide open** a competition, election, etc. that is wide open can be won by anyone: *The presidential race is still wide open.* **3** away from the point you were aiming at: *His shot* ***went wide****.*

wide·ly /ˈwaɪdli/ *adv.* **1** in a lot of different places or by a lot of people: *products that are widely available* | *Salinger is widely known as the author of "The Catcher in the Rye."* **2** to a large degree [= **a lot**]: *Taxes* ***vary widely*** *from state to state.*

wid·en /ˈwaɪdn/ *v.* [I,T] **1** to become wider or to make something wider [≠ **narrow**]: *His eyes widened in fear.* | *The old trail was widened into a road.* **2** to become greater or larger, or to make something do this: *The gap between low and high incomes began to widen after 1974.*

wide·spread /ˌwaɪdˈsprɛd◂/ *adj.* happening in many places: *the* ***widespread use*** *of illegal drugs*

wid·ow /ˈwɪdoʊ/ *n.* [C] a woman whose husband has died and who has not married again: *She's the* ***widow of*** *the late Thomas Franklin.*

wid·owed /ˈwɪdoʊd/ *adj.* a widowed person is someone whose husband or wife has died: *my* ***widowed mother/father***

> **THESAURUS**
> **married, single, engaged, separated, divorced**
> → see Thesaurus box at MARRIED

wid·ow·er /ˈwɪdoʊɚ/ *n.* [C] a man whose wife has died and who has not married again

width /wɪdθ, wɪtθ/ *n.* [C,U] the distance from one side of something to the other: *the* ***width of*** *the window* | *It's 10 inches* ***in width****.*

wield /wild/ *v.* [T] **1 wield power/influence/authority etc.** to have a lot of power, influence, etc., and use it: *the influence wielded by the church* **2** to hold a weapon or tool that you are going to use

wife /waɪf/ *n.* plural **wives** /waɪvz/ [C] the woman that a man is married to [➡ **husband**]: *This is my wife, Elaine.* | *He had two children with his first wife.*

wig /wɪg/ *n.* [C] artificial hair that you wear on your head [➡ **toupee**]

wig·gle /ˈwɪgəl/ *v.* [I,T] to make small movements from side to side or up and down, or to make something move this way: *wiggling your toes* —**wiggle** *n.* [C]

wig·wam /ˈwɪgwɑm/ *n.* [C] a type of tent that was used in past times by some Native Americans

wild[1] /waɪld/ *adj.* **1** wild animals or plants live or grow in a natural state, without being controlled by people [≠ **tame**]: *wild horses* | *wild flowers* → see Thesaurus box at NATURAL[1] **2** showing strong uncontrolled emotions such as excitement, anger, or happiness: *a wild look in her eyes* | *wild laughter* | *The kids were* ***wild with*** *excitement.* **3** *spoken* exciting, interesting, or unusual: *Sarah's party was wild.* | *a wild haircut* **4** [only before noun] done or said without knowing all the facts or thinking carefully about them: *a* ***wild guess*** **5 be wild about sth/sb** *informal* to like something or someone very much: *I'm not too wild about his movies.* **6** a wild card in a game can represent any card that you want it to be **7** a wild area of land is in a completely natural state and does not have farms, towns, etc. on it

wild[2] *adv.* **1 run wild** to behave in an uncontrolled way because you have no rules or people to control you **2 go wild** to suddenly become very noisy and active because you are excited or angry: *The crowd went wild when the Giants won.*

wild[3] *n.* **in the wild** in an area that is natural and not controlled or changed by people [➡ **captivity**]: *animals that live in the wild*

wil·der·ness /ˈwɪldənɪs/ *n.* [singular, U] a large area of land that has never been farmed or built on: *the Alaskan wilderness*

ˌwild ˈgoose ˌchase *n.* [singular] a situation in which you waste a lot of time looking for something that cannot be found

wild·life /ˈwaɪldlaɪf/ *n.* [U] animals and plants that live in natural conditions

wild·ly /ˈwaɪldli/ *adv.* **1** extremely: *Baseball is **wildly popular**.* **2** in a very uncontrolled or excited way: *The crowd **cheered wildly**.*

wiles /waɪlz/ *n.* [plural] things you say or tricks you use in order to persuade someone to do what you want

will¹ /wəl, əl, l; *strong* wɪl/ *modal verb* **1** used in order to make the future tense: *Kathy will be there tomorrow.* | *What time will she get here?* | *I'll* (=I will) *go shopping later.* **2** used in order to say that you are ready or willing to do something: *I'll do whatever you say.* | *Vern said he won't* (=will not) *work for Joe.* **3** used in order to ask someone to do something: *Will you do me a favor?* **4** used in CONDITIONAL sentences that use the present tense: *If it rains, we'll have the barbecue in the clubhouse.* **5** used like "can" to show what is possible: *This car will seat 5 people.* **6** used in order to say what always happens or what is generally true: *Accidents will happen.* **7 Will you...** *spoken* used to give an order: *Will you shut up!*

will² /wɪl/ *n.* **1** [C,U] the determination to do what you have decided to do: *He's lost **the will to live**.* | *a woman of high intelligence and **strong will*** **2** [C] a legal document that shows whom you want to have your money and property after you die: *Grandma Stacy left me $7000 **in** her **will**.* | *Have you **made** a **will**?* **3** [singular] what someone wants to happen in a particular situation: *No one can force him to stay here **against** his **will*** (=if he does not want to). **4 at will** whenever you want and in whatever way you want: *They can just change their policies at will.* **5 where there's a will there's a way** *spoken* used in order to say that if you are determined enough you will succeed

W

will³ *v.* [T] **1** to try to make something happen by thinking about it very hard: *He shut his eyes, willing her to win.* **2** to officially give something to someone after you die: *She willed the house to her son.*

will·ful, **wilful** /ˈwɪlfəl/ *adj.* *disapproving* doing what you want even though people tell you not to: *a willful child* —**willfully** *adv.*

will·ing /ˈwɪlɪŋ/ *adj.* **1 be willing to do sth** to be prepared to do something: *How much are they willing to pay?* **2** eager to do something: *They were **willing participants** in the fraud.* —**willingness** *n.* [U] —**willingly** *adv.*

wil·low /ˈwɪloʊ/ *n.* [C] a tree with very long thin branches, that grows near water

wil·low·y /ˈwɪloʊi/ *adj.* tall, thin, and graceful

will·pow·er /ˈwɪlˌpaʊə/ *n.* [U] the ability to make yourself do something even if it is difficult or unpleasant: *I don't have the willpower to diet.*

wil·ly-nil·ly /ˌwɪli ˈnɪli/ *adv.* something that happens to you willy-nilly happens whether or not you want it to

wilt /wɪlt/ *v.* [I] if a plant wilts, it becomes soft and bends because it needs water or is old

wil·y /ˈwaɪli/ *adj.* good at using tricks in order to get what you want: *a wily politician*

wimp /wɪmp/ *n.* [C] *informal* someone who is weak and afraid: *Don't be such a wimp.* —**wimpy** *adj.*

wimp² *v.*

wimp out *phr. v. spoken* to not do something that you intended to do, because you do not feel brave enough, strong enough, etc.

win¹ /wɪn/ *v.* past tense and past participle **won** /wʌn/ present participle **winning** **1** [I,T] to be the best or first in a competition, game, election, etc. [≠ **lose**]: *Who do you think will win the Super Bowl?* | *Dad **won at** chess again.* | *Marcy's team **won by** 3 points.* | *We could not have won the war without them.*

THESAURUS

come in first – to win a competition, game, etc.
be/come in first/second etc. place – used to describe someone's position at the end of a race
be in the lead or **be ahead** – to be winning at a particular time during the competition
the winning team/horse etc. – the one that wins
If you are the **champion** or you **hold the record for something**, you are the person who has beaten all other people in a series of competitions.

2 [T] to earn a prize at a competition or game: *the joy of winning a gold medal* | *I won $200 playing poker.*

USAGE

Win means to get a prize in a game or competition: *The first person to get all the answers right will win $100.*
Use **earn** to talk about getting money for the work you do: *He earns more than I do.*
Make is a less formal way of saying **earn**: *I make $20 an hour.*

3 [T] to get something good because of all your efforts and skill [= **gain**]: *Dr. Lee's work won her the admiration of scientists worldwide.*

win out *phr. v.* to succeed after being unsuccessful for a long time: *Sooner or later good sense will win out.*

win sb ⇔ **over** *phr. v.* to persuade someone to like you or support you

win² *n.* [C] a victory or success, especially in a sport: *a record of 7 wins and 6 losses*

wince /wɪns/ *v.* [I] to suddenly change the expression on your face when you see or remember something painful or embarrassing: *I still* ***wince at*** *the memory of how badly I sang.*

winch /wɪntʃ/ *n.* [C] a machine with a rope or chain used for lifting heavy objects —**winch** *v.* [T]

wind[1] /wɪnd/ *n.* **1** [C,U] the air outside when you can feel it moving around you: *An icy* ***wind blew*** *through the open door.* | *Expect* ***strong winds*** *and rain tomorrow.* | *a* ***gust of wind*** (=a short strong wind) | *A cold* ***east/west, etc. wind*** (=from the east, etc.) *was blowing.*

THESAURUS

breeze – a light wind
gust – a sudden strong movement of wind
gale – very strong wind
storm – a period of bad weather when there is a lot of wind, rain, snow, etc.
hurricane – a violent storm with wind that is very strong and fast
tornado – an extremely violent storm consisting of air that spins very quickly and causes a lot of damage
typhoon – a very strong tropical storm
➔ RAIN, SNOW, WEATHER

2 get wind of sth to find out about something private or secret **3** [C] your ability to breathe easily: *Rae got the* ***wind knocked out of*** *her* (=was hit in the stomach and could not breathe for a short time). **4 the winds** the people in an ORCHESTRA or band who play musical instruments that you blow into, such as the FLUTE

wind[2] /waɪnd/ *v.* past tense and past participle **wound** /waʊnd/ **1** [I,T] to turn or twist something several times around something else: *Don't* ***wind*** *the cord* ***around*** *the iron.* **2** [T] **also wind up** to make a machine, toy, clock, etc. work by turning a small handle around several times: *I forgot to wind my watch.* **3** [I] if a road, river, etc. winds , it curves or bends many times

wind down *phr. v.* to gradually end: *The party started winding down after midnight.*

wind up *phr. v.* **1** to be in a bad situation or place after a lot has happened: *Most of them* ***wound up in prison.*** **2 wind** sth ⇔ **up** to end an activity, meeting, etc.: *It's almost 5:00 — we'd better wind things up.*

Wind·break·er /ˈwɪndˌbreɪkɚ/ *n.* [C] *trademark* a type of coat that protects you from the wind

wind·chill fac·tor /ˈwɪndtʃɪl ˌfæktɚ/ *n.* [U] the effect the wind has in cold weather, making the temperature even colder

wind·ed /ˈwɪndɪd/ *adj.* having difficulty breathing because you have exercised too much or have been hit in the stomach

wind·fall /ˈwɪndfɔl/ *n.* [C] an amount of money that you get when you do not expect it

wind·ing /ˈwaɪndɪŋ/ *adj.* having bends or curves: *a long winding river*

wind in·stru·ment /ˈwɪnd ˌɪnstrəmənt/ *n.* [C] a musical instrument such as the FLUTE that you play by blowing into it

windmill

wind·mill /ˈwɪndˌmɪl/ *n.* [C] a tall structure with parts that are turned by the wind, which is used to crush grain or make electricity

win·dow /ˈwɪndoʊ/ *n.* [C] **1** a space or an area of glass in the wall of a building or vehicle that lets in light: *Can I* ***open/close/shut the window****?* | *He was* ***looking/gazing out the window.*** | *I could see her face* ***in the window*** (=on the other side of the window). **2** one of the areas on a computer screen where different programs are operating

ˈwindow ˌdressing *n.* [U] **1** an attempt to make something seem better than it really is **2** the art of arranging things in a store window so that they look attractive to customers

win·dow·pane /ˈwɪndoʊˌpeɪn/ *n.* [C] a whole piece of glass used in a window

ˈwindow ˌshopping *n.* [U] the activity of looking at goods in store windows without intending to buy them

win·dow·sill /ˈwɪndoʊˌsɪl/ *n.* [C] a shelf at the bottom of a window

wind·pipe /ˈwɪndpaɪp/ *n.* [C] the tube through which air passes from your throat to your lungs

wind·shield /ˈwɪndʃild/ *n.* [C] the large window at the front of a vehicle ➔ see picture on page A12

ˈwindshield ˌwiper *n.* [C] a long thin object that moves across a windshield to remove rain ➔ see picture on page A12

wind·surf·ing /ˈwɪndˌsɚfɪŋ/ *n.* [U] the sport of sailing across water by standing on a special board and holding onto a large sail ➔ see picture on page A10

wind·swept /ˈwɪndswɛpt/ *adj.* **1** a place that is windswept is often very windy and has few or no trees or buildings to protect it **2** made messy by the wind: *windswept hair*

wind·y /ˈwɪndi/ *adj.* if it is windy, there is a lot of wind: *It's been windy all day.* | *a windy beach*

wine[1] /waɪn/ *n.* [C,U] an alcoholic drink made from GRAPES, or a type of this drink: *a glass of* ***red/white wine*** | *a fine selection of wines*

wine[2] *v.* **wine and dine** to entertain someone with good food, wine, etc.

wine·glass /ˈwaɪnglæs/ *n.* [C] a tall glass with a thin stem, used for drinking wine

win·er·y /ˈwaɪnəri/ *n.* plural **wineries** [C] a place where wine is made and stored

wing[1] /wɪŋ/ *n.* [C] **1** the part of a bird's or insect's body used for flying: *ducks* ***flapping*** *their*

W

wings **2** one of the large flat parts that stick out of the sides of an airplane and help it stay in the air → see picture at AIRPLANE **3** one of the parts that a large building is divided into: *the east wing of the library* **4** a group of people within a political party or other organization who have a particular opinion or aim [➡ **left-wing**, **right-wing**]: *the liberal wing of the Democratic Party* **5 take sb under your wing** to help or protect someone younger or less experienced than you **6 waiting in the wings** ready to be used or ready to do something: *At least two potential buyers are waiting in the wings.* **7 the wings** [plural] the side parts of a stage where actors are hidden from people watching the play

wing² *v.* **wing it** *informal* to do something without any planning or preparation: *We'll just have to wing it.*

winged /wɪŋd/ *adj.* having wings: *winged insects*

wing·span /ˈwɪŋspæn/ *n.* [C] the distance from the end of one wing to the end of the other

wing·tip /ˈwɪŋtɪp/ *n.* [C] **1** a type of man's shoe with a pattern of small holes on the toe **2** the end of an airplane's or bird's wing

wink /wɪŋk/ *v.* [I] to close and open one eye quickly, usually to show that you are joking or being friendly: *"Don't tell Mom," he said, **winking at** her.* —**wink** *n.* [C] *He smiled and **gave** her **a wink**.*

win·ner /ˈwɪnɚ/ *n.* [C] **1** someone who wins something: *The winner will receive $5,000.* | *a Nobel prize winner* | *the **winner of** the Boston marathon* **2** *informal* someone or something that is likely to be successful: *His new film looks like a winner.*

win·ning /ˈwɪnɪŋ/ *adj.* **1** the winning person or thing is the one that wins a competition or game: *the winning team* | *the winning run* | *I'm on a **winning streak*** (=continuing to win). **2 winning smile/charm/personality etc.** a feature you have that makes people like you

W

win·nings /ˈwɪnɪŋz/ *n.* [plural] money that you win in a game or competition

win·o /ˈwaɪnoʊ/ *n.* plural **winos** [C] *informal* someone who drinks a lot of alcohol and lives on the streets

win·some /ˈwɪnsəm/ *adj. literary* pleasant and attractive: *a winsome smile*

win·ter /ˈwɪntɚ/ *n.* [C,U] the season between fall and spring, when the weather is coldest: *The park closes **in the winter**.* | *I'm going skiing **this winter**.* | ***last/next winter*** (=the winter before or after this one)

win·ter·time /ˈwɪntɚˌtaɪm/ *n.* [U] the time when it is winter

win·try /ˈwɪntri/ *adj.* cold or typical of winter: *a wintry day*

win-ˈwin situˌation *n.* [C] a situation that will end well for everyone involved in it

wipe /waɪp/ *v.* [T] **1** to clean something by rubbing it with a cloth or against a soft surface: *Could you **wipe off** the table?* | ***Wipe** your feet **on** the mat before you come in.* **2** to remove dirt, water, etc. from something with a cloth or your hand: *He **wiped** the sweat **from** his face.* | ***wiping away** her tears* **3** to remove all the sound, film, or information from a tape, video, or computer DISK

wipe out *phr. v.* **1 wipe** sb/sth ⇔ **out** to destroy or remove something completely: *Fires wiped out half of the city.* **2 wipe** sb ⇔ **out** *informal* to make you feel extremely tired: *All that running wiped me out.* **3** *spoken* to fall or hit something when driving a car, riding a bicycle, etc.

wipe sth ⇔ **up** *phr. v.* to remove liquid from a surface using a cloth: *Wipe up this mess!*

wip·er /ˈwaɪpɚ/ *n.* [C] a WINDSHIELD WIPER

wire¹ /waɪɚ/ *n.* **1** [U] metal that is long and thin like thread: *a wire fence* **2** [C] a long thin piece of metal that is used to carry electricity: *a telephone wire* **3** [C] a TELEGRAM

wire² *v.* [T] **1 also wire up** to connect electrical wires so that a piece of equipment will work: *I'm almost finished wiring up the alarm.* **2** to fasten two or more things together using wire **3** to send money electronically **4** to send a TELEGRAM

wire·tap /ˈwaɪɚˌtæp/ *v.* past tense and past participle **wiretapped**, present participle **wiretapping** [I,T] to secretly listen to someone's telephone conversations by attaching electronic equipment to the wires of his/her telephone —**wiretap** *n.* [C]

wir·ing /ˈwaɪərɪŋ/ *n.* [U] the network of wires that form the electrical system in a building, vehicle, or piece of equipment: *You need to replace the wiring.*

wir·y /ˈwaɪəri/ *adj.* **1** someone who is wiry is thin but strong **2** wiry hair is stiff and curly

wis·dom /ˈwɪzdəm/ *n.* [U] **1** good judgment and the ability to make wise decisions based on your knowledge and experience **2 the wisdom of sth** used to say that you think something is not sensible: *Many experts **question the wisdom of** sending these men to prison.*

ˈwisdom tooth *n.* [C] one of the four large teeth at the back of your mouth that do not grow until you are an adult

wise¹ /waɪz/ *adj.* **1** based on good judgment and experience: ***It's wise to** leave before the traffic gets too heavy.* | *a wise decision* **2** a wise person makes good decisions and gives good advice because s/he has a lot of experience: *a wise leader*

THESAURUS

intelligent, **smart**, **bright**, **brilliant**, **clever**, **intellectual**, **gifted**
→ see Thesaurus box at INTELLIGENT

3 be none the wiser a) to not understand something even though it has been explained to you: *They sent me on a training course, but I'm still none the wiser.* **b)** used to say that no one will find out about something bad someone has done: *He could have taken the money and we would have been none the wiser.* **4 price-wise/time-wise etc.** *informal* used for saying which feature of a situation you are referring to: *It would have been a problem transportation-wise.* —**wisely** *adv.*

wise² *v.*

wise up *phr. v. informal* to realize the truth about a situation: *Corporations should wise up and realize that employees aren't machines.*

wise·crack /ˈwaɪzkræk/ *n.* [C] *informal* a quick, funny, and often slightly unkind remark

> **THESAURUS**
> **joke, gag, one-liner, pun, funny story**
> → see Thesaurus box at JOKE¹

'wise guy *n.* [C] *informal* an annoying person who thinks that s/he knows more than s/he really does

wish¹ /wɪʃ/ *v.* **1** [T] to want something to happen even though it is unlikely: *I wish they'd hurry up!* | ***I wish (that)*** *I could remember his name.* **2** [I,T] *formal* to want to do something: ***I wish to*** *make a complaint.* **3** [T] to say that you hope someone will be happy, successful, lucky, etc.: ***Wish*** *me* ***luck!*** **4 I/you wish!** *spoken* said when you do not think something is true or possible, but you want it to be: *"Steven Spielberg wants me in his next movie." "Yeah, you wish!"*

wish for sth *phr. v.* to want something to happen or want to have something, especially when it seems unlikely: *If you could have anything, what would you wish for?*

wish² *n.* [C] **1** the act of wishing for something that you want, or the thing that you wish for: *Close your eyes and* ***make a wish****!* | *Did you get your wish?* **2** *formal* a desire for something: *It's important to respect the* ***wishes of*** *the patient.* | *He left school* ***against*** *his parents'* ***wishes*** (=his parents did not want him to leave school). | *I had no* ***wish to*** *see him.* **3 best wishes** a friendly phrase that you write before your name in cards and letters

wish·bone /ˈwɪʃboʊn/ *n.* [C] a Y-shaped chicken bone that two people pull apart in order to find out who will get his/her wish

ˌwishful 'thinking *n.* [U] a way of thinking that is based on what you want to happen rather than what is likely to happen

wish·y-wash·y /ˈwɪʃi ˌwɑʃi, -ˌwɔʃi/ *adj. informal disapproving* a wishy-washy person does not have firm or clear ideas and seems unable to decide what s/he wants

wisp /wɪsp/ *n.* [C] **1** a small thin amount of hair, grass, etc.: *A* ***wisp of*** *hair had escaped from under her hat.* **2** a small thin line of smoke or cloud —**wispy** *adj.*

wist·ful /ˈwɪstfəl/ *adj.* slightly sad because you cannot have something you want: *a wistful expression* —**wistfully** *adv.*

wit /wɪt/ *n.* **1** [U] the ability to say things that are funny and smart **2** [C] someone who has this ability **3 wits** [plural] your ability to think quickly and make the right decisions: *Without a gun, he knew he'd have to rely on his wits.* | *Somehow Austin* ***kept*** *his* ***wits about*** *him* (=thought quickly and dealt with a difficult situation). **4 be at your wits' end** to be upset because you have tried everything possible to solve a problem **5 scare sb out of his/her wits** to frighten someone very much

witch /wɪtʃ/ *n.* [C] a woman who has magic powers, especially to do bad things

witch·craft /ˈwɪtʃkræft/ *n.* [U] the use of magic, usually to do bad things

> **THESAURUS**
> **magic, spell, curse, the occult**
> → see Thesaurus box at MAGIC¹

'witch ˌdoctor *n.* [C] a man who is believed to be able to cure sick people using magic, especially in some parts of Africa

'witch hunt *n.* [C] *disapproving* an attempt to find and punish people whose opinions, political beliefs, etc. are considered to be wrong or dangerous

with /wɪθ, wɪð/ *prep.* **1** used in order to show that two or more people or things are together in the same place: *She went to the beach with her friends.* | *Put this bag with the others.* | *eggs mixed with milk* | *Make sure you* ***take*** *an umbrella* ***with*** *you.* **2** having, possessing, or carrying something: *a boy with a broken arm* | *Where's the dish with the blue pattern?* **3** because of something, or as a result of something: *Connie smiled with pride.* | *The room was bright with sunlight.* **4** including: *Your dinner* ***comes with*** *fries.* **5** using something or by means of something: *Don't eat with your fingers!* | *What will you buy with the money?* **6** used in order to say what covers or fills something: *a pillow filled with feathers* | *His hands were covered with blood.* **7** relating to something: *What's* ***wrong with*** *the radio?* | *Be careful with that glass.* **8** supporting someone or sharing his/her opinion: *I agree with you.* | *You're either with me or against me.* **9** used to say who or what someone has a particular feeling toward: *She's* ***in love with*** *you.* **10** used to say which other person, group, or country is involved in an action or activity: *He's always arguing with his son.* | *the war with Iraq* **11** used to say how someone does something or how something happens: *The fuel has to be handled with great care.* **12** at the same rate as something else, and because of it: *The wine will get better with age.* **13 be with me/you** *spoken* to understand what someone is saying: *Are you with me?* **14** employed by someone: *Jack has been with the company for 25 years.* **15** used to talk about the position of someone's body: *He stood with his back to the wall.*

with·draw /wɪθˈdrɔ, wɪð-/ *v.* past tense

W

withdrew /-ˈdru/ past participle **withdrawn** /-ˈdrɔn/ **1** [T] to take money out of a bank account: *He* ***withdrew*** *$200* ***from*** *his savings account.* **2** [T] to stop giving support or money to someone or something: *Congress threatened to withdraw support for the space project.* **3** [I,T] to stop taking part in a competition, race, etc., or to leave an organization: *She was* ***withdrawn from*** *Winston Academy.* | *The third candidate has withdrawn.* **4** [I,T] if soldiers withdraw from an area, they leave it: *American troops were gradually withdrawn.* **5** [T] if you withdraw a threat, request, proposal, etc., you say that you no longer intend to do what you said or no longer want what you asked for: *We have withdrawn our offer to buy the company.*

with·draw·al /wɪθˈdrɔəl/ *n.* **1** [C,U] the action of taking money out of a bank account, or the amount you take out: *I'd like to* ***make a withdrawal****, please.* **2** [C,U] the action of moving an army, its weapons, etc. away from the area where it was fighting: *the* ***withdrawal of*** *1000 Russian tanks* **3** [U] the action of not continuing to give something: *the* ***withdrawal of*** *government aid* **4** [U] the act of no longer taking part in an activity or being a member of an organization: *Hanson's* ***withdrawal from*** *the competition surprised everyone.* **5** [U] the pain, bad feelings, etc. that someone suffers when s/he stops regularly taking a drug: *Many people have* ***withdrawal symptoms*** *when they quit smoking.*

with·drawn /wɪθˈdrɔn/ *adj.* quiet, and not wanting to talk to people: *As the years passed, he became increasingly withdrawn.*

THESAURUS

shy, timid, bashful, reserved, introverted, antisocial, retiring
→ see Thesaurus box at SHY[1]

W

with·er /ˈwɪðɚ/ **also wither away** *v.* [I] **1** if a plant withers, its leaves become dry and it starts to die **2** to become weaker and then disappear: *Our morale eventually withered away.*

with·hold /wɪθˈhoʊld, wɪð-/ *v.* past tense and past participle **withheld** /-ˈhɛld/ [T] to refuse to give someone something: *They said McShane had* ***withheld*** *information* ***from*** *Congress.*

with·in /wɪˈðɪn, wɪˈθɪn/ *adv., prep.* **1** during the period of time mentioned, or before the period of time ends: *The movie should start within the next 5 minutes.* | *Within a month of meeting him I knew I was in love.* **2** less than a certain distance from a particular place: *We need a hotel within a mile of the airport.* **3** inside an organization, society, or group of people: *There have been a lot of changes within the department since I joined.* **4** according to particular limits or rules: *driving within the speed limit*

with·out /wɪˈðaʊt, wɪˈθaʊt/ *adv., prep.* **1** not having a particular thing: *I can't see anything without my glasses.* | *They went without food and water for 2 days.* **2** not having someone with you: *Why did you leave without me?* | *We can't finish this job without Jake.* **3** not doing a particular thing: *He left without saying goodbye.* | *Suddenly,* ***without warning****, Griffin turned and ran.* **4** not showing a particular emotion: *The mayor announced his resignation without bitterness.*

with·stand /wɪθˈstænd, wɪð-/ *v.* past tense and past participle **withstood** /-ˈstʊd/ [T] to not be harmed or affected by something: *The buildings have withstood earthquakes since 1916.*

wit·ness[1] /ˈwɪtˀnɪs/ *n.* [C] **1** someone who saw an accident or a crime: *Unfortunately there were no* ***witnesses to*** *the robbery.* **2** someone who describes in a court of law what s/he knows about a crime: *He asked the witness how well she knew the defendant.* | *Michael was a crucial* ***witness for*** *the prosecution.* **3** someone who watches another person sign an official document, and then signs it also to prove this

witness[2] *v.* [T] **1** to see something happen, especially an accident or a crime: *Few people actually witnessed the event.*

THESAURUS

see, notice, spot, catch a glimpse of, make out, catch sight of
→ see Thesaurus box at SEE

2 to watch someone sign an official document, and then sign it also to prove this

ˈwitness stand *n.* [C] the place in a court of law where a witness answers questions

wit·ti·cism /ˈwɪt̬əˌsɪzəm/ *n.* [C] a smart and amusing remark

wit·ty /ˈwɪt̬i/ *adj.* comparative **wittier**, superlative **wittiest** smart and funny: *a witty young man* | *a witty response*

THESAURUS

funny, hilarious, hysterical, corny, amusing, humorous
→ see Thesaurus box at FUNNY[1]

wives /waɪvz/ *n.* the plural of WIFE

wiz·ard /ˈwɪzɚd/ *n.* [C] **1** a man who has magic powers **2 also wiz** /wɪz/ *informal* someone who is very good at doing something: *a computer wizard*

wiz·ened /ˈwɪzənd/ *adj.* old and having dry skin with a lot of WRINKLES (=lines)

wk. the written abbreviation of **week**

wob·ble /ˈwɑbəl/ *v.* [I] to move from side to side in an unsteady way —**wobbly** *adj.*: *a wobbly chair* —**wobble** *n.* [C]

THESAURUS

shake, tremble, shiver, vibrate, rattle
→ see Thesaurus box at SHAKE[1]

woe /woʊ/ *n.* **1 woes** [plural] *formal* problems

that are affecting someone: *the country's economic woes* **2** [U] *literary* great sadness

woe·be·gone /ˈwoʊbɪˌgɔn, -ˌgɑn/ *adj.* looking very sad

woe·ful /ˈwoʊfəl/ *adj.* **1** very bad or serious: *the woeful state of the economy* **2** *literary* very sad: *a woeful goodbye* —**woefully** *adv.*: *woefully inadequate facilities*

wok /wɑk/ *n.* [C] a large round pan, used especially in Chinese cooking

woke /woʊk/ *v.* the past tense of WAKE

wo·ken /ˈwoʊkən/ *v.* the past participle of WAKE

wolf

wolf¹ /wʊlf/ *n.* plural **wolves** /wʊlvz/ [C] a wild animal similar to a large dog

wolf² **also wolf down** *v.* [T] *informal* to eat something very quickly: *She wolfed down a couple of hamburgers.*

THESAURUS

eat, devour, gobble up
➔ see Thesaurus box at EAT

wom·an /ˈwʊmən/ *n.* plural **women** /ˈwɪmɪn/ **1** [C] an adult female person [➡ **man**]: *Who was that woman you were talking to?* | *Ireland's first woman president* | *single women* **2** [singular] women in general: *It's not safe there for a woman traveling alone.*

wom·an·hood /ˈwʊmənˌhʊd/ *n.* [U] the state of being a woman, or the time when a female person is an adult [➡ **manhood**]

wom·an·iz·er /ˈwʊməˌnaɪzɚ/ *n.* [C] a man who tries to have sexual relationships with many different women

wom·an·kind /ˈwʊmənˌkaɪnd/ *n.* [U] women considered together as a group

womb /wum/ *n.* [C] UTERUS

wom·en /ˈwɪmɪn/ *n.* the plural of WOMAN

won /wʌn/ *v.* the past tense and past participle of WIN

won·der¹ /ˈwʌndɚ/ *v.* [I,T] **1** to think about something that you are not sure about and try to guess what is true, what will happen, etc.: *I **wonder if** she knows we're here.* | *I **wonder how** Wendy's feeling today.* | *We **wondered where** you'd gone.* **2 I was wondering if/whether** *spoken* **a)** used in order to ask someone if s/he would like to do something: *We were wondering whether you'd like to come with us.* **b)** used in order to politely ask for something: *I was wondering if I could use your phone.* **3** to doubt whether someone or something is good or true: *I began to **wonder about** this business of his.* **4** to be surprised by something: *I **wonder why** she didn't call the police.*

wonder² *n.* **1** [U] a feeling of admiration and surprise: *They listened to Lisa's story **in/with wonder**.* **2 no wonder** *spoken* said when you are not surprised about something: *No wonder you feel sick – you ate a whole pizza!* **3** [C usually plural] something that is very impressive: ***the wonders of** modern technology*

wonder³ *adj.* [only before noun] very good and effective: *a new wonder drug*

won·der·ful /ˈwʌndɚfəl/ *adj.* extremely good [= **great**]: *Congratulations! That's wonderful news!* | *We had a wonderful time.* —**wonderfully** *adv.*

THESAURUS

good, great, excellent, fantastic, outstanding
➔ see Thesaurus box at GOOD¹, NICE

won't /woʊnt/ *v.* the short form of "will not": *Dad won't like it.*

wont¹ /wɔnt, woʊnt/ *adj.* **be wont to do sth** *formal* to be likely to do something

wont² *n.* **as is sb's wont** *formal* used in order to say that it is someone's habit to do something

woo /wu/ *v.* [T] **1** to try to persuade someone to do something such as support you, vote for you, or buy something from you: *Politicians were busy wooing voters.* **2** *old-fashioned* to try to persuade a woman to love you and marry you

wood /wʊd/ *n.* **1** [C,U] the material that trees are made of, which is used to make things: *polished wood floors* | *a table made from three different types of wood* **2 the woods** [plural] a small forest: *I went for a walk **in the woods**.* ➔ **knock on wood** at KNOCK

wood·chuck /ˈwʊdtʃʌk/ *n.* [C] a GROUNDHOG

wood·ed /ˈwʊdɪd/ *adj.* covered with trees

wood·en /ˈwʊdn/ *adj.* made from wood: *a wooden bench* ➔ see picture at MATERIAL¹

wood·land /ˈwʊdlənd, -lænd/ *n.* [C,U] an area of land that is covered with trees

THESAURUS

the woods, forest, rain forest, jungle
➔ see Thesaurus box at TREE

wood·peck·er /ˈwʊdˌpɛkɚ/ *n.* [C] a bird that uses its long beak to make holes in trees

wood·wind /ˈwʊdˌwɪnd/ *n.* [C usually plural] the group of musical instruments that you play by blowing and pressing KEYS

wood·work /ˈwʊdwɚk/ *n.* [U] **1** the parts of a building that are made of wood **2** the skill of making wooden objects

W

wood·y /ˈwʊdi/ *adj.* looking, smelling, tasting, etc. like wood: *woody plants*

woof /wʊf/ *interjection* the sound a dog makes when it BARKS

wool /wʊl/ *n.* [U] **1** the soft thick hair of a sheep, used for making cloth and YARN **2** material made from wool: *a wool skirt* | *wool blankets* → see picture at MATERIAL¹

woolen /ˈwʊlən/ *adj.* made of wool: *woolen socks*

wool·ens /ˈwʊlənz/ *n.* [plural] clothes that are made from wool

wool·y /ˈwʊli/ *adj.* made of or feeling like wool: *a wooly hat*

woo·zy /ˈwuzi/ *adj. informal* feeling weak and unsteady [= **dizzy**]

word¹ /wɚd/ *n.*

1 LANGUAGE PART [C] a group of sounds or letters that have a particular meaning: *"Casa" is the Spanish* ***word for*** *"house."* | *Write a 500-word essay about your family.* | *I know the tune, but not the words.*

2 STH SAID/WRITTEN [C] something that you say or write: *Tell us what happened* ***in your own words.*** | *Promise you won't* ***say a word*** (=not say anything) *about the accident to John.*

3 not believe/hear/understand a word used to emphasize that you do not believe or cannot hear any part of what someone is saying: *I didn't understand a word you said.*

4 STATEMENT [C] something important that someone says to you: *Mr. Gleeson would like* ***a word with*** *you in his office.* | *a* ***word of caution/advice/encouragement etc.*** (=used when you want to warn someone not to do something, give them some advice, etc.) | *Mr. Martin will now* ***say a few words*** (=make a short speech).

5 in other words used when you are repeating a statement in a clearer way: *Some people aren't demonstrative. In other words, they don't express their feelings.*

W

6 NEWS [singular, U] a piece of news or a message: ***The word is*** *the company's closing its offices in Boston.* | *Have you had* ***any word from*** *your lawyers yet?* | *The group went on television to* ***spread the word*** (=tell other people the news) *about child abuse.* | *Many people learned about the band* ***by word of mouth*** (=because someone told them about the band).

7 sb's word someone's promise or statement that something is true: ***I give you*** *my* ***word****; we'll take good care of him.* | *I trust him to* ***keep*** *his* ***word****.* | *The money's all there —* ***take*** *my* ***word for it*** (=believe what I say is true). | *He's* ***a man of his word*** (=does what he promises to do).

8 swear/dirty/cuss word a word that is considered to be offensive or shocking by most people

9 word for word in exactly the same words: *That's not what he said word for word, but it's close.*

10 put in a good word for sb to try to help someone get or achieve something by saying good things about him/her to someone else: *Could you put in a good word for me with your boss?*

11 the last word the last statement in a discussion or argument: *She's not content unless she* ***has the last word****.*

12 not in so many words not in a direct way: *"So Dad said he'd pay for it?" "Not in so many words."*

13 give/say the word to tell someone to start doing something: *Don't move until I give the word.*

14 the final word the power to decide whether or how to do something: *My boss* ***has the final word*** *on hiring staff.*

word² *v.* [T] to use words that are carefully chosen when saying or writing something: *a* ***carefully worded*** *letter*

word·ing /ˈwɚdɪŋ/ *n.* [U] the words and phrases used in order to express something: *the exact* ***wording of*** *the contract*

ˈword ˌprocessor *n.* [C] a small computer or computer software that you use for writing —**word processing** *n.* [U]

word·y /ˈwɚdi/ *adj. disapproving* using too many words: *a wordy explanation*

wore /wɔr/ *v.* the past tense of WEAR

work¹ /wɚk/ *v.*

1 DO A JOB [I,T] to do a job in order to earn money, or to do the activities and duties that are part of your job: *"Where do you work?" "I* ***work in*** *the city."* | *Heidi* ***works for*** *a law firm in Montreal.* | *I used to* ***work at*** *Burger King.* | *She* ***works as*** *a bartender in a nightclub.* | *He's* ***working with*** *children who have learning difficulties.* | *Are you willing to* ***work nights/weekends etc.****?*

TOPIC

If you work for a company or organization, you are an **employee**.
The person or organization you work for is your **employer**.
Your employer pays your **salary** or **wages**.
An organization's **staff** are all the people who work for the organization.
Your **colleagues** or **co-workers** are the people you work with.
When you reach the age to stop working permanently, you **retire**.
→ JOB

2 MACHINE/EQUIPMENT a) [I] if a machine or piece of equipment works, it does what it is supposed to do: *The CD player isn't working.* **b)** [T] to make a machine or piece of equipment do what it is supposed to do: *Does anyone know how to work the printer?*

3 BE EFFECTIVE [I] to be effective or successful: *This plan isn't going to work.* | *I hope this cough medicine works.*

4 DO AN ACTIVITY [I] to do something that needs effort in order to achieve a result: *He's* ***working***

towards *a better life for his family.* | *She's been* ***working hard*** *to get the house ready.*

5 work your way through/to etc. sth **a)** to move somewhere slowly and with difficulty: *He worked his way through the crowd.* **b)** to achieve something gradually by working: *Dave* ***worked*** *his* ***way to the top*** *of the firm.*

6 work your way through school/college to do a job while you are in college because you need the money to help pay for it

7 HAVE AN EFFECT [I] to have a particular effect on someone or something: *Unfortunately her bad grades* ***worked against*** (=caused problems for) *her.* | *Your job experience should* ***work in*** *your* ***favor*** (=help you).

8 MOVE SLOWLY [I,T] to move into a position slowly with many small movements, or to move something in this way: *Slowly he worked the screwdriver into the crack.*

9 SHAPE STH [T] if you work a material such as clay, leather, or metal, you bend it, shape it, etc. in order to make something

10 EXERCISE [T] to exercise a muscle or part of your body

11 LAND [T] if you work the land or the soil, you try to grow crops on it

work on *phr. v.* **1 work on** sth to try to repair, complete, or improve something: *Dad's still working on the car.* | *I need to work on my essay.* **2 work on** sb to try continuously to influence someone or persuade them to do something

work out *phr. v.* **1** if something works out, it gradually stops being a problem: *Don't worry. I'm sure everything will work out fine.* **2** to do a set of exercises that make you stronger: *Sue works out in the gym twice a week.* **3 work** sth ⇔ **out** to calculate an amount, price, or value: *Have you worked out how much we owe them?* **4** to cost a particular amount: *The hotel* ***works out to/at*** *about $50 a night.* **5 work** sth ⇔ **out** to find a solution to a problem or make a decision after thinking carefully: *He still hasn't worked out which college he's going to.*

work up *phr. v.* **work up an appetite/sweat** to do so much exercise that you become very hungry or SWEATY

work up to sth *phr. v.* to gradually prepare yourself for something difficult: *I started with 10 laps and now I've worked up to 20.*

work[2] *n.* **1** [U] your job or the activities that you do regularly to earn money: *Much of our work involves meeting clients.* | *Do you want to go to dinner* ***after work*** (=after you have finished working)*?* | *Hurry up or we'll be* ***late for work.*** | *I've been* ***out of work*** (=without a job) *for a year.* | *Rob's still* ***looking for work.*** ▶ Don't say "I have a work." say "I have a job." ◀ **2** [U] the place where you do your job: *I'll see you* ***at work*** *on Monday.* **3** [U] physical or mental activity and effort: *Looking after children can be* ***hard work.*** | *Stop talking and* ***get to work*** (=start working)*!* | *They've done a lot of* ***work on*** *their house.* **4** [U] the things you produce for your job, as part of a class, etc.: *We're pleased with your work.* | *an excellent* ***piece of work*** **5** [C] a painting, book, play, piece of music, etc.: *great* ***works of art*** **6 at work** doing a job or an activity: *Crews were at work repairing the roads.* **7 have your work cut out (for you)** *informal* used to say that it will be very difficult to do something **8 work clothes** clothes designed for people to work in **9 the (whole) works** *spoken* everything that is available with something you are buying: *a hamburger* ***with the works*** (=with onions, cheese, etc.) **10 works** [plural] a building where goods are produced or an industrial process takes place: *a gas works* → **do sb's dirty work** at DIRTY[1]

work·a·ble /ˈwɚkəbəl/ *adj.* a workable plan or system can be used or done effectively: *a workable solution*

work·a·hol·ic /ˌwɚkəˈhɔlɪk/ *n.* [C] *informal* someone who spends all his/her time working

work·bench /ˈwɚkbɛntʃ/ *n.* [C] a strong table used for working on things with tools

work·book /ˈwɚkbʊk/ *n.* [C] a school book with questions and exercises in it

ˌworked ˈup *adj. informal* very upset or excited: *Don't get so* ***worked up about*** *your daughter.*

work·er /ˈwɚkɚ/ *n.* [C] **1** someone who works for a company or organization, especially someone who is not a manager: *Fifty workers lost their jobs.* | *a farm worker* **2** someone who works in a particular way: *Lisa's a* ***good/hard/slow, etc. worker.***

ˌworkers' compenˈsation also **ˌworkers' ˈcomp** *n.* [U] money that a company must pay to a worker who is injured or becomes sick as a result of his/her job

work·fare /ˈwɚkfɛr/ *n.* [U] a system under which unemployed people must work before they are given money by the government

work·force /ˈwɚkfɔrs/ *n.* [singular] all the people who work in a particular country, industry, or company: *There are still more men than women* ***in the workforce.***

work·ing /ˈwɚkɪŋ/ *adj.* [only before noun] **1** having a job: *a* ***working mother*** **2** relating to work: *bad working conditions* **3 in working order** working correctly and not broken: *My watch is still in good working order.* **4 a working knowledge of sth** enough practical knowledge about something to use it effectively

ˌworking ˈclass *n.* **the working class** the group of people in society who usually do physical work and who do not have much money or power [➡ **lower class**, **middle class**, **upper class**] —**working-class** *adj.*: *a working-class neighborhood*

work·ings /ˈwɚkɪŋz/ *n.* [plural] the way something works: ***the workings of*** *government departments*

work·load /ˈwɚkloʊd/ *n.* [C] the amount of

W

work that a person is expected to do: *a **heavy workload*** (=a lot of work)

work·man /ˈwɚkmən/ *n.* [C] someone who does physical work such as building or repairing things

work·man·like /ˈwɚkmənˌlaɪk/ *adj.* skillfully and carefully done, but often in an uninteresting way: *a workmanlike performance*

work·man·ship /ˈwɚkmənˌʃɪp/ *n.* [U] the skill with which something has been made

work·out /ˈwɚk-aʊt/ *n.* [C] a series of physical exercises that you do to keep your body strong and healthy: *I started my workout with some stretching exercises.*

TOPIC

jogging, lifting weights, aerobics
→ see Topic box at EXERCISE²

work·sheet /ˈwɚkʃit/ *n.* [C] a piece of paper with questions, exercises, etc. for students

work·shop /ˈwɚkʃɑp/ *n.* [C] **1** a room or building where people use tools and machines to make or repair things **2** a meeting at which people try to improve their skills by discussing their experiences and doing practical exercises: *a writing workshop*

work·sta·tion /ˈwɚkˌsteɪʃən/ *n.* [C] the part of an office where you work, including your desk, computer, etc. → see Topic box at OFFICE

world /wɚld/ *n.*

1 the world the PLANET we live on, and all the people, countries, etc. on it [= **Earth**]: *the world's longest river* | *Athletes from **all over the world/around the world** compete in the Olympics.* | *The practice is illegal in many **parts of the world**.* → see Thesaurus box at EARTH

2 SOCIETY [singular] our society, and the way that people live and behave: *I want **a better world** for my kids.* | ***In an ideal world**, you and your sister would get along.*

W

3 AREA OF ACTIVITY/WORK [C usually singular] a particular area of activity or work, and the people who are involved in it: *the **world of** sports* | *the music world*

4 COUNTRIES [singular] a particular group of countries: *the Western world* | ***the industrialized world***

5 DIFFERENCE/CHANGE [C] used to emphasize that a difference or change is very great: *There's a **world of difference** between his public and private life.* | *We're **worlds apart**.*

6 SB'S LIFE [C] the life and experiences of a particular person or group of people: *He lives **in a world of** his **own**.* | *Hemmingway's world*

7 in the world used in order to emphasize what you are saying: *You're the **best** dad **in the world**.* | ***Why in the world** should I listen to you?*

8 the animal/plant/insect world animals, etc. considered as a group

9 ANOTHER WORLD [C] another PLANET that is not the Earth: *a world light years away from earth*

10 have the best of both worlds to have the advantages of two completely different things

11 out of this world *informal* very good: *Their ice cream is out of this world!*

12 do sb a world of good *informal* to make someone feel much better: *A vacation would do you a world of good.*

13 be/feel on top of the world *informal* to feel extremely happy

14 mean the world to sb/think the world of sb if someone or something means the world to you, or if you think the world of him/her, you love or respect him/her very much → **the outside world** at OUTSIDE²

ˌworld-ˈclass *adj.* among the best in the world: *a world-class athlete*

ˌworld-ˈfamous *adj.* known about by people all over the world: *a world-famous musician*

world·ly /ˈwɚldli/ *adj.* **1 sb's worldly goods/possessions** everything someone owns **2** knowing a lot about people and society, based on experience: *worldly young men*

ˌworld ˈpower *n.* [C] a powerful country that has a lot of influence in many parts of the world

ˌworld ˈrecord *n.* [C] the fastest time, longest distance, highest level, etc. which anyone has ever achieved anywhere in the world, especially in a sport: *He **set a** new **world record** for the marathon.* | *the 800m **world record holder***
—**world-record** *adj.*

ˌWorld ˈSeries *n.* **the World Series** the last series of baseball games that is played each year in order to decide the best professional team in the U.S. and Canada

world·wide /ˌwɚldˈwaɪd◂/ *adj.* everywhere in the world: *worldwide fame*

THESAURUS

everywhere, all over, nationwide, everyplace
→ see Thesaurus box at EVERYWHERE

ˌWorld Wide ˈWeb *n.* [singular] **www** the INTERNET

worm¹ /wɚm/ *n.* [C] **1** a small tube-shaped creature with a soft body and no legs that lives in the ground **2** a type of computer VIRUS that can make copies of itself and destroy information on computers that are connected to each other → **a (whole) can of worms** at CAN²

worm² *v.* **worm your way into/through etc. sth** to move slowly through or into a small place or a crowd: *My daughter wormed her way into my sleeping bag.*

worn¹ /wɔrn/ *v.* the past participle of WEAR

worn² *adj.* a worn object is old and slightly damaged because it has been used a lot: *worn stone steps*

ˌworn ˈout, **worn-out** *adj.* **1** very tired because you have been working or playing hard

THESAURUS

tired, **exhausted**, **weary**, **run-down**, **beat**
→ see Thesaurus box at TIRED

2 too old or damaged to be used: *a pair of worn-out sneakers*

wor·ried /ˈwɚid, ˈwʌrid/ *adj.* unhappy or nervous because you are worrying about someone or something: *We were really* ***worried about*** *you!* | *I* ***got worried*** *when you didn't call.* | *People are* ***worried that*** *they may lose their jobs.*

THESAURUS

anxious – very worried and unable to relax: *She was getting anxious about the children.*
concerned – worried about a social problem, or about someone's health, safety, etc.: *Many scientists are concerned about global warming.*
nervous – worried or frightened about something, and unable to relax: *I get really nervous about exams.*
uneasy – worried because you think something bad might happen: *I felt uneasy leaving the kids with him.*
stressed (out) – so worried that you cannot relax: *I'm getting totally stressed out about work.*

wor·ry[1] /ˈwɚi, ˈwʌri/ *v.* past tense and past participle **worried**, third person singular **worries** **1** [I] to think about someone or something a lot, because you feel nervous or unhappy about him, her, or it: *I* ***worry about*** *Dave.* | *She* ***worried that*** *she would get pregnant.* | *Parents* ***worry about/over*** *their children's safety.* **2 don't worry** *spoken* **a)** said when you are trying to make someone feel less anxious: *Don't worry, we're fine.* **b)** used in order to tell someone that s/he does not have to do something: *Don't* ***worry about*** *the kids – I'll take them to school.* **3** [T] to make someone feel nervous, unhappy, or upset: ***It worries me that*** *she hasn't called yet.*

worry[2] *n.* plural **worries** **1** [C] a problem or bad situation that makes you unhappy because you do not know how to solve it: *financial worries* **2** [U] the feeling of being anxious about something: *Her father was frantic* ***with worry****.*

wor·ry·ing /ˈwɚiɪŋ, ˈwʌr-/ *adj.* making you feel worried: *a worrying development*

worse[1] /wɚs/ *adj.* [the comparative of "bad"] **1** more unpleasant, bad, or severe, or lower in quality: *Traffic always* ***gets worse*** *after 4:30.* | *The accident could have been* ***much/far worse****.* | *Don't go see her; it will only* ***make matters/things worse****.* **2** sicker or in a condition that is not as good: *Do you feel any worse?* | *His hearing has* ***gotten worse****.* | *He seemed* ***none the worse*** *for his ordeal.* **3 go from bad to worse** to continue getting worse: ***Things went from bad to worse*** *and finally we got divorced.*

worse[2] *adv.* **1** in a more severe or serious way than before: *It hurt worse than anything.* **2** not as well, or less successfully: *Margo sings even worse than I do!*

worse[3] *n.* [U] something worse: *Critics are wrong to say the* ***changes*** *are* ***for the worse*** (=make things worse).

wors·en /ˈwɚsən/ *v.* [I,T] to become worse, or to make something become worse: *The weather had worsened.*

ˌworse ˈoff *adj.* poorer, less successful, or having fewer advantages than you did before: *There are a lot of people worse off than I am.*

wor·ship /ˈwɚʃɪp/ *v.* past tense and past participle **worshiped** or **worshipped**, present participle **worshiping** or **worshipping** **1** [I,T] to show respect and love for a god, especially by praying in a church, TEMPLE, etc.: *a church where people have worshipped for hundreds of years* **2** [T] to love and admire someone very much: *She worships her Grandpa.* —**worship** *n.* [U] *a* ***house of worship*** (=church or building where people can pray) —**worshiper**, **worshipper** *n.* [C]

worst[1] /wɚst/ *adj.* [the superlative of "bad"] worse than anything else of the same type: *It was the worst movie I've ever seen.* | *the worst snowstorm in years*

worst[2] *n.* [C] **1 also the worst** someone or something that is worse than all others: *This is the worst I've ever done on a test.* | *The cities are dirty and poor, but* ***worst of all*** *is the violence.* | *The* ***worst of*** *the storm seemed to be over.* | *What's* ***the worst that can happen****?* **2 at worst** if a thing or situation is as bad as it can be: *At worst, the repairs will cost you around $700.* **3 if (the) worst comes to (the) worst** if the worst possible thing happens: *If worst comes to worst, we'll have to sell the house.*

worst[3] *adv.* in the worst way or most severely: *Their village was worst affected by the war.*

worth[1] /wɚθ/ *adj.* **1 be worth sth** to have a particular value, especially in money: *Our house is worth about $350,000.* | *Each question is worth 4 points.* **2 be worth (doing) sth** to be helpful, valuable, interesting, or good for you: *The Getty Museum is definitely worth a visit/worth visiting.* | *It was a lot of hard work, but* ***it was worth it****.* | *Stop crying over him. He's* ***not worth it****.* | ***It is worth*** *pausing to examine this more closely.* | ***It's worth a try*** (=you might get what you want if you try doing something). **3 worth your while** valuable to you because you could gain something you want or need: *It'd be worth your while to talk to someone who works there.*

worth[2] *n.* **1 ... worth of sth** an amount of something based on how much money you spend, how much time you use, etc.: *twenty dollars' worth of gas* | *a year's worth of training* **2** [U] the worth of someone or something is how important or useful he, she, or it is: *children who have a sense of their own worth* | *The new computer system has already* ***proved its worth****.* **3** [U] the worth of something is

W

its value in money: *It is difficult to estimate the current worth of the company.*

worth·less /ˈwɚθlɪs/ *adj.* **1** not valuable, not important, or not useful: *The data was worthless.* **2** a worthless person has no good qualities or useful skills

worth·while /ˌwɚθˈwaɪl◂/ *adj.* if something is worthwhile, it is important or useful, or you gain something from it: *All that work finally seemed worthwhile.*

wor·thy /ˈwɚði/ *adj.* **1** good enough to deserve respect, admiration, or attention: *a worthy opponent | worthy achievements* **2 be worthy of sth** *formal* to deserve something: *a leader who is worthy of respect*

would /wəd, əd, d; *strong* wʊd/ *modal verb* **1** used as a past tense of "will" when reporting what someone has said or thought: *Mr. Thomas said it would be okay to go. | She told me she wouldn't* (=would not) *come.* **2** used when talking about a possible situation or about a situation that does not exist: *Dad would be really mad if he knew. | I'd* (=I would) *help you if I could. | If you had listened to me, you wouldn't have gotten in trouble.* **3** used in order to say what you intended to do or expected to happen: *I thought Caroline would be happy, but she got really mad at me. | Glenn knew he'd* (=he would) *be tired the next day.* **4** used in order to say that something happened regularly in the past: *In the evenings, we'd* (=we would) *read or play games.* **5 would not/wouldn't** used in order to say that someone refused to do something or that something did not happen even though you tried to make it happen: *Blair would not answer the question. | The door wouldn't open.*

SPOKEN PHRASES

6 would like/would love used in order to say that you want something: *I would love to see your new house!* **7 Would you...?** said in order to ask for or offer something politely: *Would you bring me that broom? | Would you like a drink? | **Would you mind** waiting until tomorrow?* **8 I would/I wouldn't** used in order to give advice: *I'd* (=I would) *try to get there early. | **I wouldn't** go by myself, **if I were you**.* **9** used before verbs that express what you think, when you want to make an opinion less definite: *I would guess that he'd bring a friend. | I would have thought you'd be tired.* **10 would (just) as soon** used in order to say that you would prefer something to happen or be done: *I'd just as soon you didn't tell her.* **11 would rather** said when you prefer doing or having one thing instead of another: *I **would rather** take a nice vacation **than** spend a lot on clothes.* **12** used in order to show you are annoyed about something that someone has done: *You **would go and** tell the teacher!*

ˈwould-be *adj.* **would-be actor/robber etc.** someone who hopes to have a particular job or intends to do a particular thing

would·n't /ˈwʊdnt/ *v.* the short form of "would not": *She wouldn't answer.*

would've /ˈwʊdəv/ *v.* the short form of "would have": *You would've liked it.*

wound¹ /wund/ *n.* [C] **1** an injury, especially a deep cut made in your skin by a knife or bullet: *gunshot wounds | Keston **suffered/received** severe **wounds** in the attack.*

THESAURUS

injury, **bruise**, **cut**, **scrape**, **sprain**, **bump**
➔ see Thesaurus box at INJURY

2 damage, problems, or emotional pain caused by something bad happening: *It will take more than an apology to **heal the wounds**.*

wound² *v.* [T] **1** to injure someone, especially with a knife or gun: *Two officers were **badly/seriously/severely wounded**.* **2** to make someone feel unhappy or upset: *She was **deeply wounded** by the criticism.* —**wounded** *adj.*

wound³ /waʊnd/ *v.* the past tense and past participle of WIND

wound up /ˌwaʊnd ˈʌp/ *adj.* very angry, nervous, or excited: *He **got** so **wound up** he couldn't sleep.*

wove /woʊv/ *v.* the past tense of WEAVE

wo·ven /ˈwoʊvən/ *v.* the past participle of WEAVE

wow¹ /waʊ/ *interjection* said when you think something is impressive or surprising: *Wow! You look great!*

wow² *v.* [T] *informal* to make people admire you a lot: *The movie has wowed the critics.*

wpm /ˌdʌbəlju pi ˈɛm/ **words per minute** used to describe the speed at which someone can write using a KEYBOARD

wran·gle /ˈræŋgəl/ *v.* [I] to argue with someone angrily for a long time: *political **wrangling over** Social Security* —**wrangle** *n.* [C]

wran·gler /ˈræŋglɚ/ *n.* [C] *informal* ➔ COWBOY

wrap¹ /ræp/ *v.* past tense and past participle **wrapped**, present participle **wrapping** [T] **1** to fold cloth, paper, etc. around something, especially in order to cover it: *I haven't **wrapped** her **present** yet. | Here, **wrap** this blanket **around** you.* **2** to hold someone or something by putting your arms, legs, or fingers around him, her, or it: *I **wrapped** my arms **around** my daughter.* **3 have sb wrapped around your (little) finger** to be able to persuade someone to do whatever you want

wrap sth ⇔ **up** *phr. v.* **1** to completely cover something by folding paper, cloth, etc. around it: *sandwiches wrapped up in foil* **2** to finish or complete a job, meeting, etc.: *Investigators hope to wrap up the case soon.* **3 be wrapped up in your children/work etc.** to give so much attention to your children, work, etc. that you do not have time for other things

wrap² *n.* **1** [U] thin clear soft plastic that you wrap around something to protect it or keep it clean: *Cover the food with **plastic wrap**.* **2** [C] a

W

SANDWICH made of a TORTILLA folded around meat, cheese, etc. **3** [C] *old-fashioned* a SHAWL

wrap·per /ˈræpɚ/ *n.* [C] the paper or plastic that covers a piece of food, especially candy: *gum wrappers*

THESAURUS

cover, **lid**, **top**, **wrapping**
➔ see Thesaurus box at COVER²

ˈwrapping ˌpaper *n.* [C,U] colored paper used for wrapping presents

wrath /ræθ/ *n.* [U] *formal* very great anger

wreak /rik/ *v. literary* **wreak havoc** to cause a lot of damage, problems, or suffering

wreath /riθ/ *n.* [C] a decoration made from flowers and leaves arranged in a circle

wreck¹ /rɛk/ *v.* [T] *informal* **1** to completely spoil something so that it cannot continue in a successful way: *His drinking problem wrecked their marriage.* **2** to damage something such as a car or building so badly that it cannot be repaired

wreck² *n.* [C] **1** a bad accident involving cars or airplanes: *Only one person survived the wreck.*

THESAURUS

accident, **crash**, **collision**, **disaster**, **catastrophe**, **pile-up**, **mishap**, **fender-bender**
➔ see Thesaurus box at ACCIDENT

2 a car, airplane, or ship that is so damaged it cannot be repaired **3** *informal* someone who is very nervous, tired, or unhealthy: *I was a wreck, physically and emotionally.* **4** *informal* something that is very messy and needs a lot of repairs: *The house was a wreck when we bought it.*

wreck·age /ˈrɛkɪdʒ/ *n.* [U] the broken parts of a car, airplane, or building that has been destroyed in an accident: *the wreckage of the plane*

wren /rɛn/ *n.* [C] a very small brown bird that sings

wrench¹ /rɛntʃ/ *v.* [T] **1** to twist and pull something from its position using force: *Prisoners had even **wrenched** doors **off** their hinges.* **2** to injure part of your body by twisting it suddenly: *Sam wrenched his back.*

wrench² *n.* [C] **1** a metal tool with a round end, used for turning NUTS **2 be a wrench** an experience that is a wrench is difficult and involves strong emotions: *It was a wrench to leave San Diego.*

wrench·ing /ˈrɛntʃɪŋ/ *adj.* extremely difficult to deal with, and involving strong emotions: *a wrenching choice* | *a **gut-wrenching/heart-wrenching** story* (=one that makes you feel strong emotions)

wrest /rɛst/ *v. formal* **wrest sth from sb a)** to take away someone's power or influence **b)** to violently pull something away from someone

wres·tle /ˈrɛsəl/ *v.* **1** [I,T] to fight by holding onto someone and trying to push or pull him/her down **2** [I] to try to deal with a difficult problem or emotion: *Several cities are **wrestling with** budget deficits.*

wres·tling /ˈrɛslɪŋ/ *n.* [U] a sport in which you try to throw your opponent to the ground and hold him/her there —**wrestler** /ˈrɛslɚ/ *n.* [C]

wretch /rɛtʃ/ *n.* [C] *literary* someone whom you pity

wretch·ed /ˈrɛtʃɪd/ *adj.* extremely unhappy, especially because you are lonely, sick, poor, etc.

wrig·gle /ˈrɪgəl/ *v.* [I,T] to twist from side to side with small quick movements, or to move part of your body this way: *A small child sat wriggling in her lap.* —**wriggle** *n.* [C]

wring /rɪŋ/ *v.* past tense and past participle **wrung** /rʌŋ/ [T] **1 also wring out** to tightly twist wet clothes, sheets, etc. in order to remove water from them **2** to succeed in getting something from someone, after a lot of effort: *The company is trying to **wring** more work **from** its employees.* **3 wring your hands** to rub and press your hands together because you are nervous or upset **4 wring sth's neck** to kill an animal or bird, such as a chicken, by twisting its neck

wring·er /ˈrɪŋɚ/ *n.* [C] **1 go through the wringer** *informal* to have an unpleasant or difficult experience **2** a machine used especially in past times for pressing water out of washed clothes

wrin·kle¹ /ˈrɪŋkəl/ *n.* [C] **1** a line on your face or skin that you get when you are old **2** a line in cloth, paper, etc. caused by crushing it or accidentally folding it: ***wrinkles in** his shirt*

wrinkle² *v.* [I,T] to form small folds in something such as clothes or skin, or to be shaped in these folds: *Linen wrinkles easily.* | *Patty wrinkled her nose in disgust.* —**wrinkled** *adj.*: *his wrinkled face*

wrist /rɪst/ *n.* [C] the joint between your hand and your arm: *She had a silver bracelet **on** her **wrist**.*
➔ see picture at HAND¹

wrist·watch /ˈrɪst-wɑtʃ/ *n.* [C] a watch that you wear on your wrist

writ /rɪt/ *n.* [C] a legal document that orders someone to do something or not to do something

write /raɪt/ *v.* past tense **wrote** /roʊt/ past participle **written** /ˈrɪtˀn/ present participle **writing** **1** [I,T] to produce a new book, story, song, etc.: *Bombeck **wrote about** family life in a funny way.* | *a poem written by Walt Whitman* | *a sign **written in** Spanish* **2** [I,T] to write a letter to someone: *Have you **written to** Mom yet?* | *I wrote her last week.* | *He finally **wrote** me **a letter**.* **3** [I,T] to form words, letters, or numbers with a pen or pencil: *kindergarten kids learning to write* | *Please write your name on the form.*

THESAURUS

make a note (of sth) – to write down information that you might need later
jot sth down – to write something very quickly
scribble sth – to write something very quickly and in a messy way

W

take/get sth down – to write down what someone is saying
fill sth out/in – to write information about yourself on a form or other official document
sign sth – to write your **signature** (=name) at the end of a letter, document, etc.
key sth in/type sth in/enter sth – to write or record information on a computer
→ READ

4 [I,T] to write stories, plays, articles, etc. to earn money: *He **writes for** "The Chronicle."* **5** [I,T] to record information in the memory of a computer, on a DISK, etc.

write (sb) **back** *phr. v.* to reply to someone's letter by writing a letter and sending it to him/her: *Write back soon!*

write sth ⇔ **down** *phr. v.* to write something on a piece of paper: *I wrote down her phone number.*

write in *phr. v.* **1** to write a letter to an organization in order to complain, ask for information, or give an opinion **2 write** sb ⇔ **in** to add someone's name to your BALLOT in order to vote for him/her

write sb/sth ⇔ **off** *phr. v.* **1** to decide that someone or something is useless, unimportant, or a failure: *Casey had been written off as a "problem student."* **2** to decide that a debt will never be paid to you, and officially accept it as a loss

write sth ⇔ **out** *phr. v.* to write all the information that is needed for a list, report, check, etc.: *Gina **wrote out a check** for $820.*

write sth ⇔ **up** *phr. v.* to write something such as a report, article, etc. based on notes you made earlier: *Doug is writing up the results of his research.*

'write-in *n.* [C] a vote that you give someone who is not on the BALLOT by writing his/her name on it

'write-off *n.* [C] an official agreement that someone does not have to pay a debt

writ·er /'raɪtɚ/ *n.* [C] someone who writes books, stories, etc. in order to earn money [➡ **author**]: *a **writer of** children's books* | *a speech writer*

W

'write-up *n.* [C] an opinion that is written in a magazine or newspaper about a new book, play, product, etc.

writhe /raɪð/ *v.* [I] to twist your body because you are suffering pain: *writhing **in pain/agony***

writ·ing /'raɪṭɪŋ/ *n.* [U] **1** words that are written or printed: *a T-shirt with Japanese writing on the back* **2** the particular way someone writes with a pen or pencil [= **handwriting**]: *her neat writing* **3 in writing** a promise, agreement, etc. that is in writing has been written down, which proves that it is official **4** the activity or job of writing books, stories, etc.: *creative writing* | *children working on a **piece of writing*** **5** books, stories, and poems in general: *European writing from the 1930s* **6 writings** [plural] the books, stories, poems, etc. that a particular person writes: *Mark Twain's writings*

writ·ten /'rɪt˺n/ *v.* the past participle of WRITE

wrong¹ /rɔŋ/ *adj.* **1** not correct, not the one you intended, or not the one you should use [≠ **right**]: *You're wrong. I was there and I know.* | *I bought the wrong size.* | *I **got** question 4 **wrong**.* | *You must have dialed the **wrong number*** (=not the telephone number you wanted).

THESAURUS

incorrect – used about facts, answers, etc. that are completely wrong
inaccurate – used about information, a number, etc. that is not exactly right
misleading – used about a statement or piece of information that makes people believe something that is wrong: *He admitted making a false and misleading statement to Congress.* | *misleading advertising*
false – used about facts that are untrue and wrong: *He used false financial statements to defraud investors.*
be mistaken formal – used about a person whose opinion about something is wrong: *No, I've never been there. You must be mistaken.*
→ RIGHT

2 not morally right or acceptable [= **bad**; ≠ **right**]: *He didn't do anything wrong!* | ***What's wrong with** making a profit?*

THESAURUS

bad, evil, wicked, immoral, reprehensible
→ see Thesaurus box at BAD¹

3 not suitable [≠ **right**]: *It was the wrong time to make such a big decision.* | *I think they're **wrong for** each other.* **4** used in order to describe a situation where there are problems, or when someone is sick or unhappy: *Ed noticed that **there was something wrong**, as his son's grades started slipping.* | ***What's wrong**, Jenny?* | *What's **wrong with** your shoulder?* **5** if something is wrong with a vehicle or machine, it is not working correctly: *What's **wrong with** the phone?* **6 be in the wrong place at the wrong time** to become involved in a bad situation without intending to **7 the wrong side of the tracks** *informal* a poor part of a town or a poor part of society: *a boy growing up **on the wrong side of the tracks***

wrong² *adv.* **1** not done in the correct way [≠ **right**]: *You spelled my name wrong.* **2 go wrong** to develop problems and stop being good, successful, useful, etc.: *Everything went wrong yesterday.* | *Something has **gone wrong with** the car.* **3 get sth wrong** to make a mistake in the way you remember or understand something: *I got the answer wrong.* | ***Don't get me wrong** – I like Benny. I just don't like what he's doing.*

wrong³ *n.* **1** [U] behavior that is not morally correct: *young people with no sense of **right and wrong*** **2** [C] an action, decision, situation, etc. that is not fair: *a chance **to right the wrongs** they have suffered* (=have a fair solution to an unfair situation) **3 be in the wrong** to make a mistake or deserve the blame for something **4 sb can do no wrong** used in order to say that someone seems to be perfect

wrong[4] *v.* [T] *formal* to treat someone unfairly or judge him/her unfairly: *They believe that they have been wronged.*

wrong·do·ing /ˈrɔŋˌduɪŋ/ *n.* [C,U] *formal* illegal actions or immoral behavior —**wrongdoer** *n.* [C]

wrong·ful /ˈrɔŋfəl/ *adj.* unfair or illegal: *a wrongful death suit* —**wrongfully** /ˈrɔŋfəli/ *adv.*

wrong·ly /ˈrɔŋli/ *adv.* not correct or in a way that is unfair or immoral: *He was wrongly accused of fighting.*

wrote /rout/ *v.* the past tense of WRITE

wrought /rɔt/ the past tense and past participle of WREAK

ˌwrought ˈiron *n.* [U] long thin pieces of iron formed into shapes: *a wrought iron gate*

wrung /rʌŋ/ *v.* the past tense and past participle of WRING

wry /raɪ/ *adj.* showing in a humorous way that you are not pleased by something: *a wry smile*

WV the written abbreviation of **West Virginia**

WWW *n.* **World Wide Web**

WY the written abbreviation of **Wyoming**

X, x

X, x /ɛks/ **1** [C,U] the twenty-fourth letter of the English alphabet **2** [C] a mark used to show a kiss: *Love, Grandma XXX* **3** [singular, U] used in order to show that a movie contains a lot of sex or violence and that it has not been officially approved for anyone under the age of 18 **4** [C] a sign used in mathematics, representing a number or quantity that is not known but can be calculated: *If 3x = 6, then x = 2.*

xen·o·pho·bi·a /ˌzɛnəˈfoubiə/ *n.* [U] an extreme fear or dislike of people from other countries

xe·rox, Xerox /ˈzɪrɑks, ˈzirɑks/ *n.* [C] *trademark* ➔ PHOTOCOPY —**xerox** *v.* [T]

XL extra large used on clothes to show that a piece of clothing is very big

X·mas /ˈkrɪsməs, ˈɛksməs/ *n.* [C,U] *informal* a written form of the word Christmas

x-ray

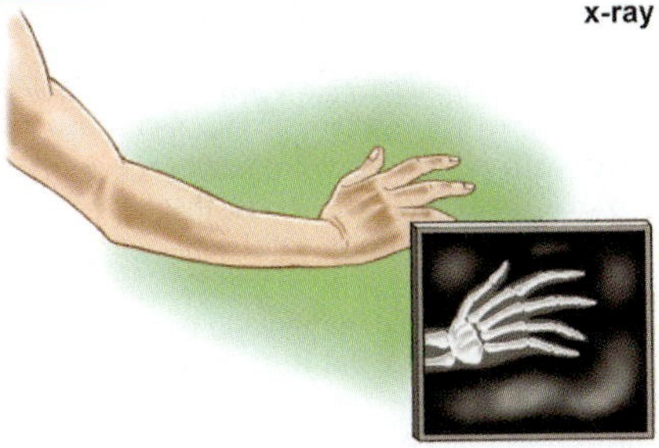

x-ray[1] /ˈɛks reɪ/ *n.* [C] **1** a beam of RADIATION that can go through solid objects and is used for taking photographs of the inside of the body **2** an x-ray photograph taken by doctors in order to search for broken bones, injuries, etc. inside someone's body: *The x-ray showed that her leg was not broken.*

x-ray[2] *v.* [T] to photograph part of someone's body using X-RAYS

xy·lo·phone /ˈzaɪləˌfoun/ *n.* [C] a musical instrument with flat metal BARS, that you play by hitting them with a stick ➔ see picture on page A6

Y, y

Y, y /waɪ/ the twenty-fifth letter of the English alphabet

ya /yʌ/ *pron. spoken nonstandard* you: *See ya later!*

yacht /yɑt/ *n.* [C] a large expensive boat used for sailing, racing, and traveling for pleasure ➔ see picture at TRANSPORTATION

yak[1] /yæk/ *n.* [C] a long-haired cow from central Asia

yak[2] *v.* past tense and past participle **yakked**, present participle **yakking** [I] *informal* to talk a lot about things that are not serious

y'all /yɔl/ *pron. spoken* a word meaning "you" or "all of you," used mainly in the southern U.S.: *How are y'all doing?*

yam /yæm/ *n.* [C,U] ➔ SWEET POTATO

yank /yæŋk/ *v.* [I,T] to pull something quickly and with force: *Kendall **yanked on** the door handle.*

Yan·kee /ˈyæŋki/ *n.* [C] **1** someone who fought against the southern states in the American Civil War **2 also Yank** a U.S. citizen – sometimes considered an insult when used by someone who is not American

yap /yæp/ *v.* past tense and past participle **yapped**, present participle **yapping** [I] if a small dog yaps, it BARKS in an excited way —**yap** *n.* [C]

yard /yɑrd/ *n.* [C] **1** the land around a house, usually covered with grass: *The kids were playing* *in the* ***front/back yard***. **2** *written abbreviation* **yd** a unit for measuring length, equal to 3 feet or 0.9144 meters: *The beach was only a hundred yards from my back door.*

ˌyard sale *n.* [C] a sale of used clothes, furniture, toys, etc. from someone's house that takes place in his/her yard [➡ **garage sale**]

yard·stick /ˈyɑrdˌstɪk/ *n.* [C] **1** something that you compare another thing with, in order to judge how good or successful it is: *a* ***yardstick*** *against which to* ***measure*** *his own achievements* **2** a special stick that is exactly one yard long, used for measuring

yar·mul·ke /ˈyɑməkə, ˈyɑrməlkə/ *n.* [C] a small round cap worn by some Jewish men

yarn /yɑrn/ *n.* [C] **1** a thick type of thread used for KNITting **2** *informal* a long story that is not completely true

THESAURUS

story, **tale**, **myth**, **legend**, **fable**
→ see Thesaurus box at STORY

yawn¹ /yɔn/ *v.* [I] **1** to open your mouth wide and breathe deeply, usually because you are tired or bored **2 yawning gap/chasm** a very large difference between two groups, things, or people: *There are yawning gaps in the medical care available to Americans.*

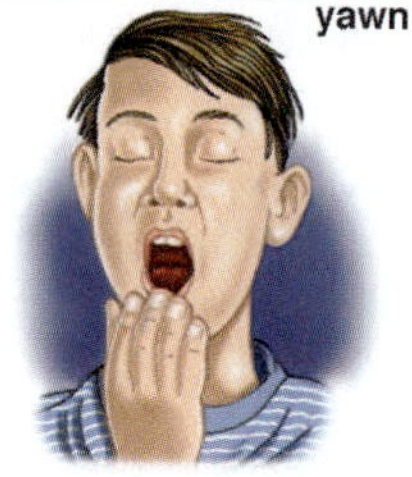
yawn

yawn² *n.* **1** [C] an act of YAWNing **2** [singular] *informal* someone or something that is boring: *The movie was a yawn.*

yd. *n.* [C] the written abbreviation of **yard**

yeah /yɛə/ *adv. spoken* yes

year /yɪr/ *n.* [C] **1 also calendar year** *written abbreviation* **yr.** a period of time equal to 365 or 366 days, divided into 12 months, beginning on January 1 and ending on December 31: *Where are you spending Christmas* ***this year****? | at the start of school* ***last/next year*** *| The museum has 100,000 visitors a year.* **2** any period of time equal to about 365 days or 12 months: *Jenny is five* ***years old****. | My passport expires* ***in a year****. | I met him a year ago. | The* ***tax year*** *begins in April.* **3 years** *informal* many years: *It's been years since I've ridden a bike. | I haven't seen her* ***in/for years****.* **4** a particular period of time in someone's life or in history: *the war years* **5 school/academic year** the period of time during a year when students are in school, college, etc.: *the 2004–05 academic year* **6 all year round** during the whole year: *It's sunny there all year round.*

year·book /ˈyɪrbʊk/ *n.* [C] a book printed once a year by a school or college, about its students, sports events, clubs, etc. during that year

year·ling /ˈyɪrlɪŋ/ *n.* [C] a young animal, especially a horse, between the ages of one and two

year·ly /ˈyɪrli/ *adj., adv.* happening or done every year or once a year: *our yearly trip to Florida*

THESAURUS

regular, **hourly**, **daily**, **weekly**, **monthly**, **annually**
→ see Thesaurus box at REGULAR¹

yearn /yɚn/ *v.* [I] *literary* to want something very much, especially something extremely difficult to get: *They* ***yearned to*** *go home. | She* ***yearned for*** *a child.* —**yearning** *n.* [U]

yeast /yist/ *n.* [U] a substance used for making bread rise and for producing alcohol in beer or wine

yell /yɛl/ *v.* [I,T] to shout or say something very loudly because you are angry, excited, or frightened: *Don't* ***yell at*** *me! | Someone* ***yelled out*** *the score. | She yelled, "Come back here!"* —**yell** *n.* [C]

THESAURUS

shout, **call (out)**, **scream**, **cry out**, **raise your voice**, **cheer**, **bellow**, **holler**
→ see Thesaurus box at SHOUT¹

yel·low¹ /ˈyɛloʊ/ *adj.* having the same color as LEMONS or butter: *yellow flowers*

yellow² *n.* [U] a yellow color —**yellow** *v.* [I,T] *The pages had yellowed with age.*

ˌYellow ˈPages *n. trademark* **the Yellow Pages** a book that lists the telephone numbers and addresses of stores, restaurants, and businesses in a particular area

yelp /yɛlp/ *v.* [I] to make a short high cry like a dog makes, because of pain, excitement, etc. —**yelp** *n.* [C]

yen /yɛn/ *n.* [C] **1** a standard unit of money used in Japan **2** [singular] a strong desire: *a* ***yen to*** *travel*

yep /yɛp/ *adv. spoken* YES

yes /yɛs/ *adv. spoken* **1** said in order to give a positive reply to a question, offer, or request: *"Is it real gold?" "Yes." | "Nancy, did you want some pie?" "Yes, please." | I'm sure Dad will* ***say yes.*** **2** said in order to agree with a statement: *"It's such a nice day." "Yes, it is."* **3** said in order to disagree with a negative statement, to say that the opposite is true: *"John doesn't like me anymore." "Yes, he does!" | "There's no bread." "Yes, there is, in the freezer."* **4** said when you have noticed that someone wants your attention: *"Linda!" "Yes?" | Yes, sir, how may I help you?* **5** said when you are very happy or excited: *Yes! I got the job!*

Y

COMMUNICATION

Ways of saying yes
yeah spoken informal
uh huh spoken informal
yep spoken informal
okay spoken informal
sure spoken informal

yes·ter·day /ˈyɛstɚdi, -deɪ/ *adv., n.* **1** the day before today: *Did you go to the game yesterday?* **2** the past, especially the recent past: *yesterday's fashions*

yet[1] /yɛt/ *adv.* **1** used in negative statements and questions to mean "at the present time" or "already": *I don't think she's awake yet.* | *Have you eaten yet?*

USAGE

Yet is used in negative sentences and questions to talk about something that you expect to happen, but which has not happened: *I haven't finished the book yet.* | *Is Mark back from lunch yet?*
Still is used to say that a situation that began in the past has not changed and is continuing: *He still lives with his parents.*
Always means "all the time" or "every time": *Her house is always clean.* | *I always see him on Tuesdays.*

2 at some time in the future: *She may change her mind yet.* | *We **have yet to** hear from them* (=we still have not heard). | *"Is Lori here?" "**Not yet**."* **3** in addition to what you have already gotten, done, etc.: ***yet another** mistake* | *I'm sorry to ask for help **yet again*** (=one more time after many others). **4 better/worse yet** used in order to emphasize that something is even better or worse than the thing mentioned before: *Respond by letter, or better yet, a telephone call.* **5** in spite of something [= **but**]: *a quiet yet powerful leader*

yet[2] *conjunction* used in order to introduce a statement that is surprising: *an inexpensive yet effective solution* | *We sent thousands of forms, yet fewer than 50 were returned.*

yew /yu/ *n.* [C] a tree or bush with leaves that look like flat needles, or the heavy wood of this tree

Yid·dish /ˈyɪdɪʃ/ *n.* [U] a language similar to German, used in many places by Jewish people —**Yiddish** *adj.*

yield[1] /yild/ *v.* **1** [T] to produce something: *One study has yielded some interesting results.* **2** [I,T] to allow yourself to be forced or persuaded to do something: *The government will never **yield to** terrorism.* **3** [I] to allow the traffic from a bigger road to go first **4** [I] to move, bend, or break because of physical pressure

yield[2] *n.* [C] the amount of profits, crops, etc. that something produces

yip·pee /ˈyɪpi/ *interjection* said when you are very happy or excited about something

YMCA *n.* **Young Men's Christian Association** an organization that provides places to stay, sports activities, and training for young people, especially in large cities [➡ **YWCA**]

yo /yoʊ/ *interjection slang* said in order to greet someone or get his/her attention, or as a reply when someone says your name

yo·del /ˈyoʊdl/ *v.* [I] to sing while changing your natural voice to a very high voice and back again many times

yoga

yo·ga /ˈyoʊgə/ *n.* [U] a system of exercises in which you control your body and mind

yo·gurt /ˈyoʊgɚt/ *n.* [C,U] a smooth, slightly sour, thick liquid food made from milk

yoke /yoʊk/ *n.* [C] a wooden BAR used for joining together two animals, especially cattle, in order to pull heavy loads —**yoke** *v.* [T]

yo·kel /ˈyoʊkəl/ *n.* [C] *humorous* someone from the country who has not experienced living in modern society

yolk /yoʊk/ *n.* [C,U] the yellow part in the center of an egg

yon·der /ˈyɑndɚ/ *adv., determiner literary* over there

you /yə, yʊ; *strong* yu/ *pron.* [used as a subject or object] **1** the person or people someone is speaking or writing to: *You must be hungry.* | *Do you want a drink?* | *I can't hear you.* **2** people in general [➡ **one**]: *You can't trust anybody these days.* | *You never know what Jim will say.* **3** used with nouns or phrases when you are talking to or calling someone: *You jerk!* | *You kids be quiet!* **4 you all** *spoken* used instead of "you" when speaking to two or more people: *What do you all want to do tonight?*

you'd /yəd, yʊd; *strong* yud/ **1** the short form of "you would": *I didn't think you'd mind.* **2** the short form of "you had": *You'd better do what he says.*

Y

you'll /yəl, yʊl; *strong* yul/ the short form of "you will": *You'll have to speak louder.*

young[1] /yʌŋ/ *adj.* **1** at an early stage of life or development [≠ **old**]: *young children* | *You're too young to get married.* | *a young country*

THESAURUS

A **small/little** child is a very young child.
A **teenage** boy or girl is between 13 and 19.
An **adolescent** is a teenage boy or girl who is changing from being a child to an adult.
→ OLD

2 seeming or looking younger than you are: *a lotion for healthier, younger looking skin*

3 designed or intended for young people: *Is this dress too young for me?*

young² *n.* **1 the young** young people considered as a group **2** [plural] young animals: *a turtle and her young*

young·ster /ˈyʌŋstɚ/ *n.* [C] a young person

your /yɚ; *strong* yʊr, yɔr/ *determiner* **1** belonging or relating to the person or people someone is speaking to: *Is that your mother? | It's not your fault.* **2** belonging to any person: *If you are facing north, east is on your right.*

you're /yɚ; *strong* yʊr, yɔr/ the short form of "you are": *You're bothering me.*

yours /yʊrz, yɔrz/ *pron.* **1** the thing or things belonging or relating to the person or people someone is speaking to: *Yours is over there. | That bag is yours, isn't it? | Is he a friend **of yours**?* **2 yours (truly/sincerely) also sincerely yours** a phrase you write before you sign your name at the end of a letter **3 yours truly** *humorous* used instead of "I": *Yes, yours truly finally quit smoking.*

your·self /yɚˈsɛlf/ *pron.* plural **yourselves** /yɚˈsɛlvz/ **1** used when talking to someone to show that s/he is affected by his or her own action: *Don't hurt yourself! | Make yourself a cup of coffee.* **2** used in order to emphasize "you": *Why don't you do it yourself?* **3 (all) by yourself a)** without help: *Do you think you can move the sofa by yourself?* **b)** alone: *You're going to Ecuador by yourself?* **4 (all) to yourself** for your own use: *You'll have the house all to yourself this weekend.*

youth /yuθ/ *n.* **1** [U] the period of time when someone is young, or the quality of being young: *Despite his youth, he was traveling alone. | She had been beautiful **in** her **youth**.* **2** [U] young people in general: *the youth of the 1960s | a church youth group | youth culture* **3** plural **youths** /yuðz, yuθs/ [C] a boy or young man, especially a TEENAGER: *A youth was arrested for stealing.*

Z

THESAURUS

boy, man, guy
→ see Thesaurus box at MAN¹

youth·ful /ˈyuθfəl/ *adj.* typical of young people, or seeming young: *youthful energy | He was youthful in appearance.*

ˈyouth ˌhostel *n.* [C] a place where people, especially young people who are traveling, can stay very cheaply for a short time

you've /yəv, yʊv; *strong* yuv/ the short form of "you have": *Okay, you've persuaded me.*

yo-yo /ˈyoʊyoʊ/ *n.* [C] a small toy that is made of two circular parts joined together that go up and down a string as you lift your hand up and down

yr. *n.* [C] the written abbreviation of **year**

yuck /yʌk/ *interjection* said when you think something is unpleasant: *Yuck! This tastes horrible!* —**yucky** *adj.*

Yule /yul/ *n.* [C] *literary* Christmas

Yule·tide /ˈyultaɪd/ *n.* [U] *literary* the period from just before Christmas until just after it

yum /yʌm/ *interjection* said in order to emphasize that you think something tastes good: *Yum! Apple pie!*

yum·my /ˈyʌmi/ *adj. informal* food that is yummy tastes very good

yup·pie /ˈyʌpi/ *n.* [C] *informal* a young person who only seems interested in having a professional job, earning a lot of money, and buying expensive things

YWCA *n.* **Young Women's Christian Association** an organization that provides places to stay, special help, and training for young women, especially in large cities [➡ **YMCA**]

Z, z

Z, z /zi/ **1** the last letter of the English alphabet **2 catch/get some Zs** *spoken* to sleep

za·ny /ˈzeɪni/ *adj.* crazy or unusual in a way that is amusing and exciting: *a zany new TV comedy*

zap /zæp/ *v.* past tense and past participle **zapped**, present participle **zapping** [T] *informal* **1** to kill, destroy, or attack something extremely quickly, especially by using electricity or a LASER beam **2** *informal* to cook something quickly in a MICROWAVE **3** *informal* to send information quickly from one computer to another

zeal /zil/ *n.* [U] eagerness to do something, especially to achieve a particular religious or political aim: *the Republicans' **zeal to** cut taxes* —**zealous** *adj.*

ze·bra /ˈzibrə/ *n.* [C] a wild African animal like a horse, that has black and white bands on its body

Zen /zɛn/ **also ˌZen ˈBuddhism** *n.* [U] a type of Buddhism from Japan that emphasizes MEDITATION

ze·nith /ˈzinɪθ/ *n.* [C usually singular] **1** the most successful point in the development of something: *This album shows Simon **at the zenith of** his powers.* **2** the highest point that the sun or a star reaches in the sky

ze·ro¹ /ˈzɪroʊ, ˈziroʊ/ *number* **1** the number 0

THESAURUS

nothing: *The score was twenty-two to nothing.*
O /oʊ/ – used to say the number zero like the letter O: *Their zip code is O two one two five.* (=02125).
zip informal: *We were behind 3-zip.*

2 the point between – and + on a scale for measuring something, especially temperature. In the Celsius system of measuring temperature, 0 is the point at which water freezes: *It was 20° below zero.*

zero[2] *v.*
zero in on sb/sth *phr. v.* to aim at one thing or give special attention to one person or thing: *war planes zeroing in on a target*

zest /zest/ *n.* [U] **1** a feeling of eagerness, excitement, and enjoyment: *a* ***zest for*** *life* **2** the outer skin of an orange or LEMON, used in cooking

zig·zag[1] /ˈzɪgzæg/ *n.* [C] a line that looks like a row of z's joined together

zigzag[2] *v.* past tense and past participle **zigzagged**, present participle **zigzagging** [I] to move forward in sharp angles, first to the left and then to the right, etc.: *a path that zigzags across the mountain*

zilch /zɪltʃ/ *n.* [U] *informal* nothing at all: *I've looked for jobs everywhere, but come up with zilch.*

zil·lion /ˈzɪlyən/ *number informal* an extremely large number or amount: *She asked a zillion questions.*

zinc /zɪŋk/ *n.* [U] a white metal that is an ELEMENT that is often used in order to produce other metals

zip[1] /zɪp/ *v.* past tense and past participle **zipped**, present participle **zipping** **1** [T] **also zip up** to close or fasten something using a ZIPPER: *Zip up your coat.* **2** [I] to go somewhere or do something very quickly: *A few cars zipped past us.*

zip[2] *n. spoken* [U] **1** a short form of ZIP CODE **2** nothing at all or zero: *We beat them 10-zip.*

THESAURUS
zero, nothing, O
➔ see Thesaurus box at ZERO[1]

ˈzip code *n.* [C] a number that you put below the address on an envelope to help the post office deliver the mail more quickly

ˈzip file *n.* [C] *technical* a computer FILE that has been made smaller so that it is easier to store and move

zip·per /ˈzɪpɚ/ *n.* [C] an object for fastening clothes, bags, etc., with two lines of small pieces of metal or plastic that slide together

zipper

zit /zɪt/ *n.* [C] *slang* ➔ PIMPLE

zo·di·ac /ˈzoʊdiˌæk/ *n.* **the zodiac** an imaginary circle in space that the sun, moon, and PLANETS follow as a path, which some people believe influences people's lives

zom·bie /ˈzɑmbi/ *n.* [C] **1** *informal* someone who moves very slowly and cannot think clearly because s/he is very tired **2** a dead body that is made to move, walk, etc. by magic

zone /zoʊn/ *n.* [C] part of an area that has a specific purpose or has a special quality: *a no-parking zone* | *the* ***war/battle/combat zone***

THESAURUS
area, region, district
➔ see Thesaurus box at AREA

➔ TIME ZONE

zon·ing /ˈzoʊnɪŋ/ *n.* [U] a system of choosing areas to be used for particular purposes, such as building houses —**zone** *v.* [T]

zoo /zu/ *n.* [C] a place where many different types of animals are kept so that people can see them: *How about taking the children to the zoo?*

zo·ol·o·gy /zoʊˈɑlədʒi/ *n.* [U] the scientific study of animals and their behavior —**zoologist** *n.* [C] —**zoological** /ˌzoʊəˈlɑdʒɪkəl/ *adj.*

zoom /zum/ *v.* [I] *informal* **1** to go somewhere or do something very quickly: *A red car zoomed past.* **2** to increase suddenly and quickly: *Inflation zoomed 123 percent.*
zoom in/out *phr. v.* if a camera zooms in or out, it makes the object you are taking a photograph of seem closer or farther away

ˈzoom ˌlens *n.* [C] a camera LENS that moves in order to make the objects you are taking a photograph of seem closer and larger

zuc·chi·ni /zuˈkini/ *n.* [C,U] a long smooth dark green vegetable ➔ see picture at VEGETABLE

Zzz used in writing to represent sleep

Irregular Verbs

This chart shows the verbs that have irregular forms for the **Past Tense**, **Past Participle**, or **Present Participle**. When a verb has more than one form that is used, the most common form is given first.

Verb	Past Tense	Past Participle	Present Participle
arise	arose	arisen	arising
awake	awoke	awoken	awaking
be	*see* **be**		
bear	bore	borne	bearing
beat	beat	beaten	beating
become	became	become	becoming
begin	began	begun	beginning
behold	beheld	beheld	beholding
bend	bent	bent	bending
bet	bet	bet	betting
bid[2]	bid	bid	bidding
bid[3]	bid	bid *or* bidden	bidding
bind	bound	bound	binding
bite	bit	bitten	biting
bleed	bled	bled	bleeding
blow	blew	blown	blowing
break	broke	broken	breaking
breed	bred	bred	breeding
bring	brought	brought	bringing
broadcast	broadcast *or* broadcasted	broadcast *or* broadcasted	broadcasting
build	built	built	building
burn	burned *or* burnt	burned *or* burnt	burning
burst	burst	burst	bursting
buy	bought	bought	buying
cast	cast	cast	casting
catch	caught	caught	catching
choose	chose	chosen	choosing
cling	clung	clung	clinging
come	came	come	coming
cost	cost	cost	costing
creep	crept	crept	creeping
cut	cut	cut	cutting
deal	dealt	dealt	dealing
dig	dug	dug	digging
dive	dived *or* dove	dived	diving
do	*see* **do**		
draw	drew	drawn	drawing
dream	dreamed *or* dreamt	dreamed *or* dreamt	dreaming
drink	drank	drunk	drinking
drive	drove	driven	driving
dwell	dwelled *or* dwelt	dwelled *or* dwelt	dwelling
eat	ate	eaten	eating
fall	fell	fallen	falling
feed	fed	fed	feeding
feel	felt	felt	feeling
fight	fought	fought	fighting
find	found	found	finding
fit	fit or fitted	fit or fitted	fitting
flee	fled	fled	fleeing
fling	flung	flung	flinging
fly	flew	flown	flying
forbid	forbid *or* forbade	forbidden	forbidding
forecast	forecast *or* forecasted	forecast *or* forecasted	forecasting
foresee	foresaw	foreseen	foreseeing
forget	forgot	forgotten	forgetting
forgive	forgave	forgiven	forgiving
freeze	froze	frozen	freezing

Verb	Past Tense	Past Participle	Present Participle
get	got	gotten	getting
give	gave	given	giving
go	went	gone	going
grind	ground	ground	grinding
grow	grew	grown	growing
hang	hung	hung	hanging
have	*see* **have**		
hear	heard	heard	hearing
hide	hid	hidden	hiding
hit	hit	hit	hitting
hold	held	held	holding
hurt	hurt	hurt	hurting
keep	kept	kept	keeping
kneel	knelt *or* kneeled	knelt *or* kneeled	kneeling
knit	knit *or* knitted	knit *or* knitted	knitting
know	knew	known	knowing
lay	laid	laid	laying
lead	led	led	leading
leap	leaped *or* leapt	leaped *or* leapt	leaping
leave	left	left	leaving
lend	lent	lent	lending
let	let	let	letting
lie[1]	lay	lain	lying
lie[2]	lied	lied	lying
light	lit *or* lighted	lit *or* lighted	lighting
lose	lost	lost	losing
make	made	made	making
mean	meant	meant	meaning
meet	met	met	meeting
mislead	misled	misled	misleading
mistake	mistook	mistaken	mistaking
misunderstand	misunderstood	misunderstood	misunderstanding
outbid	outbid	outbid	outbidding
outdo	outdid	outdone	outdoing
overcome	overcame	overcome	overcoming
overdo	overdid	overdone	overdoing
overhang	overhung	overhung	overhanging
overhear	overheard	overheard	overhearing
override	overrode	overridden	overriding
overrun	overran	overrun	overrunning
oversee	oversaw	overseen	overseeing
overtake	overtook	overtaken	overtaking
overthrow	overthrew	overthrown	overthrowing
pay	paid	paid	paying
prove	proved	proved *or* proven	proving
put	put	put	putting
read	read	read	reading
rebuild	rebuilt	rebuilt	rebuilding
redo	redid	redone	redoing
repay	repaid	repaid	repaying
rewrite	rewrote	rewritten	rewriting
rid	rid	rid	ridding
ride	rode	ridden	riding
ring[2]	rang	rung	ringing
rise	rose	risen	rising
run	ran	run	running
saw	sawed	sawed *or* sawn	sawing
say	said	said	saying
see	saw	seen	seeing
seek	sought	sought	seeking
sell	sold	sold	selling
send	sent	sent	sending
set	set	set	setting
sew	sewed	sewn *or* sewed	sewing
shake	shook	shaken	shaking

Verb	Past Tense	Past Participle	Present Participle
shed	shed	shed	shedding
shine	shone	shone	shining
shoot	shot	shot	shooting
show	showed	shown	showing
shrink	shrank	shrunk	shrinking
shut	shut	shut	shutting
sing	sang	sung	singing
sink	sank *or* sunk	sunk	sinking
sit	sat	sat	sitting
slay	slew	slain	slaying
sleep	slept	slept	sleeping
slide	slid	slid	sliding
sling	slung	slung	slinging
slit	slit	slit	slitting
sow	sowed	sown *or* sowed	sowing
speak	spoke	spoken	speaking
speed	sped *or* speeded	sped *or* speeded	speeding
spend	spent	spent	spending
spin	spun	spun	spinning
spit	spit *or* spat	spit *or* spat	spitting
split	split	split	splitting
spread	spread	spread	spreading
spring	sprang	sprung	springing
stand	stood	stood	standing
steal	stole	stolen	stealing
stick	stuck	stuck	sticking
sting	stung	stung	stinging
stink	stank *or* stunk	stunk	stinking
strew	strewed	strewn *or* strewed	strewing
stride	strode	stridden	striding
strike	struck	struck *or* stricken	striking
string	strung	strung	stringing
strive	strove *or* strived	striven *or* strived	striving
swear	swore	sworn	swearing
sweep	swept	swept	sweeping
swell	swelled	swollen	swelling
swim	swam	swum	swimming
swing	swung	swung	swinging
take	took	taken	taking
teach	taught	taught	teaching
tear	tore	torn	tearing
tell	told	told	telling
think	thought	thought	thinking
throw	threw	thrown	throwing
thrust	thrust	thrust	thrusting
tread	trod	trodden	treading
undergo	underwent	undergone	undergoing
understand	understood	understood	understanding
undertake	undertook	undertaken	undertaking
undo	undid	undone	undoing
unwind	unwound	unwound	unwinding
uphold	upheld	upheld	upholding
upset	upset	upset	upsetting
wake	woke	woken	waking
wear	wore	worn	wearing
weave	wove	woven	weaving
wed	wedded *or* wed	wedded *or* wed	wedding
weep	wept	wept	weeping
wet	wet *or* wetted	wet *or* wetted	wetting
win	won	won	winning
wind	wound	wound	winding
withdraw	withdrew	withdrawn	withdrawing
withhold	withheld	withheld	withholding
withstand	withstood	withstood	withstanding
wring	wrung	wrung	wringing
write	wrote	written	writing

Geographical Names

Name		Adjective and name of a person from this place	
Afghanistan	/æf'gænəˌstæn/	Afghan *or* Afghanistani	/'æfgæn/ /æfˌgænə'stæni/
Africa	/'æfrɪkə/	African	/'æfrɪkən/
Albania	/æl'beɪniə, ɔl-/	Albanian	/æl'beɪniən, ɔl-/
Algeria	/æl'dʒɪriə/	Algerian	/æl'dʒɪriən/
America (=the U.S.)	/ə'mɛrɪkə/	American	/ə'mɛrɪkən/
North America	/nɔrθ ə'mɛrɪkə/	North American	/nɔrθ ə'mɛrɪkən/
South America	/sauθ ə'mɛrɪkə/	South American	/sauθ ə'mɛrɪkən/
Andorra	/æn'dɔrə/	Andorran	/æn'dɔrən/
Angola	/æŋ'golə/	Angolan	/æŋ'goʊlən/
Antarctic	/æn'tɑrktɪk/	*adj:* Antarctic	/æn'tɑrktɪk/
Antigua and Barbuda	/æn'tigə, -gwə ənd bɑr'budə/	Antiguan *or* Barbudan	/æn'tigən, -gwən/ /bɑr'budən/
Arctic	/'ɑrktɪk/	*adj:* Arctic	/'ɑrktɪk/
Argentina	/ˌɑrdʒən'tinə/	*adj:* Argentinian *person:* Argentinian *or* Argentine	/ˌɑrdʒən'tɪniən/ /'ɑːrdʒəntiːn/
Armenia	/ɑr'miniə/	Armenian	/ɑr'miniən/
Asia	/'eɪʒə/	Asian	/'eɪʒən/
Atlantic	/ət'læn*t*ɪk/	*adj:* Atlantic	/ət'læn*t*ɪk/
Australia	/ɔ'streɪlyə, ɑ-/	Australian	/ɔ'streɪlyən, ˌɑ-/
Austria	/'ɔstriə, 'ɑ-/	Austrian	/'ɔstriən, 'ɑ-/
Azerbaijan	/'æzɚbaɪ'dʒɑn, ˌɑ-/	Azerbaijani	/ˌæzɚbaɪ'dʒɑni◂ , ˌɑ-/
Bahamas, the	/bə'hɑməz/	Bahamian	/bə'heɪmiən/
Bahrain	/bɑ'reɪn/	Bahraini	/bɑ'reɪni/
Baltic	/'bɔltɪk/	*adj:* Baltic	/'bɔltɪk/
Bangladesh	/ˌbɑŋglə'dɛʃ, ˌbæŋ-/	Bangladeshi	/ˌbɑŋglə'dɛʃi, ˌbæŋ-/
Barbados	/bɑr'beɪdoʊs/	Barbadian	/bɑr'beɪdiən/
Belarus (Belorussia)	/ˌbɛlə'rus/ /ˌbɛloʊ'rʌʃə/	Belorussian	/ˌbɛloʊ'rʌʃən/
Belgium	/'bɛldʒəm/	Belgian	/'bɛldʒən/
Belize	/bə'liz/	Belizean	/bə'liziən/
Benin	/bə'nin/	Beninese	/ˌbɛnɪ'niz◂ /
Bermuda	/bɚ'myudə/	Bermudan	/bɚ'myudn/
Bhutan	/bu'tɑn, -'tæn/	Bhutanese	/ˌbutn'iz◂ /
Bolivia	/bə'lɪviə/	Bolivian	/bə'lɪviən/
Bosnia and Herzegovina	/ˌbɑzniə ənd ˌhɛrtsəgə'vinə/	Bosnian Herzegovinian	/'bɑzniən/ /ˌhɜrtsəgəʊ'viniən/
Botswana	/bɑt'swɑnə/	*adj:* Botswanan *person:* Motswana *people:* the Batswana	/bɑt'swɑnən/ /mɑt'swɑnə/ /bæt'swɑnə/
Brazil	/brə'zɪl/	Brazilian	/brə'zɪliən/
Brunei	/bru'naɪ/	Bruneian	/bru'naɪən/
Bulgaria	/bʌl'gɛriə/	Bulgarian	/bʌl'gɛriən/
Burkina Faso	/bɚˌkinə 'fɑsoʊ/	Burkina *or* Burkinabe	/ˌbɚkinæ'beɪ/
Burma (*former name* *of* Myanmar)	/'bɚmə/	Burmese	/bɚ'miz/
Burundi	/bʊ'rundi/	Burundian	/bʊ'rundiən/
Cambodia	/kæm'boʊdiə/	Cambodian	/kæm'boʊdiən/
Cameroon	/ˌkæmə'run/	Cameroonian	/ˌkæm'runiən◂ /
Canada	/'kænədə/	Canadian	/kə'neɪdiən/
Cape Verde	/keɪp 'vɚd/	Cape Verdean	/keɪp 'vɚdiən/
Caribbean	/kə'rɪbiən, ˌkærə'biən◂ /	*adj:* Caribbean	
Cayman Islands	/'keɪmən ˌaɪləndz/	*adj:* Cayman Island *person:* Cayman Islander	/ˌkeɪmən 'aɪlənd/ /ˌkeɪmən 'aɪləndɚ/
Central African Republic	/ˌsɛntrəl ˌæfrɪkən rɪ'pʌblɪk/	Central African	/ˌsɛntrəl 'æfrɪkən/
Chad	/tʃæd/	Chadian	/'tʃædiən/
Chile	/'tʃɪli/	Chilean	/'tʃɪliən/
China	/'tʃaɪnə/	Chinese	/ˌtʃaɪ'niz◂ /
Colombia	/kə'lʌmbiə/	Colombian	/kə'lʌmbiən/

Name		Adjective and name of a person from this place	
Comoro Islands, the	/ˈkɑməˌroʊ aɪləndz/	Comoran	/ˈkɑmərən/
Congo, the Democratic Republic of	/ˌdɛməkrætɪk rɪˌpʌblɪk əv ˈkɑŋgoʊ/	Congolese	/ˌkɑŋgəˈliz/
Congo, Republic of	/rɪˌpʌblɪk əv ˈkɑŋgoʊ/	Congolese	/ˌkɑŋgəˈliz◂ /
Costa Rica	/ˌkoʊstə ˈrikə/	Costa Rican	/ˌkoʊstə ˈrikən◂ /
Croatia	/kroʊˈeɪʃə/	Croatian	/kroʊˈeɪʃən/
Cuba	/ˈkyubə/	Cuban	/ˈkyubən/
Cyprus	/ˈsaɪprəs/	Cypriot	/ˈsɪpriət/
Czech Republic, the	/ˌtʃɛk rɪˈpʌblɪk/	Czech	/tʃɛk/
Denmark	/ˈdɛnmɑrk/	*adj:* Danish *person:* Dane	/ˈdeɪnɪʃ/ /deɪn/
Djibouti	/dʒɪˈbuti/	Djiboutian	/dʒɪˈbutiən/
Dominica	/ˌdɑməˈnikə/	Dominican	/ˌdɑməˈnikən◂ /
Dominican Republic, the	/dəˌmɪnɪkən rɪˈpʌblɪk/	Dominican	/dəˈmɪnɪkən/
East Timor	/ˌist ˈtimɔr/	Timorese	/ˌtimɔˈriz◂ /
Ecuador	/ˈɛkwədɔr/	Ecuadorian	/ˌɛkwəˈdɔriən◂ /
Egypt	/ˈidʒɪpt/	Egyptian	/ɪˈdʒɪpʃən/
El Salvador	/ɛl ˈsælvəˌdɔr/	Salvadorian	/ˌsælvəˈdɔriən◂ /
England	/ˈɪŋglənd/	*adj:* English *person:* Englishman, Englishwoman *people:* the English	/ˈɪŋglɪʃ/ /ˈɪŋglɪʃmən/ /-ˌwʊmən/
Equatorial Guinea	/ˌɛkwətɔriəl ˈgɪni/	Equatorial Guinean	/ˌɛkwətɔriəl ˈgɪniən/
Eritrea	/ˌɛrɪˈtriə/	Eritrean	/ˌɛrɪˈtriən◂ /
Estonia	/ɛˈstoʊniə/	Estonian	/ɛˈstoʊniən/
Ethiopia	/ˌiθiˈoʊpiə/	Ethiopian	/ˌiθiˈoʊpiən/
Europe	/ˈyʊrəp/	European	/ˌyʊrəˈpiən◂ /
Fiji	/ˈfidʒi/	Fijian	/ˈfɪdʒiən/
Finland	/ˈfɪnlənd/	*adj:* Finnish *person:* Finn	/ˈfɪnɪʃ/ /fɪn/
France	/fræns/	*adj:* French *person:* Frenchman, Frenchwoman *people:* the French	/frɛntʃ/ /ˈfrɛntʃmən/ /-ˌwʊmən/
Gabon	/gæˈboʊn/	Gabonese	/ˌgæbəˈniz◂ /
Gambia, the	/ˈgæmbiə/	Gambian	/ˈgæmbiən/
Georgia	/ˈdʒɔrdʒə/	Georgian	/ˈdʒɔrdʒən/
Germany	/ˈdʒɚməni/	German	/ˈdʒɚmən◂ /
Ghana	/ˈgɑnə/	Ghanaian	/gɑˈneɪən/
Gibraltar	/dʒɪˈbrɔltɚ/	Gibraltarian	/ˌdʒɪbrɔlˈtɛriən/
Great Britain	/ˌgreɪt ˈbrɪtˀn/	*adj:* British *person:* Briton *people:* the British	/ˈbrɪtɪʃ/ /ˈbrɪtˀn/
Greece	/gris/	Greek	/grik/
Greenland	/ˈgrinlænd/	*adj:* Greenlandic *person:* Greenlander	/grinˈlændɪk/ /ˈgrinləndɚ/
Grenada	/grəˈneɪdə/	Grenadian	/grəˈneɪdiən/
Guatemala	/ˌgwɑtəˈmɑlə/	Guatemalan	/ˌgwɑtəˈmɑlən◂ /
Guiana *also* French Guiana	/giˈænə, -ˈɑnə/	Guianese	/ˌgaɪəˈniz◂ /
Guinea	/ˈgɪni/	Guinean	/ˈgɪniən/
Guinea-Bissau	/ˌgɪni bɪˈsaʊ/	Guinea-Bissauan	/ˌgɪni bɪˈsaʊən/
Guyana *also* British Guyana	/gaɪˈænə/	Guyanese *or* Guyanan	/ˌgaɪəˈniz◂ / /gaɪˈænən/
Haiti	/ˈheɪti/	Haitian	/ˈheɪʃən/
Holland (*another name for* The Netherlands)	/ˈhɑlənd/	*adj:* Dutch *person:* Dutchman, Dutchwoman *people:* the Dutch	/dʌtʃ/ /ˈdʌtʃmən/ /-ˌwʊmən/
Honduras	/hɑnˈdʊrəs/	Honduran	/hɑnˈdʊrən/
Hong Kong	/ˈhɑŋ ˌkɑŋ/	Hong Kong	
Hungary	/ˈhʌŋgəri/	Hungarian	/hʌŋˈgɛriən/

Name		**Adjective and name of a person from this place**	
Iceland	/ˈaɪslənd/	*adj:* Icelandic *person:* Icelander	/aɪsˈlændɪk/ /ˌaɪsləndɚ/
India	/ˈɪndiə/	Indian	/ˈɪndiən/
Indonesia	/ˌɪndəˈniʒə/	Indonesian	/ˌɪndəˈniʒən◂ /
Iran	/ɪˈræn, -ɑn/	Iranian	/ɪˈreɪniən/
Iraq	/ɪˈræk, -ɑk/	Iraqi	/ɪˈræki,-ɑki/
Ireland, Republic of, the	/rɪˌpʌblɪk əv ˈaɪrlənd/	*adj:* Irish *person:* Irishman, Irishwoman *people:* the Irish	/ˈaɪrɪʃ/ /ˈaɪrɪʃmən/ /-ˌwʊmən/
Israel	/ˈɪzriəl/	Israeli	/ɪzˈreɪli/
Italy	/ˈɪt̬li/	Italian	/ɪˈtælyən/
Ivory Coast (*former name of* Cote d'Ivoire)	/ˌaɪvəri ˈkoʊst/	Ivorian	/aɪˈvɔriən/
Jamaica	/dʒəˈmeɪkə/	Jamaican	/dʒəˈmeɪkən/
Japan	/dʒəˈpæn/	Japanese	/ˌdʒæpəˈniz◂ /
Jordan	/ˈdʒɔrdn/	Jordanian	/dʒɔrˈdeɪniən/
Kazakhstan	/ˈkɑzɑkˌstɑn/	Kazakh	/ˈkɑzɑk/
Kenya	/ˈkɛnyə, ˈki-/	Kenyan	/ˈkɛnyən, ˈki-/
Kirabati	/ˌkɪrɪˈbɑti/	Kirabati	/ˌkɪrɪˈbɑti/
Korea, North	/ˌnɔrθ kəˈrɪə/	North Korean	/ˌnɔrθ kəˈrɪən/
Korea, South	/ˌsaʊθ kəˈrɪə/	South Korean	/ˌsaʊθ kəˈrɪən/
Kuwait	/kʊˈweɪt/	Kuwaiti	/kʊˈweɪt̬i/
Kyrgyzstan	/ˈkɪrgɪˌstæn/	Kyrgyz	/kɪrˈgɪz/
Laos	/laʊs, ˈleɪɑs/	Laotian *or* Lao	/ˈlaʊʃən/ /laʊ/
Latvia	/ˈlætviə/	Latvian	/ˈlætviən/
Lebanon	/ˈlɛbənɑn, -nən/	Lebanese	/ˌlɛbəˈniz◂ /
Lesotho	/ləˈsoʊtoʊ/	*adj:* Sotho *person:* Mosotho *people:* the Basotho	/ˈsoʊtoʊ/ /məˈsoʊtoʊ/ /bəˈsoʊtoʊ/
Liberia	/laɪˈbɪriə/	Liberian	/laɪˈbɪriən/
Libya	/ˈlɪbiə/	Libyan	/ˈlɪbiən/
Liechtenstein	/ˈlɪktənˌstaɪn/	*adj:* Liechtenstein *person:* Liechtensteiner	 /ˈlɪktənˌstaɪnɚ/
Lithuania	/ˌlɪθəˈweɪniə/	Lithuanian	/ˌlɪθəˈweɪniən/
Luxemburg	/ˈlʌksəmˌbɚg/	*adj:* Luxemburg *person:* Luxemburger	 /ˈlʌksəmˌbɚgɚ/
Macedonia	/ˌmæsɪˈdoʊnyə/	Macedonian	/ˌmæsɪˈdoʊnyən◂ /
Madagascar	/ˌmædəˈgæskɚ/	Malagasy	/ˌmæləˈgæsi◂ /
Malawi	/məˈlɑwi/	Malawian	/məˈlɑwiən/
Malaysia	/məˈleɪʒə/	Malaysian	/məˈleɪʒən/
Maldives, the	/ˈmɔldivz/	Maldivian	/mɔlˈdɪviən/
Mali	/ˈmɑli/	Malian	/ˈmɑliən/
Malta	/ˈmɔltə/	Maltese	/ˌmɔlˈtiz◂ /
Marshall Islands, the	/ˈmɑrʃəl ˌaɪləndz/	*adj:* Marshallese *person:* Marshall Islander	/ˌmɑrʃəˈliz/ /ˌmɑrʃəl ˈaɪləndɚ/
Mauritania	/ˌmɔrəˈteɪnyə/	Mauritanian	/ˌmɔrəˈteɪniən◂ /
Mauritius	/mɔˈrɪʃəs/	Mauritian	/mɔˈrɪʃən/
Mediterranean	/ˌmɛdətəˈreɪniən◂ /	*adj:* Mediterranean	
Melanesia	/ˌmɛləˈniʒə/	Melanesian	/ˌmɛləˈniʒən/
Mexico	/ˈmɛksɪkoʊ/	Mexican	/ˈmɛksɪkən/
Micronesia	/ˌmaɪkroʊˈniʒə/	Micronesian	/ˌmaɪkroʊˈniʒən/
Moldova	/mɑlˈdoʊvə/	Moldovan	/mɑlˈdoʊvən/
Monaco	/ˈmɑnəˌkoʊ/	Monegasque *or* Monacan	/ˌmɑnəˈgæsk/ /ˈmɑnəkən/
Mongolia	/mɑŋˈgoʊliə/	Mongolian *or* Mongol	/mɑŋˈgoʊliən/ /ˈmɑŋgəl/
Montserrat	/ˌmɑntsɛˈræt/	Montserratian	/ˌmɑntsɛˈreɪʃən◂ /
Morocco	/məˈrɑkoʊ/	Moroccan	/məˈrɑkən/
Mozambique	/ˌmoʊzəmˈbik/	Mozambican	/ˌmoʊzəmˈbikən◂ /
Myanmar	/ˈmyɑnmɑr/	Burmese	/ˌbɚˈmiz/

Name		Adjective and name of a person from this place	
Namibia	/nə'mɪbiə/	Namibian	/nə'mɪbiən/
Nauru	/nɑ'uru/	Nauruan	/nɑ'uruən/
Nepal	/nɪ'pɔl/	*adj:* Nepalese *person:* Nepali *or* Nepalese	/ˌnɛpə'liz◂ / /ˌnɛpə'li/
Netherlands, The	/ðə 'nɛðɚləndz/	*adj:* Dutch *person:* Dutchman, Dutchwoman *pl. people:* the Dutch	/dʌtʃ/ /'dʌtʃmən/ /-ˌwʊmən/
New Zealand	/nu 'zilənd/	*adj:* New Zealand *person:* New Zealander	 /nu 'ziləndɚ/
Nicaragua	/ˌnɪkə'rɑgwə/	Nicaraguan	/ˌnɪkə'rɑgwən◂ /
Niger	/'naɪdʒɚ/	Nigerien	/ni'ʒɛriən/
Nigeria	/naɪ'dʒɪriə/	Nigerian	/naɪ'dʒɪriən/
Norway	/'nɔrweɪ/	Norwegian	/nɔr'widʒən/
Oman	/oʊ'mɑn/	Omani	/oʊ'mɑni/
Pacific	/pə'sɪfɪk/	*adj:* Pacific	
Pakistan	/ˌpækɪ'stæn/	Pakistani	/ˌpækɪ'stæni◂ /
Palestine	/'pæləstaɪn/	Palestinian	/ˌpælə'stɪniən/
Panama	/'pænəmɑ/	Panamanian	/ˌpænə'meɪniən/
Papua New Guinea	/ˌpæpyuə nu 'gɪni/	Papuan *or* Papua New Guinean	/'pæpyuən/ /ˌpæpyuə nu 'gɪniən/
Paraguay	/'pærəgwaɪ/	Paraguayan	/ˌpærə'gwaɪən◂ /
Persia (*former name of* Iran)	/'pɚʒə/	Persian	/'pɚʒən/
Peru	/pə'ru/	Peruvian	/pə'ruviən/
Philippines	/'fɪləpinz/	*adj:* Philippine *person:* Filipino	/'fɪləpin/ /ˌfɪlə'pinoʊ/
Poland	/'poʊlənd/	*adj:* Polish *person:* Pole	/'poʊlɪʃ/ /poʊl/
Polynesia	/ˌpɑlə'niʒə/	Polynesian	/ˌpɑlə'niʒən/
Portugal	/'pɔrtʃəgəl/	Portuguese	/ˌpɔrtʃə'giz◂ /
Puerto Rico	/ˌpɔrt̬ə 'rikoʊ/	Puerto Rican	/ˌpɔrt̬ə 'rikən/
Qatar	/'kɑtɚ/	Qatari	/kʌ'tɑri/
Romania	/roʊ'meɪniə/	Romanian	/roʊ'meɪniən/
Russia (Russian Federation, the)	/'rʌʃə/ /ˌrʌʃən fɛdə'reɪʃən/	Russian	/'rʌʃən/
Rwanda	/ru'ɑndə/	Rwandan	/ru'ɑndən/
Saint Kitts & Nevis	/seɪnt ˌkɪts ənd 'nivɪs/	Kittitian, Nevisian	/kə'tɪʃən/, /nɪ'vɪʒən/
Saint Lucia	/seɪnt 'luʃə/	Saint Lucian	/seɪnt 'luʃən/
Saint Vincent and the Grenadines	/seɪnt ˌvɪnsənt an ðe ˌgrenə'dɪnz/	Vincentian	/vɪn'senʃən/
Samoa	/sə'moʊə/	Samoan	/sə'moʊən/
San Marino	/sæn mə'rinoʊ/	Sammarinese San Marinese	/ˌsæmærə'niz/ /ˌsæn mærə'niz/
São Tomé & Principe	/ˌsaʊn təˌmeɪ ənd 'prɪnsəpə/	São Tomean	/ˌsaʊn tə'meɪən/
Saudi Arabia	/ˌsaʊdi ə'reɪbiə/	*adj:* Saudi Arabian *or* *person:* Saudi	/ˌsaʊdi a'reɪbiən/ /'saʊdi/
Scotland	/'skɑtlənd/	*adj:* Scottish *person:* Scot	/'skɑt̬ɪʃ/ /skɒt/
Senegal	/ˌsɛnɪ'gɔl/	Senegalese	/ˌsɛnɪgə'liz◂ /
Seychelles, the	/seɪ'ʃɛlz/	Seychellois	/ˌseɪʃɛl'wɑ◂ /
Sierra Leone	/siˌɛrə li'oʊn/	Sierra Leonean	/siˌɛrə li'oʊniən/
Singapore	/'sɪŋəpɔr/	Singaporean	/ˌsɪŋə'pɔriən◂ /
Slovakia	/'sloʊvækiə/	Slovakian	/'sloʊvɑkiən/
Slovenia	/sloʊ'vinyə/	Slovenian *or* Slovene	/sloʊ'viniən/ /'sloʊvin/
Solomon Islands, the	/'sɑləmən ˌaɪləndz/	*adj:* Soloman Island *person:* Solomon Islander	 /ˌsɑləmən 'aɪləndɚ/
Somalia	/soʊ'mɑliə/	Somali	/soʊ'mɑli/
South Africa	/saʊθ 'æfrɪkə/	South African	/saʊθ 'æfrɪkən/

Name		Adjective and name of a person from this place	
Spain	/speɪn/	*adj:* Spanish *person:* Spaniard *people:* the Spanish	/ˈspænɪʃ/ /ˈspænyɚd/
Sri Lanka	/sri ˈlɑŋkə/	Sri Lankan	/sri ˈlɑŋkən/
Sudan	/suˈdæn/	Sudanese	/ˌsudnˈɪz◂ /
Surinam, Suriname	/ˌsʊrɪˈnɑm/	*adj:* Surinamese *person:* Surinamer	/ˌsʊrɪnəˈmiz◂ / /ˌsʊrɪˈnɑmɚ/
Swaziland	/ˈswɑzilænd/	Swazi	/ˈswɑzi/
Sweden	/ˈswidn/	*adj:* Swedish *person:* Swede	/ˈswidɪʃ/ /swid/
Switzerland	/ˈswɪtsɚlənd/	Swiss	/swɪs/
Syria	/ˈsɪriə/	Syrian	/ˈsɪriən/
Tahiti	/təˈhiṭi/	Tahitian	/təˈhiʃən/
Taiwan	/ˌtaɪˈwɑn/	Taiwanese	/ˌtaɪwəˈniz◂ /
Tajikistan	/tɑˈdʒikɪˌstæn/	Tajik	/tɑˈdʒik/
Tanzania	/ˌtænzəˈniə/	Tanzanian	/ˌtænzəˈniən◂ /
Thailand	/ˈtaɪlænd, -lənd/	Thai	/taɪ/
Tibet	/tɪˈbɛt/	Tibetan	/tɪˈbɛt˺n/
Togo	/ˈtoʊgoʊ/	Togolese	/ˌtoʊgəˈliz/
Tonga	/ˈtɑŋgə/	Tongan	/ˈtɑŋgən/
Trinidad and Tobago	/ˌtrɪnɪdæd ən təˈbeɪgoʊ/	Trinidadian *or* Tobagonian	/ˌtrɪnɪˈdædiən◂ / /ˌtoʊbəˈgoʊniən/
Tunisia	/tuˈniʒə/	Tunisian	/tuˈniʒən/
Turkey	/ˈtɚki/	*adj:* Turkish *person:* Turk	/ˈtɜrkɪʃ/ /tɚk/
Turkmenistan	/ˌtɚkmɛnɪˈstæn/	Turkmen	/ˈtɚkmən/
Tuvalu	/tuˈvɑlu/	Tuvaluan	/tuˈvɑluən/
Uganda	/yuˈgændə/	Ugandan	/yuˈgændən/
Ukraine	/yuˈkreɪn/	Ukrainian	/yuˈkreɪniən/
United Arab Emirates	/yuˌnaɪṭɪd ˌærəb ˈɛmərɪts/	Emirati	/ˌɛmɪˈrɑti/
United Kingdom of Great Britain and Northern Ireland, the	/yuˌnaɪṭɪd ˌkɪŋdəm əv greɪt ˌbrɪt˺n ən*d* ˌnɔrðɚn ˈaɪrlənd/	*adj:* British *person:* Briton *people:* the British	/ˈbrɪṭɪʃ/ /ˈbrɪt˺n/
United States, the	/juˌnaɪṭɪd ˈsteɪts/	*adj:* American	/əˈmɛrɪkən/
Uruguay	/ˈyʊrəˌgwaɪ/	Uruguayan	/ˌyʊrəˈgwaɪən◂ /
Uzbekistan	/ʊzˈbɛkɪˌstæn/	Uzbek	/ˈʊzbek/
Vanuatu	/ˌvænuˈɑtu, ˌvænwɑˈtu/	Vanuatuan	/ˌvænuˈɑtuən, ˌvænwɑˈtuən/
Venezuela	/ˌvɛnəˈzweɪlə/	Venezuelan	/ˌvɛnəˈzweɪlən◂ /
Vietnam	/ˌvyɛtˈnɑm/	Vietnamese	/ˌvjɛtnəˈmiz◂ /
Wales	/weɪlz/	*adj:* Welsh *person:* Welshman, Welshwoman *people:* the Welsh	/wɛlʃ/ /ˈwɛlʃmən/ /-ˌwʊmən/
Yemen	/ˈyɛmən/	Yemeni	/ˈyɛməni/
Yugoslavia	/ˌyugəˈslɑviə/	Yugoslavian *or* Yugolslav	/ˌyugəˈslɑviən/ /ˈyugəˌslɑv/
Zambia	/ˈzæmbiə/	Zambian	/ˈzæmbiən/
Zimbabwe	/zɪmˈbɑbweɪ/	Zimbabwean	/zɪmˈbɑbweɪən/

Weights and measures

U.S. Customary System

Units of Length

1 inch		= 2.54 cm
12 inches	= 1 foot	= 0.3048 m
3 feet	= 1 yard	= 0.9144 m
1,760 yards (5,280 feet)	= 1 mile	= 1.609 km
2,025 yards (6,076 feet)	= 1 nautical mile	= 1.852 km

Units of Weight

1 ounce		= 28.35 g
16 ounces	= 1 pound	= 0.4536 kg
2,000 pounds	= 1 ton	= 907.18 kg
2,240 pounds	= 1 long ton	= 1,016.0 kg

Units of Volume (Liquid)

1 fluid ounce		= 29.574 ml
8 fluid ounces	= 1 cup	= 0.2366 l
16 fluid ounces	= 1 pint	= 0.4732 l
2 pints	= 1 quart	= 0.9463 l
4 quarts	= 1 gallon	= 3.7853 l

Units of Volume (Dry Measure)

1 peck		= 8,809.5 cm^3
4 pecks	= 1 bushel	= 35,239 cm^3

Units of Area

1 square inch		= 645.16 mm^2
144 square inches	= 1 square foot	= 0.0929 m^2
9 square feet	= 1 square yard	= 0.8361 m^2
4840 square yards	= 1 acre	= 4047 m^2
640 acres	= 1 square mile	= 259 ha

Temperature

degrees Fahrenheit = (°C × 9/5) + 32
degrees Celsius = (°F − 32) × 5/9

Metric System

Units of Length

1 millimeter		= 0.03937 inch
10 mm	= 1 centimeter	= 0.3937 inch
100 cm	= 1 meter	= 39.37 inches
1,000 m	= 1 kilometer	= 0.6214 mile

Units of Weight

1 milligram		= 0.000035 ounce
1,000 mg	= 1 gram	= 0.035 ounce
1,000 g	= 1 kilogram	= 2.205 pounds
1,000 kg	= 1 metric ton	= 2,205 pounds

Units of Volume

1 milliliter		= 0.03 fluid ounce
1,000 ml	= 1 liter	= 1.06 quarts

Units of Area

1 square centimeter		= 0.1550 square inch
10,000 cm^2	= 1 square meter	= 1.196 square yards
10,000 m^2	= 1 hectare	= 2.471 acres

Map

New England
Middle Atlantic States/The East Coast
Southern States/The South
Southwestern States/The Southwest
Midwestern States/The Midwest
Rocky Mountain States
Pacific Coast States/The West Coast
ALASKA
CANADA
HAWAII
MEXICO
Pacific Ocean
Atlantic Ocean
Gulf of Mexico
Rocky Mountains
Sierra Nevada Mountains
Appalachian Mountains
Grand Canyon
Great Salt Lake
Lake Superior
Lake Michigan
Lake Huron
Lake Erie
Lake Ontario
Missouri River
Mississippi River
WASHINGTON
Seattle
OREGON
Portland
CALIFORNIA
San Francisco
Sacramento
Los Angeles
San Diego
NEVADA
Carson City
Las Vegas
IDAHO
Boise
MONTANA
Helena
WYOMING
Cheyenne
UTAH
Salt Lake City
COLORADO
Denver
ARIZONA
Phoenix
Tucson
NEW MEXICO
Albuquerque
Santa Fe
TEXAS
El Paso
Odessa
Dallas
Austin
San Antonio
Houston
OKLAHOMA
Oklahoma City
NORTH DAKOTA
Bismarck
SOUTH DAKOTA
Pierre
NEBRASKA
Omaha
KANSAS
Kansas City
MINNESOTA
Minneapolis
IOWA
MISSOURI
St. Louis
WISCONSIN
Milwaukee
ILLINOIS
Chicago
MICHIGAN
Detroit
INDIANA
Indianapolis
OHIO
Cleveland
Cincinnati
KENTUCKY
Louisville
TENNESSEE
Nashville
Memphis
ARKANSAS
Little Rock
LOUISIANA
New Orleans
MISSISSIPPI
Jackson
ALABAMA
Birmingham
GEORGIA
Atlanta
FLORIDA
Tallahassee
Jacksonville
Tampa
Miami
SOUTH CAROLINA
Charleston
NORTH CAROLINA
Charlotte
VIRGINIA
Norfolk
WEST VIRGINIA
WASHINGTON, DC
MARYLAND
DELAWARE
PENNSYLVANIA
Philadelphia
NEW JERSEY
NEW YORK
New York
Buffalo
CONNECTICUT
RHODE ISLAND
MASSACHUSETTS
Boston
VERMONT
NEW HAMPSHIRE
Concord
MAINE
Augusta
0 400 km
0 250 miles
N S E W
N north
S south
E east
W west

Single User License Agreement: Longman Dictionary of American English

IMPORTANT: READ CAREFULLY

This is a legally binding agreement between You (the user or purchaser) and Pearson Education Limited. By retaining this license, any software media or accompanying written materials or carrying out any of the permitted activities You agree to be bound by the terms of the license agreement below.

If You do not agree to these terms then promptly return the entire publication (this license and all software, written materials, packaging, and any other components received with it) with Your sales receipt to Your supplier for a full refund.

SINGLE USER LICENSE AGREEMENT

YOU ARE PERMITTED TO:

✔ Use (load into temporary memory or permanent storage) a single copy of the software on only one computer at a time. If this computer is linked to a network then the software may only be installed in a manner such that it is not accessible to other machines on the network. If You want to use the software on a network or across a whole site, You need to read the Network version of the User License or the Site License. You can get these from the email address at the end of this license

✔ Use the software with a class provided it is only installed on one computer

✔ Transfer the software from one computer to another provided that you only use it on one computer at a time

✔ Print out individual screen extracts from the disk for (a) private study or (b) to include in Your essays or classwork with students

✔ Photocopy individual screen extracts for Your schoolwork or classwork with students

YOU MAY NOT:

✘ Rent, lease, or sell the software or any part of the publication

✘ Copy any part of the documentation, except where specifically indicated otherwise

✘ Make copies of the software, even for backup purposes

✘ Reverse engineer, decompile, or disassemble the software or create a derivative product from the contents of the databases or any software included in them

✘ Use the software on more than one computer at a time

✘ Install the software on any networked computer or server in a way that could allow access to it from more than one machine on the network

✘ Include any material or software from the disk in any other product or software materials, except as allowed under "You are permitted to"

✘ Use the software in any way not specified above without the prior written consent of Pearson Education Limited

✘ Print out more than one page at a time

✘ Print, download, or save any pictures

ONE COPY ONLY

This license is for a single user copy of the software

PEARSON EDUCATION LIMITED RESERVES THE RIGHT TO TERMINATE THIS LICENSE BY WRITTEN NOTICE AND TO TAKE ACTION TO RECOVER ANY DAMAGES SUFFERED BY PEARSON EDUCATION LIMITED IF YOU BREACH ANY PROVISION OF THIS AGREEMENT.

Pearson Education Limited owns the software. You only own the disk on which the software is supplied.

LIMITED WARRANTY

Pearson Education Limited warrants that the disk or CD ROM on which the software is supplied is free from defects in materials and workmanship under normal use for ninety (90) days from the date You receive it. This warranty is limited to You and is not transferable. Pearson Education Limited does not warrant that the functions of the software meet Your requirements or that the media is compatible with any computer system on which it is used or that the operation of the software will be unlimited or error-free.

You assume responsibility for selecting the software to achieve Your intended results and for the installation of, the use of and the results obtained from the software. The entire liability of Pearson Education Limited and your only remedy shall be replacement free of charge of the components that do not meet this warranty.

This limited warranty is void if any damage has resulted from accident, abuse, misapplication, service, or modification by someone other than Pearson Education Limited. In no event shall Pearson Education Limited be liable for any damages whatsoever arising out of installation of the software, even if advised of the possibility of such damages. Pearson Education Limited will not be liable for any loss or damage of any nature suffered by any party as a result of reliance upon or reproduction of or any errors in the content of the publication.

Pearson Education Limited does not limit its liability for death or personal injury caused by its negligence.

This license agreement shall be governed by and interpreted and construed in accordance with English law.

Technical support: only registered users are entitled to free technical help and advice. As a registered user, You may receive technical help by writing to elt-support@pearson.com or your local agent.

New releases and updates: as a registered user You may be able to get new releases and updates, or upgrade to a network version of the software at reduced prices.

Registration: to register as a user, please write to us at the address shown below or email us at elt-support@pearson.com

Longman Dictionaries Division
Pearson Education Limited
Edinburgh Gate
Harlow
Essex
CM20 2JE
England